FUNCTION

The WHOLE EARTH CATALOG functions as an evaluation and access device. With it, the user should know better what is worth getting and where and how to do the getting.

An item is listed in the CATALOG if it is deemed:

1) Useful as a tool,

2) Relevant to independent education,

3) High quality or low cost,

4) Easily available by mail.

CATALOG listings are continually revised according to the experience and suggestions of CATALOG users and staff.

PURPOSE

We are as gods and might as well get good at it. So far remotely done power and glory——as via government, big business, formal education, church——has succeeded to the point where gross defects obscure actual gains. In response to this dilemma and to these gains a realm of intimate, personal power is developing——power of the individual to conduct his own education, find his own inspiration, shape his own environment, and share his adventure with whoever is interested. Tools that aid this process are sought and promoted by the WHOLE EARTH CATALOG.

CONTENTS

FRONT COVER

Taken November 9, 1967, from NASA's Apollo 4 at a distance of 9850 nautical miles. This is probably the first American photograph of the "whole Earth." You're looking west over the Atlantic Ocean, with the Antarctic Continent just visible at the bottom of the crescent. The picture was released in 1967, but no one seemed to care about noticing it or publishing it. I think it was the shadow, which frightened people. There are no shadows on our maps.

INSIDE FRONT COVER

The famous Apollo 8 picture of Earthrise over the Moon that established our planetary facthood and beauty and rareness (dry moon, barren space) and began to bend human consciousness. The quote is from *Energy Flow in Biology*, by Harold Morowitz, $11.00 from Academic Press, 111 Fifth Avenue, New York, N.Y. 10003.

INSIDE BACK COVER

The photograph, courtesy Lick Observatory, shows the M-31 Andromeda Galaxy, which is considered similar to our own in structure and size. Where the thought-balloon originates is approximately the location of Earth in this galaxy. The quote is from p.464 of the extraordinary *Collected Poems* of Kenneth Patchen, 1967, 504 pp., $3.95 from New Directions, J.B. Lippincott Co., East Washington Square, Philadelphia, PA. 19105.

BACK COVER

This is the back cover that was on our first CATALOG, the Fall 1968 issue, which was 64 pages and cost $5. As most of our color covers, it was designed with Peter Bailey. The photo, the first full-Earth picture, is from the noon part of a day-long high resolution color TV film shot from an ATS satellite in November 1967. To NASA our thanks.

CATALOG Procedure

WHOLE EARTH EPILOG

The WHOLE EARTH EPILOG is a continuation of THE LAST WHOLE EARTH CATALOG—— in effect Volume II. It commences where the CATALOG leaves off, with page 449, and comprises all new material, deeper research, and a more professional index covering both CATALOG and EPILOG. Suggestions and reviews for items you think should appear in future CATALOGS are invited. We pay $10 for each short review and first-suggestion that we use; more for longer reviews and articles. Send to:

WHOLE EARTH EPILOG
Box 428
Sausalito, CA 94965

The EPILOG is 320 pages, $4 ($9.25 in hardcover library binding), and is available in bookstores or from WHOLE EARTH. The EPILOG is distributed by Penguin Books, 7110 Ambassador Road, Baltimore, MD 21207.

The CoEvolution Quarterly

Our on-going periodical, a revival of the old "Supplement to the Whole Earth Catalog." That relation has now inverted. We see the UPDATED CATALOG and EPILOG as special access-to-tools issues of The CoEvolution Quarterly. The CQ carries lengthy articles on Whole Earth themes as well as correspondence, oddments, updates of CATALOG and EPILOG, and hot news in the tool department. The Quarterly seems to focus on the current apocalypse: short-term forecasting, home remedies and ways to think about it all without losing your mind. A SUBSCRIPTION to The CoEvolution Quarterly, four issues a year—— each solstice and equinox—— costs $6/yr from:

The CQ
558 Santa Cruz Avenue
Menlo Park, CA 94025

(The address for editorial matters is Box 428, Sausalito, CA 94965).

Ordering from the CATALOG

→ Address orders to the supplier given with the item. (Or shop locally.)

→ If the price listed is not postpaid consult post office or express agency for cost of shipping from supplier's location to yours. Or have the item sent postage C.O.D.

→ Add state sales tax if transaction is within your state. (California sales tax is 6%.) You don't have to do this for periodicals.

→ Send check or money order.

If the item says or WHOLE EARTH CATALOG, you can mailorder it from:

WHOLE EARTH TRUCK STORE
558 Santa Cruz
Menlo Park, California 94025
(415) 323-0313

This service is for the convenience of readers; the Truck Store has no financial relationship to the CATALOG, (nor does any supplier).

If you're ordering from overseas, surface mail takes about two months, airmail just a couple of days.

Policy with Suppliers

Suppliers (manufacturers, creators, etc.) may not buy their way into the CATALOG. Free samples, etc., are cheerfully accepted by CATALOG researchers; response not predictable. No payment for listing is asked or accepted. We owe accurate information exchange to suppliers, but not favors.

Our obligation is to CATALOG users and to ourselves to be good tools for one another.

The judgments in the reviews are wholly sincere. They are also only partially informed, often biased, very often wishful, occasionally a temporary enthusiasm. Many are simply hasty. I wouldn't rely on them too far. Try to see through them.

Sense and Patience

Be gentle. Sometimes we carry very small companies. They often have a hard time coping with the volume of inquiries they receive as a result of their unrequested listing in the CATALOG. Especially when most of the requests for literature seem to be just curiosity. That kind of thing can break a small company. So don't write just to keep your mail box full.

The UPDATED Catalog

THE LAST WHOLE EARTH CATALOG contains some 2100 listings. Since May 1971, when we completed the CATALOG, more than half of those items have changed in price, address, sublistings, survival (many worthy endeavors went defunct), etc.

Thanks to an epic of human labor by Pam Cokeley (here pictured)— six months work contacting everyone in the CATALOG by letter or phone— this UPDATED CATALOG incorporates over 3000 changes in the original listings. In a few cases items that are no longer available have been replaced by ones that are. Mostly we let the skeletons lie there— for honor, sorrow, or warning.

The updating process goes on— current to the most recent printing (see below). Will suppliers and readers please keep us informed of significant changes? Write to WEC, Box 428, Sausalito CA 94965.

Pam Cokeley

Blackwell's Books

is a British mail order source of books that used to be cheaper than U.S. suppliers. What with the current apocalypse in Merrie England you're better off buying domestic.

Format

We used to be two publications, the CATALOG, and the Supplement. The CATALOG was formal and responsible; the Supplement wasn't. In this LAST CATALOG they are mixed. Usually material from the Supplements has a Light heading, whereas formal CATALOG items have a **Bold heading**. Both are indexed in the back. About 1/3 of the material in this LAST CATALOG is new.

Each page number has a heading indicating the section it's in, such as Whole Systems, and a heading indicating the general contents of that page, such as Funky Future.

Profits

Whole Earth is non-profit. All income from sales of CATALOG, EPILOG, or The CQ goes to POINT, an educational foundation in San Francisco.

On Getting Stuff

As Dan Schiller suggested in **Popular Photography**, the CATALOG will bankrupt you if you can't distinguish between what you need and what you wish you needed.

Start extravagant, and you'll never finish. Get the cheap tool first, see if it feeds your life. If it does, then get a better one. Once you use it all the time, get the best. You can only grow into quality. You can't buy it.

Most of the stuff in the CATALOG can be borrowed free from a library.

This issue

of the CATALOG is the last. We encourage others to initiate similar services to fill the vacuum in the economy we stumbled into and are stepping out of. We don't see how using our name or copy can aid originality, so they're not available, for love or money. Ideas we've had and evaluations we've made are free for recycling.

Preparation of the CATALOG was done on an IBM Selectric Composer and Polaroid MP-3 Camera.

Printing and binding by:
Nowels Publications, Menlo Park, California
Deven Lithographers, Inc., Long Island City, New York
Craftsman Press, Inc., Bladensburg, Maryland.

For credits, and How to Make a WHOLE EARTH CATALOG AND TRUCK STORE, see p. 434.

1st Printing June 1971—200,000—Nowels

2nd Printing July 1971—100,000—Deven

3rd Printing August 1971—100,000—Deven

4th Printing September 1971—100,000—Craftsman

5th Printing October 1971—120,000—Craftsman

6th Printing October 1971—180,000—Deven

7th Printing November 1971—100,000—Craftsman

8th Printing August 1972—100,000—Craftsman

Special British Edition June 1972—35,000—Craftsman

9th Printing August 1972—100,000—Craftsman

10th Printing October 1972—100,000—Craftsman

11th Printing May 1973—50,000—Craftsman

12th Printing February 1974—13,000—Craftsman

13th Printing June 1974—80,000—Craftsman

14th Printing September 1974—80,000—Craftsman

Understanding Whole Systems

Buckminster Fuller

The insights of Buckminster Fuller initiated this catalog.

Among his books listed here, **Utopia or Oblivion** *is now probably the most direct introduction. It's a collection of his talks and papers from 1964 to 1967, at a bargain price.* **An Operating Manual for Spaceship Earth** *is his most recent, and succinct, statement.* **Nine Chains to the Moon** *is early, and openly metaphysical.* **The Untitled Epic of Industrialization** *is lyrical and strong.* **Ideas and Integrities** *is his most autobiographical, and perhaps the most self-contained of his books.* **No More Secondhand God** *is the most generalized, leading into the geometry of thought.*

People who beef about Fuller mainly complain about his repetition——the same ideas again and again, it's embarrassing, also illuminating, because the same notions take on different contexts. Fuller's lectures have a raga quality of rich nonlinear endless improvisation full of convergent surprises.

Some are put off by his language, which makes demands on your head like suddenly discovering an extra engine in your car——if you don't let it drive you faster, it'll drag you. Fuller won't wait. He spent two years silent after illusory language got him in trouble, and he returned to human communication with a redesigned instrument.

—SB

Utopia or Oblivion
R. Buckminster Fuller
1969; 366pp.

$1.25 postpaid

from:
Bantam Books
666 Fifth Avenue
New York, New York 10019

or WHOLE EARTH CATALOG

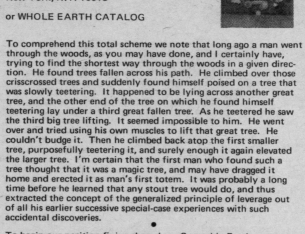

My recommendation for a curriculum of design science:

1. Synergetics
2. General systems theory
3. Theory of games (Von Neumann)
4. Chemistry and physics
5. Topology, projective geometry
6. Cybernetics
7. Communications
8. Meteorology
9. Geology
10. Biology
11. Sciences of energy
12. Political geography
13. Ergonomics
14. Production engineering

•

Here on Southern Illinois' campus we are going to set up a great computer program. We are going to introduce the many variables now known to be operative in economics. We will store all the basic data in the machines memory bank; where and how much of each class of the physical resources; where are the people, what are the trendings—all kinds of trendings of world man?

Next we are going to set up a computer feeding game, called "How Do We Make the World Work?" We will start playing relatively soon. We will bring people from all over the world to play it. There will be competitive teams from all around earth to test their theories on how to make the world work. If a team resorts to political pressures to accelerate their advantages and is not able to wait for the going gestation rates to articulate their theory they are apt to be in trouble. When you get into politics you are very liable to get into war. War is the ultimate tool of politics. If war develops the side inducing it loses the game.

•

I was born cross-eyed. Not until I was four years old was it discovered that this was caused by my being abnormally farsighted. My vision was thereafter fully corrected with lenses. Until four I could see only large patterns, houses, trees, outlines of people with blurred coloring. While I saw two dark areas on human faces, I did not see a human eye or a teardrop or a human hair until I was four. Despite my new ability to apprehend details, my childhood's spontaneous dependence only upon big pattern clues has persisted. . . .

I am convinced that neither I nor any other human, past or present, was or is a genius. I am convinced that what I have every physically normal child also has at birth. We could, of course, hypothesize that all babies are born geniuses and get swiftly de-geniused. Unfavorable circumstances, shortsightedness, frayed nervous systems, and ignorantly articulated love and fear of elders tend to shut off many of the child's brain capability valves. I was lucky in avoiding too many disconnects.

There is luck in everything. My luck is that I was born cross-eyed, was ejected so frequently from the establishment that I was finally forced either to perish or to employ some of those faculties with which we are all endowed——the use of which circumstances had previously so frustrated as to have to put them in the deep freezer, whence only hellishly hot situations could provide enough heat to melt them back into usability.

Utopia or Oblivion

Operating Manual for Spaceship Earth
Buckminster Fuller
1969; 133pp.

$1.25 postpaid

from:
Pocket Books, Inc.
1 W. 39th St.
New York, N.Y. 10018

or WHOLE EARTH CATALOG

To comprehend this total scheme we note that long ago a man went through the woods, as you may have done, and I certainly have, trying to find the shortest way through the woods in a given direction. He found trees fallen across his path. He climbed over those crisscrossed trees and suddenly found himself poised on a tree that was slowly teetering. It happened to be lying across another great tree, and the other end of the tree on which he found himself teetering lay under a third great fallen tree. As he teetered he saw the third big tree lifting. It seemed impossible to him. He went over and tried using his own muscles to lift that great tree. He couldn't budge it. Then he climbed back atop the first smaller tree, purposefully teetering it, and surely enough it again elevated the larger tree. I'm certain that the first man who found such a tree thought that it was a magic tree, and may have dragged it home and erected it as man's first totem. It was probably a long time before he learned that any stout tree would do, and thus extracted the concept of the generalized principle of leverage out of all his earlier successive special-case experiences with such accidental discoveries.

•

To begin our position-fixing aboard our Spaceship Earth we must first acknowledge that the abundance of immediately consumable, obviously desirable or utterly essential resources have been sufficient until now to allow us to carry on despite our ignorance. Being eventually exhaustible and spoilable, they have been adequate only up to this critical moment. This cushion-for-error of humanity's survival and growth up to now was apparently provided just as a bird inside of the egg is provided with liquid nutriment to develop it to a certain point. But then by design the nutriment is exhausted at just the time when the chick is large enough to be able to locomote on its own legs. And so as the chick pecks at the shell seeking more nutriment it inadvertently breaks open the shell.

•

A new, physically uncomprised, metaphysical initiative of unbiased integrity could unify the world. It could and probably will be provided by the utterly impersonal problem solutions of the computers.

•

Heisenberg's principle of 'indeterminism' which recognized the experimental discovery that the act of measuring always alters that which was being measured turns experience into a continuous and never-repeatable evolutionary scenario.

•

The gold supply is so negligible as to make it pure voodoo to attempt to valve the world's economic evolution traffic through the gold-sized needle's 'eye'.

•

Brain deals exclusively with the physical, and mind exclusively with the metaphysical. Wealth is the progressive mastery of matter by mind . . .

•

Stepping forth from its initial sanctuary, the young bird must now forage on its own legs and wings to discover the next phase of its regenerative sustenance.

Nine Chains to the Moon
Buckminster Fuller
1938, 1963; 375 pp.

Unavailable until 1972

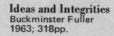

Since Yogi is a personalized art, the art dies with the person. The abstract power involved remains as real and true, always, but it cannot be made utilizable in increasing continuity for the world in general. Christ and his counterparts realized this and were unique in their refusal to apply this power to self ends. It was this personal limitation of the Yogi art which led the prosaic philosophers to search further. They sought a means of limitless articulation.

•

This phantom captain has neither weight nor sensorial tangibility, as has often been scientifically proven by careful weighing operations at the moment of abandonment of the ship by the phantom captain, i.e., at the instant of "death". He may be likened to the variant of polarity dominance in our bipolar electric world which, when balanced and unit, vanishes as abstract unity 1 or 0. With the phantom captain's departure, the mechanism becomes inoperative and very quickly disintegrates into basic chemical elements.

An illuminating rationalization indicated that *captains*—being phantom, abstract, infinite, and bound to other captains by a bond of understanding as proven by their recognition of each other's signals and the meaning thereof by reference to a common direction (toward "perfect")—*are not only all related, but are one and the same captain.* Mathematically, since characteristics of unity exist, they cannot be non-identical.

•

'Still further——over the microphone STEPPED-UP electrically this music enters a super-or-sub-sensorial wave-length frequency that makes it broadcastable, apparently BACK INTO THE UNIVERSE AGAIN, the full LATENT broadcast of which men on ships at sea, an aviator in the air, or Julia Murphy in a city hovel, or the farmer's wife, can tune in upon, without any personal-equation dissonnance by unwanted diverting human beings in their presence, and so hear the music of the universe that Bach heard years ago.

'Here is IMMORTALITY!'

'Darling,'——that radiant flash of infinite understanding had flashed between Jonesie and the X-ian——'Ican understand those houses all right.'

Untitled Epic Poem on the History of Industrialization
Buckminster Fuller
1962; 227pp.

$1.95 postpaid

from
Simon & Schuster, Inc.
630 Fifth Avenue
New York, New York 10020

or WHOLE EARTH CATALOG

However,
man unconcernedly sorting mail on an express train,
with unuttered faith that
the engineer is competent,
that the switchmen are not asleep,
that the track walkers are doing their job,
that the technologists
who designed the train and the rails
knew their stuff,
that the thousands of others
whom he may never know by face or name
are collecting tariffs,
paying for repairs,
and so handling assets
that he will be paid a week from today
and again the week after that,
and that all the time
his family is safe and in well being
without his personal protection
constitutes a whole new era of evolution—
the first really "new"
since the beginning of the spoken word.
In fact, out of the *understanding*
innate in the spoken word
was Industrialization wrought
after milleniums
of seemingly whitherless spade work.

Ideas and Integrities
Buckminster Fuller
1963; 318pp.

$1.95 postpaid

from:
Collier Books
The MacMillan Company
Order Dept.
Front and Brown Streets
Riverside, N.J. 08075

or WHOLE EARTH CATALOG

Standing by the lake on a jump-or-think basis, the very first spontaneous question coming to mind was, "If you put aside everything you've ever been asked to believe and have recourse only to your own experiences do you have any conviction arising from those experiences which either discards or must assume an a priori greater intellect than the intellect of man?" The answer was swift and positive. Experience had clearly demonstrated an a priori anticipatory and only intellectually apprehendable orderliness of interactive principles operating in the universe into which we are born. These principles are discovered but are never invented by man. I said to myself, "I have faith in the integrity of the anticipatory intellectual wisdom which we may call 'God.' " My next question was, "Do I know best or does God know best whether I may be of any value to the integrity of universe?" The answer was, "You don't know and no man knows, but the faith you have just established out of experience imposes recognition of the a priori wisdom of the fact of your being." Apparently addressing myself, I said, "You do not have the right to eliminate yourself, you do not belong to you. You belong to the universe. The significance of you will forever remain obscure to you, but you may assume that you are fulfilling your significance if you apply yourself to converting all your experience to highest advantage of others. You and all men are here for the sake of other men."

•

I define "synergy" as follows: Synergy is the unique behavior of whole systems, unpredicted by behavior of their respective subsystems' events.

(Fuller cont'd.)

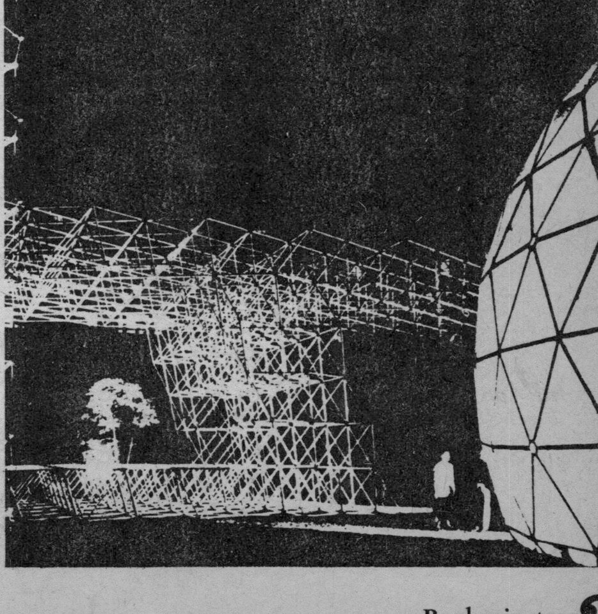

Fuller cont'd.

No More Secondhand God
Buckminster Fuller
1963; 163 pp.

$2.95 postpaid

from:
Doubleday & Co., Inc.
Garden City, N.Y. 11530

or WHOLE EARTH CATALOG

Buckminster Fuller on Hippie Hill, San Francisco, 1968.

Thinking is a putting-aside, rather than a putting-in discipline, e.g., putting aside the tall grasses in order to isolate the trail into informative viewability. Thinking is FM—frequency modulation—for its results in tuning-out of irrelevancies as a result of definitive resolution of the exclusively tuned-in or accepted feed-back messages' pattern differentiability.

I see God in
the instruments and the mechanisms that
work
reliably,
more reliably than the limited sensory departments of
the human mechanism.

And God says
observe the paradox
    of man's creative potentials
and his destructive tactics
He could have his new world
through sufficient love
for "all's fair"
in love as well as in war
which means you can
junk as much rubbish,
skip as many stupid agreements
by love,
spontaneous unselfishness radiant.

The revolution has come——
set on fire from the top.
Let it burn swiftly.
Neither the branches, trunk, nor roots will be endangered.
Only last year's leaves and
the parasite-bearded moss and orchids
will not be there
when the next spring brings fresh growth
and free standing flowers.

Here is God's purpose——
for God, to me, it seems,
is a verb,
not a noun,
proper or improper;
is the articulation
not the art, objective or subjective;
is loving,
not the abstraction "love" commanded or entreated;
is knowledge dynamic,
not legislative code,
not proclamation law,
not academic dogma, not ecclesiastic canon.

Yes, God is a verb,
the most active,
connoting the vast harmonic
reordering of the universe
from unleashed chaos of energy.

And there is born unheralded
a great natural peace,
not out of exclusive
pseudo-static security
but out of including, refining, dynamic balancing.
Naught is lost.
Only the false and nonexistent are dispelled.

And I've thought through to tomorrow
which is also today.
The telephone rings
and you say to me
Hello Buckling this is Christopher; or
Daddy it's Allegra; or
Mr. Fuller this is the Telephone Company Business Office;
and I say you are inaccurate.
Because I knew you were going to call
and furthermore I recognize
that it is God who is "speaking."

And you say
aren't you being fantastic?
And knowing you I say no.

All organized religions of the past
were inherently developed
as beliefs and credits
in "second hand" information.

Therefore it will be an entirely new era
when man finds himself confronted
with direct experience
with an obviously a priori
intellectually anticipatory competence
that has interordered
all that he is discovering.

[No More Secondhand God]

The Dymaxion World of Buckminster Fuller

The most graphic of Fuller's books (it's about his work, by Robert Marks). Consequently it is the most directly useful if you are picking up on specific projects of his such as domes, geometry, cars, demographic maps and charts, etc.
—SB

The Dymaxion World of Buckminster Fuller
Robert W. Marks
1960; 232 pp.

$4.95

from:
Doubleday & Co.
Garden City, N.Y. 11530

or WHOLE EARTH CATALOG

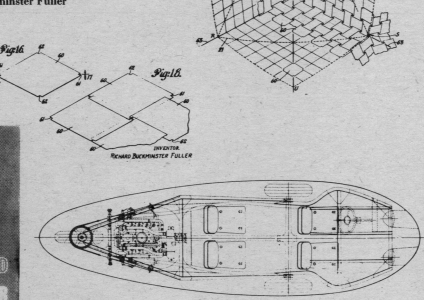

Dymaxion car 1933

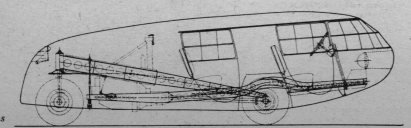

World Design Science Decade Documents 1-4

Fuller publishing Fuller (and some John McHale). Good raw material.
—SB

World Design Science Decade Documents, Vol. 1-4
R. B. Fuller, John McHale

$16.00 postpaid

from:
World Resources Inventory
P.O. Box 909
Carbondale, Illinois 62901

In the 1920's with but little open country highway mileage in operation, automobile accidents were concentrated and frequently occurred within our urban and suburban presence. Witnessing a number of accidents, I observed that warning signs later grew up along the roads leading to danger points and that more traffic and motorcycle police were put on duty. The authorities tried to cure the malady by reforming the motorists. A relatively few special individual drivers with much experience, steady temperament, good coordination and natural tendency to anticipate and understand the psychology of others emerged as "good" and approximately accident-free drivers. Many others were accident prone.

In lieu of the after-the-fact curative reform, trending to highly specialized individual offender case histories, my philosophy urged the anticipatory avoidance of the accident potentials through invention of generalized highway dividers, grade separaters, clover leafing and adequately banked curves and automatic traffic control stop-lighting systems. I saw no reason why the problem shouldn't be solved by preventative design rather than attempted reforms. My resolve: Reshape environment; don't try to reshape man.

[WDSD Document 1]

Tension and Compression are complementary functions of structure. Therefore as functions they only co-exist. When pulling a tensional rope its girth contracts in compression. When we load a column in compression its girth tends to expand in tension. When we investigate tension and compression, we find that compression members, as you all know as architects, have very limited lengths in relation to their cross sections. They get too long and too slender and will readily break. Tension members, when you pull them, tend to pull, approximately, (almost but never entirely), straight instead of trying to curve more and more as do too thin compressionally loaded columns. The contraction of the tension members in their girth, when tensionally loaded, brings its atoms closer together which makes it even stronger. There is no limit ratio of cross section to length in tensional members of structural systems. There is a fundamental limit ratio in compression. Therefore when nature has very large tasks to do, such as cohering the solar system or the universe she arranges her structural systems both in the microcosm and macrocosm in the following manner. Nature has compression operating in little remotely positioned islands, as high energy concentrations, such as the earth and other planets, in the macrocosm; or as islanded electrons, or protons or other atomic nuclear components in the microcosm while cohering the whole universal system, both macro and micro, of mutually remote, compressional, and oft non-simultaneous, islands by comprehensive tension; ——compression islands in a non-simultaneous universe of tension. The Universe is a tensegrity.

[WDSD Document 2]

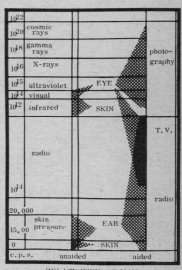

RELATIONSHIP OF MAN
TO ELECTROMAGNETIC SPECTRUM

To start off with it is demonstrated in the array of events which we have touched on that we don't have to "earn a living" anymore. The "living" has all been earned for us forever. Industrialization's wealth is cumulative in contradistinction to the inherently terminal, discontinuous, temporary wealth of the craft eras of civilization such as the Bronze Age or Stone Age. If we only understood how that cumulative industrial wealth has come about, we could stop playing obsolete games, but that is a task that cannot be accomplished by political and social reforms. Man is so deeply conditioned in his reflexes by his milleniums of slave functioning that he has too many inferiority complexes to yield to political reformation. The obsolete games will be abandoned only when realistic, happier and more interesting games come along to displace the obsolete games.

[WDSD Document 3]

World society has throughout its millions of years on earth made its judgements upon visible, tangible, sensorially demonstrable criteria. We may safely say that the world is keeping its eye on the unimportant visible 1 percent of the historical transformation while missing the significance of the 99 percent of overall, unseen changes. Forms are inherently visible and forms no longer can "follow functions" because the significant functions are invisible. . . .

[WDSD Document 4]

beware of whole systemitis.
its the lonliness awareness.
imagine you are a near sighted, bucktoothed, kid, doing
   sunflower seeds,
and somebody comes along and puts eyeglasses on you,
holds up a mirror,
then takes you out on a hilltop at night,
points up at the little winks out there,
and tells you they aren't really little winks at all,
but great big flashes,
a long way away,
then asks you if you want some more sunflower seeds.

you want to throw away the eyeglasses, but it is too late,
you are stuck,
you've seen it,
you are little,
alone,
puny,
except . . . . . .
except for a few soft flannel thoughts,
and a belief that there are others like you,
brothers like you,
and that a sunflower seed
is a whole system too.

—jd

Andromeda Galaxy

*Four color photograph posters
of Orion Crab, Trifed, Nebula
and Andromeda Galaxies.
Peerless meditation targets.*

*[Suggested by
Doug Engelbart]*

Galaxy Posters
20" x 28½"

$4.00 for set of four

from:
Edmund Scientific
100 Edscorp Building
Barrington, N. J. 08007

Cosmic View

*"The Universe in 40 Jumps" is the subtitle of the book. It
delivers.*

*The man who conceived and rendered it, a Dutch school-
master named Kees Boeke, gave years of work to perfecting
the information in his pictures. The result is one of the*

Cosmic View
Kees Boeke
1957; 48 pp.

$4.95 postpaid

from:
The John Day Company
257 Park Avenue South
New York, N. Y. 10010

or WHOLE EARTH CATALOG

*simplest, most thorough, inescapable mind blows ever
printed. Your mind and you advance in and out through
the universe, changing scale by a factor of ten. It very
quickly becomes hard to breathe, and you realize how
magnitude-bound we've been.*

—SB

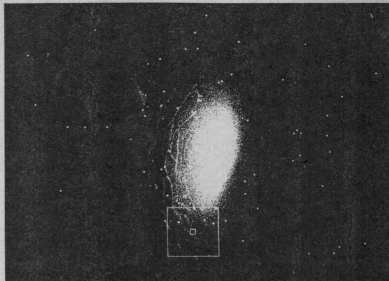

The Hubble Atlas of Galaxies

*This book is a series of superb photographs which is the
definition of Edwin Hubble's classification of galaxies.
Galaxies come in a variety of shapes from round blurry ones
through the familiar spiral in Andromeda to fantastic
blazing pinwheels like M101.*

*Hubble has lined them up in a sequence according to shape.
The meaning of this sequence has not yet been determined.
It may indicate a series of stages in the life of one galaxy
which progresses from blurred youngsters to majestic
spiral or vice versa. More likely vice versa, since the spirals
contain hot young blue stars which we know will burn out
in a few million years or so, while the blurry ones contain
many ancient red giants. It is also possible that the
sequence is not an age sequence at all, but merely reflects
conditions at that place in the universe when that galaxy
was formed.*

*But besides being a tool for scientists, this book is like a
guided tour through our own miraculous universe. When
this planet gets you down, leaf through the Atlas and
feast your spirit on galaxy after galaxy, as beautiful and
varied as snow flakes. Some galaxies are so far away that
the graininess of the photograph shows in the blow up.
Some photographs show small blurred objects in the
background which one suddenly realizes are more galaxies.*

*[Reviewed by Jenny Deupree.
Suggested by Jordan Belson]*

The Hubble Atlas of Galaxies
Allan Sandage
1961; 50 plates

$10.00 postpaid from:
Carnegie Institution of Washington
1530 P Street, N.W.
Washington, D.C. 20005

or WHOLE EARTH CATALOG

Star Maker

*A man's consciousness unwillingly departs his body and his
planet. Once in space he accomplishes willed travel in search
of Star Maker. His journey takes him into the minds of other
planetary beings; a company of these travel together and
witness countless civilizations; eventually they participate
in a combined consciousness of worlds that in time embraces
the stars as well; this leads to galactic and cosmic consciousness
and the culminating encounter with Star Maker.*

*Jordan Belson, who I trust in these matters, asserts that it is
a true vision, that Stapledon's whole life pointed at attaining
it, and that the book will be used and discussed for centuries.*

*This Dover edition includes an earlier Stapledon story, "Last
and First Men".*

—SB

Star Maker
Olaf Stapledon
1937; 188 pp.

$2.50 postpaid

from:
Dover Publications, Inc.
180 Varick Street
New York, N. Y. 10014

or WHOLE EARTH CATALOG

The sheer beauty of our planet surprised me. It was a huge pearl, set
in spangled ebony. It was nacrous, it was an opal. No, it was far more
lovely than any jewel. Its patterned colouring was more subtle, more
ethereal. It displayed the delicacy and brilliance, the intricacy and harmony of a live thing. Strange that in my remoteness I seemed to feel,
as never before, the vital presence of Earth as of a creature alive but
tranced and obscurely yearning to wake.

The sport of disembodied flight among the stars must surely be the
most exhilarating of all athletic exercises. It was not without danger;
but its danger, as we soon discovered, was psychological, not physical.
In our bodiless state, collision with celestial objects mattered
little. Sometimes, in the early stages of our adventure, we plunged
by accident headlong into a star. Its interior would, of course, be
inconceivably hot, but we experienced merely brilliance.

The psychological dangers of the sport were grave. We soon discovered
that disheartenment, mental fatigue, fear, all tended to reduce our powers of movement. More than once we found ourselves immobile in
space, like a derelict ship on the ocean; and such was the fear roused
by this plight that there was no possibility of moving till, having
experienced the whole gamut of despair, we passed through indifference and on into philosophic calm.

Though the pronoun "I" now applied to us all collectively, the pronoun
"we" also applied to us. In one respect, namely unity of consciousness,
we were indeed a single experiencing individual; yet at the same time we
were in a very important and delightful manner distinct from one another.

With unreasoning passion we strove constantly to peer behind each
minute particular event in the cosmos to see the very features of that
infinity which, for lack of a truer name, we had called the Star Maker.
But, peer as we might, we found nothing. Though in the whole and
in each particular thing the dread presence indubitably confronted
us, its very infinity prevented us from assigning to it any features
whatever.

"When the cosmos wakes, if ever she does, she will find herself not
the single beloved of her maker, but merely a little bubble adrift
on the boundless and bottomless ocean of being."

Almost certainly, the star's whole physical behaviour is normally
experienced as a blissful, an ecstatic, an ever successful pursuit of
formal beauty. This the minded worlds were able to discover through
their own most formalistic aesthetic experience. In fact it was
through this experience that they first made contact with stellar
mind.

We, or rather I, now experienced the slow drift of the galaxies much
as a man feels the swing of his own limbs. From my score of viewpoints I observed the great snowstorm of many million galaxies,
streaming and circling, and ever withdrawing farther apart from
one another with the relentless "expansion" of space. But though
the vastness of space was increasing in relation to the size of
galaxies and stars and worlds, to me, with my composite, scattered
body, space seemed no bigger than a great vaulted hall.

From all the coincident and punctual centres of power, light leapt and
blazed. The cosmos exploded, actualizing its potentiality of space and
time. The centres of power, like fragments of a bursting bomb, were
hurled apart. But each one retained in itself, as a memory and a longing,
the single spirit of the whole; and each mirrored in itself aspects of all
others throughout all the cosmical space and time.

I said, "It is enough, and far more than enough, to be the creature of so
dread and lovely a spirit, whose potency is infinite, whose nature passes
the comprehension even of a minded cosmos. It is enough to have been
created, to have embodied for a moment the infinite and tumultuously
creative spirit. It is infinitely more than enough to have been used, to
have been the rough sketch for some perfected creation."

The Atlas of The Universe

Sumptuous book. Accurate, well edited, well illustrated, well written. Does the job as no other book has, and a lot have tried.

Contents include exploration of space, atlas of the Earth, of the moon, of the solar system, and of the stars, along with a catalog of stellar objects, glossary of astronomical terms, and beginner's guide to the heavens.

—SB

The Atlas of The Universe
Patrick Moore
1970; 272 pp.

$35.00 postpaid

from:
Rand McNally & Company
P.O. Box 7600
Chicago, Illinois 60680

10 E. 53rd Street
New York, N.Y. 10022

206 Sansome Street
San Francisco, CA. 94105

or WHOLE EARTH CATALOG

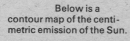

Below is a contour map of the centimetric emission of the Sun.

The Lagoon Nebula, M8 Sagittarii, is a typical emission nebula, 4850 light-years away. The "lagoon" is produced by the foreground dust-clouds. It is thought that the star producing the H-II region is of type O, and is so deeply embedded in the nebula that it cannot be observed. Globules have been detected, indicating that star formation is in process. The Lagoon is a dense nebula; there are 10^3 to 10^4 atoms per cubic centimeter in the central region—even though this density still corresponds to what we would normally term a laboratory vacuum.

Landing of Apollo 12 (above)
The lunar module Intrepid is seen descending toward the Oceanus Procellarum (19 November 1969). This photograph was taken from the command module. After Intrepid had returned to orbit, and had been abandoned, it was deliberately crashed on to the Moon setting up crustal vibrations which lasted for almost one hour.

The Galaxy *below*
The Galaxy, seen edge-on. The Sun is 30,000 light-years from the center of the system. The direction of the center is toward the rich star-clouds in the constellation of Sagittarius, but it cannot be seen through the obscuring intervening matter.

The Unexpected Universe

Loren Eiseley celebrates our grandest ignorances, the places in human experience where if you stare into them, the void stares back. City dumps; the open end of evolution; the unexplored continent in your mind; stars; a Pharaoh's dead gesture; edges of oceans. Strong useful prose from an old guy who knows something clear and bleak about regeneration.

—SB

The Unexpected Universe
Loren Eiseley
1969; 239 pp.

$5.75 postpaid

from:
Harcourt, Brace & Jovanovich, Inc.
757 Third Avenue
New York, N.Y. 10017

or WHOLE EARTH CATALOG

In the end the sea rejects its offspring. They cannot fight their way home through the surf which casts them repeatedly back upon the shore. The tiny breathing pores of starfish are stuffed with sand. The rising sun shrivels the mucilaginous bodies of the unprotected. The seabeach and its endless war are soundless. Nothing screams but the gulls. . . .

. . . The sun behind me was pressing upward at the horizon's rim—an ominous red glare amidst the tumbling blackness of the clouds. Ahead of me, over the projecting point, a gigantic rainbow of incredible perfection had sprung shimmering into existence. Somewhere toward its foot I discerned a human figure standing, as it seemed to me, within the rainbow, though unconscious of his position. He was gazing fixedly at something in the sand.

Eventually he stooped and flung the object beyond the breaking surf. I labored toward him over a half mile of uncertain footing. By the time I reached him the rainbow had receded ahead of us, but something of its color still ran hastily in many changing lights across his features. He was starting to kneel again.

In a pool of sand and silt a starfish had thrust its arms up stiffly and was holding its body away from the stifling mud.

"It's still alive," I ventured.

"Yes," he said, and with a quick yet gentle movement he picked up the star and spun it over my head and far out into the sea. It sank in a burst of spume, and the waters roared once more.

"It may live," he said, "if the offshore pull is strong enough." He spoke gently, and across his bronzed worn face the light still came and went in subtly altering colors.

"There are not many come this far," I said, groping in a sudden embarrassment for words. "Do you collect?"

"Only like this," he said softly, gesturing amidst the wreckage of the shore. "And only for the living." He stooped again, oblivious of my curiosity, and skipped another star neatly across the water.

"The stars," he said, "throw well. One can help them"

. . . It is as if at our backs, masked and demonic, moved the trickster as I have seen his role performed among the remnant of a savage people long ago. It was that of the jokester present at the most devout of ceremonies. This creature never laughed; he never made a sound. Painted in black, he followed silently behind the officiating priest, mimicking, with the added flourish of a little whip, the gestures of the devout one. His timed and stylized posturings conveyed a derision infinitely more formidable than actual laughter. . . .

We had been safe in the enchanted forest only because of our weakness. When the powers of that gloomy region were given to us, immediately, as in a witch's house, things began to fly about unbidden. The tools, if not science itself, were linked intangibly to the subconscious poltergeist aspect of man's nature. The closer man and the natural world drew together, the more erratic became the behavior of each. Huge shadows leaped triumphantly after every blinding illumination. It was a magnified but clearly recognizable version of the black trickster's antics behind the solemn backs of the priesthood. Here, there was one difference. The shadows had passed out of all human semblance; no societal ritual safely contained their posturings, as in the warning dance of the trickster. Instead, unseen by many because it was so gigantically real, the multiplied darkness threatened to submerge the carriers of the light.

. . . Out of the depths of a seemingly empty universe had grown an eye, like the eye in my room, but an eye on a vastly larger scale. It looked out upon what I can only call itself. It searched the skies and it searched the depths of being. In the shape of man it had ascended like a vaporous emanation from the depths of night. The nothing had miraculously gazed upon the nothing and was not content. It was an intrusion into, or a projection out of, nature for which no precedent existed. The act was, in short, an assertion of value arisen from the domain of absolute zero. A little whirlwind of commingling molecules had succeeded in confronting its own universe.

Here, at last, was the rift that lay beyond Darwin's tangled bank. . . .

I picked up a star whose tube feet ventured timidly among my fingers while, like a true star, it cried soundlessly for life. I saw it with an unaccustomed clarity and cast far out. With it, I flung myself as forfeit, for the first time, into some unknown dimension of existence.

Around me in the gloom dark shapes worked ceaselessly at the dampened fires. My eyes were growing accustomed to their light.

"We get it all," the dump philosopher repeated. "Just give it time to travel, we get it all."

Men, unknowingly, and whether for good or ill, appear to be making their last decisions about human destiny. To pursue the biological analogy, it is as though, instead of many adaptive organisms, a single gigantic animal embodied the only organic future of the world.

Every time we walk along a beach some ancient urge disturbs us so that we find ourselves shedding shoes and garments, or scavenging among seaweed and whitened timbers like the homesick refugees of a long war.

It was the failures who had always won, but by the time they won they had come to be called successes. This is the final paradox, which men call evolution.

The Character of Physical Law

If you look larger or smaller than the skinny realm of life, all you see is physics. It is our substratum and superstratum. These famous Feynman lectures introduce the subject as no other book has.

—SB [Suggested by Lyle Burkhead]

The Character of Physical Law
Richard Feynman
1965; 173 pp.

$2.45 postpaid

from:
M.I.T. Press
50 Ames Street, Room 765
Cambridge, Mass. 02142

or WHOLE EARTH CATALOG

○ Moon

water pulled partly away from earth by moon

earth pulled partly away from waters by moon

x ○ y

actual situation

The water at y is closer to the moon and the water at x is farther from the moon than the rigid earth. The water is pulled more towards the moon at y, and at x is less towards the moon than the earth, so there is a combination of those two pictures that makes a double tide.

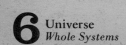

We do not realize what we have on Earth until we leave it.—JAMES M. LOVELL

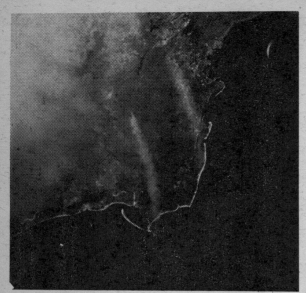

Figure 16 An infared photo of the Gulf coast showing two plumes of smoke from forest fires December 7, 1965

from *Ecological Survey From Space*

From an astronaut's vantage point, one can gaze down into the tremendously deep chasms of the Hindu Kush range in the Himalayas. The sky above the white crowns of snow on the peaks was clear when this photo was taken, but clouds filled the valleys. Temperatures as well as altitudes vary widely in this part of the world. When the morning Sun warms the highlands, fierce cold winds rush down the mountain sides to increase the rigors that men must endure to climb them.

from *This Island Earth*

NASA Earth Photo Books

You're too close. Back off and survey the big picture and old mysteries will clear up for you, and other mysteries will arrive (what is that enormous gyre in the Salton Sea?).

The earliest of the NASA color photo books, **Earth Photographs from Gemini III, IV, and V,** *and* **Earth Photographs from Gemini VI through XII,** *are the purest, least edited and evaluated. Hundreds of full page color photos of North Africa, the Himalayas, New Mexico, ocean cold fronts. If they were Sierra Club books, and they could be, they would cost $25 each. They cost $7 and $8.*

Exploring Space With a Camera *takes you up through Apollo 7, with good putting-it-all together text.* **Ecological Surveys From Space,** *still plenty beautiful, gets into big picture grit of how and where our systems affect each other. Invaluable information, which we're still learning how to interpret.* **This Island Earth.** *The most recent NASA book photographically places Earth in the Solar System.*

Among the discoveries in these books is that this lovely place is scarcely inhabited, and scarcely inhabitable.

—SB

Earth Photographs from Gemini III, IV, and V
NASA
1967; 266 pp.

$7.00 postpaid

Earth Photographs from Gemini VI through XII
NASA
1968; 327 pp. OUT OF PRINT

$8.00 postpaid

[Suggested by Steve Woodcock]

Exploring Space With a Camera
NASA SP-168   (1968 O-292-583)
1968; 214 pp.

$4.25 postpaid

Ecological Surveys From Space
NASA
1970; 75 pp.

$1.75 postpaid

[Suggested by Frank Rowsome, Jr.]

This Island Earth
NASA—SP250
1970;182 pp.

$6.00 postpaid

all from:
U.S. Govt. Printing Office Bookstore
710 North Capitol Street
Washington, D. C. 20402

U.S. Govt. Printing Office Bookstore
Rm. 1463, 14th Floor
Federal Office Building
219 S. Dearborn Street
Chicago, Illinois 60604

U.S. Govt. Printing Office Bookstore
Rm. 135, Federal Building
601 East 12th Street
Kansas City, Missouri 64106

U.S. Govt. Printing Office Bookstore
Federal Building
450 Golden Gate Avenue
Rm. 1023, Box 36104
San Francisco, California 94102

or WHOLE EARTH CATALOG

Full Earth

In November 1967 an ATS satellite whose funds phenomenally had not been cut made a home movie. It was a time lapse film of the Earth rotating, shot from 23,000 miles above South America. (This is synchronous distance. The satellite orbits at the same speed the Earth turns, so it remains apparently stationary over one point of the equator.) Color photographs of the Earth were transmitted by TV every ½ hour to make up a 24 hour sequence. The shots were lap dissolved together to make the movie. You see darkness, then a crescent of dawn, then advancing daylight and immense weather patterns whorling and creeping on the spherical surface, then the full round mandala Earth of noon, then gibbous afternoon, crescent twilight, and darkness again.

A 16mm 400-foot silent color print of the film includes several forms of the 24-hour cycle and close-up cropping of specific sectors as their weather develops through the day.

The film (NR 68 - 713) costs   **$48.94**

from:
National Audiovisual Center (NACT)
Nat'l Archives & Records Service (GSA)
Washington, D.C. 20408

Checks payable to the Nat'l Archives Trust Fund (NAC).
The price ($48.94) *includes Parcel Post shipping charges.*

Full Earth

Mandala Earth, the high noon color image shot from a synchronous satellite over South America in November 1967, is available as a poster from WHOLE EARTH CATALOG for $2 postpaid. It's 22" x 27". An order of five or more gets 50% discount.

—SB

Whole Earth Rising

Bigger and Better color Earth Posters than ours. Good ones are: Giant Earth *(shown below) and* Earth Over Moon.

—SB

OUT OF PRINT

The Biosphere

Our yard, the turning processes that keep it refreshed, and where balance is most fragile to our mistakes. This book was a single theme edition of Scientific American in 1970; it's well up-to-date.

—SB

The Biosphere
1970; 142 pp.

$3.25 postpaid

from:
W.H. Freeman and Company
660 Market Street
San Francisco, CA. 94104

or WHOLE EARTH CATALOG

Evolution fitted the new species together in ways that not only conserved energy and the mineral nutrients utilized in life processes but also conserved the nutrients by recycling them, releasing more oxygen and making possible the fixation of more energy and the support of still more life. Gradually each landscape developed a flora and fauna particularly adapted to that place. These new arrays of plants and animals used solar energy, mineral nutrients, water and the resources of other living things to stabilize the environment, building the biosphere we know today.

•

The available evidence suggests that, in spite of the much larger area of the oceans, by far the greater amount of energy is fixed on land. The oceans, even if their productivity can be preserved, do not represent a vast unexploited source of energy for support of larger human populations. They are currently being exploited at close to the maximum sustainable rate, and their continued use as a dump for wastes of all kinds makes it questionable whether that rate will be sustained.

•

Malnutrition, particularly protein deficiency, exacts an enormous toll from the physical and mental development of the young in the poorer countries. This was dramatically illustrated when India held tryouts in 1968 to select a team to represent it in the Olympic games that year. Not a single Indian athlete, male or female, met the minimum standards for qualifying to compete in any of the 36 track and field events in Mexico City. No doubt this was partly due to the lack of support for athletics in India, but poor nutrition was certainly also a large factor. The young people of Japan today are visible examples of what a change can be brought about by improvement in nutrition. Well-nourished from infancy, Japanese teen-agers are on the average some two inches taller than their elders.

•

This year the U.S. will consume some 685,000 million million B.T.U. of energy, most of it derived from fossil fuels. (One short ton of coal has a thermal value of 25.8 million B.T.U. The thermal value of one barrel of oil is 5.8 million B.T.U.) Industry takes more than 35 percent of the total energy consumption. About a third of industry's share is in the form of electricity, which, as of 1960, was generated roughly 50 percent from coal, 20 percent from water power, 20 percent from natural gas and 10 percent from oil.

Environment, Power, and Society

Beautiful work. Energy language is the simplifier we've lacked to see our systems whole. When the cosmic yum comes by, you get the ONE! all right, but that may not particularly help you work with connectedness. The terms and understandings in this book can.

Odum's point is that the macro-view of our energy systems must be clear to all of us——accurate grand images, adapted mores and laws, and responsive religions responsible to biospherical ethics——or however right in detail we shall be wrong big.

—SB

Environment, Power, and Society
Howard T. Odum
1971; 331 pp.

$5.95 postpaid

from:
John Wiley & Sons, Inc.,
605 Third Ave., New York, N.Y. 10016

or WHOLE EARTH CATALOG

ENVIRONMENT, POWER, AND SOCIETY

HOWARD T. ODUM

the Biosphere

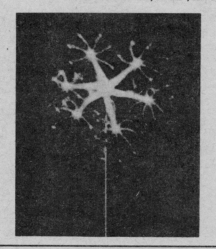

The nation's homes use almost as much energy as industry does. A major consumer is space heating, which for the average home requires as much energy as the average family car: about 70 million B.T.U. per year, or the equivalent of 900 gallons of oil. The other domestic uses are for cooking, heating water, lighting and air conditioning.

•

All together, in order to support one individual in our society, something like 25 tons of materials of all kinds must be extracted from the earth and processed each year. This quantity seems certain to increase considerably in the years ahead.

The earth's thin film of living matter is sustained by grand-scale cycles of energy and chemical elements. All of these cycles are presently affected by the activities of man

INTACT NATURAL ECOSYSTEM is exemplified by a mature oak-hickory forest that supports several stages of consumers in the grazing food chain, with from 10 to 20 percent of the energy in each trophic level being passed along to the next level. The symbols represent different herbivore and carnivore species. Complexity of structure regulates population sizes, maintaining the same pattern of energy distribution in the system from year to year.

DEGRADED ECOSYSTEM has a truncated grazing chain. The annual production of the sparse grasses, herbs and shrubs fluctuates (*shaded area*). So do populations of herbivores and carnivores, which are characterized by large numbers of individuals but few different species. Under extreme conditions most of the net production may be consumed, leading to the starvation of herbivores and accentuating the characteristic fluctuation in populations.

In this book energy language is used to consider the pressing problem of survival in our time——the partnership of man in nature. An effort is made to show that energy analysis can help answer many of the questions of economics, law, and religion, already stated in other languages. Models for the analysis of a system are made by recognizing major divisions whose causal relationships are indicated by the pathways of interchange of energy and work.

•

One self-stimulating principle of the primitive group was to allocate control of the energy flow of the group to individuals in proportion to the work they did to increase that flow. Such energy rewards took various forms, such as control of property, political power, and status influence. The economic system was simple, and economic reward often reflected the energy control gained.

•

How many persons know that the prosperity of some modern cultures stems from the great flux of oil fuel energies pouring through machinery and not from some necessary and virtuous properties of human dedication and political designs?

•

Bit by bit the machinery of the macroscope is evolving in various sciences and in the philosophic attitudes of students. The daily maps of worldwide weather, the information received from the high-flying satellites, the macroeconomic statistical summaries of nations and the world, the combined efforts of international geophysical collaborations, and the radioactive studies of cycling chemicals in the great oceans all stimulate the new view. Whereas men used to search among the parts to find mechanistic explanations, the macroscopic view is the reverse. Men, already having a clear view of the parts in their fantastically complex detail, must somehow get away, rise above, step back, group parts, simplify concepts, interpose frosted glass, and thus somehow see the big patterns.

•

With the turning of the earth, the sun comes up on fields, forests, and fjords of the biosphere, and everywhere within the light there is a great breath as tons upon tons of oxygen are released from the living photochemical surfaces of green plants which are becoming charged with food storages by the onrush of solar photons.

•

The system of man has consumption in excess of production. The products of respiration——carbon dioxide, metabolic water, and mineralized inorganic wastes——are discharged in rates in excess of their incorporation into organic matter by photosynthesis. If the industrialized urban system were enclosed in a chamber with only the air above it at the time, it would quickly exhaust its oxygen, be stifled with waste, and destroy itself since it does not have the recycling pattern of the agrarian system. The problems with life support in 1970 on the space flight of Apollo 13 dramatized this principle to the world.

•

The biosphere with industrial man suddenly added is like a balanced aquarium into which large animals are introduced. Consumption temporarily exceeds production, the balance is upset, the products of respiration accumulate, and the fuels for consumption become scarcer and scarcer until production is sufficiently accelerated and respiration is balanced. In some experimental systems balance is achieved only after the large consumers which originally started the imbalance are dead.

DARWIN-LOTKA ENERGY LAW

Thus, whenever it is necessary to transform and restore the greatest amount of energy at the fastest possible rate, 50 percent of it must go into the drain. Nature and man both have energy storages as part of their operations and when power storage is important, it is maximized by adjusting loads. . . .In the last century Darwin popularized the concept of *natural selection,* and early in this century Lotka indicated that the maximization of power for useful purposes was the criterion for natural selection. Darwin's evolutionary law thus developed into a general energy law.

Money flows in the opposite direction to the flow of energy and the concept of price which operates among human bargains adjusts one flow to be in proportion to the other. Thus a man purchasing groceries at a store receives groceries in one direction while paying money in the opposite direction. The heat losses of these transactions are small since the work involved is small.

LOOP SELECTION PRINCIPLE

In ecological studies there is the positive feedback loop through which a downstream recipient of potential energy rewards its source by passing necessary materials back to it. For example, the animals in a balanced system feed back to the plants in reward loops the phosphates, nitrates, and other compounds required for their growth. A plant that has a food chain which regenerates nutrients in the form it needs is therefore reinforced, and both plant and animal continue to survive. Species whose work efforts are not reinforced are shortly eliminated, for they run out of either raw materials or energy. They must be connected to input and output flows to survive.

Stability allows complex diversity and uniqueness of individuals. As in Augustinian Rome, there may be golden eras—if men can be satisfied with small causes, for energies big enough for new causes would have to be diverted from older endeavors. This in turn requires a willingness to discard activities.

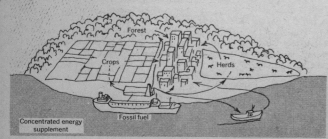

1000 kilocalories
concentrated fossil
fuel energy

4000 kilocalories
sunlight

Man's activity

Caloric food

Sea
Forest
Field crops
Range grass

Fish
Herds

Energy flow per
square meter
per day

5000 calories
heat energy

Forest
Crops
Herds
Concentrated energy
supplement
Fossil fuel

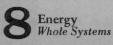

Man's Domain

I scarcely believe it. An inexpensive, paperback, lightweight but complete World Atlas that skips all the political planetary persiflage and goes straight to the guts: climate, minerals, agriculture, population, languages, land forms, ocean forms.— all the remorseless factors that have been invisible to most of humanity until recently. Nice work, McGraw-Hill, you whipped Rand-McNally and Hammond at their own game. —SB

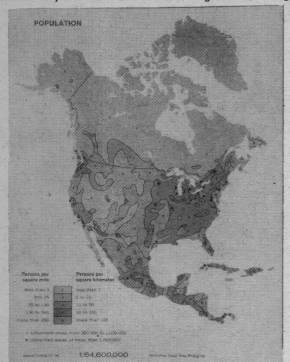

POPULATION

Man's Domain
General Drafting Co.
1968; 75 pp.

$3.95 postpaid

from:
McGraw-Hill Book Co.
Princeton Road
Hightstown, N. J. 08520

Manchester Road
Manchester, Mo. 63062

8171 Redwood Highway
Novato, CA 94947

or WHOLE EARTH CATALOG

The Times Atlas of the World

'A world remade must be a world remapped.' That intelligent dictum was issued at the end of World War I by Lord Northcliffe, then proprietor of The Times of London. He didn't wait for someone else to do the job; The Times Survey Atlas of the World, with cartography by John Bartholomew of Edinburgh, was issued in 1921, and was recognized immediately as one of the finest atlases ever printed. The tradition has been continued, and the latest Times Atlas——the Comprehensive Edition——is the best place for an English-reading person to find where in the world something is located. The book also has a unique ability to convey the feel of the world. It measures 18'' x 12½'' x 2'', weighs 11 pounds, and contains 468 pages, of which 240 are double-page maps of superb accuracy and beauty. The index-gazetteer includes more than 200,000 entries, incomparably more than any other atlas of the world, and the entries are keyed not only by individual map coordinates, but by latitude and longitude as well (a feature offered by no other atlas). Despite the huge number of place names the maps are extraordinarily legible, and they are mercifully free of the pink-purple-yellow political emphasis offered by lesser cartographers. Some of the place names may look strange to American readers, because the atlas follows the rules of the Permanent Committee of Geographical Names. This supra-political body sensibly believes that places should be called what their occupants call them. In cases where the generic name is unfamiliar, the traditional anglicized name is also given, in parentheses.

The Comprehensive Edition of The Times Atlas of the World is published in the United States by Houghton Mifflin Company, Boston, Massachusetts. It is dedicated, by gracious permission, to Her Majesty Queen Elizabeth II, and bound in appropriately regal bright red linen, gold-stamped. It costs $29.95, and it will make anything else on your coffee table seem puny, as the whole world should.

[Suggested and reviewed by
Dr. Morton Grosser]

Times Atlas of the World
Comprehensive 1 Vol. Edition
1968; 568 pp.

$29.95 postpaid

from:
Quadrangle Books Inc.
10 East 53rd Street
New York, N.Y. 10022

or WHOLE EARTH CATALOG

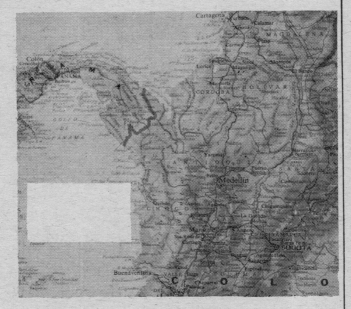

Human Use of the Earth

To get a handle on your future you've got to get outside yourself, because only from outside can you see your space-time environment whole. One way is to identify out into another culture, Indian or whatever (this is Jim Nixon's idea). Another way is to take Philip Wagner's trip into fascinated objectivity about Earthly doings. In this book he merges some of the best of geographical and anthropological perspective into a detailed treatise on the Earth as tool, how it is used and how to understand it better to use it better. —SB

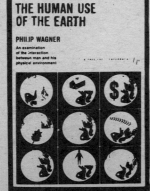

THE HUMAN USE OF THE EARTH

PHILIP WAGNER

An examination of the interaction between man and his physical environment

The Human Use of the Earth
Philip Wagner
1960; 270 pp.

$2.45 postpaid

from:
Free Press
Macmillan Company
Front and Brown Streets
Riverside, N. J. 08075

or WHOLE EARTH CATALOG

As we shall see, one of the strategies by which supplies of goods and services become available for actual use is the movement of the would-be consumers themselves to the sources of goods or services. There are even objects that act as containers of man himself, which move over land, across water or through the air, delivering the individual to the places at which he can obtain goods he desires, or where he will be served as he wishes.

The modern inhabitant of a commercial country does not make his world; he buys it. The material circumstances of his life are not the outcome of his individual encounter with the natural order, but arise out of his relations with the social order.

Those same features of the most complex human communities which indicate their ecological advantages also suggest an unusual degree of inherent ecological risk. Such communities are complex and delicately balanced, and depend utterly upon their artificiality. They and the individuals in them are threatened by the same biological penalties that attend any highly specialize system or species. Their very technical perfection may destroy them in time as other high specializations have destroyed many former species of animals and plants.

The individual organism must, on the one hand, be specialized enough in function to exploit some particular conditions in the habitat, so as to occupy a niche that no other organism can contest with it; and it must, on the other hand, possess enough versatility to adapt to any conditions of environment that may impinge upon its life activities. These two requirements may be thought of as polar extremes of a continuous scale, and every species may be placed somewhere along the scale between specialization and versatility. Some of the disadvantages of commitment to either specialization or versatility are overcome by aggregation of organisms into larger groups within the community.

Divine Right's Trip

Our story thus far

by Gurney Norman

PART ONE

DIVINE RIGHT'S BUS, URGE

I was a fairly straight '63 VW microbus till Divine Right got me, a good clean red and white seven passenger job with five new re-capped tires and near perfect upholstery. The only bad thing that ever happened to me was the Muncy's youngest kid use to puke on my seats all the time. The Muncys bought me new in Germany when the old man was stationed over there in the army. He was a Master Sergeant in an infantry outfit, a little old for that kind of work maybe, but he liked it well enough to volunteer for Vietnam when that war heated up. They brought me to the States when the sergeant went to Vietnam, and after he got blown up by a land mine, his wife Marie traded me in on a Falcon.

Two days on a car lot is a long time when you're not used to it. It was hot and damn boring, so even though this guy Divine Right looked pretty weird, I was so eager to get on the road again I felt grateful to him for buying me, although it did piss me off when the dealer let me go for only five hundred and fifty dollars. Divine Right paid the man with cash he'd got from a big grass score that morning, and if I could whistle I'd have whistled when we drove away together.

Which goes to show you how much I knew about freaks in those days. I hadn't gone five hundred miles with that son of a bitch before I'd of given my fuel pump to be back on that parking lot. That bastard drove me from Boston to Chicago to St. Louis to Cincinnati without once checking my oil. I found out later he didn't even know where my damn oilstick *was*. Drove non-stop too, all day, all night, the only time I got even a little rest was when he'd slow down long enough to refuel or buy a rat-burger. If his brother-in-law in Cincinnati hadn't noticed I was a quart and a half low I'd probably have thrown a rod as soon as we hit the next freeway.

D.R. doesn't seem to like them much, but his sister and brother-in-law are nice people. Doyle understands about cars. He's a mechanic, he knows how to take care of machines. He tried to tell D.R. about preventive maintenance, but D.R. was too stoned to pay attention. He was on speed that trip, out of his skull on ritilin and benzedrine. He told Doyle he had to split in order to make the Ultimate Rendezvous. Doyle said what's an Ultimate Rendezvous? But D.R. just grinned and started my motor and drove away.

So you get some idea of where D.R.'s head was at. He was the kind of guy who never had the faintest idea how he affected things. He could fuck over a nice '63 VW microbus he'd just paid five hundred and fifty dollars for and never blink an eye. I don't know what was the most humiliating, having my working parts ignored, or all that stupid paint sprayed all over my body. Inside and out-side, I suffered both places. It's one thing to go around feeling bad because you're low on oil; but when you have to *look* like a made-up whore it gets to be a bit much. Housepaint, Day-Glo, fingernail polish, you name it and I got smeared with it. Some-times he'd pull off into the emergency lane of some big inter-state and start painting on the spot. Said God was sending him directions how to do it. Sometimes he'd pick up hitch-hikers and tell them to lean out the window and paint while he drove. By the time him and his weird friends got through I looked like a watercolor that got rained on. It was awful.

But I survived. I don't know how but I did. Well, yes I do know too. It was Estelle. There's no doubt about it, that little lady saved my ass from the junkyard. She was one nice person, that Estelle. There was something kind of sad about her, it seemed like she cried a lot. But she sure knew how to be nice to an old broken-down bus. She'd wash me, and empty my ash trays. Sometimes D.R. would be too stoned to drive and Estelle would take over, and it would just be so fine, just me and her cruising quietly across the country through the night. That was the thing about Estelle. She understood cruising, she understood roads, and traffic, she knew how to flow with things in motion. I never did understand what she saw in D.R., but I guess it's not my place to have opinions about people. My job was to carry them around from place to place while they acted out their story, and although I resented it most of the time I did my best. It was painful, but I do have to say that it was interesting, and instructive. On some level I'm sure I'm a better bus for it. I kind of wish I could have a voice in this narrative to tell my side of the story, but Gurney says there's too many points of view already to clutter it up even more with a talking car. So this is the only chance I'll have to speak my mind. It ain't much, but, when you've been down as long as I have, you get grateful for small favors. So goodbye. If you're ever rambling around down in the Kentucky mountains, come by and see me sometime.

Bless you all.
Urge

Geology Illustrated

An artist of aerial photography, Shelton uses some 400 of his finest photos to illuminate a discussion of the whole-earth system. Not a traditional textbook, but a fascinating exploration of the problems posed by asking "How did that come about?" Worth buying for the photos and book design alone, but you'll probably find yourself becoming interested in geology regardless of your original intentions.

[Reviewed by Larry McCombs]

As a means of communicating geological concepts, the pictures are fully as important as the words that accompany them. On most pages the photographs represent the facts, the words supply the interpretation. Many of the illustrations will, therefore, repay a little of the kind of attention that would be accorded the real feature in the field. In keeping with this, almost no identifying marks have been placed on the photographs and very few on the drawings. The text (which almost invariably concerns an illustration on the same or a facing page) serves as an expanded legend for the picture; if, while reading it, it is necessary to look more than once to identify some feature with certainty, this is no more than Nature asks of those who contemplate her unlabelled cliffs and hills.

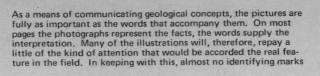

Surface Anatomy

This book is included as a companion piece to the Earth picture books. The whole lovely system of the human creature, seen from without, surface by surface, is here. One of its main revelations is how cliché ridden our usual views of ourselves are—we are still not good with mirrors (satellites were up 10 years before we got a full view of the Earth). Posing friends and neighbors, with a simple light set-up and a 35mm camera, Joseph Royce has shot the most beautiful human album I know.

It also teaches anatomy.

—SB

Geology Illustrated
John S. Shelton
1966; 434 pp.

$12.95 postpaid

from:
W. H. Freeman & Co.
660 Market Street
San Francisco, CA 94104

or WHOLE
EARTH
CATALOG

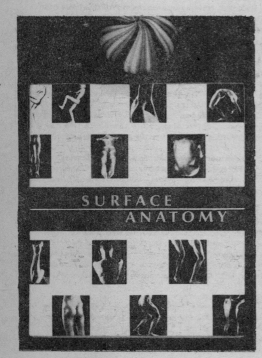

Surface Anatomy
Joseph Royce
1965; 124 photographs
and some diagrams

$12.50 postpaid

Now also in paperpack

$5.00

from:
F. A. Davis Company
1915 Arch Street
Philadelphia, PA. 19103

or WHOLE
EARTH
CATALOG

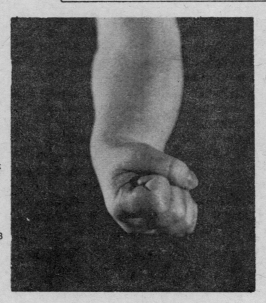

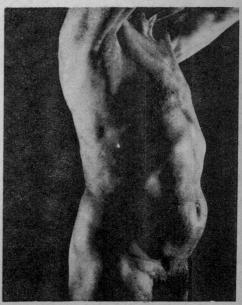

The World from Above

Close-up glamor shots of the Earth. Mystery shots (What is that? What's our altitude above it, 10 feet or 10,000?) (Fold out captions tell all.) Good traffic flow pattern shots: surface anatomy of civilization. Not a bad compendium; it'll do until they reprint E. A. Gutkind's Our World From the Air.

—SB

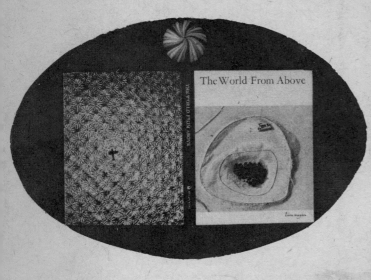

The World from Above
Hanns Reich
1966; 88 pictures

$8.50 postpaid

from:
Hill and Wang, Inc.
141 Fifth Avenue
New York, N. Y. 10010

or WHOLE EARTH CATALOG

Cloud Studies in Colour

If you really don't know clouds at all, there's another side—namely recognition and knowing what's going on in your part of the atmosphere. This lovely book of color photos and detailed descriptions can help.

—SB

Cloud Studies in Colour
Richard Scorer and Harry Wexler
1967; 44 pp. #11710-4

$10.00 postpaid

from:
Pergamon Press Inc.
Maxwell House
Fairview Park
Elmsford, N.Y. 10523

or WHOLE EARTH CATALOG

Kalliroscope

Nine square inches of divine turmoil. Rotating on its spinner or cooking on its stand, the Kalliroscope models the action on the surface of the Earth and in all the waves and fires and (probably) in your head.   —SB

Last 400 Kalliroscopes available by mail for $15; in Coral, Plum, Pearl, Red, Jade and Sea Green. Also four new flexible Kalliroscopes which sell for $3 each, more for playing with but show true currents and are not entirely without serious intent.

from:
Paul Matisse
Kalliroscope Corporation
145 Main Street
Cambridge, Mass. 02142

or WHOLE EARTH CATALOG

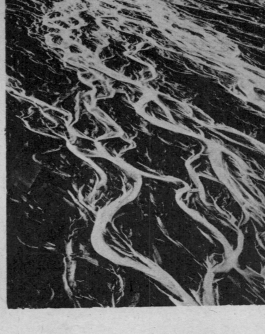

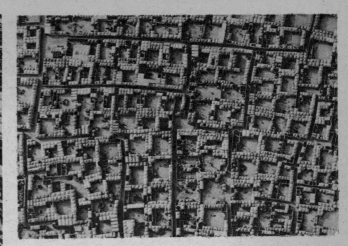

ST. GEORGE AND THE DRAGON

Here comes D.R. Davenport, Divine Right he calls himself after that incredible stoned-out afternoon when the words Divine Right formed in the clouds above the meadow where he was lying in the grass looking up and breathing deeply in awe of how really simple everything is when you come right down to it; Divine Right he calls himself, D.R. for short, driving along the highway now through a dark and rainy night in his VW microbus, Urge.

When all of a sudden Urge's headlights pick up a hitch-hiking freak on the road ahead.

I sure don't want to pick that guy up, D.R. told himself. I wish I didn't have to. He was into a radio talk show out of Los Angeles. This strange woman had called in to comment on dress styles and wound up on the Turner thesis and the American westward movement. D.R. was listening to her rap, even talking back from time to time, shaking his finger, agreeing and disagreeing, (but not too loudly; Estelle was asleep in the back of the bus somewhere and he didn't want to disturb her). Estelle was another reason not to pick the freak up but, out there the poor fucker was, sitting on his backpack holding out his thumb, with a little black dog huddled against his feet. So. D.R. dimmed the headlights and turned the radio down and pulled off the road just past where the guy was sitting.

"Get in," said Divine Right. "We're just, you know, rolling along, digging it, the windshield wipers, rain on the roof, this weird westward movement lady's on the radio, how far you going, how long you been sitting out there?"

The hitch-hiker hassled his gear in and stuffed it on the floor. He was a little old feller, just barely strong enough to lift his pack inside. But finally he managed it, and his dog Salvadore leaped in behind him. Salvadore didn't even bother to sniff out his new scene. He just curled up on the floor next to the emergency brake and lay completely still.

D.R. said, "Davenport's my name, Divine Right Davenport. Like, this radio guy says KCBR, sort of sings it you know, says KCBR, Wayne Dixon here may I have your name please? And I say Divine Right is my name and weirdness is my game, what's yours?"

Meaning, of course, his passenger, who was pissing D.R. off just sitting there. D.R. was a word man, you see, he liked to talk and to be talked to, and thirty seconds into their ride together his passenger hadn't said a thing. All he did was nod and grin and look at the wet highway stretching out in the long beams of light up ahead. After a mile or two D.R. was wishing he'd minded his own business and left the silent bastard sitting by the roadside, rain or no rain.

He turned the radio back up.

" . . . all I mean is that genocide against the Indians was the official policy of every American President after Andrew Jackson."

The announcer was aghast. "Are you saying our government had a policy . . . "

"Absolutely. It's a well known, I mean you're in radio, it's common knowledge among informed people."

"It's common rumor, maybe . . . "

"Rumor, hell," D.R. said. "The lady's right. Every word she says is true." He turned the radio down then and leaned across to stare at his passenger. "And I'll bet if you'd say something, it'd turn out to be true too, I know it would."

When the hitch-hiker didn't answer, D.R. started slowing down. "What I want to know, fuckhead, is how you're gonna keep dry when I dump your ass out in the rain about half a mile from now."

And when there was still no reply, D.R. brought Urge to a full stop, and leaned across again to look his passenger full in the face. He was surprised to see how young the freak was. Fifteen, sixteen at the most. D.R. was only twenty one himself, but the kid made him feel like an old man. He had a goatee of scraggly whiskers, twenty three long blonde hairs sticking out of various little blotches on his skin. His eyes were pale blue, streaked with red.

"Far out," said Divine Right. "Did you know you had red, white and blue eyes?"

No longer smiling, the kid opened the door and got out in the rain. He left his pup on the floor while he got his pack on, and settled his floppy, widebrim hat back on his head. Finally he was ready. As he reached in to get his dog he looked up at D.R. and said, "Did you ever read about St. George and the Dragon?"

D. R. said he hadn't.

"It's far out shit," said the kid. And he closed the door and started walking down the highway toward where ever they'd just come from.

Laws of Form

The laws of form have finally been written! With a "Spencer Brown" transistorized power razor (a Twentieth Century model of Occam's razor). G. Spencer Brown cuts smoothly through two millennia of growth of the most prolific and persistent of semantic weeds, presenting us with his superbly written **Laws of Form.** *This Herculean task which now, in retrospect, is of profound simplicity rests on his discovery of the form of laws. Laws are not descriptions, they are commands, injunctions: "Do!" Thus, the first constructive proposition in this book (page 3) is the injunction: "Draw a distinction!" an exhortation to perform the primordial creative act.*

After this, practically everything else follows smoothly: a rigorous foundation of arithmetic, of algebra, of logic, of a calculus of indications, intentions and desires; a rigorous development of laws of form, may they be of logical relations, of descriptions of the universe by physicists and cosmologists, or of functions of the nervous system which generates descriptions of the universe of which it is itself a part.

*The ancient and primary mystery which still puzzled Ludwig Wittgenstein (***Tractatus Logico-Philosophicus***, A. J. Ayer (ed), Humanities Press, New York, 1961, 166 pp.), namely that the world we know is constructed in such a way as to be able to see itself, G. Spencer Brown resolves by a most surprising turn of perception. He shows, once and for all, that the appearance of this mystery is unavoidable. But what is unavoidable is, in one sense, no mystery. The fate of all descriptions is ". . . what is revealed will be concealed, but what is concealed will again be revealed."*

At this point, even the most faithful reader may turn suspicious: how can the conception of such a simple injunction as "Draw a distinction!" produce this wealth of insights? It is indeed amazing——but, in fact, it does.

*The clue to all this is Spencer Brown's ingenious choice for the notation of an operator ⏋ which does several things at one time. This mark is a token for drawing a distinction, say, by drawing a circle on a sheet of paper which creates a distinction between points inside and outside of this circle; by its asymmetry (the concave side being its inside) it provides the possibility of indication; finally, it stands for an instruction to cross the boundary of the first distinction by crossing from the state indicated on the inside of the token to the state indicated by the token (A space with no token indicates the unmarked state). Moreover, these operations may operate on each other, generating a primary arithmetic, an opportunity which is denied us by a faulty notation in conventional arithmetic as pointed out by Karl Menger in "Gulliver in the Land without One, Two, Three" (***The Mathematical Gazette***, 53, 24-250; 1959).*

These operations are defined in the two axioms (no other ones are needed) given on pages 1 and 2. They are:

Axiom 1. The law of calling

The value of a call made again is the value of the call.

That is to say, if a name is called and then is called again, the value indicated by the two calls taken together is the value indicated by one of them.

That is to say, for any name, to recall is to call.

(In notation:

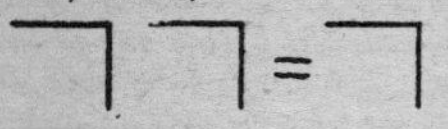

the "form of condensation".)

Axiom 2. The law of crossing

The value of a crossing made again is not the value of the crossing.

That is to say, if it is intended to cross a boundary and then it is intended to cross it again, the value indicated by the two intentions taken together is the value indicated by none of them.

That is to say, for any boundary, to recross is not to cross.

(In notation:

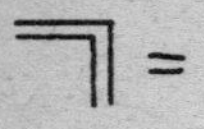

the "form of cancellation".)

For instance, take a complex expression

E = 

Then, by the two axioms

E =

In the beginning this calculus is developed for finite expressions only (involving a finite number of ⏋), simply because otherwise any demonstration would take an infinite number of steps, hence would never be accomplished. However, in Chapter 11, Spencer Brown tackles the problem of infinite expressions by allowing an expression to re-enter its own space. This calls for trouble, and one anticipates now the emergence of antinomies. Not so! In his notation the classical clash between a simultaneous Nay and Yea never occurs, the system becomes "bi-stable", flipping from one to the other of the two values as a consequence of previous values, and thus generates time! Amongst the many gems in this book, this may turn out to be the shiniest.

Sometimes the reading gets rough because of Spencer Brown's remarkable gift for parsimony of expression. But the 30 pages of "Notes" following the 12 Chapters of presentation come to the reader's rescue precisely at that moment when he lost his orientation in the lattice of a complex crystal. Consequently, it is advisable to read them almost in parallel with the text, if one can suppress the urge to keep on reading Notes.

In an introductory note Spencer Brown justifies the mathematical approach he has taken in this book: "Unlike more superficial forms of expertise, mathematics is a way of saying less and less about more and more." If this strategy is pushed to its limit, we shall be able to say nothing about all. This is, of course, the state of ultimate wisdom and provides a nucleus for a calculus of love, where distinctions are suspended and all is one. Spencer Brown has made a major step in this direction, and his book should be in the hands of all young people——no lower age limit required.

[Reviewed by Heinz Von Foerster.
Suggested by Steve Baer]

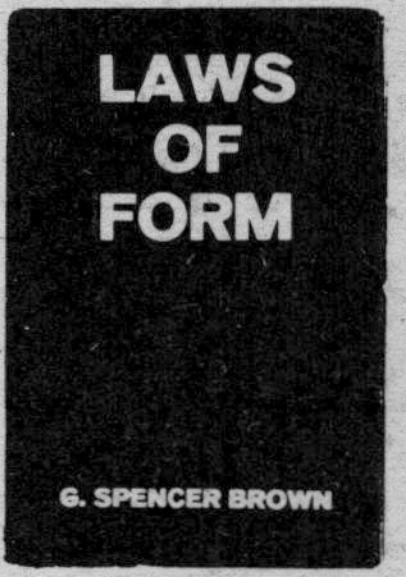

Laws of Form
G. Spencer Brown
1969; 141 pp.

$2.25 postpaid

Bantam Books
666 Fifth Avenue
New York, N.Y. 10019

or WHOLE EARTH CATALOG

無名天地之始

CONSTRUCTION
Draw a distinction.

CONTENT
Call it the first distinction.
Call the space in which it is drawn the space severed or cloven by the distinction.
Call the parts of the space shaped by the severance or cleft the sides of the distinction or, alternatively, the spaces, states, or contents distinguished by the distinction.

INTENT
Let any mark, token, or sign be taken in any way with or with regard to the distinction as a signal.
Call the use of any signal its intent.

•

In all mathematics it becomes apparent, at some stage, that we have for some time been following a rule without being consciously aware of the fact. This might be described as the use of a *covert* convention. A recognizable aspect of the advancement of mathematics consists in the advancement of the consciousness of what we are doing, whereby the covert becomes overt. Mathematics is in this respect psychedelic.

•

One of the most beautiful facts emerging from mathematical studies is this very potent relationship between the mathematical process and ordinary language. There seems to be no mathematical idea of any importance or profundity that is not mirrored, with an almost uncanny accuracy, in the common use of words, and this appears especially true when we consider words in their original, and sometimes long forgotten, senses.

•

The main difficulty in translating from the written to the verbal form comes from the fact that in mathematical writing we are free to mark the two dimensions of the plane, whereas in speech we can mark only the one dimension of time.

Much that is unnecessary and obstructive in mathematics today appears to be vestigial of this limitation of the spoken word.

•

Any evenly subverted equation of the second degree might be called, alternatively, evenly informed. We can see it over a subversion (turning under) of the surface upon which it is written, or alternatively, as an in-formation (formation within) of what it expresses.

Such an expression is thus informed in the sense of having its own form within it, and at the same time informed in the sense of remembering what has happened to it in the past.

We need not suppose that this is exactly how memory happens in an animal, but there are certainly memories, so-called, constructed this way in electronic computers, and engineers have constructed such in-formed memories with magnetic relays for the greater part of the present century.

We may perhaps look upon such memory, in this simplified information, as a precursor of the more complicated and varied forms of memory and information in man and the higher animals. We can also regard other manifestations of the classical forms of physical or biological science in the same spirit.

•

There is a tendency, especially today, to regard existence as the source of reality, and thus as a central concept. But as soon as it is formally examined (cf Appendix 2), existence [*ex* = out, *stare* = stand. Thus to exist may be considered as to stand outside, to be exiled.] is seen to be highly peripheral and, as such, especially corrupt (in the formal sense) and vulnerable. The concept of truth is more central, although still recognizably peripheral. If the weakness of present-day science is that it centres round existence, the weakness of present-day logic is that it centres round truth.

Throughout the essay, we find no need fo the concept of truth, apart from two avoidable appearances (true = open to proof) in the descriptive context. At no point, to say the least, is it a necessary inhabitant of the calculating forms. These forms are thus not only precursors of existence, they are also precursors of truth.

It is, I am afraid, the intellectual block which most of us come up against at the points where, to experience the world clearly, we must abandon existence to truth, truth to indication, indication to form, and form to void, that has so held up the development of logic and its mathematics.

•

Tao Teh King

Reviewing the **Tao** *is like reviewing the* **Bible.** *As soon as you presume, it just giggles and rains on you. Nevermind.*

The **Tao Teh King** *is a very old book (500 B.C. is one date) written by a legend named Lao Tzu. It describes how the universe is and makes an excellent case for harmony as the only survival technique that works. This translation by Archie Bahm is straightforward.*

[Suggested by Jack Loeffler]

Tao Teh King
Lao Tzu; Archie Bahm
? B.C., 1958; 126 pp.

$1.95 postpaid

from:
Frederick Ungar Publishing Co
250 Park Avenue South
New York, N. Y. 10003

or WHOLE EARTH CATALOG

Everyone says: "Nature is great, yet Nature is simple."

It is great because it is simple.

If it were not simple, long ago it would have come to little.

Nature sustains itself through three precious principles, which one does well to embrace and follow.

These are gentleness, frugality and humility.

When one is gentle, he has no fear of retaliation.

When one is frugal, he can afford to be generous.

When one is humble, no one challenges his leadership.

But when rudeness replaces gentleness,

And extravagance replaces frugality,

And pride replaces humility,

Then one is doomed.

Since a gentle attack arouses little antagonism,

And a gentle defense provokes little anger,

Nature predisposes to gentleness those most suited for survival.

•

Intelligent control appears as uncontrol or freedom.

And for that reason it is genuinely intelligent control.

Unintelligent control appears as external domination.

And for that reason it is really unintelligent control.

Intelligent control exerts influence without appearing to do so.

Unintelligent control tries to influence by making a show of force.

•

It is because we single out something and treat it as distinct from other things that we get the idea of its opposite. Beauty, for example, once distinguished, suggests its opposite, ugliness.

And Goodness, when we think of it, is naturally opposed to badness.

In fact, all distinctions naturally appear as opposites. And opposites get their meaning from each other and find their completion only through each other. The meanings of "is" and "is not" arise from our distinguishing between them.

Likewise, "difficult and easy," "long and short," "high and low," "loud and soft," "before and after"—all derive their meanings from each other.

Therefore the intelligent man accepts what is as it is. In seeking to grasp what is, he does not devote himself to the making of distinctions which are then mistaken to be separate existences.

In teaching, he teaches, not by describing and pointing out differences, but by example.

Whatever is exists, and he sees that nothing is gained by representing what fully exists by a description—another lesser, diluted kind of existence.

If something exists which cannot be wholly revealed to him with his viewpoint, he does not demand of it that it be nothing but what it seems to him.

If some one else interprets him, he does not trust that interpretation as being equal to his existence.

If some part of him stands out as if a superior representative of his nature, he will not surrender the rest of his nature to it.

And in not surrendering the whole of his nature to any part of it, he keeps himself intact.

This is how the intelligent man preserves his nature.

We cannot escape the fact that the world we know is constructed in order (and thus in such a way as to be able) to see itself.

This is indeed amazing.

Not so much in view of what it sees, although this may appear fantastic enough, but in respect of the fact that it *can* see *at all*.

But *in order* to do so, evidently it must first cut itself up into at least one state which sees, and at least one other state which is seen. In this severed and mutilated condition, whatever it sees is *only partially itself*. We may take it that the world undoubtedly is itself (i.e. is indistinct from itself), but, in any attempt to see itself as an object, it must, equally undoubtedly, act so as to make itself distinct from, and therefore false to, itself. In this condition it will always partially elude itself.

•

To *explain*, literally to lay *out* in a *plane* where particulars can be readily seen. Thus to *place* or *plan* in *flat* land, sacrificing other dimensions for the sake of appearance. Thus to *expound* or *put out* at the cost of ignoring the *reality* or *richness* of what is so put out. Thus to take a view away from its *prime reality* or *royalty*, or to gain knowledge and lose the kingdom.

Report From Gurney's Organic Garden

Part Two: Reward

From the outset I was determined to avoid relating to the garden abstractly, in terms of "poetry," or "ideas." My usual tendency is to reduce my experience to metaphors, then render the metaphors in words, and I wanted to beat that rap this time. Food, chewed and swallowed, was what the garden was all about, and nothing less than that was going to satisfy. I wanted the experience to come alive outside my head, in the concrete world, and achieving that of course was the prime reward.

But the thing I'm pleased to discover, now that the garden is a fact, is that I'm not as nervous as I was about abstractions. Abstractions built out of other abstractions can lead to actual sickness, I believe. But abstraction derived from the concrete is like the other side of the coin, yin and yang. It feels good to talk about gardening, now that the work is done. Feels the best in a long time, in fact. Like dessert, after a good meal. It's amazing what a little honest, sweat-producing work can do for a nervous head.

So stuff has been occuring to me: talk, for instance. The difference in the quality of talk that grows out of true experience, against talk that grows only out of other talk. Talk among people who never do anything but talk, vs. words between people who have other things to do with themselves. Drawing room conversation dependent on other drawing rooms, against conversation among people who've just come in from the world. Political opinions based on other people's political opinoins, against a politics growing from the life you've personally lived. It's all like the difference between a wax apple, and one just dropped off a tree.

And this: rules. How we've all gone around crazy the past few years in revolution against rules because they are rules; discovering some rules that are bad, deciding all rules must be bad, so what the world needs is anarchy. Head filled with such cheap crap, then coming up against something like a garden, entering into the work of it as if: this is my scene; I decide the processes of this garden because I'm a free man and I'm going to do my thing. So you thing is to spray water around. "Express" yourself in water. It's so... esthetic. The curve of the spray is so... poetic. It's a veritable art form, no less, the avant-garde of agriculture. Jackson Pollock with a green thumb. Spray here, spray there, spray all over God's whole creation cause I'm going to do my thing.

Well, do tell. Because what's happening, the reason all those beans and tomatoes and carrots are, like drooping a little is that you've damned near drowned the things. And so you learn: the gardener doesn't make up the terms of his relationship to the garden. He doesn't invent them out of his precious head, change them around according to his petty whim. The terms exist before he gets there and they'll still exist long after he has gone. It's like the plants are saying: "Give us none of your hip esoteric shit; we want water, and we want it in precise amounts, according to the varying root systems of each plant. We want fertilizer, and if you don't know how much, find out. Find out about nitrogen, about phosphorus, about potash. For if you expect anything from this garden, you must know what the garden expects of you. There's a reality among these rows, stuff is going on bigger than all of us, so dig it. You are only a part of what is happening here. Fit yourself into the scheme. Abide by the law, and maybe you'll be pleased that you did."

Then this: pick up a radical newspaper, see a picture of the entrance to an Army post. Fort Dix, probably. And above the gate and the M.P.'s helmets is a sign that reads: "Obedience to the law is freedom." It's one of the philosophical highlights of the gardening season to read those words in political terms, and shudder; then read them again in terms of the natural world and think: how true, how true.

From The *Free You* Volume 3 September 1969

Sand County Almanac

"Classic" it's called now, because it was published in 1949 and still has bite. Wherever the ecologist looks the world weaves a wild story. This one looked at Sand County, among other places, and was led to propose a Land Ethic.

—SB

[suggested by everybody]

A Sand County Almanac
Aldo Leopold
1949; 295 pp.

$ 0.95 postpaid

from: Ballantine Books, Inc.
101 Fifth Ave.
New York, N.Y. 10003

or WHOLE EARTH CATALOG

American conservation is, I fear, still concerned for the most part with show pieces.

•

Perhaps the most serious obstacle impeding the evolution of a land ethic is the fact that our educational and economic system is headed away from, rather than toward, an intense consciousness of land. Your true modern is separated from the land by many middlemen, and by innumerable physical gadgets.

•

A thing is right when it tends to preserve the integrity, stability, and beauty of the biotic community. It is wrong when it tends otherwise.

Solar Journal

its sure hard to put a handle on this book.
a strange overview, maybe,
or fluid bingo.
richard grossinger brings a gnat's ass
and a cannonball
together,
makes them fit,
shows how they are connected,
then takes a long skinny oecological finger
and gently tweaks the reader's nose. . . .
learn from him.

—*jd*

Solar Journal: Oecological Sections
Richard Grossinger
1970; 130 pp.

$4.50 postpaid

from:
Black Sparrow Press
Box 25603
Los Angeles, California 90025

or WHOLE EARTH CATALOG

In the beginning there was only the unity of the Ice Sheet. Then followed the unity of the March thaw, and the northward hegira of the international geese. Every March since the Pleistocene, the geese have honked unity from China Sea to Siberian Steppe, from Euphrates to Volga, from Nine to Murmansk, from Lincolnshire to Spitsbergen. Every March since the Pleistocene, the geese have honked unity from Currituck to Labrador, Matamuskeet to Ungava, Horseshoe Lake to Hudson's Bay, Avery Island to Baffin Land, Panhandle to Mackenzie, Sacramento to Yukon.

By this international commerce of geese, the waste corn of Illinois is carried through the clouds of the Arctic tundras, there to combine with the waste sunlight of a nightless June to grow goslings for all the lands between. And in this annual barter of food for light, and winter warmth for summer solitude, the whole continent receives as net profit a wild poem dropped from the murky skies upon the muds of March.

•

I was young then, and full of trigger-itch; I thought that because fewer wolves meant more deer, that no wolves would mean hunters' paradise.

•

We all strive for safety, prosperity, comfort, long life, and dullness.

•

So in his article on sanctity and adaption, Rappaport cites two essential tautologies: that every living being is connected to every other living being, and that the environment is so complex that we cannot predict the total consequences of any action. So the supernatural world, in which all beings, visible and invisible, are connected by the great spiritual thread, in which the consequences are never seen yet always critical, is not just similar but identical to the natural world. It is science which operates with an imaginary environment, an environment it imagines it can control, in which it believes its own predictions, setting limits on just how far it will trace a poison or follow a river. Who cares if insecticide in Iowa pollutes the Great Lakes, who cares if the poisonous wastes from the potato factory in Maine pour into New Brunswick, as long as the crud passes political boundaries? Who cares if the microorganisms are poisoned, the algae and snails choked, these are not men's delicacies? Who cares about the supernatural, the world we cannot see? Who cares what happens to the skeletons of the fish after the fish are eaten, when every house has a garbage disposal; except during a garbage strike in New York the people forget that there is waste and the waste goes somewhere, motorboats killing off everything in a lake during successive Memorial Days and July 4's and Labor Days? And every living organism shares in the consequences, and the consequences are collective, only civil wars says the astronaut looking down at Earth, only civil wars even as the hunter downs the bear, the fish are caught in the Bella Coola trap. And everyone is simultaneously the benefactor and the victim; we are all victimized by what we are made out of, by, in fact, that we are made out of anything. The consequences never cease but pass and rebound, and this is the story of light in the universe, a sun whose powers flood on beyond Earth, beyond planets, an Earth which receives the decay of other stars.

•

NOTE ON SPELLING: *Oecology* is the etymological spelling of *Ecology*. The *logos* of *oikos* is the *law* of the *house* in the deepest sense: meaning the speech by which the house is known to itself, meaning that the house is subject to the proportions of its rule. It's house rules I'm talking about, just and unjust, or finally JUST. I want to recall to you the house, of which planet is one aspect, language is another, body is another——house in the sense that oeconomy is the management of the house and Oikumene is the known, inhabited, LIVED IN world.

LOOKING FOR DOPE

Urge's wipers wiped and wiped and wiped and wiped and wiped and wiped and wiped, and still D.R. could barely see through the windshield. It hadn't bothered him the first few hours, but as the rain kept falling and the night wore on and his eyes got sore and tired, the world outside the windshield gradually turned into such a visual mush D.R. had trouble keeping Urge on the road. What Urge needed was a new set of windshield wipers, and what D.R. needed was some food and a good night's sleep. But short of that the next best thing of course was a good hit of grass to kind of bring things into focus.

Sorry old bus, he said to Urge as he felt his shirt pocket for a J.

And he meant that too. One of Divine Right's convictions was that it was possible to turn a vehicle onto dope if only the right means could be found. One time just before crossing the Canadian border he'd stashed an ounce of prime Afghan hash in Urge's crank case and Urge had obviously loved it. Within a mile Urge's headlights had started flashing on and off, his horn spontaneously bleated tones of joy. At least it had seemed that way. D.R. was pretty stoned himself at the time and it may have been that those were only things he wanted Urge to do. At any rate, the bus began to cough and choke and gasp for breath after a while, and he'd had to take the hash back out. But that's okay, Urge old buddy, D.R. said, feeling his shirt for a J. That's all right. I'm working on it. One of these days I'll come up with a formula to stone you with so fine, so right you'll think: divine.

The joint D.R. had put in his shirt pocket was gone. All he found was a tattered book of matches. He looked in the glove compartment and felt in his leather-belt-pouch, but it was the same. So at a wide place at the end of a bridge D.R. pulled off the road and started to rummage around the bus in search of dope.

"What is it?"

"Shhh. Go back to sleep."

"What is it?" Estelle sat up and rubbed her eyes. She was in a sleeping bag, lying cross-ways on the mattress near the back of the bus. The bus wasn't wide enough for her to stretch out fully, but there was so much junk scattered around there wasn't any other place to lie. In spite of having to twist herself into an S to lie down, she'd slept so deeply for seven straight hours that now she was having trouble getting her eyes to stay open.

"Go back to sleep."

"No, I'm awake. Where are we?"

"Fuck, I don't know. Somewhere out west."

(continued)

On Growth and Form

A paradigm classic. Everyone dealing with growth or form in any manner can use the book. We've seen worn copies on the shelves of artists, inventors, engineers, computer systems designers, biologists.

—SB

On Growth and Form
D'Arcy Wentworth Thompson
Two volume edition
1917, 1952

$45.00 postpaid

Abridged paper edition
1917, 1961; 346 pp.

$4.95 postpaid

from:
Cambridge University Press
510 North Avenue
New Rochelle, N. Y. 10801

or WHOLE EARTH CATALOG

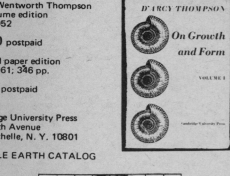

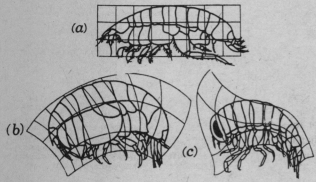

Fig. 143. (*a*) *Harpinia plumosa* Kr.; (*b*) *Stegocephalus inflatus* Kr.; (*c*) *Hyperia galba.*

When Plateau made the wire framework of a regular tetrahedron and dipped it in soap-solution, he obtained in an instant a beautifully symmetrical system of six films, meeting three by three in four edges and these four edges running from the corners of the figure to its centre of symmetry. Here they meet, two by two, at the Maraldi angle; and the films meet three by three, to form the re-entrant solid angle which we have called a "Maraldi pyramid" in our account of the architecture of the honeycomb. The very same configuration is easily recognized in the minute siliceous skeleton of *Callimitra.* There are two discrepancies, neither of which need raise any difficulty. The figure is not rectilinear but a *spherical tetrahedron,* such as might be formed by the boundary edges of a tetrahedral cluster of four co-equal bubbles; and just as Plateau extended his experiment by blowing a small bubble in the centre of his tetrahedral system, so we have a central bubble also here.

This bubble may be of any size; but its situation (if it be present at all) is always the same, and its shape is always such as to give the Maraldi angles at its own four corners. The tension of its own walls, and those of the films by which it is supported or slung, all balance one another. Hence the bubble appears in plane projection as a curvilinear equilateral triangle; and we have only got to convert this plane diagram into the corresponding solid to obtain the spherical tetrahedron we have been seeking to explain.

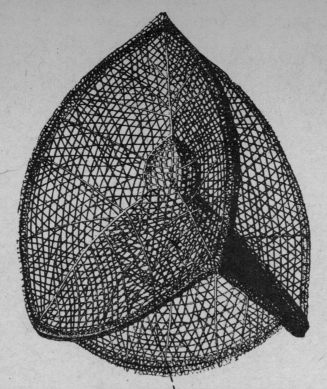

The geometry of the little inner tetrahedron is not less simple and elegant. Its six edges and four faces are all equal. The films attaching it to the outer skeleton are all planes. Its faces are spherical,

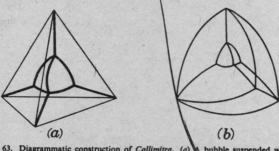

Fig. 63. Diagrammatic construction of *Callimitra.* (*a*) A bubble suspended within a tetrahedral cage; (*b*) another bubble within a skeleton of the former bubble.

and each has its centre in the opposite corner. The edges are circular arcs, with cosine $\frac{1}{3}$; each is in a plane perpendicular to the chord of the arc opposite, and each has its centre in the middle of that chord. Along each edge the two intersecting spheres meet each other at an angle of 120°.[1]

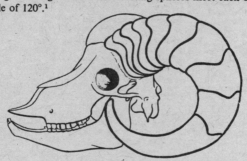

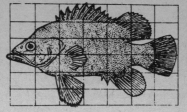

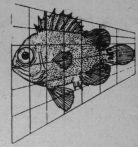

Fig. 150. *Polyprion.*

Fig. 151. *Pseudopriacanthus altus.*

The engineer, who had been busy designing a new and powerful crane, saw in a moment that the arrangement of the bony trabeculae was nothing more nor less than a diagram of the lines of stress, or directions of tension and compression, in the loaded structure; in short, that Nature was strengthening the bone in precisely the manner and direction in which strength was required; and he is said to have cried out, "That's my crane!"

Antigonia capros.

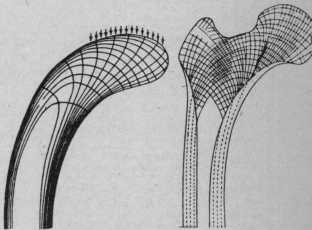

Fig. 101. Crane-head and femur. After Culmann and J. Wolff.

Purposive Systems

You're a purposive system. So am I. We're very good at it, and not as good as we'd like to be. Humanity, as a whole, is lousy at it, and worried. This collection of recent cybernetic thoughts can cheer you up and give you better concepts to worry with.

—SB

Purposive Systems

Ed.: Heinz von Foerster, J. D. White, L. J. Peterson, J. K. Russell
1968; 179 pp. from
Spartan Books
432 Park Avenue South
New York, N. Y. 10016
or
WHOLE EARTH CATALOG

$10.00

We have not yet built into our educational system any recognition of the points where precision is essential, and yet we are living in a society where one mistake can dislocate the lives of thousands of people, wreck distribution systems, and distort life-history data, and subsequent career lines.

There is no basic reason why one cannot design a control memory with a different technology, a technology which would allow the computer itself to alter the information stored in the control memory. Thus we would have a computer that could alter its own character as required. To my knowledge very little conceptual work has been done in thinking through the implications of this extremely powerful possibility. The possibilities are so staggering and deep. The poor harried souls responsible for trying to understand the classical computer as we now know it wish this idea would go away.

The act of choosing a representation for a problem involves the specification of a space where the search for solution can take place. Such a specification involves the choice of a language—and its use—for expressing problem conditions, properties of solutions, and knowledge of regularities in the search space.

If we detach the concern of survival from computers, as is generally the case, they can learn abilities more useful to man than the struggle for existence.

•

A friend of mine once gave what I regard as a nice shorthand formula. When in a dilemma, introduce novelty.

•

Exaggerated politeness is a powerful source of misunderstanding.

•

Regularity seeking activities that seem to be generally useful include the detection of symmetries, the identification of 'critical points' (key points through which the search must go to get a solution), and the recognition of redundant information in problem descriptions.

Aspects of Form

This is a well-used collection of insights by venerable initiates of form study.

—SB

Aspects of Form

Lancelot Law Whyte, ed.
1951; 249 pp.

$2.45 postpaid from
Indiana University Press
10th and Morton Streets
Bloomington, Ind. 47401
or
WHOLE EARTH CATALOG

Fig. 2 Copperhead Snake——illustrating the effectiveness of disruptive contrast in relation to background configuration

A man may learn by experience to associate two series of events between which any connection seemed at first wildly improbable. For such associations to be possible, provision must be made for every signal entering the nervous system to be relayed to every part, not merely to the specialised receiving zone. Thus from the knot of an event is generated a web of speculation; when two series of events are perceived together they form the warp and woof of a shimmering fabric into which is woven the pattern of the probability that the two events are significantly related.

An 'image' in this biological sense, then, is not an imitation of an object's external form but an imitation of certain privileged or relevant aspects. It is here that a wide field of investigation would seem to open.

We know that there are certain privileged motifs in our world to which we respond almost too easily. The human face may be outstanding among them. Whether by instinct or by very early training, we certainly are ever disposed to single out the expressive features of a face from the chaos of sensations that surrounds it and to respond to its slightest variations with fear or joy.

Synthesis of Form

Christopher Alexander is a design person that other design people refer to a lot. This book deals with the nature of current design problems that are expanding clear beyond any individual's ability to know and correlate all the factors. The methodology presented here is one of analysis of a problem for misfits and synthesis of form (via computer-translatable nets and hierarchies) for minimum misfits.

—SB

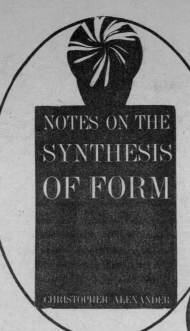

But if we think of the requirements from a negative point of view, as potential misfits, there is a simple way of picking a finite set. This is because it is through misfit that the problem originally brings itself to our attention. We take just those relations between form and context which obtrude most strongly, which demand attention most clearly, which seem most likely to go wrong. We cannot do better than this. If there were some intrinsic way of reducing the list of requirements to a few, this would mean in essence that we were in possession of a field description of the context: if this were so, the problem of creating fit would become trivial, and no longer a problem of design. We cannot have a unitary or field description of a context and still have a design problem worth attention.

Notes on the Synthesis of Form
Christopher Alexander
1964; 216 pp.

$2.25 postpaid

from:
Harvard University Press
79 Garden Street
Cambridge, Mass. 02138

or WHOLE EARTH CATALOG

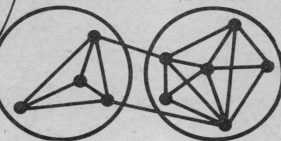

Indeed, not only is the man who lives in the form the one who made it, but there is a special closeness of contact between man and form which leads to constant rearrangement of unsatisfactory detail, constant improvement. The man, already responsible for the original shaping of the form, is also alive to its demands while he inhabits it. And anything which needs to be changed is changed at once.

A subsystem, roughly speaking, is one of the obvious components of the system, like the parts shown with a circle round them. If we try to adjust a set of variables which does not constitute a subsystem, the repercussions of the adjustment affect others outside the set, because the set is not sufficiently independent. The procedure of the unselfconscious system is so organized that adjustment *can* take place in each one of these subsystems independently. This is the reason for its success.

In the selfconscious situation, on the other hand, the designer is faced with all the variables simultaneously.

The greatest clue to the inner structure of any dynamic process lies in its reaction to change.

The Mousgoum cannot afford, as we do, to regard maintenance as a nuisance which is best forgotten until it is time to call the local plumber. It is in the same hands as the building operation itself, and its exigencies are as likely to shape the form as those of the initial construction.

The selfconscious individual's grasp of problems is constantly misled. His concepts and categories, besides being arbitrary and unsuitable, are self-perpetuating. Under the influence of concepts, he not only does things from a biased point of view, but sees them biasedly as well. The concepts control his perception of of fit and misfit—until in the end he sees nothing but deviations from his conceptual dogmas, and loses not only the urge but even the mental opportunity to frame his problems more appropriately.

The solution of a design problem is really only another effort to find a unified description. The search for realization through constructive diagrams is an effort to understand the required form so fully that there is no longer a rift between its functional specification and the shape it takes.

Two misfits are seen to interact only because, in some sense at least, they deal with the same kind of physical consideration. . . . .
It is such a physical center of implication, if I may call it that, which the designer finds it easy to grasp. Because it refers to a distinguishable physical property or entity, it can be expressed diagrammatically, and provides a possible non-verbal point of entry into the problem.

The Sciences of the Artificial

Simon says: we have generalized methods of obtaining elegant information from nature. We don't have generalized methods of making elegant things to add to nature; we lack a science of design. He's right and he doesn't waste much time being right, but proceeds to make useful suggestions— lots of them probably wrong and useful anyway. His notion of sub-system stability in evolution is beautiful.

—SB

The Science of the Artificial
Herbert Simon
1969; 123 pp.

$1.95 postpaid

from:
The M.I.T. Press
Room 765
50 Ames Street
Cambridge, Mass. 02142

or WHOLE EARTH CATALOG

The Evolution of Complex Systems

Let me introduce the topic of evolution with a parable. There once were two watchmakers, named Hora and Tempus, who manufactured very fine watches. Both of them were highly regarded, and the phones in their workshops rang frequently—new customers were constantly calling them. However, Hora prospered, while Tempus became poorer and poorer and finally lost his shop. What was the reason?

The watches the men made consisted of about 1,000 parts each. Tempus had so constructed his that if he had one partly assembled and had to put it down—to answer the phone, say—it immediately fell to pieces and had to be reassembled from the elements. The better the customers liked his watches, the more they phoned him and the more difficult it became for him to find enough uninterrupted time to finish a watch.

The watches that Hora made were no less complex than those of Tempus. But he had designed them so that he could put together subassemblies of about ten elements each. Ten of these subassemblies, again, could be put together into a larger subassembly; and a system of ten of the latter subassemblies constituted the whole watch. Hence, when Hora had to put down a partly assembled watch in order to answer the phone, he lost only a small part of his work, and he assembled his watches in only a fraction of the man-hours it took Tempus.

Most of the complex structures found in the world are enormously redundant, and we can use this redundancy to simplify their description. But to use it, to achieve the simplification, we must find the right representation.

If a complex structure is completely unredundant—if no aspect of its structure can be inferred from any other—then it is its own simplest description.

The Artifact as 'Interface'

We can view the matter quite symmetrically. An artifact can be thought of as a meeting point—an 'interface' in today's terms—between an 'inner' environment, the substance and organization of the artifact itself, and an 'outer' environment, the surroundings in which it operates. If the inner environment is appropriate to the outer environment, or vice versa, the artifact will serve its intended purpose. Thus, if the clock is immune to buffeting, it will serve as a ship's chronometer. (And conversely, if it isn't, we may salvage it by mounting it on the mantel at home.)

I should like to point to evidence that there are only a few 'intrinsic' characteristics of the inner environment of thinking man that limit the adaptation of his thought to the shape of the problem environment. All else in his thinking and problem-solving behavior is artificial—is learned and is subject to improvement through the invention of improved designs.

D.R. was on his knees next to Estelle, digging in a duffle bag. A light would have helped but Urge's overhead light was out, and D.R. didn't know where the flashlight was.

"Here, honey, light this candle," said Estelle, and she handed him a candle.

But somehow climbing through the general debris to get to the back, D.R. had lost the matches. He yelled goddamn it! as loud as he could yell.

"Shhh, honey, it's all right. What are you looking for?"

"I'm looking for the goddamn dope that I had in my goddamn hand not six goddamn hours ago. That's what I'm looking for." And he lifted the duffle bag by its bottom and dumped its contents on top of the other stuff already scattered over the mattress.

Estelle found a match and lit it. The whole wild interior of the bus came alive for a moment, but quickly began to fade. "Give me the candle," said Estelle.

"Where is it?"

"I handed it to you."

D.R. felt around his knees and legs, and in the pile of stuff he'd just dumped out. But all he could find was a broken screw driver. He held it up, looked at it, then threw it as hard as he could toward the front. "Fuck it!" he yelled, and strangled himself on the yell. It was as if something had seized his throat and choked him. Falling onto his side D.R. grabbed the handle of the side doors and threw them open, then tumbled in a heap outside into the rain. Estelle was out of her sleeping bag by the time he hit the ground.

"Honey, what's wrong?"

"I can't _breathe_!" he gasped. "That _space_ in that _bus_ . . ."

"Honey, it's fine in here. Come on back in, you're getting wet."

D.R. got to his feet and tried to wipe the mud off his knees. But that only smeared it more. "What a goddamn mess."

"Get in, baby, lie down. I'll drive awhile, and you can get some sleep."

D.R. did not seem persuaded, but he obeyed. Estelle closed the door behind him, then guided him toward the far end of the mattress.

"Where's my sleeping bag?" D.R. asked.

"Get in mine. Come on, now."

"I want mine." he whined. "Where is it?"

"It's on the floor half full of pork and beans, that's where. Now come on back here."

D.R. was too confused to argue. Estelle pulled off his sandals and got his feet pointed into the sleeping bag. He wiggled on down inside, feeling the dark warmth of Estelle's body become his own deep in the interior of the bag.

General Systems Yearbook

Good thinking, rotten publishing. The usual graphic output in this yearbook is three pallid diagrams. And you know that the mothers who wrote the articles are forever whacking away at their blackboards, but because typewriters don't draw, all that vivid stuff gets left in the author's private experience. Man, there's something suspect about General Systems Theory if the practitioners are this far out of intelligent communication. Here's part of the contents of a recent volume, which may help to vindicate matters.

—SB

General Systems

Ludwig von Bertalanffy, Anatol Rapoport, Richard L. Meier, eds.

$20.00 postpaid per volume

from
Society for General Systems Research
12613 Bunting Lane
Bowie, Md. 20715

Understanding whole systems is knowing how to fly. You can rise above local circumstances, travel with blurring speed, and set down in a place wholly distant, strange, and wonderful. Or maybe not so wonderful, in which case you best know how to take off in a tight situation, and remember where home is.

The price you pay for the understanding is the grim knowledge of trade-offs in design. That you can have an airplane that goes fast or one that lands in 200 ft. but not both. That to save these people you may have to starve those people.

By and by you dwell in a wilderness of conflicting considerations. If you survive your wishful solutions——and there's usually margin——you may become a wily and sky-hooked metaphysician. The solutions are always meta. The means always funky field expedient.

—SB

Dynamo and Virgin Reconsidered

Here in one sharp little book are noted many of the large-scale turns of history and culture that we are visibly and invisibly making in one evolutionary blink of time. Unlike most overviewers, White does not concern himself with so much pace of change as he does with origins and directions. His 1967 essay "The Historical Roots of Our Ecologic Crisis" (chapter 5 in this book) is already a much-reprinted classic. I suspect that Chapter 11, "The Necessity of Witches" will become one.

—SB

Dynamo and Virgin Reconsidered
Lynn White, jr.
1968; 186pp.

$1.95 postpaid

from:
The MIT Press
50 Ames Street
Cambridge, Massachusetts 02139

or WHOLE EARTH CATALOG

From the kaleidoscopic and iridescent record of mankind, we can learn chiefly this: the possible range of human thought, emotion, organization, and action is almost infinite. In facing today's problems, we must therefore liberate ourselves from presuppositions as to what may or may not be possible. Knowledge of history frees us to be contemporary.

Perception and Change

John Platt is an astute scientist (physics, chemistry, biology) in the process of becoming an astute social inventor. He's got some novel understandings and some promising routes out of the good old over-specialized, under-diversified deadly hole we're in. . . and into the green forest of what a "we" is, or an "I".

—SB

Perception and Change
John R. Platt
1970; 178 pp.

$7.95 postpaid

from:
University of Michigan Press
615 E. University
Ann Arbor, Michigan 48106

or WHOLE EARTH CATALOG

One reason why some fields are overstudied these days is our present system of government grants.

•

Enrico Fermi once said that a scientist should change fields every 10 years; that, in the first place, his ideas were exhausted by then, and he owed it to the younger men in the field to let them advance; and that, in the second place, his ideas might still be of great value in bringing a fresh viewpoint to a different field.

•

Why should someone not make us a single suit that would shed rain and that we could ruffle up for comfort in any weather, as a bird ruffles its feathers? A bird needs no suitcase.

•

Many who have made the jump to the subjective have ended by treating the objective as small and unimportant. Solipsist tyrants, believing that their will, like their eyeballs, could move mountains, have come to believe that it should trample over these small annoying figures in their visual field.

•

Prophecy is rash, but it may well be that the publication of D.T. Suzuki's first *Essays in Zen Buddhism* in 1927 will seem in future generations as great an intellectual event as William of Moerbeke's Latin translations of Aristotle in the thirteenth century or Marsiglio Ficino's of Plato in the fifteenth. But in Suzuki's case, the shell of the Occident has been broken through. More than we dream, we are now governed by the new canon of the globe.

•

Francis tried to depose man from his monarchy over creation and set up a democracy of all God's creatures. With him the ant is no longer simply a homily for the lazy, flames a sign of the thrust of the soul toward union with God; now they are Brother Ant and Sister Fire, praising the Creator in their own ways as Brother Man does in his. . . I propose Francis as a patron saint for ecologists.

Good living is with a tribe. At the Marine Biological Laboratories at Woods Hole, Massachusetts, where I have spent several summers, the boundaries between the generations seem to disappear, as well as the boundaries between work and play and between indoors and outdoors and between man and environment. Children and students and teachers walk barefoot in and out of the laboratories, arguing science and studying the odd creatures brought up from the sea. All night they watch the fish embryos developing in the dishes, and they go out before dawn together to catch the big striped bass. The 4-year-olds solemnly examine frogs, the 10-year-olds sell their catch of dogfish to the labs, the 15-year-olds listen to the DNA arguments on the beach or play savage tennis with the senior scientists.

•

As perception theory now suggests, each of us stands at the creative, choosing focus of a moving web of past antecedents and future consequences that branch out from our present choices and actions, propagating and amplifying themselves indefinitely. We interpenetrate the universe; it responds to our every breath.

•

It seems to me that the new rights for which a demand is arising in our time, I think in an irresistible way, revolve primarily around *the right not to be treated as an object.* We are co-subjects in our society.

It is said that after the ceremonies dedicating the great telescope on Mount Palomar, someone remarked to an astronomer, "Modern astronomy certainly makes man look insignificant, doesn't it?" To which the astronomer replied, "But man is the astronomer!"

•

There was a period in our own society when we needed witches and had them in enormous numbers. It began about the year 1300, ended somewhat after 1650, and is usually called the Renaissance. This was a time of torrential flux, of fearful doubt, marking the transition from the relative certainties of the Middle Ages to the new certainties which dominated the eighteenth and nineteenth centuries.

The Human Use of Human Beings

A proper sequel to his Cybernetics, this book is social, untechnical, ultimate in most of its considerations. Its domain is the whole earth of the mind.

Norbert Wiener is one of the founders of an n-dimensional inhabited world whose nature we've yet to learn.

—SB

The Human Use of Human Beings
Norbert Wiener
1950, 1954; 288 pp.

$1.65 postpaid

from:
Avon Books
250 West 55th Street
New York, N.Y. 10019

or WHOLE EARTH CATALOG

It is the thesis of this book that society can only be understood through a study of the messages and the communication facilities which belong to it; and that in the future development of these messages and communication facilities, messages between man and machine and between machine and machine, are destined to play an ever-increasing part.

•

Messages are themselves a form of pattern and organization. Indeed, it is possible to treat sets of messages as having an entropy like sets of states of the external world. Just as entropy is a measure of disorganization, the information carried by a set of messages is a measure of organization. In fact, it is possible to interpret the information carried by a message as essentially the negative of its entropy, and the negative logarithm of its probability. That is, the more probable the message, the less information it gives. Clichés, for example, are less illuminating than great poems.

•

I believe that Ashby's brilliant idea of the unpurposeful random mechanism which seeks for its own purpose through a process of learning is not only one of the great philosophical contributions of the present day, but will lead to highly useful technical developments in the task of automatization. Not only can we build purpose into machines, but in an overwhelming majority of cases a machine designed to avoid certain pitfalls of breakdown will look for purposes which it can fulfill.

•

We are not stuff that abides, but patterns that perpetuate themselves. A pattern is a message, and may be transmitted as a message.

It is the great public which is demanding the utmost of secrecy for modern science in all things which may touch its military uses. This demand for secrecy is scarcely more than the wish of a sick civilization not to learn the progress of its own disease.

•

It is illuminating to know that the sort of phenomenon which is recorded subjectively as emotion may not be merely a useless epiphenomenon of nervous action, but may control some essential stage in learning, and in other similar processes.

The Next Development in Man

Books. Lancelot Law Whyte, The Next Development in Man, Mentor paperback, 60¢ (may be more now). Written in 1948 but still relevant. Whyte wants to change the processes of thinking from static concepts to fluid developments. In order to do this he first has to redefine the whole language to replace our usual noun-name centered ideas with verb-action-process emphasis. Most of the book is a long, head-wrenching reinterpretation of Western history, seen as the working out of what Whyte calls the universal formative principle. But where we are now represents a blocked, one-sided aspect of this principle, hence the requirement of the development of process thinking and unitary man. The failure we are living with now Whyte recognized in 1948, the value of the book is its display of a vast and essentially complete metaphysical system that is in fact a philosophic program for the future.

No longer available   Cary James
                                     Mill Valley, Calif.

"Form is the recognizable continuity of any process." p. 15

"Anything which facilitates the development of characteristic organic form is called proper to the organism." p. 23

"The poverty of language in process concepts compels unitary thought to use 'process' as both noun and adjective. Formation, growth, development, destruction, decay, are process concepts; god, idea, number, matter, energy, are static concepts lacking the asymmetry of the time sequence and implying permanence." p. 27

"...the one God was a jealous God. With the ideal of universality appeared intolerance." p. 76

"More comprehensive processes than those of the conscious mind control human destiny." p. 118

"The final elimination of the dualism can only come about through the realization that the need to formulate ideals, and in so doing split man asunder, is itself an expression of the very human but futile desire to escape the uncertainty of process and find spiritual security in the aim at least of a permanent harmony. Unitary man can achieve this realization, and see himself as a whole, because he is ready to accept his personal life for what it is, a transient development through changes which cannot be foreseen." p. 210-11.

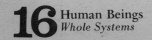

Man's Role in Changing the Face of the Earth

This book of almost 1200 pages is the result of a major conference held in 1955, sponsored by the Wenner Gren Foundation for Anthropological Research. More than 50 scholars submitted papers, covering almost every imaginable point of view related to man's capacity to transform his physical environment. Though first presented nearly 15 years ago, the facts and insights are richly rewarding today. In my opinion in fact, it is an unsurpassed achievement in assembling pertinent, insightful information of interest not only to serious students of the planet Earth, but to non-trained readers as well.

The three sections of the book are: I. "Retrospect", an historical background; II. "Process", methods and agencies involved in man's interactions with the land; and III. "Prospect", the effects and future implications of man's habitation of the Earth. Some typical subjects covered within these sections include: fire as the great force employed by man; origins and decline of woodlands; man and grass (sic); ecology of peasant life; harvests of the seas; ports channels and coastlines; and sewerage (don't belittle sewerage——society is structured around it).

This book rewards a reader like me because of its minimum of moralizing and its abundant substance. Edgar Anderson, director of the Missouri Botanical Garden in St. Louis and without whom such a book as this would be certainly incomplete, pointed out that the average thoughtful person has little inkling of how man has reclothed the world. Even professional biologists have been tardy in recognizing that a significant portion of the plants and animals surrounding us are of our own making. For example, neither Kentucky bluegrass nor Canada bluegrass is native to those places, but came from Europe. The corn belt is a very obviously man-dominated landscape, but the casual observer might never realize that even the grass covered and oak-dotted stretches of what looks like indigenous California vegetation came uninvited from the Old World along with the Spaniards.

[Reviewed by Richard Raymond]

Generally speaking, the plants which follow man around the world might be said to do so, not because they relish what man has done to the environment, but because they can stand it and most other plants cannot.

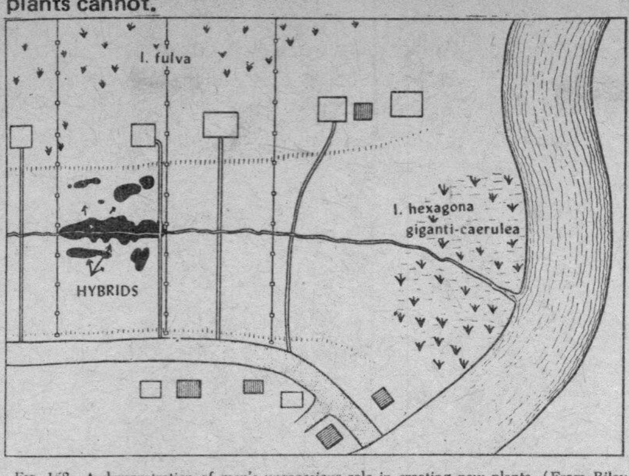

FIG. 153.—A demonstration of man's unconscious role in creating new plants. (From Riley, 1938.) At the far right one of the minor bayous of the lower Mississippi Delta. At right angles to it and running nearly across the figure is the abandoned channel of a former stream, now drained by a ditch. The natural levees of the stream are slightly higher than the surrounding country. Their sharp inner edges are indicated on the map by hachures. The road has been run along the lower levee, and houses have been built along the opposite one. The property lines (as in many old French settlements) produce a series of long narrow farms, which for our purposes serve as so many experimental plots. Each farm has its house on a low ridge with a long entrance drive connecting it across a swale to the public road on the opposite ridge. The farms (including a score of others which are out of sight to the left of the figure) were originally essentially similar. At the point where the ditch joins the bayou is a large population of *Iris hexagona giganti-caerulea*. Behind the levee on which the houses were built, *I. fulva* grows on the lower ground as well as farther upstream along the ditch. The key fact to be noted is that the hybrids are on only one farm, that they are abundant there, and that they go up to the very borders of the property on either side. Nature is evidently capable of spawning such hybrids throughout this area, but not until one farmer unconsciously created the new and more or less open habitat in which they could survive did any appear in this part of the delta. (See Anderson, 1949, pp. 1–11, 94–98, for a more complete discussion.)

Man's Role In Changing the Face of the Earth
William L. Thomas, Jr., ed.
with Carl Sauer, Marston Bates, Lewis Mumford
1956; 1193 pp.

Vol. 1 **$4.75** postpaid

Vol. 2 **$5.95** postpaid

from:
University of Chicago Press
5801 Ellis Ave
Chicago, Illinois 60637

or WHOLE EARTH CATALOG

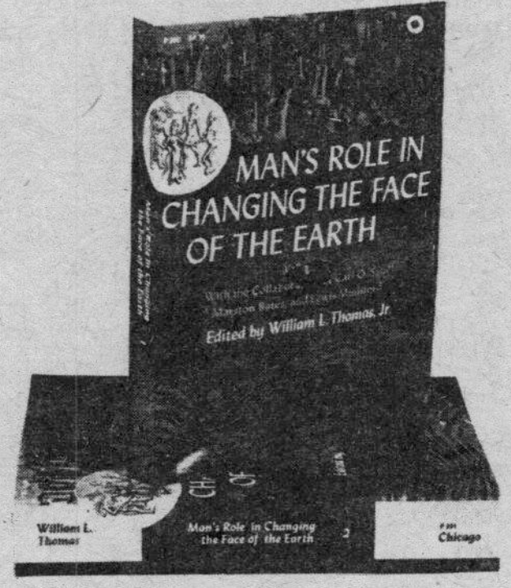

THE SOCIAL REVOLUTION

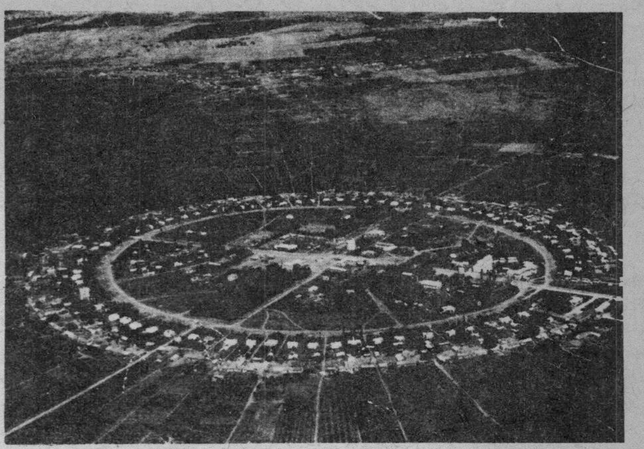

Almost every change in environmental conditions which man can make results in some change in the water economy or water budget at the earth's surface.

> The pressure for beef supply from the grasslands is very rapidly depleting the potential for protein. Where the plow went ahead of the cow, we have been able to measure the reduction in soil capabilities. The protein content of the wheat now grown on the eastern edge of the grassland area has been dropping decidedly. Where once it ranged from 19 to 11 per cent, it is now 14–9 per cent.

These are all very good ideas, but I've got something else that is very much more important. Every time you get where there is one of these populations of plants, find a large, flat rock, in the shade if necessary; sit down upon it for at least fifteen minutes by your wrist watch; and do not try to think about your clematises. Just think what a nice day it is, how pretty the flowers are, and the blue sky. Think how lucky you are to be doing this kind of work when the rest of the world is doing all the awful things they do not want to do. Just let your mind alone. Now, I am not joking. Please do this, by the clock if necessary.

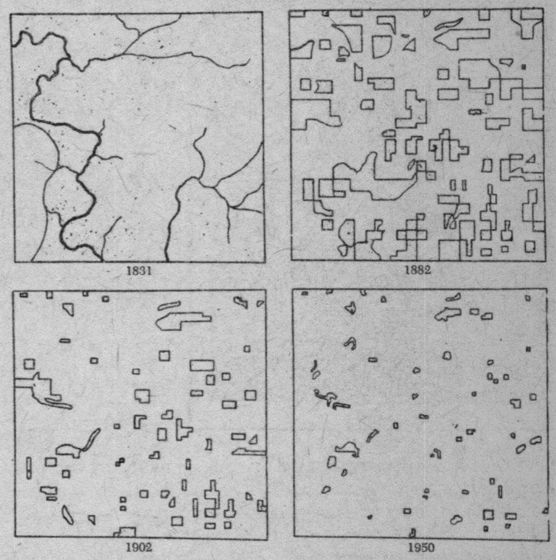

FIG. 147.—Changes in wooded area of Cadiz Township, Green County, Wisconsin (89°54′ W 43°30′ N.), during the period of European settlement. The township is six miles on a side and is drained by the Pecatonica River. The shaded areas represent the land remaining in, or reverting to, forest in 1882, 1902, and 1950.

So Human an Animal

Dubos has a combined medical and evolutionary perspective that prepares him perfectly to diagnose and prescribe for the new ills of mankind, the macro-maladies of cities and pollution and panic. Unlike other Generalsystem Practitioners, he supports his thoughts with a wealth of fascinating facts and anecdotes presented with a good cheer that makes health look quite attractive.

—SB

So Human an Animal
René Dubos
1968; 267 pp.

$2.45 postpaid

from:
Charles Scribner's Sons
597 Fifth Avenue
New York, N. Y. 10017

or WHOLE EARTH CATALOG

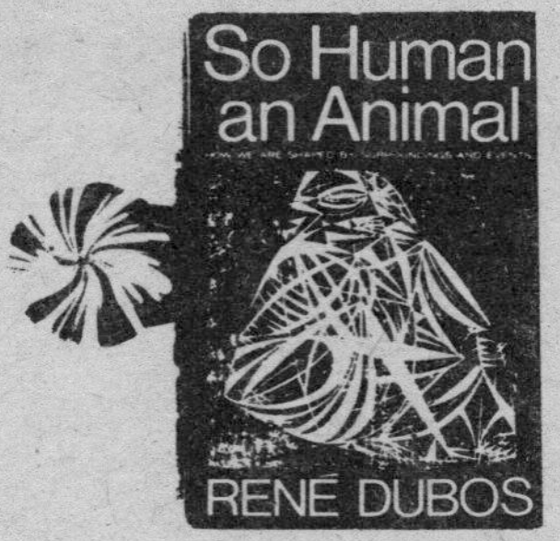

As the year 2000 approaches, an epidemic of sinister predictions is spreading all over the world, as happened among Christians during the period preceding the year 1000.

•

We behave often as if we were the last generation to inhabit the earth.

•

If the rebellious young succeed in discovering a formula of life as attractive as that of the troubadours, we may witness in the twenty-first century a new departure in civilization as occurred in Europe after it recovered from the fears of the tenth century. To be humanly successful, the new ages will have to overcome the present intoxication with the use of power for the conquest of the cosmos, and to rise above the simple-minded and degrading concept of man as a machine. The first move toward a richer and more human philosophy of life should be to rediscover man's partnership with nature.

•

Considered broadly, evolution always involves learning from experience. The learning may take place by storage of genetic information in the chromosomes, by accumulation of knowledge and skills in the individual organism, or by transmission of practices and wisdom in institutions or in society as a whole.

•

History shows that cultures of a sort can emerge from the most improbable ways of life, provided these last long enough to become integrated into an organic whole. The emergence of a new culture is rarely if ever the result of a conscious choice with a definite goal in mind.

The Human Condition

At the end of a peyote meeting, in the morning, food and water are brought in by a woman designated to be Peyote Woman. Indian women are not supposed to speak up much on general subjects, and during a meeting the women are silent participants. But at dawn Peyote Woman has the floor and the power. She speaks of fundamental things like water and birth and nourishment with all the authority of the Earth and with awesome perception.

Hannah Arendt does the same in this book. Her subject is the elements of the human condition. Her perspective, the threshold of travel away from the Earth.

—SB

The Human Condition
Hannah Arendt
1958; 385 pp.

$3.25 postpaid

from:
University of
Chicago Press
11030 South Langley Ave.
Chicago, Ill. 60628

or WHOLE
EARTH
CATALOG

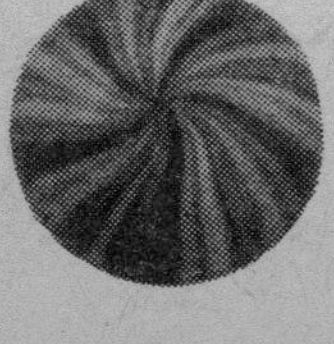

The task and potential greatness of mortals lie in their ability to produce things—works and deeds and words—which would deserve to be and, at least to a degree, are at home in everlastingness, so that through them mortals could find their place in a cosmos where everything is immortal except themselves.

•

It is true that one-man, monarchical rule, which the ancients stated to be the organizational device of the household, is transformed in society—as we know it today, when the peak of the social order is no longer formed by the royal household of an absolute ruler—into a kind of no-man rule. But this nobody, the assumed one interest of society as a whole in economics as well as the assumed one opinion of polite society in the salon, does not cease to rule for having lost its personality. As we know from the most social form of government, that is, from bureaucracy (the last stage of government in the nation-state just as one-man rule in benevolent despotism and absolutism was its first), the rule by nobody is not necessarily no-rule; it may indeed, under certain circumstances, even turn out to be one of its cruelest and tyrannical versions.

•

Love, in distinction from friendship, is killed, or rather extinguished, the moment it is displayed in public. ("Never seek to tell thy love/ Love that never told can be.") Because of its inherent wordlessness, love can only become false and perverted when it is used for political purposes such as the change or salvation of the world.

•

Without actually standing where Archimedes wished to stand (dos moi pou sto), still bound to the earth through the human condition, we have found a way to act on the earth and within terrestrial nature as though we dispose of it from outside, from the Archimedean point. And even at the risk of endangering the natural life process we expose the earth to universal, cosmic forces alien to nature's household.

•

The Cartesian removal of the Archimedean point into the mind of man, while it enabled man to carry it, as it were, within himself wherever he went and thus freed him from given reality altogether—that is, from the human condition of being an inhabitant of the earth—has perhaps never been as convincing as the universal doubt from which it sprang and which it was supposed to dispel. Today, at any rate, we find in the perplexities confronting natural scientists in the midst of their greatest triumphs the same nightmares which have haunted the philosophers from the beginning of the modern age.

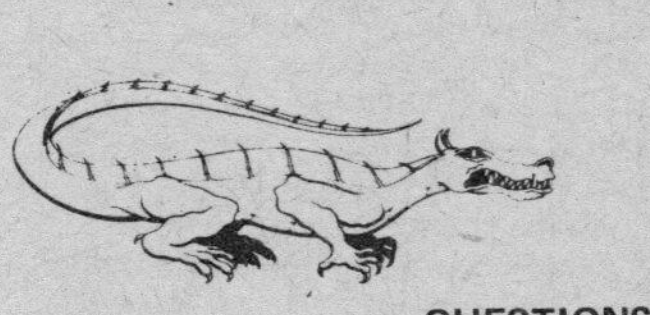

QUESTIONS

Did he dream about dragons? Did he dream about deer? Did he whisper the names of friends who were near? What songs did they play, and how far away? Why did he whisper, why did she scream? What does the sound of a screen door mean? Who walks in the pasture? Who talks on the hill? Who goes to the cellar, can you feel the chill? Where does the river, when will the wind? How far are the mountains? Where do they end? Why would the church? Did the service begin? Tell me who died, and tell me who cried. Help me to hide in the skin of a deer, my zippered-up bag in the mouth of a stag so swiftly I go through rows of does, it flows, it flows, it flows, it flows all over the hill where the green grass grows.

Man and His Symbols

Carl Jung did a nice thing just before he died. He helped with a British effort to bring all of his work together in one richly illustrated introduction to the breadth of his realm. This book covers his concepts of the unconscious, myths, individuation, the visual arts, dreams, and analysis. Why aren't all psychology books illustrated?

—SB

Man and His Symbols
Carl G. Jung
1964; 320 pp.

$1.50 postpaid

from:
Dell Publishing Co.
Dag Hammarskjold Plaza
245 E. 47th St.
New York, N.Y. 10017

or WHOLE EARTH CATALOG

A still more subtle manifestation of a negative anima appears in some fairy tales in the form of a princess who asks her suitors to answer a series of riddles or, perhaps, to hide themselves under her nose. If they cannot give the answers, or if she can find them, they must die—and she invariably wins. The anima in this guise involves men in a destructive intellectual game. We can notice the effect of this anima trick in all those neurotic pseudo-intellectual dialogues that inhibit a man from getting into direct touch with life and its real decisions. He reflects about life so much that he cannot live it and loses all his spontaneity and outgoing feeling.

Oh, come, lonely hunter in the stillness of dusk.
Come, come! I miss you, I miss you!
Now I will embrace you, embrace you!

Come, come! My nest is near, my nest is near.
Come, come, lonely hunter, now in the stillness of dusk.

He throws off his clothes and swims across the river, but suddenly she flies away in the form of an owl, laughing mockingly at him. When he tries to swim back to find his clothes, he drowns in the cold river.

The sign is always less than the concept it represents, while a symbol always stands for something more than its obvious and immediate meaning.

Abstract mandalas also appear in European Christian art. Some of the most splendid examples are the rose windows of the cathedrals. These are representations of the Self of man transposed onto the cosmic plane. (A cosmic mandala in the shape of a shining white rose was revealed to Dante in a vision.) We may regard as mandalas the haloes of Christ and the Christian saints in religious paintings.

A car is another kind of possession that is usually feminized—i.e., that can become the focus of many men's anima projections. Like ships, cars are called "she," and their owners caress and pamper them like favorite mistresses.

When an individual makes an attempt to see his shadow, he becomes aware of (and often ashamed of) those qualities and impulses he denies in himself but can plainly see in other people . . .

If you feel an overwhelming rage coming up in you when a friend reproaches you about a fault, you can be fairly sure that at this point you will find a part of your shadow, of which you are unconscious.

The archetypal sacred marriage (the union of opposites, of the male and female principles) represented here by a 19th-century Indian sculpture of the deities Siva and Parvati.

Psychological Reflections

The selection and editing of paragraphs from Jung's writings by Jacobi is done with an informed sense of continuity, so that the book is readable in sequence or by bits.

—SB

Psychological Reflections
C. G. Jung [ed. Jacobi]
1945, 1953, 1961; 340 pp.

$2.95

from:
Princeton University Press
Princeton, N.J. 08540

or WHOLE EARTH CATALOG

The man who would learn the human mind will gain almost nothing from experimental psychology. Far better for him to put away his academic gown, to say good-bye to the study, and to wander with human heart through the world. There, in the horrors of the prison, the asylum, and the hospital, in the drinking-shops, brothels, and gambling hells, in the salons of the elegant, in the exchanges, socialist meetings, churches, religious revivals, and sectarian ecstacies, through love and hate, through the experience of passion in every form in his own body, he would reap richer store of knowledge than text-books a foot thick could give him. Then would he know to doctor the sick with real knowledge of the human soul.

A neurosis has really come to an end when it has overcome the wrongly oriented ego. The neurosis itself is not healed; it heals us. The man is ill, but the illness is an attempt of nature to heal him. We can therefore learn a great deal for the good of our health from the illness itself, and that which appears to the neurotic person as absolutely to be rejected is just the part which contains the true gold which we should otherwise never have found.

The secret of the earth is not a joke and not a paradox. We need only see how in America the skull and hip-measurements of all European races become Indianized in the second generation. That is the secret of the American soil. And every soil has its secret, of which we carry an unconscience image in our souls: a relationship of spirit to body and of body to earth.

The greater the contrast, the greater is the potential. Great energy only comes from a correspondingly great tension between opposites.

No one develops his personality because someone told him it would be useful or advisable for him to do so. Nature has never yet allowed herself to be imposed upon by well-meaning advice. Only coercion working through casual connections moves nature, and human nature also. Nothing changes itself without need, and human personality least of all. It is immensely conservative, not to say inert. Only the sharpest need is able to rouse it. The development of personality obeys no wish, no command, and no insight, but only need; it wants the motivating coercion of inner or outer necessities. Any other development would be individualism. This is why the accusation of individualism is a cheap insult when it is raised against the natural development of personality.

It is naturally a fundamental error to believe that if we see an anti-value in a value, or an untruth in a truth, the value or the truth is then invalid. They have only become relative. Everything human is relative, because everything depends upon an inner polarity, for everything is a phenomenon of energy. And energy itself necessarily depends on a previous polarity without which there can be no energy. There must always be high and low, hot and cold, etc., so that the process of adjustment which is energy, can occur. The tendency to deny all previous values in favour of their opposites is therefore just as exaggerated as the former one-sidedness. Where generally accepted and undoubted values are suddenly thrown away, there is a fatal loss. Whoever acts in this way ends by throwing himself overboard with the discarded values.

The gigantic catastrophes that threaten us are not elemental happenings of a physical or biological kind, but are psychic events. We are threatened in a fearful way by wars and revolutions that are nothing else than psychic epidemics. At any moment a few million people may be seized by a madness, and then we have another world war or devastating revolution. Instead of being exposed to wild beasts, tumbling rocks, and inundating waters, man is exposed today to the elemental forces of his own psyche. Psychic life is a world-power that exceeds by many times all the powers of the earth. The Enlightenment, which stripped nature and human institutions of gods, overlooked the one god of fear who dwells in the psyche. Fear of God is in place, if anywhere, before the domination power of psychic life.

No doubt it is a great nuisance that mankind is not uniform but compounded of individuals whose psychic structure spreads them over a span of at least ten thousand years. Hence there is absolutely no truth that does not spell salvation to one person and damnation to another. All universalisms get stuck in this terrible dilemma.

Anthropology Today

If revising human affairs is your concern, or adapting to harsh social/environmental changes, the anthropological perspective can be enormously useful. Much of the value of Gary Snyder, Kurt Vonnegut, Carlos Castaneda is attributed by them to their study of anthropology. When understanding spans remote cultures, it's powerful understanding, seldom chauvinistic.

This book from the Psychology Today *folks will do for introduction.*

—SB

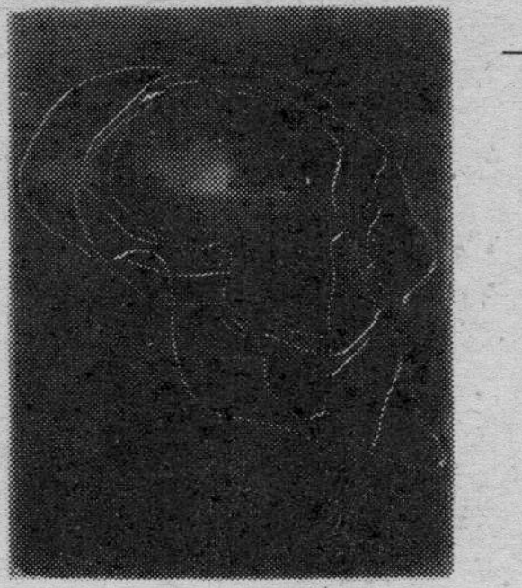

Anthropology Today
1971; 566 pp.

$12.95 postpaid

from:
CRM Books
1104 Camino Del Mar
Del Mar, CA. 92014

or WHOLE EARTH CATALOG

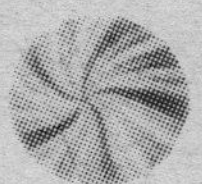

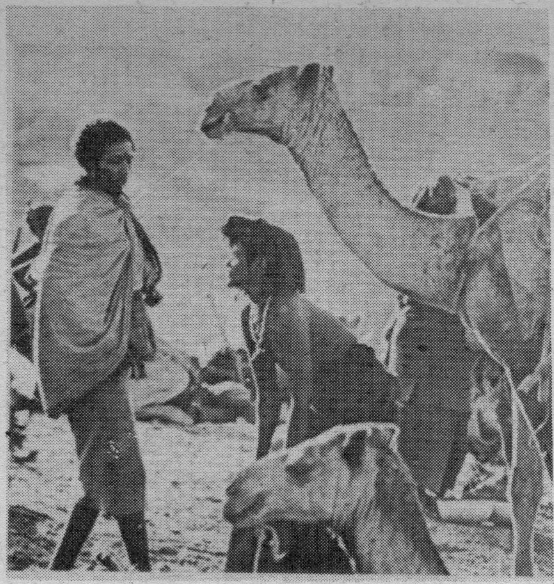

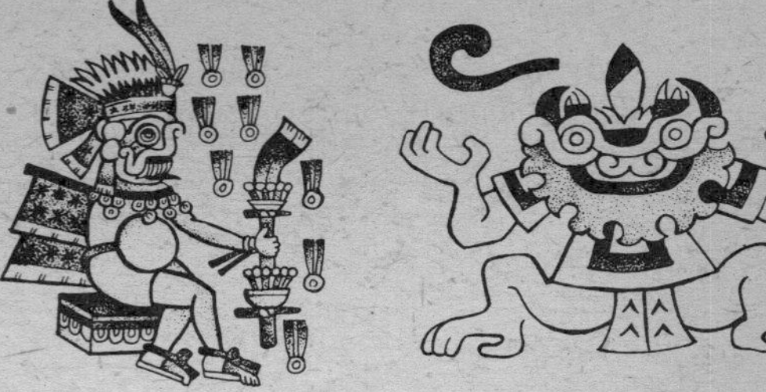

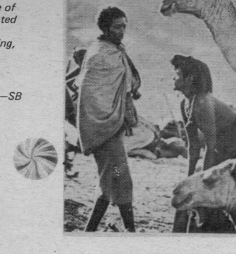

"A laughing outsider once said that anthropology is only an excuse for not specializing; a humanist remarked that a good anthropologist was the last Renaissance man. . . ."

•

These Anharic nomads of Ethiopia prefer the freedom of mobility to the accumulation of wealth practiced by the Danakil, with whom they trade in the village of Bati. Proud of their heritage, the Anharic invoke Owen Lattimore's words, "the pure nomad is a poor nomad."

Among the modern Cree, there is conflict between the traditional Cree expectation associated with the "good man" who may counsel but never coerce and the Canadian government's expectations of a chief that he must gain compliance with their orders.

Tristes Tropiques

Unlike many a French thinker, Claude Lévi-Strauss has done field work. His account of tribes in Brazil galvanized budding anthropologists all over the world. Find here the inelegant roots of elegant structuralism.

—SB

[suggested by Michael Harner]

Tristes Tropiques
Claude Lévi-Strauss
1955, 1970; 403 pp.

$3.25 postpaid

from:
Atheneum Publishers
122 E. 42nd St
New York, N.Y. 10017

or WHOLE EARTH CATALOG

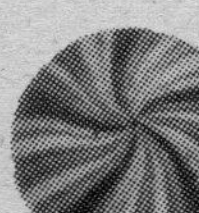

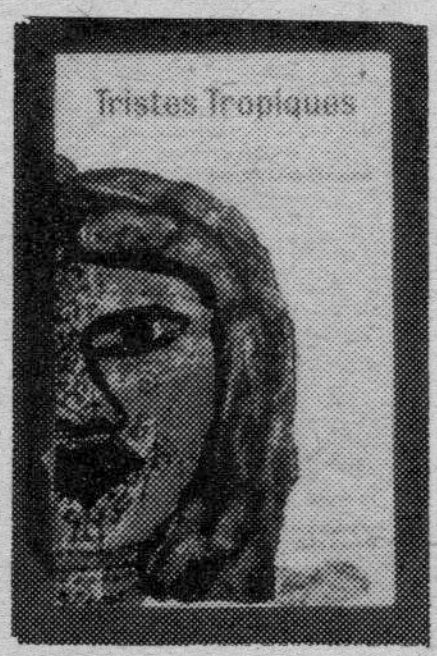

That the object of our studies should be attainable only by continual struggle and vain expenditures does not mean that we should set any store by what we should rather consider as the negative aspect of our profession. The truths that we travel so far to seek are of value only when we have scraped them clean of all this fungus.

•

And then there was that strange element in the evolution of so many towns: the drive to the west which so often leaves the eastern part of the town in poverty and dereliction. It may be merely the expression of that cosmic rhythm which has possessed mankind from the earliest times and springs from the unconscious realization that to move with the sun is positive, and to move against it negative; the one stands for order, the other for disorder.

•

The ensemble of a people's customs has always its particular style; they form into systems. I am convinced that the number of these systems is not unlimited and that human societies, like individual human beings (at play, in their dreams, or in moments of delirium), never create *absolutely:* all they can do is to choose certain combinations from a repertory of ideas which it should be possible to reconstitute.

•

What we call 'natural' sentiments were held in great disfavour in their society: for instance, the idea of procreation filled them with disgust. Abortion and infanticide were so common as to be almost normal—to the extent, in fact, that it was by adoption, rather than by procreation, that the group ensured its continuance. One of the main objects of the warriors' expeditions was to bring back children. At the beginning of the nineteenth century it was estimated that not more than one in ten of Guaicuru group were Guaicuru by birth.

•

No society is perfect. Each has within itself, by nature, an impurity incompatible with the norms to which it lays claim: this impurity finds outlet in elements of injustice, cruelty, and insensitivity. How are we to evaluate those elements? Anthropological enquiry can provide the answer. For while the comparison of a small number of societies will make them seem very different from one another, these differences will seem smaller and smaller as the field of investigation is enlarged. It will eventually become plain that no human society is fundamentally good: but neither is any of them fundamentally bad; all offer their members certain advantages, though we must bear in mind a residue of iniquity, apparently more or less constant in its importance, which may correspond to a specific inertia which offers resistance, on the level of social life, to all attempts at organization.

•

When we make an effort to understand, we destroy the object of our attachment, substituting another whose nature is quite different. That other object requires of us another effort, which in its turn destroys the second object and substitutes a third—and so on until we reach the only enduring Presence, which is that in which all distinction between meaning and the absence of meaning disappears: and it is from that Presence that we started in the first place. It is now two thousand five hundred years since men discovered and formulated these truths. Since then we have discovered nothing new—unless it be that whenever we investigated what seemed to be a way out, we met with a further proof of the conclusions from which we had tried to escape.

The Bible of the World

A collection of the essential writings of the eight major religions—Hindu, Buddhist, Confucianist, Taoist, Zoroastrian, Judeo-Christian, and Mohammedan. Super for dipping into as literature & poetry; more than adequate at conveying the essential sameness, rather than the differences between religious philosophies. Softly mind-expanding.

[Reviewed by Diana Shugart]

The Bible of the World
Robert O. Ballou, editor
1939; 1415 pp.

$4.95 plus $.15 postage

Avon Books
Order Dept., 8th floor
250 West 55th St.
New York, N.Y. 10019

OR WHOLE EARTH TRUCK STORE

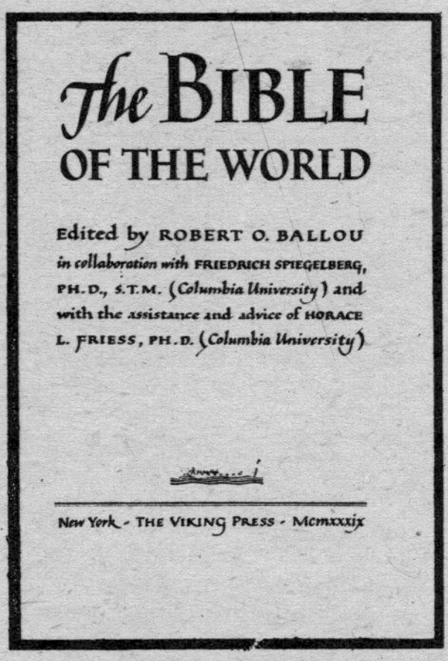
The BIBLE OF THE WORLD

Edited by ROBERT O. BALLOU in collaboration with FRIEDRICH SPIEGELBERG, PH.D., S.T.M. (Columbia University) and with the assistance and advice of HORACE L. FRIESS, PH.D. (Columbia University)

New York · THE VIKING PRESS · Mcmxxxix

(Death concludes his discourse)

There is that ancient tree, whose roots grow upward and whose branches grow downward—that indeed is called the Bright, that is called Brahman, that alone is called the Immortal. All worlds are contained in it, and no one goes beyond.

Whatever there is, the whole world, when gone forth from the Brahman, trembles in its breath. That Brahman is a great terror, like a drawn sword. Those who know it become immortal. From terror of Brahman fire burns, from terror the sun burns, from terror Indra and Vayu, and Death, as the fifth, run away.

If a man could not understand it before the falling asunder of his body, then he has to take body again in the worlds of creation.

As in a mirror, so Brahman may be seen clearly here in this body; as in a dream, in the world of the fathers; as in the water, he is seen about in the world of the Gandharvas; as in light and shade, in the world of Brahma.

Having understood that the senses are distinct from the Atman, and that their rising and setting, their waking and sleeping, belong to them in their distinct existence and not to the Atman, a wise man grieves no more.

The Upanishads

•

In hewing the wood for an axe-handle, how do you proceed? Without another axe it cannot be done.

Confucianist Scriptures

•

We sacrifice unto the undying, shining, swift-horsed Sun.

When the light of the sun waxes warmer, when the brightness of the sun waxes warmer, then up stand the heavenly Yazatas, by hundreds and thousands: they gather together its glory, they make its glory pass down, they pour its glory upon the earth made by Ahura, for the increase of the world of holiness, for the increase of the creatures of holiness, for the increase of the undying, shining, swift-horsed Sun.

And when the sun rises up, then the earth, made by Ahura, becomes clean; the running waters become clean, the waters of the wells become clean, the waters of the sea become clean, the standing waters become clean; all the holy creatures, the creatures of the Good Spirit, become clean.

Zoroastrian Scriptures

•

Then the Lord answered Job out of the whirlwind, and said, Who is this that darkeneth counsel by words without knowledge?

Gird up now thy loins like a man; for I will demand of thee, and answer thou me.

Where wast thou when I laid the foundations of the earth? declare, if thou hast understanding. Who hath laid the measures thereof, if thou knowest? or who hath stretched the line upon it? Whereupon are the foundations thereof fastened? or who laid the cornerstone thereof: when the morning stars sang together, and all the sons of God shouted for joy?

Job

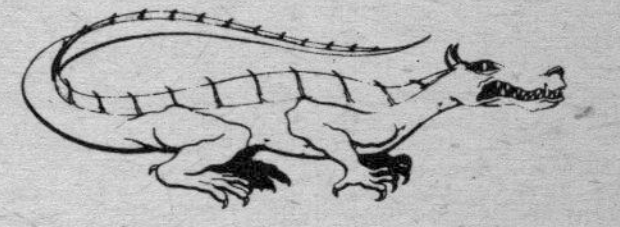

EAGLE ROCK

Sometime between first light and actual sunrise Estelle turned onto a dirt road and followed it three miles to Eagle Rock State Park, where the sign said there was a campground. They really didn't have time to stop and camp. They were almost out of money and the only chance they had of getting any any time soon was in St. Louis if they could get there by Tuesday. D.R.'s buddy Eddie owed him sixty dollars. Eddie had promised to pay D.R., but Tuesday night he was splitting St. Louis for Mexico to score a big bunch of grass. If they were going to get to St. Louis by Tuesday they certainly couldn't afford to lose a whole day camping, but, as Estelle figured it, they couldn't afford not to stop either. D.R. was getting freakier by the mile and Estelle thought she felt a cold coming on. They were both wiped out and Urge was an impossible mess. Maybe if they stopped and rested for a day, straightened up their gear and got some sun they'd both feel strong enough to make St. Louis in one more non-stop push.

There was a chain across the drive-way at the park entrance but it was easy enough to drive around it. If the ranger didn't come around later in the day to collect the camping fee, Estelle had just saved two whole dollars. It was a good omen. Stopping was the thing to do all right. As she cruised the graveled driveway looking among the assorted tents and trailers for a place to park, she began to feel really happy. The campground was incredibly crowded, but at last she found an empty space in the corner farthest from the river, a narrow slot between a GMC pickup with a great hulking camper rig on top, and a green Porsche parked in front of a red pup tent. There were beer cans all over the place, and someone had left an enormous turd lying cross ways on the metal grill above the fireplace. But Estelle was so glad to be someplace in particular she didn't let it bother her. She picked the shit up on a piece of cardboard and buried it under some leaves. In fifteen minutes she had most of the trash picked up, which included a plastic bag with some old apples in it good enough to wash and eat. I could even cook 'em, she told herself. Cooked apples. Goddamn. Her taste buds went to work on an image of apples steaming in a pot as she walked off in search of a restroom.

Parable of the Beast

if you are into molecular memory, chemical communication, slime mold colonies, time pulse perception, third eyes, acid, serotonin, intramural aggression, and other types of meta-mysticism, then bleibtreu probably has something for you, too.

he's trying to put instincts back into science and take a little of the speculation out of the name "Homo sapiens", through an introduction to the study of ethology.

readable, maybe reliable.

[Reviewed by J.D. Smith. Suggested by David Schwartz]

The Parable of the Beast
John N. Bleibtreu
1968; 304 pp.

$1.50 postpaid

from:
Collier Books
866 Third Avenue
New York, New York 10022

or WHOLE EARTH CATALOG

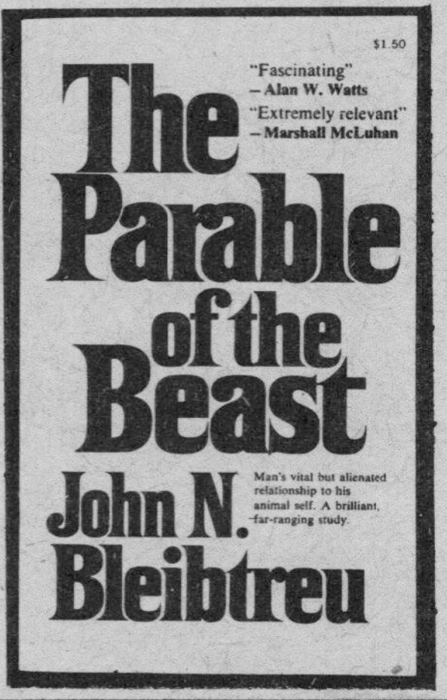

There is no longer any doubt whatever that among existing vertebrates anatomical structures are homologous, and that those two bones––the radius and the ulna––are homologous in the wing of a bird, the foreleg of a dog, and the arm of a human. The whole science of ethology is committed to the accumulation of sufficient behavioral data from all animal phyla, so that theoretical models of the evolution of behavior may be constructed.

•

Our technological control of our environment puts us into an ambiguous relationship with that environment; similar to that odd and destructive relationship that arises between a jailer and his prisoner. It seems as though the more control the jailer exercises, the more a strange kind of perverse love, a love that thrives on injury, grows between him and his charge. As the relationship develops, the prisoner often becomes the stronger of the two, inflicting by his very passivity the greater hurt.

So we, as we control the environment, have gradually become the victims of our own control. The role of cycles in our lives, being natural, should be a joyous source of strength. Generally, however, we do not acknowledge their existence at all, and when we do, we see these cyclical changes in ourselves as impediments to our efficiency.

•

The act of sharing food with one another seems to be one of the principal bases for creating societies, whether they be of the insect or human variety. It was over this ancient issue of sharing food that human beings in twentieth-century America suddenly found themselves behaving more like insects than like creatures in God's image and endowed (at least by Linnaeus) with sapience.

White Americans did not want to include Negroes within *their* society, and they understood at some infinitely deep intuitive level that if they went so far as to share food with the Negro, they could no longer effectively exclude him from the societal organism.

•

In ordinary human affairs, a breakdown in communication is generally considered catastrophic. But from the point of view of the taxonomist something new and different can only begin to occur just at that moment when communications finally do break down for good, when a splinter portion of the population finds itself so alienated from the parent group that it turns away and in upon itself, and in the process develops some new and special characters.

•

That traces of territorial marking instincts still persist among humans can be established by a wealth of detail. For example the "Kilroy Was Here" drawings of World War II are undoubtedly territorial markings. The keepers of public monuments fight a losing battle against the scrawled, carved, scratched legends that visitors leave. But perhaps the most directly territorial marking by humans is the urinal graffiti. As with animals, it is the male of the human species who is the most ardent marker; and the compulsion to mark insulting legends on the walls of urinals seemingly transects all economic classes and educational levels.

•

It is as one ascends the ladder of psychological complexity, as one observes animals up through the class of mammals, up through the order of primates, finally reaching man, that one finds what seems to be a progressive blurring of that which is innate, or given by the genetic heritage, and what is the individual response to individual experience.

But "blurring" is a poor metaphor; it seems more like an alternation, or oscillation––an oscillation between the historical past embedded within the very flesh and bone, and the perceived existential present. At each moment of our becoming (becoming older, wiser, other than what we were in the previous moment) we are being acted upon alternately by a pulse of autochthonous existence and a pulse of consciously perceived and intellectually evaluated existence; each alternating pulse modifying the next, so that, as with the sound of a flute, we are conscious, finally, only of the continuum, the thin, beautiful, and resonant sound of the self––the self, alive.

Dover Publications

Nearly every area of study has an original madman behind it. Some guy who put his life on the line to validify his notion of the universe. His value to you is that by going straight to his writings you can get some of the original juice that may have been diluted by later doctrine. Furthermore you have access to the side-thoughts that doctrine culls out. It fits you out better for your own pioneering than the tidy given-ness you get from 3rd generation interpreters.

Dover makes a practice of reprinting original work, kinks and all, in a wide variety of fields. If you're into a variety of things you might as well have their free catalog. Postage and handling for one book is $.25; $.50 for two or more.

—SB

Catalog
free

from:
Dover Publications, Inc.
180 Varick Street
New York, N.Y. 10014

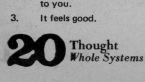

THE HUMAN FIGURE IN MOTION, Eadweard Muybridge. "Unparalleled dictionary of action for artists" (American Artist) contains more than 4500 stopped-action photographs, in series, showing undraped men, women, children jumping, lying down, running, sitting down, throwing, wrestling, carrying objects, and similar actions. Taken by the great 19th-century photographer, Muybridge, these are among the finest action shots ever taken. 4789 photographs. xvii + 390pp. 7⁷/₈ x 10⁵/₈. 20204-6 Clothbd. **$12.50**

THE UPANISHADS, translated by Max Müller. Twelve classical upanishads: Chandogya, Kena, Aitareya, Kaushitaki, Isa, Katha, Mundaka, Taittiriyaka, Brhadaranyaka, Svetasvatara, Prasna, Maitriyana. 160-page introduction, analysis by Prof. Müller. Total of 826pp. 20992-X, 20993-8 Two volumes, Paperbd. **$7.00**

THE INDIANS' BOOK, recorded and edited by Natalie Curtis. Lore, music, narratives, dozens of drawings by Indians themselves from an authoritative and important survey of native culture among Plains, Southwestern, Lake and Pueblo Indians. Standard work in popular ethnomusicology. 149 songs in full notation. 23 drawings, 23 photos. xxxi + 584pp. 6⁵/₈ x 9³/₈. 21939-9 Paperbd. **$5.00**

YOGA: A SCIENTIFIC EVALUATION, Kovoor T. Behanan. Scientific but non-technical study of physiological results of yoga exercises; done under auspices of Yale U. Relations to Indian thought, to psychoanalysis, etc. 16 photos. xxiii + 270pp. 20505-3 Paperbd. **$2.50**

THE BEAR THAT WASN'T, Frank Tashlin. Delightfully humorous, yet with serious implications; a fable for our time and an utterly charming children's story. In sum, a book that defies classification. Profusely illustrated. v + 51pp. 20939-3 Paperbd. **$1.00**

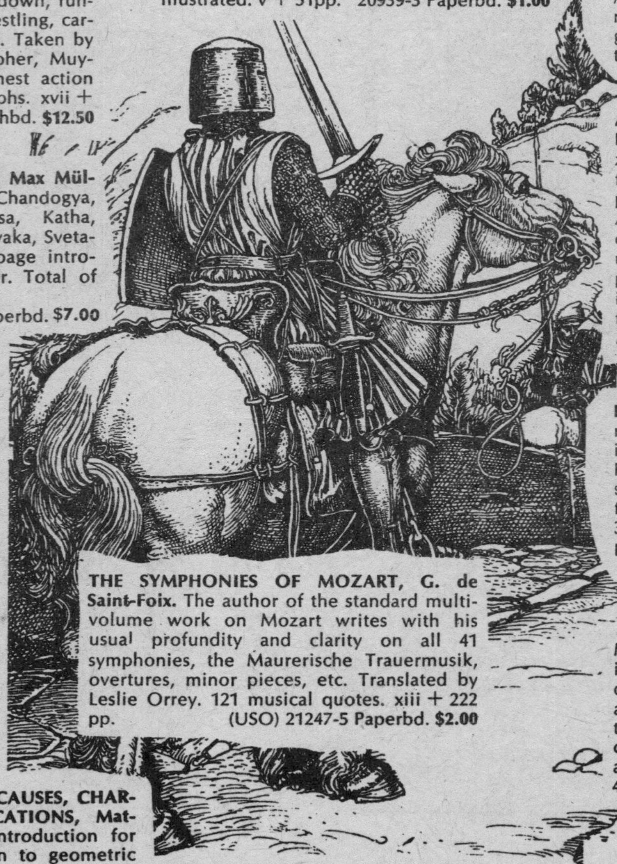

THE SYMPHONIES OF MOZART, G. de Saint-Foix. The author of the standard multi-volume work on Mozart writes with his usual profundity and clarity on all 41 symphonies, the Maurerische Trauermusik, overtures, minor pieces, etc. Translated by Leslie Orrey. 121 musical quotes. xiii + 222 pp. (USO) 21247-5 Paperbd. **$2.00**

FROM MAGIC TO SCIENCE: ESSAYS ON THE SCIENTIFIC TWILIGHT, Dr. Charles Singer. Foremost medical historian on topics in history of medicine, related areas. Medicine in the Roman Empire, the Dark Ages, School of Salerno, early English magic and medicine, herbals, St. Hildegarde and migraine visions, etc. 122 illustrations. xxxi + 253pp. 20390-5 Paperbd. **$2.75**

ABSOLUTELY MAD INVENTIONS, A. E. Brown and H. A. Jeffcott, Jr. Inventions—zany, absurd, hilarious, useless or merely fanciful—all of which have been granted patents by the United States Patent Office. An edible tie pin, a balloon propelled by eagles and vultures, and a locket to hold used chewing gum, are but three of the proposed devices, all illustrated with the inventors' drawings and descriptions. 57 full-page illustrations. Formerly *Beware of Imitations.* 125pp. 22596-8 Paperbd. **$1.50**

PRIMITIVE ART, Franz Boas. America's foremost anthropologist surveys textiles, ceramics, woodcarving, basketry, metalwork, etc. Patterns, technology, creation of symbols, style origins. All areas of world, but very full on Northwest Coast Indians. More than 350 illustrations of baskets, boxes, totem-poles, weapons, etc. 378pp. 20025-6 Paperbd. **$3.00**

MECHANICS, J. P. Den Hartog. A classic introductory text or refresher. Hundreds of actual applications and design problems are used to illuminate fundamentals of trusses, jacks, hoists, loaded beams and cables, gyroscopes, etc. Over 550 diagrams and drawings. 334 answered problems. x + 462pp. 60754-2 Paperbd. **$4.50**

VISUAL ILLUSIONS: THEIR CAUSES, CHARACTERISTICS, AND APPLICATIONS, Matthew Luckiesh. Thorough introduction for psychologists, artists, laymen to geometric and perspective illusions; size and shape distortions; illusions of color, of motion; natural illusions; psychology involved. Also uses of illusions in arts, magic, science. Introduction by William H. Ittleson. 100 illustrations. xxi + 252pp. 21530-X Paperbd. **$2.00**

SNOW CRYSTALS, W. A. Bentley and W. J. Humphreys. Over 2,000 beautiful, clear snowflakes (and occasional ice formations) enlarged from photomicrographs. Brief text on methodology of research. Can be used for decoration in many contexts. 202 plates. 226pp. 8 x 10¹/₄. 20287-9 Paperbd. **$5.00**

AN INVESTIGATION OF THE LAWS OF THOUGHT, George Boole. Classic in symbolic logic, still most useful as an introduction showing use of algebraic methods, calculus of probabilities, and similar material. Reprint of 1854 edition. xi + 424pp. 60028-9 Paperbd. **$3.00**

How To Win Games and Influence Destiny I & II

Youthful elderly wisdom. Nicely put together.

—SB

How To Win Games and Influence Destiny, Vols. I & II
Rick Strauss
1969; 69 pp.

OUT OF PRINT

Gryphon House
Box 2537, Toluca Station
North Hollywood, CA 91602

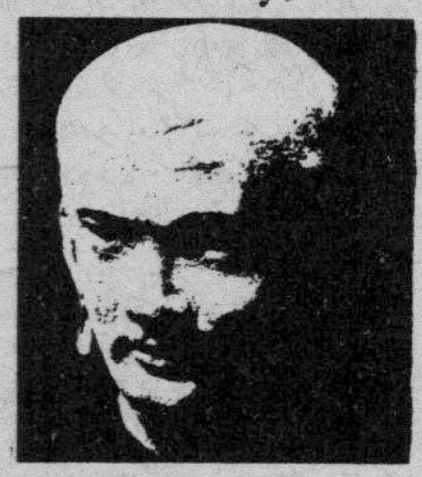

No man enters a relationship except on purpose. The question is always, "How do I best stay alive and happy?"

The answer is eternally the same. "No matter how hard you work to better yourself, you can't possibly be happy while the people around you are down. It's plain common sense then *to start out with making others happy.*" Now you can relax.

•

HOW TO TELL UP FROM DOWN

There are 3 characteristic signs which appear when you're headed in the right direction:

1. There's an immediately noticeable improvement in the style of your daily existence.
2. You gradually assume conscious control over what happens to you.
3. It feels good.

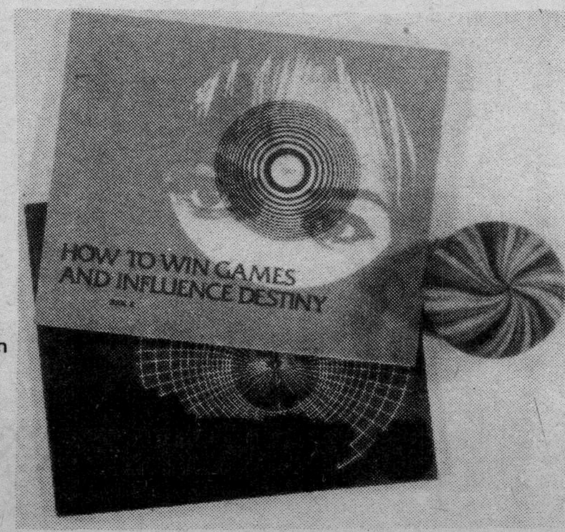

Ecology and Revolutionary Thought

To sum up the critical message of ecology: If we diminish variety in the natural world, we debase its unity and wholeness. We destroy the forces making for natural harmony and stability, for a lasting equilibrium, and what is even more significant, we introduce an absolute retrogression in the development of the natural world, eventually rendering the environment unfit for advanced forms of life. To sum up the reconstructive message of ecology: If we wish to advance the unity and stability of the natural world, if we wish to harmonize it on ever higher levels of development, we must conserve and promote variety. To be sure, mere variety for its own sake is a vacuous goal. In nature, variety emerges spontaneously. The capacities of a new species are tested by the rigours of climate, by its ability to deal with predators, by its capacity to establish and enlarge its niche. *Yet the species that succeeds in enlarging its niche in the environment also enlarges the ecological situation as a whole.* To borrow E. A. Gutkind's phrase, it "expands the environment", both for itself and for the species with which it enters into a balanced relationship.

"Ecology and Revolutionary Thought"
Lewis Herber
Anarchos, Feb 69

PO Box 466
Peter Stuyvesant Station
New York, N. Y. 10009

The Rise of the West

One humanity, one history, one fat little book. Some familiarity with world history will not help you to avoid mistakes, but it may help you recognize them and thus move on to more original ones.
—SB

[Suggested by Jib Fowles]

The Rise of The West
W. H. McNeil
1963; 896 pp.

$4.25 postpaid

from: University of Chicago Press
5801 Ellis Avenue
Chicago, Illinois 60637

or WHOLE EARTH CATALOG

In the New World, the so-called "classic" period of the Amerindian civilizations continued in full bloom for several centuries after 600 A.D. In Guatemala and adjacent parts of Mexico, classic Mayan cult centers increased in number and complexity. Then, about the middle of the ninth century, Mayan temples began to be abandoned, one by one, and jungle grew back over the vast courtyards, roadways, and steps pyramids. Yet there is no reason to suppose that the Mayan populations abandoned the region. Perhaps raids from the north destroyed the prestige of gods who failed to protect their people from merely human enemies. Or invaders may have captured and sacrificed the corps of ritual experts, thus preventing the continuance of the old elaborate cults, even if the common people still retained full faith in them. But, in view of the absence of any signs of violence at the deserted sites, it is more probably that the priestly specialists simply failed to prevent the spread of a simpler, popular religion that allowed individual farmers to assure the fertility of their maize fields by appropriate private ceremonies, thus rendering the priests' costly ritual services otiose. In the sixteenth century, European intruders found just such a private cult among the Mayan peoples, which (whenever it was introduced) obviously made the elaborate temple centers of an earlier age permanently unnecessary.

The fact that even the best laid plans for directing human affairs still often fail may turn out to be humanity's saving grace.

Once their intellectual curiosity had been aroused, Westerners discovered that the Moslems possessed a sophistication of mind and richness of learning far surpassing that available in Latin. Regular schools of translators therefore set eagerly to work to bring the treasures of Arabic learning to the Latin world. Toledo became the principal seat of this activity; but parallel work was done also in Sicily and, on a smaller scale, at Salerno, Salamanca, and Venice. The translators sought useful knowledge and were little concerned with belles-lettres. Hence they concentrated on works of medicine, mathematics, astronomy, optics, philosophy, and encyclopedic collections of information about the natural and supernatural world.

Men some centuries from now will surely look back upon our time as a golden age of unparalleled technical, intellectual, institutional, and perhaps even of artistic creativity. Life in Demosthenes' Athens, in Confucius' China, and in Mohammed's Arabia was violent, risky, and uncertain; hopes struggled with fears, greatness teetered perilously on the brim of disaster. We belong in this high company and should count ourselves fortunate to live in one of the great ages of the world.

A Year From Monday

John Cage is bright, original, and cheerful. Reading him makes me feel the same. His subject these days is "How to Improve the World (You Will Only Make Matters Worse)". Practical hints, slipped past like a puck behind the goalie's back.
—SB

Everything we come across is to the point. **Living underground because there was no money.** **Arizona land and air permitted making mounds, covering them with cement, excavating to produce rooms, providing these with skylights.** **For anyone approaching, the community was invisible.** **Cacti, desert plants: the land seemed undisturbed.** *Quantity (abundance) changes what's vice, what's virtue.* *Selfishness is out; carelessness is in.* *(Waste's*

A Year From Monday

A Year From Monday
John Cage
1963; 167 pp.

$2.45 postpaid

from: Wesleyan University Press
Middletown, Conn. 06457

or WHOLE EARTH CATALOG

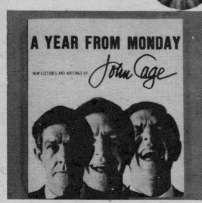

to wait. XXXVI. *Weather feels good. Isn't.* *More rain is needed.* *Water. He played two games, winning one, losing the other.* *He was continually himself, totally involved in each game, unmoved by the outcome of either.* *What's the nature of his teaching?* *For one thing: devotion (practice gives evidence of it).* *For another: not just playing half the game but playing all of it (having a view that includes that of the opponent).* *Suddenly a clam rose to*

Liberations

Visiting Fellows at Wesleyan in 1969-70 searching Humanities in Revolution. More John Cage, Fuller, Ihab Hassan, Daniel Stern, Harold Rosenberg, etc. Substantial green intellectualizing.
—SB

Liberations
Ihab Hassan, ed.
1971; 215 pp.

$3.95 postpaid

from:
Wesleyan University Press
100 Riverview Center
Middletown, Connecticut 06457

or WHOLE EARTH CATALOG

Most men of fifty or so are more intimate with another revolution, with the peculiar timebound apocalypse (for so we now see it) of the Thirties. There was almost pathetic testimony to this at a conference on The Future held at Rutgers University in 1965, where the discussion, dominated by well-known writers from New York, got stuck in the Thirties, as if the only true basis for prediction was in that period. I was never myself subjected to any experience comparable to the cauldron of New York left politics, but I could understand the fixation; my late teens were dominated by the Depression and the Spanish Civil War and the Moscow Trials and the Ribbentrop Pact. It is difficult, and probably useless, to go into this with the young. The Marxism of the time was cruder, the economic predictions on which we founded our certainties of disaster and renovation were wrong, and we all made, without thinking, certain reservations about our own roles in a transformed society which now seem naive or even dishonest. But there are, for all that, resemblances between then and now. It seemed quite certain that after the crisis there would be a wholly new state of affairs, not a modification of the old one.

Zipf

Zipf, George Kingsley.
Human Behavior and the Principle of Least Effort,
New York 1965. LC 65-20086
indefatigably interdisciplinary
irreverent infuriating
but where else can you find a book which contains:
a table of 'voiceless aspirated fortes
and voiceless unaspirated lenes stops
in present-day Peipingese' (p. 101)
a discussion of 'Death as an
economic convenience and not as a
biological necessity' (p. 236)
and the application of logarithmic
functions to anything and
everything that can be quantified
from Joycean vocabulary to
obituary notices in the N Y Times
not to everybody's taste
perhaps not to anybody's taste
but in his own way Zipf is as
mavericky as B. Fuller

$13.95, Hafner

Alan Ritch
Laguna Beach, CA

People speak of literacy. But I, for one, can't read or write any computer language. Only numbers I know are those based on ten. I'm uneducated. Home in Wayzata, Minnesota's very much like a home near Sitges (just south of Barcelona). Now we're itinerant there's no reason to go on, for instance, picking fruit. Since we live longer, Margaret Mead says, we can change what we do. We can stop whatever it was we promised we'd always do and do something else. CXXXII. He is one of my closest friends. He asked me for help. I gave it. He couldn't use it. TV Guide tells what's going on, doesn't tell what we're obliged to look at. Where you are limits what channels you can receive. (Hearing sounds before they're audible is not the way to hear them.) Imitate the telephones of your

ESTELLE'S SHOWER

It was at the Eagle Rock State Park campground that Estelle took the most delicious hot shower she'd ever had in her entire life. It was like a dream. The water pounded her neck and shoulders and folded her up in great hot clouds of steam. I'm a taco, she thought, a hot tamale cooking in a pan. The water sprayed into her mouth, the steam filled her ears and nose and seeped in at the corners of her eyes. After a night of cold rain on the open road, here she was in hot rain in a room, a steam room that at five fifteen in the morning belonged to her alone. She ran out of the shower for a minute to turn on all the other showers. In the corner stall she found a brand new bar of Dial soap, and as the bathroom filled with steam, Estelle washed herself all over, then shampooed her hair. She stayed under the water till her fingers began to wrinkle. Finally she managed to draw away from the shower stall into the cloud outside, where she used her shirt for a towel. When she was dry she went to the door and looked out, holding her clothes in her hand. The camp was sound asleep. Not even the birds were stirring yet. Laughing out loud, Estelle skipped naked down the gravel street to dear old Urge, stopping off along the way to steal some firewood from a shed that was selling it on the honor system for seventy five cents a bundle.

The Year 2000

Is Herman Kahn the bad guy (as liberal opinion would have it) or a good guy (as in some informed opinion)? Kahn will hang you on that question and while you're hanging jam information and scalding notions into your ambivalence. He does this best with a live audience, but this book is a fine collection of the information he uses.

Here is most of the now-basic methodology of future study—multi-fold trends, surprise-free projections, scenarios, etc. And here are their results. It's the best future-book of the several that are out.

In my opinion, it is not particularly an accurate picture of the future but the most thorough picture we have of the present—the present statistics, present fantasies, present expectations that we're planning with. We are what we think our future is.

—SB

The Year 2000
Herman Kahn and Anthony J. Wiener
1967; 431 pp.

$9.95 postpaid

from:
The Macmillan Company
Front and Brown Streets
Riverside, Burlington County
New Jersey 08075

or WHOLE EARTH CATALOG

The Futurist

In part because the Future is a new field of methodic study this is a lively newsletter. It reports bi-monthly on new books and programs having anything to do with social forecasting. Future study is like education: everybody thinks they're good at it. The newsletter has some of that diluted flavor, but it doesn't matter. Useful pointing at useful activities done here.

—SB

The Futurist

$10.00

for one year (bi-monthly)

from:
World Future Society
4916 St. Elmo Avenue
Washington, D.C. 20014

Maslow's Hierarchy of Needs

Abraham Maslow, a Brandeis University psychologist, has postulated that all men share certain basic needs which can be arranged in a hierarchy of five levels, from the most fundamental physiologic needs to the needs of intellectual and spiritual fulfillment. The five levels are:

1. *Physiological needs:* To survive, man needs food, clothing, shelter, rest. As the imperative requirements for staying alive, these represent the most elemental needs.

2. *Safety or security needs:* When physiological needs are satisfied, man wants to keep and protect what he has. He starts to try to stabilize his environment for the future.

3. *Social needs:* As his environment becomes more stable, he seeks to be part of something larger than himself. He has social needs for belonging, for sharing and association, for giving and receiving friendship and love.

4. *Ego needs:* These are the needs that relate to one's self-esteem (needs for self-confidence, independence, achievement, competence, knowledge) and one's reputation (needs for status, recognition, appreciation, deserved respect of one's peers).

5. *Self-fulfillment needs:* Finally comes the need for growth, self-development, self-actualization. As the capstone of all his other needs, man wants to realize the full range of his individual potential as a human being.

At each level, needs determine values and patterns of behavior. At the survival level, for instance, man values food, clothing and shelter most highly. It is important to note that a satisfied need is not a motivator of behavior. (Once hunger has been satisfied, it no longer has much motivating force.) Furthermore, higher level needs operate only when lower level needs continue to be met.

A Generation Looking for "Munich" May Be Followed
by a Generation Looking for "Vietnam"

There was, once upon a time, a generation whose consciousness was formed by Munich, and that generation has been walking around looking for Munich ever since. Among them are the guys who got us into this crazy disaster in Vietnam, because they were looking for Munich and they thought they had found another one.

Try to think what it is going to mean to have millions of Americans looking for Vietnam the rest of their lives. That is: the first thing they say about an American President is: "He is probably lying to us." Not the last thing. Not the thing you come to through great suffering. But the first thing you say is: "That son-of-a-bitch is probably lying, because every American President I can ever remember has been lying to us."

That is going to cut very deep, because if you are living in a society in which a big chunk just doesn't believe the government is legitimate, or thinks it probably isn't, and you've got to prove to them with great labor that it is, that is a very strange event in American history.

—Arthur I. Waskow

Changes in value systems will be the major determinant of social, political and economic developments on the domestic scene.

It may well be that identifying value changes will become the single most important element of environmental forecasting. For, if these changes can be identified and analyzed, then it will be that much more feasible to predict the course of the major currents in our society.

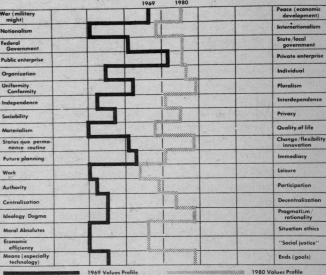

Profile of Significant Value-System Changes: 1969-1980
as seen by General Electric's Business Environment section

1969 Values Profile	1980 Values Profile
War (military might)	Peace (economic development)
Nationalism	Internationalism
Federal Government	State/local government
Public enterprise	Private enterprise
Organization	Individual
Uniformity Conformity	Pluralism
Independence	Interdependence
Sociability	Privacy
Materialism	Quality of life
Status quo permanence routine	Change/flexibility innovation
Future planning	Immediacy
Work	Leisure
Authority	Participation
Centralization	Decentralization
Ideology Dogma	Pragmatism/rationality
Moral Absolutes	Situation ethics
Economic efficiency	"Social justice"
Means (especially technology)	Ends (goals)

One way of anticipating probable changes in values, attitudes and behavior is to view them as the consequences of a progression, on a national scale, up Maslow's hierarchy of needs. Since man is a creature of seemingly endless needs, we can predict that, when one has been satisfied, another will appear in its place. Furthermore, when one level of needs has been satisfied, he will proceed to the next level. The levels are progressively less essential in terms of sheer survival, and more important in terms of living at one's fullest human potential (which seems to be the ultimate level of aspiration).

Mankind 2000

Politicians seldom invent things. They respond to pressures by reaching into the current social invention bag and finding whatever looks like the most promising program for this day our daily conflict.

So who makes the inventions? A motley crew is who. Political aids, academes, business entrepreneurs, artists, liberal scientists, and occasionally a grass root and friends. Some of their thoughts get published; some purely happen.

Whether you're an inventor or a piece of the pressure, you may want to know what's in the bag so far for the rest of this century. This book has a good range of the published ideas and expectable pressures, some lovely, some harrowing, all impinging on your very own personal world to come.

—SB

Mankind 2000
Robert Jungk, Johan Galtung, Ed.
1969; 368 pp.

$10.00 postpaid

from:
Universitetsforlaget
P. O. Box 142
Boston, Mass. 02113

or WHOLE EARTH CATALOG

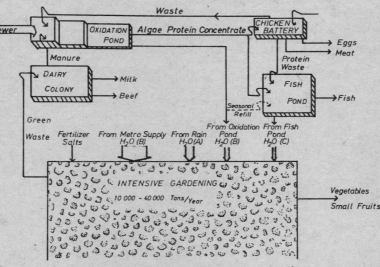

Fig. 3. *Production of perishable foods in urban village*
(Population up to 35,000 persons)

The neatest case is the sit-ins, where the civil rights movement said, "Our desirable-achievable future is that we want to be able to eat in integrated restaurants. We will not petition legislatures to require integration, we will not petition the owners of the restaurants to integrate, *we will simply create the future*. This is, we will integrate the restaurants, and it will rest upon those who have the power of law and the power of ownership in their hands, to decide how to respond to that creation. So we will build *now* what it is we want to exist in the future, and society will have to react to that. It will have to let us build it, or it will have to punish us for building it. If it punishes us for building it, we believe we can build support around that vision of the future, and can, therefore, mobilize people into action to achieve that future."

Arthur I. Waskow

We might be able to create "future gaming" centers which could offer experience in "living" alternative futures to people who are fed up with the present but have no feel for a workable or desirable society.

Arthur I. Waskow

Sewage-produced algae would be fed to chickens and fish (cattle do not need the protein) according to minor modifications of existing art in these forms of husbandry (Fig. 3).

Altogether, about two thirds or more of the weight and at least a quarter of the caloric intake of the urban diet can very likely be produced economically inside the city itself using present knowledge.

Richard L. Meier

Even in advanced countries, futurology is not necessarily identical and, moreover, can be roughly divided into three groups:

European type
US-Soviet type
Japanese type

Yujiro Hayashi

In the times of Antipatro the Macedonian, the first water-driven mills made people exclaim, "The Golden Age is returning!"

Silvio Ceccato

Tuesday's Child

All through the riots of '72 we watched, itching to leave the city but somehow still attached. I mean, we knew. We knew as early as '67, but it was so science-fictiony that we just kind of dreamed happily over it, making incredibly detailed lists, playing with the Ouija Board, studying astrology and making predictions in an off-handedly superior way. We got disillusioned in '68, and went on a lot of sidetrips, falling in love, losing it, moving, practicing all kinds of odd crafts, having babies. We knew what was happening by '69. We had our Whole Earth catalogs, and our stash of Acapulco and Panamanian pot seeds, and we were desperately raking bread, working, trying to get it together.

It was a communal trip at first, and gradually it got thinner, down to the family, and the family seemed to be a lot smaller than we'd thought. Government pamphlets, nightsoil, organic gardening, Diesel engines, music, meditation and chauvinism mounted. We decided to leave in secret.

All the mediums, most of the astrologers, some of the psychics, and even some political economists agreed that we were eating the earth into Armageddon. So we still waited, planning, collecting. In '73 we got into our bus and split for Oregon. We drove all night and the better part of the day, slept just in time to hear on the car radio that Red China had started bombing somebody, but not us yet, thank God. We woke and drove again, through the night, and finally we got there, and fell out, exhausted. In the morning the baby started to cry.

We got up. Outside the curtained windows of our bus, through the trees and the virgin country, we saw seven tepees, three Volkswagen busses, two school busses, one Renault Dauphine with a pup tent on top of it, a half-hewn cabin, two chemical toilets, several dogs, more cats, a fire somewhere off in the distance, and standing around us were ninety-seven people. They looked hungry. They all had long hair. Nobody was smiling.

We ate the ones over thirty first.

Later, the soldiers came.

What's wrong with this story?

from *Tuesday's Child*—Vol. 1, No. 1

1616 North Argyle Ave.
Hollywood, CA 90028
$6/yr.

It is as impossible to appeal to a neutral principle to determine the rationality of competing systems, as it is to invoke a neutral vocabulary to characterize a language. It is in the name of one kind of logic that one rejects the logic of another. Arnold Nash illustrated this "irrational prejudice" of reason very well in the story of a doctoral examination. The candidate, who submitted a study on Mormon history, was asked whether he, being a Mormon, regarded himself sufficiently unprejudiced to write a thesis on Mormon history. The student replied, "Yes, if you, not a Mormon, consider yourself unprejudiced enough to examine it."

•

An important difference exists between "having-no" knowledge and having "no-knowledge." The former is merely a state of ignorance; the latter is one of ultimate enlightenment and universal sensibilities. To the confirmed rationalist, no-knowledge may appear to be the hugger-muggery of the mystagogue. Nevertheless, it is precisely its ineffability that lends force to its reality. The mysteries of nature appear to be mysteries only to those who refuse to participate in them. . . .

With rational knowledge, the scientist is a spectator of nature. With no-knowledge, he becomes a participant in nature. There is a communion of understandings, of many individuals, who "fear of finding oneself alone," as André Gide describes it, "and so they don't find themselves at all."

The Emerging Japanese Superstate

After some uncomfortable years with the old cliché —— California Is The Future——I welcome the new cliché—— Japan Is The Future. After a visit there last year, I do believe that all futurists should do some time in industrial Japan. Not just awesome statistics, as Kahn cogently points out, but a whole national psyche is cooking there. A sense of Manifest Destiny that dwarfs Israel's. Generational conflict like and oddly unlike our own. Ecological practice far worse and far better than anyone else's. The damndest loyalties. Insatiable resource hunger. Desire for nuclear weapons. Planetary impact, and maybe leadership.

It'll be nice to have California merely quaint again.

—SB

The Emerging Japanese Superstate
Herman Kahn
1970; 274 pp.

$2.45 paper edition

from:
Prentice-Hall, Inc.
Englewood Cliffs, N.J. 07632

or WHOLE EARTH CATALOG

MATSUSHITA WORKERS' SONG

For the building of a new Japan,
Let's put our strength and mind together,
Doing our best to promote production,
Sending our goods to the people of the world,
Endlessly and continuously,
Like water gushing from a fountain.
Grow, industry, grow, grow, grow!
Harmony and sincerity!
Matsushita Electric!

The Tao of Science

No high-minded bridging of East and West, this. But a successful director of research showing how valuable an informed and experienced Taoist sense of harmony can be to the conduct of science. It can help balance the scientist, and it offers an avenue to balancing the application of what the scientist learns. Good medicine for over-specialization.

—SB

The Tao of Science
R. G. H. Siu
1957; 180 pp.

$2.45 postpaid

from:
The M. I. T. Press
50 Ames Street, Room 765
Cambridge, Mass. 02142

or WHOLE EARTH CATALOG

. . . This all-embracing applicability of no-knowledge makes it a valuable tool for the executive. It provides him with a common ground of all situations. It is his means of transcendence over specific experience of which he has not yet tasted. Versed in no-knowledge, he is at home under otherwise strange conditions; he always finds familiar strains in his management of assorted enterprises.

The scientific West adopts the positive method and the Taoist East the negative. In the positive method the item under question is intentionally pointed out and described. In the negative method, it is specifically not discussed. By not dissecting the ineffable x in question but merely restricting discourse to objects that it is not, the features of the x are revealed in our dim consciousness.

Communal. In nearly all activities and issues the Japanese traditionally think of themselves as members of a group, and their satisfactions are largely expected to come through group fulfillment of group objectives. In traditional Japanese culture, and to an amazing degree today (despite a nominal emphasis on democratic individuality and other erosions of traditional patterns and ties), one of the worst of all sins is to display an egoistic disregard of, disinterest in, or resistance to group mores, attitudes, taboos, totems, traditions, or objectives——or often just to display any individualism at all.

•

Traditionally every Japanese is part of a hierarchical structure. There are people who rank above every individual, except the Emperor and the shogun, and except for the youngest daughter of a member of the outcast Burakus, there are people beneath. To say in Japan that certain people are equal generally implies they are in equal distance from some common superior——i.e., they are equal in the way two privates or two generals are equal. Both have common rank in a pyramidal hierarchical structure.

It should also be noted that in probably no place in the world but Japan are such songs sung voluntarily and for fun. Certainly not in China, where there is a grim compulsion about singing them and where pleasure and voluntarism are the last two words one would use to describe the situation. It was interesting to me that at one time in Vietnam, when the Viet Cong took over a village they often made the people sing such songs for an hour or two. And when the Saigon government took over a village they too made the villagers sing songs for a half hour or so. However, when the villagers were queried, "What do you want?" the answer was almost invariably, among other things, "We want to quit singing."

The point I wish to make is the contrast between the high morale of present-day Japanese culture——in at least this matter of production——and the very low morale in the West on almost all issues.

GNP, Billion 1967
U.S. Dollars

[Graph: Line chart plotting GNP in billions of 1967 U.S. Dollars (logarithmic vertical axis from 30 to 1,000) against years 1950 to 70 along the horizontal axis. Lines labeled: U.S., U.S.S.R., Japan, W. Germany & W. Berlin, France, U.K., Mainland China.]

Note: Purchasing power exchange rates are used.

THE LONE OUTDOORSMAN

About eight o'clock a man in a red hunting cap came out of the camper parked next to Urge and began dismounting the yellow trailbike from the front end of his GMC. He was short and overweight but you could tell by the way he wore his cap and held his pipe between his teeth that he took himself pretty seriously. His face was absurdly handsome. His face could have been in a TV ad for pipe tobacco, or a men's cologne. Probably in some previous incarnation the Lone Outdoorsman had been the best five foot, five inch high school halfback in the conference. He had on a black and green wool shirt, army boots and fatigue pants faded to a pale green. Dangling from the army web belt around his waist were a canteen, a compass, a long sheath-knife, a first aid kit, survival kit, snake bite kit, sewing kit, and a kit to repair flat tires with. He banged and rattled like a mobile hardware store, and yet he smoked his pipe and worked on his bike like any neighborhood family man out waxing his car on a Sunday afternoon.

From time to time the Outdoorsman would glance over his shoulder and peek at Divine Right and Estelle through the overhanging trees. They were sitting on the ground in front of the fireplace, eating hot apples and talking quietly. He didn't mean to pry. He was just, you know, checking things out, looking to see if there was any crime going on over there among the hippies. He noticed they were both eating out of the same dish, out of a stewpot, as a matter of fact. That was irregular, to be sure, but not quite an infraction, nothing to call the Lone Outdoorsman into action yet. He glanced at the two young people every few minutes until he got the bike dismounted. Then he got on, started 'er up, and rode off to the bathroom a hundred yards away.

Think Little

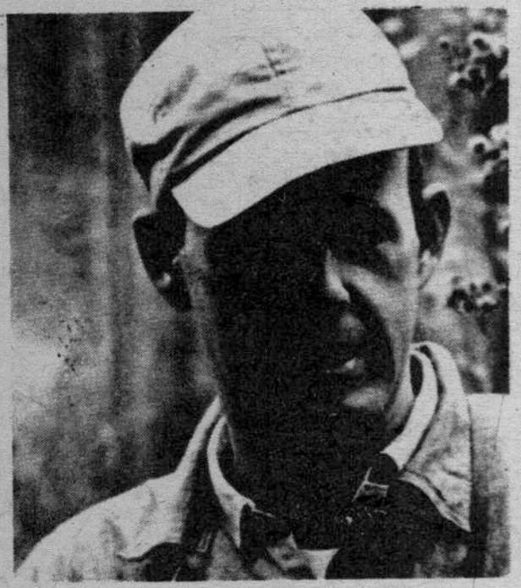

by Wendell Berry

First there was Civil Rights, and then there was The War, and now it is The Environment. The first two of this sequence of causes have already risen to the top of the nation's consciousness and declined somewhat in a remarkably short time. I mention this in order to begin with what I believe to be a justifiable skepticism. For it seems to me that the Civil Rights Movement and the Peace Movement, as popular causes in the electronic age, have partaken far too much of the nature of fads. Not for all, certainly, but for too many they have been the fashionable politics of the moment. As causes they have been undertaken too much in ignorance; they have been too much simplified; they have been powered too much by impatience and guilt of conscience and short-term enthusiasm, and too little by an authentic social vision and long-term conviction and deliveration. For most people those causes have remained almost entirely abstract; there has been too little personal involvement, and too much involvement in organizations which were insisting that *other* organizations should do what was right.

There is considerable danger that the Environment Movement will have the same nature: that it will be a public cause, served by organizations that will self-righteously criticize and condemn other organizations, inflated for a while by a lot of public talk in the media, only to be replaced in its turn by another fashionable crisis. I hope that will not happen, and I believe that there are ways to keep it from happening, but I know that if this effort is carried on solely as a public cause, if millions of people cannot or will not undertake it as a *private* cause as well, then it is *sure* to happen. In five years the energy of our present concern will have petered out in a series of public gestures——and no doubt in a series of empty laws——and a great, and perhaps the last, human opportunity will have been lost.

It need not be that way. A better possibility is that the movement to preserve the environment will be seen to be, as I think it has to be, not a digression from the civil rights and peace movements, but the logical culmination of those movements. For I believe that the separation of these three problems is artificial. They have the same cause, and that is the mentality of greed and exploitation. The mentality that exploits and destroys the natural environment is the same that abuses racial and economic minorities, that imposes on young men the tyranny of the military draft, that makes war against peasants and women and children with the indifference of technology. The mentality that destroys a watershed and then panics at the threat of flood is the same mentality that gives institutionalized insult to black people and then panics at the prospect of race riots. It is the same mentality that can mount deliberate warfare against a civilian population and then express moral shock at the logical consequence of such warfare at My Lai. We would be fools to believe that we could solve any one of these problems without solving the others.

To me, one of the most important aspects of the environmental movement is that it brings us not just to another public crisis, but to a crisis of the protest movement itself. For the environmental crisis should make it dramatically clear, as perhaps it has not always been before, that there is no public crisis that is not also private. To most advocates of civil rights racism has seemed mostly the fault of someone else. For most advocates of peace the war has been a remote reality, and the burden of the blame has seemed to rest mostly on the government. I am certain that these crises have been more private, and that we have each suffered more from them and been more responsible for them, than has been readily apparent, but the connections have been difficult to see. Racism and militarism have been institutionalized among us for too long for our personal involvement in those evils to be easily apparent to us. Think, for example, of all the Northerners who assumed——until black people attempted to move into *their* neighborhoods——that racism was a Southern phenomenon. And think how quickly——one might almost say how naturally——among some of its members the peace movement has spawned policies of deliverate provocation and violence.

But the environmental crisis rises closer to home. Every time we draw a breath, every time we drink a glass of water, every time we eat a bite of food we are suffering from it. And more important, every time we indulge in, or depend on, the wastefulness of our economy——and our economy's first principle is waste——we are *causing* the crisis. Nearly every one of us, nearly every day of his life, is contributing *directly* to the ruin of this planet. A protest meeting on the issue of environmental abuse is not a convocation of accusers, it is a convocation of the guilty. That realization ought to clear the smog of self-righteousness that has almost conventionally hovered over these occasions, and let us see the work that is to be done.

In this crisis it is certain that every one of us has a public responsibility. We must not cease to bother the government and the other institutions, to see that they never become comfortable with easy promises. For myself, I want to say that I hope never again to go to Frankfort to present a petition to the governor on an issue so vital as that of strip mining, only to be dealt with by some ignorant functionary ——as several of us were not so long ago, the governor himself being "too busy" to receive us. Next time I will go prepared to wait as long as necessary to see that the petitioners' complaints and their arguments are heard *fully*——and by the governor. And then I will hope to find ways to keep those complaints and arguments from being forgotten until something is done to relieve them. The time is past when it was enough merely to elect our officials. We will have to elect them and then go and *watch* them and keep our hands on them, the way the coal companies do. We have made a tradition in Kentucky of putting self-servers, and worse, in charge of our vital interests. I am sick of it. And I think that one way to change it is to make Frankfort a less comfortable place. I believe in American political principles, and I will not sit idly by and see those principles destroyed by sorry practice. I am ashamed and deeply distressed that American government should have become the chief cause of disillusionment with American principles.

And so when the government in Frankfort again proves too stupid or too blind or too corrupt to see the plain truth and to act with simple decency, I intend to be there, and I trust that I won't be alone. I hope, moreover, to be there, and with a sign or a slogan or a button, but with the facts and the arguments. A crowd whose discontent has risen no higher than the level of slogans is *only* a crowd. But a crowd that understands the reasons for its discontent and knows the remedies is a vital community, and it will have to be reckoned with. I would rather go before the government with two men who have a competent understanding of an issue, and who therefore deserve a hearing, than to go with two thousand who are vaguely dissatisfied.

But even the most articulate public protest is not enough. We don't live in the government or in institutions or in our public utterances and acts, and the environmental crisis has its roots in our *lives.* By the same token, environmental health will also be rooted in our lives. That is, I take it, simply a fact, and in the light of it we can see how superficial and foolish we would be to think that we could correct what is wrong merely by tinkering with the institutional machinery. The changes that are required are fundamental changes in the way we are living.

What we are up against in this country, in any attempt to involve private responsibility, is that we have nearly destroyed private life. Our people have given up their independence in return mostly for the cheap seductions and the shoddy merchandise of so-called "affluence." We have delegated all our vital functions and responsibilities to salesmen and agents and bureaus and experts of all sorts. We cannot feed or clothe ourselves, or entertain ourselves, or communicate with each other, or be charitable or neighborly or loving, or even respect ourselves, without recourse to a merchant or a corporation or a public service organization or an agency of the government or a style-setter or an expert. Most of us cannot think of dissenting from the opinions or the actions of one organization without first forming a new organization. Individualism is going around these days in uniform, handing out the party line on individualism. Dissenters want to publish their personal opinions over a thousand signatures.

The Confucian **Great Digest** says that the "chief way for the production of wealth" (and he is talking about real goods, not money) is "that tne producers be many and that the mere consumers be few. . ." But even in the much publicized rebellion of the young against the materialism of the affluent society, the consumer mentality is too often still intact: the standards of behavior are still those of kind and quantity, the security sought is still the security of numbers, and the chief motive is still the consumer's anxiety that one is missing out on what is "in." In this state of total consumerism——which is to say a state of helpless dependence on things and services and ideas and motives that we have forgotten how to provide ourselves——all meaningful contact between ourselves and the earth is broken. We do not understand the earth either in terms of what it offers us or what it requires of us, and I think it is the rule that people inevitably destroy what they do not understand. Most of us are not directly responsible for strip mining and extractive agriculture and other forms of environmental abuse. But we are guilty nevertheless, for we connive in them by our ignorance. We are ignorantly dependent on them. We do not know enough about them; we do not have a particular enough sense of their damage. Most of us, for example, not only do not know how to produce the best food in the best way——we don't know how to produce any kind in any way. And for this condition we have elaborate rationalizations, instructing us that dependence for everything on somebody else is efficient and economical and a scientific miracle. I say, instead, that it is madness, mass produced. A man who understands the weather only in terms of golf is participating in a chronic public insanity that either he or his descendents will be bound to realize as suffering. I believe that the death of the world is breeding in such minds much more certainly and much faster than in any political capital or atomic arsenal.

For an index of our loss of contact with the earth we need only to look at the condition of the American farmer——who must in our society, as in every society, enact man's dependence on the land, and his responsibility to it. In an age of unparalleled affluence and leisure, the American farmer is harder pressed and harder worked than ever before; his margin of profit is small, his hours long; his outlays for land and equipment and the expenses of maintenance and operation are growing rapidly greater; he cannot compete with industry for labor; he is being forced more and more to depend on the use of destructive chemicals and on the wasteful methods of haste and anxiety. As a class, farmers are one of the despised minorities. So far as I can see farming is considered marginal or incidental to the economy of the country, and farmers, when they are thought of at all, are thought of as hicks and yokels, whose lives do not fit into the modern scene. The average American farmer is now an old man, whose sons have moved away to the cities. His knowledge, and his intimate connection with the land are about to be lost. The small independent farmer is going the way of the small independent craftsmen and storekeepers. He is being forced off the land into the cities, his place taken by absentee owners, corporations, and machines. Some would justify all this in the name of efficiency. As I see it, it is an enormous social and economic and cultural blunder. For the small farmers who lived on their farms *cared* about their land. And given their established connection to their land——which was often hereditary and traditional as well as economic——they could have been encouraged to care for it more competently than they have so far. The corporations and machines that replace them will never be bound to the land by the sense of birthright and continuity, or by the love which enforces care. They will be bound by the rule of efficiency which takes thought only of the volume of the year's produce, and takes no thought of the slow increment of the live of the land, not measurable in pounds or dollars, which will assure the livelihood and the health of the coming generations.

If we are to hope to correct our abuses of each other and of other races and of our land, and if our effort to correct these abuses is to be more than a political fad that will in the long run be only another form of abuse, then we are going to have to go far beyond public protest and political action. We are going to have to rebuild the substance and the integrity of private life in this country. We are going to have to gather up the fragments of knowledge and responsibility that we have parceled out to the bureaus and the corporations and the specialists, and we are going to have to put those fragments back together again in our own minds and in our families and households and neighborhoods. We need better government, no doubt about it. But we also need better minds, better friendships, better marriages, better communities. We need persons and households that do not need to wait upon organizations but who can make

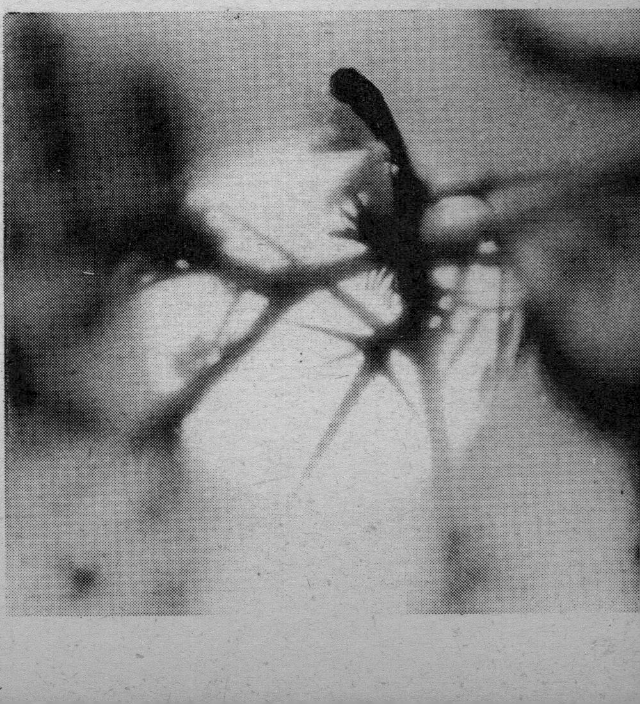

necessary changes in themselves, on their own.

For most of the history of this country our motto, implied or spoken, has been Think Big. I have come to believe that a better motto, and an essential one now, is Think Little. That implies the necessary change of thinking and feeling, and suggests the necessary work. Thinking Big has led us to the two biggest and cheapest political dodges of our time: plan-making and law-making. The lotus-eaters of this era are in Washington D.C., Thinking Big. Somebody comes up with a problem, and somebody in the government comes up with a plan or a law. The result, mostly, has been the persistence of the problem, and the enlargement and enrichment of the government.

But the discipline of thought is not generalization; it is detail, and it is personal behavior. While the government is "studying" and funding and organizing its Big Thought, nothing is being done. But the citizen who is willing to think little, and, accepting the discipline of that, to go ahead on his own, is already solving the problem. A man who is trying to live as a neighbor to his neighbors will have a lively and practical understanding of the work of peace and brotherhood, and let there be no mistake about it—he is *doing* that work. A couple who make a good marriage, and raise healthy, morally-competent children are serving the world's future more directly and surely than any political leader, though they never utter a public word. A good farmer who is dealing with the problem of soil erosion on an acre of ground has a sounder grasp of that problem, and *cares* more about it, and is probably doing more to solve it than any bureaucrat who is talking about it in general. A man who is willing to undertake the discipline and the difficulty of mending his own ways is worth more to the conservation movement than a hundred who are insisting merely that the government and the industries mend *their* ways.

If you are concerned about the proliferation of trash, then by all means start an organization in your community to do something about it. But before—*and while*—you organize, pick up some cans and bottles yourself. That way, at least, you will assure yourself and others that you mean what you say. If you are concerned about air pollution, help push for government controls, but drive your car less, use less fuel in your home. If you are worried about the damming of wilderness rivers, join the Sierra Club, write to the government, but turn off the lights you're not using, don't install an air conditioner, don't be a sucker for electrical gadgets, don't waste water. In other words, if you are fearful of the destruction of the environment, then learn to quit being an environmental parasite. We all are, in one way or another, and the remedies are not always obvious, though they certainly will always be difficult. They require a new kind of life—harder, more laborious, poorer in luxuries and gadgets, but also, I am certain, richer in meaning and more abundant in real pleasure. To have a healthy environment we will all have to give up things we like; we may even have to give up things we have come to think of as necessities. But to be fearful of the disease and yet unwilling to pay for the cure is not just to be hypocritical; it is to be doomed. If you talk a good line without being changed by what you say, then you are not just hypocritical and doomed; you have become an agent of the disease. Consider, for an example, the President, who advertises his grave concern about the destruction of the environment, and who turns up the air conditioner to make it cool enough to build a fire.

Odd as I am sure it will appear to some, I can think of no better form of personal involvement in the cure of the environment than that of gardening. A person who is growing a garden, if he is growing it organically, is improving a piece of the world. He is producing something to eat, which makes him somewhat independent of the grocery business, but he is also enlarging, for himself, the meaning of food and the pleasure of eating. The food he grows will be fresher, more nutritious, less contaminated by poisons and preservatives and dyes, than what he can buy at a store. He is reducing the trash problem; a garden is not a disposable container, and it will digest and re-use its own wastes. If he enjoys working in his garden, then he is less dependent on an automobile or a merchant for his pleasure. He is involving himself directly in the work of feeding people.

If you think I'm wandering off the subject, let me remind you that most of the vegetables necessary for a family of four can be grown on a plot of forty by sixty feet. I think we might see in this an economic potential of considerable importance, since we now appear to be facing the possibility of widespread famine. How much food could be grown in the dooryards of cities and suburbs? How much could be grown along the extravagant rights-of-way of the Interstate system? Or how much could be grown, by the intensive practices and economics of the small farm, on so-called marginal lands? Louis Bromfield liked to point out that the people of France survived crisis after crisis because they were a nation of gardeners, who in times of want turned with great skill to their own small plots of ground. And F. H. King, an agriculture professor who traveled extensively in the Orient in 1907, talked to a Chinese farmer who supported a family of twelve, "one donkey, one cow, . . .and two pigs on 2.5 acres of cultivated land"—and who did this, moreover, by agricultural methods that were sound enough organically to have maintained his land in prime fertility through several thousand years of such use. These are possibilities that are very readily apparent and attractive to minds that are prepared

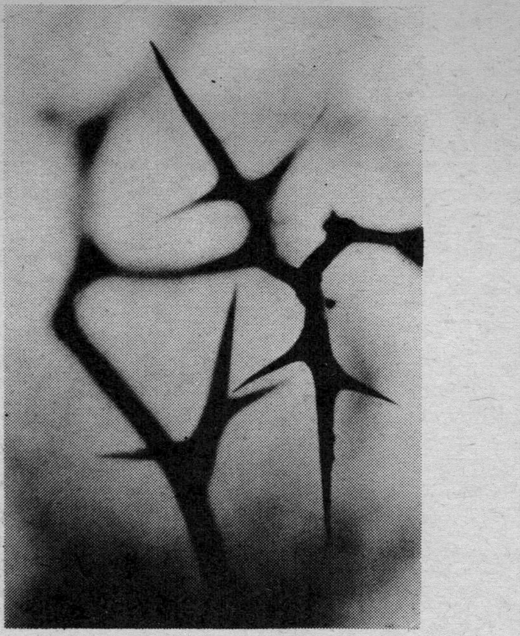

to think little. To Big Thinkers—the bureaucrats and businessmen of agriculture—they are quite simply invisible. But intensive, organic agriculture kept the farms of the Orient thriving for thousands of years, whereas extensive—which is to say, exploitive or extractive—agriculture has critically reduced the fertility of American farmlands in a few centuries or even a few decades.

A person who undertakes to grow a garden at home, by practices that will preserve rather than exploit the economy of the soil, has set his mind decisively against what is wrong with us. He is helping himself in a way that dignifies him, and that is rich in meaning and pleasure. But he is doing something else that is more important: he is making vital contact with the soil and the weather on which his life depends. He will no longer look upon rain as an impediment of traffic, or upon the sun as a holiday decoration. And his sense of man's dependence on the world will have grown precise enough, one would hope, to be politically clarifying and useful.

What I am saying is that if we apply our minds directly and competently to the needs of the earth, then we will have begun to make fundamental and very necessary changes in our minds. We will begin to understand and to mistrust *and to change* our wasteful economy, which markets not just the produce of the earth, but also the earth's ability to produce. We will see that beauty and utility are alike dependent upon the health of the world. But we will also see through the fads and the fashions of protest. We will see that war and oppression and pollution are not separate issues, but are aspects of the same issue. Amid the outcries for the liberation of this group or that, we will know that no person is free except in the freedom of other persons, and that man's only real freedom is to know and faithfully occupy his place—a much humbler place than we have been taught to hink—in the order of creation. And we will know that of all issues in education the issue of relevance is the phoniest. If life were as predictable and small as the talkers of politics would have it, then relevance would be a consideration. But life is large and surprising and mysterious, and we don't know what we need to know. When I was a student I refused certain subjects because I thought they were irrelevant to the duties of a writer, and I have had to take them up, clumsily and late, to understand my duties as a man. What we need in education is not relevance, but abundance, variety, adventurousness, thoroughness. A student should suppose that he needs to learn everything he can, and he should suppose that he will need to know much more than he can learn.

But the change of mind I am talking about involves not just a change of knowledge, but also a change of attitude toward our essential ignorance, a change in our bearing in the face of mystery. The principle of ecology, if we will take it to heart, should keep us aware that our lives depend upon other lives and upon processes and energies in an interlocking system which, though we can destroy it completely, we can neither fully understand nor fully control. And our great dangerousness is that, locked in our selfish and myopic economics, we have been willing to change or destroy far beyond our power to understand. We are not humble enough or reverent enough.

Some time ago I heard a representative of a paper company refer to conservation as a "no-return investment." This man's thinking was exclusively oriented to the annual profit of his industry. Circumscribed by the demand that the profit be great, he simply could not be answerable to any other demand—not even to the obvious needs of his own children.

Consider, in contrast, the profound ecological intelligence of Black Elk, "a holy man of the Oglala Sioux," who in telling his story said that it was not his own life that was important to him, but what he had shared with all life: "It is the story of all life that is holy and it is good to tell, and of us two-leggeds sharing in it with the four-leggeds and the wings of the air and all green things. . ." And of the great vision that came to him when he was a child he said: "I saw that the sacred hoop of my people was one of many hoops that made one circle, wide as daylight and as starlight, and in the center grew one mighty flowering tree to shelter all the children of one mother and father. And I saw that it was holy."

Wendell Berry's newest book of poems, Farming: A Hand Book, *has just been published by Harcourt, Brace and Jovanovich.* The Hidden Wound, *a book-length essay about racism, $1.25 (paper) from Ballantine Books.*

Think Little *was originally presented as an Earth-Day speech last April. It was previously published in* blue-tail fly, *a Kentucky underground newspaper.*

blue-tail fly
210 W. Third St.
Lexington, Ky. 40507
Published monthly, 25 cents a copy

Photos accompanying **Think Little** *by James Baker Hall.*

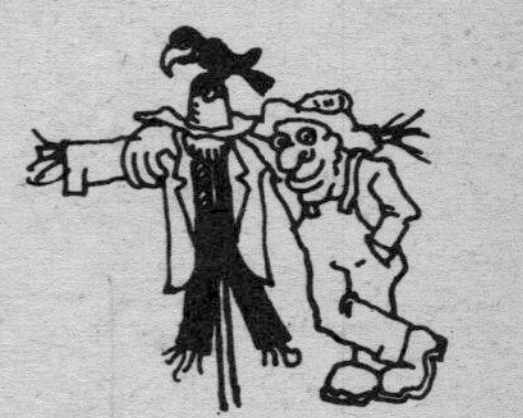

MANIFESTO: THE MAD FARMER LIBERATION FRONT

For Jack and Mary Jo

Love the quick profit, the annual raise,
vacation with pay. Want more
of everything ready made. Be afraid
to know your neighbors and to die.
And you will have a window in your head.
Not even your future will be a mystery
any more. Your mind will be punched in a card
and shut away in a little drawer.
When they want you to buy something
they will call you. When they want you
to die for profit they will let you know.
So, friends, every day do something
that won't compute. Love the Lord.
Love the world. Work for nothing.
Take all that you have and be poor.
Love someone who does not deserve it.
Denounce the government and embrace the flag.
Hope to live in that free
republic for which it stands.
Give your approval to all you cannot
understand. Praise ignorance, for what man
has not encountered he has not destroyed.
Ask the questions that have no answers.
Invest in the millennium. Plant sequoias.
Say that your main crop is the forest
that you did not plant
and that you will not live to harvest.
Say that the leaves are harvested
when they have rotted into the mold.
Call that profit. Prophesy such returns.
Put your faith in the two inches of humus
that will build under the trees every thousand years.
Listen to carrion—put your ear
close, and hear the faint chattering
of the songs that are to come.
Expect the end of the world. Laugh.
Laughter is immeasurable. Be joyful
though you have considered all the facts.
So long as women do not possess
great power, please women more than men.
Ask yourself: Will this satisfy
a woman satisfied to bear a child?
Will this disturb the sleep
of a woman near to giving birth?
Go with your love to the fields.
Lie easy in the shade. Rest your head
in her lap. Swear allegiance
to what is nighest your thoughts.
As soon as the generals and the politicos
can predict the motions of your mind,
lose it. Leave it as a sign
to mark the false trail, the way
you didn't go. Be like the fox
who makes more tracks than necessary,
some in the wrong direction.
Practice resurrection.

—Wendell Berry

Biology and the Future of Man

Where we are today technologically (and thus politically) is largely the product of several specific scientific revolutions that gathered steam early in the century—most notably mass medicine, nuclear physics, and investigation of materials. Since World War II the Information Sciences (computers, cybernetics, organization theory) have wrought considerable havoc and promise. Now we're in for biology, says everybody, probably right. Molecular biology, already mature, has only begun to hit the fan. Ecology, though in great demand, has short supply so far. The glamour light, long in molecular biology, may now be migrating into brain science, the very heart of darkness. Still waiting for systematic study is the big version of brain science. The participation of consciousness in evolution.

This book probably supports few of my assertions above. It is an authoritative up-to-the-year report on the state of biology by the leading biologists, with emphasis on unanswered questions and promising leads and possible impact of all this on society in the near future. It's a heavy book, implying no lightsome future. Technology marches on, over you or through you, take your choice.

—SB

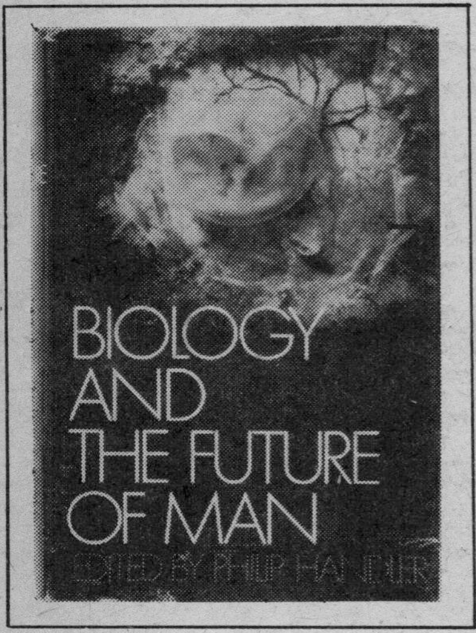

Biology and the Future of Man
Philip Handler, ed.
1970, 936 pp.

$5.95 postpaid

from:
Oxford University Press, Inc.
1600 Pollitt Drive
Fair Lawn, N.J. 07410

or WHOLE EARTH CATALOG

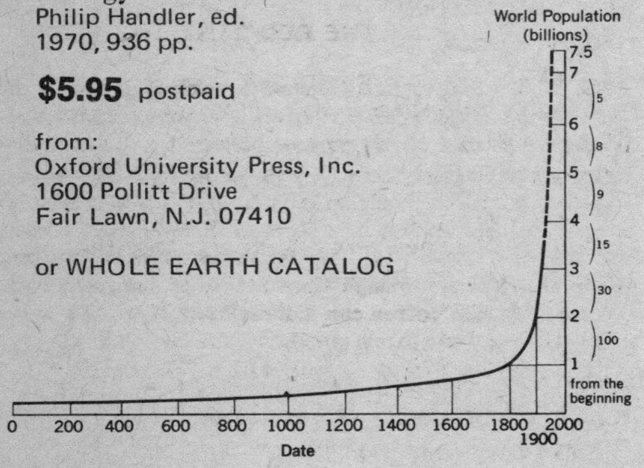

Figure 20-2. World Population Growth (Projected with assumption of constant fertility levels and declining mortality).

•

. . . any desired number of genetic twins could be produced. It would require the collection of unfertilized eggs from the oviducts of many women, removal of the egg nuclei, and replacement by the nuclei of body cells of the chosen man or woman. This would be followed by return of the eggs to the uteri of women who then would undergo normal pregnancies. In this way one could produce multiple identical copies of any person judged admirable.

•

At the present moment of extremely dangerous population growth, social pressures are best directed to lower reproduction, in general, without qualitative considerations. But one day, when populations are stable, world peace is the norm, and man's social and political institutions are sufficiently mature to assure that biological understanding will not be utilized to perpetuate injustice or strengthen dictatorship but, rather, to expand human potential, man will be free to guide his own evolutionary destiny. . . Man's view of himself has undergone many changes. From a unique position in the universe, the Copernican revolution reduced him to an inhabitant of one of many planets. From a unique position among the millions of other species which evolved from one another. Yet, *Homo sapiens* has overcome the limitations of his origin. He controls the vast energies of the atomic nucleus, moves across his planet at speeds barely below escape velocity, and can escape when he so wills. He communicates with his fellows at the speed of light, extends the powers of his brain with those of the digital computer, and influences the numbers and genetic constitution of virtually all other living species. Now he can guide his own evolution. In him, Nature has reached beyond the hard regularities of physical phenomena. *Homo sapiens*, the creation of Nature, has transcended her. From a product of circumstances, he has risen to responsibility. At last, he is Man. May he behave so!

The Second Genesis

What I like about the threat of total human control in the near future is that it obliges us to figure out fast what we are about. We got the power; here comes the responsibility. Whether you prefer to embrace it, or flee it (some should, for safeguard), or stay trembling where you are, you might as well have some detailed idea of what's looming.

This book, by the Science Editor at LIFE, *does good journalism on three spooky areas: Refabrication of the Individual; Exploration of Prenativity; Control of the Brain and Behavior.*

Hypothesis: changes this radical outdistance the laws but not the economy. Control diminishes for governments and increases for consumers. The outlaw area of rapid change. Witness dope.

—SB

•

Coming: The control of life. All of life, including human life. With man himself at the controls.

Also coming: a new Genesis—The Second Genesis. The creator this time around—man. The creation—again, man. But a new man. In a new image. A whole series of new images. What will the new images be?

They will have to be quite different from the images we have known—the images that have led us to Vietnam, to turbulent racial conflict, to nuclear confrontation, to the threat of a polluted and overpopulated planet.

But all these things have come about—have they not?—with man at the controls, more or less. If he is acquiring awesome new powers—and he is—with immeasurably greater controls, does this not accelerate us all, at uncountable G's, toward the inevitable Dead End—a hundred bangs, followed by three billion whimpers?

If we believe so, yes.

But man's new images may offer us surprising alternatives. Their creation will require the energetic projection of the best minds of the race to the farthest reaches of their imaginations.

Futile effort?

Anything but. What we <u>believe</u> about man, what we want for man, will profoundly influence what actually happens to man.

•

What would you like: Education by injection? A catalog of spare body parts? A larger, more efficient brain? A cure for old age? Immortality through freezing? Parentless children? Custom-ordered body size and skin color? The ability to convert sunlight directly into energy, just as plants do, without utilizing food as an intermediary? Name it, and somebody is seriously proposing it.

In sober scientific circles today, there is hardly a subject more commonly discussed than man's control of his own heredity and evolution. And the discussions seldom leave much doubt that man will acquire this control. It is a matter of when, not if.

•

The late Dr. J. B. S. Haldane, always intrigued by the bizarre, wrote in 1949: "If King Charles I's or King Louis XVI's head had been stuck within a minute or so [after their executions] on a pump which supplied oxygenated blood to it, it would almost certainly have come around, after half an hour or so, enough to open its eyes and move its lips, and would probably have recovered consciousness. I hope that if I have an inoperable cancer this experiment will be tried on me."

•

Could anyone ever replace a dead-but-frozen ruler? As billions of people were frozen in every generation, the dead might ultimately own all the property and hold all the important offices. Barring the return of some sort of ancestor worship or a cult of the dead, would the unfrozen population put up with it? With life so overabundant and so easy to produce anew, why should anyone want to go to all the trouble and expense of reviving all that competition? Those piled-up frozen corpses might in fact be fiercely resented. If the planet became desperately overpopulated, with prevailing undernourishment and contempt for life, their very presence might even encourage a drift toward cannibalism.

•

"There is no doubt," says Richard R. Landers in <u>Man's Place in the Dybosphere</u>, "that machines as a group will dominate man as a group, and eventually, individual machines will dominate individual men.

"By dominate I mean control, regulate, restrain, influence, pervade, direct, guide, prescribe, etc., by virtue of superiority in all aspects of tasks demanding a leader."

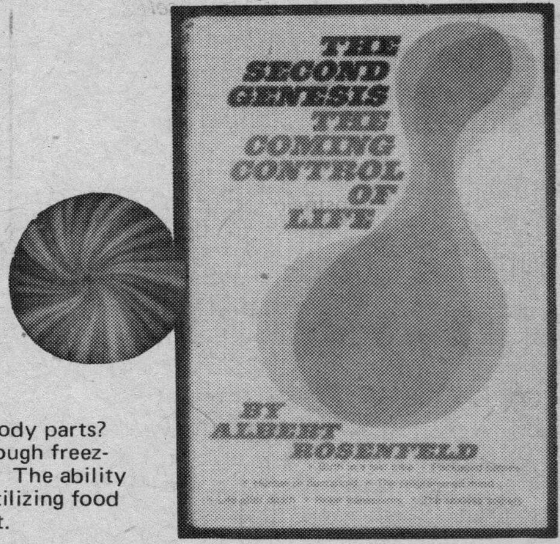

The Second Genesis
Alfred Rosenfeld
1969; 327 pp.

$1.95

from:
Pyramid Publications
9 Garden Street
Moonachie, NJ 07074

Jarfalla: City of the Future

STOCKHOLM—The first city of the future will be built in Sweden. It will be called Jarfalla, have about 100,000 residents, and be accessible by subway or highway from Stockholm, just 12 miles away. No gasoline-powered vehicle will be allowed. Noiseless electric minibuses moving at a soothing 20 miles per hour will pass within 150 yards of everyone's house, carrying passengers and baggage free. Rolling platforms something like horizontal escalators will carry downtown shoppers on their rounds, underground heating will melt snow as it falls to the sidewalks, garbage will be collected by vacuums installed in each residence and transported through tunnels by compressed air to incinerators 30 miles away. Heat and hot water will be supplied by a single thermonuclear plant, the temperatures regulated by individual thermostats. The air will be pure, the smog-free light dazzling, the water delicious and wholesome, the streets impecable, the only sounds those of music and children at play. It will cost an enormous amount of money.

Alas, we cannot be all Swedes, nor can all Swedes live in Jarfalla. By the time there are 7 billion of us milling around the planet, 30 years from now—or 9 billion, 20 or 30 years from now— our lives are likely to be arranged quite differently. Futurologists hold out a considerable range of repellent prospects.

Among the most cheerful is Nigel Calder, former editor of New Science in England, whose ideas go something like this:

Those of us still living on land may be enclosed in anything from towns of 50,000 completely under glass to supercities of 50 million commanding nearly a million square miles—the size of Western Europe. But the majority of the human race will be settled on the sea, in floating towns reaching deep under water so that disturbance due to surface winds and waves—seasickness, that is—will be negligible. More likely than not, these towns will take the form of iceships, ice being unsinkable, easily landscapable, and relatively cheap to make and preserve (one doesn't like to think of a possible power failure, but Mr. Calder assures us we needn't worry). The icetowns would be protected against wind by geodetic domes, perfumed and decorated by thoughtfully contrived sights and sounds, air-conditioned to a year-round spring-like temperature, and supplied with food by ocean gardens grown either on imported soil or in enclosed and cultivated tanks of sea water.

Limited as such nourishment may be to the palate, we might go down on our knees in gratitude for it, considering the possible alternatives. About 4 or 5 billion people would be facing starvation, few of us could permit ourselves the luxury of real fruit and vegetables (a cucumber, say, or a watermelon). Scientists having discovered that yeast can be grown on petroleum, vast quantities of this cheap protein source can be grown to feed animals destined in turn to feed us. Three main production lines for animal protein would then operate side by side.

In one, cattle, pigs and poultry would be raised on plant material for meat and eggs. In another, milk would be formed continuously by a culture of milk-producing glands, intended for drinking and making butter and cheese. In a third, beef muscle would grow continuously in long tubes, extruding itself for chopping into steaklike portions. A complex of smaller works would turn out a selection of prepared foods — soups, sausage, bread, beer and so on—for national or regional distribution. Vitamins and flavors from national suppliers would be added as required. Orange and lemon juice could be produced from cultures, with chemical processing of fibrous materials to add "bite." The very rich could buy natural fruit and vegetables from millionaire market-gardeners; the very poor could sustain life with combinations of plant and yeast material reinforced with vitamins—comparable, perhaps, to having all of one's meals supplied by a domestic airline, with vitamins added.

Mr. Calder does not go very deeply into the psychological side-effect of all this.

If the effects on human beings may not be altogether foreseeable, we are already getting some idea of what may happen to the animals we'll be counting on, nutritionally speaking. The latest method of pig-raising, for instance, already makes use of the production line, the pigs arrayed in rows before conveyor belts moving at a carefully calculated pace with carefully dosed food rations designed for optimum fattening at minimum cost. The one hitch is an inclination on the pig's part to go crazy; thus, the otherwise automated system requires a highly paid attendant whose only function is to watch for early symptoms of insanity and snatch the unfortunate patient from his place at the conveyor belt, replacing him with another identical in appearance, within five minutes at most, before all the rest go wild.

—Times/Post News Service

Moving On

One early evening in my senior year at Holy Cross College, Worcester, Mass., just before stepping onto the crossover into Loyola Hall, I stopped stoned. Like lightning, I "wanted a want"—a big one, sharp, and jagged. I wanted to swallow the whole wide world in one gulp. To get to the last alley in the world and meet the last person walking down it. Ah so!

Frankly, I haven't pulled it off. But I've tried.

At least, the long looking has made me lean, lean as a needle with a hole in it. My eyes have gone gimlet, legs gone skinny. Add New England bones, 4 years in the Iraqi Deserts, a dozen years in the Great Tramp Territory west of Denver to the Pacific. No matter how you mix it, it comes out a slim stew.

You say—like you really cared—"What in the world have you been looking for?"

"Don't laugh. I'll tell you. A horse. A horse named Freedom. 'Freedom,' says Matthew Arnold, 'is a horse but a horse is meant to go somewhere.' He sure is, has."

When I stood years ago in front of Loyola Hall with my mouth open, the horse was at an easy trot. Long since he'd finished his pioneer walk from Plymouth Rock to the Pacific, dragging that covered wagon behind him. As a reward for that Grand Tour, the people built him a big red barn. Time since has proved him right in not settling so cheap. That kind of pioneer paradise can now be produced by a pushbutton.

From the 'solid', 'thingy' walk, Freedom shifted into a 'thinking' trot. Not only by the sweat of our brow but by the cleverness thereof, would we eat bread. Much bread. The great American draam became Things & Think, Inc.—everything under control and a few beautiful people at the controls. As a trotting reward, the Corporation has built a beautifully decorated baroque stable. BUT THE HORSE HAS SPLIT OUT! Once again, off and running down the cold cement. The only thing now left behind is the empty stable, the 'soiled' straw, and the bad smell.

Now, 1969, no other when, the horse named Freedom is about to break into a full gallop, third gear. Up until now, in the walk, the trot (1st and 2nd gear), the harness, the bit and bridle have been in control. The control has been from without. Horse and rider, freedom and people, just puppets pulled on a string.

In the full gallop, both horse and rider are running free in the wind, glued into one shared spirit. You and I, not the horse, then drop the blinds from our eyes. Things, thoughts, stones, tree, dogs, that man in the last alley whatever his color—the whole world racing by—is caught up in the shape and mass of a single Big Man. The control is from within.

Freedom at full gallop is Celebration. The Big Man's general dance. Red barns full of oats won't hold him. Nor corrals built by cleverness. The entire range of America from Atlantic to Pacific would still cramp his style. Oppenheimer, the physicist, says "the universe has become a wild windy place." Only the swift spiral of Celebration is big enough to swallow the world at a single gulp.

We're all waiting for the shift into third: Czechoslovakia, Vietnam, the black man, students, ghettos, Wall Street, Roman Curia, hippies and housewives. The little ones, the beautiful people, are coming out of the highways and the hedges. The whole world has become one big waiting room, a Greyhound Bus Terminal at 3 A.M. The stranded sitting by pitiful little piles of luggage in the fluorescent emptiness.

The clutch is in. Who has not somehow felt it grabbing at his entrails? The shift can hardly be smooth and easy. The world is not a Volkswagen. The only way to get into third gear may be a violent grinding slam.

In all the doubt, despair, violence and madness, we have somehow to take our eyes from the clutch on the floor and fix them instead on the Celebration ahead. Even the worst kind of madness has a ring of reason to it. The best reason I know for this one of 1969 is:

The Big Man is in a hell of a hurry to get to his wedding on time! And you know what? This wild, silly, mixed-up bitch of a world is his bride. How about that!

Moving On
$2/yr
P. O. Box 1349
San Francisco, CA 94101

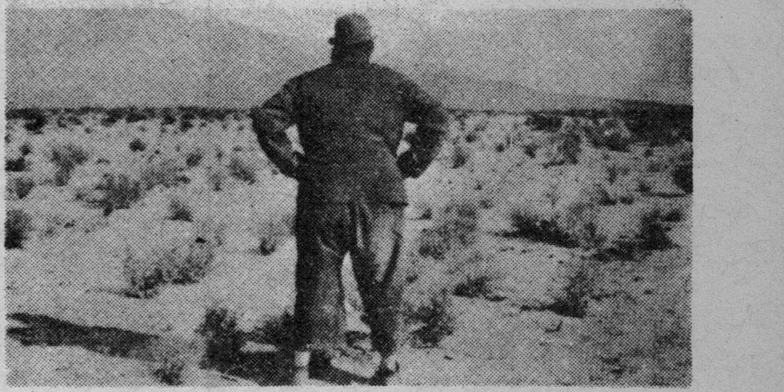

Challenge for Survival

Jesus, there are a lot of ecological anthologies coming out. This one's value is that it focuses on the devil himself. The city.

—SB

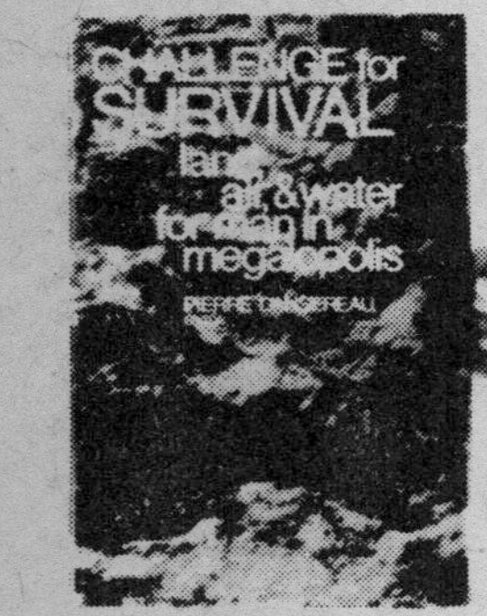

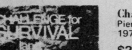

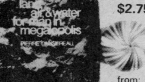

Challenge for Survival
Pierre Dansereau, Ed.
1970; 235 pp.

$2.75 postpaid

from:
Columbia University Press
440 West 110th Street
New York, N. Y. 10025

or WHOLE EARTH CATALOG

What will be left of the plant world if we allow the basically village culture, founded on a close symbiotic partnership between man and plants, to disappear? For some twelve thousand years, all the higher achievements of civilization have rested on this culture, one devoted to the constructive improvement of the habitat and the loving care of plants——their selection, their nurture, their breeding, their enjoyment. That culture, as Edgar Anderson suggested, originally made some of its best discoveries in breeding by being equally concerned with the color, the odor, the taste, the flower and leaf patterns, the sexual functions, and the nutritive qualities of plants, valuing them not only for food and medicine, but for esthetic delight. There are plenty of people working in scientific laboratories today who, though they may still call themselves biologists, have no knowledge of this culture, except by vague hearsay, and no respect for its achievements. They dream of a world composed mainly of synthetics and plastics, in which no creatures above the rank of algae or yeasts would be encouraged to grow.

Teg's 1994

We're generally down on Utopian thinking around here, holding to a more evolutionary fiasco-by-fiasco approach to perfection. Thus **Walden Two, Island, Stranger in a Strange Land,** *and Rimmer's stuff have not been listed. They're well known enough anyway. One publication——relatively unknown—— with a more structural brand of speculation is Theobald & Scott et al's* **Teg's 1994**. *The "book" is an on-going process that invites your participation.* —SB

[Suggested by Robert Theobald]

Teg's 1994
Robert Theobald & J. M. Scott
1969; 115 pp.

$2.50 postpaid

from:
Swallow Press, Inc.
1139 South Wabash Ave.
Chicago, Ill. 60605

During her year of travel as an Orwell Fellow, Teg learns that her contemporaries' concept of the "communication society" is increasingly flawed by interaction failures between diverging communities. A full expression of each community's sub-culture, or myth, has been achieved only at the cost of increasing mutual incomprehension, and even a re-emergence of an aggressive community ethnocentricism.

•

Some of the longer-term residents have begun to question this community myth of sea-use, and are proposing a change to a myth of sea co-existence. They wish to convert to a vegetarian sea-diet and prevent the eating of fish. Given the fact that pisciculture is presently essential to protein adequacy throughout the scarcity-regions the other residents think this is unrealistic.

There are also a few residents who want to change over completely to a myth of sea-adaption. They propose surgical conversion of the human-being for water-breathing.

The View from the Barrio

What a refreshment this book was after reading a handful of "future" books—scholarly radical technological inflated prophetic advice gas—which left me with a depressed feeling that the future is just words.

The real future will be made of much that is reported in this book (and approximately unknown to the scholars). Namely rural Third World people in newly rich economies and new planned cities, subverting the planners and transforming their own lives.

La Laja is a barrio in the planned Venezuelan city of Ciudad Guayana. Dr. Peattie was there for 2½ years with her family, taking part in barrio life and paying structured attention to what was going on. Social life around her was loose, fluid to a swiftly changing environment and economy. People were self-organizing only around critical community issues such as water or sewers. From the barrio it was a huge impassable distance to the planners, so when something came down that was intolerable they would beef futilely for a while and then plant dynamite under it. Nothing romantic. Just making do, getting by.

It dynamited my depression.

—SB

The View from the Barrio
Lisa Redfield Peattie
1968; 147 pp.

$1.95 postpaid

from:
The University of Michigan Press
615 East University
Ann Arbor, Michigan 48106

or WHOLE EARTH CATALOG

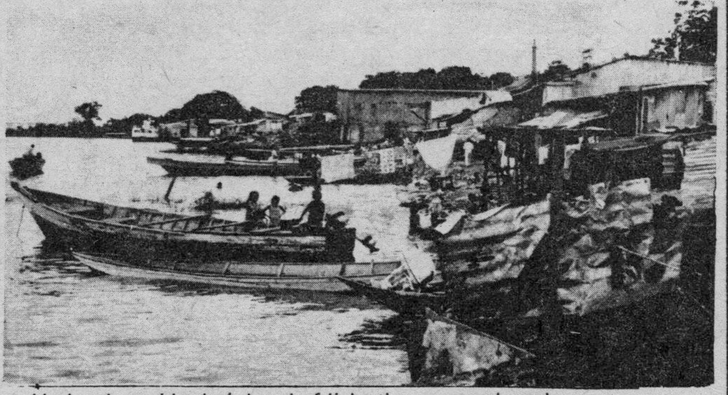

Under that wide sky's bowl of light the new roads and new concrete buildings—rows of developer houses, apartment buildings, commercial structures—seem to erupt from the dusty-dry earth which bulldozers have scraped clear of vegetation. Elsewhere, the improvised housing of the poor, of sheet aluminum or pressed-board, looks as if it had been thrown together by a hurricane. It is a city of bulldozers, of engineers who wear boots and dungarees and carry shiny briefcases, of noisy bars and holes in the streets, and of new traffic interchanges; it is a city of building and of disorderly entrepreneurship; it is a city which lives in the future.

•

Another part of La Laja's natural environment consists of the strip of unimproved land just beyond the Iron Mines fence. This land, covered with brush and cactus, is often used for toileting, especially by children; debris may be dumped there, and children collect certain wild fruits in the brush. Some medicinal plants (from an extensive folk pharmacopeia of herbal remedies) are collected there by adults. Some men of the barrio shoot birds in this piece of monte. Boys hunt birds and sometimes rats with stones, either thrown or projected with a sling shot; their accuracy is astonishing by American standards.

•

The general development planning and urban design functions of the CVG were being carried out far away from the people of La Laja, on the thirteenth floor of the Shell Building, 350 miles away in Caracas. Some individuals in San Félix—the priests, certain political and economic leaders—from time to time made visits to these offices, but to my knowledge no resident of La Laja had ever been there, and certainly the overwhelming majority had no conception of that far-off world in which La Laja appeared on maps as an area encircled by the planners' "Magic Marker" or zipatone symbols.

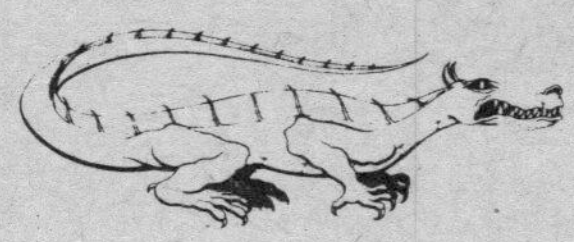

THE RED TENT

D.R. and Estelle had finished breakfast and were into cleaning out the bus when a woman from the red tent and the Porsche next door came over to borrow some sugar. She looked to be in her thirties somewhere, a very tanned athletic woman wearing a leather vest and a pair of chic brown riding pants. She was European. Her accent was so thick Estelle at first didn't understand what she wanted. But finally she heard "shu-ger" and after they'd gone through the routine of scooping some brown sugar out of the coffee can Estelle kept it in, the woman began to come in a little more clearly.

"You arrive very late," she said.

"No, no," said Estelle. "Very early. We got here just at dawn."

"You must come far."

"Very far," said D.R. "Very, very far. And we've still got a long way to go."

"We have come far too. From Amsterdam to New York, from New York to here."

D.R. asked the woman where she got her red tent.

"You like it?"

"I've never seen a tent like that before."

"Would you like to see inside? It is very lovely."

Estelle was knee-deep in the shit they'd unloaded from Urge and she wanted to get on with the work. But D.R. was fascinated by the red tent, and so he followed the woman past the Porsche over to her camping place. Another woman about the same age as the first, but who turned out to speak no English at all, was just coming out the front flap as they walked up.

"These nice people loaned me sugar," said the first woman, speaking European. "He admires our tent."

Her companion smiled and nodded and held the flap open for D.R. as he entered.

D.R.'s first hit was off the fantastic quality of the light inside. It was mid-morning by now. The sun was above the tree-line, shining directly into all the little clearings on the western side of the campground. It filled the red tent with the most completely restful light he'd ever seen before. A whole tension that had screwed his face tight all morning went away as his eyes gulped the quiet rose of the tent's interior. It wasn't large at all. There was only one place a person could half stand up, and two sleeping bags side by side would cover most of the floor. Yet somehow it struck D.R. as the most spacious, elegant room he'd ever been in. It was immaculate. In the corners of the tent near the entrance were two rolled sleeping bags. On top of each bag were small blue and white flight bags, both neatly zippered, the carrying straps arranged just so. Except for a strip of grass down the middle, the ground was covered by two straw mats. On each mat was a rubber air mattress, deflated and folded into a perfect square and stashed in the far corner of the tent. In the middle of the far end stood a short, three-legged table with a candle on it, and a single wildflower of some kind, in a glass of water. D.R. was amazed. He hadn't smoked any dope in over twelve hours now, and yet he felt completely stoned on the perfect arrangement of the small red world around him. He glanced over his shoulder to see if the two women were watching. When he saw them through the tent flap doing something over at the picnic table, he stretched himself out on one of the mats and stared up at the slanting red roof above him.

Ecology and Resource Management

Okay World Gamers. Stop doing public relations and get into it. Kenneth Watt has, and it's technical business. Complexity, trade-offs, elaborate models that are still too simple, formulas that work once, unavoidable jargon. Did you think it was going to be a breeze?

—SB

Ecology and Resource Management
Kenneth E. F. Watt
1968; 450 pp.

$14.50 postpaid

from:
McGraw-Hill Book Company
330 West 42nd Street
New York, N.Y. 10036

or WHOLE EARTH CATALOG

Large-scale biological systems are dynamic phenomena of great complexity, embracing lag effects, cumulative effects, thresholds, interactions between variables, large number of variables, and nonlinear causal relations. Because of this complexity, we must concede at the outset that even mathematical models based on oversimplified and hence unrealistic assumptions would be insoluble using traditional paper-and-pencil methods. Therefore the emphasis is shifted from ingenuity of mathematical manipulation to realism of description, with computer simulation being substituted for paper-and-pencil solution. This does not lead to less complication in the mathematics. Rather it leads to complexity of a new type. The requirement now is for depth of insight into the character of the processes dealt with, in order that computer simulation studies can in fact mimic nature.

•

Considerably more ambitious and information-hungry are models that attempt to describe population processes in some detail, while still assuming a constant extrinsic environment. Such models consider not only the numbers of animals present at each age, but also their growth rate. The most elaborate, widely applied, and discussed model of this type was proposed by Beverton and Holt, (1956, 1957) for use in the understanding and management of commercially exploited stocks of oceanic fisheries. This model was developed as follows.

Consider the rate of change of biomass yield, Y_w, with respect to time t. The average weight of fish of age t is given by w_t, and F denotes the instantaneous fishing (or harvesting) mortality coefficient, where N_t is the number of t-aged fish still alive in the typical year class, then

$$\frac{dY_w}{dt} = FN_t w_t$$

gives the rate of change of biomass yield for the typical year class with respect to its age. The problem is to evaluate N_t and w_t.

Resources and Man

A fugue of finiteness, this just-published work portrays the true size of our North American yard. How much of the depletables there is, and how long they will last at present or projected rates. Some indications of the levels of exploitation where the "non-depletables" start to give up on regeneration. For what might have been a dry book, the writing has considerable hair on.

—SB

Resources and Man
Cloud, Bates, Chapman, Hendricks, Hubbert, Keyfitz, Lovering, Ricker
1969; 159 pp.

$3.25 postpaid

from:
W. H. Freeman and Co.
660 Market Street
San Francisco, CA 94104

or WHOLE EARTH CATALOG

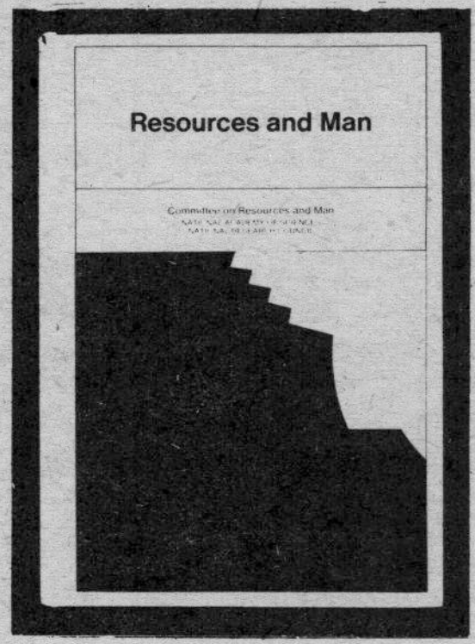

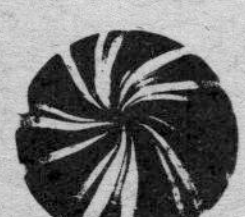

That the fossil fuels be conserved for uses which cannot be met by other sources. The fossil fuels (petroleum, natural gas, coal) are needed for petrochemicals, synthetic polymers, and essential liquid fuels, for which suitable substitutes are as yet unknown. They might also play a part in synthetic or bacterial food production (although such a use is also limited). They should not be spent in the generation of electricity, for heating, and for industrial purposes where substitutes can qualify. The Department of the Interior should be authorized and directed to develop and institute a practicable and effective hydrocarbon conservation program.

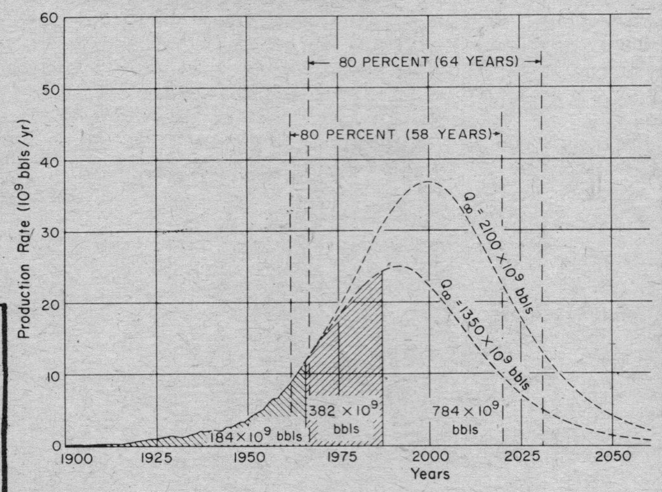

FIGURE 8.23
Complete cycles of world crude-oil production for two values of Q_∞.

"In the West, our desire to conquer nature often means simply that we diminish the probability of small inconveniences at the cost of increasing the probability of very large disasters."

Kenneth E. Boulding

•

Man's Impact on the Global Environment

Most recent, most methodic study so far of the price we're paying for this spree, and explicit recommendations for tapering off.

—SB

Man's Impact on the Global Environment
Study of Critical Environment Problems
1970; 319 pp.

$2.95 postpiad

from:
M.I.T. Press
Massachusetts Institute of Technology
50 Ames St., Rm. 741
Cambridge, Mass. 02142

or WHOLE EARTH CATALOG

'Population Control' through Nuclear Pollution

Low-dosage radiation effects, the appalling pin in the nuclear energy bubble. Two technically savvy critics take on the self-promoting AEC.

—SB

[suggested by Larry Kimmett]

'Population Control' through Nuclear Pollution
Arthur R. Tamplin, John W. Gofman
1970; 242 pp.

$6.95 postpaid

from:
Nelson-Hall Co.
325 W. Jackson Blvd.
Chicago, Illinois 60606

or WHOLE EARTH CATALOG

Oil and World Power

The brutal heart of the matter, by an Englishman not as irrational on the subject as Americans are.

—SB

Oil and World Power
Peter R. Odell
1970; 188 pp.

$3.25 postpaid

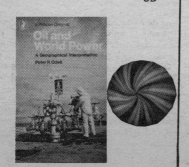

from:
Peter Smith, Publisher Inc.
6 Lexington Avenue
Magnolia, MA. 01930

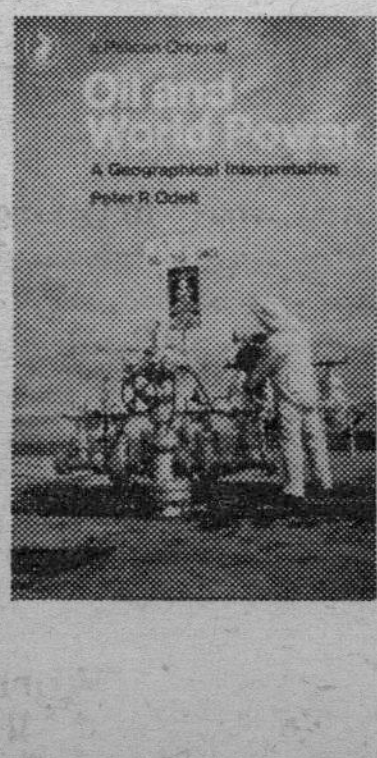

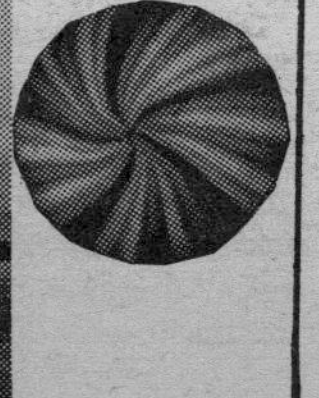

Economics and the Environment

A technical book, suggesting that accounting be applied to items formerly considered "free", such as air, water, waste. The transition from open to closed economics looks bitter.

—SB

Economics and the Environment
Kneese, Ayres, D'Arge
1970; 120 pp.

$2.50 postpaid

from:
Johns Hopkins Press
Baltimore, Md. 21218

or WHOLE EARTH CATALOG

The hunter is camped on a great plain with a small fire providing a flickering light and intermittent warmth. Tiny wisps of smoke ascend into a vast, clear night sky. Tomorrow the hunter will move, leaving behind ashes, food scraps, and his own excreta. After ten steps these are lost from sight and smell, probably forever. With them he leaves too his brief speculation about sky and earth, brought on by the loneliness of night, and he peers toward the horizon in search of prey.

The Administrator of the World Environment Control Authority sits at his desk. Along one wall of the huge room are real-time displays, processed by computer from satellite data, of developing atmospheric and ocean patterns, as well as the flow and quality conditions of the world's great river systems. In an instant, the Administrator can shift from real-time mode to simulation to test the larger effects of changes in emissions of material residuals and heat to water and atmosphere at control points generally corresponding to the locations of the world's great cities and the transport movements among them. In a few seconds the computer displays information in color code for various time periods—hourly, daily, or yearly phases at the Administrator's option. It automatically does this for current steady state and simulated future conditions of emissions, water flow regulation, and atmospheric conditions. Observing a dangerous reddish glow in the eastern Mediterranean, the Administrator dials sub-control station Athens and orders a step-up of removal by the liquid residuals handling plants there. Over northern Europe, the brown smudge of a projected air quality standards violation appears and sub-control point Essen is ordered to take the Ruhr area of sludge incineration for 24 hours but is advised that temporary storage followed by accelerated incineration—but with muffling—after 24 hours will be admissible. The CO_2 simulator now warns the Administrator that another upweller must be brought on line in the Murray Fracture Zone within two years if the internationally agreed balance of CO_2 and oxygen is to be maintained in the atmosphere.

World Game Note

There's something funny going on round here.

Right in the middle of the March one dollar issue is Gene Youngblood's article on Fuller's World Game. It's exciting, inspiring even. Here are all these guys with all the best intentions about to wire up the globe so that by the year 2000 (if not sooner) everybody will have enough of everything. He really makes you feel like it's within reach, once we get off the merry-go-round of local politics. Though NASA has promised $12 million, how much more will Fuller get when the feds discover that he really intends to put them out of business?

Anyway, once the world is all wired up, everybody will live at least as well as we do now. All the people, that is.

Right at the end of Youngblood's piece you slip into the Ecology section. The first thing to hit my eye was the quote from Lynn White, "The victory of Christianity over paganism was the greatest psychic revolution in the history of our culture . . . Christianity . . . not only established a dualism of man and nature but also insisted that it is God's will that man exploit nature for his proper ends. . ."

But what do you call wiring up the earth? Far out. Maybe Fuller is the first of the really big Christians.

Are we to be total Whole Earth technocrats, insuring only our own survival? (If you read closely you will note that Youngblood — like Fuller — talks about minerals and such, and makes no mention of organic things except what people can eat.)

Or are we to be Ecology Action pagans, trying to scramble back to a sense of union with the planet that created us?

The ecology people say we gotta change our whole culture, or we won't survive. The Fuller people say we've only got to make our culture really efficient not only to survive but to get a whole lot better.

You know, the problem goes a lot deeper than just, will we survive, and how? No doubt we can with Fuller mold and shape and wire the earth toward the compleate human habitation. We will change and even destroy a lot of things, but Fuller believes we have the thrust of evolution on our side, and that people are really a lot more important than the brown pelican (to use an unfair example).

But it's not just a matter of "Christian American saying can't. I need the money." Money really isn't important, especially in America. How much did we spend just to have a couple of guys walk on the moon, for "the spirit of exploration", for "national prestige"? How much do we pump daily into Vietnam, for "the defense of democracy" even as we search for "an honorable peace"? We struggle and fight for abstract ideas, and the money really doesn't matter.

Now Fuller obviously has the best technique for survival, given the human desire to avoid changing basic ideas. Fuller is a catalogue of 1700 years of Christian ideas. Up against this, the ecology freaks really have no chance, because all they are talking about is survival, too.

But ecology really demands another psychic revolution. Like you say, a holy war. We need to believe we are one with the whole earth. And not just to survive, but because we really are. And that means, at least in the beginning, a new religion, a new faith.

Only through belief do you really change people's heads. And right now we believe in rationalism, in the technical method, in the validity of abstract numbers. Even the piece about the sacred earthworm is full of the scientific things earthworms are and do, like 30 tons of this, 1800 species of that, 15 years of something else.

Somewhere I read an old Chinese parable about a farmer who refused to take the technologic step of making a waterwheel to water his crops, even though he knew how. The rhythms and cycles of his life were the important things. He would not, he said, subject his body to a machine merely for the gain of efficiency. In medieval China this was the highest wisdom.

The distance between that view of life and our own is almost unbridgeable, but it is that step ecology asks us to make. Can we make it? In thirty years?

So you have an answer? I don't. I'm afraid we had better light our candles to St. Buckminster.

Cary James
Mill Valley, CA

I figure our best chance lies in ecological pagans, and the world game, and critical letters, and the rest of it. So long as stuff is getting tried, and there's lots of different stuff, and the stuff knows about each other, once it's in the world, evolution can sort it out.

—SB

The Pentagon of Power

It's easy to O.D. on Fuller, Kahn, and other technological prophets. Mumford is a fine, careful antidote. He examines the unexamined premises that lead to excess.

—SB

The Pentagon of Power
Lewis Mumford
1970; 496 pp.

$12.95 postpaid

from:
Harcourt, Brace & Jovanovich, Inc.
757 Third Ave.
New York, N.Y. 10017

or WHOLE EARTH CATALOG

Western man not merely blighted in some degree every culture that he touched, whether 'primitive' or advanced, but he also robbed his own descendants of countless gifts of art and craftsmanship, as well as precious knowledge passed on only by word of mouth that disappeared with the dying languages of dying peoples. With this extirpation of earlier cultures went a vast loss of botanical and medical lore, representing many thousands of years of watchful observation and empirical experiment whose extraordinary discoveries——such as the American Indian's use of snakeroot (reserpine) as a tranquilizer in mental illness——modern medicine has now, all too belatedly, begun to appreciate.

Scientific truth achieved the status of an absolute, and the incessant pursuit and expansion of knowledge became the only recognized categorical imperative.

Now, if the history of the human race teaches any plain lessons, this is one of them: *Man cannot be trusted with absolutes.*

Technics and Civilization

I first read this book in 1957 then again in 1963 and then part of it in 1969.

Here is the first paragraph of the book.

During the last thousand years the material basis and the cultural forms of Western Civilization have been profoundly modified by the development of the machine. How did this come about? Where did it take place? What were the chief motives that encouraged this radical transformation of the environment and the routine of life: what were the ends in view: what were the means and methods: what unexpected values have arisen in the process? These are some of the questions that the present study seeks to answer.

Lewis Mumford is an unusual man. He is not an engineer or a scientist, he isn't an historian or sociologist, you can't identify him as a business man or a literary man or an academic. He seems beyond all those roles. This made him especially attractive to me when I was 19 because his style smelled of the place I wanted to go. He is profound, poetic knowledgeable. He takes care of the large and small things in his books.

Technics and Civilization is a good book to start with; if you like it, there are many others of his to turn to. Myth of the Machine, Arts and Technics, The City in History, Transformations of Man.

How I have used him: all through my twenties I used him as my guide.

[Suggested and reviewed by Steve Baer]

Technics and Civilization
Lewis Mumford
1934, 1962; 495 pp.

$3.95 postpaid

from:
Harcourt, Brace & Jovanovich, Inc.
757 Third Avenue
New York, N. Y. 10017

or WHOLE EARTH CATALOG

The Ghost in the Machine

Koestler's latest book seems to be sharing the fate of Norman O. Brown's Love's Body: the book after the big influential one (Act of Creation, Life Against Death) is considered too far out, fragmented, excessive . . . and sells half-heartedly.

Nevermind. Koestler here is doing useful dirty work: savaging rat psychology, exploring broader implications of biological systems research, and foreseeing our imminent demise unless we organize our brain-use better. Which brings him to drugs. He proposes research to find a chemical which will voluntarily disengage old-brain from new-brain—the interior emotional kill-heavy unreprogrammable stuff from exterior rational flexible stuff. Our paranoia is accidentally designed in, he suggests, and may be designed out.

Get to it, outlaws. No nation is going to support this research.

—SB

The Ghost in the Machine
Arthur Koestler
1967; 384 pp.

$3.45 postpaid

from:
Henry Regnery Co.
114 West Illinois Street
Chicago, Illinois 60610

or WHOLE EARTH CATALOG

Unfortunately, if "meaning means association," as Gray Walters observes, then dissociation and non-intercourse must result in a decrease of shared meanings. Thus in time, specialized knowledge, "knowing more and more about less and less," finally turns into secret knowledge——accessible only to an inner priesthood, whose sense of power is in turn inflated by their privileged command of 'trade' or official secrets.

2: The printing press was a powerful agent for producing uniformity in language and so, by degrees, in thought. Standardization, mass-production, and capitalistic enterprise came in with the printing press; and not without irony, the oldest known representation of the press, shown here, appeared in a Dance of Death printed at Lyons in 1499.

DRAW BACK TO LEAP

It seems that this retracing of steps to escape the dead ends of the maze was repeated at each decisive evolutionary turning point. I have mentioned the evolution of the vertebrates from a larval form of some primitive echinoderm. Insects have in all likelihood emerged from a millipede-like ancestor—not, however, from adult millipedes, whose structure is too specialized, but from its larval forms. The conquest of the dry land was initiated by amphibians whose ancestry goes back to the most primitive type of lung-breathing fish; whereas the apparently more successful later lines of highly specialized gill-breathing fishes all came to a dead end. The same story was repeated at the next major step, the reptiles, who derived from early, primitive amphibians-not from any of the later forms that we know.

And lastly, we come to the most striking case of paedomorphosis, the evolution of our own species. It is now generally recognized that the human adult resembles more the embryo of an ape rather than an adult ape. . . . .

The salutary truth of the old proverb 'Haste Makes Waste' was over-ridden by the new principle: 'Haste and Waste Make Money.'

Most of the important inventions and discoveries that served as the nucleus for further mechanical development, did not arise, as Spengler would have it, out of some mystical inner drive of the Faustian soul: they were wind-blown seeds from other cultures. After the tenth century in Western Europe the ground was, as I have shown, well plowed and harrowed and dragged, ready to receive these seeds; and while the plants themselves were growing, the cultivators of art and science were busy keeping the soil friable. Taking root in medieval culture, in a different climate and soil, these seeds of the macine sported and took on new forms: perhaps, precisely because they had not originated in Western Europe and had no natural enemies there, they grew as rapidly and gigantically as the Canada thistle when it made its way onto the South American pampas. But at no point—and this is the important thing to remember—did the machine represent a complete break. So far from being unprepared for in human history, the modern machine age cannot be understood except in terms of a very long and diverse preparation. The notion that a handful of Brisith inventors suddenly made the wheels hum in the eighteenth century is too crude even to dish up as a fairy tale to children.

A tent, he thought. A room of space. It starts here by my left arm, goes up then down and ends over there on the far side of the other mat. That is what this room is, and that is all it is, no more and no less. This is its total size and shape and full dimension: a room of space marked off and set aside by these walls of red canvas that weren't here yesterday probably and probably won't be here tomorrow, but they are here today and I am here too inside the particular space they enclose. This space has always been here. But it has not always been a room, at least not this room, because it has never been enclosed by this particular tent before. The space is here. The time is now. And they are intersecting in a way that no other tent has ever caused before. This very space where I am lying has been tented over before, closed up in other canvas rooms. And so the question seems to be: would another tent around this same space re-create this room, or does this room disappear forever once this red tent has been removed and taken somewhere else? And what about when this tent is pitched in another place? If you pitch it in the Blue Ridge Mountains, take it down and put it up again in the Rockies, has the same room been in both places? Or is it another brand new room every time you pitch the tent again?

"Comfortable, eh?"

The woman's voice startled D.R. and caused him to sit upright. But her smile was so friendly and there was such charm in her strange voice, D.R. relaxed again and invited the woman to come in. The idea struck her as very funny. Giggling, she called to her companion. Soon both women were in the tent with Divine Right, sitting cross-legged on the other mat, drinking tea and smiling back and forth at one another, and at D.R.

"I mean," D.R. was saying, "I mean, like, if you take this tent down, you know, take the poles down, fold the whole thing up, and move it fifteen yards . . . I mean, I'm just saying, if you move it, if you take it down and set it up again, where does the room . . . I mean, like, we're in a room, right? The room is these walls. And these walls are here. They're here, and they're here now. And so the question seems to be . . . the question seems to be, where does the room go when you take these walls down and fold them up and put them in your car?"

The lady who didn't speak English had begun to look a little troubled, perhaps even a little afraid. But when her friend interpreted she began to nod. Both women nodded and said, "Yes. Yes."

"Do you really know what I'm talking about?"

"Of course," said the woman who had borrowed the sugar. "You're talking about space and time."

"Far out!" D.R. exclaimed. "Far out!" Suddenly he had to get out of the red tent, and go and tell Estelle. Hastily he mumbled his thanks and his goodbyes, and crawled to the opening. Outside, he was so excited he tripped over a tent stake and fell on his ass.

Nature and Man's Fate

THE introduction to theoretical and applied evolution. Hardin is further than anyone in blending the insights of evolution and cybernetics into what may be an embryonic science of general development. Still it's a completely earthly book. The specific history of Darwin and his idea. The specific application of evolutionary understanding to human survival now. —SB

Nature and Man's Fate
Garrett Hardin
1959; 320 pp.

$1.25 postpaid

from:
The New American Library, Inc.
1301 Avenue of the Americas
New York, N. Y. 10019

or WHOLE EARTH CATALOG

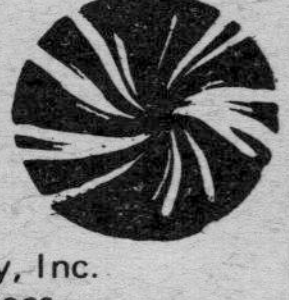

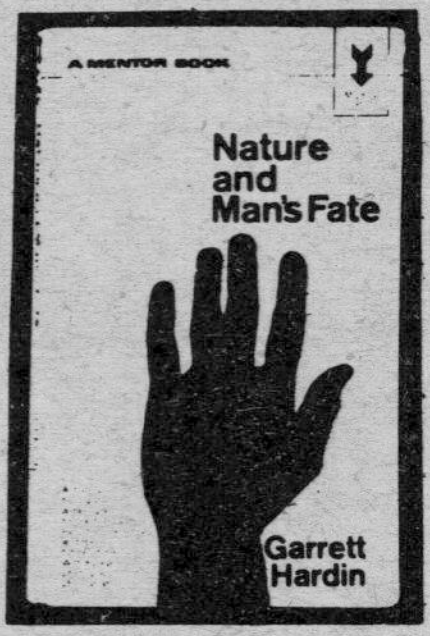

So we see that the concept of progress, for all its historical importance in sheltering the idea of evolution, is not easily applicable to facts of biology.

•

All men are, by nature, unequal—this is the censored truth of our century. We are as afraid of the consequences of admitting this truth as the Victorians were of the consequences of admitting that men are animals. Yet surely history will ultimately show that, in both instances, the consequences are good and compatible with human decency.

•

As early as 1920, the philosopher, Bertrand Russell, spelled out the nightmare qualities of the Russian dream in terms that he never needed to revise in the light of later facts. For his pains and his honesty Russell was quietly ousted from his position as the philosophic spokesman of the liberal elements. (Since he was patently unfit to speak for the conservatives either, he was henceforth a philosophic man without a party. This position may not be the most comfortable of all positions, but for a living philosopher it has its advantages.)

•

As a species becomes increasingly "successful," its struggle for existence ceases to be one of struggle with the physical environment or with other species and comes to be almost exclusively competition with its own kind. *We call that species most successful that has made its own kind its worst enemy.* Man enjoys this kind of success.

•

It is one of the few rules of evolution that extreme specialization results in eventual extinction. Environmental changes are inevitable, and the specialist-species is too strongly committed to one way of life to be able rapidly enough to "back up" genetically and take off in another "direction." All the evidence of comparative morphology and paleontology, fragmentary though it is, indicates that each great new group of organisms arises from very unspecialized species of the group "below" it, not from the conspicuously specialized ones.

•

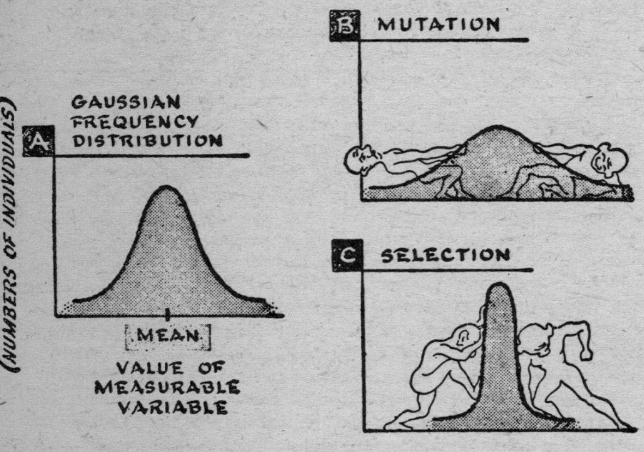

Fig. 7. The effects of mutation and selection on a Gaussian ("normal") distribution curve.

It is not easy to define "play" precisely, but whatever it is, it is something that is in some sense non-competitive, non-rational, non-economic. It is also productive of novelty in viewpoints, opening a path to new ways of doing things that would often never be discovered if only direct, completely rational, wholly efficient approaches were employed. Play, for many men, is by no means confined to childhood; it extends into the adult state, only changing its form. Freud has said, "The child has toys; the mature man has art and science." Out of the play called science—which is possible only to a society rich enough to suspend partially the laws of competition—out of the economically non-competitive intellectual play called science there comes, in fact, a competitive weapon of the most powerful sort, technology. Competition has its own dialectic.

•

In order to make a perfect and beautiful machine, it is not requisite to know how to make it. Quite so.

... To Darwinians, Design emerges from blind Waste. "To be an Error and to be cast out is a part of God's Design," said William Blake.

•

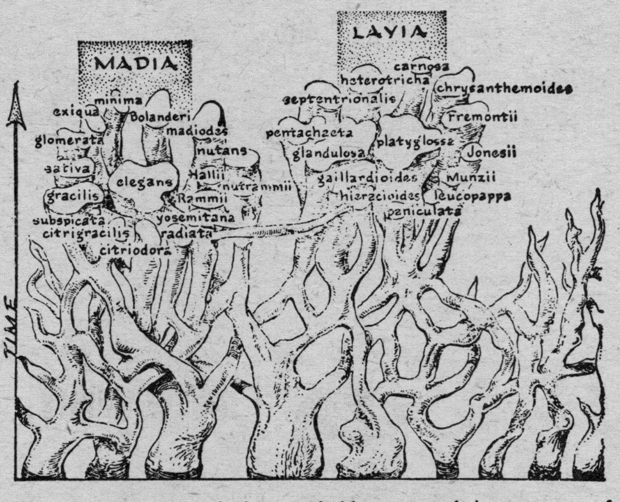

Fig. 12. Evolution, as it has probably occurred in a group of plants: showing how "nature is too disorderly" for those who seek to find clean-cut "phylogenetic trees" and unidirectional evolution everywhere. (From Clausen, *Stages in the Evolution of Plant Species,* Cornell University Press, Ithaca, N. Y.; 1951. By permission.)

The Competitive Exclusion Principle. No two organisms that compete in every activity can coexist indefinitely in the same environment. To coexist in time, organisms that are potentially completely competitive must be geographically isolated from each other. Otherwise, the one that is the less efficient yields to the more efficient, no matter how slight the difference. When two competing organisms coexist in the same geographical region, close examination always shows that they are not *complete* competitors, that one of them draws on a resource of the environment that is not available to the other. The corollary of the principle is that where there is no geographical isolation of genetically and reproductively isolated populations, there must be as many ecological niches as there are populations. The necessary condition for geographical coexistence is ecological specialization.

•

And concepts themselves occur in various grades of generality, forming a hierarchal complex that has not yet been explicitly described. Language is a wondrously subtle and complicated tool; by far the greater part of it is to be found only in mathematics. That which most men call "language" is only a small part of man's concept-handling machinery, scarcely the ABC's of it.

•

For more details on organic evolution, see Ernst Mayr's recent classic *Animal Species and Evolution* (1963; 797 pp. $11.95 postpaid from Harvard University Press, 79 Garden Street, Cambridge, Mass. 02138). The promising, if heretical, hypothesis that evolution may be directly affected by changes *within* the cells is presented in Lancelot Law Whyte's *Internal Factors in Evolution* (1965; 120 pp. $4.00 postpaid from George Braziller, Inc., 215 Park Avenue South, New York, N. Y. 10003). For a non-too-satisfactory but still tantalizing look into cultural evolution, see Sahlins and Service, *Evolution and Culture* (1960; 131 pp. $3.95 postpaid from The University of Michigan Press, 615 East University, Ann Arbor, Michigan 48106).

Among the impotence principles of socio-biology is surely this: *competition is inescapable.* That species which has succeeded in eliminating all other species as competitors, ends by becoming its own competitor. The world, in spite of comic-strip science, is a limited one. Man, freed of the population-controlling factors of predators and disease organisms, must—willy-nilly, like it or not—control his own numbers by competition with his own kind. By taking thought he can elect the kind of competition he employs; but he cannot escape all kinds. This is not to imply that the election is a trivial matter.

•

To the biologist it is clear that the best chances for man's long-time survival depend on the fragmentation of the species into well-separated populations. But it would be foolhardy to say what form the separation should take. It might be a matter of nations, as we know them; or some sort of caste system, that would permit genetic isolation with geographic unity; or—far more likely—some new kind of communities that are neither nation nor caste nor anything that has yet been conceived of.

•

The crowd-diseases—smallpox, cholera, typhoid, plague, etc.—are, by the ecologist, labeled "density-dependent factors," whose effectiveness in reducing population is a power function of the density of the population. No growth of population could get out of hand as long as the crowd-diseases were unconquered, which means that man did not have to sit in judgment on man, to decide who should have a cover at Nature's feast and who should not. With the development of bacteriological medicine, all this has been changed. Now, the feedback control is man himself.

•

Darwin's life is symbolic. His *Autobiography* clearly and unconsciously reveals two elements that are needed to produce any creative genius: irresponsibility and alienation. ...

He who is to see what other men have not seen must, in a real sense, become alienated from the crowd. The manner in which this alienation occurs is subject to an infinity of permutations. ...

The wealthy eccentric is a nearly extinct dodo. The man of wealth is now an other-directed man. He may become a lawyer or a doctor. But not a scientist. He is too much a part of the world to achieve the alienation required to be creative. (What millionaire today would have the nerve to do what Darwin did—retire to a "non-productive" life in the country *to think?*)

... We can hardly expect a committee to acquiesce in the dethronement of tradition. Only an individual can do that, an individual who is not responsible to the mob. Now that the truly independent man of wealth has disappeared, now that the independence of the academic man is fast disappearing, where are we to find the conditions of partial alienation and irresponsibility needed for the highest creativity?

•

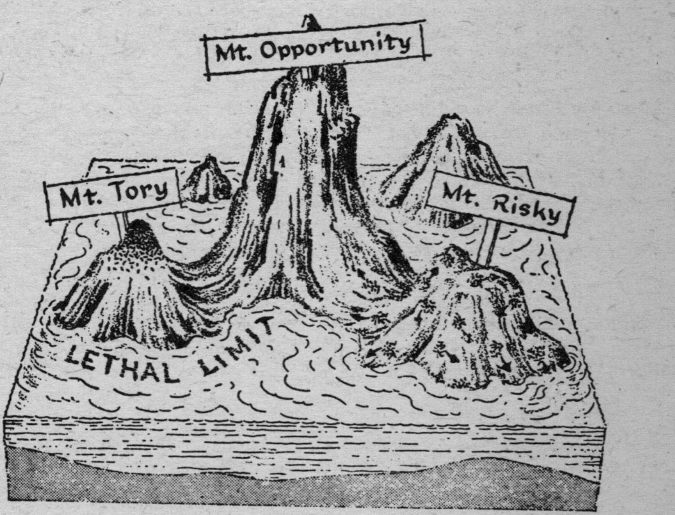

Fig. 25. A large population, which is very sensitive to selection pressure, is narrowly confined to an adaptive peak (Mount Tory). A species broken up into many separate small breeding populations is much less responsive to selection pressures; its populations will wander widely from their adaptive peak (Mount Risky)—some to perish, some, perhaps, to find the way to new adaptive peaks like Mount Opportunity. As before, the water represents the threatening natural selection.

The Step to Man

I'll be damned. I thought this was another yessir-things-are-changing technological social treatise thing. No such. It's a manual of strategies for changing the world, if you have a mind to do that. Not heavy stuff about what is terrible or what should happen, but how to remake life and stay alive in the process. Strategies like multiple working hypotheses so you don't get infatuated with your first idea. Like seed operations where one phone call makes the whole thing happen. Like self-stabilizing provisions so a process is safe from its own too-quick successes. —SB

[Suggested by Steve Baer]

The Step to Man
John R. Platt
1966; 216 pp.

$7.50 postpaid

from:
John Wiley and Sons Publishing Co.
1 Wiley Drive
Somerset, N. J. 08873

Western Distribution:
1530 South Redwood Road
Salt Lake City, Utah 84104

or WHOLE EARTH CATALOG

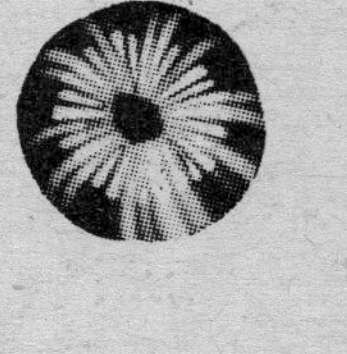

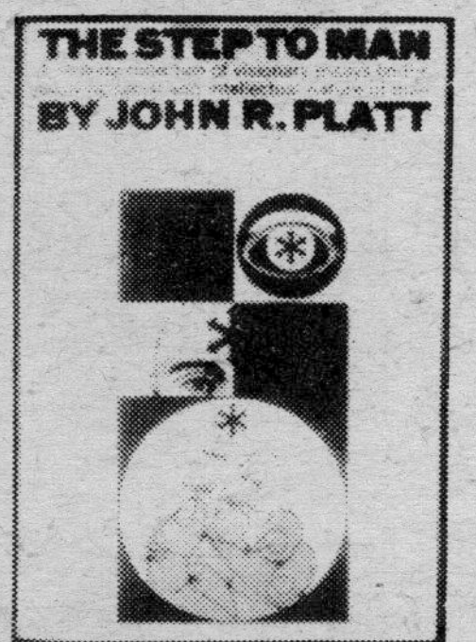

Beware of the man of one method or one instrument, either experimental or theoretical. He tends to become method-oriented rather than problem-oriented. The method-oriented man is shackled; the problem-oriented man is at least reaching freely toward what is most important. Strong inference redirects a man to problem-orientation, but it requires him to be willing repeatedly to put aside his last methods and teach himself new ones.

•

In order to carry out any great project, the future good of the group must be anticipated and turned into present and individual good, into a reward for every step that is taken in the right direction.

•

I am beginning to believe that in any social endeavor, it is the analysis of chain-reacting social processes that will enable us to choose the best course and will indicate the most effective ways for our intelligence to multiply its feeble energies. The future is waiting to respond to a touch, if it is the right touch. It is ingenuity we need, not lamentations. The world's future becomes almost plastic in the light of these possibilities.

•

We begin to realize that our brains are the most complex and self-determining things in the known universe. After all the measurements of atoms and galaxies are folded into laws in some corner of our networks, there will still be universes of interrelationships in the rest of our networks to be discovered. If this property of complexity could somehow be transformed into visible brightness so that it would stand forth more clearly to our senses, the biological world would become a walking field of light compared to the physical world. The sun with its great eruptions would fade to a pale simplicity compared to a rosebush. An earthworm would be a beacon, a dog would be a city of light, and human beings would stand out like blazing suns of complexity, flashing bursts of meaning to each other through the dull night of the physical world between. We would hurt each other's eyes. Look at the haloed heads of your rare and complex companions. Is it not so?

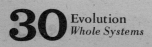

Man Adapting

The focus of this book is the human individual, what he has to deal with in this life, and what means he has to do the dealing with. Dubos is a superdoctor, so you get a damned well-informed medical perspective on questions of environment, population, health, nutrition, adaptation, etc. that subverts many a popular opinion.

—SB

The concept of perfect and positive health is a utopian creation of the human mind. It cannot become reality because man will never be so perfectly adapted to his environment that his life will not involve struggles, failures, and sufferings. Nevertheless, the utopia of positive health constitutes a creative force because, like other ideals, it sets goals and helps medical science to chart its course toward them. The hope that disease can be completely eradicated becomes a dangerous mirage only when its unattainable character is forgotten. It can then be compared to a will-o'-the-wisp luring its followers into the swamps of unreality. In particular, it encourages the illusion that man can control his responses to stimuli and can make adjustments to new ways of life without having to pay for these adaptive changes. The less pleasant reality is that in an ever-changing world each period and each type of civilization will continue to have its burden of diseases created by the unavoidable failures of adaptation to the new environment.

The paradoxical truth is that the phenomenal increase in world population during the past 50 years has coincided with great epidemics, two world wars, several minor ones, and deep disruptions of social and economic life everywhere. Furthermore, as is well known, the most destitute and disease-ridden populations of the world are precisely the ones that are increasing the fastest.

"In most cases, man's responses are determined less by the direct effects of the stimulus on his body fabric than by the symbolic interpretation he attaches to the stimulus. Human beings may suffer and even die under circumstances which seem highly favorable to physiological performance, whereas paradoxically others will prosper even though conditions appear almost incompatible with the maintenance of life."

"The negative aspects of biological interrelationships are not the most common in nature, nor are they the most important in the long run. Under natural conditions, a state of equilibrium is commonly reached between various living forms when they have long been associated in a given area. This equilibrium is achieved through biological and social mechanisms that permit the survival and perpetuation of all species involved."

The truth is, that improvements in the general nutritional state began when prosperity and greater facilities for the transportation of food made it possible for many people to afford at least one square meal a day; likewise, the mortality of many infections began to recede in a dramatic fashion in Western Europe and North America long before the introduction of specific methods of therapy, indeed before the demonstration of the germ theory of disease.

Man Adapting
René Dubos
1965; 527 pp.

$3.75 postpaid

from:
Yale University Press
149 York Street
New Haven, Conn. 06511

or WHOLE EARTH CATALOG

The Age of Discontinuity

How come Peter Drucker has so much good sense and perspective, and still remains so cheerful? Traditionally considerations such as his—economics, organizations, the future—turn a prophet's soul terrible and dark or at least partially wiggy. The only other intact floater on this ocean I know of is Marshall McLuhan. You sense that both of them have a backyard in their mind that resides somewhere else, some time else. (It would be worth pursuing this. How To Think Big and Stay Sane.)

The Age of Discontinuity takes notice of the remarkable continuity of the last 50 years in building on the technological breakthrough of the Victorian era. Now, says Drucker, we are in for some hard changes, particularly around new technologies (of information, materials, oceans, megalopolis), global economics, and redistribution of responsibility in large organizations.

—SB

The Age of Discontinuity
Peter F. Drucker
1969; 401 pp.

$7.95 postpaid

from:
Harper & Row
49 East 33rd Street
New York, N. Y. 10016

or WHOLE EARTH CATALOG

Since the computer first appeared in the late 1940's the information industry has been a certainty. But we do not have it yet. We still do not have the effective means to build an "information system." This is where the work is going on, however, The tools to create information systems may already exist: the communications satellite and other means of transmitting information, microfilm and the TV tube to display and store it, rapid printers to reduce it to permanent record, and so on. There is no technical reason why someone like Sears Roebuck should not come out tomorrow with an appliance selling for less than a TV set, capable of being plugged in wherever there is electricity, and giving immediate access to all the information needed for schoolwork from first grade through college.

Yet though IBM is now shipping computers at a rate of a thousand a month, we do not have the equivalent of Edison's light bulb. What we are lacking is not a piece of hardware like the light bulb. What we still have to create is the conceptual understanding of information. As long as we have to translate laboriously every set of data into a separate "program," we do not understand information. We have to be capable of classifying information according to its characteristics. We have to have a "notation," comparable to the one St. Ambrose invented 1,600 years ago to record music, that can express words and thoughts in symbols appropriate to electronic pulses rather than in the clumsy computer language of today. Then each person could, with very little training, store his own data within a general system, that is, in what the computer engineers call a "routine." Then we shall have true "information systems."

The Phenomenon of Man

*Reading **The Phenomenon of Man** is a bit unnerving: Teilhard de Chardin manages to say most of the things many of us are trying to say. He said them in 1938. Was no-one listening?*

The Phenomenon of Man *deals with evolution—the ascent to consciousness. The plan of the book is*

Pre-life: Life: Thought—three events sketching in the past and determining for the future (survival) a single and continuing trajectory, the curve of the phenomenon of man.

His aim is to try to see (and to help us to see)

to try to develop a homogeneous and coherent perspective of our general extended experience of man. A whole which unfolds.

Teilhard de Chardin's vision and expression of that vision are beautiful—of man evolving a super-abundance of mind; in the noosphere where the All and the Person are one. The only way to put all this together without feeling bullshitted is to read **The Phenomenon of Man.**

Only one reality seems to survive and be capable of succeeding and spanning the infinitesimal and the immense: energy—that floating, universal entity from which all emerges and into which all falls back as into an ocean; energy, the new spirit, the new God.

hominisation...noogenesis...cosmogenesis...when Teilhard de Chardin uses a simple word like homogeneous something magical happens to it.

The Omega point is where man is God and God is man, where all layers of the noosphere become involuted, fusing and consuming the All and the Person integrally in itself.

The mind is essentially the power of synthesis and organisation.

Underlying the beautiful presentation of man's ascent towards consciousness is a hard core of science:

Man, in nature, is a genuine fact, falling...within the scope of the requirements and methods of science.

*[Reviewed by Dave Evans.
Suggested by Julia Brand.]*

The Phenomenon of Man

Teilhard de Chardin
1959; 320 pp.

$1.95 postpaid

from:
Harper & Row
49 East 33 Street
New York, N. Y. 10016

or WHOLE EARTH CATALOG

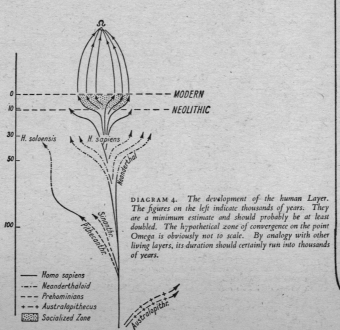

DIAGRAM 4. *The development of the human Layer. The figures on the left indicate thousands of years. They are a minimum estimate and should probably be at least doubled. The hypothetical zone of convergence on the point Omega is obviously not to scale. By analogy with other living layers, its duration should certainly run into thousands of years.*

— Homo sapiens
-·-·- Neanderthaloid
--- Prehominians
+·—·+ Australopithecus
▦ Socialized Zone

**A PLACE FOR EVERYTHING
AND EVERYTHING IN ITS PLACE**

Estelle everything's by god I really believe it is. You can tell it, you can feel it, the signs are all around. This is here and we are now and the intersection of time and space is just special as hell, and I'm going to find out some things we need to know. I believe there's going to be better relations between east and west. I believe if we get organized, a place for everything and everything in its place, books in a book box, clothes in a clothes box honey you've done a wonderful, you have now, and I love you for it and take heart and determine to be better than I've been in a long time. Those women understood every word I said. When we get to St. Louis. Are these crackers any good? Where's the tape recorder? Where'd I put the casettes? When we get to St. Louis I'm going to get some car polish and wax old Urge all over. Is this to throw away? Ain't this box any good? We need all the boxes in St. Louis I'm going to get ten cardboard boxes of identical size and label them with what they're supposed to hold. Books in one, look at this shit on my Whole Earth Catalog. Fuck, I was going to order some stuff out of there. Books in one box, tape shit in another, every goddamn thing we got's going to have its proper place. You've done a wonderful thing here honey, you really have. You ought to see their tent. From now on. When we get to St. Louis. Here, let me lift that for you. Wait! Don't throw that glass away. Here, I'll wash it out after while, I want to put a wildflower in it. I got into this rap about space, you know? I was afraid. But they knew exactly and I believe the world's getting to be a better place. I receive that from somewhere in my mind. I think love and gentleness and neighborliness and human harmony are going to prevail. I think the stars are moving into very particular cosmic arrangements. And we've got to do our part. I believe it all depends on everybody doing his part. Look at this bus, goddamn I bet old Urge is proud.

The Subversive Science

"So God created man in his own image, in the image of God he created him; male and female he created them. And God blessed them, and God said to them, 'Be fruitful and multiply, and fill the earth and subdue it, and have dominion over the fish of the sea and over the birds of the air and over every living thing that moves upon the earth.'" Genesis 1, 27-28.

And we have been fruitful, and we have filled the earth and subdued it, and we have dominion over every living thing. And what is subversive about ecology is that we know now we must turn aside from that ancient narrow edict, and live with, and not upon, the earth.

The Subversive Science *is thirty-seven essays on the shape of life. By its very breadth it creates a depth of truth no single point of view could ever make. There is a new world view within this book, a new sense of ourselves and our position on and within this earth. It is rigorous and scientific and yet in its vibrant complexity almost mystic.*

[Reviewed by Cary James]

Igloos, tepees, prairie sod-huts, hogans, pueblos—have ecology in their roof-lines.

These shelters for families, like such individual protectors as sunbonnets, sombreros, serapis, are oriented to a landscape, to weather, and to local materials.

Ecology

There are two major components to ecological study: quantitative and cybernetic. The cybernetic——control relationships——is most interesting, but the only reliable research avenue to that understanding is through grueling quantitative investigation. This book is a concise and reliable introduction to the science.

—SB

Ecology
Eugene P. Odum
1963; 153 pp.

$4.25 postpaid

from:
Holt, Rinehart & Winston, Inc.
383 Madison Ave.
New York, N.Y. 10017

or WHOLE EARTH CATALOG

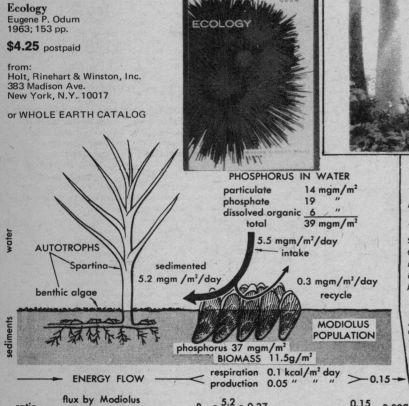

PHOSPHORUS IN WATER

particulate	14	mgm/m²
phosphate	19	"
dissolved organic	6	"
total	39	mgm/m²

5.5 mgm/m²/day intake

sedimented 5.2 mgm/m²/day

0.3 mgm/m²/day recycle

phosphorus 37 mgm/m²
BIOMASS 11.5g/m²

ENERGY FLOW

| respiration | 0.1 kcal/m² day | |
| production | 0.05 " " | 0.15 |

ratio $\dfrac{\text{flux by Modiolus}}{\text{amount in environment}}$ $P_{pa} = \dfrac{5.2}{14} = 0.37$ energy = $\dfrac{0.15}{20} = 0.008$

Fig. 4-4. The role of a shellfish (mussel) population in the cycling and retention of phosphorus in an estuarine ecosystem. The population has a major effect on the distribution of phosphorus even though the species is but a small component in the community in terms of biomass and energy flow. (Based on data from E. J. Kuenzler, *Limnology and Oceanography*, Vol. 6, 1961.)

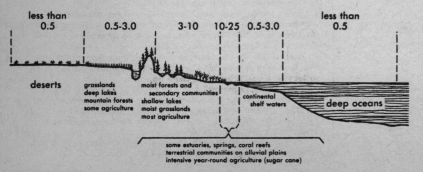

| less than 0.5 | 0.5-3.0 | 3-10 | 10-25 | 0.5-3.0 | less than 0.5 |

deserts

grasslands
deep lakes
mountain forests
some agriculture

moist forests and
secondary communities
shallow lakes
moist grasslands
most agriculture

continental
shelf waters

deep oceans

some estuaries, springs, coral reefs
terrestrial communities on alluvial plains
intensive year-round agriculture (sugar cane)

The Subversive Science—
Essays Toward an Ecology of Man
Paul Shepard
Daniel McKinley, eds.
1969; 453 pp.

$6.50 postpaid

from:
Houghton Mifflin Co.
Wayside Road
Burlington, Mass. 01803

or WHOLE EARTH CATALOG

We who were close to the Indians watched the disappearance of boys from public view. Even their father saw them no more. After sometimes a year, sometimes eighteen months, the boys returned—from the underground kivas, from the pathless areas of the Sangre de Cristo range, from the hidden crag where perhaps burns the mystical everlasting fire. Radiant of face, full-rounded and powerful of body, modest, detached: they were men now, keepers of the secrets, houses of the Spirit, reincarnations of the countless generations of their race; with "reconditional reflexes," with emotions organized toward their community, with a connection formed until death between their individual beings and that mythopoeic universe—that cosmic illusion—that real world—as the case may be, which both makes man through its dreams and is made by man's dreams.

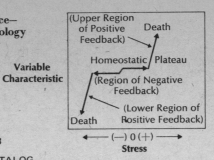

Variable
Characteristic

(Upper Region of Positive Feedback)   Death
Homeostatic   Plateau
(Region of Negative Feedback)
(Lower Region of Positive Feedback)
Death

⟵ (—) 0 (+) ⟶
Stress

"This is the dog that bit the cat that killed the rat that ate the malt that came from the grain that Jack sprayed." (Reproduced by permission of *Punch*.)

Concepts of Ecology

There is a crusade called Ecology. And also a science called Ecology. And they're not as distinct as they think they are.

This book is about the science, unhindered by rhetoric. Its subject is energy flow, cycles, populations, ecological communities, and man's place in the system. The emphasis is on theory and observation rather than math. Areas that are still poorly understood get due attention. I wish this book had been around when I studied ecology. —SB

Although the original coining of the term is an uncertainty, there is consensus that the German biologist Ernst Haeckel first gave substance to it in the following statement:

By ecology we mean the body of knowledge concerning the economy of nature—the investigation of the total relations of the animal both to its inorganic and to its organic environment; including above all, its friendly and inimical relation with those animals and plants with which it comes directly or indirectly into contact—in a word, ecology is the study of all the complex interrelations referred to by Darwin as the conditions of the struggle for existence.

The climax community results when no other combination of species is successful in outcompeting or replacing the climax community. In part, this is to be explained by the tolerance limits and optimum requirements inherent in each species. But stability of the climax is certainly not so simply explained. The answer lies in an as yet not fully understood property—diversity.

The desire to maintain __absolute__ constancy in any system must be recognized as deeply pathological. Engineering theory indicates that excessive restraints can produce instability. In psychiatry also, the desire for complete certainty is recognized as a most destructive compulsion. And in the history of nations, attempts to control rigidly all economic variables have uniformly led to chaos. The psychologically healthy human recognizes that fluctuations are unavoidable, that waste is normal, and that one should institute only such explicit controls as are required to keep each system on its homeostatic plateau. We must devise and use such controls as are needed to keep the social system on the homeostatic plateau. On this plateau—but not beyond it—freedom produces stability.

Perhaps the most serious obstacle impeding the evolution of a land ethic is the fact that our educational and economic system is headed away from, rather than toward, an intense consciousness of land. Your true modern is separated from the land by many middlemen, and by innumerable physical gadgets. He has no vital relation to it; to him it is the space between cities on which crops grow.

When we think in terms of systems, we see that a fundamental misconception is embedded in the popular term "side-effects" (as has been pointed out to me by James W. Wiggins). This phrase means roughly "effects which I hadn't foreseen, or don't want to think about." As concerns the basic mechanism, side-effects no more deserve the adjective "side" than does the "principal" effect. It is hard to think in terms of systems, and we eagerly warp our language to protect ourselves from the necessity of doing so.

Whether you will or not
You are a King, Tristram, for you are one
Of the time-tested few that leave the world,
When they are gone, not the same place it was.
Mark what you leave.

Concepts of Ecology
Edward J. Kormondy
1969; 209 pp.

$5.25 postpaid

from:
Prentice-Hall
Englewood Cliffs, N. J. 07632

or WHOLE EARTH CATALOG

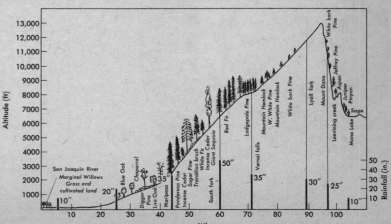

Redrawn, from B. O. Hughes and D. Dunning. 1949. Pine Forests of California. U. S. Department of Agriculture Yearbook.

Fig. 5-2. Profile of central Sierra Nevada showing altitudinal distribution of principal forest types.

Environment and Man

This is a pretty complete introductory text, well-illustrated, on all the ecological issues. There's quite a few of them, and to respond right we do need to know about all of them, or a solution to one problem may accelerate six others.

—SB

Environment and Man
Richard H. Wagner
1971; 491 pp.

$7.50 postpaid

from:
W. W. Norton & Company, Inc.
500 Fifth Avenue
New York, N.Y. 10019

or WHOLE EARTH CATALOG

When species diversity is reduced in natural ecosystems, either willfully or inadvertently, the same kinds of problems seen in monoculture begin to arise. But a natural ecosystem cannot be treated like a cornfield and routinely sprayed to control some beetle or caterpillar. For a biocide that might be tolerated in a cornfield could so scramble the food web in a woodlot that the original problem would be lost in the ensuing chaos. Moreover, while we can afford the energy input to maintain a field of corn because of the value of its yield, we cannot possibly afford the economic burden of maintaining natural ecosystems that have maintained themselves until disturbed by man. Consequently, until we know exactly the role of *every* organism in an ecosystem, how it controls or is controlled by others, we cannot abandon any species as superfluous, not even that pitiful flock of seventy whooping cranes. If we do we run the risk of having to cope with future population explosions of fungi, insects, rodents, or whatever, that might well dwarf any problems seen to date.

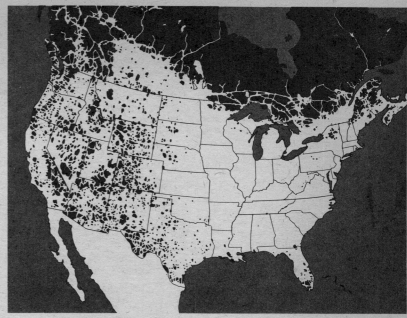

Figure 4.7 The areas in black are over five miles from the nearest road, railroad, or navigable waterway. This is America's remaining wilderness. (From C. Tunnard and B. Pushkarev, *Man-Made America*, Yale University Press, 1963.)

Science and Survival

Scientific and technological critics are significantly rare and much needed. Barry Commoner is a good one——prestigious scientist, active administrator, capable writer, committed critic.

Reading his anthology of technological blunders, I am led to wonder if the success of death-fear-driven science merely changes the size of the package that death comes in. There's less of piecemeal local, "natural" dying, and more of massive "caused" dying. I think I prefer the old way. Is anybody working on establishing friendlier relations with Death? Maybe he's a good guy who's had bad press.

—SB

[Suggested by Peter Montague]

Science & Survival
Barry Commoner
1966; 150 pp.

$1.25 postpaid

from

from:
Ballantine Books, Inc.
101 Fifth Ave.
New York, N.Y. 10003

or WHOLE EARTH CATALOG

The trouble began with the failure of a relay which controlled the flow of electricity from the Sir Adam Beck No. 2 power plant in Queenston, Ontario, into one of its feeder lines. The remaining lines, unable to carry the extra load, shut down their own safety switches. With these normal exits blocked the plant's full power flowed back along the lines that tied the Queenston generators into the U. S. - Canadian grid. This suden surge of power, traveling across New England, quickly tripped safety switches in a series of local power plants, shutting them down. As a result the New England region, which until then had been feeding excess electricity into the Consolidated Edison system in New York, drained power away from that city; under this strain the New York generators were quickly overloaded and their safety switches shut off. The blackout was then complete. The system had been betrayed by the very links that were intended to save local power plants from failure.

•

The new hazards are neither local nor brief. Air pollution covers vast areas. Fallout is worldwide. Synthetic chemicals may remain in the soil for years. Radioactive pollutants now on the earth's surface will be found there for generations, and, in the case of carbon-14, for thousands of years. Excess carbon dioxide from fuel combustion eventually might cause floods that could cover much of the earth's present land surface for centuries. At the same time the permissible margin for error has become very much reduced. In the development of steam engines a certain number of boiler explosions were tolerated as the art was improved. If a single comparable disaster were to occur in a nucler power plant or in a reactor-driven ship near a large city, thousands of people might die and a whole region be rendered uninhabitable——a price that the public might be unwilling to pay for nuclear power. The risk is one that private insurance companies have refused to underwrite. Modern science and technology are simply too powerful to permit a trial-and-error approach.

Sometimes, in moments of impending crisis, we are aware only that the main outcome of science is that the planet has become a kind of colossal lightly triggered time bomb. Then all we can do is to issue an anguished cry of warning. In calmer times we try to grapple with the seemingly endless problems of unraveling the tangle of nuclera physics, seismology, electronics, radiation biology, ecology, sociology, normal and pathological psychology, which, added to the crosscurrents of local, national, and international politics, has become the frightful chaos that goes under the disarming euphemism "public affairs."

RETURN OF THE LONE OUTDOORSMAN

The birds in the treetops hushed their singing as the Lone Outdoorsman came into Divine Right's camp. But D.R. was too deep into his monologue to catch the warning. He was too deep into it even to realize that Estelle had left the camp and gone for a walk. Before he could prepare himself in any way, there the Outdoorsman was, standing above him with his hands on his hips, staring at D.R. like a teacher or a cop. As he became aware of the Lone Outdoorsman's presence, D.R. went silent as the birds. The music that had filled his head changed from harps to kettle drums, and he wondered where Estelle had gone, and why.

"Afternoon," said the Outdoorsman.

"Good afternoon," said Divine Right.

"How're you?" asked the Lone Outdoorsman.

"Okay, I guess," said D.R.

"Yeah, Well, I noticed you over there in the tent with them foreign ladies, and I just wondered if anything might be wrong."

"No," said D.R. "Nothing wrong, as far as I know."

"Yeah. Well, just checking. I noticed you over there in the tent with 'em. You never know. Cleaning out your bus, looks like."

D.R. nodded. He had been kneeling among the stuff from the bus when the Outdoorsman first came over. Now he was on his feet, and following the Outdoorsman as he walked around the bus, looking at the paint job.

"You paint all this stuff on your bus?" asked the Outdoorsman.

"Some of it," said D.R.

"How come you to do it?" said the Outdoorsman. "Messed up a good paint job. What's that there?"

The Outdoorsman was pointing at a large yellow moon on Urge's side, with a crab walking across it, leaving tracks.

"That's a moon with a crab on it," said D.R.

The Outdoorsman looked D.R. in the eye. "You say it is, huhh?"

D.R. nodded.

"How many horsepower this thing have?"

"I don't know. Fifty, maybe."

"Fifty, huh. Yeah. Well, my GMC over there's got four hundred and fifty. Of course, the rig weighs it down some, and my boat, But it'll still outrun a bus like yours any day of the week, you better believe that."

D.R. asked the Outdoorsman why he was telling him that. The Outdoorsman said you never know. Then he told D.R. to let him know if anything came up.

"What do you mean?"

"Well. You know. Trouble."

D.R. nodded. His heart was pounding. He watched the Outdoorsman light his pipe, then carefully crush the match against his knife handle.

"You remember what I told you, now," he said, and he turned and jingled off through the trees to his own camp.

Not So Rich As You Think

Once upon a time, men lived in trees high above the forest floor. It was a gay, carefree life—your food grew right in your house and when you had eaten your fill you tossed the garbage down through the leaves. The same with your shit, and even your body when you died. The forest scavengers and processes of decay speedily disposed of all refuse.

Man came down from the trees long, long ago and created for himself a less carefree way of life. But he remains the filthiest animal around, treating his environment as if it were still magically gobbling up everything he discards. This book documents the folly with the gross disheartening facts. From human excrement to nuclear fallout, with smog, DDT and the junkyard on the way.

—HH

[Suggested by H.R. Hershey, Sr.]

Not So Rich as You Think
George R. Stewart
1968, 70; 176 pp.

$6.95 postpaid

from:
Houghton Mifflin Co.
Wayside Road
Burlington, MA. 01803

or WHOLE EARTH CATALOG

Ecology Center Reprint Series

A number of recent ecological statements have acquired 'classic' status. You can search through three libraries for them, or you can get them straight and simple from Ecology Center.

—SB

No longer available

Eco-Catastrophe, Dr. Paul Ehrlich

The Four Changes, Anonymous

Tragedy of the Commons, Garrett Hardin

The Tragedy of the Commons Revisited, Beryl L. Crowe

The Historical Roots of Our Ecologic Crisis, Lynn White Jr.

Toward an Ecological Solution, Murray Bookchin

The Politics of Population, Aldous Huxley

All About Ecology, William Murdoch and Joseph Connell

What We Must Do, John Platt

Humanistic Biology, Rene Dubos

Blind Faith In the Omnipotence of Technology, Richard Merrill

Outwitting the "Developed" Countries, Ivan Illich

Life Is an Endless Give-And-Take With Earth and All Her Creatures, Rene Dubos

Man's Eco-System, Lamont C. Cole

from:
Ecology Center Confederation
13 Columbus
San Francisco, Calif. 94111

The Population Bomb

There's a shit storm coming. Not a nice clean earthquake or satisfying revolution but pain in new dimensions: world pain, sub-continents that starve and sub-continents that eat unable to avoid each other. The consequences will dominate our lives. In the heart of the problem are the solutions, and the sooner we're clear about what's happening the sooner the solutions can work their way out. This book is the best first hard look that's around. The author is a well-regarded young population biologist and ecologist who freaked out of his lab and into the media with the bad news. Besides freaking well he reports well.

—SB

The Population Bomb
Dr. Paul R. Ehrlich
1968; 223 pp.

$.95 postpaid from
Ballantine Books, Inc.
c/o Simon & Schuster, Inc.
630 Fifth Avenue
New York, N. Y. 10020
or
WHOLE EARTH CATALOG

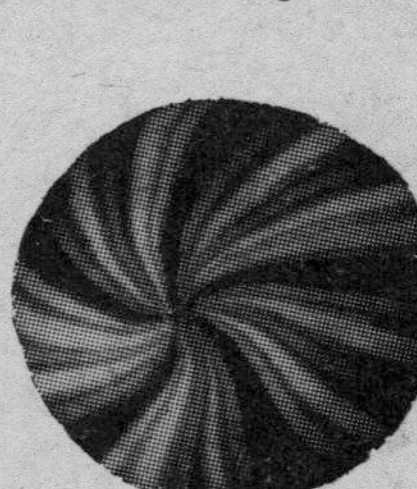

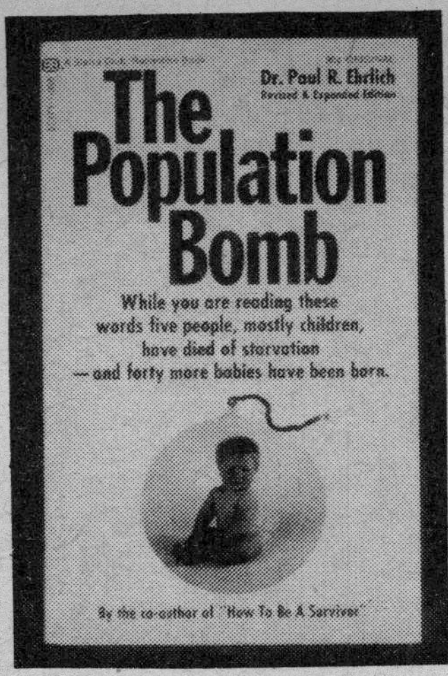

It is, of course, socially very acceptable to reduce the death rate. Billions of years of evolution have given us all a powerful will to live. Intervening in the birth rate goes against our evolutionary values. During all those centuries of our evolutionary past, the individuals who had the most children passed on their genetic endowment in greater quantities than those who reproduced less. Their genes dominate our heredity today.

The reproductive function of sex must be shown as just one of its functions, and one that must be carefully regulated in relation to the needs of the individual and society. Much emphasis must be placed on sex as an interpersonal relationship, as an important and extremely pleasurable aspect of being human, as mankind's major and most enduring recreation, as a fountainhead of his humor, as a phenomenon that affects every aspect of his being.

The battle to feed all of humanity is over. In the 1970's the world will undergo famines—hundreds of millions of people are going to starve to death in spite of any crash programs embarked upon now. At this late date nothing can prevent a substantial increase in the world death rate, although many lives could be saved through dramatic programs to 'stretch' the carrying capacity of the earth by increasing food production. But these programs will only provide a stay of execution unless they are accompanied by determined and successful efforts at population control. Population control is the conscious regulation of the numbers of human beings to meet the needs, not just of individual families, but of society as a whole.

Nothing could be more misleading to our children than our present affluent society. They will inherit a totally different world, a world in which the standards, politics, and economics of the 1960's are dead. As the most powerful nation in the world today, and its largest consumer, the United States cannot stand isolated. We are today involved in the events leading to famine; tomorrow we may be destroyed by its consequences.

•

Remember also that in virtually all underdeveloped countries, people have gotten the word about the better life it is possible to have. They have seen colored pictures in magazines of the miracles of Western technology. They have seen automobiles and airplanes. They have seen American and European movies. Many have seen refrigerators, tractors, and even TV sets. Almost all have heard transistor radios. They know that a better life is possible. They have what we like to call 'rising expectations.' If twice as many people are to be happy, the miracle of doubling what they now have will not be enough. It will only maintain today's standard of living. There will have to be a tripling or better. Needless to say, they are not going to be happy.

A ship has hit the rocks and is sinking. The passengers scream for help. Some jump overboard and are devoured by the circling sharks. A group of distinguished scientists is on board. One of their number suggests that they can help man the pumps. 'Oh, no!' shout the others. 'That might hurt the captain's feelings. Besides, pumping is not our business. It's outside our field of competence.' You can guess what they do. They appoint a committee to study the problem, with subcommittees on marine engineering and navigation. They announce to the passengers that in two or three years the committee will produce a wonderful report which will be acceptable to the passengers, the captain, and the steamship line. Not so passive are the politicians. Some jump up to say that the passengers don't understand the political realities of the situation. Other more progressive politicians grab thimbles and start bailing, stopping every few seconds to accept praise for their valiant efforts.

•

Careless overuse of DDT has promoted to 'pest' category many species of mites, little insectlike relatives of spiders. The insects which ate the mites were killed by the DDT, and the mites were resistant to DDT. There you have it—instant pests, and more profits for the agricultural chemical industry in fighting these Frankensteins of their own creation. What's more, some of the more potent miticides the chemists have developed with which to do battle seem to be powerful carcinogens—cancer-producing substances.

•

The old idea that industry could create the mess and then the taxpayers must clean it up has to go. The garbage produced by an industry is the responsibility of that industry.

Population, Resources, Environment

In **Population Bomb** *Ehrlich spared us the customary statistics and graphs, and he was accused of being no scientist. So here are the statistics and graphs and much besides——a 400-page textbook on the population-ecology crisis. Don't bother taking a course. The lab is the world.*

—SB

Population, Resources, Environment
Paul R. Ehrlich, Anne H. Ehrlich
1970; 400 pp.

$9.95 postpaid

from:
W. H. Freeman and Company
660 Market Street
San Francisco, CA 94104

or WHOLE EARTH CATALOG

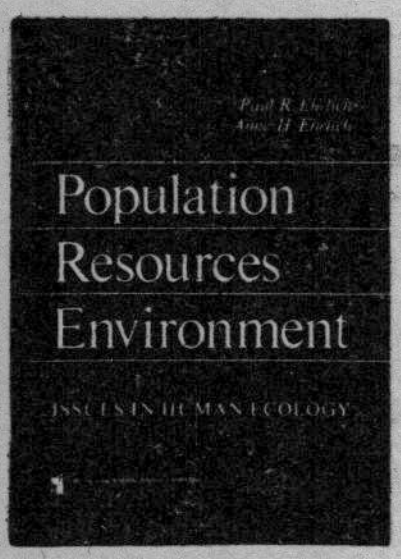

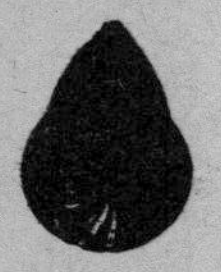

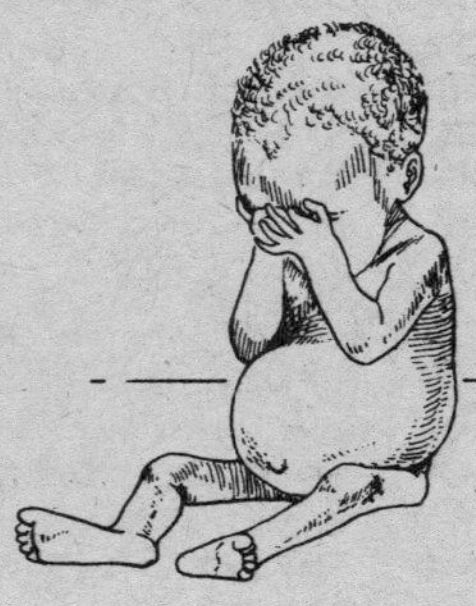

The global polluting and exploiting activities of the DCs are even more serious than their internal problems. Spaceship Earth is now filled to capacity or beyond and is running out of food. And yet the people traveling first class are, without thinking, demolishing the ship's already overstrained life-support systems. The food-producing mechanism is being sabotaged. The devices that maintain the atmosphere are being turned off. The temperature-control system is being altered at random. Thermonuclear bombs, poison gases, and super-germs have been manufactured and stockpiled by people in the few first-class compartments for possible future use against other first-class passengers in their competitive struggles for dwindling resources——or perhaps even against the expectant but weaker masses of humanity in steerage. But, unaware that there is no one at the controls of their ship, many of the passengers ignore the chaos or view it with cheerful optimism, convinced that everything will turn out all right.

•

1877-1878 *North China.* "Appalling famine raging throughout four provinces [of] North China. Nine million people reported destitute, children daily sold in markets for [raising means to procure] food. . . . Total population of districts affected, 70 millions. . . ." The people's faces are black with hunger; they are dying by thousands upon thousands. Women and girls and boys are openly offered for sale to any chance wayfarer. When I left the country, a respectable married woman could be easily bought for six dollars, and a little girl for two. In cases, however, where it was found impossible to dispose of their children, parents have been known to kill them sooner than witness their prolonged suffering, in many instances throwing themselves afterwards down wells, or committing suicide by arsenic.

•

All flesh is grass. This simple phrase summarizes a basic principle of biology that is essential to an understanding of the world food problem. The basic source of food for all animal population is green plants——"grass." Human beings and all other animals with which we share this planet obtain the energy and nutrients for growth, development, and sustenance by eating plants directly, by eating other animals that have eaten plants, or by eating animals that have eaten animals that have eaten plants, and so forth.

•

Because, as indicated in the acknowledgments, the various drafts of our manuscript were thoroughly reviewed by a large number of critics who are competent in the various areas covered, we believe that the factual basis of the book is sound throughout. We do not believe that such minor errors as may be revealed in any of our figures, estimates, or interpretations will change the thrust of our major conclusions. In many areas, of course, it is impossible to determine exactly what has happened, or to know what the significance of certain trends may be. Data are often unreliable or unavailable, and our understanding of the complexities of ecological systems and human behavior is still fragmentary. But in dealing with the population-resource-environment crisis, it is important to recognize that people are going to have to learn to make decisions in the face of such uncertainty. Possible benefits will have to be weighed against possible risks, and a great deal of thought given to possible future events which may seem unlikely *but which will be catastrophic if they do occur.* It would be a major step forward for mankind if all people could know the general state of the world and could be informed as to just what chances are being taken with their lives and the lives of future generations.

From the almost limitless number of subjects which might have been included in this book, choices of those that were to be treated in detail had to be made. We have tried to emphasize those which seemed to us to be of the most general importance, and we make no apology either for our selection of subjects or for the personal style and approach we have used throughout. We have not attempted to give equal weight to both sides of all controversial issues; where we think one side is correct we have so indicated. We also make no claim to having tried to detail all exceptions to general rules. We hope that this book will provide concerned readers with enough background to enable them to make informed political decisions about environmental issues and to combat what C. P. Snow has referred to as the "excessive unimplicity" which, in his words, "crops up whenever anyone makes a proposal which opens up a prospect, however distant, of new action. It involves a skill which all conservative functionaries are masters of, as they ingeniously protect the status quo: it is called the 'technique of the intricate defensive.' "

Population, Evolution, and Birth Control

Once you've woken up to the population squeeze and the blindness of most of your fellow men, it's worth looking around. Garrett Hardin has assembled a strong selection of eyes to look around with. Here are the ingredients for understanding. Now, how do we get the mule's attention?

—SB

The closed earth of the future requires economic principles which are somewhat different from those of the open earth of the past. For the sake of picturesqueness, I am tempted to call the open economy the 'cowboy economy,' the cowboy being symbolic of the illimitable plains and also associated with reckless, exploitative, romantic, and violent behavior, which is characteristic of open societies. The closed economy of the future might similarly be called the 'spaceman' economy, in which, therefore, man must find his place in a cyclical ecological system which is capable of continuous reproduction of material form even though it cannot escape having inputs of energy.

Kenneth E. Boulding

•

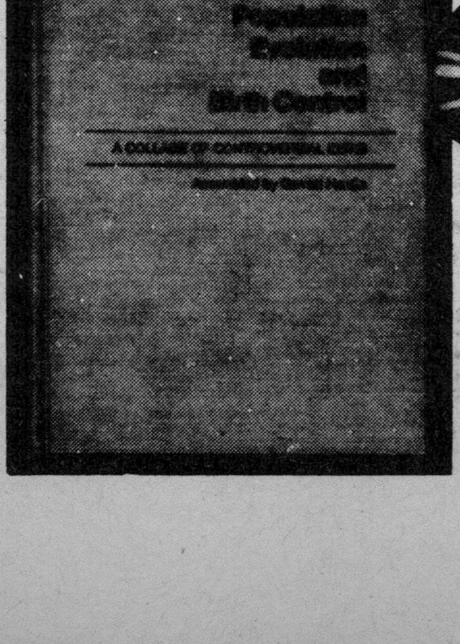

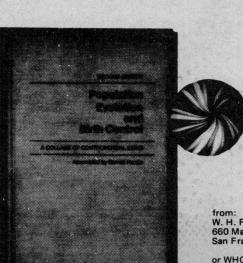

Population, Evolution and Birth Control
Garrett Hardin, ed.
1964, 1969; 386 pp.

$3.50 postpaid

from:
W. H. Freeman & Co.
660 Market Street
San Francisco, CA 94104

or WHOLE EARTH CATALOG

If the food supply is falling short, or a new disease threatens us, inventions to relieve it must be made before famine and pestilence have done their work. Now, we are far nearer to famine and pestilence than we like to think. Let there be an interruption of the water supply of New York for six hours, and it will show in the death rate. Let the usual trains bringing supplies into the city be interrupted for forty-eight hours, and some people will die of hunger. Every engineer who has to deal with the administration of the public facilities of a great city has been struck with terror at the risks which people are willing to undergo and must undergo every day, and at the complacent ignorance of these risks on the part of his charges....

Norbert Wiener

•

The rest of the night I lay there sleepless, trapped between the quavering human cry in the night and the cold fact that forced me to know I could not save him or the thousands of others whose cries I could not hear. The next morning they came and told us that the beggar was dead.

Gerald Winfield

Game design

We are talking about how to be able to change the games that Peoples play.

The strategy of game change is: you don't change a game by winning it or losing it or refereeing it or observing it. You change it by leaving it and going somewhere else and starting a new game from scratch. If it has appeal it will gather its own energy. (Fighting a system, however, merely strengthens the system, which accounts for a lot of bitter revolutionaries, including victorious ones.)

Whatever plays the game, the game is played on the field of the physical. Mind points don't count unless something happens physically. Pain penalties are of no consequence unless something adapts physically. Move the molecules, or admit you're a spectator.

As mind grows mightier, and physicality stays what it is, the world may manifest a subtler and subtler play of elements, wielded with enormous finesse by intellection largely invisible, but ever held to this world by the mundane leash. I like the rule. (Margaret Fuller said, "I accept the universe." Thomas Carlyle said, "She'd better.")

There are lots of ways to organize social behavior. The advantage of working with games is that they are regenerative, if they work. The fun of playing sustains the game from within, from the pleasure of the players. Instigators need not be leaders; the game generates its own leadership and succession.

• • • • • • • • •

Liferaft Earth

The event we did recently called Liferaft Earth was designed as a game. Its intent was to make very personal the matter of population control. The stadium was the news media, so a certain amount of theater (i.e. plot) was designed in.

The few rules, announced far in advance of the event, were: a lot of people stay publicly together for a week without eating. Anybody may leave anytime but may not return; their departure is considered a death.

The bait for the media, besides the noble cause, was suspense. Who would come to the event? How many would last the week? Who would they be? What kind of stuff would go on with hungry people penned up together?

An additional unexpected question was, Will the sponsors find a place to hold the event? We went into our press conference to announce Liferaft Earth still without a site for it. [Nobody wanted the unknown in *their* yard, not the University of California, Stanford, Berkeley, San Francisco, Tilden Park, San Mateo County. Everybody loved the idea, somewhere else.] So the press conference consisted partly of us asking for a place to hold our noble event. And it went pretty well—Jerry Mander had not given much information in the press releases, so press had to come to get the news. We had some attractive names helping with the announcement: Stephanie Mills, Dr. Eugene Schoenfeld, Don Aitken of Friends of the Earth, Dr. Sheldon Margen with nutritionist credentials at Cal, and Wavey Gravy (in his last days as Hugh Romney) dressed as a hamburger. Further visual interest—useful for TV and wirephotos—was provided by Earth posters, the door for the event with its sign "Are You Ready To Die", and a splendid model of the inflated 10,000 sq. ft. polyethylene pillow that we planned to hold the event in. Even though the reporters distrusted us for not having a site, the item was carried on local TV and newspapers, and the wire services. Thank the popularity of environmental issues for that.

LIFERAFT EARTH PHOTOS BY BONNIE-JEAN ROMNEY

Under the Press Conference gun.

The following five pages chronicles a week-long event sponsored and organized by the CATALOG in October 1969.

Richard Brautigan saw the end of it. The beginning of it was three days I spent alone on a train with excellent hash and Paul Ehrlich's **Population Bomb.** Ehrlich had been a teacher of mine, back in his butterfly and my tarantula days, so I knew to believe him.

LIFERAFT EARTH

• • • • • • • • •

Site-finding was getting truly desperate when a phone call from Hayward in the East Bay came through. A guy named Bill Goetz, head of a poverty program office in Hayward, said he had seen us on Channel 2 and did we want to hold the event in his parking lot. I went and looked, and it was all wrong, too small, all at a weird angle on a hillside, out of anybody's mainstream, into a different population than us—old folks and Spanish and social workers. . . . It was perfect. So was Goetz and his staff. So, it turned out, was Hayward.

Hayward's city manager was an old acquaintance of the head of Portola Institute. That meant that from the top there was trust. We got nothing but friendly cooperation from the city fire department, police department, health inspectors, and press. After what we'd been through, Bill Goetz and Hayward had our vote as All-American City of the Year.

Who were the cast by now? Most active was Wavey Gravy, who had signified for the Hog Farm's participation way back during the summer. Now he was inviting people left and right, buying toys like jacks and plastic fruit, hustling around. Frantic work was going on by the Southeast Inflatoenvironment group (initially Charlie Tilford, by now mostly Andy Schapiro and Joe Hall)—they were building a net to hold down the vast pillow and getting kicked off test sites. Slack polyethylene burns like napalm; inflated poly doesn't: try telling that to a Fire Marshal. Dick Raymond of Portola Institute was placating our insurance company and all the others who needed hourly placation. Stephanie Mills was on her Planned Parenthood phone inviting and reassuring. Jim Burleigh of People's Architecture in Berkeley was still hoping to find a way to do it in Berkeley. Dan Rosenberg of Sierra Club, out of the blue sky had volunteered to help find a site (Dan is the model of something every business should have, a company good guy, who's paid to go out and find good that needs doing, and do it). Back East Charlie Tilford was camped in the Union Carbide offices trying to get us a pillow of non-inflammable vinyl. Bill Goetz was busily soothing the concerned environs of his parking lot.

Since confirmation of the site came only 2 days before the event, we distributed map press-releases to the media, and made them available to participants through offices in Berkeley, San Francisco and Menlo Park. The last words of instruction were:

To make the event as easy as possible on the community we're asking that participants who plan to starve-in not park in the immediate vicinity of the site. Have someone drop you off, or park a long distance away. If you are a temporary visitor, please do what you can to reduce traffic near the event. There are many people living and working in the neighborhood of the site who did not ask for a public show on their street. They deserve every courtesy.

The Hunger Show begins on Saturday, Oct 11, with the door closing on the pillow at 6 pm. Whoever's inside at that time is in the show. No one else comes in. Anyone can leave anytime (no return). Participants should have their own sleeping gear and clothing to accommodate warm days and chilly nights. No food in the pillow. There is water. Persons with kidney troubles or other ailments that might be made worse by malnutrition should skip this token famine and wait for the real thing in 19??. There will be an MD on hand for emergencies throughout the event. No children fasting please; not yet. Participants will be asked to sign a terrifying release form which signifies that you're on your own in terms of liability and that you don't mind being filmed. Regarding legal/illegal, bear in mind that you are very visible in the pillow, and visible lawbreaking is punishable by endless inconvenience. Changing that requires some other kind of event. The subject of this one is: you are what you eat.

Believing him, I began to wonder what belief was made of. Clearly, some form of personal experience, such as knowing an author, or knowing hunger and overcrowding. How many of us arrogant world-shapers <u>knew</u> hunger? Could we learn it and teach it at the same time? The Hunger Show took shape.

Publicly it was a failure. We lost the focus of the plastic pillow and we lost the focus of staying in one place. But internally among the starvers, we connected with our bodies, with each other, with the Depression generation, with the Third World, and with the future in ways and depths that we're still sorting out.

—SB

This is the inflatable pillow, 100 ft x 100 ft of 4 mil polyethylene, that the Fire Marshall wouldn't let us use for Liferaft Earth. It was designed by Charlie Tilford. A month later the Fire Marshall okayed the structure for public use because a physicist told them it was "self-extinguishing", which it is.

•
•
•
•
•
•
•

Liferaft Earth

Robert Frank's 37-minute 16mm color sound film of the Hunger Show staged last October by Portola Institute may be rented from the POINT Foundation, Box 99554, San Francisco, CA 94109. "I'm sorry, Leon," said Bonnie Jean. "I'm hungry and I'm crazy."

• • • • • • • • •

Before saying how this Hunger Show went, I want to suggest what could be. Muster a travelling troupe of skilled improvisational actors and divide it into two or three sub-troupes. Set up a tour through college campuses with pre-publicity and all that. Starting on a Monday at each campus a hunger show begins in the theater, with the participants—one sub-troupe of actors and however many voluntary students from the college—confined behind chicken-wire on the stage. Let 'em starve all week, building publicity, to a paid-audience performance on Saturday night. Now the troupe cuts loose, laying in every kind of stress and issue, trying to burn or pray their way to the center of the population madness. Let whoever was the "leader" have a cowardly death and departure. Serve food to the audience. And so on. For the last day, Sunday morning, let audience in admission-free for what I can assure you is holy communion—the first food for the starvers.

→

There were as many Hunger Shows as there were participants (170, counting those starving on the Hog Farm buses travelling from New Mexico during the event). So rather than try to solo a description I'd rather ride tandem with Rick Field's account and Tari Reim's mid-week report for the *Berkeley Tribe.*

From *Berkeley Tribe*, Oct. 17-23, 1969

The highly public place turned out to be a parking lot for a motel turned poverty center in Hayward, California. The Southwest Electric Campfire nomad architects circled the concrete with a polyethylene air-filled wall about four feet high. It had been planned to hold the show inside a giant space-egg of the same semi-transparent membraneous material. But the fire chief declared it a fire hazard, so the wall was a last-minute innovation. Not until it was fully inflated did we realize it looked exactly like the bulging sides of a rubber raft.

Inside we had ourselves, a sound system, television, water, chemical toilets and whatever anybody brought. We flew world flags, the ones showing earth as seen from a satellite. About one-hundred twenty weighed in before the supposed one-way door closed at 6 P.M. Saturday.

People kept arriving as late as Wednesday. It was decided to let each new-comer ask every-one on board for permission to join. They spoke to us from outside the wall, using a microphone. The crew then voted yes or no, usually by voice.

No one was denied. Though a sizable minor-ity wanted to stick to the dead-line.

The first division appeared here: some took the Liferaft as a vow, and wanted to play the game close. Others didn't like the role of insider refusing outsider; they pushed for the opening up of the Liferaft game. A familiar commune problem, population pressure, how not to close off and yet not be swamped. We, however, had enough room—at least we did as long as we stayed in Hayward. And we had no problems feeding everyone. There was enough plain water, ice, and even an occasional treat of hot water, "tealess tea." We had none of the kitchen problems of large groups. No hassles about diet, cooking, cleaning. (Though we did have our share of talk about food, especially diet.) But neither did we have the unifying ceremony of a common table.

When you don't eat you have nothing but time. One corner of the raft was given over to the technology of communication and time-filling. Running this Liferaft brain-center was our jestor of ceremonies, Wavey Gravy, Hugh Romney of the Hog Farm Family.

The first days records were played when-ever no one was speaking over the sound system. Imaginary, usually elaborate, meals were read for breakfast, lunch and dinner. Games were played with prizes of plastic fruit. Newscasts kept us informed of events inside and outside

← The inflated surround was a wonder. Ideal minimal barrier. A product of desperation, it couldn't have been invented better. It was pure vulnerability—you could fall over it or cut through it easy as pie. We were contained by will and barely anything else.

Signing in Saturday afternoon was a ceremony. You weighed yourself on this funky scale and signed your weight and name with a pen embedded in a plastic asparagus into a big impressive Hog Farm book. Bonnie Jean conned and supervised. This ceremony and the many others were the product of Wavey Gravy's insistence on dramatic forms, hard edges to the game. "Play hard and play fair" is a place where he lives. It can un-fuzz your mind.

A hundred or so people. It wasn't enough. We weren't crowded. (Goodbye, expectations, you never had a chance.) And we weren't reflected on ourselves; open sky inhaled everything from us. All we had in common was plastic fence, the mike and sound system, and only gradually hunger. Without the open mike the event would have been nothing. The sound system was our mutual con-sciousness, however cluttered.

Who was there? An odd lot. A scoutmaster and his wife. Calvino, 52. High school girls. A guy, never identified, who looked like the vice-pres-ident of an electronics firm, and made it through to the end. Ecological politicians (no offense): Keith Lampe, Stephanie Mills, Gene Schoenfeld, me I guess, others. Hog Farmers, hard core and fringe—the substance of our population (Bukovitch, Tom Law, Reno, Ruffin, Sunshine, Danny, Gloria, &&). A blind girl. The filmakers Robert Frank and Danny Lyon. Student pres. from SF State. One of the staff from the poverty offices. Dick Raymond from Portola Institute. No narcs.

the raft. Six medical students had started fasting in Salt Lake City. The Hog Farm convoy of seven buses was on route to join. Sixty of them had begun to fast on Saturday.

We also watched a UN starvation movie on a sheet hung from the poverty center balcony, and listened to a tape of Kafka's "Hunger Artist."

The light-heartedness and activity were helpful, but beneath it all there was the growing awareness that the sound was never off. Since the raft was wall-less there was no escaping. Noise pollution of our own environ-ment by our own entertainment. The ampli-fication was using us more than we were using it.

Some Liferafters left because of this. But those who left without first trying to bring up the problem via the open microphone—it was there for anyone to use—did not grasp that we Liferafters could change anything we wanted to change.

Had the model of Liferaft as Earth been more deeply felt, there would have been more active caring. We create our environment. We cannot pretend the world is not our environment—an object outside—for we cannot leave it. It follows us even as we des-troy it.

Thus leaving the Liferaft because of not liking its environment was like leaving the earth—an impossibility. Yet many left, giving up the game and the vow.

Quite simply, the Liferaft depended on the people in it. Some saw this. Others treated the event more passively. They came out of curiosity and stayed as long as things were "interesting." Not seeing that the "interest-ingness" of Liferaft depended on the people in it. Stewart Brand, the inventor of the Liferaft idea, was conspicuous by his silence. More interested in what would/could happen than in making it happen.

*****

On Sunday ABC-TV arrived. They were filming a special on ecology activists. They were on our side. Could they film us from within?

Another division: some Liferafters were dead against mass media; they were the enemy. Others felt we could use them. Still others felt we could convert them, by being open and friendly.

The decision was to let them come in if they fasted with us. ABC pleaded. They had impor-tant work to do, useful work. They couldn't spare the time. So they filmed us over the wall. Anyhow, we had our own media inside, Robert Frank with an empty stomach filmed ABC filming us.

Since the door was closed at 6 pm Saturday, the music, the color TV, the four microphones, have been blaring away.

Saturday night, Reno-the-jacks-coach held the World Series of Jacks. After exhausting preliminary matches, Susy B. upset the much-lauded Gloria, much to the delight of Hayward fans watching from the perimeter.

← Rick, I was wasted. As much cogency as I could muster was sliding out over the telephone lines to the reporters who kept calling. Stephanie and I were the names they knew to ask for, and what-ever we said on that fucking phone is what appeared in the newspapers—it shouldn't be that way, but that's how it was, and it drained us.

It was far better with the TV people, because they had to come to the scene and would interview more people. More important, they saw us, and saw us diminish, and began to identify. That never happened with the newspapers and radio interviews.

If news is as important to social consciousness as everybody says, how come there's so much sloppy reporting? Associated Press (via phone) conjured the news that Dr. Schoenfeld was denying people aspirin for their headaches, and that fiction was printed throughout the United States. Some of the underground coverage was better, some much worse. You pays your money and you takes your chances when you read a newspaper.

Liferaft Earth
Whole Systems

LIFERAFT EARTH

With the arrival of the TV crew we felt how exposed we were. Flat parking lot concrete. Hot sun. Cameras. The good citizens of Hayward peering at us over the wall, as if they had never seen fasting long-hairs before. Some of us got uptight, tried to find a spot as far away from the eyes as possible, but finally there seemed nothing to do but become transparent, get used to it and continue living.

A question about getting high. Some people smoked grass, as discreetly as possible. For others, the paranoia level was too much—all those people watching. Others preferred meditation, yoga. The first three days we did group breathing exercises. (Meditation and yoga seemed good survival skills; it was easier to survive the noise, tension, nothing to do time; it gave moments of solitude in a week of constant social living.)

Truly, The Eyes of Hayward were upon us. But it was all right. Most spectators had never had the chance to observe tribal ways so closely.

The transparency phase didn't last long. Kids invented the game of punching holes in the raft. A Hole Patrol was armed with tape. It became clear that most spectators didn't know what we were doing. Some Liferafters wanted to go outside the wall and talk to people. Some wanted to let spectators wander around inside. Most of us felt exposed enough. Again, the open/closed division. Gandalf said, If you can't get through to people over the wall, you can't get through to them outside it. The end result was that more of us spent more time in communication yoga, rapping with spectators over the wall.

It was twenty-four hour parking-lot theatre; the main action was not eating. Suspense was supplied by how long we would last. It was hard for many spectators to see the connection between our "game" of not eating and getting along with each other and our "message". It was hard for some of us to see the connection also. Anyone who didn't was welcome. And some came just to fast, as self-purification, as a joyous, positive act. To some the link of fasting to starvation ecology politics was a bring-down.

The political/spiritual dichotomy was always present. Yet for many of us it was not real. Some learned what it was like to fast; some learned what it was like to be hungry; most of us learned both.

Fasting to get high, to purify, to understand the root fear of infant helplessness when the breast did not come on time; did not cancel out fasting to know hunger, to call human attention to present and future starvation of food and space and silence.

"Political" and "spiritual" were not only not mutually exclusive. They were mutually interilluminating, as interdependent as the life-support system. The Liferaft experience was a continuum, a sliding wave-length between the two conceptual extremes.

*****

Tom Law and Reno led the yoga breathing exercises. It meant a lot to do something with the body that was growth, not further shrinkage. We were doing something in unison, and that meant a lot.

On Sunday, the crew built a swimming pool and we spend the day lounging in the sun at our microcosmic Country Club.

The following day remained cold and cloudy and the crew kept warm with football, frisbee, flying kites, darts, and yoga.

We also tried a Hog Farm specialty, the Gong-Bong. A group of people get in a circle, hold hands tightly, then squatting, breathe deeply 14 times. Slowly stand up, raise your arms, holding the last breath. Then let out any sound that your lungs make. It's a very strange high. I fell to my knees dizzy, the dude next to me passed out.

Then, gong-bonged, we stayed in the circle and the microphone was passed around for each person to say who he was and why he was on the Liferaft. Wavey's right: this should happen at every event where people are staying together. What people said was strong clear stuff. By the time the mike came around I had to talk through a considerable lump in my throat.

By the second night crew members were asking other crew members for permission to leave the raft, keep the fast on the outside, and then return. By this time we had evolved a method of decision making: we would make no decision about future policy. Leave if you want and ask for permission to re-enter when you get back. In practice, people left and came back without much trouble. Maybe five, give or take a few. But there was a growing group feeling that people should not leave and then return because it was becoming clear that the difficulty was not only fasting but staying in this often insane place with the same people. (Most of us had not known each other before. We ranged from age 16 to 52, from scout-master to beyond description.) What it came down to was, if you felt people shouldn't leave, you didn't leave.

We were not in a beautiful spot. We sat, walked and slept on concrete. Longing for trees. Calvino talked about organic gardening. Maybe we could bring some earth into the raft. At least the sky was there, if you lay back.

Hayward was the kind of place you get marooned in while hitchhiking. Cars slow down just to look at you, never to stop. But as far as the ecological consciousness of Liferaft—it was perfect. A hungry crowded concrete future. And the people could step right up and see it, for free. It was also good for us, to be out there in the middle of parking lot shopping center america, talking to people far from hip ghettos. It was intensified by that empty spaced-out lighter than air feeling of hunger. And it was funny, how many of them were impressed by our not eating. We were Fools but we were doing something that was beyond them. Some heads got opened. Not making a big serious deal of fasting was our best Fool's way. We gave the microphone to somebody munching a hamburger. Spectators—a few—wanted to know what they could give us. Since food was out there wasn't much. Some of us struggled through Ehrlich's "Population Bomb", to know what we were talking about. (It was hard to read after the second day; eyes kept slipping off the page.)

*****

Rain clouds on Tuesday. We inflated our common shelter—a smaller version of the original space-egg. A warm drowsy secure nest. But it was called a fire hazard, even though it was raining. Soon we had a shanty town of scrounged plastic and wood lean-tos. Private property. The common one-sky-one-roof feeling disappeared. Small groups invisible behind their plastic. No longer could you spend time just drifting around the parking lot, bumping into people, picking up on what was happening.

Originally, this "Hunger Show" was scheduled for a nice grassy place somewhere in San Francisco. But with city officials uptight and no one willing to offer enough space, we've ended up in an asphalt parking lot in Hayward, thanks to Hayward's Poverty Director, Bill Goetz.

Bill is one of those rare people who can work in and out of both sides of the social spectrum. Fully aware of the problems we're faced with, yet with the ability to solve some of those problems by dirtying his hands with government agencies.

So on second thought this parking lot in Hayward, stereotype suburbia, couldn't be more appropriate for this ecology protest called "Liferaft Earth."

In case
there's some question
what
Liferaft Earth
was about,
it was about
this

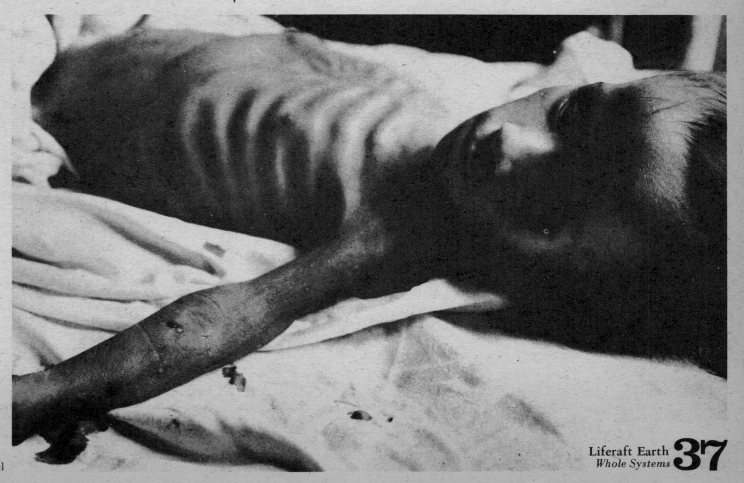

[photo: Oxfam]

Tuesday, getting bleak.

The rain that night was just too heavy. We found shelter in the poverty center office. People and sleeping bags soaked through. Started the morning with chanting. Rain continued. People left. Report that Liferaft was sinking because holes could not be patched because of wet plastic. Report that a stop sign had been thrown into Liferaft during the night. Decision to abandon Liferaft—we couldn't stay in Center office—and continue Liferaft in back room of Whole Earth Truck Store. (No place else to go.)

Many of us left during the move. Everytime condition/place changed we lost people. Keeping open to moving and change was harder than fasting for many. We were wet, tired, funky. The room was warm and dry and much much too small. We covered the floor with dry sleeping bags and the walls with wet clothing. Again, the model of a crowded hungry future, too many people living in insect closeness. Of course for a while it was nice and cozy, close comfortable groups laying around, taking it easy. But. The TV in the corner reached every ear. Cries of Turn it down. Cigarette smoke duplicated L.A. air. Many, able to stop eating, were unable to stop smoking. If you took a step, you had to step over somebody. After a few hours of this more and more people died.

A general goofy punch-drunkeness. Some avidly read cookbooks, especially savoring the big glossy illustrations. A TV crew arrived. Wavey Gravy passed out all the toys he had left. During an interview with Brand some crew member blew bubbles in front of the television camera.

We took stock. The three days in Hayward were over. We had plenty of publicity—on the news every night, talked to too many reporters. Now when TV or radio men came most people hardly stirred. Nor was there much interest in watching ourselves on TV. The Log was hopelessly out of date since people were leaving without bothering to weigh-out.

Roy Sebern, artist.

With the sky gray and threatening, like a scene from the Old Testament, with the fourth day of hunger producing weird and mellow hallucinations, the entire Liferaft Earth seems more surrealistic and more absurd.

But sitting here, looking out across the "Hunger Show", sitting here in Liferaft Earth looking across the desolation of this Asphalt-Parking-Lot in-Hayward-Wasteland, I can still remember that this macabre and absurd scene does not surpass the outside world I came from.

Tuesday night. The rain kept coming down that sloping asphalt. ("No rain this week" the weather bureau had said.) People were 3-days weak and now were soaked. ("Two more days of rain" the weather bureau said now.) The Pneumonia Show. I started waking people up and sending them into the plastic tube—it wasn't dry enough, and the Fire Department would chase them out. We'd have to leave the enclosure. I stood by the door "ARE YOU READY TO DIE" for two breaths, and pushed on out. The key I had to the big building didn't work; I called Goetz and he came down to open his office. Warm dry office, gradually filling wetly with people. Wavey comes in. His wife Bonnie Jean comes an hour later nearly hysterical; she's been searching for him all this time in every pile of junk in the enclosure. I go back out to get the final refugees. Rain and wind. What I hear, walking through the debris, is "This is the way the world ends . . . sooner than expected", only not that dramatic. Just a caption.

It was impressive, that people as weak and fucked-up as we were could clean up the parking lot and move out so efficiently. We kept discovering that, how as you get weaker you still can do what you have to, only you do it better. You get kind of simple-minded, I think. It makes for good press interviews: you're too weak to tell anything but the middle of the truth.

Robert Frank stopped by to tell us he'd died driving over from Hayward. He felt the movie he'd been trying to make had been in the parking lot. If we'd stayed there, stuck it out . . . He obviously didn't feel too good. We'd watched his last movie, "Me and My Brother," staring Julius Orlovsky, in Hayward, projected on a sheet; it was depressing to lose him.

The seven Hog Farm buses arrived that night. Painted with "Liferaft Earth Hunger Show", driving from New Mexico through breakdowns and hamburger highways. It was now Thursday. Sixty or so had managed to stay alive, driving, feeding kids. Others hadn't started the fast or had died along the way.

Back in the Hayward parking-lot—hearing that they were now in Reno, that they had to fix a clutch in Las Vegas—we had talked of the energy we would receive when they joined us. How beautiful it would be. The vision of sixty more Liferaft people coming as our numbers dropped.

But we did not run out into the rain and embrace them. Instead we stuck stubbornly to our remaining structure—probably because it had in fact fallen apart and we were doing our best to keep going. But we went through the whole trip of our game: Stop at the door, are you alive or dead, weigh-in, and so on. One by one. Since many Hog Farm people were dead, having eaten, and needed to get out of the rain, see friends, dry off, stretch, use the bathroom—the game at this point was just in the way. Living and dead from the Farm all

had the same living problems. The pure Liferaft of only fasters was, by necessity, a thing of the past. But we held on tight to our conception of what we were doing; or our conception held on tight to us.

Understandably, many brothers and sisters from the Farm were unhappy. Thoughtlessness and our weary apathy were received as negative vibrations. Farm people felt a come-down from their cross-country bus-life Liferaft. Not that it was all bad. A lot of what happened was just fine, embraces, smiles, sharing. But there were just too many people in the room. Kids and dogs running around. More people kept coming in to the room from the buses. Before our eyes our population exploded. Out of overcrowding, misunderstanding. Arguments over the microphone. Some trouble within the Farm. Somebody wanted to discuss the wording of the original Hunger Show leaflet. Finally twenty-five of the newly arrived Farmers walked out and died across the street in a Chinese restaurant. Wavey Gravy, torn between communes, said *he* was leaving because so many of his Family were leaving. He looked miserable. Somebody said, But you can't go, weren't you one of the *organizers.* Somebody answered, That's the trouble, there aren't any organizers, it's what all of us do.

Wednesday, the full catastrophe.

At this shock-point one Hog Farmer took the microphone, and said, Listen, I have this book, you ask it questions, and there was suddenly instant agreement. Bring in the Book of Changes, to help us through our changes.

A call for silence. People meditating, going into themselves, quieting down. We passed the bundle of yarrow stalks around. Over ninety people touched them, held them, heavy with potential. We all placed our hearts in the straight-crooked stalks, falling apart, coming together. Intense highly charged stale late night air.

"The Arousing: Thunder repeated: the image of shock. Thus in fear and trembling the superior man sets his life in order and examines himself." Changing to The Receptive: "Since there is something to be accomplished we need friends and helpers in this hour of toil and effort . . . to find friends means to find guidance." The words flashed away our weary collective stupidity. There was no discussion afterwards. The whole room began breathing normally. Wavey Gravy took to heart the section dealing with the leader, that " . . . this is also a time of planning and for this we need solitude . . . In this sacred hour he must do without companions, so that the purity of the moment may not be spoiled by factional hates and favoritism." Wavey Gravy returned to his air mattress and announced that he would not speak until the same time tomorrow. Thus he signed off.

*****

The police in Menlo Park also thought the Truck Store was overcrowded. Our third and final move was to a house in the mountains. It seemed a reward for going through all the rest. Walking through the forest, under clouds, pine-needle ground, hunger-sharpened taste buds feasting on fresh air, remembering I haven't been alone since the fast began. Please, People, let there be trees and space enough for space.

The scene Wednesday at the Truck Store was harrowing. This was my most protected research haven. With wall to wall people in it I was flat freaked. Now we *were* reflected on ourselves. "This is it", said Wavey, "This is the 21st Century." With the arrival of the Hog Farm buses that night (still raining), it began to get really interesting—jammed with people now, and tempers rising and procedures fraying: everything from this point on is news because nobody knows what happens next. We never found out. A long slow reading of the I Ching put everybody to sleep. The next morning Menlo police came and said to leave.

That was a strange scene. I was in the parking lot of my own store raving at a cop, wondering if I was going to slug him. He was no polite cop and I was no polite citizen. I didn't hit him, but was going to do it in the press, when Dick Raymond (who'd left and eaten, because of a death in the family) came up with an original thought. Let the cops be. Hippies against cops is a boring and useless story. Go to Portola's place in the mountains, Ortega Park, and don't tell the media where we're going. Keep the fast, but get some rest. And that's what we did. A reporter from Channel 7 said as we departed, "Is there anything else I can do for you, besides leave you alone for a few days?"

All of us are here. The Hog Farm, fasters as well as non-fasters, visitors who can find us. Robert Frank returns, asks to rejoin, resumes not eating, and brings out his camera. All Structure has disappeared. No games, no news reports, no hard and fast line between living and dead. Energy comes for clear headed moments, then evaporates, then returns. Non-fasters cook elaborate meals constantly. More people die due to proximity of food but most of them don't leave. Someone proclaims, "There is no difference between the living and the dead." A comfortable wandering chaos. One radio station reports we've given up, another, closer to the truth, says we're in hiding. We wait and take showers. Wavey Gravy, in all day silence, covered with balloons, ceremoniously presents a glass of water to everyone as they arrive from the Truck Store.

Thursday, Friday at Ortega. People who had "died" were cooking constantly in the kitchen, eating four or five meals a day in front of close friends who were starving. They weren't doing it meanly, more as if with so much hunger around, someone had to do a lot of eating. I have a feeling that this is happening in the world—under-eating in one place matched by over-eating in another to compensate.

The return of Robert Frank and Danny Lyon. "I woke up this morning," said Robert, "and I felt terrible. I had to come back." Danny commented, "I'm glad Robert had some food. He couldn't carry the camera any more." During the week Tom Albright had an article in the San Francisco Chronicle about Robert's involvement in the Hunger Show, titled "One Man's End to Cynicism."

*Friday, final meeting
on the final issues.*

My mother is right, at last at last
So Eat! Eat!, so fast & fast
In India, China & Peru
The last meal has got to be you.

DDT & a BM
The teeth of reason grind again
Fuck no more for heavens sake!
Save the world from the old fuck quake.

$1.10 and I'll make you sterile
Get your rocks off the moon
    (balls of beryl)
Kids are made by fools like me
But only the pill can make you free.

Man is a mucker (Cain mucked Abel)
Don't throw your beer cans under the table!
God's in his penthouse——all's right with the world
He's got a Dispozall for all things soiled.

Make room for God! (Heah come de judge!)
In a crown of garbage, with a scepter of sludge
Man the mucker at his right hand side
And Dr. Filth his sinister bride.

Envoi:
Breathe while you can & fuck while you may
Species pass another day
Yez dont take yer choice so yez pays yer fee:
The earth a desert & death home free.

—Tuli Kupferberg
From "Earth Read-Out"
439 Boynton, Berkeley 94707

We meet and try to discover an end to what had a beginning. Survivors decide to all sleep upstairs, then break the fast together. Press is invited. People give up their fantasy dinners and agree to break fast on stewed tomatoes with a little salad later, as suggested in a book.

Frank takes movie and tape snapshots of all survivors; some speak; some just look into the camera.

*****

Sentient beings are numberless, starving and driven mad by over-crowding; vow to save them all.

A vow is making a choice not to choose at each changing moment whether to stay or not.

Survivors took the experiment as a vow.

Here Liferaft opens out, game into world. Because there is no denying the vow of birth, of living with this world; it follows us where-ever we go, what-ever we do; there is no other choice for living because there is no other place to live.

The TV newsman said, "Well, now that you've made it through this week and I see you're having some food, how do you feel?" The same guy who answered with a simple heartfelt murmur, "This is Christmas," was the guy who had nightmares for a week that the Hunger Show was continuing, and shat pale and painful. That was me. That was my end of it.

The one Richard Brautigan saw happened back on Wednesday, around noon, after everybody had taken their sopping gear and split to Menlo Park. Brautigan surveyed the empty parking lot with its smelly outhouses and outline of deflated plastic. He poked around in our tidy pile of trash, noted the abundance of children's toys. He stood by the still-standing doorframe and listened to the sound of the rain on the plastic. While every so often the are-you-ready-tö-die door swung slowly open and blam shut in the wind.

Fasting at Ortega was simple: endurance. Bonnie-Jean was now unable to walk, and Wavey carried her from room to room. Tom Law and Reno were hustling around organizing their Sympowowsium. "The yogis," said Bonnie-Jean, "are man-mountains."

Friday afternoon was a big last meeting, partly on Hog Farm business, partly Hunger Show. Wavey was making his farewell address to the Hog, signifying a new period for him of "fast yoga", on one quick bus, next destination the Chicago 8. For the Hunger Show, it was finding a way to bring a loose show back together and end it formally Saturday morning, on schedule.

Saturday morning, the first bite of food—a squeeze of lemon, some avocado, stewed tomato—went off like fireworks in the body. Everybody's smiling, everybody's chewing. We had a kind of diploma printed up for those who made it through, and people are signing each others diplomas like high school yearbooks. "Best of luck in '69. Patty-cake."

Who are the survivors? Gandalf is manning the logbook and the scales and has the total: 52 survivors. Quite a crew. The hairiest and quietest of the starters. Lot of girls. Roy, Calvino, Rick, Amy, Wavey, Bonnie-Jean, Ruffin, Tom, Reno, Steven, Marsha, Peter, Jim, Bob Redhat, Dick Duncan, Tim, Buffalo Bob, Gil, Eban, Jerry Lamb, . . . roll-call of the living.

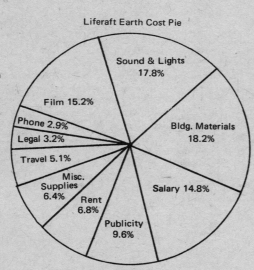

Liferaft Earth Cost Pie

Sound & Lights 17.8%
Film 15.2%
Phone 2.9%
Legal 3.2%
Travel 5.1%
Misc. Supplies 6.4%
Rent 6.8%
Publicity 9.6%
Bldg. Materials 18.2%
Salary 14.8%

total cost $2357.61
no income
paid for by customers and subscribers
of Whole Earth Catalog

*Saturday, Pigasus, Wavey Gravy
(scrawny gravy—down 20 lbs.)*

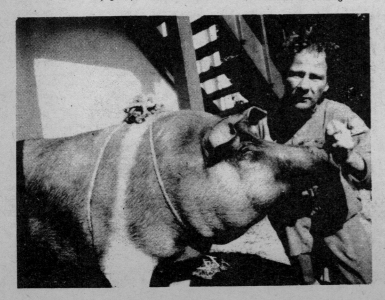

Time release

A year ago, when you did <u>Liferaft</u>, I felt a little surprised that you were putting energy into a paranoid trip. I was also a little curious, a little envious, as I watched people leave here to go and participate. I had never fasted. Six days ago I began a fast, my first; and as I began I knew it would last at least seven days, because <u>Liferaft</u> had been seven days.

I sat today for a long while under a green tree looking up at the sky through the leaves. There were many different shades of green and as the sun moved the patterns of the leaves changed; it was very beautiful.

For some reason I found myself remembering a sentence from a science book I'd been reading: "Probably 300 million children in the world today are so undernourished that they are suffering permanent brain damage."

Since I came to live in the country I have been keeping useless information out of my head. I don't want to listen to horror stories when I could be chopping wood or canning blackberries or telling a story to the kids. I refuse to worry about something that I can't do anything about. But this sentence didn't feel like that. There I was, under a tree, surrounded only by good things, and yet I knew that on this planet children were hungry, real children, children that I could easily reach in a days time (given enough money and a passport). They were inside my head, and it was right that they were inside my head.

I don't know where to go on from here. It feels like I am climbing aboard the <u>Liferaft</u>, a year late.

Elaine
Cave Junction, Oregon

AT HOME WITH THE LONE OUTDOORSMAN

So far that day the Lone Outdoorsman had motorcycled to the toilet and back, and hiked around Section B of the Eagle Rock State Park campground. His plan had been to stop off at his camper for a beer and a bar of pemmican, and then go hunting over in the park amplitheater with his new AR-15 semiautomatic double-barrel over-and-under. But after he'd noticed the hippie queer bothering the two foreign ladies in the red tent, he decided he'd better hang around the campsite just in case.

He wanted a beer really badly by now, but as an act of discipline he kept his cooler closed, and satisfied his thirst with the warm water in his canteen. He considered foregoing a beer as an act of sacrifice for the ladies. As women, alone in the wilderness, they had a right to expect that much of him. He owed it to them, to the cause of westward settlement and civilization in general, to keep alert and ready until the threatening element among them had been dealt with in some sure and final way. Maybe it had already been dealt with. Maybe that little show of force right there in the hippie queer's own campground would be sufficient to keep him from running amuck. The Lone Outdoorsman hoped it would. He sincerely hoped it would.

For he was a peaceable man. He'd fought the war to make the peace. It was his most fervent hope that peace would in fact endure, so that women and children could be safe in their homes, to grow and learn and become good citizens, so that people like these two foreign ladies could come to America and witness the magnificence of this great land from sea to shining sea in freedom and safety. Let the foreign people come to America, he thought. Let them experience our great mountains, our flowing rivers, our abundant wildlife, our historic monuments, our magnificent parks, both state and federal and our majestic canyons, deserts, plains and lakes, both fresh water and salt. Let peace reign, he thought. Let the people come, and enjoy, and be free. And let the freaks and queers and Jews and motorcycle gangs be goddamn careful when they fuck with the Lone Outdoorsman.

The Lone Outdoorsman took another pull from his canteen. As he holstered it again he peered through his curtains and saw a suspicious thing: the threatening element next door was trying to sneak away, to rendezvous with a band of confederates over by the river. The Outdoorsman reached for his AR-15 semiautomatic double-barrel over-and-under and prepared to fire. But then he lowered the weapon and through clenched teeth muttered, "I think I'll follow that son of a bitch." He hung the rifle on the wall and got his .357 magnum pistol out of a drawer and hitched it to his web belt.

As Divine Right disappeared into the trees in the rear of Section C, the Lone Outdoorsman stealthily trailed behind him.

The User's Guide to the Protection of the Environment

The consumer has more power for good or ill than the voter. All of us ecologically-concerned citizens have frets of creeping hypocrisy when we enter the supermarket all unknowing or half-knowing about the effect of our purchases and refusals to purchase.

This book is a fret-reducer. It defines daily virtuous behaviour toward ecological Good. —SB

The User's Guide to the Protection of the Environment
Paul Swatek
1970; 312 pp.

OUT OF PRINT

Ballantine Books, Inc.
101 Fifth Avenue
New York, NY 10003

Earth Tool Kit

From Environmental Action in DC comes a handy guide for political action toward eco-good. Pretty skilled information here.

—SB

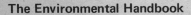

Earth Tool Kit
Sam Love, ed.
1971; 366 pp.

$1.25 postpaid

from:
Environmental Action
Room 731
1346 Connecticut Ave, N.W.
Washington, D.C. 20036

or WHOLE EARTH CATALOG

The Environmental Handbook

The Environmental Handbook as "the bible" of New Conservation. Paul Ehrlich, the others, as prophets predicting the literal end of the world. Ecology Action, the others, as young disciples working zealously to save it. The Survival Walk from Sacramento to L.A. as a modern version of the crusades. The public outcry against pollution as an evangelical call to cast out evil. San Jose State students actually burying a devil alive, in the form of a new Maverick.

While Lynn White Jr. says: "Human ecology is deeply conditioned by beliefs about our nature and destiny——that is, by religion. . . . The victory of Christianity over paganism was the greatest psychic revolution in the history of our culture. . . .We continue today to live, as we have lived for about 1700 years, very largely in a context of Christian axioms. . . .Christianity, in absolute contrast to ancient paganism and Asia's religions. . .not only established a dualism of man and nature but also insisted that it is God's will that man exploit nature for his proper ends. . . .[Christians] are superior to nature, contemptuous of it, willing to use it for our slightest whim."

Conservation asking Christian America to quit being Christian America, America saying can't, I need the money.

Psychic revolution. Beginnings of religious war. Christ a space-age anti-Christ. Battle in the cockpit. Veer left, veer right 66,000 miles an hour. Off course! Quick! Somebody grab the wheel!

[Reviewed by Gurney Norman]

Ecotactics

The Sierra Club's paperback Ecotactics was published two months after Friends of the Earth brought out The Environmental Handbook. The difference shows, but not enough to hurt. If The Handbook hadn't got there first, Ecotactics would be a hot item indeed. It's not quite as punchy as The Handbook but it's got a lot of good stuff in it, most of it by ecology writers I hadn't heard of before, which I consider a virtue. I mean, I've heard Paul Ehrlich and Rene Dubos and other big guns who appear prominently in The Handbook. I know what they have to say. It's encouraging to see just how many good young writers the whole ecology thing is producing. Since both books cost only 95 cents, the serious ecology revolutionary by all means ought to have copies of each. They complement each other, sort of fill in each other's holes. For example, The Handbook contains Gary Snyder's now famous environmental manifesto, "Four Changes", while Ecotactics presents a short article about Snyder himself, as a man, poet and a naturalist. Both statements deserve wide audiences. So do both the books as wholes.

[Reviewed by Gurney Norman]

WATER CONSERVATION IN THE HOME

Minimize the amount of water you use and the waste burden you impose on the sewer system.

Fix leaky faucets and tiolets. The steady flow uses up a considerable considerable volume.

Food waste disposal units are about as ecologically unsound as an appliance can get. A disposal unit will increase the load you impose on the sewage system by 25%......

Plant lawn covers and shrubs that will be able to get along with a minimal amount of sprinkling.

Don't move where the water is scarce.

Don't use your sink as a dump. Refrain from washing garbage, detergents, and chemicals (*e.g.* Drano) into the sewers as much as you can.

Never use pesticides in such a way that they could contaminate either ground or surface water.

Don't use salts in the winter to free walkways of ice. This practice is ruining a growing number of wells in New England.

●

". . .If the options are traveling in an old jalopy with two passengers and a driver, taking a half-full bus, a half-full plane, or a half-full train, the options would rank: train (12 gm/100 passenger miles), bus (27), jet (160), and auto (2666) in terms of CO emissions. . ."

The press release is, in effect, a news article. It must be clear, interesting, readable and to the point. In its first sentence (the lead), five questions should be answered——who, what, when, where, and why. Reporters will essentially be rewriting a press release for their articles if there are no other facts at hand, and everything they need should be included. If the lead is clear and informative, local radio stations may also use it in their hourly reports.

To be effective, the press release must also be timely. One of the media's strictest rules is the deadline, and this must always be taken into account. For morning papers, the deadline is around 7:00 P.M.; for evening papers, around noon; and for evening television news, about 4:00 P.M. Reporters should receive releases substantially ahead of the deadline, preferably by several days if the information is available. Releases should be marked "press release" and should include a release date, or a time when they are to be announced. Groups must also include on every release the name and telephone number of a person who can be contacted for further information or any questions. For best results, the envelope should be addressed to the attention of a sympathetic newsman.

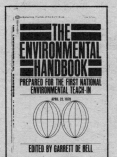

The Environmental Handbook
Garrett De Bell, editor
1970; 365 pp.

$.95 postpaid

from:
Ballantine Books
101 Fifth Avenue
New York, New York 10003

or WHOLE EARTH CATALOG

The phrase, "health of the environment" is not a literary convention. It has a real biological meaning, because the surface of the earth is truly a living organism. Without the countless and immensely varied forms of life that the earth harbors, our planet would be just another fragment of the universe with a surface as drab as that of the moon and an atmosphere inhospitable to man. We human beings exist and enjoy life only by virtue of the conditions created and maintained on the surface of the earth by the microbes, plants and animals that have converted its inanimate matter into a highly integrated living structure. Any profound disturbance in the ecological equilibrium is a threat to the maintenance of human life as we know it now.

Rene DuBos

Ecotactics
1970; 287 pp.

$1.95 postpaid

from:
Simon and Schuster, Inc.
630 Fifth Avenue
New York, New York 10020

or WHOLE EARTH CATALOG

Youth must develop an investigative approach to the problems of pollution. It is one of the most basic prerequisites. Not only must there be a close analysis of corporate statements, and periodicals, annual reports, patents, correspondence, court records, regulations, technical papers, Congressional hearings and agency reports and transcripts, but there must be a search for the dissenting company engineer, the conscience-stricken house lawyer, the concerned retiree or ex-employee, the knowledgeable worker and the fact-laden supplier of the industry or company under study. They are there somewhere. They must be located.

Ralph Nader

The Voter's Guide to Environmental Politics

Read this book if you intend to recycle wastes, write letters to politicians and business leaders, testify in court actions, design posters, raise and donate money, use public transportation, walk precincts, limit the size of your family, and vote intelligently.

[Reviewed by Richard Raymond]

The Voter's Guide to Environmental Politics
Garrett De Bell, ed.
1970; 314 pp.

OUT OF PRINT

Ballantine Books, Inc.
101 Fifth Ave.
New York, N.Y. 10003

The Friends of the Earth chart on how your congressmen vote on critical environmental issues, reprinted in this book, is available as a wall chart at 50¢ from Friends of the Earth, 917 15th Street N.W., Washington, D.C. 20005. Evaluations of congressmen are done by many other organizations and you would do well to get the ones from any organization which you feel represents your interests. All of these voting record analyses must be used with discretion because of the problems, discussed in the chapters on Congress in this book, that many key votes are not recorded and congressmen often change their vote when they know it will be recorded as a roll call vote. Hopefully, the bill now in progress to require all votes to be recorded as roll call votes will pass before the end of this Congress so you can know your congressman's position more fully.

Several complicated measuring and monitoring devices exist to detect the presence of lead, boron hydrides, arsine, hydrogen floride, combustible gases, and other potentially harmful substances. Some other companies which should be contacted for information are:

Foxboro Company
367 Neponset Avenue
Foxboro, Mass. 02035

Mast Development Company
2212 East 12th Street
Davenport, Iowa 52803

Technicon Industrial Systems
Dept 104
Tarrytown, New York 10591

Analytic Instrument Development, Inc.
250 South Franklin Street
West Chester, Pennsylvania 19380

Micronesian "out-islander" in particular—that is, those who live across a hundred miles or more of sea from any neighboring islands, and whose contact with the rest of the world is limited to the few souls who arrive on the eighty foot government boat every six months—simply don't think about infinity, or to put it more accurately, the idea that everything is possible.

In order to survive out there by themselves, they've had to gain a pretty good feeling for pacing the breadfruit production and the coconut eating. In some of those places the highest crime is cutting down a coconut tree without communal permission.

Jerry Mander

By conventional bookkeeping methods, for example, the coal compani strip-mining away the hillsides of Kentucky and West Virginia show a handsome profit. Their ledgers, however, show only a fraction of the true cost of their operations. They take no account of destroyed land which can never bear another crop; of rivers poisoned by mud and seeping acid from the spoil banks; of floods which sweep over farms and towns downstream, because the ravaged slopes can no longer hold the rainfall.

John Fischer.

Clear Creek

Out of Rolling Stone *came* Earth Times, *which died. Out of* Earth Times *comes* Clear Creek, *which looks sturdier. Lively careful journalism with departments like Environmental Law, Earth Hero, Life Form of the Month. I'll bet this and* Environment Monthly *are the only eco-periodicals I keep up with when I quit being an editor.*

—SB

Clear Creek
Pennfield Jensen, ed.

$5/yr (monthly)
   $6 Canada
   $8 Overseas & Mexico

from:
Clear Creek
617 Mission St.
San Francisco, CA 94105

The Environment Monthly

A terse publication with some of the solidest information we've seen on environmental issues, especially as they relate to architecture and land-use.

—SB

The Environment Monthly
William Houseman, ed.

$35 /yr (monthly) $12.50 students

from:
The Environment Monthly
420 Lexington Ave.
New York, N.Y. 10017

THE PEACE CORPS FINDS A NATURAL OUTLET FOR ITS ENERGIES: Flagging in purpose over the last couple of years, the Peace Corps has recently found new stimulus in the environmental sphere. Teaming up with the Smithsonian Institution, the Corps will encourage men and women of all ages experienced in the management of natural resources to sign up for constructive service in many countries that have already formed a waiting list. Among them: Philippines, Thailand, Micronesia, Costa Rica, Brazil, El Salvador and Columbia. For information write: *Robert K. Poole, Director of Environmental Programs, Peace Corps Headquarters, Washington, D.C. 20525.*

Environment

A more professional journal of applied ecology. Dry but thorough articles.

—SB

Environment

$10.00 /yr. (10 times per year)

from:
Environment
438 North Skinner Blvd.
St. Louis, MO 63130

ZPG National Reporter

I do believe that better publications are those that start quietly. . .gradually-carefully gathering resources and readers and substance until they are an organic force. This may be one.

—SB

Membership in ZPG, $15/yr, $8/yr Students
ZPG National Reporter (subscription only) $5.50/yr

from:
Zero Population Growth, Inc.
1080 Fabian Way
Palo Alto, CA. 94303

Sperm Bank for men contemplating vasectomy who would like to have a reserve of their own semen should take after their existing plans. For information: Genetic Laboratories, Suite 700, Medical Arts Building, Minneapolis, Minn. 55402.

ENVIRONMENTAL LAW

Turn off the lights; in the silence of your darkened home you can hear a thousand rivers whispering their thanks.

Environmental Action

Environmental Action is the biweekly growing out of the national environmental lobbying group by the same name. The mag is the tangible benefit of your support, but lobbying is the real name of their game. They aim at: banning throw-away beverage containers, passing a bill allowing people the right to sue polluters in court, passing a bill placing a steep tax on poor-gas-mileage autos, busting open the Highway Trust Fund to give more money to mass transit, preserving the Clean Air Act. Several regular feature departments. My favorite—Debunking Madison Avenue, which fires squarely on the unholy alliances between industry and environmentalists.

Environmental Action
Peter Harnik, ed.

$10.00
/yr (bi-monthly)

from:
Environmental Action, Inc.
Room 731
1346 Connecticut Ave. N.W.
Washington, D.C. 20036

Can this be sewage? Winter irrigation with the treated sewage effluent in this forested area produced a fairyland of ice. Because effluent is produced year round, some special distribution techniques had to be developed for operating the system during sub-freezing temperatures. Several methods were tried including open trenches, perforated pipes, and revolving sprinklers. But the best performance was obtained using a stationary deflecting sprinkler-head developed specially for the project. Although the new sprinklers operated continuously under all conditions, the distribution pattern was not completely satisfactory, and research is continuing to try to improve them.

Children in Small Families tend to be:
   brighter
   bigger and taller
   more creative
   more mentally stable
   more independent
Parents of Small Families tend to be:
   happier
   more emotionally stable
   better off financially

•

The best way to avoid any hint of genocide is to control the population of the dominant group. If this means an increase in the proportion of dark-skinned people in our society, so what? If blacks and whites cannot learn to enjoy their differences instead of using them as a basis for hatred, there will not be a world worth living in.
Paul Ehrlich & Richard Harriman

eco-tage (ē'-ko -tazh or ĕ -ko -tazh), n. [MnE. *ecology* and *sabotage*, from Gr. *oikos*, a house, and *logy*, to study; and *saboter*, to damage machinery with wooden shoes], the branch of tactical biology that deals with the relationship between living organisms and their technology. It usually refers to tactics which can be executed without injury to life systems.

BY THE RIVER

The rock Estelle was on was one of several boulders near the river, all of them gray and half as big as houses. It was already dark on the ground around the rocks, and cold enough to make you want a sweater. But the sun was still shining in the trees overhead, and as D.R. climbed he thought: climbing for Estelle is climbing for the sun. It warmed him to think that. And he was warmed all over again when he saw Estelle lying on her bright Mexican serape on the broad, flat surface of the rock.

Estelle had her shirt off, rolled under her head for a pillow. Her skin was naturally dark, a sort of pale olive that was always consistent in its tone no matter how much or how little sun she got. Estelle's hips and her thighs were too thick for anyone ever to call her figure "beautiful" in that plastic sense that Miss America is considered "beautiful." And her face was too much the face of the average girl in a crowd for, say, a TV camera man to ever zoom in on and freeze as something special. And yet Estelle was a truly beautiful girl. She had dark hair and very large, dark brown eyes. Her breasts weren't especially big, or little, or round, or pointy or any of those magazine-writer tit-fetish cliches. They were just nice boobs on a nice woman, absolutely real like everything else about her. Goddamn, D.R. thought. Tears came into his eyes. He could hardly believe the loveliness of the moment his painful walk across the campground had led him to. The sun was just going down behind the cliffs across the river, shining orange through the trees and across Estelle's naked skin. Shielding her eyes with her hand, she looked up and smiled at D.R., then patted the rock beside her with her hand. D.R. lay down and snuggled his face in her hair.

"I've been having the loveliest visions," said Estelle. "I've been seeing wonderful feathered horses, flying through the sky. And wheat fields that would turn to wings and fly away."

D.R. asked Estelle what she thought the visions meant.

"Nothing," said Estelle. "At least I hope they don't mean anything. I like them just exactly as they were."

They lay quietly for awhile. The sky was full of light and still a brilliant blue. But the rock and the river valley and the cliffs on the other side were all in shadow now, and it was getting cool. Estelle turned on her side and moved closer to D.R., laying her arm across him. Her breast tumbled precisely into D.R.'s hand, and for a time the reality between them was simply hand on breast, hand folded in the flesh of breast, pressing and rubbing and smoothing like patting down a pillow. Then their mouths came together in a long and dreamy kiss.

What To Do? What To Do!

*if you know someone
who doesn't know yet
that there is an environmental problem,
give them this book
for groundhog day.*

—jd

What To Do? What To Do!
Robinson Poliat Holmes
1970; 90 or so pp.

OUT OF PRINT

from:
What To Do
Jo Robinson
Cadenza Farm
Star Route #1
Clatskenie, Ore. 97016

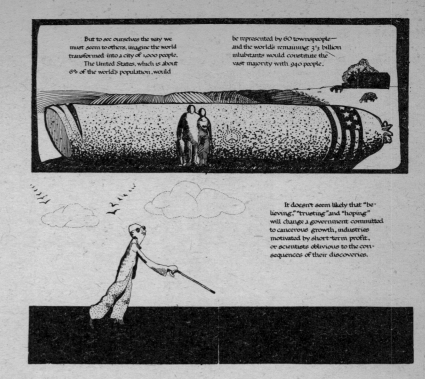

But to see ourselves the way we must seem to others, imagine the world transformed into a city of 1,000 people. The United States, which is about 6% of the world's population, would be represented by 60 townspeople— and the world's remaining 3½ billion inhabitants would constitute the vast majority with 940 people.

It doesn't seem likely that "believing," "trusting" and "hoping" will change a government committed to cancerous growth, industries motivated by short-term profit, or scientists oblivious to the consequences of their discoveries.

Eco-action Lists

What to Do! (above) has a list of home and public deeds in good ecological conscience. Others, each with some original suggestions:

If You Want to Save Your Environment
56 pp

$0.75 postpaid

from:
Environmental Handbook
Station A, Box 11321
Palo Alto, CA 94306

What You can do...
Malcolm Wells, 8 pp

$0.10 postpaid

from:
World Wildlife Fund
910 17th St. N.W.
Washington, D.C. 20006

Do It Yourself Ecology
23 pp.

$0.25 postpaid

from:
Environmental Action
Rm 731
1346 Connecticut Ave. N.W.
Washington, D.C. 20036

Eco-tips 1 & 6
$1.00 for a complete set

Concern
2233 Wisconsin Avenue, N.W.
Washington, D.C. 20007

A Survey of Environmental Science Organizations in the USA

Comprehensive list of all the groups and publications now working.

—SB

A Survey of Environmental Science Organizations in the USA
J. Y. Wang, Raymond Balter
1970; 59 pp.

no longer available

from:
Ecology Center Press
13 Columbus
San Francisco, CA 94111

Environmental Pollution

A highly technical journal with articles like "Experimental Secondary Methyl Mercury Poisoning in the Goshawk". British publication, international purview.

—SB

Environmental Pollution
Kenneth Mellanby, ed.

$15.60 /yr (quarterly)

from:
Elsevier Publishing Co., Ltd.
Ripple Rd.
Barking, Essex
England

NATURE CONSERVANCY

Patrick Noonan, President
1800 N. Kent St., Suite 800
Arlington, VA 22209
(703) 524-3151

The Nature Conservancy is a member-governed organization created for non-profit educational and scientific purposes. Projects are conducted to preserve outstanding natural areas of the U.S. The main thrust is focused upon developing public awareness of natural area problems, fostering regional and community planning for preserving parks and open spaces, and advising and supporting local groups in actual projects. The Conservancy's goal is to direct the growth of our civilization so that we may live more nearly in harmony with our environment.

Food from Waste

An inkling of the broad vision and planning needed comes from a sleepy little Mississippi town called Bay St. Louis. There, a National Aeronautics and Space Administration facility was scheduled to be phased out. But government officials and Louisiana State University [Baton Rouge 70803] representatives worked out a plan to use the buildings, scientists, and a fraction of the usual budget for a fantastic new idea of food production. Using a bacteria strain discovered in a sugar cane field by an LSU associate professor of microbiology, the scientists attempted to convert cellulose waste products—corn cobs, grass, leaves, sugar cane residue, and even logs—into high protein food.

They succeeded. In contrast to a 1,100-lb grazing cow, which produces about 1 lb of protein a day, 1,100 lb (much more than they now have working) of their busy microbes could turn waste products into 12,000 lb of protein each day—and do it without adding to the environment's burden of pesticides and nitrogenous fertilizers.

"The stuff doesn't taste bad at all—something like egg yolk with a little salt in it," says Dr. Clayton D. Callihan, LSU associate professor of chemical engineering and director of the project. It analyzes down to 50% protein, and the rest cellulose, carbohydrates, and fat."

Dr. Callihan is jubilant: "I know we already have some good cattle feed. If we ever get FDA approval, we could have human food. And we've found we can convert old books, rags, newspapers, and magazines, too."

[Item from unknown magazine sent to us by Phil Less in Berkeley]

Environment Information Access

*Environment Information Access
124 East 38th Street
New York, N.Y. 10016*

ACCESS is an indexing, abstracting and information retrieval service that covers published and non-print information on environmental pollution, conservation and related fields. ACCESS provides subscribers with an overview of the environmental reporting of more than 400 scholarly, scientific, industrial, technical and general periodicals and major newspapers; important environmental radio and television programming, films and filmstrips, books, corporate publications and major conference publications.

ACCESS is made available to subscribers in four steps:

1. *Indexing and abstracting services, published bi-weekly (26 times per year) ensure timely coverage of important information; abstracts summarize contents, and describe type of information provided.*

2. *Information Retrieval Services allow subscribers to order copies of needed items, in hard copy or microfiche.*

3. *Semi-annual cumulative indexes, provide cross-referenced coverage of past ACCESS information.*

4. *On-call research services assist subscribers in locating special items, assembling data or bibliographies, obtaining literature surveys, summaries or other research.*

ACCESS can be used to monitor:

- *general developments affecting the environment.*
- *horizontal environmental categories such as water pollution chemical and biological contamination, solid waste disposal, or water pollution.*
- *specific aspects of horizontal categories such as eutrophication, compaction, or metal poisoning.*
- *coverage of timely environmental issues such as mercury pollution, SST, DDT, Project Rulison, Trans-Alaska pipeline, or Trans-Florida barge canal.*
- *vertical industrial categories such as Agricultural chemicals, paper industry, utilities.*

ACCESS can be used as starting point for literature searches and as a reference tool for articles, congressional hearings, position papers, research reports, speeches, state of the art papers or theses; as a tool to keep abreast with professional reading; to alert superiors, peers or subordinates to important environmental information or developments; or to obtain advance notice about environmental books, radio and TV programs and films. Certain items can be ordered directly through ACCESS.

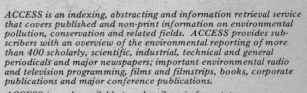

LEGEND

▽ CHLOR-ALKALI PLANTS WITH MERCURY CELLS

▼ PULP MILLS USING MERCURY SLIMICIDES

▽ PULP MILLS THAT DISCONTINUED USE OF MERCURY SLIMICIDES LESS THAN 10 YEARS AGO

km
0 100 200 300 400 500

Fig. 2. Distribution of important sources of mercury contamination of water in Canada's eastern provinces.

How to be a Survivor

Lest the population issue become the property of the Establishment, who would probably blow it, this book by Ehrlich and Harriman establishes the radically-based theory and practice it must take to evade the ultimate population crunch.

—SB

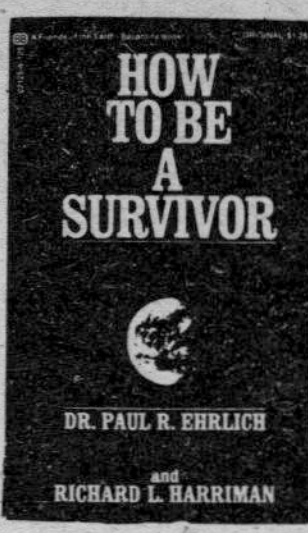

How to be a Survivor
Paul Ehrlich, Richard Harriman
1971; 207 pp.

$1.25 postpaid

from:
Ballantine Books, Inc.
101 Fifth Ave
New York, N.Y. 10003
or WHOLE EARTH CATALOG

No matter how you slice it, the resources of the planet are finite, and many of them are non-renewable. Each giant molecule of petroleum is lost forever when we tear it asunder by burning to release the energy of sunlight stored in it millions of years ago. Concentrations of mineral wealth are being dispersed beyond recall, senselessly scattered far and wide to where we cannot afford the energy to reconcentrate them. Precious stores of fresh ground water, accumulated over millennia, are being drained much more rapidly than natural processes can replenish them.

•

A less discriminatory and therefore potentially more effective program might be simply to cut the income tax in half for each woman for each year she did not reproduce, with a similar tax break going to guardians of girls who do not pay taxes. Since most of the poor have little or no income tax liability, the system would discriminate against the prime villains: the middle class. The effect on the rich, however, would probably be negligible, since the present tax structure is largely a swindle perpetrated by the rich at the expense of the middle class and poor. Replacement of our regressive income tax system with a truly progressive one would help in this area as well as in many others.

•

Europeans live a pleasant, reasonably affluent life on somewhat less than one-half the per capita electric power consumption of Americans, and with careful planning their level of consumption could also be greatly reduced. Amazingly, though, the American power industry wants to *increase* our per capita consumption at a rate that will double our national use of power every decade.

Defending the Environment

Even more direct than boycotting the bastards is sueing the bastards or toughening the laws they must abide by or just enforcing the laws they're presently ignoring. Citizen action. Sax shows why and how.

—SB

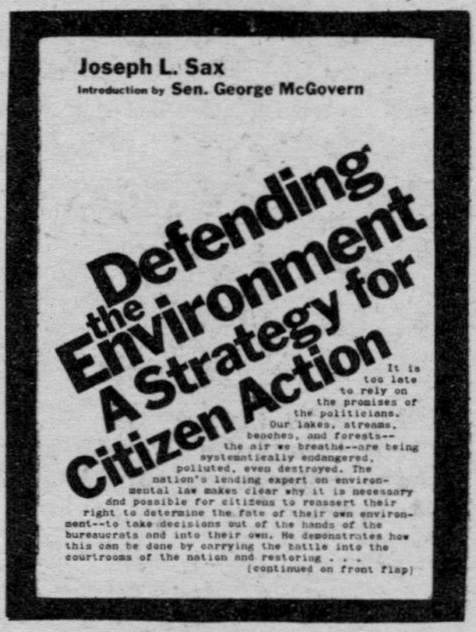

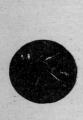

Defending the Environment
Joseph L. Sax
1971; 255 pp.

$1.95 postpaid

from:
Random House, Inc.
457 Hahn Road
Westminster, Md. 10022
or WHOLE EARTH CATALOG

This book deals principally with preventive injunctions, designed to stop environmentally dangerous projects before they get underway.

•

Lawsuits seeking money damages for the public, by and large, are of secondary importance in environmental controversies. Most of the interests sought to be protected could not be easily compensated in damages in any event. Clean air and water for public use, scenic vistas, and the maintenance of fisheries and recreation areas, even where demonstrably harmed, rarely matter in significant dollar amounts to any particular identifiable citizen. The effects of environmental conditions are diffuse both in space and time, and rarely will a damage suit achieve the results sought. This is not to assert that such suits should be banned——only that they are not appropriately at the cutting edge of the movement for environmental quality. The prospect of damage suits may have some deterrent effect, but they tend to drag on interminably, with little result.

•

There is no good reason why we should hesitate to adtop a theory of public rights to environmental quality, enforceable at law, nor is there any reason to think we cannot adjudicate the reasonable accommodations needed to protect against unnecessary threats to the environment.

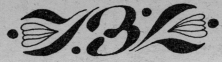

THREE LAWS

EVERYTHING IS CONNECTED TO EVERYTHING

EVERYTHING'S GOT TO GO SOMEWHERE

THERE'S NO SUCH THING AS A FREE LUNCH

Shake hands with tomorrow

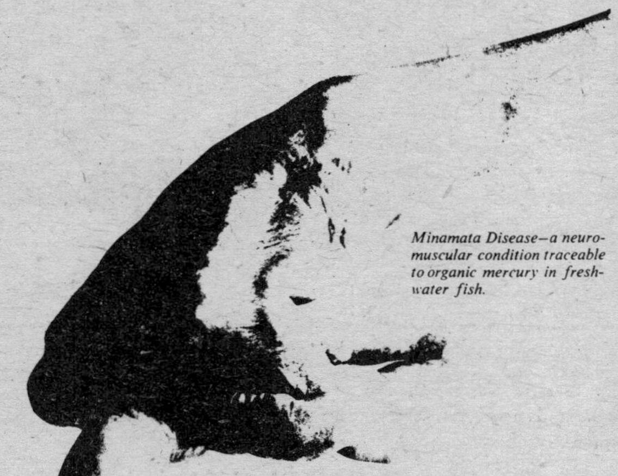

Minamata Disease—a neuro-muscular condition traceable to organic mercury in fresh-water fish.

or fight pollution today.

MANNENSHA INTERNATIONAL INC. ad, reprinted in *Environmental Action.*

Four good organizations
Four good newsletters

Clear Creek *reminded us:*

Sierra Club
Sierra Club Bulletin $15/yr
Mills Tower
San Francisco, CA 94104

Friends of the Earth $15/yr, $7.50 students
Not Man Apart **$5/yr for subscription only**
529 Commercial Street
San Francisco, CA. 94111

Wilderness Society
The Living Wilderness
$7.50/yr, $4 students
1901 Pennsylvania Ave. N.W.
Washington, D.C. 20006

Environmental Defense Fund
Newsletter $15/yr
162 Old Town Road
E. Setauket, N.Y. 11733

The Environmental Defense Fund, a group of scientists and lawyers attacking a broad range of environmental problems by incorporating science into new law and pushing for the enforcement of ecologically sound but politically unattractive existing legislation. I think a lot of Catalogue readers would like EDF. Its life style is not as funky as some ecology action groups, but it has been extremely effective in its short lifetime. EDF also has a newsletter which unspins legal and bureaucratic webs as exotic as nature herself. In that sense, affiliation with EDF is a dynamic encounter with some of the most pervasive and influential forms of our civilization.

John Woodcock
Bloomington, Indiana

Environmental lawyers will be interested in the Environmental Law Institute *(Suite 614, 1346 Connecticut Ave., N.W., Washington, D.C. 20036) a policy center and clearinghouse for information about environmental law. The library and staff can provide facts, model pleadings for environmental lawsuits, and suggested approaches to environmental problems. The Institute publishes the* **Environmental Law Reporter,** *a monthly going into its fourth year. For $175.00, subscribers receive all previously published materials, 4000 "cure pages" comprising the basic documents of statutory, administrative and decisional law, together with articles and comments to help interpret key developments.*

[Suggested by Gordon Andreus]

Know Your Local Polluters

and boycott the bastards. "The garbage produced by an industry is the responsibility of that industry." (Ehrlich). Individual buyers have far more control over economic behavior than voters. Regardless of how you feel about the profit motive (I like it fine), most of the polluters are bound by it, except government ones. If you hurt their sales because they hurt your air or water, then they or their competitors will do anything to get your business back. High-mindedness doesn't have to enter into it, just choice for value.

However, beware of false labeling. Ecology is fashionable, and there's a lot of pretense going on, especially in the ads. This is where the ecology organizations can be invaluable. They are best equipped to determine who the real polluters are (and who are making real efforts to clean up their cycles), and they can shout it from the rooftops.

A compendious list of ecology (etc.) organizations has been compiled by Ecology Center and Planned Parenthood:

—SB

Grass Roots
Feb. 1970; 50+ pp.

Not available

from:
Ecology Center
2179 Allston Way
Berkeley, CA 94704

or

Planned Parenthood
482 West MacArthur Blvd.
Oakland, CA 94609

Consumer Alliance

Consumer Alliance will represent the combined purchasing power of several million customers organized on a nation-wide basis to demand the right to have safe, functional, durable, and recyclible products which have been manufactured in an ecologically sound manner.

The address for free copies of the Declaration of Consumer Rights, membership applications and information is: Consumer Alliance, P.O. Box 11773, Palo Alto, California 94306. Annual membership is $5.00; junior memberships are available. Consumer Alliance is tax-exempt and tax-deductible.

Richard Harriman

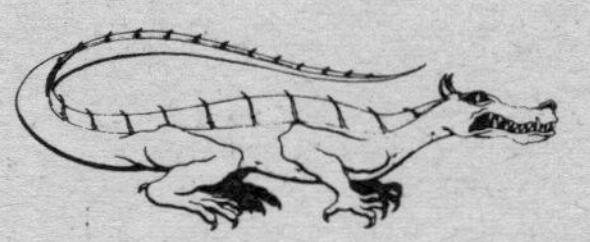

FALLING

Estelle and D.R. hadn't had many times like this one lately. They'd fucked a time or two coming down through California, but it seemed like there just wasn't enough leisure on this trip for any real love-making. Exhaustion was the theme so far. Exhaustion had been catching up to them for a long time now. In a way their whole experience together since Altamont had been a steady descent into exhaustion; a drop that gained momentum as they went along, like falling. When D.R. felt particularly tired, and dirty, and locked up in his mind, it was like he was the one who was falling, with Estelle being dragged along behind. That wasn't accurate, of course. That was just stuff in D.R.'s head, a product of the same weary fever that produced the sense of falling in the first place. There was a way in which Estelle had already fallen further than D.R. had, already knew stuff that he had yet to learn. In a way, she was coming up as he went down, and reaching out a hand to save him from what she already knew. The thing that overwhelmed D.R. when he thought about it that way was how utterly generous that was of her, and how dangerous for her. Danger was everywhere, it seemed, and in more guises than he could account for. Sometimes D.R. felt like he had some kind of disease that Estelle was sure to catch if she stayed with him long enough. As a matter of fact, he'd given her the clap the very first week they were together. As a man who dealt heavily in signs and omens, he had seen that as a forewarning, a metaphor of other and worse things yet to come. It hadn't bothered him all that much at the time. In the beginning, Estelle had been just another cunt by the roadside as likely to give the clap to him as the other way around. But that was a couple of months ago, or three, or four, he wasn't sure any more just how long ago it had been. His sense of time was all internal now. The only things he measured were miles and micrograms, and even then he had little use for precision. But however long ago it had been since he'd first found Estelle, it was long enough for him to come to depend on her so much it threatened him. He hated depending on someone as much as that, and the fact that she depended just as much, or more, on him only made it that much worse.

But it wasn't a thing that he could choose by now. It was like there was a power over his life that wasn't his to wield, a power so large and mysterious all D.R. could do was yield.

Wield to yield, now there's a nice play on words for you. I'll have to work on that. Wield and yield. Shield and dealed.

"I've just writen a poem," said D.R.

"Tell it to me," said Estelle.

"Wield and yield and shield and dealed."

Estelle laughed and rolled onto her back so she could take her pants off. "That's a good poem."

D.R. started undressing too. When they were naked Estelle pulled D.R. on top of her, and for almost an hour they made love.

CHANGES CHANGES 4 CHANGES CHANGES

CHŌFŪ

Drawing of Evolution Valley by Judy Daniel for '4 Changes' poster by Noel Young.

I. POPULATION

THE CONDITION

Position: Man is but a part of the fabric of life——dependent on the whole fabric for his very existence. As the most highly developed tool-using animal, he must recognize that the unknown evolutionary destinies of other life forms are to be respected, and act as gentle steward of the earth's community of being.

Situation: There are now too many human beings, and the problem is growing rapidly worse. It is potentially disastrous not only for the human race but for most other life forms.

Goal: The goal would be half of the present world population, or less.

ACTION

Social/political: First, a massive effort to convince the governments and leaders of the world that the problem is severe. And that all talk about raising food-production—— well intentioned as it is——simply puts off the only real solution: reduce population. Demand immediate participation by all countries in programs to legalize abortion, encourage vasectomy and sterilization (provided by free clinics)——free insertion of intrauterine loops——try to correct traditional cultural attitudes that tend to force women into child-bearing——remove income tax deductions for more than two children above a specified income level, and scale it so that lower income families are forced to be careful too——or pay families to limit their number. Take vigorous stand against the policy of the right-wing in the Catholic hierarchy and any other institutions that exercise an irresponsible social force in regard to this question; oppose and correct simple-minded boosterism that equates population growth with continuing prosperity. Work ceaselessly to have all political questions be seen in the light of this prime problem.

The community: Explore other social structures and marriage forms, such as group marriage and polyandrous marriage, which provide family life but may produce less children. Share the pleasures of raising children widely, so that all need not directly reproduce to enter into this basic human experience. We must hope that no woman would give birth to more than one child, during this period of crisis. Adopt children. Let reverence for life and reverence for the feminine mean also a reverence for other species, and future human lives, most of which are threatened.

Our own heads: "I am a child of all life, and all living beings are my brothers and sisters, my children and grand-children. And there is a child within me waiting to be brought to birth, the baby of a new and wiser self." Love, lovemaking, a man and woman together, seen as the vehicle of mutual realization, where the creation of new

selves and a new world of being is as important as reproducing our kind.

II. POLLUTION

THE CONDITION

Position: Pollution is of two types. One sort results from an excess of some fairly ordinary substance——smoke, or solid waste——which cannot be absorbed or transmitted rapidly enough to offset its introduction into the environment, thus causing changes the great cycle is not prepared for. (All organisms have wastes and by-products, and these are indeed part of the total biosphere: energy is passed along the line and refracted in various ways, "the rainbow body." This is cycling, not pollution.) The other sort is powerful modern chemicals and poisons, products of recent technology, which the biosphere is totally unprepared for. Such is DDT and similar chlorinated hydrocarbons—— nuclear testing fall out and nuclear waste——poison gas, germ and virus storage and leakage by the military; and chemicals which are put into food, whose long-range effects on human beings have not been properly tested.

Situation: The human race in the last century has allowed its production and scattering of wastes, by-products, and various chemicals to become excessive. Pollution is directly harming life on the planet: which is to say, ruining the environment for humanity itself. We are fouling our air and water, and living in noise and filth that no "animal" would tolerate, while advertising and politicians try and tell us we've never had it so good. The dependence of the modern governments on this kind of untruth leads to shameful mind-pollution: mass media and most school education.

Goal: Clean air, clean clear-running rivers, the presence of Pelican and Osprey and Gray Whale in our lives; salmon and trout in our streams; unmuddled language and good dreams.

ACTION

Social/political: Effective international legislation banning DDT and related poisons——with no fooling around. The collusion of certain scientists with the pesticide industry and agri-business in trying to block this legislation must be brought out in the open. Strong penalties for water and air pollution by industries——"Pollution is somebody's profit." Phase out the internal combustion engine and fossil fuel use in general——more research into non-polluting energy sources; solar energy; the tides. No more kidding the public about atomic waste disposal: it's impossible to do it safely, and nuclear-power generated electricity cannot be seriously planned for as it stands now. Stop all germ and chemical warfare research and experimentation; work toward a hopefully safe disposal of the present staggering and stupid stockpiles of H-Bombs, cobalt gunk, germ and poison tanks and cans. Laws and sanctions against wasteful use of paper etc. which adds to the solid waste of cities——develop methods of re-cycling solid urban wastes.

Re-cycling should be the basic principle behind all waste-disposal thinking. Thus, all bottles should be re-usable; old cans should make more cans; old newspapers back into newsprint again. Stronger controls and research on chemicals in foods. A shift toward a more varied and sensitive type of agriculture (more small-scale and subsistence farming) would eliminate much of the call for blanket use of pesticides.

The community: DDT and such: don't use them. Air pollution: use less cars. Cars pollute the air, and one or two people riding lonely in a huge car is an insult to intelligence and the Earth. Share rides, legalize hitch-hiking, and build hitch-hiker waiting stations along the highways. Also——a step toward the new world——walk more; look for the best routes through beautiful countryside for long-distance walking trips: San Francisco to Los Angeles down the Coast Range, for example. Learn how to use your own manure as fertilizer if you're in the country—— as the Far East has done for centuries. There's a way, and it's safe. Solid waste: boycott bulky wasteful Sunday papers which use up trees. It's all just advertising anyway, which is artificially inducing more industry consumption. Refuse paper bags at the store. Organize Park and Street clean-up festivals. Don't work in any way for or with an industry which pollutes, and don't be drafted into the military. Don't waste. (A monk and an old master were once walking in the mountains. They noticed a little hut upstream. The monk said, "A wise hermit must live there"—— the master said, "That's no wise hermit, you see that lettuce leaf floating down the stream, he's a Waster." Just then an old man came running down the hill with his beard flying and caught the floating lettuce leaf.) Carry your own jug to the winery and have it filled from the barrel.

Our own heads: Part of the trouble with talking about DDT is that the use of it is not just a practical device, it's almost an establishment religion. There is something in Western culture that wants to totally wipe out creepy-crawlies, and feels repugnance for toadstools and snakes. This is fear of one's own deepest natural inner-self wilderness areas, and the answer is, relax. Relax around bugs, snakes, and your own hairy dreams. Again, farmers can and should share their crops with a certain percentage of buglife as "paying their dues." Thoreau says: "How then can the harvest fail? Shall I not rejoice also at the abundance of the weeds whose seeds are the granary of the birds? It matters little comparatively whether the fields fill the farmer's barns. The true husbandman will cease from anxiety, as the squirrels manifest no concern whether the woods will bear chestnuts this year or not, and finish his labor with every day, relinquish all claim to the produce of his fields, and sacrificing in his mind not only his first but his last fruits also." In the realm of thought, inner experience, consciousness, as in the outward realm of interconnection, there is a difference between balanced cycle, and the excess which cannot be handled. When the balance is right, the mind recycles from highest illuminations to the stillness of dreamless sleep; the alchemical "transmutation."

III. CONSUMPTION

THE CONDITION

Position: Everything that lives eats food, and is food in turn. This complicated animal, man, rests on a vast and delicate pyramid of energy-transformations. To grossly use more than you need, to destroy, is biologically unsound. Most of the production and consumption of modern societies is not necessary or conducive to spiritual and cultural growth, let alone survival; and is behind much greed and envy, age-old causes of social and international discord.

Situation: Man's careless use of "resources" and his total dependence on certain substances such as fossil fuels (which are being exhausted, slowly but certainly) are having harmful effects on all the other members of the life-network. The complexity of modern technology renders whole populations vulnerable to the deadly consequences of the loss of any one key resource. Instead of independence we have over-dependence on life-giving substances such as water, which we squander. Many species of animals and birds have become extinct in the service of fashion fads——or fertilizer——or industrial oil——the soil is being used up; in fact mankind has become a locust-like blight on the planet that will leave a bare cupboard for its own children——all the while in a kind of Addict's Dream of affluence, comfort, eternal progress——using the great achievements of science to produce software and swill.

Goal: Balance, harmony, humility, growth which is a mutual growth with Redwood and Quail (would you want your child to grow up without ever hearing a wild bird?)——to be a good member of the great community of living creatures. True affluence is not *needing* anything.

ACTION

Social/political: It must be demonstrated ceaselessly that a continually "growing economy" is no longer healthy, but a Cancer. And that the criminal waste which is allowed in the name of competition——especially that ultimate in wasteful needless competition, hot wars and cold wars with "communism" (or "capitalism")——must be halted totally with ferocious energy and decision. Economics must be seen as a small sub-branch of Ecology, and production/distribution/consumption handled by companies or unions with the same elegance and spareness one sees in nature. Soil banks; open space; phase out logging in most areas. "Lightweight dome and honeycomb structures in line with the architectural principles of nature." "We shouldn't use wood for housing because trees are too important." Protection for all predators and varmints: "Support your right to arm bears." Damn the International Whaling Commission which is selling out the last of our precious, wise whales! Absolutely no further development of roads and concessions in National Parks and Wilderness Areas; build auto campgrounds in the least desirable areas. Plan consmuer boycotts in response to dishonest and unnecessary products. Radical Co-ops. Politically, blast both "Communist" and "Capitalist" myths of progress, and all crude notions of conquering or controlling nature.

The community: Sharing and creating. The inherent potness of communal life——where large tools are owned jointly and used efficiently. The power of renunciation: if enough Americans refused to buy a new car for one given year it would permanently alter the American economy. Recycling clothes and equipment. Support handicrafts, gardening, home skills, midwifery, herbs——all the things that can make us independent, beautiful and whole. Learn to break the habit of unnecessary possessions ——a monkey on everybody's back——but avoid a self-abnegating anti-joyous self-righteousness. Simplicity is light, carefree, neat and loving——not a self-punishing ascetic trip. (The great Chinese poet Tu Fu said "The ideas of a poet should be noble and simple.") Don't shoot a deer if you don't know how to use all the meat and preserve that which you can't eat, to tan the hide and use the leather——to use it all, with gratitude, right down to the sinew and hooves. Simplicity and mindfulness in diet is a starting point for many people.

Our own heads: It is hard to even begin to gauge how much a complication of possessions, the notions of "my and mine," stand between us and a true, clear, liberated way of seeing the world. To live lightly on the earth, to be aware and alive, to be free of egotism, to be in contact with plants and animals, starts with simple concrete acts. The inner principle is the insight that we are inter-dependent energy-fields of great potential wisdom and compassion——expressed in each person as a superb mind, a handsome and complex body, and the almost magical capacity of language. To these potentials and capacities, "owning things" can add nothing of authenticity. "Clad in the sky, with the earth for a pillow."

IV. TRANSFORMATION

THE CONDITION

Position: Everyone is the result of four forces: the conditions of this known-universe (matter/energy forms and ceaseless change); the biology of his species; his individual genetic heritage and the culture he's born into. Within this web of forces there are certain spaces and loops which allow total freedom and illumination. The gradual exploration of some of these spaces is "evolution" and, for human cultures, what "history" could be. We have it within our deepest powers not only to change our "selves" but to change our culture. If man is to remain on earth he must transform the five-millenia-long urbanizing civilization tradition into a new ecologically-sensitive harmony-oriented wild-minded scientific/spiritual culture. "Wildness is the state of complete awareness. That's why we need it."

Situation: Civilization, which has made us so successful a species, has overshot itself and now threatens us with its inertia. There is some evidence that civilized life isn't good for the human gene pool. To achieve the Changes we must change the very foundations of our society and our minds.

Goal: Nothing short of total transformation will do much good. What we envision is a planet on which the human population lives harmoniously and dynamically by employing a sophisticated and unobtrusive technology in a world environment which is "left natural."Specific points in this vision:

* A healthy and spare population of all races, much less in number than today.
* Cultural and individual pluralism, unified by a type of world tribal council. Division by natural and cultural boundaries rather than arbitrary political boundaries.
* A technology of communication, education, and quiet transportation, land-use being sensitive to the properties of each region. Allowing, thus, the Bison to return to much of the high plains. Careful but intensive agriculture in the great alluvial valleys; deserts left wild for those who would trot in them. Computer technicians who run the plant part of the year and walk along with the Elk in their migrations during the rest.
* A basic cultural outlook and social organization that inhibits power and property-seeking while encouraging exploration and challenge in things like music, meditation, mathematics, mountaineering, magic, and all other ways of authentic being-in-the-world. Women totally free and equal. A new kind of family——responsible, but more festive and relaxed——is implicit.

ACTION

Social/political: It seems evident that there are throughout the world certain social and religious forces which have worked through history toward an ecologically and culturally enlightened state of affairs. Let these be encouraged: Gnostics, hip Marxists, Teilhard de Chardin Catholics, Druids, Taoists, Biologists, Witches, Yogins, Bhikkus, Quakers, Sufis, Tibetans, Zens, Shamans, Bushmen, American Indians, Polynesians, Anarchists, Alchemists. . . the list is long. All primitive cultures, all communal and ashram movements. Since it doesn't seem practical or even desirable to think that direct bloody force will achieve much, it would be best to consider this a continuing "revolution of consciousness" which will be won not by guns but by seizing the key images, myths, arche-types, eschatologies, and ecstasies so that life won't seem worth living unless one's on the transforming energy's side. By taking over "science and technology" and releasing its real possibilities and powers in the service of this planet——which, after all, produced us and it.

The community: New schools, new classes, walking in the woods and cleaning up the streets. Find psychological techniques for creating an awareness of "self" which includes the social and natural environment. "Consideration of what specific language forms——symbolic systems——and social institutions constitute obstacles to ecological awareness." Without falling into a facile interpretation of McLuhan, we can hope to use the media. Let no one be ignorant of the facts of biology and related disciplines; bring up our children as part of the wild-life. Some communities can establish themselves in back-water rural areas and flourish——others maintain themselves in urban centers, and the two types work together——a two-way flow of experience, people, money and home-grown vegetables. Ultimately cities will exist only as joyous tribal gatherings and fairs, to dissolve after a few weeks. Investigating new life-styles is our work, as is the exploration of Ways to explore our inner realms——with the known dangers of crashing that go with such. We would work with political-minded people where it helps, hoping to enlarge their vision, and with people of all varieties of politics or thought at whatever point they become aware of environment urgencies. Master the archaic and the primitive as models of basic nature-related cultures——as well as the most imaginative extensions of science——and build a community where these two vectors cross.

Our own heads: Is where it starts. Knowing that we are the first human beings in history to have all of man's culture and previous experience available to our study, and being free enough of the weight of traditional cultures to seek out a larger identity.——The first members of a civilized society since the early Neolithic to wish to look clearly into the eyes of the wild and see our self-hood, our family, there. We have these advantages to set off the obvious disadvantages of being as screwed up as we are——which gives us a fair chance to penetrate some of the riddles of ourselves and the universe, and to go beyond the idea of "man's survival" or "the survival of the biosphere" and to draw our strength from the realization that at the heart of things is some kind of serene and ecstatic process which is actually beyond qualities and certainly beyond birth-and-death. "No need to survive!" "In the fires that destroy the universe at the end of the kalpa, what survives?"——"The iron tree blooms in the void!"

Knowing that nothing need be done, is where we begin to move from.

•

THE HUMANITY OF THE LONE OUTDOORSMAN

There were at least three things the Lone Outdoorsman could have done in response to the filthy crime he saw happen on the big rock by the river. He could have shot big holes in the young couple's arms and legs and heads and backs with his .357 magnum pistol. Or he could have gone to his camper, got his rubber life raft out of his fourteen foot aluminum motorboat, launched it a mile upstream and staged an amphibious assault upon the little beach near the rocks and captured them before they knew what was happening. Or—— and admittedly this is a big or; it's big because, as it turns out, the Lone Outdoorsman is far from your ordinary, everyday one-dimensional heavy; the thing that redeems the Lone Outdoorsman is a refreshing mental complexity of a kind you don't ordinarily run into in folktales. All mixed in with his gory mental images of bullet-riddled bodies and heroic assaults upon beachheads was a commendable impulse to be nice to these kids, to befriend them and hopefully influence them in some constructive way. In short, the Lone Outdoorsman could either shoot these kids, assault them from the river and take them captive, or else be a good neighbor and invite Divine Right and Estelle over to his place for supper.

And so when D.R. and Estelle had finished balling, had dressed and folded the serape and walked back through the darkening campground to their own scene, they found the Lone Outdoorsman leaning against Urge's front, waiting for them.

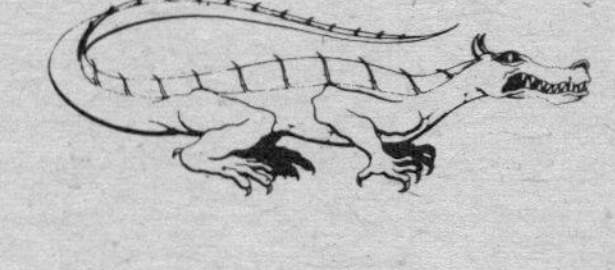

THE INVITATION

"Well," he said, "how are you young folks this evening. Feeling all right? What I thought was the two of you all might like to come over and eat supper with me, I mean it looks like you all have been traveling pretty hard, and maybe not eating too well, and since I've got these steaks, yes sir, four of the juiciest steaks you ever sunk your fangs in, buddy, that ain't no lie. And I'd be mighty pleased to have your company, you know I've got a niece and a nephew about your age, my brother's kids, the wife and me, we had a kid but he died, but my brother's kids, now, I tell you, they're all right. They come out from Little Rock about once a year, and we appreciate seeing 'em, I declare we do. You know, a lot of the older folks now, they ain't got much patience with young people these days, they object to the way they behave. And I guess in some things I do too. But my grandfather was a big influence on me, and what he believed in was giving people a second chance. I take after Granddaddy in that respect. I guess when it comes to being with people and judging 'em, I'm what you'd call a liberal. For I find a lot of good in young people nowadays, I declare I do. Why shit, all the young people need is to get out in the hills and romp around some. I grew up on the land and I know how good it is for you. Why when I was a kid I could hunt and track, why I'd go out by myself for days at a time when I was ten and twelve years old. I loved it, there just wasn't anything greater than getting off to myself in the hills with my gun. I've always said I was born a hundred years too late. I ought to of been a pioneer. The wife, she don't like to get out much, so two or three times a year I just cut loose by myself and go live out in nature a few days. As my granddaddy would say, nature's good for what ails you. Ain't that what you all say?"

Estelle mumbled that that was what she said too. Divine Right said something and the Lone Outdoorsman said something else. But five minutes later they didn't have the faintest idea how the conversation had ended. The vision of steak crowded everything else out of their head except the smoke from the horrendous joint D.R. rolled, in celebration of the party. Giggling, tumbling around in the bus trying to get dressed and smoke dope and hug and kiss all at the same time, D.R. and Estelle were ecstatic. Every kink in them had been ironed out by their wonderful hour on the rock. And now here they were, getting all dressed up and stoned, about to go eat free steak with their neighbor. Steak! Goddamn. It would be their first real meal since they'd left the Anaheim Flash's house in California. When they had their outfits on, Estelle in her ankle-length gingham dress and D.R. in his pioneer outfit of leather pants and shirt and coonskin cap with tail, they paused long enough to hold each other tightly for a moment. Then D.R. took the last drag on the joint, ate the roach as the first hors d'oeuvre of the evening, then set out with his lady to call on the Lone Outdoorsman.

Land Use

An Agricultural Testament

The first "organic gardener" I ever ran into was a man who ended all his sentences "thus saith the Lord." The Lord, it turned out, had been in the habit of speaking in a very conversational manner to this fellow, and had given him all manner of helpful hints on gardening—among other things, a recipe for fertilizer. I noticed that the Lord's side of the conversation tended to be most flattering to my new acquaintance, and most decidedly threatening to all the neighbors—a gang of villains, who were going to die of cancer because of such sins as listening to the wrong prophets, and cooking with aluminum pots.

Now I would be the last to deny the possibility that a man might receive the word from on high and speak beyond the usual powers of his head. But I am exceedingly mistrustful of a man who depends on divine revelation to show him what is obvious about the ground under his feet. This man deservedly belongs in "the lunatic fringe" of a discipline that demands respect and attention not because it is far out or esoteric or mystical, but because it makes good sense.

The principles of organic agriculture are not derived from mystical insight or revelation, but are based upon observation. They have been established in our part of the world in our time by men who were excellent observers, and who were moreover accomplished and respectable scientists. The scientific respectability of organic methods has been obscured for us both by those who have insisted upon making a cult of the obvious and by the affluence and glamor of the technological agriculture—the agriculture of chemicals and corporations.

The pioneer book of organic agriculture in modern times is King's Farmers of Forty Centuries, *which proposed no innovation, but only provided new access to the ancient tradition of organic practice in the Orient. King was no cultist or food faddist. He was a professor of agriculture, an eminently practical and observant man, well enough trained that he fully understood what he saw, in terms of the history and culture of Asia, and in terms of its potential usefulness to the West, King's is one of the most important books I have ever read. If it is allowed to remain out of print I believe that will be a tragedy and a great loss, for it can provide indispensable insights into the causes and the possible remedies of our environmental crisis.*

King's most famous reader and follower was probably Sir Albert Howard, who in thirty years of research and experimentation established scientifically the soundness of the ancient methods. Howard's An Agricultural Testament *is another extremely important book. Howard's work is based upon the premise that good agricultural practice is based upon the observation and the use of natural processes. King's book, Howard thought, demonstrated that an agriculture based upon natural processes could thrive for an unlimited time, whereas an agriculture that contradicts or ignores natural processes can only exhaust the land, and in its failure assures the failure of the society.*

Howard's thinking proceeds from one cardinal fact: "The forest manures itself." He later elaborates this observation in an agricultural metaphor:

> *The main characteristic of Nature's farming can therefore be summed up in a few words. Mother earth never attempts to farm without live stock; she always raises mixed crops; great pains are taken to preserve the soil and to prevent erosion; the mixed vegetable and animal wastes are converted into humus; there is no waste; the processes of growth and the processes of decay balance one another; ample provision is made to maintain large reserves of fertility; the greatest care is taken to store the rainfall; both plants and animals are left to protect themselves against disease.*

And so the task Howard set himself was first to understand those processes and interrelationships by which the natural world sustains and renews itself, and then to work out methods by which people could use the land in cooperation with nature. He realized—and I think it would be hard to overestimate the importance of this—that the specialized analytical approach of "scientific" agriculture was creating more problems than it solved:

> *Instead of breaking up the subject into fragments and studying agriculture in piecemeal fashion by the analytical methods of science, appropriate only to the discovery of new facts, we must adopt a synthetic approach and look at the wheel of life as one great subject and not as if it were a patchwork of unrelated things.*

He insisted that quality was a more important evaluative standard than quantity. He saw that the soil was more a process than a substance, that its life was more important than its analyzable contents, that its health was not a matter of inert proportions but a balance of live forces, and that therefore "the correct relation between the processes of growth and the processes of decay is the first principle of successful farming."

Howard's discoveries and methods and their implications are given in detail in An Agricultural Testament. *They are of enormous usefulness to gardeners and farmers, and to anyone else who may be interested in the history and the problems of land use. But aside from its practical worth, Howard's book is valuable for his ability to place his facts and insights within the perspectives of history. This book is a critique of civilizations, judging them not by their artifacts and victories but by their response to "the sacred duty of handing over unimpaired to the next generation the heritage of a fertile soil."*

A matter of considerable interest to me is that, written within the context of more knowledge and from the perspective of a more urgent time, An Agricultural Testament *can be read as a confirmation and elaboration of Jefferson's belief in the supreme importance of the small farmer—the man devoted in final terms to his own piece of his homeland, who makes of the life of the land a human way of life.*

[Suggested and reviewed by Wendell Berry]

An Agricultural Testament
Sir Albert Howard
1940; 253 pp.

$7.95

postpaid from:
Rodale Press
Emmaus, Pa. 18049

or WHOLE EARTH CATALOG

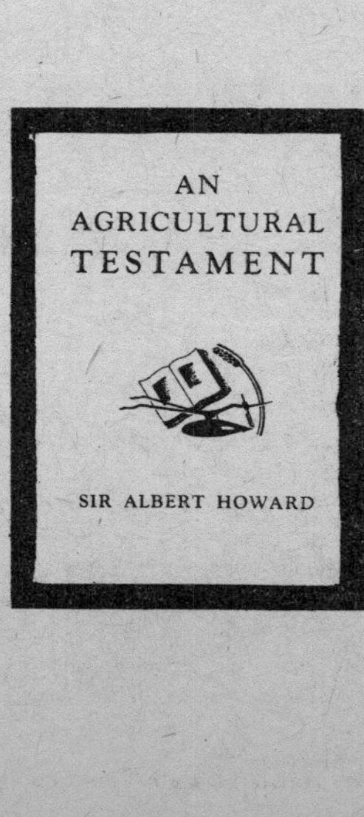

Farmers of Forty Centuries

I have come more and more strongly to believe that the ultimate moral goal, even the moral necessity, of the American people must be to become the aborigines of the American land. An aborigine, my dictionary says, is 'an indigenous inhabitant. . .as contrasted with an invading or colonizing people.' An indigenous people is one 'living naturally in a particular region or environment.' In general, aborigines are preservers of their land, whereas invaders or colonizers are the exploiters and destroyers of theirs. White Americans have for the most part remained the invaders and colonizers of the American continent; their relationship to the land has remained economic, exploitive, superficial, destructive. American history is to a fearful extent the history of a group of mercenary nomads, exhausting the land as they have moved over it.

A great mistake has been to assume that people could become American in any sense that would be meaningful and ennobling by means of the souped-up emotions of public patriotism, nationalism. The fact is that meaningful native Americanism would have to involve a complexly reverent and knowing and preserving attitude toward the land; it would manifest itself not only in public fervor but in private behavior; and it would be based on methods of land use. No matter how 'sophisticated' and urban our society becomes, our basic relation to the land will continue to be agricultural. And if we are ever to have a decent relation to our land, we will probably have to begin by converting from agricultural methods that are exploitive and wasteful to methods that are preserving. For this we will need more than the scientific expertise that we have relied on so far; we will need models.

A great deal in the way of models and examples is to be learned from the American Indians, for their relation to this part of the earth seems to me to have been exemplary. Our assumption that we could learn to live here, ignoring their example, is a cultural disaster as well as an ecological one. But we have a great deal to learn from all truly indigenous peoples. The agricultural practices of primitives and peasants ought to be particularly instructive to us, for these people have farmed the land with a sense of profound unity with it; their ways, formed slowly over generations out of an intricate knowledge of the land and its needs, have tended to preserve it.

One of the richest sources of information about peasant agriculture is a book called Farmers of Forty Centuries *by an American professor of agriculture, F. H. King. In 1907 King traveled in Japan, Korea and China, looking closely at the local practices of agriculture and land management everywhere he went. He talked with experts and with peasants. He was full of interest in the knowledge and the life of farming. His book is loaded with details of the life of the people, observed sharply, and put down with delight and sympathy.*

The question that King bore in mind throughout his travels was how these people had preserved their land, which after thousands of years of intensive use was as fertile as ever. The answer involved a complexity of methods and practices and traditions, but what it amounted to was that the taking of produce from the land was always balanced by a return of organic matter. The sewage of towns and cities, instead of being flushed out to pollute the waterways as with us, was brought back to the fields; the mud dredged from the canals was carried to the fields; no organic waste of any kind was ever thrown away, but always worked back into the soil.

King has a lot to say about the methods of composting, intertillage, crop rotation, irrigation, green manuring, and so on. He has a scientist's respect for statistics and he supplies plenty of them. But he also gives the sort of lively information that he could only have got by talking, by 'passing the time of day,' with the people he met in the fields. He writes of practices, tools, materials, dimensions. His book is the best sort of manual; it is one of the pioneer books on organic farming. And for the same reasons it is the best sort of travel book; he talks occasionally about how the plants are cared for around some temple or shrine, but for the most part avoids 'tourist attractions;' the life of the ordinary people, its sources and ways, was what fascinated him. There are more than two hundred photographs, not the work of a gifted photographer, certainly, but informative and useful.

This is a book that can suggest things for you to do, if you have a piece of ground to do them on. Whether or not you have a piece of ground, it is a book that can change your mind.

[Suggested and reviewed by Wendell Berry.]

Farmers of Forty Centuries
F. H. King
1911; 441 pp.

$7.95 postpaid

from:
Rodale Press
Emmaus, Pa. 18049

or WHOLE EARTH CATALOG

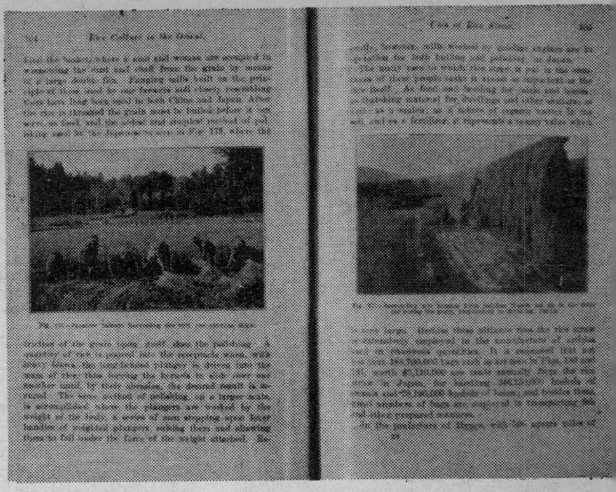

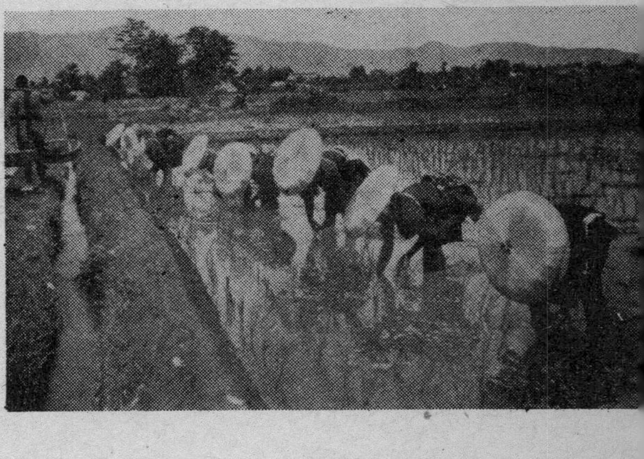

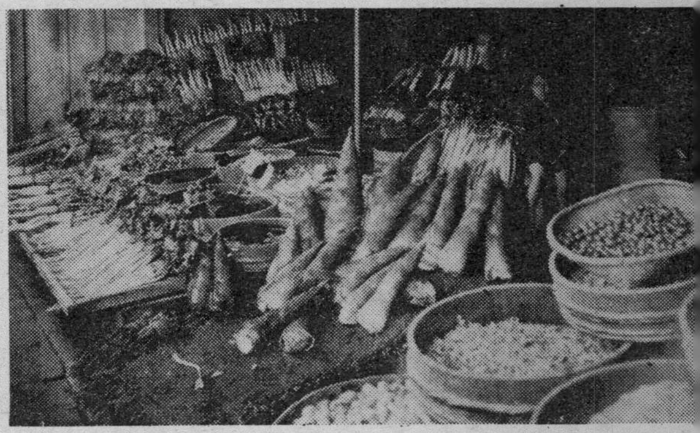

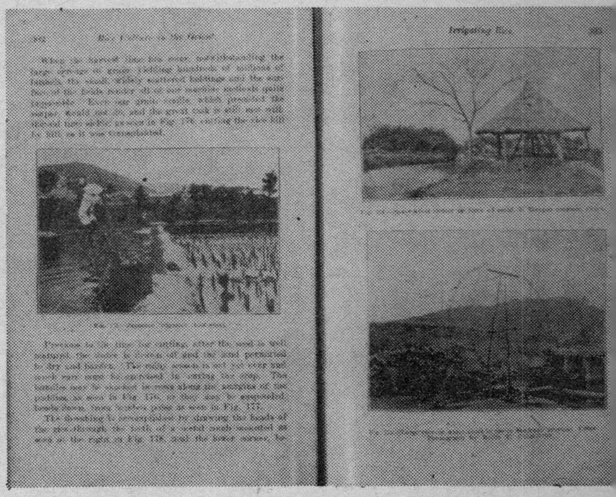

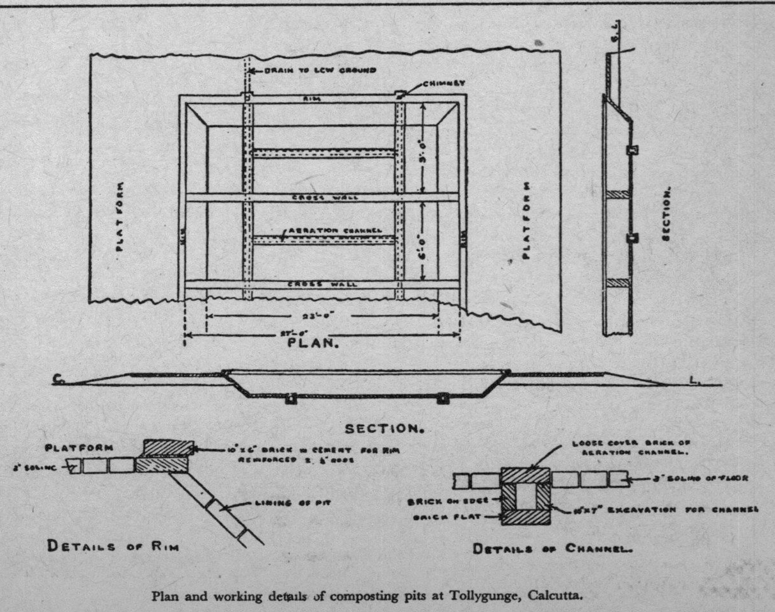

Plan and working details of composting pits at Tollygunge, Calcutta.

Living the Good Life

Some decades ago Scott Nearing gave up as an academic and retreated to the Vermont woods, where he promptly began to rediscover for himself how to stay alive in the North Temperate Zone. His advice is in this book. He invented a method for building stone houses very cheaply, he perfected a way of living into the winter on crops taken in the summer from ingeniously constructed gardens, and he relied––perhaps more than anyone today will care to rely––on a division of his labors between the hands and the head. He was a one-man community. He never wasted anything (it will drive you mad to hear his paeans of praise for used motor oil), he tried to ignore machines wherever possible, he tried to live on a cash-less basis (and largely succeeded), and he annoyed his old-timey Vermont neighbors by living in a more down-to-to-earth life than they ever could and showing them how to maple-sugar and farm. He beat them at their own game, and for thirty years it lasted––until the ski crowds began to turn utopia into suburbia. Nearing fled to Maine where, presumably, he's started all over again. Lots of sawy advice in here, and a good picture of how it works in practice to turn your back on advantages that you know are right out there waiting for you. Nutrition freaks will find the Nearing diet a new challenge. Nearing is no spring chicken, and so if nothing else this book will shame you into getting up and getting moving.

[Reviewed by Stephan Chodorov]

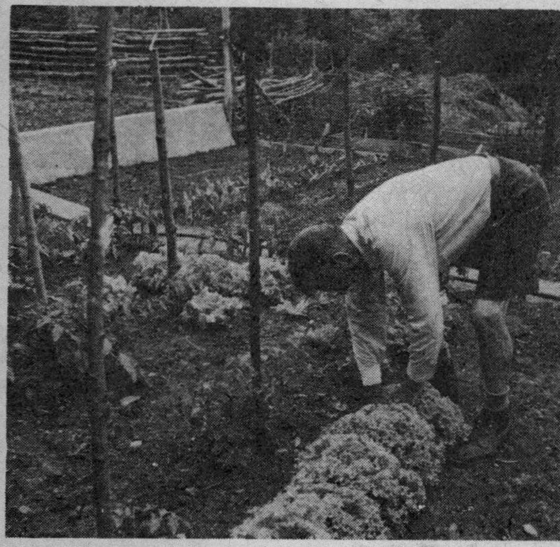

Scott Nearing tending a vegetable garden.

Living the Good Life
Helen and Scott Nearing
1954, 1970; 214 pp.

$1.95 postpaid

from:
Schocken Books
67 Park Avenue
New York, New York 10016

or WHOLE EARTH CATALOG

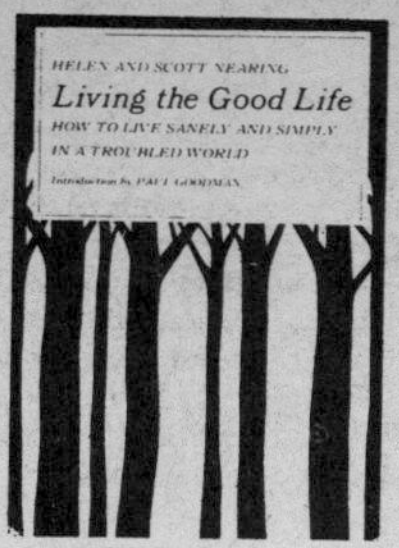

We chose stone for several reasons. Stone buildings seem a natural out-cropping of the earth. They blend into the landscape and are a part of it. We like the varied color and character of the stones, which are lying around unused on most New England farms. Stone houses are poised, dignified and solid–sturdy in appearance and in fact, standing as they do for generations. They are cheaper to maintain, needing no paint, little or no upkeep or repair. They will not burn. They are cooler in summer and warmer in winter. If, combined with all these advantages, we could build them economically, we were convinced that stone was the right material for our needs.

•

. . . we soon discovered that after the building was finished, the different rate of expansion for concrete and wood pulled the two apart at times, leaving a small crack between the frame and the concrete wall. We remedied this in later construction by cutting a square groove all around the outside of the frame and inserting a small strip of wood which projected ¼ inch or a little more beyond the center of the frame into the concrete. Later we improved this method still more and cut a groove half an inch deep with a bench-saw and set a piece of galvanized metal ¾ inch wide into the groove. This took less time than inserting the wood strip and served the same purpose of bridging the crack between frame and concrete.

•

We would attempt to carry on this self-subsistent economy by the following steps: (1) Raising as much of our own food as local soil and climatic conditions would permit. (2) Bartering our products for those which we could not or did not produce. (3) Using wood for fuel and cutting it ourselves. (4) Putting up our own buildings with stone and wood from the place, doing the work ourselves. (5) Making such implements as sleds, drays, stone-boats, gravel screens, ladders. (6) Holding down to the barest minimum the number of implements, tools, gadgets and machines which we might buy from the assembly lines of big business. (7) If we had to have such machines for a few hours or days in a year (plough, tractor, rototiller, bull-dozer, chainsaw), we would rent or trade them from local people instead of buying and owning them.

Walden

This edition is the one, I believe, that Thoreau would have bought. It costs seventy-five cents. The prime document of America's 3rd Revolution, now in progress.

–SB

Walden (and 'Civil Disobedience')
Henry David Thoreau
1854; 256 pp.

$0.75 postpaid

from:
New American Library, Inc.
1301 Ave. of the Americas
New York, N.Y. 10019

or WHOLE EARTH CATALOG

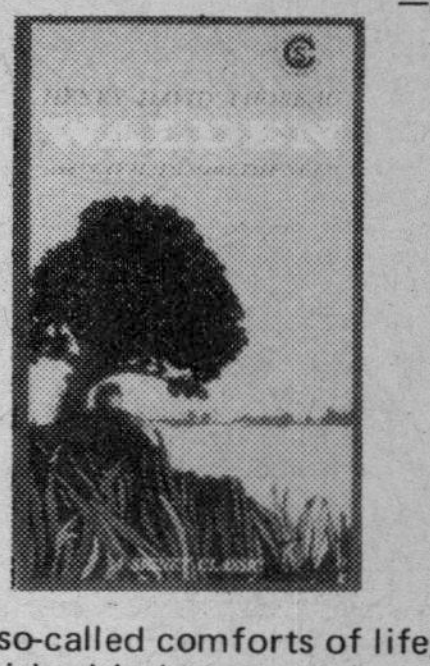

Most of the luxuries, and many of the so-called comforts of life, are not only not indispensable, but positive hindrances to the elevation of mankind. With respect to luxuries and comforts, the wisest have ever lived a more simple and meagre life than the poor.

•

The customs of some savage nations might, perchance, be profitably imitated by us, for they at least go through the semblance of casting their slough annually; they have the idea of the thing, whether they have the reality or not. Would it not be well if we were to celebrate such a "busk," or "feast of first fruits," as Bartram describes to have been the custom of the Mucclasse Indians? "When a town celebrates the busk," says he, "having previously provided themselves with new clothes, new pots, pans, and other household utensils and furniture, they collect all their worn out clothes and other despicable things, sweep and cleanse their houses, squares, and the whole town, of their filth, which with all the remaining grain and other old provisions they cast together into one common heap, and consume it with fire. After having taken medicine, and fasted for three days, all the fire in the town is extinguished. During this fast they abstain from the gratification of every appetite and passion whatever. A general amnesty is proclaimed; all malefactors may return to their town.

"On the fourth morning, the high priest, by rubbing dry wood together, produces new fire in the public square, from whence every habitation in the town is supplied with the new and pure flame."

•

I learned this, at least, by my experiment: that if one advances confidently in the direction of his dreams, and endeavors to live the life which he has imagined, he will meet with a success unexpected in common hours. He will put some things behind, will pass an invisible boundary; new, universal, and more liberal laws will begin to establish themselves around and within him; or the old laws be expanded, and interpreted in his favor in a more liberal sense, and he will live with the license of a higher order of beings. In proportion as he simplifies his life, the laws of the universe will appear less complex, and solitude will not be solitude, nor poverty poverty, nor weakness weakness. If you have built castles in the air, your work need not be lost; that is where they should be. Now put the foundations under them.

Malabar Farm

Bromfield was a Pulitzer Prize-winning author who at the start of Hitler's war returned to his boyhood home in north central Ohio, bought several worn-out farms, established something which would probably be called a commune if it were done today (it wasn't called that then, as Bromfield and the people associated with him were ultra-respectable), and proceeded to use good conservation practices and numerous innovations to restore his land to fertility and health.

[Suggested and reviewed by Pat Patterson]

Malabar Farm
Louis Bromfield
1947, 1970; 470 pp.

$1.25 postpaid

from:
Ballantine Books, Inc.
101 Fifth Ave.
New York, N.Y. 10003

or WHOLE EARTH CATALOG

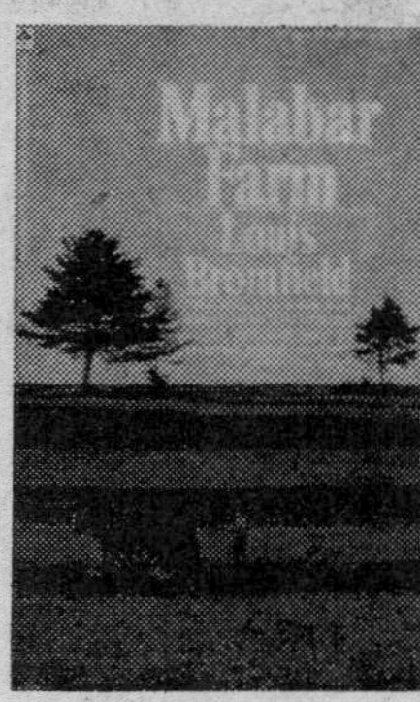

All our contour plowing, cover crops, and strip cropping have paid us great dividends. Throughout the drought when farms all over Ohio were hauling water, our springs kept up their flow, because the methods we took to stop erosion and the run-off of surface water had stored up great quantities of water underground. When we came here about 80 percent of the water in a heavy rainstorm ran off the place; today we keep on the place 80 to 90 percent of the rain that falls, trapped by sod, contours, and strips. It sinks deep into the earth to replenish the reservoirs in the great crevasses in the underlying sandstone rock.

•

The proper use of the land plus a simple program of game food and cover has certainly paid big dividends in fish, birds, and game. Everywhere at Malabar, since we established the farm as a game propagation area, the population of wild life has doubled and redoubled, again and again. Once the area becomes saturated, the excess population moves off inot the neighboring territory where it provides sport for hunters. We do not shoot on the farm and allow no shooting but the sportsmen benefit enormously by the closed season on this large area. Big fox-squirrel, fox, raccoon and rabbits are especially abundant. Of course there is always plenty of quail (on which in Ohio there is no season) and some grouse and pheasant although the foxes kill off the latter pretty rapidly.

•

The whole theory of the ability of healthy plants grown in organically balanced and complete, mineralized soils to resist disease and even to some extent attacks by insects is not altogether new, either in the field of research among highly skilled market gardeners or among intelligent amateurs, but it is largely unknown in general agriculture. The theory of putting into the soil the means of resistance rather than applying it externally by dusts and sprays is much more revolutionary and comparatively little research has been done along these lines.

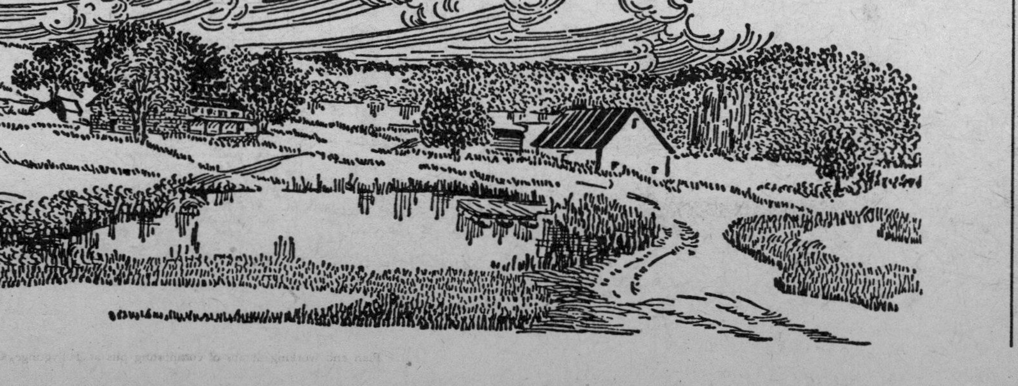

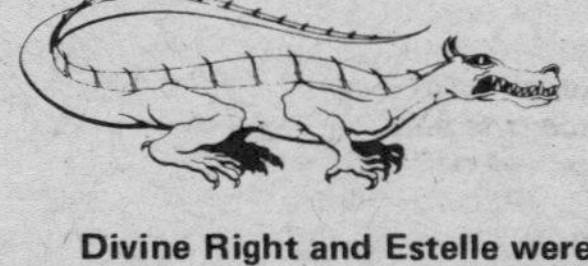

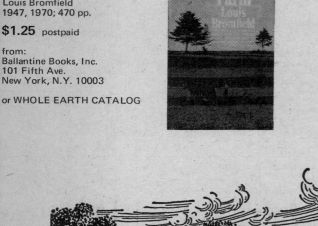

THE LESSON OF THE DEER

Divine Right and Estelle were sitting in folding chairs drinking beer and eating cashew nuts while the Lone Outdoorsman grilled steaks over a charcoal fire. Like Estelle and Divine Right, he had dressed for the occasion too. He had on a cowboy hat and cowboy boots, a pair of levis, a flannel shirt with a vest and, while he cooked, a knee-length apron that was white everywhere it didn't have blood stains on it. Now and then a breeze would swirl the smoke up in a cloud around his head, momentarily decapitating him so that it appeared that there was only his wide, round body in cowboy clothes tending the slabs of meat on the charcoal fire. It was a surreal scene all right, but D.R. and Estelle were both so stoned it struck them as the most ordinary of domestic occasions. It was dark by now and so far there wasn't any moon. The trees around the camp framed the entire universe, as far as they were witness. What they saw was all there was anywhere in all creation, and for heads as awash with dope smoke as D.R.'s and Estelle's, that was quite enough.

"I'm a cancer," D.R. suddenly called out to the Lone Outdoorsman. "My sign is the crab. I get where I'm going by walking sideways."

The Lone Outdoorsman nodded as he turned the steaks. "Yeah. I'm in the Fin, Fur and Feather Club myself, great buncha guys."

"Got him!" Estelle exclaimed, swatting a fat mosquito on her arm.

"Yeah," said the Outdoorsman. "They're pretty bad tonight. We'll go in soon as these steaks are done. Time for Westward, Westward anyhow.

"You got TV?" Estelle asked.

"Sure. It's a little one, but you can see it all right."

"Far out! Can we watch it too?"

The question pained the Outdoorsman. He turned to look at his guests. "Of course you can. You're my guests, ain't you?"

"Fantastic!" Estelle and D.R. were so excited by the prospect of TV they leaned their chairs together and gave each other little hugs.

"We haven't seen TV since we left Oregon."

"How long ago was that?" asked the Outdoorsman.

"I don't know," said D.R. "When did we leave Oregon?"

"Three weeks ago tomorrow."

"Three weeks ago tomorrow," D.R. said to the Outdoorsman.

"Shucks. I drove here from Phoenix in a day and a half."

"Yeah, well, you see," said D.R. and he got out of his chair and walked closer to his host. "You see, I'm a Cancer, my sign is the crab, I get where I'm going by walking sideways."

"I plan to take a different route back to Phoenix myself," said the Outdoorsman. "See some new country. That's the great thing about America, there's always some new country to see."

(continued)

Long-Legged House

Wendell Berry is the Sergeant York charging unnatural odds across our no-man's-land of ecology. Conveying the same limber innocence of young Gary Cooper, Wendell advances on the current crop of Krauts armed with naught but his pen and his mythic ridgerunner righteousness. One after the other he picks them off, from the flying bridges of their pleasure boats as they roar through his native Kentucky rivers, from beneath the hard hats in the Hazard County strip mines, from the swivel chairs in the Pentagon where they weigh the various ways to wage war on all forms of enemy life beyond the end of their own friendly chin. He's a crackshot essayist, and, for those given to capture, a genial and captivating poet. He boasts a formidable arsenal of novels, speeches, articles, stories, and poems from his outpost in one of the world's most ravaged battlefields where he writes the good fight and tends his family and his honeybees. Consider him an ally. Here are some samples from **The Long-Legged House**.

[Reviewed by Ken Kesey]

The Long-Legged House
Wendell Berry
1971; 213 pp.

$1.25

Ballantine Books, Inc.
101 Fifth Ave.,
New York, N.Y. 10003

OR WHOLE EARTH CATALOG

For do not all our rights have as their ultimate expression and meaning the right of a man to be secure in his own home? When this right is no longer defended by a power greater than himself, his days begin to come to him by accident, in default of whatever caprice of power may next require his life.

•

Man cannot be independent of nature. In one way or another he must live in relation to it, and there are only two alternatives: the way of the frontiersman, whose response to nature was to dominate it, to assert his presence in it by destroying it; or the way of Thoreau, who went to the natural places to become quiet in them, to learn from them, to be restored by them.

•

The years I spent between childhood and manhood seem as strange to me now as they did then. Clumsy in body and mind, I knew no place I could go to and feel certain I ought to be there. I had no very good understanding of what I was rebelling against: I was going mostly by my feelings, and so I was rarely calm. And I didn't know with enough certainty what I wanted to be purposeful about getting it. The Camp offered no escape from these troubles, but it did allow them the dignity of solitude. And there were days there , as in no other place, when as if by accident, beyond any reason I might have had, I was deeply at peace, and happy. And those days that gave me peace suggested to me the possibility of a greater, more substantial peace——a decent, open, generous relation between a man's life and the world——that I have never achieved; but it must have begun to be then, and it has come more and more consciously to be, the hope and the ruling idea of my life.

•

In a blundering, half-aware fashion I was becoming a writer. And, as I think of it now, school itself was a distraction. Although I have become, among other things, a teacher, I am skeptical of education. It seems to me a most doubtful process, and I think the good of it is taken too much for granted. It is a matter that is overtheorized and overvalued and always approached with too much confidence. It is, as we skeptics are always discovering to our delight, no substitute for experience or life or virtue or devotion. As it is handed out by the schools, it is only theoretically useful, like a randomly mixed handful of seeds planted in one's pocket. When one carries them back to one's own place in the world and plants them, some will prove unfit for the climate or the ground, some are sterile, some are not seeds at all but little clods and bits of gravel. Surprisingly few of them come to anything. There is an incredible waste and clumsiness in most efforts to prepare the young. For me, as a student and as a teacher, there has always been a pressing anxiety between the classroom and the world: how can you get from one to the other except by a blind jump? School is not so pleasant or valuable an experience as it is made out to be in the theorizing and reminiscing of elders. In a sense, it is not an experience at all, but a hiatus in experience.

What has interested me in telling the history of the Camp is the possibility of showing how a place and a person can come to belong to each other——or, rather, how a person can come to belong to a place, for places really belong to nobody. There is a startling reversal of our ordinary sense of things in the recognition that we are the belongings of the world, not its owners.

Farmer's Almanac

The almanac for weather forecasting (a year in advance), astronomical information, holidays, planting and cultivating, hunting and fishing, cooking, nautical information, livestock and poultry farming, and various other necessities of rural living. It includes astrology, entertainments (essays, poems, puzzles), practical information, old superstitions, and New England "pleasantries." It's main emphases, however, are on weather forecasts, farming data, and astronomy.

[Reviewed by David Marston]

The Old Farmer's Almanac
Judson D. Hale, ed.
176 pp.

$0.60 (published every Fall)

from:
The Old Farmer's Almanac
Dublin, New Hampshire 03444

or WHOLE EARTH CATALOG

SEPTEMBER hath 30 days. [1971

This is the month in which the world began,
A much better cradle than cold, frozen Jan.
How joyous our harvest, our blessings and future
If we might start now our hopes to nurture

When I was a boy, Dad and I often took a Sunday walk over his land, about 200 acres of oak and pine, a spring brook, swamp and pastures. A single big path went directly through it. One Sunday Dad said, "We need another path. Go ahead and make it." I knew well enough how to use my axe, the big brush cutters, and the pruning saw, though I'd never cut a path.

But the next day, all excited, I went down past the big pine and along the orchard wall to where the cows had their own path through the berry bushes. I went in and tramped back and forth blazing to the special places I wanted my path to see—the spring, down the brook to the white birches, the porcupine rock and the dens, and along the pine knoll where you found the lady slippers and the May flowers and the hobble bush in springtime.

Dad hadn't said anything about the path wandering, but it was going to sure enough, a little wandering path the sun looked into and the trees arched over.

When I was cutting, by mistake I had cut beyond two of my special places. So I made two little extra paths to them. "Sight seeing paths," Dad called them. But he liked it all, and I was proud as punch.

I remember this now, for my grandsons, who live over the hill from us, are cutting their own path to our house.

The Harvest Moon is the one nearest the equinox, so this year it comes Oct. 4

Countryside Small Stock Journal

In September 1972, Dairy Goat Guide *joined* Rabbit World *and* Countryside *to form* Countryside Small Stock Journal.

—SB

Countryside
Jerome Belanger, ed.

$3 /yr (bimonthly)

from:
Countryside Small Stock Journal
Waterloo, WI. 53594

Here's a good example of how availability increases consumption (and waste).

When water has to be carried from a well, average usage is 8 gallons per day. When a pump is put at the kitchen sink, consumption increases to 10 gallons per person per day. Put in a faucet and that figure goes up to 12 gallons. Introduce hot water in the kitchen and you'll use 18 gallons a day.

Cities Aren't Places Any More.

Practically everybody I know in California is talking about "the land thing." The visions I hear, almost daily, range from buying the northeast third of New Mexico, to getting a three-acre spread in Maine. People with access to half a million dollars of the old man's loot are in the same dream with people saving three dollars a week in a glass jar. Land. Rural land. Land in the direction of east. Western drive has brought us here. Eastern serenity, or the desire for it, is nudging us back again.

Probably everybody into "the land thing" would explain his motives in different, or at least personal, language. But I think the theme running through any variety of language would be the same. I think the thing we're talking about is no more or less than to understand than the simple desire to have a home. A home, and a sense of home that can only grow out of a sense of place. Cities aren't places any more. They're scenes, projected on screens, then bulldozed away, neighborhood by neighborhood, like cancelled TV shows. People who are tired of scenes are leaving, or wanting to anyway, longing for a place, torn between the joy of getting out of town, and a vague despair that maybe there aint no such thing as place after all, that maybe all there is to do is ride around in outfitted buses, floating along the bloodless traffic arteries of the world.

I guess the essential thing that sustains me as I try to live in the California suburbs is the sense I carry around in my mind that, in fact, there are some places left in the world that are very nice, places left over from how the world used to be, continuing in a kind of time-warp that surrounds them like a shield. I'm sure there are similar places in every state. But the ones that I know about are in Kentucky, certain towns, certain counties that go on, and on. There's a social fabric in those places intact from their very beginnings as towns and counties, and what I wish is that that fabric could somehow be declared a national treasure, and given protection, like the mountain lion, or the California condor. That won't happen, of course. The fabric is already badly torn by new freeways and the coal industry, with strip-mining as its cutting edge. So I guess the best that one can hope for is that the surviving old places be studied as models for the new places about to create themselves.
Gurney Norman

The Conservationist

It's hard to imagine how the subscription price covers the production cost of this high quality "official publication" of the New York State Department of Environmental Conservation. New York State flora, fauna, history and lore, superbly illustrated.

—AF

$2/yr., $5/3 yrs. (bimonthly)
from:
The Conservationist
P.O. Box 2328
Grand Central Station
New York, N.Y. 10017

Fabric of the Hudson

New York's Farmland

Master Plan for the Adirondacks

Remembering Rural America

Boiling Pond and a Hermit

Noah John Rondeau

Weather and the Deer Population

Nighthawks, Southbound

(Please don't ask for reprints— subscribe!)

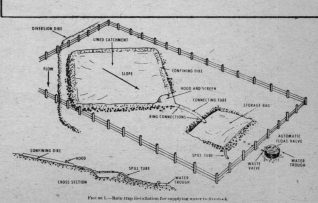

Figure 1.—Rain trap installation for supplying water to livestock.

But——put in a complete plumbing system under pressure, and usage increases to 30 gallons a day. This includes anywhere from 8-20 gallons each time the bathtub is used, 3-5 gallons each time a toilet is flushed, and 1-2 gallons each time a bathroom wash basin is used.

Brooklyn Botanic Garden

This is an outstanding source of information on nearly everything useful relating to plants, greenhouse, vines, pruning, the lot. And a fine periodical.

—SB

Plants and Gardens

$4 /yr (quarterly)

from:
Brooklyn Botanic Garden
1000 Washington Avenue
Brooklyn, N.Y. 11225

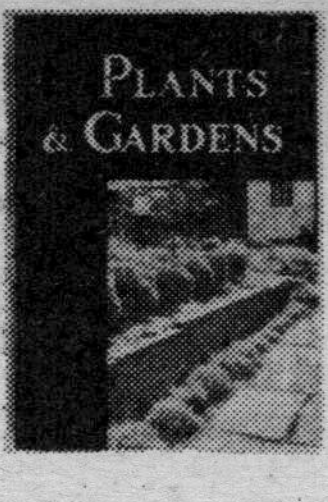

EACH ONE A COMPLETE, CONCISE MANUAL, 64 TO 112 PAGES, PRINTED ON QUALITY BOOK PAPER
(These Handbooks are separate editions of special feature issues of PLANTS & GARDENS)

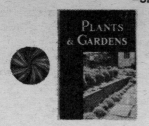

10. **Rock Gardens** $1.50
125 pictures of the best; ideas on design, construction, and care; appropriate plants
13. **Dwarfed Potted Trees— The Bonsai of Japan** $1.50
answers important questions on selection, training, pruning, care; over 100 pictures
14. **Vines** $1.50
how and where to use; cultivation and care, extensive blooming schedules
19. **Flower Arrangement** $1.50
how to use basic rules of color and design, making attractive containers, dried flower pictures, Christmas and other decorations
20. **Soils** $1.50
kinds of soils; how to build up and maintain good soils for different ornamentals
21. **Lawns** $1.50
how to establish and maintain lawns, best kinds of grass to use
22. **Broad-leaved Evergreens** $1.50
culture and use of hollies, rhododendrons, magnolias, and other broad-leaved evergreens
23. **Mulches** $1.50
best kinds to use in various regions, when and how to apply, new materials available
24. **Propagation** $1.50
seeds, hardwood and softwood cuttings, layering, grafting, use of plastics, plant hormones, propagating with mist
25. **100 Finest Trees and Shrubs** $1.50
descriptions and pictures of 100 of the world's best trees and shrubs for temperate climates; culture, hardiness, landscaping
26. **Gardening in Containers** $1.50
using containers for gardening on roofs and terraces, in city gardens, in difficult localities; hanging baskets, window boxes and moss-walls; new kinds of containers
27. **Handbook on Herbs** $1.50
featuring an illustrated dictionary of 68 different herbs; propagation; mints, geraniums, thymes; growing herbs indoors
28. **Pruning Handbook** $1.50
methods and effects of pruning woody ornamentals, fruits, and many tender plants
29. **Handbook on Gardening** $1.50
everything for beginning gardeners, experienced gardeners, too; how to select and care for plants; scores of "how-to" pictures
30. **Handbook on Breeding Ornamental Plants** $1.50
how to cross-pollinate many kinds of garden flowers and ornamentals, select good parents, raise new plants from seed. Basic genetics
31. **Bulbs** $1.50
when and how to plant all kinds of bulbs; best uses in the garden; indoor forcing; over 60 kinds illustrated
33. **Gardens of Western Europe** $1.50
a copiously illustrated guide-book for garden-minded travelers
34. **Biological Control of Plant Pests** $1.50
a handbook on the control of plant pests by parasites, predators, and other natural means
35. **Fruits in the Home Garden** $1.50
the best varieties of fruits and nuts for utility and beauty, how to grow and spray
36. **Trained and Sculptured Plants** $1.50
essentially a beautifully illustrated guide book on specialized training and pruning
37. **Japanese Gardens and Miniature Landscapes** $1.50
traditional and contemporary gardens and their application to Western culture; also tray landscapes and garden accessories
38. **Gardening with Native Plants** $1.50
how to know them and grow them. Informative articles from all parts of the U. S. A.
Same, cloth bound, hard cover $1.50
39. **The Environment: A Handbook of Ideas on Conservation for Every Man** $1.50
how to embark on anti-pollution and many other projects in communities, in short, constructive solutions for ecological problems that face man today
40. **House Plants** $1.50
150 pictures of outstanding kinds, their culture and ideas for using
41. **Flowering Trees** $1.50
crab apples, dogwoods, magnolias, cherries, others; how to select and grow them
42. **Greenhouse Handbook for the Amateur** $1.50
greenhouses of all types; plants to grow in them, how and at what temperatures
43. **Succulents** $1.50
where to obtain and how to grow American cacti, South African flowering stones and others. Illustrated dictionary of succulents
44. **Flowering Shrubs** $1.50
landscape uses, succession of bloom and care of 200 kinds, with selections by geographical region and topographic situation
45. **Garden Construction** $1.50
walks and paths, fences, walls, paved terraces, steps, garden pools, benches
46. **Dye Plants and Dyeing** $1.50
a handbook on dyes derived from plants; how to use them for dyeing yarns and textiles; many recipes; four pages in color
Same, cloth bound, hard cover $1.50
47. **Dwarf Conifers** $1.50
culture and uses of dwarf evergreens; 800 varieties described, 60 illustrated
48. **Roses** $1.50
a mine of information on landscaping, planting, pruning, hybridizing, exhibiting roses
49. **Creative Ideas in Garden Design** $1.50
83 fine photographs of well-designed gardens for outdoor living and for viewing
50. **Garden Pests** $1.50
how to control plant diseases and pests
51. **Bonsai: Special Techniques** $1.50
52. **Handbook on Weed Control** $1.50
53. **African-Violets and Relations** $1.50
54. **Handbook on Orchids** $1.50
55. **Origins of American Horticulture** $1.50
56. **Summer Flowers for Continuing Bloom** $1.50
57. **Japanese Herbs and Their Uses** $1.50
58. **Miniature Gardens** $1.50
59. **Ferns** $1.50
60. **Handbook on Conifers** $1.50
61. **Plants for the Shade** $1.50
62. **Gardening Under Artificial Light** $1.50
63. **1200 Trees & Shrubs— Where to Buy Them** $1.50

Order by name and number. Make checks payable to Brooklyn Botanic Garden
1000 Washington Avenue, Brooklyn, New York 11225

Plants, Man & Life

The classic on the domestication of plants, by a damned interesting man. Bless him, he annotates his bibliography.

—SB

Plants, Man & Life
Edgar Anderson
1952; 251 pp.

$2.65 postpaid

from:
University of California Press
2223 Fulton St.
Berkeley, Calif. 94720

50 E. 42nd St., Suite 513
New York, N.Y. 10017

or WHOLE EARTH CATALOG

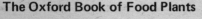

Few Americans realize how completely our American meadow plants came along with us from the Old World. In our June meadows, timothy, redtop, and bluegrass, Old World grasses all three, are starred with Old World daisies, yarrow, buttercup and hawkweeds. The clovers too, alsike and red and Dutch, all came from the Old World. Only the black-eyed Susans are indigenous. An informed botanist viewing such a June meadow may sometimes find it hard to point out a single species of plant which grew here in pre-Columbian times.

•

Ever since I first saw acres of wild sunflowers blossoming in gold and green confusion all down the back slopes of Dago Hill in Saint Louis, I have been intoxicated with sunflowers. They happen to be of key significance in the story of plants and man; if they were not I should be tempted to tell you about them anyway. I wish it were possible fully to communicate my enthusiasm for these lusty brilliant flowers, these coarse and resinous weeds which have been so closely tied up with man during his varied history on this continent. Crop plant, garden flower, roadside weed, growing unasked but seldom unwanted on vacant lots and rights of way. I wish one could in a few sentences paint the full pageant of them in any one year. The colonies of them in railroad yards in our larger eastern cities, the thousands upon thousands of acres in the Great Plains, long golden rows of them bordering roadsides and drainage ditches throughout the West, regular lines of them planted as windbreaks in some of the irrigated valleys, little bunches of them in neat Hopi gardens below the mesa tops, acre after acre grown for oil in western Canada. Or the fields of them in Peru and in Europe, single rows of them in allotment gardens at the fringes of cities, masses of them in Hungary and the Ukraine where they are grown for cooking oil. But with all my enthusiasm for them, with all my understanding of their high yield, I do not advise you to try growing them on an American farm year after year in efficient mass production.

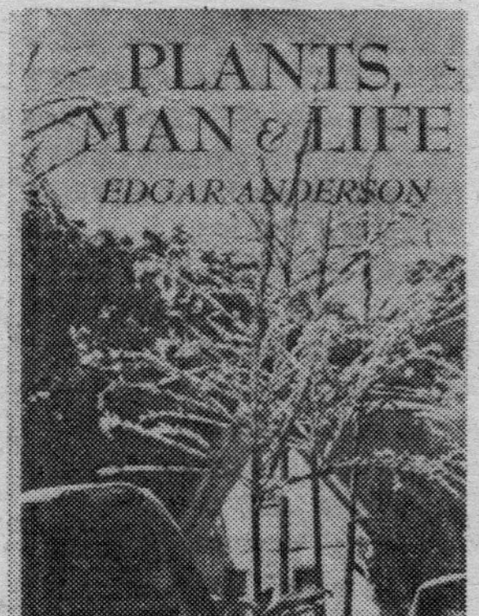

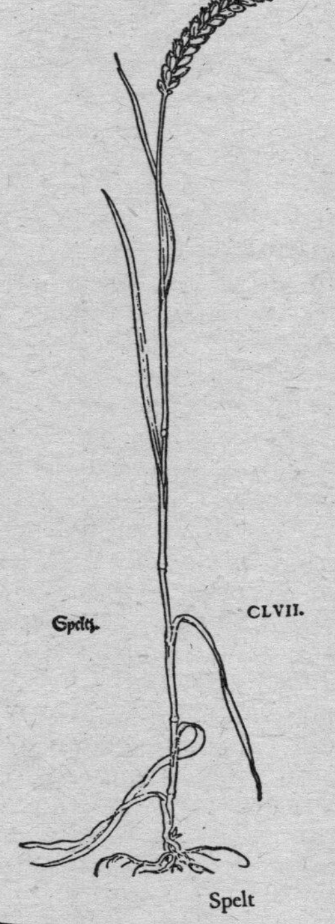

Spelt

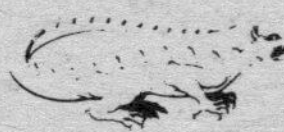

Estelle asked the Lone Outdoorsman if he lived in Phoenix. She'd come over to the fire and was holding a plate while he piled the steaks on. Hungry as she was, she was already plotting in her mind to stash part of their supper in her bag so they'd have something to eat the next day. She'd already scored a can of beer and a handful of cashew nuts. What she wanted now was half a steak and at least one baked potato. She would have scooped a potato off the platter then and there if the Outdoorsman had given her a chance. But he said, "I'll help you with that," took the platter and led his guests around the truck and through the narrow door of his camper.

"Yeah, I'm from Phoenix," the Outdoorsman said. "My grandfather helped settle that place in the 70's. Came out with the United States Cavalry, chasing after Proud Person, the Apache renegade."

"Did he catch him?" D.R. inquired.

"Well sir," said the Outdoorsman. "As a matter of fact, he did."

"Far out. What did he do with him."

"Took him to jail. Made him promise to quit bothering people, then let him go."

"Did Proud Person keep his promise?" asked Estelle.

"He did. Proud Person was a good Indian from then on. My grandfather was proud of that. He used to talk about it a lot. He got out of the Army and settled there in Phoenix as a grocer. Proud Person used to come in from the Hills about once a year and trade with him. They became life-long friends. My grandfather was a tough old codger, but that's one thing you can say for him, he was always a believer in giving folks a second chance."

The Outdoorsman was quiet then as he chewed a bite of steak. When he'd swallowed he set his plate aside and got up to turn the TV on.

The television set was a little portable with a four inch screen. It sat on top of the refrigerator toward the rear of the camper. Estelle and the Outdoorsman were seated on bunks on either side of the little room, with Divine Right between them sitting on a stool at the end of a table that folded out of the wall. Behind and above D.R. was a sleeping space that ran crossways of the cabin. On either side of the entrance to that space were the mounted heads of two small deer, both of them does. D.R. noticed them as soon as he came in. He didn't want to sit under them but he didn't want Estelle to have to either. Somehow the two does reminded him of Estelle, and he didn't like the thought. If he hadn't been on the crest of a good mood at the time, the two sad-eyed deer would have depressed him terribly. But Divine Right was about two steps back from his ordinary responses now, and the two mounted deer were no more than a minor weight upon his consciousness. He was even able to laugh when he asked the Lone Outdoorsman where he'd bagged the deer and the Outdoorsman said he'd run over them with his truck.

"Both of 'em at once?"

"No. But within a week of one another. It was the strangest thing. Soon as I got my truck fixed from hitting the first one, I was out in the hills again, and I'll be damned if another one didn't crash right into my fender."

D.R. laughed. "Sounds to me like those deer were trying to tell you something."

"Could be," said the Outdoorsman. "Cost me four hundred dollars to get my front end fixed."

The Oxford Book of Food Plants

A beautiful book, for looking and for reference. Color plates as illustration of every plant, emphasizing the part which supplies food. Arranged in a practical way—plants are grouped according to the kind of food they produce: fruits, herbs, leaf vegetables, oil crops, sugar crops, root vegetables, etc. Common and botanical name included, and an index which lists both, plus a glossary of descriptive botanical words. Descriptions of each plant tells its use, history, countries of origin and regions where it grows, along with a physical description accompanied by a drawing, food value, and economic value.

[Reviewed by D. Smith]

The Oxford Book of Food Plants
G.B. Masefield, M. Wallis,
S.G. Harrison, JB.E. Nicholson
1969; 205pp.

$13.95 postpaid

from:
Oxford University Press
16-00 Pollitt Drive
Fair Lawn, New Jersey 07140

or WHOLE EARTH CATALOG

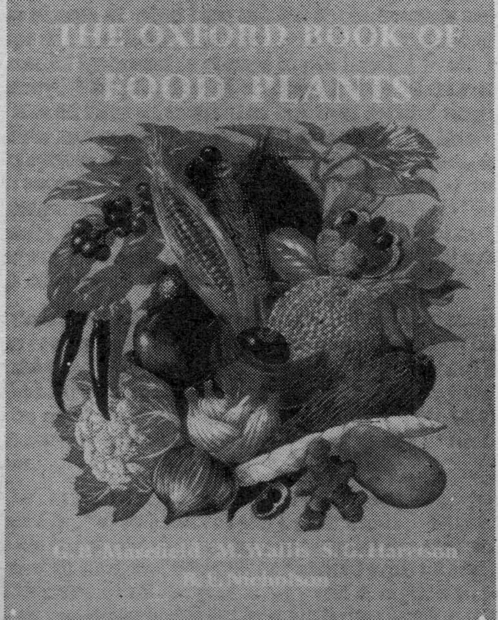

The Organic Gardening Books

When I first started gardening three seasons ago, I considered **How to Grow Vegetables and Fruits by the Organic Method** *as the first and last word on raising your own food. And I still believe that if you intend to own only one gardening book, that's the one to have. In addition to all the facts you need about soil, compost, mulch, and most domestic fruits and vegetables grown in North America, the book contains beautiful statements by individual gardeners, and by the editors themselves, that add up to an eloquent testimony in behalf of the organic idea. It is these statements, these images of gardeners as people trying to make their very lives organic, that gives the book its strength and true distinction. It's a book to turn a person on to the organic idea in the first place, and then go on to show him in precise detail ways to put that idea into practice. The book is an indispensable guide for the beginning organic gardener.*

The thing I have discovered through further reading and continued gardening, however, is that, as good as it is, **How to Grow Vegetables and Fruits** *is neither the first or the last word on the subject. There's a new book out now called Grow Your Own, by Jeanie Darlington, that to my mind comes closer to being the first word. And two other sources,* **The Encyclopedia of Organic Gardening** *and all of Ruth Stout's work in general, strike me as being closer to final statements.*

All I mean by "first" and "last" is that **Grow Your Own** *is for gardeners who are absolutely just beginning, and not only beginning, but beginning in a city at that, right up there on the very front lines where conditions come closest to impossible; while the other sources I mentioned are for people who have had gardening experience and are out to improve upon, rather than discover, their individual methods.*

Grow Your Own *is by a young Berkeley, California woman who did the whole organic trip in a plot ten feet by ten feet outside her home, paid close attention to what was going on, did careful homework, and then turned it all into a lovely little paperback book. It's an extremely personal book, sort of like a letter to close friends, charming and informational. (Of ladybugs, Jeanie says: "Imagine Volkswagens humping. That's what ladybugs look like when they mate"). The first audience for* **Grow Your Own** *is other beginning gardeners in the San Francisco Bay region, because much of the information on soil, weather and sources of organic supplies are of a local nature. But it is by no means a purely "local" book. It's a community book, but the community Jeanie is speaking to, and for, is scattered everywhere, and geography will not greatly diminish the book's practical usefulness. As the book serves the community with facts, it also helps create it in spirit. It establishes Jeanie as a kind of hero, in that by effort she has gained the experience of a professional without sacrificing the joyous spirit of the amateur. She's a freak, but she's a competent freak, and competent freaks just may be the most important people in the entire culture at this nervous point in its development.* **Grow Your Own** *is a solid achievement that everybody in the community can not only benefit from, but feel proud of.*

A lot of experienced gardeners find the **Encyclopedia of Organic Gardening** *more useful than* **How to Grow Vegetables and Fruits**, *and this is understandable. Once you're deep into gardening, past the point of needing to be convinced and wanting only to get on with the work at hand, the* **Encyclopedia** *does stand as a handier, more efficient tool. There's no table of contents. The subjects are not laid out in categories. It's all there in alphabetical order, crabapple followed by crabgrass; tobacco followed by tomato; lima beans, lime, lime tree, limonium, linaria and linden. Virtually any question you'd like to ask a master gardener is anticipated and answered here, and beyond that, a lot of questions that wouldn't have occurred to you are asked on your behalf and then answered. You wind up with a lot of accidental knowledge, browsing in this volume, and that's always fun and frequently immediately useful. I can best sum up my feelings about the* **Encyclopedia** *by simply saying that after three seasons as a gardener, I'm about to buy a copy, instead of borrowing any more, out of an impulse to acquire literature on gardening to match my own level of competence and curiosity.*

If you were to chart a course from **Grow Your Own**, *through* **How to Grow Vegetables and Fruits**, *on into the* **Encyclopedia**, *you'd wind up, of course, in Ruth Stout's garden watching her ignore practically everything you just learned from all those books as she grows stuff twice as good and ten times as easily as you do. Well, not really ignoring it. Just seeming to, in the same way that your grandmother ignores the printed recipe as she sort of unconsciously mixes a lot of stuff together and throws it in a coal stove oven to make the best Sunday dinner you ever sat down to. Ruth Stout is a master gardener who's been refining her procedures for decades now. She's sort of like an elderly Zen priest, an old roshi who after years of work and study has distilled a large burden of "knowledge" into a single gem of wisdom which he renders in a single haiku. Just at the point that I felt like I was really catching on to making compost and feeling kind of proud, I found out that Mrs. Stout doesn't fool with compost anymore. Too much trouble. Doesn't fool with tools much either. Doesn't fool with anything much, actually, except mulch. Just spreads a lot of hay around, plants by poking a hole in the ground with her finger, and when it is time, goes out and picks the produce and eats it. I'm confident that if I were to do everything in my garden that she does in hers, mine would still fail while hers would flourish, simply because I'm too young and foolish to get along without some rules. It's the difference between wisdom and knowledge, between having correct information and knowing the truth. I'll be needing "the facts" for a long time to come, but Mrs. Stout assimilated all of that long ago. She just . . . does it, and her accounts of doing it are among the very best statements on organic gardening that you're likely to come across.*

The thing to remember about organic gardening is that it's a movement, a national energy that since its beginnings early in the 1940's has grown into a force so potent by now that it contains serious political implications. The books I have mentioned are landmark documents. But more central to organic gardening as a movement is a monthly magazine published by the same Rodales who brought out the **Encyclopedia** *and* **How to Grow Vegetables and Fruits**, *called* **Organic Gardening and Farming**. *It has occurred to me that if I were a dictator determined to control the national press,* **Organic Gardening** *would be the first publication I'd squash, because it is the most subversive. The whole organic movement is exquisitely subversive. I believe that organic gardeners are in the forefront of a serious effort to save the world by changing man's orientation to it, to move away from the collective, centrist, super-industrial state, toward a simpler, realer one-to-one relationship with the earth itself. Most of the current talk about "ecology" in America is simply the noise that accompanies all fads. It's obviously doomed to go the way of hula-hoops and the fifty-mile hike. The thing I like to remember is that even when all the froth has blown away, and the rhetoric of pop-ecology has drifted off to join the other forms of pollution in the sky, the gardeners are going to still be gardening. They're going to quietly go on composting and tilling and planting, and then reaping all the good things they have sown.*

[Reviewed by Gurney Norman]

The Basic Book of Organic Gardening

For $1.25 get Rodale's basics.

—SB

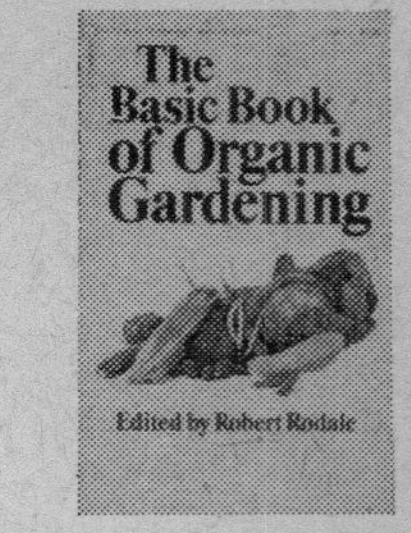

The Basic Book of Organic Gardening
Robert Rodale, ed.
1971; 377 pp.

$1.25 postpaid

from:
Ballantine Books, Inc.
101 Fifth Ave.
New York, N.Y. 10003

or WHOLE EARTH CATALOG

1. Perennial crops such as asparagus, strawberries, and rhubarb should be located at one side of the garden.
2. Tall-growing crops, such as corn, must be kept away from small crops like beets and carrots to avoid shading.
3. Provide for succession crops—a fall garden, small fruits, and overwintered crops to mature early in the spring. In this way, space for spring crops which will be harvested early, may be used again for later crops. Examples: tomatoes after radishes; cucumbers after spinach.
4. Early planted, fast-growing, quick-maturing crops should be grouped together. Examples: radishes, lettuce, early cabbage, scallions, etc.
5. Provide plenty of vegetables for canning, freezing, and storing.
6. Do not overplant new varieties, vegetables which the family does not like, or too much of any one vegetable at one time.
7. Rows should follow across the slope (on the contour) in hilly areas.
8. Make sure the plan provides the best spacing between rows for the method of cultivation that you intend to use (hand, tractor, horse).
9. Run rows north and south if possible to prevent plants from shading one another.
10. Long rows save time in care and cultivation. Several crops may be planted in the same row if the distance between rows is the same.

•

Where to Order Natural Controls

Ladybugs
Bio-Control Company
Route 2, Box 2397
Auburn, California 95603
L. E. Schnoor
Rough & Ready, California 95975

Praying Mantises
Eastern Biological Con. Co.
Route 5, Box 379
Jackson, New Jersey 08527
Gothard, Inc.
P.O. Box 332
Canutillo, Texas 79835
Robert Robbins
424 N. Courtland
East Stroudsburg, Pennsylvania 18301

Lacewings (Aphid lions) and Trichogramma Wasps
Vitova Insectary, Inc.
P.O. Box 475
Rialto, California 92376
Trik-O (Trade name for Trichogramma)
Gothard, Inc.
P.O. Box 370
Canutillo, Texas 78935

Milky Spore Disease
Doom
Fairfax Biological Laboratory
Clinton Corners, New York 12514

Bacillus Thuringiensis Disease
Thuricide
International Minerals & Chemical Corp.
Crop Aid Products Dept.
5401 Old Orchard Rd.
Skokie, Illinois 60076
Biotrol
Kobes Dist. Co.
Orange City, Iowa 51041

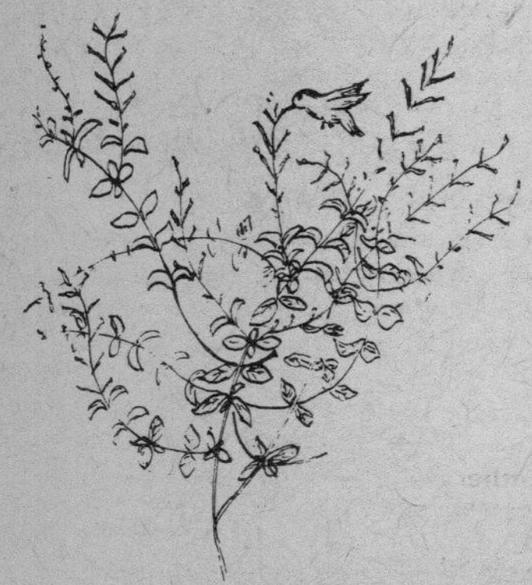

Hummingbird in the Pineapple sage

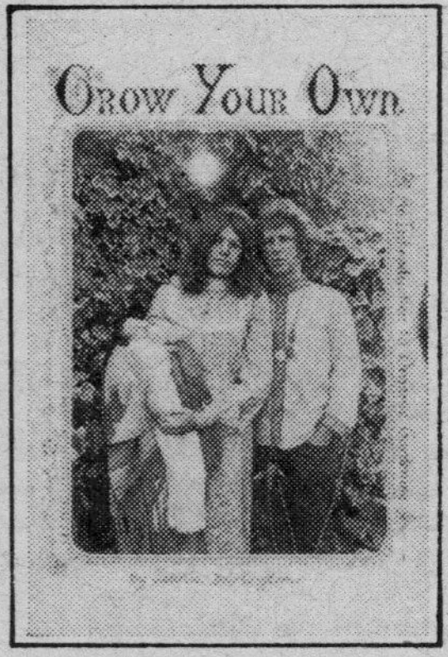

Grow Your Own
Jeanie Darlington
1970; 87 pp.

$1.75 postpaid

from:
Bookworks
c/o Random House
Westminster, Maryland 21157

or WHOLE EARTH CATALOG

Chemical fertilizers put your soil on a speed trip. The normal component balance of the soil is disturbed by the availability of more plant food than can be accepted. For a short time, everything that is living in the soil gets pushed way beyond its normal rhythm of life and of course the humus stores are depleted. A chemically treated soil is almost devoid of soil bacteria and earthworms. The structural strength of the soil is lost, and hardpans form that make it hard for water to penetrate deeply. This causes dust storm and erosion problems.

A forest is an ideal example of good soil structure. The leaves, twigs, and everything else that falls to the ground, act as a mulch and gradually decay, leaving a spongy rich layer of humus just below the surface. It is well balanced in all the nutrients necessary to the soil below and to all the living things in it. All the reserves are there mainly in an insoluble form, and they are gradually released by the action of the weather, the bacteria, the earthworms, and all the other micro-organisms in the soil.

Birds are good friends to the organic gardener. If you feed them seed this winter, they'll stick around and eat their share of bug kingdom baddies next summer.

Sweet Peas. The climbing variety, 5-7 feet, is great for hiding a wall or making a screen. Use trellis netting.

Nasturtiums. Great for hot, dry, poor soil areas. The leaves, which are peppery and high in Vitamin C, taste great in salads or cream cheese sandwiches. The flowers are good to eat too, and the green seed pods can be pickled in vinegar with a touch of mace, allspice, 1 clove and salt. They resemble capers.

The first step in pest control is to have healthy plants growing in fertile soil that is rich in organic matter. Then they are more resistant to virus and to insect invasion.
Step Two: Restore the balance of nature. The reason there are so many aphids in relation to other bugs, is that DDT has wiped out all their predators. So encourage and import predators into your garden. Ladybugs, praying mantids, ichneumon flies, lacewing flies, toads, lizards and birds all like to eat a wide variety of insects.
Step three: Outwit the insects. Here's where your ingenuity comes into action. Companionate planting is the first thing to consider.
The idea is that certain smelly flowers and herbs repel insects when planted next to susceptible plants. The flowers: marigold, calendula, nasturtium, geranium and chrysanthemum. The herbs: tansy, wormwood, chives, onions, garlic, sage, savory, coriander and hemp.

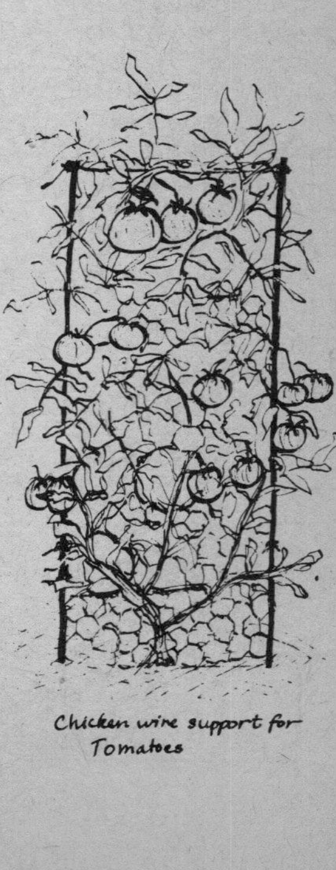

Chicken wire support for Tomatoes

How to Have a Green Thumb Without an Aching Back
Ruth Stout
1955; 160 pp.

$1.45 postpaid

from:
Cornerstone Library Publications
630 Fifth Avenue
New York, New York 10020

or WHOLE EARTH CATALOG

A New Method of
MULCH GARDENING

How to Have a Green Thumb Without an Aching Back

The liveliest book ever written on mulch gardening.
—Bernardine Kielty, Ladies Home Journal

"It isn't often that we get this excited about a new book."
—Organic Gardening and Farming

by Ruth Stout

I stopped short as a thought struck me like a blow. One never plows asparagus and it gets along fine. Except for new sod, why plow anything, ever?

Why plow? Why turn the soil upside down? *Why* plow?

I AM NOT GOING TO. I AM GOING TO PLANT!

I don't suppose I actually shouted the words aloud, but they were making a deafening uproar in my head and even in my heart. The things in me which had, at one time and another, been subjects of comment for those who bothered to notice—my extremism, radicalism of various kinds, ignorance of and indifference to convention, to the status quo, to the written word, to the "established" fact—all of these unfashionable qualities rushed in now and took over. I would ask no one's advice or opinion, I would tell no one until I had done it, but just as sure as God made rebels and nonconformists I was going to ignore custom and tradition and I was going to plant right now.

How to Grow Vegetables and Fruits by the Organic Method
J. I. Rodale & Staff, editors
1961; 926 pp.

$11.95 postpaid

from:
Rodale Books, Inc.
33 East Minor Street
Emmaus, Pennsylvania 18049

or WHOLE EARTH CATALOG

The dirt made by building a compost pile is a very desirable thing to have, but the man who goes through all the antics necessary to make this pile is to be pitied unless he has a great deal of time and energy he wouldn't know what to do with otherwise. He is like a man, let us say, who is suffering from a physical ailment and knows of a plant, growing on a far mountain, which will cure him. He makes the long, hard journey, finds the plant and is cured.

He is well satisfied until he returns home and finds that this plant also grows in his back yard. He had no way of knowing that until he saw the plant on the mountain and compared the two.

And so it is with those who build compost piles; they don't know any better way to make rich dirt. Now you are hearing of an easier, better way; you need no longer climb a mountain for your compost. It is yours for a small fraction of that labor.

METHODS OF TRAINING BLACKBERRY PLANTS

1. Trained to a stake.

2. Two-arm system trained to one wire.

The Encyclopedia of Organic Gardening
J. I. Rodale & Staff
1968; 1145 pp.

$12.95 postpaid

from:
Rodale Books, Inc.
33 East Minor Street
Emmaus, Pennsylvania 18049

or WHOLE EARTH CATALOG

A Tier-Shelf Bed for Mushrooms

Organic Gardening and Farming

$6.85 for one year, monthly

$.70 per copy

from:
Rodale Press, Inc.
33 East Minor Street
Emmaus, Pennsylvania 18049

The Amazon, however, has disappointed settlers in the past, and is likely to continue to cause immense problems, despite the technological tricks of advanced scientists.... The potential Amazon farmer looks at "a veritable wall of brown-green vines and emerald-colored trees reaching 250 feet into the blue sky." Seldom is such abundant production of plant matter seen anywhere else in the world. The new farmer clears the jungle (at considerable expense) and finds that the land produces good crops for a few years. But then comes ...a "shocking discovery." The Amazon land, after a few seasons of direct exposure to the relentless tropical rains, *hardens up like a brick.* Without the protective jungle cover as an umbrella, the basic life elements in the soil are leached out. Potassium, iron, calcium, magnesium, and aluminum are washed away.

The stone wall that neighbors helped build is to the right behind the iris in the rock garden. Six years after the project started, the author writes that she is "still hauling stones . . . but it's worth it!"

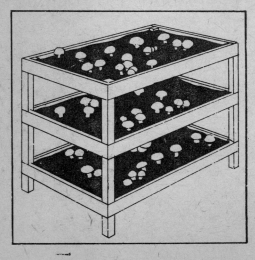

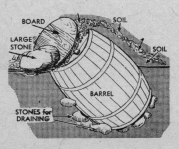

A BARREL ROOT CELLAR can store all or most garden produce in a fresh state over the winter. A strong, well-made barrel should be used and cleaned carefully before being set in trench.

Uses Manure Both as Fertilizer and Medicine

To keep my flower garden looking good, I use another natural resource, manure, both as a fertilizer and a medicine for every plant in our yard. I prefer horse manure for its light texture, and it makes a very nice mulch when dry. If a plant looks sick, it gets a dose of manure tea, and a new mulch of manure. I have found this a sure cure in our yard for rot in iris rhizomes, thrips in glads, and scale in lilacs. I haven't lost a birch tree since I started to mulch them with manure.

Compost Science

*magazine concerning itself
with teaching the world to compost
instead of dump or trash. full
range of ideascope from city conversion
down to pressing and storing chickenshit bricks.
good community awareness, printed by rodale.*

—jd

Compost Science
Jerome Goldstein, editor

$6.00 per year (bimonthly)

$1.00 single copy

from:
Rodale Press
33 East Minor Street
Emmaus, Pennsylvania 18049

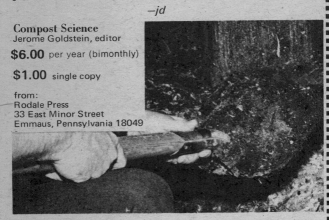

The use of composting to convert organic solid waste into a fertilizer, soil conditioner or nutrient source, is a topic of discussion and controversy. Actually the real value of this process is disposal of solid waste with the production of a usable aesthetically non-objectionable and hygienically safe residue. In this process, carbon in a high energy form and nutrient elements are returned for reuse in the ecological cycle rather than destroyed as done by incineration. Various modifications of the basic process are used throughout the world for the disposal of night soil, sewage sludge and refuse. In the United States, the interest in composting has been rather limited. It has been stated that the lack of enthusiasm for composting in this country follows from the American tradition of putting wastes "out of mind" which in effect obstructs any interest in reclaiming organic solids. Recently, some cities have recognized its potential as a method of refuse disposal as other methods of treating solid waste become uneconomical.

Past attempts to produce and market compost have met with limited success. Failure is often due to the inability to market the compost competitively with chemical fertilizers. The high paper content of a typical urban solid waste makes the material resistant to degradation by composting microorganisms. Consequently, with the limited technology available, existing compost plants operate inefficiently and cannot stabilize the organic material rapidly or completely.

Swedish Composter

Looks like it could be made as a do-it-yourself kind of kit — the inventor is looking for someone in U.S. to manufacture — any suggestions?

(Suggested by Ernest Rimerman)

CLIVUS IS NOT TO BE CONNECTED TO WATER OR SEWER SYSTEMS

The waste decomposes added by the supply of air and the inherent moisture (urine, wet garbage, etc.). Water vapour and carbon dioxide rise through the exhaust duct after leaving the waste mass which decreases considerably in volume and moves slowly towards the lowest chamber where the final products (soil, humus, nutritive salts) accumulate. They can be utilized as fertilizer — normally first after about 2 years and with intervals e.g. of 1–2 years.

Clivus is designed to meet the need for convenience and a hygienic and natural means of diminishing household waste and converting remains to soil restorer on the site.

A household with Clivus needs drainage for bath, dish and laundry water only (purification separately by method suited to local conditions — information concerning valid regulations can be obtained from the health authorities). Since Clivus takes kitchen waste normally poured down the drain, the sewer is relieved of such matter.

Through purification on site: transportation (vehicles, sewers, etc.) of refuse can be reduced or eliminated; outflow and spreading of contaminated matter in ground and water is prevented; the quantity of pure water used solely for the transport of excrement and refuse in the sewage network can be put to better use.

Methane Gas Production——Harold Bate

CHICKEN MANURE FUEL: "Put a chicken in your tank" may never match the zap of Esso's "Put a tiger in your tank" slogan. But British inventor Harold Bate will tell you that chicken power will run your car faster, cleaner and better than gasoline.

Bate has found a way of converting chicken droppings into gas——and runs his automobile on it.

By processing methane gas from rotted chicken manure and feeding it to the engine through a special device he invented, Bate says he has managed to drive his 1953 Hillman at speeds up to 75 m.p.h. without the use of gasoline.

At his farmhouse in Devon, Bate, 62, told an ENQUIRER reporter:

"This is the thing of the future. . .all you need is a couple of buckets of manure, a tin drum and my carburetor conversion device, and you're in business."

Bate's "chicken coupe" has been investigated and upheld by the British Ministry of Transport.

"We've looked into it," Frank Standing, information officer for the ministry told the ENQUIRER, "and the device works perfectly.

"However, as to mass use, that seems doubtful. There is simply not enough of a supply of chicken manure to provide fuel for autos on a mass basis."

Bate says he has been running his car and five-ton truck on the methane gas—as well as heating his home with it——for years.

"The method is really very simple," Bate said. "You just put about three buckets of manure into a sealed oil drum. Put a small oil heater under the drum to keep the manure at a steady 80 degrees.

"There are two microbes in the manure which, when heated, eat each other——this produces the gas.

"You can collect the gas in bottles or in plastic balloons for storage. Then all you do is feed the methane through an adapter into your carburetor——and you've got chicken power.

"I keep replenishing my manure supply every 2 or 3 weeks."

Bate said the conversion from gasoline to methane power can be made in two hours and requires no special tools. The only engine alteration required is the installation of Bate's patented device which feeds the methane from the bottle to the carburetor.

The gas, sucked into the engine by the cylinders, is ignited in the usual manner by the spark plugs to produce power.

Methane is not only cheap and efficient, said the inventor, but it is better for your car——no carbon deposit on your cylinders and no engine wear and no poisonous carbon monoxide fumes.

(Taken from NATIONAL ENQUIRER June 1970)

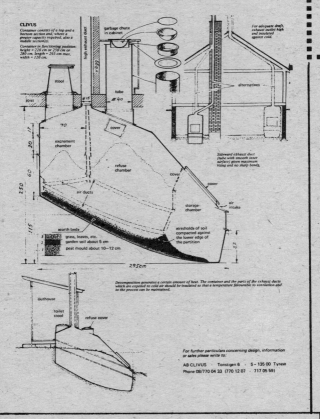

The Device is ready for connecting to the engine and is complete with Instructions and Drawings--also Instructions and Drawings for Methane Gas Production from Chicken-Pig-Cow--Sheep--Horse and Human manure--also the construction of Methane Gas Digesters of all sizes and costing from £5 upwards. The price is $55 which included the Device and the two sets of Instructions and Drawings--also the Postage by Air Mail to any part of the world.

Thanking you;
I Am Yours Sincerely;
Harold Bate.

Pennyrowden
Blackawton
Totnes—Devon
TQ 9.7 Dn.
England

Conversions by Earth Move

Since 1971 we have supplied an improving 'all-our-own-work' convertor based on the same British-made components as Harold Bate's, but with American engines in mind. Earth Move's conversion kit booklet now tops 100 pages and is set to double again during '74.

'Home-brew' gas—clean and fuel free—can be digested out of all kinds of so-called wastes . . . not just chicken manure. And methane plant design has moved from the bottom of the garden into housing, homesteads, farms, feedlots . . . until even city garbage dumps start to look like natural resources. Earth Move has become a clearing house for all these kinds of mechanical wizardry and—more recently—research-backer and test bed too. If the limits are there, we don't see them yet.

The Earth Move gas conversion will fit into any car; run on home-brew methane, propane (LPG), natural gas—and some we haven't tried yet—at pressured from zero to 200psi without a regulator. You can switch off and go back to gasoline too.

Mention model and year when ordering and please state number of carburetors or barrels. The package price of $35.00 includes delivery . . . anywhere on Earth.

*Earth Move
P.O. Box 252
Winchester, M.A. 01890*

Where to Get Compost Makers

I suggest that the WHOLE EARTH CATALOG list and describe the various Shredder/Grinders used for composting. Attached is a list which I have compiled of several manufacturers who advertize in the magazine *Organic Gardening and Farming.*

List of Companies Manufacturing Shredder-Grinders

Amerind-MacKissic Incorporated
Box 111, Dept. O
Parker Ford, Penna. 19457

California-McCulloch Equipment Co.
Box 3068
Torrance, California 90510

Gilson Brothers Company
P.O. Box 152, Dept. C
Plymouth, Wisconsin 53073

Kemp Company
602 Kemp Bldg.
Erie, Penn. 16512

Red Cross Mfg. Corp.
Bluffton, Indiana 46714

The Roto-Hoe Company
Dept. 2
Newbuty, Ohio 44065

W-W Grinder Corp.
2957B No. Market
Wichita, Kansas 67219

James G. Hupp
Orinda, CA

Microphor Sewage

Hark the crises of waste water disposal. . .and Behold this ecologically and biologically sound contraption:

"The Microphone Sewage Treatment System." This is a self-contained treatment plant designed to replace the septic tank for a small installation such as home(s), school, motel, small industry, etc. It uses redwood bark as a substrate for biological degradation of suspended and dissolved wastes, i.e., its three chambers perform the equivalent of primary <u>and</u> secondary treatment giving an effluent usable for agriculture, etc.

Being tried by
Joe Brennan
Moss Beach, CA

Information available from the inventor:

Edward Burton
Microphor, Inc.
452 East Hill Road
Willits, CA 95490

Bardmatic Garbage Eliminator

If you have a washing machine, you may have the money and desire for the convenience of this ready-made trouble-free kitchen garbage digester-composter.

—SB

Bardmatic Garbage Eliminator System

$70-80

from:
Bardmatic Corporation
Box 1306
Evanston, Illinois 60204

Methane Production in India

For more detailed information on methane production from various organic wastes, send request and a large stamped return envelope to:

Ram Bux Singh
Gobar Gas Research Station
Ajitmal (Etawah) U.P.
INDIA

Composter in the Sky

My wife & I recently moved to Ben Lomond from Atlanta & are unaccustomed to trash & garbage disposal problems, although we had some difficulties in Atlanta. We've been very interested in a composter, & my wife, Sandi, believes she's found the best. It's maintenance free, accepts any food scraps——except coffee grounds, which go to the ivy, is absolutely odor-free, rather handsome & extremely convenient. It's the California Blue Jay. It's only drawback is the noise factor. My wife has tried lubricating with meat grease but that had no apparent effect.

Really, Sandi says the blue jays eat anything——she puts all the garbage on an old redwood stump on the hill in back of our cabin & the jays have it cleaned up in a few minutes. If anyone knows how to make them run silently, please let us know.

Dave & Sandi
Ben Lomond

Biodynamic Gardening

"They plant by the moon."

"Some European mystic is behind it."

"A lot of weird theories. Nothing proven."

"They surely know their plants."

I have yet to see a 'respectable' formal evaluation of the 'biodynamic gardening' inspired by Rudolf Steiner. All I know is, the most sensational gardens I've seen all claim they owe something to biodynamic notions of soil nutrition, companion plants, and the year cycle.

The Philbrick's Gardening For Health and Nutrition looks to be the most practical entry into biodynamic gardening. Next level in: Companion Plants or The Pfeiffer Garden Book. Then Steiner's own Agriculture, with the farthest-out illustrations (in color) ever seen in a garden book.

—SB

Gardening for Health and Nutrition
John and Helen Philbrick
1963; 93 pp.

$1.25 plus $.25 postage

Companion Plants——and how to use them
Helen Philbrick, Richard Gregg
1966; 107 pp.

$4.95 postpaid

Pfeiffer Garden Book
1967; 199 pp.; also available in paperback for $2.75 plus $.35 postage

$4.25 postpaid, cloth

Agriculture
Rudolf Steiner
1958; 174 pp.

$6.50 postpaid

all from:
St. George Book Service
P.O. Box 225
Spring Valley, N.Y. 10977

They pay postage on all orders $5 and over when payment is sent with order.

Transplanting cabbage seedlings in Chadwick's incredible biodynamic garden at UC Santa Cruz, the main reason a lot of longhairs are attending the school. This photo from Cry California, Winter '71.

Gardening for Health and Nutrition

Companion Plants in a Biodynamic Garden

CABBAGES — SAGE | CHIVES — TOMATOES

path

LETTUCE — SWEET BASIL | central path | SHALLOTS — BROCCOLI

Gardening for Health and Nutrition

DANDELION (*Taraxacum officinale*) This is an important bio-dynamic plant, used to make one of the six Compost Preparations. The growing plant produces a fine neutral humus, encourages earthworms, and is a good influence among the vegetables, so do not weed them all out. Do you know how good its young leaves are in early spring salads; that its roots may be brought indoors in late fall like endive, the leaves cut off to the crown and new ones grown for winter greens? Or the roots may be dried, chopped and used like coffee. Many people enjoy dandelion wine made from the blossoms. The cultivated variety of dandelion known in Europe is used in all these ways, but that seems difficult to start here. Wild dandelions grown in a biodynamic garden are fully as satisfactory. Their deep roots bring up calcium and other minerals from the soil.

Pfeiffer Garden Book

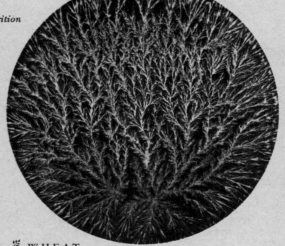

☸ WHEAT
A picture made with Pfeiffer's sensitive crystallization method

Companion Plants——and How to Use Them

Agriculture

Suburban and Farm Vegetable Gardens

For 40¢, this has a lot of basic information. Maybe all you need.

OUT OF PRINT

—SB

Suburban and Farm Vegetable Gardens
Robert Wester
1967; 46 pp.

no longer available

from:
Superintendent of Documents
U.S. Government Printing Office
Washington, D.C. 20402

or WHOLE EARTH CATALOG

Plants grown in the hotbed or greenhouse without being shifted from the seedbed to provide more room and those shipped from the South usually have very little soil adhering to the roots when they are set in the garden. Such plants may require special care if transplanting conditions are not ideal; otherwise, they will die or at least suffer a severe shock that will greatly retard their development. The roots of these plants should be kept covered and not allowed to dry out. Puddling the roots, that is, dipping them in a thin mixture of fresh cattle manure and clay, or even clay alone, helps greatly in bridging the critical transplanting period. Planting when the soil is moist also helps. Pouring a half pint to a pint of water, or less for small plants, into the hole around the plant before it is completely filled is usually necessary. A starter solution made by mixing ½ pound of a 4–12–4 or 5–10–5 commercial fertilizer in 4 gallons of water may be used instead of plain water. It is usually beneficial. Finally, the freshly set plants should be shaded for a day or two. Small branches a foot or two long from trees with heavy foliage, stuck into the soil on the south side of the plant row, serve the purpose.

Figure 18.—*Black plastic film conserves moisture, controls weeds, warms the soil, and hastens maturity of a number of vegetable crops.*

Garden Way Publishing Company

Books for Self-Sufficient Living

Free list of Publications

from:
Garden Way Publishing Company
Charlotte, Vermont 05445

WHERE IT IS STILL PLEASANT TO LIVE IN THE USA

This booklet recommends seeking a place outside of the 224 Standard Metropolitan Statistical Areas, as defined by the Bureau of the Census. These are cities of 50,000 or more with their economically attached suburban communities. The SMSA's occupy only 10% of the land area of the United States. It discusses in detail a checklist of factors to be considered in selecting an area and gives the method of finding the answers to each of the questions. $1.00, paperback.

THE BUG BOOK: HARMLESS INSECT CONTROLS
by John and Helen Philbrick

A useful compilation of imaginative methods used by practicing bio-dynamic gardeners to combat insect and animal pests. The bugs are arranged alphabetically with accompanying sketches and descriptions for easy identification. Remedies are suggested, and in the back is a listing of effective brews and potions. An invasion of blister beetles can be checked, say the authors, by calling in the neighbors and tromping through the garden beating the bushes and waving sticks and scaring them off. 143 pp., $3.50, paperback.

WESTWARD, WESTWARD

On the TV screen the world's tiniest wagon train began inching its way across what was surely the world's smallest prairie, and Divine Right and Estelle cracked up immediately.

But the Lone Outdoorsman didn't see anything funny about it.

"What do you mean?" he argued. "Look at it, why it's two miles long or more. Count the wagons. I see fifty right there."

"No! No! No!" D.R. cried. "The screen itself's only four inches wide."

"But this is a movie," the Outdoorsman protested.

"I know it's a movie," said D.R. "That's the point!"

To settle the argument, Estelle got up and held her finger against the TV screen. "I officially pronounce this wagon train we see before us worming its way across the west as being precisely one and three-fourths inches long, no more and hopefully no less otherwise it will disappear altogether."

D.R. was in hysterics. He laughed so hard he fell over backwards off his stool. And even the Lone Outdoorsman was amused now. He didn't know why, exactly. He was a little put out by the irreverence of his guests, but their mirth was contagious. He grinned. And then he laughed as hard as D.R. did when the first line of dialogue on Westward, Westward turned out to be the wagon master saying "Shut up and sit down," to a lady wagon driver.

"Stuff it up your ass," Estelle replied. When the wagon master started to answer, Estelle turned his volume down so low nobody could hear what he said.

"Turn it up, turn it up!" D.R. and the Lone Outdoorsman yelled. Estelle turned it back up and sat down to eat her steak as the lady wagon driver said to the wagon master, "Have you no feelings? Don't you care about anything except your stupid westward movement? I hate the westward movement. I wish I'd never left St. Louis.'

And the lady wagon driver began to cry.

(continued)

The Organic Way to Plant Protection

A mine of specific information: This disease or pest with this plant, do this in response. Use the friendly bird, bug, herb, barrier, trap, mild chemical.

—SB

The Organic Way to Plant Protection
Organic Gardening Staff
1966; 355 pp.

$7.95 postpaid

from:
Rodale Books, Inc.
33 E. Minor St.
Emmaus, Pennsylvania 18049

or WHOLE EARTH CATALOG

Aside from birds, there is another, more prosaic but effective insect eater——the toad.

True friend of the gardener, nearly 90 percent of the toad's food consists of insects and other small creatures, most of which are harmful. In 3 months a toad will eat up to 10,000 insects, 16 percent of which are cutworms. Mr. Toad delights on slugs and mole crickets. And golf course operators are aware of this fact. One Southern club pays for a children's Saturday movie matinee every spring. Price of admission? A toad.

The toad relishes other pests too. Yellow jackets, wasps, rose beetles, spiders, ants, moths, caterpillars, flies and squash bugs are all on its menu. In parts of Europe, toads are collected and brought to market, where they are bought by horticulturists. And before the advent of insecticides, tidy housewives kept a few toads in the house to eat cockroaches and other insect pests.

Toads, like people, feel there is no place like home, and possess a certain amount of homing instinct. So if you import yours from a distance, keep them penned up for a while so they can adjust to their new environment. After a spring rain, small toads can be found and collected in swampy, marshy lands and around shallow ponds.

Friendly insects may help the gardener in his fight against the cabbageworm-butterfly. Trichogramma, commercially obtainable parasites, attack many worms of the Lepidoptera order, which includes the cabbageworm. The trichogramma lays her eggs inside the eggs of the harmful insect by the use of her pointed egg-laying apparatus. When the trichogramma egg hatches, the young parasite proceeds to eat out the contents of the egg in which it lives, causing the egg to become black and preventing it from producing a harmful insect.

Yellow jacket hornets have been found to thrive on cabbage worms, and their presence should not be discouraged. The Braconid wasps, *Macrocentrus ancylivorus* and *Agathis diversa*, are extremely helpful control agents. The gardener can encourage *M. ancylivorus* by planting strawberries, as it feeds also on the strawberry leafroller. *A. diversa's* alternate host has not yet been discovered. Avoid using poison sprays which will kill these and most helpful insects.

Until this natural help arrives, the gardener can control the cabbageworm by the use of many homemade, non-toxic sprays. Dorothy Schroeder of Lyons, Colorado, has made her cabbages distasteful to the cabbageworm and the cabbage butterfly by spooning a little sour milk into the center of each cabbage

Organic Gardening Without Poisons

A thin, padded, over-priced book with an excellent appendix of sources for organic pest control aids.

—SB

Organic Gardening Without Poisons
Hamilton Tyler
1970; 111 pp.

$7.50 postpaid

from:
Van Nostrand-Reinhold Books
450 W. 33rd St.
New York, N.Y. 10001

Also available in paperback
Simon & Schuster
1 West 39th Street
New York, N.Y. 10018

$1.50

plus $.25 postage and handling

Harnessing the Earthworm

Harnessing the Earthworm, by Thomas J. Barrett, Wedgewood Press, Boston, Mass, 1959. A small (166 page) book about how everyone can help save the Earth a little bit by raising earthworms to make all the good new top soil that everyone knows all about (hopefully). You can raise them from egg cases in culture beds that Mr. Barrett shows you how to build & everything. Book is in two sections: "The Earthworm & Its Environment" and "The Earthworm Under Control" and you have this man speaking in terms of hundreds of thousands——millions!——of worms per acre, each processing his own weight in dirt daily resulting in the super-rich organic material that can "turn a barren desert hillside into a luxuriant paradise", like the book jacket says. It's all there, and he's done it. I'm sorry I can't give you anymore information on price & address, but I found it in the library and you know the way they insist on cutting off the price.

Eric Wurzbacher
Temple Hills, Md.

54 Pests
Land Use

BENEFICIAL INSECTS ON THE JOB

The ladybug is a veritable nemesis to aphids and also helpful in controlling scales and other troublesome insects.

Good & Bad Insecticides

Commercial insecticidal preparations which are relatively safe for the environment:

Antrol African Violet and House Plant Insecticide Bomb
Black Flag Ant and Roach Killer
d-Con Double Action Ant-Roach Killer and Repellent
d-Con House and Garden Spray
Flea Collars (all brands)
Formaldehyde Fumes
Green Thumb Insecticide Spray
Hartz Mountain Cat Flea and Tick Killer
Hartz Mountain Dog Flea and Tick Killer
Hartz Mountain Rid Tick
Hartz Mountain Rid Tick Shampoo
Johnson's No-Roach
Ortho Isotox
Ortho Malathion 50
Oxalic Acid (any brand)
Raid Flying Insect Spray
Raid House and Garden Spray
Raid Rose and Flower Spray
Real Kill Household Spray
Roaches' Last Meal
Sal Soda (any brand)
Scope Insecticide Granules
Sears Sevin
Sergeant's Flea and Tick Powder
Sergeant's Flea and Tick Spray
Shell No-Pest Strip (should not be used in rooms with infants or invalids)
Spectracid
Terro Roach Killer

BENEFICIAL INSECTS FOR BIOLOGICAL CONTROL

Raising insects, or even gathering them, for biological control use is difficult. As a result, there is a great deal of specialization. Most firms try to work with more than one control insect but are often short in supply of the second group. Some of the basic suppliers are:

Bio-Control Co.
10180 Ladybird Dr.
Auburn, California 95603

Ladybug beetles gathered in the Sierras from winter colonies; two species; sometimes mantis cases.

Ecological Insect Services
15075 W. California Avenue
Kerman, California 93630

Consultation and control for both farms and gardens; sells retail.

Dead Drunk Slugs

In the February 9, 1970 issue of *Time* on page 46 is a short article on "Dead Drunk Slugs". Entomologist Floyd F. Smith found that beer, fresh or otherwise, attracted and killed 300 slugs compared with 28 slugs for a metaldehyde/arsenic mixture. The small amounts of alcohol used in such traps as "poison" would not harm small children or pets who sometimes find and eat poison bait. This new "poison" is easy to get and safe to handle. Of course, some bird might get drunk by eating an insect killed in a trap of this type but I think that is much better than dying slowly from DDT. This new "poison" can be used for almost anything. I can remember my Grandfather telling of how he got rid of unwanted pigeons by feeding them rum soaked cracked corn and dropping the drunk birds off on the other side of town.

Yours Truly,
David Smith
Mendham, N. J.

In another example of how natural controls can offer effective protection, an attacking grasshopper is destroyed by the sting of the tiny red ant.

Beware of preparations containing the following. They are the compounds most likely to accumulate and cause damage to the environment and people. Know your enemy.

Aldrin	Endrin	Methoxychlor
BHC	Heptachlor	Perthane
Chlordane	Heptachlor epoxide	Strobane
DDD (TDE)	Hexachlorobenzene	Telodrin
DDE	Kelthane	Toxaphene
DDT	Kepone	
Dieldrin	Lindane	

Commercial insecticidal preparations which may accumulate and eventually cause environmental damage.

Antrol
Antrol Ant Trap
Comfy-Pet Flea and Tick Killer
d-Con Ant Pruf
d-Con Roach Pruf
d-Con Stay Way
Hartz Mountain Cat Flea Powder
Hartz Mountain Dog Flea Powder
Hide
Ortho Ant and Roach Spray
Ortho Chlordane Spray
Ortho DDT-25
Ortho Dormant Spray
Ortho Lawn Spray
Ortho-Klon 44
Ortho Triox
Paket Ant Bait
Raid Ant and Roach Spray
Raid Moth Proof
Raid Yard Guard
Science Kelthane
Sears Ant Killer
Sears Flying Insect Killer
Sears Insect Spray
Terro Ant Killer

Prepared by Indiana University Biology Dept. for Crisis Biology Series Lectures

Sent in by
Barbara K-G
Bloomington, Indiana

Gothard, Inc.
P.O. Box 370
Canutillo, Texas 79835

Specializes in trichogramma wasps

Mincemoyer's Nursery
R.D. 5, Box 379
New Prospect Road
Jackson, New Jersey 08527

Mantis egg cases, both native and Chinese

Rincon Vitova Insectaries Inc.
P.O. Box 95
Oak View, CA. 93022

Raises control insects for farm work. Write for free insect and price list.

Fountain's Sierra Bug Company
P.O. Box 114
Rough and Ready, California 95975

Ladybugs only
They ship from early March to late September. Delivery to California customers made through United Parcel Service, should include **6%** sales tax.

Bug Heartburn

If you have a garden you probably hate things like cutworms and aphids but are also afraid of giving yourself that last dose of chlorinated hydrocarbon that will do it. Solution: plant things like garlic, onion and chili pepper along the border of your garden and through the middle if it's wide. Bugs don't like these plants and will avoid them. Consequently they will also avoid your garden. If they don't then crush a chili carefully into about a quart of water, add a crushed clove of garlic and sprinkle or spray the stuff on your plants. This will give all the bugs heartburn and they will vow never to patronize your garden again. Good bugs to have in your garden are lady bugs, ants, wasps, bees, and spiders. Even safe insecticides will kill them, so beware. Cutworms and other caterpillars aren't numerous and should be piecked off by hand.

Piece and undermining,
RD and JL Hamilton

Troy-Bilt Roto Tiller

***$513-$543 (Direct factory orders get discount from 10% in** the spring to 22% July thru September) You'll save enough on beer in ten hot days to pay the difference between this machine and some suburbanite deluxe.*

Your 14-year-old daughter may never take the Troy-Bilt over and plow under the neighbor's cornstalks with it (though it has happened) but you can still work 10 acres easier & better with this tiller than with any garden tractor in sight. Gear-driven, powered wheels––you can guide it with one hand and not come trampling along thru the seed bed. It also cultivates, furrows, plows snow and chops in virtually anything but trees for direct composting. Front-blade tillers break your back and shake your skin loose–– it would be easier to keep mules. Troy-Bilt has blades behind the wheels, so in rough going (asphalt, maybe? I've never run into any "rough going") you could lean on the handles instead of lifting the wheels off the ground. Engineering miracle, no? They are also just plain nice people to deal with.

This review is not intended to replace the one of the Graveley tractor . Graveley is a fine machine, will last almost forever, and will do just about anything (with extra cost attachments.) But it costs twice what the Troy-Bilt does and I don't think it will do twice as much. Maybe on a larger acreage. . .but at least in the Midwest almost any implement lot or farm sale will produce an old tractor, disc, harrow, buzz saw for wood cutting and brush clearing, snow blade, etc. for less than the price of a complete Gravely outfit. None of it is the latest but with some mechanical sense and a little judicious rapping at the implement dealers, , you learn what to watch for and you won't get junk either. And remember, you can't ask questions if you don't know a plow from a pump jack. Get the basics from a book––or a friendly farmer (who will probably try to sell you every piece of scrap iron on his place)––or go to a garden tractor shop and pretend you're suburbanites.

As marginal farmers follow Good Life consumption hype off the land it's only right we should take up this smaller machinery even as we use those small scraps of land that **don't fit into corporate food factories. Going at it this way, $1500 will buy the same machines your uncle used to** *farm a half section––or two Troy-Bilt tillers, a chain saw, pump, and snow shovel––or the Gravely tractor outfit–– and any of them will turn your 20 acres into Eden with no strain at all. But for a simple tilling/composting machine, the Troy-Bilt roto tiller is the best thing around.*

[Suggested and reviewed by
Bob Kirk]

Brochure from:
Troy-Bilt
102nd St. & 9th Ave
Troy, N.Y. 12180

Gravely Tractor

I own an old one––and my 5 acres is more like 35. We mow, plow, cultivate, cut brush, saw wood, pump water, plow and blow deep snow, clear ice, haul, etc., with it. No belts and plenty of power. (Don't try to help it–– it's stronger than you are.) Rotary plow turns organic debris under and leaves a ready-to-plant seed bed in one operation.

How did you miss it so long? Not cheap, first cost, but it will outlast them all and does a better job easier.

[Reviewed by George D. James, Jr.]

Brochure from:
Gravely Corporation
Gravely Lane
Clemons, N. C. 27012

2-wheel tractors	$544-$937
Rotary plow	$147
Rotary mower	$330
4-wheel tractors	$796—$2,038

these items no longer available

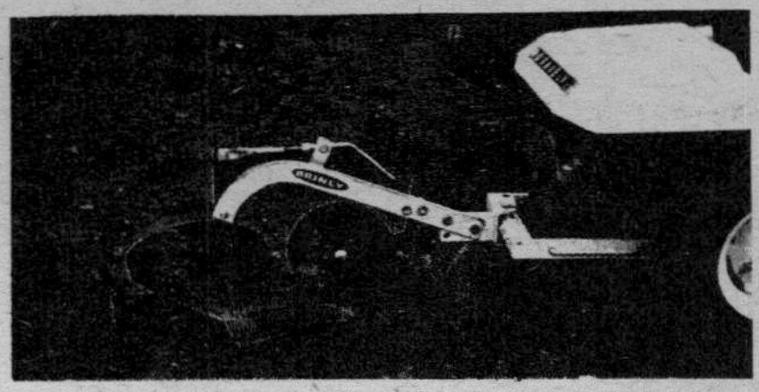

Soil Test Kit

A soil test kit enables you to test your garden soil for acidity/alkalinity, nitrogen, phosphorus, and potash. A test will show what is present and what is lacking. There are test tubes, chemicals, and a color chart to gauge results. Be sure to ask for "The Organic Supplement" prepared by **Organic Gardening** *magazine in case " . . . you have decided to work with Nature's own methods of fertilization." Feed the soil, not the plant.*

—Lloyd Kahn

Sudbury Soil Test Kit
Send for descriptive literature

Kits: **$6.95 - $42.95**

from:
Sudbury Laboratory, Inc.
Box WE74
Sudbury, Mass. 01776

Mushroom Growing For Everyone

Apparently the main effort in growing mushrooms is having, or making, marvelous compost to grow them on. Beyond that they're a low-maintenance grow-em-in-corners item. This British book has the details.

—SB

Mushroom Growing for Everyone
Roy Genders
1969; 216 pp.

$7.50

from:
Transatlantic Arts, Inc.
North Village Green
Levittown, N.Y. 11756

or WHOLE EARTH CATALOG

A crop of mushrooms may be produced in boxes beneath the kitchen sink, in a cellar or in a garden shed. They may be grown in a cupboard beneath the stairs, or in an attic room, where perhaps no more than two or three boxes may be planted with spawn; these would take the minimum amount of time to care for, just a few minutes each day. When the crop came into bearing and, provided the temperature did not fall below 45°F (7°C) there would be a few mushrooms each week for possibly three months or more. Artificial heat is not necessary for mushrooms, but the beds (or boxes) will not bear if the temperature falls below 40°F (4°C). Though the beds may become completely frozen, no harm will be done, and the crop will begin again as soon as the air temperature rises. This is another advantage in growing mushrooms in comparison with plants which may be damaged by hard frosts. Indeed, the best quality mushrooms will be obtained where the temperature does not rise above 55°F (13°C), and a cool place is better than one which is too warm, when pest and disease will be at a minimum.

It is important that the compost attains a temperature of at least 160°F (71°C) in the heap so that the spores of vert-degris disease and brown plaster mould are killed. A high temperature will also drive any mushroom midges to the surface, where they may be killed by one of the mushroom fly sprays. It should be said that, where animal manures are excluded, relying entirely upon the activator and possible a little poultry manure for composting, the incidence of introducing disease spores will be minimised.

The wagon master was moved. Behind the stern set of his huge jaw his face showed real emotion. He stood above the weeping woman, trying to figure out what to do. Finally he thought of something. He took off his hat. But the woman cried on as before, and the wagon master showed more and more real emotion. At last he sat down beside her and picked up a stick and began drawing in the dirt.

"Aw shucks, mam," he began. "I didn't mean tuh make yuh cry. It's just that, well, out here on the trail, it seems like there just ain't no time much for payin' attention tuh people's feelings. Life's hard out here, mam. And it makes a man hard. Whatever good comes out of this westward movement's going to have to be carved right out of the dust, and it ain't a gonna be easy. People get hurt, and people get bitter, and some people get killed. But I believe a great thing will come out of it all someday, mam, a brand new world where folks'll stand tall and be free and independent. Every day more people are headin' west, mam. And once you set out, there ain't no turnin' back. They've got a vision, mam. They're a very special kind of people, almost a new kind of people, you might say. People that want something more outa life than just comfort and security and money. This wagon train's made up of people like that, mam, people willin' to work and sacrifice and give up the old things so they can learn how to do what the new world requires 'em to do. That's the kind of person you are, mam. And I mean that. It's people like you who're gonna make this new world into what it's going to be. And I'm proud to help out some. I know I make a lot of mistakes, mam, mistakes that a woman like you is bound to notice and get upset by. So I apologize, mam, for upsetting' yuh. I'll try to keep it from happenin' again. If we don't run into any redskins, we'll be in Fort Leary in a couple of days. Everything'll be all right then."

The lady wagon driver dabbed her eyes with a hankie. Then she looked up and managed a smile through her tears. "I don't know why I'm telling you this," she sniffed, reaching to take his hand in her's. "But after what you just said, I feel compelled to. Tom, I've admired you greatly, ever since we left St. Louis. I know I haven't shown it. I know that I've been silly, and a nuisance. I've been confused, but now I think I understand, and I must speak my heart to you. All these weeks on the trail together, long days of dust and thirst and the ever-present danger of Indians, and these cold nights when the wolves howl and the moon lights up the emptiness of the lonely prairie, all the long, hard weeks since we left St. Louis, Tom, I've believed that I was in love with you. And the thing I realize now is that I'm not. I admire you too greatly for that. To love you would only be to tie you down. You've got a great work in front of you, Tom Ginsberg, a great role to fill on behalf of all the people who are to follow you west to help build the new world of freedom and opportunity you spoke of. It's not people like me who keep alive the promise of the westward movement, Tom, it's people like you. You've got dragons to slay, great heroic deeds to perform. I know that now. And knowing it somehow fills me with the deepest peace I've ever known."

The wagon master didn't know what to say. He just sat there scratching in the dirt with his stick. Finally he reached over and shook hands with the lady wagon driver. Then he went over to the chuckwagon and told the cook to fix her a buffalo steak.

WELCOME TO WESTERN COUNTRY

"Welcome to Western Country," said a fag in a cowboy suit as he held up a package of cigarettes. "Welcome to the clean, fresh taste of the great outdoors." As the fag took a Western out of the package and lit it, the camera pulled away to show a bunch of guys branding calves and generally horsing around the corral. Then the camera closed in on the fag again as he took a deep drag on his Western. He filled his lungs, and then without exhaling he seemed to fill his lungs again. Two, five, ten seconds and more went by and still he didn't exhale. As his face turned red and his eyes began to bulge he looked straight at Divine Right and grinned. D.R. laughed and gave him the V-sign. At last the fag blew the smoke out and holding up the cigarettes one more time he said, "Won't you have a Western?"

"Thanks," said D.R. "But I just had one."

Laughing, Estelle said "Them Westerns is all right cigarettes."

The cigarette commercial was followed by one about Stud pickup trucks. The picture showed a new Stud pickup rolling across the prairie chased by a herd of wild mustangs. A closeup showed how the independent front suspension absorbed the shock of the rocks and holes while the passengers rode in total comfort.

(continued)

Seeds, Vegetable and Fruit

Mrs. Stout swears by Harris' 'wonderful' Sweet Corn. Mr. P.N. Shrup raves over Burpee's 'Big Boy' tomato. There's a good many seeds and companies to develop your own opinions among. Send 25¢ for the catalogs.

CORN

5 lb. Minimum Order

Barbecue—A midseason early, high quality hybrid for home garden or market use. Ears 8½" long with 12-14 rows, well filled with excellent husk protection.

Per lb. Thick Kernels

5 lbs. 65¢	25 lbs. 55¢	100 lbs. 51¢
500 lbs. 49¢		

Per lb. Flat Kernels

5 lbs. 68¢	25 lbs. 58¢	100 lbs. 54¢
500 lbs. 52¢		

Butter & Sugar (78 days)

Per Lb. Thick Kernels

5 lbs. 83¢	25 lbs. 73¢	100 lbs. 69¢
500 lbs. 67¢		

Per lb. Flat Kernels

5 lbs. 86¢	25 lbs. 76¢	100 lbs. 72¢
500 lbs. 70¢		

Herbst Bros.

6123 Burpee's Big Boy Giant Hybrid ◉

78 days. A heavy producer and the largest of our hybrid tomatoes. Many weigh 1 lb. and more, some 2 lbs. and more. Unlike other large fruited varieties, Big Boy is perfectly smooth, deep globe to deep oblate in shape and very firm. Fruit is scarlet-red with thick walls and bright red, meaty flesh of fine flavor.
Pkt. (30 seeds) 50¢; 2 pkts. 95¢; 3 pkts. $1.35; ¹⁄₃₂ oz. $2.25

GOURDS

Your Choice Any 4 Pkts. of Gourds $2.75

Ornamental and Useful   ORNAMENTAL FOR TABLE DECORATION

Gourds. The various types of gourds make very interesting annual climbers which rapidly cover fences, trellises, or any unsightly objects which one might wish to obscure from view. The ornamental fruits which they bear are very attractive, many of which make delightful toys for children.

	Pkt.	Oz.
426 Shumway's Finest Mixed	85 cts.	$2.00
427 Dipper	85 cts.	$2.00
428 Sugar Trough	85 cts.	$2.00
429 Nest Egg	85 cts.	$2.00
430 Hercules Club	85 cts.	$2.00
431 Calabash	85 cts.	$2.00
432 Dish Cloth or Vine Okra, edible pods	85 cts.	$2.00
425 Vegetable Gourd. Ornamental and Edible	85 cts.	$2.00

VEGETABLE OR EDIBLE SOY BEAN, BUSH

96 days for use as green shelled beans. The plants are erect, bush-like and literally loaded with pods, each containing 2 or 3 oval-shaped, bright green beans which are delicious cooked as green shelled beans. When fully matured, the dried beans are nearly round, green and may be cooked like lima beans. Pkt. 35c; lb. $1.50

Natural Development

145 Harris' WONDERFUL Sweet Corn
A special experience in good eating. Wonderful's sweetness, flavor and tenderness are second to none. It ripens in mid-season, yielding abundantly over a considerable period. Long tapered ears with 12-16 rows of perfectly delicious, creamy golden kernels. Our customers award it their highest praise.

56 Seeds, vegetable and fruit
Land Use

Burpee is the biggest, fastest and most efficient of the seed catalogs. Send for the catalog in January or August (they're always out of them by April). Burpee designates some seeds for certain areas, which is handy.

W. Atlee Burpee Co.
Riverside, CA 92502

Natural Development Company has Lloyd Kahn's recommendation as best source of seeds. They also carry organic fertilizers and insecticides. Prices like Burpee.

Natural Development Company
Bainbridge, Pennsylvania 17502

Vita Green has seeds that are "untreated, natural, old-fashioned, unhybridized, uncrossed". The founder is moving to cleaner land in Australia, but the business will keep going.

Vita Green Farms
P.O. Box 878
Vista, CA 92803

Shumway deals particularly in bulk seed, has somewhat lower prices and nice engravings in its catalog.

R. H. Shumway Seedsman
P.O. Box 777
Rockford, Ill. 61101

Gurney has the best seed and tree guarantees. More cold climate seeds.

Gurney Seed & Nursery Co.
Yankton, South Dakota 57078

Harris seems like Abercrombie & Fitch, dignified, good quality, not cheap.

Joseph Harris Co.
Moreton Farm
Rochester, N.Y. 14624

Stokes has a large catalog, similar to Burpee.

Stokes Seeds, Inc.
Box 548, Main Post Office
Buffalo, N.Y. 14240

Rohrer's has low prices, will send untreated seeds, if you ask.

P. L. Rohrer & Bro. Inc.
Smoketown, Pennsylvania 17576

Field's has a big catalog with low prices.

Henry Field Seed & Nursery
Shenandoah, Iowa 51601

De Giorgi is 'organically oriented', has a plain catalog and low prices.

De Giorgi Co.
Council Bluffs, Iowa 51501

Olds is cheaper than Burpee and Shumway, more expensive than Fields.

L. L. Olds Seed Company
P.O. Box 1069
Madison, Wisconsin 53701

Park is recommended by some of the organic gardeners.

George W. Park Seed Co.
67 Cokesbury Rd.
Greenwood, S.C. 29647

Herbst is a catalog for professional growers. Good prices, no pictures, minimum order $25. Vegetables, flowers, shrubs, trees, and grass.

Herbst Brothers
1000 N. Main St.
Brewster, N.Y. 10509

Farmer looks like another catalog.

Farmer Seed & Nursery Co.
Faribault, Minnesota 55021

Stark Brothers is an excellent source for fruit trees, dwarf, semi-dwarf, and regular. 150-year-old nursery. Leaning organically.

Stark Brothers' Nurseries and Orchards
Louisiana, Missouri 63353

Miller also has fruit and nut trees.

J. E. Miller Nurseries
Canandaigna, N.Y. 14424

Kitazawa is a supplier of oriental seeds such as Chinese cabbage, Japanese onion, edible burdock, etc.

Kitazawa Seed Co.
A 356 W. Taylor St.
San Jose, California 95110

—SB

[Suggestions and evaluations by Lloyd Kahn, Craig Harris, R. Ruiz, Pierce Jones, Fred Gaines, Marc Lerner, Carnegie Schensted]

Seeds are exquisitely designed instruction capsules for an orderly rearrangement of the elements. The gardener plays only a small role in the process——the seed tells the soil nutrients, air and water to organize into exactly what is described on the seed packet. Automation——and an example of what we've been given to work with on our planet.

—Lloyd Kahn

a seed is a little plant in a box with its lunch. write to these addresses for free catalogs and brochures.

—jd

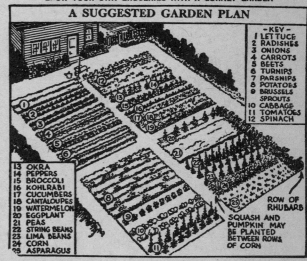

This Is The Year To FIGHT INFLATION AND THE HIGH COST OF LIVING GROW YOUR OWN GROCERIES WITH A GURNEY GARDEN

A SUGGESTED GARDEN PLAN

—KEY—
1 LETTUCE
2 RADISHES
3 ONIONS
4 CARROTS
5 BEETS
6 TURNIPS
7 PARSNIPS
8 POTATOES
9 BRUSSELS SPROUTS
10 CABBAGE
11 TOMATOES
12 SPINACH
13 OKRA
14 PEPPERS
15 BROCCOLI
16 KOHLRABI
17 CUCUMBERS
18 CANTALOUPES
19 WATERMELON
20 EGGPLANT
21 PEAS
22 STRING BEANS
23 LIMA BEANS
24 CORN
25 ASPARAGUS

ROW OF RHUBARB

SQUASH AND PUMPKIN MAY BE PLANTED BETWEEN ROWS OF CORN

Gurney

TOBACCO.

Shumway

#757, Pkt. $.75

492 Oak Leaf

40 days. Improved strain of an old favorite loose leaf variety. Forms a tight bunch of medium green leaves which are deeply lobed. Very tender, long standing and of excellent quality. Pkt., 50 cts.; oz., $1.50, ¼ lb., $3.50, postpaid.

Shumway

- - - - - - - - - - - - - - - - - - - -

Vegetables for Survival

Clyde Robins now offers a "Survival Garden" — especially long lifed seeds vacuum-sealed in a can for use in emergencies, etc. The catalog description:

After special treatment to prolong their life and their power to germinate with vigor, these superior seeds were immediately deposited in this sanitary container. Here their added vigor remains and their life span is greatly increased as they lie unmolested, figuratively, "Out of This World," ready to produce abundantly when the can is opened.

Seeds sealed by our method have been found very good after more than ten years. Our experience with them only goes this far.

Sealed in this container are:

4 oz. Beans	4 oz. Peas
1-1/4 oz. Beets	1/2 oz. Spinach
1/2 oz. Cabbage	1/2 oz. Squash
1/2 oz. Carrot	1/8 oz. Eastern Tomato
4 oz. Corn	1/8 oz. Western Tomato
1/2 oz. Onion	

Complete instructions for planting are included.

Enough seed to feed a small colony the essential vegetables for survival are contained in this can.

. . . Shipped anywhere in the United States . . . $3.25

from:
Clyde Robin
P.O. Box 2091
Castro Valley, CA 94546

Clyde Robin

Wildflower & Wild Tree Seeds. Gardeners and food growers—and maybe hunters and gatherers too—should check out Clyde Robin's seed catalog. It offers not only wildflowers, which grow easily without too much attention, but also many weird and unusual seeds of flowers, trees, shrubs, herbs, and vegetables, plus occasional information on their culture, appearance, uses, etc.

The Special Roadside Mixture grows in places where you thought only weeds would, and makes a really gaudy show in early Summer. After it has bloomed you cut it all down to the ground and the California poppies grow back and flower again. Grow catnip and turn your cats on—it grows easily from seed but you have to start the seedlings inside a small protective wire cage (which the plants will grow up through and out of) otherwise those dope-crazed cats rub out the young plants entirely.

[Suggested and Reviewed by David Noton]

Catalog
$1.00

from:
Clyde Robin
P.O. Box 2091
Castro Valley, Ca. 94546

Schumacher *is a catalog for professional nurserymen and foresters, but don't be shy. If you know the Latin name of the tree you're after, you can find a good deal in this catalog.*

—SB
[Suggested by Carnegie Schensted]

F. W. Schumacher
Sandwich, Mass. 02563

California tree seeds available from:

R. S. Adams
P.O. Box 561
Davis, CA 95616

Gardens of the Blue Ridge *is a pretty catalog of eastern U.S. wildflowers, trees, shrubs, and bulbs.*

Gardens of the Blue Ridge
Ashford, N.C. 28603

The 3 Laurels *has a smaller catalog of wild flowering plants:*

The Three laurels
Marshall, N.C. 28753

California wildflowers also from:

Theodore Payne Foundation
10459 Tuxford St.
Sun Valley, CA 91352

You can buy a forest, or all kinds of seedlings from:

Musser Forests Inc.
Indiana, Pa 15701

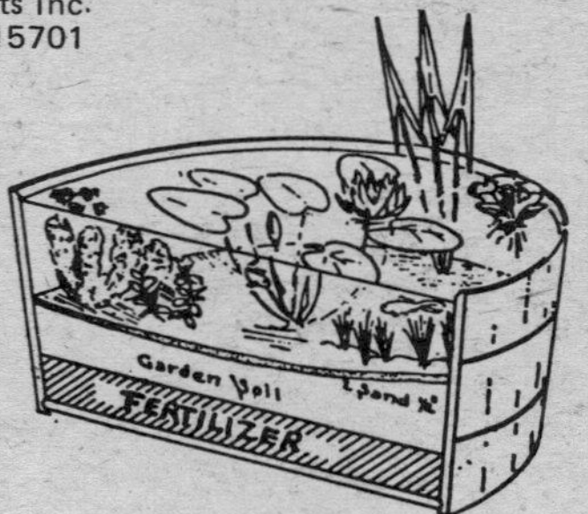

TUB GARDEN

Lilies and Lotus

The Van Ness Water Gardens carries a wonderful selection of water lilies—both hardy and tropical and also the sacred Lotus—they will send you a catalog on request and therein you will find beautiful pictures and descriptions of the lilies and lotus they offer.

Also in this catalog you will find complete instructions on growing lilies, their requirements and information also on building lily ponds——curing them——planting and natural balance of a pond. They also sell many beautiful goldfish——water plants and snails. There is a list of helpful books in there also!

In my limited dealing with them they have been very nice to me and very pleasant to deal with. You can visit the Gardens between 8:00 A.M.-5:00 P.M. any day except Sunday and Monday when they are closed because of packing and shipping because they ship all over the world.

Van Ness Water Gardens
2460 N. Euclid Avenue
Upland, California 91786

They also are familiar with the organic growing method and practice it also.

Having a frog pond gives such joy and serenity! Visiting the Zen Temples in Kyoto gave such an indescribable feeling especially the peaceful ponds! I hope this information opens new experiences for people.

Paul & Toni Goldenberg
La Habra Heights, CA

"The Stud," said an unseen baritone. "Everybody wants one."

The Lone Outdoorsman asked Divine Right if his VW had independent front-end suspension. D.R. said he didn't know.

"It's a good thing to have if you're going to do any cross-country driving."

"I guess it is," said D.R.

"We're driving cross-country," said Estelle.

The Outdoorsman turned and looked at her. He was on his feet now, looking for some ketchup in a cabinet near the TV set. "No kidding? You all drive around in the boonies?"

"No," said Estelle. "We stay on the highway. But we're driving across the country.

"I've driven across the country fourteen times in the last two years," said D.R.

"Oh," said the Outdoorsman. "That's not what I mean. I mean out in the boonies, where you'd take a trail-bike, or something. You know. Cross-country."

Divine Right asked the Outdoorsman if he'd ever driven across the country.

"Well now," said the Outdoorsman. "Do you mean cross-country, or across the country."

"I mean across America," said D.R.

"The nation, in other words," said the Outdoorsman.

"But the nation is the country," said Estelle.

Pine, Cypress, Fir, Redwoods, Eucalyptus

Davis Headquarters Forest Nursery, 580 Chiles Road, Davis, California 95616. The state of California's distribution center for trees for reforestation, erosion, windbreaks. A long form of course, but they mail pines, cypress, fir, redwoods, eucalyptus in quantities of 100-1,000 or more. One year old bare-root trees (4-10" height) are as little as $13.50 per 500 (for distribution in California only).

Growing Wildflowers

I might point out that the growing of desirable wildflowers involves a great deal more than turning them loose. If you live in suburbia the idiot who built the place dug the topsoil out to form your basement and then thoughtfully graded the subsoil over top of the existing topsoil. You can remedy this as I did by "digging the soil up two feet down", and throwing it out. Replace this with leaf-moldy soil from the nearest woods, add a ton of peat moss, the contents of your compost pile, and some well-manured soil from your vegetable patch and you're all set to go, provided you have adequate shade and moisture. Also since chlorine and flouride are fatal to native orchids, obtain water from a non-polluted source. Do this and you will be growing ladyslippers, trailing arbutus, trilliums, what have you, even as I am.

I do not recommend growing wildflowers from seed to the beginner, unless the species is otherwise unobtainable, is a biennial or annual, or is grown rather easily. It is a lot easier to collect a few specimens from your locality, and obtain desirable plants which do not grow in your area from dealers. A plant which will not survive transplant when in bloom will move with utmost ease when dormant. So place little flags on the plants you want and come back later. New plants will soon replace what you have collected if you fill in and cover the soil. If you take no more than a couple plants, the station is safe till the bulldozer arrives, and a collection of wildflowers in cultivation can restock the wild following depredation. I wonder if anyone would care to engage in a plant exchange, agricultural regulations notwithstanding.

The very best wildflower dealer I know of is Mr. Paul Leslie, 30 Summer Street, Methuen, Mass. He has obtained his entire stock by growing it from seed, without removing one specimen from the wild, which is more than I can say for myself. He also digs his plants from the ground the day he sends them to you, whereas some others use cold storage facilities. He is also more knowledgeable and takes more professional pride in his work than some others. Catalog 25¢. Also good (and less expensive) sources of plants are C. Robbins' Gardens of the Blue Ridge, Ashford, N.C. and The Three Laurels, Marshall, N.C. Although many of their plants are nursery-grown, both of these dealers sell plants collected directly from the wild. Catalogs free.

There are three firms which might be of interest to you because they offer plants which are simply not obtainable in the U.S.A. I recommend Sutton & Sons, Limited, Reading, England for vegetable seeds, Thompson and Morgan, Ipswich, Ltd., Ipswich, England for flower seeds, and C. J. van Tubergen, n.v., Zwanenburg Nurseries, Box 116, Koninginneweg 86, Haarlem, Holland, for bulbs. The last-mentioned are wholesalers, and charge 50% extra on orders under $100. Also don't let them airmail something which doesn't need it, and place your order well in advance. You will obtain superior bulbs by ordering from them, however. I wish some people in New Mexico would get together and grow their Onco-cyclus and Regelia series of Iris species; they are of unique beauty but require a hot, dry summer I cannot provide.

All three offer free catalogues.

Donald Hackenberry
Reedsville, Pa.

The Outdoorsman wrinkled his brow and thought about that as he spread ketchup on the remnants of his steak. "The nation is America," he said. "What the country is is all the land, and the rivers and things."

D.R. had stopped eating altogether. Leaning toward the Outdoorsman, and emphasizing with his fork, he said, "Do you mean you don't think America and the country are the same thing?"

"Of course not," said the Outdoorsman. "Ain't you ever read any history?"

"I've read history," said Estelle.

The Lone Outdoorsman swallowed some more steak and went on as if Estelle hadn't said anything. "Now you take these people on the wagon train. They're traveling across the country, right?"

"Right," said D.R.

"Okay. They're traveling across the country, but they're not traveling across America. Because the country where they're traveling hasn't been taken into the nation yet, if you see what I mean. There's no statehood there on the plains yet, therefore that country they're in isn't part of America. Now if where they are was a state, say Kansas, or South Dakota, then you could say they're traveling across America. But since they're not, why then thry're traveling cross-country."

"So you mean the people on Westward, Westward are not traveling in America, but just traveling in the country, because America and the country are two different things."

"Something like that. America, you see, is yet to come on Westward, Westward. Of course by now it has come. Westward, Westward's just a story, don't you see. It's about something that's been over a long time. I mean, the westward movement is something my grandfather helped do. Him and the others took the country, and turned it into America, if you see what I mean."

"Well, I don't, actually," said Divine Right.

The Lone Outdoorsman chewed the last of his steak, and sopped up the gravy with a piece of bread. "Well," he said. "You're young yet. You will one of these days."

TOM GINSBERG'S I CHING

By the time the Outdoorsman and his guests had finished their steaks and cleaned the table off for dessert, the wagon train had been surrounded by about a thousand Indians, and Tom Ginsberg had been wounded twice. He could still shoot a pistol but the lady wagon driver had to load for him. She loaded while he shot and he shot while she loaded, and the bodies made a little border around the circled wagons. Now and then the camera panned around the circle and showed other people firing at the Indians. But it was clear that the outcome of the battle really depended on how well Tom and his lady friend did with their guns. And in spite of the stack of bodies beyond the wagons, you could tell by the desperate expressions on their faces that they didn't think they were doing very well.

"Poor old Tom looks sort of undecided, don't he?" said the Outdoorsman.

Estelle laughed. "Maybe he ought to throw the I Ching," she said.

D.R. leaped to his feet. "Perfect!" he yelled. "Perfect!"

The Outdoorsman asked what was perfect but D.R. was moving too fast to answer. He bolted past Estelle, stumbled out of the camper and ran through the dark to his own campsite where Urge was patiently waiting. Half a minute later he was back in the Outdoorsman's camper, carrying his battered, leather-covered copy of the I Ching.

"What are you doing?" asked the Outdoorsman.

"We're throwing Tom Ginsberg's I Ching," said D.R.

"What's an I Ching?"

"Never mind," said D.R. "Just toss these coins."

Quickly they tossed the coins, two times each, and Estelle drew the hexagram.

Chien.

Obstruction.

Trouble.

"Uh oh," said D.R. "It looks heavy."

Indeed it did. Nearly everybody in the wagon train was dead now except Tom and the lady. Indians had penetrated the inner circle and were systematically scalping the slain white folks while still other Indians battled the remaining survivors.

D.R. began to read Tom's Ching aloud: "The hexagram pictures a dangerous abyss lying before us and a steep, inaccessible mountain rising behind us. We are surrounded by obstacles."

As D.R. said that, an arrow pierced the lady wagon driver's heart.

"Difficulties and obstructions throw a man back upon himself," D.R. went on. "While the inferior man seeks to put the blame on other persons, bewailing his fate, the superior man seeks the error within himself, and through this introspection the external obstacle becomes for him an occasion for inner enrichment and education."

The screen was filled with the face of a hideous savage, advancing on Tom with tomahawk upraised. Tom shot him with his pistol but instantly two more savages appeared, armed with knives and tomahawks.

"When threatened with danger," D.R. read, "one should not strive blindly to go ahead, for this only leads to complications. The correct thing is, on the contrary, to retreat for the time being, not in order to give up the struggle but to await the right moment for action."

"Retreat, hell!" shouted the Outdoorsman. "Stand your ground, Tom. Die with your goddamn boots on!"

The camera closed in on Tom's tense face. In spite of the blood oozing from the gash in his forehead his eyes blazed with courage and determination. Gritting his teeth, Tom struggled to get to his feet. Leaning against the wagon wheel, his left arm dangling useless at his side, Tom raised his right arm and pointed his pistol at the advancing Indians. Then he disappeared and was replaced on the screen by fifteen Dalmatian pups gorging themselves on Fido Dog Food.

Herbs

I would like to turn people on to herbs. You can grow herbs in the corner of your vegetable garden, in a patio box, in a window, in a window, in a flowerpot. You can be an agriculturalist with only a few square feet of ground and prepare yourself for that land you ultimately hope to gain part or all your livelihood from. You can use your herbs for flavoring cooking, for salads, for making things smell nice, for dying cloth, for curing yourself of all sorts of illnesses, for making magic and casting spells, for alchemy. And herbs are beautiful, simple plants, most of which grow and flourish even in the poorest soil. You can even grow your own I Ching yarrow stalks.

I haven't investigated many herb books as yet; maybe some of the other readers can recommend some good ones; anyway, better to start with the herbs and get to the books later. One interesting one I've seen is NATURE'S MEDICINES—The Folklore, Romance, and Value of Herbal Remedies really lays down a lot of lore. Another good one is HANDBOOK ON HERBS published by the Brooklyn Botanical Gardens, Brooklyn, N.Y., which is enough to get you hooked on herbs all by itself. The Brooklyn Botanical Garden, by the way, publishes a wonderful bunch of books on all phases of gardening, all of which sell for either $1.00 or $1.50 (the herb one is $1.00) Free list available from them.

As an example of herb lore, someone told me that when he gets a bad case of poison oak, he uses a leaf of comfrey to scratch with, rubbing it freely over the itchy spot, and wipes out the poison oak in a few days. However, he says, if you use a comfrey poultice on an infection or wound, don't bind the leaf directly to the skin, as it's so effective in promoting the growth of epithelial cells that it may actually grow to the skin. The Nature's Medicines book has a lot more rap on comfrey.

A problem with growing herbs is that there are seldom more than a few of the most common types in the local nursery. So I talked to someone who is really into herbs, spices, gardening, essential oils, gourds, and all that useful vegetable stuff, and asked her where to get herbs, etc. She sent me a list of addresses, I sent for their catalogs, and the following is all about that.

Nature's Herb Co., 281 Ellis St., San Francisco, Calif. They sell dried herbs and spices by the pound, ingredients for potpourris and sachets, prepared herbal remedies, and essential oils. Also various herbal tea mixtures for both enjoyment and medicine.

Herb Products Co., 11012 Magnolia Blvd., North Hollywood, Calif. 91601. Much the same as the above, with the addition of some far-out cosmetics. They are very much into ginseng, and can tell you something about that. Their prices tend to be a little higher than Nature's Herb Co., but each has things that the other doesn't

Indiana Botanic Gardens, Inc., Hammond, Indiana 46325. They will send you a very far-out catalog and an herbalists almanac, which will tell you the best days to plant, what the weather will be like for all of 1969, and other useful tidbits. They sell teas and medicines, herbs and spices, seeds, beans, nuts, gums, resins, oils, vitamins, cosmetics, perfumes, formulas to cure liquor addiction. tobacco habit, and tobacco chewing, and tell you what grateful users write about rectal ointment no. 103.

Tradewinds Candle Shop, 1224A Fillmore Street, San Francisco, Calif. I throw this in just for the hell of it. They sell candles, but their scene is magic. I was last there several years ago, and it appeared to be an old established business, run by an elderly white-haired man who looked like a Suth'n Cuhn'l, and his wife, who looked like a Haitian voodoo lady. They sell the usual oils, powders, etc., but I think they may also handle other things they don't list in their catalog. They will also give intelligent advice on how to change your luck, make money, make your love love you, etc. They make no outrageous claims, but will answer questions. I tried them once, and their advice worked, but I don't think I'd do it again. Handle at your own risk.

None of the above deal in things for gardening.

Meadowbrook Herb Garden, Wyoming, Rhode Island 02898. Their catalog is a beautiful piece of printing and caligraphy. They don't ship live plants, but will deliver if you live within forty miles. They sell herb teas and tea herbs, spices, seeds, toiletries, books, supplies, and miscellany. They seem to be into Anthroposophy and something called Bio-Dynamics.

Carl Odom, Pinola, Mississippi 39149. He will send you a very down-home two-sheet catalog on newsprint, telling you all the groovy things you can do with gourds. I won't say anything about it and ruin it for you. He also sells vegetable and flower seeds.

Nichols Garden Nursery, 1190 North Pacific Hwy., Albany, Oregon 97321. They will send you an incredible 44-page catalog that will require every ounce of your willpower to keep you from making a hundred dollar order on the spot. Seeds for vegetables and herbs, growing plants, dried herbs and spices, mushroom spores, wild-flower seeds, house plants, gourd seeds, books, supplies, brewing and winemaking stuff, and all sorts of other oddments. They specialize in the unusual, like very large, very tasty, or very different vegetables. Their catalog is mimeographed because, they say, "modern, high speed presses could probably do the job better, but we believe that people are more important than machines, and for that reason will continue to resist automation." I bought some live plants from them, they arrived in good condition and are now growing well.

Woodland Acres Nursery, Crivitz, Wisconsin 54114. They specialise in wildflowers and ferns, many of which have herbal uses, and sell mostly live plants.

Greene Herb Garden, Greene, Rhode Island. Getting their catalog is like hearing from your nice aunt that lives in the country. Full of news about their family, spring in New England, and gentle conversation about herbs. They sell only herb seeds and bulbs.

Vita Green Farms, P.O. Box 878, Vista, California 92083. They sell vegetable and herb seeds, vegetables, fruits, and preserves. If you want organic produce and are not near a good health food store, their vegetables might be worth investigating. Expensive, but I'm sure they're excellent. All vegetables are organically grown, seeds are "un-treated, natural, old-fashioned, un-hybridized, un-crossed." Their tone is a little stern, but anyone who raises organic produce for a living is bound to be a fanatic and a crusader. I sent for some of their seeds, and they came virtually before I put the letter in the mailbox. They are also pure water maniacs, and sell various types of home filtering units.

Walnut Acres, Penns Creek, Pennsylvania 17862. They sell nothing for gardening, but have the most complete selection of organic foods and related products I've ever seen, including every conceivable organic grain. Prices are high, but they have all sorts of stuff I've never seen before. They also seem like very beautiful people who love and are concerned about the world around them.

That's all for now. I'll keep in touch. Keep up the good work.

Love,
Roland

A Modern Herbal

This is far and away the most complete (and expensive) information on herbs.

"The medicinal, culinary, cosmetic and economic properties, cultivation and folk-lore of herbs, grasses, fungi, shrubs and trees with all their modern scientific uses . . . "

Over 160 useful plants are listed—the history, description, constituents, medicinal uses, preparation, dosages, and even recipes of each.

It is a two-volume set, with a meticulously complete index of the common names of the plants, followed by a service index of Latin binomials.

[Reviewed by Alan Schmidt]

A Modern Herbal
Mrs. M. Grieve, F.R.H.S.
1931 . . . 1967; 2 Vols, 888 pp.

$10.00 postpaid

from:
Dover Publications
180 Varick St.
New York, N.Y. 10014

or WHOLE EARTH CATALOG

Comfrey leaves are of much value as an external remedy, both in the form of fomentations, for sprains, swellings and bruises, and as a poultice, to severe cuts, to promote suppuration of boils and abscesses, and gangrenous and ill-conditioned ulcers. The whole plant, beaten to a cataplasm and applied hot as a poultice, has always been deemed excellent for soothing pain in any tender, inflamed or suppurating part. It was formerly applied to raw, indolent ulcers as a glutinous astringent. It is useful in any kind of inflammatory swelling.

. . . The reputation of Comfrey as a vulnerary has been considered due partly to the fact of its reducing the swollen parts in the immediate neighbourhood of fractures, causing union to take place with greater facility.

Nettle.

It is a strange fact that the juice of the Nettle proves an antidote for its own sting, and being applied will afford instant relief.

From a culinary point of view the Nettle has an old reputation. It is one of the few wild plants still gathered each spring by country-folk as a pot-herb. It makes a healthy vegetable, easy of digestion.

The young tops should be gathered when 6 to 8 inches high. Gloves should be worn to protect the hands when picking them. They should be washed in running water with a stick and then put into a saucepan, dripping, without any added water, and cooked with the lid on for about 20 minutes . . . they thus form a refreshing dish of spring greens,which is slightly laxative. In autumn, however, Nettles are hurtful, the leaves being gritty from the abundance of crystals they contain.

An efficient hair tonic can be prepared from the Nettle: simmer a handful of young Nettles in a quart of water for 2 hours, strain and bottle when cold. Well saturate the scalp with the lotion every other night. This prevents the hair falling and renders it soft and glossy.

The Herb Grower

A quarterly for grow-your-own herbalists with articles by same, plus herb prints, recipes, herb history and book reviews.

—HH

The Herb Grower

$5.00 per year (quarterly)

from:
The Herb Grower
Falls Village, Connecticutt 06031

Stalking the Healthful Herbs

Euell Gibbons (more on p. 82) has maximum information on finding herbs, and cheerfulness to match.

—SB

Stalking the Healthful Herbs
Euell Gibbons
1966; 295 pp.

$2.95 f.o.b., Long Island City, N.Y.

from:
David McKay Company, Inc.
750 Third Ave.
New York, N.Y. 10017

or WHOLE EARTH CATALOG

GINSENG

Some more herb suppliers:

Rocky Hollow Herb Farm
Lake Wallkill Rd.
Sussex, New Jersey

$1.50 for catalog

Capriland's Herb Farm
Silver St.
Coventry, Connecticut 06238

Mail Box Seeds
Shirley Morgan
2042 Encinal Ave.
Alameda, California 94501

herb seeds

Greene Herb Gardens
Greene, Rhode Island 02827

Common and rare herbs and herb seeds. From Borage and Chervil to Lovage, Sweet Cicely and Woad. Seed packets, three for $1.00. Brochure.

Meadowbrook Herb Garden
Wyoming, Rhode Island 02898

Organically grown herbs and seeds. Teas, seaweed meal and herb books. Catalog $.50.

Oak Ridge Herb Farm
R.R. #1, Box 461
Alton, Illinois 62002

Also completely organic. Rare herb seeds, plants, roots and bulbs. Teas. Free catalog.

Northwestern Processing Company
217 North Broadway
Milwaukee, Wisconsin 53202

A young company just getting into the mail order business. High quality spices, reasonable prices, coffees, teas, nuts, and herbs. They'll do their best to get rare herbs and products you can't find anywhere else. They also have a wholesale outlet, **Kettle Creek Company.** *Free catalog.*

Wide World of Herbs
11 St. Catherine Street East
Montreal, Canada

Besides being an excellent source of plants for dyes (see p. 98) they stock over 2000 different herbs, roots, barks, gums, berries and seeds. Canadian-grown Ginseng Root. Free catalog.

D. Napier & Sons
17, 18 Bristo Place
& 1 Teviot Place
Edinburgh EH1, SCOTLAND

Low low prices and some unusual herbs and herbal products, like Barberry bark powder, Dandelion coffee, Slippery Elm Bark Soap and Unicorn Root Powder. Free brochure.

[Suggested by Dr. Duncan Pepper]

Nichols Herb & Rare Seeds

Nichols and his wife who seem to have just popped out of the Black Forest. The whole place is one room of cardboard boxes and pigeon holed walls and odd notes tacked up all over the place. He is basically a mail order business and sells wine making supplies, beer making supplies (and ingredients) and rare seeds and herbs and plants and all sorts of weird stuff. He also printed his own recipe book which is fantastic for sourdough stuff, wine & beer making, and baking with malt syrup and hops also lots of recipes for yeast.

They are really beautiful old souls who send you home with extra goodies that you are to try and accept as gifts.

Needless to say—they're organic. They have a fairly complete catalog that they will send and their seeds really are superior.

[Reviewed by Mrs. K.E. Sturdevant]

Nichols Garden Nursery
1190 N. Pacific Hwy.
Albany, Oregon 97321

Growhole

A Growhole is a big hotbed. You cut a level trench back into a south-facing slope, cover it with two layers of clear vinyl, and grow vegetables all winter. A poster describing all this by Steve Baer, Day Charoudi, and Steve Durkee costs 50¢ from:

—SB

Biotechnic Press
P.O. Box 26091
Albuquerque, N.M. 87125

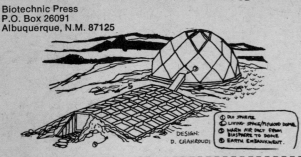

DESIGN:
D. CHAHROUDI

INTERIOR DURING 1st PLANTING

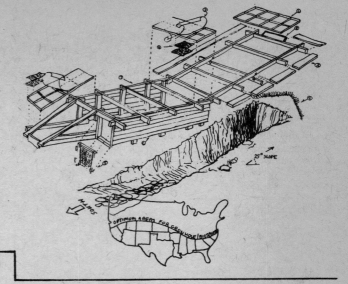

Technology Review

This space in the earlier editions listed an article on food supply research in the March '69 Technology Review, which the staff at MIT MIT reports has now been completely sold out to the Catalog readers who preceeded you. A year's subscription brings eight issues reporting developments in subjects such as the origins of planets, marine pollution control, earthquake-resistant structures, corporate social responsibility, parapsychology and generally an imaginative potpourri of applied technology, well written and documented.

—AF

Technology Review
Room E19-430 $1.50 per copy
MIT $10.00 per year
Cambridge, Mass. 02139 $11.00 Canada & foreign countries

Indoor Greenery

For those who are still in the city but are attempting an indoor green revolution to freshen air, eyes and soul, may I suggest the following sources of info., plants and materials:

The really best book on "how to" is Ernesta Drinker Ballard's *A Garden in Your House*, Harper & Row. An excellent & unusual feature of this book is that it contains lists of plants especially suited to specific indoor environments.

Indoor plants by mail:
Logee's Greenhouses, Danielson, Conn.
Catalog $1.00. 34 p of Begonias, 9 of geraniums, lots of herbs.

Merry Gardens, Camden, Maine 04843
Price list $.25. Offers a wide variety of plants—and specially wide variety of fuschia, begonias, scented geraniums and herbs. They also sell herb seeds.

Julius Roehrs Co., Rutherford, N.J. 07070
Exotic Plant Collectors list $.25
These are really groovy & unusual plants from one of the largest greenhouse complexes in the US. It's worth a visit if you're anywhere near NYC——NJ side of Lincoln Tunnel on Patterson Ave. This is the only source of "specimen size" plants by mail I know of. Most deal in plants in 2"-3" pots which are easiest to ship—— and relatively inexpensive to acquire.

Materials & supplies——particularly for growing things under lights
House Plant Corner
PO Box 810
Oxford, Maryland 21654
Catalog $.25 the 1st time.

Peace & Strength

Libby J. Goldstein
Philadelphia, PA

Algae

I notice in your September 1970 $1 WEC, p. 17, you refer to some algae production experiments. Ideas of this sort have been around for quite a while. Most of them date back to Vannevar Bush, who proposed in the mid-1940's that the U.S. should "grow algae and feed the world." In 1953, the Carnegie Institution of Washington, D.C. issued their Publication No. 600, "Algal Culture from Laboratory to Pilot Plant." This book has been reprinted several times, most recently in 1964. Price is about $5.00. The Japanese microbiologists have also been very active in this field. There is a French company researching the area, but they regard both their organism and their process as proprietary, and refuse to release any detailed information (a violation of scientific etiquette). However, the real pro's in this business at present are the Czechs. In the Annual Reports of the Laboratory of Algology of the Institute of Microbiology of the Czechoslovak Academy of Science for 1966, 67, and 68 (issued at Trebon, Czechoslovakia), they describe a method of producing large quantities of algae, outdoors, using natural illumination plus artificial nutrients and pumping facilities. One clever adaptation, not previously used so far as I know, is that they let the algal suspension flow down over large inclined sheets of glass, with interposed barriers to increase flow turbulence and promote mixing. The algae are exposed to sunlight. In the winter, when it gets cold they shut down the algae operation and use the sheets of glass as the top of a greenhouse, and grow ordinary plants inside the space used in summer for pumping and storage. These Annual Reports were free at last notice, but their budget is minimal; and people shouldn't request them unless they can really use them. Much of the information is detailed and highly technical, not to be skimmed over in a weekend

Pat Patterson
Austin, Texas

Hydroponics

*growing things without soil . . .
remember the avacado pit suspended on four toothpicks over the glass of water on the top of the refrigerator? or half a potato scumming away in some dark corner? that all has a name. here's a complete set of short booklets on hydroponics.*

—jd

Hydroponics is the opposite of Land Use. Ever since Skinner's Walden Two it's been with us in the pop culture as some kind of solution to things. And if you're living in a Soleri city, or floating Fullertown, or mountaintop, or moon, it might well be.

—SB

Soilless Culture
T. Saunby
1953; 104 pp.

$4.95 postpaid

from:
Transatlantic Arts, Inc.
North Village Green
Levittown, N.Y. 11756

Hydroculture, inc.

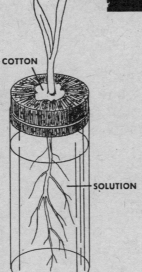

COTTON

SOLUTION

A simple method for growing plants in solution.

Hydroponics as a Hobby

$.25

from:
University of Illinois
College of Agriculture
Extension Service in Agriculture
and Home Economics
Urbana, Illinois 61801

Hydroponics supplies, chemicals, hardware, information from:

Hydroculture, Inc.
P.O. Box 1655
Glendale, Arizona 85301

Hydroponic Chemical Co.
Box 4300
Copley, Ohio 44321

The Hydroponics Company
P.O. Box 3215
Little Rock, Arkansas 72203

Hydroponics Corp. of America
745 5th Ave.
New York, N.Y. 10022

J. W. Davis Co.
Box 768
Bettendorf, Iowa 52722

Flagler Hydroponics
3255 W. Flagler St.
Miami, Florida 33100

Kelley Clark, Inc.
411 North Lincoln
Loveland, CA 80537

Pan American Hydroponics, Inc.
Dallas, Texas 75200

Hydroponic Culture of Vegetable Crops
M.E. Marvel

free   [Suggested by James J. Berryhill]

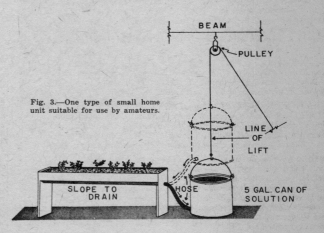

Fig. 3.—One type of small home unit suitable for use by amateurs.

BEAM
PULLEY
LINE OF LIFT
SLOPE TO DRAIN
HOSE
5 GAL. CAN OF SOLUTION

DEPARTURE

If D.R. had done what he wanted to do right then he would have leaned across the table and turned the television off.

If he had done that, and the Outdoorsman had then done what he wanted to do, he would have leaned across and turned the TV on again, which very likely would have resulted in an argument between him and D.R. about the difference between stupidity and heroism.

If there's to be a fight, D.R. reasoned, the courageous thing is to retreat before it begins, as the I Ching so wisely advises.

And so D.R. stood up, held out his hand to the Lone Outdoorsman and announced that he and Estelle were leaving.

The Lone Outdoorsman took D.R.'s hand.

Then, realizing what D.R. had actually said, let it go again and began pleading with them to stay for dessert and the rest of Westward, Westward.

No, said D.R. We must continue our journey to the east. We have to be in St. Louis by Tuesday in order to meet Eddie. We have a long, hard trip ahead. But we sure thank you for the food and the hospitality.

Estelle told the Outdoorsman thanks, and goodbye, and stepped out the door, with D.R. close behind.

From the ground D.R. turned to shake hands with the Outdoorsman again, and again to tell him thanks for the food and the very pleasant evening.

The Outdoorsman said that they certainly were welcome, and urged them again to stay on for dessert and the rest of Westward, Westward.

But D.R. said no, they had to be on their way, that it was going to be hard to make St. Louis by Tuesday as it was.

The Outdoorsman said he understood, and walked with them to their bus.

As D.R. and Estelle drove away the Lone Outdoorsman stood in the empty campsite waving, until Urge's red taillights were swallowed by the night.

Then he went back to his camper and wrote this letter to his wife, while drinking a beer:

Dear Lucille,

How are you? Fine I hope. I'm having a good time in the big woods. Ha. There are not as many people at Eagle Rock this year as last year but at Pine Point there were more people this year than last year. Rig doing fine. Tell Charley he was wrong in all his predictions of mechanical failure and he owes me five bucks. Ha. Food good tho not like you can cook it. Ha. Met a young traveling couple here at Eagle Rock, nice kids. Lucille you take care of yourself call Wanda any time necessary, you be sure to call her if you have to. I'll be home a week from Monday.

Sincerely yours,

William F. Dixon

Nasco Farm and Ranch Catalog

part of the trouble with going back to the farm, just like going into a new job or hobby, is that the technology of gadgets must be looked into, so the new farmer will be able to tell whether he really needs a master artificial vagina, liquid semen refrigerator, and trans-jector electronic ejaculator, or whether he is going to believe in a little more organic process.

the nasco catalog sits smack in the middle of farmy equipment consciousness, and carries all of the above mentioned goodies. but, nasco also carries the more staple farm tools, like crank forges, seed sowers, cant hooks, load binders, pulaskis, lopping shears, and post hole diggers.

if you are a windowshopping farmer, or farmy window-shopper, write for the catalog. prices look reasonable.

—jd

Nasco Catalog

Free

from:
Nasco,
Fort Atkinson, Wisconsin 53538

or

Nasco-West
Box 3837
Modesto, California 95352

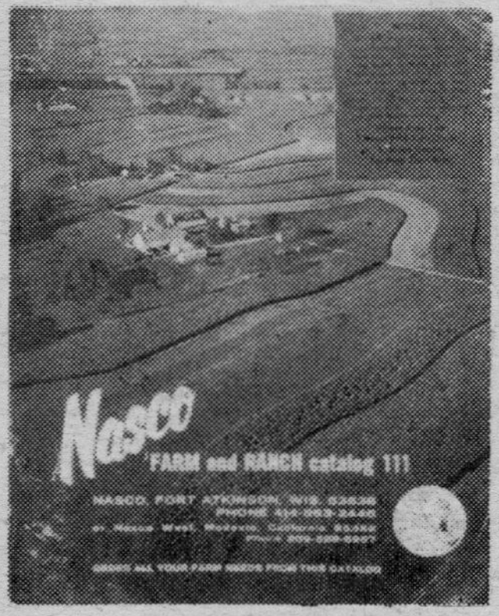

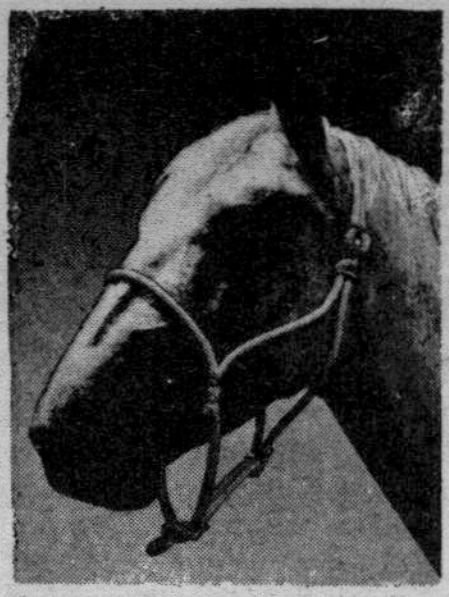

9. **GOLDIE HALTER**
A most beautiful halter . . . one that really sets the pace and rightfully belongs on the Champion.

Brilliant white polypropylene with gold threads woven into it and all gold hardware. Wool nose band. Nothing else like it on the market, and you'll want to be the first to have it.

Like all other Johnson halters, top quality and design have gone into this outstanding and unusual horse halter. Sh. wt. 1½ lbs.

C2443N-21-12 For 1100 lb. to 1500 lb. horse . . No longer available
C2444N-22-12 For 800 lb. to 1100 lb. horse 5.95

FARM POND HARVEST
This unique publication is exactly what pond owners and farmers interested in a pond have been looking for . . . a magazine dedicated to farm pond planning and construction — pond management — fishing and harvesting. Here are some typical articles from past issues: Build a Better Fish Pond; Stocking Private Ponds; Is Your Pond Clear or Muddy?; Trout in Farm and Ranch Ponds; How to Control Weeds in Your Fish Pond; The Mute Swan and Your Pond; The Raising of Channel Catfish in Cages.

Each and every pond requires management, and to be managed properly, the owner must be aware of the principles involved. Farm Pond Harvest will help you to achieve a well managed and productive body of water . . . and keep you up to date on all of the latest news pertaining to farm ponds. If you own a farm pond, plan to build one in the future, or contemplate entering the fish-farming market, you won't want to be without Farm Pond Harvest.

Z4927N 1 year subscription (4 issues) $3.00
Z4928N 2 year subscription (8 issues) 5.00

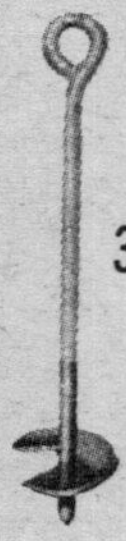

3.

3. **EARTH ANCHORS**
Constructed of high strength steel. Plate is arc welded to rod. Formed loop is welded shut. Screw in to install. Makes effective temporary or permanent anchor for many applications.

ANCHOR WITH 3" DIAMETER PLATE. Length 30", will hold 1,000 lbs. Sh. wt. 1½ lbs.
E234N-330 Each . . . No longer available 12 or more, each . . . No longer available

ANCHOR WITH 4" DIAMETER PLATE. Length 48", will hold 1,500 lbs. Sh. wt. 4 lbs.
E233N-448 Each . . . No longer available 12 or more, each . . No longer available

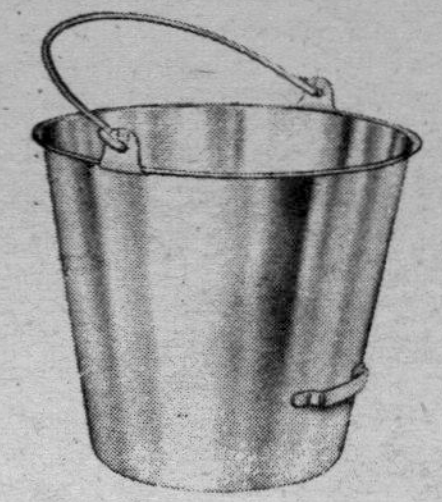

1. **STAINLESS STEEL UTILITY OR DAIRY PAILS**
With Tilting Handle
Tapered design for easier pouring. Made of extra heavy, high polished, stainless steel with thick, flat sanitary rim. Smooth and seamless. — no crevices to catch dirt. Handy tilting handle. Extra thick bottom.

16 QT. CAPACITY. 12¾" top dia., 7⅞" base dia., 12⅛" deep. Sh. wt. 5¾ lbs.
B291N-5816-1 . . . . $22.85

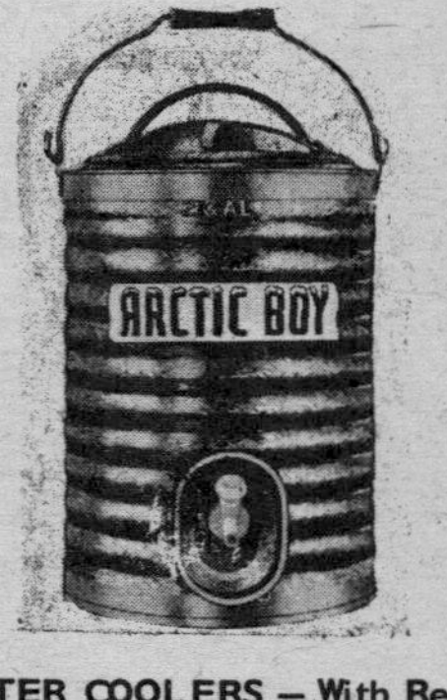

1. **PORTABLE WATER COOLERS — With Recessed Spigot**
Now deluxe Arctic Boy portable water coolers feature two exclusives!

Hot-dipped inset is galvanized after forming to eliminate chips and cracks in zinc coating. Galvanizing after forming fills lap joint completely, eliminates possible leaks, corrosion points and dirt catchers! Smooth, gleaming interior can be cleaned in seconds! No rough edges, no exposed metal, bottom rounded for free cleaning access!

Impregnite 90 — plastic on steel interior. Permanent sanitary bond. No odor — no taste.

They're made of quality materials throughout to take rugged abuse in the field . . . everywhere men work. Ideal for hunters and fishermen, too.

M1013N 2 gal. size. Sh. wt. 8¼ lbs. . . . . . . No longer available
M1014N 5 gal. size. Sh. wt. 14 lbs. 5 oz. . . No longer available

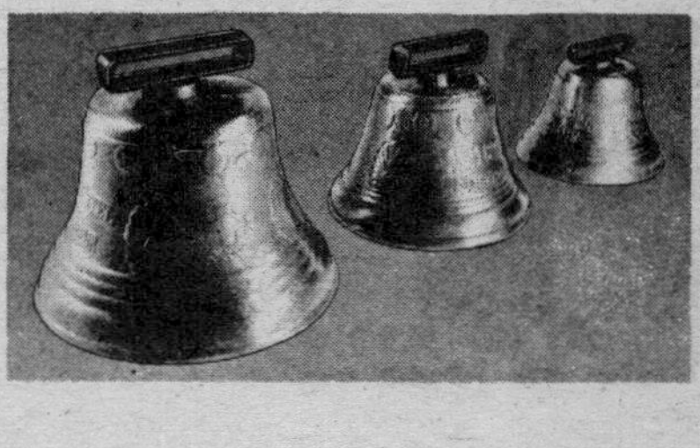

2. **TUNED IN HARMONY — SWISS SHEEP AND COW BELLS**
Very best Swiss bell metal. The kind of pleasure they give is what makes farm life really worthwhile. You can afford their small luxury. Set of three cow bells size 4", 5" and 6¼". Sheep bells are 2⅜", 3" and 3-5/16". Complete with handsome leather straps. Sh. wt. 8 lbs and 4 lbs.

C132N-A Cow Bells. Set of 3 . . . . $44.00
C167N-D Sheep Bells. Set of 3 . . . . 16.50

Agricultural Extension Services

Each of the 50 states provides agricultural advice and services through county or area offices of their Agricultural Extension Service. These services are twofold:

1. Farm Advisors, extension agents, or county agents—depending on which state you live in, staff personnel under one of the above names are available for consultation or house calls in any area or agriculture or related fields such as turf care, home gardening, livestock, pest or rodent control and soil & water conservation to name a few. Most staffs usually also have a home economist.

2. Publications—a wide range of publications are also available through the AES or the U.S. Dept. of Agriculture. Some are for sale, but most are free. They are non-scientific & are written for the lay person. These publications cover a wide range of subjects of interest in commercial agriculture. home gardening or homemaking. Most states will have a catalog of their publications, such as the two from the University of California. You may either order publications by mail or pick them up directly at the county office. If you have specific questions, it is often best to pick up brochures at the county office so that you may consult the farm adviser at the same time. Agricultural Extension Offices are normally listed in the phone book under the county listings.

[Reviewed by Ed Johnson]

Agricultural Publications

free

from:
local county office

Agricultural Publications

Free information on farming, livestock, forestry, soil science, etc. On general requests not more than one copy each of 10 publications is sent. Justification is required if you want more.

No longer available

The Farmer and Wildlife

A farm that encourages wildlife is much more of a self-balancing low-maintenance system than one without. Also it's less boring. Encouraging wildlife mostly consists of not discouraging it so much, like leaving your brushpiles instead of burning them, damming the gully instead of letting it erode, leaving a bit of woodlot instead of stripping the land.

—SB

The Farmer and Wildlife
Durward L. Allen
1949, 1969; 63 pp.

Free

from:
Wildlife Management Institute
Wire Bldg.
Washington, D.C. 20005

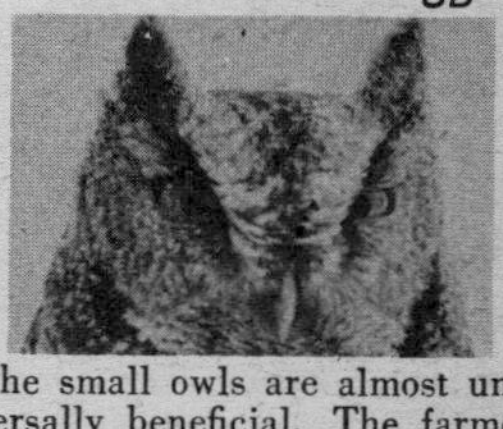

The small owls are almost universally beneficial. The farmer will do well to protect them.

A grazed woodlot is neither a good woodlot nor a good pasture. The farmer will profit by making it one or the other.

•

Formerly it was assumed that brushy fence lines might harbor crop pests. More recently we have learned that they are much more likely to serve as cover for birds, predaceous and parasitic insects, and insect-eating small mammals. An Ohio biologist whose work was mentioned before showed that there were 32 times as many songbirds in brushy fencerows as in open cropfields. Such field borders also contained 60 times as many aphid-destroying lady beetles as sodded fence lines.

In addition to songbirds, a strip of brush between fields is attractive to skunks, weasels, and birds of prey which feed upon the meadow mice in hay and grain fields. The small animals that live in shrubby fencerows are for the most part either beneficial, like the shrews, or of kinds like the woodmouse which do not commonly destroy crops. Sodded field borders are likely to harbor heavy populations of destructive meadow mice, which spread into cropfields. These animals do not live in thick brush.

Soil Conservation Service—USDA

Most rural areas of the US are incorporated into Agricultural Conservation Districts. This situation offers two services you should be aware of.

1. Soil conservationist & engineers—

The services of these people are available to you through your local district office. If you need a livestock pond or watering sites for wild game, they'll do the engineering for you. They can also help out if your basement floods, your soil is blowing away or the creek is eating away the bank under your pad.

2. Agricultural Credit & Production—

ACP, as this program is referred to, is a cost sharing program for land owners or users sponsored by the US Dept. of Agriculture. If you are located within a conservation district, you may be eligible for government money to help you develop springs, seed pasture, build fences or stabilize stream banks.

[Reviewed by Ed Johnson]

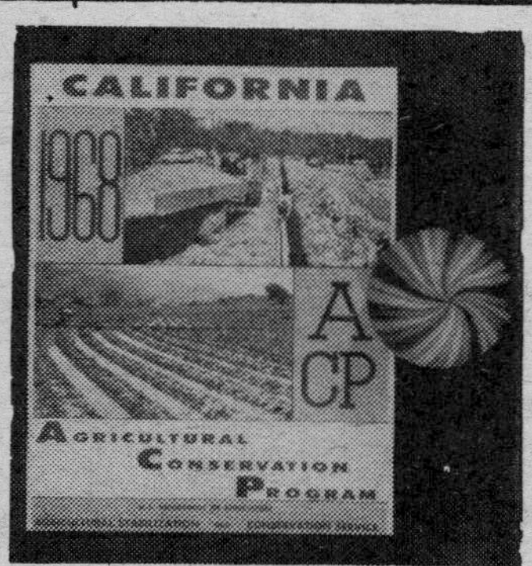

For information, write:
In California:
California ASCS State Office
2020 Milvia Street
Berkeley, CA 94704
Other states:
look in phone book under U. S. Govt. . . . Agriculture, Dept. of, Soil Conservation District.

The Negev

If you're into really dry farming, you can talk to Hopis or to Israelis. The Hopis haven't done a book yet. These Israelis have, and it's fascinating business, involving detailed desert study, reconstruction of ancient agricultural techniques—terraces, cisterns, measuring weirs, plant adaptation—the careful life with minimum water.

—SB

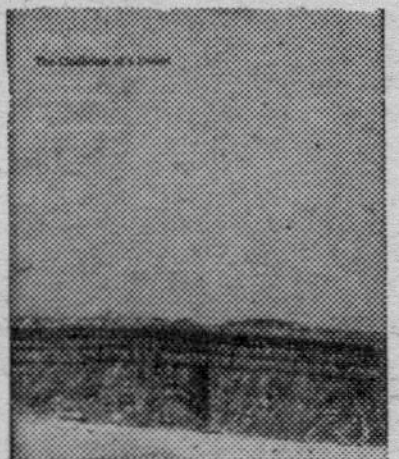

The Negev—The Challenge of a Desert
Michael Evenari, Leslie Shanan, Naphtali Tadmor
1971; 345 pp.

$15.00 postpaid

from:
Harvard University Press
79 Garden St.
Cambridge, Mass. 02138

or WHOLE EARTH CATALOG

The native wild oats (*Avena sterilis*), once established, was shown to have extremely high yields under water spreading in fertilized seed beds—yields equaling those of seeded hay crops in a humid region. After satisfactory inoculation by symbiotic bacteria had been reached, several medick and vetch species developed and yielded well under conditions of runoff agriculture; their yields approached or surpassed that of the control oats and thus were as high as or higher than those of commonly used unirrigated forage crops in more humid areas.

•

It often happens that not the whole plant but only some of its branches die. Other branches retain just as much green photo-synthesizing matter as can be supplied with the available water and this suffices to keep a few branches alive. Sometimes in extremely dry localities in years of great drought only a single branch out of many survives in this way. During the following years the plants may slowly regenerate themselves from dormant renewal buds. This is a fascinating phenomenon which shows that, paradoxically, when death is partial it becomes a means of survival.

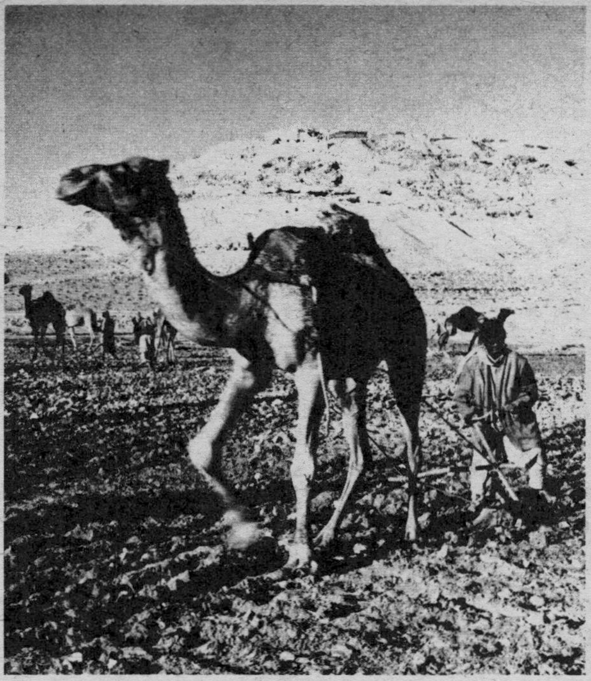

Cross section and ground plan of the cistern

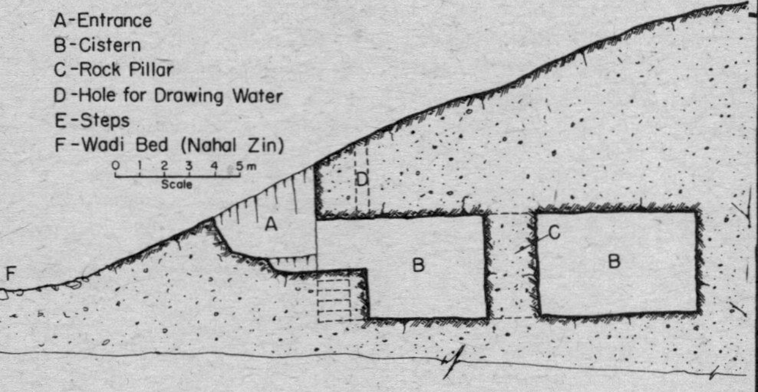

A New Technology for Dry Land Farming

India's efforts against recurrent famine have led them into sophisticated new farming techniques for marginal land. They're the only farmers I've ever heard talk about synergy.

—SB

A New Technology for Dry Land Farming
1970; 189 pp.

$1 plus shipping (about 1 lb)

from:
Ak Sherma
Indian Agricultural Research Institute
New Delhi 12
India

To cite two examples, deep ploughing has been recommended for dry areas. This practice, however, is important only in areas where the subsoil has a highly compacted zone, thereby preventing the infiltration and movement of water and penetration of roots. Hence, before a particular tillage practice is advocated, a detailed study of soil structure would be essential. Also, it is obvious that if deep ploughing using suitable iron ploughs is to be adopted, the bullocks in that area must be better-fed and made to gain the needed strength. Thus, if in 1971 it is proposed to introduce the practice of deep ploughing in a village, high-protein *bajra* fodder and other high-quality fodder crops should be introduced in 1970. Ignoring such interactions has often been in the past the cause of condemning some of the implements designed by our agricultural engineers.

•

Retention of rainfall as soil moisture mainly depends on the infiltration characteristics of the soil, time available to the surface water to infiltrate, and the moisture storage capacity of the soil. Studies at the I.A.R.I. have shown that infiltration rates could be significantly increased by improving the structure of the surface soil and by adopting suitable cultural practices. Cultural practices such as wheat-maize or wheat-*Sorghum* rotations, deep ploughing and incorporation of roots, stubbles and green stalks of cereal crops into the soil were found to be most beneficial in improving the structure of the top soil. Inclusion of a legume crop in the rotation would also considerably improve the structure of the surface layers.

Pruning Handbook

This booklet starts with a basic description of the way plants grow, lists pruning tools and their uses, and describes pruning systems for ornamental and fruit trees, berries and grapes, roses and vines.

[Suggested by Fred Richardson]

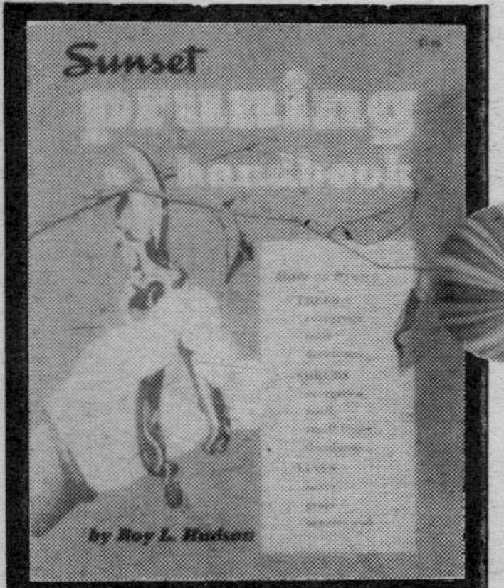

One way to learn the fundamentals of pruning is to study the mistakes that other gardeners make.

General objectives of pruning have to do with modifying the growth of the plants to adjust it to the conditions of the garden.

Pruning Handbook
Sunset Editors
1972; 96 pp

$1.95 postpaid

from:
Lane Magazine & Book Company
Menlo Park, CA 94025

or WHOLE EARTH CATALOG

Heavy pruning of the apricot is essential to insure regular fruit production. One-year old shoots produce a portion of the crop, but short-lived spurs carry the major portion. As these spurs are usually good for only three years, they must constantly be renewed. The tree, in suitable areas, is a very lush grower and a heavy bearer. Unless kept in severe check, it will rapidly become too large and will bear its fruit high in the tree where it cannot be thinned or picked easily. The lower spurs will be shaded out by the lush foliage and new ones will not form. In short, you would have a fine shade tree but a very unsatisfactory fruit tree. The necessary pruning for good fruit production does not always develop a graceful garden tree.

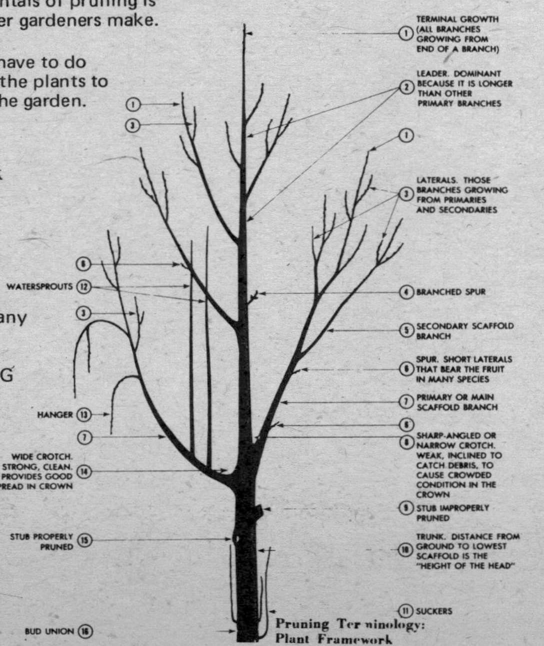

Pruning Terminology: Plant Framework

PART TWO

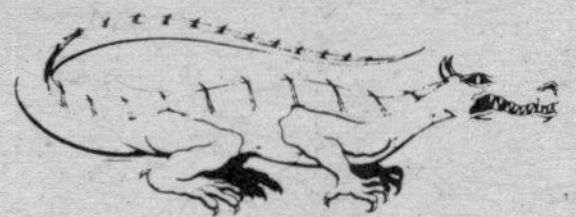

THE FISHER OF MEN

About two o'clock in the morning Divine Right and Estelle passed through a little town that was absolutely unlit except for a light shining on the front of a funeral home, and a neon sign in front of a church across the street that said, "Dope is the Only Answer. Surrender Now." Actually the sign said that Christ was the only answer, but somebody had crossed out "Christ" and with a crayon written the word "Dope" just above. It was crude lettering but the message was clear enough for D.R. to dig it, and he took three hundred micrograms of acid on the spot.

Half an hour later, the first messages from God began to float up through his soul. Feel good, God said. Feel what your eyes can see as smooth and soft and rounded. Let all the world around you sigh, let go and start to breathe. Let the steering wheel melt to bread dough and bake a donut in your hands. Guide Urge around the curves by leaning with your body, go with Urge as a sighing sleigh, riding high and far away, beyond the desert, behind the moon, you won't be coming back anytime soon.

An image of his grandfather chopping kindling flashed on the movie screen of his mind as Urge's headlights caught the gleam of animal eyes on the road ahead. D.R. blew the horn so hard and long it turned into a roar, then whooshed on out of hearing like a jet plane passing by. The plane became a bug that flew into his ear, but when he probed his finger punched on through and scratched his brain instead, causing sparks to fly out of his eyes and turn to dragonflies. The flies swarmed, flew apart all over the inside of the bus, then came together in a cloud of smoke above a burning world in front of D.R.'s eyes. Fire was everywhere. Urge's headlights were darts of flame, the center-strip down the highway was a stream of molten red. In every grate in every room of every old house he'd lived in fires hissed and licked and brooded like inflamed sick eyes of some old ancient man. Water, D.R. yelled, someone bring some water! He leaned and guided Urge from room to crowded room, swaying with his body steering Urge past people singing hymns on Sunday mornings as they warmed before the fire in grates in all the separate rooms. He rode into a kitchen where someone was making donuts in a coal stove. He wanted one, and took it, but his mother jerked it from him saying, "Honey, no, come on now, you'll have to let me drive."

D.R. tried to say no, but his tongue ignored his mind and babbled stupidly on its own like a baby's. He was crying like a baby now. Crying was the only words he had and D.R. had oh so much to say. He wanted to say the kitchen, and his grandfather building fires. He wanted to say the river he had been baptized in, and swimming in that river with other people who had not lived. He was on a riverbank now, casting far out in the stream. The sun was shining on him, he was naked in it, but a shadow lay upon the water from a bank of tall sycamores on the other side. D.R. reeled in and stuck another dragonfly on his hook, and cast again, upstream this time near an old snag of a tree where the water seemed to spin a little as it flowed. The hook sailed through the sunlight and plopped into the water a few feet from the snag. Instantly a giant catfish took hold and pulled so hard D.R. fell on the muddy riverbank and slid into the water, where an unseen current sucked him far into the river and dragged him down below. Air! he tried to call, Breath, give me breath! But his lungs were full of water now and he could make no sound. Deeper and deeper he sank in the dark and murky river. Nothing he could do would help him rise again. Nothing he could think would give him air. The chill of death entered at his fingertips and toes and slowly flowed up through his body to his throat to gather in a pool. D.R. was drowning in the pool that filled his throat and choked him. He felt his life go out, and turn into a fish with gills and scales and fins and tail, tempted by a powerful light that dangled from his brain. The light scared him but he nosed around it, lured and terrified. Against his will he nibbled at its edges. As soon as his lips touched the light a three-pronged hook snagged his throat and yanked him up. Blood filled his throat and ran out of his gills and eyes and asshole and spilled upon the sand. He struggled to ease the pressure of the hook against his flesh, but the fisherman only laughed and dangled him up and down. At last when he could stand no more the fisherman gave the line a jerk and ripped D.R.'s tongue out by the roots and dropped him bleeding to the sand. Words rose up inside him to protest but they could get no farther than his throat. Words that started deep inside him lifted through his system to collide and fall apart in heaps of jumbled a b c's. Words he'd said in childhood came charging into words he'd heard old preachers say in sermons long ago, words of preachers, words of teachers, words mysterious kin folks uttered over Sunday chicken dinners into words he'd muttered to himself in saying who he was and might become all crashed against the roadblock and piled up in a grave of words as dry and hard as bones. D.R. picked up a bone shaped like the letter W. He smelled it, licked his tongue across it, and held it to his ear. He tried an O, and R, and a broken D, but they were all the same. Dead. Dead. All the words were dead, not one had lived to tell what happened, none survived that knew the tale. Tell it! said the fisherman, but all he could do was cry. Tell it! said the fisherman, but all he could do was cry. The fisherman cursed and roughly kicked D.R. back into the river. The water scalded his wound as it mixed with blood and made a soup for bones of broken letters D.R. clutched at for support to keep from drowning.

The Cultivator's Handbook of Marijuana

How to grow good pot. The best book on the subject.
—SB

The Cultivator's Handbook of Marijuana
Bill Drake
1970; 88 pp.

$2.00 postpaid

from:
Augur Publishing Co.
454 Willamette
Eugene, Oregon 97401

or WHOLE EARTH CATALOG

Many writers have picked up on a piece of misinformation which holds male plants to be useless for drug purposes. It is substantially true that males have a much lower potency than females, but that is not the reason that they are pulled up and destroyed by professional growers. They are pulled primarily because if the male is allowed to go to maturity and pollenate the female, she will lose considerable potency because much of her energy will then be turned to nourishing the fertilized seed. What might be gained, then, in terms of overall bulk at harvest time by keeping the male plants will be lost in per-unit potency of female plants. So it becomes a trade-off situation where you have the option of lots of leaves (both male and female plants harvested) with lowered potency per unit of yield, or less yield (destroy the males and keep only females) with a higher per-unit potency. It is up to the individual cultivator to make the decision.

Another common source of death and destruction among indoor Cannabis plants is tobacco smoke. It is with a heavy heart, my fellow Americans, that I announce tonight that the smoking lamp is not lighted during grass cultivation. If smokers are using the same air supply which the plants must breathe, you must try to filter the air somehow or take great risks with the plants' survival up until the third week, and with their health beyond that.

Acapulco Gold, Panama Red and other strains of grass are reputed to be particularly potent because of a fortuitous combination of climate and soils. Actually, soil has nothing to do with potency, except that it contributes to the plant's health, and certain mineral deficiencies do cut down on resin potency (see page 31). Climate has a similar relationship with potency. It is the genetic properties of grass which determine potency, and these genetic properties vary from strain to strain, but can be easily manipulated by cultivators.

*Below: Female flowers
Left: Male flowers*

If the seedlings are to be transplanted at any point, it will be helpful to germinate them in containers making transfer to the planting soil easy and non-traumatic. Germinating the seeds in ice-cube trays or similar devices allows easy transfer of the seedlings in their original soil. The ball of soil can either be popped out at transplant time; or each depression in the tray can be lined with foil or plastic before the germinating soil is added, making transplantation a matter of lifting out the ball of soil intact and placing it in the receiving soil equally undisturbed. The foil or plastic film can be removed easily prior to placing the seedling in its new home.

The Maple Sugar Book

My family had a sugar bush in Michigan, so we always had a cellar-room full of gallon cans of pure maple syrup, which solved most Christmas-giving problems and saddled me with an early addiction.

This book by the Nearings (of Living the Good Life*) continues their fine philosophical rap and lays out the definitive information on maple-sugaring. You don't have to have maple trees to enjoy it, but if you do. . .*

—SB

The Maple Sugar Book
Helen & Scott Nearing
1950, 1970; 273 pp.

$2.50 postpaid

from:
Schocken Books, Inc.
200 Madison Avenue
New York, N.Y. 10016

or WHOLE EARTH CATALOG

General Viticulture

This book includes everything needed to know by anyone really interested in grapes. It is mainly concerned with vineyard production but it contains valuable information for small arbors and home gardening as well. Winkler deals with soils, propagation, pruning, irrigation, diseases, pests, raisins, wine grapes, table grapes and even includes a detailed appendix of costs involved. This book is the only complete work on grape production, it is a U.C. text, make your own raisins.

[Suggested and reviewed by Ron Pietrowski]

General Viticulture
A. J. Winkler
1962; 633 pp.

$16.50 postpaid

from:
University of California Press
2223 Fulton St.
Berkeley, Calif. 94720

50 East 42nd St., Rm 513
New York, N.Y. 10017

or WHOLE EARTH CATALOG

For best development the *vinifera* grape requires long, warm-to-hot, dry summers and cool winters. It is not suited to humid summers, owing to its susceptibility to certain fungus diseases and insect pests that flourish under humid conditions. Neither will it withstand intense winter cold. A long growing season is required to mature the fruit, and, since the green parts of growing vines are likely to be frozen at temperatures below 30°F., areas subject to late spring and early fall frosts must be avoided. Rain is desirable during the winter, but deficiencies in rainfall can be made up by irrigation. Rains early in the growing season make disease and pest control difficult, but are otherwise not detrimental to the growth of the vine. Rains or cloudy weather during the blooming period may result in a poor set of the berries, especially in some varieties, and rains during ripening and harvest permit much damage through fruit rot. Where raisins are to be produced by sun-drying between the vine-rows, as in California, a month of clear, warm, rainless weather is essential after the grapes are mature. Higher humidity can be tolerated in cool regions than in warm regions.

Wild Rice

Lord god, imagine having enough *wild rice.*

I always thought that Indians had some kind of legal monopoly on this expensive staple-delicacy. Maybe not. Maybe you can grow the expensive staple-delicacy in your own fresh-water shallows.

—SB
[Suggested by Ron O'dor]

Wild Rice
William G. Dore
1969; 84 pp.

$3.00 postpaid

from:
Queen's Printer
Daly Bldg.
Mackenzie & Rideau
Ottawa, Ontario
Canada

or WHOLE EARTH CATALOG

All the wild-rice sold today comes from untended stands that grow in streams and other waterways. There have been attempts to control the supply and level of the water, or to create new impoundments in localities where this is possible, but cultivation in a paddy has been done only on an experimental scale. Most of the grain is still harvested by hand from canoes. The operation of harvesting, however, is conducted in a much larger scale than formerly, and, in some regions, it follows a well-organized plan.

Wild-rice forms thick productive beds in some small rivers in southern Ontario if these rivers have rushing floodwaters in the spring. In midsummer, stands occupy all the shallow water, leaving only a narrow mid-river channel. A patch of perennial plants, including cattails and pickerelweeds, is at the right of this picture, taken near Dalrymple, Victoria County, Ont. (Photo by W. J. Cody)

Softwood in the sugar brush cuts off sunlight. Sunlight is vitally essential to sap flow, especially in the early days of a sap season. First-class sap runs, early in the season, often occur entirely on the south side of the trees.

•

If syrup is of proper consistency it will keep from one season to another without deterioration, except that fresh-made syrup possesses a delicate tang and bouquet that old syrup invariably lacks.

•

Here is a typical case in our neighborhood. The household is made up of a man, his wife, and five children, the oldest a boy of fifteen. Sugartime comes in late February or early March. The snow is so deep in the woods that logging and wood cutting (the usual winter occupations) are difficult or impossible. In the homestead there is little to do beside the regular chores. The family has a sugar bush, a sugarhouse, 1,500 buckets, covers, and spouts, an evaporator, a gathering tank, a team of horses standing idle in the barn, a supply of sugar wood. Not a single cash outlay is involved in the entire sugar operation. School allows the children a three-week "sugaring vacation." The man and his family tap out. All gather. He boils and she puts up the syrup. In the course of five or six weeks, if weather is favorable, the household can produce 350 to 400 gallons of maple syrup. If the syrup is put into steel drums, provided by one of the companies that buy syrup, there is not a nickel of necessary cash outlay, unless there are replacement parts for worn-out equipment.

ABC and XYZ of Bee Culture

The first edition of this authoritative book was written in 1877 by Mr. A. I. Root. The current edition, the 34th, is edited by Mr. E. R. Root, with the help of H. H. Root and J. A. Root. You get the picture.

We've been told by several people that bee-keeping is one of the easiest ways to make extra money with little effort and a certain amount of down-home adventure. If you are what you eat, food from flowers is hard to beat.

From whatever standpoint—commercial, nostalgic, or amateur scientific—this is a fascinating and useful book. The Roots also have a catalog of bee supplies, a beginner's book (Starting Right With Bees), and a magazine (Gleanings in Bee Culture)—monthly, $4.00 per year.

—SB
[Suggested by Tassajara Zen Center]

ABC and XYZ of Bee Culture
1877 . . . 1966; 712 pp.

$6.50 postpaid from A. I. Root
or WHOLE EARTH CATALOG

Starting Right With Bees
100 pp.

$1.10 postpaid from A. I. Root
or WHOLE EARTH CATALOG

Catalog
free

from:
A. I. Root Company
Medina, Ohio 44256

Fig. 1. Round Dance

MARKETING HONEY.—The bee-keeper with four or five colonies of bees will have no difficulty in selling honey to his neighbors. It soon becomes known that he has a few hives of bees and the people in the vicinity, feeling that they can buy "real honey," will go to the neighbor and pay good prices furnishing their own utensils. If the honey is of first quality there is no trouble about selling the entire crop from the doorway.

Walter T. Kelley Bee Supply Super Market

mail order bee supplies

Catalog
Free

from:
Walter T. Kelley Company
Clarkson, Kentucky 42726

We have assembled here the necessary items that you need in starting with one hive of bees, including the bees, necessary tools and a book of instructions. After the beginner has worked with this equipment a short time he will be able to order intelligently his future requirements.

Cat. No. 367. KELLEY'S COMPLETE BEGINNER'S OUTFIT as above
Wt. 38 lbs. F. O. B. Clarkson. Each............................ **$30.00**

Nylon Mesh ➡ Ventilator

Our gloves are of supreme quality. The cowhide is extremely soft and pliable so that you can handle the frames rapidly. The top gauntlet is treated duck that will outwear the gloves. We are installing stiff nylon mesh now in place of the screen wire and with the edges folded over the top gauntlets will not pull out. An elastic at the top makes them bee tight. We can furnish these without the mesh ventilator at the same price.

Per Pair **$4.50**

Animal Traps

If you're getting rid of a pest without being too mean about it, or if you're after a wild pet, these traps will catch sundry small animals alive. Raccoons, possums, mice, turtles, sparrows, quail, fish, rabbits, crabs, rats, pigeons. Havahart is the best known. Catalogs free.

—SB

Havahart

Havahart
120 P. Water St.
Ossining, N.Y. 10562

Johnson's
Waverly 17, Kentucky 42462

Mustang Mfg. Co.
Box 10880
Houston, Texas 77018

Tomahawk Live Traps
Box 323
Tomahawk, Wisconsin 54487

How to Adopt a Colony of Bees

This magical method may be used for removing bees and their honey from an attic without the use of pesticides or other violence, or for adopting a colony from a bee-tree. All the entrances, into the colony must first be carefully stopped up with plaster, calking compound or other goop. A single 3/4" diameter hole is left, over which a bee escape (one-way exit) is placed. Following this, a bee hive is strategically located within its entrance as close as possible, preferably within a few inches, of the bee escape. The hive may then be enticingly smeared with honey or sugar syrup on its landing strip and entrance. The bees will come out of their old home and will form a large swarm within a few days. At this point, a queen bee, in her cage, with courtiers, is suspended within the new hive. When the other bees learn of her presence, they will all go into the new hive, eat out the plug of sugar which seals the entrance to her royal residence, and liberate her. One then has a going colony of bees in the new hive. After a few weeks, the original colony will be quite depleted or almost entirely absent. At this point, the entrances to the attic or tree may be completely opened and the bees from the new hive will then go back, take all the honey out, and bring it into the new hive, which may then be moved to any convenient location.

I tried this method on a colony of bees in my attic with partial success. Unfortunately the bees found a new way to get back into the attic under the shingles which I had not adequately blocked, and I was left with two competing colonies. However, I think the colony in my hive is now getting stronger, and I will eventually have all the bees in it. It would seem desirable to do this in the spring when flowers are blooming, since in the autumn I have found the bees are less energetic and have to be fed with sugar syrup. A reliable source of bee supplies is the Sears Roebuck Suburban and Farm Catalog. In order to get a catalog, one must first place an order at a Sears Catalog Order Desk, and if they think you look like a good potential customer, they will give you a free catalog to take home. Supplies arrive by mail or parcel post in less than a week, but queen bees are sent only from April 15 to Oct. 1, and take about a week and one-half to two weeks to arrive.

P.S. If it is necessary to move the beehive less than two miles, it must be done in two steps: first the hive is moved more than two miles away and the bees are allowed to get settled in that location, and then it is moved back to where you really wanted it in the first place, which can be closer than two miles to their original location as long as it is more than two miles from the intermediate place.

David Collins, M.D.
San Diego, California

Wildlife Nurseries

If you got open water, you can plant various goodies that will attract ducks, as well as muskrats and fish. This is a catalog of the goodies, as well as some items for upland game birds and deer.

—SB

Wildlife Nurseries Catalog

$0.50 postpaid

from:
Wildlife Nurseries
P.O. Box 399-W
Oshkosh, Wisconsin 54901

Giant Wild Rice is easy to grow when fully-ripe, sure-growing seed is used. Many areas throughout the U.S. and Canada where Wild Rice does not grow, provide conditions suitable for it, and such places could and should be planted with Giant Wild Rice. Briefly stated the conditions required for its successful growth are fresh water streams, lakes, ponds or sloughs having a change of water (such as an inlet or outlet), soft mud bottom being best, but will thrive on sand, and in water from 6 inches to 3 feet deep. Sunny sheltered bays or covers where planting will not get the full current or direct wash of waves are ideal for it.

Near the seacoast it will grow along the streams 25 to 50 miles above where they enter the sea, where the water is not salty to taste and the tide not over four feet. Spots where fresh water brooks or springs enter the stream are more fresh and better suited for it. Wild Rice thrives best north of San Francisco, Memphis and Savanah; however under ideal conditions we have grown seed in the "Deep South."

GIANT WILD RICE
(Zizania aquatica)

PRICES––PREPAID

1 bushel, (25 lbs. net wt.)	$75.00
1 peck	20.00
2 quarts	6.50
Sturdy young Wild Rice Plants— 1,000 will plant one acre June delivery	
1000	$80.00
300	27.00
200	10.00

WAMPEE — DUCK CORN

(Peltandra virginica)

Excellent D u c k food — especially a t t r a c t i v e to W o o d Ducks and other Marsh Ducks. Produces an abundance of large rather fleshy s e e d s (berries), as large as kernels of c o r n, making food late into the season.

PRICES — PREPAID
"WILD LIFE" Nature-ripened pure seed
10 lbs., $19.00 - 5 lbs., $10.00 or $2.25 per lb.

WHEN MORNING GUILDS THE SKIES

When morning guilds the skies   my heart awaking cries out the night sky   light blossoms yonder where the roll is called out to a weary traveler looking for his home   among the desert sand dunes   stained glass pictures of holy desert ground   pale cactus set against an earth of waving blonde   up toward the sun about to rise behind Mount Sinai   so vast and barren   yet something lush about it   something cool   promises to satisfy whatever thirst it causes weary travelers looking for a home among the desert sand dunes   rolling up as wings and fly away   What building is this window in   Would it hurt if I would touch it   Would it shatter into pieces   Would the artist ever know and if so would he mind   How heavy walk on holy ground   how far burlap by my face   a burlap bag of knitting stuff to carry Estelle's in   burlap weaves of pieces full of burlap holes around the seams of burlap   weave together for a bag of knitting stuff to knit together into things that keep you warm   and dry   and hold together parts of wholes   a million teeny holes to smell leather through   leather smell old gloves in someone's pocket smell leather harness over mule sweat   smell sweat and miner's leather belt flashing on your ass smell leather in my nose of leather rows of leather doeskin smell and feel the leather strap get tightaroundmyhead.

Goat Husbandry

The definitive goat book.

—SB

[Suggested by Steve Durkee]

Goat Husbandry
David Mackenzie
1967; 368 pp.

$16.75 postpaid

from:
Transatlantic Arts
Trade Dept.
North Village Green
Levittown, L. I., N. Y. 11756
or WHOLE EARTH CATALOG

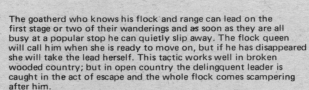

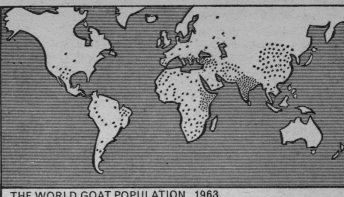

THE WORLD GOAT POPULATION 1963
One dot=one million goats

Because goats are dairy animals, they must have dairy characteristics. Check to see that the doe has a feminine head, thin neck, sharp withers, well-defined spine or backbone and hips, thin thighs, and rather fine bones. The skin should be thin and fine over the ribs. Look for a wide spring of rib and roomy barrel. This will help you to know how much feed she can eat. The constitution, or physical nature, is an important item shown by the depth and width of the chest. It's important to look at the udder, too. It should be large when full of milk and very much smaller when empty. A large udder does not always mean a high milk yield.

The goatherd who knows his flock and range can lead on the first stage or two of their wanderings and as soon as they are all busy at a popular stop he can quietly slip away. The flock queen will call him when she is ready to move on, but if he has disappeared she will take the lead herself. This tactic works well in broken wooded country; but in open country the delingquent leader is caught in the act of escape and the whole flock comes scampering after him.

Under such conditions the goatherd must use plain language to tell his flock when he has ceased to be their king billy. Mere rudeness won't suffice; king billy's manners are not of the best; a push and a grunt and a show of displeasure convey his warning to the flock to obey and follow him more closely. But king billy doesn't throw sticks or stones; the performance of such an act is a special characteristic of man and monkey which is peculiarly repulsive to all other species. So long as it is carried out calmly and ceremonially, so as not to be mistaken for mere rudeness, the flock will turn their backs on the goatherd, will go their way and leave him go to his. The popular use of effeminate males has produced flocks of half-witted goats which may be incapable of finding amongst themselves a flock queen of sufficient independence of character to accept even so broad a hint as the thrown stick. If such a flock refuses to be content without a king billy to lead them, the only cure is to give them a real one.

Dairy Goat Journal

monthly goat gab, latest in goat gear, goats for sale, goat cheese recipes, goatkeepers' classifieds. get your goat.

—jd

Dairy Goat Journal
Kent Leach, editor

$4.00 per year (monthly),
$10.00 — 3 years

from:
Dairy Goat Journal
P.O. Box 1908
Scottsdale, AZ 85252

Goat Buying

Goat owners are a lot like horse traders. Be careful. Seek out experienced advice. If possible, have someone whose opinion you trust along with you when buying a goat. If you are paying fifty dollars or more, as is sometimes necessary, for your goat, invest in a vet's inspection and opinion if at all possible.

My preference is unquestionably Toggenburg. A three year old doe whose milking and kidding record is available is most desirable. Toggenburg crosses cut the price in half and by selecting bucks you can breed back to almost pure strain in a few years. (Toggenburg on the doe's side as that's who determines milk production.) A last word: if you are in the market for goats you probably already like them. They are almost all beautiful animals. When I first got into goats I bought a nice three year old Alpine doe just drying up. She looked like an antelope. Beautiful. She did dry up shortly. I bred her, fed her for five months. She had trouble kidding and her milk production was poor. Nothing I could do in the way of feeding and milk schedules helped. I still had a beautiful pet goat but awfully expensive. Somehow I like the good milkers more.

Steve Katona

64 Goats Land Use

Dairy Goat Guide

In September 1972, **Dairy Goat Guide** *joined* **Rabbit World** *and* **Countryside** *to form* **Countryside and Small Stock Journal** *but sections on rabbits and goats maintain their identity.*

Countryside and Small Stock Journal
Jerome D. Belanger, Editor

$3 /yr. (10 a year)

from:
Countryside Publications
Waterloo, Wisconsin 53594

Lesson one about dairy goats——don't expect them to "mow" your grass for you.

Goats don't care much for grass,

But they are crazy about trees and bushes——especially fruit trees, shade trees, rosebushes, raspberry bushes, any other large woody plants you or your neighbors treasure.

A goat will strip a young fruit tree to a bare stub faster than you can run from house to orchard to stop her.

Several goats will chew enough bark off a good-sized shade tree to kill it in a single season.

If trees hang over their pens, the goats will dance about on their hind legs and trim the leaves evenly 4 to 6 feet above the ground. Makes the place look like a park.

Even innocent-looking baby kids will strip the bottom branches of an ornamental evergreen——before they have really learned to eat hay!

Moral of this is——before you get goats, get some good goat fencing. Four foot high seems necessary. They will climb on the fence to reach trees on the other side, so make it sturdy. Take care with gate latches. Bored goats scratch their heads on things which stick out——like gate latches. They have a habit of opening gates. Then they head for the fruit trees.

A length of chain and a snap hook makes a nice auxiliary latch on your gates.

About that Grass——

Most goat raisers find it necessary to mow pastures and barn lots from time to time——to keep the grass short and neat-looking.

Goats can make good use of pastures——especially if you have planted legumes such as alfalfa and clover. Good farmers mow pastures just to keep the plants young and growing for more protein.

But goats are not by nature good grasseaters. If your interest in goats is a well-mowed lawn, we suggest sheep instead.

Dairy Goats

This book bridges the gap between the 4-H pamphlet and the $15 goat book. It covers everything you should know before and when you get into goats. You can skip the analysis/amplification (if you want) of how a goat's stomach works, the manufacture of proteins, etc. and just discover that one half pound of good dairy mix grain for each pound of milk produced is what you want.

Perhaps the person who already knows a bit about goats will find that the most interesting and valuable part of the book is the last two pages which lists breed clubs, goat journals, books, and other literature.

Addendum: My friend and fellow goat husbandman, Don Symanski tells me that the one he went to the book for wasn't there——a goat's normal temp. I'll tell you, it's 101 to 102 degrees F.

[Reviewed by Steve Katona, Suggested by Al Ames]

Dairy Goats——Breeding/Feeding/Management
Byron E. Colby
77 pp.

$1.00 postpaid

from:
The American Dairy Goat Association
P.O. Box 186
Spindale, North Carolina 28160

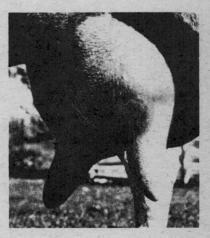

Good udder

Feeding the Kids

Giving kids a proper nutritional start without expensive goat milk is a good practice; particularly if you can sell the goat milk for a higher price than necessary to buy cow's milk for the kid. Goat's milk is ideal for growing out a kid, but you lose your income during this time. If you intend to rear the kid without mother's milk, never let him nurse. Milk the colostrum or first milk from the mother and feed it at body temperature to the kid from a nipple bottle. Continue this for three to four days. The colostrum is laxative, high in carotene, protein, and other nutrients, as well as antibodies which are so necessary to the newborn kid's digestive system and developing tissues. The nipple bottle is usually preferred over pan feeding of milk as it is more natural for the kid and less air is gulped which can cause digestive upsets.

The small fat globules and the soft curd of goat's milk contribute to its ease of digestibility. Some persons who are allergic to cow's milk can consume goat's milk readily, due largely perhaps to its easier digestibility. In a great many cases goat's milk has proved especially valuable for infants and invalids.

Livestock and Poultry Production

*if you were never in FFA or 4H, and
if you think a polled hereford is a female cow standing on stilts so she can eat the leaves off trees, then you could probably stand to read this textbook. although aimed at the beginning animal husbandry major, so that there is a morbid interest in the industrial aspect of raising to slaughter, there's a lot of useful information here about cattle sheep hogs and poultry. look past the "agriculture makes our country strong" bullshit,
and don't be put off by the questions at the end of every chapter.
should serve as an introduction to animal science.*

—jd

Livestock and Poultry Production
Bundy and Diggins
1968; 723pp.

$13.00 postpaid

from:
Prentice-Hall Inc.
Englewood Cliffs, New Jersey 07632

or WHOLE EARTH CATALOG

A ton of raw garbage formerly produced 50 to 80 pounds of pork. With the changes that have come about in kitchen and restaurant management, a ton of garbage today may produce only from 20 to 30 pounds of pork. Unless considerable grains are fed with the garbage, a poor carcass will be produced.

Garbage-fed hogs were responsible for the rapid spread of vesicular exanthema during the past few years, and cases of trichinosis have been prevalent in some communities where raw garbage was fed to hogs. In feeding garbage, extreme care should be taken to maintain sanitary quarters. Concrete feeding floors are recommended, and the yards should be thoroughly cleaned and disinfected regularly. Thorough cooking of pork products is necessary to kill any disease organisms which may be prevalent in the meat.

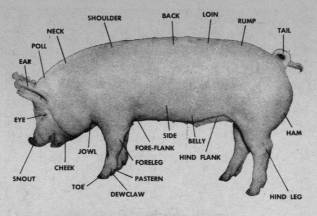

POLLED HEREFORDS. In 1900, Warren Gamomn of Iowa wrote to nearly every breeder of Herefords in the United States asking if they had any cattle which did not develop horns. He succeeded in securing 13 head of purebred Herefords that were polled. From this small beginning the polled Hereford breed was established.

The breed has become very popular among breeders who desire the Hereford form but dislike the horns. Polled Herefords originating from registered Hereford stock may be registered in both breed associations.

In form and characteristics, the polled Herefords closely resemble their ancestors, the Herefords. The distinguishing difference is the absence of horns.

PASTURES. The natural feed for dairy cattle is pasture. The pasture season should be made as long as possible. Fall-seeded rye provides early spring pasture, in areas where it is adapted, and may be followed by native grasses, or a legume and grass mixture. Sudan grass, or a sudan grass and soybean combination, makes an excellent summer and early fall pasture. In general, a legume and grass combination provides more grazing per acre of highly nutritious forage than any other common pasture crop. Pastures recommended for beef cattle are suitable for dairy cattle.

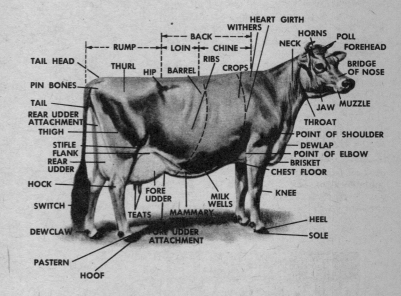

Veterinary Guide for Farmers

how to keep them healthy down on the farm.

—jd

Veterinary Guide for Farmers
G.W. Stam
1963, 69; 384pp.

$7.95 postpaid

from:
Hawthorn Books, Inc.
70 Fifth Avenue
New York, New York 10011

or WHOLE EARTH CATALOG

HERE'S THE WAY MANY SURGEONS TIE A KNOT

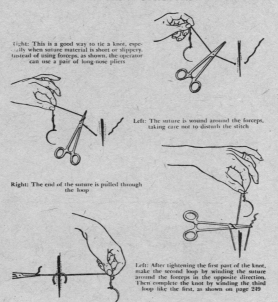

Right: This is a good way to tie a knot, especially when suture material is short or slippery. Instead of using forceps, as shown, the operator can use a pair of long-nose pliers

Left: The suture is wound around the forceps, taking care not to disturb the stitch

Right: The end of the suture is pulled through the loop

Left: After tightening the first part of the knot, make the second loop by winding the suture around the forceps in the opposite direction. Then complete the knot by winding the third loop like the first, as shown on page 249

FEVER AS A SYMPTOM

The temperature of an animal's body, rises above normal when more heat is produced than is given off. This happens naturally under a number of conditions, such as during exercise, after eating, in very hot weather and among cows in the later stages of pregnancy.

When the temperature of an animal rises without apparent reason, it is generally caused by illness or injury. That is why the presence of fever is of great importance in the diagnosis of disease, especially those that affect the internal organs.

An increase in temperature is not the only symptom of fever. Sometimes when the temperature goes up rapidly, chills may occur, and these in turn are accompanied by trembling muscles, cold skin, erect hair coat and arched back.

A strange thing about fever is that the legs, ears, nose and base of the horns in cattle and sheep become alternately hot and cold even though the internal temperature of the animals remains uniform.

One ear may be hot while the other is cold. Later these conditions may be reversed, or both ears may be hot or both cold. The same thing holds true of legs and other extremities.

Other signs of fever are dry muzzles and snouts, loss of appetite, indigestion, constipation, increased thirst, decreased urination and mental depression.

Chills do not occur with all fevers but with disease where microbes or toxins are in the blood stream. Among them are anthrax, shipping fever and maladies accompanied by pus formation. Once the body becomes used to a higher temperature, chills cease. But they will come back if the animal is taken to a colder place.

Veterinary Supplies

three companies selling serums, vaccines, instruments, and drugs, by mail.

—jd

Catalog

free

from:
Kansas City Vaccine Co.
Stock Yards
Kansas City, Mo. 64102

Catalog

free

from:
United Pharmical Company
8366 LaMesa Blvd.
LaMesa, California 92041

Catalog

free

from:
Eastern States Serum Co.
1727 Harden Street
Columbia, South Carolina 29204

Rid lice in winter Flies in summer

ROPE CHAIN OILER—This cattle oiler combines many of the finer features of other oilers. Wick is heavy hemp hawser, providing smooth, sure flow of insecticide-in-oil. Heavy chain is wrapped entire length of hawser, fitting between strands of hemp to give greater strength, longer life and coarser hide-cleaning action. Five-gallon reservoir is fitted with automatic valve actuated by rubbing action of cattle so that insecticide is given down only when cattle are working on it. Action thus is entirely automatic, requiring attention only in filling reservoir. This is our finest oiler and the newest addition to our line. Wt., complete, 26 lbs................................ $39.00

BALLING GUN

Balling Gun. Takes 00 and 000 capsule. All brass construction—nickel plated. One piece head. Length 12 inches.

Wholesale $1.60

Pig Tooth Nipper

Chrome Plated
Special forged steel with well sharpened blades. Spring Loaded 4¾" long.
(wt. 7 oz.) $3.55

SIGNS

Signs along the freeway, rolling selling telling messages from someone's head to mine. Someone wrote them, someone hoped and sent them to the billboards and stuck them to the walls of everybody's memories down old forgotten halls. Eat somewhere and sleep somewhere, we plead for you to eat and sleep and buy our gas and oil. You love us and we'll love you, the town of Lone Oak up ahead invites you to its food and sleep and oil and gas and friendly hospitality from Mayor Andrew Hess.

Welcome said the Civitans, welcome said the Lions. Welcome said the J.C.'s, there's room in all our inns. Pioneer Ho-tel, Frontier Motel, Dizzy Burger French Fries Cole Slaw Blue Skies, Tumbleweed and Dragonflies, we've got it all in Lone Oak, Welcome To Our Town.

FLIPPING THE DIAL

Estelle turned the radio on and began to flip the dial MICHELLE MY BELLE IN THE FIRST GAME OF A WEEKEND DOUBLE-HEADER WITH THE VOLUME UP ONE MILLION NINE HUNDRED THOUSAND JOYS AWAITING ALL WHO SUFFER WITH CHRIST ON SALE NOW FOR ONLY NINETEEN NINETY FIVE SINGING BLUE MOON OF KENTUCKY SHALL BE DIFFUSED BY PRESIDENT NIXON AT A PRESS CONFERENCE WHO SAID THE MIDDLE LETTER IN THE WORD SIN IS "I" but she couldn't find anything she liked so she turned it off.

Rabbits

Here are some good books on rabbit raising. If you raise rabbits you can eat them and tan the hides for clothes to keep you warm.

[Suggested and Reviewed by Martin K. Rorapaugh]

The Purina Rabbit Book, available from your feed store or probably from Ralston Purina Company, Checkerboard Square, St. Louis Mo. 63199. This one is free (they might appreciate postage if you send for it I don't know) and gives all the information you need if you just want to eat the rabbits. It gives cage dimensions, good breeding practices (for the rabbits), and feeding suggestions. The best part of this little book is that it gives a calendar system so that you can keep track of when to do what. Its a good easy thing to follow. The same people also offer pamphlets on rabbit diseases, and cage plans.

Selecting and Raising Rabbits, Agricultural Information Bulletin 358. Available from Superintendent of Documents, U.S. Govt. Printing Office, Washington, D.C. 20402 cost 15 cents. Covers basics but doesn't cover diseases or tanning hides. It's cheap but not much better than the free one above.

Commercial Rabbit Raising Agricultural Handbook No. 309, U.S. Dept. of Agriculture. Available from Superintendent of Documents for 30 cents. This is a *good* cheap book. It covers *all* the basics like how to select a breed, feed and manage the herd etc. It also tells how to use the manure (as if you didn't know) and cure rabbit skins. This is a *goodie* for the price.

Domestic Rabbit Production by George S. Templeton (He's a real genuine expert). If you want the *best* and don't mind paying money this is it. It is *complete.* Covers everything the others cover plus rabbit diseases (thorough and easy to follow), tanning the hides, rabbit recipes, and get this, quantity recipes adjusted for 25, 50 or 100 souls. Its published by the Interstate Printers & Publishers, Inc, Danville, Illinois.

Domestic Rabbit Production
George S. Templeton

$6.95 cash must accompany order

from:
Interstate Printers & Publishers, Inc.
19-27 North Jackson Street
Danville, Illinois 61832

More Rabbits

Rabbit raising:

In addition to the books you have already listed previously here are some more:

American Rabbit Breeders Association
Box 348
Bloomington, IL 61710
25 ¢

Albers Milling Co.
800 West 47th St.
Kansas City, Missouri 64112
Raising Rabbits (free, I think)
Commercial Rabbit Raising 50 ¢

Glick Manufacturing Co.
1595 Almaden Road
San Jose, Calif. 95125
Catalog & Book $1.00

Commercial Rabbit Growers Discount Club
P.O. Box 5693
San Jose, Calif. 95150
Catalog free

With four does and one buck and less than $85, you can eat good and in two years break even if...you sell your surplus to a commercial dealer. A good way to live if you aren't a vegetarian.

T.G. Crouthamel
Spotswood, N.J.

Books About Rabbit Raising

Domestic Rabbit Production,
George S. Templeton

I Choose Rabbits, E.H. Stall

Selecting and Raising Rabbits
Agricultural Info. Bulletin #358, Office of Information, Dept. of Agriculture, Wash., D.C. 20505
$.15

Magazines

National Rabbit Raiser, 241 W. Snelling Ave., Appleton, Minn. 56208

Countryside and Small Stock Journal
Waterloo, Wisconsin 53594

The Rabbitman, Auburn, Ala. 36830
36830

Additional Booklets

Commercial Rabbit Raising, USDA Handbook No. 309, 70 pages, July 1966, Supt. of Documents, Wash, D.C. 20402, 45 cents

Rabbit Production, USDA Bulletin No. 1730, 1950, 20 cents

Common Diseases of Domestic Rabbits, USDA Bulletin No. 45-3

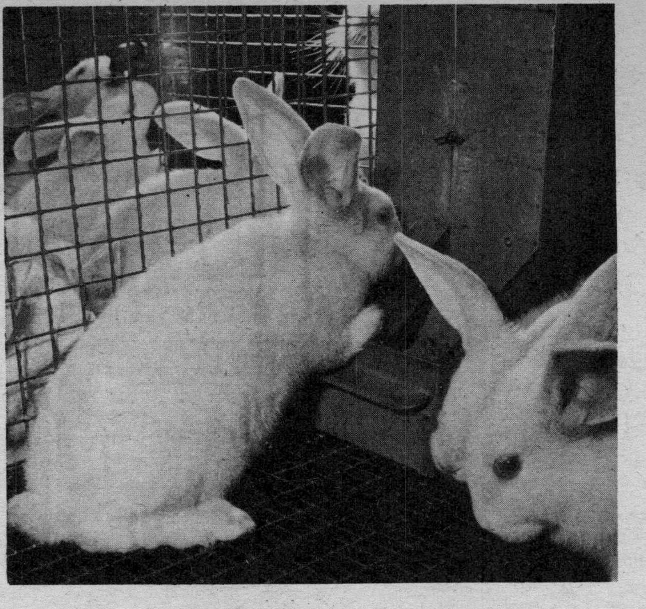

Litters range from 6 to 18 young, depending upon the breed, age of the doe, and the season. The ideal number to leave for the mother to wean is seven. If you have two or more does kindling at the same time, litters can be balanced by taking youngsters from one mother and giving them to another on the first or second day after they are born. When the young are no more than 2 days old, neither doe will mind the transfer.

Rabbit Raising

$0.45

from:
Boy Scouts of America
North Brunswick, New Jersey 08902

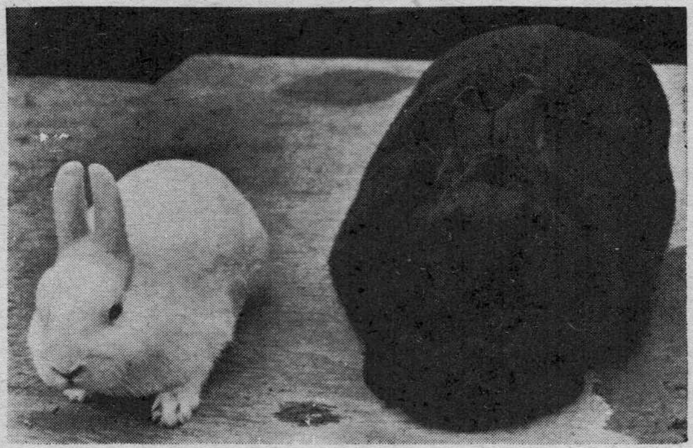

New Zealand Black (right)
Ruby-Eyed White Polish (left)

Rambling Rabbit Rap

I spent most of this past summer with a farmer friend of mine who raises rabbits as a main source of table meat for his family. Six does and a buck kept in hutches at the edge of the garden provide regular meat for his family of four. Other than the heavy work of removing the manure as it accumulates, the rabbits are in the care of my friend's twelve-year old daughter, who feeds and waters them as part of her daily chores. Her father does the slaughtering as the young rabbits mature. The meat is kept in the freezer, and eaten at the rate of about one, sometimes two, a week.

I'd tasted wild rabbit before, but I didn't remember much about it, except that the occasion was loaded with an atmosphere of muted guilt, or at least an uncomfortable degree of self-consciousness. I was a kid at the time and I don't remember who the adults were, cooking and serving the meat. But I do remember the almost compulsive talk that went on among them about how wild rabbits were sometimes dangerous to eat, about how we probably ought not be eating this one, but let's just take a bit of him anyway, and see. I took my bite, but what I tasted was the general misgivings about the whole thing. And those misgivings stayed in my head for 25 years, until this very summer when we were eating rabbit as a regular staple.

And it was great! It was at least as good as fried chicken, and maybe even a little better, depending on whose chicken you've been eating. My friend said that as far as the work of meat-production is concerned, rabbits are far less trouble to keep than chickens. He keeps chickens, but mainly for the eggs. (He raises beef and pork too, as well as a fantastic organic garden, all on twelve rather hilly acres. Working together, he and his wife and their two children come as close as anyone I know to total organic self-sufficiency).

We talked some about the question of animal slaughter, of killing other creatures to feed on them. He said that in the beginning he had some trouble killing his rabbits, but that he finally overcame it when he quit thinking of them as "bunnies" and looked upon them as simply a source of protein. That attitude will no doubt trouble the more committed vegetarians; but not many farmers putting in 10 and 12 hours work a day are vegetarians. If a rabbit is a fellow being, so is a corn stalk. Creatures eat creatures. Some day worms will eat us all, and whatever debt we may owe the carbon-nitrogen cycle will no doubt then be paid in full.

So went our dialogue. Or one chapter of it, anyway. One of the great things about the summer on the farm was the kind of running conversation we had, picking up hours and even days later where the talk left off before. Farmers certainly work a good deal more than they talk, but when they do talk, it's grand to listen in. The language of men working together in a field is a rare and special thing. Men who work together, summer after summer, for years, have a common body of lore, a mutual frame of reference that underlies everything they say. When its best is when the words begin from a concrete subject, rise into a grand abstraction, convolute a time or two then return to earth again. Our talk about rabbits was like that. We talked about them as "bunnies," against rabbits as food to eat. That got us into talk about the esoteric loveliness of a wagon wheel as a thing you paint and display in your front yard, against the loveliness of a wheel on an actual wagon that's helping you do the work necessary to your livelihood. Then we got into the difference between vocation and avocation, of the unhappiness that comes when a person's play is too far removed from his work. Raising rabbits is play, it's fun, a hobby. But it can also be work, good, productive work of the kind that contributes to health and vigor by getting good home-grown food on the table.

And so we got into the organic life as an ideal, a life in which opposites like "work" and "play" are reconciled. When your life is one of daily, personal "creation," of work that satisfies like play does, you're less in need of purchased, artificial re-creation. The average industrial worker does a job he hates in order to buy the things he loves, like food, and entertainment. His vocation is one thing, his avocation another, and never the twain shall meet. This split ultimately leads to the deadly division between city and country. And in the same way the modern vocation, or industrial job, is deadly to the individual worker's creative spirit, the city has become the deadly enemy of the countryside. To satisfy the appetites of the city, the countryside is pillaged by industrial, mechanized farms for food and strip mines for fuel for electric power. How neurotic, how divided our culture against itself!

And thus we came to the question, can the lowly rabbit possibly come to the rescue? We decided it could. Rabbits can be raised in any back yard, as food, primarily; but they can also be raised as a metaphor of a new and simultaneously old possibility, the possibility of cottage economy. They can be raised as a metaphor of opposites reconciled, of cultural schizophrenia overcome. They can stand as an image of country stuff happening in town, of town style stretched to embrace country substance, of work become play and play become work, which, after all, is not far from Adam and Eve's set-up in the Original Garden. I don't plan to hold my breath till the Golden Age arrives. But I do plan to raise some rabbits in my suburban backyard this year, and to eat the little morsels one by one when they are grown.

—Gurney Norman

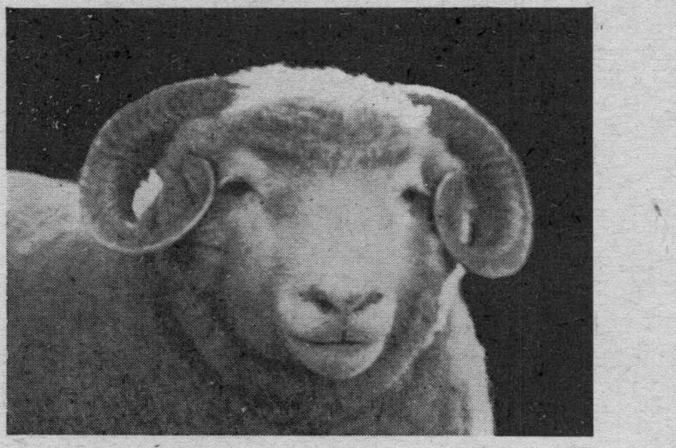

Sheep

I would like to spread the word about the joys of raising sheep. They require almost no work and very little money to care for. In return you get enough wool for yourself, your friends, as well as some extra to sell; excellent manure for your garden (second only to chicken manure in nitrogen content), and, if you're into it, a cheap source of mutton or lamb which, like all home grown foods, is far superior to anything in the store.

In the winter, you'll need some hay, corn, and a shelter for them to sleep in. In the summer, you'll need nothing but a grassy field (they're great to trim the grass around your house). Also, since they can't reach very high and are unable to climb at all, they don't wreak destruction to all your small bushes and trees as goats do.

If you're interested in raising a small flock, may I recommend the Horned Dorset. They are a good breed for producing wool or meat and are by far the most beautiful of domestic breeds. The main practical advantage of the Horned Dorset is the high frequency of twins produced during lambing. They are able to lamb twice a year, so you can usually count on three or four lambs a year from each ewe.

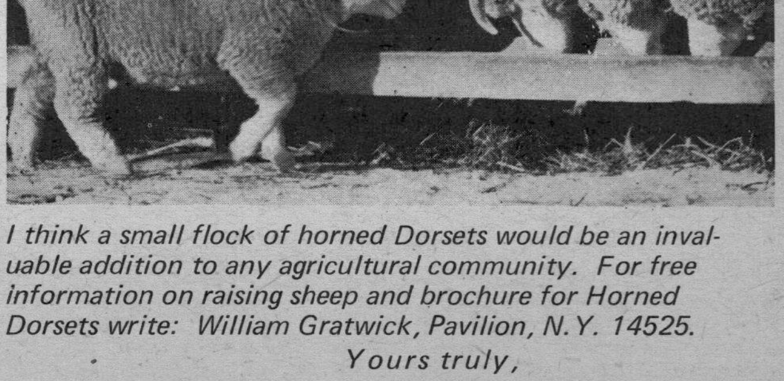

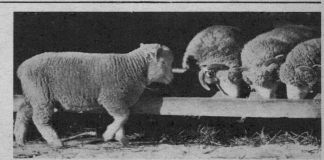

I think a small flock of horned Dorsets would be an invaluable addition to any agricultural community. For free information on raising sheep and brochure for Horned Dorsets write: William Gratwick, Pavilion, N.Y. 14525.

Yours truly,
Ned Nisson
Pavilion, N.Y.

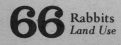

Stromberg's Chickens

For non-killed protein nothing beats milk and eggs. For ordinary chickens go to local sources. For particular chickens, fancy ones, and geese, ducks, pigeons, turkeys, partridges, peacocks——Stromberg's.

—SB

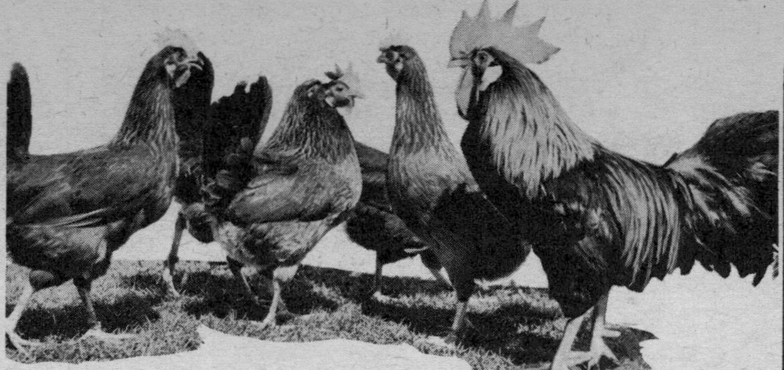

950 Picture Pet Hobby Supply Catalog

$.50

from:
Stromberg Hatchery
Box 717
Fort Dodge, Iowa 50501

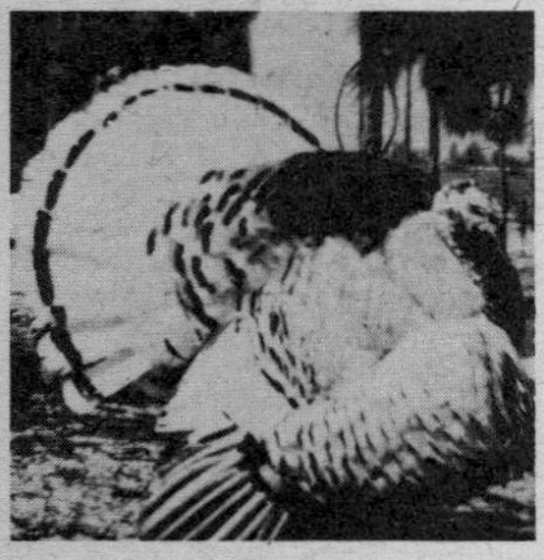

Royal Palm Tom

Genuine CANADIAN HONKERS

THE PRIDE AND JOY OF SPORTSMEN

You and your friends will be thrilled to see a pair or more of these dignified Canadian onkers about your country place. They are also a challenge to the devoted and dedicated waterfowl raiser. Mating is by pairs only—their choice of mates is a very serious matter with them. While they mate for life, should one die there is a chance they will take another mate. Still, on the other hand, they may never take another mate — especially older stock. This stock has exceptional long life, and have been known to reproduce up to 65 years of age, with some attaining an age of 85 years. Though listed in the American Standard of Perfection to encourage exhibiting, they are not a domestic but a truly wild fowl. A Federal Permit is required to ship.

STANDARD WEIGHTS

Adult Gander ....12 lbs. Young Goose .... 8 lbs.
Young Gander ....10 lbs. Adult Goose ....10 lbs.

HOW TO OBTAIN A FEDERAL PERMIT

There is no charge for the Federal Permit to raise Migratory Fowl such as the Canadian Honkers, Blue and Snow Geese. In the event you do not have this permit, write for your application to: U. S. Department of Interior, Fish and Wild Lofe Service, Bureau of Fisheries and Wildlife, 1006 West Lake Street, Minneapolis 8, Minnesota, or the same Department in Washington, D.C.

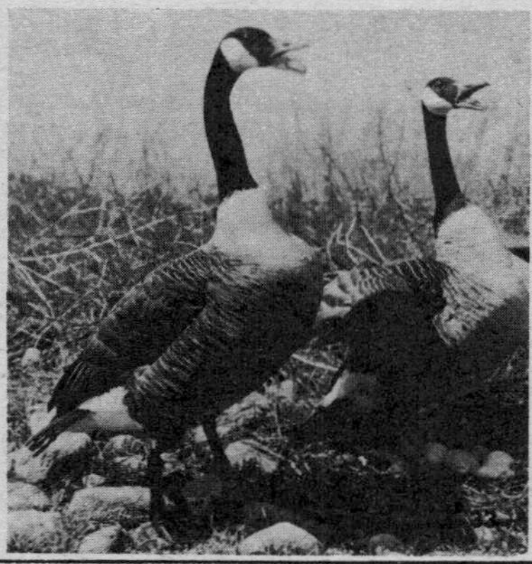

Farm Horses

The best way to learn about farm horses is to work with someone who uses them. If you're still curious, try this British handbook.

—SB

Farm Horses (and other English farming handbooks)
47 pp.

Three shillings sixpence plus postage

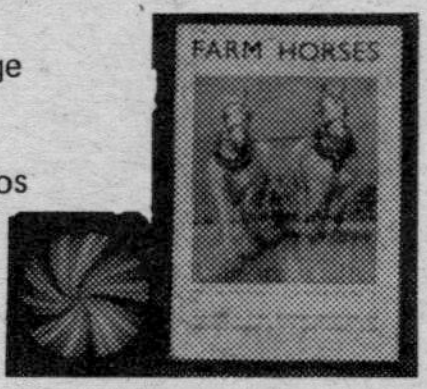

from:
National Federation of Young Farmers Clubs
National Agricultural Centre
Kenilworth, Warwickshire CV8 2L6
England

In many stables it is the custom during the winter to give the horses a bran mash, in place of the usual bait, once a week. This is usually done on Saturday evening before the Sunday rest. The purpose of this is to clear the horses' bowels (for a bran mash is *laxative*) and to lighten the diet at the weekend when there is less work for the horses to do. For if horses are hard at work and are being highly fed on oats, maize, beans or similar concentrates, they may become very ill indeed if their work suddenly stops and their rich feeding continues. The concentrates must be reduced and gran given as a mash instead. Horses have died as a result of the wagoner neglecting to reduce their feed in this way.

Horseshoeing

where i grew up they didn't shoe horses,
ground was so sandy that they didn't need to.
horseshoes were used for pitching at stakes
after the picnic.
this book tells how to shoe horses.

—jd

[Suggested by Roberta Becker Marshall]

Horseshoeing
A. Lungwitz
1966; 216pp.

$6.00 postpaid

from:
Oregon State University Press
Corvallis, Oregon 97331
or WHOLE EARTH CATALOG

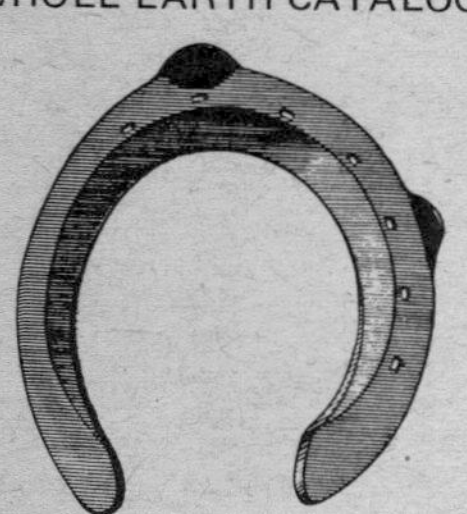

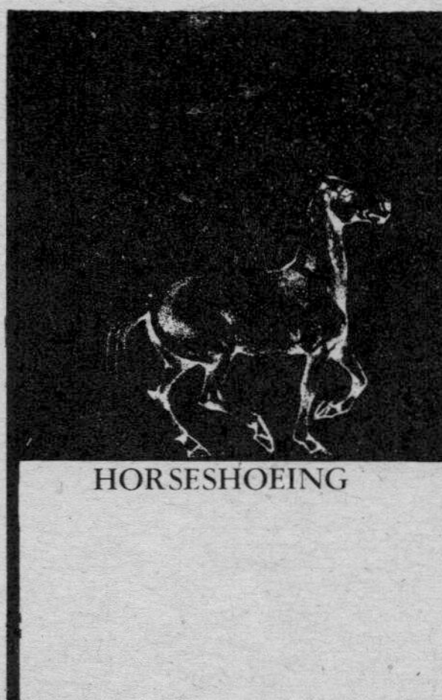

The object of shoeing is,—

1. To protect the hoof from excessive wear, and thus render the horse continuously serviceable upon our hard roads.
2. To prevent slipping and falling during the winter season.
3. To so far remove the disadvantages of faulty positions of the limbs that horses may render good service, and, in some cases,
4. To cure or improve diseased or defective hoofs or feet.

Horseshoeing, though apparently simple, involves many difficulties, owing to the fact that the hoof is not an unchanging body, but varies much with respect to form, growth, quality, and elasticity. Furthermore, there are such great differences in the character of ground-surfaces and in the nature of horses' work that shoeing which is not performed with great ability and care induces disease and makes horses lame.

Veterinary Notes for Horse Owners

an old standard. semi-technical, exhaustive, reference guide. i can't see much application for the book if you don't own a horse, but if you do, it could save you a few hundred dollars in vet bills.

—jd

[Suggested by Peter Ratner]

Veterinary Notes for Horse Owners
M. Horace Hayes
1877;1970; 656pp.

$15.00 postpaid

from:
Arco Publishing Company
219 Park Avenue South
New York, New York 10003

or WHOLE EARTH CATALOG

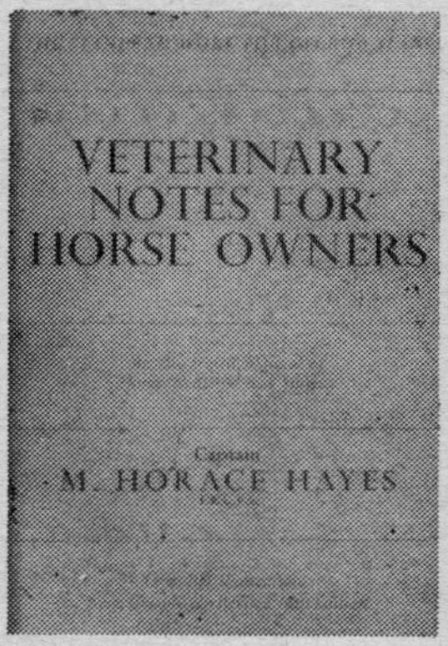

Working mares are more apt to conceive than the fat and idle, while a working stallion will often succeed in impregnating mares which have proved barren to several successive sires; this is one of the reasons why farmers use an indifferent sire in their own neighbourhood, instead of a high-priced animal who leaves no foals behind him. The method of trying a mare over a gate, and the conclusions arrived at, are not always reliable, as in the case of a mare the writer had, and for whom a suitable sire could not be found, till chancing to meet a friend's cob, he took the mare out of harness and got her covered in a neighbour's barn, much against her will, with the result that she brought a splendid foal, and 7 days afterwards conceived to another horse. The 9th day after foaling is very generally agreed to be the most successful time for impregnation, and the case mentioned is to show how great this is a departure from the received traditions of breeders is yet consistent with impregnation. This little mare never at any time showed the ordinary signs of being in use, on both occasions resented the visit of the sire, was at no other time stinted, yet proved a most jealous mother and brought up both foals. The mere fact of a stallion coming through the village was the sole reason of her being served on the 7th day.

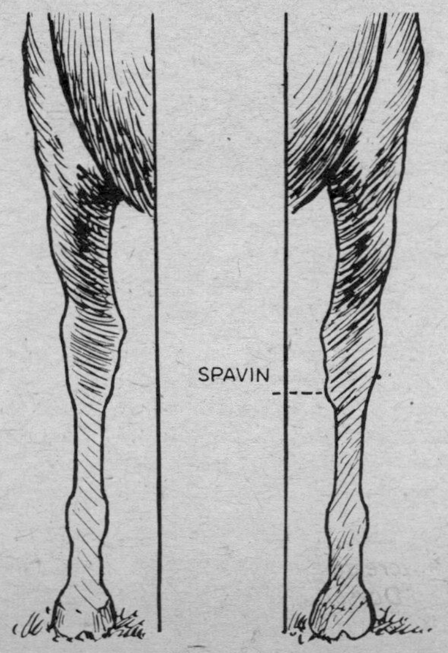

FIG. 69. Examination of the hocks from each shoulder. The near (left) hock is 'spavined'.

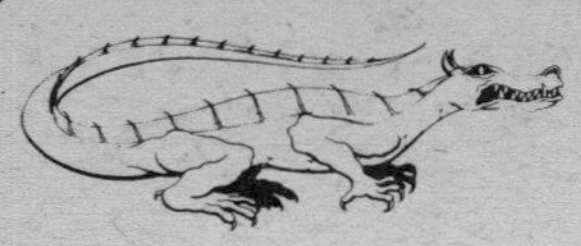

OASIS

Estelle had been driving since about two in the morning and by ten she was exhausted. She might have been able to go another hour or two if she hadn't drunk the beer she'd swiped from the Lone Outdoorsman the night before. But she did, and it wiped her out completely. Divine Right had been in a trance for over an hour now, but she couldn't spare the energy to worry about him yet. She felt it was a major achievement just to get Urge off the freeway into the little town of Lone Oak before she passed out at the wheel. Her neck and back were killing her, and she could barely keep her eyes open to look for a Chevron station. She had to find a Chevron station because they were traveling on the Anaheim Flash's credit card, and they only had three dollars and a quarter left out of the twenty dollars they'd set out with. Lone Oak was just a one-street spot on a two-lane road, but if it had a Chevron station it would be an oasis indeed. Estelle held her breath as she slowly cruised the street. At last she saw the blessed red white and blue sign, and gratefully pulled up under the canopy.

"Good morning miss, how are you today?"

The service station man was an older fellow who walked with a limp, but he gave off the nicest vibe Estelle had found at a station in more stops than she could remember. As soon as he got the gas pump going he went right to work scraping bugs off the windshield and checking Urge's tires. Estelle was so used to taking crap from service station people the old fellow's manner made her want to just stop the trip and hang around the station all day. Or even just live here, she thought. God, would I ever like to have a nice, clean service station to call my home for ever, ever more. Her sense of welcome, and relief, was so complete she decided to celebrate and blow fifteen cents on a Coke.

"Don't drink that stuff," a man's voice behind her said. "Try some of this."

Estelle turned around to face two freaks, a man in a Greek athlete costume and a girl in a drab outfit of dirty jeans and work shirt with the tail hanging out. Her expression was very spacy. She looked a little older than Estelle, but her eyes were so weird it was hard to read anything very definite in her face. After she'd looked Estelle up and down, she turned and sat on the curb in the lotus posture and stared off into the east. The Greek, however, stayed right there with Estelle, looking into her eyes very intensely, smiling broadly as he held out a small brown bottle of stuff for her to drink. Estelle glanced at the bottle, then up and down at the guy's costume. He had on a white toga, a leather thong for a belt, leather sandals that laced up to his knees, and a leather band around his upper arm. Estelle disliked him immediately, although she wasn't exactly sure why.

"What is it?" she asked.

"This, my dear, is acidophilus," said the Greek taking the lid off his bottle.

Estelle asked what acidophilus was.

"It's the source of everything good for your tummy. People have been drinking it since before recorded history. You really ought to try some."

Estelle asked if it got you stoned.

"Absolutely," said the Greek. "It stones you on health, vigor and enthusiasm for the pure-food way of life."

Estelle nodded and said no thanks and turned around to buy her Coke. The Greek pleaded with her not to buy the Coke, and when she went ahead and bought it anyway he lectured her on its evil properties as she drank it. To hush him, Estelle asked if they were traveling.

"Oh yes," said the Greek. "By all means, we are traveling. We are traveling along the Middle Way enroute to a land where nothing has a name. And we'd also like to get to Oklahoma City, if you happen to be going that way."

"Can you drive?"

"Drive like a champion," said the Greek. "I have many talents for the many circumstances, situations and occasions one encounters as he journeys along The Way. I've also got some good food in my bag here, in case you happen to be hungry."

Estelle positively disliked the Greek by now, but she knew she was going to give the people a ride and so she tried to come on to him as neutrally as she could. If he would drive and let her rest it would probably be okay. Ideally Estelle would have liked to simply pass out and wake up in St. Louis some time during the night, but she knew that was too much to hope for. An hour or two of sleep while they made a few more miles was the realistic prospect, but it was enough. She told the people to go over to the bus, that she'd be there as soon as she went to the bathroom.

"Who's that in back there?" asked the Greek when Estelle got back to the bus.

"My old man. He's a little strung out right now, but he'll be all right. You ready to drive?"

"Who painted this thing?" asked the Greek's girlfriend. Her name was Frieda. It was the first time she had spoken. There was something beligerent in her tone, and for a second it pissed Estelle off. But when she looked at Frieda again her anger went away and turned to something close to pity. Something about her eyes, what was it? She looked so lost, so far away in her mind. As gently as she could, Estelle replied, "Different people."

"Different people, huh."

"Yeah. You know. Friends."

"Friends, huh."

Estelle nodded and said yeah, and turned to pay the man for the gas and oil.

"Goodbye," Estelle said to the Chevron man. "I really enjoyed your station."

"Stop in again," said the man. "All of you, come back and see us, you hear?"

The Greek started Urge's motor. Estelle crawled in back and stretched out next to Divine Right. By the time they were on the freeway again, she was sound asleep.

VITA

Volunteers in Technical Assistance is the only source of specific practical information on small-group technology and non-industrial farming that we've found. But what a source. Find here how to make the tools that make life. Well digging bits, glue, no-ice refrigerators, water purifiers, water wheels, well construction, plows, water lifters, stoves, washing machines.

Funktional.

—SB

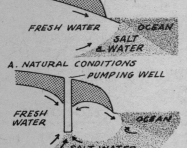

FIGURE 5

FRESH WATER — OCEAN
SALT WATER

A. NATURAL CONDITIONS

PUMPING WELL

FRESH WATER — OCEAN

SALT WATER

B. SALT INTRUSION CAUSED BY PUMPED WELL.

Village Technology Handbook
1963, 1970; 387 pp.

$7.00 postpaid

from:
VITA
3706 Rhode Island Ave.
Mt. Rainier, MD 20822

FIGURE 4

15 CM OF EARTH
LAYER OF STRAW
DIRT REMOVED FROM TRENCH

1.2M

3M TO .6M OF SLOPE PER 1.2M DEPTH OF SILO WALL

FLOOR CROWNED FOR BETTER DRAINAGE.

SPRUNG STRIP CONSTRUCTION

Economical alternative

Bamboo strips sprung over poles

Tied to face

Pole

Post

Plaster 1st coat

Plaster or stucco

Finish coat

Brick or stone base

FIGURE 22
HEAVY BIT FOR DRILLING ROCK

Bit for Drilling Rock

The bit described here has been used to drill through layers of sedimentary stone up to 11 meters (36') thick.

Tools and Materials

Mild steel bar: about 7 cm (2-3/4") in diameter and about 1.5 meters (5') long, weighing about 80kg (175 pounds)

Stellite (a very hard type of tool steel) insert for cutting edge

Anvil and hammers, for shaping

Steel rod: 2.5cm x 2cm x 50cm (I" x 3/4" x 19-3/4") for bail

Welding equipment. . .

Drilling Mechanically

A method for raising and dropping the bit mechanically, not used on the project but used successfully elsewhere, is:

1. Jack up the rear wheel of a car and replace the wheel with a small drum.
2. Take the rope which is attached to the bit and come from the tripod on the pulley and wrap it loosely around the drum.
3. Pull the unattached end of the rope taut and set the drum in motion. The rope will move with the drum and raise the bit.
4. Let the end of the rope go slack quickly to drop the bit.

It will probably be necessary to polish and/or grease the drum.

VITA International Division — provides technical support for both individuals and groups in Asia, Africa, and Latin America who are directly involved in the development process. Specific technical questions on power, farming, manufacturing process, marketing, sanitation, housing, etc. are submitted to individual volunteers or volunteer panels. National programs in Central America, the Dominican Republic, Kenya, and Brazil utilize local volunteers in providing site consultation. Services are free to eligible requestors.

VITA USA Division — offers free technical assistance to agencies sponsoring Vista volunteers in the Eastern Southern, and Midwestern parts of the U.S. VITA volunteers offer skills in hard and soft technology in areas such as rural transportation, self-help housing, cooperatives and credit unions. VITA also provided volunteer assistance to Early Childhood Education projects (daycare centers).

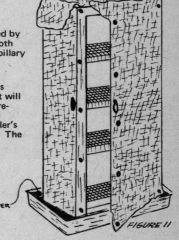

WATER

The evaporative food cooler is cooled by the evaporation of water from its cloth cover. The cloth is moistened as capillary action moves water from the pans through it.

If the climate is dry and the cooler is kept in a breezy spot in the shade, it will cool food considerably below the prevailing temperature. To be safe, the cooler must be kept clean. The cooler's cloth cover keeps flying insects out. The water-filled lower pan discourages roaches and other crawling insects.

WATER

FIGURE 11

Solar Stills

Solar stills purify seawater, hard or brackish water using heat from the sun. Sunwater Co. has done extensive work in Baja California, in one case providing drinking water for a home 200 miles from the nearest source of fresh water.

The Solarstil is a small unit, primarily designed as a boat water purifier.

——Lloyd Kahn

from:
Sunwater Company
10404 San Diego Mission Road
San Diego, CA 92129

New Sources of Energy

Well, they aren't new sources; they're the oldest: sun, wind, earth heat (geothermal). But OK, to us they're new, and indeed they're exciting. The prospect of truly self-contained habitable energy systems is romantic country. There you are with your friends on your hill putting sun and wind through useful changes that are not only apparent to you but an integral part of your living.

Michael Rosenthal first hipped us to this remarkable set of U. N. documents which arose from a conference in Rome in 1961. If you're deeply into solar or wind energy there's lots of stuff here unfindable elsewhere. Japanese solar pillows —simple elegant water heaters up on the roofs, thoroughly described in volume five. Traditional Dutch drainage windmills with suggested adaptations for other early-technology applications in volume seven. And so on. A trove.

[Suggested by Michael Rosenthal]

Solar Water Heaters in Japan

Proceedings of the United Nations Conference on New Sources of Energy

Vol. 4—Geothermal Energy $20.00
Vol. 5—Geothermal Energy $16.00
Vol. 6—Geothermal Energy $16.00
Vol. 7—Wind Power $16.90

from:
United Nations Publications
Room 2300
New York, N.Y. 10017

or WHOLE EARTH CATALOG

Solar House

Page 38 of the Fall 1970 Whole Earth Catalog shows the interesting and useful books United Nations Conference on New Sources of Energy. I felt that figure 1 on the same page labeled "a cross section of a solar heated house" was an unfortunate choice of diagrams. I saw the diagram and thought, "Wow, a solar heated house!" Went to the library, found the books and eventually found the article from which the diagram was taken. It was not a real solar heated house but was a model of one used by a group of Canadians for studying various problems involved in solar heating. All this is rather petty but what I'm trying to say is that there is, from a different article, a diagram (have enclosed a copy) that would arouse more interest because it is a cross section of a real and practical solar heated house. This solar heated home in Washington, D.C., built by Harry E. Thomason in 1959, (he has since built others) required only $11.05 worth of auxiliary fuel for the years 1959-60.

Jack McKee
Portland, Oregon

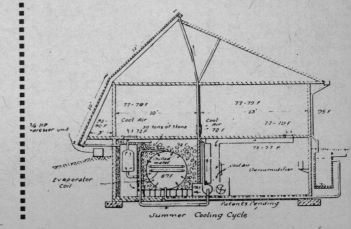

Summer Cooling Cycle

Windmills & Watermills

Lots of good ideas if you are building a windmill or water-wheel. But no plans and few really useful details. Historical approach, beautifully done, and expensive. Get your library to order it.

[Reviewed by Fred Richardson]

– OUT OF PRINT

Windmills & Watermills
John Reynolds
1970; 196 pp.

$13.95 postpaid

from:
Praeger Publishers, Inc.
111 Fourth St.
New York, N.Y. 10003

or WHOLE EARTH CATALOG

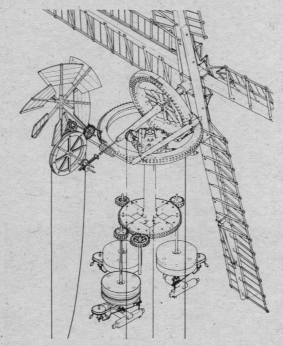

The working surfaces of the stones required careful preparation, and skilled stone dressers were craftsmen in their own right. When dealing with a new stone it was necessary first of all to produce a perfectly smooth surface. A laminated wooden straight edge was used with 'raddle', a composition of red oxide, to detect the high spots, and these were rubbed down with a fragment of burr stone. An extraordinary degree of accuracy was required, and achieved, in this operation. The dresser tested the edge of his wooden staff from time to time against a proof staff of cast iron, which was kept carefully protected from damage in a wooden case. The final aim was to achieve a surface very slightly dished, or hollowed, towards the central eye, ready to receive the system of 'furrows' which performed the actual operation of grinding. These were set out in patterns established through years of trial and error to suit the particular use to which the stone was to be put. In common dressing, the surface was marked out into ten equal 'harps' or sectors, divided not by true radii, but by lines drawn at a tangent to the eye of the stone. This basic method of division, to be seen on Roman millstones, was to remain in use until the end of the traditional corn mill. Each 'harp' was subdivided into alternate 'lands' and 'furrows', the latter cut to a depth which varied between one half and three quarters of an inch, and finished with a sharp arris on one side, an even slope up to the 'land' on the other. Finally a system of fine parallel grooves, the 'stitching' or 'cracking', was added to the surface of each land, a process calling for both skill and precision, experienced men being able to cut as many as 16 'cracks' to the inch. The dressing was so arranged that when the stones were in their working position, face to face, the 'furrows' crossed at each revolution, cutting the grain with the action of scissor blades. As the stones became dulled with wear they ceased to grind efficiently, and frequent re-dressing was required. This involved the deepening of 'furrows' and the renewal of 'stitching', and with a pair of French burrs, might become necessary every two or three weeks.

Wind and Batteries

I would like to comment on a comment on p 39 January (I think) p 7 March Re: small power plants for electricity generation.

The plants (wind) I've seen in operation all used banks of storage bat—teries. These batteries of the common lead acid type used in cars will last several years more than usual if taken care of (feed rain water and keep charged up). Direct current is of course produced and some sort of inverter would have to be used to get AC out of the system. I recall a rancher saying the company who sold him his system guaranteed the batteries 10 years; lots of technical data is available on batteries since telephone exchanges use them for emergency power.

The use of batteries with either water wheel or wind generation systems allows large surge power output; with only a few watts charging on the average thousands of watts can be drawn intermittently.

Car alternators can be used for either water wheel or wind installations; I recall seeing that VITA was working on such. They also had a design for a wind type which had a propeller made by cutting a 55 gallon drum along its axis and then offsetting the halves so that it became a two cup anemometer like rotor (I don't know how successful this was but suspect they may have had starting up problems when the wind died down all the way). When you use a car alternator you can use the regulator to keep the battery charged correctly too. The maximum output of a car alternator is in the 300-600 watt range.

On large wind plants flywheels have been used to store energy between gusts; to make the whole thing efficient several transmissions must be used and it's pretty complicated.

I think the aesthetics and ecology make gasoline fired power plants unattractive. Rural electric lines not only cost every month but often there is a line building charge on the order of a dollar or more per foot. A single auto battery will store enough to run a 40 watt flourescent lamp 10 hours; or a small radio transmitter etc. Don't expect wind fired plants to run the electric heaters and other garbage. Washing machines are made with gasoline engines; refrigerators are made that run on kerosene. Solar electric cells are still too expensive (unless you happen to run into a heap NASA threw out!). We should all learn to live with less power use. Even if it is superficially cheap.

I'd be happy to try help with small generator problems but I don't know anything much about propane conversions! Less power to ya.

John K. Green
Boulder, Colorado

P.S. Windmills still used a lot for water pumping.

Dunlite

Australian wind-driven electric plants, wind chargers. A wide variety of wind generator equipment and appliances. They need detailed information on your wind situation and power needs before they can quote a price for you. Write to: F. W. Davey & Co. Pty. Ltd.
Box 120
Oakleigh,
Victoria, 3166
Australia

Three-blade, wind-driven power plant fitted with Automatic. Variable-pitch Propeller. Two models available.

Solar Devices

How to Make a Solar Still (Plastic Covered), by A. Whillier and G. T. Ward, 9 p., January 1965. $0.90.

How to Make a Solar Steam Cooker, by A. Whillier, 6 p., January 1965. $0.50.

How to Heat Your Swimming Pool Using Solar Energy, by A. Whillier, 2 p., January 1965. $0.90.

How to Build a Solar Water Heater, by D. A. Sinson and T. Hoad, 10 p., February 1965. $0.90.

How to Construct a Cheap Wind Machine for Pumping Water, by A. Bodek, 12 p., February 1965. $0.90.

How to Make a Solar Cabinet Dryer for Agricultural Produce, by T. A. Lawand, 9 p., March 1966. $0.90.

Instructions for Constructing a Simple 8 Sq. Ft. Solar Still for Domestic Use and Gas Stations, by T. A. Lawand, 6 p., revised September 1967. $0.90.

Plans for a Glass and Concrete Solar Still, by T. A. Lawand and R. Alward, 9 p., December 1968. $3.50.

from:
Brace Research Institute
MacDonald College of McGill University
Ste. Anne de Belivue 800
Quebec, Canada
Hpx 3Mi

Wind Generators

Two U.S. sources of wind generating equipment, less sophisticated than Quirk's.

Bucknell Engineering Co.
10717 E. Rush St.
South El Monte, California 91733
Information for $3.00

Dyna Technology, Inc.
P.O. Box 3263
Sioux City, Iowa 51102

THE GREEK'S FIRST RAP

As soon as the bus began to roll the Greek launched into his first monologue of the day. It was actually his tenth one, but the first that Divine Right had heard, and it blew into the middle of his acid high like a rock band showing up at your house for supper. Estelle was so sleepy the words merely pricked her awareness, like flies flitting about on her skin, but the words were like sudden good music to D.R.'s mind. They energized and charged him up at the same time they smoothed out his waking, day-long dream. D.R. had never heard a voice like the Greek's before. He'd never heard anyone speak that confidently that rapidly. The rap was two or three minutes old before D.R. even realized that a strange man and woman had taken over the bus and was driving them away. If it had been a silent fellow mysteriously behind the wheel, acid-paranoia would have overwhelmed and terrified D.R. But this was a talker, a speaker, and D.R. trusted him implicitly. For a long time he lay there next to Estelle, taking in the Greek's words as he would a song. But he felt like moving about, and although he was weak and shaky he made his way to the front of the bus and situated himself on a box of stuff just behind the front seats.

"What I envision," the Greek was saying, "is a world entirely free from mucus. I'm convinced that if mucus can be overcome then everything else will fall into place. War. Poverty. Racism. All second-level stuff in the gross dimension, and absolutely avoidable if people would only give up their attachment to mucus-making foods.

"Now I know a lot of people are on a dairy-protein trip. You hear a lot about yoghurt, cheese, eggs, and brown rice these days. And it's true that protein is essential. But what's got to happen is that people must quit accepting mucus as the price of protein in their bodies. As anyone who has studied the sex and dietary habits of the ancient Sumerians can tell you, there's lots of protein available in non-mucus-making foods. But the thing about people in the west is nobody's interested in what he eats, now, let alone people in ancient cultures. Since the industrial revolution, people have become mere spectators of their own lives, eating what's sold to them, thinking what's told to them, never giving a thought to life after the arbitrary cut-off point the mucus propagandists have established as natural. That's why eighty is considered extremely old in places like the United States. It's due to nothing other than the American mucus conspiracy, business men, capitalists, money-mongers of the lowest order, out to make money peddling food that causes mucus that causes people to die when they're about seventy-five or eighty."

Sanitation and Health

The World Health Organization publishes three excellent books on water supply and waste systems.

Excreta Disposal for Rural Areas and Small Communities *is 189 pages of privies, latrines, and septic tanks. It's a book for health officials, and gives good information on outhouse-type waste disposal, as well as water-carried methods (5 gallons each flush).*

The most complete information we've seen on building a methane generator is in the book **Composting,** *which devotes a whole chapter to the subject. Manure and shit are placed in a sealed tank, and the anaerobic decomposition produces methane gas, which can be used for heating, cooking, lighting, and to power small engines.*

The book deals with the reclamation and recycling of wastes, explains the decomposition of organic matter, and stresses the importance of sanitation in the process.

[Suggested by Craige Schensted]

A few years ago, I spent some time looking for a good book on water systems and couldn't find one. **Water Supply for Rural Areas and Small Communities** *was just what I was looking for. Excellent information on wells, pumps, distribution systems, developed springs, and treatment.*

The World Health Organization publishes this book and apparently directs it toward underdeveloped areas. Some of their reasons for not recommending certain methods and equipment for outlying areas seem to me to be applicable to developed areas. For instance, treatment is recommended only as a last resort because of the necessity for trained operators and often expensive equipment. They have found many cases of impure water in communities where treatment was supposedly taking place, but for one reason or another, wasn't happening. Often, no one worries about water pollution if the water is being treated.

Many of the methods and equipment described are not much used in the U. S. There is very good information on low cost wells. Hand dug, drive point, and jetted. Also information on hand pumps.

[Reviewed by Fred Richardson]

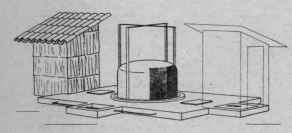

SKETCH OF MANURE GAS PLANT WITH LATRINES

The use of anaerobic digestion of organic waste materials, such as farm manure, litter, garbage, and night-soil, accompanied by the recovery of methane fuel, has been an important development in rural sanitation during the past 10 to 15 years. This development is basically an extension of the anaerobic process for sludge digestion used in municipal sewage treatment to small digestion-tank installations on farms. These farm plants comprise one or more small digesters and a gas-holder. Manure and other wastes are placed in a tank which is sealed from atmospheric oxygen, and are permitted to digest anaerobically. The methane gas, which is produced during the anaerobic decomposition of the carbonaceous materials, is collected in the gas-holder for use as fuel for cooking, lighting, refrigeration, and heating, and for other domestic or agricultural purposes, such as providing power for small engines.

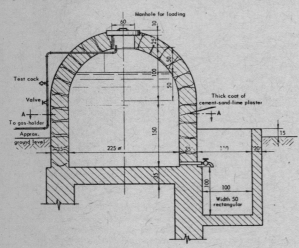

CROSS-SECTION OF INDIVIDUAL DIGESTER UNIT

Composting
Harold B. Gotaas
1956; 205 pp.

$6.00 postpaid

Excreta Disposal for Rural Areas and Small Communities
E. G. Wagner & J. N. Lanoix
1958; 187 pp.

$8.50 plus $.75 postage and handling

Water Supply for Rural Areas and Small Communities
E. G. Wagner & J. N. Lanoix
1959; 340 pp.

$9.00 plus $.75 postage and handling

all three from:
Q Corporation
49 Sheridan Avenue
Albany, New York 12210

or WHOLE EARTH CATALOG

A reasonably safe way for a villager to prepare excreta for use as fertilizer is for him to compost it in a privy pit. After the required period of composting, the pit can be emptied, thus eliminating the handling of the raw excreta. . . .

1. Dig a pit of required size, the bottom of which should always be above ground-water level.

2. Before the slab is placed, cover the bottom 50 cm (20 in.) of the pit with grass cuttings, fine leaves, garbage, paper, etc.; but allow no rubbish such as metal cans, glass bottles, or similar materials to be deposited therein.

3. Place slab, and complete superstructure, keeping in mind that they will both be moved periodically to another site.

4. In addition to depositing human excrement, throw the daily garbage into the pit, along with cow, horse, sheep, chicken, and pig manure, as well as urine-soaked earth or straw. The latter materials are important, as urine is rich in nitrogen, an essential plant nutrient.

5. About once a week throw a few kilograms of grass clippings and fine-texture leaves into the pit. After some experimentation, one can arrive at a pit mixture which will provide a good fertilizer.

6. When the pit's contents reach a level of 50 cm (20 in.) below ground, a new pit is dug 1.50-2 m (5-6.5 ft) away (more if desired), and the superstructure and slab are moved over it. The first pit is leveled, finally, with 15 cm (6 in.) of grass clippings and leaves, and the top 35 cm (14 in.) with well-tamped earth.

7. When the second pit is filled as indicated above, the first pit is uncovered and the compost removed. It should be stable, and will provide a good fertilizer which can be applied immediately to the fields or stored. . . .

Before applying or recommending this method in a rural area where it is not familiar, it is desirable to try it first on a pilot scale under adequate control in order to determine the proper operating schedule and materials suitable and available in the area under consideration. The collaboration of agricultural officials and of local leaders among the farmers of the area is necessary.

Excreta Disposal

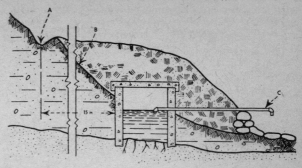

Fig. 33. PROPERLY PROTECTED SPRING (I)

A — Protective drainage ditch to keep drainage water a safe distance from spring
B — Original slope and ground line
C — Screened outlet pipe : can discharge freely or be piped to village or residence

Springs can offer an economical and safe source of water. A thorough search should be made for signs of ground-water outcropping. Springs that can be piped to the user by gravity offer an excellent solution. Rainfall variation may influence the yield, so dry-weather flow should be checked.

Hand-dug wells naturally have certain limitations. While successful wells have been sunk in special circumstances to depths of over 120 m (400 ft), half that distance is usually considered the limit of practical sinking.

•

The first consideration, then, in designing a well is its diameter; neglecting for the moment large-diameter wells built for special purposes, the size of a completed well represents a compromise between economic and practical considerations. It has been found that the cost of a lined well varies almost exactly with its diameter, taking into account the increased thickness of lining necessary in a larger well. The minimum diameter is limited by the room available for a man or men to work; experiments show that a diameter of about 1 m (3¼ ft) is necessary for one man and about 1.3 m (4¼ ft) for two men. It has been found that the efficiency of two sinkers working together is more than twice that of a single man, and consequently a 1.3-m (4¼-ft) diameter is a convenient standard size. Other considerations affecting this decision are the greater natural ventilation of the larger hole, the more efficient size of the kibbles (hoisting buckets) and other equipment which can be used in it, the additional room for concreting operations and insertion of caisson rings, and the possibility of using orange-peel grabs if desired. On the other hand, an increase in diameter beyond 1.3 m (4¼ ft) does not appear to give any great constructional advantages.

•

The quantity of water from a spring can very often be substantially increased by digging out the area around the spring down to an impervious layer to remove silt, decomposed rock, and other rock fragments and mineral matter (usually calcium carbonate) sometimes deposited by the emerging ground water. In doing this, particular care should be taken, especially in fissured limestone areas, to avoid disturbing underground formations to the extent that the spring is deflected in another direction or into other fissures.

•

Energy which Nature has provided, such as the wind, should be taken advantage of whenever possible. In many Northern European and Western Hemisphere countries, wind energy is used for pumping water for farms, homes, and small communities. This method is excellent for obtaining a steady flow of water from a well at a very low cost.

For proper operation, the following conditions must be met:

(1) winds of more than 8 km per hour during at least 60% of the time;

(2) available windmill equipment;

(3) wells that can be pumped for many hours' duration each day;

(4) storage capacity of three days' supply (or more) to take advantage of long pumping periods and to provide for calm periods when there is no wind;

(5) clear sweep of wind to the windmill. This can be obtained by the use of a tower to raise the windmill 4.5-6 m (15-20 ft) or more above the surrounding obstacles.

Water Supply

The Canadian Department of National Health and Welfare puts out a free simple book on sanitation, intended for remote northern areas. It has good clear diagrams of septic tanks, privies, and chemical toilets. There is also information on heating, lighting, water supply, and sanitation. Funky.

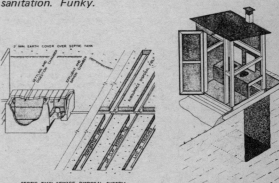

SEPTIC TANK SEWAGE DISPOSAL SYSTEM

Sanitation Manual for Isolated Regions
1967; 64 pp.

free

from:
Department of National Health and Welfare
Ottawa, Ontario, CANADA

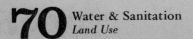

Well Drilling Operations

The Army has done it. A good cheap book on wells. The most useful parts are on auger-bored, driven, and jetted wells. Covers percussion and rotary drilling with military equipment. Useful section on well development and redevelopment of old wells, testing for yield and recognition of strata.

Even a section on "Arctic Methods of Well Construction" (jet with steam!).

The WHO Book on water supply (p.72) has much better information on dug wells and spring development.
[Reviewed by Fred Richardson]

Another simple method of testing is to pour water into the well. If the well point is in dry sand, all of the water added will drain into the sand. If the well point is in water-bearing sand, the added water also will seep out but only to the static level or the water table elevation. When the well point is in water-bearing sand, the quantity of water that can be poured into the well continuously is a rough measure of the rate at which the well can be pumped, since the saturated sand yields water about as freely as it absorbs it. Sometimes raising or lowering the well point a foot or more brings a greater length of the screen into contact with the water-bearing sand and a greater yield results.

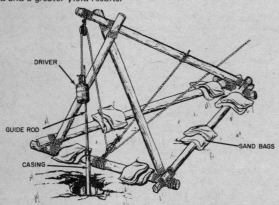

Figure 28. Expedient support for driven well.

b. In constructing bored wells, small rocks or boulders may be encountered that will prevent further penetration. When this occurs, lift the auger from the hole, remove the cutting bit, and replace it with a spiral or ram's horn auger. This tool is then lowered into the hole and turned in a clockwise direction. The spiral will usually twist around the rock so that it can be lifted to the surface. The regular bit is then replaced and boring continued. If an extremely large boulder is encountered and it cannot be removed with the spiral auger, the hole will have to be abandoned and another one started elsewhere.

Well Drilling Operations
Army & Air Force Technical Manual
TM 5-297 AFM 85-23
1965; 249 pp.

Out of print

from:
U.S. Government Printing Office
Division of Public Documents
Washington, D.C. 20402

or WHOLE EARTH CATALOG

Leffel Hydraulic Turbines

if you have a good head of water nearby, a creek, river, reservoir, dam, then you can build a electrical system powered by the water. There are homemeade methods, and used turbines, but it helps if you understand what it takes to change the creek into a lightbulb. Leffel has been doing this industrially for a hundred or so years, but they also have single family systems. Ask for Pamphlet A and Bulletin H-49.
—jd

[suggested by Pete Schermerhorn]

Information

free

from:
The James Leffel Company
Springfield, Ohio 45501

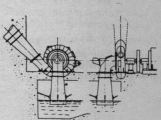

Monitor Pumps

elbow grease hand pumpstands

Information

free

from:
Baker Manufacturing Co.
Evansville, Wisconsin 53536

Rife Hydraulic Rams

a mechanical magic way of pumping water.

[Suggested by Pete Schermerhorn and S. Hamill Horne]

Information

$.25

from:
Rife Hydraulic Engine Manufacturing Co.
Box 367
Millburn, New Jersey 17041

USUAL METHOD OF INSTALLING A RIFE HYDRAULIC RAM. THIS MAY BE VARIED, DEPENDING ON LOCAL CONDITIONS.

Hydra-Drill

looks like a good way to get shallow water, tap springs, bore blasting holes. priced around $389.00.
—jd

Information

free

from:
Deeprock Manufacturing Co.
Box 870
Opelika, Alabama 36801

The HYDRA-DRILL is designed to drill water wells approx. 3½" diameter and up to 200' deep. Because it is economical, portable and easy to use, many contractors and prospectors use it for coring and other test drilling.

The HYDRA-DRILL is powered by the latest model TECUMSEH 3-H.P. engine featuring needle bearings thru out. A thumb-bar throttle control affords total operator control. The rugged 36:1 gear reducer converts the 3,600 engine rpm to 100 rpm for the hi-torque required for hard drilling.

"Now I realize that not very many people can dig on this. But it's actually an established fact that our national leaders are dedicated to the pro-mucus ethic. They consciously and maliciously intend people to get hooked on mucus-causing food as a means of keeping them in bondage and servitude, so they'll buy anything that promises to keep the specter of age eighty at a safe distance. You take the Food and Drug Administration. Big time outfit, right? Big federal scene up there in Washington. They're into mucus like the State Department's into hydrogen bombs. It's like the President's got these two big heavy numbers he's laying on people, hydrogen bombs and youth-cult mucus promotion as a means of subjecting the world--not just this country, mind you, that's old nineteenth century hat--but the whole entire world to a mucus-loving servitude. That's what's behind the eighteen year old vote shuck. And the Peace Corps. Big youth-cult mucus oriented shuck.

"It's like these friends of mine. I had these friends used to be in the Peace Corps, over in Africa, trying to turn the spades onto mucus. Stayed over there two years pretending to help the people, and all the time he was trying to get 'em hooked on mucus. And the poor people in Appalachia, down there in Kentucky, and West Virginia, and in the slums, giving away all those food stamps won't buy anything except a lot of pasty mucus-making food. And the Middle East. What do you think all that friction over in the Middle East is really about, if not mucus? A whole big goddamn mucus plot run right there in Washington, D.C. by the Food and Drug Administration. Trying to stop drugs that might help enlighten the people about the evils of mucus-making food, and promote mucus-spreading foods all because our national leaders are determined to stamp out health and spirituality, and because they're against people getting old naturally and gracefully.

"Look at the state of old people in America. Look at what America reduces old people to. People in the western world are absolutely terrified of getting old. That's because instinctively they understand, although intellectually they reject it, that man's true sexual possibilities don't even begin till around the age of ninety. It's a fear of sex, and for sex read natural health and vigor, disguised as a fear of death. Shit. Do you know what the average life span was among the ancient Sumerians? A hundred and sixty-two years. The average, mind you. Their elders lived well over two hundred years, and death at a mere hundred was considered tragically premature. Those people knew, man. They knew about everything. Western people can't even conceive the kind of sex trip those dudes were into. Western people are fuck-gluttons, just like they're food-gluttons. Got to have it, got to have it, and it's all just one big energy-wasting, mucus-oriented scam, shaped and defined and made into policy, as I say, by the American federal government, with the Food and Drug Administration as the principal architects. The Western idea is to get people to ball two or three times a week, and eat a lot of mucus-producing food so their minds won't ever wonder how it would be without all that mucus. The Sumerians knew better. All they ate were walnuts, and they only fucked once a year.

(continued)

Water in the Service of Man

OUT OF PRINT

"Water, that's our life," a Navaho told me once. This book details how the man-water relationship is played— ancient techniques, theory, flow in pipes and channels, waves, pumps, turbines, wells hydrology. A neat package.

—SB   [Suggested by Steve Baer]

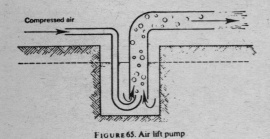

Compressed air

FIGURE 65. Air lift pump

Waves in deep water generally travel in groups or trains, separated by patches of comparatively calm water, rather than in a continuous series. A peculiar feature of the travelling groups is the successive disappearance of the leading waves and the corresponding appearance of fresh waves at the rear of the train. This results in the group advancing with a velocity that is only half the velocity of the individual waves. The newly created rear wave gradually works its way through the group to the front and then disappears. Perhaps there is some human analogy in this birth of a wave, its advancement through the group, and its ultimate death.

Aermotor Windmills

about everyone at home used aermotor,
pitmans,
pitman guides,
well points,
water sand,
home brew in the water tanks.

—jd

Aermotor Information

free

from:
Braden Industries, Inc.
Broken Arrow, Oklahoma 74012

AERMOTOR PUMPING CAPACITY								
Diameter of Cylinder (Inches)	Capacity per Hour, Gallons		Total Elevation in Feet SIZE OF AERMOTOR					
	6 Ft	8-16 Ft	6 Ft	8 Ft	10 Ft	12 Ft	14 Ft	16 Ft
1¾	105	150	130	185	280	420	600	1,000
1⅞	125	180	120	175	260	390	560	920
2	130	190	95	140	215	320	460	750
2¼	180	260	77	112	170	250	360	590
2½	225	325	65	94	140	210	300	490
2¾	265	385	56	80	120	180	260	425
3	320	470	47	68	100	155	220	360
3¼		550			88	130	185	305
3½	440	640	35	50	76	115	160	265
3¾		730			65	98	143	230
4	570	830	27	39	58	86	125	200
4¼		940			51	76	110	180
4½	725	1,050	21	30	46	68	98	160
4¾		1,170				61	88	140
5	900	1,300	17	25	37	55	80	130
5¾		1,700				40	60	100
6		1,875		17		25	38	85
7		2,550				19	28	65
8		3,300				14	22	50

Dowsing

Finding water is serious business. So is dowsing. This is the only how-to book I've ever seen. If you have a talent for this, how would you know but by trying?

—SB

Dowsing—The Key to ESP
Gordon MacLean, Sr.
1970, 1974; 46 pp

$2.00 plus $.35 postage

from:
Gordon MacLean, Sr.
30 Day Street
South Portland, Maine 04106

This pamphlet represents the experience of many experienced dowsers which they willingly share with others at the conventions of the American Society of Dowsers, Inc., held at Danville, Vermont the first weekend of October of each year.

These experiences have been collected by Gordon MacLean, Sr., a Chemical Engineer, a member of the American Chemical Society, the American Institute of Chemical Engineers and is a Fellow of the American Association for the Advancement of Science.

As president of the American Society of Dowsers, Inc. for 1968 and 1969 he was in a favorable position to make this collection. As a Trustee of the Society he continues his interest in this fascinating field which he hopes you will share with him.

Address any correspondence to him at

30 Day Street
South Portland, Maine 04106.

This is not an official publication of the American Society of Dowsers, Inc., since it represents the opinions and practices of individual dowsers which may not necessarily be those of the Society.

FIGURE 39. Water-supply pipeline. Practically all of the difference, h, in level between A and B represents energy expended by the water in overcoming pipe-flow resistance.

Water in the Service of Man
H. R. Valentine
1967; 221 pp.

OUT OF PRINT

from:
Penguin Books
3300 Clipper Mill Road
Baltimore, Md. 21211

or WHOLE EARTH CATALOG

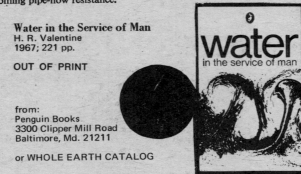

Dempster Windmills and Pumps

Information from:

Dempster Industries Inc.
P.O. Box 848
Beatrice, Nebraska 68310

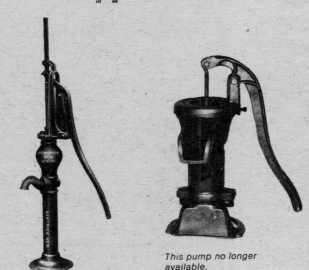

This pump no longer available.

An outfit that uses a magnetic divining device with a pretty good record is Accurate Water Location. You can get a franchise from them if you want to go into business, or you can get the address of their man nearest you. Fee for home water search is $200 plus his travel. Commissioned rates on request. Franchises scattered across the U.S.

—SB

Accurate Water Location Inc.
Route 376
Poughkeepsie, N.Y. 12603

Heller-Aller

windmills, towers, pumps, and so forth

—jd

Information

free

from:
The Heller-Aller Company
Corner Perry and Oakwood
Napoleon, Ohio 43545

The company was organized by John Aller and Frederick Baker. Sam Heller, a dry goods merchant, joined the company in 1904. The company's mills still bear the trademarked name "Baker" on their fan blades.

The development of gasoline and electric water pumps shrank the market and the competition after the 1920's, Mr. Selhorst said. Where there were once almost 20 concerns making windmills, now there are only two others competing with his, the Braden Aeromotor Corporation of Broken Arrow, Oklahoma, and the Dempster Mill Manufacturing Company of Beatrice, Nebraska. Before the decline the Heller-Aller Company was selling 4,000 windmills a year.

Despite the efficiency and speed of new water pumps, windmills still serve a useful function, particularly on large ranches where distances prohibit the continual service and refueling that gasoline and electric pumps need.

All a windmill needs, Mr. Selhorst said, is wind and about a half-gallon of lubricating oil a year. The mills, which last 20 to 40 years, cost from $265 to $500, plus $200 to $1000 for a tower, and require no money for operation.

New York Times

SIZE FT.	MODEL NO.	STROKE (Inches)	APPROX. SHIPPING WT. LBS.	LIST PRICE
6'	12	5	280	$304.00
8'	12A	5-1/2 & 7-1/2 .	388	$420.00

Swimming Pools as Reservoirs

Water being a basic necessity for life, especially in the country where it doesn't just run out of faucets, we'd like to pass along an idea for water storage, that we have been using for over a year. A swimming pool——the kind you assemble yourself with aluminum frame and plastic liner——makes a totally adequate storage tank.

When we were planning our water system, we investigated the various ways of storing water, ranging from homemade cement tanks (tricky to build so they don't crack) to expensive redwood tanks (approximately $600 for 5000 gallons and you have to keep them full or the wood gets screwed up & leaks). Finally, and luckily, we hit upon the idea of a swimming pool. We got ours (15 ft. diameter, 5500 gallons) during a Monkey Wards Spring Catalog Sale for about $160——a real buy, but even at regular prices (up to $200) this beats the redwood tanks by quite a bit, and it's easier to install than a cement tank. Sears and Western Auto also carry similar models.

We installed ours on a hillside above our house (after leveling and shoring up a 15 ft area), and we siphon the water to our house and garden using good old gravity (the tank is high enough above us so we have adequate pressure). The plastic liner (very good heavy duty) imports no taste to the water, and can be replaced for about $40. The plastic cover you can buy to go with the pool (about $12) is worthless, so we bought heavy black plastic, draped it over a cone-shaped frame we built of 2x4's (to keep the plastic from hanging down in the water——it's heavy!), and secured it around the circumference with the nylon rope that came with the original cover.

If you're going to use a siphon, curve the pipe (we used a length of copper pipe connected to our regular plastic pipe) up off the bottom of the tank 6-10" and cover the opening with screen to keep out the silt (which settles to the bottom), bugs, & frogs.

If you install this tank on a hillside, try to find a spot that has a couple of big trees or a large stump on the downhill side (our tank butts up against an old burned-out redwood), so that if the earth shifts the whole pool won't slide downhill——an unlikely occurrence, but you'll sleep better!

Upkeep is minimal. We emptied ours completely after a year to clean the liner, and found that it really wasn't necessary (the plastic looks grungy, but isn't really dirty). We "fill" ours about once a month (more often in the summer)——we don't let it get completely empty or the siphon wouldn't work. It costs us less than $2 per month in electricity to pump water uphill from our spring (if you're smart you'll put your spring above your tank—— but we didn't have a choice).

Hope this suggestion will solve someone's water-storage problem as well as it solved ours. Will be glad to answer any questions we can.

Ron & Liz Peck
Star Route Box 83
Myers Flat, CA 95554

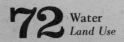

Manual of Individual Water Supply Systems

water supply,
gets into hand dug wells,
a little stiff on heavy electric motors.
—jd

Manual of Individual Water Supply Systems
U.S. Dept of Health Education and Welfare

$.60 postpaid

from:
Superintendent of Documents
Government Printing Office
Washington D.C. 20402

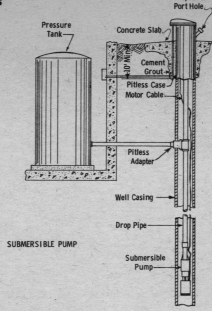

TYPES OF WELLS
Wells may be classified with respect to construction methods as dug, bored, driven, drilled, and jetted.

Drilled wells may be drilled by either the rotary or percussion method.

Each type of well has distinguishing physical characteristics and is best adapted to meet particular water-development requirements.

The following factors should be considered when choosing the type of well to be constructed in a given situation.
1. Characteristics of the subsurface strata to be penetrated and their influence upon the methods of construction.
2. Hydrology of the specific situation and hydraulic properties of the aquifer; seasonal fluctuations of water levels.
3. Degree of sanitary protection desired, particularly as this is affected by well depth.
4. Cost of construction work and materials.

Climates of the States

Specific climatological data on each state: rainfall temperature, freeze occurences, winds, etc. Not all the states are covered.
—SB

$0.25 /state

from:
United States Government Printing Office
Division of Public Documents,
Washington, D.C. 20402

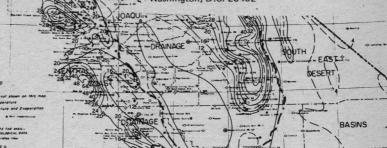

Normal Annual Total Precipitation (Inches) -- California

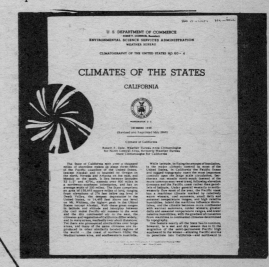

Prospecting and Operating Small Gold Placers

When I was panning gold one summer up along the Feather River a few years ago, there were still a couple of old left-overs from the Depression living meagerly off of placer gold, but Jesus that's thin hard work. Nobody pushes you around though. And just down the river from my claim a couple of college kids cleared several thousand $ out of an unlikely sandbar. This book gives you the working rudiments.
—SB

Prospecting and Operating Small Gold Placers
William F. Boericke
1933; 145 pp.

$6.95 postpaid

from:
John Wiley & Sons, Inc.
605 Third Ave.
New York, N.Y. 10016
or Whole Earth Catalog

The placer miner who is obliged to rely solely on the pan for treating the gravel must realize that it will be *only* the exceptionally rich gravel that will yield him day's wages, and he must therefore try to find pay-dirt that is far above the average. Just a few colors to the pan, however consistent, will not pay out, because it is not physically possible for him to put through unaided enough yardage by panning alone, though the gravel might pay handsomely by some more ambitious plan of working.

– – – – – – – – – – –

For pamphlet Staking a Mining Claim on Federal Lands
send 15¢ to:

No longer available

U.S. Government Printing Office
Division of Public Documents,
Washington, D.C. 20402

Rocking creek gravels in California.

ATLAS OF LANDFORMS
by James L. Scovel et al. A terrain study atlas compiled essentially from the series of 100 topographic maps illustrating typical landforms published by U. S. Geological Survey. Text material, aerial photographs and diagrams. Effective guide to land form study. 14½x12½, 168 pp, 1965, Flexible binding. $10.95

Water and Land

Another thing to think about. Any community must have water. The U. S. Geologic Survey publishes ground water surveys of many parts of the country, these include information on the availability of water, How deep it is and how much water can be expected.

Another service of the benevolent uncle is through the extension service of the various states. Usually with the Agriculture Dept. I know in N. J. they will send a representative to talk to you or supply information about soil analysis, plants, bugs, anything in that. Usually straight, but into the land and very helpful, good people.

Steve Schlossman

Underwater Prospecting Techniques

A vote for goldwater is a vote for fun.
—SB

Underwater Prospecting Techniques
Vaugn M. Greene
1960; 65 pp.

$2.00 postpaid

from:
Vaugn M. Greene
548 Elm Avenue
San Bruno, CA 94066

Miners Catalog

Mack Taylor, head of Exploration Laboratories, says this is the only Miners Catalog. We're glad it's a good one.
[Suggested by Mack Taylor]

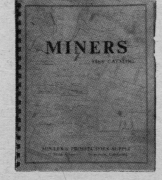

Miners Catalog   free
42 pp.

from:
Miners and Prospectors Supply
177 Main Street
Newcastle, California 95658

All they ate were walnuts, and they only fucked once a year. Once a year, that was all, but it was enough, you see.

Because what they had were these fantastic folk rituals where everybody over ninety got together in the temple at the summer solstice and balled, seventy-two hours non-stop. It was far out. Of course the younger people did it a little more often than that. But even they knew, at incredibly young ages, like nine and ten and twelve, that there were laws in life, and that if you learned them and obeyed them, learned how to orchestrate your impulses properly within the limits set by Sumerian law and folk custom, you became capable of genuine spiritual enlightenment.

Yes sir. The Sumerian line of nut-eaters remained unbroken right on up till almost modern times. That's a little known fact, but it's true. There's a good book about Sumerian nut culture by a guy named Agolt you ought to read. Dr. F. Wong Agolt. Fantastic book. It really changed my life.

MODEL G1717 ENGINEERING COMPASS. Similar to Model G1719 Geological Compass except that it does not have pendulum clinometer, level bubble or extension rule. This is a fine instrument for most engineering measurements.

The compass and optical clinometer scales permit rapid reading of horizontal and vertical angles with a precision unusual in a hand-held compass. Weight with case 9 ozs. Complete...................... $72.50

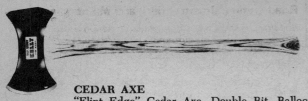

CEDAR AXE
"Flint Edge" Cedar Axe. Double Bit, Balloon Pattern. Head Weight 2 lbs. 26" Straight Handle.

No. 160780 .... $8.10

Price
$14.40

Ben Meadows

a beautiful catalog of real touch them tools.
ben meadows sells them.
great quality,
great variety,
goodie gumdrops.

—jd

[suggested by Sally Mathay]

Ben Meadows Forestry and Engineering Supplies Catalog
536 pp.

$3.00 postpaid ($3 credit with first order over $25)

from:
Ben Meadows Company
P.O. Box 8377
Atlanta, Georgia 30306

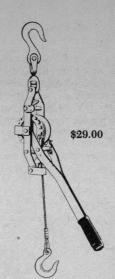

$29.00

ELLIPSE CURVE IN PERSPECTIVE
A combination of useful ellipse curves and radii points for pattern and illustrative layout work.
No. 040506 — Ellipse Curve $3.00

$4.55

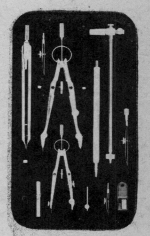

COMPACT TUBULAR STEEL UTILITY SAW TRUE TEMPER

$5.29

Compact tubular steel frame, chrome plated. For camping, nursery, farm and general home use. Light, easy to handle. Exclusive cushion grip. Easy tension take-up prevents blade twist and gives full blade exposure. Tempered blade is easily replaceable.
No. 150272 — 15" blade $2.95
No. 150273 — Replacement blade $1.15

**RELIABLE
SET NO. 020084**
$18.25

ALTIMETER
Fine quality movement. 12,-000 foot level. Size 1¾" diameter. Chrome case. Each in attractive leatherette case. Made in Germany.
No. 102108 .... $35.95

HAT WITH LEATHERETTE BAND		
Cat. No.	Price	Color
131200		Aluminum
131202		Red
131204		Blue
131206	$4.50	Green
131208		Bronze
131210		Gold

Handyman Jack

Basically the Handyman Jack is a super heavy duty bumper jack but it bears no resemblance to the inadequate things that Detroit supplies with their inadequate automobiles. It weighs 28 pounds, has a capacity of 3 tons, is four feet tall, and has a lift of three feet. The jack is guaranteed for 18 months, and complete repair parts are available should they ever be required.

I've used mine for lifting my truck, stretching shrunken plastic water pipe, and a number of odd lifting and spreading jobs, and wouldn't part with it for anything.

WARNING: Beware of handle, or EAT TEETH.

[Suggested and reviewed by Douglas Canning]

$26.95 (30 lbs.)

Harrah Manufacturing Company
46 West Spring Street
Bloomfield, Indiana 47424

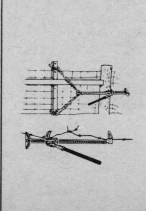

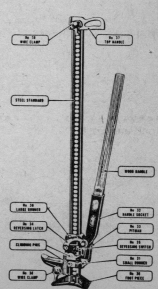

Tractor Supply Company

OK, so you've got this new community in Niobrara County, Wyoming, half way between Dull Center and Bright. You've got 20 people, 5 assorted dogs, a hen (but no rooster), and 12 cats, several of which are pregnant. You've also got: 1 glacier tent, 1 yurt, a Red VW Microbus camper with a noisy rear end, a 15 speed racing bike, and a 1947 John Deere "A" tractor.

There being no roads within 40 km., the Poppin' Johnny is the only transportation in or out. (I told you to get a horse.) Except "It" just broke a rear axle (I told you not to try those 20 ft. jumps) and it's a long, long, way to your Friendly Local John Deere Dealer. Who probably doesn't have the parts in stock anyway. And 1) won't come get your tractor; 2) doesn't want to sell you a repair manual.

There is only one general mail order house that I know of that deals in tractor parts: TRACTOR SUPPLY COMPANY.

[Reviewed by Curtis Cole]

Catalog

free

from:
Tractor Supply Company
4747 North Ravenswood
Chicago, Illinois 60640
An NII Affiliate

Moving the Earth
Modern Techniques of Excavation

The beauty of this tome, and its abridged edition, is that it does not stop after postulating optimum conditions like a "long enough lever and a firm place to stand." After suggesting ways to clear land, remove tree stumps, or lay out an access road using rented machinery like dozers and dump trucks, it goes on to explain many other ways to get it done when the "proper" equipment is not available. Most conceivable snafus are dealt with. Not just how to use a dozer so it doesn't turn over, and rig a winch so it doesn't snarl; but how to get your dozer back on its treads without calling the AAA, and how to unsnarl your winch. All is explained in text and again in eminently understandable drawings.

[Suggested and Reviewed by Alan Kalker]

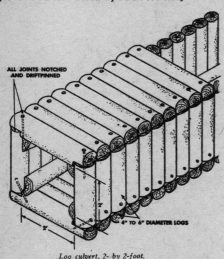
Log culvert, 2- by 2-foot.

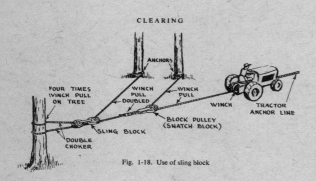
Fig. 1-18. Use of sling block

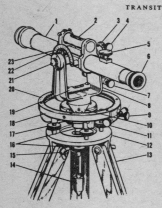
Fig. 2-6. Parts of level transit

1. Telescope
2. Telescope Bubble Assy
3. Vertical Clamp
4. Vertical Clamp Screw
5. Focusing Screw
6. Eyepiece Cap
7. Vertical Tangent Screw
8. Telescope Support
9. Horizontal Clamp Screw
10. Horizontal Circle
    Vernier Plate
11. Horizontal Tangent Screw
12. Tripod Head and Base Plate
13. Tripod Leg
14. Plumb Bob
15. Tripod Wing Nut
16. Center Screw
17. Leveling Screw
18. Leveling Head
19. Support Level Tube
20. Horizontal Circle Scale
21. Telescope Trunion
22. Vertical Arc Pointer
23. Vertical Arc Scale

Transits & Levels

A free booklet entitled "How to Use Transits and Levels for faster, more accurate building" is prepared by C. L. Berger & Sons, Inc. of Boston and can be obtained from Catalog Service, P.O. Box 1656, Dept. 88, Richmond, Va. 23213. One is to ask for the above named booklet. My first concern was whether it would be written in language for the non-technical reader and I was pleased to find it prepared in an elementary method with few assumptions taken concerning the reader.

101 uses for a transit and level are given and a select few are exemplified. It illustrates the method of squaring foundations and establishing straight lines for numerous uses. Straight crop rows are laid out with a transit which doesn't sound like a necessity but it can be helpful to the mule pulling the plow.

Wayne Wooten
Wilbar, N.C.

Rock and Dirt

Getchyer used D-8 cat, your 6 x 6 2-1/2 ton truck, your surplus half-track, your 1800 x 24 tires, your tower crane, your 8 pound sledge, your 80 ton diesel locomotive. Snort.

—SB

Rock and Dirt
Crossville, Tennessee 38555

(U.S.A. and Possessions)

	3 Mo.	6 Mo.	12 Mo.
Air Mail	$6.00	$12.00	$32.00
First Class Mail	3.50	7.00	24.00
Third " "	....	2.00	5.00

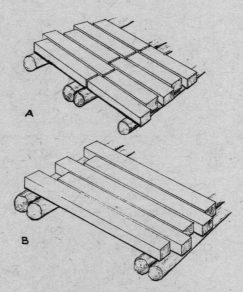
Fig. 3-10. Railroad ties for truck road

Brunton Pocket Transit

Great for rough topographical mapping necessary for planning and laying out water systems, roads, you name it.

Basically a high quality sighting compass with 1º graduations, it has an integral clinometer for vertical angles 1º to 90º with a vernier reading to 10 minutes. Very rugged.

Hand-held, it is hard to make use of its full capabilities, so there is a ball and socket head available for use with a tripod or Jacobs staff. The Brunton is available graduated in either quadrants or degrees and with or without induction damping.

[Reviewed by Fred Richardson]

Brunton Pocket Transit

$64.00 w/o damping

$75.00 w/induction damping

Instruments or literature from:
Brunton Company
500 S. 7th Street
Riverton. Wyoming 82501

Road Design, Construction, and Maintenance

Not how to build a road, but how to design it. For minimum maintainance and maximum service. Useful from driveways up. From dirt surface to pavement. Some bad stuff like calcium chloride too.

[Reviewed by Fred Richardson]

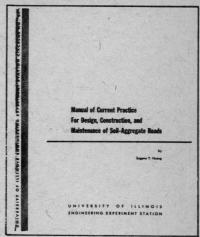

Manual of Current Practice for Design, Construction, and Maintenance of Soil-Aggregate Roads
Eugene Y. Huang
1959; 145pp.

$3.00 postpaid

from:
Engineering Publications
112 Engineering Hall
University of Illinois
Urbana, Illinois 61801

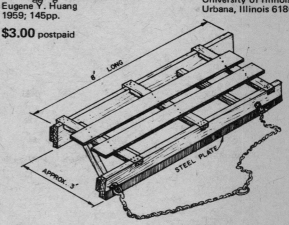
Fig. 5.4 Road Drag Constructed of Sawed Lumber

HUSH, LITTLE BABY

Estelle resisted the irritation of the Greek's rap for perhaps a hundred miles. But gradually she moved into a thinner sleep dimension which his voice pierced like claws. When she absolutely couldn't stand any more she leaned up on her elbow and yelling asked the Greek please to hush a while.

"Hush, you say," said the Greek, also yelling so Estelle could hear him above the VW's whirring engine. "Hush. Now there is one of the more peculiar words in all the English language. Hush. Notice how simple that word is, yet how loaded with implication, and strange music. Hushhhhh. Hear that whisper? Hear that sigh? It's like wind through Sycamore trees. It's the audial equivalent to wheat swaying in a Van Gogh painting. Hushhhhhhh, little baby. There's only one vowel in hush, but notice how the whole word hangs on it, sort of pivots on the U, how it seems to clutch at either side of the U and just hang there in perfect balance. Notice, too, how the word is at once imperative, <u>hush your mouth</u>, <u>hush that noise</u>, but also a noun. <u>A hush settled over the audience as the maestro walked onto the stage</u>. Hush. Hush, now. A marvelous word, hush."

When the Greek had finished, Divine Right broke into applause. He tried to say "Bravo!" but he was so stoned, his tongue was so uncontrollable, the word came out as a kind of growl, like some moron's, or an ape's. The slurpy nonsense of D.R.'s "Bravo!" caused him and the Greek both to break into hysterical laughter.

"Stop the car," said Estelle. She had scooted forward to sit next to D.R., just behind the Greek and Frieda.

"What?" said the Greek.

"What?" D.R. tried to say, but it was such a goofy sound he and the Greek roared with laughter again.

"Excuse me, honey," said Estelle to Frieda as she elbowed past D.R. and crowded into the little space between the two front seats. When she was situated she told the Greek once more to stop the car.

"Stop," said the Greek. "Now there is truly one of the interesting words in our language. When you analyze the word stop . . ."

Estelle grabbed the steering wheel and jerked Urge violently to the right. Gasping in mid-sentence, the Greek yelled "Are you crazy?" and fought to keep the bus from going off the road. Estelle said nothing. She waited till the Greek had the vehicle under control, then grabbed the wheel and yanked Urge toward the edge again. When she did it two more times the Greek at last got the idea and began slowing down. A mile or two later they left the freeway and pulled up at a roadside rest area.

Surveying

surveying is the human way of pissing on all the corners of your property, so you know what's yours and what is theirs. it is also a way of leveling, finding corners, mapping. if you are going to use land, chances are you'll run into a survey. this book seems to cover the discipline and use of the surveyor's tools.

—jd

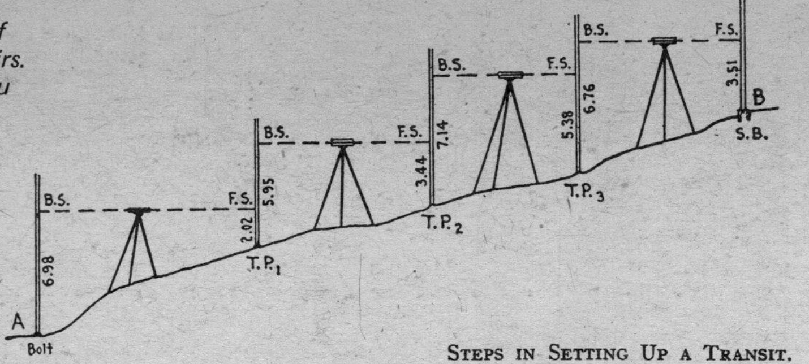

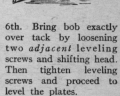

Point	B.S.	F.S.	Remarks
A	6.98		Bolt in S.W. Abutment High St. Bridge
T.P.1	5.95	2.02	
T.P.2	7.14	3.44	
T.P.3	6.76	5.38	
B		3.51	N.E. corner stone bound in sidewalk at #32 High St.
	26.83	14.35	
	14.35		
Diff.	12.48	B above A	

Fig. 51. Differential Leveling.

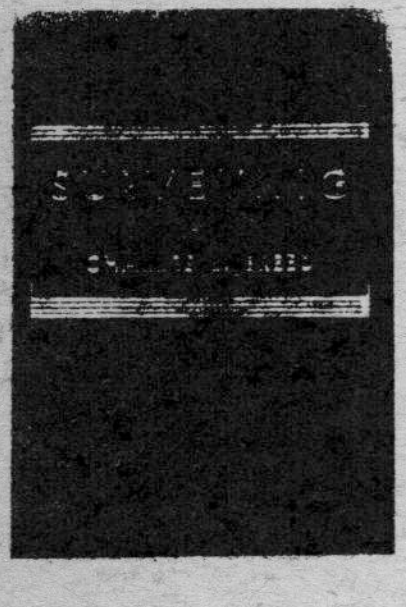

Surveying
Charles B. Breed
1971; 3rd ed.

$9.95 postpaid

from:
John Wiley and Sons
605 Third Avenue
New York, New York 10016

or WHOLE EARTH CATALOG

Steps in Setting Up a Transit.

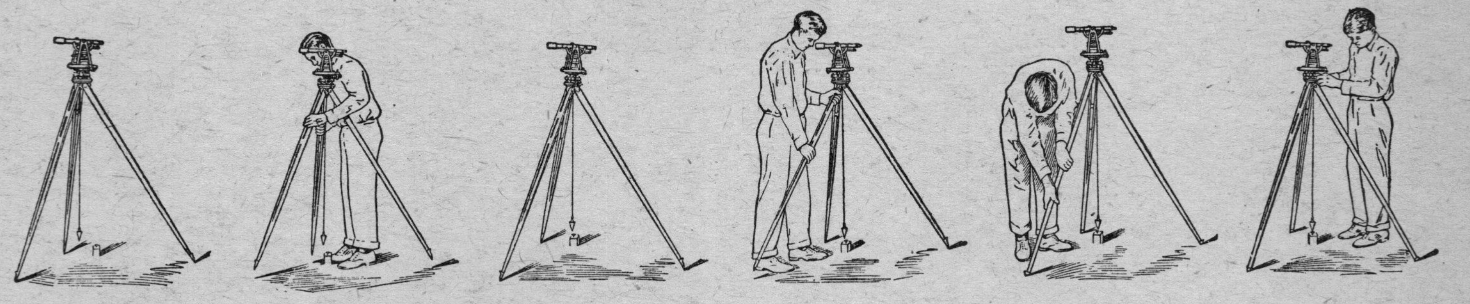

1st. Set instrument on ground near point, with legs spread to give convenient height. Without reference to point, move legs so that plates are nearly level. Tripod leg screws should be firm but not binding.

2nd. Pick up instrument bodily without disturbing relative position of legs and head.

3rd. Place down again with plumb-bob within 1″ of point and bring bob to within ¼″ to ½″ of point by shifting legs slightly.

4th. Swinging one or more legs in arc of circle will approximately level head without changing materially the position of bob.

5th. Press each leg firmly into ground about same amount, watching position of bob so that it will finally return to within ⅛″ to ¼″ of the tack. Plates should still be nearly level.

6th. Bring bob exactly over tack by loosening two *adjacent* leveling screws and shifting head. Then tighten leveling screws and proceed to level the plates.

Blasting

Explosives are a cheap, highly portable, concentrated source of energy, an industrial and agricultural tool and as such useable and useful to the amateur who has need of such tools. Dangerous? Yes, but only a small hazard with reasonable care.——consider as no more, NOR LESS, dangerous than a gun which has no safety and is never unloaded. Treat accordingly——particularly with regard to whom you allow to handle them! Can YOU use explosives?... Yes——with care. Will YOU be ALLOWED to?...Probably, but there ARE regulations and they vary too widely for generalisations.

What would you want them for? The possible answers to that question would surprise most people——the uses of explosives range from the moulding of NASA hardware to the manufacture of diamonds! For the amateur though the most likely uses will lie in the making of access roads, foundations, land clearance and drainage. For instance, $25 worth of explosive will break up 150-400 tons of rock, or lift out and break up a dozen large stumps, or blow a ditch four feet deep, twelve feet wide at the top, tapering to four at the bottom and one hundred feet long. It is often, in outlying areas, cheaper to use explosives for a small drainage or creek diversion project than to pay the cost of getting a backhoe to the site. Also explosives can be used anywhere a man can go, which is often to places machines can't. Even for a simple job like digging a trench for a culvert, a few dollars worth of dynamite used merely to loosen hard-packed soil can easily make the difference between man days of pick work and man hours of shovel work.

The next question is: Where do you go for more information? And the answer to that is...your phone book, under "Explosives" in the yellow pages. Try first the nearest big company; du Pont has the most literature, Hercules seems the most helpful. Then try your nearest dealer, your local police, fire chief and Highway Patrol, in that order. Know before you pick up the phone what you want to do and simply ask for advice and help with the regulations to enable you to do it. It is, however, normal to find that about half the latter have little idea themselves, so persist until you have read your local regulations for yourself, if necessary writing to your state capital. It goes without saying that the most useful information anyone can give you is the address of a neighbor who is experienced in handling dynamite. If you are unlucky and have to work entirely from the book, don't worry too much——there isn't any reason why you shouldn't do so safely, with no more than common sense AND RIGID ADHERENCE TO THE BOOK'S INSTRUCTIONS' Without knowledge of the reasons behind the regulations and the book's "Do's and Don'ts", you must not deviate in the slightest. In particular your local regulations for transport, storage and use will be framed to reflect local conditions and hazards——every little detail MUST be scrupulously observed.

Practical literature is restricted to handouts from manufacturers and, for those who have $6 to invest, Blaster's Handbook *from E. I. du Pont de Memours, Wilmington, Delaware or Canadian Industries Limited, Montreal, Quebec. Imperial Chemical Industries, Limited, Nobel Division, Stevenston, Ayrshire, Scotland, also provides a handbook entitled* Blasting Practice. *Whilst the handbooks admittedly contain everything, they necessarily therefore only devote a small fraction of their space to the needs of the amateur; moreover, being aimed at the professional, they are neither well laid out nor well written for anyone else.*

There is a pamphlet which, despite its small size and vaguely apologetic foreword, is a class above anything else in its field and a model of terse lucidity——"Efficient Blasting through the proper care and use of Safety Fuse" from the Ensign-Bickford Company, Simsbury, Connecticut.

Two final points: if you want to blast near rail, power, phone, or pipe lines, contact the owner; and if you have charged up your first blast and want to know how far to retire and discover that the books become suddenly vague at that point——well, half a mile is a nice round figure...

[Suggested and reviewed by Keith Britton, Advanced Blasting Company]

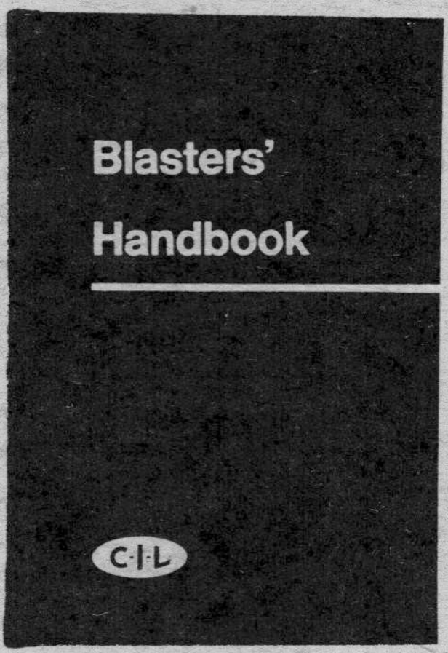

CIL Blaster's Handbook

$6.00 postpaid

from WHOLE EARTH CATALOG

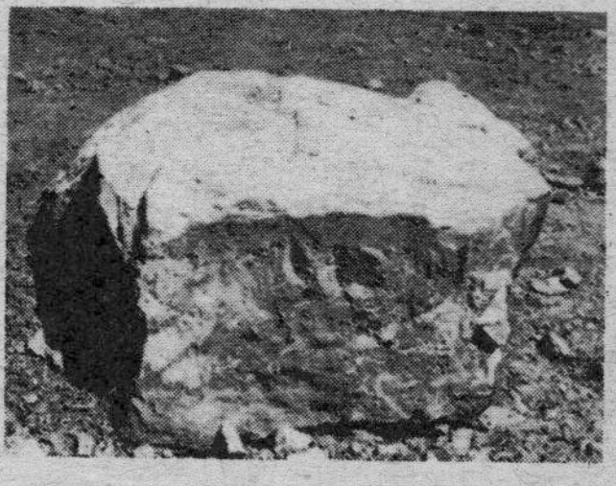

Fig. 254 A 1.3 cu. yd. boulder before mudcapping.

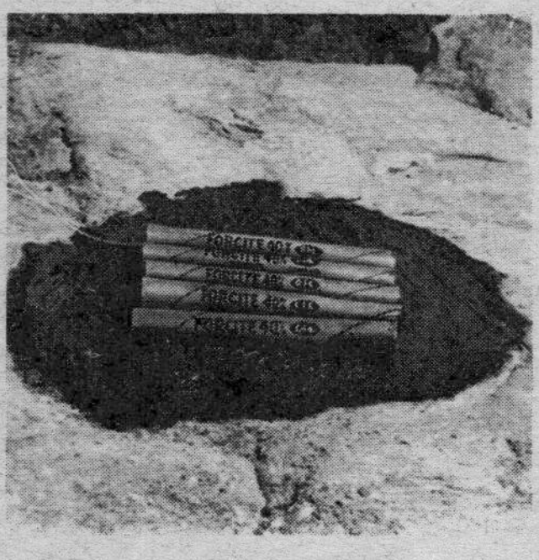

Fig. 255 Embedding the cartridges of explosive in a thin layer of clay increases the efficiency of the charge.

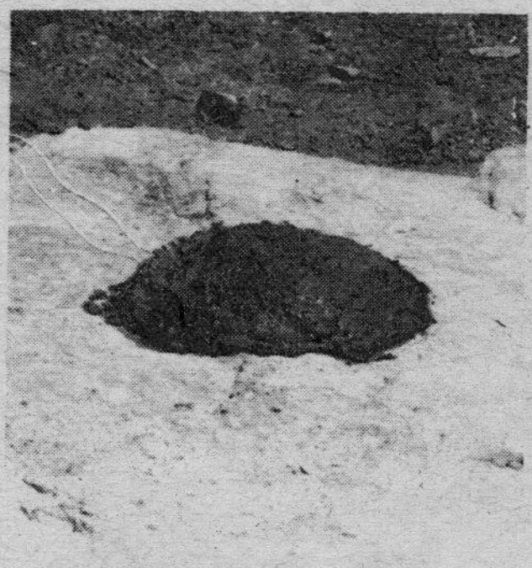

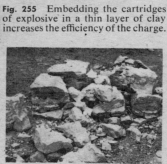

Fig. 256 Mudcap charges should be covered with a generous coating of mud or sand before firing.

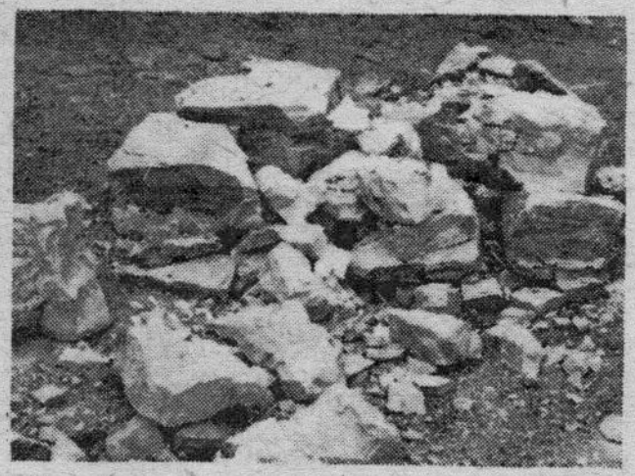

Fig. 257 Results of an efficient mudcap charge.

If several charges in close proximity are to be shot at the same time, firing must be carried out by means of B-Line Detonating Fuse or E.B. caps because all charges must detonate simultaneously; otherwise the first charge to fire might dislodge those on adjacent boulders. Where a single charge is to be fired, a fuse and cap may be used.

Rock varies greatly in hardness, density, cleavage planes, etc., thus charges from two to six 1¼″x8″ cartridges per cubic yard may be required. If the rock is very large or its width greatly exceeds its height, the charge should be divided into two or more parts and placed so that they will have the maximum effect. In the case B-Line Detonating Fuse or E.B. caps should be used for simultaneous firing.

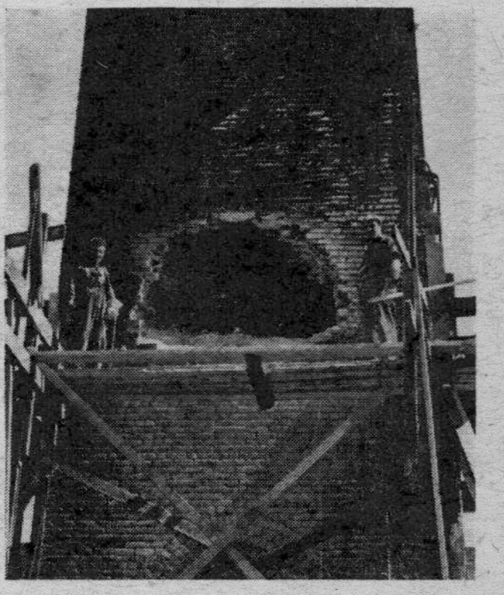

Fig. 289 An opening notch is first blasted in the 14′ x 14′ base of a 127-foot brick stack.

Old stacks, of both round and square section, whether constructed of brick or concrete, can be rapidly and economically felled by blasting where there is sufficient room. Further, they can be made to fall in the desired direction, or "on line."

The "falling notch" principle a lumberjack uses when he cuts a notch at the base of a tree, is the method employed. This involves blasting an opening cut out of that side of the stack in the direction of fall, and subsequently widening this cut by blasting successive holes, or rows of holes, on each side of it. It is essential to shoot the corresponding holes, or rows of holes, one on each side of the opening cut, simultaneously. In this way the final blast undermines each side of the stack at exactly the same instant and thus it topples over in the desired direction. Sometimes it is of assistance to drill a row of closely spaced holes on that side of the stack opposite the direction of fall. These holes are not blasted but provide a line of weakness so that the masonry will part readily and allow the stack to break away from its foundation when the undermining has been completed.

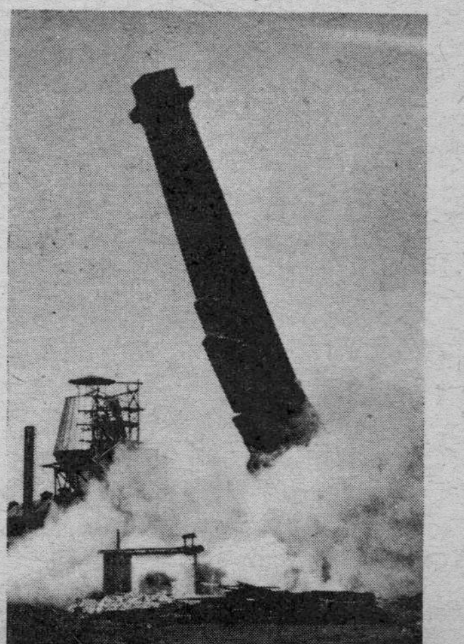

Fig. 290 Final blast brings down stack shown in Fig. 289 "on line".

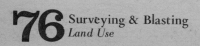

Knowing Your Trees

The encyclopedia of trees in America, with descriptions and illustrations. There are photos of leaves, seed pods, bark, and the natural shape of each type tree. Lovingly presented, in print for over 30 years.

　　　　—Lloyd Kahn　[Suggested by Rodger Reid]

Knowing Your Trees
G. H. Collingwood & Warren D. Brush
Rev. & Ed. by Devereux Butcher
374 pp. 1974

$7.90

from:
The American Forestry Association
1319 - 18th St. N.W.
Washington, D.C. 20036

or WHOLE EARTH CATALOG

Chainsaws

mac and homelight are the ford and chevvy of chainsaws. dealerships abound in timbered country, parts are easily found, and the saws are fairly simple, hard working, tools. i've used both, and, being a ford man, prefer the McCulloch, for no particular reason other than that they seem to run a little better, work a little harder. both companies make a full range of sizes, from the teeny six pound, compression release, backyard loggers saws, right on up to the big mothers, with thirtysix inch rollernose bärs, bearclaw dogs, and multiple hernias.
　　　　—jd

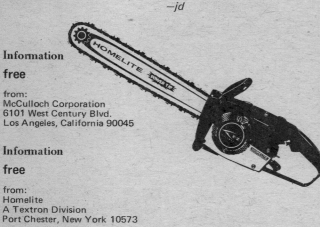

Information

free

from:
McCulloch Corporation
6101 West Century Blvd.
Los Angeles, California 90045

Information

free

from:
Homelite
A Textron Division
Port Chester, New York 10573

Alaskan Mill

This is a roller attachment for a chain saw that enables you to make boards from trees. You need a minimum of 6 horsepower and a 16''-24'' bar to power the one-man mills, and we're told that 12-15 h/p is needed for cutting any quantity of lumber.

There are two one-man attachments, and three two-man models.
　　　　—SB
　　　　[Suggested by Elias Velonis]

Granberg Alaskan Chain Saw attachment (one man)
No. G-758: $81.50, F.O.B. Richmond
Slightly larger model, G-759: $91.50.
Two man versions range from $336-$405.

from:
Granberg Industries
200 South Garrard Blvd.
Richmond, California 94804

Mobile Dimension Saw

Two issues ago you carried a good report on the "Mighty Might" saw mill from Portland, Oregon. It's a good saw, but big and costly compared to its main competitor, the "Mobile Dimension Saw"

The reason for this is that Jim May who first developed the saw, has several patented (and I must say very ingenious features in his "Mobile Dimension Saws" that for most of your readers are very advantageous. Namely these features result in considerable reduction in overall weight and add correspondingly to its flexibility. And it does this without any sacrifice in performance potential. There is also a very significant savings in cost.

My dad and I looked into both saws before we bought our large model "Mobile Dimension Saw". We have been very pleased with it. Jim May's son-in-law, Ron Harriman, who runs the company now, produces excellent workmanship and comes through with fast and dependable parts and service.

I suspect that for most commune type of situations, the smaller models would more than suffice, and pay for themselves with some outside jobs. Here in the Northwest, logs that are left laying in the forest by loggers for various reasons are often very salvageable with these saws.

[Suggested and reviewed by Fritz Mishler]

Alpine Fir

SILVER FIR or Pacific silver fir, as it is also called, is so named for the striking silvery white appearance of the under side of its needles. Another name applied to it is lovely fir ——implied by *amabilis*——because of its beautiful pyramidal or spire-like form in comparison with the usually dome-like crown of noble fir and lowland white fir, with which it is often associated. The pleasing form of silver fir shows to best advantage in open situations where it is densely clothed to the ground with comparatively short branches. These branches sweep downward and outward in graceful curves.

Seed pods of *Black Locust.*

The redwood and its close Sierra relative, the giant sequoia, *Sequoia gigantea*, are the largest, and almost the oldest, life forms in North America, if not in the world.

Accurate ring counts cannot be secured without destroying the tree, but it is assumed that redwoods 300 feet high and twenty feet or more in diameter may approach an age of 2,000 years. Most of the redwoods cut in commercial operations are from 400 to 800 years old. These are from three to ten feet in diameter, and 200 to 275 feet tall.

Fan-shaped leaf of *Ginkgo* tree is found in no other plant.

Tree Finder

For fast unromantic identification of trees, these shirt pocket books are excellent.
　　　　[Suggested by Catherine Yronwode]　—SB

Master Tree Finder (for area east of Rockies)
$0.75 postpaid

California Tree Finder
No longer available

Winter Tree Finder (east of Rockies)
$0.75 postpaid

Pacific Coast Tree Finder
$0.75 postpaid

Rocky Mountain Tree Finder
$0.75 postpaid
all from:
Nature Study Guild
Box 972
Berkeley, CA 94701

Zip-Penn

Low-cost chains and parts for chain saws.

They also have plastic wedges——you don't wreck the chain if you hit the wedge.
　　　　[Suggested by Tom Duckworth]

Catalog

free

from:
Zip-Penn Catalog Office
Box 43073
Middletown, Ky. 20243

Mighty Mite

*transportable sawmills,
expensive,
industrial,
but a possibility,
if you have more money or trees
than you care to have.*
　　　　—jd

Information

free

from:
Mighty Mite
International Enterprises of America, Inc.
P. O. Box 20066
Portland, Oregon 97220

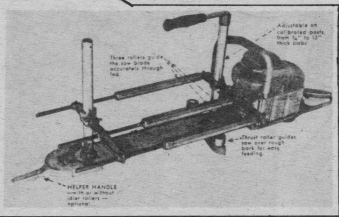

$8,400

ONWARD CHRISTIAN SOLDIERS

Oh joyous joy of wondrous joys, look at the lovely world.
The sky, the clouds, and feel the wind whipping little dusts against your skin.
A minute ago I bent over to pick up a rock the size of a nickel, but when I touched it it scurried away on the tiniest little footprints I ever saw.
A beautiful intrusion quadruples the illusion.
Confusion.
Confucian.
Ha!
What I'm trying to do is get from here to over there but it's a long, hard way of going, let me tell you.
Oh joyous joy of wondrous joys, look at the lovely world.
The world has a blue ceiling and no walls anywhere to be seen.
And a sandy-colored carpet with a parking lot painted on it.
The bright sand is painful to my eyes, and wondrous to behold.
I've got some sunglasses, but who knows where they are?
Estelle would know, but where's Estelle?
Playing in the dunes.
If I were to call to her she couldn't hear me, because of the constant wind, blowing through my mouth to take my breath away.
Trudge, trudge, trudge. Onward Christian soldiers, over the wasted land. Through heat, sun and wind, in spite of loneliness, fear, isolation, and a twisted tongue he goes on, on, forever on toward the Concrete Picnic Tables, ancient relics of a culture long forgotten, buried by the desert sand.
"I'm coming; you guys. Wait for me, I'm coming!"

MODEL 12

Mobile Mfg. Co.
Rt. #2, Box 22A
Sundial Rd.
Troutdale, OR 97218

$4,250

Finding and Buying Land

The trick is, helping the seller find you. The best way to do this is advertise. Find out what the land owners read, and advertise there. It may be the bulletin board at the general store or the six ranchers' journals of the north-western states (find at libraries in the area).

Say in your ad what kind of land you're looking for and what you're willing to pay, e.g., "WANTED TO BUY, mountain land, south slope, timber, year-round flowing water, prefer no improvements and minimum roads; 200-600 acres, in northern Oregon or Washington state; will pay $60/acre if suitable, good cash terms. Mortimer Head, 1111 A St., Portland, Ore., 16161, (007) 242-4242."

This procedure largely by-passes the real estate agents, and good riddance. Most are a foul breed, though one in twenty is all right and can help you.

To find out what land you want takes some research. Shop around locally and get a feel for the terminology and considerations of land buying (clear title, developed springs, grass for 200 head, adjoining National Forest, county road, mineral rights, water rights, NE ¼ of section 28 R 17 T26, taxes last year, six-months option, etc.) Visit friends who have land and see what they like and don't like about it. Tell everybody you talk to that you're looking for land and let them rattle on.

Finding an area to suit you is partly a matter of maps and partly visits to see how the climate and vibrations are. Write for United Farm and Strout Catalogs for rough (high) land values in various areas.

The most important source of information on a piece of land besides visiting it is the USGS (US Geological Survey) topographical map of the area. Order the index map for the state(s) you're interested in, have someone show you how to use Range and Township to locate yourself, and buy the appropriate maps. At 50¢ apiece they are an outstanding bargain.

Once you get to seriously considering a piece of land go to the County Assessor's office to find out what the County knows about it. They will have records showing what was paid the last time the property was bought and when the sale took place. They also will have maps showing who your neighbors are and where they can be reached. If you're trying to find the owner of a piece of land, that's the way. (Incidentally, wandering around in pretty country falling in love with various sites is no way to get land. It always either belongs to the Government, who won't sell, or some guy who won't sell.)

Bear in mind there is a rural land boom going on. Land that was $50/acre last year is $60-70/acre this year. Stay away from developers and their prices. They buy a big hunk cheap and sell little hunks dear. They and the neighbors they'll get you are a pain in the ass.

When you buy land in a place and start living there, you become a citizen of the county and state. Don't be surprised if the other citizens are interested in you. Wouldn't you be?

—SB

U.S.G.S. Maps

Get state indexes and maps from:

Map Information Service
U.S. Geological Survey
12201 Sunrise Valley Drive
Reston, VA 22092

United Farm and Strout

These catalogs will feed your land mania.

—S.B.

United Farm Agency

Strout Realty

Plaza Towers
P.O. Box 4528 gs
Springfield, MO 65804

Free

from:
United Farm Agency
612 West 47th St.
Kansas City, Missouri 64112
and the other local offices

Free

from:
Strout Realty
521 E. Green Street
Pasadena, California 91101
and other local offices.

Aerial Photography

You can get aerial photographs of any place in the U.S. To find which agency has the picture, get a photoindex.

—SB

Free

from:
Map Information Office
U.S. Geological Survey
12201 Sunrise Valley Drive
Reston, VA 22902

THIS VALLEY FARM is just one of the many high-yielding farms that are found in the rich and diversified agricultural "horn of plenty" in Washington.

ON KICKAPOO RIVER

No.174—103 acres, $16,500. Scenic valley recreation farm with ¼-mile frontage on Kickapoo River! 103 acres, 40 tillable, balance wooded. 4-acre corn base, 2 springs, deep well. Old buildings need extensive repair—6-room house, barn, corn-crib, granary. 2 miles to town. Destined to please at $16,500, excellent terms. UNITED, Boscobel, Wis.

ALPINE MOUNTAIN CABIN

No.199—10 acres, $20,000. Rustic mountain cabin located in alpine valley setting of pines and aspen. Spectacular scenery . . . combination of exotic rock formations, tall whispering pines, white-barked quaking aspen. 10 acres with 650-ft. frontage on rushing mountain TROUT STREAM. Good spring for domestic water supply. Direct private access to national forest, 2 miles of fishing streams and West Elk Wilderness area. 19 miles to college town. Can be yours for $20,-000, LOW down payment. UNITED, Gunnison, Colo.

HIGH COUNTRY JEWEL

No.470—5 acres, $6,000. Surrounded on 3 sides by national forest land and within 6 miles of winter ski area. 5 beautiful acres crossed by year-round rushing creek. Covered with aspen, blue and silver spruce trees. Many choice creek-side building sites for your cabin or home. Just below timberline, on good Forest Service road. 11 miles to town, 66 miles DENVER. In heart of excellent deer and elk hunting, very near several high country lakes for top trout fishing. Rare find at only $6,000, low down payment. UNITED, Conifer, Colo.

Caretaking

Tips on familiarizing yourself with an area——we did this when we moved into Lake County. Read Yellow Pages, cover to cover. The phone book also has other good parts too. Also, want ads and local paper provide much information of interest to the newcomer.

We lucked into a fantastic scene——we are CARETAKERS on a 5 acre farm on Clear Lake. We get free house, utilities and a salary of $125 per month and also all the fruit and nuts we can eat from the orchard. Fish from the lake, our own garden etc. I report this because I am amazed at the number of CARETAKER POSITIONS open in this area. Check the Santa Rosa PRESS DEMOCRAT——there are usually several caretaker ads at any given time. Our particular "feudal landlord" is a dream——he is only here once or twice a month for a couple of days. Rest of the time place is ours. He is particularly kind to longhairs. Some are not, of course, and generally owners prefer retired couples. But give them a good rap about "youth having more energy and creativity" and they might hire you. Worth a try. We got a garden of Eden——you might too!! We don't want to stay here indefinitely, but it makes a great "half-way-house" between city and community.

Larry Kelley
Kelseyville, CA

Tax Property

About the item in your Spring '69 issue about acquiring tax delinquent property; it will work, I believe, as set forth, but the title could end up being a "shakey" one, and there is always the chance you will just end up paying someone else's taxes and improving his property gratis.

Better deal and more straightforward, is to locate several tax delinquent properties, contact the owner or heirs and offer to buy at a low figure.

Also, in California, tax delinquent property is deeded to the state after a few years (5, I believe) and then sold off yearly at a tax sale auction.

Anyone acquiring property in the above fashions (and intending to keep it) should sometime "search the title" and issue a non-guaranteed "preliminary report" at low cost, anticipating that they will later insure the title. Title companies are also sometimes a source of free plat maps and other information.

Some factors to be considered when doing the land thing: government assessments (taxes & improvement districts) easements, rights of way, zoning, liens, "chain of title" and covenants, conditions and restrictions.

Researching can be done at various offices at the county court house or hall of records. Friendly real estate brokers can also be a big help.

A lot can be learned by phone.

Alex Gough
Atascadero, CA

How To Locate In The Country—Your Personal Guide

We haven't seen it, but here's some advice on How To Locate In The Country—Your Personal Guide.

$3.00

from:
Garden Way Publishing Company
Charlotte, Vermont 05445

Ruined Dinner

Wrote to the Office of Land Management in Alaska about homesteading. Prompt reply states, all homestead land indefinitely withdrawn —— ruined my dinner. Very nice Xerox form letter though.

Skip Whelan
San Diego, CA

CLOSED

Alaska

***For Facts About Alaska Lands** write to:*

Alaska Dept. of Natural Resources
Division of Lands
323 E. Fourth Ave.
Anchorage, Alaska 99501

Anybody living at all rough in Alaska (or elsewhere) can use the invaluable publications from University of Alaska Extension. Well-handled subjects like "Canning Moose & Caribou", "Sourdough", "Fruit Trees in Your Yard", "Greenhouses in Alaska", "Fur Parka", "General Pelt Care", "Game is Good Food", "Wild Berry Recipes".

Write to:

Cooperative Extension Service
University of Alaska
Fairbanks, Alaska 99701

Free to Alaskans, $.25 per copy on all publications mailed outside the state. Wild Berry Recipes an additional $.50.

Alaska State Land

I don't know so much about Fed. land up here in Alaska, but the state has a deal going where anyone who wants to take the trouble of coming up here and doing the footwork can stake out 5 acres along interior rivers and isolated coastal areas around Kodiak, the Alaska Penn., Kenai Penn, and "south-eastern." You must be 19 or over, and the land must be surveyed and bought. Costs run around $200/acre plus surveying (another $1,000?). I sure hope that anyone who comes up here please doesn't pollute the place, it's bad enough already.

Daniel G. Leen
Fairbanks, Alaska

If You Could Live Here a Year

One can buy land privately from individuals who may or may not be speculators. One can buy and lease land from the State. We are going up to Palmer in a couple of weeks and big on five acres of wilderness. The minimum the state wants for this five acres is $675.00. One hears about these land auctions through a publication called Alaska Land Lines, which is published by the State Department of Lands, *and sent only to Alaskan addresses.* Some of their land goes by lease. You can have it five years and then another five, and then if you want to own it you have to hire a surveyor. This is expensive.

Also, there are mineral lands to be had from the U.S., but again you have to have proof of "color", that there are minerals, before they let you use it. You never own these, and you have to go in yearly and do $100.00 worth of work on your claims (I think that is right. It has been a long time since I took the course at Community College).

Alaska is 500 miles from north to south, and 1500 from east to west. There are parts of it that have not been surveyed, or even walked on. Alaska is not for an "effete snob". If you can't face realities you couldn't stand to live here. Because the realities are harsh. We have bears, and each year the magistrates go into the bear caves looking for buttons, to declare so-and-so dead. We have had 40 sightings of bears in an around Anchorage this year so far. I am scared of bears. We have horrible weather in the winter. Sometimes. The winters are sometimes cold and long—always long, and sometimes cold. I remember one winter when it stayed less than 30 below for 3 weeks straight. I made the mistake of turning the car handle with a bare hand. Now each winter the palm of my hand hurts where it was frostbit. We lose people to the elements. There was a guy—a GI—here three weeks at Fort Richardson a couple of years ago. He went for a little hike and got lost. He died less than 100 yards from the entrance to the Fort. They called it exposure, but it was just plain fright, from being lost in the wilderness. I knew a guy that goes on rescue missions. He says all the people he has rescued are out of their heads from fright by the time he finds them—that is, the ones who are still alive.

I have been down to the Land Office a couple of times and I see young long-haired people looking over the maps of what is available for lease or purchase from the State, and I am glad to see this. In spite of the putdown of young people that is going on in some places—and some places there, too—I hope they can winter through. It has always been a saying that if you could live here a year you could stay and would stay. It is possible to live off the land yet, but takes planning and the knowhow.

Peacefully yours,
B. Duffy
Anchorage Alaska

Jobs in Alaska booklet

It's very businesslike so's not 2 offend the locals who forget that they too were once strangers here — but having gone thru the job hunting scene here myself in summers 65, 6 & 70, I can say this would have been a handy & welcome tool. (Do you have any idea how hard it is for someone w/ a college education to find any outdoor job? Of course you do . . .)

I would also suggest that the jobbee have many Form 57's (standard U.S. Govt. employment info. form which one may pick up at any lg. post office) filled out in advance (partially, so you can b.s. your experience to fit the application, and in full, so you can just drop it off and not have to sit in the personnel offices) as that will save much time which could be used legging down other jobs.

Thank you and many etceteras,

Scott Semans
Anchorage, Alaska

Jobs In Alaska

$2

from:
P. O. Box 1565
Anchorage, Alaska 99501

Daniel Leen's octagonal cabin near Fairbanks.

Canada

Agricultural Information

New Canadian immigrants who are setting up farms or looking for suitable sites should acquaint themselves with the publications of the various Departments of Agriculture. In addition to the Canada Dept. of Agric. each province has a department of its own. Most publications are free. The quality however, is subject to great variability. Some are excellent, some are disappointing. The subjects covered range from very general ("Farming in Canada") to very specific ("Control of the Purple Backed Cabbage Worm in Newfoundland").

The Canada Department of Agriculture will send copies of up to ten publications free to individuals. The List of Publications is available from: Information Division, Can. Dept. Ag., Ottawa. They also offer for sale at $2 each a great series of soil surveys—very useful to anyone considering buying land for farming.

Each province has its own Department of Agriculture. In Ontario the provincial dept. will send up to ten free publications to each adult resident who requests. The list of publications is available from: Information Branch, Ministry Ag. and Food, Parliament Buildings, Toronto.

Mr. and Mrs. Peter Ruppell
Hearst, Ontario

SELECTIONS: Canada Department of Agriculture publications

1296	Farming in Canada. 60 pp. Illus. 1966
1224	Climate of the Upper Peace River region. 20 pp. Illus.
868	Manures and compost. 16 pp. 1962
———	Catalogue of Plans: Sheep housing and equipment. 28 pp. Illus. 1965
1019	Sunflower Seed production. 24 pp. Illus. 1967
849	Plums for cold areas of Eastern Canada. 16 pp. Illus.
1217	Culture of cigarette burley tobacco. 8 pp. Illus. 1964
1205	How to grow mushrooms. 16 pp. Illus. 1965
1127	Swine Breeding. 36 pp. Illus. 1962
1023	The dairy goat. 16 pp. Illus. 1957
861	Mushroom collecting for beginners. 32 pp. Illus. 1958
1192	Gardening in the Yukon. 32 pp. Illus. 1963
1322	Booklice. 1 pp. 1967
1362	How to grade furs. 96 pp. Illus. 1968

ONTARIO Ministry of Agriculture and Food

128	Beekeeping in Northern Ontario—unavailable
487	The Grape in Ontario
502	Table Turnips—unavailable
94	Cultured Dairy Products—unavailable
193	Tractor Transmission Systems—unavailable
476	Farm Water Supply—unavailable
321	Wine Making in Small Quantities
283	White Grubs—unavailable
226	2,4—D Can Damage Crops

Monthly Seasonal Fruit and Vegetable Report

British Columbia Land

These folks are compiling an information book about land acquisition in British Columbia. Write to:

Statement of Intent
17 Boyd St.
Victoria, B.C.
Canada

The job market in Alaska is difficult for strangers to understand, since a vast amount of rumor and wildly inaccurate information abound. Get-rich-quick stories are the most common, and few of them are true. Wages and salaries are significantly higher than in the Lower 48, but the high cost of living in Alaska erodes much of the difference. In most ways, the economy of Alaska is similar to that of the rest of the United States. If, however, you want to earn a lot of money in a short time, and are willing to work long and hard, then there are *some* opportunities in Alaska.

One way to get rich quick in Alaska is to get on the payroll of a company which is willing to pay overtime premiums for long hours of work needed to complete projects on a rush basis. The majority of these jobs, however, are located in "the bush," which is anywhere outside the state's major cities and towns. (In-town construction usually proceeds in a normal daily manner.) Construction projects are the most likely places to have the jobs which pay a lot of overtime, but most of their positions are filled by trained, experienced, union workers.

Other seasonal jobs, such as working on a fishing boat or in a cannery, may offer large amounts of pay for work lasting a relatively short time, but the money will be well earned through gruelingly long hours of very hard work.

Crown Lands

The Acquisition of Crown Lands in British Columbia (Land Series Bulletin No. 11) is the official word on procedure, regulations and the access to further information on obtaining government lands in B.C. (I'd guess that the other provinces publish similar bulletins.) Get it free from the Government Printing Bureau, Victoria, B.C. Comes with 2 maps of B.C. (back to back): No.1—Land Recording Districts and a list of Land Series Bulletins Nos 1-10 (each is reputed to give info on physical features and economy of subdivisions of the province.) No. 2—Index to Provincial Land Status Maps.—each divides available from non-available lands in a small area of B.C.

The procedures for obtaining gov't land in B.C. sound arduous and in all cases except outright purchase, access is limited to British subjects or immigrants. Nonetheless, far more cheap land appears to be available in Canada than in the States. We'll be checking these rumors, gathering information and looking for land this year. We'll keep you informed.

Bill Dickinson
Marysville, WN

Immigration

The canadian immigration department practically requires that a prospective immigrant have assurance of a job, evidenced by a letter from the employer, along with a bank statement (savings book, etc.) showing sufficient funds to support ones self and family for a year or so, a couple of thousand will do. some folks have done this by borrowing such a sum, depositing it in a bank, getting a statement to that effect, then withdrawing the sum, returning it to the owner and retaining the bank statement for immigration purposes. also, ownership of land is another point in your favor. Even a small parcel (a city-type lot) which are available cheaply through tax-land companies can help establish your sincerity in becoming a useful, purposive canadian subject, which is what the immigration dept. wants.

–Tracy

RITUAL

"I'm coming, you guys, wait for me, I'm coming!" is what D.R. tried to say, but only garbled idiocy came out. And even if it hadn't been garbled idiocy the people he was calling to could not have understood what he said, because of the ceaseless wind. They were in a paved rest area just off the freeway, a hard, treeless place with white lines marking off the parking places, and concrete picnic tables permanently established beyond a curb. At the far end of the paved area a big trailer-truck was parked parallel to the curb across a couple dozen diagonal parking lines. Near it a family surrounded a picnic table, eating food. The Greek had established himself seven or eight tables down the line from the family, where he was preparing to do his daily food ritual. He usually did the ritual at sundown, but since they had stopped, and because everybody's nerves seemed a little on edge, the Greek felt a soothing ceremony was called for, to cool the vibe a little, and bring everybody together.

When they first stopped Estelle wandered off by herself among the dunes, but when she heard D.R.'s yell and saw him having trouble negotiating his way from the bus to the table, she went back to help him along. His arm around her neck, carrying him like a drunk, they staggered up to the table in time to observe the Greek setting up his scene.

It was a simple scene to set up because the only food involved was walnuts and water, and no dishes or utensils were involved. The Greek carried his walnuts, already hulled, in a leather bag about the size of a woman's purse. The water was in a gallon plastic jug with a label on it that said, "Pure-O Artesian Drinking Water. Rich in Natural Minerals." The Greek unfolded a black cloth about the size of a pillow case and spread it on the table. He set the jug on the eastward corner of the cloth, and placed the nut bag diagonally across from it with the open top laid out toward the west. As he picked up his first walnut the Greek bowed three times to the east, and then three times to the west as he picked up the jug and drank from it. When he'd chewed and swallowed the walnut he closed his eyes and held his palms together in front of his face in an attitude of prayer.

"F . . f . . f . . f," D.R. stammered. "F . . f . . f."

The Greek opened his eyes to see who was speaking. Although he'd only been praying about five seconds he frowned as if he'd been disturbed from a deep sleep.

"What's he trying to say?" the Greek snapped.

"He's probably trying to say far out," said Estelle. "D.R. says far out a lot."

"Why doesn't he go ahead and say it, then?"

"I don't know," said Estelle. "Ask him."

"Hey," yelled the Greek. "Get away from those walnuts."

D.R. had turned away from the Greek and was grooving on the leather walnut bag. The rough side of the leather was out, so that when you rubbed your finger across it, it made a pattern that seemed to D.R. extraordinarily beautiful. He heard the Greek tell him to stay away, but it surprised him when the Greek took him roughly by the arm.

"You're not supposed to get into the walnuts until we've prepared our hearts and minds," said the Greek. "Kindly wait."

The Greek closed his eyes and folded his hands and began again to prepare their hearts and minds to receive the walnuts. Stoned as he was, D.R. felt like his heart and mind were already prepared, but he certainly did not want to disrupt the ritual. The ritual was beautiful to D.R. The Greek was beautiful, the walnuts were beautiful, all the world around was beautiful, beautiful. Inhaling deeply, D.R. folded his hands and closed his eyes, and listened to the Greek's prayer.

Stalking the Wild Asparagus
Stalking the Blue-Eyed Scallop
Stalking the Good Life

Euell Gibbons honestly makes you wonder why we haven't been nibbling cooperatively at the wild Earth all our lives. We'd rather fight and hassle over manufactured products than dine directly on what we can't prevent from flourishing freely around us. Take a congenial trip with Gibbons to the woods, to the beach, anywhere except the parking lot, and let him feed you, tum and head.

—SB

Stalking the Wild Asparagus
1962;70; 303pp.

$2.95 FOB Long Island City, N.Y.

Stalking the Blue Eyed Scallop
1964;70; 332pp.

$2.95 FOB Long Island City, N.Y.

Stalking the Good Life
Euell Gibbons
1971; 248 pp.

$6.95 FOB Long Island City, N.Y.

from:
David McKay Company
750 Third Avenue
New York, New York 10017

or WHOLE EARTH CATALOG

Edible Wild Plants of Eastern North America

Everything east of the Great Plains and north of the Florida peninsula that you can eat. It's a technical sort of book, with a sweet attitude.

—SB

Edible Wild Plants of Eastern North America
Merritt Lyndon Fernald, Alfred Charles Kinsey, Reed C. Rollins
1943, 1958; 452 pp.

$10.95 postpaid

from:
Harper & Row Publishers, Inc.
10 E. 53rd St.
New York, N.Y. 10022

or WHOLE EARTH CATALOG

Edible Native Plants of the Rocky Mountains
H. D. Harrington
1967; 388 pp.

$10.00 postpaid

from:
University of New Mexico Press
Albuquerque, New Mexico 87131

or WHOLE EARTH CATALOG

Russian Thistle

The young shoots make a very good potherb. Served with salt, pepper and lemon or vinegar we found it to be mild, pleasant and crisp tasting, making one of the very best potherbs we have ever tasted. They can be dressed up with fried bacon and boiled eggs like spinach or creamed and served over toast. Because of the bland taste they can be mixed to an advantage with more tangy plants such as mustard.

Wild Edible Plants

there is a need for a good, big, colorful book on the wild edible plants of the united states, north america, planet, and so forth. so far no one has wanted to tackle the job, mainly i suppose because a book like that would be so expensive to produce that getting the price down for someone who wanted to forage for edible goodies would be tough. this book is neither colorful nor planetary, but if you are going to peck around some natural produce from the rocky mountains west, you should be able to use it to help you both identify and cook your meals. the line drawings are abundant, precise, carefully executed.

—jd

Wild Edible Plants of the Western United States
Donald Kirk, Janice Kirk
1970; 307pp.

$3.95 postpaid

from:
Naturegraph Publishers
Healdsburg, Ca. 95448

or WHOLE EARTH CATALOG

For the number of different kinds of food it produces there is no plant, wild or domesticated, which tops the common Cattail. In May and June the green bloom spikes make a superior cooked vegetable. Immediately following this comes the bright yellow pollen, fine as sifted flour, which is produced in great abundance. This makes an unusual and nourishing ingredient for some flavorful and beautifully colored pancakes and muffins. From fall until spring a fine, nutritious white flour can be prepared from the central core of the rootstocks for use as breadstuff or as a food starch. On the leading ends of these rootstocks are found the dormant sprouts which will be next year's cattails. These can be eaten either as a salad or as a cooked vegetable. At the junction of these sprouts and the rootstock there is an enlarged starchy core the size of a finger joint. These can be roasted, boiled or cooked with meat. In the spring, the young shoots can be yanked from the ground and peeled, leaving a tender white part from six to twelve inches long which can be eaten raw or cooked.

CATTAIL

COLD DRINKS

In this group are included the various home-brewed drinks such as birch-beer, and the simple summer drinks prepared from acid fruits and used like lemonade. We have not entered the very extensive field of distilled liquors, and there are some people who might object to indication of the ingredients of birch-beer, root-beer and other mildly alcoholic beverages, but no one can object to pink lemonade prepared by bruising Sumach-berries in water or from the juice of Prickly-Pears or Barberries. The number of these refreshing cold drinks is larger than we should have imagined; they may be prepared from the following:

Spruce (for beer), p. 80
Hemlock (for beer), p. 80
Sandbur (grain), p. 107
Chufa (tubers), p. 108
Cat-brier (roots), p. 142
Birch (for beer), p. 153
May-Apples, p. 206
Barberries, p. 208
Mountain-Ash (berries), p. 230
Raspberries, p. 236
Dewberries, p. 236
Blackberries, p. 236
Cherries, p. 240
Honey-Locust (pods in beer), p. 243
Locust (flowers), p. 248
Crowberries, p. 261
Sumach (berries), p. 262

Red or Black Mulberries, p 163
Mountain-Sorrel (leaves), p. 169
Sorrel (leaves, p. 171
Sea-Purslane, p. 189
Maple (sap), p. 269
Grapes, p. 272
Prickly-Pears, p. 276
Soapberries, p. 277

Buffalo-berries, p. 277
Spikenard (root), p. 282
Wild Sarsaparilla (root), p. 283
Pipsissewa (leaves), p. 305
Bog-Cranberries, p. 317
Persimmons, p. 321
Yellow Bedstraw, p. 344
Elderberries, p. 349

Edible Native Plants of the Rocky Mountains

This book is an excellent listing of the edible plants of the Rockies. It provides recipes for the preparation of beers and wines, jams and preserves, the cooking of greens and the preparation of dyes, as well as brief histories of the plants' use by historic and prehistoric peoples. The book contains drawings of the plants in their flowering or fruiting stage and lists them by common name as well as scientific name for ready reference.

For anyone seriously considering living off the land, trying his hand at new and exciting dishes or cutting down on the grocery bill, this book is a must.

[Reviewed by Patricia Roberts]

Green Sea Urchin.

You must develop skills in finding these perfect and formerly unused campgrounds. One way to do it is to get off the beaten track. Study the map and find a small road that leads off the one you are following, then a smaller road that leads off of it, and finally a still smaller road trailing off that. On this last little road one is almost certain to find an ideal camping spot where permission is either not required or easily obtained.

•

I don't guarantee to make the shelling of black walnuts easy, but I have found that it gets progressively easier with practice. If you stand the nut pointed end up on a solid surface and hit it a sharp blow with a hammer, it will crack into two halves. Stand each half, again pointed end up, and strike it again, and you will have broken it into quarters. Strike each quarter again on the pointed end, and it will break crosswise into eighths this time——at which point the nutmeats will fall out.

FIG. 60, MAY-APPLE

Tragopogon species (4) (Sunflower Family)
Goatsbeard, Salsify, Oyster Plant

Preparation and Uses: The fleshy roots may be eaten raw or cooked, tasting like oysters or parsnips, according to whom you are speaking. When only a few inches high the young stems, along with the bases of the lower leaves may be used as potherbs.

The coagulated milky juice of these introduced plants was used for chewing by various Indian groups. The juice was considered a remedy for indigestion. In olden times in Greece, Italy, and other Old World areas linen pads were soaked in the distilled juice and applied to bleeding sores and wounds. Pliny records that the juice, when mixed with woman's milk, is a cure-all for disorders of the eyes. *T. porrifolius* is the cultivated Salsify or Oyster Plant.

Habitat and Distribution: The Goatsbeards are found in open ground throughout the West.

Description: These plants are tall, stout, biennial or perennial herbs with fleshy tap-roots, and entire, grasslike, clasping leaves. The yellow or purple flower heads are borne on tall, leafy stems: the matured head resembling a fluffy, giant, dandelion head.

144
Tragopogon dubius
Yellow Salsify

Mushroom Hunter's Field Guide
Savory Wild Mushroom

Finding a strange, slimy, luminous colored growth on dark rotting wood is surprise and pleasure; to extend that experience into identifying it and possibly EATING it is even better. For the beginner one batch of mushrooms can occupy a whole day, from finding them, through waiting for a good spore deposit and making a decision, to cooking them. An efficient guidebook is essential to avoid frustrations.

The McKenny book is compact, but not especially well organized for use. It contains clear and concise descriptions of 83 varieties of fungi, some of them peculiar to the Puget Sound region, the rest common throughout the U.S., and 33 black-and-white and 48 color photographs. There is also an article on mushroom poisons and the many fine recipes make one want to rush to the woods and immediately gather baskets of Chanterelles, Morels and Ceps. Not so easy!

Smith's book, which I prefer, is more technical in language and scope, although, as a field guide, it avoids identification methods involving microscopes and chemicals. It is much more complete, covering 188 varieties with a black-and-white photo of each plus 84 color photos, and it is organized in keys which are super to use if you like being methodical. It is not necessarily true, however, that it is quicker to follow the system in thumbing through either book, as in wandering in the woods, luck and perseverance further.

[Suggested and reviewed by Sandra Tcherepnin]

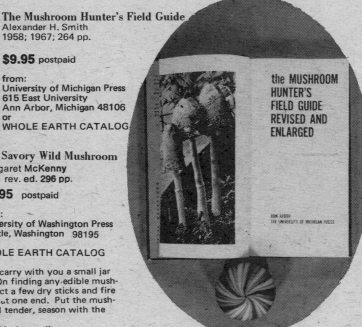

The Mushroom Hunter's Field Guide
Alexander H. Smith
1958; 1967; 264 pp.

$9.95 postpaid

from:
University of Michigan Press
615 East University
Ann Arbor, Michigan 48106
or
WHOLE EARTH CATALOG

The Savory Wild Mushroom
Margaret McKenny
1971 rev. ed. 296 pp.

$4.95 postpaid

from:
University of Washington Press
Seattle, Washington 98195
or
WHOLE EARTH CATALOG

On a tramp through the fields and forests, carry with you a small jar of butter, creamed with salt and pepper. On finding any edible mushroom (except morels or elfinsaddles), collect a few dry sticks and fire them. Split a green stick (alder or willow) at one end. Put the mushroom in the cleft, hold it over the fire until tender, season with the butter. Eat from the stick.
from "The Savory Wild Mushroom"

Less than natural size

164. COPRINUS ATRAMENTARIUS (Inky Cap)
Edibility. Edible, but some people experience a peculiar type of intoxication from eating this species and afterward drinking an alcoholic beverage. I have now discovered three people in Michigan with this type of sensitivity.
from "The Mushroom Hunter's Field Guide"

A Key to the American Psilocybin Mushroom

magic mushroom information, not found in normal mushroom guides.

—jd

Psilocybe quebecensis

A Key to the Psilocybin Mushroom
Leonard Enos
1972; 80 pp., color plates

$5.00 postpaid

from:
The Youniverse Project
8135 Lincoln Street
Lemon Grove, California 92045

or WHOLE EARTH CATALOG

Edible and Poisonous Mushrooms of Canada

The world is full of them. They grow in lawns and woodlots, by roads and rivers, in parks and pastures, but most abundantly in the piney woods in the fall. Most people do not see them. They are there, but invisible; outside the range of conscious awareness. Once you become aware of them, they seem to spring up in droves.

For the beginning pot-hunter, The Savory Wild Mushroom (Margaret McKenny, U. of Wash. Press) or the Mushroom Hunter's Handbook (Alexander Smith, U. of Mich. Press) are excellent non-technical guides. Pretty soon you can spot an Amanita, Agaricus, Russula or Coprinus or such off-beat types as Chantrelles and Boletes. But there comes a day when, after an afternoon's ramble thru a park or forest you come home with about thirty different species, most of which are not in the book. Now what?

There are a number of older and more technical manuals which can usually be found in libraries. The Mushroom Handbook by Louis Kreiger has been reprinted by Dover in paperback and so is readily available, but is rather difficult to use.

On a recent trip to Canada I found what I think is the best new book on the subject, Edible and Poisonous Mushrooms of Canada. It is authoritative, but still readable, though you might have to keep one finger in the glossary at first. There are new and simplified keys for tracking down over 400 different species, and best of all, most of them are illustrated with color photos taken in the field. With this book, and a lot of patience, you should become a local expert.
[Reviewed by Walt Downing.
Suggested by Barbara Kirshenblatt-Gimblett]

Edible and Poisonous Mushrooms of Canada
J. Walton Groves
1962; 298 pp.

$11.70 postpaid

from: Queen's Printer
Information Canada
Publishing Division
Ottawa, Ontario
Canada

or WHOLE EARTH CATALOG

Figure 266. *Mycena alcalina.*

All but one of the species have revealed an interesting and striking chemical characteristic that is very constant in fresh specimens. When the Fruit are scratched, bruised by handling, or injured in any way they stain blue, or, if the surface color is yellowish, green or greenish blue. This harmless phenomenon is apparently caused by the oxidation of an enzyme in conjunction with the psilocybin and is a main point of identification. Certain chemical reagents are known to accelerate this bluing. The best, of these indicators, p-methylaminophenol sulphate or metol, gives a constant and strongly positive reaction on the flesh of the stem, becoming very deep violet within 1-30 minutes. This chemical, which is in crystal form, is inexpensive and can be prepared from any chemical house or photographic shop that handles darkroom supplies. Metol will dissolve in about 20 times its weight of distilled water, and the solution must be used immediately since it is unstable. A canteen of distilled water and a small plastic bottle are all the tools needed to make up the solution in the field. Be sure to shake the solution vigorously to shorten the dissolving time.

Mycological Societies

Your coverage of mushroom identification books is fine, but I have graduated from Smith and McKenny (both of which I have) to *A Guide to Mushrooms and Toadstools* by Morten Lange and F. Bayard Hora, Dutton. It is very complete and has color painting instead of photographs, which I like, and every species is shown in color. I belong to the San Francisco Mycological Society and I recommend that anybody who is interested in mushrooms join the nearest mycological group for help with locating and identifying. Write to the North American Mycological Association, 4245 Redinger Road, Portsmouth, Ohio 45662, for the address of the nearest group.

Sent by

Mary Schooner
San Francisco, CA

Fruits of Hawaii

After due research I can report that it's true, you can live off the land in Hawaii for very little. Fruit grows everywhere, and this book is an excellent guide to which of it is edible and where to find it and how to cook it. If you liked the early 60's, you'll love Hawaii.

—SB

Fruits of Hawaii
Carey D. Miller, Katherine Bazore, Mary Bartow
1965; 229 pp.

$6.00 postpaid

from:
University of Hawaii Press
535 Ward Ave.
Honolulu, Hawaii 96814

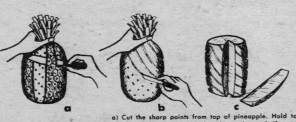

a) Cut the sharp points from top of pineapple. Hold top firmly in left hand and, with a large, heavy knife, start peeling strips from top downward until entire rind is removed. (The top may be removed before cutting off rind.)
b) Remove the eyes by cutting diagonal grooves around pineapple.
c) Cut off top and slice fruit lengthwise into wedges. Each serving then has some of the sweetest and most desirable portion of the fruit. The core may be removed from each slice.
d) If larger pieces are desired, cut entirely through the peeled fruit lengthwise and serve the slice whole.

PRAYER

The Way is uncharted. The map cannot be spoken. Names are in words, but nature lives only in nature. The source of creation is nameless, but the matrix of all is named. The secret eludes eyes clouded by longing. Prejudiced eyes must stop cold at the surface. The secret is self-contained.
May we be mindful of these truths. May we become pure enough to pass through the gate to the root of the universe.

Design with Nature

Ian McHarg is a landscape architect, and as a problem solver, he has taken on the huge challenge that ecology obviously represents to the land planner, making a positive constructive step towards a resolution. From his extensive knowledge of both landscape architecture and the biological science of ecology he has developed a methodology that no responsible land planner, city planner, or large land developer can overlook (nor any affected citizen allow to be overlooked). Through a systematic (and easily reproducible) method Mr. McHarg investigates the relevant ecological restraints inherent in any large planning area. Physiography, hydrology, geology, topology, flora and fauna ecologies, and other natural restraints are individually mapped for the area under consideration. These restrained portions of the area are mapped in varying transparent shades according to the degree of restraint the consideration warrants. By overlaying these numerous graded maps, a final map is evolved which designates where to not develop, where light development is compatible with the land, where specifically restrained development is permissible, and where other types of development (recreational, medium and high density) would be least objectionable.

Mr. McHarg realizes that the great "scabs" appearing on the face of the Earth, and the "puss" that resides within these sores are a tremendous threat to Earth's existence. But, he also realizes that growth is going to take place. To meet this growth with only derisive criticism will do little. Only by developing the attitude of "steward" towards Earth and acquiring the tools and knowledge that are needed to properly care for her, will we survive.

Interspersed with chapters demonstrating the power of his method (including examples of projects his firm has done for clients and cities all over the country), the author describes his experiences and attitudes in moving chapters that express his love for Earth, and the profound reasons behind this love.

It is a beautiful book, beautifully written and illustrated, demonstrating that enlightened man can properly care for his life giver, Earth.

[Reviewed by Vic Conforti]

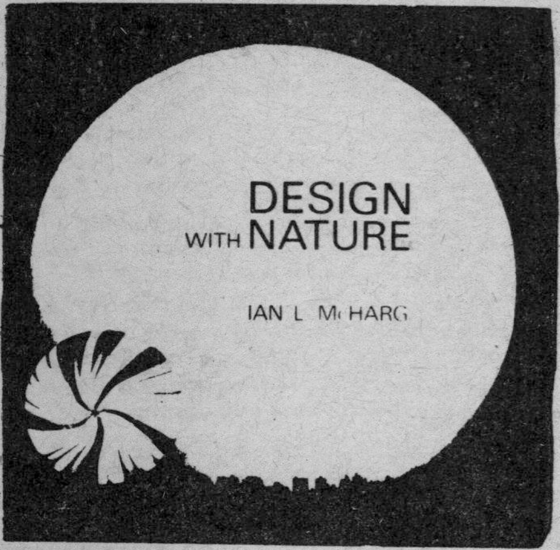
DESIGN
WITH NATURE
IAN L. McHARG

Design with Nature
Ian L. McHarg
1969; 197 pp.

$5.95 postpaid

from:
Doubleday & Co., Inc.
501 Franklin Avenue
Garden City, New York 11530
or WHOLE EARTH CATALOG

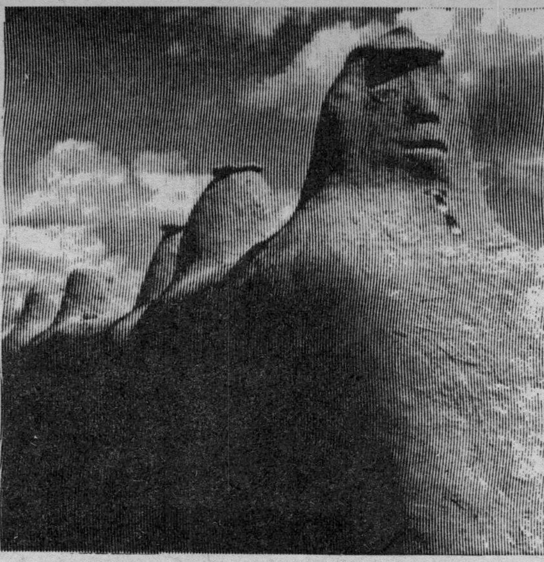

PHENOMENA	RECOMMENDED LAND USES
Surface water and riparian lands	Ports, harbors, marinas, water-treatment plants, water-related industry, open space for institutional and housing use, agriculture, forestry and recreation.
Marshes	Recreation
50-year floodplains	Ports, harbors, marinas, water-treatment plants, water-related industry, agriculture, forestry, recreation, institutional open space, open space for housing.
Aquifers	Agriculture, forestry, recreation, industries that do not produce toxic or offensive effluents. All land uses within limits set by percolation.
Aquifer recharge areas	As aquifers.
Prime agricultural lands	Agriculture, forestry, recreation, open space, housing at 1 house per 25 acres.
Steep lands	Forestry, recreation, housing at a maximum density of 1 house per 3 acres, where wooded.
Forests and woodlands	Forestry, recreation, housing at densities not higher than 1 house per acre.

One cannot predict the fate of such a book as this. But on its intrinsic merits I would put it on the same shelf that contains as yet only a handful of works in a similar vein, beginning with Hippocrates, and including such essential classics as those of Henry Thoreau, George Perkins Marsh, Patrick Geddes, Carl Sauer, Benton MacKaye, and Rachel Carson. This is not a book to be hastily read and dropped; it is rather a book to live with, to absorb slowly, and to return to, as one's own experience and knowledge increases. Though it is a call to action, it is not for those who believe in "crash programs" or instant solutions: rather, it lays a fresh course of stones on a ground plan already in being. Here are the foundations for a civilization that will replace the polluted, bulldozed, machine-dominated, dehumanized, explosion-threatened world that is even now disintegrating and disappearing before our eyes. In presenting us with a vision of organic exuberance and human delight, which ecology and ecological design promise to open up for us, McHarg revives the hope for a better world. Without the passion and courage and confident skill of people like McHarg that hope might fade and disappear forever.

Lewis Mumford

•

This book is a personal testament to the power and importance of sun, moon, and stars, the changing seasons, seedtime and harvest, clouds, rain and rivers, the oceans and the forests, the creatures and the herbs.

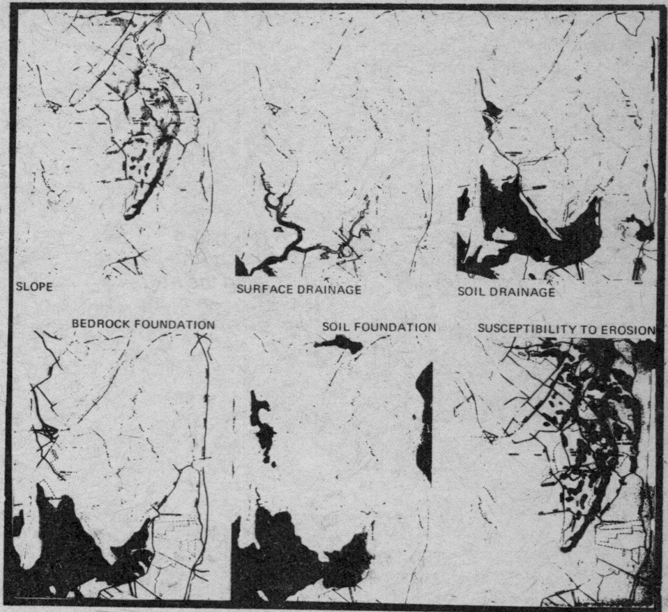
SLOPE
SURFACE DRAINAGE
SOIL DRAINAGE
BEDROCK FOUNDATION
SOIL FOUNDATION
SUSCEPTIBILITY TO EROSION

These indispensable creatures, performing their vital role in the nitrogen cycle, deserve to be household words, man's great heroes. Yet sadly those who named them had no thought of public honor and familiarity and called them Azotobacter and Clostridium, Rhizobium and Nostoc.

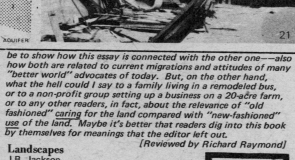

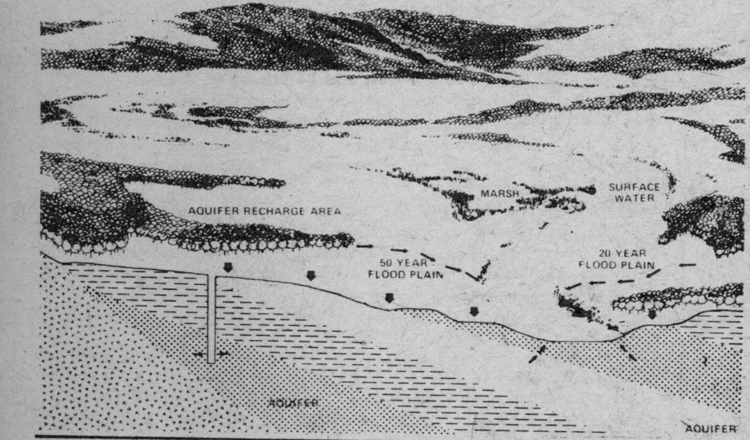
AQUIFER RECHARGE AREA
MARSH
SURFACE WATER
50 YEAR FLOOD PLAIN
20 YEAR FLOOD PLAIN
AQUIFER
AQUIFER

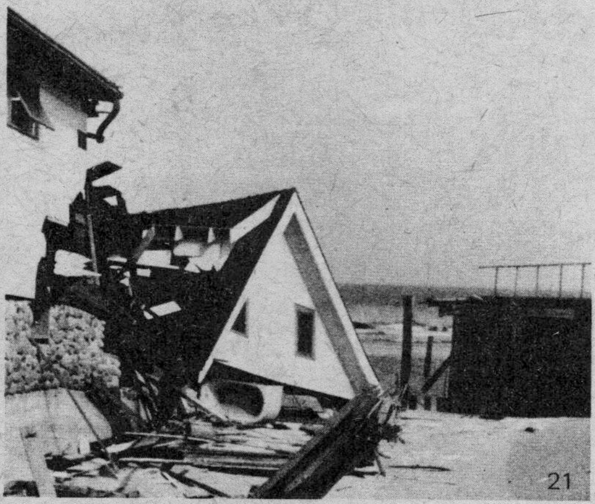
21

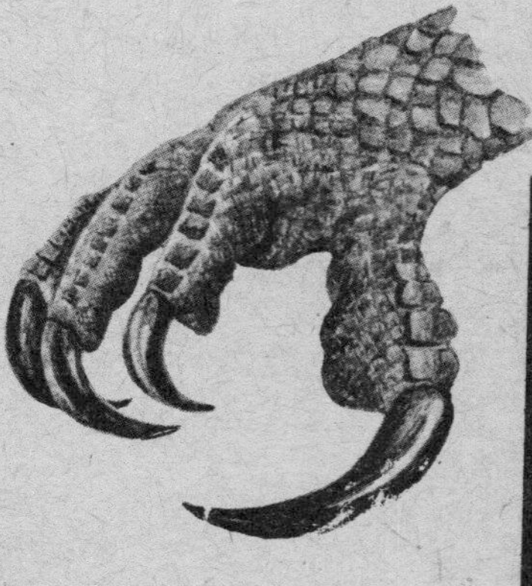

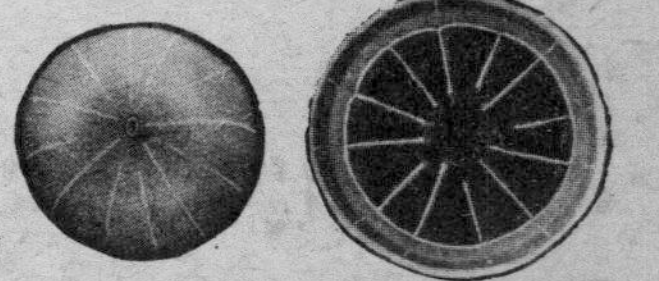

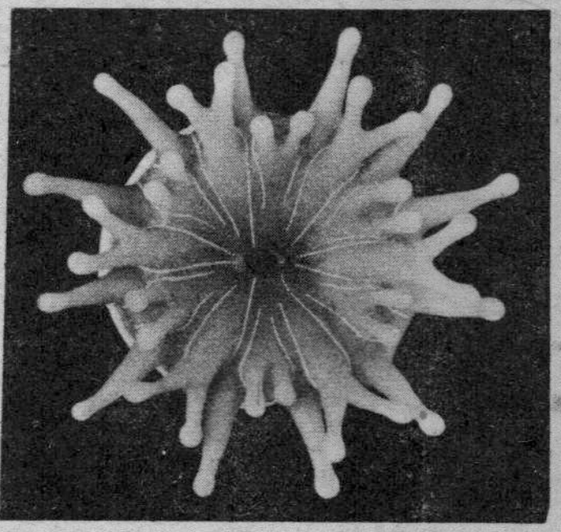

George Wald once wrote facetiously that "it would be a poor thing to be an atom in a Universe without physicists. And physicists are made of atoms. A physicist is the atom's way of knowing about atoms." Who knows what atoms yearn to be, but we are their progeny. It would be just as sad to be an atom in a universe without ecologists, who are themselves organisms.

Landscapes

Despite its title, thank God this book isn't another moralistic planner talking about landscapes.

Rather, it is more like a rural historian, who is philosophical, talking about suburbs, highways, shopping centers, neon signs, and poverty, not as enemies, but for what they are: "They are us."

Though it isn't mentioned until p. 132, the important focus of the book (especially for Whole Earth Catalog readers) is the following reality:

> At present, fifty-eight percent of our population lives in towns of 50,000 or less; more Americans live in towns of 10,000 or less than live in all of the cities of a million or more; and one out of every four Americans lives in a place with less than 2,500 inhabitants. Most of us, in brief, still live in a small city or in a semi-rural setting, and the chances are that even in 1975 the proportion will still be sizeable.

If I had been the editor of this book, I would have wanted to arrange the chapters differently and put some extra passages in between Jackson's essays. For example, in one essay, he makes a fascinating distinction between (1) farmers, (2) rural residents, (3) wilderness recluses, and (4) city dwellers, using quotes from Thoreau and T. Jefferson. And in another essay (which was the most absorbing one for me), called "The Westward-moving House", he traces an American family through 300 years of home-building history, beginning in the late 1600's in New England (Nehemiah Tinkham, with wife, Submit Tinkham, and six children), through Pliny Tinkham of Illium, Illinois, and concluding in the 1900's with Ray Tinkham of Bonniview, Texas. And my impulse would be to show how this essay is connected with the other one——also how both are related to current migrations and attitudes of many "better world" advocates of today. But, on the other hand, what the hell could I say to a family living in a remodeled bus, or to a non-profit group setting up a business on a 20-acre farm, or to any other readers, in fact, about the relevance of "old fashioned" caring for the land compared with "new-fashioned" use of the land. Maybe it's better that readers dig into this book by themselves for meanings that the editor left out.

[Reviewed by Richard Raymond]

Landscapes
J.B. Jackson
Ervin H. Zube, ed.
1970; 160 pp.

$2.50 postpaid

from:
University of Massachusetts Press
P.O. Box 429
Amherst, Massachusetts 01002
or WHOLE EARTH CATALOG

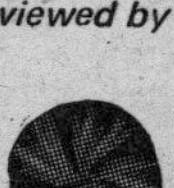

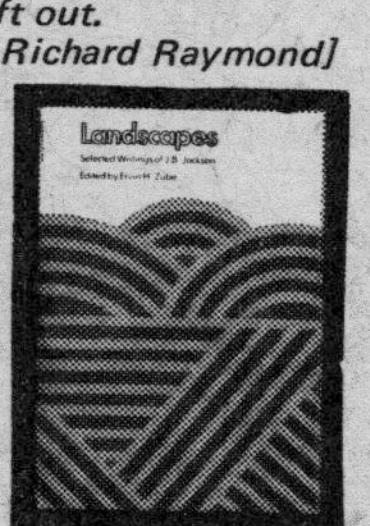
Landscapes

Somewhere (over western Kansas, perhaps) it begins to grow dark and at first all one can see is a dark mottled brown world under an immaculate sky of deep blue steel; then one flies over some small rectangular pattern of scattered lights——a farm town——and out of it, like the tail of a comet, stretches a long sinuous line of lights of every color and intensity, a stream of concentrated multi-colored brilliance, some of it moving, some of it winking and sparkling, and every infinitesimal point of color distinct in the clear night air. The stream pours itself into the black farmlands, into the prairie, and vanishes. This of course is the roadside development seen from an altitude of several thousand feet; the most beautiful and in a way the most moving spectacle the western flight can offer, because for the first time you see that man's work can be an adornment to the face of the earth.

•

Every sizeable community exists partly to satisfy the outsider who visits it. Not only that; there always evolves a special part of town devoted to this purpose. . . .

. . .Some urban geographer will be able to explain why the Stranger's Path becomes more respectable the further it gets from its point of origin; why the flophouses and brothels and the poorest among the second-hand shops (now euphemistically called loan establishments——the three golden balls are a thing of the past), the dirtiest and steamiest of Greasy Spoons tend to cluster around those first raffish streets near the depot and bus and truck terminals, and why the city's finest hotel, its most luxurious night club, its largest restaurant with a French name and illustrated menus are all at the other end. But so it is; one terminus of the Path is Skid Row, the other is the local Great White Way, and remote though they seem from each other they are still organically and geographically linked. The moral is clear: the Path caters to every pocketbook, every taste, and what gives it its unifying quality and sets it off from the rest of the city is its eagerness to satisfy the unattached man from out of town, here either for a brief bout of pleasure or on some business errand.

•

Many factors have helped preserve this kind of communal life in Santa Fe. The city fathers have had nothing to do with it, and there is a large and vociferous element that is ashamed of the town's informality. But it is lucky in possessing a population which is gregarious, and at the same time hostile to police regulation, and which remains loyal to a long-established tradition of group pleasures. Yet something of this color and vitality could be introduced to many other American cities; it is merely a matter of establishing (or re-establishing) the principle that streets are not intended solely for motor traffic but were made for any and every kind of outdoor group activity, from children's games to funeral processions and endless loitering in the sun. All civic architecture is essentially nothing but an appropriate background for this life; and city planning is chiefly justified when it helps preserve and foster informal communal activities.

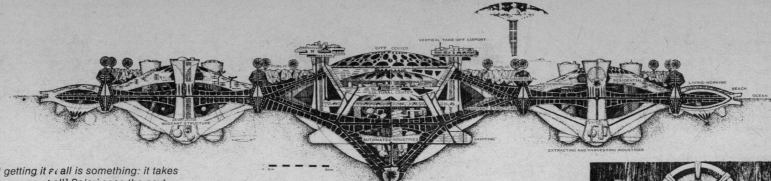

Arcology

It I get it right [and getting it at all is something: it takes either lots of work or none at all] Soleri sees the next step in evolution as man's job. He sees that step manifested in an organism and that organism is the city. Soleri says that the first part of his book is the most important. But on seeing the second part it's very difficult to muster much time for the first part. It pays, though, nicely. Soleri refers to Teilhard de Chardin in approaching the understanding of man as a cosmic problem by ascending from physics, chemistry, biology and geology, Western man must rise from his technology and one (I think) way is by being aware (of it) but ignoring it at the same time. The manifestation of a process like this is, I think, a series of drawings like that of the second part of the book. These drawings are like doorways, they're fantastic cities, wholly improbably but obviously, cosmically, possible. In fact, they are made real just by their presence in one place (the book) and by the interrelatedness of one project to the next, page to page, with seminal sketches appearing in the corners here and there. What's most fascinating are the next obvious steps: the Cosanti and Arcosanti buildings in Arizona. He's not starting all at once, big money style, but the way cities have always started: little by little. Like Nieuw Amsterdam on the tip of Manhattan Island or whatever city began at whatever river crossing or natural harbor, Soleri is beginning at a crossing of cosmic consciousness.

[Reviewed by Ron Williams]

Novanoah I, floating city for 40,000

Arcology: The City in the Image of Man
Paolo Soleri
1969; 121 pp.

$16.95 cloth

$8.50 paper

from:
The Cosanti Foundation
6433 Doubletree Ranch Road
Scottsdale, Arizona 85253

or

The M. I. T. Press
50 Ames Street, Room 765
Cambridge, Massachusetts 02142

or WHOLE EARTH CATALOG

Plan of Arcodiga (dam site)

To introduce living and working into the masonry of the dam means to transform a monolithic, noncellular system into one that is articulated and cellular. For equal mass the cellular system, not randomly given but structurally conceived, is stronger because it allows selectivity of orientation and dimensionality.

If one then considers the 1: 7 ratio of redundance in the safety coefficient in the dams built in the United States, one can see the wealth of schemes that can effectively and magnificently transform the blind mass into a singing environment.

Sketchbooks of Paolo Soleri

If you're into Soleri very much you'll want to get into his head. His notebooks will do it for you. The man dreams and schemes cloudbursts of passionate structure.

—SB

Sketchbooks of Paolo Soleri
1971; 418 pp.

$27.50 cloth postpaid

from:
Massachusetts Institute of Technology
Publications Office
28 Carleton St.
Cambridge, Mass. 02142

or WHOLE EARTH CATALOG

THE PORCH IS NOW OPEN ON INFINITY, NO MORE ON THE BUSY-BODIES OF MORE OR LESS TAILORED DIMENSION, WHICH CLOSENESS & NEED-SENTIMENTS ARE INALIENABLE BUT ONLY PART OF SUCH INFINITY ONE COULD SUGGEST THAT AS AN OPENING THE DOOR ON THE HOUSE OF WORSHIP ONE EXPECTS & FIND A PLACE OF SOMEHOW RARE PARAMETRES TO WHICH LIFE LENDS MORE OF AN ABSTRACTION THAN ANY PARTICULAR: SO THE TOTAL ONE SIDE OF THE DOME "WINDOW" OPENS ON THE INFINITUM HOUSE OF WORSHIP WHICH

CATHARTIC MOMENTUM IS IN REASON OF LIGHT & SEASON—HOURS—ATMOSPHERE—WEATHER. . . . .& SPACE & SPACES

The Climate Near the Ground

This appears to be the definitive text on microclimatology: the climatic conditions within 6 feet or so of the earth's surface. The climate in this narrow stratum differs significantly from the overall climate, and the book analyzes, in some detail, the relation of soil, water, vegetation, topography, man and animals to the microclimate.

—Lloyd Kahn

[Suggested by Steve Baer]

The Climate Near the Ground
Rudolf Geiger
1966; 611 pp.

$15.00 postpaid

from:
Harvard University Press
79 Garden Street
Cambridge, Mass. 02138

or WHOLE EARTH CATALOG

The risk of bringing about a deterioration of climate by human intervention depends on the type of climate, and is greatest where plant life is fighting for its existence because of a shortage of water or heat. It is possible for very limited intervention into the water balance to produce far-reaching results in the bordering regions of arid zones. Great "regeneration areas" have been laid out around the town of Broken Hill in Australia, the great mining center for silver, lead, and zinc, situated in the middle of arid desert land. Wise foresight indicating that the original sparse vegetation in the area would have to be removed by the inhabitants, a comparatively luxuriant type of vegetation was grown in surrounding fenced-in and irrigated areas, improving the climate of the town, providing recreation spaces, and offering protection against dust storms in summer.

Irrigation has a double purpose: to further the optimum growth of plants by giving them the supplies of water they need, and to increase air humidity during the hottest hours of the day in a dry period; this has the effect of reducing, as far as possible, the passive transpiration of the plant, which is its method of protecting itself against high temperatures, but which makes unnecessary demands on energy. The first of these aims is achieved by watering at night, the second by watering during the day with as fine a spray as possible. The period of watering, its duration, the quantity and temperature of the water must all be adjusted to suit the type and age of the fruit to be protected, and the weather at the time. Irrigation techniques must therefore go hand in hand with micro-climatology.

LOVE

"Amen."

The Greek bowed to the west and he bowed to the east, and came up filled with love for everything in the universe. When he saw D.R. leaning against the picnic table with what he took to be a forlorn look on his face he felt apologetic for coming on to him so hard during the ceremony. To make amends he went over and hugged him.

"I love you, man," said the Greek. "I love you, and you and you too, you're all just lovely, and I love you. I love the bus, I love those people down there at the other table, I love that big truck, and its driver, and the drivers of all those cars going by. I love the desert, I love the sky, I love the mountains in the distance, the oceans beyond the mountains, and all who dwell in the lands beyond the oceans. I love all sentient beings everywhere, regardless of their race, color, creed, place of national origin, or species.

"Now perhaps you wonder how it is that a mere mortal such as I have become capable of such boundless love for everything in all creation. I mean, how is it, do you suppose, that a single individual is able to sustain a feeling of love for absolutely everything, twenty-four hours a day, every day, all his life? The answer, my friends, is simple. You all of course know what the ego is. How it is first developed out of the formless void that is the childhood psyche, and then, through strength of the adult will, through ceaseless practice of the yogic disciplines, it is at last obliterated so that that which was torn asunder by the trauma of leaving the mother's womb has been reconciled and made whole again, where all is one and one is all, where the twain not only meet but embrace and join together in eternal union of individual consciousness with the cosmic life force. Well, love is bound up in the workings of the ego in a funda- mental and inextricable way. A lot of people are confused by this point, because they are confused by the apparent contra- diction built into the notion of coming to consciousness by abandoning the quest for consciousness. The great yogis and mystics and teachers of The Way have all enjoined us as disciples to abandon self-consciousness in striving for total awareness, and yet, as a means of gaining the strength to bring about that abandonment, we are simultaneously enjoyed to become more self-aware. How then do we practice self-forgetfulness at the same time we are asked to cultivate self-awareness? A lot of seekers have been defeated by that contradiction, and this is tragic because the way out is actually so simple and easy to see you really feel embarrassed when it finally dawns upon you. The answers to all the great questions are really very simple, just as the simple way of life is the proper path enroute to the Greatest Question. Simplify! Simplify! Simplify! cried Thoreau, and he was right.

(continued)

Shelter

Evolution and Design in the Plant Kingdom

Live dwellings——how soon? Houses of living vegetable tissue. The walls take up your CO_2 and return oxygen. They grow or diminish to accommodate your family changes. Add a piece of the kitchen wall to the stewpot. House as friend. Dweller and dwelling domesticate each other. Society for the Prevention of Cruelty to Structures.

Engineering lately has been inspired by bionics, the analysis of living systems for their technological accomplishments that might be borrowed by us. So far, plants have been overlooked.

Hey! Plants.

Start with this systemic lovely book and the nearest seed pod.

—SB

Evolution and Design in the Plant Kingdom
C. L. Duddington
1969; 258 pp.

$2.95 postpaid

from:
Thomas Y. Crowell Company
201 Park Avenue S.
New York, N.Y. 10003

or WHOLE EARTH CATALOG

Fig. 45.
Climbing hooks of
Ancistrocladus

Architecture Without Architects

Troglodyte caverns, 40 feet high treehouses, sculptured Iranian sail vaults; rare photos of man working in conjunction with nature. A book for architects and builders to meditate upon.

—Lloyd Kahn

Architecture Without Architects
Bernard Rudofsky
1964; 160 pp.

$4.95 postpaid

from:
Doubleday & Company
Garden City, N. Y. 11531

or WHOLE EARTH CATALOG

Fig. 10.
Longitudinal section of part of a tracheid of the yew, showing the tertiary thickening bands that give the wood of the yew its great strength and elasticity

The mechanical stresses that occur in the branch of a tree may be presumed to be the same as in any other cantilever. The material towards the top of the branch is in tension, while the material near the bottom is in compression. If it is to keep a straight course the wood must resist both these stresses equally. How it maintains its apparently predetermined course we do not know.

If we study the wood on the lower sides of branches of coniferous trees, or on the upper sides of branches in broad-leaved trees, we find that it has a distinct structural difference from the rest of the wood. This wood is called 'reaction wood', and it differs from normal wood both anatomically and chemically. In conifers, where it is called 'compression wood', it is darker than normal wood, and the walls of the cells are more heavily impregnated with lignin. The tracheids are shorter than usual, and the wood is denser. The secondary lignified cell wall which is laid down inside the primary wall consists of three layers in normal wood, but in compresion wood there are only two layers, the innermost layer missing.

In branches of broad-leaved trees there is no compression wood, but the wood laid down on the upper side of the branch, known as 'tension wood', shows modifications in structure. The vessels are narrower, and the fibres have a thick inner layer——the gelatinous layer——which refracts light very readily and is composed mainly of cellulose instead of lignin.

Recent work has indicated that the formation of reaction tissue is not limited to the wood, for the secondary phloem, the cortex and the cork cambium may also show modified growth.

The study of reaction wood is a relatively new branch of botany, and much remains to be found out before we shall be able to claim to understand its formation fully. Its function, if any, in the life of the plant is at present uncertain, but several prominent workers in this field have expressed the opinion that reaction wood is in some way responsible for the fact that branches do continue growing in the direction in which they start, and do not change their direction of growth as a result of the stresses set up by their own weight.

•

Water is not sucked up from the leaves, nor is it hoisted from below by root pressure, except, perhaps, in small plants. Our third possibility, that it is pumped up by some intermediate cell mechanism, also appears to be without foundation. One is tempted to say that it gets up by the grace of God, but scientists are chary about calling upon divine intervention in order to explain awkward facts. We must look again at our various possibilities (or impossibilities) and see whether we have missed something.

Turning once more to the theory that water is raised from above we can see at once that there is plenty of force available for the job, for transpiration sets up an osmotic gradient in the mesophyll of the leaf with pressures well above the ten or twelve atmospheres that we need for raising water even to the top of a *Sequoia*. The trouble begins when we try to see how it is applied. Suction just will not do, for we cannot get around the fact that the water barometer cannot exceed thirty-three feet. Some other phenomenon must be involved; something that can enable the pull in the leaves to reach right down into the roots and haul the water up. The answer to the problem seems to lie in a theory first put forward some time ago by Dixon and Joly, known as the 'cohesion theory'. A solid

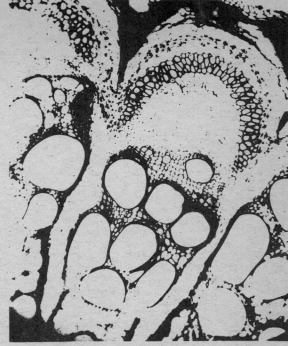

Longitudinal section of part of a tracheid of the yew, showing the tertiary thickening bands that give the wood of the yew its strength and elasticity.

substance is held together by forces of cohesion between its molecules, which form a rigid crystal lattice that resists being broken. In a liquid the forces of cohesion do not hold so closely. The molecules can slide about over one another but they are still held by cohesive forces and prevented from escaping altogether. Only when a molecule gathers to itself sufficient kinetic energy (energy of movement) to overcome the force of cohesion does it fly away completely——in other words, vapourize.

•

According to the Dixon cohesion theory, the water in the vessels forms an unbroken column from the roots up to the topmost leaves. The cohesive forces in this column of water resist breaking, so that when the osmotic gradient set up by transpiration exerts a pull on the top end of this column of water, the whole column moves upwards just as the oil dipstick of a motor car comes up when you pull the top end of it. Notice that we have now got rid of the idea of suction and the difficulty of the water barometer. The force that pulls the water up is an osmotic one, and it is transmitted down the stem by the cohesion between the water molecules.

Fig. 50.
The dodder (*Cuscuta europaea*) growing on willow

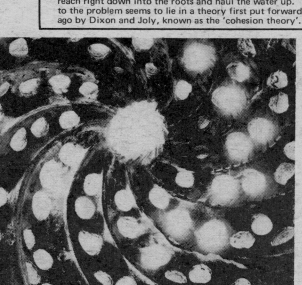

Cupola of a Turkish bathhouse—a whirlpool of bright stars, arrested, as it were, in its movement. The luminous disks embedded in the dome are thick, lenselike glass blocks. Iznic, Turkey. Othmanli period.

Many so-called primitive peoples deplore our habit of moving (with all our belongings) from one house, or apartment, to another. Moreover, the thought of having to live in rooms that have been inhabited by strangers seems to them as humiliating as buying second hand old clothes for one's wardrobe. When they move, they prefer to build new houses or to take their old ones along.

Antoni Gaudi

If everybody's so inspired by Gaudi, like they say they are, how come there's no new buildings around that look like his?

God damn architects who bore and stifle and preen their chickenyard feathers. Give us more jungle birds like this one. If their buildings are inconvenient, good.

—SB

Antoni Gaudi
James Johnson Sweeney, Joseph Lluis Sert
1960; 1970; 192 pp.

OUT OF PRINT

from:
Praeger Publishers, Inc.
111 Fourth Ave.
New York, N.Y. 10003

or WHOLE EARTH CATALOG

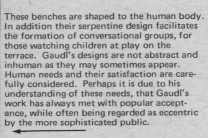

These benches are shaped to the human body. In addition their serpentine design facilitates the formation of conversational groups, for those watching children at play on the terrace. Gaudi's designs are not abstract and inhuman as they may sometimes appear. Human needs and their satisfaction are carefully considered. Perhaps it is due to his understanding of these needs, that Gaudi's work has always met with popular acceptance, while often being regarded as eccentric by the more sophisticated public.

Views of vaulting in the *Güell Colony chapel*. This type of construction recalls that used on the roof of the *Milá house*. The ribs are brick partitions that achieve structural efficiency without bulk. The construction of such vaulting requires expert craftsmanship, and careful direct supervision. There are scarcely any repetitive elements; but the application of the same directive principle and a use of warped shapes throughout make the work simpler.

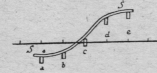

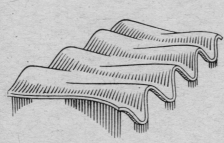

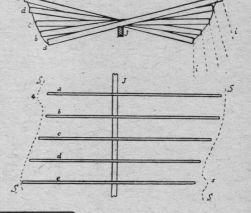

Writings and Buildings

I read this while I was in the Army, where our bugle calls came on scratchy records.

Frank Lloyd Wright's reveille is still ringing.

—SB

Writings and Buildings
Frank Lloyd Wright
Edgar Kaufman, Ben Raeburn, eds.
1960; 346 pp.

$3.95 postpaid

from:
New American Library
1301 Avenue of the Americas
New York, N.Y. 10019

or WHOLE EARTH CATALOG

So——the first thing to do was to get rid of the attic and, therefore, of the dormer and of the useless "heights" below it. And next, get rid of the unwholesome basement, entirely——yes, absolutely——in any house built on the prairie. Instead of lean, brick chimneys, bristling up from steep roofs to hint at "judgment" everywhere, I could see necessity for one only, a broad generous one, or at most, for two, these kept low down on gently sloping roofs or perhaps flat roofs. The big fireplace below, inside, became now a place for a real fire, justified the great size of this chimney outside. A real fireplace at that time was extraordinary. There were "mantels" instead. A mantel was a marble frame for a few coals, or a piece of wooden furniture with tiles stuck in it and a "grate," the whole set slam up against the wall. The "mantel" was an insult to comfort, but the *integral* fireplace became an important part of the building itself in the houses I was allowed to build out there on the prairie. It refreshed me to see the fire burning deep in the masonry of the house itself.

Simplicity in art, rightly understood, is a synthetic, positive quality, in which we may see evidence of mind, breadth of scheme, wealth of detail, and withal a sense of completeness found in a tree or a flower. A work may have the delicacies of a rare orchid or the stanch fortitude of the oak, and still be simple. A thing to be simple needs only to be true to itself in organic sense.

Style is a free product but, still, a by-product: the result of the organic working in, and out of, a project entirely in character, altogether and in one state of feeling.

In Japanese architecture may be seen what a sensitive material let alone for its own sake can do for human sensibilities, as beauty, for the human spirit.

Whether pole, beam, plank, board, slat, or rod, the Japanese architect got the forms and treatments of his architecture out of tree nature, wood wise, and heightened the natural beauty of the material by cunning peculiar to himself.

The possibilities of the properties of wood came out richly as he rubbed into it the natural oil of the palm of his hand, ground out the soft parts of the grain to leave the hard fiber standing, an "erosion" like that of the plain where flowing water washes away the sand from the ribs of the stone.

To the young man in architecture, the word *radical* should be a beautiful word. Radical means "of the root" or "to the root"——begins at the beginning and the word stands up straight. Any architect should be radical by nature because it is not enough for him to begin where others have left off.

To acquire technique study the materials of which the product is made, study the purpose for which it is produced, study the manhood *in* it, the manhood *of* it. Keep all this present in your mind in all you do, because ideas with bad technique are abortions.

Beware of the architectural school except as the exponent of engineering.

Go into the field where you can see the machines and methods at work that make the modern buildings, or stay in construction direct and simple until you can work naturally into building-design from the nature of construction.

Immediately begin to form the habit of thinking "why" concerning any effects that please or displease you.

Take nothing for granted as beautiful or ugly, but take every building to pieces, and challenge every feature. Learn to distinguish the curious from the beautiful.

Get the habit of analysis,——analysis will in time enable synthesis to become your habit of mind.

"Think in simples" as my old master used to say——meaning to reduce the whole to its parts in simplest terms, getting back to first principles. Do this in order to proceed from generals to particulars and never confuse or confound them or yourself be confounded by them.

"And that's why I'm concerned about you, my friend. I have the feeling that the answers to the great questions that are obviously troubling you are as plain as the nose on your face, but you are just too ego-centered and self-involved at this point to realize that. I've got the feeling that the Word you are so in need of hearing is sounding in the atmosphere this very minute, but that you are too full of the static of your petty mind to hear. I think the first thing we ought to do by way of helping you to find some relief for your condition is to help you forget your name. I've forgotten mine. I don't have the slightest idea what my name is, and its the most wonderful sense of liberation there is. It's like the rebirth that follows the spiritual death necessary to true illumination. One must suffer many deaths on the road to illumination, some actual, some only symbolic. Giving up your name is only a symbolic death, but for many people it is so painful it could well be likened to an actual death. What they fail to understand is that after death is the resurrection, the restoration to life that all the great spiritual leaders have experienced. This experience is available to every individual on one level or another, on planes both gross and subtle, if the individual is truly committed to his quest for the Ultimate Way. So what I need to know before we go any farther is exactly what your full name is. And your place of birth, your astrological sign, your height, weight and rate of heartbeat. Since you are having trouble speaking, perhaps you could just write all of that down in this little notebook here, and then we can get started."

The Greek handed D.R. a worn notebook with the yin-yang symbol drawn on the front in blue ink, and the word "love" written about fifty times on the back. The book had about a hundred pages in it, and nearly all of them were full of writing, and drawings and weird little scribbles too obscure to make out thumbing through. The book excited D.R. tremendously. He wished there was some way he could ask to read it. But that was not the purpose now. D.R. flipped to near the end where the blank pages began, and with the Greek's ball point pen wrote down: "Divine Right (David Ray) Davenport. Finley County, Kentucky. Cancer. Five Feet, Ten inches tall. 158 pounds. I don't know my heartbeat."

"Well, a close estimate will do," said the Greek. And he took D.R.'s wrist in his hand, located his pulse, and began to count it as he watched the seconds tick off on his wrist watch.

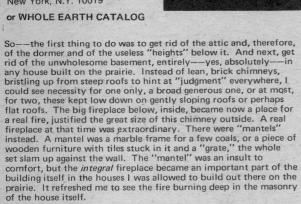

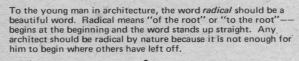

The Japanese House

Without getting all sentimental and exotic we're still going to agree that Japanese make better houses than anybody else (they also have the fastest growing economy in the world, but that's another story — or is it?). If you're going to build your own house and don't mind some inspiration on the subject, this book was laboriously made for you. It's a great big Christmas present of a book full of yummy photos and diagrams and details of technique, all of which seems right within reach: I-can-do-it. Nice cure for nothing-can-be-done-because-it's-too-damned-big industrial blues.

[Suggested by Zen Mountain Center]

$27.50 may choke you up, in which case get Japanese Homes and Their Surroundings, $2.50 from Dover Publications—straight information on how to hand-make a lovable environment.
—SB

SECLUSION IN BUILDING is an essential instrument for establishing, or preserving, the freedom of man. For, only in solitude can man escape from the coercion to which he is subjected when among the masses.

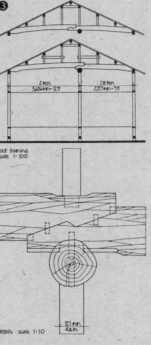

Fig. 167. — Kitchen in old Farmhouse at Kabutoyama.

Shōji paper is the "glass" of the Japanese house. Its qualities, however, are of a different nature, and, thus, also are its effects. The light, broken already by the broad overhang of the eaves, is diffused by the paper and creates a characteristic light condition comparable to twilight. This situation does not change basically even if the evening or winter sun hits the paper directly. No glare, no shadows; a general gloom creates a soft, emotional atmosphere. With artificial light in use, the shōji paper shows its reflective-diffusing ability, and at night with lights turned out, might even offer an interesting shadow play the moon has staged with the old weather-worn pine tree. As time passes, the paper darkens. Here and there, a torn piece is carefully cut out and replaced by new, lighter paper. The paper pattern becomes, though irregular, more interesting and lively. The paper ages, as does man.

The Japanese House— A Tradition for Contemporary Architecture
Heinrich Engel
1964; 495 pp.

$35.50 postpaid

from:
Charles E. Tuttle Co., Inc.
Rutland, Vermont 05701

or WHOLE EARTH CATALOG

Japanese Homes & Their Surroundings

Edward S. Morse
1886, 1961; 372 pp.

$3.00 postpaid

from
Dover Publications, Inc.
180 Varick St.
New York, N. Y. 10014

or WHOLE EARTH CATALOG

Shelter and Society

Almost all the books you ever see on architecture are concerned with monumental building, a result of the relationship between architects and wealthy patrons. Seldom do you see anything on buildings by the people, of local materials and in simple harmony with the surrounding landscape.

Here's an exception. On the cover is what at first glance appears to be a primitive Portuguese fisherman's house. On closer inspection, it's a picture of one of Drop City's domes, colorful, funky, having sprung from the trash of "...a wasteful society."

10 types of dwellings are covered, by different writers. A comparison of the pueblo and the hogan, the walled city of Old Delhi, the Norwegian Laftehaus, Villages on the Black Volta, and a fine article by Bill Voyd on funk architecture at Drop City. Many of the photographs are too dark, but you won't find them elsewhere.

It's more of a book on the functions of the buildings than on the external aesthetics.
—Lloyd Kahn

"All is as it should be", says one of the beings. "Nothing is complete," returns the other; "look at those creatures below this mountain, whom we see assembling, then disbursing, looking about, and betaking themselves to shelter."
From the Prologue to *The Habitations of Man in All Ages* by Viollet-le-Duc, translated by Benjamin Bucknall, Architect. 1876.

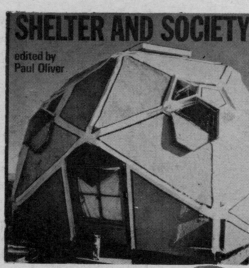

Shelter and Society
Paul Oliver, ed.
1969; 167 pp.

$12.50 postpaid

from:
Frederick A. Praeger, Publisher
111 Fourth Avenue
New York, N. Y. 10003

or WHOLE EARTH CATALOG

To the Egyptians, shelter for the dead was more important than shelter for the living; our factories, he argued, suggest that shelter for machines is better served today than that for men or gods: "Shelter seems, indeed, to have been a minor consideration in many of the early cultures."

•

For the very congruity and harmony which is so frequently a source of admiration and comment in architectural writings on vernacular shelter is evidence of the integration of the building in the life of the community as a whole.

•

The close link between dwelling and land expressed in the resemblance of the pueblo to a land-form seems to reflect the overall harmony of man and nature. The house is sacred, and so is the whole landscape and everything in it. Corn was more than a food, it was a symbol of life, and corn growing was regarded as a religious activity. Among the Tewa, for example, the greater part of religion centres around corn and, by extension, around agriculture in general. This attitude must influence the form of the pueblo and particularly its siting and relationship to the land; it helps to explain why the pueblo seems such an inevitable part of its surroundings.

Sun movements and solstices are extremely important, being related to ceremonial cycles. The pueblo is carefully orientated: it is related both to mountains ("Life comes from the mountains") and to the six cardinal points and the sacred directions of East and North.

The Office: a facility based on change

Nobody involved in this book is an architect, which is pretty interesting, because most of its implications are architectural. The design principles here apply splendidly to any work or living area which traffics in information or human interaction, from offices to small communities. It's a fine presentation of new theory, and Herman Miller, Inc. now has a line of office hardware behind it. We bought the book and hammered our own furniture out of scrap doors and 2x4's.

—SB

[Suggested by Dave Evans]

OUT OF PRINT

The Office: a facility based on change
Robert Propst
1968; 71pp.

OUT OF PRINT

from:
Taplinger Publishing Co., Inc.
29 East Tenth Street
New York, N. Y. 10003

or WHOLE EARTH CATALOG

Structural Design in Architecture

Scope: Load determination, material characteristics, design of beams, frames, cables, arches, plates, thin shells, membranes, space frames.

This is a book of tested formulas that give back-of-the-envelope solutions that are good to within a few percent. Nothing revolutionary. Just very well done. The book is set up in useable fashion——derivations that give a good feel for what's going on, relevant formulas, and realistic examples. Salvadori is a real-world man: he knows where precision is required and where it is not, and that most architects and builders can only handle algebra and trig, maybe a little calculus. So he makes the right simplifying assumptions on complex problems, to produce a book that architects can USE: many structures can be completely designed, and larger, more complex structures can be checked for feasibility.

[Suggested and reviewed by Charles Tilford]

Structural Design in Architecture
Mario Salvadori and Matthys Levy
1967; 457 pp.

$15.00 postpaid

from:
Prentice-Hall, Inc.
Englewood Cliffs, N. J. 07632

or WHOLE EARTH CATALOG

A balloon built by means of two flat, identical spherical sectors with a radius of 160 ft and an opening angle of 30°, supports a live load $q = 30$ psf and is to be prestressed with a safety factor of 4/3.

The two halves of the balloon are tied to a compression ring by radial cables. Determine the prestressing pressure, the maximum tension in the balloon and the compression in the ring, neglecting the dead load of the balloon.

Fig. 15.3.1

The Elements Rage

Every so often larger than normal pieces of cosmic energy lean on human affairs. The community dies, and is reborn, and ever after tells what the face of maelstrom looked like. Here are hair-raising photographs, intrepid accounts, hammerhead tragedies, and a seven-page scale of the energy gradient from a baseball homerun to the mass energy of the M31 galaxy. Classic.

—SB

[Suggested by Jordan Belson.]

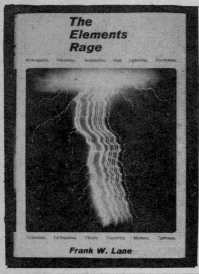

The Elements Rage
Frank W. Lane
1965; 346 pp.

$7.50 postpaid

from:
Chilton Books
201 King of Prussia Rd.
Radnor, PA 19089

or WHOLE EARTH CATALOG

Before Johnstown there were several small communities. The flood practically washed them out of existence, like a steamroller crushing toy villages. A stone viaduct was snapped in two as if made of dry clay, then ground to pieces. An iron bridge high in the valley was torn from its foundations by a blow from the edge of the flood. Dozens of locomotives and passenger carriages, hundreds of freight cars, and miles of track were swept forward as the monstrous river pounded down the valley. All these added immeasurably to the battering effect of the water.

The classic photograph of a tornado, taken near Jasper, Minnesota, on July 8, 1927. Lucille Handberg

Around us was an awesome display. Marge's eye was a clear space 40 miles in diameter surrounded by a coliseum of clouds whose walls on one side rose vertically and on the other were banked like galleries in a great opera house. The upper rim, about 35,000 ft. high, was rounded off smoothly against a background of blue sky. Below us was a floor of low clouds rising to a dome 8,000 ft. above sea level in the center. There were breaks in it which gave us glimpses of the surface of the ocean. In the vortex around the eye the sea was a scene of unimaginably violent, churning water.

During a hurricane on Puerto Rico on September 13, 1928, a ten-foot pine board measuring three by one inches was shot through this Royal Palm tree.

A tornado, like thunder, is heard many miles away. As it approaches, there is a peculiar whistling sound that rapidly changes to an intense roar, reaching a deafening crescendo as it strikes. The screeching of the whirling winds is then so loud that the noises caused by the fall of wrecked buildings, the crashing of trees, and the destruction of other objects is seldom heard.

After each strike we moved in silence for a while, with only the tearing wind and slashing rain. Then the rocks would begin a shrill humming, each on a slightly different note. The humming grew louder and louder. You could feel a charge building up in your body. Our hair stood on end. The charge increased, and the humming swelled, until everything reached an unbearable climax. Then the lightning would strike again—with a crack like a gigantic rifle shot. The strike broke the tension. For a while we would grope forward in silence. Then the humming would begin again [quoted by Colin Fletcher.]

The most serious health problem in offices is its sedentary nature. Compelled by lack of choice, we are forced to conduct most office activity in a sitting position. The result, as medical studies and insurance data make clear, is a steady decline in vitality, energy and general body tone.

Of even greater significance is the importance of sight as a window to mental recall. An office with no relevant visual display deprives the human performer of a spectacular recall tool: the human eye as a receptor for the mind.

Three sides with a slightly widened opening appears to be the best enclosure of all as a generality. There is good definition of territory or domae . . . privacy is well expressed and the ability to survey or participate is well maintained.

The management of symbolic representation of reality is the function of offices.

The office in its short evolution has adopted every kind of communication abstraction. Resultantly, we are concerned with reality simulation.

Face to face across a surface maintains formality and a tone of discretion. Ninety degree location, the most natural of all conversational positions, encourages exchange. Side by side positioning allows joint viewing of papers or objects intelligibly.

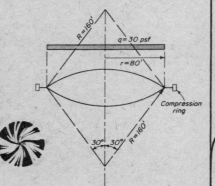

ESTELLE'S COMPLAINT

As desperate as she was for someone to help her drive, and generally hassle the whole bummer of a scene on to St. Louis, Estelle wished she was by herself again. The girl Frieda seemed okay, actually. At least she was cool enough to simply settle into the motion of the journey and keep whatever trip she was on to herself. But the Greek was such an asshole Estelle could not bear to stay in hearing of his voice. What Frieda saw in the Greek Estelle could not begin to imagine, but whatever it was, she hoped she did not hear about it. Frieda was a sad, forlorn little chick, obviously in need of some sort of help, but Estelle just did not have the psychic energy to go messing with her head. Maybe later, if things cooled out a little, they could manage a little chit-chat, but for the time being the only thing Estelle could think about was getting as far away from the Greek as possible.

At two o'clock on a hot afternoon in the middle of the desert she didn't have much appetite for walnuts. But if walnuts were what fate was serving up that day she guessed that was what she'd have. She reached into the Greek's leather food bag, got a handful of nuts, and eating them strolled off toward the dunes she'd walked on a while ago.

The thing that particularly bugged Estelle was the way Divine Right was zapping on the stupid Greek. There he'd been in a stupor for eight hours, sometimes huddling in her arms like a baby, and as soon as he comes out of it what does he do but fall in love with the first wise-man to come along and lay a heavy word trip on him. They were only a few minutes into it together, D.R. and the Greek. But Estelle had seen it happen so many times before she knew exactly what was coming down, and it was a drag. In her mind she saw the next five hundred miles unfolding in a stream of blather from the Greek while D.R. sat beside him doting on his every word.

Oh D.R., Estelle thought. You're such a goddamn child.

When he was right, when he was clear and cool and up and unhassled, D.R.'s mind was as beautiful to see in operation as anybody's that she knew. And yet he craved other people's words about "truth" and "life" like some poor junkie craving dope. If it was a habit D.R. had, there certainly wasn't any shortage of junk on the circuit they traveled in. As far as Estelle could see there were at least twice as many wisdom-pushers as dope dealers in the world, so how come the cops never got uptight about them? If she'd kept notes on all the philosophies, theories, schemes and plans to bring the world to a state of grace and love and enlightenment she'd heard in the last eighteen months she'd have enough recorded bullshit to fertilize the cosmic compost pile. There'd been a time when she was young, way back there a year or two ago, when other people's enthusiasms could excite her a great deal. But because enthusiasm was all it usually amounted to, Estelle didn't get much out of it anymore. Because D.R. still did, because he was so willing to devalue what was already in his own head and credit fast-talking assholes with some sort of superior wisdom, it divided them, and left them in different places. If she could have believed that he was over there at the picnic table grooving on the food freak simply because he was stoned on acid and <u>everything</u> he saw and heard seemed groovy, it would have been one thing. But Estelle knew that wasn't what it was. D.R. would have homed in on this dude stoned or sober and that was why it bothered Estelle so much. She knew that left out a lot about D.R. She knew there was a lot more to it than that. But right now she wasn't able to consider much that was in his favor. She was pissed and jealous and weary and depressed. If D.R. had any virtues that redeemed him she preferred not to think about them right now.

Architectural Design

This is the only architectural magazine we've seen that consistently carries substantial new information, as distinct from the stylistic eyewash characteristic of most architecture journals.

After a year of watching and using AD, it's clear that this is much more than an architectural magazine. It prints lots of news of American creative doings months before any U. S. publication. Its coverage of developments in cybernetics, structure systems, philosophy, use trends (e.g., communes), etc. is extraordinary.

—SB

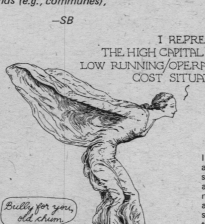

Guadi's Parque Guell—"one of the most cybernetic structures in existence."

Architectural Design

$24.10 postpaid
for one year
(monthly)

from:
Architectural Design
26 Bloomsbury Way
London W.C. 1

I REPRESENT
THE HIGH CAPITAL COST,
LOW RUNNING/OPERATING
COST SITUATION

Bully for you, old chum

Ford

Peter Brookes/Dad

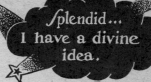

AD

DESPITE POPULAR DEMAND...

It is worth noting that the piezoelectric effect has been observed in a number of organic materials, among them wood, bone, tendon and skin and the argument has been put forward by Shamos and Lavine and others that the piezoelectric properties of these fibrous polymeric materials function as stress-sensing devices in living organisms and could account for the evolutionary and self-organizing structural characteristics of living things. In wood, stress concentrations due to wind loads would produce an electric potential proportial to the stress in any part of the tree, which might act as a growth signal, causing greatest growth in the parts that are stressed most.

As a combined sensor/effector device the possibilities are even more exciting. The most obvious and immediately valuable—if vaguely banal—proposition is that of producing a compression structure with infinite stiffness.

This Graded Universe—Lancelot Law Whyte

You should have seen the look on his face when God solved the problem of making an endlessly varied universe. He had already made two. The first was an ideal gas near to maximum dynamical disorder. That was dull; any differences he put into it soon vanished. It was an entropy victory, without order, form, or life.

Splendid... I have a divine idea.

His second was a world of perfect crystals. That was fun; there were 230 different types, all aesthetically intriguing. But each crystal was homogeneous, and therefore rather inert. It was a cold world (near zero), and left him dissatisfied. What he wanted was a blend of order and diversity, enough order to be pleasing and enough diversity to be continually forming new patterns, its fertility born of differences. Then he thought 'Splendid. I have a divine idea. My next universe will be the scene of two competing tendencies: morphic[2] processes generating three-dimensional geometrical order, and entropic processes leading towards dynamical disorder. That will make for unending variety, and when they're fluctuating nearly in balance something extraordinary will occur. The morphic processes will keep building ordered units and forming a great hierarchy of structural levels, from parts to wholes, while the entropy processes will tend to disperse the hierarchy. This subtle fluctuating balance will be called "life" by systems that display that vitality in a special mode to be called by them "thinking".'

Beyond Habitat

We've carried Buckminster Fuller, Paolo Soleri, and Christopher Alexander, so here's Moshe Safdie's first book. His first project, Habitat, was a major attraction at Expo '67 in Montreal and established him as a boy wonder in a field that usually requires decades of tooth toughening to succeed. The book is interesting for his ideas of high-rise village life, but even more valuable to the budding genius is his account of the political and economic pressures that shape a project and squash the designer and betray that original sweet idea.

(For an even more revealing perspective on Big Project success, try Albert Spear's Inside the Third Reich. Spear, at 29, was Hitler's architect. I used to think The Fuhrer was a frustrated architect. Turns out he was a successful one.)

Safdie's Student Union for San Francisco State College was initiated, guided, and funded by the students. The building was stopped by asshole trustees.

—SB

Looking back I find it incredible that fifteen thousand students who were prepared to pay for their own building, and who had support from the president, the faculty senate, the advisory committee, and some of the most respected members of the architectural profession in San Francisco, could be frustrated by sixteen trustees who met once a month to run eighteen colleges. And that in a state where Reagan was elected on a platform of "conservatism," which we are told supports decentralization and community control of community functions. This was a project that surged on the constructive energies of students over a period of five years—a campus effort to get a building built with their own money. If the building had gone ahead at that point, it would have involved the whole campus, had everyone working together creatively. We were going to buy looms and all the textiles in the building were to be woven by the students. Students were going to become involved in planting the building in collaboration with the department of botany. Students were going to make the furniture, and make the graphics, all kinds of things. So what do the trustees do? They say "No." And then they're surprised when the campus blows up.

Habitat, and crane that lifted the cast modules into place.

This was another moment when Habitat sat poised between life and death. At that point Churchill could have backed down before Lapointe's pressure. He could have said, "It's your property, you paid towards making it, and you have some rights to it . . . " or "What do you think we should do with it?" Instead, he turned round and asked, "Are you prepared to build it? Are you prepared to finance the whole project?" La pointe said, "No." Churchill said, "When you give money to the government you give it without any strings attached. The government owns what is done with the money you have donated. This is our plan. The Corporation owns it."

That was when I realized how strong Churchill really was. He had dealt with the private sector as a government official; there had often been attempts to push him around before, and he wasn't taking it. Right there he saved the project from drifting into the potential problems of the cement companies' uninvolved involvement.

Moshe Safdie
Beyond Habitat

Beyond Habitat
Moshe Safdie
1970; 244 pp.

$2.95

from:
MIT Press
50 Ames Street
Cambridge, Mass. 02142
or WHOLE EARTH
CATALOG

Proposed San Francisco State Student Union

Sweet's Files

It's a shame some of the best tools are the hardest to get to. Though Sweet's are free, they are given only to Public Libraries in cities of more than 250,000 people and to the 10,000 most active architectural firms in the U.S. It's often possible to talk a local architect out of last year's edition if you speak for it early. They do not become obsolete just because they are a year or two old.

Sweet's is essentially a catalog of catalogs, a filing system in a yard of volumes which binds, lists and cross-references catalogs of manufacturers. It covers six areas that I know of: Industrial, Residential and Commercial Construction and Product, Interior and Plant Design. Each file in these areas is a separate entity. The commercial construction file is the one most architects have and for any one building, it is the most useful. It is very helpful when improvising details for it provides a full spectrum of what is already available for the ready made answers to most problems. Manufacturers usually do a pretty good job with the material they include in the files so there's not much left to question as to how their product works. If there is any question, the manufacturer's representative is usually listed, with his phone number and address. He'll usually bend over backwards to help you if you say you saw it in Sweet's.

[Suggested and reviewed by ONYX]

Sweet's Files
Sweet's Construction Division
McGraw-Hill Information Systems Company
1221 Avenue of the Americas, 21st floor
New York, N.Y. 10020

NOTES:
1. Economic minimum only relative to flat roof Dubl-Panl
2. Preliminary design available for rise/span ratios of 1/5.

3" Corr. Roof Panel
Dubl-Panl Strut System
Rise Varies (Note 2)
3" Corr. Ceiling (gage varies)
Detail Y
Clear Span—250' to 1000' (Note 1)

TWO HINGED CIRCULAR ARCH

Structural angle assembly—Load transfer from panel chords to foundation base pin.
Pin & Base Plate assembly at 41 inch centers
DETAIL Y

BASE DETAIL

Architectural Graphic Standards

If Sweet's is a kind of magic lamp in many architects' and builders' libraries, the genie might well be 'Graphic Standards. This volume has been around for years; its latest edition is its fifth. Whenever the office expert hasn't got the answer, 'Graphic Standards usually does. It is the how-to-do-it book of construction. It doesn't cover domes but if there's anything else you have in mind, it's probably in there. Older construction techniques (stone masonry, etc.) are covered as well as relatively newer techniques; it's very useful in remodeling and repair work. Everything is done with a minimum of verbiage and a maximum of illustrations and very useable charts and graphs. 'Graphic Standards is so taken for granted by any architecture student or office that it's almost become a challenge to stay away from it; ultimately, however, there's seldom a building built without reference to it in the U.S. today. TOOL.

[Suggested and reviewed by ONYX]

Architectural Graphic Standards for Architects, Engineers, Decorators, Builders, Draftsmen and Students
Charles G. Ramsey and Harold R. Sleeper
1970, 6th ed., 695 pp.

$44.95 postpaid

from:
John Wiley and Sons
Publishing Co.
1 Wiley Drive
Somerset, N. J. 08873

Western Distribution:
1530 South Redwood Rd.
Salt Lake City, Utah 84104
or WHOLE EARTH CATALOG

Archigram

Archigram is the "Captain Billy's Whiz Bang" of architecture, with lots of imitators by now and still no equals. Dream architecture, joke architecture, blasphemy architecture, science fiction architecture, adolescent wet dream architecture, leather architecture. Sin. Fun. For a while.

—SB

Archigram
Peter Cook, ed.
No. 9, maybe 10, maybe 11

$1.25 each postpaid

from:
Archigram
59 Aberdare Gardens
London NW6
England

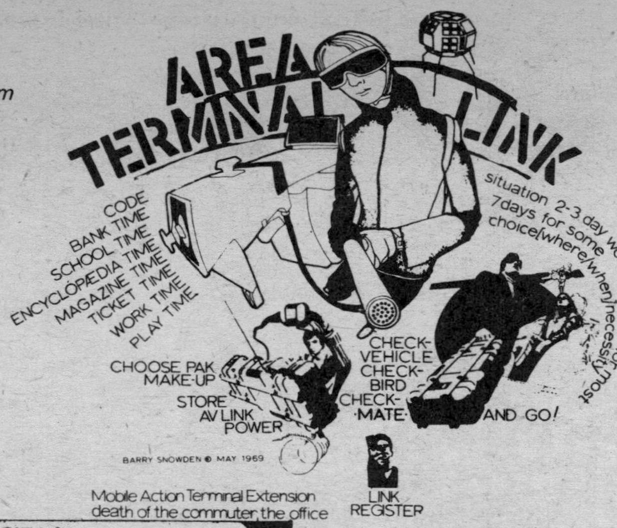

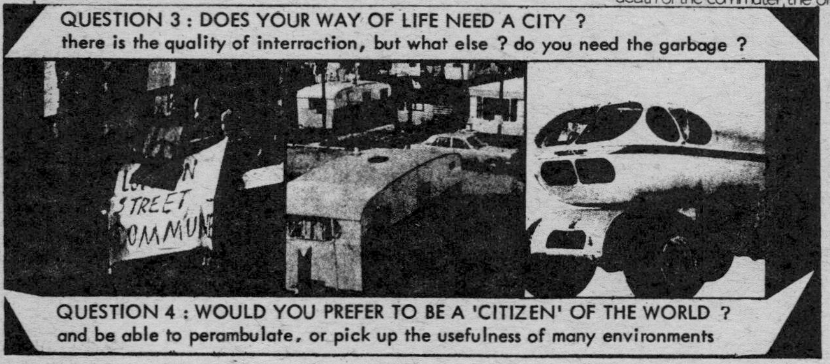

Culture Breakers, Alternatives, and Other Numbers

A thin book about inexpensive easy-to-make little function domains. Inside-out rooms, houses.

—SB

[Suggested by
Cloud and Ronald Paul]

Culture Breakers, Alternatives, and other Numbers
Ken Isaacs
a square little book with no page numbers or copyright

$5.00 postpaid

from:
MSS Educational Publishing Co. Inc.
19 East 48th St.
New York, N.Y. 10017

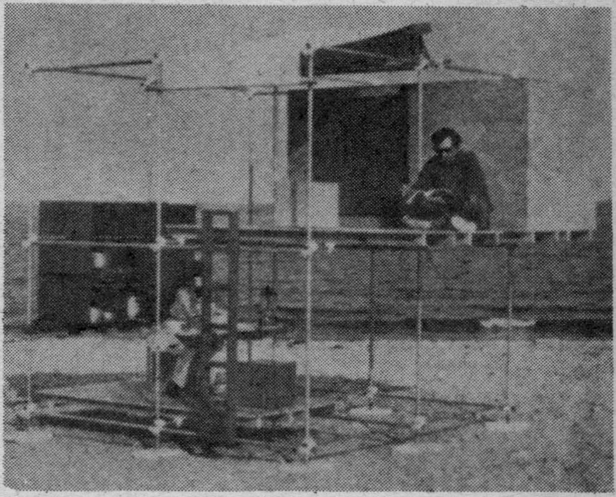

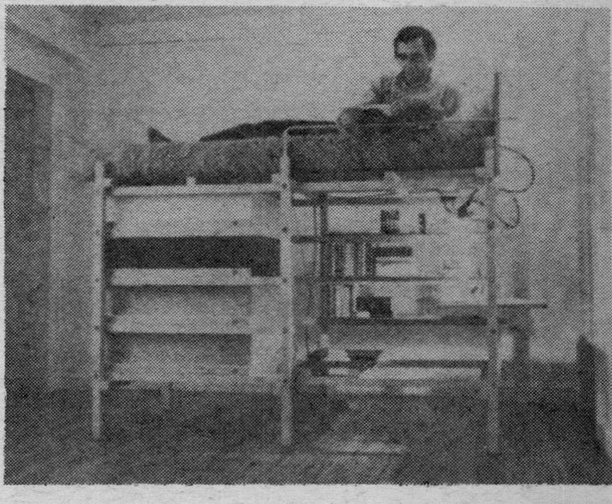

You'll Build Your Next House of Molasses

Molasses used to be an ingredient of cookies that mother made or something to put on hot cakes if you couldn't get maple syrup.

But today, if you visit our laboratory, you can hardly turn around without bumping into molasses. Beyond festoons of Spanish moss behind our home is an entire building made of molasses. It houses the machinery for making more molasses products. To get to it, you walk along a molasses driveway that looks, feels and acts like "black top." Here and there, molasses building bricks are drying in the sun. Inside the building, you walk on a molasses floor, examine samples of hard or flexible molasses sewer pipe that rest on a laboratory table top made of molasses. There are samples of molasses plaques flexible as rubber, molasses plaques as hard as rock.

The 50-foot molasses black-top driveway you walk on would cost the average homeowner about $50. Less if he did it himself. A five-room house built with molasses adobe brick on a molasses slab, finished with molasses stipple spray outside, troweled molasses plastic inside, would cost a man less than $1000, exclusive of electricity and plumbing. What's more he'd have a house that would stand a hundred years or more—moistureproof, soundproof, self-insulated, termiteproof. It's the cheapest building material in the world.

Naturally, to make these things you don't just take a barrel of pure molasses and start gumming everything up with it. Powdered molasses is the basic ingredient of a new thermosetting plastic that does the trick. By mixing this powdered molasses with plain bunker fuel oil and certain catalysts, we have come up with a thick black Plastic Bitumen we call Plastic B concentrate. By altering the formula slightly, we have made it in three different grades to produce different degrees of hardness.

Plastic B, mixed with clay and sand, produces a waterproof adobe brick hard as concrete. A different mixture of the same ingredients makes a cheap, quick-hardening paving material for driveways, highways, parking lots, tennis courts and landing airplane strips. Substitute clay and a fibrous filler for the clay and sand, and a brand-new plastic is formed, Plastic C. This can be mixed with water and sprayed outside a building to give it a tough stucco finish that won't crack or come loose. Troweled like plaster, Plastic C makes smooth inside walls, floors, ceilings and impervious table tops. . . .

The real secret of Plastic B is the dehydrator, which takes the sticky blackstrap molasses and makes a dry granular substance of it—like brown sand. We had a tough time devising a drier to do the job. Centrifuges gummed up in no time. Freeze driers solidified the stuff in gobs. Hot air only did half the job, and if heat was boosted the molasses caught fire.

Today, in the pilot plant, the blackstrap molasses goes into a hot-air drier of our own invention. Blackstrap molasses is pumped into the top of the big drumlike drying chamber under pressure. There it passes through an area of high heat in a split second. It's powdered before it knows what happened, and falls to the bottom of the drier like snow. But it didn't happen overnight. For instance, until we put in strong, stainless steel pipe, feedlines burst under the tremendous pressure. Hot molasses would geyser all over everything. We spent weeks cleaning molasses out of our hair and scraping it off the walls and ceiling.

Once mixed with oil and catalytic agents, the powdered molasses flowing from the drier becomes a regular polymerized plastic with remarkable properties. Anyone can make Plastic B-brick himself. Take a regular mortar-mixing box, and hoe up what looks like cement. It's actually 65 percent plain sand, 30 percent clay and 5 percent liquid Plastic B. Water is sprinkled on and hoed in until the mixture has the consistency of stiff mortar. The man trowels this into wooden forms, one measures 4 by 8 by 16 inches, or about eight times the size of a regular red brick. The other is 4 by 8 by 8 inches. Off come the forms immediately and oddly enough, the wet bricks stay set. In three days they're dry enough to stand on end. They are laid the same way as conventional bricks.

There's nothing new about adobe bricks, but there's something new about these. The Plastic C acts as a binder and makes them as rugged as concrete. Plain adobe has never been practical in wet country because rain washed it away. Plastic B makes the brick waterproof. We have set bricks in water for 30 days beside other brick. Plastic B-brick absorbed two percent moisture, cement brick eight percent, and regular red ceramic brick twelve percent. Plastic B-bricks have been lying all over the yard in rain, frost and heat for a year. They still look and test as good as new in the jaws of the pressure jack in the laboratory.

We contend that since the bricks are dirt, "they're cheap as dirt." We have determined that it takes 3050 of the big bricks to make a one-story adobe house of five rooms. You'd need a dozen barrels of Plastic B at $24 a barrel to do the job. That's $288 for the main shell of your dwelling. You'd set it on a waterproof, Plastic Bized adobe slab. Then, used Plastic B spray on the walls and ceiling—and on the exterior if you want a stucco-type finish. You'll have to buy 2 by 6 rafters and joists. But the whole house should not cost more than $150 a room, exclusive of plumbing and electricity.

And about that driveway? You can make that yourself, too, if you like and no one will ever be able to tell it from black top. Fifteen pails of plain beach sand to one pail (about two gallons) of Plastic B, and you've got about a square yard of driveway. In 24 hours, it's ready to use. No heavy compacting machinery is necessary, though the more compacting the harder the surface.

We compacted our own driveway with an ordinary lawn roller. Just rake out the Plastic B as you would an asphalt mix, and start rolling. . . .

Probably the most versatile of all the molasses products is Plastic C—which is simply Plastic C mixed with clay and a filler. This can come ready-to-use in 10 gallon moistureproof bags, which can sell for about 60 cents a gallon.

Thinned with water, it can be sprayed on the outside of an old house like stucco, troweled on old uneven floors to level them and give them a continuous surface like rubber tile, spread on table and counter tops to give them a flat surface impervious to acids and alkalis, laid on interior walls like plaster or molded into forms. Since it's waterproof, it's ideal for lining anything from showers to old-farm outbuildings. Eventually, the material will come impregnated with a variety of color, so no painting will be necessary. . . .

To show how it can work on an old building, a 150-year-old cookhouse was falling apart. Using the spray, we have put a complete new surface over the inside walls and ceiling, using about $6.00 worth of Plastic C. We also troweled the thick material on the old, uneven wood floor. You use a mixture of mostly sand to fill in the low spots. Then a thin layer of standard Plastic C is laid on top. When the floor of the cookhouse is finished, the outside will be sprayed—right over the old shiplapping.

We usually nail tarpaper and fine chicken wire over the surface, so we don't have to fill in all the hollows and consequently use three or four times as much Plastic C.

When complete, the old cookhouse will be tight as a battery box upside down—sealed inside and out against weather, termites and moisture. All for a materials cost of about $25.

Besides its unique qualities, we expect the demand for this molasses plastic to be high largely because of its low price—which we believe will always be low. Blackstrap molasses has jumped in price per gallon since we started. It's still cheap. But if it gets any higher, we'll switch to wood molasses, which is just as good and much cheaper. Sure it will be synthetic molasses, but Plastic B is synthetic asphalt. How synthetic can you get? As synthetic as necessary.

A number of people have questioned us about the wisdom of using sugary substance like molasses for building material. One woman wanted to know what we'd do to prevent ants and flies from eating her molasses driveway. We told her all Plastic B driveways and roads would have to be posted with ant-sized signs saying "Please Do Not Eat the Highway."

Actually, since the molasses has been completely polymerized, there is no sweetness or food value to be found in it. The experimental driveway only has a normal quota of ants and none of them look like they're eating it. But, you've got to admit that a molasses house really would be "Home, Sweet Home."

Very truly yours,

Robert Morse
15-20 202nd St.
Bayside, N.Y. 11360

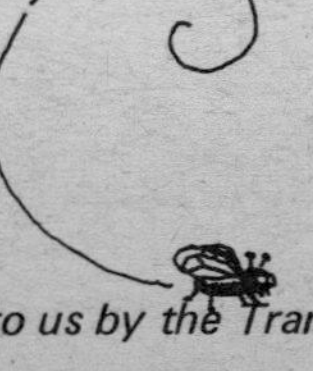

Sent to us by the Transformer.

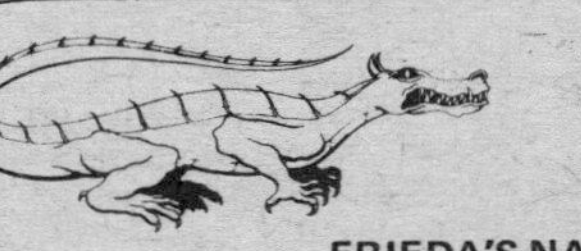

FRIEDA'S NAME

So everybody around the old picnic table has something to do now except Frieda. The Greek is teaching D.R. how to do alternate nostril breathing, and Estelle is off brooding among the dunes. That leaves Frieda to entertain herself, and so what she decides to do is work some more on letting go of her name. As we know, the Greek has forgotten his name completely. It took him six months of concentrated effort, but he made it. Frieda is not as strong in the mind as the Greek. She has been at it over nine months now, and where she is at is that delicate halfway point between being totally identified with her name, and forgetting it all together. She has managed to forget how to spell it; it means nothing to her to see the word "Frieda" written down. But when she hears it, the imprint is restored in her mind and her effort is set back a frustrating distance. Becoming nameless in a world where everything is named is a complicated process requiring the utmost diligence and perseverance, but she is committed now. That is the legacy of being the girl friend of the Greek for over a year.

The only thing wrong with that legacy, though, is that now she is known as the girl friend of the Greek. Where is that at? she asks herself. How is that better than being known as Frieda? It has slowly been dawning on her that it isn't better, that, in fact, it is a good deal worse, and suddenly she is resolved:

She stands up, dusts off her pants with her hands, glances at the Greek who is busy teaching D.R. the bellows breath, walks with great dignity over to the picnic table where the family is eating, and asks if she can ride away with them when they go. At first the family is a little uptight about this strange request, but when the girl explains to them that she has been kidnapped and held for ransom, they understand. The big fat momma of the family especially understands. She was never kidnapped, but she was an orphan as a child, and in her heart she carries a vast reservoir of love, pity and protective concern for all waifs and strays. She is also one very tough big fat momma. She offers to go over and beat up on the poor girl's tormentors, and take them before the law. But Frieda says no, that merely to escape will be enough. So the family, the Willitts family, of Oklahoma City, abruptly begins to pack up the food and load into the two-tone green and white Pontiac nearby. Momma shepherds the whole gang in before her, the Greek's former girl friend, two boys about eleven years old, a little girl about six, an old grandfather, and of course Poppa Willitts, who drives. It's crowded, but they manage. Momma Willitts gets in last, and the Pontiac, sagging drastically, eases out of the rest area onto the freeway, headed west.

The Technique of Stained Glass

Alright, you dome builders, now that you've got the sunlight working for you, how about getting it to play for you. There's livelier routes to color than car tops. Stained glass technique, ancient and modern, is here in depth. List of suppliers given. —SB

[Suggested by Stephen B. Siegal]

The Technique of Stained Glass
Patrick Reyntiens
1967; 192 pp.

$15.00 postpaid

from:
Watson-Guptill Publications
1 Astor Plaza
New York, N.Y. 10036

or WHOLE EARTH CATALOG

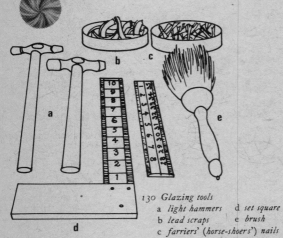

130 *Glazing tools*
a *light hammers*   d *set square*
b *lead scraps*   e *brush*
c *farriers' (horse-shoers') nails*

Whittemore Durgin Glass Company

stained glass supplies,
everything you need
to change your view of the neighbors
into a flyeye leaded splendor.
i met a fellow on a train,
once,
who paid for his bumdom,
by packing around two suitcases
full of glassworkers tools,
fixing leaded windows,
here and there.

—jd

[Suggested by Renee Gallery & Randy Street]

Catalog

$.25

from:
Whittemore Durgin Glass Company
Box 2065
Hanover, Massachusetts 02339

Besides lead came and the usual type of cathedral glass most people would associate with such work (including even——shudder!!—— "kits" for beginners), Whittemore-Durgin——for reasons known only to themselves——carry such goodies as World War II Meat Rationing Tokens, antique dog license tags from Bedford, Pennsylvania, old buttons, stop light lenses, and seemingly endless quantities of beads and antique hatpins! (They even operate a hatpin approval service.)

Even if you hate stained glass (though I can't imagine why anyone would bother hating it), whose day would not be brightened by the news that he can obtain

QUIZZICAL YELLOW FISH EYES ON WIRE——*As a result of a bad trip (to our attic) we have become almost sole owner of all these glass fish eyes. We can only describe these particular eyes as being mildly interested, but not exactly cordial. It would be of considerable benefit to our general mental outlook if this silent majority (observing us from every angle) could be reduced somehow! That's where you come in. They were made in the early 20's for use in fish lures. The wire can be cut easily, leaving a stub for pressing into soft material such as wood, cork, or tapioca pudding. You can certainly think of many devilish uses for these fine specimens. They would make interesting swizzle sticks, but the wire tastes like Post Office ink. 3/16" to ¼" diameter. 25¢ each. 10 for $2.00 postpaid.*

Gary Craig
Columbia, Missouri

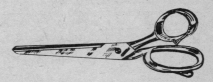

#861 SCHABLONENSCHEREN (double bladed stencil shears) Available after July 1st, 1970. Be a Schablonenscherenmeister! This scissors cuts out paper stencils and eliminates 1.75 m.m. of paper between the blades to allow for the lead came. Used by stained glass studios since early times, it is almost indispensable for any intricate pattern work.
$21.00 postpaid.

#889 SHEET LEAD For silhouettes and other intricate exercises. A pure lead which will readily solder to cames. Easily formed or shaped for work on lempshades, etc. Usually painted black.
12" wide sheets only, sold per running foot, up to 6 feet long.
$3.00 per running foot. Add for postage at the rate of 4½ lbs. per running foot.

#890 LEAD WIRE 1/8" diameter pure lead wire for various decorative effects on stained glass ornaments.
5 foot length, 75¢ postpaid.

Stained Glass Lore

I would like to help you people include another building material in your Whole Earth Catalog. Stained glass.

S. A. Bendheim Co., Inc.
122 Hudson (Corner of No. Moore)
New York, N.Y. 10013

Almost all the other stained glass shops buy their glass from Bendheim or someone who did so avoid the mark-up.

If you can't visit Bendheim's and spend hours looking at thousands of varieties of glass, it's best to know something about glass varieties. There is no good book about this and the best way to learn is by pilgrimage.

There are four basic types:

1. imported antique style
2. domestic rolled pattern
3. opalescent
4. dalles

The first three are thin sheet glass for leading and the last is thick slab glass for cementing into walls. The antique is hand blown and is usually in bright colors that have a life about them. They are the most expensive sheet glass. German selenium reds and oranges are **especially fiery. The French glass often comes flashed**—a thin layer of a second color. Then there is reamy (bumpy) and streaky (the color is streaked like marble cake). Best glass for fine art windows.

Domestic rolled glass has colors less vibrant. In quantity, it doesn't cost much more than plate glass. Some patterns are double rolled cathedral——covered with small bumps. Seedy——filled with air bubbles. Flemish——large scoops like an apple piecrust. And a flower pattern, etc. Best glass for artsy dangles.

Opalescent glass is the Victorian stuff that looks like someone mixed milk in it or painted heavy enamel on it. It is best suited for Tiffany lamp shades since it distributes the light, especially if the inside of the shade is flashed opal.

The dalles glass is about 8" x 10" x 1". It is generally broken up according to a pattern, laid on a table where epoxy is poured around the pieces. When dry, a stained glass wall is obtained. It is the most expensive. The slab is at least $4. But can be the most impressive.

So now you are ready to order glass. Request free of charge catalog from Bendheim.

Leading is best obtained from White Metal Rolling & Stamping Corp., 80 Moultrie St., Brooklyn, N.Y., except minimum order is around $75.00

The best book available, still not adequate, is Techniques of Stained Glass by Patrick Reyatiens——a $15 book from England. Another English book in paperback is Stained Glass by Laurence Lee, Oxford U at $1.25.

Peter Grant
Kingston, N.Y.

Working with Stained Glass

T. Y. Crowell is publishing Working With Stained Glass by Jean Jacques Duvall this Fall (1971) for about $8.95. Duvall also runs a stained glass workshop at 666 Fifth Avenue, New York, N.Y. 10019.

Thomas Y. Crowell Company
201 Park Ave. So.
New York, N.Y. 10003

June 7 '1970

dear whole earth,

Enclosed is a snap shot of my just about completed house. i am in great need of a used left arm. could you please ask your readers to keep on the look out for same. winter is almost here and i'm getting a draft from the pit. Thanks, nodrog.

Trailer Life

First, let me thank you for the Catalog. I and my friend my dog & cat are exiled to a carnival in Michigan and your catalog is like a bigwarm letter from the whole counter-culture. My reason for writing is to share with you something of our life style that might help others.

All the families on the show have house trailers and each week we set up our little village in a different (and sometimes a little hostile) place. Like fairground, behind gas stations, ball parks. For this one needs a truck to pull trailer (or heavy car), lots of hoses and electric cords, "Y's" (an object shaped [like a Y] used to connect untold numbers of trailers to the same water hookup.), a shovel to dig a hole if you don't have a self-contained bathroom.

We have a 27 foot 1957 trailer that has been our year-round home for over a year and it's just like an apartment but better. It needed a paint job so we all got stoned and did it pink, yellow, and orange. And I've got the outdoors all around.

It cost $900 and the only money that we had to spend was for travel, i.e. hitch $200, tires $100. The rest has gone for rugs, sound systems, posters orange light bulbs and lots of contact. But its a home and its beautiful. The new trailers are more expensive ($3,000 & up for one our size) and very sterile.

I don't know about California but the Mid West is full of old trailers & so is Florida. The old folks in the retirement parks trade in sometimes. The only drawback is our neighbors. Carnival people are a sub-culture but not ours. Trailer parks are full of nice middle class folks. But if a group of friendly freaks decided to get back to nature, I think a trailer is easier for the city folks than building a log cabin.

Susan Sullivan
Flushing, N.Y.

Dome Cookbook

A new art form is evolving in the southwest desert. Multi-colored cartop domes, put together with whatever's lying around. Free heat from the sun. Behind much of this innovating stands Steve Baer, a young inventor who generates enough energy to get others moving too.

This tabloid contains the crystallographic theory and junkyard practice behind Baer's domes: from how to distort a polyhedron without affecting connector angles to how to chop the top out of a car without losing your foot. From all we can determine, Baer's theory is unique in architecture. So is his practice; instead of dying of dissertation dry rot, his notions stand around in the world bugging the citizens.

The Dome Cookbook, now in its third printing, is published by Lama Foundation, an experimental community in New Mexico.

—SB

Dome Cookbook
Steve Baer
1968; 40 pp.

Lama/Cookbook Fund
P.O. Box 422
Corrales,N.M. 87048

Zome Primer

Gone beyond Dome Cookbook, Baer's investigation of further uses of five-fold symmetry leads toward a kind of universal truss, infinitely flexible in shape and dimension, but finite and handy in connecting hardware. The book is technical. With it and one of Baer's models you can take some surprising trips through the labyrinth of structure where just often enough you meet yourself coming back, elegantly.

—SB

Zome Primer
Steve Baer
1970; 35 pp.

$3.00 postpaid

from:
Zomeworks Corp.
P.O. Box 712
Albuquerque, New Mexico 87103

or WHOLE EARTH CATALOG

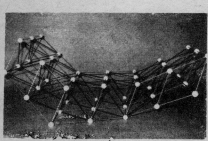

**Truss turning corner
8 A cells - 4 B cells**

Order in Space

A new book by an experimental mathematician on order in space. " . . . space defining, distribution patterns, space filling properties, packing & stacking, economy grids and communication linkages."

There are exciting insights into structure in nature, and exploratory diagrams of the functions possible in space.

—Lloyd Kahn

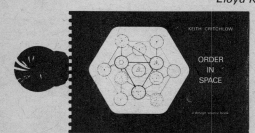

Order in Space
Keith Critchlow
1969; 120 pp.

$8.95 postpaid

from:
The Viking Press
625 Madison Avenue
New York, N. Y. 10022

or WHOLE EARTH CATALOG

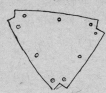
painted side up

panel, cut, drilled and broken

panel cut and drilled

When you are putting up a dome panel by panel you often have to use poles to support the wobbly sides as they close in toward the center. When we were putting up the second to last panel in the shop dome we had three poles in strategic spots to hold the wobbly overhanging panels from collapsing. The poles were nailed at the top so they wouldn't fall away if during a moment's strain the load were lifted up and off of them. The panel was an 8' by 19' and extremely heavy. We put it up with an inadequate crew, two men and two women. We struggled for an entire afternoon the last few inches Albert Mahler pushed from on top of a spool resting on top of the cab of his pickup which we had driven into the dome. It was touch and go, a clamp might slip, Albert might collapse, the poles might buckle. Each one of many failures seemed equally as probable as getting the monster joined to the neighboring panels. A huge shove, some quick work with the crow bar and clamps—Albert eased off and it still held, I took a few more turns on one clamp and added another one—it was a sure thing, we had it in place!

I felt as if the panel had been lifted into place by some incredible wave we had created that now washed back as we put down tools and Albert got down off the cab. But there was one last thing to check—the poles, were they dangerously bowed under this new load. The entire sensation in my head began for a moment to turn inside out when Holly yelled "look at them" but then I saw what it was—the dome was finding its shape, it had lifted all three heavy poles off the floor, they were hanging from where they had been toe nailed at their tops, swaying slowly. Three important pillars transformed in one moment into three dangling slow swinging pendulums.

RHOMBIC ENNEACONTAHEDRON

The geodesic dome, if it is large and composed of many different edges and joints, has many different edge lengths. It is complicated in structure and simple in shape. Zomes are simple in structure and complicated in shape.

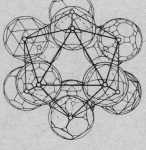

THE GENERATION OF THE BASIC POLYGONS
Pattern of unfolding or degrees of order in space

Right: The triangle is the prime polygon and only structural shape, followed by the square, pentagon, hexagon, octagon, decagon and dodecagon. The broken lines indicate relationships of concord between the polygons.

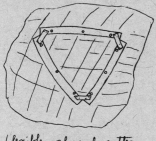
KISSING   FUSED

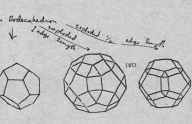

flexible plywood pattern on car top

Regular Dodecahedron
1 edge length   Exploded ½ edge length

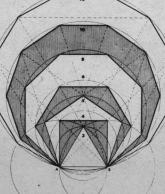

FAMILY REUNION

When Estelle saw the girl go up to the family at the picnic table she figured something weird was going on. And when the girl got in the car and drove away with them Estelle decided she'd better go back to the rest area and find out what was wrong.

D.R. was sitting on the picnic table, gurgling and groaning with his eyes closed. The Greek was peering into D.R.'s open mouth like a dentist, trying to see why he couldn't say "OM". Estelle came up behind the Greek and watched him operate for a minute or two. Then she walked around so he could see her and ask him if he had seen Frieda leave.

"Just a minute," said the Greek. He probed D.R.'s throat with his finger till he gagged. "Now try it," said the Greek. "Just sort of hum it, go 'OMMMMMMMMMMMMM.' " As D.R. swallowed and warmed up for the try the Greek looked up at Estelle and said "Yeah, I saw her. Looks like she's headed west again."

"But didn't she <u>say</u> anything?" asked Estelle. Do you know <u>why</u> she left?"

The Greek shrugged. "Everybody splits sooner or later," he said. "This was just her time, I guess."

"Awwww," D.R. intoned. "Awwwwrrrr."

"<u>Mell</u>ow," said the Greek, stroking D.R.'s throat. "Make it mellow. It's a prayer, not some sort of challenge."

The Greek turned toward D.R. again, but Estelle leaned and stayed in front of him. "But how do you <u>feel</u> about her going," she said. "Don't you care? I mean, doesn't it make any difference . . ."

"I'm very happy for her is all," said the Greek. "It was time she went. I'm pleased she was clear enough to recognize it."

"She didn't seem very clear to me."

"And what is that supposed to mean?" asked the Greek.

"Nothing. I just feel a little more concerned than you seem to. She seemed very fragile to me."

The Greek laughed. "I'm sure she did."

"And what is <u>that</u> supposed to mean?"

"Well, it's obvious, isn't it? You see Frieda as this helpless little creature who couldn't possibly get along on her own. And I'm sure you think you might have been able to do something for her if she'd stayed around."

"That's bullshit."

"Of course it is. It's all bullshit."

"No it's not," said Estelle. "It's not all bullshit."

"And I would agree with that, too. It's not all bullshit."

"Jesus," said Estelle. "You are really full of shit, did you know that?"

The Greek smiled. His white teeth were as big as thumbnails. His blonde hair glinted in the sun. "Of course I know it. Do you realize that you are full of bullshit too?"

"Yap yap yap," said Estelle. "That's all you do."

"Awwwrrr," D.R. gurgled. "Awwwrrrr."

"<u>Mell</u>ow," the Greek said to D.R. "Make it mellow. Make it mellow. Make it a prayer."

But "awwwwrrrrr" was the best D.R. could do.

"Poor old D.R. Do you realize he can't make a single vowel sound?"

"I've seen him in worse shape," said Estelle.

"You really are a bitch, aren't you?" said the Greek.

"You're a son of a bitch," Estelle hissed. "A goddamn phoney superguru son of a bitch."

"Right on," laughed the Greek. "God, is that ever right on. You're a bitch, and I'm a son of a bitch. Hello, Mother. Welcome to the family reunion."

Geodesics

This is the first book wholly devoted to geodesics. Good text, clear drawings, introductory text on the basic principles of Fuller's geodesic domes.

Shown are domes of wood, metal and plastic, most of them produced industrially; along with the various domes are detailed sections of hubs, construction methods, and assembly sequences.

The brief text discusses
—polyhedra
—orientation
—breakdown
—frequency
—base truncation
—chord factors (the constants necessary for calculation of different diameter domes.)

—Lloyd Kahn

[Suggested by Onyx]

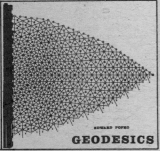

Geodesics
Edward Popko
1968; 124 pp.

$4.00 postpaid

from:
University of Detroit Press
4001 West McNichols Road
Detroit, Michigan 48221

or WHOLE EARTH CATALOG
Orders less than $15.00
must be prepaid.

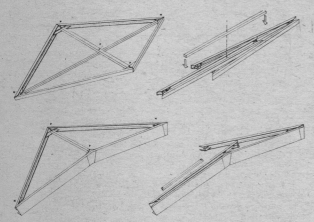

Diamond packaging sequence, an ingenious pin and hinge system allows diamond components to partially disassemble reducing packagin volume, typical diamond and base support shown. A Fuller Research Foundation Project.

O'Dome

The O'Dome is a lightweight circular structure that can be transported in a station wagon and erected in three hours. Even though the manufacturer seems to be aiming it at Playboy readers for beach cabanas——"instant vacation house"——it looks like a low cost highly portable, well designed unit that could easily be trucked into the woods for quick shelter.

It is of stress panel design (the bend-over sections are the framework as well as the membrane), and modular, meaning you can connect one to another. Tension rings top and bottom hold the panels together.

Different color panels, different sizes, options as to amount of glass.

I assume it's waterproof.

—Lloyd Kahn

15' diameter	$1200
20' diameter	$2000
25' diameter	$2500-3500, depending on amount of glass

from:
Tension Structures, Inc.
419 East Main Street
Milan, Mich. 48160

Space Grid Structures

A space grid is a means of spanning great distances with little weight, and a few immediate supports. Buckminster Fuller's Octetruss at the Museum of Modern Art in 1959 was 35' wide and spanned 60' one way, 40' another from one column of supports. It was fabricated of 2" pipe.

Space grids consist of two parallel planes, forming a floor and ceiling; "web" members in between connect them in such a way that external loads are distributed in all directions.

This book is ". . . an exchange of information about what has been done recently in the development of flat space grid structures." There are photos, drawings, models of structures and joints. The three sections of the book deal with flat double-layer space grid structures, stressed-skin space grids, and fine clear drawings of space grid geometries. Also an extensive bibliography. Very little text; it's not needed as the drawings and photos are excellent.

—Lloyd Kahn

Space Grid Structures
John Borrego
1968; 200 pp.

$4.95 paper

from:
The M.I.T. Press
28 Carleton St.
Cambridge, Mass. 02142

or WHOLE EARTH CATALOG

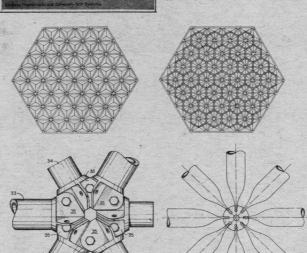

Dyna Domes

There are about a dozen Dyna Domes on the outskirts of Phoenix. Each new one built gets a little closer to the city limits, and it's the hope of domebuilder Bill Woods to have the city fathers wake up one morning, find themselves surrounded by domes, and admit the new creatures under the wings of the building codes.

These are good quality, low cost plywood domes, with fiberglass exterior, and polyurethane foam insulation sprayed on the inside. Wood struts are put together with patented metal connectors, seams are filled with high-strength caulk, then taped with fiberglass.

You have the choice of having a dome erected (within 500 miles of Phoenix), buying a kit, or purchasing just the connectors with plans.

Woods has been experimenting for some time with foam-fiberglass buildings, has built a machine that produces the sandwich panels, and is about to market a foam dome.

—Lloyd Kahn

Brochure **free** from:
Dyna Dome
22226 North 23rd Avenue
Phoenix, Arizona 85027

Complete dome, erected on concrete floor within 500 miles of Phoenix: approx. $4.00 per sq. ft. floor space.

Complete kit with instructions for erection: approx. $2.00 per sq. ft. floor space.

Hub connectors, with plans for building it yourself: $2.00 per strut.

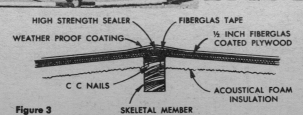

HIGH STRENGTH SEALER
WEATHER PROOF COATING
FIBERGLAS TAPE
½ INCH FIBERGLAS COATED PLYWOOD
C C NAILS
SKELETAL MEMBER
ACOUSTICAL FOAM INSULATION

Figure 3

Space Enclosure Systems

subtitled "identification and documentation of cell geometries", wood's book presents both tabulated and graphic analysis of twenty-three volumetric geometrical forms, or, as he more effectively describes them, "space enclosure systems". the result is a beautiful, clear cut little TOOL that can liberate the designer, architect, educator, sculptor, mathematician, and ambitious spirit.

wood has taken this presentation just far enough. his information is formal, clear, simple, good and useful. what stimulates appreciation for what he has presented is what he has omitted. the book is void of the cliche "author's sketches" of possible futuristic applications that too often infringe or undermine the user's imaginative potential. wood allows the application of his data to be- the reader/user's choice and opportunity.

[Reviewed by thomas casey]

Wood has written a second volume (OSU No. 205) subtitled "The variables of packing cell design", which does the same thing with a whole new set of solids.

 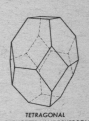

TETRAGONAL ORTHOTETRAKAIDECHEDRON

Space Enclosure Systems (No. 203)
Donald G. Wood
1968; 52 pp.

$3.50 postpaid

Space Enclosure Systems (No. 205)
Donald G. Wood
1968; 59 pp.

$3.50 postpaid

both from:
Engineering Publications
College of Engineering
The Ohio State University
2070 Neil Avenue
Columbus, OH 43210

or WHOLE EARTH CATALOG

A = 90°	
B = 112° 30'	
C = 135°	
D = 63° 26'	
E = 116° 34'	
VERTICES = 24	
EDGES = 36	
DIHEDRAL ANGLES = 114° 18'	
	131° 24'
	130° 0'
	99° 44'

FACES

 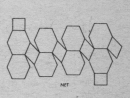

NET

Futuro

Finland, famed for its forests, and finely-crafted wooden structures, has produced the first well-detailed, commercially available foam fiberglass dwelling.

Now being manufactured in the U.S., the Futuro——a shiny elliptical pod——looks like it just landed. It can be dropped in by helicopter (expensive though) and requires no site preparation. It's structurally strong, well insulated, and has retractable stairs. Interior looks plastic and shiny and badly needs some madras bedspreads and non-plastic human touches.

——Lloyd Kahn

Futuro House

$13,200 for shell
$16,700 for completely equipped house
F. O. B. Philadelphia

from:
Casa 2 Corporation
1902 Rittenhouse Square
Philadelphia, PA 19103
215/735-7644

Domebook Two

This is an instruction manual for builders and a story book of some new communities in America. It is the beginning of an information net of people making their own shelters.

It contains instructions——as detailed as we could pull together——on a dozen different types of domes, each with much variation possible. Everything worthwhile from Domebook One is included, there are details on domes we've built since then, and there is feedback from people who built domes from Domebook One.

There are visual and mathematical sections on geodesics, a very complete chord factor section, elliptical geodesics, instructions on models, a section on trace-over paper models and take-off points for various trips.

The building information is better than Domebook One—— corrected, modified, clarified. There is now good information on sealing, floors, windows and other construction details. There are fairly complete instructions on foam and aluminum domes we have built, a five page section on domes built at the Ananda community in Grass Valley, a description of a ferro cement dome on a wood frame in Iowa, a beautiful shake dome on a lake in Washington. There are cautionary words on shiny plastics as building materials——don't be afraid to use them, but be aware-beware-of all qualities of the particular plastic and where it comes from before you decide to use it. There is emphasis on building with trash ("our only growing resource"), used materials, whatever is lying around. Funk building, the architecture of necessity.

This book is not so much specifically about domes as it is a call to get you moving, to take things in your own hands, to act. Most important to us in this process is to communicate as we learn, and in the future we'll act as a funnel of incoming shelter information. We plan another book by 1973, probably to be called Shelter, and we may put out supplementary data in between now and then. If you want us to let you know what we do next with shelter, film, video, publications——send us a postcard with your name and address.

[Reviewed by Lloyd Kahn]

Domebook Two
1971; 128 pp.

$4.20 postpaid

Shelter Publications/Mountain Books
P.O. Box 4811
Santa Barbara, CA 93103

Random House
Westminster, Md. 21157

or WHOLE EARTH CATALOG

Windows and Doors

2 X 4's are used to frame in the windows and the doors. The door is made by dropping perpendiculars to a base triangle. The door can be made to swing either in or out.

A very pleasing window pattern is with three windows in a row. The center window can be made to open and close. We made this window smaller by running the 2 X 4 frame parallel to the struts and hinging it at the top.

Cardboard can be fastened with tabs. They should be as large as you can manage. The slots should be a jam fit. Pinch the tip of the male part before inserting.

We decided on a long arc of window area to follow the sun, 2 doors(full triangles) and full triangle windows at the bottoms of 3 of the pentagons. Right now the windows are covered with 12 mil vinyl. Send us glass!

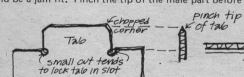

DESIGNING THE FERRO ARMATURE

A. Geodesic Frames

From the foregoing we see that a ferrocement dome can be structured as a self-supporting spherical shell, without formwork. However perhaps the simplest and safest way to describe the domical enclosure is by a geodesic net of wood or metal struts which support the mesh that gets ferrocemented.

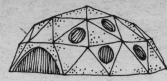 

Regardless of the size of the dome, a higher frequency geodesic net will result in a more nearly "spherical" shell, and a lower frequency will give a more "faceted" polyhedron. Although little experimental experience is available, it doesn't seem to matter critically to the ferrocement how spherical it is.

If the mesh is abundant and continuous, and if the application technique is sound, then the ferrocement skin will transfer stresses across the dihedral angles of the triangular planes without cracking. (The skin may tend to sag between the struts when loaded with wet cement, giving a tentlike effect.) Therefore, it might be just as good and a lot more convenient to use a low frequency frame of fewer and larger struts, as did the Jensens.

The Bevel Gauge

The builder's best friend at this stage of the game is the trusty bevel gauge. This is necessary because all the 2 X 4's needed for framing in windows and doors have compound angles. A short picture course in finding these two angles:

The most important trick is to make sure which length you are measuring and to be consistent in relating the angles you are finding to that length. If you have never done this before then it is a lesson in patience. It usually takes cutting a few too short and backwards to catch on. Even though we made mistakes we miraculously found a use for all the wood.

HOW TO DRAW AN ELLIPSE

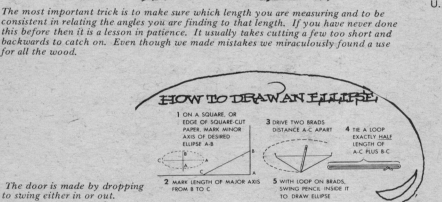

1 ON A SQUARE, OR EDGE OF SQUARE-CUT PAPER, MARK MINOR AXIS OF DESIRED ELLIPSE A-B

2 MARK LENGTH OF MAJOR AXIS FROM B TO C

3 DRIVE TWO BRADS DISTANCE A-C APART

4 TIE A LOOP EXACTLY HALF LENGTH OF A-C PLUS B-C

5 WITH LOOP ON BRADS, SWING PENCIL INSIDE IT TO DRAW ELLIPSE

No plans were ever drawn for our domes, only a few sketches. Our blueprints have been mathematics. As you read the rest of the book, it may be helpful for you to know of the following general categories of dome construction:

Sun Domes. The Sun Dome was a swimming pool cover dome published by Fuller through *Popular Science* in 1966. For some time, this was the only geodesic geometry available to anyone wanting to build a dome. The Sun Dome is made of triangles on frames that bolt together to make the dome. Some examples are Sun Dome, p. 14; Big Sur Dome, p. 16; Aluminum Sun Dome, p. 29; and Portable Pillow Dome, p. 44.

Struts/skin domes. First the framework is put up, usually with various vertex connectors, then a skin applied. See Pacific Dome, p. 20.

Flanged panel dome. Skin and struts are one-piece, with skin flanged over to form strut. Assembly is like the Sun Dome, usually with bolts, or rivets. Example: Aluminum Triacon Dome, p. 26.

Monolithic skin domes. Dome skin is applied in liquid form, hardens to make a one-piece rigid skin. See Egg Domes, P. 35; Muslin Foam Dome, p. 40; Ferro Cement Dome, p. 66.

Tent Domes. A one-piece skin is either hung from, or draped over a frame. See Tent Domes, p. 48.

The first section of the book was mathematics. What follows are our building and living experiences, and communication from other builders throughout the U. S. and Canada.

Dome Model Kits

The Dome East kit costs $5, consists of nifty hubs and struts. The Domecile kit costs $10, consists of geometric plastic panels. Models help you visualize somewhat. They may help on rudimentary structure. They also glorify trivial problems and obscure serious ones. Buildings built too scrupulously from models tend to look like models. Build buildings first, then models.

—SB

Dome East
Wendell Enterprises
Box 922
Hicksville, N.Y. 11802

Domecile Kit Co.
Box 954
Mendocino, CA. 95460

THE KEY

Estelle was so furious she went to the bus intending to just get in and drive away and leave D.R. and the Greek to their stupid games. Leave leave leave was all she could think about. Go. Go. Go. Same old story. Same old broken record. Same old thorny point on the never-ending cycle.

She was crying now. That seemed like a broken record too. God, she thought. Do I ever cry a lot. Am I ever one whiny tearful bitch.

Cry. Cry. Cry.

Go. Go. Go.

But Estelle couldn't go because the Greek had taken the key.

"You son of a bitch, give me that goddamn key!"

She was about fifty yards from the Greek, and the wind was still blowing.

"What?" called the Greek. "I can't hear you."

Estelle ran a few yards toward the table. "I said you've got the goddamn key!"

The Greek grinned and nodded his head vigorously. "I know it," he called back. "I've always had the key."

"You slimy bastard!" Estelle screamed. She glanced around the ground for a weapon of some kind to kill him with. But her eyes were too full of tears to see. She blanked out for a moment then. The whole world went black as night and Estelle forget everything she knew. When she came to again she was in the bus with the pill box in her hand, looking for a downer.

The Owner-Built Home

Ken Kern makes a unique offer to anyone thinking about building his own home: for $10 he furnishes a preliminary house design, as well as a copy of The Owner-Built Home, which is about the most useful book on building available.

For the design, send him a sketch of your building site, along with space requirements and personal likes and dislikes; or you may prefer to get the book first and read the first chapter on 'Site and Climate' before sending in the information.

The book is sound advice on the best low-cost building techniques from around the world: Africa, India, Israel: countries that cannot afford U.S.-style waste. Much of it is not in print elsewhere.

A 1" concrete floor with loading stresses of 450 lbs per sq ft; houses built of earth, woven bamboo and bottles, as well as of conventional materials. How to hook up your plumbing in a simple central core.

Good dope on concrete-proportions, additives such as sawdust or emulsified asphalt for 'comfort cushion' floor. Details on wood framing, how stud wall houses are overbuilt, the strength of threaded nails.

There is much good data on building with rock and earth; how to make a sliding form for rammed earth and a discussion of the strength of rammed earth and soil cement. Why don't you hear anything these days about earth wall buildings?

Inasmuch as there is nothing in bare earth to *sell*, no commercial group can be found to extol its merits.

Lots more, with a bibliography at the end of each chapter for further reasearch.

—Lloyd Kahn

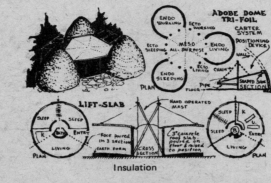

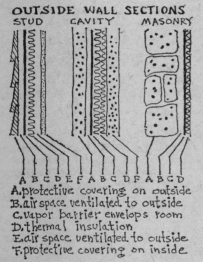

OUTSIDE WALL SECTIONS
STUD CAVITY MASONRY

A B C D E F A B C D F A B C D
A. protective covering on outside
B. air space ventilated to outside
C. vapor barrier envelops room
D. thermal insulation
E. air space ventilated to outside
F. protective covering on inside

The Owner-Built Home and preliminary house design (send sketch, etc.)
Ken Kern
1961; 300 pp.

with preliminary design

$15.00 postpaid

from:
Owner-Built Publications
P.O. Box 550
Oakhurst, CA 93644

without preliminary design

$7.50 postpaid

from:
WHOLE EARTH CATALOG

Although air is a very poor conductor of heat, the insulating value of an ordinary air space is rather small, on account of the large transfer of heat by convection and radiation. Radiation is largely responsible for the ineffectiveness of air spaces bounded by ordinary building materials, such as are found in frame or other hollow walls. The low insulating value is often erroneously attributed to convection; but, as a matter of fact, from 50 to 80 per cent of the heat transfer across air spaces of ordinary sizes takes place by radiation. If the air spaces were bounded by bright metallic surfaces, the transfer of heat by radiation would be greatly diminished, since clean metallic surfaces are much poorer radiators than non-metallic surfaces, such as brick, stone, glass, wood, paper, etc.

Reflective metal foil (copper, aluminum, or steel) costs less than 3 cents a square foot and can be easily installed. One should remember to keep the shiny side out (or up) and leave a ventilated air space inside (or below), and at least ¾-inch between the foil and the surface it faces.

About 70% of the sun's heat rays can be reflected from the house by installing a white or light-colored roof. A thin layer of quartz gravel or marble chip, backed by aluminum foil on a built-up tar-and-felt roof is by far the best type of surface for regions suffering a high incidence of summer heat.

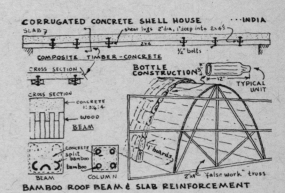

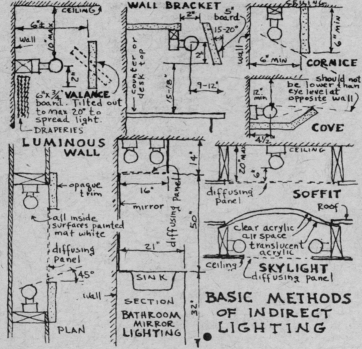

BASIC METHODS OF INDIRECT LIGHTING

Your Engineered House

'To begin this book, and the day, what does it take to get the morning sun into the kitchen?'

A delight to read before designing or building your own home. General ideas on light, heat ventilation, house placement, acoustics, financing. Specific building tips on all aspects of building but mainly post and beam houses.

This is an easy way for a beginner to frame a house (as opposed to stud-wall construction), and it gets a roof over your head right away to keep the rain off while you finish the walls. Most of this information is seldom considered by architects, and is culled from the author's building experiences. You are encouraged and told how to pick up pencil and paper and design your own home—tailormade to your own specifications, aspirations, and finances, and, although not in great detail, how to build it yourself. A discussion and treatment of homes as human environments and a good place to start if you have no design or building experience.

—Lloyd Kahn

If I am doing work with my hands, and am right-handed, I will prefer the major light source to be at my left and the minor source at my right. If I am left-handed, I will of course reverse the sources.

Your Engineered House
Rex Roberts
1964; 237 pp.

$4.95 postpaid

from: J. P. Lippincott Company
East Washington Square
Philadelphia, Pa. 19105

or WHOLE EARTH CATALOG

Scenery is what you see from where you live. If your scenery is to cost you nothing, you will leave it where it is, and if that scenery already has character, you will make only minor modifications. You will move yourself around, move the house around, but you will not move the scenery around until you have lived with it for a while as it is.

As a machine designer, I say that when we treat the window as a machine, asking it to perform multiple functions—admit light, admit air, or exclude it according to the weather, keep out bugs in summer, never mind the bugs in winter—and do all this at the twist of a crank without leaking or sticking—the window is bound to become expensive.

If we give the window one function and one only, to admit light, we can have all the windows we want at no extra charge. It is inexpensive to fix panes of glass permanently in place. Any smart carpenter can build a wall of glass about as quickly as he can build a wall of anything else.

As for the ventilator, it's a wooden door on the simplest of hinges, rigid, unbreakable, easy to weatherstrip, easy to screen. One frame does the whole job.

If we keep windows and ventilators separate, we wind up with more light, better ventilation, less trouble, less maintenance, and lower cost.

The habit of building a house in a certain way is not proof that the habit should be continued. Many of our present building methods are wrong, expensively wrong. I have tried to suggest building techniques which are inexpensively right.

37. How to build doors and windows
Here is the way the ordinary door is fitted:

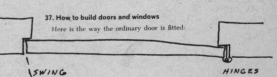

How well this door keeps the wind out depends on the accuracy with which it is fitted into a frame. In warm, wet weather, when there is no need for a tight fit, the door swells up and

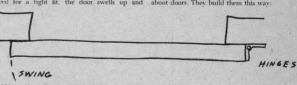

sticks. In cold weather everything shrinks and the door admits an invigorating breeze.
Refrigerator manufacturers are much smarter about doors. They build them this way:

144 How will it be built?

The moment you stop to consider it, I think you will agree this is the sensible way to build a door. It doesn't have to fit anything. It just closes, flat to flat; and there you are.
The domestic hardware people don't seem to

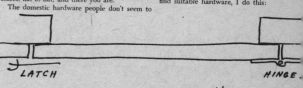

have heard about the refrigerator-type door or you will probably run into trouble getting hinges and latches that will work. When I find suitable hardware, I do this:

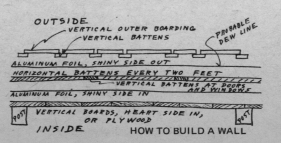

Canadian Wood Frame House Construction

*best way to learn to become a carpenter
is to get some wood and a few tools and
put them together somehow, however you can,
practice, know the material and what
you are trying to do with it. (a crosscut on a
2 by 12 is a good exercise) then, when you
are ready to build something, either find someone
who has built something, or take a good long look at what
you are living in now, or read a book. we carry a bunch
of carpentry books. their main worth is in the diagrams.
from them you can figure out how other builders do IT.
but don't be bound by rectilinear bullshit. read a
wooden boatbuilding book (page 113) and figure out
how to bend wood, build a snailshell house out of
warped one-by. good and free.
or read this book. good and free.*

—jd

[Suggested by Ian McKinnon]

Canadian Wood-frame House Construction
197pp.

out of print

from:
Canadian Central Mortgage and Housing Corporation
650 Lawrence Avenue West
Toronto, 7, Ontario, Canada

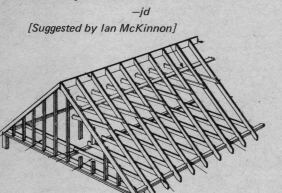

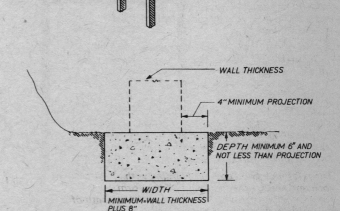

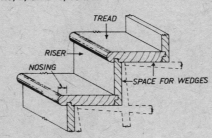

FIGURE 4.—One method often used to determine size of footings.

Low-Cost Wood Homes

*An excellent manual, with 100's of good drawings, on wood
house construction. Details on pole house construction,
and all aspects of wood frame buildings.*
—Lloyd Kahn

**Low-Cost Wood Homes for Rural
America—Construction Manual**
L. O. Anderson
1969; 112 pp.

$1.45 postpaid

from:
Superintendent of Documents
U.S. Government Printing Office
Washington, D.C. 20402

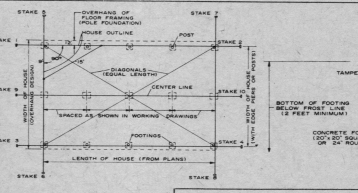

FHA Pole House Construction

*Pole type houses are easy to construct on steep hillsides,
they're inexpensive, aesthetically pleasing, and ecologically
sound (no need to bulldoze the landscape to construct a
level platform). The holes can be dug by hand. Roof goes
up first to keep your head dry while you build the floor
and walls. The pamphlet says you can use regular old
telephone poles. . .hmm. Bibliography too.*

*[Suggested and reviewed by
Kenny Rothstein]*

Free

OUT OF PRINT

U.S. Dept. of Housing and Urban Development
Federal Housing Administration
Washington, D.C. 20410

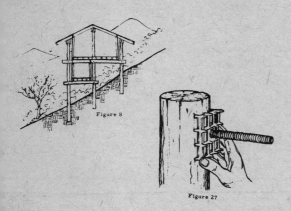

POLE FRAME: When the poles are used to support the roof as
shown in Figure 8, the roof can be installed early to keep the
rest of the construction process dry. The extra pole length also
helps to brace the structure. With two or three-story structures,
the heavy timber frame will take concentrated loads and also
reduces fire hazards. It allows flexibility in placing, and possible
relocation, of walls.

SPIKE GRIDS: Heavy timber connections standard in bridge and
warehouse construction, are less familiar to the house builder. A
single curved spike grid, Figure 27, inserted between the pole and
the beam substantially increases the strength of the bolted connection.

American Plywood Association

*What makes plywood such a desirable building material
is its extremely favorable cost/strength ratio. Also, it's
quick to install, as each piece you nail down covers 32
square feet.*

*The American Plywood Association has hundreds of pam-
phlets available on different uses of plywood: roofs, walls,
floors; cabin plans, pole buildings, barns.*

Write, asking for lists of publications:

*Residential Construction Literature Index
Agricultural Literature Index
General Construction Literature Index
Industrial Literature Index
Consumer and Do-It-Yourself Literature Index*

free
—Lloyd Kahn

from:
American Plywood Association
1119 A Street
Tacoma, Washington 98401

	Form No.
Concrete Forms	
Guide to Plywood for Concrete Forms (Sweet's insert)	S69-90
Curved Panels	F67-1020
Nailed Plywood Box Beams	62-180
Plywood Truss Designs	64-650
(Describes new plans for King-Post and W-type trusses on spans 20' to 32'-8")	
Floors	
2-4-1 Tongue and Groove Plywood	60-40
Guide to Plywood for Underlayment (Sweet's insert)	S68-50
Umbrella Structure (22' wide shelter)	63-80
Plywood and Poles for Farm Buildings (Data sheet)	67-126
A-Type Hog House (6' x 6' portable units)	61-430

Small Homes Council

*A truss can be made of relatively small pieces of wood, is
light, cheap and therefore a more economical means of
spanning distances than a solid wooden beam. Complete
clear plans of 14 different types of trusses are available,
50¢ each. Also, publications on various building techniques,
and a set of circulars, 15¢ each, on subjects such as
Selecting Lumber, Chimneys and Fireplaces, Plumbing, etc.*
—Lloyd Kahn

Brochure on publications

$.25

from:
Small Homes Council-Building
Research Council
University of Illinois
1 E. St. Mary's Road
Champaign, IL 61820

COMING DOWN

Maybe D.R.'s acid trip ain't so groovy anymore. Maybe he
wonders where Estelle has gone, and why. It's funny stuff, acid.
It'll make you laugh, it'll make you cry. It'll make you wonder
where your woman is, and why. It'll give you something new to
say, but take away your words to say it with if you're not careful.
D.R. tried to say "Estelle!" but it came out as a moan. He tried
to say, "Forward, on to St. Louis!" but his tongue flapped useless
in his mouth.

If in the beginning was the word and the word was with God
and the word was God, what are you when you're speechless?
Pretty fucking depressed, if you want to know.
Depression is a rocky land-ing. Depression is your parachute
not working after a weird re-entry.
Wham.
Grounded.
And it's stony fucking ground.
She's not there to know you're hurt, you can't call for help
because your tongue won't work, he don't see your signals be-
cause he's talking all the time.
Maybe D.R.'s acid trip ain't so groovy anymore.
Maybe that steel band around his head's a headache after
all.
Maybe that stained window of the countryside's an actual
desert after all.
Maybe the wind is really blowing, maybe the sky is actually
overhead.
Maybe Estelle was really crying.
Maybe the time came.
"Has the time come?" asked D.R.
"Mellow," said the Greek. "Mellow.'

Fundamentals of Carpentry

Better know something about tools and materials before you start on this book. (Hand Woodworking Tools, How to Work with Tools and Wood, p. 144). Lots of meat for the beginner as well as the professional. The kind of stuff you might learn working with a good carpenter.

Mostly rectilinear construction, but with ingenuity, the methods are applicable to most wood structures.

Nice appendix with a list of Associations and Institutes, and an excellent list of reference books.

[Reviewed by Fred Richardson]

Fundamentals of Carpentry, Vol. 2
W. E. Durbahn, E. W. Sundberg
1948, 1970; 504 pp.

$7.40 postpaid

from:
American Technical Society
848 E. 58th St.
Chicago, Ill. 60637

or WHOLE EARTH CATALOG

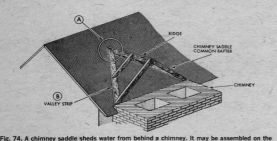

Fig. 74. A chimney saddle sheds water from behind a chimney. It may be assembled on the ground and installed after the roof is sheathed.

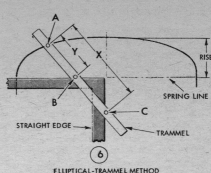

Fig. 28. Compression type bridging is equivalent to wood bridging in strength. (Timber Engineering Co.)

Fig. 29. Compression type metal bridging is installed with a few hammer blows. (Cleveland Steel Specialty Co.)

ELLIPTICAL-TRAMMEL METHOD
Straight edges are placed on the spring and center line. Nails are driven in trammel at points "A", "B" and "C". Dim X = 1/2 span. Dim Y= rise. As nails "B" and "C" follow straight edge, nail "A" will make ellipse.

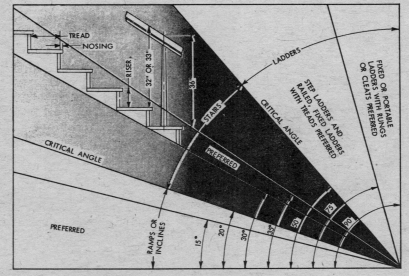

Fig. 74. Preferred and critical angles for stairs, ladders, ramps, and inclines.

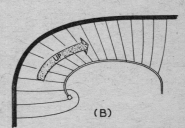

(B) elliptical stair.

Simplified Carpentry Estimating

When building, you'll do well to pre-calculate all materials and ask local lumber yards for competitive bids. This handbook, with short-cut tables, helps you quickly estimate all materials for conventional buildings: concrete, lumber, hardware, as well as labor hours.

—Lloyd Kahn

Simplified Carpentry Estimating
J. Douglas Wilson and Clell M. Rogers
1962; 320 pp.

$6.95 postpaid from:
Simmons-Boardman Books
350 Broadway
New York, N. Y. 10013

or WHOLE EARTH CATALOG

Wood Handbook

This bargain collection of technical data will be of use to anybody who works seriously with wood, for whatever purpose.

—SB

Wood Handbook
1955; 528 pp.

out of print

from:
U.S. Government Printing Office
Division of Public Documents
Washington, D.C. 20402

Simplified CARPENTRY ESTIMATING
By J. DOUGLAS WILSON and CLELL M. ROGERS

4. CEMENT CONTRACTORS' METHODS

A practical method used by cement contractors will give quite accurate results. This rule automatically allows for shrinkage.
Proceed as follows:
Rule: a. Find cubic feet contents of footings, walls and piers.
b. Divide the cubic footage by 15. Result equals tonnage of concrete aggregate (sand and rock combined). Material dealers will furnish concrete aggregate in several proportions, such as 50-50 or 40-60, etc.
c. To find sacks of cement multiply tonnage of aggregate by a constant selected from table III.

TABLE III
AGGREGATE TABLE

Mix	Aggregate Mix	Constant
1-2-3	1-5	4
1-2-4	1-6	3½
1-3-4	1-7	3
1-3-5	1-8	2½

TABLE 46.—*Recommended minimum net retentions of creosote and solutions containing creosote for various wood products* [1]

Product and service condition	Coal-tar creosote	Creosote-coal-tar solutions	Creosote-petroleum oil solution
	Lb. per cu. ft.	*Lb. per cu. ft.*	*Lb. per cu. ft.*
Ties (crossties, switch ties, and bridge ties)	8	8	9
Lumber and structural timbers:			
For use in coastal waters:			
Douglas-fir (coast type)	14	14	
Southern yellow pine	[2] 20	[2] 20	
For use in fresh water, in contact with ground, or im-			
portant structural members not in contact with ground			
or water	10	10	12
For other use not in contact with ground or water	6	6	7
Piles:			
For use in coastal waters:			
Douglas-fir (coast type)	14	14	
Southern yellow pine	[2] 20	[2] 20	
For land or fresh-water use	12	12	14
Poles	8		
Posts	6	6	7

Practical Handbook of Plumbing and Heating

Most plumbing books are either too old or too detailed for use by a novice home builder. This book, however, gives you enough basics to be your own plumber. It explains the use of plastic and "no-hub" pipe——both systems avoid the difficult process of melting lead for cast-iron drain pipe connections.

——Lloyd Kahn

OUT OF PRINT

The Practical Handbook of Plumbing and Heating
Richard Day
1969; 130 pp.

$4.95 postpaid

from:
Arco Publishing Company, Inc.
219 Park Avenue South
New York, N. Y. 10003

or WHOLE EARTH CATALOG

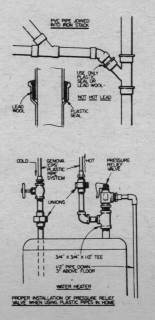
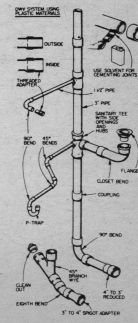

Audel Guides

I've just read a dozen or so Audel Guides, and these are some I felt were particularly useful. Some of the Audel books are quite obsolete, but much to my surprise, many have been written within the last ten years. Several have poor indexes, and some completely lack an index. The books are usually written by experts in the areas or trades described. The information in general seems to be very good.

If you are working with more or less typical American water and sewage systems, either maintaining or building, **Domestic Water Supply and Sewage Disposal Guide** *should be a rather useful book. Wells, springs, tanks, pumps (including hydraulic rams!), treatment, septic tanks, water heaters, it's all here, including many useful tables. The book is weak on the sewage end and has incomplete information on things such as hand dug, jetted and driven wells. Get the WHO book for that.*

Vol. I of **Masons and Builders Guide** *deals with clays, brick making, mortar, tools, brick laying, bonding, corners and rectangular openings. Vol. II covers arches and anchors, foundations, chimneys, fireplaces, repairs, estimation, and tile work.*

These seem very good if you want to get into traditional brick work. The chapters on fireplaces and chimneys seem particularly useful to me. I never could get behind brick work for new construction, though.

Carpentry and Building *fascinated me. Written in question and answer style, it covers many problems encountered in construction and remodeling work. Seems that these are questions that the author has received while acting as an engineering consultant for a trades magazine. Excellent sections on insulation and vapor barriers, acoustics, noise transmission and sound resistant partitions, and a beautiful miscellaneous section dealing with things like the pressures in grain bins. Good index.*

Building Maintenance *is intended for maintenance men in office etc. buildings. Looks like it would be very good for them, less useful for the home handyman. Information is included on painting, plumbing, concrete, carpentry, roofing, glazing, sheet metal, heating and air conditioning. Gives good, brief, and simple directions and assumes that the reader has at least some sense and native intelligence.*

No special knowledge is required to use the two-volume set, **Do-It-Yourself Encyclopedia.** *If you can get around the projects (!!) in questionable style (style?), there is a lot of good stuff relating to home improvement and home maintenance. A little hard to find your way around in until the second time through, it is actually fairly well organized. Far-out 1950's pictures.*

Reviewed by Fred

Domestic Water Supply and Sewage Disposal Guide
Edwin P. Anderson
1960; 440 pp.

OUT OF PRINT

Masons and Builders Guide, Vols. I, II,
Frank D. Graham
1924; approx. 300 pp. each

$5.95 each, postpaid † or

$11.25 for the set

Do-It-Yourself Encyclopedia (2 vols.)
1968; 1012 pp.

$9.00 /set, postpaid

Carpentry and Building
Harry F. Ulrey
1966; 434 pp.

$5.95 postpaid †

Building Maintenance
Jules Oravetz, Sr.
1966; 437 pp.

$5.95 postpaid †

from:
Theodore Audel & Co.
A Division of Bobbs-Merrill
4300 West 62nd Street
Indianapolis, Indiana 46268
or WHOLE EARTH CATALOG

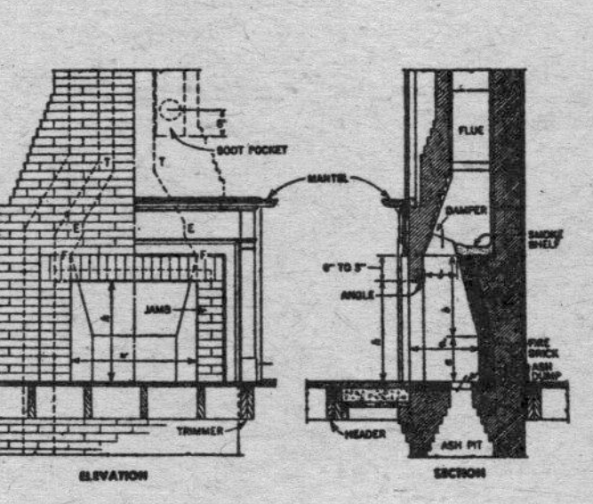

Expert foresters . . . advise that, although the hickory is a sturdy and persistent grower, a tree which has grown and matured under forest conditions cannot tolerate a disturbance of its root system; also, there may be danger of injuring the tree described if the roots are cut closer than approximately 25 feet along one side. Normally, from a circle immediately outside the crown, the main feeder roots extend outward and downward at an angle of approximately 45 degrees, and sometimes these roots go very deep. In addition, a system of very shallow roots, approximately 12 to 24 inches beneath the surface of the ground, extends outward in all directions. These roots also carry water to the trunk of the tree, and serve to anchor the tree upright in the soil. These are the roots that will be injured by digging for the foundations of the house.

Actually, there is no way to accurately foretell the reaction of the trees. Stay away from the trees as far as possible. The disturbed trees should be supplied with plenty of water and heavy feedings of fertilizer for some time to enable them to regain the loss of strength occasioned by disturbing the roots in the affected areas of the root system.

Carpentry and Building

Water Dowsing.—Although numerous persons consider the forked stick method of locating underground water as a mere "fanciful illusion" the fact still remains that extractable water has been found by this simple method throughout the ages.

Water dowsing consists essentially of the carrying of a forked twig of peach, apple, or maple over the area where the search for water is to be made. The process is performed essentially as follows:

Grasp the ends of the twig (one in each hand) with palms upward. When commencing to walk, the butt of the stick should be pointed upward. As moving water is approached, the butt end of the stick begins to dip downward until the moving water is intercepted at which location the butt end points straight down. At this particular time the forked twig has turned through an arc of 180 degrees. The stick will in some instances break under the grip as the butt dips downward. Pliable twigs will bend down despite the effort to hold them straight.

Most dowsers believe this unique ability or power comes to a person with birth. They also believe that this occult faculty can be developed and its use expanded by constant study and practice. It is, of course, a fact that many people have this ability without knowing it, never having had the reason for the experiment. Some students of the matter believe about one person in a thousand has some dowsing ability, although perhaps only about ten per cent of these latter have the ability to become good dowsers.

It cannot be too strongly emphasized that no scientific explanation exists for the location of extractable underground water by means of dowsing. The proof exists however, in thousands of usable wells which actually have been discovered by this uncanny method.

Domestic Water Supply

A well designed and properly installed damper is regarded as essential, particularly in cold climates. When no damper is used the throat opening J, should be 4 inches for fireplaces not exceeding 4 feet in height.

Placing the throat well forward has another advantage, namely that of forming a smoke shelf at the damper level. This shelf aids in stopping the down drafts which will almost invariably occur if the back of the fireplace be made to rise vertically, in the same plane as the back of the flue.

The opening above the smoke shelf should be "gathered" or *contracted* to the size of the flue by *corbelling,* this being done with the least height practicable. Up to the level of the clay flue lining, the brickwork should not be less than 8 inches thick, because the space immediately above the damper is the hottest place of the chimney.

In small fireplaces, a depth of 12 inches will permit good draft if the throat be properly constructed, but a minimum depth of 16 to 18 inches is advised to lessen the danger of brands falling out on the floor.

In construction of a fireplace the following essentials should be attained. They are:

1. That the flue have the proper area.
2. That the throat be correctly designed and have a suitable damper.
3. That the chimney be high enough for good draft.
4. That the shape of the fireplace be such as to direct the maximum amount of radiated heat into the room.
5. That a properly constructed smoke chamber be provided.

Masons & Builders Guide

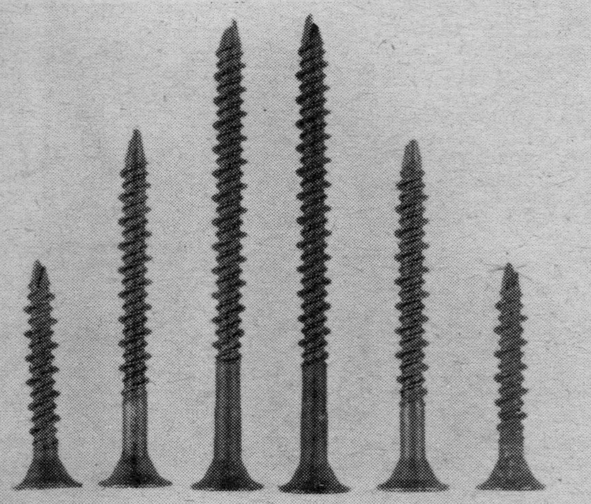

Screw Appreciation

You will see by my enclosure that the subject of this letter is screws. Since this is probably too commonplace a title to attract much attention lets call them fastening devices. This particular device is a combination of so many improvements on the standard wood screw that I'll be surprised if someone else hasn't brought it to your attention. In case no one has, here goes.

It's a Sheet Rock Screw. They are made to attach sheet rock to metal studs. They are designed to be driven with a power screw gun. They can be driven by hand, of course, and in fact are easier to drive than ordinary screws. Ideally, however, one should use a good quality variable speed and reversable drill. In the hands of the woodworker the applications are unlimited.

To appreciate the screw, one must break it down to its components:

1. It has a self tap point. No awl is required to mark the location and keep it there. It zips into wood or thin metal.

2. There are two threads. The hi thread is at 30 degrees instead of the normal 60 for faster penetration. The lo thread reduces wobble and provides lateral pressure.

3. The shank is reduced in size giving greater thread exposure and gripping power. I'm told that it holds better alone than the same number of regular screws and glue. My experience with them seems to verify this, but I can't prove it. The narrow shank also eliminates the need to pre-drill in all but the hardest woods and thicker metal. There are minimum splitting problems.

4. The finish is an attractive gray created by a zinc phosphate coating with baked-on linseed oil. It is supposed to be corrosion resistant.

5. The head is a patented shape called "Bugle" head. For the woodworker, the advantage is no countersinking. It pulls down flush with little or no surface damage.

6. The slot is a #2 Phillips, the advantages of which are well known. The pros use magnetic bits and don't even hold the screw to guide it as it's being started. The steel they are made of is so tough it's almost impossible to damage even the appearance of the slot with a spinning power bit.

7. Since the awl, drill and countersink have been eliminated, the speed in driving with power or by hand is obvious. They are equally easy to extract if you make a mistake, want to disassemble your work and/or salvage the screws.

If the above sounds like the manufacturer's sales pitch, it is. I copied most of it from the specifications, omitting the many other advantages that are probably only of interest to the sheet rock people. They are made by U.S. Gypsum Company, 101 S. Wacker Drive, Chicago, Illinois 60606. They come in various lengths and styles. There are variations for plastic, trim, sheet rock to wood, and a plain point for wood only, to mention a few.

After using them, their superiority is so apparent that one feels cheated if he has to use the old kind again. If all this is so, why isn't everybody using them? Why can't you buy them in the neighborhood hardware store? I don't really know. Anyway, I get mine at a building materials supply house that specializes in sheet rock, lath and plastering supplies, etc. They cost between $8.00 and $22.00 per thousand. I don't recommend them for the novice or occasional do-it-yourselfer. But for the guy who is "always building one thing or another" they are fabulous and worth obtaining. Instead of being the specialized fastening device they were designed to be, they are damn near universal. The only place I would hesitate to use them would be on a job where shear was important, such as a gate hinge.

Fred Barrett
Portland, Oregon

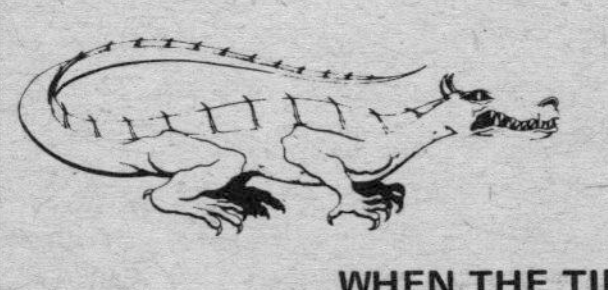

WHEN THE TIME CAME

When the time did come, the Greek did not delay. He put the items he'd used in the food ritual back in the leather bag, and carried it and the jug of water to the bus, D.R. following behind. D.R. started to get in the back where Estelle lay sleeping, but the Greek directed him to sit in front with him. D.R. obeyed, although he was uncomfortable in the front. He was close to true distress now. He was confused because he didn't know how stoned he was; he didn't know how far to trust his mind's version of things. He felt a little afraid of the Greek now, but he didn't know if that was just paranoia or his straight mind picking up real warnings from actual stimuli. He very definitely felt threatened, but he could not be sure what by, and that made the moment seem more sinister than ever. His mind was very neatly divided in two. Half of it was clear and half of it was muddy, but it was hard to keep up with which side was which because both sides claimed to be clear, and each denied that it was muddy. The sense was that of being surrounded and infiltrated by enemies, within and without. But the enemies were all unseen, and the clear half of his mind understood that very likely he was imagining the whole thing.

If Estelle had been awake she would have cooled D.R. in an instant. She would have seen that he was feeling freaky, and told him it was okay, to go ahead and feel freaky, that she would remain there before him as a living, concrete presence in a weird and abstract world. But Estelle was asleep and the sound of Urge's motor didn't disturb her. D.R. didn't learn until later that Estelle had dosed herself heavily on downers, but just looking he could tell that her sleep was very deep, that that was only Estelle's body lying there, that her life and soul and spirit were somewhere far away, and unavailable to him. D.R. felt a powerful urge to go to her, though for whose sake, his or her's, he wasn't sure. But everytime he so much as glanced back at Estelle the Greek looked at him out of the corner of his eye in a strangely intimidating way, and froze D.R. in his seat.

Wiring Simplified

other than that this book is a most useful tool for the home electrician, the thing i like about it is that it has a hole punched all the way through it, for hanging over a nail. that is a kind of practicality that all american publishers should learn. everything you'll need to wire your home yourself.

—jd

Wiring Simplified
H.P. Richter
1968; 143pp.

$1.00 postpaid

from:
Park Publishing Company
Box 8527
Lake Street Station
Minneapolis, Minnesota 55408

or WHOLE EARTH CATALOG

Fig. 4-25. In soldering, do not drop hot solder on cold wire. Heat the wire until it is hot enough to melt solder.

In residential and farm wiring, one of the wires is always grounded, that is, connected to a water pipe or driven ground rod. The grounded wire is known as the *neutral* wire; all other wires are known as "hot" wires. It is most important that you remember the following four points:

1. The grounded neutral wire is *always* white in color.
2. The grounded neutral wire must run direct to every 115-volt device to be operated (*never* to a device operating only at 230 volts).
3. The grounded neutral wire is *never* fused.
4. The grounded neutral wire is *never* switched or interrupted in any other way.

With one exception (which will be discussed later) white wire may never be used except as a grounded wire. Other wires are usually black but may be some other color, but not white (with the one exception just mentioned) or green.

The white wire must run to every 115-volt device *other than a switch*; the other wire is usually black but may be some other color, but not white or green. Examine a socket or similar device carefully and you will find that one of its two terminals for wire is a natural brass color, the other is a white color, usually nickel-plated or tinned. *The white wire must always run to the white terminal.* In the case of sockets, the white terminal in turn is always connected to the screw shell and never to the center contact of the socket. Switches for controlling lights, etc., never have white terminals.

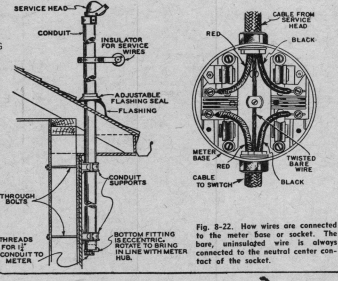

Fig. 8-22. How wires are connected to the meter base or socket. The bare, uninsulated wire is always connected to the neutral center contact of the socket.

National Electrical Code 1968
Guide to the 1968 National Electrical Code
Electrical Code for One- and Two-Family Dwellings

The Code is not law, except as adopted by local ordinances, but its requirements should certainly be met as a minimum in all wiring. Check with your local building department for their code or revisions, and permit information if you want your wiring to be legal. In any case, use the Code as a minimum.

The regulations set up seem to me to be quite reasonable and based mostly on safety. It is somewhat hard to use as a reference because it has a poorly organized index. The index is very complete if you can get into its system.

Following the Code strictly will produce a safe installation. Producing one that is convenient, efficient, practical, and allows plenty of room for expansion requires planning and study of wiring books such as Sears and Wards electric wiring books (50¢), or Wiring Simplified.

The Audel Guide to the 1968 National Electrical Code is a non-official interpretation and clarification of the NEC. It is not intended to replace the NEC, but in most cases it would be usable by itself. Its greatest handicap is that it has no index.

For people working only in residences, the new Electrical Code for One- and Two-Family Dwellings is much easier to use than the NEC, from which it is excerpted.

Suggested and reviewed by Fred

National Electrical Code 1968
1968; 466 pp.

$3.00 postpaid

Electrical Code for One- and Two-Family Dwellings
1969; 133 pp.

$1.75 postpaid

both from:
National Fire Protection Association
60 Batterymarch Street
Boston, Mass. 02110

or WHOLE EARTH CATALOG

Guide to the 1968 National Electrical Code
Robert E. Palmquist
1968; 461 pp.

$6.95 postpaid (cheaper from Silvo or U. S. General)

from:
Bobbs-Merrill Company
4300 West 62nd Street
Indianapolis, Indiana 46206

or WHOLE EARTH CATALOG

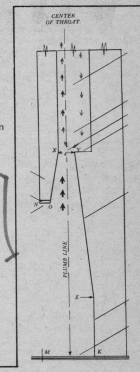

Wood (Coal, Oil) Cook Stoves

Here's a company that makes good, big, old-fashioned wood burning kitchen ranges as well as pot-belly coal stoves in five sizes, huge wood burning furnaces, Franklin stoves, parlor stoves, ship stoves, and more stoves.

These appear to be really well made expensive major appliances. Most are convertible for using wood, coal, oil, or gas as fuel. The cook stoves offer water reservoirs or coils for heating water, warming ovens, extra large ash pans and all sorts of accessories.

[Reviewed by Fred Richardson
Suggested by Gordon Breckenridge]

Literature and stoves from:

Portland Stove Foundry Co. (They may have dealers in your area.)
Sales Office
Box 59
Sterling Junction, Massachusetts 01565

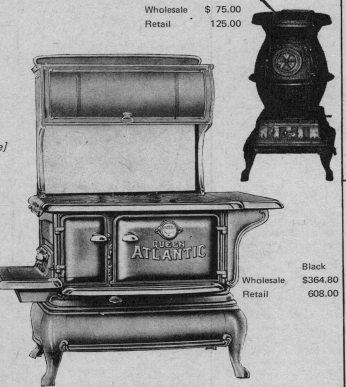

| | Wholesale | $ 75.00 |
| | Retail | 125.00 |

		Black
	Wholesale	$364.80
	Retail	608.00

For Wood ONLY

	Stove	W/Reservoir
Wholesale	$123.00	$172.20
Retail	205.00	287.00

F.O.B. Portland, Maine

Wood Cook Stoves

When I found I could get a used, "pretty good" wood stove for 20 bucks I gave up the new ones. Maybe that's what a lot of folks do. They're plentiful and cheap in used condition in northern Michigan. Probably all over. Run an ad in a newspaper.

Peace,

*Gordon Breckenridge
Alpine, Michigan*

Superior Fireplace

Seems sensible. Get this metal fireplace, and let the fire heat air in all directions, get warm air flow going in the room. It should be easy to lay masonry up around the metal shell.

—SB

ECONOFORM Not Available
Warm Air Circulating Fireplace Unit

Write for information on the new Heatform fireplace, which has replaced the Econoform.

From:
Superior Fireplace Company
4325 Artesia Avenue
Fullerton, CA 92633

$84

For single-opening fireplaces

The Forgotten Art of Building a Good Fireplace

About a year ago I became interested in the mechanics and skills necessary for the construction of super-functional living entities and the reconstruction of colonial homes. Recently, during a visit to New England, I took a trip to the Vermont Country Store in Weston, Vermont and happened upon a really funky book by the store's owner, Vrest Orton, on the art of building a good fireplace, one that throws the heat out and does not smoke. The Forgotten Art of Building a Good Fireplace is an earthy treatise on the dynamics of fireplace design.

An inquisitive inventor, Count Rumford of England, formulated the basic and seemingly immutable principles of fireplace design in 1795. These fundamentals have remained virtually unchanged since that time——a span of 176 years. Rumford was a probing fellow, having discerned convection currents and having invented the photometer and a method of boring cannon. He was the first to understand the qualities of radiant heat and used Ben Franklin's observations on fireplaces, especially on the dissipation of smoke.

This quality paperback joyously and simply tells how to design a total, functional fireplace, much unlike today's squat, low abortion, which does not radiate heat properly. Rumford's fireplaces radiate heat warmly into a room's atmosphere and assure that the smoke is drawn upward with ease. Highly recommended for anyone interested in fireplaces.

[Suggested and reviewed by Stephen Lessels]

The Forgotten Art of Building a Good Fireplace
Vrest Orton
1969; 60 pp.

$2.00 postpaid

from:
Yankee, Inc.
Dublin, New Hampshire 03444

Look at *Diagram A*. About twelve inches above the lower edge of the lintel or arch (*at point Y*), on the back wall of the chimney or throat, there must be constructed a small shelf, called the smoke-shelf. This brick shelf, projecting from the slanting back of the fireplace wall, out toward the front, is about three to four inches wide, *toward Point X*. It is laid horizontally, of course, completely across the entire back wall. This is the air-mixer, the function of which can easily be seen by the arrows in *Diagram A*, showing movement of air.

This is one of the most important features of Rumford's principles. This three-to four-inch deep opening is standard and must not vary, no matter how big the fireplace.

Aladdin Kerosene Lamps

Coleman lamps are terrible——they hiss and clank and blind you, just like civilization.

Aladdin is the answer if you need good light and 117ac isn't around. It is bright, silent, and requires no pumping. (It does require some babying to keep the mantle from smoking up; it's like not burning toast.)

British made and effectively designed, the lamps are available in this country from:

—SB

Aladdin Industries, Inc.
Kerosene Lamp Division
Nashville, Tennessee 37210

or WHOLE EARTH CATALOG

Some of the Aladdins are rather ornamental
The simplest designs are:

B—165 Font Lamp (aluminum, w/o base)

$24.50 shipping weight 2.5 lbs.

B—140 Table Lamp (with base)

$25.50 shipping weight 2.7 lbs.

and B—223 Hanging Lamp

$30.50 shipping weight 3.5 lbs.,
shade extra

Parts:

N—6400	White shade	$5.25
N—103	Chimney	$2.60
N—150	Mantle	$1.15
N—198	Wick	$1.45

Aladdin Heater

You listed the Aladdin Kerosene lamps in the Fall 1970 catalog, but not the Aladdin Kerosene heater (Model "Blue Flame" $44.95), which was used by Sir Francis Chichester on Gypsy Moth IV and by me on Kodiak Island last winter.

Daniel Earle
Anchorage, Alaska

Aladdin Tips

The lamp's efficiency and utility can be increased by taking two steps, which I've not seen reported anywhere else "in the literature." First, it is not as bright as a pressure lantern; this deficiency can be resolved by taking a second Aladdin Chimney and slipping it down over the first. This increases the overall height with no loss of stability; it just sounds a little awkward. (It's much brighter!)

The second drawback is that the d—mned thing does get blackened up if you turn the heat too high. One way to clean the charcoal off the mantle is to turn the wick very, very low and slowly, very slowly burn it off. This takes, as I recall, from twenty minutes to an hour. The second I learned from an African teacher who walked into my house about three months before I was going to depart and, noting that the lamp was turned too high, casually picked the salt shaker off the table and sprinkled a little salt down into the chimney. The mantle cleaned itself in seconds. I don't know why it works, all I really am sure of is that I hated him for that gratuitous display of African technological superiority for at least the ramainder of the evening.

The second chimney, by the way, can be an old one with a few cracks or a small piece broken off. I loved that lamp, especially after the night I tried to catch a Coleman-type lamp from falling off the table. I carried scars for over a month. The Aladdin is a cool burning, lovely piece of machinery.

Guy M. McBride
Nashville, Tennessee

Aladdin discount

We sell Alladin Kerosene Lamps at 30% off the suggested retail price, and 20% off on parts too. There is a $1.50 shipping charge per lamp but we pay all postage on parts. We'll replace for no charge any goods that arrive damaged or defective. We want to turn folks on to a clean, bright light at a reasonable price. Write for all information and prices . . .

Richard
The Lamp Company
Box 197A
Summertown, Tn. 38483

Eagle Kerosene Lamp

If you're reading by kerosene light, and you aren't up to an Aladdin, you probably could use a reflector and wall bracket. They come with this lamp.

—SB

Eagle Kerosene Lamp (with reflector and wall bracket)

$5.49 plus shipping

from:
Thermwell Products Co., Inc.
150 E. 7th St.
Paterson, New Jersey 07524

CAPTIVE AUDIENCE

So this is the situation in the bus as they drive out of the rest area: Estelle is asleep in the back seat, Divine Right is some sort or psychic prisoner sitting in the front seat beside the Greek, and the Greek, in charge of the bus now, driving east across the barren, windy plain toward Oklahoma City, is talking on and on about health, truth and love as destinations along the Middle Way. His rap began as soon as they hit the freeway again with a final lecture to D.R. on breathing, and the holy sound of OM, and continued into an explanation of the concept of karma and ways in which images like the Third Eye reconcile Zen and the mystic point of view with all modern psychology from Freud through Reich to Jung. Within fifty miles the Greek had ascended into a description of the physiology involved in the experience of Unitive Consciousness, and within a hundred miles of that he had called D.R.'s attention to the I-Thou theme in the Secret Songs of the Hindus and analyzed the personal aspects of the relationship between Ouspensky and Guirdjieff, which amounted, of course, to a kind of rambling introduction to the Greek's abbreviated version of his own life story.

We'll get into that life story a little later on, but before we do it's important to understand what was happening with Divine Right as he told it. The Greek said, "The problem, of course, is that young people have grown up oriented to a Twentieth Century Einsteinian concept of unitive time while their elders remain stuck in Nineteenth Century industrial time, which is fragmented." D.R. nodded and gurgled a few nonsense sounds But his attention was not on the Greek. He was thinking about Estelle, asleep on the mattress behind him. D.R. was desperate to get back to her. He wanted to wake her up and hold her in his arms and tell her that he was sorry, that he was going to be a lot better from now on. He wanted her to open her eyes, and recognize him, and include him in her world again. It was awful, feeling excluded. D.R. did not feel in her world or the Greek's, and he had no world of his own to occupy. He was in a vast, dark limbo somewhere and suffering terribly in his mind.

Ashley Thermostatic Wood Burning Circulator

This is a unique wood burning stove. It has a thermostat which controls air intake, thereby burns much less wood than an ordinary stove. Will go up to 12 hours without refueling. In cold climates people build just one fire a season, adding wood 2-3 times a day. It takes any type wood, up to two feet long.

One kept us warm when we lived in a chicken coop with cold concrete floors and now an Ashley is the only heat we have in a 900 sq. ft. house with high ceilings.

The firebox is airtight and there is a lever on the air intake you can set for the desired temperature. A temperature-sensitive device (bi-metal helix coil) then automatically regulates air flow to keep heat at the setting you've chosen.

—Lloyd Kahn

This is a mighty good little hard-heatin' cheap working wood stove.

—Ken Kesey

Contact Ashley-Spark Distributors or the factory for complete pricing information. (Prices lower the closer you are to the factory in Alabama).

Architects and Hot Water

Charrette Corporation of 2000 Massachusetts Avenue, Cambridge, Mass.   02140

Describes itself as "EVERYTHING The Architect Needs For Drafting Design, Presentation, & Model Making."

CATALOG on request. From my experience they have the finest quality, are reliable, good prices on all items, overwhelming volume of stuff in stock. They were set up about 5 years ago to fill a need, bringing drafting and architectural supplies and technology up-to-date. When you see their store you know they have done it.

Landam Corporation, 2211 Broadway, NY, NY 10024

makes and sells a hot water heater that plugs into the pipe very simply, and heats your water as it runs out. There's a limit to its total effectiveness, as far as total volume goes, but for a campsite, or house, or trailer living, it does a grand job. It weighs less than two pounds, needs electricity, and costs *about* $35.

Medium Flow

HOT

T. H. Neel
Cambridge, Mass. 02140

The Indian Tipi

Tipis are cheap and portable. To live in one involves intimate familiarity with fire, earth, sky and roundness. The canvas is a shadow-play of branches by day, people by night. Depending on your body's attitude about weather, a tipi as dwelling is either a delight or a nuisance. Whichever, you can appreciate the elegant design of a tipi and the completeness of the culture that produced it.

The Laubin's book is the only one on tipis, but it is very good. All the information you need, technical or traditional, is here, and the Laubins are interesting people.

—SB

The Indian Tipi
Reginald and Gladys Laubin
1957, 1970; 208 pp.

$1.65

from:
Ballantine Books, Inc.
101 Fifth Avenue
New York, N.Y. 10003

or WHOLE EARTH CATALOG

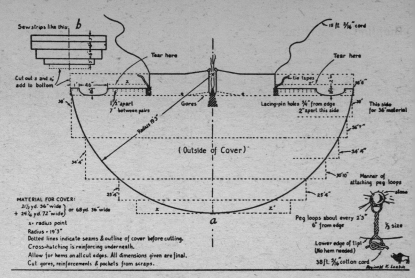

FIG. 1. *Pattern for Sioux Tipi (18-foot).*

Cheyenne

Indians had definite rules of etiquette for life in the tipi. If the door was open, friends usually walked right in. If the door was closed, they called out or rattled the door covering and awaited an invitation to enter. A shy person might just cough to let those inside know he was waiting. If two sticks were crossed over the door, it meant that the owners either were away or desired no company. If they went away, they first closed the smoke flaps by lapping or crossing them over the smoke hole. The door cover was tied down securely and two sticks were crossed over it. The door was thus "locked," and as safe in Indian society as the most strongly bolted door would be in our civilization today.

Later we discovered that the idea of a ventilating pipe underground to the fireplace is the very best way of insuring a clear lodge and the most heat.

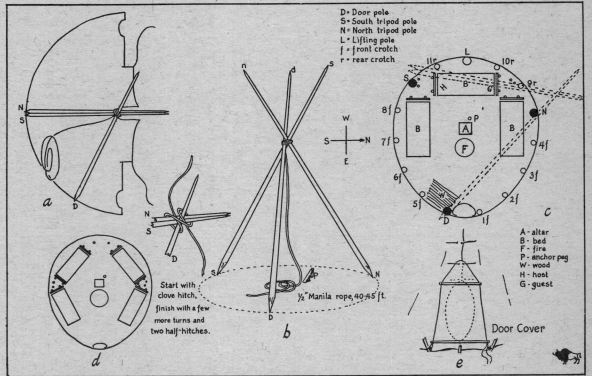

Tipis

We have word about three sources in the U.S. of ready-made tipis, and so far Goodwin-Cole is still the best——best construction, lowest cost. They also have tipi liners, which you will need if weather is wet or cold. Sew-it-yourself-kit available.

—SB

Goodwin-Cole Company
1315 Alhambra Boulevard
Sacramento, California 95816

or WHOLE EARTH CATALOG

For the following, shipping weights are undetermined. Inquire, or have the item sent shipping cost C.O.D.

10-foot is suitable for nomadic couple; 14-foot for small family. 20-foot for extended family or occasions. Flame-treated is unpleasant; law requires it in some places. Tipis of green, blue, orange, red, or yellow drill are available. Poles are available if you're that lazy.

TIPI SIZE	10 OZ. S.F. DUCK NATURAL	12 OZ. S.F. DUCK NATURAL	FLAME RESISTANT CALIFORNIA CODE 6½ OZ. DRILL BLUE-ORAN. RED-YELLO.	10 OZ. ARMY DUCK WHITE	WOOD POLES 14/SET UNPAINTED	PAINTED DESIGNS AROUND BASE	TIPI LINER 5' HIGH 10 OZ. S.F.
10'							
12'			NO LONGER AVAILABLE				
14'	$77	$84		$129	$50	14 @ $29	$35
16'	$88	$94		$155	$53	16 @ $31	$38
18'	$97	$107		$172	$57	18 @ $33	$42
20'	$107	$119		$202	$60	20 @ $35	$45
22'	$117	$134		$236	$63	22 @ $37	$52
24'	$137	$154		$285	$68	24 @ $39	$62

Door Cover $8.50
Two Designs add $10

8' Front Pole
40' of ½" Rope

TERMS OF SALE Prices are F.O.B. our Sacramento plant. All orders subject to acceptance by Home Office, Sacramento. New customers are asked to send check with order. One-half deposit required on C.O.D. orders.
$3
$4 Prices subject to change without notice.

The Indian way of attaching peg loops, as illustrated, is not only ingenious but easy and sturdy——far better than either sewn or stamped grommets. Insert a pebble about 3/4 of an inch in size on the under side of the cover about six inches above the edge, at a seam wherever possible, and around this pebble tie a piece of 3/16-inch cord. Double the cord, tie it in either a square knot or a clove hitch about the pebble, then join the free ends in a square knot. Marbles will do if you cannot find smooth round pebbles.

Note: The Nomadics people are heavily back-ordered on their ready-made tipis. They urge you to get their Sew-it-Yourself-Tipi-Kit, which they can ship in 7 days from order.

Another home-crafted tipi you can get is made in Florida, costs $85 for 13-1/2 ft. (10 oz. duck) to $145 for 18 ft (10 oz. duck). From: Woodcraft, 1921 Atapha Nene, Tallahassee, Florida 32301.

—SB

It is a joy to be alive on days like this, and when we come back to the tipi, after a long ride or a hike in the mountains, the little fire is more cozy and cheerful than ever. The moon rides high in the late fall nights, and when it is full, shines right down through the smoke hole. Its pale white light on the tipi furnishings, added to the rosy glow of the dying fire, is beautiful beyond description.

Nomadics Tipi

a new tipi company, family, tribe, 16 to 22 foot tipis, in eight and twelve ounce double fill canvas, and eight ounce acrilon. lock teeth brass grommets, sailmaker's lock stitching, dacron thread, good prices, good people.

—jd

Nomadics
Star Route
Box 41
Cloverdale, Oregon 97112

— nomadics

tipi size	8 oz.d.f.*Kit**	8 oz.d.f.	8 oz. acrilon	6'liner
16'	$60	$80	$140	$35
18'	70	90	155	38
20'	80	97	180	40
22'	90	105	212	47

*double fill

**Nomadic Tipi Kit: We send pre-cut tipi cover ready to be sewn together including all grommets, peg loops, and thread, with complete instructions.

Tipi size, listed in feet, is the actual side slope of the tipi or radius of the tipi cover when lying out flat.

For continuous nomadic living we personally recommend the twenty foot eight ounce Acrilon tipi with the six foot ten ounce Permasol liner.

Complete assembly instructions are sent with tipi.

Send 50% of cost with order if you wish C.O.D. delivery. Allow two weeks for delivery

Building a Log House

somewhere,
between missoula and great falls,
is the most beautiful house
in the whole earth,
a two-storey log cabin,
up on a knoll,·
smiling.
for two bits this book
will put you there.

—jd

NO LONGER AVAILABLE

Building a Log House
1914, 1965; 43pp.

$1.25 postpaid

from:
Cooperative Extension Service
University of Alaska
Box 1109
Juneau, Alaska 99801

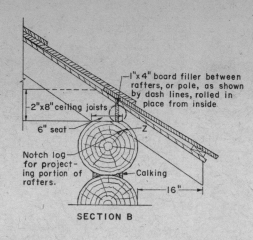

I"x 4" board filler between rafters, or pole, as shown by dash lines, rolled in place from inside

2"x8" ceiling joists

6" seat

Notch log for projecting portion of rafters.

Calking

16"

SECTION B

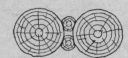

FIGURE 19. — Pole chinking.

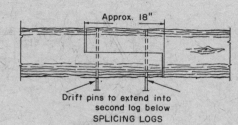

Approx. 18"

Drift pins to extend into second log below
SPLICING LOGS

The Wilderness Cabin

For more details on log construction, site selection, use of heavy timber tools. This gent has built some cabins.

—SB

Cabin on the Yukon River at 50 degrees below zero.

But an even better and more direct method than personal search is to go to the county seat in the county where you want to build. Ask the county auditor for a list of tax-delinquent properties, and the descriptions and plats of each location. During your first free weekend, examine the sites. If you find something you like, pay the back taxes.

When the original owner has failed to pay the taxes for a certain number of years—in many states the period is five years—and you pay the back taxes, you can get what is called a 'tax assignment' from the county. Your final ownership paper is about equivalent to a quit-claim deed. This is good enough while you personally own the site. Should you finally sell the property, it is best to have an attorney obtain a Torrens title for you, or procure a warranty deed through legal formality.

The Wilderness Cabin
Calvin Rutstrum
1961; 169 pp.

$1.95 postpaid

from:
The MacMillan Company
Front and Brown Streets
Riverside, N.J. 08075

or WHOLE EARTH CATALOG

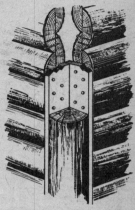

The V-Plank Corner

Method of Setting In Floor Joists of Round Logs

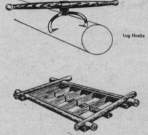

Method of Setting In Floor Joists of Planks

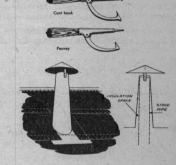

Yurt

A friend of ours got interested in the yurts used by nomadic people of Central Asia. Yurts are round buildings (tents) made out of a lattice work of sticks covered with sheets of felt. The roof is a truncated cone. The opening serves as skylight and smoke hole.

After building a number of yurts similar to the Mongolian ones out of different materials, Bill decided that he would like to build one out of milled lumber. I helped him construct one similar to the one in the plan. It is not difficult and certainly cheap. I do not know how easy it will be for someone who knows nothing about yurts and carpentry to build one, but Bill usually answers letters and I am sure he will be able to answer specific questions about the construction. He is currently revising and up-dating the plan, incorporating what he's learned in the past year.

[Suggested and reviewed by Jur Bekker]

Yurt Construction Plan

$3.00 postpaid from:
Bill Coperthwaite
Bucks Harbor, Maine

Home's Where Yurt

A funky newsletter of yurt construction and living trips for $1.00. From (send postage at least):

Dawes Hill Commune
Box 53
West Danby, N.Y. 14896

Cheap and Speedy Finish

SPEEDY FINISH A penetrating wood finish developed by the U.S. Department of Agriculture is applied super-fast with a weed sprayer. It makes up in a gray-green shade only, but can cover a barn in two and a half hours. Researchers estimate that it will protect wood for four years. It's recommended for fencing, summer cottages and other structures built of low-grade lumber. The product isn't available commercially, but you can have the formula free of charge. Write the USDA Forest Products Laboratory, Madison, Wisconsin 53705 and ask for: Research Note FPL—0134, "Experimental Chromate Finish." I found this bit in 'Woman's Day'. Maybe ECF would make a community look like a gray-green prison compound, but it sounds cheap and good. Worth looking into?

Dorcas Hebb
Bridgton, Maine

THE SCHEME

The Greek said, "Some say that God is merely a compromise between the time it takes light to travel across the Einsteinian universe, and the time it takes light to cross a neutron, that space is merely a snapshot of time, and time is space in movement. Personally . . ."

D.R. nodded and mumbled. But what he was thinking about now was his tape recorder which lay in a pile of junk behind the driver's seat. D.R. had a scheme. His muddy mind kept saying the scheme would not work, but his clear mind was convinced that it would. The scheme was to bring the tape recorder into the front seat to listen to the Greek while D.R. sneaked to the back with Estelle. D.R.'s muddy mind insisted it could not work, but his clear mind was convinced the Greek would not know the difference. Surely it was worth a try. The problem was maneuvering the recorder to the front seat without attracting the Greek's attention. All he needed was three seconds. All he had to do was edge off his seat, lean and reach behind the Greek and he would have it. Two seconds, even. Two seconds would be plenty.

Ahead of them on the freeway just then were two big semis making simultaneous emergency stops to avoid hitting a Rambler that was trying to avoid hitting a sheep that had wandered onto the freeway. The trucks were very near to crashing, and it took the Greek five full seconds to hassle the emergency, to slow down and pull into the outer lanes and then speed up, and by the time he had Urge lined out and cruising smoothly again, D.R. was back in his seat with the recorder on the floor at his feet. After that it was a simple matter to turn it on and tune it in to the Greek's voice, and then steal away to the back. The Greek talked on, suspecting nothing.

Earth for Homes
Handbook for Building Homes of Earth

*these two together give all the grit on the subject.
practical, non-historical (here's how pithecantropus
did it) get out and do big mudpies approach.
a lump of clay,
live with it.*

—jd

Earth For Homes: Ideas and Methods Exchange PB 188918

$3.00 postpaid

from:
Superintendant of Documents
Government Printing Office
Washington, D.C. 20402

Handbook for Building Homes of Earth PB 179 327

$3.00 postpaid

from:
Superintendent of Documents
Government Printing Office   OUT OF PRINT
Washington, D.C. 20402

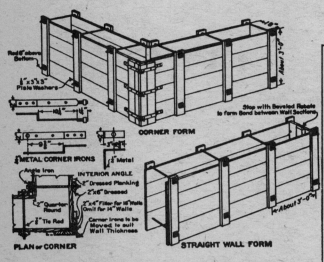

Corner and Straight Wall Forms for Rammed Earth.

Cinva-Ram Block Press

As you probably know, this machine is manufactured in
Bogota, Columbia, by Metalibec Ltda. We are handling the
complete importation of this unit into the United States
and pay all the importation charges, such as customs duties,
ocean freight and marine insurance, plus forwarding fees
and handling charges.

Our selling price for this CISVA-RAM press is $US 175.00,
F.O.B. our warehouse, Akron, Ohio. The freight charges
from our warehouse to ultimate destination will be on a
"freight collect" basis. The press comes equipped with
three wooden inserts to produce different types of blocks
and tiles, plus an operations manual. The unit weighs 140 lbs.
net, 155 lbs. gross (crated for shipment) and has a gross
cubic measurement of 3.05 cubic feet each. With the cost of
importation, freight, insurance, customs duties and handling
charges which we must pay in bringing these presses into
the United States, we are unable to extend any discounts of
any kind for the CINVA-RAM block press.

Shipment can be made immediately upon receipt of your
Purchase Order, together with your check or money order
payable to Bellows—Valvair. Please address your order to:

Bellows-Valvair
200 W. Exchange Street
Akron, Ohio 44309

I built two houses here using CINVA—RAM——where the owners
made the bricks using my machine. Both buildings were a success
and the machine certainly has its place.

However, I cannot afford to produce the block because of the big
labor factor: it is only economical for owner-builder construction.
(Which is great!) I still prefer the monolithic wall, and use a Magdiel
form and soil-cement mixture. All this info can be found in the
2 chapters of my book *(Owner-Built Home, p. 94).*

Sincerely,
Ken Kern

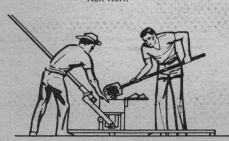

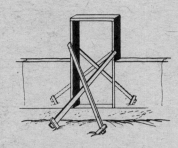

How to Dig a Dome

Our first dome is almost completed. Name Rana Grande from the
arched windows that weere thought to look like frog eyes. Tomorrow
we finish off the first third of the pur and then decorate the dirt
dome. Wednesday we expect to carve the mound. Weds afternoon
to the vigil. Thursday we finish Rana Grande & let it cure for the
grand excavation & dedication Saturday.

The dome of Rana Grande is 12 ft In diametrr & 9ft high. It is
more or less a hemeshere with the front sliced off. (Dont worry
about the spelling. I know how to spell but this typewriter doesn't
& I dont give a damn.) It is a mound of earth upon which we are
puring a 6 to 4 inch shell of cement. Saturday we will excavate
the dirt mound and reveal the completed room. It has a fireplace
poured at the same time.

This dome method should have real applicability to the alternative
community because it is cheap, artistic, organic, romantic, practical.
This one is taking fifteen sacks sement @ 1.50, 10 tons concrete mix
@$2, & 15$ worth of reinforcing bars, screen door (from the dump,
and window $5. Total about $65.

Another advantage is that there are no skills needed. See one and
build one. Simple. You dont even have to be artistic. Tools
needed are shovel, wire pliers (for wiring reinforcing bar together),.
Concrete mixer not, strictly, required. Do it (mixing) in a box. So
the other tool you'd need would be a concrete mixer or hoe with
mixing box.

Our domes are built into the side of a hill. Much of the structure
will be below grade level when finished. Some of excavated dirt
to be used to form a terrace in front.

See diagrams for more explanation.

Virgil Byxbe
Sweets Mill, CA

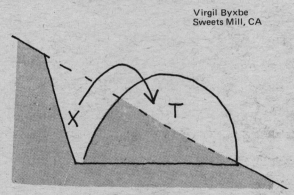

Dirt from X(cavation) is thrown on top of hill to finish off dome.
The mound is formed partly by excavating a ditch away from a
central circle & partly by thowing the excavated material on top.

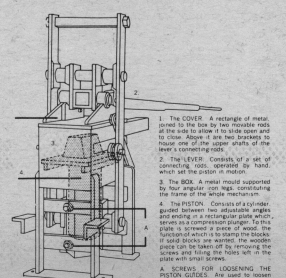

1. The COVER. A rectangle of metal.
joined to the box by two movable rods
at the side to allow it to slide open and
to close. Above it are two brackets to
house one of the upper shafts of the
lever's connecting rods

2. The LEVER. Consists of a set of
connecting rods. operated by hand.
which set the piston in motion.

3. The BOX. A metal mould supported
by four angular iron legs. constituting
the frame of the whole mechanism.

4. The PISTON. Consists of a cylinder.
guided between two adjustable angles
and ending in a rectangular plate which.
serves as a compression plunger. To this
plate is screwed a piece of wood. the
function of which is to stamp the blocks.
If solid blocks are wanted. the wooden
piece can be taken off by removing the
screws and filling the holes left in the
plate with small screws.

A SCREWS FOR LOOSENING THE
PISTON GUIDES. Are used to loosen
the piston if it fits too tightly between
the guides, or vice versa

Fig. 36   CINVA-RAM moulder for the production of soil cement blocks. explanatory sketch.

Soil-Cement—Its Use in Building

*A well-detailed booklet on the stabilization of earth with
cement, and describes all aspects of using the Cinva-Ram
earth moulder.*

—Lloyd Kahn

Soil-Cement—Its Use in Building

1964; 87 pp., 93 illustrations

$3.50 postpaid

from:
United Nations
Sales Section
New York, New York 10017

FORMS IN WHICH SOIL IS USED:

Soil is used in construction in the following forms:
(a) In the form of rubble, cut from the surface of the earth, in pieces
or blocks of soil.
(b) As bricks, made in wooden forms or molds with soil moistened
to the required degree.
(c) Moistened soil compacted *in situ* in suitable rigid frames to form
monolithic walling (rammed earth).
(d) As stabilized soil, by combining it with an agent in order to
improve its constructive properties.

Soil-cement roofing

If it is desired to use soil-cement as roofing for a house, the following
methods may be used: (a) laths or reeds are laid on the roof truss or
joists and nailed down; a plastic mortar of cement and (sandy) soil in
the proportions of 1:7 by volume, with vegetable fibres 3 cm in
length added as a reinforcement in the proportion of one part to four
parts of mortar, is spread over the laths or reeds. The layer of mortar
should be 3 cm deep, duly compacted, and its surface is
smoothed with a trowel. After the material has had time to dry and
harden, two or three coats of bituminous material are brushed over
the surface in order to make the roofing waterproof.

Slow, Heavy, and Sweaty

First off, thanks for a lovely review of my book, Stone Shelters *in
Spring, 1970. It's had other flattering reviews, but your anonymous
reviewer read it and understood it, which was not true of some of
the others. You even picked the absolutely best passages to quote.
Seems I must have a brother out there someplace.*

*Secondly, I am probably one of only a handful of your readers who
have actually built earth houses. (Mine was in Orinda, Cal., 1963).
I have some words of caution about building with dirt:*

1. *It's more work than with any other material, bar none. It's
    slow, heavy, and sweaty. You move tons of stuff every day
    to make a few square feet of wall.*

2. *Rammed earth and adobe are the most work. They make
    good walls, but not roof structure, so you don't save very
    much money. Not usually worth it, unless you happen
    to like the solidity of those big, thick walls.*

3. *Earth is great in warm climates, but in any moderate or
    cold climate it'll give you the rheumatism by thanksgiving
    time.*

4. *I built using an African technique that lets you build
    domes and vaults without formwork. Thus the whole
    house, roof and all, is dirt, and that's cheap (about $1/square
    foot for materials). None of your references cover this
    sort of thing. Two troubles remain, however:*

    a) *It still breaks your back and takes forever.*

    b) *This type of construction shrinks and cracks a lot more
        than adobe or rammed earth——a real problem.*

*Edward Allen
Wellesley, Massachusetts*

For Stone Houses

I read the letter about rocks for building purposes [p. 21 in the March
Catalog]. I'm a geology major, and think I can help a little.

First, he says the land is covered with volcanic rocks. These will fall
into three types:

1. Dark, heavy, fine grained basalt.
2. Glassy massive obsidian, various colors.
3. Light weight cellular pumice or scoria.

Of these three, the basalt is the best for building. It's tough, very hard,
and weathers slowly. The obsidian is essentially glass, and though
stronger than steel, it is easily broken. It is strong enough to build
with, but may be too non-porous and smooth to mortar together. It
also weathers slowly. The pumice and scoria is no good for uses requiring standing weight, such as a wall. However, it will make an excellent insulator for hollow walls or sub floor fill.

If the rocks are of many different types, you will have to examine each
type for three necessary characteristics:

1. It should be hard and heavy.
2. It should be fine grained.
3. It should not weather appreciably.

To check weathering, break the rock and match the fresh surface to the
old surface. Only a slightly faded appearance on the old surface is permissable. A different color on the outside as compared to the inside
is indicative of severe chemical weathering. Also check the hardness
of the weathered surface. If it is flaky or crumbly, it's no good.

Also check the well rounded rocks in any stream beds which may
be on the property. These rocks are often the most resistant and hardest

Roy. L. Porter
Virginia Beach, Virginia

Stone Shelters

This is an utterly beautiful book, a study of the people, history, geography, and vernacular architecture in a small area in southern Italy known as the Murgia of Trulli.

The several different types of stone shelters of the region are covered extensively, including cave dwellings hewn from solid stone, unmortared stone domes called trulli, *and arches and vaults built with "ragbag patchwork technique" by the masons of Cisternino.*

The book is primarily concerned with how the architectural forms came into being and how the building techniques derived from the needs of the builders.

Descriptions and text are clear, photos superb.

—Lloyd Kahn

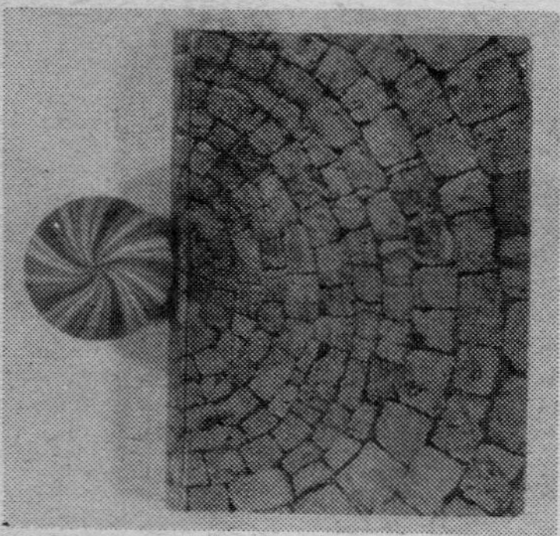

Stone Shelters
Edward Allen
1969; 199 pp.

$4.95 postpaid
New paper edition

from:
The M.I.T. Press
50 Ames Street, Room 765
Cambridge, Massachusetts 02142

or WHOLE EARTH CATALOG

The making of a cave is the antithesis of the usual construction process. A cave is space produced directly by the subtraction of a relatively small amount of solid material from a very large mass. A more conventional shelter, whether it be a *trullo*, a vaulted stone townhouse, or the reader's own dwelling, is space produced indirectly by its enclosure with pieces of solid material added together.

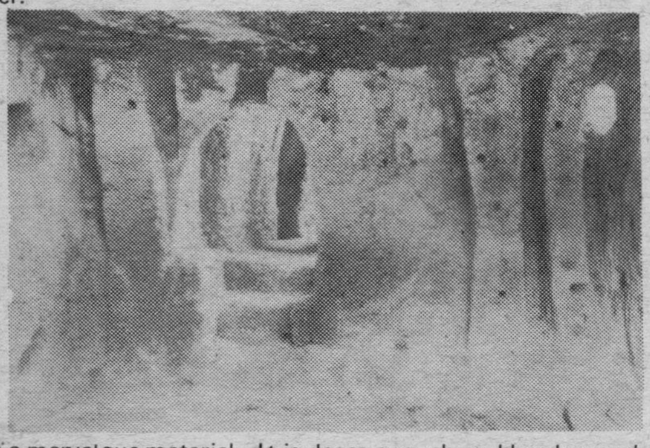

Tufo is a marvelous material. It is dense enough and hard enough to have served as both exterior and interior finishes, yet soft and fine-grained enough to have been cut into almost any shape for any purpose. Because of the immense height, length, and thickness of the *tufo* cliffs, great freedom of planning was possible.

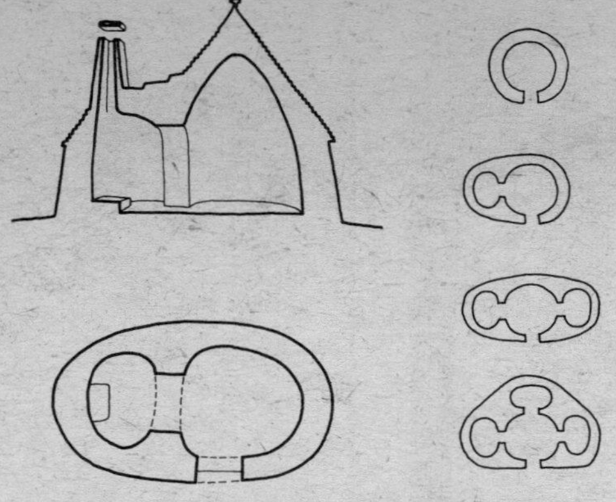

A transitional form of *trullo* field shelter, nonrectilinear in plan. A main space is joined to a smaller one housing a fireplace. Such shelters are often found with two or three smaller spaces attached to the main space, as illustrated in the small sketches. (Plan and section courtesy *Byggekunst*, redrawn by the author.)

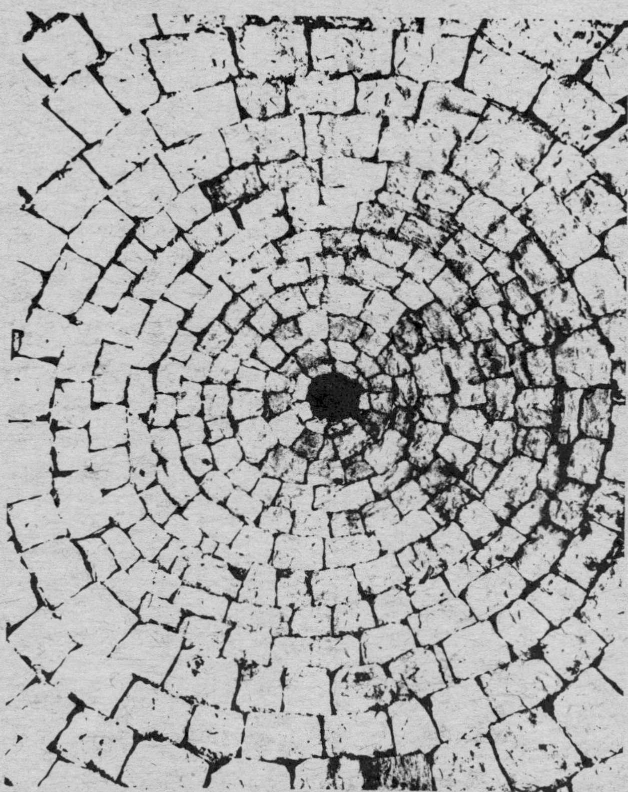

The raw material for a *trullo* could come from several possible sources. Loose stones from the field were one; quarried stone another. Often a large rainwater cistern or wine tank would be excavated in the rock beneath a *trullo*-to-be, and would yield a large quantity of good building stone. In later times especially, agricultural transformations were carried out, with great expenditure of labor, to make previously untillable land suitable for crops. The thin topsoil would be carefully removed and piled to one side, laying bare the limestone bedrock beneath. Then the limestone would be broken out in chunks to a depth of two or three feet. The best stones would be saved for construction, and the rest replaced over the still unbroken strata of the limestone, with the coarsest pieces on the bottom and the finest on the top. Following this back-breaking procedure, red *bolo* soil from a neaby depression would be carried to the field in baskets and tamped over the loose layers of broken limestone to a depth of fifteen or twenty inches. Finally, the original topsoil would be spread back over the *bolo*, and the land would be ready for cultivation. The heavy but sometimes infrequent rainfalls would be absorbed eagerly by the shallow topsoil and thick cushion of *bolo*, and once these soils had reached saturation the excess water would filter into the loose bed of broken rock beneath, from which, retained by the impervious bedrock, it could be slowly reabsorbed by the soil and roots above when needed. This continuous bed of limestone fragments, in addition to acting as an underground reservoir, served to furnish continual chemical fertilization to the soil from beneath, to complement the organic fertilizer added from above.

•

Sewage was distributed over the fields, working with the natural lime to increase the yield of the crops. . . .

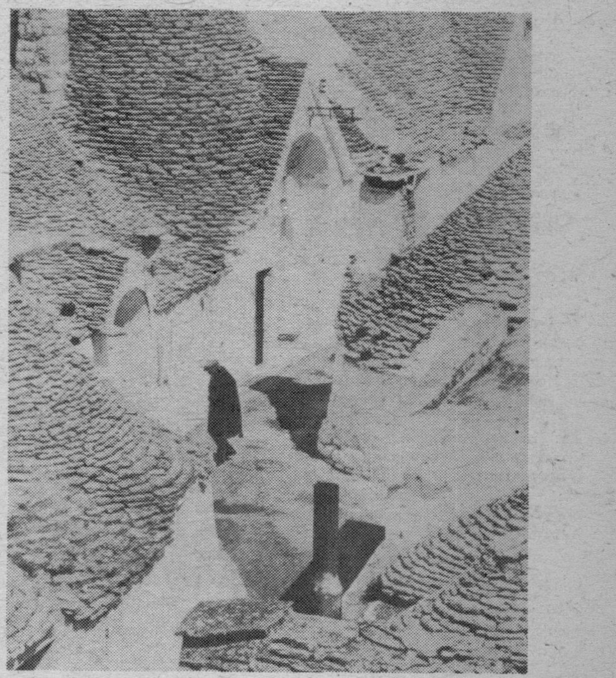

The masons of Cisternino were men of exceptional ingenuity. They sometimes laid up walls of regular stone blocks, but in other cases made walls by compacting irregular stones and mortar between wood forms. Their combinations of arches and vaults were often graceful and correct, but more often were brutally expedient, and were most often full-blooded, lusty, folk-art inventions that made some charmingly naive concessions to grace and correctness. Nothing was sacred to the masons but the sheer physical stability of what they built. A half-arch could support a stair, a tilted barrel vault could cover it. A round barrel vault could be intersected by pointed-vault dormers. A triangular piece of vaulting could support a diagonal balcony front if held at its vertex on a projecting stone bracket. A buttress to a building across the street could resist the excessive thrust of a roof vault, or of a too-ambitiously cantilevered balcony. An irregular room shape was easily covered with a skewed vault. Almost anything could be supported or spanned by cutting, twisting, tilting, truncating, or combining the standard forms of vaulting in non-standard ways.

Stone Works

Stone walls & buildings. These are actually weaker than they look. It was the wood frame houses that survived the Alaskan earthquake. Cement got no give like wood & stonework is much slower than carpentry.

Still it looks like all time and we went ahead. In planning make sure your foundation extends deeper than the frost will. Here in Maine frost heave is a prime consideration for a stone building could easily be cracked to bits.

Surround the foundation with rocks of any size & type up to grade to allow for movement. Don't pack dirt in there.

As for type of rocks to build with, granite is best. Save your really square stones for corners. Stratified, slate, etc. (I don't know the geological terms) are no good. These sedimentary types are porous and the water they suck up will expand/contract and you're in trouble. If you toss it down on the pile & it shatters there you are. But don't slam it cause anything would crack from that.

Use forms to get the straightest walls. Within these you can lay up vertically faster than without, but time saved is lost putting the forms together so the outside surface should be the consideration for forms. Our walls are straight enough to sight down tho it's a personal aesthetic.

Even with forms, don't just toss the rocks & mortar in. A strong beautiful wall is laid up rock by rock. No other way. I worked with a mason of 60 years to learn to lay fieldstone. Practice is the way. Knowing which rock to choose from your pile. Like a puzzle with no two parts the same. Choosing the wrong rock means that your work comes down on your feet. (So don't be barefoot! Also cement contains lye that burns like brimstone. Wash the stuff off afore it eats your very hide. After a few weeks you'll have to wear rubber work-gloves as your hands will be most tender.) An old Maine stonemason told me that "Even a round rock has a flat side if you can find it."

After building a while you'll understand this. Lay up a rock for strength always thinking of the rock that will rest atop it. Don't be cheap with the mud (cement) but learn what it won't do. Sometimes a rock will get a better bite on another when they're dry & just have cement around their edges. Like bricks only more tricky. If you decide to eyeball it (build without forms) stretch 2 strings down your outside dimension & lean over & sight down. When you only see one string that's your limit. Careful that a rock doesn't protrude & throw your line off. It's easy to build it too wide.

Have a large pile of rocks to choose from. Tiny to fist size stones are what you need to trig up the biggies that wobble. Little triangular shapes are best. Build a wall that rests on rocks tho, not tiny trigs or cement. The old timers here built walls without any kind of mortar (!) but just skill in laying. Those walls are still solid 130 years later. So LAY up your rocks, don't glue them up.

Progress right around your foundation a layer at a time so that when you come back to the starting point you'll be laying on dry or almost dried wall. This isn't possible if you're using forms. This because you have to build right up several feet & then move this whole rig down the line.

We built a building 30x36x11 with foundations 4 feet deep on a 1 ft. poured concrete footing. Wall thickness was 1½ ft. up to grade & a foot above ground. Solid enough for Maine but you might scale this down a great deal in a milder climate. (By the way, if you're building stone walls around an existing building it would be most simple, for you already have your forms. Accordingly if you plan to have studded interior walls go ahead & put up your studding & then cover the outside with plywood & build along that. The plywood could be removed when the cement dries & shifted for use again.)

We used an old gas engine to run our mixer. Keep cement from the motor & you'll be ok. Rocks are plentiful in Maine. For special rocks try the seashore or a tombstone dealer for scrap. We got lots of colored marble & granite for a six-pack of Shlitz. Some states forbid selling old tombstones but we got some fragments for the walls. Neighbors consider any messing with tombstones goulish so turn the lettering to the inside. You may have the sheriff's grandmaw's rock.

Lay your heaviest rocks around your feet, as lifting gets hard above your chest. Favorite, sentimental, or mystical rocks stand out from eyelevel to about eight feet up. Don't bury that romantic special thing at ankle level. We tried to get a piece of the moon for our wall but NASA never came through. A few meteors might be astrologically favorable for your project. Since our walls went up eleven feet we laid from the flatbed of a 2-ton truck above 5 or 6 feet. This proved to be an ideal mobile staging with room for two masons, mortar box and a large rockpile.

When the walls are finished go back and point up around your rocks. Pointing is a mason's signature. Use pointing cement only in small batches (a mixer full will dry out before you could use it) & a small trowel. The stuff is quick drying & sticks when you flip it in the cracks.

Look around at good walls before you start. Observe or work with a mason if possible. Don't get discouraged. It takes a bit of laying to make those rocks stay up there but you can do it if you can dig it. Consult the *I Ching* on any major problem.

Mark Mendel
Dixmont, Maine

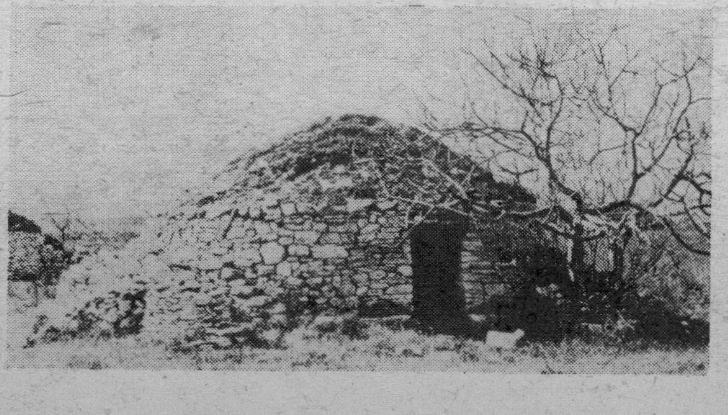

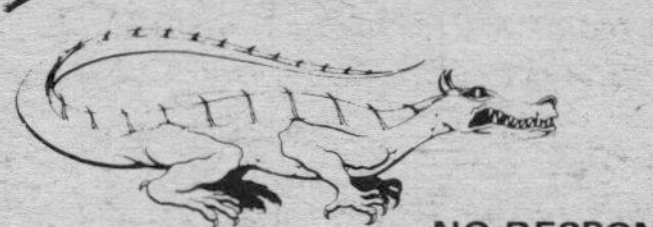

NO RESPONSE

Sad to say, however, D.R.'s clever maneuver did not have the result he was so desperate for. Estelle would have nothing to do with him when he lay down beside her. She wouldn't wake up, nor would her body respond to his as it usually did when they lay down together. D.R. shook her, and lifted her eyelids with his finger. But there was no response, except once, when he tried to hold her in his arms and she moaned and frowned and drew away to the far side of the mattress. D.R. thought he would go crazy when she did that. He sat up in the bed and pressed his hands to his head as if his skull was about to fly apart. In his mind he showed himself a little movie in which Estelle sailed away on a raft while he was drowning. He swam after her but words from the Greek's incessant talk filled the sail and pushed the boat further and further away. If he could have managed it, D.R. would have sneaked back to his seat in front and been the Greek's listener again. But he knew he couldn't bring it off. His muddy mind convinced him he could never bring it off without getting caught and reprimanded by the Greek's accusing eyes. There wasn't anything to do but lie down and try to sleep.

To D.R.'s relief, sleep came almost immediately. It was about four in the afternoon now; it had been fourteen hours since he'd dropped the acid, and of course he was exhausted. His brain felt like it had been washed and hung out to dry. Sleep was the best thing that could have happened to him then, and mercifully it came. He didn't hear a word of the Greek's life story as the Greek was telling it. But later that night, deep in Oklahoma, after the Greek got out and bade D.R. good luck and farewell, D.R. took the wheel and listened to the tape of the Greek's story as he drove non-stop to St. Louis.

Concrete Manuals

Three informative pamphlets on concrete from the Portland Cement Association:

Cement Mason's Manual for Residential Construction *is primarily for home patios and walkways, with fundamentals on use of the transit, and instructions on finishing.*

Concrete Improvements for Farm and Ranch *is a good basic instruction manual, with details on many rural applications; how to build forms, tilt-up construction, water troughs, floors, etc.*

Design and Control of Concrete Mixtures *is an engineering bulletin, very detailed, on all aspects of quality control of concrete mixtures.*

$2.40 postpaid
[Suggested by Fred Richardson]

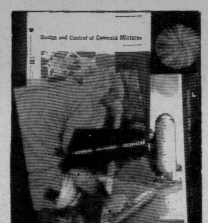

from:
Portland Cement Association
Old Orchard Road
Skokie, Ill. 60076

HARDENED STATE OF LIGHTWEIGHT CONCRETE

Compressive Strength

Lightweight concrete with 28-day compressive strengths of 3,000 to 4,500 psi can generally be produced in the laboratory with cement contents of 425 to 800 lb. per cubic yard, depending on the particular lightweight aggregate being used. Certain lightweight aggregates can be used to make concretes with strengths of 7,000 to 9,000 psi and with cement contents of 565 to 940 lb. per cubic yard. The rate of strength development for lightweight concrete is approximately the same as that for normal-weight concrete.

[Design and Control of Concrete Mixtures]

Tilt-up concrete construction is accomplished by casting wall panels on a concrete floor or other relatively smooth bed and then tilting them to a vertical position. To prevent bond with the wall panel, the floor slab is covered with plastic film or a sprayed-on chemical. Wall panels are usually tilted by a tractor or other lifting equipment. The panels are braced and reinforced concrete columns are cast at the panel junctures to tie them together.

[Concrete Improvements]

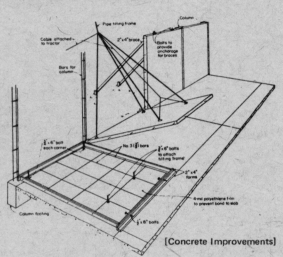

[Concrete Improvements]

Power Joint Cutter

Another method of cutting joints in concrete slabs is with an electric or gasoline-driven saw fitted with a shatterproof abrasive or diamond blade. A power cutter produces a narrow joint that minimizes the possibilities of spalling at the joint due to traffic. The joint is cut in the concrete surface 4 to 12 hours after the concrete has hardened or as soon as the concrete surface will not be torn or damaged by the saw.

[Cement Mason's Manual]

Concrete and Masonry

For a buck this is a lot of information, especially about large-scale concrete work. Good masonry introduction not as thorough as Audels (p. 97).

—SB

Concrete and Masonry
U.S. Army TM5-742
1970; 200 pp.

$1.75 postpaid

from:
U.S. Government Printing Office.
Division of Public Documents
Washington, D.C. 20402

OUT OF PRINT

or WHOLE EARTH CATALOG

1 Random rubble masonry

Laying Rubble Stone Masonry

Workmanship in laying stone masonry affects the economy, durability, and strength of the wall more than any other factor.

A. Rules for Laying

1. Each stone should be laid on its broadest face.
2. If appearance is to be considered, the larger stones should be placed in the lower courses. The size of the stones should gradually diminish toward the top of the wall.
3. Porous stones should be moistened before being placed in mortar in order to prevent the stone from absorbing water from the mortar and thereby weakening the bond between the stone and the mortar.
4. The spaces between adjoining stones should be as small as practicable and these spaces should be completely filled with mortar and smaller stones.
5. If necessary to remove a stone after it has been placed upon the mortar bed, it should be lifted clear and reset.

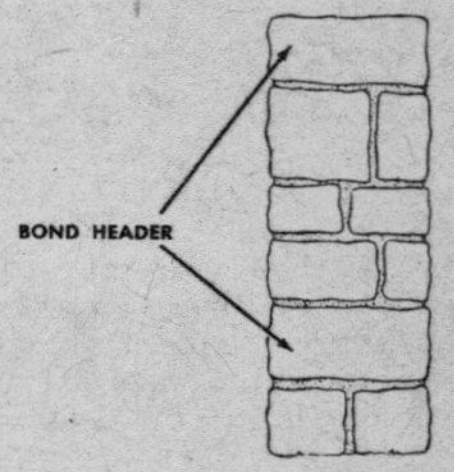

B. Footing.

The footing is larger than the wall itself. The largest stones should be used in it to give the greatest strength and lessen the danger of unequal settlement. The footing stones should be as long as the footing is wide, if possible. The footing stones should be laid in a mortar bed about 2 inches deep and all space between the stones filled with mortar and smaller stones.

Figure 8-21. Rubble stone masonry wall showing bonding stone.

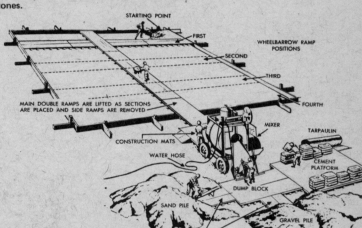

Figure 5-4. Typical organization of mixing equipment and materials.

Goldblatt Tools

An amazing catalog of specialized builder's tools. All manner of trowels and concrete tools, stilts, brick hammers and chisels, concrete saws, scaffolds, knee pads, wheel barrows, hods, tool pouches. Good prices.

—SB
[Suggested by Robert McElroy]

Goldblatt Trowel Trades Tools
Free

from:
Goldblatt Tool Co.
511 Osage
Kansas City, Kansas 66110

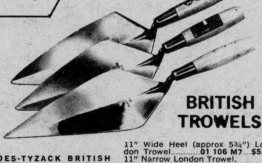

BRITISH TROWELS

● **BRADES-TYZACK BRITISH TROWELS**—Finest imported British steel, cleanly forged and heat treated to make the smoothest handlin trowel you've ever owned. Sho t post and low English "hang" mak these the trowels preferred by the most skilled masons.

11" Wide Heel (approx 5¾") London Trowel............01 106 M7...$5.75
11" Narrow London Trowel.
01 103 M7...$5.75
12" Narrow London Trowel.
01 104 M7...$5.95
13" Narrow London Trowel.
01 105 M7...$6.10
11" Philadelphia Pattern Trowel.
01 110 M7...$5.75

DEEP BIT

● **DEEP & THIN GROOVERS**— Thin, deep groove prevents spike heels from catching in pavement. These three groovers have 6"x6" body, with thin, ⅛" wide bits on ¼" radius to make grooves to state and municipal specs.
2" Groover......06 217 M7.... $6.30
1½" Bit Groover..06 216 M7... $5.80
1" Bit Groover......06 215 M7...$5.30
● **PAVER'S GROOVERS**—These are 10" x 3½" heavy duty stainless steel groovers.
1⅜" bit, ¼" rad 06 207 M7....$6.30
½" bit, ⅜" rad 06 210 M7....$6.25

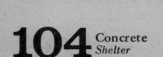

$34.95

● **BRICK & TILE BARROW**—Carries up to 120 bricks. Made of rugged, seasoned hardwood for long service. The ribbed dash is adjustable. Steel wheel guard adds rigidity to this heavy-duty barrow; wide-spread legs make it tip-proof, even fully loaded. 2-ply pneumatic tire. Bearings are self-lubricating. Weight, about 72 lbs. F.O.B. Kansas City or Harrisburg, Pa.
11 570 E2...$34.95

● **MORTAR HOE**—Two hole, 5½' handle, 10" Blade
07 228 H7...$8.80

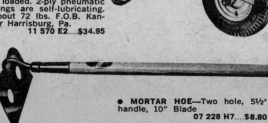

Concrete Boatbuilding

Ferro cement is a super strong ¾" thick fireproof material used for boat hulls, consisting of a mixture of sand and cement plastered over a wire framework. It is cheaper and easier than conventional boat-building techniques and very few special tools are needed. This is a textbook on building a ferro cement boat where the authors share details of their considerable experience. There is a fine concise section on how to build, and chapters on reinforcing, mortar mixing, and finish work.

Ferro cement should work well on land . . . let us know if you hear of any F. C. domes.

—Lloyd Kahn

(a) A rough and ready rowboat can be built from beach sand and cement as follows. Although not in the best tradition of ferro-cement, the form of construction is beautifully simple and inexpensive. It could conceivably have a military application.

(b) First form a mould of damp beach sand. Mix in a little fast-setting cement for the outer layer. Cover with polythene cut and taped where needed.

(c) Next cover with approximately four layers of ½" chicken netting. Wire tie at overlaps and hold at gunwale with a band of No. 8 fencing wire. Additional bands of fencing wire over the hull add stiffness. Wire mesh to these.

(d) Finally plaster with beach sand and quick setting cement mixed 2 to 1 with a minimum of water. Plaster layer of approximately ½", thickening to an inch at the gunwale, more at the keel. After two days, lift hull from mould, patch up inside and where possible sink boat to cure concrete for a few days.

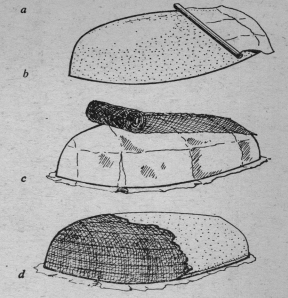

Fig. 10—Shoestring rowboat

Concrete Boatbuilding
Its Technique and Its Future
Gainor W. Jackson
W. Morley Sutherland

$9.95 postpaid

from:
John de Graaf, Inc.
34 Oak Street
Tuckahoe, New York 10707

or WHOLE EARTH CATALOG

Tongue-in-Groove Bricks

Good design on an old idea: stacking blocks--concrete, with grooves and ridges which lock the whole thing together. No mortar required, since everything interlocks. Also makes the blocks reusable. If you move--take your house apart and move it with you. Blocks are sold by franchised dealers Wedge-Block, Inc. 10439 Garibaldi, St. Louis 63131 but the molds for do-it-yourself should be simple to make.

Tom Cryar
Pittsburgh, Pa.

Stack Sacks

Between adobe bricks and formed concrete walls is this other way. You take gunny sack halves, sew them into narrow bags, fill them with sand and some concrete, stack the dry bags up like bricks, pound re-bar down through the bags, frame doorways and such with re-bar, then wet the whole wall with a hose or a rainstorm, let cure, put on the roof (maybe with wet-concrete-dipped gunny sacks for shingles). Trowel on wet concrete for a smooth wall if you want it.

According to Holly Baer, who told us, the main source of information is:

Dicker Stack Sack International
2600 Fairmont Street
Dallas, Texas 75201

They are getting a patent on the device that turns out filled bags. Apparently local franchises can deliver an order of stack sacks to your door. Some people dip them in water, then place them wet.

IL 1

This is a quarterly review of the work being done at the Institute for Lightweight Structures, University of Stuttgart. Frei Otto is director. This issue (the first) is concerned with the experimental determination of minimal nets. The subject is carefully defined, and the ingenious devices for measurement are explained in detail. The results of the explorations are presented in a series of good photographs. The whole publication has the feeling of disciplined investigation that you see in scientific periodicals such as Science. If Frei Otto's work interests you, IL is the way to keep up with what's going on. The next IL will be "Biology and Building". It should be good. — 7 issues so far, $4.50 to $27.50
[Reviewed by Jay Baldwin]

IL 1
Frei Otto, Berthold Burchhardt
1970; 56pp

$4.50 postpaid

from:
Wittenborn & Co.
1018 Madison Ave.
New York, N.Y. 10021

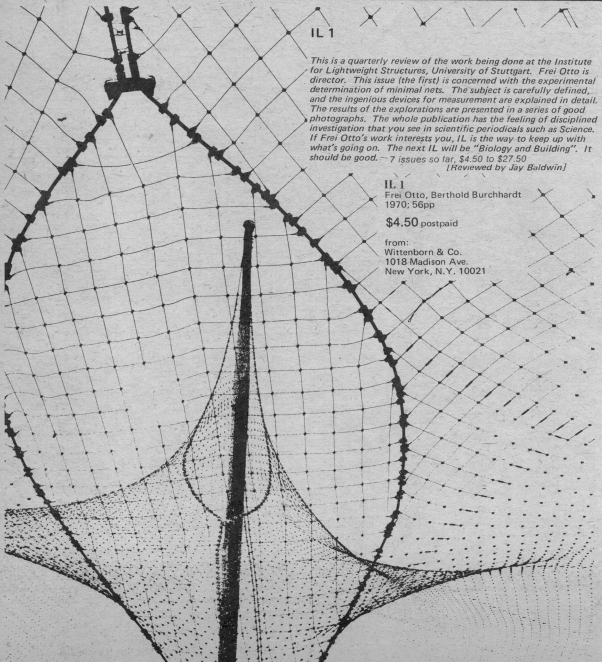

THE GREEK'S LIFE STORY

Before I tell my life story I want to explain where I'm going, and why. My destination is Norman, Oklahoma. I used to be a student at the state university in Norman, and I'm on my way there now to destroy a certain manuscript that I wrote and left there in the library, for posterity. I didn't have any way of realizing it at the time, but leaving that manuscript behind on that campus was one of the worst mistakes I've made in a lifetime filled with mistakes, and the most important thing I have to do at this point in my life is correct that mistake be getting hold of the manuscript and destroying it.

It's got to be destroyed because the story of my life from 1930 to 1955 is told on those pages. Except for that record, that whole early phase of my life is totally lost to memory. I don't remember anything that's in the manuscript, and I've forgotten the name of the person that manuscript is about. It's taken me fifteen years of constant labor to arrive at my present state of mind and I'm proud of that achievement. Yet I can't relax in my condition of forgetfulness because I know that one glimpse at that manuscript would bring it all back again, and my efforts these last years would all have been for nothing. I realize it's pretty unlikely that I would ever accidentally find myself reading the manuscript. There's only the one copy, gathering dust all these years in the stacks of the University library. But as long as that manuscript exists, intact, the possibility exists that I might see it, and I am haunted by that possibility. The very worst thing that could happen to me is to have the knowledge of my early life re-implanted in my mind.

(continued)

Tensile Structures, Volume One

The only pavilion of Expo 67 more beautiful than Fuller's U.S. Dome was the West German tent, designed by Frei Otto. He is currently the master of structures whose flexible skin is the prime structural element. Volume One of his 2-volume work is devoted to Pneumatic Structures——air houses plus. Every designer we know who's seen this book has commenced to giggle and point, jump up and down, and launch into enthusiastic endorsement of Otto, design, being a designer, and look at this here. The book is comprehensive in its field, technically thorough, beautifully presented.

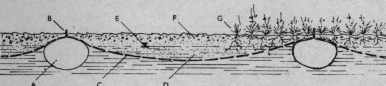

Small floating balloons may carry fertile soil in nets or perforated foils.

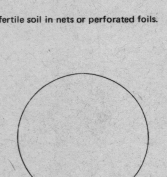

**Tensile Structures, Vol. One
Pneumatic Structures**
Frei Otto
1967; 320 pp.
1660 illustrations

**Tensile Structures, Vol. Two
Cables, Nets and Membranes**
Frei Otto
1969; 171 pp.

$22.50 postpaid

both from:
The M. I. T. Press
50 Ames Street
Cambridge, Mass. 02142

or WHOLE EARTH CATALOG

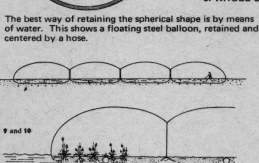

The best way of retaining the spherical shape is by means of water. This shows a floating steel balloon, retained and centered by a hose.

9 and 10

Figure 9 is a section through a greenhouse set on sandy soil and covered by a transparent membrane with internal drainage. A membrane is also laid beneath the humus layer, and is positively connected with the roof membrane at the inner drainage points and along the outside edge.
The humus layer thus forms a simple anchoring weight.

The floor membrane simultaneously permits moisture control of the soil.

The roofing of such cultivations by pneumatically tensed membranes with internal drainage is seen from the side in Fig. 10. A net of small open mesh floats on the water and carries the humus layer; it is supported both by inflated balloons and by the roof membrane itself which spans the floating fields and is immersed to a depth of approximately 15 cm at the edges.

Tensile Structures, Volume Two

Tensile Structures is the complete story on tents and cable nets and like volume one the entire subject is covered in minute detail. The book is intended to show where the thinking and practice on the subject is at this time in history. There is an overview of the whole field, then specifics on cable, net and membrane structures. Each is thoroughly discussed and illustrated with photographs and drawings although graphics here are not as intriguing as in volume one. The last third of the book contains calculations on load-bearing abilities and design. For many readers this will be too technical to understand, much less use. But tensile structures are very exciting at this time, and the book is great for getting people started on experiments and construction. Canvas is a cheap building material. There's a lot to learn here. The forms are very organic, and coverage is complete.

[Reviewed by Jay Baldwin]

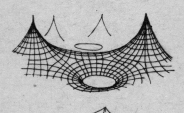

Guyed masts consist of one-dimensional central elements subjected to compression and surrounded on all sides by one- or two-dimensional tension-loaded elements. They thus form three-dimensional systems most suitable for mobile structures. Many contemporary designs of high cranes for wide reaches are variations of this basic system. An elastic central rod can be bent by varying the lengths of the guys (Fig. 3). For this, all cables must be adjusted simultaneously; this is done by synchronized hydraulic presses located at the anchoring point. A similar, but much more mobile system is shown in Fig. 4. A thin elastic central strut carries cantilevers connected to the ground by means of cables.

In living nature the spine of a vertebrate (Fig. 7) is a guyed mobile system, approximately as shown in Fig. 4. A multiple articulated, highly flexible central rod, capable of taking up large compressive forces, is surrounded by a tension-loaded system consisting of many members, which secures the central rod against buckling and bending, while ensuring its complete mobility.

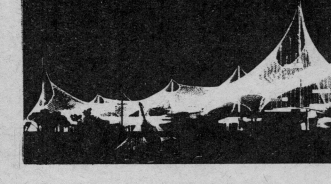

Frei Otto: Tension Structures

This is a comprehensive collection of the stretched-membrane and pneumatic structures made or proposed by Frei Otto and his friends from 1953 to 1967. The many projects actually done or modelled are shown in photographs (many rather dark). Proposals, and explanations of the structures are shown in drawings and diagrams. The text explains things in a non-technical language. The math is not discussed. There are a number of structures shown that were news to me, and as usual they excited me a lot. Can you dig a dam made of cables and a membrane? Tension structures are economical and graceful, and we will probably be seeing a lot of them soon. If you want to understand them, this book is a good place to start. It's claimed to be the only single volume collection printed in English. The price is something else.

[Reviewed by Jay Baldwin]

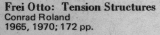

Frei Otto: Tension Structures
Conrad Roland
1965, 1970; 172 pp.

from:
Praeger Publishers, Inc.
111 Fourth Ave.
New York, N.Y. 10003

$22.50 postpaid

or WHOLE EARTH CATALOG

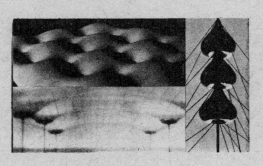

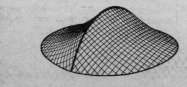

For roofs over large areas it is usually necessary to employ structures of relatively low height. Because of the large radius of curvature, large-span pneumatic domes of low "rise" have high membrane stresses. If, on the other hand, the membrane is anchored to the ground not only at the edges but also at one or more points in the interior, then the spans, the radii of curvature and therefore also the membrane stresses are reduced. While retaining the same average height, pneumatic roof structures with low points can be extended at will. They are among the most economical structures for covering large areas and are independent of the structure of the ground over which they span, inasmuch as tension anchorages may be given any desired length and be formed in all manner of soils and even under water. Such roof surfaces have to discharge their rainwater at the low points (structures of this kind are, in principle, conceivable also as vertical or steeply sloping wall surfaces.

Inflatocookbook

An inflatable is an event, like circus tents used to be. Dogs bark, kids gather, old ladies get up tight, cops drift by, youths take off their clothes.
Inflatables are trippy, cheap, light, imaginative space not architecture at all. They're terrible to work in. The blazing redundant surfaces disorient; one wallows in space. When the sun goes behind a cloud you cease cooking and immediately start freezing (insulation schemes are in the works). Environmentally, what an inflatable is best at is protecting you from a gentle rain. Wind wants to take the structure with it across the county, so you get into heavy anchoring operations.

To give inflatables their well-earned due, they are wonderful recreational structures. High and scary but thoroughly safe. Like an immense water bed, or slow-motion trampoline, or squishy mountain. Person-flinging giddiness maker.

This book of Ant Farm's has all the basic design and materials information to puff up your own dream sky hill.
—SB

Inflatocookbook

$3.00 postpaid

from:
THE ANT FARM
Box 471
San Francisco, Calif. 94101
or WHOLE EARTH CATALOG

If your inflatable is going to be up outdoors in any wind, it will need an anchoring system. For small volume (500 sq. ft. of floor area or less) interior weights should work; these could be sand bags or water bags. Larger structures require heavier anchoring. There are a number of ways of doing it: integrally made tie downs, buried edge, weighted edges, taped edge, or tension net anchors. Buried edge is good for a semi-permanent installation where you can dig a trench. A taped edge is good for a small installation on a smooth floor; tie downs and tension nets are good for sites with existing things to tie to (trees, fire hydrants), or where it would be easy to drive tent stakes or augers.

The anchoring system must withstand not only windloading but also the internal air pressure of the structure. Precise structural calculations should be left to 2 engineers, 3 Ph.D. mathematicians, and a computer, but a little rough math can give you a close enough estimate of what anchors to use. We will deal first with inflation pressure and second with wind loads.

<u>40' VINYL PILLOW</u> Dielectrically welded vinyl pillow with double blowers, net, and earth-augur anchors. 2 doors, variety of colors and weight vinyl. $2,000–2,500. Rents for $150/day. Other sizes and shapes (see pentapus) made to order.

WARNING:
FUNKY GENERATORS EAT FAN MOTORS

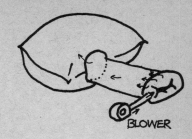
BLOWER

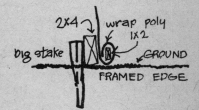

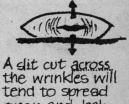

A slit cut across the wrinkles will tend to spread open and leak air. Not recommended

Products for Inflatables

Roberts Valves Catalog
Halkey-Roberts Corporation
Spring Valley Avenue
Paramus, New Jersey 07652

<u>The</u> valves for small inflatables——cheap, hi-tech like 4¢ apiece. The 660 KD is an airtight valve that goes on with a brass grommet & steel pressure die, i.e., no heatsealer. The die costs $17; it works fine in an arbor press, OK with hammer. Vacuum cleaner tube goes over outside of valve

Smith-Dixie Industrial Fabrics
North Side Drive
Box 1203
Statesville, North Carolina

Catalog has sample swatches. New & seconds, & government reject, vinyl-coated nylon fabrics at good prices. A small company; I haven't ordered yet, but people I've talked to seem pleased with their service.

Love & Peace to all

Charles Tilford
New York, N.Y.

Vinyl Cements

I have been developing a portable, collapsible, insulated shelter in which I have been using a nylon reinforced vinyl requiring a suitable adhesive.

I would like to advise the person who refers to himself as the 'Virginian' in Pax River, Maryland that Bostik Adhesive Specialists, a subsidiary of USM Corp. in Middleton, Mass., produces an excellent adhesive for vinyl. It is referred to as 4067 a nitrile rubber base adhesive and 7130, a synthetic resin base. Both are excellent and are often used industrially for vinyl inflatables.

James W. Smith
Providence, R.I.

The Latest Inflatables

Here's what we've been doing with inflatables recently——at the Media Conference at Goddard, many of us (Cosmic Labs, Southcoast) lived in poly bubbles in the woods (300' extension cord) and stayed dry through three days of rain. Very functional and nice.

I've been doing a series of Water-Bubbles for the NYC Parks Department. Their Festival Truck goes to street fairs and provides stages, PA, lites, and Bubbles. We lay down the red carpet (non-woven polypropylene, $1.75/sq. yd. from Ozite Corp.), inflate zoomy 16 guage vinyl bubbles with 5000 CFM blower mounted on the truck, tie the anchor ropes to parking meters, lite poles, fire hydrants, etc., attach 1" hose to fire hydrant & 3-way distribution system: one to overhead sprinkler hoses, one to floor sprinkler hoses, one to 4-way direct spray. Add 150 kazpos, cowbells, claves, tambourines ——and turn the kids loose inside. They really give it a workout—— the carpet protects the bubbles and the kids when they slide and fall. I try to get them involved in putting it up and down. Some do, some don't. The first model was in 8 guage vinyl——it almost worked, but would usually rip after a few hours. I really hate to tell them "Don't . .". I think the new model will take about anything except knives. Even in Hunt's Point and Lower East Side, no knives attacked it.

Now we're in Columbia Maryland working on the Antioch project to put this campus in a 1-acre inflatable using the Goodyear system ——12 guage vinyl reinforced with steel cables with internal drainage points. The site slopes 15%. We'll do earthwork——direct ramming and CINVA Ram——to form an earth berm and interior spaces. Probably also have foamed interior structures. Soutcoast is here working on a prototype. Some hassles in zoning, air conditioning, financing——we're working on a grant from Educational Facilities Labs, (Ford Foundation). Project has a fairly high reality-feel about it. I'm working on getting the vinyl metalized——to cut down heat gain. Maybe put silver mylar on the vinyl. The structure will have a double skin for insulation. This makes some problems on duct connections. But it opens up the possibility of sculpting the "ceiling" at will by varying the skin spacing. Goodyear is opening up their research department to us. The whole thing is an order of magnitude of complexity higher than the poly bubbles. But it's still more and better for less.

FINE tape source:
Arista Custom Tapes
Foot of Farm Road
Secaucus, New Jersey
Phone 201-864-3131

Mr. Zymler has been most cooperative and friendly. The tape we usually buy is 5 mil vinyl, $1.20 per inch of width for 36 yard rolls, in many colors, all good (red, yellow, blue, green, white, black, orange, and others) in case lots. He'll sell as few rolls as you need---15% more for less than a case---fast service---2 days by UPS in NYC area, and ships by air. The tape can be cut in any width. I've been ordering 3" and taping both sides, for heavy-use stuff.

A source for screw-in earth anchors:
A.B. Chance Co.
210 N. Allen Street
Centralia, MO 65240

$7.10 for an 8" helix on 1" x 60" shaft, will hold 10,000 lbs in normal soil.

Charlie Tilford
Inflatoenvironmentologist

The personal history that's still alive in my memory begins when I was twenty-two. When I was twenty-two I thought that what I wanted more than anything in all the world was to be a scholar, a student of literature, an expert on the metaphysical poets with particular emphasis on John Donne. I had a bachelor's degree but that didn't seem like enough. I felt like I'd got that degree without ever really reading anything, without ever really learning <u>how</u> to read. I wanted to read, to study, to experience the words of the masters. It seemed like such a <u>gentle</u> thing. The library, the department, the lectures, all were images of utmost quiet and tranquility to me then, and I wanted nothing more than to be quiet, to read and write and think, to live the classic life of the mind right here in the middle of the Twentieth Century.

Graduate school was good the first year. I did okay in the classes, and I was into some personal writing that satisfied me. I didn't take myself seriously as a writer, you understand. But I enjoyed it, it was expression, and I felt like I had a whole lot to express. I remember writing a short story about a flower, a daffodil that learned how to sing. Every afternoon the daffodil would give a concert for all the other flowers in the meadow. The story was published in the campus literary magazine and a lot of people told me they thought it was pretty good.

The problem with my career as a scholar was the Master's Thesis. I did well in the lecture courses and seminars, but I just couldn't hack that thesis. The reason I couldn't hack it was I really didn't want to write a thesis. I'd sit down and try to write about the metaphysical poets and every time I'd wind up saying stuff about myself. I worked over a year on that paper, and when I'd finished I had three hundred pages that simply told my life story from birth through graduate school. Of course I knew the professors wouldn't accept the manuscript as a thesis, so what I did was have it typed up professionally, and bound to look like all the other theses on the shelf. And one day I sneaked into the stacks and when nobody was looking I slipped it up on the shelf and left it there. Then a few weeks later I left the University, I left Norman altogether and entered the next phase of my life's adventure.

(continued)

Plastics for Architects and Builders

Whereas architects and builders are comfortably familiar with the "classic" building materials that come more or less directly from nature, plastics, with so many complicated names and such complex manufacturing processes, have not been as readily understood.

Most books on plastics are by and for specialists. Here, however, is a primer on plastics, clear and orderly, that gives the builder, designer, or architect enough basic knowledge to begin thinking of design with the new sophisticated materials.

It begins with a simple description of the molecular structure of plastics——one of the principal keys to their behavior. Once the designer understands this, he is ready to begin exploring the array of materials available.

Then there is basic information, pictures, many drawings on the properties, end-use applications, composites, and manufacturing processes. The designer can then begin to understand what plastics can & cannot do.

—Lloyd Kahn

Plastics for Architects and Builders
Albert G. H. Dietz
1969; 129 pp.

$7.95 postpaid

from:
The M. I. T. Press
50 Ames Street, Room 765
Cambridge, Mass. 02142

or WHOLE EARTH CATALOG

There is no escaping the conclusion that design with plastics is design at a sophisticated level.

Light Transmission: Thin structural plastics can transmit a high percentage of incident light, thus providing structure, enclosure, and illumination——a combination unique among structural materials.

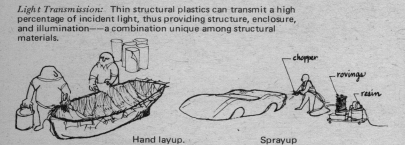

Hand layup.   Sprayup.   Preform.   Matched die molding.   Bag molding.

Cellulosics: One class of chain polymers is made by modifying cellulose, a natural high-polymer chain:

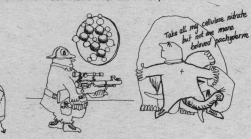

Various acids will react at the OH points of the cellulose to give a series of "esters" (the organic analogue of salts in inorganic chemistry). The oldest is cellulose nitrate, often thought of as originating the plastics industry when first proposed for billiard balls to save the African elephants from decimation for their ivory.

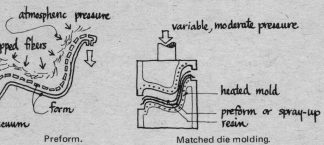

Stabilizers: Plain plastics, such as polyethylene pipe or polyvinyl chloride sheet, may degrade when exposed to some environments such as sunlight. They must therefore be fortified by stabilizers, such as ultraviolet absorbers and antioxidants. Carbon black, for example, converts polyethylene from a quickly degrading material to one that stands up extremely well to sunlight and general weathering. Other stabilizers accomplish their purpose without necessarily coloring or making the plastic opaque. Care should be exercised to select a properly stabilized plastic for a particular purpose unless it is inherently stable. The subject is far too complex to be treated here. The architect should insist upon assurance that the plastic will have the necessary life for his application.

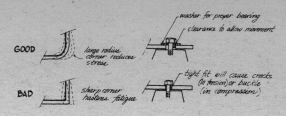

Thermal Response

Expansion and Contraction: Like all building materials, plastics expand and contract with rising and falling temperatures, but for many plastics the extent of change is appreciably larger than for many other building materials. Allowances in design must therefore be made for these dimensional changes, either by accommodating them in the shape of the component or by providing expansion joints. A curved section, for example, may bulge or flatten slightly without affecting its usefulness. Framing around glazing should allow room for expansion and contraction, and the sealants employed should accommodate such motion.

Design: Expansion and contraction can lead to severe stresses at sharp bends or at points of restraint, such as tight bolts and pins. Repeated stresses caused by temperature changes can lead to fatigue, cracking, and failure. Generous radii and fillets should therefore be provided, and holes for fastenings should be large enough to allow for movement with changing temperatures. Restrained flat surfaces may wrinkle upon expanding and in extreme cases may crack or tear upon contracting. Curved or folded surfaces, properly designed, overcome these problems.

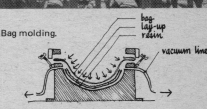

Plastics in Building

With all the sealants, plastic pipes, foams and the like coming into prominence in the building industry, it's handy to have a book like this, which describes the properties and characteristics of the many plastic materials now in use.

There is introductory information on reinforced plastic shell structures, adhesives, roofs, coatings, and reports on the use of plastics in other countries.

—Lloyd Kahn

Both the plastics chemist and the architect are designers of structures. The architect builds with units that the eye can see and the hand can weigh. The chemist's building blocks are tiny molecules, far smaller than one-millionth of an inch, which he strings together to make aggregates called <u>polymers</u>. These little chains, barely discernible by electron microscpe, are entwined and sometimes tied together to give us the plastics.

Sprayup (Figure 5-11)
The sprayup process lends itself particularly well to the manutacture of large structural polyester based panels. In this process, chopped fibers and resin are deposited simultaneously against a mold surface. The unit used for this deposition consists of a chopper and dual spray nozzles. Continuous strand is fed into the chopper where it is cut to length. Fiber length can be varied from about ½ to 2 inches. (The longer fibers are desirable for structural panels because they impart higher mechanical properties.) The fibers are fed into thepath of the dual spray nozzles. Separate reservoirs supply one nozzle with catalyzed resin and the second nozzle with accelerated resin. The resin formulation is tailored such that neither component is highly reactive, and therefore, each may remain in the reservoirs for at least several hours. When the products leave the dual elements of the spray gun, they intersect and intersperse, and pick up the chopped fibers before striking the mold. The resin mixture is then ready to cure at a convenient rate as predetermined by the concentration of catalyst and accelerator.

Plastics in Building
Irving Skeist, Ed.
1966; 466 pp.

$20.00 postpaid

from:
Van Nostrand-Reinhold
450 East 33rd Street
New York, N. Y. 10001

or WHOLE EARTH CATALOG

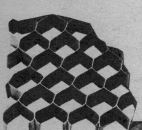

FIG. 8B-2. Sandwich panel with honeycomb core.

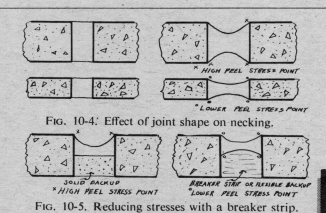

FIG. 10-4. Effect of joint shape on necking.

FIG. 10-5. Reducing stresses with a breaker strip.

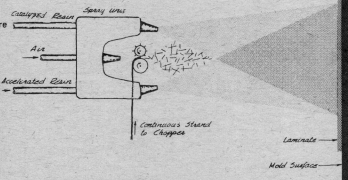

FIG. 5-11. Schematic of sprayup process.

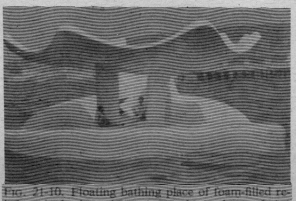

FIG. 21-10. Floating bathing place of foam-filled reinforced plastics. *(Courtesy Bath Academy of Art)*

JOINT SHAPES

The shape of the joint has considerable effect on the success of the joint sealant. As a joint moves, stresses are imposed on the sealant that may be more or less severe, depending on the natural or original shape of the joint. The deeper a sealant is in a given joint for a given width, the more "necking" and internal stress occurs in the sealant as the joint opens. As is seen in Figure 10-4 a joint ½ inch wide X 1 inch deep "necks" or pulls up within itself far more than a joint ½ inch wide X ½ inch deep. Consequently, there is a greater chance for cohesive failure with the deeper joint. A similar problem is solved when a sealant is used in a joint in which there is no breaker strip at the bottom or back of the joint, so that the sealant is in contact with three sides of the joint with only the face of the joint exposed. This, again, puts a greater strain on the cohesive strength of the sealant. The obvious recommendation here is to employ a breaker strip or type of backing which will not restrict or restrain the sealant, but will move with it as the joint moves (Figure 10-5).

Shrinkage is another characteristic whose importance varies with the use of the sealant. If the sealant is applied in a corner joint as a fillet, shrinkage actually may be desirable in order to have the joint become concave. On the other hand, a sealant put in the ¼-inch joint between two adjacent porcelain enamel panels cannot have excessive shrinkage or it will shrink into the joint providing an unsatisfactory appearance and also reducing the amount of sealant in the joint, possibly to an unsatisfactory amount. Sealants are available with shrinkage rates ranging from practically 0 to 50 per cent. If a very low order of shrinkage is required, a two-part chemically curing compound will provide shrinkages in the order of 0 to 2 per cent. If a modest amount of shrinkage is permissible and other characteristics unique in the compound are desired, solvent-release type compounds are available with shrinkages ranging from 10 to 20 per cent. For certain applications, sealants with 40 to 50 per cent solven, providing about that amoung of shrinkage eventually, may be entirely satisfactory, e.g., for needle glazing and other small joints where a concave finished joint is not harmful.

Several plastic coatings, including epoxies, urethanes and polyesters, have established themselves as extremely durable surfaces with excellent bonding characteristics. These coatings form their films by chemical action rather than oxidation or evaporation as in the case of the paints. A urethane coating was used for the car shelter and breezeway panels of the South Bend house. This two-part system promises excellent weather resistance and color retention. One clear coat of the formulation was plant applied during fabrication of the sandwich panels. After the initial color coat was mixed and brush applied at the site, an additional coat which contained a pure silica sand for texturing finished the surfaces. The coating has performed well and appears to be particularly able to conceal plywood grain raising and checking.

Fig. 19A-3. Extruded vinyl waterstop. (Courtesy Cementa A.S. Copenhagen, Denmark)

A remarkably designed extruded vinyl (Figure 19A-3) waterstop is being used as a peripheral insulation. The diamond-shaped center portion serves as a mechanical spring. When the concrete expands, the diamond collapses; when the concrete contracts, the diamond expands pushing the fins tightly into position.

Structural Potential of Foam

Plastic foams are entering the building industry. Shot from guns, poured into molds, or vacuum formed, foam is produced by mixing two liquids which expand to form the cellular structure.

Recent technological advances with urethane foams in application, fabrication, and product control have led to the current wave of experimentation. Designers such as Douglas Deeds and Felix Drury are working on structural applications of foam, hoping to achieve free-form buildings.

Equipment for spraying is expensive: a foam rig is $1,500-7,000, and foam itself runs about 10¢ per board foot (1" x 12", one inch thick) if you're doing your own application, and buying bulk materials. Its biggest applications now are in roofing and as insulation.

This book describes a government sponsored project to determine the potential use of foam for housing in under-developed areas. It may well be that building codes, unions, lumber lobby interests, etc., will hold up foam development in the U. S., and that the real advances will be made in other countries. Details are given here on several years of testing various structural applications of polystyrene and polyure-thane foams. There are pictures, construction details, drawings, graphs and charts on test results. Since this work was done several years ago, recent improvements in foams may have superceded some of the conclusions.

—Lloyd Kahn

[Suggested by Ron Brooks & Ron Swenson]

Architectural Research on Structural Potential of Foam Plastics for Housing in Underdeveloped Areas
Architectural Research Lab.
1966; 224 pp.

$5.00 plus postage from:

Publication Distribution Service
University of Michigan
615 East University
Ann Arbor, Michigan 48106

It is clearly to the interest of the plastic industry in the United States to enter the housing field on such a global scale. As the section on marketing aspects brings out, the industry is caught in a squeeze between steadily increasing surplus production capacities and a falling price curve for the basic chemicals. Housing looms as a most attractive mass market—chemicals would be bought by the ton, not just by the pound—but attempts to penetrate the housing field in the United States have been frustrated because of local building code restrictions and the opposition of established interests in the conventional way of building. In entering the housing field, the plastics producers will find better opportunities for success if initially they turn to the emerging countries where the building codes are less restrictive (if indeed any exist at all) and where there is consequently more freedom to develop a new kind of building industry.

All the shells were coated with liquid elastomer before being exposed to the weather. Two approaches were used. One was the use of the two-coat system, neoprene and Hypalon, and the other the use of two coats of Hypalon.

The shells were moved to the site by rolling each one like a giant wheel.

The shell was suspended and loaded with 20 lb sand bags to simulate uniform loading.

Petroleum is becoming increasingly the raw material for plastics intermediates.

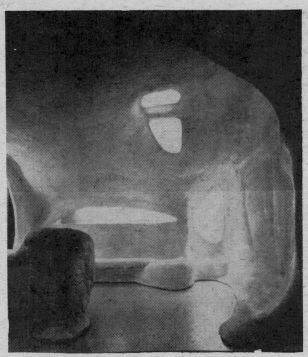

Office room transformed into grotto by designer Douglas Deeds, San Diego. Deeds built foam up in layers, as coils of clay are used to form a pot.

Vacuum forming: ABS foam, marketed by U.S. Rubber Co. under the name 'Expanded Royalite'...in sheet form is clamped in a stationary frame, heated, and then drawn into a female mold by vacuum....

The fewer the joints, the fewer are the problems the structure will have to face...lightness in structures can lead to some special problems of anchorage.

The cellular plastics admittedly have certain technical limitations. For instance, they have a low moduli of elasticity and high creep characteristics. These properties definitely restrict the way they can be formed or shaped, if they are to be used as independent structural materials.

Closed cell foam plastics offer excellent thermal insulation (with K-factors usually varying from 0.12 to 0.30) low water absorption and low moisture permeability.

Plastic materials, particularly the foam plastics, unquestionably have a high potential for housing use in the developing areas of the world.

Spray techniques have good possibilities for the construction of total structures using either air-inflated structures or lightweight armatures as form work; the present crude appearance of sprayed foam products can be overcome by mechanizing the spray gun or by using extremely skilled operators.

Plastic Hinges
This tough hinge was flexed 1,000,000 times without breaking. Comes in rolls, about 30¢ per foot. Fact sheet "Polyhinge" from:

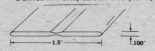

Stokes Molded Products
75 Taylor Street
Trenton, N. J. 08604

Lock and Key Extrusion
A simple way to install glass or plastic windows in wood or metal panels. Information from:

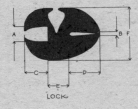

Alasco Rubber & Plastics Corp.
839 Malcolm Road
Burlingame, CA

Foam Guns
Guns & pumping systems for epoxy, urethane foam, elastomers and silicons. Information from:

W. E. Mushet Co.
725 Bryant Street
San Francisco, CA 94107

FP-10 $57.75
10 Cubic Feet, 120 Board Feet
Consists of:
1— Twin Pak carton container
2— Pressurized Component Tanks (1 "A" and 1 "B")
6— Mixer Nozzles (3 ea., 3 Tan)
2— 6' Lengths ⅜" I.D. Hose w/⅞6"-20 Connections
1— Gun type dispenser w/Valve Protectors
1 Carton — Ship. Wt. 27 lbs.

Low-cost, small-job home foam dispensers.

Foam Design

Deeds Design Associates
1706 West Arbor Drive
San Diego, CA 92103

Construction Bargaineer

Just like Rock and Dirt (p. 71). Heavy equipment, used and surplus.

—SB

Construction Bargaineer

$5 /yr (24 issues)

from:
The Construction Bargaineer
P.O. Box 1061
St. Paul, Minnesota 55105

CARGO TRAILERS
—2 WHEEL—

5,000# Cap. - Metal Body w/Front & Rear Drop Gate Air over Hyd. Brakes - 1100x20 or 900x20, 12 ply Tires - Front Caster - Body Dim. 110" L, 74" W. Wt. 2300# Excellent! **$139**

4 x 4 PICK UP

3/4 TON
● Similar to a Jeep but twice the size!
● Very Low Miles   ● Excellent

SPECIAL! While Quantity Lasts! . . . **$1,250** EA.

REO 6 x 6 w/AUGERS
6 Avail
Good Oper. Condition. **$4,500**

Adhesive Engineering Company

these guys are doing what construction people never figured could be done. they take structures like collapsed concrete bridges, jack them back into place, inject some adhesive, and the bridge is stronger than before it collapsed. They print a pamphlet called Construction Adhesives Coatings and Sealants, and they provide information and survey to about every possible application of industrial gluing. alan kalker suggested it, through herb grubb. alan's idea was that there might be an application here for prepoured concrete dome sections. just pour the sections, hoist them inplace, and stick them together.

—jd

Information

free

from:
Adhesive Engineering Company
1411 Industrial Road
San Carlos, California 94070

For the first time in my life I began living without a plan. Time and space went out of my mind as concepts as I worked to let go of every memory of my early life. It was a period of wandering, alone, traveling light, sometimes with only a pack on my back, hitch-hiking when I was broke, driving old cars when I could afford to buy them. I would drive the old cars till they fell apart, then hitch-hike again till I got enough money together to buy another old car. I was insane a lot in those days. Half the insanity of my life came from watching my cars fall apart around me, and being unable to fix them. And yet, it was fascinating. I learned much from the experience of those cars. Those cars gave me my first important insights into how all things are made of separate parts, and how those parts come together as wholes. I'd buy a car and drive it thinking that I had bought one thing and then go crazy when it would turn out I hadn't bought one thing at all, but a hundred things, a thousand things that had to fit and work together or they couldn't work at all. Fuel pumps, water pumps, head gaskets, oil filters, coils, tires, tubes, king pins, bushings, rocker arms, brake linings, horns, lights, steering wheels, transmission systems, a thousand parts that needed oil and grease and special measuring of lengths and widths and timings in between

I couldn't cope with that realization at first. There were times when a fuel pump would go out and all I could think to do was walk away, just abandon the entire car. I had no mechanical skill, and no patience to learn any. As I brooded about this idea, as that long string of broken cars forced me, literally <u>drove</u> me into this painful experience of the separate parts of machines, I began to see how everything is made up of parts, how the whole world, the whole <u>cosmos</u> is nothing but an incredibly large heap of parts. And it was then that I went truly crazy. For if all the world was a heap of parts, then where was the guarantee that all those parts would keep on working? Where was the guarantee that the one necessary part that held it all together, the screw or the pump or the axle or the philosophical theory the world just <u>had</u> to have to keep going, was not going to break or wear out or get lost at precisely the moment the world needed it the most?

I think the insight that finally broke me and made me voiceless, took away my very power to utter words, was the recognition that language itself is made of parts, little bits and pieces we call vowels and consonants, verbs, nouns, adjectives, conjunctions, the <u>parts of</u> speech, you see.

The Parts!

(continued)

RIGID SKIN MATERIAL

Fome-Cor board, type 327W .200" thick flat sandwich laminate of unicellular polystyrene foam between 2 layers of paperboard. 4' X 8' sheets $5 per sheet in 20-sheet quantities, $3 in 200-sheet quantities. Brochure Fome-Core Board's tech bulletin No. 6113A:

Fome-Cor Board
Type 327W
Monsanto Company
200 N. 8th St.
Kenilworth, New Jersey 07033

Steel foil corrugated board (up to 70" width) being produced in widths 30"-34", lengths 24"-96", with larger sizes available on special order. Cost about $80 per thousand sq ft. This company is experienced at scoring, slotting, joining techniques and can do same in plant with sufficient instructions; ask for sample:

First Container Corporation
Box 303
Fort Worth, Texas 76101
Attn: Don S. Leaman, President

Fiberglass structural panels-doors, skylights:

Sanstruction **PLEASE SEND FOR PAMPHLET.**
702 North Bend Rd.
Cincinnati, Ohio 45224

Silicone coated plywood—architectural specs and application instructions from

Weyerhauser Company
Box B
Tacoma, Washington 98401

Glass reinforced thermoplastic sheet "Azdel"—very strong, developed for autos:

G. R. T. L. Company
No. 1 Gateway Center
Pittsburgh, Pennsylvania 15222

Reinforced acrylic structural sheets, tensile strength 12,000 psi. Information from

American Acrylic Corporation
173 Marine Street
Farmingdale, Long Island, New York 11735

Rigid vinyl—fascinating brochure from Goodrich, "Designing with Rigid Vinyl." Comes in rods, extruded shapes, pipe, sheets and molded shapes. Sheets come in thicknesses from a few mils to several inches, many colors, and can be *heat-welded* with hot-air guns. You might be able to weld together a dome membrane at triangles' edges:

B. F. Goodrich Chemical Company
3135 Euclid Avenue
Cleveland, Ohio 44115

Acrylic Plastic sheet, Kydex 100, Kydex 5,000, resistant to ultraviolet. Technical data from

Rohm and Haas Company
Independence Mall West
Philadelphia, Pennsylvania 19015

Teflon, Plexiglas, fiberglass, Mylar, vinyl, foam guns, etc. A complete catalog of plastic materials and prices:

Plasticraft, Incorporated
2800 North Speer
Denver, Colorado 80211

Best plywood for domes: Duraply flat panel siding is exterior Douglas Fir plywood with phenolic resin-fiber surface, designed for severe weather exposure. Guaranteed against delamination for life of building. Brochure from

U. S. Plywood Corporation
777 Third Avenue
New York, New York 10017

GLASS TOPS FOR SKYLIGHT PURPOSES.
Leaded and Colored Glass.

WINDOWS

Plexiglas information (see also pp. 92-93)

Rohm and Haas
Independence Mall West
Philadelphia, Pa. 19105

Polycarbonate (Lexan) information (see also pp. 92-93)

General Electric
One Plastics Ave.
Pittsfield, Massachusetts 01201

Butyrate information from

Eastman Chemical Products Incorporated
Kingsport, Tennessee 37662

Flexible vinyl:
—4 mil optically clear, lasts about 1 year in direct sun, 6¢ sq ft, can order by mail:

Wards Farm Catalog.

—15-20 mil, wavy clarity, lasts several years in sun, 8-10¢ sq ft, depending on quantity:

Transparent Products Corporation
Box 15924
L. A., California 90015

Transilwrap West Corporation
1579 Custer Avenue
San Francisco, California 94124

—both of the above companies have a number of different window materials—aluminized mylar, Lexan, plexiglas, etc.

Clear UPVC rigid vinyl, flexible plasticized vinyl from

Scranton Plastic Laminating, Incorporated
Plastic Sheet Products
3216-18 Pittston Avenue
Scranton, Pennsylvania 18505

Skylight Designer's Handbook—excellent booklet on glass and plexiglas details: **My Specialty is Artificial Light.**

O'Keefe's Incorporated
75 Williams Avenue
San Francisco, California 94124

FLEXIBLE SKIN MATERIAL (FOR TENT DOMES)

Armor Shell—dacron or nylon fabric coated with .004 mil PVC. Rolls 54" wide, 100 yards long. Somewhere between 10-20¢ per sq ft. Sample book from

Cooley Incorporated
7300 Artesia Blvd.
Buena Park, California 90620

Weblon—similar to Armor Shell, info from

Astrup Weblon Industrial Fabrics
Cleveland, Ohio 44113

Shelter-Lite—vinyl coated fabrics with polyester substrate. Materials 7026, 7124, 5022 seem appropriate for skin material. 10,000 yards of No. 3022 were used for the double skin of a geodesic dome at a New York World's Fair. Heavy duty, relatively expensive. Info from

Domestic Film Products Corporation
M. L. MacKellar Associates
16250 Meyers Rd.
Detroit, Michigan 48235

Swirles and Company
900 N. Alvarado
L. A., California 1 90026

Coated fabrics (ripstop nylon, vinyl coated fiberglass, silicone rubber coated dacron, etc.) Brochure: "Coated Fabrics for Industry" from

3M Company
Film & Allied Products Division
1601 South Shamrock Avenue
Monrovia, CA 91016

Parachutes: 24 ft. diameter canopies, white and in good condition. $22.50 plus postage and tax from

Security Parachute Co.
P. O. Box 3096
San Leandro, CA 94578

All types of mylar and other skins. Laminates of mylar with dacron scrim, rip stop nylon with metallized mylar one side, etc. Exotic and expensive stuff. Info from

G. T. Schjeldahl Company
Northfield, Minnesota 55057

Glue for fabrics—Belt Bonding Cement

Power Lines
245 W. 25th St.
NYC, New York 10001

Plastic-reinforced industrial fabrics:

Sun Chemical Corporation
185 6th Ave.
Patterson, New Jersey 07524

—See also, Wards and Sears catalogs for canvas.

—See yellow pages for awnings, industrial covers, pool covers, etc.

Acetate, Rayon, Nylon, Saran, Chromspun, etc. information. List of manufacturers and basic principles of manufacturing and use. Brochures, "Man-Made Fiber Fact Book" and "Guide to Man Made Fibers" from

Man-Made Fiber Producers Association
350 5th Avenue
New York, N. Y. 10001

Electric Elevator
The Strongest Natural Cement Manufactured in America.
Remember Well This Address.

FOAM

Good source for low cost foam and good advice on proper technique:

Lloyd Fox
Douglas and Sturgess
730 Bryant Street
San Francisco, California 94107

Pour and spray foam; Speedhide latex fire retardant paint with flame spread of 10, can be sprayed on foam. Pittsburgh Plate Glass is one of the foremost and knowledgeable foam manufacturers. They have some excellent free information on foams and foam paints. Technical information bulletins on Selectron Resin Products and Selectrofoam Resin Products. Brochure "Selectrofoam Rigid Urethane Foam" has comparative chart of all insulating materials. Information from

Materials Supply Company
Box 28307
Sacramento, California 95828   FIRE-FELT

Or PPG Industries
One Gateway Center
Pittsburgh, Pennsylvania 15222
Attn: Resin Products Sales

Ask Dow for information on 3 types of rigid foam: styrofoam, Thurane (polyurethane), and Dorvon.

Dow also makes Deraspan Room Liners, a sandwich panel of styrofoam, faced on both sides with plywood, asbestos board, al aluminum, glasbord. Information and samples from

The Dow Chemical Company
Construction Materials
Midland, Michigan 48640

Rigid foam insulation

Western Foam
464 Victory Avenue
South San Francisco, California 94080

Rigid foam boardstock:

Apache Foam Products
Division of Millmaster-Onyx Corporation
1005 North McKinley Road
Belvidere, Illinois 61008

General Plastics Company
3481 South 35th Street
Tacoma, Washington 98409
Attn: L. W. Schatz

SEALANTS

Thiokol Joints Design Digest for Polysulfide Base Compounds

from Thiokol Chemical Corp.
Box 1296
Trenton, N. J. 08607

Technical data: Extrusion chart shows how much caulk is needed per lin ft of joint; coverage chart shows coverage per gallon for various film thicknesses.

from Harold A. Price Co., Inc.
P. O. Box 1389
Richmond, CA 94802

Brochure: "Seven Steps to Sure Sealing", on Dow Corning 780 Building Sealant

from Nearest Dow or Price

Access info on silicone, polysulfide, polyurethane, and acrylic caulks on p. 90.

Elastron rubber foam coatings

United Paint Manufacturing, Incorporated
1130 E. Sprague Avenue
Spokane, Washington 99202
attn: Technical Coatings

Closed cell neoprene tape 3/16" X 1", stickum one side about 7¢ lin ft, from **Boiler and Pipe Coverings**

A. B. Boyd Company
1235 Howard St.
San Francisco, California 94103

Weatherban one-part sealant, Scotch Seal Metal Sealant, other information from

Adhesives, Coatings and Sealers Division
3M Company
2501 Hudson Rd.
St. Paul, Minnesota 55119

TAPES FOR DOME SEAMS

Fab-Dek: 35 mil Hypalon impregnated with neoprene. 3" wide roll, 11¢/lin ft. Adhesive $4.50/gallon. F.O.B. plant

Miracle Adhesive Corp.
27279 Industrial Boulevard
Hayward, CA 94545
or
250 Pettit Avenue
Bellmore, L.I., N.Y. 11710

Fiberglass tape with isopthalic resin. Brochure from

TAP
1710 E. 12th Street
Oakland, CA 94606

Over 100 various pressure-sensitive tapes. Brochure: "Tapes for Industry" from

3M Company   *Send for Samples.*
320 Shaw Avenue
South San Francisco, CA

Elastron rubber foam coatings and tape for dome seams:

United Paint Manufacturing, Incorporated
1130 E. Sprague Avenue
Spokane, Washington 99202
Attn: Technical Coatings Division

Celastic tape is used by Geodesic Structures, Inc. of Bound Brook, New Jersey for sealing plywood domes. Info on tape from

Degusso Company
No. 2 Pennsylvania Plaza
Madison Square Center
New York, New York

Cybond 4546 polyurethane contact adhesive can be used to adhere flexible tape or thin rubber, then painted with Polane polyurethane paint, from

Fiberlay, Incorporated
1158 Fairview North
Seattle, Washington 98109

Catalog of pressure sensitive tapes. Vinyl, polyethylene, double faced tapes, electrical tape, etc. from

Arno Adhesive Tapes, Incorporated
Michigan City, Indiana 46360

FIBERGLASS

Fiberglass, polypropylene, other fabrics, tapes, resins:

Abe Shuster Fiberglass
6211 Telegraph Avenue
Oakland, California 94609

Excellent fiberglass info, polypropylene, Dynel fabrics, different resins, useful data. Marine Buyer's Guide, 75¢ from

Defender Industries, Incorporated
384 Broadway
New York, New York 10013

*Colossal Bronze Statuary, Tablets, Gates,
Vault Doors, Grilles, Catacomb Fittings, etc.*
FOR PERFECTLY VENTILATING BUILDINGS OF EVERY CHARACTER.

MISCELLANEOUS

Strap and strapping tools:

A. J. Gerrard and Company
400 East Touhy Avenue
Des Plaines, Illinois 60018

Check yellow pages (*strapping*) for closest location, or other companies.

Rust-proof MONEL staples, staple guns:

Duo Fast California
1465 Third Street
San Francisco, California

Extrusions: rubber and synthetic, about 40¢—$1 per ft, making the mold is surprisingly cheap, as low as $40. This means you can design an extrusion tailored to your needs. From

Wefco Rubber Manufacturing
1655 Euclid Avenue
Santa Monica, California 90404   95% Fine

INDUSTRY

Workers of the world, disperse.
Fred Richardson 1970

The report from ALLOY (Spring 1969) is reprinted here in full because the event turned out both significant and unique. A number of personal and inventive journeys made a lasting turn there. Certain issues came clear and common: coyness about money, the uses of structure in events, the bonding of mutual hardship, coherent action without subservience, and our wealth of knowledge and wealth of ignorance about processes closest to us. A faith was built: we have the juice.

—SB

The presence of the world is in us all the time. You don't need television or newspapers to know about the war. You can feel it.

Catch-22 says you can't live in a temporary structure.

You know it isn't working for them when they give it away for people to try out.

Love is joy. Joy is love.

The framework is made of fencepost pipe they cut to size at the factory. We flattened the ends in a vise and bolted them together. The frame for the whole dome cost about $180.

Except temporarily.

There's some far-out pitfall beyond that solution.

The world is one big blank working out its destiny as fast as it can.

So there she was with a 2-day-old baby hanging off her tit directing the construction of the dome.

If there's one thing we're good at, it's painting stuff up.

It's amazing that a hundred hippies could come together and even eat at all.

ALLOY

New Mexico is the center of momentum this year, and maybe for the next several. More of the interesting intentional communities are there. More of the interesting outlaw designers are.

ALLOY was their first programmatic gathering. Conducted at an abandoned tile factory near La Luz, N.M. between the Trinity bomb-test site and the Mescalero Apache reservation, the conference lasted from Thursday to Sunday, March 20-23: the Vernal Equinox.

The event was initiated and organized by Steve Baer with Berry Hickman. Ray Graham donated the use of the land. Baer had in mind a meld of information on Materials, Structure, Energy, Man, Magic, Evolution, and Consciousness, so he invited individuals with amateur or professional interest in these areas to take responsibility for their coverage in the discourse. He also invited

performances by Libre, Drop City, Bill Pearlman's theatre group from Santa Fe, and the Whole Earth Truck Store.

150 people were there. They came from northern New Mexico, the Bay Area, New York, Washington, Carbondale, Canada, Big Sur, and elsewhere. They camped amid the tumbleweed in weather that baked, rained, greyed, snowed, and blew a fucking dust storm. Who were they? (Who are we?). Persons in their late twenties or early thirties mostly. Havers of families, many of them. Outlaws, dope fiends, and fanatics naturally. Doers, primarily, with a functional grimy grasp on the world. World-thinkers, drop outs from specialization. Hope freaks.

Among the voices here are J. Baldwin, Lloyd Kahn, Steve Baer, Dave Evans, Gandalf, Berry Hickman, Stewart Brand, Steve Durkee, Peter Rabbit, Dean Fleming, and brother anonymous.

How can you exchange with 150 people?

It can't get out of control because it already is out of control.

No one wants to be an audience. You can talk if you give them a dessert at the end. You need some way of recording it, otherwise it devolves into an endless circle of rap.

The mike is a ploy to create structure. It doesn't have to be plugged in.

Everybody's assuming the human potential is a static thing.

We're in some incredible bind that we can't even move around enough to know that we're in it. Maybe the only way you can get in the right place is by rattling. If this thing we're doing isn't a big rattle, I don't know what is.

The whole system is going the wrong goddamn way. We're not investigating what we should be investigating.

These relationships between people have not been based on some kind of appreciation of what the structure of the world is.

We want to change ourselves to make things different.

Materials

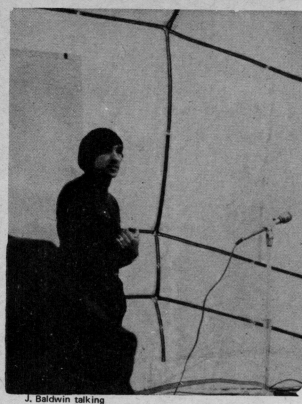

J. Baldwin talking

A temporary structure only needs to meet certain building codes.

You can buy foam crusts really cheap, like 50 cents a pound.

Check out the Encyclopedia of Modern Plastics. McGraw-Hill publishes it.

You could program a structure with built-in squishy places.

Ferro-cemento weighs over 10 pounds a square foot.

The curing is very delicate. It has to cure for like a month.

As it cures it contracts or expands. Concrete will cure under water.

It's fantastically strong stuff. An F-C boat hit a rock going at 12 knots and it smashed the rock.

Have you heard about Maybeck's experiments with gunny sacks? You dip them in concrete and lay them up on the screen like shingles.

The price is starting to come down on foam. The gun is getting better. The fire resistance is getting better.

We've been using silicon car wax on any surface we don't want the foam to stick to.

These foam buildings. They very slowly flow.

Union Carbide can be scrounged for materials.

With Bini-Shell technology you can inflate your foam dome from the ground.

One way of getting a design is by asking the question: How do you use the new materials you have?

There are new kinds of cardboard that approach plywood in strength.

You can stamp out houses like cardboard toys, really cheap. A cardboard house for a family of four would cost $35 for the shell.

So a $35 house breaks down in five years...

With cardboard you can do large things quickly, can do 3-D sketches without drawing plans.

Cardboard is cardboard, not plywood, so if you're going to make something out of cardboard, treat it as cardboard.

If you want to find out about tape, don't ask 3-M; find a man who's taping something together. Manufacturers are the last to find out about their products. Once you've tried something you can sell the information back to them.

As the temperature changes the tape walks.

Black builder's poly lasts 10 times longer than clear poly.

Lloyd Kahn speaking

Structure, energy

Everyone at first feels this kind
of awe for domes and things.

When you talk about energy you talk about the
sun. It's difficult to talk about the sun because
we're in it all the time. You have to feel it in
order to utilize it. One of the real characteristics
of energy is that it comes in lumps, and it takes a
bunch of people to trap it.

Glass isn't clear. It isn't.

What do you mean the sun doesn't go around us?
It's obvious it goes around us.

I have a particular joy in dealing
with things like this.

All your parts have to be in accordance with
those sacred lines or it won't fit together.
The sacred line is no more than an agreement.
It's very helpful if you can describe those
things ahead of time.

You can't patent geometry but
you can patent linkages.

We want to have a factory. We want to put this
cost-rose on everything we produce. What it
cost us. How it was made.

If you can just see into something. You don't
need expensive equipment, that's for sure.

Here I am bullshitting you all. I don't have a
bicycle. I also don't solar heat my house. And
I don't live in a dome. I think maybe I'll sit
down for a while.

Steve Baer talking

I'll tell you anything you want to know and show you anything you want me to show you about domes, but you probably won't build it because you're too lazy.

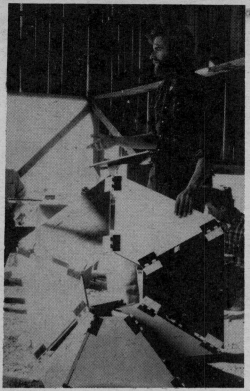

'It does different things.'

What sort of research do we do to use the technology in order to improve our own minds?

We are trying to develop computers that will help human beings to develop computers. The human and computer work symbiotically.

A lot of what goes on in our heads is dictated by what goes on outside. And what goes on outside is subject to our control.

We think there's a whole world open to the human being where he can represent outside himself the symbols and patterns he needs so he can get where he wants.

We've got a new technology for representing symbols.

So all of your thoughts that you had are in there just as you had them when you had the flash.

You've got to know when to stop going in little bits and save yourself up and make a big jump.

Geology means earth logic.

Money is the way that I can easily transfer my energy to you. Economics is the study of transfer of energy in the society.

Robert Frank filming

Dave Evans talking

Man, Evolution, Consciousness

Trust is the reality of the road being cleaned, the trash being emptied.

We're after profit. But we're after the kind of profit we're getting here. Think about what the word profit means for five seconds.

I want to get in and find out what money means. It can make you nervous.

Money makes the transfer so easy that the transfer itself becomes an obsession.

I pray for money.

Kesey says he used to cast his bread on the waters. Now he's saying you got to pick your waters.

How are you going to get money? The thing is that it's fluid. It has to pass between bodies. It doesn't have to be held onto. We're in a transitional world. I've tried to prepare the best water for money to float on.

I smoke therefore I am.

We were brothers before we were dopers.

You can get flashes all kinds of ways. I got a flash once when my parachute didn't open.

You can use dope as a pure design tool.

You don't have to take dope to do things.

You're just saying that there is in reality no guarantee that life will continue. The right to live is a fiction. It's a pretense at a political reality.

Try to understand that although we are different we are all trying to do something. People won't stick with it. This is the tough point. This is the hinge. What are we really doing together. Is it connected? Where is it connected? How is it connected?

Is it possible to be able to have access so that one person is not the only person in the position to know or to do things?

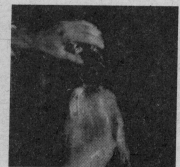

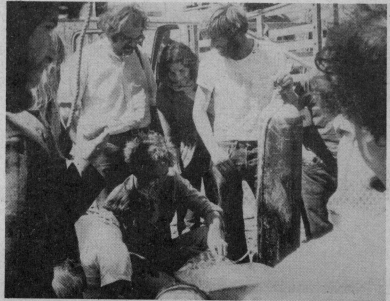

We're involved in an action-reaction game. A lot of the talk is empty cups pouring themselves into one another. Like this. Or what if your cup is full and you try to pour water into it? Look. We assume that we know everything, rather than emptying our cup. Teach me, for I know nothing.

Magic is the manipulation of matter by unseen forces. You can see unseen forces if you want to take the time. How many people here could build a car?. How many could refine gas? Could you take care of yourself on the lowest, simplest level? Before we go solving the world's problems I think it's important to know right where we are on this ground.

Steve Durkee blowing helium bubbles

If you've got to junk everything that's been written in order to find yourself in the world, do it.

Am I this 6-foot body or am I something else that could exist beyond it? If we could get enough information maybe we could go beyond the flesh envelope.

You've got to be dissatisfied. You have to know that it's not good enough. It's not giving the juice, you know? The other thing is you have to know there is a possibility. You can grasp the living rod.

The sly man takes the pill. The problem with that is you may be the sly man who opens the door, but there may be nothing there when you open it.

There's a lot of people who want the Apocalypse. Instead of looking at it as the death force, there's a possibility of the emergence of something new, a re-shuffling of the deck.

In times this turbulent the world is ready to follow any man who feels good.

Evolution is at work here as strongly as anywhere.

The main design element of evolution is variability. The times are wierd and a lot of the old forms are hanging on stiff and tight. All of us are going out and trying different things. Each community has its own notions of how to do its own civilization. The more communities the better. Big ones, little ones, urban, rural. travelling, money, no-money. With a lot of them happening, some sets do better than other sets.

You can study the evolution of man by the evolution of his tools. You can study the evolution of tools by the evolution of man.

There's a paradox. Isolation leads to over-specialization. But you have to isolate yourself somewhat in order to make your scene different than the others. Maybe it's a balance. Maybe discrete mixing events like Alloy can help.

You can randomize your behavior a little. Everybody has a notion of who they are, their character, and all their decisions converge toward that notion as if they meet at the grave. With some decisions, why not flip a coin?

Take the path you haven't taken before.

That was the Holy Grail step. When the knights left the Round Table in search of the Holy Grail, each man entered the forest where it looked most impassible to him.

Whatever frightens you, do it. That fear is a valuable key.

Evolution is any dynamically self-organizing system. The process improves itself without external influence. Everything's inherent. Every misfit carries some of the load of making the whole more fit.

Evolution and cybernetics are going to come together. This is the edge of knowledge right now, and it's right at the heart of education, and the schools don't know it.

There you are sawing away on your violin, and every now and then you catch a piece of the symphony. The trick is, when that happens, not to drop your violin.

Intention is a wierd thing in evolution. I don't think anybody understands it, but we're doing it a lot. We're increasingly putting our finger in the pie, and we are the pie, and the finger, and the putting.

It's all those choices that we make. Then we give those to the next people.

If you want to try a new way, you've got to build something.

What is Design?

There really is no better introduction to all that is admirable in design. Baer had to remind me of the book: I had forgotten how much I owe to it. It is full of the kind of lore and wisdom that you immediately take for your own.
—SB

The book is wonderful. Here is a man trying to tell the truth about design and about our lives and civilization. I never heard of him, when I read his book I can't understand why.
Steve Baer

What is Design?
Paul Jacques Grillo
1960; 238 pp.

OUT OF PRINT

from:
Paul Theobald and Company
5 N. Wabash Avenue
Chicago, Illinois 60602

Don't work for success, whether success to you means a degree, position, money, or honours. You cannot reverse the process of nature: since no fruit in spring can produce flowers in the fall, you cannot visualize the harvest before the seed matures into a healthy, full-grown plant. A hot house may grow faster products, but none that can compete with the authentic product of the soil. This attitude will force you to give "no" for an answer more often than "yes", if you are concerned only with the integrity of your production. Then your "YES" will be uncompromisingly sincere. The worst lie is the lie you give to yourself as an excuse for success.

Burn your idols once in a while, and start all over again.

Flout the rules as often as you can in a masterly way. Recipes are for poor cooks. Great chefs make them. The canvas of rules and codes that you have had to learn must be transgressed with vision for any art to be born.

Finally, during all your life as an artist, learn through painstaking experimentation, exercise, and practice, how to acquire a masterly knowledge of your craft.

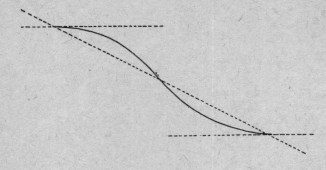

IN DESIGN, THE SHORTEST DISTANCE BETWEEN TWO POINTS IS NOT THE STRAIGHT LINE, BUT THE SLALOM

Slaloms are curves of natural acceleration and deceleration that represent trajectories *constantly controlled by man.*

A ballistic missile obeying only initial thrust and gravity will describe an orbit mathematically perfect of the conic section family. But as soon as man sits at the controls, he will make his own orbit, his *slalom.*

Curves described by a man in movement——a car, a bicycle——on a flat surface, are two dimension slaloms, or curves of the second order that may be approximately analyzed in quadratic equations.

A moutain climber, an airplane, a submarine——as well as a skier—— describe third order slaloms that may be analyzed in cubic equations.

The interest of slalom curves for the designer lies in the fact that they are all *curves of least effort,* and thus represent the most *economical* pattern of flow.

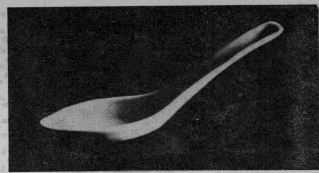

You may buy this eternally contemporary piece of design in any authentic Chinese hardware shop.

prevailing winds

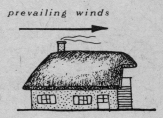

The Normans, great seafarers before settling down to farming, have devised their farmhouses exactly like the hulls of their ships, anchored them upside down on the land, the bow to the wind and the stern sheltered toward the east. They are like ships that heave-to in a gale. The single chimney crowns the western end of the roof and draws at the least breeze, while the eastern end is wide open like the captain's quarters in the stern of a galleon.

The Ganges Shark (Platypodon gangeticus)

McDonnell Voodoo F-101A (1954)

Design Methods

The discipline of design is misunderstood by many people. This book is going to help explain things. The author briefly presents some of the obvious design failures in our industrial society, such as traffic congestion, noise pollution, etc., and says. . . ."These need not be regarded as accidents of nature or as acts of God, to be passively accepted: they can instead be thought of as human failures to design for conditions brought about by the products of designing. Many will resist this view because it places too much responsibility on designers and too little upon everyone else. If such is the case then it is high time that everyone who is affected by the oversights and limitations of designers got in on the design act."

The book outlines traditional approaches. It then goes ahead and gives a really useful review of thirty five recently developed strategies, a brief description of each, and a way of determining which will likely be most useful to you. Many of the strategies are ways of organizing your information so that your intuition can be well enough informed to act. Several of the strategies are mainly concerned with preparing your head so that it may intuit effectively. Methods of analyzing the results are also presented.

As far as I know, this book is the only overall collection and review of strategies. I see it as a truly useful tool. I've ordered one myself.

[Reviewed by Jay Baldwin]

Design Methods
J. Christopher Jones
1970; 407 pp.

$14.50 postpaid

from:
John Wiley & Sons, Inc.
605 Third Ave.
New York, N.Y. 10016

or WHOLE EARTH CATALOG

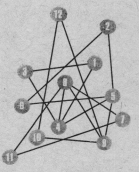 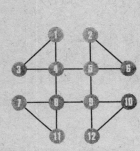

The complicated pattern of the network on the left can be transformed into the simple pattern on the right by re-arranging the nodes. This is analogous to the "change of set" which can enable one to solve a previously insoluble problem.

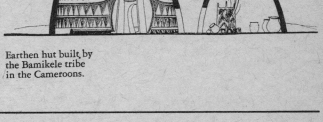

Earthen hut built by the Bamikele tribe in the Cameroons.

'I remember a priest explaining the zig-zag arch to me: "Evil is like a rhinoceros. It always charges in straight lines. We break the line of the bridge so that evil cannot cross, but falls over the edge to drown in the deep water in the middle".' From A Portrait of Japan, Laurens van der Post, 1968.

Thinking from Several Viewpoints

This is similar to 'thinking in parallel planes' but is directed at the solution to the design problem instead of at the process of finding it. At its most elementary it seems to be the stating of objectives by describing the product as something that 'provides a means' of doing something else.

(a) study the design situation

(b) provisionally identify the needs that the design is to satisfy

(c) identify and analyze the Primary Functional Need (this is the need that if not properly satisfied makes the fulfilment of all other needs pointless)

(d) explore alternative principles upon which a means of satisfying the primary need could be based

(e) complete, in outline only, a design capable of satisfying both primary and secondary needs

(f) review the functional effectiveness of this design

(g) review the material and work content in producing the design

(h) review component quality, i.e. freedom from welding distortion, refinements, etc.

The Design of Design

It's superficially a book for design engineers, but should be useful to anyone engaged in the design of physical objects or strategies. Simple and basic. More advanced treatment of design techniques gets you into computers and very sophisticated decision making theory. The main trip is concentrated on getting your head straight so that design decisions of any sort can be made intelligently. There's a good bit of practical advice concealed in a slurry of English Humour. The only book of its type that we know of. Among the better points:

Concentration and then relaxation is the common pattern behind most creative thinking.

Beware of intrinsic impossibilities.

Beware of pseudo-technical words. [He means words like "sturdy," "big", "beautiful", etc.]

Define problems in figures or configurations.

Aim at continuity of energy.

He really gets to the center of the modern-technology-versus-New-Mexico-Funk argument:

If the design of a particular machine or production line is based on the way the process was originally done by hand, it is unlikely to be the final form. The feeding forward by mechanizing a style that was handy when only hands were available is doomed, in the long run, to be superceded by the feeding back of ideas and materials from the physical sciences. Beware of well-dressed arts and crafts.

[Reviewed by J. Baldwin]

The Design of Design
Gordon L. Glegg
1969; 93 pp.

$7.95 postpaid

from:
Cambridge University Press
32 East 57th Street
New York, N. Y. 10022

or WHOLE EARTH CATALOG

Invention	Inventor
Safety razor	Traveller in corks
Kodachrome films	Musician
Ballpoint pen	Sculptor
Automatic telephone	Undertaker
Parking meter	Journalist
Pneumatic tyre	Veterinary surgeon
Long-playing record	Television engineer

You are taken out to lunch and everyone is anxious to hear you tell them how a "few adjustments" or possibly "some electronics" will solve all the difficulties. You have to break it to them that everything is wrong in principle.

cart wheel   bicycle wheel

the Forth bridge   the Severn bridge

Suspension bridge designers thought at first that the major problem would be the load, and learned by spectacular experience that it was really the stability.

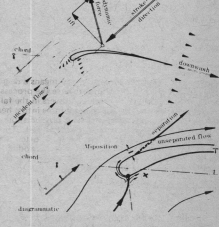

Structure, Form and Movement

The usual procedure is that R&D comes up with a new process, it's implemented for several years, and then some biologist says Hey did you know porpoises did that? (or snakes did that, or bees or elm seeds). And everybody says My, my, ain't Nature smart.

Herr Hertel and colleagues are trying to reverse the order, learn from nature first, save time and stay humble. (This approach now has a name, "bionics"; a book by that title that's around is terrible.)

This book may be too expensive for its direct usefulness, but it thoroughly displays the approach that research may take to bugs, birds, fish, etc. for yield in navigation, flight, streamlining, etc.
—SB

Fig. 52 Beginning of take-off = wing stroke forward and down
Incident flow - downwash - forces.
Below: stagnation point; flow around the leading edge.

Golden eagle. Leaping off. Legs flexed at left, extended at right

The hand remiges of birds are masterfully perfected to obviate flutter:
—The hollow cross section of the supporting frame consisting of the feather quill is continuous over the entire lenth and approximates a cylinder, which resists torsion well. This cross section also improves resistance to bending.
—The ultralight construction of the vanes ensures minimum moment of mass about the quill axis.
—Variations in aerodynamic forces during oscillation affect 25% of the profile depth. Consequently, the form of the remiges, with narrower anterior vane sections and broader posterior vane sections, is appropriate for aeroelastic reasons. In the primary feather shown in figure 65, the resultant of aero—dynamic forces lies behind the shaft.

Structure, Form and Movement
Heinrich Hertel
1963, 1966; 251 pp.

$19.95 postpaid

from:
Van Nostrand Reinhold Co.
450 W. 33rd St.
New York, N.Y. 10001

Design for the Real World

Industrial design is in deservedly bad odor lately, and this book will give you many of the reasons——most of them having to do with pandering to self-exaggerating marketplace fashion, the disposable environment.

Victor Papanek is a Bush Designer. He prefers to hang out in Third-World places, where the problems are physical and serious, and where native design genius can be learned and applied to them using industrial materials. This book works on distinguishing between real and phoney design problems, and their solutions.

—SB

Design for the Real World
Victor Papanek
1971

$2.25 postpaid

from:

Bantam Books Inc.
666 Fifth Ave.
New York, N.Y. 10019

or WHOLE EARTH CATALOG

Artificial burrs, 40cm long, made of bio-degradable plastic and coated with plant seeds and a growth-boosting solution. To reverse errosion cycles in arid regions. Student designed by James Herold and Jolan Truan, Purdue University.

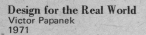

An ambulance can cost as much as $28,500. Where are well designed, low cost inserts that would convert any station wagon to ambulance use during a national emergency? With the number and prices of ambulances now, this particular national emergency began about 20 years ago!

Radio receiver designed for Third World usage. It is made of a used juice can, and uses paraffin wax and a wick as power source. The rising heat is converted into enough energy to power this non-selective receiver. Once the wax is gone, it can be replaced by more wax, paper, dried cow dung, or anything else that will burn. Manufacturing costs, on a cottage industry basis: 8 cents. Designed by Victor Papanek and George Seeger at North Carolina State College.

For a long time, I don't remember how long, but it was years, literally years, I could not get all the parts of speech together. Or if I could get them together, I could not get them together in the proper sequence. One week I could speak sentences that had everything in place except the verbs. I just could not remember verbs. I couldn't say, "I am going to town." "I am town," was the best that I could do, and it was maddening. The next week it would be nouns, or adjectives, just . . . missing, that was all. Like not having enough tools or parts to finish putting something together with. And so I would just not say anything to anybody. I wandered lonely through the world muttering "Cheeseburger" now and then, or "Where?" or "When?" or "Why?" Of course my silence was not true silence. In my mind there was utter chaos. My mind never stopped. Day and night it went on and on and on, remembering everything that ever happened, every conversation I had ever heard, playing them over and over, with new embellishments and adornments each new time.

The year it was at its worst I lived in San Francisco. There was supposed to be an earthquake that year. All the talk was of earthquakes, earthquakes. I was into earthquakes in this really heavy way. Earthquakes and Edgar Cayce. I was convinced there was going to be an earthquake, that California was going to tumble into the sea. And my trip was, I wanted it to happen. I wanted California to fall into the sea, and I wanted to fall in with it, to be swallowed up by a thing so big, so huge, so utterly enormous that I would disappear into absolute nothingness. I wanted to see heave and slide and fall with the greatest roar and rumble the world had ever known. And I wanted to go down with it because then I wouldn't have to think about the parts of things. If the parts would not come together and function for me, then let them fly apart, scatter and be gone weightless through the universe. Let freedom reign! Let nothing matter! That was my belief.

Well, of course, as we all know, there was no earthquake, California didn't fall into the sea. I was disappointed but sobered a good deal by the months I spent in anticipation of it. My head felt clearer. I began to speak simple sentences again. I got interested in art. I got interested in the possibility of Atlantis rising again, and I wondered what I ought to do about it. I even sat down one day and wrote a little pamphlet called, "What To Do If Atlantis Rises," and had a few hundred copies printed up. I tried to sell the copies, and when no one would buy them I started giving them away to people passing on the street.

(continued)

Science and Civilization in China

Joseph Needham is a renowned biologist who travelled into unexplored regions of Chinese technological history and became a yet more renowned historian and interpreter of what is for most of us the back of the planet. His series is awesome in size and depth; he's done the mining, but you've got to refine the ore to suit your own purposes. One purpose I know was Vic Lovell's, who found in Vol. I a rich lode of information on Taoism and how its influence helped the Chinese discover and utilize some technology long before the West and also overlook or never utilize other stuff that the West seized on. Another purpose might be taking some of the mechanical inventions of old China—from man-kites to water-wheels—and applying them to the hand technology of intentional communities. There's no source like the source in these matters.

The quotes and illustrations to the right are from Vol. IV, Part 2: Mechanical Engineering. All the volumes are available from the publisher and WHOLE EARTH CATALOG.

—SB

Science and Civilization in China

Joseph Needham
Vol. I   Introductory Orientations, 1954: $17.50
Vol. II   History of Scentific Thought: $32.50
Vol. III Mathematics and Science of the Heavens and the Earth, 1959: $47.50
Vol. IV   Pt. 1 Physics. 1962: $27.50
          Pt. 2 Mechanical Engineering, 1965.
          $39.50 postpaid

from:
Cambridge University Press, 32 East 57th St., New York, N.Y. 10022
or
WHOLE EARTH CATALOG

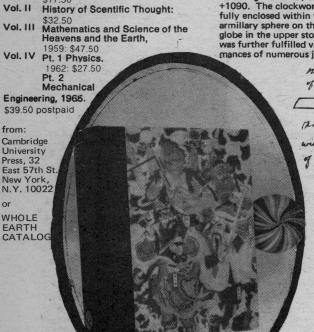

Fig. 650. Pictorial reconstruction of the astronomical clock-tower built by Su Sung and his collaborators at Khaifeng in Honan, then the capital of the empire, in +1090. The clockwork, driven by a water-wheel, and fully enclosed within the tower, rotated an observational armillary sphere on the top platform and a celestial globe in the upper storey. Its time-announcing function was further fulfilled visually and audibly by the performances of numerous jacks mounted on the eight super-imposed wheels of a time-keeping shaft and appearing at windows in the pagoda-like structure at the front of the tower. Within the building, some 40 ft. high, the driving wheel was provided with a special form of of escapement, and the water was pumped back into the tanks periodically by manual means. The time annunciator must have included conversion gearing, since it gave 'unequal' as well as equal time signals, and the sphere probably also had this (see p. 456).

Su Sung's treatise on the clock, the Hsin I Hsiang Fa Yao, constitutes a classic of horological engineering. Orig. drawing by John Christiansen. The staircase was actually inside the tower, as in the model of Wang Chen-To (7).
The historical significance of the mechanical rotation of an astronomical instrument (a clock-drive) has already been discussed in Vol. 3, pp.359ff.;cf. also p.492 below.

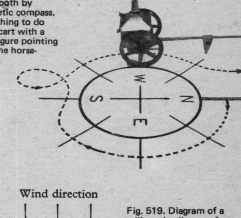

Allusion has already been made to the 'south-pointing carriage' (chih nan chhe) in Sect. 26i on magnetism, since it was long confused, both by Chinese and Westerners, with the magnetic compass. We know now, however, that it had nothing to do with magetism, but was a two-wheeled cart with a train of gears so arranged as to keep a figure pointing due south, no matter what excursions the horse-drawn vehicle made from this direction.

Fig. 707. Page of drawings sent by Cayley to Dupuis-Delcourt in 1853 illustrating an improved Chinese heilcopter top which would mount more than 90 ft. into the air. From Hubbard & Ledeboer (I). This was the direct ancestor of the helicopter rotor and the godfather of the aeroplane propeller.

Fig. 689. Typical Chinese horizontal windmill working a square-pallet chain-pump in the salterns at Taku, Hopei (king, 3). The fore-and-aft mat-and-batten type sails luff at a certain point in the cycle and oppose no resistance as they come back into the eye of the wind (see diagram on p. 559)

Fig. 519. Diagram of a sailing wheelbarrow from van Braam Houkgeest (+1797), showing the batten sail and multiple sheets so characteristic of Chinese nautical pratice.(cf. Sect. 29g below).

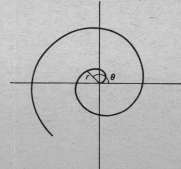

Science and Civilization

My favorite vol. of Needham (Sci & Civ in China) is Vol II which has the chapter on Taoism (not Vol I as you have it in the Fall 69 Catalogue) That chapter tells everything from how to perform coitus interruptus (haven't tried it but the directions are clear) to the origin of won ton soup (used to be an alchemical elixir)

Mark Engel
Ben Lomond, CA

A Dictionary of Named Effects and Laws in Chemistry, Physics and Mathematics

This is the closest thing to a shortcut to fundamental science that we're likely to find. A book of purest ingredients, the grand or peculiar connections that were so new and special that they got a word to themselves, the name of the finder.

A truck full of mental axes, chisels, sewing needles, screwdrivers, nail clippers, chainsaws, calipers, sand paper, coffee urns, telescopes, dynamite, and glue.

—SB

A Dictionary of Named Effects and Laws in Chemistry, Physics and Mathematics
D.W.G. Ballentyne, D.R. Lovett
1958, 1961, 1970; 335 pp.

$9.50 postpaid

from:
Halstead Press
One Wiley Drive
Somerset, N.J. 08873

or
Halstead Press
Western Distribution Center
1530 South Redwood Road
Salt Lake City, UT 84104

Gibbs' Paradox

Experience suggests that as two diffusing gases become more and more alike the change in entropy due to diffusion should get smaller and smaller, approaching zero as the gases become identical. The fact that this is not the case is known as the Gibbs' Paradox. Bridgman explained it in the following fashion: in principle at least it is possible to distinguish the dissimilar gases by a series of experimental operations. In the limit, however, when the gases become identical there is a discontinuity in the operations in as much that no instrumental operation exists by which the gases may be distinguished. Hence a discontinuity in a function such as change in entropy is to be expected.

Hubble Effect

Distant galaxies show, in their spectra, red shifts which increase proportionally with the distance of the galaxy. This effect is consistent with the hypothesis of an expanding universe.

Huygens' Principle. (Huygens-Fresnel Principle)

Every point of a wave can be considered as the centre of a new elementary wave. The resultant wave produced by the interference of all these elementary waves is identical with the original wave.

Archimedes' Principle

When a body is immersed in a fluid there is an apparent loss in weight which is equal to the weight of fluid displaced.

Archimedes' Spiral

A point, moving uniformly along a line which rotates uniformly about a fixed point describes a spiral of Archimedes. The equation is: $r = a\theta$.

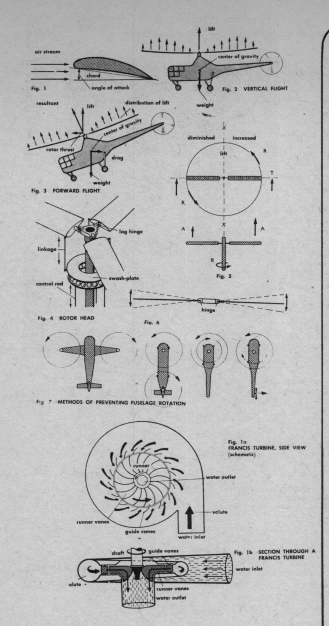

The Way Things Work

Best book for the bathroom we've seen. Nibble your way to knowledge of technology. Each two pages of the book is a bunch of text and a bunch of diagrams on all the big and little gadgets and processes you can think of, ball-point pens to data-processing. If you develop time travel, it might be interesting to take this book back to the sixteenth century and leave it under some European's pillow. (Now think about contact with alien civilizations.)

—SB

The Way Things Work
1967; 590 pp.

$9.95 postpaid

from:
Simon & Schuster
630 Fifth Avenue
New York, N.Y. 10020

or WHOLE EARTH CATALOG

The Engineers' Illustrated Thesaurus

I like this book better than **The Way Things Work**
It lists concepts, structures, and processes strictly by function instead of by object. So as you page through, the elements start adding up in your head in bizarre combinations. Let's see: if we attached a mercury switch to a geared-down rotator on the windmill and connected it to a strobe light, then whenever our heads kaleidoscoped we'd know the wind was blowing 20 miles an hour and we'd halt all traffic on the pedestrial suspension bridge before it went harmonic and tossed all our visitors in the canyon.

—SB

[Suggested by Steve Durkee]

The Engineers' Illustrated Thesaurus
Herbert Herkimer
1952; 557 pp.

OUT OF PRINT

from:
Chemical Publishing Co., Inc.
200 Park Ave. So.
New York, N.Y. 10003

or WHOLE EARTH CATALOG

And then one night a strange thing happened. I was walking through that little park on Clay Street in San Francisco, that steep one with all those old Victorian houses around it, and I gave away a copy of my pamphlet and wound up in conversation with the guy who took it, this young spade kid who had the most intense brown eyes I have ever seen. And before long a couple of other people came up and joined us, and there I was, sitting on a park bench with six or eight or maybe even ten or twelve people around, some of them on the ground, some of them just standing with their arms folded, listening to me come on about Atlantis, about my experience with the earthquake, and my difficulties with language. And they listened. And when I tried to quit talking they wouldn't let me. And finally they invited me over to someone's pad, and I kept on talking. I have no idea now what I said, but I talked all night. By morning when someone served tea and toast, there must have been fifty people in that apartment, and it was as if we'd all come through a magnificent thing together. They were as amazed as I was. No one knew what had happened, and yet, everyone knew. And it was a grand and beautiful thing. All I did was talk. I didn't know what I was saying myself, half the time. It was as if the Lord had taken my tongue and used it Himself, as if I was but a mere vehicle for His message. I said wild stuff, crazy stuff, stuff no one had ever said before, and the people just could not believe what they were hearing.

They began to come to me individually for advice, and I advised them to do incredible things. One young man came and said he was having sexual problems, and he asked me what he should do. I knew instantly. He should run for political office. I told him that, and it changed his life overnight. I don't know why I told him that, and I don't know for sure if he went away and ran for office. But I did see him some months later and he said everything was fine, just fine, and he shook my hand and he hugged and thanked me for the advice. A middle-aged black man who had come into a good deal of money came to me just fraught with worry and asked how he should spend it. I asked him where he had grown up. Dothan, Alabama, he said and I said good. Take that money and hire five hundred other black men, and all of you go rent or buy the finest black suits, with black hats, black canes, and black top coats and black sun glasses, and starting on a Monday morning begin drifting into Dothan one at a time, every hour or two another one of you just sort of amble in and walk down the street, and just kind of look in the windows as if nothing much is going on, and don't speak to each other, act as if the town is not slowly filling up with five hundred well-dressed spades, a few at a time, maybe seventy-five a day, and do that for a week, until by Saturday there's all five hundred of you there on Main Street, walking around. And this spade _did_ that. He actually did it, and I saw him about a year later and he came up and shook my hand and said Man, you are fantastic.

By then, of course, I began to believe I was. People would come and listen to me, and later pat me on the shoulder and say to me, trust it, man, whatever far-out thing it is that you've got going, trust it. And that's what made the difference. I got so I could trust it. It was like having a big bully who's always picking on you, pushing you around, snatching your cap off your head and getting into your lunchbox and now and then actually beating up on you on your way home from school suddenly turning out to be your best friend. It was like help from some source you never had counted on before. It was like getting access to some demon that's always scared you so bad you've kept a tight lid on his cage. And then somehow you go so crazy you lose your grip on his cage door and out he comes, ripping and snorting, only instead of eating you up or beating your ass he says hello boss, whose ass would you like me to whip for you today. And off you go, the two of you, heading down the road looking for some action. And what you know as you go along is that no matter what the action is, you're going to be good at it, you know you're going to come out on top of whatever you run into because you've got this big demon out there working for you because he digs you for letting him out of his cage.

It's like this kid, comes up to me one time in Seattle and says his family has kicked him out because they thought he was queer. He asked me what I thought he ought to do. Without hesitation I told him I thought he ought to go and read _Finnegan's Wake_ into a tape recorder, then call his family up long distance and when they answer turn the record on and walk away and leave them to deal with it. And that kid did that, and I saw him some time later and he shook my hand and gave me this big grin and said _thank you, man, thank you._

It's a far-out thing, having people come up to you and say thanks for helping them. I guess one of the reasons my life went sour again was I got to liking that part of it too much. I got so I waited for it to happen, and when it didn't it would bug me. There was a recognition I wanted from people that was almost like having a name again, and sourness was the only possible consequence of such craving to be named. That wonderful period of my life went away, and was followed by another time of despair. It was that despair that drove me on into a truly committed effort to forget my name, to forget everything I could recognize myself by. It's painful, laborious work to lose your attachment to identify, but I believe that once I destroy the manuscript telling my early history, I will have gone past the last serious obstacle to becoming Infinitely Nameless. I don't want to say that categorically. To say it categorically would be a speculation upon the future, and the future is of no concern to one who is truly nameless. I can say—— and this is a confession—— that I have got this close to destroying that manuscript twice before, and each time was unable to go through with it. In 1962 I got to the front entrance of the library and couldn't go in. In 1966 I made it to the very stacks where the Master's Theses are kept, and turned around and left empty-handed. So it's not for me to say how this new effort to burn the manuscript will turn out. All I know is that I'm on my way to the University again, that I'm still trying, and that I believe that if one perseveres in a righteous cause, he must eventually succeed.

Introduction to Engineering Design

Out of a whole section of books on design in the Engineering Library at Stanford, this book looked far the best. Recently Steve Baer (dome and solar designer) came across it on our editing tables, sat down and paged, then got up and hurriedly wrote a letter to a friend about the book and its author. I asked Steve to pick out some useful quotes and pictures and he wouldn't. "Look anywhere you open it," he advised, then ordered a copy.

Contents of the book include: The Engineering Problem Situation, Design Project Organization, Information and the Need Analysis, Identification of the Problems, Information Sources, Synthesis of Alternatives, Estimation and Order-of-Magnitude Analysis, Engineering and Money, Preliminary Design, Engineering Problem Modeling, The Iconic Model, Conceptual Representation, Expansion of the Criterion Function, Checking in Engineering Design, Optimization, etc., etc.

—SB

Introduction to Engineering Design
Thomas T. Woodson
1966; 434 pp.

$12.50 postpaid

from:
McGraw-Hill Book Company
Princeton Road
Hightstown, N.J. 08520
Manchester Road
Manchester, Missouri 63062
8171 Redwood Highway
Novato, Calif. 94947

or WHOLE EARTH CATALOG

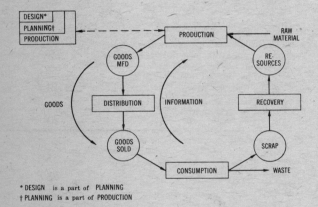

* DESIGN is a part of PLANNING
† PLANNING is a part of PRODUCTION

Fig. 3.7 The production-consumption cycle, showing the place of engineering design.

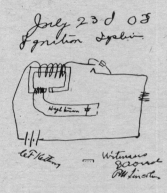

Fig. 6.2 A sketch that changed automobile ignition. (Courtesy General Motors Corp.)

WATER SUPPLY FOR MOUNTAIN CAMP

For another simple example, let us estimate how we would bring water from a running stream into a tank (let's say a 50-gallon gravity tank) to supply water for a vacation cabin in the woods. A natural supply point is 100 ft away upstream, guaranteeing among other things a clean, continuous water supply. Our problem is transport. Shall we use pipe, an open rock-lined channel in the ground, or a wooden flume or trough? See Figure 7.4. As we think about this, we discard the open channel in the ground as too easily contaminated. The pipe could be laid on the ground; and the wood flumes could be suspended from tree trunks and possibly covered as shown by the dashed "board" in the illustration. Thus, we have two reasonable ways of doing this job; the questions now concern cost and convenience.

Next we check the sizes needed. If we wanted the 50-gal. tank filled in 15 min, we would need a flow of about 4 gal/min. This is a stream of water about as big as a person's finger when the water is flowing two feet per second, as shown by the equation in the footnote† deriving the cross-sectional area, A, of the stream.

This area would require a pipe one inch in diameter. If we were using the wood "vee" channels, we would need two boards each about three inches wide to avoid splashing over, or one-half board-foot per running foot of channel (per foot of channel length). (A board-foot is one square foot of wood, one inch or less thick.)

Now we need to arrive at costs. The most convenient reference is a broad-coverage catalog (such as that of Sears, Roebuck) in which wood, metal, and other supplies can be found listed at retail prices. Of course, one can also phone the retail plumbing or lumber suppliers. In any case, we find

Wood: 15¢—20¢ / board-foot in the sizes we need
1 in. iron pipe: 30¢ / ft
¾ in. copper pipe: 58¢ /ft (One size smaller than iron pipe for the same flow rate.)

Assuming one-half board-foot for each running foot of wood channel, the comparisons are

Wood: 10¢ /running foot, materials only
Iron: 30¢ /running foot, materials only
Copper: 60¢ /running foot, materials only

Since we would do the work ourselves, the cost of labor is disregarded, and it seems that wood should be our choice. On one final check though, we ask whether these are all the choices. Someone suggests plastic pipe, so we look that up: It is corrosion-resistant, flexible, easily connected, sanitary; it has a smooth interior; it could be in one piece and simply laid on the ground. It seems to be a natural choice. The price of ¾-in. diameter plastic pipe is 10¢ /ft; 1-in. diameter is 16¢ /ft. Considering the labor needed with wood or iron pipe, or the cost of copper tubing, and the plastic's sanitary advantages, the plastic pipe (high-density polyethylene) is certainly the preferred choice.

Thus our final estimate is the use of this plastic tubing, probably ¾-in. diameter at 10¢ /ft.

† A = Q/V (area = flow/velocity)
where
Q = 4 gal/min = 1000 cu in./min (1 gal - 231 cu in.)
V = 2 ft/sec = 24 in./(1/60 min) = 1500 in./min

$$A = \frac{1000 \text{ cu in./min}}{1500 \text{ in./min}} = 2/3 \text{ sq. in.}$$

Fig. 7.4 Possible water channel sections. Water supply project for mountain cabin.

Technology and Change

The subtitle of this book is "The impact of invention and innovation on American social and economic development" The author studies this area in the light of experience in several industries, one of which is the building industry, where change has been slow in coming. This book will be of interest to its intended readership in industry. But on a larger scale, it offers an answer to that teeth-gnashing question: "Why does the 'establishment' resist change?" Or for that matter, "Why does everybody resist change?" This is one of the neatest and best explanations I've seen (perhaps because it so closely matches my experiences as a Professional Designer). It will be interesting for those who wish to better know their Corporation As An Enemy as well as to those who wish to equip themselves and their organization to better deal with inevitable and intentional change. One of his more interesting points is that "revolutionaries" are often a reactionary force instead of being truly revolutionary; they are the conservatives, especially where technological change is concerned. Lots of subversive stuff here. Recommended reading for changebringers.

[Reviewed by Jay Baldwin.
Suggested by Steve Baer]

no longer available

Technology and Change
Donald A. Schon
1967; 248 pp.

$2.25 postpaid

from:
Delta Publishing Co., Inc.
750 Third Avenue
New York, N. Y. 10017

or WHOLE EARTH CATALOG

The crucial form of experiment demanded by the technological, institutional and normative changes of our time is experiment in norms and objectives. The erosion of the objectives of the Technological Program leaves us with more information than we can handle and requires the attempt to create situations in which new objectives can emerge.

Unexpected success is no less destructive of the rational view of corporate activity than is unexpected failure. When the addition of carbon black turns out to increase the strength of rubber; when the book-mending tape turns out to have a multiplicity of unexpected consumer uses; when the new plastic, designed for a cheaper molding process, turns out to perform well in a completely different application—the corporate manager can only react with a wry smile. In ways he did not understand, and was unable to state before the fact, things have gone well; but what has he learned that will prepare him to cope with the *next time*?

Corporate behavior is based on regular, orderly, linear, predictable processes——the extension of the industrial manufacturing process itself. How is it to absorb invention?

What used to be stable divisions in our community are no longer stable:

—the division between education and work, and with it, the view of the young as learning and the old as established;
—the division between labor and business;
—the old regionalism;
—the old divisions between race and race and class and class;
—the division between the change-oriented outcasts (inventor, poet therapist) and the stable society;
—the division between "good" creative private enterprise and "evil" controlling Government.

The call to Revolt has as much appeal as the call to Return. It is an alternate response to the destruction of the myth of stability. In effect, it says that the old objectives are hollow and inadequate. There is oppression, slavery, humiliation, constraint and injustice. There is no Promised Land in sight. Revolt against these things! The call to revolt need not produce its own image of a Promised Land. It takes its image from the present against which it reacts. It gets its concreteness from the life it refuses to accept and is, in this sense, *a form of conservatism*.

If we cannot be inattentive to change of objectives in our society and cannot accept the silent calls of return and revolt, what is left? How do we ever tolerate and stand up to change in objectives?

Ideas, Inventions, and Patents

Patents are one of those facets of the establishment that both baffle and infuriate people. It's a complex business. This book gives the clearest and most comprehensive explanation of the whole patent bit that I have ever seen. It is at the same time, a reference book intended to help you understand patents, and an unintentional denunciation of the whole process. The author shows why we have to have patents, what good they do, and how to get one. He also shows how to get around patents, how long you have to wait, and how much it will cost. He reveals the human biases involved in the patent office, and admits that the government is so poorly organized that they may issue conflicting patents to two different parties at the same time! The book is indexed in a way that permits you to easily find answers to questions. If you need to know something about patents, this is it.

[Reviewed by Jay Baldwin]

Ideas, Inventions, and Patents
Robert A. Buckles
1957; 270 pp.

$12.50 postpaid

from:
John Wiley & Sons, Inc.
605 Third Ave.,
New York, N.Y. 10016

or WHOLE EARTH CATALOG

As to what constitutes prior knowledge of an invention in this country, the courts interpret the term "invention" here in its restricted legal sense as meaning a completed and operable device or system. Mere knowledge of the conception of an idea for an invention is not sufficient prior knowledge to defeat an applicant, or patent, of one who is the "first inventor" in the true sense of being the first person to make or complete the invention in operative form. This interpretation was handed down by the United States Court of Customs and Patent Appeals in a test case brought to clarify the meaning of this section of the Patent Act of 1952.

•

As soon as the invention is conceived the inventor should sit down and write out a detailed description, complete with a drawing where the subject lends itself to graphical representation, and as soon thereafter as possible he should disclose and explain his invention to someone who can understand it and who will sign his name and the date at the end of the written description, as a witness to the disclosure on that date. Very often this will be the earliest date that the inventor can prove, even though he may have conceived the invention in his mind much earlier.

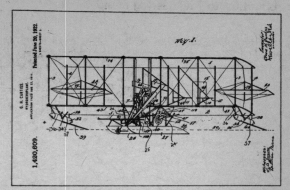

Drawings from two patents later issued to Glenn Curtiss when courts finally decided that he was the inventor of the Flying Boat.

Human Engineering Guide

Buy this book and keep it at hand at all times if you design or build anything that will be used by, for, or come in contact with people. Concise statement of ideas both through the informative writing and clear illustrations. The authors have followed their own guidelines and produced a device (this book) which will do well what it was designed to do, transfer a large amount of information between people. If you want information on human engineering, design of equipment and work space, vision, audition and body measurement, it's all in this book chapter by chapter. The above categories are a partial list of actual chapter headings. This book should be used by all design engineers, but it is not necessary to be a design engineer or even an engineer to use it. Really fundamental ideas clearly stated can be understood by anyone.

[Reviewed by F. Le Brun]

Human Engineering Guide
for Equipment Designers
Wesley E. Woodson, Donald W. Conover
1954,66; 473pp

$13.75 postpaid

from:
University of California Press
2223 Fulton St.
Berkeley, Ca. 94720

or WHOLE EARTH CATALOG

Where possible, work should be held by jigs or vises so that hands may be free to operate.

Hesitation -- or the temporary and often minute cessation from motion -- should be analyzed; its cause should be accounted for and, if possible, eliminated.

When a click in one ear leads that in the other by about 0.03 millisecond, the sound just begins to shift toward the first side; when there is a time difference of 0.65 millisecond or more, the sound appears completely localized on the side of first arrival, this localization remaining until the time difference becomes so great (3 milliseconds or more) that fusion is lost and the sound is heard separately in the two ears.

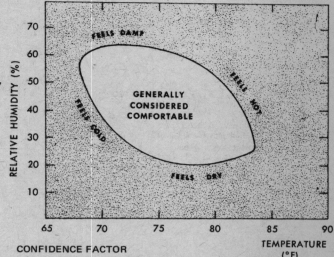

Since humans are used to evaluating things with "all their senses" from the time they are born, it is natural for them to expect this. Each of the sensory inputs, in fact, raises the level of confidence of the operator in what he is receiving – thus the converse of this, i.e., lack of certain inputs, tends to reduce the operator's confidence in the information he is receiving.

Jigs & Fixtures for Limited Production

This book is a manual of tactics for making inexpensive jigs. It's intended mainly for machine shops, but it can be quite handy for anyone who has to make a number of similar parts, such as for a dome. Jigs are also handy when a single part has to be done with high accuracy. Anyone who is into making things are repairing various artifacts could learn a bag of tricks from the book. The author shows how to convert commonly available objects into jigs; a vice into a drilling jib. There's a chapter on making epoxy tooling. The language is non-technical, with most of the terms being defined. For most makers, it won't be bedtime reading, but will be a good reference when the problems get tough.

[Reviewed by Jay Baldwin]

Jigs & Fixtures for Limited Production
Harold Sedlik
1970; 136 pp.

$10.00 postpaid

from:
Society of Manufacturing Engineers
20501 Ford Rd.
Dearborn, Michigan 48128

or WHOLE EARTH CATALOG

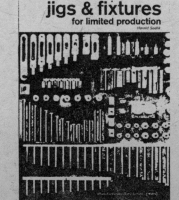

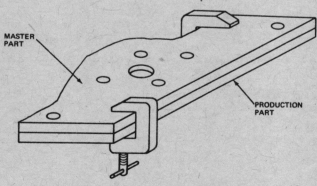

Fig. 2-4. Master part method of transferring hole locations.

If an item does not warrant special tooling, there may be an economic advantage in using the master part system. The system, as the name implies, uses a simulated or actual part fabricated to slightly closer tolerances than the intended product and used as a template or jig.

When a master part is used as a jig for locating holes, the master and the part to be worked are clamped together as shown, and the hole locations are transferred from the master to the part with a duplicating punch. If possible, hardened bushings are inserted into the master part, making it possible to transfer holes directly by drilling. The addition of drill bushings improves accuracy and increases tool life.

PART THREE

EDDIE'S FUNERAL

The mourners were lying around the room on mattresses, smoking hash between hits on nitrous oxide. Nearly everbody there was a St. Louis dealer, and since Eddie had been a dealer The Native thought it would be nice if sample's of everybody's stuff was done, in honor of Eddie's passing. Somebody do grass. Somebody else do acid. Somebody else do DMT. Somebody else do IT-290. Somebody else do STP. Somebody else do peyote. Somebody else do mescalin. Somebody else do psyciolocybin. Somebody else do reds, and everybody share the laughing gas to tie the whole thing together, in honor of Eddie's passing.

But that was just The Native coming on, just The Native doing his usual thing. The Native got his name because he was always talking about how nobody's a native anymore. Nobody lives where he was born, nobody's got real roots any more, and that's why people are so unhappy. The Native grew up in the Ozark Mountains of Missouri. He was so homesick most of the time, all he ever talked about was his family and his old home place back in the Ozarks. People at home have got identity, said The Native. They've got a history, and their lives are full of the most beautiful rituals. The Native loved rituals, and he wanted Eddie's funeral to be one, an elaborate ceremony where everybody would take a different kind of dope and then do communal things like chant and sing and mourn poor Eddie's passing.

But none of the others were up to it. There were eleven people at the funeral, besides The Native. Blue Ox was there, and Gilded Lilly. Chuck, Friendly Persuasion, City Girl and the Crosstown Rivals, plus Reed and Winston and Divine Right Davenport and his chick who had just blown in from somewhere. They had all been Eddie's friends, and they were all just as sorry as The Native that Eddie was dead. But the hash and the nitrous oxide and three TV sets all going at once were all that they could handle right then.

"Give me the hose," said Bert of the Crosstown Rivals. Bert's rival, Norton, had been sucking on the laughing gas almost two minutes now, and Bert was getting antsy. His last flash had been all about time, it had taken him down the passageway to the very door of the rose garden, but as he was about to go in the flash had started to wear off. Against his will he'd come reeling up the same passage he had taken down, and that was a disappointment. If he could have gotten the gas hose when he was supposed to, he could have made it back down in time to keep the dream intact, for even though he'd become conscious again the footprints still echoed clearly in his memory and showed the way back to the garden. But stupid Norton had the greeds and wouldn't let go of the hose.

(continued)

Direct Use of the Sun's Energy

The best book on Solar Energy that I know of.

Any curious and intelligent person can learn a great deal about our planet and ourselves by reading this book about ways of using sunlight. There are many numbers in the book but the math never goes beyond 8th grade arithmetic. The book is clear and simple whether talking about heating water——

For general domestic use of hot water for bathing and washing dishes a temperature of 135°F (57°C) is considered adequate and 20 gal per person per day is a reasonable consumption. In many sunny climates these requirements can be met with an insulated storage tank and solar radiation absorber which has an area of 0.75 ft^2 gal^{-1} of hot water. A family of four would need a tank of 80 gal and a solar absorber of 60 ft^2.

or photochemical reactions——

The photo dissociation of iodine (I$_2$) molecules into atoms absorbs most of the visible light of the sun with a considerable amount of energy which cannot be retained. It is immediately evolved as heat during the exposure to light.

I read the book on a Greyhound bus in Texas two years ago and it has changed my life and my way of thinking.

[Reviewed by Steve Baer]

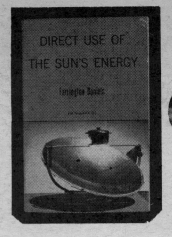

Direct Use of the Sun's Energy
Farrington Daniels
1964; 374 pp.

$1.95 postpaid

from:
Ballantine Books Inc.
457 Hahn Rd.
Westminster, M.D. 21157

or WHOLE EARTH CATALOG

Inexpensive solar water heater. A. Filling with cold water. B. Emptying hot water with suction syphon. C. Side view, showing position of end of hose.

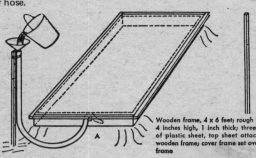

Wooden frame, 4 x 6 feet; rough lumber 4 inches high, 1 inch thick; three layers of plastic sheet, top sheet attached to wooden frame; cover frame set over base frame

a. Top cover, clear Mylar or polyethylene
b. Black polyethylene floating on water
c. Water layer, 2 inches deep
d. Clear polyethylene floor

Top cover (a) attached to wooden frame

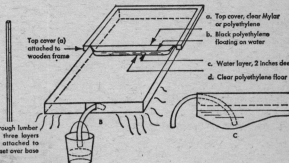

11. World wide distribution of solar energy in hundreds of hours per year. [Adapted with permission from *Solar Energy*, cover, 1, no. 1 (1957).]

32. Tilted plastic still of simple construction.

18. Method for drawing a parabola.

Solar Energy Society

More on solar energy: there is a Solar Energy Society, an "international professional organization devoted exclusively to the science and technology of solar energy applications", to quote their statement of purpose. They disseminate information on solar energy applications through the quarterly journal Solar Energy. Regular membership in the Society is $20 per year, which includes a subscription. Alternately, subscriptions can be ordered at $30 a year from the Subscriptions Manager, Pergamon Press, Headington Hill Hall, Oxford, England. The Journal is of high scientific quality and the technical articles are probably a little too technical for the layman. The Society just moved its world headquarters from Arizona State University, Tempe, to the National Science Center, 191 Royal Parade, Parkville, Victoria, Australia. There is a newly-formed US section, c/o Smithsonian Radiation Biology Laboratories, 12441 Parklawn Drive, Rockville, Md. 20852. Write there for membership info in the USA.

Steve Sargent
Research Assistant
Solar Energy Laboratory
Madison, Wisconsin 53706

Tools for Progress

Great Britain does it again (I'm beginning to feel like a Loyalist) way ahead of the let-General-Motors-do-it U.S. Here in one tasty catalog are all the 'equipment and materials for small-scale development available in The United Kingdom.' Pictures, descriptions, prices, and detailed access information on all manner of do-it-ourself tools, from hand ploughs to air houses. There may be some outrageous bargaining here, or not, I don't know—find out for yourself; a pound equals $2.40 these days.

—SB

Tools for Progress
1968; 192 pp.

$2.64 surface postpaid to U.S.
$5.00 air postpaid to U.S.
$2.10 in London

from:
The Intermediate Technology Development Group Ltd.
9 King Street
Covent Garden
London, W. C. 2
ENGLAND

WATER SUPPLY, Storage and Purification

Butyl Products Ltd

The Butank Family Rainwater Tank provides a ready supply of water for the household and ensures ample water supplies during the dry season. Rainwater runs off the collecting basin straight into the tank and is suitable for washing, for watering the vegetable garden and similar uses.

The tank consists of a long-life butyl rubber-bag, lined with a novel, simple-to-make form of concrete, laid in plastic tubular skins. The tank is covered to prevent loss by evaporation and to keep the water clean.

Three sizes of tank are available:
1,000 gal (4,546 l), 2,000 gal (9,092 l), 3,000 gal (13,638 l).
The Butank is supplied in a do-it-yourself kit and can be constructed by unskilled labour under limited supervision.
Illustrated instructions adjacent

Long-life butyl rubber is flexible, completely unaffected by any weather conditions, chemical or mould. Other important butyl applications: low cost reservoir linings, water channel liners, river training, dams, weirs and static or transportable storage tanks for water and chemicals.

Rural Industry

This guide catalogs several hundred tools, all manufactured or distributed by CeCoCo (Central Commercial Co.), and all applicable to what they term "cottage industry". In quaint English translation CeCoCo editors spell out the small scale cottage industry concept:

In almost all developing countries in the world, there are determined efforts to achieve material economic progress and emphasis is being carried out to induce a shift in the structural pattern of the economy from one basically agricultural to one that is agro-industrial in character to assure an increasing level of national production within the framework of economic and social stability which does not require much of foreign exchange to insure its growth. That is very important to select such industries which do not need foreign exchange in obtaining raw materials.

AGRICULTURE, Cultivation

Ransomes Sims & Jefferies Ltd

The Emcot
Many thousands of these oxen draught ridging ploughs are being used in developing countries where crops are grown on the ridge to combat soil erosion.

The Emcot ridging plough is used for crops such as groundnuts, cotton, tobacco as well as for cattle feed and vegetables.

The Emcot has replaceable earth wearing parts and is of solid construction for long life.

The high cost of living in the urban areas, nevertheless reduces the workers' real income. Money incomes in the rural areas is lower than those in cities but the cost of living is equally lower compared with urban living. The full development of cottage industry in the rural areas, can provide additional forms of incomes on the part of rural families, which could reduce the influx of population to cities in quest for employemnt. This ultimately would minimize social problem in urban centers.

The tools listed in this catalog are absolutely fascinating. One spends hours studying specifications, diagrams and photos of CeCoCo "making" machines. (In the Wire Products section, for instance, one finds Paper Pin Making Machine, Staple Pin Making Machine, Hair Pin Making Machine, Safety Pin Making Machine, Snap Button Making Machine, Nail Making Machine, Barbed Wire Making Machine, Chain Making Machine, Zip-Fastener Making Machine, Etc.)

CeCoCo was established in 1916, but refers to an association with a manufacturer of animal-drawn farming implements since 1863. They maintain an exhibition and demonstration farm center at Ibaraki. On the back cover of their guide book one sees photos of dignataries from all countries of the world visiting CeCoCo center.

[Suggested and Reviewed by Ken Kern]

Guide Book for Rural Cottage and Small and Medium Scale Industries
158 pp.

$10.00 airmail
$7.00 seamail

from:
CeCoCo
Ibaraki City
Osaka Pref.
JAPAN

Adana (Printing Machines) Ltd

The Adana "Eight Five" Printing Machine
Universally acknowledged to be the finest hand platen printing machine in the world. Smooth, rapid and easy in operation it produces printing of the highest quality. Sturdily built to stand heavy and constant use, it is small enough to occupy only a minimal space and light enough to be easily portable.

The Adana is so simple to use that even a beginner with no previous knowledge of printing can soon be producing first class work at speed.

Chase 8 in. × 5 in. (20.3 cm × 12.7 cm) inside.

Two composition inking rollers. Duplex roller runners fitted with two diameters to counteract atmospheric changes and for heavy or light contact with type face.

Uses standard printers' type.

Weight complete: 33½ lb (15.2 kg)
Overall size: 23 in. × 13 in. × 19 in.
(58.4 cm × 33 cm × 48.3 cm).

Price ex works: £25.10.0.
complete with fully illustrated instruction book.

Knots

Don't buy the definitive **Encyclopedia of Knots and Fancy Ropework.** *Buy* **Knots and Splices** *(95¢) if you want to graduate beyond tying your shoe into being useful with rope and string. Once that book gets you into working regularly with rope, move on up to* **Handbook of Knots** *and become a journeyman knot-tyer comfortable with cable and occasional fancy work. If you want to tell stories while you tie, or connect up with history and other possibilities, get* **The Ashley Book of Knots** *and start smoking a pipe. Now you're ready for* **Encyclopedia of Knots and Fancy Rope Work** *(includes far-out macramé).*

Knots are profound things, you know.

—SB

Handbook of Knots
Raoul Graumont
1945; 194 pp.; 428 good knots

$2.50 postpaid

from:
Cornell Maritime Press, Inc.
Box 109
Cambridge, Md. 21613

or WHOLE EARTH CATALOG

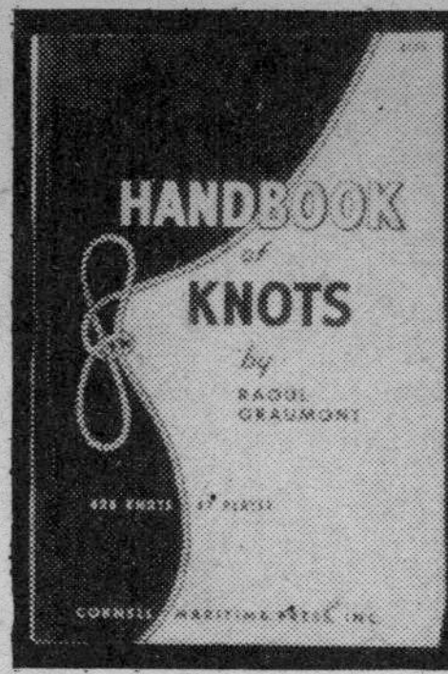
HANDBOOK of KNOTS
by RAOUL GRAUMONT
CORNELL MARITIME PRESS, INC.

Fig. 108 A: The Single Fisherman's Knot is ordinarily used to tie gut, which is less likely to slip when tied with this form of knot than when joined with a reef knot or sheet bend. It is tied with the underhand loop on the left overlapping the underhand loop on the right in the manner shown. The bight is then pulled through as the drawn in line indicates.

B: Illustrates the knot after the operation has been completed. This knot is often called an Englishman's, true lover's or waterman's knot.

Fig. 109 A: The Tom Fool's Knot or Arizona Handcuff Hitches, also known as a Conjurer's Knot, is said to have been used as a rope handcuff in the early days of the West. It can also be used as a jar or pitcher sling. It is tied by forming a loop in the manner shown, with one part of the line crossing over and the other part crossing under the knot. The bights are then pulled through as indicated.

B. The completed knot is shown here.

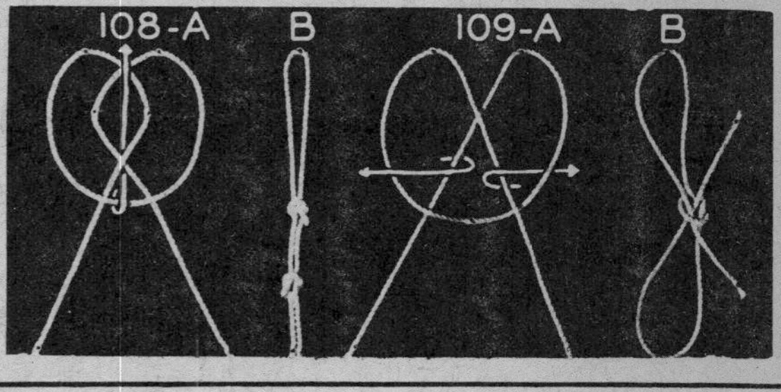
108-A
B
109-A
B

Knots and Splices
Percy W. Blandford
1962; 79 pp.; 80 good knots

$0.95 postpaid

from:
Arco Publishing Company
219 Park Ave. South
New York, N.Y. 10003

or WHOLE EARTH CATALOG

For dragging, you can get your shoulder into a bowline at the end of the rope, but if someone is needed to help you, you have to make a loop in the rope without using its ends. This can be a *man-harness knot.* Take up enough for the loop (Fig. 4C), and start to make an overhand knot in it (Fig. 4D). Instead of completing the overhand knot, grasp the opposite side of the loop through the part-knot and pull it through (Fig. 4E). To keep the knot in shape while doing this, hold one part of the rope under your foot while pulling upwards on the other part, and outwards at right angles on the loop.

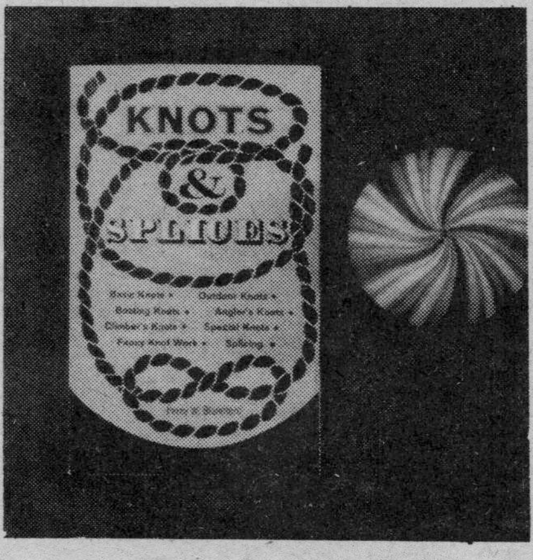
KNOTS & SPLICES

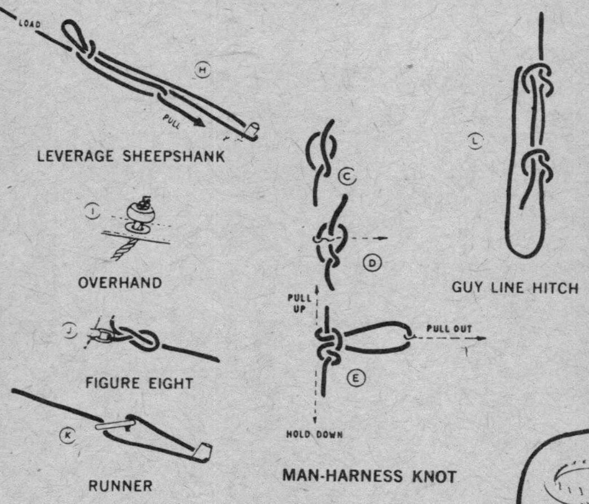
LOAD
PULL
LEVERAGE SHEEPSHANK
OVERHAND
FIGURE EIGHT
RUNNER
PULL UP
PULL OUT
HOLD DOWN
MAN-HARNESS KNOT
GUY LINE HITCH

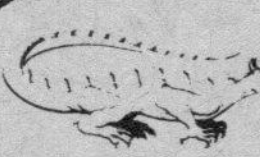

"Give me the goddamn hose!" said Bert. He reached to take it out of Norton's hand, but Norton, although he was unconscious by now, held it in a slobbery death-grip, and Bert was too stoned to fight him. As usual City Girl had to mediate. Gently she worked Norton's hands loose, and gave the hose to Bert as Norton fell over in City Girl's lap. Bert put the hose in his mouth and inhaled until he flashed. He wanted the rose garden again, but all he got was Billy Graham silently rapping at him on the top left television screen.

The three TV's were in the corner of the living room opposite the entrance to the kitchen. The big set on the bottom was a brand new color one that Eddie had bought only a week before he was killed. The other two were black and white, and small enough to sit side by side on top of the big set. The sound on the top left TV was torn up, but that's the one Billy Graham was on, and nobody wanted to hear him anyway. He was okay to look at, but the picture everybody wanted sound to was the quiz show on the big TV, in which newly-wed couples got a lot of free stuff if they knew the right answers.

The competition on the newly-wed show was between three young couples, the Morrisons, of Buffalo, New York; the Littons, of Oneonta, New York, and the Baileys, of Maryville, Tennessee. The funeral party was instantly unanimous in its hatred of the Baileys, because it was so obvious that their highest aim in life was to get to Knoxville where Charles would run for city attorney, and Rita would be an active Vol booster. As Rita pointed out when she introduced herself, she was a graduate of the University of Tennessee, where she had been very active in extra-curricular affairs. When she mentioned "extra-curricular affairs," the audience laughed. Rita blushed but laughed too. "I didn't mean it that way," she said. Every time Rita and Charles said anything the people at the funeral hissed and booed and called them stupid motherfuckers.

Everybody was kinder to the Morrisons. They dug Mrs. Morrison especially because she was so straight-forward and upfront in her manner. Her manner said: okay, by god, I'm on TV now, and I'm going to win every goddamn thing I can while I've got the chance. The people at the funeral liked Mrs. Morrison for that, and until the mid-program commercials Blue Ox, Gilded Lilly and Winston rooted hard for her and her husband to win.

As the program went on, however, the group sentiment slowly shifted to the Littons of Oneonta, and by the end of the program everybody at the funeral was solidly behind them. They were the truly engaging couple. Roger Litton was short and, at twenty-seven, a little jowly already, and Betty was having her weight problems too. They were handsome enough in the face, but there wasn't any getting around it, the Littons of Oneonta were fat, and because the Morrisons and Baileys, particularly that prissy Rita, were trying to come on so chic and "now," the people at the funeral loved the Littons all the more. They were fat, and they were modest, and they were also damn clever. The subject of the day was World Religions. The Littons weren't theologians or anything, but they knew that Buddha was enlightened under a bo tree, and that it was Jesus who'd said, "Straight is the gate, and narrow is the way, which leadeth unto life, and few there be that find it." The Morrisons and the Baileys didn't know shit about world religions. When the question man asked Mr. Morrison what country was most closely identified with Zen, he guessed Persia. When he asked Rita Bailey who was the author of the Bhagavad-Gita, she said, "Mahatma Ghandi?"

When the scores were added and Roger and Betty Litton pronounced the winners, of a new Maverick, fifty cartons of Marlboros, a fur coat for the Mrs. and a set of golf clubs for the Man of the House, plus a year's supply of parakeet food and a forty-eight hour vacation in Barcelona, everybody at the funeral applauded except Divine Right and Estelle, who had sort of withdrawn from it all and were sulking quietly in separate corners of the room. Roger and Betty hugged each other. As the program credits streamed across the screen they walked arm in arm off the stage into their new life together.

"Turn to channel four," said Chuck. "It's time for the hypnotism man."

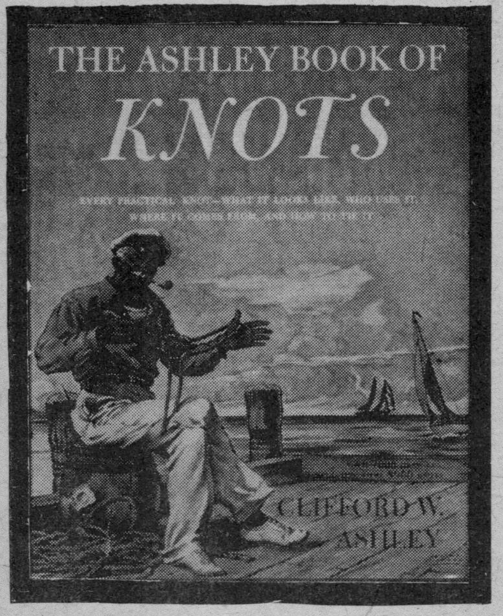
THE ASHLEY BOOK OF KNOTS
CLIFFORD W. ASHLEY

A knot having been tied or projected, the next thing in order is to 'work' it, which means to draw it up snug while molding it into proper shape. The slack should be worked out very gradually. This is a matter of no less importance than correct tying, and often presents a more difficult problem, requiring both patience and practice. Carefully fair the knot, and, once having arranged the cord in symmetrical form, never allow it to become distorted, even momentarily.

The Ashley Book of Knots
Clifford W. Ashley
1944; 260 pp.; 3900 incredible knots

$16.95 postpaid

from:
Doubleday & Co., Inc.
501 Franklin Avenue
Garden City, N. Y. 11530

or WHOLE EARTH CATALOG

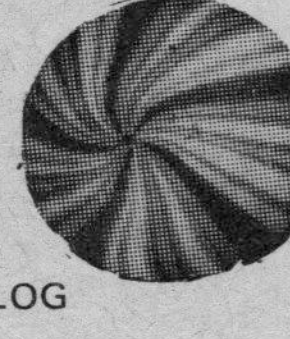

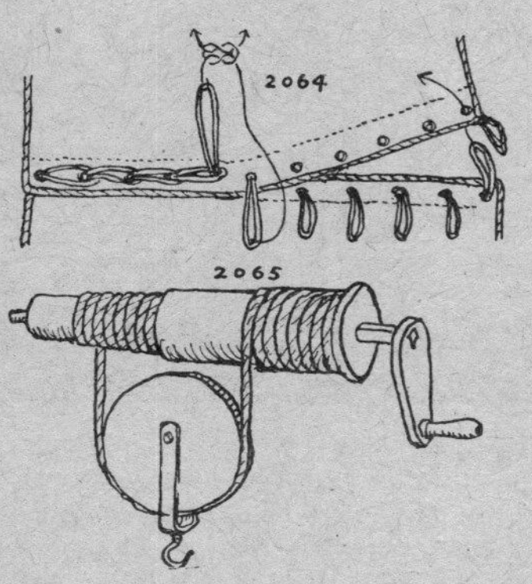
2064
2065

143. To break a heavy cord or string, take a turn of the cord around the left palm. Revolve the left hand so the cord is twisted in front of the palm, and wind the standing part several times around the fingers. Wrap the end (which is longer than illustrated) several times around the right hand; hold everything firm and jerk stoutly.

In each of the two methods given the string crosses itself at right angles, one part being held rigidly while the other part is strongly jerked.

My first impression was that the weakening effect of this harsh crossing was the important factor in causing the string to break invariably at this point. One of the "laws" quoted in dictionary and encyclopedia knot discussions is that "the strength of a knot depends on the ease of its curves," and of course a right-angle crossing provides the uneasiest curve that is possible within a knot.

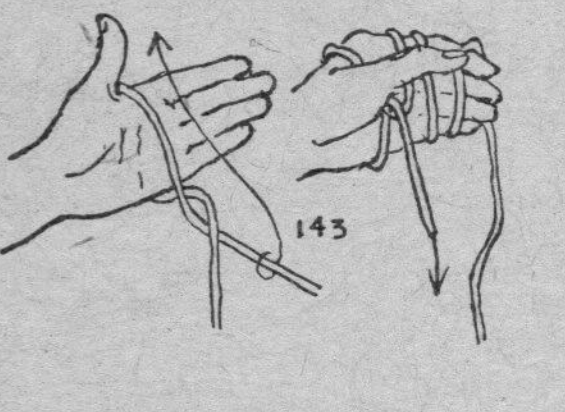
143

2064. *Latching* is an old method of attaching a drabbler to a jib, or a bonnet to a fore and aft sail. Nowadays it is the method employed by circuses in assembling the canvas sections of the tents. A series of eyelets in the upper section of the sail are opposite a series of loops, termed "keys," in the headrope of the bonnet. Starting at one side, a key is rove through the opposite eyelet and hauled to the next eye. The next key is rove through its opposite eye and through the key that was first led. This process is continued until the center is reached. The process is then repeated, beginning at the other edge of the sail. The two center loops, being twice as long as the rest, are reef knotted together. Captain John Smith described them in 1627, calling them "latchets."

2065. The *Chinese windlass* is the grandfather of the present-day differential chain hoist. One end winds, while the other unwinds, and the right end of the barrel, being larger than the left, winds or unwinds a greater length of rope than the left end, with each revolution of the crank.

Ropework, Knots, Rigging

The definitive text is Encyclopedia of Knots and Fancy Ropework *by Hensel and Graumont available from the Cornell Maritime Press, Cambridge, Maryland.* The Ashley Book of Knots *is comprehensive and charming; however, the* Encyclopedia *is comprehensive and usable (i.e., diagrams are clearer and instructions are easier to follow). I own* Ashley *and if I had it to do over again I'd buy Graumont. Also, the last time I looked the* Encyclopedia *was $12.00 at least $2.00 cheaper than* Ashley. *Actually, all most folks will ever need is* Handbook of Knots *by Graumont, $2.00 from Cornell Maritime. It handles every working knot of general use and then some. If it is splicing that is of special interest* Splicing Wire and Fiber Rope *by Graumont and Hensel is all you need (plus a fid, serving mallet, assorted marlinespikes) to splice, worm, parcel and serve. I've spoken to several master riggers from Eleventh Avenue in Manhattan to Glouchester all of whom spoke highly and exclusively about this book. It is in hard cover for $3.00 also from Cornell Maritime. It is printed on high quality glossy paper to withstand the constant use by greasy hands, a book that's a real tool.*

Speaking of rigging, there is a terrific future for qualified riggers. Ski lifts all have their cables spliced and all the tent and net structures of the larger type currently on the drawing boards will have to use wire cable which must be spliced in order to maintain the strength specs (knotting cuts down as much as 50% wire bolts as much as 25% on stated strengths, a well executed transmitional splice will leave over 95% strength). Rigging is a demanding and exacting craft with a long and honorable tradition. It may be the second oldest profession as rope (hemp) was one of the earliest invention of man.

On macramé, which I always thought was square knot fancywork, there is a store in Brooklyn, C.E. Herwig, where you can see the best of fancy ropework and get all the supplies you need like different size, quality, color twines. I think they're on Clinton Street in the Brooklyn Heights section.

Harvey Kalmeyer
Taos, New Mexico

Encyclopedia of Knots and Fancy Rope Work
Raoul M. Graumont, John Hensel
1939, 1942, 1943, 1952; 690 pp.

$15.00 postpaid

from:
Cornell Maritime Press
Cambridge, Maryland 21613

or WHOLE EARTH CATALOG

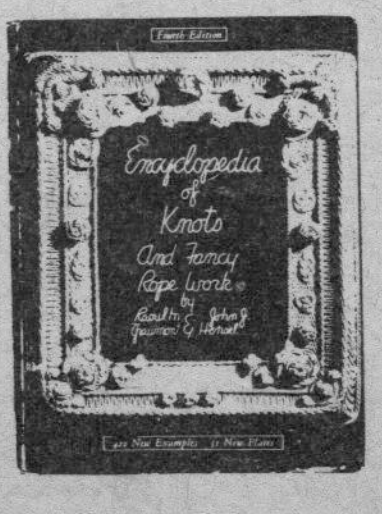
Encyclopedia of Knots and Fancy Rope Work

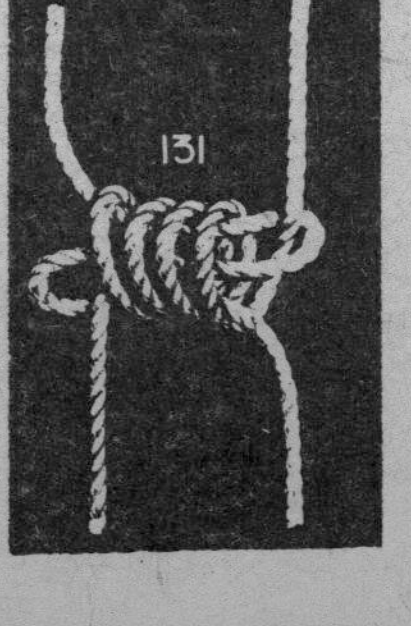
131

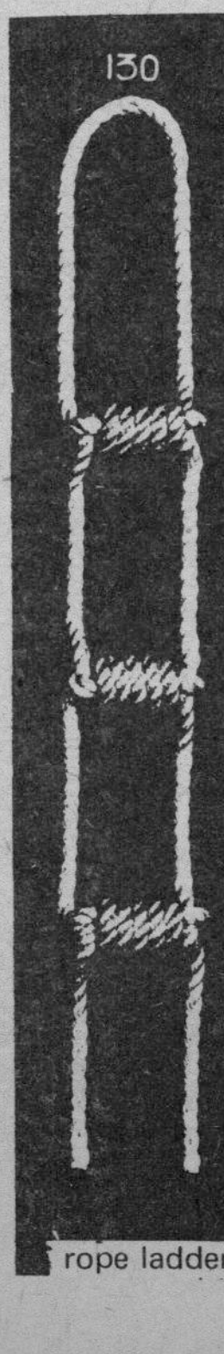
130

rope ladder

Scientific American

Good old Scientific American.

—SB

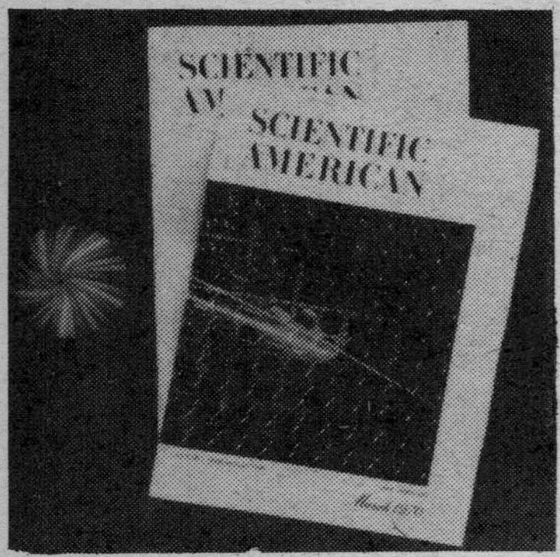

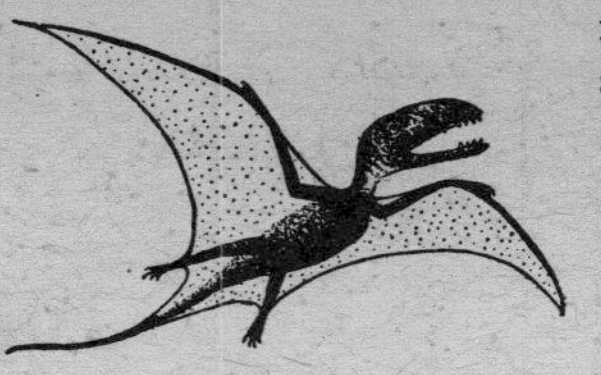

PTEROSAURIA
(DIMORPHODON)

Scientific American

$10.00 for one year (monthly)

from:
Scientific American
415 Madison Avenue
New York, N. Y. 10017

or most newsstands.

If we look at man's use of energy, the future of fossil fuels or fission is measured in centuries; only deuterium or sunlight can carry us through a long history of industrial life. Our history is now marked on a time axis by one single pulse of fossil energy, rising from the axis and falling back to it again in about a millennium. We are in the first fourth of that pulse today. Right now men add as much heat to the earth's surface as the natural flow of heat by convection and conduction from the earth's hot interior does, and we face a tenfold rise in man's activities. For the first time in so central a parameter as energy men will have worked on a geologic scale. (Of course, the sun sends 1,000 times more heat to the earth's surface; we shall not cook ourselves that way!) Still, our myriad stacks and tailpipes aggregate to more heat than Krakatoa, Etna and the Valley of Ten Thousand Smokes.

Globe-Trotter's Peril

The painful, nauseating but feverless disease known as "traveler's diarrhea" has often been blamed on a change in water or climate, on chilled drinks and on other dietary indiscretions. Its actual cause now seems to be known; it appears to result from the sufferer's ingestion of the intestinal bacterium *Escherichia coli*, but a bacterium that belongs to a strain different from those he already harbors.

Murder at Thank God Bay

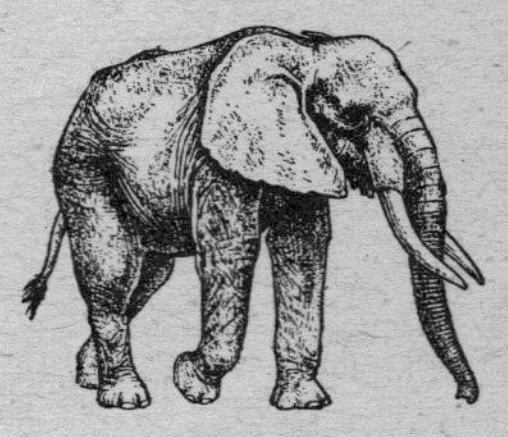

PROBOSCIDEA

New Scientist

New Scientist *is the best evidence we've seen that there are new scientists in the world, young, politically aware, irreverent, active. Every week here's yet another* New Scientist *(if you get behind reading, it's hopeless), full of actual news, critique, and gossip of the research world. The magazine is British, so you get perspective on U. S. accomplishments (flattery nonetheless), and report of world-wide activities unreported in most American journals. The Ariadne column is a gem.*

—SB.

[Suggested by Steve Baer]

New Scientist

for one year (weekly)

$34.00 airfreight

from:
New Scientist
128 Long Acre
London W. C. 2

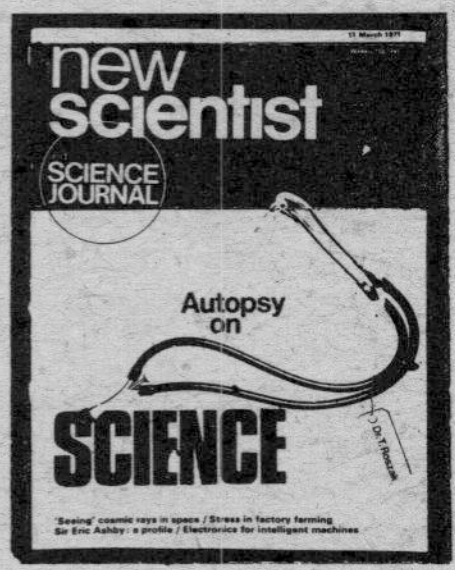

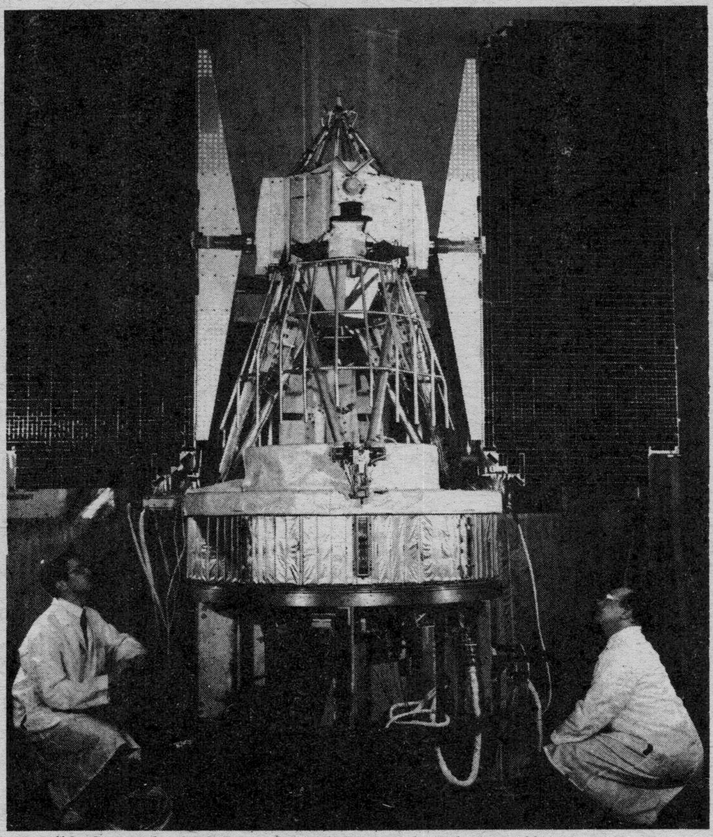

"O thou, who in former times didst wondrously magnify our appropriations, that the Marxites might be humbled; cut not back the sustenance of thy servants in the days of tightness which are upon us; but grant, we beseech thee, a renewal of thy support, that we may reap such a harvest of peaceful uses and spinnings-off as will move the people to glorify thine administration. Amen."

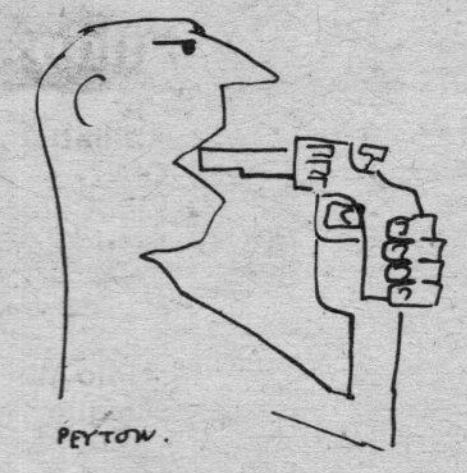

Internal pollution is being brought about in three ways: by the ingestion and inhalation of the products of our already polluted external environment; by our daily intake of chemical additives and impurities pre-packed into the food we eat and drink; and by the vast number of medicaments with which we regularly dose ourselves——more often than not unnecessarily. That some realization of the danger of this last factor is dawning was conveyed to me recently when in the United States. Among the seemingly endless mundane daily television commercials I was agreeably surprised to find one sponsored by the Blue Cross-Blue Shield Health Insurance Company, going something like this. "Got a headache? Why wait? Take an aspirin. . .Indigestion? Quick! an antacid. . . Can.t get to sleep? A pill will help you. . .Feeling down? Take a . . . ." The voide fades——pause——deep voice concludes with slow measured emphasis. "Have you thought that you might be killing yourself?" For once, advertising was used to say something that showed not only unexpected foresight, but something meriting constant repetition.

A weird case coming before the court at Oakland, California, results from the discovery that a computer was emitting more data than it had been asked for. After investigation police suggested that an unauthorized program had been run through the computer at the coded command of another computer belonging to a different company. The police obtained a warrant to search for electronic impulses in the memory of the suspect machine. The case (involving trade secrets) and its outcome should make legal history.

Science

I have to acknowledge I've gotten more useful tips from this magazine than any other technical or scientific journal.

—SB

Membership $18.00/yr

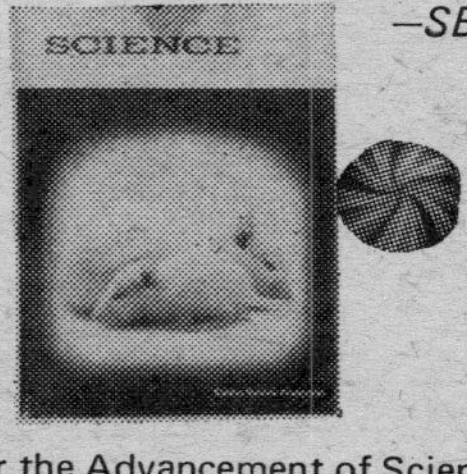

Science

$30/yr (weekly)

from:
American Association for the Advancement of Science
1515 Massachusetts Avenue, N. W.
Washington, D. C. 20005

Grassland used as a car park can easily degenerate into a quagmire. British Ropes Ltd. has made a one-inch mesh polypropylene net which can be used as an inexpensive way of stopping land from becoming boggy and rutted through use by cars, caravans etc. The net is spread over grass and pegged down. The grass will grow through the net, and can even be mowed without damaging the net. The net has been tried out at Sywell Aerodrome near Northampton and has helped keep the airport open under conditions which would previously have lead to damage to the surface. Polypropylene nets might also be useful on river banks and they could help stabilize other earthworks and protect freshly seeded areas.

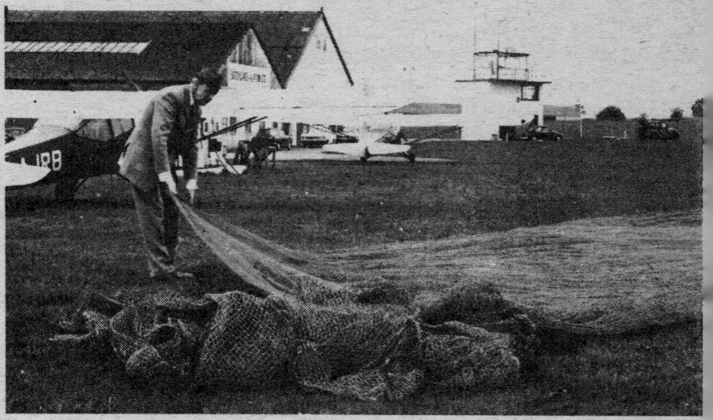

Our Fragile Environment

The quality of the environment, ecology, and pollution problems have recently become matters of concern everywhere. My own personal explanation for this outburst of interest may be peculiar to myself, but I would like to know whether my explanation sounds a responsive chord in the minds of others. I date my own reawakening of interest in man's environment to the Apollo 8 mission and to the first clear photographs of the earth from that mission. My theory is that the views of the earth from that expedition and from the subsequent Apollo flights have made many of us see the earth as a whole, in a curious way——as a single environment in which hundreds of millions of human beings have a stake.

One view in particular is awe-inspiring——with Africa in the foreground and the whole profile of the Mediterranean very clear. One stares at the whole Mediterranean, looking from outer space much as in an atlas, but *not as a drawing*. Much of our most commonly taught history centers around that little sea, a mere patch of the hemisphere, which once seemed to its inhabitants to be the whole world.

Looking at the blackness beyond the sharp blue-green curve, trying to see even the place where the thin envelope of atmosphere and the solid earth meet, the curious word "fragile" comes to mind. To be on the earth and think of it as fragile is ridiculous. But to see it from Out There and to compare it with the deadness of the Moon! I suspect that the greatest lasting benefit of the Apollo missions may be, if my hunch is correct, this sudden rush of inspiration to try to save this fragile environment——the *whole* one——if we still can.

John Caffrey
American Council on Education
Washington, D.C. 20036

If we were to judge by the sales of Spock's books, we would have to conclude that many parents of nonactivists must have put the Spock advice on their bookshelf, if not into their practices. But the studies of young activists suggest that their parents (often trained in, or well read in, social science fields where Freudian theory and Spock's advice held considerable sway) reacted more favorably to this advice than did the parents of nonactivists. Parents of activists expressed more frequently than others a belief that their own parents had been too harsh, too remote, too unfriendly, too strict, and too arbitrary. They indicated that they hoped to make things different for their children, and they expressed a belief in the efficacy of Spock's advice. Concomitantly, activists, more frequently than nonactivists, described their parents as lenient or not strict.

Thus the suggestion is that the young activists of the 1960's were "Spock marked." More pertinently, several studies in child psychology suggest that the love-oriented methods of discipline advocated by Spock tend to foster close identification of the child with the parent and corresponding acceptance by the child of his parents' values and expectations.

A contradiction of popular beliefs about activists is indicated here, for this evidence suggests that the young activists of the 1960'S, far from being the rampant deviates that they were often said to be, were, in fact, conformists. They were conforming, through identification, to a model presented by their parents. . . .

When we look to the studies for such signs of psychopathology as excessive anxiety, neurotic preoccupations, general paranoid beliefs, delusional thinking, diminished self-esteem, loss of self-control, excessive dependency, flattened affect, irresponsible interpersonal relations, lack of drive, hysteria, depression, extreme hostility, and psychopathy, we fail to find that such behaviors were any more common among activists than among comparable samples of nonactivists. Moreover, in the direction of positive mental health, the evidence indicates that activists were relatively high in self-respect, self-sufficiency, intellectual orientation, and concern for others and realtively low in ethnocentrism, possessiveness, and dependency.

There is a need, a transient need, a violent need for being just yourself, restating, recreating, talking in your own terms about what you have learned from all the cultures, scientific and non-scientific, before you and around you. During that period you want to be almost alone, with just a few friends. You want to be undisturbed. You want to be free to think not for an hour at a time, or three hours at a time, but for two days or two weeks, if possible, without interruption. You don't want to drive the family car or go to parties. You wish people would just go away and leave you alone while you get something straight. Then, you get it straight and you embody it, and during that period of embodiment you have a feeling of almost divine guidance. Then it is done, and, suddenly, you are alone, and you have a need to go back to your friends and the world around you, and to all history, to be refreshed, to feel alive and human once again. It is this interplay between all that is richly human and this special, concentrated, uninterrupted mental effort that seems to me to be the source, not only of science, but also of everything that is worthwhile in life.

Edwin H. Land

Free reprints

Bill Dickinson says you can always get free reprints of articles in Scientific American, New Scientist, etc. by writing to the authors. They all have hundreds of copies.

Popular Science

Of the three, Popular Science, Popular Mechanics, and Mechanics Illustrated, consistently the somewhat better is Popular Science. It's a good source for current applied science reporting and basement technology. Most of the tool sources we list advertise in the magazine.

—SB

[Suggested by Jay Baldwin]

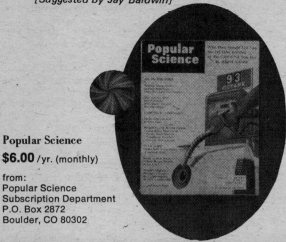

Popular Science

$6.00 /yr. (monthly)

from:
Popular Science
Subscription Department
P.O. Box 2872
Boulder, CO 80302

Clandestine shortwave stations you may hear

Frequency (mHz)	Station	Affiliation	Listener Area
3.900, 4.365	Unknown	CIA	S.E. Asia
2.440, 3.900, 4.365	Radio Liberated Army	Viet Cong	S.E. Asia
11.0 7, 9.555	PeyK-e-Iran	Radio Sofia (Bulgaria)	Middle East
9.555, 11.410	Kiss Me Honey (music jammer)	Radio Baghdad	Middle East
8.340	Radio Portugal Libre	Radio Moscow	North America
13.200, 13.300, 15.000, 15.100	Radio Euzkadi	Basque Region of Spain	Europe, N. America
17.700, 6.950, 7.050	Radio Espana Independiente	Radio Moscow	Europe
1.406, 7.305	Radio Liberated, LaVoz Anti-Com		South, Central America
9.300, 11.865, 15.050	Ministros de America	Unknown	
1.157, 6.000	Radio Americas	CIA	Central, South America
6.135	Radio Havana	Cuba	Central, South America
10.030, 10.015	Radio of S. Vietnam, Front for Liberation	Viet Cong	S.E. Asia
7.345	Free Transmitter of Czechoslovakia	Czech Nationalists	Europe, North America

---

Product Engineering

Roy Sebern pointed out the main satisfaction of reading Product Engineering: in the usual magazines such as Popular Science, everything has the tone of "I-wish-they'd make . . ."; whereas in Product Engineering it's "We are making . . ." The magazine has good reporting and excellent editing. Increasingly it is going beyond the question of how to make stuff into why make stuff. Departments include Research & Technology, Mechanical Design & Power Transmission, Hydraulic/Pneumatic Power & Control, Materials & Manufacturing, Product Planning & Management, and the Engineer & His Profession.

—SB

Product Engineering

$20 /yr (monthly)

from:
Morgan Granpian, Inc.
16 West 61st Street
New York, N.Y. 10023

Product Development and Design

Product Development and Design *monthly magazine, 200—400 items reviewed descriptively each month, 600 or so ads for unusual items related to developing all sorts of products. Info and samples are available on check-off card type access system. Subscription free to qualifiers which must mean anyone in any type research; they sent it to us and we seem mainly to be researching our own heads and we didn't ask for it. It is really a mind blow for the "mechanically inclined" or short-cut freak. In the last few years everything you ever thought would be a helpful little gadget or variation has been manufactured and is available. This is one place you'll find out about it. Especially if it's new. It must be invaluable to investment freaks cause it's good access to technology's rate of growth and the movement or dynamics of it in the small item part of the spectrum. It really seems to supplement the Thomas Registers and is full of useful stuff often available in sample form for free or a small charge to stimulate use of the item and a market for it. Product Design & Development, Bala-Cynwyd, Pa. 19004. Reader (subscriber) qualifying application form on request.*

*Recommended by
Ron Williams-
ONYX
New York, N.Y.*

Picture fuddling by computer

Can you identify this face? It's a well-known President who freed the slaves and was shot in Ford's theatre. Still stumped? Try viewing it at arm's length, or squinting, or jiggling the page rapidly. This picture represents a Bell Labs experiment to learn the least amount of visual information a picture can contain and still be recognizable—of some concern to designers of Picture-

phones. Here a computer has riven a portrait into 200 squares, each rendered in an even tone of gray along an intensity scale from one to sixteen.

Have parka, will travel

Are you a post-doctoral scholar, graduate student, or upper-division undergraduate "between 20 and 30 years old, of even disposition, with some knowledge of electronics"? Would you like to train for a one-year stint manning scientific instruments in the fields of gravity, seismology, meteorology, or terrestrial magnetism? And would you, incidentally, like to spend that year at the South Pole? Then there just might be a job for you. Inquire of the Institute of Geophysics and Planetary Physics, U. of California, Los Angeles 90024. Hurry!

Things That Go Bump

The center of the galaxy may be emitting intense bursts of gravitational radiation, according to evidence reported at the recent annual meeting of the American Physical Society by Joseph Weber of the University of Maryland. . . .

If Weber's detectors are indeed responding to gravitational radiation, what could be the significance of emanations predominantly from the center of the galaxy? Einstein's general theory of relativity predicts that gravitational waves should be produced by matter that is accelerating with respect to the observer. "Evidently," says Weber, "matter in the center of the galaxy is either collapsing or being rearranged on a grand scale."

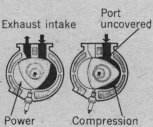

Exhaust intake — Port uncovered

Power — Compression

A stove that will burn almost any type of coal without giving off smoke has been developed by the South African Council for Scientific & Industrial Research. The aim, of course, is to reduce air pollution. In addition, council says, the new stove cannot overheat, yet develops temperatures for ordinary cooking and uses less fuel than a conventional stove.

Basic features of the stove are a firebox grate with a set of front bars only 4 in. high, to make sure the fuel bed is shallow (with a thick bed, the upper layers of fuel receive air robbed of its oxygen by the lower layers, and smoking results); a hot plate that is actually the upper surface of the horizontal flue; and a single door that serves both as fire door and ash door. The door has a novel variable-size air opening in its lower half. This opening admits air to the underside of the fire and makes it possible to cut the air supply down to bank the fire, or to increase it to achieve the optimum working temperature.

To prevent overheating, the stove is designed so, when the door is opened to add fuel, excess air enters above the fire and the draft is reduced. Thus, opening the door to increase the heating rate above the optimum point will result in cooling the stove down rather than heating it up.

Popular Mechanics

Equal Time for Responsible Spokesmen . . .

Gentlemen:

I have not had the pleasure of seeing your catalog, nor of communicating with you previously. I have, however, seen the page from the catalog in which you say *Popular Science* is "somewhat better" than *Popular Mechanics.*

This doesn't anger me, because you have a right to your opinion. But it does concern me, and I'd be interested in knowing what caused you to arrive at such a conclusion.

I have been the editor of both *Popular Mechanics* and *Popular Science,* so I know the editing philosophies of both magazines. I won't take anything away from *Popular Science,* which continues to be an excellent magazine. (Their star contributor, Dr. van Braun, is a holdover from my regime.)

However, *Popular Mechanics* has long been Number one in circulation, including newsstand, and in advertising. When I became editor of *Popular Mechanics* five years ago, I considered it a step upward.

We think we do a better job in reporting and illustrating science, inventions, aerospace, exploration and the like. We're sure we do a better job on ecology (including a monthly "Pollution Fighters Newsletter"), outdoor recreation, home repair and workshop ideas.

Although *Popular Science* has recently adopted the slogan, "The What's New Magazine," and now groups all new products in an 8-page section, I believe an item-by-item count would show that *Popular Mechanics* runs at least as many news items, scattered through the magazine. And we have come up with such important "scoops" in the past year as General Electric electric garden tractor, Perry Submarine's 2-man "Shark Hunter," Sylvania's Magicube flash bulbs, and Polaroid's recently patented shutterless camera.

I am sending you several recent issues of *Popular Mechanics.* I hope they will cause you to change the opinion expressed in your catalog. If they don't I'd still be interested in your reactions.

Sincerely yours,

Robert P. Crossley
Editor

*Popular Mechanics
Box 646
New York, N.Y. 10019
$5.97/yr, monthly*

THE HYPNOTISM MAN

The hypnotism man was a little old sawed-off Jew with a goatee who stood with his hands folded at his chest like a teacher about to say "now children." He spoke in a wonderfully deep and resonant voice, but he wasn't nearly as handsome and pleasant to look at as Billy Graham. So The Native, ritual-freak and prankster that he was, decided to rearrange things a little. What he did was fuck up the picture image on channel four so that you could hear the hypnotism man without seeing him, while you looked at Billy Graham on channel three of the top left TV. As a kind of sub-plot, some bulldozers were hacking down a mountain in a strip-mining operation in Kentucky on channel seven of the TV next to Billy Graham.

"Far out," said Reed.

"Groovy," said Bert of the Crosstown Rivals.

"Move your fucking knee," said Bert's rival, Norton.

After some stirring and shifting around and some goings and comings to the bathroom, everybody settled back onto the mattress for another half hour of good funeral.

"Good afternoon," said Billy Graham. "And welcome to today's session in self-hypnosis. I hope you've done your homework since yesterday, because today's lesson will require considerable strength of mind if you are to complete it successfully. You will remember that yesterday I asked you to practice being very quiet, all by yourself, for at least half an hour. I hope that most of you did that, for you will find, as you continue in self-hypnosis, that several minutes a day of simple quiet will add greatly to your capacity to count yourself into a trance. Being quiet for a few minutes each day is like planting a little seed in your mind that can grow and grow all through the day, and help you to stay calm and alert. So if you did not practice since yesterday's session, I urge you most strongly to sit quietly for at least half an hour before tomorrow's session.

(continued)

Handbook of Chemistry and Physics

Among handbooks this one is unusually wealthy in basic information. Its 6-figure math tables are the standard (they're obtainable separately: $6.50 from Chemical Rubber). Its chemistry and physics tables constitute a comprehensive inventory of invisible effects. It doesn't teach you how to use or even read the inventory, but if you know-how, here's the know-what tool chest. —SB

[Suggested by Lloyd Martin]

Handbook of Chemistry and Physics
Robert C. Weast, ed.
1918 . . . 1968
(54th Edition); 2436 pp.

$25.95 postpaid

from:
CRC Press
18901 Cranwood Parkway
Cleveland, Ohio 44128

or WHOLE EARTH CATALOG

WATER AGAINST AIR

Temperature °C	Surface tension dynes/cm.	Temperature °C	Surface tension dynes/cm.	Temperature °C	Surface tension dynes/cm.
−8	77.0	15	73.49	40	69.56
0	78.4	18	73.05	50	67.91
0	75.6	20	72.75	60	66.18
5	74.9	25	71.97	70	64.4
10	74.22	30	71.18	80	62.6
				100	58.9

INTERFACIAL TENSION
Surface Tension at the Interface Between Two Liquids
(Each liquid saturated with the other)

Liquids	Temperature °C	γ	Liquids	Temperature °C	γ
Benzene--Mercury...	20	357	Water--Heptylic acid	20	7.0
Ethyl ether--Mercury	20	379	Water--n-Hexane....	20	51.1
Water--Benzene....	20	35.00	Water--Mercury.....	20	375.
Water--Carbon tetrachloride	20	45.	Water-n-Octane.....	20	50.8
Water--Ethyl ether..	20	10.7	Water-n-Octyl alcohol	20	8.5

Cheaper Handbook

You list the CRC Handbook of Chemistry and Physics and show the standard price of $24.95.

I understand that CRC offers the Handbook each fall through college science departments at a great reduction. Last December I ordered the 50th edition for $8, and I suspect that 50¢ of that was a contribution to the local chemistry students society. It is stamped "college edition" but as far as I can tell contains all the standard contents.

If this is indeed an annual CRC offer it is certainly worth waiting for.

Deborah Young
San Diego, California

Machinery's Handbook

If you make things out of metal you need Machinery's Handbook. This thick, comprehensive guide to shop and engineering practice was originally designed to fit in the tall center drawer of a machinist's chest. Machinist's chests have stayed the same size, but the shaping of metal has become more and more complicated. Machinery's has coped with the squeeze heroically; the current (18th) edition contains 2293 pages printed on fine India paper, and it still fits the drawer. You can find in it things like tap drill sizes for S.A.E., metric, and Whitworth threads, what welding rod to use for which metal, and how much weight you can hang on a rope if it goes around a fat (or thin) barrel. You can also look up logarithms, area, volumes, and centers of gravity, and learn how to design helical gears, replace bearings, grind a lathe bit, and do many other useful and not-so-obvious things. The book is divided into thirteen main sections, indexed, thumb-indexed, and bound in tough, satisfyingly archaic industrial green with gold stamping.

[Suggested and reviewed by Dr. Morton Grosser]

Machinery's Handbook
1914 . . .1970; 2293 pp.

$19.00 postpaid

from:
Industrial Press, Inc.
200 Madison Avenue
New York, N.Y. 10016

or WHOLE EARTH CATALOG

The Starrett Book for Student Machinists

This is an excellent reference and introduction to machining. It can be used in place of the Machinery's Handbook by many people, although it does not pretend to replace it. Chapters like: Reading Working Drawings; Facts About Fits; Drills and How to Use them; Jigs and Fixtures; and Lathe Work. The book is well bound and small, making it an easy volume to keep.

[Suggested and reviewed by Fred Richardson]

The Starrett Book for Student Machinists
The L.S. Starrett Co.
1941 . . . 1952; 184 pp.

$2.90 postpaid

from:
The L.S. Starrett Co.
Athol, Massachusetts 01131

or WHOLE EARTH CATALOG

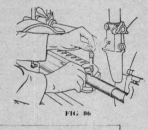

FIG. 86

Box Column Type Upright Drill Press

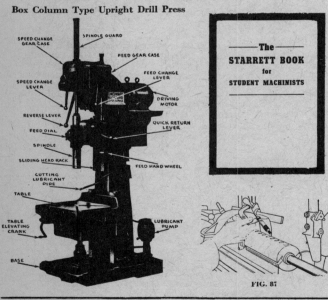

FIG. 87

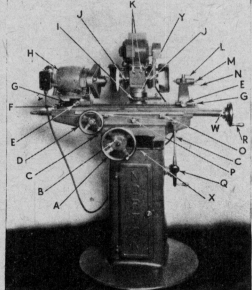

GEOMETRY
Geometrical Constructions

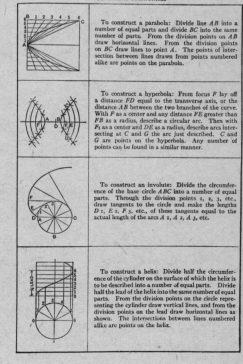

To construct a parabola: Divide line *AB* into a number of equal parts and divide *BC* into the same number of parts. From the division points on *AB* draw horizontal lines. From the division points on *BC* draw lines to point *A*. The points of intersection between lines drawn from points numbered alike are points on the parabola.

To construct a hyperbola: From focus *F* lay off a distance *FD* equal to the transverse axis, or the distance *AB* between the two branches of the curve. With *F* as a center and any distance *FE* greater than *FB* as a radius, describe a circular arc. Then with *F₁* as a center and *DE* as a radius, describe arcs intersecting at *C* and *G* the arc just described. *C* and *G* are points on the hyperbola. Any number of points can be found in a similar manner.

To construct an involute: Divide the circumference of the base circle *ABC* into a number of equal parts. Through the division points 1, 2, 3, etc., draw tangents to the circle and make the lengths *D₁*, *E₁*, *F₁*, etc., of these tangents equal to the actual length of the arcs *A₁*, *A₂*, *A₃*, etc.

To construct a helix: Divide half the circumference of the cylinder on the surface of which the helix is to be described into a number of equal parts. Divide half the lead of the helix into the same number of equal parts. From the division points on the circle representing the cylinder draw vertical lines, and from the division points on the lead draw horizontal lines as shown. The intersections between lines numbered alike are points on the helix.

The Tools and Rules for Precision Measuring

A good basic book for "mechanics, hobbyists and home workshop owners." The title describes it well. Being a Starrett publication, it naturally shows only Starrett tools, but the information is good for almost all makes. Its information is primarily on Micrometers, Dial Indicators and Gage Blocks, although it covers other tools briefly. Has several useful tables in the back.

[Suggested and reviewed by Fred Richardson]

The Tools and Rules for Precision Measuring
The L. S. Starrett Co.
1965; 80 pp.

Free from:
The L. S. Starrett Co.
Athol, MA 01331

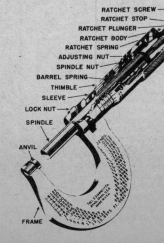

RATCHET SCREW
RATCHET STOP
RATCHET PLUNGER
RATCHET BODY
RATCHET SPRING
ADJUSTING NUT
SPINDLE NUT
BARREL SPRING
THIMBLE
SLEEVE
LOCK NUT
SPINDLE
ANVIL
FRAME

In effect, a micrometer caliper combines the double contact of a slide caliper with a precision screw adjustment which may be read with great accuracy. It operates on the principle that a screw accurately made with a pitch of forty threads to the inch will advance one-fortieth (or .025) of an inch with each complete turn. As the sectional view shows, the screw threads on the spindle revolve in a fixed nut concealed by a sleeve. On a micrometer caliper of one inch capacity, the sleeve is marked longitudinally with 40 lines to the inch corresponding with the number of threads on the spindle. Every fourth line is made longer and is numbered 1,2,3,4, etc. to indicate one-tenth inch, two-tenths, etc. while other lines are staggered for easy reading.

Man is a tool-using animal. Weak in himself and of small stature, he stands on a basis of some half square foot, has to straddle out his legs lest the very winds supplant him. Nevertheless, he can use tools, can devise tools; with these the granite mountain melts into light dust before him; seas are his smooth highway, winds and fire his unwearying steeds. Nowhere do you find him without tools. Without tools he is nothing, with tools he is all.

Thomas Carlyle (1795-1881)

Table 8. — .....erigan Standard 300-Pound Steel Flanged Fittings

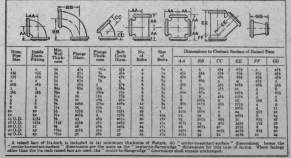

Polyester & Fiberglass

Fiberglass is a cheap strength material, comparable to wood & steel. It is weatherproof, land or sea, & is colored or translucent. The fabrication is very different, however. Since the material is applied as a glass cloth & a liquid plastic, it assumes complex & curved shapes almost as easily as simple shapes. This enables a breakaway from the lines & planes that wood & steel come in into free form & organic shapes. Since fiberglass is formless, a mold is usually necessary. Making a mold is cheap but time consuming & the mold can be used many times. A boat hull or a chair are naturals for fiberglass. We used it to make a 5' diameter parabolic dish for a mirror. It would be a cheap & effective way to turn Frei Otto's (see Vol II, Tensile Structures, of WEC) incredible shapes into houses.

This is a nitty-gritty book. It tells you what to ask for at the store. It has names for all the mistakes we made. It enables you to learn so much from your first fuck-up that the second one works. It comes as close to someone standing there showing you how to do it as a book can, which is perhaps not so close. The lack of emphasis on safety procedures is a perhaps a fatal flaw. An aspirator should always be used when sanding fiberglass & the liquid resin should never come in contact with your skin—use rubber gloves.

[Suggested and Reviewed by Day Chahroudi]

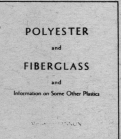

Polyester & Fiberglass
Maurice Lannon
1953, 69; 126pp.

$4.50 postpaid

from:
Gem-O-Lite Plastics Corp.
5525 Cahuenga Blvd.
North Hollywood, Ca. 91601

It is now used for making automobile bodies (Chevrolet's "Corvette" has an all-fiberglass body), and for making a permanent boat coating. Many manufacturers are using it to produce washing machine agitators, vacuum cleaners, "glass" fishing rods, dent-resistant tanks for chemicals and acids, protective safety helmets, Marine bullet-proof vests that weigh only eight pounds and will stop most shrapnel and small-arms fire, electrical insulation, laminates, precision-molded housings for machinery, skis, fishing tackle, chairs, futuristic furniture, garden furniture (Impervious to rain and sun), trailers, bathtubs, even coffins. And *you* can make any of these!

POLYESTER PLASTIC RESIN is a thick viscous liquid about like corn syrup to which a catalyst (and sometimes an accelerator) is added. It sets up hard and stiff yet has the resiliency to resist repeated hammer blows when used with fiberglass. Polyester alone is brittle in thin sheets. Fiberglass adds strength.

There are many different formulations of Polyester on the market. The variety of properties that can be obtained from this one plastic is amazing, but as there are many Polyester manufacturers, of course there are many different Polyesters, each made for laminating and/or casting, but with properties that vary slightly, and with several different manufacturer-recommended catalysts and accelerators. It is always wise to follow your dealer's recommendations on the catalyst system to use. Then experiment with other systems if you want to.

Plastics

How does a person who becomes interested in plastics find out all there is to know about plastics? One solution may be to spend the rest of your life walking from plastic company to plastic company finding out what each are doing. This would be OK if you were looking for something to do for a long period of time. But if you are longing for a comprehensive review of the world of plastics and/or some good solid reference material on the subject, then i suggest **Plastics in the Modern World.** *It is an interesting little Pelican Original pocket book by two Englishmen; E.G. Couzens and V.E. Yarsley. Part one contains: the Theory and Practice of Plastics which discusses the physical, chemical and behavioral aspects of plastics, while also explaining the manufacturing processes involved in plastics production. Part two of the book concerns itself with the domestic application of plastics and the utilization of plastics by industry.*

[Suggested and Reviewed by Michael Rosenthal]

A special application of plastics is in concrete mixing; the addition of 4 per cent of epoxy resin to coat the sand and aggregate particles before water-mixing is said to increase the tensile strength 2½ times. Reduction in shrinkage and crack tendency can be effected, along with an increase in tensile strength by using a 32 per cent aqueous dispersion of vinyl chloride, or styrene-butadiene copolymer, while an acrylic liquid modifier, known as 'Sonocrete', is used for producing a surface resistant to water and salt. The most recent development in the use of plastics concrete mixes is known as 'Estercrete', a general name given to products made by mixing unsaturated polyester resins, ethylenically unsaturated monomers, and Portland cement.

New Science of Strong Materials

Why does glass sometimes shatter and other times bend like a spring? A new field of science involves the study of materials as a whole, rather than in their special chemical, physical, and engineering aspects. Scientists have been investigating the atoms and molecules upon which the mechanical properties of materials depend, and this book is a clear explanation of some of the discoveries being made. Nothing beyond high school math, and a very palatable treatment of an exciting new science.

*[Suggested by Steve Baer.
Reviewed by Lloyd Kahn]*

New Science of Strong Materials
J. E. Gordon
1968; 269 pp.

$7.50

from:
Walker & Co.
720 Fifth Avenue
New York, N. Y. 10019

or WHOLE EARTH CATALOG

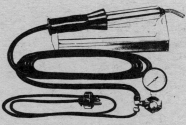

Electric Plastic Welder
yes, you can weld plastic.

—jd

$95.00 plus postage
(information free)

from:
Seelye Plastics
9700 Newton Avenue South
Minneapolis, MN 55431

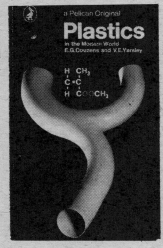

Plastics in the Modern World
E. G. Couzens, V. E. Yarsley
1941, 1956, 1968; 386 pp.

$1.65 postpaid

from:
Pelican Books
7110 Ambassador Road
Baltimore, Md. 21207

or WHOLE EARTH CATALOG

The choice of adhesive is determined by price, the nature of the substances to be joined, the strength of the bond required, and the appropriate glueing process. Thus phenol-formaldehyde and urea-formaldehyde glues are used chiefly for bonding wood, especially plywood; they may be either hot- or cold-setting according to the composition used, and P.F. resins give joints resistant to boiling water. The phenol glue gives the stronger joint, but leaves a dark glue line. The urea resis are cheap, colourless, easily handled, and extensively used in furniture, where moisture resistance is not important. They can also be applied in separate layers, that is with the resin on one surface and the hardener on the other, and where heating is required, radio-frequency heating of the 'glue line' can be employed. In general plastics glues have the advantage over screws and nails that they avoid local stresses and give joints of great strength.

If easy, cheap production of sufficient accuracy can be achieved by small units then we may be able to reverse some of the centralizing trends of the Industrial Revolution and perhaps, in part, to set ourselves free from the worst tyrannies of mass production. There may then be more room for individualistic skills and for individual tastes – perhaps we shall all feel better for it. However there is very little research going on along these lines at present and I am afraid that the Satanic Mills have still quite a long future before them.

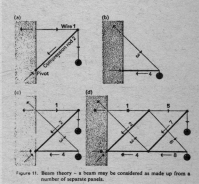

Figure 11. Beam theory – a beam may be considered as made up from a number of separate panels.

The first thing we discovered was that we could get high strength from almost anything from Epsom salts to sapphire. Provided it was in the form of a thin whisker, it did not matter what the chemical nature of the stuff was or by what method the whiskers were grown. We must have worked on well over a hundred different substances and there was absolutely no doubt about it.

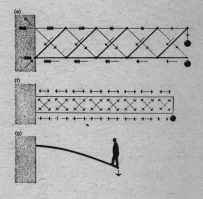

The worst sin in an engineering material is not lack of strength or lack of stiffness, desirable as these properties are, but lack of toughness, that is to say, lack of resistance to the propagation of cracks. One can allow for lack of strength or stiffness in design but it is much more difficult to allow for cracks which catch the engineer unawares and are dangerous.

"Now. Today we are concerned with time expansion. A lot of people have different notions of what time expansion is, and they approach the phenomena in a variety of different ways. But the thing that all the ways have in common is that time expansion implies a more intense experience of the present, the here and now. I'm sure that many of you sitting there listening to my voice are still not actually <u>here</u> in this moment, with me, <u>now</u>, as I talk to you. Your minds are filled with thoughts of other people and other places, of experience that has already happened or that you are waiting on to happen, or that you wished had happened or would happen. This is very common. Indeed, it is the way most people go around in their minds all the time. And it is a most wasteful, and actually harmful, destructive way to conduct your mental life. What we are going to do today is play a little self-hypnosis game that, once you master it, can be useful to you in helping you to learn how to live in the present in a natural, vital way.

"So, if you will, lie down now, and make yourself comfortable on the floor, or on a mat, or mattress, or whatever you are lying on. Let your body sink and relax into the floor. Feel the relaxation begin in your toes and flow up through your legs, into your thighs, feel it flood your mid-region and swell on up through your chest. Relax your hands, relax your elbows, and your arms and your shoulders. And let the tensions go out of your neck, and your jaw muscles, let your entire face relax and settle naturally against your bones. Feel the relaxation flowing through you from your toes right up through your scalp, and feel your breath going in and out evenly and without effort.

(continued)

Thomas Register of American Manufacturers

Let it all hang out: 7 volumes, 10,000 pages, 50,000 product ads, 70,000 classifications. It's the great American industrial yellow pages—and like the yellow pages, an education. If the Sears Catalog will tell you where American consumption is at TR tells you what's happening in production. And if you're trying to make the switch toward production, TR can help you find what you need.

—SB

Thomas Register
published annually in the summer

$44.75 postpaid

from:
Thomas Register
Sales Division
310 East 44th Street
New York, N.Y. 10017
also available in most libraries

KIND OF INFORMATION T. R. WILL FURNISH
For every industry, every manufacturer, every product, anywhere in the U. S. A.

VOLUMES 1, 2, 3, 4, 5 and 6

1—Does anyone in Alabama make Cast Iron Pipe?
2—Are Induction Coils manufactured in Wyoming?
3—Who makes Electric Motors in Michigan?
4—Is there a large manufacturer of Rubber Hose in Connecticut?

VOLUME 7

5—Trademark Section.
6—Where are the plants of the Allis-Chalmers Mfg. Co.?
7—Who succeeded the Acme Rubber Mfg. Co.?
8—Where is the home office of the Bristol Brass Corp.?
9—How many products does General Electric make and what are they?
10—Is Novo Pump & Engine Co. a parent company or subsidiary?
11—Where are the branch offices of the Star Expansion Co.?
12—What is the capital rating of the Western Supply Co.?
13—Who are the officials of the Erie Foundry Co.?
14—What is the cable address of Acme Visible Records, Inc.?
15—What companies does Howmet Corp. own or control?

Last Year Cheaper

Thomas Register can often be gotten FREE (also last year's) by approaching industrial libraries, or even the local Public Library, who generally get swamped by everybody's old edition. Big businesses make a real thing out of keeping up to date and Thomas doesn't update with supplements—new 7 volumes every year.

Peter Heinlein
Yonkers, N.Y.

Clearinghouse

Its full name is "Clearinghouse for Federal Scientific and Technical Information," it's managed by the U. S. Department of Commerce, and it's quite a service. All current unclassified R&D (research and development) done for or by the Government is available through Clearinghouse; this amounts to 30,000 new documents each year. Specific accesses are: U. S. Government Research and Development Reports (December 1,000 new documents twice a month), $22/year; Fast Announcement Service, for as many as 57 subject areas, delivered constantly, $5/year; and Technical Translations, twice a month, $12/year. These are indexes. Once you find what you want you order a paper copy (hard copy) for around $3 or micro-film (microfiche) for around $.65. The following examples of listings are from the Fast Announcement Service.

[Suggested by Jon Dieges]

Noyes Data on Industrial Equipment

When you're shopping for big industrial goodies like Waste Water Cleanup Equipment, Desalinization Plants, Artificial Kidneys, Superconducting Materials, Freeze-Drying processes, Air Pollution Devices, Soundproof Building Materials, Solar Cells, etc. . .these big books ($35 for each subject) will give you the technological specs, operating principles, etc. for comparison shopping.

—SB

Noyes Data Corporation
Noyes Building
Park Ridge, New Jersey 07656

International Yellow Pages

Wes Wilson was asking about listings of manufacturers in Europe. May I suggest International Yellow Pages. Look for it in the library. When he finds the countries he is interested in then approach the telephone company as he has done before.

The International Yellow Pages is now at least three times as big as 2-3 years ago. Fascinating reading.

There are many other sources of the type of material he wants. Most of it has a price tag but usually not too much for what is covered.

How about contacting Chambers of Commerce located in this country? As an example: Swedish American. While in the library find a New York, San Francisco, or any large city telephone or city directory for a list of such Chambers of Commerce.

Have fun.

V.A. Emery
Keene, New Hampshire

FAST ANNOUNCEMENT
CLEARINGHOUSE
ANNOUNCEMENT

Write for free information and order forms to:

U. S. Department of Commerce
Clearinghouse for Federal Scientific
and Technical Information
Springfield, VA 22151

AD-691 231 -- THE INFORMATION THEORY ASPECT OF TELEPATHY, I. M. Kogan, U.S.S.R., 1969, translated from Russian, July 69, 26p.

AD-677 116 -- A SOLAR-ILLUMINATED ALGAL PHOTOSYNTHETIC EXCHANGER, R. L. Miller et al., Martin Co., Denver, Colo., for the Air Force, June 68, 26p. . . . . Describes a continuous culture system for studying the use of solar energy for algal growth and photosynthetic gas exchange.

. . ORDER: PB-180 051 -- TRITON CITY - A PROTOTYPE FLOATING COMMUNITY, Triton Foundation, Inc., Cambridge, Mass., for the Dept. of Housing and Urban Development, Nov. 68. 131p.

↖ Fuller's floating city

AD-683 047 -- WHAT IS MEMORY THAT IT MAY HAVE HINDSIGHT AND FORESIGHT AS WELL, H. Von Foerster, Univ. of Illinois, Urbana, for the Air Force, Jan. 69, 61p. . . . . Discusses the phenomenon of physiological memory from the viewpoint that memory is embeded into the totality of cognitive processes and considered as a computational operation rather than a storage and retrieval problem.

AD-681 752 -- A FIFTEEN-YEAR FORECAST OF INFORMATION-PROCESSING TECHNOLOGY, G. B. Bernstein, Naval Supply Systems Command, Washington, D. C., Jan. 69, 187p. . . . . Uses SEER (System for Event Evaluation and Review), a technique that incorporates the consensus of participatent experts, to produce a technological forecast of what is expected to occur in the information-processing industry.

PB-180 665 -- THE INFLUENCE OF DESIGN ON EXPOSED WOOD IN BUILDINGS OF THE PUGET SOUND AREA, E. W. Schein, USDA, Pacific Northwest Forest and Range Experiment Station, Portland, Ore., Sept. 68, 50p. . . . . Identifies the best existing design solutions to exposure hazards.

AD-680 168 -- SPIRAL GENERATION OF BUILDING SHELLS FOR MILITARY CONSTRUCTION, A. N. Collishaw and R. D. Graham, Dept. of the Army, Ohio River Division Labs., Corps of Engineers, Cincinnati, Ohio, Nov. 68, 30p. . . . . Discusses immediate and potential applications of the spiral generation construction process to military construction. Included are permanent, semi-permanent, and temporary construction.

PB-182 401 -- BUILDING CLIMATOLOGY, PART IV: NOISE, National Swedish Institute for Building Research, Stockholm, 1968, 86p. . . . . Annotated bibliography of literature dealing with the following aspects of noise: (1) subjective reactions to sound, noise, and vibration, (2) objective methods of registering sound and noise, (3) noise situations, (4) fighting noise (technical and legal steps to improve noise climate) and sound insulation, (5) acoustic planning, and (6) theory of sound propagation.

AD-678 571 -- TAN-O-QUIL-QM TREATMENT FOR FEATHERS AND DOWN, G. Cohen, U.S. Army Natick Labs., Natick, Mass., Aug. 68, 80p. . . . . Describes a process for treatment of feathers and down that uses a tanning agent and a water repellent and is applicable to both landfowl and waterfowl feather filling materials. Feathers treated by the process have increased filling power that is durable to laundering, are free from dust, are exceptionally clean, and will not develop an odor even when wet.

AD-685 850 -- WATER SUPPLY IN COLD REGIONS, A. J. Alter, Cold Regions Research & Engineering Lab., Hanover, N. H., Jan. 69, 94p. . . . . Discusses the influence of a cold environment on sanitary engineering works and services, water supply engineering in cold regions, and water supply during military field operations. Report includes a bibliography.

AD-688 132 -- POLYURETHANE FOAMS: TECHNOLOGY, PROPERTIES AND APPLICATIONS, A. H. Landrock, Picatinny Arsenal, Dover, N. J., Jan. 69, available in paper copy only, $15.50, 257p. . . . . Discusses state-of-the-art of urethane foams. Topics covered are: chemistry of urethane foam process; types of polyurethane foam; methods of manufacture; toxicity of raw materials; adhesives and other methods of joining; surface coatings; foam properties; test methods; military and space applications; economics and costs; comparative properties of other foams; specifications and standards; trade designations; and definitions of terms. Report includes a bibliography of over 700 references from the open literature, government project and contract reports, commercial bulletins, and conference papers.

AD-686 723 -- WIND SURFING--A NEW CONCEPT IN SAILING, J. R. Drake, RAND Corp., Santa Monica, Calif., Apr. 69, 23p. . . . . Describes various board and sail configurations used in wind-surfing. The hand-held fully articulated sail is an entirely new means of propulsion and control.

↑ This one is great, a stand-up surfboard with a ball-joint flexible-boom sail. Surf in, then turn around and surf out. Design and instructions.

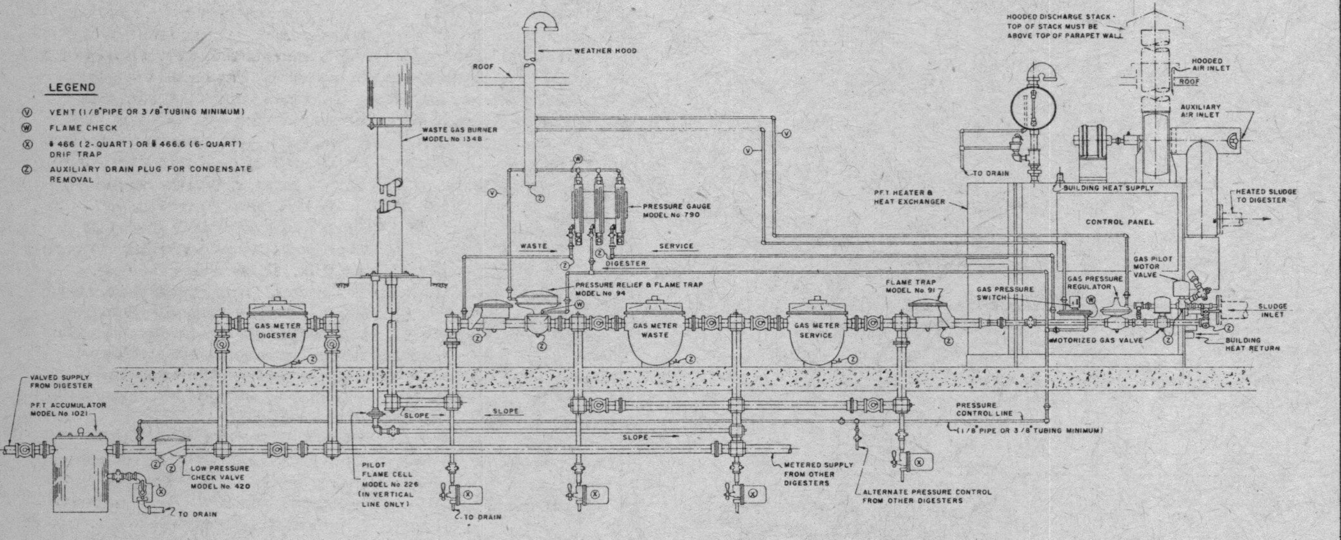
LEGEND
Ⓥ VENT (1/8" PIPE OR 3/8" TUBING MINIMUM)
Ⓦ FLAME CHECK
Ⓧ #466 (2-QUART) OR #466.6 (6-QUART) DRIP TRAP
Ⓩ AUXILIARY DRAIN PLUG FOR CONDENSATE REMOVAL
WEATHER HOOD
ROOF
WASTE GAS BURNER MODEL No 1348
PRESSURE GAUGE MODEL No 790
WASTE
SERVICE
DIGESTER
PRESSURE RELIEF & FLAME TRAP MODEL No 94
GAS METER DIGESTER
GAS METER WASTE
GAS METER SERVICE
FLAME TRAP MODEL No 91
HOODED DISCHARGE STACK - TOP OF STACK MUST BE ABOVE TOP OF PARAPET WALL
HOODED AIR INLET
AUXILIARY AIR INLET
TO DRAIN
P.F.T. HEATER & HEAT EXCHANGER
BUILDING HEAT SUPPLY
HEATED SLUDGE TO DIGESTER
CONTROL PANEL
GAS PILOT MOTOR VALVE
GAS PRESSURE REGULATOR
GAS PRESSURE SWITCH
SLUDGE INLET
MOTORIZED GAS VALVE
BUILDING HEAT RETURN
VALVED SUPPLY FROM DIGESTER
P.F.T. ACCUMULATOR MODEL No 1021
SLOPE
LOW PRESSURE CHECK VALVE MODEL No 420
TO DRAIN
PILOT FLAME CELL MODEL No 226 (IN VERTICAL LINE ONLY)
METERED SUPPLY FROM OTHER DIGESTERS
ALTERNATE PRESSURE CONTROL FROM OTHER DIGESTERS
PRESSURE CONTROL LINE
(1/8" PIPE OR 3/8" TUBING MINIMUM)

Lefax Data Sheets

Since 1910 Lefax Publishing Company has been producing data sheets on an enormous number of technical subjects ranging from athletic fields, dimensions of, to 1,3-butadiene, thermodynamic, properties of. Some are useful and some seem useless. The best part of the Lefax system is that you only buy the ones you want. Anything from 14 pages on Steam Boilers (30¢) to a complete library with a file cabinet ($140). Even single pages are obtainable, but you must buy 25 of each at 15¢ each. The best buys seem to be broad topic loose leaf binders like the Handi-Fax do-it-yourself home owners manual which cost $5 to $10 for 200 to 500 pages. Data books on such topics as Diesel Engineering, Machine Design, Home Heating, Piping Data, Lumber Data, Surveying Tables, A.C. Motors and Generators, Mining Geology, etc. at $2 each also look reasonable. Much of the data is ageless, but some seems rather outdated. This isn't always a disadvantage, though, since "old-fashioned" methods are often more useful to the amateur than "modern" methods. All data sheets are 3-3/4 in x 6-3/4 in., a convenient size to carry around and are loose leaf so you carry only the useful ones. Catalog is free from Lefax Publishing Company, 2867 East Allegheny Avenue, Philadelphia, PA 19134. *I guarantee you'll find information you didn't know you needed.*

[Suggested and reviewed by Ron O'Dor]

Lefax Publishing Co.
2867 East Allegheny Avenue
Philadelphia, PA 19134

BUILDER'S DATA (#628)
Contents include: Fireplaces; Stair Building; Wall Framing; Concrete Guide; Heating Systems; Brick Construction; Plumbing Systems; Interior & Exterior Doors; Floors; Girders; Sills & Joints; Heating & Ventilating Charts; Automatic Wall Measurement Tables.

THERMODYNAMIC TABLES AND CHARTS (#634)
Contents include: Freon 22; Refrigerants; Dowtherm A; Water Vapor; Petroleum Oils; Compressed Air; Properties of Solid & Saturated Carbon Dioxide; Properties of Ammonia; Specific Heat of the Elements.

WELDING DATA (#645)
Contents include: Wire Gauges; Pipe Welding; Copper Welding; Welding Wrought Iron; Fusion Welding of Aluminum; Standard Terms & Definitions; Temperature Conversion Tables; Weldability of Metals by Electric Arc.

All at $2.50 each

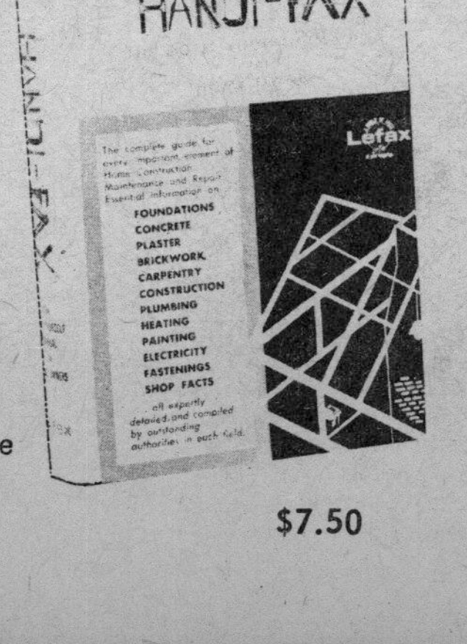
HANDI-FAX
Lefax

Essential information on ....
FOUNDATIONS
CONCRETE
PLASTER
BRICKWORK
CARPENTRY
CONSTRUCTION
PLUMBING
HEATING
PAINTING
ELECTRICITY
FASTENINGS
SHOP FACTS
.... all expertly detailed and compiled by outstanding authorities in each field.

$7.50

How to Invent

Last month, when I visited you in Menlo Park you invited me to write about inventing, and what I would have liked to read that might have been helpful when I started inventing 15 years ago.

I'm enclosing some material on my most recent work, a so-called "patent network" in which a direct relationship exists among four inventions. Each of the inventions is illustrative of a different kind of invention in the sense that each was arrived at in a different way:

The SunBird kite was developed accidentally in an effort to work out a method of preventing kites from diving out of control. (An example of trying to invent B and coming up with A.

The compression tension kite that turned into a cabana is an example of simply recognizing that something that my hands had done was an invention.

The stressed skin structure is an invention which I regard as inexplicable insight (except that, in retrospect, it is the logical relative of a claim in my compression tension patent).

The modular building system was a deliberate attempt at compromise; an effort to combine a multiplicity of stressed skin modules into a cohesive unity, but the selection of the octant as the basic module was intuitive.

Most investigators of the "creative process" seem to agree that invention is non-sense. . .a subconscious, alogical activity which is the unique output of the human random-access memory when triggered by appropriate stimuli. It's nonsense when it happens, but after the fact it makes very good sense indeed.

Since the memory is involved it follows that the broader and deeper the experiences recorded in the memory, the greater the arsenal which can be drawn upon by the subconscious for its synthesizing activity. A rather long-winded way of saying, "if you're going to invent, it's a good idea to have a broad understanding of how the real world is put together; how things work; how things are made; and how the hands and their extensions, tools, make them."

The best inventor I know is Mother Nature. She holds most of the basic patents, (maybe all of them), so perhaps evolution is one way to get the job done.

Another way is accident. I've heard it said that an average chimpanzee turned loose on a typewriter, would eventually turn out every word in the Bible, and I suppose that his cousin, turned loose in my workshop, would have eventually put together both the SunBird Kite and the Modular building.

I just couldn't wait. Time's growing short.

Don Gellert

During the research which preceded final development of the Sun-Bird, the inventor explored the work of Alexander Graham Bell, (who was a pretty serious kite flyer himself), and developed a compression-tension modification of Mr. Bell's tetrahedron kite.

While the structure was not notably successful as a kite, a pair of Siamese cats took up residence in the prototype, and led the inventor to the development of a new modular housing system on which three patents have been issued during the last 18 months.

Figure 3 shows the fabric tetrahedron as modified into a compression tension structure.

A variation of this structure, using a curved spine and semi-rigid surfaces (instead of fabric surfaces) without the external compression members is shown in Figure 4.

Figure 5, an interlocking dome system using the same module.

A FULLY CONTROLLABLE TETHERED GLIDER

If you hear talk about a kite that can: write your name in the sky; dive, loop, spin, hover on command; plunge into the water swim around and take off again; fly in formation; dance to music. . .and stuff like that the gadget that actually performs that way is a SunBird Aerobatic Kite.

A two-part invention which was developed more or less by accident, the SunBird consists of a delta wing kite, with independently movable wings, and a control reel that handles each of the two control strings and allows them to be payed out or reeled in simultaneously.

Kite flying is a sport, and the SunBird is a piece of durable precision engineered sports equipment. It takes skill to use it, and time to develop that skill but after a dozen flights or so, when you've mastered the control system it's the nearest thing to a tree-eating kite there is.

While the SunBird Kite included in the kit is considered to be the best controllable kite ever developed, the SunBird Control can be attached to almost any kite, and instructions for attachment to other kites are included together with full instructions for handling the Control System.

These designs have been rendered in fabric, urethane-covered fabric, cardboard, aluminum and urethane covered aluminum, freestanding urethane, plywood panels, steel-lath-and-concrete. The largest span to date is 26 feet (for a single module and was fabricated as a free-standing urethane panel.)

The advantages of the system lie in its power to develop, out of plane surfaces, extremely strong, thin shell structures with curved surfaces imply.

Readers interested in experimenting with the structure are invited to correspond with the inventor. Background theory material and representative designs are being assembled for reproduction and will be available at $2.00 per copy together with a license to erect experimental structures. Commercial applications may be arranged on an individual basis.

Figure 1

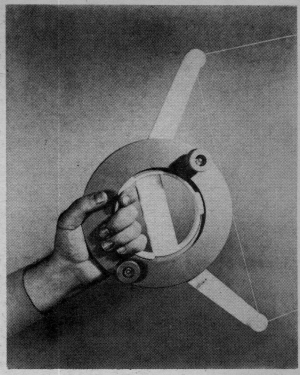

Figure 2

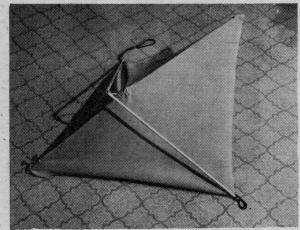

Figure 3

Figure 4

Figure 5

"As your body has settled into deep rest, your mind has been relaxing too, emptying itself until now it is cool and clear and free of all images except those I will suggest to you with my voice. Your mind is like a wall with absolutely nothing on it, no shape, no form, no color. It is empty and at rest, ready to receive the image of three boxes, three simple boxes sitting side by side in the middle of the empty space of your mind. The boxes are all the same size, and they are sitting in the same positions, with their fronts toward you, so that you can read the words written on the front of each box. Except for these words, the boxes are just alike, three neat boxes, very simple and clean of line, sitting next to each other in your mind. On the front of the box on the left is the word 'Past.' The box on the right is labeled, 'Future,' and the box in the center is labeled 'Present.' Keep seeing all three boxes sitting there together, now, but pay particular attention to the box on the left, the 'Past' box. Think about that box a minute, and think about the word 'past.' And as you think about the word 'past' begin to put into the box all those things in your mind that you ordinarily associate with the word past. All your memories, all your recollections, all your backward longings. everything in your mind that has anything at all to do with the past put it into the box on the left, and when you have done this, close the lid.

"Now you have closed the lid on the box marked 'Past.' Continue to see all three boxes in a row, but turn your attention now to the box on the right, in particular, the one marked 'Future.' Think about the word 'Future,' and as you think about it, begin to fill up the box on the right with all those elements in your mind that have anything at all to do with the future. All your ambitions, all your plans, every forward longing, every expectation, the very concept of the future, put in the box now, and when you have it all in, close the lid. The past and the future are now closed. You don't have to think about either of them again. The three boxes are still there, side by side in your mind, but the only one you are interested in now is the one in the middle, marked 'Present.' Turn all of your attention to the box in the middle marked 'Present.' Concentrate your entire mind on everything you can grasp that belongs to this particular present moment of your life. Everything that is, now, put in the box marked 'Present,' and watch, notice how the box in the middle is beginning to grow in size. You continue to put in it everything that you can possibly get hold of in this moment, this now, but as you do the box is growing, getting larger, it is swelling in length and heighth and breadth. You continue to put in it all the elements of the here and now that you can get hold of, but as you find them and put them in, you discover more and more of the present that should be included in the box.

"And as the middle box grows, the other two boxes on either side get smaller and smaller in proportion. They get smaller and smaller as the box in the middle gets larger and larger. And gradually the box in the middle begins to crowd the other two boxes out of your mental picture. Their place is being consumed by the box in the middle, which you continue to fill with every stray possibility out of the world of here and now. The two boxes on the sides are so small now you can barely see them. And now they are gone.

"Now there is only the box in the middle, the 'Present,' box, still swelling, still growing, getting larger and larger with every breath you breathe.

"And now the edges of even this box begin to disappear into the limits of your picture. It is beginning to lose its form, its identity as a box, it is turning into pure space now, pure light, and inside it is every aspect, every partical of now, of here, of this single, living breathing, on-going instant of your life."

Meccano

Meccano, originated by Frank Hornby, a Liverpool inventor, in 1901, was the prototype minature metal construction system. American children are familiar with Erector, European kinder with Trix and Marklin, but they all spring from Hornby's original brainchild. Meccano is sold today from open stock, and in sets ranging in price from $3.00 to $300.00. There are hundreds of extra specialized parts available, and power units including two sizes of clockwork motors (these are genuine governor-controlled drives, not flimsy windups), four different electric motors operating on 4½ volts D.C. to 240 volts A.C., and a reversing steam engine. Meccano gears are machined brass with setscrews; most other parts are stamped and plated steel. Auxiliary sets are available for making gear transmissions, mechanisms such as intermittent drives, and generators. Plans for many complex models are available from the factory, and there is a quarterly Meccano Magazine with projects such as regulator clocks described in detail.

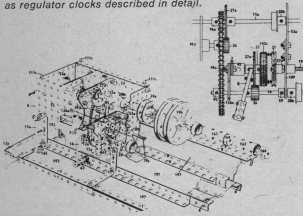

The point of all this is that if you want to breadboard an invention or a machine, Meccano is a tested, economical way to do it. Many laboratories in England carry stocks of Meccano parts to build test models with. Meccano is available in a few stores, such as Sears, in the United States, but you are better off ordering it from major British toy suppliers such as Beatties of London, 10 Broadway, London N. 14, or Manley's, Lombard Road, Merton, London S.W. 19. After more than half a century Meccano is still a viable mechanical system. It's also a pretty good toy.

[Suggested and reviewed by Dr. Morton Grosser]

Formulas, Methods, Tips and Data

Toothpaste, soap, detergent, chemical cleaners for drainpipe & toilet bowl; paint stripper, radiator quick flush, paints, dyes all have cookbook, electric mixer & stove & mixing bowl behind their shiney marketable exteriors. You eliminate several steps in the cycle between your natural resources and your products when you brew them at home. Some things (like soap) can be better quality than you buy. Some are less expensive. Unities emerge at the level of chemical ingredients which are not at all visible in the supermarket. And even if you go back to shelf-ware at some point in the future you do so with different eyes.

[Reviewed by Doug Gunesch]

Formulas, Methods, Tips and Data for Home and Workshop
Kenneth M. Swezey
1969; 691 pp.

$7.95 postpaid

from:
Harper and Row Publishers
49 East 33rd Street
New York, New York 10016

or WHOLE EARTH CATALOG

BASIC SOAP FORMULA. To make 9 pounds of pure, hard, smooth soap suitable for toilet, laundry, or soap flakes, follow this simple recipe:

Cold water	2½ pints
Pure flake lye	1 13-oz. can
Clean fat (tallow or lard, or combination)	6 pounds
6 pounds of fat is about 6¾ pints of liquid fat.	

Slowly pour the lye into the water in a Pyrex, iron, or enamel vessel (*Caution:* Don't spill lye solution on your skin, clothing, or furnishings, as it is extremely caustic). Stir until the lye is completely dissolved. Then let it cool to the correct temperature as shown in the table to follow.

Melt fat to clear liquid and let cool to correct temperature as shown in table, or until the fat offers resistance to the spoon. Stir occasionally to prevent crystals from forming. Pour the lye solution into the fat in a *thin, steady stream with slow, even stirring.* (Rapid addition of lye solution or hard stirring is apt to cause a separation.) A honey-like consistency is formed which becomes thick in from 10 to 20 minutes.

Meccano available in the United States from:

Ava International, Inc.
6500 Depot Drive
P.O. Box 7611
Waco, Texas 76710

Automat Engineering Sets

Mechanical prototyping kits. Frame system, gear systems, and variable speed motors. Presumably precise; not cheap (kits $275-$920).

—SB
[Suggested by Alan Kalker]

R. C. Distributing Company
6001 Dexter St.
Commerce City, Colorado 80022

PIC Design Corp.

Precision components. Gears, shafting, clutches, dials, differentials, and a precision 522-page catalog.

[Suggested by Fred Richardson]

Catalog
free

from:
PIC Design Corporation
477 Atlantic Avenue
East Rockaway, N. Y. 11518

6842 Van Nuys Blvd.
Van Nuys, CA 91405

Henley's

Henley's was first published in 1907, and is a fascinating mixture of obsolete and still useful formulas and processes as advertised. Some are useful but obscure (formulas for fire-eating); Some are useful but who cares? (formulas for furniture glue not as good as what you can buy); Some are frighteningly incomplete (the section on explosives); Some are bizarre (a hair pomade containing Spanish Fly); Some you can get better elsewhere (ceramic glazes); Some are funny (remove frost from windows by swabbing them with sulfuric acid); Many brews require chemicals not easily available, but sources are given (mostly in New York) and there is a glossary or outmoded terms. Some of the formulas might be of historical interest (how to make harness grease). It's not a pretty book; every copy I've seen has printing flaws, probably due to worn plates. I've been happily thumbing through my copy now and then for many years. I've never used anything from it.

[Suggested and Reviewed by Jay Baldwin]

Pour the thickened mixture into a wooden box that has been soaked in water and lined with a clean cotton cloth wet in water and wrung nearly dry. Place in a protecting pan. Cover with a board or cardboard, then with an old rug or blanket to retain the heat while it is texturing out. Leave it alone for 24 hours.

To remove the soap from the mold, lift it by the ends of the overhanging cotton lining. Cut into bars by wrapping the soap with a fine wire and pulling the wire through. Place so air can reach it, but avoid drafts and cold. Aging improves soap. In 10 to 14 days it is ready for use.

TEMPERATURE TABLE. Follow these temperatures closely:

Type of fat	Temp. of fat	Temp. of lye sol.
Sweet lard or other soft fat	98 degrees F	77 degrees F
Half lard and tallow	105 degrees F	83 degrees F
All tallow	125 degrees F	93 degrees '

Unistrut

Unistrut is great stuff. You can make houses, furniture, partitions, stage sets, boat trailers and just about all sorts of things out of it, and can take them apart later and use the Unistrut again. It comes in several sizes, in several metals and finishes, and is completely adjustable. I've used it for such diverse things as tables, store interiors, pack frames, animation stands and camera dollies, telescopes. Unistrut is distributed nationwide, but locally there may be competitors that offer cheaper prices and different finishes. Good for space frames such as Fuller's octet truss.

Similar in use but not in sophistication is "Giant Erector Set" slotted angle that goes under a number of trade names. It's usually called "slotted angle" or "metal lumber" in the Yellow Pages. It's particularly good for shelving and camping bus interiors, where 2 x 4's are not really suitable. A good brand is AIM (for list of distributors, write Frank Bonneville, Interlake Inc., 761 Port Chicago Highway, Pittsburg, CA 94565. It costs about the same as finished lumber and takes no skill at all to use. Comes with bolts and nuts and a simple table to calculate loads. Also Good Stuff.

[Suggested and reviewed by Jay Baldwin]

Unistrut Catalogs
free

from:
Unistrut Corporation
4118 South Wayne Road
Wayne, Michigan 48184

AIM

Dexion

Dexion is another brand of metal lumber. —SB

[Suggested by Rick]

Dexion
39-27 59th St.
Woodside, N.Y. 11377

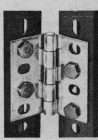

3" x 3" galvanized steel hinges, bolt directly to Dexion Slotted Angle 140, 160, 225 and 260 sections.
Each .... **$.95**

Henley's

1907 . . . 1957; 867pp.

$6.95 postpaid

from:
Embassy Sales
Box 67
East Elmhurst, New York 11369

or WHOLE EARTH CATALOG

Anti-Freezing Solution for Automobilists.—In the average size (20 qt.) automobile engine radiator, if 1½ gallons of ethylene glycol is used, together with 10 oz. of sodium chromate, the radiator and engine block will be protected to −20° F., and the cooling system will at the same time be protected against destruction by corrosion.

Anti-Freezing, Non-Corrosive Solution.—A solution for water-jackets on gas engines that will not freeze at any temperature above 20° below zero (F.) may be made by combining 100 parts of water, by weight, with 75 parts of carbonate potash and 50 parts of glycerine. This solution is non-corrosive and will remain perfectly liquid at all temperatures above its congealing point.

Anti-Frost Solution.—As an excellent remedy against the freezing of shop windows, apply a mixture consisting of 55 parts of glycerine dissolved in 1,000 parts of 62 per cent alcohol, containing, to improve the odor, some oil of amber. As soon as the mixture clarifies, it is rubbed over the inner surface of the glass. This treatment, it is claimed, not only prevents the formation of frost, but also stops sweating.

FIRE EXTINGUISHER (For Automobile):
Mix well together:
98 Parts of Carbonate of Soda
2 Parts of Oxide of Iron

When this mixture is thrown on a fire carbonic gas is liberated. This gas being heavier than air, smothers the fire.

RED FOR WOOL. For 40 pounds of goods, make a tolerably thick paste of lac dye and sulphuric acid, and allow it to stand for a day. Then take tartar, 4 pounds, tin liquor, 2 pounds 8 ounces, & 3 pounds of the paste; make a hot bath with sufficient water, and enter the goods for ¾ hour; afterwards carefully rinse and dry.

Small Engines Service Manual

*pretty complete diagrams on
repair of all types of small gasoline engines. if your
chainsaw is lugging down,
your pump sputtering,
your washingmachine clunking,
your lawnmower rusting away,
this book will help.*

—jd

Small Engine Service Manual
1973; 304 pp.

$5.95 postpaid

from:
Howard W. Sams Co.
4300 West 62nd Street
Indianapolis, Ind. 46206
or WHOLE EARTH CATALOG

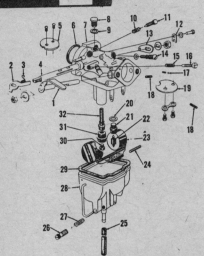

**Fig. HN1-1 — Exploded view of the Keihin
float type carburetor used on Honda industrial engines. Refer to Fig. HN1-2 for cross-
sectional view of carburetor, and to Fig.
HN1-3 for view showing method of checking float level adjustment.**

File Filosophy

*Nicholson has been making files for 106 years, so it is
only right that they publish a book about files called
File Filosophy. If you ever use files, the book is worth
getting, the more so because it is free.*

*Nicholson also has Sawology, about power and hand metal
cutting. Again free.*

[Reviewed by Fred Richardson]

File Filosophy
1956; 46pp.

free

from:
Nicholson File Co.
Providence, Rhode Island 02940

Velodur

The following is from a Navy report.

—SB

DESCRIPTION

Velodur-metal is a molecular bonding metal that can be used to bond
materials together without heat or energy. Its components are macro-
molecular substances and atomized steel and aluminum particles
which form a metallic bond. It can be used on steel, aluminum,
copper, brass, zinc, concrete, tile, glass, wood, rubber, cast iron, and
synthetics. Two or more unlike metallic materials may be bonded
together with no electrolytic action taking place. Velodur-metal is
nontoxic, nonflammable, it has unlimited shelf life, will resist heat
up to 570 degrees F, and will not conduct electricity. The standard
bonding metal consists of two components, an activator and a base.
These two components are mixed by volume on a 1 : 1 ratio. The
curing time is 3-4 hours; after this time Velodur-metal may be
drilled, threaded, machined or ground. Velodur-metal also comes
in a rapid form, mixed on a 1 : 1 ratio also, that allows repairs on
tanks, piping systems and other pressure vessels while still under
pressure. Velodur rapid cures in 4-5 minutes. However, the Velodur
rapid will not hold up as well as the standard Velodur. After using
the Velodur rapid to stop the flow of pressure the Velodur standard
metal should be applied over the rapid for the best and lasting
results.

USS NANTAHALA (AO 60) — Butterworth heater, upper level,
forward engineroom, expansion joint was badly deteriorated along
bottom and continually leaking due to several holes. Welding or
brazing were impossible. Velodur-metal was applied using fiberglass
cloth as a void cover with excellent results. The operating pressure
and temperature of this heater is 125 psi and 400 degrees F.

Velodur Metal Technical First Aid Kit Contains:

2½ lbs. Velodur Metal Standard
½ lb. Velodur Rapid
1 bottle Special Cleaner
1 yard reinforcement tape
1 spatula
¼ pt. Velodur Fluidizer
1 measuring cup

Complete kit . . . **$93.00**

from:
American Velodur Metal, Inc.
P. O. Box 156
Scituate, Mass. 02066

F.O.B. Scituate, Mass.

Electric Motors

*This book gives a few principles on motor operation funda-
mentals, then describes in more detail several types of ac
and dc motors and the control and starting devices needed
to run them. Some curves of operating characteristics and
a brief trouble-shooting guide are given for each type of
motor. There is enough information to get a feel for the
differences between the many types of ac and dc motors
which exist, but it would probably be difficult for a layman
to use this book to select the proper motor for a given
application without outside help. It is probably also necessary to have a basic understanding of simple electricity
theory (see the Basic Electricity series by Rider Publications)
before reading Electric Motors. Nevertheless, it is a fairly
complete survey of available motor types, all under one
cover.*

[Reviewed by Marv Vickers]

Electric Motors
Edwin P. Anderson
1968; 432 pp.

$5.95 postpaid from Audel's or Whole Earth Catalog

from:
Theodore Audel & Co.
Division of Howard W. Sams & Co., Inc.
4300 West 62nd Street
Indianapolis, Indiana 46206

or WHOLE EARTH CATALOG

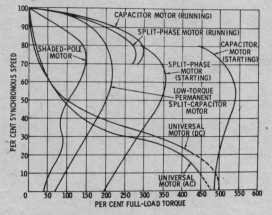

Fig. 20. Speed-torque characteristics of common types of fractional-horsepower motors.

Right

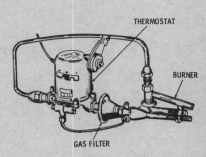

Filing Block. A piece of hard, close-
grained wood having grooves of varying
sizes upon one or more of its sides. Used
for holding small rods, pins, etc., in the
jaws of the vise while being filed. Also a
block of zinc, copper or other fairly soft
metal as one of a pair of "protectors"
placed between the vise jaws to prevent
work becoming damaged while being held
for filing.

Popular Mechanics Projects

*Popular Mechanics offers a list of reprints of innumerable
homey projects, priced 15¢ to a dollar per project.* —SB

[Suggested by Tom Duckworth]

Plans, Publications and Projects

$.25 postpaid

from:
Popular Mechanics
Box 1014
Radio City Station
New York, N.Y. 10019

X12 **Alternator,**
getting to know it 3/63-174, $1.45
X14 **Amplifier for your**
pocket 10/66-198, 65¢
X15 **Amplifier, guitar** 11/57-160, 75¢
X16 **Antenna boosts FM reception**
11/63-199, 25¢
X17 **Antenna, UHF yagi** 6/59-144, 55¢
X18 **Antiques, turning**
reproductions into 7/66-116, $1.05
X19 **Aqua-sled** 7/66-138, 45¢
X20 **Arbor press**
for small shop 7/53-189, 65¢
X21 **Arbors & trellises** 4/51-188, 85¢
X22 **Arc welder** 9&10/48-205,213, $1.85

Home Appliance Servicing

*This is the most useful book on home appliance repairing
that I have seen. It is intended for the serviceman, but it
is written clearly enough to help anyone who knows how
to use a screwdriver. Covers small and large appliances
like ranges (gas and electric), refrigerators, & air conditioners.*

*Reading the appropriate section before calling a repairman
would be good insurance against padded repair bills.*

[Suggested and reviewed by Fred Richardson]

Home Appliance Servicing
Edwin P. Anderson
1965; 600 pp.

$6.95 postpaid from Audel or Whole Earth Catalog
(cheaper from Silvo or U.S. General)

from:
Theodore Audel & Co.
Division of Howard W. Sams & Co., Inc.
4300 West 62nd Street
Indianapolis, Indiana 46206

or WHOLE EARTH CATALOG

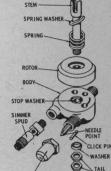

With top lighters, pilot flames generally should be adjusted so that
the top of the flame does not come in contact with any part of the
lighter. An impingement of the flame on cold metal will usually
produce either an undesirable odor from the incomplete combustion
of the gas or an undesirable carbon deposit. Pilot outage and odor
are sometimes experienced with lighters that have a solid top lighter
hood; these conditions are caused by an accumulation of carbon and
dirt in the dome and around the air ports of the hood and can usually
be corrected by drilling a ½-inch-diameter hole in the top of the hood.

Float. Sometimes used to refer to the
coarser grades of single-cut files when cut
for very soft metals (like lead) or for wood.

Overcut. The first series of teeth put
on a double-cut file.

Point. The front end of a file.

DIVINE RIGHT'S BOXES

I get the boxes all right but they won't stay shut I get 'em
set up in my mind side by side and just alike and I get the
labels on But they won't stay shut I put stuff in the past box
like saying sometimes I go whole days at a time and never even
think about Estelle but it never has been in my mind as a concept
that we'd split up till I put her in the future box I mean I
depend on knowing how a thing's going to come out and that's
a terrible I mean that's really a limitation I put that kind of thing
in the future box and close the lid and I put past stuff in the
past box stuff about Eddie dead about taking acid with Eddie
in the Grand Canyon in 1966 and then I look at the present box
and try to make it swell But all I can get the present box to do
is be an extra container to put in the stuff that crawls out of past
and future when those two boxes blow their lids off And they
always blow their lids off They won't stay on no matter what
I do I try to make the present box grow but Eddie's body comes
crawling out of the future box two bodies dead and rotten out
of past and future boxes swarm all over my present box and mix
in with me hating it hating it that we ever went to look at
Eddie's body His face looked like a wax apple They'd cut his
hair beyond all recognition I try to stuff the hair and the apple
in the past box but the lid won't stay on it flies off and stuff
swarms out and mixes with calling up my sister in Cincinnati
and asking her for money swarming out of my future box and
all I see is poor old Eddie dead Eddie dead Eddie dead
Eddie dead I called Eddie from this shopping center out in this
subdivision and City Girl said hello I said hey Eddie Divine
Right is my name and weirdness is my game what's your
And City Girl said Eddie's dead She said he's dead She said
they shot him in an alley two blocks from the bus station She
said he was shot dead in an alley two blocks from the bus station
and I said who Who she said Eddie Eddie had been shot dead
in an alley two blocks from the Greyhound station to come on over
if I wanted to some of the others were going to spend the weekend
together in Eddie's apartment It was Eddie's apartment all
right but it was in City Girl's name The cops didn't know Eddie
lived there or they would of busted it yet Eddie was all over that
apartment you could feel him in it you could smell him
you could see him in those weird dragons he drew on the wall and
that big color TV god was that big TV ever Eddie City Girl's
voice crawled out of my past box and swarmed with Eddie in his
coffin Her voice made worm tracks in the dust on Eddie's rose

(continued)

Colter-Curtin-Matheson

A nationwide distributor of professional lab equipment, from Abbe refractometers to Zimmerli vacuum gauges. Their 1111-page catalog costs them $15 each, so consult with a salesman at their office nearest you: if it appears you'll be a regular customer you get the catalog free. Minimum order $20.

—SB

[Suggested by Walt McIntosh]

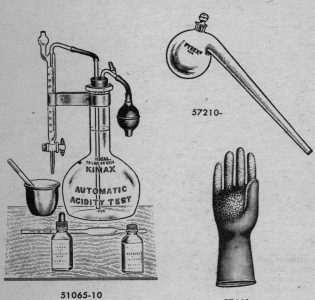

51065-10

57210-

57460-

On Jerry Stoll's advice, I painted ¾ inch plywood with this Carboline paint (clear) and made a darkroom sink impervious to all evil. Next time, a bathtub.

PAINT—Carboline Protective Coating, Vinyl, Series K.

A strongly adhering self priming top coat for wood, metal or concrete. It is easy to apply and the dry film retains good flexibility and provides excellent abrasion resistance. Thin films afford exceptional protection in moist atmosphere and are recommended for dark room and laboratory maintenance. Series K paint is primarily a maintenance protective coating for general use in mildly corrosive atmospheres. It is easily applied with brush or by spraying, dries rapidly, keeps idle time of facilities to a minimum and requires no separate primer for surfaces in good condition. Dries to a glossy finish when used over Carboline primers and provides maximum protection when so used.

May be applied directly to wood, metal or concrete. Galvanized and non-ferrous metals require priming with 53082-10 wash primer and 53083-10 intermediate primer to assure best adhesion and longest top coat life. May also be used as a refresher coat over other vinyl coatings. In many cases it may be applied directly over well oxidized coatings of other paints but a test application should always be made first to check for compatability.

Coverage, 320 square feet per gallon in a 1 mil coat. Recommended film thickness 3 mils. Thickness per coat 1½ mils (dry). Drying time to touch, 10 to 15 minutes; to over coat, 2 to 4 hours. For thinner see 53080-75.

Cat. No.	Mfrs. No.	Color	Pkg. size	Each
53080-15	K-23	Black	1 qt.	$2.05
53080-20	K-23	Black	1 gal.	6.10
53080-45	K-63	White	1 qt.	2.60
53080-65	K-83	Clear	1 qt.	2.05
53080-75	TP-92	Thinner	1 qt.	1.40

57840-

CATALOG 200

LABORATORY APPARATUS EQUIPMENT

MATHESON SCIENTIFIC
A DIVISION OF WILL ROSS, INC.

Chicago
Elk Grove Village, Ill. 60007
1850 Greenleaf Ave.
312-439-5880

Houston, Texas 77001
P.O. Box 1546
713-923-1661

Kansas City, Mo. 64111
3160 Terrace Street
816-561-8780

San Francisco, CA.
Brisbane, CA. 94005
470 Valley Drive
415-467-1040

Thorofare, N.J. 08086
Mid-Atlantic Industrial Park
1571 Imperial Way
609-848-1500

Washington, D.C.
Beltsville, Md. 20705
10727 Tucker Street
301-345-9550

International Division
Houston, Texas 77001
P.O. Box 3163

Boston
100 Commerce Way
Bldg. #1
Woburn, MA. 01801
617-935-8888

Cincinnati, Ohio 45246
12101 Centron Place
513-671-1200

Cleveland, Ohio 44125
4540 Willow Parkway
216-883-2424

Detroit, Michigan 48216
1600 Howard Street
313-965-6422

Fountain Valley, CA. 92709
18095 Mount Shay
714-963-6761

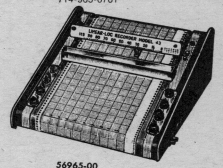

56965-00

Laboratory Supplies Co.

This company is geared for smaller orders and more amateur equipment than Matheson.

—SB

[Suggested by M. A. Klotz]

Catalog to bonafide scientists only

from:
Laboratory Supplies Co., Inc.
29 Jefry Lane
Hicksville, N. Y. 11801

AA573 Epoxy glue — World's strongest adhesive. It handles the toughest bonding jobs. Comes in handy two-tube package. The great strength of the glue is achieved by a chemical reaction of the resin and hardener when they are mixed in equal quantities. Glue will bond all metals, wood, leather, masonry, pottery, rubber and most plastics to themselves or each other. It is transparent, flexible and waterproof. Sets in 4-6 hours. ½ oz. tube kit (1 resin, 1 hardener) Kit $1.10

AA322 Handy Memo Timer. Here is a pocket-sized, Swiss made 2 hour time alarm. Easy to use. Set the dial from 5 minutes to 2 hours. A gentle buzz sounds when the time period is up. Only 1½" in diameter and weighs about 1 ounce. Easy to read with clear gold figures and a red indicator against a handsome black background. Has convenient key holder on strap.

Each $6.95; Dozen $70.00

AA39 Instant Cold, a product designed primarily for first aid purposes but can be used when it is desired to cool a specimen where ice or refrigeration is not readily available. The chemicals necessary to get the cold are packaged in a plastic pouch. By squeezing the pouch, the chemicals are mixed and in about two seconds 20° cold is created in the pouch. Stays cold for about 30 minutes. The plastic bag will conform to the shape of many items. Does not deteriorate on the shelf. These bags are excellent for use in first aid to control swelling, reduce internal bleeding, reduce pain, etc. These are for one time use only.

Per carton of 4 $ 3.96
Per case of 4 cartons of 4 12.00

AA40 Instant Heat, a product similar to above but with the reverse property of being able to provide heat when you are not near a source of heat. Will provide heat for about one to two hours.

Per carton of 4 $ 3.96
Per case of 4 cartons of 4 12.00

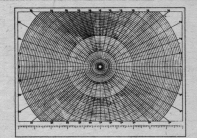

AA415 Plastic graph sheets. New gridded sheets are laminated so that the printing is permanent. One side has a matte finish for pencil plotting. The lamination and matte finish features permit unlimited reuse of the same gridded sheet. Each sheet is approximately 8½" x 11", punched for standard ring binder. Grids are printed in red for good contrast between the grid and the plotted data.

Model	Type of ruling
A	4 x 4 to the inch
B	8 x 8 to the inch
C	10 x 10 to the inch
D	20 x 20 to the inch
E	10 x 10 to the centimeter
F	Log- 1 x 1 cycle
G	Log- 2 x 1 cycles
H	Semi-Log- 1 cycle x 60 divisions
J	Semi-Log- 2 cycles x 190 divisions
K	Polar coordinate chart

Each $.75   Assorted Dozen $6.00
Assorted Gross $5.40/doz.

Beware of HyLab

I am a cameraman working for a film company on location in Colorado, and am a California resident. I am writing in regard to a very unfortunate incident which has recently happened to me.

In your March 1970 Supplement you listed the HyLab Company, Box 8625 Chicago, Ill., and described them as selling chemicals to small laboratories. Because my son has a chemistry set and I often have need for chemicals in my profession, I wrote them at the end of May requesting a catalog and/or price list. I received a letter from them in the middle of July in which they explained they were sorry but they were out of business and could not help me. Last week a friend fo mine that is a deputy sheriff in this town informed me that the town marshal had received a letter from "a chemical company" informing him that I was ordering chemicals to make LSD and that I should be placed under observation.

This allegation is absolutely untrue and I consider it a flagrant violation of my civil rights and an invasion of privacy. In the light of recent activities of the FBI in libraries, the action of the special police unit in Santa Barbara, the Kent State incident, just to name a few, I am very concerned. I don't know if this company is an FBI or police front but I don't like it. I am very upset that you would list a company like this in your catalog without a more complete investigation of it. I wonder how many of your readers (without better contact with their local police than I have) have innocently written this company and are now on police lists or are under surveillance as potential subversives. I would hope that you could print some kind of warning to your readers to avoid this company.

We appreciate and enjoy your catalogs but now we must wonder if we write for anything that might be considered illicit such as books on drugs or pot, political books, chemicals, etc. that we may end up on the same or other police lists for observation.

If you should decide to investigate I hope we hear from you.

I am also writing Senator Alan Cranston, HyLab company, and my lawyer.

Larry G. Logan
Telluride, Colorado

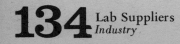

Ace Scientific Supply

Another behemoth lab supply house, from alkalimiters to wire gauze. A big expensive catalog you must be a customer to get.

—SB

Mailing Address:
Ace Scientific Supply Co., Inc.
P.O. Box 127, Linden, N.J. 07036

12-2993

12-2993 MICRO SURGERY SET

For delicate work in micro surgery, experimental research and veterinary surgery. Complete in plush-lined fitted leatherette case.

NOTE

The entrapment described above is being investigated. Would anybody who ever received a catalog from Hy Lab Chemical Company please send a copy to:

Craig Vetter
10th Floor
919 North Michigan Ave.
Chicago, Ill. 60611

17-8140

17-8140 DEMINERALIZER—Water, La Motte Filtrion

Designed to supply small amounts of chemically pure water where elaborate equipment is impractical. It can be attached to a faucet with its own flexible connection. Fifteen pints per hour can be demineralized, with a capacity of 120 grains.

Modern Plastics

Issued monthly and technically oriented, it covers the latest plastic products, manufacturing, and engineering. It's full of ads, and there is a free product literature card at the back of the magazine: you circle the appropriate number and the manufacturer mails you information.

Included in your subscription is the annual **Modern Plastics Encyclopedia,** *the most comprehensive text available on plastics. It is mailed out each October & consists of a summary of the year's trends in plastics, information on polymer science, a textbook of fundamental plastics, a directory of 3600 companies, & reference data on plastic properties & characteristics. The* **Encyclopedia** *also has free product literature cards.*
—Lloyd Kahn
[Suggested by Michael Rosenthal]

PVC film provides airtight lining for the inflated Fuji pavilion.

Modern Plastics
(Magazine & Encyclopedia)

$12.00 /yr. (monthly)

from:
Modern Plastics
Fulfillment Manager
P. O. Box 430
Hightstown, N. J. 08520

Giant polyester balloon

Construction will soon start on a 34 million-cu. ft. balloon that will require more than 13 acres—well over a half-million sq. ft.—of ⅓-mil polyester film.

Dacron polyester threads, bonded to the film (Du Pont's Mylar), reinforce it to make the balloon capable of lifting a 7-ton instrument payload. A foot-wide section of the reinforced film is said to be able to support a 1000-lb. load. Fabricating the balloon will require that some 37 miles of seams be sealed with a thermoplastic adhesive.

The balloon will be constructed by G.T. Schjeldahl Co., Northfield, Minn., under a $400,000 NASA contract. It will be sent aloft by the U.S. Air Force in New Mexico next fall, and will supply a stable support for cosmic ray detection equipment and monitoring devices at a constant altitude of approximately 20 miles.

Pocket-sized tent
Folding your tent and stealing away in the night is a simple maneuver with a new one-man shelter that uses no poles, stakes or ropes. Called Inflat—A—Tent, the all-film tent has sealed-off sections that form supporting ribs when inflated by mouth. It weighs 28 oz., forms a shelter 7 ft. long and 40 in. wide with a full floor. Deflated, it is easily rolled up and stowed. Produced by Ute Mountain Corp., Englewood, Colo., to retail at $9.95, the tent is heat-sealed with film made of Union Carbide's high-impact copolymer resin, DQDA-1824.

New honeycomb construction panels
A new RP sandwich panel for curtain walls and other interior and exterior applications is produced with a choice of paper or aluminum honeycombs. Called Glamoursdale Unicomb by its producer, Dimensional Plastics Corp., Hialeah, Fla., the lightweight panels are 5/8 in. thick, with both surfaces simulating cleft slate.

Standard sheet size for the panels is 4 by 10 ft. They are available in a variety of colors and veining.

Prefabricated plumbing wall. A conceptual "wet plumbing wall" of modular design (John A. Stahl, B. F. Goodrich Chemical Co.) incorporates rigid PVC piping, rigid urethane foam, glass/polyester faces, rigid and flexible PVC extrusions, and vinyl-jacketed electrical wiring. Fundamental is the concept that all plumbing connections are made into the pipe-bearing wall.

The likelihood of an anti-air-pollution ban on lead additives in gasoline at some time in the 1970's could drastically affect the demand for and the supply and price of propylene, an important feedstock for making polypropylene and a variety of other plastics. The additional propylene would be required in gasoline to replace lead additives.

Tamco Plastic Supplies

This company makes or supplies lots of plastic laboratory & commercial stuff: graduates, trays, pipe, plexiglass sheet, sewer & water pipe etc. The catalog is free, honest. I have bought a little from them and shipment has been prompt and the goods as advertised.

[Suggested and reviewed by Brooke Elgie]

Catalog

free

from:
United States Plastic Corp.
1550 Elida Road
Lima, Ohio

Acrylics: new look for church windows

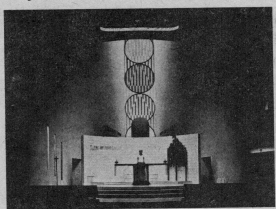

Panels of colored acrylic make up translucent chancel window in Denver church. Circles are 10 ft. in diameter, window is 50 ft. high. Acrylic skylight admits daylight to altar area.

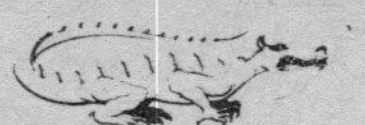

Urethane foam is sprayed onto cloth 'tents' draped over inflated weather balloons. Openings for windows and skylights are cut with hand saw. Walls are 2 to 4 in. thick.

POLYETHYLENE FLEXIBLE PLASTIC PIPE

MODERN-LINE
AVAILABLE IN BLACK ONLY
CLASS 75

Nominal Pipe Size	Nominal I. D.	Recom'd Working Pressure 74°	Approx. Weight Per 100 Ft.	STANDARD COILS Length	STANDARD COILS Outside Diameter	List Price Per 100 Ft. MODERN-LINE
½"	.622	100	5	400-100	3'-4"	$ 3.68
¾"	.824	80	7.5	400-100	3'-4"	5.95
1"	1.049	80	12	300-100	3'-4"	9.51
1¼"	1.380	80	23	300-100	4'-8"	15.79
1½"	1.610	80	31	250-100	5'-9"	20.86
2"	2.067	80	51	200-100	6'-0"	37.74

Kerodex Barrier Cream

I have been using Kerodex Barrier Creams by Ayerst Laboratories, Inc., New York, N.Y., for years with excellent results. These creams are applied to the hands <u>before</u> you start working with irritating chemicals. I find them especially useful when working with paints and concrete. With paints the solvents don't hurt my hands and paint does not stick to them as much as it does without. With concrete I can work the concrete with my bare hands (being less than expert with trowels) without having the skin dry out and shrink.

They are also supposed to be very good for protection when working with resins or liquid plastics. I've never used them for these substances. I have used them when working fiberglass insulation with good results. Also have pulled poison oak with only the cream as protection.

Comes in two types: No. 51 for dry work; if you get it wet you must reapply at once. No. 71 for wet work like concrete.

Available in most drugstores here. There is a complete list of things it protects against included in the box.

Glen A. Twombly
Pomona, N.Y.

Cadco Plastics

Sheet, rod, pipe, tape, rod, film, adhesives. Vinyl, polyethylene, nylon, mylar, polypropylene, ABS, PVC. Comprehensive stock, offices nearly everywhere. —SB
Inquire to headquarters:

[Suggested by Fred Borcherdt]

Cadillac Plastic and Chemical Co.
15841 Second Avenue
P. O. Box 810
Detroit, Michigan 48232

Bag Balm

Check into *Bag Balm,* an antiseptic medication for cows udders, teats, whatever, which happens to be the most fantastic hand lotion ever made by anybody anywhere. Used by dishwashers, clam diggers, and lobstermen up here to change cracked caloused skin into beautiful soft flesh overnight! No shit. 10 oz. can for $1.50.

Contact:

Dairy Association Co., Inc.
Lyndonville, Vermont

Charles Miller
Monhegan Island
Maine

And Estelle crying and she had never even met Eddie before She cried and swarmed with herself crying out of my future box because she was dead too and mounted on my wall Seeing Estelle lonely wandering around at Altamont crawls out of my past box and mixes with me and Eddie hiking with down the canyon wall the first time I took acid in 1966 Eddie Eddie Dead I called my sister in Cincinnati this morning She's going to send me fifteen dollars by Western Union I have to wait here till it comes My sister said that Uncle Emmit was sick and might not live him about to die alone at the old homeplace in Kentucky My sister said they had plenty of room and for me to come on I didn't tell her about Estelle But I don't know if that goes in my future box or the past It doesn't go in my present box because my present box has been taken over by swarms of past and future I mean I called yesterday that's past but the money won't come till this afternoon that's future but I am here waiting now that's present watching me swarm out of my past box yesterday when I applied for a job at the Save-More Store City Girl said Eddie had been shot dead in an alley near the bus station all I could think to do about it was go and apply for a job at the Save-More Store I went in the Save-More Store and applied for a job while Estelle waited outside in the bus I only got half way through the application form I wrote down my name and my game and this guy comes up and jerks the pencil out of the hand and says never mind never mind come on and help unload these shoes They hired me on the spot to set up a display of shoes thousands of shoes millions of brand new shoes they're desperate for help to get set up on display pay me a dollar sixty-five an hour plus ten per cent off anything in the store Four hours at the Save-More Store I cleared five dollars after taxes and social security and spent four of it on Kentucky Fried Chicken for me and Estelle Ise sat thinking about the Greek popping up through the mashed potatoes saying don't eat that greasy food it'll make mucus It'll make mucus It'll make mucus Eddie is dead I say and we want to eat meat and potatoes and gravy because we're weak and hungry and tired and beat and maybe don't have any place to stay tonight because still in the future box at the time was whether or not we'd crash at Eddie's place with these other people.

(continued)

Welding Craft Practice

If you have access to either a gas or an electric unit then all you need is the correlated volumne of Welding Craft Practice and alot of patience (whilst your hands learn what your ole brain says they should be doing) to begin transmutting the base metals. These books give a complete description of the equipment used in oxy- and arc welding plus a detailed accounting of the methodology from lighting the blowpipe to testing the strength of the finished weld. The potentially dangerous situations in storing transporting and welding with gas under pressure, and the precautions necessary for using electric arc are outlined in clear competent british prose. If youre going to learn welding on your own read the safety sections of the book first and return to them so that your safety consciousness is well programed before picking up the stri ker.

[Reviewed by Doug Gunesch]

Welding Craft Practice Part 1, Volume 2 Electric Arc Welding and Related Studies
N. Parking and C.R. Flood
1969; 182pp.

$2.40 postpaid

from:
Pergammon Press Inc.
Maxwell House
Fairview Park
Elmsford, New York 10523
or WHOLE EARTH CATALOG

Welding Craft Practice Part 1, Volume 1 Oxy-acetylene Gas Welding and Related Studies
N. Parkin and C.R. Flood
1969; 159pp.

$2.40 postpaid

from:
Pergammon Press Inc.
Maxwell House
Fairview Park
Elmsford, New York 10523
or WHOLE EARTH CATALOG

Solidox Welding Torch

A medium lightweight welding torch that uses pellets for oxygen. Very portable, nice to have as your bus torch. Solidox torch now available in hardware stores, home-improvement centers and do-it-yourself stores across the country. 5000° hot.

—SB

Solidox Welding Torch

$39.95 postpaid

Cleanweld Products
4000 Medford Street
Los Angeles, California 90063

The Art of Blacksmithing

A warm book that makes me want to learn blacksmithing. Bealer presents the history and methods of smithing in a fashion very useful to a person learning the trade. An excellent coverage of tools, most to be made by the smith himself. Bealer collected this material from many old smiths and then tried it himself in his own forge.

[Reviewed by Fred Richardson]

The Art of Blacksmithing
Alex W. Bealer
1969; 425 pp.

$10.00 postpaid

from:
Funk & Wagnalls
53 West 77th St.
New York, N.Y.

or WHOLE EARTH CATALOG

LIGHTING UP BLOWPIPE

Turn on both gas supplies and set correct pressures as before. Slowly open acetylene control on blowpipe until it is purged of air and acetylene is issuing freely (note and remember the pungent smell of the gas), and light at the tip of the nozzle using a spark lighter. The resultant diffused, luminous, but sooty flame is pure acetylene burning in air. Turn up the fuel gas supply until the smoke vanishes from the tail of the flame and the nozzle is now working at its normal capacity with a suitable gas velocity. The flame now, although cleaner, is still of a relatively low temperature. Open the blowpipe oxygen-control valve slowly and note the change in the character of the flame as the oxygen is introduced. The body of the flame turns blue with the formation of a hazy white zone which decreases in size with the development of a small greenish-white cone at the end of the nozzle. Continue increasing the supply of oxygen until the white "feather" of excess acetylene just disappears, leaving a clearly defined inner cone. This is a correctly adjusted neutral flame consuming equal quantities of acetylene and oxygen from the welding gas supplies and a further amount of oxygen from the atmosphere.

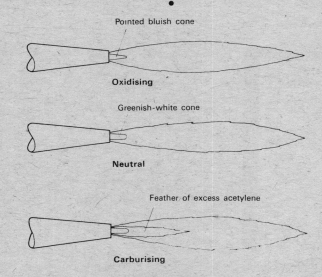

Pointed bluish cone

Oxidising

Greenish-white cone

Neutral

Feather of excess acetylene

Carburising

Fig. I.18. Types of flame.

Wright Winch

In March 1970 $1 Cat. (p. 16) Jimmie Silverthorne Suggested a cable winch for getting unstuck. ABSOLUTLY!!! and I reccomend the "Wright Type 'R' Pull-a-way, Model 2 B" at about $35. Over seven years, mine has loaded nearly all the timbers to frame a two-storey house with oak, hauled both my VW and ½-ton pick-up from ditches, bogs, brooks, muddy fields, snow-banks and the ocean, (all would have been call-a-tow-truck jobs without it), removed and installed numerous VW and detroit engines, loaded and unloaded heavy shop machinery, and done many dozens of other useful things for me. Its beginning to show a little wear now, but not too much.

Its cast Aluminum and so light enough to pack into the woods, as well as rust-proof. Works covered w/ snow without binding up, and all moving parts can be worked w/ mittens on so you dont get frozen to it when, say. . .you want to release it. One minor shortcoming: The release-pawl spring wears out at about one every two years. Order two or three spares of Part No. R043, Spring, at about 35¢ ea. at the same time you order the winch.

Its made by WRIGHT HOIST DIVISION, American Chain & Cable Co. Offices in York, Pa. Also Atlanta, Chicago, Denver, Detroit, Los Angeles, N.Y., Phila, Pittsburgh, S. Francisco, & Bridgeport, Conn.

Far superior to all other makes I've used, which is about five.

Michael Spencer
Italy Cross, Nova Scotia

Smith Welding Equipment

Professional welding equipment.

[Suggested by Jerome Skuba]

Tescom Corporation
2600 Niagara Lane N.
Minneapolis, MN 55441

STRIKING THE ARC

Select a 10-gauge electrode for your first practice at striking the arc. Set the current regulator to 117 amperes. For material use 3x3/8" mild steel flat bar approximately 7 in. long (flat bar is more suitable than plate because it is much easier to cut, either with shears or power saw). Next, direct the tip of the electrode towards the practice plate. Do this a number of times with the current switched off. When the electrode touches the material, quickly draw away to about 1/8" from the surface. Do not worry about the correct angle of electrode at this stage. When this exercise has been practised a number of times and one has the "feel" of the electrode, switch the current on and practice striking the arc. Remember to keep the welding screen in front of your eyes and, when the electrode touches the plate, very slightly scratch the surface. When the arc burns quickly draw away to approximately 1/8". The arc will still continue to burn if the electrode is 1 in. or more away from the surface of the plate but the arc must be kept short in order to control the deposition of the weld metal.

Should the electrode "stick" to the plate, do not snatch and twist to try and free it as this will only result in the piece of flat bar being lifted from the bench still attached to the end of the electrode. The correct procedure is as follows: keeping the screen in front of the face, switch off the welding set at the switch fuse, which should be located on the wall of the welding bay. Then give the electrode holder a sharp twist, which will free the electrode from the plate. The electrode and the plate may be hot, so exercise caution if attempting to touch either of them. Before continuing after the electrode has been freed, inspect it to ensure that the coating at the tip is not damaged, as in most cases the coating will be broken. The arc is very difficult to strike with a bare wire and a fresh electrode should be taken if damage has occurred.

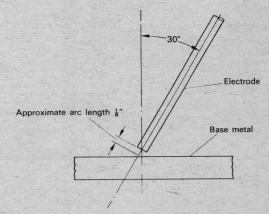

30°

Electrode

Approximate arc length ⅛"

Base metal

Fig. II.9. Electrode angle arc length.

Yankee Winch

Well,

I'm finally writing a letter to an institution (that is to say something that is not a friend or one of the relatives at Christmas.)

I'd like to tell you about a thing I just got. It's called a Yankee Winch. It is manufactured by Yankee Mechanics Inc. in Newport, N.H. They cost for the large one $150. It is a hand operated winch that is rated a 1-1/2 tons. The tests on it done by some laboratory in N.Y. showed the winch could lift 8,500 lbs without damage to the unit. A lot of other really impressive stuff.

Winch comes with 60 ft of cable.

I don't know how the company is as to catalogs or service because the owner of the company is a friend of the family. His name is Bill Ruger, is the owner also of Sturm Ruger & Co. Inc, a firearms manufacturer. Anyone who knows about these guns know that they are built with quality.

I'm a C.O. so not too big on them still the man believes in quality in his products so I'm sure that the company is as top notch as his winch.

Hope I've helped you fuckin long hairs.

Zip McCann
Putney, Vermont

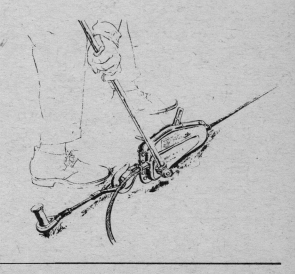

[1]

[2]

Welding: [1] where to place blows for a lap weld, [2] how to hold iron on anvil before the first blow.

Generally, I have tried to describe and illustrate only the fundamental techniques of the trade, and show how these techniques were used on a few familiar items. I hope that others may find my material interesting enough to acquire the tools of the smith and actually practice his techniques to the point that some of the ancient techniques and tools will be rediscovered for the benefit of modern man. If the ancient aurochs can be reconstituted through selective breeding of modern domestic cattle, it seems possible that the ancient smith may be waiting within a few modern men.

Master Mechanics Mfg.

Jacks 'n pumps 'n motors 'n gadgetry.

Catalog —SB

$.10

from:
Master Mechanics Mfg. Co.
P. O. Box A
Burlington, Wis. 53105

P. O. Box 65
Sarasota, Florida 33578

5 TON PUNCH PRESS 289.00

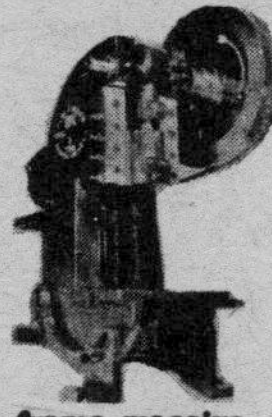

Industrial five ton bench press frame, massively reinforced with vertical, internal ribs extending the full length of the press. 65lb. precisely balanced flywheel requires less originating power is operated by single pin repeat or non-repeat clutch of new Synchronized design. One screw, quickly removed from collar, changes clutch to repeat action. Ram guides have 6" length, ram stroke 1-1/4". (other strokes available) Die bed area: 10" right to left and 6-1/2" front to back. Press operates at 280 strokes per minute, takes 1/2 HP electric motor, (not included).

C142a, 5 Ton Press, Factory Price FOB Missouri

No Longer Available

AC ARC WELDER

20-125 AMPS — Complete with Kit as shown

Only **$94.50**

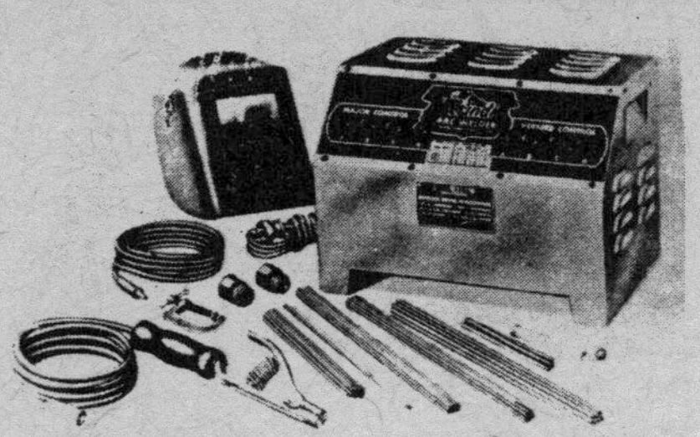

Heavy Duty Model. For light production and hundreds of repair and construction welding jobs. Gives 20 to 125 amp. output Lightweight, long-lasting electric arc welder always ready for instant action. Constructed for fast, dependable welding, brazing, soldering and cutting on iron, steel, brass, bronze and other metals from 24 gauge to 1/2 in. thick. Has 16 heat stages, uses 1/16 to 5/32 in. welding rod. Sturdy, welded steel cabinet. Welder guaranteed for 1 year. Operates from 110-220 V 60 C., AC line. Overall size 12-1/2x16x11 in high. Complete with welding kit. List price $149.50.

G26 Wt. 100 lbs.. with kit. $94.50

Cutawl

Peace. . .
I wish to recommend a tool: the Cutawl, model K-11, from The Cutawl Corporation, Bethel, Connecticut 06801.

The company calls it "a high-speed, portable precision cutting machine for all types of sheet materials". It is a sort of a 'super saber saw', but instead of rotating the whole tool with the Cutawl you rotate the blade only with a large thumb knob. It uses over a dozen different blades some of which are saws, some chisels, some knives.

It is used mainly in the display, theater and sign trades for cutting such things as large letters, outlines of drawings, valances, etc. from materials like homosote, foamcor, plywood, and plexiglas. It will also cut other things like asbestos, leather, linoleum, cloth (2-1/2" thickness of wool), paper, cork, thin metals (up to 30 gauge carbon steel). The manual lists over 100 materials.

A circle cutting attachment is available (about $13) with which you can cut perfect circles from 3/4" to 48".

The Cutawl is expensive ($245 plus $3 postage) but with even minimal care it will last for years. There are some still in daily use after 30 years. Also, if you contact one of the service centers you might be able to pick up a reconditioned one. (I understand the Model 10 would go for about $135.)

I plan to build my house next summer and will use a Cutawl for forming molds and jigs for the casting. It is a great tool and I love mine. Peace. . .

Keith Richards
Philadelphia, Pa.

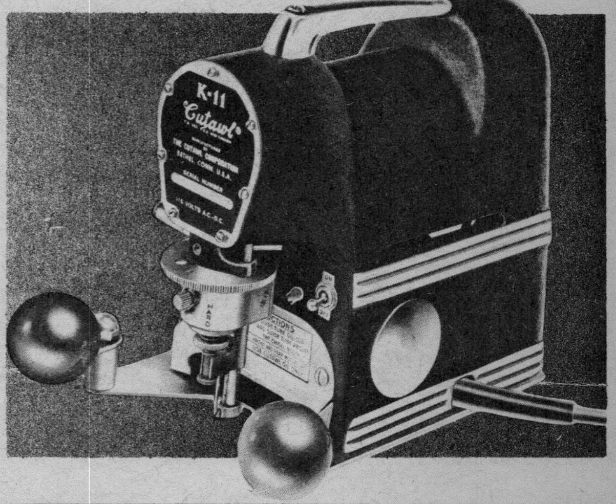

Lesto Orbital Action Jig Saw

Expensive but worth it. Follows a scribed line as accurately as a jig saw, cutting "smooth as a baby's ass" with no jumping around. Uniquely, it also can cut as rough and fast as a sabre or bayonet saw, humming through the toughest wood (up to 2-3/8" thick), soft steel (up to ¼"), and a remarkable assortment of other stuff. It does this without any change in speed or power, changing only the kind and nature of the cutting stroke. Its hard to explain how this works, but it does. The fastest cuts are done with the easily adjustable orbital movement set for full swing, similar to the sort of rocking motion you use with a large hand saw for rough cuts. The minimal swing is like the motion used in cutting thin stock or accurate cuts. Almost 40 different blades are available, saw types as well as knife and rasp types, fitting it for reinforced plastics, laminated fabrics, soft rubber, asbestos cement, wood-metal laminations, and the usual and unusual metals and woods. Should be perfect for dome freaks. Lighter and more compact than ordinary sabre saws, it also can be used for hours without your arm feeling like it was dropped in a mixmaster and without your ears stuffed with cotton.

This Swiss goodie is hard to find since it is distributed as an "industrial power tool" through specialized distributors who service factories and wholesale hardware stores who sell to the construction industry. . . 20% off "Industrial Net [List] prices" is usual from the latter if you insist. While most of the so called "industrial power tools" may be irrelevant to our uses (e.g., demolition hammers), it is disturbing to find some of the best tools, designed for long trouble free use and low operator fatique, being available only to those "in the trade." Perhaps other CATALOG readers know of similar small "industrial" tools that should be better known.

[Suggested by Don Boyce.
Reviewed by Alan Kalker]

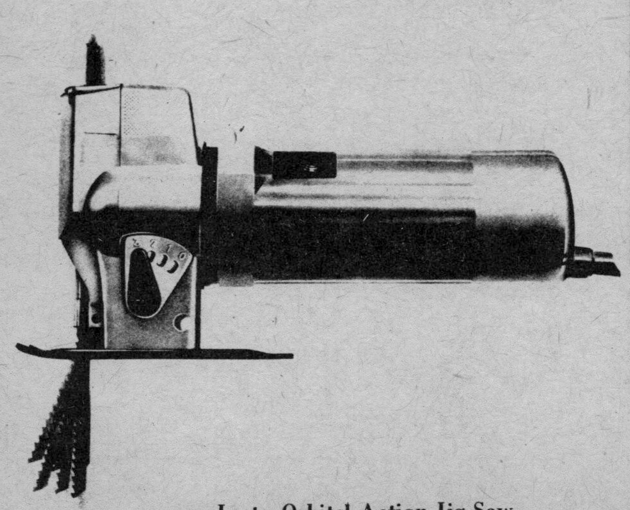

Lesto Orbital Action Jig Saw
Model 8554

$126.00 industry net [list] price, postpaid

from:
Robert Bosch Corporation, Distributor
345 E. Grand Avenue
South San Francisco, California 94080

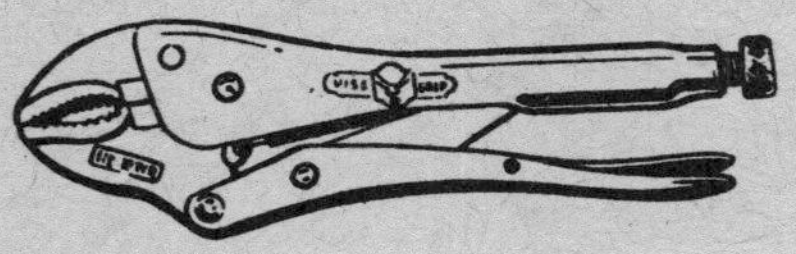

Fred says—

Buy "Vise-Grip" *brand.* None of the other similar locking plier wrenches are as good. The other sizes of Vise-Grips are just as good as the Jr.

"Vise-Grip" is like "Channellock". Brand name, not a generic term. Both better than others.

Loctite Technology

Mechanics, especially those working on old, frapped-out machinery, will dig Loctite. Anything threaded will stay together and not vibrate loose if you use the stuff. This is God's gift to the motorcycle fixer. The same company also makes a glop that you can use to make gaskets with right on the part; and for those engaged in putting new bearings in VW transmissions, they make a bearing seating compound that enables you to use wobbly old transmission cases instead of throwing them away. It works.

[Suggested and reviewed by Jay Baldwin]

Loctite Technology Catalog
free

from:
Loctite Corporation
North Mountain Road
Newington, Connecticut 06111

Cheaper Than Loctite

On page 48 of Fall 69 four dollar catalog a review of Loctite products. Being a professional motorcycle mechanic for six years, I'd like to suggest a cheaper alternative to keeping nuts & bolts from falling off. 3M weather stripping cement. Whereas if Loctite primer is not used first, Loctite won't stick. Every trace of oil and dirt has to be removed. 3M can be used as a gasket, if flowed onto the gasket surface and allowed to set up first (but not recommended—only in emergency) and as a cement to keep loose handlebar grips from falling off etc. etc. The one drawback to using 3M on nuts & bolts is the yellow color. If looks not important 3M easy and cheap. Loctite products very good but expensive, especially for home repair, and must be used carefully—with primer everytime.

Dick Tetz
San Francisco, CA.

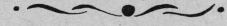

Go-Jo NO-LOK

The counterpart to Loctite. Anyone who has ever put a machine back together in imminent fear that the garped-up old threads are going to jam & that he's then going to twist the head off a bolt, or anyone who has ever had to apply lots of Liquid Wrench & swearing to get a bolt off will dig it. You put it on the threads of a bolt and that bolt just slips in and won't ever lock up. I was amazed the first time I used it; makes bolts feel like brand-new. I'm not sure if it makes things more prone to coming loose from vibration — in motorcycle applications it may be best to use lockwashers or safety wire.

Price varies; my father paid 95¢ for a little can; I paid $2.00 for a really big one. Best obtained through auto parts supply houses. A little hard to find; in some places contacting jobbers or distributors may be necessary.

Bill Houghton
Fairfax, CA

Another brand is Never-Seez.-*Fred.*

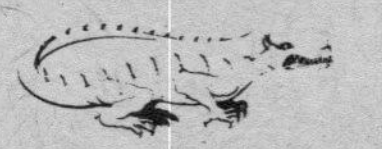

The place is in City Girl's name I didn't understand how that could be with Eddie dead although I'm rested and feel better and it's clearer now than it was We found the apartment and I called my sister and asked her to send me fifteen dollars and she said fine that Uncle Emmit was sick at the homeplace and might not live that she had plenty of room and for me to come on And then out of my past box comes us going down that long hallway in the funeral home crawling out of my past box over toward the future like some future corridor we'll all walk down some day And then Eddie's place and these same people being hypnotized and City Girl is there in my past box presiding and she says Eddie was shot dead in an alley not far from the bus station Stay away from bus stations Death lurks in bus stations posing as the candy man Ask the people who've been killed there they'll tell you ask Eddie Ah the mystery of it all the questions gone unanswered Where is Eddie's spirit now What's happening in his body Lying there in its high school graduation suit hands all folded a stupid rose in his lapel and dust upon his rose and half a haircut on his head Goddamn Momma give him a crewcut rather than half of nothing Why did you go halfway He's dead You want him back as your baby boy Why didn't you take him Why didn't you go through with it Give him the full cosmetic treatment and be satisfied Eddie would have dug that He wouldn't have given a shit Eddie dug you Momma And I did too and still do and it's very sad to see you standing here so sad like this weeping over the body of your darling baby boy shot down in an alley I stayed at your house Do you remember me Stayed there with Eddie four days one time fighting hepatitis Eddie's old man couldn't dig it He disappeared into the news and let us swirl around him like a wind But you Momma You were all right You were Eddie's Mom

Eddie's Mom recognized me at the funeral parlor But she wasn't glad to see me because of Eddie's hair Goddamn Momma if you wanted it short you should have had it cut full short You should have given that boy a crewcut like you wanted You're the one who's living now You should have pleased yourself before anybody else How long has it been since you pleased yourself Since anybody pleased you You tried to half please yourself and half please Eddie and now nobody's pleased but it's not too late to do something about it.

I swarm out of my future box with a foot-long pair of scissors right into that funeral parlor to open Eddie's box His last and past and present future box And give him a good short haircut like his Momma wants Let's do it Momma it's not too late Right there it sits Right there it is What's left of Eddie's in that box and we could do it if we tried Eddie's mother says what are you doing now I say working at the Save-More Store Oh Do you live in St. Louis now I say yes mam for a little while anyway I sure am sorry about Eddie And she cries some more and City Girl says Eddie had been shot dead in an alley not far from the Greyhound bus station and all I could think to do all I could think to do was go out was go out and get a job and work four hours at the Save-More Store and buy fifteen pieces of Kentucky Fried Chicken with my earnings.

Snap-On Tools

Outstanding very expensive mechanics tools. If you're professional they're worth it. Otherwise no. Check yellow pages, call, and they'll send delivery truck of samples.

—SB

[Suggested by Morton Grosser]

Snap-On Tools Corporation
Kenosha, Wisconsin 53140

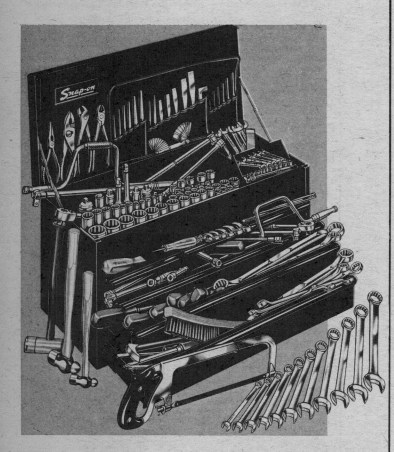

Hardware Products Springs

Hardware Products two-page catalog of springs contains more useful data than a dozen handbooks. It lists actual, stock springs of varying wire diameters, outside diameters, and lengths, with spring rate (the increase in pressure per inch of squeeze or extension) and the price per spring, postpaid! The charts make it easy to select the right size spring, compression or extension, for whatever job you have.

[Suggested and reviewed by Stephen P. Baldwin]

Hardware Products Company
84 Fulton Street
Boston, Massachusetts 02113

CATALOGS

a bunch of catalogs for catalog's sake.
people learn from catalogs.
if there was only one way to do a thing,
then there wouldn't be any reason
to choose between this and that;
catalogs are wishbooks,
where you can match
what you want
with
what you need;
catalogs are dictionaries
where you can learn the vocabulary,
talk shop.

—jd

Grainger's

Motors and fans primarily. Plus melange of other industrial and home tools. Branches all over U.S. Wholesale only; you better have letterhead and/or resale number.

—SB

[Suggested by Don Buchla]

W. W. Grainger, Inc.
5959 Howard St.
Chicago, Ill. 60648

36" 2-SPEED CEILING FAN
Quiet, Draft-Free, 3630/2585 CFM Air Movement

EMERSON **$57.00**
Lots 4

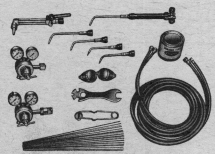

2-STAGE HEAVY DUTY WELDING & CUTTING **$130.05**
No. 2Z357

TRUCKS

E **$30.55** F **$38.40**
Lots 3 Lots 3

Harry M. Smith

Harry sells precision tools and gages, mechanical inspection equipment. "If it can be measured, it can be made."

Brown & Sharpe, Eclipse, Helios, Lufkin, Mitutoyo, Scherr-Tumico. Lots more.

They sell Gerstner Tool chests.

Free manufactures' catalogs. Send postage—they are heavy.

[Reviewed by Fred Richardson]

Catalog
$1.00

from:
Harry M. Smith & Associates
1341 Old County Road
Belmont, California 94002

B&L DOUBLE LENS MAGNIFIER

A widely useful magnifier originally designed for fine engraving and die work. Lens size 1⅝" covers up to 2¼" field. Power 3½X with good correction because of double lens construction. Plastic mount allows easy, hand-held use.

Cat. No.	Each
81-34-75	$4.95

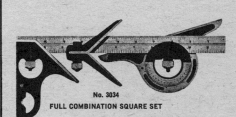

No. 3034
FULL COMBINATION SQUARE SET

No. 193 Mauser Stainless Steel Vernier Caliper

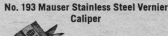

Campbell Tools

Machinist's stuff. Carries the low-cost Mitutoyo line of precision instruments.

Catalog
$.50

from:
Campbell Tools Co.
1424 Barclay Road
Springfield, Ohio 45505

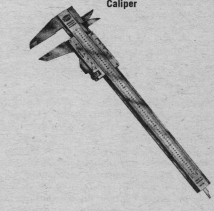

513-104

DIAL TEST INDICATORS

RANGE	NO.	GRADUATION
.04"	513-102	.001"

Set includes
Stem (102036) & Point (102039)
    already installed. Plus
Bars (102043) & (102045)
Points (102040) & (102041)
Stem (102081)
Clamp (102051)
Wrench (102037)

	PRICE
Complete with Holders and Points	$19.50

GOV'T SURPLUS

[All reviews by Alan Kalker]

GOVERNMENT SURPLUS FOR NON-PROFIT GROUPS
There is, in theory, a very special deal for local government and private nonprofit educational groups. Government property is available for donation to tax-supported or tax-exempt and not-for-profit educational and public health groups. In order to qualify you must be a college, university, school for the mentally retarded or physically handicapped, radio or television station licensed to operate as educational, or public library which is tax-supported, tax-exempt and non-profit. Some public health organizations eligible too. A State Agency handles the transfer of lands at a nominal cost (to cover service and handling charge representing its cost in getting and giving the property).

"Donation" Information Packet

free

from:
U.S. Department of Health, Education and Welfare
Office of Facilities, Engineering,
and Property Management
Surplus Property Utilization Division
Washington, D.C. 20201

•

```
MACHINE TOOLS: Various types and sizes, including
cutting tool holders, dog lathes, V-block and
taper shank sockets.
Inside - Unpacked - Used - Poor Condition
Total cost  $800
Est. total wt.  50 lbs.          1 LOT

BODY AND FRAME, JEEP, UTILITY: 1/4 ton, 1952, Willys
M38A1, S/N 22659.  With the following major compon-
ents attached:  engine block, transmission, transfer
case, radiator, rear end and 4 wheels and tires.
USA 20963498.
Outside - Used - Poor Condition
Total cost  $1000
Est. total wt.  1750 lbs.          1 EACH
```

•

DEFENSE SURPLUS Much of the surplus you see in your neighborhood Army and Navy store may have come from a nearby Department of Defense retail store where you can buy small quantities from Uncle exactly as the store owner did. While intended to be open to all, the retail stores are becoming more difficult to find and visit. Your neighborhood store owner probably will not help. Many Defense Surplus Sales Offices (a list of these come when you request a Department of Defense Surplus Bidder application [below]) have retail stores, but they may not know of retail stores in nearby Defense installations. There seems to be no central list. You can try asking for "surplus property disposal officer" at all local large Army, Air Force, etc. bases. If you get someone, ask the day and time the retail store is open as well as the building number. Competitive bid bulk lot sales are basically simple once you get into them, but none of the information the Government sends you will allow you to believe a non professional can figure it out. "Sale by Reference," a Department of Defense term for non retail sales, includes methods no more esoteric than an auction. The only way to find out easily about these non retail sales is to put your name on the DOD mailing list for sale announcements.
For the DOD there is one central address for the continental United States. You must ask specifically if you also want announcements of sales in Alaska, Morocco, etc. In exchange for your name and address to the below central office, you will get a bidder's application form asking which kinds of things you are interested in purchasing and which geographic regions you will purchase from. Check every type of thing you conceivably may need, since adding another category will take at least six weeks. Check at least two nearby geographic regions, and all geographical regions if you are interested in vehicles, boats, regions, aircraft. When your "bidder's application" is returned you will receive a pamphlet entitled "Sale by Reference" containing page after page of impenetrable small print, DO NOT CHUCK IT OUT, save it for yea shall need it. Also, save the sale catalogs for "sealed bid" sales for about 6 months. Get in the habit of looking at the mailing label on your sales announcements. Every two months or so the numeral 2 will appear in the middle of the first line, and you must send back a post card saying you are still interested in receiving the announcements. If you forget, it will again take at least six weeks to get back on the mailing list.

Bidders List Application

free

from:
Property Disposal Service
Federal Center
Battle Creek, Michigan 49016

this is a page or so of alan kalker's research on the paperwork necessary to get ahold of those fifty dollar jeeps we've all wetdreamed for so long. individuals can indeed buy things at the same price that straight-shooting ralph pays to stock them in his aceydeucy bargaincenter armory and good deal warehouse surplus outlet.
read carefully, follow alan's steps, because it has to be done correctly to work.

—jd

The following pamphlet is a bit sketchy, but it seems to be the only general guide around. It will at least give you current addresses for fuller information on special problems.

How to Buy Surplus Personal Property

$.25 postpaid

from:
Superintendent of Documents
U.S. Government Printing Office
Washington, D.C. 20402

•

```
TRUCK, PICKUP:  1/2 ton, 1960 Ford model F100, S/N
F10J0R50863, 4x2, 6 cylinder gasoline engine. Parts
missing including instrument panel and ignition
coil.  FSN 2320-752-9452.
Outside - Used - Poor Condition
Total cost  $1255
Est. total wt.  3550 lbs.          1 EACH

BUS:  37 passenger, 1960, International Harvester
model B163-238WB, S/N SB127352E, 4x2, 6 wheels with
tires, dual rear, wheel size 20", 238" wheelbase.
Standard transmission with electric shift, air
hydraulic  brakes, 6 cylinder gasoline engine model
BD-264, S/N 716275.  Wayne body model 02509X, S/N
308850.  Parts damaged including window, entrance
door glass, cushion and wiper motor.  Parts missing
including coil and glove compartment door. #91-02098.
Outside - Used - Poor Condition
Total cost  $6450
Est. total wt.  9000 lbs.          1 EACH
```

•

DEFENSE SURPLUS BID ABSTRACTS The most formidable DOD sale by reference technique is the "sealed bid." You must mail a written offer in before a certain date, but unlike an auction you will have no idea of what others have bid since all bids are unsealed simultaneously. There is a commercial service that can at least give you a starting point. Suppose you see an announcement for a sealed bid sale for 600 lbs of assorted rotary, toggle, and sensitive electrical switches, unused, excellent condition, that cost the government about $9,000; what would you bid? If you had been keeping the last six months of DOD sealed bid catalogs, you could find similar items in a past sale. Then write Bidder's Service Company for an abstract, which you will receive by airmail, and find the winning bids. In the example: $56.79 for the whole lot. Interested in a bus? 29 passenger buses in fair condition go for $590 (1957) Chev to $690 (1961 Ford); 1961 Dodge 37 passenger models in poor condition fetch $378-455. While the Kelley Blue Book might be some help in the case of vehicles, the abstracts indicate what the pro dealers will bid for all of a similar model. The abstracts now give not only what every bidder offered on every item in a particular sale catalog, but the name and address of each bidder, so you can pick out the pro's. In addition you might want to contact the sucessful bidder to buy part of a lot. With the abstract you will know exactly what he paid for it.

Bid Abstract Service

$5.00 each, postpaid

first two for new subscribers **$2.50** each

from:
Bidder's Service Company
Drawer 1790
Fort Stockton, Texas 79735

GSA (CIVILIAN) SURPLUS The General Services Administration has charge of getting rid of all government junk now owned by the Department of Defense. They sell an incredible variety of stuff. Not only old Post Office vans, but also Forest Ranger's old horses, and kilns from closed Job Corps Centers. GSA tends to be more diffuse than DOD. Except for vehicles, sale items are often scattered about in remote locations, a procedure that dissuades the professional surplus buyer. GSA does not seem to have any retail stores, but is experimenting with fixed price sales of Post Office motor scooters. GSA puts a price between $37.50 and $175.00 on the scooters depending on their condition. After an inspection period of about a week, the doors fly open at 9:00 am on a specified day and it's first come first served. Remnants are offered following days until sold. Since the ½ ton walk-in Post Office vans currently go for from $120 to $180 at GSA spot bid sales, it is difficult to know why anyone would want the scooters. Particularly when scooters in operable condition are often set at more than $100.00. The walk-in vans have 110 cubic feet enclosed bodies and with some thought could almost be a camper. Spot bid sales are the favored method of GSA sale. While bids are submitted in writing like a sealed bid sale, they areopeneditem by item in your presence and the winner announced as in an auction. When, for example, 10 identical vans are sold, you will know the winning bid on the first before you must submit your written bid for the second. There is no single central office for GSA sales information. You must request each geographical regional office to put you on the list.

Surplus Personal Property Mailing List Application

free

from:
General Services Administration
Property Management and Disposal Service
Sales Branch, Personal Property Division

at the following regional addresses:

JFK Federal Building
Boston, Mass. 02203

26 Federal Plaza,
New York, New York 10007

7th and D Streets, SW
Washington, D.C. 20407

1776 Peachtree Street, NW
Atlanta, Georgia 30309

219 South Dearborn Street
Chicago, Illinois 60604

1500 East Bannister Road
Kansas City, Missouri 64131

819 Taylor Street
Ft. Worth, Texas 76102

Denver Federal Center, Building 41
Denver, Colorado 80225

1150 San Mateo Avenue
South San Francisco, Calirornia 94080

Federal Office Building
909 First Avenue, Seattle
Seattle, Washington 98104

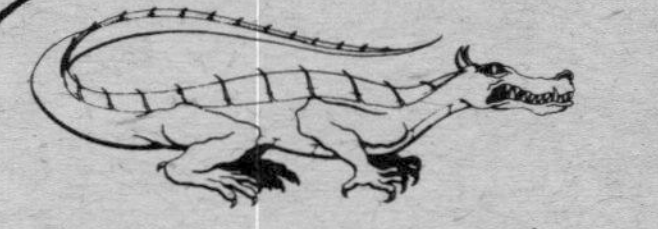

REINCARNATION

One by one, the people at the funeral sat up and rubbed their eyes. The hypnotism program was only half an hour long, but everybody had the feeling that two or three hours had gone by. The TV sets were off now. The cool, blank tubes were as much a surprise to whoever had turned them off as they were to any of the other mourners at the funeral.

"Who turned the TV's off?" asked Winston.

"I don't even remember them going off," said Norton.

"I think you turned them off," said Norton's rival, Bert.

"No, man," said Norton. "I don't know who turned them off."

"We have a mystery in our midst," said City Girl.

For a little while the room was quiet, except for the sound Estelle made as she flipped the pages of a book on Etruscan art.

"M..m..maybe it was Eddie's g..g..ghost," D.R. stuttered.

Everybody in the room except Estelle turned to look at Divine Right. It was the first time he had spoken since the night before. His silence had become such a fixture in the room it was as if a piece of furniture had been moved out when he spoke.

"I can dig that," said Chuck.

"I can dig reincarnation," said Winston. "But I don't believe in ghosts."

"It's all the same shit," said Reed.

"No it isn't," said Gilded Lilly. "Reincarnation is an established fact."

"I had a dream once about reincarnation," said The Native. "I dreamed I was a lizard in a previous life."

Friendly Persuasion asked The Native what that had felt like.

"It was pretty weird. I mean, I liked it. I liked crawling around that close to the ground. I liked the point of view. When I die, I hope I'm a lizard the next time around."

Bert shook his head. "It don't work that way," he said. "You're never the same thing twice."

"Bullshit," said Norton. "Sometimes you're the same thing three or four times in a row."

Bert started to argue with Norton. But as he was about to speak, his energy suddenly failed him. Arguing with Norton about reincarnation just didn't seem worth the trouble right then, so he kept quiet. For a while everybody kept quiet. Finally City Girl got up and went to the kitchen. For a moment it seemed as if her departure might produce some kind of conversation. But it didn't. Ten or fifteen minutes went by. The only sounds in the whole apartment were Estelle shuffling pages and City Girl clinking dishes in the kitchen.

Silvo Hardware

Tools tools tools tools. Brand names. Mostly good stuff. Several quality levels on almost all items. If you know what you want, it is probably here. Prices good, sometimes not as good as U. S. General. I have been pleased by their service on returned items. Takes about two and a half weeks to West Coast. Minimum order $10.00. Silvo is a place you can go to. U.S. General is not.

[Reviewed by Fred Richardson]

Silvo Catalog
196 pp.

$1.00

from:
Silvo Hardware Company
Dept. UEC
107 Walnut St.
Philadelphia, PA 19106

HEAVY WORKSHOP VISE

No longer available

Heavy-duty channel steel front jaw beam covers screw. Extra large back jaw anvil and anvil horn. Cold-rolled steel screw. Handle balls forged from handle stock. Replaceable malleable iron nut. Acme thread. Replaceable heat-treated steel jaw faces. Permanent pipe jaws, positive "Tri-Grip" design. Positive locking swivel base, slip-handle lock nut. Polished jaws and anvil, bright red finish.

Jaw Width	Open			
312-44E4230...	4"	5"	27 lbs.	$29.90
312-45E5360...	5"	6"	38 lbs.	37.60

NO LONGER AVAILABLE

Helios Vernier Caliper — Stainless Steel ● Reading accuracy .001" ● With leather case. ● Thumb lock. ● Hardened ground stainless steel. ● Satin-chromed finish. ● Inside, outside, depth measurements.
TL-6F-F6 0"-6" by .001", 0"-6" by 1/128" $12.70
TL-6H-F6 0"-6" by .001", 0-17" cm. by 1/20 mm. $15.75

Fox Valley Compression Tester—Single unit tester provides readings to 300 pounds per square inch and fits ALL 18 MM. and 14 MM. spark plug holes, either gasketed or tapered seat. 19 inch hose is resistant to gasoline, oil and manifold heat.
C19A-F8 P—1 lb. $13.95

Wiss Leather Shear—Polished blades, black handles. High carbon inlaid steel blades provide the keenest, longest lasting edges made. Hot drop-forged.
Serrated blade; for all belt and leather cutting operations.
8BLT-W8 P—8" long x 2¾" cut $7.70

Stanley Layout Tape — Powerlock — "Write on blade" — mark measurements directly on special blade. Wipe off marks readily with finger. Insures accuracy, saves time.
61312-S19 P—12 ft. x ¾". . $3.75

Stanley Mitre Box—7¼" Capacity at 90°—4¾" Capacity at 45°—**No. 60MB** has 24" x 4" Back saw—Can be set to cut any angle from 45° to 90°. Catches hold saw above work. Lifting Spring raises saw out of kerf cut. Adjustable stops to control depth of cut. Adjustable vertically. Adjustable for saws of different thickness.
60MB-S19 P—24 lbs. with Saw $42.98

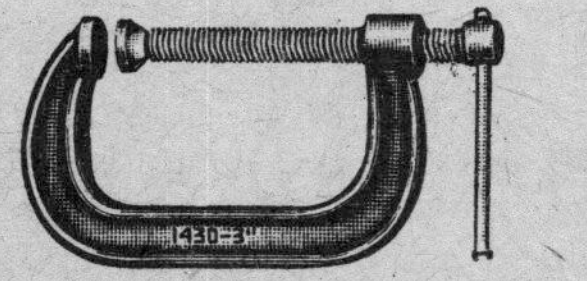

Cee Clamps—Made by Pony—Slid-in Pin Handle. Strong malleable iron frames; carefully fitted steel screws; permanently attached swivels; smooth finish.
Size shown = open in in. x Depth in.

1410-A2	1 x 1⅛"	.32
1420-A2	2 x 1¾"	.40
1422-A2	2½ x 1⅞"	.76
1425-A2	1 lb. 2½ x 2½"	.85
1430-A2	1 lb. 3 x 2"	.86
1440-A2	2 lbs. 4 x 3"	$1.60
1450-A2	3 lbs. 5 x 3¼"	$2.05
1460 A2	3 lbs. 6 x 3½"	$2.30
1480-A2	4 lbs. 8 x 4"	$3.58

Ridgid Tubing Cutters — for Copper, Brass, Aluminum Tubing and Thin-Wall Conduit.
10-R4 P—1 lb.—cuts ⅛" to 1"
O.D. tubing $4.10
15-R4 P—2 lbs. — cuts ¾₆ to 1⅛
O.D. tubing $5.25
20-R4 P—2 lbs. — cuts ⅝ to 2⅛
O.D. tubing $9.45

No. T-50—Arrow Gun Tacker—Powerful! Shoots heavier, longer, wedge pointed staples up to 9/16 (.050 wire). Excellent for ceiling tile, industrial users, etc.
T50-A12 P—3 lbs. $9.45

Lancaster Handyman Chain Saw — power packed to get the job done in a hurry. Most popular with the occasional woodcutter, excellent for the suburbanite or farmer for cutting fire wood fence posts and general all purpose use. Comes with 3 different Guide Bars — **TS** — Standard — **AN** — Armored noze — **RN** — Roller Nose. Power products engine — 4.0 H.P. — 4.7 Cubic inch displacement — Net weight 19 lbs. — Multi Position carburetor — Cutting chain is ⅜" x .063
40IL-L1 BF-24 lbs.—16" size—
RN—Model—$118.35 . . . TS-model—$110.70
401L-L1 BF—24 lbs.—19" size—
AN Model—$123.00 . . . . RN Model—$125.65
TS Model—$117.98

No longer available

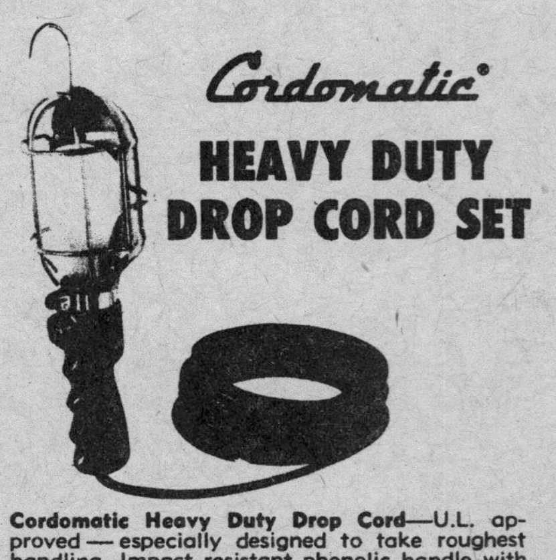

Cordomatic®
HEAVY DUTY DROP CORD SET

Cordomatic Heavy Duty Drop Cord—U.L. approved — especially designed to take roughest handling. Impact resistant phenolic handle with electric outlet built in . . . built-in strain relief post for cord . . . sturdy hanger hook . . . swing open guard. Fully guaranteed.
125DC-C20 2 Conductor Cord — push thru switch — 18 ga. SJ Cord — 7 amps. — 25 ft. long — 3 lbs. $4.25
225DCG-C20 3 Conductor Cord — grounding type — with levolier toggle-action switch — 16 ga. SJ Cord — 10 amps. — 25 ft. long — 4 lbs. $7.50

Stanley Bench Planes — Made of the finest iron castings with sides and bottoms machined true. Mouth opening can be made wider or narrower as desired.
Cutter adjusts for thickness and evenness of shaving. Lateral adjusting lever permits very fine adjustments. Handles and knobs made from the finest hardwood.
Stanley Smooth Bottom Planes —
3-S19 P—4 lbs. 8" x 1¾" cut $9.69
4-S19 P—4 lbs. 9" x 2" cut $9.65
5-S19 P—5 lbs. 14" x 2" cut $10.29
5¼-S19 P—4 lbs. 11½" x 1¾" cut $10.50
6-S19 P—7 lbs. 18" x 2⅜" cut $16.45
7-S19 P—8 lbs. 22" x 2⅜" cut $19.80

No. 652 Arco Hole Saw — With Extra Long Blades — 2¼" Long. 7 Hole Saws in One. Fits any electric drill, drill press, lathe. Exclusive "Slug-Elector" pops out slug immediately — therefore works 3 times as fast as other hole saws selling for twice as much. Cuts 1", 1¼", 1½", 1¾", 2", 2¼" & 2½" holes thru any 2" stock. Metal-cutting blades whiz thru wood, plastics, steel & other metals, formica, etc. Includes 7 blades & 3/8" drill bit with ¼" shank.
652-S6 P—2 lbs. $9.45

U. S. General Supply Corp.

Again tools, tools, tools. Brand names, catalog number is the manufacturer's model number. More junk than Silvo, and I think they sell their mailing list. At least I get lots of junk mail that I trace to them. Prices sometimes better than Silvo, service somewhat worse. Good to compare the two, as they have different prices and different things.

Net costs are coded into the item number. Divide the numbers following "E" by two. Audel books are 15-25% cheaper than publisher prices.

[Reviewed by Fred Richardson]

Catalog

$1.00 refundable

U.S. General Supply Corp.
100 General Place
Dept. WE
Jericho, N.Y. 11753

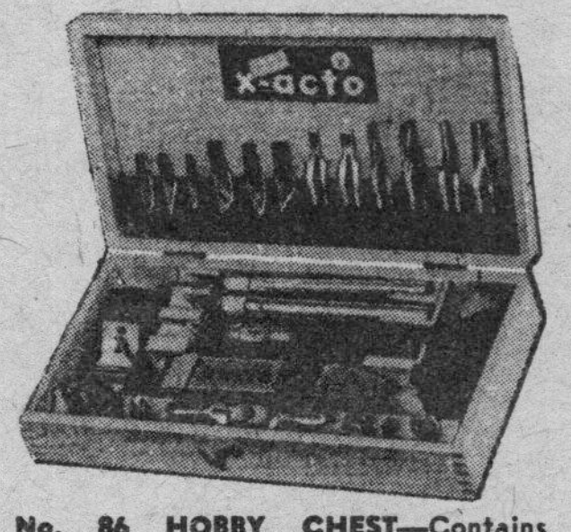

No. 86 HOBBY CHEST—Contains Nos. 1, 2, 5 Knives and complete asst. of blades, gouges, routers, punches. Has X-acto Planer, Sander, Spokeshave, Balsa Stripper, Steel Rule. In fitted wood chest.
86-X1 P—3 lbs. $10.98

Crescent 20 Piece Master Socket Set — ¼" sq. drive — Contains: 8—6 pt. sockets ³⁄₁₆" to ½", 7—6 pt. deep sockets ¼" to ½", Spinner, 2" and 6" extensions, Ratchet, Univ. joint and Steel case.
LMB20-C14 P—3 lbs. 20 pc. set . . . $15.75

"LIFE GUARD" RULES
Yellow "Life - Guard" finish protects surface . . . markings last 20 times longer. In 16ths and inches. Brassed joints, tips.
200-6LGE390 6-foot ... $2.85
As Above, with 6" extension.
200-X6LGE570 6-foot $4.40

SPECIAL WHITE TAPE
⅜" wide tempered spring steel tape is white, marked at 8ths in black. Heavy case.
604-950E480 50' $4.00 (2.40)
604-9100E700 100' 6.00 (3.50)

TANG CHISELS

STANLEY with light butt, steel caps. Alloy steel blades

Hand-forged, ground blades. Shock, fire-resistant plastic handles.

200-60-14E480	¼"	$3.39
200-60-38E500	⅜"	3.55
200-60-12E500	½"	3.59
200-60-58E520	⅝"	3.75
200-60-34E520	¾"	3.75
200-60-1E560	1"	3.99
200-60-114E630	1¼"	4.55
200-60-112E710	1½"	5.10
200-60-2E850	2"	6.10

STANLEY 100 PLUS LEVELS
Aluminum
6 vials fully adjustable in pairs or singly at any point in the circle or any angle for degree of pitch to the foot. Protective cover.
200-233-24E1720 24" $12.35

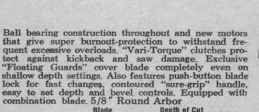
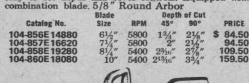
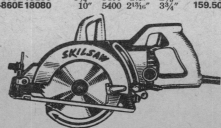

Ball bearing construction throughout and new motors that give super burnout-protection to withstand frequent excessive overloads. "Vari-Torque" clutches protect against kickback and saw damage. Exclusive "Floating Guards" cover blade completely even on shallow depth settings. Also features push-button blade lock for fast changes, contoured "sure-grip" handle, easy to set depth and bevel controls. Equipped with combination blade. 5/8" Round Arbor

Catalog No.	Blade Size	RPM	Depth of Cut 45°	Depth of Cut 90°	PRICE
104-856E14880	6½"	5800	1¾"	2⅛"	$ 84.50
104-857E16620	7½"	5800	2"	2½"	94.50
104-858E19280	8¼"	5400	2³⁄₁₆"	2⅞"	109.50
104-860E18080	10"	5400	2¹³⁄₁₆"	3¾"	159.50

STEELMASTER
Finest Hammers Made

Stanley's finest hammers . . . the Steelmaster line. A new precision-engineered all steel hammer with custom contoured grip of neoprene . . . always feels comfortable, yet cannot slip. The entire head, face and claws are specially heat-treated to give long life. Tempered rim minimizes chipping. Tubular shaped chrome alloy handle is permanently locked into the head . . . cannot break. Choice of sizes.
200-ST2E1020 13 oz. Claw. $7.29
200-SS1½E1000 16 oz. Claw. 7.15
200-ST1E1120 20 oz. Claw. 8.05
200-SS½AE1000 16 oz. Rip. 7.15
200-SS1AE1070 20 oz. Rip. 7.80

Palley's

There are many so-called "surplus" stores, most with some sort of specialty. They usually have started as war surplus, but now include all manner of industrial surplus, some of which is surplus for good reason. Some stores also carry cheap shoddy junk and "seconds" that are not at all bargains. Shopping for surplus can be tricky, but if you know what you are doing you can often do very well. It is helpful to know something about the merchandise in question and what it would cost at a straight supplier. It is better to shop in person rather than by mail because some examples are in better condition than others, and the catalog descriptions are often incomplete. It is also easier to haggle. You should keep in mind that there may be repair parts problems with surplus machines, and that it is unwise to depend upon a certain item being always available. Some otherwise succulent tidbits may turn out to work only on 27 volts DC; a bummer. Keep in mind that the "it may not be here tomorrow" feeling in a surplus store can hypnotically lead the unwary to bringing home a bunch of junk that "may come in handy later". Ingenious persons can often work wonders with aerospace stuff.

Palley's is known as the largest surplus house in the country. The most recent catalog lists mostly industrial surplus. Pumps, generator sets, storage tanks, fans, switches, power tools, vehicle winches, and gasoline engine powered carpenter saws and drills are among the items useful to the commune. They can get you specific stuff, and will haggle quantity prices.

[Reviewed by J. Baldwin]

Palley Supply Co. Catalog

$1.00

from:
Palley Supply Co.
2263 E. Vernon Avenue,
Los Angeles, CA 90058

HIGH PRESSURE TANKS

(G) Round bottom tank measures 5" dia. x 13-3/4" long. 1800 PSI. Complete with flood valve. Empty weight is 10 lbs. 12 oz., full weight is 13 lbs. 9 oz. ICC-3A1800.
OB18-UY2   **$3.95**

TACHOMETER INDICATOR

Indicates the number of revolutions per minute at which the engine crankshaft is revolving. Used with tachometer generator. Mfr: Kollsman, Type E-21A. Black face with luminous markings. Range is 50 to 5000 RPM. Overall size 3" dia. x 5-1/4" length.
INST-184-D17   **$12.95**

U.S. MARINE FIELD COOKING UNIT

Ideal for hunting, fishing and Boy Scout camps. Released by the U.S. Marines, this is an outstanding bargain for anyone needing a portable cooking outfit. Burns non-leaded gas, kerosene, fuel oil or Navy diesel oil. Unit consists of fire unit with air pump, hose, tank, and two 18-1/2" x 18-1/2" steel griddles which rest on iron grates. All you furnish is the utensils and food!
CA-61SU   **$21.00**

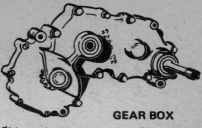

GEAR BOX

Right angle drive through. A 10 to 1 gear ratio. A 4" extended input shaft operates gear chain to a 2", 14-tooth beveled gear power output. Overall length, 12-1/2".
GB-8-SU   **$10.95**

HEINEMANN CIRCUIT BREAKER

AC TYPE
Operates on 117.5 volts, 1.25 amps, manual reset.
EL-CB84SU   **$2.50**

Type 122-954. Mfr: Leach. Coil voltage—24 volt DC. Resistance —185 ohm. Purpose—2 pole single throw. (N.O.—N.C.) Continuous duty.
EL-CB85SU   **$2.50**

"GREAT LAKES" AIR COMPRESSOR

Reciprocating power driven air compressor . . . 2 stage. Horizontal design. Puts out 2.3 CFM at 85 PSI. Operates on 27 volts DC, 8.7 amps and rated at 1/6 HP. Complete with 4000 RPM Delco motor. Overall size 11" x 5-1/2" x 4-1/2". Motor No. A9354, compressor 100-627-2.
AC-4   **$19.88**

Surplus Center Equipment Catalogs

Not only are these catalogs handy to the man who may need such parts, but they can also serve as idea-generators for solving certain mechanical problems——thumb through the pages. Some of the parts are better hunted locally where you can see, try, discuss with salesmen and haggle. Some are rare and good deals. Best suited to the mechanically hip, especially away from big city sources. All "surplus" is risky stuff unless you're familiar with it.

[Reviewed by J. Baldwin.
Suggested by Lama Foundation]

Catalog

free

from:
Surplus Center
Box 82209
Lincoln, Nebraska   68501

Battery Operated Truck-Boat Winches

MOTOR ALONE COST GOV'T OVER $275.00

Standard Drum Non-Remote Control Model Illustrated

CAPACITY 2000 LBS.

With Standard Switch Control
(ITEM #311-A)
$98.75

Remote Control Equipped Unit
(ITEM #323-A)
$110.75

Prices F.O.B. Lincoln

SPECIFICATIONS (Standard Drum)
- Ball bearing gear motor
- For 12-volts
- Capacity @ 12-volts, 2000 lbs.
- Cable speed, 15 to 20 f.p.m.
- Fully reversible
- On-Off reversing switch
- Drum capacity:
  50-ft. 5/16" cable
  90-ft. 1/4" cable
  125-ft. 3/16" cable
- Size 19" x 9" x 7"
- Shipping weight 65 lbs.

1-Ton Capacity Hoist-Winch-Puller

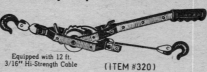

Equipped with 12 ft. 3/16" Hi-Strength Cable
(ITEM #320)

LIST PRICE $24.95
$23.95 F.O.B. Lincoln

- (ITEM # 320) -- Wherever you have a lifting, stretching, pulling, hoisting job you can do it easier, faster, and more safely with one of these HAND HOIST units. This handy, powerful, bantam weight hoist-winch-puller operates in any position with safety as there are no ropes or chains to tangle.

- Automatic let-down feature enables operator to release the load one notch at a time giving him complete and safe control of the load. This unit is extremely useful and popular with utilities, body shops, contractors, farmers and ranchers, tree trimmers, and by many governmental agencies.

SPECIFICATIONS
- Capacity 2000 lbs.
- Maximum lift 144"
- Leverage 20 to 1
- Automatic let-down
- Hi-strength steel frame
- Drop forged steel hooks
- Cadmium plated
- Heat treated steel
- Shipping weight 8 lbs.

Weatherproof Dial Telephone

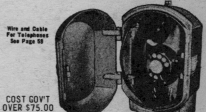

Wire and Cable For Telephones See Page 59

COST GOV'T OVER $75.00

(ITEM #780-A)   No longer available

- (ITEM #780-) -- Government surplus, Western Electric, excellent condition. Can be used on commercial telephone system (where permissable) or as intercom phone. Complete common battery dial telephone with hang-up handset enclosed in a cast steel case with cast steel door to provide complete, weatherproof protection. Heavy spring latch holds door closed securely and prevents wind or vibration from swinging it open.

- Phones are complete with brackets for mounting on wall or pole. Equipped with ½" pipe thread openings for conduit connection. Size 12" x 9" x 7". Shipping weight 27 lbs. (Available with or without lock and key on door.)

Airborne Sales

Airborne Sales Company is not the usual surplus melange. Emphasis seems to be on electrical, electronic, pneumatic, hydraulic and mechanical systems and attendant parts and pieces. Their stock includes both new and used, marine specialties, tool room items and "hard-to-find" things and stuff. Pumps and motors for a variety of applications and power sources are available. Tired of your smog producer? Develop your own electric car with motor No. 1893 (their 1965 catalog), a $259 Westinghouse product for $29.75. Gauges, tools and fittings are available for much of the pneumatic, electronic, hydraulic and mechanical systems common to aeronautic and space programs.

[Suggested and reviewed by C. P. Christianson]

Airborne Sales Catalog
95 pp.

$.35

from:
Airborne Sales Company
8501 Stellar Drive
Culver City, CA 90230

COMPLETE WELDING UNIT

NOT A KIT — THIS IS READY TO USE!

MERELY BELT TO YOUR TRACTOR, TRUCK, CAR OR OTHER POWER SOURCE. COMES COMPLETE AS SHOWN WITH CONTROL UNIT.

With 200 amp. generator internal cooling fan type. Ship. wt. 85 lbs.
No. 83

Same as above less generator. Ship. wt. 45 lbs.   No Longer Available
No. 84

TURNBUCKLE MIX

Copper plated brass barrel. Copper plated steel ends. Length open from 5" to 10". Approx. Govt cost $35.00. For boats and all outdoor and indoor installations. Ship. wt. 4 lbs.
No. 1337 SET OF 20   No longer available

FUEL SHUT-OFF VALVE

Knife type, slides in and out. Illustrated in half-open position. Handle has a full open or closed position. May be set at any point between. Aluminum construction with a stainless steel knife. 5" L x 2¾" W. Valve opening is 1-5/16". NEW. Govt. cost $103. each. Ship. wt. 2 lbs.
No. 2422   **$4.95 each**

TRIPS WITH EDDIE

Again it was Divine Right who broke the silence.

"The first t..t..time I ever had acid was in the G..G..Grand C..C..Canyon, with Eddie," he stuttered. "We were d..d..driving from L.A. to Shockey's p..p..place in Taos and stopped off at the C..C..Canyon and Eddie said let's go down in the fucker and drop acid. We called it our G..G..Grand Canyon trip. About every half hour Eddie'd say, what k..k..kind of canyon trip you having, D.R.? And I'd say g..g..grand, man, g..g..grand."

Friendly Persuasion was rummaging in her bag for a cigarette. Without looking up, she asked D.R. what was grand about it.

D.R. had to think about that. If his tongue had been healthy it would have been easy to rattle off a whole monologue about the Grand Canyon acid trip with Eddie. But his tongue was not healthy. D.R. had his voice back now, but he had to be careful with it. He had to conserve his words, spend them carefully, or else stuttering would take him over completely and reduce his words to mere babble again.

Speaking very slowly, looking at Friendly Persuasion, who had stopped fishing in her handbag while he answered, D.R. said, "Because we were t..t..ten million years d..d..deep in the earth, by that r..r..river."

Friendly Persuasion looked thoughtful a minute. Then she said, "Anybody got a cigarette?"

"I've got some, wait a minute," City Girl called from the kitchen. And she came into the living room carrying a tray loaded with cups and milk and honey to put in tea. She set the tray on the floor in the middle of the room, and went back to the kitchen to get the teapot. Before she sat down she got a package of cigarettes off a shelf behind the TV sets. As she settled cross-legged on the floor by the tray, Blue Ox got a clear look up her dress at her pubic hair.

(continued)

National Camera, Inc.

All manner of tools for fine work. Not limited to camera repair at all.
[Suggested by Jay Baldwin]

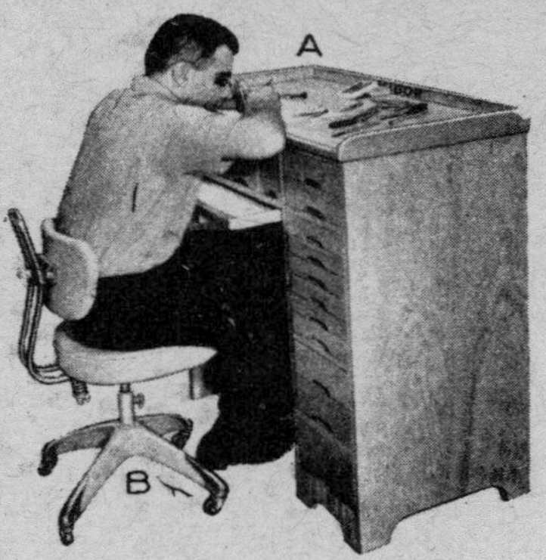

Catalog

$1 /yr (quarterly)

Free sample catalog on request

from:
National Camera, Inc.
Englewood, Colorado 80110

"ENDLESS" HACKSAW REACHES TIGHT SPOTS

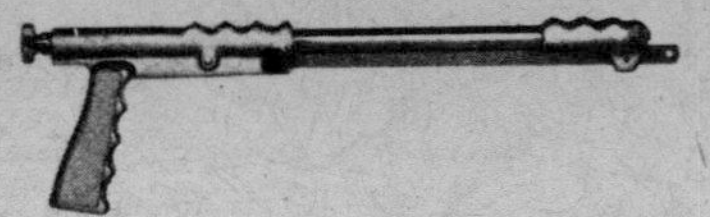

Simple-to-use, revolutionary, strong-built "Flexibar Saw" cuts flush in tight spots ... inside pipes and tubing ... also handles steel plate, corrugated iron, plastic and panelboard. No fragile holding pins to bend or break. Enclosed spring automatically returns the blade after every forward stroke. Saw is supported in front casing by three hardened steel balls to reduce blade breakage. Uses conventional 10" or 12" blades by means of locking screw. One blade—18 teeth per inch—included.

NC No. H-0300 **Not Available**

SAVE ON KITS

Rugged, easy to carry pouches containing the most useful lap joint pliers and nippers

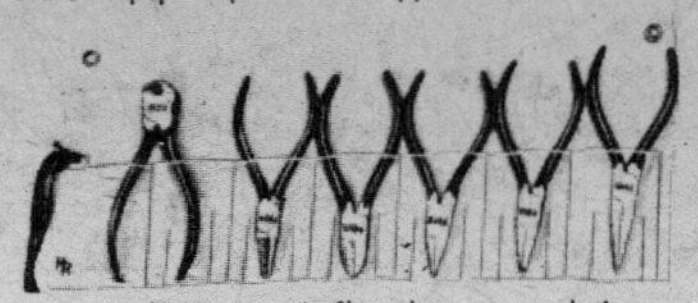

Contains chain, round, flat, long nose chain, diagonal nipper and end nipper

NC No. K-3583 Set of 6 **$23.20**

SOCKET WRENCHES

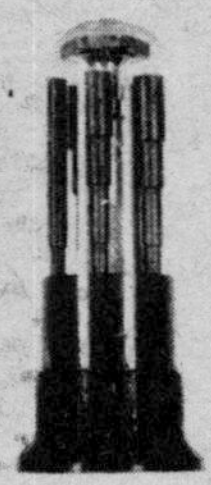

Five interchangeable box or socket hex wrenches -- sizes 5/64", 3/32", 7/64", 1/8", 5/32". Thread sizes #00, #0, #1. Choice of handles.

(Magnetic Handle)
NC No. S-1665 **$5.50**

(Non-magnetic Handle)
NC No. S-1670 **$5.00**

MILLIMETER DRILL SET

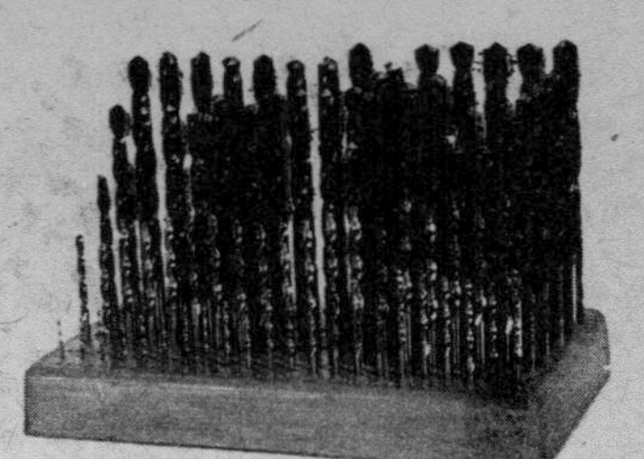

Millimeter drill set from 1.0mm (.0394 in.) to 10mm (.3937 in.) in increments of .1 mm (.0039 in.). A total of 91 drills in a newly designed handy plastic holder stand. In addition to using these drills as their nominal millimeter size, the tool maker can now drill from less than 3/64" in increments of approximately .004 in. This is a very economical way to fill in decimal dimensions which the fractional, number and letter size drills do not cover. Premium high speed steel-straight shanks. The index case is a convenient way to store drills for immediate use. Complete with a millimeter to inch decimal conversion chart.

NC No. S-1303 **Not Available**

Brookstone Tools

If precision tools are what you need, this company has nice ones.
—SB

Brookstone Catalog
64 pp.

$.50 / 6 issues

from:
Department C
3 Brookstone Building
Peterborough, N. H. 03458

HAND SABRE SAW GETS IN WHERE OTHERS CAN'T

Exceptionally handy miniature sabre saw solves many problems in model making, pattern making, jewelry work, other small-scale projects. Cuts straight or curved.

Usefully shaped Swedish steel blade is .018" thick, has 26 properly set teeth per inch. Extends 1¼" from holder. Cuts wood, plastics and soft metals including aluminum, copper, brass, etc.

Comfortable hardwood handle. About 7" long over all. Complete with two blades.

M-1685 Sabre saw & 4 blades $1.75
Three & up .... Each $1.50
N-1686 Spare blade .... Each 30¢
Per 6 blades .... Each 25¢

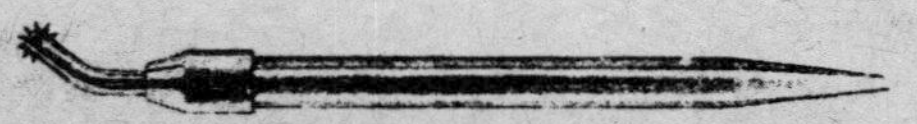

PATTERN TRACER IS TIME SAVER

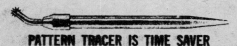

Pattern tracer or "pounce wheel" is for transferring paper drawing or other design or pattern onto work. Just draw tool along lines. Toothed wheel makes series of tiny perforations thru pattern, resulting in easy-to-see series of tiny dots in workpiece. Eliminates layout errors. Dots don't smudge or rub off to cause mistakes.

Used by dressmakers, tailors, artists, model makers, sign painters, designers, many others.

Modelers: Wheel marks on wood, cardboard, foil, etc. resemble row of miniature rivets.

¼" diam. free-turning steel wheel. 21 teeth per inch, for finest work. Swivels for caster action to follow intricate curves. Locks for straight work. About 5" long over all. Brushed aluminum handle 5/16" diam.

S-1394 Pounce wheel & handle $1.95

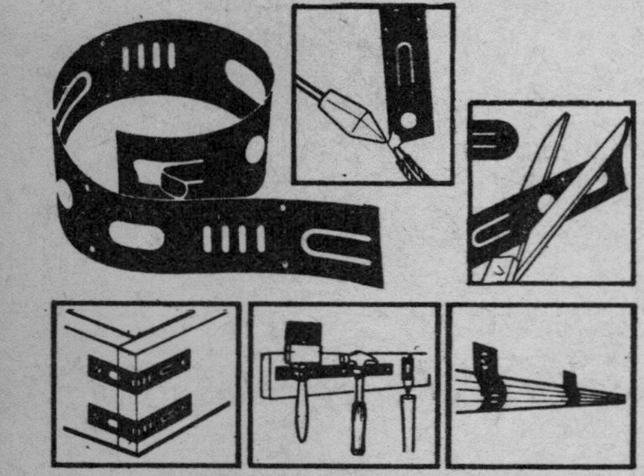

STRIP-STRAP DOES 1000 JOBS

Handiest steel strapping made. Can be bent, curved, twisted, shaped to meet any need. Clever locking tabs make it self-securing. Or you can nail it, bolt it, screw it or even solder it.

Makes clips, clamps, hangers, brackets, reinforcements, in a flash. Cut it with scissors!

Soft steel, ¾" wide x 0.017" thick x 7 ft. long. Zinc plated against rust.

T-1684 Coil of STRIP-STRAP .... 60¢
Three coils & up .... Each 50¢

UNAVAILABLE

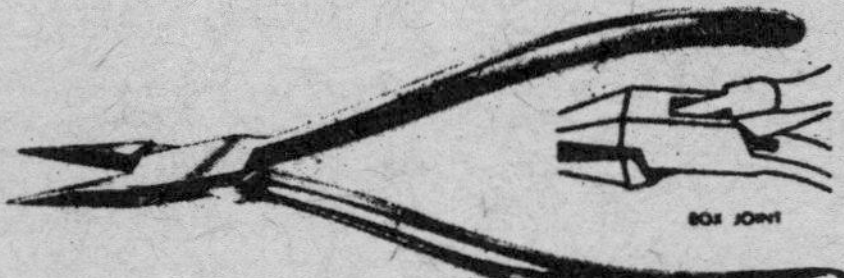

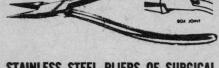

STAINLESS STEEL PLIERS OF SURGICAL INSTRUMENT QUALITY

True surgical instrument quality. Forged of AISI 420 surgical stainless steel, heat treated to Rockwell C50-55 hardness for maximum toughness. Beautifully mirror polished all over.

Box joint for permanent jaw alignment. Finely serrated jaws for firm grip. Special grooves in jaws hold washers, other objects, edgewise without slippage.

Jaws taper to fine points about 1/64" wide for finest miniature tasks. So precisely fitted that they'll grip a single hair.

M-1666 Stainless steel pliers, 6¼" $6.95

NOW, WIND YOUR OWN SPRINGS

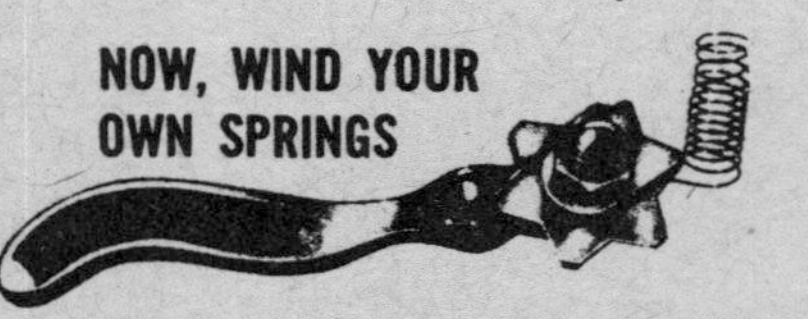

Here's a simple tool of unusual versatility. Winds extension, compression, torsion springs. Any diameter, length or pitch. Any gage of spring wire up to about 1/16" dia. Use round, flat or square wire.

Use it with a vise or lathe or drill press. Complete instructions included. (Spring wire is available at most large hardwares.)

About 4¾" long. Entirely of iron and steel.

N-1694 Spring winder $5.95
Three & up .... Each $5.30

Bartlett

Tools for watchmakers, jewelers, instrument makers, engravers, and other elves. (See also jewelers supplies on p. 156). Bartlett has several catalogs; tell them what you have in mind.
—SB
[Suggested by Jerome Senba]

Bartlett & Co., Inc.
5 South Wabash Ave.
Chicago, Illinois 60603

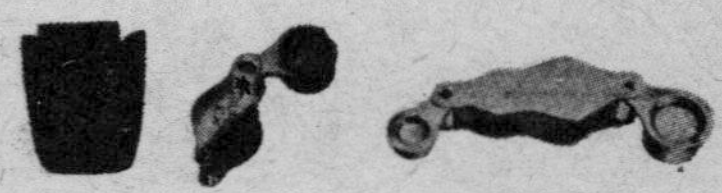

22-012 22-063

IMPORTED MAGNIFIERS

Economically priced magnifiers with spaced doublet lenses that provide distortion free viewing. No. 22-012 has leather carrying case.

No.	Style	Working Distance	Power	Price
22-012	1 Lens	1"	10X	$1.35
22-063	2 Lenses	1" & ½"	10X & 15X	2.40

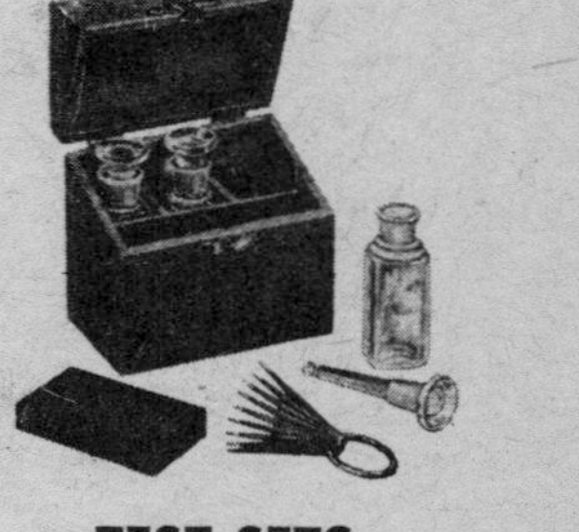

TEST SETS

For testing gold, silver platinum, etc.
Contents:
3 — Bottles
1 — Test Stone
1 — Set Test Needles
(In polished wood box)
TS-800 .... Complete $19.75

CYANIDE

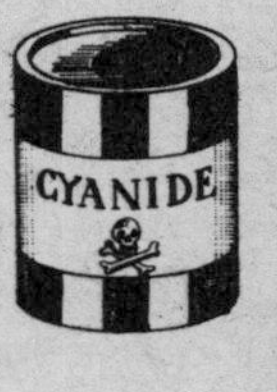

A very efficient cleaner for movements as well as jewelry. Kept in sealed, friction top cans.

SODIUM CYANIDE (EGGS)

One egg in one quart of water makes an effective cleaning solution.
CL-520 — 1 Lb. Can .... Ea. $1.50

POTASSIUM CYANIDE (GRANULAR)

Used for the same purpose as Sodium Cyanide but stronger and quicker acting.
CL-525 — 1 Lb. Can .... Ea. $2.35

SWIVEL BENCH VISE

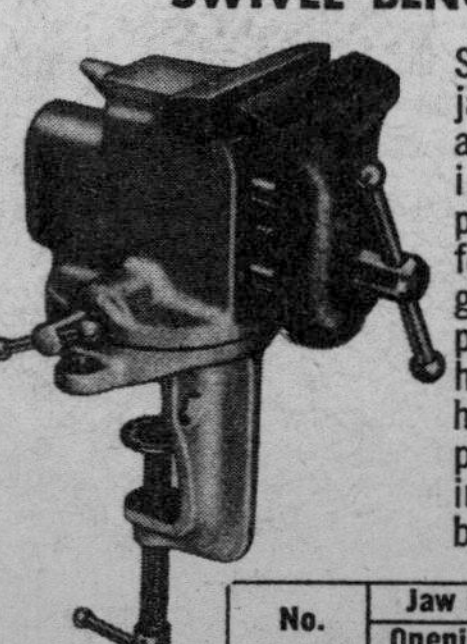

Swivel base permits jaws to be swung to any angle and locked in place. Jaws are polished and milled for close fitting. Twin guide rods assure parallel action. Body has a small anvil and has been enameled to prevent rust. Clamping device will fit on bench up to 2" thick.

No.	Jaw Dimensions		Each
	Opening	Width	
48-464	2¼"	2½"	$9.95

Jensen Tools

Primarily stuff for electronics and precision assembly. List prices, postpaid. Good deals on kits (make up your own). Excellent service.
—SB

Jensen Catalog
65 pp.

free

from:
Jensen Tools and Alloys
4117 N. 44th Street
Phoenix, Ariz. 85018

JTK-2

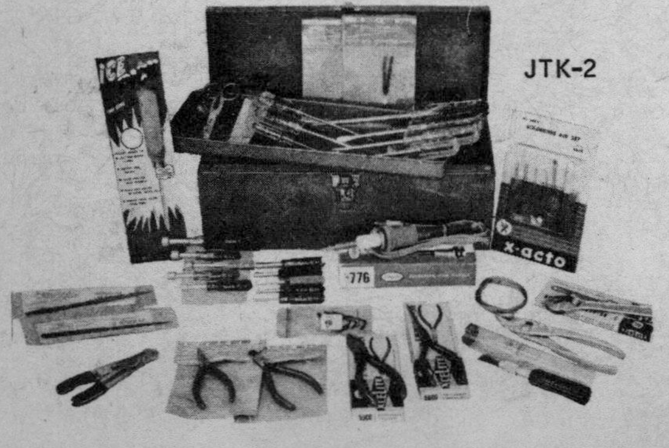

$44.50

This kit is the result of careful research and consultation with tool engineers. It was originally developed to meet the needs of large electronic-assembly plants employing many technicians, engineers, and scientists. It contains all of the tools necessary to accomplish 99% of the jobs, yet it is priced below the individual cost of the tools it contains. There is no sacrifice of quality—only the tools of well-known, preferred manufacturers (mostly American) are included. The tools are furnished in a steel, hammerloid finish tool box with catch and padlock eye.

How to Borrow Tools and Keep Friendship

If a man can trust you with his tools, there isn't a hell of a lot more he has to know about you. How trust is made:

When you borrow the tool, have him check you out on it, even if you know it cold. That'll encourage him and insure you.

Agree on a time it will be returned by. Return it by then.

Return it either to his hand or to the exact place you picked it up from.

Use it carefully. If you break it, replace it immediately, preferably with a better one.

When you're finished, service it. Sharpen it, oil it, fuel it, fix it. If his tool comes back improved, he'll let you have anything he's got.

If you make him loan you something out of guilt, you'll be sorry.

—SB

Tashiro Hardware

mailorder source for japanese tools,
—jd

Information

free

from:
Tashiro Hardware Co.
109-113 Prefontaine Place
Seattle, Washington 98104

Gerstner Tool Chests

If you enjoy reading this catalog you are probably the kind of person that is seized by an irresistible urge to open all those beautifully fitted little drawers in antique cabinets. You can satisfy the urge in your own home thanks to H. Gerstner & Sons, Inc.

They make superb wood cases that will hold small interesting things of almost any size and shape: machinist's chests, medical instrument cases, boxes for artists, photographers, dental hygienists, and so on, ad infinitum. The thing that sets Gerstner apart from their competitors is their concern with quality. You can buy a box from them that will stand with perfect aplomb on your Chippendale end table. Their cases are made of polished quartersawed oak, American black walnut, or can be covered with black leather or vinyl. Prices range from $36 to $123, and one look will convince you that their products are a rare bargain in an injection-molded age. Their service is personal and quick; illustrated literature is available. You can get factory seconds at reduced prices (less 20% plus ½ freight) too.

[Suggested and Reviewed by Dr. Morton Grosser]

Write to:
H. Gerstner & Sons, Inc.
20 Cincinatti Street
Dayton, Ohio 45407

POLISHED WALNUT	POLISHED OAK	ART LEATHER	OUTSIDE SIZE	SHIPPING WEIGHTS
No. W42	No. 042	No. 42	20" x 15¾" x 9½"	30 lbs.
No. W52	No. 052	No. 52	26" x 15¾" x 9½"	34 lbs.

The Japan Woodworker

For exquisite woodwork and exquisite woodcarving tools, the Japanese have it. This is a new importing store in Berkeley. They have a book, The Care And Use of Japanese Tools by Kit Mesirow, available by mail.

—SB

The Japan Woodworker Catalog 18 Nov 74

$0.50

from:
The Japan Woodworker
1806 Bancroft Way
Berkeley, CA 94703

日本指物師処

The Japan Woodworker
fine quality woodworking tools from japan

We have personally traveled to Japan to select Quality tools. These tools come from Miki city in the Kansai area of central Japan. Miki city toolmakers have made tools for Japanese carpenters for over 500 years in this same area.

Japan has a long history of wood construction and the carpenters perfected their craft at a very early date in history. These carpenters raised their craft to what is considered by many today to be an art in itself. The tools they used were of the highest quality and ingenious in design. The steel used in high-quality Japanese tools is of the finest grade found anywhere. This steel is to this day hand forged and tempered by a process that was known as early as the 13th century in Japan and not equaled in Europe until the 19th Century. The characteristics of this steel is a hard, sharp edge that remains extremely sharp even after repeated use. However, these tools must be used with care and for their intended purpose as the edges are more brittle than the softer, less sharp steel used in lower-quality tools.

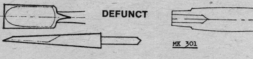

DEFUNCT

MK 301

MK 301 Heavy duty Chisels: Sets of nine or ten chisels each, ranging in blade width from 1/8" to 2" wide. The tang is heavy duty and the sturdy oak handle has a steel ring to prevent splitting from normal pounding. These durable chisels are good for mortising and general woodwork.
No longer available

Home and Workshop Guide to Sharpening

Make a distinction. Call it the first distinction. (See p. 12.) Minds do this (mine needs sharpening, judgement dull) and blades do this. Slice: two.

This book shows how to sharpen everything, to make your distinctions fine.

—SB

Home and Workshop Guide to Sharpening
Harry Walton
1967; 160 pp.

$2.50 postpaid

from:
Harper & Row Publishers, Inc.
49 E. 33rd St.
New York, N.Y. 10016

or WHOLE EARTH CATALOG

Tool Chests

A note on the Gerstner tool chests. In the old days, craftsmen made their own tools and tool chests. When they went for a job, they didn't turn in a resumé, they hauled their tool chests in and the boss looked them over. On the basis of the quality of the work, he was hired or not. Tools and tool chests were very personal things.

Max Pepke
New York, N.Y.

Leather Cases

Ray Gfellor, casemaker, Polson, Montana. Mr. Gfellor makes very good leather pouches and case. Most of his equipment it designed for geologists, but he lists a number of leather pouches that can be carried on a strap over your shoulder.

His cases are the best I've seen. The leather is very heavey and everything is riveted. You just look at them to see how good they are. They just look it and feel it.

I ordered a map case which fits on my belt. It carries a foldup, pencils and rulers. After juggling everything it pack you appreciate it. His prices appear fair: $18.00 for the case I just described.

He has a pamphlet catalogue available from him directly

Steve Schlossman
Belchertown, Mass.

Japanese Saws

Traditional Japanese saws have a variety of forms to facilitate their elegant joinery. But all cut on the pull stroke using two hands (foot holds wood). Many are double-edged, one rip and one cross-cut. They are light, thin, precise, and tireless.

To use a typical western saw after trying one of these is to induce nightmares of two-hundred pound marines hopping through rice paddies on one foot.

Can you help locate a source of Japanese tools for those who like to walk quietly through the woods?

Ken Freidus
Warren, Maine

P. S. I think there is an importer in Seattle.

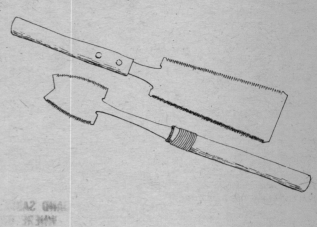

Japanese Saws

I noticed one of your correspondents was looking for Japanese Saws PP50, March cat. The only source for Japanese Saws in the East, but no mail-order business.

In Peace & hope
Chris Wolff
Berkeley Heights, New Jersey

PS Soaking an Ax handle in water is fine for a temporary job, but when the wood dries it will shrink more, & flying Ax heads result. (A BUMMER)

Blue Ox poured himself some tea. "One time me and Eddie and Winston were stoned on peyote, out in the desert," said Blue Ox. "And the goddamn stars attacked us. You remember that, Winston?"

Winston nodded and grinned a little as he dipped a spoonful of honey into his tea.

"I mean," said Blue Ox. "I mean, like, where do you run to when the whole fucking Milky Way is after your ass, answer me that?"

"You could close your eyes," said Bert.

Norton snorted. "Close your eyes. That's exactly what you'd do is close your stupid eyes."

D.R. leaned across the mattress and touched Estelle's shoulder. "You want some tea?"

Estelle shook her head and flipped another page.

"One time over in Afghanistan," said Reed. Reed was wrestling with a pillow, trying to fold it so it would support him as he drank his tea. "One time over in Afghanistan, me and Eddie had gone over there, to be big time dealers. We had four thousand dollars between us, and the plan was to score this incredible amount of hash, bring it back and sell it for a million dollars and retire from this fucking shit. So there we are fucking around goddamn Kabul, and who do we run into but this really spaced out American cat who says the best hash deal in the country is in this other town about fifty miles away. So he turns us on and shows us around a little, and tells us how to get to this other town. Of course we're all hot to go, but the thing is, his directions are pretty fucking weird. Like, I don't know how many roads there are going out of Kabul, but the one he put us on was this fucking dirt trail going north across this totally empty country. Not a house, not a roadsign, not a goddamn thing except this fucking rut they call a road going north into the country out of Kabul, just me and old Eddie bouncing along in this old taxi this other friend of Eddie's had scored somehow and left it there for us to use because he was going to be gone, some shit like that, I never did understand that car and I was too stoned at the time to care. So anyway we're on this dirt trail, bouncing along looking for this fork in the road see, and this guy who's supposed to be out there giving directions.

(continued)

How to Work with Tools and Wood

Famous for years when it was published by Stanley Tools, this comprehensive introduction is now a pocket book bargain.
—SB
[Suggested by Al Ching]

How to Work with Tools and Wood
Robert Campbell
1952, 1955, 1965; 488 pp.

$1.25 postpaid

from:
Pocket Books
A Division of Simon & Schuster, Inc.
630 Fifth Avenue
New York, N. Y. 10020

or WHOLE EARTH CATALOG

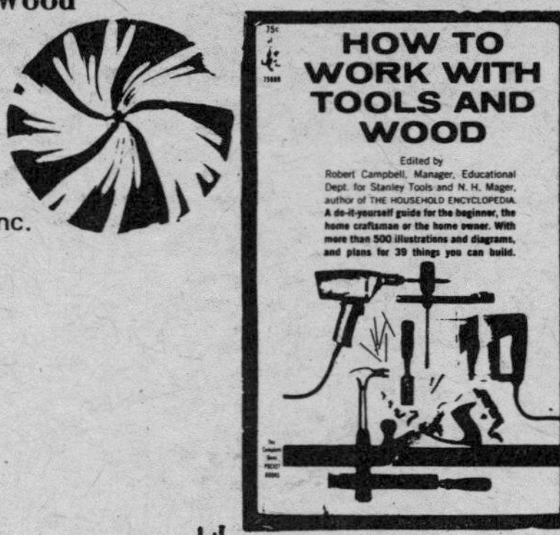
HOW TO WORK WITH TOOLS AND WOOD

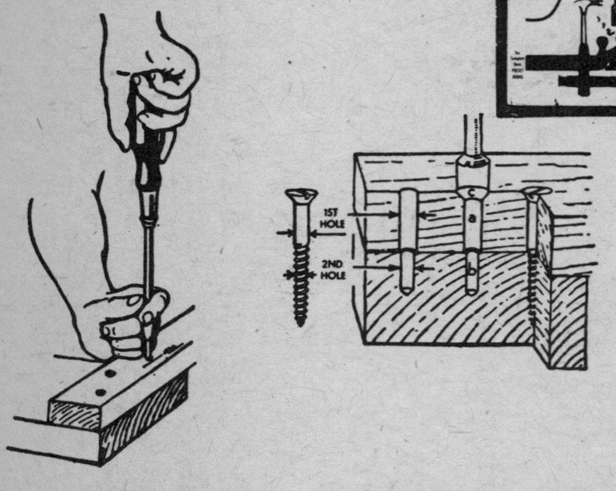
1ST HOLE
2ND HOLE

Use the longest screwdriver convenient for the work. More power can be applied to a long screwdriver than a short one, with less danger of its slipping out of the slot.
Hold the handle firmly in the palm of the right hand with the thumb and forefinger grasping the handle near the ferrule. With the left hand, steady the tip and keep it pressed into the slot while renewing the grip on the handle for a new turn.
If no hole is bored for the threaded part of the screw the wood is often split or the screw is twisted off. If a screw turns too hard, back it out and enlarge the hole.
A little soap on the threads of the screw makes it easier to drive.

Basic Hand Tools

A good, basic hand tool book (like the title says) and cheap. Covers machinists, wood working, and metal working tools. Use, care, and sharpening.
[Reviewed by Fred Richardson]

Basic Hand Tools
1963; 227 pp.

OUT OF PRINT

from:
U.S. Government Printing Office
Division of Public Documents
Washington, D.C. 20402

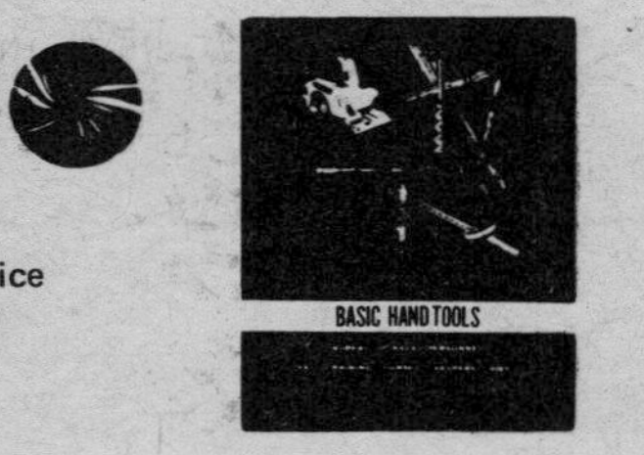
BASIC HAND TOOLS

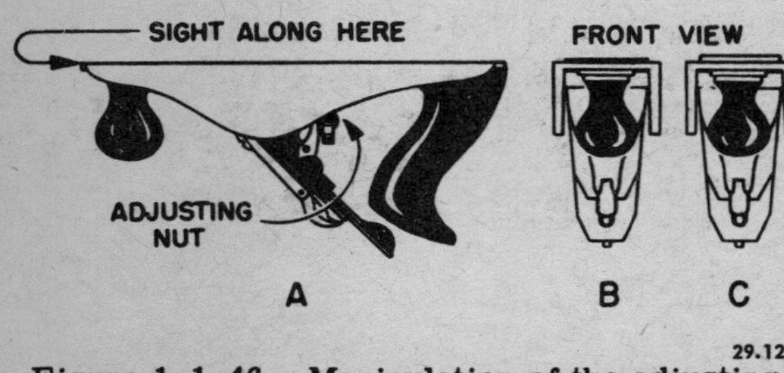
SIGHT ALONG HERE
FRONT VIEW
ADJUSTING NUT
A
B
C
29.12C

Figure 1-1-46.—Manipulation of the adjusting nut moves the plane iron up or down.

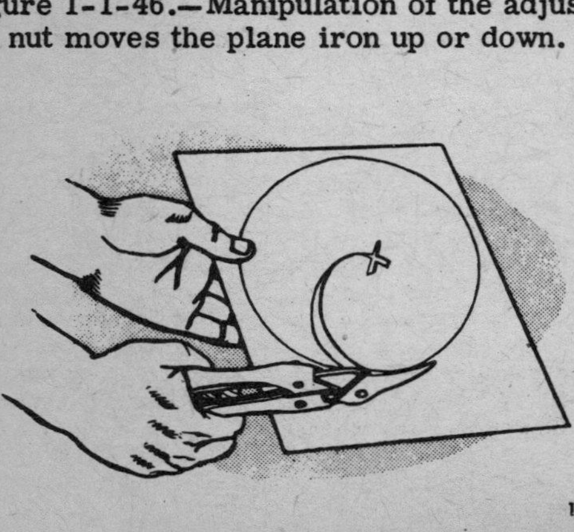
11.253X

Figure 2-6-9.—Cutting an inside hole with snips.

Notes on Simple Hand Tools

In a $1 Catalog I saw someone give out that you should tighten the loose head of a hammer by soaking the hammer in water overnight. Later, someone corrected this, noting that the wood would again shrink, leaving the head loose and ready to fly off without warning. It was then suggested that the remedy was to use a 6-penny nail with the head cut off as a wedge. NOT TRUE! I buy most of my tools used, from junk dealers. This is a good method——even with only limited experience with tools, you will find it easy to tell when most tools are merely damaged and salvable——or destroyed beyond reapir. And I have plenty of used hammers. Almost every used hammer I've ever seen has been 'fixed' with a nail driven into the haft, and this is one reason why the market is flooded with used hammers. The nail ruins the handle——ruins it. And doesn't do a good job of tightening, either. If your handle is loose, it can easily be fixed by soaking the hammer in Righteous Linseed Oil. Or you can go get a wedge, for chrissakes. If you can't get a wedge, make one. Just carve it out of hardwood and pound it in with a wooden mallet.

Axes. Keeps them sharp. Never pound on them with anything. Never use the poll (head) as a hammer. Ruins the axe by slowly mashing it out of shape. It also sometimes causes the axehead to crack right through. You then have a loose axehead that can fly off and kill. When splitting big logs, use a wedge inserted in the split——hammer on that.

Chisels and plane irons. To test for sharpness, do not use fingertips or try to shave your forearem. Instead, draw edge of fingernail across the edge of chisel lengthwise. This sensitive but neglected instrument will communicate with you instantly if it runs across a rough edge or dull spot. Try it. Needless to say, keep all edge tools sharp at all times. Saves time and money, prevents injuries. Naturally, you will have to take some time to learn to sharpen your tools properly and quickly. Few people do. But if you do, you will never go back to dull tools again unless you feel a distinct need to punish yourself.

Screwdrivers. For driving screws only, please. Drop this book right now and run down to nearest junk dealer. Purchase from him a large (8-12") old screwdriver that has been mutilated by misuse, abuse, ignorance and stupidity. Take it home. Pass it among your kinsmen while gathered in a circle. Fondle and recognize this tool. Burn Incense and repeat this mantra:

This is the tool for opening paint cans.
This is the tool for prying up planks.
This is the tool for chopping at plaster.
This is the tool for breaking down crates.

Repeat until everyone realizes that that is what the old dead screwdriver is for. Indeed, it no doubt came to be dead because it was used for just those purposes. If you use it in like way, you will contribute mightily to the longevity of many other screwdrivers. When buying good screwdrivers, here is the quickest way to spot a bad one: bad screwdrivers almost universally have skinny, grooved plastic handles with hard sharp edges on the grooves. You want a fat, generous handle at all times. Generally avoid chrome-plated screwdrivers too——cheap metal underneath.

Wrenches. Why do mechanics buy expensive assortments or dozens of one-size-only wrenches when it would be cheaper and more convenient to buy one big good happy adjustable wrench? Because they values their knuckles more than gold. Also, even the best adjustable wrench is easily maladjusted by a stray finger touch. Then it slips off, buggering the work and clobbering your knuckles. The high initial expense will eventually pay for itself by eliminating costly bandages.

Rusty tools can often be salvaged by use of Naval Jelly (trade mark). This is a gooey poison jelly that eats rust. Expensive, so try to get it by the gallon in big hardware stores fo better quantity price. The worse the rust, the longer it takes, but it will eat almost any rust you feed to it. Smells, but can apparently be used in closed spaces——label doesn't say not to. Read label anyway——you'll want to know what to do if it gets somehow in your eyes and stomach. Apply it thick and puddly——if you let it dry on the rust it's almost as bad as the rust. If you don't let it dry on the work, you just rinse it off with water, presto.

Please wear goggles. Please wear face mask. Please wear work apron. Not all the time, naturally, but whenever you realize that you won't be able to see for the wood or paint chips, breathe for the dust, or survive for getting clothes caught in the sawmill. Incredible how many people maim themselves because of neglect in this area. Don't you do it. You hurt more than just yourself, you also become a burden on your community, interrupting their work as well as your own. We are all living on the edge of a precipice: it is the responsibility of each of us not to fall off——OK?

Tape measures, yardsticks and rulers can be troublesome. First off, measure everything every time, and you will significantly reduce the chances of reading 3/8" for 3/16" or some other such dumb-ass humiliating error because you will become increasingly familiar with your tool. Use only one measuring device on a job. They are not all the same, and if you construct the frame of a four-drawer dresser using a simple, six-inch machinist's rule (highly recommended by skilled cabinetmakers), and then make all the drawers with a Stanley tape measure because you lost the machinist's rule——the drawers won't fit, that's all.

Don't get casual with power tools——they are as or more dangerous than loaded firearms. After the electric drill——a true little beauty——most common is the handheld portable circular saw——usually a 7" blade, 1/3-1/4 HP motor. Capable of slicing lumber all day, capable of wreaking incredible and irrevocable carnage in a second of careless use. Basically a primitive tool, please remember that all of the sophistication of modern medicine can do little for power saw wounds except to stop the bleeding. With all power tools, great awareness is needed. You MUST be able to see, simultaneously and at all times, BOTH of your hands, the business end of the tool, the switch and the power cord, and people who may blunder into your way. A lot to cope with; extreme care and concentration recommended.

Screws go easily into even hardwoods if 1) you ream out a pilot hole with a drill bit of correct size or, preferably, a screw-mate (a screw-shaped drill bit) and 2) scrape a little soap or candle wax onto the thread of the screw.

Handsaws. Buy the best you can get. Cheap ones are shit——although they may not smell, they are stinkers to work with. Cheap or dull saws will exhaust you, and fast.

Glue is handy and effective if you read the directions. Gluing without applying pressure by clamps or even 3 dozen phone books is a waste of time and materials.

Cultivate old heads. Use modern technology too, but not when old methods are simpler, cheaper, better, stronger. Old heads——pipe fitters, plumbers, carpenters and the like——have often learned many things handed down to them, or discovered by themselves when they had to make do on short notice and shorter cash. (Old heads with Depression experience and prepowertool experience, for example, are storehouses of beloved information.) Many of these old craftsmen have no one in their families who want to know about old outmoded crap like helping onesself, and will often willingly impart knowledge to you. Seek them out——you will do yourself——and them——a great service by it. Most of what I know of tools was taught to me by a grand old head, George Kelm, who took me into his workshop and helped me learn things that have since provided endless hours of usefulness and pleasure.

Bill Marsano

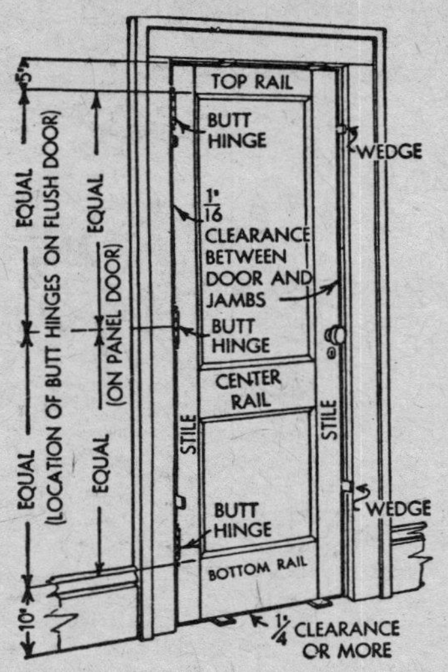
TOP RAIL
BUTT HINGE
WEDGE
1/16" CLEARANCE BETWEEN DOOR AND JAMBS
BUTT HINGE
CENTER RAIL
STILE
STILE
BUTT HINGE
WEDGE
BOTTOM RAIL
1/4" CLEARANCE OR MORE
EQUAL (LOCATION OF BUTT HINGES ON FLUSH DOOR)
EQUAL
EQUAL
EQUAL (ON PANEL DOOR)
EQUAL

Hand Woodworking Tools

Best book on hand woodworking tools I have seen. Detailed information on care and maintenance, including sharpness, for each tool covered. Goes into individual tools much more thoroughly than more general books like the Stanley book Has a very clear section on transit-levels and builders' levels.
[Suggested and reviewed by Fred Richardson]

Hand Woodworking Tools
Leo P. McDonnell
1962; 294 pp.

$5.20 postpaid

from:
Delmar Publishers, Inc.
50 Wolf Road
Albany, N.Y. 12205

or WHOLE EARTH CATALOG

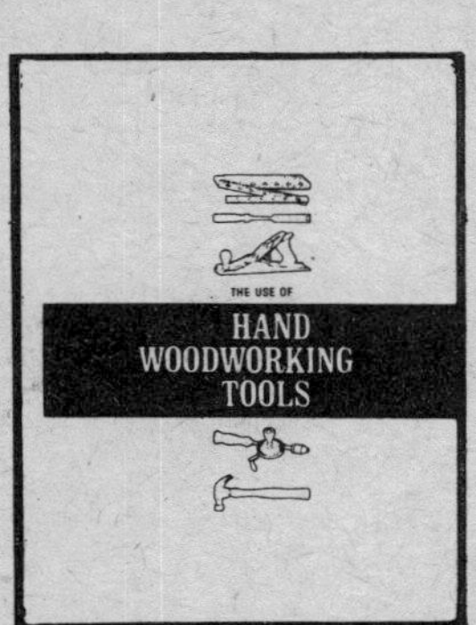
THE USE OF
HAND WOODWORKING TOOLS

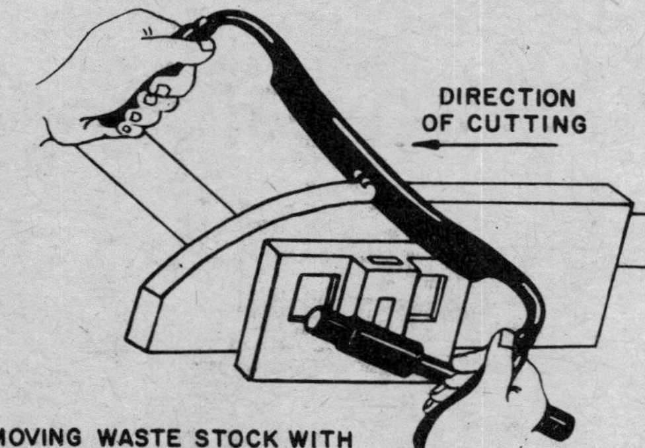
DIRECTION OF CUTTING

REMOVING WASTE STOCK WITH A DRAWSHAVE

How to Sharpen the Cutters on an Auger Bit

1. Select an auger bit file. A good "second cut" half round or three cornered file may also be used providing its size fits the surfaces to be reduced.
2. Rest the bit on a board with the screw down. Tilt the bit so that the cutter can be sharpened (see Fig. 10-14).
3. Apply the flat serrated side of the file to the under side of the lips, the side toward the shank. Never file the side toward the screw. Use forward strokes to produce the filing action. File well back into the throat. Do not leave the edge too blunt, the ideal to seek is a gradual taper from a keen edge.
4. Reposition the bit and file the opposite cutting edge in a like manner. Both edges should be filed to the same level to produce chips of equal thickness.

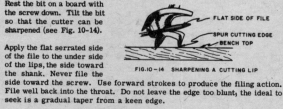

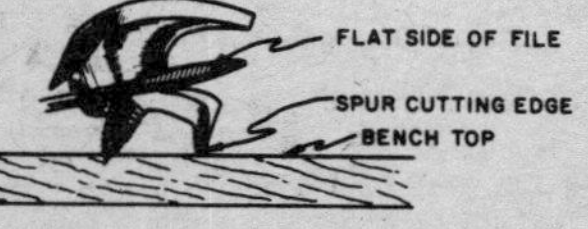
FLAT SIDE OF FILE
SPUR CUTTING EDGE
BENCH TOP

FIG. 10—14 SHARPENING A CUTTING LIP

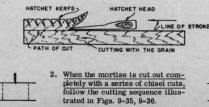

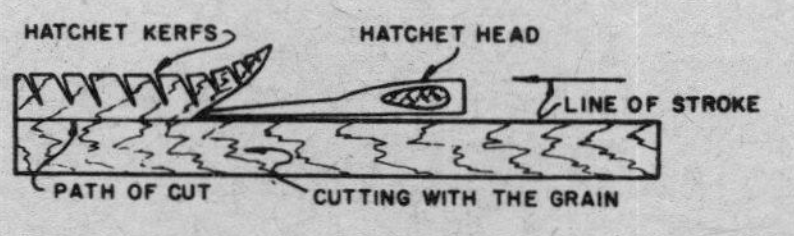
HATCHET KERFS
HATCHET HEAD
LINE OF STROKE
PATH OF CUT
CUTTING WITH THE GRAIN

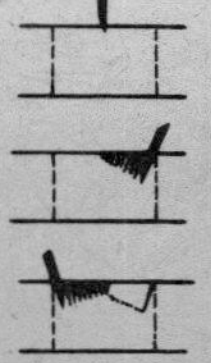

FIG. 9—35

2. When the mortise is cut out completely with a series of chisel cuts, follow the cutting sequence illustrated in Figs. 9-35, 9-36.

NOTE: Force is applied with a mallet for the roughing out operation. Use a chisel which is 1/8" less in width than the finished mortise width. Finishing to size is accomplished with a series of paring cuts.

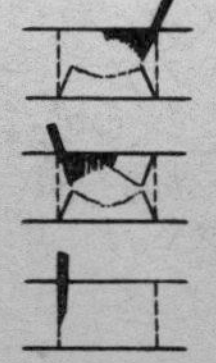

FIG. 9—36

144 Tool Use
Industry

Cabinetmaking & Millwork

Here is a big expensive book for all you woodworkers. Combine this with Hand Woodworking Tools and assorted other specialized books like Planecraft and you will have just about all you can get into books about cabinetmaking and finish carpentry. Heavy on power tools and machine tools.

[Suggested by Carl Nortenson.
Reviewed by Fred Richardson]

Cabinetmaking and Millwork
John L. Feirer
1967; 928pp.

$23.50

from:
Charles Scribner's Sons
Vreeland Ave.
Totowa, N.J. 07512

or WHOLE EARTH CATALOG

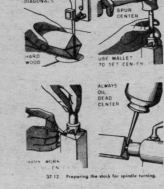

37.12 Preparing the stock for spindle turning.

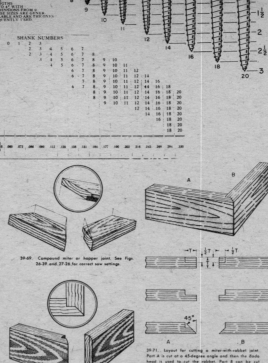
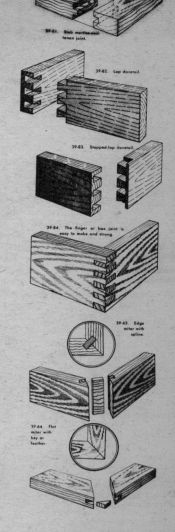

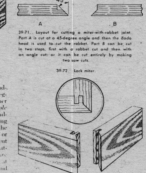
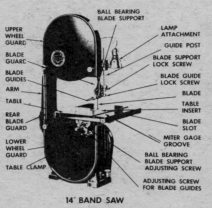

12"-14" RADIAL SAW

27-5. On this machine there is an arm track under the overarm. This track can swing in a 360-degree circle for making angle cuts.

OVER ARM
COLUMN
BLADE GUARDS
ADJUSTABLE FENCE
TABLE

TRACK LOCKING LEVER
MICRO-SET STOPS
QUICK-SET STOPS
ARM TRACK
HANDLE
SAWDUST SPOUT
FRONT GUIDE FENCE CONTROLS
MOTOR CONTROL
ELEVATING CRANK

14" BAND SAW

28-3(a). Parts of a 14" band saw.

UPPER WHEEL GUARD
BLADE GUARD
BLADE GUIDES
ARM
TABLE
REAR BLADE GUARD
LOWER WHEEL GUARD
TABLE CLAMP

BALL BEARING BLADE SUPPORT
LAMP ATTACHMENT
GUIDE POST
BLADE SUPPORT LOCK SCREW
BLADE GUIDE LOCK SCREW
BLADE
TABLE INSERT
BLADE SLOT
MITER GAGE GROOVE
BALL BEARING BLADE SUPPORT ADJUSTING SCREW
ADJUSTING SCREW FOR BLADE GUIDES

Mortise-and-Tenon Joints

There are many kinds of mortise-and-tenon joints in frame construction, leg-and-rail construction, and many other types of assembly. The *blind or simple mortise and tenon* is used in leg-and-rail construction. Fig. 39-71. In making this joint it is necessary to decide if the mortise will have square corners or rounded ends. For square corners the cut is made on a mortiser or mortising attachment. Fig. 39-73. Rounded ends are cut on a router. The mortise should be at least 5 16" from the outside face and...

Planecraft

If you work with planes and enjoy woodworking, Planecraft is a book to read. It gets into hand planes, their uses, care, and sharpening in a depth I didn't know was possible.

The book teaches methods for hand making joints I thought were practical only with machines. These methods are relatively simple and fast, but require skill.

[Suggested and reviewed by
Fred Richardson]

Planecraft
C. W. Hampton, E. Clifford
1934 . . . 1959; 255 pp.

$4.50

from:
Woodcraft Supply
313 Montvale Avenue
Woburn, Massachusetts 01801

Sharpening for Plastics. Plastics, Perspex, Formica, plywood having resin type cements and so on are notorious for their quick blunting of plane blades. Where only small amounts are to be planed, or when this type of work occurs only infrequently, the ordinary sharpening can be used, the quicker blunting of the blade being accepted as a necessary nuisance. If the work comes frequently, however, it is worth while keeping a blade specially for that work, grinding and sharpening it at a blunt angle somewhere near 80°-85°. An edge of this type will last sharp longer than a normally sharpened one. Special steels have been tried for the work but they are relatively expensive and cannot ordinarily be sharpened by the user, and hence have been ruled out. Instead of sharpening all the angle from one side, one user at least has been very successful using a blade sharpened at the normal angle, and then a grinding taken off the face side of the blade, thus making a cutting angle approximating to the one recommended above.

Fig. 327.

To the cabinet-maker, the Circular Plane is of great service in the making of circular frames and serpentine work; and to the carpenter in making circular frames for windows and doors. To the wheelwright, of course, it is indispensable.

Gilliom Power Tool Kits

Gilliom is a company which sells and manufactures plans, kits and parts for power tools. They carry a 12 inch and 18 inch Band Saw, a Belt Sander, a 9" tilt table bench saw, a shaper, a 10" tilting arbor floor saw, and a combination drill press-lathe. Can buy either the plans ($2.00) or the kit. The plans and kit make it possible to build your own power tools with Gilliom parts at a fraction of what a pre-assembled tool would cost. The metal parts are included in the kit and you can build the housings out of 3/4" plywood. The plans are simple to follow.

[Suggested and reviewed by
Marc Lerner]

Information

$.25

from:
Gilliom Manufacturing Co.
1109 N. 2d St.
St. Charles, Missouri 63301

9" Tilt Table Saw

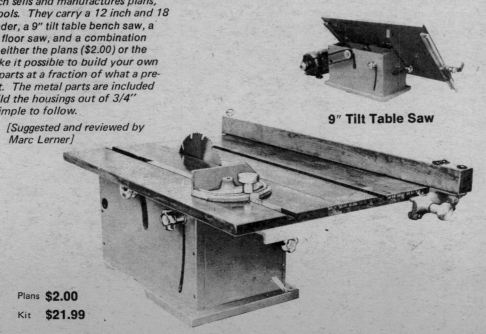

Plans **$2.00**
Kit **$21.99**

Rent It

Dear WHOLE EARTH CATALOG:

A very important tool that I think should be mentioned are rental companies. They will rent ANYTHING, tables, saws, trucks, etc. Ask about insurance, transportation clauses, and read ALL the fine print. On some large equipment like dump trucks, cranes, you may need to hire an operater and also trailers are needed for some stuff. The type, kind, and quality vary greatly so go easy. Check your Yellow Pages or ask at the local hardware store. The companies go under names like U-Rent-It, Rent-A-Tool, U-Haul, etc.

Yours Truly,

David Smith
Mendham, N. J.

That was his job. He was a roadsign. Every day this guy goes to the forks of the road, and he sits there, and people coming by ask him which road to take to where ever they want to go, and this guy tells them. The government pays him and that's his job. Only when me and Eddie get there see, the guy ain't there. He's gone. We're at this crossroads out in the middle of nowhere, three roads going three different directions and the guy who's supposed to be the roadsign ain't around. We hang around all day waiting for him to show up, but he never does. It blew out. That fucking Eddie wanted to toss a goddamn coin, or throw the Ching or something, and just <u>take</u> a road and see what happened. But it was too freaky for me, man. It pissed Eddie off but I couldn't help it. I mean, I was really counting on that guy being there and when he wasn't, the first thing I thought was nark. Maybe even CIA. I didn't want no part of that shit. We wound up not even buying any hash in Afghanistan, except just some to have around and smoke. It was heavy shit.

Reed sipped his tea as everybody laughed at his story. Most of the people at the funeral had heard it before, had heard Eddie tell it, in fact, and so the laughter was muted, very gentle and low-keyed. Reed lifted the teapot to refill his cup, but nothing came out.

"I'll put some more water on," said Gilded Lilly. She got to her feet and tip-toed through the people to the kitchen.

Craft

Woodcraft Supply

Some years ago, a large, dour Scot, Mr. Eaton by name, was trying to teach Boston schoolboys how to cut a clean mortise with machine-made carbon steel chisels. He couldn't, and being a Scot and stubborn, he began to import fine hand tools from across the water. He had to buy more than he needed, and he sold the surplus, reluctantly, from a dark cobwebbed shop on North Washington Street. To his surprise, he found that other craftsmen had also thrown shoddy tools through cellar windows in fits of frustration. North Washington Street has been torn up, and Mr. Eaton has passed on to the great workshop in the sky, but his company has become the Woodcraft Supply Corp., 313 Montvale Avenue, Woburn, Massachusetts 01801. It is a unique enterprise that operates contrary to the accepted principles of American business. As any hardware store owner will tell you, no one today will pay $47.50 for a nickel-plated fitted wood case. You can buy one from Woodcraft—if you are willing to talk about it for an hour and enjoy a good cup of home-brewed tea. Have you ever had your forearm shaved as clean as a baby's with a 1-pound paring gouge? You're not likely to have the experience many other places. The same personal touch is apparent in everything handled by this unusual company. (They sell a German cabinet-maker's bench of polished red beech that is seven feet long, weighs 300 pounds, is fitted with two built-in vises, and would make most furniture companies blush with shame. $235.) Woodcraft Supply publishes a large-format illustrated 30-page catalog full of tools that you will never see anywhere else. It costs 25 cents, and you will be a rare craftsman if you don't order something after one pass through it.

[Suggested and Reviewed by Dr. Morton Grosser]

Woodcraft Supply Catalog

$.50 postpaid from

from:
Woodcraft Supply Corporation
313 Montvale Avenue
Woburn, Massachusetts 01801

CARPENTER'S MALLET

No. 7715. Carpenter's MALLET. Angled faces of this beechwood mallet reduce wrist and arm fatigue. The handle comfortably fits hand and the increasing taper towards the head eliminates chance of head working off. Size 5½". Mailing weight 4 pounds. **$5.50**

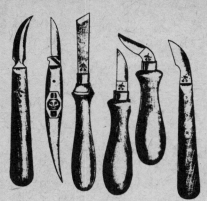

No. 7715

CHIP CARVING KNIVES

No. 600(6). Set of ten knives as shown at the left. Length 5 to 6¼ inches. Mailing weight 1 pound. **$19.75**

Individual knives as shown at the left. Order by stock number as indicated. Mailing weight 1/4 pound. **$2.40**

620　617½　619　624　623　622

QUICK ACTION CABINETMAKER'S VISE

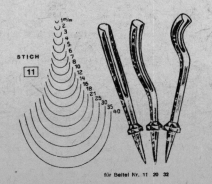

No. W52½D. Extra high grade. Sliding bars are solid steel and work in accurately machined housings. Has bench stop locked by thumb screw. Continuous action. Width of jaws 9 inches, open to 13 inches. Weight 35 pounds. Mailing weight 40 pounds. **$49.75**

ADZ HEADS

The following two adz heads are usually used with hatchet length handles. Sorry but we cannot furnish handles to fit, they are for those who are willing to improvise their own handles.

No. X23. Adz Head, straight 3¼" blade. Mailing weight 3 pounds　**$10.85**

No. X25. Adz Head, curved gouge type, about 2¾ inches across. Its degree of arc is that of a 3-inch circle. Mailing weight 3 pounds.　**$12.50**

GENERAL SMOOTHING PLANE

No. HW2. General Smoothing Plane. Beech body with hornbeam shoe. With striking knob. Length about 9 inches, iron 1-7/8 inches. Mailing weight 3 lbs.　**$16.40**

Replacement Cutter. Mailing wt. 1 pound.　**$3.90**

BROAD AX

No. 2210-14. Broad Ax. At last a true broad ax which is used for hewing timbers from logs. Head weight approximately 4 pounds. Without handle. Mailing weight 5 pounds.　**$21.75**

Paxton Lumber

Beautiful woods, good information, wholesale only.
[Suggested by Fred Borcherdt]　—SB

Booklet *Beautiful Woods*, 50 pp. **$1.00** postpaid
Set of 46 different sample woods, **$5.50** postpaid

Frank Paxton Lumber Co.
5701 W. 66th Street
Chicago, Illinois 60638

TEAK, Genuine	Small Orders Per 100 Ft.	500 Ft. Or More Per 100 Ft.
● KILN DRIED, Rough		
1" First Class European	$153.00	$147.00
1¼" First Class European	154.00	148.00
1½" First Class European	155.00	149.00
2" First Class European	156.00	150.00

Besides a treasured wood for furniture of the highest class, Teak is the criterion by which all other woods are judged for marine usage. It offers beauty of a unique sort; a well made project of Teak will last practically forever. Should be planned only for advanced students, as Teak is quite difficult to work.

Frank Mittermeier

Fine carving, sculpting, and engraving tools.
[Suggested by Jerome Scuba]　—SB

Catalog

free

from:
Frank Mittermeier, Inc.
3577 East Tremont Avenue
Bronx, New York 10465

The fastest cutting tools for wood, plastic, etc., and metals up to the hardness of mild steel.
Surform Round File **$2.95**

Spoon Gouge No. 105¼
Width from 2 to 10 mm................. each **$2.85**

Long Bend Parting (V) Tool No. 106½
Width from 1 to 8 mm................. each **$3.00**

Spoon Parting (V) Tool No. 106¼
Width from 2 to 8 mm................. each **$3.15**

German Woodcarving Tools

Several months ago I began looking for high-quality woodcarving tools at a reasonable rate. I found that the availability of any tools was not very good (at least in Salt Lake City) and that those available were very expensive.

A German neighbor who may be considered a Master of the Art, gave me this address and said that the quality couldn't be higher:

Carl Heidtmann
563 Remscheid - Hasten
Unterholzfelder Str. 46
West Germany

I ordered eighteen tools and eighteen handles and sent them $35.00. There was no duty charged me, but I'm told that sometimes (supposedly according to the amount ordered, but in fact the customs agent seems to be the determining factor) a small fee is charged. Eight weeks after I placed my order I received the tools in the mail, well wrapped in wax paper, and $3.50 credit towards further purchases.

For those who aren't in a great hurry, the quality of the tools seems well worth waiting for.

Send two International Reply coupons (about $.44) and your catalog will be sent airmail.

Sincerely,
James Jones
Salt Lake City, Utah

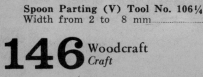

STICH
11

für Beitel Nr. 11　20　32

About Woodcarving

In any locale suitable wood may be found for woodcarving. Suitable scraps may be obtained——often free——from lumber yards and furniture making shops. Trees that are "sacrificed for progress" at the hands of real estate developers may be excellent if discovered shortly after being felled. They should be cut to desired sizes, and thick trunks are best when quartered, with wedges & ax or with a chain saw. Fresh wood should have all naked surfaces sealed with parafin so that slow, controlled drying occurs to prevent checking. Leave the bark in place. The time required for adequate drying will vary with the type of wood, the size of the piece, and the ambient humidity. For the impetuous who can't wait for completely dry wood, coat with linseed oil after each carving session. This seals the wood and also provides a nice, low-gloss natural finish but at the same time precludes the use of stain, varnish & shellac. (I think shellac gives carvings a cheap plastic look anyway.)

Tools

Obtaining good carving tools may be a hassle, especially outside large cities. I have found several good sources for tools:

1) *Ashley Iles, Ltd.*
Fenside
East Kirkby
Spilsby, Lincs.
England

2) *Woodcraft Supply Corp.*
313 Montvale Ave.
Woburn, Mass. 01801

3) *Craftsman Wood Service Co.*
2127 Mary St.
Chicago, Ill. 60608
(tools and wood)

4) *Brookstone Co.*
Dept. C.
4 Brookstone Bldg.
Peterborough, New Hampshire 03458

All the above will send catalogs on request. Ashley Iles has the best prices but the selection varies with what is in production at the moment and the service is slow.

A round-headed mallet is essential. It allows the carver to devote full attention to the cutting edge of his chisel or gouge. It's hard to miss with a large, round mallet, and even if you do, the blow is softer than that from a claw-type hammer.

A. Dover, M.D.
Atlanta, Georgia

Craft

wyatt frydenland,
a student of mine,
once said
"do it right the first time."
now, that's a little bit tightass
when applied to homedone things.
maybe it should read
"practice until you can
do it right the first time."
or
"a thing worth doing is worth doing."
or
"just go ahead on and do it,
whatever it is,
and learn from your mistakes."
or
"find somebody who knows something
and learn it from him."
or
"through industry we prosper,"
and all that craft.

—jd

Whittling and Woodcarving

remember sitting by the monkeycage
at the alliance zoo, (two male
spidermonkeys with piles) and
watching a gandydancer (must have
been a gandy . . . wasn't an indian,
it was the middle of the day,
and he wasn't at work) whittling
on a chunk of two by four. it
took him about two hours to carve
it down into a cage with three balls locked inside.
i've tried whittling away montana
nights. turned out a double-ended
wooden spoon and made the bandaid
people thirty cents richer.
should've read the book.

—jd

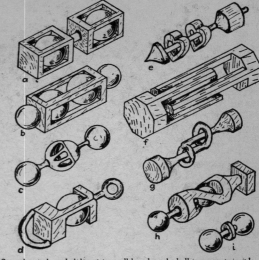

FIG. 94 · Several swivels and sliding joints, all based on the ball-in-a-cage principle

Whittling and Woodcarving

E.J. Tangerman
1936, 62; 293 pp.

$2.00 postpaid

from:
Dover Publications Inc.
180 Varick Street
New York, New York 10014

or WHOLE EARTH CATALOG

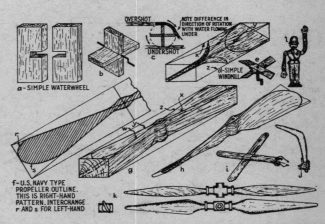

a - SIMPLE WATERWHEEL

f—U.S. NAVY TYPE PROPELLER OUTLINE. THIS IS RIGHT-HAND PATTERN. INTERCHANGE r AND s FOR LEFT-HAND

THE WHITTLER'S MASTERPIECE

Constantine's Wood Catalog

Lots of things for woodworking. Prices are high, but if you can't get it anywhere else. . . . Lots of fancy woods and finishes. Guitar materials. Fancy cabinet hardware.

[Reviewed by Fred Richardson]

Catalog
84 pp.

$.50

from:
Albert Constantine and Son, Inc.
2050 Eastchester Road
Bronx, New York 10461

Kind of Wood	Source	Color	
Avodire	West Africa	Light straw	Priced by the sq. ft.
Bubinga	West Africa	Reddish brown	
Ebony* (Gaboon)	Africa	Black	Write for current catalog prices.
Limba	Africa	Cream	
Padouk (Vermilion)	Africa	Bright red	
Purpleheart	Dutch Guiana	Purple	
Rosewood	Brazil	Brick red, black	
Rosewood	E. India	Deep red, striped purple	
Satinwood	Ceylon	Light yellow	
Teakwood	Burma	Cocoa brown	
Zebrawood	West Africa	Tan, brown stripes	

Sh. wt. per sq. ft. ¼".......2 lb.   ½".....3 lb. 6 oz.
All prices F.O.B. New York

CHOICE BRIAR BLOCKS FOR SMOKING PIPES

Make your own pipe!
You can carve a rustic-finish pipe, or you can lathe-turn the smooth style.
For popular natural finish of this beautiful briar wood, application of clear-glass high buffing pipe lacquer is recommended. After lacquering, apply polishing compound and buff to high polish on buffing wheel.
BRIAR BLOCK size R-2¼ for bents or straight.
No. 108 x 202 Each, $1.30; Two Blocks, $5.00 Sh. wt. 8 oz.
STRAIGHT BITS. Most popular style. Narrow bit; doesn't roll. Hard rubber. 11/16" diam. Length 3" shank.
No. 108 x 203 Bits, each 39¢; Two for 70¢ Sh. wt. ea. 5 oz.
PIPE LACQUER 1 pint $1.25 Sh. wt. 2 lbs.

APPROX. 3 in.

B—Jorgensen Band Clamp. Indispensable for clamping all round and irregular shapes with pre-stretched canvas of 2" width. Length of band 15 ft.

No. 50C11 (sh. wt. 5½ lb.) $21.75

B

Craftsman Wood Service

Much the same stuff as Constantine's Wood Catalog. Some things cost less, others more. Craftsman has some things Constantine doesn't, and vice versa. If you use one of them, you really need both. Craftsman has almost anything you could think of for fine woodworking, from the wood itself to books telling you how, and including tools, cabinet hardware (more kinds of hinges, for example, than you could imagine), and upholstery supplies. If you would like to try your hand at making a violin, they can provide you with an instruction book and all the materials (no ready-to-assemble kit, praises be).

[Suggested and reviewed by Edwin L. Powers]

Catalog
$.50

Craftsman Wood Service Company
2729 South Mary Street
Chicago, Illinois 60608

LIGNUM-VITAE MALLETS

Lignum-Vitae is the hardest and heaviest wood in the world. These mallets will outlast ordinary wood mallets many times over. Hickory handle is 9" long and wedged in tightly.

No. 5. Head 2" x 4". Wt. 7 oz. $2.89
No. 3. Head 2½" x 4½". Wt. 17 oz. 3.50

Genuine Honduras Mahogany

Mahogany from Honduras is generally recognized as the "King of the Mahoganies."
You can buy Mahogany grown elsewhere for less money but it cannot be compared with this beautifully grained wood from Honduras.

Thickness S2S	< ⅛"	¼"	⅜"	½"	¾"
Price per sq. ft.	$0.43	$0.52	$0.60	$0.73	$0.92
Per 100 sq. ft.	41.00	49.00	57.00	70.00	89.00

White Northern Hard Maple

(5" to 7½" Wide)

Has the same characteristics as birch. Texture slightly harder.

Thickness S2S	⅛"	¼"	⅜"	½"	¾"
Price per sq. ft.	$0.33	$0.38	$0.43	$0.52	$0.59
Per 100 sq. ft.	30.00	35.00	40.00	49.00	56.00

¾" Maple Shorts assorted random widths and lengths — 18" to 36" long — per sq. ft. $0.40

SOFT MAPLE (Northern) ¾" S2S Price per sq. ft. $0.53

ASH—¾"—Price per sq. ft. $0.43

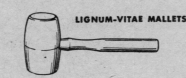

WHAT WOULD YOU HAVE DONE?

"What would you have done?" Friendly Persuasion asked The Native.
"What do you mean?" said The Native.
"At the crossroads. What would you have done?"
"Do you mean would I have gone with Eddie?"
"What would you have done, Winston?" asked Friendly Persuasion.
"I would of gone with Eddie," said Winston.
"I would of thrown the I Ching first," said Chuck. "They should have thrown the Ching and gone with it."
"Not me, man," said Norton. "I would of gone with Reed straight back to Kabul and got my ass out of there."
As people began to talk about what they would have done or not done in Afghanistan, Divine Right looked around the room for a copy of the I Ching. Chuck's mention of it gave him the idea to throw it, then and there. He didn't have anything in particular he wanted to ask. He just felt like it would be a good idea. When there was an opening in the conversation he asked City Girl if there was a copy of the I Ching in the house.
"There's Eddie's copy," said City Girl.
"You going to throw the Ching, man?" asked Reed.
"Yeah," said D.R.
"Groovy," said Gilded Lilly as she came in the room with fresh tea. "Let's ask it which road they should have taken in Afghanistan."
"I'd rather ask it what Eddie's been reincarnated as," said Blue Ox.
"I'd rather ask it how you get a job like the roadsign guy had." said Chuck.
"Oh man, wouldn't that be far out?" said Norton. "Wouldn't that be a fantastic job."
"Shit," said Gilded Lilly. "Just sit out there and give people directions, send them this way, send them that way."
"Yeah," said The Native. "And people you didn't like you could send them the wrong way. Have a whole network of your buddies in charge of all the intersections, fucking cops come up and say, which way is Kansas City? and you'd say that way, motherfucker, and send 'em to Gallup, New Mexico."
"Yeah," said Chuck, "but good dudes, send them to the grooviest places there is. Have this big farm, see, have this incredible big spread in fucking Oregon, or Colorado, or some place. And when a really good cat would come along, that's where you'd point 'em."
"I'd rather ask who killed Eddie," said Norton. "Some son of a bitch killed Eddie and we don't even know who it is."
"You can't ask shit like that," said Bert. "You can't ask specific questions."
"The fuck you can't," said Norton. "I ask it specific questions all the time."
"If you're not going to ask which road to take in Afghanistan, I don't want anything to do with it," said Gilded Lilly.
"I'm going to watch TV myself," said The Native. And he rolled across the floor and turned on the color television.
As the sound of television began to grow in the room and people quit talking about Afghanistan and the I Ching, City Girl motioned for D.R. to follow her. Together they stood up and picked their way across the people scattered around on the mattresses and disappeared behind the bedroom door.

How to Build Your Own Furniture

Unlike most books on do-it-yourself furniture, **How to Build Your Own Furniture** *by R. J. DeCristoforo contains no plans on how to build your own furniture. What it does contain is information on what should go into the design of a given piece of furniture to make it function properly. If you have ever built a table that wobbled or a drawer that wouldn't open, you will appreciate this book.*

The book gives a wealth of information and illustrations on techniques and methods of quality furniture craftsmanship. There are chapters on materials and general design and construction with separate chapters on each of the different categories of furniture (such as tables, chairs, desks, chests, etc.). The book is very concise and the instructions and illustrations are easily understandable. This is definitely a standard work for the designer-craftsman.

[Suggested and reviewed by Lloyd Martin]

How to Build Your Own Furniture
R. J. De Cristoforo
1965; 176 pp.

$1.95 postpaid

from:
Barnes & Noble
c/o Harper & Row
Keystone Industrial Building
Scranton, Pennsylvania 18512
or WHOLE EARTH CATALOG

Choose from a wide variety of hinges to suit a specific project . . .

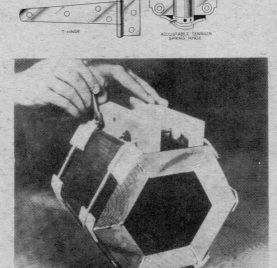

Improvised setup for clamping irregualr work. The "clamp" consists of two hardwood bars, two nuts and bolts and a couple of lengths of line.

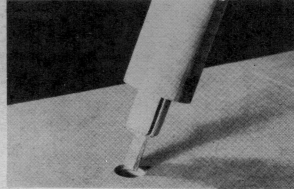

Tenon inserted in a slab can be considerably reinforced by a wedge in a slot cut in the tenon to spread the tenon tightly in the hole. Don't make the wedge too thick or you will have trouble getting tenon to "seat".

The Wheelwright's Shop

Wow. All you want to know (almost all) about wheelwrighting. Selecting trees, cutting and seasoning lumber, choosing the pieces for the various parts, shaping the stocks, spokes felloes (rhymes with bellies). Tyreing, bending, boxing, etc. Plus much about building waggons and carts.

All this through the eyes of a man, caught up by Ruskin with the idea that man's only decent occupation was in handicraft, running a wheelwright's shop through the 1880's. Interesting view of machines displacing skilled craftsman.

[Reviewed by Fred Richardson]

The Wheelwright's Shop
by George Sturt, 1923 - 1963

from:
Cambridge University Press
32 East 57th Street
New York, New York 10022

$3.75

or WHOLE EARTH
CATALOG

The special problem the sawyers knew how to tackle looks simple enough at the outset. What was it, save to get the timber —the oak, the ash, the elm, the beech—slip or slithered into sizes that experts might handle afterwards? Experts already had thrown the timber; others had carted it to the yard; another still—the master-wheelwright—had marked it into lengths and was at hand to direct the sawyers throughout; and what else was there for them to do, except supply mere brute strength? That looked about all they were fit for, with their stupid brains and brawny arms.

Yet, in point of fact, they themselves, you found, were specialists of no mean order when it came to the problem of getting a heavy tree—half a ton or so of timber—on a saw-pit and splitting it longitudinally into specified thicknesses, no more and no less. What though the individuals looked stupid? That lore of the English tribes as it were embodied in them was not stupid any more than an animal's shape is stupid. It was an organic thing, very different from the organized effects of commerce.

Stortz Cooperage Tools

Barrel-making is a craft with its own tools. Here they are, expensive and indispensible if you're making barrels.
—SB

Catalog
$1.00

from:
John Stortz & Son, Inc.
210 Vine Street
Philadelphia, Pennsylvania 19106

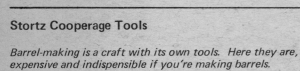

COOPERS' ADZE

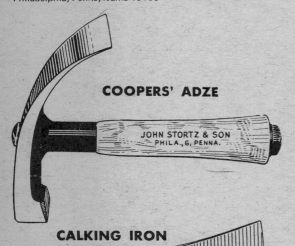

CALKING IRON

BARREL HEAD RAISER

FLAGGING IRON

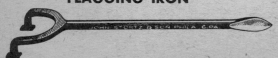

Cohasset Colonial Furniture Kits

If you're not going to make your own furniture, you can at least assemble it. These are well-crafted antique reproductions with a clean spare quality to them.
—SB

Catalog
$0.50

from:
Cohasset Colonials
Cohasset, Massachusetts 02025

Length 19½"; width 8½"
Kit $22.95 — wt. 5 lbs.

37½" hi., seat 17½" x 21½" wi.; rockers 26"
Kit $52.95— wt. 19 lbs.
Parcel Post or United Parcel Service.

OUR furniture comes to you as a *complete* "kit." Everything is accurately handcrafted and sanded ready for assembly. All necessary glue, screws, hardware, sandpaper, stain and assembly instructions are included.

Bamboo

The adoration and utilization of a towering weed.

Civilization as seen by a material.

Every single thing that plastic isn't.
—SB

Bamboo
Robert Austin, Dana Levy, Koichiro Ueda
1970; 215 pp.

$16.50 postpaid

from:
John Weatherhill Inc.
720 5th Ave.
New York, N.Y. 10019

or WHOLE EARTH CATALOG

Bamboo is one of the most extraordinary plants that exist. It flowers perhaps once in a hundred years, and then it dies. It grows faster than anything in the world. In fact, it is sometimes possible to *see* it growing, just as one can see the hands of a large clock moving: there are recorded instances of bamboo's growing four feet in a single day. In a grove in spring the vitality of the surrounding green pillars is almost palpable. While the stem is growing above ground, the root stops: when the stem has finished, then comes the turn of the other. Bamboo also possesses the characteristic of making its complete growth in about two months only. Thereafter it remains the same size as long as it lives.

But bamboo is interesting for much more than this: it is the most universally useful plant known to man. For over half the human race, life would be completely different without it. The East and all its peoples can hardly be discussed without bamboo's being taken into account. Accepted as a mere fact of life or prized for aesthetic reasons, it touches daily existence at a thousand points which vary as widely as its employment in literary metaphor and its use in the walls of houses. It serves the most mundane purposes, and the most refined: dwellings are constructed from bamboo; it is widely used for eating and drinking utensils and for countless other household implements. Ubiquitous, it provides food, raw materials, shelter, even medicine for the greater part of the world's population. The interlocked roots of a bamboo grove restrain the river in flood and during earthquakes support the insubstantial dwellings of country villages.

Dish scourer of split bamboo

Regarded as a material to work, bamboo shows itself "grateful"—to use the artisan's term. It is flexible yet tough, light but very strong. It can be split with ease, in one direction only, never in the other; it may be pliant or rigid as the occasion demands; it can be compressed enough to keep its place in holes; after heating, it can be bent to take and retain a new shape. It is straight and possessed of great tensile strength.

Conestoga Wagon

You can still see their ruts on the American land and the American consciousness. Something about spacious skies and twenty more miles and men who feared God but not six straining horses. Six h.p. for freight across the Rockies, can you do that Detroit?

This is a buff's book. A definitive admiration of the wagon, its gear, its construction, its routes, its use, its beauty.
—SB

Conestoga Wagon 1750-1850
1964-1968; 281 pp.

$16.00 postpaid

from:
George Shumway, Publisher
R.D. 7
York, Pennsylvania 17402

or WHOLE EARTH CATALOG

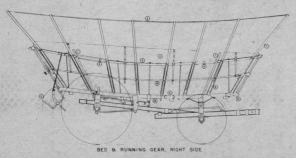

BED & RUNNING GEAR, RIGHT SIDE

So one piece after another was carved out. Now a new pleasure—to fit those pieces together to make the whole complete. The wheel was given the proper "dish"—an arch effect, the tire was the "shew back" and the hub the "keystone," thus giving greater strength to the wheel to carry the greater strain when on the low side of the road; the axles were tapered so that the spokes would stand vertically from the hub down and carry the load and all the angle given from the hub upward; also the wheels were given sufficient "lead" to prevent the hubs from running hard against either the collar or the linch pin.

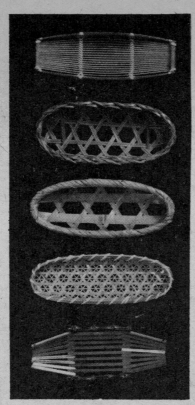

Bamboo is valuable in controlling soil erosion in areas that are poorly adapted for other crops. It grows well both on steep hillsides and along the banks of rivers, its most important features being the interlocking root system, the mulch it produces from its leaves, and its habits of propagation without attention. The sympodial types are best suited for this purpose.

Perkins Reedcraft

reedwork takes time.
that's probably why there are so many
cane bottom chairs sitting around with
the bottoms poked out.
my dad learned how to weave reeds a few years ago,
had a lot of trouble finding literature on the craft.
the perkins people sell reed and provide the newcomer
with good lessons on the basic weaves as well as
carrying a complete line of weaving materials.
—jd
[Suggested by Judy Rock]

Catalog
free

from:
H. H. Perkins Company
P.O. Box 1601
New Haven, Connecticut 06506

**FIGURE C
RAFFIA**

No. 2'-DOLLS CRADLE

Dolls cradle: made on 7 x 15 cradle base. This is a very attractive gift when lined. Base and rocker only $1.25

Materials Complete, Postage 1 lb.
$2.00—Doz. $20.00

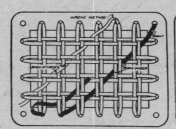

Cathedral ladder back rocker kit $13.50

BEDROOM SCENE

City Girl lay down across the mattress and reached for some books on a little stand next to the far wall. She straightened up again with Eddie's I Ching in her hand.

"I don't want to throw it right now, but if you want to, this is Eddie's."

And she held the book out to D.R.

D.R. took it, but his mind was on City Girl now. Without having anything in particular to say, he felt like he wanted to talk to her, or at least to sit there in the room with her a little while. Something like that was on her mind too, because when D.R. sat down on the mattress beside her, City Girl put her arms around his neck and hugged him. They sat holding each other a moment. Then they fell over on the mattress and lay together a long time locked in a very tight embrace. It wasn't a sexy embrace. It was, actually, but the sex was only one element of something else that was going on between them. City Girl didn't have on any underwear, and D.R. could fell her plainly against him. His leg more or less on its own wedged in between her legs right up into her crotch, and her great breasts pillowed roundly against his chest. And yet it was all just a part of this other, larger thing between them that was going on. City Girl kissed D.R. two or three times on the mouth, and once he kissed her very deeply with his tongue. But nothing led to anything. It was just a crushing physical hello between two people who had a special bond betwen them, and when they'd said that hello they drew apart and lay on the mattress looking at each other.

Finally City Girl sat up and pushed her hair back and leaned on a pillow propped against the wall.

"I guess we're going to talk about Eddie being dead," she said.

"I g..g..guess so," said D.R. "Is that what you want to d..d..do?"

"Fuck, I don't know what I want to do. All I know is Eddie's dead, and that's just the farthest out thing I ever heard of in all my life."

"How sad d..d..do you feel?" D.R. asked.

City Girl shook her head. "I don't know. Not very, I guess. I don't get sad much."

"I'm fucked up in the head m..m..most of the t..t..time," Said D.R.

"Are you sad now?" asked City Girl.

"Yeah."

"You look sad. You look damn beat up, if you want to know the truth. And that chick, what's her name?"

"Estelle."

"Jesus. Where'd you get with her?"

"Altamont."

"I was at Altamont."

(continued)

Colonial Craftsmen
Colonial Living
Frontier Living

Are these fine Edwin Tunis books really practical? No, not on the face of it. They tantalize you with detailed sketches but sketchy details of old crafts and tools, those very crafts which have long been obsolesced by machinery.

So what's the value? The value to the CATALOG is nostalgia. These books service the desire of our market to back the hell out of 20th Century confusion.

And just now, nostalgia may not only be powerful, but in the big picture very practical, if carried out. One educational route out of a dead end is indeed back. Go back, start over where it feels good, get it right this time. Not for everybody, for sure; just enough to unstack the deck a little, enhance the variety of mistakes and opportunities available.

The dolphins went back, and they're doing all right. —SB

[Suggested by Pat R. Matlock, Bruce Gifford and Kieth Gilbert]

Frontier Living
Edwin Tunis
1961; 166 pp.

$6.95 postpaid

Colonial Craftsmen
Edwin Tunis
1965; 159 pp.

OUT OF PRINT

Colonial Living
Edwin Tunis
1957, 156 pp.

$6.95 postpaid

all three from:
The World Publishing Co.
2231 West 110th Street
Cleveland, Ohio 44102

or WHOLE EARTH CATALOG

The Chandler

A colonial housewife never threw away any fat. She rendered it and stored it in pottery crocks. In very early days the family burned it in grease lamps for light, but it was a smelly, smoky light and candles were better. The mistress could make "taller dips" by repeatedly dipping wicks into hot tallow and cooling, between dips, what adhered. Some families owned tin molds that would cast as many as a dozen candles. The traveling chandler brought along his own big molds that cast six dozen at once. He strung them up with the loosely spun tow-linen candle-wick that the house provided, melted down some of the harder fat, and cast a year's supply of candles. The softer fat the chandler turned into soap by boiling it, outdoors, with lye. As he boiled, he stirred with a wooden paddle, always in one direction because of a superstition that the soap would fail if he didn't.

Casting lead pipe

Colonial Craftsmen

A Museum of Early American Tools

Behind making your own stuff there's another level: making your own tools to make your own stuff. This book gives detailed design information and fine illustration of America's pre-industrial tools, plus how to use them. Whistle while you work and revel in nostalgia. Tell the twentieth century to go jump.
—SB

[Suggested by Robert V. Allen]

A Museum of Early American Tools
Eric Sloane
1964; 108 pp.

$2.00

from:
Ballantine Books
457 Hahn Road
Westminster, MD. 21157

or WHOLE EARTH CATALOG

Wolf trap

Wattle-and-daub cabins supported on "crotchets"

Colonial Living

One way to corner a squared-log house so the joints will drain

Once temporary shelters had been set up and the "wolves who sat upon their tayles and grinned at us" had been driven back a little into the woods, the next order of business was to give land to each settler. At Plymouth they tried holding all the land in common, but it didn't work. At Salem and Boston and other later towns, a space was set aside for the church and a large area as a common pasture; what remained was divided up as building sites. The choice locations went to the governor, the ministers, and the other elite in strict order of precedence, the rest being distributed by lot among the common folk.

Frontier Living

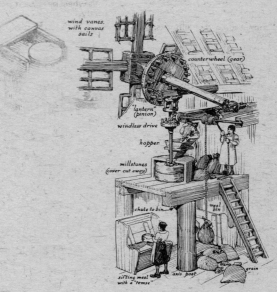

The interior mechanism of a windmill

Colonial Living

Where there are no official police, any group of people will make shift to police itself. The pioneers were beyond the reach of law, but they managed to restrict misbehavior within certain limits. They were especially severe with anyone who injured the group. Minor offenders, like petty thieves or those who shirked their share of community work, were "hated out." They cut the culprit out of all social activities, but they by no means ignored him. On the contrary, they conferred unpleasant nicknames on him that were not merely whispered behind his back. One and all told him loudly what they thought of him any time they met him.

The top social occasion of the backwoods, even more popular than a funeral, was a wedding. The festivities began at the bride s home and there seems never to have been a church ceremony. Indeed, there is no mention of religion at all in any of the old accounts except one note that marriages were sometimes postponed until a parson showed up.

The Ring-tailed Roarers and their female counterparts had full scope at weddings. Those who were not invited were likely to ambush the groom's party and attempt to kidnap him en route to his nuptials. The women often made a similar attack on the bride. We aren't told what happened when these forays succeeded. By established custom, the bride's father set a quart of whisky on his cabin doorstep, and from a mile away the male guests staged a wild horse race to get it. The winner carried it back in triumph to give the groom the first swig.

Frontier Living

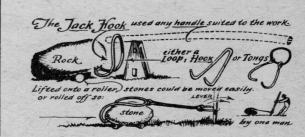

The Jack Hook used any handle suited to the work.

Rock

either a Loop, Hook or Tongs

Lifted onto a roller, stones could be moved easily, or rolled off so:

stone

LEVER

by one man

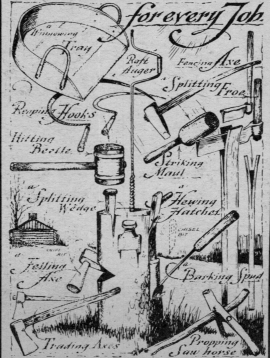

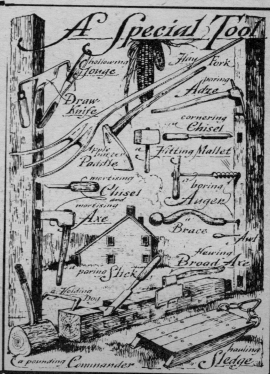

The Book of Country Crafts

Most craft books, I've noticed, either treat you as a retarded fifth grader or as an ambitious acolyte to The Craft of whatever. This book is by a man who grooves on doing his own stuff at his own place, and he makes you feel the same and shortens the route into doing it. —SB

[Suggested by Jude Harris]

The Book of Country Crafts
Randolph Wardell Johnston
1964; 211 pp.

$3.98 postpaid

from:
Routledge & Kegan Park
9 Park Street
Boston, MA. 02108

or WHOLE EARTH
CATALOG

The wheel shown is made of odds and ends. The shaft is an old Ford axle. At top and bottom are the original ball bearings of the car. The flywheel is from an old circular saw and is filled with cement. The wheel head is a clutch plate fitted tightly on the shaft end, and filled with plaster. The plaster was next turned true and recessed to hold bats of a certain size, by nailing a temporary tool rest across and turning the plaster as if it were wood on a lathe. The rounded front guard is half of an old paint pail. And the seat is one of the older style, made of cast iron, from a hay rake. The cast iron ones are much superior to the pressed steel variety. I show this wheel because it has proven very handy.

KINDS OF STONE
Of all the stones used by the colonists for grave markers none has better resisted the weather than slate. The neat inscriptions on slabs of polished slate show even the light scratches that served as guides to the letterers. Artists should consider this when selecting stones on which to work. Slate is a pleasant material to carve. I have carved a full-size portrait relief in gray slate, direct from life, and I found it possible to use a wooden mallet and wood-carving chisels on the stone. To be sure it took the finest edge off the chisels, but not much more than this. A fine toothed claw chisel is good for roughing out. One soon becomes accustomed to the grain. Files, rifflers, sandpaper, and pumice all help in finishing.

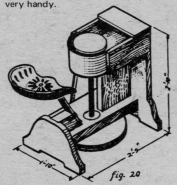

fig. 20

Collectors News

scavenge,
prepare yourself for harder times,
work over a junkpile
collect the bright shiny goodies
and broken bb guns,
save them from the fires,
and chances are
somebody else
will be collecting them,
too.

[suggested by my folks]
—jd

Collectors News
monthly

$5.00 /yr (monthly)

from:
Collectors News
P O Box 156
Grundy Center, Iowa 50638

Selling Antiques

Aunt Maud may have died penniless, but consider her attic. Better still, do it while she's healthy.
—SB

The Antique Trade Price Guide to Antiques
John Mebane, ed.

$4.00 (quarterly)

from:
The Antique Trader
Box 1050
Dubuque, Iowa 52001

What's It Worth & Where Can You Sell It?
Jerry Mack
1970; 94 pp.

$3.95 postpaid

from:
Educator Books, Inc.
P.O. Drawer 32
10 N. Main
San Angelo, Texas 76901

MARBLES

What's It Worth

Types of Mineral Waters Bottles

Andirondack Spring, Westport, N.Y., green, quart	$70.00
Blount Springs, blue, pint	23.00
Clarks & White, olive green, quart	26.00
Congress & Empire Hotchkiss' Sons, emerald green, quart	30.00
Congress Spring Co., S.S. N.Y., green, pint ...	25.00
Congress & Empire Springs, green, pint	22.00

Price Guide

Traditional Country Craftsmen

English country craft, that is. Thatching, basket making, tanning, stone masonry, wheel making. The lot. Cottage industry for the nostalgia market or the total-independence seeker. Make your own goddam barrels. —SB

[Suggested by Marjorie Posner]

Traditional Country Craftsmen
J. Geraint Jenkins
1965; 236 pp.

$7.75

from:
Frederick A. Praeger
111 Fourth Avenue
New York, N. Y. 10003

In many Welsh tanneries it was customary to keep one or two large mastiff dogs, and it is said that as soon as market hides were delivered to the tanyard, each one was pegged to the ground so that the dogs could bite off any fats and flesh that adhered to the skins. The mastiffs were, of course, useful to guard the premises and to keep control of the vast number of rats that always infested tanneries. In addition the dogs' excreta when mixed with hot water was essential for treating certain types of soft leather before tanning.

The Method of Dry Stone Walling.

They didn't say anything else for a minute, and in the silence D.R. looked around the room. The room wasn't much bigger than the mattress on the floor, but it had so much shit on the walls it looked like an infinite universe. Eddie had only lived there with City Girl a couple of weeks, but in that time he had painted serpents and dragons on every wall and ceiling. Behind a tall, skinny plant of some kind in the corner Eddie had painted a jungle of green leaves on the wall, with a vine running through them and little orange and purple dragons crawling up and down the vine. There was a red dragon on the ceiling. On the wall opposite the window a long yellow snake stretched from the corner near the floor to a corner near the ceiling, diagonally across. Light streaming through the strings of colored beads hanging down over the window made the whole place seem like an exotic tent in a curiously happy and benevolent jungle. The pictures were recognizably Eddie's, but something about them was very different from other stuff of Eddie's D.R. had seen. There was a precision in them, an order in the general arrangement of things. The place said something about Eddie that was not familiar to D.R. It looked as if Eddie had intended to stay in this apartment a while, and D.R. could not get used to that idea. He wanted to ask City Girl what she and Eddie had had going, but he couldn't bring himself to. What he wound up saying, without actually deciding to say it, was that he had gone to look at Eddie's body in the funeral home the night before.

"You said you might do that," said City Girl.
"Yeah. M..m..me and Estelle went."
"How was it?" asked City Girl.
"A bummer."
City Girl asked D.R. how Eddie had looked.
"F..f..fucked over."
"Did he have a ring on?" asked City Girl.
"I d..d..didn't see one."
"I guess his mother took it off."
"The undertaker m..m..might have t..t..taken it off."
City Girl shook her head. "No. It was her. She wasn't going to bury little Eddie-boy with that ring on his finger."
"D..d..did you give it to him?"
City Girl nodded.
"I m..m..might b..b..be able to get it b..b..back for you," said D.R.
"Nah," said City Girl. She scooted across the mattress and stood up. "Nah. Fuck it. It was just a ring. You got the book?"
"Right here."
"You can have that book if you want it," said City Girl.
"D..d..don't you want it?" said D.R.
"I think you're the one ought to have it," City Girl said. "Eddie told me about you. Eddie talked about you a lot. Hey, you want something to eat? I'm hungry."
D.R. shook his head.
"Okay," said City Girl. As she left the room, she leaned over and touched D.R.'s face with her fingertips.

Foxfire

Probably no region in the country has been written about, "explained" and "interpreted" any more than the Southern Appalachian highlands, that mountainous area embracing parts of Georgia, North Carolina, Tennessee, Virginia, Kentucky and on up into West Virginia. And yet, no region is as little known or more misunderstood. Most of the writers and film documentarians who have paid attention to Appalachia have suffered from one social/economic bias or another, or, what's worse, a pasty sentimentality inherited from romantic writers of the John Fox Jr.-James Lane Allen school. Even native writers all too often fall victim to the same stereotypes and cliches that have marred so much of the reportage in the national media.

There are, however, scattered here and there through the Appalachians, a few small journals who are truly in touch with the place they claim to represent. And one of the best of these is Foxfire.

Foxfire is a quarterly publication concerned with researching, recording and preserving Appalachian folk art, crafts and traditions. A typical issue contained articles on quilting, chairmaking, soap-making, home remedies, mountain recipes, feather beds and home-made hominy, plus regional poetry and book reviews. One issue was devoted entirely to log cabin building. These are not superficial "feature" articles, but definitive, detailed treatments of traditional skills and crafts that have come close to dying out of our culture.

Foxfire would be a credit to a group of professional folklorists. But when you consider that it is edited and published by high school kids at the Rabun Gap-Nacoochee School in Rabun Gap, Georgia, it becomes impressive indeed. The thing I like most about it is the way these kids are looking immediately around them for their inspiration, instead of taking cues from New York and California. In their own way, these people are as hip and sophisticated as any young people putting out a magazine on either coast. More so, even. They're cooler, more adult. Next to Foxfire, most "underground" papers seem written by children shrieking at Daddy (or cops, or Nixon) because he wont let them smoke grass or smash store windows. Foxfire's editors and writers (and some excellent photographers) seem to me as aware of what's wrong with the world as anyone. The thing that distinguishes them from their shrill counterparts in the cities is the absence of fad, slogan and cliche as they set out to improve the world. These kids in Georgia are living in a real world, studying real things, and in consequence they are creating a wonderfully real publication in Foxfire.

[Reviewed by Gurney Norman.]

FOXFIRE

$6.00 /yr (quarterly)

from:
The Foxfire Fund, Inc.
Rabun Gap
Georgia 30568

POTATO CANDY

Peel and boil one large white potato. When done, mash up with a fork, add a little salt, and pour in a box of confectionate sugar. This makes a stiff dough.

Roll out on a dough board that has been well floured in a layer ¼ inch thick. Spread peanut butter all over top. Roll up like a jelly roll (make two rolls if you like). Put this in the refrigerator.

Cut with knife. Serve. Good any time.

•

The churner said the chant in time to the up and down movements of the dasher as indicated below. The arrows indicate the dasher movement:

```
            ↑
Come butter come
            ↑
Come butter come
      ↓     ↑
Peter standing at the gate
   ↓        ↑
Waiting for a butter cake
      ↓     ↑
Come butter come.
```

Plate 3: Legs are shaped with a shaving horse and drawing knife.

Choose a tall maple, the trunk of which is about 8 inches in diameter and slightly curved. This curve will produce the sloped back obvious in Figure 2. If you would rather the back be straight, choose your maple accordingly.

Saw a 3'6" length out of the curved section of the trunk for the back posts; a 1'8" length out of the straight section for the front posts; and a 1'4" length out of the straight section for the backs.

At the same time, choose a tall, straight-grained white oak 4"-6" in diameter. From the trunk, cut one 16" length, two 14" lengths, and save the rest for splits.

Quarter the maple sections to be used for posts. Split out the heart. Then round the quarters off using first an axe and then the shaving horse. (Plate 3.)

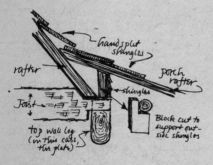

rafter

hand split shingles

porch rafter

shingles

Joist

top wall log (in this case tin plate)

Block cut to support outside shingles

Nature and Art of Workmanship

Seems like just about everybody I know is making things lately—pots & dishes & clothes & bags & belts & blouses. I read in Newsweek or somewhere that this is the New Rennaissance—Mebbe so. But it doesn't feel good to see a lot of home made things when they are also poorly made. Romanticizing the hand-made is a naive reaction to the problem of a machined-plastic environment. The Nature and Art of Workmanship is an attempt to define the asthetics of craftsmanship in a classical scholarly mode. It has clear insight and sound criteria for judging the quality of the objects that surround us without the blanket rejection of technology that is trapping many people in an alternative life-style of shoddy creativity.

[Reviewed by Terry Gunesch]

The Nature and Art of Workmanship

Nature and Art of Workmanship
David Pye
1968; 101pp.

$2.75 postpaid

from:
Van Nostrand Reinhold Co.
450 West 33rd Street
New York, N.Y. 10001

or WHOLE EARTH CATALOG

There is a very present danger that, as the kinds of medium-scale diversity which free workmanship used to impart to building become less readily available, what little can be had in that way will be over-played and in the end travestied. We do not want every piece of concrete to show board-marks, every piece of paving to be cobbled, every piece of masonry to be random rubble, every piece of brickwork to be left unplastered. There is a place for all those things, but such elephantine capers unaccompanied by diversity at smaller scales become merely ludicrous. What we want is diversity which begins at the smallest visible scale and develops continuously upwards from that; and even then we do not want it always and everywhere. Vitamins are necessary to life, but only in small amounts. Take them in large amounts and they make you ill. So I believe it is with diversification in workmanship. I do not suggest it is more—or less—than a vitamin: not a diet: not a panacea: merely something which, though we may not take much notice of it, we need to have.

It is now time to choose the placement of the inside walls. If you wish to have a wall running the length of the house, its first log should be laid in place next. If the wall is to run the entire length of the house, cut a log to that length, hew it down to 4" in width, and cut dovetail notches in the ends.

First partitioning inside wall log (notched to fit end log)

First sleeper in place

First end log

end of sill

Don't worry about the placement of the inside doors. They will be cut after the wall is completed.

Can you wash your clothes in it? "Yeah, you can. Just take that, y'know, like we used to——we took our clothes and put our soap on 'em and rub 'em and boil 'em. People don't do that now. And I ain't afraid t'wash my hands in it! That there lard kills th'lye." Why do you stir it so much? "It requires it. It wouldn't make if you didn't dissolve it good. You got t'get it thick like jelly y'know. Y'can't leave jelly 'till it gets right."

Branch Lettuce

Mertile Lamb: "Well, there is one kind we call branch lettuce. It's kindly a long leaf thing, and it grows in the wettest damp places like where moss grows. As it gets older, it has a red cast to it. And you take it and cut it up like you do the tame lettuce, and put your onions in it, and pour your hot grease on it. It tastes just like tame lettuce."

Ruskin said 'If we build, let us think that we build forever'. Shall we say 'If we build, let us remember to build for the scrapheap'? Shall we make everything so that it goes wrong or breaks pretty quickly? I think not. Men do not live by economics alone. There is a question of morale involved. A world in which everything was ephemeral would not be worth working for. There are overwhelming social and aesthetic arguments for durabiility in certain things even if, as we are told, there are no economic ones. These are:

First of all, the things we inherit from the past remind us that the men who made them were like us and give us a tangible link with them. This is a thought to set off against the knowledge that life is short. Hitherto it has been inconceivable that any one generation should discard all the equipment it has inherited and replace it completely. That may yet become possible. Even if it does, it will still be imperative for each generation deliberately to make some of its equipment so that it lasts and survives its makers.

Secondly, if you are making a thing so that it goes wrong or breaks, then, however honestly you state the fact, two other facts remain. One is that you are putting as little into the job as you decently can. The other is that you are in a fair way to force its user to spend his money on replacing that thing instead of for some other purpose. He may be glad to replace it, in an age of materialism and the passion for novelty. But why should we all be compelled to keep spending money on renewing our car, our cooker and our refrigerator? These things for some people are merely means to other ends in life. Why should we not save the money so as to pursue those ends the better: altruistic, learned or artistic ends, say? Things which are made to fail early should be made maintainable and reparable, so that a man who cares for something other than novelty and status-symbols can make them last his time respectably while he gets on with his life. Optional durability is what we want.

Buddhist Economics

The Buddhist point of view takes the function of work to be at least threefold: to give a man a chance to utilize and develop his faculties; to enable him to overcome his ego-centredness by joining with other people in a common task; and to bring forth the goods and services needed for a becoming existence. Again, the consequences that flow from this view are endless. To organize work in such a manner that it becomes meaningless, boring, stultifying, or nerve-racking for the worker would be little short of criminal; it would indicate a greater concern with goods than with people, an evil lack of compassion and a soul-destroying degree of attachment to the most primitive side of this worldly existence. Equally, to strive for leisure as an alternative to work would be considered a complete misunderstanding of one of the basic truths of human existence, namely that work and leisure are complimentary parts of the same living process and cannot be separated without destroying the joy of work and the bliss of leisure.

From the Buddhist point of view, there are therefore two types of mechanization which must be clearly distinguished: one that enhances a man's skill and power and one that turns work of man over to a mechanical slave, leaving man in a position of having to serve the slave. How to tell the one from the other? The craftsman himself, says Ananda Coomaraswamy, a man equally competent to talk about the Modern West as the Ancient East, 'the craftsman himself can always, if allowed to, draw the delicate distinction between the machine and the tool. The carpet loom is a tool, a contrivance for holding warp threads at a stretch for the pile to be woven round them by the craftsmen's fingers; but the power loom is a machine, and its significance as a destroyer of culture lies in the fact that it does the essentially human part of the work." It is clear, therefore, that Buddhist economics must be very different from the economics of modern materialism, since the Buddhist sees the essence of civilization not in a multiplication of wants but in the purfication of human character. Character, at the same time, is formed primarily by a man's work. And work, properly conducted in conditions of human dignity and freedom, blesses those who do it and equally their products. The Indian philosopher and economist J.C. Kumarappa sums the matter up as follows:

"If the nature of the work is properly appreciated and applied, it will stand in the same relation to the higher faculties as food is to the physical body. It nourishes and enlivens the higher man and urges him to produce the best he is capable of. It directs his freewill along the proper course and disciplines the animal in him into progressive channels. It furnishes an excellent background for man to display his scale of values and develop his personality."

If a man has no chance of obtaining work he is in a desperate position, not simply because he lacks an income but because he lacks this nourishing and enlivening factor of disciplined work which nothing can replace. A modern economist may engage in highly sophisticated calculations on whether full employment "pays" or whether it might be more "economic" to run an economy at less than full employment so as to ensure a greater mobility of labour, a better stability of wages, and so forth. His fundamental criterion of success is simply the total quantity of goods produced during a given period of time. "If the marginal urgency of goods is low," says Professor Galbraith in *The Affluent Society*, "then so is the urgency of employing the last man or the last million men in the labour force." And again: "If . . . we can afford some unemployment in the interest of stability—a proposition, incidentally, of impeccably conservative antecedents—then we can afford to give those who are unemployed the goods that enable them to sustain their accustomed standard of living."

From a Buddhist point of view, this is standing the truth on its head by considering goods as more important than people people and consumption as more important than creative activity. It means shifting the emphasis from the worker to the product of work, that is, from the human to the sub-human, a surrender to the forces of evil.

While the materialist is mainly interested in goods, the Buddhist is mainly interested in liberation. But the Buddhism is "The Middle Way" and therefore in no way antagonistic to physical well-being. It is not wealth that stands in the way of liberation but the attachment to wealth; not the enjoyment of pleasurable things but the craving for them. The keynote of Buddhist economics, therefore, is simplicity and non-violence. From an economist's point of view, the marvel of the Buddhist way of life is the utter rationality of its pattern—amazingly small means leading to extraordinarily satisfactory results.

Sent in by John K. Green

Resurgence
published 6 times yearly
25 pp. single issues (U.S. 80 cents)
£1.80 per year (U.S. $5.00) post free

from:
275 Kings Road
Kingston, Surrey
England

Satish asked me to add that Resurgence is a magazine of decentralization, de-urbanisation, libertarian technology and alternative life style.

—PC

The Book of Tea

this book is not just about tea.
—J.D.

The Book of Tea
Kakuzo Okakura
1964; 76pp.

$1 postpaid

from:
Dover Publications
180 Verick Street
New York, N.Y. 10014

or WHOLE EARTH CATALOG

Tea began as a medicine and grew into a beverage. In China, in the eighth century, it entered the realm of poetry as one of the polite amusements. The fifteenth century saw Japan ennoble it into a religion of aestheticism,—Teasim. Teaism is a cult founded on the adoration of the beautiful among the sordid facts of everyday existence. It inculcates purity and harmony, the mystery of mutual charity, the romanticism of the social order. It is essentially a worship of the Imperfect, as it is a tender attempt to accomplish something possible in this impossible thing we know as life.

The Philosophy of Tea is not mere aestheticism in the ordinary acceptance of the term, for it expresses conjointly with ethics and religion our whole point of view about man and nature. It is hygiene, for it enforces cleanliness; it is economics, for it shows comfort in simplicity rather than in the complex and costly; it is moral geometry, inasmuch as it defines our sense of proportion to the universe. It represents the true spirit of Eastern democracy by making all its votaries aristocrats in taste.

•

When will the West understand, or try to understand, the East? We Asiatics are often appalled by the curious web of facts and fancies which has been woven concerning us. We are pictured as living on the perfume of the lotus, if not on mice and cockroaches. It is either impotent fanaticism or else abject voluptuousness. Indian spirituality has been derided as ignorance, Chinese sobriety as stupidity, Japanese patriotism as the result of fatalism. It has been said that we are less sensible to pain and wounds on account of the callousness of our nervous organization!

Why not amuse yourselves at our expense? Asia returns the compliment. There would be further food for merriment if you were to know all that we have imagined and written about you. All the glamour of the perspective is there, all the unconscious homage of wonder, all the silent resentment of the new and undefined. You have been loaded with virtues too refined to be envied and accused of crimes too picturesque to be condemned. Our writers in the past,—the wise men who knew,—informed us that you had busy tails somewhere hidden in your garments, and often dined off a fricasse of newborn babes! Nay, we had something worse against you: we used to think you the most impracticable people on the earth, for you were said to preach what you never practised.

•

In joy or sadness, flowers are our constant friends. We eat, drink, sing, dance, and flirt with them. We wed and christen with flowers. We dare not die without them. We have worshipped with the lily, we have meditated with the lotus, we have charged in battle array with the rose and the chrysanthemum. We have even attempted to speak in the language of flowers. How could we live without them? It frightens one to conceive of a world bereft of their presence. What solace do they not bring to the bedside of the sick, what a light of bliss to the darkness of weary spirits? Their serene tenderness restores to us our waning confidence in the universe even as the intent gaze of a beautiful child recalls our lost hopes. When we are laid low in the dust it is thye who linger in sorrow over our graves.

Sad as it is, we cannot conceal the fact that in spite of our companionship with flowers we have not risen very far above the brute. Scratch the sheepskin and the wolf within us will soon show his teeth. It has been said that man at ten is an animal, at twenty a lunatic, at thirty a failure, at forty a fraud, and at fifty a criminal. Perhaps he becomes a criminal because he has never ceased to be an animal. Nothing is real to us but hunger, nothing sacred except our own desires. Shrine after shrine has crumbled before our eyes; but one altar forever is preserved, that whereon we burn incense to the supreme idol,—ourselves. Our god is great, and money is his Prophet! We devastate nature in order to make sacrifice to him. We boast that we have conquered Matter and forget that it is Matter that has enslaved us. What atrocities do we not perpetrate in the name of culture and refinement!

Craft Shops/Galleries

Craft Shops/Galleries USA *is a directory of workshop show-rooms, galleries and shops selling American crafts. It contains the names and addresses, regular exhibitions, and crafts media handled by over 600 outlets. This is a potentially invaluable guide to: 1) craft collectors; 2) craft makers; 3) shopkeepers or future shopowners who would like to hear from No. 2 and reach No. 1. (All shops interested in being contacted by craftsmen are marked with an *.) Additionally, it contains other sources of information on craft exhibitions.*

This booklet is published by the American Crafts Council, a non-profit organization founded in 1943 to stimulate public interest in and appreciation of the work of craftsmen.

[Suggested and reviewed by Judith Greer]

$3.95
$3.00 to members

American Crafts Council
44 W. 53rd St.
New York, N.Y. 10019

GEORGIA

Atlanta

THE CO-OP CRAFT STORE OF ATLANTA, 140 Spring Street, N.E. (Zip 30573) 10-6, Mon.-Sat. Owned by the Georgia Mountain Arts Products Cooperative. Appalachian pottery, ceramic sculpture, wood accessories, rugs, woven accessories, leather, silk screen, dolls, mountain novelty crafts. Craft demonstrations every other weekend.

★■ THE SIGNATURE SHOP AND GALLERIES, 3267 Roswell Road. (Zip 30305, Tel. 237-4232) 9:30-5:30, Mon.-Sat. Blanche Reeves, Sally Adams, owners. Pottery, wood accessories, jewelry, holloware, flatware, metal sculpture, wall hangings, rugs, woven accessories, glass, enamels. Occasional exhibitions.

Craft Horizons

Craft as Art.
—SB

Craft Horizons
Rose Slivka, ed.

$12.50 /yr (bimonthly)

$22.50 2/yr

Single copies are $3.00

from:
The American Crafts Council
44 West 53rd St.
New York, N.Y. 10019

Two year subscription includes admission to the Museum of Contemporary Crafts of the American Crafts Council, and makes you a member.
For subscriptions outside U.S.A. add $1.00 per year postage.

ESTELLE AGAIN

D.R. started to throw the I Ching by himself when City Girl went out, but he didn't have any coins on him. He was focused so well on what he was about to do he didn't much want to interrupt it to go outside to ask somebody for some coins. But then he considered that maybe that was part of it, that maybe his not having any coins on him was crucial to the reading somehow, and so he yielded to that and went into the living room.

The scene had changed a good deal since he and City Girl had left. Everybody except Estelle was drawn up in front of the TV to watch an old Charlie Chan movie called The Big Secret. Friendly Persuasion and Winston had a joint going back and forth between them that nobody else seemed much interested in. They were all into the number Charlie Chan was doing with the Door to the Mystic Palace. The door was about twelve feet high, and made out of some kind of shiny metal, with a big dragon embossed upon it. You could tell just by looking at it that a tank would have a hard time breaking it down. And yet, by fiddling around with the eyeballs of the dragon, old Charlie was about to spring the whole thing and enter the Mystic Palace. Everybody was so into the program D.R. didn't want to disturb them, so he did the next best thing and went over to Estelle in the corner.

"Have you got any coins?" asked D.R.

Estelle looked up at D.R. It was the first time their eyes had met in what seemed like days. D.R. and Estelle had been waging some kind of silent combat ever since his acid trip, and the business with the Greek. Neither of them knew what the issue was, but they both knew that it was serious, whatever it was. Except for the four hours D.R. worked at the Save-More Store they had stuck close together ever since they got to St. Louis, but their minds were in separate, and hostile, galaxies. They had only been in St. Louis thirty six hours, but that, too, seemed like days. Eddie being suddenly dead had lifted St. Louis out of time onto a plane where each moment is forever. Death is an infinity, and so is thirty-six hours of life in St. Louis when you're not speaking to someone you ostensibly love. I ostensibly love you, Estelle, thought D.R. And ostensibly I love you too, thought Estelle. The meeting of their eyes was filled with cold, ostensible love and both thought what in god's name is happening.

(continued)

Craftool

More than other craft suppliers, this outfit has whole-system supplies. A spinning wheel as well as looms. Various hand presses. A whole paper-making mill ($3,650). And the best line we've seen of beginning kits.   —SB

[Suggested by Julia Brand and Cynthia Mathews]

**Catalog
$1.00**

from:
The Craftool Company
1421 West 240th St.
Harbor City, CA 90710

Woodworking/Craft Kit $125.00
Gem Stone/Tumbling & Jewelry Making Kit $49.95
Batik/Fabric Dyeing Kit $24.95
Bookbinder's Repair Kit $17.95
Clay Modeling & Sculpture Kit $24.95
Woodcarving & Sculpture Kit $48.95
Graphic Arts/Etching & Block Printing Kit $69.95
Jewelry Making Kit $99.95
Stone/Sculpture Kit $99.95
Printing Press/Outfit $155.94

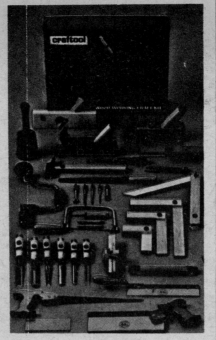

The ART PRESS $175.00

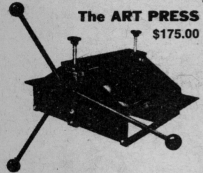

CRAFTOOL COMPLETE BOOKBINDING OUTFIT
All the basic equipment and tools necessary for the bookbinding craftsman.

Standing Press	Hand Drill
Stitching Frame	2 Knives
Lying Press	Drills
Book Saw	Nipper
Book on "Bookbinding"	Glue Brush
Shears	Bone Folder
Needles	Wax
Backing Hammer	

No. 11489 — Tools and equipment only —
less bench and top   **$250.00**

Sax Art Supplies

Big catalog, sort of school oriented, wide range of art and craft supplies.   —SB

[Suggested by Karen Shuler]

**Catalog
$1.00**

from:
Sax Arts & Crafts
P.O. Box 2002
Milwaukee, WI 53201

BATIK FORMULA WAX
Special formula wax.

No. 12738. . . . . $1.90 lb.
10 or more lbs. . . . 1.80 lb.
50 or more lbs. . . . 1.60 lb.

STONEWARE CLAY CONES 4–8.
A true stoneware clay, when fired at the recommended temperature of Cones 4 to 8 bisque, is a warm buff peppered throughout with dark specks. Interesting textures. Amaco High Fire Glaze recommended for this stoneware body. Specify No. 48-M (Moist) or No. 48-D (Dry).

5 lbs. $1.00
50 lbs. $6.50

5158

5159

Arts & Crafts

This catalog looks like it's more for the school trade. Good prices on a wide range of tools and materials.   —SB

[Suggested by Mrs. W. B. Mohin]

**Catalog
free**

from:
CCM: Arts & Crafts, Inc.
321 Park Avenue
Baltimore, Maryland 21201

CONTENTS
List of Major Classifications

MOULAGE

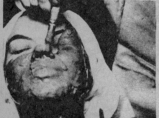

A mold material for taking impressions from life — for reproducing valued antiques when an ancient patina must be preserved, too delicate to submit to being molded in plaster, rubber or gelatine. Moulage will not adhere to anything — molds can be made on human hair or the most delicate skin. Apply warm with brush and palette knife. Captures minutest details. Reuse it approximately 150 times. Complete instructions helps beginners succeed on first project.
No. 7678 Moulage, per 2 lb. can............................$4.95

Art Consultants

Stuff for sculpture and ceramics.   —SB

**Catalog
free**

from:
Art Consultants
100 East 7th Street
New York, N.Y. 10009

All Prices Plus Postage

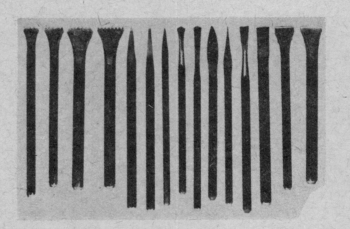

$1.70

ea.

Hand Forged Stone Carving Chisels

Professional tools forged of finest steel, tempered for marble, limestone, sandstone. Sculpture House craftsmen know how to forge and temper cutting edges that last and last; for this reason professional carvers purchase Sculpture House tools exclusively. Order by number.

#BAZ Basic Carving Set Tools Nos. 1, 6, 11, 13 plus H-17 Hammer ....**$1.70 each**
#1AZ Complete Set of 13 Tools plus H-20....**$24.95**

Average Length 8 inches

D-A MONZINI

1 quart (including hardener) ....$ 5.00
1 gallon (including hardener) 15.00

D-A MONZINI FILLER
For adding to D-A MONZINI when a thicker consistency is desired and for initial build-up.

1 quart ....$ 7.50
1 gallon 22.50

GENUINE PULVERIZED BRONZE
For fusing to final surface of D-A MONZINI or other material.

1 lb. can ....$ 4.00
5 lb. can 17.50
10 lb. can 30.00

**12 FOOT DOLPHIN
MADE WITH
D-A MONZINI**

Handcraft House

A western Canada supplier. Leclere looms, Indian spinners, procion dyes, oils, brushes, books.

—SB

Northwest Handcraft House Ltd.
110 West Esplanade
North Vancouver, B.C.
Canada

Catalog $.50.
Free brochure on two-year textile school.

154 Craft Supplies
Craft

CIBALAN DYES FOR WOOL

Blue 8G (Turquoise) all prices for 1 oz.	.65
Blue BRL	.90
Brilliant Blue GL	.95
Kiton Red B2R (HOt Pink)	.55
Red 2 GL	.80
Brilliant Red BL	1.00

Craft Tool Plans

You do not seem to hit the pattern sources, I suppose your readers don't really need these detailed plans like my readers do. But one example will suffice perhaps.... For $2 one can secure a detailed, dimensioned plan to build a 4-harness, 6-treadle jack loom. Pattern Catalog No. 396 and it includes a materials list. Order from Mr. N. Rockler, Craftplans, Rogers, Minnesota 55374. A catalog showing the plans he has patterns for is available for 25 cents, same address. He includes three types of spinning wheels and a sundial packet as well as the more usual jig-saw jiggers and clocks and more or less standard subjects like bars of little interest to Whole Earth people. But for a catalog of plans I'd put Craft Patterns Studio, Elmhurst, Illinois 60126 first on the list—they have more in greater variety and though their catalog is more (50 cents the last time I heard from them) their plans are generally cheaper.

Lura LaBarge
Newton, New Jersey

Step-by-Step Craft Series

A fine, low-priced series of introductory craft books. Each one has a thorough list of relevant periodicals, books, material suppliers, and schools which give courses in the subject. It's an intelligent way to begin——light, quick, and real. —SB

[Suggested by Jan McClain]

Step-by-Step Jewelry
Thomas Gentille
1968; 96 pp.
$2.50 postpaid

Step-by-Step Weaving
Nell Znamierowski
1967; 96 pp.
$2.50 postpaid

Step-by-Step Macramé
Mary Walker Phillips
1970; 80 pp.
$2.50 postpaid

Step-by-Step Printmaking
Erwin Schachner
1970; 80 pp.
$2.50 postpaid

from:
Golden Press Division
Western Publishing Co., Inc.
850 Third Avenue
New York, N. Y. 10022

or WHOLE EARTH CATALOG

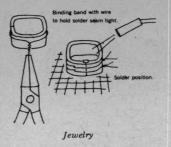

Binding band with wire to hold solder seam tight.

Solder position.

Jewelry

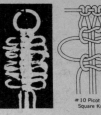

10 Picot with Square Knots

Macramé

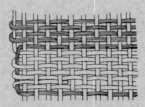

When weaving with two colors, the color not in use is carried along the selvedge until used again. This is a method for narrow color repeats. Note the start of the filling thread tucked back into shed.

Weaving

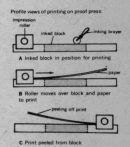

Profile views of printing on proof press.

A Inked block in position for printing

B Roller moves over block and paper to print

C Print peeled from block

Printmaking

Allcraft

Excellent catalog of tools and materials for jewelry work and enameling. Also stained glass.

—SB

Catalog

$1.00

from:
Allcraft Tool & Supply Co.
215 Park Ave.
Hicksville, N.Y. 11801

$3.95

2N-5   FORMING HAMMER - 4-1/8", flat face 1", round face 1" - 3/4 lb.

108
112
124
143
208
164
169
170
16

1H-16 HOME WORKSHOP OR SCHOOL GRADE
Available in styles 5, 6, 7, 10, 17, 101, 181, 126, 108, 112, 208, 16. $1.75 each

E4-469
MORTARS AND PESTLES for grinding enamels to a consistency for painting and special effects.
a. Wedgewood 3½" dia. $5.15
b. Wedgewood 4" " $5.95
c. Wedgewood 5" " $6.95

3A-1
Chasing Tools

$18.00 Set of 25

E4-753
BROKEN GLASS ASSORTMENT
Random sized pieces ranging up to approximately 3" x 2". Each assortment contains 12 or more colors. $1.50   2 lb. box

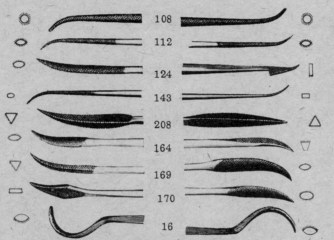

$149.50

Shown with 3-jaw Chuck

Dixon Tools & Supplies

A beautifully engraved hard cover catalog of splendid jeweler's and engraver's tools. (See also p. 142.) —SB

William Dixon, Inc.
Carlstadt, New Jersey 07072

Fig. 156-2

COPPER BOILING CUP

2" diameter by 1" height; furnished with
$3.60   and without cover.

No. 1 With Cover   No. 2 Without Cover

Fig. 101-4 with Handle, ¾" Face $5.90

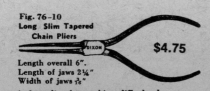

Fig. 76-10
Long Slim Tapered Chain Pliers

$4.75

Length overall 6".
Length of jaws 2¼".
Width of jaws ⅜".
A fine plier for reaching difficult places. Jaws make it adaptable for electronics.

Otto Frei-Jules Borel Co.

Jeweler's and engraver's supplies.

—SB

Otto Frei-Jules Borel Inc.
Box 796
Oakland, CA 94612

PEER MAGNIFIERS
Imported high quality magnifiers with specially corrected lenses that give good distortion free viewing.

No.	Style	Working Distance	Power	Price
22-011	Doublet	1"	10X	$7.00
22-016	Coddington	¾"	15X	$8.25

ANTI-RUST SOAP

Prevents rust caused by perspiration from your hands. Simply wash hands twice daily using this soap.

No.	Description	Each
52-771	Cake	$1.30

GOING THROUGH CHANGES

The I Ching was what was happening. Estelle took three pennies out of her bag, handed them to D.R., then turned back to her book. The way she did it, the way she fished in her bag for the coins and handed them to him as if he was collecting for the Heart Fund or something, infuriated D.R. He came close to throwing the coins right in her face. His next impulse was to jerk the book out of her hand and fling it across the room.

Fuck it! he yelled inside his mind. Fuck it!

In the bedroom with the door shut D.R. took his place on the mattress again and worked at cooling his mind with some of the breathing exercises the Greek had taught him. He tried to do alternate nostril breathing but he was so stirred up he didn't have enough patience to hold his breath for sixteen counts. Bellows breathing was easier. Huffing and puffing, doing them in sets of twenty, then twenty-five and finally thirty-five, D.R. stoned himself on breathing, his mind joined him on the mattress and at last he felt cool enough to toss the coins.

He didn't feel that way long. The first goddamn throw came up fucking Stagnation and he didn't want to read about it. He knew it was a sin not to accept the reading but he didn't give a shit. He threw the coins again. It came up Adversity and Weariness. He threw them again. It was The Estranged this time. Opposites. Fuck opposites. He threw them again. It was Ku, Decay, with changes in the third, fifth and sixth nines which gave him Abysmal, The Abyss. Fuck it. It was Eddie's I Ching, it was Eddie's room, fuck it, Eddie's dead, and Divine Right threw the book across the room, then burst into the living room and told Estelle to get off her ass, they were going to the Western Union office.

Estelle looked up at D.R., half expecting to be afraid. But she wasn't. She got up and went out with him, but she definitely wasn't afraid.

Metal Techniques for Craftsmen

If you read this book, you'll know more about metalworking than just about anybody you know. International in scope, it covers an incredible collection of techniques from many countries and cultures. The various techniques are presented with a complete set of instructions for each one and are illustrated by excellent photographs, often of native craftsmen doing their thing. Tools are described and illustrated in detail. Everything is described in detail. Reading this book will take you right up to that point where you'll have to do it awhile yourself to get into it any further. This is a real assembly of diverse information, some of it hard to find, and a metal-crafter-jeweler should be into new things within an hour of getting his hands on it. This is one of those rare and super books written by someone that wanted to lay his trip on others. Well worth the money. The "definitive text", as they say.

[Suggested by Claudio Marzollo.
Reviewed by J. Baldwin]

A craftsman of Tanjore, India, securing an encrusted silver ornamental medallion on a brass plate in the "nagas" or "swami" process of metal decoration.

Metal Techniques for Craftsmen
Oppi Untracht
1968; 509 pp.

$19.95 postpaid

from:
Doubleday & Company
501 Franklin
Garden City, New York 11531

or WHOLE EARTH CATALOG

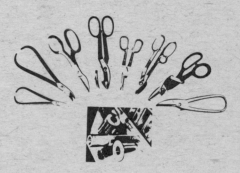

Forge welding is the oldest welding process. Wrought iron and mild steel can be welded in forging by heating the parts to be joined till they are brilliant white-hot and emitting sparks. The metal at this point has reached a condition of surface plasticity. The parts are then brought into contact quickly, on top of each other, and hammered together. They fuse into one unit. Butt joints can be welded by first upsetting the ends to be joined, to thicken them, then reheating the ends to welding temperature, placing them together, and hammering them. The original thickness is maintained. If the metal is absolutely clean, free of oil or cinder, *no flux is necessary,* because the slag in wrought iron acts as a flux. The force to be exerted by the hammer depends on the mass and size of the parts being joined.

SAND CASTING OF ALUMINUM. Sand casting is the best-known and most frequently used casting process. (For a procedural discussion, see page 325.) The method used for aluminum is the same as that used for other non-ferrous metals, with care taken for temperature control. In small sand castings, a section of 3/16 of an inch is considered the minimum possible. The surface of sand castings depends for its character on the fineness of the sand used. For large castings, coarser sand is advisable. Aluminum sand castings generally have smoother surfaces than other sand cast metals, partly because of the lower melting point required of the metal, and partly because the sand does not burn into the surface of the casting.

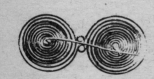

Greek bronze wire fibula, "spectacle type," tenth-eighth centuries B.C. (Geometrical Period). Back view. Length: 5 5/16 inches. This pin, including the pinstem and catch, is made entirely of one continuous piece of wire. Metropolitan Museum of Art, New York. Fletcher Fund, 1937.

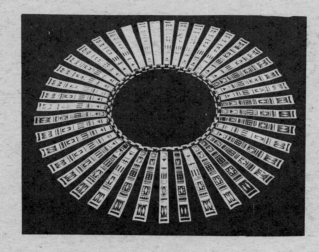

Sterling silver necklace utilizing 18-gauge metal, by Mary Ann Scherr. Length: 16½ inches; each unit: 3½ inches by ½ inch. The intaglio pa pattern was created with an etching solution of half nitric acid and half water and was then oxidized.

Jewelry Making and Design

superfloral middlefinger rock rings, grandma's brooches.
reprint of design manual from about fifty years ago.
studies in geometrical patterns
and better yet,
suggestions for lifting design
from shell, bud, leaf, bug, snow crystal, finger, and so forth.
fairly complete metalworking how-to illustrations and procedural techniques for modeling, casting, piercing, enameling, carving.
cheap too.

—jd
[Suggested by Joseph R. Coelho]

Jewelry Making and Design
Augustus F. Rose and Antonio Cirino
1918. 67; 304 pp.

$2.75 postpaid

from:
Dover Publications Inc.
180 Varick Street
New York, New York 10014

or WHOLE EARTH CATALOG

There are different ways of approaching the subject of jewelry making. Some begin by having the student or beginner take for the first problem one that calls for the use of wire bending and soldering. Others give a problem calling for the introduction of a variety of processes in one piece. Experience shows that the best and most satisfactory results are obtained both from the student's point of view and the consideration of the finished product when the student is led to advance from the simple problem to the more complex by a series of elementary problems carefully graded. The beginner has not only to learn the processes involved in the making of a piece of jewelry but also to master the various tools used and to learn the limitations of his material. Although the number of tools used in jewelry making are few, it seems best for the beginner to take them up one or two at a time and plan his problem accordingly.

The Processes involved in jewelry making are as follows: Sawing, Filing, Bending, Carving, Embossing or repousse, Soldering, Stone Setting, Polishing, Coloring, Pickling, Modeling, Casting, Annealing.

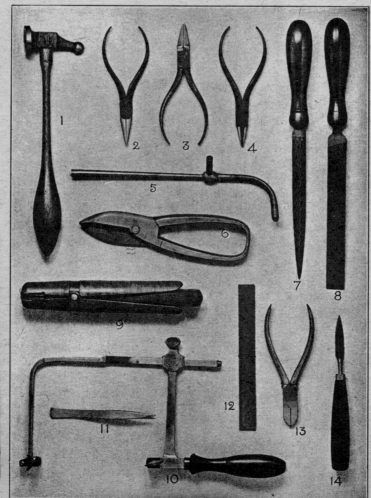

Minimum essential set of tools for jewelry making

Creative Glass Blowing

This well-illustrated and carefully written book begins with the statement "Any one can learn to blow glass." To a large extent, the authors, one of whom is a professional glass blower, succeed in making that statement believable. However, the first 50 pages are concerned with the tools of the glass blower and I found myself wondering, "Yes, but can anyone learn to be a pipe-fitter, metal worker, carpenter, and electrician?" If you can do those things, there is little doubt that this book (and several hundred dollars worth of tools and related supplies) will enable you to blow glass—probably creatively.

Don't expect to take up glass blowing casually, with just this book, but if it is a hobby to which you can commit yourself seriously this book would be an excellent investment, for starters.

There is a page at the end that lists sources of tools and materials. Unfortunately, there are only a few suppliers mentioned, all of whom are in the East. Alas, we westerners need a special supplement, obviously.

[Reviewed by Richard Raymond]

Creative Glass Blowing
James E. Hammesfahr, Clair L. Stong
1968; 196 pp.

$9.00 postpaid

from:
W. H. Freeman & Company
660 Market Street
San Francisco, CA 94104

or WHOLE EARTH CATALOG

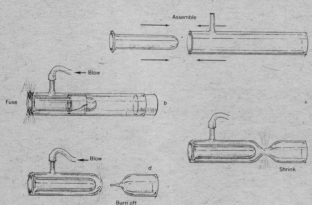

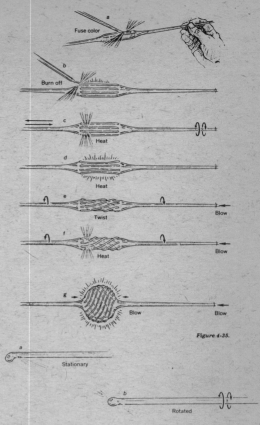

Figure 4-35.

Stationary

Rotated

Here, then, is the first skill you must develop in the course of becoming a glass blower: the knack of rotating hot glass at a rate that precisely counteracts the force of gravity. The trick is not difficult to master if you follow a few simple rules. First, never soften more glass than you need for making a desired form. If you intend to impart a rounded shape to the the end of a rod, heat only the tip. Second, never soften the material more than necessary to accomplish your objective. Obviously, stiff glass is easier to control than runny glass. Watch the work as it softens and changes form. Alter its position in the fire to take advantage of gravity, or to offset the effect of gravity, as the case may be. This is accomplished by rotating the work.

Glassworks

studio equipment for glaziers, marvers, and gaffers . . . kilns, furnaces, day tanks, benches, tables, blowpipes, all hand built.

—jd
[Suggested by Bruce McDougal]

Catalog
$0.25

from:
The Glassworks
Box 202
Warner, New Hampshire 03278

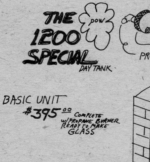

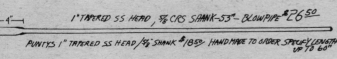

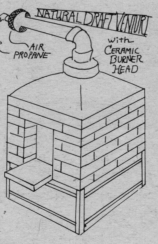
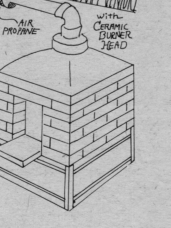
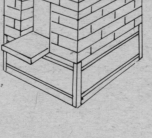

Working With Glass

There aren't many books on working with glass. W.E.C. lists only one and that is mostly about glass blowing. May I recommend: "The Encyclopedia of Working With Glass", Milton K. Berlye, 1968. Oceana Publications, Inc. Dobbs Ferry, N. Y. $12.50. It covers the entire subject very well, including fiberglass.

A. W. Griffin
Van Nuys, CA

ANGEL'S FARM

The money from D.R.'s sister turned out to be twenty-five dollars instead of the fifteen he had asked for. At some earlier point in their trip together such a delightful surprise would have sent D.R. and Estelle into little dancing ecstasies and racing to the nearest candy store to buy a bag of jelly beans. But they were so far from joy right then that ten times that amount could not have given them pleasure. D.R. put the money in his pocket and went outside where Estelle was waiting, leaning against a telephone booth.

"I want to call Gail," she said.

"C..c..call?"

"I want to call Gail. Give me a dime."

D.R. felt in his pocket. The Western Union lady had given him some change but it was all in quarters.

"Give me a quarter, then. I'll get it back. I'm calling collect."

D.R. handed Estelle a quarter. She went in the phone booth with it and slammed the door. A few minutes later D.R. saw her bang the receiver on the hook and storm furious out of the booth.

"Shit?"

"Wha..wha..what . . . "

"Her old man answered and refused to accept the charges. Shit."

"Let's p..p..pay for the c..c..call. We can af..f..ford it."

"Fuck it," said Estelle. "Let's go."

"Let's c..c..call the Flash," said D.R. "He'll accept it."

Estelle shrugged. She was leaning against the bus now, her arms folded across her chest, looking at the sidewalk. "Call him," she said. "I don't care."

D.R. went in the phone booth and asked the operator to connect him with the Anaheim Flash in Anaheim, California. He listened to the phone ring, he listened to the Flash tell the operator he would accept the charges. He heard the Flash's soft, laconic voice say, "Hey man, what's up?"

"N..n..nothing," D.R. stammered. "N..n..nothing's up. We just wanted to call somebody. We're in St. Louis."

"What's wrong, man?" asked the Flash. "You sound like you got epilepsy or something."

"N..n..no," said D.R. "It's this th..th..th**ng**, it's my t..t..tongue. It's getting b..b..better. Listen, d..d..did you hear about Eddie?"

"Yeah," said the Flash. "Fucking bummer."

"We g..g..got here after it happened. We b..b..been in St. Louis t..t..two days."

"That's two days too long for me," said the Flash. "You better get back out here to the land of sun and fun. Where's Estelle?"

"Right here," said D.R. "You want to sp..sp..speak to her?"

"Sure. Put her on. I've got a message for her from Angel."

(continued)

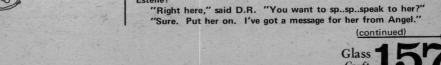

Plastics

These two books give a good idea of what's possible in art with super-versatile plastics. Newman is more comprehensive and has an excellent materials chart. Roukes has some unique techniques and more inspiring pictures. Both list suppliers.

—SB

[Suggested by Jim Robertson and Audrey M. Simurda]

Sculpture in Plastics
Nicholas Roukes
1968; 176 pp.

$12.50 postpaid

from:
Watson-Guptill Publications
165 West 46th Street
New York, N. Y. 10036

or WHOLE EARTH CATALOG

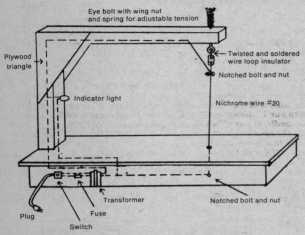

Cutting intricate forms from Styrofoam and other cellular plastic foams is easy with this 6 volt hot wire cutter, which you can make at home if you are handy. As the diagram indicates, you can make the entire structure out of wood, plus the following parts, available from your local radio parts store and hardware store: transformer, filament 6.3V @ 10 amps; switch, double pole, single throw; red indicator light; fuse holder and fuse; insulator; nickel chrome wire; plug and rubber coated wire; notched bolts and nuts; spring.

A Sculptor's Manual

This book is a well organized presentation of the basic processes behind sculpture. Detailed processes are made to seem simple, but not oversimplified; it remains obvious that a good deal of patience will be required to cast a bronze by the lost wax method. People who do not know what technique will suit them best and who want a solid footing from which to experiment, will find A Sculptor's Manual most useful. It encourages you to attempt the forms you have imagined, by showing you how.

The nine chapters cover plaster usage; foundry practice; flame and electric welding; plastics; cement; stone and wood; repetition casting; general construction; finishing; and surface coatings. Cross referencing, a glossary, and 27 diagrams make the book all the more usable. British sculptors will find a buyer's guide at the end of each chapter. Americans are referred to the yellow pages, Bernard Klein's "Guide to American Directories" and the "Thomas Register" (see p. 23 of the CATALOG) to find sources for materials.

At the back of the book is a section of 22 photos of finished sculpture, just enough to intrigue and egg you on without being pushy.

[Reviewed by Joe Bonner]

The development of plastics has been continuing since the end of the last century and the term plastics now covers a complex of materials of which those dealt with here form a small and relatively simple part.

Firstly, there is the vast range of thermosetting plastics materials which are manufactured as liquids in two or three component parts. These are the polyesters and epoxy resins. They require reinforcement and are formed in a one-way process.

Secondly, there is an even larger range of thermoplastics, manufactured in powder or chip form and fabricated into very thin sheets which are subsequently laminated to provide whatever thickness may be required. They are structural materials—either flexible or rigid—and are formed under heat in a reversible process: raise a thermoplastic object carefully to the

Plastics as an Art Form
Thelma R. Newman
1964, 1969; 403 pp.

$12.50 postpaid

from:
Chilton Book Company
Customer Service Dept.
Chilton Way
Radnor, PA 19089

or WHOLE EARTH CATALOG

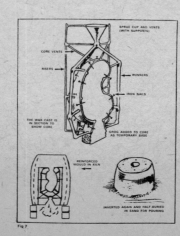

A Sculptor's Manual
Geoffrey Clarke & Stroud Cornock
1968; 158 pp.

$8.95 postpaid

Studio Vista Ltd.
Blue Star House
Highgate H171
London 19, England

or
WHOLE EARTH CATALOG

temperature at which it was formed and it will revert through the sequence of forming operations back into a sheet.

Thermosets are built up with glass-fibre reinforcement over female mould surfaces and subsequently painted if required, though mass-pigmentation can be effected before lay-up.

Thermoplastics can be bent and formed when hot, either freely or by mechanical forming, e.g. they can be injected under pressure into moulds. These materials can be bonded with adhesives, welded together by high-frequency vibration, screwed over a frame or welded with hot gas and a filter rod. It is possible to vary the mass-pigmentation of various thermoplastics by laminating a screen-printed surface onto the rigid sheet.

Adhesive Products

Silicone molding rubber (cast anything!) at low prices & Monzini epoxy based casting compounds. 20th Century materials.

[Suggested and reviewed by Jeff Schlanger]

Brochure & pricelist

free from:
Adhesive Products Corp.
1660 Boone Avenue
Bronx, N. Y. 10460

1½ Pt. Kit (1½ lbs.)
Consisting of 1 lb. ADRUB RTV and ½ lb. ADRUB RTV
Rubber Hardener .... $ 6.00

4530 MONZINI IRONZINI

5 gallons	$ .55 per pound
1 gallon	$ .65 per pound

Eduardo Paolozzi   Hagim 1967
Chrome—plated steel. 2½ in. by 11¾ in. by 6 in.
Hanover Gallery, London   photo: Howards Studio

Lost Wax process or cire perdu.
A lenthy and complex process. Join all wax runners, risers, etc., with a wax knuckle by modelling with a hot spatula. Reinforce grog with chicken wire. Before removal from kiln, reinforce surface with plaster and scrim. Keep sprue clear of sand, etc.

The process has changed little since the Greeks brought it to a pitch of achievement, and it is still so demanding that very few foundries exist. Their services are very costly. If you have a sculpture in clay, wax or plaster, and it is of a nature that demands faithful reproduction, there is no doubt that bronze—far denser than aluminium. cast by the Lost-Wax process—quite different from sand-casting—presents the only method of preserving the form and texture accurately.

This is an extremely complex and variable method, though large works can be cast more cheaply if it is followed up to the point at which the wax has been cored— or just to the production of the wax (without runners or core)—and the result is then given to a foundry for casting. If the foundryman produce a bad result, however—it will be your fault.

Candlemaking

I've been making candles for about a year now as a supplementary income for family of me, wife and bouncy baby boy, and I think I can make some useful suggestions and at the same time do a review of some candle supplies.

First——wax. *Don't buy wax in the grocery store.* It comes in one lb. boxes for sealing jelly and is prohibitively expensive. I used to buy wax from a local hobby store (American Handicrafts——if you don't have anything against using names), until I noticed that their supplier was in Phila. So I went to the supplier and got it much cheaper. Until someone told me about getting wax from the oil companies which have refineries in Phila. So now I get wax from Atlantic-Richfield, delivered to my door (300 lb——five 60 lb cartons; six 10 lb. slabs per carton minimum order for free delivery) for only 12¢/lb. Compare that to the hobby store price of 11 lb. for $3.50 = 32¢/lb. So try getting wax from oil companies near you.

Next——molds. American Handicrafts has molds which work pretty well, but they are somewhat limited in variety. Another source of molds——somewhat higher in price but also excellent quality is the Pourette Mfg. Co., 6818 Roosevelt Way N.E., Seattle, Wash. 98115. They also carry dyes, scents, wick, etc. etc. You can also use things like milk cartons, wine bottles, light bulbs, shampoo bottles, or sand to mold candles. Or if you have access to materials—— sheet metal——and rods——soldering iron. and sheet metal press——make your own molds.

Third——dyes. The best place I've found for dyes is the

J. & E. Polish Co.
1036 Monrello St.
Brockton, Mass.

They have about thirty colors——inclding shrimp, sunshine yellow, cherry, red red, and mandarin to name a few neat names. The dyes are 1/2 oz. cakes of "concentrated" candle colors (at $3.50 per dozen) and are advertised as coloring 10-15 lbs. of wax but I've done much more sometimes.

J. & E. Polish also makes the best concentrate perfume oils I've used. They have about a dozen scents including hollyberry, coconut, apple blossom & cinnamon. (And the coconut really smells like coconut!)

Pourette carries the widest variety of wick I've found. I don't advise using string——candle wick is woven with a single tight strand so it bends over and burns right and is also treated chemically I think.

I think that's about all——wax, wick, dyes & scents. One warning—— candle making can be a messy process if you spill wax around, so put down newspaper. Another warning——heat wax in a double boiler——*never directly over a flame.*

Go to a restaurant or cafeteria and get empty cans. If you're lucky,. they will have both 4 & 5 quart cans, which will make great free double boilers.

I forgot to say that you will probably have your choice of melting points if you get wax from an oil company. After experimenting with several I have found 143-148° wax the most versatile stuff.

If I'm not careful this is going to turn into a book on candle making so I think I'll stop here.

Pax,

David Inouye
Swarthmore, Pa.

The Japanese Art of Miniature Trees and Landscapes

This is the ultimate in model-making. Tiny trees in tiny scenes, and a careful, happy person hovering in the sky nearby. This book is really thorough on the science and the art of bonsai. The standard work.

—SB

The Japanese Art of Miniature Trees and Landscapes
Yuji Yoshimura and Giovanna M. Halford
1957; 220 pp.

$10.25 postpaid

from:
Charles E. Tuttle Company
28 S. Main St.
Rutland, Vermont 05701

or WHOLE EARTH CATALOG

Fig. 17.—Removing old soil and trimming roots. **A)** Before beginning. 1) Lines mark two-thirds of old soil to be removed in 2nd Step of cleansing. 2) Lines mark one-third of lateral roots to be trimmed away. 3) Lines mark one-half of old soil to be removed in 3rd Step, and, in the case of deciduous trees only, of bottom roots to be trimmed away. 4) Line marks bottom roots to be trimmed from evergreen needle trees. **B)** After finishing. 5) Remaining nucleus of old soil. 6) Alternating slices of old soil removed this potting in 4th Step. 7) Slices to be removed next potting.

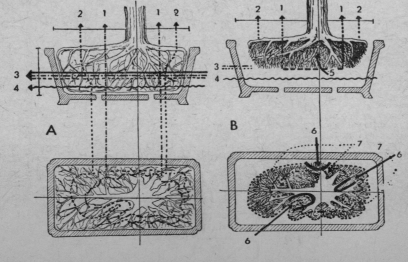

Modern Art of Candle Creating

There's lots of wimpy books on candle-making, and this is one of them. But it is better than the others—more and wider technique.

—SB

Wick Too Large

Proper Sized Wick

Wick Too Small

Wick Far Too Small

Modern Art of Candle Creating
Don Olsen
1963; 152 pp.

$7.50 postpaid

from:
A. S. Barnes & Co.
Box 421
Cranbury, N. J. 08512

or WHOLE EARTH CATALOG

RULES TO REMEMBER

To get the most out of your mold, abide by the following rules:

Never strike it with a hard object.

Never place it in an oven with a temperature exceeding 175 degrees.

Never scratch the interior with a sharp instrument or abrasive.

Never loan to friends unless they know how to care for it.

Store in a warm, dry place to prevent rust; keep covered to protect interior from dust.

If you should find it necessary to clean your mold of contiminated or "stubborn wax," use one of these methods:

Easy Method. Pour your next candle with the wax at 230 degrees. This usually cleans the mold and absorbs stubborn wax.

Celebration! Candle Supplies

We have a candle "factory" and shop here in Northern Michigan. In our attempt to produce the best quality candle at the lowest cost we have experimented with many dye and scent manufacturers, wick making companies, mold makers etc. We now have excellent sources for our materials and find that, since it is cheapest to buy them in large quantity we are in a position where we can break the supplies down into smaller quantities and resell them. Not only are our supplies better than anything we've found available to the general public, we can under cut everyone else's prices.

Here, for example, are how our prices compare to others: Dye—— we can provide enough dye to color 20 lbs. of wax for 35 cents. Pourette, a national candle supply pusher, will sell you enough to do 10 lbs for 25 cents. American Handicraft, a chain store——I don't know if they are on the West coast or not, will sell you dye for 12 lbs. for 39 cents——and it's very poor quality. Michael's, an other craft chain sells dye for 50 cents——they don't say how much it will color but from the way it looks and feels I know it won't color 20 lbs. Even the local "head" shops dye is 39 cents for 12 lbs worth of dye. And let me stress that our dye is of a much higher quality than any of the above. I've enclosed samples of our orange and lemon yellow——we have many other colors.

Scent runs much the same:

    Celebration! – 1 oz. for $1.25

    Pourette – 1/2 oz. for 75 cents.

    Am. Handicraft – 1/2 oz. for 79 cents;

Again our scent is of a higher quality. Most craft companies dilute the scent before they sell it and this damages potency. Both American Handicraft and Pourette say their 1/2 oz. will scent 3-4 lbs of wax——figure our 1/2 oz. will scent 6-8 lbs of wax.

Wick——we have an excellent source of wick. The most important part of a good burning candle is the wick——we have a fine metal core wick which we use in everything from our 3" diameter candles up to our 7" diameter candles. In our 3" candle it consumes all the candle, in our 4" diameter and larger candles it burns a well down into the candle——with the proper amount of steric acid (we can sell for $1.10 a lb compared to Am. Handicraft—69 cents for 4 oz.) this wick will not flood out. It's great. We can sell it for 10 cents a yard——Pourette is 15 cents a yard and Amer. Handicraft is even more——and of disgusting quality. We have other sizes also but this is best.

We also have molds but currently I can't estimate those prices—— but they will be good.

Because our prices are cut to the bone we will have to charge for postage——but Pourette and American Handicraft both do that even with their high prices.

Due to the fact that we are currently renovating one floor of a beautiful old building to move our shop into and making the dirty, old, big basement over as a new location for our "factory", plus we have back orders for wholesale candles——and on top of that I am trying to finish up my undergraduate crap at Michigan State University, I have not gotten the catalog of our supplies together yet. This is why I am sending you the above information, and samples, instead of our catalog. I think from the information I've included you can see that we are trying to do a good thing. If you think we might fill the need for a candle making materials supplier in the Whole Earth Catalog it would be wonderful. You could run our name and address telling people to write to us for our catalog. If you could also ask people to send 25 cents to cover printing costs it would really help us out a great deal.

Thank you for taking the time to read this. I hope it works out. Thank you also for doing the Whole Earth Catalog——you have really fulfilled a need. I'll miss you when you stop but I think your idea of "stopping" would be a good one for others to follow.

Peace,

Bill Decker

Celebration! Candle Supplies
P.O. Box 28
Pentwater, Michigan 49448

D.R. stepped out of the booth and handed the phone to Estelle.

"Hi baby," said the Flash. "How's your life?"

"Fucking miserable," said Estelle. "How's yours?"

"Better than yours, obviously. What's going on?"

"It's too long and too weird to tell," said Estelle. "What's happening in California?"

"Angel bought a farm in Oregon," said the Flash. "Two hundred acres. Her and Speed. They're into goats and bee hives."

"Far out," said Estelle. Suddenly she was smiling, and there was genuine cheer in her voice. "Far fucking out. They really did it."

"Two hundred acres," said the Flash. "I was up there the other day, it's really a neat scene. She was asking about you."

"Fantastic! Tell 'em hello, okay? Tell 'em I'll come see 'em."

"Will do," said the Flash. "Any other news, comments, hits, reports or flashes from the hinterlands?"

"It's grim," said Estelle. " 'Nuff said."

"Well," said the Flash. "Every cloud has a silver lining, and the darkest hour is just before dawn, and such like bullshit."

"You're stoned," said Estelle.

"Ah, yes, the blessed stated. As a matter of fact, the old fire is waning a bit, I better go stoke it up a little. But listen you guys, call me again, you hear? I'm interested in your fate."

"Sure," Estelle laughed. "We'll give you a weekly casualty report. Listen honey, it's nice to talk to you. Take care, okay?"

The Flash said he would take care. Estelle hung up then, and as soon as she did the smile vanished from her face. Without saying a word to each other, D.R. and Estelle went back to City Girl's apartment to get their stuff, and to tell everyone goodbye.

Pioneer Pottery

*michael cardew is a big gun, careful man,
good potter, and the book is complete in a systems way.
he starts in giving lessons in geology for potters, puts
the reader's head down into the earth with the clay,
and then runs through most of the materials tools
techniques forms receipes and principles i've ever heard
mentioned. an honest book, looks you right in the eye.*

—jd

[suggested by Jeff Schlanger]

Pioneer Pottery
Michael Cardew
1969; 327pp.

$15.00

from:
St. Martin's Press
5 South Union Street
Lawrence, MA. 01843

or WHOLE EARTH CATALOG

Michael Cardew

Practical potters have always had an instinctive knowledge of clay, and were able to make good pots with it although they (like the rest of the world) did not really know what it was. But during the past forty years a great deal of fundamental research on clays has been done, throwing a flood of new light on a field in which previously there had only been fogs, obscurity, guesswork—and mud. Potters, it is true, cannot hope to be scientists; but unless we try to learn something about all this new knowledge, we shall remain for ever at the 'animistic' level, with no real enlightenment on the ancient problems of why some clays are unpredictable and temperamental, while others are reliable and cooperative.

•

Let us begin with Geochemistry. The Earth, the warm-hearted fertile *Magna Mater* in whose bosom we all live, has been described by one geochemist as 'a projectile of nickel steel, with a slaggy crust.' The general picture of the earth presented by geochemistry is a slightly kinder one than this, since it provides a hydrosphere, an atmosphere and even a 'biosphere' to clothe the slaggy crust—the lithosphere—with decent verdure. It is estimated (1924) that the upper ten miles of the lithosphere or crust consist of:

    95 per cent igneous rocks
     4 per cent shales
    0.75 per cent sandstones
    0.25 per cent limestones

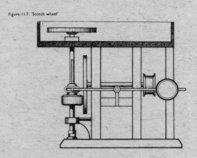

Figure 11.7. 'Scotch wheel'

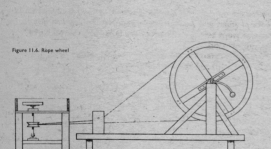

Figure 11.6. Rope wheel

Figure 10.8. Two-chamber downdraught kiln (section)

Free Fire Brick

I don't know anything about kilns except that fire brick is very expensive stuff. Noble Jasper Brinton solved this problem whilst reducing waste at the same time. He sought out and made friends with some engineers at a glass factory a few miles from his home. He was able to persuade the company officials to let him prowl in their dump. Every few years, many glass companies must tear down a kiln because the intense heat is literally eating the bricks up. The old bricks are thrown on the dump, going to waste, but Jasper says they are still perfect for ceramics kilns. Like I say, I know nothing of kilns, but I've seen a kiln that Jasper built with old fire brick, and it sure as hell looks like it works.

Bill Marsano
Radnor, Pa.

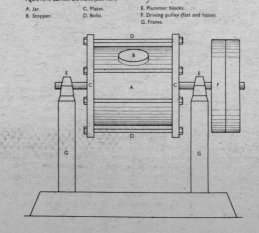

Figure A7.4. Ball-mill and frame (side view)

A. Jar.   C. Plates.   E. Plummer blocks.
B. Stopper.   D. Bolts.   F. Driving pulley (fast and loose).
                              G. Frame.

A Potter's Book

*we've carried this book as a little footnote
to our pottery section. after talking with
a few potters, and looking at the book a little,
we've decided, i've decided, it has been decided,
maybe it hasn't been decided,
that this is the best all around pottery book.
leach pretty well covers the field, with
good emphasis on japanese techniques,
particularily sound on glazes,
ample diagrams,
kiln plans,
nice advice.*

—jd

A Potter's Book
Bernard Leach
1967: 294pp.

$12.75 postpaid

from:
Transatlantic Arts
Trade Department
North Village Green
Levittown, Long Island,
New York 11756

or WHOLE EARTH CATALOG

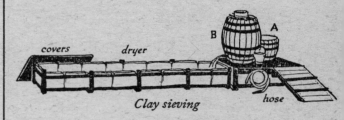

Clay sieving

This book is the outcome of thirty-three years' experience of making pots by hand processes in the Far East and in England. During twelve of those years I had unique opportunities of gaining an insight into the spirit and methods by which early Oriental pottery was made. Here I have attempted to state these simply and openly, and to relate them to our Western need, primarily for the sake of other potters who suffer inevitably from the almost entire loss of our own birthright of traditional craft lore. But this book is also intended for students and teachers, for lovers of good pots and sound craftsmanship, and finally for those to whom the cultural meeting of East and West is the prelude to a human society. Out of my dual experience I have tried to formulate a criterion by which good pots may be recognized in a manner similar to that by which an ever-changing but nevertheless continuous classic standard encourages the appreciation of fine architecture, painting, writing and music.

•

Raku has two disadvantages which should be mentioned together with those qualities which obviously recommend it to the artist, the craftsman and the school; it is porous when new, and it is comparatively fragile. With use the pores of the body and the crackle of the glaze gradually fill up, so that even a raku vase will eventually cease to leave a damp mark behind it even on a polished surface. Its fragility, due to low temperature firing, necessitates the making of pieces with fairly thick walls, handles, and spouts. For this reason it is not advisable to make thin table-ware of raku. A harder preliminary firing of the biscuit will strengthen the body, but at a sacrifice of the peculiar soft character of the glaze and its crackle. The Japanese do make pottery of this kind, using soft coloured glazes over stoneware biscuit, and call it 'Kochi' (Cochin China ware), but it requires a kiln which will go to high temperauress.

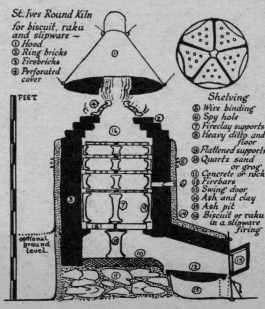

*St. Ives Round Kiln
for biscuit, raku
and slipware —*
① *Hood*
③ *Ring bricks*
⑤ *Firebricks*
④ *Perforated
cover*

Shelving
⑥ *Wire binding*
⑨ *Spy hole*
⑦ *Fireclay supports*
⑧ *Heavy ditto and
floor*
⑩ *Flattened supports*
⑪ *Quartz sand
or grog*
⑫ *Concrete or rock*
⑬ *Firebars*
⑭ *Swing door*
⑮ *Ash and clay*
⑯ *Ash pit*
⑰ *Biscuit or raku
in a slipware
firing*

FEET

St. Ives round up-draught kiln

Pottery

Authoritative and scrupulously organized with concise explanations accompanied by 388 lucid photos, Pottery presents an exceptional technique of throwing.

The rudiments seem preferable to those redundant techniques I learned. In addition are many finer techniques I never thought of.

Teach yourself to throw with this book or use it as I would to cleanse myself of bad habits. This is the only appealing pottery book I have ever seen, but it only covers throwing.

[*Reviewed by Joe Bonner*]

Pottery
the technique of throwing
John Colbeck
1969; 159 pp.

$10.00 postpaid

from:
Watson-Guptill
Publications
2160 Patterson Street
Cincinnati, OH 45214

**or WHOLE EARTH
CATALOG**

Two main pressures tend to centre the rotating mass of clay:

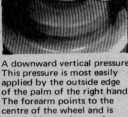

A downward vertical pressure. This pressure is most easily applied by the outside edge of the palm of the right hand. The forearm points to the centre of the wheel and is steadied by resting on the edge of the wheel tray. This pressure exerted alone tends to displace the clay into a wider form.

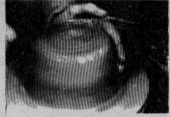

An inward horizontal pressure. This pressure is most easily exerted by the wrist end of the palm of the left hand. This forearm also points to the centre of the wheel and is steadied by resting on the edge of the wheel tray. This pressure exerted alone tends to displace the clay into a taller form.

In practice these two pressures are only rarely applied singly. Small and medium sized pieces can generally be centred by the simultaneous application of the two pressures.

The two pressures isolated in the two previous photographs are here shown combined. Every opportunity should be taken while centring of achieving additional steadiness through contact of the hands with each other.

There are other centring holds than the one illustrated. All involve an application of the same two pressures.

The clay is squeezed between the index finger and any one of the first three fingers of the right hand. This method is used much less frequently than the previous two but beginners do find it useful for gaining additional steadiness. Two variations are possible; if the pressure inside is applied by the ball of the index finger the main pressure can be applied by any one of the fingers and can be varied, the fingers not applying pressure outside can exert a slight steadying pressure to control the form either above or below the main point of pressure; or, if the side of the index finger is used inside pressure can be spread through all three fingers, the point of main pressure usually being in the lowest finger outside and the ball of the inside finger.

Throwing is the process of shaping an even mass of soft plastic clay by hand on a wheelhead revolving at speeds varied by the thrower.

Turning is the process of paring away excess clay from a leather hard form.

•

Trimming with a needle or pin

The revolving wall is gripped lightly between the fingers and thumb of the left hand. The right hand holding the needle is steadied on the left thumb.

The needle is pushed through until it touches the fingers of the left hand.

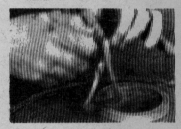

The left hand then grips the clay slightly more firmly and both hands rise forwards and upwards.

Kilns

The definitive book on kiln construction and use. If you can build a pot you can build a kiln. —SB

Kilns
Daniel Rhodes
1968; 240 pp.

$9.95 postpaid

from:
Chilton Book Co.
Customer Service Dept.
Chilton Way
Radnor, PA. 19089

or WHOLE EARTH CATALOG

Also of interest

Clay and Glazes for the Potter
Daniel Rhodes $12.50 from Chilton

Stoneware and Porcelain
Daniel Rhodes $3.95 from Chilton

Ceramics: Potter's Handbook
Glenn Nelson $10.95 from:
Holt, Rinehart & Winston
383 Madison Avenue
New York, N. Y. 10017

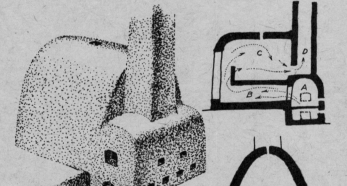

Design for a wood burning kiln with double crossdraft circulation. The bottom section is used for "Bizen" effects where a lot of flashing is desired, while the upper section is relatively free of direct flame and fly ash, and can be used for regular glazed wares.

Refractory blocks, slabs, skewbacks, arches, or door blocks may be made on the job using castable materials. In fact, it is possible to make the whole kiln from a castable material. Refractory castable mixtures are made from a suitable aggregate, such as firebrick grog, insulating firebrick granules, vermiculite, or perlite bonded with calcium aluminate cement. Calcium aluminate cement is similar to portland cement, and when mixed with water will set up in a hard, solid mass. But unlike portland cement, it is refractory and may be heated to red heat or higher without exploding or melting. Most brands of calcium aluminate cement may be used at temperatures in excess of 1300° C.

To cast a shape, a form must first be made. Forms may be made of wood or plywood, securely fastened at the corners, or in the case of curving forms, of bent plywood or masonite suitably reinforced. The forms may be given a light coat of grease to prevent sticking. The aggregate is prepared by crushing old firebrick or fragments of used insulating firebrick. The aggregate should be made up of particles of various sizes, from about ¼ inch in diameter to grains as small as sand or smaller. The proportion of very fine particles should not be too great, however. The aggregate is then mixed dry with 1/5 of its volume of cement. Water is added to this, and the mass is mixed in a mortar box until it is of plastic consistency. It should be well moistened, but not so wet as to flow. The mixture is then shoveled into the mold and rammed into place so as to leave no air pockets. The material will set in a few hours and may then be removed from the mold and cured in a cool place for several days. When thoroughly dry, cast shapes may be incorporated into the kiln structure.

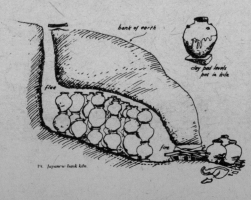

LEAVING ST. LOUIS

Gilded Lilly and the Crosstown Rivals had split while D.R. and Estelle were gone, and the others were asleep or half-asleep in odd places about the room. City Girl had gone into the bedroom by herself and closed the door. The only person who was on his feet was Reed, in the kitchen looking for stuff to make a sandwich out of.

"Get your money?" he asked.

D.R. nodded. "I g..guess we'll t..t..take off now. Anybody want to g..g..go to Cincinnati?"

"Somebody going to Cincinnati?" said a voice in the living room. It was Friendly Persuasion. She'd been asleep in the corner where Estelle had sat earlier. She was sitting up now, yawning and scratching herself through a hole in her sweater. "Somebody going to Cincinnati?"

"We are," said Estelle. She was in the living room, looking around to see if they were forgetting anything.

"Far out," said Friendly Persuasion, and she leaned over and shook The Native, who was stretched out next to her. "Hey. Wake up. You want to go to Cincinnati?"

The Native opened his eyes long enough to say sure. Then he closed them again and turned over. Friendly Persuasion got to her feet and went to the kitchen where D.R. had joined Reed scrounging for food.

"Hey," said Friendly Persuasion. "No kidding? You got room? You got room for The Native too?"

"Sure. We g..g..got a b..b..bus."

Friendly Persuasion looked at Reed. "Do I want to go to Cincinnati?"

"Nah," said Reed. "You don't want to go to Cincinnati."

"But I do! I know a lot of people in Cincinnati."

"You don't want to see those people," said Reed.

"Don't I? No shit?"

"Nah. Go on back over there and go to sleep." Reed had made a sandwich out of rice and some old chili. He took a bite, then held the sandwich out for Friendly Persuasion. She took a bite, and went back to the living room to talk it over with The Native.

"Hey, wake up," she said. "We got to decide."

"Decide what?" mumbled The Native.

"Are we going to Cincinnati or aren't we?"

"Sure," said The Native. "We're going to Cincinnati."

"I don't think I want to go," said Friendly Persuasion. And suddenly she knew for sure that she didn't. "Hey," she said to Estelle. "Hey, honey. Thanks, but we're not going, we changed our minds, okay?"

"Whatever's right," said Estelle.

"Yeah. I was just there a month ago. Fuck it." And Friendly Persuasion lay down on the floor beside The Native and soon went back to sleep.

Estelle snapped the duffle bag shut and set it beside the door. D.R. and Reed came in from the kitchen, eating chili and rice sandwiches. D.R. handed one to Estelle, then picked up the duffle bag and threw it over his shoulder.

"Well, see you around," D.R. said to Reed.

"Goodbye," said Estelle.

"Yeah, wow, man," said Reed. "Good to see you guys. Carry it on, okay?"

"We'll see you around," said D.R.

They left then.

Reed closed the door behind them.

Potter's Wheels

An outstanding kickwheel, by all accounts.

—SB

Klopfenstein

brochure

free

from:
H. B. Klopfenstein & Sons
Route Two
Crestline, Ohio 44827

price $195 f.o.b. Crestline, Ohio 240 lbs.

Reversible throwing head $15

Adjustable hip rest $15

Brent

brochure

free

from:
Robert Brent Potter's Wheels
1101 Cedar Street
Santa Monica, CA 90405

Prices	HP	Speed	
Model CX	1	0-220	$350.00
Model C	1/2	0-220	$275.00
Model C kit	1/2	0-220	$245.00
Kick Wheel			$110.00
Kick Wheel with motor inst.	1/4	175 max	$175.00
Kick Wheel kit			$ 39.50
Kick Wheel Motor kit	1/4	175 max	$ 49.50

[Suggested by Mary Crawford]

Unpainted	$200	Unpainted	$255
Painted	$225	Painted	$280

Pacifica

I used the Pacifica Crafts (Luitweiler) wheel. Main goodie is the fiberglass flywheel that you can fill with gravel to regulate the weight; empty it and it weighs about 19 lbs.; whole wheel breaks down into components for easy transport.

—jd

Pacifica Woodcrafts
P.O. Box 1438, Dept. W.
Blaine, Washington 98230

Makit A	$ 57.00
Makit AW	$ 98.00
Nordic Model	$148.00
Sierra—Standard	$148.00
Wide	$158.00
Adjustable	$168.00
Stallion Electric	$265.00

Soldner

brochure

free

from:
Soldner Pottery and Pottery Equipment
Box 90
Aspen, Colorado 81611

Unpainted	$345	Unpainted	$420
Painted	$370	Painted	$445

Lipton Kickwheel Kit

$40 for plans and mechanical parts.

Paul Lipton
1624 Virginia St.
Berkeley, CA 94703

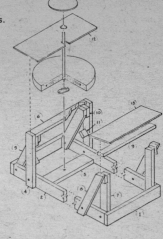

Estrin

Send $0.10 for brochure

from:
Estrin Mfg. Ltd.
3651 Point Grey Road
Vancouver 8, B. C.
CANADA

Basic wheel with 1/4 hp motor	$150
Less motor	109

Jon Kaplan on Wheels and Kilns

As a potter, I thought I'd give you some thoughts about some materials, equipment, books, etc., which people might find useful.

Potter's wheels: The kick wheel made by Pacifica Wood Crafts which you had in Spring 1970 is a fine piece of equipment. Its reasonably cheep, durable, and a good tool. I know people who have them and they have a lot of good things to say about them. The only bad thing though is the cost——the standard wheel is now above $100 plus shipping. Check the latest issue (number 6) the Mother Earth News for wheel plans which I developed along with a potter friend. Total cost——about $65.

Estrin Wheels——a Canadian corporation which also has other potter's equipment. They offer four wheels of different flywheel weights, with or without motors, from $109 to $164 plus a $6.00 crating charge on all models.

Oak Hill Industries——1301 North Utah Street-Davenport Iowa 52804. They offer a standard kick wheel in a kit form. You can get fly wheel weights of 80, 110, and 140 pounds. It has a plywood frame with a cast aluminum wheel head. You can either buy it as a kit or preassembled. It seems like a good wheel.

Westwood Ceramic Supply——14400 Lomitas Ave., City of Industry, California 91744, has a dynamite electric wheel with an automatic feed back circuit which proportions out the amount of electricity relative to the force being generated by the potter on the clay. Its an electric wheel with gear reduction system. Seems like a fine tool. Unfortunately, their catalog doesn't have a price for the wheel. Catalog $1.00.

Skutt Ceramic Products——2618 East Steele Street, Portland, Oregon 97202. They make one electric wheel for $324.95 which is a pretty heavy price. I have used one and know other potters who have and its really beautiful, except for the price.

Oscar Paul Corporation 522 West 182 Street, Gardena California 90247. They make three electric wheels which have different motors in them. Prices range from $275 to $350. Has a nice mechanical drive system.

Randall Pottery Inc. Box 774 Alfred New York 14802. They make perhaps one of the finest kick and motor driven wheels around today, except for the price. They have a standard kick wheel for $305 which can be motorized for an additional $180 so the grand total comes to $485 for their motorized wheel. I have used a Randall electric for a long time previous to the one I built now and it is a really fine wheel, except for its price.

Kilns: If you're into gas kilns, build your own. Don't buy a gas kiln cause you'll be ripped off by its overwhelming price. You can get 1000 K-23 insulating fire brick for about $300, or less if you shop around for seconds. I got 1000 of these for half price. You can make your burners out of standard pipe fittings and use a vacuum cleaner for forced air. For burner plans, write to Alfred University, Alfred New York 14802 (Ceramic Dept) and ask for the schematic for the "Alfred Burner". They will charge you for a Xerox copy (probably). You can get burners from Pyronics Incorporated 17700 Miles Ave. Cleveland Ohio 44128. You can pretty much get a burner designed to your specifications cause they have a lot of designs. I bought two of their 10ET torches with pilots, safety switches, and some other garbage for a total of about $160 which was the most expensive part of my kiln.

Books: The only trouble with Rhodes Kilns is that it leaves a lot out which you either have to find out for yourself or find out by trial and error. Other than that, it is quite good. Clay and Glazes for the Potter by Rhodes is a fine book, and that's about all you should really know. Nelson's Ceramics a Potter's Handbook is ok if you'd like a historical development of the art included with the technical.

Other ditties: If you're into building a kiln, write to the A.P. Green Company, 1018 East Breckenridge St., Mexico, Missouri 65265 and ask for their Pocket Refractories Catalog. Its free and has tables, product information, details of constructions, etc., all about refractories, and is about 200 pages for free.

Peace

Jon Kaplan
Cleveland, Ohio

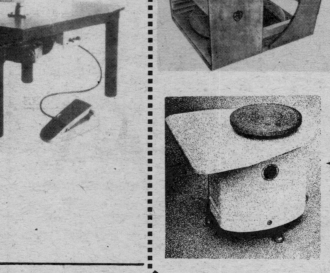

Ceramic Supplies

most of this information was given to us by bruce mcdougal, who runs big creek pottery, davenport, california, 95017, his studio looks like a fine place to learn and work pottery.

—jd

You asked for some comments on pottery suppliers and gear: And I have some opinions, so here you are . . . The enclosed is a list of suppliers that I am more or less familiar with, some of whom I do business with regularly, others I just know about. There are many more good ones I am sure, and if I've missed any that's because I don't know about them.

—Bruce McDougal

Westwood Ceramic Supply
14400 Lomitas Avenue
City of Industry, Ca. 91744

Complete line of clay, glazes, glaze materials, chemicals, tools, wheels, kilns, etc. Good service & prices. Write for catalog $1.00

Western Ceramic Supply
1601 Howard Street
San Francisco, Ca. 94103

Complete line of materials, clay, wheels, etc. Prepared glazes. Excellent source for enamels at good prices. They have a good kick wheel. Write for catalog (free). Also, new cone 10 lead-free glazes.

W.E. Mushet Co.
725 Bryant
San Francisco, Ca. 94107

Kilns, repairs & service. Refractory materials & equipment.

Ceramics & Crafts Supply Co.
490 5th Street
San Francisco, 94107

Clays & Glazes (westwood—at better small lot prices than you can get from L.A.) Materials of all kinds. Lockerbie wheels. Write for catalog (free)

Leslie Ceramics Supply
1212 San Pablo
Berkeley, Ca. 94706

Clays, glazes, kilns, wheels, chemical materials, tools. An excellent all-around source in the East Bay.

Thorley Pottery Supply
1183 Industrial Avenue
South Gate, Ca. 90280

Kiln shelves, and I don't know what else. An excellent source for fired clay shelves in large sizes that will take cone 10-11 reduction firings without trouble, at about 1/3 the cost of Silicon Carbide. Also excellent posts.

Electro Refractories
18765 Fibreglass Road
Huntington Beach, Ca. 92647

Also excellent shelves that will go to c/10-11 at a fraction of Silicon Carbide. Ask for Comp 104. They do not have the range of large sizes that Thorley has. Compare prices in your size.

Pyro Engineering
200 South Palm
Alhambra, Ca. 91801

Thick slabs for floor plates, etc. (mine are 2'' thick)—I don't know what else they have—I suspect shelves also, and etc.?

Denver Fire Clay Co.
3033 Blake Street
Denver, Colorado 80205

Complete line of kilns, wheels, glaze materials, etc. Excellent *small* power wheel. One of the original kiln builders. Bought out Dickenson years ago & now makes that kind also. Catalog (free)

Castle Clay Products, Inc.
1055 South Fox Street, Unit No. 2
Denver, Colorado 80223

Catalog free.

American Art Clay Co.
Indianapolis, Indiana 46200

An old company, making kilns, wheels, & selling all kinds of supplies. Oriented toward schools, their kilns are built massively & with all kinds of safety controls available to satisfy the most picky fire marshal. More expensive than some. Write for catalog (free)

The Craftool Co.
1 Industrial Road
Woodridge, N.J. 07075

Tools for ceramics & many other crafts. Catalog. $1.00

Kemper Mfg. Co.
P.O. Box 545
Chino, California 91710

Kemper specializes in making hand tools for the potter & sculptor. They do a good job, have a wide selection, and offer quantity discounts for direct sale. Write for catalog (free)

Sculpture House
38 East 30th Street
New York, N.Y. 10016

Hand tools for sculptors & potters—a complete line. Catalog (free)

A.D. Alpine Inc.
353 Coral Circle
El Segundo, Ca. 90245

Kilns, mainly—also wheels and other ceramic gear. Their kilns have for many years been the poor potters friend, because they have sold so many that they are easier to find second hand than almost any other (at least in the west) They take a little experience to fire, but are excellent, reliable and long-lived. Catalog (free)

Duncan Ceramic Supply
5649 East Shields
Fresno, Ca. 93727

This is reported to be a remarkable place, well worth visiting if you are in Fresno. They have an excellent line of low fire glazes, and other supplies. I don't have their catalog, but they come highly recommended, and I think they probably have one. (free???)

Jack D. Wolfe

Another ceramics supplier, lowest prices in New York area. They have a jet black clay.

[Suggested by Joan Newman]

Jack D. Wolfe Co., Inc.
724 Meeker Ave.
Brooklyn, N.Y. 11222

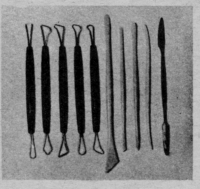

10 PIECE CERAMIC TOOL KIT

No. 96AZ—10 piece ceramic tool kit consisting of 5 double end wire tools; 4 plastic modeling tools; 1 steel scraper tool—packaged in plastic pouch..................**$6.90**

CONE HOLDERS

Jack D. Wolfe

Per Set of 4 pcs $.30

DESCRIPTION	Price Per Pound			
	1 lb.	5 lb.	10 lb.	25 lb.
Alumina Hydrate, Dense	.35	.28	.24	.20
Alumina Oxide, Calcined	.50	.35	.28	.25
Antimony Oxide	3.50	3.00	3.00	3.00
Barium Carbonate	.50	.35	.28	.24
Barium Sulphate	.50	.35	.28	.24
Bentonite	.35	.24	.21	.19
Bone Ash	.45	.35	.30	.25

Standard

TOGGLE CUTTER — Used to cut and slice lump clay or for cutting pots from wheel head. Two hardwood handles with braided nylon cord for clean cutting.

Standard   **$.50 each**

Jon Kaplan on Clays and More Kilns

Clays:

The Fenton Foundry Supply Company
134 Gilbert Avenue
Dayton, Ohio

Has the cheapest prices on all bentonites, and super cheap prices on Redart Clay ($2.50 cwt.) and Jordan Stoneware ($3.50 cwt.) They are nice people to deal with. (free brochure)

Cedar Heights Clay Company
50 Portsmouth Road
Oak Hill, Ohio 45656

They mine and manufacture the Cedar Heights brands of clays, including Redart, Goldart, Fireclays, etc. If you pick up the clay at their place, prices are good——Goldart $27.00 a ton, Redart, $40.00 a ton. (free catalog and samples)

George Fetzer Ceramic Supply Company
1205 Seventeenth Ave.
Columbus, Ohio 43211

Fetzer is a really fine person with really low prices. He used to have the lowest prices for clays and glaze materials last year, but they have gone up a few cents, but still are some of the cheapest I have found. He has a grand selection of glaze materials, clays, some tools, and some other things like cones and Tyler screens. (free catalog)

Standard Ceramic Supply Company
P.O. Box 4435
Pittsburgh Pa. 15205

Standard is a huge operation and their prices are really good. They have perhaps the most complete line of clays and glazes, next to Fetzer. They do a lot more business than George, mostly to schools, but a lot of my potter friends and I do some business with Standard. They carry a lot of tools, Randall wheels, Alpine Kilns, and a lot of good stuff. (free catalog)

Rovin Ceramics Supplies
6912 Schaefer
Dearborn Michigan 48216

Rovin is a bunch of freaks with a lot of stuff, medium prices. Have low priced wrap portable gas, gas and Crusader electric kilns and are distributors of the Pacifica Kick Wheel Kits, Pacifica, Max and Shimpo Electric wheels. A catalog for $.50 (free to schools).

Other things:

Engineered Ceramics
Division of Sola Basic Industries
P.O. Box 1
Gilberts, Illinois 60136

They just had a run on kiln shelves, cone 15 and way above. They were seconds, at $5.00 each and are outasight, I bought a whole bunch. They make high temperature refractories, like saggers, setter tiles, etc. One of the nicest companies I have dealt with. The shelves are far superior than silicon carbide, and new are pretty cheap. The seconds, if any are still left, are like new, with perhaps a little chip or an iron spot. (free brochures—Hycor Alumina—ask for)

Pyronics, Incorporated
17700 Miles Avenue
Cleveland Ohio 44128

Manufacturer of combustion equipment for industry, kilns, etc. I have two of their burners on my kiln with blowers and safety valves, etc., cost me about $150.00 total. Put out a 200,000 BTU flame of 20 inches long. (Free catalog I think)

Johnson Industrial Furnaces and Burners
Johnson Gas Appliance Company
Cedar Rapids, Iowa 52405

Some blower equipment. Don't know much about it. (free catalog)

Killam Gas Burner Company
1240 Sout Bannock Street
Denver Colorado 80223

More burners, better than Johnson, more selection. (Free catalog. ask for drawing No. M-957-D, also P-12 and P-8 burner info.)

Peace

Jon Kaplan
Cleveland, Ohio

PART FOUR

THE FIGHT

Driving through Vincennes that night D.R. and Estelle had their worst fight since they had been together. The immediate issue was whether or not they would spend the night in a motel in Vincennes. Estelle wanted to, was desperate to in fact. But D.R. wanted to keep going. Once the quarrel over motels began, all of Estelle's latent frustrations and grievances toward D.R. surfaced and for about fifteen miles she shrieked and cried and cursed like a mad woman, and when D.R. just sat there not responding she became almost hysterical. At one point she started beating on him yelling, "You clutz, you bastard, answer me!"

D.R.'s response was to turn the radio on and tune in an Indianapolis talk show. "I don't know, I just don't feel very balanced," a man was saying.

Estelle snapped the radio off. With a final "I hate you!" she crawled through the bus onto the mattress in back and covered her head with a sleeping bag.

All weaver's books and supplies edited with Sarah Kahn (and Carole Beadle advising).

The Unicorn

Mail order only, The Unicorn offers a free, comprehensive and invaluable catalog of books for weavers and needle-workers. Only source for many of the titles listed. Books from all over the whole earth on hand-weaving, spinning, dyeing, loom-building, knitting, rugmaking, macramé, embroidery, tapestry, lace-making, knots and knotting, textile design. Newly revised and expanded catalog includes select titles in related fields: textile printing, batik, tie-dye, costume design, folk and primitive art and crafts, bead-work, color theory. Each book is well reviewed / catalog is thoroughly indexed / service is prompt and personal / books may be returned if not found suitable.

—Sarah Kahn

Catalog
$0.50

from:
The Unicorn
Box 645
Rockville, MD 20851

Byways in Handweaving

The book is concerned with rare weaving techniques and patterns from ancient Egypt & Peru, modern Guatemala, Scandinavia, the South Pacific, Atlas Mountains and various American Indian tribes. Most of the weaves are for narrow bands but many may be adapted for wider fabrics.

There has been a great resurgence of interest in both card-and inkle-weaving since this book was first published in 1954. Both sections include clear text, many pattern diagrams & fine color illustrations of finished pieces. The rest of the book is concerned with a number of other little-known techniques; "primitive" only in the aspect of being non-loom, or requiring only the simplest of materials. There are examples of twined weaving as practiced in many parts of the world as remote from one another as Persia, the Subarctic & the South Seas. A fascinating chapter on braiding & knotting includes a group of Indian, Egyptian, Chinese & Peruvian braids, belt-braiding, Osage braiding. Another section deals with some very subtle and beautiful belt-weaves of Peru, Estonia & Guatemala.

Included in the book are techniques ranging from those simple enough for a child or for use in occupational therapy to some rather difficult & intricate methods which should be quite stimulating to experienced weavers.

—Sarah Kahn

Byways in Handweaving
Mary Meigs Atwater
1954, 1967; 128 pp.

$7.95 postpaid

from:
The Macmillan Company
Front and Brown Streets
Riverside, Burlington County, N.J. 08075

or WHOLE EARTH CATALOG

Osage Braiding

Weaving is for Anyone

Rich & inspiring, the theme & theory of this book is that anyone can weave on almost anything. Included in one volume are instructions for making simple and inexpensive looms and a variety of techniques for weaving on these looms. There are directions for looms made of cardboard, picture frames, boards & nails, boxes; there are round looms, bag & backstrap looms. There is a discussion of Peruvian, Chilkat, Salish, Navajo, Ghanaian & Coptic weaving & beautiful illustrations of these techniques and the looms on which they are woven. There are illustrated definitions of weaving terms. A chapter entitled "Weaving from Nature" suggests that a walk in the garden or woods can yield some fine weft material. Over 230 drawings & photos. A good general sourcebook, full of both turn-on and good practical information.
—Sarah Kahn

[Suggested by Ann Marie Goldstein]

Weaving is for Anyone
Jean Wilson
1967; 144 pp.

$8.95 postpaid

from:
Van Nostrand-Reinhold Co.
450 West 33rd Street
New York, N. Y. 10001

or WHOLE EARTH CATALOG

Sarah's Pick

Byways in Handweaving, Mary M. Atwater. 1954, 67. $7.95
New Key to Weaving, Mary E. Black $12.
Creative Design in Wall Hangings, Lili Blumenau $6.95
The Techniques of Rug Weaving, Peter Collingwood $17.50
A Handweaver's Pattern Book, M.P. Davison $8.75
Textiles of Ancient Peru and Their Techniques $25.00
    (probably the most beautiful book ever made on weaving)
Warp and Weft from Tibet, William A. King. $3.50
Navajo Shepherd and Weaver, Gladys A. Reichard $8.00 (1936, 68)
Spider Woman, Gladys A. Reichard $8.00 (1934, 68)
Weaving is for Anyone, Jean Wilson $8.50
Shuttle Craft Guild Monographs by Harriet Tidball: (Craft & Hobby can furnish list)
The Textile Arts, Verla Birrell $12.95
Your Handspinning, Elsie Davenport $3.95
Dye Plants & Dyeing——A Handbook, Brooklyn Botanic Gardens $1.65
Hopi Dyes, Mary-Russell F. Colton $2.50
The Dye Pot, Mary F. Davidson $2.00
Crewel Embroidery, Erica Wilson $7.50

All available from The Unicorn

$6.00 /yr (quarterly)

from:
Handweaver & Craftsman Inc.
220 5th Ave
New York, N.Y. 10001

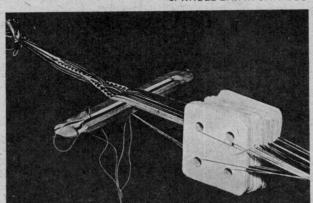

Card Weaving Cards
$2.75 /100 cards

from:
Lily Mills Co.
Shelby, N. C. 28150

or WHOLE EARTH CATALOG

Handweaver and Craftsman

the lapidary journal of weaverdom
lotta different yarn companies and loommakers advertise in this quarterly, piles of books are mentioned. downhome articles by people doing weaving emphasis on natural things. fine forum.

—jd
[Suggested by Sandra Koechin]

Handweaver & Craftsman

Handweaver and Craftsman
Harriet Hagerty, editor

$9.00 per year (bimonthly)
$1.75 single copies

from:
Handweaver and Craftsman Inc.
220 5th Ave.
New York, N.Y. 10001

New Key to Weaving

A one-book weaver's library. A comprehensive textbook covering all aspects of loom-weaving. Incredibly packed. Section on tapestry weaving alone is worth the cost of the book.
—Sarah Kahn

[Suggested by Victoria Becker]

New Key to Weaving
Mary Black
1945, 1949, 1957; 573 pp.

$12.00 postpaid

from:
The Bruce Publishing Co.
c/o Macmillan
866 Third Ave.
New York. N.Y. 10022
or WHOLE EARTH CATALOG

TEXTILE GUIDEBOOK

The trademark/generic class/description/source for nearly 2000 man-made fibers are listed alphabetically in this informative guidebook. These fibers are also listed generically as to group, by trademark & by source. Textured yarns are also included. The third edition of this guidebook is bound in a handy flexible cover.

Guidebook to Man-made Textile Fibers by Adeline Dembeck, 6 by 9, 345 pages, $11.00. The United Piece Dye Works, 111 W. 40 Street, New York 10018.

The Techniques of Rug Weaving

Here at last and it's ALL here! Like some fantastic teacher—gives you just what you need to know—being thorough, comprehensive, scholarly, inspiring (I'M GOING TO WEAVE A RUG!) Over 400 lucid diagrams, 174 illustrations, only 4 in color but how much can one ask? Detailed coverage of every aspect of rug weaving from fundamentals to most advanced & formerly obscure techniques; from ancient methods to Collingwood's own inventive technical developments. As further application beyond rugs can be made for most of the weaves, this is a book for all weavers. Formidable!

—Sarah Kahn

The Techniques of Rug Weaving

Peter Collingwood
1968; 480 pp.

$17.50 postpaid

from
Watson-Guptill Publications
165 West 46th St.
New York, N.Y. 10036

or WHOLE EARTH CATALOG

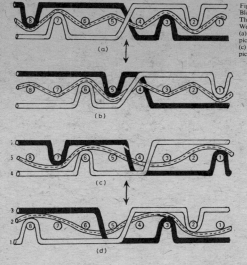

PETER COLLINGWOOD
The Techniques of Rug Weaving

The Mannings

Good source of rug materials (sturdy Swedish backing, various yarns, etc.), also weaving and macrame equipment and materials.

—SB

Catalog

$0.50

from:
The Mannings
RD 2
East Berlin, Pa. 17316

Make Your Own Rug

You can weave a tough rug (see Peter Collingwood), or you can knot a tickly deep one. This simple book has basic Smyrna, Finnen, Rya techniques of rug knotting.

—SB

Make Your Own Rug
Dietrich Kirsch, Jutta Kirsch-Korn
1969; 56 pp.

OUT OF PRINT

Watson-Guptill Publications, Inc.
165 W. 46th St.
New York, N.Y. 10036

Simple Smyrna Knot

For this time-saving knot you will need cut lengths of yarn 2-1/2 to 2-3/4 inches long. Lay the ends of one exactly together with finger and thumb and pull the loop over the latch hook.. (1) Then push the hook upwards under two cross-threads of the canvas (2).

Lay the ends of teh yearn over the latch into the hook and pull the hook downwards, which will make the eye close (3). When the ends of the yarn have been pulled right through the loop the knot is completed. Tighten it by pulling the ends of the yarn (4).

The photograph shows a row of this simple Smyrna knot. To make a square yard of rug reckon 40 to 45 hours of work. Dreher canvas is suitable for Smyrna technique.

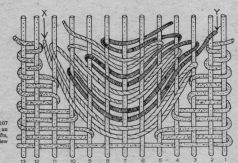

Fig. 293
Block Weaves based on Three-Weft Double-Faced Weaves.
(a) and (b) Cross-sections of picks in Fig. 292(a)
(c) and (d) Cross-sections of picks in Fig. 292(c)

Fig. 107 Kilim. Weaving an oval with two wefts, detailed view

Speed Tufting Tool

Dearest Earth,

I realize it ain't polite to turn someone on to a hooker——but I felt it my duty to do so.

You may have already heard of this device——but just in case ya ain't

I bought a rug hooker which finishes off a 2' x 3' carpet in about 4 hours in your own design, and in different lengths. And fer all those capitalists, a 2' x 3' rug can be made for under $5 & I've sold 'em for as much as $30! So.

The dojabber is a mere $11.95! Can you dig it? I didn't think so.

Check phone directory or write for name of store nearest you.

The Rug Crafters
3895 S. Main
Santa Ana, CA 92707

Dean Chapman
Sun Valley, Calif. 91352

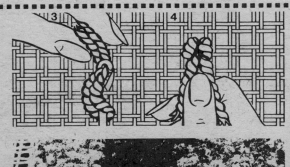

The Ruggery

Good assortment of backings, yarns, dyes, frames, hookers, slitters, and advice.

—SB
[Suggested by Bora Roka Jackson]

George Wells
The Ruggery
Glen Head, L.I., N.Y. 11545

Speed Hookers

All Speed Hookers work from the back. This reverses your design in the finished rug. Backing must be stretched on a frame for all speed hookers

Columbia Minerva Punch Needle, Postpaid $2.75

We use this Punch Needle with yarn only, but it is sometimes used with cloth strips. It is the most practical and versatile punch needle we know. Most of the rugs made at the Ruggery are made with this Punch Needle. Comes with 2 size points. Adjusts to give 10 different length loops from 3/8" to 7/8". Good for quiet sitdown work.

Instructions for making rugs or wall hangings with a Columbia Minerva Punch Needle. Diagrams. A booklet by George Wells, $1.00

Covers everything from threading the needle and spacing of stitches to backgrounds and finishing. With these instructions and no lessons you can make good rugs. Punch needles have proved to be the most popular method for "hooking" with yarn.

Susan Burr Shuttle Hooker, postpaid $5.25

Wooden handles——shaped like a guitar. Works better with "rags" than it does with yarn. It is not adjustable for height of loop. Rag loops approximately 3/8", yarn hooks slightly shorter.

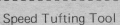

CINCINNATI

At the edge of Cincinnati D.R. pulled into a Gulf station and parked around the side by the tire rack. Since their argument the night before, and the cryptic statement over the radio by the guy who didn't feel very balanced, D.R. had been into balance as a concept. About to enter Cincinnati, he wanted to stop at the station and spend some money so his wealth would align with the inner grammatical logic of the city he was coming to. D.R. had lived in Cincinnati, and in the smaller towns north toward Dayton-- Middletown, Hamilton, Franklin, Miamisburg--the last ten years of his life, and yet this very day was the first time he had ever really flashed on the word Cincinnati. There he was, driving along, considering the concept of balance while Estelle slept furiously in the back, when suddenly the word "Cincinnati" popped up on a highway sign. Fantastic, D.R. thought.

Cin
Cin
Nat
I.

How balanced, how smooth the word Cincinnati. Both in form and content. Content equals sin two times, add one natty. Natty sin. Four vowels in Cincinnati, three i's pierced by a single a.

Cin
Cin
Nat
I.

Four syllables. Four vowels and four syllables, ten letters in the word all together. Four and four are eight, plus ten is eighteen. I've got eighteen dollars and eighty cents, an imbalance of eighty which it won't take me a jiffy to rectify if this old boy will wait on me.

"Excuse me," said D.R. "How much are those fuses there?" He was looking at a sign above a box of fuses that said, "Why be helpless when fuses blow? A few cents spent for a box of fuses will save you possible delay or danger later on."

"Do which?" said the attendant in a high, nasal, hillbilly whine. He was busy making coffee on a hotplate over by the roadmaps.

"Those fuses. How much are they?"

"Twenty cents apiece," said the attendant.

"Good," said D.R. "I'll take four."

The attendant picked out four fuses and stepped with them to the cash register, yawning as he rang them up. It was about five in the morning, barely sunrise. It was hard to tell if this was an all-night station or the start of a brand new business day.

As the attendant pecked the various keys, D.R. felt a deep sense of well-being glowing inside him. Eighty cents from eighteen eighty left eighteen exactly. How perfect, how balanced, how lovely the word *exactly*. Ex. Act. After the act. It reminded D.R. of the I Ching hexagram called After Completion, the one about the importance of tuning the flame beneath the kettle exactly right, so that it burns with a precise intensity. Precision, D.R. thought. Precision and intensity. Those are the keys.

"That'll be eighty-three cents," said the attendant, yawning again.

D.R. looked at him. "How much?"

"Eighty-three cents."

"Why the three cents?" D.R. asked, and when the attendant said sales tax D.R. thought: fucked in the ass by a tax.

D.R. was not enlightened by any of this experience, but it edged him a little further along the way.

Your Handspinning

THE book on handspinning.

The book commences with a discussion of wool & sheep, then come chapters devoted to sorting a fleece, learning to make a continuous yarn & the art of carding & spinning wool. There is an excellent section on the construction, use & maintenance of spinning wheels & hints on buying a wheel. There is information on the cultivation & preparation of flax, and the spinning of fibres such as silk, angora rabbit, camel & other animal hairs. There is a chapter on plying & the making of fancy yarns and a section devoted to the preparation of spun yarns for use——washing, bleaching, etc. The book concludes with a chapter on machine spun yarns: counts/ qualities & defects/ fibre identification. Illustrated with many line drawings. —SB

[Suggested by Victoria Becker]

Your Handspinning
Elsie Davenport
1953, 1964; 130 pp.

$4.25 postpaid

from:
Select Books
P. O. Box 626
Pacific Grove, CA 93950

or WHOLE EARTH CATALOG

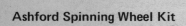

Dog Combings, etc.

Many dogs yield combings or clippings which can be spun into useful yarns by whichever method is best suited to the length and character of the fibres. Poodle clippings, for example, make a very pleasant "woollen" yarn while the lustre of Spaniel hair needs a worsted spin. The addition of a little oil prior to combing or carding may make spinning easier.

Combings or clippings should be stored until wanted in an air-tight container in a cool place, preferably with a moth deterrent such as paradichlorbenzine.

No instance of the use of cat's hair for spinning has ever come to light but it would be quite possible to spin combings of a fine haired Persian, especially carded with suitable wool. The author's experiments with a mixture of Siamese and camel are not to be recommended!

The Indian Spinner

If you are looking for an interesting new type of spinning wheel which is relatively inexpensive compared to the standard antique or new wheels, consider an "Indian Spinner". They are much easier to learn to spin on, especially if you can spin yarns with a spindle. The nicest feature is the ability to handle very thick yarns as well as the thin threads you get with a standard wheel. Its design is simple and functional, being similar (if you are familiar with the parts of a spinning wheel) to that of an enlarged "mother-of-all" of the standard wheel. The Bobbin holds a great amount of yarn. The spinner head can be attached to an old type treadle sewing machine or purchased with a wood treadle to match the spinner. The Spinner Head alone costs about $34, with a treadle base $68. These prices are for the plywood spinners; they also come in fancier woods at fancier prices. They are available through the Handcraft House, 110 West Esplanade, North Vancouver, B.C., Canada. They publish a small catalogue for $.50.

[Suggested and reviewed by Carole Beadle]

Ashford Spinning Wheel Kit

I thought I tell you something about the Ashford Spinning Wheel Kit. I am a "spinner" from way back and this wheel—— it took about 6 months to get here——is just great, well balanced. It is easy to put together and finish. Even the inexperienced spinner will have few problems with it. I am zipping off the skeins like nothing even to real fine weaving threads.

By the way it is quite worthwhile to wait for the items from New Zealand. The price alone Spinning Wheel $57 as compared to old or new ones here none under a $100.

[Reviewed by Ursula Schramm]

Ashford Handicrafts Ltd.
P.O. Box 12 - Rakaia
Canterbury, New Zealand.

Note: Delivery time only 3 months now. Write first for current literature.

—SB

Handspinning

Another THE book on handspinning.

A dense well-done technical up-to-date treatment of the subject. Customize your yarn with nubs, slubs, partially blended colors, heart. If you recall, this was Ghandi's approach to revolution.

—SB

Handspinning—Art and Technique
Allen Fannin
1970; 208 pp.

$12.50 postpaid

from:
Van Nostrand-Reinhold Books
450 W. 33rd St.
New York, N.Y. 10001

or WHOLE EARTH CATALOG

Garnetting. The use of previously spun yarns, which have been broken up or garnetted, as it is called, is another way to design yarns with texture. This method is generally not employed by handspinners, though it no doubt should be. The system of using fiber that has been reprocessed or garnetted from spun yarns, and then respun is primarily used in a mill situation for producing lower-quality goods. However, as a design device, there is much potential for the handspinner.

The flyer wheel. (A) stock (B) legs (C) treadle (D) pitman (E) drive wheel (F) drive wheel posts (G) drive band (H) flyer assembly (I) tension adjustment.

Made-Well Spinning Wheel

This company is run, I am told, by an Indian tribe. It is located in a very small town in Canada. The company doesn't have a phone; I tried to call once. They make excellent quality products.

Spinning Wheel ea $52.

Cards $7 a pair

Carding machine (crank model) ea $57.

All prices F.O.B. Sifton, or, postage extra.

These are approximate Canadian prices. They are subject to change periodically. There is also duty when having them sent into the U.S., but I consider the wheels and cards of better quality than any I have seen and worked with. The prices (even with duty) are less than wheels manufactured in the U.S. They have no outlets the wheels must be ordered direct.

[Reviewed by Diane Senders. Suggested by Brucie Adams]

Made-Well Manufacturing Company
Sifton, Manitoba
Canada

For low prices, high quality spinning wheels, also check Swedish suppliers, p. 169.

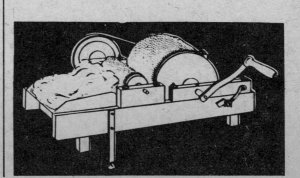

The first fibers of the fiber supply caught to the yarn.

Vegetable Dyeing

It has 144 pages 6 x 9 & 4 pages of color charts, a bibliography, a very handy reference chart and index. What I like about it is that it is listed by colors, gives more information on the process of dyeing, when to gather, how to gather, store and make fast vegetable dyes than any other book I've seen including the Botanical Garden's book, and the reference chart is very handy——

[Reviewed by Anne Popperwell]

Vegetable Dyeing
Alma Lesch
1971; 144 pp.

$7.95 postpaid

from:
Watson-Guptill Publications, Inc.
2160 Patterson Street
Cincinnati, OH 45214

or WHOLE EARTH CATALOG

Blackberries with tin mordant on cotton

Cochineal with chrome mordant on wool

Elderberries with alum mordant on wool

Logwood with alum mordant on wool

DYE SUBSTANCE	APPROPRIATE MORDANT	COLOR RANGE	SUITABLE FIBER	COLOR FASTNESS
Acorns	Alum	Tans	Wool, silk	Excellent
Alkanet roots	No mordant	Gray-blues	Wool	Good
	Acetic acid	Red-purple-browns	Wool	Good
	Alum	Red-tans	All natural fibers	Good to fair
Annatto	Alum	Oranges	Wool, silk	Fair
Annatto and red onion skins	Tin	Dark yellows	Wool, silk	Good to fair
Barberry plant	Alum	Tans	All natural fibers	Excellent
	Blue vitriol	Greens	All natural fibers	Excellent
	Copperas	Dark greens	Wool	Excellent
	Copperas	Blacks and grays	Jute	Excellent

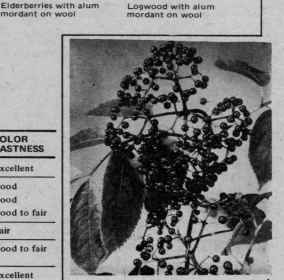

Fruits of the native elderberry (*Sambucus nigra*) will give lilac blue with an alum mordant, violet purple with chrome. The leaves alone give various tones of yellow, according to the mordant.

Dye Plants and Dyeing

This book I consider about the best that is available on its subject and would make an excellent basic handbook for the beginner. It contains historical information as well as the basic steps to dyeing, recipes, and articles about dye plants from various regions and countries. So, no matter what part of the country you live in, you will find a variety of plants and recipes which you would be able to use. There is enough information in this book which should enable you to start your own dyeing and end up with satisfactory results . . . which is not true of all natural dye books. The one difficulty in using it, however, is that there is no index.

[Reviewed by Carole Beadle]

Dye Plants and Dyeing
100 pp.

$1.50 postpaid

from:
Brooklyn Botanic Garden
Brooklyn, N. Y. 11225

or WHOLE EARTH CATALOG

How to prepare the dye solution by chopping, then soaking and boiling the plant parts, and straining them out before adding their color to the dye bath, is told on pages 13 and 14. Briefly, here are the basic directions for the actual dyeing of wool:

Have wool clean and moist.

For each pound, use 4 to 4½ gallons of dye bath.

Enter wool when dye bath is lukewarm.

Heat slowly to simmering point and let simmer half an hour (longer if required), moving wool gently back and forth.

If dye bath gets low, lift wool, add hot water, mix in well, and return wool to pot.

Rinse dyed wool first in nearly boiling water, then in several waters of gradually lowered temperatures.

When rinsing water is clear, squeeze moisture out of wool and dry in shade.

Dyes

The best are Ciba Dyes (Cibalan for wool, Chlorantine for rayon, cotton, linen). Some suppliers in eastern U.S. carry these. Putnam and Cushing are good also.

For _natural dyes_, the finest supplier is:

Comak Chemicals Ltd.
Swinton Works
Moon St.
London N1
England
[Suggested by Carole Beadle]

and the next best on natural dyes:

C. D. Fitz Harding-Bailey
15 Dutton St.
Bankstown, NSW 2200
Australia
[Suggested by Memory Holloway]

FH-B also carries wool, mohair, and weaving and spinning equipment. "No importation formalities."

Natural (Organic) Dyes	Free airmail price list upon request.	Packs
Natural Indigo		2 ozs.
Fine Ruby Cochineal (rare)		2 ozs.
Carmine Cochineal		2 ozs.
Madder		4 ozs.
Weld		4 ozs.
Victorian Walnut		4 ozs.
Cutch		4 ozs.
Logwood		4 ozs.
Red Sandalwood		4 ozs.

Procion (pronounced with a 'sh') dyes, with us only since 1956, are popular with some for being bright, simple, and fast. The manufacturer/dealer in New York has inspired complaints by short-changing on weight.

—SB

Pylam Products Co., Inc.
95-10 218th St.
Queens Village, N.Y. 11429

Note: Ms. Ella I. Roewer, Sales Manager, says dyes are sold strictly by weight in the one pound and up sizes. Introductory kits containing two oz. jars are filled by volume.

Fezandie and Sperrle

colors,
analine colors,
artists colors,
batik colors,
cement, even concrete colors.
tie dye your sidewalks.

—jd
[Suggested by Janet Sherman]

Catalog

free

from:
Fezandie and Sperrie, Inc.
103 Lafayette Street
New York, New York 10013

Try Tintex

Larry Koenigsberg's letter on pg. 7 of the January Supplement concerning Rit dyes are my sentiments exactly. A while back I dyed a T-shirt in Rit dyes. The colours were O.K. till I washed it and wow did it ever fade. I've found Tintex dyes to be more reliable — they hold their colour when washed and are brighter to begin with. They work great on cottons (even if it's stay press material), silks and linen. Tintex dyes are quite a bit cheaper than the Procion dyes Larry suggested (35¢ for a 2-1/8 oz. box), and due to the fact dyeing has become so popular they now come in a wide variety of brilliant colours (now one doesn't have to mix colours as one had to produce brighter colours). This saves time and money as well.

There are some of the new colours that I've found are exceedingly good:

Butterscotch
Tiger Lily — a brilliant orange
Cranberry Red
Plum — a beautiful purple

If you don't want your colours to run or fade when you wash them put them in vinegar or very salty water before you wash them. I've found it helps a great deal.

Marc Silberman
Indianapolis, Indiana

Wide World of Herbs

natural dyes
a complete selection,
cheap.
had trouble finding annatto seeds?

—jd
[Suggested by Michael Wells]

Catalog

free

from:
Wide World of Herbs Ltd.
10 St. Catherine St. East
Montreal, Canada

	For Dyeing Fabrics 5 lbs.		
	per lb.	1 lb.	½ lb.
Indigo roots	2.00	2.15	1.20
Madder roots	2.40	2.55	1.30
Cochineal	6.50	6.65	3.40
Alkanet roots	2.20	2.35	1.20
Logwood chips	1.25	1.40	.80
Cudbear	6.50	6.65	3.40
Quercitron bark (oak)	1.25	1.40	.80
Black walnut hulls	1.25	1.40	.80
Black walnut leaves	1.25	1.40	.30
Red santalwood chips	1.80	1.95	1.10
Henna leaves	1.40	1.55	.85

THE COACH'S PANTS

D.R. didn't feel like going out to his sister's place till things got a little more balanced, so they drove into downtown Cincinnati and parked around the corner from the Greyhound bus station. They figured that a cheap place to eat, and besides that, D.R. wanted to change clothes and wash up some. He didn't want to disguise himself in cleanliness for his sister's sake, and her family's, but he didn't want to scare anybody either. He looked pretty freaky for Cincinnati. He and Estelle had been drawing stares since the streets began to fill with people going to work. What D.R. really wanted was for his appearance to not be a factor one way or another. That wasn't very likely, considering his hair, but maybe a change into more or less straight clothes would at least keep the whole how-you-look thing at some low plane out of everybody's way. If that could happen he figured he stood a good chance of bringing this day into balance after all.

D.R. fished around in his duffel bag for the shirt and pants he'd bought at the Goodwill in California. The shirt was gray with little blue pin-stripes up and down it. It had wide, french cuffs and a button-down collar, although when he put it on he didn't button it down because the button on the left side was gone. The pants were brown, frayed at the pockets and shiny at the ass and knees. They'd probably been part of a suit worn by the manager of a discount store, or perhaps by a small town high school coach about to leave athletics and go into administration. Probably he coached about four sports. Leaving it to go into administration would mean going back to college, of course, and finishing up the old M.A. Probably he would do it in summer terms. Ten or twelve summer terms, ten or twelve more football, basketball, baseball and track seasons and he'd be all set. Maybe he would even get a new suit somewhere along the way and build his wardrobe again, after the loss of his brown pants.

Suddenly it occurred to D.R. that the reason the pants had wound up in the Goodwill on sale for twenty cents was that the coach had died. A heart attack, most likely, maybe cancer. D.R. didn't like to think about the coach being dead. The thought of him being dead put things out of balance again. To keep from thinking about the coach D.R. read the graffiti on the walls of the toilet stall as he rolled his old dirty clothes up in a wad.

Suck on this one, Hard Hat America, someone had written in ink. I'm over thirty, college educated, liberal, have long hair, and make $45,000 a year.

Next to it someone had replied, in crayon: When they aren't sucking a big dick, all Long Hairs are skin divers for Roto-Rooter.

Above the toilet paper container someone had scratched with a knife: If you've got it all together, what's that all around it?

And then as D.R. was leaving the stall he read on the door: There are times when the wolves are silent and the moon is howling.

That one sort of got him. He stood there looking at it a long time, wondering if it would make things more balanced or less for him to write something on the wall. Finally he took a stub of pencil out of his pocket and wrote: I am a balance freak in a dead football coach's pants.

Schacht Looms

Would you please consider the inclusion, in your spring catalog, of the weaving equipment being manufactured by the Schacht Spindle Co., 1708 Walnut Street, Boulder, CO 80302.

As a long-time weaver, and author of weaving books, I can recommend the four harness loom. It is especially helpful because of the portability, and possibility of a long warp. This equipment is very well made.

Enclosed, brochures and a photograph of three of the pieces of equipment made by these people.

Thank you.

Very truly yours,

Jean Wilson

P.S. Am also enclosing a brochure and announcement of my first book, Weaving Is For Anyone, *and the second one, due out any week now——*Weaving is Fun. *A third book is now at the publishers, and a fourth one is being prepared. (Book 3,* Weaving Is Creative, *all of the Weaver-controlled weaves.)*

Wind Bell Inkle

May I pass on to you and your readers some information regarding inkle belt weaving which I found very helpful? The Wind Bell Inc., 5714 Kennett Pike, Centerville, Delaware stocks an American style (table model) inkle loom for $10. Having had friends who have paid up to $30 for inkle looms, I was rather dubious about this model, but have completed the 18th belt on it and find it outstanding.

There is also a wonderful little book entitled Weaving Inkle Bands, *by Harriet Tidball, ($4.00, Craft and Hobby Book Service, P.O. Box 626, Pacific Grove, California 93950) which illustrates in easy to understand fashion the various patterns one can use in weaving these belts.*

Carol D. Westfall
Baltimore, Maryland

Katy and Don Dawson have three dozen looms left — cut, drilled, kiln-dried Douglas fir, all necessary hardware and twine for heddles. This inkle loom is for weaving narrow bands or belts. It's a great frame for cardweaving too, 31" long, 12" high, and 10" wide. $10 plus postage ($2 west of the Rockies, $3 between the Rockies and the Mississippi, $4 east of the Mississippi). Also, complete instructions on building your own for $.50 and a stamped, self-addressed envelope.

Dawson Inkle

from:
Katy & Don Dawson
379 Hull Ave.
San Jose, CA 95125

Nelson Waist Loom

For weaving up to 24" wide, do it in your lap with a backstrap and save. 13" loom $6.00, 18" loom $12.75, 25" loom $12.00.

Robert C. Nelson
R.R. 2, Box 540
Newport, N.H. 03773

Good Karma Loom

We're writing to turn you on to a hand-loom——the 18" Good Karma Continuous Warp 4-Harness Loom with Tension Adjustment. This is a superior hand-loom, very high quality and low cost. It's hand-crafted and hand oil-rubbed, obviously made with loving care. It's constructed of hardwood members pegged together with wood pegs to create a very rigid, esthetically pleasing and extremely versatile hand-loom. The only metal necessary is two wing nuts on the tension adjustment bar.

This loom may be used for controlled tabby or four-harness pattern weaving, Rya, tapestry, lace weaves, rug making and other weaving where a reed is not necessary. The warp goes directly on the loom. Heddles are attached last and may be changed with ease. This loom weaves fabric up to 18 inches wide with warps either four feet, seven feet or ten feet long. It comes with complete instructions and a 20 inch tapered hardwood shuttle.

It is easy to operate, making it ideal for beginners, yet offers a myriad of possibilities in weaving complex large pieces. This loom is for the whole family. Your kids will want to weave too——ours are doing quite well. They have their own loom now so we can have a turn, yet despite the use, the quality is such that they'll be in use in the family for years.

The price is $30.00 postpaid from Neal Patterson; Good Karma Looms; 440 W. 4th; Chadron, NB 69337. Neal guarantees it completely——if anyone is dissatisfied, they can return the loom undamaged and postpaid within a month after purchase, and he'll give a complete refund.

He does other good things with looms, too, including a 9 inch Super Inkle which we especially like. His future plans include floor looms and traditional style spinning wheels. He's really open to new ideas and wants to supply what the people need. I'm sure he'd send you any information you want, but you might enclose a self-addressed stamped envelope, as he personally handles all inquiries.

Up here in the Colorado mountains we've been learning to spin wool on a hand spindle and are beginning to size up the dogs and the goats for shearing!

Sher Herdt and Dale Kellogg
Boulder, Colorado

Pioneer Loom

A breakthrough. Table looms 10", 20", or 25"; available with 2, 4, 6 or 8 or 12 harnesses. A unique warping system which saves time and permits great flexibility in design. Since the heddles & reed are open, and the frame is extendable, the warp can be one continuous thread taken from a ball of yarn. The usual warping sequence is simplified into one operation that takes only minutes to complete. No extra equipment is needed; the loom itself can displace warping board, lease sticks, hook & raddle.

Because the warp can be one continuous thread (or several continuous threads used alternately), design can occur spontaneously without previous exacting calculations. Warp threads can be adjusted from one dent to another & from one heddle to another even after weaving has begun.

Why haven't looms always been made like this?

Prices range from $109.50 for 10" 2-harness "Sampler" to $229.50 for 25" 12-harness "Super."

[Suggested by Rose Sargant. Reviewed by Sarah Kahn]

Loom or additional information from:

Northwest Looms
Route 4, Box 4872
Bainbridge Island, WA 98110

If you're thinking about getting a loom, this is a good introduction to what that means. And if you're poor but crafty, you can move right into a substantial two-harness with these diagrams and some work.

—SB

To Build or Buy a Loom
Harriet Tidball
1968; 38 pp.

No longer available

from:
Craft & Hobby
Box 626
Pacific Grove, CA 93950

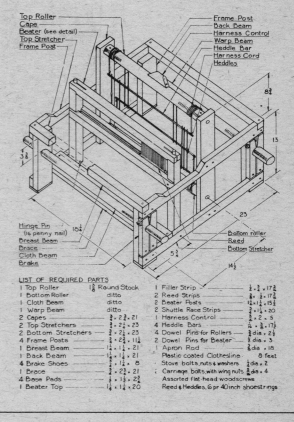

LIST OF REQUIRED PARTS

1 Top Roller	1½ Round Stock		1 Filler Strip	¾ x 2 x 17¼
1 Bottom Roller	ditto		2 Reed Strips	⅜ x 1 x 20
1 Cloth Beam	ditto		2 Beater Posts	1¼ x 1¼ x 15¼
1 Warp Beam	ditto		2 Shuttle Race Strips	⅜ x 1 x 20
2 Capes	¾ x 2½ x 21		1 Harness Control	½ x 2 x 5
2 Top Stretchers	¾ x 2½ x 23		4 Heddle Bars	¼ dia x 17½
2 Bottom Stretchers	¾ x 2½ x 23		4 Dowel Pins for Rollers	⅜ dia x 2½
4 Frame Posts	1¼ x 1¼ x 11¼		2 Dowel Pins for Beater	⅜ dia x 3
1 Breast Beam	1¼ x 1¼ x 21		1 Apron Rod	⅜ dia x 18
1 Back Beam	1¼ x 1¼ x 21		Plastic coated Clothesline	8 feet
4 Brake Shoes	¾ x 1¼ x 8		Stove bolts, nuts & washers	¾ dia x 2
1 Brace	¾ x 2½ x 21		Carriage bolts with wing nuts	¾ dia x 4
4 Base Pads	¾ x 1½ x ⅜		Assorted flat head woodscrews	
1 Beater Top	1¼ x 1¼ x 20		Reed & Heddles, 6 pr 40inch shoestrings	

Swearingen Loom Kit

A kit for a full-size tapestry loom that weaves up to 2' x 6'. The kit with string hole & slot heddle is $17.50, with rigid hole and slot heddle is $25. Or you can get just the detailed plans for $5.

—SB

John Swearingen
P.O. Box 153
Ashland, Oregon 97520

Additional loom sources suggested by Jerome Skuba:

Handcrafters
521 West Brown Street
Waupun, Wisconsin 53863

Norwood Loom Company
Box 272
Baldwin, Michigan 49304

Bailey Manufacturing Company
118 Lee Street
Lodi, Ohio 44254

15" Pioneer "Designer" model with 8 harnesses

Gilmore Looms

. . .Lastly, you are advertising LeClerc Looms, which are not the best, merely the most advertised. I am an experienced weaver and have woven on most brands. I heartily recommend GILMORE for anyone who is actually interested in weaving, rather than just playing-like. They are less expensive, better made, and much more efficient both for set-up and during weaving. The harness frames lift right out for quick heddle changes between weaving projects, a unique warp advance system is used, the rising shed is sure and versatile, workmanship is unsurpassed. When speed is important these features are vitally important. I have an 8-harness 46" very heavy rigid Gilmore ($350) [or compact $315]. LeClerc's comparable model Nilart 8-harness 45" is $457 (!) and inferior. Grok on that and send for a brochure: Mr. E. E. Gilmore, Gilmore Looms, 1032 North Broadway, Stockton, California 95205.

Truely,
Don & Mikal Deese
Vancouver, B.C.

Gilmore

40" 4-harness compact rigid loom, $360.00.
Delivery in late 1975 and in 1976. Waiting time now close to 30 months.

E. E. Gilmore
1032 North Broadway
Stockton, CA 95205

Macomber Ad-a-Harness

32" 10 harness

L. W. Macomber
166 Essex Street
Saugus, Massachusetts

Newcomb

Free Catalog
45" 4-harness, $230.
FOB Davenport
Newcomb Loom Co.
Davenport, Iowa 52808

Loom shipped crated approximately 12 weeks after receipt of order.

[Suggested by Mrs. Terise A. Schaffner]

Lorellyn

After shopping for a floor loom at a decent price I've come to the conclusion that making one is the only cheap way out. However, an alternative might be a product of Lorellyn Weavers who are located near Grass Valley, California. Mr. Crandall makes a quality loom at about half the price of many others I looked at. He is a good conversationalist and loves to answer weaving problem questions if you drop in. Go pick up your loom and learn a lot. Crandall has been into weaving for way over 30 years.

14 inch, two harness table model	No longer available
20 inch, four harness floor model	$70.00 (stained dark),
	$75.00 (natural finish)
30 inch, four harness floor model	$90.00 (stained dark),
	$95.00 (natural wood)

Prices are F.O.B. Chicago Park, California. Crating charges run $5.50 to $6.00.

Free brochure:
Lorellyn Weavers
Box 56
Chicago Park, CA 95712

Kam
Nevada City, CA

Looms From Sweden

These are fine looms that are cheaper than equivalent looms on this continent. Cheaper, including shipping and customs (there seems to be no tariff catagory applied directly to looms so persuade customs officer to classify it as a sewing machine which is the lowest rate conceivably applicable. If he's nice he'll do it automatically). Not only does this firm offer good quality equipment:——these looms are built in more or less the traditional swedish loom design (weaving having been long a prime activity in Sweden); and with the high degree of wood craftmanship Sweden is noted for (in case you didn't know, Sweden is noted for wood craftsmanship, along with all else) Therefore they are damned good to look at & just have sit around when not being worked upon (maximum wood/minimum metal). Also available are the standard weaving accessories: warping racks, etc. and spinning wheels and tapestry looms. Profusely illustrated catalog available——specify English supplement or know Swedish.

Glimåkra Västvols Fabriken
Glimåkra
Sweden

Carole Beadle says an absolutely prime source of all manner of Swedish weaving equipment is:

Gunnar Andersson
Vävskedsverkstad
792 00 Mora
Sweden

Catalog $2.00
Cash or Check

Mainland Cottage Crafts

I was dismayed to read in your March supplement about the unhappy experience of Karl Smiley in his search for a loom; and I thought some information about a loom designed and made in Vancouver might be of help to him and some of your other readers. The maker of the loom is H.C. Harris, of North Vancouver, B.C., Canada, and the looms can be ordered from Handcraft House. 110 West Esblanade, North Vancouver. The table model, 22 inch, 4 harness, sells for $78.00. Anyone living out of Vancouver would have to add shipping costs which I have been advised would not exceed $10.00, and persons living in the U.S.A. would have to find out about customs, but even with these added costs the loom is a bargain, sturdy, attractive and well designed.

Jean Mallinson
West Vancouver, B.C.

TERMINAL

As D.R. came out of the men's room he was flashing on the word <u>terminal.</u> T—E—R—M—I—N—A—L. I am in a terminal. The end of a line. Three vowels, an e, an i and an a. And three syllables, three very neat and pungent syllables each with a vowel nestled in its middle like a jewel. How balanced. How very balanced is the word terminal, in content as well as form. At a terminal people arrive and depart, they begin new journeys even as they are ending old ones. Both things happen at a terminal, it goes both ways. It's like calling graduation <u>commencement.</u> Commencing as you end. Indeed, because you end. Like living because you die. That's a very religious idea. Bus terminals are very religious places. Look at this room. A waiting room. People gathering in off the streets to wait together for the next thing in their lives. A place to come and wait. Waiting as a form of worship, sitting in these pews. Estelle is there in a pew. She could very well be praying. Praying and waiting, waiting and praying, how balanced, how even.

I wonder if she'll like my outfit.

"How do you like my outfit?" D.R. asked Estelle.

He had come up from her blind side, down the lane between the rows of pews, and his voice startled her and made her jump. She looked around at him, and smiled. But it was a feeble smile. Estelle seemed confused. Then D.R. noticed there were tears in her eyes. He sat down and put his arm around her and asked her what was wrong.

Estelle shrugged his arm away. "Nothing's wrong," she said.

"But you're crying."

"I'm not crying," said Estelle.

"But you are, honey. I see the tears in your eyes."

"Please don't say I'm crying when I'm not," said Estelle. "I'm all right."

"But honey . . . "

"Oh!" Estelle exclaimed angrily. And she got to her feet and moved several seats away.

D.R. followed her and tried to put his arm around her again.

"Estelle, something's wrong . . ."

"You're <u>hassling</u> me is what's wrong!" Estelle turned to look D.R. in the face then, and when she did the tears spilled over and she really began to cry. She looked awfully sad to D.R. then, quite weak and helpless and worn down, and he wanted more than ever to take her in his arms. But the same pleading that had been in her voice was in her eyes now. She truly wanted to be left alone. D.R. leaned back in his seat and gazed around the room. A minute or two later he leaned over and whispered that he would be right back. Then he got up and walked to the row of telephones by the wall on the far side of the room.

Condon Woolen Mills

Excellent source of high quality 100% virgin wool yarn available in broad range of colors and sizes for use in weaving, knitting, crocheting, rug hooking, afghans. Yarn sizes include 1-ply single for weaving and knitting fine garments, 2-ply fine & medium, 3-ply, and 5-ply bulky for rug hooking, heavy sweaters. Of special interest to color-fiends: Condon offers several yarn colors which are not to be found anywhere else. Service is good—West Coast orders usually arrive in a week. Prices including duty are $3/lb natural colors, $3.20/lb dyed.

—Sarah Khan

Color cards

free

from:
William Condon & Sons Woolen Mills
P. O. Box 129
Charlottetown, P.E.I.
CANADA

Lily Mills

Good yarns.

Lily Mills Company
Shelby, North Carolina 28150

Art. 814—Lily Rug Weave Yarn

Fast Colors

Skeins — Approx. 80 Yds. — PRICE 37¢ PER SKEIN

1 White	22 New Orange	62 Emerald Green
2 Black	26 Lt. Blue	70 Lavender
3 Cream	28 Delft Blue	75 Purple
4 Natural	29 Dark Blue	86 Lt. Gray
10 Yellow	36 Turquoise	87 Gray
11 Canary	41 Salmon Rose	90 Beige
12 Chartreuse	46 Rose Pink	95 Red
16 Flamingo	47 Lt. Pink	105 Wine
17 Bright Gold	55 Lt. Green	120 Brown
18 Antique Gold	58 Hunter Green	124 Dk. Brown
20 Orange	59 Dk. Green	129 Rust
	61 Med. Green	171 Avocado

More Yarns

Knitting, Weaving and Crochet Yarns

Someplace, 2990 Adeline Street, Berkeley, has 28 beautiful rainbow colors of pure wool as well as mill ends (good value), odd lots, macrame embroidery and weaving supplies. Send $.50 for a sample chart of standard stock colors. New emphasis is on bobbin lace-making . . . they have a book Bobbin Lace, the twisting of cords. Also a 24" x 30" pine tapestry loom with automatic shed-changing feature, ready-to-assemble, $7.50.

Jeanie Darlington
Mirando, Calif.

Icelandic Yarn

At about 1/2 the price sold for in this country——if you can get it. For weaving and knitting. Exceedingly warm, soft, and durable. Hand washed, carded, and spun natural (undyed) wool. In six shades (code Nos for ordering appended):

White	Farve 54	Pärti 145
Light grey	56	2
Med. grey	57	47
Rusty brown	66	275
Tan	53	56
Dark brown	52	244

The color of the wool is the color of the sheep. Which is a nice thought.

Name & address:
Rammagerdin
Hafnar Straeti 5 & 17
Reyk Javik
Iceland

CUM Yarn Samples

Though one can stockpile free & usually mediocre yarn catalogs, $3 sent to CUM brings a large binder filled with sample-cards of handweaving yarns of finest quality, large color range, yet cheaper than dime-store knitting worsted.

CUM is now set up to handle U.S. orders; their catalog/price list is in English, gives price per pound in dollars, unlike other European yarn houses. Samples include 1 & 2-ply woolen yarn, rug, tapestry & knitting yarns, worsted, cotton & linen yarns, rug warps, twine. All yarns are mothproofed; prices average less than $3/lb. for yarns of high quality, esthetically and structurally. Delivery time approx. 6 weeks by ship, less than 2 weeks by air.

—Sarah Khan

Catalog & samples

$3.00 postpaid

from:
CUM Textile Industries, Ltd.
Römersgade 5
1362 Copenhagen K
Denmark

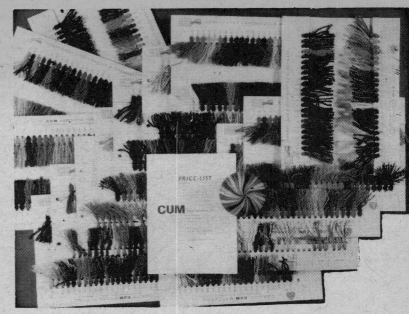

Yarns

You may be interested in the following yarn manufacturers for the Whole Earth Catalog or whoever can use them.

Countryside Handweavers, Inc.
Box 1225
Mission, Kansas 66222

Swiss goatshair, cowhair, swiss linens, Swedish rug yarns (wool). Beautiful yarns, high quality. Will send samples and prices.

Frederick J. Fawcett, Inc.
129 South Street
Boston, Mass. 02111

Beautiful linens, all weights, natural or dyed (the natural dyes very well). Will supply samples & prices. Very good quality.

Multiple Fabric Company
Dudley Hill
Bradford, 4, England

All beautiful yarns . Wool, camel hair, mohair (heavy weight) horse hair. Really fine yarns. Will send samples & prices.

Briggs & Little Woolen Mill, Ltd.
York Mills, N.B. Canada

Weaving & knitting wools, good quality——natural wools dye very well——also may order color yarns. Will send samples & prices.

Craft Yarns of Rhode Island, Inc.
603 Mineral Spring Ave.
Pawtucket, Rhode Island 02862
(Formerly Troy Yarn)

All beautiful yarns, wool & synthetic. These yarns have fantastic colors. Will send samples (25 cents each) and prices. Linens, loop mohair, mohair, etc.

Mexiskeins
c/o Sharon Murfin
1741 Allston Way
Berkeley, Calif. 94703

Handmade wools——all beautiful but very expensive from this supplier. Will send sample cards & prices.

The Mannings Creative Crafts
East Berlin, Pa. 17316

They sell seconds from other manufacturers—also have a good book list and other supplies—will send everything you need. Good prices on yarns. Samples available for $.50.

Pat Eckard
Hickory, North Carolina

Four suppliers of wool and spinning equipment, heard from at the last minute.

Colonial Textiles
The Sheldon's
2604 Cranbrook
Ann Arbor, Michigan 48104

Greentree Ranch Wools
Route 3, Box 461
Loveland, Colorado 80537

Great Lakes Wool Growers Corp.
901 Sentry Drive
Waukesha, Wisconsin 53186

Yarn Primitives
Box 1013-C
Weston, Connecticut 06880

Japanese Yarns and Threads

Very good, very cheap; beautiful samples. Embroidery primarily.

[Suggested by Sarah Kahn]

Olympus Thread Mfg. Co. Ltd.
8-9, Nishiki 3, Naka-ku
Nagoya
Japan

Cambridge Wools Ltd.

a new zealand wool source.

—jd

Catalog

free

from:
Cambridge Wools Ltd.
Box 2572
Auckland, New Zealand

Scoured Wool 46/50S Quality. Crossbred 4 to 5 inches.
AUST. 65c lb. U.S.A. $1.00 lb.
N.Z. 55c lb U.K. 6/-lb. CANADA $1.00 lb.

Natural.
As shorn from sheep. Medium quality (50S) 5 to 7 inches.
AUST. 60c lb. U.S.A. $1.00 lb. N.Z. 50c lb
U.K. 5/—lb CANADA $1.00 lb.

Black/Grey U.S.A./CANADA $1.20 lb.

SHEEPSKIN RUGS:

AUST. $9   U.S.A. $12   N.Z. $7.50
U.K. £5.10.0.   CANADA $13

Natural Yarns

I would like to suggest handspun yarn from Paula Simmons. Yarn like this really makes it worth one's while to weave or knit. Undyed, unbleached yarns that come in many shades and mixtures of cream, red, brown, grey and black——the Simmons sheep grow that way. I once saw a pelt from one and am sure it could double for costly fur.

Will's brown sweater is super warm, soft, nearly waterproof and BEAUTIFUL.

The yarns are in many thicknesses so you can make a bear sweater or a delicate baby garment. Mrs. Simmons also weaves from her yarn and sells the product as well as giving you advice on knitting or weaving with it yourself.

Peace,
Janet Bloch
St. Louis, Missouri

Paula Simmons
Suquamish, Washington

Price is 92 cents per ounce, plus postage. Yarn is completely pre-shrunk, in center pull balls.

Imported Wool

Unusual yarns from Iceland, Canada, Finland, Norway.

Elizabeth Zimmerman, Meg Swanson
Box 57
Trumansburg, N.Y. 14886

The Complete Book of Progressive Knitting

*This is the most complete knitting book that I have seen. It discusses yarn, its qualities and history, and gives clear instructions on the basics of knitting. Where other books only give directions cryptically written as 'K1, *Y.O., K2 together *K1 repeat this row for the desired no. of rows,' this book tells you how to figure out the desired number of rows for all types of garments from sweaters to suits. The only real drawback I could see was the book's illustrations.* *[Reviewed by Lois Brand]*

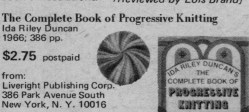

The Complete Book of Progressive Knitting
Ida Riley Duncan
1966; 386 pp.

$2.75 postpaid

from:
Liveright Publishing Corp.
386 Park Avenue South
New York, N. Y. 10016

or WHOLE EARTH CATALOG

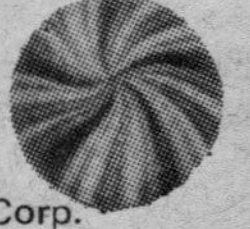

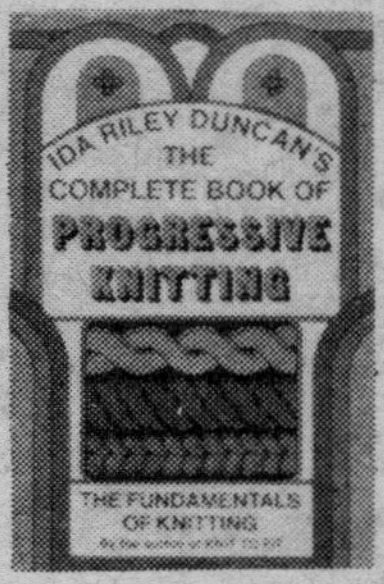

The knit stitch is the foundation of all knitted fabrics.

Position of the Hands. The needle containing the loops to be knitted is held in the left hand with the needle underneath the hand as in Plate XVI. The other needle is held in the right hand as one would hold a pen or a pencil. There are many ways of holding the yarn to be worked over the fingers, but whatever way is used there should be no tensed muscles and no stiff fingers. Knitting for relaxation requires no tension. It is preferable that the yarn be fed over the fingers of the right hand. This is the only way different colored yarns may be worked in a pattern without having a long loop at the back of the work.

The yarn passes over the index finger of the right hand, around the middle finger and is held by the other fingers. It is the way in which the yarn is held that makes the tension of the stitch. There should be absolutely no gripping of either the yarn or needles. The knitting should be worked with ease and the yarn drawn smoothly through the fingers.

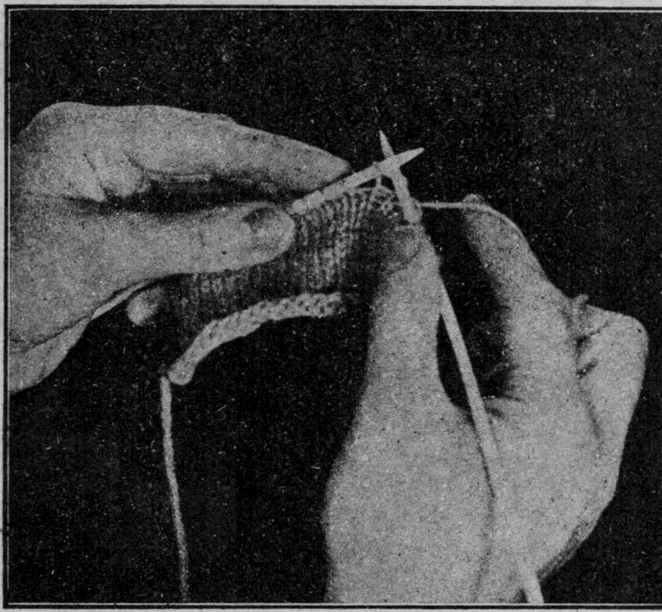

PLATE XVII.

Buttonholes are knitted as the fabric is being made, not slashed as in sewing. Therefore, it is advisable when knitting garments, to knit the side on which the buttons are to be fastened first. In this way the position of the buttons may easily be ascertained and marked, and hence be a guide for the buttonholes. This is important especially where the last buttonhole should be at the neck line. Decide upon the size of the button. If bands are used, the buttonhole is made in the center of the band. The width of the band usually depends upon the size of the buttonhole, that is, if a buttonhold requires 4 stitches, the band should be at least 8 stitches wide, allowing ½ the width of the button on each side of the buttonhole.

Method. The position and size of each buttonhole having been ascertained, bind off the necessary number of stiches at this point. Continue to complete the row as previously, and back again to where the stitches have been bound off. The stitches are added the same way as the second method in the Chapter on Fundamentals.

Note. Turn the work to the wrong side to add the stitches and back again to the right side after they have been added.

After the garment is completed, the buttonholes should be finished with buttonhole stitches, using the same yarn if possible, or should be reinforced with binding on the wrong side.

Garments of pure wool yarns are hard to ignite even with an open flame, because wool is slow to oxidize. This is a great protection in the home, especially where there are young children.

Wool may be knitted or woven into fabrics of delicate sheerness, unsurpassed by any other fiber, and lightness is one of the essentials of modern attire.

Armhole Formation

The shoulder to shoulder measurement is 13½ inches.
13½ × 6 sts to the inch 81 sts.
An even number of stitches is always better in calculating any change of shape in knitting, therefore we shall use 82 sts for the required number across the shoulders.

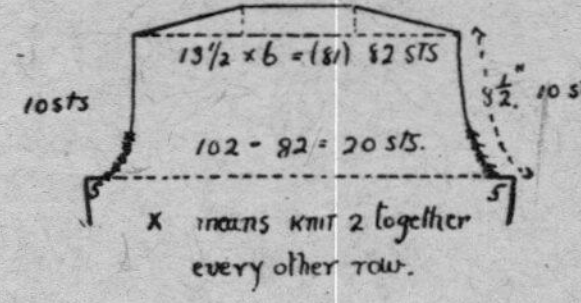

America's Knitting Book

Did you know that sweater sizes aren't standard? I didn't. Gertrude Taylor tells you how to choose your correct size by glancing through the pattern direction: Add the no. of stitches in the complete bust line and divide by the stitch gauge. This will give you the correct size. Be warned to add 3 inches to your actual measurement for ease.

America's Knitting Book *contains all the information needed for a beginner in an easy to understand style.*

"Do not hold needles like a pencil. Perch up on top of the needles." How many people quit before starting because it was too hard to hold needles like a pencil?

The instructions are good and the graphics don't look like 1940. There is also lots of stuff that's far too advanced for me to really comment on except to say that I felt that I could do it with the instructions given.

[Reviewed by Lois Brand. Suggested by Ann Hresko]

America's Knitting Book
Gertrude Taylor
1968; 288 pp.

$9.95 postpaid

from:
Charles Scribner's Sons
Vreeland Avenue
Totowa, N. J. 07512

or WHOLE EARTH CATALOG

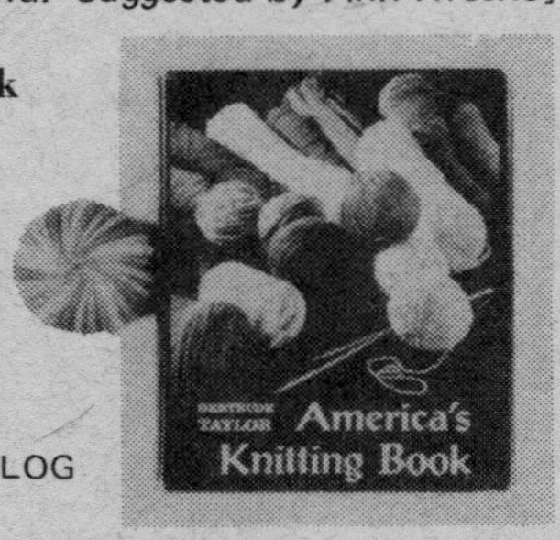

The Improved Horizontal Buttonhole

Starting at the front edge, work two stitches (or whatever your pattern calls for), bind off the next four stitches (or whatever your pattern calls for). Work to the end of the row. On the next row, work until you come to the hole, then turn your work around and "knit on" four stitches as in making the regular buttonhole, *then* pick up the front loop of the first bound off stitch and slip it onto the needle next to the knit-on stitches. Then turn your work around again and work to the end of the row (2 stitches). On the following row, work two stitches then knit together the "picked-up bound-off stitch" and the last stitch of the knit on stitches.

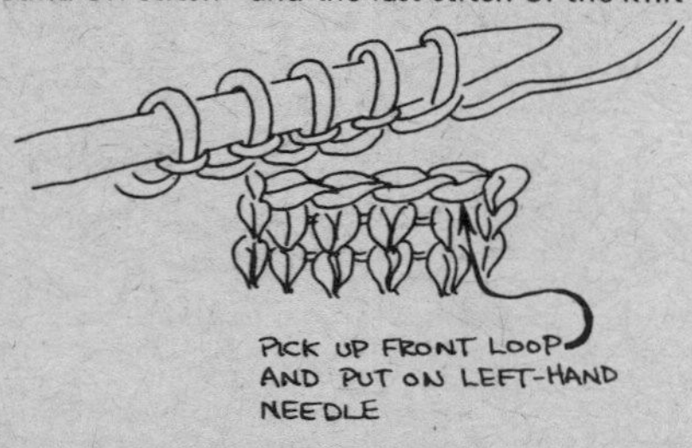

This buttonhole may be used whenever you are working with knotty or nubby yarns and cannot plan on hand-finishing the buttonholes. If you are working with smooth yarn, you will be hand-finishing the buttonholes, and it is not necessary to use this improved buttonhole.

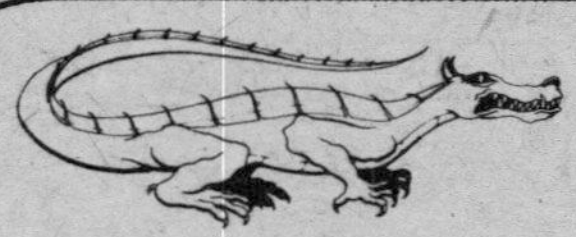

TELEPHONE CALL

D.R. dropped two nickels in the pay phone and dialed his sister's number. But as soon as he heard it ring he hung up and took his nickels back when they came clanging down the shoot. Then he was so pissed at himself for not completing the call he hit himself on the leg with his fist. As the force of the blow spread outward through his thigh and turned to pain it made him feel so one-sided and imbalanced he had to hit himself on the other leg to keep it all from toppling over.

There weren't many people in the bus station that hour of the morning, and no one was using any of the other booths. So D.R. stayed in his booth after his aborted call to think things over. He guessed that was what Estelle was doing too. Thinking things over. Her pose even resembled that of The Thinker. D.R. saw her through the window in the door of the phone booth. She hadn't moved since he left her. She sat turned to one side, one hand propping up her forehead, her elbow on her knee. She looked very unbalanced sitting like that, very awkward and unnatural. To balance it, D.R. sat up very straight in the phone booth, with both feet flat on the floor and his hands on his thighs, palms down. That did it for a minute or two. But then D.R. realized that his left nostril was stopped up, and that his breathing was very unbalanced as a result. His solution was to move his right foot until the heel was off the floor, getting the right foot out of phase as compensation for his malfunctioning left nostril. That felt pretty good. He held the position the next few minutes as he tried to think things over.

What in the goddamn hell's going on? In the long run I really couldn't say, but in the short run, to tell the absolute truth about it, what's going on is I want to leave Estelle here and go on out to Marcella's by myself. To check things out, you dig? I want to go see where it's all at with them see what kind of vibes I get, sort of break the whole thing in easy-like, and bring Estelle out later. Marcella doesn't know about Estelle. I didn't mean to hold the information from her. I just more or less didn't tell her I was travelling with a chick. And I don't want to go busting into their house with a lot of weirdness and heavy vibes and freak everybody out, that's all. It's very simple.

D.R. eased his pose then, and slumped over, relaxed. His little rap with himself wasn't at all conclusive, but somehow he felt better for it. The thing to do was call Marcella and tell her where he was and that he'd be coming on out after while. That was the thing to do.

Encouraged, and determined this time, D.R. put the nickels in the phone again and started to dial. He put his finger in the hole, he felt the cold metal of the thing you dial against his finger, he put his finger right up there in the old hole and started to dial. And then didn't. Instead he placed the phone on the little metal shelf, ran to the next phone booth to get that number, then came back to the first booth and dialed it. When the phone in the next booth rang he went around and answered it.

It was for Estelle. "Hold on a minute, please," said D.R. and he went over to the seats and told Estelle she had a phone call. Slowly she lifted her head to look at him. She wasn't crying now. Her eyes were red, but they were dry, and very clear. When D.R. took her by the hand and tugged, she did not resist. She followed him to the phone booth and went into it as he directed. Then D.R. went to his booth, picked up the receiver and after clearing his throat said, "Hello, Estelle? This is Divine Right Davenport. I want to talk to you."

Knitting Dictionary

The best book that I have found on knitting and crochet stitches is:

Knitting Dictionary: 800 Stitches, Patterns, and knitting, crochet, jacquard technics. ($1.98)

This is the most complete book that I have found. It is well organized and explains things so that if you know the basic knitting stitches you can follow it. Besides being all the above it is small enough to be easily carried with you. When I was in Vancouver B.C. over Christmas I found one there and latched on to it. Upon returning to school in Ohio, I went to a bookshop downtown and there was a whole stack of them. It's really great!

The Knitting Dictionary *is distributed by*

Crown Pub. Inc.
419 Park Avenue So.
New York, N.Y. 10016

$1.98

Basketry

Who knows about basketry? What do you think of this book?

(We asked that two years ago and received not one reply. Hello? Hello?)

—SB

Basketry
F. J. Christopher
1952; 108 pp.

$1.25 postpaid

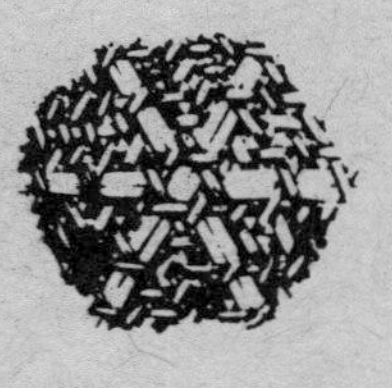

from:
Dover Publications, Inc.
180 Varick Street
New York, N. Y. 10014

or WHOLE EARTH CATALOG

Space—considerable work space—is needed for the practice of basketry, and it is a rather messy operation because of the necessity for keeping material damp. It is therefore not a craft that can be pursued in a corner of the living room (while looking at television). It also calls for a patient and careful temperament.

Most kinds of reedwork last a very long time, if they are well made in the first place, but naturally they do not stay clean indefinitely. Reed and willow can be brushed or washed in clear warm water. Soap should not be used as it tends to lodge in the cracks. Raffia work can be washed with soap and water. It should be allowed to dry naturally away from a fire, though if it is left out in the sun, it will become slightly bleached.

Silk

Silk yardage from Thai Silk Company, 311/6-7 Surawongse Road, Box 906, GPO, Bangkok, Thailand

I don't know that the item warrants a review as such. It is just the most beautiful fabric I've ever seen. When you see it you know you must wear it. I've never seen their incredible colors in any other fabric. Comes by the yard, 40" width, 3 or 4 different weights, solids (which are really made with warp & weft of different, sometimes complementary, colors) and gingham-type plaid (1" or 2" checks.) When I wrote, ca. 2 years ago, they would send generous samples for 1 genuine U.S.A. quarter.

Charles Eby
Laurel, Md.

The Illustrated Hassle-Free Make Your Own Clothes Book

We have a new game in our commune which consists of shouting, at appropriate moments, such inventions as "Right arm!", "Outta touch!" and the like. Revolution takes all sorts of forms these days, & making your own clothes is one way to play fiddle-fuck-around with fashion-sexism, consumption-pushing, & related evils. Not to mention such personal benefits as being comfortable, feeling good, & looking however you want to. This simple & charming book sure seems to give you all the basic information you'll need to get into it, plus numerous patterns & ideas. And probably sufficient inspiration to carry you into lots of new creations on your own. Outta style! Right size! and so forth.

[Reviewed by Diana Shugart]

The Illustrated Hassle-Free Make Your Own Clothes Book
Sharon Rosenberg, Joan Wiener
1971; 154 pp.

$1.25

from:
Bantam Books, Inc.
666 Fifth Avenue
New York, NY 10019

OR WHOLE EARTH CATALOG

my espadrilles

Sharon was in Formentera without a pair of shoes and the sand so hot on her feet. Under the porch of Mark and Juilia's house was an abandoned pair of espadrilles with a hole in the right toe. They fit but she didn't dig the hole. She sewed it up with some wool Julia gave her but thought, "That looks silly." Unbeknownst to her, she had used the Overcast Stitch (see p. 17). So, what she did next was sew a flower onto the shoe. This was her first attempt at embroidery. Then she sewed a butterfly on the left toe to balance out the effect. When the espadrilles wore to nothing, she put the butterfly in a plastic bag which sits in our sewing room in San Francisco.

At some time or other, everyone has had an indispensable pair of pants——jeans or chinos. And just like Roy Rogers when Trigger died, they are loathe to part with them until the irreversable moment when these pants rip at the knee. Rather than stuffing them ——as was Trigger's alleged fate——the pants can be turned into cut-offs by a mere snipping off at the knee. This, then, is re-cycling in its most common incarnation. Just as organic wastes are re-cycled, clothing scraps can be used again, old clothes can be magically transformed by a bit of imaginative remodeling, rips can be repaired and all sorts of things can be re-made into perfectly pleasureable, wearable garments without having to be thrown out.

Mariposa Codpiece

Enough of these stupid blouses. Sew a sensible codpiece. Sew a feather on it.

—SB
[Suggested by Anthony Dubovsky]

Codpiece pattern (with history)

$3.00 postpaid

from:
The Giant Dwarf
Box 77011
San Francisco, CA 94107

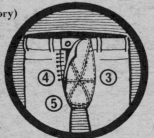

Sincere's Sewing Machine Service Book

Get an old Singer. Among new machines people seem to favor Viking, Elna, or Bernina.

Just thought you'd like to know there's a sewing machine fixit book.

—SB

Sincere's Sewing Machine Service Book
William Ewers
1968, 1970; 205 pp.

$9.95 postpaid

from:
Sincere Press
Box 10422
Phoenix, Arizona 85018

Coats & Clark's Sewing Book

There's a lot of sewing books. This is the best one. Good information, best price.

—SB

Coats & Clark's Sewing Book
1967; 224 pp.

$3.95 postpaid

from:
Golden Press
c/o Western Publishing Co.
P.O. Box 700
Racine, WI 53404
or WHOLE EARTH CATALOG

Successful Sewing

1. Contains a good list of equipment with reasons for having each item.
2. Contains a good chapter on the selection, use and care of a sewing machine for you.
3. Contains a clear explanation of sewing processes generalizing whenever possible, and not creating a lot of special cases.
4. Contains a complete section on fabrics, fibers, and finishes including background, use, properties and home laundering instructions.

[Reviewed by Lois Brand]

Successful Sewing: A Modern Guide
Nesta Hollis
1969; 206 pp.

$2.95 postpaid

from:
Ballantine Books
457 Hahn Road
Westminster, MD 21157

or WHOLE EARTH CATALOG

Practice sewing straight. If you have never used a sewing machine before, it is a very good idea to start by sewing practice lines, angles and curves. One sewing machine manufacturer, Viking Husqvarna, produces practice sheets (domestic science teachers and college lecturers can make block applications for classroom use) and they have given me their permission to reproduce two of them here. . . . Sew along the lines keeping as accurate as possible. Do not watch the needle but keep your eyes on the sewing line. If you wish you may sew without thread on these practice squares, though it is perhaps more encouraging if you do use thread.

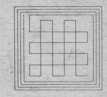

Practice patterns.

There is more than one kind of smocking. What we give you here is English smocking, in which the fabric is first evenly gathered on the wrong side, and gathers (pleats) are held together by embroidery on the right side. Evenness in gathering is essential. Striped (1/8") or checked (1/8" or 1/4") fabric provides a built-in guide, and is highly recommended, especially for beginners. With striped fabric, horizontal guidelines must be added on wrong side with pencil and yardstick, placed to correspond more or less with the embroidery pattern.

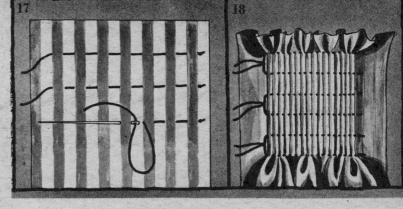

FOR MARKING

*Dressmaker's Carbon Tracing Paper and Tracing Wheel (11)——For transferring pattern markings to fabric. Paper comes in several colors. Wheels come with or without teeth. See MARKING.

*Tailor's Chalk (12)——Also used for transferring pattern markings to fabric. Clay chalk comes in red, white, and blue, in squares or in pencil form.

French seam. This is the traditional seam for fine, hand-sewn lingerie, but whether sewn by hand or by machine, a French seam can also be extremely useful for other garments, and especially for fine garments for babies and young children, where frequent washing might cause an unfinished seam to fray or unravel.

Like the flat fell seam, the French seam is produced the "wrong way" ——the wrong sides of the fabric are placed together for stitching, so that the raw edges appear on the right side of the fabric.

Instead of stitching on the seam line, stitch nearer to the raw edges of the fabric——say about 3/8 in. from the edge of the fabric. Trim the seam allowance slightly; turn article to the wrong side. Fold along the stitched seam line so that the right sides of the fabric are touching. Press along the fold, and make a line of tacking stitches 3/8 in. from the fold. Then stitch. No raw edges should be visible on the right side of the fabric; nothing looks worse than a French seam where strands are trapped in the seam, and there is almost no way of getting rid of these untidy ends once the seam has been stitched. Finally, open and press.

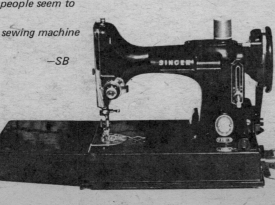

The Standard Book of Quilt Making and Collecting

*i can remember the feelies,
the little yarn tie-together things,
on my baby quilt,
and lying there,
wherever,
twisting them,
between thumb and nosepicking finger,
like i would a nipple,
now,
ah, quilts.
this book is the only one i know of that really
gets into quilting.
illustration and patterns for about two hundred
different beauties.*

—jd

In general, the following materials are a good selection for any patchwork quilts:
Body of quilt. Muslin (first choice), linen, broadcloth, cambric or percale.
Designs. Gingham, percale, calico, shirting, or broadcloth.

Of course you may make your quilt of silk, woolen, or sateen. The block background and pieces in the design must be of the same material. One last word of warning: measure all your materials carefully and be sure that you have too much rather than too little. Colors are exceedingly hard to match, even in the same shade from another bolt.

The Standard Book of Quilt Making and Collecting
Marguerite Ickis
1949; 59; 273 pp.

$3.00 postpaid

from:
Dover Publications, Inc.
180 Varick Street
New York, New York 10014

or WHOLE EARTH CATALOG

RUNNING STITCH

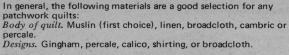

JOSEPH'S COAT

MORNING STAR

One Hundred Embroidery Stitches

For those of you who want to learn how to do embroidery rather than gaze upon lovely & expensive color photographs of how someone else did it this is the best and only necessary booklet. It contains schematic diagrams of the most popular & useful stitches with short suggestions for their application to various embroidery situations. I've "taught" several people embroidery & my first lesson is "buy this book." with the lowest price-per-stitch rate of any text on the subject it is invaluable.

[Suggested and Reviewed by
Peter & Catherin Yronwode]

One Hundred Embroidery Stitches
Coats & Clark's Book No. 150
1964; 34pp.

$.35

from:
Coats & Clark's Sales Corporation
430 Park Avenue, New York, New York 10022

Herringbone Stitch and Threaded Herringbone Stitch

Bring the needle out on the lower line at the left side and insert on the upper line a little to the right, taking a small stitch to the left with the thread below the needle. Next, insert the needle on the lower line a little to the right and take a small stitch to the left with the thread above the needle. These two movements are worked throughout.

Fig. 1

Maltese Cross

This decorative motif is worked in a way similar to Interlacing Stitch. The intertwining of the Herringbone Stitch must be worked accurately, otherwise the interlacing cannot be achieved. Bring the thread through at (A) and take a stitch

Handbook of Stitches

200 embroidery stitches, with descriptions, diagrams & samplers. Compact handbook, good for beginners.

Handbook of Stitches
Grete Petersen and Else Svennas
1959, 1966, 1970; 76 pp.

$3.95 postpaid

from:
Van Nostrand-Reinhold
450 West 33rd Street
New York, N. Y. 10001

or WHOLE EARTH CATALOG

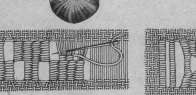

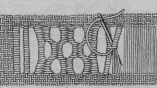

N34 NEEDLEPOINT $7.95

Hope Hanley. The author writes: "This book is intended for the person who wants to do more than just fill in backgrounds of needlepoint canvases with the half cross stitch. It is intended for the person who wants to use needlepoint as his personal art medium. In this book you will find designing techniques which apply to needlepoint. There are over fifty needlepoint stitches here for you to try. Experiment with them, combine them. Mix them as YOU please." Fully illustrated. 87 stitches and variations. 158 pages, 8 x 10 1/2. 1964.

from: Charles Scribner's Sons   or WHOLE EARTH CATALOG
Vreeland Avenue
Totowa. N.J. 07512

Quilt Making

In answer to the section on quilts in the Fall 70 issue of the catalog.

1. $2.50 is too much for Mt. Mist. You can get it cheaper by writing Mt. Mist. We only pay 92 cents a roll.

2.   Don't use cotton or dacron batten, and tie your quilt together. After 3 or 4 washings the cotton balls up and separates into wads. A good quilt must be made to last at least 10 years.

3.   For the same reason, we could not advise using old clothes. You can't tell how they will hold up. Use an old army blanket or some such blanket.

4.   Quilt patterns are regional. In isolated places like Appalachia you can run into patterns you cant find other places. Eaton's Book of Southern Highland Crafts lists many. Mt. Mist lists generally known ones. Many patterns also are known locally by different names. The quilt pattern you show in the catalog above the needle is an Hawaiian adaption of quilt patterns taken over by the missionaries, then adopted by the Hawaiians into land, sea-flower patterns—and then later taken back over here in that form. When we were demonstrating quilting at the Smithsonian Craft Festival last summer in Washington, D.C.—a Hawiian lady rushed up to us, and asked where we had gotten the Hawaiian pattern. Mrs. Johnson, who had made the quilt—just knew it as a pattern "from accross the waters." I later wrote to the Honolulu Academy of Fine Art and they sent a catalog listing some of these patterns.

5.   There are other ways to quilt other than tie or completely quilting a quilt by hand—

1.   Quilting every other block. You can do this in the evening while sitting in a rocker.

2.   Quilting by machine—either quilting the quilt with a straight or zig zag stitch after the quilt is finished,—or to quilt the square in the machine, then join the squares together and finish the raw edges (which should be top side) with a finishing strip of cloth. I am enclosing a picture of a finished quilt made in this method. A beginning machine quilter might find it easier to quilt like this in small squares, rather than tackling the whole quilt.

6.   Don't limit yourself to traditional patterns. Create your own. One of our most successful quilts is a tie-died sheet or large piece of muslin hand quilted in the patterns the tie dye has made. Anybody can piece together a pattern, but care should be given to figuring out what you want to do, cutting a pattern out of cardboard, and then getting all your pieces cut just right. I always think that the hardest thing to do about quilting is to cut the pieces ahead.

7.   Patchwork skirts are easily made from 1/2 a full bed size quilt top. I don't recommend a cotton batten filler, it makes the skirt too heavy. We put in a muslin lining, the same as the quilt, and then hand quilt a pattern in alternating squares.

8.   Quilting patterns common here:

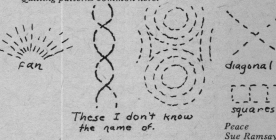

These I don't know the name of.

Peace
Sue Ramsay
Hellier, Ky.

THE CONVERSATION

D.R. said, "Estelle, we've got to talk."

Estelle didn't reply immediately. She was looking out her window at an old lady buying something at the magazine stand. She was the oldest looking person Estelle had even seen in a place like a bus station and she was fascinated. The lady had on a long winter coat and a furry hat with two white feathers on the side. She carried an umbrella on her right arm, an enormous pocket book on her left, and leaning against her leg was a large shopping bag running over with stuff. She'd been standing at the counter long enough to buy reading matter for a year but when she turned away, after going through a very complicated money routine with the clerk, all she had was a candy bar.

"Hey, Estelle? You there?"

"I'm watching a lady buy a candy bar," said Estelle. "Do you see her?"

D.R. hadn't noticed the old lady, but now he looked toward the magazine stand. They watched as she stooped over to put the candy in her shopping bag. The bag was so full of stuff she had to shift the parcels on top just to make room for the candy. Estelle held her breath for fear the bag would tear and spill its contents all over the floor. But it held, and after a good deal of ruffling and shuffling and hassling with her umbrella and pocket book, the old lady finally got herself together enough to pick up the shopping bag and walk around the corner toward the loading zones.

"Wasn't she beautiful?" said Estelle.

"She was very far out," said D.R. "Estelle, listen. We've got to talk."

"What do you want to talk about, D.R.?"

"I don't know," said D.R. He had to clear his throat. He cleared it twice, but it was still raspy when he said, "It just seems like everything's getting weird, that's all. I feel totally weird."

"Maybe it's something you ate," said Estelle.

"It's not anything I ate. It's this sense I've got. It's this feeling."

"You sound very far away," said Estelle. "Is this a long distance call?"

"You're the one who sounds far away," said D.R.

"I sound far away?" said Estelle.

"Yes. You're talking to me very weird."

"I'm talking to you weird?" said Estelle.

"Yes you are. And you know it too. You're fucking me up is what you're doing."

(continued)

Step-By-Step Macrame *(p. 155) has sold 500,000 copies in about 2 years. Does that many people tied in knots reflect some enormous cats-cradle of American psyche going on?*
—SB

Macramé, the Art of Creative Knotting

Although designs for knotted pieces differ according to locale and use, there are very few individual knots. Virginia I. Harvey has collected photographs of traditional knotted pieces throughout the world and presents them in a book called Macramé, the Art of Creative Knotting. *She carefully diagrams the half-knot, square knot, double half-hitch, diagonal double half-hitch, vertical double half-hitch and other knots. The basic knots are described in detailed instructions for making a sampler. Following the pattern for the sampler will give the beginner experience in doing the knots, and show how combining just a few types of knots can offer large pattern variation.*

This book is the best reference manual of knotting technique available. It offers information on all facets of macramé, including discussion on planning, mounting, shaping and finishing a knotting project. Tools and materials are displayed. There are photos exhibiting how different fibers worked in the same pattern can vastly alter visual and textural effects. The pictorial history of macramé and examples of contemporary knotting projects offer plenty of design ideas for more advanced macramé craftsmen.

Knotters interested in explicit directions for traditional macramé purses can obtain patterns by sending $1.10 to: Pesch Art Studio, 28 Colonial Parkway, Dumont, N. J. 07628 with a request for "Macramé Bags," Booklet A.

[Reviewed by Sue Boyle.
Suggested by Alexandra Jacopetti]

Macramé, The Art of Creative Knotting
Virginia I. Harvey
1967; 128 pp.

$3.95 paper

from:
Van Nostrand-Reinhold Co.
450 West 33rd Street
New York, N. Y. 10001

or WHOLE EARTH CATALOG

Virginia I. Harvey, author of Macramé, announces the new quarterly publication, Threads in Action, *a technical publication on non-loom techniques.* Macramé *will be the principal subject with occasional articles on stitchery, bobbin lace, netting, knotless netting, sprang, knitting, crochet, and others.*

Subscriptions are **$8.50**/year 3rd Class Mail
$10.50/yr 1st Class Mail
from:
Threads in Action
Box 468
Freeland, Washington 98249
Individual copies are **$2.50**

[Suggested by Helen Bitan]

Also you can get some macramé supplies from:

Let's Knot Co.
702 Fifth St.
Oregon City, OR 97045

Macramé

Virginia Harvey (above) is friendly and very helpful. Dona Meilach is trippy and very helpful, and paperback.
—SB

Macramé——Creative Design in Knotting
Dona Z. Meilach
1971; 212 pp.

$3.95 postpaid

from:
Crown Publishers, Inc.
419 Park Ave. South
New York, N.Y. 10016

or Whole Earth Catalog

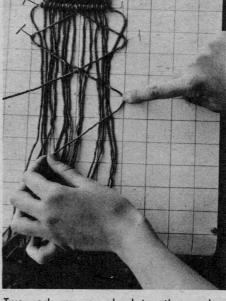

Two cork squares glued together and covered with paper marked off into 1" squares helps keep lines and angles of cords even. Pins are used to hold cords in place as they are worked.

Beads are an important Macramé adjunct. They provide a surface enrichment compatible with the raised knot shapes and a relief to straight knotting. One problem is to find interesting beads with holes large enough to accommodate double, triple, and more cords required for knotting. There are several ways to overcome the bead problem. Some suppliers are beginning to create beads with large holes. If these are not available, buy strung Indian beads, Hippie beads, or bamboo curtain beads and cut them apart. You can easily create your own ceramic and papier-mâché beads. When bead holes offer resistance to threading, use a fine wire for stringing or dip the ends of teh cords into melted wax, shape the ends to a point, and let the wax harden to make stringing easier.

Square Knot Handicraft Guide

*by any other name, macramé,
this book antedates the current enthusiasm about knotting homemade goodies.
well illustrated,
providing enough projects to get you through this winter, at least.*

—jd

Square Knot Handicraft Guide
Raul Graumont and Elmer Wenstrom
1949; 212pp.

$3.95 postpaid

from:
Random House Inc.
457 Hahn Road
Westminster, MD. 21157

or WHOLE EARTH CATALOG

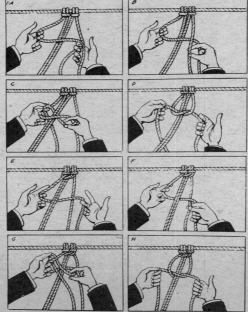

PLATE 1   Illustrated Construction of the Basic Square Knot

P. C. Herwig Co.

Calls itself Square Knot Headquarters, has cords, belt buckles, rings, beads.
—SB

P. C. Herwig Co.
Route 2
Milaca, MN 56353

DREADNAUGHT CORD No. 120

Highest Tensile Strength

Macramé & Weaving Supply

Sisal, heavy jute, colored braided nylon, linen, waxed linen, rattail, cotton and nylon seine . . . pewter, epoxy, bronze plated zinc buckles. Catalog and samples $1.00.
—SB

Macrame & Weaving Supply Co.
63 East Adams
Chicago, Ill 60603

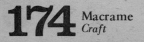

Tie and Dye

This is the only book on tie-and-dye that is available in this country. A few other books briefly discuss tie-and-dye, one of the simple means of fabric design, suitable for school-children, blah, blah, blah. But Ann Maile treats tie-and-dye like an ancient and complex folk art. Not that she is pedantic. She very clearly explains how to accomplish all the traditional and intricate effects possible with limited materials and free-flowing organic imagination. Tie and dye is such a simple art form that many people have already discovered it, and are doing it without any books to tell them how. So why buy a book?

You can buy bolts of machine printed tie and dyed drip proof, smear dry never iron cotton, . . . pretty far out. But the question isn't to be or not to be far out. The question is whether you are into the craft of tie and dye in order to create beautiful objects or just weird artifacts. If you want to really get into it, the book seems really useful and inspiring. If not——well, . . .

[Reviewed by Terry Gunesch.
Suggested by Madge Gleeson.]

Tie and Dye
Anne Maile
1963, . . . 1969; 182 pp.

$2.95 postpaid

from:
Ballantine Books, Inc.
101 Fifth Avenue
New York, N.Y. 10003

or WHOLE EARTH CATALOG

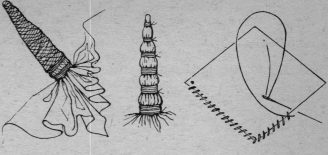

Textured squares

SEWING TECHNIQUE OR TRITIK

Outlining Shapes in Oversewing

Oversewing or whipping stitch can be used very successfully to outline any shape drawn on the sample. Whether further stitching or binding is added within the shape is a matter of choice. This way of outlining does not bunch the cloth up to quite the same extent as a running stitch outline. The scale of the actual stitching may be quite small, about 1/8 in. across, using single or double Sylko, or up to 1/2 in. wide, with double thread. The width of the stitches, that is the amount of cloth picked up on the needle, each time it is inserted into the cloth, decides the thickness of the outline, and their density determines the tone. For instance, a clear-cut resist outline will need more stitches per inch than a medium toned contour.

Variation in the thickness and tone of the lines should be exploited in working out designs.

It is almost impossible to get fine delicate designs on coarse fabric, but, on the other hand, with fine cloth any degree of fineness or coarseness in a pattern is possible.

Method

Draw or trace the design on cloth. Decide which are to be made thick dominant lines and which not so outstanding. With the appropriate cotton or thread, single or double, knotted at one end, begin to sew a little to one side of the line. Take each stitch over and under it at any angle between 30 deg. and 60 deg.

Helio Batik Dyes

Batik dyes from Canada. (Also see p. 167)

—SB

Helio Dyes
2140 West 4th Ave.
Vancouver 9, B.C.
Canada

Aiko's Art Materials Import

a source of batik dyes and tools, japanese artists supplies, books on oriental culture, collage papers, gardening literature.

—jd

[Suggested by Bob Pullman]

Catalog
$.25

from:
Aiko's Art Materials Import
714 North Wabach Avenue
Chicago, Illinois 60611

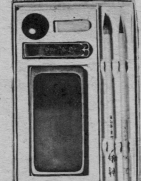

MIYAKO DIRECT DYE . . . A unit of 6 jars or more: $3.30 (at $.55 a jar)
A chemical dye of acid substance in many brilliant colors mostly made up of sulfonic acid and readily soluble. In fine powder form, easily soluble and capable of penetration to many types of fabrics. Responds better in high temperature, therefore it is primarily used for boiling although it is also used successfully for cold-dyeing such as in the case of batik—then, the process should be completed by steaming. Comes in twenty one colors individually packed in small jars for convenient use. 2/3 ox. in a jar, enough to dye 3 yards of fabric in dark color.
Burnt Sienna, Pink, Yellow, Burnt Umber, Maroon, Orange, Olive, Red Violet, Sepia, Blue, Light Blue, Red, Crimson, Violet Ultramarine, Indigo, Green, Prussian Blue, Deep Madder, Black, Grey.

JAPANESE SHEARS

Made of high carbon steel
Just grip them in palm of your hand
Left or right as you please and press points together
Between thumb and bent index finger
No finger holes to get caught

JS. . . .4¼" long

D7 BATIK, THE ART AND CRAFT   **$5.80**
Ila Keller. Japan. The author takes the reader through all aspects of making a batik, from a simple dipping, or tie-dying, to sectional dyeing, and the more intricate 5 or 6 color patterns. Basic materials, fabric mixtures, wax temperatures, etc. are discussed fully. Here is a book of batik literally giving you the "tricks of the trade." 15 Full Color Plates. 72 black and white illustrations. 1966.

D9 BATIK ART AND CRAFT   **$3.95**
Nik Krevitsky. Profusely illustrated with examples of a wide variety of batik and related processes. Step-by-step photographs show the reader how various results are achieved. Work by students and well-known artists is included, most of it created with a minimum of tools and equipment. Besides true batik, the book includes material on direct painting on fabric, crayon-resist drawing and wax-resist egg decorating.

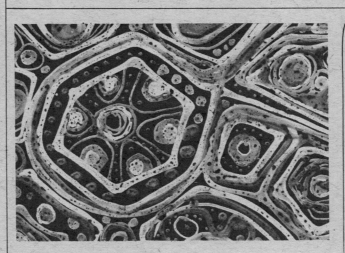

Batik for Beginners

Batik-dyed cloth looks like a stained glass window, when it works, and like the dog was sick, when it doesn't. This is a reasonable beginning text. For even simpler information, Stephen Blumrich at 1200 Meadowview Road, Junction City, OR 97448, has a $1.50 pamphlet, plus 2 first class stamps, Resist Dye Technique.

—SB

Batik for Beginners
Norma Jameson
1970; 104 pp.

OUT OF PRINT

Watson-Guptil Publications, Inc.
165 W. 46th St.,
New York, N.Y. 10036

Another difference between working on paper and working on material is that cloth is pliable and therefore the wax is liable to bend and crack as it is put into the dye. You will have noticed this. It is a characteristic of batik, and one of the recognized techniques, that you use this quality of cracking to add richness and pattern to your design. The cracks may be ordered, to a definite pattern or area, or they may be random cracks used to give a cracked texture over the whole or part of the surface.

To 'crack' the design, the whole surface of the cloth is waxed and left to go cold. In frosty weather a few minutes out in the cold air is sufficient to make the wax brittle. If the wax is brittle, the cracks will be clean and fine. If it is not cold enough outside, put the waxed cloth into cold water for a few minutes.

"I'm fucking you up?" said Estelle.

"Yes, I feel entirely fucked up. I feel like I'm going out of my goddamn mind if you want to know the truth. And you're giving me all this shit over the telephone."

"I'm giving you shit?" asked Estelle.

"Yes!" D.R. yelled. "Yes! You are."

"Well listen, D.R. Do you mind if I ask you a question?"

"Ask me anything you want to," said D.R.

Estelle said, "Do you think you're giving me shit too, by any chance?"

"If I am I don't mean to," said D.R.

"You mean you don't know if you are or not," said Estelle.

"I mean I don't mean to, if I am. But you mean to. You're really fucking me up."

Estelle said, "What if I told you you were fucking me up just as bad?"

"Well, I'd probably talk to you about it," said D.R. "At least I'm trying to talk to you."

"That's very good of you," said Estelle. "That's very decent. I appreciate it."

"Jesus, Estelle, you're really coming on to me weird, did you know that?"

"I think the whole conversation's weird," said Estelle.

D.R. waited before he spoke again. He cleared his throat, then cleared it again. "Well see if this makes it seem any weirder to you."

"What?" asked Estelle.

"I said see if this makes it seem any weirder to you."

"See what?"

"I haven't said it yet. I'm getting ready to say something."

"Oh," said Estelle. "Excuse me."

D.R. cleared his throat. "I'm thinking the thing to do is for me to go on out to my sister's house by myself. Before I take you."

"What's so weird about that?" asked Estelle.

"Doesn't that seem sort of weird to you?"

"Not really. You want to go check it out, is that right?"

"Yeah. Just check it out. Kind of ease into it with them."

"That seems cool to me," said Estelle. "Why did you think that was so weird?"

"I don't know. Now that I've said it, it doesn't seem so weird any more."

"Is that all you were going to tell me?" asked Estelle. "Is that why you got me on the phone?"

"That's it," said D.R.

"Can I come out of the phone booth now?"

"You're free to go anywhere you like," said D.R.

"Thank you," said Estelle. She hung up then and came out of her booth. But D.R. stayed in his to call his sister Marcella and tell her he was coming out to see her after while.

Osborne Tools

always wanted to be a saddlemaker.
closest i've come so far is drugstore cowboy sandalmaker.
try cutting a sole bend with a pocketknife,
or punching holes with a screwdriver,
and you begin to appreciate good leatherworking tools.
osborne is the best.

—jd
[suggested by Michael J. Green]

Catalog and list of distributors

free

from:
C.S. Osborne and Company
125 Jersey Street
Harrison, New Jersey 07029

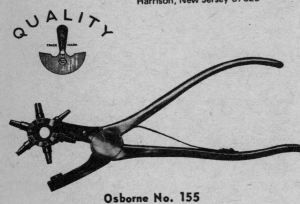

Osborne No. 155

Revolving Punch, 6 Tube. Forged steel frame, fully polished. The threaded cutting tubes are hardened and tempered. Length of punch 8½". Furnished with tubes sizes 0, 1, 2, 3, 5, 7.

Price each **$16.50**
Extra tubes each **$1.10**

Cheap Leather

A friend of ours wanted leather but couldn't afford the $25 or so for the hide and ended up buying a fresh hide from a local slaughter house for $3 or so and ta.ned it himself. We personally don't feel inclined towards doing such a thing but he came out monetarily and is richer for knowing how to do it.

Dennis and Becky Crowe
Warrenten, Oregon

How to Make Cowboy Horse Gear

A highly practical book on the uses of rawhide. Included is a section on how to cure "green leather" and make your own rawhide. When braided, leather is strong and durable. This book illustrates the use of rawhide for "horse gear"; there are certainly other situations where leather braiding can be used to advantage.

[Reviewed by Mary McCabe.
Suggested by Gary Snyder]

How to Make Cowboy Horse Gear
Bruce Grant
1953; 186 pp.

$4.00 postpaid

from:
Cornell Maritime Press
Box 109
Cambridge, Md. 21613

or WHOLE EARTH CATALOG

Sonny Strong has passed over the Great Divide, but his way of making rawhide lives on.

This is it: When the hide or skin is taken off the carcass and while the body heat is still in it, spread it out flat with the flesh side up and salt it down with 40 or 50 pounds of fine stock salt. This is for a mature hide. For a yearling or calf skin use half the amount of salt. Spread the salt evenly and fold the hide over so the hair side is out and the flesh sides are together.

Leave the hide in a shady, dry place for from a week to ten days. It is important to salt the hide while the body heat is still in it, Rickman emphasizes. So if you do not actually remove the hide yourself, get the person who does the work to salt it down for you. The salt runs the blood and glue out of the hide before it congeals and Rickman feels this is important in keeping the hide pliable.

THE SKIFE   Osborne No. 925

Makes a remarkably easy job of skiving. Increases both speed and accuracy. This essential tool is fitted with a Schick razor blade.
Price each   **$1.65**

SCRATCH AWL
Osborne No. 478

Sharp pointed, tempered blade 2" long - for piercing leather, sewing. and a variety of uses.

Price each   **$0.36**

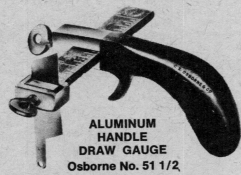

ALUMINUM HANDLE DRAW GAUGE
Osborne No. 51 1/2

Hollow handle draw gauge. Used for cutting leather strips. All metal. Polished head, slide and blade. Japanned handle. Cuts straps any width up to 4".

Price each **$14.50** Extra blades each **$1.20**

Leather Braiding

met a guy named Joe Ria at a rodeo.
he had a traveltrailer full of fancy braided horse gear
done by Yaquis somewhere in the southwest,
and was making his go as a middleman.
beautiful work, mostly in rawhide.
bruce grant has written other leatherwork books,
among them, the cowboy horsegear book that has
been carried in the catalog. i think this is
his best book. deals with the fundamentals of cutting,
braiding, knotting, lacing, and applique in leather.

—jd

Leather Braiding
Bruce Grant
1950; 173pp.

$4.00 postpaid

from:
Cornell Maritime Press
Box 109
Cambridge Maryland 21613
or WHOLE EARTH CATALOG

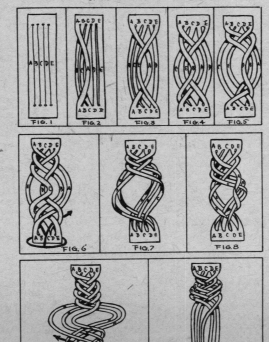

MacPherson Leathercraft Supplies

you've probably heard of tandy's.
if you haven't, look them up in the yellow pages,
(there is one close to you,
if you are close enough in to have yellow pages.)
well, macpherson's is like tandy, only a little better.
some all-in-one do-it-yourself quicky professional type
leathercraft kits, and some professional quality tools.
they mailorder good leathers at decent prices. (ask for
leather price lists) if nothing else, you can get an idea
of what you will need.

—jd
[suggested by Jack de Swart]

Catalog

free

from:
MacPherson Brothers
P.O. Box 395
San Francisco, California 94101

REX RIVET SETTER - A solidly built rivet setter with almost no breakable parts. Will set either split or tubular rivets.
T-88................... $6.20

GENUINE WISS SHEARS INDUSTRIAL WEIGHT

20 W 10 inch **$10.00**
22 W 12 inch **$12.50**

EDGE CREASER
For creasing curves as well as straight lines. Available in sizes as illustrated.

T-21   **$1.75**

Leather Notes

You list Osborne leather tools (C.S. Osborne & Co., 125 Jersey Street, Harrison, New Jersey) as the best available. Unfortunately this is true; they've been the best for many a long year——I'm still using tools my grandfather got from them 50 or so years back and they're still better than anything I can find now——including Osborne. They are living on reputation and a corner on the supply of most serious hand tools for leather. Many of the illustrations in the latest catalog bear only passing resemblence to the tool now turned out. If anyone knows where to get good English or German tools, I'm told these do exist of the old quality, I'd like to see it in the WEC in addition to Osborne and (grimace) Tandy. Good small diamond stitching awls are especially hard to come by. Also a source for a quality stitching horse which is to a leather smith what a loom is to a weaver.

Also would like to recommend Modern Leather Design by Donald Wilcox, Watson-Guptill Publications, N.Y. as a good intro for leather work. It's a 12.50 monster and there are more complete instruction manuals like General Leathercraft by Raymond Cherry (Tandycraft for about $2) but Wilcox catches the essence of leatherlove... "Leather is Sensuous. It has a texture, a color, and smell; to feel it, to see it, to smell it, is to excite the senses. Of all the raw fabricating materials known to man, leather is perhaps the most sensuous. A fabric that can, of its own, stimulate the senses has an exciting potential for hand craftsmanship." "Alright, so maybe you'll say that everybody doesn't respond to the same thing. I agree. You've got a point. But I sill insist that you test your own sensory responses to leather. If you don't respond to leather, then you'll have a real problem working with it. If leather says nothing to you, if it leaves you cold as being simply a pile of dead animal material heaped upon a tabletop, then chances are that you've got nothing serious to offer it as a material for your own design exploration." This guy loves the stuff and is great for instilling (rejuvinating) the spirit in you. Covers all essentials of techniques—especially good section on tools,— and also provides a good list of other books and sources (East Coast mainly) for materials. Read it!

Peace be with you
Robt. Klahn
Leathersmith

Community

The Joyful Community

Who ought to review this book is Ramon Sender, who grew up in a Bruderhof community in New England, and honors his education there. Ramon is the most thorough commune personality I've known. A consummate tape-music composer and grass-reed musician, for five years he's been the gentle fiber of Morning Star and Wheeler Ranch, two of the wooliest anybody-come communes ever. Did Bruderhof give him his skill and his joy? I now believe it.

Ramon's out of reach of telephones, so I'll have to make my own assertion: This is the best and most useful book on communes that's been written.

—SB

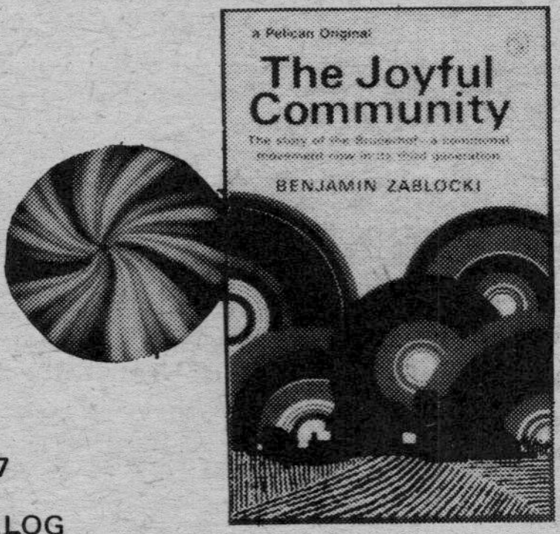

The Joyful Community
Benjamin Zablocki
1971; 537 pp.

$1.95 postpaid

from:
Penguin Books
7110 Ambassador Rd.
Baltimore, Maryland 21207

or WHOLE EARTH CATALOG

The Bruderhof is a community unlike any I have ever seen. When I first visited it in the winter of 1965, I felt as if I had wandered in a dream into a medieval village, or into a world outside of history where neither time nor space existed. Never before or since have I felt the presence of brotherly love so permeating a place that I felt I was breathing it. I have visited close to a hundred contemporary communes and studied the history of those of the last century. The Bruderhof can be classified with neither the new nor the old. It is not at all a typical case. I present this study not as a key to the understanding of some larger social movement, but because I feel that the problems that it raises and the solutions that it offers are fundamentally related to our society's quest for *fraternité*.

•

The Bruderhof is a federation of three colonies located in New York State, Pennsylvania, and Connecticut. The colonies are known as *hofs* (rhyming with the English word 'loaf'), which is German for 'dwelling place', and Bruderhof means 'dwelling place of brothers'. The total population of the community numbers about 750 men, women, and children holding all goods and property in common. The Bruderhof supports itself through a communal industry——the manufacture and sale of high-quality and expensive wooden toys, most of which are bought by schools. In 1970 the community is celebrating its fiftieth birthday. It was founded in Germany in 1920, and has since undergone migrations to England, Paraguay, and finally, in 1954, to the United States. It is held together by its common religion——a radical, fundamental Anabaptist Christianity.

A most striking thing about the Bruderhof is the people. Here are no rugged, bearded Amish peasants transplanted from another age but, for the most part, sophisticated, middle-class, college-educated individuals. The population is highly diversified in background——ex-millionaires and ex-tramps, holders of post-graduate degrees and grade-school dropouts, a dozen nationalities, and as many religions. Unlike the Hutterians and Amish, the Bruderhof has never become a blood-related ethnic group. The community still has some of its original members and is beginning to raise a fourth generation of *'sabra'* children but it has remained constantly open to a stream of new members from the outside world. At the time of this study, the majority of Bruderhof members were converts who had joined within the past ten years. This combination of survival through at least three generations with a continually open membership policy is a major accomplishment, often striven for but rarely achieved among communitarian groups.

•

Many communes eventually reach some sort of compromise between anarchism and the need for structure. But a few do a surprising flip from anarchism to authoritarianism, instead and place themselves under the power of some charismatic leader. This dramatic reversal cannot be explained entirely by the need for structure. It very likely has something to do with the dangers inherent in releasing feelings which has been long repressed.

•

The absence of money gives a storybook atmosphere to Bruderhof villages. People seem more colorful, more involved in each thing they are doing, because they are doing it for its own sake, not with the thought of some abstract reward. Even the money that does sometimes come into people's lives takes on something of a magical character. A communal treasurer, called the Steward, keeps track of financial affairs and disburses small sums when needed. When two Brothers were chosen to represent the community in an anti-war demonstration in Washington, D.C., I went with them. They spoke to each other of what an adventure it was to be driving a car of their own, with money jingling in their pockets, thinking about what kind of restaurant to choose for supper. Children sell worms to fishermen along the river. The pennies thus earned become a precious secret and a source of prestige in the peer group. But I met one nine-year-old girl at Woodcrest who didn't know what a dime was when I showed her one.

Economic decisions are made by the Brotherhood or by executives with authority delegated by the Brotherhood, as are all other Bruderhof decisions. When the new Woodcrest dining room was built, samples of various shades of paint were put on a wall and a Brotherhood meeting was called. After a long debate, no opinion could be reached. So they decided to paint one wall the color that the majority favored and then re-evaluate the situation. After the dissenters saw how that one wall looked, they decided to go along with the majority. On the other hand, when new curtains were needed for a communal meeting room, the Housemothers and a few women from the Sewing Room chose the cloth.

Kibbutz: Venture in Utopia

This book is a straightforward description of one Kibbutz. It is the history, the problems, and the moral codes of a community which began in 1920 and has grown steadily since that time. Over a span of several generations it has grappled with problems, both economic and social, which are similar to problems faced by the community movement in the United States today.

The book examines critically and sympathetically the issues of poverty, marriage, education, comfort, and communication as it has been dealt with over the various periods of this Kibbutz.

While the book is of limited practical value as a how-to-do-it text, it offers a long term perspective on the difficulties and advantages of the community way of life.

[Reviewed by James Fadiman]

Kibbutz: Venture in Utopia
Melford E. Spiro
1956, 1963; 266 pp.

$2.75 postpaid

from:
Schocken Books, Inc.
67 Park Avenue
New York, N. Y. 10016

or WHOLE EARTH CATALOG

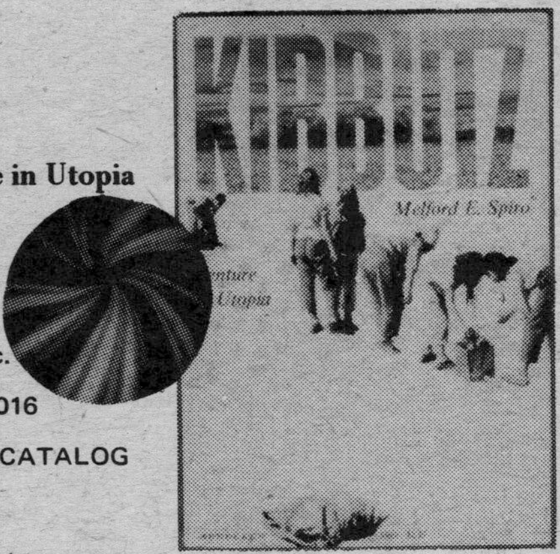

This is a community which was founded, for the most part, by middle-class intellectuals who deliberately chose to be workers. . . . Instead of aspiring to "rise" in the social ladder, they aspired to "descend.". . . This Tolstoyan attitude toward work could be evolved, it is not hazardous to say, only by romantic, urban intellectuals.

•

But this emphasis on youth and on the equality that exists between the young and the old create a potentiality for a condition of inequality—an inequality in which the young assume the superior, and the old the inferior, status.

•

The kibbutz, it will be remembered, was originally conceived as a means to an end—the creation of the new man. Instead of the selfish, agressive personality created by urban capitalism, there would emerge, as a result of the new social order, a kindly, altruistic personality. This end has not been achieved.

•

Instead of cooking and sewing and baking and cleaning and laundering and caring for children, the woman in Kiryat Yedidim cooks OR sews OR launders OR takes care of children for eight hours a day. She has become a specialist in one aspect of housekeeping. But this new housekeeping is more boring and less rewarding than the traditional type.

Communitas

This book has been around for a good while, and it's still holding its own as a lucid gathering of the elements to think and design with on the subject of community.

—SB

Communitas
Paul and Percival Goodman
1947, 60; 248 pp.

$1.95 postpaid

from:
Random House
Westminster, Maryland 21157

or WHOLE EARTH CATALOG

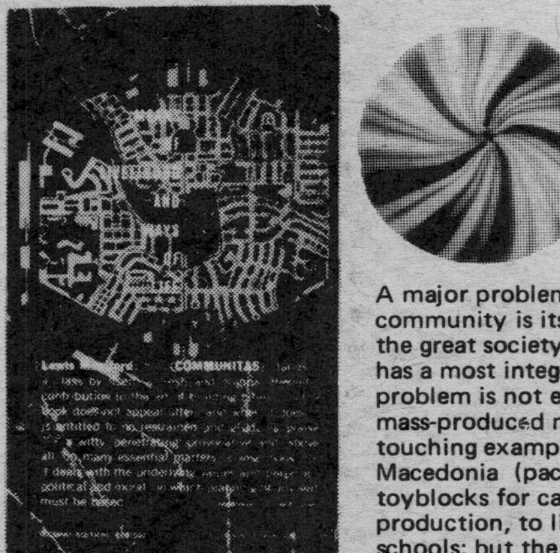

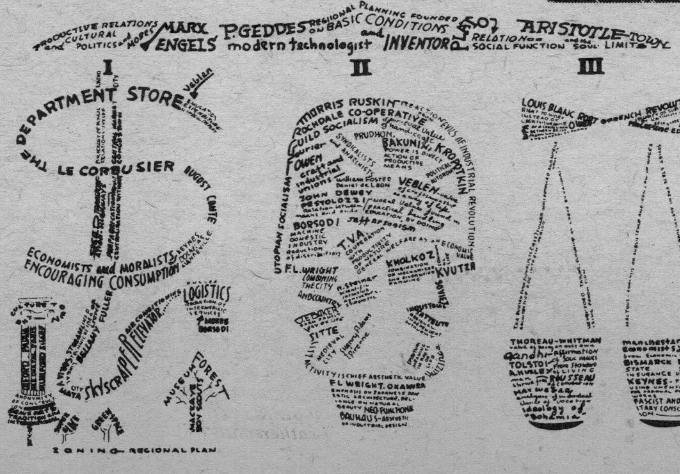

A major problem of every intentional face-to-face community is its 'cash-crop,' its economic role in the great society that has no integral way of life but has a most integrated cash nexus. Usually the problem is not enough money or credit to buy needed mass-produced machinery. But let us mention a touching example of a contrary problem. The Macedonia (pacifist) community made pedagogic toyblocks for cash, and distributed them, at cost of production, to like-minded groups like progressive schools; but the blocks became popular and big commercial outfits wanted a large number. Macedonia was then faced with the following dilemma: these commercial jobbers would resell at a vast profit; yet if Macedonia itself charged them what the market would bear, the community would itself be contaminated by commercialism.

•

Yet perhaps the very transitoriness of such intensely motivated intentional communities is part of their perfection. Disintegrating, they irradiate society with people who have been profoundly touched by the excitement of community life, who do not forget the advantages but try to realize them in new ways. People trained at defunct Black Mountain, North Carolina, now make a remarkable little village of craftsmen in Haverstraw, N. Y. (that houses some famous names in contemporary art). Perhaps these communities are like those 'little magazines' and 'little theaters' that do not outlive their first few performances, yet from them comes all the vitality of the next generation of everybody's literature.

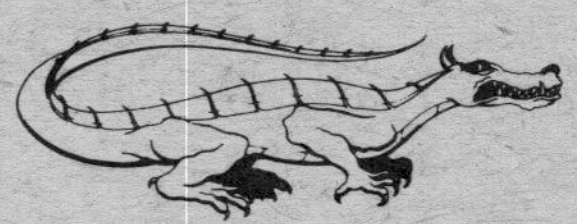

ARRIVAL

If your niece is on one arm and your nephew is on the other, does that automatically balance it? Or do their actual weights have to be accounted for? If their weights have to be accounted for, it's hopeless. But if you can go by how it feels, if a nephew automatically balances a niece, out of their own internal, organic, cosmic, natural reasons, then it's cool and doesn't matter if this particular nephew knocks me and my niece and all of us on our asses.

"Herschel you stop that?" Marcella yelled from the kitchen. She was just coming out with a tray of Pepsi Colas for D.R. and the kids. Herschel had started wrestling with D.R. as soon as he got out of the bus in the driveway. He was nine and about three sizes too big for his age. He wasn't fat, he was just big and husky, in the mold of his father Doyle, who was six feet three. Herschel wrestled with D.R. coming through the house, as he hugged Marcella and gave his niece Debbie a lift and a brief ride across the kitchen, and then he continued to wrestle him right on out the back door and into the yard. When Debbie wanted to join in, D.R. suggested they not wrestle any more, but play the lift-and-swing game like in the old days. That was okay for a minute or two. Herschel swung from the right arm and Debbie swung from the left, and for a minute or two the lift-and-swing game was cool. But then Herschel decided that what he wanted to do was lift and swing and wrestle at the same time, which he proceeded to do by getting a firm lock around D.R.'s waist with his legs as he hung suspended from D.R.'s sagging forearm. That was when Marcella mercifully appeared with the Pepsis.

"You stop that I said," Marcella snapped at Herschel. Then, her voice softer as she placed the tray on the little green metal table, "Your Uncle David is tired, honey. He's been traveling."

(continued)

Drop City

Peter can write fine. Drop City was the first of current crop of weed patch communes. The first dome-funk display in the U.S. The first nose-tickle of America's country sneeze.

How to risk your life repeatedly and keep laughing. It's a good story.

—SB

Drop City
Peter Rabbit
1971; 163 pp.

OUT OF PRINT

WHOLE EARTH CATALOG

Drop City is a fucked-up mess, Drop City is completely open, completely free; I own it, you own it, because we know that all energy comes from the same place. Ten domes under the skydome, overshadowed by the Rockies; silverdomes, domes that are paintings, multicolored cartopdomes and one black dome.

Droppers live out of the garbage dump. We know about garbage. The people of Trinidad call us Dump City——they know where it's at. They call Droppers when they want garbage picked up. It delights them to watch us rummaging around in the schmutz; it delights us too. An incredible number of people can live off the garbage heap of the U.S. Drop City is built on the garbage dump of a dying town of ten thousand strung-out coalminers. Think what can be done with L.A.——N.Y.——San Francisco——Des Moines——Dallas! The most beautiful place in Drop City is the dump, the garbage dump of the garbage pickers. It's our greatest resource.

•

Luke Cool taught Droppers to design domes, build solar heaters, make dwellings in which a family can live in comfort and beauty. Luke Cool is the king of the junkheap, teaching Droppers and the world how to USE things. Jump up on top of the car with an axe and chop'um out, all around the edges just like a can opener, stomp, pop out the back glass, use it for a window, slip off the mirrors, use them for a solar cooker, pull out the insulation, use it, USE IT; make a honeycomb sandwich out of beer cans and plywood——fantastic strength——and USE IT.

•

So they had us, A.C.L.U. and all. But Curley and I couldn't resist going down to the welfare office for a final confrontation. We sat down with the supervisor and laid our heaviest rap on him about what welfare *really* means. That we're *all* on welfare, absolutely dependent on every other human being, plant, animal, earth, air, fire, water for our welfare and we'd fucking well better start looking out for our collective welfare or there isn't going to be any welfare to look out for.

As we put it on him, the supervisor's face got redder and redder. He started chomping and puffing his fat cigar faster and faster, and when we got up to leave, he was in a blind fit of rage. He began pounding his desk with both fists, bouncing and clattering pencils, pens, paperclips and ashtrays with every blow, adn screamed like a little girl having a tantrum, "YOU HAVE NO RIGHT TO BE POOR!!!"

We fell out the door laughing hysterically.

And B. the moneyman. The hardest gig of all, the moneyman——everyone is always hitting on you. Your face disappears and is replaced by a dollar sign. Everyone is determined to help the moneyman on his road to enlightenment by relieving him of some of his material goods. The Droppers were no exception.

One Christmas Ishmael wrote a play. All of Drop City was to be the set, all the Droppers would be the cast. It was gonna be good.

Ishmael tacked a casting list on the bulletin board in the Complex. The Droppers were to choose their own parts, and they did. Everyone accepted his role.

The hardest time in a commune, particularly Drop City, is the time after the building gets done. While everyone is working together on actual construction the energy is centered, there is fantastic high spirit, everyone knows what he is doing all the time. But after the building is done comes a time of dissolution. There's no focus for the group energy, and most hippies don't have anything to *do* with their individual energy.

Handling time, learning what to do with total leisure, is one of the most important lessons to be learned in a commune. What we do with our time is our choice; there's no compulsion to work or play or *anything* anymore. We have to learn how to really use time——every second——because if we decide to lay around on our asses, it isn't long before time gets heavy. Rebuilding a world is a full-time job, a continuous job. We've got to learn to be conscious of the Great Work all the time.

In a way the time of dissolution was good; a period of service. But instead of going higher, we were on the merry-go-round. Curley and Drop Lady left, Clard and Suzie left, John McHale said, "Who Pays For The Rain," and I suddenly realized what Curley had been trying to tell me all along: It's all free, it all flows from the Cosmic Forces, all energy comes from the same place and it's free ——but I'd learned it too late. Instead of a community of people dedicated to getting it together on the highest possible level, Drop City became a decompression chamber for city freaks.

Living on the Earth

this may well be the best book in this catalog.
this is a book for people,
so,
if you are a person,
it is for you.
if you are a dog,
for instance,
and you can't read very well,
it just might be for you too,
because of the drawings.
alicia
alicia
alicia.
she's our very own bradford angier.

—jd

Living on the Earth
Alicia Bay Laurel
1970; a bunch of pages

$3.95 postpaid

from:
Random House
Westminster, Md. 21157

or WHOLE EARTH CATALOG

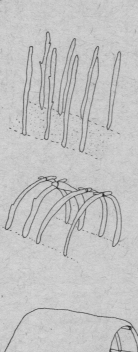

shelter...

clear and make level a floor space. dig holes 2 feet deep along the sides and insert tall poles. choose a site out of wind and possible falling trees

bend poles to meet as arches. lash them together. lash one long pole along the top of all the arches and additional poles along the sides

cover with a tarp or some plastic or an old tent or even a blanket

turn the cover under the bottom transverse pole (which is lashed to the outside of the frame) and sew it together.

if rain is imminent: cover with plastic with 2 feet extra on the sides. dig a ditch extra plastic and bury so rain will run off top and into ditches.

15

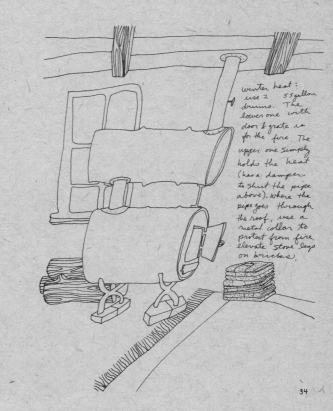

winter heat: use 2 55 gallon drums. The lower one with door & grate is for the fire. The upper one simply holds the heat (has a damper to shut the pipe above). where the pipe goes through the roof, use a metal collar to protect from fire. elevate 'stove' legs on bricks.

34

earthworms turn decay & waste into rich odorless humus earth. They are the best compost shredders going. To greatly enrich your garden's topsoil, set up a worm colony in your compost box. keep it moist & shady. start with sifted dirt & well rotted organic compost and you will gradually get to where you can give them fresh organic garbage & they will take care of it. See the earth worms turn garbage into treasure.

a gardener's allies

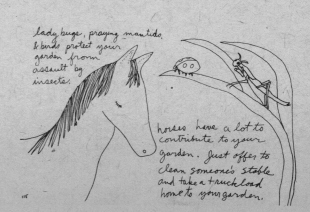

lady bugs, praying mantids, & birds protect your garden from assault by insects.

horses have a lot to contribute to your garden. Just offer to clean someone's stable and take a truckload home to your garden.

Suwanose

Gary Snyder has written of Suwanose Commune which clings to a (live) volcanic island off the south of Japan, and of Nanao who wanders around injecting energy and absurd purpose into fellow humans. Nanao visited Libre, in Colorado, a while ago. So last summer Dean and Linda Fleming from Libre visited Nanao's Suwanose. These are three of their letters home.

—SB

AFTER HITCH HIKING 10 DAYS SWEATING & STARVING WE ARRIVED IN KAGOSHIMA HOPING TO REST & GATHER SUPPLIES FOR SUWANOSE. WE FOUND THAT THE BOAT LEFT IN 3 HOURS. WE RAN THROUGH ALLEYS LOOKING FOR RICE & SOY BEANS & FINALLY BOARDED THE SHIP. THE 26 HOUR TRIP WAS ALL ROCKING & SWAYING——WITH NO FOOD & MASHED WITH PEOPLE. THE ISLANDS WE PASSED ARE INCREDIBLE & BEAUTIFUL. ONE IS COMPLETELY DESERTED & IS VERY FAR OUT LOOKING. IF YOU KNOW ANYONE WHO IS INTERESTED LET US KNOW.

FINALLY AT SUNSET——SUWANOSE! WHAT AN INCREDIBLE COLOR DISPLAY, MUCH LIKE LIBRE BUT ALL REFLECTED IN THE WATER WITH 6 SMALL ISLANDS IN VIEW. WE'RE LIVING IN A BAMBU HUT THAT NEEDS THATCHING ON THE ROOF, SO WE'RE CUTTING BAMBU & TYING IT TOGETHER WITH VINES. IT'S INCREDIBLE HOT IN THE MID DAY SO ALL WORK STOPS & EVERYONE WORKS ON HIMSELF DURING THAT TIME.

THERE ARE 9 BUZOKU & DEAN, LIA & I. THERE IS A FARM—FIELDS OF CUCUMBER' SQUASH' WATERMELON' ONIONS' BEANS & NOW HOPI CORN TUCKED IN THE BAMBU FOREST. MUCH HARD WORK, THE SOIL IS VOLCANIC ASH & VERY POOR FOR GROWING. WE MUST HAVE COW SHIT IN BASKETS FOR FERTILIZER. ALL MEALS ARE EATEN TOGETHER & EACH DAY IT IS SOMEONE'S TURN TO COOK. ONE BUZOKU IS AN INCREDIBLE SWIMMER WHO CATCHES MANY FISH EACH DAY, VERY GOOD.

SUWANOSE IS A TOUGH PLACE TO LIVE.

WE'RE NOT PARTICULARLY WELCOME & WE MUST MAKE A PLACE FOR OURSELVES. WE HAVE NO MATERIAL OBJECTS, A 3 TATAMI HUT THAT IS FALLING IN, CANNOT SPEAK JAPANESE, & MISS THE MOUNTAIN LIFE, BUT WE ARE LEARNING MUCH ABOUT OUR NAKED SELVES. WE ARE ALSO LEARNING ABOUT NAKED COMMUNITY & RELATIONS WITH OTHER PEOPLE. EVEN DEAN WANTS TO HAVE COMMUNAL MEALS & LIVE IN THE SMALL DOME MAYBE WHEN WE RETURN. THE DOME KNOWLEDGE' FAM KNOWLEDGE & LIFE STYLE ARE OF NO USE HERE. IT IS COMPLETELY DIFFERENT IN CLIMATE & AVAILABILITY OF BUILDING MATERIALS. ONLY THE KNOWLEDGE OF HAVING DONE THESE THINGS IS OF HELP & THE STRENGTH DEVELOPED THROUGH PERSEVERENCE. TAKE CARE OF OUR HOME, GARDENS & MOUNTAINS & ABOVE ALL EACH OTHER.

Love,
Linda

BELOVED LIBRE—— HIJO DEL CHINGADO! WE'VE BIT IT OFF THIS TIME——FOUND A SCARCELY LIVABLE PHENOMENA——MAKES WALKING ACROSS THE SAHARA A MIDDLE—CLASS DREAM! EVERY INSTANT OF EVERY DAY IS THE SEVEREST OF TESTS BOTH MATERIAL AND SPIRITUAL . INCREDIBLE HUMIDITY ALL DAY, MOSQUITOS AT NIGHT, ROARING CRATER, TEMPTIMG MAD SWAYING IMPENETRABLE BAMBOO JUNGLE, TWISTED BANYAN ROOT TREES MOCKING SANITY , CRYSTAL SEA OF SHARKS, JAGGED CORAL-COVERED LAVA WITH CURRENTS LIKE THE HANDS OF GOD TRYING TO DROWN, MAD BLACK EX-JAPANESE FREAK TRIBESMEN LIVING TOTALLY SELF—SUFFICIENT PRIMEVAL EXISTENCE OF EXTREME KHARMA YOGA (MEANING UNCEASING WORK). A BIT HEAVY BUT EXTREMELY RICH IN LEARNING POTENTIAL. ASHRAM FINDS 3 OF US A REAL MYSTERY AS WE SPEAK NO JAPANESE, LEARN BY WATCHING, KEEP VERY QUIET. LIA LAUGHS AT US ALL——ROCK BABY! CLIMBED, BEFORE DAWN, TO TOP OF CRATER TO PAY HOMAGE TO ONOTAKE (GOD OF EVERYTHING HERE——MATES WITH THE SEA ON FULL MOON) PEERING INTO IMMENSE, ROARING INFERNO OF SULPHUROUS GASSES FROM EARTH'S OWN BOWELS. IF GREENHORN IS THE GREAT GRANDMOTHER, THIS IS THE BABY! LEARNING TO SKIN DIVE, TRIBESMAN SATAN MY TEACHER——EVERYDAY WE CONSUME HEAPS OF SASHULI (RAW FISH). HOPI CORN WE PLANTED LEAPT FROM THE GROUND IN + DAYS! NOW VERY TALL——WE PRAY. LINDA AND I CLIMB OUR FAVORITE LAVA BOULDER AT SUNSET, MAKE LOVE, SING, READ TO EACH OTHER FROM BOOKS OF CONSCIOUSNESS, PAINT & DRAW. LIA HAS A HAPPY SWING IN BANYAN GROVE' WE ARE BLACK FROM SUN, GETTING CLEAR, LEARNING ABOUT LIBRE! HOLD TO LOVE MORE, BE CLOSER TOGETHER. WE WILL RETURN, PROBABLY IN OCTOBER——GAVE OUR MONEY TO ASHRAM BUT HAVE AIRLINE TICKETS AT LEAST TO CALIF. SO MUCH WE MISS ALL DETAILS OF OUR LIBRE LIFE YOU CANNOT IMAGINE. WE ARE WORKING, VERY HARD, ON IT ALL AND SHOULD BE ABLE TO CHANGE FOR THE BETTER SOON. THE REST OF JAPAN, AS A PLACE TO WANDER AND LEARN, VERY RAPIDLY BECAME OBSOLETE IN THE FACE OF THIS ASHRAM——MUCH THE WAY THE U.S. BECOMES, RELATIVE TO LIBRE, ONLY MORE SO——I VISITED THE OTHER BUZOKU AND THIS IS THE ONLY TRUE ONE——HONTO! GOD IS LOVE. EVERY DAY A TEST, AT NIGHT MORE SO! UNPOLLUTED, VIOLENT, NEVER RESTING, HUT CAVING IN ON OUR HEADS, PRIMITIVE ASS—BUSTER! ! IN FACT I CAN'T IMAGINE A MORE OPPOSING PLACE TO CLEAR INANE COBWEBS OF APATHETIC CONSCIOUSNESS. YES AND YES! ! ONOTAKE MAY YET LEARN TO LOVE US——OR VICE VERSA AS EVERYTHING HERE IS! KNOW THAT WE LOVE YOU & WILL BE BACK SOON.

Dean

LIBRES——ON THE MOVE AGAIN AFTER 4 WEEKS ON THAT VOLCANO. WE WERE CHASED OUT BY THE GODS IN NO UNCERTAIN TERMS. AN EARTH-RIPPING TYPHOON CAME, FLATTENING OUR LITTLE HOUSE AND BURYING EVERYTHING WE OWNED IN MUD. FORTUNATELY, THE RAIN LEAKED IN SO THOROUGHLY THAT WE HAD MOVED TO A COW BARN BEFORE SHE WENT DOWN BUT IN THE BARN, FLOATING IN PISS AND DEBRIS, WE WERE ATTACKED BY MITES SO HIDEOUS AS TO MAKE THE EVER—PRESENT MOSQUITOES SEEM PLEASANT. THEN THE HEAT RETURNED AND THE VOLCANO SCREAMED SHOOTING BLOOD—RED CLOUDS UP THOUSANDS OF METERS IN THE SCORCHING SKY. THE TRIBE, I'M SURE, WAS RELIEVED TO SEE US GO, AS THEIR GUILT OVER OUR TRIBULATIONS, ESPECIALLY LIA'S, WAS MOUNTING. FIRST WE HITCH TO THE PRAYING MANTIS TRIBE THAT LIVE ON AN OLD FARM WITH RIVER NEAR NICHIMAN IN SOUTHERN KYUSHU, ABOUT 20 BUZOKU WERE THERE WORKING HARD IN THE HEAT EVERYDAY AND GORGING ON GOOD FOOD AND GETTING VIOLENTLY DRUNK ON SHACHU EVERY NIGHT. SHADES OF MEXICO AND QUITE UNLIKE THE NEW AUSTERE ASHRAM. WE STAYED AS LONG AS WE COULD BUT THE PACE WAS TOO GREAT FOR US AFTER FALLING OFF A FEW CLIFFS AND DANCING THRU THE FLOOR' MUCH GOOD SPIRIT HERE, MORE NANAOS DREAM THAN HEAVY PRESENT-DAY SUWANOSE, BUT ALL THAT BOOZING IS TOO MUCH. SO OFF WE HITCHED OUT OF KYUSHU, UP THE WEST COAST—NOW IN KYOTO TAKING A SHORT 2 DAY BREAK WHICH, IN TRUTH, WE HAVE NOT HAD SINCE LINDA AND LIA ARRIVED. WHATEVER IDEAS WE HAD ABOUT THE BEAUTIFUL JAPANESE LANDSCAPE (WHICH IT SURE IS) HAVE NOW BEEN SOMEWHAT COLORED BY THE INCREDIBLE INTENSITY OF HEAT AND BUG AND MAD BUZOKU. TOMORROW WE ARE HITCHING TO HOKAIDO TO SEE THE MOUNTAINS AND RIVERS AND RUGGED COASTLINES, TO EXPERIENCE A COOL EVENING OR SEE LAND WITHOUT PEOPLE, TO BE ALONE TOGETHER FOR THE FIRST TIME SINCE VIGIL. WE HOPE TO LIVE CHEAPLY ENOUGH TO BE ABLE TO STAY UNTIL OUR AIRLINE TICKETS ARE VALID ON OCT. 1ST AND THEN COME FAST TO OUR OWN LAND AND OUR OWN PEOPLE LIBRE!!! MEANWHILE, IN FACT, THIS IS A VERY FAR OUT EXPERIENCE FOR ALL THREE OF US AND FULL OF TRULY GOOD PEOPLE AND PLACES. WE HAVE SEEN AND BEEN ACTED UPON BY THE EXTREME SOUTH AND NOW WE MUST SEE THE NORTHERNMOST TIP OF HOKAIDO TO GET A FULL IMAGE. THE PHENOMENA OF LINDA AND LIA'S ADJUSTMENT HAS BEEN IN ANSWER TO MY PRAYERS. LINDA IS NOW STRONG, COMPLETE & DIGGING HITCH HIKING——PAINTING TOUGH LANDSCAPES—— LIA HAS BEFRIENDED A THOUSAND JAPANESE, OLD & YOUNG, SPEAKS WELL, HAS OUTGROWN ALL HER CLOTHES AND EVEN TASMANIAN——SHE IS NOW A GOOD HITCHHIKER! ! LOVE THEM! LOVE YOU!

Dean

Japan Kibbutz Association

tetsu kishida runs the japan kibbutz association, 2-5-7 chome, akasaka, minato-ku, tokyo-to (runs it but watched over by financial godfather), tel. 03-583-3280; he speaks english, has lived on kibbutz in israel, helps run an exchange program where at least 100 japanese go to israel for kibbutz living each year, he has a list of japanese communal farms and will help arrange for foreigners to visit (and work and live) on these farms. ——self-addressed envelopes, with international postage coupons would facilitate response. also some knowledge of japanese (sam martin's pocket books easy japanese and english-japanese dictionary helpful and cheap) before arrival is helpful. tetsu's wife, kyoko, wants to do a japanese whole earth catalog and would appreciate help from any source——and a japanese whole earth catalog would be really something! your friend, michael howden, san francisco

"Where have you been traveling?" asked Debbie. Debbie was four. She wore glasses, watched TV and drank a lot of Pepsis.

"Well, all around," said D.R. "East. West. North. South. All around, actually."

"How come you're so tired?" asked Herschel. Herschel had always been D.R.'s big buddy on previous visits. But he was in Little League this year, and was so good at it he'd gotten a little arrogant.

"Well," said D.R. "Let's just say traveling can be pretty hard work sometimes."

"I've traveled, and I don't think it's hard," said Herschel.

"I've traveled all the way to Kentucky," said Debbie.

"That's enough, now," said Marcella. "You kids go on around in front and wait for daddy."

Debbie leaped at the suggestion. Carrying her Pepsi in both hands she ran around the house yelling "Daddy, Daddy!" Herschel was a little more cool. He went away, but not so far that he couldn't hear what was being said by the grownups.

"Go on," said Marcella. But Herschel sat down where he was and began to play with the ice in his glass.

"Lord I think I'm the one's tired," said Marcella. She filled her glass from the quart-size Pepsi bottle and carried it around to the front of her chair. Slowly she eased herself backward and down, moaning under her breath as if every bone in her body pained her terribly.

Marcella was only twenty-eight, but one of her games was pretending to be about three times that old. She and Doyle had been married nearly ten years, but she didn't look any older than most twenty-eight year old women with two children. She was tall and rangy and rather flat-chested. In high school she had been famous for her legs. Girls still played high school basketball in Kentucky in those days. She had been quite a good athlete, but it was her long, trim legs that made her truly distinctive on the floor. Men had always been hot for Marcella because of her legs although she had never allowed herself to acknowledge that. In the old days in the mountains she had seen herself as a big goof. Now she saw herself as some sort of senior citizen with a sense of humor. She and Doyle only had the two children, but Marcella made it seem as if she was an ancient matriarch of an enormous brood that had used up her life and left her a feeble old crone before her time.

"Lord but it's awful to get old," she said as she settled back in her chair. "I wouldn't ever do it if I was you David. I declare I wouldn't."

"You always say that," said D.R.

Marcella grunted. In a voice trembling with mock decrepitude she said, "You better listen to an old woman's advice now, child. I declare you better."

She laughed at her role and her lines. Then she took a sip of Pepsi, turned to Divine Right and with a sad expression on her face told him about their Uncle Emmit, who was close to death at the homeplace in Kentucky.

Communes

I'd call this the hardest-working, most effective of the commune publications. More than others it fosters variety, it carries detailed reports from working communes, it gets into substantial how-to information. It's British, with right worldly perspective.

—SB

Communes

$4.50 /yr, $7.50 airmail

from:
Commune Movement
Bit,
141 Westbourne Park Road
London W11
England

Not an Escape but a Confrontation

In an amplifier negative feedback is applied to improve the stability and the quality. This is done by taking a sample of the output and applying it in opposition at the input. It is very effective and its only disadvantages are, it lowers the gain slightly and necessitates a feedback loop.

This may be used in analogy when considering the function of a commune in society. The aim is the betterment of society, the isolation from society is very relative and more geographical and cultural than economic.

When an individual becomes disenchanted with society he tends to become a floater, society waste, as he no longer contributes: he drops out. This dropping out allows a period of quiet, a first taste of freedom— freedom from the duties imposed from without. Duties from parents, teachers, employers and society-in-the-mass. This kind of freedom is enjoyed for a while until further disenchantment occurs, being a limited freedom and realisation of this brings about the discontent.

To enter into society once again in such a sensitive state would be self-ruinous and self-effacing. To do this is accepting defeat and once again to run with the herd resulting in a half-hearted way of life once again, but more conscious sorrow. The alternative is to form your own closed circuit of life—sustaining activity, to have a creative aim.

Not knowing how one can fit into society in a creative manner a further period of quietude is necessary, but one in which the struggle for survival doesn't become all encompassing. To do this one must become economically independent and the purest way to this end is to live without luxury, with sufficiency and no more. This can be done most effectively in a group and naturally in a group entertaining a similar search would be the ideal.

A community.

Eventually people covering such a protracted project will mature into their own creative mood and a suitable mode of activity will surely result. Such an individual will then know his own most effective life-loving waywardness and on returning to society will not be caught up in the swirl of events but will be able to produce real individual action, from within what he has created as himself, instead of outside influenced micro-patterns of society-at-large.

This is negative feedback, though its net result is positive.

A mental institution provides positive feedback. As its small output reinforces the original input and causes excessive diharmonious action resulting in an unstable society of low quality.

Tentative Group

The Tentative Group has run into difficulties and no longer exists as a group.

•

FISH-FARMING COMMUNES

This is a suggestion only, as yet, so I will open up the discussion of the idea's value as I see it. There are three big factors: (a) For those interested in rural communities, reasonable arable land is or can be expensive— as we all know who owns the wealth and it ain't us— taking it off them may require revolutionary force— but there is something one can do quite cheaply (by comparison) in the meanwhile, as part of the process. (b) There is a world food shortage (or at least a "Third-World" food shortage; we should grow more of our own in Europe and import less from outside. (c) There are, in this country, many hundreds of smaller streams, still unpolluted on cheaply available semi-moorland ground (even near industrial areas) which with a series of small dams that would drown a minimal amount of the natural environment, would make an excellent cooperative fishing industry. Fish ponds are very important in the food economy of thickly populated countries like China, Japan and Indonesia. If you're one of those vegetarian extremists who don't believe in eating fish, the best fed parts of the World are those who have access to large scale fishing resources, i.e., Kerala in India, Coastal China, the Greek Islands, and the sea-going parts of Western Europe. The ancient Celts used to belie= ve 'gods' lived in the sea and that to kill fish was a dire act of sacrilege; this belief died out, not only because of religious changes, but because human population increase meant that land resources available were inadequate for supporting it by themselves!

Dune

***Dune** is rich re-readable fantasy with clear portrayal of the fierce environment it takes to cohere a community. The metaphor is ecology. The theme revolution, the hard-won return to balance.*

—SB

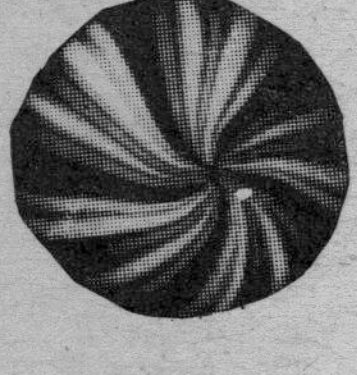

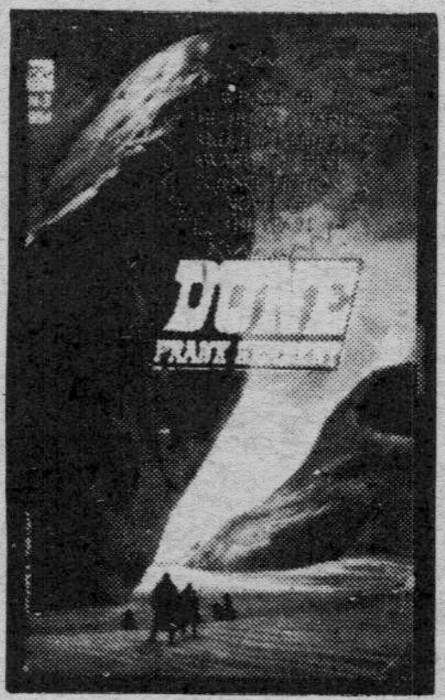
DUNE

Dune
Frank Herbert
1965; 544 pp.

$1.50 postpaid

from:
Ace Books, Inc.
1120 Avenue of the Americas
New York, N. Y. 10036

or WHOLE EARTH CATALOG

"These things are so ancient within us," Paul said, "that they're ground into each separate cell of our bodies. We're shaped by such forces. You can say to yourself, 'Yes, I see how such a thing may be.' But when you look inward and confront the raw force of your own life unshielded, you see your peril. You see that this could overwhelm you. The greatest peril to the Giver is the force that takes. The greatest peril to the Taker is the force that gives. It's as easy to be overwhelmed by giving as by taking."

"And you, my son," Jessica asked, "are you one who gives or one who takes?"

"I'm at the fulcrum," he said. "I cannot give without taking and I cannot take without . . ." He broke off.

Modern Utopian
Alternate Society

These two seem to just barely stagger along from issue to issue. **Modern Utopian** *is American, somewhat theoretical, and occasional source of useful news from particular communes.* **Alternate Society** *is Canadian, somewhat political, an occasional source of useful news from particular communes. Both rely heavily on reprints.*

—SB

Modern Utopian
Dick Fairfield, ed.

$10 /yr (quarterly, plus other stuff)

from:
Alternatives!
P.O. Drawer A
Diamond Heights Station
San Francisco, CA 94131

Alternate Society
Gary, ed.

$5 /12 issues

from:
Alternate Society
47 Riverside Dr.
Welland, Ontario
Canada

Perhaps the largest area yet to be settled in North America is Northern Ontario, comprising over 360,000 square miles of territory with a population of only a little more than half a million. Northern Ontario is as varied in terrain as it is large in size. Covering some 1000 miles between the Provinces of Quebec and Manitoba, and extending north from North Bay to James and Hudon's Bay, Northern Ontario is a land of tens of thousands of clear lakes, rugged hills of Precambrian rock, endless tracts of timber and an almost limitless freedom to exercise ones own abilities in creating a better life.

While much of Northern Ontario is unsuited to any kind of agriculture, being either too cold or rocky, numerous areas exist within Northern Ontario that offer excellent possibilities. One such area is NEAR NORTH. The "near north" or southern extremity of Northern Ontario is approx 300 miles wide, covering the distance from Ottawa River on the east to Lake Superior in the west and extending for 50 miles north and south of that line. Largely lowland, many tracts of good farmable land exist, and in some places, have been developed. The entire area is well served by all forms of transportation and has within its boundries, one third of Northern Ontario's population.

Alternate Society

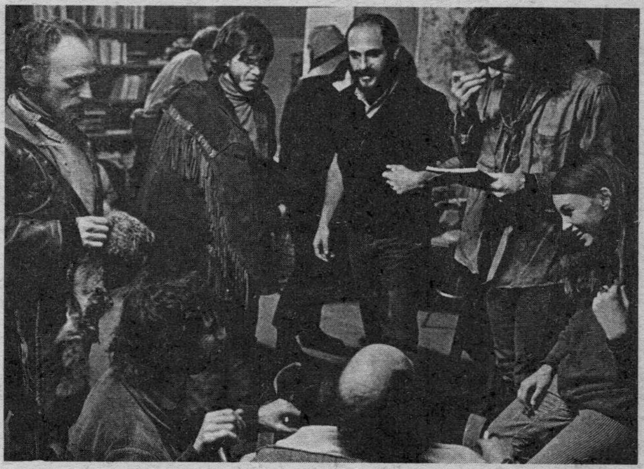

In economics, Sun Hill received some money through donations, but by far the bulk of its income came from the performing of "outside" jobs, either individually or in groups.

Most of the money earned was pooled. Members contributed what they could and drew what they needed. Petty cash was kept— at the inspiration of Heinlein's *Stranger in a Strange Land*— in an open box by the main door, from which members took what they required, and recorded on a wall-hung paper what they had spent, and for what they had spent it. Though this door-box system may be ideal in a situation as described in "*Stranger*" (where money was incoming freely and in adequate surplus of needs) our meager income (and the resultant need for tighter budgeting) eventually forced the curtailment of this practice. We had resolved that each adult member be entitled to receive a minimum of $2/week "personal money" for purchases exclusive of necessities. Actually this was rarely dared to be drawn from the precarious amounts of money on hand.

One might conjecture that great and hot disputes arose from so casual and communal a system of sharing money, but somehow they did not. I suppose this was because, in our zeal for Community, such matters were not given great weight, and each member was fairly conscientious and reasonable in his handling of his finances.

Initially, little effort was made to accurately anticipate expenses and make assurances of sufficient income to meet them. Money was simply spent as needed until it was gone, and then everything waited until more was available. No ',reserve" was ever attempted, and unexpected large bills (such as auto repairs) usually automatically meant going further into debt. Eventually, we evolved an adequate system of accounting and financial planning. Money was segregated for different anticipated uses. We could then be assured that, when an urgent (anticipated) expense came up, the money earned for it was unspent. Money that was spent was noted on the ',expense" sheet and, at the end of the month, broken down into categories to help us anticipate future needs in each category. At the beginning of the month, projected income and outgo for the coming month was compared, and our money-earning-and-spending activities adjusted to suit.

Sun Hill's most successful economic ploy was not in making money but in contriving not to spend it. Monetary expenses were generally contained by obtaining our material needs in as crude and unprocessed form as possible, supplying our own labor wherever possible, and— largely— by simply doing without. Were it not for the savings thus realized (and the collectivization of consumption) Sun Hill would have undoubtedly "gone under" financially, for income was always meager.

Modern Utopian

New Alchemy Institute

Here is a fantasy proposing to integrate solar heating, aquaculture, and agriculture in projects in New Mexico and the tropics. Technologically knowledgeable. The booklet probably costs something from:

The New Alchemy Institute, East
Box 432
Woods Hole, Massachusetts 02543
or
Box 376, Pescadero, CA 94060

Fraser Darling, in his perceptive studies of remote Scottish peoples, showed how self-sufficiency was a positive force in their lives. The most independent communities were far more diverse and socially alive than the single industry towns and those heavily dependent on a life-line to the outside. He also found that they coped far better in their dealings with the world at large. Equally important, the independent communities cared for their environment and were less prone to despoil it for short term monetary gain.

WINTER GARDEN GALLERIES

COMBINING SUNLIGHT CONCENTRATION, EARTH HEAT RETENTION, HEAT FROM DECOMPOSITION OF COMPOST AND MINIMIZATION OF HEAT LOST TO THE WINTER SKY

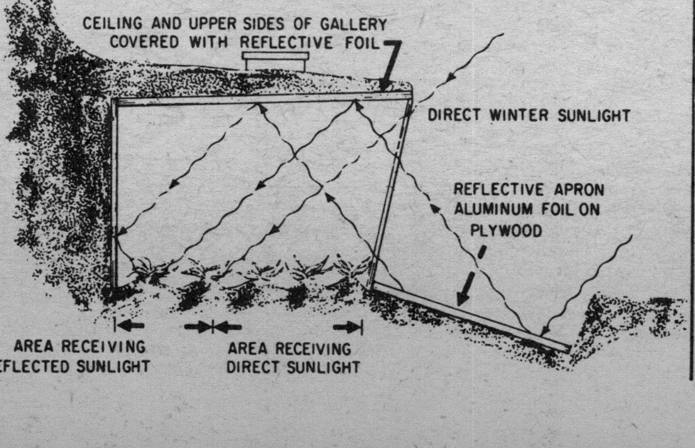
CEILING AND UPPER SIDES OF GALLERY COVERED WITH REFLECTIVE FOIL
DIRECT WINTER SUNLIGHT
REFLECTIVE APRON ALUMINUM FOIL ON PLYWOOD
AREA RECEIVING REFLECTED SUNLIGHT
AREA RECEIVING DIRECT SUNLIGHT

A Clue That Communes Are Real

Have you noticed that recent commune life in various areas of the U.S. is strongly reminiscent of Indian life in those places? The political Iroquois and Cherokees of the East Coast. The easy-going defenseless West Coast Indians. The structural, mystical pueblos of New Mexico.

—SB

Stock Letter No. 1

My wife, unborn child and I are looking for a place to get back to God. We have looked at what is offered by U.S. and Canadian society and don't feel it has what we are looking for. I went two quarters at the U. of Wash. and from my own experience plus talking to others don't feel that a formal education is what I'm seeking. Work is fine, but only when constructive and meaningful; jobs that are these are few.

What we are looking for is a communal farm that could use two healthy human beings. (almost 3)

What we have to offer is youth (both 19), a will to learn and grow and faith.

Our financial situation is quite good as I am from an uppermiddle class background.

We have been vegetarians for more than a year now and believe in the organic way.

If you can help us in any way we shall be eternally grateful.

> Love and Peace,
> Jim and Penny Kelso
> Seattle, Washington

Stock Answer No. 1

All the communes are crowded and seldom can use newcomers unless they have money to dispense or unusual pratical skills.

Community is a matter of making, not finding. Start your own.

> Whole Earth Catalog

Stock Letter No. 2

Gentlemen.

I am a graduate student at the University of California, Davis, and am working on a project involving "Intentional Community Organization." After looking at the Spring 1969 edition of the Whole Earth Catalog, I realized that you might be able to assist me. At present, I am trying to compile a list of communes, collectives, hip colonies, and other forms of communal organizations in the northern California area. The list will serve as a population from which a sample will be selected to be used in a study of child rearing and socialization.

The geographic area which I am interested in is northern California and western Nevada bounded on the south by Big Sur and Fresno.

I am specifically concerned with the items listed on the attached sheet, but any information or leads you might be able to supply would be of great benefit. If, at a later date, any of my findings become pertinent to your interests, I would be happy to share them.

I think the Whole Earth Catalog is relevant and interesting. I hope you'll be able to keep publishing it for a long time

Your time and efforts are very much appreciated.

> Peace,
> Frank Nicassio
> Davis, California

Stock Answer No. 2

Communes aren't too interested in being studied, unless you feel like paying them.

> Whole Earth Catalog

Comment

The Whole Earth Catalog is staying out of lateral communications among communities, yearning communers, social scientists, reporters, etc. for two reasons. (1) the job is massive; we can't handle it. (2) communities are beleaguered enough without us adding to the load.

> —SB

CLAP CLAP FOR PATTICLAPE

Patticake had her strange bladder pain diagnosed in town the other day. Yes, Yes, we have genuine gonorrhea right here on the farm. It was a riot watching her trying to get up the gumption to tell George that she had given it to him the night before. Ha Ha.

We don't want a commune. We want a community.
Ken Babbs 1969

The Commune Lie

One reason we promote communes is that there's no better place to make all the wishful mistakes, to get your nose rubbed in your fondest fantasies. (Sometimes a mistake works; that's gravy, and an obligation. The CATALOG was a mistake that worked.) Everybody has his own version of The Commune Lie, for example:

We'll let other people take care of us.

We'll let God take care of us.

Free lunch. (Robert Heinlein)

The Tragedy of the Commons (Garret Hardin)

We'll all be honest.

We'll all be selfless.

No rules.

Possessions are bad. Privacy is bad. Money is bad.

We've got the answer.

All lovely pitiful lies, and so, surely, is their denial. Do you know of any better, more rewarding labyrinth? And speculation won't get you around even the first turn.

Here are artifacts recovered from the midden heaps of the commune summer at Ken Kesey's farm, from the Hog Farm's first year in New Mexico, and from WHOLE EARTH correspondance.

> —SB

Food food food food
crisis crisis crisis crisis

The people in the kitchen, hard-ass Paula in particular, say there just isnt any food worth mentioning for supper or any other meal in sight. Here is what we need quick:

salad vegetables except lettuce
cooking vegetables
brown sugar
honey
non-instant powdered milk
don't waste money on fucking peanut butter

Course this food thing is really a drag, y'know, takes money, takes labor to cook it, why down at the store we can get pop-top lunch for $1.25 per six cans. The little babies like it in their bottles, and we can all cook those 200 pounds of brown rice in it, mmmmgood.

The Mormons were saved by Seagulls.

Think Dirty———

Things grow in dirt
The underground movement is necessary if you're going to plant stuff and grow it.

FREEDOM RINGS LOUD
(in our poor ears)

GEORGE'S ART OBJECT

George is way out in front in the All Asshole Farm Aesthetic Cotillion for the day: He discovered a bedpan with a turd floating in it on the bathroom floor. Good Hunting, George.

I DID NOT WASH MY DISH

Discipline on The Hog Farm

People think love is an emotion. Love is good sense.
Ken Kesey 1967

ALL ASSHOLE FARM EXPOSE

I hope that this week is the Farm's lowest point for the summer, because if it gets any lower I don't have a decent place to live. Dear reader, if I should mention some detail of fucked-up-ed-ness, you can match me with some detail you have observed; so don't fight me, you are as uncomfortable and as displeased as me. But, you may not feel as bad about this place as I do: you may have just arrived and found a slightly sloppy free summer camp, where you can fuck without your mother finding out, there are no annoying counselors and no schedule.

But I think of this as my (at-least) temporary home. And I like my home to be clear of broken glass and papers, my tools and supplies put away, I like to keep track of my guests, take care of my animals, keep my clothes hung up out of the way, and keep the equipment running.

But this farm is far from that. When you see a chocolate milk carton lying in the driveway, how long has it been there? And how many people have passed it thinking nothing, seeing nothing or else maybe saying "That's the twenty-ninth chocolate milk carton I seen today, if I picked them up, that's all I'd be doing all day.

Our average Farmer (Asshole) says to himself: "I'm here visiting (for a day, a week, a month or a year) and I'm not really a part of this farm, just a guest, so I can't do anything really effective about the Farm's condition." But, who are the non-guests, the permanent residents? Well, Page & Nadine, Gordon & Nancy. The rest of you can't be expected to take initiatives because you're not going to be here long. But while you are here you are living in shit, slop, cold, hunger, and bedlam. I gues you'll stay as long as you can stand it.

I'd like to see a group of 10 or so people cooperating, taking initiatives, picking up the chocolate milk carton, putting away food that's out, cleaning up, helping other people, fixing things, closing the gates, taking care of the equipment. I believe the key to the problem is: STABILITY LEADS TO A FEELING OF COMMUNITY.

We have very little sense of community here, except in desperate moments when everybody *must* help. Most of the time, most of us are "pigs at the trough": if you don't eat fast, your sty-mate will get more than you do. And if you don't avoid chores, you will be doing more work than your sty-mate. I believe everyone who is here for more than a few days falls into this pattern: the place just causes it. Because there is no sense of community, each person is "right" in grabbing the goodies and avoiding the work. This is, maybe, DECAY.

This is social decay: where the natural forces of the family (helping, loving, working together) are driven out by selfishness and the fear of working on a bad project.

I believe that the decay, the pigs-at-the-trough feeling, is caused by the INSTABILITY. When a stable group of ten lives together for weeks, natural forces work for community feeling. When the Farm is more than 20% tourists, when the family feeling is broken up every day or two by departures and arrivals, I see no hope.

SO YOU WANTA FUCK THE EARTH?

(an editorial)

Got your rocks off yet, Hippies?
Had your belly fill of goodies?
Have you looted your fill?
If so, take a gawk at the mother lode.
Messy, ain't it?
Yeah, that's right, man, you been
Fucking the earth rotten.
Now clean it up and take care of yours.

EMMIT'S CONDITION

David I don't know if you remember the Godsey family or not, but they use to run that little store where the post office was there at the mouth of Trace Fork when me and you was kids. Mr. Godsey was the postmaster in those days. After he died they give it to Mrs. Godsey, and she's run it and the store ever since, although the Lord only knows why Trace Fork would have a post office, they ain't over three families lives on that creek anymore. They've stripped that whole holler and then auger-mined it and most of the people that lived there when me and you did's moved away. But, Mrs. Godsey's there, and it's her that's been writing me letters about Emmit. She written me twice in the last two weeks, and I written her once and sent her our phone number. I told her to call me collect any time she thinks I need to know something about Emmit, and so yesterday she called and said the poor old feller's worse off than ever. She's really a dear woman, Mrs. Godsey is. She's known us I don't know how many years. She was Grandma's age. She remembers when Grandma and Grandad first moved to Trace Fork when they was just a young married couple. You ought to remember her, David, you use to go in there and buy candy from her when you wasn't any bigger than Debbie. Kind of a skinny woman, with the sweetest little voice you ever heard. Well, anyway, the poor thing, she's none too well herself, and I don't think she's actually been up to the homeplace to see Emmit. But she sends her boy Leonard up, and from what Leonard says, Emmit's so weak now he barely can get out of bed. Said he can get up enough to do his cooking, and goes out to feed his chickens and his rabbits. Emmit keeps rabbits now Leonard said, and manages to feed 'em. But said he couldn't garden, and when something goes wrong around the place he can't fix it, and that he's just going to have to have some help or be moved out of there, if he lives at all. I told Mrs. Godsey on the phone that we'd try to see about helping him someway, but I swan I don't know of a thing any of us can do. He won't leave the place, he's the contrariest old man that ever was. I'm worried sick about him, and Doyle is too. Mrs. Godsey's letters are in the house. After supper I'll get 'em out and let you read 'em.

The Hidden Dimension

"Don't try to reform man," says Fuller, "reform the environment." This book tools you to do it. Here is fascinating information on how we relate to space and each other through space. If you know how you want to feel and act, you can design a place to ensure that, or, equally, to make it impossible.

—SB

[Suggested by Bernie Sproch]

The Hidden Dimension
1966; 201 pp.

$1.95 postpaid

from:
Doubleday & Company, Inc.
501 Franklin Avenue
Garden City, New York 11530

or WHOLE EARTH CATALOG

. . . To increase the speed of motorists in tunnels, it is necessary to reduce the number of visual impacts that flash by at eye level. In restaurants, libraries, and public places, cutting down on movement in the peripheral field should reduce the sense of crowding somewhat, whereas maximizing peripheral stimulation should build up a sense of crowding.

•

. . . The Aivilik have at least twelve different terms for various winds. They integrate time and space as one thing and live in acoustic-olfactory space, rather than visual space. Furthermore, representations of their visual world are like X rays. Their artists put in everything they know is there whether they can see it or not. A drawing or engraving of a man hunting seal on an ice floe will show not only what is on top of the ice (the hunter and his dogs) but what is underneath as well (the seal approaching his breathing hole to fill his lungs with air).

•

. . . corner situations with people at right angles to each other produced six times as many conversations as face-to-face situations across the 36-inch span of the table, and twice as many as the side-by-side arrangement.

•

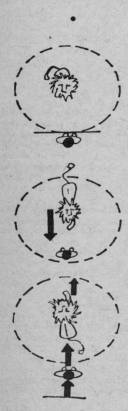

Although man is a self-domesticated animal, the domestication process is only partial. We see this in certain types of schizophrenics who apparently experience something very similar to the flight reaction. When approached too closely, these schizophrenics panic in much the same way as an animal recently locked up in a zoo. In describing their feelings, such patients refer to anything that happens within their "flight distance" as taking place literally *inside themselves*. That is, the boundaries of the self extend beyond the body. These experiences recorded by therapists working with schizophrenics indicate that the realization of the self as we know it is intimately associated with the process of making boundaries explicit.

•

In discussing olfactory messages with a psychoanalyst, a skillful therapist with an unusual record of success, I learned that the therapist could clearly distinguish the smell of anger in patients at a distance of six feet or more. People who work with schizophrenics have long claimed that they have a characteristic odor. Such naturalistic observations led to a series of experiments in which Dr. Kathleen Smith, a St. Louis psychiatrist, demonstrated that rats readily distinguish between the smell of a schizophrenic and a non-schizophrenic. In light of the powerful effect of chemical message systems one wonders if fear, anger, and schizophrenic panic may not act directly on the endocrine systems of nearby persons. One would suspect that this would be the case.

182 Considerations
Community

Village Planning in the Primitive World

Successful small community design must fit the local physical environment and at the same time render clear the community's social system and its religious system. This book has 78 pictures and eight detailed written accounts of village systems that have worked for bushmen, Cheyenne Indians, Trobriand Islanders, the Yoruba, Mbuti pygmies, and others. The systems are diverse, compelling, and mind-opening for approaching the design of one's own community.

—SB

7. Reconstruction of Pueblo Bonito. Chaco Canyon Canyon National Monument, New Mexico.

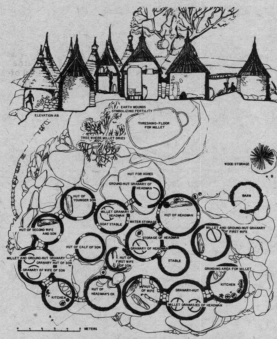

54. Plan of Matakam homestead. Cameroun, Africa.

Village Planning in the Primitive World
Douglas Fraser
1968; 128 pp.

$2.95 postpaid

from:
George Braziller
One Park Avenue
New York, New York 10016

or WHOLE EARTH CATALOG

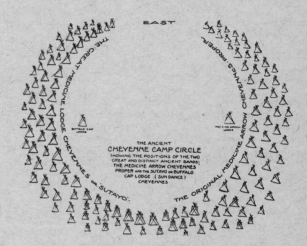

20. Plan of ancient Cheyenne camp circle. Western Plains, United States.

Gary Snyder

The Back Country $1.75

Regarding Wave $1.75

Earth House Hold $1.95

from:
J.B. Lippincott Co.
East Washington Square
Philadelphia, Pennsylvania 19105

or WHOLE EARTH CATALOG

21 August

Oiling and stowing the tools. (artifact/tools: now there's a topic.)

When a storm blows in, covering the south wall with rain and blotting out the mountains. Ridges look new in every light. Still discovering new conformations——every cony has an ancestry but the rocks were just here.

Structure in the lithosphere/cycles of change in rock/only the smallest percentage sanded and powdered and mixed with life-derived elements.

Is chemical reaction a type of perception??——Running through all things motion and reacting, object against object/there is more than enough time for all things to happen: swallowing its own tail.

[Earth House Hold]

REVOLUTION IN THE REVOLUTION IN THE REVOLUTION

The country surrounds the city
The back country surrounds the country

"From the masses to the masses" the most
Revolutionary consciousness is to be found
Among the most ruthlessly exploited classes:
Animals, trees, water, air, grasses

We must pass through the stage of the
"Dictatorship of the Unconscious" before we can
Hope for the withering-away of the states
And finally arrive at true Communionism.

If the capitalists and imperialists
are the exploiters, the masses are the workers.
and the party
is the communist.

If civilization
is the exploiter, the masses is nature.
and the party
is the poets.

If the abstract rational intellect
is the exploiter, the masses is the unconscious.
and the party
is the yogins.

& POWER
comes out of the seed-syllables of mantras.

[Regarding Wave]

The Effective Executive

Wherever there's a bunch of people doing something, somebody is bearing executive relation to the group, usually badly, so that he's unhappy and the group is unhappy, and nothing much is going on besides frustration. But some leaders are good, and with them a lot happens and everybody feels good. This book takes a deep look into how "good" executives behave in common. The generalizations that emerge are useful to anybody with responsibility, from the honcho of a commune to the goddam Pope.

—SB

The Effective Executive
Peter F. Drucker
1966; 178 pp.

$5.95 postpaid

from:
Harper & Row
49 E. 33rd St.
New York, N.Y. 10016

or WHOLE EARTH CATALOG

1. Effective executives know where their time goes. They work systematically at managing the little of their time that can be brought under their control.

2. Effective executives focus on outward contribution. They gear their efforts to results rather than to work. They start out with the question, "What results are expected of me?" rather than with the work to be done, let alone with its techniques and tools.

3. Effective executives build on strengths—their own strengths, the strengths of their superiors, colleagues, and subordinates; and on the strengths in the situation, that is, on what they can do. They do not build on weakness. They do not start out with the things they cannot do.

4. Effective executives concentrate on the few major areas where superior performance will produce outstanding results. They force themselves to set priorities and stay with their priority decisions. They know that they have no choice but to do first things first—and second things not at all. The alternative is to get nothing done.

5. Effective executives, finally, make effective decisions. They know that this is, above all, a matter of system—of the right steps in the right sequence. They know that an effective decision is always a judgment based on "dissenting opinions" rather than on "consensus on the facts." And they know that to make many decisions fast means to make the wrong decisions. What is needed are few, but fundamental, decisions. What is needed is the right strategy rather than razzle-dazzle tactics.

These are the elements of executive effectiveness—and these are the subjects of this book.

•

The definition of a "routine" is that it makes unskilled people without judgment capable of doing what it took near-genius to do before; for a routine puts down in systematic, step-by-step form what a very able man learned in surmounting yesterday's crisis.

•

We know very little about self-development. But we do know one thing: People in general, and knowledge workers in particular, grow according to the demands they make on themselves. They grow according to what they consider to be achievement and attainment. If they demand little of themselves, they will remain stunted. If they demand a good deal of themselves, they will grow to giant stature—without any more effort than is expended by the nonachievers.

•

To tolerate diversity, relationships must be task-focused rather than personality-focused. Achievement must be measured against objective criteria of contribution and performance. This is possible, however, only if jobs are defined and structured impersonally. Otherwise the accent will be on "Who is right?" rather than on "What is right?" In no time, personnel decisions will be made on "Do I like this fellow?" or "Will he be acceptable?" rather than by asking "Is he the man most likely to do an outstanding job?"

The least-known of the great American business builders, Theodore Vail, was perhaps the most effective decision-maker in U. S. business history. As president of the Bell Telephone System from just before 1910 till the mid-twenties, Vail built the organization into the largest private business in the world and into one of the most prosperous growth companies.

That the telephone system is privately owned is taken for granted in the United States. But the part of the North American continent that the Bell System serves (the United States and the two most populous Canadian provinces, Quebec and Ontario) is the only developed area in the world in which telecommunications are not owned by the government. The Bell System is also the only public utility that has shown itself capable of risk-taking leadership and rapid growth, even though it has a monopoly in a vital area and has achieved saturation of its original market. . . .

"Our business is service" became the Bell commitment as soon as Vail took over. At the time, shortly after the turn of the century, this was heresy. But Vail was not content to preach that it was the business of the company to give service, and that it was the job of management to make service possible and profitable. He saw to it that the yardsticks throughout the system by which managers and their operations were judged, measured service fulfillment rather than profit performance. Managers are responsible for service results. It is then the job of top management to organize and finance the company so as to make the best service also result in optimal financial rewards. . . .

Vail's third decision led to the establishment of one of the most successful scientific laboratories in industry, the Bell Laboratories. Again, Vail started out with the need to make a private monopoly viable. Only this time he asked: "How can one make such a monopoly truly competitive?" Obviously it was not subject to the normal competition from another supplier who offers the purchaser the same product or one supplying the same want. And yet without competition such a monopoly would rapidly become rigid and incapable of growth and change.

But even in a monopoly, Vail concluded, one can organize the future to compete with the present. In a technical industry such as telecommunications, the future lies in better and different technologies. The Bell Laboratories which grew out of this insight were by no means the first industrial laboratory, not even in the United States. But it was the first industrial research institution that was deliberately designed to make the present obsolete, no matter how profitable and efficient.

•

There is serious need for a new principle of effective administration under which every act, every agency, and every program of government is conceived as temporary and as expiring automatically after a fixed number of years—maybe ten—unless specifically prolonged by new legislation following careful outside study of the program, its results and its contributions.

The Peter Principle

The principle is: a person rises to his highest level of incompetence and then stays there forever because nobody likes to fire the formerly competent. *Now you don't need the book, which is mostly a witty dance through ramifications of the principle. Once you're caught in a Peter Principle blind alley, some escapes are: 1) stop pressing up and go sideways, 2) slide back a bit and change direction, 3) quit completely and start over, 4) put curtains and tasteful paintings on the walls of your alley and wait it out.*

—SB

The Peter Principle
Dr. Laurence J. Peter and Raymond Hull
1969; 169 pp.

$1.25 postpaid

from:
Bantam Books, Inc.
666 Fifth Avenue
New York, N.Y. 10019

or WHOLE EARTH CATALOG

Miss Totland, who had been a competent student and an outstanding primary teacher, was promoted to primary supervisor. She now has to teach, not children, but teachers. Yet *she still uses the techniques which worked so well with small children.*

Addressing teachers, singly or in groups, she speaks slowly and distinctly. She uses mostly words of one or two syllables. She explains each point several times in different ways, to be sure it is understood. She always wears a bright smile.

Teachers dislike what they call her false cheerfulness and her patronizing attitude. Their resentment is so sharp that, instead of trying to carry out her suggestions, they spend much time devising excuses for *not* doing what she recommends.

Miss Totland has proved herself incompetent in communicating with primary teachers. She is therefore ineligible for further promotion, *and will remain as primary supervisor, at her level of incompetence.*

•

The difference between cases of Pseudo-Achievement Syndrome and Final Placement Syndrome is known as *Peter's Nuance.* For your own guidance in classifying such cases, you should always ask yourself, "Is the person accomplishing any useful work?" If the answer is:

a) "YES"—he has not reached his level of incompetence and therefore exhibits only the Pseudo-Achievement Syndrome.

b) "NO"—he *has* reached his level of incompetence, and therefore exhibits the Final Placement Syndrome.

c) "DON'T KNOW"—*you* have reached *your* level of incompetence. Examine yourself for symptoms at once!

Up The Organization

This book has an amazing amount of truth, some of it pretty radical truth, about how to run an enterprise, whether it's a business, a school, a commune, or a government.

—SB

Up the Organization
Robert Townsend
1970; 202 pp.

$1.25 postpaid

from:
Fawcett Publications, Inc.
67 West 44th Street
New York, N.Y. 10036

or WHOLE EARTH CATALOG

A lesson very few have learned: If you want to approach the head of XYZ Corporation, call him cold. Tell him who you are and why you want to talk to him. A direct and uncomplicated relationship will follow.

The common mistake is to look for a mutual friend—or a friend's friend on his board, in his bank or investment bank or law firm—to introduce you. This starts all sorts of side vibrations and usually results in a half-assed prologue by the intermediary, who is apt to grind both edges of his own ax.

•

All decisions should be made as low as possible in the organization. The Charge of the Light Brigade was ordered by an officer who wasn't there looking at the territory.

There are two kinds of decisions: those that are expensive to change and those that are not.

•

If you can't do it excellently, don't do it at all.
Because if it's not excellent it won't be profitable or fun,
and if you're not in business for fun or profit, what the hell are you doing here?

•

Admit your own mistakes openly, maybe even joyfully.

Encourage your associates to do likewise by commiserating with them. Never castigate. Babies learn to walk by falling down. If you beat a baby every time he falls down, he'll never care much for walking.

•

Hiring. To keep an organization young and fit, don't hire anyone until everybody's so overworked they'll be glad to see the newcomer no matter where he sits.

DEPARTURE

Ordinarily the talk about their Uncle Emmit would have led D.R. and Marcella on into a general rap about other relatives, and the old days as children in Kentucky. But there were too many distractions for them to go very far with it that afternoon. D.R. was thinking about Estelle waiting at the bus station, and Marcella kept interrupting herself to hassle her children. About fifteen minutes into their conversation Herschel spilled his Pepsi and came demanding more, as Debbie started wailing around in the front yard. Marcella waited for Debbie to come running around the house to be comforted, but when she kept on crying where she was, Marcella jumped to her feet and ran around to see what was the matter. D.R. poured Herschel's glass full of Pepsi, and started to refill his own. But then he decided the thing to do was go in and call Estelle and see what was going down back at the old bus station.

"Herschel old friend, why don't you stay here and guard this Pepsi Cola while I go in the house and use the telephone. Okay?"

"Who are you going to call?" asked Herschel.

"I've got to call a man about a dog."

Herschel said, "You do not."

D.R. said, "I'm going to call the weather man and ask him to send us some rain."

"You're a turd," said Herschel.

"That's no way to talk to your friend."

"You're not my friend," said Herschel.

D.R. said, "I thought me and you were good old buddies."

"You're a queer," said Herschel. "Why don't you go somewhere and have a car wreck?"

"If I did that we wouldn't be able to wrestle any more, now would we?"

Instantly Herschel leaped onto D.R.'s lap. Together they fell out of the lawn chair onto the ground. D.R. started tickling Herschel in the ribs which made him squeal with laughter, but fight back twice as hard. Herschel crawled onto D.R.'s back as D.R. struggled to his feet. Together they staggered toward the house, scuffling and laughing, both red in the face from the effort.

By the time D.R. and Herschel had wrestled their way back in the house Marcella had evacuated Debbie to the bathroom, where she was having Medi-Quik sprayed on a not very badly damaged knee. Even without Debbie's commotion in the bathroom it would have been impossible to make a phone call with a nine year old orangutang on his back, so D.R. told Marcella he was going out to a pay phone to make a long distance call. Marcella tried to get him to use their house phone, but when D.R. said he wanted to go out she told him about a pay phone over in the shopping center. At the mention of the words "shopping center" Herschel started screaming and yelling for permission to go along. When it was clear he wasn't going to be allowed to he yelled "I hate you," at D.R. and slammed the door as hard as he could. As soon as D.R. got in the bus he fished a roach out of the ash try, and by the time he found the phone booth in the shopping center he was blessedly stoned.

Far-out is fine. Who's minding the store?
Gordon Ashby 1966

☐ I am...
☐ Someone else

Community Market

A growing clearing-house for communities practicing cottage economy. Serves as a mail-order catalog for the 36 groups listed. There are only a few noteworthy products, like hammocks, snowboots and papoose carriers, but there's an interesting variety of communities represented, from the Appalachian South Folklife Center to the Christian Home-steading Community.

—Hal Hershey

Directory of Community Market

$0.25

from:
Community Market
P.O. Box 268
Deerfield, Massachusetts 01342

WOODEN TOYS: Made of Pine or Fir (non-toxic)

Painted Hardboard Inlay Puzzles 10" x 12". Flowers in the Sun . . . . [32-L. $5.];
Farm Animals . . . . [32-M. $5.];
Geometric Shapes . . . . [32-N. $5.];
Word or Name—9-letter spaces per line/3 lines maximum. [32-O. $5.]

TOLSTOY FARM, Davenport, Washington 99122

Liberty House

One of the most together endeavors going; poor people from Mississippi, Louisiana, Florida, Georgia, Alabama, Africa, Mexico Guatemala and Canada making leather goods, bags, clothes, dolls, toys, basketwork, jewelry, It all seems to have a special hand-made quality.

—Hal Hershey

Catalog

$0.25

from:
Liberty House
P.O. Box 3468
Jackson, Mississippi 39207

Oven Glove: Real protection against burned hands, with a sense of humor. Well padded pockets cover both hands. Color: turquoise, yellow or red denim with multi-color lining. Indicate which. 36" long by 9" wide [21-F. $4.95]

Hand Puppets: Frog, Fish, Rabbit and Mouse. For dramatic play. Made in sturdy denim for durability. Indicate which. 10" long . . . . [21-H. $1.25]

Accounting For Everyday Profit

I do wish we'd had this invaluable book when we started business. Instead we fumbled around, lost track of things, invented procedures, got hints and requirements from Portola Institute, hired people with some experience, and after two years arrived at an excellent bookkeeping and accounting procedure which is just like what's in this book.

—SB
[Suggested by Francine Slate]

OUT OF PRINT

Accounting For Everyday Profit
J. K. Lasser
1970; 127 pp.

$1.45 postpaid

from:
Simon & Schuster
1 w. 39th St.
New York, N. Y. 10018

or WHOLE EARTH CATALOG

. . . From earliest times, whenever men gathered together in a community, some form of accounting has been necessary. And as cities and nations grew, accounting became one of the invisible connective tissues that gives any society a functioning shape. . . .

Twin Oaks Community, Louisa, Va., 23093,

From Our Doll Shop

Dolls, completely hand-made in small home-style work-shop, are stuffed with dacron polyester and guaranteed machine washable (except for clothes which should be hand-laundered separately). Each 10" tall. Indicate whether White or Negro desired. Price is same.

Girl . . . . [4-A. $5.50] **Boy** [4-B. $5.50]
Extra Set of Clothes . . . . [4-C. $1.75]

CAMPHILL VILLAGE, U.S.A. Copake, New York 12516

ASSETS			— LIABILITIES	
Cash on Hand	$	750	Accounts Payable	$ 20,000
Cash in Bank		27,000	Notes Payable	15,000
Accounts Receivable		90,000	Taxes Payable	3,000
Notes Receivable		15,000	Mortgage Payable	70,000
Inventory		35,000	Bonds Payable	35,000
Machinery and Equipment		40,000	Total Liabilities	$143,000
Land		20,000	*Capital*	
Buildings		195,000	Preferred Stock	$ 50,000
Prepaid Insurance		2,000	Common Stock	200,000
Supplies on Hand		500	Paid-In Surplus	2,000
			Earned Surplus	30,250
			Total Capital	282,250
Total Assets		$425,250	Total Liabilities & Capital	$425,250

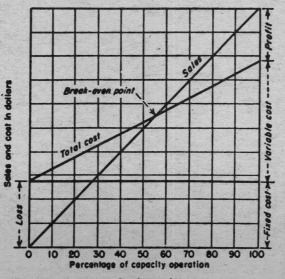

Breakeven chart.

Moonlighting means having a second job. Lots of people don't have a first job or want one. Birds of this feather flock economically together and pool resources for rent, food, dope, etc.—which still requires some modest income. Moonlight-type work may be the answer. Most of the income-sources in this book are part-time, or do-at-home, and involve low commitment of psyche (an advantage they have over stealing or dope peddling). The book includes a good list of technical training schools. —SB

300 Ways to Moonlight
Jerry LeBlance
1969; 176 pp.

No longer available

from:
Paperback Library
315 Park Ave. S.
New York, N.Y. 10010

or WHOLE EARTH CATALOG

BE A LOCKSMITH

Picking locks, installing them, or making keys, freeing people from locked rooms, or getting them into their locked homes and cars, is an art that mystifies most people, thus making the locksmith in any town a respected craftsman. But actually, almost anyone who can work with tools and has a steady hand for dealing with tiny objects can master this craft and make a secure and profitable living from it. Generally this is a job for a self-starter, whether he pursues it full time or part time. The more than three hundred tools of the trade are the secret; they really do the work.

Earnings

Some beginners report averaging $3 to $10 an hour in their spare time, while learning, and those who set up their own shops, either in their homes or in a small, rented downtown store, come closest to the higher figure. And it's almost 100 per cent profit.

Hours

Variable. This job can be placed on a regular workday basis if you concentrate on installing and replacing locks and key-making, and there are always many jobs that can be done in spare time at home. But there will always be emergency calls, too, and these can mean an hour's rush work at any time of day or night.

Requirements

If you can concentrate on simple diagrams, follow instructions and handle small tools, you can learn this trade quickly, studying in your free time at home and gaining practical experience by working with actual car locks, home locks, safe locks, and padlocks. You'll also need a car for transportation, of course.

Future

Some large-traffic supermarket and department stores are glad to set up a locksmith with the space he needs, just for the service to their customers, although they will expect a commission or rent for their ideal situation. But opening your own shop is a distinct future calling, and you can double your earnings by selling locks, keys, and safety devices, too.

For Information

Write Locksmithing Institute, Little Falls, New Jersey
07424.

American Tuning School, Gilroy, California 95020. Home study in piano tuning.

Anderson School of Scientific Massage, Princeton, Illinois. Professional massage taught by mail; diploma awarded.

Small Business Administration

The Small Business Administration publishes over 70 bibliographies that deal with differing businesses and functions. These can prove extremely useful to those people contemplating a part time store of their own and single copies are available free from the administration. Small Business Administration, Washington, D.C., 20416.

Mark McCain
Salem, New Hampshire

Credit Union

HOW TO BUILD A MONEY RE-CYCLING DEPOT FOR $30
OR
DO YOU KNOW WHERE YOUR SAVINGS ARE TONIGHT?

Remember when they burned the Bank of America in Isla Vista, California? Well, they're burning it again in IV right now, only this time the Bank isn't going to be able to re-build so easily. This time they're burning it legally, in fact they've got a charter from the federal government to do it —— by forming a "credit union."

IV's Community Council has started the Isla Vista Community Federal Credit Union as sort of a *money co-op*. Members save there just as they would at a bank —— their deposits earn dividends and are insured up to $20,000. But instead of lending money to defense-disoriented conglomerates or agri-mega-businessmen, the credit union makes loans *only to its own members*. The idea is to build up the economic vitality and self-sufficiency of the Isla Vista alternative community by creating a co-operative "people's bank."

Loans must be OK'd by a credit committee elected by the members. The money can be used for anything from buying a truck to defraying medical expenses to paying tuition to financing a tractor. A brochure from the Credit Union National Association suggests what kind of loan criteria are used: "For a community credit union, making loans on character happens to be especially easy, because it is a friendly association of neighbors. The members know each other. They do not have to investigate each other . . . Hence, whenever a loan application is being considered, the members of the credit committee can concentrate on the question, 'Will this loan help the borrower?'" And because the credit union is a non-profit, tax-exempt association, it can make loans at easy-money interest rates.

The IV credit union operates out of a corner of the Community Council's office. It pays its manager $25 a week to keep office hours Monday through Saturday, two hours a day. In its first six weeks it signed up 120 members, with share deposits of $25,000. About $5,000 has been loaned out to members so far —— one loan, for example, went to finance the inventory of a text-book co-op. Another was to help a member buy tires for his truck. The credit union has contracted with the county welfare department to sell food stamps. The county will pay IV's people's bank $1.00 every time a member buys stamps! Eventually, the credit union's board hopes to do a bail bond service and finance co-operative housing.

The Counter-Economy seminar at the Free University of Berkeley, which we co-ordinate, has formed an organizing committee to apply for a charter for a credit union of the members of the Free U. (Every credit union must be

Officers of the Isla Vista Credit Union go over accounts. left to right, J.C. Simmons (President of the Board), Rosemary McLeod (Chairman of Credit Committee). Mike Tejeda (Vice-President of Board and Chairman of Educational Committee), seated Marla Mercer (office manager).

formed among a group of people who share a "common bond" —— work for the same employer, belong to the same church, labor union, fraternal, professional, co-operative or other association, live in the same community or neighborhood, etc. The class has laid out $30 in fees, which will be reimbursed as soon as the credit union begins to wail. The class polled its 23 members and discovered that all together they had $7,910 (!!!!!) sitting in banks doing nothing socially, morally, existentially, or esthetically justifiable —— money that could be easily liberated and sluiced back into a community of friends and neighbors. This credit union will consolidate the economic resources of people who belong to the Free U. and use them to fund potentially self-sustaining co-operative businesses —— an automobile repair service, for instance, and a dressmakers' co-op —— by making loans to members. Ultimately it could serve as the clearing-house for a labor exchange that would make it unnecessary for us to be constantly handing each other government forms with numbers all over them every time the roof needs fixin'. The "People's Bank" founded by our anarchist friend Pierre-Joseph Proudhon in Paris in 1849 was, after all, designed to *eliminate* money!

There's one problem with credit union loans —— they can only be made to members who are likely to repay —— they aren't grants. The class discovered that Leopold's, Berkeley's non-profit record store, raised a $2,500 grant for a legal defense fund during the Cambodia-Kent State crisis by asking people to pay a "voluntary tax" of 25 cents an album. The class has discussed the possibility of collecting a "voluntary tax" at the credit union ——25 cents per transaction, say —— toward an "alternative community chest" that would be allocated by proportional vote of the membership to community institutions that won't be able to pay the money back, like the Free Clinic.

If you're interested in setting up a credit union as a focus for economic experimentation, write Credit Union National Association, Box 431, Madison, WI 53701. They will provide you with literature and refer you to the local office of your state's Credit Union League, which will send a consultant to speak with your group and, after the cash begins to recycle, supply all kinds of technical help and logistical support.

If you'd like to check out the Isla Vista Credit Union Newsletter, send a self-addressed stamped envelope to 970 Embarcadero Del Mar, Goleta, CA 93017.

Craig & Alison Karpel

United Security Accounts

WRITE CHECKS ON YOUR SAVINGS ACCOUNT; EARN INTEREST ON YOUR CHECKING ACCOUNT

United Security Accounts is for real. Ask any banker.
They all go tut tut and look envious.

—SB

United Security Accounts® are a combination of savings and checking accounts. Interest-bearing savings (4½%) serve as collateral for 15 to 45-day free check loans, with the obvious advantage that money spent is effectively earning interest. The accounts offer unlimited free checking with no minimum balance (a $100 deposit is required to open an account but need not be maintained); in return, you have to watch out for a few tricky features. When the free loan period is up, a loan starts costing you 9%, retroactive to the writing of the check, and savings are *not* automatically withdrawn to cover it. You can withdraw savings and apply the money to the loan yourself, though you may lose several month's interest if you do; but the accounts are most satisfactory if you deposit enough each month to cover the previous month's checks. A deposit intended to cover a check-loan must reach the bank after the check has cleared; otherwise it goes to the savings account and the loan will remain outstanding.
The checks come with an identification card and look quite distinctive. Probably as a result, they are almost as easy to cash as local checks.

The bank says the accounts are released in blocks and are not always available. I don't know how much trouble they may be to get (I had no wait at all). Don't send a deposit, just a letter of inquiry, to

Citizens Bank and Trust Company
Chicago, Illinois 60648
Duane Small
Louisville, Ky.

Far as I can see, you've covered *Everything* but this:
This check is written on a checking account which provided free printed checks, free postage for deposits, free, comlpete monthly statements that anyone can understand and...get this...*Maximum Savings Account Interest* on my MAXIMUM account balance. All this plus Federal Deposit Insurance.
My account has been with them for years, and I won't tell you how much interest they've paid me for my *Checking Account* money! Top that!
George D. James Jr.
Unadilla, N.Y.

Atlas Shrugged

This preposterous novel has some unusual gold in it.
—SB

Atlas Shrugged
Ayn Rand
1957; 1084 pp.

$1.75 postpaid

from:
New American Library
1301 Avenue of the Americas
New York, N. Y. 10019

or WHOLE EARTH CATALOG

"Did you really think that we want those laws to be observed?" said Dr. Ferris. "We want them broken. You'd better get it straight that it's not a bunch of boy scouts you're up against—then you'll know that this is not the age for beautiful gestures. We're after power and we mean it. You fellows were pikers, but we know the real trick, and you'd better get wise to it. There's no way to rule innocent men. The only power any government has is the power to crack down on criminals. Well, when there aren't enough criminals, one makes them. One declares so many things to be a crime that it becomes impossible for men to live without breaking laws. Who wants a nation of law-abiding citizens? What's there in that for anyone? But just pass the kind of laws that can neither be observed nor enforced nor objectively interpreted—and you create a nation of law-breakers—and then you cash in on guilt. Now that's the system, Mr. Rearden, that's the game, and once you understand it, you'll be much easier to deal with."

A VERY DIFFICULT DAY

"Hello?"

"Hello, Estelle? This is David Ray Davenport, the famous truth seeker. I'm calling to see if you or any member of your immediate family might have a truth to tell today."

"Where are you?" asked Estelle.

"Ahh," said D.R. "A good question. A very good question. Right now I'd say I'm cruising at about ten thousand feet. And what's that I spy below me there, off to the right, nestled in a little cluster of twenty-one thousand dollar suburban houses on the outskirts of Cincinnati? Why, I do believe its one of those hippie buses, painted up all garrish and weird, surrounded by children and a smattering of curious adult on-lookers. But wait! That curious on-looker smashing the headlights with his fists. That's no adult. That's a kid! A two-hundred-pound, nine-year-old kid. And look! Oh my God! The kid! He's gone wild! He's beating the poor hippie about the head and ears, he's hitting him with a Pepsi Cola bottle. Help, help, someone! Someone call for help!"

"Where are you?" asked Estelle.

"Mam, I regret I am unable to give out that kind of information. Heavy stuff is going on. Mad villains are everywhere. Insanity rules, and only a total clamp on all information will save the day. I can, however, reveal this much: my nine-year-old nephew is actually a dwarf with incredible supernatural powers. Only an hour ago, before my very eyes, right in my own hand, by god, he transformed a Pepsi Cola bottle into a turd. Imagine. A turd. It was awful. It was disgusting. And then, you'll never believe what he did next. There I am sitting in the back yard of this little twenty-one thousand dollar suburban home with a big piece of shit in my hand, and he says: you're going to have a car wreck. He lays this curse on me right there, he says, Motherfucker you are about to crash! It's been really heavy, mam. I've really had a very difficult day.

Understanding Foundations

It tells you some about how to raise money and a lot about where to look.

—SB

[Suggested by Larry McCombs]

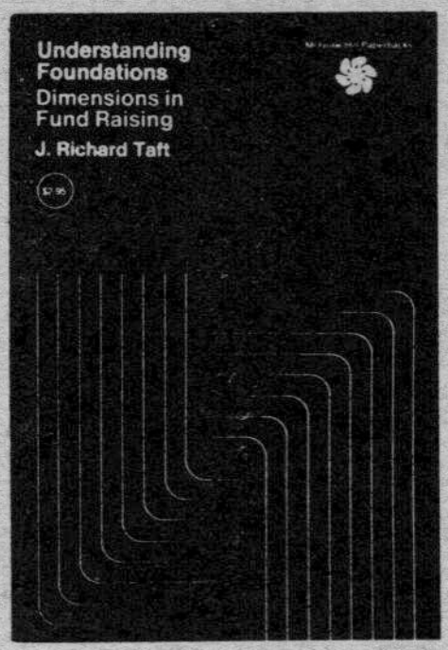

Understanding Foundations
J. Richard Taft
1967; 205 pp.

OUT OF PRINT

McGraw-Hill Book Co.
Princeton Road
Hightstown, New Jersey 08520

Manchester Road
Manchester, Missouri 63062

8171 Redwood Highway
Novato, Ca. 94947

Perhaps the greatest, most time-consuming, and least productive activity among fund raisers today is random foundation door-knocking. Amateurs, especially, are guilty of this. But professionals, who should know better, are offenders too.

•

Everyone who has ever applied or is about to apply to a foundation for a grant wonders whether there is some magic formula for a successful application. If there is one, it is simplicity.

The desks of foundation officials around the country are piled high with applications characterized by verbosity, pomposity, and vagueness. Make your application short, simple, and clear, and it will stand out.

Most foundations have no standard form which applicants fill out. A good approach is a simple letter of one or two pages (even the most complex subjects can be boiled down to this length) or a short proposal accompanied by a covering letter of introduction. Sometimes it is worth calling a foundation first to discuss your project before going to the trouble of preparing a proposal.

•

Don't hem and haw on money. State figures and try to stick with them. If you need staff, you will need to pay them. How much? If you need office space and equipment, check out all costs before going to the foundation. If materials, transportation, or other items are involved, include them. If it is a one-time grant, say so. If not, make it a two-year, or three-year, or more, request. Foundation officials are money handlers and, as such, are most concerned with sound fiscal management. They cite poor financial administration as a key factor in grants rejection.

•

Every applicant wonders whether or not he should include endorsements in his proposal. By all means, if there are reputable people in the field who are familiar with your work, the organization, and its programs, endorsements are valuable. Foundations have a high regard for expertise. The backing of respected people puts a useful stamp of approval on any project.

•

After making your proposal or writing your letter, don't expect quick response. Most foundations are extremely busy and take a good deal of time before responding to letters or applications. Certainly do not expect an early grant. Foundations generally have board meetings several times a year, at which time those proposals which have passed the scrutiny of the executive director, the program administrator, or the person concerned with applications, are considered. It is infrequent that an applicant will receive funds in less than six months' time after his application.

The Foundation Directory

The reference book of foundations. Gives addresses, finances, officers, purposes and activities. Foundations are listed by state, which is intelligent, since grants are usually given locally.

—SB

The Foundation Directory
Marianna O. Lewis, Ed.
1967; 1198 pp.

$15.00 postpaid

from:
Columbia University Press
Stock Department
Irvington-on-Hudson, N.Y. 10533

Many foundations have accepted the doctrine that their limited funds should be used chiefly as the venture capital of philanthropy, to be spent in enterprises requiring risk and foresight, not likely to be supported by government or private individuals. In their fields of special interest they prefer to aid research, designed to push forward the frontiers of knowledge, or pilot demonstrations, resulting in improved procedures apt to be widely copied.

Support for current programs, if it comes at all from foundations, must usually be sought from the smaller organizations, and especially those located in the area of the agency, well acquainted with its personnel and its needs. Most small foundations, and some larger ones, restrict their grants to the local community, or state. Immense variety exists; the interests and limitations of each foundation need to be examined before it is approached.

Where there is evidence that the applicant has not bothered to find out the field of interest of the foundation, or has made a general mailing, the cost of even a formal declination is scarcely warranted; wastebaskets are available in any required size.

•

Sample listing:

San Francisco Foundation, The
351 California Street
San Francisco, California 94104

Community foundation established in 1948 in California by resolution and declaration of trust.

Purpose and Activities: Grants principally for welfare and welfare planning, hospitals, education, health and mental health, culture and the arts, and conservation in the San Francisco area unless otherwise specified by donors. Report published annually.

Financial Data (year ended 30 June 1965): Active capital, $6,736,824 (L); gifts received, $686,287; expenditures, $681,325, including $639,793 in grants.

Officer: John R. May, Executive Director and Secretary.

Distribution Committee: S. Clark Beise, Chairman; Daniel E. Koshland, William H. Orrick, Jr., Vice-Chairmen; William R. Hewlett, Treasurer; Christian de Guigne, Mrs. Alfred McLaughlin, Emmett G. Solomon.

Trustees: Bank of America, The Bank of California, Commonwealth National Bank of San Francisco, Crocker-Citizens National Bank, First Western Bank and Trust Company, Golden Gate National Bank, The Hibernia Bank, Pacific National Bank of San Francisco, United California Bank, Wells Fargo Bank.

On Free Money

From my limited experience, the realm of foundations and grants is one of the most cynical in the American economy. Generally when you approach a foundation they are friendly and half-receptive. They consider your project promising if a little naive, and they'd like to you write up a proposal on it. You spend a month learning how to write proposals and a month writing this one. They keep it six months. Your idea has died of dry rot. Then they request that you re-write the proposal to accommodate (whatever) and it might go through next time the board meets. Do this three times, and you have died of dry rot.

Most actual grants I know of were initiated by the donors, not the donees. The most effective way to get grant money is to be Highly Visible.

I don't know why foundation and government money is so often toxic to projects. Maybe because the process becomes so easily dishonest. Do me no favors, and I'll tell you no lies. Or is it the belief that there's such a thing as a free lunch that is the root lie?

—SB

On Getting by Without Money

Disassociation with the economic bag of any society is difficult unless you are very rich or a Trappist monk. This article is for those who have no savings, no inheritance no trust funds and no desire to remain in a money-oriented rut (there are so many other ruts to explore).

What I have to offer here is not all-inclusive—just merely information that I have acquired firsthand as my family (wife and 2 kids) and I have tripped along.

When we first started on the trip, our first concern was food—a needless concern in this country—we went to the local grocery store and asked for the vegetable and fruit discards. Everyday in this country grocery stores—all of them—throw away about 4 garbage cans full of edible food. Food that is 'spotted', 'overripe', 'bruised', or ugly. The quality and quantity of the throw-away food depends very much on the type of ownership of store and its clientel. One man operations or family owned stores keep everything—chain operated stores throw away good food all the time. The easiest way to get vegetables from a store is to ask for them. Sometimes you score, sometimes not. The store I got vegetables from gave me enough to feed 31 people, 10 chickens and start a good compost pile—2-3 boxes everyday. Stores catering to the elite of this society have the most throwaways—no blemishes or bruises allowed.—but they tend to be selfish with their garbage. Stores like Safeway, etc. are best bets.

Another source of food is Government Surplus Food obtained from your local welfare office. In Santa Cruz County (Calif.), a married man with 1 child earning less than $200 a month is 'entitled' to 20 lbs. of flour, 3 lbs. of oatmeal, 5 lbs. of corn meal, 1 lb of bulgar, 3 lbs. of rolled wheat, 3 lbs. of rice, 5 lbs. of butter, 10 lbs. of powdered milk, 3 lbs. of lard, 2 lbs. of dried peas, 1 lb. of peanut butter, 5 lbs. of cheese, plus canned vegetables, dried fruit and fruit juice.—each month. These foods are good trade items—we traded for eggs and non-food items. —examples—made arrangements with a group living on a farm. They didn't 'qualify' for welfare food but had an abundance of barnyard stock. We traded. We had food, another made sandals. We traded. We had cornmeal, someone raised a lamb—we had meat, they had meal. The best way to trade is to give it all away—when it's time, it will come back.

Next to free food, you need cheap food. Most bakeries sell day-old bread—we used to get about 13 loaves of french bread and 5 dozen rolls for $1.00. (This helped feed the chickens too.) Egg Ranches sell flats of eggs below market value—we got cracked eggs for less than 1¢ each (cheap enough to feed the dogs, along with the canned welfare meat). Also, farmers markets and flea markets are good places for cheap good produce. Most important of all—bulk purchases of wheat and rice are very wise investments.

Cheap clothes are available at the Goodwill, Army Surplus Stores, Rummage sales and Flea markets. Rent is the real bummer and we never solved it completely until we moved into our camper. However, rent can be lessened on a trade for rent basis. I got 3 weeks free rent in agreement to clean up the house I was moving into. One friend got a big house for 3 months in exchange for repairs. Another got a year's free rent—the first 6 months in exchange for repairs and the last 6 months in trade for a sculpture he did. With the camper, rent is not the problem it once was.

I built my camper for about $125.00. I got nearly all of the lumber at the city dump and at construction sites (you could start a lumber company from their scrap pile). The stove in the camper came from a trash pile and I traded a window for the sink. The icebox was given to me. The $13 foam rubber mattress on our bed cost $5 at the Flea Market. Four of the five tires on my truck were free—I got them from behind the Santa Cruz County auto maintenance building. They use tubeless tires and they don't repair them. They throw them away—it's covered by taxes. Service stations and department stores sometimes throw away usable tires.

Transportation is hard—mostly luck.. I've been given 1 car, 1 truck and I bought an excellent running car for $20 trade.

Medicine. In emergency, go to the county hospital, look for trade situations. I know of a dentist who did work at cost or trade for long-haired people. Another friend worked at a Veterinary Hospital to pay for his dog's operation. Look behind the doctor's office. I found 700 tranquilizers at the dump.

Tools and furniture may be gotten at Goodwill, flea markets and rummage sales.

If you look around, you may be able to find a mechanic who will work for exchange of things other than money—there are lots of things you can do.

You don't have to be rich to drop out—but it helps.

Tom Duckworth

Organic Shopping Guide

Rodale Press has compiled a comprehensive list of Organic Food Sources in 46 states and Canada, and complemented it with essays on the state of natural foods today, safe detergents, and other juicy lists of sources for natural fertilizers, ecology action groups, and organic gardening groups.

—Hal Hershey

The Organic Directory

Jerome Goldstein and M.C. Goldman, editors
1970; 116pp,

$1.95 postpaid

from:
Rodale Press, Inc.
Emmaus, Pennsylvania 18049

or WHOLE EARTH CATALOG

NEBRASKA

Brownville Mills
Brownville 68321

Nebraska Fertilizer Co.
P.O. Box 100
S. Omaha 68107
Phone: 731-8200

KENTUCKY

Clair W. Stille
130 N. Hanover Ave.
Lexington 40502
Phone: (606) 266-8066
Fertosan organic compost maker. 100% organic liquid compost concentrate. Sell retail, wholesale, make out-of-state shipments.

IDAHO

Carl C. Brutsman
Banks 83602
Phone: 462-3794
Vegetables in season. Eggs. No shipping.

7th Day Adventist Organic Food

COLLEGEDALE DISTRIBUTORS, is run by seventh day adventists, very nice people and this is their wholesale list. I haven't used it personally, but I do shop at their retail outlet and am very pleased with their service and quality of merchandise. A really nice thing about these people, is that health foods is a part of their religion, and their retail outlets in this area are really mind busters. Aisles of good food, all at reasonable prices, and without the stench of hypocondria that I've encountered in some health food stores, (as well as the high prices). In general, if you are new in a neighbourhood, and you're interested in eating right, the best people to go to are the Seventh Day Adventists and ask them where they get their food. There was a Buddhist monk that came up here to live several years ago with a little house and a back yard on the outskirts of town, and coming from Hong Kong did not know the various ways of gardening here in the US, and it was the Seventh Day Adventists that taught him organic gardening. They have a restaurant near this wholesale outlet where we eat occasionally and they are very nice.

Bruce Rodarmor
Sewanee, Tenn.

That's right.
—SB

Write to:
Collegedale
Tennessee 37315

Feed is cheap food

Items such as brown rice, whole wheat flour, wheat germ, cracked wheat, rye flour and dried beans are available at most supermarkets, but they are cheaper at farmers' co-ops and feed and seed dealers. To locate one of these outlets, check the yellow pages under headings Feed Dealers, Seed Dealers or Grain Dealers.

Here's a comparative list of prices obtaining now in the Pacific Northwest. Obviously availability and pricing will vary locally and regionally.

Item	Supermarket price per pound	Feed Dealers' price per pound
Brown rice	25¢	18¢
Wheat germ	50-75¢	20¢
Whole wheat flour	14¢	10¢
Whole wheat flour	14¢	10¢
Rye flour	20¢	10¢
Pinto beans	25¢	16¢
Small red beans	17¢	17¢
Large red kidney	33¢	33¢
Split peas	21¢	17¢
Pearl barley	25¢	14¢

Marilyn Thompson
Eugene, Ore.

Foods by Mail

Sources for foods that are not treated with DDT, fumigants, etc. Most of these outfits are family affairs, and dedicated to supplying customers with real foods, mostly by mail.

Arrowhead Mills, Inc.
P.O. Box 866
Hereford, Texas 79045

Organically grown Deaf Smith County wheat, raised in the mineral-rich area of Texas, tests between 15.5 and 17.5% protein, high. Roots go 8 ft. into the ground.

Case of 12 two lb. Cracked Wheat Cereal	$4.00
Case of 12 two lb. Whole Wheat Flour	4.00
Case of 10 five lb. Whole Wheat Flour	7.00
Case of 2 twenty-five lb. Whole Wheat Flour	6.00
Bag of fifty lb. Whole Wheat Flour	5.00
Case of 12 two lb. White Corn Meal	4.00
Case of 12 two lb. Yellow Corn Meal	4.00
Case of 10 five lb. White Corn Meal	7.00
Case of 10 five lb. Yellow Corn Meal	7.00
Case of 2 twenty-five lb. White Corn Meal	6.00
Case of 2 twenty-five lb. Yellow Corn Meal	6.00
Bag of fifty lb. Whole Soybeans, Cleaned	5.00

Arrowhead Mills

Ted A. Whitmer & Son

Erewhon Trading Company, Inc.
342 Newbury Street
Boston, Massachusetts 02115
or
8003 Beverly Boulevard
Los Angeles, California 90048

Good source of natural foods for the East Coast. Free brochure.

Erewhon ships out by truck, UPS, and other means, but does not mail order. Bulk orders are best to get wholesale prices.

El Molino Mills
345 N. Baldwin Park Blvd.
City of Industry, CA 91746

Has good wide selection (catalog free) and a good $1.50 cookbook.

Jaffe Brothers
28560 Lilac Rd.
Valley Center, CA 92082

Cheap, good nuts, seeds, dried fruit. Also organic lemons, oranges, and avocados (10 lbs. for $4).

The Food Mill
3033 MacArthur Blvd.
Oakland, California 94602

Large stocks of bulk foods. Gallons of avocado honey, fresh peanut butter. Free leaflet.

Brown rice again?

I think it would be good for catalog readers to know where to buy Koda Brothers brown rice——by far the best grown in the U. S. and costing only $12.20 per hundred pounds. We use only this brand at Tassajara:

Nomura and Co.
151 Industrial Way
Brisbane, California

Mutual Trading Co.
431 Crocker Street
L. A., Calif. 90013

Erewhon
342 Newbury Street
Boston, Massachusetts 02115
or
8001 Beverly Boulevard
Los Angeles, California 90048

These addresses are for wholesale only.

Mottel Sugar & Bakers Products, Inc.
451 Washington Street
New York, N.Y. 10013

Japan Food Corp.
11-31 31st Avenue
Long Island City, N.Y. 11106

Infinity Foods
171 Duane Street
New York, N.Y. 10013

L.E. Robert Company
792 Union Street
Brooklyn, N.Y. 11215

Take Care,
Bill Shurtleff
Zen Mountain Center
Carmel Valley, Calif.

See p. 227 for a short rap by Fred about wholesale buying.

Walnut Acres Mill & Store

Penns Creeks, Pennsylvania 17862

Best, most reputable source in the United States. Foods like you've never tasted: unrefined corn germ oil, raw peanut flour, creamed papaya juice. If you can order with friends, bulk orders are economical. Free catalog.

FLOURS, GRAINS, SEEDS

	10 lb.	5 lb.	3 lb.	1 lb.
ALFALFA SEED — (for sprouting or tea)	9.70	4.90	3.03	1.05
Alfalfa Powder — carefully dried	13.50	6.80	4.17	1.43
Alfalfa Leaves — for tea (see Beverages)				
ANISE SEED —	9.90	5.00	3.09	1.07
ARROWROOT STARCH —	5.80	2.95	1.86	.66
BAKING POWDER, BAKING YEAST — please see Non-Conforming Items, Page 16				
BARLEY, whole, hulled, for soups	2.20	1.15	.78	.30
Barley Grits, medium - soups or cereals	2.70	1.40	.93	.35
Barley Flour, excellent for baking	2.80	1.45	.96	.36
Beale's Seeds for Sprouting —	20. oz. — $2.00			

15 packets of a variety of seeds — radish, mung beans, green soybeans, red clover, fenugreek, sesame seed, oat grains, buckwheat — to mention a few!

Walnut Acres

Some sources of organic food by mail that we don't know much about yet.

Green Acres Organic Foods
1338 Westheimer
Houston, Texas 77006

Old Town Natural Foods
174 Bridge
Las Vegas, New Mexico 87701

OMbilical Cord
611 N. Blackstone
Fresno, CA 93701

—Lloyd Kahn, Hal Hershey, SB

THE DIFFICULT DAY CONTINUES

"It sounds like it," said Estelle.
D.R. asked Estelle what kind of day she was having.
Estelle thought it over. "Kind of thoughtful," she said.
"Kind of thoughtful, eh?" said D.R.
"Yeah," said Estelle. "I've been doing a lot of thinking.
D.R. asked her what she'd been thinking about.
"Different things."
D.R. asked her to tell him about one of them.
"I guess I've mainly been thinking about us not stopping in Vincennes last night," she said. "Do you remember that?"
"Where?" asked D.R.
"Vincennes. I wanted to stop and get a motel, and rest some. I wanted to take a bath, sleep in a good bed, we talked about it, do you remember?"
"Sure," said D.R. "I remember that. That was in Vincennes."
"Well," said Estelle. "That's what I've been thinking about.
"All day?" D.R. asked.
"Just about," said Estelle.
"What have you been thinking about that for?"
"I don't know," said Estelle. "I guess I just really wanted to stop at a motel in Vincennes. I guess I was just awfully disappointed that you didn't want to, and it's just stayed on my mind."
"I'll be darned."
"You'll be what?" asked Estelle.
"Darned."
"Darned, did you say?"
"Yep," said D.R. "I'll be darned."
"What else will you be besides darned?"
"I don't know," said D.R. "What else is there to be?"
"Quite a lot of things, actually," said Estelle.
"Well," said D.R. "Don't tell me about them."
"I wasn't going to," said Estelle.
"Yes you were," said D.R. "But don't. I don't want to hear about it."
Estelle asked D.R. what he did want to hear about.
"I don't want to hear about a goddamn fucking thing."
"Well, I guess the thing for me to do is hang up, then," said Estelle.
"Where are you, a phone booth?"
"I'm at the ticket counter, D.R. you paged me, remember?"
"Are there people around?"
"A few."
"Can they hear you?"
"Probably."
"There are people around me too," said D.R. "But they can't hear me, and I fucking well can't hear them, and I like that very much."
"Are you in a phone booth?"
"I'm in a fantastic phone booth."
Estelle said, "Well I'm not. And I think I'm probably disturbing the ticket man, although he is certainly being very nice about me using his phone. So I guess what I'm going to do, D.R. is hang up now, and if you come down here after while I'll see you. Okay?"
"That sounds about right."
"Well goodbye then."
"Yeah. So long, Estelle."
"Goodbye honey," said Estelle.
D.R. sat in the booth a long time, listening to the dial tone.

Protein

Nutrition for humans is primarily PROTEIN. People short on it get sick and despondent. And dead. In the big picture there's a shortage of protein. Here are two sources.

Meals for Millions puts out a powdered protein that works as a supplement or additive.
— SB

Modern Protein Food
1800 Olympic Blvd.
Santa Monica, CA 90404

Instant Protein (which is 80% protein). FDA won't let them sell in larger lots than one pound.

1/4 lb. and cookbook	$1.25 postpaid
1 lb. can	$3.00 postpaid

from:
A. G. A. Inc.
Marine Biochemicals and Drug Division
70 Oak St.
Norwood, N. J. 07648

"**Instant Protein**" the first FDA-approved food grade fish protein concentrate to appear on the market will be available to household consumers in mid-May.

Alpine Geophysical Associates, Inc. manufacturers of Instant Protein say they plan to market the product initially in New York and New Jersey supermarkets, and branch out into New England later.

The light colored powder has only a faint aroma of fresh fish, its makers say. Blended with many foods, it adds no fish flavor, but fortifies them with animal protein at a low cost per serving.

Consumer testing of Instant Protein has shown that it blends successfully with flour products, such as cakes, breads, rolls and cookies, and with rice products. Mixed with these materials at about the ten per cent level, it produces almost no change in basic cooking characteristics. In most cases, all that is noticeable is a slightly intensified color.

The powder can also be added to a basic spaghetti sauce, its makers say, to produce meat-type sauce stock that provides about half a person's daily animal protein requirement for around six cents.

John McClaughry
Lyndonville, VT

Composition of Foods

Since natural food does not come with a list of ingredients on the label, the Department of Agriculture has kindly prepared this authoritative analysis of everything edible. If you're serious about nutrition, it's a buy. — SB

[Suggested by Tassajara Zen Center]

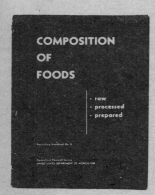

COMPOSITION
OF
FOODS

- raw
- processed
- prepared

Composition of Foods
Bernice K. Watt and Annabel L. Merrill
1963; 190 pp.

$2.35

from:
Superintendent of Documents
U.S. Government Printing Office
Washington, D.C. 20402

or WHOLE EARTH CATALOG

The Fish Protein Story

Dear folks:

A reply to reader Don Symons (January, p. 46).

Fish protein concentrate has a long and dismal history. It was invented by an elderly, idealistic scientist, Dr. Ezra Levin of the VioBin Corporation, Monticello, Illinois, who thought he had a handle on curing the protein deficiency problems of the world.

FPC uses trash fish, entrails and all. After a patented process of chemical washings, the product is a gray odorless tasteless powder that lasts forever without refrigeration, contains a very high percentage of animal protein, and is cheap cheap cheap compared to the protein equivalent price of beef, say.

Unfortunately, an unholy combination of Dr. George Larrick, then (1965) administrator of the Food and Drug Administration; Hoard's Dairyman and other milk producers interests; and midwest wheat growers, fearing its use as an additive to breads, etc. branded the stuff "filthy" and unfit for an FDA indentity standard. Four years of political battles followed, involving the National Science Foundation (or Academy of Sciences), Bureau of Commercial Fisheries, Interior Secretary Udall, etc.

I think the Catalog is great. I may be the only right wing nut who thinks so. Up here I am viewed as sort of a combination Paul Goodman and Max Rafferty, if you can figure that one out.

Yours,

Rep. John McClaughry
Jeffersonian Republican, circa 1790
House of Representatives
Montpelier, Vt.

Fish protein concentrate, once heralded as the big weapon in the war on hunger, remains an illusive dream despite the best efforts of Government and private business to produce it commercially.

About two months ago the Agency for International Development quietly canceled a $900,000 contract with the Alpine Geophysical Corporation to produce 970 tons of the flour-like food additive for Biafra and Chile.

Contract penalties of $6,000 a month were running against the producer when it proposed termination late in November.

The feasibility of commercial production of the odorless and tasteless additive made from whole fish and with a protein efficiency ratio of 80 per cent had been demonstrated in the laboratory of the Interior Department's Bureau of Commercial Fisheries at Beltsville, Md., about five years ago.

But bad weather and worse luck plagued Alpine from the contract signing in the fall of 1968 until its termination. Severe winter storms throughout New England delayed the delivery and installation of new equipment at the New Bedford, Mass., plant for three months.

A short harvest of Atlantic hake and hake-like fish then pushed up the price of the raw product to double the level expected. Finally, much of the ultimate product did not measure up to the standard set in the contract specifications. By that time it was Nov. 1, after which hake is not available.

Still, Alpine is not thinking of giving up. It hopes eventually to realize something from its $3-million investment. With the aid of Federal and university scientists the company is now trying to discover what went wrong with its process. Only 70 of the 265 tons of the concentrate inspected could pass the test of contract standards for protein efficiency.

The New Bedford plant was closed a month ago but will reopen Feb. 1. By that time Alpine hopes to have a solution to the problem of lack of uniformity in the separate batches produced by the same process.

from:
The New York Times, Jan. 15, 1970
sent in by Herb French

Insect-Food

Re: Recipes for eating insects.

This recipe comes from parts of Asia and Africa. Insert fried peanuts into crickets' abdomen (preferably cleaned). These prepared crickets are then fried. They are supposedly very tasty to those whose palate accepts them.

James Do (J.D.)

On page 49 of your July catalog, "J.D." asked for recipes for eating insects. I found this one in *Science Digest* for June, 1970, page 21. That's volume 26, number 6. I quote:

> 1 pint termites
> 1 Tablespoon vegetable oil
> ½ teaspoon salt
>
> Remove termite wings, if any. Spread termites on stone to dry in sun. Put oil in pan and spread dried termites on it. Toast over hot coals until almost crisp. Sprinkle with salt.
> "It helps the flavor, say those who have tried the recipe, if you eat the termites in handfuls."

Science Digest credits the Bantus with this recipe and reminds readers that there is "lots of vitamin B" in termites. Termites aren't all that plentiful in most of the U.S., but I suppose that the recipe would be just fine for ants.

Frank Walsh

Grasshopper Jam?

There's a bright side in the battle against the bugs, which is one front in the larger war against pesticide pollution and worldwide hunger.

"If we can't beat 'em, we'll eat 'em," cherrily predicts Dr. Howard A. Schneiderman, dean of the school of biological sciences at the Irvine campus of the University of California.

"In the event we start to lose the battle, the war itself is not really lost," he says, "for insects themselves are an excellent source of protein. . .Eating bread fortified with insect meal (is) no different than eating bread fortified with fish meal."

Proteinwise, that is.

This is not a recipe, per se, for insects but it does imply that insects are very good and could be used to eat; probably should be used to eat!

Pam Newbury

Perma-Pak

The best source we've seen for storeable foods is this outfit in Utah which caters to keep-a-year's-supply Mormons. The prices are remarkably good and they have a "Year's Food Supply" deal for $378.55 (477 lbs., FOB Salt Lake City). — SB

[Suggested by Gary Snyder]

Catalog

free

from:
Perma-Pak
40 East 2430 South
Salt Lake City, Utah 84115

CRISIS KITS

CHOW BELT, complete	2 lb.		4.35
FAMILY CRISIS KIT (See Camplite	18 lb.		33.95
KARRY-KIT order list for	12 lb.		12.95
TWO-DAY FOOD SUPPLY	2 lb.		1.95

Perma-Pak   Total 7 _____

Calorie Cost Table

Dear Friends,

You might be interested in my latest creation Calorie Cost Tables. It is based on the data in Composition of Foods and Pantothenic Acid, Vitamin B_6, and Vitamin B_{12} in Foods, but the data is presented in a different way. The tables give the number of calories of a given food one would have to eat to get 70 grams of protein, the number of calories for 800 mg of calcium, etc. The idea is that the number of calories one eats per day is nearly fixed, so that a food with lots of vitamins and lots of calories may not be as good as a food with less vitamins and very few calories. In addition since one food may be fairly rich in many nutrients and another may be very rich in one but poor in others, I have given a single "overall" figure to facilitate a general comparison of foods.

The low calorie costs of vegetables have induced Irene and me to move in the direction of vegetarianism. For those who have gone further in this direction the vitamin B_{12} column should be of special interest. Since vegetables have almost no vitamin B_{12}, vegetarians often have a deficiency. The strict vegetarians who avoid even milk and eggs are really in trouble unless they take a B_{12} pill.

We plan to sell the tables at $3 postpaid.

Neo Press
Box 32
Peaks Island, Maine 04108

NUTRIENTS IN THE EDIBLE PORTION OF 1 POUND OF FOOD AS PURCHASED

Food and description	Refuse Percent	Food energy Calories	Protein Grams	Fat Grams	Carbohydrate Total Grams	Calcium Mg.	Phosphorus Mg.	Iron Mg.	Sodium Mg.	Potassium Mg.	Vitamin A value Int'l Units	Thiamine Mg.	Riboflavin Mg.	Niacin Mg.	Ascorbic Acid Mg.
Cake mixes and cakes baked from mixes— continued Marble:															
Mix, dry form	0	1,928	22.2	61.2	342.9	590	1,225	4.5	1,728	853	Trace	0.13	0.41	2.0	Trace
Cake, made with eggs, water, boiled white icing	0	1,501	20.0	39.5	281.2	354	776	3.6	1,175	553	410	0.10	0.38	1.0	Trace

How to Buy Food

A collection of U.S. Dept. of Agriculture publications including information on fresh meat, fish, dairy products, fruits and vegetables and frozen and canned goods. Also has sections on what government gradings mean; pointers on when higher quality is worth the price, on storing food—where and for how long, and seasonal bargains. All in all informative and full of reassuring rules of thumb.

[Reviewed by Laura Besserman]

How to Buy Food
Valerie Moolman, editor
1970; 160 pp.

$1.00 postpaid

from:
Cornerstone Library, Inc.
630 Fifth Avenue
New York, New York 10020

or WHOLE EARTH CATALOG

Salmon

Briggs-Way Company
Ugashik
Alaska 99683

*This is a small family-type business that seems really dedicated to a quality product. They catch and pack within hours, fresh Alaskan salmon that is so tender and delicious it's fantastic——it comes in case lots of 12, 24 or 48 jars (1/2 lb glass home-canning jars) for about $1 pr jar. Absolutely no chemicals are used and great care is taken to see that the salmon doesn't come in contact with anything contaminating. Even their salt, when they use it, is sun-dried. Their service is extra-ordinary. Case of 12 jars $14.96 plus postage and insurance.
Shipping weight 13 lbs.*

[Suggested and reviewed by Renais Faryar]

EMORENE BRIGGS with freshly caught red salmon, which generally weigh between five and eight pounds.

Herbs

Two new herb suppliers. Lhasa Karnak has a more limited line, but it has some you can smoke.

—SB

Catalog
$0.25 from:

Aphrodisia
28 Carmine St.
New York, N.Y. 10014

Lhasa Karnak Herb Co.
1803 Euclid St.
Berkeley, CA 94704

Also see p. 58 for more herbs.

Yeast

for M/M Peter Ruppell
Hearst, Ontario

who inquired about making yeast for bread in the Jan. Catalog

2 oz hops	(Takes 4 days) Boil hops in the water for ½ hr. Strain & cool to lukewarm. Place in earthen bowl, add salt & brown sugar. Mix flour with part of the liquor then add the remainder. Let this stand until 3rd day. On 3rd day add potatoes which have been boiled & mashed fine.
4 qts water	
½ cup salt	
6 med. potatoes	
1 qt flour	
½ cup brown sugar	

Let stand a day, strain & bottle. The mixture should be stirred frequently & kept warm throughout this process.

After the fermented mix has been tightly bottled, stored in refrigerator or cool place, it will keep about 2 mos. Shake mix before using—— allow ½ cup mix for one commercial cake or pkg of yeast.

1 DAY METHOD

Add 1 qt water to 1 pt hops. Simmer 20 min. Add cornmeal until of thick mush texture. When cool, work more corn meal in & pat into cakes. Dry & store.

These are from *Rare Recipes & Budget Savers,* a compilation from a Wichita Ks paper column, "Home Town News." It has a lot of funky homespun items like Root Beer, Shoo Fly Pie, Hand care for cement workers, Curing feathers for hats, etc. $1.50 or 3 for $4.00 postpaid from Wichita Eagle & Beacon Home Town News, Cookbook, P.O. Box 820, Wichita, Kans. 67201.

Sherry
Oakland, CA

Sourdough Starter

You need it to make sourdough bread and other treats.

—SB

Sourdough Jack's Starter
$1.25 postpaid

Sourdough Jack's Cookbook & Starter
$4.25 postpaid

from:
Sourdough Jack's Kitchen
2901 Clement St.
San Francisco, CA 94121

Apple Cider

I think the New World needs a cider press like my father's daddy used. I will tell you how to use it. Can you tell me where to buy it?

It's important that you get cider apples from trees that were not sprayed. You can't wash or peel apples if you want good cider. You wouldn't want cider from sprayed apples anyway.

The little dirt you will have on "natural" apples assures that the cider will become tart. That's the first sign you can have the hard cider that made Thanksgiving in the Virginia mountains more than a pious holiday.

Choose Jonathans, Virginia Beauties, or other tart and not-so-large apples. Grind them up——the press usually comes with a grinder—— or chop them if you have patience but no grinder. The ground apples are called pumice.

Dump the pumice into the wooden drum of the press. Turn a screw on top and a piston forces the juices down out of the mash.

Strain the juice with a seive or a milk-strainer. Do not collect it in galvanized pails. You may be poisoned if you do. Glass jugs are best.

Do not bother to drink it yet. It's still just juice.

Aging, which takes from a couple of days to a week or more, makes the juice into cider. As the juice ages, a sediment forms near the bottom. Don't drink the sediment, but don't filter the next batch to eliminate it, either, because it's necessary for the hardening process.

Even if you don't take alcohol, you probably will like the bite cider made this way has when it has begun to age.

Keep check on the aging. When the cider is as strong as you like it, you may strain it through a cheesecloth, chill and serve. Cider can age too long to be palatable. Straining stops the fermentation.

It is possible to make "clean" cider like you see by the roadsides in Virginia and Michigan, but for the work you're going to have to do anyway you might as well pay a buck. "Sold" cider must be pasteurized in some states, which keeps it from hardening. I think that makes a fine breakfast drink, but is not much for heartiness.

Love,

John Hopkins
Chicago, Ill.

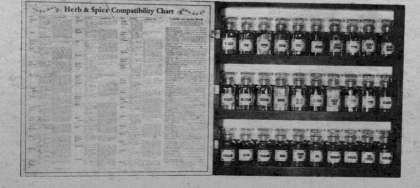

About Tea, Coffee, & Spices

I SUGGEST:
About Tea, Coffee & Spices by John A. Murchie
(catalog)
FREE from:
Murchie's
1008 Robson Street
Vancouver 105, B.C.

REVIEW:

That tea is useful and relevant to education is beyond doubt. If its *good* tea. This delightful mail-order catalog list a variety of teas, coffees, & spices. I've been drinking their tea for years and can swear to the following: IT's quality is better than the "gift teas" (Ming, Spice Islands, etc.) which come in fancy boxes and run about $5/lb or so. And their prices are better: $2 50/lb for the highest grade of most teas.(plus some postage) Their service is good. Tea arrives in Portland in less than a week. I haven't tried their coffee or spices. It's refreshing to see somebody keep a family tradition (since 1894) of quality.

SHORTER REVIEW:

Good tea at a good price. Good service.

In the Name of the Earth

Peter Dvorak
for the Free Underground
Portland, Oregon

McNulty's Tea & Coffee

Distinguished tea and coffee. They are drugs you know.

—SB

Catalog

free

from:
McNulty's Tea & Coffee Co., Inc.
109 Christopher St.
New York, N.Y. 10014

Specialty Coffees

McNulty's often obtains rare and exotic coffees such as Jamaican Blue Mountain, Tanzanian Altura Coatepec, etc. These are generally posted in our store when available. You may request notification of the arrival of any coffee you are particularly interested in.

Mail order customers may arrange to have unusual coffees sent regularly, each mailing a different coffee. A great gift.

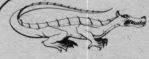

DIAL TONE

I'm sitting in a phone booth on the sidewalk in a shopping center in Cincinnati, Ohio, listening to the dial tone. I am also counting the little holes in the ear and mouthpiece of the phone but that is only a secondary activity the dial tone is the soundtrack for. As far as I'm concerned, this dial tone is the most important activity going on in this whole shopping center right now, although that dumb fuck in the T-shirt and bermuda shorts who just now peered in at me as he walked by would no doubt disagree. What that dumb fuck needs is to get his brain reamed out with the dull end of a dial tone some day and maybe he won't be so goddamn nosy. Goddamn nosiness anyhow. I don't give a goddamn what any of 'em out there do, I'm not nosy. As far as I'm concerned it's every bit one enormous colossal fucking goddamn bore. As far as I'm concerned, these sights I'm seeing through all these little windows in my brain are just bad movies projected from somewhere on the other side. I'm in a little room where the walls are movie screens, a very futuristic idea, you dig? Like, you don't go to movies anymore. You don't go in some big room with a lot of other people. You just drop your dime in the slot and go in a little one-man booth by yourself and they project weird movies onto the walls, play movies all around you, under your feet, over your head, and what you do is sit on this little seat and pick up the sound track over a telephone, and what the sound track is today ladies and gentlemen is pure, uninterrupted dial tone.

Yes sir. Stick with us and we'll show an ever-changing panorama to your eyes while your ears are soothed by wonderful dial tone. It's like a long column of dark blue smoke winding through your ear and down all the little avenues of your brain. It curls, it winds, it coils, there's something very snakelike about a dial tone. It's smoky, but there's a lot about it that makes you think of snakes as well. It's like a snake so long it's head and tail are completely lost, all you can see is his long smooth body rippling around your brain, sliding in it and through it and up it and down it, along all the secret avenues and hidden passageways and tunnels of your brain. Don't be nervous about this snake. Treat this snake right and he'll do the right things inside your head, watch him and he will show you places in your brain you didn't even know were there. And yet, it's just a sound, an ordinary dial tone on the telephone, it's just a simple sound tract for the movie about a very angry lady standing around outside the theater, waiting her turn inside.

Joy of Cooking

Adele Davis and Ohsawa to the contrary, I'm of the school that dietary schemes are out-front paranoia. A healthy mind insures a healthy body & vice versa; and what's needed more than special diets are common sense and good cooking. No food badly prepared is good for you. If you simply insure that all you eat is fresh, unpoisoned, and well prepared, the vitamins and proteins will take care of themselves. Rombauer's Joy of Cooking *is the American bible of food & is essential in any household where food is enjoyed. Not only are her recipes enjoyable, but she goes into the basic structure of food & food preparation techniques that give the novice a good idea of what's happening in the kitchen.*

*[Reviewed by Johan Mathiesen.
Suggested by Charlotte A. Wolter.]*

Joy of Cooking
Irma S. Rombauer,
Marion Rombauer Becker
1931 . . . 1974; 2 volumes

$1.95 per volume
postpaid

from:
New American Library
1301 Avenue of the Americas
New York, N.Y. 10019

or WHOLE EARTH CATALOG

Certain vegetables and fruits should not be stored together. Apples give off an ethylene gas that makes carrots bitter, for example, and onions hasten the spoilage of potatoes. Watch for other such relationships. Do not wash vegetables until you are ready to use them and then do not soak them, except as indicated, because moisture tends to leach away the water-soluble vitamins.

•

If you are willing to cut down on refined starch and sugar items, especially fancy baked goods, bottled drinks and candies, a higher percentage of the diet dollar will be released for dairy products, vegetables and fruits. Do not buy more perishable foods than you can properly store. Use leftovers cold, preferably. To reheat them with minimal loss, see page 139.

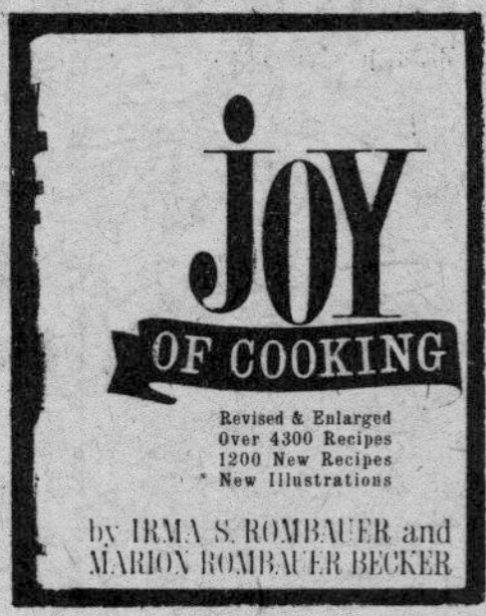

A new therapy for the treatment of small burns about the hands is to plunge the burned area into cold water.

•

Climate and age also change protein requirements. The colder the climate the greater the need. And no matter what the climate, growing children, pregnant women and nursing mothers need a larger proportion of protein than the average adult.

•

Cooking in mountainous country is an art all in itself. If high altitudes are new to you, watch for the high altitude cooking symbol which will give you formulas for adjusted ingredients or temperatures.

ABOUT HERBS

Confucius, a wise man, refused to eat anything not in season. Everyone who has tasted the difference between food served with fresh rather than dried herbs knows how wise he was. Few herbs can be bought in a fresh state at market, but the most important ones can be easily grown in a small sunny plot. We know, for we have grown and used all the culinaries in this section. Therefore, we beg you to exercise your green thumb at least on those whose evanescent oils deteriorate or almost disappear in drying. Chervil, borage, burnet and summer savory suffer the greatest losses. And those mainstays—chives, tarragon, parsley and basil—can never in their dry form begin to approach the quality of their fresh counterparts. Even the flavor of sage when fresh can be so delicate as to be almost unrecognizable.

FINES HERBES

This classic phrase connotes a delicate blend of fresh herbs suitable for savory sauces and soups, and all cheese and non-sweet egg dishes. Fines herbes are usually equal parts of parsley, tarragon, chives and chervil—although some other milder herbs may creep in. Their charm lies in their freshness and the quality they achieve when minced together with a sharp knife and added the last minute to the food being cooked, so their essential oils are not lost.

Purefoy Hotel Cookbook

My thing being cooking--I'm letting you in on something that your conscience MUST compel you to share.

Several years ago I was browsing through the high-priced cookbooks in a large Department store. In several expensive books on Southern cooking I found most of the better recipes were credited to the "Purefoy Hotel Cookbook". My mother is from Alabama and I knew she had the original. I wrote to the small town in Alabama wherein it originated to see if there were any old copies around. Ho! The little unassuming classic is not for $10-20 but $3.25 from:

*Mrs. Robert P. Purefoy
P.O. Box 98
Talladega, Alabama 35160*

This book is the real thing and if you ever wondered what happened to old-fashioned cooking and household knowledge--it's in this little book. This is the Old South, meaning fancy cleaners (that pollute) weren't available and "store bought" goods are limited. Included hints on cleaning, sewing, making wines, etc. and has the rather unusual virtue of being authentic. Also excellent tips on stain removal--great for those of us who can't or won't just throw away and replace.

One note--The basic ingredients called for are generally "unprocessed", esp. hams. The hams in the book refer to hard "country" hams, now considered a luxury. (By the way--for those who are involved in raising everything--in the Old South, everyone didn't have a smokehouse. Hams and bacon were often "plain", i.e. sugar cured. They were rubbed down daily with a 50/50 sugar and salt mixture and shelved for air to circulate around until hardening. After each rub--sprinkle well with pepper.)

Also: The Joy of Cooking; I suggest that people try to find old editions, preferably WW II vintage. The recipes include many extras on saving money due to rationing. Besides, it's cheaper used.

*Jerry & Maria Merchant
Tampa, Fla.*

INDIAN CORN STEW

2 medium onions, chopped fine
½ green pepper, chopped fine
2 tablespoons butter
1 pound ground beef
1 No. 2 can whole kernel corn (2 cups)
1 medium can tomatoes
2 teaspoons sugar
1 teaspoon salt
2 tablespoons flour blended with 2 tablespoons cold water
1 can cream of tomato soup

Cook onion and green pepper in frying pan with butter for 5 minutes. Add meat and allow to brown well, stirring frequently. Add corn, soup, sugar and salt. Simmer for about 15 minutes, stir in blended flour and water, cook for a few minutes and then serve. This is a very delightful luncheon or supper recipe. Serve together with a mixed fruit or vegetable salad.

PUREFOY FRIED CHICKEN

1¾- to 2-pound chicken is nice size to fry.

Pick, wash and cut in pieces the size you wish. Salt and pepper a few minutes before frying in order for the seasonings to go through. Beat an egg and pour over it.

Have your fat hot but not so that chicken will scorch easily. Dredge in flour, piece by piece (do not let it lie in flour as that will make it gummy) and fry nice and brown, turning it twice while it is cooking.

Fry chicken in a heavy iron skillet with a tight fitting lid. This holds the steam and cooks it better. Any good grade of vegetable shortening will do. Have fat deep enough to cover about half the chicken.

HOMEMADE SOAP

Melt 5 lbs. fat and strain through cheese cloth. Dissolve 1 lb. can of lye in 1 qt. cold water and let stand until cool. Add fat slowly, stirring constantly. Mix together 3 tablespoons borax, 1 teaspoon salt, 2 tablespoons sugar, ½ cup cold water, and ¼ cup ammonia. Add to first mixture. Stir all until thick and light colored. Pour into a pan lined with cloth. Mark into bars before soap becomes hard. When hard, break pieces apart and pile so soap may dry out well.

TO SHARPEN MACHINE NEEDLE

When sewing machine needle becomes dull, just sew across sandpaper several times and result is a sharp needle.

A TIP TO CANDLELIGHT LOVERS

Place your candles in the refrigerator for about 24 hours before you intend using them. This will keep them from burning down so fast or dripping so badly.

Fannie Farmer Cookbook

Fannie Farmer is considered by many to surpass Joy of Cooking *in the quality of its recipes. It's not quite as comprehensive. It is printed in paperback.* —SB

[Suggested by Cappy McClure and Lois Brand]

Fannie Farmer Cookbook
1896 . . . 1965; 648 pp.

$1.50 postpaid from:
Bantam Books, Inc.
666 Fifth Avenue
New York, N. Y. 10019

or WHOLE EARTH CATALOG

POTATO PANCAKES

Grate and drain
3 medium-sized raw potatoes
Add
1 tablespoon flour *or* 2 tablespoons dry bread crumbs
1 tablespoon cream, sweet *or* sour
1 egg, beaten light
1 teaspoon salt
Grated onion *or* onion salt to taste
Stir well. Cook by spoonfuls in
Hot bacon or other fat
turning once. Or cook in one big pancake. Serve with meats, with
Applesauce, cranberry sauce *or* sour cream
to spoon over the pancakes. *Serves 4 or 5.*

POPOVERS

A perfect popover is crisp on the outside, tender and moist inside. The secret of success is simple—do not overbeat the batter, and be sure the popovers are thoroughly baked when you take them from the oven. Test one to be sure.

Set the oven at 450°. Butter muffin pans or glass or pottery custard cups. Beat until light
2 eggs
Add
1 cup milk
1 tablespoon melted butter
1 cup all-purpose flour
¼ teaspoon salt

Beat until evenly blended (30 seconds in an electric beater). The batter should be like heavy cream. Add more milk if necessary. Pour into the pans, having them ⅓ full. Bake 20 minutes. Reduce the heat to 350° and bake about 20 minutes longer. *Makes 8 to 12.*

Bacon Popovers. Add to the batter ¼ cup crumbled cooked, crisp bacon.

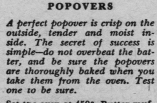

CREAM OF PEA SOUP

If the peas are very young and tender, cook a few pods with them.

Cook together for 5 minutes
2 tablespoons butter
1 tablespoon chopped onion
Add
2 cups fresh or frozen peas
⅓ teaspoon salt
1 teaspoon sugar
2 cups water
Cook until the peas are soft (about 20 minutes). Put through a sieve or whirl in an electric blender. Add
1 cup top milk *or* milk and cream
Heat slowly. Season to taste with
Garlic salt *or* mace
Pepper
Sprinkle with
Chopped parsley
Serves 6.

Quick Pea Soup. Use cooked or canned peas the same way, but cooking will not be necessary after the onion is cooked.

PEANUT BUTTER COOKIES

Set the oven at 350°. Cream together
½ cup butter *or* margarine
½ cup peanut butter
Beat in
½ cup white sugar
½ cup brown sugar

Stir in
1 egg
½ teaspoon vanilla
½ teaspoon salt
½ teaspoon baking soda
1 cup flour (preferably pastry)
Arrange by teaspoonfuls on cooky sheets. Press flat with a floured spoon or mark with a floured fork. Bake until firm (about 10 minutes). *Makes 60.*

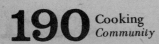

Quantity Recipes

In a commune I lived in in New Mexico we had two major problems: food and sex. This book will go a long way to helping you solve the first. What a drag to take down the Joy of Cooking, find something really groovy to fix for yourself and friends and have to spend a half an hour multiplying all the ingredients by seven or eight knowing that you couldn't possibly need a cup of oregano in the chili, but that's what your figures say. We ate some pretty bad experiments and several of the women and men shied away forever from anything but the lettuce salads. Enormous pots of food take a certain skill or they become enormous pots of glop.

In my opinion the recipes are basic, that is, I would add here and there seasonings, etc. to make the food special, new, hopefully an experience and not just another meal. Like all cookbooks this finally becomes a guide rather than a road but it will show you a road and act as a guide until the process becomes intuitive. Also, after a few weeks, or months, cooking creatively can get a bit strained. Cookbooks will pull you through with the advantage of this one already being adjusted for a large group. One of the best tools a community could buy.

[Reviewed by Steve Katona]

While you're at it, get their free catalog of Bulletins, which lists innumerable titles on food, kitchens, shopping, clothes, flowers, etc., at low cost.

[Suggested by Roger Knights]

Quantity Recipes
Marion A. Wood, Katharine W. Harris
1945, 1966; 233pp.

$1.75 postpaid

from:
Cornell Home Economics Extension
New York State College of Human Ecology
Mail Room
Building 7, Research Park
Cornell University
Ithaca, New York 14850

Another means of decreasing the cost of a recipe is by extending the more expensive items with cheaper ones. Meat stew is used as an example:

MEAT AND VEGETABLE STEW
Yield: 50 servings

3 servings per pound of meat		Price per unit	5 servings per pound of meat	
15 pounds beef	$10.65	$0.71/pound	10 pounds beef	$7.10
1 cup onions	.01	0.03/pound	1 cup onions	.01
2 quarts carrots	.14	0.06/pound	3 quarts carrots	.21
2 quarts potatoes	.12	0.04/pound	3 quarts potatoes	.18
1 quart celery rings	.09	0.13/bunch	1½ quarts celery rings	.14
1½ quarts (2½ pounds) peas, frozen	.45	0.18/pound	2½ quarts (4 pounds) peas, frozen	.72
Total cost	$11.46		Total cost	$8.36
Cost per serving $0.23 ($11.46 ÷ 50)			Cost per serving $0.167 ($8.36 ÷ 50)	

The cost of left-over foods used in recipes should be included when figuring costs.

Average serving size and cost of serving, 1966, are given in the appendix.

The Natural Foods Cookbook

Since one of the prime problems of the switch-over from supermarket foods to real foods is where to find them— this book begins appropriately with a check list of basic natural foods followed by a list of supply sources From there on it's one fine and healthful recipe after another: basics (how to make yoghurt & cheeses, yeast, sprouts, whole grains) to Delights (herbed mushroom casserole, lemon-honey jelly with a few geranium leaves.) Concludes with a list of suppliers of appliances (grinding mills, vegetable steamers, yoghurt incubators).

—Lloyd Kahn

The Natural Foods Cookbook

Beatrice Trum Hunter
1961; 368 pp.

$0.95 postpaid

from
Pyramid Publications, Inc.
444 Madison Avenue
New York, N. Y. 10022
or
WHOLE EARTH CATALOG

The Tassajara Bread Book

You'd expect Americans to have a particularly reverent attitude toward bread—it's been in our history since early colonists learned corn bread from the Indians. Trappers had their hard tack, gold miners their sourdough. No such attitude seems to have survived. Instead, bakeries today offer us tasteless cotton-textured white conglomerations and little else.

Here's a breadmaking guide that stands on profound respect for simple, wholesome ingredients and a "ripening, maturing, baking, blossoming" process, that turns a glob of dough into a fragrant food fit for any man's meal. Good bread is always magically more than the sum of its ingredients.

There are recipes for breads yeasted and unyeasted, fruit-filled loaves, sourdough, pancakes, pastries, muffins, and various favorite snacks from the Tassajara kitchen. This Zen cook knows the true nature of bread.

—Hal Hershey

The Tassajara Bread Book
Edward Espe Brown
1970; 146pp.

$3.50 postpaid

from:
Shambhala Publications, Inc.
1409 5th Street
Berkeley, California 94710

or WHOLE EARTH CATALOG

BAKED INDIAN PUDDING

1 quart milk	½ teaspoon ginger, ground
⅓ cup cornmeal	½ cup molasses
2 tablespoons soy flour	3 tablespoons nutritional yeast
⅓ cup sweet cider	
½ teaspoon salt	½ cup dried fruit, chopped (optional)
½ teaspoon cinnamon, ground	

Scald milk in top of double boiler over direct heat. Make paste of cornmeal and soy flour in cider. Blend with milk, cover and cook over hot water for 20 minutes. Add rest of ingredients. Remove from heat. Turn into oiled casserole. Bake at 325° F. for 2 hours or until set. Serve hot, topped with yoghurt. *Serves 6.*

SQUASH-CHESTNUT SOUP

1 quart stock	1 bay leaf
1 cup squash, cubed	1 cup milk
1 onion, chopped	½ cup milk powder
¼ cup celery and tops, chopped	1 teaspoon soy flour
¼ cup carrots, cubed	3 tablespoons nutritional yeast
½ pound chestnuts, shelled and boiled	1 sprig parsley, minced

Heat stock. Add vegetables, chestnuts and bay leaf. Cover. Simmer until vegetables are tender. Remove bay leaf. Blend milk, milk powder, flour and yeast. Add to soup mixture. Heat thoroughly. Serve garnished with parsley. *Serves 6.*

WALNUT-CHEESE LOAF

1 cup walnuts, ground	juice of ½ lemon
1 cup hard cheese, ground	2 eggs beaten
½ cup wheat germ	¼ teaspoon salt
¼ cup soy grits, soaked in ½ cup stock	3 tablespoons nutritional yeast
2 onions, chopped and sautéed	1 teaspoon caraway seeds, ground

Combine all ingredients. Turn into oiled loaf pan. Bake at 350° F. for 30 minutes. Serve with favorite sauce. *Serves 6.*

TASSAJARA YEASTED BREAD

The fundamental Tassajara Yeasted Bread recipe. (Four loaves)

I.
6 c lukewarm water (85-105°)
2 T yeast (2 packages)
1/2-3/4 c sweetening (honey, molasses, brown sugar)
2 c dry milk (optional)
7-9 c whole wheat flour (substitute 2 or more cups unbleached white flour if desired)

II.
2-1/2 T salt
1/2-1 c oil (or butter, margarine, etc.)
6-8 c additional whole wheat flour
2-4 c whole wheat flour

Dissolve yeast in water.
Stir in sweetening and dry milk.
Stir in whole wheat flour until thick batter is formed.
Beat well with spoon (100 strokes)
Let rise 60 minutes.
Fold in salt and oil.
Fold in additional flour
Fold in additional flour until dough comes away from sides of bowl.
Knead on floured board, using more flour as needed to keep dough from sticking to board, about 10-15 minutes until dough is smooth.
Let rise 50 minutes.
Punch down.
Let rise 40 minutes.
Shape into loaves.
Let rise 20 minutes.
Bake in 350° oven for one hour.
Remove from pans and let cool, or eat right away.

TIBETAN BARLEY BREAD

The only bread you need to know how to make, the greatest. (One large loaf)

2 c barley flour
4 c whole wheat flour
1/2 c millet meal (or roasted sunflower seeds or roasted sesame seeds)
1-1/2 t salt
2 T sesame oil (for flavor and lightness; if no sesame oil, you can use all corn oil)
2 T corn oil
3-1/2 c boiling water

Pan roast barley flour in 1 T sesame oil until darkened. Mix flours together with salt. Add oil, rubbing flour between hands until oily. Add boiling water, using spoon to mix until dough begins to form, then mixing with hands, keeping hands cool by dipping them in bowl of cold water. Mix until earlobe consistency. Knead until smooth. Place in oiled pans. Cut tops lengthwise. Proof 2-6 hours or overnight. Bake at 500° for 20 minutes on middle shelf, then 450° for 40 minutes on top shelf. Crust will be tough but inside tender. If at first you don't succeed, don't be discouraged. Try baking at 350° for 1-1/2 hours.

CALLING THE FLASH

It was such a good movie, in fact, D.R. couldn't resist calling the Anaheim Flash and telling him about it. He pressed the lever down, let it up again, put in two nickels, dialed 0, and when the operator answered he asked her to put him through collect to the Anaheim Flash in Anaheim, California.

"Where are you now?" asked the Flash.

"I'm at the movies in Cincinnati, Ohio," said D.R.

"Far out," said the Flash. "What's on."

"Well," said D.R. "Right now it's a short subject about this lady waiting outside a phone booth for this freak to quit talking and come out."

"That sounds like a pretty good movie," said the Flash.

"Listen," said D.R. "You obviously ain't heard the latest yet. Cincinnati is the new film capital of the world. There's been an incredible revolution here. I mean, like, it's so new it's only about half an hour old. I mean man you talk about interface, I mean, like Cincinnati is fucking Frontier City. You know what they got here? This is no shit. They got these little one-man theaters all over town. Pay your dime, go in, sit down, and the whole thing comes alive with movies from every which direction. It's really heavy stuff, man, I mean, like this lady, I mean she's about to go crazy right on the fucking sidewalk. It's super far-out."

"What about yourself?" asked the Flash.

"You mean me?" said D.R.

"Yeah," said the Flash. "You don't sound too goddamn sane yourself. What are you on, anyway?"

"What am I on?" said D.R.

"Yeah," said the Flash. "It's an ordinary enough question."

(continued)

The Impoverished Students' Book of Cookery, Drinkery, & Housekeepery

A brief intelligent introduction to cheap food preparation.
—SB

[Suggested by Derek Shearer]

What to Do with Left-Over Bread

Never throw out any dry, left-over bread. Slice it, dip it in a mixture of egg-milk-sugar-vanilla-and a dash-of-salt, fry it in butter and you have French Toast. Cube it, sprinkle with melted butter and garlic salt, brown it under the broiler, and you have Croutons. Roll or grind it into crumbs, put them in a plastic bag, and refrigerate, and you'll never have to buy bread-crumbs. Or just use it dry as a doorstop.

The Impoverished Students' Book of Cookery, Drinkery, and Housekeepery
Jay F. Rosenberg
1965; 48 pp.

$1.50 postpaid

from:
Doubleday & Co.
501 Franklin Avenue
Garden City, Long Island, NY 11531

or WHOLE EARTH CATALOG

Heloise

If you can get by the "little-wifey-in-the-kitchen-where-she-belongs" atmosphere of these books, there really are many useful hints. In keeping with the little wifey bit, a goodly proportion of the hints are directed towards things that might not interest younger people these days. How many of us worry about cleaning lampshades? On the other hand, using a plumber's friend as a washing machine is fine, and I've cleaned up many an oil spill with Kitty Litter. How about using a sewing machine with no thread and a big needle to punch the holes for hand stitching leather? Ants won't cross a chalk line in your floor, flies won't visit a garbage can with old crankcase oil in the bottom, Epsom salts in beer will frost a window, a light rub with shortening after defrosting will make the next defrost a quick affair. But. . .chocolate toast? Read em standing at the newsstand.

[Suggested and reviewed by Jay Baldwin]

Heloise's Kitchen Hints
1963; 180 pp.

Heloise's Work and Money Savers
1967; 241 pp

each **$0.95** postpaid

from:
Pocket Books, Inc.
1 W. 39th St
New York, N.Y. 10018

or WHOLE EARTH CATALOG

From Maine: "This is a good hint for wives who have tried to DRY OUT HUNTING BOOTS overnight. I used to hang them upside down over a furnace, stuff them with paper and the like but they were still almost impossible for my hunter to pull on for the next hunt. Then I found that if I reversed the vacuum hose on my vacuum cleaner (so it would blow), inserted it in the boot and let it run, the boots would be bone dry within minutes. Much comfort for him and what a time-saver for me!"

How about THAT? It also works on wet shoes. NEVER try to dry boots over heat of ANY kind. RUINS leather! I know. I tried. They curled up and died.

From Nevada: "How about licking the CORNER OF THE ENVELOPE instead of licking the stamp? I just don't like glue."

It's so! You won't believe it, but try it next time you want to put a stamp on an envelope. Sure keeps the nasty tastes away. Many people have asked why they don't put cherry, chocolate, or lemon flavor in glue on stamps. Most say the flavor they taste when they lick a stamp has yet to be identified——except that it "ain't" good.

WILD, BUT IT WORKS!

Frozen peas can be shelled very fast with a wringer-type washer. Put a pan on one side of the wringer to catch the peas and the pods go on through. You will think peas will go through the wringer and be mashed the moment the pod hits the wringer, but they will pop out *before* they go through. A very fast job can be done this way.

Let's Cook It Right

I'd recommend Let's Cook It Right *just for plain easy delicious recipes, down-home-style, even if it weren't for the nutritional advice, which is also well worth getting ahold of. Sure, Adelle Davis is kind of a fanatic, but I've learned a lot from her in the past year about how to cook without destroying food value. As it turns out, this often means cooking quicker and tastier anyway. Since she explains the nutritional principles behind her methods, you can easily learn to apply her methods to recipes from other cookbooks. I particularly like the sections on variety meats, which are often neglected, and on baking (though it's a shame she chickens out on cakes). And it's extra nice the way she watches out for your budget.*

[Reviewed by Ellen Hershey. Suggested by lots and lots of people.]

Let's Cook It Right
Adelle Davis
1947, 1970; 576pp.

$1.75 postpaid

from:
New American Library, Inc.
1301 Avenue of the Americas
New York, N.Y. 10019

or WHOLE EARTH CATALOG

Parsnips are often disliked largely because of the abominable method of cooking them in water, which they soak up like a sponge. They are most delicious if not touched with water after they are thoroughly washed. Even when they are steamed, sugar quickly dissolves out; if overcooked only a few minutes, the pulp becomes waterlogged and mushy. Parsnips cook quickly; hence recipes which advise cooking them twice should be avoided. Since the sugar in parsnips burns easily, the heat should be kept low after they have been heated through.

LIVER WITH APPLES

Mix together well:

3 chopped unpeeled cooking apples	**¾ teaspoon salt**
1 chopped large onion	**freshly ground black pepper-corns**

Place in oiled baking dish:

1 pound sliced baby beef, pork, or veal liver

Cover liver slices with apple-onion mixture; top with:

4 slices bacon cut in half	**generous sprinkling paprika**

Add:

¼ cup hot water

Cook in moderate oven at 350° F. for 20 minutes.

Gourmet Cooking for Free

What to do with your beavertail, moosenose, wild strawberries, fiddleheads, mussels, crayfish, and other non-supermarket provender.
—SB

Gourmet Cooking for Free
Bradford Angier
1970; 190 pp.

$4.95 postpaid

from:
Stackpole Books
Cameron & Kelker Streets
Harrisburg, PA 17105

or WHOLE EARTH CATALOG

GRILLED TROUT

The smaller the trout or other fish, the hotter the grill should be. If the fish breaks or sticks when you turn it or take it up, then odds are that you didn't let the metal get hot enough at the onset. Too, grease the grill well at the start.

Either salt the inside and outside of the trout up to an hour before broiling, or sprinkle the inside with freshly ground black pepper and lemon juice just before it goes on the heat. Whole fish may be split or not, depending on the size and on your preferences. Even when the fish has a thick skin well cushioned with fat, brushing frequently with melted butter will add to the flavor. Once the translucency of the flesh has clouded to opaqueness, the fish will be ready for serving.

Paprika butter melted over grilled trout enhances both appearance and flavor. This can be easily prepared beforehand by melting in a skillet, proportionately, a tablespoon of butter, mixing in 1/2 teaspoon of powdered onion, and cooking over low heat until golden, constantly stirring. Allow this to cool, cream with a teaspoon of paprika and butter, shape into about 1-teaspoon portions and relegate to the refrigerator.

FRIED MUSSELS

Mussels, widely available in both fresh and salt water, afford considerably more food than a similar amount of clams or oysters because their shells are so thin. One of the tenderest and most delicate of shellfish, mussels can be deliciously cooked in all the ways oysters and clams are prepared. If you live along the California coast, though, be sure to avoid them when they are quarantined from May to October because of their eating a plankton poisonous to humans during that period.

All you have to do to prepare mussels is scrub them well, preferably with a wire brush and either pull off the beard (the stringy piece connected to the inside of the shell by which they cling to rocks), or cut it off with the point of a small, sharp knife. Don't use any that stay opened when handled. Incidentally, if you steam your mussels and any have remained closed, discard these without opening them, as the shells will be filled with mud.

For temptingly fried mussels, briefly steam them with a small amount of water in a covered pot until they open. Then discard all black parts, and if you haven't already bearded them, do this now. Dip in beaten egg. Then roll in either fine cracker or bread crumbs that have been salted and prepared to taste. Fry very lightly in butter until a creamy golden yellow.

SEA MOSS BLANCMANGE

The seaweed called Irish moss (*Chondrus*), common along the Atlantic shores of Canada and the United States where it can be gathered at low tide, cooks up into a delicate blancmange which is so digestible that many drug stores stock it for invalid diets. You can harvest this moss at any season, wash it well in fresh water, and then dry it for future use. Spread out in the sun, it bleaches a pearly white.

When ready to cook, soak 1/2 cup of this iodine-rich marine alga, also called carrageen moss, for 20 minutes in enough cold water to cover it. Then drain and pick out any discolored bits. Add what is left to a quart of milk in the top of a double boiler. Cook over boiling water for 30 minutes. Then strain the milk.

Stir 1/4 cup sugar, a teaspoon vanilla, and 1/4 teaspoon salt into the strained milk. Turn into cups or molds that have been immersed in cold water, chill in the refrigerator until firm, and then serve with cream and sugar. A topping of wild strawberries really sets these off.

Cooking High

For those of us living over 5,000 ft up — BAKING AT HIGH ALTITUDE, cake, cookie and quickbread recipes adjusted for cooking about 5000 feet and adjusted again for over 7000 feet cooking. IT IS FREE. Put out by the University of Wyoming. Write for: Bulletin 427
Write to:
Agricultural Experiment Station
University of Wyoming
Laramie 82070

Tom Duckworth
Embudo, NM

The Grub Bag

I wouldn't be too surprised if somebody has already reviewed this book. I got it about four hours ago at a bookshop that had just gotten it in. Until now I didn't believe there was such a thing as a book that couldn't be put down. (With all due respect, I didn't even read the Catalog in one sitting). Now that your appetite is thoroughly whetted, the book is called The Grub Bag, by Ita Jones. She's written a series of food columns for the Liberation News Service, but as far as I know, this is her first book.

This isn't the first time that a cookbook has been written with philosophy and politics lacing the recipes, but it is the first one I've seen that doesn't look as though the recipes are the author's but the wit and wisdom are somebody else's.

Ita Jones seems to have a slightly different attitude towards food than most cookbook authors. She reminds me of a physics prof I used to have who wanted his students to consider the full range of possibilities of a physical concept instead of cranking through problems to which the concept obviously applied. (For instance, did you know that a good way to figure out if you're in a space station or not is to jump off a chair? Man is at least as sensitive to the angular rotation of a space station as he is to variations in gravity—your head would feel as if it had been kicked by a mule). Anyway, Ita Jones has that same kind of open-mindedness. If you were writing a book about cooking, would you think to include a chapter on cannibalism? Even if you had read Stranger in a Strange Land?

Some of what I thought were the more memorable things she said appear below. As an exercise, in reading the book yourself, you may want to look for something that occurred to me—her writing reminds me just the least little bit of Thoreau's writing in Walden. (reincarnation?)

For most Americans, eating has become truly one-dimensional, instead of the amazing art of combining the fruit and flesh of the earth into experiences worth remembering.

•

Eat a meal and know that it was eaten a thousand years ago, and tasted close to what it tastes like now to you. Know that what was used in this dish was used not by choice but because it lived or grew in the area (even in life the ingredients were inter-related), that those who lived in the desert ate that which arose from it and returned to it, and that those who lived by the water ate that which was part of it, and that we have lost this link (among others) between ourselves and our surroundings because in Colorado we eat fish, and near the harbors, lamb.

•

Pineapple tops can become beautiful strange plants. Slice off the crown and place it, cut side down, in a saucer of water. After it has begun to grow again, plant it in sandy compost and keep in the sun.

The seeds of grapefruit, oranges, lemons, and tangerines are usually tossed away, but even these grow into shiny plants which are happy indoors. Wash the seeds and plant them, three or four to a pot, in sandy soil. Keep in a warm, dark corner until they have sprouted. Then move them to a window sill. If you put them outside in the summer, the woody parts will develop, giving you small graceful trees.

Another thing I'd like to mention is that this book is definitely for those of us who need step-by-step instructions just to boil water. Absolutely nothing is missing from her directions.

I suppose it's also worth mentioning that none of the recipes require things that are really hard to get or expensive. There isn't any of this jazz about "procure the hind toes from twenty willow ptarmigans. . ."

I think that even people who have been cooking for fifty years could find some things to interest them. For instance, there are recipes for home-made yogurt and home-made curry powder, which aren't all that difficult to make but just don't appear in the average cookbook.

[Suggested and reviewed by Lou Bjostad]

The Grub Bag
Ita Jones
March 1971; 258 pages

$1.95 postpaid

from:
Random House
Westminster, Md. 21157

or WHOLE EARTH CATALOG

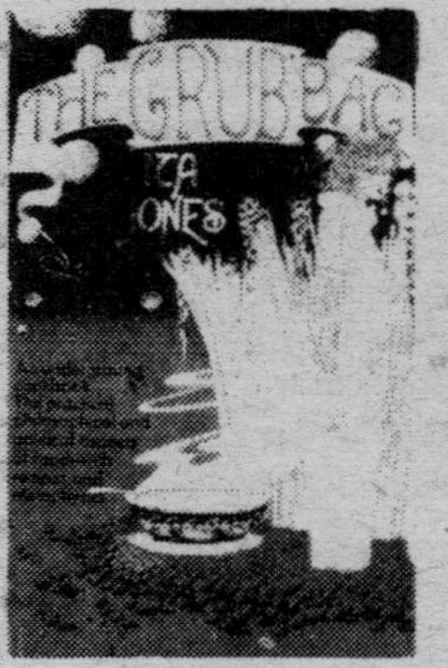

HOMEMADE CHRISTMAS SOUP

1. Heat a few tbsp. oil in a large pot and in it brown one meaty soupbone and one large chopped onion.
2. Add just enough turmeric to make the onions yellow, 1½ tsp. salt, pinch of pepper, 5 or 6 whole cloves, 1 bay leaf, ¼ tsp. thyme and generous pinches of allspice and sage, and sauté for a few minutes.
3. Add 1½ to 2 qts. water, part of which can be liquids saved from canned or cooked vegetables (corn juice is especially good) and about 4 tbsp. barley.
4. Cover and simmer very slowly for around 2 hours.
5. Now add 3 medium raw potatoes peeled and cut into small pieces, a couple of carrots cut up, and any leftover vegetables or noodles you have on hand. A bit of leftover cooked oatmeal is also very good. Add a small can of stewed tomatoes or a ripe tomato, chopped, and 1 pkg. of dehydrated vegetable soup, which can be omitted if you can't find it. Simmer another half hour or until the vegetables are tender.
6. While the soup continues to simmer for a few more minutes, remove the bone from the pot, and when it's cool enough to handle, cut off all possible meat, dice and return meat to the soup. Turn off the heat.
7. Let the soup "stand" for at least 5 minutes before serving with a simple salad and good cheese and bread. Cheap red wine goes well with soup, probably because it is the staple drink in countries where this sort of soup has long been made.

Goodcookbooks

Larousse Gastronomique *in English*

the history of the civilized use of food
articles on all kinds of Western food & a little oriental
full access to the secrets of the ultimate in Western cooking
not for "the modern housewife"
read about what you are eating at the dinnertable!
"It is very difficult to think about anything but food when eating."—Gertrude Stein

(Please include a word of caution about Rambauer-Becker next time: the instructions are over-simplified; the recipes are hodge-podges; there are a great many obvious errors in the use of the symbols & you have to refer all around in the book. Also, the OLD Fanny Farmer should be reprinted. Classical American cooking, for the faint-hearted)

How to Cook a Wolf—*by M.F.K. Fisher*

A humanistic survival book for periods of shortage and extreme poverty (such as WWII in Europe) (when it was written) in Western societies.
Very funny & a little sexy.
World—publisher, Cleveland. Still in print??

"To work! to Work! for Heavens sake! The Wolf is at the door!"

(do you hate the French? You have hardly anything French in your whole thing. They are great. [Yeah. —SB]

Frederick Ted Castle
New York, N.Y.

"What am I on," said D.R. "I think that what I am on is intensity. Intensity and precision. I feel very intense and precise today."

"Is that what they're dealing in Cincinnati?" asked the Flash.

D.R. laughed. "Yeah. You get it out of the vending machines in these little theaters."

"Well," said the Flash. "It sounds like old Cincinnati is really where it's at."

"Most definitely," said D.R. "Without question. Most definitely."

"Listen," said the Flash. "Where's Estelle?"

"The bus station. Hey Flash, listen: is it cool that I called? I mean, I know this is on your bill. But you got money, right? You still got all your money?"

"Still got it," said the Flash.

"Okay, and you can stake me to this call, right? I mean I don't want to impose it . . ."

"Carte blanche, man," said the Flash. "You sound to me like you need a friend."

D.R. laughed. "Well, we all need friends, Flash. But I'm all right. I've just got stuff on my mind. A lot of new stuff is going on. I mean, two days ago I couldn't even talk. I've been kind of bummed out, but I feel pretty good now. Hey Flash?"

"Yeah, man."

"Listen, I really thank you for the use of that card. It really saved our ass."

"No sweat," said the Flash. "What's Estelle doing at the bus station?"

"Hanging around. Hey Flash, guess what my nephew said this afternoon. He's this nine year old jockstrap in the Little League, see, really far-out kid. I come in, our first conversation he says, 'You're a turd.' And then he says, 'You're a queer, why don't you go out and have a car wreck?' "

"Nice kid," said the Flash.

"No man, I mean he's far out. It's pretty wild around here."

"So you've already seen your sister."

"Yeah, I was out there. Say, man, what time is it anyway?"

"It's eight o'clock in California. Listen, old friend, I'm worried about you. No offense, but it sounds to me like Cincinnati ain't no healthy place for a righteous dude to be."

"Ahh," said D.R. "It's all just a movie. It's just another quadruple feature happening simultaneously all around, it's okay."

"That's what you say," said the Flash. "But that ain't how you sound. I'm afraid you're not trusting in the Lord enough."

D.R. laughed. The Anaheim Flash asked him what was funny.

"What you said. I heard that as a line of dialogue from the lady in the movie. It's pretty funny."

The Anaheim Flash asked D.R. how the lady was getting along.

"Not too good, I'm afraid. The freak won't get out of the phone booth. She's got her nose up against the screen now, peering right in on him."

"Why don't the freak kiss her?" said the Flash.

"Flash, you're a genius," said D.R. And D.R. puckered up and leaned forward and kissed the movie screen as the woman, horrified, drew away.

"Did he kiss her?" asked the Flash.

But D.R. was laughing too hard to answer. He laughed so hard and so long he finally had to tell the Flash it didn't look like he was going to be able to go on with the conversation. The Flash said he guessed he'd hang up then.

"But listen, man, stay cool, you hear? You take care, and tell Estelle she's much loved, okay? Tell her Angel really wants to hear from her."

"Right," said D.R. "And I thank you for talking to me, I really do."

"Anytime, man," said the Flash.

The Anaheim Flash hung up then, and D.R. went on listening to the dial tone.

Zen Macrobiotic Cooking

A good place to start with Macrobiotics (the philosophy of eating as a means to vitality and rejuvenation).

This book is more recent, pleasantly readable, liberal and digestible than the writings of the system's founder-master Georges Ohsawa. However, once you read this, you may get into the others. Also a monthly publication.

[Reviewed by Lloyd Kahn]

In Japan it is known as yin and yang. Here, in America, it goes by the rather chemical terms of acidity and alkalinity. For instance, you eat something acid and have heartburn; common knowledge tells you to take something alkaline, Alka-Seltzer, perhaps. Acid foods are rich in potassium; alkaline, in sodium.

A few do's and don'ts

Learn above all to cook rice and to cook it well. One condition is to use a heavy cast-iron pot. Prior to cooking, wash the rice with cold water in a strainer. While cooking, never stir the rice, and keep it covered.

Sometimes when you cook rice, the bottom of the pot is slightly scorched. This part is yang. It is very rich in minerals and very good for yin people.

Zen Macrobiotic Cooking
Michael Abehsera
1968: 223 pages

$1.25 plus $.15 postage

from:
Avon Books Mail Order Dept.
250 West 55th Street
New York, N.Y. 10019

or WHOLE EARTH CATALOG

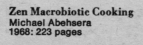

Remember—

Yogurt

Here it is! The definitive yogurt recipe, courtesy of me. No special equipment, no watching the pot for hours & fussing about keeping it a special temperature—AT ALL.

Equipment:
1 large pyrex (or otherwise heat-proof) mixing bowl
Measuring cups, spoons
Jars to store the yogurt in
Oven

Ingredients:
3 cups instant powdered milk
½ tsp. unflavored gelatin
1 tbsp. sugar (optional)
1 large can evaporated milk
3 tbsp. yogurt
Water

Instructions:
Soften the tsp. unflavored gelatin then add boiling water to make 1 cup, Add 1 tbsp. sugar (this takes the "edge" off.) and let the mixture cool a bit.

Preheat the oven to about 275º. (250-300º range is O.K.)

Mix 3 cups instant powdered milk with 3 cups water. Add 1 large can evaporated milk, 2 more cups tepid water, and the gelatin mixture.

Add 3 tablespoons yogurt and stir thoroughly.

Cover the bowl, put it in the oven, and TURN THE OVEN OFF.

Leave it overnight, or about 8-10 hours.

Makes about 2 quarts, and is "foolproof".

J. Lundquist

Applause

Help!! Please! I found a fantastic and easy yogurt recipe in your catalog (not the latest, but the one before that. I have been using it for a couple of months, but when I went to look for it last night, I couldn't find it anywhere!! Do you think you could help me get another copy? There were two on the same page——the one I want used powdered dry skim milk, evaporated milk, gelatin, water & 1 T of sugar. I would really appreciate anything you could do to help, as this is what I've been giving my husband for lunch & it's the first yogurt he would not only eat but ask for. Thank you, thank you.

Karen Barnes
N.M. Bch., Fla.

How to Make Butter and Cheese

Chr. Hansen's Laboratory, *which sells vegetable-base butter coloring, cheese color tablets and cheese rennet tablets, have some great illustrated charts on Butter and Cheese making.* They're all free. We've reproduced the essential steps here. Goat Husbandry (page 64) has several good recipes for butter and cheese using goat's cheese. —SB

How to Make Butter on the Farm Chart

How to Make Cheese on the Farm Chart

FREE

Enclose 10¢ for postage

from:
Chr. Hansen's Laboratories, Inc.
9015 West Maple Street
Milwaukee, Wisconsin 53214

HOW

Baking Soda

For 15 cents, you can buy a humble tool that replaces a lot of fancy-priced ones: Arm and Hammer baking soda.

Potential uses--
1) *Toothpaste.* Mix soda with salt, for the kind of toothpaste oldtime Texas dentists used to say was better than storebought.

2) *Acid indigestion tablet substitute.* Just take a little soda with a glass of water.

3) *Scouring powder.* Especially good in refrigerators, because it deodorizes.

4) *Sunburn ointment substitute.* Spread on paste of soda and water.

5) *Putting out kitchen fires.*

6) *Maybe even baking??*

anonymous

Bibble Ledbetter adds:

For those who still smoke you can put some on your car ash trays to absorb the odor and safely snuffs your cigarette out.

It's a great refresher when added to your bath.

Use it when I clean my iron skillets, cutting boards, knives, etc. It not only helps to remove baked on foods but it does not leave a detergent taste to the equipment like the above that tend to absorb odors.

Plus a pound costs only 21 cents.

Bibble Ledbetter
Washington, D.C.

Safer Than Shell Pest Strips, Easier Than Swatting

*Another suggestion: Fly * Paper. Absolutely non-toxic and it works almost as well as pest-strips. The type I use is Aeroxon which is made by Aeroxon products, New York, N.Y. and which I bought at my local hardware store.*

Tom Davenport
Delaplane, Va.

1 Ripen Cream, If Desired
Butter may be made from either sweet or sour cream, both of which should be free from any off flavors. Butter made from sweet cream has a mild, creamy flavor. But if a more flavorful product is desired, allow the cream to ripen at 65-75 degrees F. until thick and mildly sour.

2 Bring Cream to churning temperature
In summer: Usually 52-60 degrees F.
In winter: Usually 58-66 degrees F.
Sweet Cream: Keep cool as possible until just before churning.
Sour Cream: Hold 2 hours at churning temperature.
Churning Temperature is correct when butter "comes" in 30-40 minutes. If cream is too cool, churning will last too long, and give hard butter. If too warm, churning period will be too short for complete churning, and soft, greasy butter will result.

3 Rinse Churn with scalding water; then rinse and chill with cold water
Treat butter ladles, paddles, worker and printer the same way and place all but the worker in a pail of cold water until needed.

4 Strain Cream into churn
In order to work efficiently, the churn should be only about one-third full, or at least not over one-half full. If too full the churning period is prolonged.

5 Pour Butter Color into cream [sic]
Measure the amount of Butter Color needed and pour it into the middle of the churn, without letting the color touch any wooden parts. The quantity needed varies with the season, is highest in spring just before cows go on pasture when 2-3 teaspoons of "Dandelion" Butter Color per 10 gallons of cream may be needed (cream with 20%-30% butterfat).

6 Close Churn and start turning
Start churn at speed to produce the greatest concussion, which can be determined by the sound—about 60 revolutions per minute for the common barrel type of churn.

Crunchy Granola

We have not read all of the supplements so we don't know if you have have printed recipes for crunchy granola. If you haven't—here is one:

MIX
4 C	rolled oats
1½ C	shredded unsweetened coconut
1 C	wheat germ
1 C	chopped nuts
1 C	hulled sunflower seeds
½ C	sesame seeds
½ C	flax seed
½ C	bran
1 C	ground roasted soybeans

HEAT—
½ C	oil (soy, sesame or corn)
½ C	Honey
½ t	vanilla

ADD
honey-oil mixture to dry ingredients and mix (mixture will be very dry)

SPREAD
mixture on oiled cookie sheet or jelly roll pan (cookie sheet with sides) & bake at 325 degrees about 15 min. until light brown.

All measurements are approximate and it's nice to improvise with ingredients, too. However, you make it, it will be much, much better than any commercial varieties.

I would like to know of good books on vitamins, lecithin, pollen, ginseng, jujubes, etc. (I can't even spell them but am interested to know what they do for you.) Everyone I ask explains them a little to esoterically for my plasticized head.
Thank you.

Philip & Elizabeth Schnazerson
Berkeley, Calif.

Applause

We've been using the Granola recipe sent in by P. & E. Schnazerson. It's been working fine. We've made up to 15 lbs at a time (at 35 cents to 45 cents per) (to get 15 lbs of granola you have to multiply their recipe by 6 .) Our next batch will be about 75 lbs because it's almost become a staple in our houses. We may also sell it. With anywhere from 3 to 6 people mixing, spreading, turning etc. we've gotten the whole process down to an art. Everyone knows their job. The hardest part is cooking because you have to turn it over every 3-5 minutes. Important!: turning granola on the cookie sheets (same as you'd turn earth) is most important near the end of the 15 minute cooking period. So you may wait 5 minutes from when you first put it in the oven, then 4 then 3 then 3 again then maybe 1-2. People should figure it for themselves, tho, vibration cooking is where its at.

We've been using the Corona Mill with great satisfaction. Whole wheat kernels (from a local grainery) cost about 4 cents a lb. The kernels can also be boiled like rice or beans (first soaked overnite, tho) for an interesting meal.

David I. Schuchman
Grand Rapids, Michigan

P.S. Flax seeds in recipe should be ground, or chewed very well.

7 Permit Gas To Escape
After a few revolutions, stop churn, bottom up; remove cork to permit the escape of gas. Repeat this 2-3 times during early stages of churning.

8 Churn until Butter "Comes"
Wait for the change in the sound of the cream, and for thick mushy mass to appear on glass in churn. Then turn churn several times more, and stop to examine butter granules.

9 Stop Turning when granules are size of wheat grains
When sound of cream in churn changes watch the granules through the glass and stop churning when the butter granules are the size of grains of wheat.

10 Draw Buttermilk
Let the buttermilk out of the churn through the hole at the bottom of the churn. Run through a strainer to catch any particles of butter.

11 Wash Butter
While the last of the buttermilk is drawing off, prepare the wash water: Pure, clean water, twice the quantity of the buttermilk, and about the same temperature. After all buttermilk is drawn off, replace cork and pour one-half the wash water into churn. Replace cover and turn churn rapidly about four times. Draw off wash water and repeat washing.

12 Salt and Work Butter
Rinse "worker" once again with hot and then with cold water, leaving worker wet. Weigh butter. Spread butter with ladles on worker, in a layer about 2 inches thick. Sift salt onto butter—¾oz. salt per pound butter, or more or less according to taste. Press butter (do not rub or smear it) into thin layer, fold into a pile and press again. Continue working until salt evenly distributed and butter has desirable grain and body. If you do not have a butter worker, you can still do a good job by working the butter with your ladles or paddles right in the churn or in a large wooden bowl. This should be done by gathering the butter into the form of a ball, pressing it into a thin layer and then repeating this process over and over again until the salt and moisture are well worked in.

Vegetarian Cookbooks

For the Giant Computer if It wants It. Here are the best vegetarian cookbooks I know of right now, being good tasting, wholesome, full of life, and good loving food. Not all of them are entirely vegetarian, but I've found them all good books when it's time to eat.

A Good Cook. . .Ten Talents
Frank and Rosalie Hurd, 354 pp., ring binders, colour pictures, $7.95 from:

Allegan Health Clinic
120 Cutler Street
Allegan, Michigan 49010

Big natural food cookery and uncookery Bible: ". .What you need is less temporal food and much more spiritual food, more of the bread of life. The simpler your diet, the better it will be for you."

Tried and True Vegetarian Recipes
Shilla Judd, 66 pp., $1.95 from:

Shilla Judd
P.O. Box 75
Potter Valley, CA 95469

Mouth-waterers, some of them incredibly delicious.

Gar Shu Vegetarian Cookbook
Sanctilean, 94 pp., ring binders, $3.50 from:

Upland Trails Press
c/o Della Haney
P.O. Box 1686
Coolidge, Arizona 85228
make checks payable to "Della Haney"

Gar = sun shine
Shu = vegetal

Cosmic Cookery
Katherine Ash, 44 pp. hand drawings, out of print

Messiah's World Crusade
234 Hawthorn Avenue
Larkspur, Calif. 94939

Hygienic Cookbook and Vegetarian Recipe Book
276 mimeographed 8 x 11 pages, $5.50 from:

Health Research
70 Lafayette Street
Mokelumne Hill, Calif. 95245

Eight old-timey turn of the century books in one. . .totally wholesome. . .one of the best.

Cooking with Grains and Vegetables
29 pp., 8 x 11, out of print

Cooking Good Food
35 pp., 8 x 11, out of print

Erewhon Trading Co.
8001 Beverly Blvd.
Los Angeles, Calif. 90048

or

TAO
303-B Newbury Street
Boston, Mass. 02115

Yogi Cookbook
Yogi Vithaldas, Susan Roberts, 126 pp., $.95 from:

Pyramid Publications
Mail Order Dept., 9 Garden St.
Moonachie, N.J. 07074

"Discover the amazing health secrets of the ancients. ." Indian curries, sweetmeats, and spicey stuff.

Cookless Book
Mrs. Richter, 88 pp., $2.00 from:

Tobe's
P.O. Box
St. Catherines, Ont.
Canada

Raw food recipes and fruit jumbles, salads. . .cookless.

Tassajara Bread Book
145 pp., $2.95 from:

Shambhala Publications, Inc.
2010 7th St.
Berkeley, CA 94710

Make it whole, and chew it up, bread that tastes, and feels good to make.

Vegan Kitchen
43 pp., rings, $2.00, from:

American Vegan Society
Box H
Malaga, New Jersey 08328

Completely non-animal, no meat, fish, fowl, dairy products, honey, only stuff that grows on the earth.

Zen Cookery
74 pp., rings, $1.95 from:

Tao
303-B Newbury St.
Boston, Mass. 02115

Practical macrobiotics, traditional eating way Japan country rivers brown rice.

Food Combining Made Easy
Herbert Shelton, 71 pp., $1.00 from:

Jaffe Brothers.
P.O. Box 636
Valley Center, Calif. 92082

Learn what mixes with what, so it can get digested without too much hassle.

Scientific Nutrition and Cookbook
(for those interested in the vegetarian way of life), Donna Grey Kelley, about 100 pp. (mimeo, 8 x 11), $3.50 from:

Donna Kelley
1305 Palm Ave.
Beaumont, California

Tells what's what in nutrition, why, and how, Yummy recipes, and sage advice for children of Light.

Vegetarian Cookery
Dr. Pietro Rotondi, $5.00 from:

Dr. Pietro Rotondi
1916 Vista del Mar Ave.
Hollywood, Calif. 90028

The Soybean Cookbook

This cookbook is listed because too many vegetarians I know are looking too unhealthy. It's particularly poignant when said vegetarian is pregnant and brain-starving the child. Soybeans are extra rich in protein; they're cheap, and not hard to grow. Now would some professional nutritionist let us know if they flat-out replace animal protein? Steve Durkee got laid up for a month last summer because of too little protein in the diet at Lama. They're on vegetable protein now. Is it working, Steve?

—SB

[Suggested by Barbara Kirshenblatt-Gimblett]

Note: Lama now has goats and a cow.

The Soybean Cookbook
Dorothea Van Gundy Jones
1963; 240pp.

$1.45 postpaid

from:
Arc Books
219 Park Avenue South
New York, New York 10003

or WHOLE EARTH CATALOG

HOW TO MAKE SOY CHEESE
Soy Cheese From Milk
Soy cheese is made by allowing soy milk to sour and curdle. When it is made commercially, lactic, tartaric, or citric acid is used; but acid is not necessary when a small amount of cheese is made at home. Set the soy milk in a warm place to sour and thicken. When thick, cut it into chunks with a knife, place these in a pan, cover them with water, and bring to the boiling point. Strain through cheesecloth, wringing the curds as dry as possible. Season with salt and a small amount of soy sauce. The fresh cheese can be used like cottage cheese and can be stored in the refrigerator for several days.

Soybeans are an excellent means of making a low-cost diet nutritionally safe. They are one of our cheapest sources of nutritious protein. A few cents' worth of dry beans will serve four to six persons and give them the food value of greater quantities of meat or fish. Soy flour or grits, at the cost of a few cents, can step up the protein content of a dish to equal the more expensive animal protein foods.

Soy

...Finally a word about soybeans. As a pediatrician I'm able to pass on the word to you from the professional nutritionist friends of mine about the relative value of soybean compared to animal protein. Flat-out on a weight for weight basis soybeans have more protein and more essential amino acids than sirloin beef. Period. "Normal and Therapeutic Nutrition," by Corinne H. Robinson, 13th. Ed., pp. 822 and 825, NY 1967. The problem is more complicated, however, because the above superiority of bean over beef is with whole beans, and does not take into account such goodies as how the foods are prepared (boiling, for example, destroys some amino acids) or if the beans are in the form of a milk or flour. Soybeans despite their superiority over beef in the Proudfit-Robinson data are rather poor in methionine, for example, and in no way should they be considered a kind of miracle food capable of meeting all human nutritional needs.

The take-home lesson of the day is that whole populations have done quite well on diets that were largely vegetable, but that the proper nutrition was accomplished by the mixture of supplementary vegetable proteins, such as barley, wheat, and soy proteins. Corn, for example, is terrible in lysine. Soybean, on the other hand, is fairly good in lysine, and experiments have shown that corn and beans are better utilized when they are taken together. It is not necessary to ingest large amounts of first class, All American Boy proteins like meat, milk, eggs, and fish, providing you take in mixed amounts of supplementary vegetables, as the majority of the people in the world do, such as cereals, millets, legumes, nuts, oilseeds, common vegetables, and leaf and grass protein. I'm sorry to hear one of your friends in Lama fell ill while on a vegetarian diet. But in no way should this be construed as an indictment against the vegetable. There is emerging increasing evidence that the only feasible solution to global malnutrition in the seventies is the development of cheap, high protein plant mixtures, with considerably less rape of the ecosystem. Hope I helped.

Sincerely,
Henry Abraham, M.D.
University of Arizona
Tuscon, Arizona

Soy and Sprouts

Good simple info: **Recipes for the Use of Soybeans** *and* **Sprouting** *for one self-addressed stamped envelope from:*

Sterling H. Nelson & Sons, Inc.
525 South 4th West
Salt Lake City, Utah 84110

Totally recommended, every recipe tastes like it tastes. . .they all work.

Get some feedback from the mothers of the nation, the good cooks, put this data through the computers, and if it fits, send your dollars or commentaries to:

Banyen Bookshop
2739 West 4th Avenue
Vancouver 8, B.C.
Canada

In cases of supreme emergency, the bookshop above named stock the books above named. Boieo!

"Meat"

Have you ever published a recipe for home-made wheat gluten? This is a basic meat substitute and very easy to make, forming the basis of many of the commercially produced, canned substitutes, notably Worthington and Loma Linda vegeburger, vegetable skallops, dinner cuts, vege-cuts, etc.

Mix 2½ to 3 cups of water with 8 cups of flour (gluten flour is easiest, but ordinary white flour will do), enough to make a firm ball. Soak under water overnight. The next day, keep kneading the dough under water and pouring off the starchy liquid, replacing with fresh cold (tap) water until water is clear during kneading (no more starch — this is where gluten flour was nice). You now have Wheat Gluten (the protein of flour) in the form of a large, rubbery ball.

For eating, slice into thin steak size, roll in batter, and grill or fry; chop into fine pieces and use in stews; or put through meat grinder and you have vege-burger, which can be used in many of the same ways as hamburger (ground beef).

As the gluten is tasteless, much like a hunk of sponge, disguises are necessary. Yeast extract, soya sauce, vegetable salts, wines, and, in general, anything you can think of, improve flavor considerably. (Perhaps you can find someone to tell you about preparing tofu as well.)

Ann Liston
Burnaby, B.C.
Canada

DOYLE

When D.R. left the phone booth he intended to go directly back downtown to the bus station. But then when he passed Clark Street he figured since he was that close he'd pop in on Marcella and see what those people were up to. When it turned out that what they were up to was supper D.R. didn't see any way to leave gracefully without eating something, especially since Marcella had fixed a place for him and had served smoked ham and chow-chow in celebration of his arrival. The family was already seated at the table in the kitchen when D.R. walked in, except for Marcella who was stirring something on the stove. Doyle was at the head of the table browsing through the Enquirer when he looked up and saw D.R. in the doorway.

"Dadburn your hide, where you been?" Doyle shouted. He scooted his chair back and got to his feet so hard the dishes on the table rattled. "I come home early on account of you and there you was out and gone already. How you doing, Buddy, I declare it's mighty good to see you."

Doyle came across the floor like a coal truck and gathered D.R. into his arms. Then he stepped back and took D.R.'s hand in both his own and pumped vigorously up and down.

"I said to Mars I said dadburn the like of him anyhow, me taking off work early to come and see him, and then him not even be here. Where you been, boy, you 'bout to miss your supper."

"Don't listen to him, David," said Marcella. "He's tickled to have you as an excuse to quit early."

"Daddy home early," said Debbie.

Herschel got out of his chair and crossed the room to where the two men were standing. As they talked he tried to worm in among their legs and stand between them.

"Here now, you little sneak, you sit down, we're getting ready to eat."

"I want to sit next to Uncle David," said Herschel.

"You sit where you always sit," said Doyle. "David's place is all laid out."

Herschel made a face of disappointment, but he obeyed his father. He dropped to his hands and knees, crawled under the table and came up on the other side.

"Feistiest thing ever was," Doyle said proudly. "He's turned into a regular devil"

"You neen to brag about it," said Marcella.

"I ain't a bragging," said Doyle. "I'm just stating the plain facts. Ain't that right David?"

"That's right," said D.R. "Doyle's just telling the facts."

"What I want to know is how that bus of yours is running," said Doyle. "I told Mars when you called the other day, I said I bet that boy's got car trouble. She said you'd of said so if you had and you know what I said? I said shoot, the thing about David with his cars is he don't know when he's got trouble and when he ain't."

Doyle broke out laughing at his joke, and D.R. laughed too. Doyle was a mechanic, and partners with his cousin Vernis in a filling station and garage. The year before, when D.R. had stopped off at Marcella's and Doyle's, Urge had had a burned valve and D.R. didn't know it. That anybody could drive a car with a burned valve and not know it amazed Doyle, and fascinated him at the same time. Doyle had given Urge a valve job for free, and Vernis had banged a few dents out of the body. If they'd known at the time that D.R.'s intention was to use his bus to help Eddie transport about a zillion bricks of marijuana to Chicago they'd have been less generous with their work. But the general freaky appearance of the bus, and indeed, of Divine Right himself, had disturbed them not at all. Doyle understood that his brother-in-law was some sort of mild outlaw. But he assumed, as Marcella assumed, that whatever it was D.R. was into was only a phase, as Doyle's own youthful outlawry had been a phase, and it never occurred to any of them to withdraw their affection just because the kid was in a phase. Till Doyle was drafted into the army, back in the 1950's, he had terrorized the roads of Eastern Kentucky as a coal truck driver. In the army he'd been court-martialed twice for going Awol, and general insubordination. He spent eight weeks in the stockade at Fort Hood, Texas and described them later as the best eight weeks of his entire army career. Doyle was a settled family man now, a father, a tax-payer and, as of the previous month, a member of the Church of God. But there was a natural empathy between him and Divine Right, and in spite of the widening differences in their lives they remained among each other's favorite people.

The Wok—A Chinese Cookbook

Gary Lee knows chinese cooking and his book for the beginner presents all the great techniques and traditional ways in a well-designed readable format. The wok is the central tool in any Chinese kitchen and its quick-fry principles are here explained clearly. Double-frying, steaming, and the lesser known traditions of the looo and dah-bin-lo are covered. I'm really impressed by this book; it tells more about Chinese cooking than any other Chinese cookbook I've investigated. Lee says he's going to write another book about the fancy dishes, although I wouldn't consider beef and lettuce soup, sweet and sour fish, or steamed minced pork with salted eggs to be drab fare.

—Hal Hershey

The Wok
a chinese cookbook
Gary Lee
1970; 178 pp.

$3.95 postpaid

from:
Nitty Gritty Productions
Box 457
Concord, California 94522

or WHOLE EARTH CATALOG

STEPS IN CHINESE-FRYING

1 - Wok must be very dry and clean. If not it will burn before coming to the right high temperature.

2 - In all Chinese dishes there are two basic parts; the principal and the compliment. The principal is the meat, and the compliment is usually a vegetable. In Chinese-frying you always cook the compliment first.

3 - Calculate the amount of oil you will need to cook the compliment (1 tablespoon is usually enough for a small portion). Preheat wok to a very high temperature, put oil in wok and then add compliment immediately. This is very important, do not heat the oil in the wok before adding your compliment otherwise the food will stick to the wok. The term used for this by professional cooks is "hot wok — cold oil".

4 - When the compliment is almost 3/4 done, take it out, set aside, and keep it warm.

5 - Clean the wok with a paper towel, reheat to a very high temperature again and add about 3 tablespoons of oil to cook the principal.

6 - Note: Only 1/2 of the seasonings will be added to the marinade — the other 1/2 will be added when the principal and compliment are combined. In this way, the seasonings will be well blended.

7 - When the principal is about 3/4 done, add the compliment and remaining seasonings. Never add your seasonings before this time or the food will become soggy - except in cooking tough vegetables such as cabbage or green pepper. In that case, add a very small pinch of salt only when first cooking them.

8 - A very short period of time (about 2 - 3 minutes) is all that is needed for a good Chinese-fry. You will not have time to measure all the seasonings when you want to add them. Therefore, it is very important that you have them all ready beforehand. Use five or six very small containers (small saucers, pieces of paper, etc.), measure out the seasonings you will use, and place them on these containers before you start to cook anything. Place them within easy reach in the order in which you will use them.

9 - Add the seasonings separately with an interval of at least five seconds between each addition, mixing constantly and gently yet swiftly. Bring the food from all directions to the center so that it will be evenly blended and cooked.

10 - When the recipe calls for water, you can use chicken broth instead. You do not always need to use all the water called for in a recipe - only what you need to make a little gravy. Some vegetables have sufficient natural moisture to necessitate only a little water.

11 - The sesame oil is always added last. Its function is to give a pleasant aroma to the food - if it is included too soon, the aroma is lost. It should be added immediately before the food is served.

Wok

The wok is too good a tool to pass up. We're carrying a 16" spun steel one with a handy (practically essential) steel ring base to sit on gas burners.

Wok (with ring base and lid)

$17.50 postpaid

$15.50 in the store

from WHOLE EARTH CATALOG

■ ■ ■ ■ ■ ■ ■ ■ ■ ■ ■ ■ ■ ■ ■ ■ ■ ■ ■

Chinese Food and Utensils

Those wishing to get Chinese food by mail and also certain utensils may obtain same from Cathay Food Products, Inc. 107 Mott St., New York, N.Y. 10013. Catalog sent on request.

Neil & Lorraine Wolf
Ketchum, Idaho

■ ■ ■ ■ ■ ■ ■ ■ ■ ■ ■ ■ ■ ■ ■ ■ ■ ■ ■

Useful Odds & Ends

For those unable to afford a flour mill—an old food mill—the kind everybody's mother has—can be purchased 2nd hand for less than a dollar, is a pretty good substitute. The flour is like a combination of wheat germ & flour—makes an excellent bread—and is very economical. The grinding keeps you strong.

For flesh eaters who believe in bearing the remorse for their actions—hang some california bay (laurel) in the carcass to keep away the flies. or use it as a flea collar or in your dog's sleeping quarters. Hang it on the wall, pop it in the soup.

Weave rags & old clothes into rugs on a frame with nails on either end in lieu of a loom. Weaves up fast if cut in inch strips. Makes a beautiful covering for floors & walls & keeps out wind & wet. Using string for warp, cost is about 10 cents a rug. Results with colors & designs unlimited.

Polyethylene sheeting a phenomenal material for all occassions. Put it under flooring for a dry, draft free floor use it as extra insulation on walls & windows when its cold. Put a water tank atop your house covered with black polyethylene—hook up pipes & fixtures—voila hot running water on gravity pressure. Polyethylene makes an excellent green house over a 2x4 frame certainly cheaper than glass.

Boil eucalyptus leaves in water and use the resulting infusion on poison oak. A very good astringent.

Ann Ligosky

NEW STYLE GRIDDLE

No.	Diam. of Bottom			Wgt. Each		
6	8	in.		2	lbs.	$2.48
7	9	in.		2½	lbs.	$2.66
8	9½	in.		3	lbs.	$2.90
9	11	in.		4	lbs.	$3.20
10	11¾	in.		5	lbs.	$4.10

Dutch Oven

A very handy item for the tipi dweller or commune is the dutch oven. A low cast iron cooking pot with three short legs and a flat lip-edged cover. It is used in the hot coals of your camp fire or buried with hot coals in the ground. The results are fantastic! A source for dutch ovens: Lodge Mfg. Co. A paperback book on dutch oven cooking, Old Fashioned Dutch Oven Cookbook by Don Holm.

[Suggested and reviewed by Reed Plankenhorn]

Old Fashioned Dutch Oven Cookbook

Don Holm
1970; 106 pp.

$3.95 postpaid

from:
The Caxton Printers, Ltd.
Caldwell, Idaho

or WHOLE EARTH CATALOG

The camp Dutch oven, either iron or aluminum, can be permanently damaged by pouring cold water into a hot oven, or uneven heating such as putting only half the oven or lid on the coals, by careless packing while traveling (the legs can be broken off or pushed up through the bottom by too much jostling), and by rust and corrosion.

The lid, turned upside down on the coals or on the pot, can be used for frying eggs, bacon, or grilling hot cakes. When using more than one oven, the second can be stacked on top of the first without the necessity of spreading more coals on the ground.

One should probably call the aluminum model the *contemporary* Dutch oven, which has some advantages and some disadvantages when compared with the traditional cast-iron model. The aluminum model is the only one that can be backpacked by a hiker. It costs about the same as the ironware. But it has a much lower fuel requirement, which can lead to trouble. The trick is to use from one half to two-thirds less fuel or heat to start with and control the heat more carefully.

The old camp Dutch oven evolved through centuries of experience. It was designed for cooking complete meals on open fires without the need for other appliances. (A shovel, pothook, and grease swab come in handy, though.) Its thick construction distributes the heat evenly and thoroughly from a small bed of coals assisted by the tight-fitting, flanged lid.

It can be hung over an open fire, set down in the fire, or buried in a pit of coals. It is at once a kettle, a frying pan, an oven, a pot, and even a stove, all in on portable utensil.

On a camping or hunting trip you can prepare a roast or stew, or even sheepherder bread, go away for a half day or so, only to return bone-tired and happily find a rib-sticking meal waiting for chow down.

For hole-in-the-ground cooking, dig a pit larger and deeper than the camp Dutch oven. Line it with small stones or aluminum foil to prevent loss of heat through the ground. (Be sure to select a site that is pure mineral soil and not full of humus, or you may be the cause of a forest or range fire, which will make you extremely unpopular in most parts, podner.) Build a fire in the hole and let it burn briskly an hour or so, or until there is nothing left but hot coals. Remove some of these, place oven in pit with the rest, and rake the coals back over the oven.

Cover the whole ball of wax with fresh dirt in a blanket about four inches thick. Most dishes require from four to eight hours cooking in this way. The cooking can be hurried along by building another fire on top of the dirt.

CAMP DUTCH OVEN AND LID

Size Inches	Capacity	Depth Inches	Approximate Weight Pounds	
8	2 qt.	3	7	$ 5.50
10	4 qt.	3¼	12	7.00
12	6 qt.	4	17	8.80
14	8 qt.	4	23	12.00
16	12 qt.	4¾	30	17.00

Lodge Manufacturing Company
South Pittsburg, Tenessee 37380

Home Canning of Fruits and Vegetables

You can buy a book on this subject for $5, or you can get these perfectly adequate Government booklets at 20 cents apiece.

—SB

Home Canning of Fruits and Vegetables
Home & Garden Bulletin No. 8
1965, 1969; 31 pp.

$.35 postpaid

Home Freezing of Fruits and Vegetables
Home & Garden Bulletin No. 10
1965, 1969; 47 pp.

$.50 postpaid

both from:
Superintendent of Documents
U.S. Government Printing Office
Washington, D.C. 20402

Peaches can be peeled easily if they are dipped in boiling water, then in cold water.

Storing Vegetables and Fruits

This booklet will be valuable to anybody living in areas where the temperature in winter averages 30 degrees or lower. Storing without refrigeration relies on cold outdoor air to cool the stored products. "Basements, cellars, outbuildings and pits" are explained and diagrammed, with specific instructions for different vegetables and fruits. A bargain.

—Hal Hershey

Storing Vegetables and Fruits
in basements, cellars, outbuildings and pits
Home and Garden Bulletin No. 119
18 pp.

$.15 postpaid

from:
Superintendent of Documents
U.S. Government Printing Office
Washington, D.C. 20402

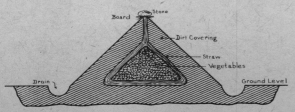

FIGURE 3.—Cone-shaped pit showing details of construction.

Ball Blue Book

Though this guide to home canning has been in print since 1909, it easily avoids the Grandma image and gets you into your own canning. It has illustrated, step-by-step directions and recipes and handy guides for jar estimating. When something goes wrong, there's trouble-shooting guides. If you have a good growing summer, this book can help you have a well-fed winter. A buy. —SB

VEGETABLE	PREPARATION FOR FREEZING	SCALDING TIME IN MINUTES*
Asparagus	Sort stalks according to thickness. Wash thoroughly. Cut in jar-size or 2-inch lengths. Scald. Chill. Pack, leaving no head space.	Small 1½ Medium 2 Large 3
Beans, Lima or Butter	Shell. Wash. Sort according to size. Scald. Chill.	Small 1 Medium 2 Large 3
Beans, Snap, Green or Wax	Wash. Remove ends. Cut as desired. Scald. Chill.	3
Beets	Wash and sort according to size. Trim tops, leave ½ inch of stems. Cook until tender. Chill. Peel and cut as desired.	Small 30 Medium 45

Ball Blue Book
1972; 112 pp.

$.50 postpaid from:
Ball Corporation
Muncie, IN 47302

Soap, etc.

TO DRY CORN FOR WINTER USE

Sweet corn is the best. Husk it. Have a pot of boiling water— put your corn in & let it boil 3 min— then cut it from the cob & put it in pans in a warm oven. It must be stirred frequently, when perfectly dry, put away in bags. When wanted for use, soak it all night, next day boil it an hour with a little salt; before serving stir in a little flour, pepper & butter.

TO FRESHEN WALNUTS

When Walnuts have been kept until the meat is too dried to be good, let them stand in milk & water 8 hrs. and dry them— fresh as new they will be.

TO MAKE AN IMPROVED CANDLE

Make the wick about half the usual size, & wet them with spirits of turpentine; dry them, before dipping, in the sunshine & the candles will be more durable, emit a steadier & clearer blaze.

WATERPROOF BOOTS

A pint of boiled linseed oil, half a pd. of mutton suet, six ounces of clean beeswax, & four ounces of rosin, are to be melted & well mixed over a fire. Of this, while warm, but not hot enough to shrink the leather, lay on plentifully with a brush over new boots or shoes, when quite dry and clean. The leather remains pliant. The New England fishermen preserve their boots water tight by this method, which, it is said, has been in use among them over 100 years. They can stand in water hour after hour without inconvenience.

TO MAKE SOAP FROM ASHES

To prepare a lye for soap, take a barrel without a bottom & place it on a board that has a trough to convey the water into another vessel; cover the bottom with straw, then sprinkle over a couple quarts of lime; fill the barrel with ashes; turn on cold water, a pail at a time— slowly! Continue to turn on water, at intervals of 3-4 hours the 1st, 3rd & 5th days. When the lye becomes strong enough to bear up an egg, put to 15 gal of it, 11 pds. of grease, heated to the boiling point. Stir it for 5 min. every day, till it forms soap. If it doesn't in 1 week, add a pailful of soft water.

Albert & Cindy
Bass Lake, CA.

WRITE FOR FREE DIRECTIONS FOR SOAP MAKING FROM:
Household Products Dept.
Penwalt Corporation
3 Parkway
Philadelphia, Pa. 19102
or

U.S. Dept. of Agriculture
Agricultural Research Service
Clothing & Housing Research Branch
Washington, D.C. 20525

Madeline G. Salmon
Menlo Park, Calif.

NOTES ON SOAPMAKING

1. Never use lye on aluminum utensils (lye acts upon them). For small batches of soap, enameled or granite ware is suitable and for larger batches, an iron kettle may be used.

2. All grease should be pure and clean to obtain soap with a clean, wholesome odor.

3. Measure accurately. Be careful about temperatures.

4. Ammonia, kerosene, carbolic acid, etc., when added to soap help it little, if any, as the lye usually neutralizes them. They increase cost and may make soap harsh on skin.

5. Coldness makes a hard, brittle soap.

6. Excess lye makes a coarse, flinty soap that will crumble when shaved. Soap should have a smooth, velvety texture that curls when shaved. It should not bite the tongue when aged.

7. Use the all-purpose soap for toilet soap, a shampoo, for washing prints, lingerie, fine and other delicate fabrics.

8. The following fats (for soapmaking) are listed in the order of their desirability: Tallow, lard and their combinations, olive oil, other vegetable oils. Mineral oils will not make soap.

9. Poultry fat should be combined with other fats, as soap made from it alone is soft and spongy.

10. Aging always improves soap. Soap made from lard or soap that has been boiled requires longer aging before it becomes hard and ready for use.

11. Instead of storing rinds and meats scraps, extract the fat; store in a tightly covered container in a cool, dry place.

12. Make the fat into soap as it accumulates and let the soap age rather than allow the fat to get too old and rancid.

13. There need never be a failure in soapmaking. If separation occurs, it can be reclaimed.

14. Where you find your grease has become rancid or contains materials other than fats, boil in large quantity of water, allow to cool, skim off grease, and then follow the directions in the recipe for soapmaking.

SALVATION

When everybody was seated they bowed their heads while Doyle asked the blessing. D.R. had never heard his brother-in-law ask the blessing before and he couldn't resist keeping his eyes open to watch him. Marcella had been a church goer all her life, and the kids had been going to Sunday School since they could walk. But the blessing had never been part of mealtime in their house before, and D.R. was a little astounded. What was surprising was the quality of Doyle's prayer. It was short and simple, but, for Doyle, strangely articulate and obviously sincerely felt. He thanked the Lord for the food they were about to eat, for the house they lived in and the comforts they enjoyed. He especially thanked Him for David's safe arrival, and for the privilege of gathering together as a family once again. Doyle seemed to sense that the ritual surprised D.R., for when he had said Amen and Marcella started serving the food, he began talking about his recent conversion and baptism into the church Marcella had been attending for years.

"Of course," said Doyle, "I'm new in it, there's a lot I don't understand. But as far as feeling good about something, David, I never felt any better about a thing in my whole life than I do this."

"We've already got him taking up the collection," said Marcella.

Doyle laughed. "I'm surprised they trust the likes of me with their money."

D.R. laughed at that, and went on to congratulate Doyle on his decision. "But I have to say I'm pretty surprised," he added. "I mean . . . "

"Honey you ain't a bit more surprised than I am, let me tell you. Why sometimes I even forget I've gone and done it. At work I'll rip out a big cuss, and along about four in the afternoon I get to thinking how good a big old beer would taste after work. But then I'll find myself in church on Sunday morning, singing hymns and listening to that little preacher, and it's sort of like waking up out of a dream."

D.R. asked Doyle to tell him how he came to his decision. The question embarrassed Doyle a little, and he took a big mouthful of food to keep from having to answer right away. D.R. watched him as he chewed. Doyle had always been very lean as a young man, but in the last few years he'd begun to accumulate flesh around his middle, and in his neck and cheeks. His face was losing its angularity and taking on a roundness that made him seem boyish and middle-aged at the same time. Doyle was thirty-four now, but as he bit down on his food the tendons in his big jaw flexed beneath his skin, and for a second the old toughness, and even meanness, of his youth was restored to his face, and for some reason D.R. found that very moving. He loved Doyle. And he loved Marcella. When he wasn't with them he really didn't think about them all that much. But now, sitting with them in their kitchen, sharing food, looking at their faces, at the faces of the children, smelling the raw, familiar odor of their home and hearing the old familiar notes in their strange voices, D.R. suddenly felt a little overwhelmed. It was a rush, a strange high that caused tears to work behind his eyes, and some deep longing to stir inside his chest. If D.R. had been called on to speak just then he wouldn't have been able to. Doyle was having his own difficulties speaking, but at last he swallowed his food and in a low and more serious tone he began to tell about the process of his salvation.

Passport to Survival

If these are your fat years, read this book and lay aside some wealth for the lean. If these are the lean years, here's how to survive them till the circle turns again.

The four foods for survival are wheat, powdered milk, honey and salt——they will keep indefinitely when properly stored. Mrs. Dickey bases her survival diet on these ingredients and enhances them with 40 more supplementary foods varying in degrees of storability and nutritional value. Then she gives more than a hundred recipes that almost all use only these four basic survival foods and water.

There's no question but you'd eat well on this diet. From wheat flour, honey and warm water you can grow yeast and thus make bread. Derive wheat gluten from wheat kernels and eat a very high-protein, incredibly versatile meat sub-stitute. Everything from spaghetti and tacos to puddings and taffy is produced rather miraculously. Supplementing with yogurt (from powdered milk) and bean and seed sprouts gives a fairly rounded regimen.

Emergency procedures and the forethoughts stored here will serve you come holocaust, catastrophe, or unemploy-ment.

[Reviewed by Hal Hershey]

Passport to Survival
Esther Dickey
1969; 180 pp.

$3.95 postpaid

from:
Bookcraft Publishers
1848 West 2300 South
Salt Lake City, Utah

or WHOLE EARTH CATALOG

Fat-free powdered milk, when kept dry and reasonably cool, stores with little change for over 15 years.

●

Honey has other virtues,. . .As it is essentially a concentrated extract from the plant kingdom, it undoubtedly contains numerous minor components which contribute in some degree to man's nutrition. It will come as a surprise to many to learn that a tablespoonful of honey contains as much vitamin C as a medium-sized apple, and that this same quantity has three times as much iron as the apple. It also possesses the same quantity of protein and nicotinic acid as the apple and a somewhat higher content of riboflavin. Never-theless it must be recognized that honey, like the apple, is far from a complete food. Its greatest virtue lies in its pleasing flavor.

No. 19. Creme Gluten A La Emergency

Gluten No. 12b   Wheat grass No. 6
Cream Sauce No. 70

Form the gluten in marble-size balls. Bake and simmer in stew broth No. 77. Mince wheat grass grown in soil and cut when 1-1/2 inches high. Add gluten balls and grass to cream sauce and serve immediately.

Chapter 7 Menu — Saturday Breakfast

Variations:

(1) Mix wheat grass in blender, using as small an amount of water as possible. Strain, and add a small amount of the green liquid to the cream sauce. (2) Wrap wheat stems in tiny bundles with noodle strips. Serve in a casserole, covering with cream sauce.

Packaging the four survival foods— wheat, milk powder, honey and salt— in five-gallon cans has been a project of different groups who have been awakened to the need for emergency storage. Each can contains one month's food supply for one adult person: 27 lb. of wheat, 5 lb. of powdered skim milk, 3 lb. of honey, up to 1 lb. of salt.

Butchering, Processing and Preservation of Meat

Vegetarians may turn their heads. (Some visited Kesey while he was slaughtering a cow. "They like to watch the blood gush just like everybody else.")

One advantage of doing your own butchering, you get to thank the animal personally, and see him personally all the way through what you're doing together. There's nothing abstract about it. This book has the whole story. Farm animals, game, fish, canning, smoking, making sausage. How to eat your friends and waste nothing.

—SB
[Suggested by Jim & Sue Walton]

**Butchering, Processing and Preservation of Meat——
A Manual For the Farm and Home**
Frank G. Ashbrook
1955; 318 pp

$4.95
from:
Van Nostrand-Reinhold Books
450 W. 33rd St.
New York, N.Y. 10001

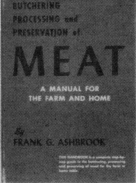

The ease with which lambs and sheep can be dressed makes them a convenient source of fresh meat for family use. Lamb is the flesh of young sheep. Handy-weight 25- to 45-lb lamb carcasses yield comparatively small cuts. The entire carcass is small enough so that with home refrigeration a family can consume the meat before spoilage occurs. Portions of lamb can also be frozen or canned. Some cuts can be cured satisfactorily. It can be kept as an emergency food reserve or as a source of variety in the diet.

A lamb carcass chills quickly and cures easily. Lambs generally dress out about 50 per cent, which means that an 80-pound lamb will make approximately a 40-pound carcass. The trimmed leg roasts from a 40-pound carcass will weigh about 6 pounds each; and the shoulder roasts, about 5 pounds apiece. There will be about 7 pounds of breast and neck and 8 pounds of loin and rib to be roasted or cut into 30 medium-thick chops.

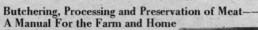

F<small>IG</small>. 16. Homemade beef hoist. A simple method of hoisting a beef carcass is illustrated in these sketches. A fork or rake handle or gas pipe is slipped through incisions between tendon and shank bone; ropes are suspended from tree limb or other support (wide apart at top) to height of hocks below. To free ends of rope are tied short sticks, as 2-foot pieces of broom handle or equally strong material. These are placed inside the shanks and are used as levers for winding up ropes around fork or rake handle, as shown. Two men wind up the rope around pipe or handle. When beef is at right height, another pipe or handle is laid across between ropes and ends of sticks to prevent un-winding. As the beef is raised the legs are spread farther and farther, as desired.

Comment on Ashbrook

If you are going to go native or at least semi-fringy, you had better figure out a way of beating Safeway to the price of a pork chop. In other words, if you are going to beat the system, Ashbrook's book will show you how. (At least in the meat department).

Want to butcher a steer? He tells you how to do it in the minute detail you need if you have never done something like this before. Same goes for hogs, sheep and lambs, game animals and poultry and wild fowl.

After you have the animal cut up he tells you how to freeze it, can it, salt it and even smoke it. Want to make your own sausage? He tells you how.

This is the most complete book I've ever seen on the subject. From how to select the right knife to what to do with all the left-over fat (make soap with it— he shows you how).

Ashbrook knows what he is talking about, 40 years as animal husband-man and biologist with the U.S. Dept. of Agriculture and Interior. You can forget about all those 15 cent pamphlets from the USDA, this one book is all you need.

Arthur Keim
Colfax, Washington

F<small>IG</small>. 69. Sawing the backbone.

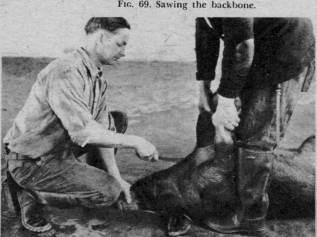

Fig. 27. Sticking the hog on the ground. The feet and legs of the man holding the hog are pressed against the shoulders of the animal to prevent it rolling.

A Complete Guide to Home Meat Curing

Brief run down on butchering, details on various curing methods. Morton also has various sugar cures, meat pumps, etc.

—SB

A Complete Guide to Meat Curing
1969; 42 pp.

$1.25 postpaid

from:
Morton Salt Company
110 North Wacker Drive
Chicago, Ill. 60606

Cured Domestic Rabbit. Rabbits can be cured whole or cut in pieces. Wash rabbit and place in a clean container. Make a curing brine by mixing 1/2 cup of Tender-Quick in 2 cups of water. Pour enough brine into the container to completely cover the rabbit.

Allow to cure 24 hours, then take it from the brine, wash, and it is ready to cook. If it is not to be cooked immediately, place in the refrigerator and cook within 3 to 5 days after it is cured. Cured rabbit may be fried, broiled, baked or stewed.

Tender-Quick brine draws out the blood, firms the meat and improves the flavor.

Wild rabbits and small game placed in Tender-Quick brine before being cooked will have an improved flavor and it helps reduce the strong game taste.

Quaker City Hand Grain Grinder

We've switched our loyalty from Bell Grinders (good meal, but no flour) to Corona Mill (flour on two grindings) now to Quaker City. The new champ, better bits, finer adjustment.
—SB

$11.95 plus postage

from:
Nelson & Sons, Inc.
P.O. Box 1296
Salt Lake City, Utah 84110

or **$15.00** postpaid
from WHOLE EARTH CATALOG

Atlas Juicer

I want to inform you and hopefully through you, your readers of a top quality tool for sustenance and nourishment. I enclose descriptive material on both models manufactured by Juice Master who is a little-heard-of firm that produces top quality farm equipment.

Either the Atlas Juicer or the Atlas Princess are far superior to any of the juicers now on the market such as Braun. The Atlas costs more but the value is there in terms of materials used (no plastic) and the construction (a 10 year guarantee on the Princess and a lifetime guarantee on the Atlas Juicer).

We now have used a Princess model for one year and find ourselves appreciating fruits and vegetables in a new and exciting way. Our diet has been improved manyfold and we now savor drinks ranging from carrot and cabbage juice to grape and apples juice.

For people living together it will be a useful piece of equipment.

Note, that although the retail price is high, it is extremely fair given the quality of the item. In addition you can buy either model at a discount if Juice Master does not have a sales representative in your area. Further reductions in price are available if you qualify to become a dealer—by simply ordering three units.

[Suggested and reviewed by B. L. Faber]

Atlas Juicer

$149.50

from:
Juice Master Mfg. Co.
407 Franklin Street
East Peoria, Ill. 61602

Tutti-Frutti Steam Juicer

One nice advantage of steam-juicing fruit and vegetables is that the residue is still palatable. So's the juice.
—SB

Tutti-Frutti Steam Juicer
Aluminum **$35.00** postpaid

Stainless Steel **$65.00** postpaid

from:
Mrs. Rex Ashdown
769 West 3650 North Street
Ogden, UT 84404

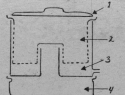

Lee Electric Flour Mills

The best bread is made from wheat ground just before baking.

This is a small electric grain grinder manufactured by an old dependable company. A unique feature of this machine is that it grinds the entire grain kernel, including the germ and bran, into fine flour. (Other mills generally discard the germ). You fill the hopper and an automatic feed admits the proper amount of grain into the stone grinding chamber. The carborundum grinding stone never needs redressing, the mill does not get warm enough to impair the nutritional value of the flour, and fresh stone ground flour . . . pass the bread!

[Suggested and Reviewed by Lloyd Kahn]

Meadows 8" Household Stone Burr Mill

Considering the cost of an electric mill such as the one sold in the store this item is high. However the Lee mill will grind only a small amount of flour and is slow for use in a community mill such as this mill would be ideal for. It will grind a hundred pounds of fine flour an hour. Such a community mill or a small co-op could supply a community with organic whole wheat flour for 6 to 8 cents a pound, depending on their source of wheat berries. Deaf Smith County wheat berries are 6 cents a lb. FOB Hereford, Texas. Freight on wheat is funny. The best I can figure out is that it would cost about $1.00 per 100 to ship it from Hereford to SF; if and only if you buy one complete truck load as only wheat can be in the truck if the truck contains wheat. Trucking companies say wheat is "exempt" and when you deal with wheat you are dealing indirectly with the Govt.

[Suggested and reviewed by Jerry Walker]

$355.00

Meadows Mill Co.
North Wilkesboro
North Carolina 28659

Big Bell Grinder

You might be interested in the C.S. Bell mill model 2 (2MC). In your very first issue you showed the small Bell mill and then later replaced it with the Corona grain mill. The Corona is far superior to the small Bell mill but the big Bell (No. 2) is far superior to the Corona. And far more expensive: about $30.00 as opposed to $13.00. But well worth the money. On the East Coast it is distributed by the Erewhon Trading Company.

And an excellent book is The Soil and Health *published by Devin-Adair. This is a classic work in the field of organic farming by Sir Albert Howard. Howard also wrote* An Agricultural Testament *and was the major influence on J.I. Rodale among others. Along with Plowman's Folly and Farmers of Forty Centuries (and the long out of print Topsoil and Civilization) one of the indispensible written works in the field.*

Jimmy Silver
Boston, Mass.

(See p. 46)

German Steam Juicer

I have something you might be interested in—I had been looking for it myself, ever since we survived on it after WWII in Germany. It is most ingenious. We used it on an iron stove—in the clipping it gives two prices—one for gas, one for electric—but I am sure it can be used on a woodburning or whatever other stove as well. We even sliced or chopped sugar beets and used this juice maker to draw out the juices completely, then we simmered these to make a great sirup, without all the extra water to boil out, as you would if you cooked the beets the conventional method. This juicer is so simple: in the upper part goes anything you want to juice—it just simmers away, and out of the siphon tube comes the clear natural juice as it is, no sugar. It can be canned right into glasses or bottles. Rhubarb is delicious, even to people who usually don't like Rhubarb.

I noticed a California Concern imports (manufactures?) these, so I am not trying to translate the German but if you want you can send for the english brochure and directions from them.

Hoping you can use this—I am sure using mine.

Inge Chase
Red Oak, Iowa

Fassungsvermögen : 10 Quart (11,36 Liter Früchte).
Sofortige Lieferung.
Für nur $24.95 für Gas Herd. Nur $28.95 für Electro
Herd mit schwerem Boden einschl. Porto und Versich.

ROBERT'S MERCHANDISE CO.
951 Howard Street   San Francisco, Calif. 94103

Catalog

free

from:
Lee Engineering Co.
2023 West Wisconsin Avenue
Milwaukee, Wisconsin 53201

OUTPUT PER HOUR

Model	Motor Size	Fine Flour	Coarse Meal	Price
500	1/6 hp	3 to 5 lbs	not adjustable	$95.00
600	1/6 hp	3 to 5 lbs	20 to 25 lbs	$125.00
S-500	1/4 hp	6 to 10 lbs.	not adjustable	$145.00
S-600	1/4 hp	6 to 10 lbs	40 to 45 lbs	$170.00

Operating Voltage	115 AD-DC
Current Draw	3.0 amperes
Overall Height	20 inches
Shipping weight	20 pounds

DOYLE'S STORY

"I think the thing that finally got me serious about it, David, was my brother Clarence getting killed in a rock fall, down home, back in the spring. I don't know if you ever knew Clarence or not . . ."

"I remember him," said D.R. "He used to work at Blue Diamond."

"That's him" Doyle went on. "Older than me, and not so long, as he used to say it. Of course it's been a while since he worked at Blue Diamond. They shut down over there right after we all moved up here, I remember that because Clarence come up here to live a while, but he never liked it enough to stay, and for the last nine, ten year he's been in and out of them little old dog-hole mines, mostly over on Second Creek, and for a while there on Trace Fork till they stripped it. He was working for the Combs brothers over on Second Creek last March when a piece of rock fell on him. The whole roof caved in and crushed him, just like that. He never drawed another breath after that rock caught him."

"I didn't know that, Doyle," D.R. said solemnly. "I'm sorry to hear it."

"Well, it was a sad time, I tell you it was," said Doyle. "It like to broke poor Mommy's heart. She was his favorite, you know. He was her first, and he lived there next door to her, and doted on her, and took care of her, him and Carlene. It was just the worst thing that could have happened in Mommy's life, and there it was, him dead just all of a sudden, and there wasn't a thing on earth anybody could do about it except bury him."

"Clarence's funeral was the saddest time," said Marcella.

"Awful sad," said Doyle. "Just awful sad. We went home for it of course. You remember the church there at the mouth of the creek, I guess. I doubt they's over twenty members of that church left around there, so many's moved away. But for Clarence's funeral it was full, people come from far away as Hyden, and Hazard. He was one of his old army buddies from Pike County heard about it and come. Brother Fugate preached, and there was singing, and old Mr. Stacy got up and preached some too. What was bad about it though, as far as Mommy was concerned, was Clarence never had been saved. And so naturally there was a lot of talk about the rest of us. Mommy cried and cried, and pleaded with me, and my brother Lee. She cried all weekend and pleaded with us to join the church. I don't know if you remember Lee or not, David . . ."

"I remember him," said D.R. "I remember all these people. Brother Fugate baptized me and Marcella right there in Trace Fork, I sure remember him."

"Well," Doyle went on. "You can imagine how it was then. To please Mommy, and ease her all I could, me and Lee promised her we'd think about it. I don't know what Lee's done, I ain't heard from him since the funeral, but I got back up here and that whole business was all I could think about. But the funny thing is, although I wouldn't want Mommy to know this, it really wasn't anything that she said that made me change my mind."

Doyle paused then to eat some more, and take a drink of milk.

(continued)

Paprikás Weiss Gourmet Shop

If a bunch of people are eating out of one kitchen where you are, it may be worthwhile to treat yourself to some gourmet equipment. Whether your scene is a logging camp, movie company, revolutionary cell, or country commune, the best way to attract and keep good people is with outstanding food.

—SB

[Suggested by Lank Felsen]

Catalog

$.25 postpaid

from:
Paprikás Weiss Importer
1546 Second Avenue
New York, N.Y. 10028

POT STRAINER
Chrome plated, black plastic handle.$1.98   **No. 5220**

FRENCH STYLE INSTA-BREWER MAKES REAL COFFEE IN 30 SECONDS
Measure in coffee. Pour in boiling water. Insert pressure plunger. Let stand from 30 seconds to 2 full minutes, depending on desired strength. Push plunger to bottom and pour. It's as easy as that with the Insta-Brewer. Made of heatproof Corning glass with stainless steel working parts, it also makes superior tea, can be used as a martini pitcher. 1 to 6 cups.
No. 201 $15.98 each

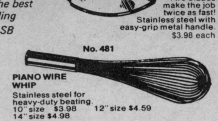

No. 391
DOUBLE-BLADED CHOPPER
Two blades make the job twice as fast! Stainless steel with easy-grip metal handle.
$3.98 each

No. 481
PIANO WIRE WHIP
Stainless steel for heavy-duty beating.
10" size $3.98   12" size $4.59
14" size $4.98

HOW TO GET A CHERRY STONED!

AMAZING CHERRY STONER PITS EVERY CHERRY ON AN ASSEMBLY LINE BASIS
It looks like a Rube Goldberg contraption and operates with the efficiency of a push-button machine. All you do is fill the hopper with cherries and turn the crank. The stone rolls out the end and the pitted fruit pops out from the center. Cherries are never bruised. And not a single pit is missed. Heavily-tinned metal won't rust. $16.98 each
No. 500

TURKISH COFFEE MAKER—Imported   **No. 197**
Authentic equipment for making thick, aroma-laden Turkish coffee. Polished Heavy-weight Aluminum long handle.
3 cup $6.68
6 cup $9.98

COUSCOUS° COOKER
This is a modern adaptation of the traditional North African djefna° used to prepare this famous native delicacy. The upper part holds the semolina° granules and the lower part the boiling water.
6-quart size $29.98

No. 353.
HEAVY DUTY SAUSAGE STUFFER AND FRUIT PRESS
A home sausage factory in one heavy steel machine! Designed to fill and case sausages with one turn of the handle. No air can ever enter casing —nothing goes in but your own stuffing. Can also be used as a fruit press. 6-Quart capacity. $105.00 each

TINNED SAUCEPANS — 704153 1½ pint size $5.98; **704138** 1 quart size $7.98; **704139** 2½ quart size $9.98 Preferred by chefs because of their excellent heat-conducting qualities, these pans add to the home cook's skill also.

No longer available

French Cookware

Equipment: No matter what kind of cooking you do, French cookware is unsurpassed both from a scientific and aesthetic pt. of view. E.G. Pots are 1/8 in thick copper, tin lined. Why: High heat conductivity (little heat wasted in heating the pot compared to iron, even heating (no burning on the edges like aluminum) Good enthalpy (keeps warm for a while after cooking etc.) Mail sources (sorry these all E. coast) La Cuisiniere, 903 Madison Ave. N.Y., N.Y. 10021. Bazaar de La Cuisine Inc. 160 E 55th St. NY, NY 10022; Basar Francais 666 6th Ave. NY, NY 10010. All three shops issue free catalogs.

Surprised that with your emphasis on self-education, you don't have 10 pages on correspondance schools. You leran at your own pace, the schools take all the work out of separating the wheat from the chaff in any field. The teacher nows you by name. Etc. A possible good first entry: National Camera Repair School 2000 W. Union Ave. Englewood Colorado 80110 Also: ICS, Scranton, PA 18515. Over 400 courses including a lot on construction which WEC'ers seem to be interested. The accrediting agency of correspondance schools is National Home Study Council 1601 18th St. NW, Washington DC 20009. It issues a free list of accredited schools.

D. Mayerson
Flushing, N.Y. 11355

ETS. E. DEHILLERIN. There are kitchen-equipment freaks, just as there are stationery freaks, and we should indulge them. Dehillerin indulges them beautifully (and, by the time you finish paying the freight, expensively). But write to 18 Rue Coquilliere, Paris, and see what happens. Sieves, grinders, broilers, boilers, whisks, spatulas, deep pots, shallow pots—anything you have ever wanted is there. They'll send out a kind of packet of loose pictures that looks like a child's alphabet primer.

Stephen Chodorov
New Milford, Conn.

Country Kitchen

Some of their stuff is eye-wash junk. Some is good.
—SB

Catalog **$1.00**

Country Kitchen
270 W. Merrick Rd.
Valley Stream, NY 11582

From: Iron Ware

UNIVERSAL SHARPENER
European import that sharpens every known type of blade: Serrated, scalloped or straight.
2969—Sharpener $1.19

Cross Imports

Another gourmet cookware catalog. Looks like good prices.
—SB

[Suggested by Muffy Anderson]

Catalog

$0.25

from:
Cross Imports, Inc.
210 Hanover St.
Boston, Mass 02113

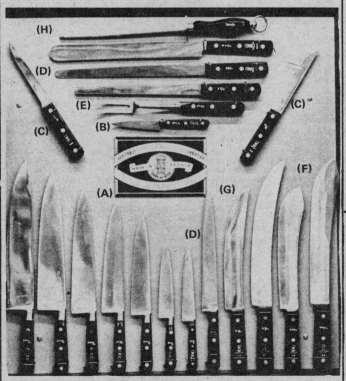

(H)
(D)
(E)
(C)
(B)
(A)
(C)
(G)
(F)
(D)

TOMATO MACHINE

801 — extra heavy with an extra large strainer $22.95
809 — large size $18.95

Iron Ware

No. 1 item in my kitchen is my iron ware. I wouldn't be without it. Frying pans all sizes, some with covers (they have both glass [$2.00 to $4.00 ea] and iron. I recommend iron for financial reasons, the glass breaks easily.), griddles, chicken cooker, deep 3" frying pan & cover, dutch oven with cover.

It is easy to care for & with proper care they will last a lifetime or more. I'm using my mothers frying pan which is now 45 years old.

Ironware is available in most large discount stores and in most surplus stores. The surplus stores usually have the best selection but are sometimes higher priced.

The two major producers are Griswold Manufacturing Co. and Wagner Ware both of Sidney, Ohio. They both have fine brochures and instruction sheets for care and use. They are glad to send these on request. Here is an info sheet (extra) from a pan in my local Alpha Beta.

No. 2 is cookie/bread sheet. It is steel and does not buckle in oven like aluminum. They are available through Country Kitchen, 270 W. Merrick Rd., Valley Stream, NY 11582. They sell for $3.50. You do not have to grease but they are not teflon. Browns so evenly and beautifully. C.K. carries all types of kitchen ware some expensive & not really necessary but others unique and reasonable.

Edie Litle
Laguna Beach, CA.

Roth

Nifty gourmet items.
—SB

H. Roth & Son
1577 First Ave.
New York, N.Y. 10028

Q

(Q) No. S320 Bread Mixer. The easy way to mix dough for bread, recipes inc. 3 gal. cap. $14.98.

Braun Appliances

As far as "things" are concerned. . .I think that BRAUN appliances are out of sight. . .they are very streamlined, practical and usually inexpensive by comparison to other products of the same type. For example. . .their $50 juicer (juicer) sp? really works as well as other $150 models on the market. They are made in Germany. A main outlet is

Braun North America
55 Cambridge Parkway
Cambridge, Mass. 02142   (catalog free)

Jo Ann Algiers
Sun Valley, Idaho

Fleming Bottle and Jug Cutter

The bottle cutter makes a practical tool. By following the instructions and with some practice anyone can turn out interesting glasses, mugs and vases. The kit will cut anything from an eight ounce bottle to a 5 gallon jug. We don't even take back bottles with deposits anymore. Wine bottles make interesting pilseners. Beer bottles make excellent glasses in sets of six, plus you get to drink the beer. We've given them as wedding presents and people really dig them. If you hate the thought of all that wasted glass like I do, you'll write to Floyd Fleming. His instructions are personable and informative.

[Suggested and reviewed by Pat Milberry]

Jug & Bottle Cutter

$9.95 postpaid

from:
Fleming Bottle & Jug Cutter
P.O. Box 6157
Seattle. Wash. 98116

or WHOLE EARTH
CATALOG

The trick is to tap the bottle from the inside; that way the bottle doesn't break. (L to R): cutting, tapping, finished product.

James Clothes Washer

I don't know anybody who's used one of these. It looks like it would do the job. May need a little bracing, the legs are flimsy.

—SB
[Suggested by Reed Plankenhorn]

James Washer $49.80
Wringer **$21.00** (plus shipping)

from:
S&H Metal Products
RR No. 1 Box 57
Topeka, Indiana 46571

Canadian residents write to:
Elmer S. Kuepfer
Route 1
Newton, Ontario, Canada

Hand Washers

A BEAUTIFUL WASHING MACHINE IS MADE OUT OF USING A "PLUMBER'S HELPER"—PUMPING IT UP AND DOWN IN ANY SUDSY LAUNDRY CONTAINER FROM BUCKET TO BATHTUB

NORMAN SOLOMAN
BERKELEY CALIF.

We asked Dale Fritz, a Peace Corps agricultural specialist and former Volunteer for Technical Assistance (VITA), who has years of experience overseas.

As it turned out, Fritz himself is the father of a simple hand-operated washing machine that has been featured for years in the Agency for International Development's (AID) *Village Technology Handbook*. What is the operating principle of the machine, we asked Fritz.

"Agitation, just agitation," he replied.

"You could take a stick and stand there and stir it," he added, "It's just the motion of the water. The clothes don't even have to move at all . . . It's just the water moving back and forth through the clothing that does the cleaning. The soap breaks down the dirt; and the water carries it away."

Well, we asked, if that is the principle, are there any other solutions to the washing problem that are simpler than yours?

Sure, he said. If you have a vehicle, throw your clothes into some kind of a closed container—like a milk can—add soap and hot water and put the container onto the back of your machine. Leave it there all day as you make your rounds—preferably over the roughest available roads—and when you get back in the evening you'll have a load of clean clothes.

That method has been used by bachelor ranchers in the western United States for years.

From *Volunteer Magazine*
Published by the Peace Corps

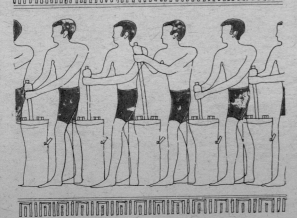

Ice Cream Freezer

I'm sure there are many lovers of home-cranked ice cream (and who isn't one?) who have been somewhat dismayed at the chinsy ice cream freezers now being turned out with their predominately plastic parts. These people can now write for info and prices to the White Mountain Freezer Co., Winchendon, Mass. 01475 and be sure of getting a solid, quality piece of machinery that will last for years. There are two models available, the Mod. 643 White Mountain triple-motion, in sizes from two to 20 quarts and whose folder I have enclosed, and the Mod. 642 Arctic double-motion in 2, 4, 6, and 8 quart sizes.

I have never seen these freezers sold in the mainland U.S. though when I was in Puerto Rico in 1964 on a school trip I saw them in various hardware stores along with kerosene lanterns and stoves, and treadle-driven Singer sewing machines (new ones!). Often in San Juan one would see a street vendor with two of the large 20 quart freezers mounted on his pushcart selling nickel cups of ice cream to passers-by.

William M. Fetcher
CINC PAC FLT Band

Garbage Diverter

One of the handiest gadgets in electric kitchens, as any upper middle class housewife can tell you, is the garbage disposer. Chuck onion peels , egg shells, moldy yoghurt, etcetera into it, flip the switch, and presto! All the stinky wet garbage disappears down the drain, born by clean water.

As the ecologically enlightened know, that stinky garbage is also potentially rich garden soil. There is something in my Scot's cells that rebels against this kind of waste. So the other day I asked a mechanic friend to create for me a device I had designed to capture the ground-up organic material before it goes down the drain. He did it. Now I am using the disposer's ground-up output plus the water in my garden instead of running it out into Bolinas lagoon.

I call the gadget Margot Doss's Little Jim Dandy Garbage Diverter and have applied for a patent.

The gung-ho back-to-nature buffs may shriek:

1. That it uses electricity
2. That you can do the same thing in a blender
3. That composting does the work in time

The answer to all these is yes, of course. Apart from that, a blender must be cleaned after every use, and the gunk that comes out of the Diverter is ground so fine it speeds up the composting considerably. I hope the Little Jim Dandy Garbage Diverter will introduce a lot of people to the mystique of organic gardening.

If your readers seem interested, I will also sell the plans for one sawbuck. Anyone who wants a reservation on this trip should send a self-addressed legal sized envelope and $1 to Little Jim Dandy Garbage Diverters, Box 447, Bolinas 94924.

Cordially
Margot Patterson Doss
Bolinas, California

Ultra-Sonic Dishwasher?

The home dishwasher probably wastes as much or more water than a garbage disposal unit. Certainly it can be improved. Watchmakers and jewelers are beginning to use small "sonic cleaners" that clean watches and suchlike with high-frequency sound waves. Why can't a dish washer be built on the same principle?

Bill Marsano
Radnor, PA

"Doyle started having dreams," said Marcella.

"I did," said Doyle. "It was the unusualist thing that ever was. After we got back from Clarence's funeral I commenced to dream about him ever night. And if it wouldn't be him it would be somebody else that had died. My father, your all's father, or somebody in my acquaintance whose death I knew something about. It was just death ever where I looked, it was all I could think about. I got afraid I was going to die, or Marcella, or one of the kids, you can ask Marcella here, it was really an awful thing to go through. Nothing like that had ever happened to me before, and I just couldn't understand it. Ever night I'd go to bed and lay there all night thinking about death and dead people and dying and I'd think: well surely I'll get over this tomorrow. But then when I'd get to work there it would be, right up in front of my mind. I couldn't hardly work. Vernis noticed it and asked me about it. Some of our customers even noticed something was wrong. This all went on I guess a month or more till finally I just had to do something about it. And so Marcella called her preacher up and asked him to come over and talk to me about it."

"He's a real nice man, David," said Marcella. "He's from Kentucky too, just smart as a tack. You'd really like him."

"Half of Cincinnati's from Kentucky," said Doyle. "This is briar-hopper country sure enough."

"How well I know," said D.R.

"I'd say it improves the place about five hundred per cent myself," said Marcella, and everybody came out of their seriousness to laugh hard at that.

When they'd hushed, D.R. asked Doyle what he had said to the preacher.

"Shoot. I just told him the truth of it. I told him I thought I was going crazy. I said I was having dreams and couldn't sleep and couldn't work, and terrible headaches. I told him I was afraid I was about to die. But that little preacher was the sweetest to me that you ever saw. I was about half embarrassed to be talking to somebody about that kind of stuff, but I mean he seemed to know what was going on in me even before I told him. He asked me if I was a Christian. I said no. He asked me if I'd like to be one. I said I hadn't thought about it. You know what he did when I said that? He bust out laughing. Just laughed and laughed and laughed, I didn't know what to think. Then he said, oh yes you have. I said what do you mean? He said oh yes you have been thinking about it. Then suddenly he quit laughing and looked me right in the eye and said, what are you afraid to die for? I said ain't everybody? He said we ain't talking about everybody, we're talking about <u>you</u>. What are you so scared to die for? What makes you think that's so awful? And just about the time I begun to wonder if he was crazy why he got out his bible and commenced to read about Jesus, and about dying, and about being re-born, and I begun to see what he meant. He must of talked to me two or three hours that night. And the next night, and the next."

"He stayed till two o'clock in the morning one time," said Marcella.

"He can just talk rings around you. He can say stuff you think ain't never been said before, he's really clever. He come over the to:: th time on Friday night, and guess what he said. He said he wasn't going to come see me no more. He said if I wanted to know what he had to say he was preaching ever Sunday morning at eleven o'clock, and for me to be there. And I ain't missed a Sunday si: :e. And after three times I confessed, and then about a month ago they baptized me, and I've slept good ever since."

Winemaking

*At some time in everyone's life he's collected together raisins, sugar and baker's yeast in a gallon wine jug and eagerly awaited the product. More often than not this resulted in an overly sweet, low power, cloudy "amber brew" that discouraged him from further efforts at wine making. Amateur wine making though long practiced is only slowly evolving from the "word of mouth" phase. These two British books are the best that I've seen; however, one does not learn wine making by reading books––he learns good habits and a feel for the techniques of wine making. From there on it is a matter of how much imagination one has, since amateur wine makers have made many delightful wines out of the most unlikely ingredients (Flowers, potatoes, parsnips, rose hips, rhubarb, etc.). Bravery's book (**Successful Winemaking at Home**) is scientific and meticulous with details. He says all wine recipes in his book have been tested personally and are of excellent quality if you follow his general rules for making good wine––and I believe him. However, they are for single (Imperial) gallons (5 quarts) which I feel hardly makes it worth the trouble unless it is a very special recipe. Five gallon spring water bottles are more convenient sizes for tested recipes and thirsty friends.*

*Berry's book (**First Steps in Winemaking**) is worth while because he has many photos and diagrams of apparatus which I feel is essential to one's initial concept of the process. He has a lot of "hints" and so forth, many of which are sound, but if there's a discrepancy I would stick to Bravery's interpretation. Both books and many others not mentioned have recipes which should get you started. Wines can be made all year if you are willing to experiment.*

A few things to remember: Read the principles of wine making carefully; wine and yeast are gentle things and they have to be cared for. Wine yeast is very important and well worth purchasing from dealers. (If you have an idea of sterile transfer techniques and the knowledge that it only takes one little yeast cell you can devise ways of making one commercial culture of yeast grow two years worth of wine.) Equipment can be expensive at specialty stores but wine is easily made in 10-20 gallon polyethylene garbage cans, "clipped" five gallon water bottles (at 1.50 per) at spring water dealers, fermentation locks of the plastic variety, a J shaped siphon to avoid "racking the lees. Tempeature is very critical and I recommend a thermostatically controlled heater or room or perhaps an immersible fishtank heater. Tap water has yeast killing chlorine in it: to remove it boiling is probably the easiest, tho if you're doing 20 gallons it can become tedious––chlorine will escape if left to the air for a day or so. Add Sodium Bisulfite (Sodium metabisulfite & Campden to the British); it is an inhibitor to all wild yeasts and many bacteria, but wine yeasts are resistant to it, so you encourage your special yeast's growth and avoid spoilers. It also allows you to avoid heating to sterilize the whole batch. A stronger solution can be used very nicely for sterilizing clean bottles, etc., without affecting the taste of the wine. Lastly one should call the Feds and register (it's free) and avoid a possible hassle.

[Reviewed by Dr. James Fox. Suggested by Tom Wellman]

Dr. James Fox says that you can use sodium bisulfite as a sterilant in wine recipes. This is not true. . .bacteria and fungus find $NaHSO_3$ such good food that it's hard to keep a solution on the shelf. Sodium metabisulfite has no other common name, and is $Na_2S_2O_5$, and i recently bought a pound of Baker Reagent Grade "Sodium meta-Bisulfite" for $1.50, this being enough to treat 1750 gallons of wine.

He also states that Bravery's recipes are for 5 quart gallons. . Bravery says, "The reason for using 5 quts of water in these recipes is that we are using enough ingredients for a gallon of wine. If we used only one gallon of water we would end up with about three quarts of wine because about a quart will be lost during boiling and other operations." (p. 55, Successful Winemaking. . .)

This last isn't very important, but the metabisulfite bothers me, because only a chemist could catch the error, and most of your readers are likely to be mislead, with possibly unpleasant results.

Sincerely,

Frank Deis
Richmond, VA.

Berarducci Brothers

You may have reported on the products shown in the Berarducci Brothers Manufacturing Company catalog (McKeesport, Pa., 15132).

If not, it might interest your readers to have a source of crocks, Barrels, Fruit crushers and wine presses, Pizelle irons, various graters, sausage stuffers, coffee roasters, ravioli machines and noodle machines. Berarducci winery equipment is also shown in most other winemaking supply catalogs, but is less expensive from this source.

Ralph Auf der Heide
Santa Barbara, CA

Many old recipes advocate far too much sugar, with the result that the winemaker is disappointed when the yeast fails to use most of it up, and he is left with a syrupy, almost undrinkable concoction.

As a good rule of thumb, remember the figure 3––3 lbs. to the gallon of liquor for a medium wine. Half a pound less will usually produce a dry wine, half a pound more a sweet. Below 2 lbs. of sugar to the gallon the wine may not be strong enough to keep, above 3½ it may well (although not always) be sickly sweet.

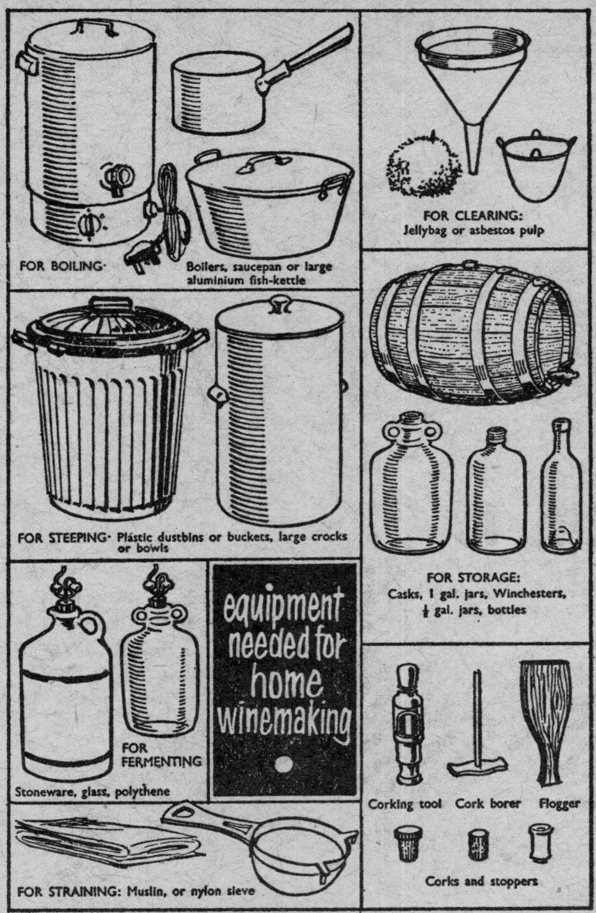

FOR BOILING
Boilers, saucepan or large aluminium fish-kettle
FOR CLEARING: Jellybag or asbestos pulp
FOR STEEPING: Plastic dustbins or buckets, large crocks or bowls
FOR STORAGE: Casks, 1 gal. jars, Winchesters, ½ gal. jars, bottles
equipment needed for home winemaking
FOR FERMENTING
Stoneware, glass, polythene
Corking tool
Cork borer
Flogger
Corks and stoppers
FOR STRAINING: Muslin, or nylon sieve

First Steps in Winemaking
C. J. J. Berry
1960; 160 pp.

$1.95 postpaid

from:
Semplex of USA
Box 12276
Minneapolis, Minn. 55412

or WHOLE EARTH CATALOG

Rose Hip Wine

One of the finest of all home-made wines; its flavour is unique and it has body and bouquet that take a lot of matching. Rose hips abound in early autumn and it matters not whether they are gathered from your own rose trees or from the hedgerows. They should not be used until they have taken on their winter coat of red or orange according to the type.

4 lb. rose hips, 3 lb. sugar, 1 gal. water, 1 oz. yeast.

Wash the hips well in half a gallon of water in which one Campden tablet has been dissolved. Crush the hips with a mallet or chop them. Put them in the fermenting vessel and pour on half a gallon of boiling water. Boil half the sugar in a quart of water for two minutes and when cooled a little add to the rest. Add the yeast and ferment the pulp for seven days.

Then strain out the solids and put the strained liquor into a gallon jar. Boil the rest of the sugar in the remaining water for two minutes and allow to cool well before adding to the rest. Cover as directed or fit fermentation lock and leave to ferment in a warm place until all fermentation has ceased.

Successful Wine Making at Home
H. E. Bravery
1961; 151 pp.

$.95 postpaid

from:
Arc Books
219 Park Avenue South
New York, N. Y. 10003

or WHOLE EARTH CATALOG

NOTE: Unlawful to build in many countries.
May require licensing in others.

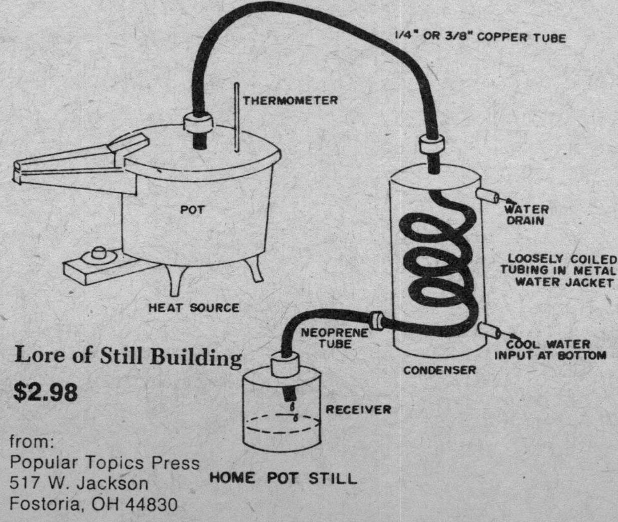

1/4" OR 3/8" COPPER TUBE
THERMOMETER
POT
WATER DRAIN
LOOSELY COILED TUBING IN METAL WATER JACKET
HEAT SOURCE
NEOPRENE TUBE
COOL WATER INPUT AT BOTTOM
CONDENSER
RECEIVER

HOME POT STILL

Lore of Still Building

$2.98

from:
Popular Topics Press
517 W. Jackson
Fostoria, OH 44830

Home Brewing Without Failures

It's an interesting book, but awfully hard to use in this country, because it's very difficult to get decent materials for brewing. It is, after all, against the law to make your own beer (at least in California). Wine is legal; up to 200 gallons a year may be made by the head of a family (a real Italian law). In Berkeley, for instance, you can buy Blue Ribbon canned malt extract at most large grocery stores, also probably corn sugar (dextrose) in most. You can buy a bottle capper and bottle caps, and a decent yeast starter at a winery. But Bravery's recipes call for a number of pretty esoteric ingredients.

There are two places to buy brewing supplies through the mail that offer a really good selection. One is Wine-Art Sales Ltd., 1108 Lonsdale, North Vancouver, B.C. This is the nicest mail order house I've ever dealt with. They have a free catalog of beer and wine making supplies. When you order from them, you send no money. They send you the stuff, and a bill, with a discount for American money, and you send them the remittance. I hope no one burns them, because it's really nice to establish such a basis of trust in the cold mail order world. Shipping charges are not expensive, except on heavy stuff, and the wait is only about two weeks (to Calif.).

I would suggest that anyone who wants to get into beer making should use Bravery's book as a point of departure, maybe order some of those nice yeasts, particularly the liquid ones, and other small stuff from Canada or England, but make do with canned malt extract, locally available sugars (yellow-D is a good one, though beer made with it is sometimes a little hard to start), maybe some molasses for extra body.

You should know that Bravery's recipes generally make very, very heavy beer. The heavier the better for me, but it's a long way from Lucky Lager, or even Heinekens and Tuborg. If you like light beer, use less sugar (use corn sugar, too), less malt, and more water. If you use a hydrometer, as Bravery recommends, you can figure out the alcohol content of your beer before you start it with the yeast.

Contrary to what a lot of people believe, a home brewer of at least thirty years experience told me to never save a yeast starter from batch to batch, but to start with a new and good one every time. Yeast gets contaminated with wild spores very easily, and your batches are likely to get worse and worse instead of better and better. Also, he says, you should ferment your beer at low temperatures, 60 degrees or lower, as at higher temperatures, the yeast starts producing alcohols you don't want, like toluene and acetone.

In general, the best way to brew is to experiment, and keep notes, so you can duplicate a really good batch when it comes along.

[Suggested and reviewed by Roland Jacopetti]

Home Brewing Without Failures
H. E. Bravery
1965; 159 pp.

$.95 postpaid

from:
Arc Books
219 Park Avenue South
New York, N. Y. 10003

or WHOLE EARTH CATALOG

Bravery's Super Stout

2 lb crystal malt
2 lb patent black malt
1 lb black treacle
3 lb white sugar
3 oz hops
2 small level teaspoonfuls salt
½ oz citric acid
yeast
nutrient

Bring seven quarts water to 150°F. Pour into polythene pail and add the malts at once. Put in immersion heater, cover vessel with sheet polythene as directed and wrap vessel in blanket to conserve warmth. Switch on heater and maintain mash at 145° - 150°F. for eight hours. At this stage you may carry out starch test if you want to. Strain mash into boiler and add salt and two ounces hops. Bring to boil and simmer gently for forty minutes. Add remaining hops and simmer hard or boil for a further five minutes.

Put sugar, treacle and citric acid into the fermenting vessel and strain the mash on to it through fine muslin. Stir well, making sure all sugar is dissolved and make up to four gallons with boiling water.

Cover with sheet polythene as already directed (p. 51) and leave to cool to 65° - 70°F. Add yeast and nutrient and leave to ferment for six-eight days.

If using hydrometer, take readings after five days until 1.005 is recorded and then bottle. If hydrometer is not being used, allow fermentation to go on until beer becomes "flat" and then prime – add sugar to recommence fermentation – and then bottle. If draught beer of this sort is wanted merely bottle the beer when it has gone "flat". Improves with keeping for six or more weeks, though it may be used as soon as all yeast has settled and the beer is clear.

OAK BARRELS for fermenting. Adds an air of "the good old days" home brewing operation.
PARAFFINE LINED BARRELS does not add wood taste as charred barrels do, but is easier to clean and doesn't leak.

1920	one gallon	10.00
1921	two gallon	11.00
1922	five gallon	12.90
1923	ten gallon	16.90
1924	fifteen gallon	18.30
1925	thirty gallon	28.20
1926	fifty gallon	41.50

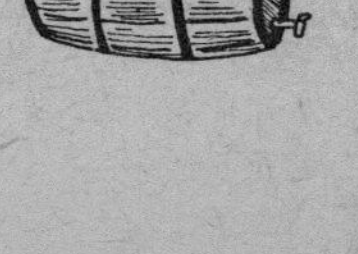

NO LONGER AVAILABLE

The Wyne Table

How To Make Booze

Reading this book, I start to yearn for a wine cellar, 10 ceramic crocks, cupboards full of dry and fresh ingredients, long wooden stirring spoons, mead tables and friends enough to provide for partying every night, starting out with the light beers and finishing up on the floor with the dark wines. This book is, not counting the historical references and mythological stories, entirely practical. Written by a former(?) student of no doubt many serious years and some wisdom who says about the book's purport: ". . . the idea was a simple one: to write a book about wine making and brewing based on the thesis that the person reading the book could actually do it."

He tells you the ingredients needed, the equipment necessary, and half necessary and slightly necessary, and how to make it, then the procedure to follow, how long to ferment, how long to age, what to do if something screws up at a point in between, how to bottle, where to get EVERYTHING the cheapest, what ingredients make it taste this way, what fruits that, heresay and incorrect rumored procedures. Covered are home brew, white lightening, wine, mead and distilled spirits, bathtub gin; at the end are remedies for hangovers. Drawings by the author of equipment to use.

[Suggested by Peter Ratner. Reviewed by D. Smith]

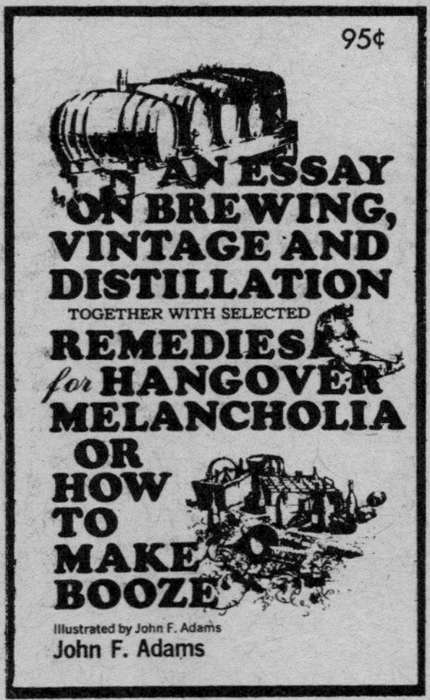

An Essay on Brewing, Vintage and Distillation, Together with Selected Remedies for Hangover Melancholia or How to Make Booze
John F. Adams
1970; 108pp.

$.95 postpaid

from:
Doubleday & Co., Inc.
501 Franklin Avenue
Garden City, New York 11531

or WHOLE EARTH CATALOG

. . . members of the Vast Unwashed resort to additives—chiefly varieties of resins, powdered isinglass, gelatin—added either to the crock or to each bottle. Ineffectual. Live with the sediment as you live with sweat and labor. Ours is a postlapsarian world. Open each bottle carefully and pour slowly, and when the sediment begins to move to the mouth of the bottle, stop. Pour quarts into pitchers if practical. About a quarter of an inch of each bottle will be wasted, but consider this your tithe. It is little enough, and full of tares anyway.

•

Mead may be purchased even today in this country at the larger liquor stores, usually imported from Denmark. All imported mead I have bought has proved to be quite unsatisfactory, and resembled only distantly what mead really should taste like. If you want good mead—and once you have tasted it, you will—you must make it yourself. Fortunately, it is simple to do so.

•

Wine, that universal beverage, became an alcoholic beverage almost through the back door. Basically, wine is a food, and its alcoholic content is primarily a preservative. (And there is much to recommend it over monosodium glutamate.)

•

. . . it probably should be pointed out that equipment of almost incredible variety is offered for sale by supply houses specializing in such truck. . . Also, in most large cities there are malt shops which sell large varieties of malts, yeasts, and sugars, as well as crocks, barrels, patent syphoning devices, etc. . . Of course, anything you buy through such speciality outlets carries a premium price. Bottle caps, for example, cost about three times the price charged by your local hardware or grocery store. Malt syrup—the same brands you find on the supermarket shelves—cost about twice the supermarket price when you buy them from "brewers' supplies."

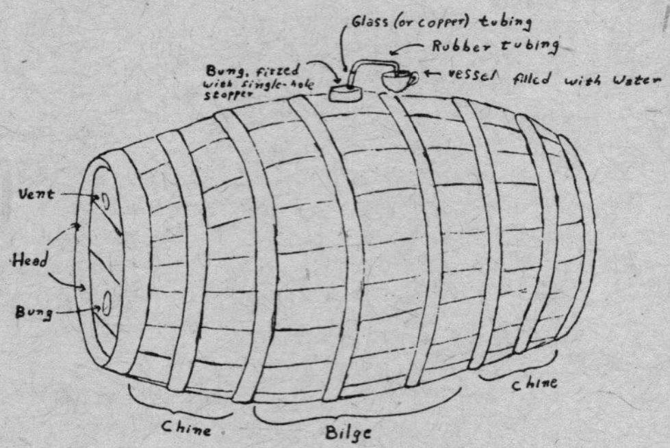

How to Lessen the Damage of Booze

Alcohol (and speed) causes brain damage, they're sure. [No certain rap on other light dopes, but those they're sure of.] Alcohol robs the brain of B vitamins, and cells die. You can counteract the effect by eating manufactured white bread, which is fortified with B vitamins. Of course, if you're into juice to get drunk and a little deader and well hungover, watch out for bread.

From Jim Fadiman
who got it from researchers
at Stanford

Balloon Wine

We made a gallon of wine once without saccharimeters, vapor locks, wine cellar or any other special apparatus. It wasn't exactly a 1961 Chateau Margaux but it was potable and fun. Friends will ask of the gallon jug near your heat register, "why is there a balloon on that bottle?" to which you can respond with all sorts of nonsense.

The wine will be a sweet concord sort. If too sweet you can cut the sugar by ½ or one cup but you can't go much beyond that because all that sweet stuff is your assurance of proper fermentation.

This is all there is to it. Thaw one large (12-13 oz.) can of frozen grape juice concentrate. Combine it with 4½ cups of sugar and one package of dry yeast. Put into very clean gallon jug and fill to the shoulder of the bottle. Mix it thoroughly. Then tie a heavy (maybe 10 cent) balloon over the mouth of the jug. Let it all stand at room temperature (maybe near the heater in winter) for 21 days. The balloon will erect and then expand. If it deflates before 21 days your vintage is ready. If the balloon blows off, just tie on another. At the end of 21 days the hooch is ready whether the balloon goes down or not. Crazy, yes? We got the idea from a Delmer Robinson who wrote it up in the National Observer. *He said when he published the idea in his local paper, town stores quickly ran out of balloons!*

Kam
Nevada City, CA

Supplies

Aetna Bottle Co., Inc.
708 Ranier Avenue South
Seattle, Washington 98144
[Suggested by Duana Matterson]

The Bacchanalia
273 Riverside Ave.
Westport, Connecticut 06880
[Suggested by Patrick N. Baker]

E.S. Kraus
P.O. Box 451
Nevada, Missouri 64772

Presque Isle Wine Cellars
9440 Buffalo Road
North East, Pennsylvania 16428
[Suggested by John C. Wilson]

Semplex of U.S.A.
P.O. Box 12276
Minneapolis, Minnesota 55412
[Suggested by Tom Wellman]

Wine Art West
4324 Geary Blvd.
San Francisco, California 94118

The ...ble DEFUNCT
P.O. Box ...
Norman, Okla... 3069

Vino Corporation
80 Commerce Drive
Rochester, N.Y. 14623

Wine, Beer and Cheesemaking Supplies

Wine Hobby
P.O. Box 428
Laguna Beach, CA 92651

Rockridge Laboratories
P.O. Box 2842, Rockridge Sta.
Oakland, CA 94618

(also has book *Guidelines to Practical Winemaking,* $4.50)

Winemakers Ltd.
Box 321
Saugatuck, CT 06880

[Suggested by Steve Sanders]

For the full picture get **General Viticulture,** *p. 62.*

Each of these supply houses has free catalogs or price lists. Semplex of U.S.A. *(American agent for a very good British firm) and* Presque Isles Wine Cellars *have very good reputations.*

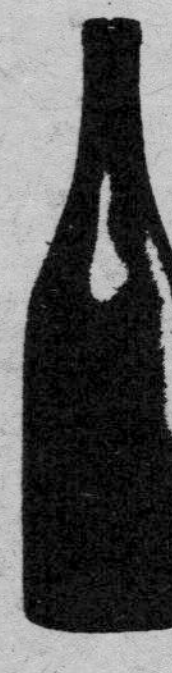

Burgundy

Claret

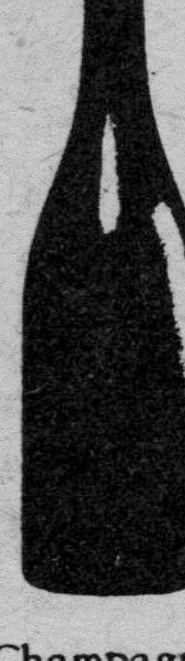

Champagne

More on Semplex

Everything for anybody into his own wine, or thinking about it. Homemade wine is good, cheap; fun to make and drink.

Semplex of USA is the American agent for a very good English firm. Most of their material is imported (nobody in the USA makes it) and expensive compared to English prices, but cheaper than available anywhere else I've found. Their service is excellent and personal.

They supply everything from pure strains of wine yeast (cheap and really necessary for good wine) to chemicals and incidentals for the more advanced freak. They also carry an excellent stock of books on winemaking from England, Germany and the USA. (I recommend "First Steps in Winemaking" by C. J. J. Berry, $1.95)

Anyone can easily make a really good (not merely a non-poisonous) wine for about $1.40 a *gallon.*

[Reviewed by Tom Wellman]

MONTRACHET WINE YEAST:
A new product put out by a large company which supplies many commercial wineries. It is in active dry granulated form and is sealed in a foil envelope under inert nitrogen gas to increase it's shelf life. It is a high quality product and each envelope is adequate for 5 gallons of must. Can be used for any type of wine and is very simple to use because it can be added directly to the must without prior starting.

Per packet.....25¢ **5 for $1.00**

Semplex of USA

Bottle Prices	At Store 1–9 cases	Shipped
Burgundy, 5ths, case of 24	3.75	4.10
Claret, 5ths, case of 24	3.95	4.30
Claret, 10ths, case of 24	3.50	3.85
Champ., 5ths, case of 12	2.95	3.30

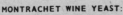

Button Corker. Sanbri. Lever squeeze. Button drive (to be struck with a mallet.)

Aluminum	**BC-1**	**4.50**
Bronze	**BC-2**	**8.75**

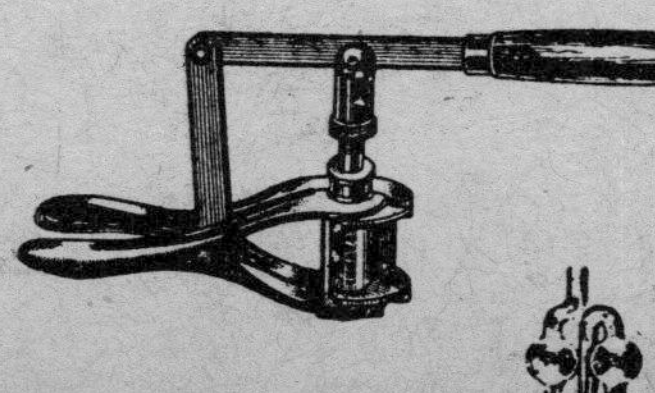

Presque Isle

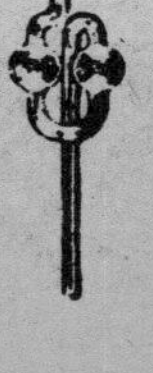

These are beautifully hand blown locks from England. They are made of thick, tough glass. Handle by the stem only.

Glass, Busby
GLB 1.15

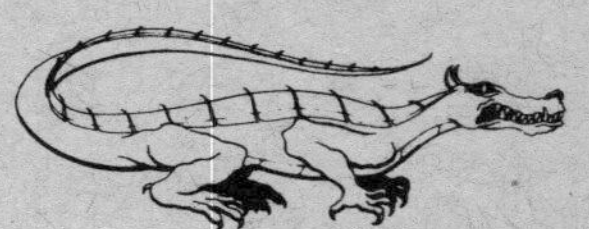

THE SECOND DEPARTURE

When D.R. got ready to leave the house again after supper he didn't tell Marcella and Doyle he was going to the bus station. He said the call he'd tried to put through earlier in the afternoon hadn't happened, and that he wanted to go out to a pay phone and try again. Doyle laughed, thinking he understood: D.R. was going out to call up his sweetheart in California, and he didn't want a bunch of prying kin folks listening in.

"I don't blame you," said Doyle. "You can't get any privacy with nosy people like Marcella around."

Marcella put her hands on her hips. "I beg your pardon." Then she doubled up her fists and put up her dukes and said she guessed she'd just have to teach Doyle a lesson. Doyle made a fist too, and swung it at Marcella slowly enough for her to grab his arm and commence to bite it. "I'll eat you up if you're not careful," she said.

"Not in front of everybody," said Doyle, and he winked at D.R. as Marcella blushed and tried to kick Doyle in the ass.

"You big goof, you get out of the kitchen."

"Ha," said Doyle, leaping out of the way. "See how mean she is, David? You're going to have to tame down while David's here, Miss Pritchet. Me and David just might beat you up good."

"Shoot," said Marcella. "Kin folks sticks together where we come from, don't they David?"

Doyle said, "Get her, David. Let's just beat the tar out of her."

Doyle moved toward Marcella then. She squealed and ran to the corner of the kitchen and grabbed the mop. D.R. laughed and for a moment pretended he was going to help Doyle whip Marcella.

But then he backed away and said he better go on and make his telephone call. Doyle walked him to the door.

"You need any money or anything?" said Doyle.

D.R. shook his head. "No. It's cool."

"We'll see you after while then," said Doyle.

D.R. waved and Doyle closed the door behind him.

PARKING

There were several empty parking places near the entrance to the bus station but D.R. felt like putting Urge back where he had been that morning, just for old time's sake. He circled the block and pulled into what he thought was the same space, but once he turned the motor off he wasn't so sure that was it. Maybe it's the next one, he told himself, and he backed up one space and turned the motor off again. This one felt a little better, but it still wasn't right. It wasn't balanced. That morning there had been a Fiat in front of Urge and a Ford behind, and D.R. was sorry they had been moved. If the Fiat and the Ford had remained in place they would have balanced it, but with them gone there just wasn't anything out there for a fellow to depend upon. When D.R. really wished for in his heart of hearts was to see a sign that said, "This is where you parked this morning." As it was, there was no indication of any kind that D.R. had ever been on that street before, except the memory of it in his mind which he just didn't feel like trusting at all right now. D.R. moved the bus three more times before he finally just arbitrarily chose two lines to park between. It seemed like a very reckless thing to do, but he was so late getting back to the bus station as it was he really didn't have much choice.

Nippa Sauna Heater

The Japanese-type bath, with a wood-burning firebox, is excellent, but the fireboxes are hard to make and impossible to buy from Japan. The Japanese bath also uses a lot of water, which can be a problem if you have to pump or carry water any distance.

One answer is the sweat-lodge/sauna. An earth-lodge will do, or better a cedar-lined room with a high bench and a drain in the floor. Carrying hot rocks can be tiresome; the best arrangement we've found is this wood-burning sauna stove made by the Nippa company in Michigan. We use the WC 22 model, holds a lot of wood, heats 15 gallons of water to a rolling boil in 20 minutes, heats the rocks on top at the same time, doesn't use much wood actually, and keeps the sauna room hot for hours. Expensive, but will last several lifetimes and keep maybe 2 dozen people clean & happy.

Out of 25 companies contacted, this is the only wood-burning sauna heater located.

[Suggested and reviewed by Gary Snyder]

WC-18 18" deep **$169.95**
WC-22 22" deep **$189.95**

Brochure

free

from:
Nippa Sauna Heaters
Bruce Crossing
Michigan 49912

Aboriginal Sweating

Your suggestions for outdoor living have been extremely enlightening. One suggestion — the aboriginal sweat house or sweat-lodge has a long history in N. America and most likely has its adaptive advantages. The Finnish and other similar Scandinavian saunas are perhaps the only extant parallels in the Western World — and unfortunately are costly and require a certain amount of skill to construct. However the aboriginal sweat house takes many forms — all of them easy to construct and if done right have nearly the efficiency of an expensive sauna. I have personally constructed two — after Nez Perce practices — and have surprised many of my friends with their heat-holding capacity. The sweat house ritual is varied and complex — some groups separate the sexes, i.e. don't sweat together (Nez Perce for example); others sweat communally. The social, psychological and physiological advantages of sweating are numerous and not to my knowledge adequately researched (Finnish data is best). This Nez Perce (contemporary) sweat house will sweat four to six:

You need:

- 5-7 green, usually deciduous, poles, approx. 15' length
- 1 ball sturdy twine or if a purist, rawhide strips
- blankets — Nez Perce uses blankets of wool, old coats, clean gunny sacks, any pliable insulating material of cloth will do, get plenty!
- 2 pitch forks
- One 20 gallon can — not absolutely necessary
- 2 18'-20' sticks, 1' or so in diameter

First — you will need a location near water (usually a stream) — cleared of all brush and undergrowth. An area 30' in diameter will do depending on local conditions. Stream must be deep enough to allow submergence of one's body.

Next — shape of wickiup type lodge will be semi-hemispherical about 8' or so in diameter. Construct frame by holding green poles in proper shape over a fire (small) and slightly dry poles which will hold curved shape better. Tie poles together with twine thereby maintaining shape.

DIAGRAM #1

Next — Cover frame with insulating material — 3 or 4 layers will suffice. Leave no spaces! Lodge must be nearly air-tight. I use an initial layer of plastic tarping to aid in heat retention — although I dislike its negative appeal. Leave a door just big enough to enter — you can hitch a cross-piece to the frame of the lodge and hang several blankets off it making sure an adequate seal is formed.

Next — dig a small depression inside the door and to the right — this becomes the receptical for the red-hot rocks. Should be 10' deep and 25-30' in diameter. Line this hole with good rocks (see definition of a good sweat rock, which follows).

Next — gather 30 or so sweat rocks. A good rock is hard to find. My best luck has been with slightly vesicular basalt, subangular and about twice the size of a brick. Test rocks by heating over fire to a red hot glow — sprinkle over with water. If the rocks spit and hiss but do not explode or crack — you may have a good rock. River rocks have been my best source, i.e. subangular basalt cobbles. Granite is too heterogeneous.

Next — gather wood — the best wood is usually the hardest to procure. Most deciduous wood burns hotter but is harder to find. I use anything I feel right about. Never cut a green tree for firewood or for any stupid reason. Use dead wood, stumps. You need a lot. Build your fire place next to, but not too close to, your sweat lodge, which is hopefully next to, but not too close to, the water. Stack your fire logs, crosscrossing to achieve a sturdy and fairly flat top, on which you evenly distribute your rocks. Fire is fairly big and hence you will need adequate precautionary measures.

DIAGRAM #2

Next — light fire — usually takes 45 minutes to an hour or even longer depending on wood. The rocks fall thru to the ground and become ash-covered. This is where the pitch forks come in. The rocks should actually be red hot and you will need them to pass the rocks into the house. One individual must receive and arrange the rocks in the receptacle pit so he will need the two sticks. By the way, the house is only about 3½' high in the center so this individual is on his knees. The pitch fork will facilitate cleaning burning ashes and embers from the rocks in the transferring process — these ashes would cause smoke in the lodge. Line floor of lodge with clean gunny sacks — cheap and available at any feed store.

Next — after rocks are all in place, all can climb in (naked of course) and enjoy. The host tends the rocks by sprinkling small amounts of water on top which cause increased humidity. I use pungent water, made by using certain roots; these cause a delightful fragrance I groove on. Sweat house lore says you should be serious or at least not too playful. When you are well heated and feel ready for the water — do indulge. Most serious sweaters consider the plunge into the water and the accompanying sensations to be the best part of sweating. Three times in the sweat house should be enough — an effective contraceptive too.

An existing sweat house:

DIAGRAM #3

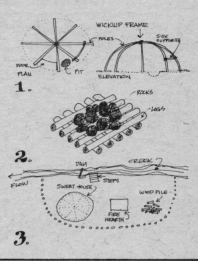

Greg Cleveland
Albuquerque, N.M.

TYP. JOINT   **TYP. SPLINE JOINT**

Communal Bath

We have been using a "Furo" (Japanese Bath) or (Japanese Bath Ritual) for some time here in Hawaii. The Furo is as old as fire itself for it consists of a large body of hot water and a bucket! The basic principles are as follows:

1. Wash by first wetting oneself with a bucket of water outside the tub.
2. Soap up luxuriantly with soap (as in a shower).
3. Rinse with another bucket of water.
4. Then slip into the furo for a therapeutic spacious bath in sparkling clean water of about 100° Farenheit.

The unique advantages of this method of bathing are many. However, the most important are—water economy (5 to 10 gallons per person), the ability of a furo to accomodate several bathers at one time, the establishment of communal bathing rituals so important for the spirit as well as the body.

The sketches and details I've enclosed are one cheap and simple way to build a Furo for a community. If manufactured fuel is not readily available, a copper bottomed Furo can be built for wood or coal heating.

If additional information regarding the construction of communal baths is needed, please write to CBS and Associates, Inc. and we'll be glad to help in any way possible. Also, any suggestions, improvements or information on other existing installations would be appreciated.

Aloha,

Nick Carta
P. O. Box 1041
Kealakekua Kona, Hawaii 96750

TYP. FURO INSTALLATION

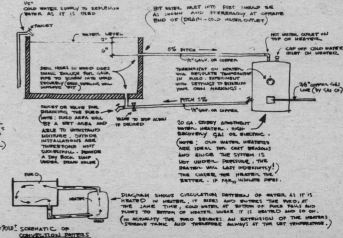

SCHEMATIC OF TYP. GAS HEATED FURO

The Massage Book

For home, not hospitals (I mean hospitals too if they can afford to get personal). For splendor in the grass. A friendly, exact book from a professional, with all the surrounding information as well as the warm heart of the subject. You don't know what a good massage means until you've had one, and then you want to give one.

—SB

The Massage Book
George Downing.
1971; 200 pp.

$3.95 postpaid

from:
Bookworks
c/o Random House
Westminster, Md. 21157

or WHOLE EARTH
CATALOG

Sauna

The only book available on Saunas: what they are, their history, how to use and enjoy, and how to build one. Although the construction details are not extensive, there is a list of about 20 Sauna manufacturers who will send you free construction plans, in hopes that you'll buy a heating device from them.

—Lloyd Kahn

[Suggested by Stan Gould]

Sauna: The Finnish Bath
Viherjuuri
1965; 87pp

$2.95 postpaid

from:
Stephen Greene Press
120 Main Street
Brattleboro, Vt. 05301

or WHOLE EARTH CATALOG

The simplest form of the family sauna is a one-room hut built of logs, with a large rudimentary stove upon which rocks are placed . . . The heat of the sauna is non-radiant: that is, it does not radiate directly toward the bather but rather is absorbed by the stones which emit the heat into the air. The indirect heat is gentle and constant . . . . The stones are heated until they become red hot . . . ideal temperature 190-200 degrees . . . water is thrown on the stones but the air remains dry because moisture is instantly absorbed by the wooden walls . . . traditional sauna includes beating with leafy birth branches, washing, and a plunge in a nearby lake or roll in the snow outside. Then follows a necessary rest while the body cools down completely.

BUILDING A FINNISH SAUNA

A practical arrangement: 1) small stools used as steps; 2) steps; 3) rail for propping up feet; 4) platform; 5) headrest.

Interior walls and ceiling are often built of kiln-dried, unfinished redwood, which does not shrink, does not warp, and is a poor heat conductor. Another excellent wood is cedar, which not only shares redwood's good properties but also emits a pleasant odor and does not stain with moisture.

Nailing should be done with hot-dipped galvanized nails to avoid stains from rust; nails should be counter-sunk whenever it is likely that a bather will touch them in the hot room. Tongue-in-groove paneling disposes of this problem in wall construction; benches can be screwed from below.

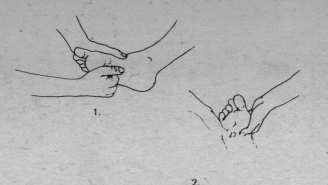

1.

2.

The foot is a "map" of the entire body. No muscle, no gland, no organ whether internal or external, is without a set of nerves whose opposite ends are anchored in the foot. And what does this mean? Simply that when we massage the foot we stimulate and affect all the rest of the body as well! So critical, in fact, are these groups of nervous correspondences between the foot and everything else in the body, that an important means of medical diagnosis and healing through foot massage, commonly called "zone therapy" by practitioners, has been built entirely upon it. I will have more to say about zone therapy in a later section. Enough for now that you be aware that while massaging the foot you are giving an extra "shadow massage" to the rest of the body as well. So do good work— a little here goes a long way.

The strokes for the foot are much like those for the hand.

I. First make a fist with your right hand. Steady the foot with your left hand, and with the knuckles of your right hand massage the sole. Move your knuckles in small circles; press hard. Be sure to cover the entire sole, including the bottom of the heel.

II. Next go over the same area with the thumbs of both hands. Hold the foot in place with your fingers and work both thumbs at once in small circles. Again cover the entire sole. Go slow. Be thorough. Remember those thousands of nerves connecting the foot with the rest of the body.

III. Next work the top of the foot, using your thumbs in the same way. Again be vigorous and be thorough; don't let any tiny patches escape unmassaged. When you reach the lower half of the foot— in other words when you near the ankle and the heel— you will find it easier to use the tips of your fingers. Circle the ankle bone itself— the round bony protruberance about the width of a half dollar on either side of the ankle— several times with your finger tips, doing both sides at once.

IV. When you finally reach the lower end of the heel, gently lift the foot from beneath the ankle with the left hand and work the bottommost edge of the heel with the tips of the finger and thumb of the right hand. Press hard.

V. Next look at the top of your friend's foot and find, just as you did for the hand, the long thin tendons running from the base of the ankle to each toe. Run the tip of your thumb, pressing firmly, down each of the valleys that lie in between these tendons. Start at the base of the ankle and end at the tiny flap of skin between the toes. As for the hand, you may, if you wish, gently squeeze this flap of skin by pressing the tip of your forefinger against its underside as your thumb passes over its top. Do each valley one time.

VI. Now the toes themselves. With your left hand hold the foot steady; with the thumb and forefinger of your right hand grasp the base of the big toe. Then gently pull, twisting from side to side in a corkscrew motion, until your thumb and forefinger slide off the tip of the toe. Do each toe in turn.

VII. Finish the foot just as you did the hand. Clasp the foot between your hands, one palm along the sole and the other along the length of the top, and for a moment allow yourself to be still. Center yourself and become aware of your breathing. Try by breathing into your hands to allow the energy circulating in your own body to mingle with that of your friend's.

Kama Sutra Oil

This material lubricates, warms, feels good, smells good, and tastes good. It's for making love with.

—SB

Kama Sutra Oil
4 oz. bottle

$4.25 postpaid

from:
Kama Sutra Oil
1041 N. McCadden Place
Los Angeles, CA. 90038

or WHOLE EARTH CATALOG

3.

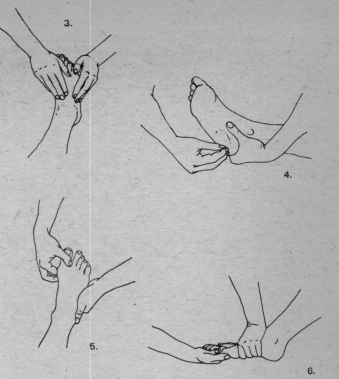

4.

5.

6.

THE SEARCH IMAGINED

As D.R. pushed through the heavy doors of the terminal he made up a little drama in his mind about how it would be if Estelle was not there waiting for him. He saw himself entering the big waiting room and first looking toward the seats they had occupied that morning. Estelle was not there. The only person in that whole row of seats was a woman with two children, one of them a baby asleep in her lap. D.R. walked by her to the seats they had sat in and paced up and down in front of them, looking at them thinking: Estelle sat here, and I sat there. He looked at the seats, and all around the big room for some sign of Estelle. He considered asking the woman with the children if she had seen a girl in jeans and a Mexican shirt, but she looked as if she didn't want to be disturbed. Her baby was asleep, and she was half asleep herself. For a second in his fantasy the woman with the children turned into Estelle. She didn't stay Estelle very long but for a moment it was very convincing. She had Estelle's dark, round eyes and her skin was dark and mellow like Estelle's. She looked up at D.R. once, sort of blankly, perhaps wearily. Then she was no longer Estelle, which was good because if she had stayed Estelle the fantasy would have ended without the kind of freak-out D.R. wanted to go through over his lost love. He glanced at the half-asleep mother again, then walked away quickly to look for Estelle in the coffee shop.

Estelle was not in the coffee shop.

She was not at the ticket counter.

She was not at the magazine stand, or over by the lockers, nor was she outside in the loading zones, leaning against a post. The whole big sleepy bus station yawned Estelle's not being there and closed its eyes again. D.R. tried to wake it up. He tried to force its eyelids open with sticks, and when it yawned he tried to stir it by pouring tar into its mouth. But the mouth slammed shut and swallowed everything that had ever happened until that moment. The hours D.R. and Estelle had been together in that bus station slipped down its long esophagus into subterranean bowels, and no amount of screaming would bring it back again.

D.R. was muttering little fretful cries by the time he went into the phone booth Estelle had occupied. First he went into his own booth, then into her's. But Estelle was not there. He tried calling her, he memorized the number, went back to his booth and dialed. But Estelle didn't answer, and D.R. sat there on the stool muttering little fretful cries. He thought about calling the Anaheim Flash to tell him Estelle was gone, but somehow he didn't have the energy. But then suddenly he did have the energy, and he put in a dime and told the operator to get him the Anaheim Flash in Anaheim, California. The operator got the Flash's number, but a strange woman answered. The Flash was out. D.R. said it was an emergency. The woman asked if she could take a message. No, said D.R. There wasn't any message. But when the woman started to hang up he shouted Wait! Wait! Yes, there is a message. Tell him Estelle's gone. Tell him to find her and take care of her and tell me where she is. The woman said she would give the message to the Flash. D.R. said thank you and hung up, then sat there muttering little fretful cries as he tried to imagine where oh where in the whole wide world Estelle might have gone away to.

The only place left to check out was the ladies restroom, and D.R. strolled around to it, and began pacing back and forth outside the door. As women went in and out he tried peering through the door but he couldn't see very much, and the women looked at him suspiciously. Then he thought of a scheme. He watched four women go in, then waited until they came out again. One, two, three, four. Obligingly they came out as they went in, one behind the other, and when number four was out D.R. made his move. He threw open the door and yelled Estelle! He yelled it again, Estelle! Estelle! as he ran the length of the ladies room, stooping to peer under the stalls. But Estelle wasn't there, and the only thing D.R. could think to do was go in the coffee shop, order a Coke, play a sad hillbilly song on the jukebox and feel his heart break into pieces.

BASIC Y. The players alternate turns. On his turn a player fills in one region of the board with his color (the two players use different colors). Each player tries to get a "Y" in his color, that is, a continuous area in his color which touches all three edges of the triangular board. The player who succeeds in this wins. Figure 2 shows the final position in five games played on the board shown in Figure 1. In each of the five cases ▨▨ has won by getting a "Y" in his color.

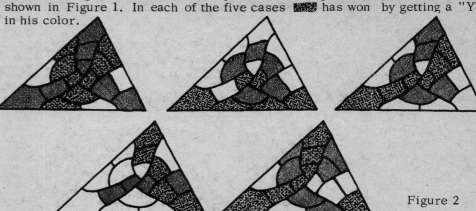

Figure 2

Sep 10, 70

Dear Friends,

When I opened my July catalog to Fun & Games on p.42 and saw the recommended books for Go my hand reached for my forehead and my mouth said "Oh, no!". Now while I owe a debt to Lasker & Smith for teaching me something of the game of Go, much better books have become available in English in the decades since then. Sadly, if you look in the local bookstore or in Books in Print you are likely to come to the conclusion that the books listed in the July catalog are the only books available.

The better books are available from JAPAN PUBLICATIONS TRADING CO., INC. (and a few bookstores also carry them).

JAPAN PUBLICATIONS TRADING CO., INC.
1255 Howard St.
San Francisco, CA 94103   Telephone
415-431-3394

The book to learn from is **How to Play Go** by Kaku Takagawa, # 4 95. Takagawa is one of the greatest modern Go players, so that what he says is reliable. Although this book is elementary, if you truly master it you will be able to play a decent game of Go. An important thing to remember when reading it is that if at any point you think what Takagawa is saying is not true, then it is time for you to study the situation in more detail until you find out why it is true.

The next book to study is **Go Proverbs Illustrated** by Kensaku Segoe, # 6 95. Go proverbs are a painless way to absorb a wealth of information which will raise your strength considerably.

These two books will cover your needs until you get serious. When you get serious, the major literature is in Japanese, although there are a few more things in English. There is **Vital Points of Go** by Kaku Takagawa, # 7 25. Takao Matsuda offers (or at least offered 7 years ago) an excellent correspo course with his text and personal instruction. The American Go Association could supply Matsuda's address. I understand there is also a translation of a book by Sakata, another of Go's greats.

If you live in a large city look up the Nippon Club or the Nihon Kiin in order to locate some good players. One should play the best players he can, as playing against other beginners will develop bad habits. Go has a handicap system which allows players of considerably different skill to play.

Lest you think that Go is only a game let me tell you my favorite Go story. Several years ago when I was in Princeton, one of the most promising young professional Go players visited this country to encourage Go playing. He told us the story of how he got to be a professional Go player. When he was a young boy he played much Go and became very good. He decided that he wanted to become a professional; so, he went to see a Go master in order to become his student. This Go master played him one game to see if he really had talent. Deciding that he was indeed a promising Go player, he took him on as a student. After that master and student had many sessions together, but Go was never discussed. The subjects of conversation were politics, art, philosophy, etc. Presently the master said that their conversations indicated that the young man now had the depth of view to become a professional Go player. To make certain, they played one more game and, as the master had expected, his student was indeed of professional quality.

In the big envelope I have included my contribution to strategic games. I like to think that Y is inherently even a better game than Go. However, Go has many centuries of people devoting their lives to exploring its possibilities. This gives Go a richness that no newly developed game can ever match. A few centuries from now, who knows?

The rules for Y are all on one page. By all means play the game before reading the rest of the text.

Peace,

Craige Schensted

Craige Schensted
Ann Arbor, MI 48104

American Go Association
Box 41, GPO, New York, N.Y. 10001
Also permanent sets (book, boards, beautiful glass stones), $10.00

Get book of _Mudcrack Y_ for $1.50 postpaid from:

Neo Press
Box 32
Peaks Island, ME 04108

Boffers

We hereby nominate Jack Nottingham for a Nobel Peace Prize for the first significant advance in weaponry since the encounter group. As Gerd Stern used to say a lot, "contact is the only love," and these foam swords permit contact—with an un-pulled punch and no corporal damage. However the release of interpersonal energy is only one of the uses of boffers. They are a fine game, builder of psychic and physical skill. For one thing you learn about temper: it's an obstacle and a hazard—you get cut to pieces every time. You learn about other stuff as well, no teacher required; the wisdom is inherent in the doing. As the inventor proclaimed at the end of a public boffing match at the Fillmore West: "The sword is mightier than the pen."

—SB

[Suggested by Heliotrope]

Boffers
(2 foam swords, 2 hand protectors, 2 goggles)
$12.50 plus $1.00 postage
(Calif. residents add 6% tax)

from:
Boffers
P.O. Box 3120
Berkeley, CA. 94703
415-654-6486
or WHOLE EARTH CATALOG

Note. I'd rather boff than eat. If you have some skill and we're together somewhere, would you accept my humble challenge?

—SB

Homemade Cosmetics

Here's an addition for your next catalog: "Here's Egg on Your Face or How to Make Your Own Cosmetics" by Beatrice Traven published by Pocket Books for 95 cents. NY Times says B. Traven is an alias because author doesn't want publicity or the talk-show route. . . just thinks people can make good use of it. I've tried the Bath Oil . . .very good/given the Basic After Shave to an unbearded friend. . . good reviews/ Pousse Café Lotion. . .very much like Alexana Lotion of Alexandra de Markoff. . .very good. None of this is miracle-stuff it just feels and smells good, uses simple grocery and drugstore ingredients and tools. . .and you save a bundle of dough. Yes roughing-it is fine but even the caveman and women had a few niceties just for pleasure's sake.

*Cordially
Margolith Rotman
Chicago, Ill.*

Libre

MAKE AN ALLOY
MAKE AN INVENTORY
COME TOGETHER WITH YOUR PEOPLE
FIND OUT WHAT EACH PERSON CAN DO
        IS WILLING TO DO FOR THE COMMUNITY
LET EACH MAN USE HIS BROTHER
LET EACH OF US BE USED
IN AN ALLOY ALL THE BEST QUALITIES OF ITS
INGREDIENTS ARE FUSED INTO A NEW SUPER STUFF

THE STRONG EGOS BLEND
COMING TOGETHER
ALL ONE

MAKE AN ALLOY
MAKE AN INVENTORY

TO STOP POLLUTION EACH MAN-WOMAN MUST CLEAN
UP HIS OWN CYCLES

THE NETWORK OF PEOPLE DOING <u>GOOD</u> WORK GROWS
IT IS UP TO US TO MAINTAIN CALM & PURE ENERGY
NEGATIVE THOUGHTS POLLUTE OUR SURROUNDINGS

BUILDING YOUR OWN DOME

To build a dome first you find the spot/make sure it is your spot/the best place for you to be/then you drive a stake into the ground in the centre of your spot/tie a string to the stake decide what the radius of your home is to be/measure the radius on the string/scribe a circle on the earth using that radius/if you are building a 2 phase dome divide your circle into 10 equal parts (for a 4 phase dome divide circle into 20 equal parts)/drive a stake into each of the 10 or 20 divisions on the circumference of your circle/dig a hole 2½ to 3 feet deep at each of the 10 or 20 points/the best way to dig holes—drive 1¼ + 1½ inch pipe into ground 3 feet deep at each stake with sledge hammer/put ½ stick 40% dynamite primed in hole made by pipe/boom—nice hole/clean out with post hole digger.

Get creosoted RR ties or telephone poles/these can be scrounged/place one in each hole set one piling perpendicular to earth using level/drive nail ½ way into top center of set piling/measure from nail in set piling to set second piling and so on around the circle. Use string level to level piling.

Porta-Shower

A good bus shower, or for scarce-water situations, or where the river's too cold. You pump up air pressure on the water (5 quarts), and then it sprays you for a while (6-7 minutes).

—SB

Porta-Shower $39.95 postpaid

Shower curtain hangs from any overhead projection.

Free Standing Porta-Shower (illustrated) $49.95 postpaid

from:
Porta-Showers
999 Commercial St. Suite 5W
Palo Alto, CA 94303

Waterbaths

It seems silly to me that bathtubs, into which we place our fragile frames, if we have bathtubs, should be made of such hard materials as porcelain & enamel. If we can have waterbeds, we ought to be able to have bedbaths— sort of waterbeds turned inside-out. Do you know of any suitable soft materials, fabrics that will stand repeated wet-dry cycles and still stay soft, cuddly, and clean?

*Joe Sonneman
Juneau, Alaska*

Decide how you want your floor/where you want plumbing—drains—etc. to be/put pilings where necessary to support floor/floor support pilings don't have to be set as deep as perimeter pilings/nail floor supports (joists—2 x 6's or bigger) to floor support pilings deck with whatever's available—we used cull (bark on one side) 2 x 4's good side up.

Cut 3" PUC pipe into 4" lengths/drill 3/8" holes at 5 or 6 equal points on PUC for pentagonal and hexagonal hubs/cut 2 x 4 structural members to proper lengths and angles/drill ¼" holes in centers of angled member ends.

Use 3/8" x 2"lag bolts with washers to fasten hubs to members/let bottom members 'float' until entire structure has been erected/use ratchet wrenches to screw hubs to members/4 or 5 people can center dome structure on floor/spike dome down to floor.

Cut skin material (exterior plywood—tempered masonite—sheet metal—celotex (very risky) into proper triangle sides/nail skin material to structural members/ring shank nails are best/3/8" skin material is good enough/2" is really good/4" is risky.

Sealing is hardest part of building dome/many methods may be used/we haven't got a perfect answer so maybe you should experiment with sealers and calks—etc./fiberglass strips and epoxy works pretty good but is brittle and expensive/tar and membrane works pretty good but has to be redone every 2 years and is very funky to work with and looks funky/silicone sealant works good but it is very expensive/hypalon and neoprene calks work pretty good but are expensive/the hypalon and neoprene calks are easiest to work with since they are applied with guns/we've just heard of a material used to cover calked fishing boat decks called HI-BALL you use it like fiberglass except burlap is used rather than fiberglass calk/we've also just heard about ferrocement which sounds like the best system yet/it can be sprayed on/the plastics are imperfect yet but much work is being done in that direction/plastics will soon evolve into the best and cheapest dome materials.

We use rock wool insulation/full thick (3 5/8") batts/stapled to the structural members and the exterior skin/one community used pearlite for insulation/fiberglass batts also work but aren't as efficient as rock wool batts.

Use ¼" sheet rock for [obliterated] /seams may be taped and spackled or not.

Put in doors and windows any way you like, using structural members as supports for glass and alter structural members to accommodate doors/in all the domes we've had anything to do with, the doors have been different/so there seems to be no set formula for doors and windows.

For covering the exterior skin use epoxy paint—or Alumination (a trailer paint made of powdered aluminum—asbestos fiber and tar)—or a really high quality paint.

For ventilation put 3 or 4 hinged flaps in triangles around bottom layer of dome/these flaps can be sealed in winter/also there should be a vent in the top of the dome (a skylite that opens and closes is one way—a revolving vent is another way) to prevent condensation from forming on inside skin of dome.

Good Luck!!!!!

THE SEARCH

But that was all just a little trip in D.R.'s mind as he pushed through the front doors of the terminal. It wasn't real. D.R.'s heart was not really breaking. His head was, but not his heart. His head was shattering into splinters but his heart was beating on nice and strong as always. He went in the station, checked out the waiting room and the coffee shop, glanced around the magazine stand, and out into the loading zones. He looked around the bus terminal for ten or fifteen minutes, and when Estelle didn't turn up he got in his bus and drove on back out to his sister's house.

Koehler Method of Dog Training

What you *train your dog to do and not do is up to you.* How *to train him is this book's entire concern.* Koehler is over-argumentative, but his method is well-regarded for effectiveness.

—SB   [Suggested by Raul's Pet Center]

Koehler Method of Dog Training
W. R. Koehler
1962; 108 pp.

$5.95 postpaid

from:
Howell Book House Inc.
730 Fifth Avenue
New York, N.Y. 10019

or WHOLE EARTH CATALOG

All is in readiness: you've got the mental equipment to start training a dog and to deal with those who would confuse you; your dog is at least six months of age (the old bromide to "wait till he's a year old" [and the house has been destroyed] has been debunked). So regardless of breed, there is no reason to delay training.

Make sure that your command is really a command, not a request, and that it is simultaneous with your first step. Again, he cannot learn to start on command if you stand there looking at him after you've told him to heel. You're moving, so keep your mouth shut and don't look back. No second commands, no invitational tugs; lock your leash hand to your body, keep your left hand off the leash, and walk. Yakking, backward glances, and coaxing gestures would merely postpone the lesson that your dog must ultimately learn—THAT HE MUST SOMETIMES DO THINGS THAT HE DOESN'T WANT TO DO. So, if you love your dog, let him learn this inescapable fact early and in the simplest way. Whether it goes against your teddy bear instincts or not, it's the truth.

•

POISON PROOFING

The vile names that his deeds call forth are probably taken as a compliment by the twisted mind of a dog poisoner. Convictions seem altogether too few and the sentences for the crime too light. The only source of satisfaction for a dog owner lies in poison-proofing his dog.

The materials you'll need are a low-priced battery-operated fence charger, and enough light, insulated wire to run from where you will conceal the unit to the different areas where you want to proof your dog against eating food. Regardless of the spots where you set the charger, the dog shouldn't see it or hear it and be warned that something strange is taking place. Both the fence charger and suitable wire can be obtained at a hardware store for a price that is small to one who feels the need to protect his dog.

At a place where the dog is particularly vulnerable to a poisoner, we'll make our first set-up in your yard. Lock your dog up so he cannot watch. Set the fence unit in a place of concealment, attach the ground wire to a pipe or a rod in the ground, and the live wire to the place designated. Run the other end of the charged wire to the spot where you feel someone might be likely to toss a bit of poisoned food. Bare half an inch or so of the end of this wire. On this bare end, stick a bit of meat, or other moist food that would appeal to your dog. Starting an inch back from the food, bend a couple of angles in the wire so that the bare part and the food will be held free of contact with the ground. Turn on the fence charger. Let the dog out into the yard.

Eventually your dog will find the food. If you are watching at his moment of discovery, you'll see that his first sniff will be met with a fat spark. He'll not be apt to try the second sniff, but keep some bait on the hot wire for at least two days. Then change the set-up to another part of the yard. If possible, conceal the wire in heavy grass or cover it with dirt, allowing the tip to protrude to hold the tid-bit free of the ground. This will make the food appear just as though it were tossed over the fence.

When your dog has had opportunity to develop resistance to food found in all areas where a poisoner might toss it, you can supply experience that will make him form an equal aversion to any food offered by hand. You'll need an outsider to help you. Possibly you can exchange services with another dog lover who might want to protect his pet. As with the case of something being found on the ground, run the bare tip of the live wire into the tid-bit. Now, however, it is offered in the person's hand, insulated from his skin by a rubber glove or a bit of cardboard, plastic, or other non-conductive material. Change situations and strangers until you feel that in or out of the house, no one could coax your dog to eat anything he might offer.

King Solomon's Ring

The classic animal book. Lorenz is a famous student of animal behavior as well as a famous pet-haver.

—SB

King Solomon's Ring: New Light on Animal Ways
Konrad Z. Lorenz
1952; 202 pp.

$1.25 postpaid

from:
New American Library
1301 Ave. of Americas
New York, N.Y. 10019

or WHOLE EARTH CATALOG

Why has the dog the inhibition against biting his fellow's neck? Why has the raven an inhibition against pecking the eye of his friend? Why has the ring-dove no such "insurance" against murder? A really comprehensive answer to these questions is almost impossible. It would certainly involve a historical explanation of the process by which these inhibitions have been developed in the course of evolution. There is no doubt that they have arisen side by side with the development of the dangerous weapons of the beast of prey. However, it is perfectly obvious why these inhibitions are necessary to all weapon-bearing animals. Should the raven peck, without compunction, at the eye of his nest-mate, his wife or his young, in the same way as he pecks at any other moving and glittering object, there would, by now, be no more ravens in the world. Should a dog or wolf unrestrainedly and un-accountably bite the neck of his pack-mates and actually execute the movement of shaking them to death, then his species also would certainly be exterminated within a short space of time.

The ring-dove does not require such an inhibition since it can only inflict injury to a much lesser degree, while its ability to flee is so well developed that it suffices to protect the bird even against enemies equipped with vastly better weapons. Only under the unnatural conditions of close confinement which deprive the losing dove of the possibility of flight does it become apparent that the ring-dove has no inhibitions which prevent it from injuring or even torturing its own kind.

Animal Veterinary Products

Health products for dogs and cats.
—SB

Animal Veterinary Products, Inc.
Box 1491
Springfield, Illinois 62705

Bill Boatman & Co.

Hunting dog stuff. Collars, pens, training devices, medicines, and coonhunting paraphernalia, such as super flashlights.

[Suggested by Charley Kroner]

Catalog

free

from:
Bill Boatman & Co.
Bainbridge, Ohio 45612

Why try to guess which worm is bothering your dog? Rid him of all three major types——tapeworms, roundworms (Ascarids), and hookworms——quickly, conveniently, and completely. These Kaps are specially prepared in easy-to-use capsule form. Each capsule contains the proper dosage of tetrachlorethylene, arecoline hydrobromide, and mineral oil.. Handily packaged in unbreakable, bubble-type container of 12 capsules for easy dispensing. Complete, detailed instructions included:
No. 339 Dog Kaps (for medium breeds, less than 40 lbs.) 85c pkg.
No. 343 Dog Kaps (for larger breeds, 40 lbs. or more) $1.95 pkg.

SURGEON'S NEEDLES
3/8 Circle E. Per Dozen $3.50

VIP ANTI-MATING SPRAY
Masks odors that attracts male dogs.
Per Can $1.05

NATIONAL ANIMAL TRAIL SCENTS

Be it rabbit, bobcat, opossum, squirrel, coyote, deer, skunk, mink, bear, fox, lion, or coon, National Animal Trail Scents are the next best thing to the real McCoy. Leaves a "hot", live game trail that enables you to quickly train even a "city" dog to trail and be "straight" on anything from a coon to a lion. Simply apply to a weighted canvas and drag for a trail; when at the end of the trail, hang in bush, or tree where it is out of reach of the dogs. Many leading trainers have said, "It's one of the trainers greatest aids." In ordering, specify type of animal scent desired. Comes in easy to handle, non-breakable Polyethylene squeeze bottle.
Large Size $2.50

TOPICAL FREEZE ANESTHETIC

A safe topical anesthetic for lancing and minor surgical procedure.

6 oz. Size each $1.95
Six $9.95

ACOUSTICALLY ENGINEERED STETHESCOPE EARPIECE

Weighs only 3½ oz.

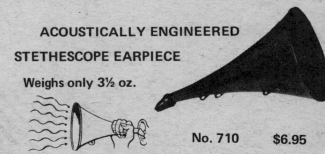

No. 710 $6.95

For those of us whose hearing ain't what it used to be!

You'll be surprised how much better you can hear your hounds. How much further away, too. This amazing device picks up your hounds voices loud and clear. Channels the sound right down the tapered horn to a stethoscope like earpiece. Works like an old time ear trumpet. Scientifically designed to increase your foxhunting pleasure. Made of tough plastic, 10" long. Easy to carry, weighs only 3½ oz. *Young and old fox and coon hunters alike can now thrill to more "music" of the pack. Order yours today.*

No. 711 Snap-on Nylon Shoulder Safety Sling $1.00

HEAVY CHROME PLATED HEAVY DUTY CHOKE

Designed for powerful, stubborn dogs. The extra strong, twist link chain gives control over strongest dog. 12 to 24 inch length, specify size.

No. 476 $1.29

The Goshawk

Those who enjoyed the falconry scenes in **The Once And Future King** *will not be surprised to know that White learned it all from a hawk. This book chronicles one of the damnedest duels there is between species, as memorable as the longest swordfight of screen history at the end of which James Mason salute and dives out the castle window into the waiting moat.*

Is it strange that out of battle this intense comes sympathy this intense?

—SB

The Goshawk
T. H. White
1951; 215 pp.

$2.25 postpaid

from:
Viking Press
625 Madison Ave.
New York, N.Y. 10022

or WHOLE EARTH CATALOG

In teaching a hawk it was useless to bludgeon the creature into submission. The raptors had no tradition of masochism, and the more one menaced or tortured them, the more they menaced in return. Wild and intransigent, it was yet necessary to 'break' them somehow or other, before they could be tamed and taught. Any cruelty, being immediately resented, was worse than useless, because the bird would never bend or break to it. He possessed the last inviolable sanctuary of death. The mishandled raptor chose to die.

So the old hawk-masters had invented a means of taming them which offered no visible curelty, and whose secret cruelty had to be borne by the trainer as well as by the bird. They kept the bird awake. Not by nudging it, or by any mechanical means, but by walking about with their pupil on the fist and staying awake themselves. The hawk was 'watched', was deprived of sleep by a sleepless man, day and night, for a space of two, three, or as much as nine nights together. It was only the stupid teachers who could go as far as nine nights: the genius could do with two, and the average man with three. All the time he treated his captive with more than every courtesy, more than every kindness and consideration. The captive did not know that it was being kept awake by an act of will, but only that it was awake, and in the end, becoming too sleepy to mind what happened, it would droop its head and wings and go to sleep on the fist. It would say: 'I am so tired that I will accept this curious perch, repose my trust in this curious creature, anything so I may rest.'

This was what I was now setting out to do. I was to stay awake if necessary for three days and nights, during which, I hoped, the tyrant would learn to stop his bating and to accept my hand as a perch, would consent to eat there and would become a little accustomed to the strange life of human beings.

•

TRAINED GOSHAWK "GAIETY GIRL"

And oh! the agony of patience, the brooding and godlike benevolence which had been exerted. At the thousandth bate in a day, on an arm that ached to the bone with its L-shaped rigidity under the weight of the bird, merely to twitch him gently back to the glove, to speak to him kindly with the little mew which of my conversation he seemed to like best, to smile past him at space, to re-assure with tranquillity, when one yearned to beat him down—with a mad surge of blood to the temples to pound, pash, dismember, wring, wrench, pluck, cast about in all directions, batter, bash, tug, and stamp on, utterly to punish, and obliterate, have done with and finally finish this dolt, cow, maniac, unteachable, unutterable, unsupportable Gos.

•

To fly: the horrible aerial toad, the silent-feathered owl, the hump-backed aviating Richard III, he made toward me close to the ground. His wings beat with a measured purpose, the two eyes of his low-held head fixed me with a ghoulish concentration: but like headlamps, like the forward-fixed eyes of a rower through the air who knew his quay. The French called him *rameur* as well as *cuisinier.* Too frighteningly for words (when I had taken him up to bring him to the well— and given him the shred of beef with which he was always rewarded for a voluntary jump— he had flown to my shoulder and fixed his talons in the unprotected flesh, taking me by the scruff of the neck), too menacingly he flew, not toward the at-right-angles-held-out beef, but directly toward my face. At five paces nerve broke. I ducked, still holding the beef at the stretch of my arm, and stayed cowering for two beats of the heart.

•

Falconry is as old as Babylon. It has never been a dead sport, and it does keep on developing. At the present moment it is developing in America, where young and enthusiastic and progressive falconers are doing wonders by not fussin. If a good American falconer would come over to Europe and show us how he does things, it would make the old fogies blink.

Stromberg's Beginner's Falconry Bulletin

If you're seriously interested in hawking, this is a most practical $1.25. A quick summary of what you're in for, an annotated list of books, suppliers of falconry equipment and falcons, and falconry clubs.

—SB

Stromberg's Beginners Falconry Bulletin

$1.25 postpaid

from:
Stromberg's
Box 717
Ft. Dodge, Iowa 50501

Stromberg's Pets

They don't have buffalo, but they have wild turkeys, ocelots, Mexican burros, ravens, monkeys, wood ducks, Belgian hares, exotic pigeons, mynah birds, and assorted equipment.

—SB

Catalog

$0.50

from:
Stromberg's
Box 717
Ft. Dodge, Iowa 50501

ABYSSINIAN
Pet Quality $100.00 Pedigreed $150.00

BLACK BEAR CUB $150.00

WILD TURKEY TOM
Book with breeding instructions $1.25

FLYING SQUIRRELS $15.00 Pair

Page 209 of The Last Whole Earth Catalog, *in a review by SB, encourages the buying of hawks, lower on the same page is an ad offering hawks for sale. Please, please please, you are unintentionally undoing the work of hundreds of U.S. Falconers who distinctly discourage the commercial trafficking of birds of prey.*

If you need confirmation of this contact the North American Falconer's Association, the largest and best falconry establishment on the continent. They have a large number of people in the Bay Area.

The problem is that hawks are decreasing in numbers due to pesticides, shooting, and habitat destruction, while would-be falconers are increasing. The only way an inept falconer can get birds is by buying them from people like the Florida Animal Dealers who supply sick, imported or stolen birds (and often totally wrong types of hawks) to beginners who have no idea of how to properly treat a raptorial bird. The result is a good number of dead hawks every year.

Falconry is a time consuming, exacting and very difficult sport. There are few good falconers. Advertising the sport can only end in harming the declining populations of the birds and the reputation of falconry. I urge you to withdraw your falconry ads as soon as possible from further printings of the Catalog. Or at least rap with somebody down there who knows about hawking —please!!

—Bud Anderson, Seattle

The Art and Practice of Hawking

I gather from **Natural History** *that falconry is flourishing in the U.S., possibly to the detriment of some of the wild hawks who are becoming endangered species. Many falconers feel bound to capture wild birds; they are not helping the situation. If enthusiasts will buy and breed hawks instead, says* **Natural History**, *they can reverse their effect and be a significant help.*

T. H. White was using obsolete books and methods with his goshawk. For more current and more effective technique this book has most of what you need.

—SB

The Art and Practice of Hawking
E. B. Michell
1900; 291 pp

$7.00 postpaid

from:
Charles T. Branford Co.
28 Union St.
Newton Center, Mass. 02159

or WHOLE EARTH CATALOG

As for passage hawks, you must remember, when teaching them to wait on, that there is much more danger than there is with eyesses. The longer they are kept on the wing, and the higher they go, the more chance there is of their espying some bird passing— perhaps some old familiar quarry, of which they have struck down scores for themselves— and making off after it. The very fact of being in the air, and feeling the free breeze as it lifts their wings, must remind them forcibly of old days of liberty, and slacken the ties which bind them to their new master. Be extra careful, therefore, in the case of all passage hawks, and most of all with the haggard, to watch for any signs of returning native wildness. Fly her in a country where chance quarry are not likely to appear. If she "rakes away," or wanders far from you in making her airy circles, call her back before it is too late. Fly her always when she is quite sharpset, even if you have to give her little or no exercise on some of the intermediate days between one lesson and the next. You may diet her now upon "washed meat." This is meat washed in cold water and squeezed dry, so that a part of the nutriment originally contained in it is lost. It is, of course, less palatable and less sustaining. But it should be used in moderation. The old falconers seem to have given it much more often than we do now. But for some reason or other the nineteenth century hawk, if at all habitually dieted on this distasteful food, seems to lose pluck and power as well as weight.

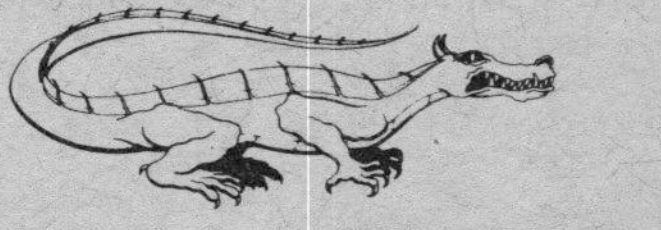

SATURDAY MORNING

Divine Right stayed in Cincinnati all day Saturday and half of Sunday, but only two things of any real interest happened to him. He watched Saturday morning TV cartoons with the kids, and then on Sunday morning received an important message straight from God. More might have happened if D.R. had been open to it. Marcella wanted to get out the family photographs and talk about the old days, and Doyle wanted to take D.R. to his shop and teach him how to give Urge a tune-up. But it was obvious that D.R. was preoccupied and perhaps even upset about something and they didn't want to impose upon him. Marcella had sensed something was wrong when she got her first look at D.R. Friday afternoon. Doyle had felt it too as they were talking during supper. D.R. didn't get back to the house after his second phone call till way after everybody else's bedtime and so Marcella let him sleep through breakfast the next morning and Doyle went on to work by himself.

D.R. likely would have slept right on till noon if the kids hadn't turned the TV up so loud when the cartoons began. Marcella was outside spraying bug killer on the roses when she heard the noise. She had specifically told the kids to keep the volume down while their uncle was asleep, and when she heard it booming through the windows she got really mad. She rushed in the house, jerked both kids to their feet and was in the process of spanking their asses when Divine Right came into the living room, yawning. Marcella snapped the television off and ordered the kids to go out in the yard and play. Debbie had begun to cry as soon as her mother burst into the room, and now she was clinging to Marcella's legs, pleading for forgiveness. Herschel almost cried but at the crucial moment he got hold of himself and stomped his foot on the floor instead.

"Shoot," said Herschel. "I wanted to watch Johnny Hero."

"I'm going to Johnny Hero your little butt if you don't get out of here," Marcella snapped. Then, to D.R., "I'm sorry, David. This place is a madhouse this morning."

"That's all right," said D.R. "I feel pretty crazy myself." He was sleepy and groggy but he smiled and gestured with his hands to show that everything really was okay. It wasn't okay with Marcella yet. She was debating whether or not to whip Herschel for stomping the floor, and Debbie was being a perfect nuisance clawing at her legs.

But the moment passed. Marcella bent over and picked Debbie up, and held her, and Herschel, who had been lurking in the doorway, slunk back in and sat down beside D.R., and very close to him, on the couch. Marcella told D.R. there was coffee made, and juice, and to call her when he was ready for breakfast. D.R. thanked her and said he would. Marcella carried Debbie outside with her, and when the storm door slammed, Herschel ran to the TV and tuned in Johnny Hero again.

All I saw finally at   was crowds, great crowds, ever ever growing, and all getting even with mummy, I WON'T clean my room, I WON'T pick up my toys, I WON'T wipe my ass! Filth, unbelievable, hepatitis, and puppy black shit, burning axe handles as you told me of. It's wonderful, wonderful (I guess) getting it all out into the open, free, or whatever, but I do prefer a modicum of elegance, cleanliness, frequent bathing, showers are really wonderful. This is called rambling, what comes up, no offense intended, heh, none accepted? We of course we all of us ARE what you might call different, clean, patronising them, black shit puppiers all. So here then am I, hair getting shorter, clothes getting neater, though it'll take a great deal to sew me into shirt and tie water coolers daily commute train with ulcers and heartburn, but who needs that, there are other possibilities, eventualities, have one's cake, eat it, save it, store it, and also give some away to the needy.

It is, of course, Subud which has driven me insane, has reduced me to the wreck you are now reading with growing horror and apprehension. But it was grass before that, nicht war, drugs of all sorts, speed nitrous oxide, amyl nitrite, nitroglycerin tablets sublingually, desoxyn for the lovely speedy float, hash and alcohol rendered cannabis, romilar tablets and syrup, the odd terp and codeine for inner and outer coughing spells, DMT, STP, those initials we all know well, peyote eating, and all the jollies of my early years when, from heights unguessed, I looked into the future and thought: what kind of groovies will we be swallowing fifty years from now? Can it get any better than this? Answer: I don't know. But then, after the umpteenth acid trip and the billionth joint, I thought: Hmmmmmmmmmmmmmmmmmm. I....have to....go out and ....I don't know....sit or....read a book on....zen? And where doesn't it end up, pernicious thoughts like this? I have given up nearly all visible vices and am now attacking the invisible ones, which are even harder. How do I know they're vices? I don't. But, when I do them, a gigantic mailed fist or smiling face or great roaring tide goes KERRRRRRRRRRWHOPPPPPP! and I soon get the idea. So my urge toward the participation mystique is now directed into this organic Indonesian brotherhood of which I am a part.

Additionally, there is/are/will be little children, of whom I see several around whenever I go home at the close of the day. I have seen them in their numbers all about me through the turning years, little and snotty, trailing after mummy in the orgiastic revel, tagging after dad who's dealing grass in the haight, dancing their little scared dances with the big folk at the Fillmore, neglected in the corner with diaper full of shit, 'Now listen, honey, there's peanut butter in the cupboard there's toys in the backyard, now for chris sake go and GROOVE, will you? Make your scene? (sotto voce) God, they're wonderful aren't they? So pure and unspoiled.' The little tads grooving with their secret illicit cap guns like their squarer

BRAIN DAMAGE IS WHAT WE HAD IN MIND ALL ALONG. CHROMOSOME DAMAGE IS JUST GRAVY.*

brethren in secret play with their weenies. Everybody's got their hook. I knew a girl once and she was very groovy, you knew her too though I won't mention names, she often had the term 'beautiful' applied to her, would do anything for anyone, a friend in need indeed, two little kids, you know, and one of them would dictate such BEAUTIFUL poetry to her mommy and had such a BEAUTIFUL mind, you know, such a beautiful soul, except that she usually put her little friends on a very bum trip because she had such a desperate need, don't you know, to be a little girl with a mommy and a daddy and a backyard and schoolmates and games and playing doctor and being cuddly and that rap. Little brother was groovy, too, but when mommy had to go out (HAD TO) she would often lock him in a little closet for his nap, a little closet made over into a little bedroom with a little bed and little stuffed animals and a lock. . . on the door. . .from the outside. I used to think of the house burning and the little bed and the little stuffed animals and oh the little boy burning and burning together into what they and we all are made of. . . .

Is that a morbid trip? Anyway,   has an extremely regulated life, lots of regularity, regular naps, regular meals of regular food, regular old mommy and daddy and big brother and is he ever groovy . . .he laughs so much it makes me cry, you know. At any rate, this can't go on forever. Perhaps one day I will do some more stuff, maybe theater, if such exists that doesn't subtract me from my real life, which is my family. But then maybe simple anonymity, a quietus from the everlasting pressure to be an innovator, among the first, at the source, the root, the avante garde. Maybe that's all over, and all that's ahead is that quiet and regularity that   digs so much. That wouldn't be so bad.

Pipe Dreams Unlimited Pipes

There's other good ones, maybe better. These came recommended by a number of our readers for their intelligent design and cooling stoning effectiveness.

—SB

Single Hose
    Thru the Looking Glass $15.00
    The Looking Glass Suspended $25.00
    Stoneware $20.00
    Stoneware Suspended $30.00

    Pipe Dreams Unlimited
    Box 777
    Mendocino, CA 94560

Below the pipe bowl is a filter chamber which you tamp full of your favorite smoking mixture. The hot resins that normally irritate your throat and clog the insides of conventional water pipes are trapped in the filter. Thus, while the smoke loses its harshness, the smoking mixture in the filter becomes increasingly strong.

The two cooling coils are copiously perforated with aereation holes, allowing many tiny bubbles to travel thru the water delivering a moist, smooth-drawing smoke.

The wide-mouthed water chamber accommodates ice cubes to further aid the pipe's distinctive cooling properties.

The optimumly proportioned porcelain bowl reduces the burning temperature, and yet one light burns all the mixture in the bowl.

All two hose models have one-way valves which allow each hose to be used without the other having to be corked or held shut.

Hints

* Use ice cubes whenever possible.

* The water chamber should be approximately 2/3's full of equal parts water and ice.

* For the filter chamber to be effective it should be firmly packed about 3/4's full-tamp down the smoking mixture in the filter until the pipe has the draw you prefer.

To Keep Your Pipe Sweet

Between uses, empty and rinse the water chamber.

If the filter picks up an unpleasant odor, empty and rinse, then let the smoking mixture dry. (use very low heat if you use an oven)

Valtox Drug Identification Kit

In three minutes, at about a nickel a test, you can selectively identify benzedrine, dexedrine, methedrine, opium, heroin, codeine, morphine, barbiturates, cocaine, LSD, marijuana, hashish, STP, peyote, and drugs such as aspirin, antihistamines, etc. The manufacturer prefers to do business with police departments, schools, and hospitals.

—SB

Valtox Master Kit

$49.50 postpaid

from:
Valley Toxicology Service
P. O. Box 1048
Davis, CA 95616

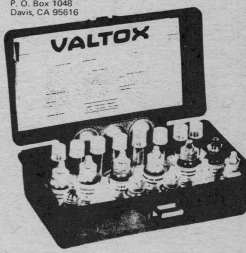

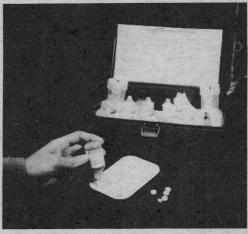

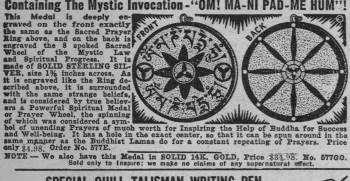
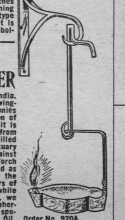

Note. After examination of the various research studies, including big ones just in, I'll stake my reputation as a former biologist on the statement: PURE LSD IN USUAL DOSAGES CAUSES NO UNUSUAL CHROMOSOME DAMAGE, BRAIN DAMAGE, CANCER, OR OTHER BODILY BREAKDOWN. The same probably holds for marijuana, mescaline, and psilocybin. Street acid is usually impure and may be harmful. Pregnant women should not be taking any drugs, including the usual drug store ones.

—SB

How To Live With Schizophrenia

Curable. With medicine. I don't mind quoting from the dust jacket of this one.

—SB

[Suggested by Trisha Masnink]

How to Live With Schizophrenia
Abram Hoffer, Humphry Osmond
1966; 177 pp.

$5.95 postpaid

from:
University Books, Inc.
1615 Hillside Ave.
New Hyde Park, N.Y. 11040

or WHOLE EARTH CATALOG

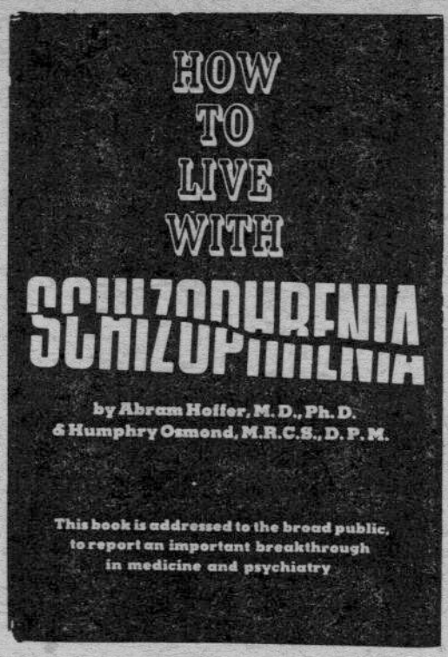

This book is addressed to the broad public to report an important breakthrough in medicine. Treatment of several hundred schizophrenic patients, during twelve years, proves beyond a shadow of a doubt that niacin or nicotinic acid speeds improvement and recovery of schizophrenics and keeps them out of hospitals. Among acute cases diagnosed in early stages the effect of niacin is usually dramatic and profound. Full recoveries are often made in a few months, hospitalized cases become well enough for out-patient care, chronic mental patients of years standing can sometimes fully recover, and extremely serious cases are improved.

Working with other scientists, the authors have established that schizophrenia is basically a physical illness caused primarily by disturbances in the biochemical balance of the body and that this is determined by genetic disposition.

Evidence has accumulated that schizophrenia may be due to a defective adrenal metabolism which results in production of a subtle poison in the blood of its victims.

In varying degrees, from mild to shattering, this schizophrenic toxin interferes with normal brain function and creates bizarre disturbances and changes in perception, mood, thought, personality so common in schizophrenia.

These two scientists also discovered a new therapy for schizophrenia which relies on a simple, harmless, cheap, and highly effective vitamin— vitamin B-3, also known as niacin, nicotinic acid or nicotinamide. Massive doses— 3,000 milligrams per day, or several hundred times the normal dietary requirement— successfully counteract the schizophrenic toxin.

Schizophrenics Anonymous, the newest idea in treatment of the mentally ill, with chapters in Canada and the United States launched at the suggestion of Drs. Hoffer and Osmond, has proven that "schizophrenics can work together toward solution of their difficulties."

Medical men and scientists have available to them publications by Dr. Hoffer, compiling information from the research in Saskatchewan, and giving results of the clinical trial of massive doses of niacin on schizophrenics beginning in 1952. Now, Drs. Hoffer and Osmond have written a pioneering work addressed directly to schizophrenics and their families, mental health workers, and the interested lay public.

In clear simple language, the noted doctors cut through the confusion, misconception and myths that have surrounded this disease, obscuring its reality and compounding its tragedies.

This book will be a godsend to many victims of this dread disease, and their families. It is bound to create a groundswell reaction which can give schizophrenics the right to be considered physically ill. Then they can benefit from a society informed and mobilized properly to treat them for their illness.

•

Treatment of Schizophrenia

Perhaps you have been depressed for the past few months. For no good reason that you can think of you suddenly burst into tears, or you have moments of panic you can't explain. Your work no longer interests you. You are fatigued and miserable.

At the same time you may be having frightening experiences such as seeing flashing lights, noticing changes in people's faces, or feeling peculiar changes in your body. Something is happening to you and no one has been able or willing to tell you what it is.

Perhaps you are now taking tranquilizers and occupational therapy at a clinic? You are possibly making regular visits to your psychiatrist for deep therapy to "root out the souce of your troubles buried in your psyche" Although you are willing to cooperate with your doctor to the best of your ability, you are frightened because you are not feeling any better, and you are convinced that you never will.

Or perhaps you have a close relative— a parent, or a child, or a sister or brother— who has, unaccountably, become very difficult to live with? Perhaps he has frequent outbursts of temper and moments of unreasonable suspiciousness? He sometimes says things which frighten you and does peculiar things which seem quite irrational to you. He may be receiving treatment for some vague "nervous" or "emotional disorder", but you have noticed little— if any— improvement.

What can you do now? Where can you go for help?

Millions of people all over the world are faced with the same dilemma you face today. There is nowhere they can go for information, and no one who can tell them why they feel the way they do, or what they can do about it. Mental health associations in England, Canada and the United States do not have any literature to which people like yourself can refer.

But for you, for your relative and those with similar problems, help is available. It is up to you to see that you get that help. We will describe here a treatment program for schizophrenia which we have developed and found effective in our own work, and which we think is the best available. We will furthermore examine what part other members of the treatment team— hospitals, nurses, family, community, and yourself— must play in this effort. For effective treatment of schizophrenia requiresall the resources that can be made available to you. . .

Phase One Treatment

You have Phase One schizophrenia if you have been sick a short time and you are still able to cooperate with treatment in your own home. It may be that you are not sure you are ill or that you are unable to take your medicine regularly because you are forgetful. You can still be given phase one treatment if you have someone in your family, or a friend who will remind you when you should take your medicine.

We suggest you take either nicotinic acid or nicotinamide as your basic medicine, as both vitamins have the same effect on you. Both substances are B vitamins; nicotinamide was once called vitamine B-3. Nicotinic acid (this is also called niacin) has an advantage which nicotinamide (also called niacinamide) does not have. It lowers the fatty substances, cholesterol and fatty acids in the blood. These substances play a role in hardening of the arteries. Since hardening of the arteries (arteriosclerosis) can lead to high blood pressure and senile changes in the brain, it may be desirable to use nicotinic acid in cases where these additional changes are present.

We have to start with one. If we start with nicotinic acid you will be given a prescription for one month's supply at a dose level of three grams per day. They are available in one-half gram tablets. You will take two half-gram tablets after each meal. The first time you take them you will probably have a marked flush. About one-half to one hour after you take the tablets you will become aware of a tingling sensation in your forehead. Then your face will turn red and you will feel hot and flushed. The flush will spread down your body. Usually it will include your arms and chest, but very rarely will your whole body flush. There is no need to be alarmed. This is a normal reaction to this vitamin. There is no change in your blood pressure and you will not faint.

You will be uncomfortable the first time and you might be wise to take the first tablets in the evening while lying down in bed. Each time you take the pills the reaction becomes less strong and, within a few days to a few weeks, you will have become accustomed to them. Eventually as long as you take the medicine regularly, you will stop flushing altogether, or it will be so mild it will not trouble you. Some patients like to take the nicotinic acid right after meals.

Sometimes patients are bothered by the acidity of nicotinic acid. If this happens to you, you can take one-half a teaspoon of bicarbonate of soda with the tablets. If, however, after you have taken nicotinic acid regularly as prescribed, and you are troubled by it, you may be advised to stop it and to take nicotinamide instead. Nicotinamide produces no flush at all, and for this reason it may be preferable for some patients. It does not lower cholesterol, but can cause some nausea.

The treatment you would be on would, in addition, depend on how old you are and what other physical complaints you may have.

Note. The use of niacin is to restore a chemical imbalance. It may take weeks or months to take effect. If it does the trick for you, you will probably need to take it for the rest of your life, like insulin for a diabetic. No drug company is getting rich off niacin (one reason for slow promotion of the treatment in the medical field); it's cheap.

Jim Fadiman told us that a good outfit to get in touch with is the American Schizophrenic Association, 56 W. 45th St., New York, N.Y. 10036. An effective service organization similar to Alcoholics Anonymous.

—SB

Megavitamin Therapy

Word has been drifting around for some while now about the use of massive doses (like 3 grams) of niacin (vitamin B-3) as a sanity drug. For example, to help terminate or lighten a bum LSD session. To alleviate anxiety states. To accomplish, with time, possible cure of schizophrenia. This pamphlet has all the basic information you need, including suppliers of niacin.

—SB

Megavitamin Therapy
20 pp.

$0.25 postpaid

from:
Aurora Book Companions
Terminal Box 5852
Denver, Colorado 80217

The megavitamin therapy is *not intended to cure vitamin deficiencies.* For that, generally, much lower dosages are needed, and natural vitamin preparations are recommended. Physicians using the megavitamin therapy know that the illnesses treated by it are not vitamin deficiencies.

The megavitamin therapy is *used for schizophrenia, neurosis, hypoglycemia, alcoholism, anxiety states, malvaria, arthritis, senility, hyperlipemia, hypercholesterolemia, coronaries and LSD poisoning.*

In the megavitamin therapy the vitamins are used to *balance the faulty body chemistry.* They were selected because they are inexpensive, can be taken orally, and have no dangerous side effects, even if taken in large dosages for a short period, or continuously in the maintenance dosages.

Alcoholics Anonymous

They're good. Check your local phone directory.

—SB

Person to Person

Barry Stevens is a lady with one of the best popularization formats going. She's taken significant papers of current action in humanistic psychology, and embedded them in a rich collection of her own non-professional living and applying. The papers are by Carl Rogers, Eugene Gendlin, John Shlien, and Wilson Van Dusen. Most of the exerpts below are from Barry Stevens.

—SB

[Suggested by Barry Stevens]

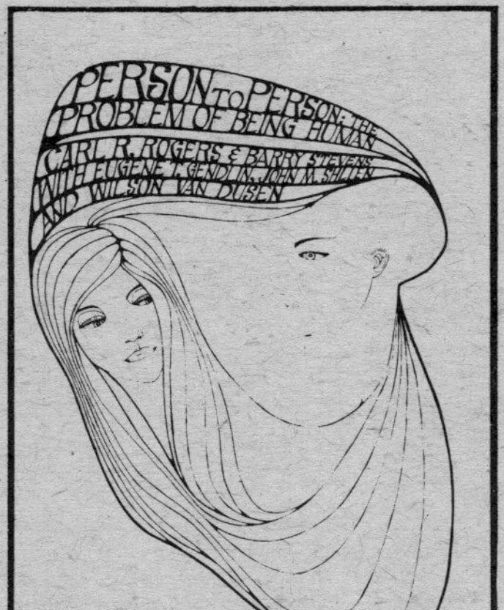

Person to Person
Carl Rogers & Barry Stevens
1967; 276 pp.

$1.25 postpaid

from:
Pocket Books
One W. 39th St.
New York, N.Y. 10018
Attn: Order Dept.

or WHOLE EARTH CATALOG

I saw the Hopi look at Cab so equally that he drew Cab down to his own level—precisely, and not one bit lower—so that they seemed to be two people eye-to-eye. I was so impressed by this that I looked up to the Hopi as though he were some sort of god. The Hopi turned to me with that same strong equalness in his gaze, and I felt myself being drawn up until we were on the same plane.

You must have a career,' they said.
I don't want a career,' I said. 'I want a careen,'....

he made the poets whom I knew seem suddenly like phoney copies of themselves, as far from real as the man who saw in a Rorschach blot where most people see two men, 'The shadows of the silouettes of the ghosts of two puppets.'

Abstract talk seems to me not only 'in front of the face' but not even in this room or this world. It is like rumors about something real.'

Sidney Cohen says 'Our visual mechanism must have evolved with the goal of keeping the organism viable rather than with the aim of seeing things as they are.' Do I sometimes see things more nearly as they are? If I do, is this 'hallucination'?

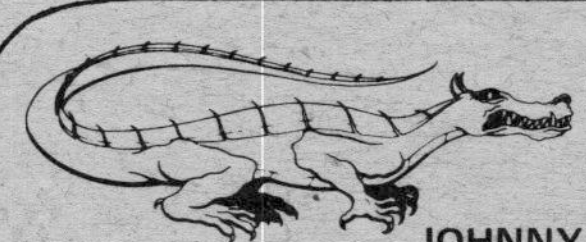

JOHNNY HERO

Last week's episode: Thanks to a timely warning by his ever-watchful guardian, Spider Woman, Johnny Hero narrowly escaped being buried alive in an avalanche caused by Trickster, the notorious henchman of the Black Dragon. In a duel fought at the very entrance to the forbidding Cave of Fear, Johnny subdued Trickster and bound him tightly with silver web provided by the ever-faithful Spider Woman. Thus did Johnny Hero overcome another dangerous obstacle in his struggle to liberate the Crystal Crown from the clutches of the Black Dragon, and lift gloom from the Land of Mee.

(continued) →

The Stress of Life

It has been suggested that this book be reviewed with the thought in ming of its being included in the WEC. Now before going into the criteria for that, it should be stated that the entertainment value, or readability of this book is high. Further note that according to a quoted review the book "...is very readable. ..." You will experience "...Dr. Selye's persuasive enthusiasm." Yet another (not quoted in the book) says it can be read "...with considerable pleasure." And thus spake (also sprach) the Library Journal: "...orchids upon this...incomparable exposition. ..."

In the reading— this applies chiefly to the first 4/5ths of the volume— a word of advice is picked up from a review quoted in the book itself and credited to the American Journal of Public Health. The book, happily, does not contain "...a mass of data of questionable relevance..." but the reader is cautioned to "...maintain balance amid Dr. Selye's persuasive enthusiasm" These words gain weight when one is apprised that they were written for the reviewing journal by Ancel Keys, one of this country's great physiologists.

Now back to the WEC. The WEC states that the criteria for listing something in its pages shall be four in number, videlicet: 1) useful as a tool, 2) relevant to independent education, 3) high quality or low cost, and 4) available by mail. This book immediately meets criteria 3 and 4.

Criterion 2 is a sort of double-barreled one that depends not only upon the nature of the book but also upon what the reader does with it. Dr. Selye epitomizes the relevance to independent education in his dedication: "This book is dedicated to those who are not afraid to enjoy the stress of a full life, nor too naive to think that they can do so without intellectual effort." So let us now say that criteria 2, 3, and 4 have now been met.

In order to determine if the book meets criterion number one as well, let us first quote the author, "I...recommend that only physicians, or readers who are at least reasonably familiar with current problems of physiology and medicine, should read this book from cover to cover." He directs the rest of us cats to first read Book V (the volume is divided into Books I-V incl.) in small installments of...ten to twenty pages at a time. Now it turns out that Book V contains "...the practical implications and applications of the stress concept in everyday life. ..."Hence, criterion number one is going to be met by the contents of Book V— a mere matter of 52 pages— or it is not going to be met at all.

Let us now diverge a bit. "The main purpose of this book is to tell...what medicine has learned about stress." It should be noted in passing that there is a glossary at book's-end to help out on the technical terms. The main subject of the book is the G.A.S. (general adaptation syndrome) which comes to be called the stress syndrome; *and conversely, the* stress syndrome, *I suppose, may be said to be a GAS. First, one should mention that a syndrome is merely a collection or constellation of related signs and symptoms which is characteristic of a disease or condition of malfunctioning.*

The G.A.S. is the sum-total of all non-specific changes that occur in the body during the time it is being acted upon by a stress-producing agent (stressor). These non-specific changes occur in three stages, 1) alarm, 2) resistance, and 3) exhaustion. Number 3 eventuates, if it continues, in death. Most stresses are only severe enough to produce stages 1 and 2. Going through 1 and 2 repeatedly in one's lifetime constitutes "adapting" to things. Various degrees of failure to adapt, Selye says, result in various disease or degenerative conditions.

Now to get back to the question of criterion number one— the use of the book as a tool. Up to page 258 it is not useful as such to the general reader. Selye says, "All we have said up to now helps to guide treatment on the part of a physician," and "...even dietary treatment must be controlled by a competent physician. All this book can do in this respect is to help the patient understand why his physician prescribes a certain regimen; it could not presume to be an adequate preparation for self-treatment along such purely medical lines." BUT, "...there are many things I have learned from the study of stress, which the physician cannot use but the patient can. I particularly want to share these lessons with you. ..." OK, reader, you are now on your own, and you will indeed find out that criterion number one is met.

[Reviewed by R. D. Chamberlain, M.D.]

The Stress of Life
Hans Selye, M.D.
1956; 324 pp.

$2.75 postpaid

from:
McGraw-Hill Book Co.
Princeton Road
Hightstown, N. J. 08520

Manchester Road
Manchester, Mo. 63062

8171 Redwood Highway
Novato, CA 94947

or WHOLE EARTH CATALOG

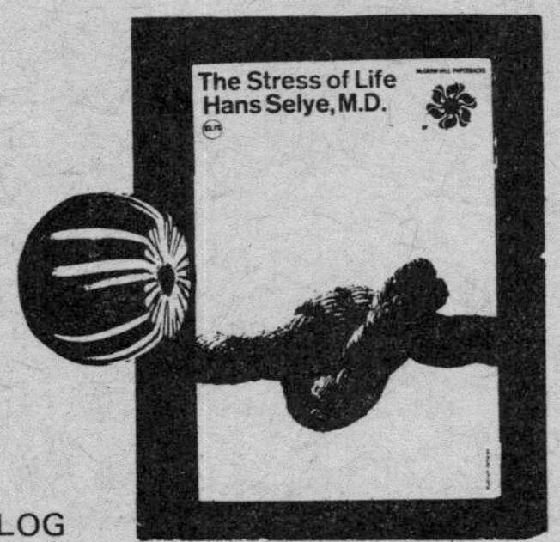

Stress is essentially the rate of all the wear and tear caused by life. It will take a whole book to explain the complex mechanisms through which the body can reduce this type of wear and tear. But let me say here, by way of an introduction, that although we cannot avoid stress as long as we live, we can learn a great deal about how to keep its damaging side-effects to a minimum. For instance, we are just beginning to see that many common diseases are largely due to errors in our adaptive response to stress, rather than to direct damage by germs, poisons, or other external agents. In this sense many nervous and emotional disturbances, high blood pressure, gastric and duodenal ulcers, certain types of rheumatic, allergic, cardiovascular, and renal diseases appear to be essentially *diseases of adaptation.*

•

The important difference between the discovery of America by the Indians, by the Norsemen, and by Columbus is that only Columbus succeeded in attaching the American continent to the rest of the world.

It is not to see something first, but to establish solid connections between the previously known and the hitherto unknown that constitutes the essence of scientific discovery.

•

Paracelsus (whose true, but somewhat bombastic, name was Theophrastus Bombastus von Hohenheim) was a famous Swiss physician who lived during the sixteenth century. In his treatise on "Diseases Which Deprive Man of his Reason," he stated that "the best cure and one which rarely fails is to throw such persons into *cold water.*"

•

Disease is not mere surrender to disease, but also fight for health; and unless there is fight there is no disease.

What is disease——not any one disease, just disease in general? This question lingered on in my mind, as it undoubtedly has in the minds of most physicians of all nations throughout history. But there was no hope of an early answer, for nature——the source of all knowledge——rarely replies to questions unless they are put to her in the form of experiments to which she can say "yes" or "no." She is not loquacious; she merely nods in the affirmative or in the negative. "What is disease?" is not a question to which one can reply this way.

Occasionally, if we ask, "What would you do if . . . ?" or, "What is in such and such a place?" she will silently show you a picture. But she never explains. You have to work things out yourself first, aided only by instinct and the feeble powers of the human brain, until you can ask precise questions, to which nature can answer in her precise but silent sign language of nods and pictures. Understanding grows out of a mosaic of such answers. It is up to the scientist to draw a blueprint of the questions he has to ask before the mosaic makes sense.

•

Fortunately, it is not so much the existence of things that we *do not know*, or about which we are too uncertain, that handicaps our research, but the existence of things we *do know* and about whose interpretation we are quite certain——although they may turn out to be false. Lack of equipment, or even lack of knowledge, is much less of a handicap in original research than an overabundance of useless materials or useless (and sometimes false) information which clutters up our laboratories and our brains.

•

The term *adaptation energy* has been coined for that which is consumed during continued adaptive work, to indicate that it is something different from the caloric energy we receive from food; but this is only a name, and we still have no precise concept of what this energy might be. Further research along these lines would seem to hold great promise, since here we appear to touch upon the fundamentals of aging.

•

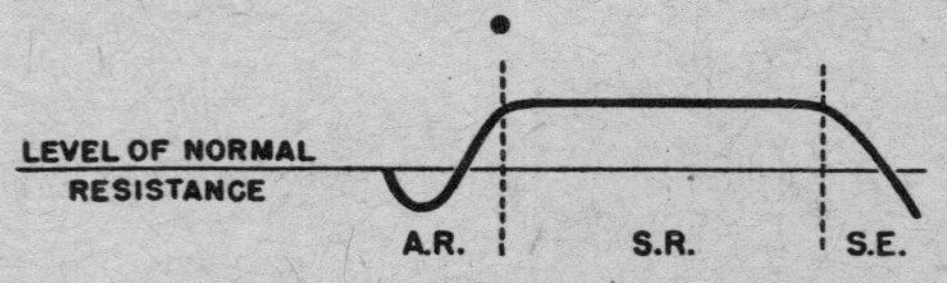

In the acute phase of the alarm reaction (A.R.), general resistance, to the particular stressor with which the G.A.S. had been elicited, falls way below normal. Then, as adaptation is acquired, in the stage of resistance (S.R.), the capacity to resist rises considerably above normal. But eventually, in the stage of exhaustion (S.E.), resistance drops below normal again.

•

Adaptability can be well trained to serve a special purpose, but eventually it runs out; its amount is finite.

•

The fact is that *a man can be intoxicated with his own stress hormones.* I venture to say that this sort of drunkenness has caused much more harm to society than the other kind.

. . . It is not easy to tune down when you have reached your stress-quota. Many more people are the helpless slaves of their own stressful activities than of alcohol. Besides, simple rest is no cure-all. Activity and rest must be judiciously balanced, and *every person has his own characteristic requirements for rest and activity.* To lie motionless in bed all day is no relaxation for an active man.

Aerobics

On the horizon the tiny figure of Johnny Hero running, on and on under a stunning sun, closeup of his surging determined face, sweat running, Johnny running, training for the big match next week; the credits roll by. That's Japanese television cartoons, every night. I was impressed. Our TV tends to show a guy in a chair eating something. Or on a table under muzzled doctors who are having an argument about surgical technique.

—SB

It turns out that the index of physical fitness is not strength, stamina, or quickness (though these inevitably follow if you're fit) but rather, the body's ability to use oxygen. I am an ardent athlete and sports freak of all kinds and spent nine years as a competitive swimmer, so I feel I can judge in these things. I also participated in the testing which resulted in the book (at Lackland AFB, Texas) while in the Air Force, so what is said is so. This tool can save a lot of time and energy to put you in top shape with about an hour's work a week. No kidding. I do about 3-4 times that but you have to do the basic or you're shortchanging yourself, your future existence, and your loved ones.

[Suggested and reviewed by Kenneth Sowers]

The New Aerobics
Kenneth H. Cooper, M.D.
1970; 191 pp.

$1.25 postpaid

from:
Bantam Books, Inc.
666 Fifth Ave.
New York, N.Y. 10019

or WHOLE EARTH CATALOG

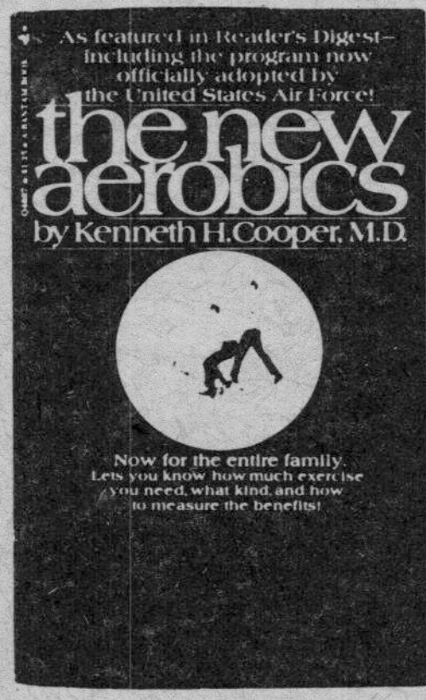

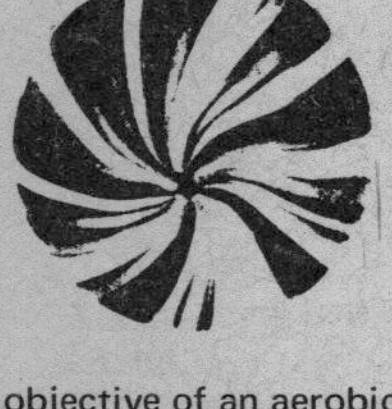

The main objective of an aerobic exercise program is to increase the maximum amount of oxygen that the body can process within a given time. This is called your *aerobic capacity.* It is dependent upon an ability to 1) rapidly breathe large amounts of air, 2) forcefully deliver large volumes of blood and 3) effectively deliver oxygen to all parts of the body. In short, it depends upon efficient lungs, a powerful heart, and a good vascular system. Because it reflects the conditions of these vital organs, the aerobic capacity is the best index of overall physical fitness.

The Israel Army Physical Fitness Book

Everybody I know's doing pushups. Kesey claims there's another wave of creativity coming, and he's doing pushups to get ready. Lloyd just finished editing his dome book, and he's doing pushups to get his head and body back in phase. I'm doing pushups out of some grotesque nostalgia for the Army (U.S.). Low-rent yoga, that's what it is. Sure enough, on a few square feet of prison cell or meditation hut, it can make you feel dedicated and well. —SB

[Suggested by Whole Earth Access Company]

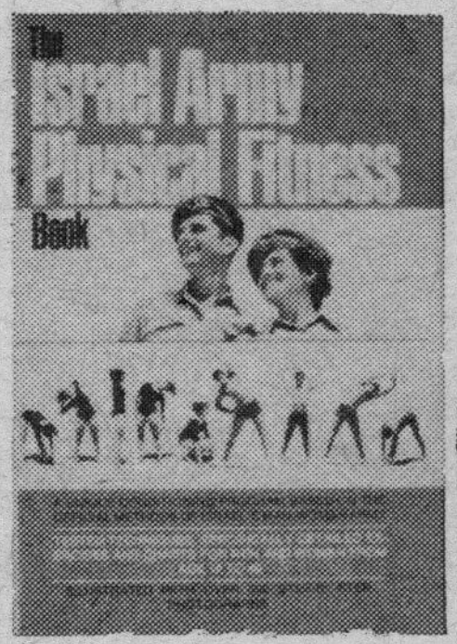

The Israel Army Physical Fitness Book
Jesse Zel Lurie and Samuel Segev, Ed.
1969; 127 pp.

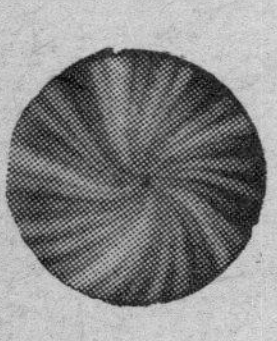

OUT OF PRINT

Grosset & Dunlap, Inc.
51 Madison Avenue
New York, N. Y. 10010

THE AEROBICS CHART PACK

RUNNING EXERCISE PROGRAM
(under 30 years of age)

STARTER *

WEEK	DISTANCE (miles)	TIME (min)	FREQ/WK	POINTS/WK
1	1.0	13:30	5	10
2	1.0	13:00	5	10
3	1.0	12:45	5	10
4	1.0	11:45	5	15
5	1.0	11:00	5	15
6	1.0	10:30	5	15

After completing the above starter program, continue with the Category I conditioning program below or, if you wish to speed up your program, take the 12-minute test of fitness. If you take the test, find your category from the table at the beginning of the chart pack (page 52). If your category is I, II, or III, continue with the appropriate category below. If your category is IV or V, follow the instructions in the note at the bottom of page 56.

* Start the program by walking, then walk and run, or run, as necessary to meet the changing time goals.

Starting Position: Stand with feet apart, trunk bent forward, arms raised sideways.

Movements: 1) Bend your back and drop your head while crossing your arms downwards.
2) Back to starting position, bringing arms up sideways.
3—4) Rest in starting position.

Explanation: In the starting position, arms should be at the sides and pulled forward, in line with the head. Eyes front. When the arms are crossed downwards they should be fairly loose. Be careful to keep knees straight.

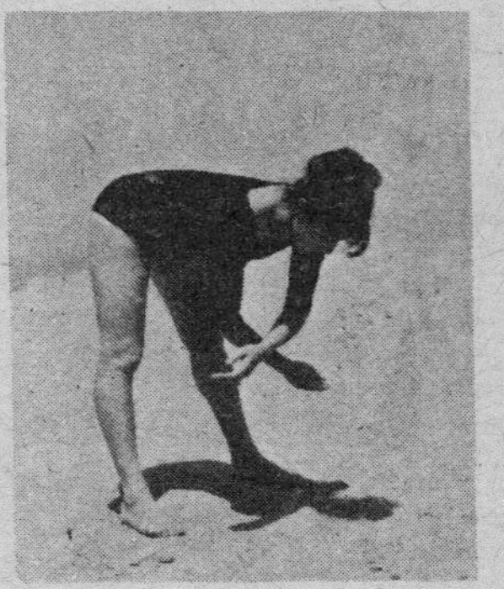

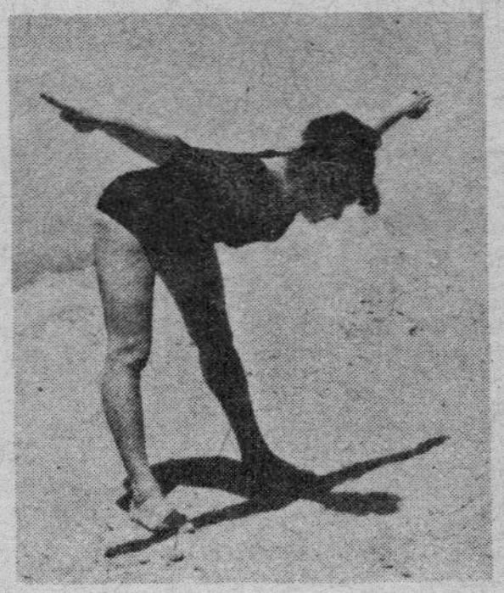

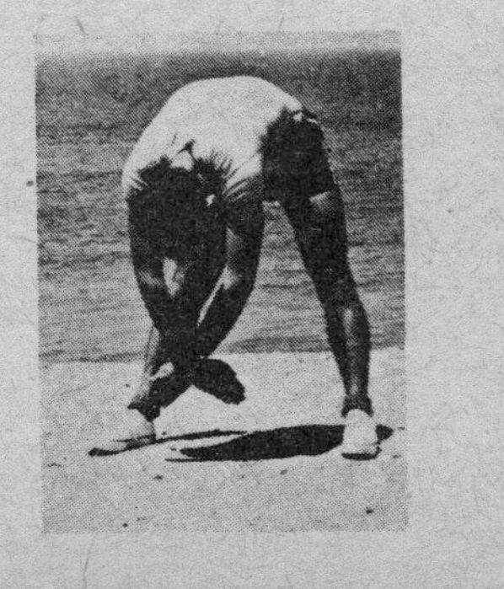

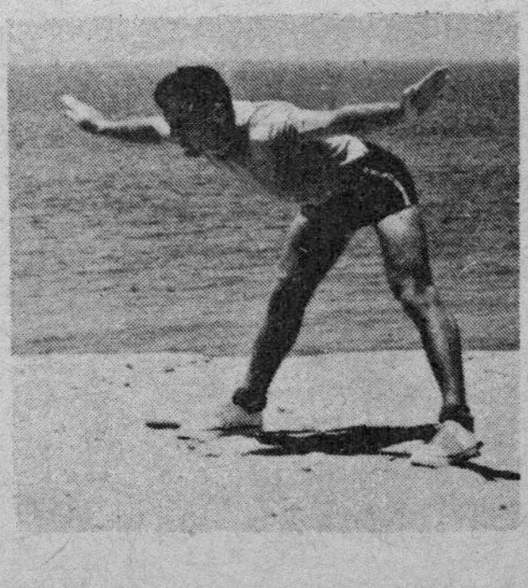

[Army Field Manual FM 21-20, Physical **Readiness Training,** *is a lot more comprehensive. Order from the Government Printing Office.* Out of print

Emergency Medical Guide

No book can substitute for a physician's care. Self-treatment of disease can be worse than no treatment at all. But the proper use of a home health manual may be invaluable in recognizing serious diseases and emergencies, rendering first aid, and treating common medical problems which do not require a physician's assistance. Outdoorsmen and members of isolated farms and communes, especially, should have on hand as much medical information as possible.

Henderson's Emergency Medical Guide *is a useful book, including illustrated sections on bandaging techniques, mouth to mouth resuscitation, injuries to extremities, poisoning, snake bites, emergencies of infancy and childhood, and home care of the ill. Emphasis is placed on the prevention of accidents and disease. Some situations are covered which are not generally considered emergencies (except by the patient) such as painful menstruation. A chapter on normal human anatomy and physiology is included in order to make the rest of the book more intelligible to those giving first aid.*

[Suggested and Reviewed by Eugene Schoenfeld]

Emergency Medical Guide
John Henderson, M.D.
1963, 1969; 556pp.

$3.95 postpaid

from:
McGraw-Hill Book Co.
Princeton Road
Hightstown, New Jersey 08520
Manchester Road
Manchester, Missouri 63062
8171 Redwood Highway
Novato, California 94947

or WHOLE EARTH CATALOG

FIG. 8–9. Procedure for reducing a simple dislocation of a finger, applying pull on each side of the affected joint.

Thumb. Do not attempt to set a dislocation of a thumb. Because of its complicated anatomy, reduction may require a minor operation. Cover the thumb with a protective compress, support the hand in a sling, and seek medical aid.

FIG. 4–1. Ejecting a foreign body stuck in child's windpipe by a sharp blow between the shoulder blades.

Home Medical Handbook

Quick and ready for all those down-home medical problems. Pretty good book.

—SB

The Home Medical Handbook
E. Russel Kodet, Bradford Angier
1970; 224 pp.

$4.95 postpaid

from:
Association Press
291 Broadway
New York, N.Y. 10007

or WHOLE EARTH CATALOG

Artificial Respiration

If the victim is not breathing, act rapidly and decisively!

1. *Have an assistant summon help* by calling the fire department *first*, then a doctor. Or ask the fire department to summon a doctor.

2. *Do not waste time with a drowning victim in trying to hold him upside down to empty lungs, etc.* A small child, however, can be held by the feet, head down, for four to seven seconds, no more, to drain lung secretions.

3. With an adult, place flat on back, with feet slightly higher than head. *But do not fuss. The positioning should not take longer than a few seconds.* Hold up the chin by supporting it with the hand, pinch the nose together, and put your mouth over the victim's mouth and blow.

Blow hard enough to make the chest rise. If the chest does not rise, it means that the chin is not being supported upward enough to clear the airway in back of the throat. The blowing should be as hard as blowing a whistle, but not so hard as blowing up a balloon. Blow twelve to fifteen times per minute.

4. With a small child, it may be impossible to pinch the nostrils together while blowing. *With a small child, then, blow over both the nose and mouth. Blow just hard enough to make the chest rise and fall.* Blow fifteen times a minute.

DO NOT GIVE UP! AT TIMES IT MAY BE NECESSARY TO DO THIS FOR SEVERAL HOURS PROVIDING THERE IS STILL A HEARTBEAT.

Closed Chest Cardiac Massage

1. RECOGNITION:

If there is a cardiac arrest— that is, heart stoppage— from drowning, a blow on the chest, electrocution, shock, insect bites, or other cause, there will be:

    a. No pulse.
    b. Dilated pupils.
    c. Shallow or no respirations, usually the latter.

2. TREATMENT:

This requires two people. Place the victim on his back on something firm. Give mouth-to-mouth resuscitation, as already described. Someone else should summon the fire department or a resuscitation squad if one is available, then a doctor.

In the meantime, put the heel of one hand on the lower one-third of the sternum (breastbone). Place the second hand on the first. Depress the chest. The sternum should move about one or one and one-quarter inches.

Exert your body weight straight downward, not toward the upper chest or abdomen. Do this forty to sixty times per minute, while someone continues to give mouth-to-mouth resuscitation.

Periodically check the eyes. If circulation is adequate, the pupils will start to get smaller. Also check the pulse for a palpable beat, and the respirations to see if they have started.

When the pulse and respirations are working, continue to watch the patient closely for twenty-four hours, at least, or until the patient is under a doctor's care. The heart may stop again, whereupon the procedure will have to be repeated as often as necessary.

Family Guide Emergency Health Care

This booklet is designed as a reference guide for use with a 65-hour free course on making like your own doctor (not first aid but for real treatment) in times of disaster. The full "Medical Self-Help Training Course" may be a bit difficult for the non straights to get into, but the Family Guide *has most of what you need to know (if you supplement it with a good technical reference).*

Apparently not available on direct sale from the Government Printing Office, but may be readily obtained by writing a fairly straight letter to your local State Department of Public Health.

[Suggested and Reviewed by James J. Berryhill]

FAMILY GUIDE
EMERGENCY
HEALTH CARE

A REFERENCE GUIDE FOR STUDENTS OF
THE MEDICAL SELF-HELP TRAINING COURSE

Family Guide Emergency Health Care
Office of Civil Defense, U.S. Dept of Defense
1965; 80 pp.

free

from:
your local
State Department of Public Health

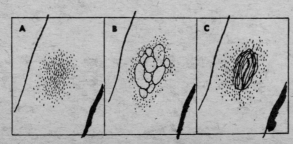

A first degree burn only reddens the skin and if it does not cover more than 25 per cent of the body, usually is not serious.

In second degree burns blisters develop and there is now the very real danger of infection. Extensive second degree burns will require giving additional fluids to the burned person. Do not apply grease or salve. Cover with sterile or clean dressing.

Third degree burns even in a relatively small area are serious. The injury is deep and the underlying tissue has been destroyed. Keep this type of burn clean to avoid infection.

EPILEPSY

It is important to keep the victim of the attack from aspirating or choking on vomited matter, but since most attacks will terminate harmlessly by themselves, regardless of what you do or do not do, just protect the victim from injury and bide your time. When he recovers, do not be unduly sympathetic—you may only embarrass him. Give him a drink of water or tea, protect him from curious onlookers, and be sure that he is well enough to go on his way or that he is taken home. If the condition is more serious, see that he gets to a hospital.

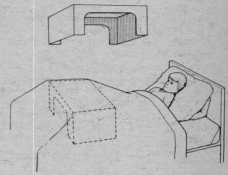

FIG. 15–1. A cradle to keep bedclothes off legs and feet, made from a cardboard carton.

As this week's story begins, we hear Johnny Hero saying to Spider Woman, "Golly, Spider Woman, it sure is dark in here."

"Here," says Spider Woman. "Eat this." And she hands Johnny Hero a magic pearl. Except for the white's of Johnny's blinking eyes, and a string of magic pearls glowing like coals around Spider Woman's neck, it is pitch dark in the cave. Spider Woman is invisible, but her presence is always known by her necklace of magic pearls. Moving across the dark now toward Johnny's eyes is a pearl which seemingly has detached itself from the string. As Johnny swallows it, a circle of light slowly illumines the Cave of Fear.

"Wow," says Johnny. "Look at that!"

He points to a pool of water bubbling and steaming in a shallow depression on the floor of the cave.

"Look!" Johnny exclaims with mounting excitement. "There's another one! And another! Look! Golly, Spider Woman, there's pools of steaming water everywhere!"

"Careful," says Spider Woman. "Those pools are the footprints of the Black Dragon. They look shallow, but actually they're a thousand miles deep."

"Golly," says Johnny. "I sure would hate to . . . fall in one!"

"You'd never be seen again," says Spider Woman. "No one has ever survived a fall into the dragon's footprint."

Suddenly Johnny Hero is seized by an idea. "But listen, Spider Woman. If those are the Black Dragon's footprints, I bet we could follow them right to the dragon's lair!"

Spider Woman is slow to reply. When she does, you can tell by the heaviness in her voice that she is troubled.

"That's right, Johnny. But there's just one thing."

"What's that, Spider Woman?"

"I can go with you no further. If you follow the footprints to the dragon's lair, you must go on alone."

"Alone!" Johnny exclaims. "But Spider Woman. Why?"

"I cannot explain now," says Spider Woman. "Are you willing to go on alone?"

"Golly," says Johnny. "I've got to go on. There's no one to take back the Crystal Crown and lift gloom from the Land of Mee but me."

"Very well," says Spider Woman. "But there are many perils along the way. You'll need these pearls."

With invisible hands Spider Woman removes the necklace of magic pearls from her neck and hands it to Johnny Hero. Johnny looks at them in astonishment.

"But Spider Woman! I shouldn't have these pearls!"

"Do as I say!" snaps Spider Woman. "There isn't much time." Reluctantly Johnny accepts the magic pearls.

"I must go," says Spider Woman. "Good luck, and godspeed."

"Thank you, Spider Woman," says Johnny. "Thanks for everything." Then, his voice trembling, he adds, "I'll never forget you, Spider Woman."

As the wind of Spider Woman's departure ruffles his tousled hair, Johnny Hero puts the string of magic pearls around his neck. With a scornful glance at the steaming pools of evil, he sets off into the cave, making a circle of light wherever he goes in the dark and murky cavern.

"I'M JOHNNY HERO!"

Herschel leaped to his feet and started running around the living room in circles shouting "I'm Johnny Hero! I'm Johnny Hero!"

D.R. yawned and stretched out on the couch.

"Not me, kid," he said, closing his eyes. "I'm so tired right now I don't even feel like David Ray Davenport."

D.R. slept on the couch all day nearly. After supper he went back to bed again and slept the whole night through.

The Merck Manual

In 1850 type-packed pages this book covers most of the possible illness and injuries that can occur to human beings. Each difficulty is described, symptoms are discussed and suggested treatments are indicated.

The writing is extremely technical and is designed as a ready reference for practicing nurses and physicians. Unless you are at ease with the unusually colorful language of modern medicine you will need a medical dictionary to fully understand this book.

While a considerable portion of the advice given is sensible and does not require a doctor's presence, much of the book will not be of use to persons who do not have access to medical supplies. This book is not intended in any sense for primitive or simple living conditions; it does not describe alternatives if medical treatment is not available nor does it suggest folk treatments in lieu of hospitalization. However, if you want to understand what is going on when a member of your family or community is seriously ill, this volume can be helpful. There is an excellent index as well as a special section devoted to specific prescriptions and special therapies. The excerpts given below illustrate both the common-sense and the technical aspects of this volume.

[Reviewed by James Fadiman]

DYSPEPSIA ("indigestion")
Treatment
General: The patient should eat a balanced diet (see DIETS, Normal Diet). At least 1 hr/meal should be allowed. Food should be chewed thoroughly without haste and not constantly "swilled down" with liquids. When possible meals should be taken in a pleasant, quiet, relaxing environment. Smoking immediately before meals should be prohibited. Food should be properly cooked, appetizing and eaten in moderate amounts. Following a meal, the patient should avoid excitement.

HEAT HYPERPYREXIA (sunstroke, heatstroke, thermic fever, siriasis)
Etiology: prolonged exposure to excessively high temperature or the direct rays of the hot sun, combined with exercise and lack of air circulation are the responsible factors. . . .
Symptoms and Signs: Onset may be sudden or may follow complaints of weakness, headache, vertigo, anorexia, nausea and precordial distress. . . . The temperature rises rapidly to 105 or 106 F. or higher. Convulsions and projectile vomiting may develop and are of serious import. . . . Treatment: heroic measures are indicated and must be instituted immediately. If the rectal temperature is 106 F. or over, an ice water tub bath or a blanket soaked in water is indicated, and the skin should be rubbed vigorously until the temperature falls. . . .

DISTURBANCES IN ELECTROLYTE (Mineral) METABOLISM
Dilutional hyponatremia will occur when excessive water is given to a patient in whom antidiuretic hormone activity (postoperatively, or in bronchogenic carcinoma, head injuries, or porphyria) or a low glomerular filtration rate is present. Movement of the water from cells in E.C.F. with a high glucose concentration may produce a temporary hyponatremia.

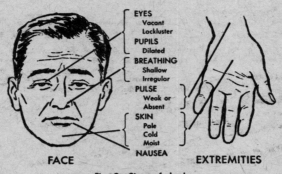

The Merck Manual
11th Edition 1966; 1850 pp.

$8.00

from:
WHOLE EARTH CATALOG

Handbook of the Hospital Corps
United States Navy

Well, we've lost the letter from Tom Scott talking about this last word in medical information, how to run a hospital (how to embalm, how to shake down a thermometer, medical chemistry, anesthetics. . .) Take it with your gang to Mars. Bargain price.

—SB
[Suggested by Tom Scott]

Handbook of the Hospital Corps U.S. Navy
Innumerable pages in enormous folder

$15 postpaid

from:
U.S. Government Printing Office
Division of Public Documents
Washington, D.C. 20402

First Aid

The fourth edition, the 37th printing, of the standard text of how to help. Time for a new edition.

—SB

First Aid
American National Red Cross   No longer available
1933, 1937, 1945, 1957; 249 pp

$1.00 postpaid

from:
Doubleday & Company, Inc.
277 Park Ave.
New York, N.Y. 10017

or WHOLE EARTH CATALOG

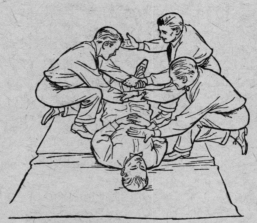

Fig. 9 Signs of shock.

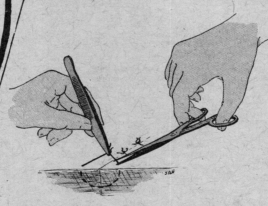

Fig. 54 Hammock carry—showing interlocking grip.

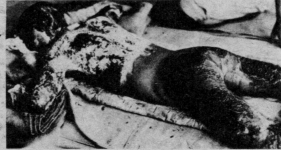

Figure 13.—Removing Sutures.   Apply traction at one end and cut thread below portion exposed on surface. Pull uncontaminated thread through tissues.

Figure 1.—"Flash Burns" of Third Degree. Partial protection of lower extremities by cloth trousers, and complete protection of abdomen by multiple layers of a cummerbund. Burns of the back where there was no clothing are sharply outlined. Photo courtesy Armed Forces Institute of Pathology.

The photo is from Hiroshima. —SB

Emergency Medical Books

Re-references to baby and birth outside of hospital. This is a tricky subject. . .however in isolated areas it could happen and not by choice. I have a Red Cross Instructor's card, but we don't teach child birth in our courses. However I was President of our local ambulance company (two Cadillac ambulances for a town of 1,500 population. . .not bad eh?) for a year or so; and also have the N.Y. State training certificate for ambulance attendant. Issued by State Health Dept. after lengthy instruction and exam. etc. Required by all ambulance attendants, drivers, etc. who work for pay but NOT required for volunteer "Free" service such as ours. And have been teaching first aid for perhaps 40 years or more in army, scouting, etc. So have collected a lot of material on the subject. Strongly recommend following for people outside range of quick medical help (2 or 3 days from doctor, etc.) This is NOT first aid. . .but "medicine".

"Emergency Victim Care & Rescue" by Div. Vocational Education, State Dept. Education, Columbus, Ohio. . . contains excellent chapter on childbirth. Costs 3 or $4 as I remember. A big volume of 327 pages. . .lots of good dope on rescue, knots, etc.

"Emergency Care of Sick & Injured". . .Manual for Law Officers, Fire Fighters, Ambulance and Rescue Sqds and Nurses" By Committee on Trauma American College Surgeons, edited Robt. Kennedy, M.D. Pub. by W. B. Saunders Co., W. Washington Sq., Philadelphia, PA 19105. A tiny book of only 122 pages and expensive—abt. $2. but very up to date and excellent chapter on child birth.

"Ships Medicine Chest and First Aid at Sea" by U.S. Dept. Health, Ed. & Welfare, Public Health Service. Obtain from Supt. Documents, Govt. Print. Office, Washington, D.C. Big cloth bound volume of 428 pages, many color illustrations, including some color plates on VD symptoms, etc. Price $3.50 and a real BARGAIN, written for captains of vessels without a doctor aboard. Good chapter on birth of baby, also covers contagious diseases very well, symptoms and treatment. A life saver for those out of reach of doctor in isolated areas.

"Being Your Own Wilderness Doctor" Dr. Kodet & Bradford Angier. Stackpole Books, Cameron & Kelker Sts., Harrisburg, Pa. 17105 $3.95 clothbound book of 127 pages. Very simply written, good on modern antibiotics, but you must get prescriptions for many of these drugs. . . excellent on kits for travel in wilderness areas. *(See p. 273)*

I could mention many more books, but these are excellent. I assume anyone interested has the American Red Cross First Aid Handbook which should be the starting point of your study. Try and needle your library into stocking some or all of these books or chip in with your group to lower cost. It is more important to study in advance than when a patient is bleeding or seriously injured. Your local Red Cross chapter can arrange to give you their first aid courses. The life you save may be your own or that of a loved one!

Maj. Lyman F. Barry
Nunda, N.Y.

The Body Politic

An attempt to reduce America's overdose of AMA. Dr. Brilliant plans to carry street and home medical information.

—SB

The Body Politic
Larry Brilliant, ed.

No longer available

from:
Medical Committee for Human Rights
558 Capp Street
San Francisco, CA 94110

HEY KID! YA WANNA SCORE SOME DRUGS?

THE PUSHER

Dear Dr. Hippocrates

Long-hairs are doing new stuff with their bodies and nervous systems that occasionally needs medical attention or perspective. Communication was blocked, however, by the social understanding that they aren't supposed to be doing that stuff. Dr. Schoenfeld and his medical advice column in the underground press cut through the blockage, and here came a spout of information as weird as it was useful. Good answers made the questions good.

—SB

Dear Doctor Hippocrates
Eugene Schoenfeld, M.D.
1968; 112pp.

$.95 postpaid

from:
Grove Press, Inc.
214 Mercer St.
New York, N.Y. 10012 0013

or WHOLE EARTH CATALOG

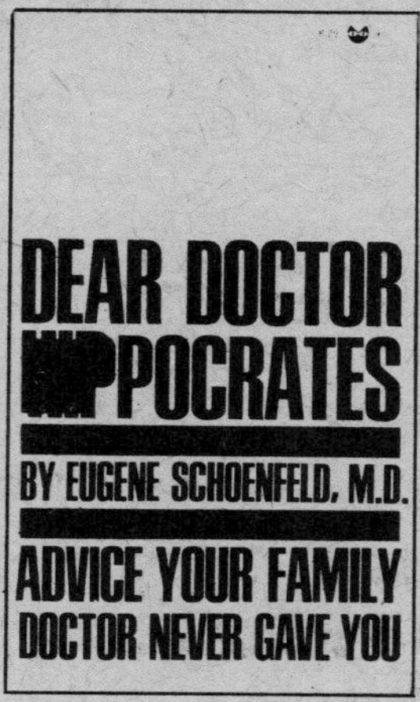

For cosmetic reasons and sex appeal, i have been interested for some time in removing my pubic hair. I initially tried scissors which left stubbles; a safety razor leaves red marks and bumps which are both unattractive and painful. An electric razor is better but still unsatisfactory. I called an electrologist who removes hair, but she found my request most peculiar and refused to undertake the work.

Can you suggest a solution to the problem? Is there any reason to believe removal of pubic hair would be either unhealthful or dangerous?

Most Middle Eastern women routinely shave their pubic hair but I leave to you and your chafed friends the question of whether this practice will enhance your sex appeal. It does not seem medically dangerous.

Cautious use of a depilatory or one of the newer electric razors would seem the best solution to your problem. I would advise against permanent removal since you might someday move to a colder climate.

Note: Judging from the volume of mail received in response to the preceding question and answer, shaving pubic hair is definitely not confined to the Middle East. Excerpts from three letters follow:

A leading manufacturer of safety razors (Gillette) recently placed on the market something called a 'Scairdy Kit.' The ad dealt with the problem of very brief bathing suits but the letter from the girl who shaves made me wonder. Perhaps she needs instructions in the use of lather or brushless cream.

She will have far better results if she uses an electric hair clipper such as the ones barbers use. The OOOO blade is the finest one and will not leave unsightly stubble, irritate the skin or cause abrasions.

For shaving, use alcohol—it eliminates abrasions and little bumps. This was told me by a psychiatrist.

•

I have seen countless old films in which Oriental bartenders slip their unsuspecting customers a "Mickey Finn" which invariably flashes them out of their skulls in about thirty seconds. Is there any such drug that, taken orally, would put a person out in less than a minute?

Two types of "Mickey Finns" were allegedly used. One was chloral hydrate, a sleeping preparation, which induces sleep after twenty or thirty minutes. Like barbiturates, it is especially powerful when given with alcohol.

Another "Mickey" favored by bartenders was a strong laxative, a favorite method for getting rid of undesired customers. But only in Hollywood do "Mickeys" work within one minute.

•

Could you please tell me if it is possible to become pregnant without coitus if ejaculation occurred outside the vagina?

Pregnancy without coitus is possible if semen is at or near the entrance to the vagina. This may occur even if a girl is wearing underpants, according to some now well-informed female sources.
Perhaps this helps to explain the phenomenon of virgin births. But it still seems a poor way to become pregnant.

•

Are there any ways to get birth-control pills besides having to go to a doctor to get the prescription?

No and for good reason. The doctor will take a medical history and do a gynecologic examination, including a Pap or cancer smear, to determine that there are no conditions which would be caused or made worse by taking birth-control pills. You should see your own physician or you may be eligible for care at your local health department or Planned Parenthood office. Doctor's aren't so bad. Some of my best friends . . .

•

(The following letter was sent air mail special delivery from New Orleans.)

Dear Dr. Schoenfeld:
Is it true that smoking incense can make you high? (I am mainly referring to the Joss incense sticks from India.)
Love,
Paul ——

Dear Paul:
I have not been aware that smoking incense could make one high. This effect would have been discovered thousands of years ago if it were true.
Are you sure it's incense you're smoking?
Sincerely,
Eugene Schoenfeld, M.D.

Complete Home Medical Encyclopedia

Just about everything that could happen to your body is discussed in this fat paperback. Acne, actinomycosis, anthrax and arthritis to sexual intercourse, thromboangiitis obliterans, and worms. Dr. Hyman combines specific treatments with clear explanations of bodily functions and how they get interrupted. I learned more here about acne than I have from any of the dermatologists I've seen. There are occasional diagrams in the alphabetically arranged text, which is written with the sensibility and humor you'd want from your family doctor. The traditional general practitioner is said to be growing scarce in the American scene, but many of the questions you might want to ask him are answered here.

—Hal Hershey

The Complete Home Medical Encyclopedia
Harold T. Hyman, M.D.
1963, 1965; 832 pp.

$1.95 plus $.15 postage

from:
Avon Books
250 W. 55th Street
New York, N.Y. 10019

or WHOLE EARTH CATALOG

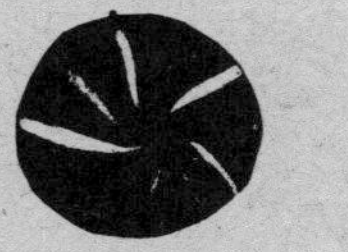

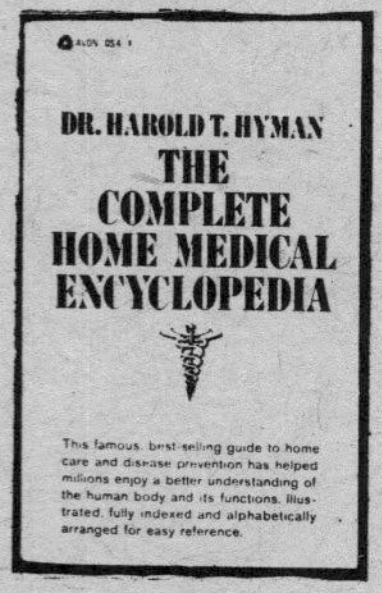

The control of acne requires a joint effort on the part of youngster and parent, usually the mother.

After a review of the nature of the disturbance, as outlined above, the parent will do well to reassure the child that no blame or shame is attached to the condition.

The child should be told that acne is not due to uncleanliness or bad habits of any description; that it is not a disease but more in the nature of a normal feature in the process of growing up. Here is a suggested outline for the home-treatment plan.

Each morning apply a lather of pure soap or a sudsing detergent (Dove) to face, shoulders and chest. Scrub vigorously with a rough towel. Give special attention to skin folds and creases.

Each afternoon or early evening, on return from school or work, repeat the scrubbing. Then, expose affected areas to ultraviolet rays, using direct sunlight, an inexpensive sun lamp (Sperti) or a bulb (RS model) that has the recommendation of the American Medical Association or a testing institute of a reliable magazine. Regulate the distance from the source and the time of exposure so that the skin is tanned but not burned, so that it flakes but does not peel.

At bedtime, apply hot towels to affected skin areas until flushed. Then, with scrubbed hands and blunt fingernails, gently but firmly extract secretions from whiteheads and blackheads and from pores in skin folds, especially those on the nostrils and between nose and cheek.

Twice weekly, shampoo with hand soap or sudsing detergent (Drene). Scrub scalp vigorously with a tough hand brush before drying.

Avoid application of medicated or cosmetic ointments and creams that may tend to plug the channels you're trying to keep open.

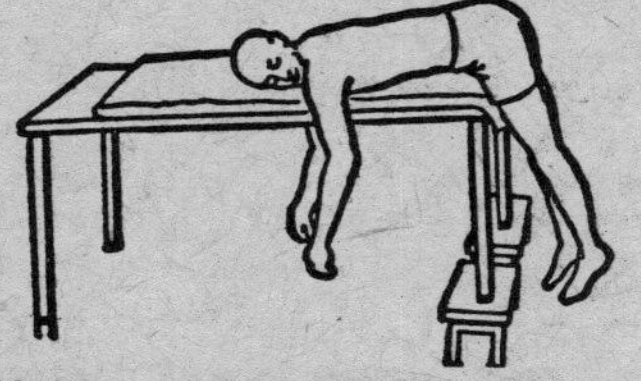

Fig. 14 Jackknife positioning for relief of acute back strain.

Crabs

I don't know if you've done this one before, but for your edification, here is a quote from the sheet of A-200 Pyrinate Liquid

Advantages of A-200 Pyrinate

1. *A-200 Pyrinate is a liquid. . .no messy salve.*
2. *It kills on contact crab, head and body lice and their eggs (nits), also chiggers (red bugs), and dog fleas.*
3. *Leaves no tell-tale odor.*
4. *Does not permanently stain clothing. Is easily removed with water— without soap.*
5. *Destroys eggs or nits, as well as parasites themselves.*
6. *Its advantages over blue ointment and larkspur lotion are obvious.*

It cost $1 in a very expensive drug store.

IT WORKS! As anyone who has sat up half the night every night crouched over a dying flashlight pursuing the pernicious phthirus pubis knows, that's the only comment that counts.

Jim Huston
Cleveland, Ohio

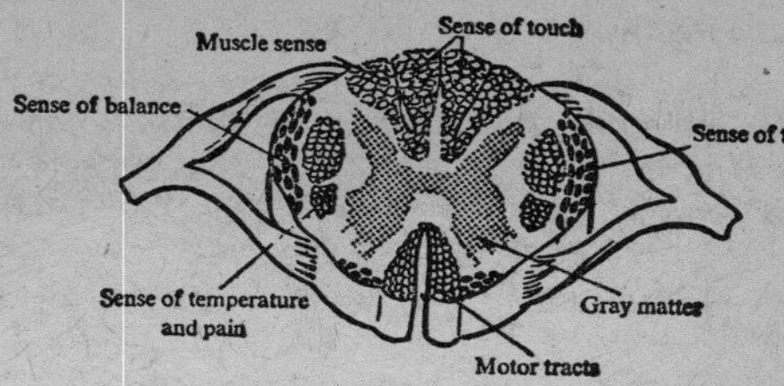

Fig. 26 Spinal cord (cross section)

Treatment of Acute Alcoholism

The best treatment of acute alcoholism is prevention. Not by absolute prohibition, but by judicious indulgence in the pleasures and uses of alcoholic beverages. Here are some hints to the accomplishment of this end:

Never take more than the equivalent of two ounces of hard liquor or of two bottles of beer at any one session. This will assure you of a safe level of blood alcohol (up to 0.05%).

If you exceed the safe limit, *don't drive your car.*

If your escort exceeds the safe limit, *take away car keys.*

If neither you nor any other member of your party is in condition to drive the car, get some sober person to drive for you. (See ACCIDENTS.)

Adopt a protective attitude toward the person who, on occasion, takesone(or a few) too many. If docile and amiable, get him (or her) to bed to sleep it off. If possible, resist efforts of well-meaning amateurs who strive to sober the patient up with large quantities of coffee and/or a cold shower.

If you are unable to contol an alcoholic, send for a physician who may succeed by giving a large dose of paraldehyde or an injection of apomorphine (vomiting within ten minutes) or a tranquilizer (Librium, Thorazine, etc.).

On awakening after a binge, take warmed fluids (tea; consommé; hot water; citrus fruit juice; clam broth; etc.). Do not add to dehydration by resorting to the conventional saline purge— with or without precedent calomel.

For relief of the hangover headache, don't take the "hair of the dog that bit." Instead, take a dose of aspirin and wash down with 250 cc. heated, charged water. As soon as stomach is tolerant, eat small quantities of warmed soft foods at frequent intervals. Choose poached egg; milk toast; warm milk and soda crackers; puree of soup; mashed potato; etc. Despite craving for cold, carbonated fluids, avoid them, since they are very apt to cause abdominal cramps and distention.

For relief of the "morning-after-the-night-before depression," take a euphoriant such as 5 mg. dextro-amphetamine (Dexedrine), 5 mg. amphetamine (Benzedrine), 25 mg. phenmetrazine (Preludin), 10 mg. methylphenidate (Ritalin), or 2.5 mg. pipradol (Meratran).

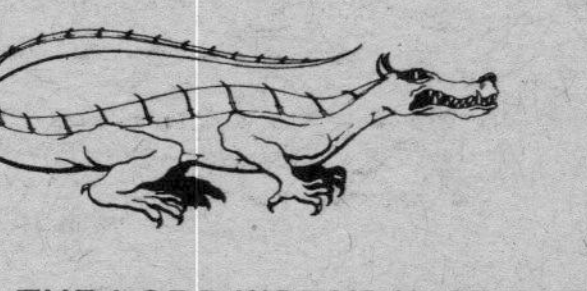

THE LORD WORKS IN MYSTERIOUS WAYS

D.R. got up and had breakfast with the family and then lay down on the couch to read the paper while Marcella and Doyle got the kids ready to go to Sunday School. It had been clear the evening before that D.R. wasn't going to feel like going to church with them, and so they left him alone to read and relax while they got dressed and ready. When the family left, the house fell into such profound silence D.R. dozed off almost immediately. But then around eleven the phone rang and woke him up and when it turned out to be God Himself calling to summons D.R. to Kentucky, alertness spread through him like a rush.

God was calling in the guise of Mrs. Godsey, Uncle Emmit's neighbor down in Finley County, but Divine Right had no doubt who it really was. Her high, nasal voice was certainly a strange one for such a weighty summons, but the Call was clear and unmistakeable: Emmit was dying at the homeplace and he must go to be with him.

Mrs. Godsey told D.R. she hated to worry him, that it might be a false alarm, but she didn't think so. She said the Lord worked in mysterious ways, that it wasn't given people to understand everything He does, that Emmit might perk up tomorrow and outlive them all, but according to her son Leonard who had been to see Emmit twice the day before, he was twice as bad off as he had been and that she just had to call Marcella and try to do something about getting somebody to go up and stay with him, or else get an ambulance to haul him out of that holler to the hospital. D.R. told Mrs. Godsey he couldn't get there before late that night, but that he would come on if she thought that was what ought to be done. Mrs. Godsey said what honey? Some fool's eavesdropping and cut out what you said. D.R. repeated what he'd said and Mrs. Godsey said she thought it would be wonderful if he would come, that it would certainly be a Christian act and a wonderful blessing for Emmit. Then she told D.R. that the last time she had seen him he was the least little old thing that ever was. She said you must be a great old big boy by now. D.R. said he was twenty-one. Mrs. Godsey said my, my, time flies don't it? She said she knew his parents, God rest 'em, would of been proud he had turned out to be such a fine young man, and that she was looking forward to seeing him again. Then she said well honey, this is costing money. D.R. told her to tell Leonard to go tell Emmit he was on his way, that he would be there late that night or tomorrow at the very latest, and Mrs. Godsey said bless your heart child, and hung up.

Handbook of Prescription Drugs

A drug ordered by brand name can cost several times as much as the same drug ordered by generic name. This book spells out the difference, its reasons, and how to get generic name prices. One way is, ask your doctor when he's prescribing a drug to prescribe the generic name.

—SB

The New Handbook of Prescription Drugs
Richard Burack, M.D.
1967, 1970; 366pp.

$1.25 postpaid

Ballantine Books Inc.
457 Hahn Road
Westminster, MD 21157

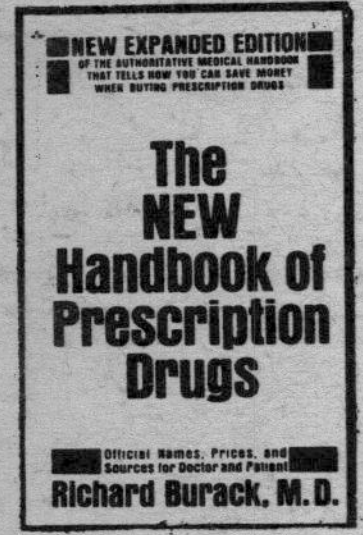

CELESTONE ® Betamethasone, N.F.
0.6 mg tablets $133.56/1000
0.2% cream 1.08/5 g tube
2.22/15 g tube

Betamethasone is a steroid chemically and pharmacologically similar to dexamethasone (Decadron®). Like dexamethasone, it is immensely expensive, and in nearly every case it can be replaced by less costly prednisone, for oral administration, or hydrocortisone, for topical administration. See Prednisone, U.S.P., and Hydrocortisone Ointment, U.S.P., in the Price Lists.

Nonetheless, in 1967 Celestone® was among the top 200 drugs prescribed to people of all ages. In 1966 it ranked 143rd among prescriptions written for the elderly; 312,000 prescriptions cost these consumers $1,526,000.

•

CODEINE SULFATE, N.F.
The manufacture and sale of this narcotic substance and also its price are rigidly dictated by the United States government: 450 grams cost approximately $350. Therefore, a single 15 miligram tablet has wholesale value of approximately one cent. A representative price to druggists is $11.80 per thousand 15 milligram tablets (Vitarine). See price list for Codeine Sulfate, N.F.

The *Handbook* lists Codeine Sulfate, N.F., rather than Codeine Phosphate, U.S.P., because the latter, being more soluble, is more bitter to the taste.

CO-HYDELTRA® Prednisolone, U.S.P.
5 mg tablets $3.25/100 Magnesium Trisilicate, U.S.P.
Dried Aluminum Hydroxide Gel, U.S.P.

Prednisone is preferable, and can be less expensive. See Prednisone, U.S.P., in the Price Lists.

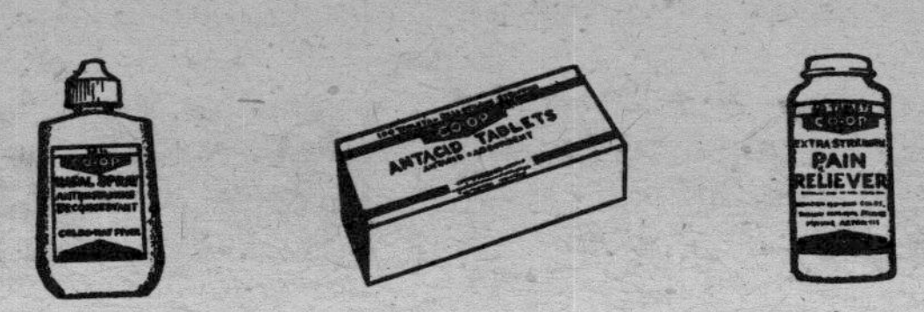

Prices on some commonly used

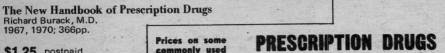

PRESCRIPTION DRUGS

If your drug isn't listed, DON'T WORRY— We fill any prescription!

Brand Name	Generic Name	Quantity	Usual Price	Our Prices: Brand Name •	Our Prices: Generic Name ••
Aldactazide	Spironolactone & Hydrochlorothiazide	100	$15.30	$13.60	$ ......
Aldomet	Methylclopa	100	10.00	7.80	......
Antivert	Meclizine & Nicotinic Acid	100	7.35	5.85	......
Arlidin 6 mg	Nylidrin	100	6.60	5.40	......
Atarax 25 mg	Hydroxyzine w/HCl 25 mg	100	11.65	9.95	......
Atromid-S	Clofibrate	100	9.75	8.70	......
Bamadex Sequels	Dextro-amphetamine SO_4, meprobamate	30	5.00	4.20	......
Benadryl 50 mg	Diphenhydramine	100	3.70	3.00	2.25
Benemid	Probenecid	100	10.00	7.50	.....
Butazolidin 100 mg	Phenylbutazone	100	9.75	7.25	......
Butazolidin Alka	Phenylbutazone	100	11.00	8.80	......
Butisol ¼ gr	Butabarbital	100	2.60	1.95	1.25
Butisol ½ gr	Butabarbital	100	3.45	2.75	1.50
Cardilate 10 mg	Erythrityl Tetranitrate	100	3.75	3.05	......

↑

Celo Direct Drug

Another thing you might like to list in a future edition is the Celo Direct Drug catalog. The Arthur Morgan School is closely associated with the co-op movement and has championed various consumer causes. For some years we operated *Celo Laboratory Products*, a project for supplying Co-op pharmaceuticals by mail at low cost. Then the Co-ops started their own mail order drug service. At this point we turned our business over to them, but edited and published their catalog. I'll enclose a copy of it. It can be had free by addressing Celo Direct Drug Service, Burnsville, N.C. 28714.

Ernest Morgan
Celo Press
Burnsville, N.C.

Vitamin C and the Common Cold

Several people around here are in a vitamin C research program at Stanford; they're pretty healthy, maybe more so than last winter. Linus Pauling has made vitamin C very popular. Linus Pauling, what do you think of, um, marijuana? *—SB*

Vitamin C and the Common Cold
Linus Pauling
1970; 122 pp.

$1.25

from:
Bantam Books Inc.
666 Fifth Ave.
New York, NY 10019

or WHOLE EARTH CATALOG

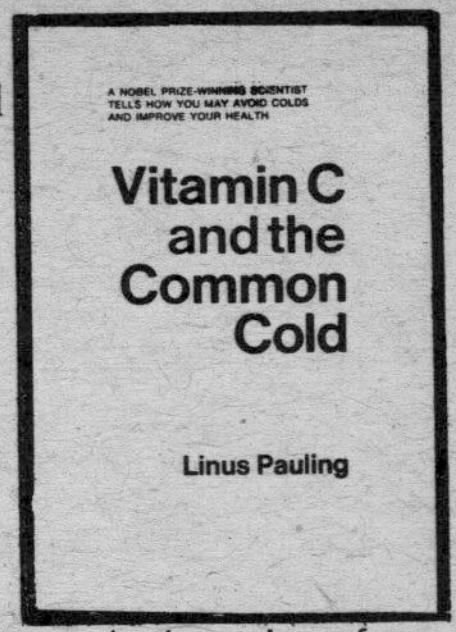

First, for good health I recommend the regular ingestion of an adequate amount of ascorbic acid. I estimate that for many people 1 g to 2 g per day (1000 mg to 2000 mg per day) is approximately the optimum rate of ingestion. There is evidence that some people remain in very good health, including freedom from the common cold, year after year through the ingestion of only 25- mg of ascorbic acid per day. The requirements of a few people for ascorbic acid may be expected to be even smaller. For some people optimum health may require larger amounts, up to 5 g per day or more.

NRTA—AARP Pharmacy

Biggest and best source for mail order drugs. Offers both prescription and non-prescription items at a great discount. Especially good for vitamins if you buy the NRTA-AARP Formula that's equivalent to nationally advertised brands. Also has a good selection of elastic stocking and hearing aid batteries.

They say their service is only for members of the National Retired Teacher's Association-American Association of Retired People. The scrupulous among us will join (they don't check) for an annual fee of $2.00. Well worth it for a confirmed pill popper. You don't have to be old, after all, to be retired.

Interestingly enough, I've been lead to believe by an official of NRTA-AARP that, despite the really good discount given, the co-op pharmacy is a real money-maker for the organization; so don't feel like you're robbing a bunch of old people by taking advantage of this. Other good things: they will give you credit with no delay for credit clearance and there are no postal charges.

[Suggested and reviewed by James Thorsen]

Catalog

free

from:
NRTA—AARP Pharmacy
1224 24th Street, N.W.
Washington, D.C. 20037

Vitamin E

about burns (july $1 catalog, pg 47), last november the gas stove in the place we were renting blue up and messed up my arm. In some places it was pretty bad (black and flacking away by the time i got to the hospital) and it hirt. i was given a shot (5 mg morphine) and the started splaching the arm with phisohex and cool water. The dr also told me to plan on skin grafting because the elbow was bad also. my old lady told me about vitamin e and i sqused some under the bandage, tood 3-4 grams a day with the same of vitamin c. IT WORKS. The only signs of the burns left show up on those occansional times when a dr gives me a through phiscal.

I forgot to say that the 3-4 grams was savesed under the bandage. I think that the oral dossage also may be important getting the stuff into the system, there by getting to the burn several ways and makeing it available over a long time, but I don't know.

I know a couple of women who squeezed Vitamin E from the capsule onto their stomachs during & after pregnancy to prevent stretch marks. They also exercized a lot & didn't get any stretch marks. They also exercized a lot & didn't get any stretch marks. We'd like to know more including natural sources for Vitamin E.

john mccarthy
denver, colorado

From a Medical Student

I did, however, register a note of dismay at the listing of *The Handbook of Prescription Drugs*. Pharmacology, in case you have not yet looked it up, may be defined as the study of the preparation, actions, and uses of drugs. Thus, although I am only a grad student, I feel obliged to comment on this book. Strictly speaking, there is no such thing as a "generic equivalent." The term should be "chemical equivalent." Most drugs currently used are so potent that doses are less than half a gram. This means that the drug manufacturer is obliged to dilute drugs so that a dosage form may be of a convenient size. In addition, if the dosage form is a tablet (commonly, but incorrectly called "pills"), then, no matter what the dosage, various agents must be added which will allow the formation of a compressed tablet. The consequence of these added or adjuvant materials is that they often affect the efficacy of the dose of the drug.

An excellent case in point is aspirin. Most aspirin tablets contain 5 gr (300 mg) of aspirin. However, the actual tablet weight is several times this. This is due to the addition of diluents, binders, stabilizers, and disintegrators. Aspirin (acetylsalicylic acid) is a very unstable compound, and in itself, even in its purest form, is a severe irritant of mucosal tissue, such as is found in the stomach and intestines. It has been estimated that about a teaspoonful (5 ml. or 1/6 oz.) of blood is lost for each aspirin tablet ingested. However, this value is only for pure aspirin, and aspirin easily breaks down in the presence of moisture to acetic acid (vinegar) and salicylic acid (used for removing corns). By this time, it should be obvious that the care and skill with which a tablet or any medication is made and the extent of testing of the final product has a direct effect on the action of the product. Thus, when you open that bottle of cheap aspirin and smell the odor of vinegar, it is advisable only to dose your sewer system, unless, that is, you feel that you have a corn in your stomach that you would like to remove.

Another interesting case is one cited in the catalog, prednisone versus Meticorten. There are several cases reported in the medical literature where a patient received, not necessarily Meticorten, but a "brand name" prednisone while hospitalized, and then was discharged with a prescription written generically. It was found that several prednisone tablets made by "generic" manufacturers were considerably less effective than the ones previously dispensed.

There are efforts being made by the AMA, American Pharmaceutical Assoc., and the Federal Government, as well as the manufacturers, to develop standards for drugs. However, these standards, when available, are basic minimums. There is no way at present of insuring anything but basic physical similarity between two "generically equivalent" medications. Thus, two aspirin tablets may both meet the legal standard of disintegration in less than thirty minutes in a special apparatus, but one tablet may take 29 minutes, while the other takes ten seconds. I have seen this happen, and I ask you which tablet you think would release its ingredient faster for more rapid absorption and consequently more rapid action? The ten second tablet was Bayer, the other was a readily available, but very cheap product whose manufacturer I shall not name.

I would like to conclude this tirade by stating that there are instances where a generic drug will be similar in action to a branded drug and that merely the fact that a drug is given a brand name does not insure efficacy. Thus, the choice of the medication by a doctor should be tempered by his experience and his faith in the dispensing pharmacist to carry a reliable line of generic drugs, in addition to the ability or desire of the patient to receive the best possible medical care. Therefore, the blanket statement that a generic prescription will save you money, while generally true on a per dose basis, may not be true if it takes more of the cheaper medication to cure you.

As I see it, the solution to the problem at present from the patient's viewpoint is twofold. First, you must choose a doctor who is not an automaton and is thus capable of discussing with you the validity of a generic prescription in your specific instance. Secondly, you must choose a pharmacy which carries products from reliable lines, and not necessarily the cheapest stuff that is available. This entails, in most cases, finding a pharmacy where the practice of pharmacy is treated as a service, rather than a business. Unfortunately, neither is very easy, thus, the problem boils down to *caveat emptor*.

I would like to add, as a footnote, that most of us closely associated with drugs avoid taking them as much as possible.

Sincerely,

Craig K. Lewis
Nashville, Tenn.

VITAMIN E

50 I.U.	100 I.U.	200 I.U.
100s..$ 1.98	100s..$ 3.25	100s..$ 4.95
300s.. 5.35	300s.. 8.78	300s.. 13.35
1000s.. 14.00	1000s.. 24.00	

NIACIN

(Nicotinic Acid)

NIACIN	100s	300s	1000s
50 mg.	$ .39	$1.05	$ 3.00
100 mg.	.69	1.86	5.50

NIACINAMIDE

(Nicotinamide)

50 mgm.		100 mgm.	
100s	$ .39	100s	$ .69
300s	1.05	300s	1.86
1000s	3.00	1000s	5.50

Wheat Germ Oil Capsules 3 minim	100s	$ .69
	300s	1.86
	1000s	5.50
Pyridoxine, 10 mg.	100s	$1.00
Pyridoxine, 25 mg.	100s	1.50
Pyridoxine, 50 mg.	100s	2.25
A & D Concentrate Tablets	100s	$ .90
A & D Concentrate Tablets	300s	2.43
A & D Concentrate Tablets	1000s	7.00
Riboflavin, 5 mg.	100s	$ .80
Rivoflavin, 10 mg.	100s	1.25

American Indian Medicine

The definitive book—all the tribes, all the medicines. The author is looking through the window of Western medicine and Western anthropology, but he is looking with detailed appreciation. Weedmunchers could find no better guide. The people who could use it best probably can't afford a doctor and drugstore and probably can't afford this book—another good reason for libraries.

—SB

American Indian Medicine
Virgil J. Vogel
1970; 583 pp.

$1.95 Paperback

from:
Ballantine Books
c/o Random House
457 Hahn Rd.
Westminster, Md. 21157
or WHOLE EARTH CATALOG

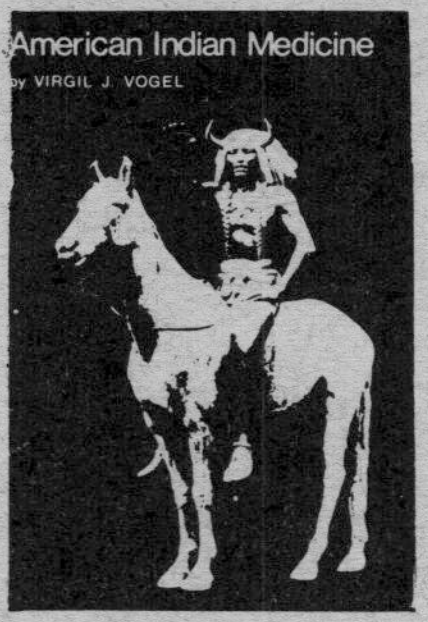

Himes concluded that "American tribes had no effective methods of preventing conception," and that they relied mainly on abortion, infanticide, and abstention to control family size.

Events have since proved how wrong Himes was, for not only have oral contraceptives come into general use in advanced countries, but Indian herbs were finally subjected to laboratory tests in the search for an effective oral means of controlling fertility, and some of them were found to be effective. Just as America was considered to be undiscovered before the white men found it, so the Indian drugs were unreal or of no account until the white men discovered them. This is one example among many of the ethnocentric attitude which has hurt the white men more than the Indian by delaying scientific inquiry into aboriginal herbal knowledge. The Cherokee drug *may* have been of no use, but what is striking here is the way it was rejected *a priori*, simply because white men knew of no oral contraceptive, and therefore, presumably, none existed. It is noteworthy that until recently it could not only be said that Indian recipes for controlling fertility had not been investigated, but that the very names of the drugs used were largely unknown.

•

Mesquite (Prosopis juliflora [Swartz] DC, and *Prosopis glandulosa* Torr.). *P. juliflora* was the *mizquitl* of the Aztecs (hence, *mesquite*), who mixed the leaves with other substances for an eye lotion when the eyes were hot and painful from sickness. Seventy years ago Bourke reported that this shrubby tree was used for the same purpose by Mexican Americans in Texas, and Hrdlicka found Indians of the American Southwest using it in a similar manner. The Mescalero Apaches ground the leaves to a powder, placed the substance in a thin cloth, added water, and squeezed the liquid on the eyes. The Pimas applied the sap to sore eyes. The Maricopas used the dried juice, ground fine, as a sore-eye remedy by applying the substance to the lids and later washing it off with warm water.

•

The skeletal remains of unquestionably precolumbian date [he concludes] are, barring few exceptions, remarkably free from disease. Whole important scourges were wholly unknown. There was no pathologic microcephaly, no hydrocephaly. There was no plague, cholera, typhus, smallpox or measles. Cancer was rare, and even fractures were infrequent. There was no lepra [leprosy] . . . there is as yet not a single instance of precolumbian syphilis. There were, apparently, no nevi [skin tumors]. There were no troubles with the feet, such as fallen arches. And, judging from later acquired knowledge, there was a much greater scarcity than in the white population of many diseases of the skin, of most mental disorders, and of other serious conditions.

The chief diseases to which the ancient Indians were subject, he added, were digestive disorders, particularly in children and older persons, pneumonia, arthritis, and localized maladies such as nutritional disorders.

•

Wild mint. This is the only indigenous species of *Mentha*. Dr. Clapp reported in 1852 that it was little used in medicine but would be a tolerable substitute for the European species when they could not be obtained.

The Cheyennes ground the leaves and stems of this species and boiled them for a medicine to prevent vomiting. Wild mint was used by all the Missouri valley tribes as a carminative, being steeped in water and sweetened with sugar for a drink. Because of its aromatic flavor, it was also used as a beverage. Among the Menominees it was combined with catnip and peppermint for a pneumonia remedy, being drunk as a tea and also used as a chest poultice. The Flambeau Ojibwas brewed a tea from the entire plant for use as a blood remedy. It was also used in the sweat bath, and the Pillagers made a tea of it to break fevers. The Potawatomis used the leaves or tops for fevers and as a stimulating tea for pleurisy. Whites have used the whole plant for its bitter, pungent, antispasmodic, antirheumatic, stimulant, and anodyne properties.

Wild mint (*Mentha arvensis*, var. *canadensis* L.) has not been official, but it contains a volatile oil from which pulegone and thymol (USP 1882-1950, NF 1950–) or carvacrol have been isolated.

•

The shock experienced by plunging into cold water after the sweat bath is parallel to hydrotherapy treatments commonly used today for patients suffering from nervous tension. Therefore it was probably effective for ailments of a psychosomatic nature.

Blind Aids and Appliances

From a design standpoint, as well as a humanitarian one, this is one of the most fascinating catalogs I've seen. Pretty reasonable prices. Braille edition of the catalog is available.

—SB

American Foundation for the Blind, Inc.
15 West 16th St.
New York, N.Y. 10011

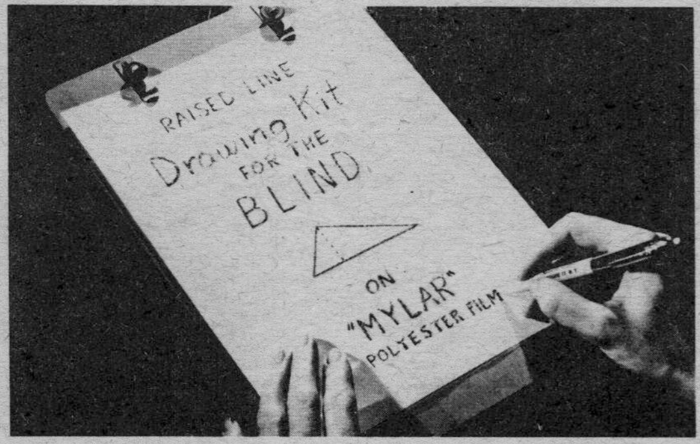

Raised Line Drawing Kit. A method whereby blind people may draw or write and feel the lines on the top surface as the lines are made. The kit comprises a rubber covered drawing board with hold-down clips for 8½" x 11" material, a ball-point pen filled with a colorless lubricant, and a package of polyester film sheets which serve as the "paper."

Heretofore, it has been necessary to turn the page over to feel the lines made with tracing wheels and the like, but with this new development, the lines can be felt on the top side of the page. The lines so made are quite easily followed by sight. (See Mathematical Aids section for description of Graph Marking Slate and Draftsman's Compass for use with kit.) **WS194—$7.10**

Polyester Film Sheets. Package of approx. 70 sheets. **WC195—$2.85**

Ball Point Pen for WS194. (Inkless) **WC196—55¢**

Braille Music. Braille music must be purchased from:

American Printing House for the Blind 1839 Frankfort Ave., Louisville, Kentucky, 40206 or Howe Press, Perkins School for the Blind, Watertown, Mass. 02172.

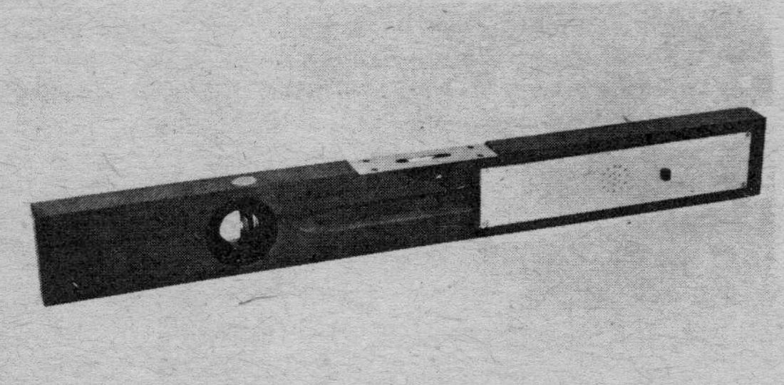

Electronic Level — AFB Model. Standard Stanley level equipped additionally with mercury bubbles to provide an audible signal. Accuracy equivalent to sight bubble. When no signal is heard, accurate horizontal or vertical measurement has been obtained. Seasoned cherry wood, 24" length. Supplied complete with 9-volt battery. (Easily obtainable replacement batteries must be bought from local supplier.)

Two types:

Horizontal measurements only. **TM325—$39.50**

Horizontal and Vertical Measurements. **TM326—$50.30**

Dig Warts

I cured my WARTS with a Swiss ARMY KNIFE. A *true* testimonial by Malaclypse the Younger of San Francisco—Plagued with Planter's Warts for over a year, and advised by the medical profession that regular medication is GENERALLY HOPELESS, I cured my WARTS with a Swiss ARMY KNIFE and voodoo. Twice a week for twelve months I cursed the warts and made them feel unwelcome. During that time, I took my stainless steel Swiss ARMY KNIFE and dug at them relentlessly. They have now more or less DISAPPEARED leaving only gaping holes and volcano-like craters on my calouses. I recommend this cure for any person with a cool hand, a knowledge of voodoo and a Swiss ARMY KNIFE. A Swiss ARMY KNIFE may be purchased at your nearest Swiss ARMY KNIFE dealer.

POEE
San Francisco, CA

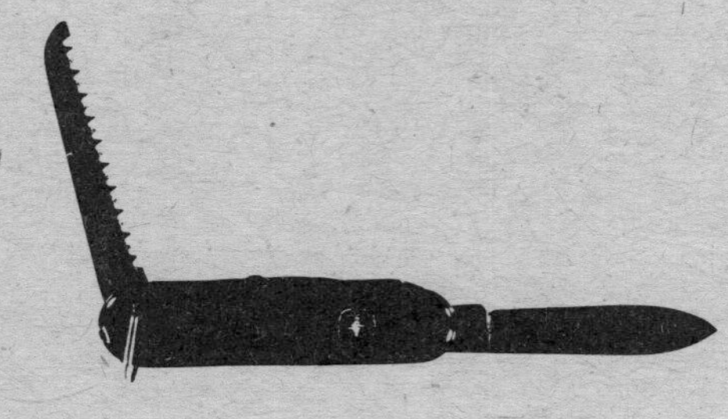

Folk Medicine

Of all the books on folk medicine that've come through our hands, this is the only one I'd trust enough to use. Seems like every other malady, Dr. Jarvis either pours honey on it or in it.

—SB

Folk Medicine
D. C. Jarvis, M. D.
1958; 192 pp.

$1.00 postpaid

from:
Fawcett World Library
67 West 44th Street
New York, N. Y. 10036

or WHOLE EARTH CATALOG

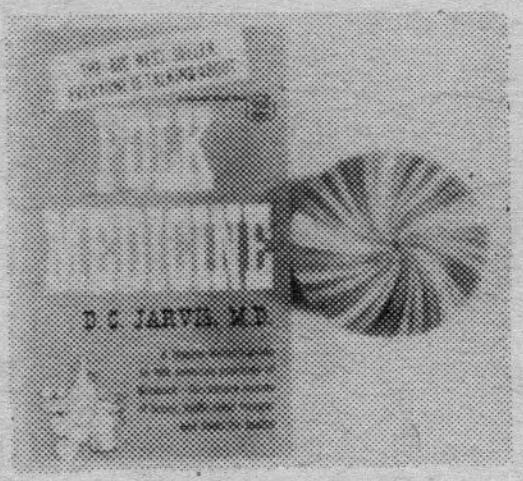

Barre, Vermont, being the largest granite-cutting center in the world, I decided to try adding granite dust which, as it comes from the dust-removing device, is fine, like flour. Granite dust contains 5 per cent of potassium, and has associated with it sixteen minerals. When I applied it to the soil around my garden plants, a number of things happened.

Among my flowers, I have 125 plants of delphinium. Each year I had been having to combat a tiny mite which caused the leaves to curl up and turn black. These harmful mites were so small that I had to use a magnifying glass in order to see them crawling on the leaves. I used a spray but it did not do away with them. When I added the granite dust to the soil around the plants, these harmful mites deserted my garden and have not returned.

•

Following the general examination, and the special examination of his nose, I gave the boy a chew of honeycomb, to learn what might happen. I wrote out directions for treatment to be followed at home and prepared drops he was to take. Before I had finished this—after about five minutes—the boy suddenly said, "My nose is open! I can breathe through it!" I gave the medicine for home use to the mother and discussed the written directions. Then I examined the boy's nose again to see what the honeycomb had accomplished.

The nose tissues had subsided, as they would have if I had used a shrinking agent in the nose. Instead of being pale, the mucous membrane was now light pink in color. One week later, at the next office visit, the boy's nose was still open and he was breathing with his mouth closed.

Wheelchairs

What do you do— and you might answer this question in your next edition— with the poor people who cannot walk and who have just enought to buy a vehicle for 100 or 200$? And who risk to be fitted into their wheelchairs like the victims of Procrustes, the figure of Greek mythology, who put his short people in long beds and long ones in short beds, stretching the legs or cutting them off accordingly.

Well, there is a good book out for those 400000 people or so, to speak only of USA. See the enclosed clipping.

Herman L. Kamenetz, M.D.
State Veterans Hospital
Rocky Hill, Connecticut

THE WHEELCHAIR BOOK: Mobility for the Disabled *by* **Herman L. Kamenetz,** *State of Connecticut Veterans Hosp., Rocky Hill.* All types of rolling chairs, stands, beds, and walkers along with the services of each are reviewed in this reference manual. Numerous illustrations with explicit legends develop an understanding of the hundreds of features of modern wheelchair design—*size, type, construction and accessories.* Contains valuable information for professionals as well as laymen. *'69, 288 pp. (6¾ x 9¾), 81 il., 8 tables, $14.75*

Charles C. Thomas, Publisher
Springfield, Illinois 62703

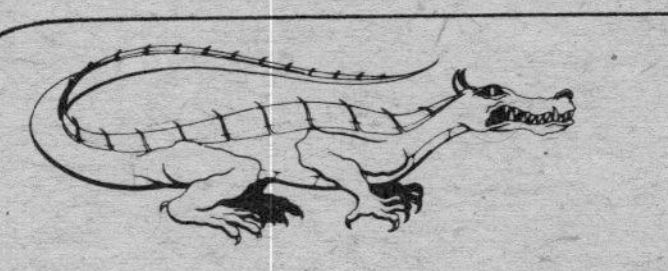

THE THIRD DEPARTURE

After God hung up D.R. sat a few minutes listening to the dial tone. But then he put the receiver down and went about getting ready to go. There wasn't much to do, actually, except put his clothes on, and leave a note on the desk for Marcella. Someone had left four dollars and some change in an ashtray on the desk. D.R. took it, and added a P.S. to his note explaining that he had. He made himself a smoked-ham sandwich, put some apples and oranges in a sack and took them out to the bus. Urge was in the worst mess he had ever been in, but mechanically he was all set to go. Half an hour after the call from God, Divine Right backed out of his sister's drive way and set out down Clark Creek for Kentucky.

Blessed Event at Cabin

THE FARM JOURNAL AND BABBS JUICE
Friday June 13, 1969 Weather: Cloudy with chance of clearing

BLESSED EVENT AT CABIN !!!!
NADINE AND PAGE PRODUCE !!!
INTREPID REPORTER ON HAND

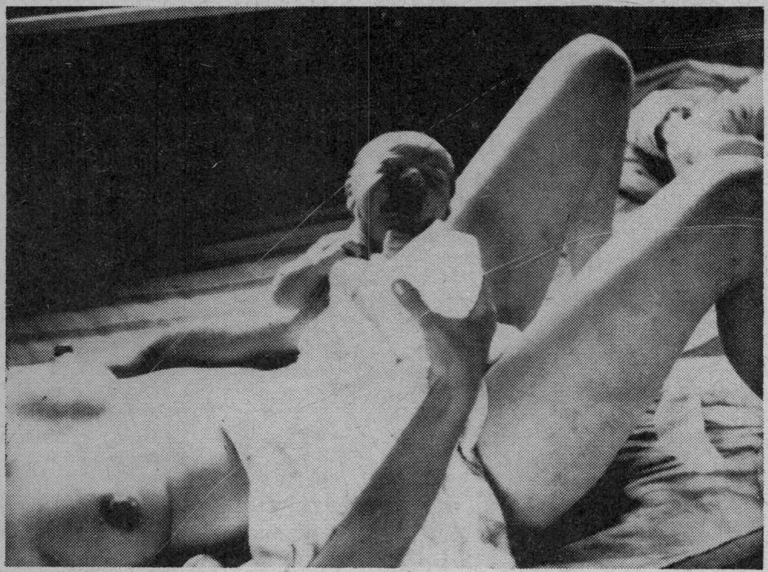

Daughter born to joyous couple sits up for pic.

HOSANNA AND HURRAH FROM THE HIGHEST TO THE LOW ON A SUCCESSFUL BIRTH

At eleven minutes before eight this morning, Nadine gave birth to a fine healthy pink skinned daughter.

Page had stepped out of the cabin for a moment.

Contractions were steady and fierce, but with Nadine directing the energy, the baby moved swiftly down the birth canal, through the cervix, and appeared at the "door."

Babbs, on hand for the occasion, broke the membrane with his finger, allowing the juices to flow freely and the head to push through.

By this time Page had reappeared.

In fact he was there for the whole thing, Nadine having the presence of mind to send Bukovich looking.

"Piped right up, didn't he," said the proud father.

"Yep." squalled like a baby.

Cassie assisted with back rubs, wet cotton balls to the lips, and solid reassurance.

Gretch provided swabs, blankets, tie ties for the cord, scissors, and kotex from Nadine's well prepared stash.

At a finely timed moment, Buko came back with hot tea for all participants.

At press time the Farmsters are gathering around the breakfast table, the afterbirth blazing merrily in the fire-place on the patio.

"That don't give up easily." says Page.

"Emergency, Says Craig. This cups broken."

Scary Event Almost at Home

I love every one of you, but I must reluctantly beg to join those who plead for less do-it-yourself midwifery unless— and this is a HUGE unless— you have a hip doctor on instant, around-the-clock ambulance call, and a girl in attendance who has been through a practical-nursing course and can (AND WILL!) put her foot down if she sees any signs of trouble.

Take me, for instance. No one could have imagined I'd get into any trouble. I'd had two babies as easy as spitting. I thought I was a perfect risk for home delivery, but my nasty old spoilsport doctor talked me out of it. "Yeah," I thought, "She wants those high hospital fees."

Nevertheless, I went into the hospital. Grousing to the last minute about all that narsty red tape and inhibition of a woman's simplest function. Who, me, have trouble? Why, I dropped babies as easy as a Chinese peasant woman. And so on, and so forth, far into the night. And farther into the night. And farther yet into the— hey, damn it, that baby should have been here a long time ago and I was beginning to feel rottener than I (a prime natural-childbirth candidate with two births behind me) should EVER have felt.

Medication— I still felt worse. X-rays; no, not twins, just one blockbuster. Anesthesia— not enough to put me out but enough to stop the screaming (and baby, I'm NOT a coward, I didn't utter yell one when I had a dislocated knee reduced without anesthesia since I can't take demerol.) To late for a Caesarean. More anesthesia. And far into the night, with my husband's face whiter than I ever saw it, the doctor dripping with sweat, and finally a "blue baby", eleven pounds, bruised and scratched and one shoulder fractured in spite of the best O.B. in Berkeley. Ten minutes of straight oxygen to bring her round, forty stitches or so and (I think) a pint or two of blood in me. (I lay there and counted the damn stitches while they put them in. You can feel them even if they don't really hurt.)

Just immagine doing that in your commune?

Yeah. One woman screaming her head off for eight or nine hours. (As I say; I didn't even moan for No. 1 and No. 2). One dead— very dead— baby, probably, at the end of it, since only incredible skill revived this one. Probably one very dead, bled-out woman, too. Six or eight nervous amateur midwives. . .all of whom would have two invonvenient corpses on their hands, and be charged with being accessories before, during and after the fact of

a) gross negligence
b) practicing medicine without a license
c) maybe even manslaughter.

Oh, brother, would you ever have your troubles. Not to speak of me and my baby— although our troubles might be strictly between us and the Keepers of the Gate to the next world!

I wonder how often it's happened that a bungled childbirth has destroyed a workable commune? Once would be too often.

So have your babies at home if you must, but for the love of God, send the girl to the local clinic for (1) prenatal care— the doctor will warn her if she's likely to have trouble. And even then it may come unexpectedly, as in my case, since I had NOT been so warned.

Send her STRAIGHT TO A HOSPITAL if she (1) bleeds, (2) has a history of swollen ankles or any signs of toxemia impending as in the Merck Manual, or (3) if her first baby has been over seven pounds or if there is more than six or eight ounces increase between her first and second babies; that means the third may be enormous. *This happens in pre-diabetic women who have no other symptoms. And finally (4) keep a telephone line open* all the time she is in labor, *so that if she manifests any trouble you can get hold of a doctor within minutes, preferably an ambulance.*

One birth in ten shows complications; one baby IN FOUR shows a birth defect— which can be aggravated if birth is hard or prolonged. Unattended births show the most serious oxygen starvation/anoxia-brain-injury which leads to mental retardation. And three births in a hundred are so complicated that without EXPERT medical help you may have a death on your hands, without warning. Don't say "It can't happen to you." I said it couldn't happen to me— but if I'd stuck to it and fled to the hills to escape that dehumanizing hospital I'd be dead, or at best seriously damaged with a dead child, or brain-injured baby to raise. Have you ever seen a badly brain-injured child? Visit your local hospital for the feeble-minded some day. Most so-called "idiots" and "imbeciles" are victims of brain injury.

I dislike many, many of the fruits of civilization. But modern obstetrics is one I'd sooner not dispense with.

Sure, having a baby is natural. So is dying in childbirth. Look in any medieval graveyard. Most men went through a few wives that way.

Love to you all,

Marion Zimmer Bradley (Breen)
Staten Island, New York

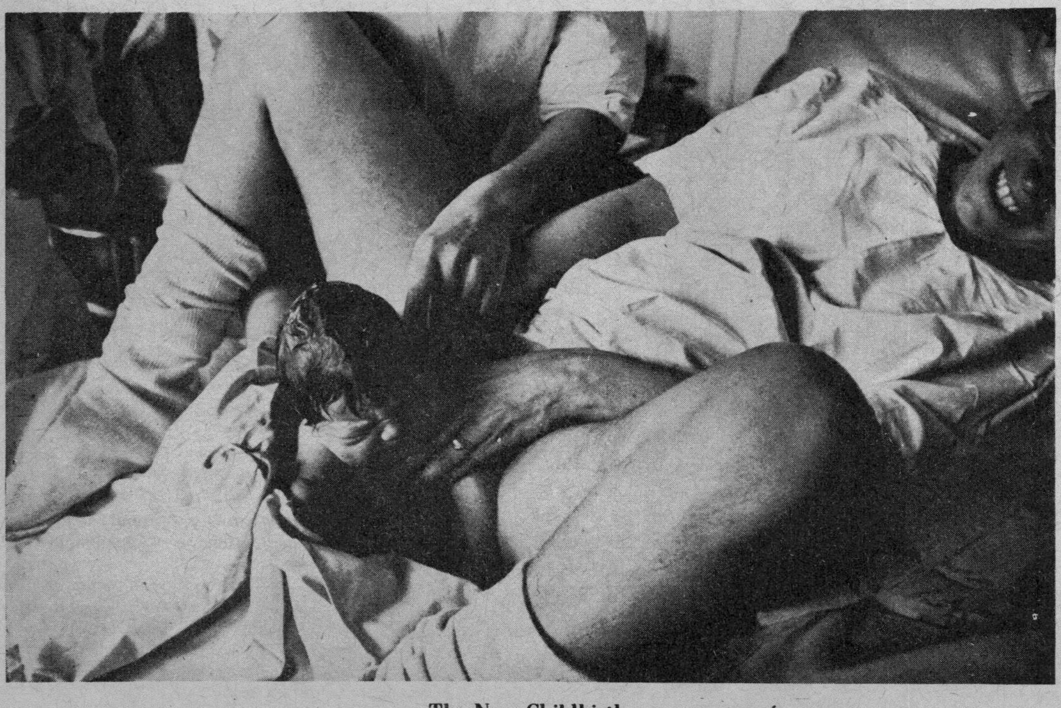

Birth at Home: The Precise Considerations

Many situations in medicine involve attempts to balance the costs and benefits of one possible course of action or inaction against the costs and benefits of another possibility, and to choose the alternative with the lowest cost/benefit ratio. Unfortunately medicine has often ignored psychosocial benefits to the patient and over-emphasized personal benefits and convenience to the doctor. Child-bearing is one such situation: the psychic benefits to the whole family of being present at the birth of a new child has largely been ignored, while the convenience to nurses, anesthetists and doctors has been over-emphasized. One result of this has been the "backlash" of interest in home deliveries, usually without the doctors approval, much less with his help. Without attempting to assess the psychic value or reduced economic cost of home deliveries, I would like to clarify some of the risk variables involved.

In the best of situations, it can be expected that about 3 to 4% of deliveries will result in either a stillbirth or a child who dies during the first week of life. This figure can result in optimism—over 95% of women will have few problems—or pessimism—nearly one in twenty women will have prenatal death *no matter how good their care.*

Because of this situation, such generalized statistics are worthless to the woman thinking of having her baby at home. Adding to the confusion is the knowledge that British and Dutch women routinely have their babies at home with apparent success judging by their lower overall infant mortality than ours. Their success however is dependent on the statistical knowledge of which situations are likely to be complicated—necessitating hospitalization and specialist care—and which are very likely to be uncomplicated—necessitating only routine measures available to a midwife in the home.

Steward Clifford, a leading expert on high-risk pregnancy, states: "it should be emphasized that in every case the identification of the high risk patient should be possible at the initial examination and at various times in the prenatal course and before labor and delivery." What are these risk factors and how can they be recognized?

First there are demographic factors. Women over forty or first pregnancies over 35 are more risky than average. Low education levels and low income are also high risk factors, even when good medical care is obtained.

Next is prior obstetric history: first births are higher risks as are fourth or greater. Infant mortality is high for patients with a previous abortion or ectopic (out of the womb) pregnancy; it is even higher if there is a history of previous premature births (weighing less than 5½lbs.),and higher still for those women with a previous history of stillbirths or neonatal deaths. A history of a large baby (greater than nine pounds) or a baby requiring transfusion is also a danger signal. Prior high blood pressure, marked swelling of hands and ankles, or protein in the urine during a previous pregnancy are further cautions.

Any woman with heart disease, diabetes (or a strong family history of diabetes) or any kidney disease should be followed closely by a doctor throughout pregnancy and delivery.

During the pregnancy there are also warning signs which preclude home delivery. Without attempting to explain the disease entities involved, suffice it to say that any vaginal bleeding after the first month of pregnancy (except very slight spotting or "show" at the beginning of labor) or any report of high blood pressure is sufficient to necessitate specialist care.

As delivery approaches there are more clues, including rupture of the bag of waters before the onset of vigorous labor; labor beginning before the thirty-eighth or after the forty-second week of pregnancy (counting from the first day of the last menstrual period). If nothing has gone wrong up to the onset of labor, but labor has progressed for eight hours without births being immanent, this is another indication to rush to the hospital.

In summary, if you are between twenty and thirty years of age, a high school graduate with a fair income and good nutrition, with one or two but not more than three previous uncomplicated births, and no medical problems, you might begin to consider home delivery as an acceptable risk. Your first step toward success is to have adequate prenatal care (mortality is much higher for women without prenatal care, mainly because of avoidable complications) beginning no later than the third month of pregnancy. You will still not be completely safe from unexpected complications, but you will have reduced the risk to proportions where the benefits to you and your family from home delivery may—for some families—be great enough to make these risks acceptable. But to fail to reduce the risks through prenatal care or to ignore any danger signal is to not only invite disaster, but also to bear the responsibility of knowing you didn't do all you could to avoid the disaster.

Bruce Ferguson, M.D.

The New Childbirth
Erna Wright
1964, . . . 1968; 246 pp.
$1.50 plus $.25

from:
Pocket Books
One West 39th St.
New York, N.Y. 10018

Commonsense Childbirth

Mrs. Hazell writes from the personal experience of having had one child under anaesthesia, another using La Maze method, and a third at home. The book covers pregnancy, birth, and care of the newborn. It is gently positive about husband-coaching and breastfeeding. There's a good chapter on home deliveries. It's written by an intelligent woman, and it doesn't needlessly complicate what is really a very simple method of controlled breathing and relaxation.

[Reviewed by Pam Smith. Suggested by Judith Bass]

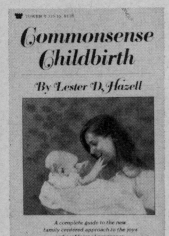

Commonsense Childbirth
Lester Dessez Hazell
1969; 243pp.

OUT OF PRINT

from:
Tower Publications
185 Madison Avenue
New York, New York 10016

or WHOLE EARTH CATALOG

My own point of view on home delivery is influenced by the fact that all my experience with it has been positive. Babies born at home seem better to me in every respect, and my students who have had both home and hospital deliveries prefer home. These babies are born crying and healthy, and with their mothers they continue in the pattern of life they have been living the last nine months.

What a mother eats has a profound effect on the outcome of her pregnancy and on her baby's start in life. A number of very convincing studies tie complications of pregnancy to a poor-quality diet. Not only do many minor annoyances of pregnancy vanish when ample amounts of necessary elements are added to the diet, but the baby is basically affected as well. One study found that 94 percent of babies born to mothers whose diet was excellent were perfect specimens, whereas 92 percent of babies whose mothers' diets were inadequate in as little as one element were defective in some way. It has been my observation that the women who feel on top of the world are usually the ones who take good food seriously and concentrate on eating types of food that contain the raw material with which to maintain health and manufacture a healthy baby. . . .

You certainly don't have to become a nutrition expert, however, to provide yourself with high-quality food. The trick is to keep your eye on how much protein you eat and at the same time to see that you get something every day from each of the four major food groups: 1) meat-egg; 2) milk-cheese; 3) vegetable-fruit; 4) bread-cereal. If we want to use a mnemonic device, we can call this the P-4 plan: Eat lots of protein in each of the basic four every day.

●

As soon as the bearing-down reflex is established, second stage is begun. For the next few contractions you push your baby down two steps, and he slides back one. This can be discouraging if you don't realize that this is the normal pattern of labor. However, when you stop to think about it, this makes good sense. In this way your passages are dilated gently and slowly by the plunger action of the baby, the baby has fluid squeezed from his lungs, his skin is stimulated preparatory to his existence in a world that will be constantly touching him, and then during the interval between contractions everyone rests.

What does the bearing-down reflex feel like? Everyone has experienced this to some degree. It is very like the pushing of a bowel movement, only more sustained and more demanding. It is far easier *not* to push when one is having a bowel movement than when one is having a baby. However, the second-stage contractions are not, as a rule, painful. In fact, they are very satisfying. You may be surprised at the noises you make. So may your family.

●

The first milk that flows is the high-protein, nonfat type. This fairly gushes into the baby's mouth. Later when the flow is slower comes the cream. The cream sticks to the baby's ribs because it digests more slowly than the nonfat milk. It is also more filling. So it is providential that while the baby is nursing vigorously in the first flush of hunger, he does not get his high-calorie dessert. Entrée before ice cream is a habit formed early!

Thus a baby knows best how to regulate how long he should nurse. He does this according to the needs of his stomach as well as for the joy of cuddling with his mother.

The let-down of the milk is a conditioned reflex. In the early days of nursing the milk flows frequently at only the thought of the baby or even the cry of someone else's baby. Later this becomes conditioned to the particular baby's sucking. Hence the working mother can go all day long and not feed her baby, and her breasts will remain flat and comfortable. As soon as her baby takes a few sucks, the milk flows in any quantity he needs.

●

We know that gross brain damage rises in direct proportion to the amount of analgesic medication given to the mother during her labor. The baby of an anesthetized and dopey mother will have been subjected to the same or greater degree (relative to body size) of anesthesia and dopiness at a time when he needs to breathe well and when his circulation should be operating at peak efficiency.

Yet the educated laboring woman finds that at every turn she must defend her position that she doesn't need analgesic medication as one attendant after another presses her to accept such nostrums. She may even have to apologize for not wanting to take medicine which she knows could jeopardize her baby.

Preparation for Childbirth

This is a thoroughly practical handbook. The suggestions if followed for carrying, climbing, lifting, breathing, and conscious relaxation are sound suggestions for the pregnant woman or anyone, for that matter. One chart on the Relief of Common Discomforts that May Occur During Pregnancy matches a discomfort with an exercise or position to alleviate it. The book does not advocate "Natural Childbirth" but rather suggests that each person is individual in his need for anesthetics; its aim (by use of many illustrations) is to make pregnancy, childbearing, and post partum as comfortable as possible.

[Reviewed by Jane Stallings. Suggested by Haru Bekker]

Preparation for Childbirth
1963, 1969; 47 pp.

$1.00

from:
Maternity Center
Association
48 East 92nd St.
New York, N.Y.
10028

ONSET OF LABOR
You may notice any one or a combination of:
    Regular contractions felt as back-
    ache, pelvic pressure, gas,
    menstrual cramp, etc.)
    Show
    Rupture of membranes
	Check signs; time contractions.
	Call doctor and report.
	If daytime continue usual light activity
	    activity,
	If night, rest.

EARLY FIRST STAGE
Cervix effacing, dilation beginning
Contractions become strong enough
    that you feel need to do something.
Dilation continuing; contractions
    becoming somewhat closer
    and stronger
 	
If contractions are causing backache
	When contractions start, breathe out
	    and relax. Continue slow deep
	    breathing through contraction.
	Try sitting positions (9).
	In between contractions rest, read,
	    watch TV, etc.
	Go to hospital as doctor directs.
	Relax as much as possible in
	    sitting or lying positions during
	    travel and admitting procedures.
	Lie on side, breathe deeply and slowly
	    while rocking pelvis very gently
	    throughout contraction (11).

Childbirth Education

ICEA is engaged in furthering the cause of family-centered maternity and infant-care and believes in closer roles for the father during childbirth and periods before and after, breast-feeding, the La Maze natural childbirth method, and generally, further education about childbirth for all concerned. They answer specific questions about childbirth, help organize classes, and "make available through the ICEA Supplies Center significant information on all aspects of childbirth education and family-centered maternity and infant care."

—Hal Hershey

Information

from:
International Childbirth Education Association
P.O. Box 5852
Milwaukee, Wisconsin

Catalog

free Booklist

from:
International Childbirth Education Association
Supplies Center
1414 N.W. 85th St.
Seattle, WA 98117

Happy Baby Food Grinder

When it comes to tools for child-rearing, this item is second only to the human breast in solving feeding problems. Better than a blender, it can easily be carried wherever parents go, to grind table foods up to proper consistency for small infants through toddlers.

[Suggested and reviewed by Mrs. Ruth Rutherford]

$6.20 First Class Mail
$6.45 Each Airmail
Happy Baby Food Grinder
$5.45 postpaid

from:
Dolly Lundberg
4036 Waterhouse Road
Oakland, CA 94602

from:
Bowland Jacobs Mfg. Co.
9 Oakdale Ave.
Spring Valley, Ill. 61362

Happy East Coast Babies

I have information regarding another supplier of the *Happy Baby Food Grinder.* It would be beneficial to East Coast readers. It is as follows:,

Bowland-Jacobs Manufacturing Co.
9 Oakdale Road
Spring Valley, Illinois 61362

Mrs. William E. Kelley
Hoosick Falls, N.Y.

Maternity Comfort Cushion

Pregnant ladies can't lie on their bellies because there's no place to put the bulges. With this cushion there is. It's well designed, and the ladies say it makes a big difference.
—SB

Maternity Comfort Cushion
Molded polyurethane cushion with brushed nylon cover

$10.00 plus $1.00 postage
from:
Maternity Products Division
Ellsworth Laboratories
Stanford P.O. Box 6101
Palo Alto, CA 94305

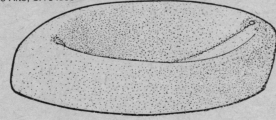

After the baby comes, "sore bottom syndrome" relieved by sitting on the cushion

Before nursing, distended breasts relieved with cushion crosswise under the breasts

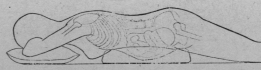

Thorax and pelvis rest on tapered ends of cushion.

PART FIVE

ACROSS THE BRIDGE

There goes D.R. Davenport, David Ray some folks call him, across the bridge into Kentucky, flipping the dial through Bill Monroe and his Bluegrass Boys to the Reverend Archie Turner saying Jesus on the main-line, tell him what you need, everybody here loves Jesus say amen. D.R. said amen and roared on across the bluegrass toward the range of hills that stretched across the windshield like the jagged spine of some old dinosaur.

Tits for Tots

I'd like to see La Leche League added to the Catalog, right in there with Dr. Spock. The League is a non-profit organization of nursing mothers, whose purpose is to encourage and counsel other women who want to breast-feed their babies. They feel that nursing a baby is an art, best learned from someone who has done it. Most women these days find their doctors, hospitals, relatives, and friends and terrifically bottle-oriented and the League can really be a help in standing up against them.

They publish a "manual," THE WOMANLY ART OF BREASTFEEDING ($3.00 paperback, $4.00 hardcover), a cookbook, MOTHER'S IN THE KITCHEN ($4.00), and the bimonthly LA LECHE LEAGUE NEWS ($2.75 a year), all available from:

La Leche
League International, 9616 Minneapolis Ave., Franklin Park, IL. 60131

Local League groups in most parts of the USA and in some other countries meet to talk over the advantages and the problems of breastfeeding and to trade experiences. The central office can tell you where the nearest group is or can tell you how to start your own; they'll give you telephone numbers of League mothers to call for help.

I'd add from my own experience that nursing a baby is a great trip and that the League, though its composition varies from place to place, usually attracts interesting women whose concern is for PEOPLE more than things or images.

Christine Mulford

The Womanly Art of Breastfeeding

Want to nurse your baby? **The Womanly Art of Breastfeeding** *prepared by the La Leche League offers a complete guide of "how to", as well as a philosophical treatise on "why to".*

Chapters include suggestions on how to prepare the breasts, how to get reluctant hospitals to cooperate with breastfeeding, how father can help, and weaning processes. In our opinion the book represents the most complete and useful information available concerning breastfeeding.

[Reviewed by Jane Stallings. Suggested by Christine Mulford]

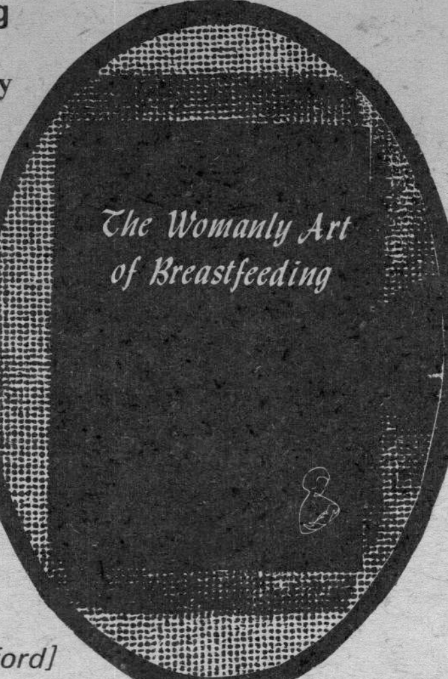

The Womanly Art of Breastfeeding
1958, 1963; 166 pp.

$3.00 postpaid from:

La Leche League International
9616 Minneapolis Ave.
Franklin Park, IL 60131

We who nurse our babies have often been agreeably surprised to note that when the rest of the family comes down with a cold or flu, the baby remains free of it, or has only a mild case. Studies have shown that breastfeeding definitely prolongs the period of natural immunity to virus diseases. These include mumps, measles, polio, some kinds of pneumonia and other respiratory infections, and some diarrhea.

•

Many studies indicate that nursing your baby will improve your chances of avoiding breast cancer.

•

Won't Nursing Spoil the Shape of My Breasts?

On the contrary; if breastfeeding has any effect, it will be to improve your figure. The bugbear here is the fear of developing pendulous breasts. Proper support during pregnancy and the avoidance of obesity (both needed whether you plan to nurse or not) are all that is necessary to keep you in good shape.

Snugli Baby Carrier

This is the most useful baby carrier I have ever seen. It can be used with a day-old baby, because of the head support, as well as a 2 year old—but not simultaneously since to enlarge the pack tucks are taken out as the baby grows.

A Snugli provides a mother with a baby carrier that allows her to have both hands free. New mothers can attend classes, work, shop, do housework, etc. without having to find a babysitter. Needless to say babies love it. If you can't stand to live with a colicky baby, put it in this pack and fix dinner or whatever.

The Snugli is of extremely high quality (will bear several machine washings and dryings per week and teething; being stuffed in purses and being left in the rain.) It is very comfortable as long as the shoulder straps are kept tight so that the weight is not carried on the small of the back.

I recommend this as second only to diapers to prospective parents.

[Reviewed by Mary Jane Markley. Suggested by Chris Brown]

Snugli Baby Carrier

$31.95 postpaid

from:
Snugli Cottage Industries
Route 1, Box 685
Evergreen, Colorado 80439

or WHOLE EARTH CATALOG

Nursing Your Baby

Nursing Your Baby *by Karen Pryor (Harper & Row 1963— $6.95) which you really ought to list by the way, has a picture of a baby carrier fashioned from 2 yards of fabric— we took 1/2 an old sheet and tied it appropriately, and discovered that it is much more confortable than even the Peterson carrier. This at a maximum cost of $1 if you buy a 2 yard remnant. My sister with her super big little boy couldn't use a back carrier once he got over 15 lbs (quite young), until she started to use a bedspread folded African style.*

So— why don't you ask the SNUGLI reviewers to try the cloth folding (which more people could afford) and see if they don't like it as well. If they do, we have a cheaper and easier to obtain tool.

Nursing Your Baby *by Karen Pryor— In my opinion is a more complete & useful compendium of information on breastfeeding than even* The Womanly Art of Breastfeeding. The Womanly Art. . *.has a sexist bias that woman's place is in the home and who would ever want time off from her baby? Karen Pryor is more realistic. 84 hour weeks get to be a drag, particularly when they are a drastic change from an autonomous, intellectual state. She has all the same facts as The Womanly. . .an more. The book is not written in such a soap opera mystical style— Aw! just read it, and you'll know what I mean!*

This is not to put down La Leche League— they are one of the greatest single forces enabling women to succeed in breastfeeding today. If you want to breastfeed, and don't have at least 2 close friends who did for at least 6 months, you stand a better chance if you'll find your local La Leche & join. Not that breastfeeding is intrinsically difficult. It's the knownothing doctors & neighbors that make it so.

Also in paperback, $1.25
Pocket Books
1 West 39th St.
New York, N.Y. 10018

Lynne Gale
Arlington, VA.

Swedish Milk Cups

For nursing mothers, these are a real boon, especially during the first few months after birth when your breasts have not completely regulated themselves to your baby's needs.

Swedish Milk Cups are made out of strong boilable plastic and are composed of two pieces. The front part looks like a hubcap with a small air hole at the top. The back part looks like a very thin warped donut. They fit together securely and fit over the nipple inside a nursing bra. What they do is collect excess milk. That means you can sleep through the night without waking up in a pool of milk, which often happens at first when your baby gives up the middle-of-the-night feeding.

I used the extra milk for mixing with our baby's cereal, or I froze it to have on hand to leave with babysitters. I wish I had had milk cups when my milk first came in, two days after birth. I was engorged (a common occurence) with too much milk and was quite uncomfortable for three days. The milk cups press lightly on the areola (the milk duct area around the nipple), and if your breasts are too full, they alleviate the situation by squeezing extra milk out.

They are also excellent to use in the treatment of sore or infected nipples because they keep pressure off the nipples and allow air circulation. And they are good for people with flat or inverted nipples. Wear them during your last month of pregnancy.

I am now in my ninth month of nursing our baby and I still wear mine occasionally. I attribute the never ending milk supply to healthy eating and nutritional yeast. Swedish Milk Cups can be ordered from Marianne Alstrom, 34 Sunrise Ave., Mill Valley, CA 94941, 388-3660. They cost $6.25 which includes tax & postage, and are worth every penny.

Jeanie Darlington
Miranda, California

Teething Biscuits

Teething biscuits: I use Milkbone Dog Biscuits, *they are not crumbly, gooey, sugary. They are the right size and shape, and are made of mere healthful ingredients. Any other dog biscuits would probably serve as well.*

Barbara Bauer Schenker

Nūk Orthodontic Exerciser

Pacifiers are something babies love and parents worry about. Most pacifiers are made in such a way which may cause the baby's mouth to maladapt as it grows, which may result in dental problems later. The Nūk pacifier was designed by an orthodontist, originally, as a theraputic tool for correcting oral abnormalities. It is constructed so that every aspect of it has a precise function, and thus aids the proper development of a baby's mouth and teeth. In addition, it is also boil-able; it contains no goo to ooze out and concern mother; and 3rdly, the shield is shaped like a happy baby smile——no more of that "plugged" look! The Nūk Orthodontic Exerciser can be found in discount department and drug stores from 44-49 cents. It is available from the manufacturer at its standard price of 59 cents (Reliance Products Corporation, Woonsocket, Rhode Island) Item No. 530.

[Reviewed by Barbara Bauer Schenker. Suggested by Lisa Law]

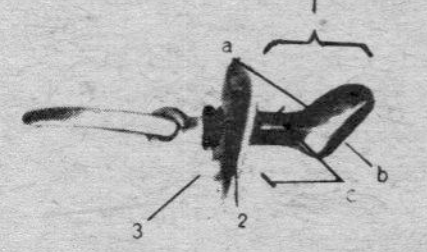

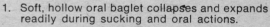

1. Soft, hollow oral baglet collapses and expands readily during sucking and oral actions.

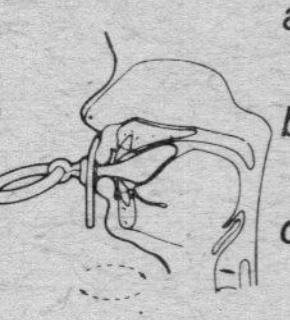

   a. *Broad, curved top (palate) side conforms to palate and arch of mouth.*
   b. *Tongue rests in proper position on bottom or concave side.*
   c. *Forward inclined planes contact upper and lower arch elements and collapse and expand during sucking.*

2. Flat passage encourages baby to close lips and helps nasal breathing.

3. Curved shield gives indirect contact with upper dental arch through firm contact with upper lip. Angled position of baglet leaves free space between lower part of shield and lower lip, thereby allowing jaw to work forward and backward.

Population Services

Here's a non-profit organization which supplies contraceptives, at low cost, by mail. Condoms and contraceptive foam are their main items, but they also have several books and publications with useful information and low prices. They have a policy of charging lower prices to young and unmarried people.

—Hal Hershey

Items: 1. We no longer have the Twentisec Pregnancy Test kit as it wasn't reliable enough. 2. We are starting up on a mail-in pregnancy test service— 2 to 4 day results depending on the mailman. 3. We had to split our non-profit and sales operation thanks to good old IRS. Sales are now through Population Planning Associates, P.O. Box 2556, WE1, Chapel Hill, North Carolina 27514. 4. We'd like to offer a ten percent reduction on all prices to all Whole Earth Catalog readers. 5. We have gotten exclusive distribution rights to two fine English condoms and now carry Naturalambs too (see enclosed blurbs). We'll be supplying a couple of more top brands soon. 6. Note our sample package——it's going good.

Peace,

Diana L. Altman
Population Services, Inc.

Information

from:
Population Services, Inc.
P.O. Box 1205
Chapel Hill, North Carolina 27514

Condoms	1 Dozen	3 Dozen	12 Dozen
Sultan, Plain Transparent	$2.45	$4.95	$14.00
Sultan, Wet Lube Opaque	$2.55	$5.25	$15.00
Koin-Pak Gold Foil Coins	$2.75	$5.50	$16.00
The Hugger Form Fit Dry	$2.75	$5.50	$16.00
The Conture Silcone Lube Formed	$3.00	$6.00	$18.00
The Trojan, The Old Favorite	$3.00	$6.00	$18.00
Foams			
EMKO Complete Foam Kit	$2.75		
EMKO Aerosol Refill (45 gm.)	$2.55		

Our Bodies, Ourselves

If anyone has any doubts left that women can really get it together, they should have a look at this book. It's written by and for women and is a masterpiece. The subject is our bodies— our relationship to them, to ourselves, to men, to each other, and to our society. It makes me feel very special but in no way unique— a warm and wonderful feeling. It's a political book in the best sense of bringing it all back home and making it clear how we got here and where we need to go. It's full of good solid information which is presented in a tone totally different from either the usual medical presentations, or the "just relax sweetie, and I'll tell you where it's at" tone of some women authors. If you don't think you have any questions about your body, you'll probably be surprised. And if you're looking for a stronger, clearer sense of yourself as a woman, you'll be satisfied. What it reminds me of most is a woman's body— intelligent, warm, soft, inviting.

[Reviewed by Diana Shugart. Suggested by Jane Pincus]

Our Bodies, Ourselves
Boston Women's Health Collective
1970; 193 pp.

$2.95 postpaid

from:
Simon & Schuster
630 Fifth Ave.
New York, N.Y. 10020

Masturbation is not something to do just when you don't have a man. It's different from, not inferior to, sex for two. It's also the first, easiest, and most convenient way to experiment with your body. It's a way to find out what feels good, with how much pressure, at what tempo, and how often. You also don't have to worry about someone else's needs or opinions of you. The more you know about your body, the easier it is to show someone else what gives you pleasure.

To masturbate you have to know something about your body, and in particular about your clitoris (klit' − o − ris). This is a small round ball of flesh located above the opening of the vagina, and it is the center of most sexual stimulation. It functions like the penis in the man. When it's rubbed up and down rhythmically, you get excited. The clitoris is where all female orgasms happen, whether by masturbation, intercourse, or fantasy.

Some women masturbate by moistening their finger (with either saliva or juice from the vagina) and rubbing it around and over the clitoris. The amount of pressure and timing seems to vary among women. Some women masturbate by crossing their legs and exerting steady and rhythmic pressure on the whole genital area. A smaller number learn by developing muscular tension through their bodies resembling the tensions developed in the motion of intercourse. Some ways of doing this is by climbing up a pole or a rope or even chinning parallel bars. Other techniques for masturbating include using a pillow instead of a hand, a stream of water, and electric vibrators. Some women find their breasts erotically sensitive, and rub them while rubbing the clitoris. It's nice sometimes to make up sexual fantasies while masturbating. Some women like to insert something in the vagina while masturbating, (like a finger or vibrator) but few women get more satisfaction out of vaginal penetration than they do from clitoral stimulation.

If you have never masturbated, don't feel you are confined to these techniques. Finding what you like to do is what it's all about.

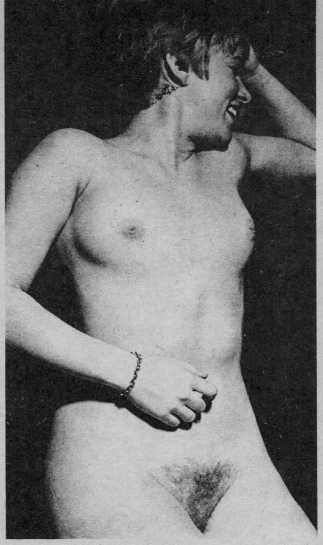

To any men who happen to read this: this pamphlet was not written for you. Please do not use it as a marriage manual; please do not "try out" the "techniques" you think have been suggested here; please do not suggest to your girl that she read it. If you do want to change your behaviour and you are living together, you might start doing half the housework. If you insist on being preoccupied with her as a sex object and want to know specifically what you can do in bed, you might try to become more open to her wants and needs. Listen to what she says, and if you can, do what she asks. In the long run you should try to change your own life, and the society, so that you can be pleased with and proud of yourself without having to exploit her. For either of the sexes to be free, both you and she must be leading worthwhile lives.

Norinyl, Ortho-Novum:

These pills are the same, just made by different companies. Norinyl contains 2 mg. norethindrone and 0.1 mg. mestranol, as does Ortho-Novum (2 mg.). The Ortho-Novum (10 mg.) contains, as the name states, 10 mg. norethindrone rather than 2 mg., and also contains 0.06 mg. mestranol rather than 0.1 mg. The pregnancy rate for both types of pills is about 0.5%. They are considered the best pills after the minipill for pregnancy prevention. Norinyl is made by Syntex Labs, Inc., Palo Alto, California, and Ortho-Novum by Ortho Pharmaceutical Corp., Raritan, New Jersey.

As these pills are androgenic, they should not be given to women with much body hair, unless those women like more hair. They produce lighter periods because they favor a thin endometrium, not very suitable for an egg to implant upon. Derived from <u>19-nor testosterone</u>.

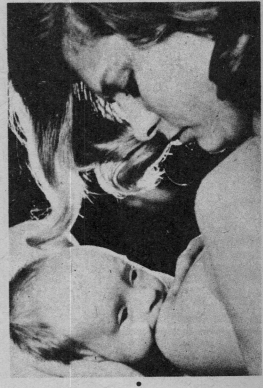

At this time our demands should include: 1) availability of life supporting mobile units to all homes; 2) doctors deliver babies at home until 3) there are enough trained midwives to take the place of doctors. We women want to have our babies in safety and in comfort. And we will not be satisfied until this is a right of all women.

A Better Pill

On the cover of our March 1969 Supplement *we printed a rumor:*

SYNTEX, DEVELOPERS OF THE PILL, HAVE DEVELOPED AN EFFECTIVE APHRODISIAC AND DON'T KNOW WHAT TO DO WITH IT.

We also printed our correspondence with Carl Djerassi of Syntex. We are even more convinced the rumor is true.

Dear Dr. Djerassi:

If inconvenience is caused by our report, I apologize. However the rumor preceded our notice of it, and identifying it as a public rumor rather than a public fact may be helpful. Any reply you care to make we are glad to publish along with the rumor and this letter.

Whether the rumor be true or false, it is maintained by desire for its truth and will probably continue until it gets what it wants: an effective aphrodisiac on the public market. The human advantages and legal disadvantages of such a drug are doubtless well-considered by you. What I would like to particularly stress, and it is the main purpose of this letter, is the public need for a double-function Pill— a combination aphrodisiac and birth control pill.

World famine versus heavy governmental controls over sex behaviour is no pleasant choice. If technology such as yours can design around the problem and encourage personal incentives to population control, there might yet be a pleasant choice. The public consequences of a cheap, legal, effective aphrodisiac would no doubt be wild and wooly, putting the psychedelic furor in the shade. But surely a revolution of pleasure-fiends is preferable to world conflict between starving populations. It's not that simple, I know, but before the Combination Pill can be realizable, some laws and attitudes are going to have to get out of its way.

Perhaps the Combination Pill could be called Make Love Not War.

Stewart Brand

Dear Mr. Brand:

I think that you have given our Syntex technology too much credit. If we have developed an effective aphrodisiac, our laboratory people have selfishly kept the whole business very quiet.

New drugs are approved for use on the basis of demonstrated relative safety and efficacy. The more serious the disease condition, the greater degree of risk is acceptable. There is nothing in the present regulatory system to accommodate the idea of the validity of drug induced pleasure, erotic or otherwise.

Your proposed oral contraceptive and aphrodisiac combination will indeed be a large pill for the FDA and the medical profession to swallow even if it has the favorable social effects you attribute to it.

Yours sincerely,
Carl Djerassi, President
Syntex Research

How to Adopt a Child

If infertility or population concerns are frustrating your desire for children around the place, adoption can be an adventurous solution. This book details what you can expect in adoption procedure, compares the adoption regulations in the various states, and lists all the U. S. adoption agencies. Roy Rogers and Dale Evans adopted a whole rainbow of kids from overseas.
—SB

In recent years, once a home is approved by the agency, placement of a child almost always follows. Further, the time necessary to determine home eligibility has been steadily decreasing. The average time necessary for a private agency to approve or disapprove a home for adoption has dropped from nine months to six months in the period 1958 to 1962. In the same period, public agency time required dropped from six months to four months.

Agencies have also grown more flexible about their age requirement in recent years. Similarly, the number of years a couple has been married is not as important as it used to be. Religion is another area where agency policy has become increasingly more flexible. Even the fact that applicants have natural or other adopted children is of declining importance. Agencies are becoming more concerned, as well they should be, with finding the proper home, one where the child can grow up in a stable and understanding environment. Of course, the adoptive parents still have to satisfy certain statutory requirements (as well as other requirements that the agency might impose), and these requirements are less susceptible to change.

To sum up, there are an increasing number of children available for adoption, and agencies are reacting to this trend by being more flexible in many critical areas.

In recent years, the number of white children adopted has been approximately ten times greater than the number of nonwhites adopted. However, nonwhite adoptions are increasing at a faster rate than white adoptions.

How to Adopt a Child
Robert A. Farmer
1967, 1968; 153 pp.

$4.95 postpaid

from:
Arco Publishing Company
219 Park Avenue South
New York, N. Y. 10003

or WHOLE EARTH CATALOG

The proper procedure for adopting a foreign orphan is by means of an authorised placement agency. Two such agencies have handled the major part of United States placements of foreign children. These are the International Social Service and the National Catholic Welfare Conference. These agencies have been able to supply foreign children to American couples in most cases for a fee of less than three hundred dollars.

BIG HILL

In the section of Kentucky where the bluegrass and the eastern mountains meet, near Berea, one of the major landmarks is Big Hill. There are several distinctive hills and knobs and rises in the vicinity, but Big Hill is the dominant land mass for several miles around. For travelers on U.S. 421, the bottom of Big Hill represents the precise dividing line between the flat lands and the branch of the Appalachian Mountains known as the Cumberland Plateau. At the bottom, the traveler headed west is entering the Kentucky bluegrass country. From the top, he faces a range of hills flowing south and east for more than a hundred miles, until they are finally broken by the broad agricultural valleys of Southwest Virginia and East Tennessee.

(continued)

Women in Communes

"In education, in marriage, in everything, disappointment is the lot of women. It shall be the business in my life to deepen this disappointment in every woman's heart until she bows down to it no longer." — Lucy Stone, 1855

The first time I picked up an ax, I felt a sense of failure. Twenty-two years of inactivity, a few isolated attempts—pretending to paint the house with water while my brother, who was only a year older than I, did the real job; or being told to do the dishes instead of mowing the lawn.

What I have learned about the ax is true of most kinds of physical work; use your head, and the ax does the work for you. I learned to hit the log first at one angle, then at another, forging a "V" into the trunk. I learned that the thicker the log, the wider the angle had to be; that the ax should come down of its own weight, guided by the hands, and that the arms and body should follow through, just as in swinging a baseball bat. The first day it was hard work—I kept missing the log, and I got tired very easily. The second day was not so bad. Now I'm no longer afraid of the ax. There are different kinds of weakness—the kind that grows in the mind, the kind that the body feels if it never has been used—and the weakness of bullshitting yourself by assuming you can't do something.

The world we live in moves so incredibly fast that it is very easy to avoid asking what we can do, and more important, what we like to do. Conditioned we are—for instance, any woman who lives in the city can pretty well write off needing to use an ax. And most white middle class women (and men) assume that such activity is beyond the scope of women's potential, calmly ignoring the trusty old pioneer women, the women in rural areas who still chop wood every day—and even the ones who live in the less affluent part of the city, who more often than not work a hard day to earn a wage that barely supports a family, then work as their own house-keepers for no pay and no recognition. The assumption that women are "weak things" is a middle class luxury. For lower class women, the opposite myth is more convenient—women are good at tedious (and physically difficult) shit work.

Certain tasks have to be done every day in nearly every living situation (although we often exaggerate addenda into the essential; furniture wax is both a luxury and a cruel oppression.), but this world never offers a us chance to "start again," with a lump of labor and a group of undifferentiated human beings, so that everyone can decide what he or she really prefers to do, and in the process become not just man or women, but human.

Something approximating such a chance occurred this summer for a small group of people living on a farm commune. There were twelve of us, give or take a few, for most of the summer, doing work which consisted of planting, weeding, pulling trees, and harvesting, as well as chopping wood, cooking over an open fire, washing clothes, and keeping the tents and the camp clean. There was no running water, which made housekeeping chores a little more difficult, and no electricity, which meant that some of the work, like washing the dinner dishes, was usually done in the dark.

Even though there was no society-dictated division of labor, even though we had complete freedom to determine the division of labor for ourselves, a well-known pattern emerged immediately. Women did most of the cooking, all of the cleaning up, and of course, the washing. They also worked in the fields all day—so that after the farm work was finished, the men could be found sitting around talking and taking naps while the women prepared supper. In addition to that, one of the women remained in camp every day in order to cook lunch—it was always a woman who did this, never a man. Of course, the women were excused from some of the tasks; for example, none of us ever drove the tractor. That was considered too complicated for a woman. We never would have had to haul wood or chop it if we hadn't wanted to.

Does this story sound exaggerated? I think it is true that even men who verbally condone the liberation of women would tend to react the same way in a similar situation, as the result of conditioning. It is true that to some extent our group was free of the dictates of society last summer—but of course we weren't free fof our cultural conditioning, which exists outside the society's institutions, and is, in fact, embodied in the individual. The men in our group were exhibiting a collective system of belief based on early training.

The women, too, had much to overcome, and we had to consciously organize ourselves to face the oppressive conditions which we were partially responsible for creating. We were a minority, and most of us were unattached; we were all between the ages of fifteen and twenty-four; all of us had thought and read, in varying degrees, about the problems which women face. We began holding private caucusses in the woods, far enough from camp so that we could feel free from any stray masculine ears. These meetings were not held in secret, though we said little about them, but they were considered a declaration of war by the men in camp, and in a sense we considered them a sign of secession from the normal order of life as pre-determined by the men, and by our own maimed outlooks.

In the meetings we discussed day to day experiences in the camp, related them to what we had gleaned from the past and the condition of women in general, and began to educate ourselves by reading and sharing general knowledge. Our strategy was a total re-orientation of our images of what we could and could not do.

One of our tactics was complete non-response to hostility on the part of the men. We had to learn to differentiate between legitimate attempts to discuss women's liberation, and sheer harassment. To the former we would willingly respond; the latter met with neutral silence. In order to forcibly shift the division of labor, we began doing other chores around dinner time. Collecting and chopping wood was an activity which was often neglected in the course of the day, so after our regular farm work, we would turn to the wood instead of the pots. We tried to discover and do things that needed to be done for the maintenance of the camp—building rather than cleaning.

If a tense situation arose, where a sister was uncertain how to react, there was usually another sister nearby, and a smile, a hand on the arm, or just the knowledge of concern, helped everyone keep calm. We felt that consistency and complete discipline in regard to our willingness to work were of utmost significance in showing the males that our intent was not to humiliate them, but to work toward a more healthy environment for everyone concerned.

Our experiment was a colossal failure. In analyzing what went wrong, it is probably unfair to place the blame on the men's inability to understand. Yet, as a woman, that is the only conclusion I can come to. a lot of dusty old myths were dragged out and shoved in our faces. . . you don't work fast enough; a man can't even get a decent meal around this place unless he cooks it for himself; before you learn to drive a tractor, learn to get the dishes clean (I don't want you fucking with *my* tractor, baby); is there something wrong with your sex life? you want to be just like a man . . .

For several weeks we lived in two separate camps. If we went gathering wood at dinner time, the men cooked—for themselves only. They washed their own dishes, but never the pots and pans that the food had come from. In the field we were a separate women's brigade—all day we worked together and talked liberation, separate from the men.

Those were happy days! Left alone, we taught ourselves, feeling free to be clumsy at first, knowing that we wouldn't laugh at each other. I think we all began to develop confidence in our ability to do things, and my own physical endurance increased tremendously—I had no reason to let a man take over, ever. I think my sisters and I learned to love and value each other as women seldom can when they are divided from each other and forced to compete for recognition by the men in their lives—forced to compete much in the same way that capitalism forces men to compete against each other. In each case, it is the best position in the pecking order that determines how people act toward each other.

The fact that half of the women involved with the farm commune project are no longer there, and that the other half are consciously compromising in order to insure the succes of the farm, is a testimony of the long fight which we all face. The inability of men to respond to our attempts to liberate ourselves seems to be an indication that now is the time to isolate, to learn, to build, and if necessary, when we have the strength, to force a change that must come if we are to be free. Cultural change, through the breaking of boundary conditions on behavior, will have to occur, and can only occur, through a conscious re-orientation of our own self-images.

By Kit Leder
Originally Published in
Women: A Journal of Liberation

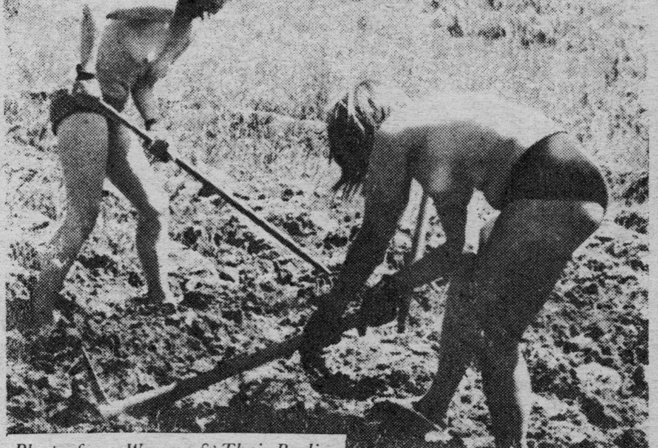

Photo from Women & Their Bodies

Diana's Rap

I successfully avoided dealing with the whole women's lib question for months. Faced with the necessity of working on these pages, I sat myself down and read Time's spread, and Life's and a bunch of other stuff. And I came to realize why I'd been avoiding it. I've been relating to all kinds of far-out movements for years, but this time, I couldn't identify. Sympathize, emphathize, yes, but the evening's reading left me feeling terribly sad and alienated from a scene that somehow should be my scene too. Nearly all the literature refers to the rare exception—the woman who has somehow "overcome" all these cultural patterns and makes her own decisions, leads her own life, does her own thing. Well, I don't at all enjoy feeling like an "exception", and I was never aware of overcoming great obstacles—male or otherwise. I've simply been leading my life and making my choices and sort of assuming everyone else was too. I have been: —a secretary, —a lab technician, —a clinical social worker, —an encounter group leader, —a wife (for one year), —a student (for six years), —a lover (-ess?), —a political activist, —a probation officer, —an editor (tress?), —paid less, always, than my male counterparts. I haven't ever been: —pregnant, —married for ten years, —a mother, —a full-time housewife, or lots of other things which I realize form some of the experience from which women's lib springs. I'll be 30 next year.

I have also never felt completely satisfied and fulfilled as a woman and as a human being. Neither has anyone else I know, and that includes men. I do remember once a woman I was working with confronting our male co-workers with a very passionate plea, "You see me as a woman, as a mother, as a little girl, as a this, as a that—I wish you'd remember I'm a HUMAN BEING!". It blew my mind, and I jumped in with my, "I feel just the opposite—you see me as a competent, talented, strong, and you forget I'M A WOMAN". Whereupon I burst into tears, having meant, of course, "I'm JUST a woman; I shouldn't HAVE to be as strong as you are; I need also to feel helpless, dependent, and weak sometimes".

Well.

I dig women's lib very much and appreciate a lot of what it's all about, and I find myself being affected by some of the thinking that's going on. I don't dig large parts of it—having spent a lot more of my life in the conventional "men's world" than in the conventional "women's world" (i.e. at home), I suspect a lot of women of over-romanticizing "the world out there". Thousands of men's jobs are at least as boring, tedious, repetitive, non-creative, and unsatisfying as housework and diapers. Nearly always there's less opportunity for physical movement during the day, for doing different things on different days, for listening to music while you work, for taking a nap, or doing a dance—in the "men's world". I have longed —get this— for the freedom of being able to regulate and choose my own schedule to some extent. For possibly having sometimes four hours to prepare a feast, when the mood strikes, instead of the hungry, post- working day quick supper. I have certainly over-romanticized the life I've never led —husband that will take care of me and deal with all that "business", babies, etc. The current sweep of women's lib inclines me a lot less toward these indulgences, and that's probably what I most appreciate. That and the theme that "this is bigger than the bot'n us" —that men suffer from their cultural roles at least as much as women do, and that the real problem lies deeper —lies, in both cases in a society and family structure which makes it very difficult for anyone to realize his full potential, or even any very close approximation.

On one level, I simply lucked out. With three sisters and no brothers and a father who is no sort of male chauvinist, I always felt there was plenty of room for me to define my own role, without a whole hell of a lot of respect for convention. I live in a commune now, with 5 men and 5 women, and we all take turns cooking. The women tend to clean up more, but the men always take out the garbage & take care of the yard. Various of us work at various times, and perhaps our strongest implicit goal is for everyone to be able to live the way they most want to, within our "family structure", and within the recognition that everyone has to do their share of the chores. The sisterhood between the 5 women is the strongest and most profound I've ever experienced—I think the same is probably true of the brotherhood of the men. I can't deny that we've all been affected by our cultural conditioning. Perhaps all I really want to say is that changes are being made, right here in river city; sympathetic male ears are available—my god, the last thing our men want is a bunch of submissive drudges around the house. Which isn't to say they aren't capable of feeling threatened by us. I experienced very peculiar feelings myself when I walked into the kitchen and saw one of my "brothers" cleaning out the refrigerator, and whistling like a lark, grinning to himself, muttering and wondering what had got into him, and really enjoying himself thoroughly. What I love most about the commune is that I feel like I can be whoever I want to be—I can wait on the men (and the women, too, for that matter) and take great pleasure in it, and I can also argue with them, be hostile, be loving, be submissive, be rebellious, do someone else's thing, do my own thing, participate in our communal vision, etc. Just like a family should be. See, the thing is, I suspect that lots women could do all these those things with their families too, if only they would. Your freedom is often, or largely, as much as you have the courage to grab for yourself. Which is to say, mine has been. And which isn't to say I can always do any, much less all, of the above. I figure I have a pretty tolerant environment, though, and it's my responsibility to get it on for myself. With a lot of help from my friends. Ok.

—Diana Shugart

SEVEN MONTHS LATER:

Wince, shudder. I wrote that six months ago, & now I want to say, "I take it all back! I didn't know what I was talking about!" I don't know very well how to describe how my head's changed around since then, but it's been a lot & in such a direction as to make me wince & shudder at what I wrote then. A lot of the women's issues are far more subtle & pervasive than I had realized, & getting into them has been an exciting & devastating experience, and still is. Becoming more aware of how we all are, indeed, oppressed, goes hand in hand with becoming more frustrated because we have so far to go. The most tolerant of environments doesn't go very far in undoing the years (centuries!) of conditioning/suffering we all carry around inside ourselves. The process of sharing & exploring with other women helps a lot. For the first time in a long time, for me, there's a kind of integration going on in my head that involves getting my own experiences together with what's happening in the world in some kind of sensible way.

A couple of books that really turned me on: Sisterhood is Powerful *edited by Robin Morgan (Vintage, $2.45), whose introduction is worth a whole book in itself. And, in a totally different line, Doris Lessing's* The Golden Notebook, *a story of two very unliberated "liberated" women.*

-Diana Shugart

Victimized

Women's Liberation convinced me with the complaint voiced by Laura: "I resent having to sleep on the wet spot in the bed, and I particularly resent being made to feel guilty about it."

—SB

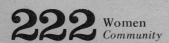

On Death and Dying

On Death and Dying establishes a psychological fact that most people close to a dying person already know, even if they can't admit it: One tends to turn away. Even from husbands, even from wives, even from one's own children. Dying people are casualties of life. Their dying, especially if it is a long, drawn-out affair, is a reminder of how vulnerable we all are, and that's something most people want to forget.

It's in our process of trying to forget that the dying person himself is often forgotten. There he is, lying there, waiting to be recognized. Doctors, nurses, friends and relatives come to "see" him every day. But what he is desperate for is recognition, and recognition is what we seem so utterly unable to give.

On Death and Dying is a powerful book, because it forces the reader into the point of view of someone dying. Suddenly you're on the other side of that glass between the living and the dying, and it's not comfortable. But, as Elisabeth Kubler-Ross points out, the point is not always to "comfort" the healthy. That tendency is a major cause of the intense psychic suffering dying people must endure, in addition to the physical failures that are killing them. This book speaks for the dying in a way they are unable to speak for themselves. It's disturbing; but then so is all education. I'd say this book is indispensable for all people who are living in the presence of someone else's gradual death.

[Reviewed by Gurney Norman]

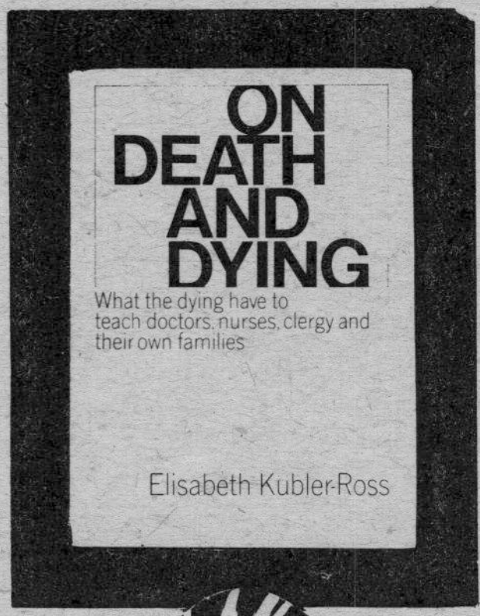

On Death and Dying
Elisabeth Kübler-Ross, M.D.
1969, 260 pp.

$1.95 postpaid

from:
Macmillan Co.
Front and Brown Streets
Riverside, Burlington County
New Jersey 08075

or WHOLE EARTH CATALOG

I remember as a child the death of a farmer. He fell from a tree and was not expected to live. He asked simply to die at home, a wish that was granted without questioning. He called his daughters into the bedroom and spoke with each one of them alone for a few minutes. He arranged his affiars quietly, though he was in great pain, and distributed his belongings and his land, none of which was to be split until his wife should follow him in death. He also asked each of his children to share in the work, duties, and tasks that he had carried on until the time of the accident. He asked his friends to visit him once more, to bid good-bye to them. Although I was a small child at the time, he did not exclude me or my siblings. We were allowed to share in the preparations of the family just as we were permitted to grieve with them until he died. When he did die, he was left at home, in his own beloved home which he had built, and among his friends and neighbors who went to take a last look at him where he lay in the midst of flowers in the place he had lived in and loved so much.

•

He was quite aware that his days were numbered, and his greatest wish was to be moved into different positions (he was paralyzed to his neck). He begged the nurse never to put the siderails up as it reminded him of being in a casket. The nurse, who was very hostile to this patient, agreed that she would leave them down at all times. This private duty nurse was very angry when she was disturbed in her reading, and she knew that he would keep quiet as long as she fulfilled this wish.

•

But I, it isn't dying alone, it's the torture that pain can give you, like you just want to tear your hair out. You don't care if you don't bathe for days because it's just so much effort, like you're becoming less a human being.

•

Everybody expected her to die soon, but day after day she remained in an unchanged condition. Her daughter was torn between sending her to a nursing home or keeping her in the hospital, where she apparently wanted to stay. Her son-in-law was angry at her for having used up their life savings and had innumerable arguments with his wife, who felt too guilty to take her out of the hospital. When I visited the old woman she looked frightened and weary. I asked her simply what she was so afraid of. She looked at me and finally expressed what she had been unable to communicate before, because she herself realized how unrealistic her fears were. She was afraid of "being eaten up alive by the worms." While I was catching my breath and tried to understand the real meaning of this statement, her daughter blurted out, "If that's what's keeping you from dying, we can burn you," by which she naturally meant that a cremation would prevent her from having any contact with earthworms. All her suppressed anger was in this statement.

Funeral and Memorial Societies

The best alternative to expensive, hastily-improvised funerals is membership in a memorial society. The Continental Association of Funeral and Memorial Societies, Inc. publishes a list of member groups in the United States and Canada. —SB

List of Member Societies

free

from:
The Continental Association of Funeral and Memorial Societies, Inc.
Suite 1100, 1828 L Street, NW
Washington, D.C. 20036

A Manual of Death Education and Simple Burial

Not everybody has an opportunity to depart this world gracefully, and those that do usually blow it. The people left behind fumble just as badly, for largely the same reasons: ignorance, fear, a lack of foresight and preparation. None but the dead can know for sure the full consequences of the failure. But even if there are no consequences for the dead, there are enough of them for the survivors in the forms of trauma and ruptured bank accounts, to make this Manual of Simple Burial seem something like a life-saver.

For this little manual of death is firmly on the side of life. As part of the literature of funerals, it's like a living rosebud in a bouquet of plastic flowers. In 64 pages it quietly tells you how to avoid the ghastly system of converting human left-overs into products packaged as "funerals." In simple language backed by intelligent sympathy, it suggests ways to surround the act of passage with appropriate rites of passage that offer real meaning to people in need of meaning.

According to the manual, the main alternative to expensive, hastily-improvised funerals is membership in a memorial society. A memorial society is "a voluntary group of people who have joined together to obtain dignity, simplicity and economy in funeral arrangements through advance planning." The manual provides a list of several societies by name and address. It also has information on cremation, autopsies, eye-banks, bequethal of bodies, and the business and legal matters that usually attend a death, as well as chapters with titles like "Interpreting Death To A Child," and "What to Do When Death Occurs."

Men choose their horrors. We choose war. We choose pollution. And, by default, we choose to make the rituals surrounding death grotesque. But what is chosen can be unchosen, once an alternative is clear. The Manual of Simple Burial describes a clear alternative to one of our chosen horrors.

[Reviewed by Gurney Norman]

You can only love life when you can love death—
The fear of death is the prime motivating force in this country at this moment.

Baba Ram Dass 1970

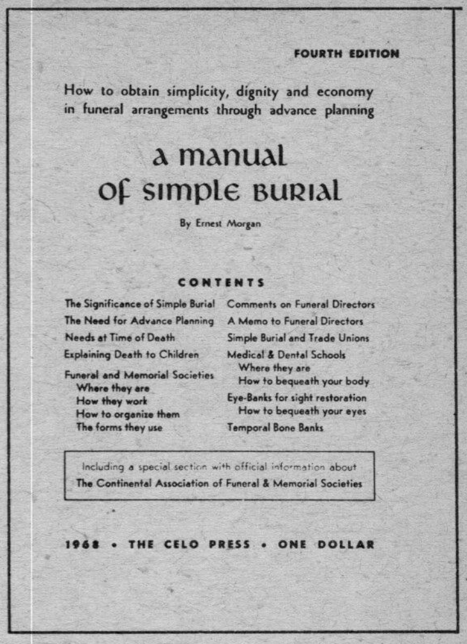
FOURTH EDITION

How to obtain simplicity, dignity and economy in funeral arrangements through advance planning

a manual of simple burial

By Ernest Morgan

CONTENTS

The Significance of Simple Burial
The Need for Advance Planning
Needs at Time of Death
Explaining Death to Children
Funeral and Memorial Societies
Where they are
How they work
How to organize them
The forms they use
Comments on Funeral Directors
A Memo to Funeral Directors
Simple Burial and Trade Unions
Medical & Dental Schools
Where they are
How to bequeath your body
Eye-Banks for sight restoration
How to bequeath your eyes
Temporal Bone Banks

Including a special section with official information about
The Continental Association of Funeral & Memorial Societies

1968 • THE CELO PRESS • ONE DOLLAR

A Manual of Simple Burial
Ernest Morgan
1968; 64 pp.

$1.50 postpaid

from:
The Celo Press
Burnsville, North Carolina 28714

or WHOLE EARTH CATALOG

Euthanasia and the Right to Death

In the midst of his terminal ordeal sustained by the hospital, my father wished to take matters into his own hands. He was not permitted. I can't see any way that that's right. He was robbed. The most law-abiding man I've known died in prison. The doctors there were friends of ours who did the best they could for him. I don't believe they are wrong, but something surely is. Some deep fault zone in our morality or our control of our technology. Whatever, I don't want that kind of exit for anybody I love. If you want to work out an elaborate scheme with lethal pills or midnight escapes, count me in. The law is wrong.

—SB

Euthanasia and the Right to Death
A.B. Downing, ed.
1969; 206 pp.

$2.45 postpaid

from:
Nash Publishing Co.
9255 Sunset Blvd.
Los Angeles, Calif. 90069

or WHOLE EARTH CATALOG

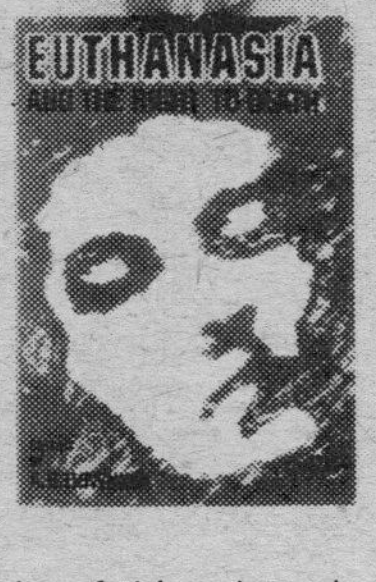

Death is both a friend and an enemy. The aim of this volume is to suggest that we have a basic human right, in certain circumstances, to decide for ourselves when it is one more than the other. When we are confronted with this fateful choice our society and our doctors must in the end allow us, suffering in life or triumphant in dying, to 'hold fast to our own discriminations'.

•

Not long ago a man came to me deeply depressed about his role, or lack of one, in his mother's death. She had been an invalid for years, requiring his constant care and attention. At last her illness reached a 'terminal' stage and she had to be taken to hospital. One Saturday after work when he arrived in her semi-private room the other patient greeted him by crying out, 'I think your mother has just passed away. See. Quick!'. His immediate reaction was relief that her suffering, and his, were now ended; so he hesitated to act on the other patient's plea to breathe into his mother's mouth in an effort to resuscitate her. Ever since, he had been troubled by a profound sense of guilt. His 'conscience' accused him. This conflict is a 'lay' version of what many doctors, if not most, feel when they forego some device that might sustain a patient's life a little longer. Some are comforted when their action, or inaction, is interpreted to them as a refusal to prolong the patient's *death*.

•

A Suggested Non-Statutory Declaration

I DECLARE AS FOLLOWS:

If I should at any time suffer from a serious physical illness or impairment thought in my case to be incurable and expected to cause me severe distress or render me incapable of rational existence, then, unless I revoke this declaration or express a wish contrary to its terms,

I REQUEST the administration of whatever quantity of drugs may be required to prevent my feeling pain or distress and, if my suffering cannot be otherwise relieved, to be kept continuously unconscious at a level where dreaming does not take place, AND I DECLINE to receive any treatment or sustenance designed to prolong my life.

I ASK sympathetically disposed doctors to acknowledge the right of a patient to request certain kinds of treatment and to decline others, and I assure them that if in any situation they think it better for me to die than to survive, I am content to endorse their judgment in advance and in full confidence that they will be acting in my interests to spare me from suffering and ignominy, and also to save my family and friends from anguish I would not want them to endure on my behalf.

SIGNED *x*

How To Avoid Probate!

It means, how to avoid lawyers, when it comes to estate, will, and all that. Life insurance is one way, the technique here is another. It's useful only if your assets are like $60,000 or more. Even if your particular situation requires a lawyer's help, he will bullshit you less and charge you less if you already know the lingo and the considerations involved. This book was a significant breakthrough in More Knowledge to the Layman, Less Privilege to the Specialist.

—SB

How to Avoid Probate!
Norman F. Dacey
1965; 362 pp.

$4.95 postpaid

from:
Crown Publishers, Inc.,
419 Park Ave. South
New York, N.Y. 10016

or WHOLE EARTH CATALOG

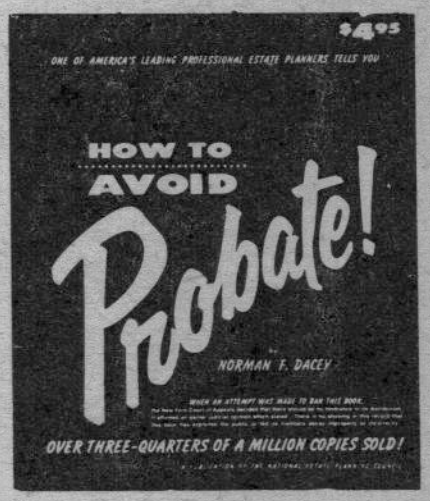

It is likely to be a long time before there is adequate probate reform in America. Don't be discouraged, though. You need not be the system's victim. There exists a magic key to probate exemption, a legal wonder drug which will give you permanent immunity from the racket.

The magic key is the inter vivos or "living" trust, a financial bridge from one generation to another. . . .Few laymen know about a living trust. Indeed, only a small proportion of attorneys know about it or understand its use. At least half of the attorneys who *do* know of it will either deny that knowledge or strongly advise against its use. The inter vivos trust, you see, is exempt from probate. Most attorneys derive a substantial proportion of their income from seeing the estates of deceased clients through probate. Seriously, now, do you expect them to tell you how to avoid probate? I would put the proportion of attorneys who know about and recommend the inter vivos trust at less than 1%.

When you set up a living trust you create it now, while you are here, not through the instrumentality of your will after you've gone. In effect, you say: "I hereby declare that I hold this property in trust for the benefit of so-and-so, I appoint John Smith as successor trustee and I direct that at my death the successor trustee shall dispose of the property as follows, etc."

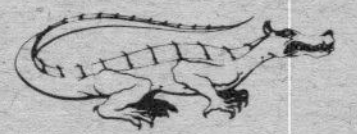

Big Hill is a special place upon the ground, and it was an important feature in the landscape of D.R.'s mind as well, because it reminded him so much of his father, and Daniel Boone. The Boone legend in Kentucky, or one version of it anyway, has it that it was from Big Hill that Boone got his first look at the lush central Kentucky plain, the fabled garden spot that had been the object of his fantasy and quest. When D.R. would ride over Big Hill with his father, his father never failed to make some reference to Boone and the Wilderness Road. D.R. had no idea how many times that might have been, but surely it was in the thousands. When his father left the coal country of Kentucky in the fifties and moved the family to Cincinnati, they came home every weekend for the next year, and almost every weekend for two years after that. And they always passed over Big Hill on their way to the homeplace up in Finley County.

(continued)

◆ The Monastic Way of Death ◆

When a monk dies here, unless it is in the middle of the night, the big bell is rung slowly for a longer period, a signal for the monks near the monastery to drop what they are doing and come pray for the Brother that he might have a good trip into eternity. Generally a large number are on hand to gather around the bed and join in the prayers. (We do the sacramental Anointing of the Sick in church for any monk getting on in years or sickly, but long before he is approaching death).

Some moments after his death, all take their leave and the Brother Infirmarian takes over. He first washes the body with care and then clothes it in a fresh habit. There is no embalming, and the only special items are that the anus is stopped up to prevent any draining, and a cloth band is wrapped around the head and under the chin to keep the mouth closed. We call the local hospital for a doctor to come out and remove the eyes for the Eye Bank, to which all the monks are subscribed, or else drive the body to the hospital if the doctor is tied up. We do not paint the face or anything like that, but simply pull his hood up over his head and fold his hands in his sleeves. If he is also a priest, he wears a stole. Then, when all is ready, the body is brought in solemn procession with the community to the monastery church. Since one of the monks is a doctor, the official declaration of his death and all the legal matters are taken care of by him and the local monk notary: the laws are quite detailed.

The body is laid out on a pallet or stretcher reserved for the purpose and is placed in the nave between the two rows of choir stalls. Then monks in turns keep watch by the body, two at a time, continuously until the burial. They watch in half-hour turns, reading the Psalms aloud to one another. The Psalms are good poetry and good prayer, and they sit well with the heart in the presence of death when you are alone with it in the deep of night. The Easter Candle is kept burning by the body as witness to our faith in the Resurrection: this is a big candle some four feet tall and as thick as your wrist. This with the large processional cross is used at all death rites. The regular Choir Services continue in the presence of the deceased monk, seven times a day, beginning at three in the morning. At such times the two by the body join the choir. The Choir Services are adapted to the event and are concerned with appropriate themes: time, eternity, death, life, resurrection.

The funeral Mass generally takes place the next morning, the Memorial Supper of the Lord. Such a Eucharist is quite filled with hope and with joy, and all eat the bread and drink the cup to faith in the life to come and in prayer for the dead Brother. After the Mass the body is sprinkled with blessed water and a thurible of smoking incense carried around it. Then the procession forms and we carry him out to the graveyard back of the monastery church.

There the Brothers have already dug a grave deep into the earth, sometimes with the help of compressed-air shovels, since there is hard clay and shale not far below. We gather around the grave and there are more prayers and readings, the grave is blessed and incensed by the Abbot. Then the Brother Infirmarian goes down into the grave by a ladder to receive the body. Meanwhile the pall-bearers have lifted the body from the pallet on the quilt mat which has three long cloth bands on each side by means of which they lower the monk into the grave. The Brother down below arranges the body, slips the quilt out so they can pull it up, pulls the monk's hood down over his face, covers him with a white sheet, and then comes up the ladder. The ladder is removed and the Abbot steps up and scatters a first handful of earth over him in the form of a cross. The pall-bearers start to fill in the grave quietly and gently, beginning at the feet. When the whole body is well covered they stop and the community leaves, after first kneeling on the earth to ask pardon for themselves and all men. A few remain to finish. Then a cross is erected over the grave and later on the name put on it.

For some weeks after his death, a cross stands at the monk's place at table in the refectory to remind all of their Brother that they may pray for him. During the days after, the monks will be praying their Psalters for him that all may be well with him in the next life.

Such a monastic funeral is very simple and beautiful. There is nothing gruesome or morbid about it, nor anything phoney or artificial. Death is recognized for what it is: the end of life on earth, and no attempt is made to hide this. The body is treated with reverence and love, but is not embalmed or falsified in any way. Nor do we use a casket or box, since the Brother is being returned to the mother which bore him and who will keep him in her depths until the last day.

Possibly the only one in the cemetery (besides an abbot who died while on a train trip) to be buried in a casket is Father Louis (Thomas Merton). He died in Bangkok and was given a military coffin and flown back to this country by the Armed Forces with other dead. Since there had been a long delay, the Abbot decided not to remove the body from the casket, no embalming having been done. The monks found the large casket in their midst somewhat incongruous, yet noted that it was perhaps fitting that the author of *The Sign of Jonas* should have been buried inside so large a fish. Father Louis was always fond of the genuine character of the monastic funeral, and we wondered that he did not in some way make it known to us that the real Jonas did not stay permanently in the belly of the whale. Other than that he had the regular monk's funeral.

Father Matthew Kelty
monk of Gethsemani
Trappist, Kentucky

—SB

The whole system of human life has been appreciated only in its ascendant aspects lately. We have entire industries— medicine, warfare— devoted to death-prevention, and a kind of pathological secrecy has surrounded the event of dying.

Dick Alpert, several years ago, proposed a Center for Birth and Dying. A place where, if you were going to die or

wanted to die, you go and do it in style, perhaps even grace. There would be whatever religious, pharmaceutical, medical aid you wanted. (If LSD has been proven to ease the departure of terminal cancer patients, why is it not in general use? What else enhances the experience of death?) The Center is also a place for natural childbirth, family supported, so that arrival and departure in this world are not estranged.

—SB

Do-It-Yourself Burial for $50

Human bodies are an organic part of The WHOLE EARTH and at death must return to nourish the ongoing stream of life. Most of the billion dollars annually which Americans pay to the undertaking industry to dispose of corpses is sheer waste, both of money and of ever decreasing living space for posterity.

Isn't there some way," I was asked by a widow," that two or three of us could dispose legally of the corpse for a few dollars? My husband's death left us badly in debt but I had to go further in debt to pay a funeral director because I didn't know what else I could do."

Contingency Planning is the essence of a Do-It-Yourself Funeral. What we need is not so much to escape the clutches of a profit-motivated business but to remove our own vulnerability by preparing to do ourselves what needs to be done. Actually in usual cases it is quite easy. Nothing very "professional" is required that any poor man or woman cannot do themselves.

If you are going to act "in place of" a funeral director you have to get prepared well ahead and take charge immediately. There is not time to learn the ropes after death occurs. One cannot just copy the writer's experience, but I can give you a close idea of what to expect. Then decide if you want to take the trouble or just pay a professional to do the work for you.

The when and where and who of death is not always very predictable. It is best to have a group plan for one's family, church, union or commune. A burial committee of 3 persons, any one of whom can take charge, can be specified in one's last instructions, just so no one is paid.

Take this example (in California):

The grandfather entered keenly into the project to set his whole family an example. When he died here is how we carried out his wishes:

1) We got out his instructions which were left handy to get at. The other grown members of the family had each completed their own set of instructions——or specified that the same ones be followed. Three of us, a son, grandson and uncle were named, any one of whom were authorized to act as his "funeral director."

2) We went immediately to our County Health Department office of Vital Statistics and obtained a Certificate of Death form, showing our authorization to do so. We had already in advance obtained a copy of the form to familiarize ourselves with the information required. We filled in the details and

3) Took it to the medical doctor who verified the facts of death to complete the technical questions. In cases requiring a coroner's action the latter would do that.

4) Then the "person acting in place of" a funeral director completed the Death Certificate and returned it to the Registrar of Vital Statistics to become a part of the state's permanent public records.

We applied for a certified copy of that Death Certificate and paid the $2 fee. For another $1 we obtained a "Permit for Disposition of Human Remains." These are needed to satisfy a hospital, possible police inquiry and to assure the receiver that he is authorized to cremate.

6) We went home and got out the six foot box which we had made long before from odd bits of plywood for $5. The cheapest wooden casket sold for $85 but why waste it? Some places do not even require a box for cremation.

7) After checking the crematory about delivery we took our box of remains there by pickup truck and handed over a check for $40, the local fee which elsewhere varies. We presented the two certificates from the County Health office and signed the authorization to cremate.

The crux of disposal is the requirement on all these forms that one must specify a legal (i.e. cemetery or columbarium) place of final interment by name and address. In practice this means another $150 or more for a plot or niche. Even strewing ashes at sea is made ridiculously complicated and costly——to discourage it. The lobby of the industry in this state has so far defeated all attempts at funeral reform which would permit relatives to keep the ashes at home or to strew them in the family garden or at a public (outside city limits) park or seashore. You may find that where you live it is perfectly legal to do this.

8) However, in this case Grandpa ordered his "funeral directors" verbally to finish his wishes as follows:

   a) fill in the name of a cemetery back in his home town to satisfy the statistical requirement.

   b) take personal custody of the ashes for delivery in a little box we made.

   c) then later scatter the ashes on the Sierra as he had privately ordered.

Most people would rather "pay the piper," even though they feel that final regulation is ridiculous and exploitative——rather than be forced to subterfuge. However, these last wishes were complied with discreetly and privately and no questions have arisen in this or other similar cases.

To complete this example I must report that two Sundays later friends and relatives gathered for a jolly memorial feast, to which all contributed, in honor of our departed. The full amount payable in "death benefits," $1000, the deceased left in a scholarship savings account for a couple of his grandchildren.

For your further study get through WHOLE EARTH CATALOG Ernest Morgan's "Manual of Simple Burial," an excellent guide to lots of other business that needs attending to at the time of a death. Also join with others who are already organized to handle death simply and with dignity. The Continental Association of Funeral and Memorial Societies at 59 East Van Buren Street, Chicago, Illinois 60605 can direct you to one of their non-profit member societies near you, to which millions of families and individuals belong. Their voluntary elected officers can help you, as they did us, to make your own family death contingency plans.

The most popular procedure up to now seems to be an arrangement with local funeral directors who co-operate with a Memorial Society in providing minimal disposal service $150 and up plus another $150 or so for a cemetery plot or columbarium niche. However, in the example given total burial costs were $48.

Anton Nelson

The death of Osceola, the Seminole January 30, 1838

About half an hour before he died, he seemed to be sensible that he was dying; and although he could not speak, he signified by signs that he wished me to send for the chiefs and for the officers of the post, whom I called in. He made signs to his wives (of whom he had two, and also two fine little children by his side), to go and bring his full dress, which he wore in time of war; which having been brought in, he rose up in his bed, which was on the floor, and put on his shirt, his leggings and moccasins— girded on his war-belt, his bullet-pouch, and powder-horn, and laid his knife by the side of him on the floor. He then called for his red paint, and his looking-glass, which was held before him, when he deliberately painted on half of his face, his neck and his throat— his wrists— the backs of hands, and the handle of his knife, red with vermillion; a custom practised when the irrevocable oath of war and destruction is taken. His knife he then placed in its sheath, under his belt; and he carefully arranged his turban on his head, and his three ostrich plumes that he was in the habit of wearing in it. Being thus prepared in full dress, he lay down a few minutes to recover strength sufficient, when he rose up as before, and with most benignant and pleasing smiles, extended his hand to me and to all of the officers and chiefs that were around him; and shook hands with us all in dead silence; and also with his wives and his little children; he made a signal for them to lower him down upon his bed, which was done, and he then slowly drew from his war-belt, his scalping-knife, which he firmly grasped in his right hand, laying it across the other, on his breast, and in a moment smiled away his last breath, without a struggle or a groan.

Catlin, *The North American Indians,*
Vo. II, p. 251n.

The Indian in America's Past,
Jack D. Forbes, $1.95 from Prentice-
Hall, Englewood Cliffs, N.J. 07632

From Newsweek

April 6, 1970

"The city person usually asks me to spare no expense in order to keep a dying relative alive," observes Dr. Robert Leachman, director of cardiology at St. Luke's Hospital in Houston. "But the rural person who has lived his life in close contact with the cycle of nature accepts death more readily as a fact of life." . . . at one Boston hospital, . . . Kastenbaum found that the terminally ill had dubbed their wing "Death Valley." the dying were kept alive with drugs till their machine ran out. In time, however, the psychologist was able to cut the use of drugs by introducing a simple humor touch: once a day, the residents of Death Valley were allowed to throw an old-fashioned beer party.

His father would say, "Right here now David's where old Boone got his first look at his new country. Stopped right over there by that mailbox, could see as far as he could see." He would grin then, and wait for David to respond. He made the joke two times every weekend, coming and going, but somehow it was always funny. David would begin to anticipate it miles before his father would say it, like a story he knew but never got tired of hearing. His father would say, "Yes sir, old Boone leaned his gun against that very mailbox yonder, and looked all around."

(continued)

How to Live on Nothing

(Our best selling book.)

This book has a lot in common with **Champagne Living On A Beer Budget** *(below), but there's enough difference between the two to make them more companion pieces than competitors. The emphasis in* **Champagne Living** *is on the cheap accumulation of necessary things.* **How to Live on Nothing** *covers some of that ground too, but its main concern is the development of personal skills to help you get free of the need to pay people like carpenters, plumbers, doctors and real estate agents to live your practical (that is to say, your "real" or "concrete") life for you.*

Of course there's no such thing as "living on nothing." The book would be more properly titled, **Living for Something.** *For in a curious, unintended, Zen sort of way, that's what this book is about: living simply to establish familiarity with the details of your world, with ordinary local mysteries and miracles such as the wiring system in your house, the fabric of the garments you wear, the truth of the food you eat, and the fuel you burn. Behind the information, the advice, the hints, and the facts, this book is about coming to see things as they are, through your own eyes, instead of the hired eyes of some expert or other. It's about training yourself to trust yourself, and trusting yourself to train yourself, until you're able to claim your right as a human to be competent with your hands.*

Finally no one is ever competent with his hands until he uses them, and flipping through how-to-do-it books can hardly be described as manual labor. So perhaps the best way to recommend a book like this is to call it literature and emphasize its inspirational value. I kind of like that idea. I've thought the same thing about the Whole Earth Catalog in general, which brings up an interesting question: if the ultimate test of a good manual is its success as art, does that mean that the ultimate test of a good novel is its uses as a manual? We'll see. Meanwhile, here's a good 95 cent how-to-do-it book that could be a help to you on your next trip, real or imagined, into the New Wilderness.

[Reviewed by Gurney Norman. Suggested by Jim Martin]

How to Live on Nothing
Joan Ranson Shortney
1961; 336 pp.

$0.95 plus $.25 handling

from:
Pocket Books
A Division of
Simon & Schuster, Inc.
630 Fifth Avenue
New York, N. Y. 10020

or WHOLE EARTH CATALOG

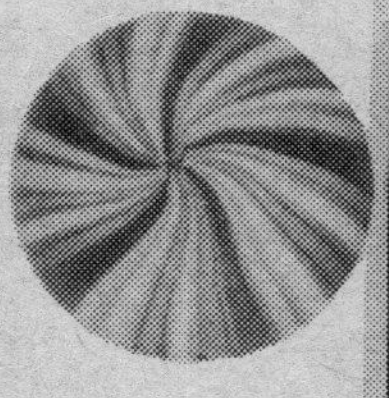

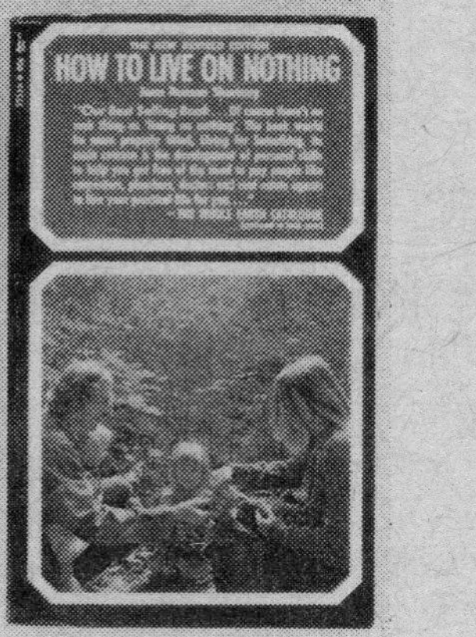

A food and nutrition chapter would not be complete without mention of a food bargain that is unknown to most of us. It is MPF, the Multi-Purpose Food, developed at the California Institute of Technology and merchandised through the Meals for Millions Foundation Incorporated, [correction: 1800 Olympic, Santa Monica, CA]. This is a non-profit organization dedicated to relieving and preventing starvation and malnutrition throughout the world. Meals for Millions supplies MPF for 3 cents a meal to famine areas.

BLACKBOARD CHALK. Leftover ends of chalk will give metals a shine when rubbed on. Also, store these ends with costume jewelry to keep it from tarnishing.

City dwellers can get many vegetables for the asking at less trouble than we who have to wander among the weeds. The grocer nowadays has a perfect passion for washing greens and wrapping them in pliofilm. If you reach his place early in the morning when he's engaged in this vitamin-robbing task, you may receive a gift of the discarded vitamin-rich outer leaves plus a stray carrot and some celery stalks. I've obtained boxfuls from a grocer in a nearby town and I use the wooden boxes for fuel while I'm preparing the greens.

CORKS. A used cork should be kept near the kitchen sink in a jigger glass or eggcup so that it is handy for scouring cutlery, etc. Used with scouring powder, it is effective and saves wear and tear on your dishcloth.

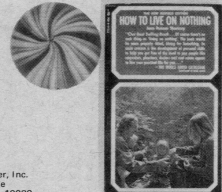

BREAKFAST WHEAT MEAL. Wash 2¼ cups (1 pound) wheat kernels. Spread on cookie sheet to dry and toast in moderate (350 degrees) oven for ½ hour. Put kernels through coffee grinder, adjusting to fine if you want meal, coarser if you want grits or groats. Makes 3 cups. Store in cool place. To make 4 small or 2 large servings and add concentrated milk values, mix ½ cup wheat meal with ½ cup dry milk solids. Mix to paste in ½ cup cold water. Add to 1½ cups boiling water with ¼ teaspoon salt. Stir over low heat 3 minutes. When smooth and thick, add a teaspoon of honey or raisins or other dried fruit or omit sweetening and serve with butter or cream as your taste dictates.

DOORKNOB. If you have no pestle for pulverizing pills and bruising seeds, mashing herbs, etc., use a doorknob in a wooden salad bowl.

If you live in the city you can usually get plenty of discarded crates for tinder, but unfortunately logs are expensive. Newspaper, however, is cheap. If you haven't enough of your own, collect your neighbors' or raid the nearest trash can. To make a log out of paper, roll the newspaper from the bottom up so that the length of the log will be no more than the width of the paper. Make a thick roll (a single Sunday edition should do it) at least 6 inches in diameter. Then fasten the roll by rolling it on the diagonal of two sheets of fully spread-out newspaper and tucking each end of this covering piece into each end of the log roll. You'll not believe this until you try it—I didn't—but this paper log burns slowly and will stretch out a scant wood supply admirably. We use these in our fireplace when it is too damp to go out for wood.

ENVELOPES, either the ones addressed to you or the ones enclosed as postage reply envelopes with ads or the ones enclosed with wedding invitations, etc., should be re-used. Open addressed envelopes carefully. Turn them inside out and reglue the seams.

Motor-driven equipment is an increasingly heavy expense as our homes become more mechanized. Most of us, however, pay for unnecessary appliance repairs through ignorance of how to avoid them. It's not necessary to try to rival the skill of a professional repairman. Simply keep him away by knowing a few rules of care and repair. Car engines aren't the only ones to suffer strain in cold weather. A hard start strains any motor. Your washing machine standing on the back porch in a temperature below 40 degrees F. must stand half a day inside in the warmth before you do the wash. If you keep your sewing machine in the cold spare room, apply the same rule. Even the motor-driven grinder out in the unheated garage needs warming before running. Vacuum-cleaner, freezer, and refrigerator motors all need warmth before starting.

Champagne Living on a Beer Budget

If your vision of an alternate life style includes a dome in the mountains, raising your own food and making your own clothes from homespun wool, you probably ought to pass this book up and wait til somebody writes **Beer Living On A Bay-Rum Budget.**

But if you are pioneering in or near a city, and if money passes through your hands with some regularity; if, that is, you consider yourself what I have come to think of as a 'suburban guerrilla,' then **Champagne Living On A Beer Budget** *would be a handy tool to have around your camp.*

(Someday, after I've lived in the suburbs longer, I'd like to write an essay about my vision of the suburban guerrilla. He's a definite phenomenon. There's a sizeable population of them here in the San Francisco Bay area, men and women out to enjoy the advantages of town life without paying the customary penalties. Every suburban guerrilla probably has his own definition of himself, but my own sense of him is this: he has a job, but not a career. He likes the comforts, but doesn't want to go into debt for them. He makes distinctions between things that are good and things that are merely expensive. He may go in for elegance, or he may dig the funky scene. Hippies, after all, are urban guerrillas. But hippies are kids mainly grooving on each other in special enclaves, and that isn't quite what I'm talking about. I'm talking about people who see the possibility of a rich and abundant adult life within the context of those same suburban communities generally condemned as such hopeless wastelands that 'real' life cannot be supported there. The suburban guerrilla I have in mind is one of the suburbs, as well as in them.

He challenges the assumption that the suburban context is hard, absolute, impenetrable, like plastic. To him, more like a piece of cheesecloth, full of holes to breathe through, and to wind in and out of, like a morning glory, or a pole bean. He borrows much of his point of view from the orientals. He realizes that life goes on in the suburbs just like every other place, even if most of the people there are too blind and deaf to see and hear it. The guerrilla lives by his wits, one day at a time. This makes him alert and alive. He has a talent for cultivating the holes in his cheesecloth. One hole might simply be the way the world is at six a.m. Another might be first-hand knowledge of all the footpaths in the neighborhood. He creates his freedom here and there and now and then, and by diligence winds up with as much as any conscious man anywhere. His landscape is small and patterned, but there are discoveries to be made on it, discoveries that can feed his own life at the same time they are important to the culture. I know of one elderly couple that subsists almost entirely on the food they raise in their organic garden in the backyard of their home in suburban Menlo Park. As far as I'm concerned, the trip those two people are on, the life they are proving possible, is the most inspiring radical activity in all of San Francisco's radical environs).

One needn't romanticize his life as much as all that, however, to find the book we're talking about a worthwhile manual. Anybody interested in bargains ought to have it. It's loaded with facts, tips and information on good deals in all the important categories. Food, clothing, shelter, real estate, automobiles, household appliances, medical things, taxation, funerals, recreation, retirement, consumer co-ops, travel, babies, insurance, charities, and more. It's entertainingly written; yet the rhetoric never gets in the way of the information. The people who wrote it obviously want to beat the money rap as much as any of us. They also want to live well. Their book will be of considerable help to other people trying to do both, simultaneously.

[Reviewed by Gurney Norman]

Champagne Living on a Beer Budget
Mike and Marilyn Ferguson
1968; 247 pp.

$1.95

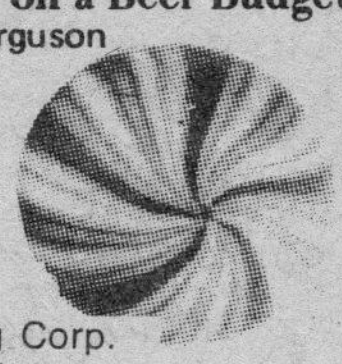

from:
Berkeley Publishing Corp.
390 Murray Hill Parkway
East Rutherford, N.J. 07073

or WHOLE EARTH CATALOG

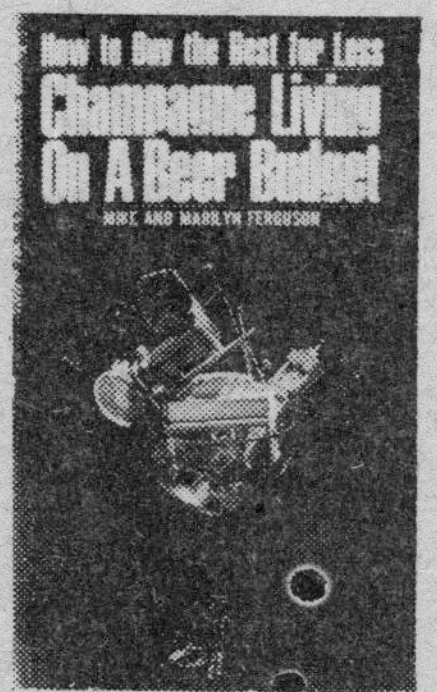

For a dollar a year, you can subscribe to Our Public Lands, a quarterly magazine telling how to buy public lands, where to hunt, fish, or camp; also details of 'Alaskan opportunities.' Order from the Superintendent of Documents, Washington, D. C. 20402

Finally we called eight establishments under Typewriters, Rental. For comparable models of a Smith-Corona electric portable, two companies wanted $25 per month; two wanted $22.50; three were asking $20; one, $15; one, $12.50. We finally rented a nearly new machine from a firm that charged $9 monthly on a two-month basis.

'Overexposed steaks' are a find for those who will literally look beyond the surface of things. The fluorescent lighting used in grocery store meat shelves darkens the steaks quite rapidly. Once a steak turns maroon, it's usually marked down by 25 percent or so—and it's fine.

Some expensive canned fruits, like Elberta peaches and fine Bartlett pears, can be bought in cans of 'chunks and pieces' for a fourth or less than you'd pay for canned halves.

Or, if you'd rather, the National Association of Housing Cooperatives, Inc., invites your query. Address: 465 Grand Street, New York City, N. Y. 10002. Latest information on new cooperative would be available from the United Housing Foundation, same address; or from the Association for Middle Income Housing, 217 Park Row, New York; or the FHC Company, 322 Main, Stamford, Conn. (FHC International, 1001 15th Street NW, Washington, D.C., is an affiliate of the FHC Company and helps develop housing cooperatives overseas.)

Homes in the paths of proposed freeways have usually been bought by the city or county and are rented on an annual lease basis until time for demolition. Friends of ours are renting a $30,000 home for $85 a month—until the bulldozers claim it. They simply called the city switchboard and asked to speak to someone about renting city-county-owned homes.

Homes being rented are often not due for demolition for eight or ten years. They're bought up far in advance of need so there won't be last-minute snags or holdouts.

Avoid the cheap $10-$17 brake jobs advertised by some service stations and shops. At the price, the linings are most likely of inferior quality, and wheel cylinders won't be rebuilt.

When it comes to air travel you can avail yourself of bargains if you'll fly major airlines on weekdays, regional airlines on weekends...fly by night...forgo the two glasses of champagne in first-class quarters...buy a 'run-of-the-airline' ticket on a regional western carrier if you live in the eastern half of the country...travel to Europe in off-seasons...fly a triangle, with a stop at an intermediate glamour city thrown in for a few dollars extra...travel a heavy-volume, frequently scheduled commuter flight...forgo reservations and fly for half fare, on a standby basis, on at least one airline...or register as a first-time airline rider on another and make any round trip in the system for $25...buy a package which wraps up hotel, entertainment, and air fare.

To locate a Memorial society in your area, or for bequeathal information, write to:

Continental Association
39 East Van Buren Street
Chicago, Ill. 60605

For $1, this nonprofit organization will send you A Manual of Simple Burial (64 pages).

For 25 cents, the Continental Association will send you Memorial Associations: What They Are and How They are Organized. The association will also be happy to inform you if any societies are newly active in your area.

Buying Wholesale

Buying wholesale is a thing lots of people can do IF it is gone about correctly. Wholesalers are interested in making a profit, as are retailers. Keep this in mind when approaching a wholesaler. Show him how he can make money by selling to you at wholesale (like, you'll go elsewhere if he doesn't). Often, a courtesy discount is given to legitimate non-profit (that means recognized by the state and Federal tax men) organizations. Courtesy discounts are usually offered only by retail establishments. They sell to you at the wholesale price and often make no money on the transaction.

Wholesalers are able to sell at lower markups and still make money by keeping down bookwork and unnecessary stock handling. That means they want to sell in quantity. So get your friends together and make up as big a list as possible. And be prepared to pay cash.

Don't expect dealer service from wholesalers. You haven't paid for it and if you ask for it, you probably won't ever be able to buy wholesale there again. Don't ask to examine everything. They can't afford to let you.

Some wholesalers will sell only to persons or firms having a resale tax license (State Board of Equalization in California). This usually requires posting a good sized bond ($50 minimum) to assure that you will pay sales tax on everything you buy. These wholesalers don't want the bookwork involved in sales tax, so they sell nothing that they will have to charge tax on.

Often, after meeting all of the above basic requirements, you still can't buy wholesale from some sources. At this point a "front" letterhead helps. Better get a city business license or DBA (Doing Business As) and stay out of trouble. These are usually free or cheap.

Buying food wholesale is more difficult, because the markup is very low. Sometimes a store will give you a special price if you buy by the case. Or buy direct from the farmer at the same price you would pay in the store. Get fresher produce and let the grower have the profit. He needs it.

Most of all, remember to show the wholesaler that he will make a profit by selling to you. That's usually all you need.

—Fred Richardson

Consumer Reports

Consumer Reports is a comfort. When the time is come to buy some goodie— color television, or a hi-fi, or a sewing machine— CU (Consumers Union) is there with the information on what's the best, or the best buy, or the healthiest of the brands available. i.e. how not to get burned (one anticipates the CU research on brand-name psychedelics). Consumer Reports *is a monthly magazine with articles on various classes of products and various cases of marketing misbehavior; the December issue is the Buying Guide— a dense compendium of all the quality/ price information, available separately for $2.65. I only wish the magazine would print ads, give the manufacturers a place to beef back, liven up the Liberal Hour.*

—SB

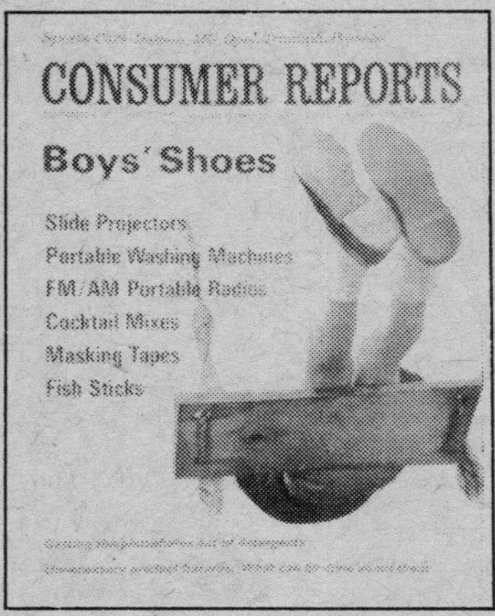
CONSUMER REPORTS
Boys' Shoes
Slide Projectors
Portable Washing Machines
FM/AM Portable Radios
Cocktail Mixes
Masking Tapes
Fish Sticks

Consumer Reports

$8.00 per year (monthly) in U.S.

$9.00 per year other countries

from:
Consumers Union
Mount Vernon, New York 10550

Consumer Reports Buying Guide

$2.65 postpaid

from:
Consumers Union
Mount Vernon, New York 10550

CU'S KEY FINDINGS

CU tested Super 8 cameras equipped with zoom lenses, automatic exposure control and, by and large, through-the-lens viewing and metering. Four earned a check-rating —the Nizo S36, the Argus Cosina 708, the Honeywell Elmo Dual Filmatic 909 and the Eumig Viennette 3. Each of the check-rated models enjoyed some distinction in addition to high overall quality. The Nizo, light and compact, was particularly comfortable to work with; the Argus provided an outstandingly wide range of zoom settings; the Honeywell could, with an optional back, take Single 8 as well as Super 8 film; and the Eumig fixed-focus camera (a Best Buy) provided optical performance comparable to the best focusing models at all but the shortest distances. The Bolex Macrozoom models also proved interesting because they can focus at extremely short distances.

CU'S KEY FINDINGS

You needn't spend a small fortune for a cartridge, or pickup, suitable for use with a high-quality stereo system. The best one we tested, the check-rated Shure V15 Type II (Improved) lists at $68 (but probably sells at closer to $50). Yet none but a perfectionist could quarrel with such a pickup as the Shure M91E, which we were able to buy at half its $50 list. And those planning a stereo system on a tight budget can buy the ADC 220XE, which should sell for under $20, or the Shure M7N21D, which lists at $18 but sells for a good deal less.

Discount Suppliers

I am just now getting around to reading back issues of the W.E.C., and have come across the letters in the July 1970 isue about "dis-unity" (page 9). Having been ripped off by Unity Buying Service a couple of years ago I would like to submit the following in hope that others might be saved the pain and financial lose.

It should be obvious that this service is a rip off. I would discourage people from using it. There are any number of more reputable and cheaper outfits. One that I have dealt with in Rochester, New York is Naum Bros., 2373 Ridge Rd. West. They operate several stores with the same type of catalogue/discount plan, without the membership or service charge. I'm not up on their mail order procedure.

I most strongly recommend another which I have come in contact with since moving to Tennessee. The name is Anderson's, 404 Bernard Ave., Greeneville, Tennessee, 37743. They have a catalogue very similar to U.B.S., and operate on the same discount procedure. There are, however, several big differences.

1. They charge no fee for membership
2. They have no handling charges. Only price + COD or postage.
3. Their prices appear to be lower. E.G., the Kodak 850 projector illustrated (pg.95 Sp 70 WEC) UBS— $144.00+ 5%; Andersons— $137.55 + nothing! CAN YOU DIG IT? !?

Anderson's belongs to a group of 35 such stores through the South-Mid West. I'm trying to get the names of the other members. One drawback is that they are very much into the Middle America/jewelry & silverplate stuff— but they have several items worth considering, especially if you are many miles from a big discount store. Also, the manager says that he will consider any requests for unlisted items (no guarantee that he can get them). They handle several limited items that they do not list, and they can get some stuff on special order.

I will personally be willing to follow up any complaints about poor service.

Harvey Williams
Greeneville, Tennessee

While I'm at it I'd like to introduce you to another friend— Jung Seed Co., Randolph, Wisconsin, 53956. They have an extremely wide variety of vegetable and flower seeds at very reasonable prices— usually 20 or 25 cents per packet. They also have prices for larger quantities (½oz. oz or pound etc), and they handle fruit and ornamental trees. Only 35 cents handling charge on orders under $10, and they pay postage on all orders (with very few exceptions— parcel post or freight charges not paid to Far West). They are very fast and cooperative. They even sent me seeds when I was in Panama and paid the Air Mail postage themselves. Not organic as far as I know.

Note their prices for fruit trees, grapes and berries are as much as ½ as much as Stark Bros.

Consumer's Research Magazine

Over the years we've found that a less well-known magazine than Consumer Reports *called* Consumers' Research Magazine *has a more ecological approach. It is published by Consumers' Research, Inc., Washington, N.J. 07882, boasts of being the original consumer's magazine and costs $8.00 for 12 issues, one of which is the 224-page October Handbook of Buying issue.*

Audrey Newcomb
Rochester, N.Y.

Moneysworth

I don't like their hard sell, nor their thinness, but they do in fact have original information on money-saving.

—SB

Moneysworth
Ralph Ginsberg, ed.

$5 /yr (biweekly)

from:
Moneysworth
251 W. 57th St.
New York, N.Y. 10019

....ROAD HOUSE: You can rent a home cheaply—if you don't mind living dangerously "Homes in the paths of proposed freeways have usually been bought by the city or county and are rented on an annual lease basis at low rates until time for demolition," say Mike and Marilyn Ferguson in their new paperback *Champagne Living on a Beer Budget* (G.P.Putnam's Sons, 75¢). "Friends of ours are renting a $35,000 house for $85 a month—until the bulldozers claim it. They simply called the city switchboard and asked for the real estate department. Some of these homes are not due for demolition for eight or ten

CALL OF THE WILD UNHEEDED: Despite increasing public interest in ecology and worsening urban pollution, jobs in wilderness management go begging. For a list of Thoreau-esque job openings, write: The Wildlife Society, 3900 Wisconsin Ave., NW, Washington 20036

Dr. R.T. Ravenholt, a State Dept. population expert, reveals to a population conference in Tokyo that the U.S. has already developed, and will soon market, a pill that enables women to induce instant abortion. The pill, based on prostglandins (which are already used to induce labor in women with overdue pregnancies), is inserted into the vagina....

The Penny Pincher's Guide

This is 50 cents worth of straight unchatty tips on beating the supermarket.

OUT OF PRINT

—SB

The Penny Pincher's Guide
Ellen Usher Durkin
1971; 96 pp.

$0.50 postpaid

from:
Bantam Books, Inc.
666 Fifth Ave.
New York, N.Y. 10019

or WHOLE EARTH CATALOG

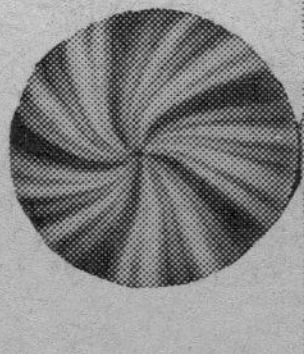

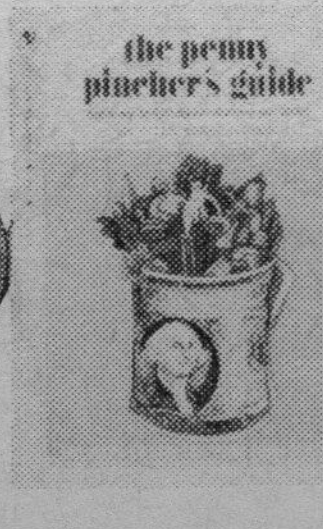
the penny pincher's guide

Cross-country, most food sales occur from Thursday to Saturday. If this is true in your area, plan to shop at the end of the week.

If you shop on Saturday, watch for reductions on foods the store doesn't want to keep over a weekend.

Shop when the selection of perishables is the freshest, usually in mid-morning.

•

Study the fine print on labels of processed food. Ingredients must be listed in descending order of quantity. This legal listing tells the true story, which product titles or handsome pictures may not. A main dish may be called "chicken with rice," but if the label lists rice before chicken, you know it's more accurately "rice with chicken."

•

Bananas may be refrigerated once they reach the brown-flecked stage of perfect ripeness. They will hold for several days, but do lose a bit of their lush flavor from refrigeration.

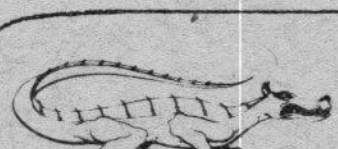

One time when Boone leaned his gun against the mailbox he found a letter in it from John L. Lewis that said DON'T COME TO KENTUCKY, BOYS, THE WORK'S TOO HARD AND THERE'S TOO DAMN LITTLE PAY' Another time there was a letter to Daniel from his brother Squire that said, "If you see a boy named David Ray Collier out in them woods, you send him home, he's too young to roam."

David said, "There was not."

"Oh yes there was too," said his father.

His father's name was Royce. Royce Collier. And in those days, before his mother's second marriage to Wallace Davenport, Collier was David Ray's last name too.

"Oh yes," said Royce. "Squire sent that very letter to Daniel Boone. You ask Doyle here if he didn't."

Doyle, the assistant driver and chief mechanic for the old Pontiac, only twenty-four then, tall and lean, fresh out of the army, sitting in the front seat beside Marcella, would nod and say that it was so, and that if David didn't believe it he could just ask Royce there. And round and round it would go, two men supporting each other's teasing lie, and sometimes it was funny and David would laugh, and sometimes they would tease too far and hurt David's feelings, and then he would sit back into the crowd of cousins in the back seat and pout the rest of the way to the homeplace.

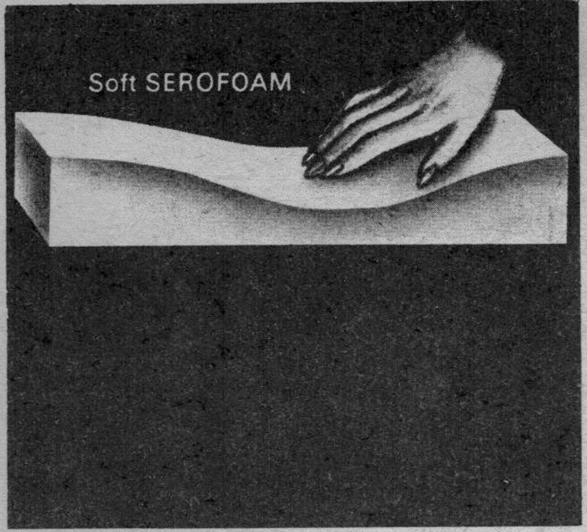

Soft SEROFOAM for relaxing comfort

Quite firm enough to keep its shape and give long service but more yielding to the figure than denser foam. Density weight, 1.25 to 1.45 lbs. per cubic foot.

Thickness	Width	Catalog Number	Shpg. wt., ft. lbs.	Shpg. wt., ft. oz.	Price per ft.
1 in.	18 in.	24 A 8892P		6	38c
2 in.	18 in.	24 A 8806P		12	66c
2 in.	36 in.	24 A 8812CP	1	8	$1.37
2 in.	54 in.	24 A 8813CP	2	4	1.99
3 in.	18 in.	24 A 8794P	1	2	99c
3 in.	36 in.	24 A 8795CP	2		1.99
3 in.	54 in.	24 A 8796CP	3		2.99
4 in.	18 in.	24 A 8797P	1	8	1.44
4 in.	36 in.	24 A 8798CP	3		2.89
4 in.	54 in.	24 A 8799CP	5	8	3.99

Pitcher-spout Hand Pump $10.50

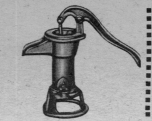

Cast-iron. Full-swing handle. Anti-freezing . . water returns to well when handle is raised. 3-in. cylinder. For 20-ft. lift. 17 in. high. 1¼-in. suction.
42 KF 2746C—Shipping weight 19 pounds $10.50

Cup Leather for Pitcher Pump. (Not shown.) Oak-tanned. Use with Lower Valve Leather (below). 3-in. cylinder, 2-in. outside diameter.
42 KF 23135—Shipping weight 1 ounce 59c

Lower Valve Leather. (Not shown.) For hand pumps and 3-inch cylinders. 3½-inch outer diameter.
42 KF 23165—Shipping weight 2 ounces 49c

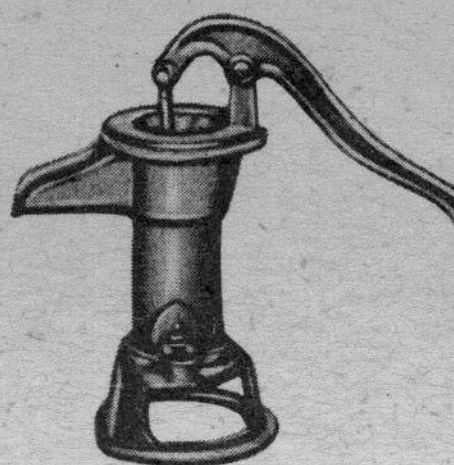

Craftsman Guarantee

It's true about Sears Craftsman tools. My Sioux brother-in-law-in-law had given me a Craftsman pocket knife that I cherished. I loaned it to Gurney, and he broke it. He took it to Sears, said "Your tool broke," and was handed a new Craftsman knife, which I still have. All right.

—SB

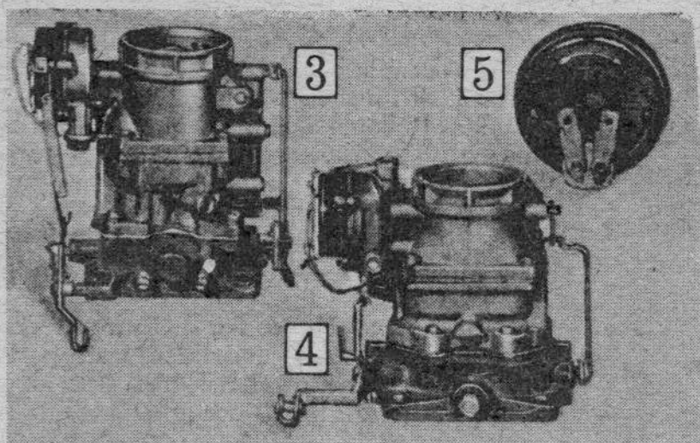

Competition Carburetors

$38.99

3 Carter "Dune Buggy Duece" Carburetors for Volkswagen. Two-barrel configuration with electric choke. For 6 or 12-volt VW engines. Mounts on manifold from Ram-induction Power Kit on facing page. For street or strip.
28 KR 4480—Shpg. wt. 9 lbs. $38.99

4 Holley Hi-Performance "Bug Spray" Carburetors for Volkswagen. Two-barrel configuration for increased power. For all 12-volt VW engines. For 6-volt engines order conversion kit below. Mounts on manifold from Ram-inductions Power Kit on facing page. For street or strip.
28 KR 4481—Shipping wt. 9 lbs. . . $38.99

5 Holley Choke Conversion Kit. Replaces 12-volt choke with 6-volt for older VW's. Bakelite® shell construction.
28 KR 4482—Shpg. wt. 8 oz. $5.99

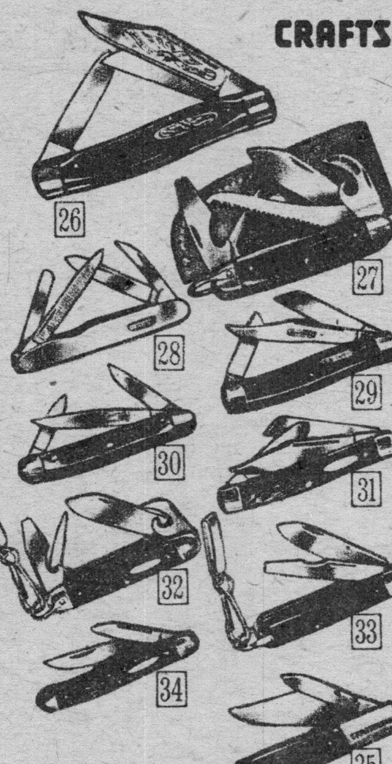

1128 CPBKM AEDSLG

CRAFTSMAN® Pocket Knives unconditionally guaranteed*

(26 thru 35) Unless stated otherwise, all these knives have high-carbon cutlery steel blades which keep their sharp edge for a long, long time . . brass-lined, unbreakable handles . . nickel-alloy bolsters. (26), (29), and (30) have DuPont Delrin® plastic handles, milled for firm grip. Length shown is with knife closed.

26 **American Eagle.** *Sears Best.* Hand crafted. 61 finishings and polishings. Nickel-alloy linings. American Eagle shield. 3 blades (long clip, sheepfoot, spay). 4 inches long. *Each knife has its own serial number.*
9 A 9500—Shpg. wt. 9 oz. $9.95

27 **Saw Knife.** Saw blade has thumb rest for fast, sure cutting—*a* CRAFTSMAN *exclusive feature.* Rust-resistant, satin-finish stainless steel blades and springs . . nickel-lined handle. 5 blades (wood-sawing, 2½-in. cutting, can opener, punch, combination screwdriver-cap lifter). 3¼ in. long. Leather sheath. Gift boxed.
9 A 9555—Shpg. wt. 11 oz. $7.95

28 **Slim Pen Knife.** For business men. 4 blades (exclusive lance blade to cut paper clippings; pen, file, screwdriver blades). Stainless steel handle. 2⅝ in. long. Carrying pouch.
9 A 9558—Shipping weight 4 oz. . . $6.95

29 **Old Crafty®.** 3 blades (long clip, sheep-foot, spay). 4 inches long.
9 A 9547—Shipping weight 7 oz. . . $6.45

30 **Stockman's.** 3 blades of rust-resistant super-razor stainless steel (pen, spay and skinning). 3¼ inches.
9 A 9553—Shipping weight 5 oz. . $5.95

31 **Stockman's.** 3 blades (long clip, sheep-foot, spay). 4 inches long.
9 A 9470—Shipping weight 5 oz. . $3.95

32 **Camper's.** 4 blades (spear, punch, can opener, combination screwdriver-cap lifter). 3¾ inches long. Belt loop and shackle for carrying.
9 A 9549—Shipping weight 6 oz. . $3.95

33 **Electrician's.** 2 blades (spear and combination screwdriver-wire stripper). 3¾ in. long. Belt loop and shackle for easy carrying.
9 A 9560—Shipping weight 7 oz. . $3.95

34 **Slim Jim.** 2 blades (pen and skinning). 3¼ inches long.
9 A 9541—Shipping weight 4 oz. . $2.95

35 **Barlow.** Old favorite, especially with boys. 2 blades (pen and clip). 3⅜ inches long.
Shipping weight 5 ounces.
9 A 9540 . . . . . $2.45

***UNCONDITIONAL GUARANTEE:** If any knife listed on this page fails to give complete satisfaction, return it and it will be replaced absolutely free of charge.

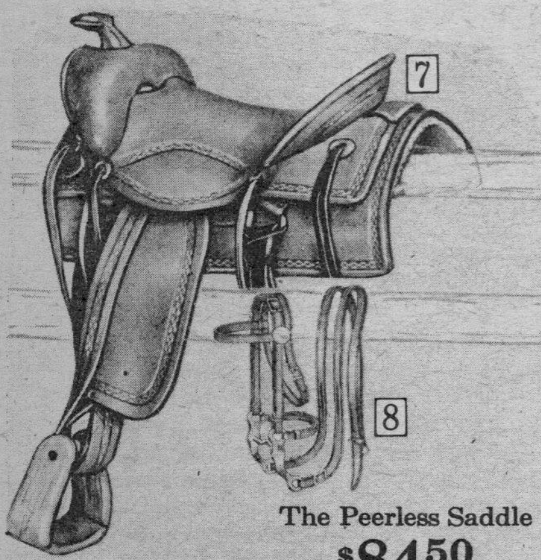

The Peerless Saddle

$84.50

7 Neat and smooth except for the beautifully embossed borders. A hard working saddle with *full double rigging,* brass-plated hardware and deep 3-inch beaded roll cantle. Skirts, 12x23 inches long. Fork, 12 inches wide. Wood stirrups with leather tread. Russet tan color.
Shipping weight 25 pounds.
32 KF 50101L $84.50

8 **Matching Bridle.** With bit and 6-foot reins. Nickel-plated hardware.
32 KF 52005—Shipping weight 1 lb. 12 oz. . . . $8.25

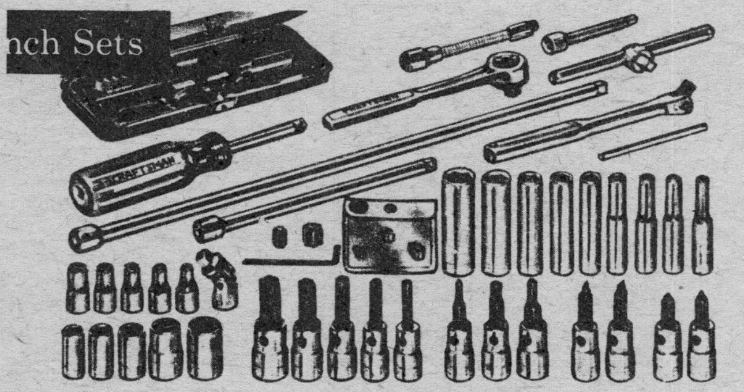

CRAFTSMAN® 48-piece Socket Wrench Set

¼-inch square drive. Ten 6-pt. sockets (³⁄₁₆ to ½ inch), nine 6-pt. deep sockets (³⁄₁₆ to ½ inch), fine tooth-quick release reversible ratchet, flex handle, crossbar, slide bar handle, 6-inch extension handle, 4-inch flex extension, three extensions (3, 6, and 14-inch), ⁵⁄₆₄-inch setscrew wrench, five hex wrench sockets (³⁄₁₆ to ⅜ inch), two Phillips screwdriver-bit sockets (Nos. 1 and 2), three clutch-head bit sockets (³⁄₃₂ to ⁵⁄₁₆ inch), two screwdriver bit sockets, universal joint, five magnetic inserts. Metal tool box.
Shipping weight 5 pounds 2 ounces.
9 AT 44392 . . . . . Set $39.99

Forged Steel Axes

7 **Our best CRAFTSMAN Axes.** Tempered and hardened. 3½-lb. tool steel heads. Enamel finish. 36-inch hickory handle tested to over 650-lb. strain . . wedgelocked. Shipping wt. 6 lbs.
99 AT 50371C—Single bit $7.49
99 AT 50411C—Double bit 8.49

8 **CRAFTSMAN Axe.** Forged 2¼-lb. vanadium steel head . . heat tempered, hardened. 28-in. hickory handle.
99 AT 5026C—Shpg. wt. 4 lbs. $6.49

Economy Axe (not shown). Single bit. 3½-pound head. 36-inch handle.
99 AT 50243C—Shpg. wt. 6 lbs. . . . $4.99

9 **Woodchoppers' Maul.** High carbon steel; polished edge. 8 lbs.
99 AT 5073C—Shpg. wt. 10 lbs. . . . $9.99

10 **Carbon-steel Wedge.** 9 in. long. Hand forged. For log splitting.
9 AT 5064—Shpg. wt. 5 lbs. 2 oz. . . $2.69

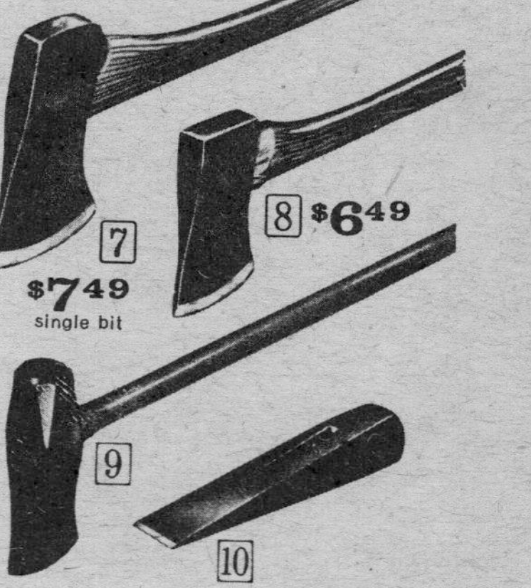

$7.49 single bit

$6.49

Heavy-duty wheelbarrows . . . sturdily built to "take a beating"

37.95 5½ cu. ft. **32.49** 4½ cu. ft.

5½-cu. ft. capacity contractors' model handles all your hauling chores. One-piece boltless tray of heavy-gauge sheet steel is leakproof, holds liquids as well as solids. Heavy-duty steel risers. Rolled edges. Channel steel undercarriage (see picture) and legs for extra support. Wheel guard allows easy dumping. Hardwood handle. 16-in. diam. ball bearing wheel; 8x4.00 tube tire.
89 FR 1118 R—Ship. wt. 70 lbs. . . . . cash 37.95

4½-cu. ft. capacity contractors' model. Has all the fine features as 5½-cu. ft. model above but with recessed bolts in tray and with wood risers.
89 FR 1117 R—Ship. wt. 65 lbs. . . . . cash 32.49

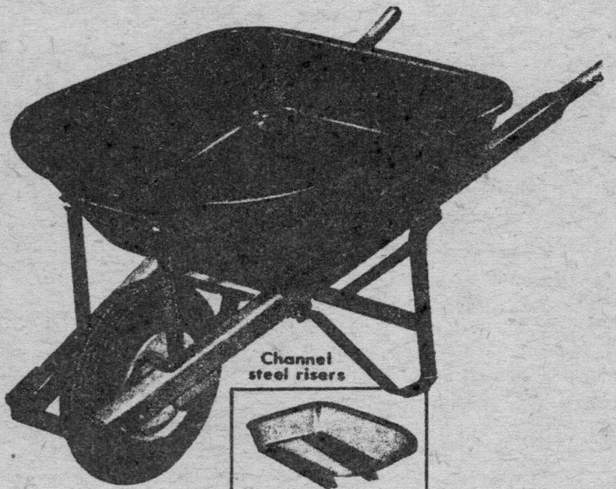

Rope hoists with double sheaves, drop-forged hooks

(10) **Self-locking rope hoists will not slip.** 4-to-1 mechanical advantage does most of the work. Requires 4 feet of rope to lift an object 1 foot. Reinforced steel construction. Drop-forged hooks at top and bottom for maximum strength. Roller bearings. Incl. 50 ft. of rope. *State size no.*

Hoist with 50-ft. rope

Rope size	Safe load	Size no.	Catalog number	Ship. wt.	Each
⅜ in.	250 lbs.	01	Z84 FR 9713 M	7 lbs.	5.79
½ in.	500 lbs.	02		11 lbs.	8.99

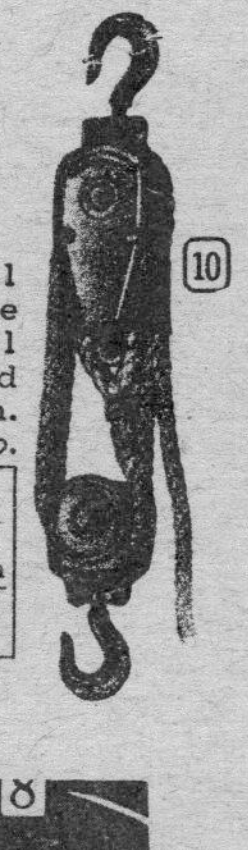

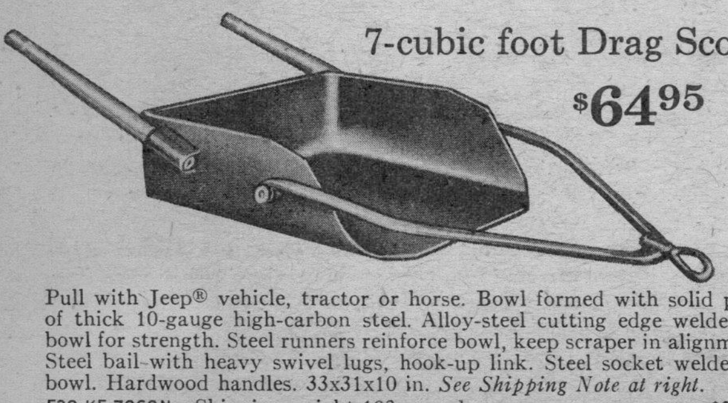

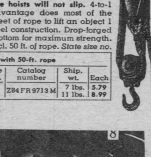

7-cubic foot Drag Scoop

$64.95

Pull with Jeep® vehicle, tractor or horse. Bowl formed with solid plate of thick 10-gauge high-carbon steel. Alloy-steel cutting edge welded to bowl for strength. Steel runners reinforce bowl, keep scraper in alignment. Steel bail with heavy swivel lugs, hook-up link. Steel socket welded to bowl. Hardwood handles. 33x31x10 in. *See Shipping Note at right.*
F32 KF 7860N—Shipping weight 102 pounds $64.95

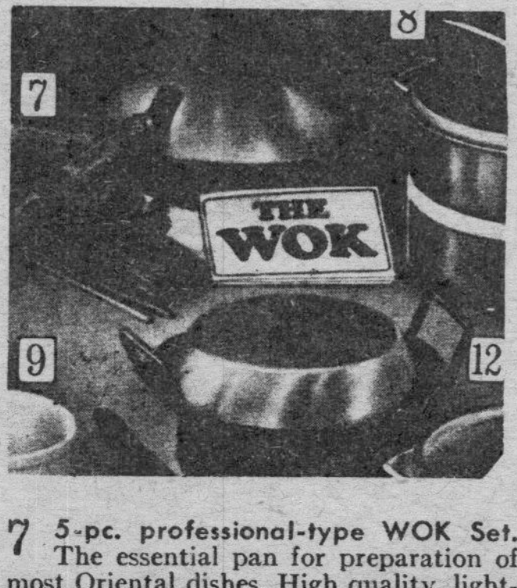

12 **Stir-fry WOK and stand.** Steel. 12-in. diameter. With lid. 3 inches deep. Shipping weight 4 lbs. 12 oz.
11 A 9206 . . . . . $6.99

7 **5-pc. professional-type WOK Set.** The essential pan for preparation of most Oriental dishes. High quality, lightweight steel for even heating. 14-in. diam. vegetable pan, 12-in. diam. braising pan for meats, also serves as vegetable pan cover. Natural pine wood handles. 12-in. bamboo whisk for cleaning, set of large stirring chopsticks incl. Reversible adapter ring of nickel-plated steel lets you cook on electric or gas stove. Use WOK for rice preparation, baking, frying, steaming in large quantities. Recipes incl.
11 A 9271—Shpg. wt. 8 lbs. 8 oz. . . $24.99

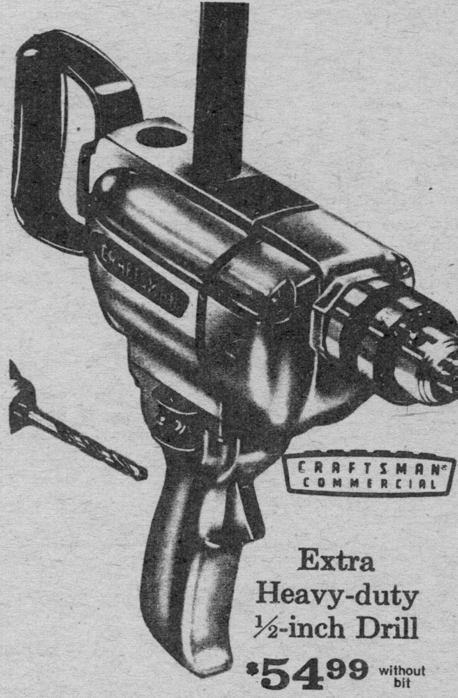

Extra Heavy-duty ½-inch Drill

$54.99 without bit

Motor develops ¾ HP . . 100% ball and needle bearings. Especially well suited for continuous-duty drilling and deep drilling in steel and concrete. Non-glare satin finish. Top handle is removable for working ease in tight places. Has a no-load speed of 600 rpm. Measures 13 inches long. Heavy-duty double-pole switch lock for continuous running. Operates on 110–120-volt, 25–60-cycle AC-DC. 8-foot length of cord. Reversing feature makes it easy to drive and remove screws . . order speed-reducer kit 9 AT 25653 on facing page and use your drill as screwdriver, nut runner, tapper, etc. *See Note below, left for other features.* CRAFTSMAN COMMERCIAL *story on page 18.*
9 AT 778—Shipping weight 9 lbs. 10 oz. . . . $54.99

Sears/Wards mail order

If you live away from cities, where telephone calls and quick car trips aren't possible, the Sears and Wards catalogs are indispensable. Clothes, tools, building materials all via mail and service is rapid. Both catalogs are intelligently organized. Although we take such for granted, the Sears catalog was on display in the U. S. pavilion at the Brussels World's Fair and continually mobbed by people of other countries.

Both have farm catalogs, with contractor's and light industrial equipment and all types of farm equipment, including live poultry. Sears has a separate catalog of Craftsman tools, which are considered the best low-cost hand tools. Most electric tools have a year's guarantee and other tools are unconditionally guaranteed. If you break a hammer handle after three years' use, they'll give you a new hammer.

Order from nearest Sears or Wards store. Two catalogs a year: spring-summer and fall-winter. **Free.** *To stay on the mailing list you must make two orders every six months.*

—Lloyd Kahn

Sears now has special catalogs on Hand Tools, Building Materials, Hunting, Toys, Old Time Movies, Business Equipment, Water Systems, Car Parts, etc. Free from Sears Catalog Sales Offices.

—SB

WARDS

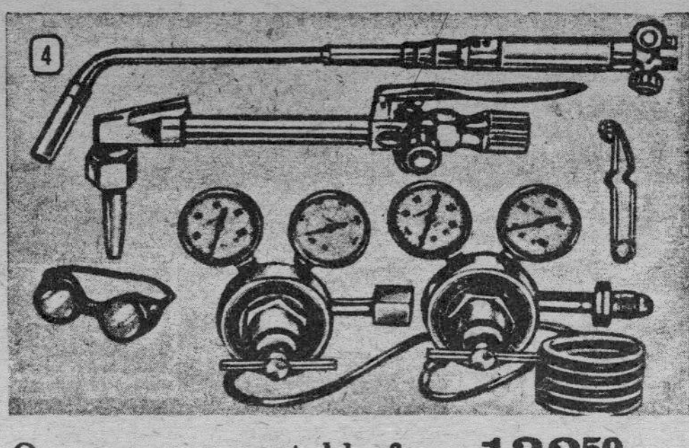

Oxy-propane portable forge 132.50

(4) **Professional outfit** handles all cutting, brazing, heating jobs. Torch produces tremendous heat for bending and straightening operations. Uses low-cost propane; fuel cost reduced 90% over acetylene when cutting. Steady delivery. Single-stage regulators UL listed. Includes: torch with brazing and heating tips; cutting attachment with No. 2 tip; industrial-size oxygen and propane regulators; twin hose; goggles; lighter, instructions and manual. Order extra cutting tips and accessories below.
84 C 5852 M—Ship. wt. 24 lbs. . . . . outfit **132.50**

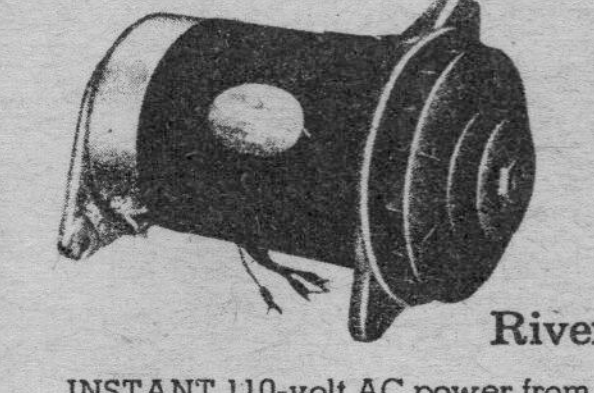
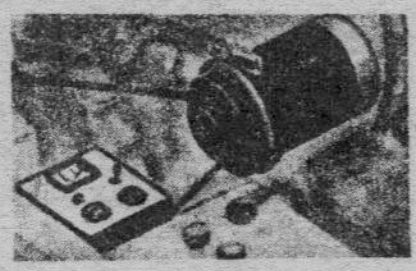

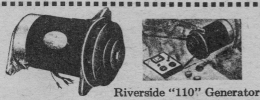

Riverside "110" Generator

INSTANT 110-volt AC power from your car, truck, boat or tractor engine. Dependable power—at the site, on the job, on or off the road—exactly where and when you need it. Isolated ground permits use under otherwise hazardous conditions. Universal mounting bracket included.

Applications: Home—operates 110-v. AC or AC/DC tools and appliances—ideal for emergency lighting in power failures. Police and fire departments—operates radios, smoke ejectors, floodlighting. Heavy equipment—use to run water pumps, blower, various electrical tools for on-the-spot repairs. Farm tractors, trucks—runs pruning saws in groves, orchards; lighting for night farming. Forged steel housing. 110-v., 27 amps.; 3500 watts peak output; 60-cycle rated frequency at 3600 RPM shaft speed. Outlet box. Ship. wt. 42 lbs.
61 C 11497 R . . . . $10 mo., Terms page 1218, or cash **198.00**

Voltage regulator—permits operation of above unit with vehicle in motion. Mailed, pay from factory in New York. Allow 7 days plus transit time. Ship. wt. 5 lbs.
X61 C 11496 K . . . . $5 mo., Terms page 1218, or cash **99.50**

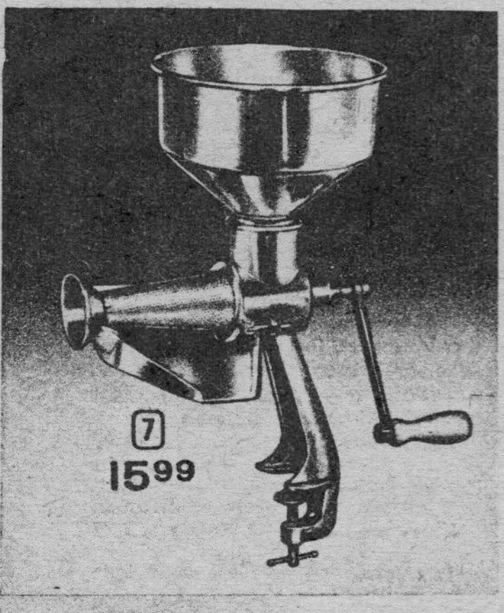

(7) 15.99

(7) **"Homemade"**—it's easy to say and easy to do when you have a Wards versatile food press in your kitchen. Squeeze your own fresh fruit juices, make purees and sauces "from scratch" in 1-gallon food press. Hopper removes for easy cleaning; sure-grip clamp. Tamper incl. 19 in. high.
86 C 5181—Wt. 7 lbs. 8 oz. . . . **15.99**

(8) 69.99

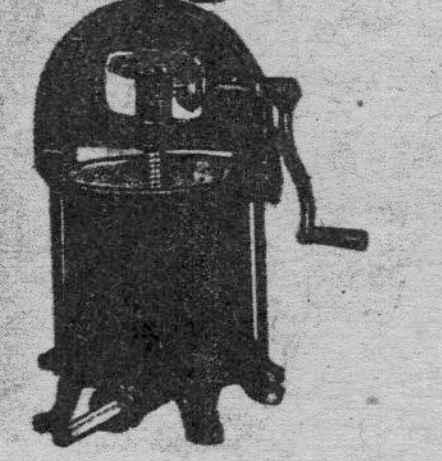

(8) **For those big jobs** you'll need this 3-in-1 heavy-duty food press. Features: plunger plate for lard; presser plate for fruit or vegetables; 3/4-in. sausage stuffing attachment. Black japanned iron cylinder has large 8-quart container—simplifies cooking for a crowd. Easy-to-use 2-to-1 gear ratio. Mailable to some locations—see page 1209. Ship. wt. 53 lbs.
86 C 5182 A **69.99**

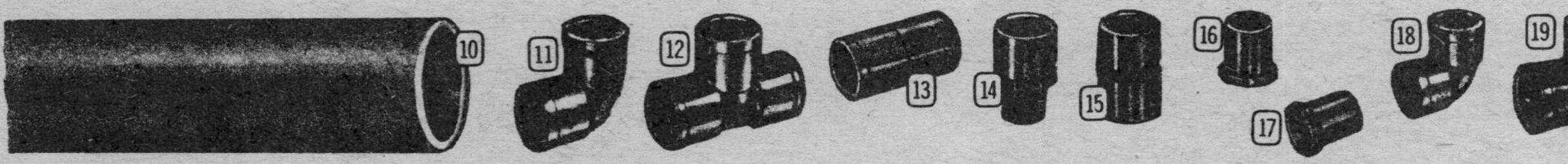

160-200 lb. Rigid PVC* plastic cold water pressure pipe

(10) ***Poly-vinyl chloride pipe—easy-to-install—can be cut with a saw.** For cold water lines only; inside, outside; above or below ground. **NSF-approved safe for use with drinking water.** In 10-ft. lengths with plain ends. Meets Commercial Standards CS 256-63. Won't rust or rot. Working pressures at 73° F.—200 lbs. for 1/2, 3/4 and 1-in. size; 160 lbs. for 1 1/4-in. size. Clean with PVC Cleaner no. 43466R. Make connections with PVC Cement 43462R or 43463R at right. To connect to steel pipe use (14) or (15). Insulate in freezing temperatures.

(10) PVC Plastic Pipe—Ea. piece 10 ft. long.	1/2-in. size			3/4-in. size			1-in. size			1 1/4-in. size		
	Cat. no.	Lbs.	Price	Cat. no.	Lbs.	Price	Cat. no.	Lbs.	Price	Cat. no.	Lbs.	Price
	81 C 43102 R	1	75c	81 C 43103 R	1 1/4	95c	81 C 43104 R	1 1/2	1.19	81 C 43105 R	2	1.89

PVC fittings	1/2-in. size			3/4-in. size			1-in. size			1 1/4-in. size		
	Cat. no.	Oz.	Price	Cat. no.	Oz.	Price	Cat. no.	Oz.	Price	Cat. no.	Oz.	Price
(11) 90° elbow	81 C 43402	2	37c	81 C 43403	2	47c	81 C 43404	2	75c	81 C 43405	3	85c
(12) Tee	81 C 43412	2	37c	81 C 43413	2	55c	81 C 43414	2	95c	81 C 43415	3	1.00
(13) Coupling	81 C 43422	1	10c	81 C 43423	1	13c	81 C 43424	1	33c	81 C 43425	2	43c
(14) Male adapter	81 C 43432	1	17c	81 C 43433	1	28c	81 C 43434	1	45c	81 C 43435	2	55c
(15) Fem. adapter	81 C 43442	1	19c	81 C 43443	1	33c	81 C 43444	1	43c	81 C 43445	2	53c

(16) Bushing—To reduce pipe 1 size	3/4x1/2-in. size			1x3/4-in. size			1 1/4x1-in. size		
	Cat. no.	Wt.	Price	Cat. no.	Wt.	Price	Cat. no.	Wt.	Price
	81 C 43452	1/2 oz.	23c	81 C 43453	1 oz.	35c	81 C 43454	1 oz.	45c

Cement, cleaner and primer

Cement for joining PVC plastic pipe and fittings (10) to (19). Clean joint area with cleaner 43466R, brush on cement, insert pipe into fitting. Allow to set. 1/2 pint seals sixty 1-in. connections.
81 C 43462 R—1/2-pint brush can. Ship. wt. 1 oz. **1.49**
81 C 43463 R—Pint brush can. Ship. wt. 1 lb. 8 oz. **2.49**

PVC Cleaner and Primer. Use to clean and prepare surface of PVC pipe and fitting. Ship. wt. 10 oz.
81 C 43466 R—1/2-pint can with dauber. **95c**

Sprinkler elbows. One end threaded for 1/2-in. nipple. Other receives PVC pipe. Wt. 2 oz.
(18) **81 C 43387—1/2 PVC x 1/2-in. thread** **37c**
81 C 43388—3/4 PVC x 1/2-in. thread **47c**

(17) **81 C 43383–Bushing.** 3/4 PVC x 1/2 thread. **21c**

(19) **Tee.** Side opening only has 1/2-in. thread.
81 C 43391—1/2x1/2x1/2-in. thread **37c**
81 C 43393—3/4x3/4x1/2-in. thread **55c**

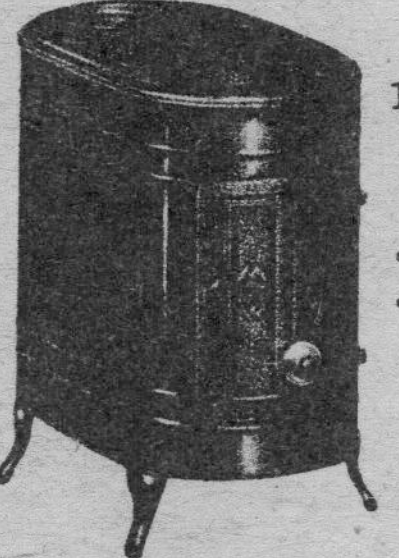

1-2 room airtight

Low as

16.95

Wards lowest price wood heater. Strong blued-steel body has double seamed top, corrugated bottom for extra strength; reinforced with steel lining for extra durability. Cast-iron feed door, frame. Nickeled screw draft control in door. Hinged top lifts easily, stays up. Rust-resistant blued steel finish. Use 6-in. stovepipe.

Large size: 17 1/2x27 1/2x31 in. high. Burns up to 24-in. wood. Shipping weight 35 lbs.
68 C 7353 R **21.95**

Small size: 15 1/2x22 1/2x27 in. high. Burns up to 20-in. wood. Ship. wt. 24 lbs.
68 C 7351 R **16.95**

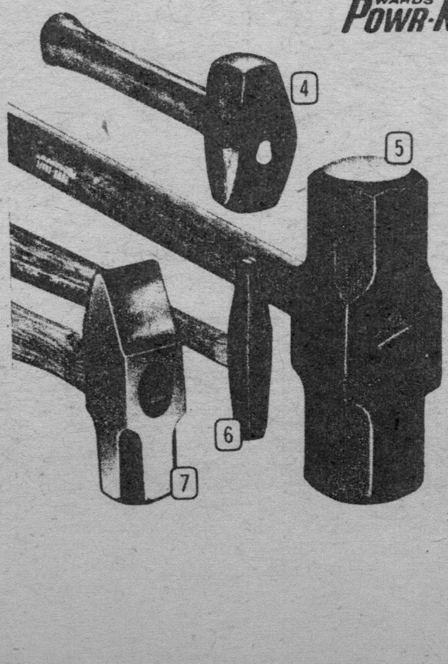

WARDS POWR-KRAFT utility hammers

(4) **Three-lb. hand hammer.** 10 3/4 in.
84 C 3695—Wt. 3 lbs. 8 oz. **4.89**

(5) **Steel sledge hammers.** Choose from 8-lb. or 10-lb. head weight. 36-in. hickory handle. Shipping weights 10 and 12 lbs. each.
84 C 3696 M—8-lb. head. **8.79**
84 C 3697 M—10-lb. head **9.89**

Extra 36-in. handle for sledge (5).
84 C 3728 M—Ship. wt. 2 lbs. **1.65**

(6) **Ten-in. magnetic tack hammer.** Magnetized to hold tacks in place.
84 C 3699—Ship. wt. 8 oz. **1.49**

(7) **Engineers' hammers.** Drop-forged heads and hickory handles. Choose 32-oz. or 40-oz. head. Shipping weights 2 1/2 and 3 1/2 lbs. each.
84 C 3692—32-oz. head. **5.99**
84 C 3693—40-oz. head. **6.49**

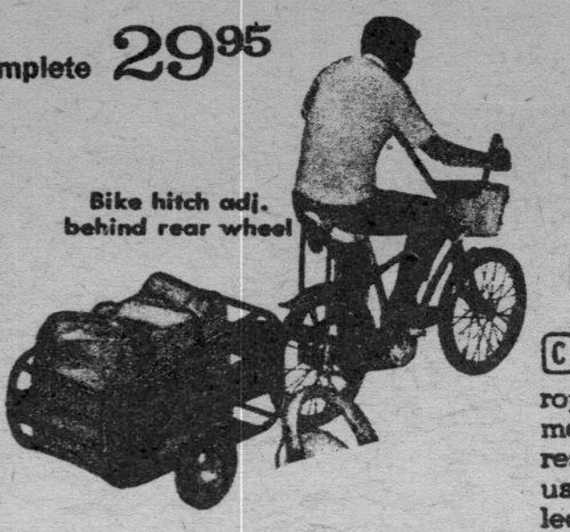

Complete 29.95

Bike hitch adj. behind rear wheel

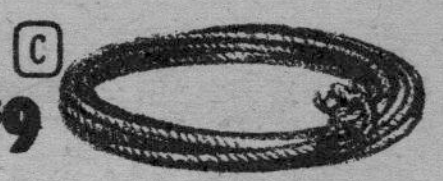

(C) $9

Professional-type lariats

(C) **Leaded nylon lariat** . . . the kind the champion ropers use! Best working rope for professionals . . . far outclasses manila in endurance, long wear. Fast, resists shock. Won't break with normal use. Will not rot or mildew. Tied-in leather honda. 7/16-in. diam., 30 ft. long.
89 FR 22475—Ship. wt. 2 lbs. **9.00**

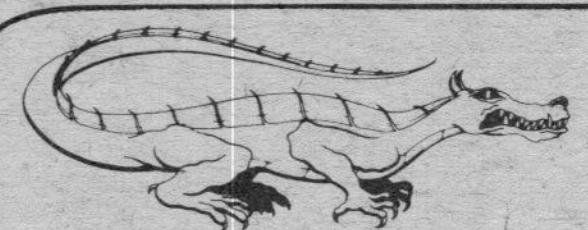

RECOLLECTION

That car of Daddy's was an old Pontiac he bought with the first wages he ever earned in Cincinnati. It had over a hundred thousand miles on it when he got it, but he never hesitated to take off in it for Kentucky. The first year we lived up there we never missed a weekend going home. Fifty-two round trips in a year, over two hundred miles each way, six, seven, sometimes eight and nine people in it every run. Every Friday as soon as Daddy'd get home from work we'd load up and head out, and drive six straight hours south on old U.S. 25, through Lexington and Richmond, east into the hills on 421, then down state route 666 to the homeplace in Finley County. In the winter time it would be dark before we even set out, but in the summers the light would hold till almost Richmond, and I remember the programs that came on the radio about that time of day. My daddy played the guitar some, and he loved hillbilly music, and so at six o'clock he'd tune in the Hillbilly Hit Parade out of WCKY in Cincinnati. I remember it started and ended with somebody's fierce picking of the Steel Guitar Rag, and then when it was over Wayne Rainey and Lonnie Glossen would come on, trying to sell harmonica instruction courses. Wayne and Lonnie were good musicians too, and when they'd get wound up Daddy would get excited and start to sing along with them, and bounce around in his seat and beat on the steering wheel with his hand. He'd cut up like that for miles and miles. He'd tickle us all so much we'd forget how uncomfortable we were, piled on top of one another in the back seat of that old car. On Fridays you wouldn't mind being uncomfortable because you knew you were on your way to some place you really wanted to be a lot, but on Sundays you'd feel so blue about having to leave the homeplace to go back to Cincinnati there wasn't any way in the world to get comfortable and Daddy would have to stop every hour or so and let people out to stretch. We hated it, coming back, but then it was only five more days till we'd go down home again, and we cheered ourselves up with that thought. The five days would drag by but finally Friday would get there, Daddy would come in from work, clean up a little and then there we'd be, on the road again. About six hours later we'd turn off at Mrs. Godsey's store and drive up Trace Fork to the homeplace.

It would be midnight by the time we'd get there and Grandma and Grandad would be in bed asleep. Grandad never let anything keep him from getting his sleep, but if Grandma was feeling well she'd get up and come in the kitchen and hug us all and start taking cornbread and beans and cold mashed potatoes out of the oven and setting them on the table. Daddy would say here now Mommy, you quit that, we've all done and eat. But Grandma would keep hauling out the food and before long we'd all be seated at the table, me and Daddy and Marcella and Doyle and usually some of Doyle's kin folks would be with us and they'd sit down too and there we'd all be, in the middle of the night at Grandma's house, eating cold beans and potatoes and blackberry jam on that good cold cornbread.

Then it wouldn't seem like half an hour till there we'd be again, sitting at the table, Grandad with us this time, the beans and potatoes hot now, the pork hot, the beets hot, the cornbread hot, the cobbler hot, and the milk cold as ice from sitting all night in the spring house. That would be Saturday dinner. Sunday dinner was always chicken and gravy and cole slaw with beans and potatoes, a big pone of biscuit instead of cornbread, and ice tea for those that didn't want milk.

Sunday dinner was considered the best meal of the week at the homeplace but I never did like it after we moved away because it was after Sunday dinner that we always had to load up in the Pontiac again and go back to Cincinnati. I was always too sad to eat much on Sundays, and what little I would eat I'd usually throw up as soon as we got back on the road. At dinner time on Saturday I'd eat like a starved horse thinking: twenty-four hours. Twenty-four whole hours to romp around the pasture and the woods, then in the evenings to hang around with my grandfather while he went about his chores. On Saturday that twenty-four hours stretched away forever, but when it was over and it was time to leave it would all seem like some strange little fifteen-second dream.

When it was time to go, Grandma and Grandad would follow us out to the car and stand around while we got in. Then Daddy would start the motor, back up to the coal pile, fight the steering wheel till the wheels turned, then ease forward down the lane, pausing in front of Grandma and Grandad for a final goodbye. I always wanted to cry at that point but I never did, except once as we were leaving, at the last second, as a surprise, Grandma tossed a Payday candy bar to me through the window and hit me in the eye. I let out a terrific squawl, and cried till it was time to get out of the car and puke. I held my eye and screeched like I was mortally wounded, but the thing nobody knew was that I wasn't really crying about being hit in the eye at all. All that was just an excuse for this other kind of crying I wanted to do, which I did plenty of on that occasion. I suffered pretty bad that trip till we got back down around Big Hill and Daddy started carrying on about Daniel Boone again. Daddy always made me laugh on Big Hill, and passing over it tonight I could feel that old familiar laugh sensation start to rumble in my guts again.

The Armchair Shopper's Guide

This cheerful book is an uncommonly practical compendium of access. Listed here are all of the major and many of the minor mail order shippers in the world. To a large extent the shippers carry items not available locally. Each source is very well described and compared with its competitors. The Armchair Shopper's Guide is more general than us, and geared to wealthier readers, but if you use the WHOLE EARTH CATALOG very much, you can almost certainly use the Shopper's Guide.

—SB

The Armchair Shopper's Guide
Delphine C. Lyons
1968; 218 pp.

No Longer Available

from:
Essandess Special Editions
Simon and Schuster, Inc.
630 Fifth Avenue
New York, New York 10020

or WHOLE EARTH CATALOG

You'll have to pay the sales tax if the mail order house is located in your own state or municipality, but you aren't required to pay it to firms in other states, nor may they charge you their local sales taxes. Although this has always held true for most mail-order houses, in the past such big firms as Sears, Roebuck and Co. made a practice of collecting the various local sales taxes from their customers and passing them on to the state or city involved. However, a recent court ruling has declared this illegal. So, if you live in a place such as New York City you can save a pretty penny (5 per cent) by buying by mail from out-of-state firms.

Katherine Smith, P. O. Box 121, Fort Worth, Texas 76101 (catalog 25 cents) offers new recordings made by old-time country and western singers, in partnership with the Bluebonnet Recording Co. In addition, she issues lists of old 78's for collectors.

•

Sunray Yarn House, 349 Grand Street, New York, New York 10002 (catalog free; yarn samples 50 cents) offers an enormous selection of discount yarns and knitting supplies, as well as some art needlework.

•

Australian Gem Trading Company, 294 Little Collins Street, Melbourne C 1, AUSTRALIA (catalog free): rough-cutting opal is available here at $1 per ounce for the lowest quality, going up to $60 and over for the more valuable types. Cut and polished stones and opal doublets are also available. In addition, there's Australian sapphire (both blue and black star), rough and polished.

•

The Putney Nursery, Putney, Vermont 05346 (catalog free) sells wild flowers by mail—not the wild flowers that have become accepted as regular garden plants, but such blossoms as harebells, trillium, wild ginger, and the like.

•

Katagiri & Company, Inc., 224 East 59th Street, New York, New York 10022 (catalog free): This well-known Japanese grocery has everything for the Japanese cuisine—dried bean curd, dried seaweed, pickled ginger, candied baby abalones and baby octopus (an 8-oz. can is 75 cents) and so on. Confections include bean jelly (16-oz. for 70 cents) and seaweed candy (6-oz. for 39 cents).

Gohn Brothers

Gohn Brothers supplies chiefly the stricter Mennonite orders and the various orders of the Amish Mennonite people all over the country. Since the Amish have managed communal living successfully for about 350 years, I figure at least some of their practices must be valid. Their clothing in particular is comfortable, durable and of low price. I can recommend from experience their broadfall work pants (no fly: broad button flap like lederhosen in front), overshirts (plain jacket with two roomy pockets on the inside) and overcoats (Heavy Dark wool, with cape). Many hard to find practical items listed, as well as a broad selection of rather plain yard goods. Service is fast and courteous. Once on their mailing list you get about four to six catalogs a year.

[Suggested and Reviewed by Peter R. Hoover]

Catalog
free

from:
Gohn Brothers
Middlebury, Indiana 46540

MEN'S BROADFALL WORK PANTS

No. 1190 10-oz. Sanf. Blue Denim.....................$6.98 pr.
No. 44 9-oz. Sanf. Grey Covert.............. No longer available
No. 55 9-oz. Sanf. Blue Saddle Denim..................$6.49 pr.
No. 66 9-oz. Sanf. Grey Saddle Denim................$6.49 pr.
No. 66 and No. 55 are solid colors. No white in it. Dressier than regular denim but make excellent work pants. Size 28, 29, 33, 42 only waist sizes left in grey covert. Also covert only available with all pockets and buttons.

MEN'S WORK SUSPENDERS
Black, 1½" wide, plain Amish.........................$1.88 pr.
Black, 1½" wide. Leather tabs.......................$1.98 pr.
BE SURE TO SPECIFY IF YOU WANT PLAIN OR TABS

Vermont Country Store

More use and less frill than other nostalgic stores. Reasonable prices, good service.

—SB

Catalog
$.25

from:
Vermont Country Store
Weston, Vt. 05161

Pot Chain

The kind grandma used, heavy steel, never wears out. For scouring and cleaning iron pans and dishes, 5½ by 9 inches. No. 11508 $1.50.* Ship. wt., ½ lb.

Farmer's Bundle of Leather

This ½ lb. bundle of leather strips (some ½" wide), thongs, ties and odd size leather pieces will meet many a need around the place. Tanned, saddle color. No. 11681 $2.00* each. Ship. Weight ½ lb.

You Can Now Make Your Own Antique Style, Scented Candles With Our Kit

You'll have fun with this kit, and what a fine gift too! With this easy-to-use kit, anyone can quickly make SIX ten-inch antique style early American candles, and later use the antique style pewter color mold for decoration. Kit consists of the 11" tall mold with six tubes and handle, and with it two 7" long blocks of wax, red and green coloring, bayberry and pine scent, and braided wicking for the six candles. Full directions, in 4 simple steps.
No longer available
SPARE PARTS. The pewter color *Metal Candle Mold* for 6 candles. No longer available

Basic Supply Set has two big blocks of wax, two coloring cubes, bayberry and pine fragrances, and enough wicking to make SIX more candles. No longer available

Braided Candle Wicking. Enough wicking to make 24 candles. No longer available

60% WOOL BLANKETLINED OVERSHIRTS

Sizes 32 to 44 chest measure. Hooks and eyes. No outside pockets. Sewn with black thread. Cut with roomy armholes and wide sleeves.
10-oz. Sanf. Blue Denim..........................$10.98
9-oz. Sanf. Grey Covert................... No longer available
AMISH OVERCOATS....................................$89.95
With Cape..$96.95
100% navy blue melton. Made in single or double breasted style. Send for samples. Complete instructions on how to measure are furnished on request.

No. 400 SHEEPSKIN VESTS ....$13.50 ea.
Zipper front. 2 patch pockets. Sizes, small, med., large, and extra large.

PROFESSIONAL RAZOR. Why does the barber always trim and shave with an old-fashioned straight razor? Because it's the quickest, gives the closest shave, is easiest to use and costs the least! Any man can learn, in ten minutes, to shave with this imported top quality German razor, full concave, double hollow ground blade, with non-slip serrated thumb rest, ivory-like handle; molded carrying case. No. 41238. $12.75. Ship. Weight 1 lb.

PROFESSIONAL RAZOR STROP. You'll learn in seconds to run your beautiful razor a few times over this fine strop of selected genuine horsehide, dark mahogany Russian hone finish with Scotch Canvas hose, all broken-in and ready to use. Individual double leather handles, gilt clincher swivel, gold stamping. No. 11644 $7.50 each. Ship. Weight 1 lb.
SHAVING SOAP. In Europe and in the best men's clubs, you'll find gentlemen still lathering up with Pears Soap, the oldest in the world. No. 669. Box of three cakes. $2.50. Ship. Weight 1 lb.

Factory Stores

The factory store is one of the first places to go if you want to get certain merchandise cheaply. This guide lists direct-from-the-manufacturer outlets for clothing and other personal and household items, but there are many other manufactured goods to be sought out in the same way. This guide is only regional, but it's listed here to stimulate bargain hunters in other parts of the country as well as readers who live in the New England area. Why couldn't someone go out and compile the same sort of valuable information for whatever area they lived in, and make it available through the community media serving the people there? You probably have enough friends, each with his own favorite source of inexpensive goods, that you'd be able to start your research with lots of good leads.

—Hal Hershey

Factory Store Guide to All New England

A. Miser & A. Pennypincher

$2.95 postpaid

Guild

from:
Pequot Press, Inc.
Old Chester Road
Chester, Conn. 06412

Fabrics

THE MILL STORE
Dorr Woolen Company
Routes 11 and 103
(Store also in Old Sturbridge Village, Sturbridge, Mass.)
Monday-Saturday, 9-5.

This is one of the most extensive and attractive fabric mill stores to be visited. Only fabrics loomed by the Dorr Woolen Company are sold here; these are available at savings of 40%. The wide selection includes solids, checks, tweeds, and Scottish plaids in both bonded and unbonded fabrics. Dress, suit, coat, and skirt weight woolens are offered, either from the bolt or by the piece.

Braid and hooking woolens are also available, as well as rug patterns and supplies. An infinite variety of shades is available for that "just-right" hooking design. Pieces suitable for braiding start at 50¢ per pound.

Trimcomb

The barbershop has been obsolete for several years. Now trimmers and hair cutters follow. This absurdly simple item uses a double-edged razor blade (one edge trims, the other dry-shaves) to sculpt your hair with simple amateur dabs at your head. It works better if your hair is wet. Trimcomb costs about $3 at most dime stores. —SB

[Suggested by Dave Evans]

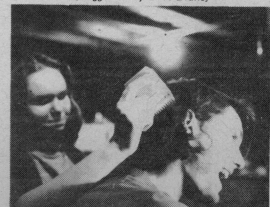

Kalsø Earth Shoe

Have you heard about the Earth Shoe? The enclosed will tell most of it. Ray Jacobs is doing the Earth Shoe thing here, working hard to improve it and make it cost less (note the price on the Danish made women's shoe). Jacobs found out about the shoe when touring in Europe and looking for relief for his wife's backache (yes). She had flat feet (no arch) and was pretty uncomfortable, I guess, but these funny shoes relieved the backache after a few weeks and now she has an arch where before. . . .Anyway, it's one of those things that seems to draw testimonials like flies. The shoes are strange to look at and stranger to wear; they hurt for the first few days but then they're dynamite.

[Suggested and reviewed by Ron Williams]

Definitely worth a mention. The straps of the wooden sandals are not so well made as the beautiful, polished bottoms, but the Kalsø people say they're working on a new version. The oxfords are the best pair of shoes I've ever worn, expensive & dearly loved hiking boots included. If you send a drawing of your foot w/your order they try to match it up with a shoe. Expensive but you don't need more than one really good pair of shoes anyway.

-Terry Gunesch

Free brochure
Kalso Earth Shoe
257 Park Ave.
New York, N.Y. 10010

Style No. 1004
LEATHER WALKING SHOE— Hand-made of top quality suede. Thick rubber sole. Available in tan and moss green.

| Women's sizes— 5-12 | Price: Women—$40.00 |
| Men's sizes— 6-14 | Men— $40.00 |

The Left Hand

A limited but useful line of left-handed stuff. Also check Anything Left Handed Limited, 65 Beak St., London W1, England. Catalog $.50.

—SB

$35.00

The Left Hand
145 East 27th St.
New York, N.Y. 10016

PORTABLE MICROFICHE READER
weighs 7½ lbs.

Product: Model PMR/50 for libraries, schools, hospitals and government operations. *Features:* Provides clear, 8½"x11" images at a finger's touch, maker reports. Measures 13"x13"x7½". Accompanying desk-top file of 4"x6" microfiche stores 10,000 pages of information. Priced at $89.50.
circle **233** *for more facts from:*
DASA Corp.
Andover, Mass.

Cheap Glasses

Some people have eye defects or disease that require prescription glasses; they should see a doctor. Most of us just get far-sighted as our muscles age, and all we need is simple magnification with a shorter focus. Certain states seem to discourage stores from stocking standard lenses in inexpensive frames on open counters. Perhaps there's an optometrist's conspiracy. But normal eye needs are no more various or peculiar than foot needs. There are standard shoe, shirt, and shorts sizes——why not standard lenses? With TV tube distortion, wrap-around windshields, and tinted sunglasses, nobody sees the real world much any more anyway. My nearsighted kid's eye examination, lenses, and frames cost $35. My own Nu-Life specs (I am farsighted and getting along) cost $3.95. Been wearing 'em 3 years, changed them once, satisfied & I Can't see any difference. Avoid plastic hinges. Outasight, intosight. Great gift for oldies who haven't seen the light.

[Suggested and reviewed by Tom Wertenbaker]

Catalog from:
free Nulife Products
Cos Cob, Connecticut

These glasses are just perfect for reading fine print and doing close work, for people over 40 who do not have astigmatism or eye disease and need the help of simple magnifying glasses. Doctors term these glasses completely safe and a highly effective aid for the natural aging of the eyes which affects the vision of most men and women after the age of 40.

Be sure to give age when ordering one of the Full Frame Magnifying Reading Glasses below as we send stronger lenses to older people.

Full-Frame
Style #U
Only $3.95

Full-Frame Style #U — Only $3.95 is a universal two-tone style with distinguished dark brow and clear lower frame. Lenses are ground to the highest standards of precision. Fits both men and women. You'd expect to pay several times the price just for the attractive frames alone.

Government Product-News

This is a goofy array of new products ranging from police equipment to seam sealant that can be applied to a wet or oily surface without cleaning it first (and whoop dee doo if that one works!) A subscription would be useful to a buyer for a school system or the like, but would be of limited value to a commune. It's one of those things that new products freaks and designers like to read once a month but isn't really worth the price of the subscription to typical private citizen. Read it at your local business library.

I dig it.

[Reviewed by Jay Baldwin. Suggested by J. Cline]

Government Product-News from:
$6.00 /yr (monthly) Government Product-News
731 Hennepin Avenue
Minneapolis, Minnesota 55403

INSTANT WAREHOUSE $895 FOB Elkhart

Get weather-proof storage capacity for your inventory, materials, tools and equipment at only $4.66 a sq. ft. — a cost far below conventional buildings. Fully assembled and ready for immediate use, sturdy Storage Wagons feature all steel structure, enameled steel exterior, painted interior with smooth board sidewalls; skylite and 110 volt prewired interior lights. Interior size 24' x 8' x 6½' high with 48"x68" high locking door and step. 37" floor height on wheels. Easily relocated. Buy direct and save! Call or write for details. **WELLS CARGO, INC.** 1503 W. McNaughton St., Elkhart, Indiana 46514/(219)264-3141 · P.O. Box 1318 · Waycross, Georgia 31501 (912) 285-8132.

WELLS CARGO ®

Thongs

Beach Walk Sandals are not so special but they are the only zoris around that last for two to four months of all-day outdoor wear and don't collapse after a few days and leave you fearfully on your heels. Cost about a buck. Buy them in Shoe Stores and Repair Shops.

Peter
Zen Mountain Center
Carmel Valley, CA

BEACH WALK ® SANDAL

Notice All Personnel

It is recommended that your headquarters screen the several hundred thousand Department of Defense field manuals, technical manuals, pamphlets, and other publications for possible inclusion in your catalog.

Thank you.

Joel Graber
Captain, US Army
APO San Francisco

Retread Your Feet

Tried and true hiking boots are a pleasure to have, and a sadness to lose. Shoe repairmen are not only expensive but their repairs often don't last very long. Here are two ways in which I've prolonged the life of my boots; they may be useful to some of you.

1) Soles from auto or truck tires

The soles on my boots were smooth and still firmly attached--just thin. If you have lug soles (vibrams, etc.) you'll have to modify this technique. If the old soles are coming off, you'll either have to take them off entirely or glue them down securely.

First, get a discarded tire. There are lots of them along back roads. I used a near-new tire (blown out) with a heavy duty tread. Cut out a section slightly longer than your boot and then cut off the side walls. Long-handled pruning shears work fine for cutting tires. Next, pry the heel off your boot and thoroughly work over the bottom of the boot and the inside of the tire with a stiff wire brush (the first key to success). Coat the two surfaces with a thermosetting resin (like epoxy) and clamp together securely (the second key to success).

Here's how I clamped mine---

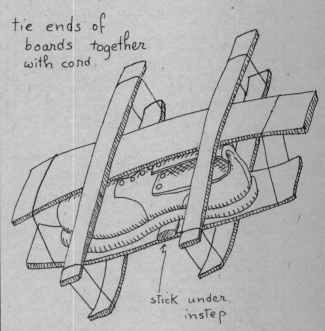

tie ends of boards together with cord.

stick under instep

Let it dry for about 24 hours, and then trim the tire to the shape of the boot. I wasn't too fussy about looks; if you don't like the sole sticking out here and there, you'll need to finish the job with a wire grinding wheel. I left the heel off and have found that it didn't make a bit of difference in how they "walk".

2) Repairing uppers with fibreglass tape and polyester resin

One of my boots was worn through at the toe. I filled the hole with fibreglass tape shredded and saturated with resin, then put a patch cut from the tape over the top and smeared this liberally with resin. Push the whole thing down until there are no trapped air bubbles. It dried hard and durable. If you don't yet have a hole, all you need do is apply a patch and soak it in resin.

I'd put on about 1,000 miles on these boots before I repaired them, and have since added another 500. If the tire manufacturer's claims are true, the soles ought to be good for another 19,500 or so. And I leave the most unique footprints around.

Roger Hope
Ruby Valley, Nevada

CROSSROADS

Traffic seemed fairly normal the first hour or so past Berea. But once he turned off 421 onto 666 D.R. went almost twenty miles without seeing another car and be began to wonder if he had got on the wrong road somehow. He wasn't lost exactly but he was afraid he might be, and at night in the mountains on the Wilderness Road it amounts to the same thing. He drove on a while longer, looking for signs, but he couldn't find any and the road got narrower and narrower. To be on the safe side D.R. turned around and retraced his path to a crossroads where there was a sign that said 666. It was a confusing intersection and he sat there a minute studying the sign, making sure it referred to the road he was on. Two other county roads came into 666 from each side near a sharp curve, and in the dark you couldn't see very far down any of them. The only marker was the 666 sign, which as D.R. read it seemed to refer to the middle road. He looked at the sign and the middle road, and finally set out down it into the night again.

(continued)

Hong Kong

If you have the time (5 weeks or so), Hong Kong offers fantastic deals in cameras, tape recorders, motorcycles, binoculars, calculators, suits, etc. Prices generally include seamail costs. You pay import duty (like $15 on a $118 Canon FT-QL—that costs $280 in the States), and Customs obliterates the trademark. Catalogs are free.

We've had exactly no complaints about any of these firms.
—SB

[Suggested by Terry Link, Thomas Dixon, Jas Hayden, Anne, Jim Kessler]

Write to:

T. M. Chan and Company
P.O. Box 7335
Kowloon, Hong Kong

Far East Company
P. O. Box 6784
Kowloon, Hong Kong

Albert White and Company, Ltd.
K. P. O. Box K-202
Kowloon, Hong Kong

Universal Suppliers
P.O. Box 14803
General Post Office
Hong Kong

Woods Photo Supplies
60 Nathan Rd.
Kowloon, Hong Kong

Mutual Funds Co.
Box K 3265
Kowloon, Hong Kong

理記靴鞋家有限公司

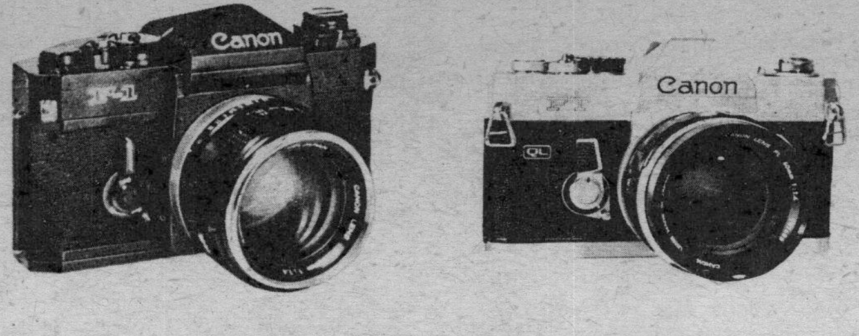

CANON F-1 (35mm) single lens reflex camera with interchangeable eye-level finder, built-in TTL meter system and leather case (in BLACK FINISH)

with Canon FD F1.2/55mm lens (Ø58mm)	295.60 (6.10)
with Canon FD F1.4/50mm lens (Ø55mm)	257.00 (5.50)

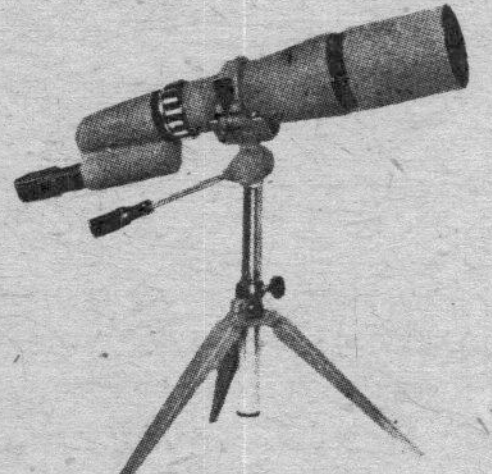

Universal Suppliers

Zoom Spottingscope with metal tripod

KENKO SPOTTINGSCOPES

20x60x60mm Zoom type (non prismatic) with metal tripod
25x50x60mm Zoom type with metal tripod . . . .
20x30x40x60x60mm 4-turret type with metal tripod . . . . .
15–50x60mm Zoom type with metal tripod . . . .
20x30x40x60x80mm 4-turret type with metal tripod . . .
20x30x40x60x101mm 4-turret type with metal tripod . . .

Hong Kong Suppliers

Friends:

Below you will find a new suggestion for Hong Kong mail order, and, if you want it, a general review for all five firms.

1. **Wood's Photo Supplies**

Wood's has the following price lists, all of which are sent by airmail:

- *A. 8 mm movie cameras & projectors*
- *B. Popular 35 mm SLR cameras & lenses*
- *C. Tuners & amplifiers*
- *D. Speaker systems, turntables & record changers*
- *E. Stereo tape recorders and decks*
- *F. Portable tape recorders.*

Wood's price lists arrived faster than any of the others. And as a company, Wood's seems to be the most personal and conscientious. Their information on U.S. import duties was most specific. All items with restricted trademarks (which must be obliterated) were noted. Wood's even suggested that I contact customs before purchasing any item.

2. Far East Company

As far as I know, Far East Company has only one catalog. It includes photographic equipment, camera accessories, projectors, binoculars, radios, tape recorders, Hi-Fi equipment and electronic calculators. The catalog was sent by airmail; and it arrived second fastest (a couple of days after Wood's).

They mentioned import duties and restricted trademarks. If you order enough Hi-Fi equipment from them, you get a discount.

3. **Albert White & Co., Ltd.**

White offers information on the following items. I sent for the camera catalog, and it arrived by airmail, third fastest (a few days after Far East Company)

1. *Photographic & Cinematographic Equipment & Accessories, Binoculars & Spottingscopes*
2. *Hi-fi & Stereo Equipment, Tape Recorders, Video-tape recorders and Transistor Radios*
3. *Seiko Watches*
4. *Electronic Calculators*

I sent for information on motorcycles six months ago, and I haven't received anything yet. They will correct the import duty and obtain the exact percentage from the Hong Kong U.S. Embassy. There was no mention of restricted trademarks.

4. **T. M. Chan & Co.**

Chan has three catalogs available.

- *A. Photographic equipment (with a few portable tape recorders)*
- *B. Catalog from the "Gents Customs Tailor Department"*
- *C. Catalog from the "Custom shirts department"*

I received the photo equipment catalog by surface mail. It arrived about three weeks after the one from White and Co.

There is absolutely no mention in Chan's catalog about import duties or trade restrictions. He says his prices are the lowest possible and invites comparison with other firms' prices, but as I have shown below, his prices are not the lowest.

5. **Universal Suppliers**

Universal has a whole slew of brochures. When I asked them for their "catalog", they sent me an aerogramme telling me that a "supply of catalogues" was being sent by surface postage. A little more than a month later, this small package arrived, weighing about 2 lbs., with all of the brochures listed below. All catalogs are sent by surface mail unless you send them money for air postage.

- *A. Cameras & accessories, binoculars, telescopes, riflescopes, sportingscopes and microscopes.*
- *B. Seiko watches.*
- *C. Rolex watches.*
- *D. Hi-Fi components, tape & cassette recorders, transistor radios, cartridge players and calculators.*
- *E. Hand embroidered tablecloths in linen, cotton or lace.*
- *F. Prescription eye glasses and contact lenses.*
- *G. Mikimoto Cultured Pearl.*

The catalog of photo equipment lists import duties on all the photographic equipment, but they make no mention of trade restrictions.

Guarantees:

1. *Wood's— makes no mention of a guarantee. They may have one and they may not.*
2. *Far East— guarantees that what you ordered is brand new*
3. *White— one year guarantee, free repair, free return by sea mail.*
4. *Chan— no mention of guarantee. Maybe so, maybe no.*
5. *Universal— same as White.*

Prices:

For camera equipment. Prices on Hi-Fi equipment seem to be agreeable with those of cameras, i.e., if prices are lowest for cameras, they are generally lowest for Hi-Fi equipment. Comments below are generalizations— they can be prefaced "on the whole".

Lowest prices— Wood's and Far East

Close third— Universal

Somewhat distant fourth— Chan

Definite Fifth— White

So, on the whole, Wood's & Far East have the lowest prices. But Universal has the lowest prices on some items. (When I say "price", I mean price of the item plus packing, handling, insurance, & sea mail shipping)

The only conclusion I'm going to make is this: If you are going to order any camera equipment from Hong Kong, write to the three top firms— Wood's Photo Supplies, Far East Company, & Universal Suppliers.

Remark: Personally, I wouldn't order any Hi-Fi equipment from Hong Kong. The prices, after sea freight charges, are not exceptionally low. They can be equalled or beaten by some of the discount houses in the U.S.

Remark No. 2— I have never ordered anything from any of the five firms above, so I don't know anything about service.

Jim Kessler
Oxford, Ohio

VIEW CAMERAS:-

Calumet (Germany) View camera	
4X5" w/16" Bellows	145.00
4X5" w/22" Bellows	178.00
4X5" Wide Field	204.00
Recessed Lensboard	12.00
Rollfilm Holder	387.00
Lensboard Standard 4X4"	8.00
Graphic Lensboard Adapter	16.00
Calumet View Camera 8X10"	370.00
Lensboard 6X6"	12.00
Lensboard adapter	28.80
Reducing Back 4X5"	74.00
Reducing Back 5X7"	68.80

Albert White & Co.

Akai (U.S. Named "Roberts") Stereo Tape Recorders, Tape Deck & Speaker System:-	
Akai Professional Tape Recorder X-360	470.00
Akai Professional Tape Recorder X-330	425.00
Akai Professional Tape Deck X-360D	405.00
Akai Professional Tape Deck 420-XD	405.00
Akai Professional Tape Deck X-33OD	380.00
Akai Professional Tape Deck 5050-XD	380.00
Akai Custom Tape Deck X-200D	255.00
Akai CustomeTape Deck X-150D	180.00
Akai Custom Tape Deck 4000D	134.00
Akai Stereophonic Tape Recorder M-10W	323.00
Akai Stereophonci Tape Recorder M-10L	312.00
Akai Stereophonic Tape Recorder X-1800SD . . .	288.00
Akai Stereophonic Tape Recorder 778-X	288.00
Akai Stereophonci Tape Recorder 1800L	222.00
Akai Stereophonic Tape Recorder 1710W	172.00

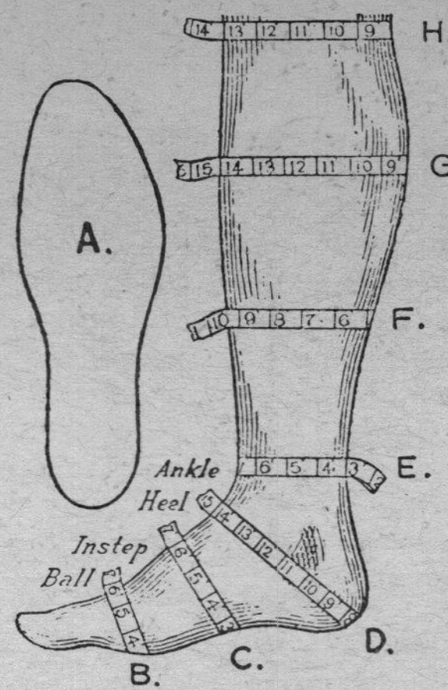
A.
B.
C.
D.
E.
F.
G.
H.
Ankle
Heel
Instep
Ball

DIAGRAM A

Lee Kee Boots & Shoes

Lee Kee Boot & Shoemaker, Ltd., Universal Commercial Bldg., No. 65 Peking Road, Kowloon, Hong Kong— will make any boot, shoe you want— send them a drawing or magazine picture & they'll do it to your size specifications. They charge for materials & not labor, so they're quite reasonable. If you'll write, they reply very speedily with price list & instructions to measuring your feet & sample sheet with range from dupont corfam to ant-eater & ostrich skin to some reasonably nice suedes & plain leathers. All leather lined. Haven't received our boots yet but have heard they do great work. See old price list enclosed. (I'm getting some knee-high brown suede lace-up-the-front high-wood heel boots for $25.00— made to fit my poor screwey feet.

Crow & Ceres Hyatt
Cedar City, Utah

Price list and leather samples, $1.00.

BOOTS

HALF-WELLINGTON BOOTS:

West German Calfskin, Scotch Grain or Rough Suede	US$13.00
West German Calfskin Top with Genuine Shell Cordovan Vamp	US$19.00
Genuine Shell Cordovan	US$24.00
Kangaroo Skin or Fine Suede	US$15.00
Du Pont Corfam	US$16.00
Italian Soft Calfskin	US$16.00

International Shopping

I would strongly suggest that anyone who wants to make any large purchases should arrange a letter of credit with a local bank. This will protect your money and will guarantee the foreign merchant his also.

Don't forget that sea mail can take an awful long time— and that air mail runs about $5.00 per pound.

You can order lists of foreign businesses from the State Dept. They will send you a catalog of countries with classifications such as machinery, textiles, etc.

For $1.00 they will send you names and addresses of specific companies (lots of them) for each classification.

From there you can write the company directly or go back to State for detailed reports on each company (assets, reputation, number of employees, language spoken, etc.).

This can be most helpful provided you have a pretty good idea of what you're after.

A.G. Willis
Washington, D.C.

All Purpose Far East

Suppose someone wants a good camera, recorder, or watch at about half the regular U.S. price. Here's a legal way with no risk. Decide the brand and model number and get a local price. Then send a 13 cent aerogramme to Mr. Tan Tieng Liat, 2 Jalan Istemewa, Singapore, 10 specifying the product desired. (Asian and European and American manufactured goods are all cheaper). Liat will refer your request to a local merchant who will reply by air mail within two weeks from the day you mail your request. They will quote a given price which will include the item, manufacturers guarantee, fabulous packing, shipping, and insurance by Lloyds of London. You then send a certified check or money order in the specified amount to the merchant. If air shipping is used, it's seven days for delivery to the U.S. Seamail takes ninety days but who'd want to ship a recorder airmail? A lens is something else.

Your postman will deliver the parcel and collect customs but you'll find a 10% rate on a $40 lens is less than the same rate on the U.S. price of $110. Singapore merchants make a profit, don't worry. But they think 10% markup is fair and Kodak has a standard 33%, Sears marks up over 40% and so on.

It's a good way to do business, and help Asia help herself by transferring capital from surplus to shortage areas.

Incidentally,— if the transaction doesn't work out, the Chinese Chamber of Commerce and Prime Minister Lee Kuan Yew of Singapore will investigate immediately on hearing from you. My US $279.00 Minolta SRT 101 cost $124.00 in Singapore. My $175 extra lens cost $80.00. I paid all the duties! I just dealt with good old Singapore merchants! In half a decade not one has ever let me down even a little.

Lloyds will send your insurance policy before the parcel arrives.

Biggest surprise to me was that I lived near Ampex in California and went to Singapore and found that Ampex stereo recorders sell for half the San Francisco price.

Wake up America. Regain the free trade heritage which initially made this country great. Save dollars for America's best products: color film for example!

James M. Oswald
DeWitt, New York

Apocalypse juggernaut, hello

As if the spirits of our ancestors weren't trouble enough, now we're haunted by the ghosts of our descendants.

Ken Kesey claims that ecology is the current handy smoke-screen for everybody's Dire Report—the voice of white-eyed paranoia. Gary Snyder (strong proponent of population control) when told of an Earth of solid people impending soon, commented dreamily "think of all that consciousness."

I tend to view the whole disaster as an opportunity to try stuff. If you take all the surprise-free projections for mankind's near future and connect them up, they lead neat as you please right into the dead end meat grinder. The only Earth we had, used up.

Unless there are surprises. Which is what we're here for. The Standard Operating Out, when a species is in a bind, is to diversify. Multiply alternatives. If you don't know what's coming, the way to evolve ahead of the changes is to try everything.

Reasonable laws made by reasonable men in reasonable times proscribe trying everything. For a good reason: people get hurt trying stuff. If you're bound to try stuff anyway, then either you're working directly for City Hall or you're an outlaw, or both.

Buckminster Fuller:

"It surprises people when you tell them that since the last ice age three-quarters of the earth has been water, and of the one-quarter that is land very little has been lived on. Ninety-nine percent of humanity has lived on only about five per cent of the earth, and anyone who went outside of it—the tiny minority that went to sea, for example—immediately found himself outside the law. And the whole development of technology has been in the outlaw area, where you're dealing with the toughness of nature. I find this fascinating and utterly true. All improvement has to be made in the outlaw area. You can't reform man, and you can't improve his situation where he is. But when you've made things so good out there in the outlaw area that they can't help being recognized, then gradually they get assimilated."

[From Calvin Tomkin's profile of Fuller, "In the Outlaw Area", *The New Yorker*, Jan. 8, 1966]

Present outlaw areas include space, the oceans, mountains, desert, northwoods and tundra, jungle, and then places like molecular biology, your mind, and other state-of-the-art frontiers whose languages are still foreign to lawmakers.

One thing we need is better outlaws. The antidote to external routine is internal routine, not sloppiness. The finding and following of your own drum. Help save the world: do something wrong today. Do it today because time is short, and capable outlaws aren't made overnight.

Is it a contradiction to design an outlaw area? In the past there was always undesignable frontier to serve, some space left over or not reached yet. If we run out of that resource, can we synthesize it, or intentionally preserve it? Or will it spontaneously bubble back up in the middle of our cities? (Oh yes.) I suggest that we must give the devil his due or he will surely extract it.

Any design fantasy is just loose talk until it happens. Here's one.

—SB

Loose Talk 1: The Outlaw Area

The specific fantasy called OUTLAW AREA is a geographical place where anything goes. Let's say it's an island.

For society it functions as a human dumping station. When a guy gets a jail sentence he has the choice of serving the sentence or being deported to the Island. He can't come back for some specific period of time, or he must meet some bureaucratic criteria to return, or the expulsion is permanent. Yessir, put all the bad apples in one bad apple barrel.

For the individual it serves as an always possible alternative to the situation he's in. He can simply split for the Island and take his chances there. No one's going to try to get him back.

For evolution it's an open end, a place for other stuff

Aquarian Haven

Photo from "Open Land: a manifesto" published recently for defense of the commune at Wheeler Ranch, Box 81, Bodega Bay, CA 94923.

to happen. High energy, minimum prior form, violent range of constant inputs; it should be wild. "In wildness is the preservation of the world."

It's difficult to imagine how it would be in the Outlaw Area. You can project some from the history of Australia, once a penal colony, or from the present underworld. Robert Heinlein has a book about the Moon as a penal colony called *The Moon is a Harsh Mistress*. It's kind of nice: they have a revolution and throw the jailers out.

Depending on the size of the island, my expectation would be either a dictatorship or warfare of rival gangs, like in old China, warlords. Maybe not though. This is a different age. The Island might become an Aquarian haven for the most useful pioneers—the cream and the dregs of society, (Kesey's notion) bending reality off into unimaginable directions with no restrictions save the harsh ones of nature.

Est

A more creative than usual call to political action.

—SB

Est— The Steersman Handbook
L. Clark Stevens
1970; 142 pp.

$1.50 postpaid

from:
Bantam Books, Inc.
666 Fifth Avenue
New York, N.Y. 10019

or WHOLE EARTH CATALOG

The definition of revolution, "the overthrow or renunciation of one government or ruler and the substitution of another" does not accord with the present continuum of events. The upheaval in America today provides a chaotic surf upon which would-be revolutionaries steal wild rides, but to define the upheaval as revolution is to fail to discern its essence. It is not organized. It has no plan. It has no doctrine. There is no pattern, no structure— no leaders and no followers. It happens. It *is.*

Guidance System

To the degree that a corporation serves the purposes of its original founder, it tends to be "humanoid." Mr. Post cared very much about Postum and personally mixed, sipped and tasted the product as his personal substitute for coffee. Henry Ford I spent much of his early life under the hood of the Model T and would tolerate no compromise in its design. Walt Disney held exact standards for his cartoon characters, and Land of Land Cameras,

participates to this day in Polaroid product as a knowledgeable inventor. Most of these originators incorporate for "tax purposes and limitation of legal liability" which means that the corporation, a structural device designed to process money, is applied to the business of producing and selling the product. The actual *kind* of product is not crucial to the corporate structure. For example, conglomerates diversify and service many products under a single, overall, corporate control. Thus, we see that the corporate structure serves as processing system and the originator serves as guidance system. When the originators, men personally and primarily concerned with the product, retire, die off or sell out, the guidance system which they embody is altered and in their stead the processing mechanism gradually dominates direction of production. To maintain apparent continuity of original guidance, the founder's name is often perpetuated through heirs, if available. In time, however, processing functions tend to over-ride guidance functions. Thus the original guidance system loses primary control. Driven now by its inherent responsiveness to profit and loss, the corporation "homes" toward money as ultimate target. The product becomes more and more of an incidental, a sort of "necessary evil" which is merely the vehicle for financial gain. This fact is plainly visible in the massive corporations of today wherein directors are rarely creator-inventors. Most of the originators have been replaced by money-managers, financiers, lawyers and accountants. In contrast, smaller business tend to retain the originator and, thereby, retain the "personal touch."

•

It is time for the Movement to defend the U.S. Constitution which is theirs by right of birth. Not a symbol like a flag or a great seal or other patriotic emblem, the Constitution is the original structure designed to guarantee the unstructured freedom of peaceful individuals. Defense of the Constitution is defense of the individual. Free U.S. citizens are not rights-beggars. Rights are not gifts given by governments. Defense of the individual is the defense of inalienable human rights: Peace, Love and Freedom. The Movement can achieve coalition within the widest disparity if it recognizes that in the Constitution there exists a chart by which to navigate continuous change. This does not suggest a global application, but for America, in the coming decade of conflict, it provides valid, familiar and necessary articles of freedom.

But ten or fifteen miles later D.R. grew so doubtful that it was right he stopped and backtracked again. It just couldn't be the right road. The farther he went the narrower it got, and there wasn't a house or a roadsign on it. D.R. went back to the crossroads, pulled off into the gravels and looked around inside the bus for a roadmap of Kentucky.

There wasn't one, of course. There must have been a dozen roadmaps scattered around, including one of the Eastern United States that showed the freeways in Kentucky. But for driving on the local roads away from the traffic mainstream there wasn't a map in the bus that showed the way and that pissed D.R. off and scared him at the same time.

His first impulse was to blame Estelle. At about the moment he realized he wasn't going to find a Kentucky roadmap he came across Estelle's knitting bag in a pile of stuff behind the driver's seat. In his mind the knitting bag, and its owner, seemed to be responsible for there being no Kentucky roadmaps. In a fury he grabbed the bag and flung it out Urge's side door. Some of the yarn fell out and tangled up around D.R.'s feet. In trying to get it off he tied his hands up in it for a second and that almost drove him crazy. He screamed through his teeth and started flinging things left and right. When he came to something that felt like Estelle's he tried to throw it out the door, but most of it caught on the door facing and piled up at the foot of the bed. D.R. picked up his cassette recorder and almost threw it too, but he caught himself and turned it on instead. The voice of the Greek filled the bus and flowed out into the night, uttering for the first time in the history of the Kentucky mountains the names of Ouspensky and Gurdjief. D.R. shouted "Fuck Ouspensky and Gurdjief," and threw the recorder hard against the back of the bus. The Greek groaned and spoke like Donald Duck for a second, then died.

(continued)

Cut The Motherfuckers Loose

Ed McClanahan found these notes by Ken Kesey in a box of stuff, two and a half years after Ken made them the night he got out of jail. The notes were made as Ken was waiting to be released. They are published here unrevised, and unedited.

—Gurney Norman

FRIDAY OCT 10,

'A'TANK,

MAYBE THE LAST TIME

And as I come in dressed in my usual street business, leather, striped pants and shoes, whistle hanging out, Derner takes one look and his already stone face freezes even harder.

"All right, Kesey, give me everything."

"What?" Usually they let the honor camp men take in anything except knives or watches.

"Everything. I don't want you in there blowing your whistle."

"Okay, then, make me out a property slip."

He gives me a steady unwavering stare through the bars. Tears a scrap of paper from a notebook and slips it in the typewriter.

"One Whistle," I say. He doesn't type. "One yellow pen." He continues to glower, stoney cold unmoveable. "Come on, I want a property slip." I'm worried about my two camp notebooks is what we both know.

"Just put it all in the trough, he says. "In fact, strip out of that jacket!" He comes out of the cage. I take off my leather jacket. "Hands on the wall. Spread 'em." He gives my feet a kick. "Now. Don't move!"

He frisks me, the whole show. Taking pens, sunglasses, handkerchief, everything. And my two notebooks, wrapped in the farewell card Stevenson made and the camp guys signed.

"Listen. I get a property slip for this stuff."

"While you're here, you do it *my* way," Derner lets me know. No malice in his voice. No anger. Just stone information and not to be argued with.

"Okay then," I hold up my two notebooks. Show them to Deputy Johnson. "Witness these?" And the rest of the men waiting in the receiving hallway. "You guys check this?" Then hand the notebook to Derner.

"You think the rest of your book will come out in *Ramparts?*" Deputy Johnson asks.

"No, it'll be a book of it's own."

"You'll have to change the title then."

"I'll bet you a carton I don't," I say, watching my pens and notebooks disappear through the cage window.

"Okay, Kesey, you can move on. Next."

I come to A Tank. Boro is still here. In blues now. But still trying to keep up that old front. One by one the other guys show up. Derner has given them each the same treatment taking cigarettes, everything.

"Sorry about that," I tell them. "I should have been way at the back so you could have gone through first. But he saw my outfit and it blew his head so he had to follow through with the rest of you."

"Yeah," Boro says. "Stir clear of Kesey, he brings you nothing but trouble."

"Kesey!" Keys jingle. "Man's here to see you." Door slides open. I follow the turnkey to where Faber waits in front. He tells me I'm getting out at midnight. Who'll be here to pick me up? Who knows.

And he wants to see my notebooks. I'm leery but I figure better him than Derner. "Go ahead."

"And you're to be in my office Monday morning at 10:30 to sign your release to Oregon."

I say okay. We talk a little more about the camp. I tell him that all the camp needs is support from Redwood City. He hems and hums. Asks me when I think The Book will be coming out. Who know? When it quits happening. "This talk will be in it. Our talk Monday morning will be in it. Your reaction to what you read will be in it. It will be finished when its all over."

And Boro shouts Kesey. "Put this down. Put this down in your fucking book. A guy——me——a guy plays pinochle 4½ months with the motherfucking brass up there——4 and one half months——and one of the deputies misses a pack of Winstons when I leave and he calls down and asks what brand of cigarettes did Boro come in with. I mean, ain't that cold, man? Ain't that a bitch?"

Weekenders——bringing the Street in to tantalize you.

You can be *made* to serve double time——now time and street-to-come time——even triple time which adds street-ago time and is called guilt. But the man who pulls straight time——now tripping is neither short or long but serves in Eternity and very close to paradise.

More Weekenders. A Tank gradually burgeoning. "Hey Deputy, we already got motherfuckers, wall to wall." Boro has a way of sniveling so it sounds like a banty crowing.

> Drunk tank full to overflowing
> Motherfuckers wall to wall
> Coming twice as fast as going
> Heads get big and the tank gets small.
>
> Dominoes slapping on the table
> Bloods playing bones in tank next door.
> Bust a bone if you be able
> Red Death stick it good some more.
>
> Three days past my kickout time
> Ask to phone but don't got the juice.
> And crime times crime just equals more crime
> Cut the motherfuckers loose.
>
> Will I make the Christmas kickout?
> Will commissary come today?
> Will they take my blood or take my good time?
> Or just rip my guts away?
>
> Some snitch has found my fucking outfit.
> They've staked a bull up at the still.
> They've found the pot sprouts I was sprouting
> At the bottom of the hill.
>
> They've punched my button, pulled my covers,
> Blown my cool and ruint my ruse
> They rehabilitated this boy
> So cut this motherfucker loose.
>
> And the fish that angles for the bull
> Let him off his heavy rod
> And you that suckers the gavel banger
> Cut him loose from playing God.
>
> Back off from Johnson all you peace freaks
> So he'll back off from Vietnam
> Cut loose the squares, cut loose the hippies
> Cut loose the dove cut loose the bomb.
>
> You the finger on the trigger
> You, the hand that weaves the noose
> You, you hold the knife of freedom
> Cut all the motherfuckers loose.

11:30

After a long talk with Braun, soft-peddling in circles and coming in Contact occasionally——back to A Tank.

Simpson: "I just don't trust Braun. I don't think he's got any balls. I think he's basically weak and I think he's trying to build his image by associating with you, Ken Kesey."

I know all that. But I'm also onto what he *wants* to be—— the strong thing he wants to be. And I'm willing to try to support that image.

...en a voice at the bars: "11:30. Kesey? Yeah. You ready? ...eady as I'll ever be. Come on then."

And into receiving where an old colored dude is excitedly getting into his clothes. Typing of forms next door. Ritual of red tape typing, gently typing at my chamber door——

The colored dude——an old shoe-shiner packs his work gear into a black cardboard box and ties it with a rag. His shirt is white and looks nice. His shoes are a sensational gloss.

"What you in for?"

"Oh I pulled a knife. Woman called the cops. Wasn't no actual fight. Well, I on my motherfuckin' way . . ." Picking up his bag and putting on his hat.

"Yessir on my way."

"Good luck to you."

"Lost some weight here. Needed to. Met some good people too. All right now . . ."

A young blood stops him, gives him his address.

"You all better print it. That the only way I can read it."

"Take it easy now, Pop."

"All right. . . ."

The kid leaves. "Damn fool tramp. Got some motherfuckers in this jail. Oh, I'm ready. City be just right. I get the right bus, that is."

Still no call to leave. He fingers a corncob full of tobacco, lights it, goes to lean at the door. "What the time?"

"12 straight up," the deputy says.

"Oh, I'm ready."

"If my people are there I'll give you a ride to the bus station."

"Appreciate it. Didn't sleep all night. I got nothin but time no way. What you in for."

"Dope. Weed."

"That a shame. That good green stuff. Make you feel good. If God hadn't wanted it on airth he wouldn't a put it here would he. That a stone shame. How much they give you."

6 months. $1500. 3 year tab.

"That a motherfucking shame."

"Well. It's done."

"I reckon."

"Rucker!" a bull's voice calls.

"I comin."

And I'm alone on the bench with his half-drunk cup of coffee, spoon still sticking out of it. His blues on the floor. The polyethelene bag his suit had hung in the corner.

"Ken."

Justice Without Trial

The social edge that the policeman patrols is highly visible these days, and all too relevant, and so ambiguous that few can bear to look at it close. But until it's looked at close, and in broader terms than one's own bust, we'll be stuck with it the way it is. This book is inherently interesting, dealing with goals and tactics and anecdotes of our closest war. It also should be interesting to those who would redesign the edge.

—SB

Justice Without Trial
Jerome H. Skolnick
1966; 279 pp.

$5.50 postpaid

from:
John Wiley & Sons, Inc.
605 Third Avenue
New York, N. Y. 10016

or WHOLE EARTH CATALOG

Whenever rules of constraint are ambiguous, they strengthen the very conduct they are intended to restrain. Thus the policeman already committed to a conception of law as an instrument of order rather than as an end in itself is likely to utilize the ambiguity of the rules of restraint as a justification for testing or even violating them. By such a process, the practical ambiguity of the rule of law may serve to undermine its salience as a value.

•

The policeman is directly antagonistic toward euphemisms. Unlike the peacetime soldier, the policeman is *always* in "combat", out on the streets, doing his job. Like the dogface, he is irritated by most manifestations of what he terms "chicken shit"——an inclusive abstraction encompassing minor organizational rules, legal technicalities, and embellished descriptions. The policeman's culture is that of the masculine workingman. It is of the docks, the barracks, the ballfield——Joe DiMaggio was a helluva good "wop" centerfielder, not an athlete of "Italian extraction," and similarly, the black man is a "nigger," not a member of an "underprivileged minority."

•

"Straight date" refers to genital intercourse. "Half-and-half" means half "French," half "straight," that is, fellatio followed by genital intercourse. "Greek" refers to anal intercourse. Other sexual acts may be purchased as well, but these are the standard products.

•

Indeed, from his familiarity with the law about possession, the nonaddict-dealer is likely to have a "stash" or a "stash pad" somewhere removed from his own residence, perhaps at the home of a girl friend, or even in any of the numerous places in the public domain that can serve as "stashes," such as trees, directional signs, the undersides of benches and so forth.

Community Profile

Interested in moving to some part of the country but never been there before? To help you examine an area, you can order a "Community Profile" on any of the 3135 counties in the U.S. Delivery takes about 3 weeks.

[Suggested and reviewed by Howard C. Wolf, Jr.]

$6.00 from:

National Technical Information Service
5285 Port Royal Rd.
Springfield, Va. 22151

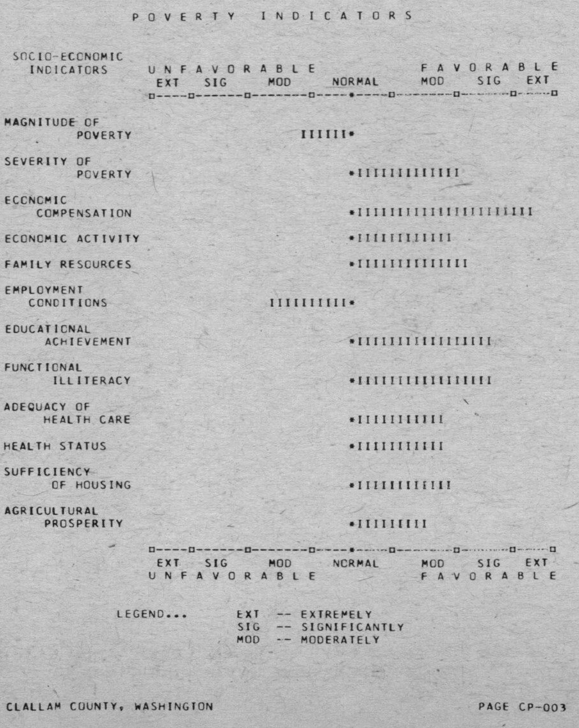

```
                    P O V E R T Y   I N D I C A T O R S

SOCIO-ECONOMIC        UNFAVORABLE                    FAVORABLE
   INDICATORS     EXT  SIG  MOD  NORMAL        MOD  SIG  EXT

MAGNITUDE OF
   POVERTY                           IIIIII•

SEVERITY OF
   POVERTY                •IIIIIIIIIIIII

ECONOMIC
   COMPENSATION              •IIIIIIIIIIIIIIIIIIIIIII

ECONOMIC ACTIVITY            •IIIIIIIIIIIII

FAMILY RESOURCES             •IIIIIIIIIIIIIII

EMPLOYMENT
   CONDITIONS         IIIIIIIIIIII•

EDUCATIONAL
   ACHIEVEMENT               •IIIIIIIIIIIIIIIIII

FUNCTIONAL
   ILLITERACY                •IIIIIIIIIIIIIIIIII

ADEQUACY OF
   HEALTH CARE               •IIIIIIIIIIIII

HEALTH STATUS                •IIIIIIIIIIIII

SUFFICIENCY
   OF HOUSING                •IIIIIIIIIIIIII

AGRICULTURAL
   PROSPERITY                •IIIIIIIIIIII

               0----0----0----0----0----0----0----0
               EXT  SIG  MOD  NORMAL   MOD  SIG  EXT
               U N F A V O R A B L E     F A V O R A B L E

LEGEND...    EXT -- EXTREMELY
             SIG -- SIGNIFICANTLY
             MOD -- MODERATELY

CLALLAM COUNTY, WASHINGTON                    PAGE CP-003
```

The Drug Bust

A very practical guide to avoid the damnedest bust we got, the drug bust. If you're smoking dope you can use this survival lore. Parents, consider this an outstanding Christmas gift for your children.

OUT OF PRINT

The Drug Bust
John Dominick
1970; 95 pp.

$1.95 postpaid

from:
The Light Company
259 W. 15th St.
New York, N.Y. 10011

or WHOLE EARTH CATALOG

—SB

Defendants in drug cases are often confronted with a form that purports to ascertain if the defendant is a drug addict. The form contains questions concerning the drugs the defendant has and is presently using. The answers to these questions constitute admissions and can be used *against* the defendant. A defendant does not have to answer these questions and should not do so, nor should he sign any form until he has consulted his lawyer.

•

The defendant has the right to remain silent and should exercise this right. Many a case has been lost before the lawyer ever met his client. The police may hint at making a deal in exchange for information. However, any deal made under these circumstances is worthless. If a deal is to be made, your lawyer is the one to make it. Let him do the talking; what he says cannot incriminate you.

•

Whenever possible a woman should step forward and speak to the officer. Whenever dealing with a policeman, respect and politeness are in order. The police are accustomed to encountering aggressive personalities they enjoy the opportunity to assert their authority. Policemen should be addressed as "Sir" or "Officer."

While maintaining this attitude one should make it as difficult as possible for the police to make an illegal search. In practice the police will do anything you let them do. And if they find drugs they'll lie in court saying they were in open sight or the defendant dropped them on the street when he saw the policeman approaching.

If a policeman approaches your car or house, you should step out, locking the door behind you. If one is going to be the victim of an illegal search, look around for a witness. Stop a passerby or summon a neighbor. Many policemen are reluctant to make illegal searches and will attempt to acquire your cooperation with a leading question, i.e., "What's inside the car?"

At this point the defendant should try politely to assert his rights. If the police ask you to open the trunk or "What's inside the car?" you should ask if you are under arrest. If the police say no, you should state, "With all due respect, I would like to continue my private lawful business. Good afternoon." If the police hint that you are under arrest, request the charge and demand to be informed of your rights, to be taken immediately to be formally charged, and allowed to contact your lawyer. Police are reluctant to make false arrests. It leaves them open to embarrassment and a lawsuit. Polite confrontation is the only way to remind them that they too are subject to the law.

Sa-So

Town equipment. Signs, trash cans, paint, flags, office supplies, auditorium stuff, playground stuff, radios, searchlights, badges, handcuffs, guns, prison stuff, uniforms, stretchers, fire equipment. Fascinating catalog.

—SB

[Suggested by Mayor of Portola Valley Sam Halstead]

SArgent-SOwell, Inc.
1185 108th St.
Grand Prairie, Texas 75050

LUFKIN
CITY LIMIT
POP. 15135

55R 175
Hand Operated Siren With
Carrying Strap.
ea. **$69.30**

55R 176   Hand Operated Siren Without Strap.
ea. **$66.00**

Perfect solution for undependable or nonexistent electric power supply. Bracket for mounting to any convenient object or use as handle for portability. Carrying strap optional. Scientific design, precision gears and bearings assure maximum sound volume for minimum cranking effort. Rated at 105 decibels at 100 RPM crank speed. Durable lacquer finish. 6¼" high, 7¼" wide, 5" deep. Shpg. wt. 5¼ lbs.

Helmet Emblems
2½ × 2½ INCH

Pressure sensitive identification emblems apply to outside of windshield or any smooth surface. 2½"x2½" in size. 10 weigh 1 oz.

50¢
ea.

23R 394   Black on White
23R 395   Black on Gold

The Bust Book

Legal First Aid (does not replace a lawyer's care) for demonstration busts, being a witness, trial strategy, bail, etc. Greasing through the machinery by knowing it. A New York book with wide application.

—SB

The Bust Book— What to Do Until the Lawyer Comes
1969, 1970; 159 pp.

$1.25 postpaid

from:
Grove Press, Inc.
214 Mercer St.
New York, N.Y. 10012

or WHOLE EARTH CATALOG

Never carry drugs in a demonstration!

If you smoke, bring a pack of cigarettes. If you get busted you'll be glad to have them for yourself, and to hand out in jail.

Never take your address book to a demonstration! If you're arrested the cops will get everyone's name.

If you're worried about having something planted on you (this is not common in New York except for Movement leadership or for addicts) have a set of demonstration clothes with the pockets sewn up or cut out.

Never carry a pen-knife or a nail file to a demonstration. You can be charged with possession of a dangerous weapon if you get busted.

You are not required to say anything to an investigator. If local cops are belligerent, and you are afraid to refuse outright to talk, tell them you want to speak to your lawyer first. The FBI will hardly ever threaten you, but they will be persistent, trying to draw you out with a "friendly" manner. They may get you into political discussions and pretend that you are winning them over as a way of getting you to talk even more. One of them may play friendly and the other tough as a way of getting you to sympathize with the friendly one and talk. You aren't required to talk to the FBI any more than the local cops— and you should clearly refuse to say anything to either one.

PRY-AXE
Forcible Entry Tool

Law enforcement officers and firefighters find this 6 lbs. of forged steel excellent for forced entry and rescue. A multi-purpose forcible entry cutting tool designed for the serious business of operating at fires, wrecks and other emergencies. Complete with operating manual and leather sheath. Shpg. wt. 6½ lbs.

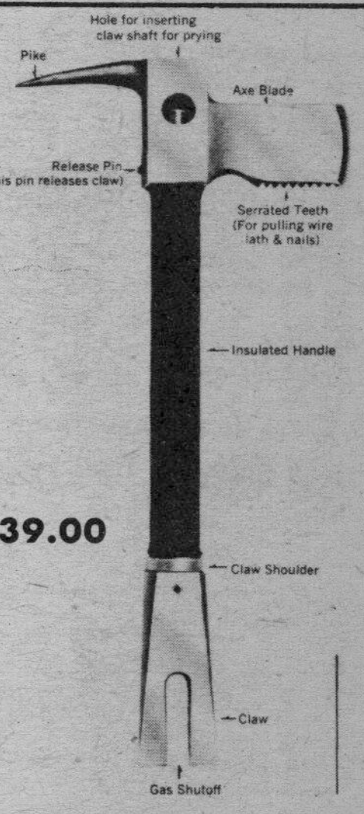

Heavy Duty   ea. **$39.00**

BICYCLE RACKS

Built for a lifetime of service. Solves that troublesome problem of parking bicycles. Sturdily constructed of 1¼" galvanized square tubing with ½" solid rods.

Allow 20-30 Days For Shipment

28R 362 5-Ft. Rack, Holds 10
Bikes, Wt. 90 lbs.......ea. **$74.10**

28R 363 10-Ft. Rack, Holds 20
Bikes, Wt. 150 lbs.... ea. **$111.10**

28R 364 15-Ft. Rack, Holds 30
Bikes, Wt. 210 lbs... ea. **$156.75**

28R 365 20-Ft. Rack, Holds 40
Bikes, Wt. 285 lbs. . ea. **$210.10**

The search for the map was so frustrating it automatically turned into a search for dope. D.R. didn't remember for sure if he even had any, and the stupidity of not having any compounded the stupidity of not knowing where it was if he did have any. That too seemed like Estelle's fault and he screamed at her as loud as he could and called her a stupid bitch. D.R. was so furious he leaped into the driver's seat and roared off down one of the three roads without bothering to close Urge's side door. Shit was falling out and crashing on the road but D.R. didn't give a goddamn. He didn't know which road he was on but he didn't give a goddamn about that either. When he'd gone ten miles and hadn't found a 666 sign he turned around and roared back to the crossroads, right on through it and down the other road across the way. He didn't find any signs on that road either. He was on his way back to the crossroads to set fire to Urge and commit suicide when a rear tire hit a chughole so hard it knocked something loose and caused the motor and headlight to cut, right there in the middle of dark nowhere. D.R. didn't even get out to see what was wrong. He just sat there behind the wheel staring through the windshield at the black shapes of mountains all around.

A Short Political Editorial

All power to the persons.

—SB

Rules for Radicals

Toward a science of revolution. Much radical literature is aimed at fighting. This book is aimed, by an expert, at winning.

—SB

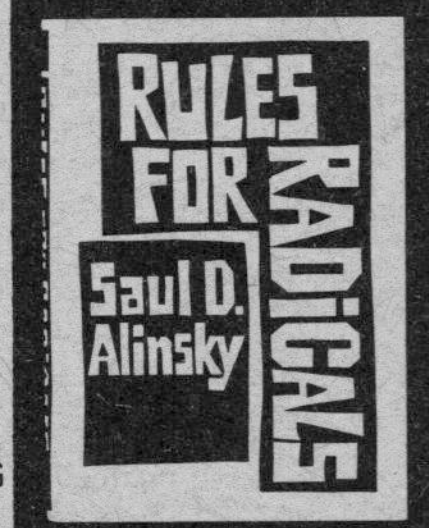

Rules for Radicals
Saul D. Alinsky
1971; 196 pp.

$1.95 postpaid

from:
Vintage Books Inc.
Westminster, Md. 21157

or WHOLE EARTH CATALOG

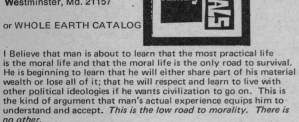

I Believe that man is about to learn that the most practical life is the moral life and that the moral life is the only road to survival. He is beginning to learn that he will either share part of his material wealth or lose all of it; that he will respect and learn to live with other political ideologies if he wants civilization to go on. This is the kind of argument that man's actual experience equips him to understand and accept. *This is the low road to morality. There is no other.*

•

Power is the right word just as self-interest, compromise, and the other simple political words are, for they were conceived in and have become part of politics from the beginning of time. To pander to those who have no stomach for straight language, and insist upon bland, non-controversial sauces, is a waste of time.

•

Tactics means doing what you can with what you have. Tactics are those consciously deliberate acts by which human beings live with each other and deal with the world around them. In the world of give and take, tactics is the art of how to take and how to give. Here our concern is with the tactic of taking; how the Have-Nots can take power away from the Haves.

For an elementary illustration of tactics, take parts of your face as the point of reference; your eyes, your ears, and your nose. First the eyes; if you have organized a vast, mass-based people's organization, you can parade it visibly before the enemy and openly show your power. Second the ears; if your organization is small in numbers, then do what Gideon did: conceal the members in the dark but raise a din and clamor that will make the listener believe that your organization numbers many more than it does. Third, the nose; if your organization is too tiny even for noise, stink up the place.

Always remember the first rule of power tactics: *Power is not only what you have but what the enemy thinks you have.*

The second rule is: *Never go outside the experience of your people.* When an action or tactic is outside the experience of the people, the result is confusion, fear, and retreat. It also means a collapse of communication, as we have noted.

The third rule is: *Wherever possible go outside of the experience of the enemy.* Here you want to cause confusion, fear, and retreat....

The fourth rule is: *Make the enemy live up to their own book of rules.* You can kill them with this, for they can no more obey their own rules than the Christian church can live up to Christianity.

the fourth rule carries within it the fifth rule: *Ridicule is man's most potent weapon.* It is almost impossible to counterattack ridicule. Also it infuriates the opposition, who then react to your advantage.

The sixth rule is: *A good tactic is one that your people enjoy.* If your people are not having a ball doing it, there is something very wrong with the tactic.

The seventh rule: *A tactic that drags on too long becomes a drag....*

The eighth rule: *Keep the pressure on,* with different tactics and actions, and utilize all events of the period for your purpose.

The ninth rule: *The threat is usually more terrifying than the thing itself.*

The tenth rule: *The major premise for tactics is the development of operations that will maintain a constant pressure upon the opposition.*

The eleventh rule is: *If you push a negative hard and deep enough it will break through into its counterside;* this is based on the principle that every positive has its negative. We have already seen the conversion of the negative into the positive, in Mahatma Gandhi's development of the tactic of passive resistance....

The twelfth rule: *The price of a successful attack is a constructive alternative.* You cannot risk being trapped by the enemy in his sudden agreement with your demand and saying "You're right—we don't know what to do about this issue. Now you tell us."

The thirteenth rule: *Pick the target, freeze it, personalize it, and polarize it.*

What do I want? I want a spring...well, I want it to run the dial, the outside dial, and of course the real problem is how to get a band out of this motion. Let me look at the motion again. How do you get inside that spring? If I...if there were an enormous spring...a spring as big as a house, and I hold onto it and it goes in and out. in and out.

What happens to me? Well, let's see, I can put a little drop of ink on the thing. Now I wind it in and out. Look. If I get a spring big enough, as the spring tightens . . . the blob of ink will move in . . . and out as the spring relaxes. . . .

"Funny . . . now I have the feeling that this thing is on its own, completely outside me . . . that the whole idea is no longer . . . no longer anything to do with being mine, my idea . . . it's just like flying now because if I put a spot on the spring and tighten it up, it performs an arc which is exactly the band I'm looking for [cf. Fig 4 (a), (b), (c)]. It's amazing, and this is no longer I . . . it's as though it was taken away from me. . . . This must be what people mean when they say you start writing a play and the people you've put in the play just go on by themselves."

Vocations for Social Change

VSC has a new magazine, Workforce, and a new direction—work liberation. They put out a good information-sharing magazine, and they're a resource directory for movement groups. How to work at changing the world.

—*Hal Hershey*

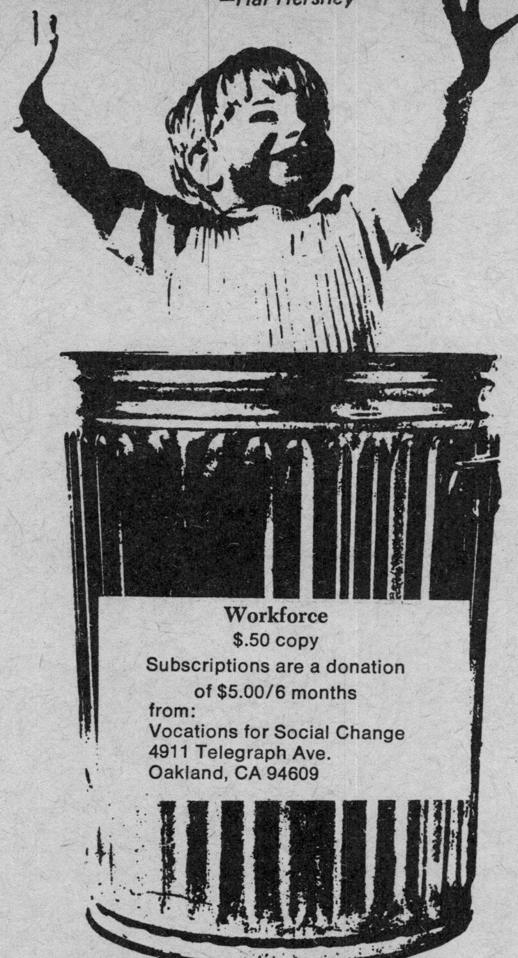

Workforce
$.50 copy
Subscriptions are a donation of $5.00/6 months
from:
Vocations for Social Change
4911 Telegraph Ave.
Oakland, CA 94609

Economic Alternatives

Co-op League, 1828 L Street, NW, Washington, D.C. 20036, publishes several pamphlets of how-to-do-it information for starting or managing a cooperative. Write for free literature lists.

(Phone: 202 628-9000)

Cooperative Services, Inc., 7404 Woodward, Detroit, MI 48202, is a big co-op service organization. They can help get co-ops off the ground.

DEVcorp, Don Newey, 26 Exeter St., Boston, MA 02116, provides a continuous buying club service to help consumers find better quality food and encourage the producers to provide better quality food. Anyone interested in either joining a buying club in your city or helping to organize one should contact them.

Foundation for Cooperative Housing, 1012 14th St., NW, Washington, D.C. 20005. Free publications, English and Spanish.

North American Student Cooperative Organization, 1500 Gilbert Ct., Ann Arbor, Michigan 48105, is a clearinghouse on cooperatives in the U.S. They have information on all forms of cooperatives: credit unions, groceries, laundries, eating clubs, etc., "as long as they are cooperative". In addition to their newsletter they publish a directory of cooperatives entitled *Crashing in North America*.

Synectics

An outline of a method for training creative groups and maintaining their creativity in the business environment. This book provides both the theoretical and experimental background and the practical details of how to put the method to work. Although written for use by business executives, the applications to other situations are obvious and important. Anyone attempting to create a commune or other group of people who will work together creatively will find many useful ideas here. The problem of interface between the creative group and the workaday world is also treated in some detail. Extensive examples of the method in operation, and a lengthy bibliography on creativity.

[Reviewed by Larry McCombs.
Suggested by Jane Burton.]

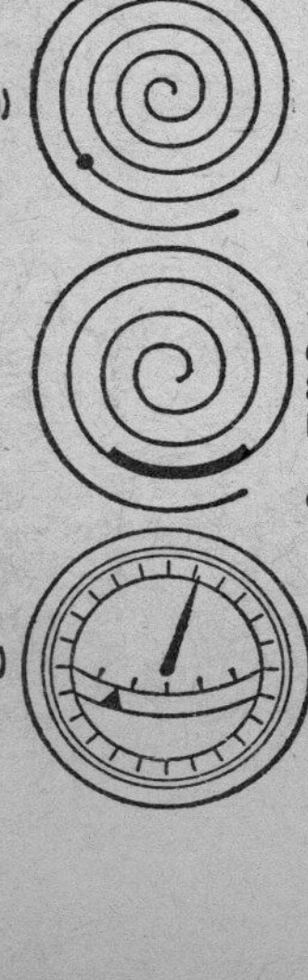

Synectics
William J. J. Gordon
1961; 180 pp.

$1.25 postpaid

from.
Collier Books
866 Third Avenue
New York, N. Y. 10022

or WHOLE EARTH CATALOG

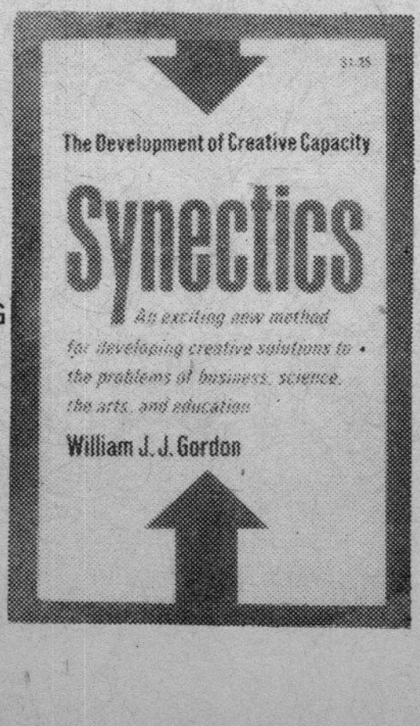

The Organizer's Manual

this book earns its buck and a quarter in its sixty-page bibliography. the other three hundred pages contain information of use to potential and polite revolutionaries, people who know they should be doing something, but don't feel right about generating unstructured change. structures and groups, rules and techniques, hints and helps for the gentle displacement of dinosaurs and pigs. like telling you to get medical attention for a bullet wound, put eggs water and baking soda on your face before the teargas attack, notify the media twentyfour hours ahead of time, watch out for chain letters, that you will get into arguments, and not to make the worker unwilling to be seen with you.

—*j.d.*

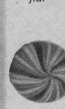

The Organizer's Manual
The O.M. Collective
1971; 366 pp.

$1.25 postpaid

from:
Bantam Books, Inc.
666 Fifth Ave.
New York, N.Y. 10019

or WHOLE EARTH CATALOG

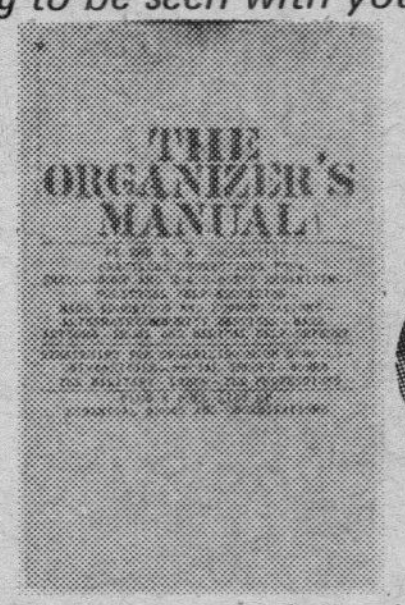

Ecology action organizations should provide the following services to the community: a regularly distributed newsletter on what has to be done and what has been done; grievances and discussion meetings and community projects. Scout troops, women's clubs, school groups, etc., are good places to plant suggestions for projects.

Within the organization itself, utilize a storefront office as a place from which to (1) publish research; (2) keep a file on local polluters; (3) document the legislative records of local congressmen and representatives to see if they match recent eco-rhetoric; (4) publicize an environmental hot line which gives the phone numbers of government agencies in your area to contact about instances of pollution; (5) lobby for legislation banning the internal-combustion engine and funding good efficient mass transportation; (6) start an ecology food store which specializes in organic food, returnable containers, and minimal packaging; (7) in conjunction with the food store, establish an ecology counseling service which develops with people ways to run an ecologically sound household; (8) send out speakers, movies, and literature; (9) distribute birth-control information and devices (check the legality so you know the situation). Demand that abortions and birth-control devices be provided free; (10) organize boycotts against local or national firms which insist on operating without regard to the environment; (11) send out guerrilla theater groups to hold mock funerals for rivers and other dying resources or hold parades for clean air complete with balloons, gas masks, drums, and coughing participants; (12) initiate campaigns to return all bottles, cans, and excess packaging to stores. Ask that it all be sent back to the manufacturer; (13) watch over, and fight when appropriate, "urban renewal" zoning, highway and airport projects, university and corporate expansion into surrounding neighborhoods; (14) set up "people's parks" in abandoned lots; conduct neighborhood cleanups (with community consent and participation).

Guerrilla Theater

Anthology of German Expressionist Drama, ed. Walter Sokel, Doubleday Anchor, 1969, $1.75.

Brecht on Theatre, ed. J. Willett, Hill & Wang, 1964, $2.45.

Commedia dell'Arte, G. Oreglia, Hill & Wang, 1968, $1.95.

Complete Plays and Prose, Georg Büchner (trans. C. R. Mueller), Hill & Wang, 1963, $1.75.

Eyes on Mime: Language without Speech, Katherine Walker, Day, 1969, $4.95.

Guerrilla Theatre Essay (pamphlet), San Francisco Mime Troupe, Dept. R., 450 Alabama St., San Francisco, Calif. 94110.

Happenings: An Illustrated Anthology, ed. M. Kirby, E. P. Dutton, 1965, $1.95.

Improvisation: Discovery and Creativity in Drama, J. Hodgson and E. Richards, Barnes & Noble, 1966, $2.25.

Modern French Drama: The Avant Garde, Dada and Surrealism, M. Benedikt and G. E. Wellwarth, E. P. Dutton, 1964, $2.75.

New Underground Theatre, ed. R. J. Schroeder, Bantam, 1969, $1.25.

Organizing a Community Theatre, S. Seldon, Theatre Arts Books, $1.75.

"Politics of Performance," *The Drama Review*, and most issues of this quarterly since 1968. *TDR*, New York University, 32 Washington Pl., New York, N.Y. 10003; $5/yr.

Radical Theatre Festival, San Francisco Mime Troupe, Dept. R., 450 Alabama St., San Francisco, Calif. 94110, $1.50. Discussion of the nature and practice of radical theater.

Stagecraft for Non-Professionals, F. A. Buerki, University of Wisconsin Press, 1955, $1.50.

Toward a Poor Theatre, J. Grotowski, Clarion, 1969, $2.45.

Ubu Plays, Albert Jarry, Grove Evergreen, 1960, $1.95.

Alternatives Directories

Movement yellow pages. Pretty handy.

—SB

Directory of Free Schools
1970; 30 pp.

Directory for Personal Growth
1970; 30 pp.

Directory of Social Change
1970; 30 pp.

$1.00 each

from:
Alternatives!
1526 Gravenstein Hwy, No.
Sebastopol, CA 97452

A Rap on Race

Some life and some light on deadly subjects like America, Race, The World, The Future, Where We Come From, What's Happening, by. . .is it a black and a white, or bright young man and a bright old lady? Foxy sweethearts.

—SB

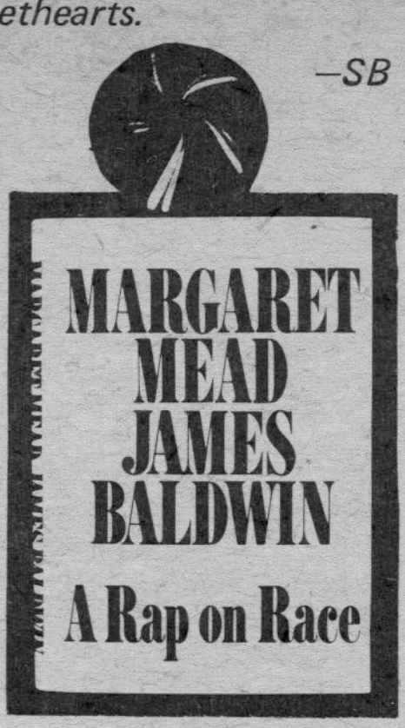

A Rap on Race
Margaret Mead, James Baldwin
1971; 256 pp.

$2.45 postpaid

from:
Dell Publishing Co.
1 Dag Hammarskjold Plaza
245 E. 47th St.
New York, NY 10017

or WHOLE EARTH CATALOG

Baldwin: This is very funny. Go on.

Mead: But I had reversed it, and my picture of rape was of a black woman raped by a white man. He was a butcher, too, and that's one of the things I thought of: he was a brutal character. So whenever I dreamt of rape, I dreamt of this black woman being raped by a white man. And our mother insisted on our calling her *Mrs.* — this is 1912. And whenever she turned up in a dream, I knew exactly what I was dreaming about. This is a straight reversal of ordinary American experience.

Baldwin: That's right. The ordinary American mythology is entirely different. I suppose that explains a lot about you.

Mead: Probably, although I'm not completely free. You see, I don't think any American— any white American— is free of a special attitude toward American Negroes. Just as you're saying there aren't any Negroes outside of America. We are often nice to other dark-skinned peoples. We treat African princes or Indians with turbans very well. When I went on. . . .My first field trip was to Samoa. Well, of course, the Polynesians are people everybody thinks are beautiful. If you look at them very closely, they are not really the most beautiful people in the world by any absolute standard. Yet everybody thinks they're beautiful. Chinese people think so, black people think so, everybody thinks so. I've now figured out why: that for maybe two or three thousand years they never saw anybody but themselves, and *they* think they're beautiful and they are so impressed with themselves that everybody else thinks they're beautiful. If you think you're beautiful, you move like a beautiful person.

Baldwin: In the name of your ancestors; let us put it that way. I have heard myself walking around the house singing a song I had forgotten, or didn't even know I knew, because I had to get through something and I had to find the only weapons I had. You reach out behind you and pick up whatever there is to confront this moment and to get past it. There is something very mysterious about it. Mystery is the only way I can define it. It is not mystical, but it seems to me that your ancestors give you, if you trust them, something to get through the world.

Handbook for Conscientious Objectors

In addition to this comprehensive guide to conscientious objection under the draft law, CCCO also publishes a variety of literature on military and draft procedures, high school ROTC, amnesty, and military recruiting deceptions. It provides legal advice and referral to military and draft counselors and attorneys. Other titles include Advice for Conscientious Objectors in the Armed Forces *($1.25),* Upgrading Discharges *($.20),* GI Booklet Series *(free), and* Guide for the AWOL GI *(free).* —PC
Suggested by many.

Handbook for Conscientious Objectors
Edited by Arlo Tatum
110 pp.; Updated frequently.

$1.50 postpaid

10/**$9.00** , postpaid

from:
Central Committee for Conscientious Objectors
2016 Walnut Street
Philadelphia, Pa. 10103

Also:
848 Peachtree St., N.E.
Atlanta, Ga. 30308

407 S. Dearborn St.
Chicago, IL 60605

1251 Second Ave.
San Francisco, CA 94122

or Rocky Mountain Military Project
1460 Pennsylvania St.
Denver, Colorado 94122

or WHOLE EARTH CATALOG

Robert's Rules of Order

If decisions are required from a group that doesn't always have consensus, these rules will organize the tangle enough to get through it.

—SB

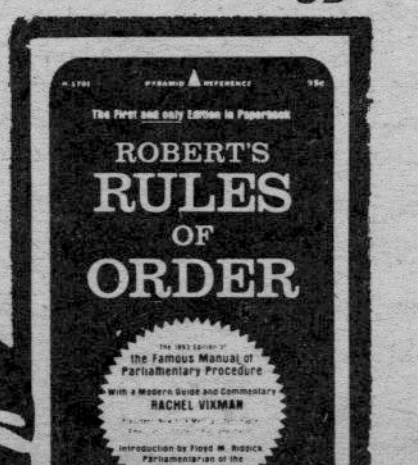

Robert's Rules of Order
Rachel Vixman commentary
1967; 204 pp.

$0.95 postpaid

from:
Pyramid Publications, Inc.
444 Madison Ave.
New York, N.Y. 10022

or WHOLE EARTH CATALOG

When Thomas Jefferson became President of the United States, he published the first American book on parliamentary procedure in 1801. This became one of the main sources for the rules in Congress and continued to be the foremost authority on parliamentary procedure until Cushing's *Manual* was published in 1844.

It remained for Henry Martin Robert, an engineer and general in the United States Army, to modify these rules to meet the needs of "ordinary societies." His first *Robert's Rules of Order*, published in 1876, soon became a handbook for organizations, clubs and schools all over the land. In a constructive way, it exposed the uselessness of attending meetings which began late and dragged on. It gave enlightenment and comfort to frustrated members who, without knowledge, were easily victimized by overbearing chairmen and ruthless small cliques. And it armed the general membership with the know-how to combat those seeking to push through controversial resolutions without proper consideration.

Black Reading List

Robin's Distributing Company lists 600 books "relating the Black Experience." Looks pretty comprehensive.

—SB

Catalog Free

from:
Robin's Distributing Company
6 North 13th Street
Philadelphia, Pa. 19107

Win

*to change people, you must communicate with them. there are a number of ways to go about changing a person's mind. walk up to him on the street, grab him by the carnation lapel, and yell "boogetyshoo, you mistaken bastard!" or catch him asleep and whisper honeydrips of sweet poison into his ear . . . "think, think, think, think, think, think, think, think." or become a soothsayer, truthsayer, set yourself up as an honest person, say what you think in a cluster of different accents, get your hand gestures down, and pretty soon people will start listening to whatever you are putting out. to work this alternative, though, you must either have a high reputation, indian chief, lawyer, god, or you must have a pile of power, the president of a large north american country. you can change society with painting, bombing, sidewalk scribbling, love, banking, unbanking, skywriting, prayer, retooling, and meditation, but, power to the people, you must change people to change society.
win tries.
it is a together magazine.*

—jd

Win
Weekly except August

$7.00 yearly

from:
Win
Box 547
Rifton, N.Y. 12471

In the ancient Runic writing, common to the Scandinavian and Celtic lands, the symbol ⅄ Signifies "Man Dying". Contained within a circle, ☮ the symbol signities "Man Dying in harmony with the established forces of Nature, to be reborn." Likewise, the symbol Y signifies "Man Worshipping." Contained within a circle, the symbol signifies "Man affirming Life in harmony with the Cosmos, the established forces of Nature." In both cases, the symbol is extremely positive, an affirmation of the place of the person in a creative Cosmos, and from this ancient use as well as from its later derivation from the Semaphore letter, it is most appropriate to signify the fact that surrounded by forces of hatred, death, and destruction we must choose love, life and creativity. In the words of the Old Testament prophet: "I have set before you this day life and death, a blessing and a curse. Therefore, choose life!"

Motive

A soft-spoken, attractive, radical magazine from the South.

—SB

Motive
No longer available

from:
Motive
P.O. Box 871
Nashville, Tennessee 37202

Our commitment to revolution must contain a recognition that we ourselves are damaged; a revolution is not a gift bestowed on others, but a process beginning with our own selves and moving outward to a fuller and more human sense of self. Blacks and women should have taught us that revolutionary politics is the effort to overcome your own victimization— this is the only lasting source. Guilt over what has been done to the Others is simply not sustaining, whatever its other noble virtues. It is urgent that we confront first the facts, then the sources of our own poisoning; and it will be as risky and terrifying a confrontation as any on the streets. We all want to believe that we can remake ourselves simply by wishing, or by some mechanical act; but could it be that the society we know to be so pernicious toward blacks and Vietnamese lets us off with a wish or a single decision?

There are a lot of specific revolutions that the movement should make in itself. Everybody has stored up his own list, but if there is a name for the attitude I would like to see, it might be *revolutionary humility*, a way of living we will have to take and make the time to struggle for. And I do not pretend that, in some sweet bootstrap operation, we can liberate ourselves if we only dissect ourselves enough. The process of liberation must remake the society as *in the process* we remake ourselves. It is said that Moses' liberation army had to undertake its 40-year-long march through the wilderness because no ex-slave would be fit to live in a new society. Do we dare now to decide that the revolution is not simply for those who come after us but for ourselves?

Imperialism is far older than capitalism. It goes back to Alexander the Great wanting to conquer the world to give it the blessings of Greek culture— and even earlier. It includes the wars unleashed by Muslims to give the world the blessings of Islam and those unleashed by the Church to convert the Infidel. Economics has sometimes been important if only because countries imagined that colonies would bring greater riches than they did. More often than not colonies have brought their mother country closer to bankruptcy than anything else. Partly because the eighteenth century English ruling class believed colonies were profitable they struggled relentlessly against American independence. To practically everyone's surprise the profits of English business on its trade with America increased fantastically after the revolution. In fact, the growth of America unleashed by the revolution was one of the most glorious things that ever happened to English Business. Liberal English economists like Huskisson argued on the basis that England should let all its colonies go. However, the glory of empire evidently moved stronger than strictly economic motives and so England held on to its colonies.

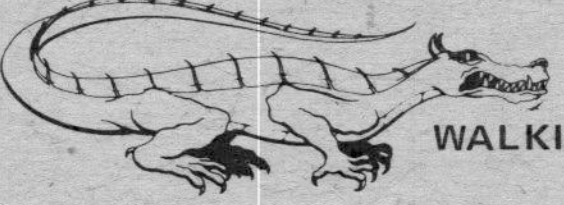

WALKING

Walking road a lonely road dark hills a starless moonless night green-smelling breeze leaves of willows sycamores down the bank I cannot see the road warm from afternoon the air cool from evening stirring leaves of willows sycamores down the bank below the road I cannot see but they are willows sycamores for there's a creek somewhere I smell it Behind the rucus of the crickets and the frogs I hear it bubbling through a shoals The air my skin and on my eyes smell animal's taste night as coal bite the coolness of the air against my skin not driving I'm not driving only walking step by step through darkness on a starless moonless night along the valley green-smelling breezes stirring in the leaves beyond the panic of the time dark the clothes my fright came garbed in the shroud of fearful ghosts that chased me driving I'm not driving now I'm being driven pulled into the night smell railroad tracks creosote and steel and splintering ties with long steel bolts into them smell it over the bank feel the road bend know the tracks bend know the creek bends into the folding of the hill smell tracks remember placing nails upon them for a train to flatten into horseshoe nails pennies into Roman gold remember boys along the tracks counting gons and waving at the man in the caboose smell a passing train from long ago smell stream hear wind in sycamores see light upon the darkness up ahead a speck a fly a lightning bug bobbing up and down and winking it's a star it's my brain shooting sparks behind my eyeballs it's some strange foxfire in the woods above the road grows larger walk slower Slower till I stop for surely stopping stop it growing larger don't jump around don't get no bigger the light is larger every step that I don't take the frogs and crickets all have hushed their singing don't get no bigger don't light up the world pupils light gets bigger coming closer I can hear it I can feel it walking I can see it just before me hissing on the forehead no please on the forehead of a man.

Wildcrafters

If you think longhairs are the only people running for the woods before the smoggy sky falls in, The Wildcrafters publications may broaden your view. They're the work of old geezers who groove on hunting and gathering food and fantasizing and opinionating about independence just like thee and me. Maybe we ought to get together and have a geezer conference. —SB

water witching
fishing tips
snow gab
future famine
nut trees
mountainmen
antique barb wire
flour mills
board warping.
a back to the sticks whole earth catalog, written by the folks who read it.
—jd

SURVIVAL HINTS
BEWARE of slipping, tripping or falling.

Back issues of
Wildcrafters are $1.00

Wildcrafters World
$1.00 yearly
Homesteaders and Landcrafters Newsletter
$2.70 per year (6 issues)
and assorted $1.50 manuals

from:
Wildcrafters Publications
R. R. 3, Box 118
Rockville, Ind. 47872

SALE OF TIMBER

If you own farm or country property with a woodlot on it, or a tract of land or large parcel on the mountain in timber country, use caution if someone comes along and wants to make a deal to cut the logs or pulpwood. Talk to your area Forest Ranger or County Agent. You can be guided by what they tell you. Also have a deposit and a contract from the lumberman. Keep in mind that it takes a lifetime to grow a logging tree, and you don't want to be cheated. We used to figure that it took 70 years for decent growth of spruce to mature. Of course, pulpwood is cut in smaller growth, large pulpwood bolts have to be split. I know of one woodlot owner that was offered $900 for the timber rights of the entire stand on his woodlot. He checked with the Forest Ranger who told him that did not seem like enough money. He gave him the name of a Timber Cruiser, the cost was not great, but the final agreement on the cutting operation was $2,800.00 I know of several other cases, but this is enough to give you an idea not to be hasty in making a deal to sell your timber. You might be given an offer that seems like a lot of money, but check into it.

Wood Heat Quarterly

The best aspect of the current resettling of the countryside is that so many of the settlers are intensely spiritual and recognize the depth of the archetypal relationship of man to earth. (That's many, I said, not all.) Such religious feeling for the agrarian life hasn't been manifested since the last century. By now, every state of the union (and many other countries) has its proportion of the new homesteaders. The Number is growing.

Wood Heat Quarterly is Vermont living, simple living, spiritual living. Practical, plain and poetic, all at once. Its articles on fuel supply, mules, soil care, herbal medicines and water witching are mixed in with the philosophy of Kirpal Singh, Wei Po-yang and the Essene Gospel. They talk about the Shakers and the Population Explosion. It's early New England transcendentalism, reborn, redefined and revitalized.

—Hal Hershey

Wood Heat Quarterly
No longer available

from:
Lowther Press
R.D. 1
Wolcott, Vermont 05680

Pyrotechnics

Homemade fireworks. Dangerous. Fun.
—SB
[Suggested by Gladney Oakley]

Pyrotechnics
George W. Weingart
1947; 244 pp.
$9.50 postpaid

from:
Chemical Publishing Company, Inc.
200 Park Avenue, South
New York, N. Y. 10003

or WHOLE EARTH CATALOG

FIGURE 66d
A Night Shell Effect

Philadelphia

In Philadelphia one day I discovered

THE HOW-TO-DO-IT BOOK SHOP
1526 Sansom Street
Philadelphia, Pa. 19102

LO 3-1516

Nice lady runs it, and she seems to have almost every howdy-do-it book ever printed. (I left with books and pamphlets on how to

        build a house or cabin
        upholster chairs
        make furniture
        start a new business
        repair a VW

May I recommend it as a place to look for the out-of-print, or not-much-call-for howtodoit book.

Judy Rascoe
Redwood City, CA

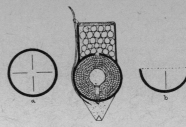

FIGURE 67
Arrangement of Smoke Stars in Shell

VOLCANO

This very pretty little device, easily made and perfectly safe for use by small children is produced by rolling a stout cone, 3 to 4 inches long and 2 inches in diameter at its base, on a former similar to that shown for sky rocket cones. The tip is cut off so as to allow an opening about 1/8 inch, into which a stout piece of quickmatch is inserted. A ramming mold is now made from a 4 inch block of wood, into which a tapering hole, of the same taper as the volcano cone, is worked. A case is inserted and rammed with the following composition:

Saltpeter	24
Sulfur	4
Mixed charcoal	4
Steel filings	10

A cardboard disk, somewhat smaller than the bottom of the cone, is now forced into the bottom of the volcano and secured with glue.

American Pyrotechnist Fireworks News

Find out what the other 7-fingered Americans are up to.
—SB
[Suggested by Rainbow People]

American Pyrotechnist Fireworks News
Peter Colonnese, Jr., Publisher; Max P. Vander Hoeck, ed.
$15 /yr (monthly)

from:
Pyro Press
Box 12010W
Lexington, Kentucky 40511

AMERICAN PYROTECHNIST FIREWORKS NEWS

A MONTHLY MAGAZINE ON FIREWORKS, & PYROTECHNICS

This completes the listing of commercial fireworks Herr Staedtler has submitted as used by the public today in Germany, but a few of his comments on several of them will be of interest. Regarding "Frogs" or "Grasshoppers", he says: "One of the most unpredictable and dangerous fireworks and one of the most unpopular for adults, for it is well known, what damages these things can cause. A paper and office supply shop sold fireworks between Christmas and Silvester and wanted to try out one of the big Frogs. They lit it and threw it out the open shop door and smiled when it blew off, but with the second bang the frog jumped back into the store and on the third bang ignited a box containing several dozen cannon crackers. With the next bang consisting of over 10 kilograms of fireworks going off and destroying the whole shop.

Kinnikinick

Available from: AMERICAN INDIAN TOBACCO & ENTERPRISES
Mohawk Nation
Via
Rooseveltown, N.Y. 13683

Write to: Kaherahare

Real and authentic Indian tobacco, several types for different tastes. I haven't tried rolling any in paper yet, but the wet type might do it if cigarettes are your bag. But, the stuff is really for pipers. The Ceremonial tobacco is by far the richest they carry, heavy and black leaf. Western Plains tobacco is in my opinion the smoothest all round stuff, mostly pure tobacco. None of the tobaccos are aromatic in the white man's sense of the word. Don't smell like mixture 79 or the like. BUT, the kinnikinick, the NON-TOBACCO leaves sold as "Chippewa Straight" is truly *the* find. No nicotine for you guys who've quit but long to puff on something that won't send you UP Also, used as a mix with other blends makes the very best smoking.

Mountain Men of the 1840's—traded very heavily for the mixture called Kinni-kinick, (Algonquian for smoking stuff) that was made best by the Chippewas of Bear Berry Leaves and Red Willow bark and other herbs. It smells like the forest. Sitting in New York, the aroma fills the apartment and for an instant, you're away. It helps. Try some.

Mohawk Blend is already a mixture of tobacco and Kinni. Northwest Coast tobacco is heavy and minty.

They'll send a sampler package of three types for $3.15 inc. post. If you want the straight non-tobacco stuff ask for sampler number two.

Otherwise just write for their free pamphlet on tobaccos.

Chuck Rapoport
New York, N. Y.

Earth Flag

A gentleman named John McConnell came into the Truck Store a few weeks ago and said that since all the nations have flags, and the UN has a flag, and states and businesses have flags, maybe there ought to be a flag that's just for people. So he got one of the Apollo Earth photographs and came up with the Earth Flag. I don't know if I'd die for it, but it's the first flag I've seen that I don't feel it somehow excludes me. The Earth Flag feels nice to wave.

—SB

Earth Flag with the Hog Farm Bus in Istanbul

Earth Flag *(12 x 18 inches)* **$2.00** postpaid
(3 x 5 feet) **$15.00** postpaid
(5 x 8 feet) **$45.00** postpaid

from:
"W.E." Inc.
19 Troutman Street
Brooklyn, New York   11206

or WHOLE EARTH CATALOG

The Country Bizarre

A hobbit-like publication from England of country hints, poems, recipes, swaps.

—SB

The Country Bizarre

Quarterly

from:
Bizarre Acres Publications
1 School Cottage
Cliffe Rd., Frindsburg Extra,
Near Rochester, Kent,
England

Paper

The other day, while cruising around Bizarre Acres, I came across a reciepe (?) for making paper. Now at first, the thought of slogging over some soggy pulp to make a few sheets of paper a dull experience but just think how nice it would be to paint or write on paper that has been produced and prepared by your own hands.

EQUIPMENT: A Stanley knife or something equivalent with which to chop up pieces of wood, one large saucepan (a pressure cooker would be better but don't worry if you haven't got one) and a rolling pin.

INGREDIENTS: Quantities of birch, pine or spruce (there's no need to hack down a tree because branches and twigs picked up from the ground will do just as well)

METHOD: Cut the wood into pieces for easy handling, remove the bark and chop into small chips. Place these chips into the saucepan, add sufficient water and boil until they have been broken down into fibres of desired length. Be careful not to let the saucepan run dry. (For the owners of a pressure cooker, cook at 15 lbs pressure.) After a few hours you will have a fibrous cellulose. At this stage, if you fancy a coloured paper, add a dash of a non-toxic dye (a vegetable dye is preferable as its non-chemical) and stir gently.

Drain the mixture carefully, roll out into the thickness you want and dry over an even heat to remove the excess moisture. When you're satisfied that the sheets are dry enough, roll into reels and leave to stand. You now have a fine matt paper ideal for all your purposes.

Should you want to work on hand-made paper but find it awkward to get things together, you can always buy some from Paperchase (half way up Tottenham Ct. Road) for about 4/6d imperial size or from Kettles (127 High Holborn, WC1, near the Art College) at roughly the same price.

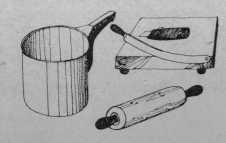

Hear the Sound of My Feet Walking
Drown the Sound of My Voice Talking

Dan O'Neill's cartoons sideswipe my head continually, and I'm grateful. The West Coast answer to Jules Feiffer.

—SB

Hear the Sound of my etc.
Dan O'Neill
1969; about 80 pp.

$3.95 plus $.50 postage and handling

from:
Glide Urban Center Publications
330 Ellis Street
San Francisco, California 94102

or WHOLE EARTH CATALOG

New Life Environmental Designs Institute

Access information and to-order research on alternatives. New Life Network and Community Designs Newsletter.

—SB

New Life Network
Bimonthly, **$6** /yr

Community Designs Newsletter
$12 /yr 6 issues

The Green Revolution

Seems to be the grandmother of the alternative culture newspapers and magazines. She's spry (been publishing since the '30's) and always has lively articles (written by Mildred Loomis and a young and young at heart staff). Wears simple, functional layout, newspaper format. Nothing called "news," though, just in-depth stories that are relevant. Latest issues have dealt with massage, pig slaughtering, rescuing trees, planting trees, defoliation, dandelions and water wheels. They're always promoting the green revoltuion, the return to the land.

—Hal Hershey

The Green Revolution

$4.00 /yr. (monthly)

from:
International School of Living
Route L, Freeland, MD 21053
or School of Living-West
4421½ Land Fair, Los Angeles, CA 90024

OFFING THE PIG

by Larry Lack

Last Saturday we lovingly liberated Ron's soul from his well-developed body. The previous day we'd transported his little sister, Laura, to a neighbor's farm so she wouldn't have to witness her brother's demise. She will remain at her new home for some time, making babies.

Ron and Laura, named for the couple who point the way in Mildred Loomis' "Go Ahead and Live," were Heathcote's pampered porkers, held in highest esteem by the entire community.

I won't attempt to describe the technics of the butchering process there: they are best observed on the spot. A few notes on the killing may be useful: several people told us that the most humane killing technique was a hammer blow to the skull prior to opening the throat and bleeding. I could not do it, and chose instead the more common method – a .22 rifle pointed just above a line between the eyes and fired point blank, I fired the shot myself, and I think it entered the brain, causing a very quick if not entirely painless death.

I chose to kill Ron myself because I strongly felt that all meateaters should come to terms with the killing their diet requires, and should assume moral responsibility for that killing by doing it themselves whenever practical.

THE GUIDE

"I thought you was a cow," said the man with the light on his cap. It was a coal miner's hat, with a burning carbide lamp on the front. "I heard you way back yonder and told myself I said that's somebody's old cow got out."

"I thought you was a ghost," said D.R.

The miner laughed. "Well now, I could have thought the same thing about you. But I've walked this road many a time at night and I learned a long time ago it's always better to tell yourself it's a cow instead of a booger."

The miner laughed some more and then set out walking again, and D.R. fell in beside him. If the miner thought it was odd that D.R. changed directions to go with him he didn't say anything about it. The miner acted as if it was a common thing to run into people on that road at night. He was perfectly at ease and confident in his direction, and when his fright had passed away D.R. was glad to be beside him.

"What are you doing out here tonight anyway?" asked the miner.

"I'm trying to get to my uncle's place in Finley County," D.R. said. "But my bus quit on me up the road here a ways."

"You a bus driver?" asked the miner.

"It's a van," said D.R. "One of those Volkswagen vans."

"Oh yeah," said the miner. "They've got a lot of them up in Dayton."

(continued)

The Realist

Paul Krassner approaches every moment in his life as a potential source of humor and moral dilemma. He is seldom disappointed. Neither are his readers.

—SB

Far away I could hear the *roar of the falls*. Catatonic and gibbering I rose to the rear. Also Butch lifted me up. We climb a final knoll and *ooweee*. Natural fuckin wonder Jim! The majesty of all that water flashing and crashing like a moving post card. Without camera or guard rail or tour guide or beercan . . . not even the plastic music that pervades most national scenery marts.

This place was special because you had to earn it. Here come Bonnie Jean and White rabbit and David LeBruan all wasted from the walk. But the falls fixes all. Quivering with dying sun shouts rose and orange. rusty like the lord's own snot she set us down to worship while the sun sunk into sleep.

•

Let's take a quick look at the blackboard. All us earth people are holding hands in a circle. Whether we know it or not. We are all dancing and chanting and making our own individual sound which makes up the whole racket of life. Now somewhere along the line the circle turned in on itself so the folks in the middle are squished and screaming like hell. Maybe that's where Hell is . . . in the middle of that circle . . . Hiroshima . . . Dachau . . . Vietnam . . . Bellevue. Just close your ears and you can hear 'em. Now what we can do is help relieve the pressure by absorbing a taste of the tug. Pass it on. Trust your neighbor. Trust your trust. Practice makes perfect and everybody wants to be practice. Open the whole thing up so everybody's comfortable. Take a deep breath and start all over.

It gets real cozy in the center when everybody's watching out for everybody else like at Yale University. In the middle of all rock and roll my brother-in-law let loose 5 live frogs . . . on cue . . . I grab a mike. *"Don't anybody move! Some nut has just let loose 5 live frogs!"* And the hunt was on . . . like looking for jumping contact lenses but we brought 'em back alive. It was a calculated risk and it worked.

Later we all laid on the floor with his head on her tummy and her head on somebody else. Not freaky at all but warm and snuggle. After a while I asked to be passed around. Over the top of the pile. Everybody lend a hand . . . and I'm skimming along at a pretty good clip and it really felt nifty. Then we sent Tooker aloft. The baby of Barry and Moe. He's maybe two and bald like the buddha. Talk about total attention. Hand over hand . . . it was really quite grand with Tooker on top of us all. We can fly with the help of our friends.

ERIC HOFFER IS A TRUE BELIEVER

The Case of the Cock-Sure Groupies
by Ellen Sander

The Trial of Abbie Hoffman's Shirt
by the United States Government

Plaster Caster samples: Jimi Hendrix (#00004, 2/25/68); a friend from school; a fellow student; Noel Redding (#00005, 3/30/68); Don Ogilure (road manager, 5/5/68).

All Watched over by Machines of Loving Grace

I like to think (and
the sooner the better!)
of a cybernetic meadow
where mammals and computers
live together in mutually
programming harmony
like pure water
touching clear sky.

I like to think
(right now, please!)
of a cybernetic forest
filled with pines and electronics
where deer stroll peacefully
past computers
as if they were flowers
with spinning blossoms.

I like to think
(it has to be!)
of a cybernetic ecology
where we are free of our labors
and joined back to nature,
returned to our mammal
brothers and sisters,
and all watched over
by machines of loving grace.

The Long Song

It saddens me that we all have never been able to make our times of functioning together really sing a long song, though maybe we are singing a long song that is more subtle that I can grasp— sometimes I suspect this, but most often I think that the subtle song thought is a bunch of shit and we're really all raving and lost in different parts of the woods. Who knows. I continue to have an enduring desire for a lot of money to enable the realization of my dreams. In any event the denouement of our movie or movies will occur and etc. I hope eventually to live in the nice-smelling pine trees in a house I've built and have a nice garden and animals and have clean streams and rivers and lakes and the hills and forests and congenial friends nearby and etc. But maybe we'll all live in plastic 21st century or maybe we'll die.

Ron Bevirt
Gardner, Colorado

Directory of Hotlines, Switchboards & Related Services

The accessor's accessor. Hotlines and the like are invaluable services. Support your local ones. If you're starting one, this is a good outfit to get in touch with.

—SB

The Communication Company
1826 Fell St.
San Francisco, CA 94117

The Communication Company has available consultants with experience in the following areas: Switchboard/Hotline crisis and information telephone services; Free Clinics/community health centers; Family planning/Problem Pregnancy/Abortion counseling and referral services; Runaway House/Juvenile social and legal services; food, housing, arts & crafts, day care, and other co-ops; newspapers, radio, television, filmmaking, and other community-oriented media projects; alternative education projects and free schools; Church renewal and reform movement; management training; drug counseling training; and several other areas. We will attempt almost anything.

check one:
□ BANG!
□ WHIMPER

Seeping through our decadence-in-the-guise-of-insight come the totally related scents of responsibility to pass on this book choice: *Efficiency in Death* (Harper & Row, $1.50), a documented analysis of 105 ordinary business firms that have been manufacturing and assembling anti-personnel weapons for the Department of Defense.

Naturally, this suggestion is offered purely as an amoral tool. Does a blunt instrument know whether it's hitting a head or a nail any more than the *Ching* intends its coincidences to be taken personally?

"Freedom's just another word"--Janis has taken her chants on that great Mercedes-Benz in the sky--"for nothin' left to lose."

--Bobbie McGee

Now a courtroom will only hold so much. The primary job of the bailiff and the law of evidence is to keep too much from happening. "We don't want any of *that* in here." But if you fill it up softly, stealthily, using the rules of evidence like the zen rules they are, you can fill it too full, just a little. Then there's the thing which can be done: the right cough or a certain question. . .Overload! Makes it harder for judge and jury to think along their old rut. (Moral: even if you blow up the courthouse, sooner or later, someday, goddamit, you're still going to have to blow the judge's and jury's minds, else it ain't revolution, only more bullshit, I'm sorry to say.)

There is another thing which can be said in a couple of ways. Bob Dylan's is the neatest: "To live outside the law you must be honest." Inside the courtroom it reads, if you lie you had better be telling another, truer, truth. Shucking and jiving won't do, for justice may have nothing to do with what goes on inside a courtroom, but it has everything to do with the people who walk in and out.

This one can't help but be a little corny when it's said; that's why you can't ever come out and say it. Understand the thing is a ritual; we don the garb of judge, juror, prosecutor and defense lawyer and become possessed, dancing out justice. The dance now is become demonic and monstrous and just a bit incredible. Maybe and only just maybe you can reach out and touch--that being no part of this particular dance--another dancer; or even a look of regret, as when two persons who wanted so much to meet, part.

The Last Supplement

The March 71 Supplement to the Whole Earth Catalog was edited by Ken Kesey and Paul Krassner. I've refrained from copying much of their material for this LAST CATALOG because The Last Supplement is really its own publication, valuable by itself. Kesey has more writing in it than has appeared anywhere since Sometimes a Great Notion. There are sundry good articles, particularly Jim Wolpman on law, Chloe Scott on feet, Paul Robertson on flute, Paul Krassner on gas. The Bible and I Ching reviewed by Kesey. R. Crumb cover. Not your usual comic book.

—SB

WINTER SOLDIER READING TOOLS

Here are some books highly recommended for your private consciousness-raising sessions:

Revolutionary Non-Violence by Dave Dellinger--morality reports that should be required reading in all high schools, colleges, communes and barracks.

No More Lies by Dick Gregory--the truth about American history (and be sure to hear his album, Frankenstein).

Sisterhood is Powerful edited by Robin Morgan--a collection which provides the kind of inspiration that transcends gender.

How to Talk Dirty and Influence People by Lenny Bruce--an autobiography of the funny prophet which makes you wonder what he'd be saying if he were alive now.

Johnny Got His Gun by Dalton Trumbo--my personal Bible.

--p.k.

Say, for example, there is the Light, and also the Way, the Prayer and the Action (and that, perhaps, the Way does not necessarily move at all times toward the Way) then we need tools in two areas. The Bible is, for me, a tool of Light and the Ching is most practical day-by-dawdling-day tool of the Way. The oracle works on the cybernetic gestalt principle that when you stand at the free-throw line that the information concerning the future and distant relationship and outcome of ball-and-basket is contained in your *physical state at the moment of the shot.* We always know *down* in our cells which fork in the road to take but the knowledge is usually not permitted audiance in the tight-assed regime of the courthouse of ego and attachment that we recognize, in a kind of diplomatic dither, as our consciousness. . .("The cells say they got a lotta useful information, Captain, but great scott! you start listening to advice from that mob and the next thing you know they'll be demanding voting rights and vacations in Atlantic City and plasma pensions and god only knows *what* all. . .!") so we are sometimes forced to rudely bypass the red-tape media garble of our city hall for some grassroots opinion. So we give the Ching a ring. Of course we can't stop the boys in the smoke=filled rotunda from tapping our line but then neither have they figured out a way to stop the call so we toss the coins and figure, What the hell; go ahead and listen, Captain. You get good advice from the Ching even when you're eavesdropping.

Rolling Stone

Primarily an emergent-music trade magazine, it has expanded to be the dominant newspaper to its Generation. The music information is still there, and so is dope notes, lengthy thorough reports on Generational heroes and events, and no-heavy-ax-to-grind-yet accounts of political occasions. The Stone's editorial standards, both on writing and graphics, are refreshingly high, and Wenner and crew have good ideas—which may save them from the cramp that Graham and the Fillmores got into with similar success in the same high-energy field.

—SB

Rolling Stone
Jann Wenner, ed.
(bi-weekly)
$12
$14/yr. Canada
$18/yr. Overseas

from:
Subscription Department
Rolling Stone
Box 2983
Boulder, Co. 80302

Spaces
Larry Coryell
Vanguard Apostolic VSD 7558

Spaces features John McLaughlin along with Coryell, and it's a guitar player's dream. Both guitarists have a strong grounding in

Funny Smell Hits Halls of Finance

BY MAITLAND ZANE

SAN FRANCISCO—Forty-five years ago in the Financial District it was hip to carry a silver hipflask and know a good bootlegger. Today, booze is for the over-40s and the younger guys brag about the supergrass their connections laid on them last week.

"What do you do? I don't know but I do it every day.
Why do you do it? I don't know: but I know I do it anyway.
I do what I do indeed I do. I do what I do every day.
(Indeed I do.)
I do what I do. I am what I am.
We are what we are. We do what we can."

—Bonzo Dog's *What Do You Do?*

Friends

This is the British equivalent of Rolling Stone (derivative; for a while they were together, then severed). It has some kinds of items we've seen nowhere else, and that's welcome.

—SB

Listen, Hippies, Look, Wake Up. You are being too hip. So you've taken your tabs of 500 microgram Orange Golden Sunshine Purple Special and you reckon you know it all, no-one can teach you anything, you got the power of Lerv, an' yer fat smiles an' yer Biba dresses an' yer seven-skin joints an' yer long lervly hair just gotta turn the natives on. Will you wear that smile right through your five year jail sentence in Malaga, Erzurum, Bombay, Tetouan? Will you grin as they stamp something strange in your passport (pity you never learnt the language and can't understand it), will you hand them a flower when they try to rape your dopey girl friend who used to sunbathe naked on the roof and say 'fuck what the neighbours think, a bit of tit won't kill them.'?

United Kingdom Whole Earth Catalogue

Every issue of Friends (above) has 2 or 4 pages of Whole Earth Catalogue U.K., which is pretty good, well-reviewed access-to-tools in England. No price for cumulative catalog yet. Edited by Colin Moorcraft.

—SB

WHOLE EARTH CATALOGUE BRITISH EDITION

Friends

from:
T.F. Much & Co.
305 Portobello Rd.
London W10, England

Wake up. Stop carrying your plastic hip culture round the world. Formentera used to be a beautiful island of sleepy farms and white-washed houses. This summer it was like the carbon-copy of the main drag in any big Western City, flashy boutiques full of ugly clothes, bars full of freaks bashing bongoes long after the owner has asked them to stop, everyone playing the same dreary games they played in Finch's bar or the Filmore East. Ask the local people what they think: they's rather have fat middle-aged German tourists who spend money than a load of penniless bums who steal from them and stir up the police while trying to turn their paradise into a psychedelic circus.

Dylon
for answers to dyeing questions
write to:
Annette Stevens,
Consumer Advice Bureau,
Dylon International Ltd.,
Dylon Works,
London S.E.26

Dylon make ultra-cheap, easy to use, effective dyes. They come in 36 different colours and work on just about any fabric — including nylons and plastics. The range includes cold-water dyes (good for batik) and liquid dyes (which are ready for use after they have simply been added to hot water).

The Organic Food Service Directory of Organic Growers & Producers
1/- (in stamps)
from:
The Organic Food Service,
Ashe,
Churston Ferrers,
Brixham,
South Devon.

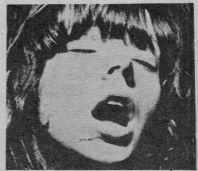

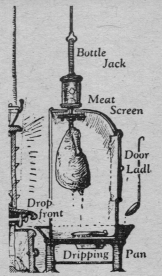

Bottle Jack

Meat Screen

Door Ladl.

Drop front

Dripping Pan

The O.F.S. Directory is continually growing and is produced once every one to two months. The idea is that you flick through the list, find your nearest grower and then go and call on him and collect what you want — thereby cutting out the middleman. A good idea. No charge (other than stamps to cover postage) is made to eaters or growers. If you grow (or know someone who grows) organic food make sure you're on this list.

"Oh, come on, mother," he muttered. "Not now. I haven't got the energy."

"Yes. Now," she said. "You've always made me feel a little ashamed whenever I criticized you, but you're not perfect, you know, and I've decided to speak up rather than let resentment grow inside me any more. You can take this any way you want to. The only time we see each other is when I invite you to my apartment. It never occurs to you that I might like to be asked out to dinner sometime. Let alone to one of your parties. I like being around young people. But you cut me off. It's not fair. I feel exploited, for example, bringing the borscht with me this afternoon, as much as I enjoy cooking for you. Can you remember the last time *you* took *me* out anywhere?"

What else could Leo say: "You're right, mother, absolutely right and I apologize. I never thought of it that way before. How about dinner next Thursday?"

"I'm busy Thursday night." She drew herself up straighter, and continued with increasing confidence. "There's more honesty in the air than ever before, in my lifetime anyway. It's simply great the way people are speaking out against injustice and prejudice. . . black power, women's liberation, gay liberation. . .people are no longer staying silent and neither will I. As wonderful as youth is today, they think they have a monopoly on the truth.

"Young people tend to discount both the interests and the opinions of elderly people. I will no longer stay silent against this form of racism. I'm thinking of starting a movement for elderly people's liberation."

Leo went over to her, kissed her on the cheek, raised a right fist, and said: "Right on, mother."

She laughed: "Up against the wall, son."

Michael Zwerin

Catalyst

The last Catalyst became the first Airmail, a directory listing information sources for artists. Publisher AIR represents 700 artists, runs visual slide library of current and experimental work available for exhibition, purchase, performance and commission.

—PC

Catalyst

$.50 once a year — airmail

from:
Art Information Registry Ltd.
Burlington House
Piccadilly
London W1V 9AG, England

Organ

Organ has the distinction of carrying new kinds of articles, new subjects instead of just new slants. That's a tough one to sustain, but editor Van der Leun has no other plans. (Editors who don't quit have my personal sustained applause; they live like Sisyphus.) This is the kind of publication that other papers cop graphics and ideas from.

—SB

No longer available

Organ

Back issues 9 for $10.

from:
Organ
Box 4520
Berkeley, CA 94794

"It's life: a game to be played for all it's worth."

L. RON HUBBARD CRUISES THE MEDITERRANEAN IN HIS YACHT APOLLO AT THIS VERY MOMENT. HE IS THE CLEAREST OF THE CLEAR. HIS CHURCH, GROSSING MORE THAN $75 MILLION A YEAR, IS COMPLETELY IN THE CLEAR. RON IS HAPPY. HE KNOWS THAT IF YOU LIKED HIS SCIENCE FICTION, YOU'LL LOVE HIS RELIGION.

At the core of Synanon is the Synanon game. The rules of the game are simple, straight forward and inviolable; no physical violence or threats of physical violence, no drugs, and, most recently, no smoking. These plus the rule that no one leaves the game until it is over are the only ones by which the players have to abide. Anything and everything else goes. Literally nothing is sacred. From these rules and the game itself comes the Synanon life style.

The students of Objectivism are filled with the wild-eyed idealism and romanticism that one normally outgrows along with pimples. A retail exec recalled, "When I think back to those in my class at N.B.I. I see them all as tall, confident, clear-eyed..." A young career woman who'd been through the mill explained, "The *Fountainhead* seemed so *moral* to me, so upright and clean and clear and logical. I read it when I was at Bryn Mawr. I was brought up a Roman Catholic and I had begun to think religion was hypocritical, full of myths. I suppose I was looking for another code, and she gave it to me. It was simple and direct. I became so involved with individualism that I was a bitch for three years, and everybody blamed it on Bryn Mawr."

D.R. asked the miner if he lived in Dayton.

"Off and on," he said. "I use to work at Frigidaire but they laid me off last year and I ain't been back. I told my wife I said if I'm going to be unemployed I'm going to be unemployed some place I care about living. So we come on home. We're staying with her people on Lower Elk right now. That's off the Poor Valley road, near the Crab Orchard."

"I see," said D.R.

As they walked on in silence D.R. tried to get a better look at his companion. He was about D.R.'s height, but much stockier. The light on his forehead went out in a jet. From the side it was hard to see his face in any detail. When the miner's face first materialized out of the dark and scared D.R. so, he had seen it from the front, and although he hadn't seen it in any detail then either, it had appeared to D.R. a very old face, weathered and deeply lined about the eyes. He had looked vaguely like an old Chinaman, but now from the side he did not look like an old Chinaman at all. He looked very young, in fact, and he certainly walked young. They'd only walked a quarter of a mile together but already D.R. was having to work at it to keep up. After they walked on in silence for perhaps another quarter mile, he asked the man where he was going.

"To join the Happy Pappys if they'll have me," said the miner. "They might not have me. It's hard to get much out of them people in town except appointments."

(continued)

Rags

Never fear, Rags is nowhere near a newsprint version of Glamour, so don't be put off by the fact that they talk about fashion sometimes. All they're really doing is talking about wearing your insides on your outsides. All of us feel that fashion can be superficial, trivial and irrelevant and it is . . . if you take it too seriously. Rags has zeroed in on fashion as just plain ole daily living and they look to the street for people who dig fashion as self-expression and not what-to-wear-when-and-why-not. They know that nobody should have to think twice about clothes or how they look except as a whimsical, trippy kind of safe-valve. Put on what you feel and you can't help but look beautiful. They print some good how-to articles, so you can pick up on all sorts of old and new recipes, beauty and otherwise, to make you feel better by doing it yourself and enjoying it all too. If your insides are being energized and revolutionized and beautified then those ole familiar outsides just have to be getting better too.

[Reviewed by Barbara DeZonia]

Rags

No longer available

from:
Rags
30 East 20th Street
New York, N.Y. 10003

Rags

CAUTION: RAILROAD RIDES MAY PULPIFY YOUR HEALTH.

T'was on the stretch of track between Starkey, Nevada and Utah that I began to learn the dangers of the rails.

I had been riding in an empty coal car with a floor that consisted of six large trap doors. Several dozen miles out of Starkey I picked up my pack and moved to another side of the car. A few seconds later there was an enormous clatter. The door I'd just been standing on had fallen open.

Sitting or lying down in my cozy coal car was impossible. The freights have no shock absorbers, a fact I'd never noticed on slower jaunts. When a train hits sixty miles an hour, the fool who attempts to sit is rewarded with a smashed ass.

Clean your boots regularly and waterproof them with Dri, Sno-Seal or a similar preparation. All reputable dealers offer resoling service.

Here is a list of boots available at various dealers (prices run about $40 a pair except for Fabiano, which is $10 less):

Leroux—Excellent French boot for real mountaineering.

Raichle—Made in Switzerland, several models from mountaineering to trail walking.

Pivetta—Italian boot sold in this country as *La Dolomite*. I own a pair and am well satisfied.

Lowa—Very good all round boot made in Germany.

Galibier—French, very fine workmanship.

Fabiano — Light weight trailboot made in Italy. Good for women.

Kronhofer — Austrian boot with hand-crafted features.

Make It

Make It

Issued quarterly, first issue, Fall 1971.

How to obtain, build, repair, recycle and renovate what you need. Dedicated to survival, economy and conservation.

Price— $3.00

Box 526, Old Chelsea Station
New York, N.Y. 10011

As soon as possible, we would like to have requests for information and projects you want.

We will also pay for suggestions and for articles describing projects you have completed.

The idea behind the periodical we're planning is pretty important, we think. Here's how it got started. I've been repairing, restoring/renovating and building things from scratch for about 25 years now, and was interested in it for a few years before that. I'll try to keep it short, but things repaired include small and large appliances like washers, refrigeration, small engines, cars of course, recording and film studio gear, radio, TV, radio and TV station gear (I have the FCC license), farm implements, steam engines and many more. I've built houses including all plumbing, wiring, finishing and cabinet making, made portland cement and bricks from clay and limestone, chemicals, jewelry, gemstones, tape recorders, recording studio consoles, radio studios, potters wheels, tools of all kinds, freezers and refrigerators, underwater photographic gear and lots more. I have considerable experience as a machinist, carpenter, mason, electrical and electronic engineer/technician, teacher, blacksmith and technical writer. My buddies have similar backgrounds.

I tell you this, not because it's some kind of a big deal— I've found that anyone with enough determination can do practically anything they want to if they take enough time— but rather to let you know where I stand and to support my belief that anyone who plans to publish or teach should know about the subjects they're talking about. And it isn't enough to have learned in an academic sense only— that may be enough for purely academic subjects, but practical subjects need to be supported by practical experience. A good way of learning a new subject is to tie it in with the related knowledge one already has learned/experienced— a craftsman can therefore learn in a very special kinetic way— by visualizing the subject as a job that will be executed to yield a finished product. If you project yourself into a job, you can predict what the order of the steps should be and what problems might come up. I'm not putting down books or even abstract or academic thinking, but when I pick up a book that claims to tell me how to do something, it should really work. It's happened to me and to everyone I know— and it must have happened to you, too— that after finding that a project from a book won't work and checking the work very carefully, you discover that the thing couldn't possibly work no matter what, because the basic concept is wrong. Then it becomes clear that the dude that wrote the book didn't try out the project, didn't have enough practical work behind him to evaluate the project, and, worse yet, didn't bother to tell the reader that the project was purely theory and therefore speculative. No good. You plan to end up with a working thing and instead you find yourself in a research project.

Our plan is to describe projects that have been done so that the idea is tested and the usual problems involved in execution can be described in a step-by-step procedure. We'll work up some of the projects ourselves, and we'll print articles from readers (paid for, of course) provided they are tested. We'll also run some abstract things or propose projects, but these will be clearly identified. The project articles will be as concise as possible, but complete enough that a newcomer to the subject can be sure that it will work if done carefully. We want to avoid the kind of abstract writing you find in survey type books where you plunk down 10 or 15 bucks for a book and get a text for an Animal Husbandry 101 class that tells you what a sheep looks like. Some books are really empty, and sadly, they may be the only thing available on a given topic. Others are written to the wrong audience. We think that homesteaders need information that applies to their needs.

An example: Instead of listing a catalog for coopers's tools, we will run an article on how to make barrels. It's important to tell where the tools can be had, as you have done so well, and it's also important to now how. We will tell how an experienced cooper makes a barrel in the classical way, where to get the tools and how to use them. We will describe how to make the tools— pretty essential when you look at the prices. Finally, we'll tell how to make barrels, using techniques that journeymen coopers don't use, but that are effective for people who want to make a barrel right the first time rather than making a lot of scrap ones as the cooper does in his apprenticeship. This will apply to all of our articles.

Max Pepke

Canadian Whole Earth Almanac

son of whole earth meets the mapleleaf mysteries
and superpress,
breeds with them,
and gives birth to
a beautiful babybeaver catalog.
thats the script.

—jd

India Trading Co. Ltd.

Located at:
113 Dupont St.
Toronto 180, Ont.

Carries a complete line of all ingredients necessary in Indian cookery. Spices, flours, rices, Dahls, chutneys, nuts, and vermicelli. Price list upon request.

Garlic—inhibits peas and beans. Garlic is very useful elsewhere in the garden as a pest repellant. A tea made with fresh garlic helps against potato blight. Roses grown near garlic have a stronger perfume

Onions—are good planted with beets and carrots. A few camomile plants (1 every 4 yds. of onions) are beneficial to the onions. Do not plant onions near peas or beans, as onions inhibit their growth.

Note: Healing and Canuck issues still available ($4.50 for both). These Canadian elves are now hard at work on a "best of" titled *Northern Comfort*. It'll be out in the Fall '74. Until then, their library is still open to everyone.

Canadian Whole Earth Research Foundation
Box 6, 341 Bloor Street West
Toronto, M55 1W8, Ontario, Canada

—PC

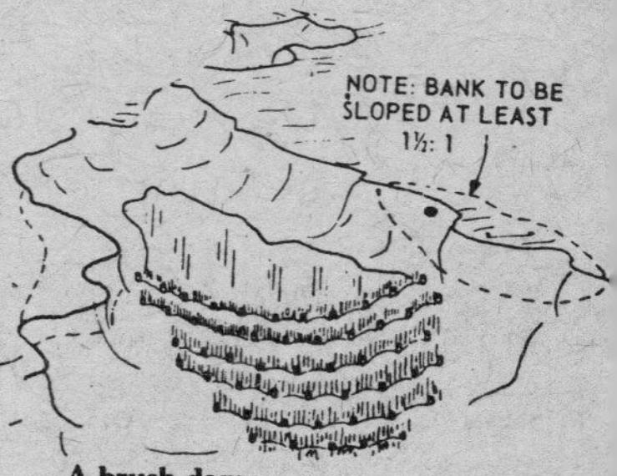

NOTE: BANK TO BE SLOPED AT LEAST 1½: 1

A brush dam

Whole Australian Catalogue

The first issue of The Whole Australian Catalogue *should be out early in 1972. At present we are negotiating with a publisher; if they print it, they will distribute it in the U.S.; if we distribute it, you can get it from us at:*

Source Books
121 Collins St.
Melbourne
Victoria
Australia

The price will be about $3.00.

Purpose: We think of Australia as one of the last frontiers. In a country so vast, the possibilities for learning, experimenting with new ways of living, and discovering untouched land and resources are still great

This catalogue is for people who live in Australia, and for those who are interested in or who want to immigrate to this part of the world.

It is a guidebook to what is available here in the way of tools, materials, information, books, land and whatever else can help us to create a new and better environment.

Contents: Dwellings: adobe; ferro cement; bark huts. Land: zoneing; prices; availability. Craft: weaving; ceramics; bush crafts. Aborigines: myths; culture; survival. Learning: experimental schools; useful tools. Ecology: conservation activity; use and misuse of land. Communications: music; film; T.V. Flora and Fauna: Australian native plants; animals; edible plants. Food: growing your own; beer and wine making. Immigration: jobs; acceptance of foreign credentials. Industry: access to materials for building, crafts. Communes: why, who, how're they're doing. Survival: in the bush, on land, at sea, in the air; outdoor activities.

Meanwhile, we might be able to offer some help and ideas for those who are thinking of coming to Australia.

Immigration: If you want to get a visa for travel only, there's no problem. Getting one for permanent residence is another thing. It can take 2 or 3 months, so you have to be patient. Also, they check lots of sources: your background, past activities, etc. Sometimes they refuse without telling you why.

Memory Holloway
David Matthews

Maine Times

John Cole is not reporting on the whole earth. The state of Maine is his beat, and the results of his focus are obvious. **Earth Times** *folded the same year* **Maine Times** *soared. Cole's weekly circulates all over the U.S., but his paper is primarily about Maine's ecological problems.* **Maine Times** *is revolutionary in that it's a straight business, dependent upon circulation and advertising revenue like most publications; and yet, it takes no shit. If the* **Times'** *editorial policy offends a potential advertiser, that's the advertiser's problem. Aside from its good work as a conservation news medium, the* **Times** *does a favor for us all by proving that power does not always rest in the hands of sons of bitches. The* **Times** *has been a central force in uniting Maine's lonely, isolated little voices for conservation into a tough political fist. It aint hippies they're uniting, and* **Maine Times** *aint a hippie newspaper, although the Freak spirit obviously dwells in the hearts of these newspaper pros. The* **Times** *lives at that difficult but special meeting place of overground and underground, with no apologies in either direction. So do a lot of other people, apparently.* **Maine Times** *circulation is climbing. Let's hope it's true, that as Maine goes, so goes the nation.*

—Gurney Norman

Maine Times
John N. Cole, Ed.

$10 /yr

from:
41 Main St.
Topsham, Maine 04086

Natural Life Styles

The Whole Earth Catalog *never became what it started out to be.* **Natural Life Styles** *comes closer. They take the time and (believe me) trouble to do a full job on subjects, like a long illustrated rambling talk with Euell Gibbons, a thorough letter on New Zealand, a comparative list of outdoor suppliers, and so forth. A hell of a lot of information for a dollar. Layout is funky but not obscure. Hang in there folks. Stay loose.*

—SB

Natural Life Styles
$9/yr (bimonthly)

from:
Natural Life Styles
Box 1101
Felton, Calif. 95108

Alpine Designs, formerly Alp Sport, PO Box 1081, 3235-45 Prairie Ave., Boulder, Colorado 80302, is a small company gone big time. They make excellent packs, pack bags, sleeping bags, tents and down clothes. Straightforward presentation with closeup of black and white photographs that give you a good idea of how the equipment actually looks.

Also from:
Gordon & Breach
Science Publications
One Park Avenue
New York, N.Y. 10016

single copies
$1.50

OUR PRECIOUS PETS by Ann Wigmore, D.D. ($.95) National Humane League, 25 Exeter St., Boston, Mass. 02116. Ann Wigmore has been known for years for the healing therapy program presented at the Hippocrates Health Institute in Boston. She offers her insights and techniques to both humans and animals alike. As a raw food, vegetarian her discoveries are quite different from any other pet publication you are apt to encounter.

Mother Earth News

Takes you a little further down the road Whole Earth Catalog *has pointed out; with complete "how-to" articles on subjects like persimmon leather, horseshoeing, free-lance cartooning, songpublishing and copyrighting, getting into Canada, recycling schoolhouses and dandelion wine.*

The entire second issue of TMEN was devoted to a reprint of The Have-More Plan, a 1944 get-back-to-the-land piece that touches on just about every problem involved in setting up a self-sufficient homestead on a few acres.

—Hal Hershey

The Mother Earth News

$8.00 per year (6 issues) $14/2 yrs, $20/3 yrs
Lifetime subscription: $120.00. Foreign: $10/yr
$18/2 yrs, $26/3 yrs
from:
The Mother Earth News
P.O. Box 70
Hendersonville, NC 28739

Mature dandelions can be trimmed to the center crown for delicious steaming.

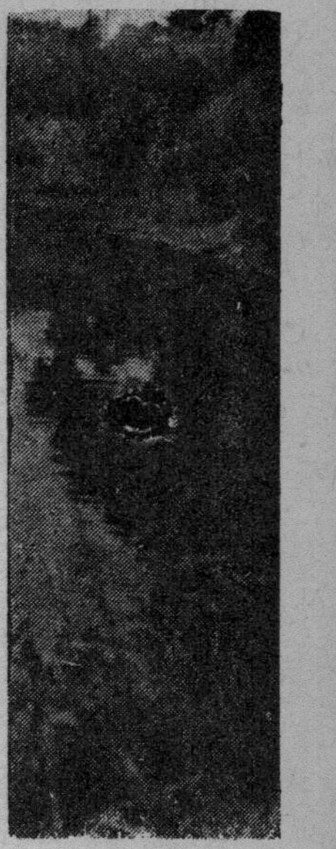

pond

I suppose the ideal location for a pond would be a half-acre (or larger) gulley or valley with clay soil, located on a gentle, grassy slope directly below a spring or artesian well. All a builder would have to do, in such a situation, is build an earth dam (with a spillway or drain pipe to control the water's depth) across the lower end of the depression and let it fill.

If you've got the gulley and slope but not the spring or well, you may still be in luck. As long as you have five acres drainage for each square foot of water that is six feet deep in your mini-lake, you can build the dam and let the rainwater runoff from the hillside fill your pond. As a matter of fact, you can get by without the gulley and slope. Even if your homestead is flat as a pancake you can still have that "private fishin' and swimmin' hole". . .by excavating.

An excavated pond is more work but it's also the most versatile (therefore, most popular) mini-lake. Such a pond can be located anywhere a source of water is available or can be made available. An excavation— instead of a dam— can even be placed in one of the gullies mentioned earlier and, so located, would probably be easier to keep full of water than a dug-out pond on level land. Most valley ponds are at least semi-excavated, as a matter of fact: the dam at the gulley's lower end being constructed, generally, of clay bulldozed out and pushed down from above.

The only minus factor (vastly overstressed in my opinion) of an excavated pond is the difficulty involved in draining such a reservoir dug into level ground. I believe, once your pond is stocked, you'll find yourself much more concerned with how to keep the water in than with how to let it out. A pond can always be speedily drained with a large pump that can be borrowed or rented if you don't have one of your own.

•

There are still other ways to get a pond constructed for very little out-of-pocket cash. If yours is to be located at least one-half mile from human habitation, blasting is a very reasonable way to remove the dirt. It's not necessary to pay for dynamite to move all that earth, either, although dynamite will be used to trigger the blast.

The main explosive element is Ammonium Nitrate saturated with fuel oil. This is the same Ammonium Nitrate farmers use for fertilizer and the fuel oil is the number two grade available at any service station. A good-sized pond can be blasted for less than ten dollars with this method. Before you try it, however, you should obtain a copy of the booklet, "*Blasting Potholes For Wildlife*" from the Wisconsin Department of Natural Resources, Box 450, Madison, Wisconsin 53701.

Vision, With Rap

I like your collective prose and the selections, under-the-skin communication. So therefore I feel called upon to criticize, no matter what your reasons for stopping publication, even of the most personal sort! I'm a new convert, and we are the crankiest!

Anyway, here are my suggestions. The catalogue and the truck store, truly beautiful in their concepts of space-mind preparations, stop short. There are other tools beside books. We do need to arm ourselves with knowledge and a clear mind to perceive, among other things the applications of knowledge. But reading is a limited way to understanding. When I came to the truck store, impatient to get there, I'd expected to find *tools,* models, materials, a community making a new design for Stores, that is——Information Centers, a place where you launch a new beginnings from. I would've like to see displays such as macrame and weaving, wind generators, plus having the wind generator working and producing, what? maybe lights and color machines, or tape music, or better yet, if we are speaking of new communities, running a motorized pump, that someone there has devised, with only available materials and his imagination. And so on. I suppose you'd need more room, but that might be exciting too! Could you go a bit farther out, close enough to urban centers, but still on the land itself, could the shape of the store change often——could people design, out of cheap materials, or plentiful materials, a changing line of Stores. I'd like to make a huge canvas shape, for instance, having it bulge and corner and dome where needed, held up by plastic rods, or aluminum poles——or another of scraps, driftwood and scrap metal. How about a small, shifting community, as people moved outward on their spiral, others come in who were interested in the Whole Earth concept, and also in spending some time in devising needed tools for where the truck store was at, putting together solar water heaters, hand made cowboy horse gear, (if of course you had horses!) organic gardens to feed this Whole Earth Truck Store Family. I think you have a lot of very committed people out here, who'd like to come together to really do things, solve common problems and learn. I think that this should happen in a real situation——there are many free university type courses, dealing well with theory and practices. I think a new book store could perhaps offer information in a more real way. That a small staff——or group—— could work out many solutions to new communities, to ecology and survival. The customers to your store could really be involved in these solutions, checking them out, offering their own, would in fact, be as neighbors concerned with the success of problems solved, not just in theory. The catalogue could, if publishing were continued become more as the supplements, be indexes of real experience (as the story of Libre, and Gary's Four Changes).

I mentioned earlier my own feeling of diet imbalance, and I know that this is not your responsibility; there are groups out in the "wilderness" learning just how one digs a well. There are many more people getting ready to go out, and not quite knowing how. I suppose we will all find out when the need hits us, soon enough! I also feel you've done a lot. So much, in fact, that I would like to see you continue. If I haven't totally turned you off by my Virgo-Vision, perhaps we can get together some time and rap about dream theories.

Thank you for creating the Whole Earth,

Sincerely,

Ann Hatch
San Anselmo, CA

I'm impressed with these ideas and moved by the vision. I expect it's not all that individual a vision, either; many of our readers and customers may have felt vague rumblings along these same lines, not to mention our own staff. We did rap with Ann——no indication yet whether she'll go any further with it. We can't do anything to actuate or realize this particular vision, beautiful as it is, and still continue the trip we're into at the Truck Store, which has its own dictates (time, energy, direction, money, space), its own pace, meaning, goals, joys, frustrations, tiresomeness, challenge and beauty. By the same token, there's nothing that would turn us on more than to see it happen. A lot of times, when people say, why don't you do such & such, we say hey that's a groovy idea, why don't you do it? We're doing our ideas and even that seems a bit much to tackle at times. I dunno, it's always seemed to me that one of the main things the CATALOG says is do it yourself, man. We dig most of the criticisms we get very much, whether or not we make changes around them. What I don't dig is the underlying feeling I sometimes get that we're being asked to do stuff that belongs by its very nature to the head that thought it up, to do it. It would be so much better ecology if some of the mental energy that gets directed toward us were directed instead towards the real and physical realization of the ideas. A lot of visions don't ever get out of the head, and that can be a waste. Some get as far as being down on paper, and that's a beginning. Only! Or get stopped after they've been rapped about, because there's a false sense that something has happened. And again, we really don't mind having visions laid on us. But I, for one, keep wishing folks would realize that we may dig it, encourage it, feed it however we can, but in approximately ten cases out of ten we aren't going to DO it. So, all you visionaries, consider, instead, laying it on your own self, and you might find out whether it's just a trip, or an idea worth realizing in your own life. I understand more and more why our collective failures so outnumber our successes. It's just very much damned harder to succeed and take the responsibility of that position. Who'll do this one?

—Diana Shugart

Journalistic Opportunity

The big question is: How do you implement a good intention or a good vision or even a good plan? If the counter culture is going to live up to its name it's going to have to shift from the role of critic to that of producer. It's going to have to produce viable examples of what it's asking for— or else invalidate its discontent. It seems to me that this need suggests a journalistic opportunity that has barely been touched: the great labor of discovering who has made a better what, and how did he do it.

Wendell Berry
Port Royal, Kentucky

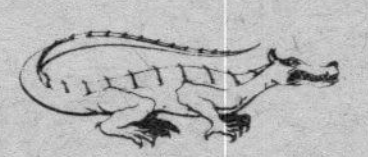

D.R. asked the man what the Happy Pappys were.

The miner snorted, and spat on the roadside. For the first time D.R. realized he was chewing tobacco. "Standing around for a dollar and a half an hour, mostly," he said. "Make work for them has got children at home." He spat again, then asked D.R. if he lived in Finley County.

"I use to," said D.R.

"Who's your people?"

D.R. said, "The Colliers. From over on Trace Fork.

"I know Trace Fork," said the miner. "Toward Blue Diamond, over yonder past Hardly. Collier, you say."

D.R. said, 'My father was a Collier. My mother married a Davenport after he died."

"Well I'm glad to know you, Collier," said the miner. "My name's Virgil Amburgey."

Virgil had got D.R.'s last name wrong, but D.R. didn't feel like correcting him. They stopped long enough to shake hands with one another. Then they set out walking again, and a while later they came to Urge, sitting like a shadow by the road.

A New Mexico Road

Dear Friends,

As the time to till the soil comes near, I think back over our time in New Mexico. Not yet a year but enough time to learn much about this beautiful land that we dreamed of so long. There is much we have learned— not in a mind blow out but rather in the joy and perfection of creative living. There is a great magnificence to New Mexico, the spacial fields the surrounding mountains and mesas, and the cultural individuality of the people. To live in this grand setting utilizing the raw materials, being close with local people and make a life time home.

Your past doesn't matter when you come but your skills do. How long you went to school is unimportant when drinking wine with the Indians and Mexicans or when carrying water from a couple of miles away because the stream froze and the water went underground. The tools you brought are probably the second most important thing. That and your ability to utilize whatever is around.

When my husband and I left the east, we had each made many scenes been many places but the peace that we were seeking always came in a natural setting. New Mexico told me that there was great wisdom to be found here. I felt this when I was last here six years ago. So we saved, without selling our souls, to get a vehicle to get us across country. We wanted to make my five year old daughter feel comfortable. So my husband built a house on the back of an old flatbed. This tin roof chicken house was able to house four people, two dogs and a cat. Seems impossible but he took out the back window and made a hole to the house so the animals and small people could move around comfortably without stopping. A fifteen year old boy from the school we taught at came with us.

Like most of our people we didn't have much money, so we wanted to take the essentials— warm clothes, tools, plenty of blankets, cooking utensils and some craft materials. We had lived in a tipi for a year and I forgot how small it closed up to. Three ft wide by 2 ft high lining and floor covering included. Our tipi was an eighteen footer. We didn't take the poles because wood would be accessible. A supply of food was necessary so we never would have to lean on friends. There are so many foods that will keep and a larder of grains, dried fruits and such could keep us going for a while.

Our route depended on where our friends lived. Stops along the way were necessary because of the physical defects of the truck. The truck became known as Blood Sweat and Tears and that is what it needed to keep it going and of course lots of oil. Actually the truck was a joke but with perseverance and cursing we somehow made it to New Mexico.

From my time on the peyote road I had friends in Santa Fe. We also knew people who ran a Summerhill school, the Santa Fe Community School. Most of the good people had headed for the hills. It was summer and the height of the hippy season. The people we talked to were so uptight about anyone new. Later I understood their situation but then information was all I was seeking. Not a place to crash or a meal just where certain communes and people were. The only information I got was where to stay. Hyde Park was a perfect place. $1.00 a day wasn't much then. The only difficulty was going down the mountain with little or no brakes. We were looking for a commune some where near Colorado named Libra that's only requirements were that you would support yourself, not build in the sight of anyone else, and you were together enough not to bring your problem to others. The scanty information we got was that it was near Chama. Of course all we need do was ask around. That didn't seem like much to go on but I didn't want to stay in Santa Fe any longer. It seemed like the place to come in the dead of winter with some hand made goods to sell. The only warmth we felt was from the shopkeeper at the Old Santa Fe Trail.

So up the trail we continued. Of course we never found Libra. But we saw another part of New Mexico. I was ready to settle among the Mexicans and sell leather goods and pottery to wealthy Texans that came hunting in northern New Mexico.

We decided to try the Taos area and see some friends at the Hog Farm before we settled. I was amazed at the help we got. Taos too was flooded with wandering people searching. Lorien Enterprizes had set up an information center where you could find out about communes, can food and a lot of other helpful things. Somehow we landed at a commune called Five Star. I liked the feeling of the people camping around. We didn't want to get too involved so we stayed on the side lines helping in the garden. The garden these people planted was plentiful. They did a great job and could have easily lived on what they produced. Even get off food stamps but there were so many people tripping by. I cooked at the big house a couple of times and there were between sixty and eighty people.

It was a favorite spot for Mexicans, Indians, Hippies and straights because of the Ponce de Leon Hot Springs. It was easy to just sit in the hot springs drinking with the people gawking at the naked chicks. But that wasn't what we were looking for. There were a few kids around that my daughter could play with. Most of the trippers were young and free and not too interested in working the garden but interested in eating. At Five Star about eight or nine people did most of the work.

As summer drew to an end we decided to put the tipi up the canyon. A friend had checked with a realtor to see if there was land available to live on free. My husband was into building a rabbit hutch for some 4-H rabbits that were laid on us. I was preparing for winter by helping canning, picking, pickling and drying foods with the Five Star Commune. A pressure cooker was essential for at this altitude vegetables had to cook for eight hours. Getting water and cutting wood was an everyday job but it was doubled when canning. That's when the Information Center came in handy again.

We had picked peaches off the ground at an orchard. Many commercial orchards will let you pick fruit off the ground. That and the wild plums, cherries and with the food Five Star had grown, canning was a full time project. The Information Center had several stoves and info about canning. They had a large kitchen. When I was there I found out about the other activities of Lorien Enterprizes.

They put out a paper called *The Fountain of Light*. Helped run a garage called M and M where you could work on your car free using their tools. Ran the General Store where you could buy and sell at reasonable prices. Most important they backed the Free Clinic that later saved many lives.

Next year they were planning to open a school. That is when I decided to apply for a New Mexican teaching certificate. No matter where we were I would probably be teaching my daughter and other kids. I talked to a hippy social worker that dealt with the communes. He said a school of any kind was desperately needed. The schools had enough trouble assimilating the Mexicans and Indians and they didn't want the problem of long hairs. They were keeping the long haired boy we brought with us out of school. So we talked about setting up a small school at Five Star. I got together with interested people and set up a schedule of what people wanted and could teach. Then we met with the kids and found out what they wanted. The kids came from the Taos area. There were only ten to begin with.

Before we got started we were hit with a plague of amoebic dysentery. It was the fly season and the mosquito season had just ended. A couple thousand people had tripped through the hot springs and the pool had never been cleaned. So my husband and a friend that lived with us started hauling water from town. Water was even more precious. The hot springs had amoebic dysentery in the algae in the pool. Many people were coming down with the dysentery. The Free Clinic was filled. I was pregnant and they insisted I go into the hospital because I too got the bug. The kids and the teachers of this new found school all came down with dysentery.

Going to the hospital was foolish— they did nothing more than I did at our tipi. My husband had just built a cook shack out of totally scrap lumber. Now sanitation had to be thought of more. So an out house was begun. It was Sept. and we were getting ready for the first snows. There was always some question about whose land we were on. Land in New Mexico has been divided up from Spanish land grants and passed down to each son in long narrow strips. Of course to listen to our Indian friend, they say that all the land around Taos belongs to the Pueblo Indians. But if you talk to a Jicaria Apache they say that land is theirs for they hunted and camped in the area.

The largest family who owned land near our tipi sight was the ______________ family. One day an Uncle of the clan from California, a cousin from up north and one of our neighbor friends happened by our tipi checking cattle. They wanted to know what our plans were. How we made our money and what we were going to contribute to the economy. When we spoke of being craftsmen they said they had their own craftsmen who needed to make a living off the tourists. The conversation left a stale air in the tipi. Somehow I knew we weren't settled yet. Even though we rarely went into Taos, I felt we were too close for comfort. So we started asking about land further away.

I won't go into the sad story of the break up of a community. Somehow we were visited every night by several people of the commune. The final push was when a group of well dressed Chicanos came and told us this was their land. We'd better get off or they would bring the sheriff. Our friend checked with the realtor and they said they could stay. But we did not want to.

We had heard about some land about a hundred miles away. It had been bought by a New York doctor and turned over to God. Our truck had broken down a long time ago and been traded for another broken down small car. So our next project was to get a truck to move us.

It was the full moon that speeded us up but still it took us four days to find an ex-Hells Angel with a classic 1937 flatbed. While some of us looked for our Angel others went to visit God's land.. They came back with beautiful stories of running fresh streams, oak groves, ponderosa pine forest and mica speckled rocks. What a picture we made when we started off with all our possessions. Our family had changed and grown to five— a lot of rabbits and dogs. This time we took the tipi poles.

It was great leaving the sage and sand behind. Going over large mountains which opened up to lush valleys with cattle and cowboys along the road. Our destination was in a valley surrounded by mountains. There were five people already here. They had been living off the apple and plum orchard and ate heartily when we arrived.

We still didn't want to be part of a community but being organized makes you a nucleus for people to come around. We set up our tipi by the stream and further away dug an out house. We agreed not to ruin the land in any way. Not to cut any living trees. Not to build in the sight of one another and try to keep cars off the land. There of course could be no rules for people who didn't believe in rules. Since new people would always be coming everything was subject to change.

First the local people were very intersted in this new population. For a town of about 100 that are all related, we were an entertainment. Cars came up at all hours, sober, drunk, before church and after church. Actually the people, whatever condition, were very nice and conserned about how we were going to make it. When they found out that we were not different from them, the traffic slowed down and we made friends with many families. We learned much from our neighbors.

The first snow was a shocking reality to many. It weeded out many crashers so we could move around a little easier. People that didn't even have a warm coat or a good pair of shoes hit the road for Taos. We realized that our supply of wood was scanty and we had best get to work. We were cooking out doors, as I usually did when we lived in the tipi. It was neater and there were now seven people sleeping in the tipi. One of the local families came with their twelve kids the first snow bringing beans and biscuits. They told us this was an early snow and were worried if we were warm enough. Thanks to all the blankets we were comfortable.

The men started to increase our wood pile and I got squaw wood. We had two axes but a well meaning tripper who didn't know what he was doing broke our ax handle. It would have been good if we had another hickory handle for there were no cars on the land. A friend of my husband's had learned the skill of making ax handles. He found a piece of oak and finished the job with a draw knife, a wood rasp and a D-saw.

The two shovels we brought were essential because the guys started to dig a house below ground. They had dug six feet in some places. Then they were told that the water level rises ten feet and we would be flooded come spring. So that project was abandoned.

A well meaning person in the town told them they could cut timber or use tree tops that couldn't be used for logging. So a week was spent in dragging down logging tops, cutting the small branches off and cutting them to the correct size for our log cabin. We then found out that even though many son, daughters, aunts, uncles, cousins and nephews own one piece of land— it is the oldest member of the family that has to give permission before anything can be taken off said land. So logs had to be found some where else.

In between all the projects of trying to build, we still needed to eat. Up until then we had not used food stamps. Somehow one of the chicks went down and gave everyone names for food stamps. Our winter supply had been depleted by the amount of people we were feeding. All time was needed for trying to build so food stamps were welcome. But we hoped we would be off them come planting season.

Every time new people came to the land it showed. So luckily only the prepared could stay. The tipi was comfortable if we had enough smokeless wood— dry cedar in combination with split dry oak and plenty of kindling. The next cozy temporary shelter were army wall tents.

The guys heard of a national forest where one could get logs that were down but couldn't cut green trees. The fiasco of getting 42 logs was unbelievable. The first part only took three days. After the second part of the trip, the local bar owner told us that we could take log tops that he had paid for and did not need. The cabin materials were coming together. The guys had gotten eleven vigas from helping tear down an old garage. Also most important were three sets of eight paned windows.

When pulling all the materials together they totaled to 16 logs— 18 feet long and 20 logs— 11 feet long. We bought three truck loads of half rounds at $4.00 a truck load. The first project in putting this large Lincoln log set together was to debark the logs with an ax. The dimensions of the cabin were 21 ft. long by 10 ft. wide. The vegas were to be used for the back wall with a stone fireplace as the center. The 18 footers were cut in half for the front leaving 3 ft. for the door. The notches were made with an ax for the lower logs and a chisel for the upper logs. After all the logs were laid, the four main roof vigas were placed. The roof was put on with tar paper and half rounds for latias. Half rounds were used for the final layers of roofing. The sloping sides were also finished with half rounds.

Adobe was a new material to work with. It was used for chinking and the fireplace. Its mixture was earth, straw and water. Everyone including my daughter could help with the adobing. The guys hauled rocks from near and far. Four hundred rocks in a jig saw puzzle had to fit tight without the adobe. The adobe for the fireplace did not have straw and was stuffed into the cracks. Snowwas threatening for the seventh time and I was expecting in a month. A full stone chimney would have taken too long. They rocked in a chimney to the edge of the roof. They then got four pieces of stove pipe and took them apart and put two pieces together to make the funnel twice as large. They were held together to make the funnel twice as large. They were held together by rivets. They found a metal earth drag and cut a hole in the top and put it on the rock chimney. Then the stove pipes were riveted to the piece of metal. An empty fifty pound lard can served as a revolving draft control.

The final projects were done inside. A wood stove had been given to us by a local family. Two sleeping lofts were built and a bunk for my daughter. Our great Christmas present was moving in before a lasting snow from middle Dec. to late Jan.

The total cost of the cabin was $14. Even cheaper than Thoreau's cabin that cost $28. It took two and a half weeks to build our new home. We felt very wealthy in many ways so we traded our tipi so others could also feel comfortable. There were three cabins on the land now all totally individual.

Now it was time to sit back, relax, create and wait. We had decided to deliver the baby ourselves. Midwifery is a dying profession and in these parts mid-wifes only speak Spanish and are very old. You have to pick them up and since we had no transportation, that would be impossible. I went in for an examination to the local clinic. They couldn't find my veins, my blood pressure and most suspiciously the fetal heart beat. This seemed strange because when I was in the hospital in Taos they also had difficulty finding the fetal heart beat. Also when ever my daughter and I would make a wish, I would wish for a healthy baby. We never listen enough to our intuition.

My water broke on a night we were invaded by ten people interested in the land. Luckily they had a car and children. So my daughter tripped off with them. We had all the necessary items ready— hot water, lots of towels, sterile gloves, gauze, cotton, bacitracin ointment in liquid form for the baby's eyes cradle clothes and some tetracyclin to prevent infection. It was a simple birth much easier than in the hospital. With each contraction I tightly held my husband's hand and drifted off into the conversation of the couple who had come to help. With a few blood curdling screams, the baby was out. I delivered the baby on my daughters bunk and practically crawled up the wall for bearing down. Breathing was essential. I had practiced both the LaMaz method of breathing and exercised during pregnancy. My husband and friend had been prepared by the doctor who owned the land on what to do. Not to cut the umbilical cord right away. Clean the baby's eyes out and not worry about the vernix caseosa. For it was most important to keep the baby warm. We had a roaring fire in the stove and fireplace. A Coleman lantern gave off so much light it almost blinded us. All seemed well; I felt great and was waiting to pass the afterbirth. My husband noticed the baby wasn't breathing steadily. After dressing the baby I held him and realized that even with my warmth and many blankets our son was cold. As much as I hated to we called the local clinic from a neighbor's store, three miles away. We wanted to give our son every opportunity for life.

A doctor and a nurse came at dawn. What a farce. He had the wrong emergency bag, didn't know how to work the oxygen tent, insisted it would require an operation to pass the afterbirth. So my husband, our baby and I went into the clinic twenty miles away. The doctor was annoyed and left a nurse in charge. I easily passed the after birth and my husband took care of the baby. He took a stethoscope and realized that breathing had stopped. As well as delivering his son he also made out his death certificate. We wanted to bury our son on the land nearby, so some red tape had to be dealt with. Luckily the visitors picked us up and we returned home.

An Indian Friend stopped by that day. he told us not to worry and forget. We didn't want to forget; we were sad then but that was natural and soon we would be able to talk about the short life of our son. There are many beautiful things in a world of nature that can cure all sorts of wounds. We had much to be thankful for.

The snow melted— we tripped— and began to build and create. An outhouse was again dug and built. That was a great luxury. In between building the guys began to hike up some of the mountains. They could see for hundreds of miles. They made all sorts of discoveries about the area. The mountain would be a source of inspiration always. My daughter and I climbed to a small ridge and sat a long time listening to the winds.

When they came down they brought a new material for working, antler. They spent many hours making antler pipes, buttons and knife handles. My husband works with leather so after having made enough serviceable clothes for himself, he started to make things to sell. I got into making candles and ordered some pottery supplies. With hand made goods and our coming garden, we should be able to be self sufficient.

The summer I'm sure will bring an onslaught of people that can't be turned away. The land can only hold so many people and we do not want to bring a city condition to such a perfect setting. So we look to the hills for the future. Land with no roads to it where we can build a stone house and live again on a new frontier.

L.

At the starting line Hugh Romney mounts his bus.

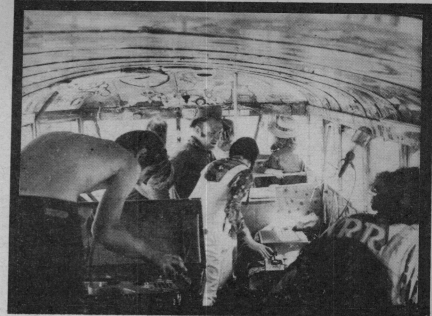

Feverish last minute preparations aboard Further.

THE GREAT BUS RACE

Winning Time 2:32. Who Won Is Debated.

Aspen Meadows, New Mexico. Summer Solstice, 1969

Hugh Romney, who mustered this 1000 in this mountain pasture, is announcing the start of the Bus Race and that a couple named John and Mary are somewhere around and must be found because they have the bubonic plague and require innoculation immediately. Everybody's pretty innoculated already; it's the spaciest part of the afternoon. The race was going to be one bus at a time against the clock, but Ken Kesey and others are maintaining that's a chickenshit race. It's got to be all at once.

The buses are Kesey's renowned Further, with a skeleton crew of Farmsters aboard, and the Hog Farm's fleet: Road Hog, Hospital Bus, Kitchen Bus, etc. The Motherfuckers' tight little bus is around but not in the race.

Everyone will go one trial run around the course: ¼ mile up the meadow, around the flag, and back downhill to the starting line. Majestically the line of buses staggers up the course. "I don't know about this," says Mike Hagen, "Further ain't got much brakes." The Hospital Bus is stalled half-way up the hill right where it's almost impossible to get around. Reportedly it also ran over a pup tent (unoccupied).

The survivors of the trial run line up. They're immense, these faded colorful wrecks filled with folly. People are climbing off, others are climbing on. It's a test of passengers as much as drivers. The mood is pure: fatalistic optimism.

And it's begun. Road Hog gets off first. Further is dragging. The buses are coming around the flag, and back downhill up the pasture like berserk pigs. As Further sways past the grounded Hospital Bus Kesey disappears over the windshield shouting orders to driver Bucavich. Over there in the bushes the Foot Swami from India is watching it all go by.

Further approaches the flag from the left. The Kitchen Bus with Romney on top is coming around the other way. They intersect, pass narrowly, and ram into opposite hillsides, then rev and back blindly toward each other. Frantic shouting gets them forward again. For a moment the entire solstice is tied in a sweet mad knot at the top of the pasture.

Bucavich gets Further around. The Kitchen Bus is still hung with a rear bumper gouged in the creek bed. Rocket, who's driving, surges again and gets it free. The buses swarm downhill. Hugh Romney's mouth is wide open, his toothless warning wailing down the pasture, "BEEE CARRREFUULLLL." At the finish line a thousand longhairs cheer and dodge.

Afterward, at the award-giving argument, Romney is saying, "A miracle. It's a pure miracle nobody was killed." Kesey is saying, "Two minutes thirty-two seconds. It's something to think about for next year."

Further ain't got much brakes.

Barrelling toward the first turn Kesey has an excellent view of the rear of the Hog Farm fleet.

Tied up at the flag, Romney and Further pass in opposite directions. Fierce bus action is visible on the track below.

The Great Bus Race May Never End
In the pursuit of truth via participatory journalism our reporter at the Great Bus Race drank fluid from a Donald Duck glass. Consequently he was too stoned to function and misrepresented some facts, such as:

* The Kitchen Bus is really the Just Bus
* The Hospital Bus is really the Us Bus
                          (Just Us Buses)
* The other bus besides Road Hog is The Queen's Midtown Tunnel of Love Bus, and was the one which broke down.
* Rocket wasn't driving the Just Bus, Bob Redhat (narcoleptic from Ann Arbor) was.
*Bucovich isn't spelled Bucovich, it's spelled some other way.

Romney had lost his notes and was starting to make up facts and the reporter sensed that once again truth was drifting. Here are some other accounts. Perhaps they converge.

And in Aspen Meadow above Santa Fe the Great Bus Further lost her silver bell to the Great Bus Road Hog in the First Annual Summer Solstice Great Bus Race.

Ken Kesey
9 Aug 69 ROLLING STONE

The Great Bus Race

c. 500 yards up the mountain, the same distance down, around a red flag marker and down past the swami's gathering place where they all sit and chant OM.

They're off we get a terrible start, next to last, 5 buses up the hill--Bucko at the wheel picks up steam, passes them all except the Road Hog—bouncing, bumping—we're scared as hell on top— the kids all love it— we lose our bell to the Road Hog— Get the Weather Vain from Just Bus. 2:29 the official record time.

Paul Sawyer

Obviously truth is not to be found in the past, nor likely in the future, next summer, when the buses race from Stonehenge to the Pyramids, maybe. Truth was good while it lasted. —SB

A few months later Hugh Romney became his own sequel, Wavy Gravy, who was last seen bussing out of East Pakistan just ahead of a civil war.

Leisure Camping

For group travel exactly nothing beats a worked-over school bus. Cheap, dependable, adaptable, and impressive. This book is the only we've seen on bus conversion, by a family man in Minnesota. It's too thin for $4, but some of the tips might pay its way for you.

—SB

Leisure Camping
1969; 53 pp.

$3.95 postpaid

from:
Camping Enterprises
923 Dodd Rd.
St. Paul, Minnesota

The school bus is a very well insulated vehicle— made of double wall construction, which also makes them very easy to remodel into a motor home. They have large radiators which give excellent cooling capacity in traveling hilly or mountainous country. They are all equipped with excellent heating plants. Most of the 1955 or newer buses have 6 foot ceilings so that you do not have to stoop while walking inside and are very comfortable to ride in.

•

You will probably get your best buy from a school that owns and operates their own bus lines and they usually keep them in better shape than the busses that are owned by individuals and leased to the schools. From a bus company that takes them in trade from schools as they purchase their new buses. . . .The best time to scout for a bus is in May, June or July. The schools are in the process of taking delivery of new buses for the school year and they are anxious to dispose of the surplus buses so they don't have to carry them over to the new school year.

•

You should also buy a "Motor Minder" for $8.95— which is a small vacuum gauge that will tell you if the motor is in good condition or not. It tells you if the rings, valves, etc., are good and can be used as a real lever in the purchase of the used bus. It is a very simple matter to hook up by removing the wiper hose line and hooking it to the vacuum gauge.

The Motor Minder is a valuable asset to your unit and as you can tell when you are driving, the most economical speed and if you are overworking your motor.

•

If you can buy a 12 to 14 year old bus for $250.00— his price should be okay, because you will probably put another $250.00 in it for repairs. A 10 to 12 year old bus should run between $200.00 and $500.00 depending on its condition. In any case, $500.00 to $600.00 should be your top dollar because if it is perfect the seller would be using it for the purpose for which it was intended.

. . . .

A good place to find nomad equipment is at the larger marine supply houses. The stuff made for boats will often adapt to land use and is likely to be of better quality. Prices are likely to be higher. Marine catalogs also list an impressive variety of pulleys, cable and rope, eyebolts, caulking compounds, and other nautical stuff that can be useful.

If you are building your own truck body, round off the front corners of all surfaces to a radius of at least 8 inches. This radius will give the least possible air drag (and consequently the best gas mileage) to a basically rectangular shape. You can make the edges of the body curved easily from sheet metal or masonite and fashion the corners from fiberglas over carved styrofoam. Funky log cabins on wheels are users.

•

AAA

If you own a car or if you're likely to be driving one much, an AAA card is worth its weight in battery charges. For $15—20 a year you get 1. Free Towing, battery jumps, emergency gas delivery. 2. The best up to date maps available for the U.S., plus booklets of camping sites, plus help in choosing travel routes. 3. Insurance discounts. 4. Bail for misdemeanor traffic charges. Our AAA has paid for itself in the first 3 months of every year we've had it.

(AAA offices in every major city.)

[Suggested and reviewed by Michael Wells]

Roadside Camping

Honda has a new 300 watt generator big enough for lighting and small appliances. It's really quiet, you can talk in normal voice with it running on your table. $185.00 They make a very nice larger one too that is exceptionally easy to operate and though it isn't as quiet as the small one, it still is remarkably quiet. 1500 watts will run Skilsaws and pumps. They are reputed to last an exceptionally long time too.

For heating a camper bus or tent there is a small but good silent heater that makes no fumes called the Therm'x. They are safe and do their job well, but use special fuel that's too expensive for heating for weeks or months. For that job the same company makes excellent propane catalytic heaters for about $75. The small Therm'x is about $20 at most camping stores.

"ADVENTURER"— #30 THERM'X SAFETY HEATER.

Made of sturdy, lightweight anodized aluminum...no rusting! Our most popular model heater for sportsmen and general use. Ideal for hunting, fishing, camping, small trailers, boats, cabins, camper units, station wagons, planes, engine heating and hundreds of other uses. Operates up to 24 hours on a filling of white gas, campstove fuel or Thermasol fuel. Minimum 3,000 BTU output; 9½" high; 8" dia.; wt. 3 lbs. Color, Hunters Red and Ivory. Suggested retail only $27.95.

CLEAN BURNING

A really good toilet for minibuses and vans or even cabins is the PORTA POTTI. It does its job as advertised for $109.00 and there is no installation chore. The same manufacturer makes nice plastic sinks for $7.50.

Honda Generators

used to be that gasoline driven generators were big clumsy oafs, but wily honda has begun to do the same thing to the generator that he did to the motorcycle. the company makes a wide variety of power models, most of them being ac-dc at the flip of a switch.

look good for auxilliary power sources, easily carried into about anywhere, fourstroke, aircooled, ten hours per gallon.

—jd
[Suggested by Les Rosen]

Information

free

from:
American Honda Motor Company, Inc.
100 West Alondra Boulevard
Gardena, California 90247

There's been some model changes in the Honda generators. The E300 was $150 as it changed to E400.

—SB

Camper trucks and busses can be made a lot more comfortable to ride in by replacing the seats with good quality bucket seats out of cars. Most junk yards charge outrageous prices for buckets, but one of the very best seats is from a Renault R8 or 10. These cost as little as $25 a pair and make a big difference. Get them tracks and all.

•

Good sunglasses can greatly reduce fatigue and headaches and also save your eyes for night driving. RayBan with g-15 gray lenses take out most of the ultraviolet and infrared rays, but pass most of the light for less eyestrain. They also don't distort colors which is nice for color freaks. These cost about $12, but are sturdy shock resistant ground glass with no distortion. They also come prescription.

J. Baldwin
Pacific High School
Saratoga, CA

Luger Camper Kits

Luger makes good kits if all you want to do is assembly. You will save some money from a new camper or trailer.

—SB

Catalog

free

from: Luger Industries, Inc.
1300 East Cliff Road
Burnsville, Minn. 55378

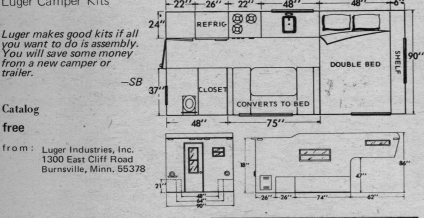

Now place fiberglass insulation included in kit within side walls and cover with factory supplied aluminum exterior covering. Covering comes complete with baked on enamel finish and factory formed seams.

Thermal Springs of the Western United States

Another over-priced pamphlet. This is a copy of part of a U.S. Geological Survey book titled Thermal Springs of the United States and Other Countries of the World, *now out of print. It was 383 pages and cost $2.75. It is public domain. This photo copy of 37 pages costs $3.*

Nevertheless it's the important 37 pages for local travel. Here are map locations of most of the known U.S. hot springs complete with information on temperature, rate of flow, mineral content, and whether commercial or wild. Some former wild springs are now power generating plants. The publishers claim they will update the book. I hope they don't.

The book fails to mention the plastic ice-water afterlife that awaits those who mess up wild hot springs.

—SB

Thermal Springs of the Western U.S.

$3 postpaid

from:
Paradise Publishers
Box 5372
Santa Barbara, CA 93103

Name or location	Temperature of water (°F)	Flow (gallons per minute)	Associated rocks	Remarks and additional references
Arizona				
Pakoon (Pahgun) Spring, on tributary of Grand Wash, 18 miles north of Colorado River.	100		Lava (late Tertiary)	Ref. 138.
Sec. 23, T. 30 N., R. 23 E., 5 miles south of Hoover (Boulder) Dam.	Hot		Lava (Tertiary)	
Lava Warm Springs, near Lava Falls Rapids in the Grand Canyon of the Colorado River.	89	6,700	Granite	Several springs. Refs. 138, 144.
Sec. 33, T. 18 N., R. 19 W., 25 miles southwest of Kingman.	Warm		Lava (Tertiary)	
Sec. 32, T. 15 N., R. 6 E., 10 miles northeast of Camp Verde.	72	50	Lava (Tertiary) overlying sandstone (Permian).	3 springs. Water used locally.
Verde Hot Springs, 0.5 mile northwest of Childs.	104	75	Lava (Tertiary)	Several springs. Resort.
6 miles south of St. Johns	74	2	Sandstone (Triassic)	Deposit of tufa.

Airstream Travel Trailer

I've lived in a 22' Airstream with wife and two cats for most of three years now. It's the only high-tech home I've found at all lovable, indeed comparable to the way some ocean-going boat owners feel about living on board. The Airstream is an elegant honest design-job. It makes us parsimonious (and conscious) about using water, gas, power. It frees us from owning land, and encourages us to live in wilder places. It is proof from fire, earthquake, floods (drive away) and mice (except what the cats bring in and lose). It's one of the few domes I know that doesn't leak. When we travel with it, wherever we go we're coming home. One more month of production and we're hauling ass and house out of here to the desert.

—SB

Therm'x Heaters

Therm'X catalytic propane heaters are neat, safe, silent, odorless, ventless, hot, and very efficient. The 6000 BTU model, enough for a typical camping bus, will run wide open for more than 100 hours on a 5 gallon propane bottle. (The usual heater of the same rating runs about 15 hours on the same bottle). They light instantly without trickery and regulate nicely to the desired output. Full heat appears a-bout a minute after it starts, is mostly radiant, and feels good. There's an eerie red glow in the dark, but it won't ignite gasoline fumes, for instance. Emissions are very small amounts of CO_2 and water vapor. We haven't had any trouble with the vapor condensing on things. The heaters cost a lot more than the local Bernz and Turner competition, but the Therm'X has the advantage of a positive automatic safety shut-off in case of trouble, and it is a handier shape to install. She also comes in a 12,000 model.

[Suggested and reviewed by Jay Baldwin]

Mark V Portable Therm'X
(3,000-12,000 BTU heat range)

$99.95 from local dealers
or
Therm'X Corporation Inc.
1280 Columbus Ave.
San Francisco, CA 94133

Therm'X Company of Canada
Box 3003 Station C
Hamilton, Ontario
Canada

Katadyn Pocket Filter

Perhaps these devices would be of interest to some of the people, especially those travelling in tropical countries.

We can vouch for the pocket filter walking through Switzerland, Italy and Yugoslavia we drank from puddles cemeteries and fetid marshes. Sometimes the water tasted like diluted cough syrup but we thrived never once having an instance of sickness.

This added up to a tremendous saving in not having to look for safe water supplies or carry so much at a time or worry.

Note that the filters only remove biological contaminants from the water— insecticides, fertilizers salt and other chemicals whose size is many orders of magnitude smaller are not filtered out.

Katadyn told us they used to have an agency in L.A. but that at the present time the simplest way to order is directly from the factory.

Write to find exact cost including postage and insurance and then send a check. They are a great firm to deal with.

John and Jane
Rochester, New York

Costs about $150 (plus shipping), pumps about a gallon in 5 minutes.

—SB

Katadyn Pocket Filter
Philmar Company
P.O. Box 35055
Los Angeles, CA 90035

Our test was run as follows: The hand operated pumping unit was taken to Missouri River where the packing house waste and sewage enters the main stream. A sample was taken from the Missouri without Katadyn treatment for control. The pump was operated on the Katadyn unit sucking Missouri River water through the unit and discharging it into a sterile bowl. We found this sample to contain no intestinal organisms of any kind after being pumped through this unit; and thus this water, after treatment, meets the standards of the Health Department for potability.

The sample that was collected from the Missouri River without treatment showed polution of intestinal organisms of all types present in extremely high numbers.

In our opinion, from the result of this test, this process would be very satisfactory for the bacterial purification of water for drinking purposes on hunting and camping trips.

Reported: T. E. COROTHERS
Bacteriologist
City of Sioux City, Iowa

If you buy in August when the sales on this year's models start, you may save $1,000 or so. For nearest dealer consult yellow pages or:

Airstream
107 Church St.
Jackson Center, Ohio 45334

15939 Piuma Ave.
Cerritos, CA 90701

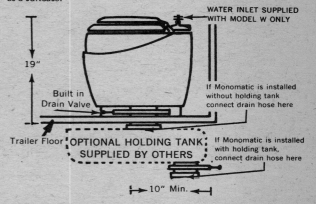

Quench Water Purifier

Here's what they say about it. We haven't used one. Recycle your piss.

—SB

MAKES CRYSTAL CLEAR, DISTILLED WATER FROM
  Sea Water
  Lake and Stream Water
  Hard Water
  Contaminated Water
REMOVES ALL SOLID IMPURITIES
AS EASY TO OPERATE AS A COFFEE POT
NO FILTERS TO CHANGE
STARTS UP IN FIVE MINUTES
COMPLETELY SAFE
MAKES UP TO 2 QUARTS OF PURE WATER EVERY HOUR
USES HEAT FROM ANY SOURCE
  Camp Stove
  Sports Stove
  Camp Lantern
  Gas or Electric Range
  Campfire (bed of coals)
  Laboratory Burner

The QUENCH Water De-Salter/Purifier supplies fresh water wherever you are. All that's needed is a source of water; any water, and a source of concentrated heat; any heat. The QUENCH De-Salter delivers up to two quarts of fresh, clear, salt and mineral free, distilled water every hour for as little as 1¢ per quart. Models with built-in electric heaters also available.

Cost: **$99.00**

Terraqua Products, Inc.
915 S. Grand St.
San Pedro, CA 90731

Monomatic Toilet

Every time you take a dump or a leak in a standard john, you flush five gallons of water out with your piddle. Five gallons in the Monomatic accomodates one hundred uses before it needs replacing. The cycling system, involving a chemical and filtration, was developed for the airlines and has spun off into general use for recreational vehicles such as campers, trailers, boats, etc. It might also be useful for water-short areas such as deserts, mountain tops, and New York.

—SB

Monomatic Toilet

$195.00 approx.

from:
trailer supply dealers or write
Monogram Industries, Inc.
10131 National Blvd.
Los Angeles, CA 90034

The chemical costs $4.75/box. The Monomatic runs on 12 volt current. I see where they have a box that disguises your toilet as a suitcase.

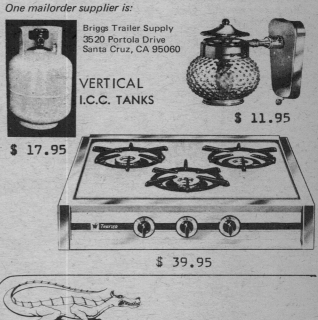

Incinerating Toilets

If you prefer fire to water, try Destroilet, which cooks the living shit out of you. No water. Requires gas and electricity. $419 from Lamere Industries Inc., 301 N. Main St., Walworth, Wisc. 53184

Monomatic Note

The monomatic-type toilets have been available here for several years. The chemicals (which keep the smell down) have caused problems since they utterly destroy all bacteria. Thus, when you dump the bucket in your friendly neighborhood sewer system, their bacteria (which eat the garbage) are destroyed which makes them unhappy.

Martin Minow
Bromma, Sweden

Recreational Vehicle Equipment

If you're outfitting a bus, camper, or trailer with lights, refrigerator, stove, furnace, windows, vents, sink, shower, toilet, etc., check on local suppliers.

One mailorder supplier is:

Briggs Trailer Supply
3520 Portola Drive
Santa Cruz, CA 95060

VERTICAL
I.C.C. TANKS

$ 11.95

$ 17.95

$ 39.95

MONKEYING AROUND

   In D.R.'s mind the bus was a total wreck and he was ready to leave it and go on to town with Virgil and find a mechanic who could fix it for him. But Virgil said let's take a look at it since we're here. About two minutes after he lifted the hood and shined his light on the problem he had Urge's motor and the headlights working as well as they ever had.

   "How did you do that?" asked D.R.

   "Oh," said Virgil. "I just said a little prayer and monkeyed with it." He laughed then and settled back in his seat as D.R. put Urge in gear and pulled back onto the blacktop.

How to Keep Your Volkswagen Alive

John Muir has written what may well be your V.W.'s best friend. In this book you are invited to "Just take the book out to the car with your coveralls on for a guided tour."

So I did. My guided tour of the car and the book's easily versed descriptions convinced me that it is the best I've encountered yet. It's written for the layman (us), and as such makes about 80% of the common V.W. ailments both clear and repairable.

If you take it literally, you will learn to "feel the car" and perform the necessary tasks with love. There are also many pages devoted to what you can do when hung up on the mud flats for one reason or another. While "Volkswagen Alive" contains more pictures of the beast, "Volkswagen Alive" is what I would prefer to have when it's time to unroll the metric wrenches.

[Reviewed by Don Burns]

OK so here's a good book on how to fix your VW written in a chummy style that will not be too amusing the second time you read it. There's a real collection of tricks and pitfalls that to my mind is well worth the money. But some of them are rehashes of old wives tales that are not true (there's a bit about the VW Understeer. What makes the VW dangerous is Oversteer: it steers more than you tell it too. Also, some of the really damnable aspects of repairing old VWs such as headlights that are about as bright as birthday cake candles, are simply and groovily dismissed without telling you how to do anything about it. HOWEVER...an idiot can actually do major repairs on his VW with the aid of this book, and that, friends, is saying a lot. I would recommend that you have this and the Elfrink book at your side. John Muir also gives lists of tools you need, which hand to hold them in, and when to stop for a morale-building smoke. He also tells you when to quit and what not to attempt. Any VW owner should be able to save the price of the book within a week of getting it. Reading it will aid you in keeping your bug out of the shop in the first place. There's a "how to buy a used VW" chapter too! And he starts out "Come to kindly terms with your Ass for it bears you." Indeed. I'd call it indispensable.

[Reviewed by J. Baldwin]

How to Keep Your Volkswagen Alive
John Muir
1969; 336 pp

$6.00 plus postage and handling ($.50)
1974 revised edition includes 411's Squarebacks and Fastbacks
Covers fuel injected engines extensively.
from:
John Muir Publications
Box 613
Santa Fe, NM 87501
or WHOLE EARTH CATALOG

Volkswagen Technical Manual

Besides Muir's book Elfrink is considered the best VW repair book. This one covers only up to 1965. For later models they have other manuals. Good prevention against getting burned by the Volkswagon agencies in Reno and Oklahoma City (name your favorite villain; those are mine) when a dismaying noise starts following you down the road and your trip shifts from 400 miles a day to nothing a week.

—SB

[Suggested by Don Burns]

Volkswagen Technical Manual
Henry Elfrink
1964; 256 pp.

$3.50 postpaid

from:
Henry Elfrink
Automotive
P.O. Box 20367
Los Angeles, CA 90006

or WHOLE EARTH CATALOG

VOLKSWAGEN TECHNICAL MANUAL

HENRY ELFRINK
ALL ABOUT THE VOLKSWAGEN

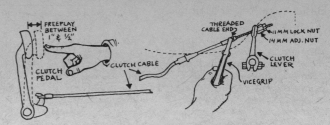

FOR SEDAN, GHIA & TRANSPORTER
HOW TO KEEP YOUR VOLKSWAGEN ALIVE
A MANUAL OF STEP BY STEP PROCEDURES FOR THE COMPLEAT IDIOT
1950 to 1969
1200 1300 & 1500
BY JOHN MUIR

Get away from the car and the owner or salesman to let your mind and feelings go over the car and the idea of the car. What has its Karma been? Can you live with the car? Walk around or find a quiet place, assume the good old Lotus and let the car be the thing. At this point some revelation will come to you and you will either be gently guided away from that scene and can start looking again, or you will still be attracted toward the car and can continue with your inspection. *It is important that you neither run the motor or ride in the car until this preliminary scene has run its course.* It also puts the owner-salesman up the wall because he has no idea of what you are doing and will be more pliable when the hard dealing time comes.

When the Volksie front end needs your tender attention, it'll let you know by feeling insecure, a not-unknown trip in any relationship. This insecurity can be evidenced in many ways: wandering mindlessly across the road, impulsively darting here and there, wearing tires out in funny patterns or making nerve-wracking noises on dirt roads. These are the symptoms and you are the doctor, at least almost a doctor. I've told you so many things to do, it's a real pleasure to tell you something not to do. *Don't rotate your tires!* It takes about 500 miles for a tire to get used to its position on a car, and changing it around just messes up its head. It will last as long or longer right where it is. The reason I tell you this now is that changing the tires around will sometimes make your front end feel insecure when there's nothing wrong with it.

The VW has often been compared to that other universal car' of many years ago: the model T Ford of which more than 15 million were built. There is a germ of truth in this comparison; both cars were built for the masses by geniuses in their field, but whereas the old model T was basically a simple car which could be repaired, so to speak by anyone with a screw driver and a pair of pliers, the VW is a high precision piece of machinery. The VW, although simple in its basic conception, actually in many ways is a subtle mechanism, as will be readily apparent after the following pages are perused.

The methods employed to boost the power output of the VW engine follow the usual speed-tuning pattern: dual carburetors, supercharging, high compression cylinderheads, high-compression pistons, long-stroke crankshafts, special camshafts, extra large cylinders and the various possible combinations of these methods.

Take the hub cap off the wheel and check the brake lining in each wheel. You can see it through the adjustment hole with the flashlight. You may have to roll the car back and forth a little to get the lining in view, and if the outside light is strong, a jacket or cloth over the fender and your shoulders will cut the daylight so the lining can be seen. If the lining is about one-eighth of an inch thick, you have plenty, but if it is less than a sixteenth, you will soon have to reline the brakes and you should know that.

Again, this doesn't apply to those who already know they're going to buy new pistons and cylinders, but you others, <u>mark the pistons.</u>

PAY ATTENTION SO YOU DON'T BANG THE PISTON SKIRT HERE

MARK PISTONS AS SHOWN BEFORE REMOVING.

With a nail or file, scratch the number on the top of the piston, through that carbon, and draw an arrow pointing toward the flywheel, like I, II, etc. Start with #1, get it out as far as it'll go, and remember the WARNING.

Western Distributors

Bug parts——at sensible prices. This small mailorder house offers the VW owner a chance to buy imported parts for his car at really fair prices. Not all parts are offered, but the ones most often replaced (cables, points, brakes, etc.) are there. Genuine Bosch sparkplugs are a bargain at 55¢ each postpaid. No minimum order, either. A few accessories, plus a VW Technical Manual complete the offering. Parts are listed for the Beetle as well as the Ghia, Bus, Fastback, Squareback, and Variant. Free catalog is offered. Service ——good. Postage——all items are shipped postpaid.

[Suggested and reviewed by Gerard Ruch]

Catalog

free

from:
Western Distributors
Box 316
Cedar Crest, NM 87008

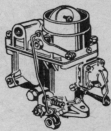 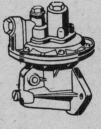

1300—1500—1600 FUEL SYSTEM

DESCRIPTION	ORDER NO.	PRICE
Fuel Pump (1300)	50-F-1	$12.95 ea.
Fuel Pump (1500-1600)	50-F-2	13.95 ea.
Fuel Pump Kit (1300)	50-F-3	2.10 ea.
Fuel Pump Kit (1500-1600)	50-F-4	2.60 ea.
Carburetor (Must have carburetor number)	50-F-5	36.95 ea.
Carburetor Kit (Must have carburetor number)	50-F-6	4.25 ea.

Another VW Book

You have in your catalogue two very good books on VWs. *How to Keep Your VW Alive* is good for technique while Elfrink's *Technical Manual* supplies sometimes very helpful extra information. However if you happen to own a 1965 Sedan (like I do) or a later model you will find that the *Technical Manual* is confusing and not complete. The latest edition of this book was published in 1965.

I have a better one. It is called *The Volkswagen Owners Handbook of Maintenance and Repair,* published by Floyd Clymer. This is a very thorough book with up-to-date and easy to understand (and to locate) exploded diagrams, and pictures. I recommend it highly to anyone that owns a '65 Sedan or later as it has sections for '65's, 1300's, '67's, '68's, and '69's.

Clymer publishes other books on VWs including one on 1600s, Transporters, Souping Up a VW, How to Drive and Road Test a VW, and even an old reprint of one of the first VW instruction books. Clymer also publishes books on many other foreign makes (Porsche, Datsun, Volvo).

Best Regards,
Steve Keleher
Van Nuys, CA

Volkswagen Owners Handbook of Maintenance and Repair
$3.00 from Floyd Clymer, 222 No. Virgil Avenue, Los Angeles, CA 90004

Baja Bug Kit

VW Owner!

Is your commune's road impassable during the winter rains; have you always wanted to drive the rough dirt roads of Baja? If you already have a VW beetle, the Baja Bug is the simplest least expensive and most versatile conversion kit on the market. You can keep your sedan and have your dune buggy too! Unlike other dune buggy kits, this one does not require chopping, shortening, and welding the belly pan or buying an expensive fiberglass body without heater, windows or top. You can do this conversion easily at home in one- or two weekends. More ground clearance, room for big wheels and tires and easy access to the engine are major advantages. Important accessories available for serious off road drivers: skid plates, air filters, high clearance exhausts, etc. VW bus owners will be interested in flared fiberglass fenders for wide tread tires.

Miller-Havens Enterprises catalog

Baja Bug Conversion Kit
Baja Bus Fender Kit

No longer available

Miller-Havens Enterprises
2944 Randolph Ave.
Costa Mesa, California 92626

Jane Nichols
Palos Verdes Estates, CA.

Basic Auto Repair Manual

This manual is intended to be an introduction to automobile mechanics and the more fearsome professional shop manuals. It contains about all the amateur mechanic needs to know in order to diagnose, repair, and maintain domestic cars and VW 1954-1965. It is assumed that the mechanic has no experience at all. All major assemblies are well illustrated and explained both in principle and specifically, with note made of quirks found in certain models. There are chapters or remarks on tools needed and how to use them, working safely, junk yard technique, on-the-road repairs, and general money saving. There is a very good chapter on logical trouble shooting. 'If this is wrong, try this first, this second, etc.' Included is most likely diagnosis and prescription. Common repairs like 'putting in new points' are covered neatly. Major jobs are presented so that the amateur mechanic can get most of the work done before calling in expensive expert help. It is clearly stated when to give up, and what not to attempt without expertise. They even tell you how much you will save, and how long it will take. This is a great book for that person trying to keep the oldie going and/or who wants to understand cars in general. It fits girls too. Well worth the money.

[Suggested and reviewed by J. Baldwin]

This is a new revised edition. Better than ever.

—SB

Basic Auto Repair Manual No. 5
1973; 384 pp.

$3.95 postpaid

from:
Petersen Publishing Co.
8490 Sunset Blvd.
Los Angeles, CA 90069

or WHOLE EARTH CATALOG

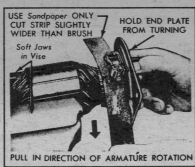

USE Sandpaper ONLY CUT STRIP SLIGHTLY WIDER THAN BRUSH

HOLD END PLATE FROM TURNING

Soft Jaws in Vise

PULL IN DIRECTION OF ARMATURE ROTATION

6. Seating Brushes

8. Distributor Lubricating Points

Address requests for automotive catalogs to:

Sears Roebuck and Co.
Local catalog order center

Montgomery Ward and Co.
Local catalog order center

Spiegel Inc.
Chicago, Illinois 60609

J.C. Whitney & Co.
1917 Archer Ave.
Chicago, Illinois 60616

Honest Charley Inc.
108 Honest St.
(P.O. Box 8535)
Chattanooga, Tenn. 37411

SA oils are non-detergent, with no performance requirements. This classification includes not only high-quality, non-detergent oils put out by major companies, but also the dregs from the local tar pit. If you want a good non-detergent oil, you will have to rely on the reputation of the maker.

SB oils have a few additives that protect against scuffing, bearing corrosion, and oil oxidation. These oils give only minimum protection.

SC oils are better. They have additives that protect against high-and low-temperature deposits, rust, wear, and corrosion.

SD oils are the best. The protect against all the conditions that the other oils do, only more so. If a car maker recommends SC oil, you will be giving your engine greater protection by using SD oil.

Mail order, as we've said, takes a little time but is an entirely satisfactory way of buying parts. The Sears, Ward, Spiegel, J.C. Whitney and Honest Charley catalogs are amazingly complete and J.C. Whitney, at least, offers to help you find a part that is not listed. All of them stock parts for a wide variety of imported cars. A further advantage is that they "guarantee satisfaction or your money back," a protection that may or may not exist when dealing with a car dealer or jobber.

Joblot Automotive

Very groovey place is Joblot Automotive in Queens, N.Y.—Address: Joblot Automotive, Inc. 98-11 211th St. Queens, N.Y.— they have an almost complete stock of spare parts for all Fords Mercury & Lincolns (including truck parts) going back at least to Model A days, and the parts are mostly original factory parts that they bought up over the years as the dealers and factory decided not to bother stocking them anymore. They have a catalogue and will mail order stuff anywhere. The last time I was there the owner told me that he started out supplying hard to get Model A parts to South America and other places where they were still widely used. When stocks of original Model A parts became scarce people in those countries began manufacturing them domestically to supply the local demand. He now imports a tremendous range of newly manufactured Model A parts and asserted that it would be possible to assemble an entirely new MINT Model A from parts. He is very helpful and should give very satisfactory service.

[Suggested and reviewed by Larry Nordell]

Catalog

$1.00

from:
Joblot Automotive Inc.
98-11 211th Street
Queens Village
Long Island, New York 11429

Carolyn Cassady: "Neal in heaven—an old car and a girl."

"Now you just dig them in front. They have worries, they're counting the miles, they're thinking about where to sleep tonight, how much money for gas, the weather, how they'll get there — and all the time they'll get there anyway, you see. But they need to worry and betray time with urgencies false and otherwise, purely anxious and whiny, their souls really won't be at peace unless they can latch on to an established and proven worry and having once found it they assume facial expressions to fit and go with it, which is, you see, unhappiness, and all the time it all flies by them and they know it and that *too* worries them no end."

Neal Cassady to Jack Kerouac

from:
Scenes Along the Road
Photographs of the Desolation Angels 1944-1960
Compiled by Ann Charters
1970; 56 pp.
Portents/Gotham Book Mart

We got our copy for $3.00 from:
Book People
2940 7th Ave.
Berkeley, CA. 94710

J. C. Whitney Automotive Accessories & Parts

A really great catalog of car parts, not all of them above suspicion as far as usefulness goes, but on the other hand very complete and especially good for older cars, is the J. C. Whitney Catalog. They stock parts for such things as model A Fords and Borgwards, Jeeps and VWs, and offer used parts.

[Suggested and reviewed by J. Baldwin]

J. C. Whitney is also known as Warshawsky & Co. (same catalog, different cover). The Whitney catalog says $1 on the cover, Warshawsky doesn't or does it by now?

—SB

Catalog

free

from:
Warshawsky & Co.
1900-24 So. State St.
Chicago, Ill 60616

A comment about the J.C. Whitney catalog:

I have been ordering from them for several years, and find their catalog an intriguing mix of good stuff and junk. Read the description of an item carefully. If an item says "No cutting, drilling or tapping" you may have to weld! The key phrases are: "Fits perfectly" or Duplicate of Original Equipment". These mean you'll have little trouble. Beware of the miracle spark plugs, "Minisuperchargers", fire injectors, and the like— they're near-useless gimmicks. They are always recognizable by a full page exhortation on what wonders they'll work. (The pitches are fun to read, though).

Sincerely yours,

*George F. Swetnam, Jr.
Reston, Va.*

VIRGIL'S RAP

"Yeah," said Virgil. "It's mighty hard times around here these days. If it wasn't for food stamps and the Happy Pappys some folks would starve plum to death, that ain't no lie. A lot of 'em are hungry like it is. Of course I've seen it when it was worse, and a man's got to count his blessings I reckon. My daddy mined coal in this county in the 1920's, no union or nothing in here then, and you talk about mean times, them times was <u>mean</u>. Of course they's not enough union left worth speaking about, but what I mean is, now, you take this Happy Pappy program. Take all this welfare stuff. It ain't nothing but a sop to keep the people from acting up. That's all in the world it is, and yet everybody wants to make so much out of it. Everybody give the President so much credit for coming in here and setting it up. All that President was doing was laying out a sop to try to keep the lid on things. And I mean to tell you, buddy, the lid was about to pop around here a year or two ago. It was like a time of war nearly. People hungry, out of work, losing their hospital cards, getting their pensions cut, little old younguns going around with worms in their bellies, some of 'em half naked in the winter time, I mean they wasn't nothing else <u>to</u> do but go to war. Big gangs of men roving up and down the highways, stopping cars, shooting, getting shot at. They was a tipple burnt ever day for two straight weeks up in your country, two or three railroad bridges went up, people's cars and houses dynamited.

(continued)

Propane Conversion

How to Propel Your Car with Propane
An Immediate Personal Action for Cleaner Air)
(reprinted from *Freedom News*, February 1970)

In addition to long range cultural change, Ecology Action is interested in immediate personal actions aimed at waging war on environmental problems. In this endeavor we attempt to practice what we preach, and to that end have begun converting the vehicles upon which we must occasionally rely to propane gas (also butane).

We have culled the following information from Imperial Rock Gas of Richmond.

If you're interested in doing something about air and water pollution now, and drive a gasoline fueled, internal combustion engine vehicle, convert to propane. Conversion is a simple, financially beneficial operation which reduces your vehicle's harmful emissions by 50%. Some estimates go as high as 75% to 80% reduction in harmful emissions.

There are other ways to reduce your personal impact on the environment, of course, and several alternatives to pouring gasoline wastes into the eco-system. Walking is the best alternative of all, and public transportation use reduces your impact.

Gas turbines, steam driven and electric engines all produce less harmful exhausts than the present gasoline engine, but these alternatives are not possible ones for most people, for a variety of reasons. Electric, steam and gas turbines cannot be made available to any significant number of persons soon enough.

Propane is different. You can go to a local propane dealer who does conversions and have your car running on propane in one day. That's how long it normally takes.

The cost is approximately $300 from which you can shave substantial amounts in a variety of ways. Labor costs about $40, but the job is simple enough so that anyone with rudimentary mechanical knowledge can do it.

How it Works: Basically: A special carburetor replaces the air filter; a heat exchanger is mounted under the hood and connected to the water hose that runs to the heater; a fuel line must be run to the tank which is usually mounted in the trunk.

This last item, the tank, is the single most expensive aspect, costing $120—$180 for a new tank capable of holding 24-36 gallons of fuel. A used tank often costs less than half as much, so shopping around for one is worthwhile.

Even with these cuts in cost, however, the average American car owner may not feel he can afford conversion. But, as economists point out, cost is a relative concept against which we must pose benefits, and the benefits of propane are substantial.

First, as previously mentioned, the use of propane cuts harmful emissions by 50%, thus reducing air pollution directly and water pollution indirectly (hydrocarbons and other exhaust products are inevitably washed off the road by rain or precipitated out of the air).

Another benefit is that the use of propane can increase the life of a new engine from 2—10 years. According to Mr. Carl Warner of Imperial Rock Gas in Richmond, forklift truckers, who have used propane for many years because of its lower emissions and the enclosed, indoor nature of much of their work, claim at least a 5—2 ratio of improved engine life. This is because, in part, the propane enters the engine as a gas, not as a liquid, and sludge and carbon are essentially eliminated.

Fuel Cost is Lower: Still another benefit of propane cost is fuel cost. Only one grade of propane is distributed: a high octane grade comparable to high test gasoline. The cost, in the Bay Area, is about twenty-four cents per gallon. Though the per gallon mileage of propane is about 3% less than gasoline, the consumer still saves a considerable amount, which, even excluding longer engine life, makes propane conversion profitable over the long run.

Cal Gas of Sacramento claims other propane benefits: cuts maintenance costs; cleaner oil; longer spark plug life——no carbon to foul spark plugs; instant cold weather starting——no flooding or choking of carburetor; fuel pump problems eliminated because there is no fuel pump.

Another consideration the potential propane converter makes is the availability of the fuel. Most cities of 50,000 or more have propane supply outlets. National and state listings are available from gas companies usually on request.

But even without careful planning the propane motorist need not fear being stranded without fuel, for the standard conversion oper-ation leaves the vehicle with a gasoline potential which may be realized by flipping a dashboard switch. Just keep a small amount of gasoline in your car.

A few other considerations: If your car is air cooled (for example, Volkswagens) about $20 extra must be spent for adaptive equipment. The higher the compression ratio of your engine the more efficiently it will run on propane (compression usually corresponds to engine size and number of cylinders but not always, so check your owner's manual).

Pressure Conversion: In addition to converting your own car, you can take a step toward lessening pollution by encouraging other individuals, industry and government to convert. Some steps have been proposed already in this area, e.g., Reagan's claim that state vehicles were to be converted and recently publicized intentions of Contra Costa vehicle conversions. Concerned individuals should keep track of these intentions.

If you want better quality air and water enough to do something, but don't think you can afford the initial cash outlay for conversion, you might consider trading in your present car for one worth about $300 less and use the difference. You'll make it back in gas savings.

Further, remember that propane is only a partial and interim solution to pollution. Even with a converted car, you still are responsible for concrete highways, noise, congestion, Santa Barbara oil leaks and Torrey Canyon shipwrecks. The answers to these problems lie with a deeper commitment to a quality life; with walking and relearning the joys of bicycle riding.

Distributed as a public service by — Ecology Action
1000 North 9th Street
Modesto, CA 95352
— 209-529-3784

I have heard of a new car dealer who is using a free propane conversion as a way to boost sales of his left over 1969 models. (Hillsdale Dodge in San Mateo, spec.) He also tries to sell a propane conversion with all new car sales ($500 per) by giving the customer a stiff lecture about civic duty and air pollution.—Fred

---

Auto Engines and Electrical Systems

There are a number of books available on how to repair automobile engines, but not many which explain so well as this one does why each part is designed as it is, why a certain repair procedure is used, or what causes the wear on a worn part. I wanted a book which would help me to understand the details of engine design and construction instead of just how to fix them; and I was extremely pleased to find that this book does both. Its explanations are clear, concise, complete, and profusely and excellently illustrated. Its authors obviously know what they are talking about, and write well. There is no bullshit and no excessive technical jargon, just good solid information. It is practically oriented, written as a textbook for mechanics, to provide the groundwork of basic knowledge a mechanic should have.

[Suggested and reviewed by Marv Vickers]

**Auto Engines
and Electrical Systems**

$10.95 postpaid

from:
Motor
250 W. 55th Street
New York, N. Y. 10019

or WHOLE EARTH CATALOG

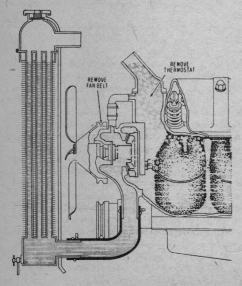

Fig. 38 Combustion leakage test of cooling system. Air bubbles in engine outlet with engine running confirms this

Books About Fords

Restoration manuals, service bulletins, buff books.

—SB

Catalog
free

from:
Polyprints
Box 31207
San Francisco, CA 94131

Hemmings Motor News

A 200 page magazine full of ads for Ford and Non-Ford cars and parts and literature and misc...that's "Hemmings Motor News!" Lots of pictures make the whole thing work while for the person with a casual interest in old cars. (Almost all the cars advertised as vintage or antique...but not all of them.) It's monthly and cheap.

The publishers have come out with a magazine called "Special Interest Autos" that looks good. Looks like it will be interesting, but you can decide for yourself. Get the "Hemmings Motor News" first and it will tell you where to send off for "Special Interest Autos." The former is the real tool, the latter looks like it might be fun.

Hemmings Motor News (monthly)

David O. Weaver
Witchita, Kansas

$12/yr.

Special Interest Autos (bimonthly)
$5.00/yr to H.M.N. subscribers
$6.00/yr to others

from:
Special Interest Autos
Box 196
Bennington, VT 05201

Would You Believe! Real, authentic captured Russian Jeep! 1966 vintage, complete. Good, restorable condition. Be the first in your neighborhood, or city, or state, or even the United States! Only $2,000.00. Aadlen Brothers, 11590 Tuxford Street, Sun Valley, California, 91352. Phone (213) 875-1400.

Truck Repair Manual

If you have a truck, chances are marvelous you spend a fair amount of your time under it or in the front end of it. Judicious use of this book might save you some down-time. It covers the gamut of trucks and tractors, 1960-69, and has better than usual illustrations of how to get at what you're working on.

Motor's Truck Repair Manual   —SB
1969; 1154 pp.

$17.00 postpaid from:
Wehman Brothers
158 Main Street
Hackensack, N.J. 07601

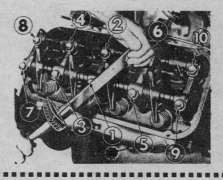

Maintenance

one way to force detroit to stop producing tinny chromedup pieces of shit is to stop buying what they produce, spend a little time operating on old terminal cases and, through the miracle of transplant, give the old '57 ford retractable another ten years of life. old cars run just as well as new ones, if the driver knows enough about his machine to keep it running. factory service manuals have the best information.

—jd

Wheels

If you are out in the woods and are needing to get into heavier vehicles a specialty magazine is Four Wheeler, not commonly available on many newsstands. You can get it for $.60 per copy when you can find it or for $5.00 per year. Road tests, conversions, accessories like winches, parts, etc.

From: PV4
                          P.O. Box 2325
Four Wheeler   FDR Post Office
P.O. Box 845   New York, N.Y. 10022
Reseda, Ca 91335 $.75 per copy, $8/yr

If you're into sports cars and some just can't get out of 'em, Road & Track is the BEST for road tests and technical stuff. Pretty bourgeois but fine photography and text. $1.00 each or $10.00 for 1 year subscription.

*Road and Track
1499 Monrovia Ave.
Newport Beach, CA 92663*

Kam
Nevada City, CA

Four Wheel Drive Handbook

Since we're getting a Dodge Powerwagon to pull our trailer into exotic places, this book came along just in time to be of excellent use. Every page has something. Including sensible warnings that 4wd may not be what you need— it's expensive, harder to service, just a bit better than 2-wheel drive. The book has an excellent list of suppliers.

—SB

Four Wheel Drive Handbook
James T. Crow, Cameron A. Warren
1970; 96 pp.

$2.95 postpaid from:

Haessner Publishing Co.
Box 89
Newfoundland, N.J. 07435

or WHOLE EARTH CATALOG

•

Low range, not used enough by 4-wheelers, lets things happen gently.

In conclusion then, here are more of our somewhat subjective opinions about the various 4wds:

Most durable vehicle: Land Rover
Most for the money: Toyota Land Cruiser
Best on/off road combination: Ford Bronco
Best for long-range off-road touring: International Travelall
Best all around vehicle: Jeep Wagoneer
Most fun to drive off-road: CJ-5 Jeep

•

There are some other driving pointers that apply almost exclusively to the snow country, such as rubbing a plug of tobacco or a piece of raw onion on your windshield to keep it clear of snow and ice (but don't use your wipers too).

•

Also as a general rule, your best tires should be on the front. Three-quarters of all tire troubles happen to the front tires in 4-wheel driving since they're the ones that reach the trouble first. It's a matter of putting your best foot forward.

At this point, we've got to say something about jacks. Here we heartily agree with the experts— always carry two jacks. There are times when two jacks may come in very handy— like the time when you want to switch a better tire to the front and use your not-so-good spare on the rear. But the primary reason, honestly, is to assure that you always have at least one jack that works.

Desert Survival

Three people died in this valley last summer. They drove in with no water. The car stalled, and they tried to walk out, arrived nowhere. Dumb tourists.

Sensible, succinct, and free, this manual from Maricopa County would have made them smart tourists with a good story to tell.

—SB

[Suggested by Mark Goodman]

Desert Survival
Information for Anyone Travelling in the Desert Southwest
1971
27 pp.
free (send postage) (organization name and postage for 2 oz. requested)
from:
Maricopa County Dept. of Civil Defense and Emergency Services
2035 North 52nd Street
Phoenix, Arizona 85008

When driving in sand or snow, traction can be increased by partially deflating tires. Drive slowly on low tires. Do not remove so much air that the tire may slip on the rim. Start, stop, and turn gradually, as sudden motions cause wheels to dig in. If you plan on driving in the desert, practice "difficult traction" in a dry wash with another car standing by to tow you out if you become stuck. Experiment with the various footings. There are certain tool and equipment requirements if you intend to drive off the main roads: one or more shovels, a pick-mattock, a tow chain or cable, at least 50 feet of strong tow rope, tire pump, axe, water cans, gas cans (both FILLED), and of course, your regular spare parts and auto tools. For rope, consider nylon rather than manila. It costs more, but has twice the strength, will last much longer, and its elasticity is highly beneficial in extracting stuck vehicles. ¾" nylon has a working strength of 2,000 pounds and a breaking strength of about 10,000 pounds. Be sure that your car is in sound condition with a full gas tank, a filled radiator, a filled battery and new (and extra) fan belts.

•

Determining Direction from Shadow: Select an object at least 3 ft. high which casts a shadow with a well defined projection. Mark the shadow tip---wait 10 to 15 minutes and again mark the shadow tip. A line drawn from the first mark through the second mark will point EAST. Effective from about 9 a.m. to 3 p.m.

QUICKSAND

Quicksand is a deposit of fine sand in combination with water. It may have the appearance of smooth dry sand, but the water underneath lubricates the grains and allows them to flow easily. There is nothing mysterious about quicksand---it acts as any thick liquid would, and if we react sensibly we can escape it. Man is lighter and will float in water, and therefore, quicksand. It has no power to suck down bodies, but frantic struggling to free the feet creates forceful downward movement which causes the sand first to move away, then quickly return to pack around the legs. The result is a firmer and deeper hold on the body. Further struggling repeats the process until the body is engulfed completely. If caught throw yourself flat on your back. You will float. Get rid of extra weight. Throw your gun and pack off quickly. Don't hold up your arms---let them rest spread out on the surface. Roll slowly to firm ground, or turn onto your stomach and do a slow breaststroke. Move slowly and carefully, and you will "swim" to safety. Avoid getting caught---look for quicksand in river beds, washes and run-off areas of recent flash floods.

Toyota Land Cruiser

The most work per dollar in a 4-wheel drive you can get this side of a truck. New soft tops run about $3,849, hard tops $4,209. For your nearest Toyota Dealer check the phone book's yellow pages, or

Toyota Motor Sales, U.S.A., Inc.
2055 West 190th St.
Torrance, CA 90501

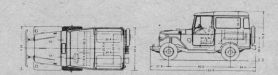

Virtuoso Handy Jack

In going over your July issue, was interested to note your mention of the Handy Jack. I have used one for year--very effective. Here are three uses for it well worth featuring:

a. In case of auto wreck and car is collapsed, insert jack and use to "unpry" the car and remove victim. Last time, I used it, man was badly crushed and was able to get some of the weight of car off him. He had skidded off road, turned upside down and roof collapsed and squeezed him. The Handyman Jack took a lot of weight off him, but I still couldn't get him out, although he was alive when I first reached him. If I had had two of these, I might have gotten him out-- but dead when our ambulance arrived and took a tow truck to lift car off his body!

b. When you skid off road in snow (or mud)...place Handyman Jack (or any bumper jack that will lift 3 or 4 ft.) under rear bumper. Raise to maximum height...then stand to one side and topple car off jack toward roadway. This will move rear end at least 3 ft.!! Repeat once or twice and you will have car wheels on road where they will get traction.

c. Getting car out of a deep mud hole...I have used this many times! Attach a lumber chain (or 3 or 4 strands of heavy rope..chain is best as it doesn't stretch) to a tree or possibly another car or truck. Attack chain to one end of Handyman Jack. Attach other end of jack to car spring or bumper if VERY securely fastened and work jack to pull car out. i.e. Jack is horizontal. This really works as jack will pull car at least 3 or 4 feet with each setting. Shorten chain and repeat as necessary. Carrying one of these jacks and a 100 ft. length of chain may save a $20 towing bill! And in some parts of this country there just aren't tow trucks or phones available.

Maj. Lyman F. Barry
Nunda, New York

Cepek Tires

Good tires, good prices, good advice. Plus other dune buggie and off-road gear.

—SB

Catalog
free

from:
Dick Cepek, Inc.
9201 California Ave.
South Gate, CA 90280

Made in U.S.A.

DICK CEPEK
"BAJA-PROVEN"

Portable Hand Spotlight
35,000 candlepower— chrome finish. Plugs into any standard auto cigarette lighter.

9' CORD
$5.95, postpaid

"And so the President comes in with all this give away. Of course now he did have to do something, let's give the devil his due. And the people did get a little something to eat out of it which they had to have, and here I am on my way to get on the Happy Pappys if they'll have me. But what I mean is, everybody talked about how good it was of the President to do that, how kind it was of him to send in the food stamps and start the Happy Pappys. Oh he was smart, you neen to doubt it. One day they was about to revolute, the next they're glad to draw a dollar and a half an hour. And top it all, here comes the President's wife down in a jet plane to show how concerned her and her husband was for all the hungry people. They lined up by the thousands just to get a look at her ride by in a big car. Parked up yonder in front of the courthouse, got up on a truck bed and made a little speech about how beautiful these old hills are. And how fine the people are, how rugged and independent and so forth all the hillbillies are. And her supposed to be so beautiful. I didn't think she was so beautiful. Why that woman was so bow-legged she couldn't hem a hog up in a pen. I felt about half sorry for her, I declare I did. Me on welfare, her richer'n Jay Goo, and I felt sorry for her because her legs was bowed. A man's got to be about half crazy to go around thinking like that, I'll swear it."

(continued) ➡

Off Road
Nomadics **251**

BMW Motorcycle

BMW motorcycles— as far as quality there is not another vehicle on the road that can touch them. Mine is 10 years old and has 143,000 miles on it. Last year I loaded it up with 430 pounds of people, camping gear and luggage and drove to Maine and then went 50 miles into the wilderness. I figure she's good for another 10/143,000. They are a bit expensive but worth every penny. If you're going to go nomadic, on or off the road, you might as well go all the way. It's the only way to travel. Western distributor is Flander Co., 200 West Walnut St., Pasadena CA 91103. Eastern distributor and sole importer is Butler & Smith, 160 West 83rd St., N.Y., N.Y. 10024.

[Suggested and reviewed by Larry Kafka]

Note. About 2 miles from here and eight months ago the reviewer Larry Kafka was killed and his wife Janet nearly killed— she's still in the hospital. It wasn't the BMW's fault, except that when the bike and a truck tried to occupy the same lane the truck driver had lots of protection and Larry and Janet none. No bike gives you protection. I ride mine slow.

—SB

Intelligent Motorcycling

A contradiction in terms. However this booklet of advice reprinted from Cycle World says more in less space about surviving and enjoying your bike than anything else I've seen.

—SB

Intelligent Motorcycling
William Kaysing
64 pp.

$2.00 postpaid

from:
Paradise Publishers
Box 5372
Santa Barbara, CA 93103

With anyone who has ever had a flat at speed on a cycle, preventive maintenance of tires and tubes rate high priority. A rider can ride a raggedy old machine with chipped paint and a smoking exhaust, but as long as the wheels are well shod, he will avoid the first and foremost hazard of motorcycling.

•

There are probably only two suitable methods of coping with rainy days as far as cycles are concerned. The first is to stay home or take your car. The second is to ride with the mental attitude that you are traveling on a sheet of oil-coated glass enhanced here and there by large patches of greased BB's. This attitude should help give you the sensitivity of response and precise control necessary to stay up on rain-slick pavement.

In the realm of spare parts, a new spark plug and a wrench to install it ranks high. . .perhaps tops. Other essentials are a spare master link, a few nuts and bolts, a roll of tape and length or two of baling wire. These items plus a screw driver and pliers taped to the frame will most often be sufficient to get a rider home from the boondocks should something fall off or poop out.

Minimum equipment for the off-the-road rider starts with an approved helmet since about 75 percent of all vehicle accidents result in head injuries. Also required for the boondock bouncer are gloves, boots, and, if possible, leather clothing or heavy denims. Remember, even when the weather is warm and heavy clothing is uncomfortable, protection for your elbows and knees will keep the skin in those areas intact.

Jawa Motorcycle

I was glad to see the BMW mentioned in the Supplement, as bikes are good tools with lots of mythic freedom meanings for most Americans; and for those who are still into the internal combustion reciprocating life style, they have the extra advantage of being: smelly, noisy, saxy, and fast.

I'd like to mention the Jawa, which is at the other end of the scale from the BMW and might be of more interest to rural/community people.

The Jawa is a 2-stroke 125-300 cc lightweight made in Czechoslovakia. Parts are easy to get in the East (a problem in the West) and the bike is dirt cheap to buy and run. Prices run about $150-$200 below Italian and Japanese machinery.

But the best thing about the Jawa is that you don't need many parts. The bike was designed to be, and is, the staple transportation device of the Communist world. It's simple, slow, reliable and strong.

Like the BMW, the Jawa is an old-fashioned "backwards" machine— unchanged since 1954. The engine is a long stroke, piston port, plain bearing low RPM single (except for the 350 twin), all of which means high torque at low speeds. It's a thumper, a tractor.

The BMW is a great road bike but as soon as you take it in the dirt you're in trouble. With the Jawa, it's the other way around. It'll shake the shit out of you on a long trip, but kick it into low and stand up on the pegs and you can chomp through anything. I like to ride mine in the sand and mud, and I'm sure I could plow with it.

I bought my new 1969 for $420! Old ones are even cheaper, as they start to rust before you even get them home. Like an East European drip dry suit, it wilts right away but wears forever. This seems like a good cheap draft horse for a community, as you can carry a lot of stuff on a bike after you get used to it, and also hook up a small trailer. I cruise Manhattan looking for firewood on mine.

Check any bike shop in the east or AMERICAN JAWA LTD. 38-15 Greenpoint Avenue, Long Island City, N. Y. 11101.

[Suggested and reviewed by Terry Bisson]

Modern Motorcycle Mechanics

ride your motorcycle;
fix your motorcycle.

—jd
[Suggested by Bob McIntyre]

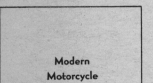

Modern Motorcycle Mechanics
J. B. Nicholson
1942-74; 760 pp.

$12.00 postpaid

from:
Nicholson Brothers Motorcycles, Ltd.
225 Third Avenue North
Saskatoon, Saskatchewan
CANADA

or WHOLE EARTH CATALOG

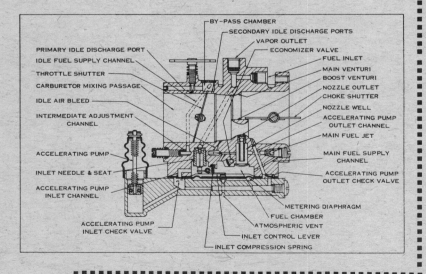

HARLEY-DAVIDSON SERVICING

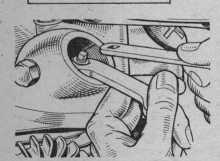

TRIUMPH TAPPET ADJUSTMENT

Adjusting screw is at valve end of rocker on all Triumph models, most B.S.A. and some other makes.

On Triumph models that require .010" tappet clearance, this can be obtained by slackening adjusting screw one-quarter turn beyond point at which it becomes free.

On models that specify .002" inlet and .004" exhaust clearance inlet rocker screws should be adjusted so that rocker is free with barely perceptible shake. Exhaust rocker should have slightly more "shake".

Bicycle Parts

How bout listing cycle parts from England. One co. I've had super service from and saved lots of money. . .fast too is

A.A. Snell & Sons
126 Boundary Road
Walthamston, London E12

Drew Langsner
San Francisco, CA

Pedal Power

Bicyclists constitute a breezy wing of the ecology movement. If you want to work on city hall, you can get advice, examples, access, etc., from:

The Bicycle Institute of America
122 East 42nd St.
New York, N.Y. 10017

Schwinn

Since the ecology drive is on, I guess there'll be more and more people riding bicycles. I used to work in a bicycle shop which carried various brands. Having worked on bicycles and having heard compliments and criticisms about different brands, I have come to the conclusion that there is only one bike worth buying; a Schwinn. Selections in frame sizes, models and colors, along with their well-built construction, are some of the reasons why I favor them. Also the availability of Schwinn parts is something many people overlook. Schwinn's guarantee cannot be excelled, (most don't even have a guarantee). I've seen Schwinns 50 years old that are in much better mechanical shape than new off-brands. Also, in your Spring Catalouge's Bicycle Page, it advises oiling the hubs and bearings. Don't! The grease that is in these hubs will be washed out when the oil quickly seaps out, leaving dry bearings.

Concerned,

PFC Palmer C. Bowen
7th Psychological Operations Group
APO San Francisco 96248

Schwinn public service brochure (free) can be had from:
Consumer Relations Dept.
Schwinn Bicycle Co.
1856 N. Kostner Ave.
Chicago, Ill. 60630

10 Speeds from Canada

I've got a good idea for traveling, and since I haven't seen anything about it in your catalog, I'll let you in on it.

Last summer, I decided to travel, going down to Boston, Cape Cod and then back thru Vermont, and then back here, Montreal.

One Problem.

I am not a rich person. So, to make a long story short, I rented a 10 speed bicycle. After cycling just 10 miles the first day, and 15 miles the second day, (had some tired muscles, but nothing really bad) the third day went 30 miles, so that at the end of the 6th day, I could do 70 miles.

Yeah.

Well, you might say: "That guy's an athlete" But no, I'm a girl, and for exercise I walk around the block once a week, so, you really don't have to be strong in any way, just a bit a patience, and around $120.00 to buy one of these things. With a 10 speed Gitane (what I recommend) you practically glide up a hill, People don't get heavy when you go thru a small town like when your hitchhiking, cause they know your leaving. . .by your own means. And you can carry loads of stuff on a saddle bag on the carrier on the back of the byke. I Can't recommend any magazines or booklets off-hand, but if you know of any, I think it would be a good idea to print it.

Also great to fight pollution, and move around faster, in the city!

SORRY ABOUT MY ENGHLISH BUT I'S A FRENCH CANADIEN, AN' YOU ENGLISH AR OWT TO GETT US.

Andrée Laparé
Ville LaSalle, Quebec

P.S. If you want to write back, feel free & we could rap about our nice facist prime-minister, our little revolutionary ideas, the kidnappings, I knew the kidnappers' sister.

Anybody's Bike Book

Ah. We have here the John Muir of bicycles. Complete cheerful information on bike use and maintenance. Good advice, reasonable price; that's nice.

SB

[Suggested by Karen Herold]

Anybody's Bike Book
Tom Cuthbertson
1971; (92 pp., 70 illustrations)

$3.00 postpaid

from:
Ten Speed Press
Box 4310
Berkeley, CA 94704

or WHOLE EARTH CATALOG

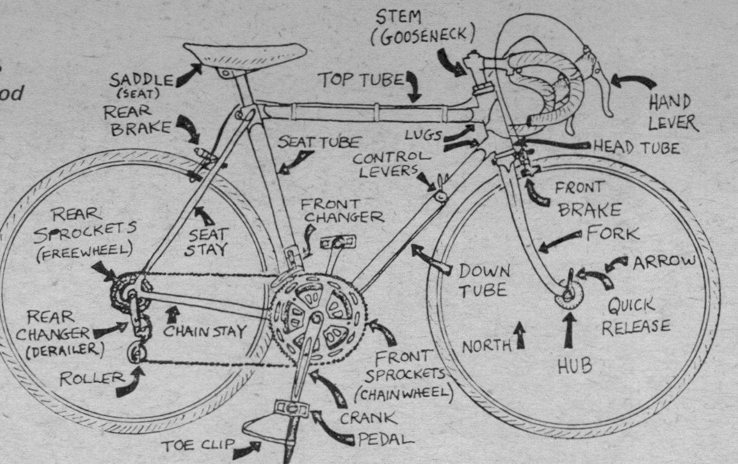
STEM
(GOOSENECK)
SADDLE
(SEAT)
TOP TUBE
HAND
LEVER
REAR
BRAKE
SEAT TUBE
LUGS
HEAD TUBE
CONTROL
LEVERS
FRONT
BRAKE
REAR
SPROCKETS
(FREEWHEEL)
SEAT
STAY
FRONT
CHANGER
FORK
ARROW
DOWN
TUBE
QUICK
RELEASE
REAR
CHANGER
(DERAILER)
CHAIN STAY
NORTH
HUB
ROLLER
FRONT
SPROCKETS
(CHAINWHEEL)
CRANK
PEDAL
TOE CLIP

Before you buy a bicycle, think about what you are going to use it for.

If you are going to ride over plowed fields, or on sand flats at low tide, or if you plan to take only short rides to the corner store, get a sturdy coaster-brake model, a balloon-tire bomber. $10-$50.00.

If you plan leisurely shopping jaunts, weekend excursions up to 30 miles, or commuting for short distances, all on reasonably even terrain, get a 3 speed. If you like a comfortable ride and maneuverability, you might try one of the newly introduced small-wheeled bikes. $50—$80.

If you plan to cover long distances over varied terrain, and if you are willing to accommodate yourself to a specialized riding position for the sake of vast improvement in cycling speed and responsiveness, get a 10 speed. $80-$300.

•

10. Find a bike shop that *cares*. They will get you hard-to-find parts, give you advice, and help you when this book can't. There *are* bike shops that care. They aren't necessarily the big and flashy ones— remember, it's the people that count. When you find a good shop, do all your business there. Tell people who want new bikes to shop there. It's the least you can do in exchange for the small-parts hunting that a good shop will do for you.

11. Cultivate a fine ear so you can hear any little complaint your bike makes, like grindy bearings, or kerchunking chain, or a slight clunking of a loose crank. You don't have to talk to your bike when you ride it— just learn to listen to it affectionately and sensitively.

12. Keep all bearings adjusted properly. Your bicycle has between 150 and 200 ball bearings. To keep them all rolling smoothly, you have to learn to adjust the *cups* and *cones* in which they run. Adjustment involves screwing the cone and cup together until they are snug on the ball bearings, then unscrewing the cup and cone slightly. The bearing should revolve smoothly, without any "play" or looseness between the cup and cone.

•

If your brake stickies are in the lever itself, you have either an unlubricated unit, a bent lever, a bent lever axle, or a misshapen post. Try a little dab of light oil on the lever axle; that's the easiest thing. No luck? The most common problem is a bent lever. Is the lever out of line? If it is, try straightening it with your bare hands, holding the post in one hand and bending the lever with the other. If that doesn't help, you can try using various metal-eating tools, such as the vise-grip.

The New Complete Book of Bicycling

This book, which contains almost everything you want or need to know about bicycling, was written by a man who rides his own 10-speed lightweight 30 miles a day in Chicago commuting between home and job. He deals knowledgeably with cycling and health, bicycling safety, choosing a bicycle, cycle touring and camping, racing, history of bicycling, accessories, and maintenance.

His advice on choosing a bicycle is quite similar to that given in the Bicycle Page of the Whole Earth Catalog, although much more extensive. Basically it amounts to this: the most satisfactory bicycle for the serious cyclist is the precision lightweight with derailleur-shifted gears. Such bikes cost about $200 or more, and the only smart place to buy one is at a reputable shop that can set it up properly when it is new and provide good service and maintenance for it as it ages.

The book has a wealth of technical detail and many good illustrations. Of special interest are the sections on choosing a bicycle and maintaining it. The former includes a thorough discussion on selecting suitable gear ratios. This important matter, unhappily, is often neglected by the inexperienced cyclist. Thus he may find— unless he is athletic and in top physical condition— that his expensive new lightweight has gear ratios better suited to road racing than to more casual touring. The book explains how to avoid this problem by ordering wider range gears.

In the section on maintenance are included detailed instructions and enough illustrations to enable the reader to do most of his own upkeep and repairs if he wants to. With this book and a few tools one could keep a bike running indefinitely at very small cost.

[Suggested and reviewed by Wallace Clements]

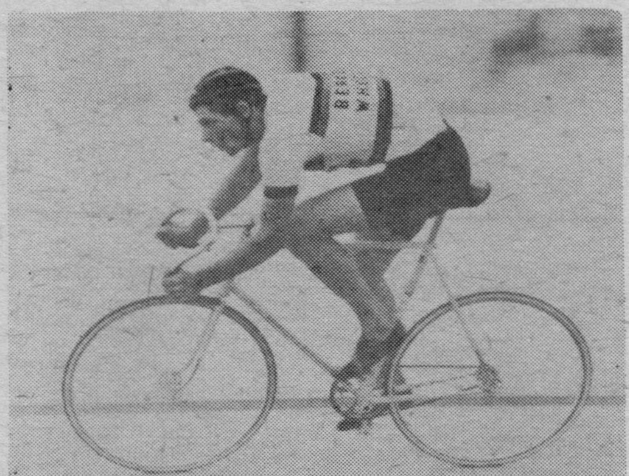

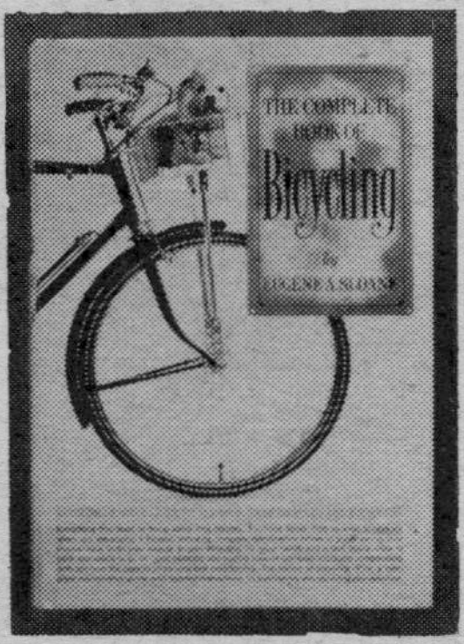
THE COMPLETE
BOOK OF
Bicycling

The Complete Book of Bicycling
Eugene A. Sloan
1970; 342 pp.

$10.95 postpaid

from:
Simon & Schuster
1 W. 39th St.
New York, N.Y. 10018

or WHOLE EARTH CATALOG

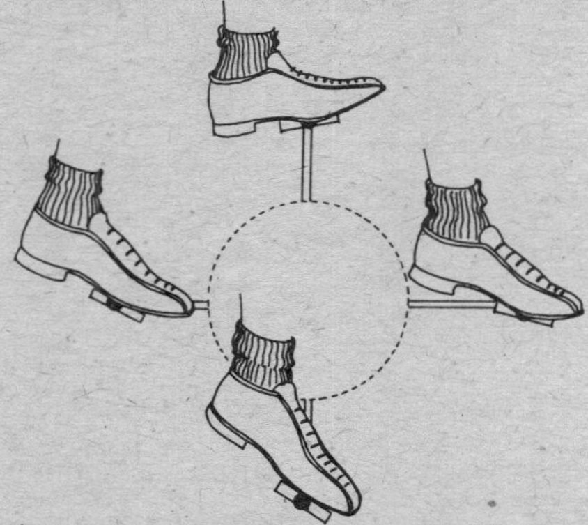

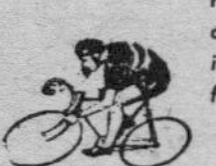

Fig. 36: Never pedal on your arch. For maximum efficiency, use ball of foot. Then ankle correctly to get maximum pedaling action, as shown here. Correct ankling technique involves ankle positions with toe pointing slightly upward at top of stroke to push pedal forward and down; downward at bottom of stroke to force pedal back and up.

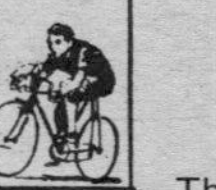

Before you buy your good machine, count the number of teeth on each of the gears on the rear derailleur. For example, the freewheel gears on the usual fine machine will start with 23 teeth on the large gear and work down in two-tooth jumps to 15 teeth on the small gear, so that you will have gears of 23, 21, 19, 17, and 15 teeth. This is a close ratio freewheel that I do not recommend for the average cyclist for cross-country tours, or for riding about in hilly country, because there is not enough variation in gear selections. You can have your bicycle dealer install a set of gears with a wider range. I recommend a rear freewheel gear cluster with these teeth: 28, 24, 20, 17, and 14, with double chainwheel of 40 and 50 teeth.

•

About horns. A mechanical horn, such as a squeeze-bulb type, takes up too much room for the noise it makes. Tinkle bells are about all you need if you do a lot of sidewalk riding. If you really want noise, try a Freon-powered boat horn, which can be heard for ten blocks. When they were new on the market, I bought one and put it in a bottle carrier on my handlebar, where I could get at it quickly. It sounded rather like a diesel freight train coming down the highway. The first time I used it, I was between a squad car and the curb, and it caused the squad car to leap forward with dome light flashing. The second time, I tried it on a woman driver coming at me from an intersection. She came to a satisfying, screaming stop. The third time, I blew it at a driver who opened a car door in front of me, and it frightened him into closing the door rather quickly. By the time he did I was long past him. But since I find my lung power about as good a horn as I need, I discarded the Freon horn and its pound of gas. In general, it's far better to be alert at all times to what's happening around you and be prepared to take evasive action than it is to count on a horn to get you out of trouble. In my opinion, any horn is just dead weight.

•

Never pedal on your arch. For maximum efficiency, use ball of foot. Then ankle correctly to get maximum pedaling action, as shown here. Correct ankling technique involves ankle positions with toe pointing slightly upward at top of stroke to push pedal forward and down; downward at bottom of stroke to force pedal back and up.

•

Tire Pumps

A pump that can be seat-tube mounted is a "must" if you tour or take trips very far from home. After having used a number of pumps, I find the Silca or the Campagnola plastic pump the best and easiest to use. These pumps can be obtained with either a Presta head for tubular tire valves, or Schrader for American tube valves. They cost about $4.00 and are well worth it. Other pumps I have tried soon fell apart or became dented and were therefore useless.

Most of the suppliers/sources here were suggested by Sage, of Turin Bicycle Co-op.

Stuyvesant Distributors
8 East 13th St.
New York, N.Y. 10003
(75¢ for catalog)

Turin Bicycle Co-op
2112 North Clark Street
Chicago, Illinois 60614

Thomas Avenia (east)
2191 Third Ave.
New York, N.Y. 10035

Thomas Avenia (west)
10205 Rio Hondo Parkway
El Monte, CA 91733

Wheel Goods
14524 21st Ave. North
Minneapolis, Minnesota 55441

Cupertino Bike Shop
10080 Randy Lane
Cupertino, CA 95014

Pleasant Valley Shop
P.O. Box 293
Livingston, N.J. 07039
(Mail order specialist for Clement cycles)

Hans Ohrt Lightweight Bikes
9544 Santa Monica Boulevard
Beverly Hills, CA 90210

Velo-Sport Cyclery
1650 Grove Street
Berkeley, CA 94709

John's Custom Bicycle Center
741 East Dixie Drive
West Carrolton, Ohio

Cyclo-Pedia
6447 Michigan Avenue
Detroit, Michigan 48210
($1.00 for 60 page "handbook & catalog")

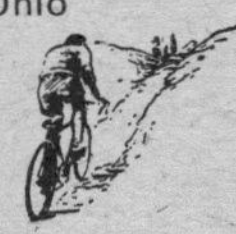

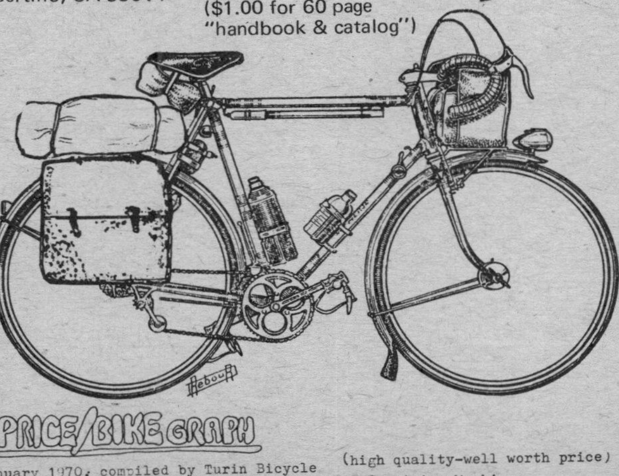

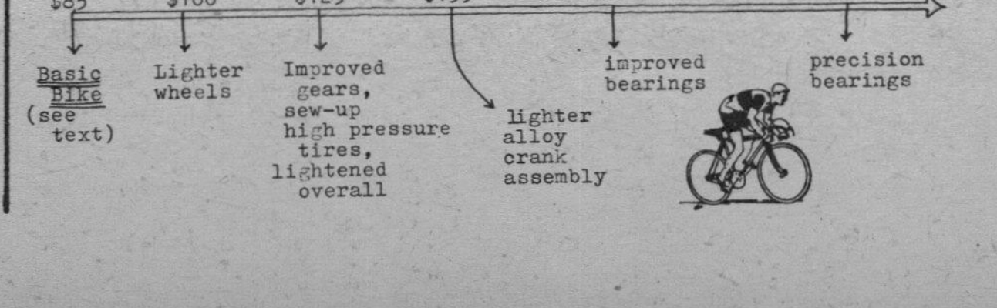
PRICE/BIKE GRAPH
(january 1970, compiled by Turin Bicycle Co-op staff with Sage)
(high quality-well worth price)
Precision Machines
$85
$100
$125
$155
$180
$240
Basic Bike
(see text)
Lighter wheels
Improved gears, sew-up high pressure tires, lightened overall
lighter alloy crank assembly
improved bearings
precision bearings

How To Improve Your Cycling

If you're getting a kid a bike, you might get this little book too.

—SB

How to Improve Your Cycling
OUT OF PRINT

from:
The Athletic Institute
Merchandise Mart, Rm. 805
Chicago, Illinois 60654

or WHOLE EARTH CATALOG

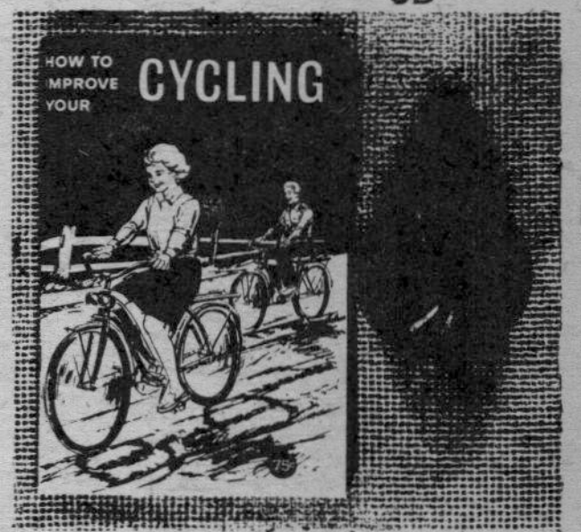
HOW TO
IMPROVE
YOUR
CYCLING

These publications are all nearly essential if you plan on checking out all available avenues before buying a ten-speed tourer.

Derailleur Lightweights— New Dimension in Cycling
available from
Schwinn Bicycle Company
1856 North Kostner
Chicago, Illinois 60639

Bicycling! (monthly magazine)
H.M. Leete & Co.
256 Sutter Street
San Francisco, CA 94108

League of American Wheelman Bulletin
L.A.W. Bulletin
19 S. Bothwell
Palatine, IL 60067

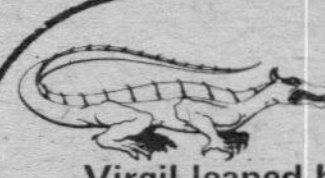

Virgil leaned his head out the window to spit again. This time he let go of his whole plug. He hawked and spat and dredged a mouthful of phlegm out of his throat and when he'd let that go too he cleared his throat and continued.

"And so what comes next but the strip mining. I mean we had some of it right along, but after that woman come in here and made her speech, seemed like it just broke out all over. Whole mountain ranges chewed up and spit right out in the river. They've done destroyed your county, Collier. Finley County's bad hit, you won't recognize that place. They say they's a strip mine bench through the Rockhouse drainage over eighty miles long, and getting longer ever day. What's worse it's a coming right my way. Man have a house and a barn, some pasture in the valley, they come right over it, the law says that's just fine. Law says a operator got a deed to the mineral, it don't matter what he does or who he does it to, it's legal to take that mineral out any way he wants to. They gouged a woman's baby right out of the grave over in Knott County, and her a looking. Said her husband had already been took to jail for brandishing a rifle at a bulldozer operator. Then they gouged up their baby right out of the grave, flung it end over end into the sky, the mother a looking. My wife's people got sixty acres on Lower Elk. Lived there thirty years. Got cows, good garden and a spring, man can live good there if he's willing to work. But they's this outfit owns the coal rights underneath, and they're on their way to get it. Eighty miles long, that bench is. Reminds me of a big serpent sneaking through the hills, big old eight miles long snake killing everything in its path. It's that way everywhere around here. Some folks call it the end of time but me, I just call it a bunch of goddamn criminals out tearing up the world.

The Way of the White Clouds

pilgrims are religious nomads,
people who go with a purpose,
think as they go,
move for a reason.
they have constancy in flux,
patterns in variety,
knowledge of the void.
this is the story of a nomad in the mountains,
a buddhist pilgrim in tibet.
-jd
(suggested by pam)

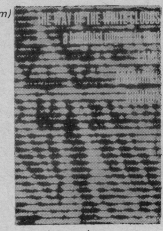

The Way of the White Clouds
Lama Anagarika Govinda
1966;70 305pp.

$3.95 postpaid

from:
Shambhala Publications
1409 5th Street
Berkeley, California 94710

or WHOLE EARTH CATALOG

To see the greatness of a mountain, one must keep one's distance; to understand its form, one must move around it; to experience its moods, one must see it at sunrise and sunset, at noon and at midnight, in sun and in rain, in snow and in storm, in summer and in winter and in all the other seasons. He who can see the mountain like this comes near to the.life of the mountain, a life that is as intense and varied as that of a human being. Mountains grow and decay, they breathe and pulsate with life. They attract and collect invisible energies from their surrounding; the forces of the air, of the water, of electricity and magnetism. they create winds, clouds, thunderstorms, rains, waterfalls, and rivers. They fill their surroundings with active life and give shelter and food to in-numerable beings; such is the greatness of mighty mountains.

•

We had crossed the feared 18,000-foot pass in perfect ease and under a cloudless sky. The sun was so hot during the ascent that I had discarded my warm things, but hardly had we entered the shadows on the other side of the pass when we were plunged into icy cold, that made me regret not having kept my warm clothing at hand. Tibet is a country where one is ever up against the unexpected and where all accepted rules of nature seem to be changed. The contrast between sunshine and shade is such that if for any length of time one part of one's body would be exposed to the sun, while the other remained in the shade, one could develop simultaneously blisters, due to severe sunburn, and chilblains due to the icy air in the shade. The air is too rarified to absorb the sun's heat and thus to create a medium shadow temperature, nor is it able to protect one from the fierceness of the sun and its ultra-violet rays.

Troutfishing in America

If it's fish you're after, go to p. 280. For headfishing, stick around.
—SB

Trout Fishing in America
Richard Brautigan
1967; 112 pp.

$0.95 postpaid

from:
Delta Books
750 3rd Ave.
New York, N.Y. 10017

or WHOLE EARTH CATALOG

The Odyssey: A Modern Sequel

This epic poem may well turn out to be the spiritual handbook of the future. In fact, our future may lie within its pages. Imminently suitable to the Whole Earth philosophy and this revolutionary generation, it traces the struggle of one hero through the successive stages of ego, race, mankind and all matter to a communion with the best post-Christian, non-Eastern concept of God I've run across yet; a struggling, ascending, evolutionary Spirit, neither Almighty, All-holy, nor pitiless, haphazard Nature itself. Odysseus finds it is his duty as the Spirit's highest, most sublime evolutionary creation to assist in the struggle; that his freedom, his salvation is concomitant with that of his God, that he must save his God to save himself, even from the illusion of salvation itself. It's a harsh, rugged phil-osophy, necessitating a joyously tragic, dionysian nihilism; but its essence is pure spiritual freedom and it places the burden of action directly on men.

On the other hand, like all great epics, it can be read first on the superficial level of great adventure, replete with battles, orgies, desert treks and primitive jungle kingdoms as Odysseus' spiritual journey takes him almost due south from Achaean Ithaca to deca-dence in Crete, political oppression in Egypt, down the Nile to its source near the mountain peak of his enlightenment, and on through Africa to freezing death in Antarctic westes. Buddha and Christ, Faust and Don Quixote put in appearances and rap with Odysseus, the famed ascetic philosopher, in various adventures after his enlightenment. The splendid verse translation is lush, organic with lots of good Nature symbolism. In short, this book's got everything and covers everything. Get it and be a believer.

[Reviewed by Thomas Edwards]

O gypsy Life, with sun-braids, with coquetting eyes,
for years I've stumbled in your light, your holy haunts,
for years been put to shame, hunting your empty shade,
thrashing my arms with rage, tearing the wild wind's hair!
Sometimes you seemed like Beauty, passion-quelling Helen,
a shadow's coolness, smell of musk, or the sea's air,
seductive dancer paid in the ecstasy of drink
to please our eyes with your adroit erotic tricks;
at times, when earth embittered me in my full youth,
you seemed, O Life, like the grass-widow Virtue, sad,
unlaughing, and I seized my spear to guard you well,
as though you ever cared, O luring siren-song,
for justice or injustice of the joys of men!
One dawn as I gleaned the mind's loneliness in vain,
I heard the seas, the heart, the earth call me for help;
God called in greatest peril, and I rushed to build
a head for him to hide in, a town in which to sleep.
Forgive me, Life, if I've so stupidly pursued
such gaudy plumes as whence we come and where we go;
I've squandered years in hunting what I thought firm flesh,
your three great shadows: Beauty, guileless Virtue, Truth;
but may these wanderings, too, be blessed that in good time
brought me to your nude body cool as warbling water.

Let Death come down to slavish souls and craven heads
with his sharp scythe and barren bones, but let him come
to this lone man like a great lord to knock with shame
on his five famous castle doors, and with great awe
plunder whatever dregs that in the ceaseless strife
of his staunch body have not found time as yet to turn
from flesh and bone into pure spirit, lightning, deeds, and joy.
The Archer has fooled you, Death, he's squandered all your goods,
melted down all the rusts and rots of his foul flesh
till they escaped you in pure spirit, and when you come,
you'll find but trampled fires, embers, ash, and fleshly dross.

There was nothing I could do. I couldn't change a flight of stairs into a creek. The boy walked back to where he came from. The same thing once happened to me. I remember mistaking an old woman for a trout stream in Vermont, and I had to beg her pardon.

"Excuse me," I said. "I thought you were a trout stream."

"I'm not," she said.

•

A little way from the shack was an outhouse with its door flung violently open. The inside of the outhouse was exposed like a human face and the outhouse seemed to say, "The old guy who built me crapped in here 9,745 times and he's dead now and I don't want anyone else to touch me. He was a good guy. He built me with loving care. Leave me alone. I'm a monument now to a good ass gone under. There's no mystery here. That's why the door's open. If you have to crap, go in the bushes like the deer."

"Fuck you," I said to the outhouse. "All I want is a ride down the river."

•

The Odyssey: A Modern Sequel
by Nikos Kazantzakis
Translation into English Verse, Introduction, Synopsis, and Notes by Kimon Friar; Illustrations By Ghika; 826 pp.
A Touchstone/Clarion paperback

$4.95 postpaid

from:
Simon and Schuster
630 Fifth Ave.
N.Y., N.Y. 10020

or WHOLE EARTH CATALOG

"Good luck," he said.

I went upstairs and there were thousands of doors there. I'd never seen so many doors before in my life. You could have built an entire city out of those doors. Doorstown. And there were enough windows up there to build a little suburb entirely out of windows. Windowville.

I turned left and went back and saw the faint glow of pearl-colored light. The light got stronger and stronger as I went farther back, and then I was in the used plumbing department, surrounded by hundreds of toilets.

The toilets were stacked on shelves. They were stacked five toilets high. There was a skylight above the toilets that made glow like the Great Taboo Pearl of the South Sea movies.

Stacked over against the wall were the waterfalls. There were about a dozen of them, ranging from a drop of a few feet to a drop of ten or fifteen feet.

There was one waterfall that was over sixty feet long. There were tags on the pieces of the big falls describing the correct order for putting the falls back together again.

The waterfalls all had price tags on them. They were more expensive than the stream. The waterfalls were selling for $19.00 a foot.

Sacred

To the Memory

of

John Talbot

Who at the Age of Eighteen

Had His Ass Shot Off

In a Honky-Tonk

November 1, 1936

This Mayonnaise Jar

With Wilted Flowers In It

Was Left Here Six Months Ago

By His Sister

Who Is In

The Crazy Place Now.

The Complete Walker

Some of them old boys are into making houses out of chicken wire and condoms. Some of them can gather you a salad right off the forest floor. Some can make you a computer out of old Stromberg-Carlson radio parts and have enough wire and tubes left over for two laser death rays and a UFO. But Colin is into walking. His two previous books are mainly about walks: In The Thousand Mile Summer *he tells about one he took up the entire Sierra range, and in* The Man Who Walked Through Time, *he walks the whole Grand Canyon. This one is about walking, not walks. It's not full of lore and woodsiness. It doesn't tell you how to get back to nature, or cast civilization from your back and wander out with a bowie knife and a jock-strap. It gives a little walk philosophy, and then proceeds to discuss, in just the right detail, how to put a nice little well-equipped house and its fittings on your back, how to be able to go out and walk for a long time without having to come back for more stuff.*

Besides just the stuff, what to take and what to leave behind, it also takes you on a trip through Colin Fletcher, which is quite an outing all by itself. It's hard to imagine a book on backpacking technique that will make you laugh out loud all the way through, but he does it. He really loves poking fun at himself. He gets completely hung up describing some gadget or technique which he then admits he's never tried. He'll spend a whole page defending what seemed at first an impossibly fussy personal idiosyncracy, and at the end you'll be dying to go out and try it for yourself. He actually has a sizable section on how to urinate and defecate in the outdoors, and it's a fine description. He includes a very complete appendix on suppliers, a list of walking organizations, and even a series of inspiring quotations to read while walking or thinking about walking.

Most important, though, its the only backpacking book I've ever seen which, if read carefully, will actually tell you how to do it in great enough detail to enable you to just go out and do it. It's also the only one that will really make you want to go out and walk for absolutely no ulterior motive.

Be sure to dig pages 45-52, 123-132, 182-186, 213-218, the whole Furniture and Appliances section, and all the illustrations.

The only adverse comment I would make is that his food preferences seem pretty sanpaku. But he also quotes the old proverb about hell being a place where the politicians are French, the police German, and the cooks English.

[Reviewed by Roland Jacopetti]

First remove any obvious and rectifiable local irritant, such as a fragment of stone or a rucked sock. Then cover the tender place. Cover it even if you can see nothing more than a faint redness. Cover it, in fact, if you can see nothing at all. Being a 'hero' is being a bloody fool. The covering may only be needed for a few hours; if you take it off at night and let the air get at the skin you may not even need to replace it next morning. But if you do nothing at the first warning you may find yourself inside the hour with a blister that will last a week.

The Complete Walker
Colin Fletcher
1969; 353 pp.

$8.95 postpaid

from:
Alfred A Knopf, Inc.
33 West 60th Street
New York, New York 10023

or **$7.95** postpaid

OR WHOLE EARTH CATALOG

There is a cardinal rule of travel, all too often overlooked, that I call the Law of Inverse Appreciation.
It states: "The less there is between you and the environment, the more you appreciate that environment."

One of the surest ways to tell an experienced walker from a beginner is the speed at which he starts walking. The beginner tends to tear away in the morning as if he meant to break every record in sight. By contrast, your experienced man seems to amble. But before long, and certainly by evening, their positions have reversed. The beginner is dragging. The expert, still swinging along at the same easy pace, is now the one who looks as though he has records in mind. One friend of mine, a real expert, says, 'If you can't carry on a conversation, you're going too fast.'

When crowds assemble in Trafalgar Square to cheer to the echo the announcement that the government has decided to have them killed, they would not do so if they had all walked 25 miles that day.

Bertrand Russell
Nobel Prize Acceptance Speech

And the Lord said unto Satan, Whence comest thou? Then Satan answered the Lord, and said, From going to and fro in the earth, and from walking up and down in it.

JOB I, 7

At this point, steam issues from the stew pot. You reduce the heat to dead-low or thereabouts (taking care not to turn the stove off in the process), stir the compound a couple of times, inhale appreciatively and replace the cover. While dinner simmers toward fruition you empty two ounces of dehydrated peaches and a little water into the small cooking pot and put it ready for breakfast, up alongside the pack. Then you jot down a few thoughts in your notebook, stir the stew and sample it, find the beans are not quite soft yet. So you study the map and worry a bit about the morning's route, put map and pen and pencil and eyeglasses and thermometer into the bedside boots, take off your shorts and slide halfway down into the mummy bag out of the wind, and stir the stew again and find all ready. You pour-and-spoon out a cupful, leaving the balance on the stove because the wind is blowing distinctly cool now. And then, leaning comfortably back against the pack and watching the sky and the black peaks meld, you eat, cupful by cupful, your dinner. You finish it—just. Then you spoon-scrape out every last possible fragment and polish-clean the pot and cup and spoon with a piece of toilet paper. You put the paper under the stove so that you can burn it in the morning. Then you put cup and spoon into the break-fast-readied small pot, pour the morning tea water into the big pot, set the big pot alongside the small one and the sugar and milk containers alongside them both, put the current day's ration bag into the pack (where it is moderately safe from mice and their. night allies) and • • •

Office-on-the-yoke

Because I so often walk without a shirt and therefore without a front pocket, I have had a five- by six-inch pocket sewn onto the front of my yoke strap, roughly where the shirt pocket comes. Into it go notebook and map, and sunglasses when not in use. Pen, pencil, camel-hair lens brush (page 233), and metal-cased thermometer (page 259) clip onto the front of it. I cannot imagine how I ever got along without such a pocket. Mine is made of ordinary blue-jean material, but anything stout will do.

For which side to put your office, see page 64.

U. S. G. S. Topographic Maps

If you're interested in buying land or visiting remote areas you'll be using any maps you can get your hands on. The United States Geological Survey publishes the most accurate and detailed maps generally available for the U. S. (and possessions). Although some are a little dated, they consistently pack a lot of information into a fairly understandable format. Besides contour intervals, these maps indicate type of earth surface, roads, train tracks and trails, buildings, mines and various land marks; plus a whole lot of other stuff.

Two series of maps are available——15 minute quadrants (approximately 1 inch equals 1 mile, with about 80 feet contour intervals, covering an area 14 x 18 miles); and 7.5 minute quadrants (approx. 2" = 1 mi., 10', 20', and 40 contour covers 7 x 9 miles). The 7.5 minute maps are more up-to-date but have not been prepared for the whole country.

[Reviewed by Drew Langsner.]

U.S.G.S. also has Distribution Centers at:
ALASKA: Anchorage, Fairbanks, Juneau and Palmer
CALIFORNIA: Menlo Park, Los Angeles and San Francisco
COLORADO: Denver
TEXAS: Dallas
UTAH: Salt Lake City
WASHINGTON: Spokane
WASHINGTON, D.C.
Canadian Topo maps from:
Map Distribution Office
Dept. of Energy, Mines & Resources
615 Booth Street
Ottawa, Ontario, CANADA K1ADE9

Maps cost **50¢** *each and U. S. G. S. provides an index map of any state* **free.**

from:
Map Information Office, Stop 507
U.S. Geological Survey
National Center
Reston, VA 22092

From Moe Armstrong

this is my third year in new mexico, the second year just living in national forest, in wickiups, this year its more like a lodge 35 feet long, 6 feet hingh. the ranger loves us, (we keep a "Model camp") and we got a jeep truck.

Moe Armstrong
Vallecitos, N.M.

the river
running south
running brown
running south
    sun setting
      on
     brown mesas
turning
  clouds
  golden
(rays like lances)
  the valley
  the river
  the sun
  the clouds
all turn
into
a feather
and
drift
  towards me

•

---

waiting
for
  the truck ride
to end
    waiting
    for
    the hiway
    to go
    someplace
    else
and me
to live
another
way
    and
    find
    something else
    to do
(with what i got)

LETTING VIRGIL DRIVE

D.R. was fascinated by all the things that Virgil was saying, but after about half an hour on 421 again he started getting so sleepy he barely could keep his eyes open. He drove through the narrow curving part of the road that had caused him to turn back before, but once into the long valley beyond the narrows, Urge's front wheels started dropping off the blacktop every mile or two, and finally D.R. had to tell Virgil they would have to stop so he could nap a while, unless Virgil would like to drive. Virgil said he'd be glad to try, but he was a little nervous about operating a car with such funny gears. He offered to just sit and wait while D.R. got some sleep, but when he thought about it that seemed pretty silly, so he pulled off the road and spent a few minutes teaching Virgil about Urge's gears. When Virgil said he thought he had it, D.R. told him it was all his, and he crawled through the junk scattered on the floor of the bus, stretched out on the mattress and fell asleep immediately.

The Last of the Mountain Men

sylvan hart lives on the river of no return,
the north fork of the salmon in idaho,
he's been there a few decades.
he builds his own tools,
grows and hunts his own food,
wears buckskin,
has a college degree,
and built a bomb shelter.
harold peterson went to visit sylvan hart,
and wrote this book about him.
a couple of friends of mine went to visit sylvan hart,
to make a film of him. turns out they didn't like him.
that shouldn't say anything about the book.
i'm hoping sylvan hart isn't the last of the mountain men.

—j.d.

The Last of the Mountain Men
Harold Peterson
1969; 156 pp.

$5.95 postpaid

from:
Charles Scribner's Sons
Vreeland Avenue
Totowa, N.J. 07512

or WHOLE EARTH CATALOG

Sylvan's pole bridge, pinned precariously to the sheer face of a cliff high above the roiling River of No Return, constitutes the only path to the outside world.

Each of these samples of his innumerable hammers, scrapers, punches, awls, adzes, gouges, and other implements was hand-made by Hart.

The guns with which Buckskin bags his trophies, trinkets, and trousers have aroused considerably more avarice than that. One handmade flintlock rifle, a particularly enviable product of loving craftsmanship, so excited a wealthy Los Angeles businessman that he offered $500 for it. "It's not for sale," Bill told him. The rich Angeleno thought a moment, offered $750. "It's not for sale," Bill repeated firmly. By this time, the man, used to having his money count, was sorely vexed. "$1,000," he snapped. "It's not worth it, but I want that rifle." "It's not for sale," Bill said, as calmly as before. The Angeleno left in a terrible temper. A week later he was back with a blank check. "Fill it out for whatever you want," he barked. "It's not for sale," said Bill. "Damn it," said the man. "You need the money. You *do* use money, don't you?" "No," said Bill. "Not where I live."

The rifle in question has a beautifully hand-bored, hand-rifled barrel, a mechanism with double cock and double-set trigger, and an ornately carved moutain mahogany stock. Bored to .45 caliber, the barrel is Swedish jackhammer carbon steel, which he had sent in to him.

Although accurately described by Buckskin as "a rotating helix drive by fingers on a headblock nailed to a table top," the machine used to make that rifle scarcely seems sophisticated enough to uncork a pop gun. As for the handmade "rifling saw" which cuts the actual groove, that looks like nothing so much as a half-inch-long bit of scrap metal. Yet if Sylvan, looking down the barrel, can find a flaw, no one else can, and the rifle shoots with deadly accuracy. "It's nothing but muscle power," Sylvan says, "but I really lay into it. That cutter comes out of there smoking."

With its light, steady touch, the firing mechanism is no less astonishing. "The interesting part is a pitiful little thing called a detent," Sylvan explains, taking a listener's comprehension for granted. "It causes the sear to ride over the half-cock notch in the tumbler."

Smoother than rosewood, the stock was simply blackened with sulfuric acid and rubbed to its lustrous deep brown finish by rubbing with the plam of the hand. It's carvings variously depict an old mountain sheep resting its heavy horns on the ground while drinking, two rams fighting, and the exact defensive deployment of a band of bighorns being attacked by eagles.

"I just make one as I need it, but I don't like to spend less'n a year making a rifle," Hart said, opening the patch button in the stock to show the orange flicker feathers inside. They are used to flick dust and lint out of the mechanism.

---

pre in FORM

one of the worst problems that we
(the MOVEMENT if you prefer)
(the Back-To-The-Land Movement, if you prefer)
have is the cost of land
if you want to stay here
(the United States of America)
land on Oahu is selling for five bucks
a square foot,
land in Montana,
about two hundred an acre,
in small pieces,
if you are lucky.
preinform gets past that bother
by advocating that we forget that
people,
the governments,
own land,
and,
just go live somewhere,
bit by bit,
dig a tunnel,
get ready to move soon,
figure on moving soon,
forget,
use,
and live,
freely.
its kinda hard to say
if these people will be there,
but if they are:

—jd

Note: pre-inform is now vonulife, a happy reincarnation.
—PC

Vonulife
$1.00
once a year
50,000 words

from:
Vonulife
P.O. Box 248
Paradise, CA 95969

Mountaineering: The Freedom of the Hills

By far the most complete and sensitive treatment of mountaineering available. Oriented around Pacific Northwest mountaineering, where trails often end miles before the peaks begin, it is particularly relevant to wilderness camping and travel. It is much more than a book on how to climb. Reflects several generations of respectful relationship with mountains. If you move (or sit) where there are trees, rocks, snow and brush, it speaks to your terrain. One limitation: little about dry, arid areas— glaciers are the local functional equivalent of deserts.

[Reviewed by Michael Templeton. Suggested by everybody.]

Mountaineering:
The Freedom of the Hills
ed. Harvey Manning
1960, 1967; 485 pp.

$7.50 postpaid

from:
The Mountaineers
P. O. Box 122
Seattle, Wash. 98111

or WHOLE EARTH CATALOG

The quest of the mountaineer, in simplest terms, is for the freedom of the hills, to be fully at home in the high wilderness with no barriers he cannot pass, no dangers he cannot avoid.

•

COOKING AND EATING UTENSILS

The least-expensive cooking utensils are tin cans in various sizes, junked (at home, not in the mountains) when rusty. Aluminum utensils cost a little more but are more durable. Bails are desirable for suspending pots over the fire, and lids to keep ashes out and steam in. Aluminum foil is versatile beyond description, under adept manipulation becoming a frying pan, oven for baking foods in a bed of coals, reflector oven for biscuits, and if need be even a cup or a pot.

•

BREAKFAST

If the climb begins in the middle of the night, breakfast is merely the first installment of lunch. A tiny can of fruit cocktail, or a doughnut and a swallow of milk, are typical menus. Some climbers are convinced their legs won't work without hot food; their neurosis can be quickly pampered with instant cereal or cocoa cooked by chemical fire.

LUNCH

As soon as breakfast is completed the climber commences lunch, which he continues to eat as long as he is awake, stopping briefly for supper. He has food in his rucksack and knick-knacks in his pockets, main courses for the summit lunch, nibbles for rest-stops, and sweets to suck while walking.

Mattresses often give a chill sleep on snow due to interior convection currents, and with age they develop leaks that let the sleeper down in the middle of the night. Convection can be reduced by inserting a few ounces of down; in this case a filter is needed on the inlet and the mattress must *not* be blown up by mouth because of the moisture thus introduced. Sheets of *foam plastic* are superior in every respect except their incompressibility and consequent bulkiness.

In recent years many a mountaineer has developed the habit or hobby of not only making his own passage invisible but of spending extra effort to obliterate evidence of his predecessors— most of whom were just ignorant and thoughtless.

If a skirmish with brush must be accepted there is no technique at all. Brushfighting is not a diversion for civilized, gentle folk. One cannot afford charity toward slide alder or devil's club; one must hate and punish and kill when possible.

The irregularity of a mountain range tends to break up a front, especially the narrow turbulence zone of a cold one. Instead of advancing in a solid line it may surge forward up a deep valley while held stationary by a high massif, this bulge perhaps being attacked by flanking air— little squalls breaking off and wandering about apparently at random. A party on one peak may experience lightning, hail, driving snow, pouring rain, and calm sunshine all within the space of an hour. On a nearby peak another party may spend the entire day undisturbed by so much as a drop of rain, using up all their camera film shooting the superb cloud structures.

Summit

The only monthly magazine published in the U. S. devoted to mountaineering fortunately covers all phases. Articles range from accounts of "treks" in Nepal and even more remote areas to logs and descriptions of spectacular climbing achievements. Of special interest has been their publication of good medical articles pertinent to conditions such as altitude, cold, and fatigue

[Suggested and reviewed by Drew Langsner]

Summit

$6.00 a year (10 issues)

from:
Summit
Big Bear Lake
California 92315

The deadly effects of hypothermia are primarily circulatory and cardiac, with rather characteristic electro-cardiographic changes, and the secondary pulmonary vascular congestion and pulmonary edema tends to simulate the entity of high altitude pulmonary edema, with foaming at the mouth. Hypothermia is generally considered to exist when the body temperature, rectally, falls below 95° F., with degrees between 90-95° F. requiring only vigorous supportive care, while temperatures below 90°F. require immediate and sometimes heroic medical treatment. In the infamous Dachau experiments on seven unanesthetized healthy human subjects intentionally chilled in ice water, death occurred between 75.2-84.2° F. with an average value of 80.6° F.

Mountain Safety Research Newsletter

When you are in the outlaw area of the mountains—on rock and snow—you want tools that will break after you do. Mountain Safety Research, Inc. is an organization that tests climbing gear and where it finds a need, designs and manufactures new equipment. It was founded by inventor-manufacturer-climber Larry Penberthy when he realized that much too of the gear on the market was shoddy. It is the closest thing to a testing service for mountain equipment that exists.

Working through existing channels in Seattle mountain climbing circles produced little support and a good deal of resistance so Penberthy started his own organization.

At any rate, Mountain Safety Research has turned up some disturbing things: carabiners and ropes that broke before their rated strengths, pitans made of metal with grain running the wrong way, and ice axes of insufficient strength. For lack of another outlet, Mountain Safety Research retails its own design of pack and frame, climbing helmet, gasoline stove, mountain tent, and many other items.

[Suggested and reviewed by David Sucher]

Newsletter and Catalog

free

from:
Mountain Safety Research, Inc.
625 South 96th Street
Seattle, Washington 98108

MSR BODY HARNESSES

East Coast Mountains

The Appalachian Mtn. Club offers a number of Trail guides, books, and maps of interest to New England hikers, climbers, and canoeists. The guides and maps are accurate and easy to read. The size of these books (aprox. 3'' x 6'') make them handy to carry on trail. Some maps are available in a weather resistant material.

Available from:
Appalachian Mtn. Club
5 Joy St.
Boston, Mass. 02108

The Appalachian Trail Conference also publish a few booklets and guides. The guides cover the entire length of the Appalachian Trail. Personally I prefer the A.M.C. guides for the A.T. in New England. The booklet Hiking, Camping, and Mountaineering Equipment lists over 400 items, including foods with descriptions, weights, suppliers (domestic and foreign), and prices.

Available for $1.00 from:
Appalachian Trail Conference
Box 236, Harpers Ferry, W. Va. 25425
General Information Packet, $.25

Anyone interested in hiking or backpacking in New York State can get information from the Finger Lakes Trail Conference. Believe it or not there is still some "wilderness" left in N.Y.! This organization is made up of various trail clubs, all are active environmental conservationists.

For info: Mr. Ervin H. Markert, Trail Chairman, Pittsford, N.Y. 14534.

Jack F. McKie
Antrim, N.H.

Manual of Ski Mountaineering

If you want the wilderness to yourself, go where it's high when it's cold. This book is a fine compendium of the technical knowledge you will need to make it.

—SB

(See p. 270)

Manual of Ski Mountaineering
David Brower, editor
1962; 1969; 232 pp.

$4.75 postpaid

from:
Sierra Club
1050 Mills Tower
San Francisco, California 94104

or WHOLE EARTH CATALOG

Two-step—One of the most useful maneuvers for attainment of speed on the level or on slight downhill gradients is the two-step, which uses the gliding ability of skis. If the two-step is to be used for long, it must be deliberate and rhythmic, slow enough to let the skier relax during the glide between thrusts.

Take a short step for propulsion, lean well forward from the waist, placing the poles well ahead, and lunge into a glide on the opposite ski by shifting the propelling thrust smoothly from the driving ski to a strong followthrough with the poles. Slowly bring the driving ski alongside the gliding ski in preparation for the next short step. Occasionally two consecutive short steps are taken to change the glide from one ski to another (this constitutes the three-step), and to tire out a new set of muscles.

Lightning and the mountain.—The urge to know more concerning the effects of lightning becomes stronger when one is on a peak with the static charge beginning to make its power felt. When every projection in the vicinity, and finally the climber himself, begins to spark and the air is filled with ominous hissing, the desire to be in camp becomes overwhelming. Since this desire cannot always be satisfied, it is well to know what to do at this time.

The reasons behind the classical warning to be off the summit and ridges in a lightning storm can be seen when the mechanics of the lightning discharge are studied.

Mountaineering Medicine

It is small enough to carry any time you go into an isolated or hazardous area; well organized, and fairly up-to-date. There are sections on various injuries, snow blindness, bites and stings, sunburn, water purification, etc.. The booklet concludes with a section on making and using a first aid kit. (You'll need a physician to write 'scrips for certain drugs listed.)

[Suggested and reviewed by Drew Langsner]

Mountaineering Medicine
Fred Darvill, Jr., M. D.
1966, 1968; 35 pp.

$1.00 postpaid from:
Skagit Mountain Rescue Unit
P. O. Box 2
Mt. Vernon, Wash. 98273

Chouinard Equipment for Alpinists

Almost everyone who goes into the mountains eventually develops an urge to try rock scrambling or climbing of some kind. It is therefore important to be aware of the best safety procedures and climbing aids available.

Alpinists Yvon Chouinard and Tom Frost design and fabricate a high quality selection of modern climbing equipment. Along with descriptions and illustrations of gear, their definitive catalog includes sections on history, use, care and precautions. There is even a beautifully illustrated article on ice climbing.

[Suggested and Reviewed by Drew Langsner]

Catalog

$1.00

from:
The Great Pacific Iron Works
P.O. Box 150
Ventura, California 93001

Fundamentals of Rock Climbing

Sure enough, the working basics.

—SB

[Suggested by Neil & Lorraine Wolf]

Fundamentals of Rock Climbing
M.I.T. Outing Club
1956; 46 pp.

$1.00 postpaid

from:
M.I.T. Outing Club
Student Center Room 490
M.I.T.
Cambridge, Massachusetts 02139

Poor, flake too thin

Bad, no support

Bad, but may have good tone

Bad, piton probably loose

Very Good, But be sure it is not just up against a dead end

Very Good

Vertical Layback

Very Good

Use for a Hag Piton

Chimney

Very Good

THE BEAST OF THE SEA

Or thought he did anyhow. It sure was wild not to know for sure. Half of D.R. was very deep asleep. It was his other half he wasn't sure about. He didn't know if what he felt around him as he lay there on the mattress, and saw, quite clearly, through the windows by the road outside, was in the actual, waking world or just a dream his sleeping half was having. D.R. felt his body rolling back and forth from side to side as Urge leaned into the curves, then straightened up again. He heard Urge's motor whirring underneath, and smelled the odor of Estelle in the mattress he was lying on. That was what he felt and heard and smelled. What he saw through the windows was the dark, lit by eerie light from slag heaps burning in a dozen different places. He saw sulphuric smoke rise from scattered fires and spread across the landscape of the night. He saw hulks of abandoned automobiles strewn about like monster corpses on some prehistoric battlefield, and he saw coal tipples by the highway like preying creatures frozen by the sudden glare of light. Animals darted off the highway as the bus approached, then gathered on the pavement when they'd gone by to stare with shining, yellow eyes. In one place the road was lined with monsters grinning wickedly. Some were merely bloody heads impaled on fence posts, or hanging by the hair from limbs of trees. Some stuck out their tongues that turned to snakes that hissed and snapped and bit as they drove by. He saw a beast from the depths of the sea, covered with weeds and ancient slime except for its head, which was adorned with jewels that glistened in the light from its own winking eyes. On the beasts' head were seven horns, and crowning each horn in rays of light was Estelle's face, distorted by a grin so evil and so knowing D.R. shuddered and pressed his face into the mattress thinking surely I'll wake up now, surely this is just another dream.

Breaking and Training the Stock Horse

Most books on, and methods of, training the western type riding horse are a collection of anecdotal tricks and clever gimmicks with which you may force or frighten the horse into doing what you have in mind. Mr. Williamson's is not.

It is a concise, orderly, and complete explanation of how, with minimum paraphernalia, to condition the horse to interpret the most subtle movements and pressures of the legs, hands, and entire body and to turn these commands into movement with the freedom and ease of an unmounted horse. A horse well trained by this method can easily be ridden without a bridle. Williamson's method develops discipline and sensitivity in the trainer as well as in the horse.

Although intended primarily for the stock horse, its basic training principles can be applied to the training of any type of riding horse, including hunter, jumper, gaited, and high school dressage. There are also chapters on horsemanship, riding, and riding a bucking horse.

Mr. Williamson has been occupied with horses all of his life——the Cavalry in the First World War, running pack outfits, catching wild horses, and training and exhibiting. He now conducts a school in horse training and horsemanship in Hamilton, Montana.

[Suggested and reviewed by Paul Bandy]

Note: Mr. Williamson says, "I bought horses for calvary but enlisted in Veterinary Corps."

Breaking and Training the Stock Horse
Charles O. Williamson
1950; 123 pp.

$8.50 postpaid

from:
Charles O. Williamson
P.O. Box 506
Hamilton, Montana 59840
or WHOLE EARTH CATALOG

A correct sliding stop on hind feet. Horse and rider relaxed, nose down, reins slack.

Contrary to the usual idea *little* equipment is necessary in the proper training of saddle horses.

A horse responds to training to relieve pressure on some part of his body. He follows you when you are leading him to relieve pressure on his poll. He goes forward when the legs are used to relieve pressure on his sides. He stops or slows when the reins are pulled backward to relieve pressure on his mouth. When he does what you want, if you do not slack and relieve pressure, he has no incentive to do the same thing again for you and finally gives up in disgust and carries you about in a listless or even defiant manner because he must.

The running W

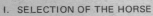
Work on the longe line. Teaching the green horse to listen to and obey the trainer and not to fear articles tied to the saddle.

Halterbreaking the green horse. Never pull a steady pull on a horse whether mounted or working from the ground. Pull and slack. Stay slack when the horse is doing what you want.

Horses

When handling horses there is no substitute for experience, but this book is as close as you can get. In the first 115 pages the author presents encyclopedic information on all phases of horse management. The last fifty pages are devoted to a brief discussion of eastern riding and showing.

[Suggested and reviewed by Michael S. Kaye]

Horses: Their Selection, Care and Handling
Margaret Cabell Self
1943; 170 pp.

$2.25 postpaid

from:
Wilshire Book Company
12015 Sherman Road
North Hollywood, CA 91605

or WHOLE
EARTH
CATALOG

I. SELECTION OF THE HORSE
   Familiar breeds of horses, how they came to be developed and for what purposes they may be used—Where to buy your horse—Tests for soundness
II. SELECTION AND CARE OF EQUIPMENT
   Types of saddles and bridles—Grooming tools and other stable equipment needed—harness—Types of vehicles—Care of tack
III. THE STABLE
   Location—Materials—Dimensions of stalls—Flooring—Stable accessories—Ventilation and lighting—The tack room—The hay loft—Paddocks and pastures—Converting a garage
IV. GENERAL CARE
   Principles of feeding and watering—Amounts and kinds of food necessary—Cost—Amount of time needed—Bedding—Grooming—Shoeing—Clipping—Vanning—Methods of tieing

V. FIRST AID
   Accidents and injuries—Treatment of lameness due to injury—Lameness due to wounds or infections—Lameness due to chronic condition or disease—Wounds—Treatment of common illnesses—For the medicine chest
VI. HANDLING THE HORSE
   General characteristics and temperament—Fundamental rules for handling and controlling in the stable—How to lead—How to back out of a stall—Working around a kicker—Catching a horse in pasture—Bridling and saddling
VII. CAUSE AND CONTROL OF VICES
   Stable Vices: Cribbing—Tearing the blanket—Weaving—Crowding—Kicking in the stall—Backing out of the stall suddenly
   Other vices: Kicking while under the saddle—Kicking while being mounted—Biting another horse—Charging in the pasture—Rearing under the saddle—Bolting—Shying—Refusing to leave his companions, or to leave the stable alone—Eating grass while under the saddle—Shying out at jumps—Getting overexcited at jumps

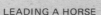

LEADING A HORSE
With neither bridle nor halter. Grasp the horse's forelock in the right hand and put your left hand on his muzzle over the nostrils. It is the latter which will give control if he tries to pull back or jerk away. Slightly pinching the nose just above the nostrils will distract his attention. With a mean, stubborn animal you may have to pinch hard enough to close the air passage. A horse cannot breathe through his mouth and will soon give up if his wind is cut off.

Practical Western Training

In an area where most of the horseshit does not come from the horses, **Practical Western Training** *is a refreshingly useful and sensible book. Dave Jones is a working western horseman and he gives the reader the benefit of years of successful, practical experience. Most important he treads the fine line between senseless counter-productive brutality and letting the horse run the whole show.*

[Reviewed by Michael S. Kaye]

Practical Western Training
Dave Jones
1968; 176 pp.

$5.95

ARCO Publishing C
219 Park Ave. South
New York, N.Y. 100(

Colt backing in draw reins. This is very good, for the pull is low. It's easy for a colt to back if his head is low, almost impossible if he's "star-gazing." Notice that Ken has his weight off the seat, which allows the horse to back fast and straight.

Some guys "knock and spur" a handle on their horses; that's one way. You won't find that kind of stuff in this book. Sure, sometimes you have to get a little rough with a rough horse, and I'll tell you how to do it. But I won't tell you how to beat up a horse.

Horses, Hitches and Rocky Trails

Right. You got your land fifteen miles into nowhere from the nearest roadhead. You deplore noisy trail bikes and ATVs, and you can't afford a helicopter. Then you're into packing. Joe Back is a packer, and talker, and illustrator, and he can help you.

—SB

Horses, Hitches and Rocky Trails
Joe Back
1959; 117 pp.

$5.00 postpaid

from:
Swallow Press
1139 South Wabash Avenue
Chicago, Illinois 60605

or WHOLE EARTH CATALOG

HORSES, HITCHES AND ROCKY TRAILS
BY JOE BACK

LEATHER HOBBLES

If you can, pick a good short-backed horse, thick in the body, with strong sturdy legs. A long-pasterned horse cripples up faster than one with short pasterns. You'll find a lot of thin, spindly-legged ponies that'll pack OK but they don't stand up well. Too heavy and too big horses slow you down and are not agile. About a 1200 lb. horse is just right for weight, although lots of smaller horses are used and stay right in the ring. The Morgan type is the boy if you can pick and choose, but don't get too choosey or we'll never get to camp.

If you don't balance each load, it's your hard luck. The handiest and cheapest tool you can buy is a fairly accurate spring or other scale that will take weights up to 100 or 150 pounds. It will last for years and you'll always use it. Some people like the style with a hook at the bottom and a ring or handle at the top. Seven or eight bucks for one will save you and your outfit a million dollars worth of grief.

Balance the two sides of each pack, being sure they weigh the same, whether they're panniers, side packs of any kind, mantied cargo, bedrolls, tents, or any daggoned ordinary pack you load.

Manila is the stuff. Most people, including me, like good manila rope for both pack and sling ropes (sling ropes 3/8 inch diameter, lash ropes 5/8 or sometimes 3/4 inch diameter: a good many times you will use a lash rope also for a picket rope, and will want it big for safety). Of course, you can use sisal, which is cheaper, and I think much weaker and less durable than manila. Cotton is good, but boy! when she gets wet and frozen you need a hacksaw blade for your knots. Nylon is a billionaire's dream, and say, Bud, try to splice one! Besides, you've seen the ads praising the stretch in milady's nylons; it's so, it never stops, you can't keep it tight.

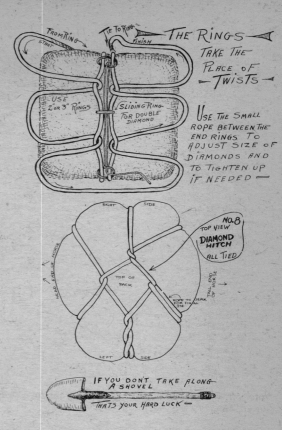

THE RINGS TAKE THE PLACE OF TWISTS

USE THE SMALL ROPE BETWEEN THE END RINGS TO ADJUST SIZE OF DIAMONDS AND TO TIGHTEN UP IF NEEDED—

NO. 8 DIAMOND HITCH ALL TIED

IF YOU DON'T TAKE ALONG A SHOVEL
THATS YOUR HARD LUCK—

The Spanish Mustang Horse

For anyone who needs a good, tough, dependable, intelligent, quick, sure-footed, little horse, the Spanish Mustang is the answer.

The horse of the Spanish conquerors, Indian pony, and original wild horse has suffered as bad a fate as his native American masters. Castrated, crossbred and shot for dog food, he is almost extinct. There is now a registry, founded by Bob and Ferdinand Brislawn, for the preservation of the mustang horse. Most of the foundation stock was caught wild in remote areas or found on Indian reservations.

They are small horses (12 to 14.2 hands). Their speed, endurance, and ability to withstand hard winters on little food is legendary. One Mustang, Yellow Fox, won the 100 mile Bitterroot, Montana, endurance ride at age eighteen. They come in conventional colors— bay, sorrel, black, chestnut— and in many others— blue and red roan, medicine hat, grulla, bluecorn, buckskin, claybank, overo paint, steeldust. . .

Kamawi, No. 115, black stallion
"His qualities are complete. Now he looks anxious; now to be losing the way; now to be forgetting himself. Such a horse prances along, or rushes on, spurning the dust and not knowing where he is."
Chuang-Tzu, Book XXIV, Part III, Section II,I Trans. James Legge

They make good pack, cart, children, saddle, or even light plow horses. Mustangs are priced from cheap ($100 to $150 for a registered colt) to expensive, depending on the breeder. Most breeders are old-timers and reasonable. We bought three last year in Wyoming and are very well satisfied. They are remarkably fast learners.

[Suggested and reviewed by Paul Bandy]

For information and breeders list write:

Information Headquarters
Bob Racicot, Exec. Secretary
Box 26, Thompson Falls
Montana 59873

IN THE FLESH

But it was not a dream. Those were really beasts outside the windows, and that was really David, sleeping there beside him on the bed. D.R. felt as if his blood was full of methedrine. Something racing through his mind increased its speed so much it disappeared completely out of sight. The half of D.R. that was sleeping was a separate, living person! It was really David, sound asleep beside him, like a child. Surely it's a dream, he thought. Surely that's me sleeping, and all of this I'm seeing is a dream. D.R. leaned up on his elbow and looked around. He breathed deeply, and smelled and listened. Urge's motor whirred beneath him, Estelle's odor rose into his nostrils from the bed. Virgil was up front at the steering wheel, guiding Urge around the curves, shifting gears from time to time, driving slowly. The world inside the bus was still in place. And David was a living person in it with him, lying there before him in the flesh.

Is he really in the flesh? D.R. wondered. Is that _really_ David there beside me, or are we somehow mixed up in each other dreams?

Touch him, D.R. thought. Touch his face and feel if he is breathing.

Don't touch him! D.R. told himself. Let him lie there, _don't_!

With the tips of his fingers D.R. touched David just below the lobe of his left ear. David stirred and smiled with pleasure, he yawned and stretched and opened wide his eyes. When D.R. started whimpering David touched his finger to his lips and whispered _shhhhhh_. He was sitting up now, looking deeply into D.R.'s face. Moving very slowly, David leaned and placed his head on D.R.'s shoulder. Don't be afraid, he whispered. I love you, and you mustn't be afraid. David kissed him then, he kissed him on the neck and lightly on the corner of his mouth. Then he took D.R. by the shoulders and pressing tried to stretch him out full length upon the mattress.

"No."

"Shhhhhh," David whispered.

"I don't care. I don't feel like lying down."

"What's that you say?" Virgil called out through the car.

"I said I don't much feel like lying down."

"Well," said Virgil. "It's just as well. I'll be getting out in another mile or two."

Regarding horses and ecology. When cars first came in, everybody said, "At last our streets will be clean and safe." As horse turds dropped off, the English sparrow population was drastically reduced.

—SB

Horse Freaks of the World. . .

As you may well realize, our planet is becoming foul. An answer, perhaps? Horses, manure is better than pollution.

I have noticed that many a freak has realized that the horse sometimes proves himself better than the car, and that since horses *can* be kept cheaper than a car, on the whole, they are really more economical.

As a horsewoman and a freak I am aware that many a freak doesn't have information at hand, and the books dealing with horses don't really go into the aspects of horses vs. the people that really appreciate the horse, more than the red neck thinks he does. Anyway, all the books you can find on the subject have a minimum requirement for owning horses; at least an annual income of $9000 or more. But this isn't necessary. There are secrets one cannot find over night in owning horses, but, if anyone would like to try they are more than welcome to write me, and I am sure, if I can get it all together, I can help them take care of their horses on a minimum of $5 a month, and have them take care of them well (a sick horse is no horse at all, remember.). To repeat, if anyone would like some enlightening answers to some puzzling questions concerning the freak and the horse, living compatably together, do write.

Love,
Gail Lusk
P. O. Box 802
Idaho Springs, Colorado 80452

P. S. In case you have any doubts about my qualifications, I used to be a Texas red neck that rode barrel racing rodeo routes. Enough.

Sioux Indian Saddle

I noticed you had a section on Horse books in the Spring catalog and thought you might be interested in the saddle we make. This type saddle was used by plains Indians warriors and is very practical. It is much lighter, cheaper, and more comfortable than a western saddle which was designed for roping cows more than for riding. It is made by hand of high quality materials and is very durable.

Your readers might also be interested in buying a product made by members of a rural crafts co-operative rather than more exploitative type factories.

These saddles retail for $55 postpaid. They are available in rust, dark brown, cedar, or beige colors.

Tolstoy Handicrafts
Rt. 3, Box 70
Davenport, WA 99122

Sioux Indian Saddle— Suede cowhide, padded with thick foam-rubber. Adjustable cinch and stirrup straps of heavy harness leather comes complete with cinch and stirrups. More comfortable for horse and rider than any other kind of saddle.

Todd's

good heavy chippewa boots and shoes.

—jd

Catalog

free

from:
Todd's
5 South Wabash
Chicago, Illinois 60603

PLAIN TOES
OUTSTANDING VALUES
FOR MEN AND WOMEN

Durable oil tanned water repellent leather, drill lined vamps, molded counters, protective hard toes, long-wear Goodyear welt outsoles and heels.

Brown & olive sizes, B 9-15, C 8-14, D 6-15, E 6-14, EE 6-14, EEEE 7-13.

Also A 8-14 in #C 6300 & C 6060

DARK OLIVE, Lightweight Neoprene cushion crepe soles
No. C 6303, 8½ inches overall, 7½ inch tops $25.95
No. C 6063, 6½ inches overall, 5½ inch tops $23.95

CEDAR BROWN, Heavy duty non-skid cork & rubber soles
No. C 6300, 8½ inches overall, 7½ inch tops $24.95
No. C 6060, 6½ inches overall, 5½ inch tops $19.95

White's Boots

White's Shoe Shop has been making hand made shoes for as long as I can remember and I say this because my Father wore them for 40 years, in every condition the Pacific Northwest has to offer, he always had three pairs at once rotating them to dry when wet also one of the pairs were elk tanned for summer. We Condras have always taken care of our feet and White's shoes are the best bar none. I've had at least one pair on hand since my feet stoped growing. The pair I have now No. 375 "Smoke Jumpers Shoe" are going on three years old, and will go more as long as you sole them etc. They aren't cheap, but if you ever spent $30.00 for a pair of shoes and only had them last a year, you'll find them a bargain in the long run. I've fought a lot of forest fires and good shoes on your feet are as much a necessity as a shovel or pulaski in your hands— if you have hard or very hard to fit feet they make shoes for you too. A nice little catalog and all the help you need with OLD fashioned quality and service.

[Reviewed by Joseph Condra.
Suggested by Daniel Vichorek]

Catalog

free

from:
White's Shoe Shop
W. 430 Main
Spokane, Washington 99201

No. 375—Vibram
8-inch top—Black, greased upper
The "SMOKE JUMPERS" Shoe

$67.15

Jungle Boots

An excellent product, expecially for those engaged in any kind of heavy outdoor labor, is the jungle boots originally made for the U.S. armed forces. These canvas and leather combat boots can be found in surplus stores for about $12 to $15 new, and about a third of that price used. Many used ones are in excellent condition, but even the ones in poor condition will last a very long time. I worked for the highway dept. last summer, along with a couple of other college students. They bought normal leather work boots for about $15 and $20 while I bought a pair of jungle boots in good condition. Both my friends wore out their boots. I can detect no wear on mine and am saving my pair for next summer, or whatever. I highly recommend this product to hikers also.

Jungle Boots Price: $15 New, $3-6 used.

—J.A.

G.I. Vietnam Jungle
Combat Boots

AVAILABLE AT LAST / Genuine U.S. Government issue Vietnam boots, vibram soled, spike proof. This is the same boot currently being issued in Vietnam. No better boot made at any price. Great for hunting, fishing, hiking and camping. Satisfaction guaranteed. Please state shoe size and width. (narrow, regular or wide).

ONLY $9.95 please add $1.00 postage.

GOLDEN STATE SURPLUS
524 W. Main St., Alhambra, Calif. 91801
Shotgun News, p. 276

CHIPPEWA RUGGED
ENGINEER & CYCLE
PULL-ON BOOTS

Famous Chippewa quality.
Extra strong and sturdy.

Premium heavy duty BLACK oil tanned water repellent leather, specially reinforced one piece tops, protective leather heel guards, heel supporting molded counters, tempered steel reinforced shanks, sturdy sweat resistant insoles, heavy duty leather midsoles, superwear Neoprene rubber outsoles, 1½ inch heels.

No. C 4666, soft toes, 11 inch tops. Men's sizes B 8-14, C 8-14, D 7-14, E 6-14, EE 6-14. FROM STOCK $34.95

No. C 7863, steel safety toes, 11 inch tops. Men's sizes C 8-13, D 6-13, E 6-13, EE 7-13, FROM STOCK $36.95

No. C 493, soft toes, 16 inch tops. Men's sizes 6 thru 14, B thru EE width. MADE TO ORDER $54.95

No. C 493-5, steel safety toes, 16 inch tops. Men's sizes 6 thru 14, B thru EE width. MADE TO ORDER $56.95

No. 75
8-inch Black

No. 75——Best Quality Calked Logger.

PRICE——Page 16. $55.75

UPPERS——Best black Kip obtainable.

SOLES——First Selection Calking Leather.

HEELS——High, set ahead, supporting the Arch.

ARCHES——Very Strong.

In stock calked only. Can be made without calks on short notice.

No. 690
8-inch top
"PACKER'S SHOE"

PRICE——Page 16. $48.85

LEATHER——Brown Elk.

SOLES——Heavy Single Oak.

HEELS——Rubber. 1¾ inches high but a little wider than the cowboy's heel.

ARCH——High and reinforced.

TYPE——Hand Sewn, Stitchdown.

USE——Designed for Riding and Walking; a shoe that fills a long-felt want.

(Not suitable for calks)

Woodman's Pal

A tool for clearing brush, where an ax is dangerous, a saw is tangled, and clippers are too small.

—SB

[Suggested by Robert Hanus]

Oley Tooling Inc.
122-26 Main St.
Oley, Pennsylvania 19547

Good Boots

Loggers, construction workers, and foresters in the Pacific Northwest need rugged boots with good grip to endure a lot of rough going. One of the boots often used by these men is the 210V built by the West Coast Shoe Company, Scappoose, Oregon 97056. This company's boots are carried by stores in the Pacific Northwest and can be ordered by mail from elsewhere. The company will send measuring instructions on request.

The 210V boot fits the foot with firm support. The boots are carefully constructed of high quality leather which is tough but soft. The leather keeps its shape and drys soft after being wet. The quality of the leather is one reason these boots keep their fit and stay comfortable while giving long service.

The 210V Boots have Vibram lug soles. It costs $43.50. Those who have worn boots with Vibram lug soles know the great traction which these soles develop. The rubber compound has a high coefficient of friction and clings to both wet and dry surfaces. The lugs give good bite on loose surfaces. Vibram lug soles get work done with less effort. They make hiking and climbing easier, safer, and more enjoyable.

The woodsman's heel is well undercut so that when a step is taken and the heel is put down the force is through the center of the ankle joint. A large flat heel produces a force behind the center of the ankle joint which must be resisted on each step by muscles in the front of the leg which is tiring.

A little care will provide a lot of wear. Mud should not be left on the boots as it will draw the oil from the oil tanned leather. An occasional rubbing with mink oil, also available from the West Coast Shoe Company, keeps the leather in good condition.

R.C. Engle
Sioux City, Iowa

Gokey

Gokey Company is in St. Paul, Minnesota. They sell junk like Abercrombie's and those mail order places and they sell custom made (hand made) (machine made with hands) shoes (and the other kind too). They sell Wallabee's (which is another story). But lately they sell fewer of their own make shoes, which is a shame; there are fewer men around who can do hand sewing and that's essential to Gokey's shoes, which are the most comfortable things I've ever owned. I walk a lot. On city streets. I've gone through every type of shoe from $150.00 Lobb to $25.00 Wallabee (and yes, that's another story) to Herman's work shoes to climbing boots & cowboy boots and finally, heaven, comfortable shoes. And besides there being fewer men around who can sew, the demand is outstripping what the available men can supply.

Gokey seems to have found the economic mean between a massed produced shoe and the hand lasted shoe. It works. They also make snake proof boots to measure. Testimonial. The important thing, however, is as Gokey say, to get more people who can work leather. This should be a fantastic opportunity...why isn't it? Or is it? It is!

[Reviewed by Ron Williams.
Suggested by Arthur Brand]

Catalog

free

from:
Gokey Co.
21 W 5th St.
St. Paul, Minnesota 55102

GOKEY BOTTE SAUVAGE PULL-ON BOOT
For Men and Women

This Gokey Botte Sauvage 9½" Pull-on Model is appreciated by sportsmen who wish a low-cut, sturdy boot that can be put on in a moment for a quick walk, ride, or any outdoor use where a service boot is required. Trousers may be either tucked inside or worn outside of boots. Made to measure only. Delivery 4 to 5 weeks after receipt of order. Use the measure sheet in center fold of this catalog when ordering.

No. 3-358. MEN'S G.B.S. PULL-ON BOOT. Price $69.00
(Parcel Post shipping weight, 6 lbs.)
No. 3-358W WOMEN'S G.B.S. PULL-ON BOOT. Price $69.00
(Parcel Post shipping weight 5 lbs.)

No. 284-B2, in oxidized metal carrying sheath **$24.95** postpaid

No. 284-CZ2, in canvas zipper carrying case with honing stone **$29.95** postpaid

Craft Manual of North American Indian Footwear

moccasinmaking. the fellow who put this book together has saved a truckload of good information from being buried in family shoestores around the world. thirty or forty designs and patterns set out, using length and circumference of whatever pretty foot to be shoed. step by step instructions for stitching and assembly can be followed by anyone who can read and use a knife and needle. not recommended for people wanting heavy-soled fringy streetshoes or patent-leather leggings. meant for people who want to build north american indian footwear like the north american indians feet wore.

—jd

[Suggested by David Morris]

Craft Manual of North American Indian Footwear
George M. White
1969; 71 pp.

$1.95 postpaid

from:
G. M. White
Box 365
Ronan, MT 59864
or WHOLE EARTH CATALOG

Yellow Knives — "Center Seam"

1. See general instructions.
2. Special instructions as follows:
3. Line L M = (length of foot + 3/4" at heel + 1/2" at toe) See general instructions.
4. A B measures circumference.
5. A'B measures leather which added to tongue insert is equal to A B or (A A' = 1/2" width of tongue.)
6. O K = 1/2 H K.
7. Draw all measurements on foot tracing.
8. Fold pattern on line L M and cut both sides symetrical.
9. See general instruction for tracing pattern on leather. Make two alike as there is no left or right.
10. Fold leather inside out.
11. Sewing: join H H' and sew to K K'. Use 1/8" stitching.
12. Sew toe with 1/8" stitch, and turn outside out.
13. Center (tongue insert. See figure 12.) on H H'. Use 1/8" stitch on insert and 1/4" on side piece as sides must be gathered.
14. Sew heel either inside out, or right side out. (See heel detail)
15. Sew on extensions. (see figure 4-a)
16. Tie strings. See figure 4-b.
17. See Figure 5 for cutting the strings.

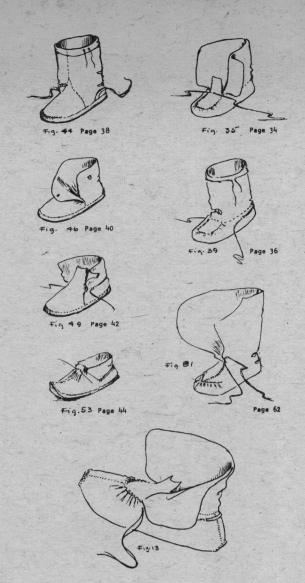

Fig. 44 Page 38
Fig. 35 Page 34
Fig. 46 Page 40
Fig. 39 Page 36
Fig. 49 Page 42
Fig. 51
Fig. 53 Page 44
Page 62
Fig 13

Sno-Seal

Sno-Seal is the most effective leather weatherproofing I have found. It costs 1/2 as much as silicone sprays and goes twice as far. Also makes shoes warmer—leather when it is not wet does not get cold as quickly as plastic.

Whole Earth Truck Store
558 Santa Cruz Avenue
Menlo Park, CA 94025
P.S. It is not grease, it is wax.

Stephen H. Nuetzel
Olympic Valley, CA

Nos. 1330, 1331 Sno-Seal

Nos. 1330, 1331 Sno-Seal. The famous original waterproofing for all leather goods. 1330 Large 8-oz. can: suggested retail price, $1.52 each. 1331 Handy 4-oz can: suggested retail price, $1.05 each.

Prices postpaid.

Mukluks

Also a real "find" for snow country is the Canadian made mukluk . . . great for hunting, shoveling snow, etc. . . and just clomping around in) Buckskin bottoms, canvas top, all waterproof. No longer available.

Factory Surplus Distributors
1300 Market St.
Denver, Colorado 80205.

Jo Ann Algiers
Sun Valley, Idaho

Walter Dyer Moccasins

A human rooster who makes tough moccasins.

—SB

Walter Dyer
7 Bearskin Neck
Rockport, Massachusetts 01966

DOUBLE-SOLED BOOT

Great, stylish and long lasting. Hand-sewn lace-up boot — blended into a double thickness, with an extra sole put on: the hard, slow way — by hand! You will own the best money can buy — why settle for less?

Men's No. 969
Price $30.95
Sizes 6-13
Widths A-EEE

Ladies' No. 969A
Price $28.95
Sizes 4-10
Widths AAA-C

Walter Dyer Moccasins

European Shoes

Buying Guide: Sturdy clothes, good walking shoes, sleeping bags, rucksacks, etc., can often be bought for less than half cost by ordering from a regular sporting equipment house in Europe, even including postage and duty. Procedure: write for catalog, for example to Sporthaus, Schuster, Rosenstrasse, Munich, West Germany (or find others by asking English, German, French and Swiss consulates, trade offices, embassies). Since catalogs come with many illustrations it isn't difficult to decipher languages once you know what you're looking for. Check with U.S. Treasury Department for information on amount of customs duty on that particular item desired. Sometimes the item will come in without any duty being charged, this is generally so on small items. You can send an ordinary American check made out in dollars; you need to know your size in the European system or send foot outline and American size and hope for best. Generally, European shoes are narrower in toes and wider in heels than American shoes.

John Christian
Buffalo, N.Y.

Kaibab boots

Kaibab boots are the real thing: traditional Indian desert moccasins. Made of deerskin and rawhide, they are light, attractive, and durable — just the right amount of improvement over bare feet. Unfortunately there are innumerable imitations of Kaibabs, all terrible. The giveaway is the seam between sole and top: if the sewing is visible on the outside the moccasins are frauds and will fall off your feet in a few weeks. Real Kaibabs will last six months of steady use, and when you finally come through the soles, you can send the tops to Tucson for new soles ($12.00) and get another six months. (One warning. Kaibabs on wet slick sidewalk are sudden death.)

—SB

When ordering, send a pencil outline of your foot.

Kaibab boots
$22.50
plus $1.00 handling

from:
Kaibab Buckskin
271 North Stone
Tucson,
Arizona 85701

Sole-Saver

"Black gick you paste on the bottom of your shoes to make them last forever. Looks particularly useful for moccasins. We like it. Marathon runners like it. Mukluks like it. I see one of the suppliers also recommends it for knee patches.

—SB

[Suggested by Leslie Schockner]

Postpaid prices:

½ Pint	**$2.80**	from:
Pint	**$4.50**	Carpet Products Company
Quart	**$7.00**	P.O. Box 5
Gallon	**$18.00**	Central Square, N.Y. 13036

Manufacturer is Edward Schlosser Associates, Inc., Ridgefield Park, N. J.

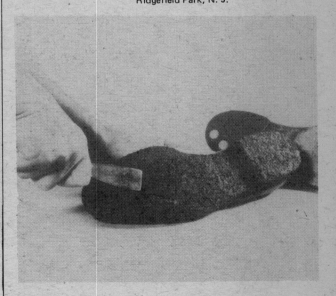

MAYBE VIRGIL LEAVES

At a junction where the road to Blaine came into 666, Virgil stopped the bus and got out, and D.R. crawled forward to sit behind the wheel. He offered to drive Virgil the three miles on into Blaine, but Virgil said he believed he'd rather walk. Light was in the sky now, but it was still a long time till Virgil's appointment at the welfare office, and he was just as glad to have three miles to walk to pass the time away. He thanked D.R. for the ride, and D.R. thanked him for getting the bus to run again, and driving as far as he had. They shook hands, and Virgil set out walking down the road toward Blaine.

Light Weight Camping Equipment and How to Make It

It's all here: design, patterns, assembly techniques, lightweight materials, and sources of the materials. Because of good information on what's needed for various environments, it's a useful book even if you aren't making your own stuff. An indispensable book if you are. —SB

[Suggested by Roland Jacopetti]

Light Weight Camping Equipment
Gerry Cunningham, Margaret Hansson
1959; 130 pp.

$2.50 postpaid

from:
Local Gerry Dealer

or WHOLE EARTH CATALOG

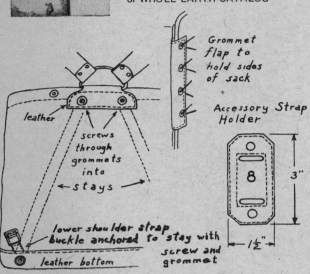

Grommet flap to hold sides of sack

Accessory Strap Holder

leather

screws through grommets into stays

lower shoulder strap buckle anchored to stay with screw and grommet

leather bottom

8   3"
1½

Sleeping Bag Materials

Since you're finishing up I guess I'd better add something now.

About making sleeping bags---

Light Weight Camping Eq. and How to Make It is instructive but careful not to give you a design for anything that would compete with their own gerry's line. You have to make your own adaptations. The basic book is still helpful.

Goose down costs a fortune from the sources listed. Most feather suppliers don't want to see you unless you can buy about 100 lbs. of down. Sometimes quilt makers will sell however. I got mine at $14 per lb. plus $.75 postage from:

J. Schachter Co.
115 Allen St.
New York, N.Y. 10002

CHECK MUST
ACCOMPANY ORDER

Nylon material is very hard to find. I was astonished to find that almost all of the fabric centers in Syracuse had no idea of what type of fiber went into their fabrics, which were strong set. All they cared about was color! After scouring the Garmet distict of N.Y.C. I happened upon a dark little store which sold "Mill Ends" or remnants. I found just what I wanted at half price--with a smile!

Fabric Export Co.
45 Walker St.
New York, N.Y. 10013

Long zippers are hard to find--long zippers which are nylon and which open at both ends such as the Waldes zipper are extremely hard if not impossible to find. Waldes does not sell retail. I still haven't found a zipper but the sleeping bag (?) is so warm that I haven't needed one yet.

David Briars
Syracuse, N.Y.

Antarctic Products

The Antarctic Products mailorder brochure contains an assortment of very high quality but low cost cold weather items made in New Zealand such as sleeping bags, parkas, sweaters, sheep skin rugs, raw wool yarn, etc. The down filled products are by the makers of the bag Hillary and Tensing used on Everest and have been chosen for dozens of world expeditions.

The prices of the items are exceptionally low for the reasons mainly that they are either high in labor or raw materials both of which are very low in cost here by U.S. standards. Mailorder also cuts out the retail markup, the import agents fees and costs, also the New Zealand government subsidizes exports (The identical sleeping bag costs $14.50 more to buy in N.Z. than the U.S. mailorder price.

[Reviewed by Warren Hayward. Suggested by Dr. Henry Mayer]

Frostline Outdoor Equipment

Frostline Outdoor Equipment is the manufacturer of do-it-yourself kits of lightweight camping equipment: tents, down sleeping bags and clothing. They also sell the raw materials for making such equipment (pre-packaged down; zippers; nylon fabrics; velcro self-sticking nylon tape fastener; Dacron thread; etc. The company's service by mail has proven prompt and dependable, all of this reviewer's orders having been filled correctly.

This reviewer has made Frostline's "Big Horn" ("Winter") sleeping bag (2¾ lb. down filled overlapping tube design with no stitched through seams), stuff sack and poncho. She found each kit to be all that the manufacturer had claimed, the catalog description scrupulously accurate.

Frostline kits are complete; all they require is assembly with a sewing machine. This reviewer used a Singer Featherweight for the purpose.

Before deciding on the Frostline kits, this reviewer compared Frostline prices and specifications with those of other companies. (The Ski Hut, Recreational Equipment Inc., Thomas Black and Sons Inc., etc.) She concluded that the Frostline kits were the most economical product without any compromise in quality.

[Reviewed by Roberta Becker Marshall. Suggested by many]

Catalog

free

from:
Frostline Kits
P.O. Box 589
Broomfield, CO 80020

$22.95

Regular	Large
Weight: 16 oz.**	Weight: 20 oz.**
No. W-10, $8.95	No. W-11, $10.95

Total Weight 6 lb.**
No. T-11L, $69.95
with lightweight floor

Weight 13 oz.**, No. P-2, $9.95

SOUTH POLAR 2 PARKA   PRICE **$43.00**

Down Filled   Duty 7%

Catalog

free

from:
Antarctic Products Co.
Box 223
Nelson, New Zealand

A pure goose down filled ski and sporting parka with dacron filled sleeves to reduce bulk. Quilted down compartments prevent down drift. Heavy duty front zipper is two way. Pockets are zip closed. Ribbed wool cuffs and belt provide good heat loss stops. Jacket weight average 1 pound 10 ounces. Please give height, chest circumference and underarm to wrist dimensions when ordering men's and women's sizes. Colors black and light blue.

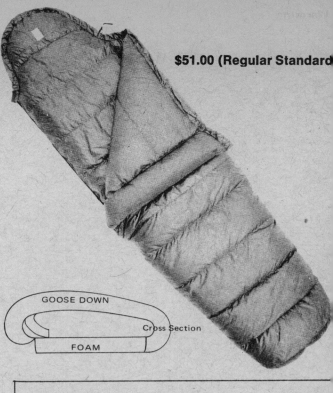

$51.00 (Regular Standard

GOOSE DOWN

Cross Section

FOAM

Barbour

Here in California, Barbour all-weather gear looks hopelessly exotic. Appropriate dress for leaning against the straining helm or sneaking into East Germany in November and other romances. Outstanding for motorcyclists. Waterproof without condensation.

—SB
[Suggested by Jerome Skuba]

Racing oversuit about $31

Catalog

free

from:
J. Barbour and Sons, Ltd.
Simonside, South Shields
Co. Durham, ENGLAND

Warmlite Tent

The Stephenson Warmlite tent is the 2-3 man tent for backpacking and mountaineering. The basic Model 6L Two Wall Tent weighs 46 ounces complete with poles. It has been designed by Jack Stephenson, an aerodynamicist and mechanical engineer, who fabricates them as a part-time operation at home. The tapered hoop shape is very stable and doesn't flap in the wind. It also provides extra interior head room compared to conventional A-frame designs. Interior thermodynamics are designed to provide good ventilation and minimize heat loss. Length is over 10 feet, width of 5 feet. Fits in small size sack. $134-$244.

[Suggested and reviewed by Drew Langsner]

MODEL 6

INSIDE MODEL 8
CHEWY — LAURA

Catalog

free

from:
Stephenson's
23206 Hatteras Street
Woodland Hills, CA 91364

Bishop Ultimate Tents

I have used the Ultimate 2-man tent & fly in a two week rain & snow spell in the Wind River Mts. It made the difference between two weeks of unpleasantness and two weeks of pleasure. When sealed, this tent will not leak and condensation does not form on the inner tent if the window is left open and the temp is above 30°. I have never before used a tent which was a joy as opposed to a hassle. As far as I am concerned, this is the tent for winter back-pack camping or camping in unpleasant weather.

I have also used the 4-man Ultimate for camping out while on a ski trip. This is the tent for 2 people & ski equipment. (I haven't tried the 6-man however, so this should be qualified.) It has the space (when used by two) to live in under extreme conditions for extended periods of time. The little "extra" makes the difference. [Barry Bishop & family (wife and children ages 4 and 2-1/2) spent 15 months living in this tent in Nepal last year (yes, 15 months). They are alive and sane.] Next time you go skiing for three weeks consider spending the $300.00 you would spend on a room on a 4-man Ultimate; at the end of the trip you have "earned" the tent.

[Suggested and reviewed by
Richard H. Goodwin]

from:
Bishop's Ultimate Outdoor Equipment
6804 Millwood Rd.
Bethesda, Maryland 20034

2-man $124
4-man $188

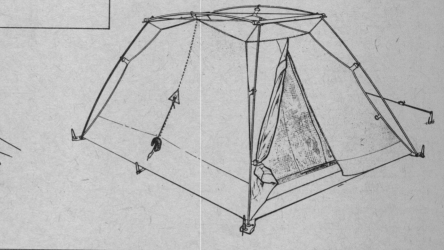

$105 rip-stop nylon

Poptent

The best roadside tent by far is the Thermos POPTENT® a dome shaped affair that erects in about one minute without ropes, poles, or stakes and will withstand bad weather remarkably well. Comes in two sizes with sewn in floor, screen door and window. Hexagonal floor about 6½ feet across the flats sleeping two and a child, and a larger one about 8½ feet and 6 feet high that will sleep four but with less wind stability. The smaller one is best, folding up into a bag 5 inches diameter and two feet long weighs 13 lbs. Prices vary from store to store, but expect to pay about $80 for the small one, $100 for the big one. Don't pay more. Cut urethane foam 2" thick to fit the floor and you have a good camp for a small car or motorcycle.

[Suggested and Reviewed by J. Baldwin]

Poptent
6½ ft. green   9½ ft.

$80 postpaid ($75 in the store) $107 postpaid ($100 in the store)

from:
WHOLE EARTH CATALOG

jacket about $7
pants about $6

Barbour +

I have some information about Barbour Suits. I have owned their heavyweight International Suit Jacket for 3 years now. (It is mostly motorcycle stuff, from my knowledge.) It is as waterproof as rubber, but on a hot day only a bit less sweaty than rubber. Mine is heavy woven cotton treated with some goo. I got an extra can of the goo for renewing the waterproofing when I bought the jacket but haven't needed it yet. This goo isn't sticky or anything, but it will rub off lightly on, e.g., another coat which rubs it a lot. And the jacket will start to have an interesting smell on hot days around the 2nd summer you have it. I prefer the jacket to leather for bike riding. The pockets (designed to be worked with gloves on), the waterproofing & windproofing and the protection are much better. I have dumped while wearing mine and it had no permanent scuffs, which leather won't do. It is not warm of itself as a lined leather jacket is, but I wear a sheepskin vest I made inside of it in winter when necessary (they sell one too). A sport coat fits comfortably under the jacket, when you have bought it properly— I wear mine to work (I teach just now). It is the standard for touring & general use for serious bike riders in Europe; worn for most competition except the road races. I have found you can wear it into a strange cycle shop (even if you don't ride a bike up) and be treated respectfully, even if you look a bit freaky otherwise, and I've had shop owners (like Moto-Guzzi M7 in 1967) apologize for not having bikes available for test driving at the moment, but if I'd care to make an appointment. . .They are very well made, and the fittings (brass) are beautiful. They are well designed for keeping out the weather, allowing for individual adjustment at the openings. I wear mine all the time, not just for riding. After I've said all this, I must tell you I haven't worn the pants, however. (I guess my enthusiasm is obvious.)

Thomas Reynolds
Pittsburgh, PA

Eureka "Draw-Tite" Tents

Eureka has been making tents since 1895, and for any use other than backpacking, they are outstanding. I have owned their 2-man "alpine" for 3 years. I have lived in it for weeks at a time, in Minnesota blizzards and -40° temps., as well as howling 2 week gales on the Bering Sea Coast. It goes up fast (anywhere), is warm, dry, and reasonably priced. I have used the thermos "Pop Tent", and the draw-tite is a better tent in all respects. The recreational equip. co-op has the best prices on "draw-tites."

from:
Eureka Tent Inc., Subsidiary of John Diversfield
Binghamton, New York
or
Recreational Equip.
1525 11th Ave.
Seattle, Wash. 98122
$53–$133.95

*Joe Bacon
Amazonas, Columbia*

Tent from Virginia Ripoff

Several issues ago you carried a letter from me asking about advertising my quonset tent design. Since it was only an inquiry I didn't include any prices for the plans. When the letter appeared I began begging requests for the plans. I was unprepared by was finally able to get copies off to all who asked. With each copy went an apology for the delay (8 weeks) and a bill for the plans ($3.00) also my best wishes.

To date (3 months later) I have received a total of $3.00, I am now only $33.00 in the hole. Since your publication concerns itself to some extent with the quality of contemporary products, I thought you might like an indication of the quality of some of your contemporaries.

John Keary
S. Haven, Mich.

TEARS

As soon as Virgil was out of sight D.R. started crying. He couldn't help himself, the tears came pouring out, and when David came up front and put his arm around him D.R. yielded. David was very cool. He didn't say a word. He just sat there with his arms around D.R. and let him weep into his shoulder as long as he had tears.

Ocaté Sleeping Bag

The ideal poor man sleeping bag, all nylon and foam and are approved fire retardant. Since it's made of polyurethane foam you've little need for a pad or air mattress, and if you get rained on you stay warm—it's like a wet suit. The material breathes okay and by adjusting the hood and strings you can adjust to temperature. I've used a space blanket in combination with the bag for temperatures down toward zero. The heavy models of the bag are 1/3 thicker and a lot warmer. Ocaté is now coming out with a double bag. Rolling the Ocaté is difficult until you get the hang: squish the bag with your knees as you roll it.

—SB

Prices on 6'2" bags

Single regular **$56** postpaid

Single heavy **$65** postpaid

Double regular **$66** postpaid

Double heavy **$75** postpaid

Zipper single or double bags also available

from WHOLE EARTH CATALOG

Also obtainable in greater variety (nylon, 5'8" & 7'2", various colors) from:

Ocaté Corporation   or: Leathers de Santa Fe
Box 2368   Box 1631
Santa Fe, NM 87501   Santa Fe, NM 87501

Yeti Sleeping Bags

i spent two months looking for a good down sleeping bag made by good downhome people at a good price.
well, that wasn't all i did for two months.
anyway, just after we threw the ching,
a fellow walked in and said he made sleeping bags, showed me one, and i bought two.
here are the specs:
made to order: send in your height and weight
100% white goose down,
ripstop nylon
nylon net baffles
nylon thread
nylon zipper
doublestitched at stress points
choice of no zipper, half length zipper, full length zipper.
from 1 to 3 pounds of down
in any of the following (or combination of two) colors:

blue, red, yellow. light or dark green, orange, aqua, black, white.
you can get two that zip together, or one big single bag to fit two people (two times the single price).
here is the price schedule for single bags:

zipper type	weight of down in pounds				
	1	1½	2	2½	3
none	$60	65	70	75	80
½ length	65	70	75	80	85
full length	70	75	80	85	90

—jd

from:
John Williams
Yeti Enterprises
P.O. Box 617
Topanga, California 90290

Fairy Down Sleeping Bags

Here are the price list and catalog of some inexpensive and well made duck down sleeping bags. Mine cost under $40 which includes all costs of shipping and insurance. It is their warmest bag. It has box-construction, chevron type down compartments, ripstop nylon covering and nylon zipper. It weighs 4 lb 2 oz including the detachable hood. It took somewhat over 2 months to get it by surface mail. By air it would arrive sooner but cost about $10 more.

[Suggested and reviewed by K. Hagadone]

Arthur Ellis & Co. Ltd.
Private Bag
Dunedin
New Zealand

The Twenty Below
Cost: About $23
Surface shipping: about $3

Cost: about $23
Surface shipping: about $4

Sierra Designs

They are very, very nice people, and I truly believe they make the best available sleeping bags. Design, workmanship, materials, aesthetic beauty, all tops. Prices are high, but not that much higher than everyone else. If you're looking for the best, they've got it.

[Reviewed by Roland Jacopetti.
Suggested by Sandra Tcherepnin.]

Catalog
$.50

from:
Sierra Designs
Fourth and Addison Streets
Berkeley, California 94710

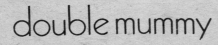

double mummy

Double Mummy is a logical choice for maximum togetherness. It is lighter, cheaper and more efficient than most combinations of zippered-together single bags. Shell fabric is 1.9 oz. nylon ripstop. A 70" nylon zipper is located on each side of the bag and each zipper slides open from either top or bottom. It is also possible to zip any of our other mummy bags to the double mummy. One size bag for persons up to 6'2" tall. STUFF SACK INCLUDED.

Loft: 4-5" +
Est. Min. Temp. 45°
Girth Shoulders: 98"
Girth Hips: 98"
Girth Foot: 63"

$175.00

Specifications:
Construction: Slant wall, 6" tube width
Fill: 39 oz. prime goosedown.

Stuffed Size:
11" x 22"
Color: Ruby Red

Can Opener

The P-38 (or GI can opener, as surplus store owners tend to refer to it) may well be the highest point to which technology has ascended and is certainly an indication of the direction in which it should be headed— away from complex, flashy gimmickry and onward into simplicity and reliability.

It weighs no more than a nickel, takes up less room than a key (I always carry mine on my keychain; you never know where your next can's going to turn up), has a breakdown factor of 0, gets better with time (as all good things should), and, should you be unlucky enough to lose it, can be replaced for just 9¢ ($.09) at the going rate.

Within my admittedly limited experience, it has also served as an effective, if frustrating, fishhook, a reasonable facsimile of a knifepoint, a tack remover, and a superb toothpick (though my dentist would probably flip his fillings if he heard me say that).

Invest a dime, slip it on your keyring (or lovebeads, depending on where you're at) by means of the thoughtfully-provided hole (it was originally meant to go on a dog-tag chain), try to forget its militaristic ancestry, and never, never be without it.

Note on can-opening with the P-38: Do not open the entire lid; leave a piece attached, fold the lid back, bend it in half, and you have a backwoods coffee cup, soup bowl, water glass, etc.

Eliot Wald
Chicago SEED
Chicago, Illinois

Kelty Packs

Famous packs.
—SB

Catalog

free

from:
Kelty Pack
1801 Victory Boulevard
Glendale, California 91202

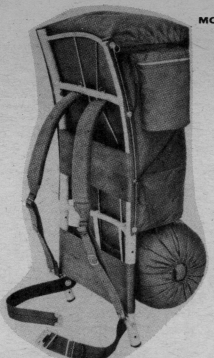

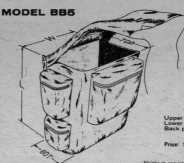

MODEL BB5

Developed primarily for expedition work, the MODEL BB5 is a very large, open-style packbag. It is made with increased profile and equipped with five large out-side pockets. Do not order this packbag model unless you actually need the capacity it offers. Model BB5 available in three sizes only — see chart.
Colors: Olive Green or Red
See Page 7 for order information.

Upper pockets: 3¼ x 6½ x 9° — 11° zipper
Lower pockets: 2¾ x 6   x 6 — 9° zipper
Back pocket: 2¾ x 11 x 14 — 14° zipper

*7½ for medium packbag

Price: $29.75

*Weight in ounces includes packbag fittings
(Hold-Open Frame, pins and wires)
Volume in cubic inches includes capacity of pockets
Dimensions, in inches, are approximate*

SPECIFICATIONS

MODEL	SIZE	WEIGHT	VOLUME	L	W	TOP	BOT.
BB5	MEDIUM	23	3090	18	14	9¾	6¾
	LARGE	25	3680	20	15	10¼	7¼
	EXTRA LARGE	26	3890	22	15	10¼	7¼

coyote call
on a dark nite

down
the
canyon

(holding
the dark
in
the shape
of trees)

first
one,
then
two,
then
several

coyote calls

Moe Armstrong

JanSport Packs

this is the review we received of JanSport packs from Dennis Hollenberg.

A remarkable system because its oval design and weldless construction allow the Jan Sport pack frame to flex when strained by shocks and heavy loads, avoiding the sad broken-parallelogram demise of some ladder types.

Each frame section of tubular aluminum is swaged and fitted in an admirably craftsman-like manner and compressed to its mate by a tensional system of webbed nylon belts. The frame system is in dynamic equilibrium, continuously accomodating the load for more dependable balance; a special model is made for the high angle freaks.

Hefty machined blocks connect the cross pieces, enabling both easy height adjustment and disassembly to fit in a suitcase for that Himalayan assault. In fact, it has more provisions for adjustment than any other unit. Packing with a Jan Sport is like getting an extra pair of arms.

—DH

we sent for a pack, tried it a little, and decided it was a quality pack, so we got in touch with Murray Pletz, Mr. JanSport, and asked him to work up a series of good packs for us. here's what he came up with. it looks to be the best deal in packs we've seen. everything in forest green.

—jd

from:
Jan Sport Company
Pain Field Industrial Park
Everett, Washington 98204

or WHOLE EARTH CATALOG

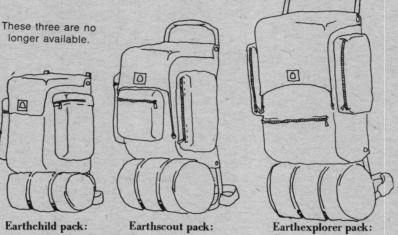

These three are no longer available.

Earthchild pack:
(for kids and little people in general)

Earthscout pack:
(middle range all purpose packing and hitchhiking)

Earthexplorer pack:
(Superpack for serious packing, putting your household on your back)

Rucksack $20 postpaid

Coleman Lanterns & Stoves

"Coleman lamps are terrible——they hiss clank and blind you, just like civilization."

Fact is: when the man says they blind you, what he's really saying is that they put out a lot of light. In most circles this is considered a plus. The big drag is that the bright light attracts everything that flies, every moth and his cousin for a radius of a mile comes to circle around your lantern. Simple remedy: buy yourself an amber glass (just $1.99 at big 5 sport stores). Softens the light, doesn't attract bugs——at least not too many.

Come to think of it, I guess Coleman lanterns, stoves, etc. deserve a praisworthy word from you folks. I've owned the same gasoline lantern for at least 15 years, and going strong. I'm about to replace the stove——with another Coleman, but that's because I'm messy, and too lazy to clean it. It is interesting to note that other companies have marketed similar products in recent years, but have not at all improved upon the original design that Coleman has been selling. Also, Coleman sells replacement parts. You can buy a new generator pipe or valve, and get another 15 years of use out of a lantern or stove. This is unusual for an American co.

Bernard Altshuler
Los Angeles, Ca

Outdoor Suppliers

Lightweight Equipment for Hiking, Camping and Mountaineering (includes list of mail order suppliers).
—$1.00 from

The Potomac Appalachian Trail Club
1718 N. St. N.W.
Washington, D.C. 20036

Adventure 16 Pack Kit

Something you might want to look at for the Nomadics; Adventure 16 backpack and trail supplies, 10056 Bert Acosta Drive, Santee, Calif 92071. Their strong point is their Kit-pak, which is what it says— bent aluminum tubing, fittings and rivits and all the nylon material, cords, zippers, grommets, etc. to make a pack. The pack is large, and there's enough material left over to make two extra pockets. In my opinion the belt arrangement is superior to Sierra Designs. There's a lot of work involved getting it together–especially if you don't know sewing-ese. But what you have upon completion is a pack that is far better than those selling for $50 and equal to those selling for $65-75. Cost of kit: $17.95 (with pattern). Plans $2.00.

Investigate!

[Reviewed by Tim Kelly]

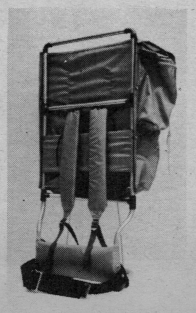

Haverhill's

Nifty items. High-rent personal turniture. Haverhill's carries sort of executive tools which because of their general lightness and handiness may be considered nomadic. The main drawback about Haverhill's is their customers, who brag a lot about the nifty little items. 'See. You turn it around and it rubs your back. Then in here it has a caché for pills. I carry it with me all the time now. Why don't you get one? It's only forty-two dollars.'

—SB

[Suggested by Alan Kalker]

Haverhill's Catalog

free

from:
Haverhill's
584 Washington Street
San Francisco, CA 94111

MAYBE VIRGIL LEAVES

After a while D.R. realized he was on the bed again, and that the bus was moving. He didn't remember leaving the front seat, but what was more confusing, it seemed dark outside again. D.R. rolled to the edge of the mattress and looked up through the window at the sky. The clouds were there, but the sky was dark as midnight, there wasn't even a speck of moon to light them up. When D.R. looked toward the front of the bus to remark about the light, he saw Virgil sitting behind the wheel, and David in the other seat beside him. D.R. almost yelled then, but before he could the bus slowed down and stopped at the junction where the road to Blaine came into 666. D.R. listened as David offered to drive Virgil on in to Blaine. Virgil thanked him, but said he believed he'd rather walk. He only had three miles to go, but it was a long time till his appointment at the welfare office, and he was just as glad to have that far to walk to pass the time away. Virgil and David shook hands. When Virgil set out walking down the road toward Blaine, David shifted gears and headed down the final fifteen miles to Godsey's Grocery Store.

Recreational Equipment, Inc.

"The Co-op" as it's called, probably offers the widest selection of camping and climbing gear available in the U. S. They carry many outstanding lines of gear; sometimes confusingly too many (their catalog shows 21 different ice axes!) I fully recommend the French Millet rucksacks (especially the ones with tough canvas sacks and leather bottoms) and their own line of Cruiser packs . . . both good values. Some of their "special imports" (from Japan) are cheap in quality besides price. For instance rubber water-proof coating peeled off scree gaters after 2-3 uses but they took them back for full credit two years later.

Membership is $2 and you get approximately a 10% dividend each year.

[Reviewed by Drew Langsner. Suggested by Roland Jacopetti.]

Catalog FREE
Membership $2.00

from:
Recreational Equipment, Inc.
P.O. Box 22088
Seattle, Wash. 98122

[A] Sierra Cup. Stainless steel, all-time favorite, wire handle, nesting.
H657C37   Weight, 3 oz. **1.20**

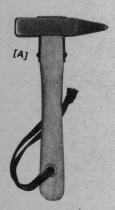

[D] Instant Tent 1-Man. A polyethylene tube 9' long, 3.2' in diameter (5' flat) with 3 grommets at each end for drawing the ends together. The polyethylene is .003" thick. Green.
E477A34   Weight, 1¼ lbs. **3.75**

Instant Tent 2-Man. A 4.8' diam. x 9' long polyethylene tube .003" thick. Color: Green.
E477A35   Weight, 2½ lbs. **5.25**

[A] Austrian Rock Hammer. With a sharp pointed head. Length 10", 4½" head. Ash handle with leather thong for carrying.
A018E1   Weight, 1 lb. **3.50**

[C] Velcro® Closures. The pull-apart closure that takes the place of a zipper. Although sold separately, both halves are needed for a closure. Grey color.
N315B14   1" hook, per foot . . . . **.35**
N315B15   1" pile, per foot . . . . **.35**
N315B16   2" hook, per foot . . . . **.70**
N315B17   2" pile, per foot . . . . **.70**

(B)

[B] French Altimeters. Watch-type instruments in plastic case, compensated for temperature, movable outside altitude scale for adjusting. With carrying case, size overall 3⅛"x3⅛".

Calibrated to 16,000'. 100' graduations.
P069A10   Weight, 4 oz. **29.00**

Calibrated to 21,000'. 200' graduations.
P069A11   Weight, 4 oz. No longer available

FILM

No dividends are paid on the films and print services listed below. When ordering, use the Kodak order number for film.

Color Film

K135-20	20 Exposure (list $2.10)	**1.68**
K135-36	36 Exposure (list $2.95)	**2.35**
KX135-20	20 Exposure (list $2.10)	**1.68**
KX135-36	36 Exposure (list $2.95)	**2.35**
KX126-20	20 Exposure (list $2.10)	**1.68**
K459	25' Roll 8 mm (list $2.95)	**2.55**
KA464	Super 8 (list $3.20)	**2.55**
K447	50' Magazine 16mm ($7.05)	**5.83**
K449	100' Roll 16mm (list $9.05)	**7.55**

FENWICK VOYAGEUR RODS

[A] Feralite Rods. Consist of four or five tubular glass sections which approximate one-piece action when assembled due to the fiberglass slip joints which eliminate the need for metal ferrule joints. Rods have full cut cork grips, anodized aluminum reel sets, are resin finished and packed in aluminum cases with screw caps. Fly rod case is 26¼" long. Spin-Fly rod case is 24¼" long.

S662B1	7½' Fly Rod, 14½ oz.	**33.00**
S662B4	8½' Fly Rod, 17 oz.	**35.00**
S662B5	7½' Spin-Fly Rod, 18⅜ oz.	**33.00**
S662B6	7' Spin Rod, 18 oz.	**33.00**

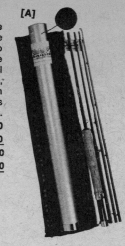

[A]

(H)

[H] Justrite Carbide Lamp. With a 4" reflector, 4½" high, brass, weight 7½ oz.

No longer available

(A)

(E)

SILVA COMPASSES

Swedish made, graduated 0° to 360°, transparent base plate and housing. All plates are ruled in inches and mm. except the Huntsman model which is in inches only. Jewel bearings. Instructions are included.

[A] Explorer. Liquid filled, luminous points, with aluminum housing, used by Scout leaders. Cord for carrying included.
P633B1   Weight, 3 oz. **10.00**

[E] Ranger. Liquid filled, sighting mirror, with declination offsetting device, luminous points, used by professional people.
P633B5   Weight, 3 oz. **19.30**

L.L. Bean

The Bean catalog is the model for the WHOLE EARTH CATALOG. Mr. Bean had a directness and integrity that shows through his catalog, his products, his service. The catalog has excellent items, especially outdoor clothing. An uncommonly pleasant company to do business with.

—SB

Catalog
free

from:
L. L. Bean, Inc.
Freeport. Me. 04032

Bicycle Panniers and Touring Bag

Lightweight compartmented panniers similar in design to the time proven packs used in horseback travel. Zippered compartments allow easy access and packing of load for controlled weight distribution. Made from waterproofed nylon.
Color, Blue. Size 18" each side x 15" x 9". Weight 1 lb. 14 oz.
Price, **Panniers,** No longer available.
Bike Touring Bag. Fits on handlebar or behind saddle. Made from waterproofed nylon, zipper closed. Large enough for lunches, extra jacket, sweater, etc.
Color, Blue. Size 6" x 9" x 10". Weight 11 oz.
Price, **Touring Bag,** No longer available.

Bean's Mountain Pants

Sturdy, two-ply twill fabric of polyester and combed cotton. Exceptionally strong and abrasion resistant with a supple finish for wearing comfort. Washable.

Two convenient bellows pockets in front measure 6½" x 8½". Ample for tackle, maps, tools, etc. Plus two hip pockets with button flaps. Double seat and knees for extra protection. Adjustable Velcro straps on lower legs for keeping out insects or wearing inside boots.
Color, Taupe.
Men's even waist sizes 32 to 44.
Inseams 28", 30" and 32".
Price, No longer available.

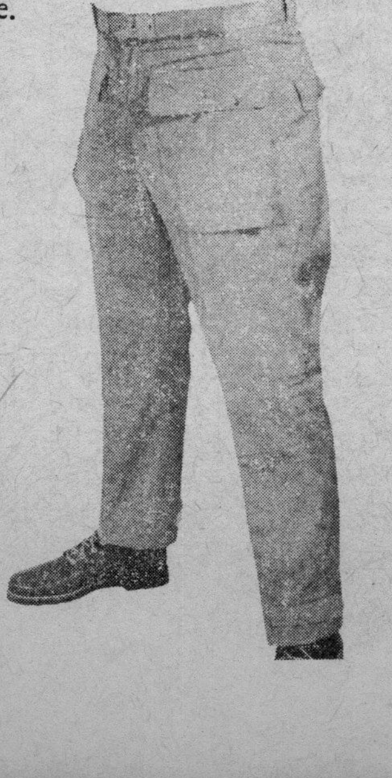

The Smilie Company

For those interested in traditional mule packing and log cabin living——or if you're just hung up on old time type stuff. Everything from sheepherders ovens to genuine heavy iron griddles. They also make those large semi-permanent encampment tents.

[Reviewed by Drew Langsner. Suggested by Jim Wayman]

Catalog
$.25

from:
Smilie Co.
575 Howard Street
San Francisco, Ca. 94105

2-3405 SHEEPHERDERS WOOD CAMP STOVE is the old time sheepherder's stove, built for hard and long use. Of heavy sheet iron (20 ga.) with 5 piece telescoping pipe (16" lengths) which packs in fire box. Oven size 5" x 8" x 11" with bakepan. Overall size 12" x 9" x 27". Can be packed as top load on pack animal. Wt. 26 lbs.
Shipping weight 35 lbs. $39.95

2-3428 4" Stove Pipe Damper
Wt. 7 oz. $1.05
2-3429 5" Stove Pipe Damper
Wt. 9 oz. $1.15
2-3426 4 1/2" Stove Pipe Tent Ring
Asbestos. Wt. 4 oz. $3.35
2-3427 5 1/2" Stove Pipe Tent Ring
Asbestos. Wt. 5 oz. $3.75
2-3425 6 1/2" Stove Pipe Tent Ring
Asbestos. Wt. 6 oz. $4.15
2-3410 Extra set Telescoping Pipe for Sheepherder Stove -5 pieces - Maximum diameter 5". Wt. 6 lb. $8.65

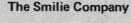

1-4952 BLANKET PINS - Large 4" safety pins for keeping covers on during cold nights, etc. Wt. 1 oz.   2/$.25

PONCHO/SHELTERS are made from completely waterproof ultra lightweight coated nylon material with a snap-up hood. Snaps are provided along each side spaced approximately 2"-3" apart so that each side can be snapped closed without side leakage as is common with ordinary ponchos. Also these snaps allow pairs of these ponchos to be snapped together with any other size, and these can be set up either as an inverted V-shaped tent or a lean-to shelter. Grommets are provided at the four corners and at the mid-points of the sides. Wear your shelter during the day as a poncho and use your poncho as a shelter at night.

6-5428 PONCHO/SHELTER, Large. Size 106" x 63", for persons over 5' 8" tall. Wt. 1 1/4 lbs. $17.50

6-5429 PONCHO/SHELTER, Long-Tailed Medium for over-the-pack. Size 106" x 52". Wt. 1 lb. $16.50

Ski Hut

A well-established supplier of outdoor goodies. Colin Fletcher, the complete walker, gets most of his stuff there. I see they're giving even dollar prices now. Good for them.

—SB

Catalog

free

from:
The Ski Hut
1615 University Ave.
Berkeley, CA 94703

EVEREST — THE WEST RIDGE. Tom Hornbein. A moving account of the 1963 American Everest Party's first ascent of the West Ridge; from its inception, through the rain forest of Nepal, to its triumphant climax on the starkly beautiful summit ridge. 90 color plates. $25.00
Abridged paperback edition $ 3.95

MUIR TRAIL. An excellent lightweight trail boot of grey abrasion-resistant suede. Fully lined in smooth calf; padded tongue and ankle section. Reinforced toe caps and heel counters. Non-skid Vibram lug soles. Doubles as an excellent climbing boot. Height 6". Sizes 4 to 14; widths AAA to D.
B101 . . . . ave. wt. 3 lbs. . . . . **$ 33.00**

SAFARI ONE-MAN COOKSET. Spun aluminum from West Germany. Includes 8" plate, 7" fry pan, 6¼" dia., pot with lid, spoon-fork combination, spring pot gripper, and plastic cup. Packs into neat unit 2½" x 8" diameter. Exceptionally lightweight and an excellent value.
U301 . . . . .wt. 17½ oz. . . . . **$ 5.85**

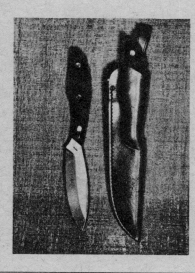

RUSSELL BELT KNIFE. This unusual knife has received many design awards for beauty and function. Handcrafted in Nova Scotia. Blade is of high carbon Swedish steel. Unequaled for holding a keen cutting edge. Rosewood handle is secured by three brass rivets. Molded cowhide scabbard. 4" blade.
J150 . . . . . . wt. 6 oz. . . . . . . **$ 17.00**

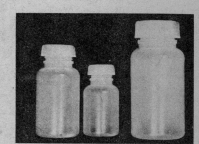

SPACE SPORTSMAN'S BLANKET. This amazing full-size (56" x 84") blanket reflects up to 80% of the body's warmth, yet folds to only 5½" x 8" and weighs a mere 11 ounces. Tough enough to take on the 1967 winter ascent of Mt. McKinley, the Sportsman's blanket has also proven itself in the jungles of Ecuador. Waterproof and windproof, it will never crack, rot, or mildew, and remains flexible at 60 degrees below zero. Pound for pound it is ten times warmer than wool; and with bound edges and grommeted corners, this versatile blanket may be used as a ground sheet, wind break, stadium or boat blanket—even a radar reflector. Colors: red, blue, or olive with silver.
E701 . . . . . wt. 11 oz. . . . . . $ **5.85**

PLASTIC WIDE-MOUTH BOTTLES. Unbreakable polyethylene. Positive sealing heavy-duty lid.
U650 ½ pt. . . . . wt. 1¾ oz. . . . $ .45
U651 1 pt. . . . . wt. 2¾ oz. . . . $ .75
U652 1 qt. . . . . wt. 5½ oz. . . . $ 1.15

Holubar

We've been slow to list Holubar because we're not familiar with their stuff. Readers who have used their stuff have been fast to advise us that we list them and prominently. Done.

—SB
[Suggested by Craige Schensted]

Catalog

free

from:
Holubar Mountaineering Ltd.
Box 7
Boulder, Colo. 80302

Inside Length	Inside Girth	Down Wt.	Total Wt.	Price
5'10"	60"	3 lbs. 4 oz.	5 lbs. 1 oz.	$130.00
6'2"	63"	3 lbs. 11 oz.	5 lbs. 10 oz.	135.00
6'6"	65"	4 lbs.	6 lbs.	140.00

MALLORY FLASHLIGHT

Two sizes now available! The handiest lightweight, non-corrosive, compact flashlights for around camp and can be easily stored in pocket, pack or glove compartment.

"EZEE" BACKPACKERS TROWEL

Made from CYCOLAC plastic, this tough, lightweight tool has many uses around camp. Trowel is marked with 5" scale.
Wt. 2 oz. $0.39

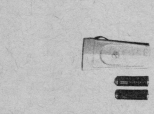

MALLORY AA MODEL (2 AA cells included). Wt. 3 oz. $1.95
AA Cells. Wt. ¾ oz. . . . . . . 2 for $1.20

MALLORY C MODEL (2 CC cells included). Wt. 7½ oz. $2.79
C Cells. Wt. 2½ oz. . . . . . . 2 for $1.60

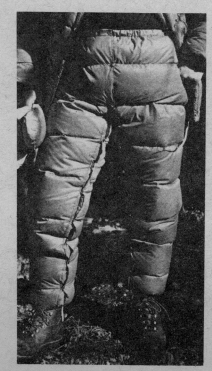

HOLUBAR "COLORADO DOWN PANTS"

A lightweight pant that is very warm for wear in extreme cold. Quilted construction with tough 11-A ripstop nylon fabric and 10 oz. of AA PRIME NORTHERN GOOSE DOWN (Garment Grade) filling. Waistband is elastic with drawstring ankle closures. Snaps along the inseams, insulated with Down-filled tubes and snaps on the overlapped fly allow pants to be put on over boots and crampons; also allows pants to be converted into a light short half bag. A perfect combination with the "COLORADO DOWN PARKA." Stuff sack included.
Colors: Blue or Orange 11-A; Navy NP-64
Sizes: State **waist** and **inseam**: Regular Inseam (28"-31"), Long Inseam (32"-35")
11-A, Wt. 1 lb. $40.00
NP-64, Wt. 2 lb. $45.00

HARDLY

By the time they got to the little community of Hardly, three miles down the road from Godsey's store, it was light enough outside to see the barns and houses they drove by. As far as David could tell, Hardly hadn't changed a bit since he used to come there on Saturdays to the stock sale as a child. Mooney's store and filling station were on the left exactly as they had always been, and beside them Harold Campbell's Feed and Grain. On the right were the rows of stock pens, and the old run-down house at the end where missionary ladies used to sell second-hand clothes. Across the road from the second-hand store was Mable's Place, and beside it, set back from the road a ways, was the old flat-roofed, red brick-sided Pentecostal Church of God. The place was so still that hour of day it looked more like a movie set of Hardly than actually Hardly itself. David wanted to stop the bus and get out and walk around.

He asked D.R. if that would be all right. D.R. was sitting in the front again, but he was sullen now and didn't have much to say. "Come on," said David. "Just for the hell of it. There's nobody out there."

But D.R. didn't want to, and David didn't want to push. He drove on, and a few minutes later pulled up in front of Mrs. Godsey's store at the mouth of Trace Fork.

Herter's

If we gave a prize for most-suggested item, we would have to award it to Herter's, the people's choice (maybe 30 suggestions, 15 or so reviews). Everybody says their prices really are low and their quality good on a truly unusual range of products. And Herter's indeed puts out the most entertaining catalog in the business ($1.00 until you're a regular customer; 656 pp.) At mail order distance it's a giggle, all those inflated boasts and fierce gun and trap write-ups and between-the-lines patriotism. We visited their showroom in Minnesota a summer ago, and in the presence of their guards and threatening signs and shoddy goods on display——well, up close we stopped laughing. [By the way, I could see people doing very similar takes on the WHOLE EARTH CATALOG——we pretend to be a consumer service, but it's just a front for fuzzy-headed apologism for dope and sex and subversive activity. No wonder I'm freaky about Herter's. We're sisters under the skin.]

—SB

Herter's Catalog
1970; 656 pp.

$1.00 postpaid

from:
Herter's, Inc.
Waseca, Minnesota 56093

HERTER'S

I realize there are many good things about Herter's. Yet I feel there are much more important things about them that should be brought to your attention. In 1970, Herter's was fined . . . $15,000 for hiring, or paying poachers for killing an almost extinct Indian bird, illegally importing them, so they could use their feathers for fishing lures. . . .

I would also like to bring to your attention that Herter's sees wildlife as a product to be consumed, not honored. This is repeatedly brought up in their own catalog, those guns and traps you talked about.

Thirdly, Herter's exploits the people who work for him by the fact that he underpays the workers, and has little if any interest in them. He doesn't even insure his help while they work for him. It seems ironic that he should produce a book on how to get out of the rat race, when he himself is making a very good living off it.

Again, I would like to tell you that I really think you have a good thing, but please make it a little better. . . .please?

A local Wasecan

P.S. I may be a farmer & can't spell well, but I also love the animals and plants that share my farm.

Thank you.

Camp and Trail

The most beloved of the New York outdoor suppliers.

—SB

[Suggested by Annie Helmuth]

Catalog

free

from:
Camp and Trail Outfitters
112 Chambers Street
New York, N. Y. 10007

No. 178— RUBBER WASH BASIN
16" Diameter, 5" deep. 2 gallons capacity
WEIGHT: 1 ¼ LBS. $8.50

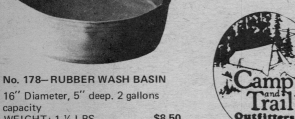

POP-TENT CAMPER
7 foot diameter, sleeps two adults. Finished size 52" high, 81" wall to wall. Folds into 30" carrying case. 13 lbs. Gray. 8.16 High count Drill, mildew and water resistant. $61.95

No. 159— Lennan Rubber Light A 2 cell waterproof, damage proof flashlight. Has a very excellent switch. Wt. empty, 8 oz. $2.95

HERTER'S COTTONTAIL RABBIT FLUSHER

FLUSH COTTONTAILS FROM ANY TYPE OF COVER

The main problem in cottontail hunting is to get them out where you can get a shot at them. Unless you have a good rabbit dog or there is fresh snow on the ground, you walk right past cottontails in brush and grass without getting them up.

Our call is loud and piercing and will get them up in about a 20 yard circle. Just right for good shooting. Takes only minutes to learn how to blow it. Shpg. wt. each 8 ozs.; per doz. 6 lbs

No.	1-4 Calls Each	5-11 Calls Each	1-5 Doz. Calls Per Doz.	6 Doz or more Per Doz
C39	$2.00	$1.60	$16.00	$14.40

HERTER'S GENUINE HUDSON BAY WILDERNESS ICE CHEST

THE ONLY ICE CHEST ENDORSED BY THE INTERNATIONAL GUIDE ASSOCIATION

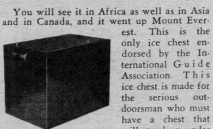

You will see it in Africa as well as in Asia and in Canada, and it went up Mount Everest. This is the only ice chest endorsed by the International Guide Association. This ice chest is made for the serious outdoorsman who must have a chest that will stand up under the hardest use and one that honestly will keep food fresh for weeks, not just days. The outside of this chest is made of durable duraluminum. The insulation is genuine epofoam a full inch thick. It gives over four times the insulation of fiberglas. The cover is also insulated with a full inch of epofoam. This cover has over six times the insulation of any ice chest. Handles are not cheap metal stampings but solid cast duraluminum handles that lock the cover tightly in place with a ball bearing roller. These handles are the only genuine heavy duty handles on any ice chest. They are made so they cannot cut your hands as you lift the chest. You can

---

Venison getting

I read that book by Francis E. Sell
that DEER HUNTER'S GUIDE
& it's pretty good if you're one of those sporty guys
he says he killed a thousand deer
1000
that's a lot of meat for a man & his family & his friends
    to eat
at Libre we killed 8 deer last year & we fed a lot of friends
    & we thought we had plenty of meat
at that rate it'd take us well over 100 years to kill 1000 deer
guess we just aint sporty enuf

It takes Francis Sell about 200 pages to tell you the same
    things
that Herter's tell you in that free 20 page pamphlet you
    get with knives & deer calls
except the Herter's pictures are better

I don't know anything about sporty hunting
I'm a good poacher
I've thought a lot about it & decided that if there's going
    to be meat on our table
I'm going to put it there
I hunt with a .22 Winchester magnum with a 4x scope
I have a blind overlooking a big block of salt in a creek
    bottom
the deer come there every morning & evening
I watch them
I call them with a Herter's Deer Call
I ask them if any among them is ready to die
I tell them that we will use the energy we get from eating
    their flesh in a way that would please them
I don't forget those words
almost always it is a doe without a fawn or a lone buck
    that tells me he will join us
I shoot them in the chest from no further than 50 yards
they die almost instantly
I feel their spirit enters me
everytime
it feels good
that's all I know about killing deer.

Joy — Love — All Blessings
Peter Rabbit
Libre, Colo.

HERTER'S COMMERCIAL FRUIT AND NUT PICKERS

Pays for itself in one season. Made of heavy lifetime galvanized wire; easily fitted to a pole or long stick. Picks apples, pears, peaches, apricots, plums, walnuts, butternuts, pecans, etc. Pays for itself for the home owner with fruit or nut trees or for persons who gather wild nuts or fruits. A great gift too.

AM6E Shpg. wt. 8 ozs. _____ **$1.00**

Eastern Mountain Sports

Glossy catalog which doubles as an information source. They're into Orienteering and X-country, don't cater to downhill skiers or car campers.

—PC

Catalog

free

from:
Eastern Mountain Sports Inc.
Dept. WE, 1047 Commonwealth Ave.
Boston, MA 02215

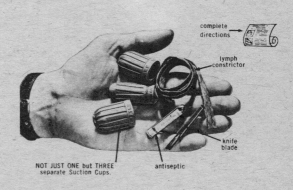

NOT JUST ONE but THREE separate Suction Cups.

CUTTER SNAKE BITE KIT

Simple and effective, this kit is one of the lightest, most widely used emergency kits for snake bite.
C02L205

BUCK KNIVES

World renowned; high carbon steel, beautifully tempered. Very tough but not brittle, will hold edge even after cutting bone. These blades are still handcrafted. All large Buck knives come with handsome full leather sheath with belt loop, including the folding "Hunter." The three small pocket models come with no sheaths.

Buck General	7½"	blade	**Model #120**
Buck Special	6"	blade	**Model #119**
Fisherman	5¾"	blade	**Model #121**
Pathfinder	5"	blade	**Model #105**
Personal	4½"	blade	**Model #118**
Skinner	4"	blade	**Model #103**
Woodsman	4"	blade	**Model #102**
Caper	3¼"	blade	**Model #116**
Buck Folding Hunter	4"	blade	**Model #110**

(arranged as in picture)

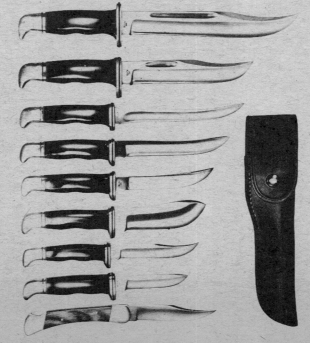

Don Gleason's Camping Equipment

A big range of stuff, uneven prices. Some unique funky items. More stuff for car camping. Good prices. Also check surplus catalogs (p. 141).

—SB

Catalog

$0.35

from:
Don Gleason's Campers Supply
9 Pearl St.
Northampton, Mass. 01060

Stop worrying about bad weather. No need to let a cold, damp sleeping bag ruin your fun. No more handling and drying heavy canvas.

VersaTarp gives you the rugged long life and dependability of canvas with the light weight and convenience of plastic.

Handy VersaTies let you rig your VersaTarp into dozens of useful protective covers and shelters. And they have greater pull out strength than conventional grommets.

Versa Tarp
COMPLETE WITH Versa Ties

SLIP   CLIP   TIE

Versa Ties
ALL PURPOSE TIE DOWNS

Use with plastic films or fabrics instead of grommets. Easy to install without tools. Place where you need them in seconds.

ONE DOZEN **$1.45**

Shpg. wt. 1 lb.

SIZE	WEIGHT	VERSATIES	PRICE
8' X 6'	1½#	12	5.50
8' X 12'	2¾#	12	9.95
8' X 16'	3¾#	24	11.50
12' X 12'	4#	24	13.90

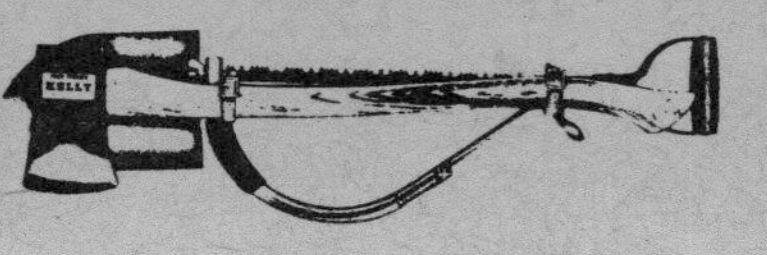

A compact three-piece set consisting of axe, utility saw and shovel. Designed especially for campers, trailer owners and vacationers. Shovel is heat treated, smooth finish blade, strong fire-hardened ash handle. Axe is famous "Kelly" quality durable heat treated head. Saw is chrome plated tubular steel frame with cushion grip. Light and strong, easy to use. Long-life blade stays sharp for fast, easy cutting. Mailable.

	17" shovel w/hatchet and saw		
Set No.		Ship. Wt.	Price
CK-2		5 Lbs.	**$12.95**
	30" Shovel w/long handle axe and saw		
Set No.		Ship. Wt.	
CK-1		8 Lbs.	**$16.95**

COLLAPSIBLE PLASTIC WATER TOTE

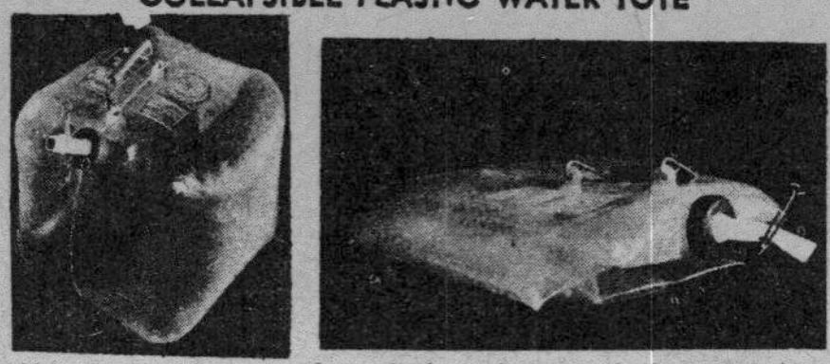

Now a water carrier designed especially for the sportsman and vacationists — made of a super-tough transluscent sanitary polyethelene — approved safe for drinking water. Lightweight and completely collapsible when empty. Easy dispensing of liquids through a white neoprene tube. Strong handle for carrying. Picture shows 5 gal. model collapsed and 2 1/2 gal. filled. Made in Canada.

Cat. No.	Cap. Size	Ship Wt.	Price ea.
88-26	2 1/2 Gal.	16 oz.	$1.75
88-27	5 Gal.	22 oz.	$2.00

It's a blanket that is ten times warmer, pound for pound, than wool. Waterproof, windproof, still flexible at 60 degrees below zero, the SPACE Sportsman's Blanket is the most versatile blanket ever made. Moreover, it is a full size 56" x 84" blanket that folds up to a compact 8" x 5 1/2" package, weighs only 11 ounces . . . comes with its own handy reusable plastic pouch. It won't crack, mildew or rot. It is extremely pliable and impervious to moisture. What's more, it is a radar reflector that's always ready to use . . . wipes clean with a damp cloth. Sh. Wt. 1 1/2 lbs.
Cat. No. 98-09

the SPACE™ Blanket

$6.50   windproof   waterproof

(Not exactly as illustrated)
MT. CLIMBER CANDLE LANTERN No. 30

Very much like the old favorite made years ago. Made in Europe. Telescopes out 11" when used and is but 4½" long when closed and slightly over 2" in diameter. Handy arrangement for installing candle wind proof glass protected windshield. Candles sold separately.

$5.25

Wt. (less candle) 4 oz.
Ship. Wt. 14 oz.
Cat. No. 80-26   3 for 25¢
Small candles to fit
Cat. No. 80-18   10¢ ea.

Black's

Said to be the largest camping equipment supplier in England, Black's has an outlet in New York state.

[Suggested by Jerome Skuba] —SB

Catalog

free

from:
Thomas Black & Sons
930 Ford Street
Ogdensburg, N. Y. 13669

SPECIALISED STRING UNDERWEAR
Very popular underwear which keeps the body at normal temperature in both hot and cold temperatures by providing an insulating layer of air next the skin. Very comfortable and light. Made in Norway.

Athletic Shirts. Weight 4 oz.	$5.35
'T' Shirts. Weight 5 oz.	$5.50
Shorts. Weight 4 oz.	$4.50
Longs. Weight 8 oz.	$5.50

Eddie Bauer

Dude catalog. Very expensive maybe very good duds. The hides of too many endangered species involved. Their down stuff has good reputation.

—SB

Catalog

free

from:
Eddie Bauer
Box 3700
Seattle, Washington 98124

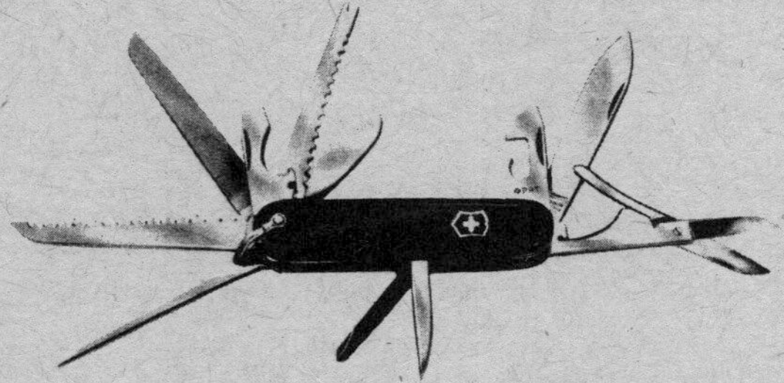

JUNIOR CAMPER Sleeping Bag
Built to Bauer Quality Standards and sized to serve most youngsters until they're into their 'teens. Measures 55-inches long; 71-inches from end to end with the hood unrolled. With Nylon zipper closed, width at top is 25-inches. Fully insulated with Bauer Goose Down quilted in Glacier Blue Rip-Stop Nylon outside and Gold inside. Comfort Range is 25° to 65°. 3-way convertible hood forms a pillow in mild weather, one side zipped up when it's windy, or fully closed with drawstrings snugged for maximum protection for head and shoulders.

This fine sleeping bag is amazingly light in weight . . . less than 25-ounces . . . and in its own tote bag the JUNIOR CAMPER compresses to a size that fits conveniently in a youngster's pack or rucksack.

0401 JUNIOR CAMPER and Tote Bag
.............ppd. **$29.95** ⑨*

3-WAY CONVERTIBLE HOOD

2-BURNER CAMP STOVE 425E499

Specifications: Burners: Two. Distance Between Centers: 9". Fuel Capacity: 2½ pints. Size Folded: 18" x 11½" x 4⅞". Shipping Weight: 12 lbs.
$20.95
Coleman's new compact, economy two-burner camp stove. New space-age contour design, plus exclusive stainless steel Band-A-Blu burners. Rugged controlled hinge action that automatically stops lid in cooking position. Strong steel case has Hi-Lustre baked enamel finish. Nickel-plated, copper-brazed, corrosion-resistant fuel tank. New hinged steel rod grate. Strong steel legs lock lid firmly in place, fold down quickly for instant set-up.
Extra Generator for 425E499 $2.50

SWISS ARMY KNIVES

Made in Switzerland from tough, rust-proof, corrosion-proof Stainless Steel. Each knife has blades, screwdrivers, punch, can and bottle openers and exotic tools in sizes and assortments that fairly boggle the mind. Traditional Red handles with Swiss Army medallion and swiveled lanyard.

5870 — 2 blades, screwdriver and cap lifter, can opener and punch.
5870 .... ppd. **$7.00** (½)*

5871 — 2 blades, screwdriver and cap lifter, can opener and screwdriver, scissors, punch, phillips screwdrive and file.
5871 .... ppd. **$11.00** (½)*

5872 — 2 blades, screwdriver and cap lifter, can opener and screwdriver, scissors, punch, phillips screwdriver and file. saw blade, tweezers, toothpick.
5872 .... ppd. **$13.00** (½)*

5873 — 2 blades, screwdriver and cap lifter, can opener and screwdriver, scissors, punch, phillips screwdriver and file, fine and coarse saw blades, fish scaler and hook disgorger, fingernail file with cleaning point, tweezers, toothpick.
5873 .... ppd. **$18.00** (½)*

Moor & Mountain

Looks like a good supplier. Plenty of cross-country ski equipment. (Also see p. 270).

—SB

Catalog

free

from:
Moor & Mountain
Chelmsford, Massachusetts 01824

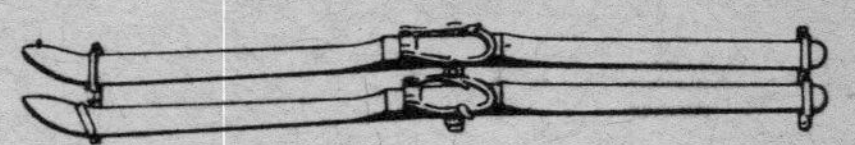

CROSS COUNTRY WAXES — There are three types of waxes for cross country skiing — base wax to be put on the bare wood to act as a binder for other waxes; hard waxes for soft and new snow from 32°F. and below; klisters for crusted or wet snow. See one of the books on cross country skiing for a detailed discussion of waxes. With the right wax you can walk up steep hills and still slide down or on the level with good speed.

REX RUNNING WAXES — For all types of snow conditions.

Cat. No. 737	Light Green hard wax	Wt.: .10 lbs	$ .85
Cat. No. 738	Green hard wax	Wt.: .10 lbs	$ .85
Cat. No. 739	Blue hard wax	Wt.: .10 lbs	$ .85
Cat. No. 740	Violet hard wax	Wt.: .10 lbs	$ .85
Cat. No. 733	Red hard wax	Wt.: .10 lbs	$ .85
Cat. No. 741	Yellow hard wax	Wt.: .10 lbs	$ .85
Cat. No. 742	Red klister	Wt.: .18 lbs	1.10
Cat. No. 743	Violet klister	Wt.: .18 lbs	1.10
Cat. No. 744	Blue klister	Wt.: .18 lbs	1.10
Cat. No. 745	Silver klister	Wt.: .18 lbs	1.10

4 DEERSKIN FACE MASK — Soft to the touch, windproof and washable. One size fits anyone; wide elastic headband; essential for frostbite protection. More compact than any other mask; will fit in your shirt pocket. Tan.
Cat. No. 651
Wt.: .11 lbs.   **$4.25**

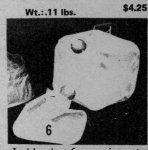

6 COLLAPSIBLE WATER JUG — tight seal with spigot for carrying water over long distances; polyethylene; can be folded flat repeatedly without damage.

Cat. No. 505	2½ gal.	Wt.: .50 lbs.	$ 2.00
Cat. No. 521	5 gal.	Wt.: 1 lb.	$ 2.50

A SENSE OF DANGER

D.R. stayed in the car while David went up on the store porch to talk to Mrs. Godsey. The store wasn't open at that hour, but Mrs. Godsey lived in the rooms behind it and David knocked on the door till she came through and answered. D.R. was so terrified Mrs. Godsey would see him he hunkered down low in his seat while she and David stood facing each other, talking about death and heaven and God.

(continued)

The New Cross-Country Ski Book

I'm really irked. your January, 1971, issue mentioned cross-country skis as being "awkward" (article on snowshoes). False. Ski touring is the best, quickest, most healthy, and most beautiful way to travel across the snow. And right now, before the big industries exploit the market, good equipment is still very cheap. A pair of cut-down army-surplus touring skis run from 50¢ to $5.00 in your local Army-Navy.

I don't know if it snows in California, but in New England half the year involves snow. Why not mention cross-country skiing, not just as a fun sport, but as the smartest way to get about during the winter months? It's a way of life in Scandinavia. Speaking of ephipanies, give touring a try. It's better than acid. And it's ecological.

The best, and still cheapest, handbook is Johnny Caldwell's Lots of pictures, and the words of an expert— the US Men's Cross-country Ski Coach, and a devout Vermont farmer in his spare time (during the Sugaring Season, anyway). All you need to know to get going and to love what you are doing. I don't care what you say, but MENTION CROSS-COUNTRY SKIING. Not all your readers are summer people!!!!!!!!

[Reviewed by Jim Townsend]

The New Cross-Country Ski Book
John Caldwell
1964, 1968; 4th ed.; 144 pp.

$6.95 postpaid
$3.95 paper

from:
Stephen GreenePress
P.O. Box 1000
Brattleboro, Vt. 05301

or WHOLE EARTH CATALOG

If you're already skiing x-c and are perfectly happy with your technique, OK; don't be dumped by this chapter. I've seen a lot of happy golfers or tennis players go sour after trying to "improve their game." Enjoyment by the participant is the most important aspect of sport, to my way of thinking. So for you at this stage, why not approach method as a means of increasing your pleasure, and not as an end in itself?

Akers Ski

Unfortunately there are still not many stores that sell cross-country equipment and those that do overprice equipment and don't have a very good selection.

Akers has a good variety of boots, skis, poles, wares, etc., at reasonable prices. They are also amazingly prompt in filling mail orders. A pair of skis we ordered arrived within the week.

[Suggested and reviewed by Jake and Andy Cook]

Akers Ski
Andover, Maine 04216

321 TOURING BINDING. Adjustable cable attaches to side of toe plate. Sizes: Men's, ladies. **$9.95** postpaid

Snowmobiles

Snowmobiles have waked the frozen north out of its hibernation. Some eskimoes have traded in their dog-sleds on snowmobiles and fashioned fuel filters out of driftwood when necessary to keep them going. Among off-road vehicles snowmobiles cause the least ecological damage provided you don't go bashing the bush tops. The worst damage they do is bringing clatter and haste to still winter woods. Manufacturers are precisely irresponsible for not quieting their engines. As soon as a quiet one is built, buy it and boycott the others.

Ski-doo is the most economical-dependable-popular of the 50 or so snowmobile makes. They have a dual track that looks good for winter hauling.

We're listing Sno-Scat here because it's the only snowmobile kit we've seen. Don't know about its performance. The manufacturer also has kits for little tractors (including caterpillar) and all-terrain vehicles.

—SB

Catalog
$0.75

from:
C.F. Struck Corp.
Cedarburg, Wisconsin 53012

Sno-Scat Kit $300
(w/7 hp engine, less hood & lights)

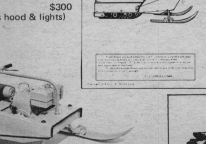

No. 19. *The x-c way to climb a hill: ski up the thing.*

Snowshoes

Winter in the woods. Snowmobiles too noisy, ugly and maybe fuck up the ecology. Cross country skis dandy but too awkward for working (Cutting trees, working in brush, etc.) Best snowshoes I've ever seen are Walter York shoes. Better made than Canadian shoes which are the most often sold. York starts by cutting and drying his own ash. Steams and bends the ash. Makes his own rawhide and his own harnesses. The shoes are fucking beautiful. Light and very strong. Good tools. He'll even sell you shoes with turned-up toes (Alaska type) but you'll have to persuade him because turned-up toes slide you backwards down hills. He also reluctantly admits that neoprene is maybe better than rawhide for webbing because wet snow don't stick to neoprene. He sells both. Prices about comparable to usual prices. Abt. $30 plus $4 for the bindingd. He custom makes shoes to order and specific need. (Heavy people need bigger shoes. Some people want a quick-release harness etc.) He says he fixes shoes too but he hates to work on Canadian ones. After using his shoes, I can't blame him.

Good luck to the Catalog & Godspeed,
Snee & Anne Ashley
N.Y., N.Y.

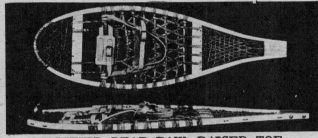

MODIFIED BEAR PAW, RAISED TOE
13 x 36 in. $26.00
Neoprene filled. $26.00
Rawhide. $28.00

Caratunk Snowshoes
Walter E. York, Mfr.
Caratunk, Maine 04925

The Off-Road Vehicle and Environmental Quality

Primarily about snowmobiles, but also dune-buggies and trail bikes. Model ordinance in back. Includes fold-out chart giving off-road vehicle regulations state by state.   —PC

$4.00 postpaid

from:
The Conservation Foundation
1717 Massachusetts Ave. NW
Washington, D.C. 20036

Dog Sleds

I grew up listening to Sgt. Preston of the Yukon on the radio. They had the finest sled-dog yelps and whistling winds you can imagine. Don't imagine. Get some. Nordkyn Thompson has sled dog equipment. Raymond Thompson has two books on sled dog training. On, King. On, you huskies.

—SB

[Suggested by Glen Rawson]

Catalog

free

from:
Nordkyn Outfitters
Mazuma, Washington 98833

Complete Cross-Country Skiing and Ski Touring

Where Caldwell comes at the subject from the perspective of the expert, Lederer and Wilson work from the beginner's view. It's a straight well-made how-to book. Either book will do it for you.

—SB

Complete Cross-Country Skiing and Ski Touring
William J. Lederer, Joe Pete Wilson
1970; 184 pp.

$6.95 postpaid

from:
W. W. Norton & Company, Inc.
500 Fifth Ave.
New York, N.Y. 10036

or WHOLE EARTH CATALOG

Complete information on ski touring, trails, clinics, and clubs can be obtained by sending $2.00 to Rudolph F. Mattesich, President, Ski Touring Council, Inc., West Hill Road, Troy, Vermont, 05868. We recommend this for all ski tourers.

•

The air should be emptied from the lungs with a great, big, powerful whooooosshh, thus emptying the lungs of the carbon dioxide which has accumulated from the strenuous physical exercise. *The skier should not even be thinking about breathing in.* If the air is forced out of the lungs, the lungs will draw the breath in quite naturally on their own and in a very comfortable and invigorating manner.

If the skier can acquire the habit of emptying his lungs in this manner thus getting rid of the excess carbon dioxide, the way his stamina in skiing will increase will be almost miraculous.

Fig. 1

Beck Neoprene Bindings

Leather bindings for snowshoes and crampons stretch and freeze up. Beck's neoprene bindings don't.

—SB

Bruce Beck
Box 3061
S. Berkeley, Calif. 94703   Catalog FREE

REGULAR MODEL makes use of the design used widely over this continent by trappers, lumberjacks, and real outdoorsmen—men who sometimes must be on snowshoes 25 hours a day. We have replaced their leather straps with neoprene-nylon, which lasts longer and doesn't stretch. We have added riveted tabs for adjustability in the arch area, and special length-adjusters where heel straps attach to snowshoe crossbar. Three buckles per shoe (heel strap buckle shown in photo No.2). All ends pointed, all holes punched clean. Standard size shown, the first item on page 1 list. 7.00 ppd.

When the dog is traveling well, he may still stop when the drag strikes an obstacle or catches on something. This is where he learns to pull. If you think he can break it loose with no assistance, use your "impatient" voice, "Rover, Okay, Okay," (or whatever forward command you use). Step forward so that there is slack in the long lead, and if the dog does not try to break loose the load, flip it in a quick throwing motion— but not letting go of the end— so that the loose line slaps against his rear. If he makes any sort of attempt to pull, the drag will usually come loose and move again, and you have accomplished your first major feat; getting the dog to pull something he thought he couldn't pull, on your command. Tell him he is a good dog; keep traveling.

Novice Sled Dog Training
Lee and Mel Fishback

Cart and Sled Dog Training
Raymond Thompson

each **$2.25** postpaid

from:
Raymond Thompson Co.
15815 2d Place West
Alderwood Manor Sta.,
Lynnwood, Washington 98036

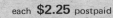

Novice Sled Dog Training

Alaska Wilderness

bob marshall's wanderings in the brooks range, with a good introduction that lays down the dangers of ramming a pipeline through the wilderness without knowing much about pipelines or wildernesses. ecology at the practical level.

—jd

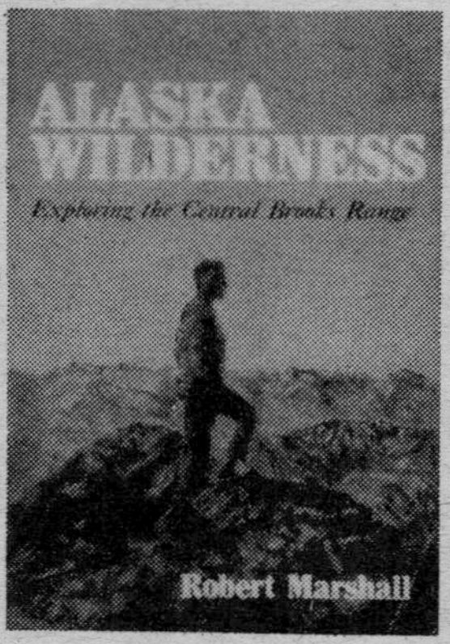

ALASKA WILDERNESS
Exploring the Central Brooks Range
Robert Marshall

Alaska Wilderness
Robert Marshall
1965, 70; 208 pp.

$2.95 postpaid

from:
University of California Press
2223 Fulton Street
Berkeley, California 94720

50 E. 42nd St.
Room 513
New York, N.Y. 10017

or WHOLE EARTH CATALOG

Our routine in camp was the result of many a night out in the deep snow. We would start with nothing but two bundled sleds, a wilderness in which a shelter had never yet been erected, and more (Ernie) or less (I) personal competence to combine the two into something safe and comfortable. Our procedure generally began by Ernie tramping down with his snowshoes a space big enough to pitch the 9 by 9 tent, with a little extra room to prevent our sinking clear to our waists the moment we stepped outside our tent. Then we usually hitched the tent to trees by ropes at either end of the ridge, and stretched out the wall ropes to trees, shrubs, or specially cut poles, whichever happened to be most handy. Meanwhile I would hack down a green spruce for blocks on which to set the stove, saving the boughs to spread on top of the snow inside the tent. Ernie would cut more boughs, and soon we would forget we were roosting on snow, unless we happened to look under the stove.

Before we started out in the morning, Ernie always filled the stove with shavings, kindling, and dry sticks of wood, so that once it was set up and the stovepipe attached at night, we would have a roaring fire in a few moments. Getting a fire started quickly was most important in really cold weather. Even in relatively mild weather the sooner the fire got going the better, because all cooking had to wait until we had melted enough snow to get the water we required. For melting the snow we used five-gallon gasoline cans, with one side cut out. Each night we used three of them, half full of water, two for cooking dog feed and one for ourselves.

But with melting the snow our nightly task was far from finished. Wood had to be cut. The dogs had to be unhitched and tied to trees. Spruce-bough bedding had to be prepared for them. Then we had to take in our own bedding and spread it out on our boughs. We had to scrape the snow from our socks, overalls, and moccasins, and hang them up to dry. When a little of the snow was melted we started the tea water, and after that the rest of the supper. While we were eating and afterward, the dog feed would be cooking. After supper there would be dishwashing, sewing, repairing snowshoes, and—most tedious of all—crawling, head first, into a sleeping bag to change films in total darkness. When the dog feed was done we would take it outside, pour it into separate pans for each dog, and let it cool. Just before going to bed we would serve it.

This may sound like a lot of work, and actually we were kept busy until ten or eleven o'clock. Nevertheless these evenings were very pleasant. Ernie was a simple but excellent cook, and the meals he prepared added real joy to our life after a day of mushing. The *piece de resistance* of our suppers was always a pot of boiled meat. Ernie believed it essential for healthy camp life to avoid too much frying, and above all to avoid burned grease. The meat was tender sheep, which Ernie had shot late in the fall. With the natural cold-storage facilities of the Arctic there was no trouble in keeping meat all winter. We varied our suppers by boiling lima beans, peas, dried vegetables, rice or macaroni with the meat. One potful lasted us for two nights. On the second night it was only necessary to thaw out and heat what was left from the first. The same was true of fruit. We always had a pot of dried apples and cranberries cooked and ready for immediate use. The only fresh cooking necessary for supper on the second night was tea, biscuits, and sometimes rice or macaroni.

Cache Lake Country

an illustrated seasonal diary of lake country tricks and tips, written by a mellow, contented, man, who loves the woods, knows his subject, and writes pretty well too. kane's illustrations are the nicest i've seen. the book makes me want to learn how to swim.

—jd

Cache Lake Country
John J. Rowlands, Henry B. Kane
1947, 59; 270pp.

$5.95 postpaid

from :
W. W. Norton & Company, Inc.
500 5th Ave.
New York, N.Y. 10003

or WHOLE EARTH CATALOG

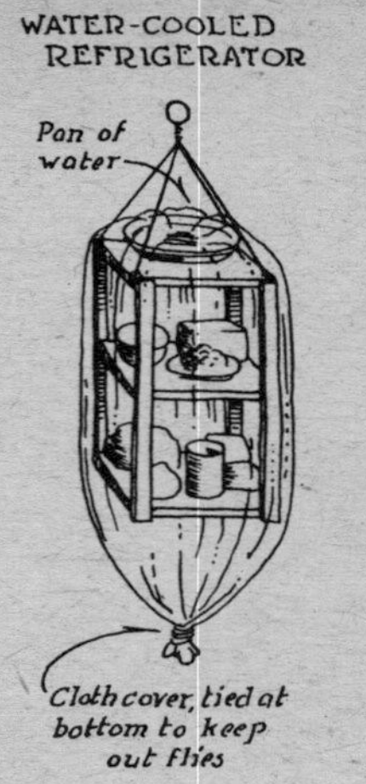

WATER-COOLED REFRIGERATOR
Pan of water
Cloth cover, tied at bottom to keep out flies

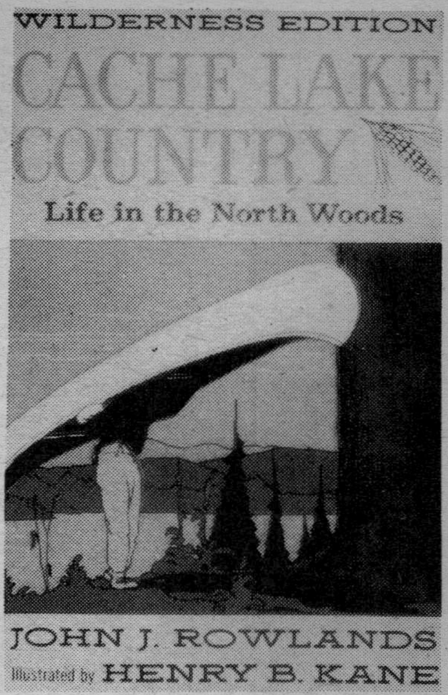

WILDERNESS EDITION
CACHE LAKE COUNTRY
Life in the North Woods
JOHN J. ROWLANDS
Illustrated by HENRY B. KANE

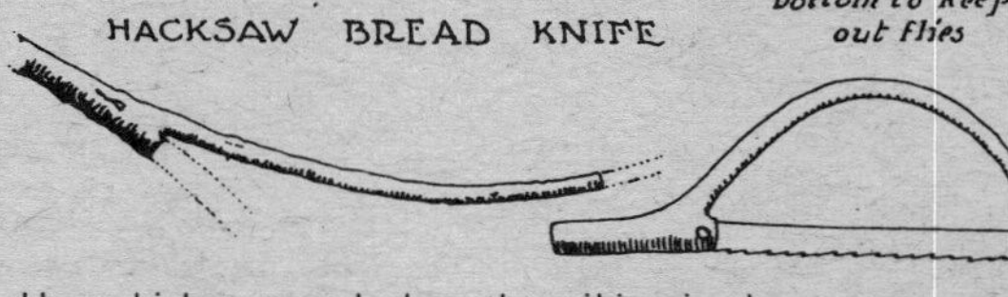

HACKSAW BREAD KNIFE

Up on higher ground where the soil is mixed with sand and well drained, I plant my potatoes early in June; for I depend on the late crop to put away for the winter. We grow very fine potatoes here in the woods and they have a flavor all their own, especially when baked in the ashes of a campfire. There is quite a trick to cut seed potatoes, for you get a better yield if you cut them so that you get the eyes on the flower end and in the middle instead of the stem end where the potato was attached to the plant. When the time comes to harvest the crop we have to watch for sudden cold rains which make the potatoes soggy. Another thing is that if potatoes lie in the sunlight for any length of time after digging they turn green and are not much good. For keeping through the winter, potatoes should be stored in a dark dry place where the air circulates freely, but they must always be protected against freezing.

Another sign that may mean stormy weather is that earthy, rainy smell you sometimes notice before a storm, especially near a muddy pond or marshy place. Some of this odor, which at times is very unpleasant, is caused by marsh gas escaping from the mud at the bottom of the pond, where it is formed by rotting vegetation. This gas is most likely to bubble up from the bottom when the atmospheric pressure is low as it usually is before a storm. When the pressure is high and the weather clear most of the gas is held at the bottom. When I was a boy I would row out on a pond and drive a pole intc the bottom and touch a match to the gas when it came to the top in the form of bubbles. Makes quite a flare for a second or so. In addition to gas, low atmospheric pressure has a tendency to keep odors close to the ground, which accounts for all kinds of strong woods scents, including the musky smell of animals just before a spell of bad weather.

Handbook for the Alaskan Prospector

longstanding fantasy: learn a little about rocks, walk, fly, out there somewhere. set up a placer claim, live happily ever after. then this book let me know that i had to know more than a little about rocks.

—jd

Handbook for the Alaskan Prospector
Ernest Wolff
1969; 460 pp.

$6.00 postpaid

from:
The Mineral Industry Research Laboratory
University of Alaska
College Alaska 99701

or WHOLE EARTH CATALOG

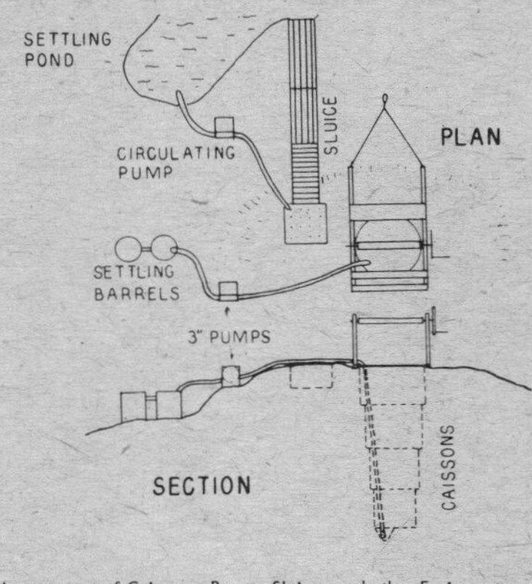

SETTLING POND
SLUICE
PLAN
CIRCULATING PUMP
SETTLING BARRELS
3" PUMPS
SECTION
CAISSONS

Arrangement of Caissons, Pumps, Sluice, and other Equipment.

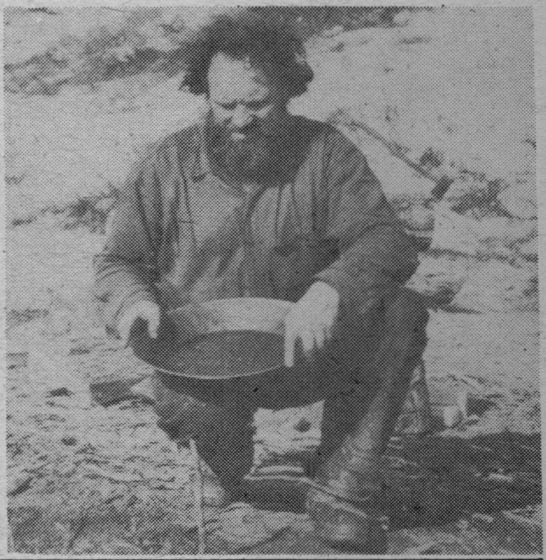

Hunters of the Northern Ice

For anyone wanting to stay alive around ocean ice this book is necessary: otherwise it is merely fascinating. Nelson was an eskimo for the U.S. Air Force. He spent four years engaged in the seal hunters' life accumulating polar survival lore and respect for Eskimo endurance and ingenuity. His report is as dense and pungent and nourishing as good pemmican. Every sentence tells you something about ice formation, ice movement, finding open water, weather forecasting, cold injury, ice camps, bird behavior, game habits, hunting techniques . . . survival in terrain without margin.

—SB

Hunters of the Northern Ice
Richard K. Nelson
1969; 429pp.

$3.95 postpaid

from:
University of Chicago Press
5801 Ellis Avenue
Chicago, Ill. 60637

Unlike the westerners with whom he has contact in modern times, the Eskimo seldom doubts what he has been told by others, especially if they are his elders. Thus, without previous actual experience in a given situation he will unquestioningly respond to it in the way that he has been told. The outsider, on the other hand, continually frustrates the Eskimos by doubting these instructions and attempting to formulate original solutions which he believes to be better. Those who live with Eskimos over a long enough period find themselves questioning less and less, and following whatever they are told to do by their more experienced native companions.

•

Returning to the ice apron after retrieving a seal with an *umiahaluąk*. The man at the left spreads his legs wide to prevent his breaking through the thin ice. He will use the hook of his unaak to draw the boat up onto the ice.

•

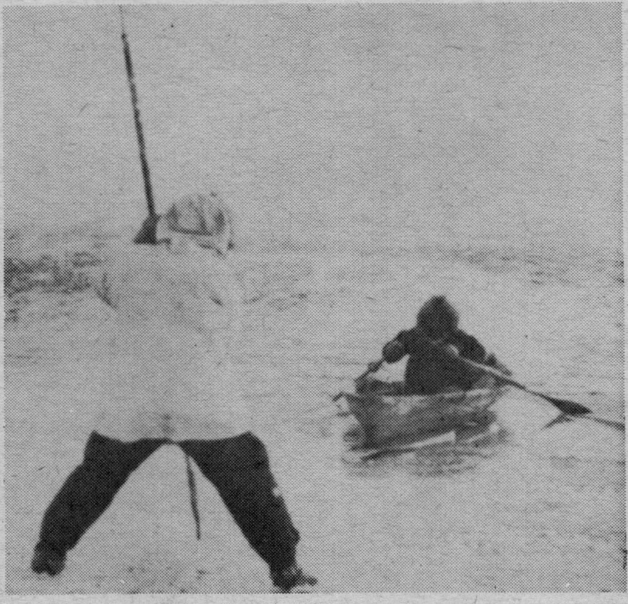

There is one other attitude of the Eskimo which seems to be adapted to his economic life. This is his ability to find genuine humor in misfortunes that befall him, or in his own errors. It is sometimes explicitly stated that a hunter should laugh when things go wrong, because anger never helps him, while laughter makes him better able to overcome setbacks. In an environment where so much can go wrong, and it is so easy to lose something that has nearly been gained, such an attitude is almost a necessity. If a hunter has shot a bearded seal, and when the harpoon is tossed it glances off just as the animal sinks, this is an occasion for laughter, not for disgust. The old hunter, Kavik, never tired of telling stories of his exploits, and he would sometimes laugh until tears glistened in his eyes when he told of his greatest and most frustrating mistakes.

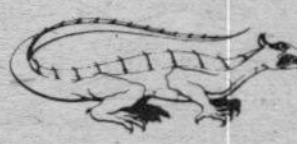

D.R. was too far away to understand all they said, but those three words ran through their conversation like a refrain. "Death," said Mrs. Godsey, and David smiled and said, "Yes mam, and God and heaven too." Mrs. Godsey's face was lined with age, but her voice and gestures were as vigorous as David's. She had long, white hair, gathered behind her in a bun. Dressed in a long, white robe, she looked like some Old Testament prophet just stepped out of the Bible she carried in her hand. "God and heaven," she said. David said, "Yes mam, and death too." David seemed to be enjoying himself immensely. He leaned against the wall, his hand spread out on a sign advertising Bruton's Snuff. "Death and heaven," he said, and Mrs. Godsey nodded and said, "That's right, honey. And God too. We mustn't never leave out God." Once when Mrs. Godsey glanced toward Urge, D.R. got so scared he lay down across the front seats and hid till David came back to the bus ten or fifteen minutes later.

"Come on," said David. "We have to walk the rest of the way."

D.R. asked how come.

"You can't get a car up Trace Fork any more. We have to walk."

D.R. said he wasn't going.

"Sure you are," said David. "Come on, it's only a mile to the homeplace."

D.R. said he refused to leave the bus till he had some kind of protection. David looked at him and asked him what he was talking about.

"You and Mrs. Godsey were up there talking about me," D.R. said.

David laughed. He'd been standing outside the bus, but now he got in and established himself in the driver's seat. "That's a very weird thing to say, D.R."

"I don't care if it is," said D.R. "It's true."

"You don't know that," said David. "And even if it is, what difference does it make?"

(continued)

Camping and Woodcraft

How could anything written in 1916 still be so useful? One, it is a masterwork. Two, in Kephart's day when you went camping you really disappeared, so there's a valid nostalgia factor. But the main thing is, the book survives on its wealth of specific practical lore. Game: find the information that is outdated, sort it from the information that is correct and available nowhere else.

—SB

Camping and Woodcraft
Horace Kephart
1917, 1921, 1967; 479pp.

$6.95 postpaid

from:
The Macmillan Company
Front and Brown Streets
Riverside, Burlington County
New Jersey 08075

or WHOLE EARTH CATALOG

Fig. 185.—Splicing thongs

Men working hard in the open, and exposed to the vicissitudes of wilderness life, need a diet rich in protein, fats (especially in cold weather), and sweets. This may not agree with theories of dieticians, but it is the experience of millions of campaigners who know what their work demands. A low-protein diet may be good for men leading soft lives, and for an occasional freak outdoorsman, but try it on an army in the field, or on a crew of lumberjacks, and you will face stark mutiny.

Rabbits are unfit to eat in late summer, as their backs are then infested with warbles, which are the larvae of the rabbit bot-fly.

Green Corn.— If you happen to camp near a farm in the "Roasting-ear" season, you are in great luck. The quickest way to roast an ear of corn is to cut off the butt of the ear closely, so that the pith of the cob is exposed, ream it out a little, impale the cob lengthwise on the end of a long hardwood stick, and turn over the coals.

Skilligalee.— The best thing in a fixed camp is the stock-pot. A large covered pot or enameled pail is reserved for this and nothing else. Into it go all the fag-ends of game — heads, tails, wings, feet, giblets, large bones — also the left-overs of fish, flesh and fowl, of any and all sots of vegtables, rice, or other cereals, macaroni, stale bread, everything edible except fat. This pot is always kept hot. Its flavors are forever changing, but ever welcome. It is always ready, day or night, for the hungry varlet who missed connections or who wants a bite between meals. No cook who values his peace of mind will fail to have a skilly simmering at all hours.

A woodsman, on the contrary, walks with a rolling motion, his hips swaying an inch or more to the stepping side, and his pace is correspondingly long. This hip action may be noticed to an exaggerated degree in the stride of a professional pedestrian; but the latter walks with a heel-and-toe step, whereas an Indian's or sailor's step is more nearly flat-footed. In the latter case the center of gravity is covered by the whole foot. The poise is as secure as that of a rope-walker.

It is not nearly so much the "make" of rifle as *the load it takes* that determines the gun's shooting qualities. So, choose first a cartridge, then a gun to handle it.

BENDING WOOD.—Small pieces of green wood can be bent to a required form by merely soaking the

Fig. 54.—Spanish Windlass (for bending wood)

pieces for two or three days in water, but if it is desired that they should retain their new shape, they should be steamed.

In Alaska, all animals leave for the snow-line as soon as the mosquito pest appears, but the enemy follows them even to the mountain tops above timber-line. Deer and Moose are killed by mosquitoes, which settle upon them in such amazing swarms that the unfortunate beasts succumb from literally having the blood sucked out of their bodies. Bears are driven frantic, are totally blinded, mire in the mud, and starve to death. Animals that survive have their flesh discolored all through, and even their marrow is reduced to the consistency of blood and water. The men who penetrate such regions are not the kind that would allow toil or privation to break their spirit, but they become so unstrung from days and nights of continuous torment inflicted by enemies insignificant in size but infinite in number, that they become savage, desperate, and sometimes even weep in sheer helpless anger.

Fig. 68.—A Masked Camp

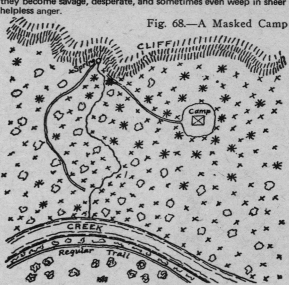

Trees and Lightning. — I have never seen, nor heard of, a beech tree that had been struck by lightning, although beeches are plentiful on many battle-scarred mountains where stricken trees of other species can be noted by the score.

One glance at a camper's fire tells what kind of a woodsman he is. It is quite impossible to prepare a good meal over a heap of smoking chunks, a fierce blaze, or a great bed of coals that will warp iron and melt everything else.

Skills for Taming the Wilds

Bradford Angier's outdoor books are generally thin, sketchy, and repetitive from book to book. This appears to be the least diluted one. Applicable mainly to north-woods, where indeed Angier has lived for many years.

—SB

Skills for Taming the Wilds
Bradford Angier
1967; 280 pp.

$1.25 postpaid

from:
Pocket Books
1 West 39th St.
New York, N.Y. 10018

or WHOLE EARTH CATALOG

When campfire or cabin smoke, after lifting a short distance with the heated air, beats downward, it is a sign of approaching storm. On the other hand, steadily rising smoke prognosticates fair weather.

Oleomargarine, largely because it keeps so well, is recommended for general wilderness use. To cut hard margarine or butter cleanly, use a knife that has been heated in hot water.

To protect yourself from popping hot fat, stop the spattering by sprinkling a bit of flour into the frypan. If the grease catches fire, throw a handful of flour on it or extinguish the flames by covering the burning fat and shutting out the air.

Water Cress (*Nasturtium*)

Stopper Knot

Pockets are so handy in the outdoors that special attention should be paid to their deepness and ruggedness when buying clothing for the woods. Because of the danger of losing your already limited essentials, it is well to get most or all of these with fasteners.

It usually requires a disproportionate amount of energy to travel straight up and down hills, as the trails of animals reveal they well know. You generally will do better in the long run either to zigzag or to slant off at a gradual pitch. Energy will be conserved if you can proceed without cutting across major drainage systems. As for resting, this is more beneficial when enjoyed frequently for brief periods. Hurrying ahead for long stretches and then taking prolonged breathing spells tends to cause the muscles to stiffen.

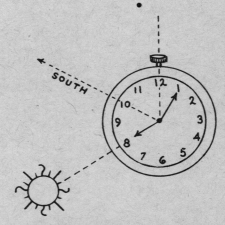

Telling Direction by Watch and Sun. When the hour hand points directly toward the sun, south lies midway along the smaller arc between the hour hand and twelve o'clock.

Wildwood Wisdom

this is the only book of wilderlore i've ever read from front to back, mainly because one third of the book is pictures, and i got sucked from one picture to the next, all the way through,
jaeger assumes that you are in the wildwood because you want to be, and that the woods dictate as much a style of living as do the sidewalks of omaha, if you are going to live anywhere, do it with style, like an indian, with decorum, simply, carefully, quietly, but with style.

—jd

Colorful blankets, striped or in plain colors, may be cut up into the patterns shown in the drawing. The front is made in two parts, the back in one. The wide circular collar is made double thickness. Large patch pockets are sewed on the front sections before the coat is stitched together. The eqauletlike pieces of blanketing at the shoulders are placed there to act as drains, so that the rain will not soak in at the shoulder seams. Coarse blanket fringe may be stitched on at the front and back, as well as the belt loops, if desired. Double-stitch the front and back together at the shoulders. Sew the sleeves and the epaulets double at the armholes, and double-stitch the circular collar to the coat proper. If a belt is wanted, sew double thicknesses of the blanket together about four inches wide. The belt may be fastened with buttons or it may be made long enough for a sash. A colored yarn tassel ball may

Wildwood Wisdom
Ellsworth Jaeger
1945;69; 491pp.

$6.95 postpaid

from:
The Macmillan Company
866 Third Avenue
New York, New York 10022

or WHOLE EARTH CATALOG

be attached to the belt ends. Buttons and buttonholes must be provided on the front and on the patch pockets.

Now stitch the sides of the coat and the sleeves, starting at the bottom and continuing upward and along the sleeves. Turn up the cuffs of the sleeves to the desired width and fasten them with a few stitches. A french-Canadian *capote*, or hood, may be added, and the illustration shows how it is made. This fits over the upturned color and may be fastened to the colar with a few small buttons, or it may be worn by itself and held with tie-strings under the chin. This briefly completes the job; and a colorful, picturesque, and very warm addition has been made to your outdoor wardrobe, one which can be worn for many years.

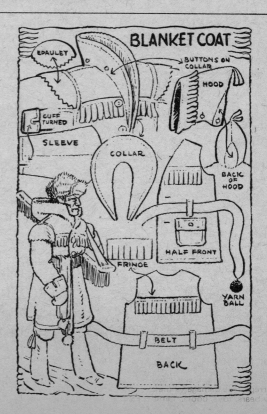

BLANKET COAT

The Golden Book of Camping

As usual, wonderfully clear information from Golden Press. I'd have put this book in the Learning section of the CATALOG only it has better camping information than the authoritative tomes here. Some tips I've never heard anywhere before. Profusely illustrated. I can hardly wait for the Golden Book of Dope.

—SB

The Golden Book of Camping
William Hillcourt
1971; 104 pp.

$3.95 postpaid

from:
Golden Press, Inc.
c/o Western Publishing Co.
P.O. Box 700
Racine, WI 53404

or WHOLE EARTH CATALOG

TO KEEP FROM BEING SCALDED, USE A MOP MADE BY TYING A WAD OF CLOTH TO A NOTCHED STICK.

CLEAN THE DISHES IN HOT WATER CONTAINING A DETERGENT OR SOAP.

1.
USE FELLING AX AS PLUMB LINE TO DECIDE FALL OF TREE.

IN LIGHTWEIGHT CAMP, PLASTIC SHEET TAKES PLACE OF HEAVY POTS. MAKE TWO RINGS OF STONES OR FRAME OF LOGS. DRAPE SHEET TO FORM TWO BASINS. PUT DETERGENT IN ONE, SANITIZER IN THE OTHER.

IF YOU SHOULD STUMBLE AND SPRAIN AN ANKLE, DO NOT TAKE OFF YOUR SHOE. INSTEAD, TIE A BANDAGE FIRMLY AROUND ANKLE AND SHOE BOTH.

European Lightweight Camping Supplies:

Thomas Black and Sons, Port Glasgow, Renfrewshire, Scotland

Bukta, Stockport, Cheshire, England

Camptors, 16 Buckingham Pallace Road, Victoria, London S.W.1, England

Lembcke, Noerregade, Copenhagen K, Denmark

Haus Altenberg, Derendorfer Strasse 1, Dusseldorf, Germany

Bantam-Camping, Hirschengraben 3, Berne, Switzerland

Moretti, Foro Buanaparte 67, Milan, Italy

Being Your Own Wilderness Doctor

My husband suggests you include Being Your Own Wilderness Doctor by good old B. Angier and Dr. E.R. Kodet. The medical guide is very uptodate, better than in How To Survive In The Woods, we feel. It is written with the problems (probably) encountered while hiking back in, etc. It is one we want to add to our personal library as soon as $ allows. In the front is a quick-reference index of stuff. While the supra-organic finks won't be too keen on it because of its emphasis on new drugs, the rest of the info provided (sprains, dislocations, fractures, stitches, etc.) certainly would be useful. I worked two years in a hospital emergency ward and to me, this is about the best emergency guide I've come across that is written for non-medical people.

Lewis
Ottawa, Ontario

Being Your Own Wilderness Doctor
E. Russel Kodet, Bradford Angier
1968; 127 pp.

$1.50 postpaid
Plus $.25 handling
from:
Simon & Schuster
1 West 39th St.
New York, N.Y. 10018

or WHOLE EARTH CATALOG

The following medicine chest should be adequate for a longer stay, or when several people will be in the party. Double or triple the quantities of drugs suggested for the light kit. Otherwise, make up as follows:

Aspirin— 100 tablets will be a good idea.

Aspirin with codeine— twenty-four.

Darvon Compound— Eighteen tablets in addition to the above codeine will be adequate.

Compazine— twelve.

Lomotil— Thirty-six.

Sulfasuxidine— Fifty tablets for one individual, one hundred for several.

Bismuth and paregoric— eight ounces, mixed in equal parts.

Probanthine— Thirty-six.

Pyridium— Eighteen. Take one every four to six hours. If this causes stomach irritation, take with food, otherwise as needed. Pyridium will stop all urinary burning and distress. It will color the urine red.

Gantrisin— Fifty. These are for treatment of a urinary tract infection, as well as for the continued treatment of strep infections, pneumonia, and the like. They can be used if only a few antibiotic tablets are carried, and the condition requires additional treatment. Some individuals are sensitive to sulfa. Gantrisin should be discontinued if there is rash, fever that comes and goes when the sulfa is used, or nausea or vomiting.

Erythromycin— Twenty-four or thirty-six tablets, depending on the remoteness and the number of people.

Pyribenzamine— Thirty-six.

Dexedrine— Twelve

Cortisone (prednisone)— Thirty.

Sterile vaseline— One tube.

Baciguent— One one-ounce tube of this antibiotic ointment should do.

Zinc oxide— One tube, for chapped lips or for mixing in equal parts with Eugenol to make a temporary filling for a tooth.

Eugenol— One-quarter ounce bottle will be adequate.

Oil of cloves— small bottle, as only a few drops are needed for toothache.

For surgical supplies, it is suggested that you take both a two-inch and a four-inch Ace or similar elastic bandage. Although optional for a short trip, these are very handy for holding splints, etc.

The amount of gauze and tape to pack along is optional, particularly as it is always possible to improvise. For a long stay, two packs of each type of suture material are recommended.

You'll want a thermometer. Check this before taking a temperature and first shake its mercury down, if necessary.

There is no absolute normal temperature. Ignore the red marks on the thermometer. They do not mean fever unless the temperature is over 99.6°. Keep the thermometer in a case and out of the sun. In most cases, a temperature taken under the tongue or armpit will suffice.

Costs

Eighteen dollars should do it for the light kits, plus several dollars more for the snakebite kit with suction cups. Add eight to ten dollars for antivenom.

Fire Without Matches and Books

A browseful hour spent with the WE catalog indicates that some readers are on the fire-without-matches kick. For what they're worth, a few suggestions.

Ordinary household steel wool, *of the kind available in any grocery store, is the best* tinder *ever invented (if you really want to go first cabin, get the extra-fine kind that cabinetmakers use). Scratch a spark into a small glob of steel wool and watch it glow! Wrap the steel wool in a fist-sized glob of dried grass (say), blow on it for ten seconds, and* presto! *Instant fire.*

And where do you get the sparks for the above process? From a cigarette lighter, *man! A cheap cigarette lighter, used without fuel, provides an* excellent *source of sparks. Some spare flints can be carried inside the lighter, down where the cotton filler is located, and you have a lifetime source of sparks— so much handier than a hunk of quartz and a broken file. Of course, you can fill your lighter with fluid if you want, but that takes all the fun out of it...*

And now a real survival item: the reflector *in a flashlight (headlight, etc.) can start a fire for you on a sunny day. Simply take your flashlight apart, aim the reflector toward the sun, and poke a bit of tinder up through the hole where the bulb fits (a cigarette works fine), extending it no more than half-an-inch (less may work better) and* presto! *again. (You don't actually get* fire *this way; what you get is a lighted cigarette which, with patience and tinder like steel wool or dry grass should make fire for you...) This, of course, is an adaptation of the "Solar cigarette lighter" that was common in novelty shops a few years ago.*

Joe Smith
Hood River, Oregon

Wilderness Camping, $4.00/yr

Bimonthly from:
Wilderness Camping
Box 1186
Scotia, N.Y. 12302

"Mrs. Godsey wants to see me dead," said D.R. "I've known that much all along."

David shook his head, as if from profound sadness. "Well," he said. "Personally, I think we ought to quit thinking about ourselves and put our minds on Emmit. He's the one we've come down here to help."

"He's probably in on it too," said D.R. "And you are too, and I know Virgil was."

David looked at D.R. grinning. "You want to know what I think?" he said.

D.R. waited for him to say.

"I think you're stoned on your ass." He laughed, but D.R. was not amused. "All I know," said D.R., "is I don't trust you for a minute, and I'm not getting out of this bus till I feel protected from all this bullshit going on."

There was a little silence between them then, and in it David's tone and manner changed. When he spoke again his voice had a new edge, a touch of cold impatience. "Let me ask you a question," he said.

D.R. waited for him to ask it.

"How'd you like it if I went in and got Mrs. Godsey, and told her to come out and talk to you about the bullshit. How would that be? I'll go in and tell her you're feeling a little bad out here and ask . . ."

D.R. didn't wait for him to finish. He had seen the evil in David's eyes, he knew for sure now that David was in on it, and that he must run to get away or he would die. Without looking at David again he flung the door open, leaped out and took off running, with David chasing after, close behind.

The Sierra Club Wilderness Handbook

Practical information distilled through years and years of Sierra Club outings. Covers a wider range (women, burros, rivers . . .) than Colin Fletcher.

—SB

The Sierra Club Wilderness Handbook
David Brower, ed.
1951, 1968; 317 pp.

from:
Ballantine Books
101 Fifth Avenue
New York, N.Y. 10003

$.95

Good pack horses and mules can carry a pay load of 200 pounds when expertly packed. One hundred and seventy-five pounds should be considered a maximum load on one's first trip. The pack train can be counted on for 15 miles a day on good trails if it keeps pushing. These animals walk at a good clip and, unless their handlers are fast hikers, all personnel should be mounted. This becomes more important as the size of the party increases. Mules are led singly by pedestrians or are tied in groups of not more than five animals and are then led by a man on horseback. This is the "string" of the professional packer.

•

In addition to standard equipment, it will be wise with preschool-age children to take along some portion of the home environment whose value is purely emotional, even at the expense of inconvenience and irreparable damage to the articles; these might be, for example, teddy bears, toys, books, familiar clothes, or eating utensils.

At Home in the Wilderness

Unusual outdoor book, written by Sun Bear, who edits a pan-Indian magazine called Many Smokes. *His lore is most relevant to North Woods and the Great Basin.*

—SB

At Home in the Wilderness
Sun Bear
1968; 90 pp.

$3.00 postpaid

from:
Naturegraph Publishers
8339 W. Dry Creek Rd.
Healdsburg, CA 95448

or WHOLE EARTH CATALOG

As a preference of weapons, I like a .22 bolt action rifle for providing the weekly meat larder with small game. I prefer this to automatic as you are not as inclined to waste shells. When deer or big game hunting, I like a 30-30 for open country and use a shotgun in brush country with slugs or buck shot. Sometimes in the brush country, when deer hunting, I still carry a slingshot for small game. Instead of old auto inner tubes, I use a surgical rubber for the slingshot. The new type of inner tube does not have the stretch that the old post-war tubes had. Many a ruffled grouse, gray squirrel or rabbit has found his way to my table, thanks to the slingshot. Back during the depression—W.P.A. days, there was hardly an Indian working on the road crew that did not carry a slingshot to get a little camp meat.

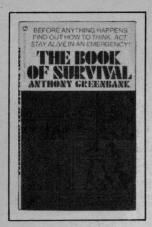

The Book of Survival and The Survival Book

One barometer of people's social confidence level is the sales of books on survival. I can report that sales on The Survival Book are booming; it's one of our fastest moving books. What's weird is that it's almost pure romance to buy The Survival Book, which is an excellent handbook for Air Force pilots downed in remote regions. The other book we list, The Book of Survival, is far more practical and far better organized. The threats it deals with are closer and realer: burning buildings, freaked humans, speeding cars, dogs, floods, electricity, poison——genuine homely hazards. From what we can see, people are less interested in survival and more interested in the return of the frontier or maybe a sudden desert island. Fat chance.

—SB

The Book of Survival
Anthony Greenbank
1967; 223 pp.

$.95 postpaid

Kidney and head protection

from:
The New American Library, Inc.
1301 Avenue of the Americas
New York, N. Y. 10019

or WHOLE EARTH CATALOG

FIGHTING DRUNK

Humor.

If involved in brawl, drunks can offer astoundingly strong grip. Hit hard in stomach and this may make him sick.

Final consolation: a REAL ghost . . .
(a) Will disappear if you approach it.
(b) Can do you no physical harm because it leaves nothing earthly——not even messages or footprints.
(c) Will not cast a shadow; will look quite substantial rather than misty; will not ignore you; will not carry its head tucked under an arm.
(d) Is all in YOUR mind anyway

FIG. 64: Making footgear

When lying on the ground and being kicked try to keep rolling, shielding parts being kicked with arms. BUT always protect head as priority. Clasp base of skull with both hands, bring wrists across ears and side of head and press elbows together. Bring knees up, crossing ankles to save genitals.

In all attacks it pays to shout/gasp/yell more than you need: Feign pain. Especially when on receiving end (lying on ground and being kicked). Attacker may be satisfied sooner when you appear in agony.

SELF-PRESERVATION
Crushed in crowd

Aim to ride like buoy in rough sea – where tide is extremely powerful. To go under means drowning from suffocation and trampling. Brace like a powerful spring (as shown).

FIG. 10: Spring and buoy position in surging crowd

The Survival Book
Paul Nesbitt,
Alonzo Pond,
William Allen
1959, 338 pp.

$1.95 postpaid

from:
Funk & Wagnalls
c/o Thomas Y. Crowell
666 Fifth Avenue
New York, N.Y. 10019

or WHOLE EARTH CATALOG

Expected Days of Survival at Various Environmental Temperatures and with Varying Amounts of Available Water

	Max. daily in shade temperature, °F	Available water per man, U.S. quarts					
		0	1	2	4	10	20
NO WALKING	120	2	2	2	2.5	3	4.5
	110	3	3	3.5	4	5	7
	100	5	5.5	6	7	9.5	13.5
	90	7	8	9	10.5	15	23
	80	9	10	11	13	19	29
	70	10	11	12	14	20.5	32
	60	10	11	12	14	21	32
	50	10	11	12	14.5	21	32
WALKING AT NIGHT AND RESTING THEREAFTER	120	1	2	2	2.5	3	
	110	2	2	2.5	3	3.5	
	100	3	3.5	3.5	4.5	5.5	
	90	5	5.5	5.5	6.5	8	
	80	7	7.5	8	9.5	11.5	
	70	7.5	8	9	10.5	13.5	
	60	8	8.5	9	11	14	
	50	8	8.5	9	11	14	

DO'S AND DONT'S FOR THE TRAVELER IN ARABIAN DESERTS

Here are a few of the most important don't's. In general they apply to the deserts everywhere.

Don't reprimand an offender in front of other people.
Don't draw sand pictures or maps with your foot—stoop down and draw with your right hand.
Don't swear at a native.
Don't expose the soles of your feet to others. Sit tailor fashion or on your heels.
Don't ask about a man's wife.
Don't throw a coin at a man's feet. That is insulting.
Don't try to gamble. It is forbidden.
And here are a couple of Do's worth remembering.
Do have patience when dealing with desert people.
Do act friendly.

Survival Evasion and Escape

Here's one for our customers who plan to jump bail or escape from jail. Thoughtfully prepared by the U. S. Army. Three-fourths of the book is about living off the land, with edible plants illustrated in color. Pretty damn good book.

—SB

Survival, Evasion, and Escape
1957, 1965; 1969; 430 pp.
FM No. 21-76

$6.05 postpaid

from:
Superintendent of Documents
U. S. Government Printing Office
Washington, D. C. 20402

or WHOLE EARTH CATALOG

FM 21-76
DEPARTMENT OF THE ARMY FIELD MANUAL
SURVIVAL EVASION AND ESCAPE
HEADQUARTERS, DEPARTMENT OF THE ARMY, MARCH 1969

Casting

Frequently the duplication of buttons, insignia, seals, medals, etc., is necessary to complete an evasion disguise. Casting these items in soft metal generally is the best method, and the procedures involved require very simple materials.

a. Lead, solder, and zinc are the easiest and most common materials to work with. Lead can be obtained from pipe or plumbing fittings, from around underground electrical wire, and from leaded window frames. Solder may be melted from the seams of tin cans. Zinc

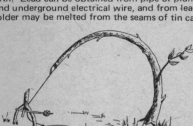

CROSS SECTION OF SNOWDRIFT
VENTILATION HOLE
DOMED ROOF
WARM AIR LEVEL
SNOW BLOCK
COOKING SHELF
DOOR
SLEEPING PLATFORM
COLD AIR LEVEL

Snow caves.

frequently is used on washbowls, metal fittings, metal containers and some window and roof construction.

b. Make a mold by using clay, soap or a large potato. The material used is cut in half, and half of the design is cut into each piece so that when fitted together the hollowed-out parts will have the form desired. In all molds, a hole must be made in one side through which to pour the metal; a small hole is made in the other side to allow air to escape. Molds made of clay should be baked to harden. After being poured and allowed to cool, finish the casting by trimming with a knife or file and painting or polishing as appropriate.

sand dunes in the Gobi Desert

West
dune
dry sand
saturated sand
East
dig for water

Life Support Technology, Inc.

The most sophisticated survival kits and equipment. Designed for bush pilots and the like.

—SB

[Suggested by Alan Kalker]

Catalog

free

from:
Life Support Technology, Inc.
4530 S. E. Roswell St.
Portland, Oregon 97206

$6.95

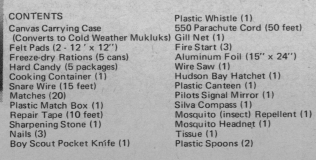

M2/f "Economy" Aeronautic Life Support Unit $89.50

CONTENTS

Canvas Carrying Case (Converts to Cold Weather Mukluks)
Felt Pads (2 - 12' x 12')
Freeze-dry Rations (5 cans)
Hard Candy (5 packages)
Cooking Container (1)
Snare Wire (15 feet)
Matches (20)
Plastic Match Box (1)
Repair Tape (10 feet)
Sharpening Stone (1)
Nails (3)
Boy Scout Pocket Knife (1)

Plastic Whistle (1)
550 Parachute Cord (50 feet)
Gill Net (1)
Fire Start (3)
Aluminum Foil (15" x 24")
Wire Saw (1)
Hudson Bay Hatchet (1)
Plastic Canteen (1)
Pilots Signal Mirror (1)
Silva Compass (1)
Mosquito (insect) Repellent (1)
Mosquito Headnet (1)
Tissue (1)
Plastic Spoons (2)

Candle (1)
Plastic Sheeting (9' x 12')
Fishing Kit (1)
Sewing Kit (1)
Surgical Tubing (4 feet)
Hacksaw Blade (1)
Pencil (1)
Rescue Blanket (1)
Slingshot Pouch (1)
"tinyMIGHT" Aerial Signaling Device w/6 Aerial Flares
Fusee Flares (2)
Wilderness Survival Manual (1)

Shipping Weight: 11 pounds

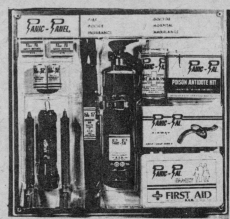

A 'Panic Panel', 20" square, weighing 13.5 lbs., containing a fire extinguishire, a first aid kit, poison antidote, a resuscitator, an aerosol spray, an emergency bar, a torch and batteries and candles and matches, is now on sale in the USA. Cost $29.95. Available from M. C. DISTRIBUTORS, 4104 N. College Avenue, Indianpolis, Indiana 46203.

Architectural Design, p. 88

Outdoor Survival Skills

olsen assumes that you get stuck out there with nothing but some knowledge, no matches, food, compass, toothpaste, or magazines. scrounge the tools food and shelter. good bunch of pictures and diagrams. sort of a purists book. for someone who is thinking about stopping along the road on the way to work some day, and just walking out into the wilderness.

—jd

[Suggested by W.H. Bayman]

Outdoor Survival Skills
Larry Dean Olsen
1973; 188 pp.

$4.96, cloth; **$2.95,** paper
postpaid

from:
Brigham Young University Press
Marketing 2050PB
Provo, UT 84602

or WHOLE EARTH CATALOG

At least once in life, every man, woman and child should know (1) the feeling of complete dependence on the bounties of nature, (2) hunger and hardship, (3) the meaning of total self-dependence, and (4) the personal inventiveness required to wrest a living from nature. Each should have the opportunity to learn the use of his own two hands in making necessary items for comfort and survival in nature.

Few of us ever depend upon our own skills and resources for our needs. We depend, instead, upon the manufactured items of our

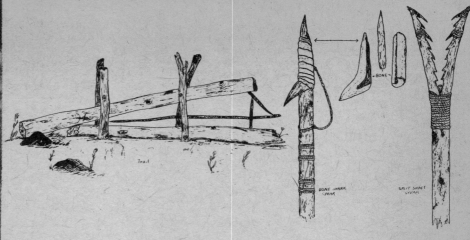

OUTDOOR SURVIVAL SKILLS
Larry Dean Olsen

civilization to the extent that it would be nearly impossible to conceive of a life without them. We marvel at the ability of Stone Age people to survive under such adverse conditions as they were usually found. We envy somewhat their ability, and deep down inside of us we hold a secret fear that somehow, someday we may find ourselves in the same situation as these primitive folks. Even worse, we may find ourselves lost in a wilderness without food, water, shelter or even the know-how to provide them. We fear the though thought of getting along without our "gadgets."

Survival Arts of the Primitive Paiutes

This book is about people living in equilibrium with their environment. They probably had no words for garbage or waste because they used everything— cattail, tule, willow, rabbit pelts, buckskin, sagebrush bark, bones, rocks. Somehow the story of how they did it, which is told with simple words and ungimmicky photographs, reflects the expanse and serenity of the Great Basin environment and is beautiful.

[Reviewed by Tony Mindling]

Survival Arts of the Primitive Paiutes
Margaret M. Wheat
1967; 177 pp.

$10.00 postpaid

from:
University of Nevada
Press
Reno, Nevada 89507

or
WHOLE
EARTH
CATALOG

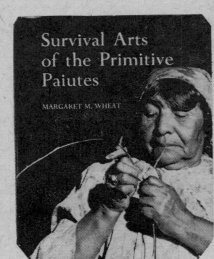

Survival Arts of the Primitive Paiutes
MARGARET M. WHEAT

Shoveling hot coals from the breakfast fire onto the small, brown pinenuts in the winnowing tray, she began immediately to bounce and turn them, keeping them in constant motion to protect the basket from becoming scorched.

When the nuts hissed and popped somewhat like popcorn, she knew they were cooked. This first roasting leaves the meat soft and translucent.

When the boat was completed, Jimmy stepped in the center to form a deeper hollow. The finished boat was eight-and-a-half feet long but so light that it could easily be lifted with one hand.

To play the game, two people on one side each concealed a pair of sticks or "bones" within their closed fists. One bone of each pair was plain, the other ornamented. The guesser on the opposing team had to choose in which hands the unornamented sticks were hidden. If the guess were correct, his side was awarded a tally stick. If not, his side lost a stick. The side winning all ten tally sticks claimed all the bets. The singers opposing the guesser shouted, waved, and beat the logs to confuse him, but he sat quietly, apparently oblivious to the distractions, concentrating on his choice. It is remarkable how often a good guesser won. Winners were never congratulated, nor were losers ever consoled. The game is still played in the Great Basin with stakes often running into hundreds of dollars.

Survival Equipment

Yerger's Supplies, Box 8138, Anchorage, Alaska 99504. Catalog contains Air Force Survival Equipment selections for light aircraft.

Survival Equipment Company, Division of Oley Tooling Inc., Oley, Pennsylvania 19547. Survival equipment for aircraft owners and pilots. Kits, tools, & books. Everything from a one-man life raft model PK—2 at $123.00 to an orange smoke bomb for $2.25. In sixteen pages this is a very complete survival equipment company. Many kits are useful for any wilderness traveler on foot or horseback, or river float trip.

Northwest Wilderness Survival Schools, Life Support Technology, Inc., 4530 SE Roswell Street, Portland, Oregon 97206. Summer Sessions $60.00. One week. They also have survival kits for snowmobiles along with a film on winter survival available for rent.

Survival Research Laboratories, 17 Marland Road, Colorado Springs, Colorado 80906.
A. Individual one man three day survival kit designed for the average Cross Country flight. $37.85
B. "Trail Kit"® for the shirt pocket $4.98
C. Special information about Alaska and Canada

Earl Palmer
Corvallis, Oregon

Survival Documents

Are you onto a book outfit in Glendale, Az, called The Adobe Hacienda; They furnish an assortment of Survival, Herbal, Medical, Military documents and books, and their mail-order service is superior. This outfit seems to be somewhere right of the Birch Bunch, and some of their offerings are pretty scary. Nonetheless they inadvertently (what right-type would do such a thing vertantly?) feed the needs and/or curiosities of The People as well. Their address is: Rt 3, Box 517, Glendale, AZ. 85301.

S. Stanton
Pacific Grove, CA

Trail Food

Thought you might like a great recipe for survival food for anyone going off into the woods for a long jaunt— cross country ski trips, hikers, mountain climbers, cycle trips, snow mobiles, etc. It doesn't spoil, tastes not too bad, and it keeps forever— well, darned near it.

2 tablespoons wild honey (tame will do, but not the flavor)
2 cups oatmeal (or bran or wheat germ)
2-1/2 cups powdered milk
1 cup sugar
3 tablespoons of water
1 package jello in your favorite flavour (I'm partial to rasberry)

Boil the water and honey together, then add jello. mix dry stuff together, stir in water mixture. Mix well— probably with your hands. You might need a drop more water but don't add too much— it has to be dehydrated. You might like to add a little grated orange or lemon peel. Now spread the stuff into a 9 x 13 cake pan and put it in an oven at about 200 degrees. Leave the door ajar and let it "cook" for about six hours. Be sure to cook it that long or it won't keep. When done, let it cool and then cut it into 2" bars. Wrap them in foil and they will keep for years— Each is packed with energy— really one makes a meal. On a camping or back-packing trip you can crumble one and add boiling water and have a hot meal.

Lee Cole
Portland, Oregon

The 10 Bushcraft Books

. . . it's sort of a how-to-do-it-in-Australia, which turned me off at first until I read it a little more thoroughly. The problem with most books on this subject which are available in this country is that they are basically diletante's manuals; they tell you how to live in the open for a week or two, but always presuppose that sooner or later you're going to go back to your Telegraph Hill apartment and take a nice hot shower. Australia, however, is a different scene, more like the U.S. a hundred years ago, when quite large numbers of people were accustomed, for various reasons, to living out of doors for most of the year. And that, I take it, is what more and more of our brothers and sisters are doing or thinking about doing (or have to do.)

[Suggested and reviewed by Roland Jacopetti]

The Ten Bushcraft Books
Richard Graves
300pp.

$3.95 postpaid

from:
Dymock's Book Arcade Ltd.
Sydney 2000, Australia

Schocken Books, Inc.
200 Madison Ave.
New York, N.Y. 10016
or
WHOLE EARTH CATALOG

THE 10 BUSHCRAFT BOOKS are:

Book 1. Ropes & Cords	Book 6. Knots & Lashings
Book 2. Huts & Thatching	Book 7. Tracks & Lures
Book 3. Campcraft	Book 8. Snares & Traps
Book 4. Food & Water	Book 9. Travel & Gear
Book 5. Firemaking	Book 10. Time & Direction

A TOOTHLESS MOUTH

Half a mile up Trace Fork from the store D.R. stopped to hide and rest a while behind a rusted hulk that used to be a '47 Ford. There was a four-room house with the roof caved in half-hidden in the weeds behind he might have gone to, but D.R. was scared to go to places he couldn't make out clearly with his eyes. He hadn't seen David behind, or heard him, in several minutes now, but he knew that he was somewhere close around. David had been right behind him the first several hundred yards, but then D.R. had left the road and plunged over the bank into Trace Fork creek and David hadn't followed. D.R. didn't stay in the creek. The banks were thick with weeds for David to hide in, and the water was slimy-yellow from the strip mining operations at the headwaters. D.R. slogged up the creek for perhaps a hundred yards, then scrambled up the bank again and hid behind the corpse of the old car.

D.R. knew he was close to the homeplace now, but the hollow the creek flowed through had been so disfigured by the strip mining he didn't see a feature on the landscape that he recognized. The ridges where the Trace Fork waters gathered were so uniformly scarred they looked like rims of craters on the moon. The guts of entire mountains had been ripped out and strewn about like so much worthless slop. Every roll and fold, every feature of the drainage that might have framed a context and established where the homeplace was had been torn away by bulldozers or smothered by fathoms of overburden. A slope that might have been the lower pasture on the homeplace was littered by shattered rocks and jagged ends of broken trees sticking up like legs of mules slaughtered in some awful no-man's land.

D.R. heard a snapping noise behind, then David yelling, 'Hey! D.R.! Where are you?'

His voice came from the old abandoned house not fifty yards away. It was as if the house itself had yelled. Its vacant windows were like eyes of some old dead man, its door a toothless mouth that never closed. "Wait up for me, okay?" yelled the mouth as David stepped through it and headed through the weeds toward D.R.'s hiding place.

Good Tools That Shoot

The recent suggestions in the *Supplement* re: black powder shooting led me to attempt laying a double of heavy thoughts on you, one on cheap shooting, and one on a couple of good buys for communes who need game (and other interested parties.)

Reloading: All right, black powder is cheap. Also messy, and damn dangerous to keep around your pad. Also, from now on, you have to register it. If you want cheap shooting with some other advantages, try handloading, using the Lee Reloader ($9.95 usually discounted to $7—$8, includes all the tools you need except some kind of hammer).

Advantages: 1.)— it's cheap; I shoot .30/06 ammunition that is just about as powerful as factory ammo only it costs me $1.57 for 20 as opposed to $5.30+ for 20 factory rounds. Using cast bullets for practice, it costs me 97¢ for 20. 2.) Hand-loads are more accurate. Want proof? All current records for accuracy were set using hand-loaded ammunition, in some cases using the 'cheap' little Lee Reloader. For me, 5 shot groups on my iron-sighted Springfield shrink from 2+" (factory) to about 1" with hand-loads. 3.) You can load weights and styles of bullets not available in commercial factory ammo. Example, the Speer 165-gr. .30/06 bullet is the best all-round bullet for the '06, combining high down range velocity like the 150-gr. and high energy like the 180- and 220-gr.

What you need to reload: Principally, some time, a little patience and capacity for taking a very pains, some freedom from distraction while actually working and a tool with maybe a few accessories;

THE TOOL is the Lee Reloader, which comes with complete instructions, in any rifle, pistol, or shotgun size you need. It includes everything you need to reload ammunition for all guns with the possible exception of relatively weak lever actions, namely the Winchester 94's which are notorious for stretching brass badly. As a guide, if you can re-chamber the fired case and re-extract and eject it, you don't have to full-length resize your brass and can use the Lee Reloader. Should you have a gun that does stretch your brass too badly, either get rid of it or get the hand-operated full-length re-sizing dies that L.E. Wilson, Cashmere, Washington sells for $9.95. Although I have some pretty complicated, sophisticated equipment, including bench press and scales, I use my Lee Reloader for almost all of my reloading because of its simplicity and reliability and effectiveness.

A FEW ACCESSORIES: The Lee Reloading manual tells you most anything you'll ever want to know about reloading for 98¢. The best reloading manuals are the Lyman ones, if you want to go big time, or load cast bullets, and they are $3.95 for shotguns and $4.95 for the combined Rifle-Pistol manual. Other worthwhile accessories include:

—The Lee Powder Measure Kit ($3.95) includes enough different scoop type measures that you can load many more different loads than you can with the single measure in the Reloader Tool.

—The Lee Priming Tool, $3.95 for rifles and pistols is quieter and easier to use than the system in the tool itself. You can get interchangeable bases too so you can then use the tool for many calibers.

—The Lee Crimp Starter for Shotgun Shells (95¢) is a MUST if you load shotgun shells with plastic bodies (and you shouldn't bother messing with paper shells unless you have to.) You will need two, the six- and eight-segment crimp starters.

While you don't really need other tools, there are two accessories that I like. One is the Pacific MESUR-KIT (8.95) which is a portable powder measure that is accurate to ± .2 grs. which is pretty good. You get a lot of versatility through combining charges (DO NOT FORGET THAT FOR EACH OPERATION OF THE MEASURE YOU SHOULD ADD ANOTHER .2 Grs. Probable Error), and it's good for large scale operations or quantity reloading and more convenient than the Lee dippers. A bullet loading block (out of plastic with holes big enough for your cases to sit in) helps operations by keeping cases segregated according to what step you are on. Finally, if you are a true accuracy enthusiast, the Target Model Lee Reloader at $24.95 contains everything you need to reload ammunition that will be about as accurate as any in the world.

Finally, a note of caution and a suggestion: Don't use powders unless you know what they are, and don't buy advertised surplus powders unless they are sold by B.E. Hodgdon because otherwise they may not be what they are advertised and you might lose your head over the deal— literally! For advice, suggestions, and pretty solid opinions on reloading and shooting, the NRA has experts who will provide about all the answers you need for $6 a year. It's a good investment, and like the man said, they do try to protect your right to have guns legally.

A SECOND SUGGESTION: Dempster on Good Gun Buys.

All right, so you've decided you've got to get a gun for some reason or other, including just the joy of owning a good tool. What you get depends on what you'll use it for. Here are some suggestions for some really good gun buys for the subsistence— dare we say pot?— hunter, the commune, and the guy who just wants a good gun.

There are two kinds of .22's and both are useful. If you only want target practice and an occasional squirrel or rabbit for the pot (yes a .22 will kill moose but don't try it), get a .22 Long Rifle. If you want a cheap varmint rifle that really does enough power for anything smaller than deer up to 125 yards, get a .22 Winchester Magnum Rimfire (.22WMR) which up to 50 yards in a rifle with a careful chest hit will (illegally) do a deer in. For cheap target practice since the magnum ammunition is expensive, use .22 CB caps made by CCI. These CB caps and .22 Winchester Special are the only other kinds of ".22 ammo" that you can safely use in a Magnum. The best and cheapest buys in .22's are the Savage-Stevens 34 (.22 Short, long, and Long Rifle) at $39.95 or 34-M (.22 WMR) at $44.95.

If I could have only one gun, it would be the Savage 24-S which has a .22 Magnum (also available in .22 LR) rifle barrel over a 20 gauge 3" magnum barrel (will fire 2 3/4" shells also). These cost $63.95, usually discounted, which is less than the price of separate rifles and shotguns. The shotgun patterns well and a 20 gauge shotgun is big enough for any bird, rabbit, etc. or even deer with readily available rifled slugs while the .22WMR gives you a pretty decent rifle. I'd get a Lee Reloader in 20 gauge to go with it.

If you reload, forget a pump or automatic shotgun. They aren't sporting or pretty or anything else anyway. A double costs a little more in a bare model, but handles better, and while digest your handloads (this is not a problem for rifles and pistols) without a bobble. The best buy is the Savage-Stevens 311 at $109.95, usually discounted, and also available more cheaply under Western Auto and Sears brand names.

Big Game Rifles: With good shooting, a 30/30 will do fine up to 150 yards on deer (black bear, antelope) and with good bullet placement, will kill an elk up to 100 yards pretty well. While the lever action Winchester 94 isn't very accurate unless you pay about $8 for a peep sight which you can put on yourself, and are willing to hand-load with the aid of the Wilson Full-Length Sizing dies and the Lee Reloader, for $55 to $75 (it lists at $99.95 but is widely discounted) it's not a bad buy, especially if you combine it with a Savage 24-S for a good two-gun battery. The best buy in a .30/30 though is the Savage 340 bolt action which will be priced from $78 to $89 depending on discount— the cheaper Springfield 840 is the same gun for less money. A more accurate fast repeater in .30/30 than the Winchester is the pump action Savage 170 which is usually discounted to $75 from $99.95. Don't ever bother with a scope for any .30/30.

If both deer and smaller game are your would-be bag, get the Remington 788 bolt-action repeater in .243 Winchester for $109.95 with a 4X Universal scope. ($99.95 or less without). If Elk or Moose are a regular thing with you, get the 788 in .308 Winchester— same prices. This is a very strong and accurate gun. Elk will fall to a .243.

The best 'expensive' all-round rifle if you hand-load and want to make do with only one rifle for everything that is good-looking is the Winchester 770 in .270 or (later this year) .25-06. The Remington competitor, the 700 ADL lists for $10 more but sometimes is discounted to a lower price. The very best Deluxe rifles are the Ruger 77 Bolt Action ($175), the Sako Finnbear bolt action ($220) and the Ruger Number One Single Shot ($285.) The only surplus rifles that I would ever trust are the British Enfield .303 British which comes in a variety of styles from a long rifle-musket to a jungle carbine (price $35-60 depending on model) and the US Enfield and Springfield (if marked Springfield Armory, the serial number should be above 880,000 or so) about $45-60. My own rifle is a Springfield which I restocked myself, and I've been very happy with it.

Good luck, good living, good hunting, and good shooting,

Shalom,

Cliff Dempster
Missoula, Montana

Golden Age Arms

This company offers reproductions of muzzle-loading firearms (pistols and rifles— BOTH percussion cap and flintlock). All parts and accessories offered.

i.e., Flintlock rifle— overall length 55½", weights 8½ lbs., .45 caliber 7 groove 13/16" barrel mounted curly maple stock. $295.00 plus $3.00 shipping.

All kinds of powder horns, flasks or the components to make your own. Bullet molds, stag slabs for knife handles or pistol grips.

Sheffield knife blanks, requires handles only. Highly polished and handhoned.

6" Bowie $3.50

4" Skean Dhu $1.50

Tricorn hats $12.00

Deerskins, patterns, tools for making hunting shirts, moccasins

Books on firearms.

The best buy is tomahawk kit, hand-forged head, hardwood handle, wedge, thong & decorative brass tacks. $4.95 postpaid. Perfectly balanced for throwing and an excellent light belt ax as well as an efficient weapon.

Tomahawk heads cast steel $5.50
cast brass $6.50

A catalog is available for $1.00 from:

Golden Age Arms Co., Inc.
P.O. Box 83
Worthington, Ohio 43085

Submitted by
Kenneth Cowing
Meriden, Conn.

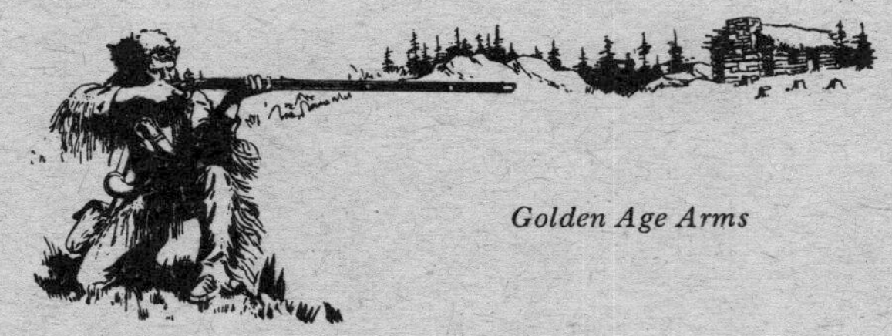

Golden Age Arms

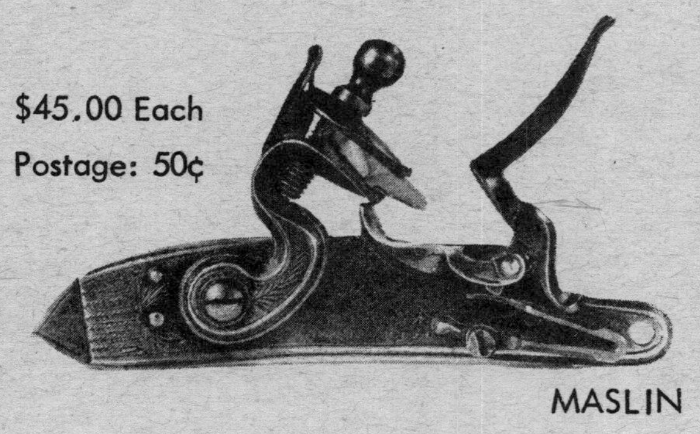

Golden Age Mountianman Rifle Kit

Flintlock $104.50	Postage $5.00
Percussion $94.50	Postage $5.00

Contains Grade-B stock; barrel and breech plug; single trigger; Hamm or Robbins lock of your choice; hand-forged butt plate; trigger guard; ramrod pipes; underpinning strip.

All This Information

All this information comes to life at the twice-summerly National Muzzle Loading Rifle Assoc. shoots in Friendship, Indiana. It is truly weird and magnificent to see a bunch of right-wing gun nuts dressed up in fringed buckskin and long hair and impossible to distinguish from visiting freaks also dressed in. . .well, you get the picture.

Carl Fleischauer
Morgantown, West Virginia

KER—PLOW! Gottim

Deer Friends,

In one issue of W.E. I saw a riff about weapons, can't recall when/ where but mentioned stuff re. crossbows, guns, flintlock/percussion muzzle loaders. Well, as it turns out if you want a weapon that's powerful fun and pretty legal there's only one way---

★★★★★★★★★★ *Black Powder (rifles & pistols)* ★★★★★★★★★★★★★★

See, these can be sent thru mail with no restrictions (check local laws tho) to anyone. To get a pistol you have to say you're 21. Big deal. Anyway, muzzle loading longarms (flintlocks and percussion) are reasonably accurate, make one fuck of a big beautiful noise. Same for pistols. Also very cheap, like maybe 1/10 cost to shoot than cartridge weapons. Calibres .36 ++++ infinity (flintlocks & shotguns). These guns are modeled after old timey (thymey?) type guns like model .36 cal Navy percussion revolver or Kentucky type squirrel guns, as examples

Sources: get a gun mag. like Shooting Times or Guns & Ammo and look at prices, descriptions, and pictures. (fetishists take particular note). OR

Centennial Arms Corp.
3318 W. Devon Ave., Lincolnwood, Ill. 60645
(price list $1.00!!) ("You can't always get what you want...")

OR

Dixie Gun Works
Dept. 1, Union City, Tenn. 38161
catalogue $2.00--250 pages!!! Lots of good stuff

OR

Any other places you might see in a gun mag.

Notes: (1) Dixie's cat. is VERY far out. They are honest!!!
(2) Centennial is good and cheap and has nifty pistols. Their pistols (Italian & Belgium) are well made for the price--like $39.95 for a steel frame 36 cal percussion pistol. Beware of pistols over .36 with brass frames, steel is stronger.
(3) NEVER, NEVER, NEVER use smokeless powder-- if you do YOU will be blown to shit. USE BLACK POWDERONLY. It is very safe--smash it with a hammer and it won't go off. Only ignites by spark (from flint or percussion cap)
(4) Make sure the weapon you buy has been "proofed" (tested) so that you can be sure it won't blow up--beware of "trade" guns. You get what you pay for.
(5) Clean your gun regularly. Black powder is CORROSIVE and can make a mess of your weapon. These guns ain't too hard (or too much fun either) to clean--find out the best way from someone who knows-- or make up your own way.
(6) When a flintlock goes off it's the most far-out. There's a snap, whoosh and a BOOM. Percussion ones just go BOOM. Anyway if you want to stay on friendly terms with your neighbors, tell them when you're going hunting, target shooting, poaching so they don't think you're playing Lawrence of Arabia blowing up trains.*
(like a cherry bomb in a 50 gal. oil drum.)*
(7) For all types of guns get a copy of Guns Illustrated 1970 by the editors of The Gun Digest. It has everything legal in it. All types of guns, pistols, derringers, etc. Unfortunately it costs $2.95. If you're serious it's worth it.
(8) Join the NRA. The NRA establishment freaks want to repeal gun laws. They're all perverts but join them it's a good cause.
(9) What the world needs now is a better Anarchy.

Peace,
Crazy Bill
Allston, Massachewsit

PLINKER PERCUSSION FULLSTOCK RIFLE KIT USING 14/16" BARREL BLANK, Calibers .32, .38, or .43. Specify caliber. **KIT # 108** **$35.35**

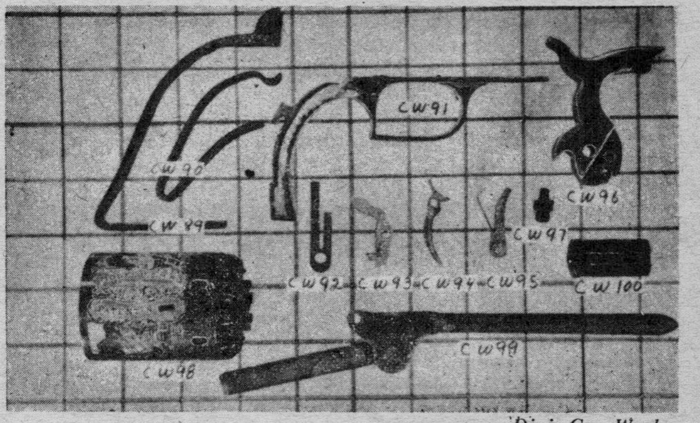

Dixie Gun Works

SPARE PARTS FOR THE REPRODUCTION COLT WALKER REVOLVER

CW78	Butt screw	$ .25
CW79	Backstrap screw	.25
CW80	Rear guard screw	.25
CW81	Front guard screw	.25

NRA

National Rifle Association is a bogey man to many people, and this is perfectly understandable. There are a lot of flag-freaks and super-patriots involved in it. They are against gun legislation. If you can stand reading any further, good information is coming.

The NRA, for all its faults, provides many valuable services, many of them free. If you must supplement community food supplies, hunting is a good way to do it, if you are not morally opposed to that sort of thing. Most of the people in the NRA are pretty reasonable types— either target shooters who damage only paper targets, or hunters who eat what they kill. Their needs are catered to in the American Rifleman, a monthly magazine that is paid for by your club dues. This journal will, every month, teach you things about hunting and shooting, cooking, storing, skinning and preparing game, the advantages and disadvantages of different pieces of equipment, field techniques, and it will keep you up to date on gun laws in all areas— even abroad. Any member needing help with something to do with guns can write to the NRA and get personal help— good help— free. Membership is $7.50 a year. National Rifle Association, 1600 Rhode Island Ave., N.W., Washington DC 20036

Bill Marsano
Radnor, Pa.

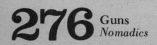

Knives

In March 1970 Catalog I noted the mention of Custom Knife maker.

As with all things there are those who demand the "best" and for these "users" or "taste at any price buffs" there is a fine selection. The post war success of "Randal" of Florida brought on dozens of Custom Knife Makers a few of whom I shall list:

Arnold Made Knives

Clyde Fisher
Rt. 1 Box 170
Victoria, Texas 77901

Buck Knives, Inc.
P.O. Box 1267
1717 N. Magnolia Ave.
El Cajon, CA 92022
(Sporting gds. stores)

Dennis F. Foreman
155 Ave. "U"
Brooklyn, N.Y. 11223
(March '70 Catalog p. 14)

Morseth Sports Equipt.
Box 406
Redmond, Washington

Randall Knives
Box 1988
Orlando, Florida

Stone Knives, Inc.
703 Floyd R'd
Richardson, Texas

Bone Knive Co., Inc.
806 Ave. "J"
Lubbock, Texas 79401

M.W. Sequine
Juneau Alaska

T.M. Dowell
139 St. Helens Pl.   Catalog
Bend, Oregon 97701 $1.00

Draper Custom Knives
Ephraim, Utah 84627

D.E. Henry
300 St. Henry Dr.
Fremont, Calif. 94538

Hibben Knives
Manti Utah 84642

W.G. Moran Jr.
Rt. 5
Frederick Md. 21701

Olsen Knife Co., Inc.
Howard City, Mich. 49329

Ruana Knife Works
P.O. Box 574   Al Fry
Bonner, Montana 59823 Perris, CA.

Shotgun News

Best paper out for gun bargains.

[Suggested and reviewed by Rainbow People]

Shotgun News

$5 /yr (bi-weekly)   Sample copy $.75

from:
Shotgun News
Box 1147
Hastings, Neb. 68901

● ● ● ● ●

Karma

Note.

We list Shotgun News *with the expectation that all you're interested in shooting is inanimate targets and food. If you buy a gun through this source for any other reason, you're loading our Karma as well as your own.*

—SB

● ● ● ● ●

Shotgun News

In case you can't get samples, here is our latest copy of "Shotgun News". Because of gun laws— some of the guns offered must be bought through a licensed gun dealer. In a small town such as ours, this can be done through a dealer who carries firearms as a sideline (i.e. Hardware Store) and they will do it as a courtesy and no money involved. I sure in larger cities some sort of deal which keeps both the dealer and the buyer happy can be worked out since they are mainly a pick up point for the gun and may have to do a little paper work to satisfy the man. But of course you will see, Shotgun News is not limited to guns.

More on the Dixie Gun Works catalog. They carry parts, machinery, books on making guns as well as antique guns. Also black power ball and cap guns are for people who feel the animal should get half a chance in the hunt since they take a little skill and find a bow not their game. They are good hunting rifle but you only get one shot.

Rainbow People

Indian Ridge Traders Knife Blades

An outfit called Indian Ridge Traders in Ferndale Michigan. IRT's specialty is a line of unfinished knife blades made by Hopkinson in Sheffield, England. IRT is a small neo-co-op organization which I have dealt with over the last couple of years. Their prices are low, the service fast and friendly, and best of all unlike other knife firms, no far right political bullshit.

Their blades are almost strictly high-carbon steel which although not as classy as 440C stainless is easy to work with and can be sharpened by hand in a finite amount of time, a characteristic not included in 440C's properties. A knife which I made for my own use from one of their blades, a rigger's knife, has seen use in and around fresh and salt water for over a year now with negligible rusting and pitting with only a minimum of care.

Their catalog lists a large variety of blades, mostly tools with only a few weapons, if you can dig the difference. Their line of kitchen blades is especially good. They also list some knife finishing materials and suggest sources for others. One source which they suggest for a variety of weird hardwoods is the back of your friendly neighborhood Oriental motorcycle dealers. Nearly all his thrown-out crates are a made of a variety of Eastern hardwoods. Their catalog is free from:

Indian Ridge Traders
P.O. Box X-50
Ferndale, Michigan 48220

[Reviewed by Larry Murray.
Suggested by Cos Newton,
John Langley and Chuck Jenkins]

Wrist Rocket

"My God! Is that far-out!", was the reaction given to a demonstration of the power and accuracy inherent to my "Wrist Rocket", an example of an old inovation, the sling shot, the creative application of a scientific principal, leverage, and a little practice can produce.

The "Wrist Rocket" is an expertly crafted piece of hand weapontry far superior to all others I have ever encountered, short of the fire-arm. It is completely rust-proof and, if in time the rubber sling should break after hard, long usage, it is easily replaceable with two matching lengths of surgical rubber tubing obtainable from your local dealer.

Price — complete Wrist Rocket $3.50 plus $.50 postage and handling on each order. Matched replacement rubbers and leather pouch assembly $1.00 (plus $.25 postage if ordered alone).
Wrist Rocket Mfg. Co., Inc.
2654 44th Ave.
Columbus, Nebraska 68601

"Joe Eddy"
Southern Illinois University

Ruana Knives

Made by a stern old fellow in his blacksmith shop in Bonner, Montana, these knives are as good as you will find anywhere. He used to make them out of old Chevrolet springs, but chevy went to coil springs and now he has to buy his steel elsewhere. None of that dude business with stainless steel or chrome blades, however, these knives are strictly for cutting. If you look closely, you may see some honest hammer marks on the blades, but they are as good as the high priced prestige models favored by knife snobs everywhere. Handles are cast aluminum over elkhorn and a full length tang, as tough and functional as you'll find. If you're in the woods and lose all your tools but one, better make it one of these.

[Reviewed by Daniel Vichorek]

Ruana Knife Works
Bonner, Montana 59823

Sharpening

To really sharpen knives, axes, and the like, with a razor edge that stays sharp you should have three sharpening stones and a piece of leather. The stones should be: a coarse or medium corundum stone, a fine India stone (these two are usually fused back to back and sold as a combination stone), and a hard Arkansas stone (expensive but worth it). Follow the directions with the stones for soaking them in oil for this prolongs the life of the stone by filling up the spaces between the particles of the stone so metal particles from the sharpening process do not lodge in these spaces and render the stone ineffective. Also oil applied to the surface of the stone while sharpening helps float the excess metal away. The purpose in going from a coarse to a fine to a hard stone is not only to form the edge but also each successive step polishes out the scratches of the previous step, and the polish is the key to edges staying sharp since the scratches are the cause of the blades getting dull fast. For a dull knife, start with the coarse or medium corundum stone to form the rough edge. When that is done go to the fine India stone, work on this stone till the large scratches from the coarse stone are worn away and the blade has a sharp edge. The knife could be used at this point but would not be razor sharp or stay sharp long. So go to the hard Arkansas stone and stay with it till the edge takes on a mirror finish. Then strop it (draw the blade back and forth) on the leather to remove the wire edge and further polish the blade— then you're done. It takes a lot of words to write it, but from dull knife to sharp knife takes only about ten minutes. Maybe this is more than anyone wants to know about sharpening.

Manufacturer of Excellent Stones

Norton Co.
50 New Bond St.
Worcester, Mass 01606
Free brochure, local hardwares etc. carry their stones

Sincerely,

David Mohrhardt
Bozeman, Montana

For Guide to Sharpening, see p. 143.

—SB

Kneubuhler

In the same bag (outfits servicing your "primitive weapons" nut) there's a amusing, illustrated 25¢ brochure of handmade hunting knives from Walter Kneubuhler. (W.K. Knives, 2835 117th St., Toledo, Ohio 43611).

Carl Fleishhauer
Morgantown, West Virginia

THE DISCOVERY

D.R. was crawling now, on hands and knees and sometimes on his belly like a worm, squirming through the weeds and briars and piles of ancient trash away from David toward the far side of the hollow. He was crying now. He tried to fight it but the tears insisted and they flowed in little channels down his muddy face. By the time he stopped to rest and get his breath behind a pile of old boards and rotting beams and rusted mining cable, D.R. was bleeding from cuts and scratches all over his face and arms. He heard David thrashing through the weeds behind him, coming closer, but he was too worn out to move. He lay down across the front seats of the bus to keep Mrs. Godsey from seeing him and listened to his footsteps running through the weeds. He ran until he fell, exhausted, so tired that only his torn hands could move. As he lay there crying, his hands started working on their own, burrowing in the earth at the edge of the old junk pile. The ground beneath the rotted boards was so dry and crumbly he pulled it loose in double-handfuls and pushed them to the side. It was like sawdust, like leaf-mold beneath an oak tree that had never been disturbed. Whole sections of rotted board fell away before D.R.'s clawing hands, until he had made a place large enough to worm his body through. Pushing with his toes, D.R. squirmed into the center of the mound, then lay still to breathe and rest his raw and aching hands, and discover something so profound and unexpected it blew a little hole right through his mind.

D.R. lay in an opening in the earth. He had crawled into the drift mouth of an old, abandoned mine. His arm was through, inside it, and now his head and shoulders, he could smell it, he felt the dark space opening out around, he felt the wind from deep inside the earth.

(continued)

"Primitive Weapons"

Compared to firearms, the so-called "primitive weapons" have several advantages: they are simple, light, cheap, and versatile in use. They require no ammunition you can't make yourself— and although you can reload some kinds of firearms ammunition, you will eventually run out of powder and primers. Except in places like New York City, you have no legal hassles over ownership or registration with "primitive weapons". These weapons are perfectly adequate for hunting (or our ancestors would not have survived), if you will practice with them. They are silent in use. In some cases, they exhibit amazingly advanced understanding of technically advanced concepts and principles— the boomerang operates on the principles of the airfoil and gyroscopic precession, etc. They are fun to play with, and if you use reasonable care and do not endanger others, you can usually play around with them in a lot of places where it is illegal to practice with firearms.

Boomerangs— As mentioned, the boomerang works on the principles of the airfoil and gyroscopic precession. This is not a toy, but a hunting and fighting weapon which works very well on small game, especially birds in flight. More fun to play with than a frisbee, but don't ever forget that it strikes with tremendous force due to the rapid rotation of the blades. The best ones I know of are made by Colonel John M. Gerrish, 4409 S.W. Parkview Lane, Portland 1, Oregon. These are plywood booms that weight the same as a baseball, and he also makes a heavier hunting type with lead weights set into the blades. His booms are about five dollars depending on the model.

Blowguns— Not to be confused with a kid's peashooter. You don't need poison darts either, at least on small game. A four foot length of half-inch aluminum tubing develops enough velocity with a light dart to give results about like a .22 rifle up to 25 yards or so. This is silent, as accurate as a rifle, and with practice can develop a high rate of sustained fire if you care about that. This weapon is so simple that you can make your own very easily— using half inch tubing and making darts out of lengths of steel (like cut off knitting needles) set into golf tees for bases. Use a mouthpiece of wood or rubber, etc. for your lips to press against. If you prefer to buy one, try Survival Research Company, 71 Ridge Crescent, Manhasset, New York 11030. Another source: the Wham-O Manufacturing Company, 835 E. El Monte Street, San Gabriel, California 91778.

Crossbows— The modern resurgence of interest in regular bows and arrows is well known, but the crossbow has been neglected for some reason. This is strange, since the crossbow is, in its usual form, much more powerful than conventional bows, more accurate (for anyone except experts with the conventional bow) since you do not have to exert muscular effort while aiming the arrow, and considerably easier to learn to use than is the conventional bow. Crossbows with steel bows cut from automobile leaf springs may be made to pull at several hundred pounds, while the conventional hunting type bows seldom run much over fifty. This means that if you are good enough, you can use a heavy crossbow to pot at that deer two hundred yards away or so. Light crossbows may be comfortably set by hand and are sufficient for small to medium game. They are silent and can be nearly as accurate as a hunting rifle within their range, which is nearly as great as that of a firearm in many kinds of terrain.

If you want to make your own crossbow, you might try to locate the "C" volume of the old Popular Mechanics Do-It-Yourself Encyclopedia, which had an excellent article under "Crossbows". This is a fairly complicated job, however, so unless you are a skilled craftsman in wood and metal, you might prefer to buy a crossbow. Wham-O Manufacturing, listed above, sells one in the $30-$40 price range. Another source: George Stevens, Huntsville, Arkansas, or Dave Benedict, 20601 Covello Street, Canoga Park, California. The crossbow is one "primitive" weapon which is efficient enough to be subject to a certain amount of legal restriction— so you might check out your local situation in that regard. Also, some states now have seasons and areas reserved for hunters using bows or crossbows, and if you are a meat hunter this could be important.

William Kirby
Portland, Oregon

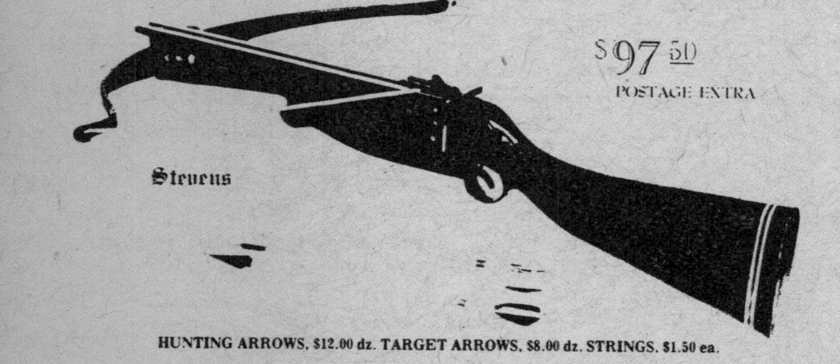

$97.50
POSTAGE EXTRA
Stevens
HUNTING ARROWS, $12.00 dz. TARGET ARROWS, $8.00 dz. STRINGS, $1.50 ea.

Zen and the Art of Archery

A fine excuse to get into either archery or zen.

—SB

Zen and the Art of Archery
Eugene Herrigel

$1.65

from:
Random House
Westminster, Md. 21157

Bow & Arrow

Well, the best book for getting into bow and arrow isn't a book it's a pretty good magazine. The ads will give you all the suppliers (there's scores), and the articles are better than most hobby magazines.

—SB

Bow & Arrow
Jack Lewis, ed.

$3 /yr (bi-monthly)

from:
Bow & Arrow
Covina, CA 91722

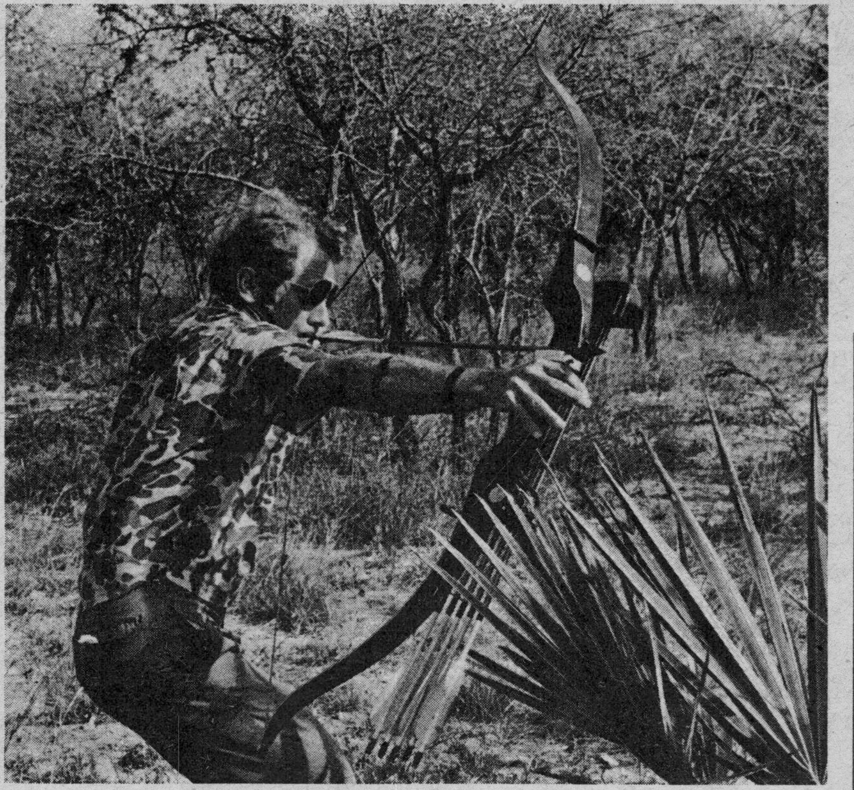

Archer's Bible

This is the catalog of Kittredge Bow Hut supplies. It has some books and kits for making your own bowhunting tackle.

—SB

Archer's Bible

$.50

from:
Kittredge Bow Hut
Box 598
Mammoth Lakes, California 93546

THE AMAZING COMPOUND BOW: The most remarkable new development in bows is an imposing-looking device called the Compound Bow, illustrated here and described fully later on in our bow section. It is just like a regular bow in principle of operation, except that the relatively stiff limbs work together, rather than separately, by means of cables strung around a pulley at the end of each limb. Because these pulleys are eccentric (axle *not in center* of pulley), peak draw weight comes at the *middle* of the draw rather than at the end. In other words, a fifty-pound bow would reach fifty pounds at mid-draw, then *actually decrease to about 38 pounds* at full draw! Result? Well, it's obviously a lot easier to hold thirty-eight pounds instead of fifty pounds. Or, thirty pounds instead of forty. But the significant feature is the blazing, unbelievable arrow speed! The Compound Bow is fifty percent faster than any other bow of comparable weight. A standard, unmodified, fifty-pound Compound Bow shot a legal broadhead nearly a quarter-of-a-mile in a recent National Flight Shoot. And, *you can adjust the draw weight* of a Compound Bow! This bow may very well revolutionize archery—particularly bowhunting, where penetration is so important.

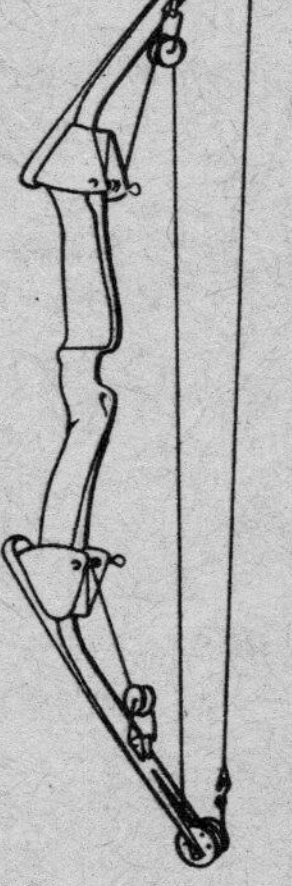

ARROW REST—SIGHT WINDOW—CENTERSHOT DESIGN: In addition to simply supporting the arrow, the arrow rest keeps the arrow away from the shooter's hand, prevents arrow feathers from hitting the shelf, and positions the arrow the same way every shot. Better bows are usually factory-equipped with an arrow rest, even if only a silencing pad of wool felt or leather covering the arrow shelf.

There are many types of arrow rests, but basically they fall into two groupings: those for hunting or all-purpose shooting, and those for serious tournament shooting. The feather rest, made with four or five pieces of feather set vertically and cut to a curved shape, is almost universally popular as a hunting or all-purpose rest. The tournament rests are too numerous to mention, but you'll find one of your choice listed in the Arrow Rest Section of this catalog.

What's wrong with modern archers is that many of them don't know the history of their sport, one of the oldest in the world.

In my collection of bows and arrows which date back to 500 BC, I have an arrow with a bone insert nock of a snap type shape identical with the Bjorn nock, a recent invention which is the favorite of many of today's experts.

I have a broadhead that is three blades with a five-degree taper insert for the shaft. It is made of bronze, and has been authenticated by museum experts as being over 2,500 years old. We rediscovered that five-degree taper, three-bladed broadhead about twenty years ago.

I have one ancient arrow with a superb broadhead. It is one-eighth-inch thick in the center and bevelled to a sharp edge from the center toward the point. It is of hardened steel, three-quarters-inch wide and one and a half inches long. It could not possibly bend if it hit a bone and was probably designed to pierce armor or chain mail. The shaft is a hollow bamboo reed similar to our modern hollow glass or metal shafts.

The twenty-two Oriental bows in my collection are from five hundred to two thousand years old. Their basic design of sinew on the back of a wood or bamboo center, with horn on the belly, dates back about 2,500 to 3,000 years ago, and is much the same as our modern bow except for the materials.

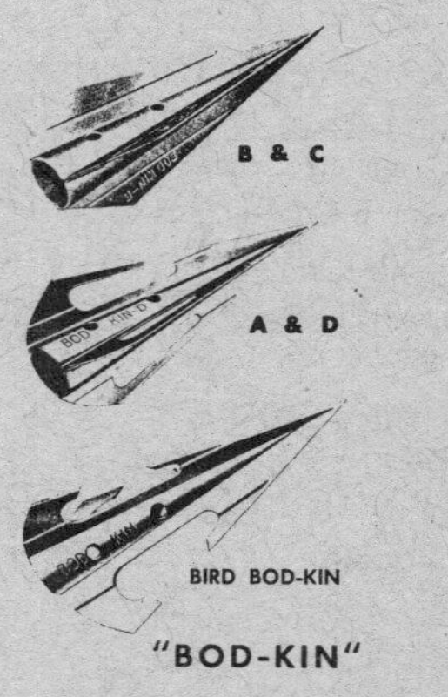

B & C
A & D
BIRD BOD-KIN
"BOD-KIN"

BOD-KIN, MODEL "A"- 3 blade design, rounded corners as illustrated, but without slotted blades. Tool steel, spot welded and furnace brazed. Holes in ferrule for pinning or forming glue rivets. 11/32" x 125 grains.
#RP-404 . . . . . $3.95/doz

BOD-KIN, MODEL "B"- Same as "A", but rear corners of blades cut to sloping angle so it will back out of hay bales when practicing. 11/32" x 112 grains.
#RP-405 . . . . $3.95/doz

BOD-KIN, MODEL "C"- Same as model "B", but 5/16" x 90 grains.
#RP-406 . . . . $3.95/doz

BOD-KIN, MODEL "D"- Same as model "A", but with slotted blades for lightness. 11/32" x 115 grs.
#RP-407 . . . . $3.95/doz

BIRD BODKIN- Designed to cut and rip; hunting small game, birds, etc. 11/32" x 130 grains.
#RP-440 . . . . $4.50/doz

BOOKS

HOW TO MAKE BOWS by Tom Jennings & Doug Kittredge: Contains complete plans and instructions for building the custom ULTRA BOW. A "must" for every bow maker who wants the latest information on building modern laminated fiberglass bows!

#BB-260 HOW TO MAKE BOWS $1.95

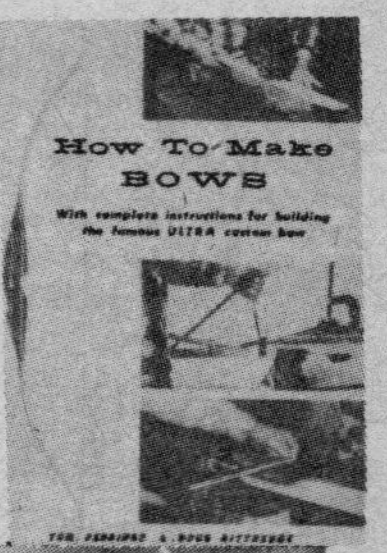

How To Make
BOWS
With complete instructions for building the famous ULTRA custom bow

HOW TO MAKE MODERN ARCHERY TACKLE by Tracy Stalker: Contains infomation about how to make bowstrings, arrows, bows, with a minimum of store bought tools. Only book telling the old way of making wood bows of the "long bow" design.

#BB-700 HOW TO MAKE MODERN ARCHERY TACKLE $1.00

HOW TO MAKE ARROWS by Doug Kittredge: Complete, detailed information on building your own arrows of wood, fiberglass and aluminum. Many tricks and secrets of the trade never before published. Fully illustrated.

#BB-252 HOW TO MAKE ARROWS $ .75

SHIPPING WEIGHT FOR ONE OR ALL BOOKS- 8 oz

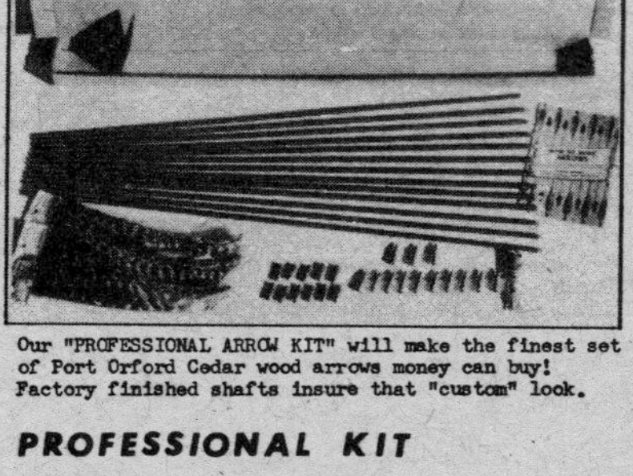

Our "PROFESSIONAL ARROW KIT" will make the finest set of Port Orford Cedar wood arrows money can buy! Factory finished shafts insure that "custom" look.

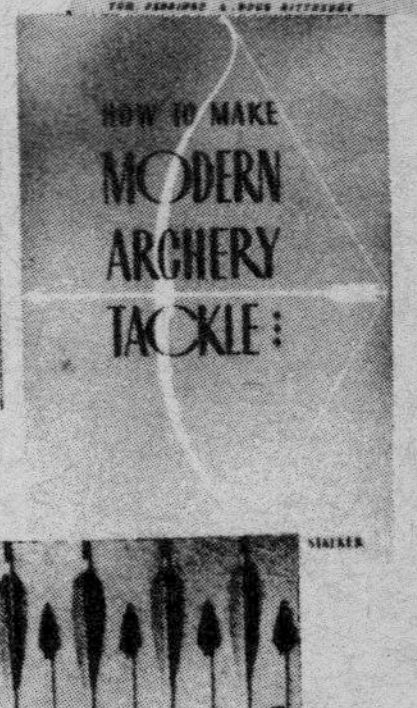

HOW TO MAKE
MODERN
ARCHERY
TACKLE:

PROFESSIONAL KIT

KIT CONTAINS:

13 - #1 MATCHED P.O. CEDAR SHAFTS. Factory finished, 2 coats lacquer, any color: Clear, White, Yellow, Red, Blue, Orange, Green. Nock Taper included.
13 - SPEED NOCKS, your choice of color.
36 - FEATHERS, Die Cut, any color or length
13 - FIELD OR TARGET POINTS, state choice.
1 - FLETCHING AND NOCKING CEMENT
1 - SET OF ARROW NUMBER DECALS, 1 thru 12
1 - INSTRUCTION BOOK: "How To Make Arrows", fully illustrated, complete detailed instruction.

IF BROADHEAD OR TAPER-HOLE FIELD POINTS DESIRED, show head wanted and add cost to arrow kit price, less 80¢

#RK-501 PROFESSIONAL ARROW KIT . . $7.95
White or Dyed White feathers, extra 1.50

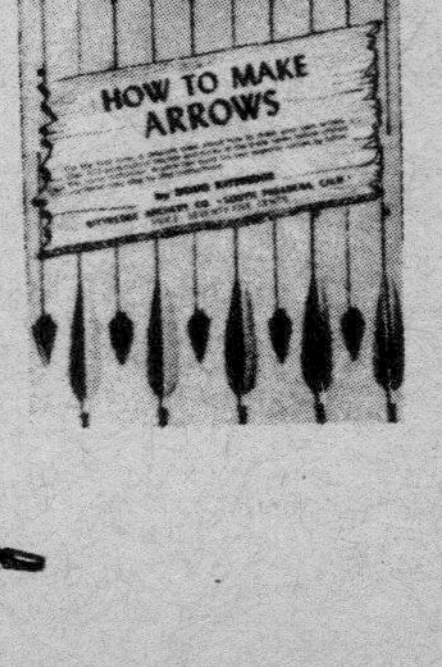

HOW TO MAKE
ARROWS

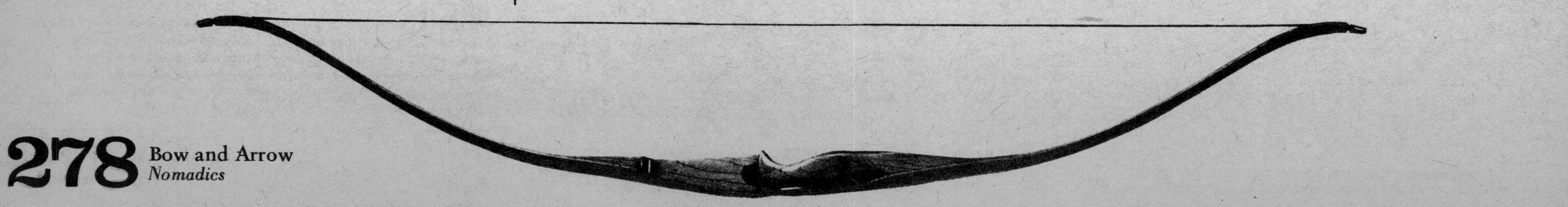

Bowhunting for Deer

A serious technical book. For successful bowhunting you've to to be a lot closer to the deer, in every way. Most states have a long bow & arrow season for deer.

—SB

Bowhunting for Deer
H.R. Wanbold
1964, 1965; 160 pp.

$5.95 postpaid

from:
Stackpole Books
Harrisburg, Pennsylvania 17105

or WHOLE EARTH CATALOG

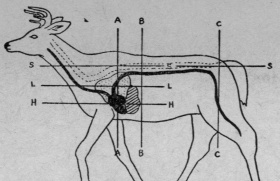

Vital Areas for Point of Aim

The heart and main anterior and posterior arteries, including the femoral artery, are shown in black; the lungs, which extend down over the heart on each side, are shown in dotted area; while the liver, low and behind the heart, is shown in striped area, with the spine shown as the broken line from head to tail.

Vertical line (A) designates the maximum forward deflective line of sighting which puts the arrow in the center of the heart-lung cluster as well as the top exit of the aortic arteries. Hits to the left or forward will strike the shoulder-bone which will prevent penetration. Vertical line (B) designates the maximum deflective line of sighting to the right or rear of line (A), which is about nine inches in distance. A hit between (A) and (B) if low or at cross-hair line (H) will result in either a heart or liver hit. If hit between (A) and (B) center at cross-hair line (L) the hit will be in the rear of the lung lobe. If hit anywhere along cross-hair line (S) between deflective line (A) to (C) the arrow will strike the spine. A hit where (H) and (A) intersect means a dead center heart shot. If the arrow enters where (L) and (A) intersect, the center of the lungs will be hit, and also a possible severance of the posterior aortic artery as well. An arrow that hits in the area of deflective line (C) down through the center of the hind ham will sever the femoral artery. With the exception of the spine hits all the other vital points will produce sufficient hemorrhage to drop the deer within reasonable yardage.

Tools for Field Repairs

A simple kit that will enable you to make minor field repairs can be carried in a small compact container. The tools and other items listed below are sufficient for changing heads, replacing broken or cracked nocks, for wrapping a nocking point on a new string, sharpening broadheads, and repairing damaged fletching.

Quantity	Item
1	Mill file (flat), 1/8-inch, with shank broken off and taped for handling protection
1	Duco cement, tube
1	Ferrule cement, stick
1	Candle stub
1	Pliers, slip-joint style
1	Dispenser, dental floss
6	Pins, common
3	Broadheads, spare
6	Nocks, spare
—	Extra bowstrings

All of the listed items will fit in an ordinary cigar box or in a small metal box of similar size. Such a kit takes very little room in your gear and is very handy in camp.

Just a note of warning. If this early-bird deer happens to be a little fellow, be cautious! Many times such a young deer acts as a sort of scout sent out by the old doe of the group to see if all is clear. If this be the case, this little guy will roam around under the tree and nip an apple or two. Then, after looking around for a while, he will bounce back into the timber. And invariably, if you have not betrayed yourself, the other deer will then step out, one by one, a few minutes later.

The Venison Book

In my experience, getting the deer is the easiest part, if most written about. The rest of the action——butchering, storing, cooking——is the subject of this economical little book. —SB

[Suggested by Barbara Kirschenblatt-Gimblett]

The Venison Book
Audrey Alley Gorton
1957; 78 pp.

$1.95 postpaid

from:
The Stephen Greene Press
120 Main Street
Brattleboro, Vt. 05301

or WHOLE EARTH CATALOG

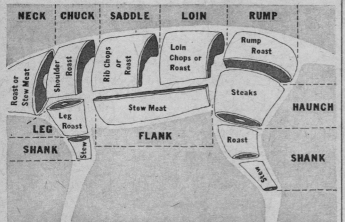

One of the first things some hunters feel obliged to do is to stab or slit the throat to bleed the carcass. This is called "sticking." Consensus among people who have experimented is that this process is entirely unnecessary and, in certain instances, definitely detrimental.

You can use any cut of meat to make "jerky." If you are just trying it on for size, though, you won't be wasting superior meat if you cut your strips from the flank.

Cut the meat *with the grain* into strips 1 inch wide and ½-inch thick. Make them any length you can. Prepare a brine of 6 quarts of water to 2 pounds of salt (the brine should be salty enough to float an egg in its shell). Soak the strips for 2 days in the brine. Remove and wipe dry. Hang the strips of meat in the sun to dry; they may be pinned to the clothesline with spring clips. When they are dry they may be smoked or simply stored as is, in an airy place well protected with netting.

Bear Archery

A glossy catalog of good archery stuff. Seems like everybody up in my part of Michigan likes Fred Bear. The catalog tells what your local dealers should have. Includes bows, arrows, quivers, accessories.

—SB

Catalog free

from:
Bear Archery
Rural Route 1
Grayling, Michigan 49738

7160 Fred Bear Camouflage Make-Up Cream
Kit of three colors. Camouflage your face, hands and bow with Bark Brown, Glade Green or Shadow Black Cream. Applies easily. Cold Cream base. Contains insect repellent.

7138 Bow Cover Camouflage
Two piece cover slips over bow limbs. Does not hamper shooting.

7670 String Peep Sight
Attaches into string; serves as rear sight for perfect alignment. Unbreakable hard vinyl. Weatherproof.

3000 Bear Converta-Bowfishing Rig
Now you can take any Bear bow, from a Take-Down to a Grizzly, fishing. The new Converta fish reel fits right into the accessory insert on all new composite Bear bows (except Bearcat and Little Bear). Outfit comes complete with reel, 50 ft. of 90 lb. test braided Nylon line, fiberglass arrow with harpoon head and instruction booklet.
3005 Same as **3000** except with **3060** easy-off point.

Professional Guide's Manual

If you're eating meat, deerhunting is about the most honest and economical way to go about it. This bargain book from Herter's——amazingly unhysterical for them——has all the information you need to find, shoot, and butcher your deer. It's also chock with tips on fishing, camping, storing stuff, and other sundry.

—SB

[Suggested by Peter Rabbit]

Professional Guide's Manual
George Leonard Herter & Jacques P. Herter
1966; 98 pp.

$.45 postpaid

from:
Herter's, Inc.
Waseca, Minnesota 56093

To use the "Back Carry" method as shown in Figure 10, slit the skin through each hind leg as the illustration shows. Through these slits put the corresponding front legs. Put sharp sticks through the front legs to lock them in place. To get the deer on your back, set the deer up on his rump in a sitting position. Spread the hind legs apart and set between them. Grasp a front leg in each hand, lean backward and swing the deer up on your back. Put both arms through the loops formed by the legs. Now go on your hands and knees and lean forward. Bring up first one foot then the other until you are erect. **Whistle and sing as you carry out the deer when using this method so no one can possibly mistake the deer on your back for a live one.**

Figure 10.

Home Tanning and Leather Making Guide

Best information on tanning we've seen. If you're eating deer or calf or dog or whatever and throwing the skin away, you don't need this book. Meathead.

—SB

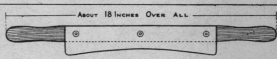

ABOUT 18 INCHES OVER ALL

TWO HANDLED SCUDDING KNIFE
Used like Slicker, curved to fit beam. Brass, copper or slate edge, to avoid rust.

Home Tanning and Leather Making Guide
A. B. Farnham
1950; 176 pp.

$2.00 postpaid

from:
Harding's Books
2878 East Main Street
Columbus, Ohio 43209
or WHOLE EARTH CATALOG

I'm in a coal mine, huddled at the face with no light, it's total black around. I can breathe all right but the air is sulphuric and stale, I have to adjust, grow a kind of gills in my neck, become a kind of fish in order to live this deep underground. It's so dark I believe I don't have eyes any more, until a prick of light comes toward me through the pitch black dark of the mine. It's like foxfire. It's like a spark from two thoughts striking one another. It's like the first star that ever was. Slowly it floats toward me, bearing a promise to bore my forehead like a breast-auger, like a mine drill. Shavings coil out like old memories, and form shapes around the light. They form my father with a carbide lamp on his head, spewing a long, thin flame. They form my mother with a shiny brooch at her throat, and then they become Jesus carrying a candle that becomes a minnow and swims away through the mine's dark river. I can't see it but I hear the river gurgling toward the drift mouth, and I panic trying to decide whether to follow or stay where I am. I huddle against the face of the coal, wondering if my eyes are open or closed. The coal is cold and hard, like a huge black diamond, my face against it, rough and cold. I think of ancient ferns, tall as tipples, a million years ago beneath the sea, fish gliding among the very ferns that have hardened into the coal my face is pressed against. In the midst of the waters I see a firmament arise, a lovely wilderness of plains and valleys and high mountains with low wavy foothills. And there in the side of one of the hills is a wound, bleeding coal that I have cut with my own hands and crawled inside for rest and safety.

NECK | CHUCK | SADDLE | LOIN | RUMP

(beef cuts chart: Neck, Shoulder Roast, Chuck, Rib Chops or Roast, Loin Chops or Roast, Rump Roast, Steaks, Stew Meat, Leg Roast, Flank, Leg, Shank, Haunch, Shank, Roast, Stew)

PROPER RIPPING OPEN CUTS FOR A CORRECT PATTERN
The dotted lines show the path of the knife, and the solid lines show the appearance of the hide when spread out.

Something on Fly Fishing —

by Michael Athay
Rocky Hill, New Jersey

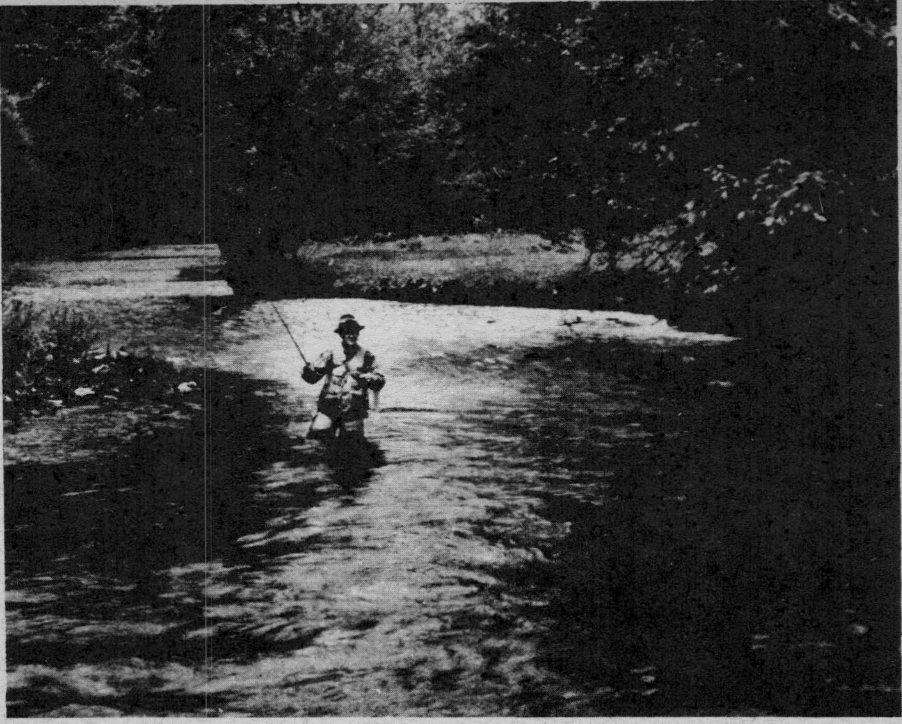

ANGLING: For trout: with artificials.

def.: A trout fly is part fur, feather, floss, tinsel, and sometimes horsehair; secured with black thread (in the jargon, 'tied') to a fishhook in hopes of replicating a bug accurately enough to fool a trout into eating it; and thereby getting caught.

Tyers of trout flies, like their quarry, come in schools. Three predominate (the authority for this classification is myself): (1) the 'exact imitation' school; (2) the 'follow a pattern' school; (3) the 'tie a pretty fly' school. The division is normative. Adherents of school (1) definitely are the elite, because they not only build bugs— they spend hours and hours crawling along muddy river and stream-banks peering at the principles through large magnifying glasses and telephoto lenses. Their object is to find out personally what insects the trout are eating this evening. They want a fur-and-feather copy of the real thing. Entomology first; fill-the-creel later. Pattern followers, on the other hand, are content to turn to pages 88 through 96 of Herter's Professional Fly Tying Manual *(revised condensed edition), where they find explicit instructions for Bumblepuppies, Nymphos, Woodruff Spent Wings, and a few score other standard fish-favorites. This* a priori *method obviously has its disadvantages: A standard fly pattern modelled on the pale watery dun common to Southern England's Chalk Streams may or may not have much to do with the day's hatch on Big Lost River above Mackay, Idaho. As for school (3), well, they just aren't serious fly fishermen. I've known these types to show prodigious technique, but how can you expect to catch real live fish on a green-hackled, purple-bellied absurdity, however 'aesthetic'?*

If I've managed to get you thinking along 'exact imitator' lines, you'll have to know something about 'fly-fishing entomology', as the initiates call it. This is an informal version of what one kind of biologists do— viz., determine, describe, and classify the kinds of bugs fish eat in different seasons and locales. The best book I've seen on the subject is John Goddard's Trout Fly Recognition. *Unfortunately for us, Mr. Goddard is an Englishman who writes about English insects. Even so, a lot of the information is of use to fishermen on this side, especially as a good introduction to insect classifications, techniques of observation, and so on. (More than one author in this area intimates that many of the bugs British fish eat have near or exact counterparts on American streams.) The best thing about Goddard's book is plate after plate of color photographs of the insects he discusses— all of them large enough and detailed enough to serve as models for tying. A little field work, or a visit to your biologist friend, will quickly establish the relevance of this book for the streams you like to fish. Goddard also provides instructions on photographing live insects, and detailed photographs and drawings of insect wings— the hardest part of the fishing fly to reproduce well.*

Several good books on insects common to American streams have been published, but they tend to go in and out of print rather quickly. Ernest G. Schwiebert, Jr's Matching the Hatch *is one sound treatise currently available. Schwiebert describes common trout flies found both in the Eastern and Western parts of the country. This alone makes the book valuable, for most books tend to deal only with East coast streams. He provides classifications of flies according to the approximate season of their appearance, and includes four color plates of drawings of mayflies. The plates are good enough to reproduce flies from.*

The classics of American fly fishing entomology are Preston Jennings A Book of Trout Flies *and Art Flick's* New Streamside Guide to Naturals and Their Imitation. *The first is a handsome hardcover volume, with copious and detailed illustrations of insects. It deals mainly with the East coast. My objection to the Flick book is its diminutive size, poor binding, and (relative to what you get) large price.*

These books will only get you started, though. If you come to take this side of fly fishing seriously, you will have to do your own entomology, for another man's investigations of his favorite streams probably will not apply very exactly to yours. Goddard's book is by far the best model for your own field work.

Pictures of bugs won't tell you how to tie imitations of them. If you are a beginner who wants instructions in the basics, I suggest the Herter's manual afore-mentioned (available, of course, from Herter's Inc., for a mere 89 cents in the condensed version— which is all you need) and J. Edson Leonard's Flies. *Herter's gives you the basics, with George L.'s usual remarks about the impossibility of doing it any other way, plus a list of patterns. Leonard's book is very detailed and complete (340 pp.), including chapters on hook design (you will be surprised how many sorts of eye, point, shank, and shape are to be found in the common fishhook), tools, and materials, as well as construction. He gives good tips on tying technique which you won't find in the Herter's manual. His dictionary of fly patterns runs some 80 pages and could keep you tying for decades. He also includes a 50-odd page chapter on entomology which serves as an adequate introduction. If you want just one book on fly tying, this is it.*

I can't imagine anyone wanting more patterns than Leonard lists, but if you do, a series of books by Britisher W. H. Lawrie certainly should suffice. Most notable is his Reference Book of English Trout Flies, *and his* International Trout Flies *(which includes some American patterns). Both are published in England, but should be available through Blackwells. The predominance of British bugs does not make them irrelevant, assuming you've given up becoming an amateur entomologist, because most of the standard patterns you find in the local tackle shop are of British origin anyway.*

Let's suppose you've done your field work on the native insects, become a master at tying technique, and stocked up on as many of the standard patterns as you can use for the next three seasons. You're all ready to go out and catch a limit, but you don't know how to cast a fly. Well, there's a book for this too. Indeed, a legion of them. I recommend just one, however, because it is excellent: The Angler's Cast, *by Capt. T.L. Edwards and E. Horsfall Turner. This book has more information on every kind of fishing rod casting — bait, spinning, ocean, etc., as well as fly casting— than you can possibly remember. The authors discuss everything from physical theory of rod action to the kind of tackle you ought to buy. The account of fly casting is detailed and pleasingly undogmatic— you needn't conform to any ideal casting patterns in order to catch fish— if a bit wordy. Pictures and diagrams show you how to do what the text tells you.*

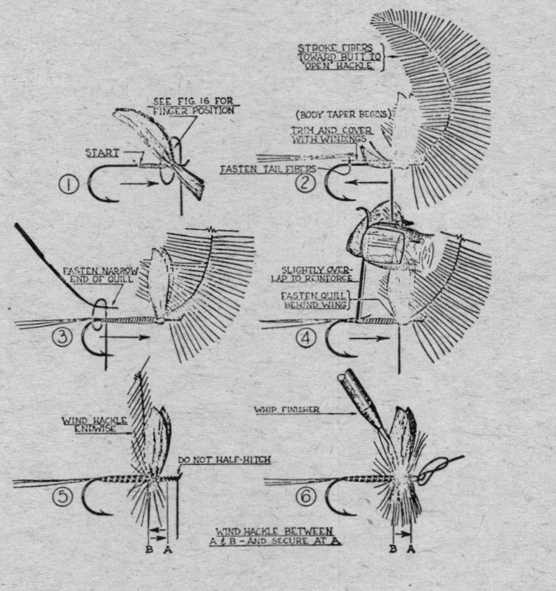

Source for fly tying tools and supplies: Herter's Inc., Waseca, Minnesota.

Books mentioned in the review:

Goddard, Trout Fly Recognition, *pub. A & C Black, London, 1966. Hardcover, available from Blackwells.*

Leonard, Flies, *A.S. Barnes & Co., New York, 1950, hardcover.*

Herter, G.L., Professional Fly Tying Manual, *(revised, condensed edition) available from Herter's Inc., Waseca, Minn.*

Edwards & Turner, The Angler's Cast, *pub. Jenkins, London, 1960; hard cover, available from Blackwells.*

Jennings, A Book of Trout Flies, *new ed. by Crown Publishers, 1970, hardcover.*

Schweibert, Matching the Hatch, *Macmillan Co., N.Y., 1955, hardcover.*

Flick, New Streamside Guide to Naturals and Their Imitation, *Crown Publishers, hardcover.*

Lawrie, W. H., Reference Book of English Trout Flies, *pub. Pelham Books (British), 1967*

Lawrie, W.H., International Trout Flies.

Spin Fishing

I'm a nut on survival and this spinning reel gadget is a beauty. Called a handline spinning reel it's a hard plastic, 6" diameter like a wheel. You hold the thing with one hand, and lariet fashion, cast with the other. The line spins off the reel as on a regular open faced spinning reel, but since this handline reel is 6" in diameter compared to 2" or 3" of a fresh or salt water reel, the line spins off faster, with less fouling, and also the retrieve is much faster. Naturally there is a lot against handline fishing. No rod to play the fish and to take the punishment the fish gives out. The pull is directly on the line and not on the rod so the line must be stronger. But I'm talking now about a cheap rig to carry anyplace with you and one that will land all kinds of fish. I've had more fun with the thing than any rod and reel combination.

As you know spin fishing (where the fish line pays off the face of the spool instead of the reel) is a very old way of fishing. Even before the invention of the bottle or can, indians fished in the spin off style using a kind of wooden shuttle. People throughout the world spin fish off bottles and cans. In Mexico it's called the Dos Equies reel after that famous dark beer. In Australia they use handline spinning reels similar to this Boone Bait Co product in three sizes going from a five inch to a ten inch. I bought one of these in Trinidad as Trinidad imports from Australia. The word on this Boone reel is that years ago the Japanese dropped off such a reel in the West Indies. The Cubans then got onto the thing and it made its way through Key West and now to Winter Park.

I like to use 25 lb monofilament line on mine although you can use from 15 to 50 lb. Fill it up (25 lb test will take about 300 yards) to within a half inch of the flange, whirl the lure along side or around your head and cast. Retrieve smoothly or in short bumps.

I'm speaking now of lure fishing. With lead and bait of course you just let it lie in position until you feel the nibble-strike. As I say I'm hung up on survival but I'm also a purist about fishing. I never use bait, only lures, and only single hooked lures, perhaps a spoon or two, but I prefer jigs. Leadheaded jigs. My favorites are: 1. The Bill Upperman bucktails. 2. The chrome headed Japanese feather jigs.

Ten years ago off a beach just north of Puerto Vallarta I was casting a Japanese white feather jig off a "Dos Equis" reel and picking up a channel bass or two and snook. But it was hot and I had already drank the beer in order to use the reel and so I took to the sea, carrying my beer can reel and line and lure with me. Thus began the most pleasure I've ever had. I call it Swim Fishing. Now these days I take the Boone reel out with me, 25 lb test mono on it, and a bucktail (¼ oz) on the end. Off the beaches in Santa Monica Bay I've caught halibut, skip jack tuna, small blue shark, leopard shark, bonito, mackeral, sand bass, calico bass, white sea bass. . .

For bottom feeders I merely kick (using swim fins) along slowly and let the lure bounce off the bottom. For bonito, etc, I swim flat out, holding the reel in one hand and in this way giving the jig action with each stroke. When the water is clear and in the kelp beds of Point Dume or Laguna Beach I wear a face plate and snorkel, dive and look for the fish. I've been in a salad of kelp and into a school of calico and placed my yellow Upperman right on the table of sand before them. Letting out line I kick to the surface. Then yoyo the lure. Wham, a strike.
I've caught great barracuda and mangrove snapper in the Bahamas, snook in Trinidad, Pompano in Cozumel and the Virgin Islands, Ulua in Hawaii and the Tuamotus, flounder off Hong Kong, jack in the Phillippines, and once I foul hooked a two ton Manta Ray off Yelapa, Mexico.

The beauty with swim fishing is that you swim the water the boats can't work. You also work ten times the water that a surf fisherman can because you present your lure parallel to shore, fishing it all the way. One of my finest experiences swim fishing was when a surf was running off Ft Lauderdale, Florida. I had my lure out behind me, resting on the bottom. I held onto my Boone reel. Here comes a wave. I body surfed it in and on the way got a big strike. I rode the wave to shore and reeled in a three pound Jack Crevalle.

Available for $2.00 plus 50¢ for shipping from Handline Spinning Reel, Boone Bait Co., Inc., Box 571, Forsyth Road, Winter Park, Fla. 32790

I've got another good gimmick for you. You ought to check it out. You can't buy it in retail stores, and I don't know why. I've never seen it for sale, always send to the source for mine. Over the past ten years I've had four of them and they are by far the best and cheapest barbq outfit on the market.

OLD SMOKEY. Looks like two galvanized tin pails sitting mouth on top of mouth. Hot smoke oven (better than that expensive but chic Japanese cooker) with two drafts for control (as good if not better than Weber and much cheaper).

I use ours for everything. No burn. No flare ups. If fat on meat does flare, just close drafts somewhat. I cook whole turkeys and chickens. Set them on lemon slices in foil boat and on grill and pop on cover and leave. No turning. Baste some. No spits needed. Sometimes I use wet smoke chips. Fabulous for salmon which I have cooked whole or in steaks. I've got both size Smokey's but use the No. 14 (14 inch diameter) more often.

OLD SMOKEY, Burkhead Mfg Co, 1920 Harrington, PO Box 4, Houston, Texas 77001

No. 14 is $9.95, No. 18 is $14.95. No shipping charges.

Ben Masselink
Pacific Palisades, CA

Spear Fishing

For $125 I have been feeding our entire community of eleven adults and four children. $125 will buy you an entire spear fishing outfit at Steeles (Telegraph, Oakland). For vegetables, flour, dope and whiskey I trade my surplus. To learn, find somebody who is an expert diver and apprentice yourself. I'm available for advice.

Alan Graham
Caspar, CA

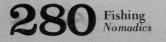

Orvis

I remember my dad's Orvis fly rod. Beautiful, flawless casts with no effort (when he'd let me use it). Bamboo plus engineering craftsmanship puts anything else to shame as far as flyrods go. Orvis also offers a good line of trout, salmon & bass fishing gear some moderately some expensively priced.

[Reviewed by Mike Goslow.
Suggested by R. Davis]

Plus very nifty and very expensive outdoor stuff.

—SB

Catalog

free

from:
The Orvis Co., Inc.
Manchester, Vermont 05254

Chase Fly Tyer's Bobbin

This one is cheerful red plastic. Keeps tension on the spool. A loose spool can slip away awfully suddenly.
T1436—(Min.) $3.50

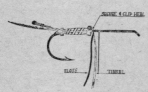

Basic Fly Tying

If it's not too late, I am sending a copy of a "book" that I produced which has had good acceptance while I was selling it through Abercombie & Fitch in San Francisco. This was a couple of years ago and they no longer have the claim to exclusive distribution.

I would like to offer my humble work, which in its original state (this is a xerox copy and a poor one at that) is a series of pen & ink sketchings on parchment. If your people and readers are interested I will be glad to mail them a copy for whatever they consider righteous.

This is a fascinating hobby and I have devoted many years to perfecting my techniques. I also want to share this with others. Thank you.

Dick B. Miller Jr.
674 Jackson Street E
Monmouth, Oregon 97361

It's a good little book. Send him some money with your request.

—SB

Fish Catalogs

I list below some sources I have not seen in your catalogues, although you may know of them. The items are all in the area of fish-catching, tying flies etc. I recommend them all highly.

Reed Tackle
Box 390
Caldwell, New Jersey 07006 (catalogue available)

Tully's (fly tying methods & materials)
Box 176
Bellwood, Illinois 60104 (catalogue available)

(If you need flourescent mallard plumage, chenille feathers, nordi hackles, Amherst pheasant tippets or skunk tails your quest is over)

E. Hille, the anglers supply house
815 Railway Street
Williamsport, Pa. 17701 (catalogue available)

(this outfit is the quintessence of every piscatorian's hidden—although not without guilt—desires. They start with Dubby Argus tail quills, continue through Baikal teal feathers and startle even the most professedly liberal with their Jungle kock plumes. From their catalogue "As an added attraction to fish, eyed jungle kock feathers are extensively used on streamers and wing pads of nymphs." E. Hille's also carries all other items to make the complete fisherman look like he knows what he is doing.)

Ross McLord Miller
Okemos, Michigan

Netcraft

Swivels, sinkers, spinner blades, bodies & hooks for making your own lures, some good prices on rods & reels. Equipment for most fresh water fishing. Fantastic offering of plastic worms.

[Reviewed by Mike Goslow]

TROUT NET

Catalog

free

from:
Netcraft Fishing Tackle
3101 Sylvania
Toledo, Ohio 43613

FLOATING TROUT NET — $1.95

Madison Bamboo Fly Rod Kit

Madison Kit complete, including poplin sack and aluminum rod case (4 lbs.) **$80.00**
Extra Tip Section, ferrule & tip top mounted (4 lbs.) **$34.00**

Cabela's

Another catalog worth looking at, for outdoor as well as fishing equipment.

—SB

Cabela's Inc.
812 13th Ave.
Sidney, Nebraska 69162

Introduction to Caving

Make your heroic journey to the underworld. Return to tell about it. This intro has an annotated bibliography if you get to liking that kind of adventure.

—SB

Introduction to Caving
John Thrailkill
1962; 30 pp.

$1.00 postpaid

from:
Alpine Rec.
Box 54
Mount Vernon, N. Y. 10552

INTRODUCTION
TO CAVING

It is quite an experience to visit a cave that is heavily decorated with speleothems, and it is quite a temptation to remove just one or two small ones as mementos of the trip. Surely, you think with all these stalactites no one will ever miss just one or two. Obviously you are right, no one will ever miss just one or two. But after a hundred people have removed just one or two, the loss of one or two hundred is all too apparent. Something beautiful has been destroyed. Utterly destroyed, for it will take many lifetimes for even the smaller stalactites to be replaced.

Falling rocks are one of the greatest hazards of spelunking. For this reason, hard hats should always be worn in caves where there is any climbing to be done. A falling pebble can be a murderous weapon, and extreme care should be taken to avoid dislodging loose rocks if there are people below. It is obvious that boulder piles should be treated gently, since they are often precariously stacked and a slide could prove disastrous to persons on and below them.

THE EIGHTH FATIGUE

There is space, but no time. There is distance, but no direction. And both space and distance are riddled with twisting shafts and caverns underground. There is endurance, but no duration. D.R. can say, I am here, but he cannot say where, and he cannot say for how long either, for that would place it in time and where he is there is no time. There is only endurance to move by, there are only fatigues to measure by, and he is eight fatigues inside the earth in a narrow, vertical shaft no larger than a hand-dug well.

The first fatigue was lined with rails and posts along the sides, and now and then a roof-bolt in the ceiling. The rails were gone by the second fatigue. The shaft dipped low to a widening curve which curved again and further on it curved and curved again. The third fatigue was when the shaft divided. Two tunnels opened off the shaft that he'd just crawled through, and a little way inside of one it divided yet again. But one of these divisions was closed off by a slate fall near its portal, and the other narrowed to a point so small D.R.'s folded hands would not pass through. D.R. backed out and probed the second tunnel. It's floor was ice-cold water that seeped above his ankles and reached up for his knees. D.R. waded blind a full fatigue, the fourth one, until the water deepened at the entrance to a chamber divided into rooms by so many pillars D.R. was quickly lost among their maze. Clinging to the rocks like a salamander, his lower body swimming through the water, he felt along the ledges of the rooms. When he could find no exits up above he dived deep into the blackness feeling for an opening in the bottom of the walls. On his third dive he found space enough to flow through, and he swam into another, stranger dark: the fifth fatigue. He could stand there. He felt the water level falling down his body to his toes as he walked out on higher, drier ground. He was going up, but not as direction, for there is no time where D.R. is, and no direction. It was up as shape, configuration, rising in the mine. There were no holds or ledges in the sixth fatigue, but once into the seventh the ascent became a gradual ramp of stone, the walls beside it coarse, like sandstone, and porous, with wind blowing through the larger holes. D.R. put his arms into the holes, he felt them out to see if they were shafts he should explore. But none were large enough for him to crawl through and he continued up the ramp the seventh and then half the eighth fatigue.

Pole, Paddle & Portage

This is the authoritative book on canoes and canoe-tripping. I paddled northern Wisconsin lakes and rivers for six summers without learning a fraction of the useful information here.

—SB

Pole, Paddle & Portage
Bill Riviere
1969; 255 pp.

$3.95 postpaid

from:
Little, Brown & Co., Inc.
200 West Street
Waltham, MA 02154

or WHOLE EARTH CATALOG

Pole, Paddle & Portage

A Complete Guide to Canoeing

By Bill Riviere

A Maine Guide

B Sugar Island

C Beavertail

Figure 18   (A) *Maine Guide blade;* (B) *Sugar Island blade;* (C) *Beavertail blade.*

Canoeing

The American Red Cross has instructions on how to make a birchbark canoe. No wonder they got into teaching lifesaving. The book has one hell of a lot of canoe information for $1.25.

—SB

Canoeing
American National Red Cross
1956; 445 pp.

OUT OF PRINT

from:
Doubleday & Co., Inc.
501 Franklin Ave.
Garden City, L.I., N.Y. 11530

or WHOLE EARTH CATALOG

One of the most frequent questions is, "How big a canoe shall I buy?" There is only one answer . . . the biggest one you can lift gracefully.

Dozens of uses are found for the rope: tying gear into the canoe, guying the tent against a stiff blow, rigging a clothes line, lining the craft through turbulent pitch, hanging food supplies out of reach of hungry critters, tying packs for portaging and emergency towing——to name only a few.

The Yukon's canoe routes are long and remote. With the reduction of commercial river traffic——most of this now going over the highways——the rivers are once more deserted. Waters in the Yukon average about 50 degrees even during a hot summer; lakes may not be ice-free until the middle of June and freezing temperatures and snow can be expected by the first of September. The rivers are large, supply points are few and far between. A canoe cruise should, therefore, include at least two, preferably three craft. Early September sees grizzlies feeding on salmon in the shallows so that the Department of Travel suggests that a rifle be carried during this period, *to be used only in emergency. . . .*

There are compensations for the difficulties, though. From Whitehorse to Dawson City, via the Yukon River, there are no portages during the 450-mile run and the river gradient is only 1 foot per mile! Since this is a former route of the majestic sternwheel steamers, there is available a published log of the river between Whitehorse and the Tanana River (see Appendix).

Because the flat surface of the paddle blades rest on the shoulders, this type of yoke is one of the most comfortable. Photo by Eleanor Riviere.

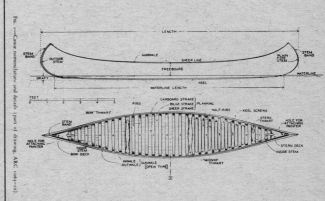

Bark Canoes and Skin Boats

Design and construction details for all native American boats. Compleat.

—SB

The Bark Canoes and Skin Boats of North America
Edwin Tappan Adney and Howard I. Chappelle
Smithsonian Institution, USNM Bulletin No. 230

$6.75 postpaid

from:
Superintendent of Documents
U.S. Government Printing Office
Washington, D.C. 20402

or WHOLE EARTH CATALOG

FIG. 6—When running rapids solo it is advisable to take a position at or near amidships as shown. This permits shallowest draft, maximum maneuverability, and maximum rise and fall of the ends of the canoe as the waves work on it. The latter is important in keeping out water when waves are large.

FIG. 8—Outrigger dugout of the Papuans of New Guinea represents types found among many islands of the Pacific Ocean. The cloth canopy protects from the hot tropical sun. The platform is built on a very narrow hull and the outrigger provides stability. (Photograph by Ewing Galloway, New York)

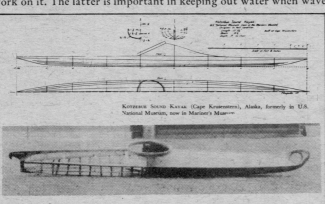

KOTZEBUE SOUND KAYAK (Cape Krusenstern), Alaska, formerly in U.S. National Museum, now in Mariner's Museum

A White Water Handbook for Canoe and Kayak

That's what it is.

White Water Handbook for Canoe and Kayak
John T. Urban
1969; 76 pp.

$1.50 postpaid

from:
Appalachian Mountain Club
5 Joy Street
Boston, Mass. 02108

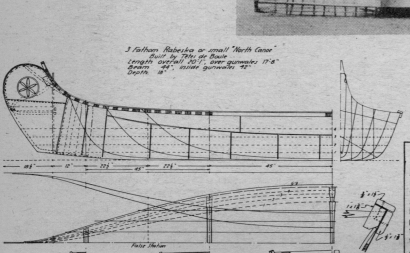

3 Fathom Rabeska or small "North Canoe"
Built by 78ter de Boule
Length overall 20'-1", over gunwales 17'-8"
Beam   44", inside gunwales 42"
Depth   18"

Eskimo roll. Apart from the direct satisfaction that it brings, mastering the roll has some specific and important benefits. Since you can cheerfully court an upset when practicing bracing strokes and crossing currents, your practice and subsequent style will not be cramped through fear of capsizing; your ability to use the paddle for balance in rough water will be much enhanced; and finally, you will be able to recover from at least some upsets on the river.

Rolling is not the rare feat it was once thought to be. In a well-designed kayak little strength is required for a properly executed roll, and some experts can roll without a paddle using two hands alone, and in some cases, only one hand.

An eddy turn below a midstream boulder, followed by a turn downstream into the current on the opposite side.

Fig. 14.

Birchbark canoes, good price

Birchbark canoes, good price

I build birchbark canoes of the Malecite Indian type so described in the book, "Bark Canoes and Skin Boats of North America." These canoes are entirely hand made using the axe, crooked knife, and awl. The woodwork is white cedar except for the thwarts, which are ash or birch. The cover is white birchbark sewn with pine root and the gunnels are root lashed and pegged. All wooden structural parts have been split from the log and shaped with the crooked knife. The canoes average about $800. for a 14', and I am usually back-ordered a couple of years.

In addition, I make fur trade canoes in lengths from 20' to 37' in various styles. 24' is $3000.

Paddles are Malecite style in cedar or birch. Birch paddles have incised line decoration on the blade and grip. Cedar paddles are $35., birch $55. Lead inlay $15. extra. There is no waiting time on paddles.

Lastly, I sell crooked knives with either a straight or a curved blade. Crooked knives are $15. Lead inlay $5. extra.

Sincerely,
Henri Vallancourt
Mill Street Box 199
Greenville, N.H. 03048

Old Town

A famous reliable traditional canoe-maker with a sporty line these days. Wood and fiberglass. Canoes and kayaks. Also a special brochure on the Eskimo roll. —SB

Catalog

free

from:
Old Town Canoe Company
Old Town, Maine 04468

Scuba diving from a 16' F. G. Canoe $385

Chicagoland Canoe Base

A good line of canoes, including Canadien fiberglass, Max Anderson mahogany, and accessories. They've been trying to teach the Midwest that they had a canoe tradition 150 years before their first covered wagon. —SB
[Suggested by Ralph C. Dougherty]

Chicagoland Canoe Base
4019 N. Narragansett Ave.
Chicago, Ill. 60634

Grumman Canoes

Generally considered the best aluminum canoe on the market. Costs about $50-$75 more than other makes but workmanship is far superior. It's well worth the price if you intend to use the boat heavily. Very durable; I got mine at a discount after it had been blown down a wooded hill during a tornado and it was fine after I pounded out the dents. Can be equipped with a sail which you can buy complete at considerable expense or buy the basic parts and make the rest yourself. Grumman sends along a complete list of franchised dealers in your states; it's wise to check with several before buying as reductions from the list price are not uncommon.

[Reviewed by Phil Schrodt]

Grumman Boats
Grumman Allied Industries, Inc.
General Sales Office
Marathon, N.Y. 13803

GRUMMAN CARRYING YOKE— Clamps to gunwales over center thwart. Two cushioned pads, scientifically spaced and positioned to rest easily on shoulders, make portaging light and comfortable. Catalog #905

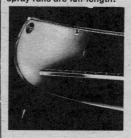

SPRAY RAIL All Grumman square-stern canoe models and the Sportcanoe™ are equipped with scientifically designed spray rails for driest operation with outboards or sailing. All Grumman spray rails are full-length!

CANOE KEEL Heavy extrusion, heat-treated, full-length keel and keelson sandwich type construction. Neoprene seal with close-spaced rivets on ⅝" centers. Built-in clips for mast step and floorboards. Easy installation of accessories and positive watertight seal.

18' Guide Special

Specifications: Guide Special Model Canoe. Wood-canvas construction. Available with reinforced plastic in place of canvas — $30.00 extra, about same weight. Stock color: Dark Green.

Length	Width	Height Bow	Depth	Wt.	Packed Wt.	Price
16'	35"	20½"	12"	70 lbs.	100 lbs.	$700.00
18'	37"	23"	12"	85 lbs.	110 lbs.	$740.00
20'	39"	23½"	13¼"	100 lbs.	135 lbs.	$820.00

	MANITOU	REGATTA
Length	16'	16'
Beam	32"	30"
Depth	12'	12"
Weight	85 lbs	85 lbs
Price	$600 FOB Chicago	$325 FOB Chicago

Quicksilver Canoe & Kayak Kits

Build it all winter. Put it in the stream when the ice breaks up. Paddle to the sea.

—SB

Quicksilver Canoes
115 McGavock Pike
Nashville, Tenn. 37214

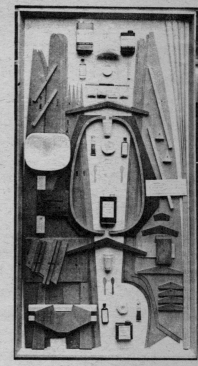

KAYEL-OTTER KIT $70
Absolutely Complete

Kit: $80

KAYEL-OTTER CANADIAN

KAYEL-OTTER SPORTS SINGLE
A 33 pound beauty.

Price
$250.00

THE SAND ROOM

He is in the well, inching down, supported by his back and feet pressing into opposite walls. His legs are aching terribly, sharp protrusions gouge deep furrows in his back, but there is no way he can reverse and climb back out again. He can't stop himself from slipping down. Every time he presses hard enough to stabilize his thighs swell with cramps and make him shift his feet around, which drop him down another inch or two. Once when he released a foot to shift he lost all control and fell scraping several feet before he caught himself again. Down. Sliding down, lowering through the tight, round passageway, pain all through his legs and back, inch by inch along the jagged walls behind him . . . disappear . . . falling falling free through empty air!

(continued)

Klepper

Klepper is the best of the folding boats and kayaks.

—SB

[Suggested by Dee Scarmon]

Catalog

free

from:
Hans Klepper Corp.
35 Union Square West
New York, N. Y. 10003

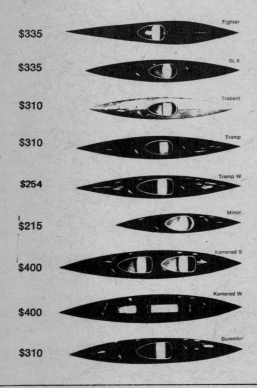

$335	Fighter
$335	SL 8
$310	Trabant
$310	Tramp
$254	Tramp W
$215	Minor
$400	Kamerad S
$400	Kamerad W
$310	Bummler

"Blauwal" $440

Texas Dory

Texas Dory Boat Plans Catalogue, by Capt. Jim Orrell. $5.00, I think, from Texas Dory Boat Plans, Box 720, Galveston, Texas 77550

A catalogue with illustrations and line drawings of plans for boats 15 to 45 feet, sail, outboard or inboard. Plans cost $10 to $15 but by careful drafting you could make your own from the line drawings.

By following one of these plans even you and I can build a strong, seaworthy boat of plywood for less than it should cost to power it. These designs are mostly modifications of the traditional dory workboat. The angular shapes make for relatively easy boatbuilding. You need a skill-saw, mitre box, a copy of Stewart's *Small Boat Construction*, a whole mess of clamps and a place to do it. I used my living room.

Tom Tarr
North Vancouver, B.C.
CANADA

Cheaper Inflatables

A suggestion. Avon makes the best inflatable rubber boats (see page 114, Spring 1970) but they are way over-priced. Recommend best buy for the money are WFR rafts (price: 4 man-$60, 6 man—$80.) Good solid construction— neoprene coated canvas as opposed to the rubber coated nylon (marketed by Sears and Wards) which is less rigid, more suseptible to tears and slippery when wet. WFR rafts are available from: Lee's Outdoor Stores, 37 West St., Annapolis, Md 21401 (phone 301-269-0600). Rafts don't have an inflatable internal cross member, but if added support is needed for white water work, a medium large inner tube works fine (on your lunch break, take the inner tube out of the boat, walk up stream and float by your friends in grand style.)

A recommendation for anyone that lives between Albany and Washington: the Youghiogheny River. One of the best stretches of white water on the East Coast. Start at Ohiopyle, Pa (20 miles east of Uniontown on U.S. 40, then 10 miles north on pa. No. 381) and get about 10 miles of great river. (Ask anyone in Ohiopyle where "they take the rafts out" and you'll get directions where to leave your second car down-river)

For the less-than-experienced, Lance and Lee Martin take groups (or individuals) down the same stretch. For about $10 a head, you get a raft, a good lunch, expert guides, and real wet. Even for the experienced, not a bad idea just to learn the river. Call Wilderness Voyageurs, 412-329-4752 (Lance's mother-in-law usually answers the phone.)

Warmest Regards,
David Abrahamson
Harwood, Maryland

British Seagull

The Seagull outboard is designed to give power rather than speed. We've used it on our 23' Ketch for both harbors and long distance and it's equally good at both. The operating manual says, "The Seagull is a pure-bred marine engine, for a hard life on saltwater... a plain, functional motor with an exceptional performance, & unlimited life requiring the simplest of maintenance at the lowest possible cost." We're being rapidly convinced that the Seagull is one thing that actually gives you what you pay for plus a little more.

[Suggested and reviewed by Judith Sawyer]

2 h.p. 'featherweight' $180
3 h.p. 'forty plus' $195
5 h.p. 'silver century' $265
6+ h.p. 'silver century plus' $305

British Seagull Co. Ltd.
Poole, Dorset
England

Seagull Marine
1851 McGau Ave.
Irvine, CA 92705

and various U.S. Distributors such as:

Inland Marine Co.
79 E. Jackson St.
Wilkes-Barre, Pa. 18701

Imtra Corp.
151 Mystic Ave.
Medford, MA 02115

The Boat Locker
1375 E. State St.
Westport, Conn. 06880

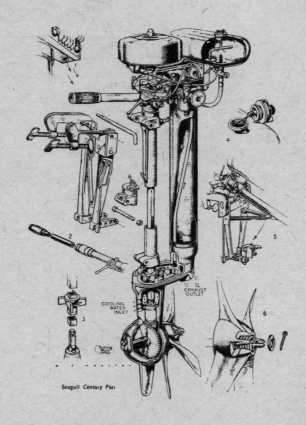

Seagull Century Plus

Avon

Avon is the best of the inflatable boats. Also an excellent liferaft kit.

—SB
[Suggested by Vaughn Greene]

Catalog

free

from:
Seagull Marine Sales
1851 McGau Ave.
Irvine, CA 92705

Inland Marine Co.
79 East Jackson Street
Wilkes-Barre, PA 18701

The Imtra Corp.
151 Mystic Avenue
Medford, Mass. 02155

$415

Pirelli Inflatables

Another high-rent inflatable. Italiano gorgeous.

—SB
[Suggested by Brooks Tenney]

Centro Pirelli
20100 Milano
Italy

$500

Water Charts

If you're travelling on the water, you're going to need something more than an Esso roadmap to tell you where you are. For United States waters the best charts (the only ones, really. All the others say something like "refer to the appropriate C & GS chart for navigation data") are the ones issued by various government agencies.

Where to get the charts depends upon where you want to go. Charts of the Atlantic, Pacific, and Gulf Coasts, and the Intra-coastal Waterway come from the Coast and Geodetic Survey. The Mississippi River and its tributaries are on Army Corps of Engineers charts, and the Great Lakes are handled by the Lake Survey.

Cost of individual charts varies, most run about a dollar or two, except for the rivers, which come in books. The Missouri River, for instance, comes in two parts and costs $2.00 a book.

Index maps for the lakes and coasts are free from the appropriate agency. It's easier for the rivers——you tell the Corps which river you want, and they sell you the whole book.

Charts are frequently revised, and you should be using a current one, because the changes can sometimes be big ones. Catalogs are available free from:

Director, Coast & Geodetic Survey
E. S. S. A. Washington Science Center
Rockville, Maryland 20852

Lake Survey Center—NOS
630 Federal Building and U.S. Court House
Detroit, Michigan 48226

There's no central source for river charts. Appended list is where each can be gotten.

Nautical charts of foreign countries are issued by the U. S. Naval Hydrographic Office, Washington, D. C. 20390. Write to them about a catalog.

John M. Ross
St. Louis, Mo.

Upper Mississippi River

District Engineer
U.S. Army Engr. Dist., St. Paul
1217 U. S. P. O. & Customhouse
St. Paul, Minnesota 55101

District Engineer
U.S. Army Engr. Dist., Rock Island
Clock Tower Building
Rock Island, Illinois 61202

District Engineer
U.S. Army Engr. Dist., St. Louis
906 Olive Street
St. Louis, Missouri 63101

Lower Mississippi River

District Engineer
U.S. Army Engr. Dist., Memphis
668 Federal Office Building
Memphis, Tennessee 38103

District Engineer
U.S. Army Engr. Dist., Vicksburg
P. O. Box 60
Vicksburg, Mississippi, 39180

District Engineer
U.S. Army Engr. Dist., New Orleans
Foot of Prytania Street
New Orleans, Louisiana

Illinois Waterway

District Engineer
U.S. Army Engr. Dist., Chicago
219 South Dearborn Street
Chicago, Illinois 60604

District Engineer
U.S. Army Engr. Dist., St. Louis
906 Olive Street
St. Louis, Missouri 63101

Missouri River

District Engineer
U.S. Army Engr. Dist., Omaha
6012 U. S. P. O. & Court House
Omaha, Nebraska 68102

District Engineer
U.S. Army Engr. Dist., Kansas City
1800 Federal Office Building
Kansas City, Missouri 64106

Kanawha River

District Engineer
U.S. Army Engr. Dist., Huntington
502 8th Street
Huntington, West Virginia 25721

Ohio River

District Engineer
U.S. Army Engr. Dist., Pittsburgh
Federal Building
1000 Liberty Avenue
Pittsburgh, Pennsylvania

District Engineer
U.S. Army Engr. Dist., Huntington
502 8th Street
Huntington, West Virginia 25721

District Engineer
U.S. Army Engr. Dist., Louisville
830 West Broadway
Louisville, Kentucky 40201

Green River

District Engineer
U.S. Army Engr. Dist., Louisville
830 West Broadway
Louisville, Kentucky 40201

Allegheny & Monongahela Rivers

District Engineer
U.S. Army Engr. Dist., Pittsburgh
Federal Building
1000 Liberty Avenue
Pittsburgh, Pennsylvania 15222

Tennessee, Cumberland, Little, Clinch, Emory & Hiwasse Rivers

District Engineer
U.S. Army Engr. Dist., Nashville
P. O. Box 1070
Nashville, Tennessee 37202

Other

District Engineer
U.S. Army Engr. Dist., Little Rock
P. O. Box 867
Little Rock, Arkansas 72203

District Engineer
U.S. Army Engr. Dist., Garrison
Administrative Building
Riverdale, North Dakota

District Engineer
U.S. Army Engr. Dist., Tulsa
P. O. Box 61
Tulsa, Oklahoma

District Engineer
U.S. Army Engr. Dist., Mobile
2301 Airport Boulevard
P. O. Box 1169
Mobile, Alabama 36601

Tennessee Valley Authority
Knoxville, Tennessee

[These last are sources for reservoirs, man-made lakes and such. There's probably some other office for lakes in the Colorado. Check with your local office of the Corps of Engineers]

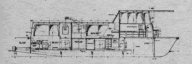

$200 mater. aver. ferro
$1400* cement

Samson Marine Design Enterprises Ltd.
833 River Road
Richmond, B.C. Canada

Boston Whalers

Jay Baldwin says these Boston Whalers are known as the best of the new small utility outboards. $890-$5180. Suitable for ocean use.

—SB

from:
Boston Whaler, Inc.
1149 Hingham Street
Rockland, Mass. 02370

House Boating

If you're shopping for houseboats this magazine will help. Houseboats are pretty nice to live on. I lived on a grounded barge with a board & batten cabin on it in Sausalito till the fleas chased me out. Probably these aluminum and fiberglass jobs don't have that problem. I bet they have others. A home to fuss with, where weather and tide concerns you, that's houseboating. Live like in a movie.

—SB

Family Houseboating
Art Rouse, ed.

$4 /yr (bimonthly)

from:
Family Houseboating
23945 Craftsman Rd.
Calabasas, CA 91302

Pontoons

We're planning on having a houseboat built, and would like to know what kind of material is best for the pontoons. . .fiber glass, aluminum, or steel? At the present time, we're thinking of fiber glass, built with seven bulkheads.

Billy V. Gibson
Whittier, California 90604

Each material has its own pros and cons, but if it were our boat we'd go with marine aluminum.

$10,950

Land N' Sea Craft, Inc.
1813 South Tenth Street
San Jose, California 95112
Land N' Sea

Sea-Space Corporation
15 Berry Hill Road
Oyster Bay, New York 11771

Deck-Line 301

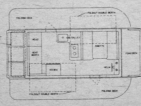

$4490

HOUSEBOAT KITS

Luger Industries, Inc.
1300 East Cliff Road
Burnsville, Minnesota 55378

Glen-L Marine Designs
9152 Rosecrans
Bellflower, California 90706

The Old Boathouse

let me recommend the old-fashioned wooden rowing & sailing dinghies sold by "The Old Boathouse", 2770 Westlake No. Seattle, 98109, as beautiful & seaworthy craft.

The Norwegian "rana" boats range in size from 9½" to 16½'. They are LAP strake, copper riveted & oak framed. They are light, yet very strongly built. The 16½' sloop is an open dinghy with a full-length skeg as well as daggerboard. This gives a directional stability lacking in fibreglass racing boats. A rana boat will beat or reach all day without a touch of the helm. She can carry as many as 6 adults comfortably & still not be overloaded. She is a great, safe family boat that sails well in all conditions & rows quite well. (Oars come with the boat.) The rana boats are a real bargain, costing far less than anything comparable in fibreglass.

"The Old Boathouse" also sells a traditional, fine lined, LAP strake rowing skiff on the lines of the famous "whitehall" skiffs. This boat is built in Minnesota &.is a wonderful example of a dying art. These boats are undoubtedly one of the most easily rowed boats in the world. The construction is white cedar planking, oak frames & copper clench nailed throughout. The boats are beautifully finished in varnish inside & out. The prices for this boat are quite high, but the craftsmanship is the highest qualtiy.

[Suggested and Reviewed by Robert Perry]

The Old Boathouse—Information

free for the *genuine* enthusiast

from:
The Old Boathouse
2770 Westlake North
Seattle, Washington 98109

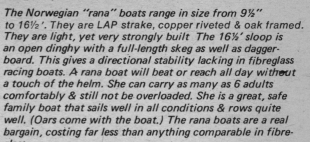

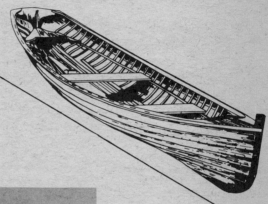

$2495

Beyer Manufacturing Co.
2978 So. Cherry Avenue
Fresno, Calif.

Uniflite, Inc.
P.O. Box 1095
Bellingham, Wash. 98225
Yacht Home

$24,795
$24,495

D.R. was falling but because he couldn't see that he was falling his sense was one of sudden weightlessness, of sudden freedom from the limits of the well, from pain from cramp from gouge in his torn back from crawl and slide from run from try to make his body pull beyond its power. Free, D.R. flew into a black he couldn't see before he landed hard enough in dry loose sand to take his wind away. Windless he felt more euphoric than hurt or terrified. He landed on his back and empty as it felt throughout the lower reaches of his lungs it was peaceful lying in the black, and he just lay there. Lying, resting. His body rested in the sand so deeply it had no wish to move even when his lungs had filled and breathed again. Except to stretch. There was rest. The longest, deepest rest upon the blackness of the sand and then: a stretch, a reaching of the sinews, utter luxury of move and stretch and feel it lengthen out the spine until the yawn and yawn and yawn from the very bottom of his spine.

(continued)

Skin and Scuba Diving

Don't expect to read this book and start scuba diving in a month or so. Scuba diving is fun and rewarding sport. But without proper training, it is very dangerous.

This book has grown in time along with the sport of scuba diving. Now in its newest edition, it is more complete than any other book ever written on this subject by anyone. So if you're interested or planning to be involved in this art, you would be best to buy this book; if you don't get it now, your instructor will tell you to later.

[Reviewed by Jay Bonner.
Suggested by Jack O'Neill]

The New Science of Skin and Scuba Diving
1974; 288 pp.

$4.95 postpaid

from:
Association Press
291 Broadway
New York, N. Y. 10007

or WHOLE EARTH CATALOG

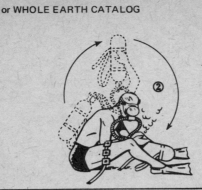

U.S. Navy Diving Manual

the navy probably knows more about water things than any other institution on earth, mainly, sadly, because they have been making war on the oceans for longer than you and i can remember. this is the manual they use to train their divers. good introductory stuff about pressure, buoyancy, anatomy, safety principles, and heavy portions of deepdiving techniques. the gear illustrated is generally navy issue equipment, but it is easy enough to make the connection between government and private manufacturing.

—jd

U.S. Navy Diving Manual
March 1970; 687pp.

Out of print

from:
Superintendant of Documents
U.S. Government Printing Office
Washington, D.C. 20201

or WHOLE EARTH CATALOG

The buoyant effect of liquids is expressed by *Archimedes' principle*. This states that *any object wholly or partially immersed in a liquid is buoyed up by a force equal to the weight of the liquid displaced.* Figure 1-17 illus* ates the following example: A diver, with his helmet and dress, weighs 384 pounds. If he inflates his dress so that he displaces 6.5 cubic feet of water, we will be buoyed up by a force equal to the weight of 6.5 cubic feet of water. Because sea water weighs 64 pounds per cubic food (1.2.4 (10)), the buoyant force acting on this diver would be 6.5x64=416 pounds. This force is 32 (416—384) pounds more than his total weight. Such an excess of buoyant force is called positive buoyancy.

Diving *without* breathing apparatus requires breath holding, and methods of prolonging the length of time the breath can be held are always of interest to skindivers and the like. The discomfort which forces a man to resume breathing arises largely from the two main mechanisms concerned with the control of breathing. Rising carbon dioxide tension directly stimulates the respiratory center, while falling oxygen tension stimulates it via the chemoreceptors. As the degree of stimulation increases, it becomes more and more difficult to restrain the urge to breathe; and at some point, the individual will break and resume breathing.

Underwater Work

If you're near the water, there's all manner of work to be done under it, and a well-paid shortage of men with the skills.

—SB

Underwater Work
John E. Cayford
1966; 258 pp.

$6.00 postpaid

from:
Cornell Maritime Press, Inc.
Cambridge, Maryland 21613

or WHOLE EARTH CATALOG

Hours	Pay Scale (Master Scuba Diver)
0—8	$ 22.50 per hour
8—12	45.00 " "
12—16	100.00 " "
16—20	250.00 " "
20—24	500.00 " "
Over 24	1000.00 " "

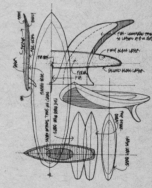

Surfer

A very well produced magazine, well ahead of its imitators, and miles ahead of most other sport/hobby magazines. Has anybody ridden clean up and around inside a curl, vertical 360, and come out standing?

—SB

Surfer
John Severson, ed.

$5 /yr (bimonthly) $5.50 foreign

from:
Surfer Magazine
Box 1028
Dana Point, CA 92629

How much planning do you do before you start into a ride?

I hardly ever organize what I'm gonna do on a wave. The only thing I do organize is probably my first turn. After that I flow with the wave, and if an opportunity comes up to try something, I do it. It's just a matter of getting onto the wave and going and seeing what happens. I like to get into the rhythm of the wave and see what comes out of it.

What do waves represent for you?

Well, they're definitely not football fields, though there are athletes in the sport who look at them that way. But then there are the other people that aren't looking at it as a sport at all. They sort of see it as an art form. To me it's a lot like dancing. I get the same feeling from moving to music as I do with moving on a wave. As a matter of fact, I went dancing last night.

•

You are often associated with "power surfing," but is that really your thing?

I don't try to be powerful. To me, to be powerful is to overwork the board and the waves. I don't think of myself as a power surfer, because it's the wave that's got me in its power. Like with skiing, the speed comes from the hill. The skier just tries to maintain.

Barry Kanaiaupuni

Surfboard Builder's Yearbook

You can't build surf when you want it. But you can build a surfboard while you're waiting.

—SB

Surfboard Builders' Yearbook
Steve Shaw, ed.
1963-1974; 64 pp.

$4.00 postpaid

from:
Transmedia
9811 Edgelake Rd.
La Mesa, CA 92041

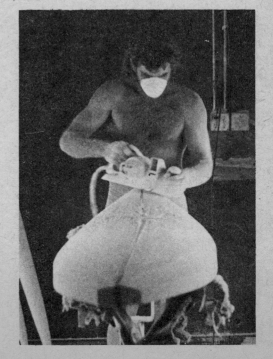

New England Divers

Skin diving (with mask, snorkel, fins, etc.) and/or scuba diving (with tanks of air) are healthy recreation which allow one to see and enter a completely different world where he is surrounded by a different medium (water) and different flora and fauna from those which he has experienced in his lifetime.

I have found the best place to buy equipment on the east coast, and I think the west coast. It is New England Divers Inc., Beverly, Mass. They are the distributors of diving equipment to the eastern sports shops and will sell to individuals, in small or large quantity, all brands of diving equipment at the same price that they sell it to the sports shops. They sell over their counter, by mail, or by phone (one can call collect from anywhere in the continental U.S. for an order over $50.).

The "salesmen" in the store are all extremely experienced professional divers. They have given me knowledgeable and honest advise with their low prices. Last spring I was preparing to go to Turkey on a deep diving underwater archeological expedition sponsored by the National Geographic Society.

When I went to their shop to discuss some personal equipment purchases with them I found they already knew about the expedition and what kind of work I'd be doing. They brought up and discussed with me the pro's and con's of various equipment, convincing me not to buy some items and to buy some others. When I was in Turkey this summer, isolated from any diving shop, I found they had been right in every detail.

One of the things I bought was a U.S. Divers Calypso "J" regulator which can be purchased in any sports shop at $141.95. These people sell it for $120.40, brand new, with guarantee (this is one of the most expensive but also the most reliable regulator).

[Reviewed by Warren Riess]

Price List

free

from:
New England Divers Inc.
42 Water Street
Beverly, Mass. 01915

U.S. Divers

U.S. Divers— for scuba is the only co. I would recommend. In 8 years of scuba diving I have used their gear time and time again and find it to be reliable and durable. Their regulators and wetsuits are for my money the best on the market. They aren't cheap but most dealers give pretty good discounts.

For shallower water (75'), which is arbitrary as to depth, Desco, Inc. makes an open-circuit-surface-supplied face-plate (the same plate is used by the U.S. Navy) that is out of sight but slightly limited as to vision for about $120. Desco also makes a complete line of heavy gear from air-hats to commercial diving dress and accessories, none of which I can say yea or nay about as I have only used their shallow water mask.

The best deep-sea hard-hat is one made by Kirby-Morgan (A Division of U.S. Divers) and is called their Standard Air Hat. If you are buying or need to buy heavy-gear, I recommend (and have bought for myself) their Standard Air Hat above all others. It has the increased port area of most commercial hats for better visibility with the ruggedness and reliability of the Navy Mark V Hat.

As far as training facilities go for commercial diving there are two in Southern Cal. and one in Oakland. I investigated all of them before enrolling and finally wound up going to Universal Divers Lmt. in San Pedro. Universal is the only school that trains a man in all phases of commercial diving. Their instructors are all commercial divers of 10 or more years diving experience each and their facilities include a fully equipped commercial grade diving barge, a 40-50 foot ocean diving boat and complete classroom facilities. The course runs 10-12 weeks and at present costs $795. It will go up to $1000 as they will be adding a section on commercial abalone diving in the near future. This is still about $250 cheaper than the other schools. As to periodicals and books on commercial diving there really is only one book and that is the U.S. Navy Diving Manuals. They are available at most dive shops and are the final authority on all phases of diving. The manual is a must for all divers, commercial or otherwise. Only one periodical is out that specializes in commercial diving and it is called Undercurrents. It is so new I haven't got its address yet but as soon as I do I will send it along.

[Reviewed by Michael Montenegro]

Catalog

$1

from:
U.S. Divers
3323 West Warner Ave.
Santa Ana, CA 92702

So, get your U.S. Divers stuff from New England Divers, at about 1/3 off.

—SB

Another supplier of underwater equipment, with some commercial diving stuff like Desco masks, is:

M & E Marine Supply Co.
Box 601
Camden, New Jersey 08101

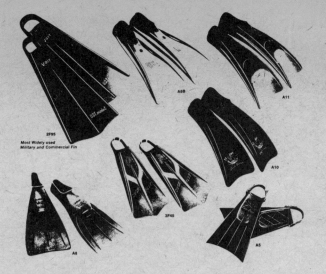

KA-13—G
MAKO COMPRESSOR
CFM 2.5, 4 HP Gasoline Engine, PSI 3200, RPM 750, Width 14", Length 34", Height 20", Weight 96 lbs. 3 stage compressor, moisture and oil separator, activated charcoal filter. Fills a 70 cu. ft. tank in 29 minutes.
Cat. No. KA-13-G **$1,386.00**

No longer available

FINS

Description		Retail	Dealer	Weight
2F95	"Regulation UDT Duck Foot" Black ML-L-XL-SXL	20.00 pr.	15.00 pr.	7 lbs.
A6B	Voit "Viking" Blue, M-ML-L	16.00 pr.	11.95 pr.	4½ lbs.
A10	"Skin Diver" Black,S-M-ML-L	11.95 pr.	8.95 pr.	5 lbs.

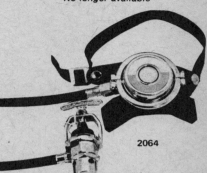

2064

HYDRO-AIR
All metal parts of chromed brass or stainless steel for maximum corrosion resistance, downstream second stage provides a maximum flow with minimum demand. Piston first stage has only one moving part. Back-up ring seals out fouling sediment. Improved contoured air exhaust valves for added safety.
Cat. No. 2064 . . . . . . *No longer available*

WET SUITS
(Single Zipper on Special Order Only)

SEA MASTER 5 ZIPPER 3/16" NYLON 2 SIDE

				Retail	Dealer	Weight
Complete Suit						
3400-00	Sm.	3401-00	Med.			
3402-00	Med. Lg.	3403-00	Lg.			
3404-00	XLg.			115.00	77.05	9
Shirts Only						
3400-01	Sm.	3401-01	Med.			
3402-01	Med. Lg.	3403-01	Lg.			
3404-01	XLg.			67.50	45.23	5
Pants Only						
3400-02	Sm.	3401-02	Med.			
3402-02	Med. Lg.	3403-02	Lg.			
3404-02	XLg.			49.50	33.17	4

No longer available

REGULATORS

CAT. NO.	DESCRIPTION	RETAIL	DEALER	WEIGHT
1070-00	Calypso "J" Regulator	124.50	83.75	3
1071-00	Calypso III Regulator	106.50	71.69	3
1072-00	Conshelf XI Regulator	89.50	59.97	3
1075-00**	Aquarius Regulator	65.00	43.55	3

Calypso "J"

The Calypso "J" regulator epitomizes the ultimate in regulator design. The completely balanced and adjustable first stage provides effortless inhalation, no matter what the depth or tank pressure. The second stage has superior magnum exhalation which allows a diver to exhale with complete ease from any position. These two stages, coupled with the "fail-safe" reserve system and the high pressure port provide the diver with the finest breathing combination available. Patented.

1083....................$141.95

DESCRIPTION	RETAIL	DEALER
1 hose	35.00	25.00
Hydro-Balance Regulator	95.00	63.65
Hydro-Master Regulator	105.00	70.00
Hydro-Dive Regulator	70.00	48.00
Ladies Zodiac Sea Wolf Watch	100.00	65.00
Hydro-Air Regulator	60.00	40.00
Pressure Gauge	15.95	11.50
Sea Wolf Watch	100.00	65.00

No longer available

GENOA AND MEDITERRANEAN FINS - Floating
Made from two compounds of high quality floating rubber. A soft compound for stretch and comfort in the foot pocket. A stiff compound along the rails and tip for strong blade action. These fins also feature a high heel for a comfortable fit with or without boots. And blades with angled length and width which combine with extremely live rubber to provide spring-like blade action for effortless dives. Though comparatively light, these fins are strong and durable.

1365 Genoa. Black 5—7 . . . . . . $11.50
1366 Genoa. Black 7 –8½ $11.50
1367 Genoa. Black 8½–10 . . . . . $12.50
1368 Genoa. Black 10–12 . . . . . $13.50
1369 Genoa. Black 12–14 . . . . . $13.50
No longer available

D.R. rolled over and buried his face in the sand, loose, smooth, clean as the purest beach. He felt it scrape the crusted mud and sweat and slime and blood from his face and neck, his forehead and his hair. He was bathing. He was a snake shedding old and stiffened skin. Grinning D.R. sat up and peeled off his matted shirt. When he pressed his chest into the sand again it felt like touching breasts with some warm woman. Smiling in the deepest pleasure he sank both arms into the sand and when he pulled them out he scraped the sand up into piles like breasts and then lay down upon them. Exalted, now, he leaped to his feet and wrestled off the remnants of his clothes. Falling forward naked he spread-eagled himself upon the clean invisible sand, embraced it close with every surface of his body. He rolled and rolled again, then wiggled, pulling through it like some amphibious creature joyous to be on land. When he was tired he stopped and nestled wiggling till he'd formed impressions for each contour of his body. Sand was under every arch, his lower back, the hollow of his knees, relieving every tired place in him, sending streams of rest through every isthmus, his mind as dark and peaceful now as the inmost silent chamber of the mine.

Sailing Illustrated

This is a little book with a lot of pictures and an unusually useful layout. It's a nice job of information packing with easy retrieval designed in. —SB

[Suggested by Don Gerrard]

Sailing Illustrated
Patrick M. Royce
1956 . . . 1968; 352 pp.

$5.15 postpaid

from:
Royce Publications
Box 1967
Newport Beach, CA 92663

or WHOLE EARTH CATALOG

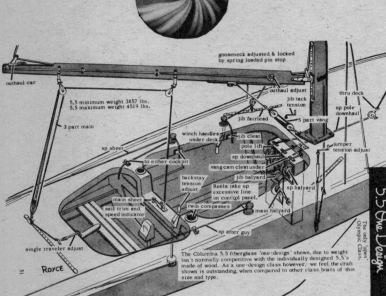

Piloting, Seamanship, and Small Boat Handling

The required book on piloting. Encyclopedia on weather, compass, charts, ground tackle, codes, etc. Strong on power boats, weak on sailing.
—SB

Piloting, Seamanship and Small Boat Handling
690 pp.; 1000 illus.
Comprehensive index
Older edition pictured

$8.95 postpaid

from: or WHOLE EARTH CATALOG
Motor Boat and Sailing
250 W. 55th St.
New York, N.Y. 10019

THREE HOURS AFTER 'SLACK, FLOOD BEGINS' AT THE RACE

Tidal Current Charts are published for certain major bodies of water. Each is a set of 12 small-scale chartlets whosing currents existing at hourly intervals throughout a complete cycle of flood and ebb.

The Glénans Sailing Manual

This is the closest we've seen to a definitive text on small-boat sailing. Clearly illustrated.
—SB

The Glénans Sailing Manual
Philippe Harlé
1961; 448 pp.

$10.00 postpaid

from:
John de Graff, Inc.
34 Oak Avenue
Tuckahoe, N.Y. 10707

or WHOLE EARTH CATALOG

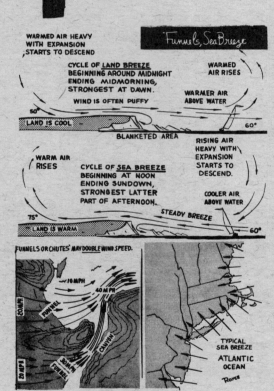

Ocean Living

For those with sea-going commune or escape-and-evasion fantasies, this newsletter is right in there.
—SB

[Suggested by Roberta Becker Marshall]

Ocean Living
William Taylor, ed.

$1 for 10 issues

from:
Ocean Living
Box 17463
Los Angeles, CA 90017

Dear Ocean Living People: We have received your OL issues via a friend. It is right on what we need and are interested in. For my objection to the Vietnam war I could choose either exile or jail. I chose "exile" in Sweden where I'm now living with my family. We are opposed to all war, a tragic human-social sickness, and we wish to affirm life and peace as much as we can. Therefore we are building a boat here, a James-Wharram-designed, 40-ft catamaran, polynesian style, of plywood. I am familiar with Charles Greene's Bungay boat kit company as you have talked about in one of your issues. This boat I'm building, called "Narai", appears, from all our study, a very good boat. It won't capsize (except in a hurricane with full sail out), has a number of safety features not found in most boats, will be our family, living-boat in which we'll cruise around the world looking for our own paradise. You can write to Miss L. Scrutton, S/C Rongo, Poste Restante, Deganwy, N. Wales; for plans of these catamarans. Mike Romano & Family, Osthammar, Sweden.

A washing machine designed for underprivileged peoples in foreign lands, the Colgate Wash 'n Go (as it is marketed in America to campers and boaters) is not in mass production— but the last we heard a limited number were still on hand in the company's New York warehouse, selling for $11.95. This one-moving-part gadget combines the principle of automatic washer rotation with the energy source of a Chinese hand laundry. We sent for one (and postage is included in the price) and Cara says it is much easier than competitive manual wash facilities— such as washboards and wringers or rocky river banks. It holds four to five gallons, three pounds of clothes, and a cup of detergent. Operation is something like churning butter. Made of extremely light-weight semi-flexible plastic. It ain't Westinghouse, but think of the electricity you save.

Kerry Thornley

The Chinese gybe:

If the sail manages to gybe before it is amidships, the bottom half of the sail gets across, while the upper half gets hung up by the cross-trees or by a batten catching on something, and stays on the original side. You can easily tear the sail. If this mishap befalls you, there is one thing to do, and only one— gybe back to get on the original tack. Anything else is bound to fail and will risk tearing the sail. *(It may be noted that the term Chinese gybe is not a reflection on Oriental seamanship, which is of a very high order; the junk rig is designed to carry out a gybe in this manner without unpleasant consequences.)*

Liberty Communes

According to AD (p. 88), Brand Griffon at Washington State University has schemes to convert mothballed Liberty Ships into community environments for 600 dwellers. The plans include use of sea resources such as plankton.
—SB

LIBERTY COMMUNES

A plan for the conversion of mothballed Liberty Ships to community environments

It's a bit hard to bullshit the ocean. It's not listening, you know what I mean?

David Crosby 1970

Knight's Modern Seamanship

If there's a single book to have on board at sea, this updated classic is probably it. Everything from mooring to an ice shelf to port-tack-yields-right-of-way to minimizing hover time for boarding helicopters.

—SB

Knight's MODERN SEAMANSHIP
14th Edition

CAPTAIN JOHN V. NOEL, JR. U.S. NAVY

Knight's Modern Seamanship
Austin M. Knight; Rev. by Capt. John V. Noel, Jr.
1901 . . . 1966; 610 pp.

$14.95 postpaid
from:
Van Nostrand-Reinhold
450 West 33rd Street
New York, N. Y. 10001

or WHOLE EARTH CATALOG

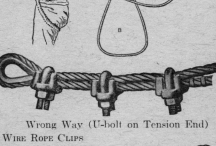

Wrong Way (U-bolt on Tension End)
WIRE ROPE CLIPS

Right Way (U-bolt on Dead End)

HANDLING WIRE ROPE

Ci 2

"MARES' TAILS"

This type appearing after cirrus and followed by thickening lower clouds, increases probability of rain within 24 hrs.

CIRRUS and cirrostratus. "Mare's tails" is the popular name given to well-defined cirrus clouds that thicken into cirrostratus, and then gradually lowering into water droplet altostratus. The clouds may resemble a mare's tail and may often be the forerunner of a storm as indicated in the old rhyme: "Mackerel sky and mare's tails, make tall ships carry low sails." The more brush-like the cirrus, the stronger the wind at that level.

Unsolved Oceanographic Problems of Interest to Mariners

How do some marine organisms used for food by man tolerate and store poisons at concentrations harmful or lethal to man?

Why is the layer of unconsolidated sediments in the deep sea so thin (average 1000 ft thick)?

Why are there no sea fossils older than 100 million years?

What is the cause of the sudden increase in radium content in the oceans about 200,000 years ago?

What are the enzyme systems that operate in the oceanic regions of high pressure and perpetual low temperature?

How do microscopic plants and animals (plankton), apparently helpless in the face of water movement, maintain themselves so regularly in their own specific regions?

Coast Navigation Schools

Has home-study courses in Coastwise Navigation & Piloting ($90). Celestial Navigation ($190), Boating & Seamanship ($165), Celestial Air Navigation ($175), Visual Astronomy ($75), Telescopic Astronomy ($125). We've heard good recommendations of the place.

—SB

Coast Navigation School
418 East Canon Perdido
Santa Barbara, CA 93102

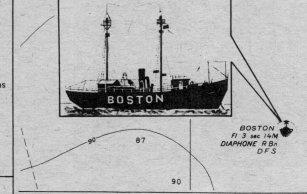

BOSTON

BOSTON
Fl 3 sec 14M
DIAPHONE R Bn
D F S

90   87

90

FIGURE 513b.—A lightship with a radiobeacon.

Coast Guard Courses

The Coast Guard Auxiliary gives free classes in things like "Basic Seamanship" (their book of the same name costs $2.50 and gives you at least what you have to know, probably more).

Joe Sonneman
Juneau, Alaska

How to Navigate Today

So long as navigation tables are printed, you need celestial navigation like you need birdwatching. Here's how to relax and use the Nautical Almanac and Navigation Tables.

—SB

How To Navigate Today
M. R. Hart
1943-1970; 111 pp.

$2.50 postpaid

from:
Cornell Maritime Press, Inc.
Box 109
Cambridge, Maryland 21613

or WHOLE EARTH CATALOG

While I have tried to give a clear picture of the necessary geometrical relations, I have avoided astronomy as much as possible. The *U.S. Nautical Almanac*, in giving S.H.A. and G.H.A. directly, entirely disposes of the former Right Ascension which immediately removes the most confusing part of the study of navigation. Therefore the discussion of Time, except in relation to Meridian Altitude, has been reduced to a minimum.

The greater ease and accuracy of navigating by the stars has been stressed and navigation by the sun has been put in its proper place as a special case of stellar navigation.

This book makes no pretense of being an exhaustive scientific study of navigation. It is not intended to discipline the mind nor train the character. It does claim to give the essentials necessary for intelligent navigation.

American Practical Navigator — Bowditch

There's an episode in Kenneth Roberts' Lydia Bailey where Albion Townsend, having helped lick Napoleon in Haiti, is sailing across the Atlantic with his common-law bride, Lydia, and they're out on deck a lot at night doing sex with Bowditch's book in hand, teaching each other navigation.

This book is big, probably lots more than you care to know about navigation, but it's authoritative, THE word, and it's cheap. Dating origins back to 1799, it has romantic associations to go with its practical lore.

—SB

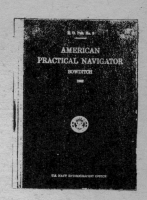

AMERICAN PRACTICAL NAVIGATOR
BOWDITCH

U.S. NAVY HYDROGRAPHIC OFFICE

American Practical Navigator—An Epitome of Navigation
Nathaniel Bowditch & U.S. Navy Hydrographic Office
1966; 1524 pp.

$18.00 postpaid

from:
U.S. Govt. Printing Office Bookstore
710 North Capitol Street
Washington, D. C. 20402

U.S. Govt. Printing Office Bookstore
Rm. 1463, 14th Floor
Federal Office Building
219 S. Dearborn Street
Chicago, Ill. 60604

U.S. Govt. Printing Office Bookstore
Rm. 135, Federal Building
601 East 12th Street
Kansas City, Missouri 64106

U.S. Govt. Printing Office Bookstore
Federal Building
450 Golden Gate Avenue
Rm. 1023, Box 36104
San Francisco, CA 94102

U. S. Navy standard micrometer drum sextant.

If the craft is to proceed out of sight of land for more than short intervals, celestial navigation equipment should be carried. This includes a sextant, an accurate time-piece, an almanac, sight reduction tables, and perhaps a star finder.

NAVIGATIONAL STARS AND THE PLANETS

Name	Pronunciation	Bayer name	Origin of name	Meaning of name	Distance*
Acamar	ā'kȧ-mär	θ Eridani	Arabic	another form of Achernar	120
Achernar	ā'kẽr-när	α Eridani	Arabic	end of the river (Eridanus)	72
Acrux	ā'krŭks	α Crucis	Modern	coined from Bayer name	220
Adhara	ȧ-dä'rȧ	ε Canis Majoris	Arabic	the virgin(s)	350
Aldebaran	ăl-dĕb'ȧ-răn	α Tauri	Arabic	follower (of the Pleiades)	64
Alioth	ăl'ĭ-ŏth	ε Ursa Majoris	Arabic	another form of Capella	49
Alkaid	ăl-kād'	η Ursa Majoris	Arabic	leader of the daughters of the bier	190
Al Na'ir	ăl-nä'ĭr	α Gruis	Arabic	bright one (of the fish's tail)	90
Alnilam	ăl'nĭ-lăm	ε Orionis	Arabic	string of pearls	410
Alphard	ăl'färd	α Hydrae	Arabic	solitary star of the serpent	200
Alphecca	ăl-fĕk'ȧ	α Corona Borealis	Arabic	feeble one (in the crown)	76
Alpheratz	ăl-fē'răts	α Andromeda	Arabic	the horse's navel	120
Altair	ăl-târ'	α Aquilae	Arabic	flying eagle or vulture	16
Ankaa	ăn'kä	α Phoenicis	Arabic	coined name	93
Antares	ăn-tā'rēz	α Scorpii	Greek	rival of Mars (in color)	250
Arcturus	ärk-tū'rŭs	α Bootis	Greek	the bear's guard	37
Atria	ä'trĭ-ȧ	α Trianguli Australis	Modern	coined from Bayer name	130
Avior	ā'vĭ-ôr	ε Carinae	Modern	coined name	350
Bellatrix	bĕ-lā'trĭks	γ Orionis	Latin	female warrior	250
Betelgeuse	bē'tʼl-jūz	α Orionis	Arabic	the arm pit (of Orion)	300
Canopus	kȧ-nō'pŭs	α Carinae	Greek	city of ancient Egypt	230
Capella	kȧ-pĕl'ȧ	α Aurigae	Latin	little she-goat	46
Deneb	dĕn'ĕb	α Cygni	Arabic	tail of the hen	600
Denebola	dē-nĕb'ō-lȧ	β Leonis	Arabic	tail of the lion	42
Diphda	dĭf'dȧ	β Ceti	Arabic	the second frog (Fomalhaut was once the first)	57
Dubhe	dŭb'ē	α Ursa Majoris	Arabic	the bear's back	100
Elnath	ĕl'năth	β Tauri	Arabic	one butting with horns	130
Eltanin	ĕl-tä'nĭn	γ Draconis	Arabic	head of the dragon	130
Enif	ĕn'ĭf	ε Pegasi	Arabic	nose of the horse	250
Fomalhaut	fō'mal-ōt	α Piscis Austrini	Arabic	mouth of the southern fish	24
Gienah	gĕ'krŭks	γ Crucis	Arabic	coined from Bayer name	72
Gienah	jē'nä	γ Corvi	Arabic	right wing of the raven	130
Hadar	hä'där	β Centauri	Modern	leg of the centaur	76
Hamal	hăm'ăl	α Arietis	Arabic	full-grown lamb	76
Kaus Australis	kôs ôs-trā'lĭs	ε Sagittarii	Ar., L.	southern part of the bow	163
Kochab	kō'kăb	β Ursa Minoris	Arabic	shortened form of "north star" (named when it was that, c. 1500 BC-AD 300)	100
Markab	mär'kăb	α Pegasi	Arabic	saddle (of Pegasus)	100
Menkar	mĕn'kär	α Ceti	Arabic	nose (of the whale)	1,100
Menkent	mĕn'kĕnt	θ Centauri	Modern	shoulder of the centaur	55
Miaplacidus	mī'ȧ-plăs'ĭ-dŭs	β Carinae	Ar., L.	quiet or still waters	86
Mirfak	mĭr'făk	α Persei	Arabic	elbow of the Pleiades	130
Nunki	nŭn'kē	σ Sagittarii	Bab.	constellation of the holy city (Eridu)	150

Handy Medical Guide for Seafarers

This here is a handy medical guide for seafarers.

—SB

Handy Medical Guide for Seafarers
R. W. Scott
1969; 86 pp.

$3.50 postpaid

from:
Fishing News Ltd.
23 Rosemont Avenue
West Byfleet
Surrey, England

or WHOLE EARTH CATALOG

a   b   c

Pinch up loose skin, insert needle, avoiding veins, and inject solution

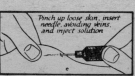

HANDY Medical Guide FOR SEAFARERS

R.W. SCOTT

THE LIGHT

D.R. did not intend to leave the Sand Room, and he wouldn't have for anything less than light. It was safe in there, and dry, and warm. He would end his journey on that sand rather than go into another hopeless maze of watery caverns.

But feeling along the high, smooth walls D.R. found an opening a vertical break that led into a narrow, winding hallway, and because the floor was also sand he decided to check it out a ways, and just beyond the second curving of the hall he saw a light.

At first he was certain it was just an image in his mind, and to be sure he closed his eyes, expecting to see the light still hanging in his mind just as he had seen it in the mine. But when he closed his eyes it went away, and when he opened them again, there it was before him, a tiny star in the farthest galaxy. Close. Open. Close. The light went out and came again as D.R. blinked his eyes, and stayed there when he held them open wide and stood still.

Breathless, he started walking toward it down the hall. Leaving the Sand Room D.R. had been careful to keep his two hands on the opposite walls, but now he was so excited he forgot to touch them, and when he thought and felt for them again the walls were gone. The hall was gone, the sandy floor had disappeared, his bare feet were on hard rock again. But the light was there in front to lead him on, growing larger as he walked heedless now of where he put his feet or kept his hands.

Boats Letter 1

International Marine Publishing Co. By the way, they have the best boat-book catalog anywhere. 21 Elm Street, Camden, Maine 04843. Put their catalog in your catalog.

OK, here's a list of good books on basics of sailing, cruising, design, and boatbuilding, with hasty comment.

On elementary sailing:

There's a flock of new books I haven't looked at. The old (1930s) classic, and I suspect still the best in many ways, is Learning to Sail, *by H.A. Calahan, MacMillan, $5.95. Calahan is clear and painstaking on rudiments, but also far wider in scope than most primers. Good material on peripheral but important matters from maintainance to moorings. Out of date with respect to modern materials (fiberglass, dacron), but that just means the old materials (wood, canvas, manila rope) are thoroughly covered. A rare virtue nowadays.*

On cruising (assuming you have the rudiments of sailing covered):

Calahan has a sequel, Learning to Cruise, *which is just as good. Again, oriented towards traditional boats, materials, and methods. You can get both Calahans (and* Learning to Race*) in a single volume called* Yachtsman's Omnibus, *MacMillan, $9.95.*

If I had to recommend only one book, it would be Cruising Under Sail, *by Eric Hiscock, Oxford University Press, $12.75. Hiscock and his wife have spent their adult lives making long voyages, including twice around the world. This is the book on how to do everything, a fantastic wealth of detail given in an orderly and practical manner.*

If bread for books is a problem, you can at least begin with Cruising, *by Peter Heaton, Penguin paperback, $1.95. This is a sketchy treatment, but a bargain. Some nice boats pictured in both plans and photos.*

About money: cruising boats are very expensive. The very cheapest boats discussed in Hiscock, Calahan, or Heaton, for instance, might easily cost ten or fifteen thousand dollars to build new today. Prices of old boats vary with age and condition. There are some good bargains around. However, the novice can get started pretty cheaply, since you can cruise, after a fashion, in very small craft. You'd be wise to start small anyway, regardless of expense, because small size reduces the scale of the mysteries to be mastered.

The smallest possible is very small indeed. Robert Manry crossed the Atlantic in a thirteen-footer. This wasn't a stunt, either, but in most respects a well-planned and competent passage. It's worth mentioning that he knew nothing about sailing beforehand, but he used his good head and systematically read every book he could find. (Many have put to sea ill-informed and ill-equipped. They always fail and are sometimes lost altogether.) Tinkerbelle, *Robert Manry, Dell paperback, 75¢.*

The Hiscock of very small boats is Cruising Boats Within Your Budget, *by John Jacob Benjamin, Harper & Bros. This covers almost everything a beginner can learn from a book about owning, cruising in, maintaining, and loving his own very small ship. Published in 1957, and dated on materials and costs. I fear, I sadly fear, that it may be out of print, but is worth looking for. In any case, I don't know the price.*

My favorite manual on cruising in very small boats is The Small Boat Skipper and His Problems, *by Eugene V. Connett, W. W. Norton Co. This too appears to be out of print, but is too beautiful to neglect mentioning. This, like Benjamin, is about life aboard boats so small that pulling on your pants in the cabin becomes a logistics and engineering adventure. Much less systematic and comprehensive than Benjamin, and so perhaps less useful.*

This book is about love.

The Compleat Cruiser, *by L. Francis Herreshoff, Sheridan House, $7.50, is a Victorian-style fiction in which a cast of tediously stuffy characters enact some cruises in various boats. Some of the dialogue is unintentionally hilarious. But Herreshoff is a cranky genius and a great yacht designer, and much lore and wisdom comes out of those improbable mouths. Don't make this your first book on cruising, but don't miss it either, somewhere along the way.*

Piloting, Seamanship, and Small Boat Handling, *by Charles Chapman, published by Motor Boating magazine, $11.95, is a really essential encyclopedic reference, used as a textbook for Power Squadron courses. Not much on sail (written primarily for motor boats), but the best single book on piloting, with excellent stuff also on weather, marlinespike seamanship, ground tackle, signalling codes, and everything else imaginable. With Hiscock and Chapman you can get pretty far.*

On design and construction:

These subjects, especially design, are important to anybody who is about to actually lay out money on a boat, even if he will never do any designing or building. As in skiing, mountain climbing, playing a musical instrument, or any such subtle and beautiful skill, you will be severely limited and inconvenienced by poor equipment. In this field, change is not always progress, and the older boats are often better than the latest fiberglass models. Many of the contemporary mass-produced, mass-marketed fiberglass racing-cruising boats have design defects as cruising craft, and your only defense is knowledge.

The real beginner could start with Understanding Yacht Design, *by Edward S. Brewer and Jim Betts, Yacht Design Institute (Brooklin, Maine 04616), 8 1/2 x 11 paperbound, $3.95. This is non-technical and elementary, in fact sometimes oversimplified at the cost of clarity and precision. There are a few controversial points which are not labelled as such, but offered as gospel.*

The Sailing Yacht, *by Juan Baader, W. W. Norton & Co., $15.00, covers an enormous range of subjects from principles of design to storms at sea, though this range leads to some superficiality. It's in part a pretty good introduction to the grosser aspects of design, with chapters on hull forms, rigs, and aerodynamic and hydrodynamic theory as applied to sailboats. Particularly useful for the large number of plans given of boats of all types.*

A somewhat more technical and far more detailed and elegant treatise is Sailing Yacht Design, *by Douglas Phillips-Birt, Adlard Coles Ltd. (London), $13.95. This may be the most useful single volume for the amateur who is really interested. Other books get deeper into certain specifics, but this covers the subject in a most lucid and orderly way, touching on history, theory, shapes, types, rigs, construction, drafting, measurement rules, and calculations.*

Yacht Designing and Planning, *by Howard I. Chapelle, W. W. Norton & Co., $10.00 reflects the state of the art in 1936, and conservatively even for then. Very good if you want to get into the actual process of designing, with a sample design worked out step by step through the book. Along the way you get valuable comments on many matters from an empirical and commonsense point of view. No theory. Superb drawings.*

American Small Sailing Craft, *Chapelle, Norton, $12.50, is the standard work on the history of all important types of small sailing craft and their evolution during the years of working sail in America. A great classic. More superb drawings.*

The Common-Sense of Yacht Design, *by L. Francis Herreshoff, Caravan-Maritime Books, $25.00, is another classic. Herreshoff, one of the great designers, is an eccentric artist, and this work is rambling, anecdotal, opinionated, insulting, entertaining, personal, and endlessly instructive. Also occasionally wrongheaded. It covers sooner or later and somehow or other most subjects of importance. Some exquisite drawings.*

Boatbuilding, *Chapelle, Norton, $15.00, is the standard text on traditional wood construction, and* Boatbuilding Manual, *by Robert M. Steward, Poseidon Publishing Company (Lakeville, Conn. 06039) is a useful and more modern supplement.*

Peace,

Mait Edey
Edey & Duff
Harbor Rd.
Mattapoisett, Mass. 02739

Edey & Duff build a nice fiberglass and wood cruising boat, the Stone Horse. Info: $1.50.

—SB

The Craft of Sail: A Primer of Sailing, *Jan Adkins, Walker & Co., NY, $5.95. Especially for kids, but superb for any novice who wants to see at a glance how and why sailboats do this or that. The text is simple and lucid, managing to convey much information in a few words. The drawings are full of character, and show a real understanding of the aesthetics of small boats.*

Cruising Under Sail

I love any book that has the balls to fully annotate its bibliography. This one does. I can see why it's the standard cruising text.

—SB

Cruising Under Sail
Eric C. Hiscock
1950, 1965; 468 pp.

$15.95 postpaid

from:
Oxford University Press, Inc.
200 Madison Ave.
New York, N.Y. 10016

or WHOLE EARTH CATALOG

Cruising teaches a man to rely on his own judgement and skill, and it is one of the few worthwhile things that can still be enjoyed today by a man or woman of independent spirit, for there are no restrictions, no organizing body is needed, and the sea is open and free for all who have the inclination to sail on it and a suitable vessel for the purpose. It may cost as much or as little as one is prepared to spend, for an old and cheap yacht, provided she is sound, may be just as suitable for cruising, though perhaps not so convenient or such fun to sail, as an expensive one of modern design and build, and a small yacht, though not so comfortable, may be just as seaworthy as a large one.

There are many different forms of the sport. One man gets his pleasure by making short day sails along the coast, spending each night at anchor, sharing with his wife and family the peace of the creeks and the novelty of life in their compact and mobile floating home. Another, who can spare the time, gets his satisfaction by making long passages in the open sea, taking the weather as it comes, and driving his yacht day and night until she fetches up in some foreign land.

•

Meeting steamers do not dread'
When you see three lights ahead
Starboard wheel and show your red.
Green to green and red to red,
Perfect safety, go ahead.
If to starboard red appear,
'Tis your duty to keep clear;
Act as judgement says is proper,
Port or starboard, back or stop her.
But when upon your port is seen
A steamer's starboard light of green,
There's not so much for you to do
For green to port keeps clear of you.

Sailing Hydrofoils

Very far out boats. All manner of designs and lore on home-makeable boats that rise up and go like a son of a bitch. The cutting edge of sailboat design. The Amateur Yacht Research Society also has literature on Self Steering, Multihull Design, Sailing Aerodynamics, Dinghy Design, etc.

—SB

Sailing Hydrofoils
Amateur Yacht Research Society
1970; 286 pp.

$8 postpaid

from:
Amateur Yacht Research Society
Hermitage, Newbury, Berkshire
England

At the moment, we are on the very verge of seeing some remarkable hydrofoil craft which fall into two classes, namely (1) the Flying hydrofoil craft where the whole boat lifts off the water, leaving only three foils to sustain it and *2) the Hydrofoil Stabilised craft, where a long lean boat is stabilised against the capsizing moment of the wind by a hydrofoil placed to leeward.

The fully flying hydrofoil sailing boat may, or may not, achieve speeds of 40 knots. Due to the limitations of hydrofoils in "cavitation," ultimate speeds of more than 45 knots are very unlikely indeed. Some development is needed, however, before such a craft is seaworthy.

The hydrofoil-stabilised sailing boat, on the other hand, if some 50 feet long could be ordered tomorrow. If built lightly enough such as in PVC foam and fibreglass sandwich, it will have a better "lift to resistance ratio" than the fully flying type up to speeds of 30 knots. It might well do 40 knots and be a fully seaworthy craft capable of righting herself from the upside down position.

Bill Prior's second flying hydrofoil

National Fisherman

The saltiest publication I know. Fishing, boatbuilding, ocean conservation, oceanography, sea news. A trade publication with a dignified nod to the sea buffs. Damn good newspaper.

—SB

[Suggested by Paul Wingate]

The National Fisherman

$6.00 for one year

from:
The National Fisherman
21 Elm Street
Camden, Maine 04843

WANTED — CREW FOR OCEANOGRAPHIC RESEARCH
Cook — Seaman
Assistant Engineer
Permanent - based Staten Island N.Y. — operating Maine to Bahamas — send information regarding education and experience.
TWIN HULL BOAT COMPANY
Box 159 Hasbrouck Heights, N. J. 07604

By D. Karl Hoppe

The Dept. of Defense in Washington has begun an investigation into the apparent dumping into the ocean of a can of DDT, a highly toxic pesticide — which may have come from a military installation.

The DDT can, painted an olive drab military color, was pulled from water 20 miles west of Bodega Bay, Calif., by Ferndale, Calif., fisherman Thomas C. Webster Jr., owner of the dragboats Havana and Franklin. Webster said that during the same trip to the southern fishing area, he and a crew of three on the Havana also netted a 2.75" aircraft rocket, which was immediately thrown overboard for fear of possible explosion.

The New World of the Oceans

Everybody says, The Ocean Is Next, and that's probably right. Every bookstore has a line of ocean popsicles for your refreshment now. This book of Behrman's has more protein than that. If you're planning to go down to the sea in science, he can let you know where science has been with the sea. He can also get you giggling proper.

—SB

The New World of the Oceans
Daniel Behrman
1969; 436pp.

$2.95 postpaid

from:
Little Brown and Company
200 West Street
Waltham, Massachusetts 02154

or WHOLE EARTH CATALOG

As one of its manifold functions, UNESCO has traditionally served as a foster home in Paris for sciences in need of a place to hang their international hats, offering a maximum of independence as long as they were willing to accept a minimum of money. (This is true of science everywhere—the amounts of independence and money are inversely related.) It is something like those little French country cafes that post signs announcing they will take customers who bring their own provisions.

•

The pendulum of scientific inquiry keeps swinging between observation and synthesis. Aristotle had to resolve such a conflict: according to Sir John Murray, editor of the reports of the Challenger Expedition, Aristotle threw himself into the whirlpool of the Strait of Euripos, separating Euboea from the Greek mainland, because he was unable to explain it.

Fish Catching Methods of the World

definitely not about sportfishing, brandt concerns himself with harvest fishing, food fishing, money fishing, desperation fishing, corporation fishing, nets, spears, traps, explosions, harpoons, diving equipment, and fishing with bare hands and teeth. its an expensive book, but i don't know of another that runs through everything the way this one does. it would be of particular use if you are going to try circumnavigating the earth on a surfboard.

—jd

FISH CATCHING METHODS of the WORLD

Fish Catching Methods of the World
A. von Brandt
1964; 191pp.

$15.00 postpaid

from:
Fishing News Books Limited
23 Rosemont Ave.
West Byfleet, Surrey
England

Fishing with hand grenades as practiced after both World Wars was particularly damaging. The hand grenade was actually called "soldier's fishhook". When a hand grenade was exploded in an experiment a diver brought up from the depths ten times more fish than was gathered on the surface.

Fishing by dynamite in Greece became rather notorious, but there it has now also been prohibited for the reasons mentioned. It happens, however, that sharks are attracted by such explosions since they have learnt that the acoustic stimulant meant that they could easily get fish for themselves! Dynamite explosions are therefore now used in some places to attract sharks.

Dynamite in small quantities, however, can be very useful for frightening the fish. Purse seiners in California use small bombs to frighten the fish before the gear is completely pursed and closed. These bombs are called "cherry-bombs" according to their original form. In the Philippines, where fishing with large dip nets is practised, a small explosive is used to stun the encircled fish and so prevent their escape when the net is lifted. This too, however, is illicit, although it is well known that the use of dynamite may possibly determine whether any particular operation is a success or not. If the fish are not bodily damaged, they are stunned only temporarily and will soon recover. This fact also explains why the loss of fish can be relatively small after underwater explosions by blastings, bombs or by firing at a lake during wartime.

Oceanography in Print

A Whole Oceans Catalog! This pamphlet is certainly of use to anyone wanting to learn about the sea. It gives access to information ranging from "elementary" to "adult technical" interests. The preface makes a claim about the ease of obtaining most of the books listed from public resources—checked out, they are easy to get.

[Reviewed by Mary McCabe]

Oceanography in Print
58 pp.

free?

OUT OF PRINT

Ricketts, Edward F., and Jack Calvin. 1952. BETWEEN PACIFIC TIDES. 3rd edition. Revised by Joel W. Hedgpeth. Stanford, Calif.: Stanford University Press.
A detailed account of the habits and habitats of the animals which live in the rocky shores and tide pools of the Pacific Coast. The book is invaluable for its reflection of the spirit of a remarkable man. John Steinbeck's foreword is also not to be missed.

What Everyone Should Know About Oceanography

A practical intro. Has all the publications, organizations, institutions, and rough information on what you're getting into.

—SB

What Everyone Should Know About Oceanography
Robert M. Snyder
1970; 50 pp.

$3.50 postpaid

from:
Snyder Oceanography Services
Jupieter, Florida 33458

Marlinspike Seamanship

Several additions to your books on knots and sailing: (all of these are published by Brown, Son & Ferguson, Ltd. 52 Darnley Street, Glasgow, S. 1. Costs are post-paid in USA) Marlinspike Seamanship by Leonard Popple is the classic text on wire-rope splicing. While he is more concerned with 1-inch diameter cable, I've used his technique on the 3/8 in. halyards on my sailboat. Since professional splicing is about four dollars per, there's more than just snob appeal involved, especially since the book costs $1.30. His other book, Advanced Ropeworking ($.80) discusses splicing large hemp rope, making fenders, etc. and is most valuable as a discussion of tools and techniques, rather than as a cookbook. Three books by Blandfors (see p. 57 of the Spring Catalog); Rope Splicing (.75), Working in Canvas (1.00), and Netmaking (.86) are all well worth their prices. The latter two should be quite valuable. to any tent-living commune that either plays tennis or poaches. A friend of mine who sailed on a five-masted bark, Antara, mentioned that the ship was completely re-rigged recently. As an "instruction book" they used Harold Underhill's Masting and Rigging the Clipper Ship and Ocean Carrier. He used the book to re-rig a Baltic Galeas (schooner with mainsail aft). Along with several other books by Underhill, these are excellent introductions to how these sailing ships "worked". (It costs $8.62) Their catalog "N" is free.

Martin Minow
Bromma, Sweden

For more knots, see p. 125.

—SB

ADORATION OF THE LIGHT

Beyond those looming shapes is brilliant light but here are only shadows reaching out across a vast and empty plain. I'm crossing an enormous floor, an ancient oceanbed so smooth I didn't even stumble when the light was far away. I'm near it now. It pours down in a shower from up above. It streams, it falls, it's a column made of light, a light that's shaped like stone and stone with light inside.

The light's a mass of molded stone hanging in a chamber like a frozen waterfall.

It's a stalactite shaped like some cathedral spire, hanging upside down, a perfect pearl of stone with light inside, shining out through jewels that cling like beads of moisture on a melting tower of ice. Above, it widens and is lost in the high, vaulted ceiling of the chamber. It narrows to a tip that points into a pool of water down below the rocky ledge where I now stand. It shines so bright above it blinds me to look up, but in front and down along the falling spire its light is soft, a comfort to my eyes. Above, the light is blinding white. Below, it's tinted by the jewels to soothing amber.

I can gaze into the amber without blinking. It bathes me in its amber, in its glow, in its love so sweet a subtle sense of danger can't intrude.

Danger tries. It makes a scraping sound behind me. But the love will not allow me to turn away.

I hear it clearly. The sense tries hard to penetrate. It bangs and clamors for attention, but my eyes will not be moved from this love they finally see.

It scrapes behind, and now it hisses, I feel it, coming close, my skin is warned and thrilled by some enormous hostile force behind. My flesh responds in tingling fear but my eyes are bathed in love and soothed by light, and in my breast is perfect adoration, without fear.

But my body must respond. My body feels it and turns itself around to look at David lurking in the shadows of the ledge. My eyes see his eyes shining in the murky dark. My stomach turns, my hair feels wild, but my adoration of the light remains serene. It's only David's eyes, and lower forehead. The rest is monster, the mouth of dragon teeth, the chin and jaws and head leading into short, thick neck and shoulders are horns and scales and fur. Oh it's true all right. He's the monster-guardian of the light. But adoration is quiet in my breast. My love can know no fear.

Leave fear to the flesh. The flesh is better terrified, stronger for the wars. Scared flesh can attack, a quick advance into the very teeth of monsters of the deep, throwing dust into their eyes swinging wildly human fingernails as claws. Oh yes, my friend. It's joined now. Slink back goddamn you hide back in your lair. My flesh is eager and my love serene. It's time, old friend. I'm here.

Boatbuilding

This is the book for the man who wants to put together a boat he can live in and with. Chapelle is full of ideas for getting the maximum use of the limited space on a boat. He is also the easiest way to avoid all the miserable pitfalls one can encounter: leaking hatches and deck seams, toilets that don't work on one tack, or back up and fill the bilge, storage that rots its contents or dumps them on the deck at the first wavelet. There is even a chapter on hand tools and how to use them. The book is generally considered the standard reference of the boatbuilder. Its single drawback is its age (first published in 1940) so it misses the latest developments in materials. Still, it's the best I've seen for staying out of trouble.

[Reviewed by Christopher E. Prael
Suggested by everybody.]

Boatbuilding
Howard I. Chapelle
1941; 624 pp.

$15.00 postpaid

from:
W. W. Norton & Co., Inc.
55 Fifth Avenue
New York, N. Y. 10003

or WHOLE EARTH CATALOG

Amateur Boat Building

A publication of kinks, crochets, tips, arguments, gossip, plans, reviewers, ads. Build a couple rowboats before you build a ship, that's the message I get.

—SB

Amateur Boat Building
Austin Cole, ed.

$6./yr (monthly)

from:
International Amateur Boatbuilding Society
3183 Merrill
Royal Oak, Michigan 48072

Chapelle

I suggest the inclusion of a book called American Small Sailing Craft, *by Howard I. Chapelle. The book was published by Norton in 1951 and copies can be obtained from*

Caravan Books   *still available from* W. W. Norton
87-06 168th Place   500 Fifth Ave.
Jamaica, N.Y. 11432   New York, N.Y. 10003
                                                    $12.50
. . .Price will vary according to condition of book, but expect in the 10-20 dollar range.

Howard Chapelle is the W.F.A. (World's Foremost Authority) on the design, construction and evolution of sailing vessels, although he presents an obvious historical-antiquarian bias. He's a marine architect and a professor of maritime history (Harvard) and is now one of the directors of the Smithsonian Institute.

His best-known works deal with large sailing ships of the XVIII-XIX centuries, and his two books on design and construction are outdated (dealing entirely with wood, pre-fiberglass and ferrocement) but American Small Sailing Craft *is a book no boat freak should be without.*

It is interesting, chavinism notwithstanding, that coastal North America has produced more and better types of small sailboats than any other culture in history. This is the importance of this book. SOMEWHERE in these pages there is a design for a sailing or rowing (auxiliary power not impossible) boat which is PERFECTLY suited for whatever work load and weather and sea conditions any sailor, boat builder or water freak may have to face. If you want to buy, build or have built your IDEAL boat for work, travel or pleasure, this is the place you should look first. There are lake boats as well as deepsea craft, Pacific and Gulf Coasters as well as Down East types discussed; and there is a detailed drawing (at least) of every type mentioned. Which is EVERY TYPE. If you happen to live in, say, Casper, Wyoming, it's a hell of an interesting book anyway. Bear in mind that marine construction techniques are applicable in many ways to land structures.

It's probable that many of the designs included in the book could be executed in ferrocement. I'm sure any of them could be done in fiberglass.

Thom Lee Wharton
Middletown, New Jersey

Amateur Yacht Research Society

Last letter to you I told you about the "amateur yacht research society" well I forgot a very important feature. A correspondence course in yacht design is offered.

In 24 lessons of about 2000 hours work, cost is $325 payable in small instalments with each lesson. For further information write Yacht Design Institute, 111 Woodcrest Avenue, White Plains, New York 10604.

The sea is the last "free range" it's your last chance to "be a cowboy"

Love,

Bill Lange
Sweden

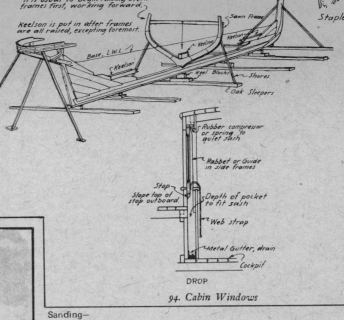

116. Scuppers

94. Cabin Windows

JOHN ATKIN—24' DAY SCHOONER
LOA 22' 4'' /LWL 20' 0'' /Beam 7' 8'' / Draft 3' 0''

S. A. 297 sq. ft. / Displ. 5,888 lbs.

Ballast 765 lbs.

Plans are $50.00 per set, glossy photograph is $2.00. Write to John Atkin, P. O. Box 3005, Norton, Conn. 06820.

DREADNOUGHT BOATWORKS
P. O. Box 221, Carpinteria, Cal. 93013

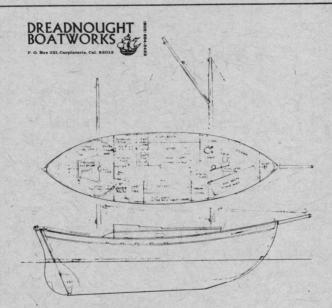

"The Dreadnought is designed for completion by a person of average ability for less than $1,000-$12,000."

Dreadnought Glass Hull

For anyone interested in a cruising knowledge of boatbuilding, there is now in production a Tahiti ketch. It is modelled after the Adios, a three-times-around-the-world traveller. For $4,260.00 you can have a hand-laminated hull of heavy fiberglass, one-piece construction. It is 32 feet long with a 10 foot beam and can be ketch or cutter-rigged. Contact:

Dreadnought Boatworks
Box 221
Carpenteria, Calif. 93013

Mr. & Mrs. Michael Gazzaniga
New York City, N.Y.

Sanding—

1. Wear a gauze mask. Most paint dust is toxic, especially dust from bottom paint.

2. Don't use steel wool. Tiny particles embedded in the surface will eventually rust through the paint.

3. Sand with the grain.

4. Don't leave bare wood exposed too long; it absorbs moisture.

5. If you have never used a machine sander, practice on scrap wood. You'll be glad you did.

6. Don't use a machine sander between paint or varnish coats.

7. Don't apply too much pressure with a machine sander as it may glaze the surface; also, frictional heat may soften the paint or varnish and "load" the sandpaper.

8. Don't sand if your neighbor is about to paint or varnish.

Boatbuilding Manual

With this in combination with Chapelle you've got boatbuilding technique just about surrounded.

—SB

Boatbuilding Manual
Robert M. Steward
1969; 220 pp.

$9.85 postpaid

from:
International Marine Publishing Co
21 Elm Street
Camden, Maine 04843

or

WHOLE EARTH CATALOG

Silicon Bronze

For every structural fastening in a boat it is hard to beat a copper silicon alloy sometimes called Everdur. It is about 96% copper and is so strong that seldom are fastenings wrung off when being driven, and, of major importance, it is highly resistant to corrosion from sea water. The use of this metal removes the risks involved with the brasses and galvanized steel fastenings and is well worth the difference in cost. When it is considered that it takes no more time to drive a bronze screw than other kinds the difference in cost is not as much as the price of the screws alone might indicate, and a point to be remembered is the resale value of a bronze fastened boat.

Practical Ferro-Cement Boatbuilding

I'd call this the funkiest and far most practical of the f.c. books. Also see p. 105.

—SB

[Suggested by Daniel Earle]

Practical Ferro-Cement Boatbuilding
Jay R. Benford, Herman Husen
1970; 216 pp.

$10.00
$.50 postage
Postage: $1.50 airmail; $3.00 Foreign Airmail

from:
J.R. Benford
Box 456
Friday Harbor, Washington 98250

Used Boats

Anyone looking for a used (and sometimes new) boat or related equipment in the Northeast should get ahold of a copy of Soundings. *Covering the coastal area from South Carolina to Maine this newspaper of pleasure and usable boats in season has as many as 5,000 classified listings for everything from ocean racers to long-boat canoes. And each month you get pages of news and features about boats and tricks of the trade in boating and sailing or canoeing and people, on and around the water.*

A years subscription $5.

Soundings
Box 210
Wethersfield, Conn.

On the West Coast the same type of newspaper is available from:

Yachtsman
Box 819
Rio Vista, California 94571

A years subscription $3
35¢ per copy
3 years $7.50

James H. Lawton
Paynes Creek, California

TRADITIONAL old English gaff ketch. Comfortable accommodation: two heads, eight berths. Interesting history. Good condition. $15,000. Contact Carib Cruises Ltd., P.O. Box 188, Castries, St. Lucia. PABC2B

(SISTER SHIP)
24' CUSTOM "Dolphin" Fiberglass Sloop, 1969. Double Vee Berth forward, Enclosed Head, Dinette converts to Double Berth. Complete Galley with Counter, Sink, Ice Chest, Alcohol Stove, etc. Dacron Main, Jib, Hood 150% Genoa; Geared Roller Reefing. Many "Extras" and much Equipment including No. 10 Barient Winches, Main Halyard Reel Winch, Jib Halyard Winch, Pulpit & Life Lines, Chrysler 9.9 Outboard in well, Dinghy, Omni Compass, etc. In Like New Condition - only 10 weeks use. Asking $7,800. Page Marine Services, Yacht Brokerage, 26 Sea Street, Camden, Maine. (207) 236-2383. PABC2B

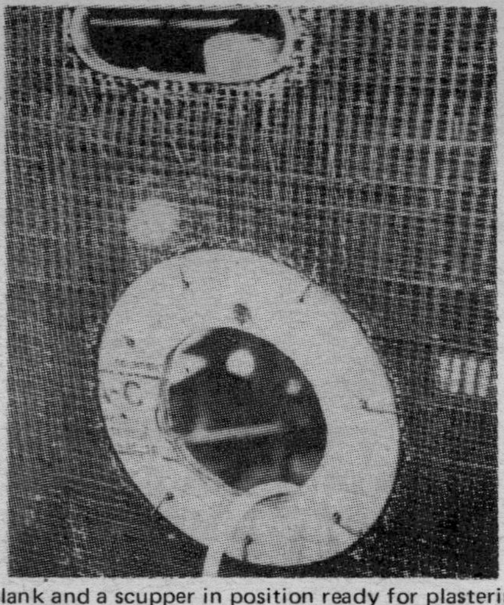

A portlight blank and a scupper in position ready for plastering day. The ends of the wires holding the blank in place are carefully turned in to prevent catching on a trowel. The hole in the hull is cut with an acetylene torch around a 3/4" plywood disc which was used as a template. The disc was conveniently held in place by a single 1/4" eye screw that passed through a hole in its center and screwed into the mesh. The scuppers were prefabricated from stainless steel half-oval, and short 1/4" rods were welded to them on the welding table.

•

Miscellaneous Comments About Plastering

Obviously, not everyone wanting to build a ferro-cement boat will live in an area where there are professional plasterers with boatbuilding experience, readily available. For an individual in such a situation, five courses of action come to mind:

a.) He could move and build his boat in an area where experienced boat plasterers are available.

b.) He could transport a crew of experienced boat plasterers to his job site.

c.) He could transport the foreman only of an experienced boat plastering crew, and fill out the crew with local plasterers (Not cement finishers who are unused to working on vertical surfaces and who do not normally use a hawk in their work.)

d.) He could employ a local crew of professional plasterers who have had no boat experience, use whatever printed material he can find on the subject as a guide, and hope for the best.

e.) He could call in a crew of inexperienced friends and proceed as in d.) above.

As one proceeds down the above list of possibilities, the probability of producing a hull with an acceptable finish diminishes. Although it may be possible for a group of careful, hard-working, inexperienced builders to plaster a hull without professional help and make it structurally sound, the finished product might be an abomination to look at.

As ferro-cement technology advances, it may be that techniques will be developed which will allow the amateur to produce an acceptable, smaller hull with only the help of some inexperienced frinds. The probable sequence of this technique would be to:

a.) produce an exceptionally fair armature,

b.) plaster in the usual fashion,

c.) scrape and broom both the inside and the outside of the hull,

d.) cure, and

e.) after the vessel has cured, glaze the outside of the hull with a glazing compound which can be sanded and shaped.

Luger Boat Kits

Luger makes a line of boat kits intended for assembly by the inexperienced amateur. They have powerboats from 14 to 32 feet, sailboats from 14 to 20 feet, all in fiberglass, and a 22 foot houseboat of wood.

The basic kit consists of all the parts needed for a bare boat. These parts are precut to size and shape so no layout and cutting is necessary. This saves you about a quarter or a third of the effort necessary to build a boat from scratch. The quality of these parts is very high and they will make a strong, safe baot. However, pay no attention to Luger's estimate of time for building the bare boat. I put in 500 man-hours on my houseboat, they predicted 125.

The instructions must be carefully read and reread, because they do contain mistakes. For example, I found I had to drill holes through a laid-up fiberglass job (Step No. 17) in order to install a bracing member (Step No. 32).

Their prices for the bare boat kits are reasonable. Their bare boat doesn't contain such "accessories" as windows, galley hardware, head, latches, hinges, trim and upholstery. Luger sells these as extras. They are generally not of the same quality as the boat itself. In fact they are mediocre and overpriced. I would advise getting your accessories from a mail order discount hardware dealer.

Luger's Customer Service Dept. is slow and inefficient, but they do stand behind their guarantee. They'll gladly give you a "no-questions-asked" refund on anything you wish to return.

Best of all, their catalog is free. It's well worth looking at it if you're seriously considering building yourself a boat.

P.S. Presently, I'm living on my boat in a marina. I think living on the water is one alternate that many people overlook. The rent is cheap (averages about $2.00/month for every foot of boat length. 22 foot boat cost $44/month for slip.) The people are friendly (they're all boat freaks, or they wouldn't be there). My 22 foot house boat cost me about $2600 to build and finish without power, which is a fairly inexpensive home. It's a good life.

[Suggested and reviewed by Stephen Schwartz]

Catalog
free

from:
Luger Industries, Inc.
1300 East Cliff Rd.
Burnsville, Minnesota 55378

$ 2000 Postpaid

Ferro-Cement Boat Construction

The establishment book. If I were building with f.c. I'd want every book on the subject. This one has excellent technical information on treating concrete, mixing procedures, curing, design factors, etc. No nonsense.

—SB

Ferro-Cement Boat Construction
Jack R. Whitener
1971; 128 pp.

$7.50 postpaid

from:
Cornell Maritime Press, Inc.
Box 109
Cambridge, Maryland 21613

or WHOLE EARTH CATALOG

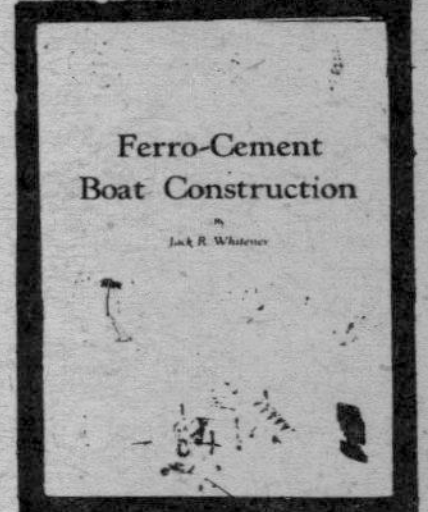

When comparing the weight of a ferro-cement hull with that of a similar wooden hull, remember both will be the same weight at around the 30-foot length. If one progresses beyond the 30-foot length, then the ferro-cement hull becomes some five percent lighter than a similar wooden one. Going the other way, the ferro-cement rapidly gets heavier than wood, unless one uses less hull thickness. The average hull thickness for this discussion will be about one inch, though on hulls smaller than 30 feet one can certainly go to a thinner hull.

Ferro-cement hulls larger than 30 feet in workboats, power cruisers, or sailboats are most economical to build when compared to wood, steel, aluminum or fiberglas. Ferro-cement gives an increase of interior space when compared to wood construction, something on the order of 12 percent. This is due, of course, to the elimination of thick beams and frames, and to greater planking thickness, especially in larger hull sizes.

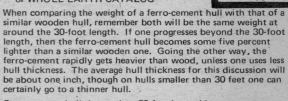

COMBAT

The dragon drew away when D.R. rushed him, but then came biting back and swiping with his claws. The dragon's rush maneuvered D.R. toward the wall, then pinned him there with furious snapping of his knife-like teeth till D.R. fell and rolled beneath the claws and came up past the monster, running for the edge. The monster howled in rage and turned but D.R. had already leaped and gained a foothold on the stalactite, and broken off a slender, jagged spire. He started to climb up the stalactite then, but the dragon slithered onto it above and trapped him on the lower, thinning levels of the shaft. D.R. braced his feet in solid clefts and held his weapon ready in his hands. When the dragon reached down to claw him D.R. stabbed it through the scales and made it scream in furious pain and slither lower to bring his teeth in range. It bit and clawed but each time D.R. struck it back, drawing blood from wounds in the monster's face and head and paws. The dragon's tail extended back across the ledge, its endless body still wound deep among the shadowed labyrinths above. The monster's writhing pushed small stones and grains of dust off the ledge into the pool below, making the green water come alive with squirming creatures. Tails and fins cut the surface, long snake-like tentacles reached into the air and felt along the edges of the pool. The monster coiled along the folds and clefts of the stalactite up above, pressing down and down, D.R. fought back as long as he had room to stand, but the monster pressed him down and down and he retreated until there was only the smooth, thin tip of the stalactite left between him and the pool. The dragon swiped at D.R. with his claw, then swiftly struck again and caught him hard upon the shoulder. D.R. thrust his weapon, but already the chamber was turning, he was falling, he felt the water close around him and the creatures thrashing as he sank deep, deep, the monster's head behind him, biting for his legs.

D.R. felt the teeth sink in, then something stirring, burning in his veins, a stinging venom. D.R. twisted and tried to pull away but the monster held him fast between its teeth and dragged him down and down. D.R.'s legs were numb now but there was strength yet in his back and arms. He saw the monster clearly in the light his spire gave off, and he maneuvered till he had a proper angle. With both hands he swung the spire and stabbed the monster in the eye. He stabbed again, and sunk the spire so deep into the second eye he couldn't pull it out again. Black blood spurted and darkened the churning water as D.R.'s own mind darkened into sleep. In his deaththroes the dragon plunged, carrying D.R.'s body and its own through endless fathoms of the deep.

Semple Steam Engines

Develop fire to twenty horsepower with wood or coal. Ride up the river. Finished engines or kits.

—SB

Semple Engine Co., Inc.
Box 6805
St. Louis, MO 63144

Semple Steam Engines

Five Horsepower (single)	
No. 34 DW 3" x 4" - wheel reverse	$256
No. 34 DL 3" x 4" - lever reverse	$320
Ten Horsepower (compound - 2 cylinders) lever reverse	$569

Semple Marine Power Units
(Engine, Boiler, Accessories)

Five Horsepower (standard)	$1830
Five Horsepower (special)	$2107
Ten Horsepower	$2893
Twenty Horsepower (dual ten)	$5403
Condenser (optional on 5 hp)	$ 97

Magazines:

"Steam Power Quarterly" — $8.00 a year
Peter Scott-Brown, Editor
636 Ralston Street
Reno, Nevada 89503

"Light Steam Power" — $7.70 a year
Kirk Michael,
Isle of Man, G.B.

"The Iron Men Album" — $4.00 a year
Box 328, Lancaster, PA 17604

Boat Owners Guide

Published yearly in the winter, this guide gives the full range of what's available in boats, what's new, what prices are, and where to order. —SB

Boat Owners Guide
1969; 320 pp.

$1.95 postpaid ($.50 more outside U. S.)

from:
Yachting Publishing Corporation
50 West 40th Street
New York, N. Y. 10036

Best Boat Buying

If some of the members choose to use boats as a more versatile survival platform, the best place to buy them seems to be Hong Kong new or England, second hand. England because they have a Lloyds broker who will inspect boats for a fee.

By using a magazine like "Yachts and Yachting" in the classified section, one could acquire a sound boat at a reasonable price.

Brian Sauer
Pointe Claire
Quebec

Yachts & Yachting

$11.42 /yr (fortnightly)

from:
Yachting Press Ltd.
196 Eastern Esplanade
Southend-On-Sea
Essex
England

ALACRITY
Well maintained and in excellent condition. 18ft. 6in. L.O.A. Beam 6ft. 11in, Draft 1ft. 10in. 3 berth, Fibreglass, pulpit, pushpit, rails and dodgers, Gaz cooking/lighting. Seagull Century Plus outboard, 2 foresails, Chemical toilet, navigation lights. Many cruising extras. Can be stored until required. £690. Dukes, Antrim Road, Belfast.

FOLKBOAT. Built in East Germany of Carvel Mahogany Strip Planking on Oak in 1967. 4 berths in 2 cabins with W.C., Galley, Hanging Locker, etc. 10 H.P. Volvo Penta 2 cyl., 4-stroke petrol engine with electric start gives good 6 knots. Hollow spruce mast with S/S fittings. Good inventory includes Echosounder, Clock, Barometer, Avon Dinghy, etc. 12 volt battery. Laid up ashore Hants. £1,950 o.n.o.

Used Sails

Bacon & Associates, Inc., 528 Second Street, Annapolis, Maryland 21403, are the best source of used sail boat sails in the United States. Bacon & Associates, on request, will send you a list or lists of used sails they have in stock. The lists run as follows.

List "AC" For centerboard type boats, sails up to 25' luff size.

List "AK" for keel type boats, Mainsails from 25' luff to 45' luff, appropriate jibs, mizzens, genoas, staysails, spinnakers, to 45' luff, all thru 7 oz. weight.

List "B" Big sails, over 45' luff; and heavy working & storm sails, of all sizes, 8 oz. or heavier.

Low $ List: Mains, Jibs, Genoas, Spinnakers, for keel boats and other large boats. Damaged Dacrons, some excellent cottons, much used synthetic & cotton sails. All sizes, weights.

"Gaff" list: Gaff-Head, gunter-rig, 4-sided sails, all sizes, all fabrics. (Usually a ½ page sheet as this listing is small)

Bacon & Associates, is a quality outfit and able to save the sailor lots of $'s. They give an excellent discription of the sail for sale and allow you a ten day examination.

A quote from their "AK" listing:

Main, 6.5 oz. Dacron by Ratsey. Luff 33' 10" x 37' 6" x 13' 9" foot. 5/8" slides on shackles on taped luff & foot. One shag patch on batten pocket. Leach draft line. 3 draft gussets on fot. Numbered. Flattener reef at foot. With bag. Excellent. $175.00

Their lists generaly run 10 to 15 pages of good, clear discriptions. The sails will be just as discribed and their service is prompt. If you know anything about sails you can read a lot into the listing and you will save money.

I hope this is a satisfactory review. If you are going to send me ten bucks for it, I will be so appreciative of the gesture that I will use three of the ten to purchase a Spring 1970 Catalog, so you can just send me $7.00 and the Catalog.

Thanks,

*F. Harris
Lahaina, Hawaii*

Jim Brown Sailing Trimarans

*nice bunch of plans.
build your own,
sail to algeria.*

—jd

Catalog: **$4.00**

Information

free

from:
Jim Brown Sailing Trimarans
Box 2291
Santa Cruz, CA 95060

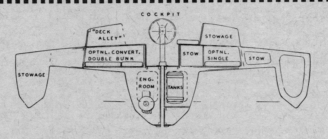

"BROWN 37"
DESIGN NO. 107

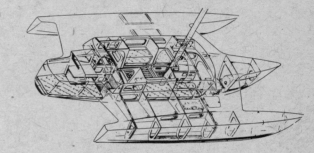

Wharram Polynesian Catamaran

I noticed in the Fall Catalog you carried a notice on Jim Brown Trimarans, which I believe are excellent designs. (They were among the three or four I would have liked to build myself.) However, there were three considerations which weighed somewhat against them in my case, and might be serious factors for other Catalog readers. No. 1— They cost much loot— lots of fiberglass, lots of resin, lots of high class lumber & fittings. No. 2— They take skill, equipment, and time to build. and No. 3— They could be pretty exciting to dock singlehanded.

I believe that if someone is unstable enough to want to cross a large ocean in a small sailboat in the first place, a Wharram design will probably provide the best, most economical, and most enjoyable, chance of survival.

Keep up the good work, and stay loose.

Sincerely,

*Ed. J. Kytta
Townsend, Mass.*

James Wharram
c/o The Long House
Milford Docks
Milford Haven
Pembs, So. Wales

ORO

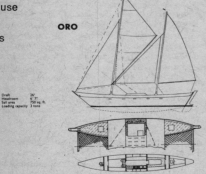

Overall length	46'	Draft	26"
Waterline length	35' 3"	Headroom	6' 3"
Overall beam	20'	Sail area	750 sq. ft.
Beam of each hull	7'	Loading capacity	3 tons

Fabulous ORO can be built and equipped for £2,000 in 1,000 working hours, designed to sail at speed averages of 8-10 knots (peak speed of 15-20 knots).

ORO has 4 private bunk cabins, each with a double bunk and an 18" deep and 6' wide wardrobe.

The 2 "working" cabins, galley and chartroom/library/office, are 7'6" long and 7' at deck level) wide. Provision for 3 extra single bunks.

The main hatches lift off as on a cargo ship, so that air and sun can enter the ship in warm weather. Designed for fast, all-weather weekend sailing for 6-8 people, ocean-voyaging for 4-6, suitable for charter work, beach chartering, sailing guests or a small expedition ship.

Jerry John

Most boat dwellers crap in the bay or the river and then wonder why the fish and the people go away. Here's a clean alternative.

—SB

Jerry John

$80

from:
Dillon-Beck Manufacturing Co.
1227 Central Ave.
Hillside, New Jersey 07205

STPA

Another marine discount catalog. —SB

Catalog

$.50 from:
Sportsman's Trading Posts of America, Inc.
Box 419
Rockville Centre, N. Y. 11571

Non-Fouling

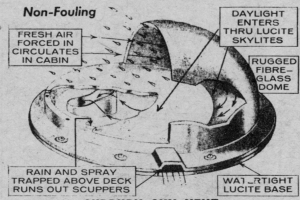

FRESH AIR FORCED IN CIRCULATES IN CABIN

DAYLIGHT ENTERS THRU LUCITE SKYLITES

RUGGED FIBRE-GLASS DOME

RAIN AND SPRAY TRAPPED ABOVE DECK RUNS OUT SCUPPERS

WATERTIGHT LUCITE BASE

SUDBURY SKY VENT

Give your boat more light and fresh air. Install this new, practical creation—the Sudbury SKY-VENT. Rugged dome, molded of laminations of tough fibre glass, never needs painting unless you want to; is set over heavy plate of thick, transparent lucite that lets in light and air, yet keeps out rain and spray.

Stock #		L.P.	S.P.	Ship. Wt.
13958	9-inch Sudbury Sky-Vent — each	42.75	29.95	4 lbs.
13959	12-inch Sudbury Sky-Vent — each	71.25	54.95	6 lbs.
13960	18-inch Sudbury Sky-Vent — each	99.95	74.95	10 lbs.

GAS VENTED TO ATMOSPHERE

FLEXIBLE HOSE

EXISTING TOILET

CHEMICAL TREATMENT SECTION

EFFLUENT DISCHARGED OVERBOARD

SOLIDS SEPARATION SECTION

Sailing Clothes

VICTORY SWEATERS, made in England, distributed in U.S. through Fulton Supply, Fulton Street, New York City. $18.95 (?)

These sweaters are made of wool with the oil left in——are very good for sailing, crusing through rain forests, or just plain potting about in. Those who have them live in them. Like a sweatshirt (with high, rolled collar), but for colder weather. Fulton supply, which puts out a free catalog, outfits both commercial fishermen and sailing people. Good place.

"TOPSIDERS," which are sailing shoes (leather & nylon & canvas), boots; both with special tread. Supplied by Sperry, somewhere in Conn. (Streeter & Quarles West in San Francisco carries the brand, and can tell you the home base) Various prices.

These shoes seem to cost twice as much as those put out by the competition struggling to break Topsiders' corner on the market. For example 11.95 for the canvas, 12.95 for the nylon sneakers. Don't know how successful the competition has been; Topsiders seem to be *the* universal sailing shoe. Have used them; they work.

FOUL (OR WET) WEATHER GEAR, made by Helly Hansen of Norway, distributed in U. S. by Canor Plarex, Inc.

1) 4200 23rd Ave W.
   Seattle, Wash 98199
2) 6 Westchester Plaza
   Elmsford, NY 10523
3) 41 Alexander Street
   Vancouver, B.C., CANADA

This seems to be the best gear around. Used by many deep water sailors. Have seen it (felt it? touched it? etc.) and it works. Very good stuff. (see p. 262)

C. Pitt
Urbana, Ill. 61801

294 Boats
Nomadics

West Products

To the boat owner/builder——or someone with a similar cramped living space such as a VW camper bus, trailer, dome or tree house——West Products offers an excellent chance to order high quality fittings, tackle, rope, etc. at extremely low prices. Compare the usual Yacht Store prices with West's for "Dacron" rope.

[Suggested and reviewed by Dr. Stephen Morris]

Catalog

free from:
West Products Corp.
P. O. Box 707
E. Boston, MA 02128

Sea Line

100% DU PONT
"DACRON"
TYPE 67 FIBER
MARINE ROPE
LAID CONSTRUCTION

Sea/Line marine "DACRON" rope is available in any length you require: all orders are put up on shipping reels. Quantity price reductions usually occur for 300 and 600 foot increments. In-between lengths are priced accordingly.

catalog #	DIA.	average breaking strength	PRICE PER FOOT			shipping wt. per 100 ft.
			1 ft. to 299 ft.	300 ft. to 599 ft.	600 ft. and over	
12-303	3/16"	1000 lbs.	3½¢	3½¢	3¼¢	2 lbs.
12-304	1/4"	1800 lbs.	4¾¢	4½¢	4¼¢	3 lbs.
12-305	5/16"	2900 lbs.	7¾¢	7¼¢	7¢	4 lbs.
12-306	3/8"	3600 lbs.	11½¢	11¼¢	11¢	6 lbs.
12-307	7/16"	5200 lbs.	15¢	14½¢	14¢	8 lbs.
12-308	1/2"	6500 lbs.	18½¢	18¢	17½¢	9 lbs.
12-310	5/8"	10000 lbs.	30¢	29½¢	29¢	13 lbs.
12-312	3/4"	14000 lbs.	42¢	41½¢	41¢	19 lbs.

STAINLESS STEEL TURNBUCKLES

At these prices, why buy bronze?

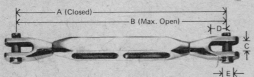

Unsurpassed for strength, durability, and appearance, these Turnbuckles are made of the most corrosion-resistant material available. Built in Sweden of Type 316 Stainless Steel and polished to a high luster to increase corrosion resistance and beauty. Even the cotter pins are of the same high grade metal through the ends as well as through the middle barrel.

WORKING DIMENSIONS						Approx. Tensile Strength
SIZE	A	B	C	D	E	
1/4"	5 3/4"	8 1/8"	1/4"	3/8"	3/16"	3,500
5/16"	6 7/8"	9 5/8"	5/16"	5/8"	5/16"	6,300
3/8"	8	11	3/8"	5/8"	5/16"	6,900
7/16"	8 1/2"	11 5/8"	7/16"	5/8"	3/8"	9,800
1/2"	9 3/8"	12 1/4"	1/2"	3/4"	7/16"	14,000
5/8"	12 3/16"	16 5/8"	5/8"	1"	9/16"	19,000

SIZE	CAT. #	PRICE	WGT.
1/4"	22-104	$10.00 ea.	1/4 lb.
5/16"	22-105	$11.50 ea.	1/2 lb.
3/8"	22-106	$13.00 ea.	3/4 lb.
7/16"	22-107	$15.00 ea.	1 lb.
1/2"	22-108	$19.00 ea.	1 1/4 lb.
5/8"	22-110	$33.00 ea.	2 3/4 lb.

FREE MASTER CHART SELECTOR.

U.S. Coast and Geodetic Survey Chart Selectors for
Atlantic and Gulf Coasts   Chart Catalog # 1 FREE
Pacific Coast & Hawaii   Chart Catalog # 2 FREE
Alaska   Chart Catalog # 3 FREE
Lake Survey: Catalog of Great Lakes charts. FREE
U.S. Naval Oceanographic Master Chart Selector for United States, Cat. Region "O", Canada-Cat. Region "1" (Other areas of the world on request.)
35c EACH

Defender Industries

If boating is your bag & you are a self-help enthusiast you need the "Defender Industries" catalog of marine hardware & accessories. If it has to do with boats, they have it: engines to dacron sails, bilge alarms to fiberglass roving. Included are pages of information on new products, application procedures for some of the materials, construction & maintenance tips for boaters and a page devoted to "How to Build a Fiberglass Boat." Defender Industries claim that they are "one of the most complete marine supply firms in the world." They say their prices are competitive and "should we be undersold on any current standard materials, you may place your order at the lower price by merely including a tear sheet from the cheaper source, and we will fill your order."

[Suggested and reviewed by C. P. Christianson]

Catalog

$.75

from:
Defender Industries, Inc.
255 Main Street
New Rochelle, NY 10801

Sea Line ROPE & SAIL SEWING KIT

Everything you need for rope and sail work, in a single heavy-duty nylon drawstring kit bag. The top quality materials include: Sea/Line Stainless Steel rigger's knife with marlin spike. ● Heavy-duty leather sewing palm (specify right or left hand). ● Swedish half-round Stainless Steel fid. ● 4 nickel-plated English "sailmaker's" needles. ● 2 Stainless Steel sewing needles. ● 2 rolls of Sea/Line waxed nylon whipping thread. ● 2 rolls of white Sea/Line nylon sewing thread. ● 2 rolls of Sea/Line utility tape. ● 1 roll of sail fabric repair tape (1½" wide).

Cat. No. 15-319 $9.00 plus postage

Knife Engraving: Max. 12 letters on one line, $1.20 (add 10c each add'l. character or punctuation. Max. total 2 lines, 20 spaces per line).

Additional Needles and Sewing Palm

4 nickel-plated steel English sailmaker's needles in a waterproof vial. Catalog No. 15-322 50c ppd. U.S.A.

Individual needles   15c each ppd. U.S.A.
2¼" Catalog No. 15-3221   2½" Catalog No. 15-3222
3" Catalog No. 15-3223   3½" Catalog No. 15-3224
Heavy-duty leather sewing palm $6.95 Ppd USA
Right-Hand Palm   Catalog No. 15-323
Left-Hand Palm   Catalog No. 15-3231

Discount Marine Hardware Ltd.

Another marine discount catalog. They claim low prices on British Seagull motors and Avon inflatable boats.

—SB

Catalog

$0.75

from:
Discount Marine Hardware Ltd.
875 A West 15th St.
Newport Beach, CA 92660

150 WATT

RAY JEFFERSON MODEL "4150A" MARINE RADIO TELEPHONE—
Eight crystal controlled channels plus standard broadcast band — ~~$499.95~~ List Price OUR PRICE
Complete with four Crystals, Microphone and **$395.00**
Universal Mounting Bracket.

PART SIX

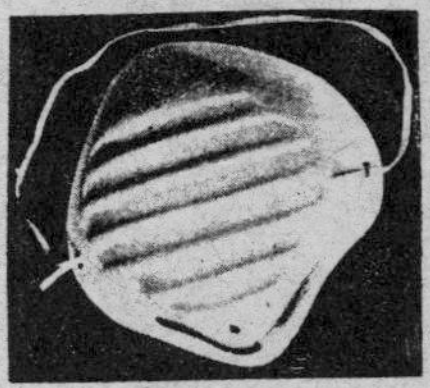

LET EVERY SOUL BE SUBJECT UNTO THE HIGHER POWERS

Mrs. Godsey was in the post office in the far corner of her store, sorting through the Tuesday morning mail. As if people had known it would be a puny delivery that morning, only Mrs. Thornton was there waiting for Mrs. Godsey to hand the letters out. Most days the store was half full of people waiting on their mail, five, six, sometimes as many as a dozen of them, sitting in chairs or leaning against the soft drink cooler, waiting and talking while Mrs. Godsey organized the mail for distribution. But this morning there was only Mrs. Thornton, and to Mrs. Godsey's mind that was just as well. The only mail in the whole batch that was in the least bit personal was a post card to Wendell Hall from his daughter in Detroit, and she was asking for money. Mrs. Back's copy of The Upper Room came, and Barry Berry got a statement from the Famous Writer's School. Old Mr. McClanahan got a brown envelope from the Social Security Administration but you could tell just by looking that it didn't have a check in it. Circulars, statements, bills, and fourteen identical blue envelopes with white writing on it, promotional literature from the Stewart Kesey Soap Company in Chicago addressed to "Boxholder", Trace Fork, Kentucky, and that was it, as sorry a batch of mail as Mrs. Godsey had seen in all the years she'd been postmistress.

"I declare it looks like that Charlene would write me," said Mrs. Thornton. "I written her twice this last month and narry a peep have I heard. I begun thinking she don't much care about her old momma any more."

Mrs. Thornton wiped a tear from her eyes with the cuff of her long sleeve.

"Now honey, you know that aint so," said Mrs. Godsey as she came out of the little cage that was the post office. "You know it aint like Charlene not to write."

"Sometimes I believe it is," said Mrs. Thornton. "Sometimes I know for sure it is."

(continued)

Stick and Rudder

Subtitle: 'An Explanation of the Art of Flying.' This book was written in 1944 and is still, I understand, the basic flying book. Writing, illustration, comprehensiveness—it's a full-throated classic. I've never flown a plane, but I've flown other stuff, and every page glimmers with useful hints for every kind of flight. Maybe some Sufi pilot would like to do an allegorical review of this profound book.

—SB

Stick and Rudder
Wolfgang Langewiesche
1944; 389 pp.

$9.95 postpaid

from:
McGraw-Hill Book Co
East:
Princeton Road
Hightstown, N.J. 08520

Mid-continent:
Manchester Road
Manchester, Mo. 63062

West:
8171 Redwood Highway
Novato, Ca. 94947

or WHOLE EARTH CATALOG

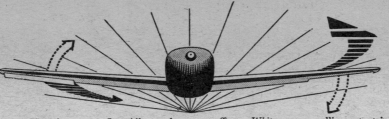

The adverse yaw effect. Ailerons have *two* effects. *White arrows:* rolling effect is what pilot wants. *Black arrows:* yawing effect is an undesired by-product of rolling effect. Here, the pilot banks to (his) left, presumably in order to turn to the left, but the airplane at the same time yaws to (pilot's) *right.* That's why this yaw effect is called "adverse." Pilot must kill this effect by using rudder.

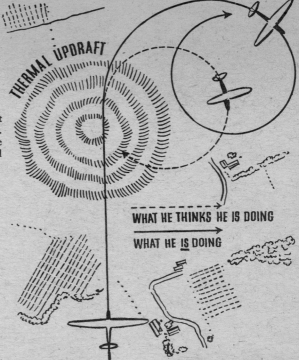

THERMAL UPDRAFT

WHAT HE THINKS HE IS DOING

WHAT HE **IS** DOING

Stick and Throttle. The so-called 'elevator' is really its up-and-down control. This is hard to believe but is one of the keys to the art of piloting.

Hence the Angle of Attack cannot be seen simply by looking out the window; in fact, it cannot be seen at all! For remember, Angle of Attack is the angle at which the wing meets the air—and we can't see air. That is perhaps largely why flying is so much *i* an art. In baseball the batter keeps his eye on the ball that he is going to hit. Flying is the art of batting the air down with our wings; but in flying, our trouble is that we can't see the air; hence we often fail to hit it right, and hence so many of us break our necks

Take your hands off a good airplane's stick, and it will do a good job of flying all by itself. Take your feet off its rudder as well, and many airplanes will even then do a fair job. The airplane has a built-in will of its own, and generally speaking it wants to do whatever is necessary to maintain healthy flight.

In actual practice most airplanes have a tendency to hunt. This means that with the controls released, the ship will not fly at constant speed but will oscillate up and down, now dropping its nose, building up speed, diving for perhaps 10, 20, 30 seconds. Then, with its essential stability and better self asserting itself, it will catch itself, raise its nose, try to get rid of its excess speed, and go into a climb. In this climb, a bit too much speed is lost, and the ship noses down again, to repeat the process.

On wings it is safe to be high, dangerous to be low; safe to go fast, dangerous to go slow. Generally speaking, if you want the airplane to go up, you point its nose up; but point its nose up a little too much, and you go down in a stall or a spin. In landing an airplane, to make it sink down on the runway and stay down, you move the controls much as for an extreme upward zoom. In the glide, if you want to descend more steeply, you point your airplane's nose down less steeply; if you want to descend less steeply, you point the airplane's nose down more steeply! And—most spectacular contrariness of all—in emergencies, when the airplane is sinking toward the ground in a 'mush' or falling in a stall or a spin, and you are afraid of crashing into the ground, the only way to keep it from crashing is to point its nose down and dive at the ground, as if you wanted to crash!

Flying is done largely with one's imagination! If one's images of the airplane are correct, one's behavior in the airplane will quite naturally and effortlessly also be correct.

The pitfall of glide control: when doing the right thing, you get the wrong result first, the right result only later. Nosing the airplane up steepens the descent, but *first* causes a temporary ballooning. Nosing the airplane down shallows the descent, but *first* causes an extra sink. Be patient for a few seconds.

As you approach the ground you must keep your vision relaxed and look all around; you must take in the whole scenery, the perspective of the hangars on the side of the field and the other airplanes on the field, the parked automobiles, the trees, the telegraph poles all around, the grass, the horizon; for it is from the perspective and apparent motion of such things that you will get a vivid perception of your height; and a staring eye will not see what matters. When you get tense, you will almost certainly stare; approaching the ground, most students do get tense; that is largely why the landing is so difficult for most beginners.

If an untutored person tries to fly an airplane and uses the controls in the manner that seems most 'natural' to him, responding most energetically and most quickly to those disturbances that 'naturally' impinge most sharply on his consciousness, the flight will almost certainly end in a spiral dive and a crash.

Weather Flying

It's a good title. You don't fly in the sky, or in just air, you fly in the weather. This book takes you through what that means, how to recognize and know ahead what you're in for, how to handle it, what to avoid, and how to survive your mistakes. A good companion book to Langewiesche.

—SB

Weather Flying
Robert N. Buck
1970; 261 pp.

$5.95 postpaid

from:
MacMillan Company
866 Third Ave.
New York, N.Y. 10022

or WHOLE EARTH CATALOG

The nature of the brain is such that we see what we have seen before, and what we have a name for. We are blind to things which have not been properly introduced. People had fronts passing over them for thousands of years, but nobody ever saw a front as *front*—i.e., as boundary between contrasting air masses. Then, 50 years ago, the Norwegians first recognized the *cold front*, described it, named it. Now everybody can plainly see many frontal passages every year. In this sense, some descriptive meterology helps the pilot fly the weather.

Lows that slow down are the nasties that really ruin a forecast. There isn't anything more difficult to figure out than a stalled front. If a cold front was supposed to go right through the East Coast but slows down and stops instead in the New York area, things go to pieces. Instead of clearing, the skies remain cloudy; wind hangs limply around the southerly quadrant, getting over to southeast perhaps; and fog and low ceilings prevail. With such a situation a kink may develop on the stalled front, a wave form, and a new low pressure area move up along the coast following the stalled front's line and putting out a lot of weather.

We've mentioned that scared or not a weather-flying pilot has to control his emotions and keep his imagination subdued or used only to advantage. The pilot has to fly carefully and thoughtfully even though his knees may tremble.

The toughest place to keep this fear under control is a thunderstorm. It is dark, it is turbulent, rain comes down in a deluge, lightning flashes close, and occasionally ozone from a nearby lightning passage can be smelled. A lightning discharge may make a brilliant flash and loud bang as it goes off the airplane. An irritating hashy noise may be tearing at our eardrums from static in the radio. It's a hell of a place for a man to be! It takes a strong will to say, "I'll watch the horizon and keep it level. I'll hold that heading and it will all turn out okay." But that's it, and the only way to do it.

If we summed up one weather rule it would always be: *Have an out!*

Fly above this kind of cloud. Beneath these cumulus it will be rough and uncomfortable; while on top the air will be clear, smooth, and cool.

The Air Almanac

Here's a book of pure data. If you need to know where sun, moon, planets, stars are, or where you are, this book is prime source. It is published quarterly for the forthcoming 3 months.

—SB

THE
AIR ALMANAC
1969
MAY–AUGUST

The Air Almanac
570 pp.

$3.75

from:
Superintendent of Documents
U. S. Government Printing Office
Washington, D. C. 20402

Aeronautical Charts

Mack Taylor is a friend who has a fondness for the blank places on other people's continents. He walks into them in his tennis shoes and makes friends with the chief and walks out and tells stories about how the main hazard in the jungle is dead-eye monkeys who shit on you from the trees. Mack says that often the only maps with information in the blanks are the ONCs—Operational Navigation Charts, available for $1.15 apiece. The Coast and Geodetic Survey Catalog of Aeronautical Charts has a map index for ONCs and sundry other flight maps and publications.

—SB

Catalog

free

from:
Distribution Division C-44
National Ocean Survey
Riverdale, MD 20840

Yay

Now, here.s why I'm writing, private aviation is beautifully compatible with the life style of WHOLE EARTH readers and not at all the straight, statusy thing many think it is.

You can get a good two passenger plane for under $2,500, a good four passenger plane for under $3,500. You can get 35 mpg and travel at more than 100 mph for about 5 cents a mile. You can be free as a bird, see the countryside as no earthling can, camp away from crowds and fuzz, be welcome on farmers' landing strips and even work on the farm for a while.

You can trade learning to fly for the instructor's use of your plane— and do the same flying-time-for-labor trade with a mechanic for maintenance. But maintenance isn't as high as generally supposed anyway. If you have a four passenger plane you can share expenses with other couples and travel almost free since their share covers gas, oil, food, etc. for the owners (the owners share covers maintenance, depreciation, insurance, tie-down— so it's really a fair (or should I say fare), (sorry about that, it was pretty bad), bargain.

I have enclosed a copy of *Trade-A-Plane* ($4.00 per year), and some aviation charts which show how many airports and landing strips there really are. I have marked some plane prices in *Trade-A-Plane* just to give you some idea of costs.

I can not here do justice to the truly far out places we've been— the deserted beaches where we've walked and slept naked in the sun, the rivers we've followed like footpaths only to land at their edge and camp when they turned to gold in the afternoon sun, nor the islands, idyllic and "ours" where we've floated and swum in water whose clarity was only surpassed by the crystal clear sky above us. We have encountered the scent of orange blossoms half a mile over Florida at night and visited Mexican villages and out of the way towns no tourist chained to a Cadillac ever will see.

To come down, pilots are kindred souls welcome at flying farmers' landing strips. (It's almost impossible to be more than 15 miles from a landing strip in the midwest— see Chicago chart). Most airport operators will lend you a car to go to the grocery store, and many airports keep several beat up VW's or similar cars around that you can use for no more than a couple of dollars placed in a cigar box in the glove compartment. Not long ago the operator at Lancaster, Pa. apologized for being out of cars and gave me the snow-plow to drive into town.

Quite apart from the bare bones super economy kind of mostly nomadic flying, one of the best buy planes for more settled and regularly working couples or singles is the early Cessna 172. A four passenger, all metal, 120 mph. tri-cycle gear plane, it can be bought for about $5,000. On time payments that would be about $500 down, $100 a month. Maintenance is low and you travel 120 miles for 8 gallons of gas at .42 a gallon.

Don.t be turned off by age of planes advertised, age really isn't a factor with a reasonably well maintained plane.

Peace,
Don Biggs
Arlington, VA.

Boo

In light of what you state as your purpose (which I whole-heartedly endorse,) I think you are way off base on a good part of your information on flying. 99% of all flying is directly government controlled, is very big business, and demands and requires formal education and training. Modern flying has been described as long periods of boredom punctuated by moments of sheer panic; if you knew what was going on in the cockpit as you circled in solid overcast for a rush hour approach to Kennedy you'd never fly again. You haven't gotten far enough away from the crap yet in the CATALOG.

Try soaring. The Schwiezer's are the only major manufacturers of sailplanes in the US. All of their ships are very tough, and while very short of performance compared to the German fibreglass ships, a lot of fun and an awful lot cheaper. The I-26, a classic sailplane, (Steve McQueen flew one in "The Thomas Crown Affair,") can be built from a kit for around $2500.00. It will be worth more than you paid for it when finished.

I'm getting very hot on ballooning, but know nothing about it. Worth looking into.

I suggest dropping the So You'd Like to Buy an Airplane *and* Used Plane Buying Guide. *You only need two things to buy an airplane: a copy of "Trade-A-Plane" for current prices, and an A&E mechanic to check it out. All that crap about checking the fabric for wrinkles doesn't mean squat if the spars are rotten. The best places to look are the little grass filled fields and short strips around your home. There are invariably perfectly good 15 and 20 year old planes sitting around for $2000-2500. Great fun and you can sell it a year later for what you paid for it.*

Stick and Rudder definitely keep in. Indeed a classic; not a bit outdated and never will be. There are several flying magazines available. If you've read one you've read them all. ("How to make safe landings ANYWHERE!" turns out to be the same old rehash about power and attitude.) There is one exception: "Private Pilot." Relatively new, struggling I suspect, and very exciting. Also very nicely put together, from a technical and design point of view. I hope they make it.

Drop the BD-4. Its not really a home-built in the "pure" sense, but a kit. It's not really a very good plane (no wing dihedral, i.e., lousy longitudinal stability, tiny tail, and flimsy gear.) It's not really cheap either. It appeals to insurance salesmen who always wanted a four seater of their own to fly the kids and the missus up to the folks but never could afford it, and never finish it. It's a bummer really. Soap inside your chocolate bar.

Pertinent addresses:

Private Pilot, Dept. PV5
3 West 57th St.
New York, N.Y. 10019

Schweizer Aircraft Corp.
Box 147
Elmira, N.Y. 14902

The Soaring Society of America, Inc.
P.O. Box 66071-W
Los Angeles, CA 90066

I'm not sure sport flying can be saved anymore in this country. I'm not sure we can afford to save it in the light of the zillions of things which need help more badly. But I would very much like to.

Sincerely,
D.J. Clausing
Thetford, Vermont

Private Pilot Study Guide

Of preparatory books for the FAA exam, this is the best. Cram, pass, fly.

—SB

Private Pilot Study Guide
Leroy Simonson
1973; 440 pp & map

$10.00 postpaid

from:
Aviation Book Company
Box 4187
Glendale, CA 91202

or WHOLE EARTH CATALOG

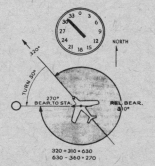

Others

Other basic books recommended by **Plane & Pilot Magazine:**

■ *The New Private Pilot*
■ *Student Pilot Flight Manual*
■ *Private Pilot Flight Manual*
■ *Flight Maneuvers Manual*
■ *Roll Around A Point*
■ *Instrument Procedures and Techniques*
■ *Airframe and Powerplant Mechanics*
■ *Pilots Guide to an Airline Career*
■ *Safety After Solo*

from *Beauty of Flight*, Manfred Curry, date unknown, John Day Company, out of print; kindly loaned to us by Jay Bonner's father.

Mrs. Godsey sighed. She wanted to commisserate with Mrs. Thornton about Charlene, and maybe pick up some late news on her in the process. But sorting the mail, as little as it had been, had given her such a headache the world was starting to spin before her eyes. She sat down on the bench facing Mrs. Thornton's chair, and appeared to go instantly to sleep. But in a little bit she opened her eyes and looked up at Mrs. Thornton and said, "Honey, I wonder if you'd do me a favor."

"Why sure," said Mrs. Thornton. "You just tell me what it is."

"Get me a R. C. out of the cooler, and some of them Goody Powders off the shelf. My poor old head feels like it's about to come apart."

Mrs. Thornton was a big woman and she had to struggle to get to her feet. She was sweating just sitting there and as she walked to the cooler Mrs. Godsey invited her to help herself to a soft drink, on the house. Mrs. Thornton said she didn't think she wanted anything right then. But once she peered into the cooler and saw the bottles standing cold and lucious in the dark water she changed her mind and took out a Dr. Pepper for herself. She opened them and got a package of Goody's off the shelf.

"I don't know what I'd do without my Goody's," said Mrs. Godsey as she fumbled with the wrapper. "Them and R. C.'s is about all that'll keep me going any more."

(continued)

Trade-a-Plane

This tabloid size yellow peril to the tranquility of aviators' home life is published three times a month out of Crossville, Tennessee, and contains thousands of classified ads for small airplanes all over the country. You may not find the plane you're looking for next door, but after a couple of weeks' reading, nobody can fake you out on prices.

[Reviewed by Don Biggs]

$4.00 /yr. (3 times monthly)

from:
Trade-a-Plane Service
Crossville, Tennessee

GUN CAMERAS

Types, N-6, operating
on 24 volt DC 22
Magazine
16 (?)
...
Price ... $27.50
Each ... Postpaid

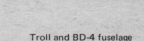

BD-4

All reports are that this is the best homebuilt airplane on the market. With the 150 hp engine it seats four, has a useful load of 870 lbs, cruising speed 170 mph, take-off run over 50 ft. obstacle 900 ft., maximum range 1,200 miles. For a new tailormade with similar performance you'd pay $10,000 more. The kit is intelligently designed.

The main hangup at Bede is slow delivery of materials. We've been waiting months for wings and engine on the BD-4 we're building at the Truck Store. Most of the kit is indeed straight-forward bolt-together, but welding on the landing gear needs professional work.

Bede is now bringing out a BD-5 kit. Very radical airplane.

—SB

[Suggested by John Shuttleworth]

BD-5

Troll and BD-4 fuselage

Complete kit with 150 hp Lycoming engine:
$6300.00 plus shipping

with 180 hp
$7200.00 plus shipping

Information kits $3.50 postpaid

from:
Bede Homebuilts
355 Richmond Road
Cleveland, Ohio 44143

NEW PLANE FROM BEDE Jim Bede has designed a new single-seat "everyman's plane" to sell as a package, materials plus construction drawings, at a "fantastically low price," he says. Called the BD-5 Microplane, it's an entirely new approach to homebuilts that can be assembled in double-quick time. The new Microplane will use a two-cycle, two-cylinder pusher engine, will be able to climb about 4,000 fpm, and will have unique construction features. Bede said that wings will be easily removable for storage. There will be two sets of wings, long ones for soaring, short ones for powered flight.

Air Progress
November 1970

Aircraft Components

Comments deleted at Aircraft Components' request.

Aircraft Components, Inc.
Benton Harbor, Michigan 49022

COMPASSES
Style 8-16 fits the standard 3-1/8" panel hole, completely remanufactured with new dial, airworthiness certificate, 90 day guarantee. Shipping Weight 2 pounds.

RUNWAY WIRE
Special Runway Light Wire—all weather-proof two conductor stranded copper with a double vinyl sheath for above or below surface. 14 gauge. Comes complete with air filter on the instrument. Lengths up to 1,000 feet. Shipping Weight 1 lb.

TURN & BANK

Stanley Type B Turn and Bank Instrument with standard 3-1/8" dial. Operates from any pump or venturi. Comes complete with air filter on the instrument. Just purchased as surplus, and checked for proper operation before shipment. In excellent mechanical condition with 90 day guarantee. Dial markings are yellow, but easily read. Quantity limited.

COMPACT HEATER WARMS ENGINE FOR QUICK STARTING
Made by the Evans Products Co. for the Air Force, this compact unit operates on gasoline, fuel oil or kerosene. Tripod legs for use on the ground or can also be hung below the engine being warmed by using the handle and hook furnished.

Output is about 50,000 BTU. This heater will start your engine in the coldest weather. Only 12" high and 9" wide. Comes complete with all fittings and full instructions on how to use. Use in ventilated areas only.

TELEX COMBINATION MICROPHONE/EARPHONE
Low-cost headset for high noise environments, features deep cavity, dual cup headphones with comfortable soft foam rubber ear cushions and adjustable head-band. Noise cancelling carbon boom microphone provides excellent performance reliability. Expressly designed for use in helicopters, spray planes, open cockpit planes and other environments with severe noise problems. Order PT-200 Push-To-Talk kit 'elow for aircraft not so equipped.

Used Plane Buying Guide

An objective rundown on what you can expect buying a used plane is what you can expect from this sensible book. Besides information on purchasing and maintenance it gives comparative data (including price range) on the common light planes in the used market.

—SB

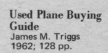

Used Plane Buying Guide
James M. Triggs
1962; 128 pp.

$2.95 postpaid

from:
Crown Publishers
419 Park Avenue South
New York, N. Y. 10016

or WHOLE
EARTH
CATALOG

USED PLANE BUYING GUIDE
by James M. Triggs
MODERN AIRCRAFT SERIES

The Joy of Soaring

like a big bird
quiet whoosh over the wings
alone
wheel
circle
lift.
manual of instruction for glider flight
—jd

The Joy of Soaring
Conway and Parcell
1969; 134pp.

$15 /yr
Associate SSA Membership
(magazine included) $9/yr

from:
Soaring Society of America
Box 66071
Los Angeles, California 90066

or

WHOLE EARTH CATALOG

THE BASIC IDEA

The glider's angle of bank and pitch attitude should be fairly well under the pilot's control, and the glider should be equipped with a variometer, airspeed indicator and altimeter. Thus prepared, the pilot can try his hand at thermaling. When the variometer reads up, the pilot commences circling, keeping a sharp eye on the instruments, the attitude of the glider and the position of other traffic. After a full turn he will know at what point of his circle the lift was best and where it was weakest. Mentally, he draws a line through these points, and then moves his circle toward the stronger lift to improve his rate of climb. When the variometer shows a constant rate of climb for a full circle, the glider is perfectly centered in the lift, so the rate of climb is best. Oh happy day! (It seldom happens.)

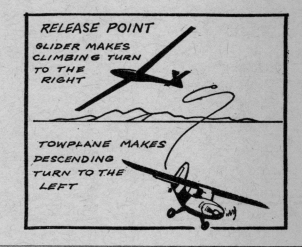

RELEASE POINT
GLIDER MAKES CLIMBING TURN TO THE RIGHT

TOWPLANE MAKES DESCENDING TURN TO THE LEFT

Bat Glider Plans

Supplier: Bat Glider Plans
P.O. Box 7115
Amarillo, Texas 79109 **$5.00**

Additional Information:

These are plans for a *man carrying* glider for soaring down from the heights. I know nothing about these particular plans yet, but the concept is quite sound. (I am a senior aerospace engineering student.) If the military doesn't find me, I will build one of these gliders and write an evaluation for you. To quote a review in March, 1970 *Sport Flying,*

How about a glider for a total outlay of about $20.00 cash? Well, if this sounds like fun, you might try this simple hand glider. It goes together in hours and will supply hours of endless fun. All you need is some bamboo or aluminum tubes, reinforced plastic tape, some plastic sheeting, and a gentle slope with a tad of breeze. A quick flying lesson is incorporated on the plans. Sounds like a gas for the adventurous. *No flying certificate required. [my italics]*

This must be the grooviest way to get high since Harry Anslinger discovered grass. Hope you can use the tip.

Stephen L. Addington
Austin, Texas

Stits Aircraft Supplies

Construction materials and supplies.

—SB

Stits Aircraft Supplies
Box 3084
Riverside, CA 92509

SAFE FLIGHT PRE STALL WARNING SYSTEM

Warns by red light and horn 5 to 10 miles per hour before the stall occurs. Detector unit easily mounts on leading edge of wing and is activated by a change in the flow of the air at the leading edge. Complete with installation instructions. Available in 12 or 24 volt; specify when ordering. List price $68.00 per set.
Sale price $58.00 per set.

2024-T3 Mil Spec QQ-A362 ALCLAD		6061-T4 Mil Spec QQ-A-327 BARE, Used for welded fuel tanks, formed parts, ribs, etc.	
Thickness	Sheet Size 4' x 12'	Thickness	Sheet Size 4' x 12'
.016	$ 21.97		
.020	26.26		
.025	29.55	.025	$ 26.77
.032	36.51	.032	32.55
.040	44.52	.040	39.79

DISCOUNTS on all aluminum sheet - 10% off on a total of 6 or more & 15% off on 10 or more sheets. Sorry, we no longer cut aluminum sheet to remnant sizes.

Soaring

A thoroughly useless sport, unless like Don Aitken you happen to be a passenger in a private plane flying over the barren Australian outback and the engine goes out and the pilot can't glide it well but you can, picking your way from thermal to thermal clear back to civilization. The magazine is nice for shopping.

—SB

Soaring
Doug Lamont, ed.

$13 /yr (monthly)
includes SSA membership

from:
The Soaring Society of America
Box 66071
Los Angeles, CA 90066

Around 10:00 a.m. the first ship stayed aloft. By the time he was well into the second turn of a thermal, I knew it was late. Time for the sneaky rush to get the ship up to the tow line before too many people saw the light. By 10:45 I was aloft and sampling the 300-fpm lift of the early thermals. The winds were all that had been promised. With thermals topping at 8000 msl (4700 feet above ground level), it would have been a chore to stay near the field. At the southeast end of the Minden Valley, Mount Siegel and surrounding ridges rise to about 9000 feet. I drifted that way and worked each thermal to its limit. Gradually, as the ground level rose, so did the thermal height, until it was possible to clear the hills and drop over into the next valley south. I sent my crew (wife Eunice and sons Bob and David) south on Highway 395 and immediately dropped below the ridge and lost direct radio contact.

Chatter on 123.3 indicated lots of activity back at the field— all of it being directed to landing the gliders aloft because of an approaching dust storm and sharply increasing winds. It was obvious that I didn't want to return in that direction even if I could— much safer and a lot more fun to outrun the front.

19-METER HP-14, N1051. Completely equipped. $7300. Phone George Thomas, (714) 646-9248; or Ned Jacoby, (714) 673-4374, evenings.

BEAUTIFUL CHEROKEE II. Sell or trade for as little as $625, $833.33, $1250 per share (¼, ⅓, ½). (213) 328-7476.

Ballooning

There's a magazine for balloonists:

—SB

Ballooning
Deke Sonnichsen, ed.

$2 /yr quarterly ($3 foreign)

from:
Ballooning
Menlo Oaks Balloon Field
Menlo Park, CA 94025

J-2 Gyroplane

A local job to go with your Lear jet.

—SB

McCulloch Aircraft Corporation
Box 1259
Lake Havasu City, Arizona 86403

Mrs. Thornton took a drink of Dr. Pepper.

"They say Joyce Jennings is taking tranquilizers now," she said. "They say since Billy Joe left she can't get any rest a tall without taking one of them pills."

"I never knowed Joyce to get any rest even when Billy Joe was home," said Mrs. Godsey. "I never knowed her to be home any night of the week before one and two o'clock in the morning."

Mrs. Thornton sighed and dabbed her eyes again. "It's her poor old mother I feel sorry for. I declare but children is a trial. They're nothing but a burden to be borne."

Mrs. Godsey nodded. "About the only one I ever knowed that wasn't is my Leonard," she said.

"He's the exception all right," said Mrs. Thornton. Him and Roxie's both good. You're lucky to have them, Mrs. Godsey. You are, now."

Mrs. Godsey was having trouble taking the celophane off her package of Goody's. She'd been picking at it ever since Mrs. Thornton handed it to her, but her hands were so stiff and arthritic she hadn't made a tear in it yet.

"Honey, let me undo that for you," said Mrs. Thornton.

"Never mind," said Mrs. Godsey. "I may be old but I aint plum helpless yet."

(continued)

The Explorers Trademart Log

This magazine is a couple years old now. After a period of initial cuteness, it's begun to focus directly on usefulness. Like, exactly how to buy good surplus jeeps. Design of the Eskimo igloo. Economics of a private plane. How to buy public lands. Evaluation of canoes. Encouraging wildlife. Winterizing your tipi.

—SB

[Suggested by Mack Taylor]

The Explorers Trademart Log

$3.00 /year (bimonthly)

from:
Explorers Trademart, Ltd.
Post Office Box 1630
Annapolis, Md. 21404

In summary, then, you can expect to get a Jeep which is close to running condition for around $600 at an open auction. In the closed bid sale, which is the usual type, you can expect to get a Jeep for around $400-$500 with a few sizeable chunks missing or around $200-$300 with some major stuff missing, like say, the engine, or an axle and the transmission. In all sales, you can expect that. a lot of minor stuff like bolts, brackets, cover plates, gearshift levers, and the like, will be missing.

The address to which to write is:
DoD Surplus Sales
P.O. Box 1370
Battle Creek, Michigan 49016

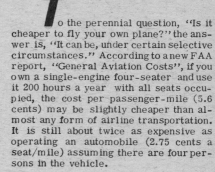

First tier of snowblocks laid in place. Note how tops of blocks are beveled inward. Hole has been dug before laying blocks to allow builder entry into igloo.

To the perennial question, "Is it cheaper to fly your own plane?" the answer is, "It can be, under certain selective circumstances." According to a new FAA report, "General Aviation Costs", if you own a single-engine four-seater and use it 200 hours a year with all seats occupied, the cost per passenger-mile (5.6 cents) may be slightly cheaper than almost any form of airline transportation. It is still about twice as expensive as operating an automobile (2.75 cents a seat/mile) assuming there are four persons in the vehicle.

National Geographic

Long live National Geographic.

—SB

National Geographic

$7.50 annual membership
($9.50 outside U.S.)
12 issues

from:
The Secretary
National Geographic Society
Washington, D. C. 20036

National Geographic publishes excellent maps at reasonable prices. We use two huge maps in the CATALOG office for geographical portrait of subscribers. Write for **free** publication list to above address.

Handbook for Expeditions

If you want excuses (i.e., income) for wandering around in the fastnesses, this British book spells them out. What to study, how to study it, how to organize your scene. Thorough book, very civilized.

—SB

Handbook for Expeditions
Brathay Exploration Group
1971; 137 pp.

$1.50

from:
The Geographical
128 Long Acre
London WC2E 9QH
England

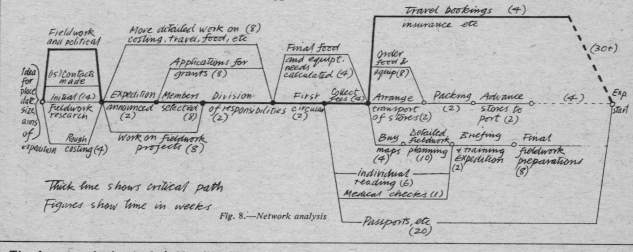

Thick line shows critical path
Figures show time in weeks

Fig. 8.—Network analysis

Fibre Cases

The last catalog should have Ikelheimer—Ernst's FIBRE PRODUCTS DIVISION reviewed. I wanted a tool box for all my VW Idiot tools and couldn't find one of those old aerial camera boxes. So I bore it in mind and one day I noticed (made real, realized) Victor Lassiter's tool box and all those telephone installer's tool boxes and all those cases with wheels that city salesmen have and then I found FIBRE PRODUCTS DIVISION. I called all the people listed under sample cases in the Yellow Pages under Sample Cases. FPD sent the most useful and most complete catalog. Some others had a few lower prices but had really messy and difficult or too specialized an interface (wouldn't want to call some of them catalogs).

We sit around and read the catalog and prices to each other. Just like the good old days only now. I remember hitching across country during the 50's and seeing the sturdy black suit-cases cowboy's traveled with; they're the same item and they are STRONG. (WOW). The tool box I bought cost me $12.05 including NYC tax and is on p. 5, no. 228A, 16" x 10½. x 5¼" and works just fine; Large screwdriver and ball peen hammer fit perfectly. The leather knob handles are the best. The sell a line of photographer's cases too but are reluctant to give out the catalog at this point for they are dropping some items from the line. The main line catalog is free but it's worth the stamps or whatever you can put together for a copy. Corduroy lining on the suitcases is nice and cheap.

I priced a custom made box for storing my prints; I need 6 of them and they quoted me $18.50 each. Note prices on the 10' leather straps. And web straps are worthwhile extra. The fibre is tough clean stuff and the fastening system used is strong (brutal) and flexible. I haven't researched the fibreboard itself yet but it has lots of promise: light weight, glueable, rivetable. I've been thinking of fitted luggage for a VW bus, liners for buses and vans; it might work real well for Domes.

[Suggested and reviewed by Ron Williams]

Ikelheimer-Ernst
Fibre Products Division
601 W. 26th St.
New York, N.Y. 10001

No. 7518 — Carousel Projector case   **$42.00**

The Amateur Archeologist's Handbook

There I was, digging around in an Illinois cornfield with an archaeologist who had hair down the middle of his back. There under the hot sun in the dry dirt we found Kickapoo Indian potshards, a clay pipe, and aha a trusty flintlock hammer. All the Illinois history bullshit I had in school simply faded. Who had lost his flintlock hammer? What was on his mind at the time?

This is a good introduction to careful archaeology (any other kind really is graverobbing, shrine-wrecking) in North America, good technique, good scan of what kind of stuff you'll find, and what to make of it.

—SB

[Suggested by Steve Pober]

The Amateur Archaeologist's Handbook
Maurice Robbins
1973; 288 pp.

$7.95 postpaid

from:
Thomas Y. Crowell Company
666 Fifth Ave.
New York, N.Y. 10019

OR WHOLE EARTH CATALOG

This book bridges the gap for the American amateur who wishes to take up the hobby of archaeology in a serious, orderly, and professional manner. Its scope is limited to the North American continent. Just enough of the prehistoric background and cultures is sketched to provide a frame of reference for, and to give meaning to, the archaeological materials that will be uncovered by methodical excavation. Many of the problems concerning cultural areas, chronology, and terminology that continue to baffle archaeologists have been omitted or have been treated quite cavalierly in the process of presenting the simplest and briefest accounts for the general reader. The amateur who wishes to extend his knowledge and fill in the missing details of the outline is urged to read widely in the literature suggested in the bibliography.

Digs

The Council for British Archaeology, 8 St. Andrews Place, London NW 1 publishes *Calendar of Excavations*, c. 50 cents per year monthly March through September. This bulletin lists archaeological digs (and field schools) planned or under way in Britain with details of salary, type of work, qualifications wanted, etc. With no previous experience a digger can often get paid 10 shillings per day by the Department of the Environment—enough for room and board. More, if you can camp. There's usually opportunity for weekends or weeks off work for hitching around. Digs generally run during the four summer months, and you can usually work all or part of the summer and thus live in England free—often in a sort of camping commune which lets you get to know people and places. With $50 cash I flew a charter flight New York-London round-trip for $210 and returned with some of my cash. Part of the plane fare investment was made up by the fact that I could buy a few "permanent" possessions there for about half what they would have cost here in the U.S. Thus the trip really cost about $100 more than living in the U.S. without an income—but living here I would have had expenses (and no job). You can quickly find out all sorts of free places to crash, travel, eat, etc. once you have a "base" in Europe. But if you want to get paid, make arrangements in advance. You *may* be able to get "room" (or tent) free if you simply show up at a camping dig, but the Department of the Environment money has to be arranged for. At the least the *Calendar* may provide a travelogue of crash pads—probably in return for volunteer labor; it's better to get a little pay, though—and fairly easy. (Digs in America are generally much less interested in volunteers or employees—they have more field student-slaves available! University anthropology departments and various state archaeological societies and *American Antiquity* may be of some help, but paying jobs are few.)

John R. Cole
Lincoln, Nebraska

Excavation of the Poole Purchase grave revealed the remains of a chief accompanied by the trinkets with which the land had been bought— a copper kettle of beans, several iron hoes, a mirror, and glass beads.

Outdoor Schools and Trips

Wilderness trips require equipment, skill, and usually, someone to go with. The best way to get into the wilderness is to find a friend who has all these, and is willing to loan you equipment and to share his knowledge with you. The next best thing is to go with a group organized by a club or professional school, camp, or guide service. Groups are organized to do every conceivable thing in the wilderness; this approach has a lot to recommend it. If you don't know people who have the skills necessary for what you want to do in the outdoors, going on a group trip will provide them and give you the opportunity to get together a few people and go off on your own the next time. Aside from not being much fun, some wilderness activities are pretty dangerous if you do them alone.

The organization that runs the trip will usually handle all the equipment and transportation problems; this can be important, particularly on long trips, foreign trips, or on trips where a lot of specialized equipment is needed. The outdoor schools also do an outstanding job of teaching you how to cope with outdoor problems, and may push you to do some things you had never thought yourself capable of doing. You will develop the skill and confidence necessary to put together your own trips.

Schools and group trips have their drawbacks, too. Most distasteful is the regimentation that is usually necessary when a group of people do something together; you are not completely free to set your own schedule and to go where you want to go. You should weigh this against the advantages before you go along on any trip. Be sure that you are ready to commit yourself to going along with whatever the group does. It can be difficult and dangerous to split from the rest of the group in the middle of the wilderness. You will probably find, though, that you have a lot more freedom than you had imagined.

The cost of a trip may range from nothing to a sizeable amount of money, depending mostly on the amount and quality of the instruction you get. Some schools, particularly the "character building" ones, have scholarships available.

Another problem caused by organized trips is the rape of the wilderness caused by hundreds of people using it. If you organize your own trip, keep the group small.

Mountaineering

There are a lot of climbing schools and guide services, each one specializing in techniques applicable to their local mountains. They're expensive at first glance, but they supply a lot of equipment, feed you while you're there, and tive you excellent instruction and a healthy outlook towards the sport. Mountaineering often presents the only way to get away from people; most wilderness valleys are overcrowded. Mountain summits are getting that way, too, but more slowly. Unless you know someone who has a lot of experience, you should probably get some professional training. As a general rule, climbing schools are better than guided climbs, since guided climbs tend to be oriented to just hauling people up a mountain rather than to encouraging them to learn how to lead the party themselves. The schools listed below are oriented to developing understanding as well as skills.

California:

Rockcraft is a school run by Royal Robbins, one of the Yosemite rock climbing pioneers. The school is located near Lake Tahoe—away from the crowds and hassle of Yosemite. He teaches big wall rock climbing techniques, but won't let you put in a whole route with bolts. (You can get a fine in Yosemite for cutting down a tree; why should drilling a hole in the rock be any different?) Write for a brochure.

Rockcraft
906 Durant Street
Modesto, Calif. 95350

Northwest:

Mt. Hood Meadows School of Mountaineering runs the most comprehensive program around. The school is run by Lute Jerstad, who climbed Mt. Everest in 1963, and also has Tenzing Norgay, the Sherpa who made the first ascent of Everest in 1953 on its staff. They run ice climbing seminars, rock climbing schools (instructed by Tom Frost, another Yosemite climber), and climbing excursions which climb 3 peaks in a week. Write to:

Lute Jerstad Adventures
9920 SW Terwilliger Blvd
Portland, Oregon 97219

Wyoming:

Jackson Hole Mountain Guides has a program of guided climbs and instructional camps in the Teton mountains. They have literature describing both their programs and philosophy of mountaineering.

Jackson Hole Mountain Guides
Teton Village
Wyoming 83025

Personal Trips or Character Building

There are a number of organizations which make use of the unfamiliar situations encountered in the wilderness to build character. It's really a great approach if you are into that sort of thing. If you go on one of these schools, you will learn to feel at home in the outdoors and will have the confidence that you can survive in whatever situation you find yourself. Outward Bound runs programs at six locations throughout the U.S. Their concept is that you can and should learn to rise to an emergency situation, so they often place you in a "sink or swim" position. They assume that you have no previous experience, yet by the time you complete the course you will have developed enough skill to spend several days alone in the wilderness. The programs are expensive, but the results are incredible. One thing you should be aware of is that they have a tendency to treat the outdoors as a foe to be conquered rather than a friend to coexist with; this is a very different concept from most of the other outdoor programs. A really turned on brochure describing all of their programs is available from:

Outward Bound, Inc.
165 West Putnam
Greenwich, CT 06830

National Outdoor Leadership School trains teachers, instructors, and counselors for outdoor programs. They also accept people who want to learn skills for their own outings and expeditions as well as those who just want an extended wilderness experience. They stress conservation and ecology during a five week summer course in Wyoming. The school is run by Paul Petzoldt, an outstanding mountaineer and outdoorsman, a Grand Teton Guide, and from all reports, a great person. Write directly to him for more information.

Paul Petzoldt
National Outdoor Leadership School
Lander, Wyoming 82520

River Trips

River running is both easy and exciting and usually takes you through wild and remote country. One of the best reasons for going on an organized river trip is that they take care of a lot of the hassle; they provide boats, life jackets, waterproof bags for your gear, etc., and get you back from the end of the river to where your car is. Otherwise you have to either find somebody who isn't making the trip with you up, or hitchhike— but many rivers start in remote country where only a few cars a day travel.

American River Touring Association is one of the oldest operator of river tours. They are a non-profit organization which runs first class trips. ARTA uses special rubber rafts rowed by one of their guides on the Colorado and a lot of other rivers. Prices are reasonable, but you have to pay extra to have your car shuttled to the end of the river. Write for a brochure listing all the rivers they run or request a spearate brochure for a specific river.

American River Touring Association
1016 Jackson St.
Oakland, California 94607

Grand Canyon Dories is the most unique of the many groups that run the Colorado. They use small wooden dories similar to the ones used by Powell on his first trip down the river. They provide air transportation back to your car.

Grand Canyon Dories
P.O. Box 5585
Stanford, California 94305

Lute Jerstad Adventures runs trips on several northwest rivers in six man rubber rafts that they teach you to row yourself. Transportation is provided from Portland, which overcomes the car shuttle hang up. Write for river trip information.

Lute Jerstad Adventures
9920 SW Terwilliger Blvd.
Portland, Oregon 97219

Bicycling

You probably won't get too far into the wilderness on a bicycle, but you can move incredible distances on one and still be outdoors and not cause pollution. Several clubs run bicycle tours through all sorts of country; they usually are accompanied by a "sag wagon", a car that carries all the baggage, which saves a lot of effort. Write to:

International Bicycle Touring Society
846 Prospect Street
La Jolla, Calif. 92037

or

League of American Wheelman (LAW)
19 So. Bothwell
Palatine, IL 60067

Backpacking

Get a copy of *The Complete Walker*, rent a pack and a sleeping bag, and go do it! Organized backpack trips are one of the major causes of deterioration of many wilderness areas. The Boy Scouts run an unbelievable number of trips, and many outdoor clubs run frequent trips with 10 to 50 people in a group. Backpacking is really an opportunity to find solitude and wilderness; don't destroy that experience for yourself and others by marching up a trail with a crowd. One of the largest conservation organizations asked that their outings not be publicized because the impact on the environment from the trips they run is becoming critical, and they would prefer that no more people attend them.

Foreign Trips

There is a lot of wilderness outside of the United States, some of it virtually unexplored. Many groups run expeditions and wilderness outings to such places as the South American jungles, the Andes, Alaska, Iceland, Antarctica, and the Himalayas. Two major problems occur on a wilderness trip in a foreign country: logistics are incredible— if you don't have experience, you can get really hung up in problems of customs, transportation to remote areas, language, hiring locals to carry your gear, and finding food; the other problem is that you may be traveling in primitive areas where westerners don't usually travel. This is a fantastic opportunity, but you have to be careful not to destroy the area for both the locals and the next traveler. Many places operate on a subsistance level economy; they don't have spare food to sell, and they probably spend most of their time raising their own food. If you hire somebody at an outrageous salary, or pay $5 for a 10¢ item, you have blown the whole economy all to Hell: Try to make arrangements for food and be as self sufficient as possible; leave your culture and economy at home. One way to be self sufficient is to travel with a group which makes all the arrangements for you.

Mountain Travel is one of the largest organizers of foreign wilderness trips. They have a catalog which lists more than 25 trips and expeditions to incredible places all over the world. Their trips are really inexpensive— usually about 20-25 dollars per day plus airfare. One way they keep prices low is by not paying their leaders a salary (they just come along for free) so they sometimes get non-professional leaders. They take care of all of the details overseas, but pre-trip information assumes that you have a lot of previous experience. Free catalog from Mountain Travel (USA)

6201 Medau Place
Oakland, California 94611.

Lute Jerstad Adventures runs climbing expeditions, and is getting into running treks to the Mt. Everest base camp and throughout the Himalayas. All trips are lead by a professional mountain guide with Tenzing Norgay accompanying the Himalayan treks; this provides an opportunity to get acquainted with the local culture—particularly in the region of Tibetan Buddhist influence near Mt. Everest where Tenzing was born. Trips are a little more expensive than Mountain Travel's, primarily because of the leaderwhip; pre-trip information includes a lot of cultural background and detailed information on what to expect on the trip. Write for trek information to:

Lute Jerstad Adventures
9920 SW Terwilliger Blvd.
Portland, Oregon 97219

—Stan Armington
Lute Jerstad Adventures

The ladies hushed talking until Mrs. Godsey got the wrapper off the package. There were four doses in it, each folded in a paper. Mrs. Godsey took out a dose, laid the box aside, then, very carefully, she poured the white powder into her R. C. Cola.

"I use to just dump it out on my tongue," said Mrs. Godsey. "But here lately it gags me to do that, so I just mix it in a dope now, and sort of sip on it as I go along. I think it's better that way. Seems to stay with me longer."

"When I was in the hospital they fed me through the veins," said Mrs. Thornton. "I laid over there three weeks and never got a bite to eat. I hated it. I've done and told Wheeler he neen to expect to ever take me to a hospital again. I told him I'd as soon pass out right there at the house as put up with that outfit over in town."

"I'm just like you, honey," said Mrs. Godsey. "I've got terrible things wrong with me, but I aint about to go to no hospital for them. I told Leonard if I get down sick to just prop me up in bed, give me some sassafras tea and let the Lord take care of the rest."

"Amen to that," said Mrs. Thornton. "The Lord's better'n any doctor I ever had anything to do with."

(continued)

Overland Guide To Nepal

An overland trip East can be a beautiful experience, but a lot of work as well. Here I attempt to give you a factual outline to make this experience even more pleasant and less confusing than it was for me.

WHEN TO GO

Firstly, it is well to start the trip in late summer from Europe: August, September and October as starting dates will give you the advantage of the best possible weather all the way to Nepal; arriving Nepal circa xmass. NOTE: The weather along the route I outline is mild from August to xmass. Eastern Turkey is cold at night in the mountains. It can be cold with light snow crossing the mountain ridge out of Ghazni just before dropping into Kabul, Afganistan. It would be impossible to cross the Hindu Kush after November and difficult to get to the ruins of Bamiyan, north of Kabul. Shrinagar, the city of houseboats in Kashmire will be very cold and possibly snowbound late November. Kathmandu valley is mild year round with a couple of weeks of freezing weather in January.

HEALTH

It is of utmost importance to keep in good health. First, a smallpox and cholera vaccination are mandatory as you will not be allowed to cross frontiers without a World Health Certificate. A large supply of multiple vitamins is strongly recommended. Your diet will lack in vitamin C. Also Intro-vioform are some help against diarrhea and dysentary. If you become seriously ill go to U.S. Consulate and a reliable doctor will be recommended. NOTE: At U.S. Embassy in New Delhi there is a clinic in the main building, and they will treat you without question.

CLOTHING

Of course, you are going to travel light. Itemizing everything isn't necessary, but it should be noted that you will need a dark sweater and windbreaker. That everyday stuff you wear, take one spare. I dye my underwear dark colors; white will never be white again and there is nothing which looks worse than dirty drawers when stripping down in front of a room full of fellow travelers.

Same goes for the girls, and pants are quite acceptable for the girls. One dress and a few tops are all that is necessary. GIRLS: Mini skirts only attract remarks and trouble. You can visit holy places in pants, but dresses higher than just above the ankle will bar you from many mosques.

PAPERS

Bartholomew maps are the best, but you can get shell and local tourist maps along the way. Take all the credentials you can get. International Student Card, $3 from Nat. Student Association, 265 Madison Ave., N.Y. A youth hostel can be obtained at any hostel in Europe and cost less than here if you tell them you want one only for foreign travel and void in U.S. hostels. A PRESS card. Try having an official looking I.D. laminated with PRESS stamped in large red letters across the whole face.

MONEY

Take some cash and save it for the Eastern money market. Some travelers checks are good for the time spent in Europe and stable currency countries. Money is unstable in: Pakistan, India and Nepal. My summation will give you an idea of expense.

GETTING TO EUROPE

Cheapest way is Icelandic Airlines: $167.50 thrift season one way to N.Y. to Luxembourg. So called work aways and other fantastic stories of cheap boats don't exist except for 1% of total travelers hunting for these bargains.

You've arrived in Luxembourg or some seaport, take my advice and start immediately for the East. Even if you have never been to Europe before save your cash for the East. If you are hitching, or driving get on the Autobahn for Munich. Now that you are on the road there are a couple of essential items for all travelers: an air mattress and a good sleeping bag. There are two things about the overland trip to Nepal which are very important: good food and good sleep. You can make the whole trip sleeping on hard floors and eating rice, but once your body resistance falls there are a number of maladies awaiting entrance to your system. An Army type poncho is also a very handy item, and a small one-burner gasoline cook stove should be seriously considered.

MUNICH

Choices for Hitch-hikers:

1. Europa bus direct to Teheran for $75 plus overnight hotel expense. A ten day trip.

2. Train direct to Istanbul, $45, a two day ride. Be sure to take food on train.

3. Hitch-hike on to Istanbul, three to ten days. Do not try to hitch the Dalmatian Coast. Route: Munich to Salzburg, Klagenfurt, Ljubljana, Beograd, Skopje and from Skopje through Bulgaria to Istanbul, or to Thessalonika and on to Istanbul. I prefer through Greece. DRIVERS: If you're not in a hurry you would do well to consider driving down the Dalmatian Coast. There are many campsites and late September or early October will still be sunny days. The route from Dubrovnik goes to Titograd, then Kolasin. Careful not to miss the turn off into the city of Kolasin and out the opposite side of town runs an unbelievably potholed dirt road. This will be the worst road of the entire trip to Nepal. It is very bad to Pec, then you continue to Prizren, and you can depend on a modern new campsite in Prizrin, then Skopje and the main road. From Skopje you can go either through Bulgaria or on to Thessalonika, Greece. In Thessalonika is a very modern campsite with free hot water showers and a private beach. The camp is actually 25 ks out of the city and signposted by International camp signs. NOTE: All travelers who plan on transiting Bulgaria will have to pay $4 for a visa at crossing point. The train transits Bulgaria so be sure and get a Bulgarian visa at a Bulgarian Consulate before starting out. Visa costs $2 at Consulate.

(Revision: Delete reference to going through Kolasin. From Kolasin you can stay on asphalt by going direction Bijelo Polje and back down to Andrijevica. When you look at this on a Yugoslavia map you will see that it is twice the distance as from Kolasin direct to Andrijevica, but that road is extremely bad. Take your pick. For those of you who are really serious about getting to India with the least amount of expense, then follow the main road through the center of Yugoslavia.)

TURKEY

Arriving from Greece, there is a campsite at border crossing in Ipsala. These modern campsites in Turkey are located at BP gasoline stations and called BP Mocamps. Arriving from Bulgaria there is a BP Mocamp at crossing town of Edirne.

ISTANBUL: BP Mocamp is on your right 8 ks before city and near airport. It is the main road leading into Istanbul so you can't miss it. This camp has a swimming pool as well as free hot water showers and free GAZ cook stoves. Cost varies depending on size of car and tent My wife and I, motorcycle and small tent ran $1.25 per day. For those arriving by public transport or hitching without tents, cheap hotels are located around the train station and the Blue Mosque. A room for two will cost from 5 to 10 lira per person per night. You may change money at the banks for an official 12 lira to $1. NOTE: if you are going to buy a ticket on an international carrier then you must change your money at the rate of 9 lira to $1 and produce receipts. Get your visa for Iran; U.S. passports: no charge. For those who elect to follow route to Trabzon, you can get a visa for Iran in Trabzon and avoid the huzzle of Istanbul.

If you are continuing by automobile the direct route is Ankara, Kayseri, Sivas, Erzincan, Erzurum, then Mako, Iran. After Ankara the roads are for the most part loose gravel to the Iranian border. NOTE: Watch out for six inch deep pot holes in surfaced road 20 or 30 miles before border.

HITCHERS: You have several choices.

1. Take boat from Istanbul to Trabzon, $4 with student discount, two nights without food. If any are on motorcycles freight is $2 and well worth missing the uninteresting drive over bad roads through central Turkey. The ship, EGE, leaves once a week on Tuesday and the office for the company is Denizcilik Bankasi located to your right just after crossing the Galata Bridge from old to new Istanbul. For student discounts you must get a Turkish student card obtainable from any of the many student organizations in Istanbul: cost $1. NOTE: if you are over 26 you might be refused student discount, but argue.

2. Train from Istanbul to Erzurum $6.50 with stu. dis., and that is a very nice second class.

3. TBT bus from Istanbul direct to Teheran $30, a four day trip with nightly stops in hotels. Expect to spend about $1.50 per day for food and lodging. Bus driver will not allow you to sleep on bus.

(Revision: Camping 50% cheaper and olympic size swimming pool at Londra (London) Camp 200 meters past B.P. east, same side of road.

If you are continuing by automobile: Istanbul-Izmit-Bolu-Ankara, then north to Samsun-Trabzon-Erzurum. This is a little longer, but the road and scenery are much better than the center road.)

TRABZON: There are several mini bus companies which will take you to Erzurum.

ERZURUM: One connects here with either a Mihan Tour or TBT bus to Teheran for $12. One can camp at the BP station.

NOTE: Where student prices quoted non students figure 30% more. If student rate not quoted then rate is fixed to all.

IRAN

You can expect to find only two more campgrounds from here on; one in Tabriz and one in Teheran. Otherwise those traveling by car can pull off the road most anywhere to overnight camp. The camp in Tabriz is signposted and easy to locate. The one in Teheran is about 10 ks out of town on the road to Saveh. It is on your right and called Camp del Sol. Cheap hotels are located in Teheran around the train station ranging from 30 to 50 rials per person per night. $1 equals 75 rials. Rials are also spoken of as Tummin. One Tummin equals 10 rials.

TEHERAN: Get your visa for Afganistan; U.S. Passports, no charge. Afganistan consulate is currently asking the rougher looking travelers to show their money, but one can pass around one person's roll. For those of you who might need a good Western type meal you can get an excellent lunch for 150 rials at Sandys Restaurant located next door to the American Express office on Takht-e-jamshid street. From Teheran the route is north to Sari and on to Meshad. This road is bad, dirt and washboard, from Shah-pasand to Meshad. For those going public transport there are both trains and buses running to Meshad. By bus it takes between twenty and thirty hours and prices vary from 150 to 400 rials. Be careful of overcharging and short changing in Iran. Gas pumps do not ring up the price. Find out the price by liter and figure up bill yourself. Price is standard as gasoline is state controlled. Iranian numbers to ten are:

1 2 3 4 5 6 7 8 9 10
۱ ۲ ۳ ۴ ۵ ۶ ۷ ۸ ۹ ۱۰

MESHAD: Cheap hotels run 30 to 50 rials. There are transit beds in bus stations but they cost as much as a place downtown. Twice a week a bus runs from Meshad to Herat, Afganistan. If you don't want to wait for that connection you can take a bus daily to the border town of Taiebat, Iran; 75 rials. From Taiebat you can hitch a ride with a tanker truck to Herat; you'll be expected to pay truck driver. If the taxi from Herat happens to be in town it will cost, after bartering, 200 Afganies per person. (75 Afs to $1.)

DRIVERS: You will leave Meshad on the road to Torbat-heydriyeh and go on this road 38 kilometers and on your left will be a dirt road leading down into a dry river bed with an old washed out bridge. That is the road to Afganistan and til now there is no sign post. This road is badly washboard for 190 kilometers to Taiebat.

HIKERS: If stuck in Taiebat you can sleep in tea house across street from customs house for one Tummin. Keep in mind that you can sleep in most roadside tea houses.

AFGHANISTAN

(Revision: Change $1 for Afgan currency in Iran. Rate is not good, but before you get to Herat there is a toll station and you cannot pass without paying a toll of 30 Afganies (.40¢) and the toll man's rate of exchange is incredible!)

From Herat you get a bus direct to Kabul with an overnight stop in Kandahar. You may break your journey in Kandahar if you wish. The price varies from 215 to 300 Afganies Herat to Kabul. Bus leaves daily. Hotels in Afganistan will run from 30 to 50 afs. per person per night. If you want to buy skins Herat is actually the best we saw. Afgan coats are running between $10 and $30.

KABUL: The bus will let you off in front of the Khyber restaurant. This is where most travelers first come and you can meet other people coming from the East and exchange information. In Kabul is the money bazaar. Here you will get 40% more for your money than the official rates of India and Pakistan. This is all illegal and you should check with current travelers as to what's going on. You can expect about 12 Indian rupees to $1 (Official rate 7,40) and 8.50 Pakistan rupees to $1. (Official rate 4.75). Get your Indian and Pakistan visas; no charge to U.S. passports. NOTE: No matter how you travel through Pakistan you will need a road permit. The two best cheap hotels are Sakhi, and Bamiyan. A bus runs daily to the Pakistan city of Peshawar for $2.

PAKISTAN

In Peshawar the youth hostel is very good and costs 1.50 rupees. It is located on your left at the University on the main road coming into Peshawar from Afganistan. Trains run regularly to Lahore. Interclass is $2. Side note: you can fly from Peshawar to Gilgit and then trek to Hunza. Flight cost $6.

LAHORE: There is a youth hostel on Ferozepore road. A bus runs daily to the Indian border. Save 1.75 rupees for bus fare.

INDIA

After crossing the frontier you take a tonga, a horse drawn cart, to Ferozepore. Don't take a bicycle as the ride is 12 ks. Train to New Delhi costs $1.50. The best way to get around India is by train. Now your student card will come in handy as students get 50% reductions and no age limits. The best class for long journeys is third class two tier sleeper. To get the reduction you go to the main administration building in major cities. For example, in New Delhi you go to the office of the Northern Railroad and tell them where you want to go and they check your student card and give you an authorization for reduction which you then take back to the railway ticket office and present it to the window of the line you wish to buy a ticket on. He will then sell you a ticket. Tickets should be reserved for a week in advance, but if you find the train sold out, then apply for a special tourist quota. For this you return to the administration building for the authorization, and most times these buildings are several kilometers apart. In other words affairs in Indian are complicated with forms and papers to fill out, but this is part of a rich experience. NOTE: Mail trains are faster than express trains.

NEW DELHI: Hotels in the center of town will run about 7 to 10 rupees per person per night. There is a 1 rupee youth hostel, but it is very difficult to find and out of two several ks. If you are approaching New Delhi by car keep asking directions to Connaught Place; the center of town. Indian meals will run 1 to 2 rupees and the best thing on the menu at Wengers restaurant, Connaught Place is 6 rupees. Wengers is a place to meet other travelers and get excellent Western meals while your tummy is getting used to Indian fare. Don't shy away from expensive restaurant hotels in India. You can usually get a full lunch and eat as much as you like for 7 to 10 rupees and you need to keep body fit on this kind of trip. We would stop at one of these luxury places once a week to rebuild our bodies with the comforts of hot water in the toilets, etc. For those travelling by car there are DAK bungalows or PWD Inspection houses scattered all over India. These cost 1 to 3 rupees a night per person, and some- per room no matter how many people are in it. Get your Nepalese visa in New Delhi.

NOTE: Way out hip types are being refused visas to several Eastern countries. That doesn't mean one can't have long hair and a beard, but if it is shoulder length and you are barefoot wearing robes you might be mistaken as a hippy.

Take the train to Raxual, the border town before Nepal. There is a government rest house there for 1.50 rupees. Begin the trip to Kathmandu early in the morning as it is a ten to twelve hour trip by truck. DRIVERS: Leave early and fill up all gas cans in India as gasoline is double priced in Kathmandu.

NEPAL

There are several hotels which are cheap. Prices vary from sleeping on the floor for 15¢ to 30¢ a night to a nice double room and patio at the Camp Hotel for $1.25 for two. Currently the blue Tibetian restaurant and Camp hotel are hangouts for travelers. However, there are many fine little hotels and the valley is not difficult to get around in. Bicycles are renting for about 75¢ a day.

SUMMATION

Public transport cost from Europe to Nepal and back circa $200. The whole trip with food and lodging should realistically cost you about $400 to $500 Europe-Nepal-Europe. Many people do it for less, but my cost estimate is based on good food and good sleep; your only health insurance in the East. Remember Europe is the expensive place.

MAIL DROPS

These are the best for a variety of reasons which six years of travel have dictated to me:

Istanbul:	Post Ristante
Kabul:	Post Ristante
Kathmandu:	Post Ristante
Teheran:	American Consulate
New Delhi:	American Express

NOTE: American Express charges $2 for forwarding mail. American consulate forwards promptly free. Post Ristante is slow to forward. Having money sent to India should be avoided, but if you need this service have your U.S. contact go to American Express office and get a demand for money which will be forwarded to American Express in Bombay or New Delhi. In any case you will not be allowed to receive foreign cash.

Liquor permits are given to tourist by the tourist office and can be illegally sold. Check with travelers as to where and going price.

No insurance is required from Turkey onwards so don't bother to get any for your vehicle. A Carnet De Passage is the easiest way to cross borders with a car. Automobile club can assist you in getting one. Not necessary for a motorcycle as you can have it entered on your passport when crossing all the borders. India, however, requires a letter from the Consulate as to your promise to re-export machine from India. Currently the U.S. Consulate in Kabul is issuing such letters, which you then take to the India Consulate in Kabul for an authorization to cross the border with the cycle.

(Revision: The U.S. Consulate is no longer giving letters certificating that you swear to re-export your machine. A Carnet de Passage is mandatory if you plan to continue to India. Carnets are only issued by the country where your machine is registered, so get it before you start out. Local Automobile clubs handle the paper work.)

A good all purpose guide is: Golden Guide to Southeast Asia.

Do not be sold on buying a dozen or more visa photos in U.S. at high cost. Cheap photos are available along the way. You can use 2 doz. small two inch photos.

My gasoline expense from London to Nepal was $65. Driving a BMW R60.

Sid Sheehy, London, England

Cheap Travel

Two undistinguished but helpful books on international travel at low cost. —SB

[Suggested by Nancy Schimmel]

Icelandic Airlines has been the pioneer of low-cost, Trans-Atlantic air transportation. Since 1952 Icelandic (Lofteidir in the Icelandic language) has consistently offered the lowest fares of any regularly scheduled airline between the U.S.A. and Europe.

•

. . . I feel Icelandic's regular round-trip New York-Luxembourg fare of $319 offered from August 4 through May 31 (to Europe) and September 25 to July 21 (returning) is a remarkable bargain and one of the best buys available anywhere. This bargain is good for a year with no minimum stay or weekend restrictions.

Air Travel Bargains

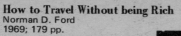

Air India Boeing 707

The new Japan Air Lines $400 round-trip Bulk Inclusive Tour fare from the U.S. West Coast to Tokyo is an incredible bargain. There will be some real money saving tours to Expo 70 based on this fare.

Air Travel Bargains

How to Travel Without being Rich
Norman D. Ford
1969; 179 pp.

$2.50 postpaid

from:
Grosset & Dunlap, Inc.
51 Madison Avenue
New York, N. Y. 10010

or WHOLE EARTH CATALOG

Air Travel Bargains
Jim Woodman
1970; 320 pp.

$2.95 postpaid

from:
Essandress Special Editions
c/o Simon & Schuster
1 West 39th St.
New York, NY 10020

or WHOLE EARTH CATALOG

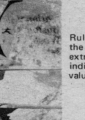

Rule: the travel value of any fare is determined by the number and variety of places you can visit at no extra cost en route to your destination. The more indirect and round-about your route, the greater value you receive from any fare.

How to Travel Without Being Rich

London–Istanbul: Direct Orient Express	$70 second class
Istanbul–Ankara: Taurus Express	5 second class
Ankara–Erzerum, Turkey: local train	10 second class
Erzerum–Teheran, Iran: TBT or Mihantour bus	12
Teheran–Meshed, Iran: rail	8 second class
Meshed–Yousouf Abad, Iran: bus	1
Yousouf Abad–Herat, Afghanistan: Afghan Mail bus service	4
Herat–Kandahar–Kabul, Afghanistan: Afghan Mail bus service	4
Kabul–Peshewar, Pakistan: Afghan Mail bus service	3
Peshewar–Lahore, Pakistan: express bus	2.50
Lahore–Ferozepur, India: local buses	1
Ferozepur–New Delhi, India: Punjab Mail train	6.50 first class
New Delhi–Calcutta, India: Toofan Express train	13.35 first class
Calcutta–Madras, India: Howrah–Madras Mail train	15.20 first class
Madras–Penang, Malaysia: B.I. Line or Shipping Corp. of India	74
Penang–Bangkok, Thailand: International Express train	25 second class
Bangkok–Kobe, Japan: Messageries Maritimes Line	155 tourist class
Kobe–Tokyo, Japan: Kodama Express train	8 second class
Total: London to Tokyo	$417.55

Michelin Maps and Guides

If you're gadding about Europe or Africa these are the standard maps ($.75-$1.50) and guides ($3-$4.50). —SB

[Suggested by Joe Godwin]

Catalogs

free

from:

Michelin Tire Corporation
2500 Marcus Ave.
Lake Success, N.Y. 11040

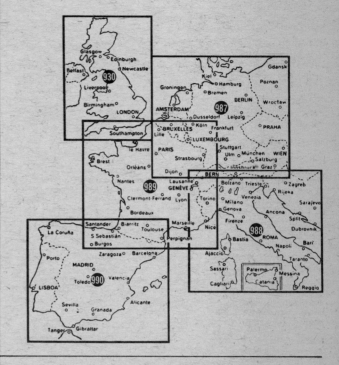

Reference Guide for Travelers

If you're going to some particular place in the world and want to know about the guide books etc. for that place, go to a library and find this excellent annotated bibliography of all travel books in print. —SB

Reference Guide for Travelers
J. A. Neal
1969; 674 pp.

free at sensible libraries everywhere

Shipping Out

Reply to a letter in the March issue in the "Other People's Mail" section, p. 22.

P.G. asks "Who's got the Straight Skinny?" concerning shipping out on merchant ships.

Firstly — get your passport and have your occupation listed as Merchant sailor (or seaman).

Second — to ship out on U.S. vessels you need a Coast Guard document which is a plastic I.D. pass with your photo and a "Z" number. You can only obtain this pass from *Coast Guard Merchant Marine Documentation* offices in all major seaports. Look in the phone book under U.S. Government.

Third — here is the hangup! The Coast Guard won't issue new documents to anyone unless they can prove that they have a job. Acceptable proof usually consists of a letter written by the personnel manager of the company who will hire you. Most companies won't hire you without you already having the required document. I include maritime unions in with companies as they, these days, are trying to limit union membership.

Fourth — your chances of shipping out on U.S. vessels are quite slim. Many people were hired to man the ships that ran to Vietnam and the Far East hauling war or war-related cargoes during the last five years. Now they are reducing the war effort and many sailors will be out of work as the government lays up ships.

Fifth — to hire out on U.S. vessels your best bet is to pester the hell out of the maritime unions —

    Sailors Union of the Pacific — Seattle, Portland, S.F., L.A. (Wilmington)
    Sea Farers International Union — East Coast & Gulf Ports
    National Maritime Union — East Coast & Gulf Ports.

Also try tug boat companies — they hire a lot of men and pay very well. Your best bet is to play a "straight" roll. Most personnel managers and Union dispatchers are straight and anti-anyone who does not also appear straight. Having got the job and the required C.G. documents and entered into the seafaring life you will find that sailors don't give a damn what you look like, or how you act.

Sixth and last — shipping out on foreign vessels is a matter of chance. Contact the consuls of each maritime nation — Norway, Denmark, Sweden, Italy, Germany, England, Panama, Liberia, Greece — in each major port city of the U.S. leaving your name, address, and phone number.

Also go to a seaport and go aboard foreign ships and ask for a job.

Also contact Steamship agents (phone book again) and drop a card to the operations manager with name and phone number.

Kevin Mercer
Seattle, WA

How To Get a Job Overseas

Most of the openings are pretty imperialistic if your conscience is sensitive to that score. The book does cover the field okay. Mainly it comes down to this, if you have a needed skill (like nursing, metallurgy, veterinary) the door is open. Otherwise you're welcome to either spend or starve but not compete with local labor. —SB

How to Get A Job Overseas
Curtis Casewit
1970; 253 pp.

$1.45 postpaid

from:
Arc Books Inc.
219 Park Ave. S.
New York, N.Y. 10003

or WHOLE EARTH CATALOG

The agency likes to get you while you're young, but older people— with special backgrounds in the sciences and technology— have made the grade, too. If you're now a highly regarded cartographer, mathematician, anthropologist, or engineer, you can also ask for application forms (write CIA, Office of Personnel), or report personally without prior appointment to 1820 N. Fort Myer Drive, Arlington, Virginia. CIA draws its staff from many racial and ethnic backgrounds, which means that you'd encounter no obstacles on that score. But don't expect to earn as much as you would in private industry. Salaries start at a low $3,889, and go up— in rare cases— to a limit of $25,044 a year.

"What people don't understand is that you've got to trust the Lord before He can do you any good," said Mrs. Godsey.

"But people aint willing to do that any more," said Mrs. Thornton. "That's what's wrong with the world."

"Let every soul be subject unto the higher powers!" Mrs. Godsey quoted. "For there is no power but of God: the powers that be are ordained of God. That's scripture, sister. Romans thirteen, one."

"People just wont accept it," said Mrs. Thornton. "People just turns away."

"They turn away from God and toward Satan," said Mrs. Godsey. "Old Satan's got a arm-lock right around ever one of their necks."

"That's the pure truth," said Mrs. Thornton. "That's the pure truth if it was ever told."

After a little pause for a sip of their drinks, Mrs. Thornton said, "But you know, Mrs. Godsey, if there is anybody that ought to be in a hospital it's surely poor old Emmit Collier. I think it's just pitiful, him a laying up there on that old hillside by himself. Me and Wheeler was talking about him just yesterday, wondering what anybody could do."

"Why honey," said Mrs. Godsey. "You're behind the times."

Mrs. Thornton's face said what do you mean?

"Emmit aint by himself no more."

"You don't mean he's died!" gasped Mrs. Thornton.

Mrs. Godsey grinned. "Oh no," she said. "His nephew David come in and's gone up there to stay with him. Drove in from Cincinnati yesterday in the paintedest old bus-of-a-thing you ever saw. Went right straight on up there to take care of him."

"Well I'll swan," said Mrs. Thornton.

(continued)

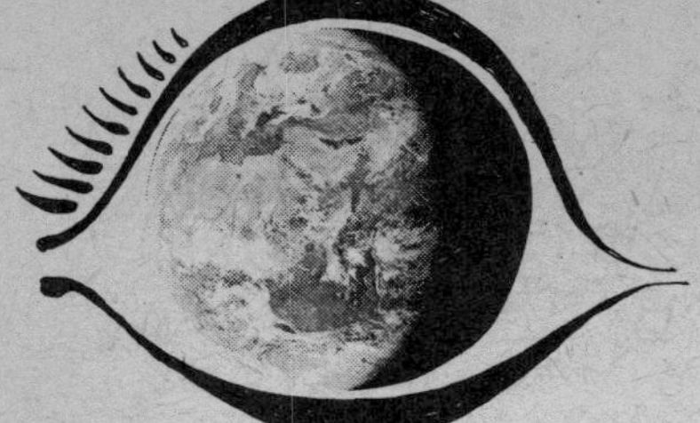

Peace Corps

We've got fine vacation news for suburban guerrillas, or for that matter, anybody up for a trip. Make Peace Corps your local travel agency at no expense to you.

If you want some time to think, adequate salary, easy and fun job, free medical care, free dental care, many profusely illustrated publications, and other gratuities, take advantage of the free offer. The U.S. government can be penetrated "like cheese-cloth". It's full of holes to breathe through.

Chances of acceptance are high, especially for people who can make things grow. If you can't make things grow you probably qualify as an English teacher. The more under-developed the country, the more loosely defined the job. If you want to make a big deal out of what you find yourself doing you can, but if you're not that type then let the Peace Corps be your reality trip. You might end up with a Maharishi in your own neighborhood.

Training usually amounts to a 6–10 week commune. Our program trained on a ranch near Rocky Mountain National Park — an instant plastic community with coop general store, nightly dancing, feasting together, mountain climbing, even our own mythology. We also learned a foreign language. The same kind of language course we got would cost a couple thou at Berlitz. Other training programs have taken place in Mexico, Canada, the Virgin Islands, and all over California. The trend in Peace Corps training programs today is to choose a salubrious place where volunteers will feel a sense of oneness.

Peace Corps employs thousands of volunteers in countries all over the world — Morocco, Afghanistan, Nepal, Micronisia, India, Peru, Sierra Leone, and other places you might like to know. It's usually no problem enjoying the better aspects of the natives and retaining what you are at the same time. If you don't dig the natives you can work along with them anyway.

Peace Corps volunteers get two days of paid vacation for every month of service. That means 48 days accumulated vacation for two years of service. During vacation you get nine dollars a day just to subsist on. One volunteer visited five countries his first year of service — Spain, Tunisia, Sicily, Italy, and Greece, spending no less than two weeks in any one country. A skillful volunteer could easily beat that. Counting local holidays, Christmas vacation, summer vacation, spring vacation, and unexpected surprises like International Moon Day or a sudden coup, a volunteer could easily push five months in days-off during a single year.

Despite recession in the states Peace Corps salaries have been going up recently. In less than a year's time our salaries have increased by 33%. With our excess subsistance allowance we've bought a lot of hand-made rugs and blankets worth thousands in the states if you need retirement money.

The necessary information is available through Peace Corps, Washington. When you read Peace Corps material, use your imagination. Don't be turned off by jargon like "volunteer spirit" and "effectiveness". In most countries lack of communications make bureaucracy virtually impossible. You are necessarily left alone. Improvise. Take a stereo and plenty of books you've been wanting to read. If the Peace Corps charters an airplane to fly your program to its site, there is practically no limit on baggage weight.

Regardless of when you leave the Peace Corps you get 75 dollars for every month of service abroad or about 1500 dollars after two years, plus free air fare back to your suburban camp. The Peace Corps will even find you another job.

And the whole two years is a free-trial period. If for any reason you don't like what you're doing, Peace Corps will pay your way home at any time.

Write Peace Corps in Washington and ask for a hand-book. Ask for special information on the country of your choice. Inquire about training programs and fields open to volunteers. Everything is free of charge. The whole trip costs you nothing.

<u>Quotations from Peace Corps literature:</u>

The change in attitude many Volunteers have after the initial novelty of living abroad has worn off is sometimes striking. The fire of enthusiasm they brought with them turns to ashes not long after they encounter the first misunderstanding, the first reluctance to change traditions based on the heritage of generations. Instead of attempting to affect the attitudes around them, however slightly, they begin in some respects to adopt these attitudes.

Going from the ordered routine of training to an unstructured job overseas has sometimes been compared to running off the end of a pier. Suddenly there is no solid footing underneath; often there is not a staff member or an instructor in sight, and it's up to you to sink or swim.

The work of a volunteer is largely a matter of individual definition.

<u>Emergencies</u>: The best advice here is to use your common sense.

Neither volunteers nor staff members may pilot air-craft during their service with the Peace Corps.

Mobius Polymers Unltd.
Tunis, Tunisia

Knapsacking Abroad

The quickest way to get to know the local folk is to let them help you, like giving you a ride or a place to camp. This is a practical collection of basic lore.

—SB

Knapsacking Abroad
Herb and Judy Klinger
1967; 95 pp.

OUT OF PRINT

Stackpole Books
Cameron & Kelker Sts.
Harrisburg, Pa. 17105

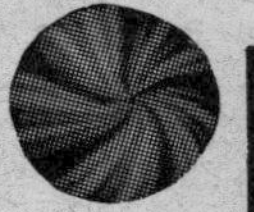

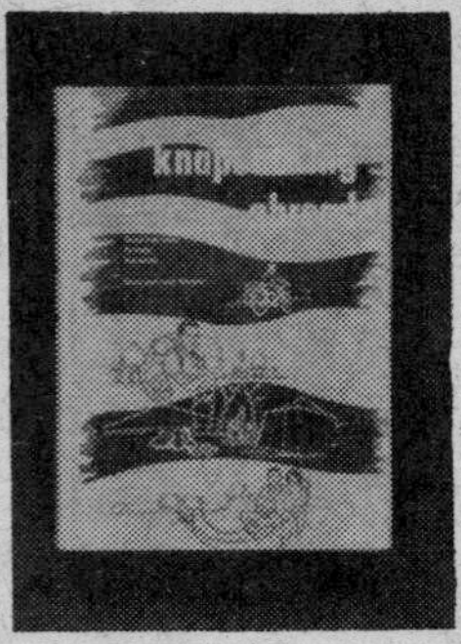

Small gifts say more than "thank you" to someone who's helped you along your way. Ingenious traders also manage to subsidize their travels by importing reasonable quantities of locally scarce personal goods for distribution in non-industrial countries. Gifts and goods needn't all be hauled from home. Duty-free shops at ports of exit, or free ports en route, invite bargain purchases as well as personal restocking.

Premium items vary with country and times. Likely to continue popular in major blocs of the world are: Kennedy half-dollars, U.S. jazz records, unusual flower seeds, nylon shirts and stockings, instant coffee, transistorized equipment, watches, cameras, liquor, lipsticks, ballpoint pens, and photos of yourself and family.

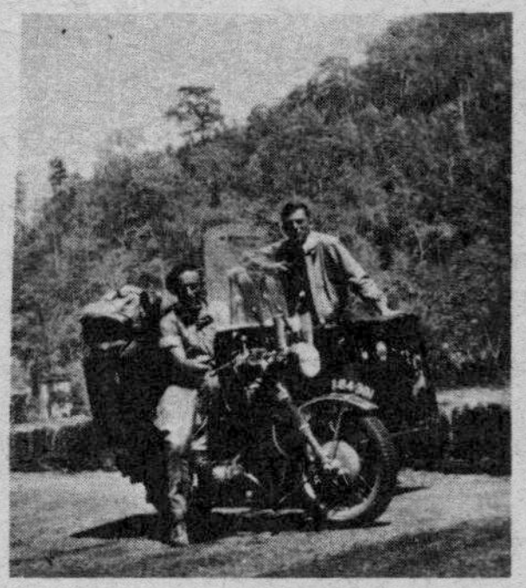

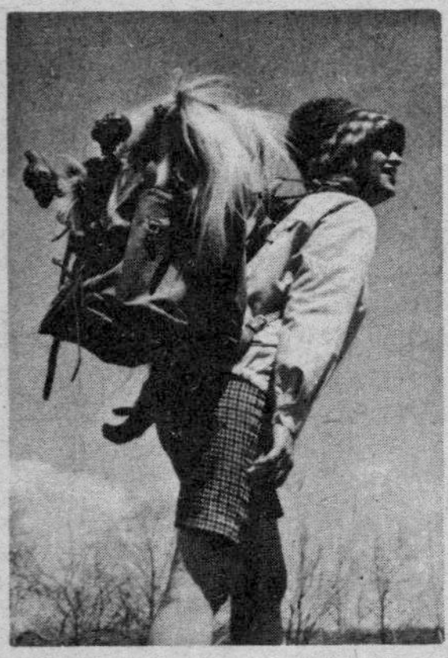

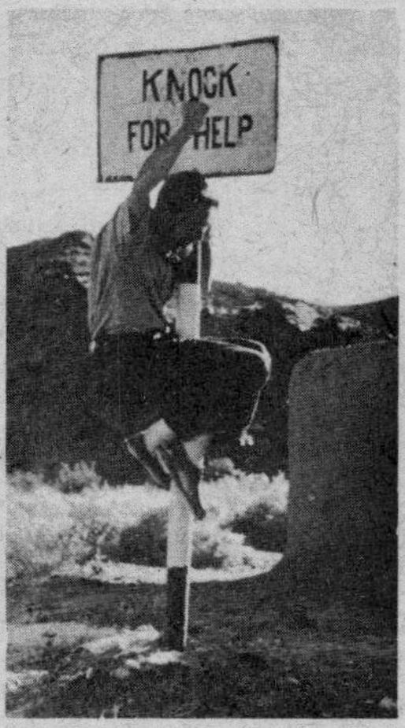

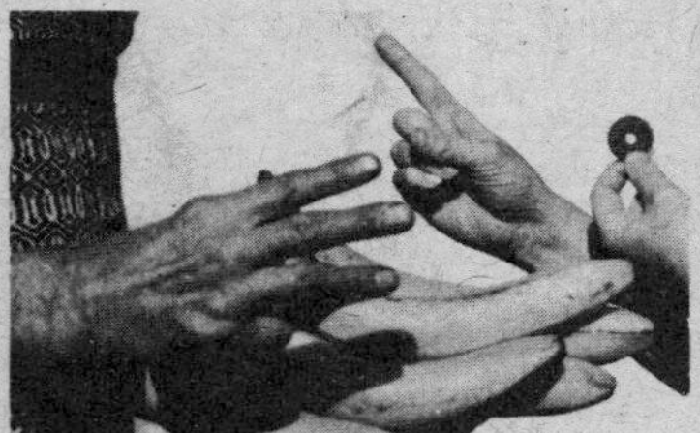

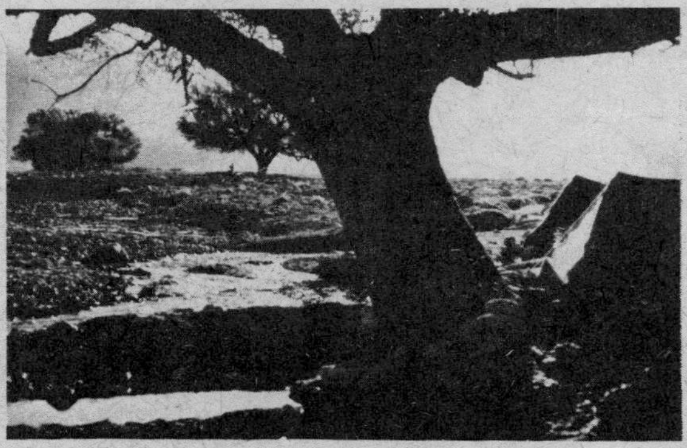

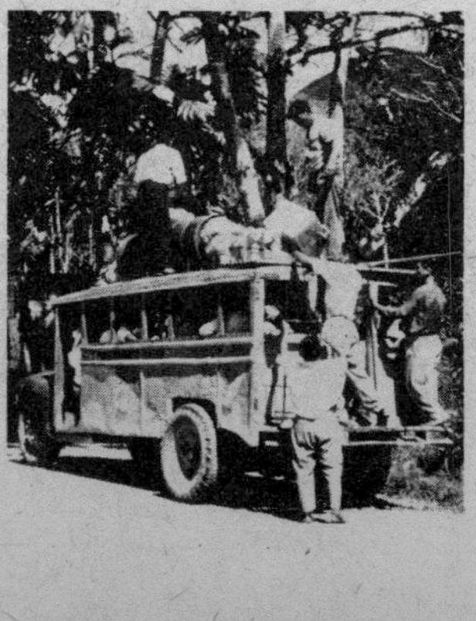

Student Eurail Pass

I have just read your Fall catalog and I noticed that you didn't have anything about the greatest bargain in traveling in Europe, i.e., Student Eurail Pass. For $125 you can ride 2nd class for 2 months on the railroads in 13 countries.

If you wish to see some more evidence of this bargain read the August 14, 1970 edition of Life Magazine.

Thanks,
Jay Buster
Peoria, Ill.

2 months/$165 — $260 non-student
Talk to a local travel agent

Youth Hostel Pass

The Youth hostel pass costs from $5 to $12, depending upon age and number in the group. It is required when staying at most of the European and American Youth hostels. The hostels in Europe generally charge from $1.50 on down per night per bed and often offer either the use of a kitchen or very cheap meals. If you plan to visit any of the bigger cities (Copenhagen, Stockholm, Amsterdam, etc.) you should reserve a couple of weeks ahead of time. When you buy your card you should also buy the guide for the area you intend to visit. They offer a fairly complete listing and rating of each hostel, and tell how to get to them via public transport in the larger cities. You do not have to sleep in a hostel to eat, wash, loaf, etc. there. Also it is a good place to use as a mailing address. I used the youth hostels in northern Europe and noticed that whole families often stayed at them. They also converted many schools into hostels during the summer. As I have written above hostels are very cheap. I stayed at the Luxembourg hostel and paid $1.25 for breakfast, supper and bed. I could have paid 50¢ more and gotten a packed lunch. The German hostels charge two marks a night or 60¢ but are very strict but clean. For more information write:

American Youth Hostels Inc.
National Campus
Delaplane, VA 22025

I am a member of the Potomac Area Council and they have lots of ecology oriented outings.

Leon Dubman
Baltimore, Maryland

P.S. Travel light and swift.

Visit USA

Another overseas bonus, "Visit USA" airline tickets. Even if you're an American citizen, as long as you reside so-many miles outside the U.S., you're eligible. The $150, 21-day deal is the best— on the feeder airlines. Forget those big promotional jobs on the trunk lines. The feeders are good and cover more ground. Since the ticket must be started within 30 days from your arrival in the U.S., get two of them and get 42 days of bombing-around for $300. There are no hitches or anti-double-back gimmicks. When you get tired, jump on the longest flight you can find. When you're hungry, look for one with a meal coming up soon. A big bonus— as of last year, Alaska Airlines was in the deal. So my kids and I flew from NYC to Nome, Alaska and back for $300 (kids are half fare until the age of 20 or 21!). We even made a side trip from Seattle to Portland and back to buy cigarettes— they're cheaper in Oregon.

Pete Schermerhorn
Aruba
Netherlands Antilles

Vagabonding in Europe and North Africa

Good specific low-rent information.

—SB

Vagabonding in Europe and North Africa
Ed Buryn
1971; 225 pp.

$3.95 postpaid

from:
Bookworks
c/o Random House
Westminster, Maryland 21157

or WHOLE EARTH CATALOG

P—R—O—V—O—Y—A is a number you dial in Paris if you want a ride out of town bound for anywhere in Europe. This is an organization that arranges rides for hitchers for a $2 registration fee. Get details from: Provoya, 16 rue de Provence, Paris 9e. I've heard of this several times but haven't used it and don't know anyone else who has. Anybody?

•

Drivers pick you up because they want something from you. Short list of wants:

1) They're bored— you're to entertain them or vice-versa;
2) They're curious— you're to provide information about something, usually yourself;
3) They want to feel charitable— you're the chosen recipient;
4) They need something tangible— you're to share expenses or help drive, etc.

•

Europe This Way by James Steffensen Jr. and Lawrence Handel (Atheneum; $7.95). New edition each year. Never mind that it's intended for students— ETW is the best all-around guidebook I've seen. The cost is high and the book is bulky, but both these disadvantages result from one considerable advantage: it is packed with information. More of it on more countries than any other guidebook, and particularly important, the information is all useful and sensible. It covers trip preparation, working or studying abroad, transportation, food, lodging, entertainment, and the advice given by the authors is consistently excellent. Its country-by-country listings are the best available between one set of covers. If you get it, consider tearing it apart to carry only the pages you need. It's too bulky to carry whole.

Hitchhiking, the homilies:

Use a sign. Have a map.

Look like who you want to pick you up.

Wait where it's easy for drivers to see you and stop.

Be of use to the driver, or at least no bother.

Don't take it personally when they don't pick you up. See it as their problem.

Stay on the curb, and off freeways. Don't rob or murder anybody; it makes it hard for the next guy.

—SB

Travelers Directory

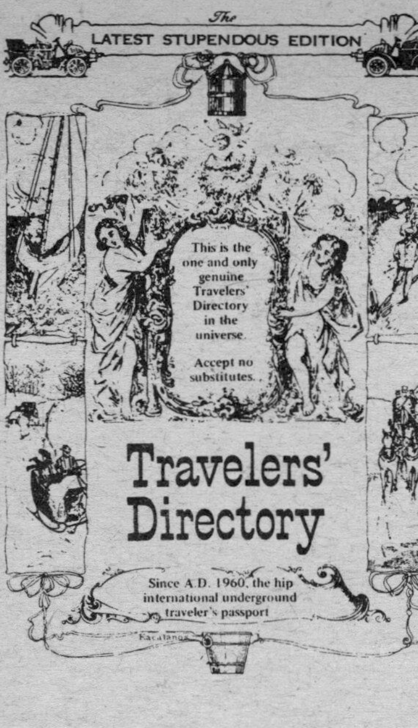
The
LATEST STUPENDOUS EDITION
This is the one and only genuine Travelers' Directory in the universe.
Accept no substitutes.
Travelers' Directory
Since A.D. 1960, the hip international underground traveler's passport

Travelers' Directory is the international registry of hip travelers who enjoy meeting others everywhere, whether around the corner or around the world. The book lists their names, addresses, telephones, ages, interests, and offers of hospitality to other travelers passing through. The upcoming Spring 1971 edition will list almost 1000 addresses in its 96 pages. New listings are now being accepted in Directory headquarters in New York City. EQUALITY readers are especially welcome, because they obviously share common interests with those already listed.

Prospective listees should submit the above information about themselves for publication in the Spring edition. (Published annually since 1960, Travelers' Directory is now being published every six months to keep pace with its rapid growth.) As always, copies of the new edition will be sent only to those travelers listed in that edition, so only listees will know who else is listed. No extra copies are ever printed, so none is available to anyone not listed. Each copy of Travelers' Directory is numbered, bears the listee's name, is neither transferable nor replaceable, and acts as each listee's "underground passport" to identify him to all the others in the book.

Ever since its first edition ten years ago, Travelers' Directory has been a non-profit labor of love. The costs of printing and mailing the Directory are shared by the editor and all the listees. Each listing is submitted with a donation of at least U.S. $3 (about 10DM) to defray some of the production expenses of the editor, who receives no remuneration at all. Donations may be sent in any currency, or by check or money order made out to Travelers' Directory. Listings arriving by 28 February will be included in the Spring edition, to be sent to all listees in March, in plenty of time to make plans for summer traveling.

Even before the new edition of the Directory is published, listees will start receiving the Directory's magazine, Trips, as a free bonus. This amusing publication is written by and for the listees themselves.It featuresarticles on their travel experiences, invitations to all listees for free weekend Directory parties in different cities, and solid advice on such subjects as hitching free rides on planes and ships, or which companies will pay you to drive their customers' cars across the country.

Such bonuses, though, are incidental to the primary purpose of Travelers' Directory. People decide to be listed mainly because they enjoy meeting others with similar interests wherever they travel. They know they have friends to welcome them in any city in the world where there are Directory listees, and that seems to be just about everywhere: London, Paris, Frankfurt, Rome, Stockholm, Bombay, Tokyo, Sydney, you name it. Listees live in almost every major country on every continent, even in such uninviting areas as Antarctica and Viet Nam. One listee recently toured much of Africa, staying with other listees in Tanzania, Uganda, Ghana, Liberia, Sierra Leone, Spanish Morocco and the Canary Islands. The country best represented in the current edition is the United States, with hundreds of listings, ranging from one to 55 addresses in each city. Although listees collectively speak dozens of languages, every one speaks English, the international language used throughout the Directory. No listee ever visits another, of course, without first phoning or writing to be sure he's welcome.

Because each listee must submit his listing himself each time he wants it published in the next edition, all addresses and offers of hospitality to compatible listees are current. No listing is ever carried over to the next edition automatically. Despite that policy, many current listees have managed to be listed in every edition since 1960. Travelers' Directory can't be all bad. Welcome aboard.

P. Kacalanos, Editor, Travelers' Directory, 51-02 39th Ave., Woodside, New York 11377

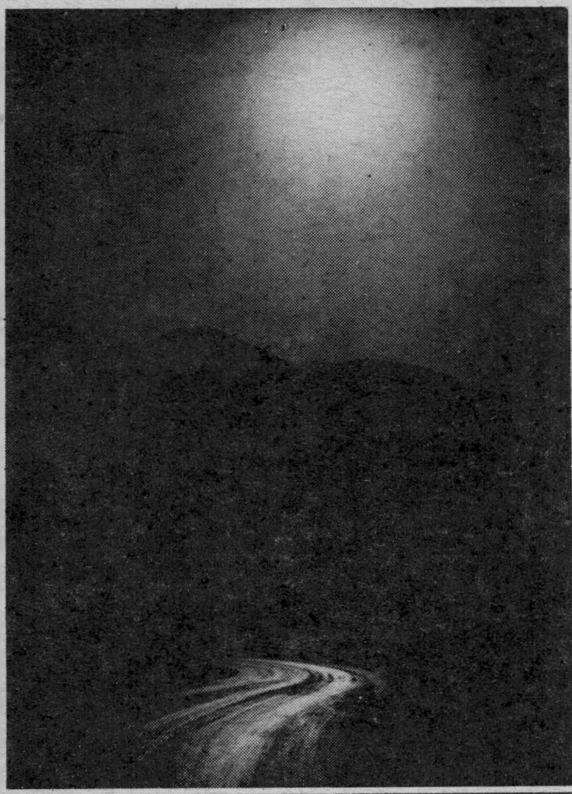

Temporary Car

Re: Survival Travel Suggestions

If you have a little bread, a good way to move from city to city is by driving a car for an Auto Transport Agency . In most big cities there are usually a number of agencies. Call up and ask if they need any cars driven near to where you want to go. If they say yes, you go to their office to fill out an application. Requirements are generally, but not necessarily, 25 years of age or over, some references, a valid driver's license, and supplementary identification. They will ask how many are driving with you. Depending on the vibes you can either tell them or say that you are driving alone. (I don't know if there are any insurance complications in this respect.)

Usually they require a deposit of $40 to $50. At the end of the trip you are reimbursed for the deposit, any gas allowance permit fees, and repair expenses you might have incurred on the road— if they were not the result of negligence. Be sure to keep your receipts. It pays to shop around. Often one car will have a larger gas allowance. Also, if you are low on cash, you want to get a car which is less likely to break down, or one that uses less gas. Rattle traps usually mean trouble. Waiting a douple of days and checking regularly with the agencies will often turn up a car.

About five western states have a commercial vehicle tax which you are required to pay upon crossing the state line. If you are stopped and do not have a sticker you are liable for a large fine. If you obey all the laws and slow to 25 when passing through the small towns, the chance of being stopped if you are driving a car is very slight. Worse odds if driving a truck, van, or obvious commercial vehicle (get a larger gas allowance for these— dicker a little, they are anxious to move them). I keep my agency sticker in my pocket. If stopped, tact and a hard luck story are advised.

Should you run out of gas money before, you can telephone collect to destination and have cash wired to you as a deduction from your deposit. Another angle is to check the Greyhound Bus Stations and see if someone cool will pay for your gas. This will usually save them cost of half a ticket. Watch out you don't get picked up for soliciting. Plan ahead.

Peace and good luck,

Arn
Sherman Oaks, Calif.

Cheap Meal in a Strange Place

Landing in a strange city with very little bread is rough; rougher even than *living* in one with very little bread. Eating is always important and should not be put off for too long in any circumstances. I may have a rung for your ladder. A good meal can be had in any hospital cafeteria in the land for from 60 cents to one dollar. Meat or fish, vegetable, salad, milk and dessert at 1/3 the price of any restaurant. No one cares what you look like either, they assume that you're a visitor and leave you alone. More often than not you might be invited into a friendly conversation since people in hospitals share a common bond.

If you are looking for a good spot to eat in San Francisco, I recommend St. Mary's Hospital on Hayes and Stanyan--- excellent ****

Dana McDill
San Francisco, Ca. 94133

Canadian Rail Cheap

I have a couple of suggestions which I hope you can use. (You probably know about this one). You can travel on the Canadian Pacific Railroad from Montreal to Vancouver for $51.00 (Canadian or $49.00 (American), coach, no meals. (For three days——who cares). I really didn't believe this so I wrote to the company and it was verified. That is so incredibly cheap & what a trip, through the Canadian Rockies, etc. Right now some friends are travelling this train and I'm dying to hear how it goes.

Love & Peace—

Margaret Cherran
Providence, R.I.

Freight Hopping

You do o.k. by hitchhiking but hardly a mention of freight hopping. In the U.S.A. this is technically illegal, but in many areas, particularly in the west, it is allowed in order to have cheap labor available for the big farmers. For example, you can catch a ride from Seattle's Interbay to Minneapolis or on to Chicago in 2 or 3 days respectively. Also from Chi-town (if you're very careful in the yards) and Minneapolis you can go down to St. Louis or Kansas City and thence to L.A. via the southwest and thence up the coast to Seattle again. There are spots where you have to be cool and awake to avoid getting kicked off a train, but you soon learn where and when. One sees a part of America few people see anymore, too. Some roads (like U.P. and a lot of southern and eastern lines) won't let you ride, but then again, this is always a relative thing, depending on who knows you're on a train, and who you ask. I advise caution in order to keep from an avoidable 30 days in the city jail and also to avoid getting cut in half or wiped out by a switch standard (if you are gonna mess with a train when its moving, you better know what you're doin', otherwise stay on or stay off till it stops). You can get up to Prince George & Prince Rupert, and east and south as you find possible, I've heard good & bad things about Dixie and Mexico (RE: freights) and don't know. Information is half of your ticket— ask the workers (particularly the switchmen in big yards) where and when a long shot is being made up for your destination. Be cool with RR dicks, they exist but sometimes you meet them in spite of intentions otherwise. "innocense" is helpful in such cases; tell 'em you didn't know you were doing anything wrong and don't want to. . .etc. I find empties (opened boxcars) the best, except in very good, warm weather. Sometimes you might even get a ride in the caboose ("crummy" its called) for a division or two. There are a lot of things that are "dangerous" like shifting loads crushing people etc. that I can't ever completely cover. Sensitivity and awareness about how the train functions is the other half of your ticket. Bring your own food, water and warmth. I guess there's a lot to it, but no more than a lot of other things. Well, as they say at Suwa-no-se Jima, Sayonara, you all! Keep on truckin'

Shanti to Alan who was able to write a personal letter about a gristmill we ordered.

Hope to see you all

Daniel G. Leen
Fairbanks, Alaska

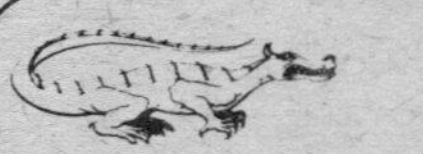

"His bus is out behind the house right now."

"Well I'll swan. Now what nephew would that be, honey? It aint Jenny's boy is it?"

"Jenny's boy'd be too young, honey. He's Royce's. You remember Royce."

"Got killed in a car wreck," said Mrs. Thornton.

"That's right. It was his woman Eva that took up with that Davenport everybody hated so bad."

"Why yes. I remember that family. Their girl went to school to my brother-in-law's wife Rona, when she taught over yonder at Hemlock."

"That's Marcella," said Mrs. Godsey.

"Well now," said Mrs. Thornton. "I remember Marcella real good, but I declare I can't picture a boy."

"He's nearly grown now," said Mrs. Godsey. "I wouldn't of recognized him if he hadn't told me who he was. You'd think he was one of them hip-eyes on television, to look at him. Kind of queer-acting but I tell you now. That child sure meant business about taking care of his uncle. I called up there to Cincinnati Sunday to say how sick Emmit was, and he answered and said he'd come as soon as he could. Just like that. Stopped in here a few minutes, then took off up that creek lickety-split. His bus is out behind the house right now. Leonard pushed it around there."

Mrs. Godsey took a sip of her R. C.

"I tell you now, honey," she went on, "I've been praying for Emmit. I've been asking a blessing for him ever since he come down sick, and I declare if it don't look like the Lord's done sent him one."

"I hope it's so," said Mrs. Thornton. "I say God bless the boy if he don't do no more than make Emmit feel like somebody cares a little something about him."

"That's right," said Mrs. Godsey, and she started to get up then. Struggling to rise, she said, "Well young 'un, I don't mean to run you off, but it's my nap time, and I'm going to go in yonder and lay down in the bed a while."

"I don't blame you," said Mrs. Thornton, and she started getting up too. "I've got to get on home myself. Wheeler'll probably kill me for being gone this long."

Mrs. Thornton was as fat as Mrs. Godsey was old, and it took them equally long to work out of their seats and stand. When they'd made it, Mrs. Godsey said, "You come back to see me, now, you hear?"

"I will," said Mrs. Thornton. "And you come up and see us some time."

"Ohh, I don't know," said Mrs. Godsey. "I guess I'm too old to be out gadding about."

Mrs. Thornton said, "Psshht. You tell that Leonard I said for him to load you in the back of that truck of his'n and haul you up to our house for dinner next Sunday."

Mrs. Godsey laughed and said she'd tell him.

"Where's Leonard at, anyhow?" said Mrs. Thornton. "I've been wanting to ask him something."

"I don't know where he's at today," said Mrs. Godsey. "But he's on the Grand Jury next week."

"The Grand Jury!" exclaimed Mrs. Thornton.

"Yep. Two weeks of it, starting Monday."

"Lordy," said Mrs Thornton. "He'll come back thinking he's a big shot."

The women laughed again and waved as Mrs. Godsey went through the curtain that separated her house from the store. Mrs. Thornton picked up the empty soft drink bottles, put them in a case beside the cooler, and then went out the door.

Communications

Diagrams

A diagram is a conceptual map. Elegantly done it can ease comprehension. Thoroughly done it can aid analysis. Done with originality it can remake your internal world. This book, the first of its kind, is a splendid survey of the range and usefulness of diagramming.

—SB

Diagrams
Arthur Lockwood
1969; 254 pp.

$15.00 postpaid

from:
Watson-Guptill Publications
2160 Patterson St.
Cincinnati, OH 45214

or WHOLE EARTH CATALOG

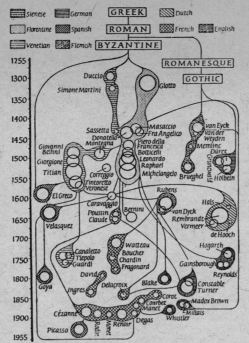

Chart from a book, showing chief schools of European painting from Giotto. Devised by Eric Newton who explains that it attempts to indicate relative importance of schools (areas of shaded masses), approximate dates, principal artists (circle), relative importance (size of circle), threads of influence between schools and artists. Eric Newton, European Painting and Sculpture, Faber and Faber

There is no attempt to give this book a historical perspective, although some of the pioneers in the effective presentation of information in visual form are included. The pioneers include magazines such as Fortune and Scientific American; firms such as the Container Corporation of America, and particularly the Isotype Institute, London, whose approach and achievement has affected all designers of diagrams even though they may not be aware of their debt.

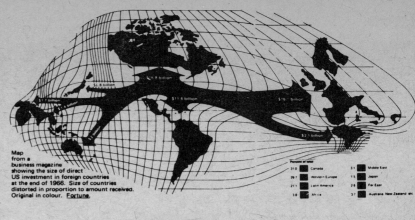

Map from a business magazine showing the size of direct US investment in foreign countries at the end of 1966. Size of countries distorted in proportion to amount received. Original in colour. Fortune.

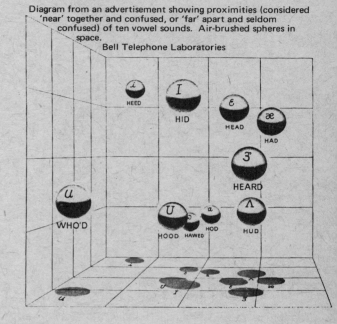

Diagram from an advertisement showing proximities (considered 'near' together and confused, or 'far' apart and seldom confused) of ten vowel sounds. Air-brushed spheres in space.
Bell Telephone Laboratories

Mapping

A map is the meeting ground of drawing, writing, and geometry. No other medium carries such a wealth of critical information at glance readiness. Students of brain and thought design are lately placing more and more emphasis on the matter of Where-Is-It—apparently much of the mind's store, retrieve, and relate systems are based on position relationships in mental space.

This book is a well-made introduction to map use, map construction, and something of the meaning of maps.

—SB

Mapping
David Greenhood
1944, 1964; 288 pp.

$2.95 postpaid

from:
University of Chicago Press
5801 Ellis Ave.
Chicago, Illinois 60637

or WHOLE EARTH CATALOG

Land-form map. Accurate information shown with vividness and grace. Drawn by Erwin Raisz for a geography textbook

Pen pressed against T square too hard

Pen sloped away from T square

Pen too close to edge. Ink ran under

Ink on outside of blade, ran under

Pen blades not kept parallel to T square

T square (or triangle) slipped into wet line

Not enough ink to finish line

Avoidable troubles of the ruling pen

We can scan the history of civilization as well as of mapping itself simply by observing which direction has topped the map. Erwin Raisz, the Harvard authority on cartography, says, "It seems to be a tendency among map makers of every country to put at the top of the map the direction toward which national attention is turned."

The Romans headed their maps as they so often did their empire-stretching ships, eastward. So did the Crusaders trying to recover the Holy Land. Many medieval wind roses have a cross as an east-mark.

Maps and charts—you may have noticed in this chapter the repetition of these two words. What's the difference in their meaning? Charts are maps with a special, practical purpose such as navigating, weather forecasting, and population studies. A chart is a map on which to work with protractor, compass, dividers, and guages—even a densitometer.

This connection between local pinpoints and cosmic points is one of the majestic relationships recognized by science. Considering how much the mere idea of a map encompasses, maps are probably more unconfusing than anything else put down on paper. A map should be regarded as an antidote to panic.

The Image

This book is by an economist enchanted with cybernetics. He's after the organizing principle in life, the image the everything comes together through. He scarcely mentions the brain, and he's right. It ain't the brain.

—SB

[Suggested by Martha Neufeld]

The Image
Kenneth E. Boulding
1956; 175 pp.

$1.95 postpaid

from:
The University of Michigan Press
Ann Arbor, Michigan 48106

or WHOLE EARTH CATALOG

The meaning of a message is the change which it produces in the image.

•

Between the incoming and outgoing messages lies the great intervening variable of the image. The outgoing messages are the result of the image, not the result of the incoming messages. The incoming messages only modify the outgoing messages as they succeed in modifying the image.

•

I have never been to Australia. In my image of the world, however, it exists with 100 per cent certainty. If I sailed to the place where the map makers tell me it is and found nothing there but ocean I would be the most surprised man in the world. I hold to this part of my image with certainty, however, purely on authority. I have been to many other places which I have found on the map and I have almost always found them there. It is interesting to inquire what gives the map this extraordinary authority, an authority greater than that of the sacred books of all religions. It is not an authority which is derived from any political power or from any charismatic experience. As far as I know it is not a crime against the state nor against religion to show a map that has mistakes in it. There is, however, a process of feedback from the users of maps to the map maker.

•

There is a strong tendency for authoritarian organizations to use violence or the threat of violence in support of the role structure, that is, in order to gain acceptance of the role on the part of the persons occupying the lower role. For a time this may be successful in maintaining the organization. It is usually, however, self-defeating because of the corruption of the communication system which it entails. The case is somewhat analogous to that of the schizophrenic or the extreme paranoid. His sense receptors are so much "afraid" of him that they merely confirm the products of his heated imagination. The terrorized information sources of the tyrant likewise tell him only what they think will be pleasing to his ears. Organizations as well as individuals can suffer from hallucinations. It is the peculiar disease of authoritarian structures.

At the other extreme, democratic structures in which there is no adequate leadership, that is, in which the feedback is destructive of the decision-making process on the part of higher roles are likewise unstable and incapable of maintaining themselves. If discussion is to be a successful process of decision-making it must exhibit a degree of convergence toward common images of the whole organization. If the feedback from the followers destroys the image of the leader instead of merely modifying it, the process is likely to be self-defeating.

•

The image acts as a field. The behavior consists in gravitating toward the most highly valued part of the field. It does not follow from this, however, that the consequences of behavior are in conformity with the image which produced them. Disappointment and surprise are a common lot of both organisms and organizations. We behave according to some image of the consequences of our acts. When, however, these consequences are reflected in information fed back to us, we find very often that beedback does not confirm the original image. Under these circumstances, as we have seen, the image may be modified or it may not.

•

In tracing the effect of images on the course of history, peculiar attention must be paid to the images of time and especially the images of the future. Curiously enough, it may not be so much the actual content of the image of the future which is important in its effect, but its general quality of optimism or pessimism, certainty or uncertainty, breadth or narrowness. The person or the nation that has a date with destiny goes somewhere, though not usually to the address on the label. The individual or the nation which has no sense of direction in time, no sense of a clear future ahead is likely to be vacillating, uncertain in behavior, and to have a poor chance of surviving. Those images of the future which are most persistent and which have had the greatest impact on human history seem to be those which are impenetrable to feedback and which maintain themselves by their own internal beauty and consistency.

Cybernetics

McLuhan's assertion that computers constitute an extension of the human nervous system is an accurate historical statement. The research and speculation that led to computer design arose from investigation of healthy and pathological human response patterns embodied in the topological make-up of the nervous system. Insights here soon expanded into generalizations about communication that permitted the building of analagous electronic devices physically separate from the Central Nervous System. But they're just one artifact of these new understandings about communication. Society, from organism to community to civilization to universe, is the domain of cybernetics. Norbert Wiener has the story, and to some extent, is the story.

—SB

Cybernetics — or Control and Communication in the Animal and the Machine
Norbert Wiener
1948,1961;212 pp.

$2.45 postpaid

from:
The M. I. T. Press
Cambridge, Mass. 02142

or WHOLE EARTH CATALOG

To predict the future of a curve is to carry out a certain operation on its past.

•

The central nervous system no longer appears as a self-contained organ, receiving inputs from the senses and discharging into the muscles. On the contrary, some of its most characteristic activities are explicable only as circular processes, emerging from the nervous system into the muscles, and re-entering the nervous system through the sense organs, whether they be proprioceptors or organs of the special senses. This seemed to us to mark a new step in the study of that part of neurophysiology which concerns not solely the elementary processes of nerves and synapses but the performance of the nervous system as an integrated whole.

•

The feedback of voluntary activity is of this nature. We do not will the motions of certain muscles, and indeed we generally do not know which muscles are to be moved to accomplish a given task; we will, say, to pick up a cigarette. Our motion is regulated by some measure of the amount by which it has not yet been accomplished.

•

I have spoken of the race. This is really too broad a term for the scope of most communal information. Properly speaking, the community extends only so far as there extends an effectual transmission of information. It is possible to give a sort of measure to this by comparing the number of decisions entering a group from outside with the number of decisions made in the group. We can thus measure the autonomy of the group. A measure of the effective size of a group is given by the size which it must have to have achieved a certain stated degree of autonomy.

•

Thus small, closely knit communities have a very considerable measure of homeostasis; and this, whether they are highly literate communities in a civilized country or villages of primitive savages. Strange and even repugnant as the customs of many barbarians may seem to us, they generally have a very definite homeostatic value, which it is part of the function of anthropologists to interpret. It is only in the large community, where the Lords ofThings as They Are protect themselves from hunger by wealth, from public opinion by privacy and anonymity, from private criticism by the laws of libel and the possession of the means of communication, that ruthlessness can reach its most sublime levels. Of all of these anti-homeostatic factors in society, the control of the means of communication is the most effective and most important.

•

The mongoose begins with a feint, which provokes the snake to strike. The mongoose dodges and makes another such feint, so that we have a rhythmical pattern of activity on the part of the two animals. However, this dance is not static but develops progressively. As it goes on, the feints of the mongoose come earlier and earlier in phase with respect to the darts of the cobra, until finally the mongoose attacks when the cobra is extended and not in a position to move rapidly. This time the mongoose's attack is not a feint but a deadly accurate bite through the cobra's brain.

In other words, the snake's pattern of action is confined to single darts, each one for itself, while the pattern of the mongoose's action involves an appreciable, if not very long, segment of the whole past of the fight. To this extent the mongoose acts like a learning machine, and the real deadliness of its attack is dependent on a much more highly organized nervous system.

•

To use a biological analogy, the parallel system had a better homeostasis than the series system and therefore survived, while the series system eliminated itself by natural selection.

We thus see that a non-linear interaction causing the attraction of frequency can generate a self-organizing system. . . .

OBJECTIVELY

Objectively, here's what happened: D. R. crawled under the ruins of the old coal tipple and about fifty yards back into the old abandoned mine.

And there in the dark and the moist cool he went ahead and freaked out completely.

That really happened.

Late that afternoon, Leonard, Mrs. Godsey's son, decided he'd walk up Trace Fork and see how Emmit and his nephew were getting along after their first day together. Leonard had been going up to see Emmit every day or two since he'd been sick. Even before he was sick he went up just to visit Emmit a couple of times a week, to take him the things he needed, and talk a while, and now and then to sip a little moonshine with him, or wine that Leonard's cousin Daniel made.

And now the nephew was there, and Leonard thought he'd just stroll up and say hello, and see if they needed anything.

And found D. R., filthy dirty, sitting in the weeds there by the fallen timbers of the tipple of the old Blair Brothers mine.

He looked like a casualty of war.

If it had been anybody besides Leonard that found D. R. like that they would almost certainly have handled it wrongly. Probably they would have run to the nearest telephone and called the doctor, and maybe even the magistrate. But Leonard was a very special man. In ways his old mother who admired him so could never in a hundred years imagine or believe, Leonard was a very special man.

A lot is said about Leonard by the fact that he could appreciate and be friends with a man as strange and eccentric as Emmit Collier. There were people around who thought of Emmit as actually crazy, but they would never have said so around Leonard, because they knew Leonard would defend Emmit, and not many people were inclined to argue with Leonard, or contradict him. Not that they were afraid. Leonard did not inspire fear in anyone. Trust was the feeling most people had toward Leonard. Trust, and confidence in him as an honest man, and strong.

He was the kind of man, the kind of mountaineer, who inevitably makes sergeant in the military, simply because it is so apparent to everybody around from private to Captain that he's the man for the stripes. The assumption happens automatically in the minds of everybody who's looking. Some men are just born with the qualities it takes to impress other men as a leader, and Leonard was one of them. During World War Two he served four years and five months in the Army, and came out a First Sergeant, with a year and a half in grade.

I mention these details about Leonard to give some indication of the kind of fellow he was. His story is as rich and complex as Emmit's or D. R.'s, and it will have to be told some day. But for now, let this much be enough, and observe him as he deals with his bizarre discovery of Emmit's nephew, sitting bewildered and filthy by a pile of rotting logs half-way up a creek that except for one old man has been abandoned by humankind.

•

Leonard speaks to D. R. gently, and looks into his eyes.

•

D. R. looks back into Leonard's eyes, and when Leonard says who he is, D. R. recognizes him, and understands where he is.

Understanding Media

Everybody talks about McLuhan, and everybody does something about him, and that makes it subjectively harder to get at him. He's got other insights than what you hear about, so it's worth the trouble to track him down, both his current sayings and his prime collections. An excellent set of recent sayings was in a Playboy interview a few months ago (he foresaw the imminent demise of language into global telepathy: 'The body of Christ). For prime collection the primest is Understanding Media.

—SB [Suggested by Gerd Stern, then.]

Said the Duke of Gloucester to Edward Gibbon upon the publication of his *Decline and Fall*: 'Another damned fat book, eh, Mr. Gibbon? Scribble, scribble, scribble, eh, Mr. Gibbon?'

As W. B. Yeats wrote of this reversal, "The visible world is no longer a reality and the unseen world is no longer a dream.'

Not only does the visual, specialist, and fragmented Westerner have now to live in closest daily association with all the ancient oral cultures of the earth, but his own electric technology now begins to translate the visual or eye man back into the tribal and oral pattern with its seamless web of kinship and interdependence.

Understanding Media
Marshall McLuhan
1964; 318 pp.

$1.25 postpaid

from—Signet—New American Library, Inc.
1301 Avenue of the Americas
New York, N. Y. 10019

or WHOLE EARTH CATALOG

Even slight changes in the environment of the very well adjusted find them without any resource to meet new challenge. Such is the plight of the representatives of 'conventional wisdom' in any society. Their entire stake of security and status is in a single form of acquired knowledge, so that innovation is for them not novelty but annihilation.

Meantime, the countryside, as oriented and fashioned by plane, by highway, and by electric information-gathering, tends to become once more the nomadic trackless area that preceded the wheel.

Eventually the method of the counting board gave rise to the great discovery of the principle of position in the early centuries of our era. By simply putting 3 and 4 and 2 in position on the board, one after another, it was possible to step up the speed and potential of calculation fantastically. The discovery of calculation by positional numbers rather than by merely additive numbers led, also, to the discovery of zero. Mere positions for 3 and 2 on the board created ambiguities about whether the number was 32 or 302. The need was to have a sign for the gaps between numbers. It was not till the thirteenth century that sifr, the Arab word for 'gap' or 'empty,' was Latinized and added to our culture as 'cipher' (ziphirum) and finally became the Italian zero. Zero really meant a positional gap.

'Work,' however, does not exist in a nonliterate world. The primitive hunter or fisherman did no work, any more than does the poet, painter, or thinker of today. Where the whole man is involved there is no work.

If the phonetic alphabet was a technical means of severing the spoken word from its aspects of sound and gesture, the photograph and its development in the movie restored gesture to the human technology of recording experience.

Man the food-gatherer reappears incongruously as information-gatherer. In this role, electronic man is no less a nomad than his paleolithic ancestors.

Everybody experiences far more than he understands. Yet it is experience, rather than understanding, that influences behavior, especially in collective matters of media and technology, where the individual is almost inevitably unaware of their effect upon him.

It is a principal aspect of the electric age that it establishes a global network that has much of the character of our central nervous system. Our central nervous system is not merely an electric network, but it constitutes a single unified field of experience. As biologists point out, the brain is the interacting place where all kinds of impressions and experiences can be exchanged and translated, enabling us to react to the world as a whole.

Communication Arts

*a slicky for graphics freeks,
and ad men,
people who cut things out of magazines,
to paste them on walls,
christmas cards,
kleenex boxes,
and catalogs.
expensive but pretty.*

—jd

Hess: Products very definitely have a life span. Proctor and Gamble knows this, and they have very tightly documented projections on each one of their products. They know two or three years in advance when they can expect that product to peak out and start its eventual decline. Perhaps some studies should be made. It would behoove publishers to take that same point of view that the package goods manufacturers do and schedule a new product or some kind of revitalization of the old product to coincide with that peak before the decline.

Coyne: You mean fire the publisher and the editor and start over?

Hess: It's an idea.

Communication Arts
Richard Coyne, editor.

$18.00 per year (bimonthly)

from:
Communication Arts
P.O. Box 10300
410 Sherman
Palo Alto, California 94303

By the Late John Brockman

John Brockman, though dead, is in his late twenties and agile in New York. His book is an interpretation of recent work in brain-study, information theory, and art. It proposes that man is dead, replaced by a superior being—once he learns this—called invisible.

—SB

Man is dead. Credit his death to an invention. The invention was the grasping of a conceptual whole, a set of relationships which had not been previously recognized. The invention was man-made. It was the recognition that reality was communicable. The process was the transmission of neural pattern. Such patterns are electrical, not mental. The system of communication and control functioned without individual human awareness or consent. The message in the system was not words, ideas, images, etc. The message was nonlinear: operant neural pattern. It became clear that "new concepts of communication and control involved a new interpretation of man, of man's knowledge of the universe, and of society." Man is dead. "We're talking."

Every movie is the first movie. The brain goes into its stereotyped movie program even before the ticket is purchased. The information received by the brain from the experience of purchasing a ticket may be enough to activate the hormonal responses of the movie experience. Buy your ticket: See the movie.

It is not necessary to say Yes to life.
No one is there to listen; no one is interested in your words.

By the Late John Brockman
John Brockman;
1969; 166 pp.

$6.95 postpaid

from:
Macmillan Company
Front and Brown Streets
Riverside, Burlington County
New Jersey 08075

or WHOLE EARTH CATALOG

The concept of ecumenical technology provides a frame of reference which points to clues about the invisible stage of evolution. The ecumenicism of technology is the unitive force that can make all brains perform the same operations simultaneously. Ecumenical technology is the key to the simultaneous universe of electronic communications. Consider that in the pre-electric age the operations of multitudes of brains in the world would function on different frequency bands. With electronics, an important event on television will mean that on the neural level millions upon millions will have a ray projected onto their retina, providing their brains with the information needed to maintain continuity. This information measures a change in the brain's activity, a frequency modulation. Every brain working the same way, on the same frequency, the same wavelength, performing the same operations simultaneously. Not brotherhood, but unity. Ecumenical technology.

It was all invisible to man. The clash of generations, the crashing down of institutions, the divisiveness—it was all invisible. Man never knew what was happening. To the invisible, it was a question of nonsynchronization of frequencies, where certain brains were unable to adapt to new rhythms of the information received within parameters consistent with continuity. It became a question of phylogenic suicide. To the invisible: out of phase. To man: out of mind. Who's crazy?

Culture is Our Business

McLuhan's best format. Each pair of pages has a reprint of an ad on the right, and fresh McLuhan aphorisms, quotes, and misquotes on the left. The resulting energy across the spread is economic and multi-directional——i.e. you make it. Pound's statement (next p.) about Chaucer and Shakespeare applies as well to McLuhan.

To me he is as valuable. His news stays news.

—SB

Culture Is Our Business
Marshall McLuhan
1970; 336 pp.

$3.95 postpaid

from:
Ballantine Books Inc.
457 Hahn Rd.
Westminster, MD 21157

or WHOLE EARTH CATALOG

Ads are the cave art of the twentieth century. While the Twenties talked about the caveman, and people thrilled to the art of the Altamira caves, they ignored (as we do now) the hidden environment of magical forms which we call "ads." Like cave paintings, ads are not intended to be looked at or seen, but rather to exert influence at a distance, as though by ESP. Like cave paintings, they are not means of private but of corporate expression. They are vortices of collective power, masks of energy invented by new tribal man.

Since Sputnik there is no Nature. Nature is an item contained in a man-made environment of satellites and information. Goals have now to be replaced by the sensory reprogramming of total environments and DNA particles, alike. The earth is an old nose cone.

Today, through ads, a child takes in all the times and places of the world "with his mother's TV." He is gray at three. By twelve he is a confirmed Peter Pan, fully aware of the follies of adults and adult life in general. These could be called Spock's Spooks, who now peer at us from every quarter of our world.

Poets and artists live on frontiers. They have no feedback, only feedforward. They have no identities. They are probes.

Silence

John Cage's seminal work that initiated us all to the uses of audible darkness. How to be undeafened. Also how to enjoy mushrooms, zen, famous people, and space-time crossword puzzles. I've never met a person who liked John Cage's music, or disliked his sunny books.

—SB

Silence
John Cage
1961; 276 pp.

$3.95 postpaid

from:
MIT Press
50 Ames St.
Cambridge, Massachusetts 02142

or WHOLE EARTH CATALOG

I BELIEVE THAT THE USE OF NOISE

Wherever we are, what we hear is mostly noise. When we ignore it, it disturbs us. When we listen to it, we find it fascinating. The sound of a truck at fifty miles per hour. Static between the stations. Rain. We want to capture and control these sounds, to use them not as sound effects but as musical instruments. Every film studio has a library of "sound effects" recorded on film. With a film phonograph it is now possible to control the amplitude and frequency of any one of these sounds and to give to it rhythms within or beyond the reach of the imagination. Given four film phonographs, we can compose and perform a quartet for explosive motor, wind, heartbeat, and landslide.

Psychically, art is valuable only when new.
COMMERCIALLY, NEW ART IS KOOKY AND WORTHLESS.
The gap between the kooky and the commercially valuable is closing fast.

"**We'll return to our commercials after this brief word from the program...**"

NBC and CBS could easily become the political "parties" of the future, just as the New York Central and the Pennsylvania railroads were once the political parties of the nineteenth century.

"Wiretapping," quoth the raven, "is a threat to identity. Why not beat 'em to the wire? Get rid of your identity now."

After a long and arduous journey a young Japanese man arrived deep in a forest where the teacher of his choice was living in a small house he had made. When the student arrived, the teacher was sweeping up fallen leaves. Greeting his master, the young man received no greeting in return. And to all his questions, there were no replies. Realizing there was nothing he could do to get the teacher's attention, the student went to another part of the same forest and built himself a house. Years later, when he was sweeping up fallen leaves, he was enlightened. He then dropped everything, ran through the forest to his teacher, and said, "Thank you."

During a counterpoint class at U.C.L.A., Schoenberg sent everybody to the blackboard. We were to solve a particular problem he had given and to turn around when finished so that he could check on the correctness of the solution. I did as directed. He said, "That's good. Now find another solution." I did. He said, "Another." Again I found one. Again he said, "Another." And so on. Finally, I said, "There are no more solutions." He said, "What is the principle underlying all of the solutions?"

In the space that remains, I would like to emphasize that I am not interested in the relationships between sounds and mushrooms any more than I am in those between sounds and other sounds. These would involve an introduction of logic that is not only out of place in the world, but time-consuming. We exist in a situation demanding greater earnestness, as I can testify, since recently I was hospitalized after having cooked and eaten experimentally some *Spathyema foetida*, commonly known as skunk cabbage. My blood pressure went down to fifty, stomach was pumped, etc. It behooves us therefore to see each thing directly as it is, be it the sound of a tin whistle or the elegant *Lepiota procera*.

Invention is the mother of necessity.

GOING, GOING, GONG

When the evolutionary process shifts from biology to software technology the body becomes the old hardware environment. The human body is now a probe, a laboratory for experiments. In the middle of the ninettenth century Claude Bernard was the first medical man to conceive of *le milieu interieur*. He saw the body, not as an outer object, but as an inner landscape, exactly as did the new painters and poets of the *avant garde*.

If nature didn't, Warner's will.

Our stretch-banded Young Thing™ bra will do it for $5. Our Young Thing girdle will do it for $8. Warner's

---

Political Buttons

Lowest prices to movement organizations. Best quality we've seen. Fast delivery—faster if requested. Union label on all. Custom-made, non-political too, if you want them. Descriptive catalog and price list available. Nice people to deal with.

from:
Printed Celluloid Buttons
Larry Fox Associates
P.O.Box 581
Hempstead, NY 11551

Karen Penner
Valley Stream, NY

list available $1.00 (refundable on 1st order)

And when Leonard says why don't you come on with me, David, and wash up some, D. R. is more than glad to follow.

•

Leonard leads D. R. on up the hill to the place where Emmit's water-pipe from the spring empties into a fifty-gallon barrel, the water point for Emmit's little garden and rabbit scene, above the old falling-down barn.

•

And he pours water on D. R. and D. R. washes himself all over the best he can.

•

Then Leonard leads D. R. around the hill and down a ways, past the barn, and along a path now to the old main house of the homeplace, where old bearded, feeble Emmit sits on the porch in a rocking chair.

•

Leonard speaks to Emmit, quietly. D. R. can't hear what he says, nor can he hear when Emmit nods and quietly replies.

•

Emmit gets up and leads D. R. into the house, into a bedroom, and smoothly without an interruption into a sleep so deep that for a long time there is no dream.

The Elements of Style

Watch a craftsman work. With a few well cared-for tools and direct unshowy motions he keeps the work moving steadily toward completion. The result looks as if it must have been easy to do,'surprisingly inevitable'. You can write like that. Here are the tools.

—SB

The Elements of Style
William Strunk, Jr., E.B. White
1959; 71 pp.

$1.25 postpaid

from:
MacmillanCo.
866 Third Ave.
New York, N.Y. 10022

or WHOLE EARTH CATALOG

10. Use the active voice.

The active voice is usually more direct and vigorous than the passive:

I shall always remember my first visit to Boston.

This is much better than

My first visit to Boston will always be remembered by me.

The latter sentence is less direct, less bold, and less concise.

•

11. Put statements in positive form.

Make definite assertions. Avoid tame, colorless, hesitating, noncommittal language. Use the word *not* as a means of denial or in antithesis, never as a means of evasion.

He was not very often on time.	*He usually came late.*
He did not think that studying Latin was much use.	*He thought the study of Latin useless.*

12. Use definite, specific, concrete language.

Prefer the specific to the general, the definite to the vague, the concrete to the abstract.

A period of unfavorable weather set in.	*It rained every day for a week.*
He showed satisfaction as he took possession of his well-earned reward.	*He grinned as he pocketed the coin.*

•

18. Place the emphatic words of a sentence at the end.

The proper place in the sentence for the word or group of words that the writer desires to make most prominent is usually the end.

Humanity has hardly advanced in fortitude since that time, though it has advanced in many other ways.	*Humanity, since that time, has advanced in many other ways, but it has hardly advanced in fortitude.*
This steel is principally used for making razors, because of its hardness	*Because of its hardness, this steel is principally used in making razors.*

•

The breezy style is often the work of an egocentric, the person who imagines that everything that pops into his head is of general interest and that uninhibited prose creates high spirits and carries the day. Open any alumni magazine, turn to the class notes, and you are quite likely to encounter old Spontaneous Me at work— an introductory paragraph that goes something like this:

Well, chums, here I am again with my bagful of dirt about your disorderly classmates, after spending a helluva weekend in N'Yawk trying to view the Columbia game from behind two bumbershoots and a glazed cornea. And speaking of news, howzabout tossing a few chirce nuggets my way?

This is an extreme example, but the same wind blows, at lesser velocities, across vast expanses of journalistic prose. The author in this case has managed in two sentences to commit most of the unpardonable sins: he obviously has nothing to say, he is showing off and directing the attention of the reader to himself, he is using slang with neither provocation nor ingenuity, he adopts a patronizing air by throwing in the word "chirce," he is tasteless, humorless (though full of fun), dull, and empty. He has not done his work. Compare his opening remarks with the following— a plunge directly into the news:

Clyde Crawford, who stroked the varsity shell in 1928, is swinging an oar again after a lapse of thirty years. Clyde resigned last spring as executive sales manager of the Indiana Flotex Company and is now a gondolier in Venice.

This, although conventional, is compact, informative, unpretentious. The writer has dug up an item of news and presented it in a straightforward manner. What the first writer tried to accomplish by cutting rhetorical capers and by breeziness, the second writer managed to achieve by good reporting, by keeping a tight rein on his material, and by staying out of the act.

ABC of Reading

In grade and high school I was taught how to hate Shakespeare, most novelists, and all poetry. College merely burnished my ignorance, adding the ability to hate in French. Ezra Pound, where were you when I needed you? Through Pound, literature becomes a place to revel, confirm, maybe even grow.

—SB

[Suggested by Frank Deis]

ABC of Reading
Ezra Pound
1934; 206 pp.

$1.75 postpaid

from:
New Directions Publishing Corp.
J. B. Lippincott Co.
East Washington Square
Philadelphia, PA 19105

or WHOLE EARTH CATALOG

It doesn't, in our contemporary world, so much matter where you begin the examination of a subject, so long as you keep on until you get round again to your starting-point.

•

Language is a means of communication. To charge language with meaning to the utmost possible degree, we have, as stated, the three chief means:

I throwing the object (fixed or moving) on to the visual imagination.

II inducing emotional correlations by the sound and rhythm of the speech.

III inducing both of the effects by stimulating the associations (intellectual or emotional) that have remained in the receiver's consciousness in relation to the actual words or word groups employed.

Style results; it does not precede.

Nothing so fits a person for a life of dedicated useless unhappiness as four years of majoring in English.

—SB

(phanopoeia, melopoeia, logopoeia)

Incompetence will show in the use of too many words.

The reader's first and simplest test of an author will be to look for words that do not function; that contribute nothing to the meaning OR that distract from the MOST important factor of the meaning to factors of minor importance.

•

'Literature is news that STAYS news.'

•

The man who really knows can tell all that is transmissible in a very few words. The economic problem of the teacher (of violin or of language or of anything else) is how to string it out so as to be paid for more lessons.

•

Men do not understand BOOKS until they have had a certain amount of life. Or at any rate no man understands a deep book, until he has seen and lived at least part of its contents. The prejudice against books has grown from observing the stupidity of men who have *merely* read books.

•

Chaucer and Shakespeare have both an insuperable courage in tackling any, but absolutely any, thing that arouses their interest.

•

The sonnet was first the 'little tune', the first strophe of a canzone, the form found when some chap got so far and couldn't proceed. Steadily in the wake of the sonneteers came the dull poets.

Literary Essays of Ezra Pound

Someone was set on a trip (Spring, 1970 Catalog) when she found that Ezra Pound had delivered unto man the only good mind-blower on language and literature in the ABC of Reading. *In the* ABC, *though, E.P. only elaborated on a much more concise and potent pronunciamento he handed down in the* New York Herald *'Books' supplement in 1927 or 1928 under the title "How to Read." That reading lesson is available in the company of thirty-five other vigorous and iconoclastic forrays by E.P. in the* Literary Essays of Ezra Pound *(also New Directions ppbk: NDP250; $3.25). For less than three times the bread for the* ABC, *E.P. will spring open your mind and ears as he lets go with some sharp barbs at "institutions for the obstruction of learning" and their inhabitants, while he lets you see and connect with those men, from the Medieval troubadours to Brancusi, who knew where and what it was and how to put it together long before we even were.*

[Suggested and reviewed by Joseph]

Literary Essays of Ezra Pound
T.S. Elliot, ed.
1935, 1968; 464 ppl

$3.25 postpaid

from:
New Directions Publishing Corporation
East Washington Square
Philadelphia, Pa. 19105

or WHOLE EARTH CATALOG

A civilization was founded on Homer, civilization not a mere bloated empire. The Macedonian domination rose and grew after the sophists. It also subsided.

It is not only a question of rhetoric, of loose expression, but also of the loose use of individual words. What the renaissance gained in direct examination of natural phenomena, it in part lost in losing the feel and desire for exact descriptive terms. I mean that the medieval mind had little but words to deal with, and it was more careful in its definitions and verbiage. It did not define a gun in terms that would just as well define an explosion, nor explosions in terms that would define triggers.

Misquoting Confucius, one might say: It does not matter whether the author desire the good of the race or acts merely from personal vanity. The thing is mechanical in action. In proportion as his work is exact, i.e., true to human consciousness and to the nature of man, as it is exact in formulation of desire, so is it durable and so is it 'useful'; I mean it maintains the precision and clarity of thought, not merely for the benefit of a few dilettantes and 'lovers of literature', but maintains the health of thought outside literary circles and in non-literary existence, in general individual and communal life.

•

No one wants the native American poet to be *au courant* with the literary affairs of Paris and London in order that he may make imitations of Paris and London models, but precisely in order that he shall not waste his lifetime making unconscious, or semi-conscious, imitations of French and English models thirty or forty or an hundred years old.

How to Need a Catalog

Wendell Berry says this letter is a fugue, It's a real letter written by a man who says what he means. It came to us through Gurney Norman.

—SB

Dear TV Star Editor

I am writing you this letter for some help from this TV Show. That I am a single man looking for a wife. I am 61 years old not never been married. I am trying to look for some women of any age and near my age 61 years old and as tall as I am tall. I am even 6 feet tall weigh 198 lbs. I am looking for some just about as tall that would weigh from 289 to 298 or better with extra very nice wide large full breast with such a pretty nice large heavy extra wide round well built legs and extra wide full size hips and very pretty well stout and filled around her legs and waist line I would like to get married to some of the colored widow and to some white German and to some Indian women. I would like to join in and go with the wild west show. I like to ride these montana and North Dakota North Western wild unbroke horses. And mares. I have been with the rodeo show since I was 13 years old. I cannot get no other kind of work around here or no construction work or any other kind of work. Because I am not a married man. But I will tell you that I am a real good man yet that can go out and do a good days work yet. I like my wild and tame mare horses and I like also my women nice and heavy set with extra wide round legs and hips around their waist and extra wide and large full size breast I would like to get some naked women without anything on there bodies. Just there bare skin. I would like to see there naked full size breast and there extra wide waist and extra round heavy legs above there knees and extra round fat arms. There full linth of there stout heavy naked body. Will you please send me a free book of all kind of women that are colored White German Spanish Indian race and all different race widow women. I do like to get acquainted with them all black white red widow women. I want there names and address from them and from you. I would like to ask you if you please help a poor man out as long as he is sick in the hospital. I am looking for some help till I could get back on my feet again. I will soon get my discharge this hospital next month in August or in the month of September of this year in 1962. I am looking for some help from you and from the widow women. I need some writing paper envelopes and some stamps so I can write you also to the women. I want them to be red extra stout and well heavy set around the legs above the knees. That would have a very nice big farm ranch plenty of wild tame hereford cows and hereford white face heifers tame and wild mare horses and if they have about 375 head of these red heavy sows and hogs and also some real heavy laying red chickens that weight 75 up to 98 pounds. I like all my women reall extra heavy with full wide large breast also with extra large full wide extra round fat legs above the knees and there widest part of the thickest of the waistline hip bones. That do measure 74 around there breast and a 78 there widest and the thickest of there thighs above the knee. And the waist line hips and extra round fat arms. Above there fore-arm extra round fat calf and the thighs of there legs. That would not weight less than 298 hundred to 398 hundred pounds. or over that weight. I want women that are extra stout full large size breast and real extra wide across there large size part of the hips and the waist line extra round fat legs down to the ankles shoe slipper of there feet. Extra round fat arms to the wrist of the hand. I do like to have some of the widow women to help me and each of them could send me about $5.00 or more. I want to come to the state of New York Because I was not in New York state at all I wish to come to New York and find myself some colored and some white also some of the indian widow women. That I could get some farm and ranch work and live with all the colored Indian white widow women I want a home with every one of the white women colored widow women and with the red Indian widow women. Will you please answer on this letter. Please send me a widow woman catalog of all colored, white and Indian women.

The Story of Language

We are ensorcelled by language. I am coming to believe that halting the all-too-unified construction of the Tower of Babel by dispersing the communication system was a good idea. Pluralism may be a nuisance, but juggernaut unanimity is a curse. One escape from the bonds of one's own language is excursion into another, or into very variousness of language usages, as this book encourages——it's a good, richly exampled trip. [Another escape is silence.]
—SB

[Suggested by Herb Childs]

The Story of Language
Mario Pei
1949, 1965; 508 pp.

$1.50 postpaid

from:
The New American Library, Inc.
1301 Avenue of the Americas
New York, N. Y. 10019

or WHOLE EARTH CATALOG

The use of Indian sign language for international purposes has repeatedly been advocated. Sir Richard Paget and the American Tourist Association, in recent times, have both advanced the possibility of "handage" to replace language.

Very close to the spoken language is also the whistling language used by the natives of Gomera, in the Canary Islands, who communicate by means of it over very long distances (some say six miles); it seems established, however, that this whistling language is based on Spanish rhythms and pitch. A similar type of whistling language is employed by the natives of Kusnoy, a village in Turkey. The sounds are described as formed with tongue curled around the teeth and lips not puckered but tensely drawn, with the palm of the left hand cupped around the mouth, and high pressure applied from the lungs. The villagers are said to speak, argue, and even woo in whistles.

Hoboes and gypsies have a way of carving symbolic messages on the bark of trees, or scratching them on rocks, for the benefit of their fellows who may follow. A pair of spectacles, in gypsy symbolism, means "Beware! Danger and trouble here!"; but a small circle inside a larger one spells out "Very kind people. Don't impose on them."

Perhaps the phonetic system of writing is not the acme of perfection after all. There is at least a talking point in the arguments of those who advocate that we go back to the picto-ideographic systems of our remote ancestors or simply adopt the ideographic writing of the Chinese. At least all the peoples of the earth, regardless of their spoken tongues, would understand one another in writing.

Economic relations depend on numerals to a greater extent perhaps than on any other factor. It therefore does not surprise linguists to find that numerals are among the oldest and best-defined words indicating connections among the languages of a given family. A word indicative of a given numeral (say "four," or "ten," or "hundred") can usually be traced without difficulty through all or most of the languages of a given group. It is as little subject to borrowing as are names of family relationship.

There are in existence only thirteen languages with 50 million or more speakers. They are, in order of numerical importance, Chinese, English, Hindustani, Russian, Spanish, German, Japanese, Arabic, Bengali, Portuguese, Malay, French, and Italian. The roughly approximate figures, which include non-native as well as native speakers, are as follows:

Chinese	700,000,000
English	350,000,000
Hindustani	200,000,000
Russian	200,000,000
Spanish	160,000,000
German	100,000,000
Japanese	100,000,000
Arabic	90,000,000
Bengali	90,000,000
Portuguese	85,000,000
Malay	80,000,000
French	80,000,000
Italian	65,000,000

Technicians of the Sacred

These are songs from the center, from the middle. (The cortex of humanity is convoluted, each fold patriotic, distinct on the outside, connected in the middle.) Superb editing by Rothenberg. A book to take with you.
—SB

Technicians of the Sacred
Jerome Rothenberg, ed.
1968; 521 pp.

$3.95 postpaid

from:
Doubleday & Company
501 Franklin Avenue
Garden City, New York 11531

or WHOLE EARTH CATALOG

the odor of death
I discern the odor of death
in front of my body

—*Namebines*
(Ojibwa)

I am using my heart
(Ojibwa)

I am still carving an ironwood stick.
I am still thinking about it.

(Bantu)

What are you saying to me & am I
in-my-senses?

(Ojibwa)

An Eskimo Poem against Death

I watched the white dogs of the dawn.

Primitive Means Complex

That there are no primitive languages is an axiom of contemporary linguistics where it turns its attention to the remote languages of the world. There are no half-formed languages, no underdeveloped or inferior languages. Everywhere a development has taken place into structures of great complexity. People who have failed to achieve the wheel will not have failed to invent & develop a highly wrought grammar. Hunters & gatherers innocent of all agriculture will have vocabularies that distinguish the things of their world down to the finest details. The language of snow among Eskimos is awesome. The aspect system of Hopi verbs can, by a flick of the tongue, make the most subtle kinds of distinction between different types of motion.

There is no one; there are no people. It is desolate; it lies desolate. There is nothing edible. Misery abounds, misery emerges, misery spreads. There is no joy, no pleasure. It lies sprouting; herbs lie sprouting; nothing lies emerging; the earth is pressed down. All die of thirst. The grasses lie sprouting. Nothing lies cast about. There is hunger; all hunger. It is the home of hunger; there is death from hunger. All die of cold; there is freezing; there is trembling; there is the clattering, the chattering of teeth. There are cramps, the stiffening of the body, the constant stiffening, the stretching out prone.

(Aztec)

Before a noise., may become a symbol, something must exist for the symbol to symbolize. So the first problem of symbolism should be to investigate the problem of 'existence'. To define 'existence', we have to state the standards by which we judge existence. At present, the use of this term is not uniform and is largely a matter of convenience. . . . It is extremely important, semantically, to notice that not all the noises., we humans make should be considered as symbols or valid words. Such empty noises., can occur not only in direct 'statements' but also in 'questions'. Quote obviously, 'questions' which employ noises., instead of words, are not significant questions. They ask nothing, and cannot be answered. They are, perhaps, best treated by 'mental' pathologists as symptoms of delusions, illusions, or hallucinations. In asylums the noises., patients make are predominantly meaningless, as far as the external world is concerned, but *become symbols in the illness of the patient.*

ALL LIVES, ALL DANCES, & ALL IS LOUD

The fish does . . . HIP
The bird does . . . VISS
The marmot does . . . GNAN

I throw myself to the left,
I turn myself to the right,
I act the fish,
Which darts in the water, which darts
Which twists about, which leaps—
All lives, all dances, & all is loud.

The fish does . . . HIP
The bird does . . . VISS
The marmot does . . . GNAN

(Gabon Pygmy)

the blue, overhanging
sky
answers me back

—*Wabezic*
(Ojibwa)

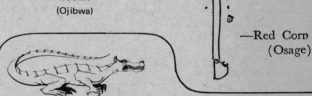

—Red Corn
(Osage)

DRAGON TRACKS

Emmit says, drink this, it's good old 'sang tea, it'll make your insides feel good.

He says, I'm going out to look at the stars, bud. Come on out if you feel like it.

D.R. would have taken him up on that if there hadn't been so much work to do. He was helping his dead grandmother with her wash day. And it would be a while before he was free.

His grandmother pulled a pair of overalls out of the churning water and started them by the bib through the black and white rubber wringers. He caught the overalls as they came through, and guided them into the tub of warm rinse water sitting on the bench beside the old machine, flat

Flat and stiff they floated like a dead man till D.R. punched them loose with his stir stick. He punched until their life came back, until they spread out soaking in the water, until the soap was rinsed away and it was time

and it was time to send them through the wringer once again, then hang them on the line outside to dry.

Let me do it.

Let me do it, D.R. said.

Let me

Get away, said his grandmother. You can't even reach the line.

Science & Sanity

Korzybski aims to help you train yourself in new semantic reactions: literally to get your head— and your whole nervous system— together. All too often we think and speak in ways that are structurally false to the events we are trying to describe, analyse, and deal with, ways that are harmful to our ability to function semantically. We use artifical aristotelian divisions such as body vs mind, objective vs. subjective, and ignore half a century's work in physics by operating on Newtonian assumptions.

Korzybski conceives all knowledge in terms of the functional structure of your nervous system, and he explores the consequences of this idea in Physics, Math, Chemistry, Neurology, "Psychology" and Education. Synthesis of this approach with newer ecological studies should provide a real start toward a gestalt understanding of the universe.

[Reviewed by C. Baird Brown. Suggested by Dave Guard]

Science and Sanity
Alfred Korzybski
1933-1958, 806 pp.

$15.50 postpaid

from:
Institute of General Semantics
Lakeville, Connecticut 06039

Further

If the roots and by-products of language intrigue you, a trusty guide for further travel is Benjamin Lee Whorf (Language, Thought and Reality, $2.95, MIT Press, 28 Carleton Street, Cambridge, MA 02142).

—SB

Intelligent Life in the Universe

Methodically blow your mind. The information in this book, mutually massaged by the American and Soviet co-authors, proceeds from superb introductions to evolutionary astronomy and biology, through a complete presentation of recent discoveries of astronomy and space science, to brilliant speculation on the parameters of inter-civilization communication. It's the best general astronomy book of recent years but that's nothing next to its impact on all the biggest questions we know.

—SB

Intelligent Life in the Universe
I.S. Shklovskii and Carl Sagan
1966; 509pp.

$2.95 postpaid

from:
Delta Books
One Dag Hammarskjold Plaza
245 East 47th St.
New York, NY 10017

or WHOLE EARTH CATALOG

But how can a natural satellite have such a low density? The material of which it is made must have a certain amount of rigidity, so that cohesive forces will be stronger than the gravitational tidal forces of Mars, which will tend to disrupt the satellite. Such rigidity would ordinarily exclude densities below about 0.1 gm/cm^{-3}. Thus, only one possibility remains. Could Phobos be indeed rigid, on the outside—but hollow in the inside? A natural satellite cannot be a hollow object. Therefore, we are led to the possibility that Phobos—and possibly Deimos as well—may be artificial satellites of Mars.

•

So, by an interesting coincidence, the distances between the stars in interstellar space, relative to their diameters, are just about the same as the distances between the atoms and molecules in interstellar space, relative to *their* diameters. Interstellar space is as empty as a cubical building, 60 miles long, 60 miles wide, and 60 miles high, containing a single grain of sand.

With 10^{11} stars in our Galaxy and 10^9 other galaxies, there are at least 10^{20} stars in the universe. Most of them, as we shall see in subsequent chapters, may be accompanied by solar systems. If there are 10^{20} solar systems in the universe, and the universe is 10^{10} years old—and if, further, solar systems have formed roughly uniformly in time—then one solar system is formed every 10^{-10}yr = 3 x 10^{-3} seconds. On the average, a million solar systems are formed in the universe each hour.

```
11110000101001000011001000000010000010100
10000011001011001111000001100011101000000
00100000100001000010001010100001000000000
00000000001000100000000101100000000000000
00000001000111011010110101000000000000000
00001001000011101010101000000001010101010101
00000000011101010101111010110000000010000
00000000001000000000000000000100011111000
00111010000010110000111000000010000000000
10000000010000000111110000001011000101110
00000000110011011110101111110001100011111001
00000000011111000000101100011111111100000
10000011000001100001000010000000011000101
00100011110010111
```

FIGURE 30-1. *A hypothetical interstellar message due to Frank Drake. The 551 zeros and ones are representations of the two varieties of signals contained in the message. The problem is to convert this sequence of 551 symbols into an intelligible message, knowing that there has been no previous communication between the transmitting and receiving civilizations.*

1. Decode this ↑
2. Into this →

3. Now decode this for physiological, astronomical, chemical, mathematical, social, historical and linguistic information.

Extraterrestrial Civilizations

A technical discussion by Russian scientists.

—SB

Extraterrestrial Civilizations
G. M. Tovmasyan
1964; 99 pp.

$4 postpaid

from:

U.S. Department of Commerce
Clearinghouse for Federal
Scientific and Technical Information
Springfield, Virginia 22151

We have no doubt whatsoever that life and civilizations exist on a multitude of celestial bodies, but we must go in some detail into the question of possible technological disparity between these civilizations. Although the Earth civilization, in the broad sense of the word, is a few tens of millennia old, the modern technological civilization has its origin no more than two hundred years in the past. It is moreover highly significant for the problem under consideration that the present-day notions on stellar systems, i.e., the conceptual approach which has suggested the multiplicity of inhabited worlds, have arisen and developed during the last two centuries. And yet, the ages of planets may differ as much as millions of years. Hence the apparent conclusion that different civilizations in the Universe may differ by millions of years in their respective developmental stages. It seems that the Earth civilization is not yet past the diapers age, and that there should be enormous disparity between extraterrestrial civilizations.

Charles Fort

SUGGESTION FOR WHOLE EARTH CATALOG

Name of item: The Books of Charles Fort. 4 volumes:
The Book of the Damned; New Lands; Lo!; and Wild Talents.
from: Ace Books, 1120 Avenue of the Americas, New York, N. Y. 10036

Review: Reading Charles Fort (1874-1932) is like getting a foretaste of Buckminster Fuller, so I asked Fuller if he had known Fort. He hadn't, but it turns out he was writing the introduction to Damon Knight's forthcoming biography of Fort. Ace has recently reprinted Fort's works in paperback; they are stacked with the psychic-and-saucer books. But don't overlook Fort. Each of his books is laden with reports of unorthodox, widely recurrent, phenomena——but he uses the material as a tongue-in-cheek, comprehensive philosopher. He throws galactic theories at you like paper airplanes, laughing at himself as often as at dogmatic orthodoxy. Some examples of his style:

Much of the argument in this book will depend upon our acceptance that nothing in our existence is real. The Whole may be Realness.
—*Wild Talents*

•

Mineral specimens now in museums——calcites that are piles of petals——or that long ago were the rough notes of a rose.

•

An early stage within the shell of an egg——and a protoplasmic line of growth feels out through surrounding substance——and of itself it is lost. Nourishment and protection and guidance come to it from the whole.

•

Or occasional falls of "manna", to this day, in Asia Minor, may be only one factor in a wider continuance. . . .
—*LO!*

Gene Keyes
Carbondale, Ill.

Almost any other of the many accounts of alleged contacts of human beings with the crews of flying saucers——follow the same pattern and stress the same points. The extraterrestrials are human, with few even minor physical differences from local cosmetic standards. (I know of no case of Negro saucerians, or Oriental saucerians, reported in the United States; but there are very few flying saucer reports made in this country by Negroes or by Orientals.)

•

Radio astronomers may be interested to know that the so-called "brightness temperature" of the Earth at television wavelengths is some hundreds of millions of degrees. This is 100 times greater than the radio brightness of the sun at comparable wavelengths, during a period of low sunspot activity.

•

Taken at face value, the legend suggests that contact occurred between human beings and a non-human civilization of immense powers on the shores of the Persian Gulf, perhaps near the site of the ancient Sumerian city of Eridu, and in the fourth millenium B.C. or earlier. There are three different but cross-referenced accounts of the Apkallu dating from classical times.

•

"Well, ladies and gentlemen," Struve concluded, "it was pretty dull on Epsilon Eridani and Tau Ceti eleven years ago."

Thought Forms

Well, for once I'm truly sorry our reviews are limited to illustrations in shades of grey. The power of these 58 extraordinary images is mostly in their color, unexpectable, unearthly, delicious. The images were seen by the authors as clear representations of human states of mind. Pioneer work.

—SB
[Suggested by Jordan Belson]

Thought-Forms
Annie Besant and C. W. Leadbeater
1901, 1969; 77 pp.

$3.45 postpaid

from:
Theosophical Publishing House
Box 270
Wheaton, Illinois 60187

or WHOLE EARTH CATALOG

Three general principles underlie the production of all thought-forms:

1. Quality of thought determines color.
2. Nature of thought determines form.
3. Definiteness of thought determines clearness of outline.

Thought form of high ambition.

Thought form of selfish ambition.

Human Biocomputer

BACK IN PRINT. After a year of absence, this landmark paper is back at a lower price (formerly $7.95, now $1.50).

John Lilly has worked for a long time with sensory deprivation, pursuing the notion that relieving the computer (mind) of many of its environmental-survival chores frees it to attend more fully to self-investigation. Of late he's added LSD to the process and has found ways to flourish and discover within this doubly floating condition.

The paper HUMAN BIOCOMPUTER is the best internal guidebook I've seen—far more practical and generalized than transcendent Eastern writings or wishful Underground notes. Though it's not the whole story by any means, it makes an open start on fresh language and powerful technique for the frontier.

An additional advantage the paper offers is the opportunity to learn and explore computers without requiring money or administrative approval. You inherited and grew everything you need, and it's free. —SB

[Suggested by Ralph Metzner]

In the analysis of the effects of LSD-25 on the human mind, reasonable hypothesis states that the effect of these substances on the human computer is to introduce "white noise" (in the sense of randomly varying energy containing no signals of itself) in specific systems in the computer . . . .

•

The increase in "white noise" energy allows quick and random access to memory and lowers the threshold to unconscious memories ("expansion of consciousness"). In such noise one can project almost anything at almost any cognitive level in almost any allowable mode...

•

The noise introduced brings a certain amount of disorder with it, even as white noise in the physical world brings randomness. However, the LSD-25 noise randomizes signals only in a limited way: not enough to destroy all order, only enough to superimpose a small creative 'jiggling' on program materials and metaprograms and their signals.

•

Programming and Metaprogramming in the Human Biocomputer— Theory and Experiments
John C. Lilly, M.D.
1967, 1970; 112 pp.

$4.95 postpaid

from:
Julian Press
150 Fifth Ave.
New York, NY 10011

OR WHOLE EARTH CATALOG

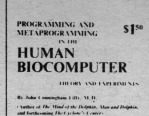

The boundary of the brain, of course, may be considered as the limits of the extensions of the central nervous system into the periphery.

•

Later with higher motivational energy the subject returned to the problem of the lock, the doors and the rooms somewhat refreshed by the experiences in the other realms.

•

In the complete physical absence of other external computers within the critical interlock distance, the self-directed and other-directed programs can be clearly detected, analysed, recomputed, re-programmed, and new metaprograms initiated by the solitudinous computer itself. In the as-completely-as-possible-attenuated-physical-reality environment in solitude, a maximum intensity, a maximum complexity and a maximum speed of re-programming is achievable by the self.

•

For example, the term 'reprogramming substances' may be appropriate for compounds like lysergic acid diethylamide. For substances like ethyl alcohol the term 'metaprogram-attenuating substances' may be useful.

The major problems of the research of interest to the author center on the erasability, modifiability, and creatibility of programs. In other words, I am interested in the processes of finding metaprograms (and methods and substances) which control, change, and create the basic metaprograms of the human computer. It is not known whether one can really erase any program.

•

I believe that by using certain methods and means some of which are presented in this work that truly talented and dedicated individuals can forge, find, and devise new ways of looking at our minds, ways which are truly scientific, intellectually economical, and interactively creative. Consider for example, the case of the fictitious individual created by the group of mathematicians masquerading under the name of "Dr. Nicholas Bourbaki"

This group of mathematicians in order to create a mathematics or sets of mathematics beyond the capacity of any one individual, held meetings three times a year and exchanged ideas, then went off and worked separately. The resulting papers were published under a pseudonym because the products of this work were felt to be a group result beyond any one individual's contribution.

•

In the maximally attentuated environment (92 to 95 degrees F. isothermal skin, salt water suspension, zero light levels, near-zero sound levels, without clothes, without wall or floor contacts, in solitude in remote isolation, for several hours), the addition of LSD-25 allows one to see that all the previous experiences with "outside screens" are evasions of deeper penetration of self (and hence are "screens" in the sense of "blocking the view behind", as well as 'receiving the projected images').

•

The essential features and the goals sought in the self-analysis is the metaprogram "make the computer general purpose". In this sense we mean that in the general purpose nature of the computer there can be no display, no acting, or no ideal which is forbidden to a consciously willed program. Nor is any display, acting, or ideal made without being consciously programmed.

•

"Mathematical transformations" were next tried in the approach to the locked rooms. The concept of the key fitting into the lock and the necessity of finding the key was abandoned and the rooms were approached as "topological puzzles." In the multidimensional cognitional and visual space the rooms were now manipulated without the necessity of the key in the lock.

The Mind of the Dolphin

Lilly knows that it is to everybody's advantage for one kind of computer to link up with another, and that's his program with dolphins. This book reports his speculations and experiments with dolphins in recent years. Included is a thorough account by a girl, Margaret Howe, who lived alone with Peter Dolphin for 10 weeks. As usual with research on communication, everything discovered has broad implications.
—SB

The Mind of the Dolphin
John Cunningham Lilly, M. D.
1967; 286 pp.

$.95 plus $.15 postage

from:
Avon Books
250 West 55th Street
New York, N. Y. 10019

or WHOLE EARTH CATALOG

Once one has been through deep experiences in tune with the vast forces of the universe, the vast forces within ourselves, we see that the need for conflict, the need for hostility, and the need for hatred become less intense. One finds the universe inside and the one outside so vast and so lonely that any other living thing that loves or shows any signs of loving is precious and close.

•

The human participant's assumptions, i.e., those of Margaret C. Howe, in her own words are as follows:

1. Dolphins are capable of communication with man on the level of high intelligence.
2. Dolphins are not only capable of this communication but are eager for it and are willing to cooperate with man to achieve it.
3. Possibly the best way to go about establishing this communication is to set up a situation where the man (woman) and a dolphin live together as closely as possible for an extended period of time.
4. This is a long process and involves many steps, each of which must be recognized and encouraged. The attempt to communicate with a dolphin in English involves two main parts: (1) the dolphin must learn how to physically say the words, and (2) he must learn the meaning of what he is saying. These two parts may be worked out individually or simultaneously.
5. One first step is the creation and the maintenance of the mutual trust and reciprocal rewards one for the other

Sometimes I feel that if man could become more involved in some problems of an alien species, he may become less involved with his own egocentric pursuits, and deadly competition within his species, and become somehow a better being.

•

We are often asked, "If the dolphins are so intelligent why aren't they ruling the world?" My very considered answer to this is—they may be too wise to try to rule the world. The question can be easily turned around, Why does man or individual men want to rule the world? I feel that it is a very insecure position to want to rule all of the other species and the vast resources of our planet. This means a deep insecurity with the "universes" inside of one's self. One's fears and one's angers are being projected on others outside of one's self; to rule the world is, finally, to rule one's inner realities.

•

Thus a given dolphin can carry on a whistle conversation with his right side and a clicking conversation with his left side and do the two quite independently with the two halves of his brain.

•

Conservatively, we estimate that the dolphin can put out ten times the sonic physical information per second that a man produces.

The information does not exist as information until it is within the higher levels of abstraction of each of the minds and computed as such. Up to the point at which it becomes perceived as information it is signals. These signals travel through the external reality between the two bodies, and travel as signals within the brain substances themselves. Till the complex patterns of traveling neuronal impulses in the brain are computed as information within the cerebral cortex, they are not yet information. Information is the result of a long series of computations based on data signal inputs, data signal transmissions to the brain substance, and recomputations of these data.

•

By long and hard work I found that the evil label "negative" should not be tied to any mode or any kind of thinking at all.

•

I found that bodily sources of discomfort, pain, or threat tend to program the mind in the negative mode and keep it there as long as the discomfort continues. As long as pain, even at a very low level, continues, the computer (which is one's mind) tends to program a negative pall.

She filled the clothesline full, twenty yards of overalls and work shirts, sheets and towels and socks and underwear, a few dresses of her own, his own small clothes sprinkled in between. They hung there all afternoon, flapping in the wind like ghosts of an entire family.

•

Emmit coughed into the curtain of the dream. D.R. heard him in the kitchen, building a fire in the coal stove.

•

He could tell by the way Emmit handled the stove lids he was being as quiet as he could to keep from disturbing him. But it was morning now and D.R. was awake before Emmit was. It was too dark yet to see but he heard him putting his clothes on across the room. He heard the spring on the screen door whine when he went outside to pee. Then he heard him in the kitchen building a fire and putting water on to boil, and D.R. lay there watching the room take shape as the dark gave way to the growth of light in the window.

•

Here he comes.

Eye and Brain

I can't think of another book as well-made as this one. It is well designed, illustrated, and diagrammed. The writing is excellent, the subject matter important and new. The book is inexpensive. Altogether Eye and Brain *lets you see how crappy most books are.*

—SB

Eye and Brain— The Psychology of Seeing
R. L. Gregory
1966; 254 pp.

$2.45 postpaid

from:
McGraw-Hill Book Company
Princeton Road
Hightstown, N.J. 08520

Manchester Road
Manchester, Missouri 63062

8171 Redwood Highway
Novato, CA 94947

or WHOLE EARTH CATALOG

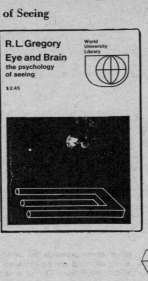

R.L. Gregory
Eye and Brain
the psychology of seeing
$2.45
World University Library

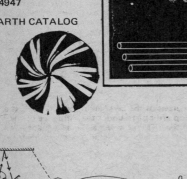

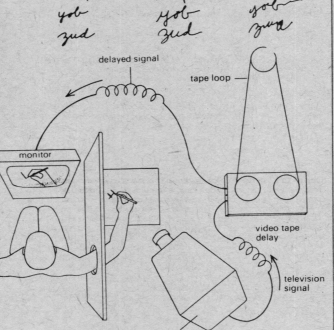

delayed signal

tape loop

monitor

video tape delay

television signal

television camera

Stratton went on to perform other experiments which though less well-known are just as interesting. He devised a mirror arrangement which, mounted in a harness, visually displaced his own body, so that it appeared horizontally in front of him, and at the height of his own eyes. Stratton wore this mirror arrangement for three days (about twenty-four hours of vision) and he reported:

"I had the feeling that I was mentally outside my own body. It was, of course, but a passing impression, but it came several times and was vivid while it lasted. . .But the moment critical interest arose, the simplicity of the state was gone, and my visible actions were accompanied by a kind of wraith of themselves in the older visual terms.

Why should the perceptual system be as active in seeking alternative solutions as we see it to be in ambiguous situations? Indeed it seems more active, and more intellectually honest in refusing to stick with one of many possible solutions, then in the cerebral cortex as a whole if we may judge by the tenacity of irrational belief in politics or religion. The perceptual system has been of biological significance for far longer than the calculating intellect. The regions of the cerebral cortex concerned with thought are comparatively juvenile. They are self-opinionated by comparison with the ancient striate area responsible for vision.

An elaboration of the television technique makes it possible to displace retinal images not only in space, but in time. Temporal delay of images is a new kind of displacement, and promises to be of the greatest importance. The method is to use a TV camera and monitor, with an endless tape loop so that there is a time-delay between the recording from the camera and the playback to the monitor. The subject thus sees his hands (or any other object) in the past; the delay being set by the gap between the Record and Play-back heads.

This situation is not only of theoretical interest, but is also of practical importance because controls used in flying aircraft, and operating many kinds of machine, have a delay in their action: if such delay upsets the skill, this could be a serious matter. It was found that a short delay (about 0·5 seconds) made movements jerky and ill co-ordinated, so that drawing became almost impossible, and writing quite difficult. Practice gives little or no improvement.

Held found that only the active kitten developed perception, the passive animal remaining effectively blind. He thus suggested that active touch is essential to perceptual development.

The Intelligent Eye

R. L. Gregory continues, this time with a book rich in visual illusions which suck the reader (viewer) into many a flickering illuminating trap. The thesis is that visual imagery is made intelligible by the eye itself. 3-D glass included with the book.

—SB

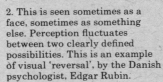

The Intelligent Eye
Richard L. Gregory
1970, 191 pp.

$2.95 postpaid

from:
McGraw-Hill Book Company
330 W. 42nd St.
New York, N.Y. 10036

or WHOLE EARTH CATALOG

2. This is seen sometimes as a face, sometimes as something else. Perception fluctuates between two clearly defined possibilities. This is an example of visual 'reversal', by the Danish psychologist, Edgar Rubin.

Retinal images are patterns in the eye— patterns made up of light and dark shapes and areas of colour— but we do not see patterns, we see objects. We read from pictures in the eye the presence of external objects: how this is achieved is the problem of perception. Objects appear separate, distinct; and yet as pictures on the retina they may have no clear boundaries. In this photograph of a spotted dog, most half-tones have been lost (as in vision by moonlight) and yet we can distinguish the spots making up the dog from similar spots of the background. To make this possible there must be stored information in the brain, of dogs and thousands of other objects.

Brain Storms

Dr. Barker presents a fascinating argument that epileptic fits and fits of creativity are very closely related and both are brought on by unusual threats to continuity in brain function, requiring a massive "storm" of re-organization in the brain. The fit is an attempt to in fact fit together incompatible considerations which have collided. I believe it, in part because Barker makes his case so well, in part because it sounds like what I've experienced.

—SB

A fit, even the grossest major convulsive fit of epilepsy, is many things happening at once. Fits are patterns of awareness and action, combinations of knowing, feeling, and doing. They are episodes of behavior and experience put together by the brain during crises in the continuity of living. Such crises are characterized by a sudden coming together of a complex of conflicting and disparate ideas, images, and impulses; fits are syntheses of such complexes that both resolve and represent their otherwise unthinkable contradictions and ambiguities. By providing more or less fitting resolutions of crises, fits serve to maintain or restore the crisis-disrupted continuity of transactions between organism and environment.

184 *The Concepts of Dysjunctive Situations*

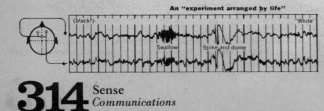

An "experiment arranged by life"
(black?)
White
Swallow
Spike and dome

Brain Storms— A Study of Human Spontaneity
Wayne Barker, M.D.
1968; 277 pp.

$2.95 postpaid from:
Grove Press, Inc.
53 East 11th Street
New York, N.Y. 10003

or WHOLE EARTH CATALOG

What we need is to let the fitting-together capacity of the human brain operate at least occasionally in freedom from the narrow, provincial, egoistic concerns of "I" and "Us." The essence of our contemporary crisis is simple: Most people in the world want to have modestly human food, shelter, and an opportunity to care decently for their children. The technological and material means for satisfaction of these wants exist. Not much of a "dream" is required to get it done. No longer will any conventional evasion or caricatured "solution" suffice. The only possible outcomes now are convulsive or creative. It all depends upon our commitment.

. . . if we can endure confrontation with the unthinkable, we may be able to fit together new patterns of awareness and action. We might, that is, have a fit of insight, inspiration, invention, or creation. The propensity for finding the answer—the lure of creating or discovering the new—no doubt has much to do with some people's ability to endure tension until something new emerges from the contradictory and ambiguous situation.

Physical Control of the Mind

I do not like this guy. He has insufferable hubris and he tramples on all my fondest notions about the independent life of the mind. The book is full of harsh physical evidence and harsh hypotheses that I have got to either surround or accept (or quit).

—SB

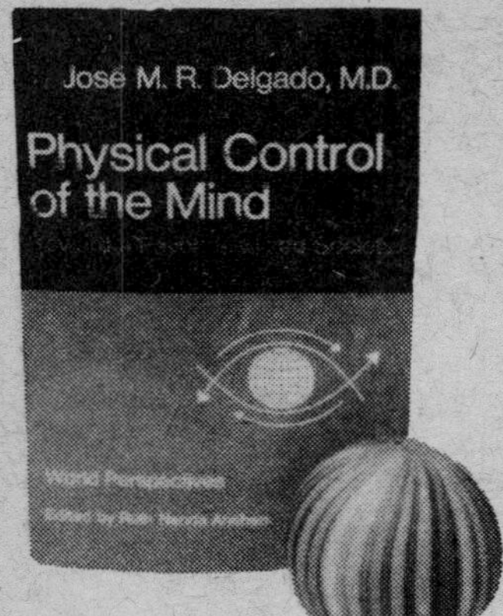

Physical Control of the Mind
Jose M. R. Delgado, M. D.
1969; 280 pp.

$2.25 postpaid

from:
Harper & Row, Publishers
49 E. 33rd Street
New York, N. Y. 10016

or WHOLE EARTH CATALOG

Pleasure is not in the skin being caressed or in a full stomach, but somewhere inside the cranial vault.

(1) Lack of predictability: When a point of the brain is stimulated for the first time, we cannot predict the effects which may be evoked. . . .
(2) Lack of purpose: In some cases the evoked response is directed by the animal in a purposeful way, but the movements and sequential responses are usually out of context, and there is no reason or purpose for yawning, flexing a hand, or walking around, apart from ESB. . . . [Electrical Stimulation of the Brain]
(3) No robot performance: Brain stimulation activates cerebral mechanisms which are organized for motor performance, but it cannot replace them. With the present state of the art, it is very unlikely that we could electrically direct an animal to carry out predetermined activities such as opening a gate or performing an instrumental response. We can induce pleasure or punishment and therefore the motivation to press a lever, but we cannot control the sequence of movements necessary for this act in the absence of the animal's own desire to do so.

•

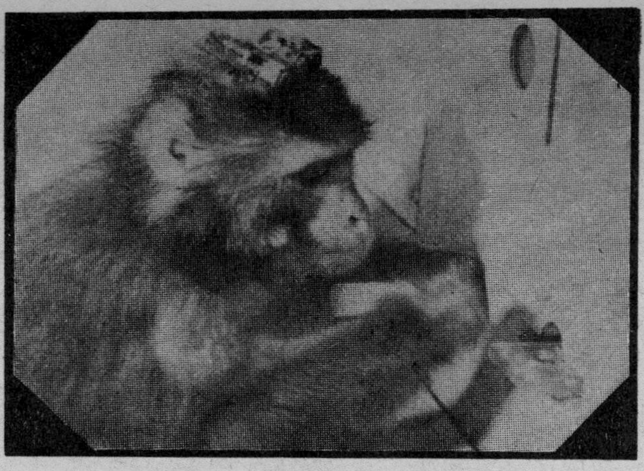

Watching a rat or monkey stimulate its own brain is a fascinating spectacle. Usually each lever pressing triggers a brief 0.5-to 1.0-second brain stimulation which can be more rewarding than food. In a choice situation, hungry rats ran faster to reach the self-stimulation lever than to obtain pellets, and they persistently pressed this lever, ignoring food within easy reach. Rats have removed obstacles, run mazes, and even crossed electrified floors to reach the lever that provided cerebral stimulation.

•

One of the moving pictures taken in this study was very demonstrative, showing a patient with a sad expression and slightly depressed mood who smiled when a brief stimulation was applied to the rostral part of the brain, returning quickly to his usual depressed state, to smile again as soon as stimulation was reapplied. Then a ten-second stimulation completely changed his behavior and facial expression into a lasting pleasant and happy mood. Some mental patients have been provided with portable stimulators which they have used in self-treatment of depressive states with apparent clinical success.

•

The brontosauri became extinct because of their extremely limited mental powers; faced with an increasingly unfavorable climate and diminishing food supply, these animals were incapable of adaptation and could not survive in the changing environment.

The fate of these giants may have symbolic value for twentieth century civilization, which is also attempting to direct tremendous potential with disproportionately small brains. While our mental faculties are incomparably superior to those of the early land animals, we still lack adequate self-knowledge and control, and natural history teaches that when underdeveloped brains are in charge of great power, the result is extinction.

•

In my opinion, without stimuli (or without the brain), the mind cannot exist; without behavior, the mind cannot be recognized. Because of its essential dependence on sensory inputs, both at birth and throughout adult life, the mind may be defined as the intracerebral elaboration of extracerebral information. The problem is then focused on the origins, reception, dynamics, storage, retrieval, and consequences of this information. The basis of the mind is cultural, not individual.

•

The newborn brain is not capable of speech, symbolic understanding, or of directing skillful mobility. It has no ideas, words, or concepts, no tools for communication, no significant sensory experience, no culture. The newborn baby never smiles. He is unable to comprehend the loving phrases of his mother or to be aware of the environment. We must conclude that there are no detectable signs of mental activity at birth and that human beings are born without minds.

•

. . . the microneurons of the cerebellum, which serve as association elements, develop after birth under the influence of the infant's behavioral activities. Therefore it can be said that the environment is absorbed as a structural part of the neurons in the developing brain.

•

When the patient was warned of the oncoming stimulation and was asked to try to keep his fingers extended, he could not prevent the evoked movement and commented, "I guess, Doctor, that your electricity is stronger than my will."

The Machinery of the Brain

Some is known about the brain, but not much. Woolridge's book is the best intro to the subject we've seen. For richer detail, get Pribram's two-volume Brain and Behavior *(each volume $2.95 from Penguin, 7110 Ambassador Rd., Baltimore, Md. 21207).*

—SB

The Machinery of the Brain
Dean E. Wooldridge
1963; 252 pp.

$1.95 postpaid

from:
McGraw-Hill Book Co.
Princeton Road
Hightstown, N. J. 08520

Manchester Road
Manchester, Mo. 63062

8171 Redwood Highway
Novato, CA 94947

or WHOLE EARTH CATALOG

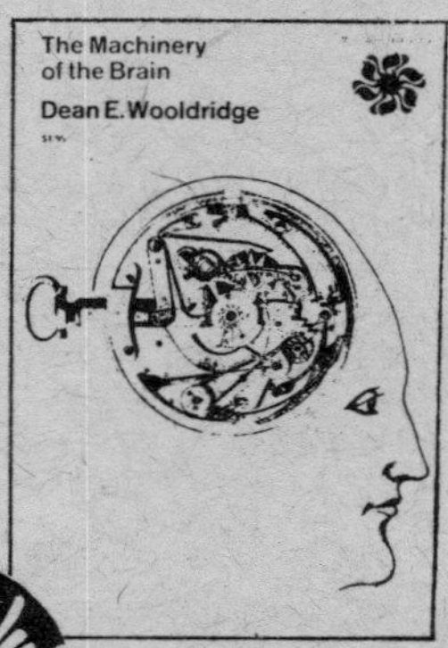

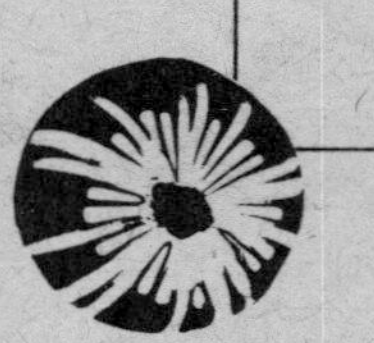

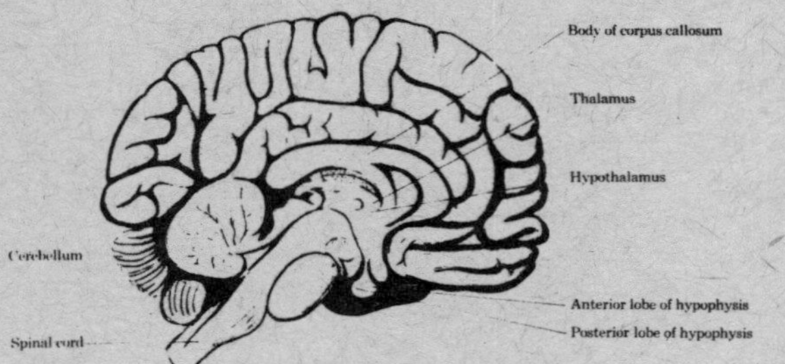

If monotonously repetitive stimuli are provided, such as a regular series of clicks or staccato tones, the nonspecific-brain-potential measurements will display the property of *habituation*: the pulse of brain potential induced by each audible stimulus will, with continuing repetition, gradually diminish and ultimately disappear. If we consider these nonspecific brain potentials as being somewhat related to the degree of attention the subject is paying to the stimulus, their gradual decline correlates nicely with subjective experience: noises that initially interfere with concentration or keep us awake may ultimately recede into the background of our consciousness and lose their effectiveness if they are monotonous and repetitive in character. Such habituation must be regarded as another basic form of learning. It is in effect a kind of negative learning, perhaps antonymous to the essentially positive learning of conditioned responses. Habituation is found throughout the animal scale, from protozoa to man. The indication is that, as in the case of learning by conditioning, habituation derives from some fundamental property of nerve tissue and does not necessarily require special complex neuronal circuits.

•

Experiments have been reported with a six-month-old baby to determine how many trials would be necessary to condition it against reaching out to touch the flame of a lighted candle. (The experiment of course was so arranged as to block the child's hand each time before injury was sustained.) The number of trials required was the same as for training the earthworm, approximately 150!

•

The optical mapping system of the human brain is of special interest and importance. Through the more than one million fibers of the optic nerve of each eye, the pattern of light and dark formed by the lens on the retina is transmitted to a specific set of neurons in the *occipital lobes* of the cortex. Although the picture that is produced by the pattern of voltages reaching these positions at the extreme back of the head is a highly distorted one, topological continuity is preserved, in the sense that adjacent points in the retina are represented by adjacent positions on the cortex. The application of an electric stimulus to any of these cortical points causes the subject to see flashes of light at the corresponding point of his field of view. Similarly, the illumination of the retina by a single bright spot of light results in the arrival of the usual train of voltage pulses at the corresponding spot of the visual cortex.

•

If subsequent work confirms the preliminary indications that pleasure and pain centers occur together, it will be interesting to learn what kind of pleasure is the negative of what kind of pain, in electrical neuronal terms.

A Model of the Brain

Inside every brain there is a model of the world. How does all the elaborate wiring help us, or any other creature, make our model of the world? A noted British anatomist, J. Z. (Jay Zed) Young has spent many pleasant summers in Naples studying the behavior of octopuses, and has also done a great deal of work on the anatomy of their nervous system. The result is a fascinating picture of how to teach octopuses to do things, and some interesting—though not yet very deep—speculation on how cybernetics might help us to relate brain structure to external behavior. Especially interesting are the many hypotheses about the building of networks which can learn. At this early stage all such models are wrong, but we learn from our mistakes. One approach to all this is mental introspection. Here, on the other hand, we learn what we can learn about learning by literally introspecting: looking inside the head of an octopus to see what networks there could possibly change as the animal learns.

[Reviewed by Michael Arbib. Suggested by David Evans]

A Model of the Brain
J. Z. Young
1964; 358 pp.

$9.50 postpaid

from:
Oxford University Press
16-00 Pollitt Drive
Fair Lawn, N. J. 07140

or WHOLE EARTH CATALOG

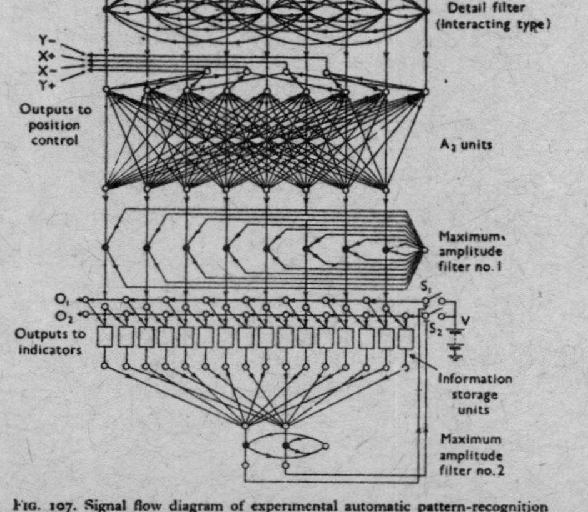

FIG. 107. Signal flow diagram of experimental automatic pattern-recognition apparatus.

The inputs to the nine detail filter terminals are supplied by photoelectric multipliers arranged in a 3×3 matrix. Patterns are centred automatically by combining outputs of the detail filter to form position controls. The filtered inputs are then connected to eight 'A_2 units', one of these will show a maximum amplitude for each pattern (Fig. 108) and this is selected by the first maximum amplitude filter. The outputs of these supply eight pulse generators and these in turn sixteen capacitor storage units.

During the teaching process the switches S_1 and S_2 are closed manually or by means of some artificial external classification system. After learning the switches are closed by electromagnets supplied by the outputs of maximum amplitude filter 2. In both cases the closed switch applied the voltage V to one of the output terminals O_1 or O_2. The same voltage is also connected to an input of the information-storage unit. (After Taylor, 1959.)

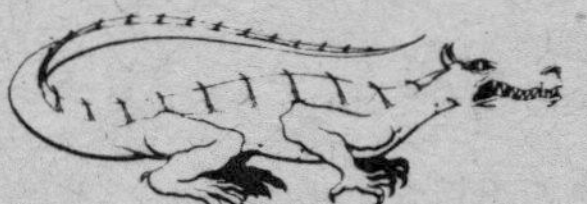

•

Emmit walks

•

stoop-shouldered, bent and drawn

Through the curtain Emmit walks, carrying a steaming cup in his hand. He stops at the window to look out and to scratch himself deep down in his pants somewhere, way down along his thigh needs scratching and Emmit gives it a good one before he goes on over to sit down on the bed and sip from his hot cup.

•

The amazing

•

The amazing thing is Emmit's beard. The whole shaggy mass of hair, all over his head. It falls across his forehead and down across his ears, sticking out in little tufts. His beard starts at his ears and covers his entire face except for his eyes and nose and cheekbones, a great thick Santa beard that hangs down like a waterfall across his mouth.

Design for a Brain

This is a reputation review. Ashby's book is found prominent in the bibliography and footnotes of every text we've seen on computers and the mind. It's technical going to read but worth it for the insights of prime work.

—SB

Design for a Brain
W. Ross Ashby
1952, 1960; 286 pp.

$3.95 postpaid

from:
Halstead Press
605 Third Ave.
New York, N.Y. 10016

or WHOLE EARTH CATALOG

This is the learning mechanism. Its peculiarity is that the gene-pattern delegates part of its control over the organism to the environment. Thus, it does not specify in detail how a kitten shall catch a mouse, but provides a learning mechanism and a tendency to play, so that it is <u>the mouse</u> which teaches the kitten the finer points of how to catch mice.

•

The development of life on earth must thus <u>not</u> be seen as something remarkable. On the contrary, it was inevitable. It was inevitable in the sense that if a system as large as the surface of the earth, basically polystable, is kept gently simmering dynamically for five thousand million years, then nothing short of a miracle could keep the system away from those states in which the variables are aggregated into intensely self-preserving forms.

•

Finding an optimum is a much more complex operation than finding a value that is acceptable (according to a given criterion). Thus, suppose a man comes to a foreign market containing a hundred kinds of fruit that are quite new to him. To find the <u>optimum</u> for his palate he must (1) taste all the hundred, (2) make at least ninety-nine comparisons, and (3) remember the results so that he can finally go back to the optimal form. On the other hand, to find a fruit that is acceptable he need merely try them in succession or at random (taking no trouble to remember the past), stopping only at the first that passes the test. To demand the optimum, then, may be excessive; all that is required in biological systems is that the organism finds a state or a value <u>between given limits</u>.

Remarks on Ashby

RE: Chis Smith's letter, January Supplement p. 42

I must rally to the defense of a valuable information source: W. Ross Ashby. *Design for a Brain* may not satisy those who seek physiological correlates of behavior but it is an excellent formulation of a very *general* adaptive *system*. It could also be called *Design for an Ecosystem*. I highly recommend, not only that you retain the listing, but that you add Ashby's *Introduction to Cybernetics.*

Ashby understands general systems & cybernetics and does a great job in careful explanation. *Intro. to Cybernetics* reviews all the math you need to understand the heavies like Shannon & Weaver.

General system theory is the new paradigm for understand ourselves scientifically. It will eventually provide for the synthesis of science and magical systems like astrology and the I Ching. Its very important to have a clear understanding of the basics, and Ashby is an excellent place to start.

An Introduction to Cybernetics by W. Ross Ashby. $6.25 trade edition, or $4.00 paper text edition. From Barnes & Noble, Inc., 105 Fifth Avenue, NY, NY 10003.

Ron Nigh
Palo Alto, CA

Brains, Machines and Mathematics

Take the theoretical-neuron work of McCulloch & Pitts, the Perceptron, von Neumann and Shannon's communication theory, Gödel's incompleteness theorem, and Wiener's cybernetics. Blend, and see how far along we are toward a "biological mathematics". The answer is not far; this is a tidy survey of how far we aren't.

—SB

[Suggested by Dave Evans]

Brains, Machines and Mathematics
Michael A. Arbib
1964; 152 pp.

$1.95 postpaid

from:
McGraw-Hill Book Co.
Princeton Road
Hightstown, N. J. 08520

Manchester Road
Manchester, Mo. 63062

8171 Redwood Highway
Novato, CA 94947

or WHOLE EARTH CATALOG

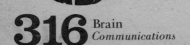

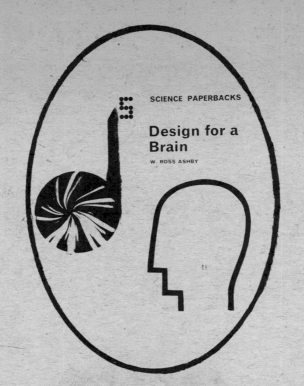

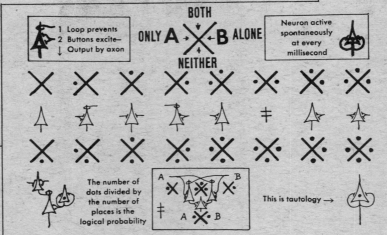

The number of dots divided by the number of places is the logical probability

This is tautology →

In these pages we coerce what is essentially still the mathematics of the physicist to help our slowly dawning comprehension of the brain and its electromechanical analogs. It is probable that the dim beginnings of *biological* mathematics here discernible will one day happily bloom into new and exciting systems of pure mathematics.

•

Reinforcement rules: There seems a great deal of evidence that humans have two kinds of memories——"short-term" and "long-term." It further appears that we have to retain an idea for quite a while in short-term memory before it is transferred into long-term memory. The time taken for this transfer has been variously estimated——one estimate is 20 minutes. It appears that if someone goes into coma, his memories of the 20 minutes or so prior to this are lost forever, i.e., they were not transferred to his long-term memory. It is now commonly believed that short-term memory is precisely that type of memory we gave our modular net——the passage of complicated patterns of electrical impulses through the net. It appears, then, that if such transient activity persists long enough it *actually changes the net.*

•

The Perceptron group has had three main modes of investigation: mathematical analysis, simulation on a digital computer, and construction of an actual machine. Each method has its own advantages. One important result of using an actual machine is that it has been found that *neither precision nor reliability of the components is important, and the connections need not be precise.*

Another interesting result is that the perceptron can "learn" *despite trainer error.*

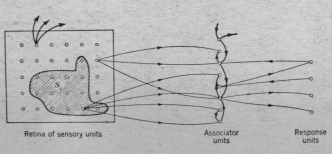

Retina of sensory units   Associator units   Response units

Figure 2.5 Schematic of a perceptron.

Embodiments of Mind

I'm not competent to review this book. I can recognize McCulloch's wisdom and humor. I can report his high standing as an Old One in the field of brain research. I can assert I've revelled in some of his insights. But I can't tell you how far he takes us toward full accountability in how nerve nets yield mind, except that he makes the question appear answerable and worth answering.

[Suggested by   —SB
Milton E. Boyd]

Embodiments of Mind
Warren S. McCulloch
1965, 70, 402pp.

$2.95 postpaid

from:
The MIT Press
50 Ames Street
Cambridge, Massachusetts 02139

or WHOLE EARTH CATALOG

Embodiments of Mind Warren S. McCulloch

Modern evidence indicates that all our acquired ideas, or learned generalizations and specifications are carried on for nearly half an hour by regenerative activity, of which there is beginning to be some electrical evidence. If this activity is interrupted during that time, no memory remains. From the evidence to date it seems that if the process had not been interrupted, and if one looks at the appropriate neurons half an hour later, one finds that there is a great rise in ribonucleic acid, and protein synthesis is under way. So, while we do not yet know how or where this building material will be distributed, we may see nature using the same trick as in the immune reactions.

Morgan's Tarot

Just as we were glad to see a guy invent a new language (aUI——see Fall 69 CATALOG), we are delighted by this thoroughly practical tarot deck based on traditions dating back nearly eight years. Two years from now it will be unusable. Twenty years from now it will be as venerable as the medieval Tarot, if anybody notices. The main limitation I see with tarot cards, astrology, any language, is that the systems close on themselves. They offer no exit, except finally an attenuated exhaustion, frustration, possible cause to bust out. Some systems are more open, more immediately and fractionally self-frustrating—— science; evolution; human life . . . and the market, where these cards are for sale.

—SB

Morgan's Tarot

$3.50 postpaid

from:
Morgan's Tarot, Rt. 1, Box 2251
Tokayana Way, Colfax, CA 95731

or WHOLE EARTH CATALOG

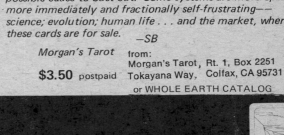

An Introduction to Cybernetics

We are migrating from a world governed primarily by the laws of thermodynamics to a world governed primarily by cybernetics——a weightless world (Fuller says "metaphysical") whose events are the impinging of information on information, whose basis is survival and direction is growth. Thought, society, economics, media, evolution

The two main entries to understanding in this realm are Norbert Wiener (see pp. 16 & 307) and Ashby. Wiener's books are wider, more inspiring. Ashby is more thorough:

—*SB*

[*Suggested by Dave Evans*]

An Introduction to Cybernetics
W. Ross Ashby
1958; 295 pp.

$4.50 postpaid

from:
Barnes & Noble, Inc.
105 Fifth Ave.
New York, N.Y. 10003

or WHOLE EARTH CATALOG

Thus there exist factors, such as "height of threshold" or "proportion of variables constant", which can vary a large system continuously along the whole range that has at one end the totally-joined form, in which every variable has an immediate effect on every other variable, and at the other end the totally-unjoined form, in which every variable is independent of every other. Systems can thus show more or less of "wholeness".

•

This earth contained carbon and other necessary elements, and it is a fact that many combinations of carbon, nitrogen, and a few others are self-reproducing. It follows that though the state of "being lifeless" is almost a state of equilibrium, yet this equilibrium is unstable, a single deviation from it being sufficient to start a trajectory that deviates more and more from the "lifeless" state. What we see today in the biological world are these "autocatalytic" processes showing all the peculiarities that have been imposed on them by two thousand million years of elimination of those forms that cannot survive.

The organisms we see today are deeply marked by the selective action of two thousand million years' attrition. Any form in any way defective in its power of survival has been eliminated; and today the features of almost every form bear the marks of being adapted to ensure *survival* rather than any other possible outcome. Eyes, roots, cilia, shells and claws are so fashioned as to maximise the chance of survival. And when we study the brain we are again studying a means to survival.

•

One way of blocking the flow (from the source of disturbance D to the essential variable E) is to interpose something that acts as a simple passive block to the disturbances. Such is the tortoise's shell, which reduces a variety of impacts, blows, bites, etc. to a negligible disturbance of the sensitive tissues within. In the same class are the tree's bark, the seal's coat of blubber, and the human skull.

At the other extreme from this static defence is the defence by skilled counter-action——the defence that gets information about the disturbance to come, prepares for its arrival, and then meets the disturbance, which may be complex and mobile, with a defence that is equally complex and mobile. This is the defence of the fencer, in some deadly duel, who wears no armour and who trusts to his skill in parrying. This is the defence used mostly by the higher organisms, who have developed a nervous system precisely for the carrying out of this method.

•

What is an amplifier? An amplifier, in general, is a device that, if given a little of something, will emit a lot of it. A sound-amplifier, if given a little sound (into a microphone) will emit a lot of sound. And a money-amplifier would be a device that, if given a little money, would emit a lot.

Such devices work by having available a generous reservoir of what is to be emitted, and then using the input to act as controller to the flow from the reservoir.

Information

The September 1966 issue of Scientific American was devoted entirely to the new technology of information. Now available as a paperbound book, it is the best introduction we've seen to computer science. Articles include: "Computer Logic and Memory", "Computer Inputs and Outputs", "Systems Analysis and Programming", "Time-sharing on Computers", "The Transmission of Computer Data", "The Uses of Computers in Technology", "The Uses of Computers in Organizations", "The Uses of Computers in Education", "Information Storage and Retrieval", and "Artificial Intelligence".

—*SB*

Information
1966; 218 pp.

$2.50 postpaid

from:
W. H. Freeman & Company
660 Market Street
San Francisco, CA 94104

or WHOLE EARTH CATALOG

The computer is almost exactly what man is not. It is capable of paying undivided attention to unlimited detail; it is immune to distraction, precise and reliable; it can carry out the most intricate and lengthy calculation with ease, without a flaw and in much less than a millionth of the time that would be required by its human counterpart. It is emotionless, or so we suppose. It suffers neither boredom nor fatigue. It needs to be told only once; thereafter it remembers perfectly until it is told to forget, whereupon it forgets instantly and absolutely.

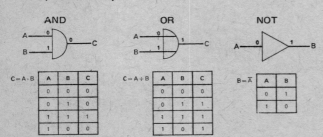

Critical Path Method

Most construction I've been around was under conditions of "The rains are due next week" or "If we don't get the dome covered by the first snow, we've blown it for the winter." Time pressure. At the miraculously complete and on-time Expo 67 in Montreal the magic ingredient was CPM—— Critical Path Method. It's the analysis of what must be done in sequence (foundation, then floor) and what can be done concurrently (while the foundation is being dug in, the girls can cut the roof panels). The maximum necessary sequence is your minimum construction time, and is the critical path. Any delays on it slow down the whole operation. A clear CPM map, using now-standard symbols, can vastly simplify coordination. The technique is useful for any group operation that's time-bound. This book is the briefest clearest on CPM.

—*SB*

Critical Path Method
A. T. Armstrong-Wright
1969; 113 pp.

$4.25 postpaid

from:
Humanities Press, Inc.
303 Park Avenue South
New York, N. Y. 10010

or WHOLE EARTH CATALOG

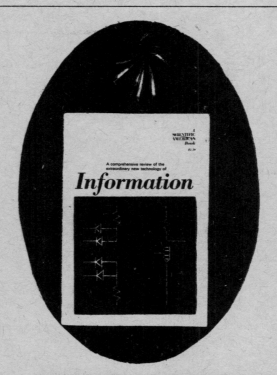

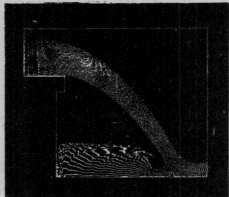

Simulated waterfall spills over the edge of a cliff and splashes into a pool in this computer experiment performed by John P. Shannon at the Los Alamos Scientific Laboratory as part of a study of dynamic behavior of fluids with the aid of numerical models.

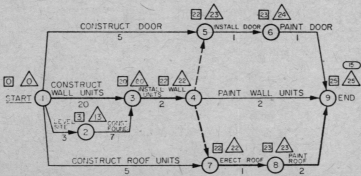

In the above example, the required time for completing the project is 25 days and the project end-event time is calculated as "day 25". Assume that the owner is anxious to complete the garage before a new car is delivered on "day 15", it will thus be necessary to reduce the critical path by 10 days if this scheduled date is to be achieved. In this case it may be a simple matter of doubling the labour on activity 1–3 "Construct wall units" in the hope of reducing the duration by 10 days.

For example of CPM in use, see p. 300.

Systems Thinking

Well, this should be in "Understanding Whole Systems". It's an excellent introduction to systems theory. It's here so you can connect it up with cybernetics and your own bodily and social open-system functioning. In the light of systems thinking statements like "He not busy being born is busy dying" have precise truth.

—*SB*

Systems Thinking
F. E. Emery, ed.
1969; 398 pp.

$2.65 postpaid

from:
Penguin Books, Inc.
7110 Ambassador Rd
Baltimore, Md. 21207

72 Fifth Ave.
New York, N.Y. 10011

or WHOLE EARTH CATALOG

In physics, the theory of open systems leads to fundamentally new principles. It is indeed the more general theory, the restriction of kinetics and thermodynamics to closed systems concerning only a rather special case. In biology, it first of all accounts for many characteristics of living systems that have appeared to be in contradiction to the laws of physics, and have been considered hitherto as vitalistic features. Second, the consideration of organisms as open systems yields quantitative laws of important biological phenomena.

It is events rather than things which are structured, so that social structure is a dynamic rather than a static concept. Activities are structured so that they comprise a unity in their completion or closure. A simple linear stimulus-response exchange between two people would not constitute social structure. To create structure, the responses of A would have to elicit B's reactions in such a manner that the responses of the latter would stimulate A to further responses.

•

But the rim of his cup finds his mouth in there somewhere and he drinks.

•

And then he wipes his mouth and drinks again.

•

"I'm awake."

•

Emmit raises

•

Emmit lifts his head, like a bird alerted.

•

He raises his bearded head and looks at his nephew in the big bed across the room.

•

He looks. For a long time he looks, and doesn't speak.

•

But then he lifts his cup in a neat salute and says you had a right smart of sleep, old bud. How long

•

How long have I been sleeping? D.R. asks.

•

About a day.

•

Then silence. Do I remember coming here?

Mathematics

As far as we're concerned, these are the pick of self-education math books. From them you can learn delight as well as method in the universal language.

Mathematical Snapshots operates by visibility. What's going on mathematically is plain as day in the diagrams and illustrations. It's like learning history by anecdotes.

Mathematical Models is a classic of 4-D technique. The whole purpose of the book is enabling you to make your own geometric forms in the world. Like learning history by psychodrama.

[Suggested by Sim Van Der Ryn]

The World of Mathematics IS history and anecdotes, an infectious multi-faceted telling of math stories—pure, applied, ancient, recent: a fine and complete collection. Math seen from outside.

Mathematics: Its Content, Methods, and Meaning. Math from inside. A Russian-compiled technical run-down of everything of concern in mathematics today.

The Graphic Work of M. C. Escher is geometry set at its own throat via the images of dreams. The subjective frontier.

The New Mathematics Dictionary and Handbook is the handiest of handy reference books.

[Suggested by Lloyd Kahn]
—SB

Mathematical Snapshots
H. Steinhaus
1950, 1969; 328 pp.

$7.95 postpaid

from:
Oxford University Press
16-00 Pollitt Drive
Fair Lawn, N.J. 07410

or WHOLE EARTH CATALOG

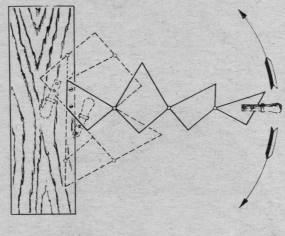

1

From these four small boards (1) we can compose a square or an equilateral triangle, according as we turn the handle up or down. The proof is given by sketch (2).

2

The patterns we observe on the shore of a river when the mud has been dried up by the sun (98) seem to be quite irregular; nevertheless as a rule they show right angles. This can be explained by assuming the cracking to be an effect of contraction; the line appearing as a fissure has, by a principle of mechanics, to make the work of disjunction as small as possible. The work is proportional to the areas of the sections and the lines must have a course such as to minimize the surfaces laid open by the fissure. This procedure gives right angles if the clay is homogeneous; the varying thickness of the layer accounts for the curvature of the lines. This remark supplies in many cases a means of deciding which line appeared earlier and which later: the older of the two splits passes right through the point of junction. Thus we can follow the genealogy of splits and eventually find the ancestors of the whole system.

Suppose the pattern was composed initially of two regions, A. and B. A new line appears, joining two points of two already existing arcs and giving rise to a new region C (100); since the new line breaks up two arcs into two parts each, the number of arcs increases by three. After n steps we have n more regions and $3n$ more arcs. Since there were initially two regions and three arcs, we now have $n+2$ regions and $3n + 3$ arcs.

Mathematical Models
H. Martyn Cundy & A. P. Rollett
1961; 286 pp.

$7.50 postpaid

from:
Oxford University Press
16-00 Pollitt Drive
Fair Lawn, N.J. 07410

or WHOLE EARTH CATALOG

PLAN:

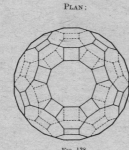

FIG. 138

F₄	F₆	F₁₀	V	E
30	20	12	120	180

POLYHEDRA

3.9.4. Great stellated triacontahedron. $V(3.\frac{5}{2})^2$

FIG. 153

The exterior perimeter of a net of a polyhedron which is all in one piece becomes a 'tree' of edges on the solid. This tree may be branched, but every edge is double and occurs twice on the perimeter of the net. It is evident that if these edges are numbered consecutively round the net every even edge will be joined to an odd edge in the final solid. This means that tabs need only be attached to the even edges. In the nets which follow, tabs are not shown unless there is special need to do so. In all other cases the rule is: attach tabs to alternate edges round the net.

There is an exception in the case of the last face, which is best left free of tabs. The missing tabs must be added to the other edges, and are best made large, so that a platform can be built up to which the last face can be stuck.

Obviously, for any model which is to be at all permanent, cardboard will be used.

The card should be white with a good surface, and fairly thin, about the thickness of a plain postcard. Thick cardboard makes ugly corners, and allowance ought to be made for its thickness in drawing the net. It is useful, however, to cut flat sheets of thick card for internal strengthening in some of the stellated and interpenetrating polyhedra.

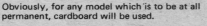

3.7   POLYHEDRA

3.7.12. Great rhombicosidodecahedron *(cont.)*

NET:

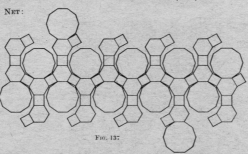

FIG. 137

When the dimensions of the model have been decided on, the net can be constructed on the cardboard. In the case of a complicated net this is facilitated by pricking through vertices from a template drawn on tracing paper, but it must be done very accurately. Tabs are then added to alternate outside edges, care being taken to ensure that the angle at the shoulder of the tab is small enough to admit of the tab's being cemented to its appropriate face. The net can now be cut out with a razor-blade and the edges scored half-through for bending. (Where edges have to be scored on the back—in the stellated polyhedra—this is indicated in the diagrams.) The face of the net becomes the outside of the polyhedron.

For joining, a quick-drying cement, such as balsa-wood cement as used for model aircraft, is essential. After the cement has been applied to a tab, the edges to be joined are brought together, and the tab can be held down with a small wire paper-fastener while the cement dries. This is particularly useful in small models when the fingers cannot easily get inside, and near the finish of any model when there are several edges to be joined at once. A thin wire probe is sometimes useful in getting the last face to adhere.

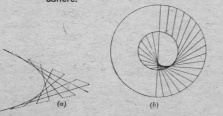

2.5. Curve-Stitching

One very old method of expression work in mathematics, and one which affords a welcome change from 'the tyranny of pencil and paper', is that of curve-stitching. It seems to have originated in a book by Mrs. E. L. Somervell, entitled *A Rhythmic Approach to Mathematics* and published in 1906. The idea has recently been revived, both in America and in this country. Basically it consists of constructing straight-line envelopes by stitching with coloured threads through a pattern of holes pricked in cardboard.

Mathematics: Its Content, Methods, and Meaning
A. D. Aleksandrov, A. N. Volmogorov, R. A. Lavrentev
1956 1963; 1144 pp.; 3 vols.

$10.00 postpaid

from:
The M. I. T. Press
Cambridge, Mass. 02142

or WHOLE EARTH CATALOG

III. There exists neither a point nor a line in the plane that is carried into itself under all the transformations of the group. Groups of this type are called plane Fedorov groups. They are the symmetry groups of infinite plane ornaments. There are altogether 17 of them: five consist of motions of the first kind only, and twelve of motions of the first and second kind.

In Table 3 we have given examples of ornaments corresponding to each of the seventeen plane Fedorov groups; every group consists of precisely those motions that carry an arbitrary flag drawn in the diagram into any other flag of the same diagram.

It is interesting to note that the masters of the art of ornamentation have in practice discovered ornaments with all possible symmetry groups; it fell to the theory of groups to prove that other forms do not exist.

Crystallographic groups. In 1890 the eminent Russian crystallographer and geometer E.S. Fedorov solved by group-theoretical methods one of the fundamental problems of crystallography: to classify the regular systems of points in space. This was the first example of a direct application of the theory of groups to the solution of an important problem in natural science and made a substantial impact on the development of the theory of groups.

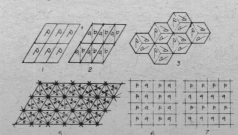

The World of Mathematics
James R. Newman

World of Mathematics
James Newman
1956; 2469 pp; 4 vols.

$14.95 postpaid

from:
Simon & Schuster, Inc.
630 Fifth Avenue
New York, N. Y. 10020

or WHOLE EARTH CATALOG

...AS our mental eye penetrates into smaller and smaller distances and shorter and shorter times, we find nature behaving so entirely differently from what we observe in visible and palpable bodies of our surrounding that no model shaped after our large-scale experiences can ever be 'true'. A completely satisfactory model of this type is not only practically inaccessible, but not even thinkable. Or, to be precise, we can, of course, think it, but however we think it, it is wrong; not perhaps quite as meaningless as a 'triangular circle,' but much more so than a 'winged lion.'

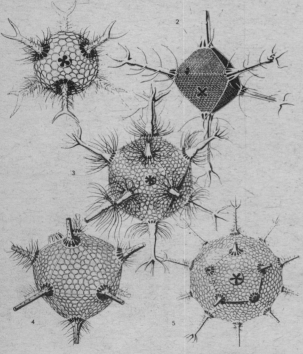

Here (Figure 45) is a page from Haeckel's <u>Challenger Monograph</u> showing the skeletons of several Radiolarians. Numbers 2,3, and 5 are octahedron, icosahedron, and dodecahedron in astonishingly regular form; 4 seems to have a lower symmetry.

1. This Book has 597 Pages
2. The Author of this Book is Confucius.
3. The Statements Numbered 1, 2, and 3 are all False

Problem 36 of the papyrus begins: "Go down I times 3, 1/3 of me, 1/5 of me is added to me; return I, filled am I. What is the quantity saying it?

FIGURE 10—Which points of the plane are inside this polygon?

The Graphic Work of M. C. Escher
M.C. Escher
1960,68; 76 plates

$3.95 postpaid

from:
Hawthorn Books, Inc.
70 Fifth Avenue
New York, N. Y. 10011

or
WHOLE EARTH CATALOG

57. DOUBLE PLANETOID, wood-engraving , printed from 4 blocks, 1949, diameter 37.5 cm

Two regular tetrahedrons, piercing each other, float through space as a planetoid. The light-coloured one is inhabited by human beings who have completely transformed their region into a complex of houses, bridges and roads. The darker tetrahedron has remained in its natural state, with rocks, on which plants and prehistoric animals live. The two bodies fit together to make a whole but they have no knowledge of each other.

The New Mathematics Dictionary and Handbook
Robert W. Marks
1964; 186 pp.

$.95 postpaid

from:
Bantam Books, Inc.
666 Fifth Ave.
New York, N.Y. 10019

or WHOLE EARTH CATALOG

VENN DIAGRAMS. Diagrams using overlapping circles to show relationships between sets; developed by John Venn (1834—1923), English logician. Each circle represents one set. Two or more may be overlapped. The areas of overlap (lens-shaped areas) indicate subsets which may contain elements common to both or all of the indicated sets. Some authors shade or cross-hatch the areas that contain members of a set; other authors use shading or cross-hatching to indicate emptiness. In the diagram below, shading indicates content.

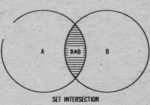

SET INTERSECTION

The shaded area represents that set of all elements that are both elements of A and elements of B.
Example: If A is the set of all students who take chemistry, and B is the set of all students taking physics, the shaded area is the set of all students taking both chemistry and physics.

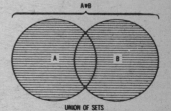

$A \cup B$

UNION OF SETS

The shaded area in the second diagram represents the set of all elements that are in A, or in B, or in both A and B.
Example: If A is the set of all men who own boats, and if B is the set of all fishermen, the shaded area indicates the set of all men who are boatowners or fishermen, or who are boat-owning fishermen.

Number Words and Number Symbols

There's lots of ways to invent things—two big ones that this CATALOG promotes both involve the return to rudiments, but in different ways. Invention-By-Usefulness is People's invention—a flock of people go live a different way: the new methods that arise to aid their different living are their inventions (subject to no prices, patents, marketability, or even notice usually). Invention-by-Inventor, on the other hand, involves a double perception by an individual—he perceives a potential usefulness for something, and he perceives the roots of a set of tools that may be adapted or combined to perform the new usefulness.

"Academic" study, of little use to the flock of pioneers, is essential to the inventor, especially the study of the origins of crafts he's working in. Take numbers. Suppose you want to help human communication to re-understand itself. So much of that understanding is wrapped up in numbers that if you penetrate the one you may have a foothold to tweak the other onto a new course. Invent language and you invent man.

This book penetrates numbers.   —SB

Number Words and Number Symbols
Karl Menninger
1958, 1969; 480 pp.

$15.00 postpaid

from:
The M. I. T. Press
Cambridge, Mass 02142

or WHOLE EARTH CATALOG

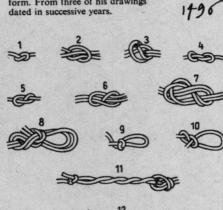

Fig. 222 Chinese fork coin, with the number 34 written in abstract place-value notation. Ca. A.D. 20.

In the seaports and market places of the Red Sea, Arabia, and East Africa, merchants have evolved a finger language that is understood in every market of every country in the region. Buyers and sellers come to terms underneath a cloth, a fold of garment or a strip of muslin from a turban, by touching the fingers of each other's hand and thus bargaining in complete privacy.

When Buddha reached the age of manhood he courted Gopa, the daughter of the Prince Dandapani. But he would be rejected unless he could show public proof of his abilities. And so, together with five other suitors, he was put through trials in writing, wrestling, archery, running, swimming, and number skills. In all these contests he brilliantly defeated his rivals. After the competition, Gopa's father commanded him to pit himself against the great mathematician Arjuna, who was to be the measure of Buddha's knowledge. Arjuna instructed him to list all the numbers (that is, the numerical ranks) above 100 kotis. Koti was the name of the seventh rank, meaning 10^7 or 10 millions. Beyond sahasra (10^3), Indians at an early date had ayuta (10^4), niuta, also called lakša (10^5), and prayuta (10^6 = a million).

Buddha answered:

koti (10^7, abbreviated 7)	hetuhila (31)
ayuta = 100 kotis (9)	karahu (33)
niyuta (11)	Hetvindriya (35)
kangkara (13)	samaptalambha (37)
vivara (15)	gananagati (39)
akšobhya (17)	niravadya (41)
vivaha (19)	mudrabala (43)
utsanga (21)	sarvabala (45)
bahula (23)	visandjnagati (47)
nagabala (25)	sarvasandjna (49)
titilambha (27)	vibhutangama (51)
vyavasthanapradjnapti (29)	tallakšana (53).

Fig. 242 Albrecht Dürer's year dates. In writing the dates of the years around 1495, Dürer illustrated the development of the 4 into its present form. From three of his drawings dated in successive years.

1292
1295
1496

Fig. 90 Miller's knots used to indicate amounts and kinds of flour.

1 2 3 4 5 6 7 8 9 and 0 — these ten symbols which today all peoples use to record numbers, symbolize the world-wide victory of an idea. There are few things on earth that are universal, and the universal customs which man has successfully established are fewer still. But this is one boast he can make: The new Indian numerals are indeed universal.

Regular Polytopes

*shel kaphan,
mathematician,
boy wizard,
bookkeeper,
bicyclist,
alpinist,
shel kaphan recommended this,
as an old standard for mathematical model builders.*

—jd

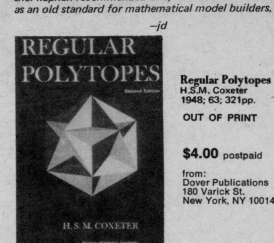

Regular Polytopes
H.S.M. Coxeter
1948; 63; 321pp.

OUT OF PRINT

$4.00 postpaid

from:
Dover Publications
180 Varick St.
New York, NY 10014

A honeycomb is said to be quasi-regular if its cells are regular while its vertex figures are quasi-regular. This definition (cf. #2-3) implies that the vertex figures are all alike, and that the cells are of two kinds, arranged alternately. To find what varieties are possible, we have the same two alternative methods as in #4-6. Either we seek (as cells) two different regular polyhedra whose respective dihedral angles have a submultiple of 2 pi for their sum; these can only be a tetrahedron and an octahedron, where the sum is pi. Or we look at the possible vertex figures, admitting the cubocta-hedron, whose edge is equal to its circum-radius, and discarding the icosidodecahedron (for which the ratio of edge to circum-radius is dodecahedron (for which the ratio of edge to circum-radius is 2 sin pi/h=2 sin pi/10=2 cos 2 pi/5). From either point of view, we conclude that there is only one quasi-regular honeycomb. Each vertex is surrounded by eight tetrahedra and six octahedra (corresponding to the triangles and squares of the cuboctahedron).

Curta Calculator

The Curta Calculator (made in Lichtenstein, no less) is one of those machine things that it would be nice to just have one around because it is so beautiful. It's tiny, but made in a way that discourages errors. It'll take poor climates without failure. Adds, subtracts, multiplies, divides, squares, cubes, takes square root, accumulates multiplications, multiplies or divides by constants. Rally navigators dig em, but so will anyone that needs a small calculator. Super in every respect. I've never talked to anyone that would part with his. Two models, $75 and $99, both about 2-1/2" x 3-1/2".

[Suggested and reviewed by Jay Baldwin]

Literature

free

from:
M. Wolf
The Curta Company
Box 275
Chatsworth, CA 91311

Indecks Information Retrieval System

What do you have a lot of? Students, subscribers, notes, books, records, clients, projects? Once you're past 50 or 100 of whatever, it's tough to keep track, time to externalize your store and retrieve system. One handy method this side of a high-rent computer is Indecks. It's funky and functional: cards with a lot of holes in the edges, a long blunt needle, and a notcher. Run the needle through a hole in a bunch of cards, lift, and the cards notched in that hole don't rise; they fall out. So you don't have to keep the cards in order. You can sort them by feature, number, alphabetically or whatever: just poke, fan, lift and catch. Indecks is cheaper than the McBee system we used to list.

We've used the McBee cards to manipulate (edit) and keep track of the 3000 or so items in this CATALOG. They've meant the difference between partial and complete insanity.

—SB

[Suggested by Ernest L. Gayden]

Catalog

free

from:
Indecks
Arlington, Vt. 05250

PAPER/THESIS DECKS @ $9.75
RESEARCH DECKS @ $9.75
STUDY/REVIEW DECKS @ $9.75
MEDICAL/SURGICAL DECKS @ $12.95
PAPER/THESIS REFILL PACKS (50 cards) @ $1.95
RESEARCH REFILL PACKS (50 cards) @ $1.95
STUDY/REVIEW REFILL PACKS (50 cards) @ $1.95
MEDICAL/SURGICAL REFILL PACKS (50 cards) @ $2.25
MULTI-PURPOSE REFILL PACKS (100 cards: 4''x6'') @ $3.50
REFILL CARTONS: 600 cards (P/T) (R) (S/R) @ $21.25
REFILL CARTONS: 600 Med/Surg cards @ $25.00
REFILL CARTONS: 600 Multi-Purpose cards @ $19.00
INDECKS NOTCHERS @ $5.85
HOLE REPAIR BELTS. (Single Row) (Double Row) @ $.95
CODE CARD PACKS (10 cards ea.) @ $.60
SORTING RODS @ $.20
INSTRUCTION BKLTS. (P/T) (R) (S/R) (M/S) @ $.60
FILE BOXES (P/T) (R) (S/R) (M/S) @ $.90

Sorting allows you to retrieve the information that has been Recorded, Coded, and Notched (Steps 1, 2 & 3).

Align the Deck at the clipped corners...

Pass the Sorting Rod through the hole with the number which matches the listed code number of the category you wish to retrieve...

Shake gently...and all cards notched at this hole will drop.

THE CARDS YOU WANT HAVE BEEN RETRIEVED

Handbook of Mathematical Functions

Designed for the person who needs but does not have access to powerful computer facilities, this Government bargain is a modernized version of the classical tables of functions of Jahnke-Emde.   —SB

[Suggested by Mrs. W. B. Mohin]

CONTENTS

1. Mathematical Constants
2. Physical Constants and Conversion Factors
3. Elementary Analytic Methods
4. Elementary Transcendental Functions
   Logarithmic, Exponential, Circular and Hyperbolic Functions
5. Exponential Integral and Related Functions
6. Gamma Function and Related Functions
7. Error Function and Fresnel Integrals
8. Legendre Functions
9. Bessel Functions of Integer Order
10. Bessel Functions of Fractional Order
11. Integrals of Bessel Functions
12. Struve Functions and Related Functions
13. Confluent Hypergeometric Functions
14. Coulomb Wave Functions
15. Hypergeometric Functions
16. Jacobian Elliptic Functions and Theta Functions
17. Elliptic Integrals
18. Weierstrass Elliptic and Related Functions
19. Parabolic Cylinder Functions
20. Mathieu Functions
21. Spheroidal Wave Functions
22. Orthogonal Polynomials
23. Bernoulli and Euler Polynomials, Riemann Zeta Function
24. Combinatorial Analysis
25. Numerical Interpolation, Differentiation and Integration
26. Probability Functions
27. Miscellaneous Functions
28. Scales of Notation
29. Laplace Transforms

Handbook of Mathematical Functions With Formulas, Graphs, and Mathematical Tables
1964, 1968; 1046 pp.

$6.95 postpaid

from:
Dover Publications
180 Varick Street
New York, N.Y. 10014

Basic Graphics

Comprehensive treatment of design graphics——tools, geometry, projection, graphs etc.——with good updating on use of computer graphics.
　　　　　　　　　　　　　　　　　—SB

Basic Graphics
Warren J. Luzadder
1957, 1962, 1968; 641 pp.

$11.50 postpaid

from:
Prentice Hall, Inc.
Englewood Cliffs, N. J. 07632

or WHOLE EARTH CATALOG

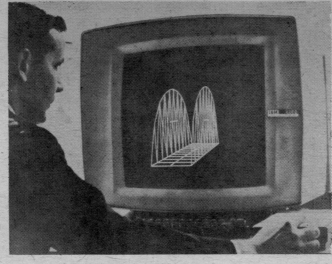

One can not ignore the fact that graphics now serves as a language for communication between man and computer.

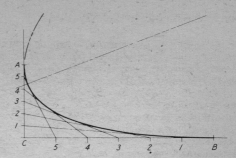

Fig. 4.49. To construct a curve of parabolic form.

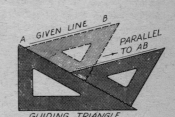

Design and Planning 2

Incredible: you actually got your hands on a computer powerful enough to generate rich graphics, and you have an employer/patron rich enough to buy you some play time on the computer. In order not to waste his money too idly splashing around in your new pool, you might check this book for a beginning inventory of some of the things you and your computer can accomplish together. It's far the most practical book we've seen on the subject, and the subject is what wizards are about.
　　　　　　　　　　　　　　　　　—SB

[Suggested by Eric Renner]

Design and Planning 2
Martin Krampen and Peter Seitz, eds.
1967; 177 pp.

OUT OF PRINT

Hastings House, Inc.
10 East 40th Street
New York, N. Y. 10016

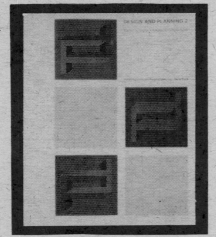

Table 3—EXAMPLES OF PROPERTIES GIVEN TO GLYPHS

Function	Remarks
TURN	3-axis rotation
PAN; ZOOM-MOOZ	3-axis translation
PERSPECTIVE-PROJECTIVE	Geometric transformations
STEREO	2-views
BLINK	Attention direction
SHADE	Optical density variations; texturing
COLOR	Associate a color with the image (parts)
PHOTO	Take a picture
MOVIE	Take a sequence of pictures
NAME	Associate a name with the image(s)
ATTACH	Join line segments
CONNECT	Special glyph linking
DRAW	Follow the light pen
SMOOTH	Apply a relaxation operator to the data
MODIFY	Some change to a display list
DIMENSION	Assign lengths (areas, volumes, masses)
ERASE	Remove the image (parts)
WRITE	Prepare for text

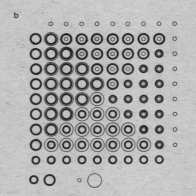

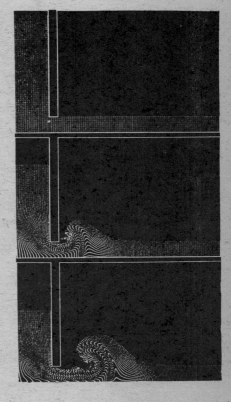

The Architecture Machine

A book of beginning efforts to domesticate computers. Good intro to life with dumb-fuck genius machines.
　　　　　　　　　　　　　　　　　—SB

The Architecture Machine
Nicholas Negroponte
1970; 153 pp.

$2.95

from:
MIT Press
28 Carleton Street
Cambridge, Mass. 02142

or WHOLE EARTH CATALOG

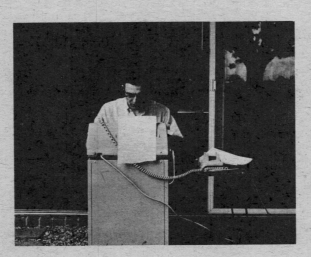

There are three possible ways in which machines can assist the design process: (1) current procedures can be automated, thus speeding up and reducing the cost of existing practices; (2) existing methods can be altered to fit within the specifications and constitution of a machine, where only those issues are considered that are supposedly machine-compatible; (3) the design process, considered as evolutionary, can be presented to a machine, also considered as evolutionary, and a mutual training, resilience, and growth can be developed.

I shall consider only the third alternative and shall treat the problem as the intimate association of two dissimilar species (man and machine), two dissimilar processes (design and computation), and two intelligent systems (the architect and the architecture machine). By virtue of ascribing intelligence to an artifact or the artificial, the partnership is not one of master and slave but rather of two associates that have a potential nad a desire for self-improvement.

Professor: What time is it?

Computer: I did not catch the last word. Or was it two words?

Professor: What is the time?

Computer: The dime is a copper coin worth one-tenth of a dollar. The word derives from the Latin decem, meaning. . . .

Professor: No. No. What is the time? The time?

Computer: It is 8:30 p.m., Thursday, December 5, 1985. We have been having some trouble with your linguals recently. Sometimes I can't tell your d's from your t's. Let's practice them. Watch the display screen for the intonation pattern, and repeat after me: Teddy's daddy toted two dead toads to Detroit.

Professor: Teddy's daddy toted. . . .

But there is just the silence of the old decaying room at early morning, no motion and no swirl. Just still and cool, the old uncle sitting on one bed, the young nephew lying in the other, craving something to drink now, feeling the pulse begin to quicken as he comes again into the world.

He says, I believe I'll have me a cup of that tea, Uncle Emmit.

And Emmit says this just hot water I'm drinking. I'll go fix you some tea.

I can

I can do it.

But Emmit is up

He's already up and gone to the kitchen to stir the fire and put the water on while he dies.

Cybernetic Serendipity

This book started life as an exhibit at the Institute of Contemporary Arts in London last year. Simultaneously it was an issue of Studio International magazine. It must have been an Event. Certainly it is the best collection of computer art yet, the only one not dismissable as engineers kidding themselves. There's been talk for years (e.g. The New Landscape, 1956) of how art and science are gonna come together, and indeed communications have improved. But there was no direct avenue, no real mutual domain. Not until computers got common enough for funky hands to lay hold of them to do tricks for funky heads. That's happening now, and this book is good evidence. Ahead, deep space

—SB

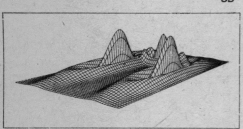

(Art, if you want a definition of it, is criminal action. It conforms to no rules. Not even its own. Anyone who experiences a work of art is as guilty as the artist. It is not a question of sharing the guilt. Each one of us gets all of it.)

Cybernetic Serendipity
1969; 100 pp.; 260 illustrations

$9.95 postpaid

from:
Frederick A. Praeger, Publisher
111 Fourth Avenue
New York, N. Y. 10003

or WHOLE EARTH CATALOG

1 Poem
    eons deep in the ice
    I paint all time in a whorl
    bang the sludge has cracked

2 Poem
    eons deep in the ice
    I see gelled time in a whorl
    pfffft the sludge has cracked

3 Poem
    all green in the leaves
    I smell dark pools in the trees
    crash the moon has fled

3 Poem
    all white in the buds
    I flash snow peaks in the spring
    bang the sun has fogged

Cybernetic Serendipity
the computer and the arts

Studio International special issue 25s

To co-operate or even to orient themselves and to engage their programmes, the mobiles must communicate. They do so in a simple but many-levelled language of light flashes and sounds. You may engage in this discourse if you wish to, though your goals may be alien to the goals of the mobiles; for example, you might be trying to achieve a configuration that you regard as pleasing.

Data Study

Information that isn't organized isn't signal in your life, it's noise. You waste yourself searching the full length of a file for something, feeling as stupid as a driver in crosstown New York, and for the same reason: your access is brute linear and laborious. This book can help you if not New York. It presents theory and practice on how to keep stuff straight, at least in terms of organization. Display is another matter, however, in which the information sciences are still poor.

—SB

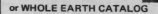

Data Study
J. L. Jolley
1968; 254 pp.

$2.45 postpaid

from:
McGraw-Hill Book Company
Princeton Road
Hightstown, N. J. 08520

Manchester Road
Manchester, Missouri 63062

8171 Redwood Highway
Novato, California 94947

or WHOLE EARTH CATALOG

The decimal system of numerals begins with 0, if its ten characters are arranged in ascending order. Binary, octal, and other systems also begin with 0, for 0 is the origin, zero, the place we start from before some change in the situation gives us some information.

Information, whose handling is the topic of this book, is generated by change, and whatever is our unit of change is our unit of information.

a mutually exclusive set	an overlapping set	a cumulative set	an equivalent (identical) set
hotel is :	hotel possesses :	hotel is :	hotel has :
in France	a ballroom	more than 50 years old	first class food
in Spain	tennis courts		excellent
in the United States	a swimming pool	more than 100 years old	cuisine
in Germany	a bowling green		top quality
in Switzerland	a skittle alley	more than 200 years old	refreshments
	a golf course		

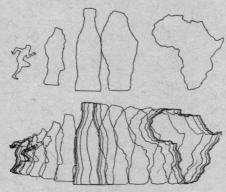

Running cola is Africa

A sustained image of the visual world around us is maintained by the brain's continual coordination of a great flux of varying sensory input. Much of this co-ordination is achieved by the series of voluntary and involuntary eyemovements which serve to scan the image of the pattern across the retina. When these eyemovements are eliminated or controlled, a remarkable collapse of the perceptual process occurs in which visual patterns disintegrate—but in non-random fashion, and according to 'rules' which appear to be common to all humans. The device, which we have called the CYBERNETIC INTROSPECTIVE PATTERN—CLASSIFIER—because that is as good a description as any—is not really the exhibit itself: it is by means of this device that the human brain can be turned into its own exhibit. People looking into the CIPC will be given a brief, bright flash of a pattern which plants an image on the retina in such a way that it can be seen, with eyes closed, for one or two minutes. Since the image is fixed on the retina, eye movements are irrelevant, and the perceptual system collapses as described above. The pattern can be seen to fragment and change its form, and these forms are probably the basic perceptual units used by the brain in recognising the pattern. This exhibit therefore allows people to watch their own cerebral processes actually in action.

Intelligent Computers

I've been bumming around the country lately, trying to see where I would lead me. And or course one of the places I eventually would up was inside my own head, the primary content of which is a lot of scientific information that I'd never really sorted through before.

My latest flash was about computers, which I do know a little about already. Specifically about intelligent computers, which nobody knows anything about. It involved assembling what I know about neurochemistry (my main field of scientific interest) with a lot of stuff about animal behavioral psychology and the history of the development of mathematics and a dash of Zen. The result was that I scared the shit out of myself and quit before I had translated it all into machine language, which I don't know anyway.

The point is that it is too valuable to lose and too powerful to let IBM or the Pentagon come up with it on their own, especially since it looks like the only way an intelligent computer could remain sane would be if it believed itself to BE the planet earth.

I would like to sit down with a bona fide computer genius with an island psychology and a bit of stock in the human race and try to work this thing through with him.

Ken Colstad
Hardin, Montana

I know just the man. Ken Colstad. — S.B.

Desk-top Calculators

The Hewlett-Packard 9100A is now $4400. If you have to deal with problems which require a considerable capacity then the Wang 700 should be a great deal better than the HP since its total memory under program control (core plus tape) will be about 70 times as much as HP's. For people that order a 700 before it is being produced Wang loans a 370 with two card readers, a system which in some ways is already better than the HP. Such a 370 system costs $4700. Deficiencies of 370 compared with HP:

*Much slower
Does not have wired in programs for trig functions and some other functions (but programs can be fed in on cards)
Can not handle as wide a range of numbers (only from about 10^{-10} to 10^{+9} instead of nearly 10^{-100} to 10^{+100})
Much less convenient to write and correct programs
Results of a computation cannot be read out onto a magnetic card or tape for later use (this can be done on the HP altho the salesman may not realize it)
Not as good a display*

*Advantages of 370 compared with HP:
Greater capacity (28 registers compared to 19 for HP with no program, with 160 step program 370 still has 28 registers but HP has only 7 —160 steps is maximum size program for 370 with two card readers without feeding cards in manually, compared to 196 for HP but another card reader would bring it up to 240)
Ability to use subroutines (but not subroutines within subroutines)—with HP a subroutine must be rewritten every place it is used in the main program thus using up precious capacity.*

The 700 should be as good or better in all these respects, except the display, as well as having some other big programming advantages—particularly indirect addressing of registers in which the computer decides which register to go to thus saving much capacity as well as making programs easier to write.

[Reviewed by Craige Schensted, 1969]

Note: Wang 700 is now discontinued.

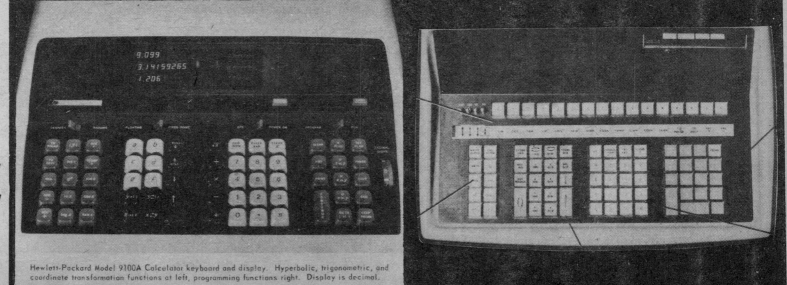

Hewlett-Packard Model 9100A Calculator keyboard and display. Hyperbolic, trigonometric, and coordinate transformation functions at left, programming functions right. Display is decimal.

Hewlett-Packard information from:
P. O. Box 301
Loveland, Colorado 80537

Wang information from:
Wang Laboratories, Inc.
836 North Street
Tewksbury, Mass. 01876

Basic Electricity

Van Valkenburgh, Nooger & Neville, Inc.
1954; 579 pp; 5 vols.

$15.95

from:
Hayden Book Company, Inc.
50 Essex Street
Rochelle Park, N.J. 07662

or WHOLE EARTH CATALOG

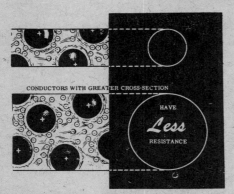

Basic Electronics

Van Valkenburgh, Nooger & Neville, Inc.
1959; 680 pp; 6 vols.

$19.20

from:
Hayden Book Company
50 Essex Street
Rochelle Park, N.J. 07662

or WHOLE EARTH CATALOG

There are many ways of controlling the amount of feedback. One method which has been used involves varying the physical position of the tickler coil with respect to the grid coil. If the coupling between the two coils is reduced by moving the tickler coil away from the grid coil, or rotating it so that its axis is at an angle to the axis of the grid coil, the amount of feedback will be reduced. When this method is used to control feedback, a potentiometer is not connected across the tickler coil.

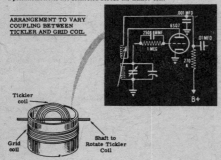

You learned that a good way for you to picture the operation of a grid in a vacuum tube was to think of the grid as a valve in a water pipe. The British are so fond of this explanation that, to this day, they call a vacuum tube a "valve." When the grid of the tube is very negative, the "valve" is closed and there is little or no flow of electrons from the cathode to the plate. When the grid voltage is changed so that it becomes only slightly negative, the "valve" is nearly wide open and there is a large flow of electrons from the cathode to the plate.

Basic Electronics

Basic Mathematics for Electronics

Nelson M. Cooke &
Herbert F. Adams
1942, 1960; 679 pp.

$10.95

from:
McGraw-Hill Book Co.
Princeton Road
Hightstown, N. J. 08520

Manchester Road
Manchester, Mo. 63062

8171 Redwood Highway
Novato, CA 94947

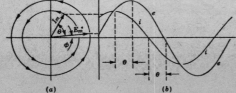

Fig. 32–8 Current i leads voltage e by phase angle of θ.

Electronics Page

Graphically illustrated and intelligently sequenced, the Basic Electricity *(vols. 1-5) and* Basic Electronics *(vols 1-6) sets from Rider are the easiest route from innocence to usefulness in electronics without an unnecessary load of math and physics. Good rudiments.*

If you plan to go very far with electronics, you will need heavier math. Basic Mathematics for Electronics *keeps matters practical.*

If you're already somewhat into electronics the Rider sets will insult you. A better route into deeper work is the well-regarded Elements of Radio.

For work with Silicon Controlled Rectifiers, the handiest device for controlling AC power to lights, motors, heaters, etc., get the comprehensive SCR Manual *from GE.*

A simple, non-technical, concrete, lucid, complete user's guide to hi-fi is High Fidelity Systems.

[*Evaluated by Marv Vickers, Fred Richardson, Les Rosen*]

Elements of Radio

Abraham Marcus and William Marcus
1965; 672 pp.

$10.40 postpaid from:
Prentice Hall
Englewood Cliffs, N. J. 07632

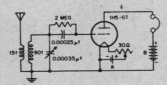

Fig. 15–14. *Diagram of the complete receiving set, using the triode as a detector. The symbol 2 MEG. over the grid leak stands for 2 megohms. The symbol 30 Ω over the rheostat stands for 30 ohms.*

Discrete transistors (where electronics was 10 years ago) are very easy to work with. It is far easier to get into construction and design with transistors than it ever was with tubes. No chassis, no heavy components to mount, no high voltage, power supply can be a battery, etc. Very cheap, too. Trying to work with "state of the art" components (wherever that is now) is very expensive, parts are difficult to get and information is often unreliable.

—Fred Richardson

SCR Manual

F. W. Gutzwiller, ed.
1967; 513 pp.

$3.00 postpaid

from:
General Electric Company
Dept. B.
3800 North Milwaukee Avenue
Chicago, Illinois 60641

High Fidelity Systems

Roy F. Allison
1962, 1965; 91 pp.

No longer available

from:
Dover Publications, Inc.
180 Varick Street
New York, N. Y. 10014

or WHOLE EARTH CATALOG

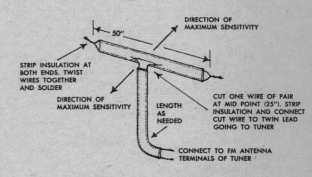

How to make a simple FM antenna which is very effective in favorable receiving locations.

Still simpler, and satisfactory in favorable reception areas, is the twin-lead antenna shown in the diagram. This can be stapled inside a closet, on the back of a cabinet holding high-fidelity equipment, along a baseboard moulding, or in any convenient location so long as it isn't very close to large bodies of metal.

One final note on hum: don't overlook the possibility that it may be mechanical noise. The power transformer of an amplifier can buzz at a hum frequency if the mounting bolts or the windings aren't tight. Cures include tightening the mounting bolts and shock-mounting the amplifier on a soft pad. Leave holes for ventilation, of course.

Acoustic feedback usually can be cured (or at least reduced to insignificance) by improving the shock mounts under the turntable. Putting the speakers on thick pads of foam rubber may help also, particularly if they rest on the floor. In some severe cases you may have no alternative to increasing the distance between the turntable and speakers.

High Fidelity Systems

D.R. saw that he was dying as soon as they went outside. They shouldn't have even tried it but the pulse was quickening now, Emmit wanted to go. He wanted to show D.R. how little there was left of what there used to be, and how many new things he had started.

Ten

Ten feet from the porch steps Emmit shook his head and said he couldn't go any further. His breath was failing. Half falling he turned and went back and sat down on the bottom step and then leaned back against the steps above, fighting for his breath.

ABC's of Short Wave Listening

I started listening to short wave when I was twelve on an old (1937) Crosley shortwave console radio I bought from Honest Ben's for $5. I replaced a few tubes and then learned to count seconds listening to WWV.

You can receive much more than the WWV time signal. Voice of America. Radio Swan. Etc. (See p. 127, Popular Science) It is fun and can be very informative.

This book is a very basic introduction to short wave. You <u>can</u> spend a lot of money on a good receiver. Or make do with an old console. Depends on what you want.

[Reviewed by Fred Richardson]

ABC's of Short-Wave Listening
Len Buckwalter
1962; 96 pp.

$2.95 postpaid

from:
Howard W. Sams & Co., Inc.
4300 W. 62nd St.
Box 558
Indianapolis, Indiana 46206

or WHOLE EARTH CATALOG

As the major piece of equipment in the hobby of shortwave listening, the receiver must convert the minute energy of a radio wave into an audible signal. How well a receiver can do this is mostly a measure of its sensitivity and selectivity. The first quality, *sensitivity*, is the ability to separate a signal from the ever present noise level created by disturbances in the atmosphere and outer space.

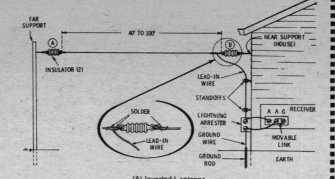

(A) Inverted-L antenna.

Table 2-1. The Radio Spectrum

Major Divisions	Frequency Ranges
VLF = Very Low Frequency	10 kHz to 30 kHz
LF = Low Frequency	30 kHz to 300 kHz
MF = Medium Frequency	300 kHz to 3000 kHz
HF* = High Frequency	3 MHz to 30 MHz
VHF = Very High Frequency	30 MHz to 300 MHz
UHF = Ultrahigh Frequency	300 MHz to 3000 MHz
SHF = Superhigh Frequency	3 GHz to 30 GHz
EHF = Extremely High Frequency	30 GHz to 300 GHz

* Most SW listening is done in this part of the spectrum.

Selectivity describes how well the receiver can pick out a signal in a crowded frequency band. It is mainly by these two qualities that a short-wave receiver may be judged. A multitude of features may appear in a given set, but these are usually concerned with operating convenience rather than operating quality.

The Radio Amateur's Handbook

10 The Radio Amateur's Handbook

10a This has been the pracitcal guide for radio amateurs for 43 years. It begins with the fundamentals of electric circuits and follows a simple development of the radio theory necessary to understand communications. There is brief section on laws governing amateurs and references to other books that are valuable aids in obtaining a license.

10b Throughout the book actual circuits are shown, always with enough information to build them. Later sections cover complete construction details for various transmitters and receivers but don't be misled by their apparant simplicity. It takes a lot of time and know-how to make these things work and unless circuit building is your thing you are better off to buy commercial equipment or kits. (Heathkit is one of the best sources for ham gear.)

The review to the left was prepared and printed on a computer by Bill English—as you can see, the fluidity of computer interaction makes spelling more casual than with direct hard print.

The Radio Amateur's Handbook may be of interest to the communities and enclaves who've been fantasizing an underground radio net. Like a night of the week or month when all the world's long-hairs are on the air, vibing to each other and the stars.
—SB

[Reviewed by Bill English. Suggested by Arthur Brand]

The Radio Amateur's Handbook
American Radio Relay League
1925 . . . 1974; 704 pp.

$4.50 postpaid

$5.00 Canada, $6.00 elsewhere

from:
The American Radio Relay League
Newington, Conn. 06111

Electronics

For technical freaks. If you are a double e ENGINEER, the articles may be of interest. Otherwise, spend your time with the ads. Learn about all the new hardware and bits and pieces. Reader service card whereby all of the advertisers will send you piles of shit on their products. Electronics Buyers' Guide is offered to U.S. and Canada subscribers if they fill out a questionnaire sent out each year.

Don't forget your title and company name. Get a subscription blank from one at the library and have no trouble.

[Reviewed by Fred Richardson]

Electronics

$9.00 a year, biweekly

from:
Electronics
P.O. Box 514
Hightstown, N.J. 08520
Subscription department

Subscriptions limited to persons with active, professional, functional responsibility in electronics technology. Publisher reserves the right to reject non-qualified requests. No subscriptions accepted without complete identification of subscriber name, title or job function, company or organization, including product manufactured or services performed. Subscription rates: qualified subscribers in the United States and possessions and Canada, $9.00 one year, $18.00 three years; all other countries $25.00 per year. Limited quota of subscriptions available at higher-than-basic rate for persons outside of field served, as follows: U.S. and possessions and Canada, $25.00 one year; all other countries $50.00. Air freight service to Japan $50.00 one year, including prepaid postage. Single copies: United States and possessions in Canada, $1.00; all other countries, $1.75.

Radio

In the March $1 *Catalog* you were wondering about how to fit electronics into your catalog better. It seems to me that electronics equipment is relevant to the very important business of communicating with one another. Radios, transceivers, hydrophones, ultrasonic translators, and tape recorders certainly are significant tools. However one of the most important communication tools, (in my opinoin) is a shortwave receiver. Listening is the beginning of all communication. With even the humblest short-wave receivers one can tune in many different nations all around the globe. Americans have neglected shortwave radio but the rest of the world (mainly other governments) is broadcasting it's opinions, viewpoints, philosophies, music, literature and drama for anyone to examine. It is free to anyone with a shortwave radio.

The simplest way to start listening is to turn on any shortwave-ready radio you have. Reception is better if you attach a long antenna and a good ground. Reception is also better after dark. You may have a good shortwave receiver in your attic or a $5 to $25 Salvation Army Store radio will serve. Almost anything made after 1932 is liable to work well . Of course if you have more money a store-bought receiver or kit would be a fine tool. I hope some of your correspondents will be reviewing receivers and listening guides.

Besides ham radio it seems to me that souls interested in underground (and aboveground) radio and tv ought to check the radio & tv trade journals for the names of brokers in used broadcast equipment. With the introduction of color tv, multiplex fm and transistors a lot of good equipment has been obsoleted. Presently much of this stuff is sold to less affluent parties overseas. Also since many police and fire departments have changed from broadcasting on 1700 kc. (which is just on one edge of the broadcast band) to vhf and uhf bands I'd bet that there is some modest power gear on the market that would be fine for am broadcasting with merely a new crystal (like $10 and a tune up.

Lee McKusick
Chimayo, N.M.

Get Your Ham Ticket

Okay, why push for all the whole earth types to get their tickets?

A) *When this country falls apart, all that portable equipment and practical electronics knowledge and all those established nets are going to be <u>the</u> tools to stay alive and coordinate with your friends.*

B) *Intelligent roundtable discussion is not only possible but enjoyable, mainly because if someone is an obnoxious bastard you can tell him so politely or go off on some other frequency and start another roundtable.*

C) *Organized amateur radio gets information spread <u>fast</u>. It doesn't matter what the information is or how far it has to go, witness Alaska hams during the big earthquake a few years ago and the more recent and controversial National Student Information Net.*

D) *Ever see a ham tv roundtable?*

Why don't more freaks and street people become hams? I think that most do not see amateur radio as the subtle tool that it is. The skills and discipline of radio in the telephone age are somewhat like the skills and discipline of the photographer who shoots 4 x 5 black and white in the Instamatic age. The price of versatility is knowledge and time.

The whopper in this whole discussion, though, is the relatively unknown but potentially enormously beneficial use of amateur repeaters. See the April 1971 issue of 73 , which lists six in the Bay area alone. With repeaters, ten watts of rf and a good antenna pointed at the repeater itself will get your signal out over the entire Bay, Los Angeles area, Chicago area, the entire state of New Mexico, most of Mass, N.H., and Vt, or coverage in most of the sizeable cities in the U.S. One at a time, of course. Repeaters are relatively easy to license in most parts of the country, but require a lot of groundwork and a good, high antenna site. Also a couple thousand dollars unless you are the scrounger supreme.

Last summer I listened to the prime Chicago repeater for a couple days and heard fixed stations over the Wisconsin border and out more than thirty miles to the south chatting with a mobile unit watching the planes take off at O'Hare and a woman walking near the loop with a walkie-talkie. I understand that one can now drive through the northeast and scarcely ever be out of range of at least one machine. Mind you that all this is taking place more or less line-of-sight on frequencies tucked between the fm broadcast band and tv channel 7.

I'll QSO any of you after my part of the war is over.

Wes Plouff WA8CBN
Eielson AFB, Alaska

Sex and Broadcasting: A Handbook on Starting Community Stations
Lorenzo W. Milam
1972; 40 pp.

$2.00 postpaid   plus $.15 postage

from:
Dildo Press—KTAO
5 University Avenue
Los Gatos, California 95030

or WHOLE EARTH CATALOG

I could spend pages, hours, days, telling you about how to fill out Form 340 (from the FCC). But since you and I are always involved in learning processes, let us look on this as such an experience. Fill it out to the best of your ability, show it to your lawyer— assuming you have one— or send a rough draft to me. I will help you out as much as I can if I am convinced that you truly want to set up a community oriented free form free forum listener volunteer station. If not: I can't help you. For I love broadcasting and radio too much to give free time and assistance to someone who will use a broadcast outlet as a stamping ground for some misshapen single-cell personality.

Heathkit

Between readymade and total do-it-yourself is Heathkit. Assembling yourself saves 25-40%, plus education, minus time. It's good electronic equipment of wide variety: color TV (14", $299.95), guitar amplifier (120 watt, $179.95), excellent AR-15 stereo tuner ($199.95), 5" oscilloscope ($119.95), CB 5 watt transreceiver ($89.95), portable short-wave receiver ($129.95), organ ($995.00), microwave oven kit ($379.95).

Heathkit Catalog
1974; 115 pp.

free

from:
Heath Company
Benton Harbor, Mich. 49022

Stout heart of the finest stereo systems: Heathkit AR-1500 Stereo Receiver $379.95 $649.95 wired

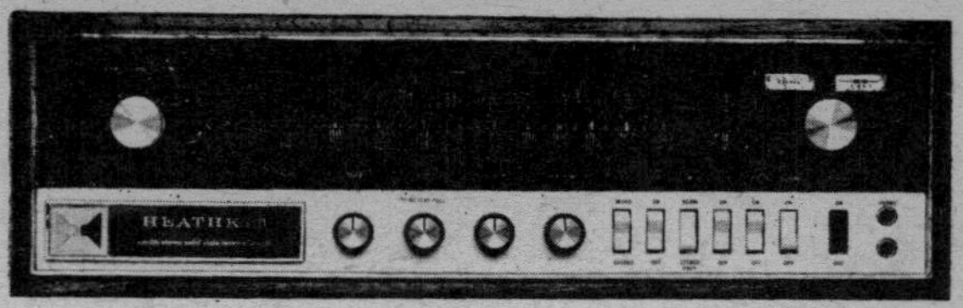

Famous Low-Cost "Benton Harbor Lunch Boxes" Compact 6 & 2 Meter Transceivers

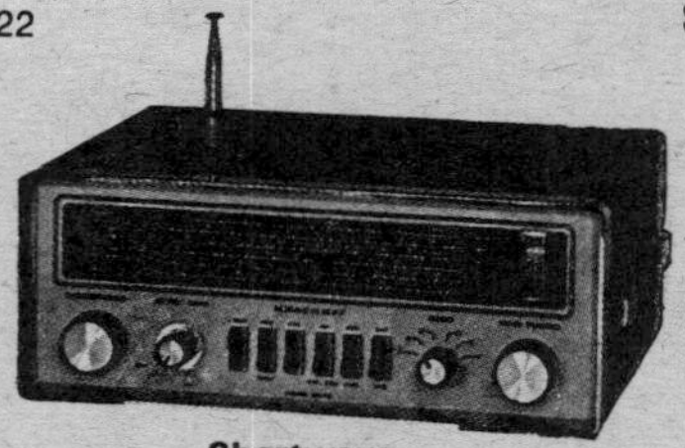

Shortwave

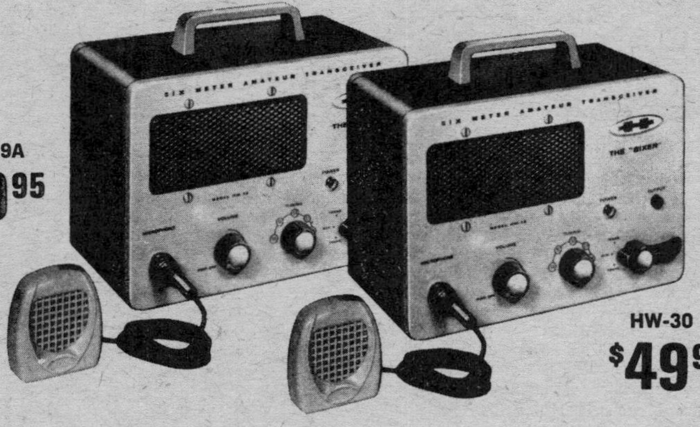
HW-29A
$49.95
HW-30
$49.95

• Perfect for the ham-on-the-go • Ideal for CAP, MARS, local net, or emergency operations • 5-watt input crystal-controlled A.M. transmitter • HW-30 2-meter model capable of operation on new USCG Auxiliary frequency 143.28 MHz

GO VHF FOR LESS . . . complete tranceivers, lunch-box size. Feature crystal controlled transmitter with straight-through final amplifier. Crystals (not supplied) are in the 8 MHz range. Receiver is super-regenerative with RF stage . . . features 1 uv sensitivity! The built-in 120 VAC power supply, speaker, press-to-talk switch on front panel, and ceramic mike included make these units ready to go on the air with your antenna. Power cables for mobile and A.C. operation are included.

Kit HW-29A (6 meter), 9 lbs., no money dn., ... **$49.95**
Kit HW-30 (2 meter), 9 lbs., no money dn., ... **$49.95**

Radio Shack

After considerable mail and discussion by CATALOG users, it seems clear that Allied (now merged with Radio Shack) is the best mail order source for electronic gear. They also print an industrial electronic catalog that is particularly rich in components, (especially noteworthy integrated circuit components). Plug in, link up, dis-corporate.

—SB

Radio Shack Catalog

or

Allied Industrial Electronics Catalog

$1.00

from:
Allied Electronics
2400 W. Washington Blvd.
Chicago, IL 60612

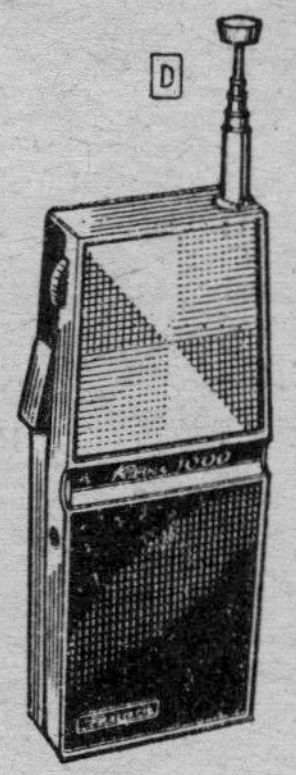
D

D 21-112 ONE-WATT ONE-CHANNEL WALKIE-TALKIE
Long-range power at a rock-bottom low price. The "Rover" has all solid-state circuit with extra-sensitive RF amplifier stage to really pull in signals. Volume control and push-to-talk switch. Slim design with rugged die-cast front. Perfect for sportsmen, yachtsmen, farmers or anyone who needs long range capability. Has 59" chromed telescoping antenna. Complete with 8 "AA" penlight cells, plug-in Channel 11 crystals and instructions, and $4.95 value carrying case. Size, 7½x3¼x1½". 910-0067. Shpg. wt. 5½ lbs. . . . .

NO LONGER AVAILABLE

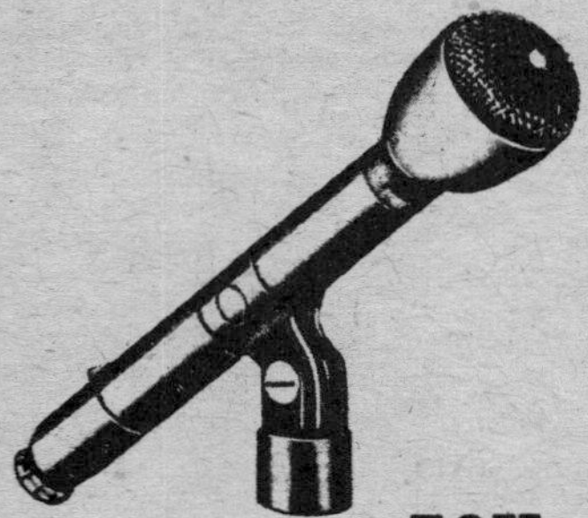

58.75 Model 635A

Performer's dynamic Mike

Model 635A. Widely-accepted professional omnidirectional mike for hand or stand use. Four-stage pop and blast filter eliminates need for external windscreen. Smooth shaped frequency response: 80-13,000 Hz Low impedance. Output: −55 dB. Magnetically shielded diaphragm, turned-steel case. Cannon XLR-3-11 connectors. Non-reflecting nickel finish. 6x1⅜" diameter. With 18" three-conductor cable and convenient stand adaptor. Shpg. wt. 1 lb.

NO LONGER AVAILABLE

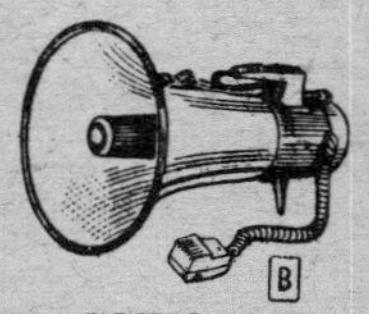
B

ELECTRO-VOICE

B 16-WATT PORTABLE MEGAPHONE
ELECTRO-VOICE PM16EAC. Battery-powered portable megaphone provides 16-watt peak power (10-watt continuous) output to cover a range of 650 yards. Has external noise-cancelling mike with on-off switch, volume control, coiled cord. Built-in siren alarm tone. Bell diameter, 11½". With shoulder strap. Operates on 8 ordinary flashlight "C" batteries.
781 X0020.

NO LONGER AVAILABLE

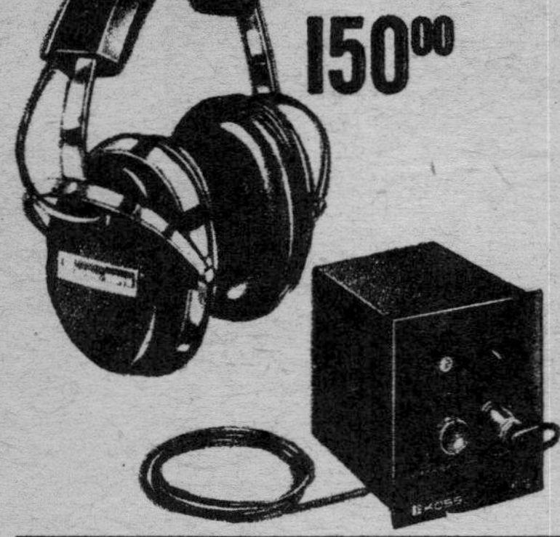

Ten octaves of sound!

150.00

Electrostatic Headphones give widest response

Model ESP-9. World's only self-energized electrostatic headphones. Give depth and breadth of sound for stereo at its best. You get the perfection of the original studio recording with no room acoustics problems. Electrostatic driver elements provide unbelievable response far beyond the limits of ordinary voice coils and cone-type driver elements. From 15-15,000 Hz, response is an amazing flat ±2 dB (full 10 octaves). Total response is a remarkable 10-47,000 Hz.

Special push-pull acoustical circuitry virtually ends distortion to give the clean sparkling sound of a live performance. Harmonic distortion is less than 0.2% at 110 dB SPL. No special amplifier or power supply needed. Separate energizer offers option of self-energizing for bias supply, or energizing through AC line. When energized through AC line precise level measurements can be made, in tape mastering machines and recording consoles for example. Energizer has speaker/headphone switch, on-off switch and AC pilot light.

Fluid-filled earcushions and lightweight design (only 19 ounces) let you listen in comfort for hours. Full 12-watt power capacity. Impedance, 4-16 ohms. With 6'4" conductor input cable that connects to amplifier output terminals. Energizer size, 4⅛x3¾x6¼".
33 B 6515. Shpg. wt. 8 lbs. . . . .

NO LONGER AVAILABLE

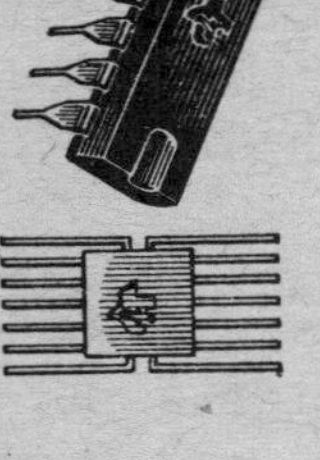

Newark Electronics

If you are at all a serious buyer of electronic parts and equipment, industrial catalogs should be much more appealing to you than the standard consumer catalogs. Industrial catalogs dwell mostly on the facts rather than promotions. Each item gets its share of space, and no more. And of course the variety is extremely broader. When building your own projects, it makes a lot more sense to use a large, factual catalog full of components rather than the typical consumer catalog. Newark's catalog fills the bill well. Don't let the word "industrial" scare you. They're prepared to handle the same kind of mail orders as the firms whose catalogs fill their first 200 pages with color photos of hi-fi equipment (one item per page) and use most of the descriptive text for promotional purposes. Newark lets the facts sell you.

[Suggested and reviewed by David Marston]

Newark Electronics Corp.
500 North Pulaski Road
Chicago, Illinois 60624

Edlie's Flyer

Beginners in electronics who don't want to be stuck with very beautiful but very unusable gadgets (and also experts who know what's-used-for-what) can get a lot of value from industrial (civilian) surplus electronics, these days.

For the "consumer" uses of electronics—music, p.a., TV, repair parts and instruments, experimenting—Edlie Electronics has the best selection and the lowest prices of any mail-order dealer I have found.

They handle everything from hi-fi components (e.g., an FM tuner from a discontinued console) to single resistors. Some of it is new, and some of it is sold "as is" (e.g. small radios and tape recorders returned to the store under a warranty.)

If you don't feel safe about repair work or experiments, though, better concentrate on getting electronic stuff with a dependable guarantee, maybe by buying from a repair shop.

[Suggested and Reviewed by John Huntley]

Edlie's Flyer Catalog

free

from:
Edlie Electronics, Inc.
2700 Hempstead Turnpike
Levittown, Long Island,
New York 11756

11 Tektronix

11a Textronix has become the electronics industry standard for oscilloscopes. They are consistantly ahead of the competition and their attention to "user" features in functions and control design make the instruments a joy to use. This catalog includes the complete line of scopes and of their other test equipment, particularly pulse generators and amplifiers, all solidly designed.

11b The equipment is expensive - $735 for the cheapest scope - but well worth its price.

[Reviewed by Bill English. Suggested by Mike Brand]

Tektronix Catalog
1971; 432 pp.

from:
Tektronix, Inc.
P. O. Box 500
Beaverton, Ore. 97005

(see p. 346)

TYPE 321A OSCILLOSCOPE, without batteries $1045

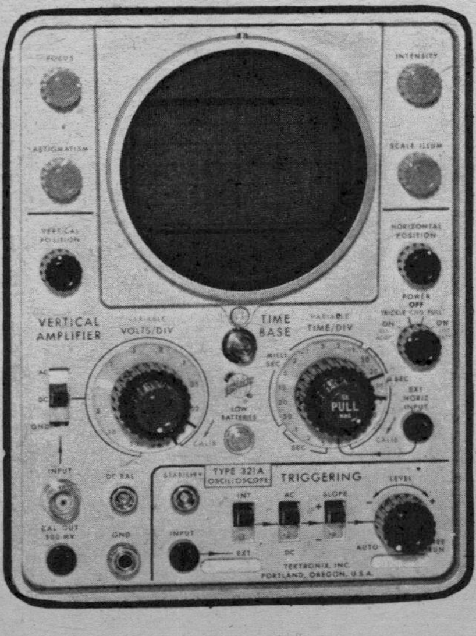

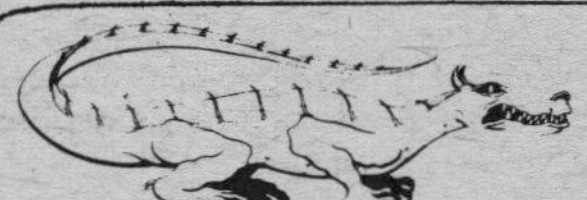

•

Right there in front of D.R.'s eyes

•

Emmit was actually dying.

•

D.R. started to ask Emmit what he should do but Emmit waved his hand and shook his head. He knew what D.R. was about to say and he didn't want to

•

hear it

•

hear what? What old voice, old time

•

For sure, Emmit didn't want the boy to say anything he would have to answer, for he was barely breathing now, working hard for every little bit of air he got.

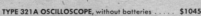

John Holt on Hi Fi

Don't know whether the Catalogue is much into the Hi-Fidelity sound business. Hi-Fidelity is an imprecise term. It is a spectrum. But the smallest and least expensive speaker that seems to me to be entitled to call itself hi-fidelity is the new Dynaco. It is really quite extraordinary. I made A-B tests of it against a KLH—6, a very fine speaker, and though in some respects the 6 was better, deeper bass, somewhat more fullness——in other respects, I felt the Dynaco was quite definitely superior. In really dense textured material, large orchestral and choral passages, the sound is somewhat better defined. Anyway, it is a fine piece of work——list price $80, discounts for less than that at some places in the east.

Some of the best European tape recorders can be bought much more cheaply from a London firm called C. C. Goodwin, Ltd., 7, The Broadway, Wood Green, London N22, England. The new Tandberg 1600X tape deck which sells here for $250, they sell for $172. To that you would have to ad cost of shipping and some duty, but the total would not be as high as $200, which is a useful saving.

Feeling rich these days. Bought a couple of Rectilinear X speakers. Tastes differ in these matters, but I haven't heard anything I like better at *any* price.

A portable tape recorder is a very good gadget for school. CONSUMER REPORTS recently recommended one from Sears. I bought one and have tried it out and it seems to work very well. Good sound quality.

An English audio outfit called Sinclair makes a little stereo amplifier called the Neoteric 60 Mark MK II. An outfit called Audio T, 16 RR, Dryden Chambers, 119 Oxford St., London W1, England, sells it for 46 pounds, which with shipping and duty it all comes to about $125.00. I took it to one of our best local hi-fi places, and they were ecstatic about it. Not only is there nothing of comparable power and quality at that price in this country, but the little gadget is so tiny you can hardly believe it. A really elegant piece of gear. The manufacturers say it has 20 watts per channel, but this is *extremely conservative*.

Best,

John Holt
Boston, Mass.

Hi-Fi Tips

Read John Holt's hi-fi letter, and concur with his rave review of the Dynaco speaker. After about 13 years as a hi-fi buff, the last 8 of them writing about the field professionally, Dyna is one of those companies whose new products I tend to trust before I see them, but in the speaker, they've surpassed themselves.

Dyna also has discovered that a good step towards the effect of a four-channel system can be achieved with existing stereo recordings and broadcasts, using only one extra speaker. Connect it across the hot leads of both stereo channels, and any instrument that was recorded out of phase in the two normal channels comes out loud and clear from this 3rd speaker (which should be in the back of the room). Other than that, stay clear of four-channel for at least 6 months, until the smoke clears. There will be lots of pseudo-quad gadgetry and some good stuff coming out in a batch between now and Fall.

The Rectilinear X John Holt mentions has been replaced by the Xa, which Rectilinear (friends of mine) say is better, as does the guy who writes their ads, and uses them at home. There seems to be some opinion that the X (and Xa) beat the more expensive Rectilinear III; I haven't directly compared them, so can't confirm, but all 3 Rectilinears sound fine to me, and I prefer the RIII to the AR-3a for most (not all) material — especially prefer RIII for piano, but AR-3a for most pop.

If I were recommending a cheap component system right now, my choice would be:

Dual 1212 changer or AR turntable.
Grado FTR ($10) cartridge — Shure M91E, if you want to spend lots more. (Also, listen to the Pickerings — I don't know how well they sound from personal experience, but the dust-brush feature is nice for people who don't clean records much)
Sony ST-5600 tuner
Sony TA-1100 amp (may be prejudiced — had them in the house while I wrote ads about them for Sony — but they seemed very good for the money: $120 each)
Dynaco A25 speakers.

Watch for Dolby-ized tape and cassette equipment later this year — it lets you get good quality on recordings you make at slower speeds (saving tape); KLH $225 tape recorder has it now, others to follow, especially in cassette. Doesn't do anything for pre-recorded tapes, though.

Roy Allison's hi-fi book from Dover publications (sugg. by Fred) is best practical guide I know; Ed Villchur's companion volume (also Dover p.b.) is best, most lucid, most accurate guide to hi-fi theory.

Ivan Berger
New York, N.Y.

P.S.: Other companies I take on faith: AR, Shure, KLH (at least, until many of their top brains went out and started Advent — now I wait and see on both companies).

P.P.S.: AR speakers sound very bass-y when sitting on the floor. If you don't like that, they make a good, cheap speaker stand — or raise your speaker on a crate (good for other speakers, too, with the same problem).

Glyph

A big tough speaker, like a diesel truck, and tone as nice as you please. Built weatherproof. Easy to ship. The first loud sound I've heard that didn't make me want to run. I wanted to stay and shake.

—SB

MN50 w/M Driver **$800.00**

Glyph Sound Systems
Berkeley, CA
(415) 524-3656

How to Build Speaker Enclosures

In order to get the best response from a speaker, the enclosure needs to be carefully designed and engineered to match the speaker being used.

If you have some knowledge and skill in cabinet construction, you should be able to use this book to build excellent speaker enclosures. It doesn't tell you how to put them together, but it does tell you how to calculate size, design baffles, and properly brace the cabinet to keep it from vibrating.

Not for the novice carpenter.

[Reviewed by Fred Richardson. Suggested by Michael Wells]

How to Build Speaker Enclosures
Alexis Badmaieff and Don Davis
1966; 144 pp.

$3.95 postpaid

from:
The Bobbs-Merrill Company, Inc.
4300 West 62nd Street
Indianapolis, Indiana 46206

or WHOLE EARTH CATALOG

Tandberg

Special price on Tandberg tape recorders. I bought my model 64 for $205 when Allied, Lafayette, etc., were quoting $495. If you buy three or more model 64's at one time, you get a $10 discount on each. But there will be freight and duty costs. Write for information to Klaus Lefdal/Co. A/S, Bekkestua Pro., Oslo, Norway. In spite of authorized U.S. dealerships, I beleive they will ship to the U.S. anyway. They also have good prices on AKG headsets. Thorens turntables, Leak amplifiers, BASF tape, and goodness-knows what else.

Pete Shermerhorn
Aruba
Netherlands Antilles

Preener

The best record cleaner is the Watts Preener.

—SB
[Suggested by Roger Knights and Jerry Minkoff]

$4.50

from:
Elpa Marketing Industries, Inc.
New Hyde Park, N.Y. 11040

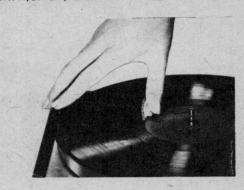

Audio Cyclopedia

The comprehensive all-purpose reference on audio everything.

—SB

Audio Cyclopedia
Howard M. Tremaine
1959, 1969; 1757 pp.

$29.95 postpaid ($35.95 ppd in Canada)

from:
Howard W. Sams & Co.
4300 West 62nd Street
Indianapolis, Indiana 46206

Dynaco Kits

Dynaco Inc. of 3060 Jefferson Street, Philadelphia, Pennsylvania 19121 manufactures a line of high quality and excellent value stereo equipment. Their equipment represents some of the best dollar value in the stereo field. They do not change models very often (almost never) which means that parts are always available and that their equipment has good resale value. They don't even change prices with inflation as does everyone else. Added bonus! All the Dynaco line of components is available as kits at substantial savings.

Dynaco kits are easy to assemble and all the critical work is done by Dynaco!. Their kits could more accurately be described as semi-kits as all the printed circuit boards are done by Dynaco and you just mount them and wire them in place. Dynaco has some of the easiest, plainest, clearest, most complete construction manuals to make sure that there is no problem in assembling their kits.

Dynaco doesn't sell and leave you on your own out in the cold, they also provide technical assistance and service for their equipment.

Ross Bernheim
Honolulu, Hawaii

Stereo Discounts

Did you recently pay full list price for stereo components or recording tape? If so, you got burned. Next time, a discount house can put a comfortable distance between you and the heat. Many discount houses advertise in *Stereo Review* and *HIgh Fidelity*, but I've narrowed the list to 6 that give the lowest prices--which doesn't mean, of course, that some more equally good ones may not spring up. These discount houses, by the way, are NOT clubs and don't charge membership fees, although there are such clubs dealing in stereo gear. To my knowledge, these clubs don't match the discounts of the discount houses. The 6 discount houses mentioned above are:

Downtown Audio
17 Warren Street
New York, NY 10007

Dixie Hi-Fidelity Wholesalers
5600 2nd St. NE
Washington. D.C. 20011

Hi-Fidelity Center
239 East 149 Street
Bronx, NY 10451

Boston Audio Co.
1 Discount Drive
Randolph, MA 02368

Rabsons 57 Street Inc.
119 West 57 Street
New York, NY 10019

Carston Studios
R.D. 3, Route 7
Brookfield, CT 06804

I've personally had satisfactory dealings with the first three. I haven't ordered from the others, but they offer equally low prices. Here as with any purchase, it pays to check each house's price on a given component. Some of available discounts follow:

Component	List Price	Discount Price
Dynaco SCA-80 amplifier, wired	$249.95	$165.00
Shure M44E cartridge	34 . 95	10.50
Superex ST-Pro–B headphones	49.95	32.00
Garrard 40B changer with base, dust cover, less cartridge	55.50	33.48
Harman-Kardon HK-50 speaker system	95.00	55.00
Watts Dust Bug	6.50	4.95

Certain brands of equipment are fair traded and theoretically can't be sold below list price, but you can sometimes get around this by ordering a fair-traded component and a non-fair-traded component together. Discounts are even better on complete systems than on individual components.

In the market for a low-cost stereo cartridge tracking at 2 to 3½ grams, such as the Shure M44-7, ADC 220X, Pickering P/AT, or Empire 909/X? Forget them--you want the Grado FTR at not $24,95, not $19.95, but $9.95 from Grado Laboratories, 4614 &th Avenue, Brooklyn, NY 11220. Or a discount house may have it for $5 to $7.

In Stereo' Review July 1969 survey of cartridges the FTR ramked a close third in sound quality behind the ADC 25 ($100) and the Elac STS-444-12 ($69.50), and ahead of cartridges costing up to $69.50 (to keep things in perspective, some of the more expensive cartridges tracked at lower forces than the FTR). Not having a pile of test equipment, I can only add that I've been using an FTR for a year and that it does what it's supposed to.

Other Grado cartridges are the FTE ($19.95 with elliptical stylus), FCR ($25), and FCE ($35 with elliptical stylus). According to Grado, the FC series cartridges are assembled more carefully than those of the FT series. However, I don't know of any test reports on them.

R. Andrews Buc
Clayton, Mo.

More Stereo Discount

One other house that offers significantly discounts on the material they do carry (they don't seem to have as big a stock as others is

Audio Sales
2745 Erie Blvd. East
Syracuse N.Y. 13224

I bought my own equipment from them $650 list. Cost me a little less than $400 including shipping.

One other note for thos who purchase tape

The Archer Av. Store
4193 Archer Ave.
Chicago, Ill. 60632

has the lowest prices for Sony tapes that we've been able to find in the country. Ex. 1800' 7" polyester PR-150-18 cost $2.79 a reel. In Phila. this costs 3.69 + 6% sales tax. They'll pay all postage on orders of $30. (That's just a doz. tapes--Get a group together) and on orders over 48 tapes offer another 5% discount if the tapes are in groups of a doz.; can be mixed as long as there's a doz. of each type. For a full list of prices just write them.

John F. Rakickas
Philadelphia, Pa.

Stereo Warehouse

Young discount crew. I'd get one of their component systems. Postpaid service to West Coast.

—SB

Stereo Warehouse
151 Casa St.
San Luis Obispo, CA 93401

"OUR CHOICE"   (System #1)

$229.95

The best medium priced system we have been able to offer

Nikko STA 301 am/fm receiver. Solid 40 watts of power into 8 ohms, with audio linear integrated circuits, FET front end, direct tape monitoring, contour control switch, 3 circuit breaker protection, tuning meters, and more.

	Regular Price
Nikko Nikko STA 301 am/fm receiver *Solid 40 watts of power into 8 ohms, with audio linear integrated circuits, FET front end, direct tape monitoring, contour control switch, 3 circuit breaker protection, tuning meters, and more.*	$159.95
Garrard 40B. Most popular model in the Garrard line. Using the famous 4-pole induction motor, and large balanced platter. 4-speed, automatic record changer with viscous cueing, and low mass calibrated tracking tone arm— for fine cartridges. Comes with oiled walnut base.	$ 44.50
Grado Magnetic Cartridge	$ 35.50 (base + cart.)
Jordan 830 Speakers. Excellent 8 in two-way speaker system. Smooth-extended fidelity, with good bass response. System is efficient, yet will handle considerable power. 8 in. woofer and 3 in. high frequency driver in beautiful oiled walnut cabinet. Approximate size is 18 in x 10 in x 9 in deep.	$119.00 (pair)
Total regular price of this stereo system is	$358.95

With the Stereo Warehouse we offer very good name brand components at super low prices. We have tried to eliminate all the disadvantages of buying through correspondence as all shipping and insurance charges are prepaid and we break our asses to ship within two days of the order. All products are factory sealed and carry the full warranty, we even supply all the necessary wire to make setting up the equipment simple and quick.

Most important of all WE CARE.

Peace

Tom Spalding
Stereo Warehouse

---

db

For those interested in audio in either a professional or semi-professional way the best source of information on the state of the art is a magazine called "db—the Sound Engineering Magazine." This is not to be confused with the so called "consumer" hi-fi books. It is strictly devoted to the recording engineer, broadcast engineer, audio-visual, theatre sound, commercial sound type of person. It contains a wealth of design, operational and trade info that just cannot be found elsewhere. If you want to know how to install a sound system in an airport, or how to operate a recording console, or are worried about sound levels effecting rock musicians hearing, or any number of purely audio oriented subjects, then db is for you.

I have spoken to the editor of db who informs me that subs are $6.00/yr in the US and $11/yr elsewhere. Sample copies are available upon request.

Hope you can use this material. Thanks very much.

[Suggested and reviewed by Fred Hahn]

db
980 Old Country Rd.
Plainview, N.Y. 11803

King Karol Records

This looks like the best mail order source of records. They send you a comprehensive Schwann catalog to order from. Fairish discounts, postage paid. They also carry pre-recorded and blank tapes, cartridges, and cassettes. Now the question is how quick and reliable are they?

—SB

[Suggested by Lloyd Martin]

Catalog

free

from:
King Karol Records
P. O. Box 629
Times Square Station
New York, N. Y. 10036

ALL ORDERS IN THE U.S.A. A.P.O. AND F.P.O. ORDERS **FREE** OF MAILING AND HANDLING CHARGES (Add 15% for all other Foreign handling and mailing—minimum charge $1.50)

SCHWANN CATALOG MAILED FREE ON REQUEST

Schwann Catalog List Prices	Your Discount Price	Schwann Catalog List Prices	Your Discount Price
$1.98	$1.55	$3.98	$2.75
2.50	1.85	4.98	3.35
2.98	2.20	5.98	4.15
		6.98	4.65

PLEASE NOTE: N. Y. RESIDENTS ADD TO THE ABOVE PRICES THE NEW YORK CITY OR STATE SALES TAX

D.R. lay his uncle down and helped him stretch out on his back. He started to take his shoes off for him but Emmit pulled his feet away. He didn't want to be fooled with.

•

Leave me alone.

•

I'll be okay, just let me catch my breath, he said. He reached for the sheet and quilt and pulled them over his shoulders and closed his eyes and sank into the pillow, and D.R. took off running.

•

Running, down the path below the house, through some half-dead trees. Downhill he ran this time, past blasted rock and broken trees and piles of rusted trash along the ruined roadside.

•

Past what was left of people living there and

•

mining

•

old hulks of cars and shells of houses,

•

past the fallen tipple he had hidden under

•

past the door of one old house whose mouth said what's the hurry,

•

Down Trace Fork all the way across the bridge

•

and there he was again, pounding on the store door. And who should answer

•

Who should answer but Mrs. Godsey, her Bible in her hand, all smiling, glad to see him, then frightened by his story.

•

And Leonard came a running.

•

He wheezed and strained and bit for air and tried to ass himself up the steps, the second,

•

third

•

Moving and breathing a little now, some air was coming in.

•

D.R. put his arm around his uncle's waist and pulled Emmit's arm around his neck and half-carried him up the steps across the porch and to the bedroom. That one, Emmit said.

•

That one, over there. The bed D.R. just got out of. They were changing places, passing one another, going opposite ways, and the pulse of things was clicking right along.

Making It With Rock

This article appeared April 4, 1969 in the Berkeley Barb.

We tried by letter and phone to get hold of the author Ed Denson to see if it was all right to reprint his piece but we couldn't find him. The article's good enough we'll just have to pirate it through and hope it's OK. What I really hope is that it's part of a forthcoming book on music entrepreneuring; we'd CATALOG that in a minute. —SB

by ED Denson

BERKELEY BARB
2042 University Ave.
Berkeley, Calif. 94704

25¢ Bay Area
$6.00 a year, published weekly
$10.00 a year elsewhere

(Editor's Note: ED Denson manages Country Joe and the Fish, and The Crabs, and other Rock bands.)

I - the band

First, of course, you'll need a band. There are over 100,000 rock bands in the United States at any given moment, or at least that's the number which participated in a national Battle of the Bands series last year. Not 1000 are making a living, so you should be a little careful when you pick yours.

More realistically, if you are interested in managing a band, probably you already have one. Deciding to be a manager is not a result of a serious conversation with your high school counselor, it's an accident like picking up the girl who is to become your wife. Probably you are sitting around one day with a bunch of your friends who are musicians and complaining. You inadvertantly mention that Atrium Burlaping and the Watercrossers are making $200 a night somewhere else, and zap, you're a manager. In that case you'll want to read this to decide whether to keep going or to forget it.

Let's start at the beginning: you as manager want a band which will do three things--make good music, make good money, and stay together for three years. These three things follow from the nature of the business you and the band are in.

Now at this point I should explain something before some nitwit begins to say "Oh wow man, music is not a business it's too beautiful", and that is this: if your band is not a business it does not need a manager. Anyone can play the guitar in his room without a manager, and when he gets tired of that he can go out into the park and play without a manager. Not everyone knows this, and it is the cause of a great deal of wasted time and energy.

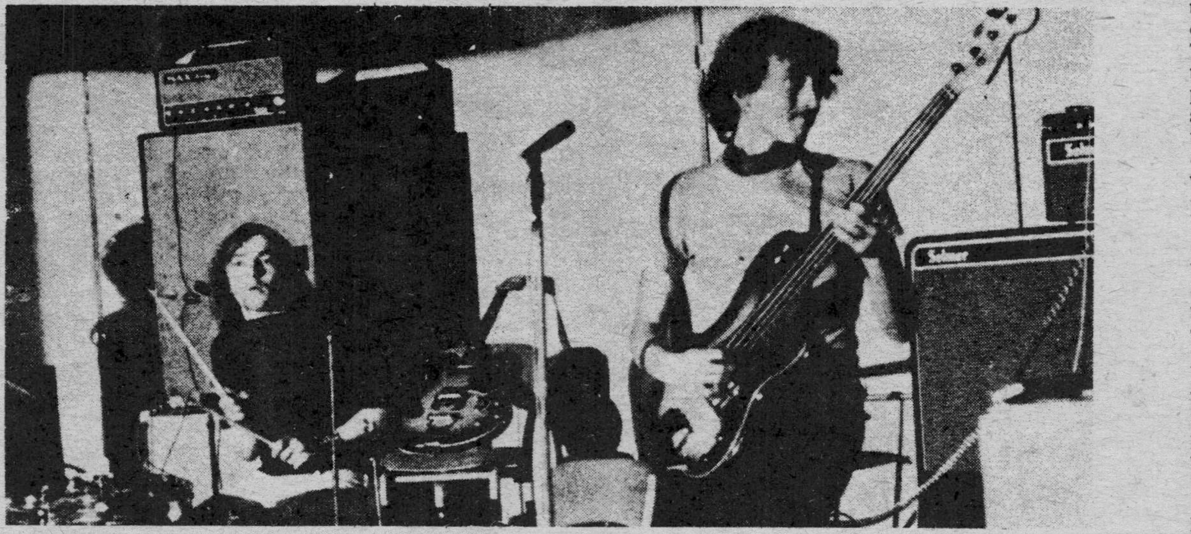

No matter what your band says to you about business, they are hiring you to make them money, and fame, and glory, and one day they are going to ask you where it is.

Now to amplify those three things which you want your band to do:

1. MAKE GOOD MUSIC: you, a human being, are a valuable person and your time is worth spending in such a way that you won't think it wasted later. If your band is not making music which you think is good, or as we say in the trade, promising, forget it. Even if you think they'll make a million, but their music is not your bag, forget it. No one is so lame as a manager who can say "It's just a business with me, like selling cars or canned peas." No one. And no one can do less for a band than a manager who feels that way. We Americans, due to a peculiar hangover from Protestant religion, believe in the back of our minds that sincerity is the touchstone of truth, and a manager who cannot sincerely say that his band is great cannot hope to get anyone to do anything for it.

Then too, no band is successful that does not make good music. But, you say, leaping to your feet in indignation, what about all those creepy straight bands with their press agent hpye and record company bullshit who are regularly crammed down the unknowing throats of the American public all of whom are idiots except me.

Forget it. There are certain delusions which you, as a member of the hip record buying public and brilliant critic of American taste, have been living with. You as a realistic hard-bitten business manager had better clean the garbage out of your head before you get going, or else your hangups will fuck up the lives of a number of people including yourself.

Try this one: Any band which successfully manages to become one of the really popular recording and performing groups in the country, does it by making good music, on well done records, giving exciting stage performances, and especially, by projecting values which their audience likes with some militance. You probably do not like their cultural values, which is not the same thing as their music being no good. However, a band, a guru, and a candidate for president all do the same thing and only those who are good at it make it.

But back to your band. Let's start with the basics. Is your band able to play in tune? And do they agree amongst themselves about rhythm? Most American bands can not both play in tune and together, and get really mad when someone points this out. If your band cannot do both it is going to take a great deal of luck, practice, and probably a couple of people fired to cure the problem. During that time nothing much can happen with their career, and they won't need you to hang around waiting.

Perhaps they can play in tune, together, and in public. Then we know they can make music, and now we wonder if they can make good music. Your taste is going to be the judge, but the question is not one that can be dodged with horseshit like "anything can be good music, it's all a question of taste." That's not true. If they are making good music, you can objectively show it.

First, there is the question of melodies, and chord and note choice. If there is someone in the band who is brillinat, and often there is, these things will be startling, and good. The band will be playing its own music, not anyone else's be it the Box Tops or Muddy Waters. If you want to work with musicians who are into playing other people's music, go work for the Symphony.

Are the songs any good? Do they make sense? Do they mean anything to you? Would you be impressed if someone walked up to you and said what these songs are saying?

Probably you don't know much about music. Probably you don't know enough to make final judgements about the questions I've just mentioned, and if you are listening to a band in a small club, probably you can't hear the music well enough to tell anyhow. To serve as a double check on your opinion, if you think that they are making good music but you are not certain, go watch them perform at a local club and see if the audience is reacting well to the performance.

Well, means applauding each number, and yelling sometimes, getting excited. If this is not occuring then the band is either not making good music, or not making good music well, or in the wrong club.

For your purposes as a manager, unless you are independently wealthy, it is necessary for your band to make music well in that the audience wants to SEE the band make that music. Major attractions have two things in common: they symbolize something important to the audience, and they put on a good show. That is ture of James Brown, that is true of the Budapest String Quartet. Perhaps your band does not want to be showmen, because that's all phoney and has nothing to do with great art. Don't let it worry you, they'll get out in the real world as soon as someone applauds them

2. MAKE GOOD MONEY: It is possible to make good music without making good money, but it is hardly possible to make good money without making good music. It is also possible to make good music, and to blow it all for non-musical reasons. This is dumb.

Making money for music is a business. Your band will be hired by people to put on a show, at a certain place at a certain time. If they don't get there on time, in a condition to play, with a put together performance, they will not get hired very often. If someone in your band is chronically late or doesn't show up for a bunch of reasons, he has to go. Or you do. Then, too, people who use a lot of acid, or juice it up, will not play well dependably. They shouldgo. Or you should. Even if they are nice guys, and you believe every human being has the god given right to take drugs and drink anything anytime they want.

We're not talking about right, we're talking about putting on a shitty performance and boring or bum-tripping the audience. If your band puts on poor performances because your brilliant drummer is out of his mind on something, the audiences who have paid money willnot like it. Free audiences will like it perhaps. But that is none of your business.

3. STAYING TOGETHER FOR THREE YEARS. May seem at the onset like a wierd thing to ask of a band--a thousand days and all that. But that's the life span of a band. It takes that long to get it together, work up the music, become known, and make a lot of money. Any shorter time is usually not really worth the effort on anyone's part.

Somethings cannot be foreseen or prevented, but most of the things that break a band up are already present when it forms, and can be avoided. Take the draft for instance: if your band has already shown a little initiative and gotten 4-Fs, fine. If not, then maybe 1-Ys. If neither, and they are 18-26, and 1-A you should check with them now and see if they have the guts to go thru the long legal hassle necessary to delay, or deter the draft board. The draft is illegal, and unpopular, but the government has the might to enforce it unless you are really determined. If your lead singer goes in at the height of his career without a fight, everyone else is fucked. If he is willing to fight, a three year delay is not unthinkable.

We've already gotten rid of the heavy heads, chronically unstable and really incompetent musicians by this time, if you recall, and the only other problem to be wary of is genius. Genius comes in two forms, brilliant workers and loud-mouthed assholes. Some of the more reputed musicians in this country presently are also loud-mouthed assholes who cannot work with other musicians past the first flush of seduction because they are just too brilliant to let anyone else take part in the creation. That is fine for their ego, but bad for your band.

From the onset everyone involved should realize that in the next three years some of the musicinas are going to receive public praise for being the brilliant men who are really making the band go, and the private advice to dump everyone else. If they are a little nuts in the start, they'll do something destructive, or flip out under the pressure. There's not a lot you can do about this except try to avoid such people Watch a couple of rehearsals and you'll know if they are present. Bon don't panic if someone there is doing most of the work, watch for ill humor.

* * * * * *

Now if you've got your band, and they are making good music well and are all ready to go out and make music for the millions, the next steop is to check your own head and be certain that you are capable of being a manager. You have no real way of knowing what you are getting into, any more than the band does at this point. All of you are babes in the woods, but there are few things you can predict.

You are going to have to work hard for three years, with few breaks and little respite. You will work more hours than your band, and you will have to be much more stable than the musicians. That's one part of your job--to be stable and to know what's happening when they forget. A good deal of money will be flowing thru your hands, and you should be able to account for it in some detail, which means you'll have to keep good records and be precise.

Moreover you are going to have to do business with a lot of people, talking about performances, equipment, recording contracts, booking agencies, etc., and usually you are not going to know what you are talking about. You have to recall that, while not letting it out. If you are one who believes that business consists of a lot of people with desks and good looking secretaries bullshitting each other and doing a lot of public relations, you are going to fail. The business you do will show up in a growing number of contracts passing across your desk and that will be based on facts. Facts like how many people came to see your band.

But the most disturbing, and dangerous aspect of management is that the band is never going to know what you are doing, or how well you are doing it. On the one hand you will be subject to their occasional paranoia, instability, incoherence, mistrust, and unless you are exceptionally fortunate, their almost complete lack of ethics. On the other hand you will receive considerable unearned praise, and in most of your business dealings with them you will have your own inexperienc and ethical state to contend with. You will do things which are dumb, and you may easily cheat everyone in sight for a few months. If you think you can work under those conditions, you're all set.

Electric Guitar Amplifier Handbook

For years my clearest image of impotence was the college student and the soft-drink machine: he has just watched his Pepsi flow by without benefit of the expected automatic cup, and he is kicking shit out of the machine. This image has gradually been replaced by the finer one of the rock musician and his audience of worshipful fans and his intermittent amp.

Avoid embarrassment, learn about the components of thy act. This is a remarkably adequate repair manual. —SB

[Suggested by Philemon Vanlangendonck]

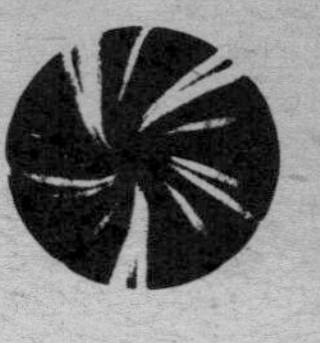

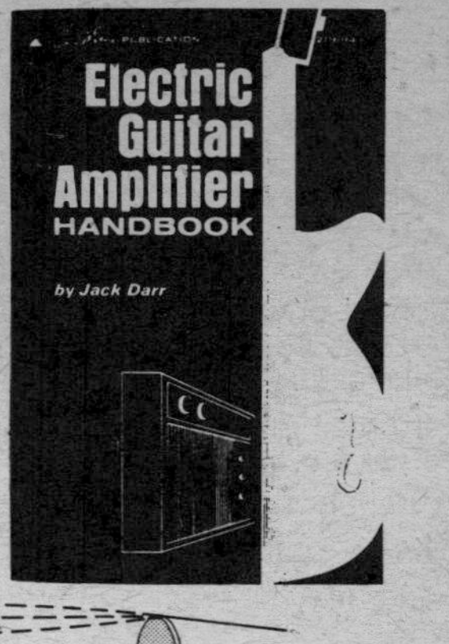

Electric Guitar Amplifier Handbook
Jack Darr
1965, 1968; 160 pp.

$6.95 postpaid

from:
The Bobbs-Merrill Company, Inc.
4300 West 62nd Street
Indianapolis, Indiana 46206

or WHOLE EARTH CATALOG

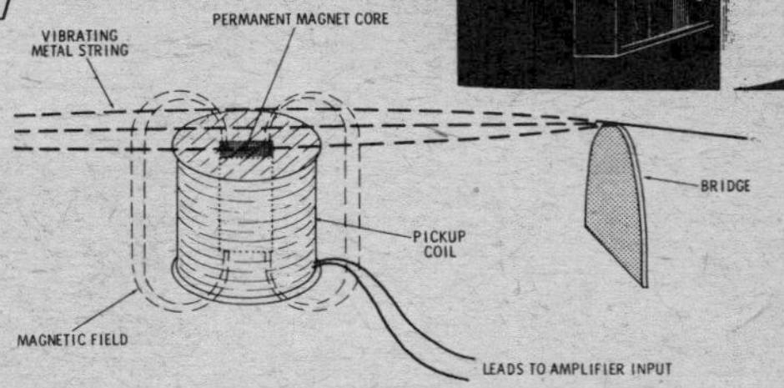

Fig. 2-2. Operation of a magnetic pickup.

The top of the heap in sound recording is Nagra. Their prices start at $1123.

For general purpose high-quality mobile recording, the Uher 4000L is still in front of everyone else for reliability and economy. The new Uher 1200 Neo-Pilot designed for sound/film synchronization, costs about $1600.00.

—SB

For Uher:

Hervic Corporation
14225 Ventura Boulevard
Sherman Oaks, California 91403

Music by Computers

Music by Computers. Goddamn right. When can we get our hands on them without having to tiptoe around some 18th century Department Chairman? This book and four records edited by the worthy Von Foerster and others assembles James W. Beauchamp, Herbert Brun, M. David Freedman, Lejaren Hiller, M. V. Mathews, J. R. Pierce, J. K. Randall, Arthur Roberts, L. Rosler and Gerald Strang. What I want to know is, can Frank Zappa use it?

—SB

Biologically speaking, all auditory systems serve primarily one and only one purpose: to infer from the sounds that are perceived the sources that produced these sounds.

In this example 'The British Grenadiers' is gradually converted to 'When Johnny Comes Marching Home' and back, a nauseating musical experience but one not without interest, particularly in the rhythmic conversions. 'TheGrenadiers' is written in 2/4 time in the key of F major. 'Johnny' is written in 6/8 time in the key of E minor. The change from 2/4 to 6/8 time can be clearly appreciated, yet would be quite difficult for a human musician to play. The modulation from the key of F major to E minor, which involves a change of two notes in the scale, is jarring, and a smaller transition would undoubtedly have been a better choice.

Only the opinions of listeners can evaluate these factors. Limited opinion sampling, with both experienced and inexperienced listeners, indicates that professional performers prefer a higher level of regularity and accuracy than nonperformers. Neither type appears to approve of the maximum level of computer 'perfection.' Listeners object to the 'electronic organ sound' or the 'machine sound' and ask for more warmth or spontaneity.

Even if extensive opinion sampling were carried out, we would know only what listeners think now, based on conventional literature in conventional performance. There is no reason to believe that such judgments will remain unchanged after listeners have been exposed to much more synthetic sound. Perhaps they prefer 'imperfection' primarily because they have never heard anything else.

Music by Computers

Heinz von Foerster and
James W. Beauchamp, ed.
1969; 139 pp., 4 records

$16.75 postpaid

from
John Wiley & Sons, Inc.
One Wiley Drive
Somerset, N. J. 08873

West:
1530 South Redwood Road
Salt Lake City, Utah 84104

or
WHOLE EARTH CATALOG

And fifteen minutes later D.R. and Leonard were running up the Trace Fork road, leading an old gray horse that pulled a wooden sled on runners through the breaks and holes and my how fast it all was moving once it started.

Breathless they stopped at the foot of the little slope in front of Emmit's house that in the old days was a grassy yard that D.R. played on. Even ruined

Even ruined, it was recognizable

but not at all familiar, up

Up the final yards to find Emmit on the floor, tangled in his quilt and dying, his head pointed toward the kitchen, barely breathing, Leonard

Leonard grabbed the quilt and all the bedding

He grabbed the quilts and blankets off both beds and ran outside to pile them

He piled them on the sled while D.R. lifted

D.R. lifted Emmit by the shoulders. His eyes were open, seeing, but he didn't look at D.R. He was looking around his bedroom, this old room

in this old house

this bedroom of this ruined house, taking in its details for what his instinct knew would be his final time

FRAP

"Flat response audio pickup." Hmmm. . .well, theoretically flat. It's response hasn't actually been __measured__ *on an instrument, but it would sound to be better than any other pickup.*

The FRAP picks up the sound of the instrument. It's an accurate vibration detector, picks up all vibrations, unlike the magnetic pick-ups that pick up only the strings. Use it on pianos, guitars, drums. It sounds like you're in a studio using separate microphones.

I wish companies wouldn't use terms like "flat response" without defining what they mean by flat. Can be highly misleading at best.

Shipping delay seems to be a month or a little more.

Transducer, preamp, adhesive wax, $160.

[Reviewed by Fred Richardson]

Information or FRAP from:

FRAP
P.O. Box 40097
San Francisco, CA. 94140

Cousino Continuous Play Tape

Cousino Electronics Copr., 1941 Franklin Ave., Toledo, Ohio. Ph. 246-3691 Makers of Audio-Vendor, offering continuous playback from recorded tape. Single spool of tape unwinds and rewinds onto itself. Avail in time playing from 3 min to 30 min. at 3-3/4 inches/sec. Used for sleep-learning and therapy, broadcasting, teaching, and sales. from $6.15 to $19.95. Free info.

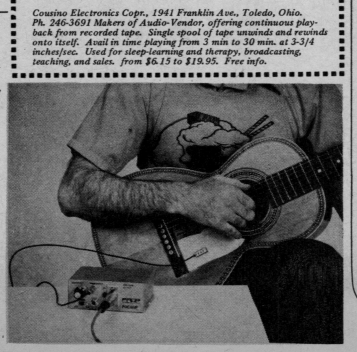

Walter Carlos on Synthesizers

Hi— This is probably either too late to write you, or my own personal ego trip, ergo: of no particular value to anyone, however, I've gotten myself off my other projects/ass long enough to realize that I've been wanting to write all of you for a long time. Also, since all those cliché cats out there keep telling me I'm like the ultimate sage in synthesizers, electronic music, and all that confetti, and since you always find at least a page to devote to "synthesizers", it does seem fair=right to write, and here it is.

If you haven't already thrown this one in that appropriate round recepticle provided for broken goods or boring papers and other worldly goods, I'll pompously introduce myself:

I am Walter Carlos, creator of Columbia Record's *Switched-on-Bach*, and the *Well Tempered Synthesizer*, currently composing instead of merely performing up a 3rd & 4th album for Columbia (since I was always s'posed to be a composer all along and those two records are more or less "learning territories"). The next will probably be titled *The View Inside*, but I'm not looking for plugs or promos.

Actually, I know of no good lit. on electronic music, and I've been stuck in it for at least a dozen years. And that's the problem. You see, I'd kinda like to turn you on to some good text or paperback on the subject, but, frankly (and excluding only the short-lived *Electronic Music Review*, which had many shortcomings) they all stink, are axe-grinding with a vengeance (like the latest stuffy, fadist & sure-to-be-successful periodical *Synthesis*) and are few-to-the-point of extinction.

Granted, I'm as prejudiced as anyone can be— I make my life in the field— but hell, I've tried all the currently available synthesizers, and none of them matches a decent Steinway or Baldwin when it comes to subtlety. Sure, they've all got their own set of gimmicks, but really— that ain't where music's at. What about nuance, phrasing, or that particular gripe of mine: control? Most of the "magic boxes" purport to simplify electronic music. The ghastly thing is that they, as a group, all do — simplify to the point of an imbecilic device which is happy to engage in cranking-out a totally unpredictable series of musical "notes", sounds, "exciting textures", whatever— what a lot of bunk. After my first record gained all its "fame" everyone was out there, hustling to either buy a *Moog* (pronouncing it like a cow, to this day, despite the numerous printed corrections I've only casually spotted) or to build a "better synthesizer" & cut into this, quote: rapidly growing field, unquote. The former hyped-up a bunch of fantastically dull records, too eager to get out de produk', instead of payin' a little dues, the latter glutted the market with that dusty heap of clatter machines & wonder toys that even W.E.C. advertizes.

Unless "Music for Non-thinkers" (thank you, RCA Victor), is your bag, it seems that warnings rather than plugs & puffs is the call of the day. Sure, the pianola is lots of fun at the right party, but Nancarrow notwithstanding, it might be healthier if we had a little less, not more activity in E.M., at least for a period long enough to let the smoke screens either vaporize or settle down into a uniform dust film over all of musicland, ecology be damned!

Enough sour grapes. Of course none of my outrage is printable or ought be. You could certainly "preach the good word: (5 letters, first is "T") "Better than I in your beautiful "Bible-for-a-new-day" (thank God even as the Bible ceased publication at some point you choose to stop prior (by at least a margin of 5 yrs. to atrophy-of-purpose settling in on yet another "groovy mag") (remember *Mad*— the old ones, still in comic-book form—?)

Look, no real damage is going to come from a few sales of *Moog*, *Buchla*, and *Tonus* synthesizers. Most of the "mini" versions are simply cash-in-on ignorance rip-offs, including the *Mini-Moog* (choke) and the *Muse*, and the *Putney*, (I've tried these toys, too) although maybe these do serve a purpose, to groups as "local color" items of the right fashionable kind. I still use a *Moog*. Its grown since S-OB, and is basically bastardized to the extent that, unlike the products for sale, it is a crude but viable musical instrument. *Tonus* will get there too, if they shake off the cancer of advisory committees (formal or informal) which threaten to turn their machines into versatile musical automatons ("Sing Along with Hal," anyone?). *Buchla* is great for a certain limited but beautiful ambience-oriented E.M. and *Moog*, in all standard packaging, is workable, nasty to keep in tune (unlike *Tonus*) and ready for the right non-standard modifications if you're interested and have the time & the bread to personalize same (ditto for *Tonus*).

And, in the final analysis, it is time and bread that enable any music to come out of these "instruments". A multi track machine (pref: 8-track or more) is, in all truth, essential. The would-be synthesist had better invest in a good mixing console (size not too important, quality is), I've used a home-made, "10-in", stereo out one for many years, only now have I scraped up the bread for an all-dolby, "18 in", "6 out" quadraphonic version & 16-track 3M to go with it. This E.M. business can be idiotically expensive. (But 24-track machines still sound to me like a put-on). (Might be good to put a Dolby-ad along with the synthesizer pix. Even the small home "type-B" made by *Advent* will keep hiss down to at least tolerable levels.) Both my old console & the new Biggy used spectra sonic active components— they're in Ogden, Utah, if you're interested.

Also, if you can find the space, I think it might be ultimately best to list a few books on audio, acoustics,electronic organs, (even), and perhaps speech & so-called "visible-speech". I'm copping-out on you, since I honestly don't have the time to look up titles— so send me no $, I insist. The point is, the very word "Synthesizer" (which is otherwise full of unfortunate connotations) suggests a fertile investigation of the whole world of sound— like: why does a trumpet sound like a trumpet & not a clarinet or a violin, etc. All I can tell you is this kind of knowledge, more than any particular hardware, is what enables me to obtain the sounds that I do.

Oh, a piece of philosophy here. Many people suggest to me that I constantly "limit myself to imitating real (sic) instruments". They say it is freer to invent "new, never-before-heard sounds". Bull shit. The easiest to obtain sounds (3 or 4 patch cords on the *Moog*, for ex.) are all those dreary "new" sounds. I've rarely tried to actually "imitate" traditional musical instruments— I've always used them as a point of departure & then veered off into subtlely different areas. It's almost more fun to invent a new woodwind sound; one which is, say, as flexible & musical as an oboe, but better, at least in context, for what you are doing at that moment. And these, be they obtained on *Moog, Tonus*, or whatever, are the very tedious, time-consuming many-interconnection-types of sounds that lead to my own bag (although to the average ear, they may be reinterpreted as "sounding-like". . .a jet plane? a trombone? an electric motor? "Gee, that Picasso paints weird "flowers", don't he?!"

Ah well, ya can't work in a field and not get highly (or lowly) opinionated & I have contracted the disease, doctor, and right now it hurts to see charlatans show off how many suckers (gee that word sounds up to date again) are born every 60 sec.

But, guess it's safe to say that although music performs no true basic function, to wit: It don't plow the fields, it don't build shelter, weave clothing, but it does sooth the human mind at times, and during sex— enough, it shall endure, and no doubt not without some electrical or electronical assist, so, E.M., be it virus or anti-biotic, looks like it has sneaked-in the life bldg. door marked "viva la" and thus my rapping here now, taking up your time & totally ruining my dreams to obtain the worst-letter-writer award for another year. But it's all your fault, you're the ones with the irresistable threat of "last call", last issue, or whatever, and since so many "blame" me & my big SOB for getting up all this E.M. interest I feel like it's only fair that I con you, at this zero (18th?) hour, to put aside a square inch or two of your valuable 500+ pages in service of this 4th or 5th order cause.

TELL THEM: That none of the existing hardware really does the job. Tell them that they should expect to get more than casually involved with the thinks behind schematic diagrams, those dumb cylindrical-bored valved up clarinet & flute & on why the gods decreed that medium-bright sounds with high energy content around 5KC (I refuse Khz, next thing rpm will be called, like 33 1/3 edisons, or eds for short; 15 ips will get 15 magnetophons or mags, for short, humbug!) should sound louder to humans but be more aurally fatiguing, and that they might prepare themselves to dissect any given musical phrase & figure out how to play only certain groups of the notes at a time, over & over into a sel-sync *Ampex* or *3M* (If this be eden) so that the final mix-down sounds phrased & shaped with lots of timbral vibrations & tactile organic electronicism, despite (oh shit) the preparation of many hours for a mere handful of seconds of music (sure kills all the magic, I think) but that in E.M. as all art, the quickest short cut is a short circuit to: short on ideas but oh my long on wind (those monsters don't have to stop to breathe, remember?) music, be it on record or on stage. Of course on stage you could get away with less. Probably have to, but if some cat & chick pluck down several of those government issued rubber bands you'd better give them something more than surface, unless proper chemical assists are available to get them so high they think your yawns & electronic pharts are sublime & majestically musical.

So, I sound square & stuffy. A regular put-down artist in cognito. The W.E.C. is a "list of tools" and the tools are out there for those who've got. I started with *Viking* tape recorders & *Heathkit* oscillators, cause in those days I didn't have. But, with the two best tools I've ever come across: my hands, I built dumb things that got music (of sorts) down & done. A mention of all the auxillary hardware that the promising new E.M. enthusiast will

The Synthesizers

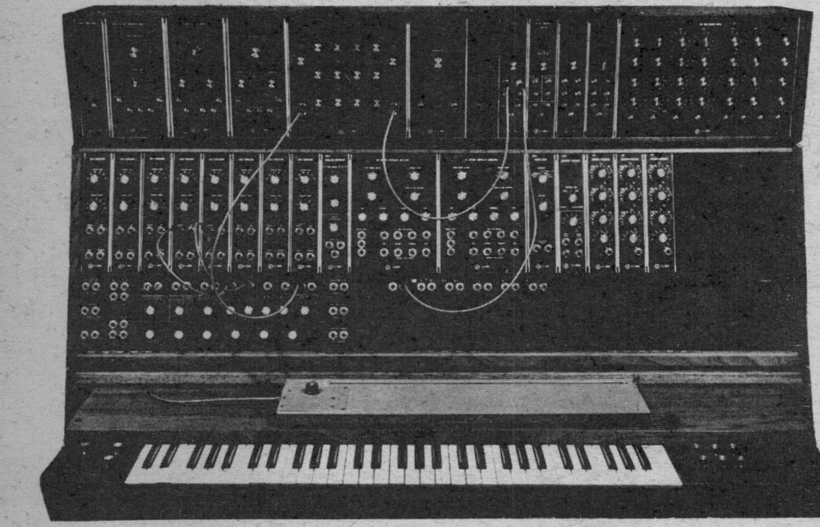

Moogs range from $3500 to $8000
Write to:
R.A. Moog Co.
Trumansburg, N.Y.

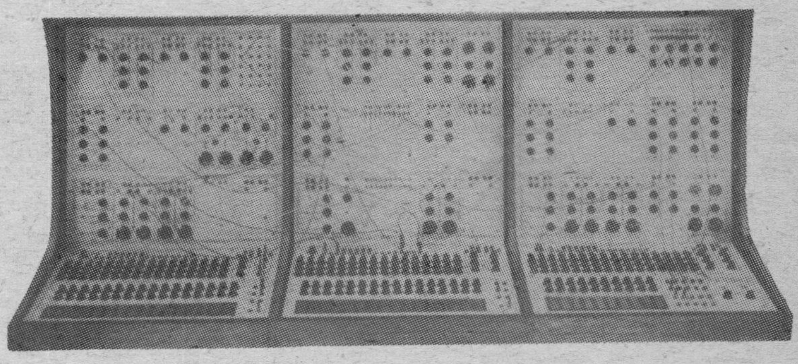

Buchla, marketed by CBS, has a handy user's guide.
Write to:

CBS Musical Instruments
Columbia Broadcasting System, Inc.
1300 East Valencia
Fullerton, California 92631

For information on new Buchla equipment (the Electric Music Box) write to:

Don Buchla
Box 5051
Berkeley, CA 94705

ARP's range from $1295 to $20,000 for complete system, with good owners manuals and instruction book. Easy to redesign/adapt. Write to:

ARP Instruments Inc.
320 Needham St.
Newton. MA 02164

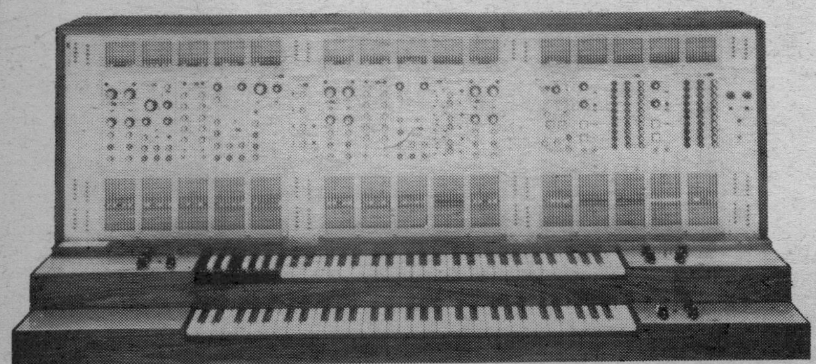

Synthesis

Dear Whole Earth People,

Concerning your question about the relative merits of synthesizers, I think it impossible to answer in less than several hours.

The January issue of a new quarterly entitled **Synthesis** *will have articles on the five major synthesizers.*

Synthesis *is a forum for electronic music and bru-ha-ha beginning in January, 1971.*

A small, free complimentary copy can be obtained by writing:

Synthesis
1315 Fourth Street
Minneapolis, Minnesota 55414

Peace, William A. Johnson
(Editor)

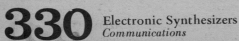

need would give a much more honest description of the game than a few promo-photos of the big 5 (approx.). Good speakers (I stubbornly build my own) & amps are, of course necessary if your tape is to sound ',as good" on someone else's stereo hi-fi. A friendship with an "edital" block will prove invaluable. It's equiv. to the editor's blue pencil. Prior to the synthesizer every note (yes, Virginia, even the 16th & 32nd kind) were assembled by the edit block & by a musician/composer who either didn't own a watch or had absolutely no regard for the units it indicated.

And, oh yes, it helps to be a bit crazy. No, let's say a lot crazy. To be sitting here in my west side brownstone in upper 80's Manhattan contemplating the multi-thousand dollars of equipment Rae Elkind & I have been organizing into our new tempi studio & then writing all these put-downs to you, in her home town, makes me feel kinda strange (and being very broke helps). Perhaps that will help the new album. I wish you were closer-by so that you could see just how involved two "art with a capital (fingers crossed) A-artists" can become in this medium. And our only hope right now? Pay the bills & get ourselves a nice quiet geodesic dome (again, thanks to you & Domebook I) down on St. Thomas & get out of N.Y.C. except now and again when that urge/appetite for noise/dirt/culture/thinking/books/concerts/activity calls.

Frankly, you all sound like our kind of people, or vice-versa if thats more right-onish, we'll miss you. Many will. I hope determination, sweat, brains, adrenalin-push, etc. get that last one out. And, if it's not too late, please help get the confusion out of the E.M. scene. Objectivity here is mostly cop-out, but lack of time & help, that I understand. If anything in this garbled mess of a rap is useful, it's yours, no strings— first time I've ever left my hermiting to do it— so; but do credit it with a simple: W. Carlos. Otherwise, all warmest regards from but two more of your fans!

W. Carlos

A P.S. page of specifics

THE MOOG— I know this unit the best— first met Bob (R.A. Moog's "R") at 1963 AES show. Purchased a small collection of his first 900 series modules & combined into my 1st prototype synthesizer. Paid most of the bill by doing a demo record for Bob & doing music & efx for T.V. commercials. Developed several ideas many now part of standard *Moog* units which are packaged with (sadly) no choice of compoents except on special order. The pix of the *Moog III* you show is 3-4 yrs old. Newer IV is more compact & less blank panels. Portamento & hold circuit originally my concept, but Bob improved it greatly. He built my two touch-sensitive keyboards to spec. and together we got them to work. They're far from good, but do allow the pressure (depth) and momentum (speed) touch of the performer to be used to give feelings of expressive & phrasing, either of the traditional kind or other kind (timbral-vibroto expressivity, for ex.) unfortunately, his keyboard supplier changed and the new kinds don't lend themselves to token sensitivity except in the horrid way the *Putney* does it (more on that later). He uses good controls (ohmite or AB "pots") and sturdy construction, but relies on patch cords except for a few basic switch available internal connections (keyboard pitch to voltage-control input on an oscillator, for ex.) in the toxic & polluted N.Y. air the cumbersome patch cords are more reliable than switches, making a *Moog* for city use a better choice than the *Tonus* which is nearly all crossbar/matrix switch–interconnected–neater but fail unsafe. *Moog's* 904 filter best voltage controlled version around. I have 3. Also his envelope generators are great, but he underestimates their need. His largest Mark III has but 3 envelope generators on it. I use 8 & still run short. Also, he's great even if slow on custom gadgets; I've got several foot buttons and toe pistons/expression pedals that he built— all good stuff. Logical layouts, too. I also am a nut about all that pretty real walnut for everything, even the custom gadgets. We also concocted a "polyphonic" generator bank, an outgrowth of one of his earlier educational contracts. It's got 49 separate little oscilators—filters—envelopers & permits chords, arpeggios, and the like. It's another one-of-a-kind thing, although he now also supplies a bank of fixed oscillators with no voltage control or enveloping or the like, but it's good for pop-style "vamping" of chords, and at least he has it up for sale. I have two keyboards but despite the 6' x 6' mass of my machine I usually use up nearly all the components on one sound leaving the 2nd keyboard without any resources, so I almost always work one-note at a time. It does give the best control— you can concentrate on one part, like a soloist, and let multi-tracking provide the chords, the density, the orchestration, etc. so far, with only an 8-track I've gotten to 32 parts, with but a few "pre-mixes". That should be enough for anyone, but I'm still eager to work on 16 tracks, more for convenience than thickness.

THE TONUS has much better oscillators than the *Moog* & gives you 2 notes at a time, with reservations. Otherwise it isn't too different from the *Moog*. Al Perlemon admits being influenced by Bob Moog. I already mentioned the hazzards of *Tonus'* switching— "caveat emptor". Also, his walnut formica is a bit less "classy" than Bob's walnut wood veneers. He has a few new ideas— somewhat better wave shape variety, but his filters are not so great, and his envelopers have a more limited range than I could work with, although throughout that range they are good. The *Arp*, then, could be better than *Moog* but is not yet, and is about the same price. But again, the biggest is about seven grand and by now my unit is worth over double that, and *Tonus* doesn't grow larger as conveniently as *Moog*, so again compromises. But, for concert use, it's probably the best choice & operates about as easily as a *Moog*, and is quickly learnable (basic techniques, not philos., natch).

The "BUCHLA Box" was built mainly to Morton Subotnick's specs & his group originally at San Francisco. It's better suited to that type of partially aleatoric/partially contrived—planned music that Mort writes. The *Electric Circus* in town here uses one for ambience, and, with all its automated sequencers it's good for that. The construction and looks are good, but his patching is flimsy and breaks under less-than-cautious handling. Prices are reasonable. However, there is no playing-keyboard of the more or less traditional type, and along with oscillators less stable & less easy-to-tune than *Moogs*, is not a good device for traditionally oriented melody/harmony/rhythm. Also, unlike *Moog's* and *Arp's* sequencers, his are usually evenly spaced leading to, for my ears, a rigid, mechanical rhythmic quality which some people seem to dig.

The PUTNEY is a real toy. It's components are highly unstable/unpredictable, and the selection made is highly gimmick oriented, and does not by any stretch of the mind permit any subtle sounds & exp. to be constructed. It also has a so-called touch-sensitive keyboard, which has to be tried to be believed, it's that awful! No feel or physical feedback at all (as there is on a piano, for example); again, another great concept worked out in ignorance (and the one I tried worked backwards: softer touch=louder sounds!) But it is small & portable & groups might like it for special effects.

The same for several other mini-synthesizers. I won't go into details, but it is sufficient to say that they are not aiming at any degree of sophistication or control. I find the lot of them dull & not worth even their modest costs. Better to save up for a *Moog* or *Arp* of moderate size & build it up with time to as large a complexity (or compoundity) as you desire.

Most of these units are not easily compatible with one another, although the hybrid idea can be made to work if one has the necessary knowledge. I'm still waiting for a better state-of-the-art before I part with any more of my bread, however.

On top of this, one must realize that the money trip has just begun, even a used *Ampex* 4 track costs nearly 3 grand, and another 2 track (preferably) is usually necessary, for at least half that. Most home machines fall flat on their capstans in this kind of work. Perhaps the small Dolby-B could help out the limited budget.

There is still a lot of garbage-talk out. The "technical—snow-session" is sadly typical. But who am I to put down folks who dig the magic/mysticism of what I feel is downright quackery? I was sorry to see that new publication jump into that fire. It's like everyone wants to join this or that "avant garde" movement, complete with secret-code type jargon & mathematics of the most pitiful sort (my B.A. in physics-math-music is showing) to "prove" that such and such a dull work is "really interesting". I'd like to see more pioneers of the independent sort, striking out with even makeshift gear to find some personal statement of truth, be it fashionable stylistically or not, but then this seems to be the problem of all music & all the arts in general; electronic music has no monopoly here.

I wish the name "synthesizer" could vanish. Who wants synthetic anything, especially music? The path we are on is (I hope) towards a useful, convenient new musical instrument which employs electronic components to do what physical components have done for years. It ought to be an outgrowth of the past; I see no skyhook to a totally new music, and the attempts I've heard seem to prove this rigorously. In the meantime I can only hope not too much damage to the image & progress of E.M. will be brought about by the "nonsense-boys", and that some talented "saviors" will find the means & bread to show the way & expose the bull-shit artists for what they are, even to the uninitiated. So, there, my sermon is done. Sorry about that. It's just so damned hard to be objective anymore.

W. Carlos

Music Synthesizers

coming into california out of montana snow a couple of years ago the truck radio started picking up a strange, synchopated, alien, version of "cripple creek." sounded like some human metronome playing a banjo with a waawaa petal inside a boxcar. turned out to be a moog. seems like the synthesizer people should stay away from old standards like "don't step on mama's roses" and develop some sound that fits the tool.

—jd

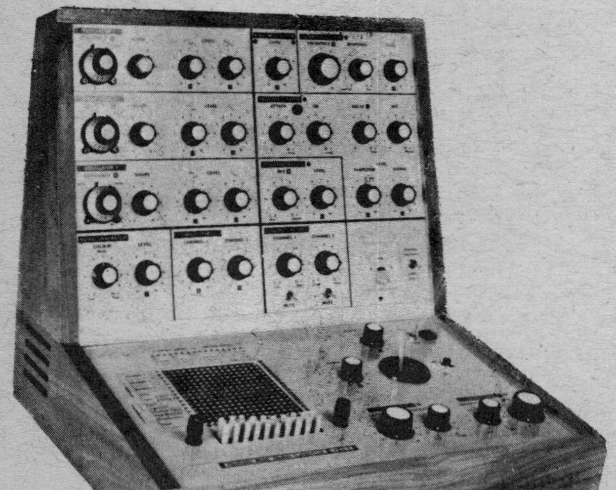

The Putney looks to be a more modest, self-contained unit, with a lower price range (around $1000). Write to:

Ionic Industries, Incorporated
128 James Street
Morristown, New Jersey 07960

Electronic Musical Instruments

A not-too-bad introduction to the rudiments of the hardware.

—SB

Electronic Musical Instruments
Norman Crowhurst
1971; 191 pp.

$4.95 postpaid

from:
TAB books
Monterey & Pinola Aves.
Blue Ridge Summit, Pa. 17214

or WHOLE EARTH CATALOG

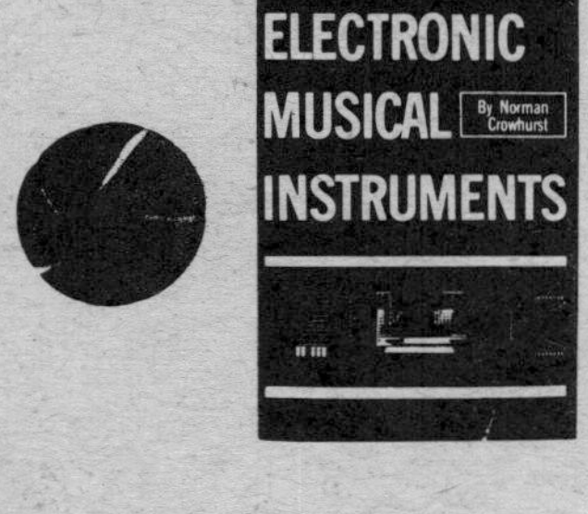

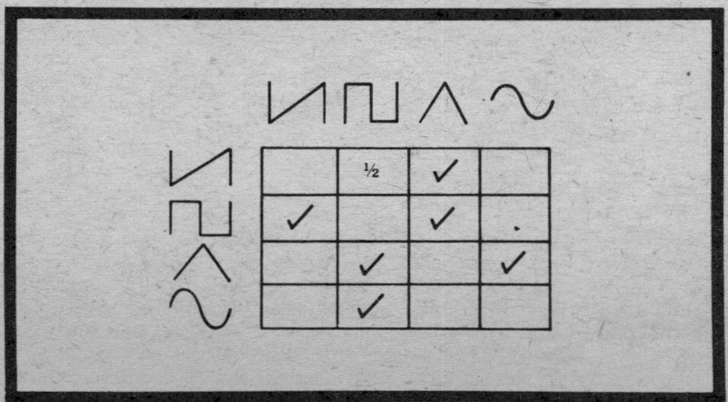

Fig. 6-25. Chart showing the possible direct transformations of the four basic waveforms.

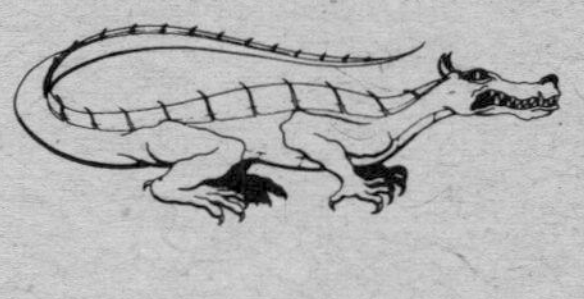

•

Breathe, Emmit. Suck you in a big lungfull.

•

Emmit heaved, he bit

•

Emmit heaved and bit and suddenly raised his head and sniffed and got some air. In, out, he breathed and breathed, and by the time they got him on the sled he had voice enough to argue.

•

I don't want to go to no hospital.

•

Well you're going to one whether you like it or not. I should have taken you in a month ago.

•

Who was that?

•

It was Leonard.

•

It's me, said Leonard.

•

Goddamn you for taking me, said Emmit. And he looked at D.R. and said goddamn you too.

•

Oh it was moving swiftly now. Oh it was happening fast. Is this how fast it goes? It's so clear, so vivid, is this how fast it happens? Emmit's final hours on earth were sweeping through D.R. like some fire, consuming him, filling all his cracks and empty spaces with its rush and flow and go.

•

There's so much work, so much to suddenly do. It's not about doing. It's not fretting doing. Not talking, nor remembering nor looking forward but DOING. Get him to the hospital, quick

•

quick,

•

off this mountain, into Urge.

Exotic Delicate Harpsichords

I'm a sculptor, actually, but I've lately become involved in harpsichords and clavichords. I got to reading about them, and then started building clavichords, and concentrating on them. I might mention briefly some of the qualities clavichords have which draw me to them. They are, as you probably know, an early keyboard instrument, very simple in principle. When played, they are so quiet as to be drowned out by 2 people talking. They can't be played with another instrument, as they are too quiet, and I seriously doubt that they could be played very satisfactorily in a city, due to traffic noise. But (the delicious but) they are the most sensitive of all keyboard instruments. You can play with a volume range down to nothing, and you can add vibrato to a note by pressing your finger gently up and down on the key. If you are sensitive, you can feel the vibrations of the string in your finger as you hold the key down. Now here's the thing. Almost everything you see on TV, or read in magazines, billboards, etc. etc. is designed to be seen or read by someone who is not too interested. Commercials must catch the guy just heading into the kitchen, must reach out and grab the listener. I guess one of the big things that turns me on about clavichords is that they make no attempt whatsoever to do this. You must come to them, and you must come on their terms, that is absolute silence. As you play, or listen to one, your level of hearing grows more acute. What sounded like a faint tinkling when you started becomes full, almost loud music. Then, if someone coughs, it sounds like dynamite. I like the idea of small sounds being appreciated, and of great sensitivity, which you must seek out, which is not rammed down your throat. If you approach a clavichord on its own terms, it has a tremendous amount to give.

Now for something of more use to you. In this whole bag of reviving old instruments, there are a number of sources of information. "Three Centuries of Harpsichord Making" by Frank Hubbard, Harvard University Press, 79 Garden Street, Cambridge, 02138, $15.00, is simply a fantastic book. It describes the technical processes used to make harpsichords (he doesn't deal with clavichords at all) and it is so thoroughly researched it makes your head spin. He spends quite a bit of time with general processes of the time (1500 to 1800) such as how lumber was cut and sold, what sizes of boards could be bought, how common pins were made (you wouldn't believe it!) the tools used, etc. Another great book is "The Modern Harpsichord" by Wolfgang Zuckermann, October House, 55 W.13th St. N.Y., 10011, $15.00. This deals with instruments being made today. He has good sections on old instruments and practices, then the main body of the book is a section listing modern makers, with addresses, photographs, cockeyed opinions, very good opinions, humorous anecdotes etc.

Makers of modern instruments are all in that book, but you might be interested in some of the more interesting among them, mostly those who make kits.

J. Witcher, Ancient Instruments, 17715 La Rosa Lane, Fountain Valley, California, 92708. This firm is a gas (run by 2 ex-underwater engineers) and they make harpsichords, virginals, clavichords, Gigues, Liri da Braccio, Citterns, Hurdy Gurdies, Epinettes des Vosges, Baroque Flutes, Baroque Oboes, Baroque Oboes d'Amour, Cornetti, mute Cornetti, Rackets, Curtals, and the famed Baroque Bassoon. Honest. Their dulcimers go for around $30 and $45. They also make a hurdy gurdy kit $75 and a table model clavichord kit ($95 or $125). Neat guys.

E.O. Witt, Route 3, Three Rivers, Michigan, 49093. He makes a very serious line of harpsichords and clavichords (including fretted clavichords--the only man I've heard of doing that, and in this crowded world if you're the only man doing anything, it's something). He has a good line of clavichords from $505 to $1025, and he says he supplies them partially made (all the tricky parts done) for about 2/3 that price. Ditto his harpsichords, at about half price. They look very good.

Herbert Burton, Box 80222, Lincoln, Nebraska 68501, makes a really neat looking harpsichord kit—prices range from $220-$795—complete with everything but liquid finishing materials. They try to ship kits same day order is received.

Zuckermann Harpsichords, Box 121, Stonington, CT 06378 is an address I'm sure you know. His hardsichord kit is $150, produces a rather ugly, squat, unversatile instrument with amazingly loud tone. He makes a clavichord kit for $100, but all you get is a keyboard, piece of plywood for soundboard, some wire and other odd bits and pieces.

Frank Hubbard, 185 A Lyman St., Waltham, Mass. 02154. Fantastic maker of instruments (all harpsichords). He makes a kit ($700 for one keyboard, $900 for two) which is precut, fitted parts to make construction easier, but which makes an instrument about as good as any you can buy (including the $4000 ones!) Top of the line stuff, for serious people only.

William Post Ross, 791 Tremont St., Room 515, Boston, 02118, though mostly a serious maker of fine harpsichords, has a virginal kit (snicker snicker) for about $560. Virginals are rectangular harpsichords, with a rounder, "tubbier", sometimes louder tone than harpsichords. They don't take up much room in a house. His kit produces a historically accurate 18th century Italian instrument.

S.R. Williams, 1229 Olancha Dr., Los Angeles, 90065, makes kits, for a small harpsichord, a triangular spinet, and one or two other things, but I've lost the brochure. They looked good, though, not too expensive.

More stuff. H.L. Wild, 510 East 11 St., N.Y., 10009, is a fantastic source for guitar supplies. He has all the woods (Deluxe German German Silver spruce etc.) necks, rosettes, fret wire, tools, books, everything. Really great. Banjo parts too!

I don't know if you want all this junk or not, but I suspect that the kind of people who want to stop killing, stop eating plastic food, stop building plastic relationships, get off the ladder of success, who want to smell trees, and hear the little noises in the world, would also like to hear and make music, and make their own instruments. If nothing else, out in the boondocks of Indiana there is a clavichord freak (who would have thought...)

Harold R. Langland
12632 Anderson Rd.
Granger, Indiana

The Art of Organ-Building

If you like the idea of combining architecture and musical instrument design, this book is the standard of pipe organ construction. Hey Baer, could we drive one with solar energy, or would it only work when the wind was blowing?

—SB

The Art of Organ-Building
George Ashdown Audsley
1905, 1965; 1358 pp.; 2 vols.

Vol. I; $10.00
Vol. II; $10.00

$20.00
per set **postpaid**

from:
Dover Publications, Inc.
180 Varick Street
New York, N. Y. 10014

or WHOLE EARTH CATALOG

TRUMPET. Ger., TROMPETE. Fr., TROMPETTE.— This is probably, taken generally, the most important reed stop in the Organ, adding richness and dignity to every combination of stops into which it enters. So important and useful is a good TRUMPET, 8 FT., that no Organ of any pretension is built without one. The proper tone of the TRUMPET is imitative of that of the orchestral instrument; and there is almost unlimited scope for the skill of the reed voicer in the production of this stop. The tubes of the TRUMPET are of metal and of inverted conical form and normal speaking lengths.

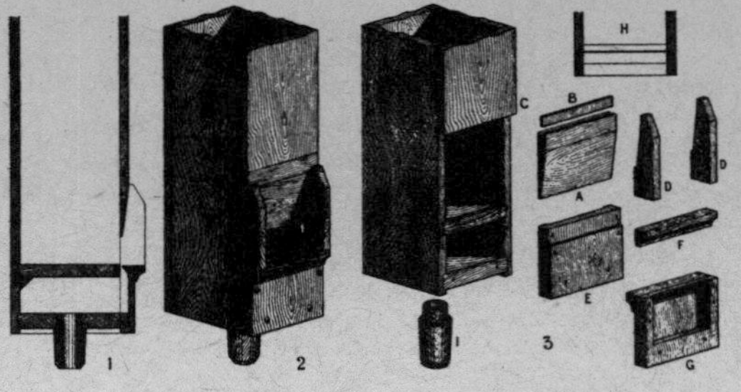

Wooden pipe of a *Principal* or *Open Diapason*, 16 ft.

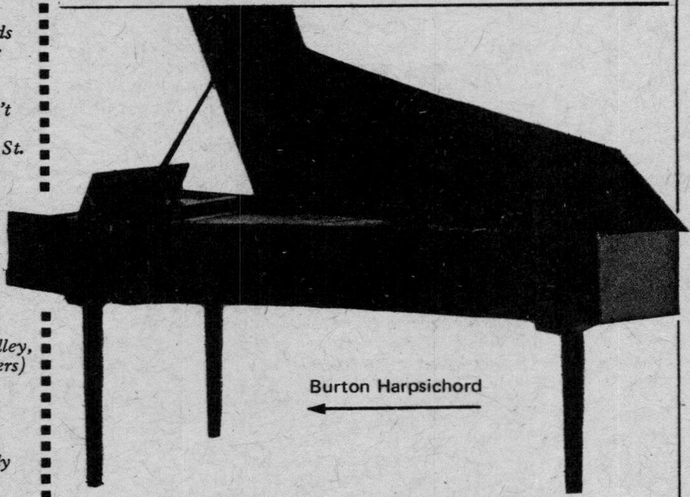

Burton Harpsichord

Three Centuries of Harpsichord Making

Have you ever heard a harpsichord? It'll make a gentleperson out of you. For some reason I have this conviction that harpsichord-makers aren't afraid of dying. This book revels in the 16th, 17th, and 18th century. The workmanship and music thereof.

—SB

Three Centuries of Harpsichord Making
Frank Hubbard
1965; 420 pp.

$15.00 postpaid from:
Harvard University Press
79 Garden St.
Cambridge, Mass. 02138

or WHOLE EARTH CATALOG

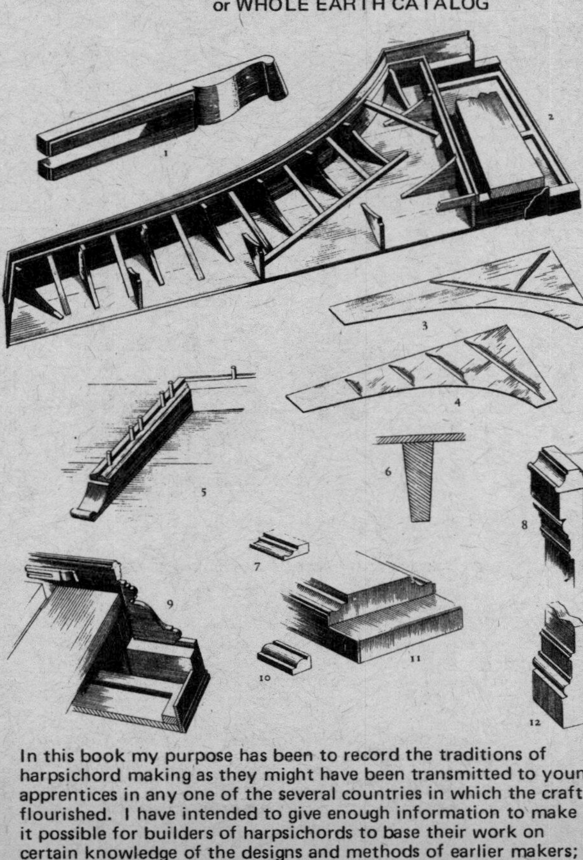

In this book my purpose has been to record the traditions of harpsichord making as they might have been transmitted to young apprentices in any one of the several countries in which the craft flourished. I have intended to give enough information to make it possible for builders of harpsichords to base their work on certain knowledge of the designs and methods of earlier makers; to guide players of the harpsichord in their search for appropriate instruments, dispositions, and registrations in re-creating the music of the past; and to serve as a useful body of information for historians and editors of early keyboard music.

Building Electric Organs

Books: **Electronic Musical Instruments** *by* ***Richard H. Dorf*** *(president of Schober) is available 1) from*

Radiofile
Box 43
Ansonia Station
New York, N.Y. 10023
and 2) from libraries. C. 1968
Frequency Divider Organs for the Constructor *(hardbound) and* **An Electronic Organ for the Home Constructor** *(hardbound) written by Alan Douglas, published in England by*

Sir Isaac Pitman & Sons, Ltd.
39 Parker St.
Kingsway, London W.C.2
England

in preparation, same author and publ; Transitor Elec. Organs for the Amateur. *Kits: from*

Schober Organ Corp.
43 West 61st St.
New York, N.Y. 10023; literature and plastic demo record on request.

Electric Organs

I. "Electronic Musical Instruments" hardbound only, $10 ppd., is 1) a buyers guide to commercially available organs and 2) an instruction manual on technical aspects of elec. organs generally. Dorf is a leading authority and received cooperation from all the companies whose organs were reviewed.

II. The two books by Alan Douglas are plans, circuit diagrams, etc. for home construction with parts bought at a radio supply store (a complete list of which is in the index). "An Electronic Organ for the Home Constructor" deals with a A.G.O. Standard organ with separate generators for all tones. "Frequency Divider Organs. . ." involves a more common modern system in which separate generators are used for the highest octave in the organ and all other lower tones are produced by division. Both books deal with tube and valve types; a solid state edition is said to be in preparation.

III. Kits: While the Douglas books all require a rather solid backing in electronics, persons who read English, solder, and have time, can probably manage any organ in kit form. HEATHKIT/ THOMAS has two models with an impressive array of gadgets and questionable use musically. SCHOBER ELECTRONICS has five models, with base prices from about $500 to $1850. Numerous money-saving (or cost-spreading) routes of purchase are open, including buying in pieces (in the order you will need them for construction), cabinet kits, buying no cabinet and receiving plans for use with lumber of your choice, addition at a later date of optional equipment (reverb, percussion, etc.) LP demo records available. Literature and plstic demo record free on request.

[Suggested and reviewed by Charles Kopp]

Harpsichord Advice

Relatively simple kits available in varying degrees of completeness: from one where you must do all the cabinet and need a reasonable woodworking shop to one that requires only hand tools. Wallace Zuckermann, Herbert Burton.

A full size concert instrument in kit form designed by one of the modern masters. (400-600 hours) Frank Hubbard.

Supplies and parts for scratch builders of harpsichords and clavichords.

Plans of Historic Instruments

B & G Instrument Workshop
318 N. 36th Street
Seattle, Washington 98103

Smithsonian Institution (MHT)
Division of Musical Instruments
Washington, D.C. 20560

Superb Custom Instruments, Harpsichords, virginals, spinets, and clavichords in elegant period cabinets. (We sell our jacks to scratch builders but no unusual kits. We do have plans and parts for a small portable spinettino but you make the keyboard. Not your screwdriver assembly kit):

B. W. M. Benn Harpsichords
4424 Judson Lane
Minneapolis, Minnesota 55435

They might also be interested in another dulcimer & psaltery kit source:

Here Inc.
410 Cedar Avenue
Minneapolis, Minnesota

Sincerely,

Bradley W. M. Benn
Harpsichord Maker

Zuckermann Harpsichord Kits

I'm an enthusiastic backer of Zuckermann kits for harpsichords and clavichords. Zuckermann levels with you about the difficulties involved, then makes it all easy with good, cheap kits and excellent instructions. The harpsichord weighs about 150 lbs and can hold its own as a solo instrument or in chamber groups. The clavichord is a suitcase-sized delight, very expressive but very soft, quick to assemble, and easy to carry along on trips or to have in a very cramped dwelling. There are more historically authentic kits available, but none that will get you into Renaissance and Baroque music more quickly, more cheaply, and with greater satisfaction. Harpsichord kits start at$150, clavichords about $125.

[Reviewed by Edward Allen]

Zuckermann Harpsichords
Box 121
Stonington, CT 06378

H.L. Wild

good wood is getting scarce.
it takes a good while to grow a mahogany tree.
wild has fine selection of instrument maker's woods,
and the plans, tools, and books to go along with them.
stamped across the front of their catalog that came
to us was, "Due to World Conditions, Prices Changed
Without Notice."
i like that way of putting it.

—jd

H. L. Wild must be the most honored dealer we list. A number of readers have written us love letters about Wild's service, prices, advice, quality woods, and quality of store-keeping.

—SB

Catalog
free

from:
H.L. Wild Company
510 East 11th Street
New York, New York 10009

Face or Top. Purchase two pieces of the Best Imported Spruce your pocketbook can afford. This is the sounding Board of the Guitar. These come in Matched Pairs 1/8" by 8" by 20", and must be joined together to make a full top. We will mark each pair how they are to be glued together with the FINE grain always in the center.

GERMAN MOUNTAIN SILVER SPRUCE.......Slow Growing
Matched Pairs........Full 1/8" thick, 7 1/2" wide 20" long
No. 177 Consert Artist Grade..............per pair $8.00
No. 176 Free Lance Grade.................per pair $7.00
No. 175 Musician Grade.....................per pair $6.00
No. 174 Vaudeville Grade..................per pair $5.00
No. 173 Commercial "A" Grade.........per pair $4.00

•

PLECTRUM BANJO NECKS
Already Carved Necks for 4 string Plectrum Banjo 27 inches long, 26-7/8" Scale, using a 19-3/8 in. Finger Board.
No. P 530 Maplewood Neck   with $6.50
No. 0 531 Mahogany Neck   Figured   7.50
No. 0 532 Teakwood Neck   Veneers   9.50
With each Neck we include enough Highly Figured Veneer to cover both sides of the Peg Head and Heel. Postage extra: $1.50

Classic Guitar Construction

This is the only adequate book on the subject in English: it is worth your money even if you don't intend to build a guitar. Every method and tool described actually works, and the design and illustration are of the quality to be expected from a professional designer.

If you can work up your courage to the point of actually starting in, the following is good advice—

1) Buy a good 18" straightedge: a ¼" x 1" dimension-ground steel bar (available from industrial supply houses) is the cheapest way. You need it to get the fingerboard really straight.

2) The fret slots must be .025" wide for most fret wire. Ebony is hard and brittle so the slots must be accurate. Most saws sold as "fret saws" won't work, so beware when buying.

3) (a) Make sure joints fit as near perfectly as you can make them before gluing.

(b) If an operation doesn't come out right, do it over. Don't let yourself get away with any shoddy work.

The experience of building a guitar is guaranteed to change you, probably for the better.

[Reviewed by David Russell Young]

Guitar sales are soaring as factories in the United States and abroad work at top speed to fill the demand. Unfortunately, fine guitars cannot be made at top speed and mediocrity is the rule. In Spain, $120 will buy a guitar of a quality that cannot be duplicated in the United States at any price except by a few private luthiers. Hand-made guitars start at about $500.

Classic Guitar Construction
Irving Sloane
1966; 95 pp.

$6.95 postpaid from:
E. P. Dutton
201 Park Avenue
New York, N. Y. 10003

or WHOLE EARTH CATALOG

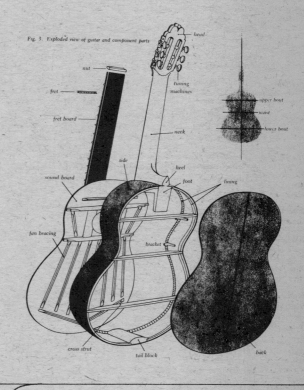

Fig. 3. Exploded view of guitar and component parts

Ratajak Clavichord

To do this properly, I should have had one of my customers "suggest" it. That would get me out of the faintly contemptible position of trying to stick my clavichords up your butt.

Nonetheless, pictured is the latest clavichord to come out of my shop. Price is $500.   The people who want them are keyboard players trapped in no-musical-instruments-allowed apartments; for these clavichords make no more noise than a lethargic bumblebee.

I also make harpsichords and virginals, both semi-kit and finished. Clavichords are available as finished instruments only.

W. P. Ratajak
1636 Brook Lane
Corvallis, Oregon 97330

Guitar Mold

Hope this isn't too late for the last Whole Earth Catalog. I have an item to suggest for guitar makers— an electrically heated mold with an electrically heated shoe for bending guitar sides and bindings quickly and accurately. They are made of cast aluminum and are thermostatically controlled. The molds were developed by Mr. A. E. Overholtzer, 618 Orient Street, Chico, California 95926, who won the annual competition of the International Violin and Guitar Makers Association in 1969. The cost of the mold and shoe is $150 plus shipping from Chico and insurance. Order from Mr. Overholtzer. I can vouch for the mold— on my first try I bent vertical grain rosewood sides perfectly and easily.

Rose-Ellen Leonard
Chico, California

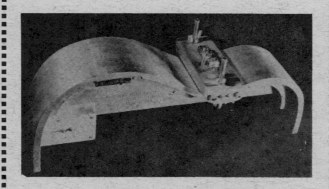

Hughes Instrument Kits

Nice cheap shoddy instrument kits. I believe I'd try a few of these before I took on a Burton Harpsichord. Dulcimers ($12-28), sitars ($25), guitars ($14-28), balalaikas ($13-35), thumb pianos ($3-7), Irish harps ($29-39).

—SB

[Suggested by Charles Benecke]

Catalog
free

from:
Hughes Dulcimer Company
815 Santa Fe Drive
Denver, CO 80204

Tune Your Piano

You can do a good job of tuning your piano with a few tools and a little information. The information is in the book How to Tune a Piano by H. Staunton Woodman. The book and the tools are available from Tuners Supply Company, 94 Wheatland Street, Somerville, Mass. 02145. The book, Stock No. 288, is $4.00. The tools are in Stock No. 5100 Basic Tuning Kit for $20.00.
To be up to pitch and in tune a piano must be tuned often. How often depends on the amount of use, seasonal humidity changes, and moving of the piano. A concert stage piano may be tuned weekly, but in a home tuning every 3 to 6 months is usually enough.

The usual charge by a piano tuner is $12 to $18. This is for placing the instrument in tune with itself, not bringing it up to standard pitch. This takes about two hours work and includes no repairs. You will be able to do the same job in about 8 hours the first time and about 4 after a little practice. But a big saving is yours if the pitch of your piano is flat and you want it pulled up to standard pitch. A tuner will not do this unless specifically ordered as it takes 2 or 3 tuning sessions with a charge to match. You can do the job over a few weeks. All pianos built in this century are designed for standard pitch (A=440) and can be brought up to this pitch with a little work and care.

Refinishing or rebuilding an old piano can give you a good instrument for a small investment. Replacements for broken or missing parts can be purchased from Tuners Supply. Also they will rebuild parts of the action for you if you do not want to tackle this yourself. They do a beautiful job of recovering white keys, one thing that can make an old piano look a lot better.

R.C. Engle
Sioux City, Iowa

What's this you're a putting me in? Emmit wanted to know.

It's a bus, said D.R. I've come from California in it. It's got a bed and everything. Emmit said

He said goddamn you both for taking me.

The doctor said what's wrong? He said, what's wrong, old timer?

They say you can't breathe.

But Emmit wasn't saying. He was captured

He was a prisoner now, he reserved the right to hold his silence, to keep all that he knew to himself, goddamn them all

goddamn

And he said no more, except madly, through drugs and semi-sleep and through the haze of death.

He never said another word he meant to say the three more days he lived.

Gurian Guitars & Lutes

Up till about two months ago it would have been impossible to even consider listing ourselves in your catalog due to the fact that our instruments were very highly priced; with a long backlog of orders. We felt at that point that we had an obligation and commitment to people other than the large money-making groups and single entertainers (i.e. Bob Dylan, The Band, Richie Havens, John Sebastian, Jake Holmes, Judy Collins, etc.); so we reorganized the shop and started training people in building fine quality, handmade guitars.

We are now in the process of having our catalog printed. For the time being we have enclosed a description and price list of all our instruments: we will try to forward some pictures to you, so that you can see and judge for yourselves our high quality standard.

Yours faithfully,
Michael Gurian
Gurian Guitars, Limited
100 Grand Street,
N.Y., N.Y. 10013

STEEL STRINGS

Size 1 Mahogany sides and back; spruce top; black ebony fingerboard; Schaller machine heads; 12 fret to the body; plays best with light or extra light guage strings; price, $250.00

Size 3 Mahagany sides and back; spruce top; black ebony fingerboard; Schaller machine heads; 14 frets to the body; plays best with light or medium guage strings; price, $325.00

Size 3 same as above, but, with rosewood sides & back; price, $425.00

Jumbo Mahogany sides & back; spruce top; black ebony fingerboard; Schaller machine heads; 14 frets to the body; plays best with medium or heavy guage strings; price, $300.00

Jumbo same as above, but, with rosewood sides & back; price, $400.00

Classical Guitars

CL 1 Mahogany sides & back; European spruce top; black ebony fingerboard; Landstorfer machine heads, when available; price, $325.00

CL 2 Indian rosewood sides andblack; European spruce top; black ebony fingerboard; Landstorfer machine heads, when available; price, $425.00

CL 3 Concert model: Brazilian rosewood sides & back; best quality European spruce top; black ebony fingerboard; Landstorfer machine heads, when available; price, $525.00

Flamenco

In keeping with the tradition of the flamenco guitar, I have developed a guitar that possesses the brightness and clarity of sound sought after by flamenco guitarists. In addition, my guitars have the sound projection of a classical guitar. For this result, I use specially selected woods for the top, back, and sides. If preferred, the traditional Spanish cypress would be used. As in the classical models, Peruvian mahogany and black ebony are used for the neck and fingerboard. The head may be fitted with friction pegs or Landstorfer machines. This model also has a handmade rosette. The price of the flamenco guitar is $750.00.

Lutes

1) Elizabethan: This model is constructed with either 7 or 8 courses, depending on personal preferences. Woods employed are Peruvian mahogany for the neck with black ebony for the the fingerboard, curly maple for the boat and spruce for the top. Rosettes are designed and handcarved in the traditional manner.
The price for this model is $850.00.

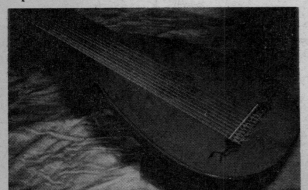

Guitars

Friends: here are a few things you might want to include in your catalog:

C. F. Martin guitars: There are a lot of things to look for in buying a guitar. Some, like the feel of the neck, are really subjective and individual with different musicians. But you also want to know that the instrument will last and improve with time and use. This is where the Martin company comes in. For a long time, they've been making honest, workmanlike guitars. I've had a D-18 for the last 6 or 7 years and it continually amazes me. The tone improves every time I play it. Martins are about the best steel-string acoustic guitars made in any quantity. They're a joy to play. They're not *too* good for riding freights/bumming because they're relatively fragile, but they hold up with proper care, for a long time.

Gibson Electric guitars: I don't dig Gibson acoustics too much—some people find them really durable but I don't like their tone very much. Gibson electrics are another story. I've had a Gibson ES 335 electric guitar for quite a while. It has a beautiful neck, and will do almost *any*thing in terms of tone production that you want from it. Things to look for in buying one are: 1) a good neck. Gibsons vary tremendously, so be careful. 2) "Humbucking" pickups are really the best on the market. Gibsons last forever. Mine's fallen off stages all over the country, & it's still good as new. If you buy a Gibson, try for one over 2 yrs old (pre-1968), otherwise examine the workmanship *very* critically.

V. C. Squier strings: These strings are *really* hard to find, which is a damn shame, because they're the best strings made in the U.S. They're smooth to play & will enhance the tone of any stringed instrument. I've only used their guitar strings, but I suspect the others they make (violin, etc.) are just as good. Bug your music store 'til they get some in. Here are some kinds they make: ES-2500: Tops! these are *smooth* roundbound strings, $5.75 a set (list) & worth it. Also in light gauge, ES-2550. They also make nylon wound electric guitar strings, which I haven't tried. These could be really beautiful strings (ES—8000)
V.C. Squier Co. 427 Capital Ave, S.W., Battle Creek, Mich 49016

Stan & Jane Davis
Denver, Colorado

Squier Strings

the reason squier strings are so scarce (and perhaps the reason they are so good) is that v.c. squier co. is a very small operation— only 6 or 8 people. as stan says, though, they are indeed the best string-makers (?) around, and from what i've heard, they offer a service available nowhere else in the country (to my knowledge at least): they will custom-make sets of strings to your specifications. i know of a fellow who gets hand-made smooth round-wound strings with an elliptical core— easy on the fingers.

any guitarist who really knows what he wants will do well to send them a letter of inquiry.

*V.C. Squier Co.
427 Capital Ave. S.W.
Battle Creek, Michigan 49016*

Mark Talaba

Stewart—MacDonald Banjo

I thought you might be interested in hearing about a company that specializes in banjo parts.

Catalog

$0.50

from: *Stewart-MacDonald Mfg. Co.
Box 900
Athens
Ohio 45701*

They carry a full line of products, have a catalog, and operate entirely by mail. They also seem to give very fast service, and the quality of their products is very good. As they add new items, they publish supplements to their catalog which are apparently sent to everyone on the mailing list.

Stephen R. Monaghan

KROLL GEARED 5TH PEG

The best solution yet for keeping the 5th string in tune. 9 to 1 gear ratio eliminates slipping.

No. 38—Polished Nickel $14.50
No. 39—Gold Plated $17.00

With Five Star tuning knob and thumbscrew—add $1.50 to the above prices.

The John Dubroff Instrument Makers List

This arrived late and unexpected, so we're jamming in a piece of it. Why don't you start a Catalog, John.
                                                            —SB

This list originally started out with the intention of being "The Great North American Musical Instrument Maker List", but intentions being subject to change without notice (what with area informants, and half the instrument makers contacted, not replying), it has ended up essentially a Promotional Directory to the Central California Way, with a few excursions to Elsewhere in the nation.

Wherever you are, there are a good many more makers of instruments near you than you think. Many of them are like mushrooms, they appear suddenly and don't stay in it, or around, long. Doesn't necessarily mean they do poor work. Scout around, go direct to the source— more fun than buying from a shop.

And catalog collectors, please spare these fellows listed here; none of them can afford your Habit.

cheers,
John

Electric Violin

California

R. Kent Albin
675 Golden Gate Ave.
San Francisco 94102

Guitars: classical, steel string, electric; Electric bass; Acoustic and electric Dulcimers; Electric Violins, violas, cellos, and quintons; Irish harps; Hummels; Lyres; Viol da Gambas; Harpsichords.

Also available are various accessories, wood, tools, and custom made cases. Catalog free. Mail order, yes.

Patrick Armstrong
3052 Telegraph Ave.
Berkeley, CA 94705
phone: 549-1604

Harpsichords and clavichords made on order for rent or sale. Payments are around $20-$50/month; $1000 for chavichords, $2000 and up for manual harpsichords; also pedal harpsichords.

Capritaurus
Box 153
Felton, CA 95018
phone: (408) 335-4478

Appalachian Dulcimers, $40 up to $150; custom models also. African Thumb Pianos, $8; made of mahogany or ash with ten keys. Dulcimer price sheet available; mail order, yes.

Haldon Chase
Rt. 1, Box 122
Paso Robles, CA.

Renaissance instruments: Lutes, Viola da gambas, Italian harpsichords. No catalog; prices vary with individual instruments. Mail order, yes.

John Dubroff
107 Grattan St.
San Francisco 94117
phone: 665-0783

Four-string Dulcimers: $90; $150. $150 model comes with either carved animal head (pictured) or carved scroll. Both models are made large for volume, so that they may be played with guitar. Plucked Psaltries: 16 strings, $60. Mail order, no.

The Dulcimer Works
1723 W. Washington Blvd.
Venice, CA 90291
phone: (213) 821-8514

Dulcimers: spruce face on all models. Walnut back and sides, $99.50. Rosewood back/sides, $150. Three or four strings. Mail order, yes. Steel string guitars soon available.

Childs Family
P.O. Box 482
Soquel, CA 95073

Traditional Appalachian Mountain Dulcimers. The two traditional shapes, three or four strings; $50 to $65. Mail order, no.

Steven Freegard
P.O. Box 377
Cambria, CA 93424

Woodwinds: flutes, recorders, double reeds. Exotic and native hardwoods are used for the woodwinds, which are made in any size or scale. When specified, they are fitted in carved wooden cases. Prices range from $25 to $100-plus. Catalog no, mail order, yes.

String instruments: All one-of-a-kind pieces, e.g. spike fiddle, large fretted drone, koto-type, etc. These are made from gourds, bamboo, hardwoods, and whatever else. Prices run from $20 to $500. Most of these string instruments are too bulky or delicate to mail.

Morris Freeman
P.O. Box 392
Paradise, CA.

Dulcimer: 3,4, or 6 strings; electric also. Sizes vary, prices also from $100 to $200. Mail order possibly.

Dennis Grace
3052 Telegraph Ave.
Berkeley, CA 94705
phone: 549-1604

Classic guitar: $600 and up. Steel strings on request. "Acoustical research in the classic guitar."

Larry Higgins
160 Noe St.
San Francisco, CA 94114

Guitars: classical, steel string, $350 to $400; electric solid body, $375 (usually set up with two thumbuckers, Tune-a-matic bridge, Schaler heads)
Dulcimers, $75 to $100.
Viols, $450
Clavichords, lutes, etc.
Mail order, no.

(continued)

George Peacock
160 Noe St.
San Francisco 94114

Guitars: classical and steel string, also electric. Lutes and Viola da Gambas. $300 to $600 for instrument w/case. Dulcimers also. Materials and supplies for sale too: rosewood and spruce, purflings and bandings, fretwire, mother of pearl and abalone, sheet tortoise shell, machine heads, etc. Mail order, no.

Robinson's Harp Shop
Mount Laguna, CA 92048

Harps: Irish, Paraguayan, "Mini-concert"; run from $295 to $435. Plans and instructions for constructing Paraguayan, $15. Kits for Paraguayan go from $130 to $260. "Mostly I sell plans, strings, hardware. Also have kits for dulcimers, thumbpianos, lyres, etc. Also several other types of harps." Descriptive sheet available. Mail order, yes.

Roy Scott
2747 Woolsey St.
Berkeley, CA 94705

Thumb pianos: Vary in size from 7-1/2 x 4", $7.50, up to 10" x 8", $18.00. All are individually hand made and decorated; all are tuneable. Decorated Ceramic Flutes: these are individually hand decorated, range from $7.00 to $10.00. Free catalog, mail order only (add 50¢ to cover postage).

Lynn B. Sears
P.O. Box 144
Loleta, CA 95551

Four string Dulcimers: made of any wood desired, exotic and native hardwoods, spruce tops. Handcarved scroll. From $55 to $110. Price list free; mail order, yes.

J. Witcher
Ancient Instruments
P.O. Box 552
(107 First St.)
Forestville, CA. 95436

Medieval, resnaissance, and Baroque keyboard, stringed, and wood-wind musical instruments and kits.

Harpsichords, Clavichords, Virginals, Spinets, ranging from $750 for Spinet to $4800 for German type Harpsichord. Table model Virginal for $275.

String Instruments: Eight different kinds; among the more familiar, Hurdy Gurdy, 10 keys: $150; Minstrels Harp, 24 strings: $75; Dulcimer, 3 string: $30 and $45; Psaltry, 13 strings: $25.

Woodwinds: 16 different kinds available, most in the area of $25 to $85.

Kits: table model Clavichord, $100; Italian polygonal Spinet, $300; Hurdy Gurdy, $75.

Catalog in process of preparation. Mail order, yes. Formerly known as Renaissance and Baroque Musical Instruments, formerly located in Randsburg, Calif.

Henry Yeaton
3230 Ellis St.
Berkeley, CA.

So-called "primitive" instruments, unusual noisemakers, African marimbas, Thumb pianos, South Indian flutes, drums. Mail order, yes. Write for more information; catalog, no.

Elsewhere:

Lynn McSpadden
Box 110
Mtn. View, Arkansas 72560

Guitars: custom made only; "D" size steel string. From $295.
Banjos: traditional fretless.
Ozark Mouthbows: $5.50 w/postage.
Mandolins: lute shape, flat back. From $95.
Psaltries: write for price/description.
Dulcimers: many models available. Run $68, $85, $95, $140. Descriptive price lists available; mail order, yes. Also available are two books, $2.95 each, containing songs (traditional) arranged for playing by the dulcimer: "Brethren, We Have Met"— hymns and carols, and "Four and Twenty", containing songs plus information on tuning and playing.

Frank Proffitt Jr.
Rt. 2
Todd, North Carolina 28684

also: Rt. 2
Vilass, North Carolina 28692

Fretless banjos, five strings, $80.
Dulcimers: hourglass and teardrop shapes, heart sound holes. Three string: $90; four string, $95. No catalog; mail order, yes; shipping fee $3. These instruments made in the patterns of the late Frank Proffitt Sr.

Dennis Dorogi
Ellicott Road
Brocton N.Y. 14716
phone: (716) 792-9012

Dulcimers: Six basic designs, 16 types overall—depending on wood used and number of strings. Start at $70 and move up to $175. A simple design, hourglass shape dulcimer available completed except for sanding and finishing, 3 string $42.50, 4 string $45. Plucked Psaltry; 20" x 7" x 3", $45 postpd, other models up to $300. Mini-psaltry: 9-1/2" x 4" x 2", $18.95 postpd. Scheitholt: five string, $125; three string, $95-$100 Information on request on other instruments: Hammered dulcimer, rebec, lyra, kantele, psaltry, aeolian harp, classical guitar. Brochure, price list available for 25¢. Mail order, yes.

Appalachian Dulcimers
232 W. Frederick St.
Staunton, Virginia 24401

Appalachian Dulcimers. $65, includes accessories, instruction booklet, carrying bag. Made of native woods, spruce top, rosewood pegs. Information sheets available. Mail order, yes.

Edward Merrifield
Merry Field Meadows
Star Route A
Inchelium, Washington 99138

"Instruments designed out of my imagination, mostly harps; reproduction of ancient instruments— Greek, Egyptian, Medieval— maybe out of your imagination. The only instrument I am on a

production basis with is a small Lyre Harp with 15 strings, hand carving and mother of pearl inlay— $200. The gourd harp pictured was on personal order, price around $400." Mail order, yes. Delivery time, two months.

Rizzetta String Instruments
4616 South 1st St.
Arlington, VA 22204
(703) 527-1829

Hammered dulcimers, oak frame $200, black walnut $300, plain hardwood, ea. $80; mountain dulcimers, $100; guitars, $400 and up; push-button harps, $160. Mail order, prefer not but will consider.

Dulcimers

I have noticed in the Supplement's to the Spring Catalog Some questions Regarding Dulcimers. the following are Four Address which make Dulcimers & Dulcimer Kits.

Here Inc.
410 Cedar Avenue
Minneapolis, Minn. 55404

Homer C. Ledford
125 Sunset Heights
Winchester, Ky. 40391

Appalachian Dulcimer Corp.
232 West Fredrick St.
Staunton, Virginia

The Dulcimer Shoppe
Mountain View, Arkansas
72560

More Dulcimers

Here are some more dulcimer makers to add to your list in the January and March Supplements:

George Pickow
7A Locust Avenue
Port Washington, New York 1Q050

George Pickow is Jean Ritchie's husband and they make dulcimers in three shapes (teardrop, traditional, and semi-diamond) and with either 3 or 4 strings. The prices range from about $40.00 to $100.00.

The Magic Mountain Workshop
Box 614
Mill Valley, California 94941

[remarks omitted by request of Magic Mountain Workshop]

William Wallace
19 26th Avenue
Venice, California 90291

He makes hammered dulcimers on request for $100.00 They come with 3 or 4 different types of hammers.

Lynn McSpadden
of The Dulcimer Shoppe
listed in the January Supplement also makes fretless banjos if anyone's interested.

If anyone is interested in making a dulcimer, Howie Mitchell's book, The Mountain Dulcimer— How to Make It and Play It— (After a Fashion) is very good. He's very good for understanding the fret structure and how the thing works. He also has stuff about chorded dulcimer playing and various instruments made from doors and a plan for making a "courting dulcimer" (one played by two people. It's available from Folk Legacy Records, either separately or with a record.

Susan Barger

The Mountain Dulcimer: How to Make It and Play It
Howard W. Mitchell
50 page book and record

$6.95 postpaid

from:
Folk-Legacy Records, Inc.
Sharon, Connecticut 06069

Homer C. Ledford

All of these addresses responded with price lists & descriptions. the prices Range from $18.00 For a Kit to $125.00+ for a completed Dulcimer. I ordered a Kit from Here Inc. It arrived within 10 Days with comprehensive instructions for Assembly. For other names of manufacturers consult Sing Out. Jean Ritchie also makes Dulcimers But I have no information concerning her at this time.

Sincerely,

Rick
Wooster, Ohio

More Dulcimers Continued

Some more dulcimer sources:

N. T. Ward, Jr.
Vilas, N.C. 28692

[Suggested by Chuck & Kathleen Miller]

Student Craft Industries
Berea College
Berea, Kentucky 40403

[Suggested by William Taylor]

Peacewood Dulcimers
Box 188, Route 1
Lawton, Michigan 49065

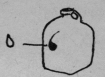

Flat Picks

Hint: The best flat picks are whittled out of old polyethylene gallon milk jugs. Firm, but not noisy.

Sincerely yours,
Marlin Spike Werner

Estelle.

Dear Estelle,

Estelle, honey,

Dear Estelle, I'm sitting by my uncle's bedside in the hospital now. In Blaine, Kentucky. This sweet little hospital where believe it or not I was born about five centuries ago. And my poor old uncle is dying, and I am tending to him while he does. It's after midnight now. We've been here since this morning. And it's a strange

Dear Estelle, I'm sitting by my uncle's bedside in the hospital now. We've been here over twelve hours, and he's dying.

Estelle

D.R. helped Emmit sit up to pee. He was having to pee every ten or fifteen minutes now. Or at least he thought he had to and each time he thought he had to D.R. had to help him up because Emmit didn't know himself until he sat up, and even if he did know he couldn't say so because he was so far gone in his mind. Drinking and pissing was the treatment. That was it, all right. Flush him out. He was drowning in his own internal fluids and the only thing to do was fill him up and pour him out and that was D.R.'s job and he tried to tell Estelle about it in between the pee times.

He yells water-time! it's water-time! and I look to see which one he means, put it in or take it out. Sometimes he doesn't know himself. Once this afternoon I held a glass up to his mouth and he peed all over the floor. And later after he'd let some out in the jar he turned it up to drink it. His eyes are yellow as lampshades now. I wonder what crazy point of view goes on behind them.

Leonard came and went. I don't know who you are! Emmit yelled. You're a mystery man, what are you doing here? Who's in charge?

I'm Leonard, Leonard said. I'm your friend. I'm your neighbor. I'm taking care of your rabbits while you're sick, do you remember them?

Kill 'em! Emmit shouted. I want all them rabbits dead, do you hear me?

Carroll Sound

Getcher Chinese Bell Tree ($38.50) your Sheng ($59.50), your 2-string oriental violin ($17.50), your shenhai ($35), your santoor ($240), your train whistle ($8.24), boing box ($40.50), lion roar ($45), horses hoofs ($4.50), and storm ($69.50), and more. Get em all and start a band.

—SB

Carroll Sound Inc.
Box 88
Palisades Park, N.J. 07650

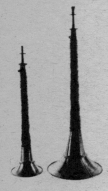

CHINESE MUSETTE (So-Na)

— A typical Chinese double-reed instrument. Wood portion is attractively scalloped and polished brass components used throughout.

C5-29-1 Chinese Musette (large) $14.95
C5-29-2 Chinese Musette (small) $12.50

M   3-tone Train Whistle   M $4.60

Homemade Harps

Gents,

I was told—by a friend at Stanford Research, that you folks might be interested in my business.

Frankly it isn't much—but I sure like it.

Robinson

ROBINSON'S HARP SHOP

P. O. BOX 141
MOUNT LAGUNA, CALIFORNIA 92048

Woodwinds, etc.

I enclose a sheet on my activities, if you can use it. Also an article on baroque shoes for your information.

I have several friends in this area who make harpsichords professionally:

—Sandy Fontuit (sp?), San Francisco
—Richard Mexandu, 1281 Hearst, Berkeley
—Thomas Haynes (my father), 1607 Webster St., Berkeley 94705.

Other early woodwind makers I can recommend:

—Friedrich von Huene, 59 Boylston St., Brookline, Mass. 02146 (I apprenticed with him)
—Sandy Lemberg, 42 Kincaid St., Cambridge, Mass. 02139
—Robert Marvin, 6 Main St., Hoosick Falls, N.Y.
—Hans Coolsina, Oude Gracht 305, Utrecht Holland (I enclose a sheet on his instruments we are importing. He also makes very good cheap recorders ($25. alto).
—Klaus Scheele, 2854 Loxstedt, Dunenfahrstrasse 40, W. Germany.
Hope this is of help to you.

Best wishes
Bruce Haynes

Bruce Haynes
Baroque Woodwind Replicas—Repairs
1260 Redwood Lane
Lafayette, CA 94549

Musical Saw

[Suggested by Scot Barner]

Musical Saw, lessons, and soft hammer,
Musical Saw, lessons, hammer, bow & rosin
Carrying case for the complete unit

Mussehl & Westphal
Fort Atkinson, Wis. 53538

Mr. E. E. Hardy, Albion, Neb., 54 years old, who writes us,"after 25 minutes practice I played 10 or more songs using the hammer."

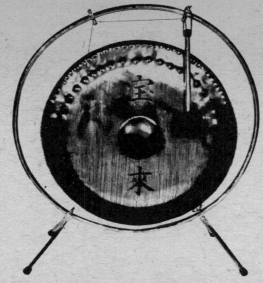

GONGS WITH STAND & MALLET FROM JAPAN (28" and 30")

— These gongs are so economically priced that they can now be added to schools and orchestras whose budgets might otherwise not have been able to afford them.

These fine gongs are every bit as good as gongs of considerably higher cost and come complete with stand and mallet.

C5-23 Bass Gong, 28", w/stand & mallet $165.00
C5-24 Bass Gong, 30", w/stand & mallet $195.00
C5-25 Bass Gong Deluxe Mallet only $ 10.50
C5-30 7" Gong on stand with mallet $ 15.00

Walton's Irish Harps

The kind of harp that is pictured on the front of the Guiness Stout bottle, on the label. The Irish Harp has had a number of interesting uses, including providing the accompanyment to which the Bard, an important part of the Celtic armies, would curse the enemy during battle. These harps were strung with steel wires, and probably sounded weird.

The Walton's company does not make steel-strung harps however, since we don't sing curses at the enemy in a war anymore. The harps they do make are very fine instruments, however. The quality is rather better than what one would expect of a comparably priced guitar. It is not necessary to be a hibernophile to like the Irish Harp, as it is very easy to learn to play, and adapts well to Simon and Garfunkel, and to most traditional Appalachian ballads. The Walton's company is all kinds of reputable, and it backs up its instruments with a degree of concern for the customer's satisfaction that I have never found in any domestic company.

[Suggested and reviewed by Louise B. Heite]

Waltons
5 N. Frederick St.
Dublin, 1
Ireland

"Brian Boru" 710/3 $199.00

Autoharps

i think autoharps are easier to play than guitars,
mainly because the chording is done mechanically.
thirty-six strings and twelve or fifteen bars of felt pads.
push down a bar,
and all the strings you don't want in your chord, are felt padded out,
so you are left to figure out how to keep thirtysix strings in tune, and what to do with the hand that isn't pushing down bars.
autoharps are cheap: thirty to forty dollars from Wards or Sears.

—jd

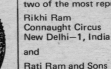

Information

free

from:
Oscar Schmidt International Inc.
Department B
Garden State Road
Union, New Jersey 07083

TABLA DRUMS

— Most popular drum of North Indian classical and theatrical music. While more properly referring to a wooden drum, the TABLA is most often taken to mean a pair of drums, one wooden and one metal. Includes rings and tuning hammer.

C6-17-1 Tabla Set. Professional $75
C6-18 Tabla Drum Case, Fiber $39

Ceramic Drums

There are a couple of long time potters in Berkeley who have begun in the last year or so to direct much of their energies towards making ceramic hand drums of all kinds. Jill Neff and Peter Overton have produced Taraboukas, Dumbakis (belly-dancer drums), African Talking drums and many primitive, tuneable drums of their own design. I guess what excited me most about what they are doing is that they are into having you come to them with your own design—and working from there. At this point they use mostly goat skin heads, but then again that can be changed by you if you so desire. Prices range from $15 to $25 per drum, less shipping charges. Write to them at 2719 Stuart'St., Berkeley, Cal. for more info and a price list. Both Jill and Peter will be out of town until Sept. 1, 1971 but will accept orders after then.

—Austin Jenkins

The Sitar Book

A surprising amount of basic sitar in a few pages.

—SB

The Sitar Book
Allen Keesee
1968; 63 pp.

$2.95 postpaid

from:
Oak Publications
33 W. 60th St.
New York, N.Y. 10023

or WHOLE EARTH CATALOG

Extra strings can be ordered from Jimmy's Music Store, Terminal Music Store, Manny's Music Store, and Eastern Music Corporation, all in New York City. For information on sitars, and in case you are brave enough to contemplate ordering one direct from India, two of the most reputable firms to deal with are:

Rikhi Ram
Connaught Circus
New Delhi—1, India

and

Rati Ram and Sons
Nai Sarak
Old Delhi, India

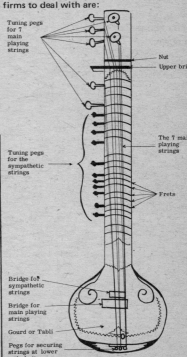

Tuning pegs for 7 main playing strings
Nut
Upper bridge
The 7 main playing strings
Tuning pegs for the sympathetic strings
Frets
Bridge for sympathetic strings
Bridge for main playing strings
Gourd or Tabli
Pegs for securing strings at lower end of sitar

Folk Style Autoharp

oak publications can get you started here's their autoharp book.

—jd

Folk Style Autoharp
Harry Taussig
1967, 70; 81 pp.

$3.95 postpaid

from:
Quick Fox
33 West 60th St.
New York, N.Y. 10023
or WHOLE EARTH CATALOG

In this chapter we will return to the development of the right hand. So far all the melody notes that have been played by the right hand index finger have been played at the same times as the right hand thumb was playing a bass notes. In other words, all the melody notes that we have played have been in pinches. In this chapter we will investigate melody notes that are not played by pinches.

Melody Flute

Musical instruments are extremely satisfying tools. However, in most cases the cost for quality instruments is restrictive. The Melody Flute is an exception. For from $1.00 to $1.75 one receives a nickel plated, six holed instrument of fine tonal quality, and an instruction manual.

It is easy to learn and a lot of fun to play.

The Melody Flute Company also sells a complete line of recorders at very reasonable prices.

[Suggested and Reviewed by Winston Fowlkes]

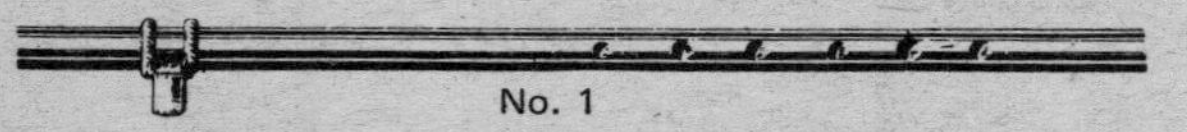

No. 1

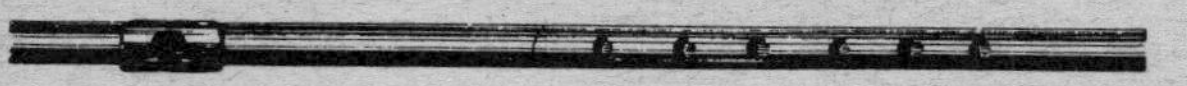

No. 2

Melody Flute

NO LONGER AVAILABLE

from:
Melody Flute Company
126 Lafayette Avenue
Laurel, Maryland 20810

No. 0—Plastic Flute C with mouthpiece 50 cents—Book $.25 total $.75
No. 1—*Metal Flute C with mouthpiece $.75—Book $.25 total $1.00
No. 1—*Metal Flute B flat with mouthpiece $1.25—Book $.25 total $1.50
Total $1.50
No. 2—*Metal Flute B flat Professional Type $1.50—Book $.25
Total $1.75

*Nickel Plated
One price—any quantity.
POSTAGE—Above prices include postage on orders amounting to $5.00 or more. On smaller orders add $.25 per order for mailing costs.
BOOK PRICES—Books alone—$.25 each—Any quantity—Postage prepaid on orders amounting to $1.00 or more. On smaller orders add 10 cents for mailing costs.

Bagpipes

For those who may be interested in bagpipes— acquiring them or playing them, there is an excellent company in Scotland:

Hugh MacPherson Ltd.
17 West Maitland Street
Edinburgh 12, Scotland

Importing them yourself is about 4 times cheaper than buying one over here. Furthermore, the quality is better and the service is extremely courteous (although slow. It takes 3 months to get your bagpipe after ordering it) It is worth it however. A full sized bagpipe— full mounted in imitation ivory costs about $84.52 in American money (at the current rate of exchange) (That's another thing they'll do for you. They'll translate their prices into recognizable money symbols for Americans) In California, a cheap Pakistani imitation Scottish bagpipe costs $150.00!!! Since MacPhersons's things are made of selected African blackwood and constructed with an old fashioned pride-of-craftsmanship, there can be no comparison. Their fanciest, a full mounted model in H.M. silver either chased or engraved costs 170 pounds. (let someone else translate that into dollars. I asked them for price translation of the low priced models.) Furthermore, they even offer a miniature bagpipe suited for indoor playing for about $50 (£22 10 0). They sell also practice chanters, instruction books, collections of the Ceol Mor, maintenance accessories and even superfluous goodies like highland costumes for performers. They will send you a catalogue (of sorts) if you write them. I highly recommend the practice chanter for starting. It costs about $8 for the simplest and will teach you the notes and let you play tunes. An excellent beginners instruction book is the College of Piping Tutor Book I, by Seumas Masneill and Thomas Pearston. Also order extra reeds with your chanter. The plastic types last a long time.

—Tiny Alice
Los Angeles, California

Mittenwald

I suggest the Mittenwald Co. of Chicago, importers of fine recorders and other instruments. The recorder, as most everyone knows, is one of the easiest instruments to learn to play while still remaining a challenge to the virtuoso. They are great fun to play in groups (in "consort"). There is a vast repertoire of music for them. They take up little room and aside from an occasional swabbing and oiling of the bore are practically maintainance free. While cheap soprano recorders are available for two or three dollars, for the person serious in getting going with them, I recommend the Adler or Moeck line of recorders. For really ambitious people there are reproductions of baroque and renaissance oboes, bassoons, shawms, rackets, cornetts, serpents etc. available on special order.

William M. Fetcher
CINC PAC flt Band

Mittenwald Company
1565 W. Howard St.
Chicago, Illinois 60626

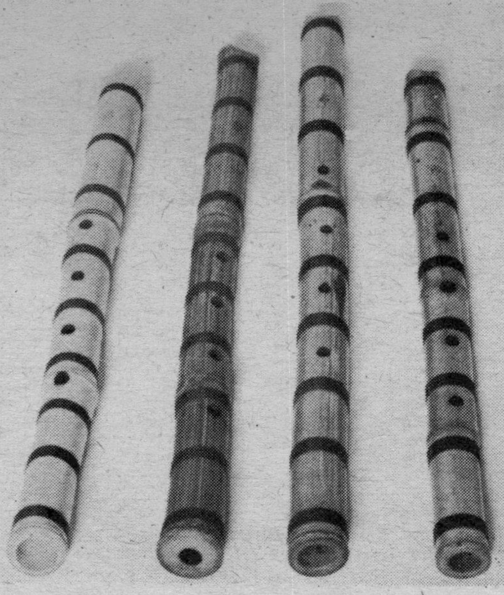

Shakuhachi

I make shakuhachi flutes. The shakuhachi is Japanese in origin, an end-blown flute tuned to a pentatonic scale. Its music— one of the major genres of traditional Japanese music— flourished during the Edo Period (1603-1867) and lasted well into the Meiji Era. It faded, finally, into relative obscurity when challenged by the pervasive absorption of Western classical forms. Only recently, in Japan, has there been a revival of traditional shakuhachi music. The effect of Western imperialist penetration on indigenous Third World cultures is especially apparent in the case of Japanese music. By the 'Twenties and 'Thirties the majority of contemporary musicians were firm in their preoccupation with Bach and Beethoven. Attempts to integrate classical Japanese forms into this scheme resulted in such perversions as grandiose emulations of Western symphonic music. Perhaps less pretentious, but just as perverse, was the incorporation (or exploitation) of traditional music into Pop Culture in Japan. Just the other day I came across a recording entitled something like The Shakuhachi Goes Latin. *Well, perhaps Xavier Cugart does play an occasional gig at a zen monastery.*

Historically, the shakuhachi went through a number of heavy trips. During different periods it was favored by men of diverse temperaments and ways of life: from mendicant Buddhist monks to lower-class Samurai (who, disarmed of their swords by the Emperor, carried the Shakuhachi as a weapon, a club) to merchants. The appeal of its subtle qualities is near universal.

Before I tell you of my experiences with this flute, I'll quote a very concise description of it by Kishibe Shigeo in The Traditional Music of Japan: *"The instrument is made from the lowest section of the bamboo. The average diametre of the pipe is 4-5 cm, and the inside of the pipe is almost cylindrical. . . .The standard length of 1.8 (Japanese feet) or 54.5 cm is used for solo pieces (when played in ensemble with Koto and Shamisen its length is varied according to the pitch of the other instruments) and the pitch of the open pipe, d, is regarded as the standard pitch. Five fingerholes, four in front and one in the back, give the following six tones in the standard pipe, d (closed), f, g, a, c, d'. By various fingerings, half-holing, and controlling the angle of the mouthpiece against the lip, all of the twelve tones can be produced. The mouthpiece at the top of the pipe is made by cutting the edge diagonally toward the outside. This type of mouthpiece makes it possible for the player to control the pitch by changing the angle, which in turn produces a delicate change intonation not possible on a Western recorder (blockflote) having a whistle type of mouthpiece. As well as the delicate changing of intonation and various kinds of portamento, the noise of blowing on the edge of the mouthpiece creates an artistic effect. Of course the mellow timbre of the rather thick bamboo pipe is the basic characteristic of the instrument." The inherent dispassion of any attempt to discribe the sound of the shakuhachi is brought home forcefully only by the sound itself. In short, one must expeience it and then create it himself. My own experience of seven or eight months has been a love affair with this sound. At times, still, it eludes me and laughs at me; at other times it caresses me. Always, however, it reflects some fundamental aspect of my being. The shakuhachi is a barometer fo the soul; it cannot be cheated. It never lies. That is, unless I do.*

To get down to business: I was turned on to the shakuhachi by some friends in Berkeley. It was magnetic: a whirlwind romance. This experience, I later discovered when selling shakuhachis, was typical. Before it was introduced to me, I had never heard of it nor read of it in books. Soon after purchasing my first flute, I tried my hand at making one. Other people who came around saw my flutes and went through the same trip I did. The idea of selling them, however, seemed absurd. Most people find it difficult to play at first, usually have never heard of it before, and are otherwise skeptical about this thing which is so simple yet so mysterious. For most people, purchasing one is more often than not an act of faith. (Out on the street selling them I can see that faith in the eyes of those few who fall in love with the sound. The look is one of assurance and certainty. About what I cannot put into words. I have no idea.) In any event, my skepticism proved mistaken. In the months that I have attempted to sell shakuhachis several people have expressed a desire to own one. There seems to be a sizeable demand for good but inexpensive flutes of this kind. But not much of an outlet. I myself know of only one or two such outlets, and they deal with a small clientele on a selective basis. The waiting lists are long; the prices are expensive. What I am proposing to do is provide good inexpensive shakuhachis to those who desire them. It's as simple as that.

One final thing which I would like to emphasize. The flutes I am presently making are not <u>authentic</u> *shakuhachis. Avoiding semantic hassles this merely means that they are not made of the root end of the bamboo. Such root pieces already aged (the optimum length of aging is three years for a piece of bamboo that is to be fashioned into a shakuhachi) are very difficult to come by. As such I have been using pieces close to the root. As far as I am concerned the basic difference between such flutes and root-end flutes is largely aesthetic. Of course, the tonal quality of a shakuhachi varies with a number of factors: the size of the bore, the length of the flute, the texture and density of the bamboo, etc. The flutes I have made resemble, in their tonal quality, the mellowness of the root-end shakuhachi. They are fashioned and tuned like authentic instruments. I am presently in the process of trying to score better quality bamboo: root pieces which I can age properly, then fashion into shakuhachis. (Perhaps I can run a request in the Catalogue.)*

That's about it. There are also a number of books about and recordings of shakuhachi music which I think people may be interested in. These too are kind of obscure and difficult to track down through regular channels. I can provide a list of them if desired.

Monty Levenson
Rt. 1 Hilltop Dr.
Willits, California 95490

Violin Repair

I learned violin repairing from a guy right out of a Breugel painting in Boston. Information which he passed along also is useful if you desire to repair a guitar. So— some how to and some where to.

1. Cracks in top or back.
on a violin you can take the top off and pull the split together— I would not suggest trying this on a guitar because of various construction differences. Best thing to do is fill crack with shaped splinters of wood (shaped to crack), spruce, or whatever the top is made of. These should be stuck in with a white glue Elmers is O.K. but "Tirebond," (which is slightly yellow (otherwise like elmers) is Best. Can be gotten at some hardware store— look around for it. More expensive but waterproof and strong. If can't find it is made by:
The Franklin Glue Company
Columbus Ohio U.S.A.
eight fluid ounce container (like elmers) @ $1.40

2. Tiny cracks can be fillered with "Tirebond."

3. Broken neck. (guitar) where neck joins body.
glue on with epoxy— drill hole and insert 1/2 inch wood (birch usually) dowel. coat the dowel with "tirebond" before you stick in. DO NOT fill hole with glue and drive in peg (dowel) this will give neat demonstration of how hydraulic pressure can split wood. If tremendous strength is necessary use a thick metal screw. (drill out first)

Broken neck other places.
Never have done it but some kind of pin, peg or dowel between the two pieces is highly recommended.

for finishing materials and glue of other types for use in guitars or furniture (either main business)
H. Behlen Bros. Inc.
10 Christopher St.
New York, N.Y. 10014

ask for catalogue and price list (they are separate) They are prompt. 1-2 weeks. (on east coast anyhow) they make a really beautiful white shellac.

Home recipe No. 1 for a good violin/guitar varnish
1. combine their "sandarac" resin in a jar with alcohol (rubbing type) enough alcohol to cover the sandarac and 1/3 more.
2. leave it to dissolve for a week (until it all dissolves)
3. drain through cheesecloth
4. combine with equal part of good quality white shellac
5. Powdered colour can be used with it. (get this at some art stores)
6. Thin with alcohol

Stephen Till
Concord, Mass. 01742

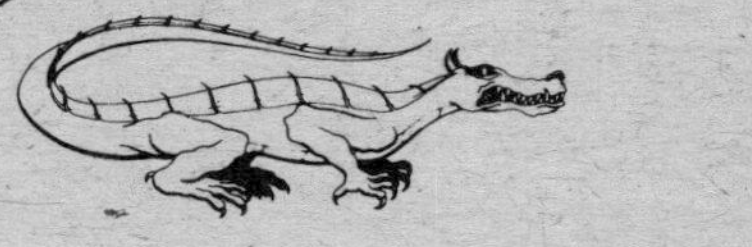

Then it was water-time again and Leonard went outside while D.R. helped his uncle up and held the jar.

•

Leonard wanted to know if there was anything he could do. I'll stay with him tonight if you want me to.

•

D.R. shook his head. I'm okay. I sleep a little, off and on. If you feed his animals I can take care of this end here just fine.

•

Leonard handed D.R. a ten dollar bill. You'll need to eat, he said. D.R. took it and thanked him and started down the hall. Hey Leonard!

•

Hey Leonard, I wonder if you'd mind calling Marcella.

•

Momma already has, said Leonard. She called her this morning.

•

I'll see you later, D.R. said.

•

And then it was time to shave him.

•

Two orderlies came in to shave Emmit, young fellows, not particularly eager for the job. The doctor wanted it done, they said. And D.R. didn't argue. I'll do it.

•

I'll do it, D.R. said, and he took the tools from the orderlies and they went away.

•

Scissors.

•

Comb.

•

Razor, shaving cream. I'm going to give you a haircut and a shave, Emmit.

•

Hunh?

Horns, Strings, and Harmony

This is a very clear and fairly comprehensive introduction to musical physics, with suggestions for experiments to be performed by the reader at home. It is a paperback of 260 pages with a good bibliography for further study. The author is a physicist and musician; the book is written for musicians and amateur physics teachers.

There are three main divisions of subject matter:

1) Theoretical discussions of the principles of vibration, Chapters II, III, and VII

*2) Practical applications,
 Chapters IV and V — the physics of hearing
 Chapters VI, VIII, and IX — instrumental design
  (strings, brass, woodwinds)*

3) Homemade wind instruments, Chapter X.

Familiarity with algebraic concepts is necessary throughout; access to musical instruments is helpful. Most of the experiments can be done at home without too much difficulty or expense (whistles, string, beads, etc.). The chapter on homemade instruments is for accomplished wind instrumentalists who are also confident with hand tools.

*[Reviewed by Peter Lynn Sessions.
Suggested by Allen Watson III]*

Horns, Strings, and Harmony
Arthur H. Benade
1960; 269 pp.

$1.95 postpaid

from:
Doubleday & Co.
501 Franklin
Garden City, N. Y. 11531

or WHOLE EARTH CATALOG

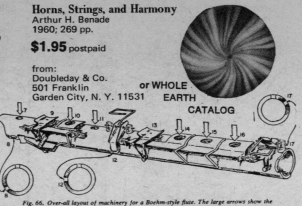

WOODWINDS

Fig. 66. Over-all layout of machinery for a Boehm-style flute. The large arrows show the finger and thumb holes, while the numbers refer to particular hole positions as explained in the text. The right-hand part of this diagram also applies to the clarinet.

Thus we see that the real test of a good violin is not in the ears of the listener, but rather in the hands of the player. If he can get the range of effects he wants, without strain, then he has a good instrument. Except in a minor way, by clearing away some of the most obvious stupidities, physics has not been able to help him very much more than has the witchcraft that has grown up lush and rank around this beautiful instrument.

Once again the flute is different from other woodwinds; it needs no bell for two reasons: first because the vibration recipe of any flute, old or new in style, is so lacking in the higher components that very little sound energy is present above the change-over frequency, and, second, the very large holes of the modern Boehm flute serve to cut off the tube so effectively that all the notes think of themselves as coming out of the end of an ordinary pipe!

Fig. 46. The size of a side hole affects a pipe's vibrational frequencies. The extent of the effect is illustrated here by comparing different hole sizes with pipe lengths that give matching frequencies. Each pipe in the lower row has a frequency matching that of the holed pipe immediately above it.

The Acoustical Foundations of Music

Here it is, folks! The hard-core treatment of the physics of music. You'll get the most out of this one if you enjoyed high-school physics. If you hated physics, skip this one and try Horns, Strings, and Harmony by Benade. You may end up with this one later.

Backus put everything into this book that he would like to cover in a college course (for musicians) but couldn't because there is too much of it for one semester. He likes to play with equations, and gives a lot of them, but I couldn't use them to compute the power output of a guitar string. Designers of instruments who want to start from the ground up should read at least parts of this book. A theoretical tool if you're into theory-building; I haven't had it long enough to see if it serves as a useful reference source.

[Reviewed by Peter Lynn Sessions]

The Acoustical Foundations of Music
John Backus
1969; 312pp.

$9.75 postpaid

from:
W. W. Norton
500 Fifth Ave.
New York, NY 10036

or WHOLE EARTH CATALOG

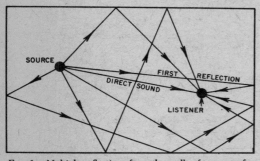

FIG. 1. Multiple reflections from the walls of a room of a single impulse produced by a sound source.

Improvising Jazz

An exceptionally clear explanation and analysis with original examples of the concepts basic to modern jazz composition and instrumental improvisation. But the title is deceptive. Modern jazz is 20th Century harmony superimposed on traditional types of chord progression, and this book should be of use to any student (or teacher) of musical practice.

The fundamental ideas of chord structure, notation, chord progression, modulation, and variation of motivic and thematic material, including a simplified chord symbolism, are presented in edible portions. The discussion of the more exotic concepts of chord/scale relationships, chord superimposition, and functional chord substitution, are among the best I have seen, including college texts. This book is a solid value that becomes more and more useful with every rereading.

[Suggested and reviewed by Peter Lynn Sessions]

What is the soloist doing when he attempts to "build"? Actually the ideal process hardly ever takes place—that is, it is hardly ever the case that a conscientious soloist plays a thinking solo for a hard-listening hearer—but when this does happen, the key process is memory. The soloist has to establish for the listener what the important POINT, the motif if you like, is, and then show as much as he can of what it is that he sees in that motif, extending the relationships of it to the basic while never giving the feeling he has forgotten it. In other words, I believe that it should be a basic principle to use repetition, rather than variety—but not too much. The listener is constantly making predictions; actual infinitesimal predictions as to whether the next event will be a repetition of something, or something different. The player is constantly either confirming or denying these predictions in the listener's mind. As nearly as we can tell (Kraehenbuehl at Yale and I), the listener must come out right about 50% of the time—if he is too successful in predicting, he will be bored; if he is too unsuccessful, he will give up and call the music "disorganized."

Improvising Jazz
Jerry Coker
1964; 115 pp.

$2.45 postpaid

from:
Prentice-Hall, Inc.
Englewood Cliffs, N. J.
07632

or WHOLE EARTH CATALOG

Kord

*i can plunk an autoharp some,
whistle a little,
used to have a trumpet lip,
but i'm tone theory blind.
Kord is a new music theory practice magazine,
for people who are trying to understand music
while they are plunking and whistling.
looks pretty useful.*

—jd

[Suggested by Peter Sessions]

Kord
Eric Kriss, ed

Defunct

from:
Kord
Box 531
Northampton
Massachusetts 01060

Oak Publications — Quick Fox

I was interested in your inclusion of autoharps, dulcimers, etc. As an old folkie this warmed the cockles of my otherwise hibernating heart. Well, if'n folks is gonna build or buy these kinda things, they's gonna hafta learn ta play em, I reckon. And for that may I suggest Oak Publications. Their list of books just keeps on growin like Topsy. Among the ones we've used and found valuable are "Note Reading & Music Theory for Folk Guitarists"—a most amazing book. Taught what and why a chord is, also how to create 'em. "Beginning the Folk Guitar," "Folk Singer's Guitar Guide Vol. 1 & 2," "Folksingers Guide to 12 string, as per Leadbelly," "The Art of Folk Blues Guitar," "How to Play 5-string Banjo by Seeger," and "The Dulcimer Book by Ritchie" have also been pretty nice to have around. Frankly, Oak's instruction books are the only ones I've ever seen that I could even RELATE to, let alone learn from, straight forward & well done.

In addition to these fine funky instructo manuals they have lotsa song collections (in case your memories a little fuzzy) for all shades of people. "Reprints from Sing Out" goes on for volumes & volumes, some bettern'n others (I mean where else can you find the words to "Plastic Jesus"?) and in addition they carry some off-the-wall collections from Russia, France, Egypt, etc. plus books on playing steeldrums (& how to make em), dulcimer, recorder, fiddle, blues harp (another goodie!), even sitar. Most of em are paper, usually illustrated, and around 2.95-3.95. But for my money Oak is THE publisher when it comes to down home funky music. Their address, by the way, is Oak Publications, 33 W. 60th St., New York, N.Y. 10023.

Love & peace

*Andi Lewis
Ottawa, Ontario*

$4.95

$2.00

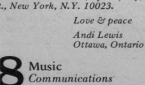

$3.95

$3.95

The expanding staff for intensity

Exploding staff for dynamics

In future issues, KORD will be publishing original compositions of a varied nature. Submissions are welcomed. Preference will be given to previously unpublished work.

Economics

All the fundamental economic principles are in this text book. It is just the thing for anyone who wants a basic familiarity with the subject. No previous knowledge of economics or any other social science or math is required. I got through an economics major in college relying almost solely on this book.

[Suggested and reviewed by Dave Shapira]

Economics
Paul A. Samuelson
1955; 1970; 868 pp.

$11.95 postpaid

from:
McGraw-Hill Book Company
330 W. 42nd St.
New York, N.Y. 10036

or WHOLE EARTH CATALOG

A good final warning in economics is this: things are often not what at first they seem. The following true statements provide examples:

1. If all farmers work hard and nature cooperates in producing a bumper crop, total farm income may *fall*, and probably will.

2. *One* man may solve his own unemployment problem by great ingenuity in hunting a job or by a willingness to work for less; but *all* cannot necessarily solve their problems in this way.

3. Higher prices *for one industry* may benefit its firms; but if the prices of *everything* bought and sold increased in the same proportion, no one would be better off.

4. It may pay the United States to *reduce* tariffs charged on goods imported, even if *other* countries refuse to do likewise.

5. It may pay a firm to take on some business at much *less than full costs.*

6. *Attempts* of individuals to save more in depression *may lessen the total* of the community's savings.

7. What is prudent behavior for an *individual* may at times be folly for a *nation.*

Let us emphasize: Each of the above statements is true; but each is outwardly paradoxical. In the course of this book, the seeming paradoxes will be resolved. There are no magic formulas or hidden tricks. It is typical of economics that anything which is really correct must seem perfectly reasonable once the argument is carefully developed.

At this point it is just as well to note that many of the above paradoxes hinge upon a single confusion or fallacy. It is called by logicians the "fallacy of composition." In books on logic, this is defined as follows:

Fallacy of composition: a fallacy in which what is true of a part is, on that account alone, alleged to be also necessarily true of the whole.

•

Why study economics, is a famous one given by Lord Keynes. The final lines of his 1936 classic, *The General Theory of Employment, Interest and Money,* consist of a famous passage:

The ideas of economists and political philosophers, both when they are right and when they are wrong, are more powerful than is commonly understood. Indeed the world is ruled by little else. Practical men, who believe themselves to be quite exempt from any intellectual influences, are usually the slaves of some defunct economist. Madmen in authority, who hear voices in the air, are distilling their frenzy from some academic scribbler of a few years back. I am sure that the power of vested interests is vastly exaggerated compared with the gradual encroachment of ideas.

•

Unless proper macroeconomic policies are pursued, a laissez faire economy cannot guarantee that there will be exactly the required amount of investment to ensure full employment: not too little so as to cause unemployment, nor too much so as to cause inflation. As far as total investment or money-spending power is concerned, the laissez faire system is without a good thermostat.

•

Limitation in the supply of money is the necessary condition if it is to have value. If currency is so unlimited in amount as to become practically a free good, people would have so much of it to spend as to bid up all prices, wages, and income sky-high. That is why constitutional powers over money and banking are never given to private groups, but are always vested in government.

•

Many writers have tried to read into economic history a linear progression through inevitable stages, such as primitive economy, feudalism, capitalism, and some form of communism. The actual facts have not agreeably stuck to such timetables; in particular, the mixed economies that dominate the Western world came into being without the permission of social prophets.

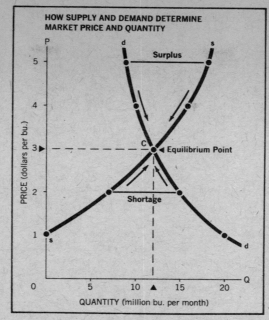

HOW SUPPLY AND DEMAND DETERMINE MARKET PRICE AND QUANTITY

FIG. 4-3. At the *C* equilibrium intersection, the amount supplied just matches the amount demanded.

At any lower *P*, the excess amount demanded will force *P* back up; and at any *P* higher than the equilibrium, the amount supplied will be excessive and *P* will be forced back down to the equilibrium level.

Beyond Economics

Since so many of you dwell on the fringes of society, I thought you might be interested in the fringes of economics where Kenneth Boulding thoughtfully paces. Those places where economics meets religion and ethics, meets general systems, social science, learning theory, evolution, and (watch it) politics.

—SB

Beyond Economics
Kenneth E. Boulding
1968, 1970; 308 pp.

$2.95 postpaid

from:
University of Michigan Press
615 East University
Ann Arbor, Michigan 48106

or WHOLE EARTH CATALOG

Similarly atoms come and go in a molecule, but the molecule remains, molecules come and go in a cell, but the cell remains, cells come and go in a body, but the body remains; persons come and go in an organization, but the organization remains. What "remains" in the midst of all this flux of components is the "role," the "place," and the relations of roles one to another. A role is a hole, an organization is a related and orderly set of holes, and one sometimes catches a fleeting and slightly night-marish vision of the scientific universe as a set of holes bounded and defined by other holes! The significance of almost anything, like that of a word, is derived largely from its context; everything, however, is the context for other things; context creates itself, *ad infinitum.*

•

Energy and matter can only be exchanged: knowledge can be *produced.*

•

The Communist society is a "one-firm" state"—that is, a society organized hierarchically into a single economic organization. It is simply General Motors (or perhaps more realistically, the Pentagon, which is in terms of national income the world's third largest Communist society) expanded to include the whole economy, with the possible exception of a few Nepmen and some surreptitious private trade. A capitalist society by contrast is "ecological" where the Communist society is "organic." A Communist society is a true Leviathan, a vast social whale; a capitalist society is more like a pond with a great multitude of interacting organisms bound together in a system of mutual exchange, or markets.

•

If a genuine learning process—the continual elimination of error in our image of the world, as well as the enlargement of this image—is to take place, there must be safeguards against rejecting inferences or rejecting the image of the past.

Fleshfeather wants to know

what is postmonetary economy?

fleshfeather

Good question.—SB

Supply and Demand

A briefer, more classic, and earlier account of economic theory is Henderson's Supply and Demand.

Bear in mind that economists are created by economies, not vice versa very much. Who does create economies? You. If you don't like the one you're in, invent and perform a better one. Do it informed or do it innocent, either one beats passive complaint.

—SB

[Suggested by Steve Baer]

I. When, at the price ruling, demand exceeds supply, the price tends to rise. Conversely when supply exceeds demand the price tends to fall.

II. A rise in price tends, sooner or later, to decrease demand and to increase supply. Conversely a fall in price tends, sooner or later, to increase demand and to decrease supply.

III. Price tends to the level at which demand is equal to supply.

It has become an axiom of business men that, while Governments can manage with more or less competence a safe and routine business like a Postal Service, their success would be unlikely to prove conspicuous in undertakings where the element of risk is great. There, it is said, we owe everything in the past to the enterprise of individual men (for even joint-stock companies have not been notable as pioneers) adventuring their own fortunes in accordance with their own unfettered judgment.

Supply and Demand
Hubert Henderson
1922; 142 pp.

$1.35 postpaid

from:
Cambridge University Press
32 E. 57th Street
New York, N. Y. 10022

or WHOLE EARTH CATALOG

•

I said I'm going to trim you up a little. Cut your hair, shave all that beard off.

•

You do and I'll chase you from star to star,

•

You can't catch me, Emmit, D.R. laughed. I'm one of them crabs, I'm on the moon, too fast for you to catch.

•

You'll see, said Emmit. You'll see how far your threats and bribes get from star to star.

•

But Emmit's eyes closed, he fell into a fifteen minute dream, and swiftly D.R. cut his hair, not much, just as much as he felt competent to do with comb and scissors. And then he cut the beard away. Scissors. Comb. And as he worked D.R. saw his father's face take shape before him. The mouth, the little cleft in the chin. They'd looked so much alike, Emmit and D.R.'s father. Royce. Somewhere there was a picture of them together in their Army uniforms, taken about 1944, home on furlough before going overseas, sitting on the front porch of the homeplace, their arms around each other and their cheeks pressed together, mugging for the camera. And they looked so much alike you couldn't tell them apart except that Emmit had on paratroop boots and Royce didn't. Emmit jumped into Holland, around Eindhoven, with the 101st Airborne, and got wounded there. A head wound. The scar is probably right down there in his hair, D.R. thought. But he had finished with the hair. There was just the beard now. Scissors, comb, he snipped and snipped, and then as Emmit slept D.R. covered his face with lather and carefully shaved him, stroke by stroke, pausing now and then to feel the smooth, clean skin as he cleared it of the stubble.

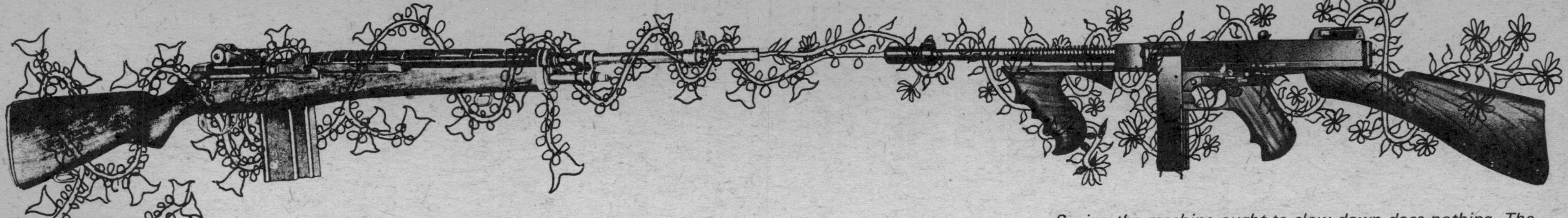

Technological Checks and Balances

As the 200th Anniversary of the American Rebellion, Declaration of Independence, Constitution, etc. comes by, we can expect some useful reappraisal of the splendid old instruments.

They were an astonishing balance of utopian and cynical, the Federalist Papers, ready to try something new in a big way, and ready to acknowledge and use the omnipresence of unenlightened self-interest.

For politics, for establishing a politically cybernetically stable system, they're still effective.

But for controlling technology, for stabilizing the economy and the drain on the environment, the American Constitution hasn't helped much. Neither has anyone else's.

Fuller suggests that by amassing the technological and resource information and computer-relating it, on-going solutions will be self-evident. I doubt if that will be adequate.

There are inter-relation forms, formulae, missing. Inventions of information structure not yet made.

Since the early 1800's economics has been fiddling around intelligently with self-balancing mechanisms, but still hasn't done the job. Economics by itself is no more of a solution than politics by itself.

It has got to be acknowledged that technology has some self-propelling dynamics of its own that unless turned on themselves will acclerate to destruction like an un-governed motor.

Saying the machine ought to slow down does nothing. The machine must be given the ability to address itself.

The whole machine: from which economics, politics, ecology, computers, and we...are not separate.

If that means new and more encompassing Constitutional models, let's get cooking.

All we have so far is the old perpetually recurrent stablizing system of internal rivalry. Our technology addresses itself by means of war. That's cool: all systems go in for it. Stable systems have rules, however, and accomplishable tokens of victory and loss. Our present World War system is short on these.

Perhaps our effort should be to civilize war rather than eliminate it.

—SB '71

Fortune

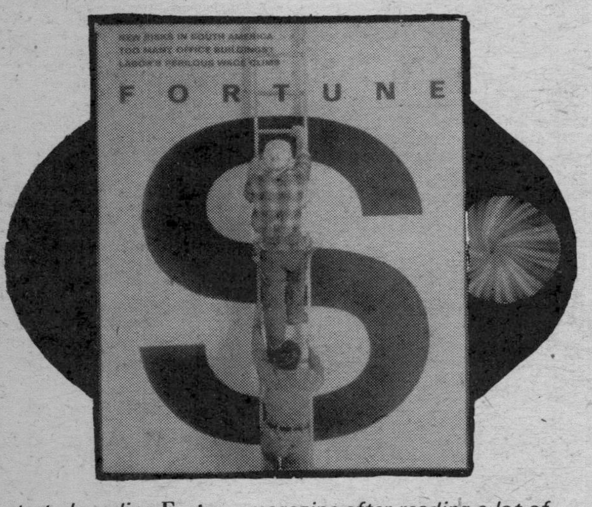

I started reading **Fortune** *magazine after reading a lot of Buckminster Fuller because it was the only periodical with regular informative articles on his level of thinking (world shipping, construction, new industrial processes, natural resources, etc.). What I found was editing and reporting that made the contents of most popular American magazines look like so much paste.* —SB

Fortune
$12 /yr (monthly)

from:
Fortune
540 North Michigan Avenue
Chicago, Illinois 60611

THE WEALTH AND POWER OF THE OVERSEAS CHINESE

Millions of expatriate Chinese knit a strong web of commerce through Southeast Asia, from Burma to the Philippines. They dominate the economic life of villages, cities, and even nations in a part of the world where the native populations, because of cultural attitudes and historical colonial policies, often lack the experience and lust for profit that the Chinese bring to business. In many of the countries where they operate, the Chinese must deal with political instability and corruption, and racial hostility that sometimes erupts into violence. Some hostility also springs from the envy of less successful local residents because the Chinese, by their very enterprise, often preempt the available business opportunities. But as a group they survive and prosper, and many international banks and corporations find the overseas Chinese to be invaluable as managers and allies.

Many of the most prominent members of this international expatriate community, some of whom are pictured in the accompanying portfolio, are men who have been driven from one country to another by war or xenophobia, and who have had to start all over again in a new setting. This ability to build a new fortune in still another strange land is a telling testimonial to their extraordinary determination, and to their acumen.

•

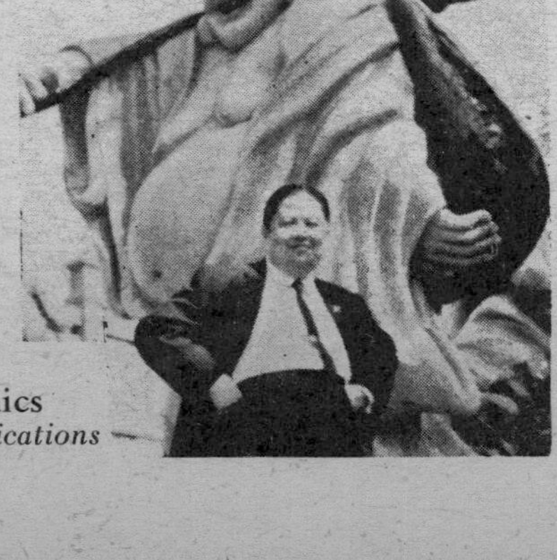

The Money Game

I have been a close stock market observer for about five years and I am still amazed at the low level and inanity of writing about the stock market. Most books are so narrow and confined as to be virtually useless.

The Money Game *is the first really good book about the market that I have found. It doesn't try to tell you how to make money or even how to play the game, but it certainly may help you avoid losing. Its great value is in stimulating the reader to think about himself and his own relationship to gambling and about mass psychology and the way it influences price movements on the market. And it is funny and enjoyable besides.*

[Reviewed by Dave Shapira]

The Money Game
'Adam Smith'
1969; 253 pp.

$1.25

from:
Dell Publishing Company
750 Third Ave.
New York, N.Y. 10017

or WHOLE EARTH CATALOG

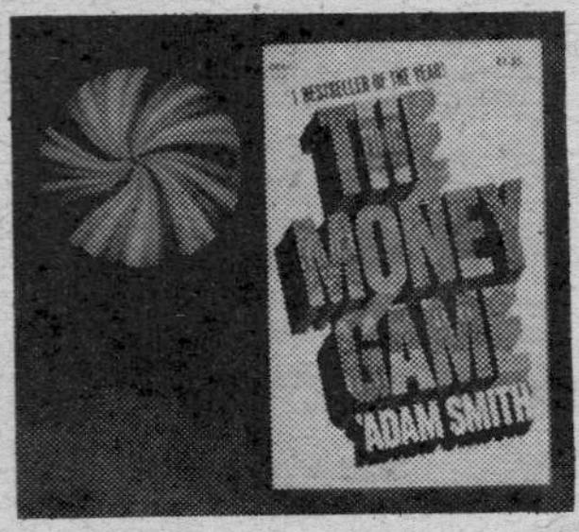

Really big money is not made in the stock market by outside investors. That may come as a shock to you. You may not even care, since by ',really big'' I am talking about multiples of millions rather than just, say, one lousy million. It is certainly possible to make ten or twenty times your money as an outside investor in the stock market given enough time, enough intelligence, enough emotional detachment, enough luck, and somebody smart on the other end of the phone. It is possible because a lot of people have done it.

Who makes the really big money? The inside stockholders of a company do, when the market capitalizes the earnings of that company.

•

Prices have no memory, and yesterday has nothing to do with tomorrow. Every day starts out fifty-fifty. Yesterday's price discounted everything yesterday. To quote Professor Fama, "the past history of the series (of stock price changes) cannot be used to predict the future in any meaningful way. The future path of the price level or a security is no more predictable than the path of a series of cumulated random numbers."

Randomness as a way of beating the market is not limited to academics, of course. Senator Thomas J. McIntyre, Democrat of New Hampshire and a member of the powerful Senate Banking Committee, brought his dart board in one day. Senator McIntyre had tacked the stock market page onto his dart board and thrown darts at it, and the portfolio picked by his darts outperformed almost all the mutual funds. (Senator McIntyre's darts thus supported the random-walk testimony of Professors Paul Samuelson of MIT and Henry Wallich of Yale, given when the Senate was considering mutual-fund legislation.)

Herman Kahn, the wide-ranging savant who heads the Hudson Institute, has observed: "When you ask a European what he does, instead of saying he's a clerk, he is likely to say, 'I'm a motor driver,' or 'I'm a mountain climber.' " Americans are tending in this direction; what a man does with his leisure is perceived, increasingly, as a key to his identity. Boating enthusiasts— nearly nine million Americans own boats— identify themselves as a breed apart from golfers, and neither resembles bowlers or Sunday painters; among boating men, moreover, the sailing fans see themselves as distinct from (and superior to) the outboard-motor crowd.

•

The psychiatrist Erik Erikson of Harvard, who is perhaps America's leading student of adolescence and youth, has suggested forcibly that the new behavior patterns of the young in the 1960's may not represent any wave of the future at all. Erikson believes that "the available inventory" of pleasure-seeking experience will be tried by the young and found only moderately satisfying, and "new boundaries will then emerge from new ways of finding out what really counts." Their judgment about what it is that "really counts" is perhaps the largest of all the uncertainties about the U.S. economy in the years ahead.

An Alternative Future for America II

What's different about this book of economics is that it was designed by graduate students. Though Theobald is the soloist, the voices of the young generation can plainly be heard. It makes you wish that every author who writes about new ways of coping with the changing world would be forced to immerse himesif in the lives of those for whom he purports to make predictions.

Because it reads like a collection of class notes and uncompleted journal articles (all of which is probably true), the book pulled me into wanting to add a chapter or two of my own. That is a delicious feeling, when you have been so many times bored by economics texts.

In fact, the book abruptly ends with a spcific invitation to its readers to take some further action. I would hope subsequent editions will continue to have such an open-ended design.

The stuff to "wow" over in the book includes Theobald's high-headed insights into computerized decision making ("There is no doubt in my mind that the computer has been one of the factors that has led us into the present disastrous situation in Vietnam"), and his list of the five traps we've laid for our social system: the war trap, *into which we have put all our ultimate sanctions for solving international disputes;* the efficiency trap, *in which we place man's human value to lie measured against the efficiency of machines;* the consumption trap— *if it's good, it must have a sales price and be advertised; and* the education trap, *in which we cement our behavior to the past. The fifth trap never gets listed— see what I mean: "unfinished journal articles"?*

Theobald's most orderly work has to do with his persuasive case for a guaranteed income, about which he has written for many years. The potentiality for his ideas during this distressed period of history are ever more dazzling. And in this book, the dazzlement is fully let loose in a series of far-out proposals for experimenting with altered life styles. It may be weeks before I stop trembling. That's why I wanted to add another chapter or two, when I got to the end of the book.

[Reviewed by Richard Raymond]

An Alternative Future for America II
Robert Theobald
1968, 1970; 199 pp.

$2.00 postpaid

from:
The Swallow Press, Inc.
1139 Wabash Avenue
Chicago, Illinois 60605

or WHOLE EARTH CATALOG

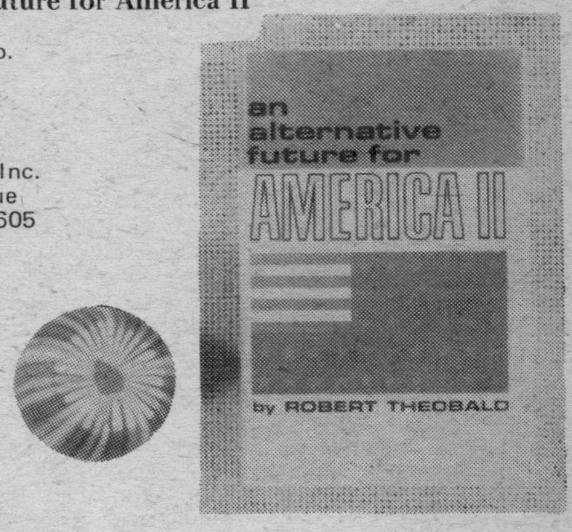

"Our key problem stems from the fact that we have made the value of a man synonymous with the economic value of the toil he performs: we fail to recognize that people should have a claim on resources even if they do not toil. The measure of destruction of our values is, I believe, shown in the fact that those living in an industrial society find it natural that people do not receive an adequate amount of food, clothing and shelter even though there is surplus food in storage and the possibility of producing more housing and more clothing if we gave people the money to buy them. We can contrast this view with that of the so-called primitive societies; in many of these it was literally impossible to starve unless the whole community was starving. George Peter Murdoch, the celebrated anthropologist, described the reaction of one group of natives when he tried to explain the problem of the poor in Western countries. There was stark disbelief: "How can he have no food? Does he have no friends? How can he have no house? Does he have no neighbors?"

•

We can anticipate the organization of what I have called "consentives": productive groups formed by individuals who will come together on a voluntary basis, simply because they wish to do so. The goods produced by these consentives will not compete with mass-produced products available from cybernated productive organizations; the consentive will produce the "custom-designed" goods and services which have been vanishing within the present economy.

How To Become a Non-Profit Tax-Exempt Corporation, and Why, and Why Not

It's not as hard as you think.

A lot of people come to Portola looking for shelter here for their educational or other do-good project. Mostly we advise them to start their own scene.

We asked the Law Commune in Menlo Park to write up the basic information, which follows.

—*SB*

SOME PRELIMINARY QUESTONS AND ANSWERS ABOUT NONPROFIT CORPORATIONS*

What is a nonprofit corporation?

A corporation is a separate legal entity which the law allows to be created for the purpose of doing business. In the eyes of the law, a corporation is a separate "person" who has its own debts, owns its property, and pays its own taxes, and who, unless dissolved by its owners, lives forever. Nonprofit means that none of the owners, or "members" receive any financial gain or profit from the work being carried on by the corporation. This does not mean that officers and employees of the corporation do not receive salaries, it means that a nonprofit corporation does not have "investors" who in the case of a regular corporation would buy stocks or bonds in the corporation and receive a dividend or some other financial return on their investment. Instead of selling stock to stockholders, who are the "owners" of a regular corporation, a nonprofit corporation sells or gives "memberships" to members. These members do not receive dividends but they do perform the acts of ownership normally carried out by the stockholders, such as electing the board of directors. The Board of Directors have the duty of watching over the business of the corporation, making the major decisions, and of hiring the officers of the corporation such as the president, general manager, and executive secretary who carry out the day-to-day business of the corporation.

What are the advantages of forming a nonprofit corporation?

The advantages of operating through a corporate structure are all based on the concept of the corporation's being a separate person. As a separate person the corporation remains no matter what individuals come and go. Most important, the corporation's liabilities are separate from those of its owners or employees. Thus the corporation's debts cannot be collected from any of the individuals connected with the corporation, unless a creditor can persuade a court that somebody set up the corporation for the sole purpose of dodging personal debts. If the corporation goes broke nobody can get at the personal possessions or money of the corporation's members. If an employee of the corporation causes serious damage in a traffic accident, the corporation will have to pay damages, but none of the other employees and none of the owners will have to pay the damages, even if the corporation itself is unable to pay.

The advantages of making the corporation nonprofit has to do with tax status. As a separate person, a regular corporation must pay its own taxes on its income, but if a nonprofit corporation qualifies under Federal standards, it does not pay income taxes. Thus if a labor union or an educational magazine, both of which are nonprofit corporations, have more money coming in than is going out, neither will have to pay the usual corporate income tax. Again, this corporate income shouldn't be confused with the salaries of individual employees which are still subject to personal income tax. Another tax advantage is that individuals who donate money to certain nonprofit corporations can receive personal tax deductions for their donations.

Another advantage of a corporation is that its very existence lends stability and respectability to your enterprise, especially in the eyes of people like bankers and local storekeepers who hand out things in credit.

What are the disadvantages of having a nonprofit corporation?

You will have the initial expense of forming the corporation. Although there are manuals available most groups will have to hire a lawyer to do the legal work and he/she will charge a minimum of several hundred dollars unless you can persuade him/her to do the incorporation as a public service (not likely). As a corporation you will have to keep careful financial records and file detailed tax returns concerning the corporation's finances. Incorporation means that you must in some way show proof of observance of specific regulations and formalities, for example, regular meetings of a board of directors; it also means someone will be watching to see that you do things like make payroll deductions, pay unemployment insurance taxes, etc.

There are other less tangible drawbacks. Persons working for the corporation will have to act with a high degree of care, since their actions can put the assets of the whole corporation at stake, for example in the traffic situation described above. Incorporation means your enterprise will have a higher degree of visibility both with the community and the government. The existence of a corporation may increase the likelihood of its being sued. For this reason, most labor unions are not incorporated. Certain people such as internal revenue agents and the state attorney general will have the right to be snooping into your affairs, if they think you are violating the purposes stated in your Articles of Incorporation or to check out any information in your tax returns.

What exactly is involved in formation of the nonprofit corporation?

As was already stated, you will almost always have to hire a lawyer to do the formation, but you should have a clear understanding of what he/she is up to. First you will have to select a name for your corporation and register it with the state—in California, specifically the office of the secretary of state. You will have to choose three or more people to act as "Incorporators". Their duties are to sign the articles of incorporation, and act as the board of directors at the first meeting of the board of directors. They may then resign and elect a new set of directors who will act as the board from then on, or they may themselves continue to act as directors. It should be noted by any potential directors, that they are required to exercise reasonable care in running the corporation and if they fail they may be held legally responsible for mismanagement.

You will also draw up Articles of Incorporation. The law requires that these articles contain the name of the corporation, the names of the incorporators, and the county where the principle place of business is to be located. Most important these articles must state the specific primary use or purposes for which the corporation was formed. These purposes must be carefully chosen since they are the most important consideration in determining whether the corporation will be granted nonprofit status for Federal tax purposes. Some time during this period, a set of by-laws will have to be drafted. The by-laws set out the rules for governing the corporation, for example, how are the directors to be elected, how are the meetings of the board called, when are meetings of the members to be called, what is the price of membership, what classes of membership are there to be, etc. In a small corporation, such questions are mostly formalities and standard forms can be used. The Articles of Incorporation should be done first since the corporation's life begins when the Articles are filed with the appropriate state agency. Sometime during this period also, you will want to apply to the Internal Revenue Service and to the appropriate state agency for a determination that the corporation will be exempt from taxes. On the average, if there are no complicated tax problems, these procedures will take about (ask Charlie).

This answer, and subsequent answers do not apply to charitable organizations such as the March of Dimes, whose regulation is both different and a great deal more detailed. Also, California considers co-operatives to be a special type of nonprofit corporation, and has special rules concerning their formation. Unlike other corporations, the state does not give the parties freedom to choose their own Articles and by-laws, instead it specifies such things as what type of officers there will be and how they are elected. However, a co-operative is also allowed to distribute some types of dividends to its members. There is another special incorporating procedure which allows the head of a religious organization to act himself in a corporate capacity. It is called a "corporation sole".

Once the corporation has been formed, you will not have to file any continuing types of reports other than tax returns. The only exception is if it becomes necessary to amend the Articles of Incorporation, which shouldn't happen unless the corporation goes through some type of major changes in its purpose for existence.

Could you explain more about the tax angles?

As was mentioned before, the Internal Revenue Service will tell you before you begin operating as a corporation whether you qualify for the various tax exemptions available to nonprofit corporations. This saves you the trouble of going through the whole procedure of formation, if you aren't going to get tax advantages.

Federal exemptions for nonprofit coporations are set up in specific categories. The most advantageous category is for "religious", "charitable", and "educational" organizations. Not only is the income of corporations within this category tax exempt, but unlike all the other categories, persons making donations to these corporations may receive tax deductions on their personal income tax. However, corporations in this category have a very important limitation on their activities; they may not participate in any political campaign, lobby for specific legislation, or otherwise engage in active political activity. This is the reason that the IRS has taken away the Sierra Club's tax exemption.

All the other categories allow the tax exemption for the corporation's income but do not allow donors to deduct their contributions. These categories include organizations dedicated to "social welfare", business leagues, social clubs, labor and agricultural organizations, credit unions, and farmers cooperatives. Exemptions from state income taxes usually are modeled on the federal laws. For most of these categories, any "unrelated business" carried on by the corporation as a subsidiary to its main purposes, for example a college bookstore, is subject to tax on its income. (Whole Earth pays taxes on its store and mail-order operation.)

In California, a few types of nonprofit corporations are also exempt from property taxes, these are, religious, hospital, charitable, scientific, and some types of higher education institutions. For all of these tax exemptions, the corporation will be required to file detailed informational tax returns showing that the corporation is not violating its exemption. Of course, if the IRS or state agency feel that the corporation has violated its exemption, it will investigate further and if not satisfied will remove the exemption for a period of time until the violation has ended.

How much of a problem is it to dissolve the corporation?

A corporation remains legally alive unless the formal procedures of dissolution are carried out. Thus if you form a corporation and later it ceases to do any business or carry out any activity, that in itself will not dissolve it. Since the members are considered the owners of the corporation voluntary dissolution can only occur when 50% of the members vote to dissolve. A formal certificate must be filed with the appropriate state agency showing that such a vote has occurred. The Board of directors must then follow a set of procedures spelled out in the laws. This process is called "winding up" and includes terminating business relationships, paying all bills, and dividing up whatever is left over among the members. The corporation then ceases to exist once a certificate of winding up and dissolution has been filed with the appropriate state and county agencies. Like formation, you will probably have to hire a lawyer to do your dissolution.

There are also several types of procedures for getting a court to order dissolution. These are generally termed involuntary dissolution, and are of course expensive since they go through a court. The directors of 1/3 of the members may ask the court to dissolve if the corporation has not done any business for a year, if there has been serious mismanagement, or if there is a serious deadlock among the directors.

What alternatives to formation of a nonprofit corporation are there?

The most important alternative form of enterprise is a nonprofit unincorporated association. The main difference is that the association has no separate legal existence. Thus any debts and other liabilities of the association can be collected from the individual active members of the association. As was noted in the case of labor unions, this may be an advantage. Futhermore, the modern trend of the law has been to give associations many of the advantages formally held only by corporations. For example, associations can now own some types of property in their own name, and can sue and be sued in their own name. Associations may apply for the various federal and state tax exemptions in the same way that a corporation would.

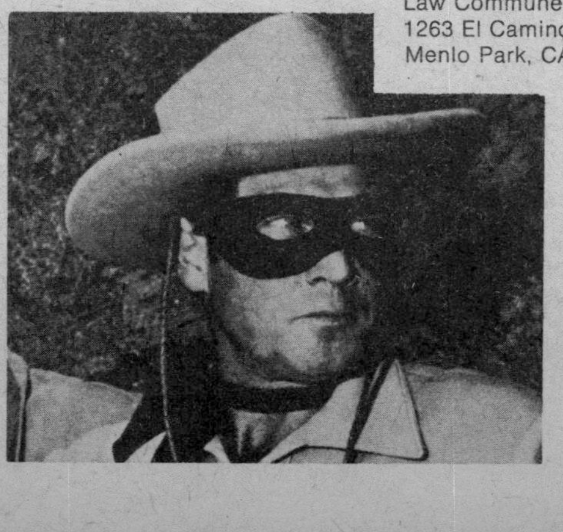

Law Commune
1263 El Camino
Menlo Park, CA. 94025

* *Except for tax questions, which concern the federal government, each state has its own laws regarding corporations. These answers are based on California law, but at least in regards to these general questions, the reader can assume that his state has similar or analogous laws.*

Ayn Rand says the dollar sign insignia was arrived at by superimposing the U and the S of United States. Means US.

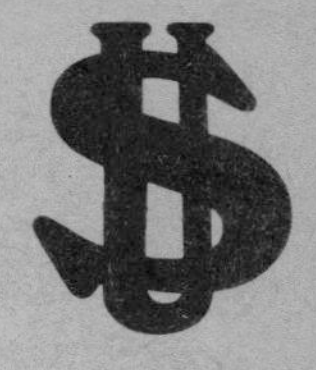

"If there are no complicated tax problems, the attorney should complete incorporation procedures within a month. A ruling from the IRS should take about three weeks more, once incorporation is completed. The most important factor in determining the length of time everything will take is how quickly your attorney works."

—Charlie

One Dollar Lawyer

Some of us choose to deal with money. The best book I have found on the subject is How To Avoid Financial Tangles *by Kenneth G. Masteller. This book is not quite as good as having a lawyer, but then I talk to a lawyer frequently and I learned a lot reading this book. Volume I deals with property problems, financial relationships, joint ownership, wills and trusts; life, auto and fire insurance. Volume II deals with taxes, gifts, and help for the widow. Volume III has ideas for retirement planning. You can do most of the legal bit yourself. $1.00 per volume from American Institute for Economic Research, Great Barrington, Mass. 01230. Please note I am not recommending their books on investing. The only complaint I have is that this used to be available for $1.00 total, and these people are always screaming about inflation.*

Walter Groch
Berkeley, Calif.

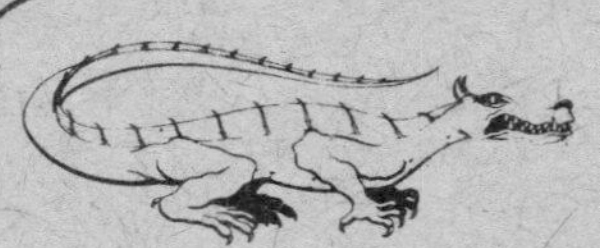

•

Emmit felt his face. He rubbed his cheek with his hand, then both cheeks at once with both his hands, and finished smiling. Did you do that? he asked.

•

Yep.

•

Are you the one in charge here?

•

D.R. said he was.

•

Can I dream away the sky?

•

You can dream away the sky and fill the gap with blossoms, Emmit. You can do anything you feel of a mind to do, old friend.

•

I'll dream the sky away and think about the honey-pond and fritter-tree, Emmit said. That's a land, you know.

•

I might dream along with you after while, said D.R. I'm pretty sleepy.

•

Don't go to sleep, said Emmit. That'd violate the other custom.

•

What custom is that, Emmit?

•

A trustworthy man on guard! said Emmit, and for the first time since they'd been there, he laughed.

•

D.R. tried to tell Estelle about it, the shave, and Emmit's face, so much like his father's. But that was too particular, too precise a thing for him to have enough words for. What he did have words for was an image of how it felt to be there in that hospital like he was. He said, one of the men in Emmit's ward has been here four months now, and another almost three, and I know that to them a day and a half can't seem like a very long time. But it's some kind of infinity for me. I haven't slept at all except little naps in my chair, and once last night for about an hour lying on a gurney in the hall. It's very informal at night. It's a small place, and nobody ever comes on heavy much. You can stretch out where ever you can at night and nobody seems to mind. I have the keenest sense of this place as a secret city hidden from the world. And all the people in it are perpetually stoned on the activity of the city, which is suffering, and coping with suffering. Some of the suffering is birth and some of it is death, and endless different points in between. After a day and a half here, round the clock, I feel as if we've all been here all our lives, together, as if we're all warm and comfortable inside this strange cloak. It's like I'm wearing this hospital, as if its atmosphere and its routines, night and day and day and night, people coming and going, the change of shifts, the long passing of the night and then the day, is all some kind of magnificent garment I've put on. And Emmit is in it with me. We're all in it, doctors, patients, nurses, visitors, secretaries, everybody, and it's as if we all like being here in one another's company, collectively

Nineteenth Century Token Coinage
W.J. Davis
1969; Seaby, London

A Tool for Experimental Economics

TOKENS

In Las Vegas and Reno, tokens (called "tokes") are the money of the casinos. On the tables and the slots they work like dollars. Turn your cash into pretty bits of plastic, and easily spend your plastic. With the forthcoming return of "silver dollars" (Ike dollars this summer), the token traffic may subside a little.

In Nevada, tokens aid irrational behavior. At a mental hospital in Illinois, tokens have proved to be a powerful incentive to sanity. By putting the patients of one ward (a picked set of "incurable" or "incorrigible" ladies) on a token economy, the experimenters found they simply solved 2 basic problems of treatment—how to reinforce (reward) sane behavior, and how to encourage real transaction between a sick patient and the real world. The patients were paid for small items of self-care (grooming, bedmaking, etc.), for chores on the ward (filling the coffee urn, setting table, assisting nurse, etc.), and for off-ward jobs (cooking, clerical, laboratory, etc.). With their tokens they could buy privacy (personal cabinet, screen, rent on preferred room, personal chair, etc.), goodies from the commissary, leave from the ward, exclusive use of the TV, etc.

The book, **The Token Economy**
A Motivational System for Therapy and Rehabilitation
Teodoro Ayllon, Nathan Azrin
1968; 288 pp
$5.20
from:
Appleton-Century-Crofts
440 Park Ave. South
New York, NY 10016
or WHOLE EARTH CATALOG

is a dry technical book but sensational if you're interested in miracle cures, social cybernetics, whole-system education, or experimental economics. It's like an X-ray of economic civilization. The crazy ladies---and all of us, once you notice--- are seen to swerve their behavior enormously with minor easily made shifts in assigned values and transactional opportunities in the ward. Yet much of what goes on is determined by derived value, by what the ladies really want. They gain a power in their formerly powerless environment. I'm grateful to Jay Baldwin for telling me of this book.

If a school or a community goes onto a token economy, they suddenly become much more of a single entity, more interrelated, and more distinct from the rest of the world. The closeness has little to do with space. One of the qualities of money is the way it spans distance and time.

Companies used to pay workers in tokens that were only good at the company store. The company profited twice. That system inside out might be a community co-op which sold at cost only to token holders, that is to sustainers of the community.

Reportedly, schools that have gone in for simulation games have had considerable success with economic games involving token money. They gradually expand from one class to incorporate the whole school and eventually the kids' homes.

I know of no examples of tokens being used for economic experimentation. But how quickly you could establish a sub-economy, directly related to the big economy, yet differently structured. It would be completely measurable, and therefore precisely adjustable. You could know exactly the relation of your mutant economic system to the normal, and gauge your wholeness and independence, or balance and success.

As for legality, the only regulations I've been able to find are: your tokens can't resemble US currency (that's counterfeit), and they can't have a dollar and cent value indicated on them. There mav be other regulations.

One good source I know of for beautiful money is Remson Wood of Riderwood, Maryland. He makes diffraction grating disks with whatever imprint you want. Rainbow money, cheap.

Subway tokens. Subculture tokens.

—SB

A state mental hospital is a severe testing ground for any theory of human behavior. Almost every conceivable behavioral difficulty can be seen there, often in its most extreme form. Senile disorders, neurological disorders, adolescent problems, employment problems, sexual difficulties, addiction, alcoholism, general disculturation, intellectual retardation, and neuroticism converge and interact in one community. To gaze upon this multiplicity of disorders and problems is to be overwhelmed by a sense of hopelessness and helplessness. Any simple answer that one might consider for the problems of one patient seems irrelevant for other patients. Theories of human behavior which have been so relevant in treating neurotics, such as psychoanalysis and nondirective therapy, flounder when encountering the institutionalized psychotic. It seems that every type of explanation has already been proposed, applied, and found wanting in its general application, including psychotherapy, group dynamics, recreation therapy, vocational therapy, drug therapy, etc. One feels compelled to do something-anything—to assist this forsaken segment of humanity. One might feel that if only the individual could be made to *talk out* his problems, then some cure might be achieved. Yet, a large segment of the patients will not listen, much less respond, to any conversation. How can we achieve therapy by having the patient reach an insight into the meaning of his hallucination when there is not even sufficient motivation for him to listen to the therapist? How can a vocational therapist pry a patient loose from his psychosis by interesting him in learning a vocational skill when it is not even possible to interest the patient in eating to stay alive? Where does one begin in imparting a sense of personal identity and worth to a patient that has been incontinent for 10 years?

...Psychologists and psychiatrists alike have fled from this graveyard of psychological theories, leaving only a small but extremely dedicated group of psychologists and psychiatrists to deal with these problems. The ratio of patients to psychologists or psychiatrists in a mental hospital, where the need is greatest, is often in the order of 1000 to 1.

...The large mental hospital is a testing ground for psychological practices as well as theories. Any general procedure that is found to be effective with the great range of problems encountered in a mental hospital will probably find great applicability in many different disciplines concerned with human behavoir. A method of controlling the aggressive outburst of the destructive patient would seem to have great relevance for the control of criminal behavior outside the hospital. Similarly, a procedure that could motivate a vegetative psychotic who has been hospitalized for 20 years might be appropriate for motivating a high school dropout to return to his school. A procedure that motivated a withdrawn patient to seek out the company of other patients will probably have some relevance in building social habits in school children. A course of action which enabled a congenitally retarded child to function in some fashion should surely have some message for developing improved methods of teaching a normal child the multiplication table in a more efficient manner. From this point of view, the mental hospital provides a challenging opportunity to devise totally new psychological and educational procedures in spite of the adversities that such an environment seems to present...

•

The procedure for adjusting the earnings for each job was in terms of supply and demand. Those jobs for which many patients volunteered were assigned a smaller number of tokens. The jobs for which few patients volunteered were assigned a sufficiently large number of tokens to ensure the selection of the job by at least 2 patients. Periodic examination of the number of individuals who selected each job led to periodic revision of the number of tokens given for it. Other considerations such as the presumed difficulty or the duration of the job were not factors in assigning a given pay to a job. In fact, some jobs that were fairly demanding physically and that required about 3 hours through the day for completion, such as sweeping the floors, earned only about 5 tokens since many patients volunteered for those positions. A job that earned a large number of tokens but for which there were few patients who qualified for it was the job of tour guide. This job required only about 10 minutes for completion yet earned 10 tokens. The procedure minimized the dangers of personal idiosyncratic evalution of what a given job should pay. If a particular job involved certain features that were considered highly desirable for a given individual, the earnings for that job were arbitrarily adjusted upward in order to ensure exposure of the patient to that job.....

•

Prices for each of the reinforcers were based primarily on supply and demand. Some kinds of reinforcers were necessarily limited because of considerations of space. Not all patients could sleep in the same well furnished dormitory room. The opportunity to go by bus to a nearby town was necessarily limited by the size of the bus. Because of time limitations not all patients could speak to the ward psychologist or the social worker as frequently and as long as they might care to. In such cases, the cost was adjusted upward to the point where the number of patients selecting the reinforcer did not exceed the supply of the reinforcers. If the reinforcing items or activities were available in a greater quantity than was being utilizied by the patients, the cost of that item was revised downward. Periodic and regular review of the number of patients requesting each item was made in order to assure the full use of all available resources and reinforcers. Some reinforcing activities had no limitation of availability. For example, as many patients as wanted could go to the movies and dances, attend religious services go on walks, etc. Consequently, most of these items were given a cost of only one token to provide maximum opportunity for the patients to obtain these reinforcers. Sometimes therapeutic objectives dictated that a given individual should be exposed to a reinforcer that he could not afford. In such cases, the cost to that individual was reduced to an amount that was sufficient to motivate the individual to select that reinforcer. For example, at one time to encourage a mentally defective patient to have more interaction with the supervising ward psychologist, the usual cost of 20 tokens for an interview was reduced to one token.

•

...The primary function of the tokens was to bridge the delay between the response and the delivery of the reinforcement. The tokens also provided an objective record of reinforcement delivery and permitted an objective check by the supervising personnel on the appropriate occurrence of the conditioned reinforcement procedure. Also, the attendants did not have to be concerned about voice tone or facial expression as they would if they were delivering a social or a verbal type of reinforcement. From the patient's point of view, the token provided an unambiguous indication of approval independent of the attendant's particular mood or whim at the time of delivery. Further, the token procedure limited the need to discover what reinforced the patient when the response occurred. It was necessary only to deliver the tokens and allow the patient complete self-expression of her individual preferences at a later time when the token could be exchanged for a wide variety of different reinforcers. (Ferster, 1961). Most important, the objectivity of the procedure guaranteed that the patient would be reinforced even for minimally useful responses, thereby freeing the attendants and the staff from the need to define what was *normal* or worthy of being rewarded.
The effectiveness of the reinforcers program was not restricted by any identifiable trait or characteristic of the patients...

Token (A.S. *tacen*, a sign, symbol): (i) A token in numismatics is a piece of metal, in size, shape, and type resembling a coin, issued usually without government authority, and generally at a time when coin of the realm is in short supply; it is intended as a pledge to be redeemed either in goods to the value it represents or in corresponding coin of the realm. It is usually of lower intrinsic value than a coin. In the Middle Ages base-metal spurious coins were imported into England from the Continent (see *Spurious*) and the brass *jetons* or *Nuremburg Tokens* (q.v.) would serve as small local change in the neighborhood of a monastery. Owing to the growth of trade in the sixteenth century, considerable inconvenience was experienced in the lack of small change. To remedy this, traders themselves started to strike small token coins in base metal.

In the time of James I, the Government took things in hand, and issued *Harrington farthings*, as an official token coinage.

These, however, were extremely unpopular. They showed a handsome profit to the instigators and no small loss to those who had to use them. During the whole period of the Commonwealth no copper coins were issued, but an enormous number of private tokens were struck by municipalities, traders, tavern keepers, etc. It is estimated that over 20,000 different types were issued from 1648 to 1672. In Evelyn's *Diary* we read of the tokens issued by every tavern

"payable through the neighborhood, though seldom reaching farther than the next street or two."

Such common inscriptions on them as FOR Y^e^ BENEFIT OF Y^e^ POORE show that they were essentially a poor man's coin. They are usually circular, but square, heart-shaped, lozenge-shaped, and octagonal tokens are common. Penny tokens are known, but the usual values are halfpennies and (more frequently) farthings. They are usually dated, and give the name and town of the issuer. Often they bear the initials of the issuer and of his wife, sometimes joined by a "true-love" knot. In 1672 Charles II issued the first regal copper coins, and the making of private tokens was prohibited by proclamation, in August of that year.

(ii) *Eighteenth-century Tokens.* Between 1755 and 1769 no regal copper coins were struck. Halfpennies and farthings were struck 1770–75, but in no great quantity, and no more copper coins were struck until 1797. In 1787 local issues by private companies and corporations began with the Anglesey penny and halfpenny (q.v.). About the same period, John Wilkinson struck his well-known "Iron-Master" Tokens, bearing his portrait, and on the reverse, a steam forge.

Eighteenth-century tokens abound in mythical types (Bladud, Prince of Bath, Lady Godiva), historical (King Alfred, John o' Gaunt, Queen Elizabeth, Isaac Newton), contemporary notorieties (Nelson, Earl Howe, William Pitt), literary characters (Shakespeare, Dr. Johnson), politicians (Thomas Hardy, Horne Tooke).

On the social side we find bathing machines, mail coaches, and ships of all types depicted. Some tokens are in the nature of advertisements (Lackington the Bookseller and his "Temple of the Muses"), vendors of boots, gloves, umbrellas, fireplaces displaying their wares. Some are architectural in type (cathedrals, shire halls, guild halls, bridges, canals, town crosses, Newgate Jail). Many of these were evidently struck more as collectable curiosities and souvenirs rather than as currency. For this reason it is easy to find pieces in uncirculated condition. PRIVATE TOKENS were also struck in limited numbers by individuals as numismatic oddities, and for gifts to friends. The large issue of regal pennies and twopenny pieces in 1797 brought the series of eighteenth-century tokens to an end.

(iii) *Nineteenth-century Tokens.* As the Industrial Revolution swept over the country, so supplies of copper coins, needed to pay the thousands of workers entering the new factories, dwindled, and in 1811 a number of private firms began striking the larger penny tokens. Such tokens were declared to be illegal in 1817, though tokens of the Birmingham Workhouse and Sheffield Overseers of the Poor were allowed to circulate for some years after this date, owing to the great quantity which had passed into circulation. Silver tokens began to be issued as early as 1804, but most of these are dated 1811 and 1812. They are mostly sixpences and shillings, though pieces of higher value were sometimes issued. (See also *Bank of England Dollars; Dollars, Countermarked.*)

In the United States large quantities of privately issued tokens were struck during the economic distress of the 1830's (see *Hard Times Tokens*). Several decades later thousands of different kinds of tokens made their appearance during the Civil War because the official coinage was hoarded (see *Civil War Tokens*).

Private tokens were widely used in Canada even after the introduction of official coinage in the nineteenth century (see *Canadian Tokens*).

Coin Dictionary and Guide
C.C. Chamberlain and Fred Reinfeld
1960; Sterling, NY

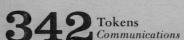

Two-Factor Theory

There is a conspicuous void in the arguments and the programs of the counter-culture groups of this country, in that they have produced no well-formulated economic theories.

Unfortunately and ironically, Lou Kelso, who has some very imaginative economic proposals, has been offering them for many years to the establishment, the dinosaur culture.

Kelso has long ago perceived the obsolescence of prevailing economic doctrine that deifies labor as the single component of capitalism. He correctly argues that machinery, land, structure (that is, capital), produce wealth in the same way that human labor does. He calls this insight "two factor" economics or "universal capitalism", and since it recognizes the emerging importance of technology, and accepts the diminishing necessity of human labor, it is an economic theory that is beautifully tailored to the values and beliefs of most CATALOG readers and those seeking alternatives to dinosaur existence.

Kelso's book struggles manfully with practical solutions, including a Second Income Plan, a Capital Diffusion Insurance Corporation, and even a proposed Full Production act of 19—-.

These proposals have been laid on presidential candidates, congressmen, newspaper publishers, leading economists, and nearly all key decision makers of the establishment over and over again.

So either Kelso is a lousy salesman or the dinosaurs are convinced their own designs will see them through.

My advice to Lou is: "Come on, Lou, grow long hair, drop all that establishment costumery, immerse yourself in the now generation, and start to work with a constituency that wants you and needs you. If you don't some bright young radical economist certainly will."

[Suggested and reviewed by Richard Raymond]

Two-Factor Theory:
The Economics of Reality
Louis O. Kelso and Patricia Hetter
1967; 202 pp.

$1.95 postpaid

from:
Vintage Books, Inc.
201 E. 50th Street
New York, N.Y. 10022

or WHOLE EARTH CATALOG

The theory of unviersal capitalism makes two assumptions about the good society. One is that its most important value is freedom. Any society seriously caring about freedom must structure its economic institutions so as to widely diffuse economic power while keeping it in the hands of individual citizens. Nor can freedom in an industrial democracy be long maintained unless the economic well-being of the majority is reasonably secure. Never in history has universal suffrage been built on a sound economic foundation; it is this defect, not the ordinary man's inability to cope with freedom, that accounts for the notorious fragility of democratic institutions.

Secondly, it is assumed that leisure is essential to a civilized definition of affluence. To venerate collectively what every intelligent man eschews individually, namely unnecessary toil for the goods of subsistence, makes no human sense. Today, in Western industrial society, we see toil advancing totalitarian claims on the whole of life at the very moment in history when technology offers liberation. Leisure and the liberal-arts tradition are giving way to the totalitarian work state which has no place for whole men, only "human resources" and servile functionaries.

•

As Harold Moulton of the Brookings Institution first pointed out in 1935, new capital does not have to be financed exclusively from past savings. It can just as easily and logically be financed from credit, by means that create new capital owners simultaneously with new capital assets. Capital produces wealth. Unlike consumer goods, it is inherently financeable. With very slight alterations the same techniques being used today to finance the acquisition of non-income-producing consumer goods can be employed (1) to vastly expand the existing economy—to build a Second Economy —and, (2) to enable noncapital-owning households to buy equity interests in new capital as it is formed, paying for it precisely as the capital owner (with rare exceptions) has always done—out of the income the newly formed capital produces.

•

Alternative is indeed the crux of the matter, and here it is that youth is vulnerable. For as the elders point out, the posture of moral superiority is easy to maintain from the sidelines, particularly when one's livelihood and education are being provided for by others. But would the young do any better under the same circumstances? *Will* they do any better when their turns come? The answer is that youth would not and cannot, given the financial and economic framework within which the elders are operating. While the moral convictions of individuals are important in the long run, it is institutions that determine the immediate course of events—particularly the institutions of finance.

Not an evil conspiracy, but defective financial institutions and the lack of alternative institutions have delivered us to the door of the total work state. This book has attempted to present the alternatives, founded on the missing logic of an industrial economy.

Not-money Money

Your piece on tokens interested me. Contrary to what you indicate, there is a law making it illegal to "utter coins intended for use as money" in the U.S., with a similar provision for paper bills. However, these provisions can be avoided by printing disclaimers like those appearing on the enclosed certificates ("Not Legal Tender For Any Purpose," "Not Intended As Current Money"). There's no effective way to prove any other intent.

These bills were the result of a weekend spent tinkering with play money and a Monday morning visit to a local fast-print place. The denominations are in decagrams of silver (One decagram equals ten grams, 454 grams equal one pound, 37 plus gram equals one troy ounce). The decagram is currently worth 50¢ to 60¢. Although silver is subject to considerable short-term price fluctuation, it is fairly invulnerable to radical, runaway inflation, and hence is a good base for an alternative unit of value to the dollar.

To validate the certificates, the issuer has only to sign them and put his address on them. If he is issuing a large quantity of these notes, and wants to protect himself against radical changes in the price of silver, he can make an appropriate deposit with the Atlantis Commodities Purchasing Service (ATCOPS, RD 5, Box 22A, Saugerties, NY 12477). This is a "silver bank" (current assets about 85,000 decagrams of silver (Decas), or $40,000 to $50,000, backed by the personal faith and credit of the owners, who are worth several hundred thousand to several million dollars). That is, it takes your dollar deposits, converts them into an equivalent number of Decas (on paper), pays 3% annual interest in Decas, and, when you want to withdraw your money, they convert it back to dollars and pay you. Thus you earn 3% plus (or minus) any change in the price of silver, and, in any case, you needn't worry about any price changes of silver screwing you vis-a-vis any outstanding decagram notes you have.

This outfit also mints Deca coins, but, by the time you add sales tax, shipping, the fact that the coins are sterling (92.5%) silver but are priced at the price of 99.9% silver, etc., etc., etc., these are of interest mainly as curios. ATCOPS is a part of Operation Atlantis, a group that is planning to found its own country in the Carribean this fall. They put out a four-page newsletter (theoretically semimonthly, but often late) at $4.50 for 24 issues. They also have, for $1.00, a pamphlet describing their premises (The Story of Operation Atlantis). All from the address above in Saugerties.

Sincerely yours,
Erwin S. Strauss
TTA Enterprises
Santa Barbara, CA.

Money, Honey

Your comments about a depression further stimulated my thinking organ. Nearly every financial analyst who correctly called the 68-69-70 stock market slump and associated phenomena now predicts a major depression, coupled with a runaway inflation and eventual devaluation of our now worthless dollar. Variations on the theme are that an increasingly intense cycle of "regression/inflation" will precede the deluge. It is also universally agreed that the best hedge against said deluge is 1. savings account in a Swiss bank in Swiss francs (more than 80% gold backed, if the dollar is devalued you will earn much, much more than the 5-6% they pay on savings); 2. silver coins (for cash you can buy coins in $1000 bags or less from Deane S. Jones, PO Box 8414, Reno, Nevada 89507), preferably in dimes and quarters (circulated) for which you will have to pay a premium over face value because the silver content is worth more than the face price. 3. leveraged silver coins, if you have a bit more to invest, the Pacific Coin Exchange, 3520 Long Beach Blvd., Long Beach, California 90807, will loan you $1100 on each $1000 bag of coins and charge you 9% interest. This means you can leverage your own $1000 up to about $5000 and risk only the premium (about $250) and interest. This risk is almost nonexistent—except that it is not at all unthinkable that the USFeds will make ownership of silver illegal as they did gold in 1933. You'd get your money back anyway. It is possible to buy silver, leveraged, through a Swiss Bank and Economic Research Counselors, 1760 Marine Dr., Suite 212, West Vancouver, B.C. Canada V7V 3P2 are specialists in helping you do this.

If you buy silver coins as a hedge against the deluge (anyone will take a good hard silver coin) it will be best to store them in a safe deposit company, NOT IN A BANK. Bank Holidays close the whole bank, and when silver is called in, goodbye! Or you can dig a hole in the ground. The lowest prediction for the price of silver (which sold for $1.78 and ounce at the close of the market the end of July) is $3.00 by the end of '71. Many factors make other predictions much, much higher.

The important thing is that WHEN (not IF) the public finally looses all confidence in its politicos and their funny paper money, dimes will spend. You must have pre 1965 coins or you will get funny copper/nickle tokens called money.

At $1.80 an ounce your coins are worth 34% more than face value; at $3.00 an ounce they are worth 121% face value.

If you have a lot of bread, and want a more easily stored and stable piece of wealth you can buy British Sovereigns (pre 1933) from Jones. Today they will cost you about $10.50 each or about $44 an ounce, which is an excellent buy. They could be used as a source of land purchase, etc., or to trade for more respectable silver. Many might think these little anxieties are the mark of old fashioned reactionary nuts; however,

1. the government always degrades money
2. politicians always lie
3. people always accept silver and gold which can be tested easily for its integrity
4. nobody has found a politician integrity test yet.

Silver and gold have become good buys because the USFeds have given all theirs away and can no longer depress the market.

Cheers,
George von Hilsheimer, himself

PS. Unless your crystal ball really works stay out of the silver commodity futures market. Only about 1% of contracts are delivered on, which means the futures games is a legal way to play craps.

More Money, Honey

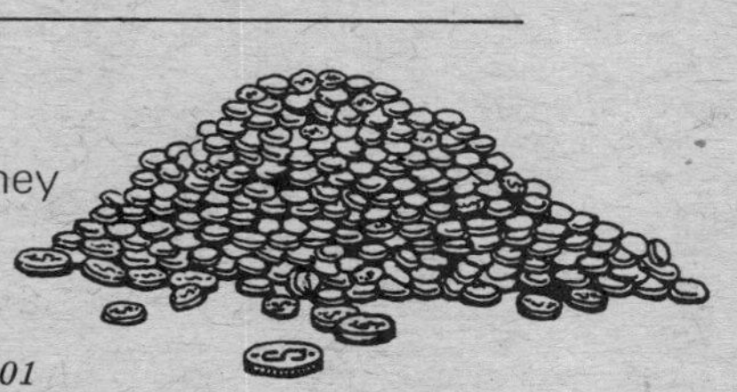

Gary Filler
Chattanooga Coin
910 Market Street
Chattanooga Tenn. 37401

is so far the cheapest interest on silver coins bought on loans (you pay the difference between face value and market value of the silver on dimes and quarters) at 7%.

To reiterate. Silver, for lots of reasons, is becoming dearer and dearer. In the event of atomic catastrophy or a quite probable economic debacle in the USA, genuine silver dimes and quarters will spend at silver value when paper or cupronickel coins will not get you anything but laughs.

A bag of silver buried on the old homestead is the nicest security blanket.

Mildly speculative investments in silver coins is about a 85% winner, in fact, my own personal attitude— measured by what our commune does with its surplus and where we have our employees retirement banked— is that its closer to a 99% winner.

In short, silver can be stole, but it can't be changed to clay by politicians promises.

George von Hilsheimer, himself
Orange City, Florida

People's Capitalism Has A Newsletter

We carried Kelso's Two Factor Theory ("How to Turn 80 Million Workers into Capitalists on Borrowed Money") in the Spring CATALOG with a review by Richard Raymond, which suggested that Kelso address himself to a younger and readier audience. The review was widely quoted in other publications, including one in England.

Kelso's scene is gathering some Movement qualities, including now a

Newsletter of the Institute for the Study of Economic Systems
111 Pine Street
San Francisco, CA 94111
Membership $10/ year
Student membership $6/year

Below is an article from Vol. 1, No. 1, October 1970

TRIBUNES ON THE MARCH

Tribunes are mobilizing to the defense of the people in the Nation's capital!
A group of Kelsonians here calling themselves the "Ninety-five Percenters" has begun an ambitious social action program designed to achieve the goals of Universal Capitalism as outlined in The Capitalist Manifesto *by Kelso and Adler. Rejecting all forms of concentrated ownership--whether in the form of class capitalism, mixed capitalism, or state capitalism—as the inevitable result of defective economic systems, the Ninety-five Percenters will appeal to the capital-less masses, and to potential allies among the five percent who enjoy exclusive access to capital ownership today.*
Starting from a nucleus of a Washington Area Free University class, this "new movement" has organized into bands of three people called "Tribunes". With "Economic Power to the People" as its rallying call, the group will take steps to contruct history's first democratic economic foundation for a free industrial society. It will strive to connect corporate economic power directly to every person in society through new ownership shares and by updating and revitalizing the institution of private property, an institution that has eroded and become misunderstood and abused as access to capital ownership was denied to the vast majority of people.
The groups chose the name "Tribunes" for its original meaning, "defenders of the people". Through bold yet constructive challenges on many fronts, they will expose the failures of the Nation's decision-makers to achieve economic justice. The Tribunes will promote the three Kelsonian principles of economic justice:
1. Everyone should have equal opportunity to participate in production through both labor and ownership of capital. (The input or "participation" principle.)
2. Everyone is entitled to the rewards of his production. (The "private property" principle of distribution.)
3. No one should produce radically more than he can consume, if this would deny others the right to participate in production. (The anti-monopoly or "limitation" principle.)
Each of the three members of a Tribune assumes the personal responsibility for forming another Tribune, to which he is an observer for communications purposes. As their numbers increase throughout the United States, the Tribunes will be organized along regional lines to conform with the Federal Reserve and Congressional districts. Each Tribune in the network will develop its own action and educational programs, guided by the spirit of the First Amendment and based on non-violence.
Separate and distinct from the Institute for the Study of Economic Systems, the Tribunes are political and social-action oriented. Their aim is to develop the political base for spreading the philosophy and programs of Universal Capitalism.
The Tribunes will bring together the expertise of individuals from varied professions and fields of interest. Regular meetings will effect a continuing exchange of information and ideas and result in practical planning for effective activism.
For information about forming your own Tribune, write to:

Rev. William Gardiner
All Souls' Church
16th and Harvard Streets, NW
Washington, DC 20009

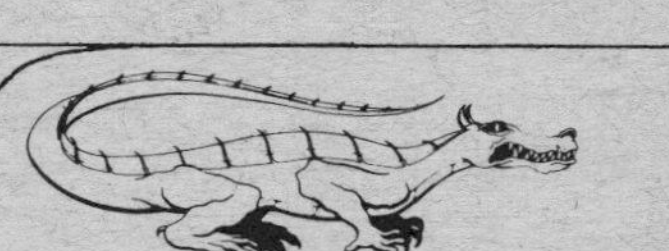

•

My job is to get liquids into Emmit, and then help him get them out again. His throat is so messed up, and his breathing, and now, since they've doped him up, his senses as well, that he can't even handle as much as a spoonful of water at a time. So what I do is sink a straw into a glass of water, or juice, or Coke, than cap it with my finger, hold the straw to his lips, than take away my finger to let it run into his mouth and down his throat. About once a minute I do that, take the water into the straw, hold it to his mouth, then let it out again. It's like feeding some little animal with a nipple. I manage less than a glass full an hour, but still it adds up because his kidneys continue to function, and Doctor Robinette says that's the key to any chance that Emmit has, which isn't very much of a chance no matter what we do. But it doesn't matter. I just keep dipping it up and dropping it into his mouth, strawful after strawful, and then a little while later here it'll come, it'll be water-time, Emmit will yell out water-time! water-time! and I'll tug him to a sitting position and help him leak it out, then lay him down again and go on dipping in and letting out.

•

How many times.

•

No one knew.

•

That was one statistic no one kept.

•

The thousands, surely. Maybe millions.

•

Maybe billions, D.R. thought. Maybe this has been going on for years and years. If you don't count the times, how can you know how many? How can you know for sure? They count the stars. The stars

Capitalism & Freedom

A New Radical's Guide to Economic Reality

Government-managed economy. Or laissez-faire. Both ends are right theoretically, wrong practically, and the middle where we live is no prize either. I personally lean with these two toward the Let It Be end of things, but I got nothing more than glands to back my arguments, which are the economics of a quack biologist: evolution is continuity plus unfettered mistakes.

Milton Friedman, distinguished Chicago-school economist, and Angus Black, hairy power-to-the-peopler. Both find government management of the economy consistently unjust, unfreeing, and usually in the dark about what's going on. They have some proposals; specific, radical ones.

—SB

Capitalism & Freedom
Milton Friedman
1962; 202 pp.

$1.50 postpaid

from:
University of Chicago Press
5801 Ellis Ave.
Chicago, Ill. 60637

or WHOLE EARTH CATALOG

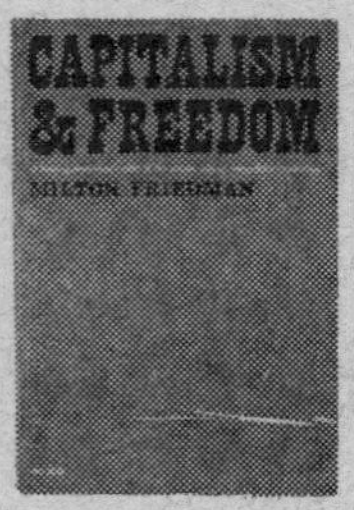

We could say to the rest of the world: We believe in freedom and intend to practice it. No one can force you to be free. That is your business. But we can offer you full co-operation on equal terms to all. Our market is open to you. Sell here what you can and wish to. Use the proceeds to buy what you wish. In this way co-operation among individuals can be world wide yet free.

•

Which if any of the great "reforms" of past decades has achieved its objectives? Have the good intentions of the proponents of these reforms been realized?

Regulation of the railroads to protect the consumer quickly became an instrument whereby the railroads could protect themselves from the competition of newly emerging rivals— at the expense, of course, of the consumer.

An income tax initially enacted at low rates and later seized upon as a means to redistribute income in favor of the lower classes has become a facade, covering loopholes and special provisions that render rates that are highly graduated on paper largely ineffective. A flat rate of 23-1/2 percent on presently taxable income would yield as much revenue as the present rates graduated from 20 to 91 per cent. An income tax intended to reduce inequality and promote the diffusion of wealth has in practice fostered reinvestment of corporate earnings, thereby favoring the growth of large corporations, inhibiting the operation of the capital market, and discouraging the establishment of new enterprises.

Monetary reforms, intended to promote stability in economic activity and prices, exacerbated inflation during and after World War I and fostered a higher degree of instability thereafter than had ever been experienced before. The monetary authorities they established bear primary responsibility for converting a serious economic contraction into the catastrophe of the Great Depression from 1929-33. A system established largely to prevent bank panics produced the most severe banking panic in American history. . .A housing program intended to improve the housing conditions of the poor, to reduce juvenile delinquency, and to contribute to the removal of urban slums, has worsened the housing conditions of the poor, contributed to juvenile delinquency, and spread urban blight.

In the 1930's, "labor" was synonymous with "labor union" to the intellectual community; faith in the purity and virtue of labor unions was on a par with faith in home and motherhood. Extensive legislation was enacted to favor labor unions and to foster "fair" labor relation. labor unions waxed in strength. By the 1950's, "labor union" was almost a dirty word; it was no longer synonomous with "labor," no longer automatically to be taken for granted as on the side of the angels.

A New Radical's Guide to Economic Reality
Angus Black
1971; 114

$2.45 postpaid

from:
Holt, Rinehart & Winston, Inc.
383 Madison Ave.
New York, N.Y. 10017

or WHOLE EARTH CATALOG

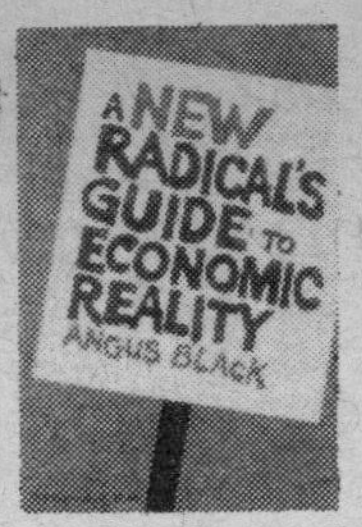

Let's quit fooling ourselves. Get rid of the progressive income tax. In its place put a flat 20-percent tax on all income over a certain minimum, while eliminating all escape clauses. We'll end up getting more from the rich than now, for it will no longer be worth it to them to cheat and look for legal loopholes with the aid of lawyers. As an added attraction, those high-paid tax lawyers will then be out of their jobs. Their salaries may suffer, and so more legal aid might be funneled to defending the poor in our rich man's system of "justice".

Getting rid of our present income-tax mess would also save taxpayers a wad. How? By eliminating the time and effort that they and their accountants spend on filing returns. In a recent study the American Bar Association came up with the estimate that we had put a preposterous $1.3 billion of effort into filing 1967 returns.

•

A highly respected member of the Budget Bureau got the figures together on how much was being spent on all poverty programs. He then calculated the total cost of direct payments to all families necessary to bring everyone above the "poverty line." The conclusion he reached was that direct income payments would add up to less than half the present poverty-help outlays! Even the Wallace asshole around the corner may be convinced by the tax savings to him that unworthy niggers, hippies, artists, and bums should all get a minimum income, too.

Another important benefit of direct minimum-income payments would be a renewed sense of dignity for the current welfare poor. We also could eliminate the numerous political connections so often tied to welfare and other such programs (as occur daily in Daleyland, U.S.A.). Think, too, of all those snooping social workers who will be forced to do something worthwhile for a change.

•

The minute you accept censorship of advertising you're paving the way for government Fascists imposing their uptight, puritanical outdated values on the rest of society. Being unduly deprived of bare tit on the tube is one thing. Big Brother is another.

•

Why don't building codes work? The answer is easy. Special-interest groups, like producers and repairmen, have concentrated, well-defined goals. They can attack with vigor any changes in legislation that will harm them. Consumers, on the other hand, have millions of goals as the buyers of products. They are a diversified group of people who cannot collect forces easily to fight legislation that may affect the production of only a small aspect of what some of them are buying.

•

For anarchy to work, however, all members of society must be fairly homogeneous. There would be open season on wops, wetbacks, kikes, niggers, hippies, polacks, redheads, and cripples if the Constitution didn't exist. Many more of us would end up like Captain Amerika and Billy. I happen to want to keep my hair long and curly. You may not want ever to wear shoes. The only way to prevent the majority from forcing us to change is to have some guarantee of our rights enforced. Anarchy is not the answer. We should therefore keep government, but reduce its power over our economic, moral, and social lives.

What should we do, then, to solve our problems? Demand only a few simple realistic programs from the powers that be— enforcement of contracts, protection of constitutional rights, a minimum income, and the distribution of educational taxes by way of certificates. Anything more complex will only give every rotten profiteer in the country a chance to fatten his purse at our expense.

My plea is clear:

less government today
even less tomorrow.

If you want something for nothing, go jerk off.
Bob Weir 1970

The RSVP Cycles

The RSVP Cycles is a scoring guide, a technical manual, highly illustrated and explicated in everyman language. It is a self-defining, singing, swinging score (S) of Halprin's own performance (P), his electric, focused stash of resources (R) from the I Ching, to a controversial Northwestern-Minnesota football play and his conscientiously objective valuactions (V),— a term he coined to suggest action and decision aspects of the RSVP cycles.

Profusely graphic and photographic, excellently designed by Barbara Stauffacher Solomon. The RSVP Cycles is a collector's item, a conversation piece de resistance, a real-time information/ slice delicacy. . .The "Driftwood Villages" story and photographs depicting experimental scoring and building of a community from available beach materials, provides precise images of the Halprins' own creative in-process use of RSVP cycles and frames perspective for the assemblage pot-latch of world-wide historical goodies in the book.

Using splendid examples such as his own project at Sea Ranch, a 10-mile long ecologically scored development on the Northern California coast and Lovejoy Plaza and Cascade, a public space in Portland, Oregon, scored for people participation, Halprin superimposes the natural geometry of his RSVP cycles against the functional perspective of his experience.

[Reviewed by Gerd Stern]

[Reprinted from Landscape Architecture, *Jan 71]*

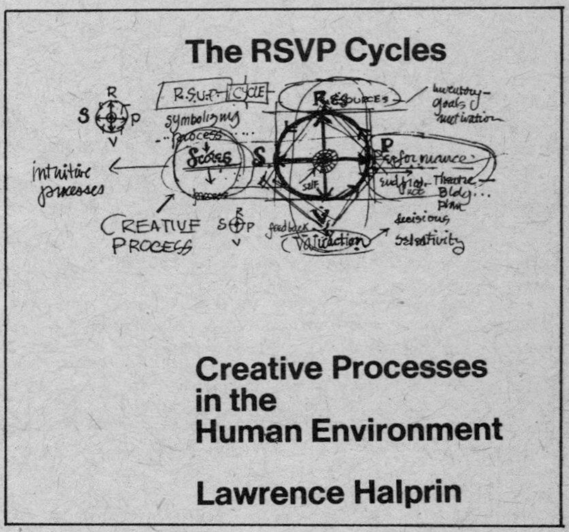

The RSVP Cycles: Creative Process in the Human Environment
Lawrence Halprin
1969; 207 pp.

$4.95 postpaid

from:
George Braziller, Inc.
One Park Avenue
New York, New York 10016

or WHOLE EARTH CATALOG

One of the gravest dangers that we experience is the danger of becoming *goal-oriented.* It is a tendency that crops up on every hand and in every field of endeavor. It is a trap which goes like this: things are going poorly (in the realm of politics or religion or building a city or the world community or a personal relationship or whatever). As thinking people we must try to solve this problem that faces us. Let us set ourselves a "goal" upon which we can all agree (most goals after all are quite clearly moralistically based and incontrovertibly "good ideas"). Having set ourselves this goal we can then proceed posthaste to achieve it by the *most direct method possible.* Everyone can put his shoulder to the wheel, and systems engineering, technology, and our leader (or whatever) will get us to the agreed goal.

It doesn't work! The results of this oversimplified approach, now coming into general vogue, are all around us in the chaos of our cities and the confusion of our politics (or other politics—fascism and communism are clear statements of this approach.) It generates tension in personal relationships by burying the real problems; it avoids the central issue of education, which is why today's young people are dropping out; it is destroying the resources and physical beauty of our planet; and it avoids the basic issue.

•

The relationship of the Tarot cards to the *I Ching* hexagrams is remarkable; both deal with universal ideas and problems facing us all in life situations. Both connect us with the subconscious activities of the human mind and with natural processes. Both deal with archetypal examples of what Jung has called the "collective unconscious." In both the divination process itself requires a letting go of the intellect—an acknowledgement of the rhythmic and unconscious forces at work in the universe. If we can give way to these forces and think of ourselves as part of the universal processes of living, of time in space, then we can release ourselves from preconceptions and hangups which prevent and block creativity. One of the important functions of scores is to make possible and accepted nonrational means of "getting at" problems. Both the Tarot cards and the *I Ching* have been used by musicians such as Pauline Olivieros and Morton Subotnik as compositional devices. Pauline Olivieros has said "I mix chance and choice somewhat scandalously" (*Notations,* John Cage).

Libertarian Periodicals

From Ayn Rand to bushy anarchists there is an occasional agreement on means called libertarianism, which is a faith in laissez-faire politics/economics. It's damn near the only specific set of radical economic proposals around. The Jan. 71 issue of **A is A** *has a directory of libertarian periodicals, scads of them. How to hate your government on principle.*

—SB

A is A
Directory Issue

$2.00 postpaid

from:
Mega
A31, 9730 Hyne Rd.
Brighton, Michigan 48116

2623 Benvenue
Berkeley, Calif.
$4.00/6. Every 2 mo.
Did not answer inquiry.
Reported to contain articles, poetry, art, photography, humor, and fiction..

Individualist
31 Parkside Gardens
London, S.W. 19, England
Edit: Henry Meulen
12 pp., 5½ x 8½
Offset, stitched.
$2.40/6. Every 2 mo. Adv.
1970 is the hundredth anniversary of this journal of the Personal Rights Association. Short notes, comments, and reviews of economic and political affairs in Britain. Laissez-faire viewpoint.
Mr. Meulen is the author of Free Banking.

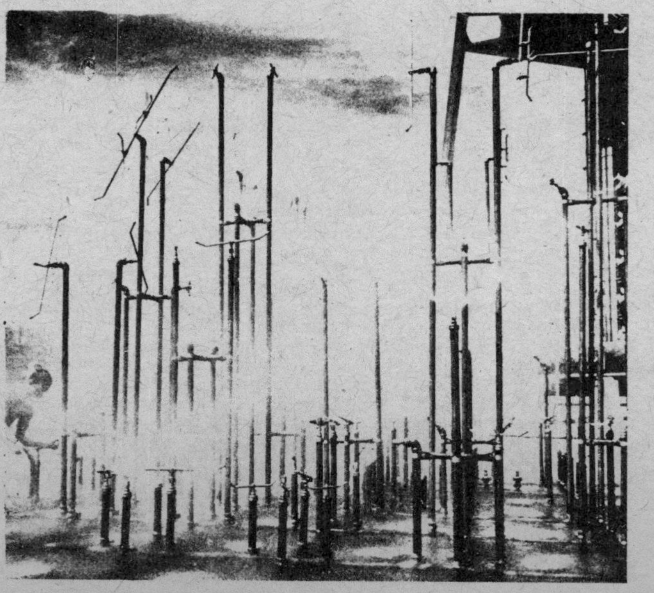

Radical Software

We get letters—saying how encouraging, enspiriting, possibility-expanding the Whole Earth Catalog is— embarrassing amount of gratitude in these letters. Well, it's how I feel about Radical Softwear; A double handful of fast young heads have entered do-it-yourself TV and gotten acquainted with each other, and now started a tabloid of mutual read-out, aiding each other's scuffle for equipment, audience, comprehension, concepts, values. They sense power (95% of U.S. homes have TV) and unexplored territory (broadcast TV still scarcely seems to know what it is) and the hard cider of dwelling on evolution's imploding edge (maybe. [always maybe.].) In a way it's about time: we have head radio, head records, head books, magazines, newspapers, head movies; very little head TV. [Beware beware of controlling all your inputs lest ye become your own caricature.] These are TV heads, getting restless, with a fine access publication. I hope it stays solvent and publishing. High content goods.

—SB

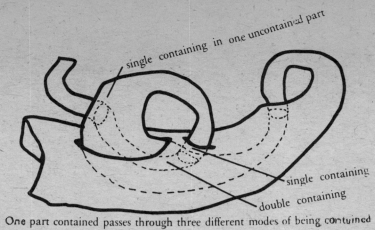

single containing in one uncontained part

single containing

double containing

One part contained passes through three different modes of being contained

Radical Software

$1.50 issue (quarterly)

from:
Raindance Corporation
8 East 12th Street
New York, New York 10003

"Water systems engineers must build city water supply systems to accommodate the drop in water pressure occasioned by the toilet-flushing during television commercials."

Vic and I recorded a conversation between us using full body shots on a split screen. We were seated facing each other. A week later we played the tape back using slow motion and no sound. We both sat facing the screen imitating the kinetics of the other on the screen and verbalizing how we felt from going through those motions. It was extraordinary. Holding my head and rocking back and forth in imitation of Vic. "Yeah, I'm listening to what you're saying, Ryan, but I'm really getting ready to strike back." Following a diminutive hand gesture "Let me make it nice and small, Ryan, so that you can understand it. " Vic was scoring on me in a similar way and we were laughing our heads off. What was even more extraordinary was when I woke up the next morning, I felt like I was wearing his body. That I had it on. I called up Vic and started telling him how I felt about the relation between his/my stomach and shoulders, stomach and head, torso and legs, etc. etc. Each time Vic confirmed I was right on. For the next few weeks I found I could recall this sense of his body when I wanted.

Relative to video infolding it is near impossible to describe in words even using klein worm graphs what I'm talking about. The following will mean little to anyone except those who have had some experience of taping with themselves at different levels.

Taping something new with yourself is a part uncontained
To replay the tape for yourself is to contain it in your perceptual system
Taping yourself playing with the replay is to contain both on a new tape
To replay for oneself tape of self with tape of self is to contain that process in a new dimension
Parts left out of that process are parts uncontained

All of this is mapable on computer graphic terminals.

At one level that of reality that is left off the tape is the part uncontained
Raw tape replayed is part contained in the head
If it is somebody else's tape you are watching you can to an extent share in this live perceptual system via the tape he took.
To watch another's edited tape is to share in the way he thinks about the relation between his various perceptions in a real time mode. This enters the realm of his intention.
If you are editing some of your tape along with tape somebody else shot and he is doing the same thing using some of your tape then it is possible to see how one's perceptions relate to another's intentions and vice versa.

Design Intelligence: The Akai has two major differences which set it apart from the other Porta-Paks. One, it uses quarter-inch tape. All the others use half-inch.

The advantage of quarter-inch videotape is that it's fabulously cheap compared to other standards. Quarter-inch is the same size as audio tape (for reel-to-reel machines) and lists for $7.95 for twenty minutes as compared to $14.95 for twenty minutes of Sony videotape. The disadvantage of quarter-inch is that it has less information storage capacity as reflected in the 200 lines resolutions of the system, the lowest of any.

The other unique feature of the Akai is that it has a small detachable monitor which clips onto the recording deck. The camera itself has an optical viewfinder which means reduced weight. Overall this means that Akai is the first system not to place a tiny TV screen between your eye and the lens in imitation of a film camera.

GUNS, KNIVES OR VIDEOTAPE* works this way. Two people, each with a portable pack and camera, face off fifteen feet apart. At a given signal they start "shooting" each other. Both roll tape continuously for five minutes. Then both tapes are played back simultaneously on two monitors set up side by side. The area should be large enough so that participants can move around. Variations are possible. Doubling up in teams of two, doing it in a mirrored room, setting up a third camera on a stationary tripod to catch the whole duel for playback with the participant's tapes.
*executed in Pontiac, Michigan

The Techniques of Television Production

I'm coming to believe that good how-to writing mostly depends on good diagramming. Millerson has mastered that, so you're inclined to believe that he knows his television. Certainly he covers the ground in a thorough fashion: studio layout, TV picture and camera, TV lighting sound, film reproduction, sets, make-up, organization, imagery, camera control, editing, sound composition, production method, titling, effects, and color. The book can make a more critical viewer of you. Or it can give you some skill to go with the power when you demand and get some control of the half-hour educational program about your scene.

—SB

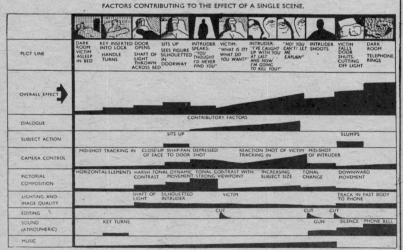

FACTORS CONTRIBUTING TO THE EFFECT OF A SINGLE SCENE.

 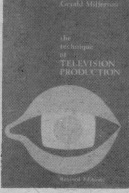

The Technique of Television Production
Gerald Millerson
1961, 1968; 440 pp.

$7.50 postpaid from:
Communication Arts Books
Hastings House, Publishers, Inc.
10 East 40th Street
New York, N.Y. 10016

or WHOLE EARTH CATALOG

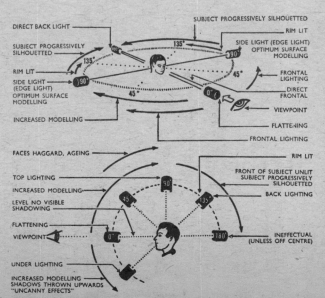

LIGHTING ANGLE. The lighting angle we choose depends on which particular features we want to display, e.g. roundness, surface-texture, relief.

D.R. was outside now, breathing and looking at the stars. When Leonard was there in the afternoon he left D.R. a half-pint whiskey bottle with about three drinks in it, and about midnight he stepped outside and downed them, one, two, three, and then stood around a while, looking up and breathing. Emmit had fallen into one of his rare sleeps about midnight, and the hospital was quieting, quieting down. The lobby was half-lit and silent except for Mrs. Hubbard shuffling papers behind the admissions desk. Dear Mrs. Hubbard. This was their second night together. It was like some kind of combat tour they'd been on, and it had drawn them close, her and D.R. He's very nice, she thought. She hadn't paid much attention to him the night before, but tonight she thought: he seems like a very nice young man, taking care of his old uncle like that. Not many people take that kind of care of dying old folks. Most just dump them on the hospital to live or die and here's one sure to die, and soon, and yet that young man is caring for him as if it was his own life at stake. The first night she hadn't offered him any coffee from her electric coffee pot, but tonight she did, a couple of times because tonight they're both into it together, staying up, awake, on the graveyard shift. D.R. drank two cups of Mrs. Hubbard's coffee, and then later went outside and sipped the whiskey Leonard brought him, and as he looked up at the stars, and smelled the coal dust in the air and listened to the trains clanging across the river in the yards, he thought about how kind all the people were. Leonard, Mrs. Hubbard, Doctor Robinette. This big cloak, he thought. This marvelous garment. As he walked back inside he picked up a corner of the garment and settled it about Mrs. Hubbard's shoulders and she smiled at him and said there'd be more coffee later on.

At nine thirty the next morning D.R. called Marcella from the drug store on Main Street. Marcella said it's bad news aint it. I'm afraid so, said D.R.

He could hear Marcella crying, not much, a sudden flash of tears, then sniffles. She could talk okay. She said how long has he been gone, David?

Just a few minutes. He died about ten after nine.

Video Goodies

The following are suggestions and reviews by the Media Access group at Portola Institute, 540 Santa Cruz Avenue, Menlo Park, CA 94025

—SB

Sony

Video is not cheap film, or a new gadget for TV "professionals." It's an information-processing tool with a built-in capacity for _feedback_, in all forms. Which opens up entirely new arenas of cybernetic work, and play.

Sony may not be the best 1/2" portable system around—don't hesitate to look into Panasonic, Shibaden, others, or wait for Ampex coming in the fall—but it's the most available, and most people into video use it. The electronics are dependable, and the source of its magic, but you can count on exasperating mechanical flaws. Such as: short-life batteries, tape snagging during recording, handles or straps breaking, tape drop-out (with every brand). Editing presents problems, too, if you're a perfectionist. A good engineer friend is a god-send.

—Allen Rucker

Sony Corporation of America/VTR Division
47-47 Van Dam Street
Long Island City, New York 11101

Sony AV-3400/AVC-3400 Portable Recorder/Camera	$1495.00
Sony AV-3600 Recorder/Playback Deck	$ 695.00
Sony AV-3650 B&W Editing Deck	$ 995.00

Cable Television

A Community Antenna or Cable Television system (CATV) consists of:
1. super antenna to pick up broadcasted signals,
2. a "head" or "headend" which processes these signals and can serve to process locally originated signals,
3. coaxial cable which is strung via telephone poles or city ducts to home TV sets.

As many as 40 (soon to be 80) channels can link your tube with all sorts of information-entertainment systems— the street, libraries, a tape bank of almost anything. New systems may adopt two-way capabilities permitting individual feedback into the system. (Big brother possibilities loom large as files of individual uses are stored on central computers.)

Half-inch video is cable-castable and systems with more than 3500 subscribers are now required by the FCC to program a "significant" amount of locally originated material.

Everyone can be a source of local life data affecting a media inversion that may clear the air.

—Richard Kletter

Selected References:

Johnson, Nicholas. _How to Talk Back to Your TV Set_. (Atlantic-Little, Brown, & Co., Boston, 1969, & Bantam Books, 95¢)

Price, Monroe E. _Content on Cable: The Nascent Expeience_. A report prepared for the Sloan Commission on Cable Communications, Sept. 1970. Write: 105 Madison Ave., New York 10016.

Smith, Ralph Lee. "The Wired Nation," in the _Nation_, May 18, 1970. Write: The _Nation_, 333 6th Avenue, New York 10014 (35¢ or 10 for $3)

Tewlow, Jules S. "Cable TV in Perspective." American Newspaper Publishers' Assoc. Research Institute Bulletin No. 1029, Sept. 25, 1970. Write: P.O. 598, Easton, Pa. 18042.

Challenge for Change Newsletter

The Challenge for Change program (and its French-speaking equivalent, Societe Nouvelle) conducts forceful media access projects in film, video, and CATV with disenfranchised Canadian groups. With no cybernetic shuck, these people are real pioneers in the information environment. Their newsletter documents their approach to decentralizing media control, and is itself a vehicle for social change.

—Allen Rucker

National Film Board of Canada
P.O. Box 6100
Montreal 101, Quebec

No charge indicated

evaluation
In March we taped a meeting of the film-VTR sub-committee evaluating the use of the video equipment. The following are quoted from that discussion.

effects on the individual
"We were not very interested in ourselves when we started."

"But it helped me a lot to know myself. You see how you function."

"It helped me gain more confidence in myself. It's important to know who you are."

"It develops your critical senses. You become two people – he who acts, and he who watches himself act."

Graphic Terminal

Enclosed is information (circled) for a review of Tektronix. The Tek. 7000 series will be the popular 'scope for the predictable future (i.e. on the order of 10 years); 'scope users would be years ahead to learn the new 7000 series rather than the 500 series. Graphic input-output remote computer terminals (as in "2001") are the way to trip, yes? They beat teletypes and CalComp mechanical curve plotters (or plodders) for speed and interaction. Graphic terminals are currently the best ('tho little used) computer-human interface for scientific/engineering (vs. accountant) problems; and graphics should replace catalogs, sales personnel, trips to the store, & maybe option-designers in the 1970's, as a home tool. Tek's T-4002 and other graphic terminals using Tek's storage CRT (TV screen), are far cheaper means of displaying large quantities (3000) of alpha-numeric characters or high-resolution drawings, than the commoner conventional CRT plus magnetic core or other storage unit.

Tektronix seems a nice environment for electronics engineers (me): lots of freedom & informality (work when the mood strikes, 24 hr. access to buildings, no suit &/or tie image), active in education of employees & community (gifts & heavy discounts to schools), as well as the usual excessive pay and excessive equipment to play with. (The universities which I know irradiate the community with free/cheap information (software), whereas they should be distributing tools/games/toys/hardware (photo film computer everything that must be actively used not passively sat-at), to everyone who enjoys playing with tools).

Larry Greisel
Gresham, Ore.

Tektronix Catalog
1971; 432 pp.

from:
Tektronix, Inc.
P. O. Box 500
Beaverton, Ore. 97005

Video Cassettes

Home video playback/record systems will soon extend a visual data bank to your personal control. Create your own television with portable recorders or watch when and where you will by simply plugging in the cartridge.

You'll get hit for an uncomfortable amount of money— looks like about $400 for the playback deck alone and at least $10 for cassettes at the beginning— but it is hoped that the content will be worth it.

Color flashes and other psychodelevision, organic video magazines and esoteric films will be coming at you— perhaps over giant wall screens. But it's all at least three years away from the home market. The early technical battles, fought by a plethora of giant corporations, will be waged in industrial and educational applications. Technical standards, distribution and maintenance support systems should be further along by the time the hardware gets to us.

—Richard Kletter

"The people we interviewed on the street – I really felt they wanted to get a message across. They wanted other people to hear about their problems, to share them. People feel pretty isolated."

"I think the people hoped their message would reach the powers-that-be. They had never had the chance, before."

"When we watch the tapes, we don't just learn to know ourselves better; we also come to understand others better. After that, it's much more fun to work together."

Videa 1000

A dense monthly fruitcake of tips about TV state-of-the-art and the future. Aimed mainly at TV advertisers, but of use to any media cowboys. Swap them info they can use for a subscription.

—SB

Videa 1000
Robert DeHavilland, ed.

$25 /yr (monthly)

from:
Videa International
54 Park Ave.
New York, N.Y. 10016

Now seeking information about corporate activity not in the public interest: the new Clearinghouse for Professional Responsibility (Box 486, Washington, D.C.) via Ralph Nader. Washington is aware that the organization could develop into something big— if the Clearinghouse idea appeals to many UNEMPLOYED professionals with a newly stimulated social conscience. Such as engineers and advertising men.

The revolution is starting. First U.S. catalogue of videocassette programs— 600 titles, about 50% in color— is now available. From CBS Electronic Video Recording Div. (For a copy, write Norman Ober at CBS EVR, 51 W. 52 St., NYC 10019.)

2-way cable TV is being tested in New York— with 10 subscribers of Manhattan Cable television. (Part of one test: viewers were asked to indicate their choice of vacation trip after watching a commercial for Eastern Airlines.) In 6 to 9 months: 500 subscribers may have new converters with special buttons to signal their "votes".

Pornography on Japanese TV. It's happening. But not officially. "Transmission leaks" from closed-circuit systems of some Japanese inns— which show porno films and tapes— are now being picked up by home TV sets in the Kansai region

This year in Japan (next year in the U.S.): a color TV camera for about $1000. Next: perhaps $500. Sony's marketing plan for its 1-gun "Trinicon" now under development. A "professional" version, reportedly suitable suitable for broadcast television markets, will be introduced at about $3000.

Videa verite— by Annette & Lesley. New, fact-packed newsletter about cartridge television: CTV News Digest. Published by Billboard Publications, 165 West 46 St., New York, N.Y. 10036. One of the best bargains in the business. For a sample copy, write Stephen Traiman, Editor.

Fast way to edit videotape to the beat of a sound track. Transfer the track to videotape via equipment that lays down a 'frame count'. Feed the audio to an oscilloscope to get a visual indication of the audio. Find location of the beat on the tape, note the frame count. . . .For more information, ask for the report, "Instant Replay No. 4" from National Teleproductions, 5261 North Tacoma Avenue, Indianapolis, Indiana 46220. (One NTP job: 32 edits in 10 seconds of tape.)

Towards a Poor Theatre

The strongest work in theater lately is Jerzy Grotowski's. This is his book. Social yoga, with balls.

—SB
[Suggested by Robert Frank]

Towards a Poor Theatre
Jerzy Grotowski
1968; 262 pp.

$2.45 postpaid

from:
Simon & Schuster, Inc.
630 Fifth Avenue
New York, N. Y. 10020

or WHOLE EARTH CATALOG

If the actor, by setting himself a challenge publicly challenges others, and through excess, profanation and outrageous sacrilege reveals himself by casting off his everyday mask, he makes it possible for the spectator to undertake a similar process of self-penetration. If he does not exhibit his body, but annihilates, it, burns it, frees it from every resistance to any psychic impulse, then he does not sell his body but sacrifices it. He repeats the atonement; he is close to holiness. If such acting is not to be something transient and fortuitous, a phenomenon which cannot be foreseen in time or space: if we want a theatre group whose daily bread is this kind of work—— then we must follow a special method of research and training.

When I take sides against half-heartedness, mediocrity and the easy-come-easy-go attitude which takes everything for granted, it is simply because we must create things which are firmly orientated towards either light or darkness. But we must remember that around that which is luminous within us, there exists a shroud of darkness which we can penetrate but not annihilate.

Contact is one of the most essential things. Often when an actor speaks of contact, or thinks of contact, he believes that it means to gaze fixedly. But this is not contact. It is only a position, a situation. Contact is not staring, it is to see. Now I am in contact with you, I see which of you is against me. I see one person who is indifferent, another who listens with some interest and someone who smiles. All this changes my actions; it is contact, and it forces me to change my way of acting.

Scenery for the Theatre

*me and carl were stage carpenters
once upon a time
and we built a good part
of what's in this book,
flats, traps, platforms, risers,
doorways, windows, parallels,
bartables, machineguns, crossbows . . .*

*the standard procedures, tools,
and tricks
for the grand illusion are here.
maybe someone can use this book,
and a little soul
and breathe some life back into
the theater,
bring it out into the streets.*

— jd

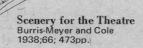

Flats

Onstage

Fig. VIII–36.
A cantilevered balcony

Scenery for the Theatre
Burris-Meyer and Cole
1938;66; 473pp.

DROPPED

from:
Little, Brown and Company
200 West Street
Waltham, Massachusetts 02154

or WHOLE EARTH CATALOG

Characteristics of the Craft. Scene construction is chiefly a specialized type of joinery. The materials and technique of the woodworker are adapted and other techniques and materials introduced for the manufacture of structures which differ from the ordinary product of the carpentry shop, cabinet shop, or woodworking mill. The nature and uses of scenery impose requirements which make scene construction a craft by itself with which the ordinary carpenter or cabinet maker is unfamiliar.

Scene carpentry differs from other forms of carpentry and cabinetwork in several respects: 1. The objects built must be demountable and portable, and yet when assembled they must show no evidence of joining. 2. Scenery is built for use during a short period of time, as compared with furniture, dwellings, etc. 3. Scenery presents only one finished side or face to the audience. 4. Scenery is never seen or examined at close range.

Scenery which has to be demountable and portable must be built in pieces which fit neatly together and which are strong enough to withstand intermittent and often rough handling. The frames must hold their shapes rigidly so that the fit is assured each time they are assembled. There can be no cutting to fit when the scenery reaches the stage. Each piece must be constructed exactly to size and shape as planned. Rebuilding of scenery, when it reaches the stage, is costly.

The fact that scenery is used for a shorter period of time than other carpentered objects allows the use of lumber of smaller cross section than is generally used in weight-bearing structures, since deterioration and constant use do not enter into the determination of the safety factors. For the same reasons and for reasons of workability, softwoods are used in scene carpentry, where hardwoods would be used in ordinary carpentry and cabinetwork.

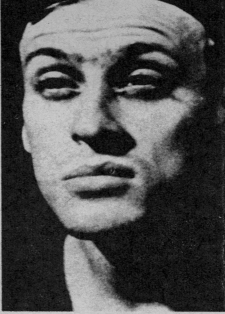

Akropolis: Masks created solely by the facial muscles (Zygmunt Molik, Zbigniew Cynkutis, Rena Mirecka). Photo: Teatr-Laboratorium.

The costumes are bags full of holes covering naked bodies. The holes are lined with material which suggests torn flesh; through the holes one looks directly into a torn body. Heavy wooden shoes for the feet; for the heads, anonymous berets. This is a poetic version of the camp uniform. Through their similarity the costumes rob men of their personality, erase the distinctive signs which indicate sex, age, and social class. The actors become completely identical beings. They are nothing but tortured bodies.

The inmates are the protagonists and, in the name of a higher, unwritten law, they are their own torturers. The merciless conditions of the extermination camp constitute the milieu of their lives. Their work crushes them with its size and its futility; rhythmical signals are given by the guards; the inmates call out in screams. But the struggle for the right to vegetate and to love goes on at its everyday pace. At each command the human wrecks, barely alive, stand up erect like well-disciplined soldiers. The throbbing rhythm of the play underscores the building of the new civilization; the work expresses the inmate's stubborn will to live, which is constantly reaffirmed in every one of their actions.

There is one absolute rule
Bodily activity comes first, and then vocal expression. Most actors work in the opposite order.
First you bang on the table and afterwards you shout!
The vocal process cannot be free without a well functioning larynx. The larynx must first be relaxed, and then the chin and jaws.
If the larynx does not relax and open, you must try to find a way to make it do so. That is why I asked the third pupil to stand on his head. If he does this, and at the same time speaks, shouts or sings, there is a good chance that the larynx will open.

Stage Make Up

In San Francisco in the days when everyone was painting their faces, it was strictly fauve: My face is gobs of color, let's ball. Except for Page Browning. Page was a Merry Prankster who wound up doing time in jail with Kesey. His particular outlaw talent, besides dope, was his face. In the Boyscouts he'd learned the rudiments of makeup/ war paint, and that skill blossomed into: Page at the Acid Tests. A black and white streamlined living skull wearing a cape. A red and blue face, one side red, the other blue. A face of flames.

I wish this book had been around then. Somebody would have got one for Page and let him go for the next higher level. He could have come as Kesey, as President Johnson, as an infant, as himself enlightened.

—SB

Stage Makeup
Herman Buchman
1971; 208 pp. 113 color plates

$15.00 postpaid

from:
Watson-Guptill Publications, Inc.
2160 Patterson St.
Cincinnati, OH 45214

or WHOLE EARTH CATALOG

Makeup bases

The makeup base is a cosmetic that creates the desired skin color. There are many kinds of bases manufactured in a variety of consistencies: hard grease sticks, soft grease paint, liquid, and pancake. In this book, you will be using practically all of them.

Hard grease paints These are available in a complete range of colors. These paints come in stick form and are approximately 5" long and about 1" thick. Although this base requires a bit more effort to apply, when done properly it has the best and longest wearing quality of any of the others.

Soft grease paints These are available in a complete range of colors for use as makeup base. Manufactured in a toothpaste type tube, soft grease paint has a creamy texture and is quickly and easily spread. Soft grease paint tends to shine excessively because of its cream content and, moreover, does not survive body heat as well as the hard grease paint.

Pancakes These are also available in a complete range of base colors. This paint is supplied in a compressed form in a flat, round container, and is applied to the face with a moistened sponge. Pancakes dry quickly and have a matte finish and, therefore, form a difficult surface for further detailed makeup work. This base is the least effective for theatrical use because it dissolves under heat and perspiration. It is much more practical for film work because it can be repaired continuously.

Liquid base colors These are available in bottles and used primarily as a body— as opposed to face— base. Liquid base dries quickly, which makes it impractical for use as a facial base.

Well honey, you've done a wonderful thing, being there with him, I know you have. And me and Doyle'll and the kids'll be on down tomorrow. When do you think

I figure about two in the afternoon, Marcella. Might as well. There wont be that many people to come, and we might as well get it done.

Well honey, listen, said Marcella. What we'll do is leave here real early in the morning, and be there about one. Does that sound okay?

That sounds fine, said D.R. I'll take care of whatever arrangements. And Leonard'll help me.

Marcella told D.R. she thought he was wonderful. They hung up then, and D.R. went to Olney's Funeral Home to buy a casket.

That happened fast too.

Expanded Cinema

We're moving out of a universe made up mostly of physical objects and emerging into one formed of a flux of energy, electromagnetic waves and invisible changes and communications. All the world's television and radio broadcasts are constantly moving through our unaware heads, along with a lot of things we've not yet tuned in to. This book is about this new universe and about learning how to live in and participate in its changing patterns.

[Reviewed by Tom Bender]

Expanded Cinema
Gene Youngblood
1970; 432 pp.

$4.95 postpaid

from:
E. P. Dutton, Inc.
201 Park Avenue South
New York, New York 10003

or WHOLE EARTH CATALOG

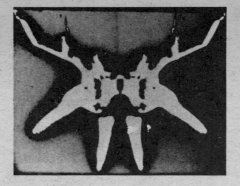

Expanded cinema isn't a movie at all: like life it's a process of becoming, man's ongoing historical drive to manifest his consciousness outside of his mind, in front of his eyes. One no longer can specialize in a single discipline and hope truthfully to express a clear picture of its relationships in the environment. This is especially true in the case of the intermedia network of cinema and television, which new functions as nothing less than the nervous system of mankind.

. . .But when you're really involved with the thing you want to experience, you stop conceiving it. Art finally becomes a barrier to accepting what IS. Art stays within its closed circle and reality never does. Art is all symbols of reality. Symbols are never going to free you. But it would be foolish to say "Stop making art."

James Whitney

The individual's ability to apprehend, capture, generate, transmit, duplicate, replicate, manipulate, store, and retrieve audio-visual information has reached the point where technology results in the rebirth of "cottage industry" as conceived by the economist William Morris during the Industrial Revolution in England— the autonomous ability of the individual to generate his own industry within his own local environment. The primary difference between Morris' pre-industrial view and today's post-industrial reality is that cottage industry and global cybernetic industrialization interpenetrate each other's spheres of influence synergetically, each benefiting from the other.

. . .However, means have been devised through which even the hologram may no longer need "reality" to exist. . . .Moreover, the ability of holography to record natural phenomena that exist beyond the range of human perception— shockwaves, electrical vibrations, ultraslow-motion events— could contribute to an experience of nonordinary realities totally beyond the reach of conventional cinema or television.

Theatre House

Lovely junky stage stuff. Reminds me of Prankster trips to Serbin's in SF to stock up on fringe, da-glo feathers, costume jewelry, face paint, tigerskin fabric, and the two trouperette spotlights that made the Acid Test Graduation work.

Catalog not available

—SB

Theatre House Inc.
400 West 3rd St.
Covington, KY 41011

No. 639 - 3" CHAINETTE FRINGE ------ yd.
Rayon - Colors: Red, Gold, Kelly Green, Light Blue, Royal Blue, Peacock Blue, Aqua, Light Pink, Candy Pink, Orange, Fuschia, Lavender, Purple, Black, Silver Gray, White

POLICEMAN CLUB
#1412 -
12 1/2" long, made of black inflated plastic.

COLONIAL MAN
Tan duvetyne knickers, purple, royal blue or ruby red jacket.
B or C size   #1108 -

MINSTREL
Cotton and duvetyne, red with green stripe, green with red stripe
A, B or C size
#1109 -

MISS LIBERTY
Red and white cotton skirt, blue satin blouse. Sizes A or B #1140 -

PILGRIM WOMAN
Gray duvetyne. Sizes A or B #1122 -

ELF RUBBER SHOES

Made of green rubber. These fit over the shoes.
#D-139 -
pair.

No. 19-S JUNIOR FOLLOW SPOT - Price, 162.00
Delivered with stand, color frame, built-in iris, 25 ft cable and plug. Has 3 lens system: 2 stationary; one with control on side of lamp to obtain either a soft edge spot or a sharp clear cut edge. Can be adjusted from 18" head spot at 100 ft. to full stage flood as controlled by following handle. Uses 1000 or 1500 watt lamps.
Accessories:
1000 watt lamp, T20 PAB, 12.50
1500 watt lamp, DTJ, 16.20

#19S

FELT HIGH HAT

Rolled brim, black only.
#1180 - 2.00 each
PAPER STAGE MONEY
Assorted denominations.
#1312 - 100 pieces - 45¢
1000 pieces - 3.50

TRICORN HAT
Black felt with gold braid trim.
#1496 - 1.00 each

Creative Theatre

Kelly Yeaton's pick of quotes:

. . .the stage is not a picture, it is a place.

. . .a new world in which every application of science has contributed to human loneliness. Our teeming presses, the motor car, the phonograph, the radio have given an enrichment that has been paid for by isolation.

. . .the new dreamers have watched the efforts of a world to restore community and have caught a vision of the theatre as peculiarly the art of community.

. . .we have for several centuries failed to discern that the theatre's essential art is motion, and that we can have no great theatre until we find it and cleave to it through all distractions.

. . .We must reaffirm our belief that the theatre has its source in the highest of mysteries and however incompetent we may be to utter these highest truths, there still dwells in it as great prophetic voice as in any other human institution.

. . .We must learn to see Shakespeare and Kalidasa as prophets no less than Job and Isaiah, and to say that Aeschylus, no less than Enoch, walked with God.

. . .They say it is a law of life that every creature is at once pupil to someone higher than himself and master to some lower, a link in a great sequence, each instructed in the measure that he instructs, and spiritually nourished in the measure that he nourishes. He is a conduit. If he is stopped below he must stagnate and can receive nothing from above.

. . .a theatre in a village at the end of the Sacred Road outside of Athens was called the Theatre of the Advent of the Earth Mother. One did not say of that theatre, "I think I'll run out to Eleusis tonight and see what they are doing." One said, "If I am patient and worthy, please God, I shall one day be admitted to that theatre."

. . .Emperors, kings, poets, philosophers and soldiers came to it from all over the known world. Its theme was the vicissitudes and triumph of the soul of man. . .and it ran on this policy for eight hundred years. When I think of that theatre all things seem possible.

Creative Theatre, by Roy Mitchell. John Day, N.Y. 1929, now reprinted by Kindle Press, Westwood, N.J. Obtainable only from Drama Book Specialists/Publishers, 150 West 52nd, New York City. Paper $4.95, Cloth $7.50.

Simon's Directory

"Of Theatrical Materials Services & Information." Where to find play leases, actors' agents, costumes, make-up, scenery, curtains, projection systems, lighting, props, sound equipment, signs, photographers, books, periodicals, foundations, and so forth. Covers U.S. and Canada.

—SB

[Suggested by Bob Shelli]

Simon's Directory of Theatrical Materials
Services & Information
1970; 320 pp.
$5.50 postpaid

from:
Package Publicity Service
1564 Broadway
New York, N. Y. 10036

Clouds and Fog to Order

We thought you might be interested in knowing about our company, which makes clouds.

Thomas R. Mee
Mee Industries, Inc.
Altadena, CA

Clouds, fog and mists have many applications in display, decoration, advertising and special effects. Mee industries can produce these phenomena in size, quantity and even color to meet your requirements.

This firm of cloud physicists has made some major breakthroughs in cloud generation so that these special effects can now be tailored to meet your requirements. One exclusive Mee Industry capability is the generation of real cloud or fog banks from pure water. This can be used to advantage where chemical additives are undesirable.

One of these "natural" clouds will grace the dome of the spectacular Pepsi-Cola pavilion at the Expo '70 Fair at Osaka. Other interesting Mee Industry capabilities include stabilization of natural fog by seeding with hygroscopic nuclei and fog making by chemical means.

Mee Industries will work with your designers, engineers and contractors to put clouds to work for you. Call for a quotation on any job with a cloud in its future.

Mailing Address: Post Office Box 365, Altadena, California 91001
Phone (213) 794-2577

The Film Director As Superstar

If you've always hated Pauline Kael anyway and you've been mildly freaked because your 5 yr old kid sister just completed her 3rd on-the-street-every-inch-true-to-life documentary, then you will find comfort as well as real hope between these covers. This is one of those rare books on film that actually comes out and says what up till now you felt only you and Godard understood: that Film is Revolution not A Wave and its credo is the novelty of just going out and doing it. Now that we have been amply and repeatedly assured that we are on the threshold of a technological and aesthetic revolution in movies which will inevitably restructure human consciousness and understanding, this book says that the new sensibility obviously would be awfully nice in 70mm Panavision but that it will work in Super 8 too. Which is just another way of saying, Hey, remember 2001 is probably the most awesome underground movie ever made ($10,500,000) before, lean and crazed, you sell your soul for a jr. apprenticeship on Mary Poppins. The 16 interviews that follow are a cross-section of independent directors— all of whom are just as interested in finding a new life style as a new film style. They are all, in one way or another, outsiders from Jim McBride (Greetings) whose $2500 1st film still hadn't been shown theatrically 2 yrs. after he made it, to Roman Polanski who says definitely that he's not obsessed with the bizarre and that his next film is going to be about the Donner Pass Cannibals, to Andy Warhol who says that he's still learning how to use a camera and that they haven't really made a "movie" yet. The book is not a defense of cinema vs. movies nor does it go through the theoretic/aesthetic trauma of The Underground vs. Hollywood. What it says is that personal films are not sprung full-blown from the head of the inspired amateur with his 16mm Arriflex and Nagra tape recorder slung over his shoulder.

[Reviewed by Barbara DeZonia]

•

Everybody's looking for young talented directors. But what they all do is: they'll take you, a young talented director, and take a young talented writer, and a young talented producer and they'll give you young talented property about young talented people and they'll put you all together and you'll make a young talented film." So they've called me up and said, "We're interested in you." And I say, "Well, I'm interested in doing this movie. I'll send you a script." And they say, "Well, we've got this famous book," or something like that. So I say, "Forget it."

[Jim McBride]

•

I don't think that it is possible for a man to spend a number of hours discussing himself and his work and his life without revealing a kind of personality profile . . . one man's evasiveness can be as eloquent as another man's candor."

A director's job in this period of filmmaking—and I know this may change as it has in the past—is to be an absolute dictator and produce a personal vision on a subject that he has chosen. He is paid too much because he has that responsibility, but what the people are buying is that personal vision."

[Lester]

Take One

TAKE ONE is a bi-monthly no nonsense film magazine that reviews a good number of low budget films, documentaries, and foreign releases which generally escape the notice of the big slicks. It has information on film festivals and some new product material. . . .so it is directed toward both the filmmaker and the filmwatcher.

[Reviewed by Ron Carraher]

computers as amplifiers of human imagination . . . graphic display systems using "light pens" . . . at which the artist can draw, ask the machine to rotate his drawing, (move it in many ways) . . . and put it on film . . . simultaneously making an electronic sound track . . . animation of drawings of great detail done in minutes . . . computer sensing systems that study the eye's movement over research material and when the eye rests on an image, the image automatically enlarges; if the eye rests for a longer time on the same material, the image changes . . . (imagine a french lesson on an electronic page full of words that are going by rapidly. you are reading from a display scope or tv screen. if a word is doubtful to you, by looking at it for three seconds it will enlarge itself above the other words; if you are still looking at it three seconds later, it will automatically change into English . . .)

Filmmakers Newsletter

The Filmmakers Newsletter is a clearing house for all and any information pertaining to filmmaking. As such, it's without any competition and fills a real need for the independen filmmaker. Each issue features an interview with the directo or cinematographer of a major motion picture on how the film was made. Regular monthly features include Videotape, Super-8, Product Reports (field-tested by the staff a la "Consumer Reports"), Technical Information, Book Review, How to Make Money in Filmmaking, Building Your Own Equipment, What's Happening (seminars, workshops, etc., around the country), Festival reviews and complete information on those upcoming, and free Classifieds. Despite its name, the Filmmakers Newsletter is an 84-page monthly magazine published 11 times a year (one summer issue). Subscription rates are now $7.00/yr., $12.00/two years.

[Suggested and reviewed by Phyllis Wilson]

Filmmakers Newsletter

from:
Filmmakers Newsletter Co.
P.O. Box 115
Ward Hill, MA 01830

The Film Director as Superstar
Joseph Gelmis

$3.50 postpaid

from:
Doubleday & Co. Inc.
Garden City, N.Y. 11530

or WHOLE EARTH CATALOG

P. Yes. The older I grow, the more I value simplicity. The more difficult it seems to me to make a simple film. I want my film to be done so the people who see it have the impression it was done without any effort. But, of course, there is a lot of effort behind it, a lot of struggle. And as for realism, the only way to seduce people into believing you—whether they want to or not— is to take painstaking care with the details of your film, to make it accurate. Sloppiness destroys emotional impact.

[Roman Polanski]

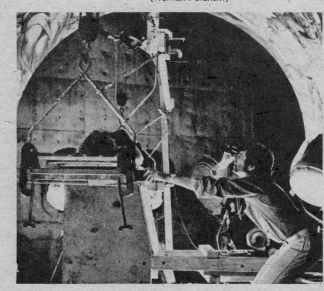

JM: Would you like to have a contract that gave you the final cut?
SP: I don't think I need one. I don't make a picture by myself, I make a picture with other people's ideas, other people's minds, other people's bodies. We make a picture together and if they don't like to work this way, then I fire them.

Take One
$5.00 /12 issues (bi-monthly)

from:
Unicorn Publishing Corp.
Post Office Box 1778
Station B
Montreal H3B 3L3
CANADA

International Film Guide

Well, as it says right on the front, this is a "record size survey of film in 32 countries with at-a-glance guide to Festivals, films on 16 mm, film books and magazines, shorts and animation, film schools and art houses." Hard to beat that except by the Saturday Review's comment: "eminently informative." Well, and then too it has lots of nice stills, in-depth articles on Anderson, Chabrol, Ichikawa, Pasolini, and Skolimowski, a world production survey with articles on new films from everywhere from Israel to Romania to Bulgaria, a list of all current film co-operatives and operating theatres around the world, and a review of all new magazines and other publications dealing with film, plus a list of film archives and film services. . .and all sorts of other stuff crammed in these fat little pages. Make friends with someone who reads sub-titles well and you'll be set no matter where in the world you are.

[Reviewed by Barbara DeZonia]

International Film Guide
Peter Cowie, editor
1970, 1974; 600 pp.

$3.95 postpaid

from:
A.S. Barnes & Company
Forsgate Drive
Cranbury, New Jersey 08512

or

WHOLE EARTH CATALOG

Anthology Film Archives

A museum of avant-garde films in New York. Monthly program $1.

—SB

Anthology Film Archives
425 Lafayette St.
New York, N.Y. 10003

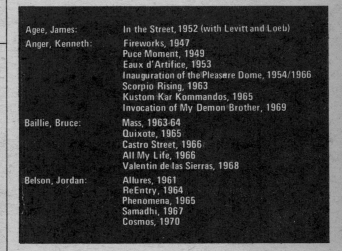

Agee, James:	In the Street, 1952 (with Levitt and Loeb)
Anger, Kenneth:	Fireworks, 1947
	Puce Moment, 1949
	Eaux d'Artifice, 1953
	Inauguration of the Pleasure Dome, 1954/1966
	Scorpio Rising, 1963
	Kustom Kar Kommandos, 1965
	Invocation of My Demon Brother, 1969
Baillie, Bruce:	Mass, 1963-64
	Quixote, 1965
	Castro Street, 1966
	All My Life, 1966
	Valentin de las Sierras, 1968
Belson, Jordan:	Allures, 1961
	ReEntry, 1964
	Phenomena, 1965
	Samadhi, 1967
	Cosmos, 1970

•

Mr. Olney didn't recognize D.R. but when D.R. identified himself he remembered. He had buried D.R.'s father and both his grandparents. And now there was Emmit's body following theirs through the same treatment in the same treatment rooms. Let it happen, D.R. thought. I hate it but let it happen anyway, there's nothing else to do.

•

Mr. Olney was a nice old man actually, but D.R. had trouble with him. He said how much is this one? and when Mr. Olney said eleven hundred dollars D.R. laughed and asked to see the cheapest thing he had. This one's two hundred and twenty, Mr. Olney said. It's our cheapest model. D.R. said I'll take it.

•

Mr. Olney sold suits and shirts and ties for thirty five dollars a set. D.R. said he couldn't afford that much, that what he'd like to do is help dig the grave and maybe get the suit half price. Mr. Olney said he believed he could manage that, and suddenly D.R. was sorry he'd acted weird toward Mr. Olney. He's just an old undertaker, D.R. thought. Be kind to the old and the dead.

•

I'll be old myself before long.

•

I'll be dead myself some day.

Guide to Filmmaking

ed pincus is a careful man, once a logician of sorts, now a cameraman. he's taught still work at the visual arts center, harvard, and now is at the mit film department.

his book is carefully done, thorough, nicely indexed, easier to use than the american cinematographers manual, and probably more useful to the student.

and it only costs a buck fifty.

its good, ed.

hi, jane.

—jd

Guide to Filmmaking
Edward Pincus
1969; 256 pp.

$1.50 postpaid

from:
The New American Library, Inc.
130I Avenue of the Americas
New York, New York 10019

or WHOLE EARTH CATALOG

16. 16MM CAMERA—FILMING WITH SOUND. Cameraman (*left*) is shooting hand-held with an Eclair NPR. Soundman (*right*) is using a Nagra III NPH tape recorder with a Sennheiser 804 shotgun microphone with a homemade windscreen. Subject is shooting hand-held with a Bolex. (*National Educational Television*)

The book is intended to give a fairly precise idea of how much it costs to do various types of films and the way to go about making these films. It is a production manual, including all the information the serious filmmaker will need about the technical side of making movies.

A whole breed of filmmakers and potential filmmakers is appearing for whom 16mm is *the* professional film and super 8mm a serious amateur gauge which someday may be a professional gauge. Much of the information for one gauge is relevant to the other. This book discusses them both, emphasizing 16mm, pointing out the differences in the narrower film.

The unedited footage is called *rushes* or *dailies*. Almost invariably there is a considerably greater amount of rushes than there is of final film. The ratio of film shot to final footage is usually between 5:1 and 10:1. But the ratio varies tremendously depending on the type of film being made and the method of filming. Peter Emmanuel Goldman's underground classic *Echoes of Silence* was done using a ratio of less than 2:1 for an hour-long film. At the other end of the spectrum, documentary filmmakers who use no script often shoot ratios higher than 40:1, which means shooting over 90,000 feet to end with an hour's length of film. Often one of the most difficult tasks in writing up a budget for a film is to estimate the amount of footage that will be needed.

When there is a script for a film, a great deal of additional footage is shot to give the editor a selection of shots and to guarantee that there will not be any continuity gaps either within scenes or in the story line. It is not unusual, when two possibilities for a story line exist, for *both* to be filmed and the final choice delayed until the film is being edited. Often the same action is filmed several times in several "takes" to get different camera angles (positions) and to guarantee that the actors have performed their task well.

In much black and white photography, correct exposure for the subject will give you a pale, washed-out, and cloudless sky. A sky darkened too much (by using a heavy filter) will have a phony, heavily dramatic quality. The bluer the sky, the easier it is to darken it and the less filtration needed. When the sky is overcast or misty, filters will not be very effective. The sky near the sun and on the horizon is often almost white and does not respond to filtration. If the film is overexposed, the filter effect may be largely lost.

If you wish to bleach a blue sky, a blue filter will do the trick.

As in all things, it is often hard to find yourself in film. For some, the way is to make their films alone. For others, film is essentially a group enterprise. In film you may be able to find yourself, understand the world, show others what the world really is, and, finally, change it.

American Cinematographer

Accurate, specific information on what's new in equipment, techniques, standards, and the attitudes of technicians using them. Also gossip and news about who's doing what where. Covers all aspects of professional filmaking from Hollywood Super Panavision 70mm to 8 mm educational loops.

The ads, fully as important as the text, are mouthwatering for those with an appetite for Eclairs and such.

If you read it regularly you'll never need Baddeley—you'll know how it's really done. Often the information is directly and simply usable; sometimes it stimulates visions of the super-cinema of the future. When in school I consulted back issues for a psychology paper on perception. The articles are really interesting and, best of all, there is no film criticism so you avoid all those negative emotions.

[Suggested by Gordon Ashby
Reviewed by Sandra Tcherepnin]

American Cinematographer

$9.00 for one year (monthly)

from:
American Cinematographer
1782 North Orange Drive
Hollywood, California 90028

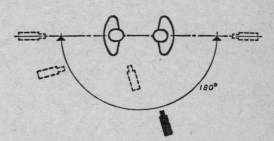

If you have been thinking of shooting your films with double-system sound, and if your camera has a synchronous motor, for about $30.00 in parts, and a little labor, you can construct a signal generator that can be used with a number of tape recorders to permit the synchronism necessary for double-system work. Furthermore, the construction is so straightforward that even if you are absolutely unhandy with tools, the labor charges for constructing the gadget should be well within the budget of even the most cost-conscious producer.

The 180° rule: If we draw a line through the main action, any camera position on one side of the line will preserve screen direction.

PROFESSIONAL MINIATURE TAPE RECORDER NAGRA SN

American Cinematographer Manual

Indispensible data book, used by American cinematographers. Expensive, because it is absolutely comprehensive, up to date, from Hollywood, and has no competitors.

[Reviewed by Sandra Tcherepnin]

American Cinematographer Manual
Arthur C. Miller, Walter Strenge, editors
newest edition 1969; approx. 600 pp.

$15.00 postpaid

from:
The American Cinematographer Manual
P. O. Box 2230
Hollywood, California 90028

Q. How can I produce a night effect in the daytime using color film?

A. This is the question we most frequently receive, and though the answer has been given many times, still the key to the question is to *underexpose two stops.* Additional techniques which assist the illusion are to photograph the scene in back-light, using lights or reflectors as fill lights on the players. When such are not available, use front cross-light. By all means avoid any white sky in the scene. You may use a 85N6 filter, but disregard its factor. The N6 (Neutral density—6 transmission) portion of this filter will reduce the light transmitted by two stops. Therefore, you judge the exposure as if you were using the normal No. 85 filter for a *day* exposure; the N6 portion cutting two stops will produce the underexposure for a night effect.

It will further the illusion if you can include in the scene some light source— such as lighted windows or street lamps. These must be boosted by using photo-flood lamps— using tracing paper or Bon Ami on the glass of the windows to diffuse the light from the naked globes.

(LEFT) The Handiola is a device for achieving instantaneous positive interlock sync. Once picture and track start-marks are aligned in their respective units, sync is maintained by simply sliding tape transport assembly 1/4-inch toward viewer. Shaft engages the viewer's sprocket for positive interlock between both media, running forward or backward; movement of either medium causes the other to move in sync. Note inching knob on front of tape transport, for precise cuing without handling tape or film. Accessory frame counter is shown installed at right. (RIGHT) Pen points to interlock shaft, at point of connection with viewer. ¼-inch movement of tape assembly establishes and releases interlock.

CAMERA SPEED COMPENSATOR

EXPOSURE INCREASE AND DECREASE
ABOVE AND BELOW NORMAL 24 F.P.S.

(The Factor for Above Normal Speeds can be used with both the Filter Factor Compensator and the ASA Exposure Index Reduction Tables)

ABOVE NORMAL SPEED		
FRAMES PER SECOND	FACTOR	STOPS INCREASE
24	0	0
32	1.5	½
48	2	1
72	3	1½
96	4	2
120	5	2¼
200	8	3
240	10	3¼
400	16	4
500	21	4¼

BELOW NORMAL SPEED		
FRAMES PER SECOND	FACTOR	STOPS DECREASE
24	0	0
16	1.5	½
12	2	1
8	3	1½
6	4	2
4	6	2½
2	12	3½

F&B/CECO

a supply house for film equipment,
rental and sales.
the catalogs are best used for pricing,
figuring production costs,
and for good listings of equipment readily available.

—jd

F&B/CECO catalogs

free

from:
F&B/CECO Inc.
315 West 43rd Street
New York, New York 10036

For professional filmmakers only

Serving the World's Finest Film Makers

MICROPHONES	Daily
Sennheisser MD 214 Lavalier	5.00
Sennheiser MKH 404 Condenser	10.00
Sennnheiser MKH 805 Directional	15.00
Sennheiser MKH 804 Directional	15.00

ECLAIR NPR 16 mm CAMERA	
With 15 and 25 mm lenses, 12V constant speed motor with built-in sync generator, battery 1-400' magazine	50.00

Superior Bulk Film

A reliable mail order service (& store) for 8 mm & 16 mm film, processing, equipment for home processing labs, & most equipment & supplies for amateur filmmakers who desire control & versatility at low-cost. Their film & processing package deals are as cheap or cheaper than any I've seen, probably more reliable than most. Also have excellent specials frequently. Discontinued film stocks, spliced reels, etc.——check it out! Good catalog available, newsheets rundown specials, new stuff, changes, etc. This place isn't one of these Jumbo-Junk Filmailer houses.

[Suggested and reviewed by Bruce Schmiechen]

Catalog, 84 pp.

Free

from:
Superior Bulk Film Co.
442-450 N. Wells Street
Chicago, Ill. 60610

ASA 25 Daylight, ASA 40 Tungsten

No longer available

A full, rich natural color film manufactured for us by one of the leading film manufacturers in the U. S. Available for both indoor (Type A) and outdoor use, this film is fully guaranteed and will satisfy even the most critical. Superior offers you greater savings on color film at no sacrifice in quality! Colors are clear, sharp and brilliant. Similar in speed and characteristics to Kodachrome II.

24-HOUR PROCESSING INCLUDED

NS-8—25 Ft. 8/8mm Spool Type . . . . Each $2.79   3 for $7.75

NS-B—100 Ft. 8/8mm for Bolex . . . . Each $9.49

NS-6—100 Ft. 16mm Spool Type . . . . Each $8.59

NS-5—50 Ft. 8/8mm Prestriped for Fairchild . . . . Each $8.39

When ordering specify Daylight or Type A

SMPTE Publications

Very technical film books.

—SB

Society of Motion Picture and Television Engineers
9 East 41st St.
New York, N.Y. 10017

Selection and Specification of Rear-Projection Screens
By Petro Vlahos. Reprinted from the February 1961 *Journal.* A detailed examination of rear-projection screens.
7 pp.   NC†

Macmillan Audio Brandon (Audio Film Center)

Rent a 16mm movie.

—SB

Macmillan Audio Brandon
34 MacQuesten Parkway South
Mount Vernon, N.Y. 10550

Macmillan Audio Brandon
2512 Program Drive
Dallas, Texas 75229

Macmillan Audio Brandon
8400 Brookfield Avenue
Brookfield, Illinois 60513

Macmillan Audio Brandon
3868 Piedmont Avenue
Oakland, California 94611

Pather Panchali   (Rental: $110)

Yojimbo   (Rental: $65)

King Rat   (Rental: $35.00)

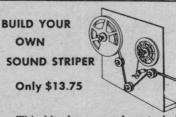

The General   (Rental: $55)

BUILD YOUR OWN SOUND STRIPER

Only $13.75

This kit shows you how to build your own sound striper. Plans and all the moving parts are included in this exclusive Superior kit that will work either with your projector or rewinds. Included are 1 roll of 400 ft. 8mm or Super 8 (specify size desired) Superstripe tape and 1 oz. bottle of adhesive. After you make this remarkable unit you can order the same accessories and supplies used on the Super-sound stripers.

MAGNETIC OXIDE STRIPING FLUID	
For use with the Argus, Perfecto or other magnetic sound stripers requiring a liquid striping	
DZ-2—1 oz.—will stripe ι800-1000 ft.	$2.75
DZ-C—1 oz. solvent for cleaning cartridge and parts	$1.50

Motion-Picture Projection and Theatre Presentation Manual
Don V. Kloepfel, Editor. This Manual details operational information for the projectionists and theatre personnel in a concise and convenient form. It is to be used as a guideline to good motion-picture presentation in the theatre.
1969   hardbound   190 pp.   illus. $7.50*

Cool Hand Luke   (Rental $65.00)

Oh far out, far out, far out. It happens with such speed, it swooshes by with such perpetual haste. There he was already, him and Leonard, helping the two guys from Olney's Funeral Home dig poor Emmit's grave. There in the family graveyard, one corner of it buried by overburden from the mining on the slopes above, rocks as big as people's heads scattered over the graves. One headstone (Daniel Hutchins Collier, D.R.'s grandfather's brother, born 1887, died 1932) had been knocked over and broken straight across the middle by a rock from the mining up above. The graveyard was at the edge of the pasture, when there had been a pasture. D.R. used to pass it all the time, going to get the cow, out walking with his grandfather on Sunday afternoons, or just in the pasture by himself at any odd time, for no reason. D.R. had been visiting that graveyard of his ancestors as long as he could remember, and now here he was again, helping to dig this time. How strange that was. How swiftly it moved along.

Leonard finished his turn digging and sat down beside Royce's grave to smoke a cigarette. Royce was buried just uphill from where Emmit was going to lie. Royce Collier, his gravestone said. Among The Angels Now. Beside Royce were his sister Blanche, and his father, who'd outlived him, and beyond his father, his mother, who'd outlived them both. D.R.'s mother wasn't in the Collier graveyard. She had died a Davenport in Illinois somewhere. Leonard sat near where she might have been if fate had willed it so, and smoking he looked up the hill toward the curve of the slope and told D.R. how the strippers had come, from left to right, peeling the trees off first, then the cut, then the blasting and finally the exposed coal seam. The only image D.R. could get was of road builders indiscriminately hacking through the pasture, and Leonard said that was pretty close to how it was.

D.R. asked Leonard if the overburden above the cemetary was stable, if rain would loosen it and let it slip on down across the graves. Leonard said there was a chance of it. He said that down behind the main house it was definitely going to slip some more but up there, maybe not.

What if it does, D.R. thought.

What difference would it make?

In the corner of the cemetary where the slide had broken through the picket fence, D.R. picked up a piece of shale that had some fossils in it, little shells of ancient creatures that millenia ago had been alive. Buried all this time and now uprooted, D.R. thought. And he thought of his father's bones, and his grandfather's.

And he thought of his own bones, too. His living hand held the ancient shale. Some day that hand itself would fossilize, and what difference does it make how deep it's buried down.

Down, they went down with Emmit's grave. Down, down. Three feet. Four. Four and six inches. Five. Right on through supper time, into evening they dug, taking turns, resting, going on again.

D.R.'s hands were blistered bad when at five feet eight inches Leonard said boys that's good enough, let's quit.

Total Picture Control

Zone System Manual

Three teachers and two books taught me photography. John Collier showed me the objective power of photographs (anthropologists with a Polaroid start far more informative conversations than anthropologists without). Minor White showed me how to go into mild trance to see directly. Jack Welpott showed me that the main obstacle to good pictures is my own ideas and arrogance (an entire class of us shot better pictures— better by every standard — blind-folded than we did in the usual way).

Total Picture Control, a good technical unimaginative book, showed me how to use lenses, filters, view cameras, settings, print papers, the whole tool kit, to get what I wanted. It displayed the basic range of possibility.

Zone System Manual, by Minor White, gave me Ansel Adams' zone system of photography in distilled form. The key is previsualization, which is looking at reality through an accurately imagined photographic print, then knowing how to make the calculations and mechanical and chemical adjustments so the print has what you saw, plus any divine grace that happened by.

—SB

Total Picture Control
Feininger
Revised edition 1970

$12.50 postpaid
from:
American Photographic Book
         Publishers, Inc.
East Gate & Zeckendorf Blvds.
Garden City, N.J. 11530

or WHOLE EARTH CATALOG

Zone System Manual
Minor White
1965, 112 pp.

$2.50 postpaid

from:
Morgan & Morgan, Inc.
25 Main Street
Hastings-on-Hudson, N.Y. 10706

or WHOLE EARTH CATALOG

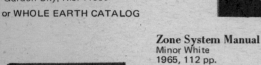

ZONE
a "Zone" as a visual unit of measurement is arrived at by altering a standard exposure by one "stop" more or one "stop" less. For example all the values in a scene exposed at f/11 at 1/25 second would print one "zone" lighter than a print of the same scene exposed at f/16 at 1/25 second. (Providing

of course that the two negatives were given identical development time and the same exposure time in the enlarger.)
This "one Stop" or "one Zone" alteration, links the "zone" to the classic 1:2 exposure ratio used in photography to calibrate shutter speeds and diaphragm openings or "stops." *(Zone System Manual)*

The composite picture at the left illustrates why straight lines must of necessity appear curved in all super wide-angle renditions. Each of its three components was taken with an ordinary camera and a lens of standard focal length. The perspective of each is "normal": with the camera in level position (center), verticals are rendered parallel; with the camera pointed upward (top), verticals converge toward the top of the picture; with the camera pointed downward (bottom), verticals converge toward the bottom of the picture. Each of these photographs encompasses an angle of approximately 47 degrees. Now, if all three were combined in one single shot encompassing three times 47 degrees, or approximately 140 degrees, how would perspective be manifest? It would appear as in the Panon shot on the opposite page which encompasses an angle of 140 degrees in which the actually straight verticals of the skyscraper are rendered as curves.

(Total Picture Control)

Extend previsualization until the negative image below can be seen in your own eye

While looking at this *(Zone System Manual)*

(Zone System Manual)

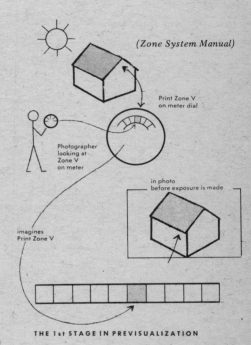

Print Zone V
on meter dial

Photographer
looking at Zone V
on meter

in photo
before exposure is made

imagines
Print Zone V

THE 1st STAGE IN PREVISUALIZATION

LIFE Library of Photography

Recently I enjoyed an airplane magazine in which all the articles were illustrated by the authors. What a difference. Instead of glamorous eye candy, the pictures were frank, densely informative, thoroughly tied in to the articles. Photography, especially professional photography, is best in the hands of skilled amateurs. Sharper than words photography is a reality medium. No specialist elite should monopolize that kind of power.

I believe these are the beginner's books I've been looking for ever since we started the CATALOG. They cover the territory— camera, printing, film, history, photojournalism, They have sensational pictures (and price to match), and fine practical information like "Camera Buyer's Guide," "Darkroom Equipment," etc.

Get a Polaroid Swinger and play around for a while. If you like the pictures to where you want to use the medium, get a 35 mm and some used darkroom equipment, develop your own film and prints, and mention the LIFE photography books to relatives in November.

—SB

The Camera
1970; 235 pp. & Camera Buyer's Guide
Light and Film
1970; 227 pp. & Guide to Camera Accessories
The Print
1970; 227 pp & Buyer's Guide to Darkroom Equipment
Photojournalism
1971; 227 pp.

Each **$7.95** plus shipping
            and handling

from:
Time-Life Books
Time & Life Building
Chicago, Ill. 60611

Polaroid Land Camera. *Sometimes thought of as an instrument designed purely for amateurs, the Polaroid Land Camera is a cherished professional tool on hundreds of weeklies and small dailies. Its almost foolproof operation enables reporters with little photographic training to get*

good pictures. The 3¼ x 4¼ pictures are large enough for a harried editor to judge without a magnifying glass, and most important of all, the instantly available prints can be sent directly to the engraver without darkroom processing—an obvious advantage under the pressure of

deadlines, aside from being a cost saver. A special film pack, usable on some models, can produce not only positives but negatives to make additional prints for presentation to local celebrities —a good-will practice sometimes followed by small papers.

Photojournalism

DUANE MICHALS: *The Illuminated Man,* 1969   *The Print*

Basic Photo Books

There is a lot of bullshit about photography; it is easily (and usually) a subject for egoistic subjectivism and it is much in the hands of the people that push consumption. But like any other art form, the thing is to shut up and get dirty learning, working feeling it. I've come this way and perhaps can help. There are a few good books:

The first book is Chas. Swedlund's A Guide to Photography. *When I last heard the book was available from him (address: 5019 W. Blemont, Chicago, Illinois 60641) for about $5. It is the best starting book; it is as simple, direct and complete as the Domebook. Women and children can use it. The mechanics of the beast are explained by a working photographer and teacher not by a streamlining book designer. Basic.*

It will get you out of the Popular Photography bullshit of one thing, one issue, another, the next. It will be enough for the person who wants a simple image— getting that consistently isn't easy. So the beginning booklist is one title.

There may come a time, though, when you wish to make love with it, form koan, fix energy. The process is capable; photography can be an art form with just as much subtlety of creation as pottery glazes, dyeing, weaving. Go to the index of the Life series on photography and look up the photographs of Ansel Adams, Brett and Edward Weston, Paul Caponigro (these are my favorites) and. . .and. . .This is the business of the fine print. And consider that reproductions almost always run a poor third to the original print.

You can do it. Hell, you can do it to yourself!!

You may want to do 35mm, perhaps large format— negatives 4" x 5" up to 11" x 14". It involves the use of the zone system of exposure and development. The knowledge won't be wasted even in 35mm. As for printing the negative you get, the more esoteric information comes largely from the same sources that will tell you about the zone system. There is one book (or rather a series) that has compass, the Ansel Adams series. True they were written nearly twenty years ago and are $5.98, but this man must know more than any other one (or many) person about da modemploi. Some find him confusing but those who work his books find it the teachings of a master— seemingly contradictory and incomplete but rich for those who will try it, work it, re-read it, understand some more, work some more. It is a book for application, not a neatly wrapped set of answers that spoil your appetite. The core of the series are The Negative, The Print and Natural Light Photography. There are others in the series. In The Print for example there is a chapter devoted to developers, on what goes in them and what those ingredients do. At the back is an appendix with a table of nearly twenty developing formulas that you can mix yourself— and play tones, print colors and contrast ranges like stops on an organ. Maybe there is space age chemicals in cans these days but a) lookit the man's pictures b) I want to fucking know the stuff I work with.

These books are the richest single source of information on how to fly with this set of wings; there is even a good part of The Negative devoted to "miniature camera", i.e., 35mm and 2¼ square. ACCESS. This man is a concert pianist, a photographer and a master. See his photographs and books. He knows how.

The Life series— it has the best set of pictures around, bar none, everything is represented. But I don't dig it. My hassle perhaps, but I find it a bit sterile. It is complete, complete,complete and very rational. Streamlined. And the questions are generally posed and answered. Spoils that appetite like a jr. high physics book. For those interested in a specific tag end to chew on, to learn from— very little. Such a thing is not a tool but an intellectual candybar. How do I make platinum prints, eh? Where do I get the chemicals, what precautions do I take? Well, maybe you'll pick up on something— and do your seeking elsewhere. It does have a damn good set of pictures.

If you wish your prints to last forever, there is the East Street Gallery permanence publication. 50¢, available from 1408 East Street in Grinell Iowa, 50112 in numberland. Says you might make it last 3000 yrs; I wish I was that important.

For those who want to get into the alchemy of mixing their own funny chemicals, you can still order most everything through Kodak via your local photo store and get a week's delivery For the really weird stuff such as Amidol or Pyrocatechin, try Dignan Photographic, Inc. 12304 Erwin Street in, yes, North Hollywood, CA. They also have an excellent publication, Booklet No. 8, Photographic Chemical Facts and Formulas. Tells you what chemicals do, is more complete and up to date (but is technical only) than Ansel. $2.50.

The Zone System hasn't been fully explained yet. Minor White's book is the most complete account, Ansel has some information about it in The Negative. Both of them are talking from the application viewpoint and it's a bit like describing the Elephant. They don't tell you how else it might be done (e.g. Minor figures development times off of zone eight, Ansel off of six) and why. Try Minor but pulleeez don't get the idea it's all that clanky. I've worked with Paul Caponigro: a lot of the time he'll merely take one or two readings and make the exposure. Fast. Simple. And you get a lot more room for creation, expression and like that.

There is a book for telling you how to do platinum, palladium and gum arabic prints. Other processes, too, all of days gone by. Interesting. They're powerful, could be a heavy trip if you've got the negatives to print out. A platinum print is a rich brown (not sepia) or glowing silver color and has an incredibly rich swimming misty depth to it. You make the paper, that is, make the emulsion and then coat a stock (of your choosing!) with it. I haven't yet done it but imagine it would be as hard as making DMT (which I haven't either). And gum arabic prints are made without silver (it's getting scarce and may disappear from the private market) and can be of any color (not just black and white). I don't know the price. It is A Handbook for Contemporary Photographers by Arnold Gassen who is an assistant professor of Art at Ohio U. in Athens, O. The Handbook is distributed by Light Impressions, Box 3012, Rochester, N.Y. 14614.

And for the technically minded, there is Todd and Zakia's Photographic Sensitometry *(Morgan & Morgan, publ.) ($9.95 list, I bought for $7.95 at the Rochester Inst of Tech. bookstore). This is a well rounded scientific treatment of light sensitive materials. Micro and macro physics, statistical mathematics, etc. While it will tell you more than you want to know, it may have valuable information. For instance, the graphics-oriented person may wish to know primarily how to twist the crittur's tail in the darkroom, being less interested in the reproduction of a visual experience than he is in the manipulation of the materials. This book would tell him a good bit about 'effects', as they're called scientifically, that he could use.*

Good luck to make it happen.

Stewart Dean
West Cornwall, Conn.

Camera

Aperture

Two magazines have consistently outstanding photographs. Camera, from Europe, has every issue a whole different kind of photographs. Of all the magazines we see at WHOLE EARTH this is the one that gets cut up and pinned to the walls. . Aperture, Minor White's magazine, carries camerawork as a mystical tool, not O Boy! God!, but how to see and see until you see through and back.

—SB

Camera
Allan Porter, ed.

$23.00 /yr (monthly)
in three languages:
French, German & English

from:
Camera
C. J. Bucher Ltd.
CH-6002
Lucerne, Switzerland

Aperture
Minor White, ed.

$14 /yr (quarterly)

from:
Aperture, Inc.
Elm St.
Millertown, N.Y. 12567

Duane Michaels, Camera

Conclusions

1. That the photographer is in a poor position to forecast how others will respond to his pictures. (a) Because he was there at the moment the exposure was made, or at least thinks that he was there. (b) Because he assumes that as soon as his camera is paid for that the pictures emerging from it are his.

2. The remedy is to learn to look at his own photographs as if they were made by some other photographer.

3. The remedy, if applied, becomes a discipline that separates the men from the boys.

4. In learning to predict responses it is better for the photographer if he has the *direct experience of gathering responses* to his pictures than to read extensively about such matters. It is better because the direct experience gives an opportunity to study himself and his work in relation to the world.

(Aperture)

Richard A. Egli, Camera

(Aperture)

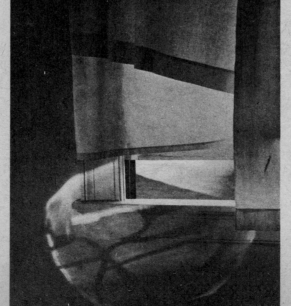
(Aperture)

On their way off the hill Leonard stopped off at the homeplace to show D.R. how to feed and water Emmit's rabbits and his chickens. There were forty rabbits in eleven hutches, and about a dozen banty chickens to feed, a half hour chore even when you knew what you were doing. D.R. worked along with Leonard, and listened to him, he wanted to learn this work.

•

But his mind was still on Emmit's grave.

•

Leonard invited D.R. home with him to eat supper but D.R. said he didn't feel like eating.

•

He said he wanted to be by himself a while, and Leonard understood.

•

As soon as Leonard was out of sight downhill D.R. went back around the hillside to the grave.

•

A grave.

•

That is a grave.

•

That dark opening

•

That dark there is a hole in the ground for Emmit's body. It's Emmit's body's home now. We're going to put it in a box and put the box in that hole tomorrow afternoon and cover it with dirt and leave it there for years and years and years. Worms are going to eat his flesh and devour the casket, and in time even his bones will turn to dust. We're going to plant Emmit here tomorrow like a seed.

•

He's worm-food now.

•

D.R. was sitting on the mound of dirt they'd thrown up, looking at the hole. Above him was his father's grave, and all around were other graves of long-dead people who had sired him, and it was dark and overhead some early stars were shining as they had the night before, how many nights before? In the ground, D.R. thought.

•

In the ground.

•

Out loud, D.R. said: in the ground.

•

And without really deciding to in his mind, D.R. scooted to the edge, then bracing across the corner of the grave he lowered himself into it, and lay down on his back and closed his eyes.

•

This is Emmit's wake, he thought.

•

This is Emmit's wake. I am waking here for Emmit.

East Street Gallery

The East Street Gallery, a cooperative community located in Grinnell, Iowa. Photography, publishing and the making of photographic equipment provide the economic base of the community.

They put out an extremely honest and thorough as can be booklet . . . it contains the results of their tests, and organizes the scattered information relating to the processing and storing of pictures for maximum permanance . . . an issue neglected by too many photographers who other otherwise care about that they are doing.

They also describe in detail their high cost, but very high quality and efficient film and print washers and timing device . . .

[Suggested & Reviewed by Will Endres]

Nearly all the negative filing devices now on the market are very destructive to silver based film emulsions. This is especially true of the common "kraft paper" and glassine sleeves. These negative containers contain excessive amounts of sulfur and other harmful chemicals. Also, many of these containers contain glue in the seams which over a period of time may cause severe damage to negatives. It may currently be assumed that no paper or glassine container is safe for long-term storage of negatives or prints.

Procedures for Processing and Storing Black and White Photographs for Maximum Possible Permanence.

$1.00 postpaid via 1st class mail

from:
East Street Gallery
723 State St.
Box 68
Grinnell, Iowa 50112

Archival Print Washer $120.75
Archival Film Washer $16
Archival Print Dryer $35
Water Collection Base for print washer $33.25

Cheap Kodachrome

For use in my teaching and for pleasure I buy a lot of Kodachrome for slides. And, after fifteen years, I've decided that Kodak is the best operation to do my developing. I order 35mm KII 36 exposure cartridges with Kodak developing mailers from an outfit in New York City. For $36.47 I get ten rolls (360 pictures) at a cost of less than a dime per slide counting postage, film, developing, and even 6% sales tax. Order from outside New York and they don't even charge sales tax.

I used to buy film at discount stores and camera shops which charge, typically, 200 per cent of my present cost and for the same product.

I order from 47th Street Photo, Inc., 67 W. 47th St., New York City, 10036. I like them. They even charge my order to my credit card number (Master Charge, or BankAmericard) and save the price of a check.

James Oswald
DeWitt, N.Y.

Index to Kodak Information L-5

Lessons in eye-hand coordination— Keys to holding your camera steady. . .learning photographic terms. . .How to record eclipses and starlight. . .choosing the right film. . . In the darkroom: theory and technique. . .photomacrography. . .graphic arts techniques. . .infrared. . .Pictures in extremes of weather (and of extremes of weather). . . Projection. . .filters. . .extra-long exposures. . .Scientific photography. . .Low prices and good mail service make it profitable to pick the brains of Kodak's researchers and staff photographers. Information useful to novice and pro alike. . . .

When you see a picture, this catalog will probably guide your hand. But first you have to SEE. . .and that is another thing entirely.

[Suggested and reviewed by Gary Braasch]

Index to Kodak Information L-5

free

from:
Eastman Kodak Co.
Dept. 454
Rochester, N.Y. 14650

KODAK Projection Calculator and Seating Guide;
9-69; $2 (S-16)

Calculator is a three-part dial for computing factors such as image/screen size, projection, distance

Bibliography on Underwater Photography and
Photogrammetry; 10-72; $.35

KODAK Master Darkroom **DATAGUIDE**; 10-72; $5.50
Data for black-and-white processing, printing, and copying.

Dignan Photographic

If you try to find information on the chemistry behind color processing you soon discover that it is hard to come by and the chemicals are equally hard to locate or purchase. Dignan Photographic can help you solve both problems. They publish a monthly newsletter which is full of information and formulas for both color and b&w. Many formulas are simplified versions of commercial brews which make them easy for the novice to use. Their C-22 for developing Kodacolor or Ektacolor film and their unicolor print paper formulas are easy to mix and use. Not only is it interesting but you can easily save 40 to 60%, sometimes more, on your chemical costs. Mixing your own also offers the possibility of doing things not possible with the commercial chemical kits. Dignan Photographic sells most of the chemicals you will need for color or b&w by mail order. Their newsletter covers many major products of Kodak, Agfa, GAF, Fuji, etc. It began being published Sept. '68 so you will want to order back issues. If you are a photographer who wants control over a large and important segment of photographic technology Dignan can help you.

[Suggested and reviewed by Terry Gritton]

Dignan Photographic Inc.
12304 Erwin St.
No. Hollywood, Calif. 91606
Dignan Photographic Newsletter
$18.00/yr
Catalog free on request.

Merit Photo Supply

Lowest prices on film. Handling charge of 75¢ on all orders. Minimum order $4.00.

—SB

Merit Photo Supply
Box 6011
North Hollywood, CA 91603

1971
(Prices effective
Nov. 1, 1970)

KODACHROME II
The universal favorite for color slides in daylight or with blue flashbulbs. Has unexcelled color quality and extreme sharpness, with moderate speed (ASA 25) and good exposure latitude.

K 135 20 exp. $1.49
K 135 36 exp.   2.10

Prepaid Processing Kodak Mailers

PK-20, for 35mm 20exp. or 126 slides
. . . .$1.29
PK-27, for 127,120,620 Ektachrome
. . . .$1.29
PK-36, for Kodachrome or Ektachrome
36 exp. $1.89
PK-59, for 8mm roll or Super-8 50ft.
. . . .$1.29
PK-49, for 16mm 100ft. roll...$3.10

Kodak Ektagraphic Carousel

I've been working with tape-slide shows, and if audience involvement is any measure, tape-slide is fully as effective a medium as film. I use two Kodak Ektagraphic projectors, with the lamp circuits rigged so that one image can be dissolved into the other. The speed of the dissolve is controlled by a switcher-fader that I designed and built from two household light dimmers and a Spirograph game. I would be happy to share my invention with any other media freaks who are interested. Just write.

You reviewed the Kodak Carousel projector in Fall 69. Please tell everyone that the Carousel is good, but not as good as its big brother, the Kodak Ektagraphic. Advantages of the Ektagraphic: 3-connector power cord is permanently attached; Model AF has remote focus control, autofocus, timer, tungsten-halogen lumenized optics, and all other features of the Carousel 860; all Ektagraphics are built more ruggedly than the Carousel; all Ektagraphics will center each slide horizontally, as well as vertically, for precise projection of lap-dissolve slides (important in tape-slide shows); all Ektagraphics have an extra fuze in the lamp circuit. The Ektagraphics are a light gray color, rather than the black of the Carousel. Cost is about the same as the Carousel. Ektagraphics are only available through audio-visual supply houses, and other establishments that supply equipment for auditorium, school, business, and industrial uses. See your local school district, or write to Kodak for dealers. Most audio-visual houses give up to 20% discount to schools and other good liars, so you can frequently horse-trade an Ektagraphic for less than the Carousel. The Ektagraphic AF has got to be the finest slide projector on the market.

I also want to tell you about the finest 35mm camera on the market— the Nikkormat FTN. I've used a lot of different 35mm cameras, including the Nikon F ($150 more than the Nikkormat), and find the Nikkormat superior to all of them. Camera buyers should ask these questions at least: How complete is the selection of lenses and accessories (who can beat Nikon, Vivatar, Soligor, etc)? How easy is it to change lenses (Canon and Pentax fall down here)? Do I have to move my trigger finger to change shutter speed? Is the thru-the-lens (the only way) meter accurate and dependable? How bulky and heavy is the camera? Is the shutter cloth, or titanium? Does the camera fire quietly and smoothly (the Nikkormat could be a little better in this category)? With a little hunting, you can get a Nikkormat with f:2 50-mm lens for under $220.

Jim Mitchell
725 West Margaret
Pasco, Washington 99301

I agree about the Nikkormat. Best prices are Hong Kong, see p. 232. A good buy on Carousels is on p. 227.

—SB

Spiratone

If you don't have much bread, or don't want to spend much, don't be put off (or put on) by Nikon prices when shopping for new photo gear. Spiratone handles almost every piece of equipment the 35mm enthusiast could want, under their own brand name. They sell lenses from a fisheye to a 500mm mirror, and virtually all lens accessories. Their prices are ridiculously low. For the same money you'd pay for a Nikon 24mm lens, you can get a Spiratone fisheye, 200mm, 300mm, and 28 mm lenses. I have owned a Spiratone 200mm lens for three years. It's gone through a lot of heavy trips— never broke down— never been to the shop. I doubt if you can differentiate, with the naked eye, my Spiratone lens prints from my Nikon prints. Even the arch-deacons of the Nikon-Leica-Hasselblad cult, Popular and Modern Photography, have periodically applauded a low-priced Spiratone innovation. (e.g., See Pop. Photog. May 1970 on Spiratone 500mm mirror lens). When I returned a defective lens, it was replaced by a brand new one, no questions asked, within five minutes.

Spiratone also sells cheaply the most complete line of photo special effects equipment I've seen anywhere, including day-glo enlarging paper, right angle lenses, starlite and multiple image attachments, and focal length and lens angle multipliers. Before you buy high, get high, and write to Spiratone for a free catalog.

Larry Lynn
Kingston, R.I.

Spiratone, Inc.
135-06 Northern Blvd.

Flushing, N.Y. 11354

Camerafreaks, indicate name and model camera, and whether you do own darkroom work.

—PC

The Art of Color

"If you, unknowing, are able to create masterpieces in color, then unknowledge is your way. But if you are unable to create masterpieces out of your unknowledge, then you ought to look for knowledge."

The same goes for seeing masterpieces. This beautifully made book is more than a text—it is a powerful tool that can help you realize the physical act of seeing as a creative act. A way to open your mind and eyes and make the connections to the world more direct and immediate. The plates are so good that there is tangible physical pleasure in seeing them. Worth the giant price if you work with color at all—worth at least a trip to the library if you don't.

[Reviewed by Terri Gunesch]

The Art of Color
Johannes Itten
1974, revised, 155 pp.

$47.50 postpaid

from:
Van Nostrand Reinhold Company
450 West 33rd St.
New York, N.Y. 10001

or WHOLE EARTH CATALOG

JOHANNES ITTEN · THE ART OF COLOR

Yellow is the most light-giving of all hues. It loses this trait the moment we shade it with gray, black or violet. Yellow is, as it were, a denser, material white. The further this yellowed light is drawn into the denseness of matter, of opacity, the more it is assimilated to yellow-orange, orange and red-orange. Our red is the stopping point of yellow, with which it is not visibly tinged. In the center of the yellow-to-red band, we have orange, as the strongest and most concentrated interpenetration of light and matter. Golden yellow suggests the highest sublimation of matter by the power of light, impalpably radiant, lacking transparency, but weightless as a pure vibration. Gold was formerly much used in painting. It signifies luminous, light-emitting matter. The golden domes of Byzantine mosaics and the backgrounds of the paintings of early masters were symbols of the beyond, the marvelous, the kingdom of sun and light. The golden aura of saints is the token of their transfiguration. The attainment of this state was conceived as an envelopment by light. This heavenly light could not be symbolized except by gold.

Foundations of Modern Art

Full of pronouncements to make you urp ("There are only three billion seconds in a century. Art? To make us forget it"). This 1931 work still serves by odd illumination. Every third pronouncement or so scratches an itch you didn't know you had. The pictures (226 of them) are splendidly peculiar— battleships, native masks, a survey of military formations, a fat lady, cubist paintings, an ancient Egyptian with glasses. I don't know if the book has much to do with art: it has plenty to do with the tension of environment and anti-environment.

—SB
[Suggested by Frederick Ted Castle]

Foundations of Modern Art
Ozenfant, Trans. by John Rodker
1952; 347 pp.

$3.50 postpaid

from:
Dover Publications, Inc.
180 Varick Street
New York, N. Y. 10014

or WHOLE EARTH CATALOG

The early youth of a man marked out for greatness reveals his later quality. His middle age is often characterised by work that is not truly representative, for self-criticism often obscures his natural virtues. Often works of this period, when technically he is most accomplished, mirror a malaise due to the fact that his intellect has not yet established full harmony with his instincts. The greatest works of art are those produced in the fifties. By then that master has drawn from his intellect all it can give, and is reaping the reward of his experiments. He discovers or rediscovers his own well-springs. Michael Angelo, Tintoretto, Renoir, Cezanne.

SUSPENSE

Our mind always tries to organize what appears unorganized or not organized enough. It also tries to resolve the discontinuous in continuous. Our mind tends to complete the incomplete or interrupted forms. We feel first suspense, then satisfaction of completion. (Phenomenon much in use in music.)

Negress seeing herself for the First Time in a Good Mirror.

VISION & VALUE series

Design! Prestige! $75!

Some years ago Gyorgy Kepes revolutionized the Design industry with a book called The New Landscape, illustrating the convergence of the scientific and artistic imagery. Since then he's been compiling a deep series of latest thought on motion, image, structure, symbol, module, so forth. It's a casket of jewels, some glass but pretty, some valuable gemstone.

—SB
[Suggested by Len Fehskens]

Education of Vision 1965; 233 pp. **$12.50** postpaid
Structure in Art and in Science 1965; 189 pp. **$12.50** postpaid
The Nature and Art of Motion 1965; 195 pp. **$12.50** postpaid
Module Proportion Symmetry Rhythm 1966; 233 pp. **$12.50**
The Man-Made Object 1966; 230 pp. **$12.50** postpaid
Sign Image Symbol 1966; 281 pp. **$12.50** postpaid
  VISION & VALUE series $75.00 postpaid

from:
George Braziller
1 Park Avenue
New York, N. Y. 10016

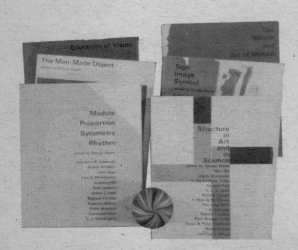

Assume for the moment that the gentleman in the bowler hat insists that he is the sole reality, while everything else appears only in his imagination. However, he cannot deny that his imaginary universe is populated with apparitions that are not unlike himself. Hence he has to grant them the privilege, that they themselves may insist that they are the sole reality and everything else is only a concoction of their imaginations. On the other hand, they cannot deny that their fantasies are populated by apparitions that are not unlike themselves, one of which may be *he*, the gentleman with the bowler hat.

With this the circle of contradiction is closed, for if one assumes to be the sole reality, it turns out he is the imagination of someone else who, in turn, insists that *he* is the sole reality.

The resolution of this paradox establishes the reality of environment through evidence of a second observer. Reality is that which can be witnessed; hence, rests on knowledge that can be shared, that is, "together-knowledge," or *con-scientia*.

Heinz Von Foerster
Sign Image Symbol

In which sense reality indeed exists for a self-reflecting organism will become clear by the argument that defeats the solipsistic hypothesis. This arguments proceeds by *reductio ad absurdum* of the thesis: this world is only in my imagination; the only reality is the imagining 'I.'"

I'm awake.

And suddenly D.R. felt Emmit in the air above him, looking down into the grave. He was flying in the cool night air, he was walking on the broken slopes above.

That's silly, D.R. thought. He's not flying. He's not walking. He's not even

He's not even Emmit any more.

For Emmit's lost his name now. He's gone free of names.

And in the cooling dark, feeling the walls of earth on either side, D.R. wondered what that could feel like, what it could possibly feel like to have no name.

To not be David.

To not be Collier. Or Davenport or Divine Right, or even D.R. I have no name, he thought.

No name, no name. I've joined the earth and turned to no-name stuff downhill from the bones of Royce, my father.

Father. I remember you, my father, lying through this wall of earth above my head. You played the guitar and sang and drove us around. I remember seeing you carrying groceries on your shoulder in a box, and one time on the courthouse lawn in Hyden eating crackers and sardines, the two of us together. Now you are bones and I am bones, and let the dead bones lie. Old fish that used to swim here have no names. Old cows that used to pasture here forgotten, without names. And people that once lived here, Indians in the rockhouses, digging hominy holes, dead, and only remnants of their living here remain, and no names. A few names fading in the headstones maybe, stones already sinking, leaning, eager to lie down. I am lying down. Down, down in Emmit's bed, trading places with him as a wake.

The Natural Way to Draw

Drawing is a deeper and wider kind of writing. It's better communication in many ways than writing, and it's much closer to your mind. (The same goes for music and speech.)

This classic work by an outstanding art teacher is not only the best how-to book on drawing, it is the best how-to book we've seen on any subject.

—SB
[Suggested by Roy Sebern]

The job of the teacher, as I see it, is to teach students, not how to draw, but how to learn to draw.

YOU SHOULD DRAW, NOT WHAT THE THING LOOKS LIKE, NOT EVEN WHAT IT IS, BUT WHAT IT IS *DOING*. Feel how the figure lifts or droops — pushes forward here — pulls back there — pushes out here — drops down easily there. Suppose that the model takes the pose of a fighter with fists clenched and jaw thrust forward angrily. Try to draw the actual *thrust* of the jaw, the *clenching* of the hand. A drawing of prize fighters should show the *push*, from foot to fist, behind their blows that makes them hurt.

In contour drawing you touch the edge of the form.

In gesture drawing you feel the movement of the whole.

THE SOONER YOU MAKE YOUR FIRST FIVE THOUSAND MISTAKES, THE SOONER YOU WILL BE ABLE TO CORRECT THEM.

The first exercise, which you are about to attempt, is planned consciously to bring into play your sense of touch and to coordinate it with your sense of sight for the purpose of drawing.

Look at the edge of your chair. Then rub your finger against it many times, sometimes slowly and sometimes quickly. Compare the idea of the edge which the touch of your finger gives with the idea you had from merely looking at it. In this exercise you will try to combine both those experiences —that of touching with that of simply looking.

The Natural Way to Draw
Kimon Nicolaides
1941; 221 pp.

$6.95 postpaid

from:
Houghton Mifflin Company
Wayside Road
Burlington, Massachusetts 01803

or WHOLE EARTH CATALOG

A gesture drawing is like scribbling rather than like printing carefully — think more of the meaning than of the way the thing looks.

Exercise 1: Contour Drawing

Materials: Use a 3B (medium soft) drawing pencil with a very fine point (sharpened on sandpaper) and a piece of cream-colored manila wrapping paper about fifteen by twenty inches in size. Manila paper usually comes in large sheets which may be cut into four pieces of that size. You may use, also, the kind sold as "shelf paper" provided it is not glazed. Fasten the paper with large paper clips to a piece of prestwood or a stiff piece of cardboard. Wear an eyeshade. Do not use an eraser until you come to Exercise 28.

Sit close to the model or object which you intend to draw and lean forward in your chair. Focus your eyes on some point— any point will do—along the contour of the model. (The contour approximates what is usually spoken of as the outline or edge.) Place the point of your pencil on the paper. Imagine that your pencil point is touching the model instead of the paper. Without taking your eyes off the model, wait until you are convinced that the pencil is touching that point on the model upon which your eyes are fastened.

Then move your eye slowly along the contour of the model and move the pencil slowly along the paper. As you do this, keep the conviction that the pencil point is actually touching the contour. Be guided more by the sense of touch than by sight. THIS MEANS THAT YOU MUST DRAW WITHOUT LOOK-ING AT THE PAPER, continuously looking at the model.

Exactly coordinate the pencil with the eye. Your eye may be tempted at first to move faster than your pencil, but do not let it get ahead. Consider only the point that you are working on at the moment with no regard for any other part of the figure.

TWO TYPES OF STUDY. The way to learn to draw is by drawing. People who make art must not merely know about it. For an artist, the important thing is not how much he knows, but how much he can do. A scientist may know all about aeronautics without being able to handle an airplane. It is only by flying that he can develop the sense for flying. If I were asked what one thing more than any other would teach a student how to draw, I should answer, "Drawing—incessantly, furiously, painstakingly drawing."

Probably you realize already that contour drawing is of the type which is to be done "painstakingly". On the other hand, gesture drawing, which you will begin today, is to be done "furiously". In order to concentrate, one can act furiously over a short space of time, or one can work with calm determination, quietly, over a long-extended period. In learning to draw, both kinds of effort are necessary and the one makes a precise balance for the other. In long studies you will develop an understanding of the structure of the model, how it is made—by which I mean something more fundamental than anatomy alone. In quick studies you will consider the function of action, life, or expression—I call it *gesture*.

Some students become self-conscious and confused as soon as they attempt to draw a face. Don't think of the head or the face as something different from any other part of the body. Draw it as you would draw a hand or an elbow or a knee.

Don't try to "get a likeness" of your model. The tendency of the beginner is to separate likenesses from drawing. Draw strangers if you can because you care less what they look like. Do not draw members of your family— or at least do not show them your drawings— because their one reaction will be to look for the likeness. Keep it clearly in mind that YOU ARE NOT MAKING A PORTRAIT. You are making a study of a head.

CHANGING THE POINT OF VIEW. It is well known that the printed or spoken word has a tendency to take on authority once it is printed or spoken. To get away from it almost takes a revolution. The same thing is true with your own drawing. The very mistakes you make, as they linger on the paper, have this tendency to become authoritative. To combat it, move about the room during the long pose, making occasional scribbled drawings. A thing is factually the same from whatever point of view you see it, but seeing it from different points of view will illuminate the meaning of the forms and lines you have been looking at.

Whenever you are uncertain as to how to begin a study think of the movement.

Art and Illusion

So much art criticism is so much a vapid waste of time that a book like this one is thoroughly a shock. Every page yields fresh information (did you know that the comic strip was singlehandedly invented by a Swiss gent named Töpfler in the 1820's?) and worthwhile hypotheses about how art and artists gradually teach themselves energies of effect. Furthermore the book is a bargain— it has 319 fine illustrations, 18 in color. —SB

Art and Illusion
E. H. Gombrich
1960, 1961; 466 pp.

$6.45 postpaid

from:
Princeton University Press
Princeton, New Jersey 08540

or WHOLE EARTH CATALOG

E. H. GOMBRICH
ART AND ILLUSION
A Study in the Psychology of Pictorial Representation

The A. W. Mellon Lectures in the Fine Arts, 1956
Bollingen Series / Princeton

Only in the realm of dreams has the artist found full freedom to create. I think the difference is well summed up in the anecdote about Matisse. When a lady visiting his studio said, "But surely, the arm of this woman is much too long," the artist replied politely, "Madame, you are mistaken. This is not a woman, this is a picture."

But no tradition of art had a deeper understanding of what I have called the "screen" than the art of the Far East. Chinese art theory discusses the power of expressing through absence of brush and ink. "Figures, even though painted without eyes, must seem to look; without ears, must seem to listen. . . . There are things which ten hundred brush-strokes cannot depict but which can be captured by a few simple strokes if they are right. That is truly giving expression to the invisible." [170] The maxim into which these observations were condensed might serve as a motto of this chapter: "i tao pi pu tao—idea present, brush may be spared performance."

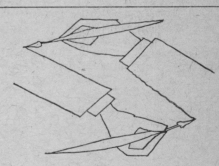

202   STEINBERG: *From "The Passport"*

Max Friedlander tells the revealing story of the bank official who insisted that German bank notes should retain a portrait head in their design. Nothing, he said, was harder for the forger to imitate than precisely the right expression of these artistically quite insignificant heads, nor was there a quicker way of discovering a suspect note than simply observing the way these faces look at you.

Rabbit or duck?

True, we can switch from one reading to another with increasing rapidity; we will also "remember" the rabbit while we see the duck, but the more closely we watch ourselves, the more certainly we will discover that we cannot experience alternative readings at the same time. Illusion, we will find, is hard to describe or analyze, for though we may be intellectually aware of the fact that any given experience must be an illusion, we cannot, strictly speaking, watch ourselves having an illusion.

Art in America

The only periodical I know that consistently makes art seem like something worth bothering with.

—SB

Art in America
Elizabeth C. Baker

$16.50 /yr (bimonthly)

from:
Art in America, Inc.
Subscriber Service
1255 Portland Place
Boulder, CO. 80302

Walter Evans talking:

It's a very exciting, heady thing. It happens more when you're younger, but it still happens, or I wouldn't continue. I think there is a period of esthetic discovery that happens to a man and he can do all sorts of things at white heat. Yeats went through three periods. T.S. Eliot was strongest in his early period, I think. E.E. Cummings seemed to go on without losing much. After all, poetry is art and these fields are related. It's there and it's a mystery and it's even partly mystical and that's why it's hard to talk about in a rational pragmatic society. But art goes on. You can defend it in spite of the fact that the time is full of false art. Art schools are fostering all sorts of junk, but that's another matter. There are always a few instances of the real thing that emerge in unexpected places and you can't stop it; there it is. Even in a puritan, materialistic, middleclass, bourgeois society like America. Because the country is like that, the artist in America is commonly regarded as a sick, neurotic man. (And tends to regard himself that way.) Until recently, true art in America was sick from being neglected. Now of course it's sick the other way: too much is being made of it. The period that's just finishing, of fame and fortune for a few artists, is outrageous. It's outrageous for a few to make hundreds of thousands of dollars while a number of very good artists cannot even make a living. It makes you sick to think about it. The art world is part of our very sick society. Think of what a man of letters is in Paris or in England and what he is here. Here he's either outrageously famous and rich, or treated as less than nothing, never understood, never honestly appreciated. In those countries everyone understands that there are many excellent, poor, almost starving artists, and they are very much respected, just as old age is respected. The unappreciated artist is at once very humble and very arrogant too. He collects and edits the world about him. This is especially important in the psychology of camera work. This is why a man who has faith, intelligence and cultivation will show it in his work. Fine photography is literate, and it should be. It does effect cultivation if there *is* cultivation. This is also why, until recently, photography has had no status, as it's usually practiced by uncultivated people. I always remember telling my classes that the students should seek to have a cultivated life and an education: they'd make better photographs. On the other hand, Eugene Atget was an uneducated man, I think, who was a kind of medium, really. He was like Blake. His work sang like lightning through him. He could infuse the street with his own poetry, and I don't think he even was aware of it or could articulate it. What I've just been saying is not entirely true. Since I'm a half-educated and self-educated man, I believe in education. I do note that photography, a despised medium to work in, is full of empty phonies and worthless commercial people. That presents quite a challenge to the man who can take delight in being in a very difficult, disdained medium.

•

Turner, of course, is played by Jagger— or rather, Turner *is* Jagger— or rather, and much more interestingly, Turner is the future of Jagger as seen by Donald Cammell and Nicolas Roeg, the codirectors of the film, and most likely by Jagger himself. Burned to a metaphysical crisp by his years in the radioactive spotlight of pop superstardom, Turner has become a glassy-eyed avatar of decayed dreams and rancid drives. He potters about his house, playing with his massive electronic equipment, exhaustedly having sex with his hip hetaira, turning on, reading Borges. Turner is a new genus— Standoff Man, a creature caught and confounded between the extreme energies that dominate contemporary life. He mumbles Nietzsche and sings the blues; he swaggers with cockney machismo and paints his vulvate mouth; he gives off sparks of violence and an effluvium of torpor. And all of this comes together in a brilliant passage when he sings *Memo from T,* the ultimate Jaggeresque dithyramb, in which Turner catapults through a series of identity changes and gender blurrings, accomplished by Jagger's satanic singing and the kaleidoscopic camerawork and editing. In this Brechtian anthem Jagger becomes the Lotte Lenya of our nihilist time.

The Way of Chinese Painting

chinese painters do more with brush, ink, inkstone and paper than western gadgeteers accomplish with their complicated mixing formulas, apprenticeship programs, and didactic traditions.
has a lot to do with thinking simply.
this book can provide you with good access to the tools and ideas of eastern brush painting,
things you can carry around in your hip pocket as you move; you provide the practice.

—jd

Kenneth Rexroth and Minor White had me use this as a photography book.

—SB

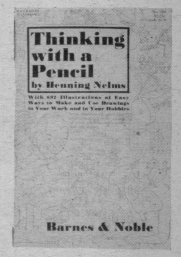

PURIFYING WHITE

In paintings, the areas where white is used often darken. Chew the heart of a bitter apricot seed, and with the juice wash these spots once or twice. The dark spots will then disappear.

The Way of Chinese Painting
Mai-mai Sze
1956, 59; 456pp.

$1.95 postpaid

from:
Random House, Inc.
Westminster, Md. 21157

or WHOLE EARTH CATALOG

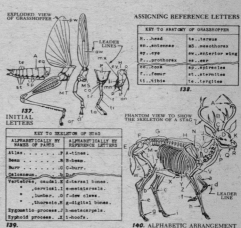

Lu Ch'ai says:
Among those who study painting some strive for an elaborate effect and others prefer the simple. Neither complexity in itself nor simplicity is enough. Some aim to be deft, others to be laboriously careful. Neither dexterity nor conscientiousness is enough. Some set great value on method; others pride themselves on dispensing with method. To be without method is deplorable, but to depend entirely on method is worse.

You must learn first to observe the rules faithfully; afterwards, modify them according to your intelligence and capacity. The end of all method is to seem to have no method.

For good supplier of Sumi ink brushes and materials (Aiko's Art Materials Import), see p. 175.

The Très Riches Heures of Jean, Duke of Berry

If you are at a place in your life where images can affect you, level this book at your head. It has 139 color plates, incomparable, exquisite, razor-edged. There is nothing like it in history.

—SB

The Très Riches Heures of Jean, Duke of Berry
1485, 1969; 139 plates and text.

$45.00 postpaid

from:
George Braziller
1 Park Avenue
New York, N.Y. 10016

or WHOLE EARTH CATALOG

Thinking With A Pencil

This book is a good pragmatic introduction to the full range of image-representation. Whether you plan to top Zap comics or use computer-generated diagrams to expand your intellect, these are basics you can use, if only to depart from.

—SB
[Suggested by Dave Guard]

Thinking With a Pencil
Henning Nelms
1957, 64; 348 pp.; 629 illus.

$2.75 postpaid (Canada $3.00)

from:
Barnes & Noble, Inc.
105 Fifth Avenue
New York, N.Y. 10003

or WHOLE EARTH CATALOG

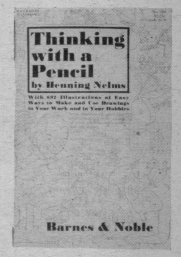

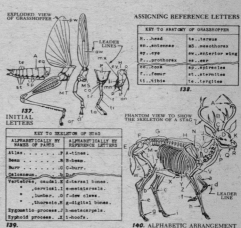

Omitting the useless is as important as including the essential. Aristotle stated a fundamental truth when he said that everything which does not add will detract.

•

Practical drawings are mental tools. Once you have learned to make them, you will find that they are as useful in solving problems as saws and hammers are useful in carpentry.

But then the night and then how soon the daylight comes, how endless are the details of the work. Busy. Busy. It's ritual time, it's tending to the dead.

•

D.R. rolled out of bed —— Emmit's bed, the big one he had slept in the first day he was there —— at six a.m. and by six thirty he was sitting in Leonard's kitchen, his wife Roxie's kitchen, eating eggs and ham and biscuits covered by thick gravy.

•

This is my wife Roxie, Leonard said. This is David, Emmit's nephew.

•

I been hearing about you, said Roxie, and Leonard said you just help yourself now, David, you make yourself right at home.

•

D.R. ate. He ate, and ate. He ate like some great tanker taking on a load of fuel.

•

We've all been hearing about you, said Roxie. Ma Godsey said your coming to take care of Emmit was a blessing from the Lord.

•

Ma thinks everything's a blessing from the Lord, said Leonard.

Catalog of Art Prints

Since 1949 UNESCO has been trying to update and internationalize the world of Art Prints. They have a central archives of prints, and a committee of experts who decide which prints to include in their catalogs. The criteria are: quality of print, significance of the painter, and importance of the painting.

There are two UNESCO print catalogs: Catalogue of Colour Reproductions of Paintings Prior to 1860 and the same of paintings from 1860 to 1965. Both are understandably limited in scope by what quality prints are available, and the choice of painters and paintings is often poor. Too much trivial or repetitive work by minor painters takes the place of better paintings by major artists. The catalog does function as a useful access device, and includes reproductions of many inspired paintings, not all of which are expensive. Each entry includes the artist's name, dates, a black & white photo of the painting, its title, date, medium, size and collection in which it rests. In addition, there are lists of publishers and printers, and information on purchasing prints.

Catalogs are trilingual in French/English/Spanish and print dimensions are given in both inches and centimeters. But price conversions are not given so you must deal with each foreign price.

[Reviewed by Joe Bonner & Annie Helmuth]

If you want good prints of Giorgione, Van der Weyden, Klee etc., see the Unesco catalogs at your library or:

Catalogue of Colour Reproductions of Paintings Prior to 1860
1968; 451 pp.
$9.50 postpaid

Catalogue of Colour Reproductions of Paintings 1860-1965
1966; 561 pp.
$8.50

both from:
UNESCO
Unipub, Inc.
Box 433
New York, N.Y. 10016

Painting, Technical Info

Two paperbacks re painting & painting materials—economical substitutes for Mayer's book.

Painting Materials
by Getters & Stout
Dover Publications, N.Y. $2.75

A Handbook on the Care of Paintings
by Caroline K. Keck
Watson-Guptill Publications
2160 Patterson St.
Cincinnati, OH 45214
$3.00

H. L. Bogdos
New York, N.Y.

The Artist's Handbook of Materials & Techniques

Written in a time when "artist" meant "painter", this classic gives detailed technique on preparation of your own materials for painting. —SB

The Artist's Handbook of Materials & Techniques
Ralph Mayer
1940, 1947; 721 pp.
$12.50 postpaid

from:
The Viking Press
625 Madison Avenue
New York, N.Y. 10022

or WHOLE EARTH CATALOG

These emulsions have been employed by experimental painters, but, because no standard tradition has been established they must be closely observed and tested before being used, to make certain that they are homogeneous mixtures miscible with solvent and that they will dry well. The presence of finely divided pigments is helpful in the formation of water-in-oil emulsions; tube oil colors can be used in their preparation.

The presence of much turpentine in an emulsion recipe definitely favors the formation of the regular, or oil-in-water type; on the other hand, formation of the water-in-oil type can be aided by omitting all volatile solvent from the mixture. I find that whole egg gives far superior results than egg yolk, in every respect.

Painter's Companion

After searching through all the books in libraries & bookstores on painting technique, methods & materials, & finding nothing but superficial, wordy, popularized presentations after the order of the Walter J. Foster series I decided that if I must I would put out the $20 or $30 necessary to buy a definitive & authoritative work on the subject. Imagine my surprise to find my every hope satisfied in a $1.95 find! It is The Painter's Companion by Reed Kay. Published in paperback by Webb Books, Inc., Cambridge, 1961. It deals with pigments, binders & diluents, oil technique, supports & grounds, water paints, tempera, casein, encaustic, cold wax techniques, fresco painting, synthetic resin paints, pastels, gilding, has a good bibliography & addresses for supplies. It has all the formulas and step by step instructions. 264 pages. A must for anyone working in painting.

We-lost-her-name
Livorno American High School
APO New York

Utrecht Linens

Utrecht Linens Company sells oilpaints, canvas, water colors, acrylics, brushes etc. at wholesale prices. If you order more than $49 you get further discounts, so get together with your friends and stop paying those high prices in art supply stores. Send for a free catalogue. There are three offices, one in NY, one in Philli and one in Boston. I have been ordering from them, the quality is professional and the service sometimes slow with backorders trailing 2 weeks behind the package. However, it is a good source.

Utrecht Linens Co.
33 Thirty-fifth Street
Brooklyn, N.Y. 11232   Minimum order $20

[Suggested and reviewed by Gudrun Scott]

Utrecht finest unprimed cotton duck canvases are carefully woven from 100% pure high grade cotton yarns. The surfaces are excellent to paint or stain directly with New Temp acrylic colors. They can be prepared with New Temp Gesso or in the traditional manner.

TYPE C.D. 70	60" WIDE

Med. Tex.: 7¾ Oz. Per Sq. Yd.

10 YD. ROLL . . .	$ 13.95
50 YD. ROLL . . .	$ 68.50
100 YD. ROLL . . .	$137.00

TYPE C.D. 12	76" WIDE

Med. Tex.: 11¾ Oz. Per Sq. Yd.

10 YD. ROLL . . .	$ 27.75
50 YD. ROLL . . .	$136.75
100 YD. ROLL . . .	$269.00

ROUNDS

Rhenish Red Sable Oil Color Brushes are made with exacting craftsmanship, and of carefully selected 100% pure red sables. The pure red sable hairs are strong, extra-long and of great resiliency, which makes for durability and professional quality. The brights are used for broad and smooth brush work, and for blending colors. The rounds are excellent for outlining, painting details, and fluid brush work. Seamless nickel ferrules with long black polished handles.

ROUNDS	No. 2	No. 4	No. 6	No. 8	No. 10	No. 12	No. 14	No. 16	No. 20
PER BRUSH	.60	.72	.90	1.05	1.35	1.80	2.55	3.30	4.50
PER DOZEN	7.05	8.45	10.50	2.30	15.85	21.00	29.95	38.75	52.75

Flax Artist's Materials

All the graphics goodies. Brushes, paints, pens, inks, paper, fabric, scissors, knives, zip-a-tone, Letraset, T-squares. Offices in Chicago, L.A., New York, San Francisco. Minimum order $5.

—SB
[Suggested by Michael R. Menkin]

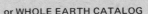

33 2.25

Flax's
250 Sutter St.
San Francisco, CA. 94108

All-Purpose Shears: Inlaid blades, enameled handles, nickel plated blades.

9141-16   #37 7" **5.50**   #38 8" **6.00**

9141-17   #39 9" (with adjustable nut) **7.25**

YARDSTICK COMPASS #108: Pivot point and leadholder fit over wood yardstick. Easily and accurately adjusted. Takes cutting blade 24 E.

Flax No.
9020-01   each **1.50**

SHIVA SIGNATURE OIL COLORS

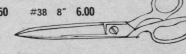

Cadmium Yellow Light	1.40
Cadmium Yellow Medium	1.40
Cadmium Orange	1.40
Cadmium Red Pale	1.65
Cadmium Red Scarlet	1.65
Cadmium Red Deep	1.65
Cadmium Purple	1.65
Shiva Yellow Citron	1.00
Shiva Yellow Pale	1.00
Shiva Yellow Light	1.00
Shiva Yellow Medium	1.00
Shiva Orange	1.00
Shiva Red Light	1.25

Dick Blick

Another mailorder art supplier. Geared to schools.
—SB
[Suggested by Samuel Soltan]

Dick Blick
Box 1267
Galesburg, Illinois 61401

Standard Rapidograph
Technical Fountain Pen
Non-clogging; always draws **constant width line** with regular drawing inks; automatic filling system. Excellent for stencils, templates, drafting, fine and commercial arts, music, lettering and general writing

RAPIDOGRAPH with 1 of 7 Points
State choice: 00   0   2   2½   3   4
B-6950   Fac 3060   Shpg 8 oz/Ea $4.70   Dz/Ea $3.90

Longwood Portable Easel

B-8472
12 or more
13 90 Each
Shpg Wt 13 lbs

82" hi when open

B-8472 LONGWOOD		
Each Easel		$16.90
2 to 11 Easels	Each	15.90
*12 or more Easels	Each	13.90

Shpg Wt 13 lbs each
*FOB Glendale, New York

RAPIDOGRAPH with 000 Superfine Point		
B-6960 Shpg Wt 8 oz/Each $5.70		Doz/Ea $5.30

Rapidograph Replacement Points
State choice: 1 Fine   3 Broad
00 Extra Extra Fine   2 Medium   4 Extra
0 Extra Fine   2½ Med broad   Broad
B-6953 (Fac 67)   Shpg 4 oz/Ea $2.30   Dz/Ea $2.00
000 Superfine Replacement Point
B-6956   Shpg Wt 4 oz/Ea $3.20   Dz/Ea $2.90

Silk Screen Books

Two excellent books for beginners and journeymen silk-screeners.

I like best:

57 How-to-do-it Charts
by Harry L. Hiett **($3.00)**

63 pp. 8-1/2 x 2 x 11 "Gives you a quick breakdown, in chart form, of all the necessary steps for making frames, producing your own films, and building your own basic equipment. Shows you how to stretch your silk, both by rope & by tacking method, & how to build jigs for 3-dimensional printing. A practical book for the professional., the student, or the technician."

The supply outlet likes best:

Silk Screen Printing
by Eisenberg & Kafka **($2.64)**

90 pp., 18 chapters. "Devoted to describing each phase of screen processing clearly w. illustrations & photographs. Step-by-step suggestions on techniques & methods, clearning of equipment, color mixing, art & lettering, multi-color screening, etc. Recommended handbook for beginners."

The prices are so reasonable, for a welcome change, I really advise getting both. My source, get their giant catalog, too, is:

WESTERN Sign Supplies, Inc.
77 8th St.
Oakland, Calif. 94607

[Suggested and reviewed by Norman Solomon]

57 How-to-do-it Charts *also available from:*

Signs of the Times Publishing Co.
407 Gilbert Ave.
Cincinnati, Ohio 45202

Naz-Dar Silk Screen Materials

Probably the most complete source of screen processing materials for printing on almost everything but soft butter. While intended primarily for the commercial market, Naz-Dar's catalogue will give you an insight into this practically unlimited medium.

[Reviewed by Carl Mueller. Suggested by Jerome Skuba]

The Naz-Dar Company
1087 N. North Branch Street
Chicago, Ill. 60622

Problems Answered

The film refuses to adhere to the silk.
The silk was not washed with both solvent and water before use. Insufficient solvent is used during adhering operation.

The film buckles while cutting.
There is an excessive humidity, hence the work must be handled rapidly and not allowed to stand around too long before adhering.

Spots appear on the print.
Pieces of dirt or lint get on the under surface of the screen and must be picked off. Fine skins from the ink have been ground into the meshes of the silk by the squeegee action, necessitating washing up of the job.

Colors on a several color job fail to register.
The film is allowed to lie around after cutting and expands on a very humid day. The guides moved during printing of early colors. The frame is loose or sprung from constant, hard use. The first colors were not printed with all sheets fed carefully to guide.

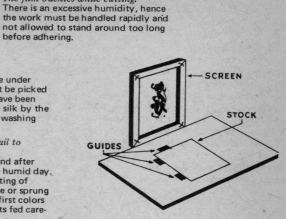

	Per Inch
No. 5100 Complete Squeegee, Black Rubber, Medium Grade	$.20
No. 5102 Black Rubber only	.15
No. 5150 Complete Squeegee, Gray Rubber, Hard Grade	.20
No. 5151 Gray Rubber only	.15
No. 5200 Complete Squeegee, Amber Rubber, Soft Grade	.20
No. 5202 Amber Rubber only	.15
No. 5420 Complete Squeegee, Extra Hard Grade	.20
No. 5421 Rubber only	.15

STENCRAFT STENCIL SILK (Price per Yard)

number	Mesh Count	Width	1-14 Yards	15-29 Yards	30 Yards
6xx	70	40"	$3.45	$3.20	$3.00
8xx	86	40"	3.60	3.35	3.10
10xx	107	40"	4.00	3.70	3.45
12xx	125	40"	4.25	3.95	3.65
14xx	139	40"	4.55	4.20	3.90
16xx	156	40"	5.60	5.20	4.85

Silk Screen Printing

Fig. 41. Back Bar Fastened With Wing Nuts

57 How-to-do-it Charts ✦

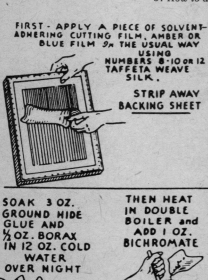

FIRST - APPLY A PIECE OF SOLVENT-ADHERING CUTTING FILM, AMBER OR BLUE FILM 9x THE USUAL WAY USING NUMBERS 8-10 or 12 TAFFETA WEAVE SILK. STRIP AWAY BACKING SHEET

NOW- GIVE THE INSIDE OF SCREEN A QUICK WASH WITH A CLOTH DAMPENED WITH SOLVENT THIS SETS THE FILM FIRMLY IN THE MESH

NOW- CLEAN FACE OF FILM WITH NAPHTHA and WHITING AND RINSE CLEAN

NOW- MAKE A SUBSTRATUM BY MIXING THE WHITE OF ONE EGG OR EQUAL AMOUNT OF DRIED ALBUMEN INTO 28 OZ. COLD WATER, AND APPLY TO FILM

SOAK 3 OZ. GROUND HIDE GLUE AND ½ OZ. BORAX IN 12 OZ. COLD WATER OVER NIGHT

THEN HEAT IN DOUBLE BOILER and ADD 1 OZ. BICHROMATE

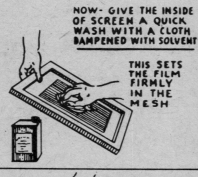

STRAIN THE HOT EMULSION AND FLOW ONCE OVER, UPON FILM SIDE PLACE STRIPS MASKING TAPE AT BOTTOM AND TOP

IMMEDIATELY AFTER FLOWING HOT EMULSION, PLACE SCREEN IN FRONT OF HEATER AND DRY

PLACE SCREEN ON PRINTING FRAME FILM SIDE FACE DOWN TO POSITIVE EXPOSE 7 MIN. AT 20 IN. with Nº 2 PHOTO FLOOD

NOW DEVELOP OUT FACE SIDE OF FILM IN MEDIUM HOT WATER THEN RINSE AND CHILL IN COLD WATER DRY USING A FAN TO HASTEN

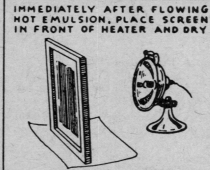

NOW- UPON INSIDE OF SCREEN, PAINT A COAT HOT LIQUID GLUE, FREE FROM BICHROMATE SMOOTH UP WITH A CARD SQUEEGEE AND LET DRY. REPEAT BOTH ABOVE OPERATIONS AND DRY

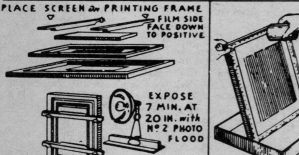

THE LACQUER FILM DEVELOPER MIX 10 DROPS OLIVE OIL INTO 8 OZ. BUTYL LACTATE WITH THIS SOLUTION ETCH LACQUER FILM. NOT PROTECTED BY PHOTOGRAPHIC RESIST. KEEP SWABBING FRESH SOLUTION WITH CAMEL HAIR BRUSH UNTIL LACQUER IS COMPLETELY ETCHED OUT

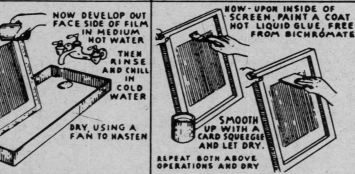

NOW - REMOVE THE PLAIN GLUE COATING, FROM INSIDE OF SCREEN WITH MEDIUM HOT WATER THEN LET DRY WITH FAN OR HEAT TO HASTEN

NOW- POUR DENATURED ALCOHOL INTO SOFT CLOTH AND WASH BOTH SIDES OF SCREEN - THIS REMOVES ANY REMAINING TRACES OF LACQUER FILM LEFT IN THE OPEN PORTIONS. IF THE PHOTOGRAPHIC RESIST IS TO BE REMOVED, USE EITHER A WEAK CAUSTIC SOLUTION or ½ OZ. 28% ACETIC ACID MIXED INTO A 32% SOLUTION FORMALDEHYDE.

Further Silk Screen

There's a good British book:

Practical Screen Printing
Stephen Russ
1969; 96 pp.

$8.95 postpaid

from:
Watson-Guptill Publications
2160 Patterson Street
Cincinnati, OH 45214

And a good expensive American book with a full list of suppliers and annotated bibliography:

Screen Printing
J.I. Biegeleisen
1971; 159 pp.

$13.95 postpaid

from:
Watson-Guptill Publications
2160 Patterson Street
Cincinnati, OH 45214

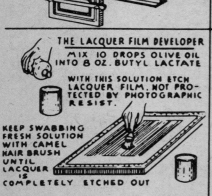

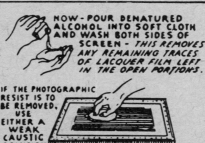

Leonard was putting on a tie. He looked strange in a suit, and yet it belonged on him too. He was tall and roughly-cut, big-boned and lean, a powerful man. Leonard was in his fifties, he was a grandfather as a matter of fact. But nobody ever deferred to him because of it. People deferred to him but it wasn't because they thought he was old or beyond his prime. He was right in his prime, and so was Roxie. Roxie was large and getting round, but she was some years younger than Leonard, barely forty. Their children were grown, most of them already married, living away in Indiana and Illinois. Their youngest son Glenn had left home just the year before. He was in the Army, over in Vietnam now. Leonard showed D.R. his picture when D.R. went in the bedroom to try on Glenn's graduation suit.

A perfect fit.

Close to it, anyhow.

Why yes, said Roxie. That suit looks fine on you.

And Leonard and D.R. went up to the church to talk to Reverend Bagby about the service.

Reverent Bagby had it all planned. Mrs. Thornton's niece Dorothy had agreed to sing Abide With Me, and Mrs. Bagby would play the piano. The message would be short, said Reverend Bagby. It was hot, and there was the work of getting the casket up on the hill to bury. It all sounded fine to D.R. He liked Reverend Bagby. He liked Mrs. Bagby. He liked Leonard and he liked Roxie. D.R. tried to hide it as best he could, but the truth of the matter was, he was really enjoying this day so far.

And then there Marcella was to help him enjoy it more.

How good, just plain good it was to see her. And Doyle and Herschel and little Debbie, my what a pretty family. Doyle grabbed D.R.'s hand and shook it as Marcella gave him a powerful hug, and Herschel began tugging at his coat pocket. Debbie hung back, and D.R. lifted her into the air as a reward for being demure. Lift me! Lift me! Herschel shouted, and Doyle took him by the hand and led him off to one side to explain why he ought not be yelling like that. Leonard stood among them as a greeter. It was proper that he do so. Everybody felt it, and in their separate ways they thanked him for it. Doyle held his hand out to Leonard and said you may not remember me, Leonard, but I'm Doyle. Leonard said why Doyle, I remember you good. You fixed a car of mine one time, a Mercury, back in the days when I drove Mercurys, don't you remember that? Doyle looked a little puzzled, then embarrassed. Now I'd plum forgot about that, said Doyle. A maroon car. Put a new coil in it for you, down there by your all's store.

Printers' Supply Book

A look at the Whole Earth Catalogue or any other piece of printing (especially "Movement" stuff) confirms that the items sold by the Kelsey Co. are obsolete—today good, cheap quick printing is done offset. And Kelsey sells only letterpress equipment. But they have a full line—everything. Good and reasonably priced.

For the holdout who still prints letterpress and wants to make some cash from stationary, business cards, billheads, invitations and announcements or just fiddle in the basement, Kelsey has the supplies. I wouldn't suggest buying a hand press from them. They are costly, especially since good used Chandler and Price or other motor-driven hand fed presses can be gotten cheaply. But they do sell all sizes of paper and will custom cut. This is a help to the person who is not employed at a printing office where he can get off-cuts or paper at cost. And they have the whole range of equipment—bodkins, line gages, composing sticks, type cases and stands, galleys, quoins, furniture, reglets—the works. A nice range of inks is listed, and they are ready to answer your letter about inking problems.

Their types cover a wide range. The job printing standbys are all there—Copperplate and Bond Gothics; Caslon, Goudy, Caramond; Egyptians; and the whole mess of ugly cursives you need to do social stationery for your aunt. Several are worthy of note. Steelplate Shaded is one. There isn't much use for this, but it is well-designed and fine-looking. A rather mundane range of sans-serif wood type is listed. Two lines of type are sold—New England and Connecticut. With the Connecticut faces (more expensive) spaces and quads are included. Fonts are sold in regular, large or all cap.

Service reputed to be good to East Coast. Can't say about other areas.

Will Powers
RFD 2
Lancaster, New Hampshire
03584

Printers' Supply Book

$.35 (refunded with first order)

from:
The Kelsey Company
Meriden, Connecticut 06450

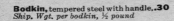

Bodkin, tempered steel with handle, **.30**
Ship. Wgt. per bodkin, ½ pound

Useful when setting or making up forms, especially forms which are too large to go in the composing stick. Also to hold forms that you want to keep set-up. **Rustproof Steel.**

From actual experience in our printing department we find these the most practical sizes.

	inches. Ship. Wgt. 2 lb	
6 x 10		.78
8¾ x 13	" 3 "	.85
10 x 16	" 4 "	1.08

Line Gage, for all printers' measurements; is made from heavy polished metal,—very plain and easy to read, graduated on one edge to picas (12 points) and ½ pica (6 points), and on the other edge to inches. **No. 2,** 12 inch, **1.65**

STEELPLATE SHADED

No. 6011	6 Point	15A $6.40—5A $3.15
WITH THIS STEELPLATE SHAD-
No. 6012	6 Point	10A $6.40—5A $4.20
AT MODERATE PRICES & 75
No. 6013	6 Point	10A $6.40—5A $4.20
USE LITTLE INK AND 3
No. 1214	12 Point	10A $9.20—5A $5.60
ADD SOME BLUE 7
No. 1215	12 Point	7A $9.20
GRAY LOOK 5
No. 1216	12 Point	6A $9.20
USE WITH 3

ABCDEFGHIJKLMNOP
QRSTUVWXYZ&,;:.-"?!
$1234567890

QUOINS:- to lock forms in chase. (C)

Kelsey, the most popular of all quoins,
per set of two pcs. **.48**
half-dozen sets, **2.30**
per dozen sets, **3.75**
Kelsey Key Wrench, **1.45**

COMPOSING STICKS (C)

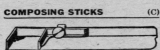

Excelsior Job, new improved model.
☐ 8 inch, (Capacity 36 picas) **3.85**
Shipping Weight, 1 pound

T. N. Lawrence

English engraver's tools and supplies.

—SB

T.N. Lawrence and Son
Catalog March 1970

free

from:
T. N. Lawrence and Son Limited
2-4 Bleeding Heart Yard
Greville Street, Hatton Garden,
London, E.C.I. England

REST ON BACK
WHEN NOT IN USE

Rollers, Soft Plastic, Transparent.

TOOLS for ENGRAVING

Gravers Lozenge, several sizes		7/- each
" Square		7/- "
Spitstickers, Fine, Medium, Broad		7/- "
Scorpers, round, Nos. 1–12		7/- "
" square, Nos. 1–12		7/- "
Tint Tools, Nos. 1–6		7/- "
Bullstickers, 3 sizes		7/- "

Fox Etching Press

I think that the equipment about which I am sending you information will surely interest a certain subset of your readers, namely, parcticing artists and printmakers. The FOX I LEVIGATOR is a unique stonegrinder. the FOX I ETCHING PRESS is far more portable, versatile and by far less expensive than any comparable professional etching press in the field. (Its closest competitor costs $500 more.)

Carlos Joly
Fox Graphics
Back Bay Annex
Box 328
Boxton, Mass. 02116

Levigator $1,200
Etching Press $1,200

Parchment

The William Cowley Parchment Works, Newport Pagnell, Bucks, England, supplies Sheepskin Parchment & Calfskin vellum for about 1.2¢ to 2.5¢ a square inch. This is 1/2 to 1/3 less than anything I have found in the US. & the quality is extremely fine.

Richard F. Wheeler
Portland, Oregon

Graphic Chemical & Ink

The best place and the cheapest to get printmaking (lithography, etching, etc.) supplies.

They supply schools and colleges around the country, also art supply stores which mark everything up 1000% or so.

What they sell is everything from Korn's litho crayons, Arches paper, and Sennefelder's Asphaltum to a $1000 Dickerson combination press.

Most of their orders are filled through the mail and are pretty big. We went out on a Saturday and purchased a staggering $30 worth of supplies, but they treated us like fuckin kings man and showed us all over the plant, where they do every-thing: they make their own inks from raw pigment, they manufacture or at least assemble their own presses, but most of all they seem to dig on showing people around. We spent at least an hour just feeling all the different kinds of paper one extremely nice dude showed us.

[Suggested and reviewed by Betsy and Ralph]

Graphic Chemical & Ink Company
728 N. Yale Avenue
P.O. Box 27
Villa Park, Illinois 60181

Tools

Etching Point, all metal, double end	$ 1.50
Litho Needle, 7" long, wooden handle	1.35
Carbide-tipped Point, suitable for dry-point work	1.45
No. 787 Double-End Pin Vise, carbide and steel tips	3.05
Diamond Point for No. 787	10.00
Lithographer's Etching Diamond:	
No. 49-B	23.50
No. 49-C	36.50
No. 49-D	43.50

Diamonds are not to be used on glass. For some reason they invariably break. We also have the "Lancer" diamond point that is set in a ball point pen barrel.

Lancer Retractable Diamond Point	6.50
Needle Burnisher (combination burnisher and etching needle)	3.25
Burnisher, tempered blade, wooden handle,	
Straight, 3" blade	1.75
Bent, 3½" blade	1.75
Straight, Triangular, 5½" blade	2.50
Bent, Fine, 3½" blade	2.50
Scraper, 3-square hollow, wooden handle	1.90
3-square flat, wooden handle	1.90
Burins, Straight or Bent, wooden handle Squares and Lozenges:	
No. 2, 4, 6, 8	1.40
No. 10, 12	1.45
Knife, No. 1, 3, 5, 7	1.25
Lining tool, 2-line, 4-line, 6-line	3.50
Chisel, No. 0, 1, 2, 3	1.25
Scorpers (round), No. 53, 57, 60	1.35
Flats, No. 38, 42, 46	1.35
Elliptic Tint Tool, No. 2, 4, 6	1.90
Burins, Boxed Set	60.00
Handles, alone, each	.20
Mezzotint Rocker	26.00
Roulette	6.65
Copper Cutter, Draw-Type	8.75
Sharpening Jig	6.75
India Sharpening Stone, 1B-64	4.10

Calligraphic Lettering with wide pen and brush

calligraphic lettering, by ralph douglass, presents a lot of different forms of lettering; italic, chancery cursive, english roundhand, spanish gothic, etc., but it's up to you to do them right. he just shows you what the letters should look like.

[Suggested by Cappy McClure
Reviewed by Ruth Wyant]

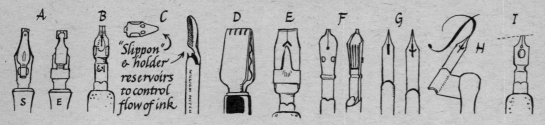

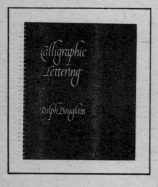

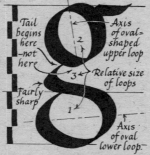

**Calligraphic Lettering
with wide pen and brush**
Ralph Douglass
1949, 67, 68; 112 pp.

$6.95 postpaid

from:
Watson-Guptill Publications
2160 Patterson Street
Cincinnati, OH 45214

or WHOLE EARTH CATALOG

A Study of Writing

Not as good as it should be, this is still the best introduction around to the growth and diffusion of language notation systems.
—SB

**A Study
of Writing**
I. J. Gelb
1952; 319 pp.

$3.45
postpaid

from:
University of
Chicago
Press
5801 Ellis Ave.
Chicago, Ill.
60637

or WHOLE
EARTH
CATALOG

Colour does not seem to play an important role in our modern writing. Although colouring schemes are occasionally used to differentiate meaning, as in charts, it is normally the black or dark colour that predominates, whether in our handwriting or book print. In older times, when all writing was done by hand, colour differentiation was found more frequently. Both the old Mexican writings and the more modern writings of the American Indians frequently employ a method of colouring the signs. Among the Cherokee Indians white colour is used for peace or happiness, black for death, red for success or triumph, blue for defeat or trouble.

HIEROGLYPHIC				HIEROGLYPHIC BOOK-SCRIPT	HIERATIC			DEMOTIC

The retrograde evolution of individual writings was frequently facilitated whenever they fell under the control of a priestly or political caste. In such cases the systems gradually became so overburdened with various artificial and baroque deflections that they grew too difficult for large masses of people to master. The final result of such degenerated writing was frequently its total rejection by the people and its replacement by an entirely new system introduced from abroad.

Short-Cut Shorthand

Writing is slower than talking, and thereby hangs a lot of problems. If you need to write fast you have approximately three choices of method: Gregg (the fastest, but really hard to learn), Speedwriting (slowest, a cinch to learn), and this (medium fast, medium easy to learn). The book is well designed for self-teaching.
—SB

Short-Cut Shorthand
S. M. Wesley
1966; 275 pp.

$3.95 postpaid

from:
Henry Regnery Company
114 W. Illinois St.
Chicago, IL 60610

or WHOLE EARTH CATALOG

PHONETIC SYSTEM. Unlike other shorthand systems, Short-Cut Shorthand follows a purely phonetic system. It has no hieroglyphic-like forms or subtle differences in lines that need to be learned and interpreted. The forms are distinctive and clear cut. Once you learn the character for a particular sound you continue to use it throughout. You just write down what you hear.

Hand Bookbinding

No longer available

There's hardly anybody around nowadays who can teach you how to bind books. Hand bookbinding is a fairly simple process that requires patience and the art of pains-taking. Although machines long ago took over the commercial phase of binding, good hand-bindings are still stronger and more durable, and almost always more beautiful.

I took a course in hand bookbinding at San Francisco State College from Dr. Green, a cantankerous craftsman who would prod, cajole, and insult us into taking time for details and caring about the work enough to redo it two or three times until it was perfect. While that kind of discipline isn't in this book, the basic processes are, clearly described and illustrated with lucid drawings by the author himself.

Principles of bookbinding have scarcely changed at all in the 1,800 years since Roman scrolls got cut up into pages, sewn together in signatures and bound between boards wrapped in leather. Most of today's books are constructed in exactly the same way. Watson presents these techniques in a series of projects, starting with an easy dust jacket and ending with slipcases— to me, one of the most difficult jobs, requiring absolute precision measurements. The first binding project is a simple one— signature book with paper covers. The most fun projects are the blank books— which make perfect journals or gifts for friends— and repairing and rebinding old books (when word gets around that you're into bookbinding, your friends will bring you all kinds of favorite dog-eared volumes, coverless and tattered and worn out from countless re-readings.)

Watson also covers handmade headbands and has a whole chapter on making your own tools and equipment, like awls, sewing frames and presses.

—Hal Hershey
[Suggested by John Meissner]

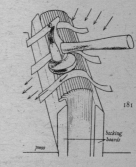

Hand Bookbinding
Aldren A. Watson
1963; 93 pp.

OUT OF PRINT

from:
Crown Publishers, Inc.
419 Park Ave., South
New York, N.Y. 10016

. And the mention of the store caused Marcella to interrupt and ask Leonard how his mother was.

•

She don't change, said Leonard. I swear, she aint a bit different than when you all use to live here, Marcella.

•

Well, said Marcella, I've been talking to her on the phone, but it's been so long since I've seen her.

•

She'll be to the church after while, Leonard said. And she'll be glad to see you all.

•

Then there she was, old Mrs. Godsey, with a hat on now, a great, white wide-brimmed hat, and a kind of cream-colored dress that reached to her ankles nearly. Her daughter-in-law Roxie was walking with her, holding her by the arm. But when she saw Marcella the old woman moved out by herself and walked toward Marcella with her arm stretched out, to shake hands. Only instead of shaking hands she hugged her, and the two women pressed their cheeks together briefly, then stood back to look at one another.

•

And these are my children, said Marcella. This is Debbie. And that's Herschel. Herschel, come and say hello to Mrs. Godsey. She's an old neighbor-friend of ours.

•

D.R. said, Mrs. Godsey knew your mother when she wasn't as old as you are, Herschel. What do you think about that?

•

Herschel didn't think much about it one way or another, but he shook hands anyway, and then retreated behind his father.

•

And then they got to talking about Emmit, how he died, and D.R. being there with him.

•

He wouldn't go to the hospital for me, said Leonard. I argued with Emmit a month to go to the doctor.

•

And then here comes this boy and packs him off the first day, said Mrs. Godsey, patting D.R. on the shoulder.

•

He didn't like it one bit either, said D.R. He cussed me and Leonard all the way to Blaine, and up two flights of stairs.

•

It had to be done though, said Leonard. It just had to be done.

Bookmaking

A textbook for book designers.

Should enable anyone from author to customer to communicate intelligently about any aspect of the design or production of a book. Probably the only existent reference for someone who needs to deal with printers and publishers, and isn't quite sure he knows an offset from a castoff. Perhaps the best thing that can be said about this book is that it is beautifully designed, but by the time you finish reading it you'll probably know enough to start criticizing its design.
—SB

Bookmaking
Marshall Lee
1965; 399 pp.

$15.95 postpaid

from:
R. R. Bowker Company
1180 Avenue of the Americas
New York, N. Y. 10036

or WHOLE EARTH CATALOG

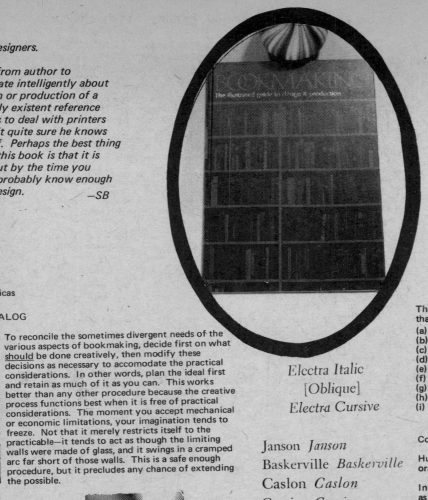

PROOFREADERS' MARKS

Marginal sign	Mark in text	Meaning	Corrected text
ℨ	Proofreading	Delete, take out letter or word	Proofreading
ℨ first	Legibility is the requirement of a proof reader's marks.	Delete and close up / Insert marginal addition / Close up entirely	Legibility is the first requirement of a proofreader's marks.
◡	Symbols should be made neatly and	Less space / Push space down to avoid printing	Symbols should be made neatly and
# eq.# ¶ no¶	in line with the text to which they refer. Place marks carefully. Paragraphs may be	Add space / Space evenly / New paragraph / No new paragraph	in line with the text to which they refer. Place marks carefully. Paragraphs may be

Illustrations scattered through text

Four kinds of development in sequence.

To reconcile the sometimes divergent needs of the various aspects of bookmaking, decide first on what <u>should</u> be done creatively, then modify these decisions as necessary to accomodate the practical considerations. In other words, plan the ideal first and retain as much of it as you can. This works better than any other procedure because the creative process functions best when it is free of practical considerations. The moment you accept mechanical or economic limitations, your imagination tends to freeze. Not that it merely restricts itself to the practicable—it tends to act as though the limiting walls were made of glass, and it swings in a cramped arc far short of those walls. This is a safe enough procedure, but it precludes any chance of extending the possible.

Circular screen

Electra Italic
[Oblique]
Electra Cursive

Janson *Janson*
Baskerville *Baskerville*
Caslon *Caslon*
Granjon *Granjon*

Spartan
Metro
Erbar Light Condensed
Optima
News Gothic
Vogue
Gothic Condensed No. 2
GOTHIC NO. 31

Memphis
Cairo

The readability of a page is affected by no less than 9 factors:
(a) typeface,
(b) size of type,
(c) length of line,
(d) leading,
(e) page pattern (which includes "margins"),
(f) contrast of type and paper (which includes color),
(g) texture of paper,
(h) typographic relationships (heads, folios, ets.), and
(i) suitability to content.

Color has 3 aspects: (a) hue, (b) intensity, and (c) value.

Hue—This is the 'color' of the color (red, blue, yellow, green, orange-red, etc.).

Intensity—This is the purity of the color (intensity is lowered as the color is grayed or 'softened').

Value—This is the darkness of the color (even in pure primary colors there is variation in value—yellow is lighter than blue, blue is lighter than red, etc.; however, an intense yellow may be darker than a blue whose intensity [and value] has been lowered by the addition of white).

There are many considerations involved in matching printer to job, but the main ones are:
(a) the kind of presses he has (letterpress, offset lithography, gravure),
(b) the size presses he has,
(c) the number of presses he has (this relates to capacity to produce),
(d) the kind of work he has done,
(e) the quality of his work,
(f) his schedule, and
(g) his prices.

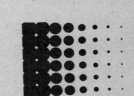

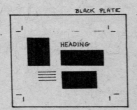

Advertising Graphics

*Who wants to make a book of just type and a few clunky illustrations? [If you do, see **Bookmaking**, above.] A richer palette is offered, and well described, by **Advertising Graphics**. Drawing, rendering, indication, type, layout, and on through the production process. McLuhan says that ads are good news. Since good news is boring, it's put the burden on advertisers to acid-coat their sugar pill. If we'd had this book back at our beginning, I suspect our $1 Catalogs would be a lot livelier to look at.*
—SB

[Suggested by Stephen Sulka]

Advertising Graphics
H. William Bockus, Jr.
1969; 251 pp.

$7.50 postpaid

from:
The Macmillan Company
Front and Brown Streets
Riverside, Burlington County
New Jersey 08075

or WHOLE EARTH CATALOG

*Also check out **Basic Graphics** (p. 321).*

BLACK PLATE

HEADING

Windowing. If your ad includes a few rectangular halftones either same size or reductions, rectangles of black or the red artist aid can be pasted in position on the black plate or base of the pasteup. When the black (line) copy is shot, the rectangles will appear as transparent windows in the black negative. After the halftones are shot they can be positioned under these windows and burned into the printing plate right with the line work. Of course if the halftones are to be reduced, the artist must figure the scaling to make certain the width and length of the pasted rectangles are proportional to the reduced halftone neg. Using a mechanical scaler is one of the quickest ways to do this.

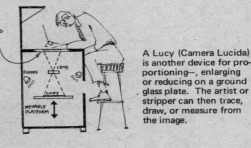

GROUND GLASS

A Lucy (Camera Lucida) is another device for proportioning—, enlarging or reducing on a ground glass plate. The artist or stripper can then trace, draw, or measure from the image.

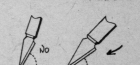
KEEP BLADE AT LOW ANGLE TO PREVENT CHATTERING

INDICATION

The layout artist must be able to imatate or simulate typography, lettering, and the human figure quickly and clearly.

Type is usually indicated by using chisel-point pencils of varying width.

CUT OUT YOUR INITIAL OR A SYMBOL FROM A BLOCK OF WOOD OR ART GUM ERASER. USE IT TO STAMP YOUR PRINTS OR STATIONERY AS YOUR IDENTIFYING "CHOP".

Alternative Press Syndicate

1.   *We, The Free Ranger Tribe, have published this booklet called, "How To Publish Your Very Own Alternative Newspaper", which contains just about all the basic information you need, such as— printing, type setting, layout, advertising, subscriptions, distribution, mailing, the police, etc. It is distributed through the Alternative Press Syndicate, Box 26, Village Station, New York, New York 10014. It is a compendium of other, smaller booklets on the subject plus the combined experience of the Underground Press Syndicate. $1.*

2.   *Enclosed is a list of all the Alternative Press Syndicate papers, their addresses, and subscription rates. I can't imagine why this has never been run before in the Catalog since this is one of the most basic things for people to plug into. Not only for subscriptions but to advertise in, to send out information and publicity to and to obtain papers from for distribution. An updated list is published periodically, available from U.P.S. A quarter and a self-addressed, stamped envelope would be nice.*

3.   *The Free Ranger Tribe publishes the A.P.S. Directory which lists papers, editors, addresses, phone numbers, advertising rates, advertising deadlines, copy deadlines, mechanical specifications, subscription rates, bulk rates, etc. $2.00 from A.P.S.*

Writing and Illuminating and Lettering

Publish your own book and let the New York madness go choke. Photo-offset on newsprint is incredibly cheap. To make up CATALOG pages we spent $150 a month for an IBM selectric composer and $850 for a Polaroid MP-3 camera with half-tone kit, and that's high-rent. With this $7 book and loving care you could hand-make a publication more personal than speech.
—SB

[Suggested by Richard F. Wheeler]

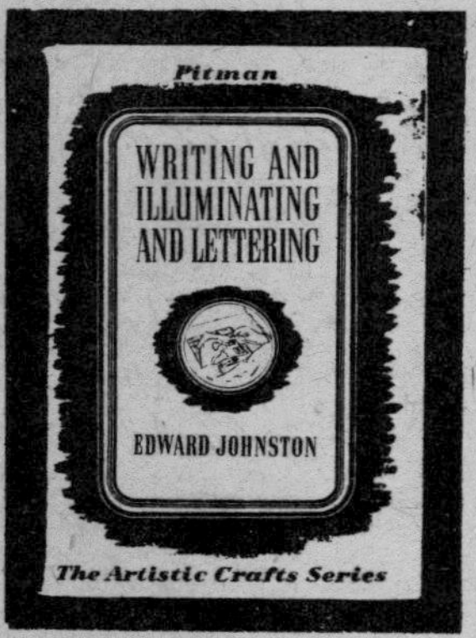

Pitman
WRITING AND ILLUMINATING AND LETTERING
EDWARD JOHNSTON
The Artistic Crafts Series

Writing Illuminating and Lettering
Edward Johnston
1906 . . . 1969; 439 pp.

$10.75 postpaid

from:
Pitman Publishing Corporation
6 East 43rd St.
New York, N. Y. 10017

or WHOLE EARTH CATALOG

Laying & Burnishing Gold

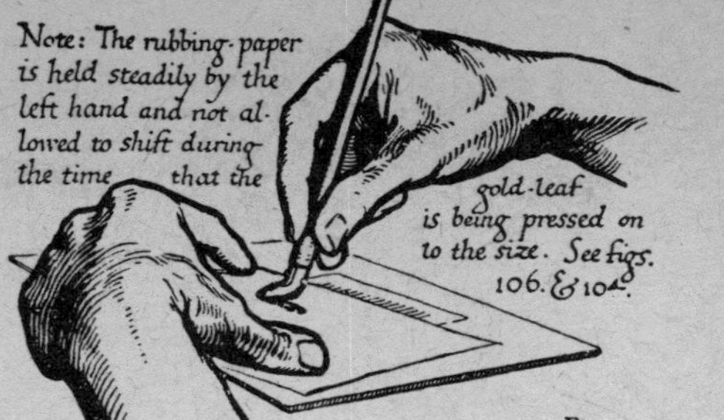

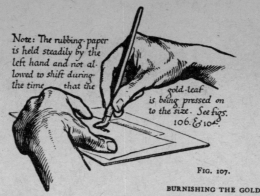

Note: The rubbing-paper is held steadily by the left hand and not allowed to shift during the time that the gold-leaf is being pressed on to the size. See figs. 106 & 107.

FIG. 107.

BURNISHING THE GOLD

OF QUILLS GENERALLY

For ordinary use the nib may be cut with a fairly steep angle, as shown (magnified) at *a*, fig. 36.

But it is better for all careful work and fine, sharp writing that the angle be made very sharp: the knife blade is laid back (much flatter than is shown in fig. 29) and the quill is cut quite thin; the knife blade is then held vertical and the extreme tip of the nib is cut off sharp and true (*b*, fig. 36).

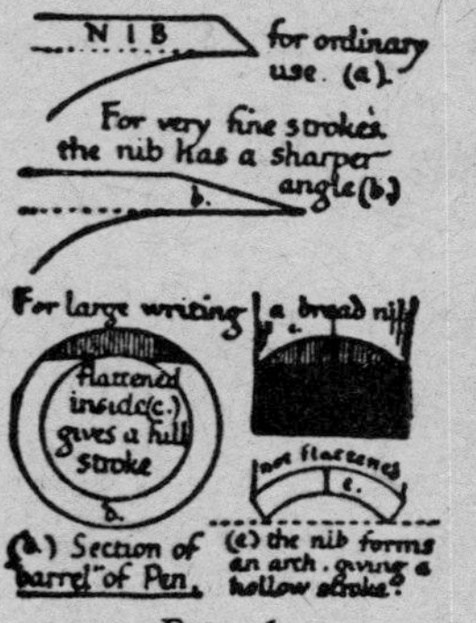

NIB
for ordinary use. (a).
For very fine strokes the nib has a sharper angle (b).
For large writing
a broad nib
flattened inside (c) gives a hill stroke
not flattened
(b.) Section of barrel of Pen.
(c) the nib forms an arch, giving a hollow stroke.

FIG. 36.

Printing It

An outline for a handbook instructing those who need printing done inexpensively and who want to do as much of the work as possible themselves. The manual deals mainly with printing on small offset presses, and particularly with methods of preparing paste-ups for offset printing. The stress throughout is on saving money without losing quality, and on building equipment and using hand work to save on the high costs of machinery and labor. Also included is a brief survey of movement printers in the San Francisco Bay Area, and their approach to these problems.

1/Basics. The kinds of printing that might be needed, and that this book will deal with (leaflets, pamphlets, posters, etc.). Terminology. How to recognize possibilities. Content and intended use determine form. Stressing what the finished product will be used for. Design.

2/Processes. Offset printing in general, and the small offset duplicator in particular, as the most convenient and cheapest method for most work. The mimeograph machine, its possibilities and limitations, and the electronic stencil device. Some thoughts on letterpress (more to come under "starting a Shop").

3/Camera Ready Copy. Advancing the notion that a tremendous amount of money and time can be saved by preparing good pasteups, and by learning tricks that can be done at the paste-up stage rather than by highly paid printers and camera men. Discussion of the nature of "photo" "offset" and the need for care and patience in producing the original, camera ready copy.

4/Materials and Equipment. Setting up a paste-up studio. What you can build; what you have to buy. The IBM typewriters. Art-Type and related transfer lettering. Typewriter correction techniques and materials. General paste-up techniques and materials. Comparison of various pasting materials— rubber cement, wax, spray adhesive, etc.

5/Aspects of the Paste-Up. The problem of photographs. Multi-color separations. Paste-up niceties, such as Bendays, acetate reverses, white lettering, etc. The use of line drawings for inexpensive art work. Advanced equipment, such as the IBM Composer, head-liner, Varityper, etc. Justified margins versus ragged.

6/Aspects of the Paste-Up: 2. Fine points. The use of ruling pens, rapidograph pens, sign pens, etc. and their possibilities. Calligraphy as an innovative and inexpensive way to do titles and headlines. Lifting printed work, starting a clip file, and recognizing problems in using printed work.

7/Paper and Ink. The right colored paper can salvage a pedestrian leaflet. The right colored ink can make it exciting. Buying paper. The understanding of paper sizes and cutting. Avoiding waste, and the uses for waste paper. The cheapest paper is not always the best. The PMS ink color system, and how and why to use it. Planning second color printing. Color ink versus color paper.

8/Binding. An area in which all time and no money can be an advantage. The reasons for not owning bindery equipment. Small office folding machines, staplers, collaters, etc. Methods. How to sew a pamphlet by hand, and decorative possibilities. How to dress up stapled pamphlets. Perfect binding, spiral binding, etc.

9/Planning Print. How to talk to printers. Know what you need, and what is possible. "Instant" printing franchise shops and how they work— why they are cheap and how to prepare for them. Rough sketches. Copy fitting. The preparation of copy for type-setting. Let your printer suggest possibilities. More designing. Printing is Practical.

10/Starting Your Own Shop. The camera as the basis of offset printing, and why it is more important to own a camera than a press. The homemade camera. Other homemade offset equipment, as seen in working shops in the Bay Area. What to look for in buying offset presses. The possibilities and economics of letterpress. Relative costs and capabilities. Sources of supply. Suppliers as sources of information.

Included within the book will be information about the availability and prices of equipment and materials, as well as rough prices for building certain pieces. These costs of course will apply primarily to the Bay Area, though an attempt will be made to include some regional comparisons.

Clifford Burke has been in the editing/designing/printing/publishing business for just over ten years. He started Cranium Press in the Haight Ashbury district in 1966, and his experience includes working as printer for the Associated Students of San Francisco State College just prior to the Black Student Union strike in 1968. He now works primarily as a book designer and printer, and operates a casual typographic beer drinking session on Saturdays.

Printing It *128 pages and illustrated by Chuck Miller is $2.95*

Inquiries to:
Book People
2940 7th Street
Berkeley, CA 94710

Printing as a Hobby

Most books that deal with printing are of a highly technical nature; aimed at the professional printer, or someone aspiring to be one. This book, on the other hand, is aimed specifically at the beginner with very little money. With this book and $10 you can set up your own private print shop. And if you want to graduate later to a small printing press, Mr. Lieberman explains the processes involved with that also.

[Suggested and reviewed by Lloyd Martin]

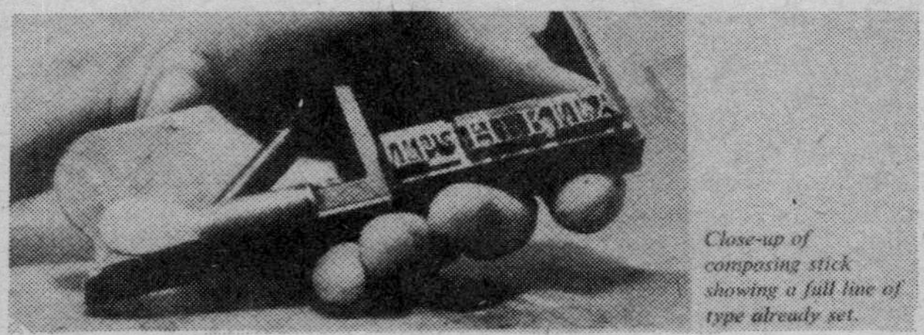

Close-up of composing stick showing a full line of type already set.

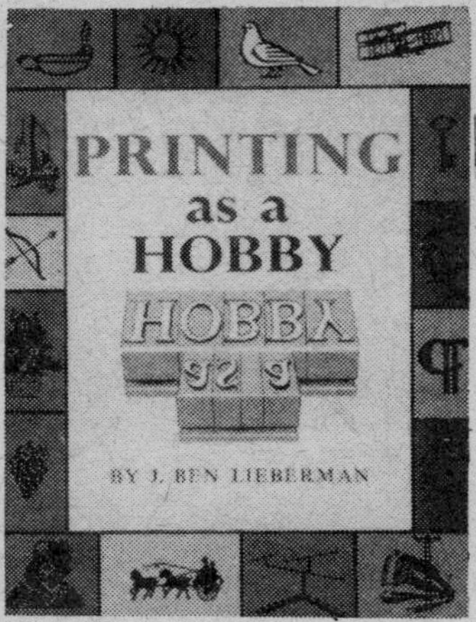

PRINTING as a HOBBY
BY J. BEN LIEBERMAN

Printing as a Hobby
J. Ben Lieberman
1963; 128 pp.

OUT OF PRINT

Signet-New American Library
1301 Avenue of the Americas
New York, N. Y. 10019

The easiest way to buy materials, therefore, is to write for the catalogue and type and paper-stock sample books of Popular Printing, Inc., 1010 South Weinbach Avenue, Evansville, 14, Indiana, U.S.A. (It has, among other kits, a special $10 starter pack [as of 1963] which includes all needed items which you cannot make or find around the house.)

ANYONE
who would
letterspace lowercase
would steal sheep
FRED GOUDY

Printing With the Handpress

A beautiful explicit book on how to hand-print beautiful books. Seeing the book makes you want to do it, and the contents can indeed get you there.
—SB

Printing With the Handpress
Lewis M. Allen
1969; 78 pp.

$9.95 postpaid

from:
Van Nostrand-Reinhold Books,
450 W. 33rd St.
New York, N.Y. 10001

or WHOLE EARTH CATALOG

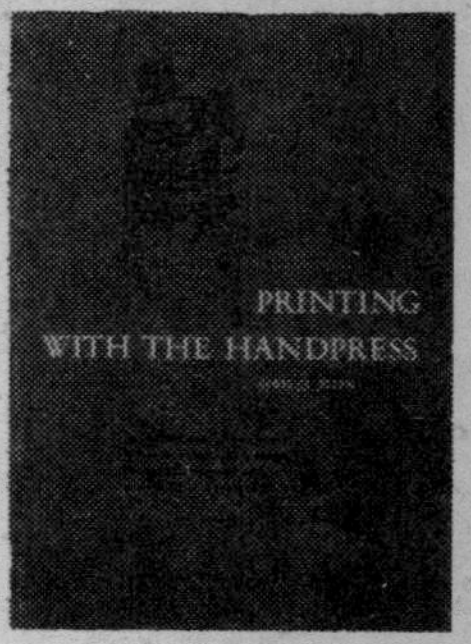

PRINTING WITH THE HANDPRESS

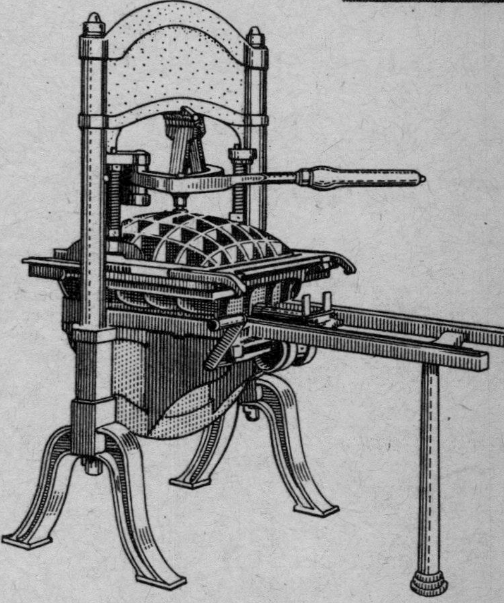

THE WASHINGTON. *The final statement in the development of the handpress. Manufactured in the United States from 1821 through 1910, thousands were produced, but today they are rather difficult to find.*

Introduction. This manual is for serious amateurs and potential professionals who wish to operate a handpress easily but expertly. However, we will not discuss in detail operations which are basic to all forms of printing— such as design, typesetting, make-ready, binding. There are many competent books on these subjects— see the Bibliography.

One of the supreme pleasures available to man is knowledge, discipline, intelligence guiding the hand to create beautiful and intellecutally desirable objects. This human and consequently expressive element is dominant in handpress printing. Such a press not only records, but glorifies because the hand-printed sheet emanates a unique liveliness and sparkle, and to the touch a sculptural character; it pleases the eye, the mind, the hand.

•

Presses. A handpress, like gold, is where you find it. Scan classified advertisements of used printing machinery in large dailies and trade journals; run a Want Ad. The best source of information is handpress printers. But the surest approach is through English companies which acquire and re-condition antique presses:

Brett & Cox, Ltd., 15 Black Friars Lane, New Bridge Street, London, E.C.4.

Cropper, Charlton & Co., Ltd., Trent Bridge Works, Nottingham.

Excelsior Printers Supply Company and Frederick Ullmer, Ltd., 63 White Lion Street, London, N.1

T. N. Lawrence & Son, 2 Bleeding Heart Yard, Londong, E.C. 4

Harry F. Rochat, Cotswald Lodge, Stapylton Road, Barnet, Hertford.

Frederick Ullmer, Ltd. (see Excelsior Printers Supply Company).

F. W. Woodroff & Company, Ltd., 137 Mile End Road, London.

(Prices run from about $350.00 for small models, to $750.00 for the large— FOB).

Cylinder Handpresses. (Asbern). The E.G. Lindner Company, Ltd., 612 East Twelfth Street, Los Angeles, California 90015

(Challenge). Gane Brothers & Lane, 1335 W. Lake Street, Chicago, Ill. 60607.

(Vandercook). Vandercook & Sons, 3601 West Touhy Ave., Chicago, Ill. 60645.

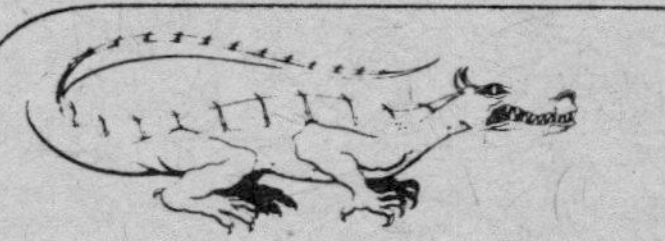

•

And then everyone got quiet because Mr. Olney drove up in the hearse, and the two fellows who'd helped dig the grave the day before, Ray and Chester, started unloading the casket. Mr. Olney came and shook everybody's hand and looked generally solemn. What D.R. realized today that he had only sensed the day before was that Mr. Olney was a very sick man himself, pitiful-looking. D.R. shook his hand warmly today, and felt responsible for him in some strange way. Mr. Olney seemed to have a burden D.R. wanted to relieve him of, and he studied the old undertaker as he walked into the church behind Ray and Chester, who were wheeling the casket in.

The Reader's Adviser (vol 2)

"A Layman's Guide to the Best in Print in General Biography, History, Bibles, World Religions, Philosophy, Psychology, the Sciences, Folklore, the Lively Arts, Communications and Travel." And, by God, it is. As access to quality, it beats college.

—SB

The Reader's Adviser (vol 2)
Winifred F. Courtney, Ed.
1969; 912 pp.

$21.00 postpaid

from:
R. R. Bowker Co.
1180 Avenue of the Americas
New York, N. Y. 10036

or WHOLE EARTH CATALOG

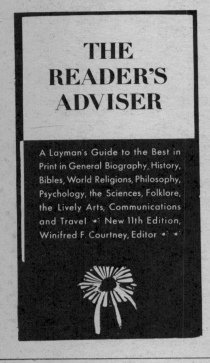

THE READER'S ADVISER

A Layman's Guide to the Best in Print in General Biography, History, Bibles, World Religions, Philosophy, Psychology, the Sciences, Folklore, the Lively Arts, Communications and Travel • New 11th Edition, Winifred F. Courtney, Editor • •

The Book Review

A good book magazine. Carries sharp reviews, information on bookmaking, and talk with authors. Unglamorous and lively.

—SB

The Book Review
Jay Bail, ed.

$4 /yr (10 issues)

from:
The Book Review
Box 14143
San Francisco, DA 94114

The most intriguing of the naturalistic justifications of death occurs in a book of short stories, entitled *T Zero*, by Italo Calvino (Harcourt). The argument, as presented by an unidentified narrator, may be summed up as this: *The risk we ran was living: living forever.*

Life, says Calvino, amounts to self repetition. When this self repetition is simple, as with the cell which does not die but merely divides and divides and divides, life extinguishes itself by overrunning the earth and exhausting the resources necessary for its continuation. Life continues only by evolving for itself the concept of seed. Once the seed has come into being, errors and improvements in genetic transmission can occur, giving rise to other species. To control these errors, life becomes sexual, in that genetic messages must to some degree 'match' before life will result. With the development of sexual reproduction, the first death of an individual occurs, and for the first time, reproduction entails bringing *another* into the world. Thus, death is to life as the concept of zero is to mathematics: it sets life free.

•

Impermanence. The sound and the fury of change. Mircea Eliade is a Rumanian, settled here in this country, who rounds out the *feeling* of a Merton and a Suzuki with a fine fire of fiction. The stories in this book— *Two Tales of the Occult* (Herder, $5)— written in the personable manner of Conan Doyle's mysteries and Maugham's adventures, stories that bend reality back on itself. Eliade usually writes academic-intellectual books concerning societal mythologies. This is his first fiction translated into English (other stories and novels of his have not yet been translated)— and these tales never stop. Always in back of, say, a pleasant chat between friends, an outing, is the structure of the Social Delusion, the falseness of time, the impermanence of people and events.

'Nights at Serampore', the first story sees three Europeans wandering through a dense jungle near Calcutta, coming across a dream-like sequence of happenings between Indians, and slowly realizing that they're seeing the past, the past within the present time field, so that time itself is whipped into a different pattern in which the past comes out vaguely different and the present, too begins mysteriously changing. . .

For more books, the American Book Association, **Publisher's** *Weekly, R. R. Bowker, etc., all the stuff the CATALOG has used, see the history/how-to section following p. 434.*

WALTON, IZAAK. 1593–1683.

The Compleat Angler: or, The Contemplative Man's Recreation. 1653–1676. *Dutton* Everyman's 1906 $2.45; ed. by John Buchan *Oxford* 1914 World's Classics 1935 $2.75

"The Compleat Angler," one of the most famous books in English, was written by a self-educated ironmonger. Walton wrote it for his own pleasure as well as that of others; it not only describes the technique of angling, but is a contemplative essay on the peace and quietude attained by the fisherman. After its first appearance in 1653 there were frequent revisions adding new material during the author's lifetime. George Saintsbury called Walton's style one of a "singular and golden simplicity." In spite of Walton's background he became recognized as a "gentleman" of cultured tastes and learning. An Anglican and Royalist, he was overjoyed with the Restoration. In his own time, Walton was known as a biographer, author of the "Lives of Donne and Herbert" (*Cambridge* $.90) and "Lives of John Donne, Sir Henry Wotton, Richard Hooker, George Herbert and Robert Sanderson" (*Oxford* $2.75).

Kenneth Rexroth wrote a charming essay on "The Compleat Angler" in the *Saturday Review* of Sept. 16, 1967, which catches the secret of its enduring appeal——and that of its author shining through it:

"Izaak Walton, above all other writers in English, owes his enormous popularity to his virtues as a man, and these virtues are what condition his style and give his work its fundamental meaning. Millions have read him with joy who have never caught a fish since childhood, if at all. Indeed, . . . in America at least, most of the kinds of fish he talks about are left to small boys. The second half of the *Compleat Angler* was added in late editions and written by Charles Cotton as a guide to trout fishing in rough water. Those who want to know how to catch fish can learn most from Cotton's additions. We read Izaak Walton for a special quality of soul . . . for his tone, for his perfect attunement to the quiet streams and flowered meadows and bosky hills of the Thames valley long ago. . . . It may sound outrageous to say that Izaak Walton wrote one of the Great Books——and that about catching fish——because he was a saint, but so it is. . . . He is, in fact, an unusual embodiment of a quietly powerful tradition, that of the contemplative laymen, St. Thomas More, Nicholas Ferrer, William Law, Gilbert White. After the eighteenth century this type is more commonly found in the sciences than in religion. And like Gilbert White's *Natural History and Antiquities of Selborne*, Walton's *The Compleat Angler* is, in a sense, a scientific work, an outstanding example of the piety of science."

Izaak Walton. By Margaret Bottrall. Pamphlet. *British Bk. Centre* pap. $.75

The Art of "The Compleat Angler." By John R. Cooper. Professor Cooper teaches English and the humanities at the University of Chicago. *Duke Univ. Press* 1967 $6.00

Demco Library Supplies

After 3 years of handling books I've come to understand and appreciate library hardware— card catalog drawers, bookends, magazine protective covers, book trucks, book repair fabric, record-keeping cards. Noble stuff, right up there with fireman's hats as far as I'm concerned.

—SB

Synergy

Extraordinary publication. It's an on-going bibliography of the Subculture for libraries. Every two months there's an issue on a new subject—Women's Liberation, Communes, Ecology, Indians—with articles, pictures, and fine annotated bibliographies, the cheery fruit of solid research. As I understand it, the service is only available to libraries: free. So bug your local library, or, hmmm, I wonder what it takes to start a library. Back issues of Synergy are worth getting. Also they answer questions on research problems.

—SB

[Suggested by William Hogan]

Synergy
via your local library

from:
San Francisco Public Library
Civic Center
San Francisco, Ca. 94102

Odum, Eugene. *Fundamentals of Ecology.* (2nd ed.) Saunders, 1959. $11.75

A compendium of interesting ideas for ecosystem management, this text is useful both for understanding some possibilities for technically resolving our conflicts with nature and, more important, for understanding actual and potential strategies employed by ecosystem exploiters.

•

Bellamy, Edward. *Looking Backward, 2000-1887.* Modern Library, 1951.

A wealthy Bostonian awakens to find himself in the year 2000 A.D. He falls in love with the great granddaughter of his Bostonian fiancee and with her tours the ideal socialist commonwealth. Bellamy's utopia had tremendous impact on social reformers and had hundreds of imitators.

Science Books

A quarterly published by American Association for the Advancement of Science (the people who publish Science*). Most of the reviews are specific and quite nitty-gritty; if they don't like a book they often cite better books on the same subject. It reviews books right on down to kindergarten level; very helpful in locating non-anthropomorphic, factual, logical, and withal delightful books for young ones.*

[Suggested and reviewed by John Lord]

Science Books

$12

from:
AAAS Science Books
American Association for the Advancement of Science
1776 Massachusetts Ave. N.W.
Washington, D.C. 20036

621.47 SOLAR ENERGY ENGINEERING.

HALACY, D. S., Jr. **Experiments With Solar Energy.** NY: Norton, 1969. 147 pp. illus. $4.14. 69-18892.

Experiments with Solar Energy is a revised and updated version of the author's *Fun with the Sun* published in 1959. Being collateral reading, it might serve as a classroom or family science project manual. Directions are given on the selection of materials, approximate cost, the construction and operation of devices utilizing solar energy; solar furnaces; cardboard cooker; solar oven; water heater; solar still; radio; and a solar-powered airplane. Emphasis is placed on the utilization of solar energy in space vehicles and its potential use on lunar stations that offers opportunities to enterprising and imaginative young people. Its expanded usefulness on earth, particularly, in arid lands is not overlooked. The value of this updated volume is enhanced by the inclusion of clear diagrams and illustrative photographs, lists of firms engaged in solar-energy applications and a subject index. A more comprehensive bibliography would have been desirable. [See also *Solar Energy* by John Hoke; Watts, 1968; *S/B* 4(1) 59.] **SH ★**

(C) Two Shelf Display. Holds approximately 75-80 books on two sloping shelves. Dimensions: 31" long, 17" wide, and 41" high, including casters and convenient handle formed by "U" shaped tubular frame. Bottom shelf 18" from floor; space between shelves 12¼"; top shelf 30¾" from floor.

41-6350 — Mist Gray **$58.50**
41-6351 — Light Beige **58.50**
41-6352 — Mellow Gold **58.50**

Demco
Box 1488
Madison, Wisconsin 53701

STEAL THIS BOOK

I grew up copping change from my mother's purse. In college I stuck a transistor in the telephone cord to get free calls. Then I entered the big time, became an Army officer, and was trained in advanced lying, cheating, and stealing until finally in disgust I turned honest. It was an abandoned act of rebellion, and lo, it freed me. I was just barely in the Army after that.

If you steal, you're in the Army. That's my perspective.

Popular theft is largely a matter of who's Fair Game. In parlous times everybody is, to somebody. In the 1770's American rebels righteously robbed Loyalists and vice versa. During the same period in stable Indian tribes theft was practically unknown within the tribe (encouraged sometimes outside the tribe). Are booksellers outside the tribe?

Most bookstores operate very near the financial edge. Reportedly one-third of all bookstores lose money, run at a loss. They're in the business for love, not money. I know enough now about book-making, selling, and using to assert that books are a fantastic bargain, like matches. Stealing books is a lot like robbing match girls, not exactly a far-out revolutionary gesture, just a lazy, military thing to do. —SB

Personalized Bibliographic Service

If you buy more than one book a year, you want to join PBS. You sign up for various categories, and each month brings a computerized printout of all new titles in those categories, including dissertations, films, records and ??

There's more. The good part. To order a book, any book in the world, you just send a card or other written transmission, to PBS; they take care of all the crap of ordering from the publisher AND (it's coming!) they split their profit on each tome with you. . .in practice, this means 10-15% off on hardbacks! You may or may not get something off on softies, depending on what the trade discount is.

They will also conduct a search with used book stores for anything that tickles your fancy but is out of print.

After years of begging, pleading and lying to publishers in an attempt to convince them that as an ally of academe I should get a "professional" discount, PBS appeared and made it automatic. . .at a time when a lot of publishers are cutting off their discounts even to faculty!

Cost is negligible— you pay $1 for the first category you sign up for, and 50¢ for the rest. . .that's your entire financial input FOR A YEAR. . .except for whatever monthly bill you manage to achieve, of course.

A very complete folder with all the poop will be sent (not exceedingly promptly, because they use 3rd class mail a lot) from:

Personalized Bibliographic Service
20434 SW Cypress St.
Santa Ana, Calif. 92707

When you write, tell them No. 390 recommended you.

Brian Weiss
Ann Arbor, Michigan

Remaindered Books

These are books ye publisher got stuck with. After a few years in the warehouse, they are unloaded at astonishingly cheap prices— mere pennies on the dollar— to remaindering houses. Two reliable remainder services are:

Marboro Books
131 Varick St.
New York, N.Y.

Marboro deals by mail catalogs— huge ones— and a card should get you on their mailing list. They also insert their catalogs in the NY Times from time to time, as they have several retail stores in NYC. Their discounts are good and their books are usually in good shape. A little slow by mail, though. Records and posters, too. Prices from 59¢ to 10-15 bucks, depending on what they think they can get. Also, they sell some books at list prices. These books are marked in the catalog by a star. Remember this, because they have recently stopped telling people what the star means— or have found a really good place to hide that information.

Publisher's Central Bureau
33-20 Hunters Point Ave.
Long Island City, N.Y. 11101

About the same as above— often many of the same books in stock, prices about the same too. By mail only.

Bill Marsano
Radnor, Pa.

C-1007. THE TIMES ATLAS OF THE WORLD: Comprehensive Edition by The Times of London in collaboration with John Bartholomew & Son Ltd., Edinburgh, Cartographers. Revision of the coveted Mid-Century Edition: 121 double-page maps color-coded for elevation, with more than 200,000 place names (indexed with map references & latitude-longitude), plus map-guides to world climate, food & food potential, minerals, energy, star charts of northern, southern & equatorial skies, solar system, world sunrise-sunset diagram, lunar map, much more. Huge 11⅞" x 17¾". Pub. at $57.50. **Only $29.50**

Publishers Central Bureau

Magazine subscription discounts

Re: magazine subscriptions— one should never subscribe through the magazine itself— do it through

Publishers Clearing House
382 Main St.
Port Washington, N.Y.

They will match any cheaper offer or refund the difference. Write for their current price list.

Donald McKenzie
Berkeley, CA

Wittenborn and Co.

When it comes to buying books by mail I've had few times when it's been really necessary. Mostly they've been when I've been away from New York and I wanted the book NOW. If the book involved the visual arts and came from anywhere in the world, I've sent the price or its approximation to Wittenborn and presto! They have always responded immediately and more than satisfactorily. They're the kind of book store that has most of the staff mailing or typing— busy— not getting in your hair if you want to browse but always helpful. We've never been able to think of a book they haven't been able to help us with; they are always ready to refer you to someone else if they can't help out. They have always been a regular stop for information recharge with us. Introducing new customers is always a charge: they get kind of watery knees as they begin browsing and suddenly bank accounts fall.

Wittenborn publishes free lists of recent arrivals on their shelves; they are mailed irregularly. They give a 10% "courtesy discount" with some arm twisting. They are the best source in the U.S. for back issues of art and architecture magazines from both the U.S. and most everywhere else. They also publish and/or distribute many small publications such as Ed Ruscha's Royal Road Test *and large publications such as* Tantra Art. *In short, it's a book freak's heaven.*

[Suggested and reviewed by ONYX]

Catalog free

from:
Wittenborn and Co.
1018 Madison Avenue
New York, N.Y. 10021

☐ **TEACHING AND LEARNING AS PERFORMING ARTS** by Robert Filliou and the Reader

A multi-book, with the participation of John Cage, Benjamin Patterson, George Brecht, Allen Kaprow, Marcelle, Vera and Bjoessi and Karl Rot, Dorothy Iannone, Diter Rot, Joseph Beuys. Spiralbound, space provided for the reader's use, German and English text, 228 p., wrappers, 1970 $9.50

The reader is free not to make use of his own writing space, but it is hoped that he will enter as performer, for this is about permanent creation and audience participation.

Introductory Ripoff

A final suggestion for other tool-gatherers who've noticed the high cost of books in general and reference works in particular: At last! *You* can make the system work for you!

Yes, you too can manipulate the Establishment! How? Simple— through the intro offers of book and record clubs.

Most every book club has come-on offers to make your mouth water—seventy-three books, all for only thirty-eight cents and two boxtops. Seriously, though, there are some good buys. The condition, of course, is that you buy a certain number of books at member prices in a given time period.

What the clubs hope for is that you stay in. What you do is get out. Fulfill your minimum obligation and resign your membership. The next time a good offer comes up, join. (It helps if you've changed your name or your adress in the meantime. If not, join your wife, your kid, your parakeet.) A friend has joined the Mainstream Book Club eight times.

Here's how he does it. Their latest ad offers five books for $1, if you buy four more books in the next two years. That's worth up to $85 when you send it in. There's almost no way four book-club books will cost you $85, so you come out ten, twenty, forty dollars to the good.

(I'd just as soon you didn't put my name down for this, if you use it, because some of *my* book clubs may get your catalog.)

Detroit, Michigan

Internews

Interesting service. For $12.00 a year you get local English language newspapers from Ireland, England, Scotland, France, Canada, Mexico, Panama, Brazil, Ghana, South Africa, Israel, Spain, Mallorca, Italy, Japan, Hong Kong, India, Bahama, Australia, New Zealand, Isle of Man, Greece, Venezuela, and Holland

[Suggested by Patrick Leavens]

Internews
$12.00 /yr.

from:
Internews Co.
P.O. Box 3138
Aspen, Colo. 81611

Hamilton Discount Books

A good source of in-print book discounts. It lists publisher's overstocks and reprints, like Publisher's Central Bureau and Marboro. 32-page Catalog is free, published six times a year.

Address is
Edward R. Hamilton, Bookseller
Box 549
Sherman, CT 06784

Government Printing Office

***The best buys in books in the U.S. is the U.S. Government, who prints all manner of fascinating non-fiction. If you're interested in a particular area you might as well get the free list of publications in that area. Or you can get the (most useful, I've found) free biweekly list of* Selected U.S. Government Publications.** *Or, for totality, for $19.50/yr, the* **Monthly Catalog of U.S. Government Publications.** *All, all from:*

Superintendent of Documents
U.S. Government Printing Office
Washington, D.C. 20402

Books from Britain

Larry Schwartz calls the readers attention to Blackwell's Books, England. (p. 2). Your readers might be interested in two other book dealers in Great Britain.

James Thin (53-59 South Bridge, Edinburgh, Scotland) is a bookseller dealing in new and used books. He can provide books in any area— he will send catalogs on request or the price of an individual book if not in a catalog— at considerably less than U.S. prices. Hardbacks cost 1/3 to 1/2 what they do here. Penguin paperbacks (for example) can be obtained at about 1/2 what they cost locally. You can open an account or send your personal check (Made out to Messrs Brown Bros. Harriman & Co., New York). Add 15% for postage & insurance (even so, still a big bargain).

Mr. Thin deals in antiquarian and other used books as well. Books dating to the 16th Century.

(The only books that are not cheaper from Mr. Thin are those published by U.S. University Presses.

The service is courteous, prompt, and personal. The time it takes from date of order to date of receipt of books varies between 4-10 weeks.

For the "Book freaks":

The Folio Society (6 Stratford Place, London WIN OBH, England) publishes books on history, belles-lettres, biography, poetry, fiction, by the world's great authors, in boxed, beautifully bound (canvas, leather, wood veneer, etc.) editions. Some of the books have illustrations directly from the wood block or soft ground etchings. Presently, books average about $3.44, including postage. The most expensive is the two volume Canterbury Tales at $8.75. Send for their catalog. Members (there is no membership fee) must buy at least four volumes per year.

James E. Buhn
Penngrove, California

Ray and Chester came back out in a minute to get the flowers they'd brought in the hearse. The flowers had been delivered to the funeral home. Six wreaths: from Marcella and her family, Leonard and his family, Mrs. Godsey, the Thornton's, Reverend Bagby on behalf of the congregation (although only five people in the congregation came to the funeral), and one wreath that was signed, simply, "hospital staff." Ray and Chester took the flowers in and arranged them in front of the casket, and at the ends, and then as a final act they opened half the coffin lid and the people who had gathered in the church filed by for one last look at Emmit, lying on the light-blue pillow, hardly recognizable without his beard, and in the suit and shirt and blue tie they'd dressed him in. His lips were puckered unnaturally but the whole thing was so unlike Emmit that detail didn't matter much. The people filed by, some of them sniffling, and then they all sat down in the front two rows, fourteen people counting children and the Reverend Bagbys and Ray and Chester and Mr. Olney and the Thornton girl who was going to sing Abide With Me.

•

Mrs. Bagby played the piano softly for a while.

•

And then the Reverend Bagby, not a tall man, kind of pale but still strong in his impression, stood up and opened his Bible.

•

He read from Ecclesiastes. The third chapter. Sweetly, and yet with power and resonance in his voice he said that for every thing there is a season, and a time for every purpose under the heaven.

•

There is a time to be born and a time to die.

•

A time to plant and a time to pluck up that which is planted.

•

A time to kill, and a time to heal.

•

A time to break down and a time to build up.

•

A time to weep and a time to laugh.

•

A time to mourn and a time to dance.

•

A time to cast away stones and a time to gather stones together.

•

A time to embrace and a time to refrain from embracing.

•

He said there was a time to get and a time to lose, a time to keep and a time to cast away. A time to rend, a time to sew, a time to keep silence and let us keep silence now.

Learning

Dr. Spock

Baby and Child Care *by Dr. Benjamin Spock is an excellent book to have handy, especially with a first child. The advice and explanations Dr. Spock gives regarding fever, rashes, coughs, innoculations and clothing for the infant is presented in simple language, somewhat wordy and repetitious, but in such a manner that you cannot misunderstand or confuse his instructions. Bathing an infant and sterilization of bottles, etc. seemed far too complicated. The chapters on illness, first aid, and special problems are excellent and probably the most read and re-read chapters in the book. Not only do you get lots of psychological guidance in the areas of toilet training, weaning, thumbsucking, and bed wetting but, as may be expected, there are sermons on agressive children, no-war toys and growing up in a bomb-oriented world. You couldn't possibly agree with everything Dr. Spock says but after reading this book you are left with the feeling that you should relax, enjoy your baby, do what seems right and natural and that Spock is speaking from experience and common sense.*

[Reviewed by Connie Duckworth]

Dr. Benjamin Spock
BABY and CHILD CARE

Baby and Child Care
Dr. Benjamin Spock
1946, 1968; 620 pp.

$.95 postpaid

from:
Pocket Books
1 West 39th Street
New York, N. Y. 10018

or WHOLE EARTH CATALOG

More babies are overdressed than underdressed. This isn't good for them. If a person is always too warmly dressed, his body loses its ability to adjust to changes. He is more likely to become chilled. So in general, put on too little rather than too much and then watch the baby. Best guide is the color of his face. If he is getting cold, he loses the color from his cheeks.

•

To some degree, the first pregnancy spells the end of carefree youth—very important to Americans. The maidenly figure goes gradually into eclipse, and with it goes sprightly grace. Both eclipses are temporary but very real. The woman realizes that after the baby comes there will be distinct limitations of social life and other outside pleasures. No more hopping into the car on the spur of the moment, going anywhere the heart desires and coming home at any old hour. The same budget has to be spread thinner, and her husband's attention, all of which has gone to her at home, will soon be going to two.

•

155. Gradual weaning from breast to cup in the middle of the first year. If a mother is producing plenty of milk, how long should she plan to nurse? Best of all, most natural of all, is to nurse until the baby is ready for weaning to the cup. Most breast-fed babies are becoming bored between 5 and 6 months.

•

A 2-year-old baby shouldn't be worrying about the consequences of his actions. This is the period when he is meant to learn by doing and having things happen. I'm not advising that you never warn your child in words, but only that you shouldn't always be leading him out beyond his depth with ideas.

It's a good idea to begin offering a sip of milk from the cup from the age of 5 months, so that the baby gets used to it before he is too opinionated.

•

Better to remove and distract him than just to say, "No, no!"

Between the ages of 1 and 5 years, children may develop fever as high as 104° (sometimes even higher) at the onset of mild infections, such as colds, sore throats, grippe, just as often as with serious infections. On the other hand, a dangerous illness may never have a temperature higher than 101°. So don't be influenced too much, one way or the other, by the height of the fever, but get in touch with the doctor whenever your child appears sick in any way.

How to Parent

So many child psychology books leave an unsure new parent more anxious or even guilty feeling. This one builds confidence.

How to Parent *is both a practicable review of child psychology and an excellent catalog of toys, books, records, equipment, parental survival, and inexpensive do-it-yourself materials and projects useful in a child's physical, emotional and intellectual development.*

The text concentrates on the different stages of development from birth to six years, offering the most basic findings of behavioral science in relation to each stage, and usable advice on how to help a child structure his self-concept to become a self regulating person. Most important, the author insists the application of these findings and advice be guided by the feel of childhood—–a contact with the child within you that you once were, and that parents must have the wisdom to follow their own hearts, no matter what the "experts" say.

[Reviewed by Faye Kesey]

SIGNET REFERENCE • Y4527 • $1.25
First Dr. Spock, then Dr. Ginott, and now
Dr. Fitzhugh Dodson
HOW TO PARENT
The revolutionary new approach to your child's formative years that puts joy back in parenthood and discipline back in child-rearing

$1.25 postpaid

from:
New American Library, Inc.
1301 Ave. of the Americas
New York, N.Y. 10019

or WHOLE EARTH CATALOG

You may be able to toilet train a child who is less than a year old, but you are going to have to pay a psychological price for training that early. Personally, I don't think the price is worth it.

•

Let's be very clear: *you cannot spoil an infant.* Cuddle your infant as much as you want; you won't spoil him. Feed him as often as he's hungry; you won't spoil him. Sing and coo to him as much as you want; you won't spoil him. Pay attention to him as often as he cries; you won't spoil him. The best things that can happen to your baby, psychologically speaking, is to have as many of his needs gratified and to have as few frustrations as possible. His ego or sense of selfhood is too tender and immature to be able to cope with much frustration now. There will be plenty of time for life to teach him about frustrations when he is older.

•

Books are far inferior in effectiveness to what a mother can do to stimulate the language development of a child. Continue the "label the environment" game that you started in the stage of infancy. You can do this wherever you are with him. Point to objects in the house and name them for him. When you are riding in the car, you can point out and name objects that you are passing: truck, tractor, house, church.

•

We may say, "Now that was a bright thing to do, wasn't it?" or "How could you be so dumb?" or "Haven't you got any sense?" Each time we unleash one of these belittling statements we are chipping away at our child's self-concept.

•

Threats deal with the future, but children live in the present. Therefore, threats are useless in improving the future behavior of a child.

•

Mother is hurt and furiously accusatory: "Willie––you promised!" She doesn't know that promises are meaningless to children. A promise, like its older brother, a threat, deals with the future. But small children live only in the present. If a child is a sensitive youngster, extracting a promise from him will merely teach him to feel guilty if he breaks it. Or, if he is not so sensitive, it will merely teach him to be cynical, and substitute verbal behavior for true behavior change.

If you get upset and angry at a child's temper tantrum you will reinforce it. Then he will know that he can get to you any time with a tantrum. Don't try to reason with a child in the midst of a temper tantrum or try to talk him out of it. He is a boiling sea of emotions. He is in no mood to listen to reason or logic. Above all, don't try to get him over a temper tantrum by the threat of a spanking. Haven't you overheard parents say to a child in the midst of a tantrum, "Shut up, or I'll *really* give you something to cry about!" That's like trying to put out a fire by pouring gasoline on it.

What should you do when your first adolescent throws a temper tantrum? What you want to convey to the child is that this tantrum is something he apparently has to go through, but that it will get him absolutely nowhere. How do you convey this to him? *You ignore the tantrum.* Each mother has to find the ways which are most comfortable for her to do this. Some mothers can stand there and say nothing and wait until the tantrum runs down of its own accord. Others will want to say: "I know you're frustrated and mad, but you'll need to go to your room until you've finished crying. Then when you're through I have something interesting to show you." Others will say sternly: "Go to your room!" Find the method of ignoring temper tantrums that suits you best and use it. But most of all, try to help your child save face by giving him a graceful way out of the situation, if at all possible.

•

The time to start a child on the road to awareness is when he is a preschooler. *A true awareness of the sensory world is his most basic foundation for thinking.*

In addition to providing a wide range of sensory experiences for our children, we need to provide a variety of materials which they can use as stimuli for their thinking— materials which your child should have between the ages of three and six. He should have available lots of paper; crayons, felt pens or watercolor pens; scissors with blunt ends; stacks of old magazines; cardboard of various shapes and sizes; a blackboard with white and colored chalk; a scrapbox for collage, containing all kinds of scrap wood, fabric and paper; glue; wooden blocks of various sizes; dress-up clothes and costumes; a record player or tape player; inexpensive records he can play by himself; good records you play for him; Lego or similar types of construction toys; playdough and clay; books. Your child should have a set of plastic, magnetic alphabet letters and numerals and a metal blackboard they can stick to. Without the above-mentioned materials, your preschooler would be as handicapped in his thinking as a college student with no textbooks.

•

There is also no reason why your child cannot continue to have an evening bottle to go to sleep by, even at this "advanced age" of two or two and one-half. Many of your neighborhood "experts" will frown on you if you do this, and say: "What— he's two and a half and he hasn't given up the bottle yet?" So what? What's the rush? If he still likes it as a security device, is there any reason why we have to insist he give it up at this age? All three of my children had a bedtime bottle. They didn't give up until they were between two and one-half and three years of age.

One of the important things about the evening bedtime ritual is that it should be a time of pleasure for your child. We want him to look forward to going to bed. He should not feel that bedtime is something unpleasant, where he is banished abruptly to a dark room, while the rest of the family does interesting things. The evening bedtime ritual should not only be a time of pleasure for the child, but for mother and father as well.

•

DR. DODSON'S WHIZ-BANG, SUPER-ECONOMY PARENT'S SURVIVAL KIT

If you have skimmed over this entire list of books, your reaction right now may be: "Wow! I'd like to buy scads of those books, but my family budget won't stand it!" I have considered that very important financial factor and come up with the following list of thirteen paperback books which will form a basic home library for parents at the relatively modest cost (considering today's inflation) of only $11.60 for all of them. Here they are:

1. *Baby and Child Care,* Benjamin Spock (Pocket Books), $.95.
2. *How to Give Your Child a Good Start in Life,* Leland Glover (Collier, 1962). $.95.
3. *The Intelligent Parents Guide to Raising Children,* Eve Jones (Collier, 1961). $.95.
4. *How to Guide Your School-Age Child,* Leland Glover (Collier, 1965). $.95
5. *Between Parent and Child,* Haim Ginott (Avon, 1969), $1.50
6. *Child Behavior,* Frances Ilg and Louise Bates Ames (Har-Row) $.95
7. *Your Child's Play,* Arnold Arnold (Essandess Special Edition, 1968). $1.00
8. *Play Therapy,* Virginia Axline (Ballantine, 1969). $1.25.
9. *A Parent's Guide to Children's Reading,* Nancy Larrick (Pocket Books, 1969), $.50.
10. *A Parent's Guide to Children's Education,* Nancy Larrick (Pocket Books, 1963), $.50.
11. *Summerhill,* A. S. Neill (Hart, 1966), $2.45
12. *Accident Handbook,* Children's Hospital (Children's Medical Center [300 Longwood Avenue, Boston, Massachusetts], 1950) $.25.
13. *A Parent's Guide to Better Baby-sitting,* Faye Cobb (Pocket Books, 1963), no longer available

TOTAL COST: $12.20

Playthings

The old standby who always comes up with nifty, new items, especially for infants is **Creative Playthings.** *Catalog free.*

Childcraft *has a good similar line, with some more elaborate toys. Catalog free.*

Preschool Things Catalog *is a nice sideventure of Sesame Street (long live), with various toys and books. Catalog $0.50.*

Constructive Playthings *has stuff especially for yards, schools and playgrounds, along with dolls, games, etc. Catalog $1.00.*

Childlife Play Specialities *has strictly yard and playground stuff. Catalog free.*

Polypops *is a British outfit with extraordinarily nifty cardboard items— rollers, furniture, little houses, etc. Catalog free.*

[Suggested by Jeremy Scott Wood]

Galt Toys *has complex, civilized, inexpensive British stuff. Catalog free? Galt Toys, 63 Whitfield Street, Guilford, CT 06437*
—SB

Galt Toys
3210 Whitney Ave. (Rt. 10)
Hamden CT 06514

Puppets

From 3 years. Simple and expressive vinyl puppets for fantasy fun. Blue whale, green frog, grey wolf, red dragon, yellow duck. Designed by Dion Porzio. $2.95 each.
Creative Playthings

Tube Rattle

From 3 months. Soft clear plastic tube for watching, touching, chewing, bending and stretching. Five stainless steel balls locked inside roll freely through the entire loop. Designed by Fredun Shapur. $2.50

Creative Playthings

Creative Playthings
Princeton, New Jersey 08540

PUNCHIN JUDY BAG

Childlife Play Specialties, Inc.
55 Whitney St.
Holliston, Mass. 01746

The perfect outlet for active youngsters' energies, our Punchin Judy Bag will take all the punishment they can deliver. Tackle or punch it, roll it or ride it— this sturdy bag comes back for more. Easily disconnected from its double rope for separate play on the floor. Designed for both indoor and outdoor use, but store inside. Length 27'', diameter 9''. Made with strong cotton duck, a heavy top strap and firm wool stuffing. Screw eyes included. Age 2½ up. (p.p. 15 lb.) $17.50

BOUNCING TUBE
This heavy-duty truck tire tube inflates to 36'' diam. and 11½'' high. The two heavy canvas covers and strong webbing supports can take all the punishment energetic bouncers can give it.
No. 2   4 lbs. $10.95

Constructive Playthings
1040 East 85th St.
Kansas City, Missouri 64131

Childcraft Education Corp.
Dept. WE
150 East 58th Street
New York, N.Y. 10022

THREADING BLOCK

Children can't resist this natural hardwood toy that invites involvement. Push the wooden needle into a hole; it comes out of a hole on another side. Changing the order in which holes are threaded creates a variety of patterns on the block. Unusually fine for developing finger, hand and eye coordination. 18 mos. — 3 yrs.
RM 163 1 lb. $4.50

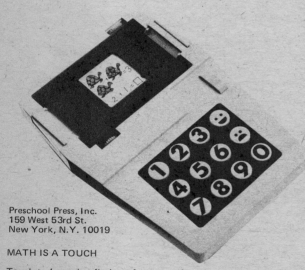

Preschool Press, Inc.
159 West 53rd St.
New York, N.Y. 10019

MATH IS A TOUCH

Touch to Learn is a find-out-for-yourself math machine. It works on flashlight batteries with visual cassettes, each stocked with 20 picture problems. Only a correct response will wind the tape to the next question. Comes with two programs, Learning to Identify Numbers and Learning to Tell Time. Six other programs available separately broaden the program to include counting, addition, subtraction and coin values.

412 TOUCH TO LEARN
Price: $8.00 (batteries not included)

413 SET OF SIX ADDITIONAL TOUCH TO LEARN CASSETTES.
Price: $6.00

Polypops
Paperchase Products Ltd.
11 Alfred Place
London WC1
England

LUNARTRACK

Articulated caterpillar track propelled by one child power. The child gets in and crawls forward in a normal manner the tank revolving round the child. The tank like action is extremely realistic and the track sill surmount small obstacles. A certain degree of skill develops with use and familiarity. Sections can be omitted to make a circumference more adaptable for younger children.
Dimensions: Width 15'' Overall length 56''
Carry Home Case: 35¼'' x 2-3/4'' x 28½''
Price £3.0.0

•

And Reverend Bagby presided over a silent prayer with his arm upraised and his hand outstretched, till finally someone among the people said amen, and Reverend Bagby concluded with verse fifteen:

•

That which hath been is now; and that which is to be hath already been; and God requireth that which is past.

•

Reverend Bagby began to speak then, and remarks about Emmit, personally, were only a part of what he had to say. He gave a little of Emmit's biography. He said that he was born there on Trace Fork, that he'd grown up there, and had gone to Finley County High School. He said that he'd served in World War Two, and been wounded, and that after the war he'd gone into the coal business for a while. He talked about Emmit living a few years in Louisville, and about his year in the Veteran's Hospital and then his return to Trace Fork when his father died. But the remarks about Emmit personally were only little decorations on a larger statement he was trying to make that D.R. listened to very carefully. It wasn't a logical statement, it was better than that. He began with the reading from Ecclesiastes, and then allowed his words to spread up and outward into a kind of song. Half the time he spoke with his eyes closed. And now and then he'd stop suddenly, hushed by some inner command, and in the church a silence would build that he in turn would use to build his song upon, reaching higher and higher and lower and lower, sometimes bridging the high and the low by lapsing into an unknown tongue, never much, and never for very long, just little shines of the pure language of glossolalia, fah lan tah, mah nah lah, fa lan tah.

•

And D.R. listened.

Play and Playthings for the Preschool Child

This book will be useful to schools, and parents and teachers of children under eight. It was originally published under the title of Play With a Purpose for Under-Sevens, *so the "preschool" in the title doesn't mean only 3 and four-year-olds. Since the author is an English nursery school teacher the book is written under English assumptions: you aren't going to run out and buy everything you need, and you're going to make use of anything you've got lying around the house anyway, like castoff car tires and coat hangers. Mrs. Matterson has a clear practical style of writing, and a lovely way of making things sound terribly easy to do. As a matter of fact, most of the equipment and toys in this book are easy to make. Besides giving instructions for making things, Mrs. Matterson says a lot about children's play: the kinds of play, its meaning to children, music, pets, natural play materials, books (there's a whole chapter on story-telling), and play for sick children. Her last two chapters are on planning a playgroup (that's an English co-op nursery school) and an open letter to child-welfare experts and school boards. There's an appendix at the end with a list of books suitable for children from 3 to 6 years old, and a list of sources of supply for play equipment. Probably the editor did the appendix, since it lists American sources of supply and information. She also must have weeded out the exclusively English terms and objects available only in England, because everything in the book seems to be universal and easy to get. In Evelyn Beyer's introduction she gives the American viewpoint on what seems to be a point of difference between parents and teachers here and in Great Britain— whether or not to read fantasy and fairy tales to young children. In England parents and teachers rarely seem to* worry about the effect on young children of wicked stepmothers abandoning children to starve, of the chopper coming to chop off your head when you play London Bridge, but here we're all awfully queasy about that sort of thing. Mrs. Beyer is in favor of "a story diet of here-and-nowness" for three and four-year-olds. (I disagree with her here— taken literally that would mean throwing out The Three Bears and Peter Rabbit)

[Suggested and reviewed by Dorothy Horn]

Play and Playthings for the Preschool Child
E.M. Matterson
1965, 1967; 180 pp.

$1.95 postpaid

from:
Penguin Books, Inc.
7110 Ambassador Rd.
Baltimore, Md. 21207

3984 55th St.,
New York, N.Y. 10019

or WHOLE EARTH CATALOG

"Basic materials (like water, earth, wood, vegetable matter, rock and metal) impose a relentless, impersonal, uniform discipline on us all. . .If your children were provided with nothing else ever, they would still be far happier and learn more than a good many children with. . .a room full of status-symbol toys."

Wooden Toys

Community Playthings has the widest variety, including a nice set of blocks. These toys are the product and income of the Rifton, N.Y. Bruderhof community. Catalog free.

[Suggested by William Ilson]

Vermont Wooden Toy has particularly lively small toys. Dune buggie and raceway. Kid-size wooden sled. Dusenberg with passengers that fall out. Catalog free.

Everdale Toys, from a community in Ontario, prices stiffer because of the border. Catalog free.

Matten Enterprises, fine toy boats. Catalog free.

[Suggested by Joeann Yellot]

Dick Schnacke has a splendid selection of traditional toys — ball & cup, Jacob's ladder, bull roarer, tops, bean bags, etc. Good prices (50¢ — $5.50). Catalog free.

[Suggested by Bob Railford]
—SB

Unit Block Family Sets

F-135 Three Year Old Set Unit Blocks.
32 blocks with 7 different shapes,
18 lbs $11.50

F-145 Four Year Old Set Unit Blocks.
55 blocks in 12 shapes. 32 lbs 19.50

F-155 Five Year Old Set Unit Blocks.
85 blocks in 15 shapes, 50 lbs 29.50

Community Playthings
Rifton, N.Y. 12471

---

an authentic mountain folk toy

Flipperdinger

One of about 75 items available.

Instructions:
—Carefully remove tape, release pith ball
—Place wired ball in nozzle of blowpipe. Blow gently on pipe and ball will float up on air stream. Try to snag the ball on the hoop!
—Now blow again, try to unhook ball and back the ball down into pipe nozzle

Vermont Wooden Toy Co.
Old High School Building
Waitsfield, Vt. 05673

Dune Buggy Raceway $11.95

Van $19.80 plus taxes

Everdale Toys
Box 29
Hillsburgh, Ontario
Canada

Dick Schnacke
Mountain Craft Shop
Route 1
Proctor, West Virginia 26055

14-inch Silly Sailor
$8.50

Matten Enterprises
The Toy Shop
Southwest Harbor, Maine 04679

Diary of An Early American Boy

A quaint account of life on an early American homestead. Its daily entries are so vividly portrayed by the author's word-pictures and ink sketches that you actually feel you are living with Noah and his family. With them, the forest is the marketplace, the creek is power, and Nature is ever in Command. With a knowledge of levers, use their ox to clear a field for corn. With a broadaxe and the help of your neighbors, erect a king post bridge over your creek. With flour ground in the mill you built, bake bread. With scraps of branches taken from fallen trees, make toys for children. And on Christmas Eve, as a blanket of snow glistens outside under the stars, sit by your warm hearth and give Thanks to the Forces that made you.

[Suggested and reviewed by Sawdust Ribiba]

Diary of an Early American Boy
Eric Sloane
1962; 108 pp.

$2.00

Ballantine Books
457 Hahn Rd.
Westminster, Maryland 21157

or WHOLE EARTH CATALOG

25: A cold and windy day. Neighbor Adams' with son Robert stopp'd by. We drank mead and mint tea. No work done this day. Father is going to the woodlot behind the barn tomorrow for floor timbers. I shall assist him.

26: A light snow fell which Father believes will be the last of the winter. We fell'd a fine oak and rolled it upon rails for Spring seasoning. Mother is joyous at the thought of a good wood floor.

In the little forge barn half-way down the bridge, Izaak had earned most of the money needed around the homestead. Not that an early American had great need for cash, as most things were traded; but a good farmer always had a cash crop or some paying trade other than farming. Izaak was a nail-maker. He had taught Noah the art of making hand-wrought nails by letting him pump the bellows of the forge as a little fellow; now and then he actually hammered or broke the iron nail rods.

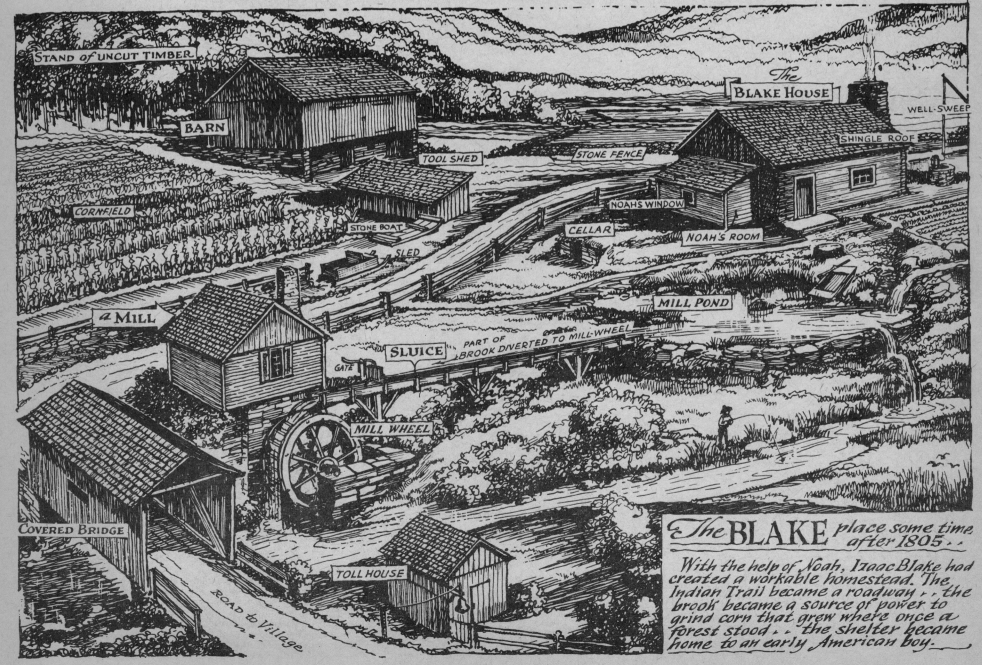

STAND OF UNCUT TIMBER

BARN

TOOL SHED

CORNFIELD

STONE BOAT

SLED

a MILL

SLUICE   PART OF BROOK DIVERTED TO MILL-WHEEL

GATE

MILL WHEEL

COVERED BRIDGE

ROAD to Village

TOLL HOUSE

The BLAKE HOUSE

WELL-SWEEP

SHINGLE ROOF

STONE FENCE

NOAHS WINDOW

CELLAR

NOAH'S ROOM

MILL POND

The BLAKE *place some time after 1805 . .*

With the help of Noah, Izaac Blake had created a workable homestead. The Indian Trail became a roadway . . the brook became a source of power to grind corn that grew where once a forest stood . . the shelter became home to an early American boy.

For more Eric Sloane, see p. 150.

Children's Books

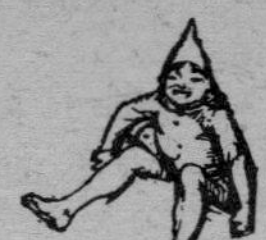

As an old children's book buff (I grew up in a family of four kids in which we read aloud every evening, and have a heavy-reading bunch of four kids myself) I feel moved to respond to your San Diego correspondent who in the January issue asks for "any sort of literature for our kids that doesn't constitute total propaganda for the establishment set." First, though, I'd have to say that I don't think it is possible to do very well on her specific request for stuff on families other than the Standard American model, since the books on "other kinds" of families (eg Reba Mirsky's *Thirty-One Brothers and Sisters*, Lois Lenski's stories about Okies and such) which are available and often not bad are written by people who are outsiders to the life they write about and have that flat and faintly didactic quality which goes with that. There are some autobiographies from other cultures which I remember liking (Youel B. Mirza, *Children of the Rooftops*, Younghill Kang, *The Happy Grove*, Mme Sugimoto, *A Daughter of the Samurai*, Camara Laye, *The Dark Child*, Wright's *Black Boy*) but none of the ones I think of are for young children. I'd imagine that the main thing she wants and what we generally want is something which encourages kids to be open and to grow into the kinds of grown-ups who can laugh and cry and wonder. Now having, as is customary, re-defined the question to suit the answer I have, I will make some suggestions along those lines. Just things which come to mind.

If my list has an idiosyncratic character, so would any child's. For kids not only have their individual tastes but also use particular books for some particular thing in that book which speaks to their particular condition. One of mine, for example, loved a book by Robert McCloskey called *Blueberries for Sal* which is about a bear mother and child and human mother and child getting scrambled and then brought back together properly again, and at a time of great stress (she'd had to have part of a finger sewed back on) had it read over and over. She would wake at night crying, and I would hit her with the *Blueberries for Sal*, and she'd go back to sleep comforted. Also, kids, like grown-ups, like from time to time to rest or rot their minds with trash.

Anyway, some suggestions.

First, for pretty young kids:

Ruth Krauss' *Bears* is perfect play, and her book *The Big World and the Little House* is a beautiful statement about being at home in the world.

Antonio Frasconi's multi-lingual woodblock picture books *See and Say* and *More See and Say* are extraordinary, and even nicer is *The Snow and the Sun.*

The tiny, precise books by Beatrix Potter may seem too old-fashioned to parents who think of themselves as advanced, but I think should be looked at. The best known is of course *The Story of Peter Rabbit* but some others are more interesting. I like especially *The Tailor of Gloucester.* (Beatrix Potter was a terribly cooped-up Victorian clergyman's daughter who wrote and illustrated these stories to keep alive; late in life she married, happily, and never wrote another line. Women's Lib take note.)

Maurice Sendak's *Where the Wild Things Are* is preferred by the Cambridge types.

I'm not sure if you can get in the U. S. Tove Jansson's *The Book About Moomin, Mymble and Little My*, but if you can get it you'll be amazed: Finnish surrealism.

Dr. Seuss, as is well known, writes splendid nonsense; for me, the one which comes off best is *If I Ran the Circus.*

For somewhat older children:

All the books by Laura Ingalls Wilder are wonderful. They should probably be read more or less in order, not only because they follow the chronology of her own life (they are autobiography) but because the scale of vision in each is that of the age level represented. The first one, *The Little House in the Big Woods,* is in its own way a sort of child's Whole Earth thing anyhow, full of careful descriptions of such things as how to make a smoke house and smoke meat in it and how to make a wood-and-leather door latch. My favorite of the lot is *The Little House on the Prairie*; the chapter in that on "Indians Going Away" is for me one of the most perfect pieces of writing in English for any audience.

E. B. White's *Charlotte's Web* is a wonderful book about the basic things—friendship, death and birth.

Randall Jarrell's *The Bat Poet* is a fine book about being a poet and has some great bat poetry; his *The Animal Family* is also the real stuff.

Saint Exupery's *The Little Prince* one might think is really for grown-ups, but my kids like it.

P. S. Beagle, *The Last Unicorn.* So sad.

Tolkien, of course.

Three books which we have loved which might not go for kids who don't know New York, are Jean Merrill's *The Pushcart War* (guerilla warfare against trucks) Doris Plenn's *The Green Song* (about being a Puerto Rican, in this case a frog, in New York) and George Selden's *The Cricket in Times Square* (on being alive at all in New York.)

Two very old-fashioned books which might or might not go for some kids in this age are Frances Hodgson Burnett's *The Secret Garden* which is about a couple of terribly neurotic kids growing into health by working together to make a garden come back to life, and George MacDonald's *At the Back of the North Wind* which is a terribly strange book, I guess metaphorically about death.

Selma Lagerlof's *The Wonderful Adventures of Nils;* travelling around Scandinavia with a flock of wild geese.

Some children like fairy stories and some don't. Those who do usually need a big supply; readily available in paper are the red, blue, pink etc. fairy books. The stories of Hans Andersen are usually listed as fairy stories, but of course they are something else than "tales."

Then there are the Homeric epics. For kids I like best the Giant Golden Book of the Iliad and the Odyssey. I have burst into tears reading aloud the Iliad to a little boy who was mystified (and re-reading Simone Weill's "The Iliad: The Poem of Force" knew why it made me cry.)

Some really good collections of poetry are: Herbert Read's *This Way Delight*; Dunning (ed) *Reflections on a Gift of Watermelon Pickle* (can be got in paper, but the photographic illustrations are so good the hard cover is worth it if you can afford it) and C. F. Moule's *Miracles* (poems by children.) Carl Sandburg's poems, *Wind Song* can be got in paper.

Having listed all this fantasy, I would like to cite also one very good book about fact: Mary Elting's *The Lollypop Factory and Lots of Others* which is about industrial organization, written in a nice no-nonsense style like those old books by Ilin. There is a Giant Golden Encyclopaedia which doesn't tell you much about anything, but is the sort of thing it is fun to browse through.

I'd also like to list one stunning biography available in paper, which I have been giving away to friends of mine: *Journey Towards Freedom: The Story of Sojurner Truth* by Jacqueline Bernard.

If you are far from libraries or bookstores, Blackwell's in Oxford has a splendid children's book catalog, and the price of books in England is so reasonable that even with postage it may be cheaper than here; they are very obliging about letting you set up an account rather than paying for each order. If you write them they will reply (or have to me) via a handwritten letter.

Now for another department. If you are going to list books on such finicky crafts as macrame, I think you should list *Cookies and Breads: The Baker's Art* by Ilse Johnson and Nika Standen Hazelton, Reinhold Publishing Corp., $6.95. Most of it consists of photographs of items in an exhibition of ornamental breads and cookies at the Museum of Contemporary Crafts, but it also has some how-to directions and we went absolutely wild here one Saturday making instant stained-glass with cookie dough and pounded-up sourballs.

I was rendered absolutely euphoric by your review of my book, *The View from the Barrio*, in the fall issue. Such a contrast to the *American Anthropologist*. They sort of liked it, but were made very uneasy by the lack of footnotes.

Loyally,

Lisa R. Peattie
Newton, Mass.

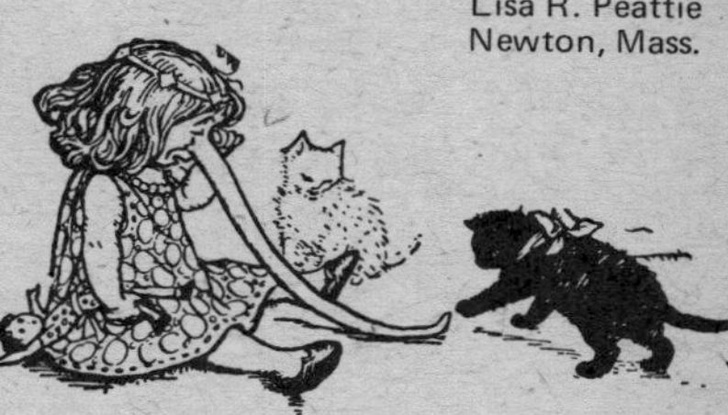

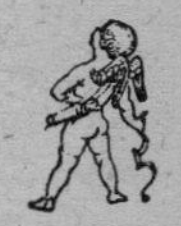

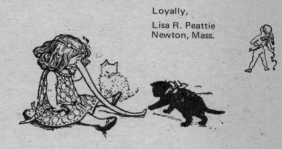

Indian Tales

About ten years ago a story went around that a beatnik girl in Sausalito wrote to Ezra Pound and asked him how to write poetry. Pound replied promptly. "Read **Indian Tales** *by Jaime de Angulo. It is how."*

De Angulo was a linguist at Berkeley, a bohemian personality in early Big Sur, and a good friend to the "primitive" Pit River Indians in Northern California. (His challenge to the notion of primitive may be found in his excellent article "Indians in Overalls", reprinted in The Hudson Review Anthology, *Vintage, 1961). He wrote these stories for his children. They are made from odds and ends of his experiences with Indian stories, language, lore, and mysterious occasions. They are the best children's stories I know, and they are more simply Indian than anything else I've read.*

(KPFA in Berkeley has superb tapes of De Angulo reading the stories. Maybe they've decomposed by now. If they were made into a record set, I'd buy them in a minute.)

—SB

Indian Tales
Jaime de Angulo
1962; 246pp.

$2.65 postpaid

from:
Hill & Wang
72 5th Avenue
New York, N.Y. 10011

or WHOLE EARTH CATALOG

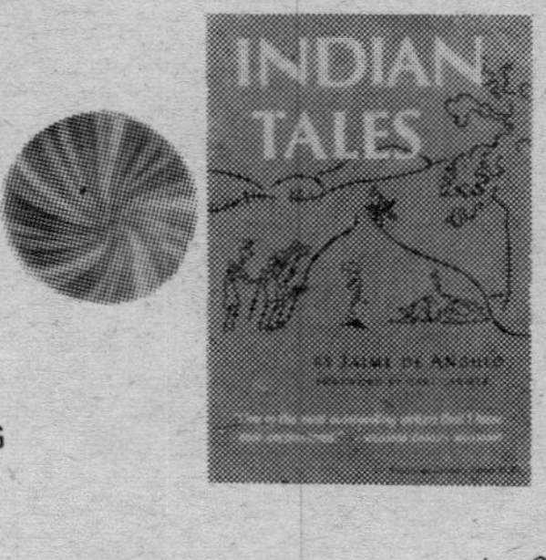

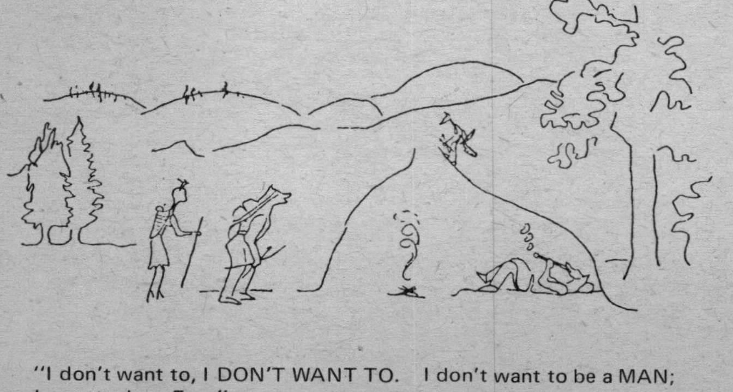

"I don't want to, I DON'T WANT TO. I don't want to be a MAN; I want to be a Fox."

"Oh, the Ha-Has again. You are reverting."

Fox was laughing. He said, "Seriously, Oriole, why did we grow up so fast? Only yesterday, when we began our story and I started to see the world with my father, who was then a real Bear . . ."

Oriole interrupted. "No, you are mistaken. He was not a real Bear yet, he was only a beginning of a bear, he was a person-bear. Now he is a bearman—I mean a man-bear . . .I mean . . . "

"Oh, keep quiet. You are getting me all mixed up again."

"No, Fox, listen to me; I will explain. The man who is telling our story, it's his fault, he has done something wrong with the machinery of time, he has let it go too fast. You see, he was supposed to take a million years to tell our story. The poor fellow, he is too old, he gets all mixed up. He should go and take a rest in the country for a while."

"Oh, my, my, my!" sighed the Fox, "the only thing to do is to start again RIGHT AT THE BEGINNING." Fox looked curiously at Oriole. "What do you mean, a MILLION years?"

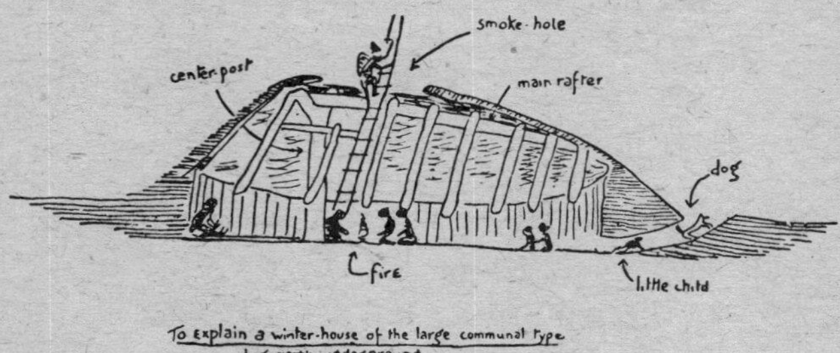

To explain a winter-house of the large communal type. dug partly underground

"Why, I mean an infinity of time, just as Tsimmu was telling in his story of the creation of the world, Don't you remember? Ten times ten times ten times ten years, *molossi molossi molossi tellim piduuwi.* When Cocoon Man was floating around in nothing but air and fog he waited a million years for that cloud to come near enough so he could jump on it."

"Yes," said Fox. "Yes, just like Marum'da, who made the world and then he went to sleep. That's an infinity of time, but it must stop somewhere—it can't go on forever. It must stop somewhere."

Oriole asked, "WHY? "

Fox thought a moment then he said, "I dunno. But listen, Oriole, what's time anyway?"

Oriole said, "Why, it's ten times ten times ten times ten years. What else do you want it to be?"

Fox said, "I dunno, I guess it's growing old."

Oriole said, "All right, then, some people grow old faster than others. You know that yourself. Just as some people walk faster than others. It all depends on who is looking at it."

"Why, Oriole, you are crazy. It depends on who is walking, not on the man who is looking at the fellow who is walking."

"No, certainly NOT. Look at that man over there walking. He seems to be just crawling along, but if you were close to him, he would be going much faster. That's the way with the man who is telling this story. Sometimes he is closer and sometimes he is farther away, so for him that makes us go faster or slower."

Fox said, "Oriole, you drive me crazy. Now I don't know whether I am standing on my head or my feet. It's like that time when we first met you and your father."

"Listen, Fox, it is not I who started this idea that there was a man telling this story, it was you. For all we know, there is no such man."

"Of course, there is not, I invented him."

"That doesn't prove anything. Marum'da invented the people, and they existed whether he liked it or not. Maybe you invented the man who is telling this story, so now he exists. It's too bad, but now you can't get rid of him."

"Yes, I will. I'll destroy him the way Marum'da did the people."

"Then you know what will happen, Mister? You won't exist any more because he is the one who is telling the story."

"Oh, oh, oh, stop, Oriole!" Fox was holding his head in both hands. Then he laughed as he pulled Oriole to her feet and they both ran down the hill.

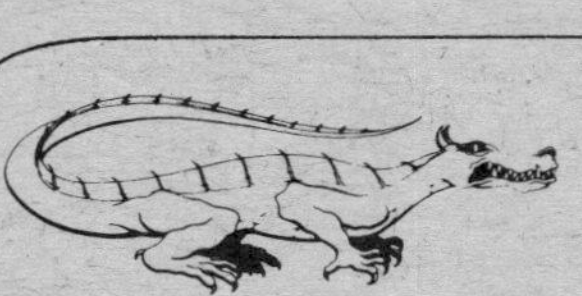

•

He heard a sweet voice sing Abide With Me.

•

And then he helped them carry Emmit in his coffin outside to where the sled was waiting.

•

And he walked with Leonard leading the horse up Trace Fork, the others coming behind, not the old folks, not Mrs. Godsey nor Mr. Olney, just those who could make it in the sun over the broken road and then across the broken hillside up the rugged slope past yellow, yellow earth of the churned up land,

•

And he helped them lower the coffin into the grave

•

And he walked with Marcella and Doyle and Leonard and the rest back down to the homeplace

•

And Mrs. Thornton had been in the old house, cleaning up, and someone had brought food, fried chicken and cakes and pies and a great bowl of green beans cooked with a piece of fat,

•

And D.R. ate with the people and talked with them and Marcella and her family stayed that night at the homeplace and it was a marvelous, far-out time they had, talking about the old days,

•

That evening in itself's a story but I'm just too tired now honey to tell you any more. I'm crashing now, falling into sleep again, here in Emmit's bed. I'll tell you the rest when I wake up, for there's oh so much to say.

Programmed Reading

If you have a pre-school or kindergarten age child who you feel is ready to learn to read but you don't know how to start, this series of programs may be your answer. The series of twenty-two books begins with a set of eight sound-symbol cards. Each 8 x 10" card has a picture and the sound (letter) it stands for.

When the child has learned all eight sounds without the help of the pictures, he is ready to begin the primer, which uses only the eight familiar sounds plus 'I', 'yes', and 'no'. Learning the sounds and getting into the primer may take a long time and plenty of help from you, depending on the age of the child and how much he can absorb in one sitting. Our children started short sessions before age four and it was several months before they reached the self-teaching level, about half-way through the primer. After that they were on their own, going through each book at their own rate and becoming fairly good readers by the time they started kindergarten.

The material in every book is presented in a highly entertaining way; drawings by Carol Andrews are funny and colorful so that learning to read never becomes a drag.

The main characters throughout the series are Sam, Ann, their little brother Walter, Nip the dog and Tab the cat. The beginning books are about their daily adventures and how they get into and out of trouble. In the more advanced books, when the mob is looking for adventure they visit the Roundabouts who live in a land where anything can happen. The last three books, also in the form of self-teaching programs, are stories from Greek mythology meaningfully written for seven and eight year olds.

Cynthia Buchanan has also written a three-part series, Programmed Geography (Macmillan) including The Earth in Space, Continents & Oceans, Latitudes and Climates. Our children were able to do this series successfully at eight years or so. Another excellent program by the Sullivan Associates is Programmed Astronomy (2 books).

[Suggested and reviewed by Gretchen Guard.]

Programmed Reading
Cynthia D. Buchanan
Sullivan Associates.

Programmed reading: The pre-reading series. 3 bks. bk. 1, Programmed pre-reader. 1966. $1.80; 2nd ed. 1968. $0.92; bk. 2,Programmed pre-reading. 1963. $2.40; bk. 3, Programmed primer, $1.32; readiness test, $2.80; teacher's alphabet cards, $3.60; student's alphabet cards, $1.84; sound-symbol cards, $1.92; teacher's guide to Pre-reader, stage 2, 1968. $2.72; teacher's guide to Reading readiness, stage 1, 1968 $2.00.

Programmed reading. 2 series. 1963. series 1. 2 vols. vol. 1, Programmed pre-reading, $1.48; vol. 2, Programmed primer, $1.24; reading readiness test, $2.40 per pkg. of 10; series 2, Programmed reading, bk. 1, $1.32; teacher's guide, $0.72.

Programmed reading. 21 bks. 3 ser. 1963-66, Teachers guide to ser.1, $2.40; bks. 1-2. $1.50 ea; teacher's guides to bk. 1, $0.72; to bk. 2, o.p. bks. 3-7, $1.68 ea; teacher's guides to bks. 3-7. o.p. pupils response bks. for bks. 3-7, $0.32 ea; test bklet, $0.96; teacher's guide, $0.96; placwment test, set, $8.00; guide to reading tests, $0.32. 7 filmstrips set, $30.00; teacher's guide to filmstrips, $0.96 ; Series 2, bks. 1-2, $1.56 ea; bks. 3-7, $1.68 ea; bks. 8-14 ea; teacher's guide to ser. 2. $2.40; pupil's response bks. $0.32 ea; Webster master's bks. 8-14, $16.00; sound symbol cards, $4.40; alphabet strips, $1.48; test bklet, $0.96; teacher's guide. $0.96; text films available; Series 3. bks. 8-21, $1.80 ea; pupil's response bks. 15-21, $0.32 ea; taacher's guide, $3.60; tests. $0.96; teacher's guide to tests,$0.96; bk. 15. 2nd ed. 1968. $1.80; programmed reading evaluation set, $130.00.

Programmed reading classroom starter set. 1967. $360.00.

from:
McGraw-Hill Book Co.
Princeton Road
Hightstown, N. J. 08520

Manchester Road
Manchester, MO 63062

8171 Redwood Highway
Novato, CA 94947

garden
breathe
trip

The next thing Ann knew, she and Mr. Roundabout were swinging in his gard___. "Oh," she said, hardly daring to ___reathe, "that was the most wonderful trip!"

"Trip?" said Mr. Roundabout, bringing the swing to a gentle stop. "Have you been on a ___rip, my dear?"

Initial Teaching Alphabet

As everyone knows, the English language is inconsistent. For instance, here are four different pronunciations of the letter A:

ape   apple   arm   all.

i.t.a. eliminates all such inconsistencies by spelling with a separate symbol for each "a" sound:

æp   appl   arm   aul

Eliminating contradictions in spelling and pronunciation makes learning to read and write a logical process. Anyone whose mind can grasp logic——and this includes three and four year olds——can learn to read with i.t.a. There are none of the complicated rules of the normal alphabet. Capitals in i.t.a. are just the regular size i.t.a. symbols written or printed a little larger. Each sound has its own symbol; there are 44 altogether.

After learning to read in i.t.a., the switch can be made to the conventional alphabet easily. The irregularities are not troublesome at this point, because the reader can read whole words at a time——not letter by letter——and can read for content.

I.t.a. is great for pre-school age children who want to read. At that age, kids get frustrated easily. The i.t.a. alphabet prevents the frustration by its consistency. We taught our 4 year old the sound of i.t.a. letters. Then we showed him how words could be made by blending sounds together. It took a while before he was able to blend the sounds by himself. But when that happened, he was then able to read.

I.t.a. is also good for teaching English to foreigners (many foreign languages also have one symbol or one group of symbols for each sound) and for remedial reading instruction. It is also a good tool for writing: once all the sounds of the symbols are learned, one can write anything he can say.

[Reviewed by Lora Ferguson

The ITA Handbook for Writing and Spelling
Mazurkiewicz and Tanyzer
1964; 50pp.

$2.00 postpaid
from:
Initial Teaching Alphabet Publications, Inc.
20 East 46th Street
New York, N. Y. 10017

or WHOLE EARTH CATALOG

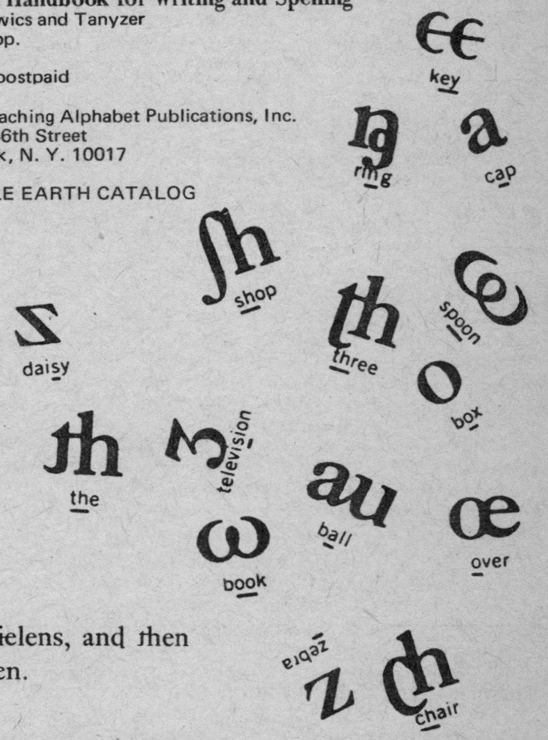

Cuisenaire Rods

The first rod is a small wooden cube with a 1 centimeter side. The second is twice as long with the same cross section. The third is three times as long as the first. Each length has its own color. With these rods, a child can learn arithmetical operations and mathematical relationships even though he recognizes no mathematical symbols. (Children are capable of grasping mathematical concepts before they have the mechanical ability to write. Therein lies one of the great advantages of Cuisenaire rods.) For example, if a child puts the first (white) and the second (red) rods end to end he can see that together they are equal in length to the third (green) rod. Once he realizes that a white and a red always equal a green, he has learned something quite general about addition and equality. If, later, the numeral "1" is associated with the first rod, "2" with the second rod and "3" with the third, he will be in a position to grasp at once that 1 + 2 = 3. But the rods have no absolute numerical value so that if the value "1" were assigned to the third rod rather than the first, the truth 1/3 + 2/3 = 1 would also be forthcoming as "proved" by the general rule that the child discovered with the rods.

What is happening here is that algebra (the general case) is being learned before arithmetic (specific cases), as logically, it should be.

This is undoubtedly one of the best pieces of teaching equipment ever invented. But it is important that you don't show children the truths that the rods demonstrate. They must be allowed to discover these themselves or it won't work.

[Suggested by Virginia Baker Reviewed by Jane Burton]

Catalog free

Basic classroom kit for 24 kids **$74.95** postpaid
Cuisenaire Home Mathematics Kit **$13.95** postpaid

from:
Cuisenaire Co. of America, Inc.
12 Church Street
New Rochelle, N. Y. 10805

Home Mathematics Kit available from
WHOLE EARTH CATALOG

þær wos næ wind tω blœ him neerer tω þe tree sœ þær hee stæd. hee cωd see þe huny, hee cωd smell þe huny, but hee cωdn't kwiet reeþ þe huny.

after a littl whiel hee caulld doun tω yω.

"cristofer robin!" hee sed in a loud whisper.

"hallœ!"

"ie þiŋk þe bees suspect sumþiŋ!"

"whot sort ov þiŋ?"

"ie dœn't næ. but sumþiŋ tells mee that þæ'r suspiſhius!"

"perhaps þæ þiŋk that yω'r after þær huny?"

"it mæ bee that. yω never can tell with bees."

From back cover of
Winni þe Pω
OUT OF PRINT

from:
E. P. Dutton
201 Park Avenue South
New York, N. Y. 10003

Free literature about i.t.a. is also available from:

Foundation for Educational Technology
World Building
Silver Springs, Maryland
20910

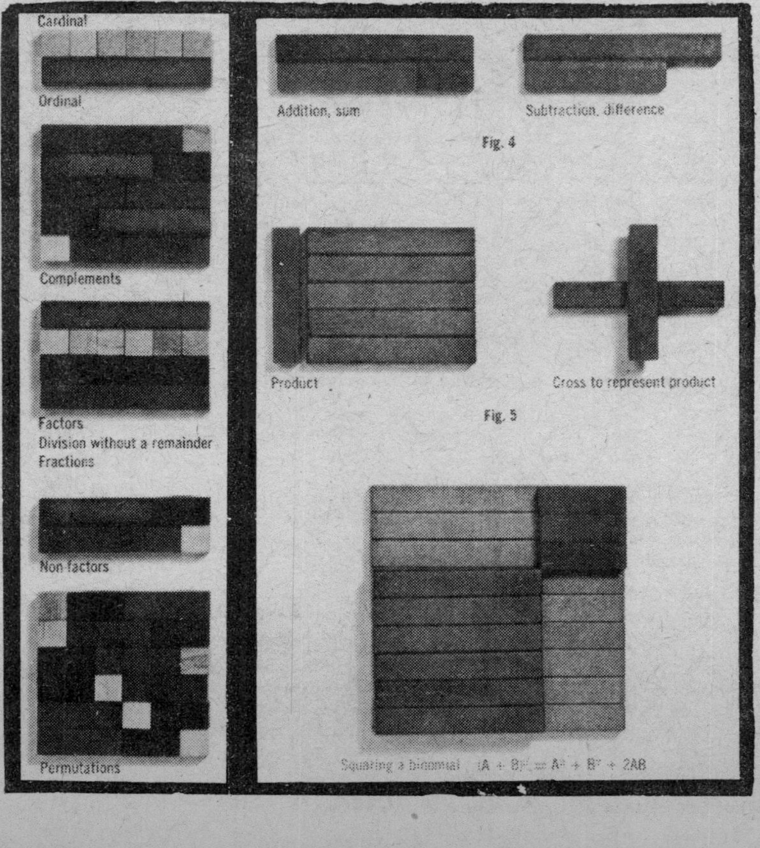

þær wos anuþer littl sielens, and þen he caulld doun tω yω agæn.

"cristofer robin!"

"yes?"

Cardinal
Ordinal
Complements
Factors
Non factors
Permutations

Addition, sum
Fig. 4
Product

Subtraction, difference
Cross to represent product
Fig. 5

Division without a remainder
Fractions

Squaring a binomial : (A + B)² = A² + B² + 2AB

I Know A Place

Good simple idea, good simple book; pure mirror: you write and illustrate a book whose subject (not object) is you. Kids groove. Me too. —SB

[Suggested by Joni Miller]

I Know A Place (Vols. 1,2,3)
Robert Tannen
1969; 134 pp.

$3.40 postpaid (20% off to schools) per set

from:
City Schools Curriculum Service, Inc.
60 Commercial Wharf
Boston, Mass. 02110 [Spanish edition is forthcoming.]

I Know a Place
I Know a Place
I Know a Place

by
and Robert Tannen

I know a person. A picture of this

person is on the next page.

The name of this person is

_____

The person was named

because

Looking and Seeing

1. Pattern and Space
2. The Development of Shape
3. The Shapes We Need
4. The Shape of Towns

This series of 4 books was designed for use in British schools. They are absolutely first-rate.

As befits such books, they are filled with excellent illustrations and the text is very explicit. While it would seem to have the 12-16 year olds in mind, the books are packed with stuff of interest to anyone who wants to know about the visual world and isn't too proud to read simple English.

The author's view is,

We have learnt to exert a certain amount of control over our world, over our surroundings and the lives we lead within them. But although we have gained much we have probably lost even more. We no longer possess the knowledge and the understanding to judge the things we make: our houses and factories, our implements and machines, our cities and roads. Because of this failure in judgement, we often find ourselves surrounded with such ugliness as would have horrified men of past ages. . . . It is now more important than ever that we should learn to understand the basic laws of the world around us, the man-made world and the world of nature.
(bk. 1, p. 2)

The illustrations are widely drawn, but are consistently relevant to man. Traditional crafts, modern building, technology, graphics, ergonometrics, D'Arcy-Thomson-like discussion of structure, social influences and industrial design are all dealt with.

One small foible——not all the illustrations are fully identified, except in the teachers' handbooks which are put out as small companions to the 4 books. These also deal with the short exercises which are set at the end of each section in the books.

[Suggested and reviewed by David and Lyn Roessler]

3

4

Looking and Seeing Books 1—4
Kurt Rowland
1966; 130 pp. each

$4.50 each postpaid

from:
Van Nostrand-Reinhold
450 West 33rd Street
New York, N. Y. 10001

Both the pine cone, **3,** *and the dahlia,* **4,** *have two sets of spirals. Count them and see if they are part of the Fibonacci series.*

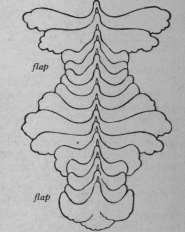

flap

flap

The same author has another excellent series, for younger children: 48 pp. each.

Learning to See *(Vols. 1-3)*
1968

$1.95 each (75¢ workbook for each available)

from:
Van Nostrand Reinhold
450 West 33rd Street
New York, N.Y. 10001

Musical Instruments Made to be Played

Dryad Press in England has a series of craft books that may be particularly apt for school kids. Their **Musical Instruments** *book has clear instructions and full-size plans for the fabrication of simple drums, shakers, xylophones, glockenspiels, dulcimers, psalteries, etc. Looks like fun. Other books of theirs we've seen include one on* **Netting** *(40¢) and one on* **Making and Playing Bamboo Pipes** *($2.70).*
—SB

[Suggested by Richard Raymond]

Tuning and Playing the Bowed Psaltery
The notes to which the strings should be tuned are given on the full size drawing on the inserted sheet. See also diagram 70 for the compass of the instrument. Tune the notes of the strings to the notes of a piano. In playing, rest the short side of the triangle against the body just above the left hip, and with the left hand, support the instrument towards the other end. Holding the bow in the right hand, bow the far end of each string. See plate 6. The diatonic scale of C is on the right. Reach over to the other side for the sharps and flats. It is necessary to lift the bow from string to string. True legato playing is impossible but it is easy to play sustained notes, and these are particularly acceptable when used with tuned percussion insturments.

SIMPLE STRING INSTRUMENTS

Musical Instruments Made to be Played
Ronald Roberts
1965; 81 pp. and plans

$7.50 postpaid from:
Dryad Press
Northgates, Leicester
ENGLAND

or WHOLE EARTH CATALOG

A pattern of instruments. In addition to showing many of the instruments described in the book, this photograph shows the frame and soundboard assembly of a Spinet and also a Fidel with its bow. Nearby lies the template for a viola back.

PART SEVEN

THE TRACE FORK NEWS
by Barry Berry
(reprinted from the Blaine <u>Herald</u>)

Well, I know a lot of you were disappointed that there wasn't any news last week. It didn't mean that nothing was going on. Something's always going on around Trace Fork and up and down Rockhouse Creek, but I just felt too bad last week to write it up. I've had a virus going on ten days now. I don't know what it was, but it sure makes you feel awful when you get it. I'm not plum over it yet but I do feel some better this week although I'm still not up to making a full report. This time next week I intend to be well enough to write half the paper full, but I'm going to take it kind of easy this week because I sure don't want any relapse of whatever it was that I've been down with.

Dolly Huff told me that Mr. and Mrs. Dwayne Holcomb were down from LaPorte, Indiana over the weekend visiting her mother, who is 88 years old.

Aunt Eunice Bartlett and her son Denver went to Lexington to visit Ira Combs, who had surgery on his leg. They report the operation was a success and that Ira should be home in a week or two. Denver drove his new Chevrolet.

Mr. and Mrs. Joseph Cooney have also been to Lexington lately. Their daughter Sarah finished nurse's training at Good Samaritan Hospital and her parents went down to the graduation. Sarah is a registered nurse now. Seems like only yesterday she was here in high school, cheerleading. Congratulations, Sarah. Why don't you come on back home and be a nurse in one of our fine mountain hospitals? We need good nurses and doctors. We need all of our young people to come back home to live.

But it seems like there's just not enough opportunity here for young people any more. I'd hate to know the figures on just how many of our fine young people have moved away in the last few years.

(continued)

The Psychology of Children's Art

An elegant masterpiece on an inelegant subject, children's art. And they mean young children ages two through ten. Rhoda Kellogg, having analyzed some one million pieces of children's art, has categorized their early scribbling patterns into seventeen consistently recognizable stages and basic shapes. She has found, and you'll see this with her through a startlingly clear picture essay presentation, that children from every part of the world go through the same artistic maturational stages in terms of the identical shapes, designs and symbols that they use. "If children everywhere are so alike, then it may be possible to build upon man's common heritage rather than to founder upon his differences." The Psychology of Children's Art is a visual treat and an educational rarity—it would be a welcome gift to new parents, old parents and non-parents.

[Suggested and reviewed by Carol Guyton Goodell]

The Psychology of Children's Art
Rhoda Kellogg with Scott O'Dell
1967; 110 pp.

OUT OF PRINT

from:
CRM Books
1104 Camino del Mar
Del Mar, Calif. 92014

or

WHOLE EARTH CATALOG

The mandala, a simple crossed circle, has always been one of man's favorite compositions. This is the finger painting of a three-year-old.

Creative Drawing

Ernst Röttger has a fruitful technique for graphic exploration (or any other kind). He gives the students a medium— usually very simple— and some harsh constraints— usually very simple— and lets them find their own way out of fresh air. I suspect that this kind of medium exploration is better the more "useless" it is. Good book.

—SB
[Suggested by Dr. Morton Grosser]

Creative Drawing
Ernst Rottger, Dieter Klante
1963; 143 pp.

$3.95 postpaid

from:
Van Nostrand-Reinhold Co.
450 West 33rd Street
New York, N.Y. 10001

or WHOLE EARTH CATALOG

Van Nostrand-Reinhold also has Röttger books on Paper Design, Wood Design, Clay Design.

In his early pictorial work, the child is just beginning to paint and draw animals. He also tries buildings, trees, flowers, boats, cars and airplanes. In child art, humans become animals when there are ears on top of the head instead of hats or hair.

The critical period in child art is between the ages of five and seven. The child who feels free to use the colors and basic shapes which please him will continue to flourish artistically when he moves into pictorial work.

BLOWN LINES

A thick line drawn on the paper with India ink. By blowing sideways at the line the ink runs over the paper at random, producing bizarre patterns. What at first seems to be an aimless blue becomes quite controllable after a little practice. If a drinking straw is used for blowing, the stream of air is concentrated and easily aimed. Patterns can be influenced in many different ways—the distance of the straw from the paper, the angle at which it is held, blowing straight, crooked, evenly or in bursts or by moving the tube. The best way of exploring the possibilities is to begin by free experimentation, then the results achieved by chance should be brought under control and used consciously. The few illustrated examples show the enormous potential variety. Formal patterns of this kind have a unique character which is quite unattainable by drawing. If colour is also employed the number of possible combinations is greatly increased.

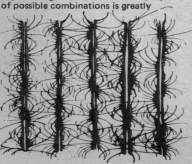

In the Kingdom of Mescal

a fairy tale for adults, with pictures, tuck somebody in, and read it out loud.

—jd

In the Kingdom of Mescal
Georg Schafer and Nan Cuz
1968, 70; 30 pp.

from:
Shambhala Publication
1409 5th Street
Berkeley, California 94710

OUT OF PRINT

They were in a strange world of pools and craters. Here and there he saw tender green shoots. Clouds of steam rose towards the sky from gaping holes and it was raining, like on earth. Then they went on.

"If you still had the serpent Time in you," said the Lord, as they stood on another mountain top, "you would have to die and be born again as many times as there are drops of water in all the seas in the world. It would take that long before you could stand on this star with me."

TOPSYS & TURVYS

A fun little book for kids by Peter Newell with 74 drawings which are topsy-turvy.

[Suggested and reviewed by Gordon Ashby]

Available from:
Dover Publications, Inc.
180 Varick Street
New York 14, N.Y.
Paperbound .$1.25

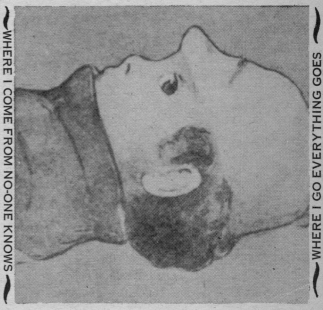

WHERE I COME FROM NO-ONE KNOWS ➤ — WHERE I GO EVERYTHING GOES ➤

Golden Handbooks

I think the handbooks and nature guides from Golden Press are wonderful, and by no means just for kids. They're economical in size and cost, intelligently researched and edited, well illustrated in color, thoroughly indexed with good bibliographies. In any of their subject areas, I'd start with the Golden book. —SB

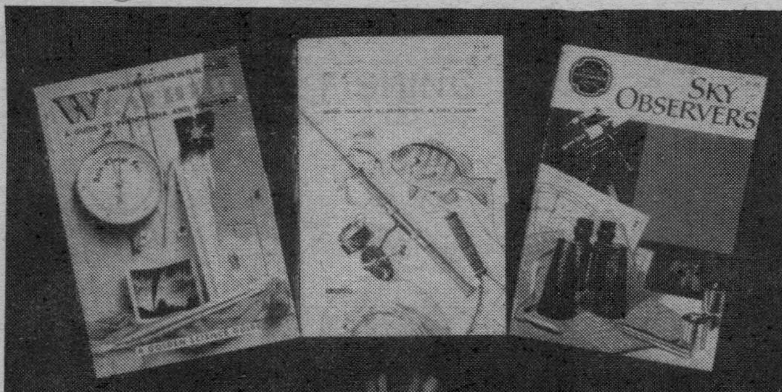

SKY OBSERVERS

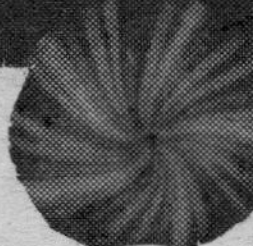

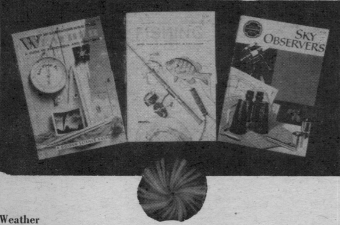

Weather
Paul E. Lehr, R. Will Burnett, Herbert S. Zim
1957, 1965; 160 pp.

Guide to Fresh and Salt Water Fishing
George S. Fichter and Phil Francis
1965; 160 pp.

Sky Observer's Guide
R. Newton Mayall,
Margaret Mayall,
Jerome Wyckoff
1959, 1965; 160 pp.

$1.50 each, postpaid

from:
Golden Press Division
Western Publishing Co., Inc.
1220 Mound Avenue
Racine, Wisconsin 53404

or WHOLE EARTH CATALOG

Other books available from The Golden Press:

Golden Nature Guides
Birds
Flowers
Insects
Trees
Reptiles and Amphibians
Stars
Mammals
Seashores
Fishes
Fossils
Gamebirds
Zoology
Sea Shells of the World
Rocks and Minerals
Butterflies and Moths
Non-Flowering Plants
Insect Pests
Pond Life
Zoo Animals
Spiders

Golden Field Guides
Birds of North America
Trees of North America
Sea Shells of North America

Golden Handbooks
Sailing
Photography
Guns
Power Boats
Camping
Henry Gasser's Guide to Painting
Skiing
Antiques
Sports Cars
Scuba Diving

Golden Regional Guides
The Southeast
The Southwest
The Pacific Northwest
Everglades National Park
The Rocky Mountains
Acadia National Park
Washington, D.C.
Israel and the Holy Land
Mexico

Weather will generally remain fair when:
The wind blows gently from west or northwest (p. 66).
Barometer remains steady or rises (pp. 85-88).
Cumulus clouds dot the summer sky in the afternoon (p. 20).
Morning fog breaks or "burns off" by noon (evidence of clear sky above).

Rainy weather or snow may come when:
Cirrus clouds thicken and are followed by lower clouds (p. 88). (Particularly true if barometer is dropping.)
There is a ring around the moon (pp. 17 & 88). (Particularly true if barometer is dropping.)
Puffy cumulus clouds begin to develop vertically (p. 20).
Sky is dark and threatening to the west (p. 85).
Southerly wind increases in speed with clouds moving from west (p. 85).
The wind—particularly a north wind—shifts in a counterclockwise direction—that is, from north to west to south (pp. 85-88).
The barometer falls steadily (pp. 85-88).

Weather will generally clear when:
Bases of clouds show steady rise to higher types (p. 85).
The wind—particularly an east wind—shifts to the west (p. 85).
The barometer rises rapidly (pp. 85 and 88).

Temperature will usually fall when:
Wind blows from—or shifts to—north or northwest (p. 85).
Night sky is clear and wind is light (pp. 9 and 14).
The barometer rises steadily in winter (p. 85).

Temperature will usually rise when:
Wind is from south, particularly with cloud cover at night or clear sky during the day (pp. 9 and 88).

Seasonal Lag

August is hotter than June even though the sun is more nearly overhead and the day is longest on June 22. In terms of solar radiation reaching the earth, May, June, and July should be our warmest months. But June, July, and August actually are. Why?

During the year the earth, as a whole, loses precisely the same amount of heat it receives from the sun. But as the sun moves north in spring, our part of the earth gains heat faster than heat is lost. On June 22 it is receiving maximum solar radiation. The heat gain continues to exceed heat loss until maximum warmth is reached, usually in late July. Heat gain continues to exceed heat loss, at a diminishing rate, until about August 31. Then our part of the earth starts to lose heat faster than it receives it, and begins to cool down. The process is like starting a fire in a stove: the roaring fire heats the room slowly, but the room will stay warm for a while after the fire has died down. The same heat lag accounts for the fact that the warmest time of day is usually about 3 p.m.——not noon, when the sun's rays are most intense.

Weather

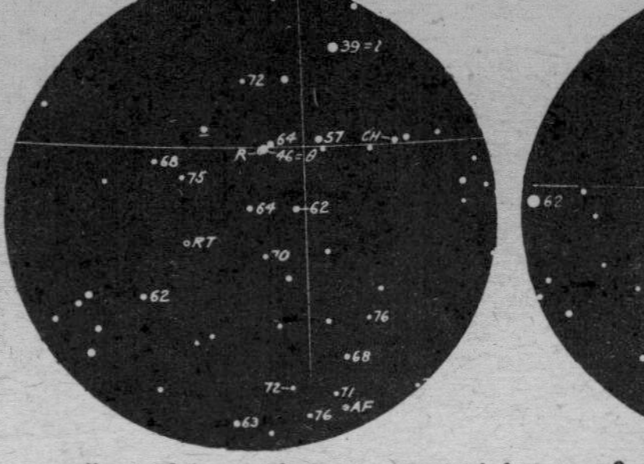

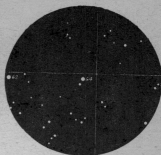

Effect of increasing power: At left is a 7° field in Cygnus as seen with 7x50 binoculars. At right, centered on the same star, is the reduced and inverted field seen through a small telescope at about 35X. Numbers on map indicate magnitudes of stars (decimal point before last digit omitted).

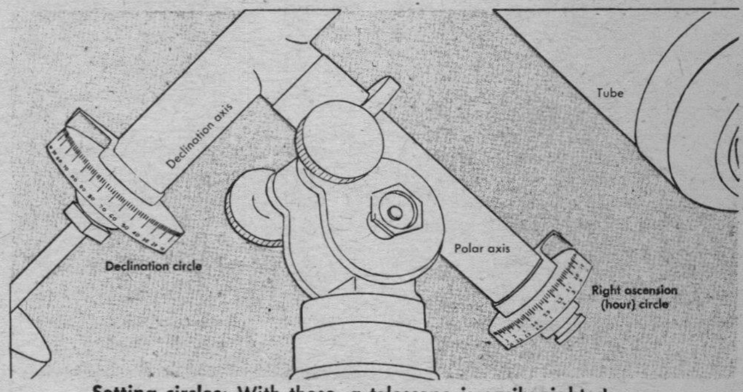

Tube
Declination axis
Declination circle
Polar axis
Right ascension (hour) circle

Setting circles: With these, a telescope is easily sighted.

Sky Observer's Guide

In summer, the surface water warms to well above 39.2°F. and floats on the heavier water below. Mixing ceases, and lake stratifies into 3 layers. Fish are found in warm top layer, which is rich in oxygen, and a few in or near the middle layer, a zone of rapidly descending temperature. The bottom layer is cold and low in oxygen.

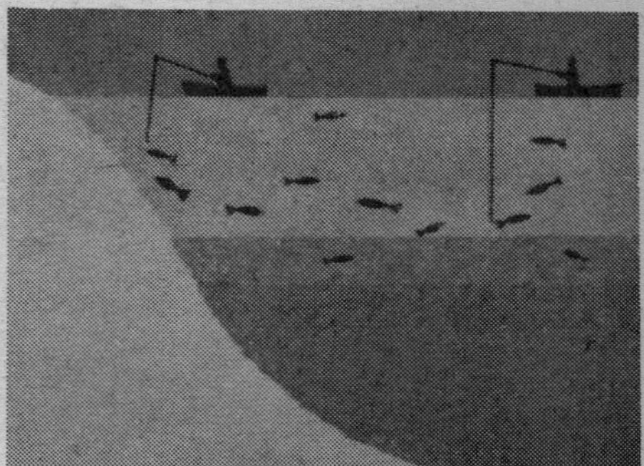

HOW TO SURF CAST

Before attempting a cast with a revolving-spool surf reel, wet your line. This prevents it from burning your thumb on the cast. Shift reel into free spool and put thumb firmly on the spool. Let out 2 or 3 feet of line, and hold the rod pointed low opposite the direction of your cast, the sinker resting on the ground. Now bring the rod up with a powerful overhead sweep, pulling downward with your left hand and pushing upward with your right. As the rod comes up past the vertical, ease your thumb pressure and let the spool turn. Let the line run out under your thumb; removing your thumb will cause a backlash. As the sinker hits the water, thumb spool hard. Surf spinning is done with same motions, using forefinger instead of thumb to control line.

Fishing

Andrew Lang Fairy Books

Everybody suggests these books, but nobody wants to review them, which I take as a good sign: it's too rich a bundle to bag. I haven't read the series. I have been paging through, and it's clear the stories (gathered and published by Andrew Lang around 1905) are made of meat and potatoes and starvation and eagles and ladies and hermits and ogres and hard changes and not cotton candy. The turn-of-century illustrations by H. J. Ford are romantic. —SB
[Suggested by Holly Baer]

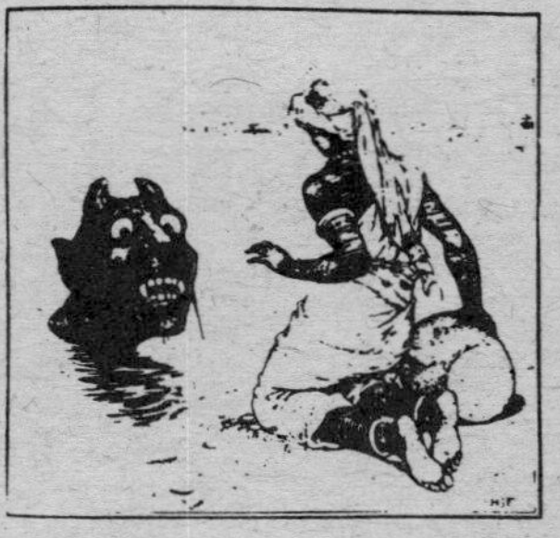

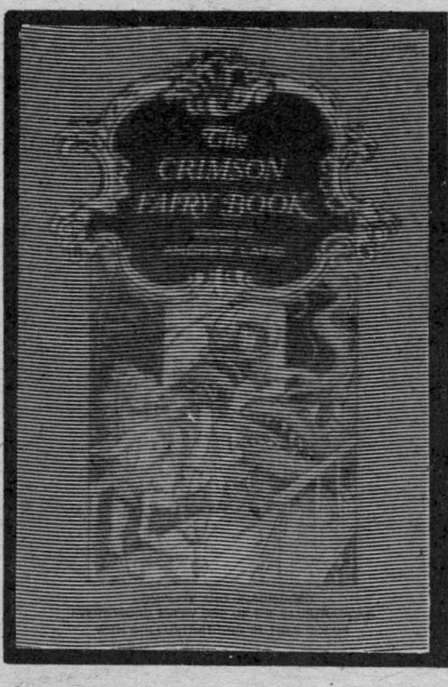

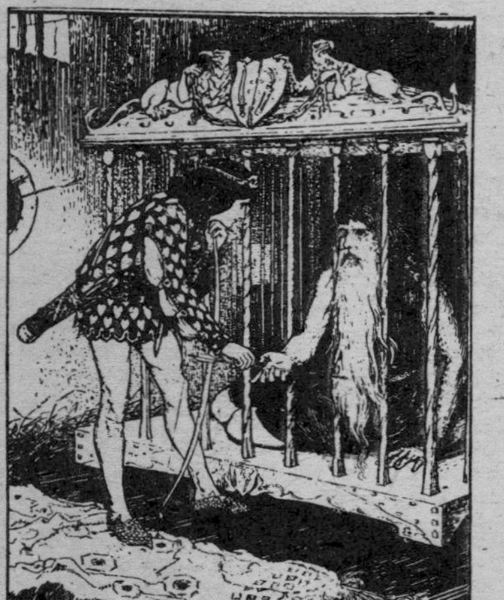

The Golden-bearded Man Gives up the Arrow

THE BLUE FAIRY BOOK. 37 tales. 8 plates. 130 additional illustrations. ix + 390pp. $5\frac{3}{8} \times 8\frac{1}{2}$. *Paperbound* $2.50

THE GREEN FAIRY BOOK. 42 tales. 13 plates. 87 additional illustrations xiii + 366pp. $5\frac{3}{8} \times 8\frac{1}{2}$. *Paperbound* 2.00

THE BROWN FAIRY BOOK. 32 stories. 30 plates, 8 in color 20 additional illustrations. xii + 350pp. $5\frac{3}{8} \times 8\frac{1}{2}$. *Paperbound* 2.00

THE YELLOW FAIRY BOOK. 48 tales. 22 plates. 82 additional illustrations. xviii + 321pp. $5\frac{3}{8} \times 8\frac{1}{2}$. *Paperbound* 3.50

THE VIOLET FAIRY BOOK 35 tales. 41 plates, 8 in color 33 additional illustrations. xii + 388pp. $5\frac{3}{8} \times 8\frac{1}{2}$. *Paperbound* 3.50

THE RED FAIRY BOOK. 37 tales. 4 plates. 93 additional illustrations. x + 367pp. $5\frac{3}{8} \times 8\frac{1}{2}$. *Paperbound* 3.50

THE PINK FAIRY BOOK. 41 tales. 34 plates. 36 additional illustrations. xii + 360pp. $5\frac{3}{8} \times 8\frac{1}{2}$. *Paperbound* 2.00

THE CRIMSON FAIRY BOOK. 36 stories. 43 plates, 8 in color 10 additional illustrations. xi + 371pp. $5\frac{3}{8} \times 8\frac{1}{2}$. *Paperbound* 2.50

THE GREY FAIRY BOOK. 35 tales. 32 plates. 28 additional illustrations. xiv + 387pp. $5\frac{3}{8} \times 8\frac{1}{2}$. *Paperbound* 2.00

THE LILAC FAIRY BOOK. 33 stories. 26 plates, 6 in color 26 additional illustrations. xv + 369pp. $5\frac{3}{8} \times 8\frac{1}{2}$. *Paperbound* 2.50

THE OLIVE FAIRY BOOK. 29 stories. 28 plates, 8 in color. 22 additional illustrations. xv + 336pp. $5\frac{3}{8} \times 8\frac{1}{2}$. *Paperbound* 2.00

THE ORANGE FAIRY BOOK. 33 stories. 25 plates, 8 in color 33 additional illustrations. xiv + 358pp. $5\frac{3}{8} \times 8\frac{1}{2}$. *Paperbound* 3.50

from:
Dover Publications, Inc.
180 Varick Street
New York, N. Y. 10014

or WHOLE EARTH CATALOG

The Yellow Fairy Book, The Violet Fairy Book, The Red Fairy Book and *The Orange Fairy Book* are $3.50 from Peter Smith, Publisher, Inc., 6 Lexington Ave., Magnolia, MA. 01930.

"Someone has told the king that I have prophesied that a child shall be born this night in the palace, who can speak all the languages in the world and play every musical instrument. I am no magician to bring these things to pass, but he says that if it does not happen he will have me dragged through the city at a horse's tail till I die."

"Do not trouble yourself," answered the stork. "I will manage to find such a child, for I am the king of the storks whose life you spared, and now I can repay you for it."

There was once a king's son who told his father that he wished to marry.

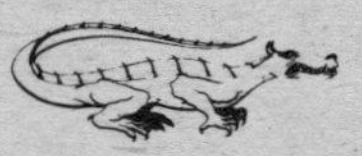

Mr. and Mrs. Elmer Hampton from Cutshin in Leslie County visited his sister, Mrs. Ruth Gordon on Ten Mile creek two weekends ago.

Phyllis and William Sims have a new baby girl. Her name is Janell. Congratulations, Phyllis and William.

I didn't get to go to church the last two Sundays but Brother Bagby says attendance has been real good.

Hagen Banks made the honor roll at Morehead University the last semester. His mother, Theda, said this was the third straight semester Hagen made the honor roll. Hagen is going to summer school so he can finish college in three years. He is studying to be a biology teacher.

Sammy Kirk has been home on furlough from Fort Knox the past couple of weeks, but he has to leave Saturday for Vietnam. I know his mother, Mrs. Cinda Banks, will hate to see him go so bad. Readers will remember that it has only been a little over a year since Cinda lost her husband Arlis in a mining accident. May the Lord watch over Sammy and return him safely to us as soon as possible.

Our community was saddened last week when Emmit Collier died. Most people didn't even know that Emmit was all that sick, till they took him to the hospital in Blaine. Leonard Godsey, who was a good friend of Emmit's, said he was bad sick for a month or more, and that he tried to get Emmit to go to the hospital, but he wouldn't. Emmit lived by himself up at the head of Trace Fork and didn't get out much. I didn't get to go to the funeral but everybody that went said it was real nice. Brother Bagby officiated, and Dorothy Thornton sang. They buried Emmit in the family cemetary up on the old Collier homeplace. The road up Trace Fork's so bad any more they had to haul the casket up in a sled.

Relatives at the funeral included Emmit's niece Marcella, and her husband Doyle Maggard, and their children, all from Cincinnati, plus Marcella's brother, David Ray, who was already here visiting.

Lee Sergeant said that his neighbor, Mrs. Lois Pope's application for a Black Lung pension on her husband, the late Kermit Pope, has been approved, and that Mrs. Pope will soon begin to receive the monthly benefits. As far as I know, Mrs. Pope is the first in this end of the county to have her Black Lung application approved. But there are many more who ought to receive those benefits if justice is to be done to all those whose health was destroyed working in the mines.

Well, that's all for this week. My head's starting to hurt again so I'm going to quit and go out on the porch a while.

Audubon

I'd call this the strongest ecological-call-to-arms publication we've got. Its illustrations (both photographs and paintings) have visceral impact. The articles are thorough and authoritative. Audubon Society is no longer just birds but all life and it's into appreciation as much as protection. Like National Geographic, it's healthy just to have around the house. I keep thinking of the canary the miners kept for warning of poison gas.

—SB
[Suggested by Ursula M. Vann]

Audubon
Les Line, ed.

$10/yr (bi-monthly)
Student membership $6 (includes magazine subscription)
from:
Audubon
950 Third Avenue
New York, N.Y. 10022

The fact is, however, that the sportsman's code of ethics just doesn't exist anymore. And if you don't believe it, examine the facts of a story that broke in *The New York Times* on Sunday, February 7th. And then watch the bang-bang books to see if they report this odious episode, complete with names and addresses of every hunter involved (which are readily available). If they do, perhaps there is some hope for the future of hunting.

The headline read, "35 Named in Raids on Bighorn Sheep," and the story told how rare desert bighorn rams were being slaughtered illegally on secret safaris into the Jacumba Mountains east of San Diego, California, not far from the Mexican border.

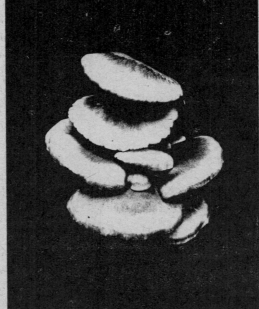

For fees as high as $3,500 apiece, wealthy sportsmen from across the country— from Washington, California, Vermont, Oregon, Colorado, Idaho, Pennsylvania, New York, Texas, Oklahoma, Missouri, Hawaii, and Canada— were led into these sere hills to shoot an animal that has been totally protected in California since 1872. Three races of the bighorn were slain, and two are on the U.S. Fish and Wildlife Service list of America's rare and endangered species.

Their guide, according to state and federal wildlife agents, was a man who until recently had been a director (and a charter member) of the National Society for the Conservation of Bighorn Sheep, who had long been one of the organization's most ardent workers in seeking better food and water supplies for this vanishing species, who for years had aided the California Department of Fish and Game on its annual bighorn census— and thus knew all of the rams' haunts.

And he not only led the expeditions, but he mounted the trophies at his own taxidermist shop. A raid there uncovered 31 skulls of bighorns, plus hides, capes, and one fully mounted ram. Forty more ram heads from the Jacumba herd have been seized by federal wildlife agents in hunters' trophy rooms in thirteen states and Canada.

The take? Thousands and thousands of dollars over a period of three years.

Smithsonian

The good old Smithsonian Institution has a new magazine, similar to Natural History, plus more Americana. Some very original articles.

—SB

Smithsonian
Edward K. Thompson, ed.

$11.50/yr (monthly)

from:
Smithsonian Institution
Membership Services
P.O. Box 2606
Greenwich, CT 06830

His chickens provide meat and eggs equally as good. The secret, Rodale is eager to reveal, is in their environment. They cluck contentedly in a chicken house unusually clean and almost odorless, thanks to another organic wrinkle. The chickens roost on a dropping pit primed with several layers of soil and rotted cattle manure. This culture, rich in bacteria, acts as a deodorizing agent on the droppings, which, as they are digested, provide a continuing source of loamy compost for gardens and fields.

Rodale also "fertilizes" with rocks and tin cans. In 16 Howard cylinders (1/1000-acre garden plots rimmed with low concrete walls), he has experimented with metals as growing aids, coming up with surprising results. For instance, he once planted string beans in all the cylinders, adding cans to four, wire mesh to another four, and cultivating eight plots normally as controls. The metal-enriched areas yielded 50 percent more beans—with higher vitamin content— than the control plots. Rodale borrows from the Chinese in growing vegetables among rocks. He bends to pull up a clump of parsley. Some of its roots cling to a rock, sucking out natural trace minerals, Rodale explains.

One Million

Working familiarity with large numbers is an acquired skill. (Until this gig I could never handle a concept like "twenty-thousand dollars" without sitting down— "How much is that in candy bars?" Or, this printing of the CATALOG is 600,000 lbs of paper; that's, let's see, 300 tons of cultural/ ecological karma.)

This well-made book of dots and notes can make formerly impossible numbers relatable to each other and to life. It's fun. Godwork.

—SB

One Million
Hendrik Hertzberg
1970; 211 pp.

Out of Print

from:
Simon & Schuster, Inc.

630 Fifth Ave.
New York, N.Y. 10020

or WHOLE EARTH CATALOG

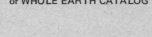

955,396—Dollars earned on costs totaling $14,293 by Western Electric on a U.S. Government contract for checking over "launcher loaders"—a profit of 6600 per cent.

955,484—Vehicles recalled by automobile manufacturers in 1968 to check for potential safety defects.

Natural History

The publication of the Natural History Museum in New York, this magazine covers wildlife, anthropology, science, archaeology, history, conservation, and more. It's always good, occasionally outstanding. Excellent bimonthly night sky map.

—SB

Natural History

$8.00 year (10 issues)

from:
The American Museum of Natural History
Central Park West at 79th Street
New York, New York 10024

The reef is perhaps the most complex community in all of nature, where plants and animals of infinite variety live together in seeming confusion. But even here there is an orderly balance and interrelationship among organisms. The gorgonians provide concealment and shelter for fish, both hunter and hunted. Brittle stars and feather stars perch in their branches, and certain crabs and shrimps make their homes nowhere else. All the species of two important families of snails— the egg cowries and the coral snails— prey exclusively on the polyps of various corals. But the most fantastic relationship of all is the partnership, or symbiosis, between minute plant cells and the corals and most other coelenterates, whose living tissue they inhabit. These plants, known as zooxanthellae, need the carbon dioxide produced by the animal, which in turn utilizes the surplus oxygen and food produced by the plants through a complex enzyme system, increase the coral's ability to deposit calcium carbonate and so make it possible for them to produce the vast framework of the reef.

•

South Vietnam approximates the size of New England; the area sprayed is larger than Vermont; the area bulldozed almost that of Rhode Island. While none of Vietnams's 43 provinces has escaped, some have been attacked herbicidally with particular intensity and frequency. Among these are the Rung Sat region in Gia Dinh Province southeast of Saigon, Tay Ninh Province (War Zone C), which is northwest of Saigon, and Long Khanh Province (War Zone D) northeast of Saigon— the last previously contained major stands of South Vietnam's magnificent virgin tropical forest.

Most forest spraying has been done with a 1:1 mixture of 2,4-D and 2,4,5-T, Agent Orange in military terminology; some with a 4:1 mixture of 2,4-D and picloram, or Agent White; and small amounts with dimethyl arsenic acid, Agent Blue. The use of Agent Orange was discontinued in early 1970, largely in favor of Agent White. Agent Orange was applied at the rate of 25 pounds of active ingredients per acre; Agent White at 8 pounds; and Agent Blue at 9.

This book is a yardstick, a ruler divided into a million parts instead of a dozen. The reader may use it to measure any quantity between one and one million: it will provide a visual equivalent thereof.

There are 5,000 dots to a page— 10,000 on each double-page spread. The progression is marked, and a little counting and multiplying will yield the dot that corresponds to any number one likes.

Notes are scattered— like mileposts— here and there in the inside margins. Each note corresponds to a number, and the dot signifying that number is readily identifiable.

955,001—960,000

Patterns of Survival

As far as I'm concerned education and evolution are conceptually indistinguishable. If you know how to evolve you're ahead of whatever game is going. For example, the way to be safe from dinosaur bites is to be little, fast, furry, warm-blooded, and smart. (The way to be in hazard of dinosaur bites is to be another dinosaur.) We're talking about education in the school of survival, which every school is, despite pastel walls.

This well-illustrated and personal book is the best introduction I've seen to the fascination of evolutionary perspective on the living and dying world we take part in.

—SB

Patterns of Survival
Lorus and Margery Milne
1967; 339 pp.

$8.95 postpaid

from:
Prentice-Hall
Englewood Cliffs, N. J. 07632

or WHOLE EARTH CATALOG

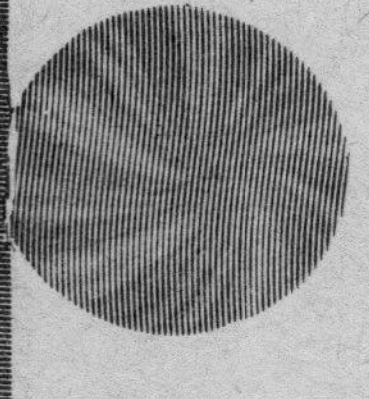

We remember that Nietzsche said: "In the architectural structure, man's pride, man's triumph over gravitation, man's will to power, assume a visible form." But should we now go the extra step and imitate the successful corals? From them we could learn that defense against gravity is not enough to give us power for survival. We might build into our urban architecture an added wealth of plant partners to clean the air and give us extra food. Perhaps rows of wheat plants and a potato vine should join the geranium flowering on the window sill, as a first step in the right direction.

•

Flea powders containing poison deadly to adult fleas were puffed into the dirty clothing and dirty homes where the parasites were numerous. But poison proved to be just a new kind of dirt. It killed only 99 percent of the fleas, or slightly more. A few of the parasites were resistant, and so were their offspring. In just a few years the fleas became as numerous as ever and virtually immune to the poison in concentrations that previously had seemed effective. So long as the creature survives, it still has a chance to evolve a little more and make a comeback everywhere.

•

Not so very long ago the eminent British biologist Joseph Bancroft of Cambridge University set down his thoughts on what he called Features in the Architecture of Physiological Function. He was impressed by the number of ways in which living things have escaped "from the tyranny" of the chemical rule shown by the equation of Arrhenius. He saw how far-reaching was the change when, instead of just slowing down as the weather chilled, the ancestors of mammals and birds began to shiver inside their coats of fur and feathers. Here was "the cold-blooded animal successfully adopting ingenious mechanisms, first biochemical, then physiological, in order to adapt its heart to the variations of its environment; the warm-blooded animal discarding what its cold-blooded predecessor has laboriously beaten out, invoking the nervous system to reverse the normal biochemical relationship and gaining a new freedom by adapting, not itself to the internal environment, but the internal environment to itself."

The Web of Life

A good anecdotal introduction to ecology. —SB

The Web of Life
John H. Storer
1953, 1956; 128 pp.

$.95 postpaid

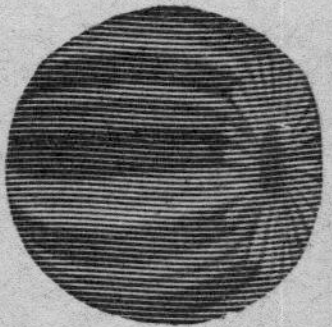

from:
New American Library
1301 Avenue of the Americas
New York, N. Y. 10019

or WHOLE EARTH CATALOG

In the White River National Forest in Colorado a heavy wind blew down several groups of Englemann spruce trees. It broke many of the tree roots, weakening the flow of sap, but left enough roots in the ground to keep the trees alive. Thousands of beetles gained entrance to these weakened trees and found a paradise to work in; for the underside of each tree, buried in a mat of crushed branches, was protected from the hunting woodpeckers. The most effective of these woodpeckers, the arctic three-toed, hunts this area chiefly in winter, but now, with the fallen trees covered by snow, the beetles were completely safe from their chief enemy and they multiplied.

First they killed the fallen trees. Then the dead trees became a focus of infection for the surrounding forest, as more beetles in search of food attacked the healthy trees nearby. The potent sap of these growing trees drove out the first attackers, but millions more followed, puncturing the bark and weakening the sap flow until later hordes gained easy entrance. These swarms outgrew the appetites of the woodpeckers, whose numbers were adjusted to a normal beetle population.

In a few years the entire forest, covering many thousands of acres, was dead or dying. Four thousand million board feet of timber stood rotting where it died, most of it wasted; for in this rough mountain country it was not worth building roads to bring it out. There was no young, productive forest left to justify the cost of these roads.

The entire forest was doomed, and all the great dependent community of living things had lost its food and shelter. This community too must go, simply because one of its smallest members had escaped its natural controls and found too much prosperity.

Never Cry Wolf

Farley Mowat is a good wolf-watcher.

—jd

Never Cry Wolf
Farley Mowat
1963; 176 pp.

$.75 postpaid

from:
Dell Publishing Co.
750 Third Avenue
New York, New York 10017

or WHOLE EARTH CATALOG

Quite by accident I had pitched my tent within ten yards of one of the major paths used by the wolves when they were going to, or coming from, their hunting grounds to the westward; and only a few hours after I had taken up residence one of the wolves came back from a trip and discovered me and my tent. He was at the end of a hard night's work and was clearly tired and anxious to go home to bed. He came over a small rise fifty yards from me with his head down, his eyes half-closed, and a preoccupied air about him. Far from being the preternaturally alert and suspicious beast of fiction, this wolf was so self-engrossed that he came straight on to within fifteen yards of me, and might have gone right past the tent without seeing it at all, had I not banged my elbow against the teakettle, making a resounding clank. The wolf's head came up and his eyes opened wide, but he did not stop or falter in his pace. One brief, sidelong glance was all he vouchsafed to me as he continued on his way.

•

Apart from the fact that there are only a fixed number of homesteads available to the wolves, their abundance is apparently further restricted by a built-in birth-control mechanism. Thus it happens that when food species are abundant (or the wolf population is scanty) bitches give birth to large litters—sometimes as many as eight pups. But if the wolves are too numerous, or food is scarce, the number of pups in a litter may fall to as few as one or two. This is also true of other arctic animals, such as rough-legged hawks. In a year when the small mammal population is high, roughlegs will lay five or six eggs in a clutch; but when mice and lemmings are scarce, they may lay a single egg or they may not breed at all.

Peterson Field Guide Series

The thing that is so nice about these guides is that everyone of them has a lot of stuff in it. The books are easy to use and well-illustrated enough so that if you look carefully you can identify most any species of bird, flower, bug, etc. that you meet up with. Too bad they aren't all paperback so that you could put all of them in your pack.

[Reviewed by Terri Gunesch]

at present, there are 19 books in the series. they are generally $5.95 each. here is the list:

* 1. **A Field Guide to the Birds** (paper $3.95) (eastern land and water birds)
1R. **A Field Guide to Bird Songs** (two 12-inch LP records)
* 2. **A Field Guide to Western Birds** ($4.95)
2R. **A Field Guide to Western Bird Songs** (three 12-inch LP records) ($14.95)
3. **A Field Guide to the Shells** (Atlantic and Gulf Coasts)
4. **A Field Guide to the Butterflies** (Eastern North America)
* 5. **A Field Guide to the Mammals** ($5.95)
6. **A Field Guide to Shells of the Pacific Coast and Hawaii** (including the Gulf of California) ($3.95)

SHORT-TAILED HAWK
Dark phase

* 7. **A Field Guide to Rocks and Minerals** ($6.95)
8. **A Field Guide to the Birds of Britain and Europe** ($5.95)
9. **A Field Guide to Animal Tracks** ($5.95)
10. **A Field Guide to the Ferns and Their Related Families** (Northeastern and Central North America) ($5.95)
11. **A Field Guide to Trees and Shrubs** (Northeastern and Central North America) ($3.95)
*12. **A Field Guide to Reptiles and Amphibians** ($5.95) (Eastern North America)
13. **A Field Guide to the Birds of Texas and Adjacent States**
*14. **A Field Guide to Rocky Mountain Wildflowers** ($3.95)
*15. **A Field Guide to the Stars and Planets** ($6.95)
*16. **A Field Guide to Western Reptiles and Amphibians** ($5.95)
*17. **A Field Guide to Wildflowers** ($3.95) (Northeastern and North Central North America)
18. **A Field Guide to the Mammals of Britain and Europe**
19. **A Field Guide to the Insects** (America North of Mexico)

* indicates those books carried by WHOLE EARTH CATALOG

these are obtainable from:

Houghton Mifflin Company
2 Park Street
Boston, Massachusetts 02107

—jd

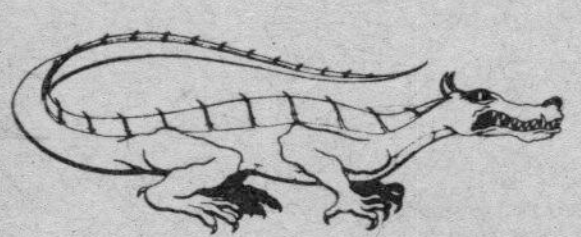

DEAR FLASH

Well, man, it's far out. In the last ten days me and Estelle split up, I've gone crazy and an uncle of mine here in Kentucky has died. I tended to him the best I could but he died, and we buried him on the hillside last Saturday afternoon. I helped dig his grave.

And now I'm living here in his house, an old house my grandfather built about 1920, a house my father grew up in, and that I lived in a while myself when I was a boy. It's an amazing scene. This hill, and all the hills around here, were strip-mined a couple of years ago. I mean, man, they've been destroyed. Bulldozers pushed the tops of the mountains into the valleys so they could scoop the coal up with machines. About eighty per cent of my grandfather's farm here is under mud now, and out behind the house there's this incredible big mound of mud, this big wall of it, about fifteen feet high, waiting on a rain to loosen it enough to flow right on through this very kitchen. I wish you could see it.

In fact, consider coming to see it. I'm going to stay on here a while and look after things and get myself together a little. The Lord has sent me to a cool place at last. I haven't ridden in a car in almost a week now. The theme here is staying put. Being still. No freeways, please. No wheels, except maybe one at a time, on a wheelbarrow. About all I want to do at this point is rest and be real quiet, and what I'm finding is that the best way to do both those things is to work hard. I've been working full days since my uncle's funeral. If you feel like resting and being quiet, come on down here and work with me a while. You can shovel rabbit shit while I water the garden.

If you can't swing that, do two other things for me. Send me some money, and find out where Estelle is. I don't need a lot, and I don't need it all at once, and whatever you send, from now on, I intend to pay you back. (I mean, like, how many freaks mooching off you intend to pay you back, Flash? This may be the start of some whole new trend). If you could send me two hundred dollars now, and a hundred dollars a month till further notice, I'd be cool. I can live on a hundred a month here easy. Food for the rabbits and myself is the only really big expense. (My inheritance includes forty seven rabbits, all hopping around and eating and shitting in hutches out behind the barn. They're part of my uncle's scheme to save the world with rabbit shit, which I will describe for you in full detail in another letter. It's very far out). If I stay the rest of the summer, I'll owe you four hundred dollars by fall. But even if I wind up staying a whole year I'd only owe you about fourteen hundred next summer. I'll figure out something else by then. What I need to do now is get some money coming in so I wont have to sweat it for a while, so please let me know pretty soon if you'll be able to carry me for a while.

Estelle. I don't know what to say, where to begin. We got really fucked up in Cincinnati. Or at least I did. It was heavy, I was heavy, and it got heavier and heavier till I really couldn't carry it anymore. It's much better now. I'm much better. At least I think I am. I feel like I am. And what I want to do is get hold of her and tell her that. And a whole bunch of other stuff too. So please try to scout her out for me Flash, get an address or a phone number and send it to me as soon as you can. Maybe Angel's heard from her. I'm sure she didn't go back to her parents place in Grayling, although maybe she did at that. I'm sending a letter to her, in care of you. As soon as you get an address please forward it to her immediately, and then let me know.

Well, old hoss, many thanks to you. I'm not rapping with anybody here much, except a little with this one guy, Leonard, who was a friend of my uncle's and who comes up to help me now and then. So I'll be laying some letters on you for a while, probably. And if you feel like it, lay some on me in return.

Peace.

D.R.

Living With Your Land

If you're a kid in a family that has some land this book will help you get family support for projects to encourage wildlife, improve the soil, build a pond, liven up the place.

—SB

Living With Your Land
John Vosburgh
1968; 191 pp.

$2.65 postpaid

from:
Charles Scribner's, Sons
597 Fifth Ave.
New York, N.Y. 10017

or WHOLE EARTH CATALOG

Exotic Aquarium Fishes

More than 70% of the Whole Earth's surface is under water, with proportional animate population, our ancestral home. Some people immerse themselves in this ecological dimension swimmingly. Others box a bit of it and stash it in their pads for observation, education, fascination, fun. Aquarists have been long aware of environmental balances and such, playing god. Aquariums are communes. How you keep your tanks will show you to be curious, careless, callous, compassionate, concerned, or what.

The dean of American aquarists is Dr. William T. Innes, whose classic manual with its exquisite color photographs, updated by assistants and now published cheaply, unfolds scientific insight, practical lore, wry humor, and humane wisdom.

[Suggested and reviewed by Tom Wertenbaker]

Exotic Aquarium Fishes
Dr. William T. Innes
1938-1966; 590 pp.

$5.95 postpaid

from:
E. P. Dutton & Company, Inc.
201 Park Ave. South
New York, N.Y. 10003

or WHOLE EARTH CATALOG

"Missionary fish" would be a fitting name for this little beauty, for it far exceeds any other species in the number of convert aquarists it has made. And many of these converts who branched out and became aquarists in a big way still keep Guppies, and still feel that, with their infinite variety of colors, they are the most interesting of all aquarium fishes. Each male is as individual as a thumbprint.

Besides its beauty the Guppy has other great merits. Scarcely any other fish combines so many cardinal points in such degree. It is a live-bearer, the most popular type of fish. It is an extremely fertile as well as dependable breeder. It is unusually active. It will thrive in close confinement. It can stand foul water. It has an extreme temperature range of 40 degrees, from 60 to 100. It will take any kind of food. It does not fight. It is not timid. It matures rapidly, an important point for those aquarists breeding for special points. It is subject to few diseases. It can be had everywhere at prices available to everybody.

The activity of the male is extraordinary. Whether flashing about in pure joy of living, or paying court to a female, he is ever the embodiment of intensity. He might well be termed "the playboy of the aquarium."

The specimens chosen for use in our color plate were selected with the idea of illustrating certain color features. Five of these color standards are shown. The fish just below the head of the female displays two of them. He has the "Peacock" or "Lace" design in the tail. The fish in the lower left corner also embodies two definite points. First it is a "Chain Guppy." This refers to the irregular dark line from the head through the body. The eye in the dorsal also makes it a "Birdeye Guppy."

The large central figure, of course, is a "loaded" female. The gentlemen craftily approaching from the rear is in typical position for action, with his gonopodium brought forward for an instant thrust.

In highly developed stocks some females appear not only showing traces of color in the tail fin, but also shiny highlights in it, as indicated in the single illustration. It is believed, but not certain, that such females throw youngsters of superior colors. Any color in female adds value to a show pair.

•

Sometimes an individual fish, possibly of a peaceful species, learns that other fishes will flee if chased. This becomes a sport with that fish, to the misery of its fellows and the discomfiture of their owner. It should either be disposed of, partitioned off, (perhaps in a corner, like a dunce), or placed in another aquarium with larger fishes, where, among strangers, it may reform. Like the rooster taken out of its own barnyard, it will not fight so well.

•

Inequality in the size of youngsters always puzzles the beginner. None can tell why it is any more than in human beings. Some fishes are no doubt born more vigorous than others. They get "the jump" by bolting the biggest and best food. Presently they become large enough to eat the smallest of their brethren. As these make the best of food, the disproportion increases. It is Nature's way. A plentiful early supply of the small live foods tends to equalize growth.

Birdhouse construction is booming. Some factory and do-it-yourself sources are pressed to keep the supply in pace with the demand. People seem to want birdhouses as badly as the birds do. Here is a gratifying and constructive trend. Obviously the clearing of a million acres of land a year for the suburbs is having its effect on nesting practices. At a time when urbanization is depriving hole-nesting birds of nesting sites, it is but prudent to fill the gap caused by the scarifying of the countryside and the removal of old trees and fence posts. It is also wise to encourage population growth of useful and disappearing species, such as practiced by Dr. Heinz Meng of New Paltz, New York. To bolster the dwindling sparrow-hawk population in his Hudson Valley area, he sets out large nesting boxes with entrance holes three inches wide. Thirteen of his 14 boxes were occupied in 1965.

COLOR PLATE PAGE 571

Lebistes reticulàtus (PETERS)
Pronounced Le-biss"tees re-tik'you-lay"tus *Popular names*, Guppy and Rainbow Fish
MEANING OF NAME: *Lebistes*, probably from *Lebias* (=*Cyprinodon*), and
istion, a sail; *reticulatus*, net marked, or mottled
Also known as *Girardinus reticulatus, Girardinus guppyi* and *Poecilia reticulata*
Trinidad, Guiana and Venezuela   Length—male, 1¼ inches; female, 2¼ inches
Western Location Map x19 to A24
Artificially introduced into many other locations

"CORKSCREW" VALLISNERIA

An attractive mutation from the tall *Vallisneria spiralis*, but instead of growing from 15 to 20 inches and sprawling on the water surface of small tanks, its charmingly twisted leaves average only 7 to 12 inches. Very popular. Prefers hard water and fairly strong light.

Plants and Man

This is a terrific book about plants and agriculture. We haven't seen the other books in the Nature and Science series from Natural History Press, but if they're as good, they've got something. —SB

Plants and Man
H. L. Edlin
1969; 253 pp.

$6.95 postpaid

from:
Doubleday & Company, Inc.
501 Franklin Avenue
Garden City, N. Y. 11531

or WHOLE EARTH CATALOG

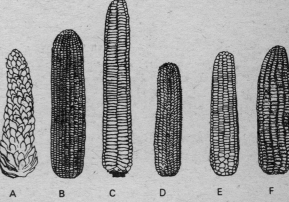

A   B   C   D   E   F

The six principal types of maize. (A) pod corn, a probable ancestor of modern corn; (B) dent corn; (C) flint corn; (D) popcorn; (E) flour corn; (F) sweet corn.

As food for humans, corn is inferior to wheat and some other cereals because it contains very little protein. The absence of protein means that cornstarch does not form gluten when it is mixed with water, and so corn bread has a rougher texture than wheat and rye loaves made from the "stretched" dough (full of air pockets) that gluten provides. Even so, corn has formed the principal diet of many peoples in Central and South America for several thousand years.

Tropical Fish Essay

Dear Sirs:

Herewith is my essay about Tropical Fish for beginners. I obtained my information from The Innes Book of Exotic Aquarium Fishes, Copyright by Aquariums Incorp., Maywood, NJ. (19th Edition revised)

The hobby of tropical fish and plants is an old and fascinating one. The beginner however, must remember that he should start with the most simple and common types of fish to insure a successful project. The best fish for beginners to start with is the guppy. It is colorful, inexpensive, and easiest to breed. In fact, it is almost too easy to breed. Most hobbyists end up with more baby guppies than he can handle. So the best thing to do is to buy only one female, and have a dealer ready to receive the fish when you no longer want it. The next easiest fishes to have are the Mollies, and the Platys, orange or otherwise. They are lively and attractive and also inexpensive. But, if you are a beginner, do not attempt to purchase a soft-shell turtle, or frog or crab. My own experiences have led me to this conclusion. Soft-shell Turtles are prone to a deadly disease known as fungus. Caring for a sick turtle is messy, hopeless, and uncomfortable for the turtle itself.

Water used in the aquarium should be treated with Di-Chlor, which rids tap water of its chlorine content. Make sure that the water temperature stays between about 67 to 88 for the fish mentioned above, but for other types of fish, consult your dealer for correct temperature ranges.

The most common and cheapest plants are: Vallisneria, Cabomba, and Anacharis. Vallisneria should be planted with the roots above the gravel, or the plant will gradually decompose and pollute the tank. One of the most common problems arising in tropical fish "communities" is the act of over feeding. This is the big mistake that many young aquarists make. Feed only once a day, and once in a while twice. You will just have to overcome the joy of watching the fish devour their lunch, breakfast, snack, dessert, etc.

The other problem that arises is diseases. If your fish is acting jittery, or lies down at the bottom of the tank, he most likely is ill. Treat him at once by placing him in a jar with about 1-1/2 teaspoons of salt, and 1 cup of water. (Float the jar in the tank) Then consult your dealer. But be sure you follow these guidelines: Do not overcrowd, do not overfeed, keep tank clean, keep the "Innes Book" on hand, keep temperature between 72 and 81, and always watch out for sick fish.

Submitted by
Elizabeth Collins, age 12
San Diego, California

All About Telescopes

If you have been putting off building a telescope because you thought it was too expensive, too difficult, or too time consuming, this is the book for you. It is the next best thing to taking a telescope building class from John Dobson of the San Francisco Sidewalk Astronomers. A high quality astronomical Newtonian telescope (reflector) can be built in one weekend if all the materials are at hand. Most other books on telescope building make the whole process sound very complicated. Therefore, many would-be amature astronomers get discouraged and give up before they get started.

This book has everything from basic optics to basic astronomy. The emphasis is on do-it-yourself and do it cheaply. Many different types of telescopes diagramed. How about a 4¼" "sky beam", a reflecting telescope made from board? Old pipes, scraps of wood and metal, bottle caps, tin cans, cardboard tubes, etc. are the materials suggested for construction various parts of telescopes. Extremely informative diagrams give you many ideas for doing things in different ways. This book will take you from grinding and polishing your own mirror through building mounts to using your telescope. One of the best illustrated how-to-do-it books ever written.

[Suggested and reviewed by Kenneth R. Lajoie]

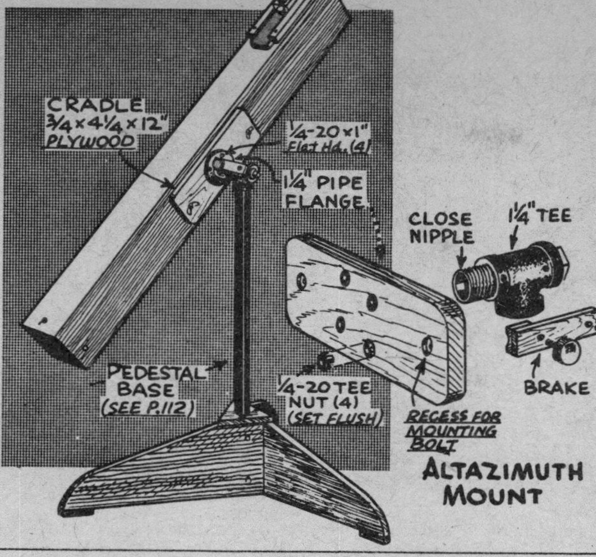

CRADLE
3/4×4 1/4×12"
PLYWOOD
1/4-20×1"
Flat Hd. (4)
1/4" PIPE
FLANGE
CLOSE
NIPPLE
1/4" TEE
PEDESTAL
BASE
(SEE P.112)
1/4-20 TEE
NUT (4)
(SET FLUSH)
RECESS FOR
MOUNTING
BOLT
BRAKE
ALTAZIMUTH
MOUNT

All About Telescopes
Sam Brown
1967; 192 pp.

$3.00 postpaid

from:
Edmund Scientific Co.
555 Edscorp Bldg.
Barrington, N.J. 08007

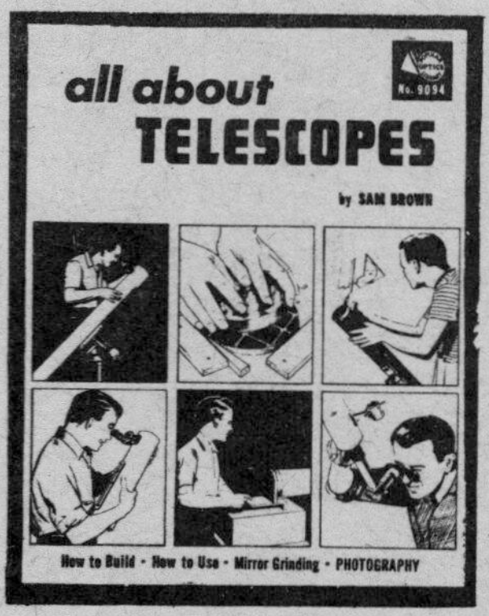

all about
TELESCOPES
by SAM BROWN
How to Build · How to Use · Mirror Grinding · PHOTOGRAPHY

Catalogs of Astronomical Photos

all kinds of spacy pictures pretty cheap((eight by ten, a buck fifty or so).

—jd

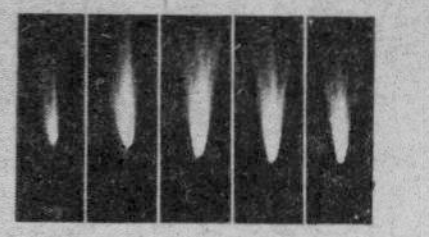

Cat. No. 295†

AREND-ROLAND COMET: five views, on a single print, taken April 26, 27, 29, 30, and May 1, 1957. 48-inch.

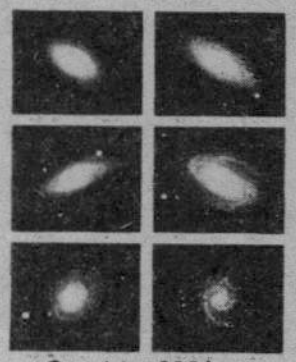

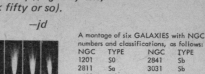

A montage of six GALAXIES with NGC numbers and classifications, as follows:

NGC	TYPE	NGC	TYPE
1201	S0	2841	Sb
2811	Sa	3031	Sb
488	Sab	628	Sc

Cat. No. 138†

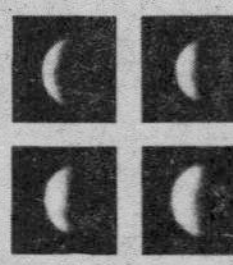

VENUS. Six views in ultraviolet light: June 6, 23, 24, 26, 30 and July 1, 1927. 100-inch.

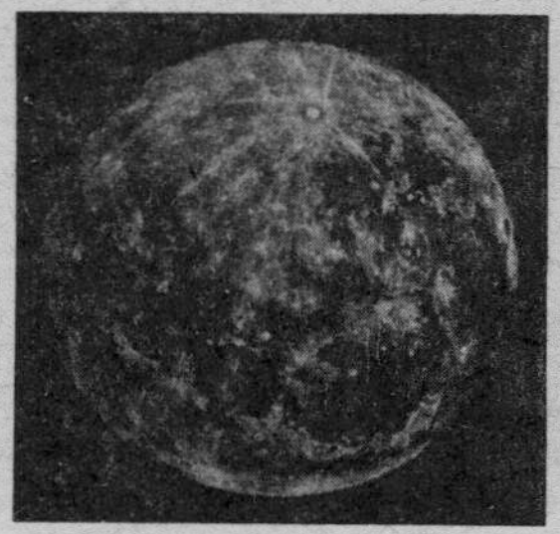

L4 Age 14 days (full)

Catalog

free

from:
California Institute of Technology
Bookstore
1201 East California Boulevard
Pasadena, California 91109

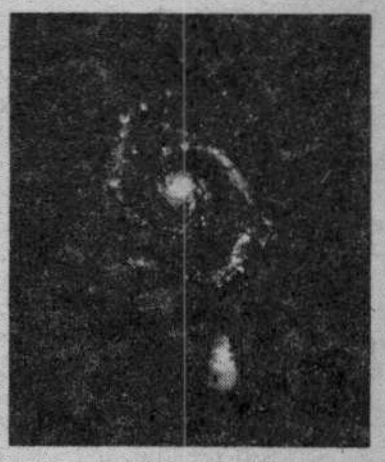

S12 The Whirlpool Galaxy in Canes Venatici (Messier 51, NGC 5194-5).

Catalog

free

from:
Lick Observatory
University of California
Santa Cruz, California 95060

The Observer's Handbook

For those who like to stare stars straight in the eye, this is the best amateur astronomer's handbook. Asteroids, clusters, constellations, eclipses, galaxies, planets, nebulae, occultations, radio sources, precession, star maps, sun spots, meteors. Published annually in November.

—SB

[Suggested by Lee Anderson]

The Observer's Handbook
103 pp.

$3.00 postpaid

from:
Royal Astronomical Society of Canada
252 College Street
Toronto, Ontario M5T IR7
CANADA

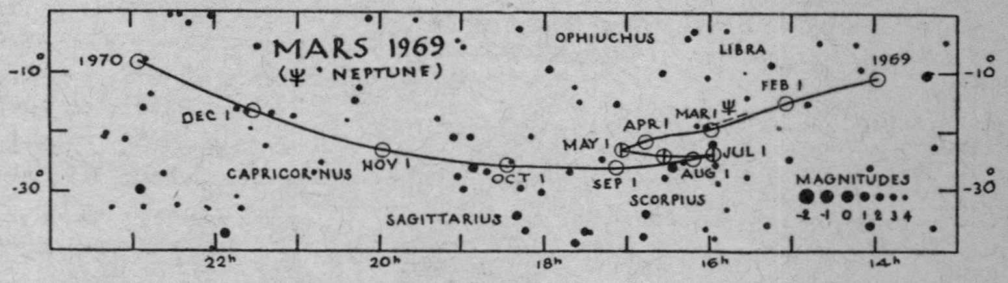

MARS 1969
(♆ NEPTUNE)
OPHIUCHUS
LIBRA
1970
1969
DEC 1
FEB 1
MAR 1
APR 1
MAY 1
JUL 1
AUG 1
SEP 1
OCT 1
NOV 1
CAPRICORNUS
SAGITTARIUS
SCORPIUS
MAGNITUDES
-10
-30
22h
20h
18h
16h
14h

Amateur Telescope Making

You left out the best books on telescope making, namely **Amateur Telescope Making.** *The set (I, II & III) are $5, $6, $7) from Scientific American Publishing. It gives explicit directions for making and designing almost any telescopic system— from 6" wooden mounted reflectors to Schneider optical systems on cast aluminum forks. They write even of how to set up your own foundry to cast the mounting. Much practical, some theoretical information, some history. One not-particularly impressive photo is one of a windmill, looking like a normally exposed photograph. Reading the text, it was Schneider's first photo with his newly designed camera, taken from two miles away in starlight with a two hour exposure. Then they tell you how to make a better camera than that one. Sort of a make-your-own-trip-through-the-universe book.*

Love,

Barry Oliver
Austin, Texas

The Attractive Universe

Soundly written, brilliantly illustrated guide to the interactive dominion of gravity. If I were orbiting the moon, I'd want my understanding to be able to swim in this element like a fish.

—SB

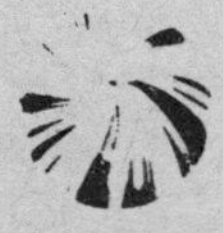

The Attractive Universe
E. G. Valens
1969; 187 pp.

$5.95 postpaid

from:
The World Publishing Company
2080 West 117th Street
Cleveland, OH 44111

or WHOLE EARTH CATALOG

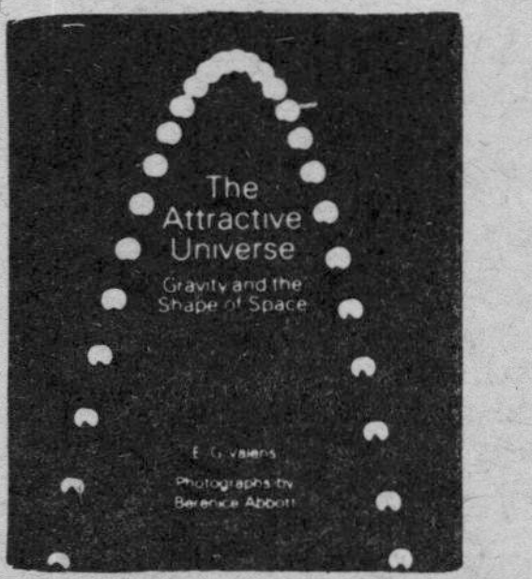

The
Attractive
Universe
Gravity and the
Shape of Space
E. G. Valens
Photographs by
Berenice Abbott

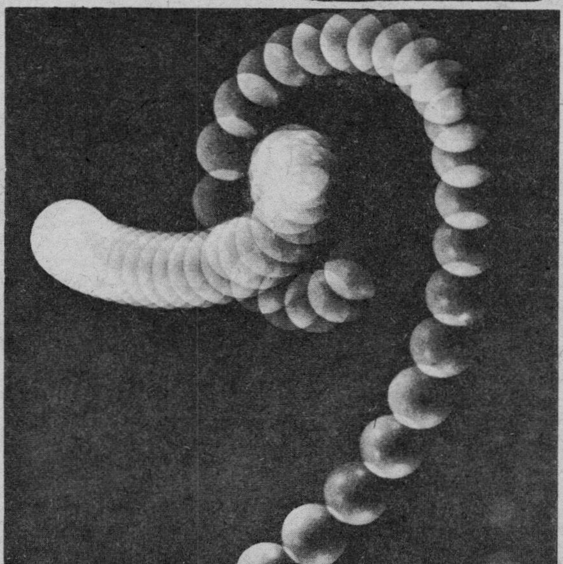

If we allow Star B to orbit for a longer time, something else occurs.

Star B is falling into an elliptical orbit, fut in addition, Star A itself begins to move. Why?

Star B responds to a bending of space caused by Star A. But Star B itself, by virtue of its very existence, causes an additional curvature in space, and this in turn affects Star A. Furthermore, Star B is moving, and it literally carries the additional curvature along with it. The shape of space is now changing constantly and the originally stationary star is thus set in motion.

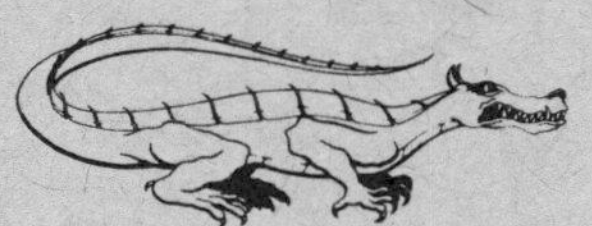

DEAR ESTELLE

I've written you about fifty pages of letter since I've seen you but it's too big a mess to send. Some time I want to read those pages to you, or let you read them, and I'd like to talk to you a long time about what's in them. Some amazing things have happened since I didn't see you in Cincinnati any more and it's probably been the same for you. It seems like adventures keep on happening to me and you, and most of the people we know, even when we don't particularly want to have adventures for a while.

What I want us to do, Estelle, is get together and talk it over. I want you to come here where I am, and be with me a good, long while, and let's get into it again and see what happens this time. That's what I want us to do. If it's necessary, and you want it that way, I'll come where ever you are. I want to hang around here a while, but I want to see you more than I want to stay here, so if you want me to come where you are, just say so.

But let me tell you a little about this place, Estelle. Let me tell you how it is here.

Mainly, it's very quiet. It's not so lovely to look at because this is coal mining country, and the hills have been pretty much fucked over, but in its way this is the loveliest place to be that I've found in a long time. Of course I always thought it was lovely. I use to be around here a lot when I was a kid, and I've got a lot of sweet kid memories of how it was in those years. But the way it's lovely now doesn't have anything to do with memory. I'm surprised that it's that way. It seems very far out to be looking at this place from such a different angle. But I'm not spending much time on my surprise. I'm too involved in this other loveliness that's here that I can't describe very well, but that I feel really strongly.

What's here is an old house, and an old barn, both of them ruined. There's a small garden that's not ruined, and water piped down from a spring. There's some chickens, and there's just one hell of a lot of rabbits living in hutches out by the barn. Most people would consider this a pretty grim and worthless place, but it holds a very large value for me that I haven't got completely figured out yet, but that emotionally I feel like I've got a pretty good grip on. There's no electricity, and you can't get a car up here, but those are both pluses as far as I'm concerned. I'm writing to you right now by the light of a coal oil lamp, and that's a plus. In a few minutes I'm going to go out on the front porch and sit in my uncle's rocking chair and look at the stars and feel the cool and enjoy this quiet Kentucky evening and that's a plus for sure.

But the really big plus would be if you were here with me. I want you to be. At the least, I want you to write to me and tell me where you are and that you're okay. I'll worry about you till you do. I'm pretty bored with worrying about myself so much, but I'll worry about you till I hear that you're okay. So please write to me just as soon as you possibly can.

Love,

D.R.

Sourcebook on the Space Sciences

If your plan includes getting off the planet, and you don't care to be just an inert passenger or dumb tourist, this book is the most useful––if a little outdated––single volume you'll find. Rockets, orbits, propulsion, guidance, Earth as planet, other planets, sun, extraterrestrial man. When you get out there where Nothing is, say hello to it, will you?

—SB

[Suggested by E. G. Valens]

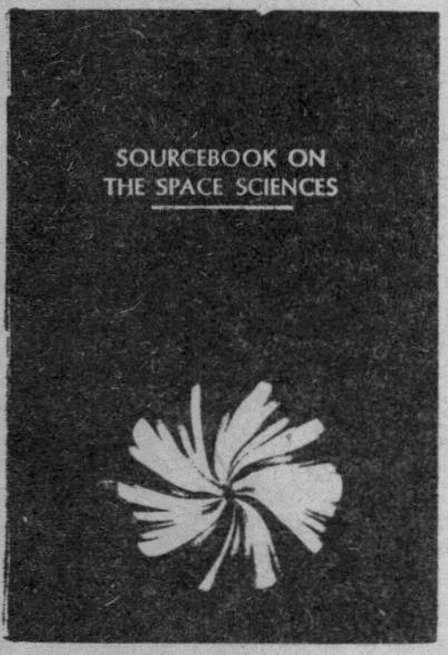

SOURCEBOOK ON
THE SPACE SCIENCES

Sourcebook on the Space Sciences
Samuel Glasstone
1965; 937 pp.

$12.95 postpaid

from:
Van Nostrand-Reinhold
450 West 33rd Street
New York, N. Y. 10001

or WHOLE EARTH CATALOG

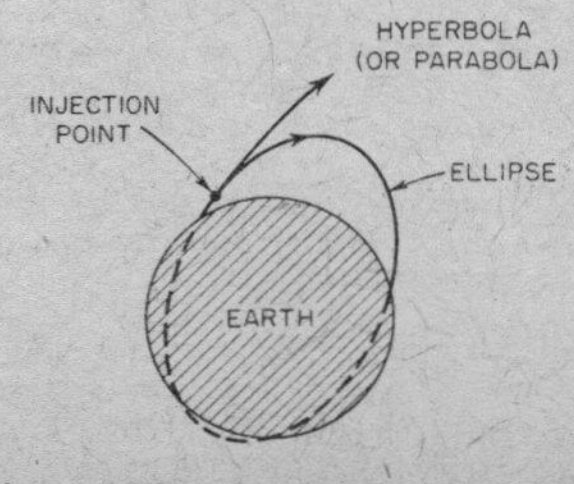

HYPERBOLA
(OR PARABOLA)
INJECTION
POINT
ELLIPSE
EARTH

If a spacecraft is launched near to, i.e., within a few hundred miles of, Earth's surface into an elliptical orbit that extends out to 10 Earth radii, $R_{peri}/2R_{apo}=1/20$; the required injection velocity (v_{peri}) is then as much as 95 percent of the escape velocity. For a launch to the Moon, some 60 Earth radii distant, $R_{peri}/2R_{apo}$ is about 1/120 and the injection velocity is over 99 percent of the escape value.

Worlds in the Making

We see all manner of books on the Future around here, and I can't think of a nicer one than this. It's a collection of readings aimed, pretty accurately, at teen-age readership. It presents the future not as a menace or a promise, but as a home, a hard and damned interesting place to live.

—SB

Worlds in the Making
Dunstan & Garlan
1970; 370 pp.

$5.35 postpaid

from:
Prentice-Hall Inc.
Englewood Cliffs, New Jersey 07632

or WHOLE EARTH CATALOG

Behind every man now alive stand thirty ghosts, for that is the ratio by which the dead outnumber the living. Since the dawn of time, roughly a hundred billion human beings have walked the planet Earth.

Now this is an interesting number, for by a curious coincidence there are approximately a hundred billion stars in our local universe, the Milky Way. So for every man who has ever lived, in this universe there shines a star.

But every one of those stars is a sun, often far more brilliant and glorious than the small, nearby star we call *the* Sun. And many—perhaps most—of those alien suns have planets circling them. So almost certainly there is enough land in the sky to give every member of the human species, back to the first apeman, his own private, world-sized heaven—or hell.

How many of those potential heavens and hells are now inhabited, and by what manner of creatures, we have no way of guessing; the very nearest is a million times farther away than Mars or Venus, those still remote goals of the next generation. But the barriers of distance are crumbling; one day we shall meet our equals, or our masters, among the stars.

Arthur C. Clarke,
2001: A Space Odyssey

Institutions established to prepare students for goals by specialist courses and credits are being rejected and even defied by their clients. The TV generation wants participation in the educational process. It does not want packages. The students want problems, not answers. They want probes, not exams. They want making, not matching. They want struggle, not goals. They want new images of identity, not careers. They want insights, not classified data.

Marshall McLuhan,
"The Reversal of the Overheated Image"

Pioneer Posters

Cheap, good, educational, weird. They're a whole other kind of history than book history and better posters than most posters. Immense variety.

—SB

Catalog

$0.25

from:
Buck Hill Associates
75 Garnet Lake Road
Johnsburg, N.Y. 12843

C35—REWARD POSTER—Pinkerton for Perry "nerviest train robber" 60¢

C36—VIGILANCE POSTER—Want list of bad-men-1868 65¢

C37—ADAMS EXPRESS POSTER—"ship gold" pictures train 50¢

C38—BUFFALO BILL WILD WEST SHOW—Illustrated poster 50¢

C39—RAILROAD POSTER—Connects Wells-Fargo coach, illustrated 65¢

C40—BATHING SUITS 1885—Styles seashore 4 ladies 50¢

C41—AUTOMOBILE CLOTHING WORN—In 1900—3 illustrated ads 55¢

C42—CALAMITY JANE POSTER—Exhibition, relates exploits 65¢

C43—REWARD POSTER—Lists train robbers and

headaches, knock out tired feeling, its all for 5¢; colorful language 5¢

POSTER—1903 — "Edison's moving ed on canvas. life-like, life-size" on x 11 75¢

AR RECRUITING HANDBILL—Flag, sol 11 x 8½ 35¢

LEE—Full length portrait engraved ave Gen. Jackson, 23 x 18, special ted, unusual value $1.25

Globe—earliest—1542 by Volpius

RULES—Written 1400 years ago by how to treat a guest; illustrated; r, social history 75¢

POSTER—1759—Quaint illustration to Philadelphia. 2 day trip; gives all rarity 55¢

WAR ORDER—1861—Provost Marshal of the enemy" to pay cash assess- ke taxation. Little known document sion 55¢

WAR BROADSIDE—Early 1861—En- s king" shows devil sitting on bale tty follows, unique 50¢

WAR POSTAL SEALS—Sheet of 24 intended to be cut apart and pasted Remember Fort Sumter." all different.

ERATE BROADSIDE—Lincoln is auc- lls all U.S. possessions for badly- l stanzas, each 8 lines. Ornamental border 17 x 5½; scarce, ridicule 10¢

C90—INSURANCE POLICY—1829—Unique protection 55¢

C57—UNCLE TOM'S CABIN POSTER—Woodcut picture Negro family, cabin, advertises book that had greatest influence in American history 55¢

Things Maps Don't Tell Us

This seductive book—each page has a big simple illustration and accompanying text—teaches you to see what's happening in a piece of landscape. The mountain range is rising or diminishing. The lakes are lined up because the strata are. The atoll is there because a volcano was, and then sank. Geology cycles slow, but big.

—SB

Things Maps Don't Tell Us
Armin K. Lobeck
1956; 160 pp.

$6.95 postpaid

from:
Macmillan Company
Front and Brown Streets
Riverside, N.J. 108075

or WHOLE EARTH CATALOG

THINGS MAPS DON'T TELL US

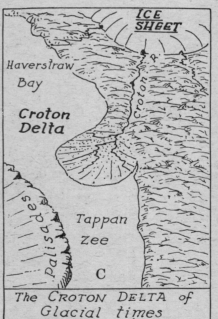

C
The CROTON DELTA of Glacial times

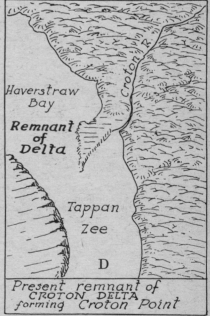

D
Present remnant of CROTON DELTA forming Croton Point

The clue to the origin of Croton Point is the Croton River. During the waning stages of Glacial Time, when this part of the continent stood somewhat lower than it does now, because of the great weight of ice upon it, the Hudson River was about 80 feet deeper in Haverstraw Bay than it is at present. The Croton River, pouring out from the melting ice front, carried great quantities of sand and gravel into Haverstraw Bay and built there a large delta which reached half way across the river. Like most deltas built into quiet estuaries, the Croton Delta was more or less round in shape, with distributary streams flowing outward in all directions toward its margins.

Following the final disappearance of the ice and the removal of this great weight, the crust of the earth in this part of the United States gradually rose above sea level. In the Croton Delta region the elevation was about 80 feet, with the result that the flat top of Croton Point stands now 80 feet above sea level. An important result of this rising was the invigorating effect it had upon the Croton River. This stream, therefore, flowed more swiftly, and eroded its valley extensively. Much of the delta was removed by the river, so that now only the northern half remains. This is clearly revealed by its present shape.

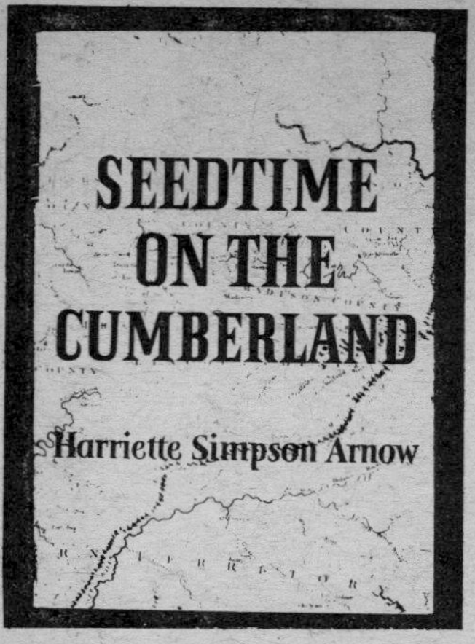

Seedtime On The Cumberland
Harriette Simpson Arnow
1960; 449pp.

$8.95 postpaid

from:
The Macmillan Company
866 Third Avenue
New York, New York 10022

or WHOLE EARTH CATALOG

Miss Arnow combines her talents of novelist and historian in Seedtime *to produce a beautifully-written account of life among the settlers on the Appalachian frontier. Her geographical focus is the Cumberland River drainage, which begins in Eastern Kentucky and sweeps south-westward into middle Tennessee. The book is loaded with details of frontier life-style which provide pictures not only of the pioneers' daily life, but their psychology as well.*

—Gurney Norman

Von Graffenried had chosen his people carefully, so that most needed skills would be represented, as many were required. There had to be carpenters, joiners, plasterers, and sawyers in order to build the only kind of home they knew to build on the rockless, clayless coastal plain—one of sawed timber. This, in addition to skilled workmen, demanded saws, hammers, nails, trowels, chisels, shingles, and lime that had to be got from the burning of oyster shells.[44] Such a house took time in the building that might have gone to clearing fields and fortifying against the Indians; and during the long weeks of its building the owner and his family had to live in some makeshift shelter such as a tent or even house of bark and boughs, thereby increasing their liability to illness through exposure to rain and cold.

The man who could with felling ax, broadax, drawing knife, auger, and froe ride into the woods and in a few days' time build an all-weather house of logs in which he could live decently, and in comfort when it was finished, was not there. The "house made of logs Such as the Swedes very often make in America,"[45] was still very much a rarity on the Carolina coast.

The New Bern settlers had brought plenty of clothing, but soon they were almost naked. They had when food got low, bartered clothes with a nearby tribe of Indians for "wild meat, leather, bacon, beans, and corn." Less than a day's journey away were game-filled woods, but there were no hunters in New Bern, and nobody to teach hunting.[46] There were in North Carolina at that time famous hunters, who could, wearing the head and skin of a deer, stalk the living animal until they could get close enough for the kill; but these were Indians.[47] The white hunter, so proficient he could make money from the selling of skins, was not yet in America; the North Carolina planters paid the Indians to hunt for them.

•

Skills alone were not enough; it is true any man who would survive on the border had to be an artist in the use of the broadax, skinning knife, scraper, hoe, froe, auger, awl, adz, and other tools, but equally important or more so was a knowledge of the woods. All borderers who lived as farmers were woodsmen. The forest was only part enemy to be pushed aside for cleared fields. It was for the Virginia or North Carolina settler a vast and seemingly bottomless widow's barrel yielding up all manner of things from walink for the newborn baby's tea to dogwood for the weaver's shuttle. The settler had to know these offerings, where to hunt a slender hickory sapling for the corn pounder sweep, lightwood for a bit of tar, cane stalk for the weaver's sleigh, a small and crooked white oak for a sled runner, but a straight one for a splitting maul. He had to know his wood-poplar for hewing and gouging, but cedar for riving, and so for several dozen: what would sink and what would float, what would bend, and what was best for a shoe peg. He was dependent upon the woods around him not only for building materials for house, barn, fence, much of his furniture, and many of his appliances from pitchfork to gunstock, but the woods gave him fuel, drugs, dyes, and a good bit of food. All new-settled farmers, even the wealthy, had, until fence could be built, to use the open range so that meat, milk, and butter came from woods pasture.

•

Years ago before the days of consolidated schools and good roads, I taught in remote sections of Pulaski County, Kentucky now part of the Cumberland National Forest. My pupils were chiefly the children of small farmers, but all around them were the woods. At that date in that community most farm animals were still on the open range so these children like earlier generations spent much time in the woods; in rounding up the forever straying animals, in going to church, school, or to a neighbor's, and in collecting herbs, fruits, nuts, fuel, and in hunting and trapping.

They had had no nature study or lessons in woodscraft, but on a Monday morning they could, with no apparent study of the either muddy or dusty road, tell all who had ridden or walked by the schoolhouse during the weekend, for they knew every shoe print, mule and horse "sign" in the neighborhood. They knew the common names as well as uses of several dozens of plants,[17] and they knew them winter as well as summer. One faint clink of a distant bell and they could tell whether made by horse, cow, or sheep, who owned the animal and what it was doing, grazing or sleeping or "hid-out." They could track a strayed mule or hog or cow for miles when there were no tracks I could see.

They, no different from the young hunters of earlier generations, ranged over rough lands and were never lost or hurt. They delighted in swinging out over creek or river and dropping into a pool of water; they climbed tall trees, explored sinkholes, caves, creek pools, rockhouses, yet I never had a school child hurt by a fall or suffer a snake bite, and though many of the boys started hunting alone at ten years of age I can recall no gun accident. Bred into them was the same caution the hunter had to have; a perch in the swaying top of a "slim" fifty-foot hickory made for good safe fun in a high wind, but only a fool would on a hot summer day stick his hand under a rocky ledge or into any hole where he could not see—that was a good place for a copperhead to be. They were forever cautious; they respected the woods, the caves, and the river as one respects honorable enemies; young children were constantly watched and guarded against the dangers there, and it was not until they were eight years old or so they were allowed to walk the paths alone.

•

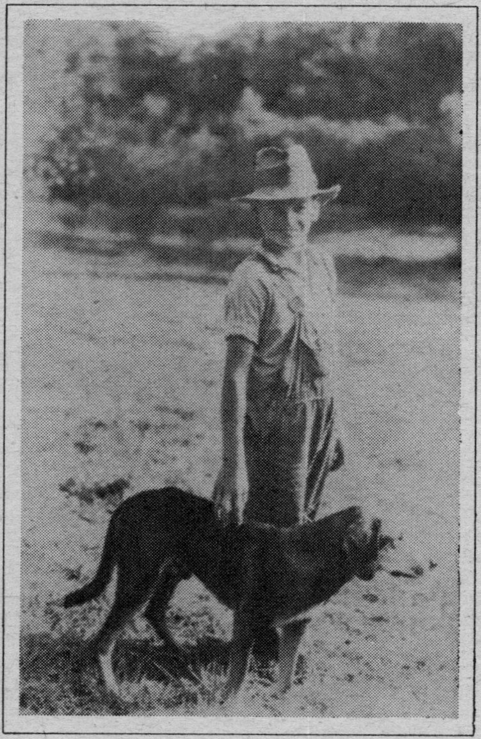

Cabins In The Laurel
Muriel Earley Sheppard
1965; 313 pp.

$7.25 postpaid

from:
The University of North Carolina Press
Box 2288
Chapel Hill, N.C. 27514

or WHOLE EARTH CATALOG

Cabins in the Laurel *is a record of Mountain life in Western North Carolina during and before the 1930's. The area has changed in this past 40 years; only small pockets of the old simple life remain but what there is is worth knowing about. At first you might take it for Americana or funk, but you soon see that the people are really far out. There is a ballad in there sung by a woman named Frankie Silvers. The song is her answer to her executioner's question: "Do you have any last words?" There is a portrayal of an ecstatic scene inside a Holiness church wherein a woman becomes a saint by dancing and wailing until the congregation joins her. These are true stories.*

[Reviewed by Dave Smith]

On Heroes

Daniel Boone had a land fantasy. He wanted to cut loose from the straight life of the settlements and go live someplace that made a greater demand on his talents and creative energies. He didn't like the economics of the settlements. Too much usury, too easy to get in debt, too hard to get out. His style and temperament were thwarted by people dealing only in the safe and known. The people in the settlements, the good burghers, were so bent on insulating themselves from the dangers of the unknown, they wound up insulating themselves from the pleasurable possibilities as well. In an easay the poet William Carlos Williams describes Boone as "a great voluptuary born to the American settlements against the niggardliness of the damming puritanical tradition." Boone was a sensualist, desperate to engage the raw, natural world directly. As a man of his own time, Boone performed the classic act of the truely modern person: he embraced the new world of possibility that lay before him, and didn't look back.

•

People who are truely of their own time are the result of a process, children of an evolutionary working that cannot much be hastened by artificial means. It took 150 years to produce Boone and the Long Hunters, men capable of looking at the wilderness face to face without flinching, without glancing back to the settlements, and to Europe, for assurance. They were the products of what Harriette Simpson Arnow, in her book Seedtime On The Cumberland, *calls "the long learning." The long learning was a period of several generations in which descendants of the original coastal settlers gradually learned to get along away from the sea, farther and still farther inland. Gradually the grandchildren and the great-grandchildren of an ocean-oriented people came to acquire the skills and attitudes a mountain man had to have. It was a slow and reluctant process, but by degrees individuals were formed whose growing expertise in the woods matched the waning of their interest in the old world of their fathers.*

•

There were many factors that accounted for this early "generation gap," but the crucial one was the willingness of the woodsmen to learn from the Indians. People before Boone's time went on expeditions in the woods, of course. But always with Indians as their guides. They hired Indians to hunt and track; it was nearly a hundred years before it began to occur to the coast-dwellers that they might learn the Indian skills themselves.

Williams says of Boone, "To Boone the Indian was his greatest master. Not for himself surely to be an Indian, though they eagerly sought to adopt him into their tribes, but the reverse: to be himself *in a new world, Indianlike. If the land were to be possessed it must be as the Indian possessed it."*

•

And so the metaphor is inescapable: today's middle-class consumer culture as a Mother Country to cut loose from; then a period of long-learning, in which modern frontiersmen gain the individual competence that allows them to do the necessary, practical things. Indians were the original teachers. They are with us still, their ways and attitudes remain as models, to emulate and learn from. But today they are joined by others who qualify as "Indians" of a sort, by virtue of their skills which allow them to function as teachers, as shamen, as knowers of The Way. Certain thinkers, certain mystics, certain far-out entrepreneurs, qualify, but so do certain small farmers and artisans, aborigines of a kind, native to their places, there on the land to be learned from by modern Long Hunters willing to range beyond the settled places in search of education and adventure.

•

The Long Hunter is the hero of his time, in any age. He is himself in a new world, Indianlike; sensuous in his relationship with the natural world around; one who has left the Mother Country intent upon being of as well as in whatever wilderness he encounters. I'm sure that's an oversimplification, but at least it's a handle on the definition. And definitions are important. As the new world unfolds around us, so a new mythology comes into being, peopled with new heroes, and new styles of heroic behavior. In trying to arrive at a new heroic definition, it's helpful to read up on heroes who have gone before. Seedtime On The Cumberland *is filled with tales of heroes. The thing you begin to realize as you read about them is that in most cases they were in actuality complex, mortal people like you and I who simply rose to the occasion that was before them, and did what they were called upon to do.*

—Gurney Norman

American Boys Handy Book

Dan Beard's **American Boys Handy Book** *was first published in 1882. Out of print for a long time, Tuttle has finally reprinted it. This is barefoot-boy-with-cheek-of-tan stuff, detailed lore on how a boy may make his own world. Extraordinary book, highly recommended for funky schools or communities, especially if woods are handy.* —SB

[Suggested by Arthur Brand]

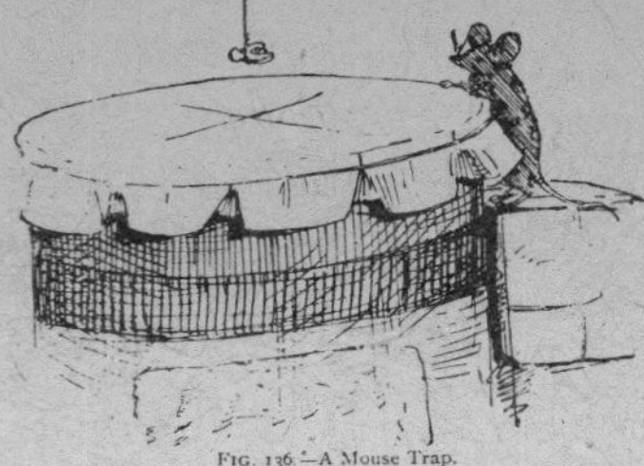

FIG. 136.—A Mouse Trap.

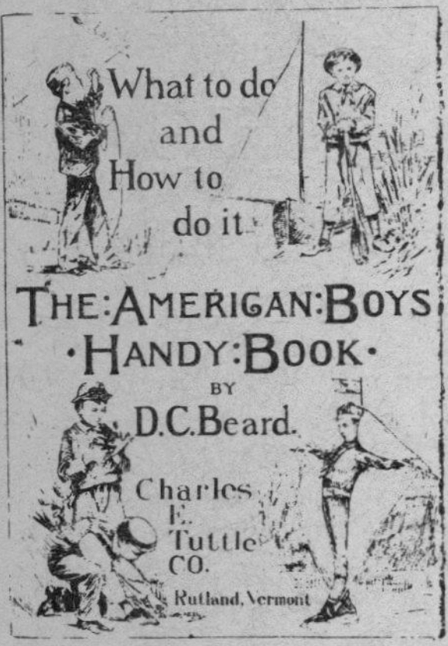

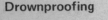

The American Boys Handy Book
D. C. Beard
1882; 391 pp.

$5.50 postpaid

from:
Charles E. Tuttle Co., Inc.
Rutland, Vermont 05701

or WHOLE EARTH CATALOG

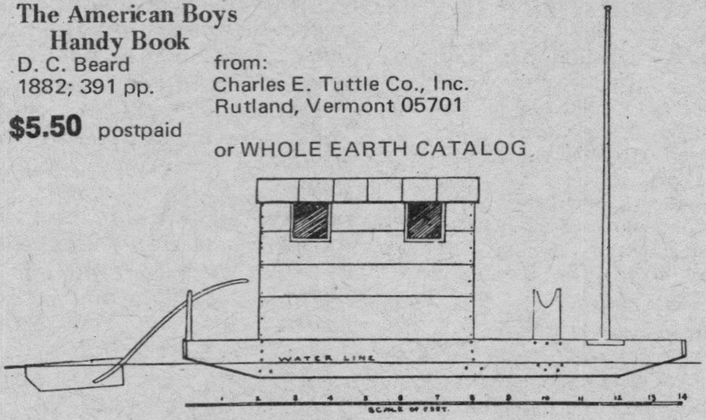

FIG. 81.—Side View of Flat-Boat.

Set a seat in front of the rowlock with a hole in it for the "jack-staff" to pass through. The jack-staff should be made so that it can be taken out and put in at pleasure.

Fieldbook

The Scouts continue their tradition of excellent feedback from an increasingly enormous membership. The Second Edition (1967) of the **Fieldbook** *may well be the best value around. Of course, the context is short term camping out in the continental U.S., but much more is afoot. In taking us sure-handedly from the root-hog-or-die survival situations through toward gourmet ecology, the* **Fieldbook** *shows how far we've come and certainly what to do next. The spirit of the Boer War appears to be giving way to that of enlightened naturalism (don't go blazing trees—the landowner will never have us back). Full of recipes, checklists, buying guides, patterns and plans, close-up photographs in how-to-do-it sequence. If you'll need to know something, it's there.*

Having put us at home outdoors, the book opens up into biology, geology and astronomy, and what to do about them. I especially like two sections: one has pictures of wild plants to eat where you're starving to death, and the page that tells you not to apply the tourniquet except as a last resort.

[Reviewed by Dave Guard
Suggested by Eugene Schoenfeld]

there's some good information here, twenty years later. the fieldbook is the most complete outdoorsy reference work at the cheapest price i know, and the merit badge series will teach just about anything from citizenship to hog production. learn from the scouts, maybe even become a den mother.

—jd

[Suggested by the Texas Hamiltons]

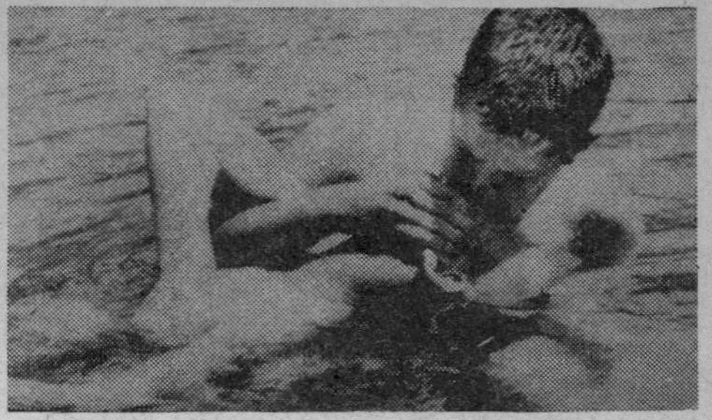

No time to wait to bring victim to shore. Start rescue breathing immediately. Tilt victim's head far back. Cradle his head with one hand and grasp his jaw with the other. Open your mouth wide and take a deep breath. Blow air into the victim through nose or mouth. Keep it up as you bring him to shore.

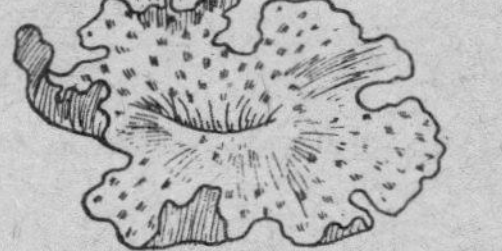

Rock Tripe (Gyrophora dillenie) can be scrambled like egg in a little water or fat.

Nosebleed is usually from a small vein in the middle partition of the nose. Fold a clean piece of paper into a pressure pad and tuck it under your upper lip. If the blood continues to flow, add to the thickness of the pad and press your index finger across your upper lip.

Fieldbook
Boy Scouts of America
1967; 565 pp.

$1.95

from:
Boy Scouts of America
P.O. Box 521
North Brunswick, N.J. 08902

Boy Scouts of America
1930 No. Mannhaim Road
Melrose Park, IL 60160

Boy Scouts of America
120 San Gabriel Dr.
Sunnyvale, CA. 94086

Merit Badge Series

$.45 each, postpaid

Number		Copyright
3304	Agriculture	1949
3301	Animal Industry	1944
3381	Archery	1941
3321	Architecture	1943
3320	Art	1944
3303	Astronomy	1944
3324	Athletics	1943
3305	Automobiling	1956
3293	Aviation	1954
3313	Basketry	1953
3340	Beef Production	1958
3362	Beekeeping	1957
3282	Bird Study	1938
3378	Bookbinding	1954
3379	Botany	1941
	Bugling (see Music)	
3307	Business	1942
3256	Camping	1946
3811	Canoeing	1952
3326	Chemistry	1957
3290	Citizenship	1953
3374	Coin Collecting	1949
3257	Cooking	1939
3341	Corn Farming	1948
3365	Cotton Farming	1953
3277	Cycling	1949
3330	Dairying	1950
3289A	Dog Care	1952
3367	Dramatics	1936
3206	Electricity	1956
3344	Farm Home and Its Planning	1930
3345	Farm Layout and Building Arrangement	1945
3346	Farm Mechanics	1958
3382	Pioneering	1942
3386	Plumbing	1953
3314	Pottery	1954
3331	Poultry Keeping	1957
3377	Printing	1944
3251	Public Health	1957
3373	Public Speaking	1944
3375	Rabbit Raising	1946
3333	Radio	1947
3292	Railroading	1954
3393	Reading	1953
3813	Reptile Study	1944
3392	Rowing	1952
3347	Safety	1958
3815	Salesmanship	1942
3384	Scholarship	1940
3322	Sculpture	1945

Number		Copyright
3349	Farm Records	1955
3287	Fingerprinting	1942
3317	Firemanship	1955
3238	First Aid	1957
3318	First Aid to Animals	1930
3295	Fishing	1954
3288	Forage Crops	1951
3302	Forestry	1956
3360	Fruit and Nut Growing	1953
3240	Gardening	1944
3284	Geology	1953
3380	Hiking	1944
3361	Hog Production	1956
3329	Home Repairs	1943
3298	Horsemanship	1958
3358	Indian Lore	1958
3348	Insect Life	1944
3812	Journalism	1943
3353	Landscaping	1944
3310	Leatherwork	1951
3278	Lifesaving	1944
3337	Machinery	1956
3338	Marksmanship	1953
3339A	Masonry	1952
3351	Mechanical Drawing	1945
3312A	Metalwork	1952
3336	Music	1953
3285	Nature	1953
3372	Painting	1954
3286	Personal Fitness	1953
3281	Pets	1957
3334	Photography	1956
3369	Pigeon Raising	1958
3332	Seamanship	1945
3370	Sheep Farming	1952
3237	Signaling	1940
3364	Skiing	1950
3283	Small Grains	1957
3291	Soil and Water Conservation	1952
3359	Stamp Collecting	1951
3327	Surveying	1960
3299	Swimming	1960
3743	Textiles	1953
3816	Weather	1943
3300	Wildlife Management	1952
3315	Woodcarving	1937
3316A	Woodwork	1952
	World Brotherhood (see Citizenship)	
3356	Zoology	1941

Drownproofing

The product of most warnings about water is: "Well, I've fallen in the water, now I'm supposed to start drowning."

New program. "No need to drown." Sinkers, non-swimmers, cripples, children; cramped, exhausted, injured, no rescue in sight. "No need to drown."

The book is sufficient for you to learn or teach the techniques appropriate for floaters, sinkers, and sundry special circumstances. Good medicine for anxious parents. Teach your kids and yourself and stop worrying. —SB

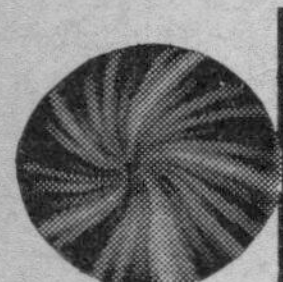

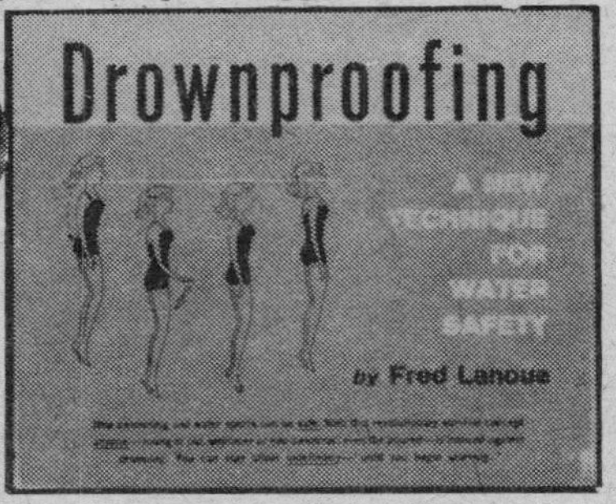

Drownproofing
Fred Lanoue
1963; 112 pp.

$6.50 postpaid

from:
Prentice Hall
Englewood Cliffs, N. J. 07632

or WHOLE EARTH CATALOG

$3.66 from Blackwell's (see p. 2)

Panic makes you throw your head back, reach up, make gurgling noises, horrible faces and kick and wave your arms frantically. None of these moves will do you the slightest good. Now is the time to learn the following, because *this is what really makes drownproofing work:*

Whether your nose and throat are full of water from lips to stomach, the stroke or the kick will *always* get you to the surface . . .

If you do it in the same manner as you had been doing it, *if* you blow out through your nose, with your lips clamped tightly together as you break the surface with another kick or stroke, whether air or water comes out, you will be somewhat relieved and you will be ready for the inhale.

If your eyes are open and *if* you inhale through your mouth, whether you end up with all air, half air and half foam, you will be better off, and *if* you continue the cycle, *no matter how much water you shipped,* things will get better much sooner than you think.

If this procedure is stuck to and mastered, 90 percent of those involuntary swallows of water will be forgotten three cycles (15 seconds) later. The other 10 percent may take 10 cycles to completely recover from, but if you force yourself to repeat the cycle properly, you are sure to be all right. What counts is that you get yourself out of trouble.

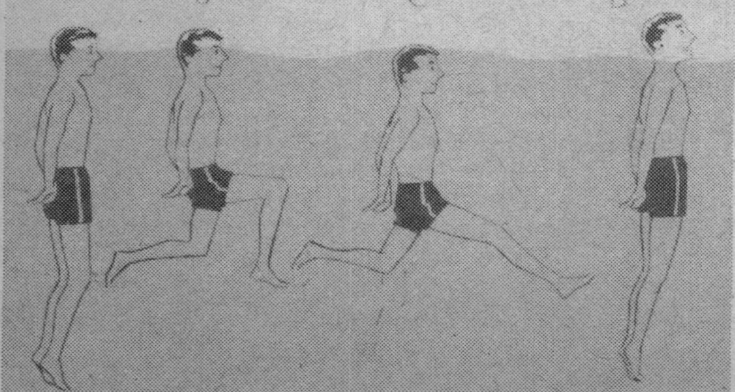

Scissors kick

Outward Bound

"I can't do that, I'll die."

But, if, for whatever horrid reason you do do it, and live, ah. Then right from your center out speculation is open about all the other things you knew you couldn't do.

This was one of the qualities of the Acid Tests administered by the Merry Pranksters. It was the only deeply useful thing I found in Ranger and Paratroop training in the Army. It looks to be the basic function of the Outward Bound *School of the Possible.*

Tuition for 26 days of Outward Bound (schools in various harsh locations) is $350-450 for people mid-teens to early twenties. There are courses for girls and older folks. According to a report in Reader's Digest, "No one who wants the Outward Bound Course is denied for financial reasons." U.S. Schools are in Texas, North Carolina, Oregon, Maine, Minnesota, Colorado and New Hampshire. For information and application forms, write:

Outward Bound, Inc.
165 West Putnam Ave.
Greenwich, Conn. 06830

26-DAY PROGRAM FOR ONE 12-STUDENT WATCH

DAY	0845-1030	1030-1215	1300-1545	1545-1730	1945-2100
1	Enroute to Rockland, Maine		12-mile boat trip to Hurricane Island	Issue Gear Quiet Walk	Director's Welcome Pledges
2	First Aid Lecture	Initiative Tests Ropes, Wall	Seamanship and Navigation Rowing Whaleboats		Navigation Lecture
3	Seamanship Small Sail Boats	Ecology First Field Trip	Drownproofing Introduction	Climbing Knots, Belays	Free Time/Duty Watc (duty watch begins at 2100)
4	DUTY WATCH: 24-hour manning of the Rescue Station and Radios Radio Procedures, Fire Fighting Techniques, Proper Use of E uipment, Weather, Logs, Mess Detail				
5	Sunday Meeting Free Time	Seamanship Peapods	Initiative Tests Ropes, Walls	Downproofing Float Test	Artificial Respiration Lecture, Demonstrati
6	Climbing Belaying, Scrambling	Downproofing Practice tied up tests	Seamanship and Navigation Rowing Drills, Intro. to Sailing		Navigation Plotting Practice
7	Three Day - Planning a Cruise, Stowing and Checking a Boat Inventories, Camp Ashore at Nigh				
8	Training Cruise: Basic Campers Skills, Boat Watches Intensive Seamanship, Night Exercises				
9	In Whale Boats: Anchoring, Man Overboard Procedures F ·wing, Sailing Navigation, Return by 1730				
10	Climbing Rappelling, Practice Falls	Drownproofing Legs Tied Test	Seamar p and Navigation Drills w· nout Instructor		First Aid Lecture
11	Seamanship Capsize Drill	Ecology Field Trip (low tide)	Community Service	Drownproofing Arms Tied Test	Free Time Duty Watch
12	DUTY WATCH: 24-hour manning of the Rescue Station and Radios. Solo Briefing after 2100 Rescue Unit, Fire Fighting, Search Patterns, Mess Detail, Casualty Handling, Logistical Support				
13	Solo Drop Off on an Island				

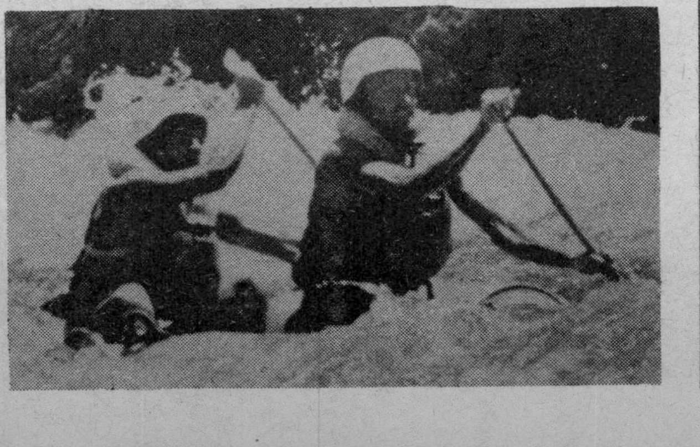

National Outdoor Leadership School

An item I believe you should consider for your catalog is the National Outdoor Leadership School located in Lander, Wyoming.

It is different from the Outward Bound Schools you list in your catalog since it teaches skills for living in the mountain wilderness rather than using it as an obstacle course or training ground . . . . . . it teaches for the environment rather than through it.

While limited to the Wind River Range of Wyoming, NOLS provides a better background for those wanting to learn about the mountain wilderness than the Colorado or Northwest Outward Bound School do. I say this from experience, having worked as an instructor at both schools. For more information you schould write to:

Mr. Paul Petzoldt, Director
National Outdoor Leadership School
Lander, Wyoming 82520

Sincerely,

Dave H. Williams
Lake Forest, Illinois

For more information on Outward Bound and National Outdoor Leadership Training, *see p. 301.*

Indian Crafts and Lore

If Boy Scouts and Germans make better Indian gear than most Indians (it's true: ask at any pow-wow), this book may be why. Thorough research and splendid illustration trip you right on in. Good book.

—SB

Indian Crafts and Lore
W. Ben Hunt
1954; 112 pp.

$3.95 postpaid

from:
Golden Press, Inc.
Western Pub. Co.
1220 Mound Ave.
Racine, Wisconsin 53404

or WHOLE EARTH
CATALOG

Good Medicine

A series of booklets with how-to info and worshipful flavor, from:

Adolf Hungry Wolf
P.O. Box 429
Fort Macleod
Alberta, Canada

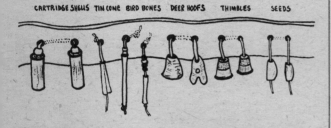

CARTRIDGE SHELLS TIN CONE BIRD BONES DEER HOOFS THIMBLES SEEDS

Indian Craft Materials

Grey Owl has mainly inexpensive, wide range of quasi-authentic stuff for making Indian outfits. Good selection of records. Catalog free.

[Suggested by Pam Wright]

Four Winds has what looks like genuine Indian goods — moccasins, cradle boards, baskets, jewelry, etc. Catalog is an unillustrated mimeographed list, costs 25¢.

Del Trading Post supplies authentic raw materials for American Indian crafts, particularly northern plains. Excellent selection of beads. Catalog $1.00.

—SB

DEL TRADING POST has been in business over 17 years. Through the years our customers have mainly been Indians and Indian lore enthusiasts but with our listing in the Whole Earth Catalog our clientele has broadened to include a wide range of people. We appreciate the increased business these "new people" have provided, but please remember, we are not Wards or Sears and we don't want to be. Del Trading Post is still basically a one man operation, ("I get by with a little help from my . . ." wife.) I'm in this business because I enjoy it. If I wanted to work and make money, I would have stayed at General Motors.

Peace,
Dennis Lessard

Del Trading Post
Mission, South Dakota 57555

41) TRADE PAINT — An early trade item used for coloring buckskin, painting parfleches, war shirts, pictographs, etc. They can be used dry or applied with a fixative depending on what you are painting. Our colors are exact duplicates of the old colors and are the finest powdered pigments available. Colors available: Vermillion, Yellow, Green, Blue, Black, White, Verdigris (bluish-green), Brick red (this is the color of red earth paint), and Ochre (this is the color of yellow earth paint).
.75 for 4 ounces of one color.

55) BUFFALO HIDES — No longer available

62) CATLINITE PIPES — Genuine Indian made "T" style red pipestone pipes with wooden stems.
Large, approx. 26" overall length — $30.00
Medium, " 20" " — 24.00
Small, " 14" " — 12.00
plus $1.00 for shipping costs

North American Indian Arts

Another excellent little book from Golden Press, illustrating as well as anything I've seen that Art and Technology are one in original North American cultures.

—SB

North American Indian Arts
Andrew Hunter Whiteford
1970; 160 pp.

$1.95 postpaid

from:
Golden Press, Inc.
Div. of Western Pub. Co.
1220 Mound Avenue
Racine, Wisconsin 53404

or WHOLE EARTH CATALOG

CHIPPING techniques were used to shape flint and other dense, smooth-textured stones into weapons and tools. Techniques are described below.

PERCUSSION CHIPPING knocks off flakes with a sharp blow. The direction and force of the blow determines the size and shape of the flake. Stone and antler hammers are used in direct percussion (1). A rest (2), to hold the flint in place, improves control. Indirect percussion (3) is used to strike off long blades with accuracy.

PRESSURE CHIPPING is used to shape and finish fine stone implements. A chipping tool of bone or antler (4) is pressed against the edge of the flint, breaking a small flake from the opposite surface (5). A crutch (6) may be used for increased pressure.

Secondary flaking is a finishing process (7). Rough pieces are retouched to even the edges and to give the blade a uniform thickness.

Pressure finishing is also used to form notches and barbs. The point may be held in the hand (7) or on a support (8) with a cushion of leather used for protection.

Nibbling with a notched antler (9) or prong (10) removes minute flakes from the edges of points and knives.

Grey Owl
Indian Craft Manufacturing Co.
150-02 Beaver Rd.
Jamaica, New York 11433

French Brass Beads

IC-104(DV) FRENCH BRASS BEADS: The real SOLID BRASS beads, and burnished to a high polish. Large opening for thong. Use for necklaces, chokers, breastplates, etc. ¼"
Per 50— **$2.25**   Per 100— **$4.10**   Per 1000— **$37.50**

Plus $.50 postage and insurance

Four Winds Trading Post
Route #1
St. Ignatius, Montana 59865

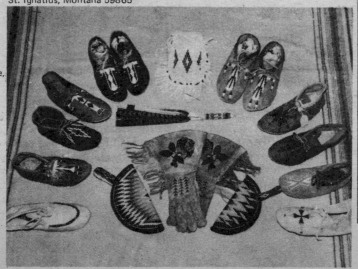

Indian House Records

Excellent LP recordings of American Indian Songs are available from INDIAN HOUSE, Box 472, Taos, New Mexico 87571. Each album contains representative songs from one tribe or one culture area. Some of the tribes now on this label are: Navaho, Taos, Ponca, Kiowa, Comanche, Kiowa-Apache, and Creek.

All sounds are recorded and produced on modern high fidelity equipment by Tony Isaacs, the proprietor of INDIAN HOUSE and a longtime student of Indian music. Isaacs has had many years of field experience recording Indian music on various reservations in the US.

An album titled "Sounds of Indian America, Plains and Southwest," has been released. This very inclusive album has music that was recorded at the Gallup Inter-Tribal Ceremonial, Gallup, NM.

Sincerely,
Frank Turley
Santa Fe, New Mexico

**IH 2501 Handgame of the Kiowa, Kiowa Apache, $5.00
and Comanche**
Carnegie Roadrunners vs. Billy Goat Hill
23 handgame songs sung by these two teams during an actual game. More than 60 singers. Recorded **live** at Carnegie, Oklahoma. Introductory notes on jacket.

**IH 1001 Round Dance Songs of Taos Pueblo— $5.00
Volume One**
16 Taos round dance songs sung by John C. Gomez, Orlando Lujan, Ralph Lujan, Benny Mondragon, Ruben Romero, and Louis Sandoval. Recorded at Taos Pueblo, New Mexico. Introductory notes on jacket.

Catalog of Indian Books

$1.00 from:
The Ceremonial Indian Book Service
P.O. Box 1029
Gallup, New Mexico 87301

Best mail-order source for Indian Books I've been able to find. They have over 2000 titles listed. Nice to deal with. Is an activity of the Inter-Tribal Indian Ceremonial Association.

Cal Knight
Pocatello, Idaho

PEOPLE AT THE STORE

When D.R. went in the store to mail the letters to Estelle and the Anaheim Flash, Mrs. Thornton saw him and headed him off at the bread rack.

"Well I'll swan," she said. "Look who finally came down off the hill."

"Hello Mrs. Thornton."

"Hello yourself is what I say," said Mrs. Thornton. "What have you been doing all week, anyhow, hibernating?"

D.R. laughed and blushed a little and scratched his head. "No mam. I've been working pretty hard."

"I'll bet you have," said Mrs. Thornton. "Sorting through Emmit's stuff I bet, God rest him."

"Yes mam. Trying to clean up a little. And keep his animals fed. There's a lot of work to do up there."

"I know just what you mean," said Mrs. Thornton. "It took us over a month to go through Wheeler's daddy's things when he died. We couldn't figure out what to do with it all."

"Is that him?" said a man's voice behind Mrs. Thornton.

"This is him," said Mrs. Thornton. And then to D.R. she said, "We've been talking about you, young 'un. Come over here and meet some people."

The man who had spoken was a pale and nearly bald fellow sitting in a wheel-chair. Grinning, he rolled himself outside of the little circle of chairs where the other people were sitting and came forward to meet D.R. and Mrs. Thornton.

"I'm Barry Berry," the man said. "I'm proud to make your acquaintance."

"Barry's the news correspondent for the county paper," said Mrs. Thornton. "He was asking me questions about you. I don't guess you've seen this week's paper yet have you?"

"No mam, I haven't," said D.R.

"Barry wrote you up," said Mrs. Thornton, and turning then she called out to Mrs. Godsey, who was in the post office cage in the far corner of the store, "Is they a copy of the paper around anywhere, Mrs. Godsey?"

"Is they what, honey?" Mrs. Godsey called back. She was reading someone's post card and did not look up when she replied.

"The paper. David aint seen Barry's article in it yet."

"I've got one in yonder," said Mrs. Godsey, still without looking up. "I'll get it for him when I get done here."

"Mrs. Godsey'll show you her'n after while," said Mrs. Thornton.

"I'd like to see it," said D.R.

"Well," said Barry. "It wasn't much, actually. I've been down with some kind of virus lately, and I didn't write much last week. It was just a little mention about Emmit was all. I sure was sorry to hear about Emmit, I'm going to miss him a lot."

(continued)

*who loned it through the streets of Idaho seeking
visionary indian angels who were visionary
indian angels . . .*

—Ginsberg, Howl

The booklist that follows comes from two intense informal
years (and five-slack ones) hanging around Indians,
reservations, anthropologists, and libraries. Long may
Indians, reservations, anthropologists and libraries thrive!
They gave me more reliable information, and human
warmth, than dope and college put together.

I'm sure that the books all by themselves cannot deliver
The Native American Experience. For that you need
time immersed in the land and neighborly acquaintance
at least with some in fact Indians. Still, an amazing
amount is in the books.

—SB

Book of the Hopi

If you're susceptible to tarot or astrology, you'll probably
revel in this book. Its business is the esoteric lore and
historical drama which lives and protects the Hopi Indians
in Arizona. They were possibly the farthest out of the
American tribes (in present times they are not as together as
Zuni, or Taos, but they are larger and so is what they
attempted). This is the mysticism not of change but of
stability, of the year cycle, of one more winter of food
obtained by the hard knowledge from uncounted prior
generations of winters and, they say, travels from world to
world and place to place to arrive finally at the center,
these bleak mesas, to here sustain forever responsibility for
the well-being of the world. Frank Waters was perhaps too
eager to write a Bible, but I can't blame him. It's that kind
of knowledge.

—SB

Book of the Hopi
Frank Waters,
Oswald White Bear Fredericks
1963; 423 pp.

$3.25 postpaid

from:
Ballantine Books, Inc.
101 Fifth Avenue
New York, New York 10003

or WHOLE EARTH CATALOG

So the people emerged to the Second World. Its name was Tokpa
Dark Midnight . Its direction was south, its color blue, its mineral
qochasiva, silver. Chiefs upon it were salavi, the spruce; kwahu,
the eagle; and kolichiyaw, the skunk.

It was a big land, and the people multiplied rapidly, spreading over
it to all directions, even to the other side of the world. This did
not matter, for they were so close together in spirit they could
see and talk to each other from the center on top of the head.
Because this door was still open, they felt close to Sotuknang
and they sang joyful praises to the Creator, Taiowa.

They did not have the privilege of living with the animals, though,
for the animals were wild and kept apart. Being separated from
the animals, the people tended to their own affairs. They built
homes, then villages and trails between them. They made things
with their hands and stored food like the Ant People. Then they
began to trade and barter with one another.

This was when the trouble started. Everything they needed was on
this Second World, but they began to want more.

Parrot Clan maiden
sitting on a plaque of
seeds during
Soyal Ritual.

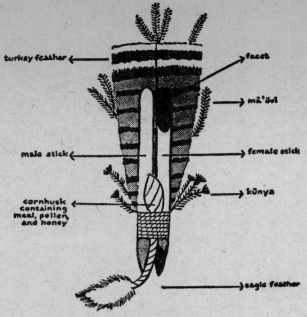

Figure 55. Male-and-female pâho

Every *pâho*, simple or complex, is made with prayerful concentration
and ritually smoked over. Then it is carried to a shrine, where it is
stuck in a cleft of rocks or hung on a bush and left until the invisible
vibrations of the prayer it embodies are slowly absorbed by the forces
of life to which it is dedicated.

The Lost Universe

The book has anthropological rigor along with its very
unusual completeness. Here is the whole life of the Pawnee,
told in a way that you could go now and live it. Here are
old solutions to problems we consider unsolvable and new.

—SB
[Suggested by Pam Smith]

The Lost Universe
Gene Weltfish
1965; 617 pp.

$1.65 postpaid

from:
Ballantine Books, Inc.
101 Fifth Ave.
New York, N.Y. 10003

or WHOLE EARTH CATALOG

The Pawnee child was born into a community from the beginning,
and he never acquired the notion that he was closed in "within
four walls." He was literally trained to feel that the world around
him was his home— *kahuraru*, the universe, meaning literally the
inside land, and that his house was a small model of it. The
infinite cosmos was his constant source of strength and his
ultimate progenitor, and there was no reason why he should
hesitate to set out alone and explore the wide world, even though
years should pass before he returned. Not only was he not
confined within four walls but he was not closed in with a permanent
group of people. The special concern of his mother did not mean
that he was so closely embedded with her emotionally that he was
not able to move about.

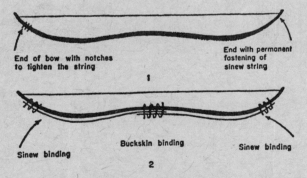

End of bow with notches
to tighten the string

End with permanent
fastening of
sinew string

1

Sinew binding   Buckskin binding   Sinew binding

2

FIGURE 51-1. (1) A simple bow of ashwood. (2) A sinew-backed
bow, *tskatstaxkasa*. Two pieces of sinew, crossed at the middle
could be permanently pasted on when wet.

•

As they continued on the move, pressures might build up between
individuals because of the closeness of the living conditions in
camp and the strain of constant migration. This was particularly
true between father-in-law and son-in-law. Theoretically, it was
the first duty of the son-in-law to serve his wife's family, but
when his father-in-law was quite old, the son-in-law often felt put
upon by the arrangement. Sometimes in the camp one could hear
people calling out, "Fight, fight!" and father-in-law and son-in-law
would be grappling with each other in a tent. People all came
running and a roughneck in the crowd would call out, "Who's
underneath?" Someone who was close to the tent would say,
"Son-in-law." In general the crowd would approve and say,
"That's good," the sentiment being with the underdog, the old
father-in-law. Such a quarrel would be ended when a brave or
other person of high social rank put a hand on each of the com-
batants and said, "I want you to stop." Out of respect for his
rank and eminence, they would separate at once and go in
different directions. Should they not respond it would be a major
insult and he would say a second time, "Didn't you hear me?"
This would certainly end the fight. Any person known to be
sensitive and to dislike violence could perform this same good office.
Violence of this kind within the village or band was considered a
serious social malfunction and people made every attempt to avoid
it or put a stop to it.

Black Elk Speaks

The Pueblo tribes don't go in for visionary solitary mystical
whizbangs. (Of all of them only Taos is into peyote very
much.) The plains tribes are something else however. Their
lives turned on their visions—solo manhood transports,
dreams, name visions, sun dance ordeals, battle ecstasy,
doctoring sessions . . . and later, ghost dance and peyote.
This book is the power vision of one Oglala Sioux, and the
extraordinary man it made. Black Elk's account, besides
affording unusual insight into Sioux life and historical
figures such as Crazy Horse, demonstrates the manner of
recognizing a serious vision and being responsible for it,
and the burden, joy and power of doing that.

—SB

Black Elk Speaks
John G. Neihardt
1932, 69; 280pp.

$1.50 postpaid

from:
Pocket Books
c/o Simon & Schuster
One West 39th Street
New York. N.Y. 10018
or WHOLE EARTH CATALOG

Crazy Horse's father was my father's cousin, and there were no
chiefs in our family before Crazy Horse; but there were holy
men; and he became a chief because of the power he got in a
vision when he was a boy. When I was a man, my father told me
something about that vision. Of course he did not know all of it;
but he said that Crazy Horse dreamed and went into the world
where there is nothing but the spirits of all things. That is the
real world that is behind this one, and everything we see here is
something like a shadow from that world. He was on his horse in
that world, and the horse and himself on it and the trees and the
grass and the stones and everything were made of spirit, and
nothing was hard, and everything seemed to float. His horse was
standing there, and yet it danced around like a horse made only of
shadow, and that is how he got his name, which does not mean that
his horse was crazy or wild, but that in his vision it danced around
in that queer way.

It was this vision that gave him his great power, for when he went in
to a fight, he had only to think of that world to be in it again, so that
that he could go through anything and not be hurt. Until he was
murdered by the Wasichus at the Soldiers' Town on White River he
was wounded only twice, once by accident and both times by some
one of his own people when he was not expecting trouble and was
not thinking; never by an enemy. He was fifteen years old when he
was wounded by accident; and the other time was when he was a
young man and another man was jealous of him because the man's
wife liked Crazy Horse.

They used to say too that he carried a sacred stone with him, like
one he had seen in some vision, and that when he was in danger,
the stone always got very heavy and protected him somehow. That,
they used to say, was the reason no horse he ever rode lasted very
long. I do not know about this; maybe people only thought it; but
it is a fact that he never kept one horse long. They wore out. I
think it was only the power of his great vision that made him great.

•

. . .Then I was standing on the highest mountain of them all, and
round about beneath me was the whole hoop of the world. And
while I stood there I saw more than I can tell and I understood more
than I saw; for I was seeing in a sacred manner the shapes of all
things in the spirit, and the shape of all shapes as they must live
together like one being. And I saw that the sacred hoop of my
people was one of many hoops that made one circle, wide as daylight and as starlight, and in the center grew one mighty flowering
tree to shelter all the children of one mother and one father. And
I saw that it was holy.
  Black Elk said the mountain he stood upon in his vision was Harney,
Peak, in the Black Hills. "But anywhere is the center of the world,"
he added.

•

When a vision comes from the thunder beings of the west, it comes
with terror like a thunder storm; but when the storm of vision has
passed, the world is greener and happier; for wherever the truth of
vision comes upon the world, it is like a rain. The world, you see, is
happier after the terror of the storm.

•

You have noticed that the truth comes into this world with two
faces. One is sad with suffering, and the other laughs; but it is the
same face, laughing or weeping. When people are already in despair,
maybe the laughing face is better for them; and when they feel
too good and are too sure of being safe, maybe the weeping face
is better for them to see.

•

I think I have told you, but if I have not, you must have understood,
that a man who has a vision is not able to use the power of it until
after he has performed the vision on earth for the people to see.

Custer Died For Your Sins

Vine is the perfect dude to write of current Indian politics. Son of a missionary, enough Sioux to be a Sioux, long experience getting Indian kids into good schools, revved up by The National Indian Youth Council stand-up-and-fight meetings of the late fifties and early sixties, levered into the key position of Executive Director of the major Indian lobby The National Congress of American Indians, and after all that he's thirty-five and still funny. He has what Alvin Josephy warned me about, "the traditional American Indian cut-throat zeal for politics." Add that to his humor and his thoroughness and you have an unusually clear summary of the Indian situation now. His recommended route for Indian survival is strong land-based tribal identity.

Since Vine addressed his book primarily to young Indians, I can't resist a remark to young white Indian-savers: you can't help anybody by saving them; that's a self-defeat program. Relax and appreciate. Custer died for your sins. Also your virtues.

A long-haired artist famous former-dope-fiend commune white person I know is busy learning from his Indian friends at the Taos Pueblo: manners.

—SB

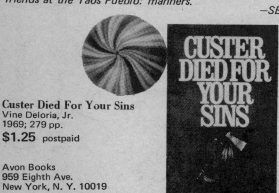

Custer Died For Your Sins
Vine Deloria, Jr.
1969; 279 pp.

$1.25 postpaid

Avon Books
959 Eighth Ave.
New York, N. Y. 10019

or WHOLE EARTH CATALOG

From 1860 to 1880, tribes were confined to reservations, as the West was in its death throes. Churches began lobbying early in the 1860's at the Indian Bureau in Washington for franchises over the respective reservations. Thus one reservation would be assigned to the Roman Catholics, one to the Lutherans, one to the Methodists, and one to the Episcopalians. Other churches were prohibited from entry on a reservation once it had been assigned to a particular church and could enter only with permission from the other church. It always bothered me that these churches who would not share pulpits and regarded each other as children of the devil, should have so cold-bloodedly divided up the tribes as if they were choosing sides for touch football.

People have found it hard to think of the Indian Bureau without conjuring up the picture of a massive bureaucracy oppressing a helpless people. Right-wing news commentators delight in picturing the Indian as a captive of the evil forces of socialism and leftist policy. Liberals view the bureaucracy as an evil denial of the inherent rights of a free man.

It would be fair to say that the Indian people are ambivalent about all this. They fully realize that with no funds for investment in social services they are dependent upon the federal government for services which the ordinary citizen provides for himself and which other poor do not receive except under demeaning circumstances. Yet they are also fully aware that the services they receive are not gratis services. Many services are set out in early treaties and statutes by which Indians bargained and received these rights to services in return for enormous land cessions.

. . . the bureau should not be characterized as paternalistic. It should be characterized as "fear-ridden," for the circle of fear that operates within it is much more detrimental to its efficiency than is its desire to paternalize.

•

Peoplehood is impossible without cultural independence, which in turn is impossible without a land base. Civil Rights as a movement for legal equality ended when the blacks dug beneath the equality fictions which white liberals had used to justify their great crusade. Black power, as a communications phenomenon, was a godsend to other groups. It clarified the intellectual concepts which had kept Indians and Mexicans confused and allowed the concept of self-determination suddenly to become valid.

•

I remember spending a whole afternoon talking with a number of hippies who had stopped in Denver on the way west. They were tribally oriented but refused to consider customs as anything more than regulations in disguise. Yet it was by rejecting customs that the hippies failed to tribalize and became comical shadows rather than modern incarnations of tribes.

Hippies, at least as I came to understand them, had few stable clan structures. They lived too much on the experiential plane and refused to acknowledge that there really was a world outside of their own experiences. Experience thus became the primary criteria by which the movement was understood. Social and economic stability were never allowed to take root.

•

Robert Thomas tells a famous story concerning the Cherokee who had a white man kill his children, steal his wife, sell his cattle, and burn his farm. The Cherokee chased the man for ten years and finally caught him. "Are you the guy who did all those things," the Cherokee asked. Yes, the white man admitted, he was the one.

"Well, you better watch that crap," the Cherokee warned.
And that is my greatest concern for the Indian people. That we will be so damn polite that we will lose everything for fear of hurting someone's feelings if we object to the way things are going.

Tales of the North American Indians

most anthropology
always seemed a little like
legalized graverobbing
to me.
this book does everything
through a cross-reference
bibliography-type distance
from the content classification system,
but the tales survive. it is a
fine readable collection of farout stories.

—jd

Tales of the North American Indians
selected and annotated
by Stith Thompson
1966; 385 pp.

$2.95 postpaid

from:
Indiana University Press
Tenth and Morton Streets
Bloomington, Indiana 47401

or WHOLE EARTH CATALOG

The beaver and the porcupine were great friends and went about everywhere together. The porcupine often visited the beaver's house, but the latter did not like to have him come because he left quills there. One time, when the porcupine said that he wanted to go out to the beaver's house, the beaver said, "All right, I will take you out on my back." He started, but instead of going to his house he took him to a stump in the very middle of the lake. Then he said to him, "This is my house," left him there, and went ashore.

While the porcupine was upon this stump he began singing a song, "Let it become frozen. Let it become frozen so that I can cross to Wolverine-man's place." He meant that he wanted to walk ashore on the ice. So the surface of the lake froze, and he walked home.

Some time after this, when the two friends were again playing together, the porcupine said, "You come now. It is my turn to carry you on my back." Then the beaver got on the porcupine's back, and the porcupine took him to the top of a very high tree, after which he came down and left him. For a long time the beaver did not know how to get down, but finally he climbed down, and they saw that this is what gives the broken appearance to tree bark.

The Eagle, The Jaguar, and the Serpent

i've had this book out of the library for about four years now, and haven't read the text yet, got my money's worth out of the illustrations.

—jd

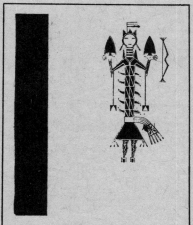

The Eagle, the Jaguar, and the Serpent
Indian Art of the Americas
Miguel Covarrubias
1954; 314 pp.

$20.00 postpaid

Alfred Knopf, Inc.
c/o Random House, Inc.
Westminster, Md. 21157

or WHOLE EARTH CATALOG

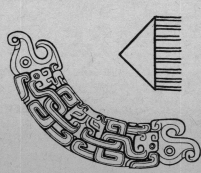

SB '64

Hola Tso

Sacred Knowledge

Will you please reveal to me what knowledge of organization the Indians taught you. I have been wondering since the article in Rolling Stone a few months ago. Hope you will find time to answer.

Love,
Eileen O'Leary
Vancouver
B.C.

Anarchistic Indians, right? So I still thought until I attended a Navaho peyote meeting. The Roadman, Hola Tso, was in charge—sat at the center behind the altar, handled all the major ceremonial changes, was aware of everything going on, had full responsibility and authority, was strict, was humorous, said very little, let most of the administrative mechanics be handled by the other officers Fireman, Cedarman, Drummer, Peyote Woman---one hand on the helm, sharp crew.

I've been to glorious meetings, with big feeling and big learning. And to loser meetings , boring, depressing. The glorious were flexible, tight. The losers, loose, "democratic", wishful, weak. That's what I saw. The difference wasn't Indian, White; it was responsibility, or not.

—SB

Alcheringa

If you like Rothenberg's Technicians of The Sacred (p. 311) you can probably use his magazine of 'World's Tribal Poetries'.

—SB

Alcheringa
Jerome Rothenberg, Dennis Tedlock, eds.

$9.50 /4 issues (2 years)
$2.50 /issue

from:
Alcheringa
600 W. 163rd St.
New York, NY 10032

"You know," Barry went on, "I don't guess I saw Emmit more than once or twice a year the last five or six years he lived, but I tell you, I was always mindful of him living up there on that hill. I use to know about everybody that lived on Trace Fork. I watched 'em move out one by one, till they wasn't a soul living up there except Emmit. Of course it's all ruined up in there now. But it seemed like as long as Emmit stayed on, the place wasn't plum dead yet. I'd been wanting to get up to see Emmit for a long time, but I just never got around to it. Of course, if I'd of known he wasn't going to be with us right on and on, I'd have made myself get around to it. But there you are."

"It really is a shame," said Mrs. Thornton. "I mean, me and Wheeler talked about going to visit Emmit too, but we just kept putting it off. It's funny, how you'll put off things you intend to do, and put 'em off and keep on putting 'em off. And then all of a sudden it's too late to do it even if you tried. I feel bad about it, I declare I do."

"We all could have done better by Emmit than what we did," said Barry. "We sure could have been better neighbors than what we was."

(continued)

Children's Games in Street and Playground

Suppose you were trying to replace war. Would you be interested in "games in which children may deliberately scare each other, ritually hurt each other, take foolish risks, promote fights, play ten against one, and yet in which they consistently observe their own sense of fair play." (dust jacket blurb). The games are not learned from adults but passed on through the generations of children. This study comes from England, which looks to have a much richer game cycle than American kids usually experience. A product of ten years' research, the book thoroughly describes the rules of play and the popularity of more than a thousand fascinating games.

—SB

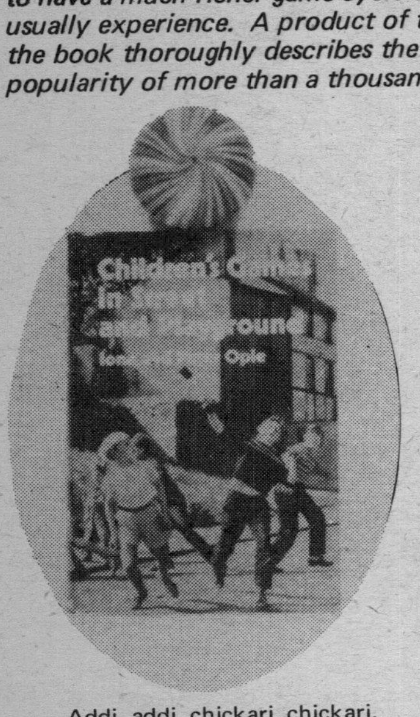

Children's Games in Street and Playground
Iona and Peter Opie
1969; 370 pp.

$10.00 postpaid

from:
Oxford University Press
16-00 Pollitt Drive
Fair Lawn, N. J. 07140

or WHOLE EARTH CATALOG

Addi, addi, chickari, chickari,
Oonie, poonie, om pom alarie,
Ala wala whiskey,
Chinese chunk.

One-erie, two-erie, tickerie, seven,
Allabone, crackabone, ten or eleven;
Pot, pan, must be done;
Tweedle-come, tweedle-come, twenty-one.

KINGY

This fast-moving game has all the qualifications for being considered the national game of British schoolboys: it is indigenous, it is sporting, it has fully evolved rules, it is immensely popular (almost every boy in England, Scotland, and Wales plays it), and no native of Britain appears to have troubled to record it.

"Kingy" is a ball game in which those who are not He have the ball hurled at them, without means of retaliation, and against ever-increasing odds, an element that obviously appeals to the national character. Anyone who is hit by the ball straightway joins the He in trying to hit the rest of the players. Those who are throwing may not run with the ball in their hands, but pursue their quarry by passing the ball to each other. Those being thrown at may run and dodge as they like, and may also punch the ball away from them with their fists. For this purpose players sometimes wrap a handkerchief round their hand, as "fisting" the ball can be painful. The game continues until all but one have been hit and are "out," and this player is declared "King." When the contestants are skilled (and boys of fifteen and sixteen readily play the game), the ball gets thrown with considerable force; it shoots back and forth across the street or playground, and the game can be as exciting to watch as a tennis match.

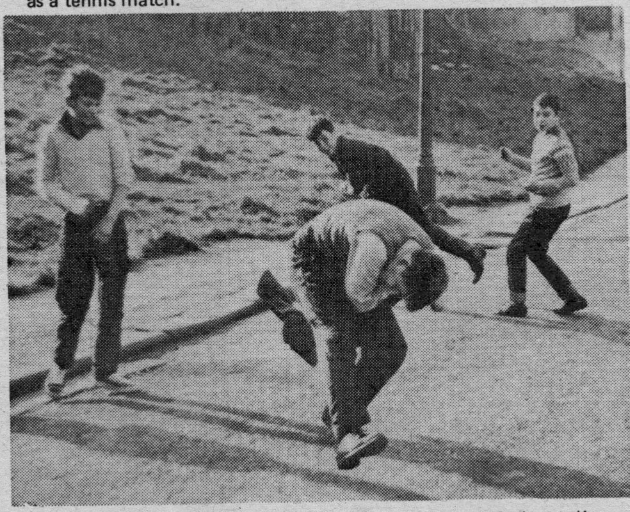

As befits a sport in which so much energy is expended, the preliminaries are sometimes wonderfully ritualistic. At Bishop Auckland, for instance, one person shouts "King" to start the proceedings, and two others follow up by crying "Sidey." The players then form a circle round the King, with the two who shouted "Sidey" standing on either side of him like heirs-apparent. The players making the circle stand with legs apart, each foot touching the foot of their neighbour on either side. The King picks up the ball and bounces it—or, as they say in Bishop Auckland, "stounces" it—three times in the ring, and then lets it roll. Everyone watches to see whose legs it will go through. If it does not roll through anybody's legs the King picks it up and bounces it again, and if his second turn fails he has a third try. If the ball still has not passed between anyone's legs, he hands it to the first sidey (the "foggy-sidey") who, as necessary, repeats the performance—for the moment the ball does pass between someone's legs that person is "on," and everyone runs. At the end of the game whoever becomes King takes the place in the centre of the ring to start the next game, and the first two people to shout "Sidey" stand beside him. . . .

The Rules. Although the ways of choosing the chaser are numerous, the game itself is played with little variation. Reports from more than fifty places have been so similar, it is as if a mimeographed sheet of rules was carried in every grubby trouser pocket. Such a set of rules would read as follows:

1. The number of players shall be not less than six or more than twenty: the best number is about twelve.

2. The boundaries of the game shall be agreed on before the game begins. A flat area of 20 x 20 yards, or a length of street of about 20—30 yards, depending on the number of players, is ample.

3. One person shall be chosen chaser, and the game shall start immediately he is chosen. The chaser shall, however, bounce the ball ten times before he throws it at anyone, to give the players time to scatter.

4. The chaser may not run with the ball; but while he is the sole chaser he may bounce the ball on the ground as he runs.

5. A player shall be "out" when the ball hits him on the body between his neck and knees (or, as may be agreed, between his waist and ankles). It shall be determined beforehand whether a hit shall count if the ball has first bounced on the ground or ricocheted off a wall; or whether only a direct hit shall count.

6. As soon as a player is "out" he shall assist the chaser in getting the other players out.

7. When there are two or more chasers they may not run with the ball, but may manoeuver as they wish by passing it to each other.

8. Players being chased may take what action they like to avoid being hit by the ball, including "fisting" it, i.e. punching it away with their fist. They may also pick up the ball between their fists and chuck it away.

9. Should a chaser catch the ball when it has been "fisted", or touch a player while he is holding the ball in his fists, the player shall be "out."

10. Should a player kick the ball, or handle it other than with his fists, he shall be "out."

11. Should a player run out of bounds when trying to avoid being hit by the ball he shall be "out."

12. The last player left in shall be "King," and shall officiate at the selection of the next chaser.

•

Some times I kill Some One and Some One kills me but my men release me and I release them Back.

•

Split the kipper

In this contest, which, as one boy admitted, "takes quite a lot of nerve, the two adversaries stand facing each other a yard or so apart, with their feet together. The first boy throws a knife, preferably a sheath knife, so that it sticks in the ground not more than twelve inches to the left or right of one of his opponent's feet. The other boy, without moving his feet, plucks the knife out of the ground, and moves his nearest foot to the place where the knife went in. In this position he makes a return throw (most boys specify that the knife must be thrown by the blade), and the first boy, likewise, moves his foot to where the knife stuck in. However, should the point of the knife not stick into the ground, or should it stick in more than twelve inches away from the person's foot ("if more than a span," says a Durham lad; "if over two knife lengths," says a Fife boy), the player does not have to move his foot, and the throw is lost. The object of the game is to force the opponent to stretch his legs so far apart that he cannot move them further, and gives in, or falls over while attempting the stretch. In this form "it is a short game and suitable for short breaks at school." But in many places, particularly in the north, a player is allowed to "split" his opponent. If a person's legs are uncomfortably wide apart, and his opponent's likewise, or at least moderately open, he may attempt to throw the knife so that it sticks between his opponent's legs, and if he succeeds in this, may close his own. Usually "splitting" is allowed only once, twice, or three times, otherwise the game can "go on for ages". Alternatively in Scotland, including the Isles, if the knife sticks between the opponent's legs, that person has to turn round, and thereafter throw less surely, and undoubtedly more dangerously, with his back to the other player.

This game, or ordeal, which is sometimes played with a dart, iron spike, or geometry dividers, has become popular only during the past decade.

World Wide Games

WWG is a small woodworking company that makes and sells games: mostly wooden; some expensive ones (up to $55); mostly inexpensive ($1 to $10). About half of their games are American (old and new); the others originated overseas. For the games they make, they sell replacement parts. The woodworking is clean, smooth, and solid.

Our family has been buying WWG's inexpensive games for several years. Their mail-order service is fast. Their catalog is free.

[Suggested and reviewed by R. W. Radl]

Catalog

free

from:
World Wide Games, Inc.
Box 450
Delaware, Ohio 43015

Complete $38.00

Extra Parts

#WWG 116-A	B. H. Stick	.35
#WWG 116-B	B. H. Puck	.15
#WWG 116-C	Instructions	.10
#WWG 116-D	Set of B. H. Parts	2.60

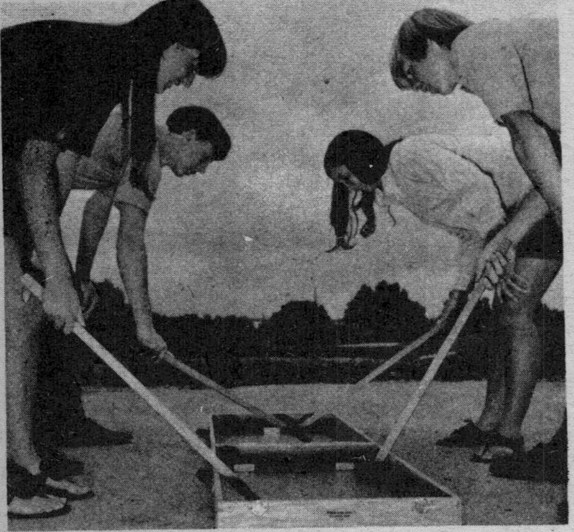

Box Hockey is an exciting and noisy game for 2 or 4 players. Each holds a stick in one hand and attempts to knock the puck through the goal to his left. Game is played on the floor — no table needed. Box Hockey is sturdily built with sides and ends of white oak lumber, bottom of hardwood plywood. It contains 6 sticks and 2 pucks. Box measures 18 x 60 inches open and folds to 18 x 30 x 6. Brass hinges and leather handles make Box Hockey an excellent carrying case for other games.

#WWG 121

Complete $13.00

#WWG 121-A	½" Steel Bearing	.15
#WWG 121-B	Instructions	.10

The Johnson Smith Catalog

If you were ever a kid, you remember Johnson Smith. But you may have forgotten just how relevant Johnson Smith could be to your present happiness, not to mention your spiritual development.

Remember their ads in the inside cover of Little Lulu? Remember the lists you used to make of all the things you wanted? Well, surprise! You'll still want the same things: secret agent pen radio, juggling kits, X-Ray Spex, Beatnik Disguise, Magic Money Maker, joy buzzers and, of course, VENTRILO ("BOYS! BOYS! BOYS! Learn Ventriloquism and Apparently THROW YOUR VOICE! Into a trunk, under the bed, under a table, back of the door, into a desk at school, or anywhere. You'll get lots of fun fooling the teacher, policemen, peddlers and surprise and fool your friends besides.")

Yes, Johnson Smith is alive and well in Detroit. Johnson Smith hasn't changed. But what about you? Get with it, kids! This is what you've been looking for and its been on the inside front cover of Little Lulu all the time.

Johnson Smith Catalog
80 pages
FREE!
35075 Automation Drive
Mt. Clemens, Michigan 48043

P.S. If you ever get the chance, pick up an *old* J-S catalog. (They've been publishing them for over 50 years). Incredible bargains: Like alligators for $1.50. Lions for $75. And pages of "indoor fireworks." Many of the old items are still listed, in the same form. (for example, page 49, "LEARN TO TAP DANCE" "Why envy the easy rhythm and fascinating grace of Step'n Fetchit.")

Peace.

Robert Goldman
Oakland, CA

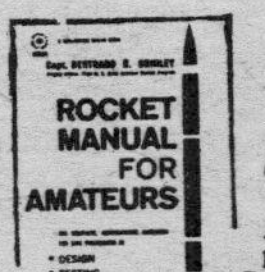

ROCKET MANUAL FOR AMATEURS

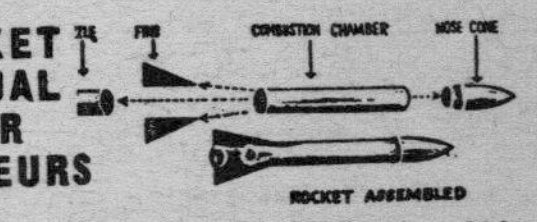

Amazingly complete and authoritative 380 page handbook that covers Rocketry

Covers: Basic Rocket Design, Motor Systems, Rocket Propellants (Solid & Liquid), Instrumentation, Safe Testing Procedure, Layout & Construction of Launching Site, Safe Firing Procedure, Tracking & Evaluation of Data, Summary of State Laws Governing Amateur Rocketry, Complete Mathematical Tables, Organization of Amateur Rocket Groups, Legal Codes and Safety Procedures, Fuel Formulas, Dictionary of Terminology, List of Other Books. 100 illustrations, diagrams, plans. Equal to books selling for $10.00 and more.

☐ 1008. Rocket Manual for Amateurs. Postpaid...$1.25

NO LONGER AVAILABLE

UNDERWATER MOTOR

$1.00

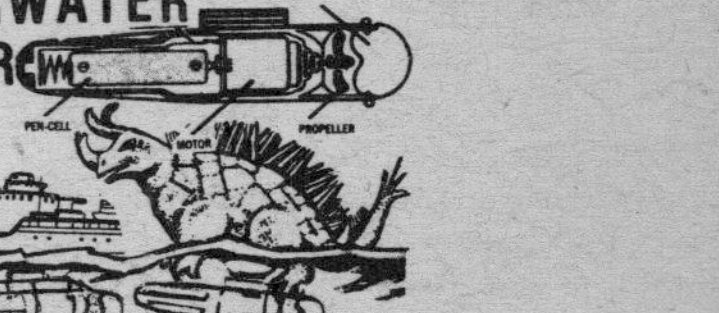

POWERS BOATS, SUBS, ANIMALS, etc. IN or UNDER WATER! Amazing imported precision submarine power unit runs hour on single pen-cell. Nearly **TEN MILLION** sold all over world before being brought to U.S. Waterproof sealed, adjustable rudder, built-in switch. 4500 RPM. 5" long. Suction cup or V-mount.

☐ 7435 Price Postpaid $1.00

50 FOOT MONORAIL

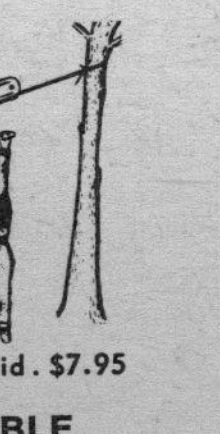

FLY THROUGH THE AIR WITH THE GREATEST OF EASE! Thrilling Monorail gives fast or slow ride, whatever you wish. Ball-bearing pulleys, comfortable handlebar grips, 50 foot line, all hardware for easy erecting on trees, house, etc.

☐ 7047. Complete Set Postpaid. $7.95

NO LONGER AVAILABLE

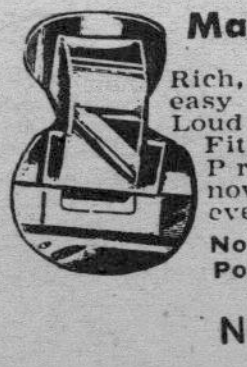

Magic Nose Flute

Rich, flute-like music easy to play.
Loud whistles, effects.
Fits over nose & mouth.
Produces the most novel effects you have ever heard!

No. 3478. Price, Postpaid............. **25c**

NO LONGER AVAILABLE

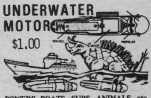

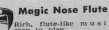

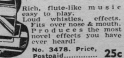

A Short Editorial on War

More war toys. —SB

Modern War in Miniature

We are enclosing a book, **Modern War In Miniature,** *authored by our son in 1964 when he was nineteen. One of its great uses is at the Wargaming table, a place to learn and understand war and its horrible effects, without experiencing its dreadful waste.*

It's also an excellent reference book and is in the libraries at West Point, the Air Force Academy, etc.

[Suggested and reviewed by Leota Korns]

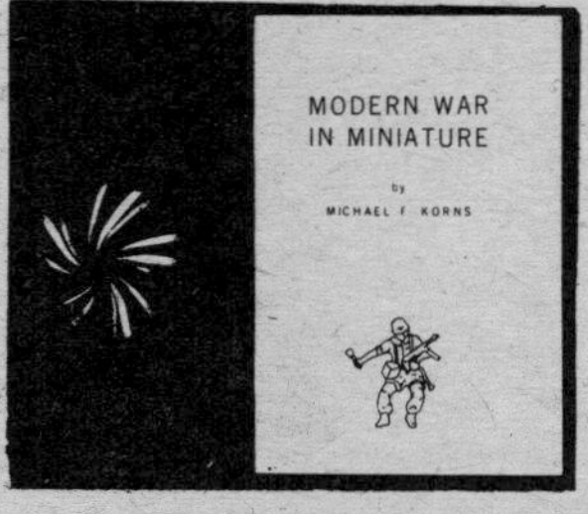

MODERN WAR IN MINIATURE
by
MICHAEL F. KORNS

Modern War in Miniature
Michael F. Korns
1964; 83 pp.

$3.95 postpaid

from:
Omega Co.
Dept. E771
Box 1617
Durango, Colorado 81301

The judges are very important. They are the only ones who need be familiar with the rules. The players only give orders as they would in actual combat. They are not allowed to see what is going on in the sand table or on the main flight board. They have only their maps with the positions of their own troops and planes, and they know only what the judge tells them that their troops can see or hear. In this way the judges are used to isolate the players within the confines of the knowledge of their troops.

•

J: THERE IS A SUB-MACHINE GUN FIRING ON THE BOARD.

J: Your schmeisser is kicking chunks out of the edge of the building all around him. . .It's hard to say whether you hit him or whether he pulled his head back.

J: an M-1 HAS FIRED ON THE BOARD.

J: That rifle round hit you in the side. It knocked you a little farther into the ditch; you're bleeding from the mouth too.

J: You can see who did it now. The American is on your left about 12 meters away running at you with his bayonet.

P: Can I still move?

J: Yes, but you are almost unconscious.

P: I'm turning around and firing the rest of my schmeisser's clip into him.

J: THERE IS A SCHMEISSER FIRING ON THE BOARD.

J: He's coming up fast. Your bullets are jerking around in an arc towards him as you turn. Seven meters, four meters, one meter. I'm afraid you're dead.

•

If a soldier is advancing on enemy positions *and is under fire* and his person is more than 20% exposed, his base chance of developing a transient reaction in any given two-second period is: r = 1/12. Of those soldiers who develop transient reactions while advancing, 30% usually exhibit manic symptoms and 70% disassociative symptoms.

If a soldier is stationary defending a position *and is fired upon* and is more than 20% exposed, his base chance of developing a transient reaction to stress in any given two-second period is: r = 1/12. Of those soldiers who develop transient reactions, about 30% will exhibit manic symptoms and 70% will develop disassociative symptoms.

Strategy & Tactics

I was once an umpire at a huge war game at Camp Drum, New York, and had a wonderful time.

Unfortunately, this magazine seems to be limited to board games using historic battles. It looks to have a cult readership related to Sci Fi fandom. But its considerations of game design, nostalgia-stroking, and bloodless conflict may be worth investigation by inventors of whatever's gonna replace war. You can be sure that peace isn't. Conflict is too interesting. —SB

Strategy & Tactics

$7.50 /year (bi-monthly)

from:
S&T
Box 396
New York, N. Y. 10009

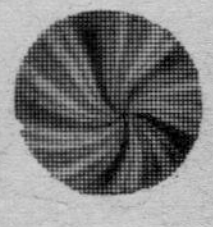

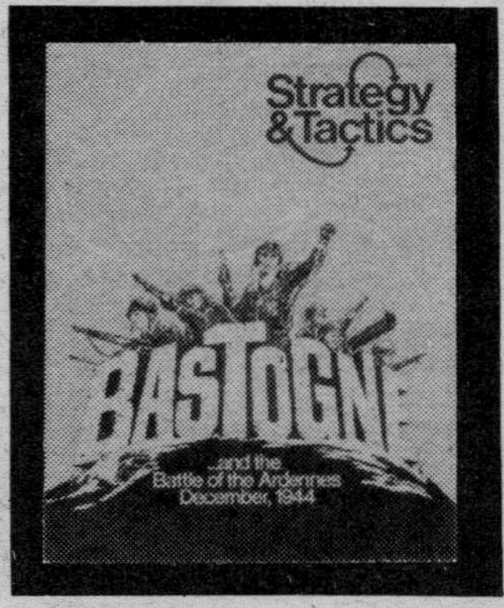

Strategy & Tactics
BASTOGNE
...and the Battle of the Ardennes December, 1944

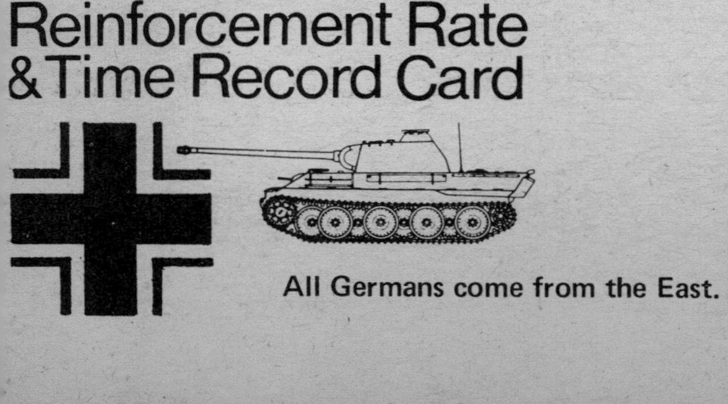

Reinforcement Rate
& Time Record Card
All Germans come from the East.

The Hand Game

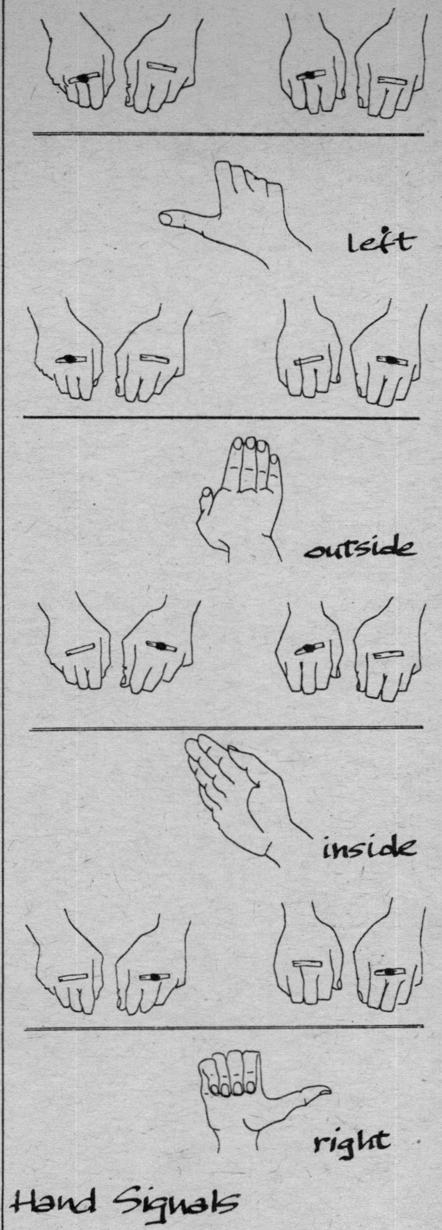

left
outside
inside
right
Hand Signals

The Bone Game is a gambling game
To Play you need
Two Tribes
A Place divided by a line
Each Tribe puts up Stakes, displayed in a Special place
Each Tribe begins with five marker sticks to keep score

There are four Magic Bones
Each small enough to be concealed comfortably in a closed fist
Two of the bones are marked by wrapping thread around them
Two bones, one marked, one unmarked, form a Set.

One Tribe begins by hiding the bones
The Tribe chooses Two Hiders
Each hider holds a set of bones, one bone in each hand
The hiders stand in front of their tribe
Close to the Line, fists closed.

The other Tribe chooses one Shooter whose task is to find the two threaded bones.

The play takes place when the Hiders have hidden their Bones
and present themselves facing the Line

Either Tribe may use any strategy they want in playing
Except the Line is not to be crossed
Nor may the Tribes touch each Other
Common Strategies Include
Chanting, Swaying
Singing
Music Making
Having Secrets
Casting Spells

The Shooter shows where he feels the threaded bones are hidden
By using a set of Hand Signals
There are four possible places the Bones can be hidden
When the Shooter is ready to shoot, he faces the Hiders across the Line, shouts HO and makes one of the Hand Signals
After the shout, the hiders open their fists displaying the bones

A shooter can capture no bones, one bone, or two bones
Every time the shooter fails to capture a threaded bone
His Tribe loses a marker stick; every time he succeeds
His Tribe wins a threaded bone.

The shooter shoots, until he has captured both threaded bones
Or lost all his Tribe's marking sticks
When the shooter has captured both bones
His Tribe chooses Hiders and hides the bones
The other Tribe chooses a Shooter

The clash is not only between the Shooter and Hiders
It is between the Spirits of the Two Tribes.

A clash is over when the Shooter has captured both bones.
A Round is over when one Tribe has taken all the Markers.
A Game is over when one Tribe has Won
The Agreed upon number of Rounds.

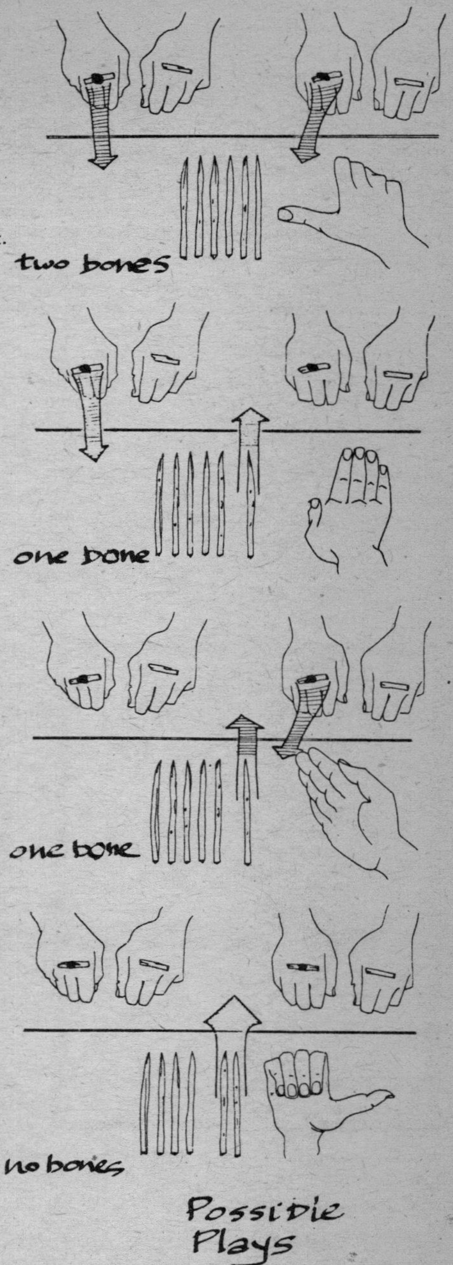

two bones
one bone
one bone
no bones
Possible Plays

All games to stay alive have to teach you something. Some games teach a lot. My three favorites are boffing, volley ball. . .and the Hand Game, which is a form of mind-war common to nearly all the North American Indian tribes. I first saw it played between the Maidus and Paiutes on a mountainside near Reno. The games went on for two days and nights, with what seemed like half the money in the county riding on the outcome. I'd wake up at 2 am and hear the steady pounding stick beat of the Paiutes when they were hiding the bones, chanting a dreamsong hiding song that sounded like ANy day now we're flying aWA-ay. ANy day now we're flying aWAY wayo maYA HA-ah ts-n-n-n-na-nah haYA-ah ts-n-n-n-na-nah! The Paiutes played men and women, steady and structured and controlled against the lolling drunken Maidu men-only team, opposite strategies evenly matched. Finally one Paiute woman single-handedly defeated the Maidus. No one could guess her. She was fantastic, a cool cruel queen of victory. She didn't hide her face like the others; she stared the shooter straight in the eye and crumpled him.

A few years ago I showed the game to Jim & Cynthia Nixon, and they showed it to Sim Van der Ryn, who came up with this nice set of instructions and illustrations on how to play. You can get copies of the poster from Sim at Box 372, Inverness, CA 94937, for $1.00.

—SB

Chicago-Chicago!'

CHICAGO CHICAGO is very similar to the more familiar wargame in that it involves conflict. It is unlike a wargame in that it does not simulate death. But then there are the "what if. . .?" situations. If nothing else it might broaden your understanding of what went on at the Democratic Convention in 1968.

DESIGNER'S NOTES

Probably the most significant "battle" fought by Americans in 1968 took place in the streets of Chicago between 25 and 28 August. This was conflict, politics waged with more than verbal violence as Clauswitz would put it. No one was killed, but the outcome of the battle, primarily the 'Police Riot' of 28 August (televised nationwide that same night), had a profound affect on subsequent American, and world, history. The embarassment of the Democratic party probably cost them an otherwise tight election. The effect of the subsequent Republication administration on the "state of the nation" were obviously different than if a Democratic administration had continued. The "What Ifs?" are manifold, but one fact stands out. The "Battle of Chicago" was a very significant event, ranking with the more 'conventional' battles of Midway, the 'Bulge' and Stalingrad as turning points in history. Ignore this fact and you'll have no one to blame but yourself when you wonder; "What the hell's going on in this country?" . . .

Putting such a situation into game format is extremely difficult. Eight months were spent on developing this game, longer than the time spent on such games as 1914 or JUTLAND. This was primarily because a new game system had to be developed. Not simply because this was not your usual "pitched battle" type conflict but more because one side was organized and the other wasn't. . .The game is based on the premise that neither side wished to avoid a confrontation. If either side had, there would have been no 'Battle of Chicago'. As it was, the demonstrators were determined to make their point and the police were determined to stop them. Thus the game becomes one of strategy, how best each side can achieve its goals. The Exposure Index reflects the accumulated 'good press' each side builds up. In the 'original campaign' the demonstrators built up a lead only late in the 'game'. What really put them in the lead was the police riot on the night of the 28th. One important point to keep in mind is that the demonstrator player is not actually 'commanding' his 'forces' in the same manner as the police player. Because there was no real organization and leadership for the demonstrators the demonstrator player is actually deciding which 'What if?' situations he would like to see played out. 'What if?' the demonstrators had done this or that? As it was, the 'demonstrator strategy' was quite simple: they should gather their strength in a remote and fairly 'safe' area (Lincoln park is the best for this) and then move downtown to a more 'exposed' (although less hospitable) area for the nitty-gritty 'confrontation'. There are, of course, many possible variations to this basic strategy.

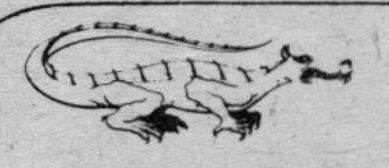

D.R. said, "Well, the thing for you all to do is come up and visit me some time. It looks like I'll be staying around a while."

Mrs. Thornton and Barry both looked a little startled. "Are you really?" said Mrs. Thornton.

"Yep," said D.R. "I thought I would. A month or two, anyhow. Maybe even longer."

Mrs. Thornton said, "Well I'll swan. Now that really is news," and turning around again she called out to Mrs. Godsey, "Did you hear that?"

"Hear what, honey?"

"David said he's going to live at the Collier place a while. Said he was going to stay on up there a month or more."

"Oh yes," said Mrs. Godsey. "Leonard told me that a day or two ago."

"Well it sure is news to me," said Mrs. Thornton, and she turned to gush about it some more to Barry and D.R.

But Barry had led D.R. over to the circle of chairs to introduce him to the other people in the store. There were two, Mrs. Whitaker, who was so shy she could only nod and say hello to D.R., and Mr. McClanahan, who was not at all shy, but who was old and could barely hear.

"Do what?" he yelled, cupping his hand to his ear.

(continued)

Paper Airplane Book

"If we knew what it was we would learn, it wouldn't be research, would it?" was the title of an ad for Scientific American's project of an international paper airplane competition. The 20 winners are photographed in full page aeronautical glory followed by a tear-out pattern for imitations. No materials are needed other than the basic one referred to in the dedication —

The authors wish to dedicate this manuscript to Capt. Fear God Bascomb, out of New Bedford, Massachusetts, who brought the first known pad of lined 8 x 11" paper from China on May 1, 1743. It may well be said of Capt. Bascomb that without him, the paper airplane as we know it would not have been possible.

and scissors and infinite doodling type patience. As a school librarian with only two copies of this wildly popular book, I was finally reduced to tearing it up page by page for an eye level wall long display for group reading and a handy supply of tracing paper for pattern copiers. Our airborn climax was the North Hillsborough, California School Paper Airplane Olympics with appropriate contests and flyers, after which we were not able to cross the school campus without shuffling ankle deep in aborted and/or terminated flight materials. The school custodian was one of the few associates not turned on by this librarian's flight of fancy (or reason, depending on your bias).

[Reviewed by Carol Guyton Goodell]

The Great International Paper Airplane Book
Jerry Mander, George Dippel, and Howard Gossage
1967; 128 pp.

$2.95 postpaid

from:
Simon & Schuster, Inc.
1 West 39th Street
New York, N. Y. 10018

or WHOLE EARTH CATALOG

How To Make and Fly Paper Airplanes

written by the winner of the Great International Paper Airplane Contest.
—jd

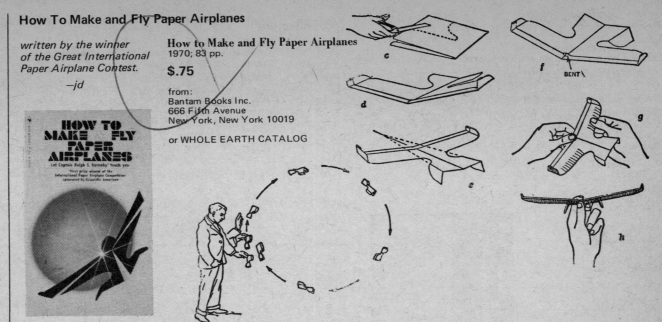

How to Make and Fly Paper Airplanes
1970; 83 pp.

$.75

from:
Bantam Books Inc.
666 Fifth Avenue
New York, New York 10019

or WHOLE EARTH CATALOG

Fishertechnik

One more item in the form of a suggestion to the Catalogue; there must be a few readers like myself who have kids (We have a six year old boy) and who travel and are often trying to answer the question of buying a worthwhile toy. Toys like art books are many and I haven't seen any in the catalogue. You ran the Tantra book because of it's obvious up front value and I feel the same way about a toy I want to tell you about.

We've taken our son everywhere we've gone and on our last trip we obtained a Fishertechnik building set which John played with day after day without ever tiring of the toy or destroying it and it took some abuse on our recent trip to Afganistan. This toy is not advertised, hence requires turning people on to it. I think it is the best building toy on the market with many applications for kids and adults. It's expensive and a German import. The sold importer is:

Fisher of America. Inc.
1317 Broad Street
Clifton, New Jersey 07013
Attn: Ted Kiesewetter

Lowell Sid Sheehy

Model Rockets

UNIQUE ROCKETRY

Model rockets, you say, what are they. . .idealizations of instruments of war? Not at all. They are idealizations of one of man's primal urges, mastery of the skies.

In practice model rocketry is safe (remote control firing, parachute recovery), inexpensive (average costs: engines— 25¢, vehicles— $2.50), scientific (limitless opportunity for creative one-man research), and great fun. Practical applications include smog sampling, weather studies and aerial photography. Model rocketry supplies became available as a safe and meaningful alternative to dangerous "Basement Bomber" activities of amateur rocket builders impressed by the first Sputniks in the late 1950's. The National Association of Rocketry was formed to promote safe and educational model rocketry activities among manufacturers and enthusiasts.

Brochure: Free
National Association of Rocketry
Box 178
McLean, Virginia 22101

Also, a NAR publication
Model Rocketeer
$6/yr. (membership)
National Assoc. of Rocketry
P.O. Box 178
McLean, VA 22101

Two new manufacturers suggested by Norman Ward at NAR:
Mr. Myron Bergenske
Aerospace Vehicles, Inc.
P.O. Box 77
Mineral Point, WI 53565

Mr. Lonnie Reese
Reese Industries
9300 East 68th
Raytown, MO 64133

There are nearly a dozen manufacturers of kits and parts to choose from, but ESTES and CENTURI are consistently the best. There are many similarities between these two, but their differences are striking. Estes is the venerable pioneer, but it stresses bold innovations such as flexible landing gear and unbelievably inexpensive kits for aerial photography cameras (Still camera: $5.95). Soon to come out with a motion picture camera suitable for use in flying models . . . less than $21.95 . . . WOW!

Centuri is noted for kits of handsomely detailed scale models and formidable power of their larger engines. Centuri, like Estes, has a well developed educational services program where free textbooks and discount prices are offered to any sort of reasonably legitimate educators such as teachers, Boy Scout leaders and Civil Air Patrolers. Both are mail order oriented, with excellent personalized service. The safe and inexpensive engines of all manufacturers are standardized and interchangeable. Estes and Centuri each send free newsletters to regular customers.

Model rocketry is a going thing, not only because it offers an opportunity for inexpensive creative research into the relatively unexplored field of sub-sonic rocketry, but because it is a fun way to participate in the Space Age.

Catalog: 25¢
Estes Industries, Inc.
Dept. 28
Box 227
Penrose, Colo. 81240

Catalog: 25¢
Century Engineering Co.
Box 1988
Phoenix, Ariz. 85001

Melville G. Boyd
Midwest City, Okla.

Kites

New Golden Handbook. All the basic information. Send up two trains of kites with spotters to keep them apart; attach a man-sized harness; goodbye.
—SB

Kites
Wyatt Brummitt
1971; 120 pp.

$1.50 postpaid

from:
Golden Press
c/o Western Publishing Co.
1220 Mound Ave.
Racine, Wisconsin 53404

or WHOLE EARTH CATALOG

The best known "general store" of kiting is the Go Fly a Kite Shop, 1613 Second Avenue, New York City 10028. An illustrated price list is available; much of their business is by mail. Andrea Bahadus is the proprietor.

Come Fly a Kite Store
900 North Point
Ghiradelli Square
San Francisco, CA. 94109
is operated by Diresh Khare, a famous Indian kiteflier.

Schubert's, 2135 Union Street, San Francisco 94123, is primarily a toy shop, but the owner is a kite enthusiast and carries a variety of ready-made models.

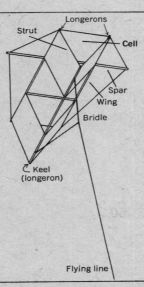

Longerons
Strut
Cell
Spar
Wing
Bridle
Keel (longeron)
Flying line

Kite Tales

For people who are into kite-flying as a hobby or a sport, I would like to suggest a listing of the American Kitefliers Association. Their mailing address is P.O. Box 1511, Silver City, New Mexico 88061. They are the only true organization of kite fliers in the world, representing all 50 states and 24 foreign countries. They publish a quarterly magazine, "Kite Tales," which contains many articles of interest on building and flying kites, as well as advertising for all different sorts of kites, probably the biggest selection anywhere. Membership costs $4 per year, $5 Canada, and $6 overseas, which includes a subscription to the magazine.

Sincerely, Pax,
Robert Williams
Worcester, Massachusetts

Regardless of what other equipment you take along on a kiteflying expedition, one should always have some type of cutting instrument, preferably a sharp knife. Perhaps the second most important item of supply is a roll of some type of self-adhesive tape to repair fabrics.

Oh, I've slipped the surly bonds of earth —

(See also p. 131)

Boomerangs

For wonderfully complete information on construction, history, throwing, purchase, and appreciation of boomerangs, write to Benjamin Ruhe at The Smithsonian Institution, office of Public Affairs, Washington, DC.

Following are excerpts from his Boomerang Workshop.

I love The Smithsonian.

—SB

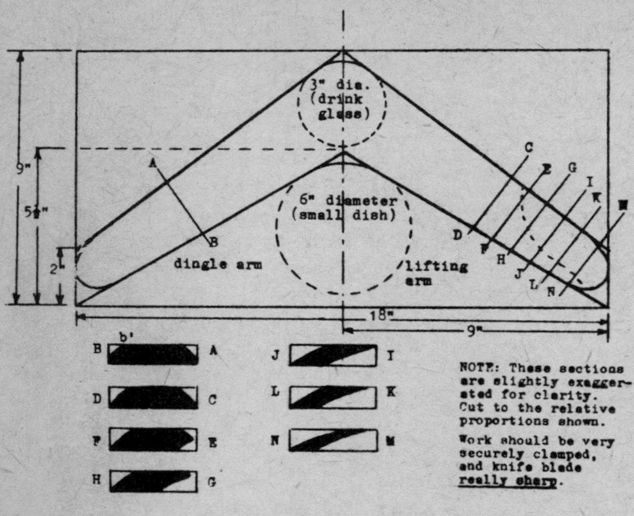

3" dia. (drink glass)
6" diameter (small dish)
dingle arm
lifting arm
9"
5½"
2"
18"
9"
b'
NOTE: These sections are slightly exaggerated for clarity. Cut to the relative proportions shown.
Work should be very securely clamped, and knife blade really sharp.

Making Your Own

Making your own boomerang is not difficult; all you need is a piece of "Three eighths" five ply (actual thickness is about five sixteenths, but to get this you usually have to ask for three eighths thickness), a sharp knife and a whetstone to keep it sharp, a couple of small "C" clamps, a sheet of 80 grit sandpaper, and a suitable saw to cut out the shape.

The boomerang illustrated is for right handed throwers. If you are left handed, all you need do is to look at the plans through a mirror so that everything is reversed from right to left.

The design of the boomerang shown below is a very simple one, selected as especially suitable for a beginner to make as it requires no previous experience and is foolproof (well, almost), giving a nice curving flight that should bring it back fairly close to the thrower. Also, because of its flexible design, it can be made with a large variety of plywoods, and the 18" size means it can be made from readily available off-cuts from a lumber yard, sparing you the expense of buying a whole sheet. It is NOT, however, a competition quality boomerang, but will give you hours of enjoyment nevertheless.

PROCEDURE

Obtain a sheet of aircraft or high-grade marine plywood (5 ply) and mark out the straight lines shown in the diagram. The actual elbow and tips should be rounded, however--do this by drawing a couple of circular arcs at the elbow with a 3-inch drinking glass or compass, and with a 6-inch dish or the equivalent. Draw the curves for the tips in freehand as shown in the figure and then cut it out, using a saw. Next clamp one arm firmly to a table or workbench, leaving the other one free to work. With straight, even strokes, slice off wood to attain the aerodynamic contours shown in the sectional drawings at the bottom of the main sketch. Make sure that the direction of the knife stroke is such that it makes an acute angle with the grain on the top layer of wood; otherwise this may tear or lift off. If you find this happening, cut from the other direction.

Do not be afraid to take wood off, but check from time to time that you are following the general sections shown in the drawing. When completed, the weight of the boomerang should not exceed four ounces. After the knifework is over, sand it down smoothly with 80 grit sandpaper and give it a few throws. If all appears to be well, finish the boomerang off by coating it with floor wax or brown shoe polish to waterproof it. If it does not return properly, but tends to run out of spin and drops in front of you, sand off a bit more material from the trailing edge of the dingle arm making the taper near "b" more sloping, until it works right, but be careful not to take too much off or you'll wreck the whole thing.

With regard to the balance of a boomerang, this is a fairly complicated thing. Suffice it to say that the important thing is not so much the static balance you see when you put it across your finger, but the dynamic balance of it when in flight. It should appear to have a hole about two inches in diameter when spinning rapidly, at the inside curve of the elbow. Actually, it is this hole that does the travelling when the boomerang is thrown, the fact that it is accompanied by the boomerang being more or less incidental.

Suitable Conditions

The boomerang should be thrown into a LIGHT BREEZE ONLY. Early morning or late afternoon usually offer the best conditions. Larger boomerangs can at times be thrown into fairly moderate winds, but generally the results are poor. Best results are obtained when a few blades of grass have to be used to indicate wind direction.
Throwing into high winds even on a large clear area is dangerous, since these conditions cause the boomerang to climb steeply, and travel with the wind a great distance, and at a great speed.

The Throw

Grasp either end of the boomerang with the thumb and first two fingers of the right hand (special boomerangs are needed for left handed people) and hold it firmly *with the flat side outward* so that the plane of the boomerang is inclined at about 60 degrees to the horizon, then give it a gentle throw with plenty of spin.

It should curve around to the left and climb slightly, turning around and finally stopping to hover in the vicinity of the thrower.

The key to success in the whole operation is the imparting of considerable spin on the throw, and this is aided by holding no more than an inch and a half of the tip of the boomerang, and by not actually releasing it but by making it pull itself out of the hand by its own impetus, pivoting around the index finger when doing so.

Architecture

I don't know that architecture is a useful term or profession any more. This book gets a kid into building stuff and some of the traditional considerations in doing that.

—SB

Architecture
Forrest Wilson
1968; 96 pp.

$6.95 postpaid

from:
Van Nostrand-Reinhold
450 West 33rd Street
New York, N. Y. 10001

or WHOLE EARTH CATALOG

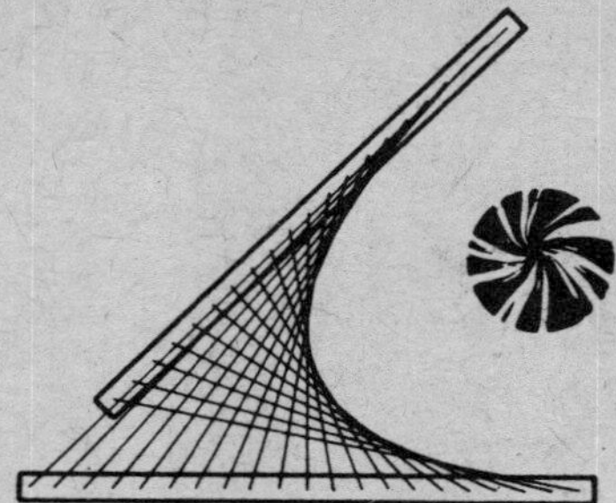

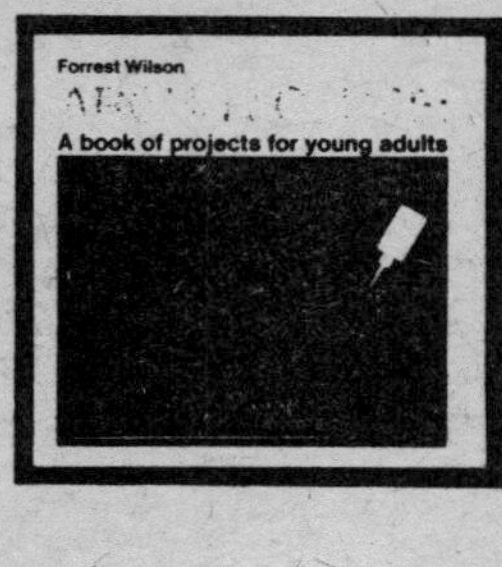

Forrest Wilson
A book of projects for young adults

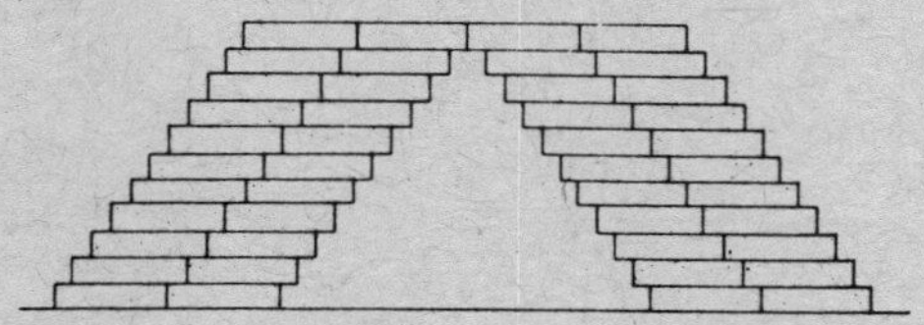

PROJECT 4 – BUILD A CORBEL

Materials: Box of sugar cubes.

Procedure: Place cubes on top of each other with the end cube of each course (row) projecting about one third of its length over the front edge of the cube beneath it. You will notice that unless there are enough cubes behind the projecting end cubes the construction will fall forward. You will also notice that it is possible to stack the cubes higher if the projection is shorter. There is a relationship of projection to height in a corbel the same as there was in the column.

If you construct two such corbels opposite each other, ten or eleven cubes high and about five inches apart so that the top cubes meet each other, you will have a pyramidal opening. This is how corbels are used to span openings.

When you have made the structure, hold it in your hand and gently squeeze. If it does not feel rigid but moves in your hand look for the configurations that move. You will find that these invariably are not triangluated. Glue toothpicks across their corners to make them rigid.

Jonathan Livingston Seagull

RICHARD BACH

A Blood woman told me "Behind the Sun is the real Sun." This book is about flight that way. Beyond perfection of technique is another perfection, a further freedom, another discipline. Jonathan eventually has to insist he is not the Son of the Great Gull.

—SB

[Suggested by Sharon Graham]

Jonathan Livingston Seagull

1970; 93 pp.

$1.50 plus $.15 postage

from:
Avon Books Mail Order Dept.
250 W. 55th St.
New York, NY 10019

or WHOLE EARTH CATALOG

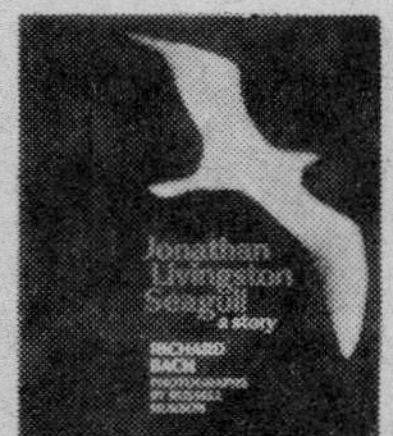

Jonathan Livingston Seagull
a story
RICHARD BACH

Here he came this minute, a blurred gray shape roaring out of a dive, flashing one hundred fifty miles per hour past his instructor. He pulled abruptly into another try at a sixteen-point vertical slow roll, calling the points out loud.

". . .eight. . .nine. . .ten. . .see-Jonathan-I'm-running-out-of-airspeed . . .eleven. . .I-want-good-sharp-stops-like-yours. . .twelve. . .but-blast-it-I-just-can't-make. . .thirteen. . .these-last-three-points. . . without. . .fourtee. . .*aaakk!*"

Fletcher's whipstall at the top was all the worse for his rage and fury at failing. He fell backward, tumbled, slammed savagely into an inverted spin, and recovered at last, panting, a hundred feet below his instructor's level.

"You're wasting your time with me, Jonathan! I'm too dumb! I'm too stupid! I try and try, but I'll never get it!"

Jonathan Seagull looked down at him and nodded. "You'll never get it for sure as long as you make that pullup so hard. Fletcher, you lost forty miles an hour in the entry! You *have* to be smooth! Firm but smooth, remember?"

•

And so they flew in from the west that morning, eight of them in a double-diamond formation, wingtips almost overlapping. They came across the Flock's Council Beach at a hundred thirty-five miles per hour, Jonathan in the lead, Fletcher smoothly at his right wing, Henry Calvin struggling gamely at his left. Then the whole formation rolled slowly to the right, as one bir. . .level. . .to. . .inverted. . .to. . . level, the wind whipping over them all.

The squawks and grockles of everyday life in the Flock were cut off as though the formation were a giant knife, and eight thousand gull-eyes watched, without a single blink. One by one, each of the eight birds pulled sharply upward into a full loop and flew all the way around to a dead-slow stand-up landing on the sand.

•

"Home I have none. Flock I have none. I am Outcast. And we fly now at the peak of the Great Mountain Wind. Beyond a few hundred feet, I can lift this old body no higher."

"But you can, Jonathan. For you have learned. One school is finished, and the time has come for another to begin."

As it had shined across him all his life, so understanding lighted that moment for Jonathan Seagull. They were right. He *could* fly higher, and it *was* time to go home.

He gave one last long look across the sky, across that magnificent silver land where he had learned so much.

"I'm ready," he said at last.

And Jonathan Livingston Seagull rose with the two starbright gulls to disappear into a perfect dark sky.

Simple Working Models of Historic Machines

Far-out ingenuity revisited.

—SB

Simple Working Models of Historic Machines
Aubrey F. Burstall
1968, 1969; 79 pp.

$3.95 postpaid

from:
The M. I. T. Press
50 Ames Street, Room 765
Cambridge, Mass. 02142

or WHOLE EARTH CATALOG

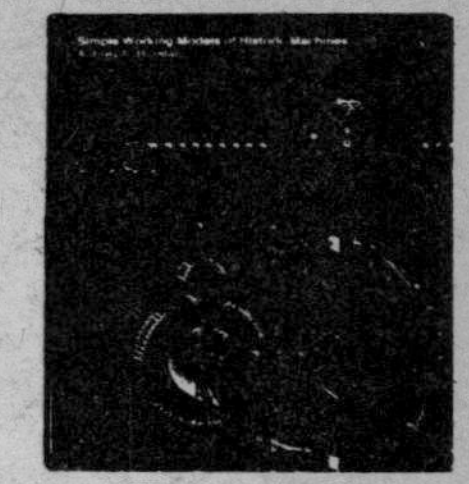

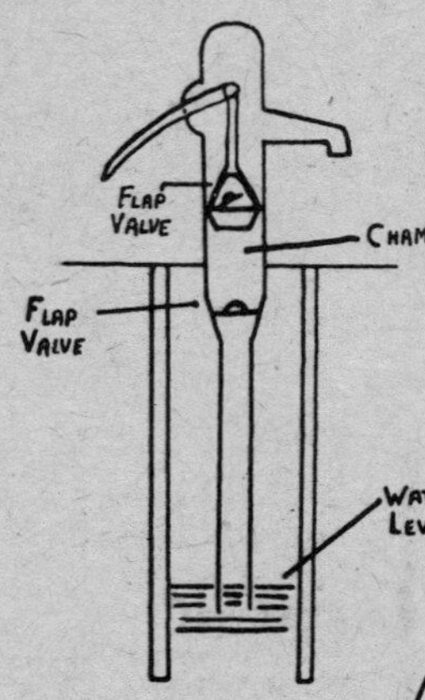

Flap Valve
Chamber
Flap Valve
Water Level

The Suction Pump.

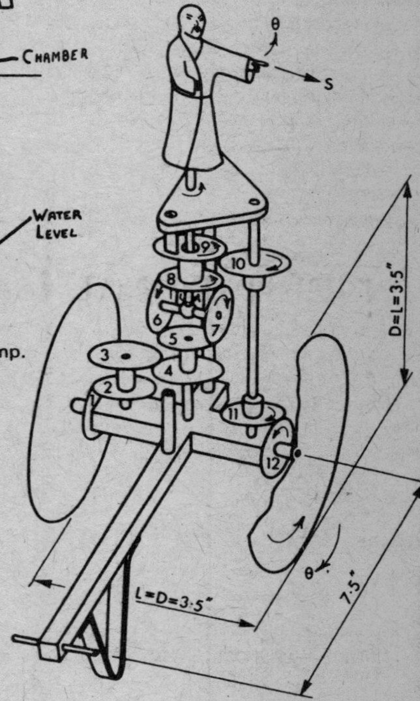

θ
S
D=L=3.5"
L=D=3.5"
7.5"
θ

Wheels 1,2;5,6,7,8;11,12:– Bevel gears,1:1 ratio
Wheels 3,4;9,10:– Spur gears,1:1 ratio

The Chinese South-pointing Chariot

A full-scale machine of this kind was used in ceremonial processions in China between A.D. 120 and 250. It seems that its purpose must have been simply to cause awe and wonder in the onlookers since whichever way the chariot was turned the figure on the top always pointed in the same direction. This intriguing result was obtained by means of differential gearing, very similar to that used in the back-axle of the present-day motor vehicle. Possibly pin gears were used in the originals, though this is not certain.

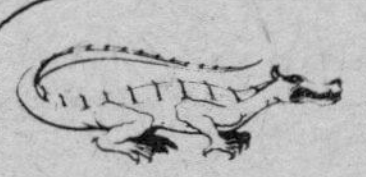

"I said this is Emmit Collier's nephew," said Barry. "David's his name."

"Cecil Agnew!" the old man shouted. "Who? What did you say?"

"Emmit Collier!" Barry yelled. "That died the other day. This is his nephew."

Mr. McClanahan heard the word "died" and suddenly it all came together in his mind. He shifted his cane to his left hand and with his right he reached out and grabbed D.R. by the leg, just above the knee, and squeezed hard.

But when he spoke, he still addressed himself to Barry.

"I knew this boy's grandfather," said Mr. McClanahan. "Me and him use to log together. Hard worker. Knew his father, too. That was a good family of people."

"David here's going to live a while at the old homeplace," Barry said.

"Do which?"

"I said, David's going to live a while up there where Emmit did. He's taking care of the place."

Mr. McClanahan shook his head. "Trace Fork used to be full of people," he said. "But they aint nobody lives up there now that Emmit's dead."

Barry smiled and nodded and let it go at that.

(continued)

700 Science Experiments for Everyone

This book grew out of a smaller volume called **Suggestions for Science Teachers in Devastated Areas** *whose production was sponsored by UNESCO right after World War II. It was meant for use in schools whose buildings and labs had been destroyed and soon found its way into the hands of people who had never had these things to begin with. Thus it solves the problem of schools, communities—people—who want to do'live' science without money or equipment. There isn't any experiment in it which would be too costly for any of us to do. The book tells you how to put together the equipment you need: real clever ways of making glass cutters, balances, burners, telescopes, microscopes, etc. A lot of what you need to do the experiments is just stuff you'd have around the house. The rest can be gotten [very low cost stuff] at the drugstore, hardware, junk yard, etc.*

Also the book is unusually well written. There's no bullshit in it and it doesn't talk down to the reader. Just very straightforward instructions with illustrations that are highly readable. In most cases you aren't told the outcome of the experiment, an aspect which makes you much more interested in doing it.

[Reviewed by Jane Burton]

700 Science Experiments for Everyone
1958; 250 pp.

$4.95 postpaid

from:
Doubleday & Company, Inc.
501 Franklin Avenue
Garden City, L.I., N.Y. 11531

or WHOLE EARTH CATALOG

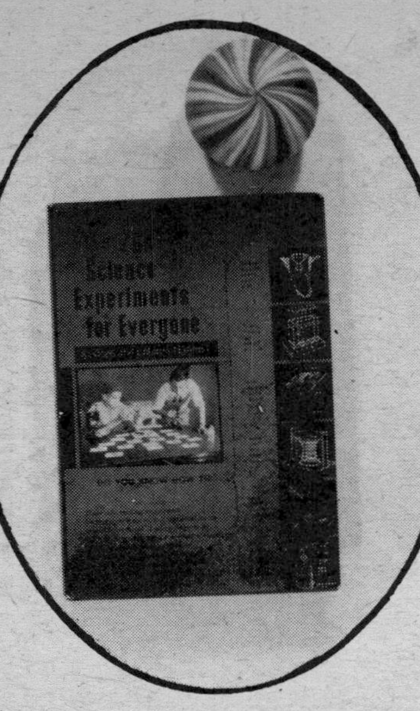

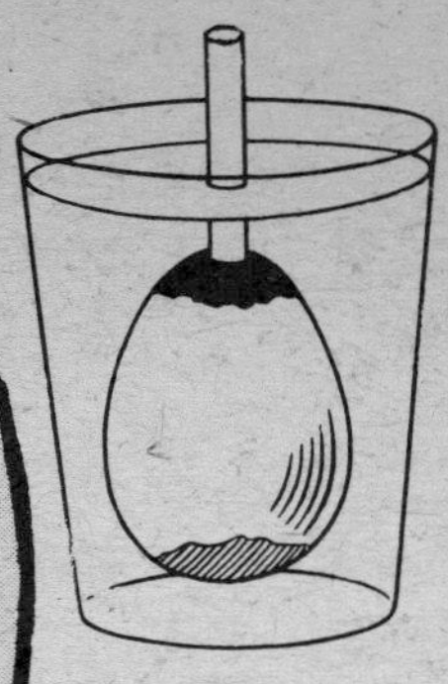

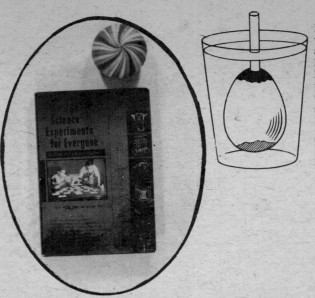

An egg osmometer

Place some dilute hydrochloric acid or strong vinegar in a shallow dish, such as a saucer, to a depth of about one centimetre. Hold the large end of an egg in the acid until the shell has been eaten away on the end leaving the thin membrane exposed. Rinse the acid from the egg. With a sharp instrument work a small hole through the shell at the other end. Insert a soda straw or a length of glass tubing through the hole into the interior of the egg. Seal the opening around the tube with household cement or sealing wax. This must be absolutely tight. Place the osmometer in a glass of water and let it stand for a few hours.

Making smoke prints of leaves

Smoke prints of leaves may be easily made by following the four steps shown in the diagrams.

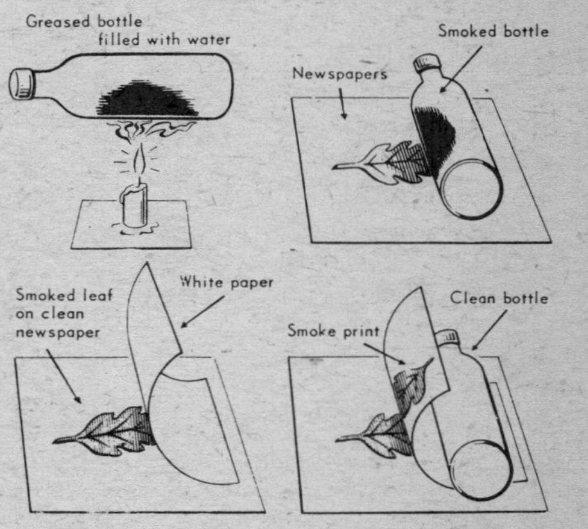

Cover the side of a smooth, round bottle with a thin layer of grease or vaseline. Fill the bottle with cold water and cork it tightly. Hold the bottle over a candle flame until it is covered evenly with soot. Place a leaf, vein side up, on a layer of newspaper and roll the sooty bottle over the leaf. Remove the leaf and lay it vein side up on clean newspaper. Cover the leaf with a sheet of white paper. Next, roll over the white paper and leaf with a clean round bottle or other roller.

Another way to show that water pressure increases with depth

Find a tall tin can. Punch holes up the side of the can about 3 cm apart. Put a strip of adhesive or plastic tape over the row of holes and fill the can with water above the top hole. Hold the can over a sink and strip the tape from the holes beginning at the bottom. Observe the streams and note the distances travelled outwards from the can.

Water pressure is the same in all directions

Punch holes around the base of a tall tin can with a nail. Cover the holes as above with a strip of tape. Fill the can with water and strip off the tape while holding it over a sink. Observe and compare the distance the streams shoot out from the holes all around the can.

Edmund Scientific

Edmund is the best source we know of for low-cost scientific gadgetry (including math and optics gear). Many of the items we found independently, such as **Dr. Nim, 700 Science Experiments,** *Geo-D-Stix, Spilhaus Space Clock, etc., turned up in the Edmund Catalog, so we were obliged to recognize that in this area we've been preceded. They list 4,500 items* —SB

Catalog

free

from:
Edmund Scientific Company
100 Edscorp Building
Barrington, N. J. 08007

EASILY BEND WIRE INTO USEFUL SHAPES

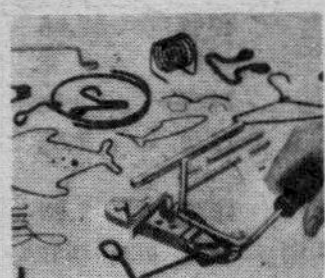

Turn wire, coat hangers, etc. into peg board hardware, stakes, springs, tools, toys, art. Cast aluminum jig with cutting blade, fulcrum & bending pins handles up to 1/4" steel wire. 100 illustrated projects.
No. 40,870 $2.95 Ppd.

HIGH-OUTPUT SILICON SOLAR CELL

"ONE OF THE FINEST I'VE EVER SEEN," says our Engr.

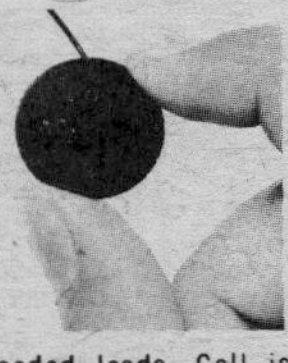

Small yet extremely powerful, this cell permits applications formerly impossible . . . use in solar powered boats, toy cars, etc. Exposed to bright sunlight this cell delivers more than 1/10 amp. current. One alone operates our ball bearing motor (No. 40,902, Pg. 72) even under incandescent illumination. Open circuit voltage 0.5v; short circuit current 100 ma; output in excess of 20 mw. Color coded leads. Cell is 15/16" in dia. and less than 1/16" thick.
No. 30,538 $11.95 Ppd.

MINIATURE MAGNETIC MOTION DEMONSTRATOR

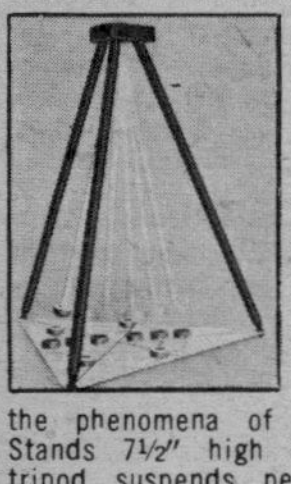

No matter what your age, the TOY MINI BOPPER will hold your attention for hours! Just arrange the 10 circular magnets into any pattern you choose, swing the magnetic pendulum over the pattern, and . . . WOW! It goes crazy as it reacts to the pattern's magnetic force field . . . circling, swinging, jumping, hovering, bouncing, accelerating, slowing and accelerating again. Make up games, try to outguess your opponent, demonstrate the phenomena of magnetic attraction and repulsion. Stands 7½" high on a metal triangle base. Plastic tripod suspends pendulum. Includes instructions.
No. 71,279 $2.00 Ppd.
No Longer Available

LARGE 9-FT. HOT-AIR BALLOON KIT

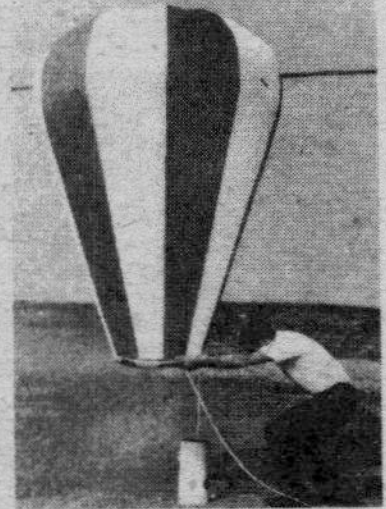

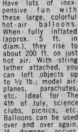

Have lots of inexpensive fun with these large, colorful hot-air balloons. When fully inflated (approx. 5 ft. in diam.), they rise to about 200 ft. on just hot air. With string tether attached, you can loft objects up to ½ lb.; model airplanes, parachutes, etc. Ideal for The 4th of July, science clubs, picnics, etc. Balloons can be used over and over again. If damage occurs, you can easily repair it. Kit includes 10 precut, red and white gores (No. 1 model paper); 6 feet of 14 ga. wire for bottom ring; top tie-off cord and instructions.
No. 60,691 $2.50 Ppd.

HAVE FUN WITH SCIENCE OF SOAP BUBBLES

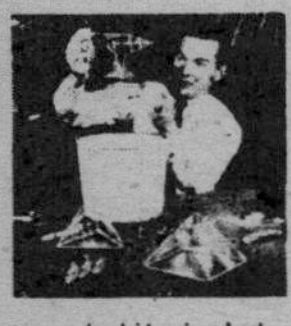

Create endless complex shapes, study and enjoy their fascinating behavior. Learn about liquid skins, pressures, jets, electrical conduction and the membrane theory of stress distribution. Chemist designed kit includes special, longer-lasting, lower-cost bubble formulation (makes several gallons). Sticks with poly connectors and wire bending jig to make bubble frames, plus 190-pg. book on subject by C. V. Boys.
Complete instructions. **No. 70,742 $6.00 Ppd.**
Formulation only. **No. 40,782 $3.00 Ppd.**
No Longer Available

NEW GAMES TEACH POLLUTION CONTROL

***SMOG* • Dirty Water**

Smog and Dirty Water acquaint 2-4 players with many of the complexities and obstacles which an administrator meets in controlling water and air pollution in his community or lake. The player who best succeeds in controlling pollutors wins.

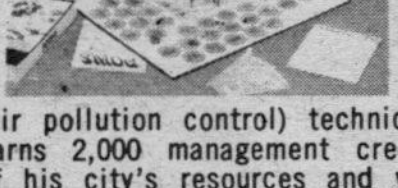

Smog illustrates the complex problem of air pollution. Each player is the "Air Quality Manager" in his city and learns about actual abatement (air pollution control) techniques. The player who first earns 2,000 management credits is the best manager of his city's resources and wins. Smog includes 19½" sq. gameboard; hundreds of pegs, smoke plumes, rings; "'Outrageous Fortune Cards"; play money; die; pad; and 11-page informative instr. booklet.
No. 71,321 $7.95 Ppd.

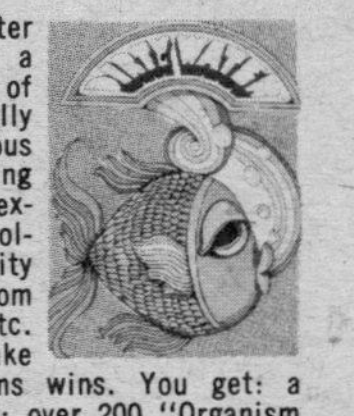

Dirty Water: Each player is a "Water Pollution Official" in charge of a lake that needs a proper ratio of certain organisms to be ecologically balanced. You learn about various types of water pollutors, each causing a specific type of pollution. You experience the problems facing real Pollution Control Officials . . . priority decisions, threats of pollution from an upstream community, finances, etc. The player who first stocks his lake with the correct ratio of organisms wins. You get: a colorfully illus. gameboard (19" sq.); over 200 "Organism Pieces" including algae, weeds, bass, etc.; die; tokens; pad; abatement cards; charts; and informative 12-pg. instr. booklet. **No. 71,320 $7.95 Ppd.**

FIRST LOW-COST AIR POLLUTION TESTER

CO_2 CO H_2S NO_2 SO_2

Quantitative results in a few minutes!

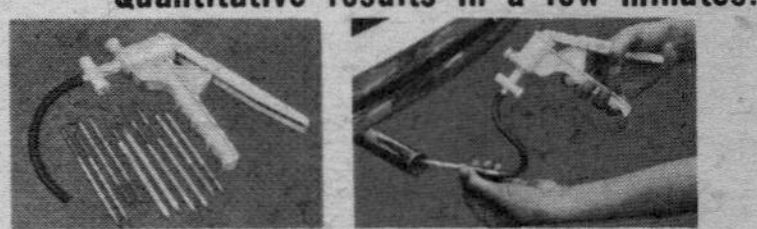

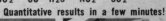

Now a low-cost, quick, easy-to-use kit for sampling and testing pollutant gases in the threshold limit ranges set up by the American Conference of Governmental Industrial Hygienists. Sensitivity, accuracy, wide measuring range, and portability of this lightweight unit, make it ideal for use by safety engineers, industrial hygienists, pollution control officers, teachers, students, and all others requiring quantitative data on air pollutants.

Kit contains sturdy plastic sampling pump; coupling tube; 10 ready-to-use, break-tip test ampoules (2 each for: CO_2, CO, H_2S, NO_2, SO_2); and complete instructions with scales for determining results. Pump draws air through ampoule containing impregnated chemical specific for pollutant. The length of the stain that appears indicates the concentration of the gas in the air. It only takes a few minutes to test for: Carbon Dioxide (CO_2) .01-10% by volume; Carbon Monoxide (CO) 10-3000 Ppm; Hydrogen Sulfide (H_2S) 1-800 Ppm; Nitrogen Dioxide (NO_2) .1-50 Ppm, and Sulfur Dioxide (SO_2) 1-400 Ppm. Kit includes enough ampoules for 2-4 tests for each gas above depending upon concentration. Replacement ampoules available below.

Complete Kit	**No. 71,349**	**$23.50 Ppd.**
(4) CO_2 Ampoules	No. P-60,833	6.50 Ppd.
(4) CO Ampoules	No. P-60,834	5.25 Ppd.
(4) H_2S Ampoules	No. P-60,835	6.25 Ppd.
(4) NO_2 Ampoules	No. P-60,836	6.50 Ppd.
(4) SO_2 Ampoules	No. P-60,837	8.00 Ppd

Guinness Book of World Records

Guinness Book of World Records

1956-1971; 608 pp

$1.50 postpaid

from:
Bantam Books
666 Fifth Ave.
New York, N.Y.
10019

or WHOLE EARTH CATALOG

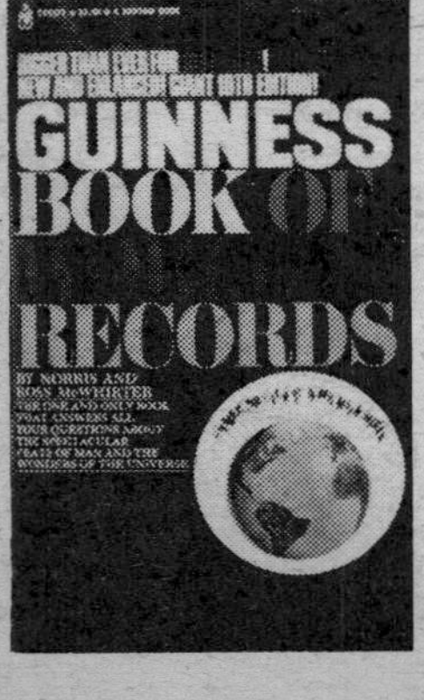

An astonishing amount of conversation in the Western World is spent agreeing or disagreeing on the extremes of experience. Maybe it's some primordial urge to know where we are in the universe. Whatever, it's deep. This book is automatic conversation; whoever's reading it has to start reading aloud. And whoever's around has to listen and respond. Weird. Painless education though. —SB

Highest Income. The highest gross income ever achieved in a single year by a private citizen is an estimated $105,000,000 in 1927 by the Chicago gangster Alphonse ("Scarface Al") Capone (1899–1947). This was derived from illegal liquor trading and alky-cookers (illicit stills), gambling establishments, dog tracks, dance halls, "protection" rackets and vice. On his business card Capone described himself as a "Second Hand Furniture Dealer." Henry Ford, the first (1863–1947) earned about $70,000,000 per annum at his peak.

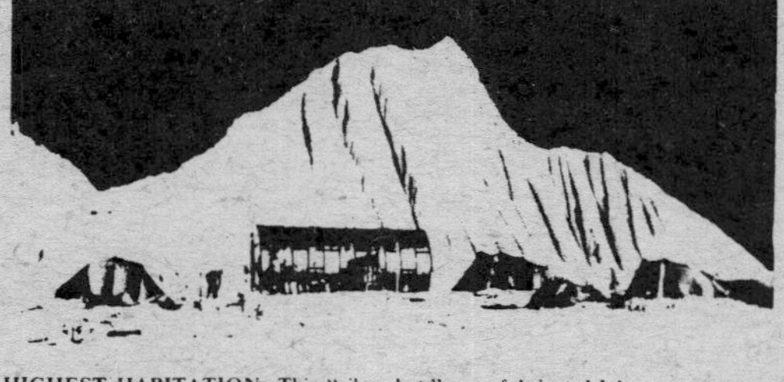

HIGHEST HABITATION: This "silver hut," a prefabricated laboratory erected at an altitude of 18,765 feet in the Ming Bo Valley of the Himalayan mountains of India, was inhabited for four months in 1960-61.

Lowest Incomes. The poorest people in the world are the 42 surviving Pintibu (or Bindibu) found in the Northern Territory of Australia in July, 1957. They subsist with water from soak holes and by eating rats. In September, 1957, Chinese Government sources admitted that in some areas of the mainland the average annual income of peasants was 42 yuans per head. In 1964, China's average income per head was estimated at $70 and the daily calorie intake at 2,200 (see page 298 for highest intake).

Return of Cash. The largest amount of cash ever found and returned to its owners was $240,000 in unmarked $10 and $20 bills found in a street in Los Angeles, by Douglas William Johnston, an unemployed Negro, in March, 1961. He received many letters, of which 25 per cent suggested that he was insane.

Handshaking. The world record for handshaking was set by Theodore Roosevelt (1858–1919), as President of the U.S.A., when he shook hands with 8,513 people at a New Year's Day White House Presentation on January 1, 1907. Outside public life, the record is 37,500 hands in 7 hours 15 minutes 18 seconds by George Borkowski, in London on February 22, 1967.

Pill Taking

It is recorded that among hypochondriacs Samuel Jessup (born 1752), a wealthy grazier of Heckington, Lincolnshire, England, has never had a modern rival. His consumption of pills from 1794 to 1816 was 226,934, with a peak annual total of 51,590 in 1814. He is also recorded as having drunk 40,000 bottles of medicine before death overtook him at the surprisingly advanced age of 65.

Hiccoughing

The longest recorded attack of hiccoughs was that afflicting Jack O'Leary of Los Angeles. It was estimated that he "hicked" more than 160,000,000 times in an attack which lasted from June 13, 1948, to June 1, 1956, apart from a week's respite in 1951. His weight fell from 138 lbs. to 74 lbs. People sent 60,000 suggestions for cures, of which only one apparently worked—a prayer to St. Jude, the patron saint of lost causes.

Sneezing

The most chronic sneezing fit ever recorded was that of June Clark, aged 17, of Miami, Florida. She started sneezing on January 4, 1966, while recovering from a kidney ailment in the James M. Jackson Memorial Hospital, Miami. The sneezing was stopped by electric "aversion" treatment on June 8, 1966, after 155 days. The highest speed at which expelled particles have been measured to travel is 103.6 m.p.h.

LIFE Science Library

After two years of looking at everybody's nifty books, I'd say that the two sets of books to have around your place for pick-up education of young and old are the Golden handbooks (see p. 373) and these science books from Time-Life. They're available only by mail, and they come one every month or so. If you don't like what you got, you can send it back. We haven't sent any back.

Most popular science books are badly behind the times. This series puts special emphasis on recent developments.

—SB

LIFE Science Library

each book **$5.95**
plus 84¢ postage & handling
from:
Time-Life Books
Dept. WEC
Time & Life Bldg.
Chicago, Illinois 60611

TWO LENSES IN ONE   Light and Vision

Bifocals—introduced to America in the 18th Century by Benjamin Franklin—help older people with rigid lens structure to focus at both near and far distances. The upper half of the spectacle lens gives slight correction for distant viewing. The lower half is for close-up work; it provides the increased refraction needed to compensate for the increasing rigidity—and the inability to focus—of the aging lens.

5200 B.C.   500 B.C.   20TH CENTURY

THE EVOLUTION OF CORN to the modern fruitful version required 7,000 years of radical change, as indicated by these three samples. The inch-long ear of wild maize *(left)*—a Central American plant now extinct—dates from around 5200 B.C.; it has only eight rows of kernels with five to six kernels on each row. By 500 B.C. Mexicans were growing four-inch-long ears called Nal-Tel *(center)* that had some 11 rows of small kernels per cob. Today, one of the most widely cultivated corn plants in Mexico is Chalqueño *(right)*, eight inches long, with 17 rows of narrow kernels.

The dangers of leaching were pointed out as recently as the 1920's, when public-health officials were puzzled by the strange pattern of malnutrition in the South. Impoverished sharecroppers there ate poorly—grits, corn mush and molasses, greens, with a bit of fatback. The diet for white and Negro sharecroppers was much the same. But, oddly enough, the whites suffered more severely from deficiency diseases; the Negroes, also ill-fed, were relatively unaffected. The mystery was not solved until the scientists learned that both whites and Negroes boiled their staple foods for long periods to improve the palatability of the somewhat tasteless provender. But then the whites threw away the cooking water; using the so-called potlikker was socially unacceptable. With the discarded liquid went the nutrients that had been leached away by long boiling. The Negroes, uninfluenced by the social stigma attached to potlikker, drank it and used it to soak corn bread, recapturing the essential vitamins and minerals.

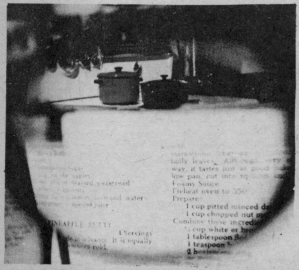

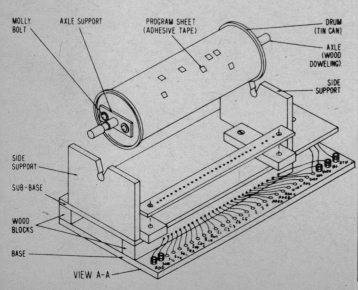

How to Build a Working Digital Computer

Since computers are ever more centrally with us, it behooves us to allow them as few mysteries as possible. A kid who's built a computer out of paper clips has a healthy handle on his relationship with high technology.

The computer you can build from this book will operate with a program of 28-bit instruction works and has a ten-instruction repertoire. It adds, subtracts, multiplies, divides, and costs very little.

—SB

How to Build a Working Digital Computer
Alcosser, Phillips, and Wolk
1967, 70; 176 pp.

$4.75 postpaid

from:
Hayden Book Co., Inc.
50 Essex Street
Rochelle Park, N.J. 07662

or WHOLE EARTH CATALOG

MOLLY BOLT — AXLE SUPPORT — PROGRAM SHEET (ADHESIVE TAPE) — DRUM (TIN CAN) — AXLE (WOOD DOWELING) — SIDE SUPPORT — SIDE SUPPORT — SUB-BASE — WOOD BLOCKS — BASE — VIEW A-A

△ **PARIS IN THE THE SPRING**

WHAT'S WRONG WITH THIS PHRASE?
At first glance, seemingly nothing. But with closer reading the repetition of the word THE becomes obvious. Because we generally read rapidly in word patterns rather than slowly a word at a time, it is easy for the eye to skip over the extra THE and register the familiar phrase "correctly."

Light and Vision

WFF 'N PROOF

The WFF 'N PROOF games came out of the ALL project (Accelerated Learning of Logic) at Yale Law School. This project was established in 1960 to develop materials to teach mathematical logic to elementary school students. The authors' first principle in designing the games was that they be fun to play.

WFF 'N PROOF is a series of 21 games. The first ones can be played by children (starting around age eight), the last ones are difficult enough to interest logicians. The first game can be bought separately under the name of just 'WFF.' It is the best game and children always like to play it. In it you learn what a WFF (well formed formula) is, and there is no nicer way of doing that. The rest of the games teach you about constructing logical proofs. They are more tedious and a good teacher can find ways of doing this which are more fun. There's no harm in getting the whole set, however, and using it as long as it works.

[Reviewed by Jane Burton]

WFF **$1.50** postpaid
WFF 'N PROOF **$8.00** postpaid
Tac Tickle **$1.00** postpaid
The REAL Numbers Game **$2.00** postpaid
On-Sets: The Game of Set Theory **$5.00** postpaid
The Propaganda Game **$6.00** postpaid

from:
WFF 'N PROOF
P. O. Box 71
New Haven, Conn. 06501

or WHOLE EARTH CATALOG

And about that time Elmer the mailman came in with the morning delivery. D.R. excused himself from the conversation and took his letters to Mrs. Godsey, behind the cage.

"He's about to miss the boat aint he Mrs. Godsey?" said Elmer as he traded mail sacks with her. "Yes sir. About to miss the last mail-boat out of China."

"Oh no," said Mrs. Godsey as she held D.R.'s two letters up to the light. "These letter's going to California, Elmer. We can't slow this mail down. Going to, what's this, honey? Anaheim? I can't make that out."

"Flash," said D.R.

"Flash. Now that's a queer name. And what's this one? Esther?"

"Estelle," said D.R. "Estelle Adams."

Mrs. Godsey stamped the postmark on the letters, then sat a minute, thinking. "Adams. That's not Felix Adams's girl from Leatherwood is it? That joined the WAC's here while back? Seems like they sent her to California."

"No mam," said D.R. "Estelle's not from around here. She's from Michigan."

"How come you're writing to her in California then?" asked Mrs. Godsey.

D.R. grinned. "Well, I was thinking she might be in California by now."

"But you don't know for sure," said Mrs. Godsey.

"No mam, I don't," said D.R.

"Sounds like this girl must be your sweetheart," said Mrs. Godsey.

D.R. laughed. "I guess I don't know that for sure either," he said.

"Well now, she either is or she aint," said Mrs. Godsey. "Aint that right, Elmer? Elmer here's a bachelor, but he knows more about women than anybody else around here, don't you Elmer?"

Elmer took the letters from Mrs. Godsey and stuffed them into the mailbag. When he'd drawn the strings on the bag together again, he looked up and pushed his cap back off his forehead.

"It's like this," said Elmer. "She either is or she aint unless you're on the outs, and then it all depends. Sometimes one can be your sweetheart but get on the outs with you, and then it's just all hurly-swirly."

Everybody in the store laughed at Elmer then, including Mr. McClanahan who hadn't understood what was said, but who was in the habit of laughing at Elmer every time he saw him at the store.

"Elmer's got more sweethearts than any man around here," said Barry.

"But I hear there's one he likes better than any other," said Mrs. Thornton.

Standing in the door now, about to leave, Elmer said, "If you all don't quit talking about me I wont bring you any more mail."

"You don't ever bring nothing worth reading anyhow," said Barry.

"I bring the Blaine *Herald* once a week," said Elmer.

"Well you *know* they aint nothing worth reading in that thing," said Barry.

Mrs. Thornton said, "Elmer, if you don't bring me a letter from Charlene pretty soon I'm going to wring both your necks."

"I'll bring you one tomorrow if I have to write it myself," said Elmer.

"I'll be looking for it," said Mrs. Thornton.

"So long," said Barry, and as Elmer went out the door, waving, Mrs. Godsey said, "We'll see you tomorrow, Elmer. You be good now."

Build-it-yourself Science Laboratory

My youthful science investigations went about as far as the tameability of wild animals and the thermo-dynamics of breaking glass. Some kids go a lot further, and this book is for them. Stay out of the lab unless invited.

—SB

[Suggested by Fernando L. Nevarez]

Build-it-yourself Science Laboratory
Raymond E. Barrett
1963; 339 pp.

$6.95 postpaid

from:
Doubleday Books
501 Franklin Ave.
Garden City, N.Y. 11530

or WHOLE EARTH CATALOG

HARMONOGRAPH

Purpose: Harmonic motion is a movement or motion that repeats itself. A pendulum is a good example of harmonic motion. When two forces work together, the result is a pattern of movement that combines the movements of both forces. The harmonograph records such movement in pleasing and unusual designs.

Materials: Wood for stand, piece of plywood, two wooden rods about 5' long, two metal collars, two cans, two clamps for the rods, four spikes, cement for the cans.

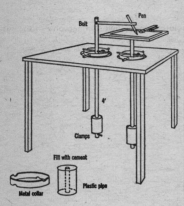

Transistors and Circuits

Home electronics.

—SB

Transistors and Circuits
W. E. Pearce, Aaron E. Klein
1966; 1971; 156 pp.

$4.95 postpaid

from:
Doubleday and Co., Inc.
501 Franklin Ave.
Garden City, N.Y 11530

or WHOLE EARTH CATALOG
(probably cheaper from Blackwell's, p. 2)

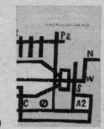

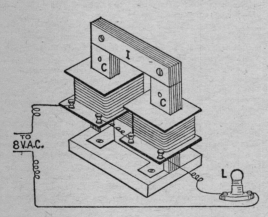

Figure 91

LIGHTNING CONDUCTORS

A lightning discharge is an electric sprak between two oppositely charged clouds, or between a charged cloud and the earth. The discharge may pass through a building with disastrous results. To prevent this, a conductor such as a copper strip is well grounded at one end near a wall and erected as high above the building as possible. At the top, a number of sharp metal points are fixed to the conductor. When a charged thunder cloud comes over the house, there is a good chance that point action will neutralize the charge on the cloud. If a flash should occur, the straight conductor offers an easy and safe path for the electricity to the ground.

In a number of electrical machines, as described later, charges are collected by the action of points. On the other hand, charges can be lost by point action. Charge the electroscope as in Figure 10, and remove the balloon. Place a grounded conductor within 1/8 inch of the points. Unless you are well insulated your hand will do as the conductor. The action is now reversed, and the electroscope loses its charge, which is grounded.

Crystals and Crystal Growing

Grow your own.
Read J. G. Ballard's The Crystal World.

—SB

Crystals and Crystal Growing
Alan Holden, Phylis Singer
1960; 320 pp.

$2.50 postpaid

from:
Doubleday and Co., Inc.
501 Franklin Ave.
Garden City, N.Y. 11530

or WHOLE EARTH CATALOG

Plate 11. An ethylene diamine tartrate crystal with unexpected crystals growing on its surfaces. Later they were identified as crystals of the monohydrate.

One of the touchstones to the true solid— a crystalline solid, in contrast to a merely "rigid" glass— is its sharp melting temperature. When you heat the crystal slowly, it remains rigid until it reaches its melting point. Then, if you keep it at that temperature, it will melt completely to a liquid. The temperature need not increase as the crystal melts; the melting point is a critical temperature for it, and there its orderliness suddenly collapses into disorder.

- -

Permanent Bubbles

I'd like to recommend for review a publication of the Franklin Institute titled "True Plastic Bubbles and How to Blow Them". It's done by the same people who caused such a stir about a year ago with their giant long-lasting soap bubbles. The resulting excitement inspired them to greater heights. This report tells how to blow bubbles up to 4 feet in diameter! The bubbles are tough, waterproof, and being made of plastic film, have an indefinite life span. The report gives brochures and sources for materials. Ask for "Plastic Bubbles Report" (No. 1) available from the Franklin Institute, 21st and the Parkway, Philadelphia, Pa. — $1.00

John Prenis
Utica, NY

- -

Home Physics

Einstein once said that physicists first knew sin in World War II. Chemists had known sin in the First World War. By this he meant that the explosives and poison gases used in W.W. I were the work of chemists. The sin of the physicists was the atom bomb. There was a time before the physicists sinned. That was also a time before large grants and appropriations existed. Then physicists were poor. They built their research equipment from whatever was cheaply available. There is a how to do it book from that period. The title is Procedures in Experimental Physics. *The author is John Strong of Cal. Tech. The illustrations are by Roger Hayward who does those fine drawings in the Amateur Scientist in "Scientific American". Published by Prentice-Hall the book costs about $13.50. The same book is published in England under the title* Modern Physical Laboratory Practice.

The first chapter in the book concerns working with glass. All the basics are covered. Several chapters have to do with making and testing mirrors, lenses, and telescopes. Others deal with heat and its measurement. Filters for light and special light sources are covered in still other chapters. If you want to go more deeply into photography than most amateur photographers do, there is a chapter for you. There are chapters on melting iron, silver, or gold and making castings with them. All these things are done with simple hand tools for the most part. In short the procedures for doing most of the things necessary to make something useful are explained in this book. In addition this book is one step above most do it your self type books, because all the procedures have references to the technical journals. With these you can go still more deeply into those items that interest you. This is an essential reference book for everyone who uses tools to make things.

Sincerely,

Daniel P. Norman
Chicago, Illinois

Test Tubes and Beakers

Home Chemistry. A little deeper than 700 Science Experiments (p. 388).

—SB

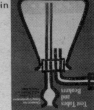

Test Tubes and Beakers
E. H. Coulson, A. E. J. Trinder, Aaron E. Klein
1963, 1971; 134 pp.

$4.95 postpaid

from:
Doubleday and Co., Inc.
501 Franklin Ave.
Garden City, N.Y. 11530

or WHOLE EARTH CATALOG

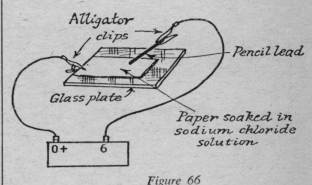

Figure 66

Electric Writing

Dissolve 1/8 teaspoon of sodium chloride in 2 milliliters of water. Divide the solution into two parts.

1. To one part add 3 drops of pheolphthalein solution. Using a bulb pipette, drop this mixture onto a 2 inch square of white blotting paper (or filter paper) until it is just wetted. Put the wet paper on a small piece of glass, and attach the alligator clip on one of your electrolysis leads to both paper and glass (Figure 66). Connect the plus end of this lead to the + pole of the battery. Fix a piece of pencil lead into the alligator clip of the other lead and connect this to the 6-volt pole of the battery. Hold the pencil lead in your fingers and write lightly on the wet paper. The writing will appear red because of the formation of alkali at the cathode. Do not go on with this experiment too long; chlorine gas is evolved at the anode which, besides being poisonous and unpleasant, will corrode the alligator clip attached to the edge of the glass plate.

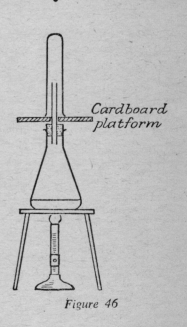

Figure 46

THE PREPARATION OF AMMONIA

Place 1/2 inch of ammonium chloride and 1/2 inch of slaked lime in a small test tube. Mix thoroughly. Gently warm in a Bunsen flame. Cautiously smell the gas evolved by waving the gas toward you. Hold a damp red litmus paper near the mouth of the tube and note any changes. The gas is ammonia. Is the gas acidic or alkaline?

To make a larger quantity of the gas, set up as shown in the diagram (Figure 46). If a piece of cardboard is fitted over the delivery tube, it will help prevent too much of this gas escaping.

Put 1 inch of strong ammonia solution or household ammonia in the flask and heat gently. As the gas is lighter than air, it can be collected by upward delivery. Collect a jar and several tubes of the gas by holding the containers over the delivery tube.

1. Observe the color and smell of the gas. The odor is hard to forget.

2. Invert one of the tubes under water and note what happens inside the tube. What does this indicate?

3. Invert the jar of ammonia and put a lighted splint into the jar (Figure 47). What is the color of the flame just above the splint before it goes out?

Scientific American Offprints

Consistently the best science writing and illustrating appears in* Scientific American. *For 25¢ you can get a full color copy of any article. The catalog of offprints is well organized (some 700 to choose from).

—SB

[Suggested by Jane Burton]

Catalog

free from:
W. H. Freeman & Company
660 Market Street
San Francisco, CA 94104

ANTHROPOLOGY

140. John Napier THE EVOLUTION OF THE HAND
1617. Bernard Greenberg FLIES AND DISEASE
1062. H. Bentley Glass THE GENETICS OF THE DUNKERS
1070. John Napier THE ANTIQUITY OF HUMAN WALKING
1091. J. M. Tanner EARLIER MATURATION IN MAN
1151. Johannes Iversen FOREST CLEARANCE IN THE STONE AGE
463. Adriaan Kortlandt CHIMPANZEES IN THE WILD
601. Sherwood L. Washburn TOOLS AND HUMAN EVOLUTION
602. Marshall D. Sahlins THE ORIGIN OF SOCIETY
603. Charles F. Hockett THE ORIGIN OF SPEECH
604. William W. Howells THE DISTRIBUTION OF MAN
605. Robert J. Braidwood THE AGRICULTURAL REVOLUTION
606. Robert M. Adams THE ORIGIN OF CITIES
607. Herbert Butterfield THE SCIENTIFIC REVOLUTION
608. Edward S. Deevey, Jr. THE HUMAN POPULATION
609. Theodosius Dobzhansky THE PRESENT EVOLUTION OF MAN
613. Jean de Heinzelin ISHANGO
614. S. L. Washburn & Irven DeVore THE SOCIAL LIFE OF BABOONS
615. Colin M. Turnbull THE LESSON OF THE PYGMIES
616. Julian Huxley WORLD POPULATION
619. William L. Langer THE BLACK DEATH
620. James Mellaart A NEOLITHIC CITY IN TURKEY
622. Elwyn L. Simons THE EARLY RELATIVES OF MAN
625. Richard S. MacNeish THE ORIGINS OF NEW WORLD CIVILIZATION
627. Richard J. Andrew THE ORIGINS OF FACIAL EXPRESSIONS
628. D. J. Mulvaney THE PREHISTORY OF THE AUSTRALIAN ABORIGINE
630. William W. Howells HOMO ERECTUS
632. Wilton M. Krogman THE SCARS OF HUMAN EVOLUTION
636. Elwyn L. Simons THE EARLIEST APES
639. Annemarie de Waal Malefijt HOMO MONSTROSUS
641. Rada & Neville Dyson-Hudson SUBSISTENCE HERDING IN UGANDA
643. Sally R. Binford & Lewis R. Binford STONE TOOLS AND HUMAN BEHAVIOR
644. Edward T. Hall, Jr. THE ANTHROPOLOGY OF MANNERS

Libraries

One of the things that struck me when I first encountered the catalog was that many of the books you have suggested or others have suggested are in the collection of even the tiny branch that I work at. The point being that Americans don't use or appreciate the libraries that their taxes support. A good strong plug for people to use the library first to find material (saves buying a book sight unseen and being disatisfied) and reference to further material and places to look for it would be an aid to those needing information. Granted one in the wilds of the backwoods has little opportunity to stroll down the block to his local library however most people still have contact once and a while with some sort of town. Now many states have a complete regional library system that allows one to borrow books from anywhere in the state. This process is only as slow as the mail and the librarian's willingness to help. I know the average person's image of librarians is of a crotchety old maid etc. and this I would have to agree with. But things are moving pretty fast back there in the stacks (how many of us were conceived there), there are hundreds of younger hip librarians and library students invading these tombs of learning. One thing they've found is the older librarians are bitchy because they are frustrated radicals from another era. The resistence to suggestion and criticism from the youth in library circles has not only been low, but the most flaming radical has been welcomed as an ally by older librarians. The concept of librarianship as custodians of books is out the window. The job is now getting information and IDEAS to the people. The smaller the branch the more the librarian is eager to help. One, he's all alone and has few colleagues to help insulate him from the outside; two younger people don't enjoy the hack work that has in the past been the librarian's excuse for lack of time to service the public. It's a good feeling when you help a person take a step closer to knowing himself and his world and librarians aren't insensitive to this. We have all the modern technology at our finger tips though sometimes we have to be prodded touse it. Like, why buy BOOKS IN PRINT when your library has it (it isn't complete either; ask anyone in the publishing industry). Virtually all libraries are your entrance to the Library of Congress.

Warren L. King
Free Library of Philadelphia
Philadelphia, PA

If you're making a library, you might be interested in library materials, on p. 364.

—SB

A Concise Guide to Library Research

In my hairiest dope-fiend days, whenever I drove past a library I'd experience waves of gratitude to those inside who were doing what I knew I could not: opening the library on time, keeping track of the books, patiently explaining again how to use the card catalog, daily dispensing invaluable free information, all without fanfare. This here is a book of what's in a library and how to get at it.

—SB [Suggested by Craige Schensted]

The Concise Guide to Library Research
Grant W. Morse
1966, 1967; 214 pp.

$.75 postpaid

from:
Washington Square Press, Inc.
1 West 39th St.
New York, N. Y. 10018

or WHOLE EARTH CATALOG

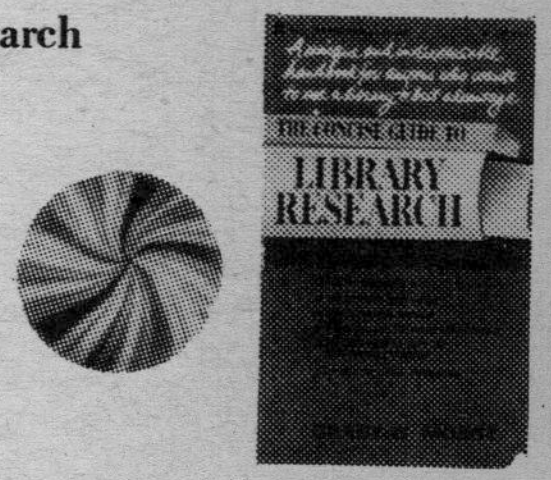

B238 *General works and histories of science*

A Guide to the History of Science, by G. Sarton, 1952, Chronica Botanica Co. Includes a classified bibliography of the subject.

A History of Technology, 5 vols., 1954—1958, Oxford. Scholarly and readable account of the development of technology from earliest times, chronologically arranged.

Introduction to the History of Science, by G. Sarton, 3 vols., 1927—1948, Williams & Wilkins. From Homer to the fourteenth century, including good biographies and bibliographies.

McGraw-Hill Encyclopedia of Science and Technology, 15 vols., 2nd ed., 1965, and yearbooks, 1961—, McGraw-Hill. Very comprehensive. One should use the index volume.

Smithsonian Institution, 1847— (annual). U. S. Government Printing Office. Very useful and authoritative.

Van Nostrand's Scientific Encyclopedia, 3rd ed., 1958, Van Nostrand.

An Introduction to Scientific Research

A practical guide for the scientific experimenter, covering experimental planning, design of apparatus, and analysis and reporting of results. Basic general information applicable to many fields. Extensive lists of references for further information. The book is clearly written and surprisingly enjoyable reading.

[Reviewed by Larry McCombs]

An Introduction to Scientific Research
E. Bright Wilson, Jr.
1952; 373 pp.

$2.95 postpaid

from:
McGraw-Hill Book Company
Princeton Road
Hightstown, N.J. 08520

Manchester Road
Manchester, Missouri 63062

8171 Redwood Highway
Novato, California 94947

or WHOLE EARTH CATALOG

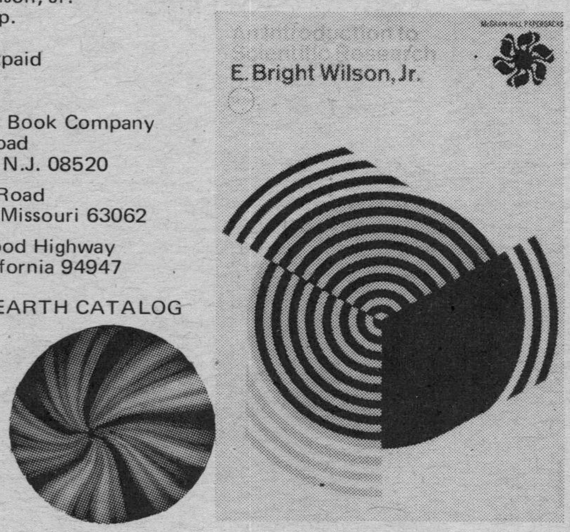

This book is an attempt to collect in one place and to explain as simply as possible a number of general principles, techniques, and guides for procedure which successful investigators in various fields of science have found helpful. The emphasis is entirely on the practical rather than the philosophical or psychological aspects.

•

There is a story of an industrialist who was unable to duplicate in a branch factory the manufacture of a chemical in a desirable crystal form. On further investigation of the process in the main plant, he found it in charge of an elderly employee who had always operated it, apparently with a perfectly simple routine. Closer examination, however, revealed that at one stage he always injected tobacco juice into the vat. This was the missing step, presumably because of surface active ingredients which influenced the growth habits of the crystals.

•

The overconservative scientist will pass by the new phenomena; the overenthusiastic one will endow commonplace events with world-shaking interpretations. Herein lies one good reason for understanding an apparatus and its quirks thoroughly. The momentary signal on the cathode-ray screen may be worth a Nobel prize; but it may also be the thermostat turning on the room heat.

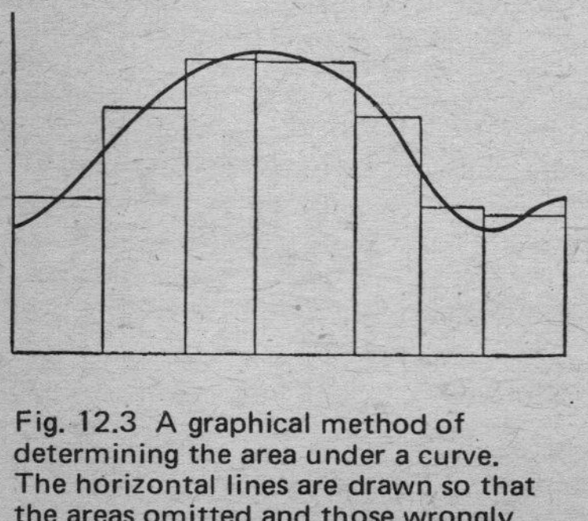

Fig. 12.3 A graphical method of determining the area under a curve. The horizontal lines are drawn so that the areas omitted and those wrongly included in each rectangle balance, as judged by eye.

A completely free rigid body has six degrees of freedom: displacement in three perpendicular directions and rotation about three perpendicular

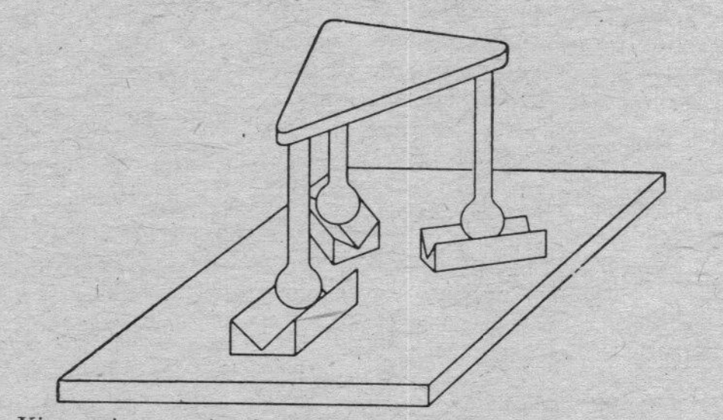

Fig. 5.13. Kinematic mounting for removable part which must be precisely located. Three ball feet make two contacts each with V grooves.

axes. The stool on the flat floor had only three degrees of freedom because its motion was restricted by three properly placed *constraints*, the three contacts of its ball feet with the floor. The stool (or platform) of Fig. 5.13 has no degrees of freedom because its supports make six suitable contacts, two for each ball foot. In general, a contact (or constraint) is needed for each degree of freedom which is to be eliminated. More may be used, as with the four-legged table, but then sag (internal strain) or rocking will occur unless the workmanship is very precise.

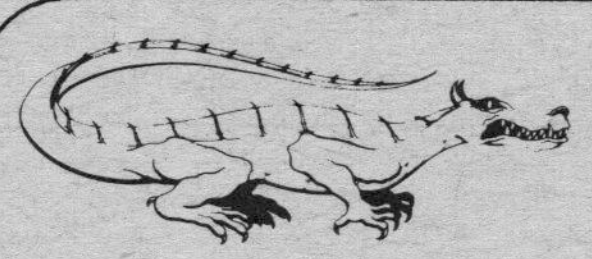

CREDIT

After Mrs. Godsey had sorted the mail and handed it out and chatted with the people a while, she told D.R. to come with her to the kitchen and she would show him Barry's article in the paper. D.R. followed and when she'd found the paper for him she asked if he wouldn't like to sit down at the table and have a cup of coffee or something while he read. D.R. said he'd like that fine, and before long he had finished reading the article and Mrs. Godsey had joined him at the table with an R.C. Cola of her own.

"That's a nice thing Barry wrote," said D.R.

"He's awful good at it," said Mrs. Godsey. "Barry's wrote books and everything."

"Has he really?"

"I don't think any of them's been printed. But he's writing one now that he says is sure to be printed, because he's made arrangements with the newspaper in town to have it done."

"That's very far out," said D.R.

"It's what, honey?"

"That's unusual. I'm impressed."

"Lord, honey, that Barry's a genius," said Mrs. Godsey. "He used to be a house painter till he fell and paralyzed hisself. That's when he took up writing. He's a pure genius at it, everybody thinks so."

Mrs. Godsey took a drink of her R.C.

"Leonard told me you quizzed him about getting credit here at the store," she said.

"Yes mam, I wanted to ask you about it."

"Nothing to ask," said Mrs. Godsey. "Emmit had credit with me for years. He never missed paying a one of his bills, and I know you wouldn't either. You're welcome to anything in my store that you want."

"Now I appreciate that, Mrs. Godsey," said D.R. "And I appreciate you letting me park my bus out back, too."

"Why, that aint nothing," said Mrs. Godsey. "I like to look at it setting out there."

"You and Leonard have been a big help to me," said D.R. "I feel like I'm in debt to you both."

"We're glad to help you, honey," said Mrs. Godsey. "We're glad you're going to be with us a while. Leonard is, especially."

"How is Leonard?" said D.R. "I haven't seen him in a day or two."

"Well," said Mrs. Godsey. "I think that old grand jury business has thrown him behind in his work pretty bad. He's been to town ever day this week, and has to do it again next week too."

"I hope he comes up to see me when he gets a chance," said D.R. "There's some things I need to ask his advice on."

"You neen to worry about Leonard coming up," said Mrs. Godsey. "Use to, they wasn't anything he liked better than to take off up that creek and hang around with Emmit half the day. He'll be up, you neen to worry."

D.R. got up to go then. Mrs. Godsey followed him into the store to help him pick out a few groceries and write them into her account book. D.R. bought canned things mostly, corned beef hash, peas, beets, turnip greens, a bag of cookies and a loaf of bread and some milk. Mrs. Godsey put it in a bag for him, and when they had bid each other good day D.R. set out walking back up Trace Fork again.

The Practical Cogitator

Every profession— science, politics, art, dope, revolution— has a fog of conventional wisdom that will narrow your life and your actions. This book can be a quick avenue out. It's not a collection of quotable quotes, but an anthology of whole ideas. If Marx or Whitehead takes six or seven pages to make his point, the editors don't mind. Neither do I.

—SB

The Practical Cogitator
Charles P. Curtis, Jr., Ferris Greenslet, eds.
1945, 1950, 1962; 692 pp.

$6.95 postpaid

from:
Houghton Mifflin Co.
2 Park St.
Boston, Massachusetts 02107

or WHOLE EARTH CATALOG

We cannot think first and act afterwards. From the moment of birth we are immersed in action, and can only fitfully guide it by taking thought.

A. N. Whitehead

●

Montaigne 1533-1592

If you have known how to compose your life, you have accomplished a great deal more than the man who knows how to compose a book. Have you been able to take your stride? You have done more than the man who has taken cities and empires.

The great and glorious masterpiece of man is to live to the point. All other things— to reign, to hoard, to build— are, at most, but inconsiderate props and appendages.

The truly wise man must be as intelligent and expert in the use of natural pleasures as in all the other functions of life. So the sages live, gently yielding to the laws of our human lot, to Venus and to Bacchus. Relaxation and versatility, it seems to me, go best with a strong and noble mind, and do it singular honor. There is nothing more notable in Socrates than that he found time, when he was an old man, to learn music and dancing, and thought it time well spent.

●

John Milton 1608-1674

And as for you, citizens, it is of no small concern, what manner of men ye are, whether to acquire, or to keep possession of your liberty. Unless your liberty be of that kind which can neither be gotten nor taken away by arms (and that alone is such which, springing from piety, justice, temperance, in fine from real virtue, shall take deep and intimate root in your minds), you may be assured that there will not be wanting one who, even without arms, will speedily deprive you of what it is your boast to have gained by force of arms. For know (that you may not feel resentment, or be able to blame anybody but yourselves) that as to be free is precisely the same thing as to be pious, wise, just, and temperate, careful of one's own, abstinent from what is another's, and thence, in fine, magnanimous and brave— so to be the opposite of these is the same thing as to be a slave; and by the wonted judgment and as it were by the just retribution of God, it comes to pass that the nation, which has been incapable of governing and ordering itself, and has delivered itself up to the slavery of its own lusts, is itself delivered over against its will to other masters— and whether it will or no is compelled to serve.

●

Walter Lippman 1889-

It was in the mediaeval doctrine that to kings belong authority, but to private persons, property, that the way was discovered to limit the authority of the king and to promote the liberties of the subject. Private property was the original source of freedom. It is still its main bulwark. Recent experience confirms this truth. Where men have yielded without serious resistance to the tyranny of new dictators, it is because they have lacked property. They dare not resist because resistance meant destitution.

●

Thoreau 1817-1862

If the injustice is part of the necessary friction of the machine of government, let it go, let it go: perchance it will wear smooth— certainly the machine will wear out. If the injustice has a spring, or a pulley, or a rope, or a crank, exclusively for itself, then perhaps you may consider whether the remedy will not be worse than the evil; but if it is of such a nature that it requires you to be the agent of injustice to another, then, I say, break the law. Let your life be a counter-friction to stop the machine. What I have to do is to see, at any rate, that I do not lend myself to the wrong which I condemn.

●

O. W. Holmes, Jr. 1841-1935

Continuity with the past is a necessity, not a duty.

How to Solve It

This is the best book I know of for lining up a problem for a logical solution. The emphasis is on math, but it is simple logic and can easily be applied to all forms of problem identification and analysis. Better yet is that the methods shown really work even on personal decision-making binds. Essentially it's a head-straightener.

[Suggested and reviewed by Jay Baldwin]

How to Solve It
G. Polya
1945; 253 pp.

$1.95 postpaid

from:
Doubleday and Co.
501 Franklin Street
Garden City, N. Y. 11531

or WHOLE EARTH CATALOG

HOW TO SOLVE IT
G. POLYA

Mathematics— A Human Endeavor

If I were going to teach mathematics, or learn it, I'd want this book. It's unusually enjoyable as well as big and thorough. Also see the goods on pp. 318–319.

—SB

Mathematics— A Human Endeavor
Harold R. Jacobs
1970; 529 pp.

$8.50 postpaid

from:
W. H. Freeman & Co.
660 Market
San Francisco, Calif. 94104

or WHOLE EARTH CATALOG

MATHEMATICS
A Human Endeavor

Would you believe this is a photograph of a wooden crate used for shipping optical illusions?

Courtesy of C. F. Cochran.

By permission of Johnny Hart and Field Enterprises, Inc.

© 1963 United Feature Syndicate, Inc.

Inventor's paradox. The more ambitious plan may have more chances of success.

This sounds paradoxical. Yet, when passing from one problem to another, we may often observe that the new, more ambitious problem is easier to handle than the original problem. More questions may be easier to answer than just one question. The more comprehensive theorem may be easier to prove, the more general problem may be easier to solve.

First.
You have to *understand* the problem.

Second.
Find the connection between the data and the unknown.
You may be obliged to consider auxiliary problems if an immediate connection cannot be found.
You should obtain eventually *a plan* of the solution.

THE GUY IN THE MIDDLE IS TOM
I'M DICK
THE GUY IN THE MIDDLE IS HARRY

Three golfers named Tom, Dick, and Harry are walking to the clubhouse. Tom, the best golfer of the three, always tells the truth. Dick sometimes tells the truth, while Harry, the worst golfer, never does.

Use deductive reasoning to figure out who is who and explain how you know. (Hint: First, figure out which one is Tom.)

●

Inflation of the value of money is a serious economic problem. In 1946, inflation of the currency was so bad in Hungary that the gold Pengo was worth 130 quintillion paper pengos. Write this number in scientific notation. (The pengo was replaced that year by another unit of money.)

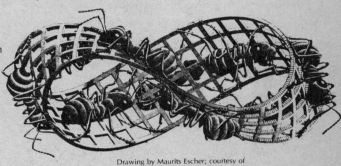

Drawing by Maurits Escher; courtesy of G. W. Breughel, Zwolle, Netherlands.

12. Snub cube

HOW TO SOLVE IT

UNDERSTANDING THE PROBLEM

What is the unknown? What are the data? What is the condition? Is it possible to satisfy the condition? Is the condition sufficient to determine the unknown? Or is it insufficient? Or redundant? Or contradictory?

Draw a figure. Introduce suitable notation.

Separate the various parts of the condition. Can you write them down?

DEVISING A PLAN

Have you seen it before? Or have you seen the same problem in a slightly different form?

Do you know a related problem? Do you know a theorem that could be useful?

Look at the unknown! And try to think of a familiar problem having the same or a similar unknown.

Here is a problem related to yours and solved before. Could you use it? Could you use its result? Could you use its method? Should you introduce some auxiliary element in order to make its use possible?

Could you restate the problem? Could you restate it still differently? Go back to definitions.

The Logic of Scientific Discovery

It has been powerful magick, the scientific method. Here is an authoritative much quoted investigation of its philosophical core. When Popper takes you around an abstruse corner, you can trust him to show you something interesting that you can keep and use.

—SB

The Logic of Scientific Discovery
Karl R. Popper
1935, 1959, 1960, 1965; 480 pp.

$3.75 postpaid

from:
Harper & Row Publishers
49 E. 33rd St.
New York, N.Y. 10060

or WHOLE EARTH CATALOG

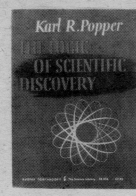

Now in my view there is no such thing as induction. Thus inference to theories, from singular statements which are 'verified by experience' (whatever that may mean), is logically inadmissible. Theories are, therefore, *never* empirically verifiable. If we wish to avoid the positivist's mistake of eliminating, by our criterion of demarcation, the theoretical systems of natural science, then we must choose a criterion which allows us to admit to the domain of empirical science even statements which cannot be verified.

But I shall certainly admit a system as empirical or scientific only if it is capable of being *tested* by experience. These considerations suggest that not the *verifiability* but the *falsifiability* of a system is to be taken as a criterion of demarcation. In other words: I shall not require of a scientific system that it shall be capable of being singled out, once and for all, in a positive sense; but I shall require that its logical form shall be such that it can be singled out, by means of empirical tests, in a negative sense: *it must be possible for an empirical scientific system to be refuted by experience.*

•

I do not wish to suggest that the belief in perfection— the heuristic principle that guided Kepler to his discovery— was inspired, consciously or unconsciously, by methodological considerations regarding degrees of falsifiability. But I do believe that Kepler owed his success in part to the fact that the circle-hypothesis with which he started was relatively easy to falsify. Had Kepler started with a hypothesis which owing to its logical form was not so easily testable as the circle hypothesis, he might well have got no result at all, considering the difficulties of calculations whose very basis was in the air'— adrift in the skies, as it were, and moving in a way unknown. The unequivocal *negative* result which Kepler reached by the falsification of his circle hypothesis was in fact his first real success. His method had been vindicated sufficiently for him to proceed further; especially since even this first attempt had already yielded certain approximations.

No doubt, Kepler's laws might have been found in another way. But I think it was no mere accident that this was the way which led to success. It corresponds to *the method of elimination* which is applicable only if the theory is sufficiently easy to falsify— sufficiently *precise* to be capable of clashing with observational experience.

The Structure of Scientific Revolutions

If you want to make a scientific revolution you might be interested in how it's done. Another well-used book.

—SB

The Structure of Scientific Revolutions
Thomas S. Kuhn
1962, 1970; 210 pp.

$1.75 postpaid

From:
University of Chicago Press
5801 Ellis Ave.
Chicago, Illinois 60637

or WHOLE EARTH CATALOG

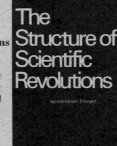

Normal science does not aim at novelties of fact or theory and, when successful, finds none. New and unsuspected phenomena are, however, repeatedly uncovered by scientific research, and radical new theories have again and again been invented by scientists. History even suggests that the scientific enterprise has developed a uniquely powerful technique for producing surprises of this sort. If this characteristic of science is to be reconciled with what has already been said, then research under a paradigm must be a particularly effective way of inducing paradigm change. That is what fundamental novelties of fact and theory do. Produced inadvertently by a game played under one set of rules, their assimilation requires the elaboration of another set. After they have become parts of science, the enterprise, at least of those specialists in whose particular field the novelties lie, is never quite the same again.

•

Lavoisier, we said, saw oxygen where Priestley had seen dephlogisticated air and where others had seen nothing at all. In learning to see oxygen, however, Lavoisier also had to change his view of many other more familiar substances. He had, for example, to see a compound ore where Priestley and his contemporaries had seen an elementary earth, and there were other such changes besides. At the very least, as a result of discovering oxygen, Lavoisier saw nature differently. And in the absence of some recourse to that hypothetical fixed nature that he "saw differently," the principle of economy will urge us to say that after discovering oxygen Lavoisier worked in a different world.

Thinking Straighter

In an era when information is going to have to replace laws, it's increasingly important to be familiar with the anatomy of bullshit (manipulation by language). Everybody does it, and that's cool; it's just when you don't know it's happening that it gets hazardous. This book does vivid, organized analysis of ads, political statements, and other bubbles of our day. How to build your own shock-proof crap detector.

—SB

Thinking Straighter
George Henry Moulds
1965; 234 pp.

$4.75 postpaid from:
William C. Brown Book Co.
135 South Locust Street
Dubuque, Iowa 52003

Thinking Straighter

DRAWING THE LINE

Meaning: Sharp distinctions are drawn where no sharp distinction exists.

Example: "Either you tell the truth or you lie."

•

The motive is the reason behind the argument; the intent is the reason ahead of the argument.

QUOTATION OUT OF CONTEXT

Meaning: Quotation out of context is a fallacy when the effect of quoting a given statement without its context is to distort the original meaning in context.

Example: Someone quotes the Bible as saying that "money is the root of all evil" but leaves out the preceding words, "the love of."

•

REPETITION

Meaning: We buy or believe because we have heard or seen the idea or the product name so often.

Example: Radio commercial: "Get up with GET-UP. GET-UP's got get up. Got it? Get it! Get GET-UP!!"

•

ATTACKING A STRAW MAN

Meaning: Your opponent either (1) restates your position falsely or (2) exaggerates the consequences that may follow from your position.

Example: (1) Smith: "I am opposed to capital punishment."
Jones: "I'm not."
Smith: "You ought to be; capital punishment is un-christian."
Jones: "I'm getting tired of people like you who oppose punishing criminals."

(2) Smith: "I am opposed to capital punishment."
Jones: "You fellows that are against capital punishment must want your daughters molested every time they leave the house."

Soviet Books

A thought. Soviet books; yes, written in Russian. One of the points the Soviets push with great and justifiable pride about their country is the easy accessibility of education——do-it-yourself or official—— especially along certain lines, which includes beautiful detailed books about peasant architecture, graphic and detailed books about the medicinal and other helpful uses of wild plants, and so forth. Some of these are set up so you don't need to know Russian at all, and others a few minutes' work with a dictionary will give plenty of access to. They sell so cheap in the Soviet Union (part of making it accessible) that even with transport and markup, they are mostly tremendous bargains in the U.S. You can get them from only a few bookstores in the U.S., among them Schoenhof's, Harvard Sq., Cambridge, Mass., 02138; Kamkin Inc., 1410 Columbia Rd., NW, Washington D.C. 20009; Four Continents Book Corp, 156 Fifth Ave., NY NY 10010; (and there's one in San Francisco, I think whose address I can't find at the moment. Also, through any one of these stores you can subscribe to a weekly service called *Novye knigi SSSR [New Books of the USSR]* (52 issues for $2.00!) which announces in advance the books that are going to be published during the coming months. Knowing Russian helps in making sense out of this, but isn't absolutely necessary——all you have to do is learn a few key words.

The bookstores themselves will send out price lists (though these are generally not broken down so much into categories, so knowing Russian is more important), and are mostly pretty good about answering questions like: "do you have anything on . . . ?"

Similar service for other Eastern European countries can be obtained from FAM Book Service, 69 Fifth Ave., Suite 8F, New York, NY 10003.

Hugh Olmsted
Brooktondale, NY

GETTING UP

About six o'clock Saturday morning D.R. heard somebody clamber up the front steps, stomp across the porch then pound on the door like the house was on fire. D.R. was already vaguely awake, but the weight of pure comfort held his body in the bed, and likely it would have lured him back to sleep again if the racket on the porch had not made him bolt up and reach for his pants and shirt.

"Who is it?" he called out.

"It's Leonard," came the reply. "I'm sorry to bother you this early."

D.R. said he'd be right there. Hobbling with one shoe on and one off, and buttoning his shirt as he went, D.R. went out of the bedroom and faced Leonard standing in the kitchen by the door.

"How'd you like to work for me today, David?"

D.R. had never seen Leonard as restless and impatient as he was now. He followed D.R. into the bedroom, then paced out again and walked around and around in the kitchen.

"I'll be glad to try," said D.R. "What doing?"

"Building a hog pen. This goddamn jury business has thrown me plum behind. I thought if you wasn't busy we might try to build that thing today."

"Nah," said D.R. "Nothing up here that can't wait to be done."

"Good," said Leonard. "Come on down and Roxie'll fix you a good breakfast."

"I like it already," said D.R.

And when he got his shoes tied he stood up and followed Leonard out the door.

Piaget for Teachers

This is a super how-to-do-it book — Piaget's thinking made concrete and applicable to the teaching of children. The theory is rich, and clearly presented, and involves mainly a concept of intelligence far more integrated, exciting, and beautiful than what we're used to. About half the book is a presentation of scores of exercises, games, and ideas for stimulating the development of real intelligence in children. Furth appears to have a soft heart and doesn't get strident about how schools are fucking it up now; he just says how education could be done a lot better. I bet he's right.

[Reviewed by Diana Shugart. Suggested by Martha LaVoie]

Piaget for Teachers
Hans G. Furth
1970; 163 pp.

$3.50

from:
Prentice-Hall, Inc.
Englewood Cliffs, N.J. 07632

or WHOLE EARTH CATALOG

Piaget
for
teachers
HANS G. FURTH

A school that in the earliest grades focuses primarily on reading cannot also focus on thinking. It must choose to foster one or the other. Historically, it has chosen reading. Undoubtedly, it once could be tacitly assumed that a child's thinking had developed adequately before he entered school and continued to do so outside of school. These assumptions were perhaps not altogether ill-founded. Schooling in the past was the prerogative of a special class and only gradually broadened its base to include a school-minded and school-ambitious citizenship within a relatively stable social and physical environment that was generally conducive to spontaneous intellectual growth. But today these assumptions are largely irrelevant for a large segment of our population.

•

. . . ask a seven-year-old child to draw you a bottle half-filled with water. When he has done this, draw the bottle—without water—in a tilted position and ask him to add the water level. Or take a match, put it half over the edge of a table, and slightly tap the overhanging part. Let a nine-year-old child observe what happens. Give him a paper on which is drawn the table and the overhanging match with the head of the match marked in solid black. Tell him to draw the successive positions of the match as it flips over and finally falls on the floor. Look at the child's drawings of the water level or of the positions which a falling match is supposed to take. I do not see how any person can observe these kinds of behavior samples and still maintain that knowing is a passive copy of "objective" facts.

•

We know that educators in a long tradition have put primary stress on such factors as personal acceptance, and I would be the last to belittle them. However, I venture to suggest that sensitivity to the "hidden" environment is not enough for a successful school. "Love is not enough" for the hungry child; he needs wholesome food on the table. Educational theories have been on a perilous swing from an extreme that stressed discipline and learning to another that focused on emotional and social adjustment. I suggest that you cannot have one without the other. A viable theory of the development of knowing will also be a viable theory of emotional and social development. A school system whose goal is geared toward healthy intellectual growth cannot but be conducive to healthy emotional and social growth. For this reason alone, my professional advice on problems of educational adjustment or motivation would be first to check the objective program that is offered to the child. If this program is psychologically or socially unsuitable to a child's developing intelligence, we should be slow in looking for secondary, indirect causes.

These few observations merely sketch ideas on the vast topic of social thinking. All I want to show you is the close organic connection between intelligence and social reality. If the school is to be for real, intellectual food must be for real, too. . . .

Teaching As a Subversive Activity

You may have noticed that schools are society's goat just now, and the blame machine revs on and on. The authors of this handy de-crisis book take a nice clean no-blame revolutionary approach to things: what works this minute and doesn't work this minute. In their experience (high-school), instruction in authoritative subject matter doesn't work very well. What does work is an experience-based inquiry approach to learning to learn and learning to selectively un-learn: i.e. basic survival strategy in an environment of change. What's nice is they aren't just threatening: they have gathered and published a strong collection of technique. —SB

Teaching as a Subversive Activity
Neil Postman and Charles Weingartner
1969; 219 pp.

$2.25 postpaid

from:
Delta Books
750 Third Avenue
New York, N. Y. 10017

or WHOLE EARTH CATALOG

Teaching as a
Subversive Activity
A no-holds-barred assault on outdated teaching methods—with dramatic and practical proposals on how education can be made relevant to today's world
NEIL POSTMAN & CHARLES WEINGARTNER

The new education, in sum, is new because it consists of having students use the concepts most appropriate to the world in which we all must live. All of these concepts constitute the dynamics of the questing-questioning, meaning-making process that can be called "learning how to learn". This comprises a posture of stability from which to deal fruitfully with change. The purpose is to help all students develop built-in, shockproof crap detectors as basic equipment in their survival kits.

•

The teacher rarely tells students what he thinks they ought to know.

His basic mode of discourse with students is questioning.

Generally, he does not accept a single statement as an answer to a question.

He encourages student-student interaction as opposed to student-teacher interaction. And generally he avoids acting as a mediator or judge of the quality of ideas expressed.

He rarely summarizes the positions taken by students on the learnings that occur.

His lessons develop from the response of students and not from a previously determined "logical" structure.

Generally, each of his lessons poses a problem for students.

He measures his success in terms of behavioral changes in students.

•

What we confront, at this juncture, is a most difficult problem in education: helping students to unlearn much of what they "know." Josh Billings said it almost a century ago: "The trouble ain't that people are ignorant; it's that they 'know' so much that ain't so." What are some of the things these students know that "ain't so?" Well, for example, they "know" that 1) the more "content" a person "knows," the better teacher he is; 2) that "content" is best "imparted" via a "course of study"; 3) that "content" is best kept "pure" by departmentalizing instruction; 4) that "content" or "subject matter" has a "logical structure" or "logical sequence" that dictates how the "content" should be "imparted"; 5) that bigger schools are better than smaller schools; 6) that smaller classes are better than bigger classes; 7) that "homogeneous grouping" (with students "grouped" on the basis of some real or fancied similarity) makes the learning of subjects more efficient; 8) that classes must be held for "periods" of about an hour in length, five days a week, for about 15 weeks in order for a "course" in a "subject" to happen.

It comes as a shock to the students that there is no evidence to support any of these contentions. On the contrary, there is massive evidence to confute them. It takes some doing, however, to help students to recognize the fact that most of their deeply internalized assumptions about "education" are based on misinformation rather than information

•

The instructor brought to class a black attaché case. He told the students that inside the case there was a small computer which was capable of producing the answer to any question anyone asked. 'What questions,' he asked, 'do you want it to answer?'

Teacher

Teacher is as unphoney, warm, and appealing as the grubby, tear streaked face of a child; it is also an important technical notebook for educators. Miss Ashton-Warner's organic approach to reading and writing is a detailed enough account to be explored further by teachers anywhere. It is of especial value to teachers working with primary children. Students with a cultural or language barrier, and adult illiterates.

[Suggested and reviewed by Carol Guyton Goodell]

Sylvia Ashton-Warner
Teacher

Teacher
Sylvia Ashton-Warner
1963; 224 pp.

$1.25 postpaid

from:
Bantam Books, Inc.
666 Fifth Avenue
New York, N. Y. 10019

or WHOLE EARTH CATALOG

Noise, noise, noise, yes. But if you don't like noise, don't be a teacher.

•

But there are two kinds of order, and which is the one we wish for? Is it the conscious order that ends up as respectability? Or is it the unconscious order that looks like chaos on the top? There is a separate world on each side of this question mark.

•

Organic reading is not new. The Egyptian hieroglyphics were one-word sentences. Helen Keller's first word, 'water,' was a one-word book. Tolstoy found his way to it in his peasant school, while, out in the field of UNESCO today, it is used automatically as the only reasonable way of introducing reading to primitive people: in a famine area the teachers wouldn't think of beginning with any words other than 'crop,' 'soil,' 'hunger,' 'manure,' and the like.

•

Backward readers have a private Key Vocabulary which once found launches them into reading.

•

The power content of a word can be determined better from a backward reader than from an average reader.

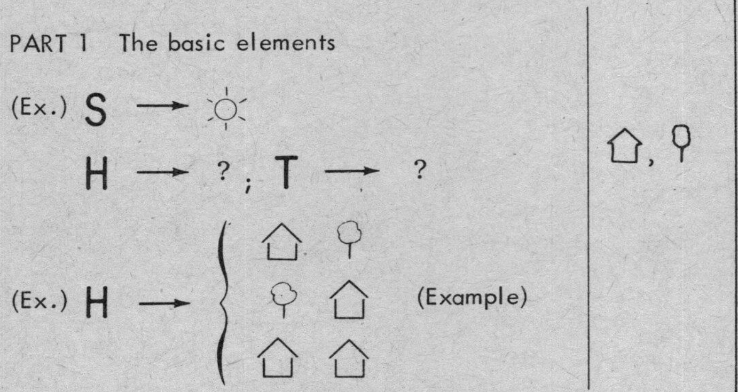

PART 1 The basic elements
(Ex.) S
H
?
T
?
(Ex.) H
(Example)

How Children Learn

This rambling series of innocent everyday happenings to a bevy of pre schoolers is described, digested, and given educational depth by an extremely observant and articulate educator, Mr. Holt. The great strength of his book is its readibility. His use of preschooler learning situations is ingenious, since it is a common reference point to all teachers and parents. Anyone who doesn't see toddlers in a different light after reading this book probably ought to write a book himself.

[Reviewed by Carol Guyton Goodell]

How Children Learn
John Holt
1967, 70; 156 pp.

$.95 postpaid

from:
Dell Publishing Company
750 Third Avenue
New York, New York 10017

or WHOLE EARTH CATALOG

HOW
CHILDREN
LEARN
by JOHN HOLT
author of HOW CHILDREN FAIL

Why does a baby begin to make sounds in the first place? Is it instinctive, like crying? It seems not to be. A puppy raised apart from other dogs will know how to bark when he gets old enough. But the few children we know of who grew up without human contact, grew up almost wholly mute. Babies in under-staffed foundling hospitals, who see very little of older people, are said, except for crying, to be almost silent. Apparently it is from hearing people speak around them that babies get the idea of "speaking." When they make their first sounds, are they imitating the sounds they hear around them? Or are they inventing, so to speak, from scratch? Perhaps at first they mostly invent, and imitate more later.

•

We must recognize that there are some teachers who like being "leader-draggers." They like to feel that they are at every moment in control, not only of the child's body, but also of his mind. They like to feel themselves the source and the sole source of all knowledge, wisdom, and learning in the classroom. Some such teachers are moved by a love of power, of which the classroom gives them plenty; others, by a deep and sometimes desperate need to feel useful, necessary, and even indispensable to their students. Both kinds are strongly threatened by any suggestion that children can and should learn on their own. Many other teachers would like to give their students more independence and self-direction, but are held back by a fear of the standardized tests by which their pupils, and they themselves, will be judged. In any school whose main business is preparing children to get high scores on achievement tests, regents' exams, merit scholarship exams, college boards, and the like, we are not likely to see much open-ended, independent student work. It must be said in fairness, too, that so far not many of the curriculum reformers and educational revolutionaries have shown much interest in it either. They tend to be so sure that the path they have marked out for their students is the best of all possible paths, that their main concern is how to lead or drag them down it as fast as possible.

•

Explanations. We teachers—perhaps all human beings—are in the grip of an astonishing delusion. We think that we can take a picture, a structure, a working model of something, constructed in our minds out of long experience and familiarity, and by turning that model into a string of words, transplant it whole into the mind of someone else. Perhaps once in a thousand times, when the explanation is extraordinarily good, and the listener extraordinarily experienced and skillful at turning word strings into non-verbal reality, and when explainer and listener share in common many of the experiences being talked about, the process may work, and some real meaning may be communicated. Most of the time, explaining does not increase understanding, and may even lessen it.

•

It is a remarkable business. We are so used to talking that we forget that it takes a very subtle and complicated coordination of lips, tongue, teeth, palate, jaws, cheeks, voice, and breath. Simply as a muscular skill it is by far the most complicated and difficult that most of us ever learn, at least as difficult as the skill required to master a serious musical instrument. We realize how difficult speech is only when we first try to make the sounds of a language very different from our own. Suddenly we find that our mouths and tongues won't do what we want. Yet every child learns to make the sounds of his own language. If he lives where more than one language is spoken, he makes the sounds of them all. How does he do it? His coordination is poor to start with; how does he manage to do what many adults find so difficult?

The answer seems to be by patient and persistent experiment; by trying many thousands of times to make sounds, syllables, and words; by comparing his own sounds to the sounds made by people around him; and by gradually bringing his own sounds closer to the others, above all, by being willing to do things wrong even while trying his best to do them right.

How to Live with your Special Child

No sweet romance here. Written mainly for teachers & mainly about children suffering from various forms of weirdness, it speaks to us all. Peculiar & powerful. Refreshingly skipping the theory in this book, he tells you what to do to make kids act better. Simple. Far out. Offensive! I ain't sure why, but I do think everyone should read it; in fact I downright ache for revolution in our schools, he makes it seem so possible, and because

> I remember all those thousands of hours that I spent
> in grade school watching the clock, waiting for recess
> or lunch or to go home.
>
> Waiting: for anything but school.
>
> My teachers could easily have ridden with Jesse James
> for all the time they stole from me.
>
> Richard Brautigan
> *Rommel Drives on Deep Into Egypt*

[Reviewed by Diana Shugart.
Suggested by George von Hilsheimer]

How to Live with your Special Child
George von Hilsheimer
1970; 272 pp.

$7.50 postpaid

from:
Acropolis Books
Colortone Building
2400 17th Street, N.W.
Washington, D.C. 20009

or WHOLE EARTH CATALOG

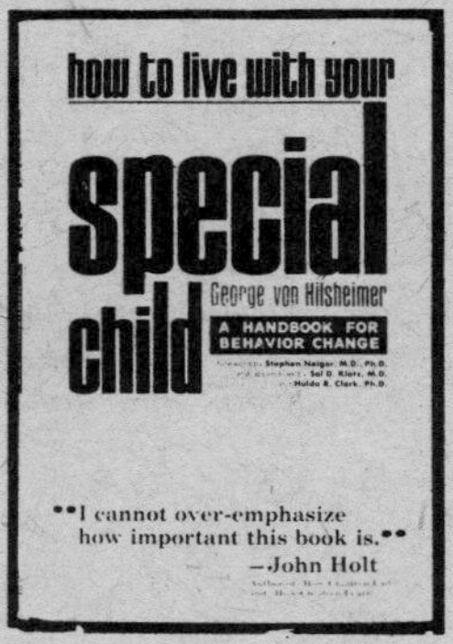

There is very good evidence that reducing the pressures on childish and adolescent offenders reduces the incidence of their failures. For example, kids who drop out of school are *arrested* more often while they are in school. Dropouts do *not* commit more crimes than kids who remain in school. There are more juvenile crimes committed on school nights than on weekends. The evidence indicates that the successful middle class child who also commits crimes carries out much more destructive and serious offenses than dropouts and lower class offenders.

•

An ideal elementary classroom has at least two teachers, and often involves as many as ten at one time (by teachers of course I mean volunteers, aides and "real" teachers——all used to advance the transactions of learning and not just for janitorial, nursing and secretarial tasks). The number of students can be more than thirty or so. The room should be large and ideally has an easily accessible half-second-story for reading and solitary quiet study or withdrawal for sleep or sloth. ("Il dolce fariente"——sweet do nothing, is really *useful* in the class.) The main room is organized with formal foci——messy corners, neat book corners, production corners and display corners. A separated or semi-separated area for noisy, messy corners, neat book corners, production corners and display corners. A separated or semi-separated area for noisy, messy, destructive and constructive shop work, biology or what have you is also ideal.

•

We have been impressed by the almost total inability of troubling adolescents to express or accept positive emotions. We have been amazed to see how seldom such children touch themselves or others, at how little physical flexibility even the best of them have, at how limited is their ability at nonverbal kinetic communication, how poor their mimetic ability, and how congested their emotions. We are often sent children with histories indicating many rage experiences. We never see this behavior more than once or twice at our centers (probably because we simply restrain and ignore it in a very blunt and matter of fact way) and the few initiating times we do see it, it appears to us much more as display and histrionics than emotional expression. . . .

We believe that touching is so important that we actually run a "love-up" rota of staff in our elementary residential programs. Even the most wooden staff member is received with delight. Each child is tickled, rubbed, fondled, patted and kissed good-night with special words of affection and joy. I am always impressed at the willingness of otherwise tough and aloof teenage criminals to accept this "baby" treatment. Our experience is sufficiently convincing that we persist in touching those teenagers who strongly reject touching. The weaker staff is not encouraged to take on these kids but strong staff members will tease and ridicule the aloofness and pursue and persist in touching.

•

The important principle is to bring new experiences, or present old experiences from a new angle. Don't wall them in with words by talking about the experience, analyzing, or introducing. Encourage the children to talk, talk, talk, describe, describe, write, write, write after the experience. Don't grade the productions. What you are trying to teach is responsiveness, transaction with the environment, observation analysis, reportage. Accuracy, style and grammar will come. Very quickly too.

Difficult children can be induced to enjoy Basic English by giving them something pompously moralistic to translate; or first show them a translation of some pompous moralizing, then give them another to have a go at. Translating the ideas of politicians and educational philosophers is always great fun.

•

Conditioned Acceleration of Responses by Relief of Aversion (CARRA). We use CARRA with a simple electric stimulator. We tell the pupil that we are going to turn on a mild tingle and then increase it. We will turn it off when the pupil makes a new response to the category we are asking for. For example: "I want you to tell me something you might say to your mother when you wake up in the morning. Each time tell me something different."

When we get a response that is not a repetition we immediately turn the current off. It can be done without electric stimulation but no one seems to mind very much and it works a great deal more quickly. For many kids, switching on a red light seems to work just as well (inward kids who are quiet, with downcast eyes, and sullen kids mostly). For others, simply driving an answer with verbal encouragement and direction will work. The advantage of electric reinforcement is that it is simple, matter of fact, unavoidable, and does not require verbal skill on the part of the teacher or aide. Also we seem to build up a tolerance for electric stimulation which in general seems to correlate quite well with general stability in the nervous system. In addition, the conditioning model is more precise and we seem to get a spill-over of conditioning for anxiety relief and a sense of being in control of the anxiety-producing stimulus.

The routine goes only about five minutes and any category is stopped as soon as it becomes a bit sticky for the student to think of something new. We are not trying to punish the child or test him.

•

Charles Stack has been having Puerto Rican janitors (preferably with little or no English) bring teaching machines into cells with young criminals. The janitor gets it across that the machine is supposed to teach the kids. He also gets it across that since it is the machine's job to *teach*, if the kid makes a mistake the machine will give him a dime for having wasted his time.

Nearly everyone rubs their eyes at this point. *The machine gives the student a dime if the student makes a mistake* because the machine has not done its job and taught him. These young criminals do not work to make mistakes or to make dimes. No one has to con these kids into the advantages of knowing. They do quite well for themselves if the social consequences and structures of the *teaching* process are changed. Many of these hoods work for hours at a time on the machines and graduate from jail to college.

•

Making the Human Garden Work

BIOLOGICAL inventory and regulation. It is stupid if not immoral to fail a hypoglycemic patient by not regulating his glucose supply. His brain had better be able to function before we offer him the choice of setting his own bedtime, regulating his own diet or learning how to read. A remedial diet often tells the whole story.

BOUNDARIES that are firm, clear, consistent and real. The child *knows* what and whom he can depend upon. It really doesn't seem to matter very much if the boundaries are actually fair, although it is nicer if they are. Sometimes, as the farmer said, a muleheaded client requires an attention-getting device like a two-by-four applied suddenly between the eyes. Tough, honest language often does it. After gaining his attention we give him a list of things to do, and we say, "Choose one." (At last analysis about ten per cent of our students were mules.)

TIME to relax, regularize, recuperate. The patient is almost certainly under chronic high arousal, has difficulty sleeping, is quick to startle, overreacts and has a badly regulated metabolism.

A good deal of doing nothing is often the first prescription.

GOOD SLEEP.

COMPETENT people who are warm, touching, friendly.

Everything else is aesthetics.

Humanitas Curriculum

School stuff from George von Hilsheimer's school. Modern Reading (a sure-learn primer or money back — $25). How Many? Math primer, $1.80). First Abacus ($1.25, and abacus $10). And a remarkable line of pamphlets on such subjects as "Eliminating The Smoking Habit", "The Self-Regulating Child", "How to Run an Effective Conference", etc.

—SB

from:
Humanitas Curriculum
A Division of Green Valley School, Inc.
P. O. Box 606
Orange City, Florida 32763

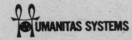

HUMANITAS SYSTEMS

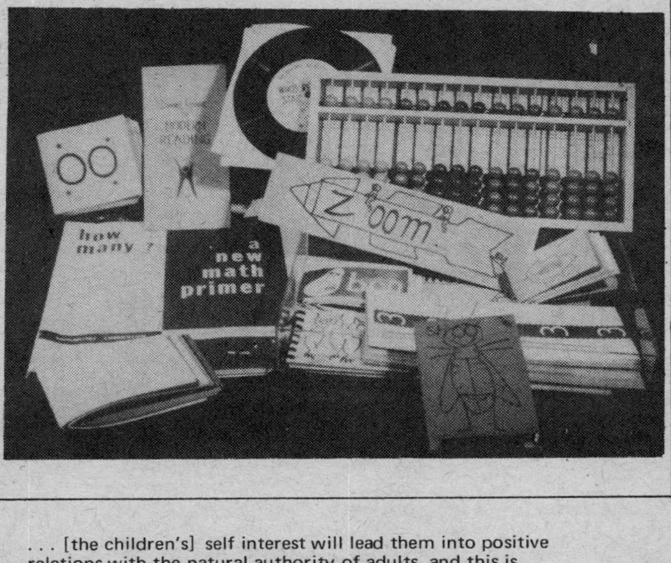

The Lives of Children

For some months, when speaking to teachers or to anyone else concerned with education, I have said that while there were many recently published books on education (my own among them) that I thought they should read, if they felt they had time for only one it should be **The Lives of Children.** *It is by far the most perceptive, moving, and important book on education that I have ever read, or indeed ever expect to. For while I hope that in years to come we may learn much about human growth and development that we do not now know, I doubt that any one book will advance our understanding as much as this one.*

It describes the lives of twenty-three children in the small private school in New York in which Dennison taught, and which has since been disbanded. They were black, white, and Puerto Rican in equal proportions. All were poor, half were on welfare, and about half "had come to us from the public schools with severe learning and behavior problems." . . . This school, spending no more money per pupil than the city's public schools, did not fail. The children got well, grew, learned.

[Suggested and reviewed by John Holt. This review is excerpted, at John Holt's request, from his review in Oct 9 **N. Y. Review of Books.***]*

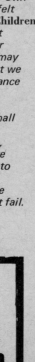

The Lives of Children
George Dennison
1969; 308 pp.

$1.95 postpaid

from:
Random House, Inc.
Westminster, Md. 21157

or WHOLE EARTH CATALOG

. . . [the children's] self interest will lead them into positive relations with the natural authority of adults, and this is much to be desired, for natural authority is a far cry from authority that is merely arbitrary. Its attributes are obvious: adults are larger, are experienced, possess more words, have entered into prior agreements among themselves . . . .

When all this takes on a positive instead of a merely negative character, the children see the adults as protectors and as sources of certitude, approval, novelty, skills. In the fact that adults have entered into prior agreements, children intuit a seriousness and a web of relations in the life that surrounds them. . . . These two things, taken together—the natural authority of adults and the needs of children—are the great reservoir of the organic structuring that comes into being when arbitrary rules of order are dispensed with.

•

Here we come to one of the really damaging myths of education, namely, that learning is the result of teaching, that the progress of the child bears a direct relation to methods of instruction and the internal relationships of curriculum . . . To cite these as the effective causes of learning is wrong. The causes are in the child. When we consider the powers of mind of a healthy eight-year-old —the avidity of the senses, the finesse and energy of observation, the effortless concentration, the voracious memory—we realise immediately that these powers possess true magnitude in the general scale of things. . . . Why is it, then, that so many children fail? Let me put it bluntly; it is because our system of public education is a horrendous, life-destroying mess.

There is no such thing as learning (as Dewey tells us) except in the continuum of experience. But this continuum cannot survive in the classroom unless there is reality of encounter between the adults and the children. The teachers must be themselves, not play roles. They must teach the child, and not teach "subjects." . . . The continuum of experience and reality of encounter are destroyed in the public schools (and most private ones) by the very methods which form the institution itself . . .

•

Jose's reading problem is Jose. Or to put it another way, there is no such thing as a reading problem. Jose hates books, schools, and teachers, and among a hundred other insufficiencies——*all of a piece* ——he cannot read. Is this a reading problem?

A reading problem, in short, is not a fact of life, but a fact of school administration. It does not describe Jose, but describes the action performed by the school, i.e., the action of ignoring every thing about Jose except his response to printed letters.

•

My own demands were an important part of Jose's experience. They were not simply the demands of a teacher, nor of an adult, but belonged to my own way of caring about Jose. And he sensed this. There was something he prized in the fact that I made demands on him. This became all the more evident once he realized that I wasn't simply processing him, that is, grading, measuring, etc. And when he learned that he *could* refuse——could refuse altogether, could terminate the lesson, could change its direction, could insist on something else . . . we became collaborators in the business of life. . . . It boils down to this . . . we adults are entitled to demand much of our children . . . The children are entitled to demand that they be treated as individuals, since that is what they are.

WATERING

Outside D.R. snapped his fingers and said, "Shit, Leonard. I've got to water the rabbits first."

Leonard looked pained. "Didn't you water 'em last night?"

D.R. shook his head. "They all still had some water in their crocks. I fed 'em. I thought I'd water 'em this morning."

Leonard was plainly pissed off, but all he said was, "Always water your stock at night, son. Don't put that kind of thing off."

Working together, D.R. carrying the bucket and Leonard dipping, they filled the crocks in all eleven hutches in ten minutes and then went on down the hill to Leonard's house for breakfast.

How To Survive in Your Native Land

I like, enjoy, learn from this book of school adventures. I can see that teaching will drive a person either crazier or saner. This book may help on the sane end.

—SB

How To Survive in Your Native Land
James Herndon
1971; 192 pp.

$1.25 postpaid

from:
Bantam Books
666 Fifth Ave.
New York, N.Y. 10019

or WHOLE EARTH CATALOG

. . . Couldn't have it! We soothed him, agreeing to tell Piston in no uncertain terms and so on. We walked outside with Lou, who had calmed down and had begun admiring the kite in retrospect, realizing that there was no way such a creation could fly (*aerodynamically speaking*, he said), and yet it did fly and this Piston or whatever his name was must be a pretty exceptional kid, and we were agreeing and realizing what a great guy Lou was for a principal even if, we reminded him, he had goofed up our schedule for this marvelous class we'd planned which had resulted in that extraordinary kite and other grand exploits, along with, we admitted, a certain amount of difficulty for him, Lou, and how well he'd handled it and supported us and . . . when Lou suddenly screamed Aaarrghhh! and fell back. I thought he'd been stung by a bee—we'd had a lot of bees that year, which also interrupted Egypt quite a bit, flying in the classroom where kids could scream with fake or real fear or try to kill them by throwing objects, often Egypt books, at them, exempt from retribution by the claim that they were just trying to save some *allergic kid* from *death*—but then he screamed There it is again! and pointed up, and there was The Monster From Outer Space, seventy-five feet up, plunging and wheeling and lurching through the thin air, a ton of boards and heavy paper and ghouls and toothy vampires leering down at an amazed lunchtime populace of little seventh grade girls, all with mothers and phones. Jesus Christ, look out! yelled Lou, and rushed for the playground, just as the giant came hurtling down like a dead flying mountain. It crashed; seventh grade girls scattered. (Their mothers reached for the phones.) Kids rushed from every direction and hurled themselves at the kite. They stomped it and tore it and killed it in wildest glee. They lynched it and murdered it and executed it and mercy-killed it and put it out of its misery, and when it was over and Lou had everyone pulled off the scattered corpse of the kite and sitting down on benches and shut up there was nothing left of it but bits and pieces of painted butcher paper and 1 x 2 boards and clothesline rope.

•

The school's purpose is not teaching. The school's purpose is to separate sheep from goats. . . .

•

. . . All of the talk about *motivation* or *inspiring* kids to learn or *innovative* courses which are *relevant* is horseshit. It is horseshit because there is no way to know if students really are interested or not. No matter how bad the school is, it is better than jail. . . .

•

A while back at Spanish Main School, it came to pass that *Immature* was out of style, and *Non-Achiever* was in. That is what drives everyone mad at a school, even if no one is aware that they are being driven mad. Humans like history, like to know why things start and end, like to have reasons for it, and the school never has any reasons. It doesn't have any because, in fact, it doesn't have any. . . .

On Federal Help

July 20, 1970

Hon. John Brademas, Chairman
Committee on Education and Labor
Select Subcommittee on Education
U.S. House of Representatives
Washington, D.C. 20515

Sir:

Thank you for the opportunity to testify before your committee.

I am delighted by the spirit behind your Environmental Quality Education Act (H.R. 14753) and depressed by every measure in it.

I'm a former ecology student, and I can report that ecology as a science is pretty boring. Definitely not for everyone.

Ecology as a movement, as a religion, is tremendously exciting, and everyone can get a piece of the fervor.

However, this voluntary mass education could be poisoned by Federal "help", as highly-intentional over-specialized application of fertilizers and pesticides has damaged other natural growth processes.

In my experience, the whole apparatus of application, approval, and funding commonly introduces a dishonesty into an operation that can never be eradicated. And if the operation is educational, dishonesty is the death of it.

I see that the bill provides for preparing information specifically for mass media use. Involvement of Government with mass communications in this manner strikes me as dangerous as re-joining Church and State.

If Federal funds are to be spent on environmental matters, let them go to:

1) The space program which has given us the anti-environmental perspective to see our planet whole and alive and in hazard.

2) The World Game of Buckminster Fuller's. This computer operation is planned to perform for the Earth as NASA's computers did for Apollo 13. (Inventory resources, assess damage, compare alternative "futures", select the most promising, constantly.)

3) Contingency planning for environmental disasters comparable to long-range planning in the military.

4) A "wet" NASA to investigate the sea and treat it like Antarctica, as a fragile, trans-national environment. (Use of the oceans must be governed from a strictly environmental standpoint by an international body with a great deal more power to act than the U.N. has.)

5) Rehabilitation for ecological disaster areas such as Lake Erie and Appalachian strip mine country.

6) Ecology Action-type groups, but only for services rendered. Do not fund them, do not tax them, do not pass laws about them. When they perform a service to Government, such as investigation of environmental crimes, pay them for the information.

7) Follow-up reports by independent groups of Federal actions affecting the environment. Do this as a built-in part of initial funding. Appropriations for a dam or a war would include money to go to the National Science Foundation or the Audubon Society or whoever to study the environmental effects of the project and report on them.

I realize that practically none of the above are the province of an Education Subcommittee.

John Holt has suggested that if we tried to teach infants to talk, they would never learn. I suspect it is the same with ecology. It must be learned. It is being learned. If you try to teach it to people, you will only teach them to hate it.

Let it be.

Stewart Brand
Whole Earth Catalog
Menlo Park, California

Push Back the Desks

Every effective teacher has had projects and ideas which really turned kids on, but most of them don't take the time to write about just what it is that makes their classes remembered by former students as 'one of the best years ever.' Albert Cullum did, and his enthusiasm and involvement with his class of elementary kids over a twenty-year span spill over to the reader in a veritable flood of ideas, theories, and teacher war stories. He is explicit enough about his projects to make them instantly available to any admirer, but the major strength of the book is its ability to awaken a hundred or so related ideas in the teachers who read it. It is teachers like Mr. Cullum who epitomize the best aspects and possibilities of the self-contained classroom for elementary school children.

[Suggested and reviewed by Carol Guyton Goodell]

Push Back the Desks
Albert Cullum
1967; 224 pp.

$2.65 postpaid from:
Citation Press
50 West 44th Street
New York, N.Y. 10036

or WHOLE EARTH CATALOG

I have found that children are interested in two things—doing and doing now. Children are looking for the unexpected, not the safe; children are looking for noise and laughter, not quiet; children are looking for the heroic, not the common.

•

Shakespeare may be for scholars to debate and discuss and philosophize over, but he is also for Corky, a fifth-grader who died beautifully as Julius Caesar. There are 'murderers' galore in the elementary schools ready to help Macbeth kill Banquo; many a fifth- and sixth-grade girl can really whip up a moment of insanity as Ophelia.

Hooked on Books

If you've wrestled with ways to teach a non-reader as a teacher, if you've wondered what you could do as a businessman to help an obviously weak reading program in your schools, or if you're the worried parent of a Book Avoider, then you'll tear through **Hooked on Books** *with a firelike fervor fed on rekindled hopes.*

Fader's program involves the saturation of students' surroundings with newspapers, magazines and paperbound books chosen because they are written on subjects relevant to the world outside a classroom. Diffusion of such materials among teachers of all subjects and the use of writing, writing and more writing as the primary ways in which to teach English is another important tenet of this program.

It is a detailed report on an exciting and practical way to teach reading, and it's laced with such well written anecdotes about the inmates of Maxey Boys Training School where this program was first tried that Big Bill, Superduck, Hogman, and Lester the Poet seem as real and as teachable as they were to the authors.

[Suggested and reviewed by Carol Guyton Goodell]

Hooked on Books: Program and Proof
Daniel Fader and Elton McNeil
1968; 236 pp.

$.75 postpaid

from:
Berkeley Medallion Corp.
390 Murray Hill Parkway
East Rutherford, N.J. 07073

or

WHOLE EARTH CATALOG

Those of us who participated in selecting the original 1,200 titles for the Maxey paperback library will never again have to be reminded how little we know about the students we teach. None of us will forget the untouched 700 titles that decorated our gleaming drugstore spinners while the boys read and reread the 500 they liked. . . . The 500 winners of our book Derby are included in the Reading List (pp. 148-173).

•

The boy turns, pulls out of his shirt Dick Gregory's From the Back of the Bus, waves it at the teacher, and shouts, "I bought it, man, I bought it! Bought four more while I was home. Didn't steal none!" Bought or stolen, those five books were the first that boy had ever owned.

How To Change The Schools

An outraged parent can hinder or help a bad school. Here's how to help, and how to hinder in the right places.

—SB

How To Change The Schools
Ellen Lurie
1970; 293 pp.

$2.45 postpaid

from:
Random House, Inc.
Westminster, Md. 21157

or WHOLE EARTH CATALOG

. . . the moral which has been indelibly stamped on my brain is that community groups must not fight each other, because when they do, only the school system wins. When the black parents demanded integration, the system labeled them irresponsible militants. When the white parents demanded educational improvements before they would accept integration, the system labeled them irresponsible bigots.

Meanwhile, in Washington Heights, busloads of black children were being transported into our neighborhood schools, only to be completely abandoned once they arrived. The schools which "received" them were given no special services; the teachers were given no special training. The black children were left to learn as best they could, and having suffered years of educational neglect, they often failed. The white children watched the black kids fail, and had all their preconceived prejudices reinforced.

It seemed almost as if the bureaucrats downtown had arranged this thoughtless program so that the white parents could fight the black parents and the black parents could fight back. And the more the parents argued and fought, the more the professionals at the Board of Education could say, of *all* parents, "You see, those people cannot be given any authority; look how irresponsible they are."

•

You and other parents might organize a campaign to have all children who have been labeled "slow" or retarded retested by *non*-Board of Education specialists. Get a volunteer team of doctors to check their eyes. Hundreds of "slow" children have turned into geniuses overnight when they got eyeglasses. Insist that all Spanish-speaking children be retested in Spanish.

•

Principals will try to "buy off" the most articulate parents in your group by assigning their children to the top classes and best teachers, or offering to transfer them to a "better school." *Don't* attack parents who take advantage of this offer. Remember their children, too, have only one chance for an education. Find ways to include these parents in your committee so you can still work together.

•

The school system destroys many many children. But, just as important, it destroys most teachers. It does not care about teachers any more than it cares about children. It does not help teachers achieve any more than it helps children achieve. The system engulfs the hopeful, energetic, often idealistic young teachers. It rapidly dehumanizes them, squeezing and twisting warmth and compassion out of them, turning them into non-thinking machines which obey and enforce automatically the rules and regulations of the bureaucracy. . . .

Media & Methods

A slick good education magazine. I can see that running a soft magazine in the hard-sell education media market is difficult, but Frank McLaughlin is doing all right.
—SB

Media and Methods
Frank McLaughlin, ed.

$9.00/yr. (nine issues)
$11.00 in Canada

from:
Media & Methods
134 North 13th Street
Philadelphia, PA 19107

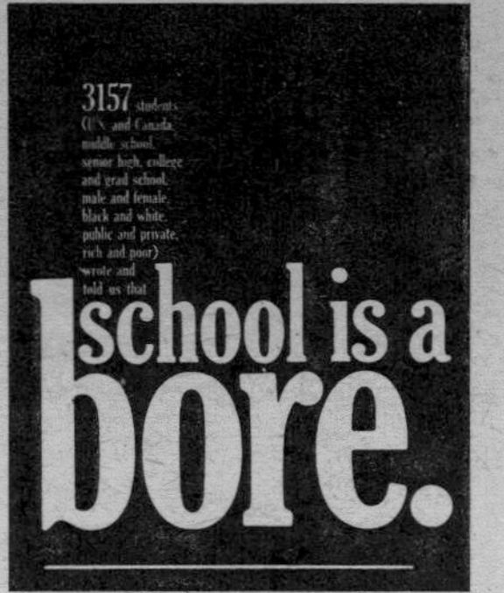

A Handy List of 16mm Distributors Suitable for Framing

Audio Film Center, 34 MacQuesten Pkwy So., Mt. Vernon, N.Y. 10550

Brandon Films, 221 West 57th Street, New York, New York 10019

Contemporary Films, (McGraw Hill/ Contemporary), Princeton Road, Hightstown, NJ 08520

Films Inc., 4420 Oakton Street, Skokie, Illinois 60076

Janus Films, 24 West 58th Street, New York, NY 10019

Universal 16, 221 Park Avenue South, New York, NY 10003

UA/16, 729 Seventh Avenue, New York, NY 10036

"The mood of students involved in simulation games is intense, purposeful and humorless, an all too perfect imitation of the real world atmosphere . . . In this way the simulation game seems more of an initiation rite than an educational experience."

•

Many different kinds of dramas are available: adventure, detective, western, spy, science-fiction, horror, mystery, soap opera, almost anything. With a series like *Gunsmoke, The Lone Ranger, Have Gun, Will Travel,* you can again stay within the students' knowledge. Shifting to the less familiar, you should find *Mercury Theater, I Love a Mystery, X Minus One, Suspense, Lights Out* and *The Whistler* of interest to any group.

•

Program Sources

1. The Longines Symphonette Society, Symphonette Square, Larchmont, N.Y. 10538.
2. Great Radio Shows, Inc., Box 254, Woodinville, Washington 98072.
3. Radio Yesteryear, Box H, Croton-on-Hudson, N.Y. 10502.
4. Wayne Field, R.F.D. #1, Meridian, Idaho 83642. Mr. Field has a large collection of shows and is willing to tape them on your blank tapes. His charge is another tape that you send along. In other words, send him two tapes; he records and returns one and keeps the other as payment.

•

Zero for Conduct, (Brandon) $32.50. (Dir: Jean Vigo) An innovative, poetic and surrealistic evocation of youth and its rebellion against the system.

Village of the Damned, (Films, Inc.) $22.00. (Dir: Wolf Rilla) An eerie tale about a group of super-intelligent and hyper-bizarre blond children who freak a peaceful English village. A simple horror story or a significant allegory, depending on your mood.

Jean Shepherd's America (Sunday night at 8 pm, beginning April 11, on PBS) is a series of "sensual essays" on the feel cities in America have. It is not in any standard sense a documentation of the U.S.A., but is rather a personal odyssey of one man as he visits Milwaukee, Colorado Springs, Honolulu, Cheyenne, Nome, Hammond (Indiana) and other places. The shows will be sprinkled with the wit and humor that has won Shepherd four *Playboy* Humor Writing Awards. He is also author of *In God We Trust, All Others Pay Cash* and the man humorist Marshall McLuhan has called "one of our only truly electronic novelists." A much sought-after performer on the college lecture circuit, Shepherd embodies in a real way Kerouac's maxim: Travel Equals Freedom. He begins his free-wheeling journey April 11. Check local listings for exact date and time.

The feeling of contempt so many college professors feel toward high school teachers and high school teachers in turn feel toward elementary teachers is shot through with irony. What has been consistently borne out in my experience is that the best teaching takes place at the elementary level (especially nursery school through 3rd grade). The best environments for learning are reflected in these "elementary" situations, the most natural employment of media are demonstrated, and the most humane relationship between adult and child exist.

The Metaphorical Way of Learning & Knowing

It's very hard to understand, after reading this book, why everyone isn't Doing It. Synectics Education Systems has workbooks for use in schools, and if the examples in this book are indicative, they are pretty far into the business of blowing (creating) minds. This one book is enough to keep an adult excited for hours, and the implications for using these trips with children are wonderful. For trips they are —— based on a very sound and well-developed theory of learning, they playfully seduce one into forgetting the old rules, and one finds oneself sitting there mind-blown, consciousness-expanded, and high.

[Reviewed by Diana Shugart. Suggested by Linda Williams]

Also check out Gordon's original Synectics, *on p. 236.*

The Metaphorical Way of Learning and Knowing
W.J.J. Gordon, et al.
1966–1971; 263 pp.

$5.50 postpaid

from:
Synectics Education Systems
121 Brattle Street
Cambridge, Mass. 02138

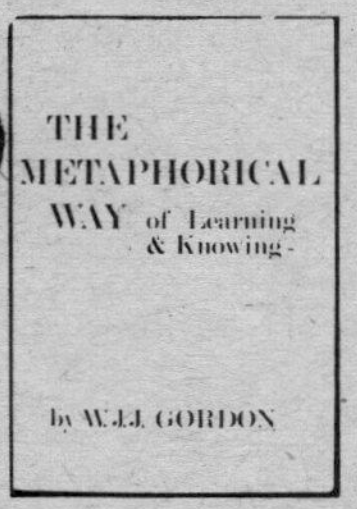

Most learning situations involving substantive material call for Making the Strange Familiar, whereas most situations that require innovation, as in problem-solving, demand Making the Familiar Strange. When the objective is to digest new substantive material, a student's learning can be inhibited by metaphors that introduce too much conceptual distance between him and the subject matter. However, when the student's objective, in language arts for instance, is to produce innovative and imaginative material; then the more distance he can introduce, the better.

•

BE THE THING. Imagine that you are a great rock. You are afraid of nothing. You are so strong that the wind and rain can't even scratch you, although during thousands of years they have worn away lesser rocks. However, one day, toward winter, a harmless drop of water trickles its way deep into one of the cracks with which you were born. Having withstood the onslaught of floods, and hurricanes through the ages, what is your attitude toward this tiny drop of water? *Oh, you tickle! You can't hurt me though. I'm much stronger than you. You can stay there if you don't tickle me anymore. It might be nice to have company. Are you sure I won't hurt you?*

From what you just wrote, pick the ONE word that compresses all your feelings toward the drop of water. Write it here: *strength.*

That night the temperature falls below 32°. The drop of water freezes. In freezing, it expands and hurts you. Nothing before in your life has been able to even mark you. How do you feel as the drop of water expands and cracks you in two?

Write a short story about the tiny drop of water defeating you, a great rock.

Improvisation for the Theatre

Somewhat like *The Natural Way To Draw* in its fundamental "process approach" to acting, games and plays. It is also similar to that amazing book in that the written instructions of the tasks are the primary method of instruction, and that the untrained person may read the instructions with reasonable confidence that they are accurate and have been tested.

Spolin's book is perhaps the one most in demand by young acting instructors today and because of its price is much stolen from libraries. It is just as much used by children's theatres and for professional training. The recent two-coast success of *Story Theatre* under the directorship of Paul Sills simply confirms the relevance of such training. (Spolin is Sills' mother and appears on the program as a consultant.)

The development of spontaneity and freedom in improvisation has applications far beyond the theatre or even the Esalen studies and psychodrama to which it has been applied. If you stop to think about it, improvisation is a necessary skill for us all . . . it is the way we all live our lives, isn't it? There is a technique used in speech training that is relevant here . . . they teach stutterers how to stutter voluntarily, to simulate their own type of stutter. By doing this they find that the stutterer develops a voluntary control over the process. Perhaps if we all learn to improvise consciously we may also attain greater control over our own lives?

Kelly Yeaton
State College, Pa.

Improvisation for the Theatre
Viola Spolin
$10.00 plus postage (2 lbs.)
from: Northwestern University Press
1735 Benson
Evanston, Illinois 60201

A Schools Booklist

Brothers,

Enclosed is a book list for all interested in open, free, anarchic, holistic education——as well as behavior change technology that works. Those marked are anecdotal, practical, and excellent guides to both the problems of cranky schools and communes. *The Peckham Experiment,* Pearse & Crocker, was probably the answer to it all.

GREEN VALLEY SCHOOL RECOMMENDED READING LIST

*Ashton-Warner, S., *Teacher,* Simon and Schuster, New York, 1963
Astrup, C., *Pavlovian Psychiatry,* Charles Thomas, Springfield, Illinois, 1965
*Bazely, E., *Homer Lane and the Little Commonwealth,* Schocken, New York, 1969
Beck, J., *How to Raise a Brighter Child,* Simon and Schuster, New York, 1967
*Burn, M., *Mr. Lyward's Answer,* Hamish Hamilton, London, 1956
Chall, J., *Learning to Read,* Grolier, New York, 1967
Coleman, M., *Adolescents and the Schools,* Basic Books, New York, 1965
Dennison, G., *Lives of Children,* Pantheon, New York, 1969
Engleman, S. & T., *Give Your Child a Superior Mind,* Simon & Schuster, 1966
Franks, C., *Conditioning Techniques,* Springer Publications, New York, 1964
Friedenberg, E., *Coming of Age in America,* Random House, New York
Dignity of Youth and Other Atavisms, Beacon, Boston, 1965
*George, W., *The Junior Republic,* D. Appleton & Company, New York, 1909
Ginnot, H., *Between Parent and Child,* Macmillan, New York, 1965
Goffman, E., *Asylums,* Doubleday, Garden City, New York, 1961
Goodman, P., *Growing Up Absurd,* Random House, New York
Compulsory Miseducation
Utopian Essays
Community of Scholars
*Hemming, J., *Teach Them to Live,* Longmans, Gram & Company, London, 1952
*Holmes, G., *The Idiot Teacher,* Faber and Faber, London, 1952
Holt, J., *How Children Fail,* Pitman, New York, 1964
How Children Learn
The Underachieving School
Ilg and Ames, *School Readiness,* Holt and Rinehart, New York, 1965
Illingsworth and Illingsworth, *Lessons from Childhood,* Livingston, London, 1966
*Jones, H., *Reluctant Rebels,* Tavistock, London, 1960
Klotz, S., *Guide to Modern Medical Care,* Scribners, New York, 1965
Kohl, H., *The Open Classroom,* New York Review, New York, 1969
Teaching the Unteachable
36 Children
Koerner, J., *The Miseducation of American Teachers,* Pelican, New York, 1965
Kozol, J., *Death at an Early Age,* Bantam, New York, 1968
Krumholz and Thorensen, *Behavioral Counseling: Cases and Techniques,* Holt, Rinehart, and Winston, New York 1969
*Lane, H., *Talks to Parents and Teachers,* Schocken, New York 1969
London, P., *Behavioral Counseling*
London, P., *Behavior Control,* Harper and Row, 1969
Modes and Morals in Psychotherapy, Holt, Rinehart, and Winston, New York, 1964
MacKenzie, R., *The Sins of the Children,* Collins, London, 1965
Escape from the Children, 1965
A Question of Living, 1963
*Neill, A. S., *Summerhill: A Radical Approach to Child Rearing,* Hart, New York, 1960
Freedom, Not License
*Makarenko, A., *Road to Life,* Foreign Language Publications, Moscow, 1951
A Book for Parents, 1954
Learning to Live, 1953
*Pearse and Crocker, *The Peckham Experiment,* Allen and Unwin, London, 1947
Richardson, E., *In the Early World,* Pantheon, 1969
Salter, A., *Conditioned Reflex Therapy,* Capricorn, New York, 1961
Scrimshaw and Gordon, *Malnutrition, Learning and Behavior,* MIT, Cambridge, 1968
Spiel, O., *Discipline without Punishment,* Faber and Faber, London, 1962
Trace, A., *Reading without Dick and Jane,* Regnery, Chicago, 1965
Ullman and Krasner, *Case Studies in Behavior Modification,* Holt, Rinehart, and Winston, 1965
Ullman and Krasner, *A Psychological Approach to Abnormal Behavior,* Prentice-Hall, Englewood Cliffs, New Jersey, 1969
von Hilsheimer, *Is There a Science of Behavior?,* Humanitas, Orange City, 1967
Watson, J. B., *Behaviorism,* Phoenix, Chicago, 1963
*Wills, D., *Throw Away Thy Rod,* Gollanz, London, 1960
Homer Lane: A Biography, Allen and Unwin, London, 1964
Wolpe, J., *Psychotherapy By Reciprocal Inhibition,* Stanford University Press, 1958
Wolpe and Renya, *Behavior Therapy and Experimental Psychiatry,* Pergamon, New York, 1969
Wolpe and Lazarus, *Behavior Therapy Techniques,* Pergamon, 1966
Wolpe, Salter, Renya, *The Conditioning Therapies,* Holt, Rinehart, and Winston, New York, 1965

Best,

George von Hilsheimer
Orange City, Florida

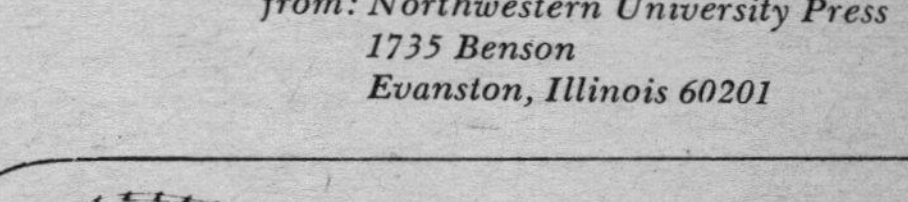

BREAKFAST

Roxie fed D.R. another big breakfast of ham and eggs while Leonard loaded his tools into his pickup truck. The barn they were going to build the hog pen onto was half a mile up the road from Leonard's house there behind the store. The barn sat on two acres of bottom land that an in-law of Roxie's had owned till he moved to Louisville two years before. The first year he was gone Leonard rented the barn and used it as a storehouse, and then later he bought it. He still used it as a storehouse, but this year Leonard decided to try keeping hogs up there. He had four, penned in a make-shift stall inside. But they were getting so big so fast they needed an outdoor place to be, and that was what he'd asked D.R. to help him build that day.

When he got the tools loaded and the truck turned and pointed out the drive-way, Leonard left the motor running and went to the back door and asked D.R. if he was ready.

Roxie said, "Let the boy finish eating, Leonard."

"I'm finished," said D.R. "One more biscuit and I'm ready to fly!" D.R. wiped the remaining egg yellow off his plate with a biscuit, stuffed it into his mouth, and washed it down with a drink of coffee as he got out of his chair. "Mighty good," he said to Roxie and she smiled at him as he went out the back door after Leonard, who was already half-way back to his pickup.

Catalog of Free Teaching Materials

The 8th edition of a constantly updated source book for teachers and other educators of free things for a class—maps written information, an occasional free sample from some company, filmstrips, charts. This edition good for 1973-76. The introduction says that "materials in this book have been evaluated by accredited teachers, and only those items which have direct bearing on the curriculum have been included." Items are listed alphabetically by subject, and annotated to provide for clear ordering instructions and information about the exact nature of the materials.

Dense, comprehensive, and clearly read.

[Reviewed by D. Smith.
Suggested by Big Rock Candy Mountain]

Catalog of Free Teaching Materials
Gordon Salisbury
1973; 365 pp.

$3.25 postpaid

from:
Catalog of Free
Teaching Materials
P.O. Box 1075
Ventura
California 93001

Catalog for Learning Things

All manner of dandy low-cost tool kits, materials, animal cages, and funky classroom furniture. —SB

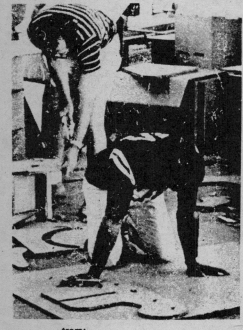

Catalog
$.50

from:
The Workshop for Learning Things
5 Bridge Street
Watertown, Mass. 02172

Several years ago, the Workshop ran across triple-thick corrugated cardboard for the first time. We began to design and build with it, wondering how many conventional building materials—lumber, plywood, masonite—it might replace. Since then, we've used thousands of sheets of it, much of it in workshops working with people using it for the first time. It has given us all a part in shaping learning environments.

This laminated cardboard is three layers thick and comes in very large sheets. It is inexpensive, compared to plywood, yet it is strong. Used with a good eye for its strengths and shortcomings, it can be as durable in a classroom as more expensive materials. Furthermore, it can be worked with simple tools and requires few or no woodworking skills. The inventory of things made by teachers in recent workshops is endless . . . chairs, carts, tables, easels, playhouses, jungle gyms, boats, giant globes, cages, aquariums, desks, carrels, seesaws, sandboxes. . . . This combination of cardboard, tools, techniques, and people we call Cardboard Carpentry

CARDBOARD CARPENTRY SMALL TOOL KIT

5 carpenter's saws	5 yard sticks
1 keyhole saw	2 wrenches
2 double-bladed hacksaws	2 spring clamps
2 paring knives	1¾" hole cutter
2 mallets	1 *The Further Adventures*
2 hole punches	*of Cardboard Carpentry*

$68.00
weighs 25 pounds

398 School Things
Learning

Children's Music Center

Music and dance instruments, records, and books for kids. Also history and contribution of black and Spanish-speaking Americans.
—SB

Catalogs
$.25

from:
Children's Music Center Inc.
5373 West Pico Blvd.
Los Angeles, CA 90019

DF35 COMPLETELY WELL
B. B. KING
12" L.P. Record 5.98
A great blues collection by "King Of The Blues." B. B. King with his blues guitar singing Confessin' The Blues, So Excited, Key To My Kingdom, etc.

DF32 IN MY LIFE
JUDY COLLINS
12" L.P. Record 5.98
Collection of songs that Judy Collins makes an inspiration for movement. Susanne (Leonard Cohen), Tom Thumb's Blues (Bob Dylan), Marat/Sade, In My Life (Lennon-McCartney).

B785 SOUL ON ICE 5.95

A collection of essays and open letters written by Eldridge Cleaver which he began writing in 1965 "to save himself." He wrote passionately and critically as a participant-observer about prison life, Watts, Malcolm X; Negro Heroes of the White Race; James Baldwin, Richard Wright, Norman Mailer; Vietnam; To Black Women from Black Men.

EC24 LET'S BE TOGETHER TODAY
12" L.P. Record 4.98
"Misterogers" relaxed songs for children and their families; Parents Were Little Once Too, I Like To Be Told, I'm Taking Care Of You, Alphabet Song, Peace and Quiet. Words on jacket.

★ **EC25 WON'T YOU BE MY NEIGHBOR?**
12" L.P. Record 4.98
Childhood songs performed in easy style by "Misterogers"; Somethings I Don't Understand, I'd Like To Be Like Dad, I'd Like To Be Like Mom, When The Baby Comes, I Like You As You Are. Words on jacket.

Kaiser Aluminum News

Don Fabun is doing very well at his job of making Kaiser appear comprehensive and futuristic. The Kaiser Aluminum News that he edits comes out several times a year, each issue devoted to one large topic, such as communication, transportation, food crisis, etc. They are excellent compendiums of current thought, vividly illustrated and laid out. Best of all, they're only $.50 if you write Kaiser for single copies.
—SB

Inquire for their list from:
Kaiser News
Kaiser Aluminum Chemical Corporation
Kaiser Bldg. 937
Oakland, CA 94643

I have yet to see any problem, however complicated, which, when you looked at it the right way, did not become still more complicated.

POUL ANDERSON

A hundred years ago a chemical theory was uncovered that retains broad significance. It is known as the "Law of the Minimum."

Under ideal circumstances, a reaction will continue until restrained by exhaustion of whatever essential ingredient is present in least supply.

What is our essential ingredient in least supply? And how much of it do we possess? We do not know.

S. P. R. CHARTER / "Man on Earth"

According to legend . . . the Worm Ouroboros ate its own tail, and thus was a symbol of a world that survives by endlessly devouring itself.

A compendium of 6 issues of Kaiser Aluminum News about the next 20 years has been published in hardcover under the title The Dynamics of Change. The book costs $8.95 from Prentice-Hall, Englewood Cliffs, N. J. 07632.

Catalogo

I should like to suggest the following catalogue for your Whole Earth Catalogue: El Centro Comercial of Box 1074, San Antonio, Texas.

Many of us who live close to the border of Mexico are bilingual. Ask for CATALOGO 1966. It's free! 66 pages and contains:

Catalogs of books for sale dirt cheap--in Spanish e.g.

Ocult Science

Music and Songs

"The head of Pancho Villa" (someone cut off his head)

"Huckleberry Finn"

Poetry

Medical Guides

Medical Plants

Sex Education

Catholic Religious Articles & Books

Guitars & Acordeon

Radio, Auto, TV Repair Books

Off Beat Books e.g. Mexican Penal Code & 1917 Constitution

Mexican Playing cards---deck of 40

Service is fair. Everything is encono-priced and of Economy quality.

J.K. Lassig
Houston, Texas

CR44 GOURD TONE BLOCK 1.50
Very deep hollow tone produced by striking, or striker can be rubbed over corrugations on wood block for gourd tones. Striker included.

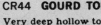

CR45 HANDCASTAS .... set of 2 pairs 1.50
Japanese finger castanets in bright colors — very easy to play to get clicking sound.

CR41 JUMBO SAND-BLOCKS .... pair .90
5" x 3" — with gripping knobs attached. Durable abrasive paper produces deep swishing sound when blocks are rubbed together.

CR112 FLUTOPHONE or TONETTE 1.00
Plastic — Key of C, Chromatic scale.

NICEM Indices to Educational Media.

The National Information Center for Educational Media has just completed publication of fourteen comprehensive volumes dealing with non-book media, including films, filmstrips, audio and video tapes, records, cartridges, overhead transparencies and slide sets, plus volumes devoted specifically to the areas of psychology, health and safety education, vocational and technical education, black history and studies, and ecology. Each index contains alphabetical listing by title and subject heading and each entry contains the size, black and white or color, with sound or silent, length, audience level, speed of rotation (for records) and the name and address of the producer and distributor. Also, a subscription service which updates everything yearly. NICEM has also done custom cataloging (free quotations and time estimate) for over 500 institutions.

The indices, subscription service and cataloging service available from:

Nicem
University of Southern California
University Park
Los Angeles, California 90007

Nicem Index to 16mm Educational Films
4th Ed., 70,000 entries

$79.50 postpaid

Nicem Index to 35 mm Educational Filmstrips
4th Ed., 42,000 entries

$58.50 postpaid

Nicem Index to Overhead Transparencies
3rd Ed., 35,000 entries

$49.50 postpaid

Nicem Index to 8mm Motion Cartridges
3rd Ed., 18,000 entries

$19.50 postpaid

Frank Kroger
Venice, California

Spoken Arts

A fine big collection of records, tapes, filmstrips of poets, stories, exotic song, drama, and so forth. Records are $6.50 each. Play Rikki-Tikki-Tavi again. Play Wallace Stevens again.

—SB

Catalog
free

from:
Spoken Arts, Inc.
310 North Avenue
New Rochelle, N.Y. 10801

Rubaiyat Of Omar Khayam
Inaugural Addresses Of Washington, Lincoln, Jefferson, Theodore Roosevelt, Read By Senator George McGovern (T)
Adventures Of Tom Sawyer by Mark Twain

W. H. Auden: Selected Poems
(C) W. H. Auden: Poems

Wind In The Willows: Grahame

The Gift Of The Magi and The Last Leaf: O. Henry
The Notorious Jumping Frog Of Calaveras County, The Professor's Yarn and The Man Who Put Up At Gadsby's: Mark Twain

Pit And The Pendulum: Edgar Allan Poe: Scourby

Just So Stories: Kipling (Volume I)
Just So Stories: Kipling (Volume II)

Brendan Behan Sings Irish Folksongs and Ballads

Pacifica Programs

Liven up Current Events with some current events. Reel and cassette, $10-$20.

—SB

Catalog
$1.00

from:
Pacifica Tape Library
5316 Venice Blvd.
Los Angeles, CA 90019

AP 1203 OVERPOPULATION AND OUR DETERIORATING ENVIRONMENT—Dr. Paul Ehrlich, author of "The Population Bomb," expands on his original thesis in a talk given February 1970 at the First Congregational Church in Berkeley. The audience was appreciative, and the program should "be heard here, there and everywhere" say the KPFA evaluators. 89 minutes. $14.00

Educator's Guide to Free Films

This is an invaluable reference if you are interested in film education. The book has indices of contents, film listings, cross-index; titles, subject, and source and availability. The source and availability index saves hours of time, although it does not indicate whether or not you need a special order form. It also indicates whether you pay mailing cost one-way or two-way. Every school or proto-school should have a copy.

[Suggested and reviewed by Chip Chappell]

Educator's Guide to Free Films
1973; 784 pp.; 4919 films

$12.45 postpaid

from:
Educators Progress Service, Inc.
Randolph, Wisconsin 53956

CONQUEST OF LIGHT   (1964) 16mm Sound 10 min.
This film tells the story of the laser (sometimes called an optical maser), a device with almost unlimited potential in many areas. Although the film explains basically how a laser works and what it is, it does so in language clearly understandable to a non-technical audience. (Not cleared for TV)

Bell System Telephone Offices

CIRCLE OF THE SUN   16 mm Sound 29 min.
This film, in full color, records one of the last gatherings of the Blood Indians of the Blackfoot Confederacy. It shows the sun dance, but it also reflects the predicament of the younger generation——those who have relinquished their ties with their own people but have not yet found a firm place in the changing world. (Available from the Boston, Chicago, Detroit, Los Angeles, New Orleans, and Washington offices. See Source Index for addresses and areas served by each.) (Not cleared for TV)

Consulate General of Canada

Follow Through Project

Educational Development Center has far the best list we've seen of recommended instructional aids, materials, and supplies for the primary grades. Prices and suppliers are given with the items. Two lists, Instructional Aids & Children's Literature, available for $1.00 each. —SB

[Suggested by John Holt]

from:
Follow Through Project
Educational
 Development
 Center
55 Chapel Street
Newton, Mass. 02160

Playground Equipment

A list of playground equipment sources is available **free** *from:*

The Parks Council
80 Central Park West
New York, NY 10023

Things **A SCHOOL NEEDS**

Desks, filing cabinets, sewing machines. Television, radios, phonographs. Typewriters, DITTO machine. Stove, refrigerator, freezer. Heaters. Cameras (moving and candid), projectors and screens. Camping equipment, musical instruments. Darkroom equipment. Good pocketbooks. Arts and crafts supplies, science equipment. Kitchenware, cleaning equipment. Gardening tools, building tools and supplies. Garbage cans. All paper products. Sod. [New Directions Community School, Richmond, CA]

AP 1168   AN ANTHROPOLOGIST VIEWS THE SOCIAL SCENE—Gregory Bateson talks at the Mental Research Institute in Palo Alto. One of his conclusions is that the commonly accepted way of looking at out world as "man versus environment" will soon prove lethal to a society with enough technology to put the idea into practice. Bateson gives mankind only a 50-50 survival chance within the next 20 years unless radical changes are made. 46 minutes. $12.00

AP 1189   CHINA OBSERVED—Neal Hunter, an Australian teacher, taught English in Chinese schools from 1965 through 1967, and was on the scene for the first year of Mao Tse Tung's Cultural Revolution. Following his return, he wrote a book of the same title as this program, and is currently in Berkeley's Center for Chinese Studies writing a second book on his sojourn in Red China. A vivid and personal glimpse of life under Mao. 55 minutes. $12.00

Puppetry Store

Has a good catalog of puppetry books, and probably other puppet stuff too.

—SB

Puppetry Store
Ashville, Ohio 43103

Cloth Diagram — Lewis Mahlmann

For those who like to sew — not the rag doll type but a shaped pattern that even permits you to change the profile of the face to change the character. Step by step, very definite instructions.

Price — $1.00

Introducing Puppets
Peter Frazier

Again, a book for the beginner, and yet a book for all.

Nothing new or unusual but the author has taken the best of many construction methods, gathered them together in a systematic way, and filled almost every page with clear, explicit drawings that anyone can understand and follow, - full pages in most cases, excellently executed.

Shadow puppets, rod puppets, hand puppets, and marionettes, - there are plans for construction of all, together with good stage plans, and many extras.

Perfect for new members just starting in puppetry.

8 x 8 — 120 pages $6.95

Puppet Theater Handbook
Marjorie Batchelder
(full 69 pages of diagrams by Doug Anderson)

The Handbook covers practically every phase of puppet construction and production. Contributions from more than 50 outstanding puppeteers make this a complete manual of construction and production. Often referred to as the Puppeteer's Bible, Bibliography and Materials Supplement. If you can only buy one book, this is it.

6 x 9 — 293 pages $6.50

THE PLAN

Leonard said, "What we want to do now, David, is fence in this place here where you see it's shady. This shade now's from the barn, but later on in the heat of the day those sycamores over there shade this same spot pretty good too, without keeping the sun out completely. I've studied this side, there's good sun late in the morning and then along about the middle of the afternoon it comes in from the road-side pretty good. If we do a good job fencing, those hogs'll have a good place out here.

"What we'll do, David, is just come right out from the two corners of the barn there, make it square on that end, come out about twenty feet on this side, and I figure about twenty six on that side over there because of that old stump. It wont be square on this end and we'll have to dig an extra posthole or two, but that'll be easier than trying to fight that old stump, and the hogs'll be glad of the extra room. I don't expect to win any architect's prize with this pen, but it'll be solid if we get the posts in good, and that's what we're interested in.

"What I'll do, David, is mark off where we want the posts to go, and work with you a little to get you started. Then while you dig I'll take the truck into Blaine and get the posts and my one-by-sixes, shit I guess I better get nails too. I'm sorry I'm so disorganized this morning, but it's just piled up on me so bad I aint thinking too straight yet. But we'll get lined out. It's a little after seven now. If we get the holes dug this morning and I get back with the fencing material by dinner time, we might not be in such bad shape after all. Get those diggers off the truck why don't you David, and I'll gouge around a little with my spade, and we'll just light right into it and hush talking about it.

Graves-Humphreys Shop Equipment

An enormous catalog of good stuff available only to schools. Wonderful prices.

—SB

Graves-Humphreys, Inc.

CRAFTOOL CARVING TOOL SET

Consists of one Veiner, one Shallow U Gauge, one Knife, one Chisel and a Sharpening Stone. All tools are equipped with varnished hardwood palm-grip handles and measure 4¾" long. Forged and heat-treated steel blades used throughout. A perfect set for doing fine carving.

No. 528AZ $7.25

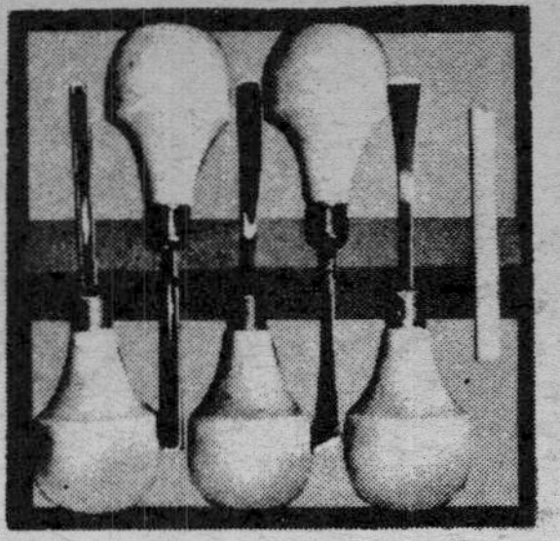

HAND PLANES
BLOCK PLANES
STANLEY

REGULAR

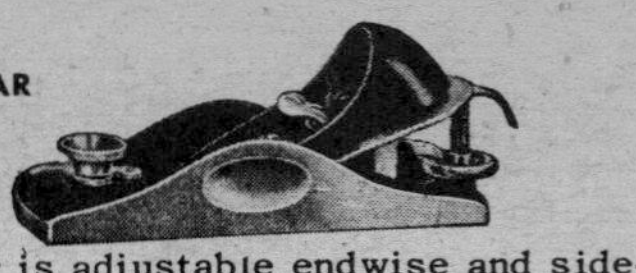

Cutter is adjustable endwise and side-wise. Adjustable throat. "Handy Grip." Sides and bottoms ground. Black trim.
No. 9¼ made without adjustable throat.

No.	Lgth.	Cutter	Price
9¼	6"	1-5/8"	$4.43
9½	6"	1-5/8"	$5.63

BLACKSMITHS' ANVILS
VULCAN

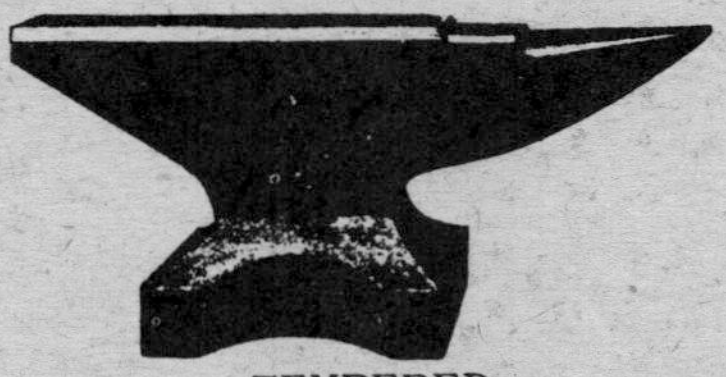

TEMPERED
SOLID TOOL STEEL FACE

The face is one solid piece of high grade steel thoroughly welded to the body of the anvil. It is accurately ground and tempered. The face is fitted with a true hardie-hole for use of anvil tools. The horn is made entirely of tough untempered steel.

Nos.	7	10
Wt. Each, Lbs.	70	100
Length, In.	18-1/2	20-1/4
Face, In.	11x3-1/4	12-5/8x3-1/2
Height, In.	8-1/8	9-1/4
Length Horn, In.	7-1/2	7-5/8
Hardie Hole, In.	1/2	3/4
Pritchel Hole, In.	3/8	1/2
Price Each	$52.80	$63.80

KELLER "JEFFERSON 601" SAW
the LITTLE GIANT of Power Hack Saws
Capacity 5" x 4"

- Pressure Relief on reverse stroke
- Adj. Hookup Bar
- Two Speeds: 120/160 spm.
- Blades: 10" or 12" High Speed Steel
- Stroke: 3-3/4"
- 1/3 HP at 1725 rpm.
- Capacity 5"h, 4"w, 4" diam. Pipe: 3-1/2", 45° Angle: 3"

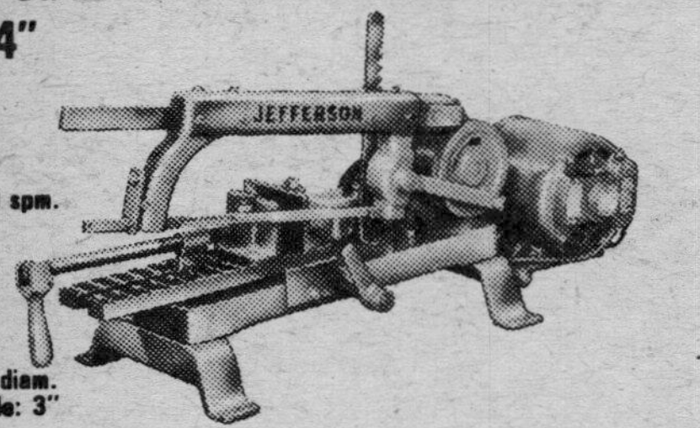

SPECIFICATIONS
Bench space .... 11-1/4" x 34-1/4"
Total height .... 15-1/2"
Ship. Wt. .... 87 lbs.

Complete with Single Phase 110V motor, Ready-to-run .... $99.50 FOB

"Jefferson 601" Floor Model — $114.50
"Jefferson 601" Portable Model — $127.50
For 3 Phase 220/440V motor and starter for any "Jefferson 601" add $30.00

MANILA ROPE

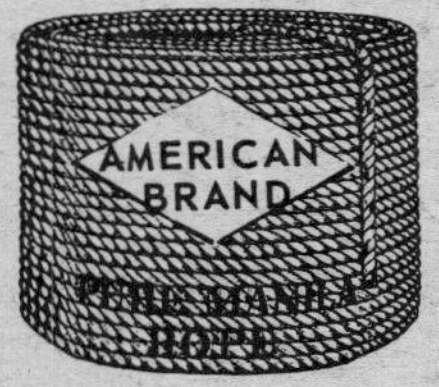

For Marine Industrial and Agricultural Use

Dia.	Test Strength Lb.	Per Ft.	Per 600' Coil
1/4"	600	$ .05	$11.90
5/16"	1000	.10	14.65
3/8"	1350	.10	23.00
1/2"	2650	.15	38.50
5/8"	4400	.20	66.00
3/4"	5400	.25	79.50
1"	9000	.30	124.00

TINNERS' SNIPS
WISS INLAID® BLADES

Polished, inlaid crucible steel blades; black enameled handles. Precision ground and specially tempered to cut hard alloy metals.

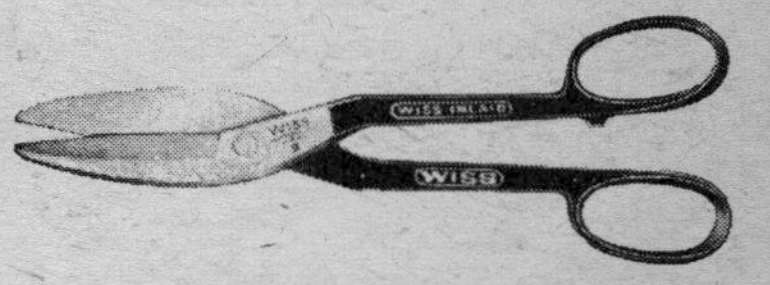

Regular Pattern

No.	Lgth., in.	Cut, in.	Wt. each, lbs.	Each
10	11½	2½	1½	$5.35
9	12½	3	1⅞	6.00
8	13½	3½	2½	6.75
7	14½	4	3⅓	7.50

Crafts Design

A school or family that's into crafts for the kids could make good use of this book. It has big well-illustrated introductions to paper, bookbinding, weaving, textiles, leather, clay, mosaic, and enameling.

—SB

Crafts Design
Spencer Moseley, Pauline Johnson, Hazel Koenig
1962; 437 pp.

$14.95 postpaid

from:
Wadsworth Publishing Company, Inc.
Belmont, California

or WHOLE EARTH CATALOG

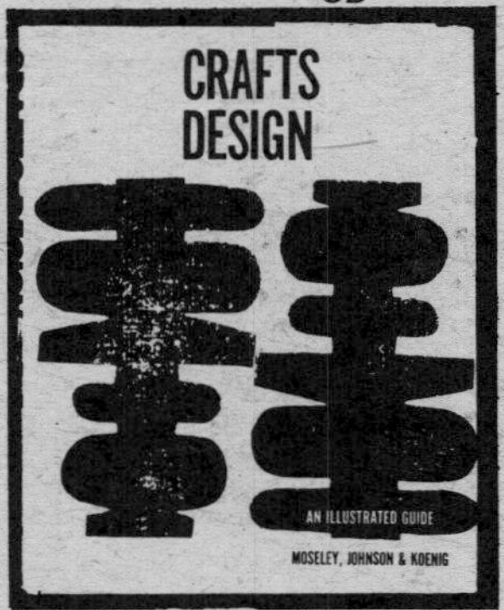

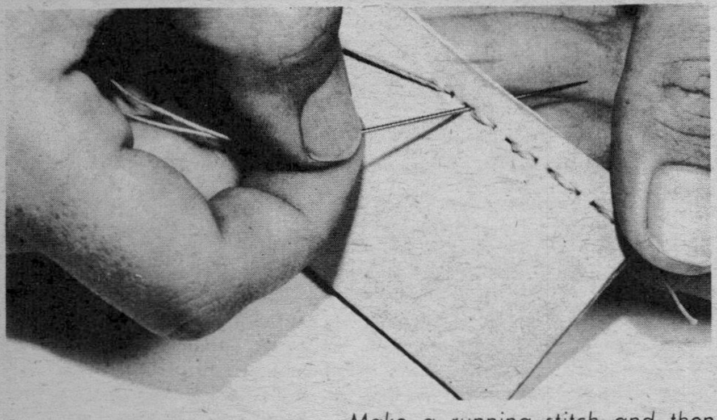

Make a running stitch and then reverse the direction, filling in the spaces between. The straight running stitch can be used for thin leathers. For heavier leathers two threaded needles may be used at one time. They go through the same hole from opposite sides of the leather, exchange positions, and return through the next hole. This process fills in all spaces between the holes.

Simple Weaving

Good simple crafty. Finger weaving, slot loom, T-D, card weaving, Indian bag loom, inkle, even a small 2-harness. I'd start weaving here with this likeable usable book.

—SB

[Suggested by Mary Madsen]

Simple Weaving
Marthann Alexander
1954, 1969; 112 pp.

$6.95 postpaid

from:
Taplinger Publishing Company
200 Park Avenue South
New York, N.Y. 10003

or WHOLE EARTH CATALOG

The T-D loom, a simple soom for weaving narrow fabric, is made from tongue-depressor blades. The loom is rather limiting to the weaver, as it produces strips of cloth only five or six inches in width; but it is so inexpensive to build and so much fun to use that everyone should try weaving on a T-D loom. A belt woven on the T-D loom makes a good beginning weaving project.

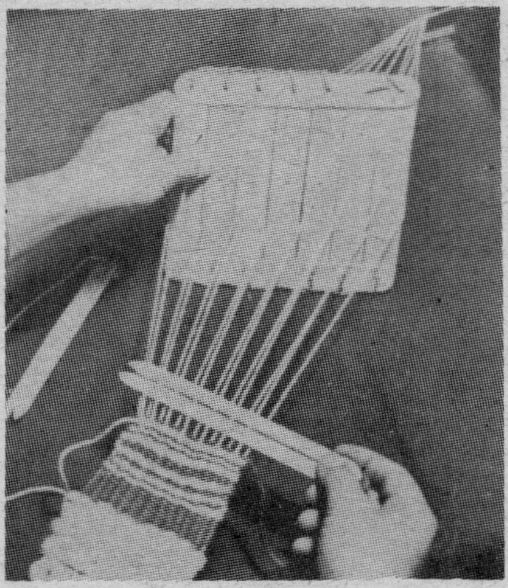

Raising the T-D Loom to Open the Shed

Roma Plastilina

This stuff has been very good to me. I've used it for my own sculpturing and in educating kids — you can let them work forever without having the stuff dry out in their hands. The softest grade is good for small children; for older kids you might want to knead together some #1 and #2, in equal parts. Then when a kid puts together a masterpiece, you can either let it stand as is or make a casting of it — Plastilina is especially good for rubber moulding.

It's also completely recycleable — as they say, it never dries out, so there's no hassle about storing it airtightly. It does, really, get better with age and use.

The kids and I both love the feel — slightly greasy, not watery, and very workable. Seems made for hands, not artificial tools. You can leave a project out on the table when you get tired, and come back whenever the muse hits again — even if it's a year later.

I don't really know how good this price is in comparison to clay — I know it's more expensive than other plastilina, but the quality doesn't even compare. I've always got mine in a store, but I believe they sell quantities by mail, and cheaper than these little packages.

A great creative play medium.

Ron Benson
Chicago, Illinois

Sculpture House
38 East 30th Street
New York, N.Y. 10016

CIDOC

Though your stated purpose is more inclined toward independent learning than formal schools, I would like to recommend to you the CENTRO INTERCULTURAL DE DOCUMENTACION (CIDOC) in Cuernavaca, Mexico. This school would, I think, provide an excellent base for those wishing to understand the third world role of Latin America. CIDOC is actually divided into 2 parts: an intensive Spanish language training school and a free form "Institute for Contemporary Latin American Studies" which includes many areas from Agrarian Reform to Youth in Cuba. Courses are taught mostly in English by men like Ivan Illich (who helped found CIDOC), Paul Goodman, John Holt, Herbert Kohl, and Edgar Friendenberg. To quote from the catalogue:

Cidoc is not a university, but a meeting place for humanists whose common concern is the effect of social and ideological change on the minds and hearts of men. It is a setting for understanding the implications of social revolution, not an instrument for promoting particular theories of social action. It is an environment for learning, not headquarters for activist planning. The main context of CIDOC is contemporary Latin America.

Cost by American standards is not great ($135 per month for the language course — 4 months are recommended for fluency, and $30 for each course plus $25 registration fee). Living quarters are up to you, though there is a service which can help you locate all types of arrangements from a room with a Mexican family to "Hawaiian Suites" with heated swimming pools. Interest free loans are available to any student who has been registered for at least one month and who states in writing that he can't continue in school without one.

Cuernavaca is a beautiful place, though somewhat of a retirement area for large numbers of American executive types and their Mexican counterparts. It is one hour by car from Mexico City with its fantastic museums (esp. modern art and anthropology) and also within a couple hours drive from the finest scenery in central Mexico (around Taxco). The town itself is an old colonial capital noted for a constant spring like climate and such sights as the crumbling garden of Maximillian and Carlotta and a Diego Rivera mural on one side of the provincial assembly building. Mexico as a whole is a warm friendly CHEAP place once you get a day's drive from the border. I have not actually attended the school so I cannot attest to how CIDOC lives up to its purpose, but its credentials are impressive. An informative, minimal bullshit catalogue is free by writing:

CIDOC
APDO. 479
Cuernavaca, Mexico

Sincerely,
John Carson Graves
Greensboro, NC

Papier Mâché

Cheap sculpture.

—SB

Papier Mâché
The Sunset Editors with William J. Shelley and Barbara Linse
1970; 80 pp.

$1.95 postpaid

from:
Lane Books
Menlo Park, California 94025

or WHOLE EARTH CATALOG

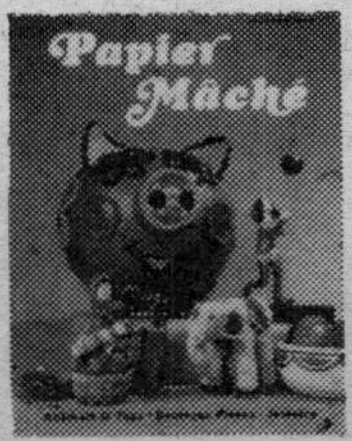

Crayons

"Stockmar Wachsfarben" (wax-crayons). I have used them both in school and privately for many years. They are very clean to use, especially important for children, and have the most pure colors I have ever seen. If you want to have a real color-experience & not only want to color objects pedantically, then these lend themselves to it. You can use them in many imaginative ways, many techniques. They come in a basic block-form or in sticks. They last a very long time.

Hanna Wilson
Detroit, Michigan

St. George Book Service
The Melnickers, Box 387
Sparrow Bush, N.Y. 12780

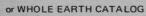

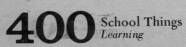

Elementary Science Study

ESS (a project of Education Development Center) had developed 56 interesting science units for elementary-school-age children. All of these are in commercial publication through McGraw-Hill. Supporting pieces in the form of highly informative and useful "working papers" are available from the EDC Distribution Center reasonably. Even some of the commercial stuff is cheap. Those units—and there are several—requiring only teacher's manuals and some ingenuity in locating materials are frequently the most interesting and the cheapest. In addition, EDC will send you their free newsletter. It usually has some feedback reports on the success (or lack of it) of their materials, good recommendations of books and stuff in the field of education, news of interesting projects tried by individual teachers, and advance notice about EDC research. For any of the above information write to:

Publications Office
Education Development Center
55 Chapel Street
Newton, Massachusetts 02160

[Suggested and reviewed by Mrs. W. B. Mohin]

Film Making in Schools

A good introductory film book at last. What's remarkable is that it gives aid in thinking film as well as making film, and all the perspective is around kids and what trips them instead of what used to trip Hollywood. The book is edited and illustrated with good film sense; it moves, and it moves you. Every other page you want to chuck it and go make film. How many instructional books do that for you?
—SB

Film Making in Schools
Douglas Lowndes
1968; 128 pp.; 353 illus.

$8.95 postpaid

from:
Watson-Guptill
2160 Patterson Street
Cincinnati, Ohio 15214

or WHOLE EARTH CATALOG

Introducing the Single Camera VTR System

A ". . . basic manual designed specifically to introduce helical scan (1/2 inch, 3/4 inch) VTR."

If your school video equipment is run by that education anomoly — the "AV boy" — a hardware freak, fluent in electronics and as open as a programmed reader — this manual will provide talk-back ammunition.

Simple definitions, good sense operating instructions, and practical maintenance tips offer the resources necessary to operate the equipment smoothly and to convince even the skeptical of your knowledge about the machines.

The technical information and equipment specs and suggestions are also very useful in piercing the bubble of manufacturers hype. But most of the exercises and production techniques are heavily scripted — suffering the patterned dullness of imitation broadcasting.

The growing video head scene can probably pass this manual up but schools without portable equipment may find the information worth the purchase.

[Reviewed by Richard Kletter]

Introducing the Single Camera VTR System
Grayson Mattingly, Welby Smith
1971; 150 pp.

$8.95 postpaid

from:
Smith-Mattingly Prod.
310 So. Fairfax Street
Alexandria, VA 22314

Guide To Simulation Games for Education and Training

Some say simulation games are good. Some say they're a fad. Maybe they're a good fad. Here's your reference guide.
—SB

Guide to Simulation Games for Education and Training
David W. Zuckerman, Robert E. Horn
1970, 336 pp.

$15.00

from:
Information Resources Inc.
1675 Massachusetts Avenue
Cambridge, Mass. 02138

The ESS materials are described and listed in the McGraw-Hill *Science Materials Catalog,* available from:

Webster Division
McGraw-Hill Book Company
1221 Avenue of the Americas
New York, N. Y. 10020

The purpose of this book is to examine the value of practical film study in the context of education. That is, to see how still cameras, movie cameras and tape recorders can be used to extend powers of observation and comment and to help young people develop an understanding of contemporary society.

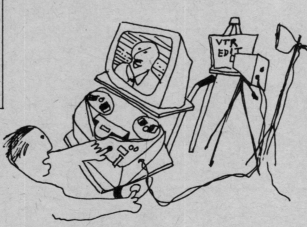

RECORDING SLIDES AND MOVIES

Slides or movies can be transferred to video tape by projecting them onto a piece of smooth white posterboard or paper. If a projector screen is used the reflecting particles on the screen are picked up by the camera and will add a grainy appearance to the slide. This may sometimes be desired. Copying sound 16mm or super 8mm films in this manner will produce a slight flutter in the picture. The expense involved in a film chain projector system ($1500 and up) will make you tolerant of the small flutter. If you have a silent film, or a sound film whose sound track is of no concern to you, you can eliminate the flutter by showing it back on a projector with a variable speed control and regulating the control to the proper speed. This will slow down the motion only slightly. Then, if your VTR has audio dubbing capability, you can add your own sound track. If you record sound from a film as you are taping it, try to feed the sound directly into your VTR. Most sound projectors have high impedance outputs which allow you to go from the ' aux audio out" on the projector to the "aux input" on the VTR via an RCA-to-RCA patch cord. If this is not possible, place the microphone in front of the projector speaker. Get the speaker as far away from the projector as possible, even in a closet or another room, so your microphone won't pick up the projector noise as it most likely will if you have to place the microphone near the projector.

Selective Educational Equipment

S.E.E. It looks like the E.S.S. stuff to me, maybe simpler and cheaper.
—SB

SEE
3 Bridge Street
Newton, Mass. 02195

Hubbard Scientific

Elaborate models, 3-D books, and gear. Here we have a demonstration of nepotism. Hubbard's a cousin of mine.
—SB

Hubbard Scientific Company
Box 105
Northbrook, Illinois 60062

Real Maps

These are called Colorgraphic relief maps and they are beautiful. They show the earth as it looked to the astronauts — but without the clouds. The only maps I know to integrate vegetation with land forms in a pictorial way.

Jeppesen and Company
Stapleton Airfield
Denver, Colorado 80207

Stephen Hopkins
Scottsdale, Arizona

Sound and Vision

First stages that link camera and tape recorder and yet cannot be considered as film production.

Stage 1

Students who have had little opportunity to use audio/visual equipment can start by comparing abstract sounds and images.

whoooooooooooooooooooooooooo

woowoowoowoowoowoowoowoowoowoo

First by recording noises and then painting or drawing the visual equivalents when the recordings are played.

The tape recorder is one of the most valuable tools in education today. Schools cannot have too many of them in service and young people should be able to use recorders with the same skill and ease that they exhibit when using bicycles for transport or power tools for woodwork.

THE WORK

They dug the first hole six inches from the corner of the barn. Leonard started it by scraping away some surface rocks and digging out some old leaves and crap that had accumulated under the eaves. Then he took the diggers from D.R. and started down. He dropped the diggers hard into the ground, spread the long handles and then lifted out the dirt in bites. The first few inches of the hole were easy, just dirt lying there waiting to be scooped up. But about a foot down the diggers banged into solid rock and Leonard told D.R. to hand him the sledge. It was hard to get at the rock with the sledge because of the narrowness of the hole, but after five or six licks he cracked it enough to get the end of the long crow-bar in to work. By the time they'd broken the rock into pieces small enough to pull out, both men were sweating and ready for a little rest. Wiping his forehead, Leonard looked at D.R. and grinned and said, "It aint like grave-digging, is it?"

D.R. automatically looked at his hands. It had been a week and a day since they had worked with Ray and Chester, digging Emmit's grave. The blisters D.R. had worn that day had all broken and hardened in that time, although after he'd worked with the diggers a while the one on his left palm near the fleshy part of his thumb opened up again and started to bleed.

"Don't force your diggers," Leonard said. "You're banging 'em down a little too hard to suit. Just sort of try to help their own natural weight along a little, if you see what I mean. That's it. Easy-like. That's right. You're getting it."

Leonard worked with D.R. about an hour, sharing the work with him, trading on and off with the various tools. By the third hole they seemed to have worked beyond the shelf of rock that made the first two holes so hard. D.R. dug most of the third one by himself, and was starting into the fourth as Leonard got ready to leave.

"I'll be back by dinner time," he said. "I'll come and get you and we'll go to the house a while."

Without breaking his motion D.R. nodded and said good enough, and Leonard drove off to town.

This Magazine is about Schools

Now THIS MAGAZINE, a socialist journal about the politics of the Canadian nationalist movement . . . also poetry, photoessays, book reviews.

—PC

This Magazine

$3.50 /yr. (6 issues) U.S.

$3.00 /yr. (6 issues) Canada

from:
This Magazine
56 Esplanade St. East
Suite 407
Toronto, Canada MSE IA8

"The Risk of Being a Social Scientist in Canada Is that One May Die Laughing."

HOW TO SOFTEN YOUR HARD SCHOOL

1. *USE THE CORRIDORS. Sell the steel lockers for scrap and use the money to buy cushions. Scatter the cushions around the corridors and let the students lie around on the floor. Have the floor cleaned very seldom but leave brooms about.*
2. *TAKE ALL THE AV EQUIPMENT OUT OF THE STOREROOM AND PUT IT IN THE CORRIDORS. Let the students use it when they feel the need for it. Let them break projectors, tape-recorders and viewers. Let them take machines home, steal tapes.*
3. *HIRE A XEROX MACHINE AND PUT IT IN THE CORRIDOR. Place no restrictions whatever upon its use. Find a kid willing to keep it running. Put a thermofax copier in the corridor too. With a mountain of paper and acetate.*
4. *OPEN UP THE LIBRARY. Take the doors off their hinges. Roll up the carpet and sell it. Let the students cut up the books with scissors. Provide scissors, paste, paper. With the money provided by the sale of the carpet, buy:*
   a. *A bucket full of magazines.*
   b. *A bucket full of comics.*
   c. *A bucket full of newspapers.*
   d. *Several incomprehensible thick medical tomes. Try McAinsh, Toronto.*
   e. *A number of books in Chinese, Japanese, Sanskrit and other languages.*
   f. *A barrow-load of old books from the Old Favorites Bookstore, Toronto.*
   g. *Photographs, maps, geological maps, plans, blueprints, research papers.*

HOW TO HARDEN YOUR SOFT SCHOOL

1. *ESTABLISH A SYSTEM FOR SUPPLYING THE SCHOOL WITH MATERIALS. On several occasions I have walked into a free school and been bitterly disappointed by the lack of materials. No school dedicated to making a decent mess should open its doors before it has obtained two truck loads, say 5 tons, of begged, borrowed and stolen information in the shape of string, glue, magnets, records, magazines, books, paints, test-tubes, chemicals, transistors, advertisements, felt pens, catalogues, newspapers, fossils, rocks, microscopes, herbs, wire, acetate, slide-rules, typewriters, tapes, film stock, stuffed owls, old pieces of machinery, cloth, thread, animals, bones, fishing flies, photographs, paintings, slides and films. Treat information like water from a tap.*
2. *PUT YOUR FINANCES UPON A SOUND FOOTING.*
3. *ORGANIZE A FEW BOOKS. Wade into the sea of information, clear a few shelves, and arrange thirty reference books in alphabetical order. Stick numbers on their spines, stamp them NOT TO BE REMOVED and chain them to the shelf. While you are in the mood, padlock a few doors and windows.*
4. *MAKE A HARD ROOM. Set aside at least one room to represent the organized side of life. If you can afford it, build a laboratory with identical stools, gas taps, electrical outlets and small sinks for washing retorts. Have a ten-week course in the laboratory for which interested students have to sign in advance and attend at regular times. If you have no science teacher, immediately appoint a meticulous chemist.*
5. *STOP CHOOSING NEW STUDENTS to fit the community. The next person whom you choose should be unlike anyone else you've ever had before.*

This Book Is About Schools

"How do you change things?" asks Satu Repo in her forward to **This Book**. *Change the schools or start new ones. Then start a magazine to help spread the word and try to find out what all the others out there are doing at their schools.* **This Magazine Is About Schools** *was started by a community of people in the Toronto, Canada area who were also working in a complex of free schools there. It is an exciting, widely-read publication and an important piece of scripture for the New Schools movement.* **This Book Is About Schools** *offers the best of the magazine and is a fine collection of essays on a wide variety of subjects. They are divided into three categories: growing up in America, the alternative school, and the institutional put-down.*

[Reviewed by Kit McClanahan]

This Book is About Schools
Satu Repo, ed.
1970; 457 pp.

$1.95

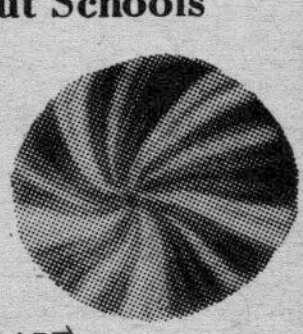

from:
Random House
457 Hahn Rd.
Westminster, MD 21157

or WHOLE EARTH CATALOG

The book presents few conclusions and perhaps more bravado than wisdom. It reflects the views of people who are pursuing a rather desperate search for life forces in our civilization. Whether it will be possible for us to combine our strong heritage of bourgeois freedom with the interconnectedness necessary to create a viable human community no one knows. The world may be pushing us too hard, forcing us to shift our priorities in such a way that the will to keep our schools together gradually is dissipated. But at the present time they give one answer — maybe too sane an answer — to the question: "What Can I Do Right Now?"

—Satu Repo

•

I can honestly say that for four months I did nothing, and I fell into my method of teaching those kids purely by accident. And it wasn't until I'd been doing this for six months that I realized that I had actually hit upon the best way of teaching them. Suddenly, after Christmas, I looked up and realized that I had created a beautiful second grade monster — fifteen of them, beautiful monsters — and I had done it by doing nothing. It wasn't because I had said, "I'm going to let them be free." They had to be free because I just, I just abdicated.

Big Rock Candy Mountain

Big Rock *is a Portola Institute publication with a format similar to WHOLE EARTH CATALOG and contents it calls Resources for Our Education. I'm close enough to it to have the same complaints I do about the CATALOG: it is too wishful, too little experienced in grimy school work, too self-indulgent in listing material of interest only to the editors. But we get some of* **Big Rock's** *mail, and I also know that its readers are glad to have it, especially when they're up against the classroom wall needing sympathy, wisdom, diversion, and tools to get through the day with.*

—SB

Big Rock Candy Mountain
Sam Yanes, ed.

No longer available

from:
Big Rock Candy Mountain
Portola Institute, Inc.
540 Santa Cruz Avenue
Menlo Park, CA 94025

Back issues available:
$4.00 for six
$1.00 each for biggies
$.25 each for skinny, newsprint ones

THE PUPPET THEATRE HANDBOOK

An excellent book. If you can have only one technical book, this it it. Originally written as an Army manual for Special Services, it is still unsurpassed. The *Puppet Theatre Handbook* covers puppet construction of all types including some experimental puppets; costume design and construction; puppet stages; scenery, lighting, properties, and special effects; and brief information on production.

The Puppet Theatre Handbook
Batchelder, 293 pp. 1947
$7.50

from:
Harper & Row
Keystone Industrial Park
Scranton, PA 18512

QUICK HARD SUMMARY OF HOW TO OPEN A FREE SCHOOL AND KEEP IT OPEN

People: If ten people will contract (written) to work to support one or two of their number to run a school, if necessary, you can open a school.

Money: Good books fanatically kept. Planned purchasing with ferocious control of buying and *nothing* retail. About $2500 for day school and $4000 for boarding. ETS in Princeton will sell you a weighting for scholarships or you can make your own simple one. *Everyone should pay something.* Get one semester up front— banks will loan readily to parents, but not to you. The nicest people will deadbeat, poor mouth, lie, cheat, and otherwise do you in. Conservatives pay their bills much more faithfully than liberals and forget about so-called radicals. Be warned. Don't go for or even want Federal or State money. It's not worth it. (Repeat 9 Billion times.)

Records: Print an honest transcript form that syas you are an ungraded school and what follows are teacher rankings of grade and class equivalents. Give them names and credit hours on the usual 16 high school hours. Give a class rank equivalent. It is a waste of time to try to convert admission offices and you owe your brats an *honest* attempt at a prediction. Use STANDARD TESTS and give HONEST scores. Academic tests are a gas in a free school, a game. Don't cheat at soccer, why cheat at test? If the kid can't play you know he's in trouble. Keep complete health records, make sure you have a waiver for hospital and doctor care on each kid from his mama and daddy. Keep an ongoing log of every sick complaint and every vitamin pill etc.

Food: make up a two or three week cycle of meals. Stick to it. Calculate from the cycle what you need and buy cheaper wholesale. If you change (you own plan not reverse) also change the plan. Expect to lose and buy two or three sets of tableware and dishes every year.

Work: teachers at a free school are mostly about cleaning, sorting clothes, carrying garbage and all that stuff most Ami's hire niggers to do. America moves on invisible black grease and when you give it up, and give up the coercions that keep juniors in line, etch! Slime-o and bubonic plague unless you rotate the schlock work and don't hesitate to seaparate yourselves from people who won't do scut work. World is full of incompetents and lazies.

Curriculum: you've got to make a formal one for the State, urp. Otherwise, tons of books, magazines, newsprint, things. Hard areas. Reference room, serious art, library, labs run like SS training camp. Books are treasures not things to be left in rain— same for microscopes etc. As long as kids are free to have acres of soft areas and lilligag, what harm? They may learn that expensive equipment is liberating if kept operating, but tyrannical if schlocked up. And you may have exceptional free school that produces some grads with competence to help save Mama Earth with green technology instead of more editors and other paper and tree users.

Officials: write every conceivable agency and invite their inspection, supervision, admonition, guidance, etc. Be as open as your heart. Cooperate them to death. Of course, as soon as possible set aside legal fund for inevitable clashes when they want you to crucify babies on 5000 year old idiocies. But don't fight the health department, nor the fire, they are really on your side, if dumb at times. Question is, is shitting on the grass a more important freedom than having happy self regulating kids? Of course you get along with these parasites better if you wear straight uniform, but those struggles are up to you. Me, I'd rather the kids be free for their childish games and me have more time for goodies than have long hair etc.

Finally: Opening and keeping open a free school has much more to do with being touch, anal, compulsive, cantankerous and agile than with love. The *real* genius at Summerhill is Mrs. Neill who sees to the kitchen, housekeeping, bills *and billing.* I cannot too strongly tell you how all those nice folks you take in for nothing will be the first to run screaming to the fuzz about how vile you are— meantime owing you for the medicine, food and clothes you bought their brat.

Them facts ain't nice, but there aren't too many free schools around and I make about six of them. There is an illusion, created by Summerhill Society, New Schools Exchange and others that the woods are just full of free schools. What the woods are really full of is dreamers— and some bastards who want the publicity but make the kids play whatever their hanger happens to be. I know one "free" school makes the babes pray over their food— out loud. Man, Jesus said not to do that!

Big Rock editors Sam Yanes, Hal Hershey, Cia Holdorf

I keep getting plaintive letters (many dittoed) asking for reading lists, histories, thoughts and other bull shit.

The way to open a free school is to open it.

The way to run a free school is to hand those parts which are kid stuff (learning) to the kids and ferociously plan and organize those things which are daddy/mommy stuff (food, shelter, tools, special care) without getting too tight abot the separation.

The way to keep a free school open is to be compulsively sure you want it open, hardnosed about business, and WORK. America's most lamented four letter word.

This is all ex cathedra from

George von Hilsheimer,
himself

PERADAM

PERADAM was an event held at the 1969 Autumn Equinox to bring people from technological and long-haired worlds together. It was styled after ALLOY, the event organized by Steve Baer in New Mexico at the Spring Equinox, and some of the same people attended. (ALLOY is on p. 111.) Peradam was assembled by Dave Evans of the Augmented Human Intellect group in Menlo Park. The gathering took place in a wooded canyon near Santa Barbara. The 3-day meeting did not have a particular program, and suffered for the lack. Also Alloy was a tough act to follow.

Participants came from SRI, Zomeworks, Portola Institute, Pacific High School, Parnassus Institute, Hog Farm, Ecology Center, Southcoast, Beckwith & Langsner, Office Design, Placitas, and etc. Steve Katona cooked.

Here's some of what was said. The strongest stuff came from students and teachers from Pacific High School.

—SB

How do you continue to live a life of learning once you escape the institutions set up for learning?

We've been forced again & again to the old religious truth.

We've become anal about our own gifts. We're afraid we might bruise ourselves.

Computers are beginning to give the mechanistic world a brain. And it's our job to give it a soul.

All I know is, when you fuck a robot, you gotta get a shot for lockjaw.

The machine doesn't solve all our problems, it gives us more problems than we'd have without it. Like the first airplanes. It'd be easier to ride a horse.

We're gonna choke on our own self-satisfaction . . . Any of the things we do have an active life of about a year. It may be on the order of a natural law. Maybe people shouldn't have a sense of failure. . . . The things that sustain us are the trickle of information, but what pushes us on are the new surges. Get what you can out of it & move on.

They zoned Soleri's place as habitable sculpture.

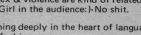

We got a lot of myths we plug into.

Tires can be made into sandals.

Sex & violence are kind of related. (Girl in the audience:)- No shit.

Something deeply in the heart of language is what's fucking us up.

Jail is the national monastic center.

You learn something different when you do it yourself.

They all crap in the same sewers. That ought to bring them together.

All that amateur radio operators do is talk about the weather and describe their equipment. Those media are really ripe for infiltration.

We're starting with an incredibly powerful technology, and what we've got so far is an incredibly primitive technique.

There's a whole mass of information stirred in the computer. It's a filing cabinet that's so fast and so together that it makes a whole different kind of difference.

Guerilla theater is usually about something that's already up that isn't satisfactory.

It takes 500 people to incorporate into a community.

30 is about the carrying capacity of most communes.

It's not enough to protest. We're trying exemplary forms.

The guys I went to high school with are just about running the country now. I didn't get along with them. Nobody here did.

We gave everybody a spoon and the rule was you couldn't feed yourself.

We called our group at first Bum Academy.

Entrance requirements: You must walk from Tokyo to north of Japan to south of Japan, with no money.

Monks from the Zen Mountain Center.

At various times the situation has become very entropic. We seem to be taking the attitude this year that there are certain kinds of urgent things that need doing. . . . We have some 20 boarding students. All the staff are living at the place. If you want a place to live you better build it, and you better find out what the design considerations are.

It isn't enough to say I am a music teacher and my door is always open. We are going to do music at a certain hour on a certain day.

Yoga. Sociology. Math. Music French. Biology. Literature—those happen to be the fields of competence of the staff who are there.

The changes that can come down in like 10 days are just real. There may have been a revolution while we're away.

The least active students right now are the new students. I guess it's right. They're going through shock.

At first there must be a dream. Then economy or technology or whatever.

On Friday we take off to places that we think might have educational value like the beach, or here.

The director was brought up in a Catholic orphanage, where his tongue developed a fine cutting edge.

We have a student who wanted to build a submarine. We have a nice lake. He took over the shop and started putting together this thing. We can't get this kid to do anything else. The fallout from the submarine completely covers the shop and the adjoining art room. He keeps assuring us that it's nearing completion.

I went back to my old high school, and the kids were just going saying fuck fuck and getting loaded. And I had changed more in a week than they had all year.

Preparing the student for "the Future". High school will prepare you for college. And college will prepare you for a job. And a job will prepare you for retirement. And retirement will prepare you for death. We call that "The Sorrowful Round." It's based on the present, not the future.

It's really far-out to look at a teacher as an overgrown student, and a friend.

The students ask to graduate. It's a privilege of the staff to decide. We huddle in a smoke filled room. We get the student in there. We have certain criteria which we hold up against the student:
3 quarters of presence (we've graduated some at less)
is 18 years of age
clear idea of what he wants to do

What's our policy on drugs? "You're not free to get the school busted." It's the same with sex.

We don't know whether we're on a 5 year thing or a 500 year thing.

It's all show. It's the life show and the show show and we're trying to get them till they're all one.

It's the problem of being an American, to be sitting here with a full belly while the rest of the world starves.

The Playboy guys came by and said they wanted to take pictures, and we said we wanted a well, and they said you got a well.

In public high school I could sort of dig the idea of being a classroom Commando. But at Pacific it's obvious you're just fucking yourself.

The hospital is right next to the stage and the kitchen is next to that. And we put the light show on the girls washing dishes and with all that energy the dishes just wash themselves.

The Open Classroom

The Open Classroom is written for anyone with the courage (or foolishness) to want to be a decent teacher within the public school system. It's a good book. It persuaded me that this is possible. It is surprisingly concrete. It describes exactly what "successful" teachers do to establish control over their classes. (These things are quite subtle, and worth knowing about. If you have a child who has to go to a typical public school, you can prepare him for the brainwashing he's going to get.) It also describes concretely what a teacher must do if he wants to have an honest relationship with his students, if he wants them to learn something (really), and he does not want to use authoritarian methods. (It's not always so easy not to fall back on authoritarian methods, no matter how idealistic we are.) It goes on to describe and warn of the problems that an "open classroom teacher" will have with other teachers, principals, supervisors. They are almost certain to be severe. It gives ways of saving your job while maintaining an open classroom, and it discusses when it is wisest to sacrifice your job.

Herbert Kohl has been through all of this himself. If you don't know what it's like inside the system, his book can tell you some things that will make your hair stand on end.

If you want to be a public school teacher, The Open Classroom is an indispensable handbook. If you don't, it's an excellent critique anyway, and it will make you feel good, because it constitutes a realistic plan for recovering some value from the public schools—from within.

[Reviewed by Jane Burton]

The Open Classroom
Herbert R. Kohl
1969; 116 pp.

$1.65 postpaid

from:
Random House, Inc.
Westminster, Md. 21157

or WHOLE EARTH CATALOG

A teacher in an open classroom needs to cultivate a state of *suspended expectations*. It is not easy. It is easy to believe that a dull class is dull, or a bright class is bright. The words "emotionally disturbed" conjure up frightening images. And it is sometimes a relief to discover that there are good pupils in the class that is waiting for you. Not reading the record cards or ignoring the standing of the class is an act of self-denial; it involves casting aside a crutch when one still believes one can't walk without it. Yet if one wants to develop an open classroom within the context of a school which is essentially totalitarian, such acts of will are necessary.

Apprenticeship Service Program

The program intends to give high school age kids an alternative to in-school learning by helping and encouraging them to find people near or far from home to study with them what they are most interested in. Once the teacher and student have met and if they feel they can work together, they can work out the details between them (length of time working together, expenses, hours, room and board or commuting, responsibilities, expected behavior —— whatever they feel is important to talk over). We are interested in the traditional crafts and trades apprenticeships and apprenticeships in such things as farming, business, politics, . . . after which a student may be competent to work in that field, and in apprenticeships to people such as doctors or lawyers where the student might still have to go to college if he wanted to work in that field, but would have a sense of what it is like to be a doctor or lawyer.

To receive high school credit the teenager and teacher would have to send us quarterly reports on their work. To receive a full year's credit the student would need to work at one or more apprenticeships (maybe some school too) for at least 180 days of the year to meet the education code. Teenagers who wish to apprentice but do not want to be enrolled in high school can apprentice themselves and between the ages of 18–21 (it varies with the state) take high school equivalency tests, which upon passing gives them the equivalent of a high school diploma. (I do not know if there is a similar test in Canada.) The cost of this program for students who wish to be enrolled in high school is $200. Scholarships are available. For those who do not wish to be enrolled we will charge $5.00 IF we find you your teacher. Eventually we hope to cover these costs out of donations. (All donations are tax deductible.)

Since we have been working on this program we have received many letters from teenagers. Some are full of wisdom and life, some full of determination and life, and some very touching pleas for help and life. We need the help of people to share their skills and knowledge and/or help finding people who will. We need people all over to open up their lives to the young and to encourage those around them to do it. If you can be a teacher, or can help us find teachers in your area — write. If you would like to be a student in this program — write. We can create a network of learning — a whole nation, a whole earth people's school.

Apprenticeship Service Program
Pacific High School
1211 Skyline Blvd.
Los Gatos, CA 95030

There are no simple ways to give up deeply rooted expectations. There are some suggestions, however:
—talk to students outside class
—watch them play and watch them live with other young people
—play with them——joking games and serious games
—talk to them about yourself, what you care about
—listen

In these situations the kids may surprise you and reveal rather than conceal, as is usual in the classroom, their feelings, playfulness, and intelligence.

•

There is a way a teacher can experiment with non-authoritarian teaching and be free of other teachers and supervisors. That way is to work with problem students——those students the school system has given up on.

WANTING TO QUIT

After the sixth hole, D.R. wanted to quit. It wasn't his body that wanted to quit. His hands were hurting a little but his strength was flowing good and his arms and back felt readier to go on with it than when he'd started. It was something else, some longing, some invitation from somewhere deep inside him to lay down the tools and just arbitrarily quit.

Not stop to rest.

Not go sit down by the barn and lean his back against the wall and sip water from the half-gallon Mason jar Leonard had left.

But quit.

For the day.

Just stop right there where he was, ten inches deep into the seventh hole, and go down to the store and hang around a while, or else on back up to the homeplace for the afternoon.

It was like some kind of sour bile swimming through his head. His hands and arms and back worked on well, but his mind, his mind was terribly dissatisfied to be there with nothing to do but observe his arms and hand and back. His mind was a message to him, it was an argument from the very depths of itself to stop this work and, at the very least, take it easy for a while.

Look how much you've already done! it said. Six holes already, look at that! That's a morning's work for any man!

Not for Leonard, D.R. said.

Fuck Leonard! the message said. You've got the whole afternoon to dig these holes. At least go sit down and rest for a couple of hours.

All right, said D.R. Soon as I finish this hole, I will.

And he dropped the diggers hard into the ground.

I'll get a start on number seven and then quit, D.R. said. Let me start number seven and I'll stop a while.

And he said the same thing again when he had finished the seventh hole, and gone on to number eight.

And then nine, and then ten. Let me finish ten, he said. This one more, and then I'll quit for the day.

D.R. finished the tenth hole. He needed the sledge on that one. Eight inches down he came into thick rock, and he needed the sledge and the bar, and the sledge and the bar together, and then the diggers, little pinches of earth and rock at a time. That one hole took him over half an hour of solid work, but he finished it, and was starting the eleventh hole when Leonard came back with the lumber.

"You getting tired?" he said.

Not "wow! look how much work you did!"

Not, "Congratulations, David, you're the most fantastic hole-digger I ever saw."

Not even, "It looks like you've worked hard while I was gone."

Just, "You getting tired?"

"Not too bad," D.R. said.

"Do that one, and one more while I unload this stuff," said Leonard. "Then we'll go see what Roxie's fixed us to eat."

Start Your Own Skool

The legal and practical rudiments. Particularly for California.

—SB

Start Your Own Skool

$1.00 postpaid

from:
New Directions Community School
445 Tenth Street
Richmond, CA 94801

Addenda: the surplus hardware program requires that you have a letter from a public school saying they accept your credits. The surplus food program does not & is beautiful. Start a lunch program; there's even food for "outdoor education programs": camping trips. // Once you're non-profit, file Form 637, exempt'n from excise taxes; i.e. Fed. gas tax (4¢ per gal.). Then talk to your friendly gas station (might have to get a credit card, or save receipts, . . .) More funancial: you must file annual info. forms for Fed. and State. In Calif., it's form 199B and is simple. The Feds will require it starting 1970 or 71. Even if you're an "unincorporated association", it's easy, once you've balanced your books.

Farallones Scrapbook

Another homemade collection of handy hints for new schools (or old schools that want to loosen up) or families that want to make things more interesting.

—SB

Farallones Scrapbook
Sim Van der Ryn, Jim Campe, et al
1971; 120 pp.

$4.00 postpaid

from:
Farallones
Star Route
Point Reyes Station, CA 94956

Outside the Net

A radical education magazine with some useful stuff.

—SB

Outside the Net

$2 for 4 issues

from:
Do It Now Foundation
6136 Carlos Avenue
Hollywood, CA 90028

Quantity orders for resale
National Media Center
P.O. Box 5115
Phoenix, Arizona 85010

Slim, the trucker, wasn't as black-hearted[1] as he seems from these statements. Because he was sorry for me he bought me a meal of two t-bone steaks and offered me a motel room when we reached Ft. Worth. I accepted the meal gratefully. Ironically enough, just before he bought me the steaks the waitress told him that Red had died on the 1st of January. Men are such a curious mixture of good and evil; black and white. Who would have thought that a lanky, tough-as-nails truck driver would burst into tears upon hearing that his killer-friend had died?

Travel is the best education. The best way to meet people while traveling is to hitch. If you decide to leave school, jam a few paperbacks in your pockets, pack a bag and hit the road. It's nearly free. You'll learn about people and places.

Summerhill Society

An information source on free school matters. It has New York and California chapters.

—SB

The Summerhill Society of California
6063 Hargis Street
Los Angeles, CA 90034

New York Summerhill Society
339 Lafayette Street
New York, N.Y. 10012

Envirom

ENVIROM is a soft ring of lightweight inflatable pillows designed to bring people together in play, seminars, groups. Used by free schools, experimental colleges, encounter and sensitivity groups. ENVIROM offers a relaxing and inexpensive alternative to institutional furniture. Constructed of heavy duty 20 gauge vinyl it withstands the toughest use. Folds to blanket size, weighs 20 lbs. Seats twenty in comfort.

[Suggested and reviewed (and designed) by Sim Van der Ryn]

Envirom

$60.00 each
plus postage
(20 lbs. parcel post)

from:
ENVIROM
731 Virginia Street
Berkeley, CA 94710

Here's what you will need/want for a hitching trip:

1 A large army-type duffel bag or a heavy laundry bag (white to be visible at night)

2 About $10 for every 1,000 miles you want to travel

3 A large piece of white cardboard (12" X 24") and a black, felt-tip marker

4 A plastic rain poncho and a good sleeping bag for long trips

5 New maps from gas stations with extra information about major cities to be traversed. Cities and national borders can be major obstacles. Persevere.

6 A few cans of sardines, some peanuts, candy, crackers, cheese, joints, etc.

Teacher Drop-Out Center

Teacher Drop-Out Center has identified (and continues to do so) schools — from pre-school to college, public and private — that have a relatively high degree of student-centered learning: few, or no, or non-compulsory classes; little, or no marking or grading; considerable student and teacher autonomy and independence; a low-pressure humane atmosphere where students can develop self-respect and a sense of dignity.

So far, they have come upon 1500-2000 such schools and they have established personal contact with these schools or are in the process of doing so. They have compiled a list of the schools and information about some is available from the Center.

Teacher Drop-Out Center acts as a clearinghouse of information on and a specialized placement service for teachers finding it difficult to function in traditional schools. They are interested in those who wish to make education relevant; those who truly believe in letting students grow into individual, alive, awake humans in an atmosphere of love and acceptance; those who breathe controversy and innovation and see schools as places for controversial ideas and innovations; those who want to be more than just babysitters or warm body in the classroom; those who feel they have to function freely as individuals with their own sense of style; those who believe that learning is an individual process best carried on by each individual exercising his own choice and going at his own pace.

They are open to inquiries from teachers or teachers-to-be. So far, they have helped and are helping hundreds of people get in touch with and find positions in schools.

Teacher Drop-Out Center
P. O. Box 521
Amherst, Mass. 01002

[Suggested by Bill Tully]

Observations from Treadmill

One of the best new publications about education, young people, etc. is Observations From the Treadmill, put out by Mort Yanow, 357 Hidden River Rd, Narberth, Pa. 19072. It is one of the most interesting, level headed, and well written things I've seen — indeed, probably the best. The issue on drugs was way ahead of anything else I've seen on the subject. Your readers should plug into this. No subscription price. Get two issues and then pay what you think it's worth, if anything. Pass the word.

Peace,

John Holt
Boston, Mass.

Rasberry Exercises

free school knowhow
with a forum format,
how to start a school
could be important collection
point for new ideas.
solid children's lib philosophy.

—jd

Rasberry Exercises—How to Start Your Own School & Make a Book
Salli Rasberry and Robert Greenway
1970; 125pp.

$3.95 postpaid

from:
The Freestone Publishing Company
Box 357
Albion, CA 95410

or WHOLE EARTH CATALOG

Insurance

It's important to have liability insurance covering all operations of the school. A good private agent can get it for you for less than $100 per year. You'll have to meet some standards to get it.

Most states require workman's compensation insurance for employees.

And be sure your car is covered for whatever use you put it to for the school.

"Pacific runs on promises — and the basic assumption is that when one makes a promise (even if only in his own self-interest), he will commit himself to that promise, and he can be comfortable in trusting that others will keep their promises as well. Everyone has to care at least that much. Thus, the whole fabric comes apart when, for reasons of apathy, or whatever, little promises are not kept..."

Amy

Teachers and Writers Collaborative Newsletter

Kid stuff runs as deep as you care to appreciate. Here is the work of kids and of teachers who know how to tap deep and get out of the way.

—SB

Teachers and Writers Collaborative Newsletter

$3/ 4 issues

from:
Teachers and Writers Collaborative
Pratt Center for Community Improvement
244 Vanderbilt Avenue
Brooklyn, N.Y. 11205

one foot, one eye, sniff sniff
is best can opener in the world.
He eats worms, rats and his special
food is fryed lobster.
Before they go to bed they sniff
each other's nose 16 times.

Unsigned
Grade 6

"I told the teachers we'd proceed exactly as if I were doing a creative writing session and they were the students. I asked each person to complete on a piece of paper and then hand to me, anonymously, the following two sentences:

'Where I live . . .'
'Last night I dreamed . . .'

"Then we read some of then aloud, in random sequence, to form a 10 line poem (lines one and two from the same person, lines three and four from another person, etc.; each completed sentence treated as one line of the poem). We talked about the effects of the random grouping, then re-ordered the lines and talked about them. . . .

Last Night I Dreamed

Last night I dreamed that I was a hippy
in the circus and everyone laughed at me.
Last night I dreamed that I was a pro ball-player.
Last night I dreamed that I had all the money in the world
and everyone had to listen to me
and I owned all the buildings and houses
and I was so happy that
I couldn't even laugh.

Mary had a stegasaurous.   It followed her to school one day.
His fleece was none at all.   Which there was no rule about.
Instead he had sharp scales,   It didn't help the school too much.
on his back   And everybody ran out.
And was very huge and tall.

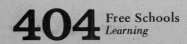

Guide to Correspondence Study

handy guide to courses given out through the mail by colleges in this country. for instance, the university of nebraska will give you arc welding, automotive mechanics, beginning woodwork, drawing and drafting, home mechanics, photography, plumbing, and roof framing, as well as the standard rot like genetics and heredity.

—*jd*

[Suggested by Emmanuel Appel]

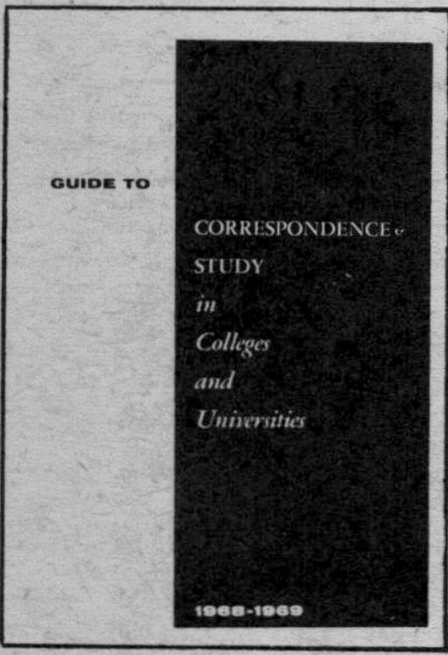

Guide to Correspondence Study in Colleges and Universities 1970

$1.00

from:
University of California Extension Service
2223 Fulton Street
Berkeley, California 94720

Directory of Accredited Private Home Study Schools

Care to study up on diamond-cutting at home? Electronic organ repair? Truck maintenance? Paper making? Penmanship? Radio? Tractor repair? Calculus? Welding? Concrete engineering? Sign lettering? Plastics? This amazing catalog lists all the subjects available and what schools carry them and where to write the school. From here on, we need your evaluation: are these correspondence courses worth it? How much do they cost? Who's best for quality or low-cost?

—*SB*

[Suggested by D. Mayerson]

Directory of Accredited Private Home Study Schools

free from:
National Home Study Council
1601 Eighteenth Street, N. W.
Washington, D. C. 20009

Cleveland Institute of Electronics, 1776 East 17th Street, Cleveland, Ohio 44114. Founded 1934. Electronics Technology; Electronics Technology with Laboratory; Broadcast Engineering; First-Class FCC License; Electronic Communications (including 2nd Class FCC License); Carrier Telephony; Electronics Engineering; Electronic Slide Rule and Operation; Industrial Electronics and Automation.

Coast Navigation School, 418 East Canon Perdido, Santa Barbara, California 93101. Founded 1966. Courses in Air navigation; Coastwise navigation and piloting; Celestial navigation; Celestial air navigation; and the Elements of boathandling, seamanship, and sailing.

Used Correspondence Courses

now this is a real recycle notion,
jobbers in used instructional materials.
when you've finished with poultry management,
and want to learn insect science, just
get in touch with one of these fellows
and swap with him. good bunch of technical books too.

—*jd*

[Suggested by Jim Toms]

Price of List $.10
Listings of items change often.

from:
Lee Mountain
Used Correspondence Courses
Pisgah, Alabama 35765

Foundry Practices, I.C.S.	4.40
Foundry Work and Tool Making, American School	7.50
Foot Culture, Stephenson Laboratory	15.00
Arch Support Making and Foot Culture Course	9.00
The Human Foot	2.95
Shoe Fitting and Orthopedics, Modern School	3.00
Foot Culture, Lincoln Institute	15.00
Practipedics, American School of Practipedics	3.00
Poultry Farming, National Poultry Institute	10.00
Poultry Book	1.00
Poultry Management	1.50
Railroad Rates Course, I.C.S.	5.75
Railroad Signaling, I.C.S.	9.00
Brakeman's Instruction, Railway Educational Association	4.00
Fireman's Instruction, Railway Educational Association	4.00
Airbrake Course, I.C.S.	15.00
Steam Locomotive, I.C.S.	9.00
Locomotive Engineering, I.C.S.	15.00
Railway Station Work, Railway Service Bureau	3.00
Sleeping Car and Train Porter	2.90
Railroad Correspondence File	2.25
Elementary Gunsmithing, Frazer	4.64
Modern Gunsmithing, Baker	6.85

Catalog

free

from:
Smith Instruction Exchange
124 Marlborough Road
Salem, Massachusetts 01970

Operation, Care, Repair Farm Machinery		1.55
Motor's Auto Repair Manual (1962)		7.50
Fordomatic - Mercomatic Transmission		1.85
Diesel Engines	*McGraw - Hill*	1.30
Illustrated Course Horse Training	*Beery*	7.75
How to Ride and Train the Western Horse		6.50
Saddle Horse Instructions	*Prof. Beery*	4.50
Diseases of the Horse	*Dept. Agriculture*	1.40
Complete Book of Horses & Horsemanship		1.90
Teaching the Young to Ride	*M. Self*	1.50
Saddlery : Equipment Horse & Stable		2.75
Sportsman Guide Horseback Riding	*Wall*	1.70
Colt and Horse Sense (2 Books)	*Bob Carson*	2.75
Out of West; New Horsemanship	*L. Taylor*	4.70
Complete Book of the Quarter Horse	*Nye*	5.60
Schooling of the Western Horse	*J. Young*	3.80
Hackamore Reinsman	*Ed Connell*	1.60
The Horseman's Encyclopedia	*M. Self*	4.20
The Horse ; Judging, Breeding, Feeding Management and Selling	*D. Kays*	6.50
Quarter Horse Breeder	*M. Lindeman*	4.50
How to Buy a Healthy Horse and Keep Him That Way	*Farmer's Digest*	5.90

Penn State Correspondence School

Penn State is Number One, at least in correspondence courses that have relevance to agriculture. Cornell University recommended them to me and am I glad. All the courses have "x" pages of written material followed by a "test" that is "graded" by someone in State College (if you desire) and returned. Naturally, with so many courses, the quality is varied. I've read maybe two dozen of them. They are extremely valuable in areas where the reader has absolutely no knowledge. The Penn State introduction obtained with no small degree of authority enables one to more intelligently choose more advanced material (which is not always necessary) without waste of too much time and money in shotgun searches through libraries and/or bookstores. I recommend particularly their survey on Poultry Keeping. [Suggested and reviewed by John E. Schultz]

Catalog **free** from:
Correspondence Courses
The Pennsylvania State University
307 Agricultural Education Building
University Park, PA 16802

Correspondence Schools

You asked for comments on correspondence schools in relation to a suggestion in your spring issue, and I happen to have a few. I worked with a reporter gathering information for a story on the subject, and the results were depressing. (The story appeared in the New York *Times* on May 31, 1970.)

The catalog suggestion was to write the National Home Study Council for information about courses. If someone is bent on taking a correspondence course, the Council is the best source of information for halfway reputable schools, because the Council is the only nationally recognized agency in the field. It has established minimum standards for business and educational operations and is supposedly held, by Federal law, to the same standards as the agencies which issue accreditation to resident-type schools and colleges. However, this does not hold up for there is little regulation by the states or the Federal government. Last fall, for example, the accrediting commission of the Council examined 6 Crowell-Collier institutions (remember your friendly Collier's Encyclopedia salesman?) and withdrew their accreditation. The major Crowell-Collier school is LaSalle Extension University of Chicago, and without its accreditation, the State of Illinois was required by Federal law to change its status. Among other things, this would have made LaSalle ineligible for any funds from any of the G.I. and Veterans education bills. But nothing was done. (An unknown number of LaSalle executives purchased tickets to a $100-a-plate political dinner for the Superintendent of Public Instruction for the State of Illinois.) Crowell-Collier also filed an anti-trust suit against the Council. Having no funds for a court fight and no encouragement from any of the Federal agencies, the Council accepted the Crowell-Collier settlement out of court, reaccrediting LaSalle and the other schools.

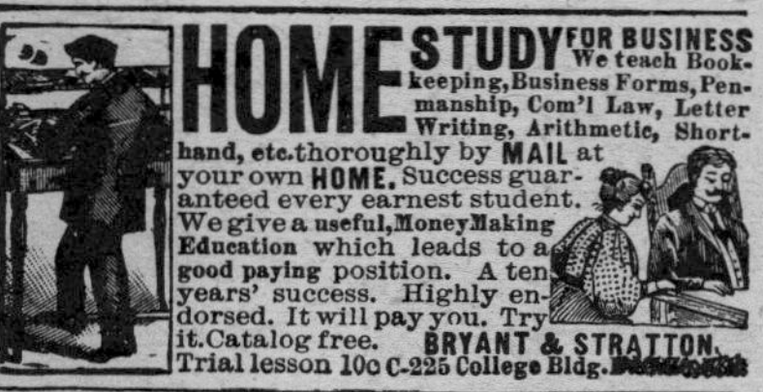

So, although the National Home Study Council has set standards, it has no way to enforce them, thus leaving the question of quality up to the individual schools. Two schools which have maintained high standards are the advanced Trade School and the American School, both in Chicago and both offering a wide range of courses. These two schools run credit checks on applicants, administer valid admissions tests, actually turning away those who fail, and pay their salesmen a salary rather than a commission based on how many people they sign up.

Many schools don't have admissions tests, and those that do often make the tests ridiculously easy to pass. Many of the schools pay no attention to the results of their tests anyway. In other words, for many courses, if you can sign on the dotted line and make the down payment, you've met all the necessary requirements.

Many of the courses are very over-priced for what is provided. Private correspondence schools charge from less than $100 to more than $2500 and the average course costs between $300 and $600.

In many places, there are less expensive alternatives available to home study courses. Many universities, colleges, local government adult education programs, churches, YM and YWCAs, civic groups, etc., offer courses in a wide variety of subjects to the general public, usually for nominal fees and/or the cost of any materials. For instance, if you live in New York, check the Photography page in the Entertainment Section of the Sunday New York *Times* for locations, dates, and costs of beginning and advanced courses in photography. Your local U.S. Department of Agriculture extension office makes available a great amount of information and demonstrations on farming. Check with local companies in your field of interest; many run their own training programs. I also know of people who have actually apprenticed themselves to local craftsmen, one to a harpsichord maker, the other to a cabinetmaker.

It is much easier to check the reputations of courses offered locally, but if nothing is available then write the National Home Study Council for a list of schools offering the course you want. Send away to all the schools suggested, and from the ensuing, and never-ending deluge of promotional mail, pick the one which seems to be the most reputable and seems to offer the exact course or training that you want.

Finally, should you sign up for a course and then find out that it isn't what it was advertised to be, send your letter of resignation by registered mail.

However, if you want to get rich quick, which is the result promised by most of these schools, and you have no scruples about ripping off unsuspecting poor people, instead of taking a correspondence course, I suggest you try selling one. All you need do is follow the advice which a Dr. Richard S. Frazer gave to members of the Association of Home Study Schools. Dr. Frazer was head of the now-defunct Christy Trade School in Chicago and he received his doctoral degree from something called the "Neotarian College."

Dr. Frazer's suggestions: Immediately offer courses in 200 subjects and decide on public response to an advertising campaign which of the 200 is the most likely best-seller, and provide that one. Select a textbook on the subject and order a gross from the publisher, then have a bookbinder split these books into 20-page units of lessons (new covers should be designed, taking care to leave space for stamping on the title and number of each "lesson"). For your promotional campaign, Dr. Frazer recommends, for example, perfumed mailings and the use of "gadgets, gimmicks, premiums, giveaways, and special formats." Then when your sales begin to level off, begin preparation of your second course.

A quick look at the advertising layouts and promotional materials of most of the correspondence schools would lead anyone to believe that large numbers of them are doing exactly what Dr. Frazer suggests. And many of them go even further—they hire salesmen who are inadequately trained and paid only a commission based on their sales, with no reimbursement for expenses. In order to make sales, these men, whether instructed by their employers or not, misrepresent the courses they sell in many ways. In other words, they tell outright lies in their presentations. (The salesman from LaSalle who called on me informed me, when I told him I worked for the New York *Times*, that "a lot of the top men there got most of their training at LaSalle. I know of one—I can't recall his name right off—who got all of his training through LaSalle." Ha.)

I could relate other examples of misrepresentation by salesmen, if you want, but I doubt you have room to run this letter as it is. You may use what I have said here any way you can. I hope I have been of some help.

Sincerely,
Adrianne Burk
Washington, D.C.

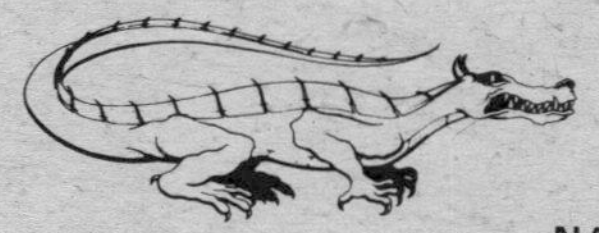

NAILS

Nail hammer <u>whap</u> <u>whap</u> nail.

Set it and hit it, drive it <u>whap</u> hit it home and nail that board to the post.

Set it in here David. Throw in some rock, fill it and tamp it, hold on now, let's get 'er straight. Reach me the level there and we'll line this baby up. There. Tamp it down, hand me the end of that one-by-six and you take the yon.

Nail. Hammer <u>whap</u> <u>whap</u> and nail. Nail it in and drive it home. This one's warped, David, hold on, let's not get ahead of ourselves. Got your's nailed? Hit it.

Nail. Hammer, <u>whap</u>. Nail, <u>whap</u>, set, <u>whap</u>, hit it and drive it, drive it and pound it

and

Leonard bears his weight down on the loose end till the warp comes out and says drive it in now son, set it and hit it, that's right, we'll teach this wood to bow.

One time David I was carpentering with this old one-armed boy over in Owsley County. Fellow by the name of Calhoun. Building a school up there, back before the war. I'd tried mining and didn't like that, so my daddy said why don't you go up to Owsley County and help 'em build that school. The boss of that job was a friend of my daddy's and he took me on. He said I could work a week and if I could drive nails faster than this Calhoun he'd let me stay on. So we worked. Side by side with old Calhoun. Him with just one arm, I figured surely I could out-work a one-armed man. But you ought to of seen him, David. He'd set nails this way: hold the head between his two fingers like this, you see, brace the head against the flat of his hammer, go <u>stick</u> like that and set that nail in the wood just pretty as you please. Then he'd rare back with that hammer in that one good hand of his and go <u>whap</u> and about two whaps later that nail'd be out of sight. Drive a sixteen penny nail in three licks when he wanted to. I couldn't keep up with him with two hands. Nobody on that job could.

But the old foreman let me stay on anyhow.

<u>Whap!</u> Nail. Set. Hammer. <u>Whap</u>.

Sweat.

Sweat all down his neck and off his ears and in his eyes.

Get us another locust post and I'll deepen this next hole a little.

Fill it. Tamp it down. That's right, stomp it right in there good. She level? Read it right, now, we want this fence preee-cise, looking too good to mess it up now. You finish here David and I'll go get us another one-by-six.

Up Against the Law

To be a teenager in the U.S. is approximately illegal. Nevertheless many survive. This revealing remarkable hard-working book can really help.

—SB

Up Against the Law
Jean Strouse
1970; 269 pp.

$1.25 postpaid

from:
Signet
The New American Library, Inc.
1301 Avenue of the Americas
New York, N.Y. 10019

or WHOLE EARTH CATALOG

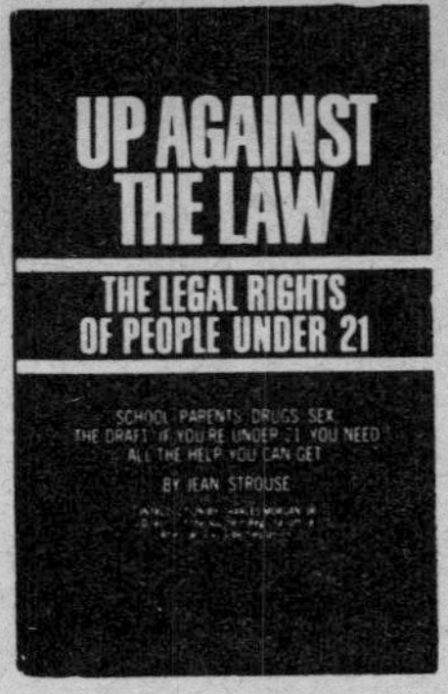

Q: You have been suspended from school for two weeks and don't know why. Do you have the right to be told what the charges are against you?

A: Yes. Any time school officials give you a punishment with serious consequences (expulsion, suspension for more than a few days — the number of days varies from place to place) they should notify you and your parents *in writing* of the specific things you have done wrong.

•

Q: If you've applied to and been accepted at a boarding school or college and your father refuses to pay the tuition, can he be forced to pay?

A: Yes, if he can afford it and the court decides it is in your "best interests."

•

AGE OF CONSENT: STATUTORY RAPE.

(If you are a girl under the age of this chart, anyone who sleeps with you may be considered guilty of statutory rape.)

Alabama	16	Montana	18
Alaska	16	Nebraska	18
Arizona	18	Nevada	16
Arkansas	16	New Hampshire	16
California	18	New Jersey	16
Colorado	18	New Mexico	16
Connecticut	16	New York	18
Delaware	7*	North Carolina	16
Florida	18	North Dakota	18
Georgia	14	Ohio	16
Hawaii	16	Oregon	16
Idaho	18	Pennsylvania	16
Illinois	16	Rhode Island	16
Indiana	16	South Carolina	16
Iowa	16	South Dakota	18
Kansas	18	Tennessee	12
Kentucky	18	Texas	18
Louisiana	12	Utah	18
Maine	14	Vermont	16
Maryland	16	Virginia	16
Massachusetts	18	Washington	18
Michigan	16	West Virginia	16
Minnesota	18	Wisconsin	18
Mississippi	18	Wyoming	18
Missouri	16	Puerto Rico	14

*Yes, seven is the age of consent on the books. But other sexual offenses against minors, such as harboring a male or female child under eighteen for purposes of sexual intercourse, are crimes though not technically considered statutory rape.

Q: If you're in a car that's stopped by the cops and there's dope in it, are you considered guilty of possession?

A: That depends on state laws. In New York, if drugs are found in a car, everyone in the car is presumed to have had the knowledge that the drugs were there—unless they were concealed on one person. This means that if the cops find dope in the glove compartment, everyone will be *presumed* to have known it was there; you may be able to present a case at trial that you did not, in fact, know the dope was there—but it will be up to you to disprove the presumption that you knew. If the dope is found concealed on one person, he's the only one considered guilty.

Other state laws vary. In California there is a case-law precedent saying that cops may search only the inside of the car incidental to an arrest—that is, they may not search the trunk or engine area.

CHIPS & FPS

CHIPS means Cooperative High school Independent Press Syndicate. FPS means whatever you want. They're a service for high school underground papers.

—SB

FPS

Six Issues **$1** high school age and younger
$2 movement groups
$5 everyone else

from:
Student Information Center
3210 Grace St. NW
Washington, D.C. 20007

The Underground Guide to the College of Your Choice

A really fantastic amount of information packed in an honest, if somewhat clichéd style. The paradox about this book is that it seems to be written for freaks —— or at least for those who are looking for alternatives to traditional academia; while the descriptions indicate how much traditional academia still prevails on most campuses. It does look very useful, though, especially in giving a real flavor and feeling for what's going on at different schools. A lot of the descriptions include how campuses are changing, too, which is very interesting in itself. I hope someone keeps it up to date, since one of its messages is that what it says now will be obsolete shortly. It makes it painfully clear that we need some new colleges.

[Reviewed by Diana Shugart]

The Underground Guide to the College of Your Choice
Susan Berman
1971; 509 pp.

$1.50

from:
The New American Library, Inc.
1301 Avenue of the Americas
New York, N.Y. 10019

or WHOLE EARTH CATALOG

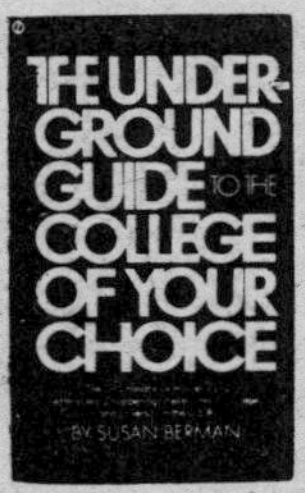

University of Illinois

Urbana, Illinois

Illinois is becoming more and more radical but still a Big Ten fraternity stronghold.

SERGEANT PEPPER SECTION:

31,267 students of which 8,500 are graduates. 15% out-of-state. Freshmen must have completed at least six semesters of high school, submit either SAT or ACT scores, and be in upper one-fourth of their class. As long as there is space open in his chosen curriculum, there is room for him.

ACADEMIC BULLSHIT:

The best departments are Engineering, Agriculture and Computer (the best computer school in the nation). In these departments the professors give the students a lot of individual help. No one seems to know of any exciting or particularly great courses or professors.

Some Pass/Fail and all you need is a professor's sponsorship to get credit for a class you want to originate. If you can't get credit, it can be a Free U course. Third World studies started in various departments in 1970. The University requires that every student take a final examination in all classes. Some study abroad.

BROTHERS AND SISTERS:

Ratio cats : chicks—2 : 1.

They have their freaks here, but most of the kids are straight—the big thing for guys is jeans or slacks, button-down shirts or T-shirts and brown loafers without socks (in the spring). No one would be caught dead wearing white socks (very gauche). The straights' hair isn't especially long, but there is a beau brummel in every crowd who dares let a stray hair or two grow. The straight chicks wear their dresses and skirts and every now and then get into some pants. Lots of people wear those ugly University of Illinois T-shirts (which in the past were mainly gray but with the whole psychedelic craze are turning up in other colors). As to the freaks (who are very few), long hair, no bra, tie dyes, jeans, hair bands, shoeless and on strike. On the whole, there isn't that much dating (there are more than 10,000 more men than women on this campus). The Greeks are deeply into the dating game—maybe 25% of the campus dates—while most everyone else is spontaneous. A date consists of going to a movie, and then to a bar or an eatery afterwards.

As for the girls being liberated—"Any girl *wants* to do it, but is *waiting* for the *right guy*." The hip chicks will do it. Not that much shacking-up here. The chicks are either just off the farm or from Chicago (so they are either naive as hell or know it all).

Intervisitation in the dorms just started about a year ago on campus—more pregnancies have been registered with the health center than in previous years. It is easier to find a chick who will have sex now than it was two years ago when things were extremely difficult—all the sorority houses lock their doors at night.

SURVIVAL:

Getting easier. Plenty of dope, sex and politics are opening up. BC pills through student health and Planned Parenthood in area. No suicide prevention center. Draft counseling by student government, and the Draft Resistors Corps in the area. It's a Big Ten school so football is still important. The campus paper is the *Daily Illinois*—a bore. Two underground papers—*Walrus* and *Greek*. No health-food stores. The closest "big city" is Chicago.

The merchants in the area are big exploiters, especially around Wright, Green and 6th Streets. Two of the dorms have "had trouble with the black community" and so lock their doors at night.

Private Independent Schools

I've been to a liberal grade school, an Archie and Veronica high school, a prestigious prep school (Exeter), a glossy college (Stanford), and the Army (Infantry). The most education happened at the prep school and the Army. This book describes private schools throughout the U.S., Canada, and overseas. If I had a kid and the money, I'd use it. If I were a kid with parents with the money, I'd use it.

—SB

Private Independent Schools
1946–1971; 704 pp.

$25.00 postpaid

from:
Bunting and Lyon, Inc.
238 North Main Street
Wallingford, Connecticut 06492

The Sidwell Friends School

WASHINGTON

THE SIDWELL FRIENDS SCHOOL is a coeducational day school, offering 14 years of education from Kindergarten through Grade 12. Administrative offices and the Middle and Upper Schools are at 3825 Wisconsin Avenue, N.W., Washington, D. C. 20016, which serves as the mailing address for the entire School. The Lower School (Kindergarten-Transition and Grades 1–4) is located on its own campus at 5100 Edgemoor Lane, Bethesda, Maryland. The telephone for all offices is 202-966-0953.

BUILDINGS AND EQUIPMENT. On the Wisconsin Avenue campus, separate buildings provide classrooms and study halls

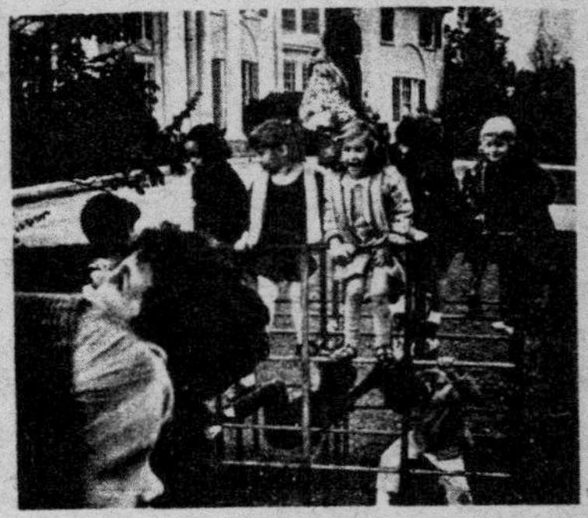

for the Upper and Middle Schools. Administrative offices are in historic Zartman House. Other facilities include the Activities Building and gymnasium, the George H. Sensner Science Building, and the Goodwin Library housing a collection of some 8000 books as well as audio-visual materials and periodicals.

FACULTY AND STAFF. Robert Lawrence Smith, the Headmaster, is a graduate of the University of California (Berkeley) and holds an M.A. from Columbia University. Before coming to The Sidwell Friends School in 1965, the Quaker educator was Assistant Dean of Columbia College. Jean Z. Jaspersen, Assistant Headmaster, holds a B.S. from the University of Pennsylvania. Prior to assuming this position, Mrs. Jaspersen was a teacher in and later Dean of The Sidwell Friends Upper School.

A Principal heads each of the School's three levels. In addition to administration and staff, the faculty includes 77 full-time teachers (24 men and 53 women) and 23 part-time teachers, holding a total of 85 baccalaureate degrees and 35 graduate degrees.

STUDENT BODY. There are enrolled (1969–70) 937 students aged 4 through 18. Each of the 14 grades is divided into sections. Class size is 5 to 25 students; median class size in the Upper School (grades 9–12) is 15 students.

ADMISSION AND COSTS. The School seeks students who meet high academic and personal standards and will distinctively contribute to the vitality of the school community. The School also recognizes the educational value of a school community that includes a variety of economic, cultural, and racial backgrounds. Special consideration is given candidates who meet the School's requirements and are members of the Society of Friends, brothers or sisters of present or former students, children of alumni and faculty. Coeducation is an important part of the School's tradition and life; and an attempt is made to maintain an even balance between the number of boys and girls in all grades. All inquiries regarding application for admission should be directed to Llewellyn W. Lord, Jr., Director of Admissions.

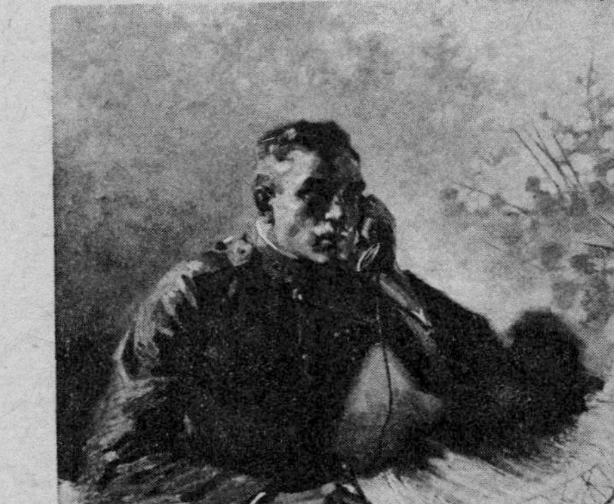

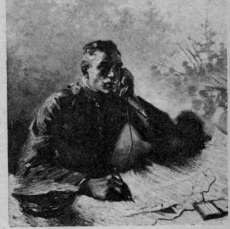

The Army

I am presently serving in the United States Army (Signal Corps) and would like to say that it (or rather certain schools it offers) is certainly relevant to independent education, your own personal feelings on militarism notwithstanding. It of course offers fine schools in electronics, diving and living off the land. If it wasn't for the war I would most probably apply for airborne training, officer candidates school and Ranger school. However, things being as they are in Vietnam, I can't see myself being a platoon leader in a Long Range Reconnaisance outfit. The thought of it scares me shitless, to be perfectly frank. I know Mr. Brand or someone who writes reviews was an airborne ranger, no offense intended.

I have the greatest respect for anyone who goes through just ranger school, I would look on someone with combat experience as a Ranger with fascination and awe.

Someone should probably review Vietnam, it is useful as a tool, since it is a medium where you can get stereo, and camera equipment, jewelry, clothes, women and VD rather cheaply.

John H. Kirck
Glenholden, Pa.

I didn't make it through Ranger School. Quit. Too cold.

—SB

The New Religions

One splendid effect of ecumenical technology is our new and deep access to top scientists from the East such as Suzuki Roshi, Meher Baba, Bapak, Krishnamurti, Tarthans Tulku, and others. Jacob Needleman, young head of the Philosophy Department at San Francisco State, has perceived their various convergent messages and assembled a thoroughly useful catalog. He's as serious as any student, and he knows more than one thing at a time. I hope he will expand a later edition of the book to include Gurdjieff, the Native American Church, and the whole Sufi number.

—SB

The New Religions
Jacob Needleman
1970; 245 pp.

$5.95 postpaid

from:
Doubleday and Company, Inc.
277 Park Avenue
New York, New York 10017

or WHOLE EARTH CATALOG

The contemporary disillusionment with religion has revealed itself to be a *religious* disillusionment. Men are moving away from the forms and trappings of Judaism and Christianity not because they have stopped searching for transcendental answers to the fundamental questions of human life, but because that search has now intensified beyond measure.

•

It has been said that every time and place has its own despair. The despair of California is the despair of people relentlessly getting what they want.

•

At Tassajara, however, one comes to see monasticism not as a flight from society, but to society. The principle difference between the monastic society and ours is surely not that ours is more real, but that in this monastery everyone has a common aim. Moreover, this aim is for themselves: each to awaken to his true nature, each to find "his own way."

In such a community, there exists a constant danger that in the name of charity and kindness someone will find my way for me, will directly or indirectly tell me what to do, what is good and what bad. As a result, I may find a way, but not my own way; I will discover a nature, but not necessarily my own nature. . .

Some people say, "If we have a perfect social construction, we will not have these difficulties." But as long as there is human nature, nothing will help us. On the contrary, the more human culture advances, the more difficulties we will have in our life. The advancement of civilization will accelerate this contradiction in our nature. When we realize the absolute presence of our contradictory nature, the way-seeking mind arises, and we begin to work on ourselves instead of the material world. Most people who are interested in Buddhism are more or less critical of our social condition, expecting a better social framework.

•

Baba was sitting on his bed. Naked from the waist up. I think there were two other men in the room. And Baba just—*beamed* at me, man, I always have difficulty talking about Baba. I mean, I'm not given to having visions or hallucinations. For me, it was just this incredible, extraordinary *light*, like his head was the center of it, like emanating in all directions. It filled everything. To the extend that tears started forcibly coming out of my eyes like a reaction to all this incredible light.

Scholarships to U.S.?

An old problem just plagued me again. There are lots of smart students in a place like Ethiopia who want to go to school in the U.S. They often ask people like me (visible "Americans") how to find schools and/or money. For schools, accesses exist, in U.S.I.S. libraries. But for finances (& schools characteristically ask 1 yrs expenses to be paid by the student — a lot of bread for all but the aristocrats in, for instance, Ethiopia) they (the students) & I am stymied.

But I know there exist breaded people who see the value of getting minds in communion world round & would personally or thru foundations to help bona fide (ie. all the test scores & recommendations) good students get it together. Is there some access info on this?

John Morgan
Village Technology
Innovation Experiment
Addis Ababa, Ethiopia

Monday Night Class

Steve Gaskin mixes acid, the East, vibes, his audience, himself, and the universe real nice. He has been doing an informal weekly sermon for the past year or so and this book is simply transcriptions of several of his raps with the people. Its simple and straight; it helps me stay loose. Printed in purple.

[Reviewed by Merce]

Monday Night Class
Stephen
1970

$1.95 postpaid

from:
The Farm
Summerton, TN 38483

or WHOLE EARTH CATALOG

Keep your attention on a single point as long as you want. You have to learn how to be loose to do it, it's not a thing you can do if you're tight, cause if you're tight your attention will tend to fidget. You gotta learn how to be just a loose observer. You have to really not give a damn too much about what's going on out there in front. You know, you gotta just look at it and dig it and see what it is and get the informational quality of it . . . Like you're supposed to groove. You're supposed to just really be grooving as hard as you can. There's a Zen master thing that says, Although my heart is on fire, my eyes are as cold as ashes. You know. So then you can keep concentration really well when you're not attached. That's a loose place you have to be to play music or to ride a bike or any of those kind of places, where you have to have that loose no-mind. . . let it do it, concentrate it there, put it there in one place. Yeah.

•

We're all like little energy transmuters. You know those things that float in swimming pools and go ssshhhwck and suck down all the leaves and bugs and sticks and stuff. That's what we are. You wander around through the world and take in all the vibes, transmute 'em through serenity and what have you, good dope, and put 'em back out, all vacuumed. The way we do it is that we absorb the body energy at this level and then transmute it . . . We do other people's homework as if it were our own. We do the homework of all the people around us. That's how we help out, you know, by just refining those vibes everywhere we go.

•

In most square folks' ground rules it's considered impolite to notice that your conversational partner is neurotic. And what you do about that's another thing. Jesus, when he was giving the instructions to the apostles, told 'em when you go into a house, feel the house, and let your peace descend on the house, and if the house accepts your peace then you're cool. You stay there. But if the house rejects your peace go forth from that house and go forth from that town and shake the dust from your feet. Because there's a whole lot of folks aching to know. Don't bother arguing with somebody that don't want to know.

•

Laughing? I think laughing's just free good karma. You know, all the time that you're laughing you're wide open, you're non-linear, non-directional . . . It may be the highest form of communication that we can do by mouth. Cause somebody can drop your cut-glass vase on the floor . . . and you can laugh and it's cool.

•

And you really got to be careful about that kind of thing, cause when someone's drunk, a lot of their consciousness is knocked out, and they're running a lot on their subconscious . . . and they're pretty telepathic and stuff at that stage, drunks and kids and people like that, don't ever lie to 'em. Don't lie to acidheads either. It's a waste of time.

•

Well, here's the thing that is one of the basic spiritual teachings that's been around for like ten or twelve thousand years . . . and it is that if you just quit paying attention to bad trips, pull your juice out of them, that they'll run out of juice, and they'll run down and stop. And they do that, because the karma is a little slower when you're not stoned, but it's the same karma and it works the same way . . . it's just a little slower, but it's not a bit different than when you're ripped. And where you cast your head you get that kind of thing. As ye sow so shall ye reap. Well, that means that in an energy relationship if you feel that somebody's on a negative trip, first you have to be accepting and free enough to say that they can do that if they want to . . . cause they got free will . . . everybody's got free will. The next thing is that you also have a choice in the matter and that's whether you pay any attention to it or not. And if you pay attention . . . this is something I've found out so many times trying to take care of people who bring me a bad trip to sort out for them—you can straighten them and let go of them and they'll dive right back into it . . . cause they're looking for it, really. People who really want help, you just make a suggestion and they do it . . . and they get straight. I've seen that happen lots of times. If you put a lot of attention and energy into a down trip, then you're stepping on a down elevator. And the vibe may be exhilarating for awhile, but it gets pretty funky the farther down you go.

Comix

These ain't your run-of-the-mill comic books. At times they are gross, beautiful, or violent. Best of all, they can be very funny, and a good reminder not to take things (such as yourself) too seriously. Who sez comic books ain't relevant?
— Steamboat

(Adults only)
Mail order lists from:

Print Mint, Inc.
830 Folger Avenue
Berkeley, California 94710   Catalog $.25

Rip-Off Press
Box 14158
San Francisco, California 94114

San Francisco Comic Book Co.
3339 23rd Street
San Francisco, California 94110

TIME

Nail. Set. Hammer. <u>Whap</u>.
Set. Nail. <u>Whap</u>.
How's your blister, David?
Not too bad. It's not on my hammer hand.
We'll get some turpentine on it when we get done here.
Done.
Get done.
Two o'clock.
Two ten.
Nail. Set. Sweat, slick, hand, <u>whap</u>.
And then it was two eleven.

Times is hot Jessie!

Everybody one bedtrice fire or another just cooks
the living shit out of us.
Some stuff never smoked into the light of day
before. You know? Out there after Further got hot.
Umber. Thunder. Boiling. Everywhere !!! ...wow.
New wideawake fires with no respect for old shit
cooking us clean.

Thing is ... what does a man do with a
brand new next job of your
idea in mind?
Despite of it, I guess, as efficiently as possible
without getting too heavy about it.

And get on with the game.
But what IS the game?
Is it the GAME? Or The Game? Or THE game?
Damned if I can say for certain. All I know is that
SOME of the question above
— and some MORE —

Now! I being decided to play on next question is:
what position?

Well, I'm glad you ask that question, neighbor, because
I got not ONE NOT TWO BUT [scribble] ANSWERS!
(completely)

1. Perfection of flat-out ME! Right?
2. Perfection of [crossed out] OTHER MOTHERFUCKERS!! the wise
   you get there miserable asses underfoot all the time disturbing
   your meditations.
3. Perfection of GOD. You might assume the accomplished
   of the first two steps would accomplish this. No Indeed, Art.
   merely brings us up to the completion of fantasies
   already outlined. while the third task is more
   interesting in foreshowing NEW fantasies. Completion
   as opposed to Creation; two separate tasks though
   our position — the action may and probably
   is simultaneous or whenever its spelled.

yeah, but WHAT POSITION???

I was getting to that, neighbor. Just keep your
blue-eyes open for some fast footwork out plans
stop execute plans STOP WORK OUT AREA FOR WORKING OUT
PLANS STOP WORK OUT HEAD WORK OUT TEAM WORKOUT GOD
IN AREA STOP. OR: PROVIDE SITUATION CONDUCIVE TO HAPPENING!!!

(love)

Sometimes a Great Notion

A strong man's argument with himself, with the false meek and the hollow strength, until the meek rings true and the strength fills up. The book is about logging. Women hate it.

—SB

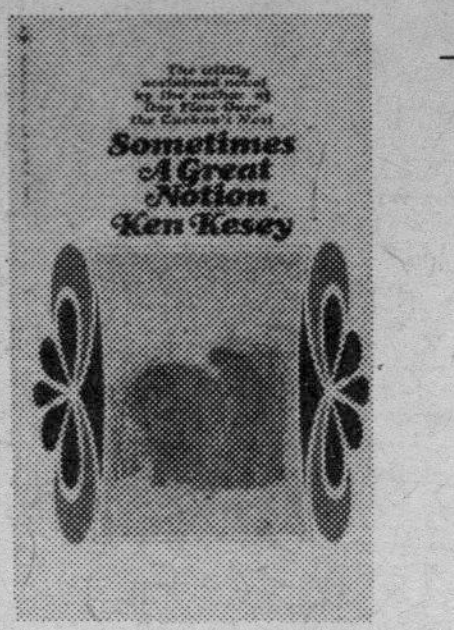

Sometimes A Great Notion
Ken Kesey
1964; 599 pp.

$1.25 postpaid

from:
Bantam Books, Inc.
666 Fifth Ave.
New York, N.Y. 10019

or WHOLE EARTH CATALOG

He moved his ear to the animal's sleek bulk and could hear her guts working. He liked the sound. He liked the cow. He liked feeling her warmth and squeezing the rhythm of milk into the pail. It was a dumb-ass thing keeping a milk-cow these days when you could buy milk cheaper'n alfalfa, but dammit a cow's tit was a nice change from an ax-handle, and the soft working of a cow's gut was a relief after the old man's snortin' and fartin' and John's bullshitting and Orland's wife's screeching. Oh, well; they didn't really mean anything by it.

The milk rang into the pail, then muffled its ringing in folds of white froth, a measured bell sounding through thick, creamy warmth.

This is Hank's bell.

On the river the motorboat gnashed at the leaf-dappled water as Joe Ben ferried the loads of people across. Cars started, spinning gravel to get back onto the highway. Henry's plaster cast thundered and rolled on the docks.

A dumb-ass thing, keeping a cow.

In the deepening sky where the spearpoint firs scratch the clouds, already a moon— like a cast-off paring from the setting sun. This is Hank's bell, too.

But god oh mighty ain't they warm to lean against?

On the docks the noisy woodpecker of a man parades up and down, shaking his plume of hair that is yellow and coarse as a bundle of broken toothpicks when seen close up; fifty yards away it is white as a thunderhead; fifty yards away at the wrong end of a telescope the drink-whipped cheeks of John glow with ruddy health, and Orland's wife steps into the waiting boat with a foot as demure and dainty as that of a thoroughbred colt. Joe Ben's poor hacked gridiron of a face shines out across the green water as pure as a cameo, and his potato-shaped wife is a swan in polka-dotted taffeta. Fifty yards away.

This is Hank's bell— secret between peaks of foam, muffled in warm white valleys— this is Hank's bell ringing

•

(I watched as Hank stood, strangely peaceful, and let the challenger deliver the first blow. It was almost his undoing. He was spun completely around and into the bar; his head struck the wood with a thick sound and he fell to his knee RUN FOOL! WATCH OUT! and the Bignewton was on him before he could rise. . .) *You see, Lee?* All every one dirty whining sniveling pricks vicious red-sweater cunts grubby faces far back I can remember blame me *Me, Lee, do you see?* (this time hitting him high on the cheekbone and rolling him face forward on the floor) assholes who couldn't pour piss outa a boot is my fault— *Oh Christ, Lee, do you see?* (and from this position he twisted his head toward me WATCH OUT! WATCH OUT! seemingly to make certain of my presence) all yelling stomp him stomp the hardnosed motherfucker— *Oh Christ, Lee!* (He looked at me from the floor, his head twisting back, asking the question now with one green eye WATCH OUT RUN! the other blinded with blood. . .) all yelling kill him because I won't run the sonsabitches *Lee! you bastard!* (. . .and, before I could think— because of the noise, the beer I'd drunk, perhaps because I wanted him beaten further— WATCH OUT, HANK! I heard myself shouting encouragement right along with Joe Ben GET UP, HANK, GET UP GET UP GET UP!) sonsabitches you think I care *please* let me hate them *Lee you see I can* (and, as though he had been waiting for my signal, he rose GET UP trailing blood HANK HANK and an awesome war cry. . .) YOU you think I care hate *I please* them! *owe them not run* (. . .to prove himself HANK YES HANK HANK! every bit as primitive. . .) *please* hate! *care do you?* Them sonsabitches! (as the prehistoric biped) THEM NOW do *you?* CARE *please* KILL THEM! (and even *more* proficient YES HANK YES a pugilist!) let me *do you* THEM kill NOW NOW NOW. . .!

Four-Gated City

An introspective woman's acquiescence to insanity to get understanding. It's about culture, the city, issues of conscience, of madness and reality, of health. Men hate it.

—SB

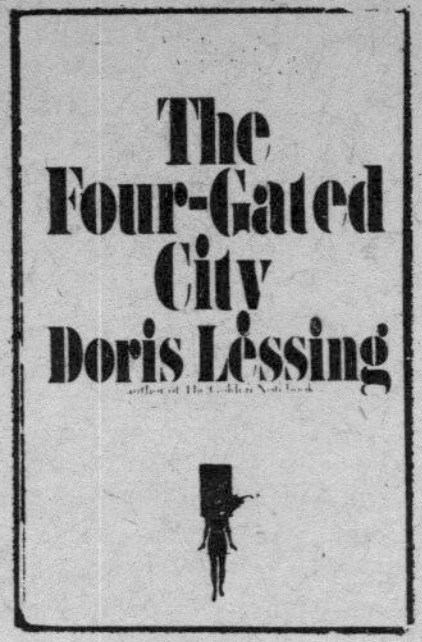

The Four-Gated City
Doris Lessing
1969; 656 pp.

$1.25 postpaid

from:
Bantam Books, Inc.,
A National General Co.
666 Fifth Avenue
New York, N.Y. 10019

or WHOLE EARTH CATALOG

The bad time continued. It was expressed in a number of separate events, or processes, in this of that part of the world, whose common quality was horror — and a senseless horror. To listen, to read, to watch the news of any one of these events was to submit oneself to incredulity: this barbarism, this savagery, was simply not possible. And, everywhere in this country, in the world, people like oneself sat reading, looking, watching, in precisely the same condition: this is not possible; it can't be happening; it's all so monstrously silly that I can't believe it . . . The war in Korea was at the height of its danger for the world, the propaganda on both sides had reached a point where no one sensible could believe a word of it, and for months it looked as if nothing could stop America using "the bomb" there. In America the hysteria had grown till that great nation looked from outside like a dog driven mad by an infestation of fleas, snapping and biting at its own flesh; and a man called Joe McCarthy, who had no qualities at all, save one, the capacity to terrorise other people, was able to do as he liked. Throughout Africa various countries fought in various ways against the white man, but in Kenya there was a full-scale war, both sides (as in Korea) fighting with a maximum of nastiness and lies.

•

This is Dali landscape. I'm plugged in to Dali mind. If I could draw, paint, then I'd paint this, Dali picture. Why does only Dali plug in to Dali country? No, Dali and me. Therefore Dali and — plenty of others. But nurse says, delusions. If ignorant, does not think is Dali country. Thinks: That's a silly picture. If educated, knows, thinks: I am a copycat. Or, that must be a Dali picture I haven't seen? (Perhaps it is.)

He couldn't have painted so many. Why not?

Plagiarism. (Think about this after when time.) Mark writes something. Then it's floating in the air. Someone can plug in. A City in the Dessert is photostatted in the photosphere. (Oh, very funny. Ha. You only deserve half a laugh for that one.)

One of them is rather weak,
And one of them is very meek.
And one of them is just a horse.
And one of them is rather coarse.
One of them would like to strangle.
Hurt and tear and bite and mangle.
And one of them is rather crude.
And one of them is just a prude.
And one of them . . .

For God's sake stop, sobbed Martha, clutching her ears as this awful da-da-da-da-da- ground in her eardrums.

Lying face down, nose in a thick plush of carpet which smelled faintly of dust, the sea of sound came down, swallowed her.

Almost.

Let Us Now Praise Famous Men

This book is the opposite of fiction. In Walker Evans' photographs and James Agee's prose and in the lives of the share-cropper South is the sound

of quiet revolution.

—SB —jd

Let Us Now Praise Famous Men
James Agee, Walker Evans
1941, 1960; 428 pp.

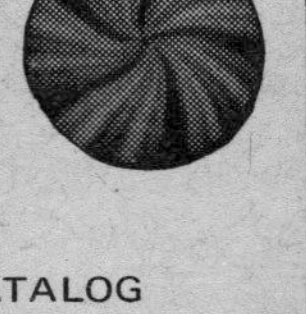

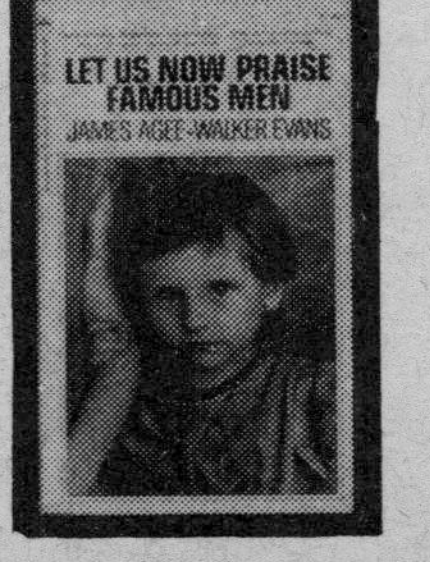

$1.65 postpaid

from:
Ballantine Books, Inc.
101 Fifth Avenue
New York, N.Y. 10003

or WHOLE EARTH CATALOG

How were we caught?

What, what is it has happened? What is it has been happening that we are living the way we are?

The children are not the way it seemed they might be:

She is no longer beautiful:

He no longer cares for me, he just takes me when he wants me:

There's so much work it seems like you never see the end of it:

I'm so hot when I get through cooking a meal it's more than I can do to sit down to it and eat it:

How was it we were caught?

•

His mother sits in a hickory chair with her knees relaxed and her bare feet flat to the floor; her dress open and one broken breast exposed. Her head is turned a little slantwise and she gazes quietly downward past her son's head into the junctures of the earth, the floor, the wall, the sunlight, and the shade. One hand lies long and flat along her lap: it is elegantly made of bone and is two sizes too large for the keen wrist. With her other hand, and in the cradling of her arm and shoulder, she holds the child. His dress has fallen aside and he is naked. As he is held, the head huge in scale of his body, the small body ineffably relaxed, spilled in a deep curve from nape to buttocks, then the knees drawn up a little, the bottom small and sharp, and the legs and feet drifted as if under water, he suggests the shape of the word siphon. He is nursing. His hands are blundering at her breast blindly, as if themselves each were a new born creature, or as if they were sobbing, ecstatic with love; his mouth is intensely absorbed at her nipple as if in rapid kisses, with small and swift sounds of moisture; his eyes are squeezed shut; and now, for breath, he draws away, and lets out a sharp short whispered *ahh*, the hands and his eyelids relaxing, and immediately resumes; and in all this while, his face is beatific, the face of one at rest in paradise, and in all this while her gentle and sober, earnest face is not altered out of its deep slantwise gazing: his head is now sunken off and away, grand and soft as a cloud, his wet mouth flared, his body still more profoundly relinquished of itself, and I see how against her body he is so many things in one, the child in the melodies of the womb, the Madonna's son, human divinity sunken from the cross at rest against his mother, and more beside, for at the heart and leverage of that young body, gently, taken in all the pulse of his being, the penis is partly erected.

And Ellen where she rests, in the gigantic light: she, too, is completely at peace, this child, the arms squared back, and palms open loose against the floor, the floursack on her face; and her knees are flexed upward a little and fallen apart, the soles of the feet facing: her blown belly swimming its navel, white as flour; and blown full broad with slumbering blood into a circle: so white all the outward flesh, it glows of blue; so dark, the deep hole, a dark red shadow of life blood: this center and source, for which we have never contrived any worthy name, is as if it were breathing, flowering, soundlessly, a snoring silence of flame; it is as if flame were breathed forth from it and subtly played about it: and here in this breathing and play of flame, a thing so strong, so valiant, so unvanquishable, it is without effort, without emotion, I know it shall at length outshine the sun.

A Hall of Mirrors

Armageddon is ours. We can trudge along, getting by, matching facades, half-escaped, and be the very wheels of the juggernaut. Kill the fuckers, kill them. Them? In an Ice Age?

—SB

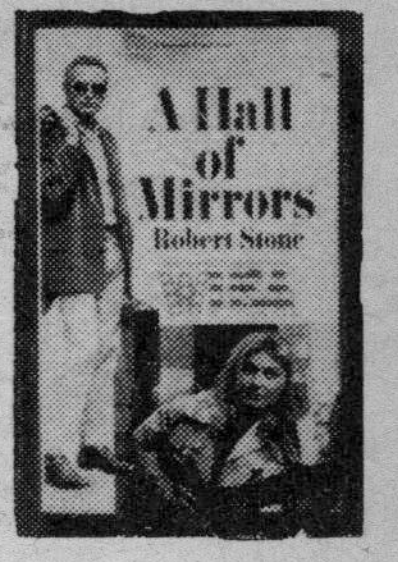

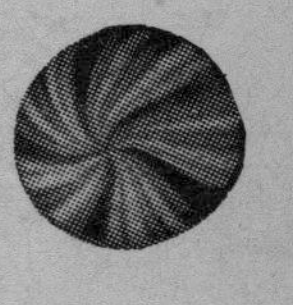

Hall of Mirrors
Robert Stone
1967; 352 pp.

$0.95 postpaid

from:
Fawcett Publications, Inc.
67 W. 44th St.,
New York, N.Y. 10036

or WHOLE EARTH CATALOG

Marvin looked from face to face and stopped at Rheinhardt. "Man," he said, "that wasn't the California you know. No mufflers. No titty-tatty. No ogla bee. No gasoline-smell grease-trap taco stand plastic supermarket shit. No fat woman drive ins. No polite killer cops. No oregano salesmen. No Northbeach. No Southbeach. No Beach Beach. It wasn't like that, man—you think it was?"

"No," Rheinhardt said. "It couldn't have been."
"It couldn't have been," Marvin said soberly. "It could not have been. And it was not."
"It was a California of the mind," the girl said.

"My God," Bogdanovich said stepping forward in wide-eyed astonishment, "what a California that would be!" As they watched, he raised his hands to describe a box and held them palms facing down. "Look," he told them, "that's your mind, dig? And here it's all gray, it's all nowhere, it's just dry and barren and terrible trips. But here, dig—at the western end there's a curving beach and white surf rolling up on it. And there's blue and purple islands and high cold mountains and forests with a carpet of pine needles. And orange juice in the clear desert."

•

"There, there, baby. Don't feel so bad. I'll tell you a little story make you feel better. See, Lester knows how you all can't tell one black person from another because you couldn't live with yourselves and all like that. He enjoys that phenomenon very much, you dig it? Well, one time they sent him down a fool like you and he walked that cat over a whole floor of his wiggy little hotel interviewing different people. All sorts and kinds and shapes of humanity. Every one of them— man, woman and child— was the same cat. It was the greatest Big Store trip ever pulled and old Lester did it sheerly for the sport."

Berry removed his shades and wiped his eyes.

"Fella's name was Archie that was all the people. Archie had a lot of talent but the day was Lester's. It was too much. That white man left with a notebook full of details and a funny feelin' somewhere way down in his head. I don't think it ever really got to him."

He was weeping with mirth, waving his shades in Rainey's face.

Rainey began to laugh with him.

"The Big Store," Rainey said, twisting his rainhat, nearly doubling up.

"That's it, that's it," Berry said, gripping Rainey's shoulder. "Too much."

"Too much," Rainey said.

•

It seemed to Rheinhardt that he had elicited a respectful silence from the stands; thus encouraged, he went on.

"The American Way is innocence," Rheinhardt announced. "In all situations we must and shall display an innocence so vast and awesome that the entire world will be reduced by it. American innocence shall rise in mighty clouds of vapor to the scent of heaven and confound the nations!

"Our legions, patriots, are not like those of the other fellow. We are not perverts with rotten brains as the English is. We are not a sordid little turd like the French. We are not nuts like the Kraut. We are not strutting maniacs like the gibroney and the greaseball!

"On the contrary our eyes are the clearest eyes looking out on the world today. I tell you that before our wide, fixed blue-eyed stare the devious councils of the foreign horde are confounded as the brazen idolators before enlightened Moses.

"No matter what they say, Americans, remember this— we're OK! Who else can say that? No one. No one else can say— we're OK. Only in America can a people say— we're OK. I want you all to say it with me.

"We're OK," Rheinhardt shouted raising his arm to invite accompaniment. Someone in the stands was heard to fire a pistol.

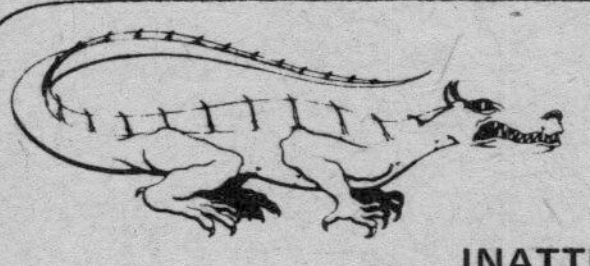

INATTENTION

But you could see it now. Taking shape. The short side was completed, and they were half way across the long front, nailing to the seventh post. An enclosure was being made. A wall, the horizontal one-by-sixes parallel, a perfect shape of empty space between them; the upright posts their roots into the ground. There was a texture now; the rough lumber like beard-stubble, splintery to the touch; there was shape and there was texture and marvelous patterned lines and angles at the posts. There was aesthetic going on, and cosmic law. It's measured space, enclosed, D.R. thought. It's a line upon the earth for the work of meat-production to go on behind. They were agents of the fence, its architects and builders; they were building fence, setting limits on the space. The space, enclosed, was inside time, it's two twenty now. . .

"Yeoww! Shit!" and D.R. dropped his hammer and grabbed his thumb and danced around in circles.

Leonard looked up and grinned as D.R. cussed.

"Be kinder to yourself," said Leonard. "Always pay attention to your work."

The Proper Study of Man

Jim Fadiman went to college and read all those books and readings in the social sciences and got acquainted with various pioneers and put together a book of all the good stuff. Now you don't have to go to college.

—SB

The Proper Study of Man
James Fadiman, ed.
1971; 481 pp.

$5.95 postpaid

from:
Macmillan Company
866 Third Ave.
New York, N.Y. 10022

or WHOLE EARTH CATALOG

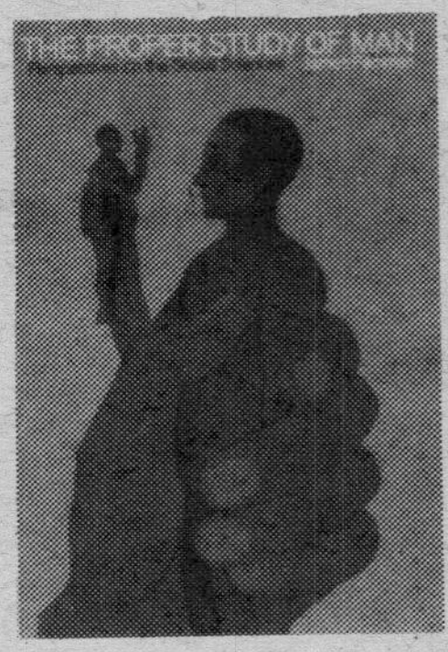

Skill

Ever since his "expulsion from paradise," man has been inclined to protest work as drudgery or as slavery, and to consider most fortunate those who seemingly can choose to work or not to work. The fact is that man *must* learn to work, as soon as his intelligence and his capacities are ready to be "put to work," so that his ego's powers may not atrophy.

The rudiments of *skill* add method to hope, will and purpose. Now, what "works" in the fabric of one's thought and in cooperative encounters: a self-verification of lasting importance. All human environments, therefore, meet this stage with the offer of instruction in *perfectable skills* leading to *practical uses* and *significant achievements*. All cultures have their logic and their "truth," which can be learned, by exercise, usage, and ritual. Where literacy is a common basis for all future specialization, the rulse of grammar and of algebra, of course, form a more abstract demonstration of the workings of reality. Thus *workmanship* and the *reasonableness* which comes from convincing experience prepare in the child a future sense of *competency* without which there can be no "strong ego." Without it man feels inferior in his equipment, and in the hope to match an ever increasing section of manageable reality with his growing capacities.

Erik Erikson, *The Roots of Virtue*

From *The Diary of Vaslav Nijinsky*

Everybody will say that Nijinsky has become insane. I do not care, I have already behaved like a madman at home. Everybody will think so, but I will not be put in an asylum, because I dance very well and give money to all those who ask me. People like an odd and peculiar man and they will leave me alone, calling me a "mad clown." I like insane people, I know how to talk to them. My brother was in the lunatic asylum.

I was fond of him and he understood me. His friends there liked me too, I was then eighteen years old. I know the life of lunatics and understood the psychology of an insane man. I never contradict them, therefore madmen like me. . .

Life is not sex— sex is not God, God is man, who fecundates only one woman, a man who gives children to one woman. I am twenty-nine years old. I love my wife spiritually, not for begetting children. I will have children if God wishes it. Kyra is an intelligent girl. I do not want her to be clever. I will prevent her from developing her intelligence. I like simple people but not stupidity, because I see no feeling in that. Intelligence stops people from developing. I feel God and God feels me.

•

Manas

These guys, whoever they are, are all for making this a better place. They don't shout and they don't make funny. But they say a lot of good stuff for $5/yr. What got me on to them was that I read somewhere that Manas *was a kind of unofficial organ of the humanistic psychology bunch. I'm not sure this fully explains them, as they don't seem to follow any party line. They've got some heroes like Gandhi and Tolstoy, too; but they don't go on and on. They comment on whoever has grist for the mill (Plato, Paul Goodman, Peter S. Beagle, Christ knows who-all). They've turned me on to a whole hell of a lot of really great stuff.*

[Suggested and reviewed by Richard Welsh]

Manas

$5 /yr (weekly, except July & August)

from:
Manas Publishing Company
Box 32112
El Sereno Station
Los Angeles, CA 90032

If buddhism were to contribute to the "Global Canon" its assumptions of "Mind Only," *karma*, and the Unity of Life, our ecological exertions within a chilling space-time continuum might gain some impetus from the emotion Einstein speaks of. But the *mahayana* has more to offer. Its last words affect man alone, as the recipient of self-consciousness. suggesting to him a peak definition of himself. For he is here sponsored as an advanced candidate for *prajna*, total Enlightenment through personal effort, in a world whose equilibriums, endlessly disturbed, are being as endlessly restored under a law of impartial justice.

But then comes the rider. Despite appearances, the effort boomerangs, the reward recedes, whenever *karuna*, compassion, is absent anywhere between the means and the end. Ruthless progress is, in fact, not progress at all.

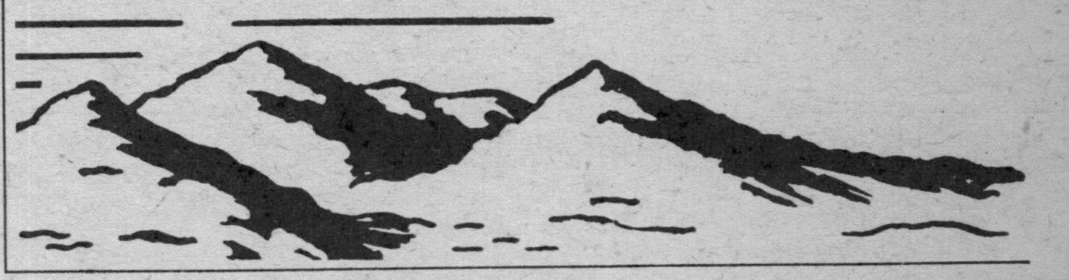

The Five Ages of Man

Educational theory presumes that cognitive and intellectual and "social" development is about all that can or need be dealt with in the schools, and the schools act accordingly.

Gerald Heard (scarcely mentioning schools) investigates a deeper education, namely emotional human development both in history and in the individual. His effort is to recognize and honor the various stages of people's relation to their own energies, and recognize and honor the requirement of recurrent further growth, and recognize and assist the hard transitions from one stage to the next.

His notion spreads out like this:

Historical stages (5 crises)	Personal stages (5 ordeals)	Initiations (5 mysteries)
Coconscious man	Birth trauma	Rebirth (Earth)
Heroic, self-assertive man	Childhood (becoming paranoia)	Catharsis (Water)
Ascetic, self-accusing man	Adolescence (schizophrenia)	Inspiration (air)
Humanic, self-sufficient man	First maturity (manic depression)	Illumination (fire)
Leptoid, post-individual man	Second maturity (involuntary melancholy)	Transformation (electricity)

What emerges from all this is pretty radical education. Depending on where a person is hung up, you ritually bury him, or half drown him, or gas him, or burn him, or send electricity through him. Mr. Heard has done much of this to himself and speaks well of the effects. I believe it. Rites of passage are rare these days, and mostly fumbled when they occur. It would be nice to know what's going on and be able to get some help when spontaneous metamorphosis has you spinning.

Says Heard, if we tend properly to all the transitions, we will enable old people to be useful and growing, as seers. Gerald Heard is 80.

—SB

[Suggested by Peter Douthit]

The Five Ages of Man
Gerald Heard
1963; 393 pp.

$8.50 postpaid

from:
Julian Press
150 Fifth Ave.
New York, N.Y. 10011

or WHOLE EARTH CATALOG

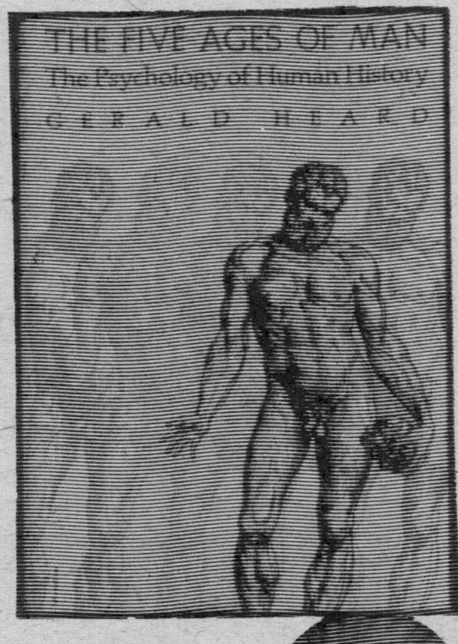

Briefly, then, this is the thesis of this book: man can train himself, and he has done so with increasing understanding. Although at first this training was implicit in a rite that worked without being consciously comprehended and, next, it was esoteric and a mystery understood only by psychophysical pioneers, today it can become explicitly exoteric, rendered in contemporary terms and applied with scientific exactitude and as a therapeutic education. Such an education can fully develop both an entire person and a complete society. It can produce a constituent able to accept and fulfill his whole personal process and also be the conscious, willing, and developmental unit of a civilization that is creatively run by a common consent and coterminous with a nonviolent mankind.

•

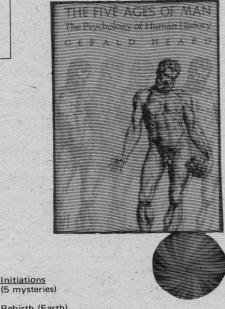

It is now clear that before historic record, but well illustrated by superb pictures, there was a culture that was preindividualistic and to some extent coconscious because it was under a comprehensive suggestion by imposed interpretation and rule. And even today there are fragmentary societies which (as in Australia and Papua) still seem to preserve much of the same cohesion and precritical amalgamation of psychological value and economic profit. Secondly, there is the Heroic Age, which helped to destroy the preindividual condition and which is itself only protoindividual; only crudely critical of the old order; childishly ignorant of its own weakness and faults; boastful, displayful, and un-self-conscious in any sense of objective awareness. It did not understand, it simply reacted. Thirdly, this second stage is succeeded by one of self-questioning and criticism that produces a desire for self-improvement, self-discipline, and finally self-reduction. Then, with struggle, this ascetic, midindividualistic condition passes into the fourth stage when individualism attains totality. At first, man's self-consciousness made him criticize only the tradition-bound group. Then it made him criticize himself. And now, in his complete self-confidence, he no longer sees any need either for boast and shame or for guilt and gratitude. He sees himself as neither condemning nor approving, as being the flawless mirror of the world that is as orderly (and so as repetitively aimless) as he is rational and inventively comprehending.

These four phases have therefore given rise to four distinctive types: (1) the nonpersonal group constituent, (2) the hero, (3) the ascetic and (4) the humanic. And that, until the beginning of this century, seemed to be the culminant end of the story.

•

For three reasons a specific treatment is required for the present dominant type, the totally self-conscious man, the person of first maturity. (1) Cut off from his own deep, intuitional mind, he must suffer increasingly from a subconscious anxiety. (2) Cut off from interior knowledge of his own body and function rhythms, he must be increasingly attacked by psychosomatic illness. (3) Cut off, psychologically, from the society whose granulation into separate cells he acutely expresses and coercively commands, he must create an international anarchy.

The bigger logs, ablaze but not yet broken up by the fire, were arranged crosswise in the trench, above the bed of flame made by the pieces that had broken down into small brands and bright charcoal. So a kind of cattle-guard or corduroy walk was made, through which grate or grill the flames rose. The priest with the wands, who had sat before the fire while it was being lit and brought to full conflagration, had now moved and sat at one end of the trench with an assistant seated at the other. They stayed sitting like this for a few moments, after which all was ready for the therapy. The first to walk the length of the trench was one of the chief priests. By then a considerable portion of the lay congregation had been brought near and lined up. Old people, the middle-aged, and youngsters—between seventy-five and one hundred persons went along the trench. Dr. Campbell himself went in his turn. He reports, "I deliberately stepped on some nice fat flames, smelled the hair burning on my legs but found the flames were cool. When I put on my socks again I found that my right ankle, which had been swollen and sore from a strain acquired at Ankor Vat some weeks before, had gone down to normal and no longer hurt. The next day I walked some nine or ten miles and the ankle was still OK. The skin of my feet had not been damaged in the least—not even reddened by the flames. . . ."

•

A meteorologist friend of Jellinek's, caught in a thunderstorm on a Swiss peak, used the method. Having braced himself against the possibility of being struck, he was hit three times by lightning. But although his clothes were torn and his skin broken, because he was prepared he was neither stunned nor did he suffer anything but the surface abrasions.

•

The emergence of second maturity, the large class of healthy grandparents, can be understood and be availed of only if we see that this fifth phase is inevitable; that it is the essential requirement for the manning of a fifth category of mankind, the fifth age of man as a race and as a person.

•

Now, with old age and at the upper end, Nature restores freedom of choice and permits, once again, that rightful irresponsibility to enquire and explore regardless of consequences. Being relieved of the armor of authority and the enforcement instruments of command, those in second maturity are once more at liberty to enquire rather than to order, and to question rather than reply.

•

Second maturity is a return to a regeneralized outlook emotionally and intellectually, a resumption of generalized response. Hence, it can be the state in which it would be natural for the capacity of seership to be attained, to re-emerge. And, with that capacity, to regain a generalized affection, good will, and anxiety-free concern and vision into the nature of time that would explicate death by uniting the mind with eternal life.

•

The actual procedure of the water initiation would, then, involve first an immersian, naked and in a tank of circulating water kept at body temperature, and wherein the body would be irrigated exteriorly and interiorly. The eyes could see, through a glass visor, the water-suffused and wavering light that should probably also have rhythmic light patterns given it by the use of a stroboscope. The ear should be vibrated by sound rhythms of a comparable frequency sent through the water, which is a better sound-carrying medium than air. In this medium and state the postulant should first be floated. But after ten minutes the water in the tank would be made to begin a pulsing, vortex movement. And against this whirlpool he would have to struggle until exhausted. At this point he should achieve a further loss of self; he should emerge into an enlarged state of consciousness.

World Game Report Two

Play the Big Game. This is good introduction to basic technique. More World Game stuff on p. 28.

—SB

[Suggested by Timmi Bushbaum]

World Game Report Two

from:
Design Department
Southern Illinois University
Carbondale, Illinois 62901

SIX SUB-SYSTEMS OF MAN'S EXTERNAL METABOLICS

Definitions

Materials Conversion— Sub-system whose function is to reduce complex or heterogeneous matter-energy into more simple or basic forms of matter.

Tool Making— Sub-system that takes pure or processed matter (from matter conversion) and makes it into more organized configurations that are to be utilized by all sub-systems (including tool making). Tool making outputs all tools and contact products (see definitions) but not services.

Power Conversion— Sub-system that transforms unutilizable matter-energy into energy utilizable by the entire technological system.

Transportation— Sub-system whose primary function is to deliver matter-energy forms and some types of information from sub-system outputs to desired inputs of the sub-systems. Transportation also performs storage functions for matter-energy and information temporarily not being utilized by the technological energy.

Media-People— Sub-system whose primary function is to accumulate, integrate, store and distribute information for all sub-systems. The effects of people occur primarily in this sub-system.

Everything Else— Those variables in universe over which man has no control (or over which man has relinquished control).

FLASH

for immediate release

GOD CREATING THE UNIVERSE

photo by Mrs. God

Dymaxion Sky-Ocean World Map Kit

$1.25 *for the punch-out kit*
(includes shipping)

from:
Fuller Dymaxion Maps
Box 909
Carbondale, IL 62901

The shiny flat maps are **$6**

from:
Fuller Dymaxion Airocean World
3508 Market St.
Philadelphia, PA 19104

or WHOLE EARTH CATALOG

Extinction

Of the innumerable topical board games that have come by lately, this is the first we've seen that is both an interesting game with some subject—fresh dynamics and pretty good education. Suppose you're a nocturnal species with a high litter size of 10 and mobility of 20; you're already over-populated and in hazard of famine or pestilence; you breed in swamps and marshes and you have water pollution resistance (water pollution just eliminated your competition in the marshes); you have defense against swift predators, but one of your opponents is crafty and you think the other one is strong since he changed genes last turn; you spin the spinner and get—watch out—migrate and reproduce; what do you do? [I would migrate out of marshes and swamps and up next to the predators before reproducing. Then spread the new individuals thin in 'unfavorable' environments, thus reducing my reproduction rate and keeping well buffered against environmental changes in my breeding grounds. Also I'd look for new genes.]

If the game could include considerations of nutrition, energy cycles, and specialization, I'd be happier with it, but the makers encourage you to add your own rules to make this flexible game closer to the Big Game.

—SB

Extinction: The Game of Ecology

No longer available

from:
Sinauer Associates, Inc.
20 Second Street
Stamford, Connecticut 06905

Systems and Education

Author: John Pfeiffer
Title: New Look at Education: Systems Analysis in our Schools and Colleges
Publisher: The Odyssey Press, N.Y.
Cost: $1.00—Paper
Total No. of Pages: 162

Books on systems are usually either loaded with statistical equations so complex that even advanced graduate students can't figure out what the author was saying, or they are specific to esoteric subject, like the hormone system of the species Ratus Ratus. Admittedly, such books are important to a very overspecialized scientific few, but for me (a layman) they take on the average of about one year to translate into everyday "living language" to be useful.

However, John Pfeiffer DID IT!!! He wrote a small book, with no excess verbage or professional rhetoric, which describes simultaneously the fascinating history, slow development, and almost karmatic application of systems analysis— all over the recent past thirty years. This in turn, is blended into a concise description of the basic elements of "the systems approach," with numerous "living" example for testimony to the naturalness of being and living with systems.

One last comment. There is fast approaching the long shadow of both individuals, and our entire society, beginning the mad scramble to discover and reset the most important priorities for personal and planetary survival. Which comes first? (Circle One!!!) Racism? Ecology? Cosmic Consciousness? Joy? Education? Poverty? Love? Population? Self-Awareness? Tools? God? Birds? Books? Man? Each group scrambles for identity and social awareness of its cause, and is eaten up by the mass media. And each person does two year stints at this or that, and not having "made it," put on another cause for another two years (with appropriate clothes.)

But what if there is no "first cause (or first sin)? What then? Where to begin?!?!? "begin at the beginning, of course!" With everything. And then decide what to do and what to believe in. Pfeiffer helps man begin, by inviting him to take a look at systems, and then to make conscious decisions, with a renewed knowledge that whatever one does is interrelated IN SPECIFIC WAYS to EVERYTHING THAT IS.

Paul R. Poduska
Amherst, Mass.

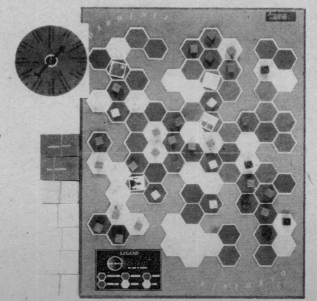

Education Automation

In this book Fuller is mainly concerned with educational access: designing ready access to comprehensive and replicable information and designing mobility as the basis of education.

—SB

Education Automation
R. Buckminster Fuller
1962; 88 pp.

$1.95

from:
Doubleday & Co., Inc.
501 Franklin Avenue
Garden City, NY 11530

or WHOLE EARTH CATALOG

I would say, then, that you are faced with a future in which education is going to be number one amongst the great world industries, within which will flourish an educational machine technology that will provide tools such as the individually selected and articulated two-way TV and an intercontinentally net-worked, documentaries call-up system, operative over any home two-way TV set.

We also find that generally speaking the geographically larger the physical task to be done, the duller the conceptual brain that is brought to bear upon the integration of the scientific discoveries and their technically realized applications. Finally, we get to international affairs, and you know what is happening today.

I would counsel you in your deliberation regarding getting campuses ready now to get general comprehensive environmental controls that are suitable to all-purposes like a circus. A circus is a transformable environment.

You don't need a detailed drawing; we do not make that kind of communication to a craftsman anymore; but all the schools go on teaching that we do. The data no longer goes to the craftsman; it goes to the tools. The idea of drafting measured details is going to become obsolete. We don't want any more measured detail drafting. What we want is the man who gets the fundamental concept, the information significance and can do some comprehensive thinking regarding that information. He will put the data into the information machines, and it will be processed by automation into physical realization of his effective thinking. We don't need many of the myriad of "things" we have had in schools.

ATTENTION

Attention drove the afternoon along outside of space and time. It drove the work along like floating free of gravity.

It lifted the work above its own resistance and its friction, like running naked after wearing heavy boots and suits of clothes.

It set the posts and tamped them firm.

It drove the nails unerringly, and ran the one-by-sixes across the front and past the dog-leg by the stump, and pointed then along the final side to link up with the other corner of the barn.

It closed the fence. It held them to their task till they had cut a door in the barnwall for the pigs to come out through, and smell out their new universe.

Reluctant, then curious, the pigs came out, cautious, one at a time, then gathered in committee in the corner to inspect D.R.'s and Leonard's work.

They approved.

Grunting, muttering little squeals, they scattered across this unexpected ground, and one pissed on it. D.R. and Leonard laughed at that, and D.R. listened carefully to their laugh. He watched closely as Leonard fed the hogs, and closed them back in their stall for the night.

On their way to the house for supper he paid attention when Leonard said: next winter when we have us some good sausage for breakfast we'll remember this day, David.

That thought thrilled D.R. and he paid attention to the thrill.

He paid attention to Roxie pouring turpentine in the wounds from his day's labor. He noticed how her hands felt on his, he paid attention to her presence, close, and to the food she had prepared.

Roast beef, boiled potatoes, beans, cole slaw heavy with mayonaise, rhubarb, cornbread, cold milk, and then banana pudding for dessert. D.R. noticed every bite he took, he paid attention to his mouth chewing, he tasted every flavor that there was, and all their exotic mixtures in his mouth. He paid attention to the coffee, and when they had finished supper he experienced himself getting up and saying he guessed he better get on up the hill and get his animals fed —— and watered — before it got dark.

He thanked Roxie for the supper, and Leonard thanked D.R. for the work. D.R. paid attention to Leonard's face and voice when he said it. Leonard offered to pay D.R. but D.R. said oh no. I owe you that much.

Leonard said, Well, when I get a little time I'll come up and give you a hand.

I'll be needing it, D.R. said.

Come down and go to church with us tomorrow if you want to, David, said Roxie.

D.R. said he didn't think he would, but he thanked her for inviting him.

We'll see you later then, said Leonard.

Yeah, said D.R. Good night, you all.

And he left then. He got home with just enough daylight left to do his chores.

Conscientious Guide to Drug Abuse

I'd call this THE BOOK to have around if you or anyone in your family is doing drugs. It has kind, quick, accurate advice.

—SB

Conscientious Guide to Drug Abuse
Vic Pawlak
1973; 48 pp.
$1.00

from:
Do It Now Foundation
6136 Carlos Ave.
Hollywood, CA 90028

or WHOLE EARTH CATALOG

quantity orders for resale from:
National Media Center
P.O. Box 5115
Phoenix, Az 85010

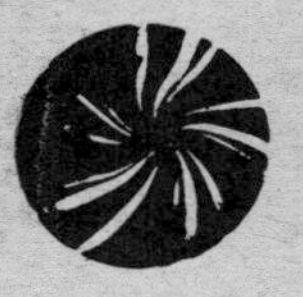

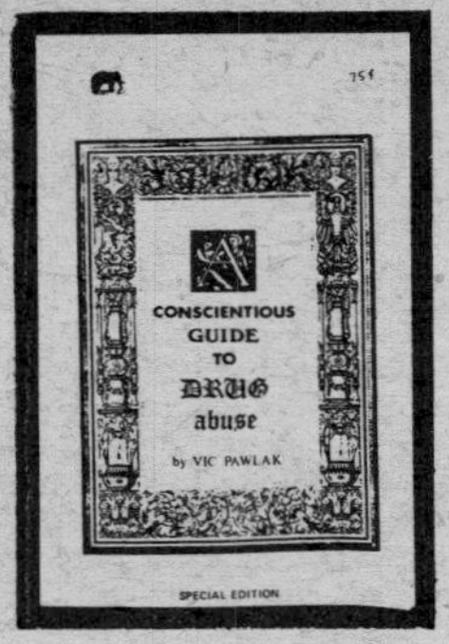

BUM TRIPS

One of the prime factors inherent in acid is the possibility of incurring a bum trip. This possibility has kept many from tripping. Over the past several years in particular, it has been nearly impossible to obtain pure acid. Most stuff is mafia-originated and cut heavily with speed and/or strychnine (rat poison). Under clinical circumstances, bum trips rarely occur unless provoked. But *when acid contains strychnine, speed or other impurities, the possibility of a bummer increases tremendously.*

The best advice to give straight or inexperienced people about dealing with bum trips is: Don't panic. Be gentle, kind, and smile a lot. If necessary to avert a traumatic chains of events, divert the person with pleasant music or a change of atmosphere (like turning off or on the lights). Most bum trips could have been prevented if the right information was only known by the person's friends ahead of time.

Clinically, Thorazine (a strong tranquilizer) has often been used to relieve the effects of a bum trip. Thorazine works by tranquilizing the system and relieving the built-up tension. Lately the use of Niacinamide has become popular in relieving bummers; this substance, buffered by Niacin or Vitamin B3, chemically changes LSD to another lysergic substance that has no effect on the body or mind.

It seems unlikely that the availability or legal staus of LSD will be changed significantly in the next few years. Slowly, as the practical uses are realized, there may be a loosening of restrictions regarding research with the drug. At best, acid may soon be recognized as a legitimate, useful chemical to be given only under careful supervision...

•

SPEED KILLS. It's true. People have been taking speed ever since it was developed before World War II. How many people have you ever met who have been taking Speed for as much as 10 years? 6 years? A few 3 and 4 year veterans are around, but not in very good shape.

Even smack addicts have a longer life span.

Speed kills. The reason most kids don't notice it is because they have young, healthy bodies that can take a lot of stress and strain before they finally give in. Speed activates the entire body and forces it to race at high rates of speed for long periods of time. The larger the dose, the greater the strain. The smaller the dose, the smaller the strain. This is why Speed can be legitimately prescribed in minute doses (in diet pills, pep pills, etc.), for several months without apparent harm. A lot of speed puts a great strain on the entire circulatory system and often causes aneurism (ballooning) in the arteries or vessels.

Appetite is non-existant. Food is a big drag and it is almost impossible to eat solids. Sleep is also very difficult, if not impossible, during the run. Both lack of appetite and inability to sleep are side effects of speed; the body becomes very wasted when no nourishment or chance for sleep-rejuvenation takes place.

The liver and kidneys, which filter impurities from the system, are forced to over-work. This creates a situation which like operating a complex water pump and filter system without water. It just burns up.

Because of the massive stimulation of the nervous sytem by Amphetamines and because appetite and sleep patterns are disturbed, an eventual state of toxic psychosis often occurs. This is usually charcterized by hallucinations, tremendous panic or fear reactions, with added waves of despondency and depression. During this period it is extremely tempting to avoid the hard comedown by shooting up again or dropping more speed. By the third or forth day of continuous use the chemical starts taking over, everything seems unimportant.

Speed actually enables years of ageing and deterioration to be squeezed into a few weeks or months.

In addition, Speed freaks often suffer an acute state of paranoia. Friends who used to take Speed imagined that people were staring at them through windows and whenever they weren't looking. The natural uneasiness-nervousness that comes from Speed is intensified by fear of getting caught or busted.

Kids who are on Speed make a big mistake that is common to this and other hard drug users. The more Speed they take, the more their heads get messed up *anyway*, and take more speed to alleviate the anxiety caused by intense confusion. Of course, the end result is only increased confusion, anxiety, and decreased mental capacies. Another proven effect of Speed is eventual damage to brain functions; people who once had full control of the English language find themselves unable to remember proper words, and even have difficulty in speaking. Not all hard drugs will do this-----but Speed will.

IN CASE OF SPEED OVERDOSE

Hospitalization is almost never necessary. The person will be *very* wired at first, eventually leveling off after several hours. Speed may be very dangerous for those with heart defects.

Besides long-term dangers of Speed itself, there are several dangers associated with using needles for the injection of the drug. The most common of these, *hepatitis*, will be discussed here:

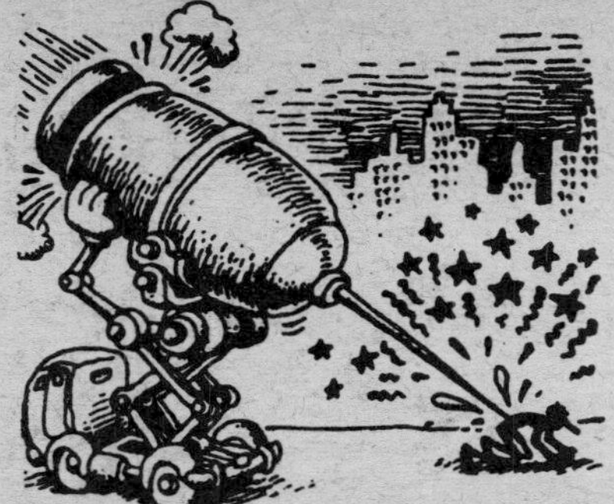

HEPATITIS

The common form of hepatitis is "viral hepatitis", caused by an unclean needle or contamination of the drug being injected. There is nausea, loss of appetite, possible vomiting, and usually a feeling of being ill similar to the flu, but on a heavier scale. Following this, jaundice, yellowing of the skin and eyes, usually occurs. After a period of weeks to months, the patient feels fairly well. But the extensive cost and good care involved with such a rehabilitation are usually too much for the average speed freak to afford.

Research that is being done suggests that the average case of hepatitis among speed users is of a more chronic type. Weeks and even months after recovery from hepatitis, blood tests from the liver show high abnormality. It may be that a more chronic disease state is still occurring; cirrhosis of the liver has been suggested by one researcher. Cirrhosis also occurs in some alcoholics; normal liver tissue dies or is choked by other, non-functioning tissue...

•

ALCOHOL

Classification: Depressant.

Overdose potential: Possible, when taken in sufficient amounts or mixed with Barbiturates.

Physical addiction: Yes.

Common methods of consumption: Ingested, liquid form.

Notes:

Alcohol is a depressant; in chemistry and pharmacology, it resembles chloral hydrate and paraldehyde.

The pitfalls are many and varied. It is among the most dangerous drugs in existence, ranking in the category of Speed, Barbiturates and hard narcotics. An estimated 6 to 7 million Americans are chronic alcoholics, or one out of 30.

The American Pharmaceutical Association, in their pamplet on "Drug Abuse Education," credits alcohol with causing "acute and chronic intoxication, habituation, physical dependence and addiction. Withdrawal symptoms (delirium tremens) result when alcohol is discontinued."

Because of the extent of the alcohol problem in the US and elsewhere, a great deal is known about treatment and cure of alcoholics. For more information or assistance, contact your local chapter of Alcoholics Anonymous.

Medical Uses: As mentioned earlier, alcohol and hashish were once used as an anasthetic during open surgery with reasonable success. Before either was widely available, alcohol was sometimes used medicinally. (Remember the Old West doctors in the movies?)

Alcohol is extremely dangerous when taken with most Barbiturates because it heightens action of the pills so much that it can create an overdose.

Magically Aborting Unwelcome Trips

About acid bummers &c.:

Assume that human beings are energy devices. Assume that your right hand is a positive pole, your left a negative (vice versa if you're left-handed). Assume that headaches, bummers & the like are symptoms of minor disturbances in energy flow. (These assumptions are not necessarily true. Just a useful metaphor, a convenient way to think, that works.)

To cure a headache, place your positive hand at the base of the sufferer's skull and your negative hand on his forehead. Imagine there is a current flowing through his head from your positive hand to your negative hand, and that this current causes the flow in the sufferer's head to straighten out & flow right, thus terminating his headache. This takes from 5 to 30 seconds.

This works, whether the operator believes it will or not, and regardless of what the sufferer believes. (Beautiful cries of "My God! It's GONE!" are commonplace.) The only requirement is the act of imagination. If you imagine it'll work, it works.

I've used the same process on about 50 acid bummers so far, with 100% success. Variations can be invented freely to suit various circumstances.

This is traditionally called "Magnetic Healing." I prefer to call it & related phenomena "Energy Transactions." Very useful in Magick & other western yogas.

Invent your own techniques. Please tell me what happens.

Relief is probably symptomatic, but saves on aspirin & similar crap.

Chester Anderson
Los Angeles, CA

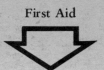

First Aid

Chemically Aborting Unwelcome Trips

The following is excerpted from a pamphlet by Naturalism, Inc., Box 8318, Chicago, Illinois. L.S.D. Rescue in Chicago is doing a phenomenal service by researching dope at the same time they're cooling bummers. Nowhere else have I seen detailed reviews of the various drugs available in the street ("THUNDER. Grey and black speckled. The Dope is saturated on strychnine pellets. It's a bad trip. BLACK DOMES. Double-domed— dynamite— good tabs.")

—SB

ABORTIVE MEASURES:

Stimulants— Give Ascorbic Acid (vitamin C) 3-6 gr; this absorbs Amphetamine in the bloodstream. Also 7 tbls. Accent (meat tenderizer) or 5 gr. Glutamic acid to relax muscles. Sedatives (Barbituate) and tranquilizers may be used to control excess stimulants.

Depresents— (Barbituates, alcohol, Tranquilizers, and narcotics). Keep persons awake by physical shaking and/or hot & cold showers. Give Caffeine, or coffee, or amphetamine if available. Maintain vital signs, i.e., pulse, blood pressure, respiration. Opiates (Heroin) may be absorbed with Lorfan (3mg-2mg. I.V. or subcut.) or Nalline.

Cannabis (Marijuana, Hash, T.H.C.) Raise blood sugar by giving honey, sugar water, maple syrup. 4-10 oz. sugar water. This causes hyperglycemia which sedates the person. Mild tranquilizers may be used to relax persons in extreme situations. "Accent" is also effective.

Serotonin type drugs— (LSD, DMT, Psilocybin) Give Niacin (B3) 1 gr./50 lbs. body weight to stop hallucinations within 40 min. Prescription abortants include: Valium 5-25mg., Vistaril 25-200 mg., Librium 10-100 mg., Seconal 100-100 mg., Carbrital 3/4-3 gr. Also "Accent" 7 tbls., is effective.

Adrenalin (Belladonna, scopalamine) Treat symptoms— give fluids to counteract dehydration. Take temperature often and bring down all fever over 104 degrees with alcohol rubs. Watch the person until the drug has worn off. In case of severe crisis (cholinergic) give physostigmine salicylate I.M. or orally 2-4mg.

Miscellaneous— (Glue) Restore consciousness if necessary. This usually occurs when fresh air is supplied to the person. Artificial respiration may be necessary. If person is conscious, have him inhale some alcohol to break down the glue.

Darvon— Treat symptoms; induce vomiting; if person convulses and respiration is depressed, give nalorphine and/or levallorphan. DO NOT GIVE AMPHETAMINE OR CAFFEINE as these will cause convulsions.

Peace Acid— Treat symptoms. Give 5g Glutamic acid to help person relax.

NOTES: Situations in which a persons life appears to be threatened are handled by a doctor or hospital. Emergency wards are much better equipped to maintain vital functions, i.e., heart, heat, and respiration, and have technical facilities more efficient than those found in the home stomach pumping and analysis of drug while most drug problems can be handled by empathetic and assuring trained friends or counselors, problems such as toxic drug overdoseage and poisoning may require professional medical care. Always when possible inform the victim when you feel that hospital attention is vital.

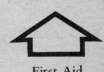

First Aid

Megavitamin Therapy

More on niacin and its curing powers on p. 211.

Psychedelic Guide to the Preparation of the Eucharist

This is a thoroughly unusual as well as an unusually thorough collection of details concerning the preparation of a number of hallucinogenic substances. There are an initial few pages that editorialize on the legal and ethical aspects of psychedelic drug usage (and some argument might be taken with the proposed dose schedules) but little fault can be found with the detailed recipes and techniques that constitute the bulk of the book. There is provided the do-it-yourself details for everything from organic gardening to organic synthesis.

On the botanical side of things, a number of comments are given concerning the growing of marijuana and its conversion to hashish or red oil. Far more unusual and interesting however are the procedures for the setting up of appropriate fungal culture media for the surface growth of Psilocybe *mycelia (for the production of psilocybin) and* Claviceps *in submerged systems (for the production of the lysergic acid precursor to LSD). Also along the nature line, the isolation of mescaline and other alkaloids from Peyote is described in extreme detail.*

Within the synthetic preparation of various substances, there is some unevenness. The preparation directions for tetrahydrocannabinol (THC) are sketchy; the details for the formation of precursors such as olivetol are clear, but the final steps are presented in outline only. It is doubtful that anyone without some chemical sophistication could successfully follow the procedures, and such a person would certainly have access to the original literature. The synthesis of mescaline, however, is described in adequate detail and several alternate processes are offered. The various indoles (psilocin, DMT and DET) are covered in good detail. Special note must be made of the section on LSD. The conversion of lysergic acid into LSD, and the final purification of the product, is given in exquisite detail. It is doubtful that such a thoroughly exacting account has ever previously been published.

A number of references are made to the scientific literature that will certainly help in filling out the missing fine points. Directions are at hand for the construction of a number of laboratory utensils, but these fall short of sufficient. The suggested modification of a refrigerator will probably not lead to a vacuum pump adequate for the described preparation of red oil from crude marijuana extract.

Finally there are warnings and admonitions advanced to the reader such as the naming of chemicals that are on the federal watched list. Of course, these chemicals to be avoided are to a large measure those that are required for the successful pursuit of the projects described in the book. This paradox is recognized by the editor, who states:

> *"It must be clearly pointed out that many things throughout this manual have recently become unlawful and no one should ever break the law. Therefore, anyone attempting to pursue the course outlined herein (in countries where prohibited) must be willing to shoulder the burden of persecution which may fall upon him. Since the religious user and chemist are unfortunately not immune to legal retribution, the editors sincerely hope that no one will be forced to martyr himself for his incorrect use of this guide-book"*

All in all this is a charming book, pleasantly illustrated, that should serve at least as an engaging conversation piece in most households.

Metacelsus

Psychedelic Guide to Preparation of the Eucharist
Robert E. Brown
1968; 60 pp.

OR WHOLE EARTH CATALOG

Linga Sharira Incense Co.
Box 4374
Austin, Texas 78765

$5.50 postpaid

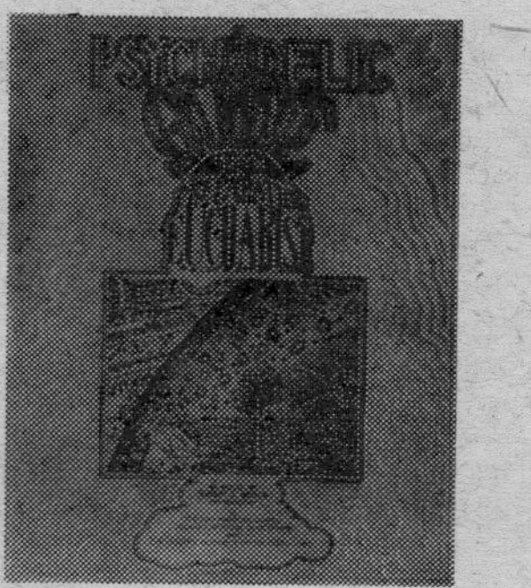

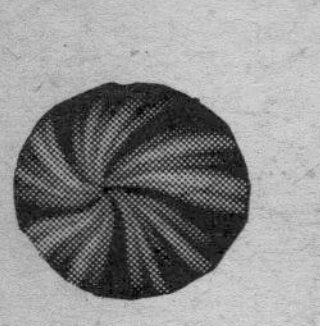

Preparation 2

Step I---Use Yellow Light

5.36 g of d-lysergic acid are suspended in 125 ml of acetonitrile and the suspension cooled to about -20 degrees C in a bath of acetone cooled with dry ice. To the suspension is added a cold (-20 degrees) solution of 8.82 g of trifluroroacetic anhydride in 75ml of acetonitrile. The mixture is allowed to stand at -20 degrees for about 1½ hours during which time the suspended material dissolves, and the d-lysergic acid is converted to the mixed anhydride of lysergic and trifluoroacetic acids. The mixed anhyride can be separated in the form of an oil by evaporating the solvent in vacuo at a temperature below about 0 degrees. Everything must be kept anydrous.

Step II---Use Red Light

The solution of mixed anhydrides in acetontrile from Step I is added to 150ml of acetonitrile containing 7.6 g of diethylamine. The mixture is held in the dark at room temperature for about 2 hours. The acetonitrile is evaporated in vacuo, leaving a residue of LSD-25 plus other impurities. The residue is dissolved in 150ml of choroform and 20ml of ice water. The chloroform layer is removed and the aqueous portions are combined and in turn, washed with four 50ml portions of ice-cold water. The chloroform solution is then dried over anhydrous Na_2SO_4 and evaporated in vacuo.

Figure 1

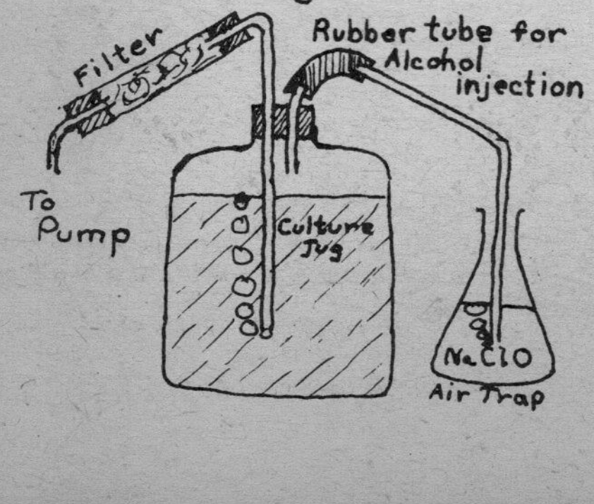
Filter
Rubber tube for Alcohol injection
To Pump
Culture Jug
NaClO
Air Trap

More dope on p. 210 and p. 62.

Psychedelic Review

***The Psychedelic Review** is back. It had stopped publication for over a year but — like its godfather Tim Leary — it is alive and well in a new location. Once again it arises to fill the gap between the bio-chemical abstracts and the yellow journalism treatments of psychedelic experience.*

The review has been the place to look if you were seriously interested in drug usage, drug effects, drug theories, and drug-oriented art and poetry. The word psychedelic, *once limited to drug-induced experience, now has expanded to include other altered states. The review has expanded as well. The latest issue has articles on the world of spirits, the use of pot in curbing alcoholism, LSD as preparation for death, and a multi-faceted view of Tim Leary's present position. Leary, Baba Ram Dass, and Leary's lawyer contribute ideas and reflections.*

***The Psychedelic Review** is the only journal to treat the literary, the scientific, and the spiritual aspects of psychedelic experience equally well. Its return is good news.*

[Reviewed by James A. Fadiman]

The Psychedelic Review
Robert Mogas, ed.

$7.50/ year (quarterly)

from:
The Psychedelic Review
4034 20th Street
San Francisco, California 94114

By an extraordinary series of circumstances a confirmation appears to have been found for one of Emanuel Swedenborg's more unusual doctrines — that man's life depends on his relationship to a hierarchy of spirits. Out of my professional role as a clinical psychologist in a state mental hospital and my own personal interest, I set out to describe as faithfully as possible mental patients' experiences of hallucinations. A discovery four years ago helped me to get a relatively rich and consistent picture of the patients' experience. Though I noticed similarities with Swedenborg's description of the relationships of man to spirits it was only three years after all the major findings on hallucinations had been made that the striking similarity between what Twentieth-Century patients describe and Swedenborg's Eighteenth-Century accounts became apparent to me. I then collected as many details as possible of his description. I found that Swedenborg's system not only is an almost perfect fit with patients' experiences, but even more impressively, accounts for otherwise quite puzzling aspects of hallucinations. I will first describe how I worked and my findings, and then relate this to Swedenborg's work.

•

It would appear that for selected alcoholics the substitution of smoked cannabis for alcohol may be of marked rehabilitative value. The drug effect of cannabis, as compared with alcohol, while having a sense of euphoria and detachment in common, lacks any other similarity except the intent for which it is taken. Excessive alcohol use produces a predictable weakening and dissolution of various superego and ego functions, whereas cannabis does not seem to have this attribute, providing, if anything, an increase in ego strength. Because cannabis does not facilitate ego alien behavior as seen with alcoholic excess, a great burden of guilt if removed, thus freeing the individual for more constructive pursuits.

The fact that cannabis did not produce symptoms of irritability upon withdrawal, nor effects on the gastrointestinal tract, as compared with alcohol, also assists in the rehabilitation of the individual. Since he is not physically sick any more, he is thus free to begin resocialization with the expansion of his consciousness to perceive the subtleties of the world beyond his needs for immediate gratification or succor. Certainly cannabis is not a panacea, but it warrants further clinical trial in selected cases of alcoholism.

DOSAGE BY WEIGHT

Drug	Light High	Experienced User	Normal	First Psychedelic	Maximum safe dose
LSD	20-50 μg	100-200 μg	300 μg	400-800 μg	1000-3000 μg
THC	1 mg	2.5 mg	5 mg	10 mg	20 mg
STP	5 mg	10 mg	22 mg	35 mg	50 mg
DMT	5-10 mg	20-30 mg	40 mg	50-60 mg	100 mg
Psilocyn	5-10 mg	20-30 mg	35 mg	40-60 mg	150 mg
Mescaline	50-200 mg	300-500 mg	400 mg	600-800 mg	1000 mg

The very light doses only give a feeling of well-being and seldom cause much hallucination. The experienced user can achieve the psychedelic effect with less of a dose, grading off to no drug at all. A person trying to experience the full psychedelic effect for the first time needs to be disconnected much more fully, therefore the larger dose. The largest doses cause a complete break with reality that few can handle pleasantly. The slight toxic side effects are not a major factor in considering the dosage because the hallucinogenic effects are so much more overwhelming at those high doses that other factors are minimized. The crude natural substances are not listed here because the amount of drug available does not follow any reliable weight percentage as the quality of these substances is not at all constant.

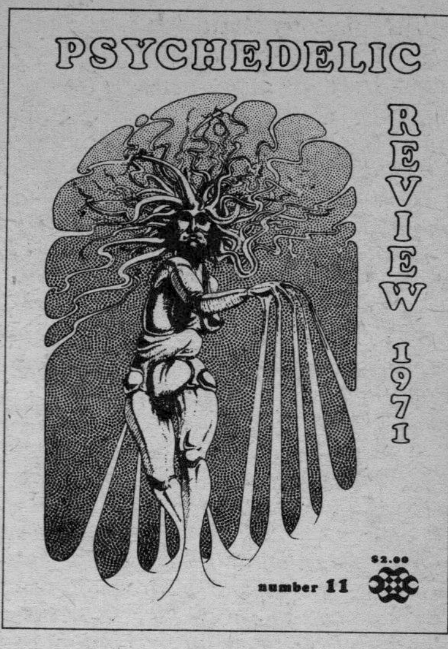
PSYCHEDELIC
REVIEW
1971
number 11
$2.00

Hemp

Hard work, but we must get there too. Also we must stop being such *heads* and learn the art of the follow-through. "Where were you? Why weren't you there? Why were you so late? Why didn't you finish it? Why don't you remember?" Hemp is a tool, not a separate universe.

Rō-non-so-te

Marijuana Review

Good current information on pot, especially towards its legalization. Research, reform, news.

—SB

Marijuana Review
Michael Aldrich, ed.

$1 per issue; or $3/4 issues

from:
Amorphia
Box 744
Mill Valley, CA 94941

STASH

Means Students Association for the Study of Hallucinogens, Very thorough, sometimes academic, information on drugs.

—SB

STASH Press
118 S. Bedford
Madison, Wisconsin 53703

When the British government was investigating the effects of marijuana on the Indian populace in the 1890's, they conducted a series of biological experiments with monkeys. One animal was trained to smoke a combination of marijuana and *Datura* and was allowed to continue this practice for a number of months. The monkey was then sacrificed and the autopsy revealed abnormally soft cerebral matter, while the other parts of the brain were in various stages of decomposition. None of these effects were seen in those monkeys trained to smoke only marijuana, and the doctors concluded that *Datura*, when used over a prolonged period of time, can directly cause organic brain damage.

•

It seems a sad commentary on the state of the present "psychedelic subculture" that the very practices of the establishment which are criticized as hypocritical (a lack of "truth in packaging" and the slick merchandizing techniques of Madison Avenue) are the same practices employed by the purveyors of our chemical sacraments. When television sells Middle America an electric toothbrush, it does not sell the toothbrush, but an entire way of living (of which the toothbrush is but one small component). In much the same manner the dealer who offers his clientele a plethora of "mind-altering goodies" (from 4-way "sunshines" to speckled psilocybin "pumpkin seeds") performs as much a disservice to the "contra-culture." Unwary and inexperienced buyers are being led to believe that if they haven't been "stoned" with Dealer X's acid, then they've never been "stoned." A mind washed in one dealer's mescaline is purported to be "whiter than white" while the head of the unfortunate user of brand X seems to display the same old discouraging collar stains. "New" and "improved" preparations are being hawked with all the fervor of the quack who sells us Anacin® on the tube.

Scores of underground chemists who have discovered that the *Life* magazine claim that anyone who received a B in high school chemistry can make good, pure LSD is a myth, have compensated by spiking their concoctions with everything from amphetamines to belladonna alkaloids. The powerful financial incentives associated with the manufacture and sale of illicit psychedelics have, unfortunately, attracted the same types of unscrupulous merchandizers who have grown rich convincing us to buy cars that are unsafe, diet drinks that cause cancer and a frightening variety of status symbols that are of no human use. As a result, many of the "freaks" who have gotten involved with the psychedelic scene in the past few years may have never had a real LSD experience. It is not difficult to comprehend the increasing cynicism of the "flower children" as they are manipulated and possibly even poisoned by people taking advantage of their implicit trust in others.

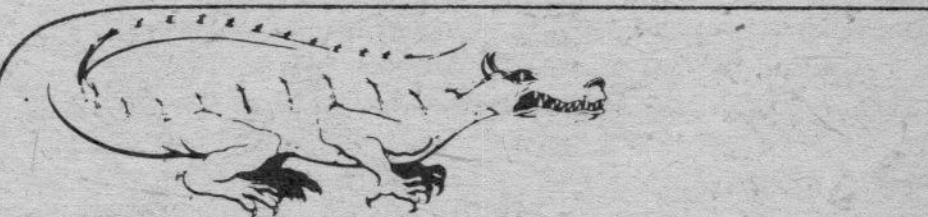

SUNDAY: THE MINE

Walking, body jolting, downhill. It's Sunday morning now and D.R. is on his way to explore the old abandoned coal mine he'd freaked out in his first day back at Trace Fork. It's been on his mind for several days to do it, to crawl back in with a light of some kind and get a real look at that place. He has passed the ruins of the tipple every time he has gone in or out of the hollow; but until this morning he has always been on some specific errand or other, and there has been no chance to stop and look around.

But it's Sunday now, his day of rest and leisure. D.R. slept till almost ten, fixed himself some eggs and fried a slice of green tomato for breakfast, and now at about the hour the other people of the community are gathering for Sunday worship at the church, D.R. has set out from the house with this very special destination in mind.

There were other things in D.R.'s mind too as he jolted down the hill, but they were bouncing around in such a chaos of broken images he wasn't paying them much attention. Pictures of the day before with Leonard, working, were vivid, and entirely pleasant to see: Leonard wiping sweat off his face, and grinning; the way the long one-by-sixes formed angles with the upright posts; and then an image of the finished pen itself, a space enclosed; all of those were pleasant scenes to see. But they flashed and flickered and jumped around so fast D.R. couldn't hold to any single one long enough to bring it into focus.

Shots from further in the past than yesterday were mixed in too. He caught a glimpse of himself walking out of Trace Fork years ago, a child among a group of people on their way to church on Sunday morning.

And then he saw Estelle lying on her back on that big rock where they'd made love that time, by the river.

He heard the sound that cars make when they pass real fast, that sudden whooshing of the wind, and he caught a glimpse of cactus by the roadside on some desert he had travelled in a car.

The Hallucinogens

You wouldn't nose out onto the freeway if you didn't know how to drive, and you damn well shouldn't go playing "eat me" and "drink me" unless you know what you're about. Here, in a book ostensibly for the medical profession, is the whole story to date: Hoffer and Osmond know more about this field than anyone else in the world, and their aim is to investigate it further. Osmond is one of the unsung sages of our times, working quietly in his own way to find out the nature of human nature. (He is a leading researcher into schizophrenia, the coiner of the word "psychedelic", the doctor who gave Huxley his mescalin, and is into a hundred other interesting things, including the reliability of the Jungian personality types. There are at least a few pages on every hallucinogen you've ever heard of, and on a lot you haven't; e.g.: the "dream fish" kyphosus fuscus, *and the plants the ancient Norse used to induce the state of "berserk" (and why it became, among themselves, illegal.) Where previous experimenters have used themselves as guinea-pigs, their diaries are reprinted, e.g.: Wasson's trips with* psilocyba *mushrooms. In most cases, Osmond has tried the stuff himself; and he is a very patient, understanding and aware guinea-pig indeed. For people who remember their college chemistry, the molecular diagrams are here, for people who want to read more an exhaustive index shows you the way. This is a source book of knowledge, but by the by Osmond has two main observations of a philosophical nature: 1) man has been looking for hallucinogens from the beginning, and has been finding them, and 2) you don't get something for nothing. You can believe this man; he has smoked with the best of them, and popped things into his mouth that haven't been tried in a few centuries.*

Warning: not reading this book may be injurious to your health.

[Suggested and reviewed by Stephan Chodorov]

The Hallucinogens
A. Hoffer and H. Osmond
1967; 626 pp.

$27.50 postpaid

from:
Academic Press
111 Fifth Avenue
New York, N. Y. 10003

or WHOLE EARTH CATALOG

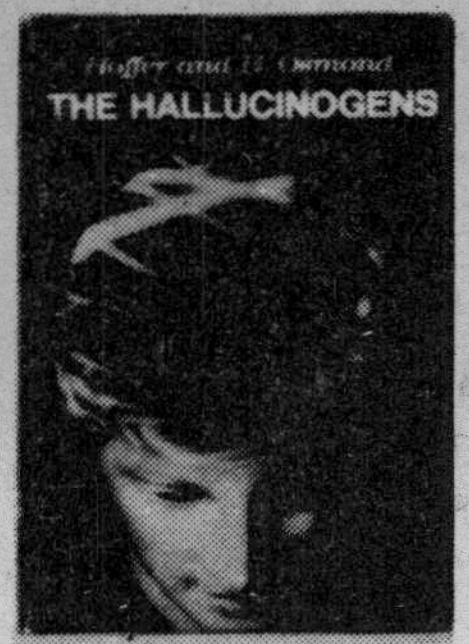

Perhaps nutmeg pastry is popular because of the myristicin it contains. A feeling of well-being, following the ingestion of these cakes, might easily lead to a conditioned reaction to this pastry. In the same way it is likely that adrenoxyl is used by surgeons because of the feeling of well-being it induces in their patients, and not because it is a valuable hemostatic agent (Hoffer and Osmond, 1960). The euphorient or relaxant properties of nutmeg and of myristicin should be examined carefully. Too little attempt has been made by modern man to discover safe plant antitension and euphorient remedies.

•

There is a difference between LSD and other hallucinogenic compounds. LSD seems in small doses to act as a stimulant not unlike amphetamines, in larger doses it seems to possess a depressant effect. Other hallucinogenic compounds tend to have depressant effects at all the dose levels.

•

We had, as we later learned, merely hit upon a solution to alcoholism which the Native American Church of North America, or its antecedent groups, had used long before. According to Slotkin (1956) the Indians believed peyote took away the desire for strong drink and claimed that hundreds of drunkards had been "dragged from their downward way." The small band of Indians in Saskatchewan who allowed us to observe their ceremonies one night, explained that their religion based upon God and the use of peyote to reach Him included three important principles: (a) The member must be a good man, (b) he must educate himself, and (c) he must not drink. Thus we can only conclude that the peyote religion is the chief variable. Several Indians related to us how they had achieved sobriety only after this church.

Acorus calamus is a plant known in Asia, Europe, and North America for its medicinal properties. It was also known as flag root, rat root, and sweet calomel. During the great depression of the 1930's it was chewed in England by people unable to buy tobacco.

Recently one of our informants well acquainted with the habits of the Indians of northern Canada, reported his personal experiences with rat root collected in northern Alberta by the Cree. He reported that nearly all the Indians over age 40 used rat root regularly but the younger Indians were unfamiliar with it and its use was discouraged by physicians who practiced there. Rat root users seemed to be healthier, and were not subject to alcoholism. The Indians used rat root (a) as an antifatigue medicine (they chewed about 1 inch of the dried root which had a diameter equal to a pencil); (b) as an analgesic for relieving toothache, headache, etc; (c) for relief of asthma; (d) for oral hygiene, and (e) to relieve hangover.

Our informant had over the years tested these medicinal qualities and generally confirmed them. It was particularly effective for alleviating fatigue. On one occasion, he walked 12 miles in the northern woods to fight a forest fire. He was out of condition and was exhausted at the end of the march. He chewed and swallowed 2 inches of rat root. Within 10 minutes the fatigue vanished and on the return march he seemed to be walking 1 foot above the ground and felt wonderful. The effect was very unlike amphetamine. On his return home he was very exhausted but after a night's sleep was normal.

•

LSD was used not only in "Island," but in Chicago to relieve pain. It has powerful analgesic properties. Kast and Collins (1964) gave LSD to a group of patients many of whom knew they were dying of terminal cancer. In addition to their relief from pain some of the patients developed a peculiar disregard for the gravity of their situation. They spoke freely of their impending death with much less depression than they had had previously. The newer attitude to death lasted much longer than the analgesic action. It is likely those who have a visionary, psychedelic or transcendental reaction may equate this with life after death. This would account for the new more beneficial frame of mind for those patients who were dying.
One of our subjects recently told us that since his psychedelic experience several years ago, he no longer feared death.

•

The bark of the root of *Tabernanthe iboga* contains about 12 alkaloids (Downing, 1962). Of these the best known is ibogaine, a tryptamine derivative. This plant, named in 1889 by Baillon, was used by the natives of West Africa and the Congo to increase resistance against fatigue and tiredness and as an aphrodisiac. Dybowski and Landrin (1901) extracted the psychologically active alkaloid which they named ibogaine. They reported that the natives considered the plant equivalent or similar to alcohol, that it was a stimulant which did not disturb the thought processes of the user.

Psychedelics

A fine collection of the best papers by the man who coined the word psychedelic. Some good research got done before the Federal ban.

—SB

Psychedelics
Bernard Aaronson, Humphrey Osmond, eds.
1970; 512 pp.

$2.45 postpaid

from:
Doubleday & Company, Inc.
501 Franklin Avenue
Garden City, N.Y. 11530

or WHOLE EARTH CATALOG

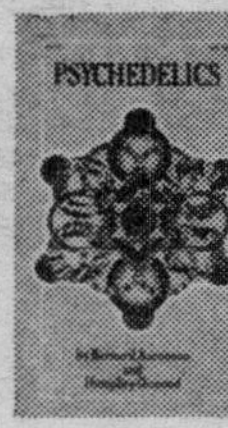

Once out of the water, I started climbing the mountain on a sacred pilgrimage. I stopped to examine small flowers and brightly colored rocks. I picked the flowers, putting them in my hair. The world shone with the joy of existence.

Again on level ground, I ran along, feeling Indian things. With virtually no plant growth in sight, I was hacking my way through jungles. I saw visions of snake gods, and received stories to take to my people. When I looked down to the oasis below, my friends, the others there, the wind caressing the water — all poignantly symbolized the human condition. Everybody should have a chance to see this vast panorama of man's existence on earth. To see the tides of nature, as I did then, seems an overwhelmingly marvelous thing in itself.

—Peter Stafford

•

Shortly after this my fellow observers left for what must have been twenty minutes or so, but it could have been as many centuries. I stayed behind with the Indians, and I became part of the worshipers. I entered their world, where for generation upon generation they had hunted the buffalo. They had lived with and on the buffalo. They were of one piece. They were the buffalo. Their lives were part of those shaggy lumbering herd beasts whose myriads roamed the great plains. On these wide prairies, where trees and hills are almost equally scarce, sound often conveyed as much as sight. So the Indians call up their past with song, with drum, and with rattle. For them, minute alterations of rhythm and pace evoke ever-changing images. Because we cannot hear as they do, the drumming and rattling seem endlessly repetitive to us. The drumming was the steady running of a man with his dog padding beside him. It was the pawing and thudding of buffalo hooves crescendoing in thunder. It was the gentle crumpling of dung falling or the soft plop of a calf dropping on turf, soundless, yet heard by the hunter. The gourd evoked the endlessly sifting wind, catching at scrub and grass as it passed. It was the hissing of an arrow as it leaves the bow or snakes by one's head in battle. It was the sizzling of buffalo meat grilling on the campfire and the creak of a hide tepee as the blizzard twists and whirls around it. The drumming was life and death, scarlet blood spurting from a stricken buffalo or from a fallen warrior. Yet it was also the first fluttering of a child inside its mother. As he sang, a young man wept, and Frank Takes Gun said, "Shed tears on mother earth that the Universal God may take pity on him."

When my friends returned, I felt that the Indians and I were one and that, for a little time, or more accurately, a different sort of time, I was of their world rather than that of my colleagues, their conquerers. It was not simply that I realized they had a point of view I could respect, but that I felt in my bones as they felt in theirs. Looking back, I do not believe that this was an illusion, for I continued to be much more aware of their way of looking at things. But how could one prove such an opinion — without fine instruments for measuring a man's system of values.

—Humphrey Osmond

•

Mr. Russell had the blackdrum passed to him. He sucked a little water from it, tautened the hide, and smoothed it with a caress. Frank Takes Gun explained the next part of the ceremony. "You have only seen three last night — the leader, the drummer, and the fireman. Now you will see the fourth. Thank God we have lived to see another day. We represent our lives: we don't imitate anything. The foundations of human life rest with our mothers who delivered us into this world." The Mother stepped into the tepee through the door flap, announced by the shrilling of the eagle's-bone whistle. She sat down by the white enamel waterpot. The tepee was dim, the fire was low, but some wisps of smoke rising from it seemed to surround her. She had a red blanket around her shoulders, a blue dress, smooth black hair, and her face seemed very broad. She was greeted by a song of welcome with voices, drum, and rattle. With the singing, she became superb mother earth, mother prairie, grass, cow buffalo, mare, and doe, the epitome of motherhood. The drum beating was not restful or sleep inducing. It was the fecund pulsing of sex, passion, generation, and death, sung without guilt and without self-consciousness. The mother was weary, patient, tender, butenduring. She stood behind all the men — drummer, fire tender, leader. In front of her were the waters of life and death.

Frank addressed her in the highest falsetto, a tearing, almost noiseless scream, the cry of the tiniest baby or of an old man breathing his last. It was unbearable. The mother could have been any age — maid, mother, or crone, from sixteen to a hundred sixteen.

"You have been good to us while we were here. You worked hard and made this possible. God knows we worship Him. God knows we respect the mothers of our children."

•

The happy, oceanic feeling so often experienced by normal subjects was also evident among preterminal patients. It could be noted up to twelve days following the administration of LSD . . . A certain change in philosophic and religious approach to dying took place that is not reflected in the numerical data presented here . . . Real terror experienced upon the contemplation of death in preterminal patients, as well as in normals, consists of fear of the loss of control of internal functions and environmental influences. It is self-evident that control can be achieved only to a very limited degree, but this small degree of control has enormous survival value. In conjunction with this actually very limited ability to influence internal and external events, goes a fantasy-feeling of power to shape one's fate and an adult elaboration of the infantile feeling of omnipotence and omnipresence. The realization of imminent death obviously deals a heavy blow to that fantasy.

During and after LSD administration, acceptance and surrender to the inevitable loss of control were noted; and this control is anxiously maintained and fought for in non-drugged patients. LSD administration apparently eases the blow that impending death deals to the fantasy of infant omnipotence, not necessarily by augmenting the infantile process, but by relieving the mental apparatus of the compelling need to maintain the infantile fantasy. Parallel to the general improvement in the patient's feelings, mood, and conflict situation, sleep patterns improved for approximately twelve to fourteen days . . .

The results of this study seem to indicate that LSD is not only capable of improving the lot of preterminal patients by making them more responsive to their environment and family, but it also enhances their ability to appreciate the subtle and aesthetic nuances of experience. This increased delicate sensitivity is as marked as that usually encountered in normal volunteers subjected to LSD. Here, however, this imagery not only gives aesthetic satisfaction, but creates a new will to live and a zest for experience that, against a background of dismal darkness and preoccupying fear, produces an exciting and promising outlook. Patients who had been listless and depressed were touched to tears by the discovery of a depth of feeling of which they had not thought themselves capable. Although short-lived and transient, this happy state of affairs was a welcome change in their monotonous and isolated lives, and recollection of this experience days later often created similar elation. Of course, these subtleties cannot be appraised in numerical terms. In human terms, however, the short but profound impact of LSD on the dying patient was impressive.

—Eric C. Kast

•

The recent impassioned discussions of the possible effects of LSD on chromosomes is paralleled by similar discussions over masturbation. It was stated with the utmost confidence that not only would the secret vice result in the collapse and insanity of those who practiced it, but should they be unfortunate enough to survive to adulthood, their children would suffer for their sins. There was no evidence for this, but it did not prevent men of the highest integrity from stating that it was undoubtedly so.

•

While not everyone might choose to die with his mind stimulated by LSD, as did Aldous Huxley (Huxley, L.A., 1968), rather than dulled by morphine, such matters call for careful consideration, for each of us owes God a death.

•

If Victor Gioscia (1969) is correct, and there is an LSD subculture, the dangers, particularly to those under thirty, require very careful consideration. Leaving out chromosome damage, perhaps the most dramatic misfortune is the development of a schizophreniform illness. There is no doubt that this can happen, though it is not clear how often it does. Certain myths current among some young drug takers increase the danger. One of the most unfortunate is that the appropriate remedy for a bad trip is another one, frequently with a larger dose than that which produced the first one. This notion is on a par with the alcoholic slogan of having a hair, or even the tail, of "the dog that bit you." The sensible response to a bad trip is not to have another, but to seek competent advice and guidance without delay. Some people, who are clearly developing schizophrenia and have disturbances of perception (Hoffer and Osmond, 1966a) combined with usually depressed mood changes, with anxiety and sometimes thinking difficulties, take psychedelics because they have heard, or hope, that they will help. The most probable outcome is a severe and prolonged bad trip, or sometimes the precipitation of a more-severe and actue illness. If these dangers were more widely known and understood, many young people would avoid trying to treat themselves by these desperate means and avoid much unhappiness and distress.

•

The sociological, psychological, political, and other consequences of psychedelic experience, however induced, occurring in the majority or even a substantial minority of a postindustrial population, is likely to affect most of us far more than a few space jaunts for carefully selected heroes and heroines. The record is merciless: practical men of sound sense are nearly always wrong about the future, though never lacking in certainty. While the winds of change strum to gale force around us, they perform their ostrich acts and proclaim that they have everything under control. But the gale does not blow itself out because of their rhetoric, and to survive, we need to set a course that carries us into the future. Some years ago one of us wrote (Osmond, 1957a):

> . . .these agents have a part to play in our survival as a species, for that survival depends as much on our opinion of our fellows and ourselves as on any other single thing. The psychedelics help us to explore and fathom our own nature.

We can perceive ourselves as the stampings of an automatic socio-economic process, as highly plastic and conditionable animals, as congeries of instinctive strivings ending in loss of sexual drive and death, as cybernetic gadgets, or even as semantic conundrums. All of these concepts have their supporters and they all have some degree of truth in them. We may also be something more, "a part of the main," a striving sliver of a creative process, a manifestation of Brahma in Atman, an aspect of an infinite God immanent and transcendent within and without us. These very different valuings of the self and of other people's selves have all been held sincerely by men and women. I expect that even what seem the most extreme notions are held by some contributors to these pages. Can one doubt that the views of the world derived from such differing concepts are likely to differ greatly, and that the courses of action determined by those views will differ. . .?

> . . .I believe that the psychedelics provide a chance, perhaps only a slender one, for homo faber, the cunning, ruthless, foolhardy, pleasure-greedy toolmaker, to merge into that other creature whose presence we have so rashly presumed, homo sapiens, the wise, the understanding, the compassionate, in whose fourfold vision art, politics, science, and religion are one. Surely we must seize that chance. . .

•

Altered States of Consciousness

If you're doing anything with meditation, dope, hypnosis, dreams, subjective exploration of any kind, this is a useful book. John Lilly borrowed our review copy and returned it with particular recommendation for these articles:

A Special Inquiry with Aldous Huxley into the Nature and Character of Various States of Consciousness	*Milton H. Erickson*
Toward the Experimental Control of Dreaming	*Charles Tart*
A Study of Dreams	*Frederik van Eeden*
The "High" Dream	*Charles Tart*
Mutual Hypnosis	*Charles Tart*
The Effects of Marijuana on Consciousness	*Anonymous*
Subjective Effects of Nitrous Oxide	*William James*
Attitude and Behavior Change Through Psychedelic Drug Use	*Joseph Downing*
Psychedelic Agents in Creative Problem Solving	*Harman, McKim, Mogar, Fadiman, Stoleroff*
Guide to the Literature on Psychedelic Drugs	*Charles Tart*
An Electroencephalographic Study on the Zen Meditation	*Kasamatsu, Hirai*
Operant Control of the EEG Alpha Rhythm and Some of Its Reported Effects on Consciousness	*Joe Kamiya*

Elsewhere in the CATALOG is a book called Direct Use of the Sun's Energy. *Tart's book is moving toward Direct Use of the Mind's Energy.*

—SB

Altered States of Consciousness
Charles Tart, ed.
1969; 575 pp.

$4.95 postpaid

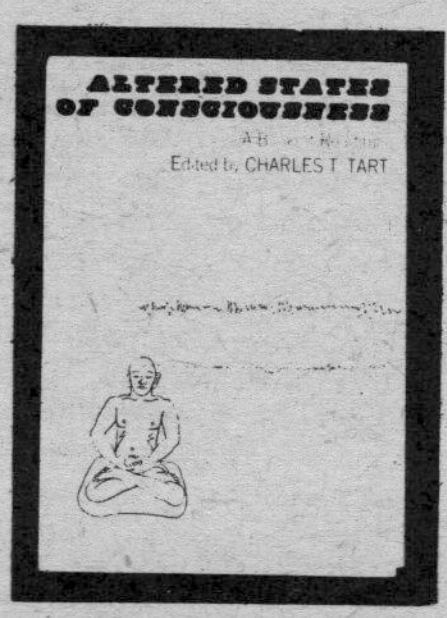

from:

from:
Doubleday & Co., Inc.
501 Franklin Ave.
Garden City, NY 11530

or WHOLE EARTH CATALOG

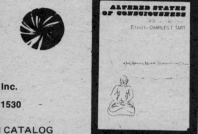

1. The first three to five hours are usually individual, to try to relax and let go.
2. Spouses' problems; usually we like spouses separate for first group treatments. If both are present, it is better if you start in different areas, but if you both want to be together, okay.
3. Don't be surprised at anything you may see the therapist doing—he knows what he is doing.
4. A person who is having trouble breaking through needs something to resist against—the therapist may hand wrestle, or be on top and have three to six others on top as well. The person then can exert all his strength to break loose.
5. Anytime you are in trouble, don't hesitate to ask for help.
6. As people make break-through you'll hear laughing, crying, screaming. Don't worry about it, or get concerned.
7. Nothing is expected of you, don't expect anything of yourself—most people have a glorious trip.
8. Try to avoid impressing anybody—you'll have a better trip.
9. Around three to four hours after beginning, a stimulant will be brought around to keep your energy level up.
10. Anytime you want to stop the trip, take some niacin, 500 to 1000 mgm at a time. Niacin is good for bad re-entry, will make it easier.
11. During the experience, if you want to come together, touch the other person or ask him. He may shake his head 'no,' or else turn and touch you. Don't have hurt feelings, or guilt if they don't want to be with you, be free to be yourselves.

•

The change that then came over Bill was dramatic. He began mumbling typical induction suggestions about relaxing, but over the course of a few minutes his voice became dramatic and forceful. He suggested that Anne see a diamond in her hand and concentrate on it and then almost immediately suggested that it would disappear and her mind would go blank. Then he very forcefully suggested physical relaxation as he counted her into hypnosis: when he reached 20 his whole manner changed and became relaxed and soothing. Anne reported a depth of 22.

Bill then began talking about a 'hallucinatory' journey that he and Anne were on together. His voice was confident, smooth, relaxed, and completely convincing that he was describing actual events that were happening rather than anything 'unreal.' They were standing on a mountain slope, in front of the entrance to a tunnel. They walked hand-in-hand down this tunnel, with the explicit suggestion by Bill that they would be going deeper into hypnosis as they walked deeper into the dark tunnel. It was quiet in the tunnel, all outside noises had vanished, and an ineffable feeling of pleasantness and significance pervaded the tunnel. Anne reported a depth of 35 after a few minutes of this, and Bill continued describing their walk down the tunnel.

The tunnel was absolutely real to Anne and Bill (and to Carol), as real as any experience in life. Although it was dark they could 'see' its walls in a strange way: Anne said it felt as if she had a 'light' coming out from under her eyebrows, and "...it wasn't illuminating anything I was seeing, yet it helped me to know that things were there without seeing them." Both Ss reported feeling the texture of the rock walls, which ranged from soft and slippery at places where it seemed moss-covered to quite hard where the bare rock was exposed.

Anne and Carol were intensely curious as to what lay at the end of the tunnel, the end that Bill would not let them reach. This resulted in an interesting aftermath. About a month after this session, Anne was a subject in a group hypnosis test. As she knew what the induction procedure was, she decided to 'go' back to the tunnel and explore it as soon as she was hypnotized but before the suggestibility test items were administered. She found herself running along the tunnel, hurrying to reach the end before the test items. At the end of the tunnel she found a cave, blazing with brilliant white light, and occupied by an old man of angelic appearance. The room was filled with music from an unseen source. Anne repeatedly asked him what this experience meant: he ignored her at first, and finally told her, very sternly, that he could not answer her question because Bill was not with her. Anne then found herself back at the group hypnosis testing.

I asked the Ss about their perceived bodies during the experience and found that they were curiously disembodied much of the time. They mentioned having heads or faces but no bodies at times, and Anne reported that they walked through each other sometimes. When Bill commanded Anne to give him her hand so he could lead her back, Anne reported that she had to "crawl back into my body, sort of. It was almost as if we were moving around with just heads. When Bill said give him my hand, I had to kind of conjure up a hand."

Anne and Bill read the transcripts over and were both shocked. They had been talking about their experiences to each other for some time, and found they had been discussing details of the experiences they had shared for which there were no verbal stimuli on the tapes, i.e, they felt they must have been communicating telepathically or that they had actually been 'in' the nonworldly locales they had experienced. This was frightening to both Ss, for what had seemed a lovely shared fantasy now threatened to be something real.

•

The most coherent and articulate sentence which came was this:

> There are no differences but differences of degree between different degrees of difference and no difference.

•

Wonderingly, but with outward calm, I undertook to arouse Huxley from the trance state by accepting the partial clues given and by saying in essence, "Wherever you are, whatever you are doing, listen closely to what is being said, and slowly, gradually, comfortably begin to act upon it. Feel rested and comfortable, feel a need to establish an increasing contact with my voice, with me, with the situation I represent, a need of returning to matters in hand with me not so long ago, in the not so long ago belonging to me, and leave behind but AVAILABLE UPON REQUEST practically everything of importance, KNOWING BUT NOT KNOWING that it is AVAILABLE UPON REQUEST. And now, let us see, that's right, you are sitting there, wide awake, rested, comfortable, and ready for discussion of what little there is."

As he watched, he became annoyed with me since I was apparently trying to talk to him, and he experienced a wave of impatience and requested that I be silent. He turned back and noted that the infant was growing before his eyes, was creeping, sitting, standing, toddling, walking, playing, talking. In utter fascination he watched this growing child, sensed its subjective experiences of learning, of wanting, of feeling. He followed it in distorted time through a multitude of experiences as it passed from infancy to childhood to school days to early youth to teenage. He watched the child's physical development, sensed its physical and subjective mental experiences, sympathized with it, empathized with it, rejoiced with it, thought and wondered and learned with it. He felt as one with it, as if it were he himself, and he continued to watch it until finally he realized that he had watched that infant grow to the maturity of 23 years. He stepped closer to see what the young man was looking at, and suddenly realized that the young man was Aldous Huxley himself, and that this Aldous Huxley was looking at another Aldous Huxley, obviously in his early fifties, just across the vestibule in which they both were standing; and that he aged 52, was looking at himself, Aldous, aged 23. Then Aldous, aged 23 and Aldous aged 52, apparently realized simultaneously that they were looking at each other and the curious questions at once arose in the mind of each of them. For one the question was, "Is that my idea of what I'll be like when I am 52?" and, "Is that really the way I appeared when I was 23?" Each was aware of the question in the other's mind. Each found the question of "Extraordinarily fascinating interest" and each tried to determine which was the "actual reality" and which was the "mere subjective experience outwardly projected in hallucinatory form."

•

When I have been flying in my dreams for two or three nights, then I know that a lucid dream is at hand. And the lucid dream itself is often initiated and accompanied all the time by the sensation of flying. Sometimes I feel myself floating swiftly through wide spaces; once I flew backwards, and once, dreaming that I was inside a cathedral, I flew upwards, with the immense building and all in it, at great speed.

Journeys Out of the Body

Many people doing drugs, meditation, or some of the occult stuff have experienced an astral projection or out-of-the-body experience. Sometimes it was marvellous, other times it scares the hell out of you. If you want to find out more about this, you'll find practically everything written is the "I've got a secret that you're not spiritual enough to hear (believe and pay and maybe I'll tell)" school. Or by people who have a system to push. This book is by a person who's clearly a sensible man and who's trying to tell it like it is, instead of what he believes about it. And willing to put himself on the line— he's worked on demonstrating his ability in my lab several times now. Techniques for leaving the body, evidential stuff (am I just crazy?), meetings with the "dead," visits to other "planes," frustrated attempts to find somebody who really understands this phenomena, astral sex (wow!). No ego trips, either. Just a solid citizen who's been "out" a thousand times now and wants to pass his experiences to others so they won't have to go through some of the confusion and terror he did learning on his own.

[Suggested and reviewed by Charley Tart]

Journeys Out of the Body
R. Monroe
1971

$6.95

from:
Doubleday & Company, Inc.
501 Franklin Ave.
Garden City, N.Y. 11530

or WHOLE EARTH CATALOG

There is a better, faster way. Happily, there seems to be built-in directional senses if their use can be mastered. The "if" is the catch. As noted elsewhere, you "think" of the person at the end of your destination— never a place, but a person— and use the method prescribed. In a few moments, you are there. You can watch the landscape move under you if you wish, but it's a little disconcerting when you rush headlong toward a building or tree— and go right through it. In order to avoid such traumas, forget about seeing during the traveling process. You never quite get over the physical-body conditioning that such things are solid. At least I have not. I still have the tendency to move in the direction of the door to leave— only to realize again the situation when my Second body hand goes through the doorknob. Irritated with myself, I then dive through the wall rather than the door to reinforce my awareness of the Second state characteristics.

In conjunction with this convenient homing instinct that is uneffected by distance, you are given a further problem. The automatic navigational system is accurate, too accurate. And that is the problem. It works by what and of whom you think. Let one small stray thought emerge dominently for just one microsecond, and your course is deviated.

•

This near area is not a pleasant place to be, albeit completely understandable from this viewpoint. It is a level or plane where you "belong" until you learn better. I don't know what happens to those who don't learn. Perhaps they stay there forever. The moment you disassociate from the physical via the Second body, you are upon the fringes of this close-by section of Locale II. It is here that one meets all sorts of disjointed personalities and animate beings, ssuch as described in Chapter X. If there is some protecting mechanism for the neophyte, it was not apparent to me. Only by cautious and sometimes terrifying experimentation was I able to learn the art or trick of passing through the area. I still am not sure precisely of all this learning process, and so have presented only the obvious. Whatever it was, I happily have not been troubled in such passages for several years.

•

You are unaware of differences in sex, you yourself as a part of the Whole, are both male and female, positive and negative, electron and proton. Man-woman love moves to you and from you, parental-child-sibling-idol and idyll and ideal— all interplay in soft waves about you, in you and through you. You are in perfect balance because you are where you Belong. You are Home.

Within all of this, yet not a part of it, you are aware of the Source of the entire span of your experience, of you, of the vastness beyond your ability to perceive and/or imagine. Here, you know and easily accept the existence of the Father. Your true Father. the Father, the Creator of all that is or was. You are one of His countless creations. How or why, you do not know. This is not important. You are happy simply because you are in your Right Place, where you truly belong.

Each of the three times I went There, I did not return voluntarily. I came back sadly, reluctantly. Someone helped me return. Each time after I returned, I suffered intense nostalgia and loneliness for days. I felt as an alien might, among strangers in a land where things were not "right," where everything and every one were so different and so "wrong" when compared with where you belonged. Acute loneliness, nostalgia, and something akin to homesickness. So great was it that I haven't tried to go There again.

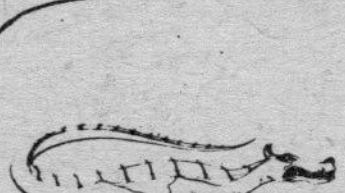

The pictures and the images squirmed in D.R.'s mind like worms in a can. His mind was alive with their flickering dance, their scatter and their swirl, and it remained that way till he had left the world of sunlight and crawled into the darkness of the mine.

The mine.

That old coal mine hidden under the fallen tipple, there by the Trace Fork road.

It was an easy entrance this time. No digging, no scrabbling. The little furrow he had made the other time was still there, an indentation in the weeds, and then the dry, rotting wood and dusty earth leading to the center of the pile of fallen boards and beams.

The old wood formed a lattice overhead, a network that allowed an ornate design of sunlight to filter through.

D.R. lay a moment, resting, looking up, peaceful in his body, the clatter in his mind already settling, slowing down.

(continued)

Psychic Discoveries Behind the Iron Curtain

The Russians are coming, the Russians are coming! Without the historical set of disbeliefs that has kept ESP research in the country limited to card guessing and tall tales, the Russians have been developing a number of laboratories and qualified people to run them. This book is a relaxed, sometimes-flamboyant tour of the Russian work as well as samples of Bulgarian, Czech, and other iron curtain researchers.

The whole book blows my mind. The Russians are years ahead of us in using and understanding clairvoyance, telepathy, auras, and related areas. The Bulgarians appear to have made and implemented fundamental discoveries in learning (not teaching rates, but getting people learning five to ten times faster). The Czechs are ahead of us in pragmatic applications of astrology (birty control, fertility, sex determination of chidren). Most of the strange and wondrous powers we were all taught don't exist are being explored, trained, extended, and researched by well-known, well-qualified, and well-financed government researchers.

One result of this book is that our parapsychologists are trying to get over there to learn how to start catching up. Another result is that this publication may force the United States government to release its own secret work (which the Russians know about but which has never been reported here). Is there an ESP gap? Who will have the first telepath on the moon? From the looks of this tour through inner space you can be sure it won't be one of us.

[Suggested and reviewed by James Fadiman]

Psychic Discoveries Behind the Iron Curtain
Sheila Ostrander and Lynn Schroeder
1970, 443 pp.

$1.25 postpaid

from:
Bantam Books, Inc.
666 Fifth Ave.
New York, N.Y. 10019

or WHOLE EARTH CATALOG

Dr. S. N. Dobronravov of Sverdlovsk reported that up to 72 percent of children had skin sight potentials. "it is most noticeable in children from the ages of seven to twelve years." Scientists at this convention agreed that the "supersensational, carnival" atmosphere whirling around eyeless sight was harming the subjects and the investigation. Work would continue quietly with subjects anonymous to the public.

Dr. Novomeisky was quietly trying to get information to help the blind. He found that blind adults didn't take to skin sight as readily as did blind children. The adults probably didn't believe that hands could see. Secondly, their acquired sensitivity of touch, and the habit of trying to "read" textures, blocked feeling of the dermo-optic sensations. But when Novomeisky put colored paper in *insulated* trays, ten blind adults suddenly got all the eyeless sight sensations that seeing students experienced. "With the insulated tray," Novomeisky reported,"we didn't find a single blind person who did not have positive tendencies toward skin sight."

•

"Our support is from the highest levels of government," said Lozanov, "the highest. The government has given us excellent conditions for our work. We never have to worry about money here. We can go ahead on any project, in any area of paranormal. Vanga is the first clairvoyant in the world to be put on the state payroll and our government has created good conditions for researching pre-cognition." Lozanov said this with considerable pride— pride in Bulgaria and her remarkable people to whom Lozanov is extra-ordinarily dedicated.

•

In actuality this is a French lesson. Against the background of Brahms or Beethoven, the voice of the teacher seems sometimes businesslike, as if ordering work to be done, sometimes soft and calming, then unexpectedly hard, commanding. Her voice repeats in a special rhythm, on a special scale of intonation, French words, idioms, and their translations. But the students aren't really listening. They've been warned *not* to pay attention, not to think about whether they hear the teacher. "Relax. Don't think about anything." Their conscious minds are to be totally occupied with the music.

Journal of Transpersonal Psychology

This is a journal that is bringing old-fashioned "all-I-want-is-the-facts-ma'm" science one step closer toward areas of fundamental concern. It publishes articles on scientific subjects such as ecstasy, transcendent education, and deep hypnosis, as well as unusual articles such as Baba Ram Dass's lecture to the staff of the Menninger Clinic and a test to see if you can tell the difference between a mystic and a physicist. If you are willing and able to go beyond **Weird Tales** *and* **Fate Magazine,** *to alpha feedback and experimental yoga this journal will make it easy to walk the distance without leaving your scientific or your telepathic friends behind.*

[Reviewed by James Fadiman]

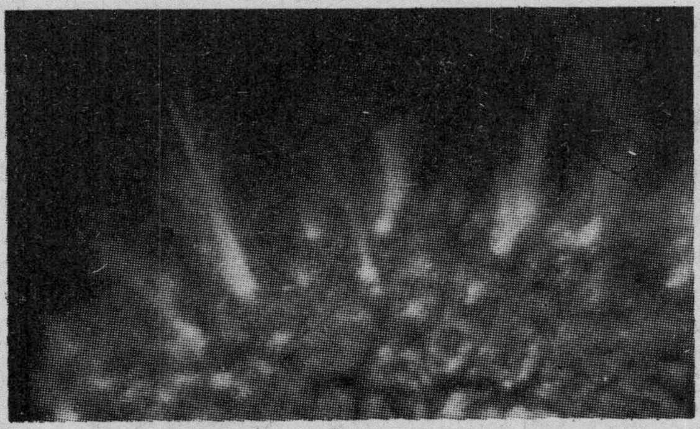

Each of these pictures shows a human fingertip magnified fifty times. Picture at top shows that of a healthy man, calm and even-tempered. Photo at bottom shows the finger of an overtired, emotionally tense individual. In a state of fatigue, more energy seems to leave the body.

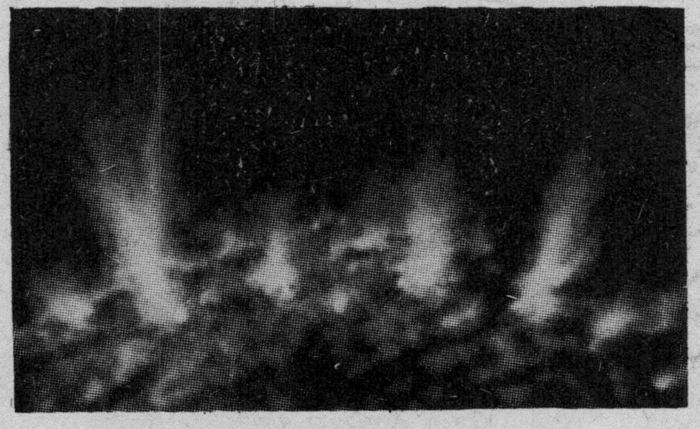

•

The next day surprised students discover that even though they were sure they'd learned nothing, they remember and can easily read, write, and speak from 120 to 150 new words absorbed during the two-hour session. In the same way the toughest part of the language course, the grammar rules, painlessly take root in the minds of music-lulled students. Within a month students with no prior knowledge of a language have accepted two to three thousand vocabulary words and have a good grasp of the grammar. Tests a year later show they still know all the material learned in this incredibly effortless way.

How does it work? Lozanov based his method, which can help you learn five to fifty times faster, on the Yoga technique of relaxation— *Savasanna*. Using suggestion and autosuggestion, muscle tension is relaxed and the brain relieved of the usual anxieties and stresses. In this relaxed "free state of consciousness," or meditative state, fatigue quickly vanishes. Freed from all distractions which hamper its functioning, the brain resembles a sponge able to absorb knowledge of all kinds. The secret of the technique is that material doesn't reach the memory in the ordinary way, because the student doesn't participate consciously in the process.

•

Journal of Transpersonal Psychology
Anthony Sutich, ed.

$7.50 /yr (semi-annual)

from:
P.O. Box 4437
Stanford, California 94305

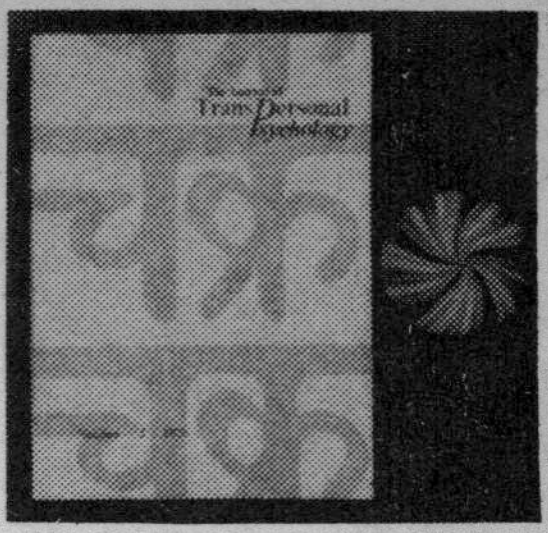

Statement of Purpose: The *Journal of Transpersonal Psychology* is concerned with the publication of theoretical and applied research, original contributions, *empirical* papers, articles and studies in meta-needs, ultimate values, unitive consciousness, peak experience, ecstasy, mystical experience, B values, essence, bliss, awe, wonder, self-actualization, ultimate meaning, transcendence of the self, spirit, sacralization of everyday life, oneness, cosmic play, individual and species-wide synergy, maximal interpersonal encounter, transcendental phenomena; maximal sensory awareness, responsiveness and expression; and related concepts, experiences and activities. As a statement of purpose, this formulation is to be understood as subject to *optional* individual or group interpretations, either wholly or in part, with regard to the acceptance of its content as essentially naturalistic, theistic, supernaturalistic, or any other designated classification.

•

. . .the reason why our sentient, percipient, and thinking ego is met nowhere in our world picture can easily be indicated in seven words: because it is ITSELF that world picture. It is identical with the whole and therefore cannot be contained in it as part of it.

. . .all phenomena and their development are simply manifestations of mind, all causes and effects, from great universes to the fine dust only seen in the sunlight, come into apparent existence only by means of the discriminating mind. Even open space is not nothingness.

. . .the stuff of the world is mind stuff.

•

Mantra gets so far out, that after I did it for two days and two nights solid in Nepal once, I stopped to go to sleep and of course it continued going. But instead of it continuing going just in *my* voice it continued going. . .what it sounded like was a cross between the Mormon Tabernacle Choir and the O Heavenly Day Chorus. It's that huge a thing except it was made up of all old voices and they stretched back in time and space in infinite direction. . .you know, distance. All I heard was *Om Mani Padme Hum* and the wind was *Om Mani Padme Hum* and the air conditioner was *Om Mani. . .*, the whole thing. I had tuned in on that place where that was all I could hear. But it was no longer my voice. I went rushing to a yogi and I said, "What's happening? I'm going crazy." He said, "You've tuned in on the *Om*, that's that place. You've tuned in on that place. There it is. That's where they're all hanging out."

•

Now it turns out— and this is the one that many of you will find hard sledding, but it's the way I understand it now, having been through this particular trip I've been through— that Freud is an absolutely unequaled spokesman and master of second-chakra preoccupation, that is, of those beings who were primarily involved in second chakra. So he could say quite honestly, because it is true at the second chakra, that religion is sublimated sex. Now it is true that in his generalized libido theories and the idea that all the body is erogenous. . .there are a lot of ways in which he slips over the edge; but his system is primarily concerned with the second chakra. Adler is primarily concerned with third chakra. Jung is primarily concerned with fourth chakra. I would point out that there are still the fifth, sixth and seventh chakras. And these are in terms of other kinds of psychic spaces and ways of organizing the universe and understanding what's happening. So that to the extent that you have "uncooked seeds" of the second chakra and you have a Freudian analyst, he's going to help you cook those seeds. He's not going to do much about where you're stuck in the third chakra, particularly. And he hasn't much to say about the fourth chakra, which is what Jung pointed out about Freud.

•

Courses on Altered States of Consciousness are being offered at Sonoma State College, the University of California at Davis, and Stanford University. Within five to ten years, it will no doubt be offered as generally as present courses on Motivation or Abnormal personality.

Psychological Exercises

Orage, who edited "New Age" in the 'thirties, knew everyone. His favorites, like Pound, Gurdjieff and Ouspensky, were certainly worth knowing. Those were the days when intellectuals thought they could change the world just by pointing out what was right and what was wrong. Hah! Anyway, Orage had a secret kick, too, and it was exercising the grey matter. For example: while reciting "Jack and Jill" write down "Mary Had a Little Lamb". For example: while you are talking to someone, or reading this, count from 100 to 0 backwards by three's. You'll find that with some practice you really can do these things, just like learning to pat your stomach while rubbing your head. And then where are you? Fun.

[Suggested and reviewed by Stephan Chodorov]

Read at sight the following unspaced passage in which each second word has been spelled backwards:

AsnoosasehtsermonsifinishedydobonpresumesotstirllitSirregoRise
nogoutfothehcruhc.Thethginkwalksnwodfromsihseatnithelec
nahcbetweenadoubleworofsihtenantstahtstandgniwobtomihon
hcaeside,dnaeverywonandnehtinquireswohsuchnaone'sefiwor
rehtomornosorrehtafdo,mohwheseodnoteesathcruhc——which
siunderstoodsaatercesreprimandotthenosrepthatsiabsent.

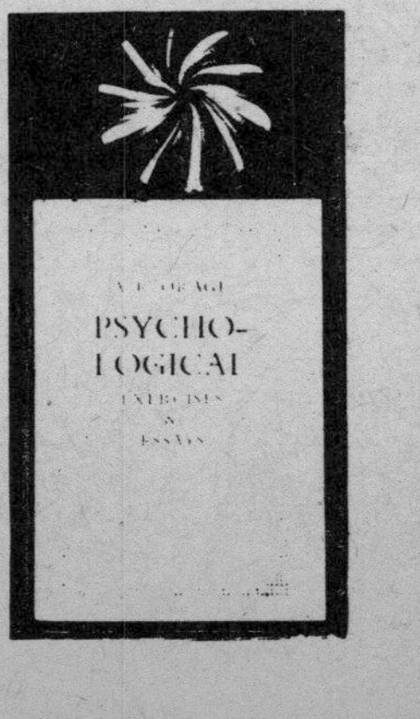

•

Psychological Exercises & Essays
A. R. Orage
1930 . . . 1968; 121 pp.

$3.50 postpaid

from:
Samuel Weiser
734 Broadway
New York, N. Y. 10003

or WHOLE EARTH CATALOG

Let some prepared incident be staged and played before a group of students, who shall afterwards report it correctly.

E.g., the lights are suddenly turned off. Student A. blows a police whistle. He scuffles with Student B. and some noisy conversation takes place between them. Student B. escapes, making some remark as he bangs the door behind him. The lights are now turned up; and the rest of the students are called upon to report fully, accurately and in proper sequence the events of the episode.

•

Arrange the following sentences in order of their intellectual content; and give reasons for your arrangement.

Where law ends, tyranny begins.
The road to Hell is paved with good intentions.
A desire in psychology has the same status as a force in physics.
Our antagonist is our helper.
The world is a comedy to those who think, a tragedy to those who feel.
Man's character is his destiny.
A stitch in time saves nine.

Lindberg Crosses the Great Water

If we can combine our knowledge of science with the wisdom of wildness, if we can nurture civilization through roots in the primitive, man's potentialities appear to be unbounded. Through his evolving awareness, and his awareness of that awareness, he can merge with the miraculous—to which we can attach what better name than "God"? And in this merging, as long sensed by intuition but still only vaguely perceived by rationality, experience may travel without need for accompanying life.

Will we then find life to be only a stage, though an essential one, in a cosmic evolution of which our evolving awareness is beginning to become aware? Will we discover that only *without* spaceships can we reach the galaxies; that only *without* cyclotrons can we know the interior of atoms? To venture beyond the fantastic accomplishments of this physically fantastic age, sensory perception must combine with the extrasensory, and I suspect that the two will prove to be different faces of each other. I believe it is through sensing and thinking about such concepts that great adventures of the future will be found.

Read the whole marvelous piece in July 4, '69 *Life* Magazine in your library.

1935, Lindberg in New Mexico with rocket inventor Robert Goddard.

1969, conservationist Lindberg.

Lucis Trust Library

Here's an unusual item; a mail library of magical books. The catalog lists 1600 titles from ABC of Jung's Psychology to Zoroastrianism: The Religion of the Good Life. You can borrow two books at a time for a month. Lucis is a nice service that subsists on contributions; it probably is fragile to exploitive use.

—SB [Suggested by Gerald Thatcher]

Catalog

$1.00 contribution

from:
The Lucis Trust Library
866 United Nations Plaza
Suite 566-567
New York, N. Y. 10017

Seven Human Temperaments, The	Geoffrey Hodson
Seven Principles of Man, The	Annie Besant
Seven Rays, The	Ernest Wood
Seven Seventy-Seven	Anonymous
Seventy-Fifth Anniversary Book of the Theosophical Society	Josephine Ransom
Sex Worship	Clifford Howard
Shadow Forms	Manly Hall
Shinto, The Unconquered Enemy	Robert O. Ballou
Shri Ramakrishna	T. L. Vaswani
Signs and Symbols of Primordial Man, The	Albert Churchward
Signs and Symbols	George Oliver
Simple Method of Raising the Soul to Contemplation, The	Francois Malaval
Simple Study in Theosophy, A	Michael J. Witty
Simple Way, The	W. Gorn Old
Simplified Scientific Astrology	Max Heindel

Big Sur Recordings

Much of the best of the Esalen Institute occasions (Baba Ram Dass, John Lilly, Fritz Perls, Joseph Cambell, Lancelot Law Whyte, Carl Rogers, etc.) are available by mail. Cost of the tapes is $10/hr Mono or stereo reels or cassettes.

—SB

Catalog

free

from:
Big Sur Recordings
Box 4313
San Rafael, CA 94903

ONE MAN'S JOURNEY TO THE EAST
Baba Ram Dass
The former Richard Alpert tells the story of his own journey from professor at Harvard, through psychedelia, to the finding of his guru in the East and the continuing changes in his own life. Includes a discussion of yoga and meditation, reincarnation, and the problem of desire   4 hours ☐ 3280

INTRODUCTORY LECTURE-DEMONSTRATION ON STRUCTURAL INTEGRATION
Ida Rolf
A discussion of Ida Rolf's methods of body alignment and balance through Structural Integration. A lecture and demonstration   1½ hours ☐ 4500

LEARNING FROM DOLPHINS
John Lilly
An attempt to communicate with another intelligent species is described, with comments on the dolphins' life styles and ethical codes   1½ hours ☐ 4340

POLITICS AS EXPERIENCE
R.D. Laing
The initial family structure splits into social and political forms, creating complex obstacles to true self-knowledge   1 hour ☐ 1181

ON BEING A "PSYCHIC"
Ann Armstrong
In this personal and informative account of a person with psychic abilities, Mrs. Armstrong describes her problems in learning to use her powers, how she first discovered them, and their changing character as they continue to emerge   1 hour ☐ 4770

PSYCHOSYNTHESIS
Robert Gerard
Inner imagery as a technique to further psychological growth, illustrated with case history material   2 hours ☐ 2060

LSD THERAPY
Stanislav Grof
Report on extensive LSD therapy from Czechoslovakia, with extraordinary findings   1 hour ☐ 1110

WORLD MYTHOLOGY: SYNTHESIS
Joseph Campbell
The relation of myth to individual evolution, to the journey of one's own life   3 hours ☐ 3399

Samuel Weiser

Weiser's is a huge mystical book store in Manhattan with a good mailorder catalog.

—SB

Catalog

free

from:
Samuel Weiser, Inc.
734 Broadway
New York, N.Y. 10003

Bailey, Alice A. *A Treatise on White Magic.* New York, 1970. 705 pp. Index. Paper. $4.00

Knight, Gareth. *Occult Exercises and Practices.* Sangreal Series No. 1. The complete beginner's guide to practical occultism with bibliography of systems of practical occult development. London, 1969. 67 pp. $3.00

Crookall, Robert. *Out-of-the-Body Experiences.* Detailed analyses of testimony of hundreds who have reported out-of-the-body experiences. New York, 1970. 219 pp. Unavailable from Weiser.

Conze, Edward. *Selected Sayings from the Perfection of Wisdom.* A selection of passages from the "Perfection of Wisdom," the basic teachings of Mahayana Buddhism. London, 1968. 131 pp.
Out of print.

Govinda, Lama Anagarika. *Foundations of Tibetan Mysticism.* Esoteric principles of Mantra explained and the differences between Hindu and Tibetan yoga clarified. New York, 1969. 331 pp. Illustrated. Bibliography. Paper. $3.75.

Knight, Gareth. *A Practical Guide to Qabalistic Symbolism.* Compendium of the symbolism of the Tree of Life of the Qabalah with especial reference to the Tarot. 2-volume set. London, 1965. 540 pp. $16.50.

TEACHINGS AND DISCIPLINES OF ZEN
Suzuki Roshi
An informal talk to Westerners by the Abbot of Tassajara Zen Mountain Center   2 hours ☐ 304-2

LP-110 $6.95

THE MUSIC OF TIBET — TANTRIC RITUALS
Huston Smith
The sound of one voice chording; multi-tone chanting, recorded and interpreted by Huston Smith. Accompanied by complete music and acoustical analyses

Toward a General Theory of the Paranormal

The title is accurate. The book offers some conceptual handles toward a communicable understanding of mystical and clairvoyant experiences. It has nice quotes from the literature.

—SB

Toward a General Theory of the Paranormal
Lawrence LeShan
1969; 112 pp.

$3.00 postpaid

from:
Parapsychology Foundation, Inc.
29 West 57th Street
New York, N. Y. 10019

or WHOLE EARTH CATALOG

Our concern is with those aspects of whatever is *out there* that constitute the *individual reality* (IR) of a specific individual. ("We must remember," wrote Werner Heisenberg in a famous statement, "that what we see is not Nature, but Nature exposed to our method of questioning.")

One is reminded here of the old Spanish proverb: "Take what you want," said God. "Take it, and pay for it."

He felt the cool air from the mine blow across his neck and face and arms.

And he smelled it, smelled the mine, the slate-taste-color flowing from the earth into his nostrils like some subtle gas that soothed and calmed his mind.

For a long time D.R. lay breathing and resting and looking at the lattice overhead.

Then he turned and eased himself into the narrow opening, underground.

And there he was, again.

Cool.

Dark.

Quiet, except for an occasional dripping, and except for the way the very silence was a kind of noise.

He was actually there, beneath the mountain, quiet in the bosom of the world. And conscious of it this time, there freely, there simply, without all that smoke and swirl. On his way down the hill to the mine his thought had been that he would go inside, maybe deep inside, and explore by the light of his candle. That impulse was gone now. Within thirty feet of the entrance D.R. found what he had come for. He hadn't known, really, just what he was going there for. But now he knew. It was just to sit a while, at rest in a cool, quiet place. That was all.

D.R. sat holding the candle in his hand, looking around him in the circle of light at the ragged posts on either side that held the roof in place.

The roof was slate, and the color of slate.

The walls were solid coal.

The floor was dusty near the walls, but in the center it was moist, with here and there a pool of water gathered from the dripping above.

D.R. sat a long time without moving. There was the roof above, the floor beneath him, and the walls on either side. And the candle, in the center of the circle of the light.

After a while, without deciding to, D.R. leaned forward and set his candle in the mud beside a little pool near his feet.

The reflection was a perfect reproduction of the real, and D.R. marvelled at it.

One above, one below, the two candles shone together in the vastness of the cavern, and D.R. sat crosslegged on the floor in total fascination.

Behind him in the dark was the entrance to the mine, and the world of day beyond.

Behind the candles was the deeper vastness of the mine.

Neither attracted him.

D.R. didn't want to go in motion either way.

He was where he was.

This was his place to be.

And that stayed true even after he blew the candle out.

Without deciding to, D.R. crawled forward and blew the candle out. And then, for longer than he knew, he sat there where he was, within and of the dark.

Sensitivity Books

What I find missing from the pages of the Catalog are tools to help groups work better together. Too often, I think, we simply assume that like-minded people can get along with each other, find constructive work patterns by instinct, and so on. We toss around a lot of words like "openness" and "honesty," but the words and the practice are two different things. Then, six months after arriving on the homestead (or buying the big communal house in the city, or whatever), fights break out around the issue of who's to do the dishes. Some folks flare and smolder; they leave a few weeks later with a bucketfull of bad memories.

Premise: we really have not learned to listen effectively, give helpful feedback to others about their here-and-now behavior, plan together for a common task, be it building a barn or living collectively. We can't build community by good intentions alone, or by imploring our brothers and sisters to be "honest." In short, we need tools.

With that lengthy preface out of the way, I want to introduce sensitivity training. Before everyone starts to groan, let me make clear what I am not talking about. I don't advocate all the stereotyped stuff now coming out in movies and novels, the scenes where people are licensed to call each other no-good S.O.B.'s for a weekend. No freewheeling ego destruction, no confessions about horrible misdeeds and terrifying anxieties. What I am talking about is the more conservative wing of the sensitivity training movement, as represented by the National Training Laboratories: training that focuses on the here-and-now aspects of group behavior, leadership, communications, and the like.

Since the sensitivity training movement has exploded into every imaginable direction, and since anybody can hang out a shingle and "run groups," folks interested in exploring this area should be wary and cautious. Even the legitimate trainers are expensive, to the tune of $100 a day for the best of the bunch. Fortunately, there are some books around that qualify as tools; here are three of the best that I know about:

(1) The Practice of Creativity, *George M. Prince, Harper and Row, 1970, $8.50. This is about Synectics, but it's much better than the other Synectics book the Catalog used to list. Prince's book qualifies as a true tool; there are a variety of suggestions for improving the creative output of small groups. The entire Synectics problem-solving process is outlined in detail, and many of its techniques, if consciously applied, really help in all sorts of situations. One example: the Spectrum Policy, which says that you're not allowed to criticize an idea until you've said something positive about it. This sounds incredibly trite and artificial, I'm sure, but its use has drastically improved half a dozen work situations that I've been in. Even the best-intentioned people are often unwittingly destructive in group situations.*

(2) A Handbook of Structured Experiences for Human Relations Training *(two volumes), J. William Pfeiffer and John E. Jones, University Associates Press, Box 615, Iowa City, Iowa 52240, 1969, $3.00 each volume. These are two small volumes of exercises in group processes. Some sample titles: "Hidden Agendas," "Status-Interaction Study," "Developing Group Commitment," "Process Intervention Practice". Not all of these will be helpful to every group, but some of the exercises have universal use. IMPORTANT NOTE OF CAUTION: These exercises are not toys; if they're to be used, they should be used only when every member of the group agrees to their use. Most of the exercises are designed for use by a trainer in a laboratory group. If, say, a commune uses some of these, the person acting as trainer should not be from that commune.*

(3) Basic Reader in Human Relations Training *(in eight mimeographed parts), Service to Dioceses, Episcopal Church Center, 815 Second Avenue, New York, N.Y. 10017, apparently free of charge. This series is what it says it is, a collection of written materials on all phases of group processes as shown in laboratory situations. The advantage is that the editors have collected many papers on the same topics, so the reader has a choice of frameworks on which to hang his understanding. The set includes a good bibliography and list of further sources.*

For people interested in exploring further, the NTL Institute for Applied Behavioral Science runs labs all over the country in various aspects of group dynamics. Their address is 1201 16th Street, N.W., Washington, D.C. 20036.

Finally, a statement from George Prince, with which he closes his book: "The conscious practice of creativity as an everyday activity is particularly valuable because it permits you to rationalize, accept, and gradually expect miracles of yourself."

Go well,
Bob Fried
Berkeley, California

Psychology Today: An Introduction

My god, they've done it——and I'm stunned. After spending more years than I care to remember dealing with this sort of subject matter, I expected to skim through this book, and I tried——for hour after hour after hour. First off, it's the most fantastic visual presentation I've ever encountered in a textbook; every page is arresting and imaginative and many are clearly and simply beautiful. It's the first time I've ever seen such consistent remembering that the subject under study is that of me and you and our fellows. This would surely be the book to start with for anyone interested in finding out what psychology is all about. There are eight major sections, each representing a main branch of the field, and each being covered clearly and thoroughly. There are two companion volumes, the Instructor's Guide, and the student's workbook, Involvement in Psychology Today. The Instructor's Guide lists appropriate films and suggests demonstrations for each section. "Involvement" is designed to do just that——the suggested projects are unusual and look like fun. There are good bibliographies here too, for those interested in pursuing particular subjects further, including a lot of wonderful books that didn't used to be considered proper.

These things about the content especially impress me: The scientific study of behavior is treated cogently so that anyone can learn the basics of scientific methodology. And this without the usual accompanying tone that only what's measurable is worth studying, a tone that so pervades many textbooks that as an undergraduate I despaired of learning anything interesting or meaningful about human beings. This stuff really turned me on to human behavior and the study of it. The sections on drugs and craziness are also impressive in that the subjects are tackled head-on; there's no evasiveness and no apparent prejudice. There is lots of good information and, best of all, a powerful feeling conveyed of what it's all about.

The authors have clearly attempted to make this book super-relevant to today's world. They have succeeded.

[Reviewed by Diana Shugart]

Psychology Today: An Introduction
1970; 707 pp.

$14.95 postpaid

from:
CRM Books
511 S. Coast Highway
Solano Beach, CA 92075

or WHOLE EARTH CATALOG

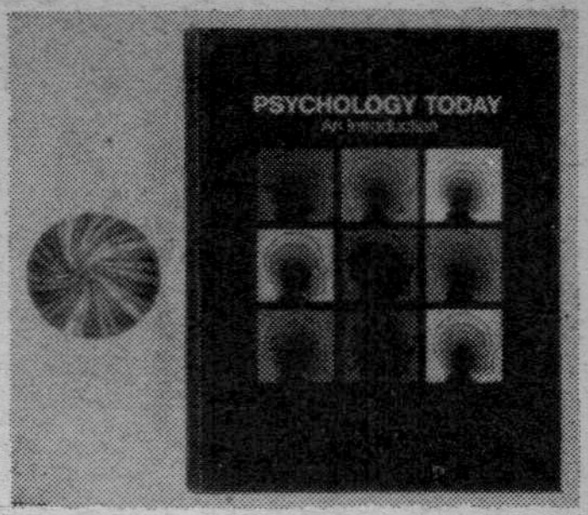

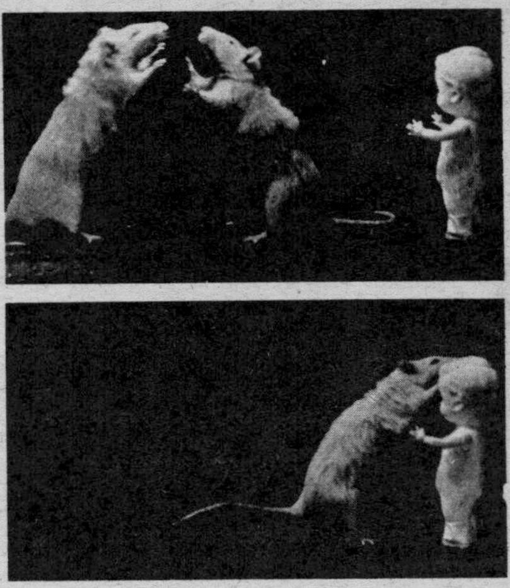

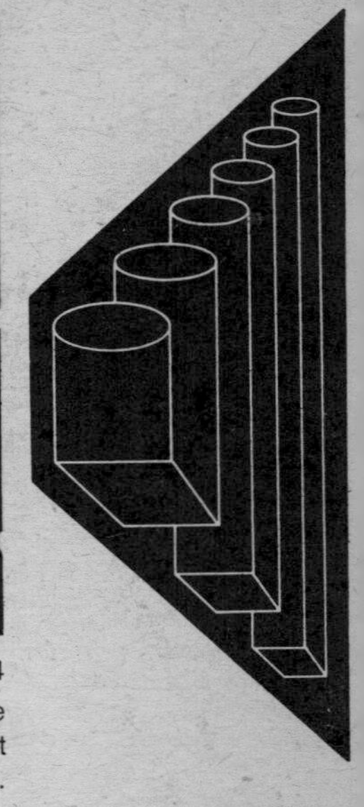

Figure 7.14
Aggression elicited by shocks may be displaced to a doll if another rat is not present.

May hypothesizes that when a culture is moving toward integration and unity, it has a system of symbols, myths, and values that give integration to the members of society, and people are then relatively free from psychological breakdown. But when a culture is in the process of disintegration, it loses first of all its myths and symbols, then its system of values that have been based on these myths. Subsequently, people in large numbers come to seek psychological help. May believes that therapy will remain a critical part of our cultural scene until society discovers new myths and symbols to replace those we are currently losing.

Developmental Psychology Today

Again, a beautiful and stimulating book, all about growing up— and around, in and out, and sideways. All the ways we grow, how we get stuck and unstuck, what we need to get it together and what happens when we don't. These CRM books really make anything else on these subjects taste like dry oatmeal and read like an abridged, unillustrated Dick & Jane.

[Reviewed by Diana Shugart]

Developmental Psychology Today
1971; 1972; 575 pp.

$13.95 postpaid

from:
CRM Books
511 S. Coast Highway
Solano Beach, CA 92075

or WHOLE EARTH CATALOG

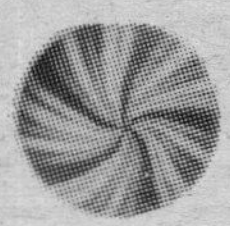

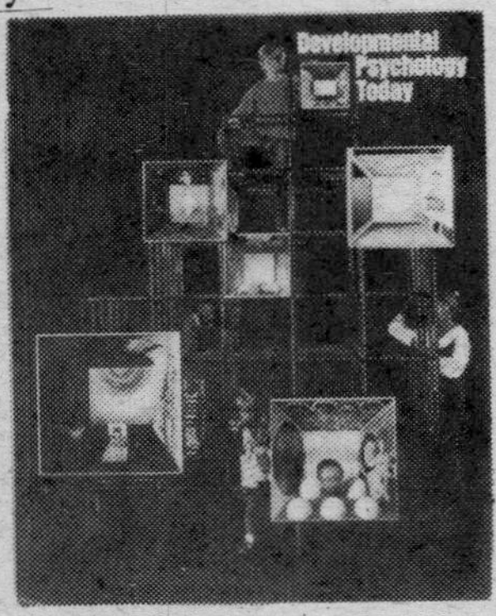

Normality

It is customary to start with definitions, but volumes have been written attempting to define the concept of normality— with very little success. Using any criteria, there is no such thing as a person who is totally normal in all respects and at all times, nor is anyone totally abnormal. Neither is there such an entity as an "emotionally disturbed child." Emotional disturbance is not a disease, like diabetes, that is either present or absent in a given individual. In current usage, "emotional disturbance" is an umbrella term that covers all degrees of behavioral problems in four major categories: antisocial aggressiveness, overwhelming fears, failures in learning, and infantile habits.

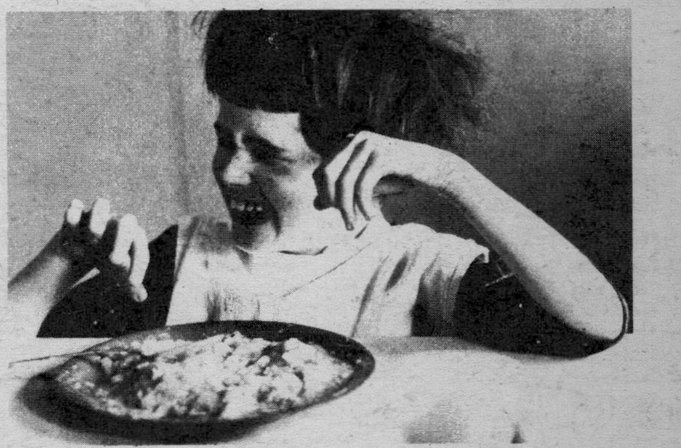

Put the personality of a child in the body of a man, furnish a need to be loved and a fierce desire to be independent, allow a need to be self-directing but leave out any idea of what direction to take, add an enormous amount of love but also the fear that it may not be accepted or returned, give physical and sexual powers without any knowledge or experience of how to use them— take these and place them in a society whose values and achievements are essentially incomprehensible and certainly unattainable and whose concerns are seemingly misplaced and insincere. Then you will have just begun to scratch the surface of adolescence.

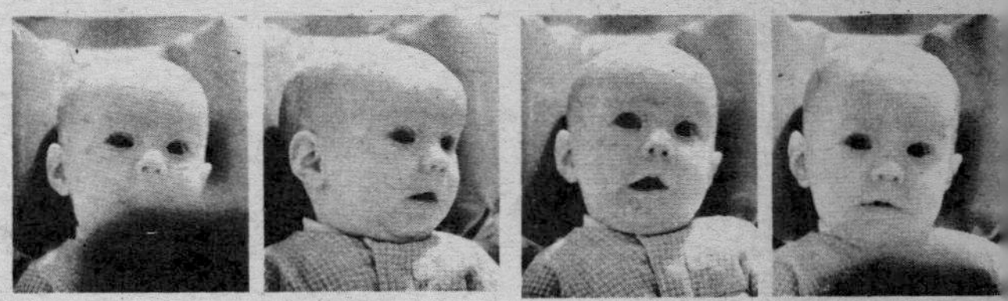

Love and Will

Here's a book to disabuse you, and you, and you of any notions you might have about there being anything very special in your sufferings; or anything terribly unique about your dilemmas and your fuck-ups. May describes our external and internal environments in their relationship to each other with a mind-~~blowing~~ accuracy that evokes recognition——"Yes, that's me, all right, and that's just the way it is these days". Far from being brought down, one feels embraced by a warm intelligence, and relieved that there are minds like May's around. A sort of psychological ecologist, May points to the price we pay for every step of "social progress", and suggests that if perhaps we have unwittingly but consistently thrown out the baby with the bath water, then maybe it's time to find the hell some other way to get clean.

[Reviewed by Diana Shugart]

If we repress the daimonic, we shall find these powers returning to "sicken" us; whereas, if we let them stay, we shall have to struggle to a new level of consciousness in order to integrate them and not be overwhelmed by impersonal power. And (what a refreshingly honest motto to put up in a psychotherapist's office!) *either way will hurt.*

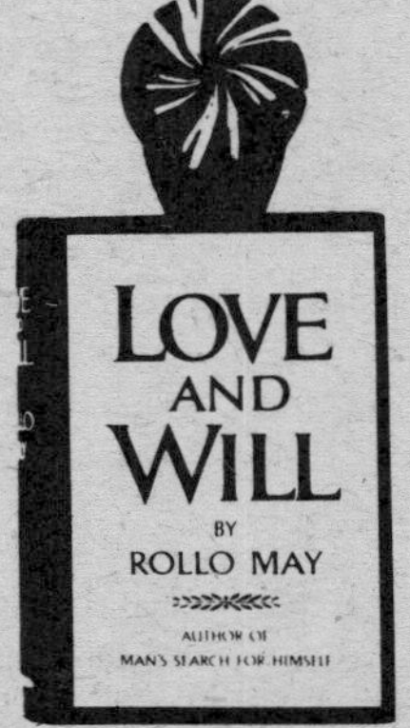

Love and Will
Rollo May
1969; 352

$1.75 postpaid

from:
W. W. Norton & Company, Inc.
500 Fifth Avenue
New York, N. Y. 10036

or WHOLE EARTH CATALOG

Just as the individual is feeling powerless and plagued with self-doubts about his own decisions, he is, at the same time, assured that he, modern man, can do anything. God is dead and are we not gods——for have we not re-enacted Genesis by splitting the atom in our own laboratories and over Hiroshima? Of course, we did it in reverse: God made form out of chaos and we have made chaos out of form, and it is a rare human being who is not, in some secret place in his heart, scared to death that we shall not be able to turn chaos into form again before it is too late.

If will remains protest, it stays dependent on that which it is protesting against. Protest is half-developed will. Dependent, like the child on parents, it borrows its impetus from its enemy. This gradually empties the will of content; you always are the shadow of your adversary, waiting for him to move so that you can move yourself. Sooner or later, your will becomes hollow, and may then be forced back to the next line of defense.

This next defense is *projection of blame.* We find an illustration in every war of this unwitting confession of failure to integrate the daimonic. In the Vietnam war, for example, Secretary Rusk and the Administration blamed the Viet Cong for the escalation, and the Viet Cong——and those in this country opposed to the war——blamed Rusk and our own Administration. The self-righteous security that is achieved by means of this blaming of the other gives one a temporary satisfaction. But beyond the gross oversimplification of our historical situation which this exhibits, we pay a more serious price for such security. *We have tacitly given the power of decision over to our adversary.*

Psychiatry and Social Science Review

This publication is Free, if you keep returning the card on the back. One need never buy a book. No need to return.

Nanna Bollnig
Philadelphia, Pa.

Psychiatry and Social Science Book Club
59 4th Ave.
New York, N.Y. 10003

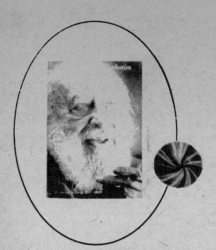

Gestalt Therapy Verbatim
In and Out the Garbage Pail

Fritz Perls is not nearly as deceased as he seems. These two books preserve his power for all to tap and use. They also, to my mind, revolutionize the book industry. Gestalt Therapy Verbatim is made of tapes from Fritz' seminars and workshops at Esalen——and seldom will you find conflict, funk, truth and accomplishment so thick in a book. In and Out the Garbage Pail is Fritz' application of his methods to himself, through the very writing. It's autobiography, theory, poetry, and Fritz' many voices hassling each other through impasse into growth. The illustrations by Russ Youngreen raise the book by at least a dimension.

But all of this is derivative from Fritz Perls' main accomplishment. His psychology and his therapy . . . work.

—SB

[Suggested by Barry Stevens]

Gestalt Therapy Verbatim
Frederick S. Perls, M.D., Ph.D.
1969; 279 pp.

$1.65 postpaid

from:
Bantam Books
666 Fifth Ave.
New York, NY 10019

or WHOLE EARTH CATALOG

In and Out the Garbage Pail
Frederick S. Perls, M.D., Ph.D.
1969; 280 pp.

$1.65 postpaid

from:
Bantam Books
666 Fifth Ave.
New York, NY 10019

or WHOLE EARTH CATALOG

Helpers are con men, interfering. People have to grow by frustration ——by skillful frustration. Otherwise they have no incentive to develop their own means and ways of coping with the world.

•

F: Okeh. Withdraw into your body, to your anxiety.
G: My——I can feel my heart pounding, and my pulse is——and my arms, and my legs, and my neck . . . Actually it's not a bad feeling.
F: Enjoy it.
G: It's a good strong heart . . . I feel the warmth of the fire on my back——that's nice, too.
F: Now come back to us.
G: I'm not so scared now——it works every time, Fritz.

•

Now let's take another step. You come up here and talk to me——just say anything. (as the person speaks, Fritz imitates his words, voice inflection, and facial expressions) Pair up and do this, and again try to really get the feel of being this other person. . . .

Now I want each one of you to transform yourself into something a little bit more different. Say, transform yourself into a road. . . .

Now transform yourself into a motorcar. . . .
Now transform yourself into a six months-old baby . . .
Now transform yourself into the mother of that baby . . .
Now transform yourself into that same baby again . . .
Now the same mother . . .
Now the same baby . . .
Now be two years of age . . .
Now transform yourself into your present age, the age you are . . . Can everyone perform that miracle?

•

Q: What is your opinion about meditation?
F: Meditation is neither shit nor get off the pot.

Look at the difference between the words "I am tensing myself" and "There's a tenseness here." When you say "I feel tenseness," you're irresponsible, you are not responsible for this, you are impotent and you can't do anything about it. The world should do something—— give you aspirin or whatever it is. But when you say "I am tensing" you take responsibility, and we can see the first bit of excitement of life coming out. So stay with this sentence.

As soon as you say, "I want to change"—make a program—a counterforce is created that prevents you from change. Changes are taking place by themselves. If you go deeper into what you *are*, if you accept what is there, then a change automatically occurs by itself.

You see how you can use *everything* in a dream. If you are pursued by an ogre in a dream, and you *become* the ogre, the nightmare disappears. You re-own the energy that is invested in the demon. Then the power of the ogre is no longer outside, alienated, but inside where you can use it.

You never overcome *anything* by resisting it. You only can overcome anything by going deeper into it. If you are spiteful, be *more* spiteful. If you are performing, increase the performance. Whatever it is, if you go deeply enough into it, then it will disappear; it will be assimilated. Any resistance is no good. You have to go full into it—— swing with it. Swing with your pain, your restlessness, whatever is there. Use your spite. Use your environment. Use all that you fight and disown.

Gestalt Therapy Verbatim

One remark that I get makes me embarrassed and angry: "When will the book come out?"

"Will you please leave me alone and let me do my thing! I am glad that I am excited and eager to write. I am glad to do something that integrates your needs and mine. So, don't push the river; it flows by itself!"

But I am holding onto my credo: "I am responsible only for myself. You are responsible for yourselves. I resent your demands on me, as I resent any intrusion into my way of being."

I know I am holding on just a bit too tight.

Topdog: Stop. Fritz, what are you doing?
Underdog: What do you mean?

Cope and withdraw, contract and expand, implode and explode—— like the heart imploding, contracting, and then exploding, opening to be filled. Permanent contracting leads to quick death, as does permanent extension.

In and Out of the Garbage Pail

The Primal Scream

. . . I read The Primal Scream. It is a long book written by a man who has stumbled upon a very valuable technique, and who still has not explored it to his total satisfaction, but who wants to communicate his whole experience and all he knows about it.

Dr. Janov says that neuroses and psychoses result from thwarted attempts made by the human organism in childhood to get what it wants. If an infant's Primal Needs (to be fed, kept warm and dry, to grow and develop at its own pace, to be held and caressed, to be stimulated) are not fulfilled, the infant must separate his needs from his consciousness, in order to avoid the pain of unfulfillment. The infant, and later the child, is forced to split into a real and an unreal self, to build a false persona which he uses in his struggle for gratification. Each time the struggle fails, each time the child is required to be other than he is in order to fulfill some aspect of his parents' needs, the resultant pain, unuttered and unrequited, is driven within, to add another drop to the Primal Pool, the reservoir of hurt.

As the assaults on the real system mount, they begin to crush the real person. One day an event will take place which, though not necessarily traumatic in itself— giving the child to a baby sitter for the hundredth time— will shift the balance between real and unreal and render the child neurotic. That event I call the major Primal Scene. It is a time in the young child's life when all the past humiliations, negations, and deprivations accumulate into an inchoate realization: "There is no hope of being loved for what I am." It is then that the child defends himself against that catastrophic realization by becoming split from his feelings, and slips quietly into neurosis. The realization is not a conscious one. Rather, the child begins acting around his parents, and then elsewhere, in the manner expected by them. He says their *words and does their thing. He acts unreal, i.e., not in accord with the reality of his own needs and desires. In a short time the neurotic behavior becomes automatic.*

Janov's cure for neurosis is simply to drain the Primal Pool, to enable his patients to feel their long-repressed pain and outrage, ". . . to feel and recognize the split, and scream out the connection that will unify the person again." It is to this goal that Primal Therapy is directed.

For the first three weeks of Primal Therapy, the patient is the therapist's only patient. Twenty-four hours before the first session, the patient is isolated in a hotel room and asked not to leave it until he reports for therapy the following day. During that time, he is asked not to read, watch TV, telephone anyone, smoke, drink, or take drugs. When the patient arrives for therapy the next day, he is asked to talk about his childhood. Then a therapist observes him closely for signs of feeling. When the feelings manifest, the patient is urged to sink into them. When he begins to invent defense mechanisms, they are forbidden him. He is told to lie on his back, arms and legs spread-eagled, and breathe deeply through his mouth. When the unrequited needs of childhood begin to rise in him, he is told to give them utterance. "Tell Daddy you're afraid!" "Momma, don't go!" The patient will begin to thrash about, experience nausea, have difficulty breathing, try to say it, as the therapist urges him to let it out.

Finally, out it will come: a scream— "Daddy, be nice!" "Mommy help!"— or just the word "hate": "I hate you, I hate you!" This is the Primal Scream. It comes out in shuddering gasps, pushed out by the force of years of suppressions and denials of that feeling. Sometimes the scream is only "Mommy!" or "Daddy!" Just saying those words brings with it torrents of pain since many "mommies" would not even permit their children to call them anything but "Mother." Letting down and being that little child who needs a "mommy" helps release all the stored-up feeling.

This process continues for three weeks, after which the patient will enter a therapy group, where for several months he will continue to experience what Dr. Janov calls Primals, his openness having developed beyond the need for exclusive attention.

So that's what happens, and I was interested to read a while ago that it was happening to John Lennon, that he and Yoko were patients of Dr. Janov in his Southern California clinic. Then a friend brought me John's new record and said, "Hey, man, here's that Primal Therapy you were telling me about." And it is. . . .

*[Reviewed by Roland Jacopetti.
Reprinted from Organ (p. 241)]*

The Primal Scream
Arthur Janov
1970; 446 pp.

$1.50 postpaid

from:
Dell Publishing Company
1 Dag Hammarskjold Plaz
245 E. 47th St.
New York, NY 10017
or WHOLE EARTH CATALOG

MONDAY: THE SCHEME

On Monday morning, D.R. went to work expanding Emmit's scheme.

He had tinkered with it and nursed it along, doing chores, in the time he had lived alone as Emmit's successor at the homeplace. But it wasn't until this particular Monday morning that D.R. took up tools to enlarge and make his own mark on the work that Emmit had begun the last year of his life.

(continued)

Man's Presumptuous Brain

Dr. Simeons spent 18 years in India (had brilliant successes with malaria there). Is that why he's written the most useful yoga book to originate in the West? It's not a yoga book, of course, it's an investigation of psychosomatic disease (which will probably kill you and is certainly killing Us). Simeons' contention is that our brains, cerebral cortex specifically, have evolved clear out of coordination with the rest of our nature, body especially. It is the arrogant cortex that permits us to burn holes in our stomachs and in each other.

The book would be worth reading just for its central theme, but a whole lot more than just that is going on in Simeons and in the book. Unique document. —SB

[Suggested by Steve Baer]

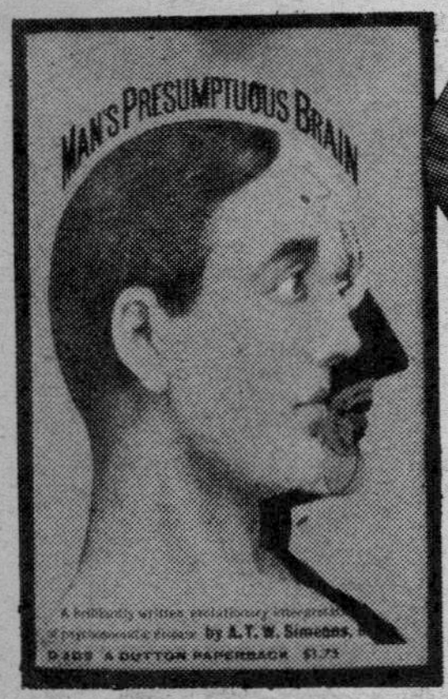

Man's Presumptuous Brain
A. T. W. Simeons, M. D.
1961; 290 pp.

$1.95 postpaid

from:
E. P. Dutton & Co., Inc.
201 Park Avenue South
New York, N. Y. 10003

or WHOLE EARTH CATALOG

Psychosomatic ailments account for the bulk of urban man's ill-health and are the most frequent cause of his death. Man shares this kind of affliction with no other living creature.

•

The reptilian brain is so organized that it must respond to all incoming messages from the senses. On the ground these messages lead to purposeful actions, for instance burrowing for food or safety; but in the trees many of these actions became pointless. A reptile's behaviour is governed entirely by automatic reflexes. Its actions are not subject to reason. It does not have to make a choice between different ways of reacting. All its actions are due to sensory messages putting an ingrained reflex into operation, and over this process the reptile has no control.

A reptile, taking to the trees, carried with it all the ancient reflexes which it had acquired in millions of years on the ground. These reflexes which the change of habitat rendered useless must have been a terrible harassment to an already overworked reptilian brain. In the slow course of evolution these reflexes would have gradually changed into more suitable ones. But so desperate was the situation of the tree-living reptile that it would have become extinct long before normal evolutionary trends could have brought about a better adjustment to the new environment. Some sort of evolutionary shortcut was needed if the species was to survive.

The shortcut was biologically evolved out of just the right mutations occurring at this dramatic moment. It consisted of a mechanism which blocked useless messages from the nose and thus prevented them from reaching those centres of the brain which would have been obliged to react to them. In the olfactory lobes a few cells took over the function of a screening device, a sort of censorship or filter by which incoming olfactory messages were either suppressed or allowed to pass, according to their vital importance. This sorting or classifying of smells relieved the reptilian brain of the exhausting need to react to every message from the nose and thus, in the trees, proved to be an efficient labour-saving device.

•

The instinct-conflicts which produce an ulcer are usually concerned with sex or family relationships. The modern cortex refuses to admit such conflicts and to expose them to the processes of reasoning. Guilt of this type, therefore, continues to build up behind the censoring screen and forces the diencephalon into the drastic action which causes the ulcer.

This interpretation of the peptic ulcers suggests an obvious psychotherapeutic approach. Censorship at the level of consciousness must be so far relaxed that the conflicting instincts, and the emotion of guilt which they engender, can be ushered into conscious awareness. Thereafter the psychological situation becomes identical with that of a person who has a guilty conscience on account of something he knows he has done, a situation which never produces an ulcer. If such a psychotherapeutic manoeuvre is successfully accomplished, ulcers may heal with surprising rapidity, often in a matter of days, and do not recur unless an entirely new guilt-provoking situation arises.

One of the most remarkable things about the growth of the cortex was the incredible acceleration of this process. While the earlier phases took tens of millions of years to evolve, the later phases were covered in a few hundred thousand years. It seems to be a general law of evolution that once a trend towards a single successful specialization has become firmly established, the speed with which this specialization develops gets faster and faster and may even develop of its own accord beyond the limits of usefulness. Meanwhile, the rest of the body continues to evolve at a slow and steady pace, so that after a while a stage is reached in which all the other evolutionary trends are left far behind the outstanding specialization.

In modern man this development has already gone so far that there are signs of an evolutionary regression in the body in favour of a still more freakish growth of the brain. Modern man's body no longer reaches its full evolutionary maturity, as it did in Neanderthal Man. Though the modern brain develops further than that of Neanderthal Man, modern man's body remains behind in an earlier embryonic stage. He carries certain embryonic features on into adult life. An example of this has already been mentioned in connection with the distribution of human hair, but there are many other instances. One that interests us here is the relationship between the brain and the rest of the body.

In the light-skinned human races the development of the body is sharply braked in the last stages of pre-natal life, while the growth of the cortex is accelerated. There is some evidence to suggest that the negro's body is better adjusted to his brain. He is physically more mature at birth, and under ideal environmental conditions he averages a larger body. From an evolutionary point of view this makes his brain-body ratio more balanced.

•

A tendency to self-destruction seems to be inherent in the over-developed human brain. It is a situation similar to that in which a parasite thrives so exuberantly that it destroys its host, thereby bringing about its own undoing. As the host can survive if the parasite's rapacity is kept within tolerable limits, so man will survive longer if he can release his body and his diencephalon from the cruel cortical grip to which civilization is increasingly subjecting him.

In psychosomatic disease urban man is already paying a heavy price for his civilization, but he now has the means substantially to reduce the price if he will but make full use of them and realize to what extent his cortical presumption, deluding him that he has full control over his animal nature, prevents him from doing so. Western man will eventually go about the solution of his most pressing biological problems through a better understanding of psychosomatic mechanisms and will not adopt the only alternative, which is to give the cortex full rein; for if he did this, all his behaviour would become governed by rigidly conditioned reflexes. His mating and breeding, his drinking and feeding and all his many emotions would then have to conform to a fixed pattern applying to everybody; this would be entirely contrary to the way of life which he has so far followed.

The Mind of Man

A good broad intelligent introduction to current work in brain science. Well illustrated.

—SB

The Mind of Man
Nigel Calder
1970; 288 pp

$8.95 postpaid

from:
Viking Press, Inc.
625 Madison Ave.
New York, N.Y. 10022

or WHOLE EARTH CATALOG

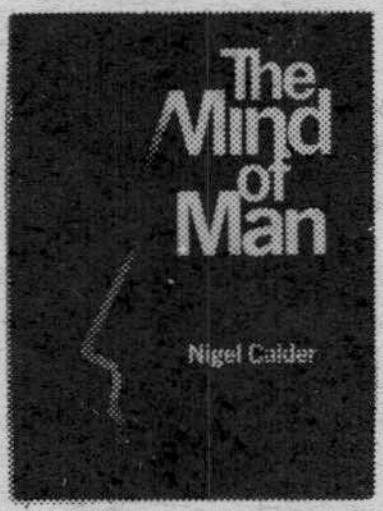

Everyone waited expectantly for the next half-hourly sample and its analysis. When it came, it showed an oxygen consumption of 2.2 litres. Ramanand Yogi had voluntarily knocked his requirement down to one quarter of the minimum supposed necessary for the maintenance of life. The *Bhagavad-Gita*, holy book of the yogis, remarks aptly:

> As a blazing fire turns fuel to ashes,
> so does the fire of knowledge turn all actions into ashes.

•

Changes in the size of the pupils of the eyes are an unconscious form of communication: large pupils denote interest and therefore make a woman seem more attractive. (Modified detail from Botticelli's *Primavera*)

•

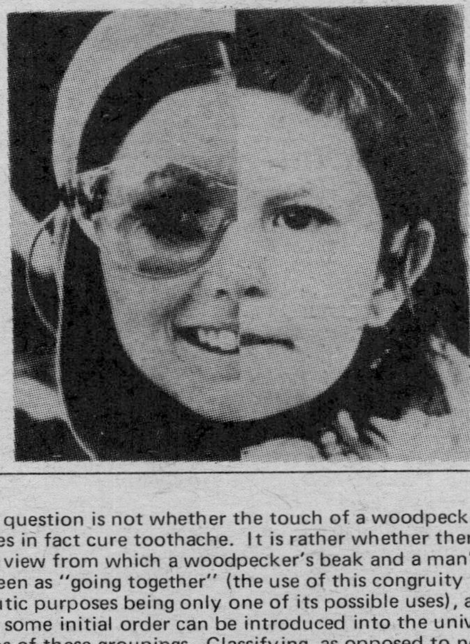

A housewife in her mid-thirties sits in a laboratory at the California Institute of Technology. In front of her is a screen and she has been asked to gaze at a spot marked in the middle of it. A strange picture appears briefly on the screen. It is a split face made up of two halves joined down the middle. On the right, as seen by the housewife, it is a young child; on the left a young woman wearing spectacles.

Next, the housewife is shown a choice of several faces, and she is asked to point with her right hand at the one she saw. She describes the old man and denies that there was anything odd about the picture.

Like the face on the screen, the housewife's brain has been split down the middle. She underwent an operation for severe epilepsy in which the surgeon cut the great bundle of nerve fibres which normally connect the two sides of the roof of the brain. The operation was successful and the woman is now able to lead a more normal life. To see her doing her housework, swimming, riding a bicycle, and so on, you would not for one moment suppose there was anything unusual about her. But the tests devised by Roger Sperry and his colleagues show that she possesses two independent minds under the one skull.

The Savage Mind

Claude Levi-Strauss is the most famous — I mean, all the anthropologists recommend — He's so — I mean, so what if he's French — The most profound — Sartre couldn't — structural anthropology was what — Primitive doesn't mean — I mean, they knew what they were doing — So when — It looks crazy to us of course — They were just abstracting in a different — But you can analyze it once you — So you see, ritual is the — If you never — The Indians always — I mean, what makes you think you're so logical?

[Suggested by Michael Harner. Not reviewed by Lily Tomlin.]

The Savage Mind
Claude Lévi-Strauss
1962, 1966; 290 pp.

$3.45 postpaid from:
University of Chicago Press
5801 Ellis Ave.
Chicago, Illinois 60637

or WHOLE EARTH CATALOG

The real question is not whether the touch of a woodpecker's beak does in fact cure toothache. It is rather whether there is a point of view from which a woodpecker's beak and a man's tooth can be seen as "going together" (the use of this congruity for therapeutic purposes being only one of its possible uses), and whether some initial order can be introduced into the universe by means of these groupings. Classifying, as opposed to not classifying, has a value of its own, whatever form the classification may take.

•

A native thinker makes the penetrating comment that "All sacred things must have their place" (Fletcher 2, p. 34). It could even be said that being in their place is what makes them sacred for if they were taken out of their place, even in thought, the entire order of the universe would be destroyed. Sacred objects therefore contribute to the maintenance of order in the universe by occupying the places allocated to them. Examined superficially and from the outside, the refinements of ritual can appear pointless. They are explicable by a concern for what one might call "micro-adjustment" —the concern to assign every single creature, object or feature to a place within a class.

Several thousand Coahuila Indians never exhausted the natural resources of a desert region in South California, in which today only a handful of white families manage to subsist. They lived in a land of plenty, for in this apparently completely barren territory, they were familiar with no less than sixty kinds of edible plants and twenty-eight others of narcotic, stimulant or medicinal properties (Barrows). A single Seminol informant could identify two hundred and fifty species and varieties of plants (Sturtevant). Three hundred and fifty plants known to the Hopi Indians and more than five hundred to the Navaho have been recorded.

•

We have had to wait until the middle of this century for the crossing of long separated paths: that which arrives at the physical world by the detour of communication, and that which as we have recently come to know, arrives at the world of communication by the detour of the physical. The entire process of human knowledge thus assumes the character of a closed system. And we therefore remain faithful to the inspiration of the savage mind when we recognize that, by an encounter it alone could have foreseen, the scientific spirit in its most modern form will have contributed to legitimize the principles of savage thought and to re-establish it in its rightful place.

Centering

Centering
M. C. Richards
1962, 1964; 159 pp.

$3.95 postpaid

from:
Wesleyan University Press
Middletown, Conn. 06457

or WHOLE EARTH CATALOG

Because I am a potter, I take my image, centering, from the potter's craft. A potter brings his clay into center on the potter's wheel, and then he gives it whatever shape he wishes. There are wide correspondences to this process. Such extensions of meaning I want to call attention to. For centering is my theme: how we may seek to bring universe into a personal wholeness, and into act the rich life which moves so mysteriously and decisively in our bodies, manifesting in speech and gesture, materializing as force in the world the unifying energy of our perceptions.

•

Our studies of Eastern philosophy teach us to let go, to drop it. To surrender our attachments, our mentation. To free ourselves from ignorance and suffering. Our studies of Western philosophy teach us to surrender our minds to perception. Pure thinking has its source at the center. Thus Idealism is our Western knowledge: to surrender reflections for the evolving forms toward which matter is continuously casting itself, a dynamic thinking which generates rather than mirrors. And Western empiricism, which brings us back always sharply to the edges of a particular moment. There is only the moment, and yet the moment is always giving way to the next, so that there is not even Now, there is Nothing. True, true. There is nothing, if that is the way to understanding how much there is.

Sense Relaxation

This is a book which _is_ an experience while it teaches you how to have additional experiences. It is a combination of simple straightforward how-to-do-it prose broken by puns (to slow down your reading) plus sensual photographs of every exercise. Your first time through this book you will only glance at the words; the pictures are so compelling. The second and third times through you will read individual sections to find out what the pictures suggest. Finally you will begin to use this book to add touch, relaxation and pleasure to your life. This book gives very specific and easily followed exercises for individuals, couples, and groups to tune in to their own bodies and to all their senses. Gunther gives suggestions and techniques to energize, to tranquillize, and above all to increase awareness. It is a beautifully designed and executed book.

[Reviewed by James Fadiman]

**Sense Relaxation –
Below Your Mind**
Bernard Gunther
Photographed by Paul Fusco
1968; 191 pp.

$1.50 postpaid

from:
Pocket Books
c/o Simon & Schuster
1 W. 39th St.
New York NY 10018

or WHOLE EARTH CATALOG

Most people are half breathers,
keeping residual air
in their lower lungs;
they are unable to take a full
deep breath even if they want to.
To breathe deeper
you must exhale more. Yelling
gets out all the old air and
some of those held-in feelings;
let yourself be open-air.

Alpha

Alpha waves are produced by the brain when it's being nice and quiet. With a sensor you can learn to produce alpha, so it can be a sort of shortcut to meditative skill. But it's a fussy problematic business to deal with the sensors.

Alpha wave sensors are like water beds. A technological step in leisure activities they are being manufactured and marketed in profusion, largely on a cottage industry basis. Some are undoubtedly better than others, but we haven't sorted them out. Here's addresses and prices. Good luck.

—SB

Alphawave kit— $26
(board of assembled electronics.
You build audio connections, electrodes,
& cabinet. Warbling audio signal for alpha.)

from:
Steve Parks
1857 West Pensacola
Tallahassee, Florida 32304

Bioscope— No Longer Available
(includes warranty. Well spoken of by our public meditator on KPFA)

from:
Bio-Meditation Society
19145 Lanark Street
Reseda, California 91335

Toomim Alpha Pacer— $195-295
(fits in a jacket pocket)

from:
Toomim Laboratories
10480 Santa Monica Blvd.
Los Angeles, CA 90025

Aquarian Alphaphone—$80-$990
(5 year warranty)

from:
Aquarius Electronics
Box 627
Mendocino, CA 95460

Bioscope

Cyberscope—$70
(cheap wired headset)

from:
Inner Space Electronics
Box 319
Fairfax, CA 94930

ETC—from $250.00

from:
Psionics
Box 1919
Boulder, Colorado 80302

Psychophysics— $45

from:
Psychophysics Labs
31 Townsend Terrace
Framingham, Mass. 01701

It was a scheme to reclaim the soil of the homeplace that had been killed by the mining on the slopes above the farm. Until Emmit started rebuilding the garden soil with rabbit shit behind the barn, the only living spot on the homeplace was the little triangle of green in front of the house, where some grass still grew and the poplar trees and the silver-leaf maple tree had leaves. It was only a matter of time before that little patch would be destroyed too, however, and the old family house along with it. For behind the house was a wall of dried mud and shale and blasted rock high as the roof in places. It had rolled down from the bench above, and then in two wet winters continued to slip until now it looked like a frozen ocean wave, waiting for another winter to melt it and send it flowing through the house and on across the yard toward the road and Trace Fork creek below.

But out near the barn, which stood a little uphill from the house and on a kind of roll in the slope, the overburden had stabilized. It had slipped as far as it was going to, and it was there that Emmit had chosen to make his effort and invest his work the last few months of his life.

The barn had been pushed off its foundation by the wash of overburden, flowing down. A rock big as a car, set rolling by a bulldozer up above, had smashed into the upper end of the barn and ripped a big hole in the wall. But in spite of the damage the barn was still a fairly solid structure, and when the mud had dried and settled Emmit had gone to work behind the barn, spreading all the manure and organic matter he could get, in an effort to create enough new topsoil to make a garden.

There'd been some old rotted manure in the stalls in the barn, left from the days when the Colliers kept cows and a work horse. Emmit had shoveled it out and scattered some spoiled hay over it, and then worked that into the spot he intended to garden. Emmit's health was starting to fail him even then. That shoveling was among the last heavy work he tried. It was then he got his idea to raise rabbits in hutches as a source of manure for the garden he intended to create below the barn.

A friend of Emmit's on Upper Rockhouse Creek who raised rabbits for meat sold him the buck and the first two does. Emmit built hutches for them out of weather boarding he ripped off the back of the old doomed house he lived in. In a year's time he built eleven hutches from lumber off the house, and his herd grew to nearly fifty rabbits. He fed them commercial rabbit feed that Leonard hauled up the creek in the sled by the hundred pound bag. It cost him, but the project was important to Emmit and he was willing to pay. Emmit received a disability pension from the government for his war wound, a hundred and forty-some dollars every month. His personal expenses were rarely more than half of that, so he could afford his herd of rabbits. Leonard said that Emmit would eat a rabbit now and then, but what he kept them for was the first-class shit they produced. As it accumulated beneath the hutches he spread it on the sterile soil, and in a year's time he had redeemed a patch twenty feet by ten, and it was now growing short, single rows of lettuce, carrots, turnips, cucumbers, potatoes, beets, tomatoes and comfrey, and two longer rows of beans.

(continued)

Self-Hypnosis

A guy from Stanford named Bob Lochridge came into the Truck Store, saw Lecron's **Self Hypnotism** *and said that it was sure enough a good book* __*about*__ *self-hypnotism, but for technique we'd be better off with Sparks'* **Self-Hypnosis.** *So we are.* —SB

[Suggested by Bob Lochridge]

self-hypnosis
A CONDITIONED-RESPONSE TECHNIQUE

Self-Hypnosis
Laurance Sparks
1962; 254 pp.

$2.00 postpaid

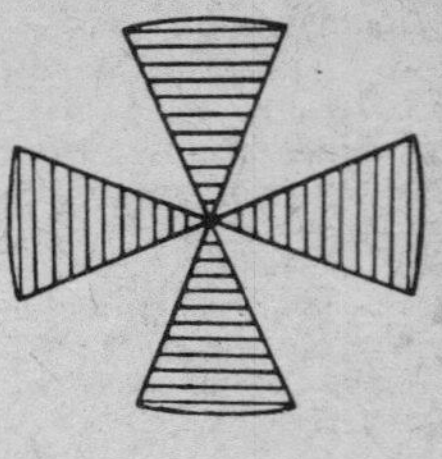

from:
Wilshire Book Company
12015 Sherman Road
N. Hollywood, CA 91605

or WHOLE EARTH CATALOG

Pre-Trance Instructions

While in a comfortable place and with eyes fixed straight ahead:
1. Think of the time you wish to "wake up."
2. Formulate your suggestion.

Trance-Induction Procedure

3. Imagine "1000-1", the symbol for evoking tiredness of the eyelids.
4. Imagine "1000-2", the symbol for evoking eye-closure.
5. Imagine "1000-3", the symbol for relaxation.
6. Imagine "1000-4", the symbol for emotional tranquillity.
7. Imagine "1000-5", the symbol denoting "hyper-suggestibility."
8. Imagine a circle enclosing an "X," then carefully erase the "X."

Deepening Procedure

9. Imagine, one by one, the letters of the alphabet, as if writing "a" in the circle, then erasing it, etc.

•

After she achieved a self-induced trance, I explained to her that she would see a movie that she had seen years ago, that it would be very clear and vivid and that she would see it upon a signal of snapping my fingers. I made a mistake, which had to do with the realization that I had neglected to give her certain instructions, and inadvertently snapped my fingers before explaining to her about the second signal. Imagine my surprise when she immediately woke up! I felt rather provoked with myself until I noticed her amazed expression, and she said, "Why, that's the most interesting thing that ever happened to me!"

"What happened?" I asked, not knowing quite what to expect.

"I just saw Gone With the Wind," she replied, laughing.

"How much of it did you see?"

"I saw the whole thing from beginning to end. It was even better than I remembered."

While I was still trying to figure out what had happened, she was telling me at great length about the picture. I found it hard to believe that she had really seen the whole picture, or even a small part of it, in such a short instant of time. But she convinced me by describing every detail of the opening scenes and dialogue, and continuing with vivid word-for-word reproduction as if she had just come from the theatre. Better, in fact, than if she had. It was clear that she had experienced imagery of the most vivid kind imaginable of a two-and-one-half hour picture in the time it took to snap my fingers—not between two signals; just during one snap!

•

"We are now going to assume that you are at the stage of 1000-5 and that we have made the suggestion that your right hand is going to move up toward your face, and when your fingers touch your face you will go deeper than ever before. While you are very deep I will go over the pattern again, and from then on you will be able to put yourself into a deep trance whenever it is safe for you to do so. You will be able to go deep any time you wish. Quickly and easily as long as it is safe. Deeper each time.

"I want you to think about your right hand now. Notice how it feels. Everyone has sensations going on in his hands continuously, but usually we don't notice these sensations. We have no need to notice them. Now, I want you to notice your right hand. Think about how it feels.
Think about whether it feels warm or cool. Think about whether it feels light or heavy. Notice whether or not you can feel the pulse beating in your hand or fingers. In a little while, perhaps already, there will be a sensation of lightness in your hand and arm. Your hand will keep getting lighter and lighter and it will be drawn up to your face. When your fingers gently touch your face you will go very deep. Deeper each time. Deeper than before.

"Keep thinking about your hand. Your fingers may have a tendency to twitch or move a little. This just means you are going deeper. This is what we want. Now I want you to think of your hand being a little bit higher than it is. Picture your hand a little bit higher and, as you do, it becomes that way. Now picture yourself writing the word 'lighter' on a blackboard. Each time you write the word 'lighter' your hand moves up higher, a little higher each time. It keeps moving higher and higher with each breath. Picture the image of your hand a little higher alternately with writing the word 'lighter' on the blackboard. Each time you do, subconscious impulses make your hand and arm lighter, and they keep moving up. Moving up. Higher and higher."

Self Hypnotism

One of the things that intrigues me most about hypnotism is that no one knows how it works—which accounts for some of its disrepute. No common factors, for example, have been found to pre-distinguish susceptibles from non-susceptibles. Black box business.

Lecron doesn't talk about any of this. He's concerned with how you can detect and de-suggest old imprinted hang-ups and suggest in new ones you like better. (One subject suggested herself larger breasts, and got them.

Possibly the most general use of this book is its clear delineation of a simple avenue __*in*__*—a meditative technique without much dogma. There's a lot of hypnosis books; this is the best we've seen.* —SB

Self Hypnotism
Leslie M. LeCron
1964; 208 pp.

$0.75 postpaid

SELF HYPNOTISM

from:
New American Library, Inc.
1301 Avenue of the Americas
New York, New York 10019

or WHOLE EARTH CATALOG

Now that you are comfortable you will listen closely to my voice and will follow all the suggestions given. This will teach you how to enter hypnosis and how to produce it yourself. Your eyes are now closed. Take another deep breath, hold it a few seconds and let it out.

The more you can relax, the deeper you will be able to go into hypnosis. Let all your muscles go as loose and limp as possible. To do this start with your right leg. Tighten the muscles first, making the leg rigid. Then let it relax from your toes up to your hip. Then tighten the muscles of the left leg. Let that leg relax from the toes up to the hip.

Let the stomach and abdominal area relax; then your chest and breathing muscles. The muscles of your back can loosen— your shoulders and neck muscles relaxing. Often we have tension in this area. Let all these muscles loosen. Now your arms from the shoulders right down to your finger tips. Even your facial muscles will relax. Relaxation is so pleasant and comfortable. Let go completely and enjoy the relaxation. All tension seems to drain away and you soon find a listlessness creeping over you, with a sense of comfort and well-being.

As you relax more and more, you will slip deeper and deeper into hypnosis. Your arms and legs may develop a feeling of heaviness. Or instead you may find your whole body feeling very light, as though you are floating on a soft cloud.

Now imagine that you are standing at the top of an escalator such as those in some stores. See the steps moving down in front of you, and see the railings. I am going to count from ten to zero. As I start to count, imagine you are stepping on the escalator, standing there with your hands on the railing while the steps move down in front of you taking you with them. If you prefer, you can imagine a staircase or an elevator instead. If you have any difficulty visualizing the escalator or staircase or elevator, just the count itself will take you deeper and deeper.

(Slowly) TEN—now you step on and start going down. NINE—EIGHT—SEVEN—SIX. Going deeper and deeper with each count. FIVE—FOUR—THREE. Still deeper. TWO—ONE—and ZERO. Now you step off at the bottom and will continue to go deeper still with each breath you take. You are so relaxed and comfortable. Let go still more. Notice your breathing. Probably it is now slower and you are breathing more from the bottom of your lungs, abdominal breathing.

In a moment you will notice your hand and arm are beginning to lose any feeling of heaviness and are becoming light. If you are right-handed, it will be your right arm, if left-handed, it will be the left. The arm is getting lighter and lighter. It will begin to lift. Perhaps just the fingers will move first, or the whole hand will start to float up. It will float toward your face, as though your face was a magnet pulling it up until the fingers touch your face someplace. Let's see where that will be. The arm begins to bend at the elbow. It is floating upward. If it has not started of its own accord, lift it voluntarily a few inches to give it a start. It will continue to go up of its own accord with no further effort. It floats on up toward your face, higher and higher. The higher your hand goes the deeper you will go. The deeper you go, the higher the hand will go. Lifting, lifting, floating up higher and higher. Going higher and higher. Now if it has touched your face let your hand go down to any comfortable position. If it has not touched yet, it can continue to float up until it does touch. You can forget about the arm while I tell you how you can put yourself into hypnosis whenever you may wish to do so.

You will use much the same method being used now. When you have made yourself comfortable, you will merely close your eyes and drift into hypnosis. But in your first three or four practice sessions it would help you if you first lit a candle and when you have made yourself comfortable would look at the flickering flame for two or three minutes. Then close your eyes.

Then you will think to yourself the phrase, "Now I am going into hypnosis." Then repeat to yourself the words, "Relax now" three times, saying them very slowly. As you do this you will slip off into hypnosis. You say nothing aloud, you merely think these words. When you have done this, take another deep breath to help you relax more and go through the relaxation just as you have done before. Tell your muscles to relax as I have done.

When you have finally relaxed your arms, imagine the escalator, elevator or staircase. Now you should count backward from ten to zero, including the zero. Count slowly. In your first four practice sessions repeat the count three times, as though going down different levels. With practice you need only count once.

Whenever you are ready to awaken all you need to do is think to yourself, "Now I am going to wake up." Then count slowly to three and you will be wide awake. You will always awaken refreshed, relaxed and feeling fine.

While you are in hypnosis if something should happen so you should awaken, you will do so instantly and spontaneously—something such as the phone ringing or a real emergency like a fire. You will awaken instantly and be wide awake and fully alert. Actually this would happen without such a suggestion being necessary, for your subconscious mind always protects you.

Now I will count to three and you will be wide awake. If convenient you should then go through this formula for self-hypnosis and put yourself back in. You will remember the formula and go through it exactly as given. Now, awaken as I count. ONE. Coming awake now. TWO—almost awake. THREE—now you are wide awake. Wide awake.

Psycho-cybernetics

This strange and gaudy volume will probably turn you off if you associate wisdom with subdued writing or humble exposition. However, if you can overcome your initial resistence to the high-pressure, breezy style and the sometimes excessive claims, it will be worth the effort. Dr. Maltz has outlined perhaps the easiest program of personality development and modification in print. It is easy because it contains nothing but the suggested exercises and the understanding that the motivation to change is still the most powerful tool.

This is not a book to read. It is a kit of tools to use in gaining control of your nature for whatever ends you desire. The author has made it clear that there is no virtue in being obscure or even in being poetic if it detracts from getting the reader off his ass and doing something about himself.

There is an assumption of a higher self or a core to one's being which tends toward realization or whatever term you prefer but understanding of this inner nature is not vital to using the book.

What we need to understand is that these habits, unlike addictions, can be modified, changed, or reversed, simply by taking the trouble to make a __conscious decision__—and then by practicing or "acting out" the new response or behavior.

Simple? Yes. But each of the above habitual ways of acting, feeling, thinking does have beneficial and constructive influence on your self-image. Act them out for 21 days. 'Experience' them and see if worry, guilt, hostility have not been diminished and if confidence has not been increased.

So, why not give yourself a face lift? Your do-it-yourself kit consists of relaxation of negative tensions to prevent scars, therapeutic forgiveness to remove old scars, providing yourself with a tough (not a hard) epidermis instead of a shell, creative living, a willingness to be a __little vulnerable__, and a nostalgia for the future instead of the past.

If the above puts you off then this is not the book for your use. If this totally western way of dealing with yourself interests you, this book is far better than most of the other pop-enlightenment books around.

[Suggested and reviewed by James Fadiman]

PSYCHO-CYBERNETICS
A New Technique for Using Your SUBCONSCIOUS POWER
By MAXWELL MALTZ, M.D., F.I.C.S.
Foreword by MELVIN POWERS

Psycho-Cybernetics
Maxwell Maltz
1960; 256 pp.

$.95 postpaid

from:
Pocket Books, Inc.
1 W. 39th St.
New York, N.Y. 10018

or WHOLE EARTH CATALOG

Inner disturbance, or the opposite of tranquility, is nearly always caused by over-response, a too sensitive 'alarm reaction.' You create a built-in tranquilizer, or psychic screen between yourself and the disturbing stimulus, when you practice "not responding"—letting the telephone ring.

You cure old habits of over-response, you extinguish old conditioned reflexes, when you practice delaying the habitual, automatic, and unthinking response.

•

You may have never been formally hypnotized. But if you have accepted an idea—from yourself, your teachers, your parents, friends, advertisements—or from any other source, and further, if you are firmly convinced that idea is true, it has the same power over you as the hypnotist's words have over the hypnotized subject.

•

Your automatic mechanism, or what the Freudians call the 'unconscious,' is absolutely impersonal. It operates as a machine and has no 'will' of its own. It always tries to react appropriately to your current beliefs and interpretations concerning environment. It always seeks to give you appropriate feelings, and to accomplish the goals which you consciously determine upon. It works only upon the data which you feed it in the form of ideas, beliefs, interpretations, opinions.

Meditation in Action

The Venerable Trungpa Rinpoche was some kind of a high abbot over a district of monasteries in Tibet, so you can expect a book of his talks to be some kind of esoteric and too profound for us surface-dwellers.

If it's esoteric, he's cleverly hidden that fact, and surface dwellers are being sucked in from all over the map. I've never seen so much good sense in so little space on the subject of meditation. As a book, it trends toward the very goal: singularity.

—SB

Meditation in Action
Chögyam Trungpa
1969; 74 pp.

$2.25 postpaid

from:
Shambhala Publications Inc.
1409 5th Street
Berkeley, California 94710

or WHOLE EARTH CATALOG

The point is that whatever one is trying to learn, it is necessary to have first hand experience, rather than learning from books or from teachers or by merely conforming to an already established pattern. That is what he found, and in that sense Buddha was a great revolutionary in his way of thinking. He even denied the existence of Brahma, or God, the Creator of the world. He determined to accept nothing which he had not first discovered for himself.

. . . He developed the creative side of revolution, which is not trying to get help from anyone else, but finding out for oneself. Buddhism is perhaps the only religion which is not based on the revelation of God nor on faith and devotion to God or gods of any kind. This does not mean that Buddha was an atheist or a heretic. He never argued theological or philosophical doctrines at all. He went straight to the heart of the matter, namely, how to see the Truth. He never wasted time in vain speculation.

•

If we are meditating at home and we happen to live in the middle of the High Street, we cannot stop the traffic just because we want peace and quiet. But we can stop ourselves, we can accept the noise. The noise also contains silence. We must put ourselves into it and expect nothing from outside, just as Buddha did. And we must accept whatever situation arises. As long as we never retreat from the situation, it will always present itself as a vehicle and we will be able to make use of it. As it is said in the Scriptures, "The Dharma is good at the beginning, the Dharma is good in the middle and the Dharma is good at the end." In other words the Dharma never becomes out-of-date, since fundamentally the situation is always the same.

•

The whole point is to cultivate the acceptance of everything, so one should not discriminate or become involved in any kind of struggle. That is the basic meditation technique, and it is quite simple and direct. There should be no deliberate effort, no attempt to control and no attempt to be peaceful. This is why breathing is used. It is easy to feel the breathing, and one has no need to be self-conscious or to try and do anything. The breathing is simply available and one should just feel that. That is the reason why technique is important to start with. This is the primary way of starting, but it generally continues and develops in its own way. One sometimes finds oneself doing it slightly differently from when one first started, quite spontaneously. This is not classified as an advanced technique or a beginner's technique. It simply grows and develops gradually.

•

Where there is an external person, a higher Being, or the concept of something which is separate from oneself, then we tend to think that because there is something outside there must be something here as well. The external phenomenon sometimes becomes such an overwhelming thing and seems to have all sorts of seductive or aggressive qualities, so we erect a kind of defence mechanism against it, failing to see that that is itself a continuity of the external thing. We try to segregate ourselves from the external, and this creates a kind of gigantic bubble in us which consists of nothing but air and water or, in this case, fear and the reflection of the external thing. So this huge bubble prevents any fresh air from coming in, and that is "I"——the Ego. So in that sense there is the existence of Ego, but it is in fact illusory.

•

Q. For meditation, would a student have to rid himself of Ego before he started, or would this come naturally as he is studying?

A. This comes naturally, because you can't start without Ego. And basically Ego isn't bad. Good and bad doesn't really exist anywhere, it is only a secondary thing. Ego is, in a sense, a false thing, but it isn't necessarily bad. You have to start with Ego, and use Ego, and from there it gradually wears out, like a pair of shoes. But you have to use it and wear it out thoroughly, so it is not preserved. Otherwise, if you try to push Ego aside and start perfect, you may become more and more perfect in a rather one-sided way, but the same amount of imperfection is building up on the other side, just as creating intense light creates intense darkness as well.

A Hidden Wholeness

No book has convinced me so directly that the life of active contemplation can be utterly wholesome. Here are indisputable photographs by Merton and by John Howard Griffon (remember **Black Like Me**? *The white who dyed himself black so he could understand). . .photographs and some calligraphy by Merton that attest something tough, pointed, and very healthy going on here that I don't understand.*

—SB

A Hidden Wholeness
Thomas Merton, John Howard Griffin
1970; 147 pp.

$15.00 postpaid

from:
Houghton Mifflin Co.
2 Park St.
Boston, Mass. 02107

or WHOLE EARTH CATALOG

Thomas Merton entered the Cistercian Abbey of Our Lady of Gethsemani in Trappist, Kentucky, on December 10, 1941, to begin his life as a Trappist monk.

Twenty-seven years later, to the day, on December 10, 1968, a few hours after addressing a religious conference near Bangkok, Thailand he died alone in his room from the effects of an accidental electric shock received when he touched a fan.

His religious life formed a single arc. From the beginning he sought to lose himself in God in the silence of Trappist contemplative life. Through all the intrusions of his celebrity as a writer and prophetic figure, that initial religious passion remained paramount and growing. At the end of his life he was in search of deeper silence and solitude and more perfect contemplation.

On the Psychology of Meditation

If you're into meditation, but think Science has something to offer the world, you've probably tried to see what scientists have said about it. And been pretty disappointed. With few exceptions, they glibly call it "self-hypnosis," and, having said the magic word that exorcises the mysterious, forget about it. This book, still in press, is the first scientific treatment of meditation that is really good. If you're a meditator and want your world-view expanded this will help. If you're a scientist and want your world-view expanded, this will do it.

Claudio Naranjo looks at the multitude of ways of meditating and finds some basic dimensions running through them. Robert Ornstein looks at meditative practices and results from a psychologist's view and finds similarities to some well-known psychological processes that make it clearer just how meditation works, even though the ultimate question of where it takes you is beyond books.

[Suggested and reviewed by Charley Tart]

On the Psychology of Meditation
Claudio Naranjo, Robert Ornstein
1971: 320 pp.

$2.25 postpaid

from:
Viking Press, Inc.
625 Madison Ave.
New York, N.Y. 10022

or WHOLE EARTH CATALOG

Aside from the difficulty arising from the esoteric nature of some practices, a fact that makes writing on techniques almost irrelevant, in the sphere of meditation that we are discussing, is that the effectiveness of any practice seems to depend, more than in another case on an extra-technical factor of "personal contagion."

The infectious nature of possession by devils throughout history is well established, and it is impressive to read documents such as those of the epidemic of Loudun, showing how even apparently sane priests sent to perform exorcisms became affected by the prevalent state.

What is true in regard to unwanted devil possession is apparently as true with regard to states that are welcomed and cultivated. Among many peoples, trance is a collective phenomenon in which the state of the more experienced is believed to facilitate that of the novices. Among the Kung bushmen of the Kalahari desert, for instance, who understand the possessing entity not as a spirit but as an energy,—originally given to man by God— the energy, also called a "medicine", is now maintained by direct *transmission* from man to man. According to Dr. R. Lee, who has studied their trance dances, the practicing curers spend much of their time implanting *medicine* into the bodies of their trainees.

•

Recall the phenomenon of habituation. A slight change in the input is enough to "dishabituate" and to return the stimulus to awareness. Similarly, slightly altering our usual "automatic" behaviors, such as tying shoes, driving cars, should return them again into awareness.

In Yoga itself there is a similar tradition called Karma Yoga. The attempt is to treat everyday activities as a sacrament and to give them full attention. This exercise performs the same function as "right mindedness", or "self-remembering", and perhaps is a less extreme version of shikan-taza.

Most schools within these traditions combine the two major kinds of awareness, exercises or meditations, using a half hour or so twice a day of the "shutting down" meditation and as much as possible of the remainder of the day in a form of self-observation.

•

That concentrative meditation is a "turning off" of competing activity does seem quite clear. We recall in Anand's study of Yoga meditation that while in meditation the brains of the Yogins did not show any response to the external world. Also recall that the repetitive stimulation of the ganzfeld and by stabilized images leads to a state equivalent to that of no external stimulation at all. The repetitive form of meditation involves a trick to turn off the nervous system, to turn off awareness of the external environment, to enter a state of "darkness", or the "void", or, in our previous metaphor, that of turning out the light of the sun.

Meditation Cushions and Mats

Traditionally designed softness for your hard edges. —SB

Catalog

free

from:
Alaya Stitchery
ZEN Center
300 Page Street
San Francisco, CA 94102

Zafu $12.50-$15.00.
Measures 7"x12", available in several colors, patterned after traditional Japanese designs.

Zabuton $12.50-$18.00. Measures 30"x34"

Futon $27.00-$34.00. Sleeping and Yoga mat.

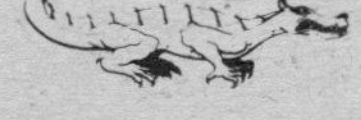

The rabbits were the central project in Emmit's scheme, but he had other things going too that he had worked at as he had the time, and strength. He had a worm pit going by one of the walls inside the barn. He'd built it when he first got his rabbits, filled it with manure and stocked it with five thousand red worms he'd ordered through the mail. A year later there were so many worms in it he was scooping them out by the pitch-fork full and planting them in the garden rows to go to work on the mulch of shit and hay. But as the garden expanded and the rabbit population increased, Emmit wanted still more worms, and the extension of the pit was one of the projects he left unfinished when he died.

D.R. intended to finish that pit, and perhaps build another one along the facing wall.

It would not be possible to breed too many worms for the work he had in mind.

(continued)

Light on Yoga

If you are into it already, and want probably the most complete Hatha Yoga book, get this book. It has over 600 pictures, 200 asanas (postures) and a warm guru-like introduction to get you straight.

[Reviewed by Merce]

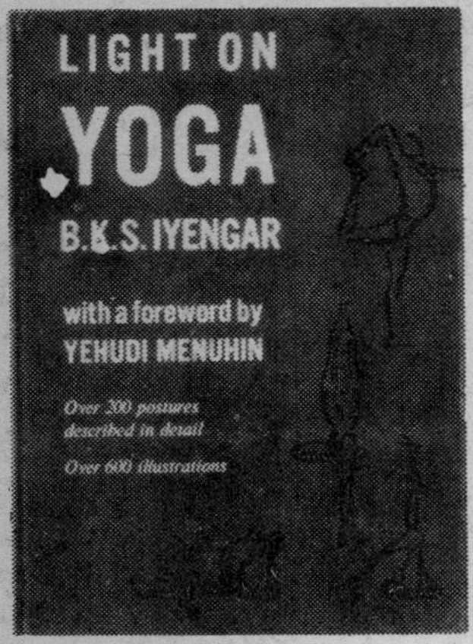

Light on Yoga
B.K.S. Iyengar
1965, 70; 342 pp.

$3.95 plus $.30 postage and handling

from:
Schocken Books, Inc.
200 Madison Ave.
New York, NY 10016

or WHOLE EARTH CATALOG

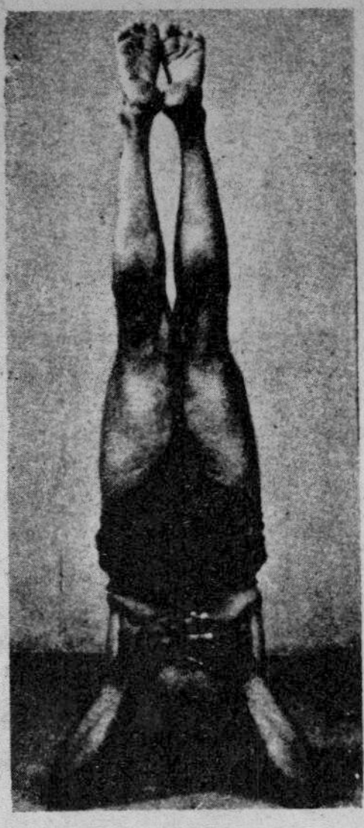

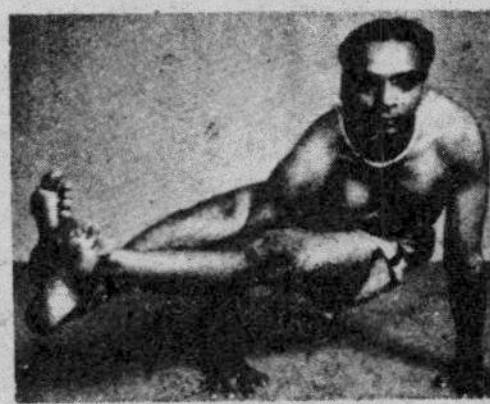

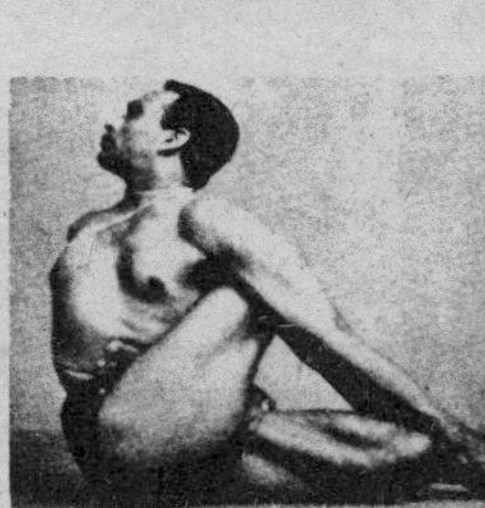

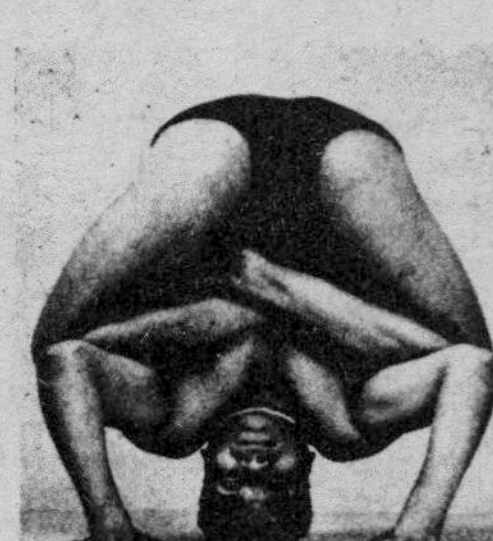

Yoga is the method by which the restless mind is calmed and the energy directed into constructive channels. As a mighty river which when properly harnessed by dams and canals, creates a vast reservoir of water, prevents famine and provides abundant power for industry; so also the mind, when controlled provides a reservoir of peace and generates abundant energy for human uplift.

•

To make life healthy, happy and peaceful, it is essential to study regularly divine literature in a pure place. This study of the sacred books of the world will enable the sadhaka to concentrate upon and to solve the difficult problems of life when they arise. It will put an end to ignorance and bring knowledge. Ignorance has no beginning, but it has an end. There is a beginning but no end to knowledge.

•

Once the sadhaka has experienced the fulness of creation or of the Creator, his thirst (tṛṣṇa) for objects of sense vanishes and he looks at them ever after with dispassion (vairāgya). He experiences no disquiet in heat or cold, in pain or pleasure, in honour or dishonour and in virtue or vice. He treats the two imposters—triumph and disaster—with equanimity. He has emancipated himself from these pairs of opposites. He has passed beyond the pull of the gunas and has become a gunatita (one who has transcended the gunas). He is then free from birth and death, from pain and sorrow and becomes immortal. He has no self identity as he lives experiencing the fulness of the Universal Soul. Such a man, scorning nothing, leads all things to the path of perfection.

•

27. When one has mastered an asana, it comes with effortless ease and causes no discomfort. The bodily movements become graceful. While performing asanas, the student's body assumes numerous forms of life found in creation—from the lowliest insect to the most perfect sage—and he learns that in all these there breathes the same Universal Spirit—the Spirit of God. He looks within himself while practising and feels the presence of God in different asanas which he does with a sense of surrender unto the feet of the Lord.

The Yoga System of Health and Relief from Tension

If you do yoga every day, you'll feel better. An uncluttered hour and Yogi Vithaldas' funky book will get you off . . . it has large print, adequate pictures, and makes you want to get out on the floor with it. A good book to begin with.

[Reviewed by Merce]

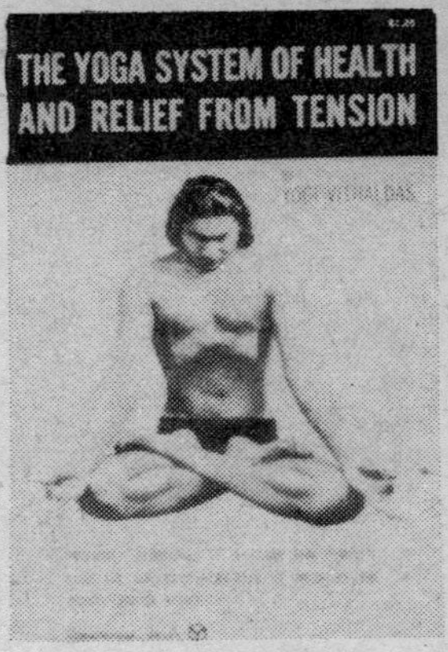

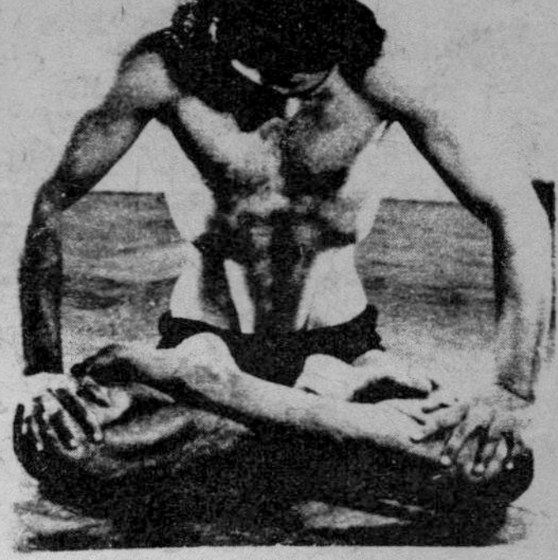

The Yoga System of Health and Relief from Tension
Yogi Vithaldas
1957; 120 pp.

$1.25 postpaid

from:
Cornerstone Library
c/o Simon & Schuster, Inc.
1 West 39th Street
New York, NY 10018

or

WHOLE EARTH CATALOG

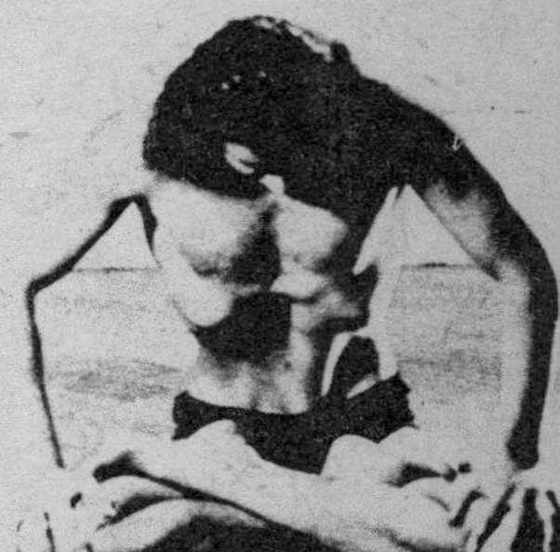

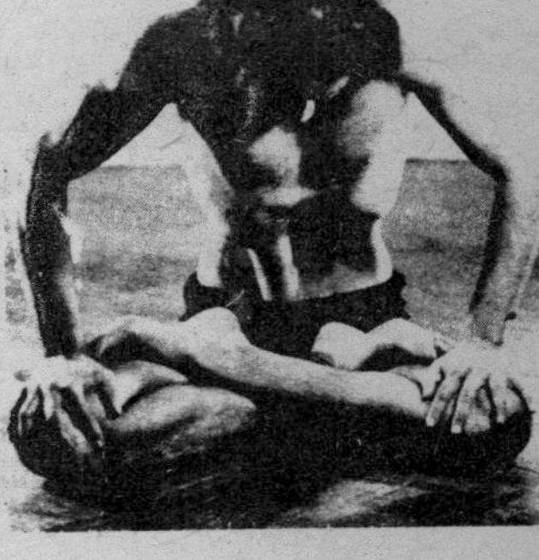

When concentrating on an object it is best to begin slowly and concentrate for thirty seconds intensely rather than three minutes in a half-controlled, disconnected fashion. Choose any object for the mind to fasten on, and make it a pleasant one—say a half-opened rose. Place it in front of you in a little vase on a level with your eyes, and think of nothing but its beauty, the soft imperceptible grading of the colours, the stalk, the thorns, and the leaf. Keep your mind on that rose until you could tell anyone every feature of the blossom, and eventually, even with your eyes closed, that rose will be so firmly imprinted on your mind that it will be as vivid for you as if you were still looking at it.

Regard the exercise as a kind of game, and have a shot at it at odd times of the day when you are waiting for a bus or for a meal. Do not waste that time by idle dreaming, but consciously direct your mind to some object, and, shortly, an admirable technique of mind-control will be established.

•

Place an acorn before you and gaze steadily at it, fixing it firmly in your mind. Know with certainty its attributes, as with the rose—its shape, colour, and any markings you can discern. Then imagine the acorn in the ground and a root shooting from its burst seed, and the first green leaf, and carry on the process to the complete tree. Leave nothing out, hurry nothing, let nothing interfere with you until in your mind the acorn has become a great tree.

•

Meditation has a positive and negative pole, or, in other words, two extremes in its practice which must be avoided. A person who erring on the positive side, avoids the great middle path, develops an assertive inner nature, and takes pride in a false superiority of power.

The student who sees no difference in receptivity and surrender of the will meditates in a negative manner, laying himself open to every passing force, desirable or not, instead of practising disciplined reception.

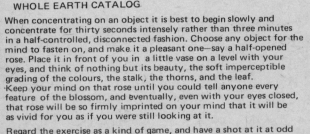

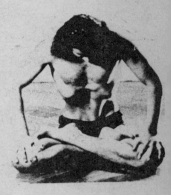

Kundalini: The Evolutionary Energy in Man

dear jerry,
the universe from the inside out,
through the meditation efforts
of an Indian government worker,
a college failure.
a story of personal contact
with the cosmos,
and what happens to a man
when, unexpectedly,
he is set apart from his friend,
by a blinding flash
of pure white enlightenment.

—jd

[Suggested by Sam Bercholz]

Kundalini: The Evolutionary Energy in Man
Gopi Krishna
1970; 252 pp.

$2.25 postpaid

from:
Shambhala Publications
1409 5th Street
Berkeley, California 94710

or WHOLE EARTH CATALOG

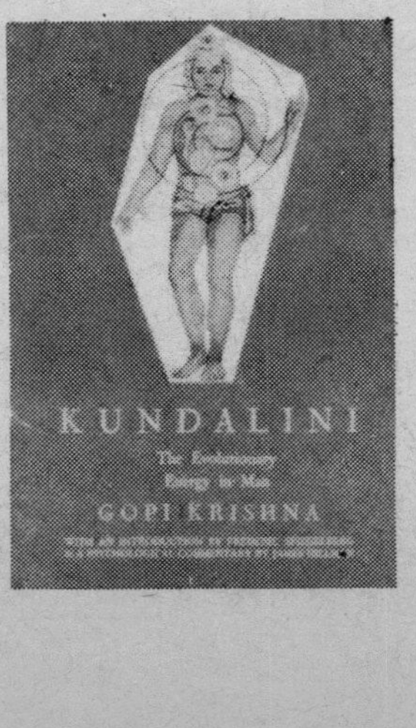

During one such spell of intense concentration I suddenly felt a strange sensation below the base of the spine, at the place touching the seat, while I sat cross-legged on a folded blanket spread on the floor. The sensation was so extraordinary and so pleasing that my attention was forcibly drawn towards it. The moment my attention was thus unexpectedly withdrawn from the point on which it was focused, the sensation ceased. Thinking it to be a trick played by my imagination to relax the tension, I dismissed the matter from my mind and brought my attention back to the point from which it had wandered. Again I fixed it on the lotus, and as the image grew clear and distinct at the top of my head, again the sensation occurred. This time I tried to maintain the fixity of my attention and succeeded for a few seconds, but the sensation extending upwards grew so intense and was so extraordinary, as compared to anything I had experienced before, that in spite of myself my mind went towards it, and at that very moment it again disappeared. I was now convinced that something unusual had happened for which my daily practice of concentration was probably responsible. . .

Entirely unprepared for such a development, I was completely taken by surprise; but regaining self-control instantaneously, I remained sitting in the same posture, keeping my mind on the point of concentration. The illumination grew brighter and brighter, the roaring louder, I experienced a rocking sensation and then felt myself slipping out of my body, entirely enveloped in a halo of light. It is impossible to describe the experience accurately. I felt the point of consciousness that was myself growing wider, I felt the point of consciousness that was myself growing wider surrounded by waves of light. It grew wider and wider, spreading outward while the body, normally the immediate object of its perception, appeared to have receded into the distance until I became entirely unconscious of it. I was now all consciousness, without any outline, without any idea of a corporeal appendage, without any feeling or sensation coming from the senses, immersed in a sea of light simultaneously conscious and aware of every point, spread out, as it were, in all directions without any barrier or material obstruction. I was no longer myself, or to be more accurate, no longer as I knew myself to be, a small point of awareness confined in a body, but instead was a vast circle of consciousness in which the body was but a point, bathed in light and in a state of exaltation and happiness impossible to describe.

After some time, the duration of which I could not judge, the circle began to narrow down; I felt myself contracting, becoming smaller and smaller, until I again became dimly conscious of the outline of my body, then more clearly; and as I slipped back to my old condition, I became suddenly aware of the noises in the street, felt again my arms and legs and head, and once more became my narrow self in touch with body and surroundings. When I opened my eyes and looked about, I felt a little dazed and bewildered, as if coming back from a strange land completely foreign to me. The sun had risen and was shining full on my face, warm and soothing. I tried to lift my hands, which always rested in my lap, one upon the other, during meditation. My arms felt limp and lifeless. With an effort I raised them up and stretched them to enable the blood to flow freely. Then I tried to free my legs from the posture in which I was sitting and to place them in a more comfortable position but could not. They were heavy and stiff. With the help of my hands I freed them and stretched them out, then put my back against the wall, reclining in a position of ease and comfort.

•

Under the action of a stronger current than that for which it was designed, any man-made mechanism, even a hundredth part as sensitive and intricate as the human frame is, would be wrecked or damaged immediately, but because of certain inherent qualities, developed by the human organism as a means of evolution, the sudden release of the serpent power, provided the blood is healthy and the organs sound, is not attended by fatal results in favourable cases because of safety devices already provided by nature to meet a contingency of this kind in individuals ready for the experience. Even in such cases it is essential that the energy be benignly disposed and that the subject take the necessary precautions to maintain the strength of the body and the balance of the mind during the subsequent period of inexpressibly severe trial. How far I was endowed with a constitution suited for the great ordeal I cannot say, but being an utter stranger to the science, taken unawares without the requisite preliminary course of physical and mental discipline, and a prey to adversity, I was buffeted unceasingly for many years partly because of my ignorance and lack of sufficient strength and partly because of the extreme suddenness and rapidity of the extraordinary development.

•

I was destined to witness my own transformation, not comparable in any way to the great transfigurations in the past, nor similar in point of results to the marvelous achievements of genius; but though simple in nature and ordinary in effect, a transformation nevertheless, attended all along by great physical and mental suffering. But what I witnessed and still witness within myself is so contrary to many accepted notions of science, at variance with many time-honoured dogmas of faith, and so antagonistic to many of the universally followed dictums of civilization that when what I have experienced is proved empirically there must occur a far-reaching, revolutionary change in every sphere of human activity and conduct.

The Job

Burroughs' domain is the interface of individual mind and social mind––control. When social controls become demented, suicidal, the individual must break from them and find his own health. This book is a discussion of the control-busting techniques Burroughs has explored: Scientology's E-meter, word-subversion, violence, doing nothing, tape recorders, apomorphine, contradictory commands. All methods of seizing the social tools and turning them against themselves.

It's important research in a critical, invisible realm. My only carp would be Burroughs' assumption of crafty, subtle, efficient intellects behind society's controls . . . which describes Burroughs but hardly describes the tired men I've seen earnestly coping with the top jobs in the Pentagon and the Department of the Interior. Their main activity is trying not to fall over their own feet.

—SB

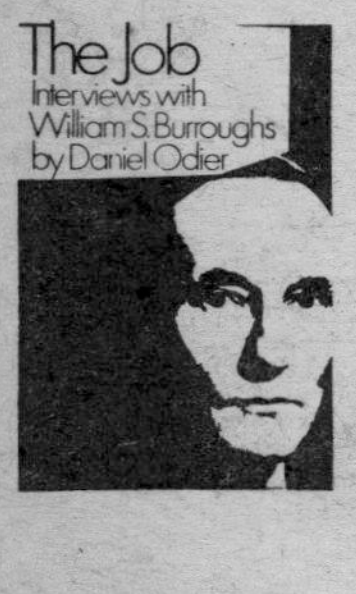

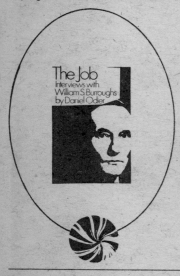

The Job: Interviews with William S. Burroughs
Daniel Odier
1970 189 pages

$2.95 postpaid

from:
Grove Press, Inc.
214 Mercer St.
New York, N.Y. 10012

or WHOLE EARTH CATALOG

"Navigare necesse es. Vivare no es necesse."

"It is necessary to travel. It is not necessary to live." These words inspired early navigators when the vast frontier of unknown seas opened to their sails in the fifteenth century. Space is the new frontier. Is this frontier open to youth? I quote from the *London Express*, December 30, 1968: "If you are a fit young man under twenty-five with lightning reflexes who fears nothing in heaven or on the earth and has a keen appetite for adventure don't bother to apply for the job of astranaut." They want "cool dads" trailing wires to the "better half" from an aqualung. Doctor Paine of the Space Center in Houston says: "This flight was a triumph for the squares of this world who aren't hippies and work with slide rules and aren't ashamed to say a prayer now and then." Is this the great adventure of space? Are these men going to take the step into regions literally unthinkable in verbal terms? To travel in space you must leave the old verbal garbage behind: God talk, country talk, mother talk, love talk. You must learn to exist with no religion no country no allies. You must learn to live alone in silence. Anyone who prays in space is not there.

The last frontier is being closed to youth. However there are many roads to space. To achieve complete freedom from past conditioning is to be in space. Techniques exist for achieving such freedom. These techniques are being concealed and withheld. In *The Job* I consider techniques of discovery.

•

Why then does the subject when he is trying most desperately to make a good impression make the worst impression possible? Because he also has the goal to make a bad impression which operates on an involuntary automatic level. This self-destructive goal is such a threat to his being that he *reacts* against it. He may be conscious or partially conscious of the negative goal but he cannot confront it directly. The negative goal forces him to react. The Reactive Mind consists of goals so repulsive or frightening to the subject that he compulsively reacts against them and *it is precisely this reaction that keeps these negative goals in operation.*

•

We take karate and Aikido training in the schools scattered through large cities of the world, our Scientology training at Scientology centers. Other courses are provided by a network of institutes and foundations often short-lived. The training is often interrupted. Three months of karate then Scientology take up all my time and just before the advanced Scientology courses I am shifted to Cairo for an intensive course in Egyptian hieroglyphs. This center is closed down by the government. After that there is a weapons course financed by a rightist billionaire in East Texas where we learn to use every weapon from a crossbow to a laser gun, a seminar in black magic of Africa sponsored by an ethnology institute in London that is always short of funds, a volunteer experiment in prolonged sense withdrawal set up the U. S. Navy which ended in a Congressional investigation of brainwashing, a free fall club in North Dakota, skin diving and just when I am getting used to the aqualung we are thrown out of Geylong where the program is and I do a Yoga stint in Northern India.

The aim of academy training is precisely *decontrol* of opinion, the students being conditioned to *look* at the facts *before* formulating any verbal patterns. The initial training in non-chemical methods of expanding awareness would last at least two years. During this period the student would be requested to refrain from all drugs including alcohol since bodily health is essential to minimize mental disturbance. After basic training the student would be prepared for drug trips to reach areas difficult to explore by other means in the present state of our knowledge.

The program proposed is essentially a disintoxication from inner fear and inner control, a liberation of thought and energy to prepare a new generation for the adventure of space. With such possibilities open to them I doubt if many young people would want the destructive drugs. Remember junk keeps you right here in junky flesh on this earth where Boot's is open all night. You can't make space in an aqualung of junk.

•

the more people we can get working with tape recorders the more useful experiments and extensions will turn up why not give tape recorder parties every guest arrives with his recorder and tapes of what he intends to say at the party recording what other recorders say to him it is the height of rudeness not to record when addressed directly by another tape recorder and you can't say anything directly have to record it first the coolest old tape worms never talk direct

•

After the baptism of silence the student moves with ease in the soundless medium but words are at his disposition when he needs them to be used with absolute precision.

•

Society makes all these criminals quite deliberately, these great concentration camps, where they dump people known as criminals. Many of them are psychopaths, that is, they are refractory to control. As soon as they become criminals, there will be no more trouble from them at all. They're right in that game of cops and robbers for life, in a concentration camp. But now they've begun extending this concentration camp, extending it and extending it, by making more laws and making more people criminals, if all the laws were enforced, they'd have practically everyone in the concentration camp, and everyone else would be necessary to guard them. They have reached an impasse: they must either admit that the whole thing is a farce and that laws are not meant to be enforced, or change them, or enforce them.

Aikido and the Dynamic Sphere

Aikido is the most recent and most brilliantly conceived of the Japanese martial arts. A superb fighting technique, it is scarcely interested in fighting––it doesn't even have matches, just training. You train to put your mind and body in the same place for once––the one-point at your center of gravity. You train to acquire and direct Ki––energy (not strength, but coherent energy: when it's flowing you don't have to move). You train to blend with your opponent and use his energy to unhinge his attack. I find this book by two Americans to be far more useful for learning aikido than the numerous texts by Japanese students of the original master Morihei Uyeshiba. The illustrations here are profoundly better than the usual photographs. They depict the mental image––which is the heart of aikido technique. An editor can use aikido, a general, an actor, a craftsman, a politician, a designer. What the body learns and practices becomes useful in any realm.

—SB

Aikido and the Dynamic Sphere
A. Westbrook and O. Ratti
1970; 375 pp.

$11.50 postpaid

from:
Charles E. Tuttle Co.
Rutland, Vermont 05701

or WHOLE EARTH CATALOG

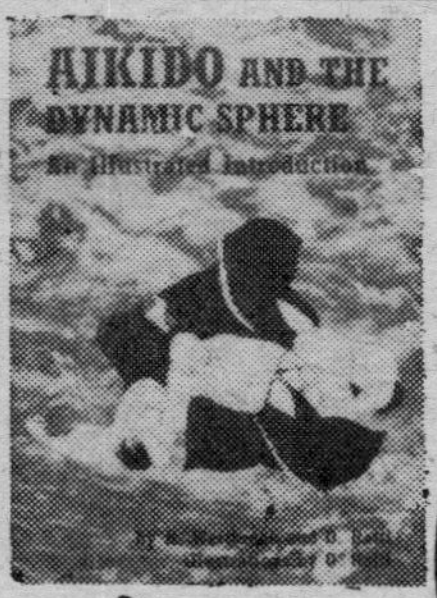

For teachers near you, get in touch with:

American Aikido Federation
142 West 18th St.
New York, N.Y.

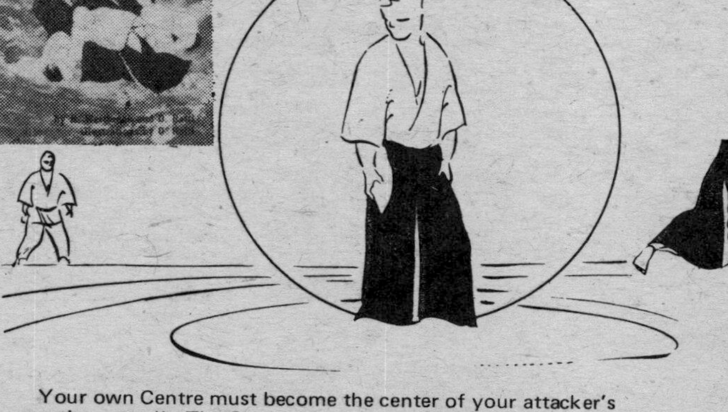

Your own Centre must become the center of your attacker's action as well. The Centre is not restricted in aikido, as we have indicated, to your personal dimension. If a man attacks you, he has lost his own point of independence and balance by the very irrationality of that act, and you must substitute your own Centre in an attempt to return the situation to normal. Thus he attacks, you evade; he plunges into a vacuum, you lead and guide him back around your own Centre and neutralize his attack.

Control the Attack by Leading it.

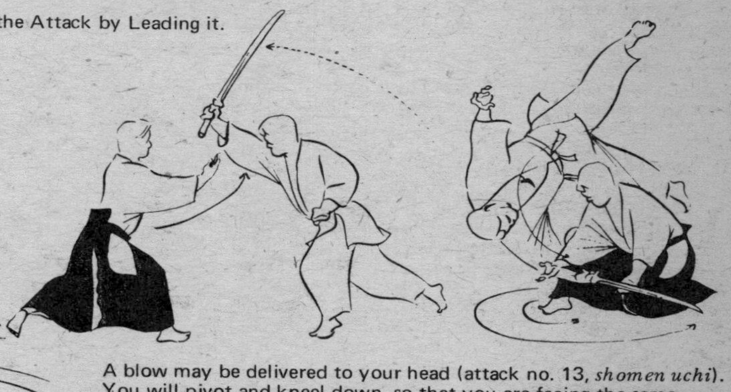

A blow may be delivered to your head (attack no. 13, *shomen uchi*). You will pivot and kneel down, so that you are facing the same direction as your opponent. Your arm(s) will not "block" in the sense of stopping his motion, but will be extended so as to protect yourself. At the same time you will guide his motion (via his wrist or even sleeve) from the inside, lead him in full, circular extension forward and then down. This can be accomplished almost without touching him.

There is no pulling, no dragging; it is just a smooth, simple, circular lead, synchronized perfectly with your attacker's own movements. It is blended dynamically with them and, therefore, almost unnoticed until he is in flight. He falls, but yet does not know precisely how he came to fall.

T'ai-Chi

i've only watched two people doing t'ai chi.
one, an old man at sunrise,
in front of a two-car garage,
swooping and turning.
the other, cathy dutton,
sun on her eyelids,
slowly working it out
on the front lawn in menlo park.
it is beautiful dance-with-the cosmos
personal movement,
meditational motion,
and maybe it can be learned from a book.

—jd

[Suggested by Jim Frierson]

For teachers near you, get in touch with:

Tai Chi Chuan Association
211 Canal St.
New York, N.Y. 10013

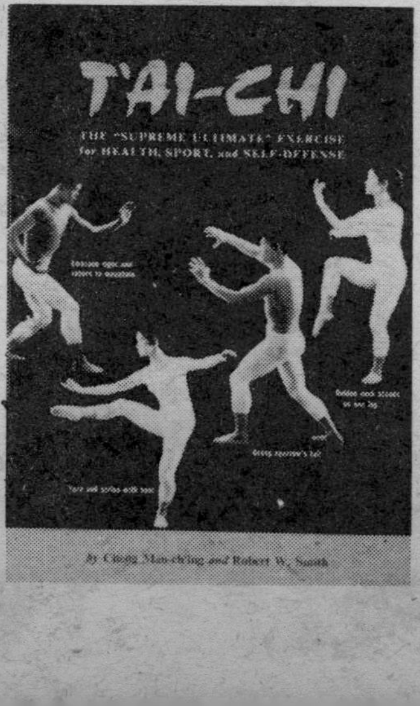

T'ai-Chi
Cheng and Smith
1967;69; 112 pp.

$9.75 postpaid

from:
Charles E. Tuttle
28 South Main
Rutland, Vermont 05701

or WHOLE EARTH CATALOG

How should a novice begin his training in T'ai-chi? He should relax completely. The aim is to throw every bone and muscle of the body wide open so that the *ch'i* may travel unobstructed. Once this is done, the chest must be further relaxed and the *ch'i* made to sink to the navel. After a time the *ch'i* will be felt accumulating for mass integration in the navel, from where it will begin to circulate throughout the body.

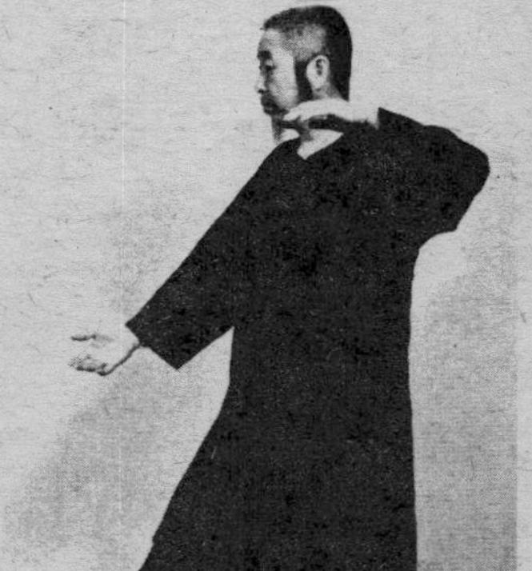

48

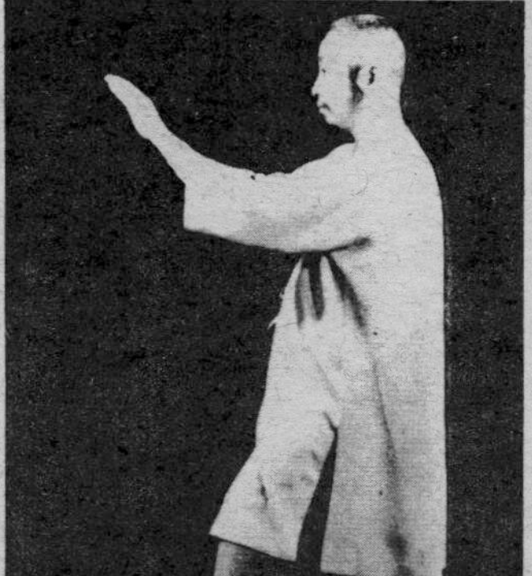

49

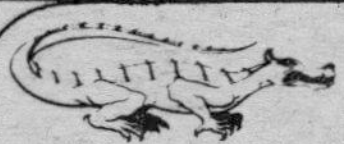

He also intended to go on dismantling the old house, to tear as much of it down for salvage as he possibly could before the coming winter's rains. Emmit had only taken boards off as high as he could comfortably reach. He had stripped the weather boarding from the lower portions of the house on three sides. With a ladder D.R. would be able to get three times as much lumber as Emmit had before he even touched the insides of the house. Emmit had worked the lumber with a hammer and a wrecking bar, pulling out the nails and trimming up their edges with a saw. As he cleaned the boards he had stacked them neatly in a corner of the barn. He had scavenged more lumber than he needed for his hutches. It wasn't clear what he had intended to do with the extra, but D.R. knew exactly what his own intentions were: he was going to remodel two of the stalls into a weather-tight room, and live in it that winter.

Two rooms, if he could get them done.

And three rooms, if Estelle would come to live there with him, and help him with the work.

If Estelle would come, they would convert one whole end of the barn into a house, and live there together by the rabbits and the worms and near the garden. They would get up early every morning and work to improve their place. If they wanted to, they could have a hundred hutches full of rabbits, and a million worms a year. They could have five hundred hutches full, and ten million worms at work in their manure, if they wanted to. If they wanted to, they could have a thousand hutches, one standing on every five square yards of that old ruined mountain, shitting pure worm food onto the ground, creating perfect lettuce beds and comfrey stands and alfalfa fields galore.

They could do that if Estelle would come to live there with him.

They'd do all of that, and more.

If she came.

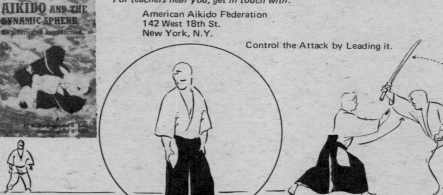

Be Here Now

Baba Ram Dick Dass Alpert has put together for us a very tasty hot fudge Sunday school (you know how hot fudge sundaes came about? It seems this little princess once demanded of the King's cooks something absolutely new to tittle her jaded pallette: "It must be both black and white and hot and cold," she pouted. Pow! They socked a sundae to her. . .) Be Here Now is western in flavor, Eastern in content and sprinkled generously with the kernels of wisdom gleaned from ten years of dedicated nutcracking. Rum Dum (as his father calls him) has over the past four or five years become a true disciple of Vedanta and Yoga, and in his box we get it all: a history, a cookbook, a bibliography and a collection of daily meditations hung together in beautiful layout. Though the book is clearly founded in Eastern Philosophy, Rum Dum's background is tennis shoes and bikes and cars and trying to get laid and gaining prestige, just like all of us, so his meditations are as familiar to us as our own bathwater. He makes the Message of the East comfortable for our coffee table studies with his references to drugs we have all taken, books we all have read and flashes we all have experienced. This warmth and dedication makes the Lama Foundation the most personal and reliable-seeming school of psychedelic thought that has so far surfaced in our hemisphere, and Baba Ram Dass shines forth from the box looking as though he may be our first true guru.

[Reviewed by George de Alth]

Be Here Now
Baba Ram Dass, Lama Foundation
1971; 400 pp.

$3.33 postpaid

from:
Crown Publishers, Inc.
419 Park Ave., South
New York, N.Y. 10016

or WHOLE EARTH CATALOG

The Base Camp

The base camp includes all the living facilities with the exception of the hermitage rooms or buildings. Participants in the base camp follow a schedule as follows:

5:30	Rise
5:45-6:30	Group silent meditation.
6:30-7:00	Chanting, reading aloud, singing.
7:00-9:00	Dancing, *asanas, pranayam*, breakfast, getting the children to school, clean up, etc.
9:00-12:00	*Karma yoga* (work) period— assignments for an entire week are usually made once a week on Saturday morning.
12:00-2:00	Bringing food and supplies to hermit and preparing and having *prasad* (consecrated food), taken in silence. Then rest or relaxation and clean-up.
2:00-4:00	*Karma yoga* period.
4:00-5:30	Group study, and exercises in consciousness.
5:30-6:30	*Pranayam, asanas*, preparing evening food, etc.
6:30-8:00	Evening *prasad* (silently) plus clean-up and relaxation, reading, etc.
8:00-9:00	Group meditation and chanting and singing.

By assigning the *karma yoga* tasks over a period of a week you can use the *karma yoga* periods in a fluid fashion. One person's *karma yoga*, for example, might include milking goats, making cheese, weaving, picking the kids up at school, getting the car fixed, etc. Also a person may design his schedule to use a few of the morning *karma yoga* periods for personal study or meditation. The use of these periods is largely dependent upon the number of participants, and the amount of man-hours required for right livelihood and community maintenance. Time not spent in fulfilling assignments should be used on inner work (study, meditation, *asanas*, singing *kirtan*).

Most activities can be carried on in silence. Groups working together on a shared project such as gardening, building, etc. can either do these tasks in silence or do *mantra* during the work. Silence is an important part of the work. Formal discussions at the base camp of the hermitage experiences of the participants can be useful. Gossip, small talk, and hanging out. . .have a limited value in breaking through the illusion.

It is well to realize that the relationships in this community are not the dominant concern. Ideally, personality falls away in the common endeavor. If you want at all costs to hold onto your personality, don't join a spiritual community. . .because no one is going to be interested. Interpersonal matters are dealt with only to the extent that they are disruptive (i.e., capture the consciousness of the group or some participants.) Such matters can be dealt with at a group meeting if necessary. . .but the moment the group gets bogged down in heavy melodrama. . .it is well to call a meditation interlude until everyone can find a center again. Melodrama sucks us in again and again, but diminishes in power if actively thwarted.

DO YOU THINK
THAT WHEN CHRIST IS LYING THERE
AND THEY'RE NAILING THE NAILS IN
HE'S SAYING,"OH MAN, DOES THAT HURT!"? HE'S
PROBABLY LOOKING AT THE GUY WHO'S NAILING HIM
WITH

ABSOLUTE COMPASSION

HE DIGS WHY THE CAT'S DOING IT.
WHAT HE'S STUCK IN
HOW MUCH DUST COVERS HIS EYES
WHY HE'S GOT TO BE DOING IT
THAT'S THE WAY IT IS
HE SAID THE NIGHT BEFORE:
"WELL, TOMORROW IS THE BIG TRIP.
YEAH-RIGHT-THESE ARE THE NAILS
WOW! LOOK AT THAT!"

AM I HE WHO IS BEING PAINED?

NO! THAT'S THE THING. ONCE YOU KNOW THAT
THEN: PLEASURE & PAIN
LOSS & GAIN
FAME & SHAME
ARE ALL THE SAME

THEY'RE ALL JUST HAPPENING

THIS WHOLE TRIP I'M TALKING ABOUT IS FRAUGHT WITH

PARADOX

THE MOST EXQUISITE PARADOX
AS SOON AS YOU GIVE IT ALL UP
YOU CAN HAVE IT ALL
HOW ABOUT THAT ONE?
AS LONG AS YOU WANT POWER
YOU CAN'T HAVE IT.
THE MINUTE YOU DON'T WANT POWER
YOU'LL HAVE MORE THAN YOU EVER DREAMED
POSSIBLE

WHAT A WEIRD THING!

AS LONG AS YOU HAVE AN EGO
YOU'RE ON A LIMITED TRIP

YOU'RE ON A TRIVIAL TRIP THAT'S GOING TO LAST
MAYBE WHAT? 60 — SAY 70 — MAYBE 80 YEARS
AND FULL WITH FEAR OF ITS END
TRYING TO MAKE ITS OWN ETERNITY.

WELL: IF 'I' AM NOT SPEAKING
IF 'I' AM NOT WHAT 'I' THOUGHT 'I' WAS
HOW DID 'I' GET INTO THIS
WHO   AM 'I'

FOR ONLY WHEN 'I' KNOW WHO 'I' AM WILL 'I' KNOW WHAT IS

POSSIBLE

₃₁₅

"Did I ever tell you about the time that Tim and I. . ."

And he'd say, "Don't think about the past. Just be here now."

Silence.

And I'd say, "How long do you think we're going to be on this trip?"

And he'd say, "Don't think about the future. Just be here now."

I'd say, "You know, I really feel crumby, my hips are hurting. . ."

"Emotions are like waves. Watch them disappear in the distance on the vast calm ocean."

He had just sort of wiped out my whole game. That was it— that was my whole trip— emotions , and past experiences, and future plans. I was, after all, a great story teller.

So we were silent. There was nothing to say.

IN GOD WE TRUST

ONE

The Hero With A Thousand Faces

*myths and man's dreamworld have,
for the past fifty years or so,
been the objects of various alchemical
attempts at synthesis. about the time i get
convinced that screaming green weenies have
some larger context than madison avenue,
someone else denies the organic connection
between them.
the hero with a thousand faces is one of
those syntheses. its about the monomyth.
campbell traces his hero right out into the
void.*

—jd

[Suggested by George & Laura]

The Hero With A Thousand Faces
Joseph Campbell
1979, 70; 416 pp.

$3.95 postpaid

from:
Princeton University Press
Princeton, NJ 08540

or WHOLE EARTH CATALOG

It is the business of mythology proper, and of the fairy tale, to reveal the specific dangers and techniques of the dark interior way from tragedy to comedy. Hence the incidents are fantastic and "unreal": they represent psychological, not physical, triumphs. Even when the legend is of an actual historical personage, the deeds of victory are rendered, not in lifelike, but in dreamlike figurations; for the point is not that such-and-such could be done on earth, this other, more important, primary thing had to be brought to pass within the labyrinth that we all know and visit in our dreams. The passage of the mythological hero may be over-ground, incidentally; fundamentally it is inward—into depths where obscure resistances are overcome, and long lost, forgotten powers are revivified, to be made available for the transfiguration of the world. This deed accomplished, life no longer suffers hopelessly under the terrible mutilations of ubiquitous disaster, battered by time, hideous throughout space; but with its horror visible still, its cries of anguish still tumultuous, it becomes penetrated by an all-suffusing, all-sustaining love, and a knowledge of its own unconquered power. Something of the light that blazes invisible within the abysses of its normally opaque materiality breaks forth, with an increasing uproar. The dreadful mutilations are then seen as shadows, only, of an immanent, imperishable eternity; time yields to glory; and the world sings with the prodigious, angelic, but perhaps finally monotonous, siren music of the spheres. Like happy families, the myths and the worlds redeemed are all alike.

The King and the Corpse

I know of no better myth-telling than this, and no better myths. You've got Abu Kasem's Slippers, and then Conn-eda and John Golden-Mouth, and four romances from King Arthur that take deeper turns than T. H. White, the King and the Corpse, and the prize: the ancient Hindu Romance of the Goddess, plumbing the involuntary creation. Collected by Heinrich Zimmer, edited by Joseph Campbell. There's few books with such a blend of extravagance and intelligence, and none that come so close to the heart of education.

—SB

[Suggested by Jim Fadiman]

The King and the Corpse
Heinrich Zimmer; Joseph Campbell, ed.
1948; 338 pp.

$2.95 postpaid

from:
Princeton University Press
Princeton, N. J. 08540

or WHOLE EARTH CATALOG

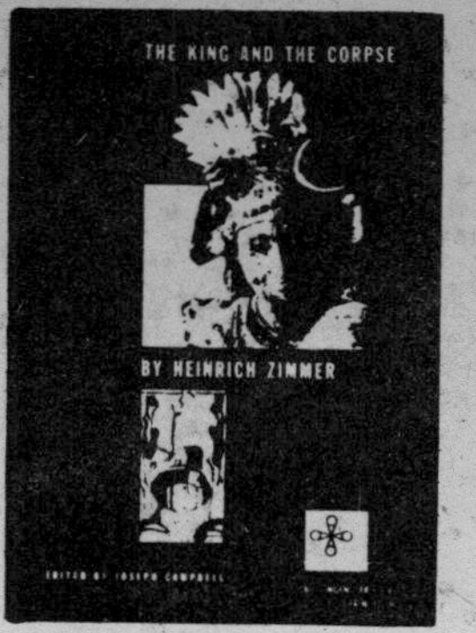

The course of the world runs awry, but therewith it goes directly to its goal. The catastrophe of the previously unforeseen is what breaks the world progression forward, and the moment the catastrophe has come to pass it appears to be what was intended all the while. For it is creative in a deeper way than the planning creative spirit supposes. It transforms the situation, forces an alteration on the creative spirit, and throws it into a play that carries it beyond itself carries it, that is to say, really and properly into play, and into a play that entrains the entirety of creation. The planner, the watcher, is compelled to become the endurer, the sufferer. Such a metamorphosis into the opposite, into the absolutely alien, is what throws the knots that reticulate the net of the living whole and mesh the individual alive into the fabric.

•

That night, in the bed, Sir Gawain could not at first bring himself to turn and face her unappetizing snout. After a little time, however, she said to him: "Ah, Sir Gawain, since I have wed you, show me your courtesy in bed. It may not be rightfully denied. If I were fair, you would not behave this way; you are taking no heed of wedlock. For Arthur's sake do kiss me at least; I pray you, do this at my request. Come, let us see how quick you can be!"

The knight and loyal nephew of the king collected every bit of his courage and kindness. "I will do more," he said in all gentleness, "I will do more than simply kiss, before God!" And he turned around to her. And he saw her to be the fairest creature that ever he had seen without measure.

She said: "What is your will?"

"Ah, Jesu!" he said, "what are ye?"

"Sir, I am your wife, securely; why are ye so unkind?"

"Ah, lady, I am to blame; I did not know. You are beautiful in my sight——whereas today you were the foulest wight my eye had ever seen! To have you thus, my lady, pleases me well." And he braced her in his arms and began kissing her, and they made great joy.

"Sir," she said, "my beauty will not hold. You may have me thus, but only for half the day. And so it is a question, and you must choose whether you would have me fair at night and foul by day before all men's eyes, or beautiful by day and foul at night."

"Alas," replied Gawain, "the choice is hard. To have you fair at night and no more, that would grieve my heart; but if I should decide to have you fair by day, then at night I should have a scabrous bed. Fain would I choose the best, yet know not what in this world I shall say. My dear lady, let it be as you would desire it; I rest the choice in your hand. My body and goods, my heart and all, is yours to buy and sell; that I avow before God."

"Ah, gramercy, courteous knight!" said the lady. "Mayst thou be blessed above all knights in the world, for now I am released from the enchantment and thou shalt have me fair and bright both night and day."

•

The involvement of the gods in the web of their own creation, so that they become, like Abu Kasem, the harried victims of their creatures, entangled in nets of not quite voluntary self-manifestation, and then mocked by the knowing laughter of their own externally reflected inner judge: this is the miracle of the universe. This is the tragicomic romance of the world. The gods, the fairy powers, are always in danger of self-enchantment. Like the youth Narcissus, they become fixed to their own reflected images—momentarily reluctant to pass with the passing of time, and critically in need of the shocking, shattering blow of the redemptive catastrophe. Man is the little world creator; God, the great. Each, surrounded by the figments of his own mirrored depths, knows and suffers the cosmic self-torment. And the fatal power that enchants them both is ever the great goddess, Māyā, self-delusion, the supreme creatrix of all the worlds.

•

Brahmā, sinking still further into the limpid darkness of his own interior, struck a new depth: suddenly the most beautiful dark woman sprang from his vision, and stood naked before everyone's gaze.

She was Dawn, and she was radiant with vivid youth. Nothing like her had yet appeared among the gods; nor would her equal ever be seen, either among men, or in the depths of the waters in the jeweled palaces of the serpent queens and kings. The billows of her blue-black hair were glistening like the feathers of a peacock, and her clearly curving, dark brows formed a bow fit for the God of Love. Her eyes, like dark lotus calyxes, had the alert, questioning glance of the frightened gazelle; and her face, round as the moon, was like a purple lotus blossom. Her swelling breasts with their two dark points were enough to infatuate a saint. Trim as the shaft of a lance stood her body, and her smooth legs were like the stretched-out trunks of elephants. She was glowing with little delicate pearls of perspiration. And when she found herself in the midst of her startled audience, she stared about at them, in uncertainty, then broke into a softly rippling laugh.

•

Shiva's visage became radiant with joy. In the presence of all the Holy Ones he lapsed, absorbed, into introverted vision. Then he permitted himself to sink to the floor, legs crossed, shut his eyes, and sank into his being to the depth of the Being Sublime. His body began to glow, so that the eyes of all the Holy Ones present became dazzled. And the moment he reached quietude in this immersion, Vishnu's Māyā fell away from around him, and his entire body burst into such a radiance that even his own hosts were unable to bear the blast. Vishnu passed into him, poured into him as the pure Light of Heaven, and disclosed within Shiva's body, to the eye of his inner contemplation, the whole lotus-spectacle of creation and the procession of the world. Blissful and serene, beyond the senses and their universes of distinctions, alone and pure, beholding everything, the abstracted one experienced within his own being the Being Supreme, that Substratum of all Unfoldments. He beheld, riveted in contemplation, how the One Substance exfoliates into all the delectations of the world.

•

Shiva, bereaved, distracted, was conducted gently by his guru, Brahmā, out of the gates of the city of his life's loss and away into the Himalayan peaks of snow. There, walking together, the two came upon a little lake of solitude, clear, and delightful to the mind. Brahmā perceived it first.

And seated here and there about the quiet shores were saints and sages in absolute meditation; two or three stood bathing in the cool crystal waters, sending ripples out across its mirroring of the blue and immobile, high, mountain sky. Many migratory birds, shrilly crying, were coming from all directions to flutter down into its lotus-bordered waters—pairs of splendid ruddy geese beautifully spreading out their great wings in exultation, cormorants with their hooked bills, gray-winged geese, and Siberian cranes, stalking about the shores, floating on the surface of the lake, peering into the waters, themselves beautifully reflected—and, occasionally, with a sudden thunderous beating of hundreds of wings, all lifting out of the lake into the sky, to circle in many companies, and presently return to settle, flutter, and preen. And beneath them, in the crystalline depths, were swimming fish of innumerable brilliant hues, visible as they darted in and out among the lotus stems. Lotus buds, lotus chalices, blue lotuses and white were abundant there; and the vegetation about the shores was luxurious and of cool shade.

The Masks of God

Want to grab history while reading mythology? Want to understand for the first time why those crazy Mayans and other South American civilizations used "Christian" symbols, attributed by European so-called Christians who came a-calling swords in hand, to works of the Devil? Want to see why Sumer and Egypt and Mexico are so similar? Want to really fumigate your fancy with the Mother Goddess and then enjoy Christmas all the more? Want to understand why the patriachism of Judaism drives a woman nuts if she's neolithic at all, and why those paleolithic hunters may have had something important to say about self experience and a coming to an understanding? Want to hear who said the voice of the Universe is as gentle as a woman's? Want to sally forth into the world of the spirit, in other words, to really dig where Lewis Mumford says it's at: humanity's penchant for dreaming?

When you come right down to it, imagination really seems to be the point: we differ from our furred and feathered fellows because we dream of things that are not and of things that never were. We believe, and in our believing brings madness and the sublime into reality.

Get Joseph Campbell and blow your preconceptions. You'll never see yourself the same again.

[Reviewed by J. A. Pollard]

THE MASKS OF GOD
Joseph Campbell

Primitive Mythology
1959; 504 pp.

$3.25 postpaid

Oriental Mythology
1962; 561 pp.

$3.75 postpaid

Occidental Mythology
1964; 564 pp.

$3.75 postpaid

Creative Mythology
1968; 730 pp.

$4.50 postpaid

from:
Viking Press, Inc.
625 Madison Avenue
New York, N.Y. 10022

or WHOLE EARTH CATALOG

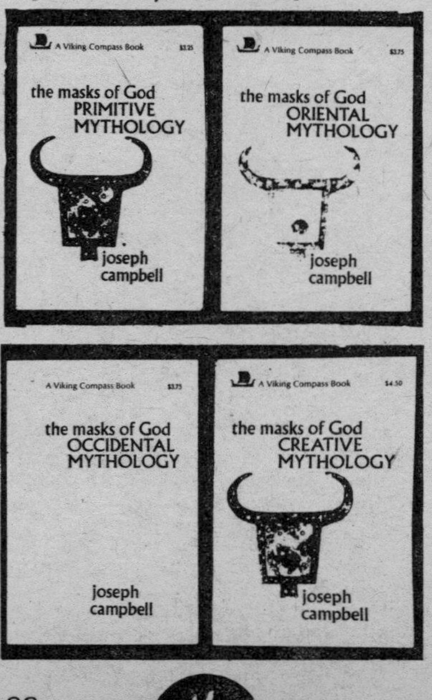

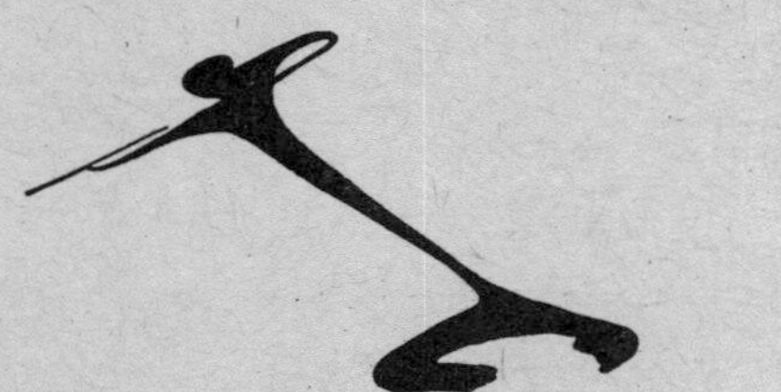

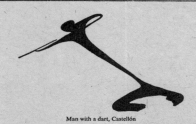

Man with a dart, Castellón

Primitive Mythology

Gawain, on the other hand, was one who had spent his life not posing in a role unearned, conferred upon him by anointment, but in quest, sincerely, for his object of desire, and when he found her — after years, not days — he was transfixed, established in his own true center, and knew exactly where he stood. She was, again, the bereaved Orgeluse. But he was no toy king. There was no threat, no fear, either of man or of spirit, that could put him off his course or freeze him to a halt. His trials were proper to his own life and he was consequently their match: hence, at one with his Lady Soul; at peace with her; and in the fair castle of love, the master of his world.

It remained only to make peace as well with the world beyond the broad stream. . . .

Sitting chatting with his grandmother at the window, Gawain with a start of joy espied on the meadow on the other shore the first of Arthur's host arriving with banners, colors, spears, and immediately setting up pavilions. With love in his heart, tears in his eyes, he watched, then ordered all his own castle company — knights and ladies, squires and pages — to make ready with their own banners and tents to cross and welcome his uncle's court. Arthur and his queen were introduced to Arnive, the king's mother, Sangive, his sister, and the sisters of Gawain. All kissed and laughed, wept and laughed and kissed again. Moreover, many a knight who had been mourning Gawain's death came smiling into his tent. But the seneschal Keie only murmured, "God surely does work wonders! Where did Gawain get all these queens?"

Next day a third host, that of Gramoflanz, arrived, and Gawain then rode forth onto a broad plain, alone, for exercise, where he saw a lone knight galloping his way, wearing armor redder than rubies. . . .

•

Humor is the touchstone of the truly mythological as distinct from the more literal-minded and sentimental theological mood. The gods as icons are not ends in themselves. Their entertaining myths transport the mind and spirit, not *up to*, but *past* them, into the yonder void; from which perspective the more heavily freighted theological dogmas then appear to have been only pedagogical lures: their function, to cart the unadroit intellect away from its concrete clutter of facts and events to a comparatively rarefied zone, where, as a final boon, all existence — whether heavenly, earthly, or infernal — may at last be seen transmuted into the semblance of a lightly passing, recurrent, mere childhood dream of bliss and fright. "From one point of view all those divinities exist," a Tibetan lama recently replied to the question of an understanding Occidental visitor, "from another they are not real." This is the orthodox teaching of the ancient Tantras: "All of these visualized deities are but symbols representing the various things that occur on the Path"; as well as a doctrine of the contemporary psychoanalytical schools. And the same metatheological insight seems to be what is suggested in Dante's final verses, where the illuminated voyager at last is able to lift his courageous eyes beyond the beatific vision of Father, Son, and Holy Ghost, to the one Eternal Light.

•

". . . in reality, Slayer and Dragon, sacrificer and victim, are of one mind behind the scenes, where there is no polarity of contraries, but mortal enemies on the stage, where the everlasting war of the Gods and the Titans is displayed. In any case, the Dragon-Father remains a Pleroma, no more diminished by what he exhales than he is increased by what he repossesses. He is the Death, on whom our life depends; and to the question 'Is Death one, or many?' the answer is made that 'He is one as he is there, but many as he is in his children here.'

Creative Mythology

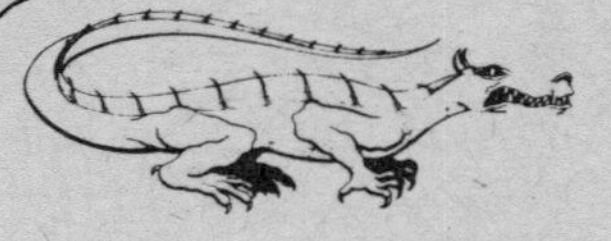

TUESDAY: THE MAGIC RABBIT

Until the work was done, Tuesday was very much like Monday.

D.R. spent the morning turning under the manure he had spread the day before. He planted the little new-ground with worms and humus from the pit, then worked a while tearing boards off the side of the house, dressing them and stacking them in the barn. Already the stack was waist-high and five boards across, enough to begin the work of converting the stalls to rooms. D.R. had an impulse to commence it then and there, but he knew he ought to talk to Leonard first. He could probably bang a room of some sort together by himself; but this was no crude project he had in mind. There are ways to go about certain kinds of work; there are rules in building and D.R. wanted to learn them. He wanted to do a good job, and know something truly useful when he was done. So he left the room alone till Leonard could come up to advise him on it, and worked some more in the afternoon on the new worm pit instead.

D.R. worked the whole day through, going from job to job. It tired his body in that satisfying way he'd come to relish the last few days, and after supper he was glad to sit in Emmit's rocking chair on the front porch and rest himself a while. His body sank into the chair and without reluctance let go of the day in anticipation of the night.

But D.R.'s mind wasn't ready for that yet. His mind was still excited, eager for some action, some outlet for the words that had built up through the day and gone unsaid. And so he went in the house and got his tablet and his pen, came back to his chair and wrote another letter to the Flash.

(continued)

Chuang Tzu: Basic Writings

a
great
long
string
of
solid
crystal
fortune cookies

—jd

Chuang Tzu: Basic Writings
Translated by Burton Watson
1964; 66; 148pp.

$3.00 postpaid

from
Columbia University Press
526 West 113 Street
New York, N.Y. 10025

or WHOLE EARTH CATALOG

Your life has a limit but knowledge has none. If you use what is limited to pursue what has no limit, you will be in danger. If you understand this and still strive for knowledge, you will be in danger for certain! If you do good, stay away from fame. If you do evil, stay away from punishments. Follow the middle; go by what is constant, and you can stay in one piece, keep yourself alive, look after your parents, and live out your years.

Cook Ting was cutting up an ox for Lord Wen-hui. At every touch of his hand, every heave of his shoulder, every move of his feet, every thrust of his knee—zip! zoop! He slithered the knife along with a zing, and all was in perfect rhythm, as though he were performing the dance of the Mulberry Grove or keeping time to the Ching-shou music.

"Ah, this is marvelous!" said Lord Wen-hui. "Imagine skill reaching such heights!"

Cook Ting laid down his knife and replied, "What I care about is the Way, which goes beyond skill. When I first began cutting up oxen, all I could see was the ox itself. After three years I no longer saw the whole ox. And now—now I go at it by spirit and don't look with my eyes. Perception and understanding have come to a stop and spirit moves where it wants. I go along with the natural makeup, strike in the big hollows, guide the knife through the big openings, and follow things as they are. So I never touch the smallest ligament or tendon, much less a main joint.

"A good cook changes his knife once a year—because he cuts. A mediocre cook changes his knife once a month—because he hacks. I've had this knife of mine for nineteen years and I've cut thousands of oxen with it, and yet the blade is as good as though it had just come from the grindstone. There are spaces between the joints, and the blade of the knife has really no thickness. If you insert what has no thickness into such spaces, then there's plenty of room—more than enough for the blade to play about in. That's why after nineteen years the blade of my knife is still as good as when it first came from the grindstone.

"However, whenever I come to a complicated place, I size up the difficulties, tell myself to watch out and be careful, keep my eyes on what I'm doing, work very slowly, and move the knife with the greatest subtlety, until—flop! the whole thing comes apart like a clod of earth crumbling to the ground. I stand there holding the knife and look all around me, completely satisfied and reluctant to move on, and then I wipe off the knife and put it away."

•

Chuang Tzu and Hui Tzu were strolling along the dam of the Hao River when Chuang Tzu said, "See how the minnows come out and dart around where they please! That's what fish really enjoy!"

Hui Tzu said, "You're not a fish—how do you know what fish enjoy?"

Chuang Tzu said, "You're not I, so how do you know I don't know what fish enjoy?"

Hui Tzu said, "I'm not you, so I certainly don't know what you know. On the other hand, you're certainly not a fish—so that still proves you don't know what fish enjoy!"

Chuang Tzu said, "Let's go back to your original question, please. You asked me *how* I know what fish enjoy—so you already knew I knew it when you asked the question. I know it by standing here beside the Hao."

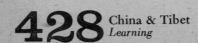
The Secret of the Golden Flower

the way it reads to me:
pass beyond the little old man
sitting on
that ledge of awareness
on which
you watch yourself making love,
become the little old man,
split him a few times,
and realize that,
because all this is possible,
the light from the golden flower
dissolves duality
into the one.

—jd

The Secret of the Golden Flower
translated by Richard Wilhelm
1962; 149 pp.

$2.35 postpaid

from
Harcourt Brace and Jovanovich, Inc.
757 Third Avenue
New York, New York 10017

or WHOLE EARTH CATALOG

Master Lu-Tsu said, When there is a gradual success in producing the circulation of the light, a man must not give up his ordinary occupation in doing it. The ancients said, When occupations come to us, we must accept them; when things come to us, we must understand them from the ground up. If the occupations are properly handled by correct thoughts, the light is not scattered by outside things, but circulates according to its own law. Even the still invisible circulation of the light gets started this way; how much more, then, is it the case with the true circulation of the light which has already manifested itself clearly.

One looks with both eyes at the tip of the nose, sits upright and in a comfortable position, and holds the heart to the centre in the midst of conditions. In Taoism it is called the yellow middle, in Buddhism the center of the midst of conditions. The two are the same. It does not necessarily mean the middle of the head. It is only a matter of fixing one's thinking on the point which lies exactly between the two eyes. Then all is well. The light is something extremely mobile. When one fixes the thought on the mid-point between the two eyes, the light streams in of its own accord. It is not necessary to direct the attention especially to the central castle. In these few words the most important thing is contained.

The Tibetan Book of the Great Liberation

toward knowing the mind
(talking to yourself)
and the liberation of realization,
nirvana,
oneness with voidness,
together,
now,
and the evaporation of karma,
poof.

—jd

[Suggested by Sam Bercholz]

The Tibetan Book
of the Great Liberation
W.Y. Evans-Wentz, editor
1969; 261 pp.

from:
Oxford University Press
200 Madison Avenue
New York, New York 10016

$2.95 postpaid

or WHOLE EARTH CATALOG

In the process of meditating introspectively upon the aphoristic teachings concerning the One Mind, the disciple will inevitably come face to face with the age-old problem of what man is. He will intuitively ask himself, Why am I? What am I? Am I a something, a self, a soul, eternally separate and different from each of the countless myriads of similarly constituted beings I see round about me in various states of existence? Is the glamorous world of appearances real? Are all these inanimate objects and all these living, breathing creatures, in the midst of which I find myself, real? Or are they, as the Buddhas declare, no more than the content of a *karmic* mirage, the stuff composing the dreams of life?

When the truth begins to come from within, very feebly at first, like the consciousness of a man awakening from the torpor of a drugged sleep, or like the first traces of dawn coming forth in an eastern sky, the disciple will realize gradually that only by transcending the realm of separateness and attaining super-consciousness of the immutable at-one-ment of all things, organic and inorganic, can the age-old problem be solved. The more the disciple meditates upon what the self has in common with other selves, the more he will discover the impersonal self common to all selves. Thence he will reach the conclusion that if one and the same factor is the core of each individual's selfhood, no individual in its true essence had individuality. There would be nothing like *my* self; there would only be the Self.

•

The One Mind being verily of the Voidness and without any foundation, one's mind is, likewise, as vacuous as the sky. To know whether this be so or not, look within thine own mind.

Being of the Voidness, and thus not to be conceived as having beginning or ending, Self-Born Wisdom has in reality been shining forever. Like the Sun's essentiality, itself unborn. To know whether this be so or not, look within thine own mind.

Being merely a flux of instability like the air of the firmament, objective appearances are without power to fascinate and fetter. To know whether this be so or not, look within thine own mind.

All appearances are verily one's own concepts, self-conceived in the mind, like reflections seen in a mirror. To know whether this be so or not, look within thine own mind.

Arising of themselves and being naturally free like the clouds in the sky, all external appearances verily fade away into their own respective places. To know whether this be so or not, look within thine own mind.

•

The Realization and the Great Liberation

Nothing save mind is conceivable.
Mind, when uninhibited, conceives all that comes into existence.
That which comes into existence is like the wave of an ocean.
The state of mind transcendent over all dualities brings Liberation.
It matters not what name may carelessly be applied to mind;
truly mind is one, and apart from mind there is naught else.
That Unique One Mind is foundationless and rootless.
There is nothing else to be realized.
The Non-Created is the Non-Visible.
By knowing the invisible Voidness and the Clear Light through not seeing them separately—there being no multiplicity in the Voidness—one's own clear mind may be known, yet the Thatness itself is not knowable.
Mind is beyond nature, but is experienced in bodily forms.
The realization of the One Mind constitutes the All-Deliverance.
Without mastery of the mental processes there can be no realization.
Similarly, although sesamum seed is the source of oil, and milk the source of butter, not until the seed be pressed and the milk churned do the oil and butter appear.
Although sentient beings are of the Buddha essence itself, not until they realize this can they attain *Nirvana.*
Even a cowherd [or an illiterate person] may by realization attain Liberation.

Zen Mind, Beginner's Mind

Suzuki Roshi says he prefers to work with American students because they are such total earnest beginners, and that is an advantage in the Zen business. Roshi is a remarkable person. During World War II in Japan he was a pacifist — unheard of. When the Americans came in the people in his town wanted to quickly tear down a war memorial statue they had; Roshi said don't do it, the Americans won't mind (they probably didn't even notice). Americans did notice during construction of the Tassajarra Zen Center when the students found that their tiny Roshi could move as powerfully and gracefully with huge boulders as he could with obstacles to understanding. This book is a nicely edited transcription of words Suzuki Roshi spoke to a beginning Zen group in a Los Altos garage.

—SB

Zen Mind, Beginner's Mind
Suzuki Roshi, (Trudy Dixon, ed.)
1970; 134 pp.

$2.50 postpaid

from:
John Weatherhill, Inc.
720 5th Avenue
New York, N.Y. 10019

or WHOLE EARTH CATALOG

Zen mind is one of those enigmatic phrases used by Zen teachers to make you notice yourself, to go beyond the words and wonder what your own mind and being are. This is the purpose of all Zen teaching — to make you wonder and to answer that wondering with the deepest expression of your own nature. The calligraphy on the front of the binding reads nyorai *in Japanese or* tathagata *in Sanskrit. This is a name for Buddha which means "he who has followed the path, who has returned from suchness, or is suchness, thusness, is-ness, emptiness, the fully completed one." It is the ground principle which makes the appearance of a Buddha possible. It is Zen mind. At the time Suzuki-roshi wrote this calligraphy — using for a brush the frayed end of one of the large swordlike leaves of the yucca plants that grow in the mountains around Zen Mountain Center — he said: "This means that Tathagata is the body of the whole earth."*

—Richard Baker

•

According to Christianity, every existence in nature is something which was created for or given to us by God. That is the perfect idea of giving. But if you think that God created man, and that you are somehow separate from God, you are liable to think you have the ability to create something separate, something not given by Him. For instance, we create airplanes and highways. And when we repeat, "I create, I create, I create," soon we forget who is actually the "I" which creates the various things; we soon forget about God. This is the danger of human culture. Actually, to create with the "big I" is to give; we cannot create and own what we create for ourselves since everything was created by God. This point should not be forgotten. But because we do forget who is doing the creating and the reason for the creation, we become attached to the material or exchange value. This has no value in comparison to the absolute value of something as God's creation. Even though something has no material or relative value to any "small I," it has absolute value in itself. Not to be attached to something is to be aware of its absolute value. Everything you do should be based on such an awareness, and not on material or self-centered ideas of value. Then whatever you do is true giving, is "dana prajna paramita."

•

I discovered that it is necessary, absolutely necessary, to believe in nothing. That is, we have to believe in something which has no form and no color — something which exists before all forms and colors appear. This is a very important point. No matter what god or doctrine you believe in, if you become attached to it, your belief will be based more or less on a self-centered idea. You strive for a perfect faith in order to save yourself. But it will take time to attain such a perfect faith. You will be involved in an idealistic practice. In constantly seeking to actualize your ideal, you will have no time for composure. But if you are always prepared for accepting everything we see as something appearing from nothing, knowing that there is some reason why a phenomenal existence of such and such form and color appears, then at that moment you will have perfect composure.

But perfect freedom is not found without some rules. People, especially young people, think that freedom is to do just what they want, that in Zen there is no need for rules. But it is absolutely necessary for us to have some rules. But this does not mean always to be under control. As long as you have rules, you have a chance for freedom. To try to obtain freedom without being aware of the rules means nothing. It is to acquire this perfect freedom that we practice zazen.

•

Galton's Walk

Associations, the mind's incessant ticking. You might get free of associations by investigating them, as this book relentlessly does.

I recall a jazz musician who kept seeing a little black dog walk by in front of him. "There he goes again," he would say. It never occurred to anybody that he was onto something.

—SB

Galton's Walk
Herbert Crovitz
1970; 159 pp.

$3.50 postpaid

from:
Harper & Row Publishers, Inc.
49 East 33rd Street
New York, New York 10016

or WHOLE EARTH CATALOG

Galton's Walk celebrates the Galton who invented the method of free association, and who first used it as he "walked leisurely along Pall Mall, a distance of 450 yards," taking careful note of all the thoughts associated with each object he saw. From that beginning Galton moved next to word associations, and concluded his observations with the remark that "our working stock of ideas is narrowly limited," and that "the mind continually recurs to them in conducting its operations."

The important word here is "recurs," for it was this idea that fired Herbert Crovitz's imagination. A basic, tractable fact of psychology, he points out, is the fact that everything recurs. It is well that it is so, for a world in which every experience was novel could hardly support intelligent life. From such basic facts, so obvious that they are easily overlooked, a scientist begins.

•

William James took the discussion of genius out of the shadows and into the laughter of sunshine. In part, he wrote, it is richness of association and in part it is ignoring "old hat." James, in one of *his* strokes of genius, brings confusion to the front. After all, he notes, confusion is mistaking the wrong part of something for the thing, while reasoning is taking the right part of something for the thing. Therefore, both confusion and reasoning partake of the same essence.

•

In class one day, some undergraduates were told to tell a story, and observe the destruction of thought. One began, "There were three men on their way to Chatham . . . (pause) . . ." During the pause, the teacher said "Chatham," and the student boggled. He froze in amazed silence, having forgotten what he was going to say. Another student said, "I went downtown to the station and sat down at the lunch counter . . . (pause) . . ." During this pause, the teacher said, "I went," which also erased whatever was to follow — not just the speech, but the intention.

•

We are now well acquainted with the idea that consciousness has the features of a plenum; that it may be entirely full of its contents, whatever they are: and, therefore, that all movement in consciousness may be cyclic. On this basis the recurrence of thoughts and actions is just what we might expect. We are now acquainted with the idea that there is something called creative thinking and problem-solving about which nothing is so clear as that it is a chancy passive pursuit.

Finally, we are acquainted with some thrashings of the awakening beast, some rousing from the long sleep of thought, some attempts to jab it, poke it, mechanize it, shatter it, reform it, and shake it awake — so that we might find a way to do the same things we do passively, as in dreaming, while we are awake and with all our wits about us.

We have seen that memory is aided by an externalized similacrum of the hidden plenum, and that a little intellectual progress can be made in taking words and separating them into a pile called content and a pile called form.

Not Even God Is Ripe Enough

Very far out African fables. Here's just the titles.

—SB

[Who sent this to us?]

Not Even God Is Ripe Enough
Bakare Gbadamosi, Ulli Beier
1968; 58 pp.

$1.75 postpaid

from:
Humanities Press Inc.
450 Park Avenue South
New York, NY 10016
or WHOLE EARTH CATALOG

Egypt

For those who want to learn ancient Egyptian:

The standard work is Sir Alan Gardiner's Egyptian Grammar, *3rd edn, 1957, Oxford($12.50). It is the best grammar for beginners in any language and also the most authoritative reference grammar of Middle Egyptian. A magnificent piece of typesetting, it uses a special hieroglyphic font and a complete sign list and vocabulary. 4to, 646 pp + xxxvi*

For the latest scholarly additions see H. J. Polotsky's "Egyptian Tenses" Jerusalem, 1965. 26 pp, 50¢.

The best and only dictionary in English is R. O. Faulkner's A Concise Dictionary of Middle Egyptian, *Oxford, 1962. 327 pp 8 vo $4.20.*

For the history and culture of ancient Egypt:

John A. Wilson: The Culture of Ancient Egypt, *Chicago, 1951. U of Chicago Press Phoenix Boox (paperback) $2.45 best & most enlightened*

Sir Alan Gardiner: Egypt of the Pharaohs, *Oxford, 1961, paperback $2.95*

Adolf Erman: The Ancient Egyptians, a Sourcebook of their Writings, *Harper Torchbacks, $2.75*

James B. Pritchard, ed.: Ancient Near Eastern Texts, *Princeton. 2nd ed. $30 ea.; $50 set.*

W. C. Hayes: The Scepter of Egypt, *Harvard, 1959. 2 vols. $30*

Prices quoted for books from England are those of Blackwell's, Oxford, England. They can be ordered there cheapest.

Enthusiasts should write for the catalogs from Blackwell's and also from Otto Harrassowitz, 6200 Wiesbaden, Postfach 349, Germany.

Note: I have listed only those works published in English. For works in other languages you can use the bibliographies in the above books as well as the book dealers catalogs.

Kenneth Konrad
Chicago, Illinois

Dear Flash,

Here's what's going on:

Saturday I helped Leonard build a new pen for his hogs.

Sunday I crawled back in an old coal mine and watched a candle burn. Then I sat a long time in the dark, just being quiet.

Yesterday I spread rabbit shit on some old dead ground, and today spaded it in and sprinkled two gallons of red worms on it.

I also ripped a lot of boards off this old house I'm living in, and cleaned them up to use building myself a pad in a corner of the barn.

This house I'm living in is dead.

There are people living who have memories of it, and things that happened here. I remember things, and my sister, and there are a few others scattered around with old home movies in their brains they filmed in years gone by.

But the house itself is dead, and within the year it will be buried by about a million tons of mud and crap piled up behind it.

The barn is where the life is now. The garden is behind it. The worms live inside it in a pit. There's a chicken lot on one side, and on two sides all the rabbits in their hutches that I told you about. They're in those hutches right this minute, Flash, wondering when I'm going to come and live there as their neighbor.

This afternoon I stuck my head in one of the hutches and breathed a while with the old momma and her litter. She's brown and white and solemn. The babies are about three weeks old, just starting to hop in and out of the nest box on their own, and sniff their mother's solid food. They're getting curious about the larger world. The old momma already knows. She's wise and proud and I think satisfied. We looked deeply into one another's eyes a time or two. I'm her bringer of food. That's my whole function in the world as far as she's concerned. As a matter of fact, it's my function in the world as far as I'm concerned too, except that what I know that she doesn't is that there's this whole larger scheme going on. What I know that she doesn't is that her produce — the manure; those thousands of little pellets that gather beneath her hutch — is food too, in this amazing scheme that my uncle started before he died, and that I'm now in the process of expanding.

(continued)

A Yaqui Way of Knowledge

This book records the experiences of an anthropology student who becomes the apprentice of Don Juan, a Yaqui indian "man of knowledge" who is also a "diablero", a black sorcerer. It is a profoundly disturbing book since it opens up areas and ideas we usually dismiss or deny. Don Juan, over a period of five years, teaches the author a little of his knowledge. He teaches through giving his apprentice various psycho-active plants: peyote, datura, and a mixture of psilocybin mushrooms, genista canariensis, and other plants. Each of these plants has its own way of teaching, its own demands and its own kind of power. For those of us who thought we understood psychedelic effects this book reveals the rudimentary state of our knowledge. For those of us who have dismissed magic as a combination of hypnotism and stage effects we are confronted with powerful and effective magic which seems irrefutable.

Don Juan himself appears as a powerful, indecipherable, wise man whose knowledge is both extensive and alien to our own. He offers to each of us the possibility of dealing with other realities, but he makes it clear that all these ways are dangerous, difficult and once entered, cannot be put aside as simply another experience.

The goal of his teaching is partially expressed as follows:

The particular thing to learn is how to get to the crack between the worlds and how to enter the other world. There is a crack between the two worlds, the world of the diableros and the world of living men. There is a place where these two worlds overlap. The crack is there. It opens and closes like a door in the wind. To get there a man must exercise his will. He must, I should say, develop an indomitable desire for it, a single-minded dedication. But he must do it without the help of any power or any man . . .

Not a book to be read for pleasure, a book which will affect you more than you may wish to be affected.

[Reviewed by Jim Fadiman]

(Why not read it for pleasure? It's frontier Boswell and Johnson. —SB)

The Teachings of Don Juan: A Yaqui Way of Knowledge
Carlos Castaneda
1968; 276 pp.

$1.25 postpaid

from:
Ballantine Books
101 Fifth Avenue
New York, New York 10003

or WHOLE EARTH CATALOG

He looked at me for a long time and laughed. He said that learning through conversation was not only a waste, but stupidity, because learning was the most difficult task a man could undertake. He asked me to remember the time I had tried to find my spot, and how I wanted to find it without doing any work because I had expected him to hand out all the information. If he had done so, he said, I would never have learned. But, knowing how difficult it was to find my spot and, above all, knowing that it existed, would give me a unique sense of confidence. He said that while I remained rooted to my "good spot" nothing could cause me bodily harm, because I had the assurance that at that particular spot I was at my very best. I had the power to shove off anything that might be harmful to me. If, however, he had *told* me where it was, I would never have had the confidence needed to claim it as true knowledge. Thus, knowledge was indeed power.

"Don't get me wrong, Don Juan," I protested. "I want to have an ally, but I also want to know everything I can. You yourself have said that knowledge is power."

"No!" he said emphatically. "Power rests on the kind of knowledge one holds. What is the sense of knowing things that are useless?"

•

Once a man has vanquished fear, he is free from it for the rest of his life because instead of fear, he has acquired clarity of mind which erases fear. By then a man knows his desires; he knows how to satisfy those desires. He can anticipate the new steps of learning, and a sharp clarity surrounds everything. The man feels that nothing is concealed.

And thus he has encountered his second enemy: Clarity! That clarity of mind. which is so hard to obtain, dispels fear, but also blinds.

•

"I say it is useless to waste your life on one path, especially if that path has no heart."
"But how do you know when a path has no heart, Don Juan?"
"Before you embark on it you ask the question Does this path have a heart? If the answer is no, you will know it, and then you must choose another path."
"But how will I know for sure whether a Path has a heart or not?"
"Anybody would know that. The trouble is nobody asks the question; and when a man finally realizes that he has taken a path without a heart the path is ready to kill him. At that point very few men can stop to deliberate, and leave the path."
"How should I proceed to ask the question properly, Don Juan?"
"Just ask it."
"I mean, is there a proper method, so I would not lie to myself and believe the answer is yes when it really is no?"
"Why would you lie?"
"Perhaps because at the moment the path is pleasant and enjoyable."
"That is nonsense. A path without a heart is never enjoyable. You have to work hard even to take it. On the other hand, a path with a heart is easy; it does not make you work at liking it."

•

You have the vanity to believe you live in two worlds, but that is only your vanity. There is but one single world for us. We are men, and must follow the world of men contentedly.

"But is this business of the dog and me pissing on each other true?"
"It was not a dog! How many times do I have to tell you that? This is the only way to understand it. It's the only way! It was 'he' who played with you."

"Let's put it another way, Don Juan. What I meant to say is that if I had tied myself to a rock with a heavy chain I would have flown just the same, because my body had nothing to do with my flying." Don looked at me incredulously. "If you tie yourself to a rock," he said, "I'm afraid you will have to fly holding the rock with its heavy chain."

•

He listened without interrupting me. I talked for a long time. Then he said:

"All this is very easy to understand. Fear is the first natural enemy a man must overcome on his path to knowledge. Besides, you are curious. That evens up the score. And you will learn in spite of yourself; that's the rule."

I protested for a while longer, trying to dissuade him. But he seemed to be convinced there was nothing else I could do but learn.

"You are not thinking in the proper order," he said. "Mescalito actually played with you. That's the point to think about. Why don't you dwell on that instead of your fear?"

"Was it so unusual?"

"You are the only person I have ever seen playing with him. You are not used to this kind of life; therefore the indications [omens] bypass you. Yet you are a serious person, but your seriousness is attached to what you do, not to what goes on outside you. You dwell upon yourself too much. That's the trouble. And that produces a terrible fatigue."

A Separate Reality

The Teachings of Don Juan *ended with Castaneda ceasing his apprenticeship, profoundly afraid to continue. In this book he is back at it, and in place of the fear prevalent in the first book now it is humor that pervades the teachings, along with some phenomenal events.*

I don't have words for the importance I consider these books to carry.

—SB

A Separate Reality — Further Conversations with Don Juan
Carlos Castaneda
1971; 317 pp.

$1.25 postpaid

from:
Simon & Schuster, Inc.
1 W. 39th Street
New York, N.Y. 10018

or WHOLE EARTH CATALOG

"Please tell me, don Juan, what exactly is controlled folly?"

Don Juan laughed loudly and made a smacking sound by slapping his thigh with the hollow of his hand.

"This is controlled folly!" he said, and laughed and slapped his thigh again.

"What do you mean . . . ?"

"I am happy that you finally asked me about my controlled folly after so many years, and yet it wouldn't have mattered to me in the least if you had never asked. Yet I have chosen to feel happy, as if I cared, that you asked, as if it would matter that I care. *That* is controlled folly!"

•

"Would I feel differently if I could *see*?" I asked.

"Once a man learns to *see* he finds himself alone in the world with nothing but folly," don Juan said cryptically.

He paused for a moment and looked at me as if he wanted to judge the effect of his words.

"Your acts, as well as the acts of your fellow men in general, appear to be important to you because you have *learned* to think they are important."

He used the word "learned" with such a peculiar inflection that it forced me to ask what he meant by it.

He stopped handling his plants and looked at me.

"We learn to think about everything," he said, "and then we train our eyes to look as we think about the things we look at. We look at ourselves already thinking that we are important. And therefore we've got to *feel* important! But then when a man learns to *see*, he realizes that he can no longer think about the things he looks at, and if he cannot think about what he looks at everything becomes unimportant."

•

"Take your grandson Lucio," I said. "Would your acts be controlled folly at the time of his death?"

"Take my son Eulalio, that's a better example," don Juan replied calmly. "He was crushed by rocks while working in the construction of the Pan-American Highway. My acts toward him at the moment of his death were controlled folly. When I came down to the blasting area he was almost dead, but his body was so strong that it kept on moving and kicking. I stood in front of him and told the boys in the road crew not to move him any more; they obeyed me and stood there surrounding my son, looking at his mangled body. I stood there too, but I did not look. I shifted my eyes so I would *see* his personal life disintegrating, expanding uncontrollably beyond its limits, like a fog of crystals, because that is the way life and death mix and expand. That is what I did at the time of my son's death. That's all one could ever do, and that is controlled folly. Had I looked at him I would have watched him becoming immobile and I would have felt a cry inside of me, because never again would I look at his fine figure pacing the earth. I *saw* his death instead, and there was no sadness, no feeling. His death was equal to everything else.

Don Juan was quiet for a moment. He seemed to be sad, but then he smiled and tapped my head.

"So you may say that when it comes to the death of a person I love, my controlled folly is to shift my eyes."

I thought about the people I love myself and a terribly oppressive wave of self-pity enveloped me.

"Lucky you, don Juan," I said. "You can shift your eyes, while I can only look."

He found my statement funny and laughed.

"Lucky, bull!" he said. "It's hard work."

•

"You think and talk too much. You must stop talking to yourself."

"What do you mean?"

"You talk to yourself too much. You're not unique at that. Every one of us does that. We carry on an internal talk. Think about it. Whenever you are alone, what do you do?"

"I talk to myself."

"What do you talk to yourself about?"

"I don't know; anything, I suppose."

"I'll tell you what we talk to ourselves about. We talk about our world. In fact we maintain our world with our internal talk."

"How do we do that?"

"Whenever we finish talking to ourselves the world is always as it should be. We renew it, we kindle it with life, we uphold it with our internal talk. Not only that, but we also choose our paths as we talk to ourselves. Thus we repeat the same choices over and over until the day we die, because we keep on repeating the same internal talk over and over until the day we die.

"A warrior is aware of this and strives to stop his talking. This is the last point you have to know if you want to live like a warrior."

"How can I stop talking to myself?"

"First of all you must use your ears to take some of the burden from your eyes. We have been using our eyes to judge the world since the time we were born. We talk to others and to ourselves mainly about what we see. A warrior is aware of that and listens to the world; he listens to the sounds of the world."

I put my notes away. Don Juan laughed and said that he did not mean I should force the issue, that listening to the sounds of the world had to be done harmoniously and with great patience.

"A warrior is aware that the world will change as soon as he stops talking to himself," he said, "and he must be prepared for that monumental jolt."

"What do you mean, don Juan?"

"The world is such-and-such or so-and-so only because we tell ourselves that that is the way it is. If we stop telling ourselves that the world is so-and-so, the world will stop being so-and-so. At this moment I don't think you're ready for such a momentous blow, therefore you must start slowly to undo the world."

•

"The sole idea of being detached from everything I know gives me the chills," I said.

"You must be joking! The thing which should give you the chills is not to have anything to look forward to but a lifetime of doing that which you have always done. Think of the man who plants corn year after year until he's too old and tired to get up, so he lies around like an old dog. His thoughts and feelings, the best of him, ramble aimlessly to the only thing he has ever done, to plant corn. That, to me, is the most frightening waste there is.

"We are men and our lot is to learn and to be hurled into inconceivable new worlds."

"There aren't any new worlds for us!" I exclaimed.

"We have exhausted nothing, you fool," he said imperatively. "*Seeing* is for impeccable men. Temper your spirit now, become a warrior, learn to *see* and then make the statement that there are no longer new worlds for our vision."

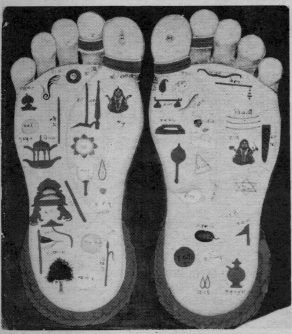

Tantra Asana

All that have seen a copy of **Tantra Art** *and its incandescent images have been tantalized by a year of rumors that a second* **Tantra** *book was coming. Here it is, more riches, tools, from what must be an inexhaustible source.*

—SB

Tantra Asana
Ajit Mookerjee
1971; 164 pp.

$37.50 postpaid

from:
Random House
Westminster, Md. 21157

or WHOLE EARTH CATALOG

Some copies of **Tantra Art** *are still available for $35 from Shambala.*

Rati is Kama's sakti representing kinetic energy. Kama is the god of love about whom it is said in the Vedas: "Desire first arose at the dawn of creation." In the Atharva-Veda, Kama is known as the creation. They remain in a union of oneness, enjoying that supreme bliss which is the highest non-duality.

"The woman you love, you must not possess"

Mysticism

The mystical event is to occupy ONE. Every time it happens it is a life enhancer and a history enhancer. Evelyn Underhill wrote this classic to gather and map the full range of Western mystical experience — Greek, Catholic, Protestant — and yours if you care to follow the steps. Each of those ONEs is unique. Each is the same. That seems pat, but this book approximately proves it.

—SB

[Suggested by James Watkins]

Mysticism
Evelyn Underhill
1911; 519 pp.

$2.45 postpaid

from:
E. P. Dutton & Company, Inc.
201 Park Avenue South
New York, N.Y. 10003

or WHOLE EARTH CATALOG

. . . Récéjac has well said that "from the moment in which man is no longer content to devise things useful for his existence under the exclusive action of the will-to-live, the principle of (physical) evolution has been violated." Nothing can be more certain than that man is not so content. He has been called by utilitarian philosophers a tool-making animal — the highest praise they knew how to bestow. More surely he is a vision-making animal; a creature of perverse and unpractical ideals, dominated by dreams no less than by appetites — dreams which can only be justified upon the theory that he moves towards some other goal than that of physical perfection or intellectual supremacy, is controlled by some higher and more vital reality than that of the determinists. We are driven to the conclusion that if the theory of evolution is to include or explain the facts of artistic and spiritual experience — and it cannot be accepted by any serious thinker if these great tracts of consciousness remain outside its range — it must be rebuilt on a mental rather than a physical basis.

Pain, then, which plunges like a sword through creation, leaving on the one side cringing and degraded animals and on the other side heroes and saints, is one of those facts of universal experience which are peculiarly intractable from the point of view of a merely materialistic philosophy.

. . . Where the philosopher guesses and argues, the mystic lives and looks; and speaks, consequently, the disconcerting language of first-hand experience, not the neat dialectic of the schools. Hence whilst the Absolute of the metaphysicians remains a diagram — impersonal and unattainable — the Absolute of the mystics is lovable, attainable, alive.

. . . "All mystics," said Saint-Martin, "speak the same language, for they come from the same country." The deep undying life within us came from that country too: and it recognizes the accents of home, though it cannot always understand what they would say.

. . . there are two distinct sides to the full mystical experience. (A) The vision or consciousness of Absolute Perfection. (B) The inward transmutation to which that Vision compels the mystic, in order that he may be to some extent worthy of that which he has beheld: may take his place within the order of Reality. He has seen the Perfect; he wants to be perfect too. . . .

. . . "Thou, my God, who art Love," says Nicolas of Cusa, "art Love that loveth, and Love that is loveable, and Love that is the bond between these twain." . . .

. . . Here the common opinion that a pious effeminacy, a diluted and amiable spirituality, is the proper raw material of the mystic life, is emphatically contradicted. It is not by the education of the lamb, but by the hunting and taming of the wild intractable lion, instinct with vitality, full of ardour and courage, exhibiting heroic qualities on the sensual plane, that the Great Work is achieved. The lives of the saints enforce the same law.

. . . To go up alone into the mountain and come back as an ambassador to the world, has ever been the method of humanity's best friends. . . .

. . . That law of the inner life, which sounds so fantastic and yet is so bitterly true — "No progress without pain" — asserts itself. It declares that birth pangs must be endured in the spiritual as well as in the material world: that adequate training must always hurt the athlete. Hence the mystics' quest of the Absolute drives them to an eager and heroic union with the reality of suffering, as well as with the reality of joy.

. . . In that remaking of his consciousness which follows upon the "mystical awakening," the deep and primal life which he shares with all creation has been roused from its sleep. Hence the barrier between human and non-human life, which makes man a stranger on earth as well as in heaven, is done away. Life now whispers to his life: all things are his intimates, and respond to his fraternal sympathy.

. . . "When the soul is plunged in the fire of divine love," he says, "like iron, it first loses its blackness, and then growing to white heat, it becomes like unto the fire itself. And lastly, it grows liquid, and losing its nature is transmuted into an utterly different quality of being." "As the difference between iron that is cold and iron that is hot," he says again, "so is the difference between soul and soul: between the tepid soul and the soul made incandescent by divine love." . . .

It's a business, actually. I mean, just this very second I flashed that this enterprise of mine is actually a business. It's called The Magic Rabbit. The rabbits are my employees. They shit all week, around the clock, and I pay them with food. Out purpose is soil redemption. Salvation! Healing, by miracles, signs and wonders. The theme song of our commercials is The Old Rugged Barn.

> On a hill far away,
> Stood an old rugged barn,
> The emblem of effort and pride.

Far out!
Come be my partner, Flash. Go find Estelle and bring her with you, and join the Magic Rabbit, Incorporated, and we'll get into soil salvation. First we'll save our own; we'll breed ten thousand rabbits and twenty million worms, and make this dead old hillside bloom. Then if other people feel like they've got a troubled soil, why let them call upon us, and we'll respond, with miracles, signs and wonders.
Faith, brother! Faith and rabbit shit, that's the theme!

> On a hill far away,
> Stood an old rugged barn,
> The emblem of effort and pride.
> How I love that old barn,
> So despised by the world,
> For the weirdness that happens inside.

You've got forty-eight hours to reply to this business proposal, Flash. Refuse it at the peril of your soil.

Your associate,

D.R.

Plans and the Structure of Behavior

What I know is that this book and Act of Creation taught me most of what I know about using my head.

The result of a year-long conversation by the authors in California in 1958-59, the book discards Stimulus-Response psychology (which never helped my head, or probably anybody's) and wades into cybernetics instead. The book is cheerful, if academicky. From it the notion of being programmed, and self-programming, emerges as a convenience rather than a threat. That Plans (programs) operate hierarchically rather than single-file is clearly an enormous saving in trouble and trivia. The constant checking of feedback loops (called TOTE units) yields a nice connectedness to the environment. The consideration of contradictory or interrupted Plans gives insight into the uses and misuses of frustration. A handy book, this, of simple concepts for understanding the subtle realm.

—SB

[Suggested by Preston Cutler]

Plans and the Structure of Behavior
George A. Miller, Eugene Galanter, Karl H. Pribram
1960; 226 pp.

$10.00 postpaid

from:
Holt, Rinehart and Winston, Inc.
383 Madison Avenue
New York, N. Y. 10017

or WHOLE EARTH CATALOG

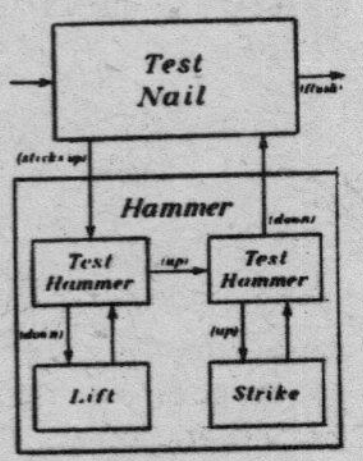

As you brush your teeth you decide that you will answer that pile of letters you have been neglecting. That is enough. You do not need to list the names of the people or to draft an outline of the contents of the letters. You think simply that today there will be time for it after lunch. After lunch, if you remember, you turn to the letters. You take one and read it. You plan your answer. You may need to check on some information, you dictate or type or scribble a reply, you address an envelope, seal the folded letter, find a stamp, drop it in a mailbox. Each of these subactivities runs off as the situation arises—you did not need to enumerate them while you were planning the day. All you need is the name of the activity that you plan for that segment of the day, and from that name you then proceed to elaborate the detailed actions involved in carrying out the plan.

Plan. When we speak of a Plan in these pages, however, the term will refer to a hierarchy of instructions, and the capitalization will indicate that this special interpretation is intended. A Plan is any hierarchical process in the organism that can control the order in which a sequence of operations is to be performed.

A Plan is, for an organism, essentially the same as a program for a computer, especially if the program has the sort of hierarchical character described above. . . .

Execution. We shall say that a creature is executing a particular Plan when in fact that Plan is controlling the sequence of operations he is carrying out. When an organism executes a Plan he proceeds through it step by step, completing one part and then moving to the next. The execution of a Plan need not result in overt action—especially in man, it seems to be true that there are Plans for collecting or transforming information, as well as Plans for guiding actions. Although it is not actually necessary, we assume on intuitive grounds that only one Plan is executed at a time, although relatively rapid alternation between Plans may be possible. An organism may—probably does—store many Plans other than the ones it happens to be executing at the moment.

Image. The Image is all the accumulated, organized knowledge that the organism has about itself and its world. The Image consists of a great deal more than imagery, of course. What we have in mind when we use this term is essentially the same kind of private representation that other cognitive theorists have demanded. It includes everything the organism has learned—his values as well as his facts—organized by whatever concepts, images, or relations he has been able to master. . . .

The central problem of this book is to explore the relation between the Image and the Plan.

•

If this description of hammering is correct, we should expect the sequence of events to run off in this order: Test nail. (Head sticks up.) Test hammer. (Hammer is down.) Lift hammer. Test hammer. (Hammer is up.) Test hammer. (Hammer is up.) Strike nail. Test hammer. (Hammer is down.) Test nail. (Head sticks up.) Test hammer. And so on, until the test of the nail reveals that its head is flush with the surface of the work, at which point control can be transferred elsewhere. Thus the compound of TOTE [Test-Operate-Test-Exit] units unravels itself simply enough into a coordinated sequence of tests and actions, although the underlying structure that organizes and coordinates the behavior is itself hierarchical, not sequential.

—Planning can be thought of as constructing a list of tests to perform. When we have a clear Image of a desired outcome, we can use it to provide the conditions for which we must test, and those tests, when arranged in sequence, provide a crude strategy for a possible Plan. (Perhaps it would be more helpful to say that the conditions for which we must test are an Image of the desired outcome.)

•

We see, therefore, that a person who is caught between conflicting Plans is in a somewhat different situation from the person caught between conflicting motives. He is almost necessarily unaware that his Plans conflict, whereas he may be painfully conscious of his incompatible desires. There is almost certain to be a large penumbra of confusion surrounding the incompatible Plans; the person seems to be deliberately frustrating himself, but cannot discover why. He knows something is wrong, but cannot discover what it is. The two Plans may be isolated from one another in such a way that it never occurs to the person to contrast one with the other.

•

Human institutions exist primarily for the purpose of executing plans that their members, as individuals, would be unable or unwilling to execute. When the plans that form their raison d'etre are taken away—finished, frustrated, outlawed, outgrown, completed, whatever—the group may disband. Sometimes they may hold reunions to swim in an ocean of emotion, but then they have become social groups with corresponding changes in the plans they execute. But many planless groups disappear and are never heard from again. In this respect groups are like computers, 90 percent plan and 10 percent image. Individuals, on the other hand are about 75 percent Image and 25 Percent Plan.

The means-ends analysis runs something like this: First, see if you know any way to transform the given into the desired solution. If no way is known, then try to reduce the difference between them; find some transformation that reduces the difference, and then apply it. Then try the first step again—see if you know any way to transform the new version of the given into the desired solution. If not, search again for a way to reduce the difference, etc. Each time the difference is reduced, the problem gets a little easier to solve.

A second very general system of heuristic used by Newell, Shaw, and Simon consists in omitting certain details of the problem. This usually simplifies the task and the simplified problem may be solved by some familiar plan. The plan used to solve the simple problem is then used as the strategy for solving the original, complicated problem.

The Act of Creation

Koestler takes his notion of bisociation to be the root of humor, discovery, and art. I take it to be one of the roots of learning, subject to applications of method (on yourself or whomever).

Koestler is a scientist of some reputation by now. He's made contributions beyond the work of others that he's generalized from. This is the book that gave him the reputation.

—SB

There are two ways of escaping our more or less automized routines of thinking and behaving. The first, of course, is the plunge into dreaming or dream-like states, when the codes of rational thinking are suspended. The other way is also an escape—from boredom, stagnation, intellectual predicaments, and emotional frustration—but an escape in the opposite direction; it is signaled by the spontaneous flash of insight which shows a familiar situation or event in a new light, and elicits a new response to it. The bisociative act connects previously unconnected matrices of experience; it makes us 'understand what it is to be awake, to be living on several planes at once' (to quote T.S. Eliot, somewhat out of context).

The first way of escape is a regression to earlier, more primitive levels of ideation, exemplified in the language of the dream; the second an ascent to a new, more complex level of mental evolution. Though seemingly opposed, the two processes will turn out to be intimately related.

When two independent matrices of perception or reasoning interact with each other the result(as I hope to show) is either a collision ending in laughter, or their fusion in a new intellectual synthesis, or their confrontation in an aesthetic experience. The bisociative patterns found in any domain of creative activity are tri-valent: that is to say, the same pair of matrices can produce comic, tragic, or intellectually challenging effects.

The re-structuring of mental organization effected by the new discovery implies that the creative act has a revolutionary or destructive side. The path of history is strewn with its victims: the discarded isms of art, the epicycles and phlogistons of science.

Associative skills, on the other hand, even of the sophisticated kind which require a high degree of concentration, do not display the above features. Their biological equivalents are the activities of the organism while in a state of dynamic equilibrium with the environment—as distinct from the more spectacular manifestations of its regenerative potentials. The skills of reasoning rely on habit, governed by well-established rules of the game; the 'reasonable person'—used as a standard norm in English common law—is level-headed instead of multi-level-headed; adaptive and not destructive; an enlightened conservative, not a revolutionary; willing to learn under proper guidance, but unable to be guided by his dreams.

The main distinguishing features of associative and bisociative thought may now be summed up, somewhat brutally, as follows:

Habit	Originality
Association within the confines of a given matrix	Bisociation of independent matrices
Guidance by pre-conscious or extra-conscious processes	Guidance by sub-conscious processes normally under restraint
Dynamic equilibrium	Activation of regenerative potentials
Rigid to flexible variations on a theme	Super-flexibility (reculer pour mieux sauter)
Repetitiveness	Novelty
Conservative	Destructive-Constructive

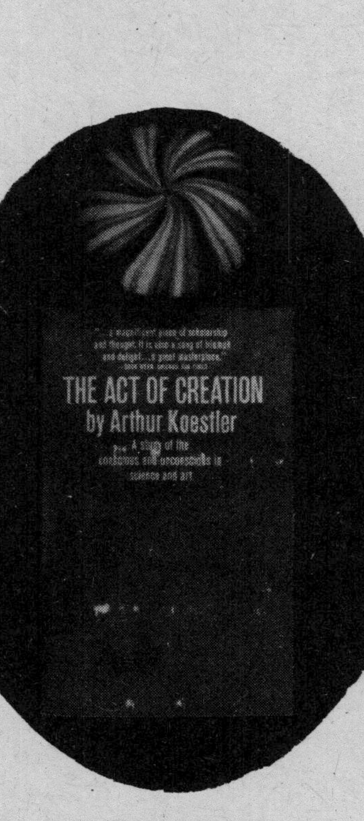

The Act of Creation
Arthur Koestler
1964; 750 pp.

$1.95 postpaid

from:
Dell Publishing Company, Inc.
750 Third Avenue
New York, N.Y. 10017

or WHOLE EARTH CATALOG

I have coined the term 'bisociation' in order to make a distinction between the routine skills of thinking on a single 'plane', as it were, and the creative act, which, as I shall try to show, always operates on

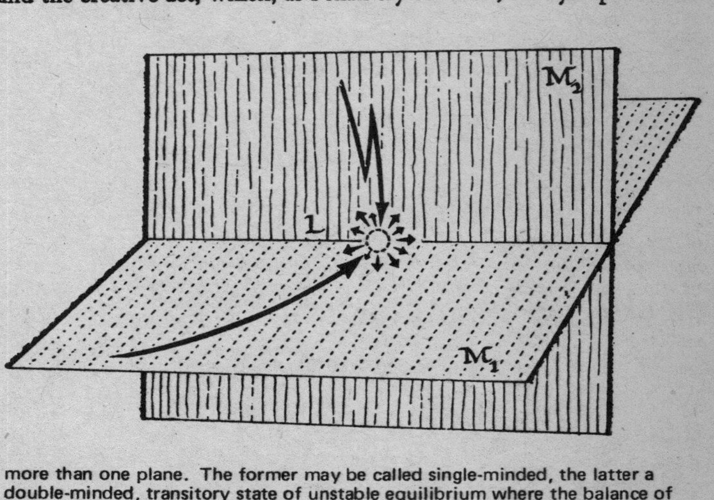

more than one plane. The former may be called single-minded, the latter a double-minded, transitory state of unstable equilibrium where the balance of both emotion and thought is disturbed.

•

In the popular imagination men of science appear as sober ice-cold logicians, electronic brains mounted on dry sticks. But if one were shown an anthology of typical extracts from their letters and autobiographies with no names mentioned, and then asked to guess their profession, the likeliest answer would be: a bunch of poets or musicians of a rather romantically naive kind.

Modern man lives isolated in his artificial environment, not because the artificial is evil as such, but because of his lack of comprehension of the forces which make it work—of the principles which relate his gadgets to the forces of nature, to the universal order. It is not central heating which makes his existence "unnatural," but his refusal to take an interest in the principles behind it. By being entirely dependent on science, yet closing his mind to it, he leads the life of an urban barbarian.

•

I must mention one specific factor which is largely responsible for turning science into a bore, and providing the humanist with an excuse for turning his back on it. It is the academic cant, of relatively recent origin, that a self-respecting scientist must be a bore, that the more dehydrated the style of his writing, and the more technical the jargon he uses, the more respect he will command. I repeat, this is a recent fashion, less than a century old, but its effect is devastating. The pre-Socratics frequently wrote their treatises in verse; the ancient Peruvian language had a single word—hamavec—for both poet and inventor. Galileo's Dialogues and polemical writings were literary masterpieces which had a lasting influence on the development of Italian didactic prose; Kepler's New Astronomy is a baroque tale of suspense; Vesalius' Anatomy was illustrated by a pupil of Titian.

The I Ching

The I Ching, the Book of Changes, is a brilliant problem-solving device. A problem (or ignorance) generally consists of being caught in local cyclic thinking. To consult the oracle, the wisdom of chance (or synchronicity, no matter), is to step out of the cycle of no-change and address a specific story on the nature of change. You now have an alternative set of solutions that owe nothing but proximity to your problem. You make the associations, you find the way out. It's prayer.

I can't think of a more important and useful book than this one. It's famously ancient, poetic, deep, esoteric, simple, involving. It has been the most influential book on American art and artists in the last 15 years.

Most people know about it. We've included it here to point at the new smaller (unabridged) cheaper Princeton University Press version of the classic Wilhelm-Baynes Bollingen edition. The oracle method is still on page 721.

—SB

The I Ching
Translated by Richard Wilhelm, Cary F. Baynes
? B.C.; 740 pp.

$8.50 postpaid

from:
Shambhala Publications
2010 Seventh St.
Berkeley, CA 94710

or

$8.50 postpaid

from:
Princeton University Press
Princeton, New Jersey 08540

or WHOLE EARTH CATALOG

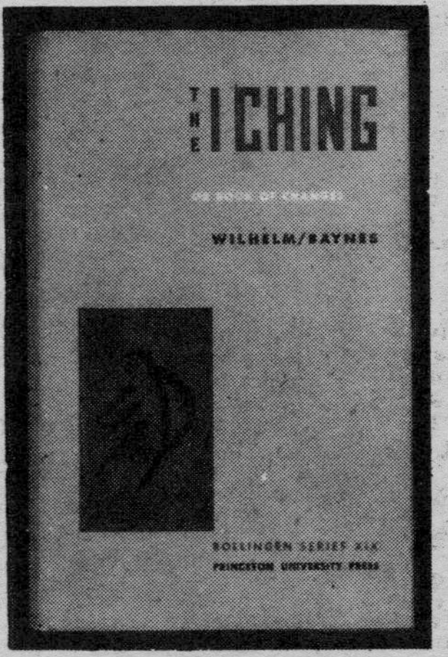

解

40. *Hsieh / Deliverance*

above CHÊN THE AROUSING, THUNDER
below K'AN THE ABYSMAL, WATER

Here the movement goes out of the sphere of danger. The obstacle has been removed, the difficulties are being resolved. Deliverance is not yet achieved; it is just in its beginning, and the hexagram represents its various stages.

THE JUDGMENT

DELIVERANCE. The southwest furthers.
If there is no longer anything where one has to go,
Return brings good fortune.
If there is still something where one has to go,
Hastening brings good fortune.

40. *Hsieh / Deliverance*

This refers to a time in which tensions and complications begin to be eased. At such times we ought to make our way back to ordinary conditions as soon as possible; this is the meaning of "the southwest." These periods of sudden change have great importance. Just as rain relieves atmospheric tension, making all the buds burst open, so a time of deliverance from burdensome pressure has a liberating and stimulating effect on life. One thing is important, however: in such times we must not overdo our triumph. The point is not to push on farther than is necessary. Returning to the regular order of life as soon as deliverance is achieved brings good fortune. If there are any residual matters that ought to be attended to, it should be done as quickly as possible, so that a clean sweep is made and no retardations occur.

THE IMAGE

Thunder and rain set in:
The image of DELIVERANCE.
Thus the superior man pardons mistakes
And forgives misdeeds.

A thunderstorm has the effect of clearing the air; the superior man produces a similar effect when dealing with mistakes and sins of men that induce a condition of tension. Through clarity he brings deliverance. However, when failings come to light, he does not dwell on them; he simply passes over mistakes, the unintentional transgressions, just as thunder dies away. He forgives misdeeds, the intentional transgressions, just as water washes everything clean.

Leisure— The Basis of Culture

This is a searching, philosophical book, examining some important questions. It first appeared 20 years ago and surprisingly few people have read it.

But that isn't the item.

Here's the item: why would an economic consultant, specializing in recreation resources, turn to this kind of philosophical tract as a sourcebook (with an introduction by T.S. Eliot, yet!), when there are dozens of current, thickly documented studies available, prepared by first rate scholars, dealing with leisure, social change, consumer economics, and all the other relevant issues consultants are paid to investigate?

That is a question I am anxious to answer, especially for Whole Earth readers, who are inclined to be, I imagine, more than superficially interested in issues as basic to these times as leisure and our culture.

Whenever I read the current literature and listen to the experts on the subject of leisure, I realize that no one has contributed much new wisdom to the field beyond what Pieper, in fewer than 100 pages, has laid out. His major contribution, in my opinion, is to set down a fundamental, no horseshit, definition of leisure, which certainly has nothing to do with motor boat sales, average hours of work, and all that statistical trash that keep so many consultants and writers employed. In Piepers's words

Leisure, it must be clearly understood, is a mental and spiritual attitude— it is not simply the result of external factors, it is not the inevitable result of spare time, a holiday, a weekend or a vacation. It is, in the first place, an attitude of mind, a condition of the soul, and as such utterly contrary to the ideal of 'worker' in each and every one of the three aspects under which it was analysed: work as activity, as toil, as a social function.

Compared with the exclusive ideal of work as activity, leisure implies (in the first place) an attitude of non-activity, of inward calm, or silence; it means not being 'busy', but letting things happen.

Leisure is a form of silence, of that silence which is the pre-requisite of the apprehension of reality: only the silent hear and those who do not remain silent do not hear. Silence, as it is used in this context, does not mean 'dumbness' or 'noiseless'; it means more nearly that the soul's power to 'answer' to the reality of the world is left undisturbed. For leisure is a receptive attitude, and it is not only the occasion but also the capacity for steeping oneself in the whole of creation.

The adoption of this definition is like adopting a religion. Your life may be permanently altered.

Leisure is not the attitude of mind of those who actively intervene, but of those who are open to everything; not of those who grab and grab hold, but of those who leave the reins loose and who are free and easy themselves— almost like a man falling asleep, for one can only fall asleep by 'letting oneself go'. Sleeplessness and the incapacity for leisure are really related to one another in a special sense, and a man at leisure is not unlike a man asleep.

•

Compared with the exclusive ideal of work as toil, leisure appears (secondly) in its character as an attitude of contemplative 'celebration', a word that, properly understood, goes to the very heart of the meaning which I am concerned to put before you. . .God, we are told in the first chapter of Genesis, 'ended his work which he had made' and 'behold, it was very good'. In the same way man celebrates and gratefully accepts the reality of creation in leisure, and the inner vision that accompanies it. And just as Holy Scripture tells us that God rested on the seventh day and beheld that 'the work which he had made' was 'very good'— so too it is leisure which leads man to accept the reality of the creation and thus to celebrate it, resting on the inner vision that accompanies it.

•

. . .In the same way, no one who looks to leisure simply to restore his working powers will ever discover the fruit of leisure; he will never know the quickening that follows, almost as though from some deep sleep. . . .Aristotle says of leisure, 'A man will live thus, not to the extent that he is a man, but to the extent that a divine principle dwells within him.'

•

Leisure, it must be remembered, is not a Sunday afternoon idyll, but the preserve of freedom of education and culture, and of that undiminished humanity which views the world as a whole.

•

. . .once again, work stops for the sake of work, and the feast is subordinated to 'work'. There can of course be games, circenses, circuses— but who would think of describing that kind of mass entertainment as festal?

It simply cannot be otherwise: the world of 'work' and of the 'worker' is a poor, impoverished world, be it ever so rich in material goods; for on an exclusively utilitarian basis, on the basis, that is, of the world of 'work', genuine wealth, wealth which implies overflowing into superfluities, into unnecessaries, is just not possible. Wherever the superfluous makes its appearance it is immediately subjected to the rationalist, utilitarian principle of the world of work. And, as the traditional Russian saying puts it: work does not make one rich, but round-shouldered.

[Suggested and reviewed by Richard Raymond]

Leisure— The Basis of Culture
Josef Pieper
1952; 127 pp.

$.95 postpaid

from:
New American Library
1301 Ave. of the Americas
New York, N.Y. 10019

or WHOLE EARTH CATALOG

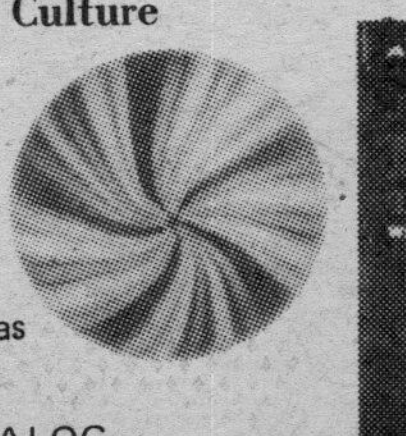

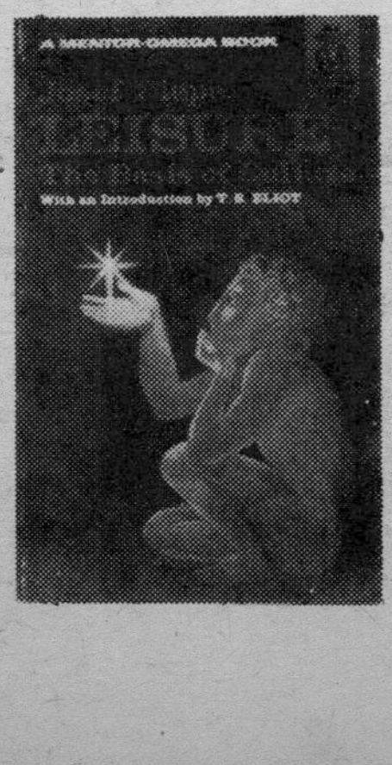

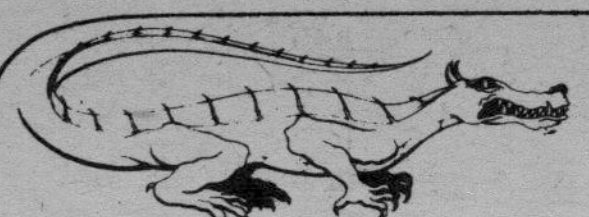

WEDNESDAY: URGE'S BATH

When D.R. went off the hill late Wednesday to mail his letter to the Flash he was almost certain there'd be a letter waiting for him at the store. From the Flash, from Marcella, maybe even, by sudden cosmic arrangement, some word from Estelle. A postcard, a note, something, from somebody.

But there wasn't, and D.R. had to fight his disappointment down.

He bought a Coke from Mrs. Godsey, and after he had drunk it he bought a few more groceries to see him through the remainder of the week. Mrs. Godsey asked D.R. how he was and he said fine, but it was clear to her that he wasn't fine, and Mrs. Godsey found herself worrying about D.R. a little. She tried to think of something to say that might make him feel better, but she didn't have any confidence in any of the words that occurred to her. She wrote his groceries up in the account book, and wished him a good day as he carried them out the door. But that wasn't enough, it wasn't enough at all and she felt bad about D.R. as the screen door slammed behind him.

Before he started back up the hill, D.R. went around in back of Godsey's store to look in Urge a minute. Urge had still not been given a thorough cleaning since he had been in Kentucky. A little at a time, D.R. had been taking stuff out of the bus and either throwing it away or carrying it with him up the hill. But the great bulk of their stuff still had not been touched, and in looking at it now D.R. felt suddenly inspired to pitch in then and there and clean it out once and for all.

As soon as he decided that's what he'd do, he felt instantly better, and better still when he started dumping junk out of the bus left and right. He spread their old stale sleeping bags on top of the bus to air. He dragged the mattress out and laid it on the grass in Leonard's yard. He collected the worst of the actual trash, the empty bottles, old apple cores, old smashed Kentucky Fried Chicken boxes, paper cups, old magazines, and grubby old paper napkins, and threw it all outside in a pile. Beside it he piled an old quilt that had had a chocolate milkshake spilled on it, and a towel too far gone to preserve. A pair of his own worn-out jeans wound up on the pile.

When he started coming to things he wasn't sure what he should do with, he began a separate pile. He found one of Estelle's blue sneakers, worn through at the little toe, laced with binder twine. He found a pair of her cut-off Levis, and three dirty socks. In a pillow-case he found two of her special outfits, the gingham frontier dress, and the tie-dyed jumpsuit she'd made out of a mechanic's coveralls. He found their kitchen stuff in a box lined with the green sports section of the San Francisco Chronicle. The pots and pans and skillet and plastic plates and bowls were piled in with the Mazola Corn Oil, a box of salt, some spices in little cans, brown sugar in a jar, some old rice. He found their mangled copy of the Whole Earth Catalog, the paperback of Stranger In A Strange Land that Estelle had made so many notes in. And then, way back under the bed, face down on the floor, opened at the hexagram called Youthful Folly, D.R. found their I Ching.

Far out.

The Ching.

It was like running into an old friend. D.R. picked it up and dusted it off, and sat for a while holding it in his hand. He had been wishing for the Ching. It was time for him to start consulting it again. And maybe he could find some shit to order from the Catalog, too. The found books pleased D.R. enormously, and lifted him past the little desire that had begun to build in him to stop working on the bus and go flake out somewhere. D.R. was suddenly filled with tenderness and affection for Urge, and he went the whole way with his cleaning job.

When he had emptied the bus completely, he went to Roxie's house and borrowed a broom, and swept everywhere in the bus the broom could touch. Roxie showed him where the outdoor faucet was, and Leonard's hose. D.R. took the sleeping bags off the top, spread them out beside the mattress, and moved Urge until the hose could reach. And then he washed him good, all over, inside and out, with soap and warm water from Roxie's kitchen, and then a cold rinse with the hose. It was the first bath Urge had had since the west coast, and you could tell by the sound of the motor how much the old bus dug it. When he went back in the store to get some cardboard boxes, Mrs. Godsey told him he could store anything he wanted to in her basement. D.R. spent the rest of the afternoon sorting through the stuff that he would keep, getting it into boxes, four of them, and then stacking the boxes on the floor of Mrs. Godsey's basement.

Leonard came home from another day with the Grand Jury in town as D.R. was finishing up and asked if he would like to stick around for supper. D.R. said no thanks. He had a whole new fund of energy now, and he wanted to get back up on the hill with it, and use it well. He gathered up his books and his groceries and set out whistling, back up Trace Fork again.

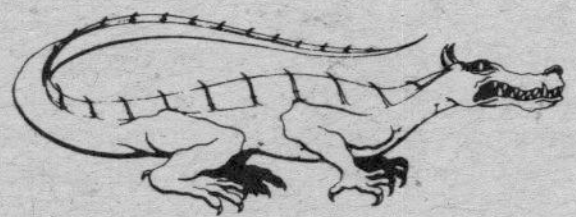

WEDNESDAY EVENING: THE BOOKS

Whole Earth Catalog: Shit, man, I want that. And that. And that! I want The Owner-Built Home. I want House Carpentry, Simplified. I want Domebook One. I want the Manual of Individual Water Supply Systems. I want Direct Use of The Sun's Energy. I want Electricity From The Wind. I want an Ashley stove. I want the Encyclopedia of Organic Gardening. I want Livestock and Poultry Production. I want Goat Husbandry. I want Human Use of The Earth. I want Rural Industry. I want Farmers of Forty Centuries. I want a Corona Hand Mill. I want The New Religions. And I want Estelle to get here just as fast as she possibly can.

(continued)

Credits

Cumulative Roster of Whole Earth Catalog Editors

FALL 68	Stewart Brand
Jan 69	SB
March 69	SB
SPRING 69	SB (with Lloyd Kahn— Shelter & Land Use)
July 69	SB
Sept 69	SB
FALL 69	SB (with Lloyd Kahn— Shelter & Land Use)
Jan 70	SB
March 70	Gurney Norman (with Diana Shugart)
SPRING 70	SB (with Lloyd Kahn— Shelter & Land Use)
July 70	Gordon Ashby (with Doyle Phillips)
Sept 70	Gurney Norman (with Diana Shugart)
FALL 70	JD Smith (with Hal Hershey— Community) [The six month's prior research was also JD's, done while he was managing the Truck Store.]
Jan 71	SB
March 71	Ken Kesey and Paul Krassner
LAST CATALOG	SB

Divine Right
Gurney Norman

Those with **Portola Institute** who we owe the most to are
Richard Raymond
Les Rosen
Larry Kline
Vern John
Eleanor Watkins
Nancy Wirth
Mitzi O'Dell

And our **agent**
Don Gerrard

Production Credits

LAST CATALOG Spring 71
Steamboat (70-71) Layout and drawings
Fred Richardson (69-71) Camera and index
Evelyn Goslow Composer
George de Alth Layout
Mike Goslow Layout
Phyllis Grossman (70-71) Composer
Laura Besserman Proofreading
Trudy Smith Composer

Mar 71 Supplement, add
Ron Bevirt Schedule

Jan 71 Supplement, add
Hal Hershey (69-71) Layout
Barbara DeZonia Composer
Bud DeZonia Field operations
Ant Farm Diversions
Lois Brand Corrections and food

Fall 70 CATALOG, add
Robin Wakeland Composer

Spring 70 CATALOG, add
Cappy McClure (69-70) Composer
Ellen Hershey Sundry
Peter Bailey (68-70) Cover

Mar 70 Supplement, add
Mary McCabe (69-70) Layout

Fall 69 CATALOG, add
Joe Bonner (68-69) Layout
Jay Bonner Layout

Sep 69 Supplement, add
Jan Ford Composer

July 69 Supplement, add
Annie Helmuth Composer

Fall 68 CATALOG, add
Sandra Tcherepnin Composer

And at **Nowels Publications**

Bob Parks

Truck Store Credits

Laura Besserman (70-71) Research and books
Lois Brand (68-71) Bookkeeper
JD Smith (70-71) Manager
Herald Hoyt (70-71) Books
John Clark (69-71) Mailorder
B. Anne Hines Bookkeeper
Francine Slate (70-71) Bookkeeper
Dudley DeZonia (70-71) Mailorder
Jerry Fihn (70-71) Subscriptions
Barbara DeZonia Mailorder
Bernie Sproch (69-71) Filing and store
Amy Fihn (70-71) subscriptions
Mary Jo Morra (70-71) Subscriptions
Diane Erickson (70-71) Store and mailorder
Soni Stoye (70-71) Lunch, flyers
Terri Gunesch (70-71) Lunch
Troll (70-71) Subscriptions, BD-4
Peter Ratner (69-71) Books
Doug Gunesch BD-4
Bob Rich BD-4
Molly Books
Paul Narewski Subscriptions
Pam Smith (70-71) Mailorder
George de Alth (70-71) Subscriptions
Austin Jenkins (70-71) Mailorder
Carolyn Green (70-71) Lunch
Hal Hershey (69-71) Manager
Diana Shugart (69-71) Research
Les Rosen (69-70) Bookkeeper
Mary McCabe (69-70) Store
Megan Raymond (69-70) Sundry
Shel Kaphan (70) Sundry
Russell Bass (69-70) Subscriptions
Leslie Acoca (70) Subscriptions
Tracy McCallum (69-70) Manager
Alan Burton (69-70) Mailorder
Barbara McCallum (69) Mailorder
Rob Gilmer (69) Mailorder
Arnold Scher (69) Mailorder
Michael Handler (69) Store

Spring 1970, left to right, front to rear: Mary McCabe, Alladin Lantern, Les Rosen, Darby, coffee cup, Mary Jo Morra, volley ball, Laura Besserman, Soni Stoye, Lois Brand, bag of money, Pam Smith, Delta Mist Smith, Diana Shugart, Earth flag, Ashley stove, Russell Bass, JD Smith, 30-30, Peter Ratner, Jerry Fihn, Austin Jenkins, boffer, Stewart Brand, Leslie Acoca, Alan Burton, Cappy McClure, John Clark, Supplement, Gurney Norman, skull, George de Alth, money, Megan Raymond, Truck Store. Photo by Sam Falk.

How To Do a Whole Earth Catalog

Take what you can use, and let the rest go by.
Ken Kesey 1969

The masked man left behind a silver bullet. The people said, "We'd rather have a scribbled diagram," and they shot him with his silver bullet. Here's our scribbled diagram.

Researching

For us this consisted of three big jobs. 1) Encouraging an incoming flow of information— spontaneous research by the readership. 2) Scanning "the literature" for promising stuff. 3) Sorting the good from the bad.

1) The incentives we laid out for spontaneous suggestions were : reward of money ($10 for published review, later $10 for any used suggestion); reward of recognition (we published the name of the reviewer and suggestor, spelled as correctly as possible); reward of honor-by-association (to the extent that we kept valid high standards, and honored the famous suggestor no more than the teenage one); reward of doing a good deed (to be a noble conduit we had to stay clean); reward of return (to the extent that we gave good, people returned it).

2) "The literature" for us consisted of Publisher's Weekly, Forthcoming Books in Print *(both from R. R. Bowker, source of all the basic cataloging information on books in the U.S.— I consider R. R. Bowker a major pillar of Western Civilization; they labor endlessly, invaluably, without bias and of course unheralded).* Science *(who lists all the books sent to them for review),* Scientific American *(the first national publication to notice us, by the way),* Popular Science *(for tools), and later our cooperative competition such as* Mother Earth News, Big Rock Candy Mountain, Canadian Whole Earth Almanac, Natural Life Styles.

Other major sources: catalogs from the publishers, bibliographies in good books (especially when annotated), big book stores, especially Kepler's, friends' bookshelves, the Stanford and Menlo Park libraries, and our own bookshelves revisited.

At the beginning of the CATALOG I ordered copies of promising titles from the publishers at 40% discount on ABA's Single Copy Order Plan. After about a year of this MIT said we didn't really have to pay for review copies from them. After that we requested free review copies from all the publishers and usually got them, at least on new books. It took some self-policing to keep from requesting "review copies" that we just wanted to have. There are some built-in conflicts-of-interest in the reviewing business.

3) Sorting. Fuller calls it "tuning out everything that's irrelevant", and considers it the core activity of thinking. It is utterly unglamorous; it is shovelling shit by the mountainload. I never spent my time reading the good stuff— whose quality was usually evident in 2-3 minutes. I spent the yellow-brown hours reading the lousy books, digging past their promising facades to the hollow within. Some of these wound up in the stove, where their publishers belonged.

Sorting requires criteria for yes and no, and sets to sort within. By angelic good fortune I thought to spell out our criteria at the beginning on page one of the first CATALOG. The sets (the section headings, devised originally as a secondary definition of our contents) also held up surprisingly well. Both the criteria and the sets became well-worn handles on the otherwise wholly unmanageable mass of information that flooded in. They also helped preserve continuity during three years of gradually migrating values.

At the beginning of the CATALOG I imagined us becoming primarily a research organization, with nifty projects everywhere, earnest folk climbing around on new dome designs, solar generators, manure converters; comparing various sound systems, horse breeds, teaching methods. . .the only product-project we ever did was build a BD-4 airplane, and I felt guilty about that because of the big expense for low yield of information.

In fact we didn't do enough research. Not the studious kind. Of our staff of about 26, only 2 or 3 were ever engaged in active search for CATALOG material. It could have been much more and better, but it never got organized, probably because of prima donna failings on my part.

Reviewing

Usually I review a book before I read it. These are almost always shorter, pithier, more positive and useful reviews. You're approaching the book from the same perspective as the reader— unfamiliarity— and you're not apt to fall into imitation of the author's style or petty argument with his views, as critics do.

So, I review the book, enthusiastically, on what I know from its title, its subject, the author, my own experience, and a hasty glance at the pages. Then I look a little more deeply to see if the review is fulfilled. If not, I either rewrite the review or discard the book.

The quickest clues to the authority of a book are its illustrations and its back pages. Cheap shit editor's-idea books puff up their illustrations. If a book has a whole page devoted to a photograph of nothing, with a nothing caption and credit to some manufacturer for the photo, throw the book. Look for photographs that contain real information related to the text, and captions that multiply the use of the picture; or diagrams that deliver complex understanding simply. In the back of the book look at the bibliography. If it's absent, or inflated endlessly, or unannotated, or oddly limited, be suspicious. The bibliography is an easy way to compare the author's judgment with your own.

The CATALOG format for reviews includes excerpts from the book (or magazine or catalog). The excerpts should expose the book— convey quickly what's in it, and deliver a few complete ideas independently useful to the reader. I always attempt to gut the book with the excerpts, extract its central value. Really good books like On Growth and Form, *or* Stick and Rudder, *or* Natural Way to Draw *will not be gutted; practically any line or picture in them can be used.*

An ideal review gives the reader: a quick idea of what the item is, what it's useful for, how it compares to others like it, and how competent the reviewer is to judge. (This last is why I stopped having unsigned reviews— the reader gradually grows familiar with the weaknesses and strengths of the various reviewers.)

The horrible temptation in reviews is to show off rather than simply introduce the item and the reader to each other and get out of the way.

Editing

The operational word on the cover of the CATALOG is access. Ultimately that means giving the reader access from where he is to where he wants to be. Which takes work, work takes tools, tools need finding, and that's where we come in.

A good catalog is a quick-scan array of tools, where you can find what you want easily, with detailed information where you're interested.

Our attempt to fulfill these requirements led to use-based section headings (Shelter, Land Use, Communications, etc.), an alphabetic index, and page-theme layout.

On each page we try to have one graphic which "keys the page", tells with a glance what's there. The hardest thing we had to learn was providing simple clear demarcation between items— an unadorned line.

We publish considerable detailed information— fine print. Sorting among that is aided by a consistent code of type-faces (reviews are always "univers italic," access is always "teeny", Divine Right is always "bold teeny", and so forth). The IBM Selectric Composer makes this an easy matter. Still we're not as consistent as we should be.

In descending order of importance, our layout guidelines are:

- *accuracy*
- *clarity*
- *quantity of information*
- *appearance*

Glamorous white space has no value in a catalog except as occasional eye rest. I figure the reader can close his eyes when he's tired.

I keep coming back to the reader/user because that's who the editor represents. I've had to feel that my obligations to Portola Institute, to staff, friends, relatives, and to myself are all secondary. So are obligations to authors, suppliers, publishers, other editors. Usually there's no conflict, but when there is the editor has to see that the reader wins.

The editor's main mechanical task is determining efficient use of production time and page space. It's like spreading hard butter on soft bread, best if you cut the task into workable hunks and distribute them evenly.

I use McBee cards, one for each item, for rough editing. I know from looking at previous CATALOGS and the new material approximately how many pages should be in the, say, Nomadics Section— 61 pp. So I take the stack of McBee cards punch-coded for that section and break them down into categories— mountain stuff, car-stuff, outdoor suppliers, survival books, etc. Then those sub-piles are put in some sensible sequence. Then on a big table the cards are separated further into 61 little page-stacks, by pairs (the reader sees 2 pages at a time, not one). The contents of those piles are written on my desk dummy. The cards are stacked in page sequence, and I've got a section rough-edited.

There are two main work governors tacked to the wall— a calendar showing days of production and a page-chart. If we have 8 weeks to do 448 pages, then we have to finish a signature of 64 pages every 6 working days, or about 11 pages a day. The signature-finished points are marked on the calendar so I know exactly how far behind we are and when we'll have to start working nights to get copy to the printer on time.

The page chart is big, a couple square inches for each page. On each page I write the basic information for the three layout people. As they finish a pair of pages they mark them off on the chart and look for the next ready pair. From the chart they get the number and name of the pages, the titles of the items (and whether they're new or to be cut out of old flats), plus the appropriate piece of Divine Right, and any headings.

In our production the editor, typist, cameraman, and three layout men work together. The editor tries to stay a couple days ahead of layout in fine-editing the pages, and the typist and cameraman a day ahead.

When a layout guy has the copy all gathered he calls me over to see what the space situation is and determine what to leave out and what to retype or reshoot so it will fit. After he's finished I'm called over again for any revisions and to try to catch the mistakes while they're easy to correct. Two other proofreaders also try (while they're indexing) before the page is flatted and sent to the printers.

Just before the signature goes to press I get page-proofs for a last chance at corrections before the karmic soup gels irretrievably.

Some publications make all their editorial decisions by continual discussion and consensus. I admire the ones who can make it work. I've gone the faster and possibly more limited route of strong central direction.

When we have a guest editor, every bit of the authority and most of the responsibility is his. Now that we're quitting, it's all yours.

Layout

We use a tabloid sized page, like the magazines in the Sunday papers. Steve Baer's Dome Cookbook *was what convinced me it's a good format. You have enough space on each page and spread (facing pair of pages) to lay out a graphic array of information with multiple visual relationships and plenty of freedom for the reader to pick his own path. Also it's an economical size for printing on a web press. The two main disadvantages are that booksellers don't like the display space a tabloid book takes up, and some readers get tired holding the big page up.*

(continued)

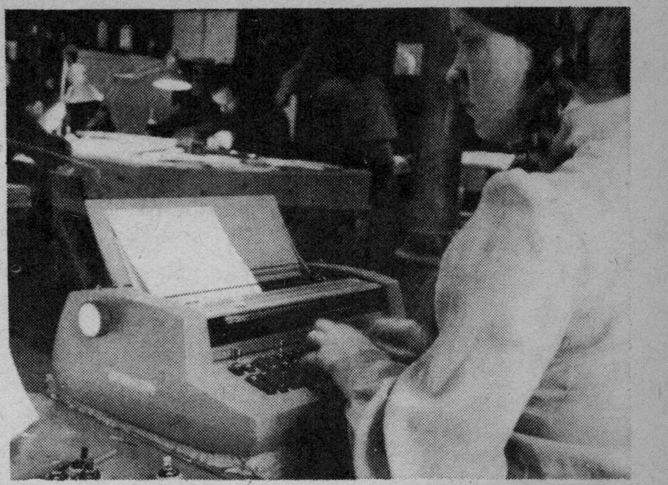

Composition. IBM Selectric Composer, Evelyn Goslow. Some type fonts are visible at lower left.

IBM Selectric Composer

As far as I'm concerned this is the tool that made our operation possible. Instead of having to send material to a type-setter— a costly, standardized, and full-of-problems procedure— we can sit down with the layout people and editors and fit copy precisely to the page, with all the options of last-minute corrections. IBM offers about 140 different type fonts from 6-point to 12-point in size (you have to buy the fonts, $30 apiece) which permits variety that would cost a fortune at a typesetter. We used 15 fonts for this CATALOG.

The Composer leases for **$150** */month, a bargain if you're using it regularly or can rent it to careful people when you aren't. There is some special knowledge without which you will wreck the machine, but IBM can teach it to you in about an hour. The machine can, in two typings, make the right hand side of your copy straight, like in newspapers, but since this saves no space and is no easier to read, I think you're wasting your time to do it.*

The Composer is a fine machine, flexible and durable (we dropped ours on the ground and ran wrong voltages through it in the desert; it kept typing). To see one, look up IBM in the yellow pages under Typewriters.

—SB

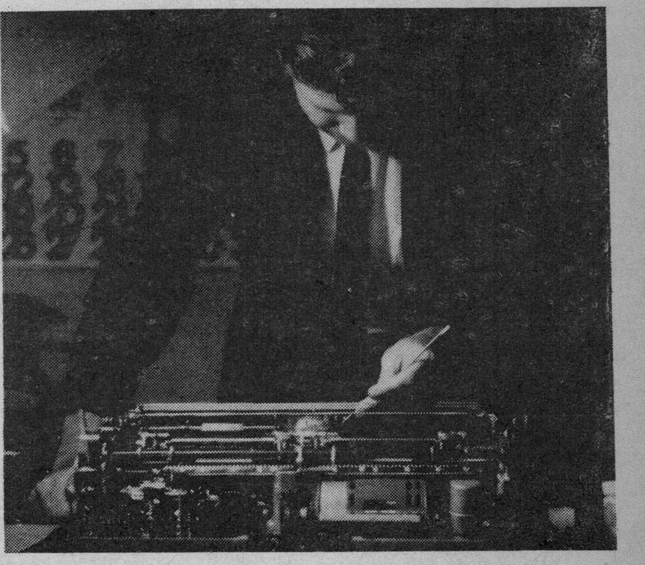

Larry Whiteside from IBM fixing the composer. Free and fast repair service is part of the lease contract. We needed to call a repairman usually 3-4 times during a production. IBM can furnish service damn near anywhere, which made travelling production a lot easier.

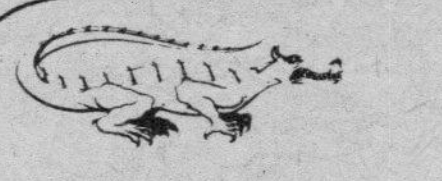

The I Ching: After supper, sitting on the porch in the final hour of light that day, D.R. threw the I Ching. He had always been ceremonious when he cast the Ching; but that evening the sense of ceremony and ritual came more naturally to D.R. than it ever had before. There were no trappings. No candles, or bells or incense, none of that. There was only D.R. on the front porch of the house, sitting on the floor with his feet two steps down, the book beside him on the floor, and the coins lying loosely in his hand. D.R. was sitting quietly, waiting for the spirit to move him, and the spirit was taking its time. It wanted D.R. to really settle now, to fit into his natural place within the flow and motion all around. The day was ending, the night was on its way. The air was fresh and thick with the settling evening dew. Over by the silver-leaf maple tree some lightning bugs were blinking. And above them in the sky the first stars of the evening were popping out. Day and night were trading times and places, easing into one another's spheres around the world.

And D.R. sat very still and allowed a similar change to happen inside him.

(continued)

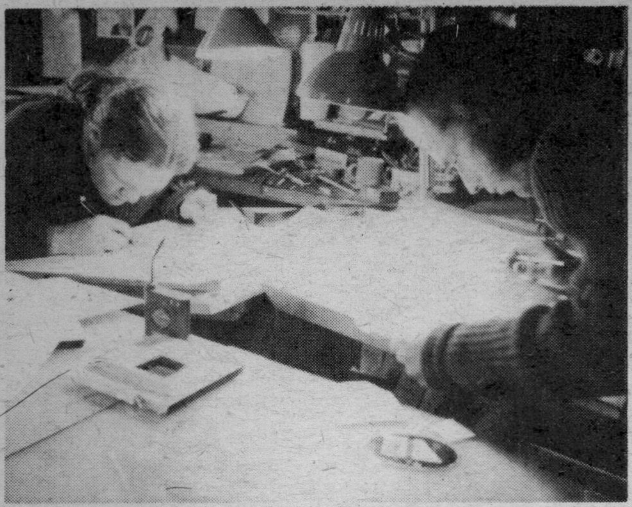

Layout. Steamboat drawing dragons. George working on pp. 422-423.

Layout (continued)

At first we laid out our pages just the way a newspaper does (the Menlo-Atherton Recorder showed us how). We used flats (blank, line 2-page-sized pieces of paper provided by the printer) on light tables (made out of plywood, fluorescent lights, white plastic, and glass). The flats were placed line-side-down on the light tables, so the lines showed through and you could align items on them but they wouldn't show on the final layout. Also like the newspaper we used beeswax (also provided by the printer) to stick the items down with— it was kept liquid in an old electric frying pan. The advantage of wax is that it's fairly easy to lift an item and restick it. After everything was in place on a page we took a little wooden roller and ran it firmly over all the copy so it would stay attached to the flat.

We made the flats so that they could be used directly by the printer for making the negatives and the plates. Thus in the first CATALOG p. 1 and p. 64 were on the same flat, p. 2 and p. 63, p. 3 and p. 62, and so forth, with the even page always on the left. On this last production we found it more convenient to layout the pages individually in page sequence, and tape together the flats for each signature when we were done (p. 65 and p. 128, p. 66 and p. 127, etc.).

We went along using light tables and wax until Gordon Ashby and Doyle Phillips revolutionized our procedure with the July 70 Supplement. They showed us that working on a portable drafting table, with a T-square and rubber cement for adhesive was really much easier and gave us better layout. We still had lines on the flats but they were on the top surface in light blue (invisible to the camera).

So now our tools are:

- *Portable drafting table and engineers lamp*
- *T-square and triangle (for horizontal and vertical lines and alignment)*
- *Exacto knives and very good scissors (for cutting copy)*
- *Rapidograph pens (for clean ink lines)*
- *Rubber cement and dispenser (jar with brush), and solvent (in a squirt can dispenser, for lifting already glued copy), and warts (sticky squares for cleaning up stray rubber cement on the page).*
- *Drafting tape (for holding paper in place)*
- *Thin white tape (for holding down bits of copy where rubber cement won't do it and for covering up mistakes)*
- *Blue pencil (for marking on the page)*
- *Template (for ruling curved lines such as around Divine Right)*
- *Letraset (burnish-down characters for page numbers and headings) and wooden stylus (for burnishing)*
- *Tuffilm (to spray on finished copy for protection)*

We still use the light tables for correcting copy. When the typist makes a mistake she simply types the line again correctly, makes a blue pencil mark, and goes on. Then on the light table it's easy to cut the copy, align the mistaken line under the previous line, stick the pieces together with white tape, and go on to the next mistake.

We used to custom-make each page with various column widths, which only led to extra trouble for us and the reader. Now we type to a basic 20-pica three-column page and everything's much simpler.

—SB

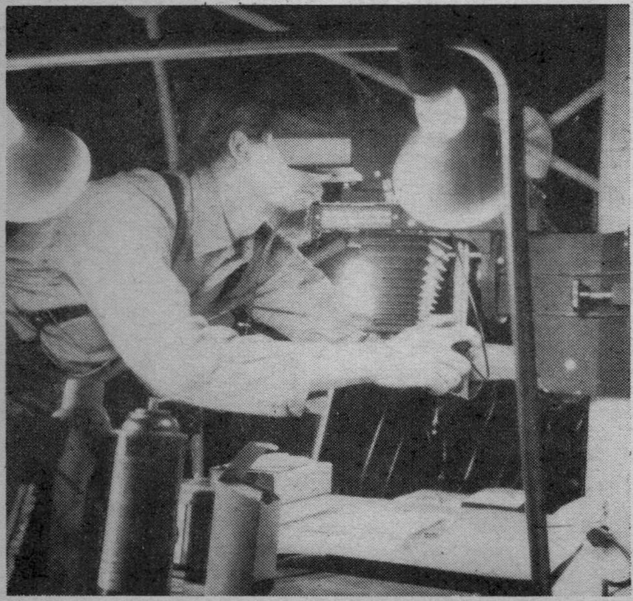

Polaroid MP-3 and Fred Richardson during January production in the desert. In the foreground are cans of Omit, pressurized air for cleaning glass surfaces.

Books

We get letters all the time asking how to start a Truck Store and Diana's quick hard summary tells you the basics. I'll try to tell you how to stock that store with books. There are a few how-to books on the subject of bookstores. The one I read is *How to Run a Paperback Bookstore* (R. R. Bowker 1962, $5.00). It tells you enough to figure out hardbacks too and if you know nothing about bookstores, get it. Even if you do know something you might enjoy it and it can help answer some questions, like, how come we're not making any money. This book helps to explain the minimum initial investment of $10,000 though they suggest $15,000. That sum may sound staggering and I do know people who've done it on $1,000 but they started 5 years ago and are still in the red. It's really not worth the headaches. Running a store that serves the community and turns people on to new ideas is a far out venture but don't forget that you've got to make a profit ("we're not in business for our health you know. . .").

Tools of the Trade

Join the American Booksellers Association and with your membership ($25 the first year) you'll get their Book Buyers Handbook. This gives addresses for all the major publishers and their discount schedules returns policies and other good stuff. It's essential. When you join, tell them you want their MANUAL ON BOOKSELLING and other free stuff (you do have to remind them).

American Booksellers Association
800 Second Avenue
New York, N. Y. 10017

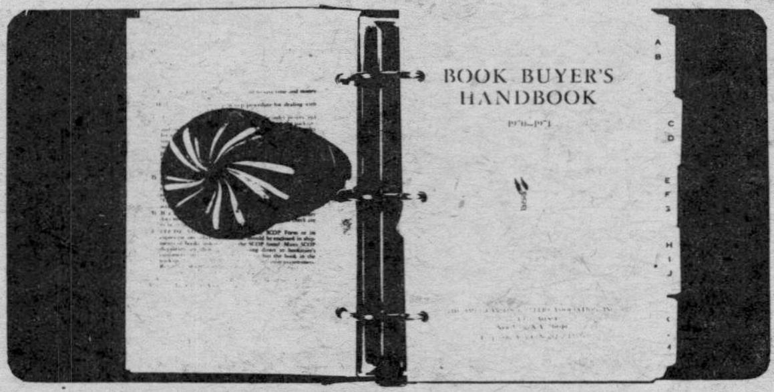

Bowker publishes the other essentials. *Books in Print* ($25.50 yearly) is two volumes, authors index and titles index of current books in print with price and publisher. Their appendix of publishers' addresses is more complete than the ABA Handbook. *Paperback Books in Print* ($29.95 yearly) has three cumulative issues in November, March and July which list current paperbacks by subject as well as alphabetically by title and author. There are also monthly editions to fill in between with reviews taken off the book's cover. *Publishers Weekly* is a great magazine and if you don't enjoy it you are probably in the wrong business. A subscription is $18.50 and aside from giving you general news of the trade, its spring, summer and fall editions are devoted to notices by publishers of the books they plan to release that season. The weekly reviews of forthcoming books are honest and entertaining. The magazine keeps you ahead of your customers. *Forthcoming Books in Print* ($19.95) supplements *Books in Print* following the same author and title format and is issued 6 times a year. *Subject Guide to Books in Print* ($23.50 a year) is in two volumes and is an index by subject. For an additional $8.95 you can get *Subject Guide to Forthcoming Books in Print* which is bi-monthly. *Publishers Trade List Manual* is a 6 volume collection of over 2,000 publishers trade lists which is pretty impressive but its main use is to check discount categories for making single copy orders and if you are not doing much of that or even if you are, you can still get by using somebody's last year edition checking price changes in BIP. The cost is $17.50 a year.

There are many more but these are the ones we have and I've listed them pretty much in the order of frequency of use. When deciding which to get, consider what services you want to provide to your customers.

R. R. Bowker
1180 Avenue of the Americas
New York, N.Y. 10036

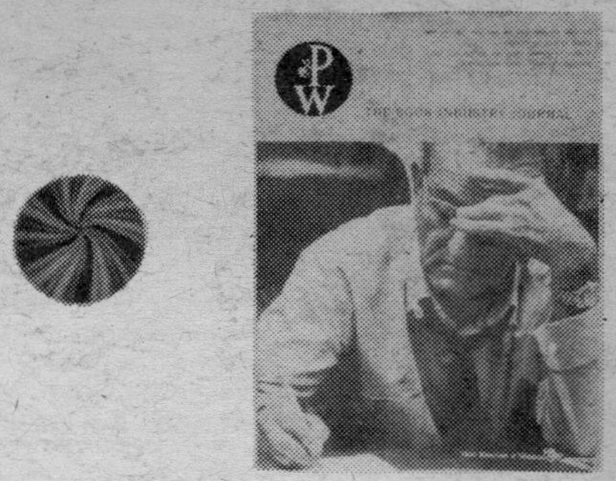

Kinds of Books

Books are not just books. There are obviously hardback (cloth) and paperbacks. There are also text, trade, and mass editions.

Text editions are not simply the books you read in school but rather are designated by publishers as texts and sold to bookstores on a very short discount, generally 20%. This small discount is the reason most stores don't carry text books. The Truck Store is an exception. Trade books are the largest category of books and they, like texts can be either hardbound or paper. Book stores get the most generous discount on these, generally 40% or better. Trade paperbacks are termed quality paperbacks. Mass books are weird and if you buy them from a distributor, which you are almost forced to do, you get only 30% discount. If you can buy direct from the publisher you get 40%, but more about this confusion later.

Where do Books Come From

You buy both direct from the publisher and from wholesalers (known also as jobbers or distributors). The best way to find out about wholesalers in your area is to ask around at friendly stores. You will find that most wholesalers deal mainly one kind of book, that is, trade hardbacks, trade paperbacks (call these guys quality jobbers) or mass paperbacks (the last are a special case and will be dealt with in their own section). You'll need accounts with all 3 kinds. At the Truck Store we do most of our business with publishers and use wholesalers only to fill in. There are advantages and disadvantages to this.

Wholesaler advantages: They are regional and thus can give faster service and shorter distance makes for less postage and freight costs. Since they are smaller operations they are easier to deal with and adjustments in billing or invoice errors are handled more quickly and returns are made with no hassle. Also there is less paper work as you are dealing with one firm rather than 20, so there's just one invoice and one bill. This saves an incredible amount of time.

Disadvantages: They either don't stock what you want or are out of it and won't back order (that is, record your order and send it when the books come in). Their maximum discount is anywhere from 36-40%. You must pay 30 days from date of invoice.

Publishers advantages: They do have the books you want and they will back order. They may say you must pay in 30 days but allow 60 to 90 without bitching. They will send you current price lists, order forms, catalogs, advance notices of new books, and a salesman once in a while. Salesmen lay raps on you about why you should buy 25 copies of everything in their line but also they help you stay on top of it, assist in getting returns permissions, and some times they'll give you free books or take you out to lunch. Publisher's most important advantage is their better discounts. They generally have a minimum order of 5 books to get a 40% discount but from there discounts go up. This schedule varies with every publisher and is fully detailed in the ABA handbook. WORKING WITH THESE DISCOUNTS IS WHERE YOU MAKE YOUR MONEY!!!

Publishers disadvantages: Unless you live in the East you have to wait at least 3 weeks for delivery and pay that long distance postage or freight, though a few publishers have regional centers. (If you are in a rush say so in red letters and ask for "special handling" book rate which is not too much more expensive and can speed delivery by as much as 10 days.) Their bills are often computerized and each account means more invoices and more bills to pay and it is a lot of paperwork. Getting returns permissions is a drag and the delay for credit on returns is slow but we feel that the better discounts we get from publishers offsets these. One other disadvantage is that there is the minimum order to earn their discount but a way to get around it is the single copy order plan (SCOP). Essentially you send in a check with your order on a special order form and the publisher gives you a better discount than he would otherwise (see the ABA Handbook for details.) We use this for the few super expensive books we stock rather than invest money in keeping them around the store collecting dust.

(continued)

Polaroid MP-3 Camera

The production photography that I do for W.E.C. includes all halftones up to 3½" x 4½" and line shots up to page size.

Our halftones are done with a screen that has 85 dots to the inch. Really fine printing on slick paper sometimes uses screens with more than 200 dots/inch. Consult with your printer to find out what he can handle with his camera/on what kind of paper/in your production.

We make all our 3½" x 4½" or smaller halftones and let the printer make the bigger ones. We do them as veloxes (positive prints on paper) and paste them down directly on the flats. On large photos that we want especially nice we have the printer do in negative and strip into the negative he does of the flat.

Why not have the printer do all of the halftones? You can. It won't cost anymore. In fact, it may cost less. We like to do our own, though, because it gives us control, reduces the problems of getting all the stuff to the printers in good shape, losing material, and getting the wrong picture in the right spot. We also get to see exactly what the page will look like.

The Polaroid MP-3 with lights, film back, halftone kit, and 5" lens costs about $800. Film, depending on type, costs $13.50 to $15.50 per box of twenty sheets (60¢–75¢ per picture). After working with the MP-3 for 1½ years, I average 2½-3 shots per good halftone, 1½ shots per good line shot. That is working with varied copy. If I have a series of originals to be done to the same size, I can arrange them by contrast and average maybe 1½ shots per good halftone.

That assumes that I have good film. I had no trouble with the Polaroid film the first year I used it, but during the last six months, quality has been extremely variable.

Stat King

We bought a Visual Graphics Stat King camera for doing work up to 11" x 17". It is a fancy photostat machine that will enlarge/reduce 200%—50%. Cost $4000. It can have prints out and dry in 5 minutes or so. We wanted to do halftones with a contact screen but it didn't work well enough (the camera lacks a vacuum back) so we use it only for line work. Fairly cheap to use, but we don't use it enough to be worth anywhere near $4000.

—Fred Richardson

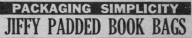

The Mass Book Racket

We have found that once you deal with a distributor of mass books the mass publishers are reluctant to sell to you. (I think it's some sort of conspiracy.) Mass distributors have some advantages in that they are everywhere there are magazines (that's the other side of their business) so there is probably one near you. This means that you can call in an order one day and can get it two days later. Delivery is cheap if not free and you can even go pick up the books yourself. Ask and maybe they will let you take a shopping cart around and pick the books off the shelves yourself (check out their nudie magazines while you're there.) Returns are also done with no hassle. None of these things do the Truck Store much good as we carry very few mass books but if you are doing a more general store you will find these things helpful. However they quite often don't stock the books you want as the bulk of their trade is traditionally with drug stores and magazine stands and they are not easily persuaded; if it doesn't sell at the corner grocery they won't stock it. THEY ONLY ALLOW 30% DISCOUNT and sometimes less which is hardly enuff to get by on. If you do mail order you can lose money.

How To Get Around This (Maybe)

If you are just starting I suggest that you set up accounts with mass publishers from the beginning telling them you are a new store. If they try to direct you toward a local distributor tell them you're not interested (ours makes deliveries before we open and many boxes of books have been rained on). Then, when you are established, see what kind of service the local guy can give you. This way at least you have an option. If you've already been buying from the distributor and want to order direct, send in an order to the publisher. The minor mass houses will be more likely to ship direct because their local distribution isn't very good but with the major publishers this probably won't work. Another tactic would be to use the order form the publishers send out with promo material (tho you might have to write first telling them to put you on their mailing list. Getting yourself listed in Publishers' Weekly as a new store accomplishes this, not a bad thing to do.) They might just fill your order automatically or they might send it back to your local distributor to fill. But if they do fill it they cannot legally refuse to ship future orders direct, though they might.

Another tactic is to get in touch with their salesman (though being regional he may be far away) and get him to send in your order or a letter okaying your order. He'll be somewhat sympathetic as more orders mean more money for him and it will look like he's really doing his job. The problem here is that he probably isn't, and you may have some trouble finding him. The main office may tell you who he is or send him your way or you could ask other salesmen, bookstores, or maybe quality distributors. I wouldn't ask the mass distributor as he may catch on that you want to take your business elsewhere.

Some distributors:

Ray Surguine (3640 Walnut, Boulder, Colorado 80302) is a western wholesaler that carries both quality and mass paperbacks. Their discounts are straight 30% on mass and 40% on quality with a minimum order of 25 books on each. They are a good firm to do business with when your local guy doesn't have what you want and you are doing battle with the mass publisher.

Book People (2940 7th St., Berkeley, Ca. 94710) is a quality paperback wholesaler. They are unique in that they carry a lot of small presses. They have a free catalog.

L & S Distributors (1161 Post St., S. F., Ca. 94109) carry a lot of the same publishers as Book People but fill orders faster and seem to have books in stock more regularly. They give good service and we use them alot.

Baker & Taylor Company has regional offices (Somerville, N.Y. 08876; Mommence, Ill. 60954; and Reno, Nevada 89502). They carry a very complete line of hardbacks, including text editions, and a limited selection of trade paperbacks.

The East Coast is full of wholesalers of all kinds of books. Check the telephone books for names of mass distributors, either under Books or under Magazines.

There are lots of things I didn't talk about, most of which are contained in HOW TO RUN A PAPERBACK BOOKSTORE. Things like stock control, checking invoices and paying bills, making returns, setting up credit and budgeting have to be learned and systemized as you go along, everyone has their own way of doing it.

One prime piece of advice to those of you who've never run a bookstore before would be to get yourself a job for a while to apprentice or if you can't do this try and hire someone who knows something about the business. If you have any specific questions you can write to us and we will try and answer them. Please don't send orders to us and expect us to fill them at a discount as we are a retailer just like you. Good luck.

—Laura Besserman

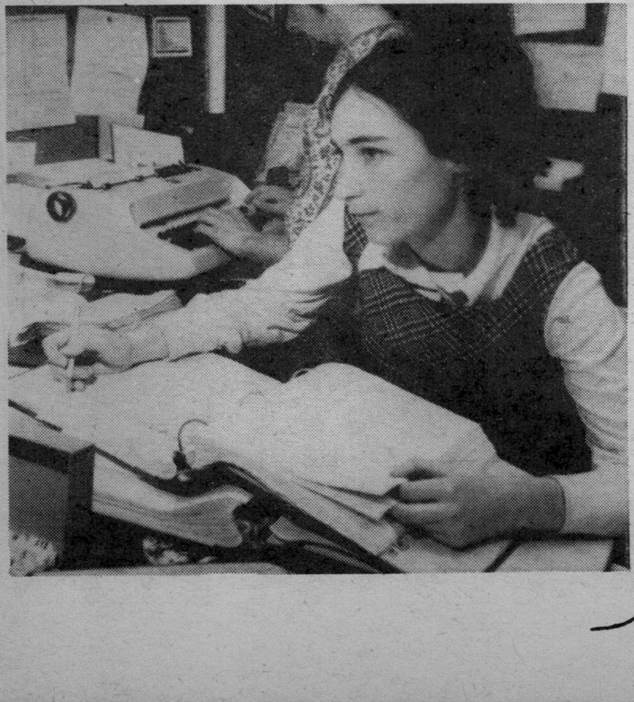

Sam Falk

The Quick Hard Summary.

In the September 69 **Supplement**, *Stewart boldly invited anyone who was thinking of opening a Whole Earth Store to write to Hal for a quick hard summary. We've since had many inquiries & various of our staff have written numerous more or less quick & more or less hard summaries. Here's a sort of composite of all that information. We've also told folks to write to the two going stores we now know of, & they've been very helpful:*

Whole Earth Access Co.
2466 Shattuck
Berkeley, CA 94704
(415) 848-0510

Whole Earth Learning Community
817 East Johnson
Madison, Wisconsin 53703
(608) 256-8828

The Quick Hard Summary

First, get lots of money to start with. Ideally, enough to run on for at least six months, preferably longer, & assuming whatever you make during the first raunchy months will go for unforeseen expenses, which there always are. A very rough minimum estimate is $10,000; it depends a lot on how much space you want to occupy & what you plan to do with it. Basic necessary expenses are: rent—often first & last months', plus cleaning deposit maybe—utilities—gas, electric, phone, water, garbage, some deposits required; insurance; equipment & supplies (possibly cash register, adding machine, typewriters), forms, paper, notebooks, files; use permit from your city—not much ($10–$50); furniture & redecorating: desks, tables, chairs, shelving, display areas, signs, etc. (A lot can be done with used stuff). If you don't have them you'll need tools—hammers, saws, etc. And paint. Salaries—possibly the largest single item, unless people work for free, which tends to breed poverty & discontent.

Now—assuming you have some bread, or think you can get some—find a place. Not too high-rent, but hopefully somewhere where people walk by a lot. Don't sign a lease until you have a friendly lawyer check it—most agencies use standard forms that are designed to screw the tenant, but you can change clauses you don't like if they want to rent the building. Next: apply to your town or city for a use permit, which often takes a while to get. Without one you can be shut down forthwith. Apply to your state for a resale permit, same reason. Invite your local building inspector & fire inspector to come inspect—before signing a lease, if possible. Because—if you're in an old building, you may be required by law to make changes in wiring, plumbing, fix leaks, etc. at your own expense. Again this is preventative—later harassment can come from these areas, & you have no recourse. Again, a good friendly lawyer can be a lot of help in knowing local ordinances, etc. Also, lots of towns are zoned so that you can only do business in certain areas. Find out about zoning before *renting.*

Hopefully when you start getting your building into shape & see how much space you have, you can start ordering stock. A good idea is to figure out how much it's going to cost you to keep the physical place & the people going for six months. Then see how much money you have left & order your stock accordingly. You'll probably have already opened a checking account. If you're going to stock books, join the American Booksellers Association —$25 gets you a manual of publishers with info on almost all publishers—their discounts, access info, credit terms, policies, etc., free advice; & so forth. You can also file a statement of your credit with their affiliated group—the American Book Publishers Council; whenever you open a new account with a publisher you just tell him your credit was established there, he looks you up, & things are speeded up considerably. Usually publishers & suppliers require payment in advance on your first, or first several orders—after a while you can order, be sent an invoice, & have 30 days to pay. The more you order at once, the better discount you get—it's a question of working up to where you're selling enough that you can afford to order in larger quantities. It takes an average of a month for orders to arrive. By the way, when opening accounts, please make it clear that you're not connected with us—we've had trouble already with publishers putting other people's accounts on our statements, because of similarity of names.

What to sell? Depends a lot on you. We do mostly books & that's what we know most about—also some merchandise (Ashley Stoves, Corona corn mill, Aladdin lamps, Snugli baby carriers, etc.) & a few magazines. A lot of the people who've written to us are interested in health food; arts & crafts, & other trips. Selling food requires special permits; that's about all we know. You can often get local arts & crafts on consignment (you pay the artist when the item is sold), which can save you some basic stock expense. A rule of thumb in ordering books is that cheap paperbacks sell the most—you can be surer of selling more of them than of the more expensive hardbacks. The Catalog *itself is our bestseller, could probably be yours too.*

OK. If you get this far—plan a gala opening for publicity—invite Everyone & serve cheap (homade!) goodies. Word of mouth is best advertising we've found. But you can put up posters, flyers, whatever. Try to get your local newspaper to do a feature on you. Smile a lot.

We'd like to see a Whole Earth Store in every town. Yea!! But before you start, be sure you're ready to do business—you will have to hassle with publishers & suppliers, keep records, mess with forms, numbers, paperwork. You will need a lot of human energy —someone has to do: ordering stuff, keeping track of what comes in, selling stuff, bookkeeping, cleaning up around the joint, correspondence, typing, filing, building or buying equipment, furniture, painting, keeping track of what you have & what you need (inventory), business with landlord & miscellaneous officials, decision-making, paying bills & payroll, etc., etc. Our aim here is not to discourage anyone, but to encourage open-eyedness about the prospects.

—Diana Shugart

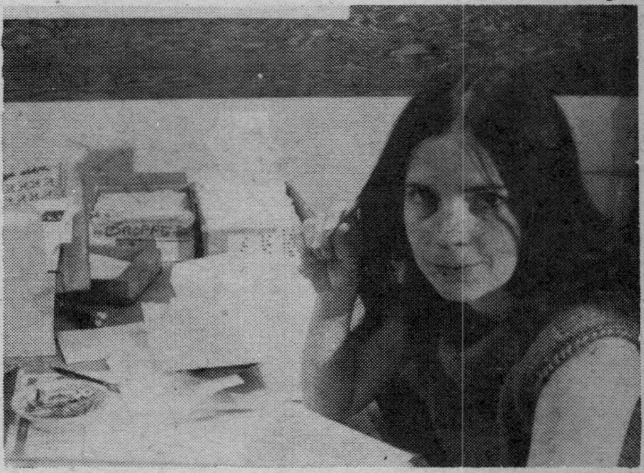

Sam Falk

AAA Adding Machine Company

I wish we'd known about this outfit when we started business. They carry used and reconditioned calculators, adding machines and cash registers at good prices.

—SB

Catalog

FREE

from:
AAA Adding Machine Company
26-09 Jackson Avenue
Long Island City, New York 11101

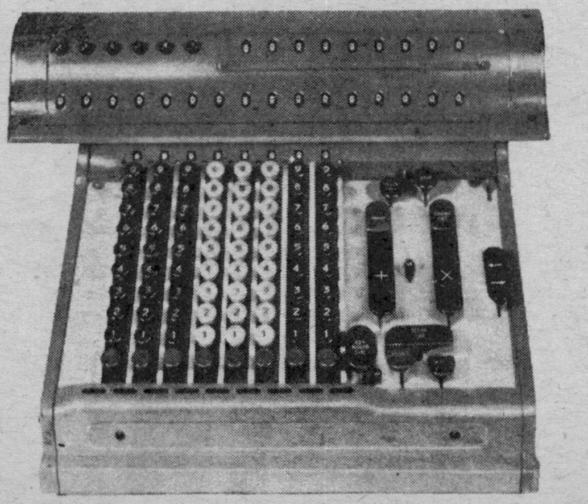

MARCHANT $99.00

Automatic carriage return • Carriage tabulation; preset decimal as well as multiplication • No repeat or non-repeat keys • Automatic elimination of 1 in division • Complete carriage carry-over • Exclusive keyboard check dial • Complete in line 3 figure proof.

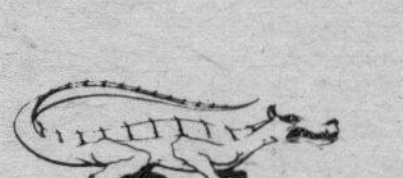

Beginning in his mind, then flowing down along his spine and outward through his body, the change came slowly over him. D.R.'s hands waited for it to be complete. Then, on their own, unhurried, they began to toss the coins. Six times they shook and dropped the coins, and the reading materialized:

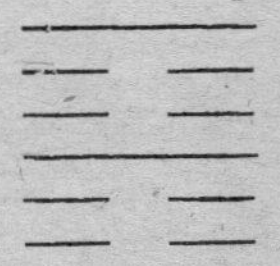

Ken/Keeping Still, Mountain

"The image of this hexagram is the mountain, the youngest of heaven and earth. The male principle is at the top, because it strives upward by nature; the female principle is below, since the direction of its movement is downward. Thus there is rest because the movement has come to its normal end.

"The hexagram signifies the end and the beginning of all movement. The back is named because in the back are located all the nerve fibers that mediate movement. If the movement of these spinal nerves is brought to a standstill, the ego, with its restlessness, disappears as it were. When a man has thus become calm, he may turn to the outside world. He no longer sees in it the struggle and tumult of individual beings, and therefore he has that true peace of mind which is needed for understanding the great laws of the universe and for acting in harmony with them. Whoever acts from these deep levels makes no mistakes."

•

Stranger In A Strange Land: D.R. tried to read that novel by lamplight after he went to bed, but he was too sleepy to pay attention.

Some other time, he said to himself.

And he blew the lamp out and went to sleep.

Money

One of the main things that drove me into business was ignorance. A liberally educated young man, I hadn't the faintest idea how the world worked. Bargaining, distribution, mark-up, profit, bankruptcy, lease, invoice, fiscal year, inventory— it was all mystery to me, and usually depicted as sordid.

I noticed that great lengths were gone to in order to prevent "consumers" from knowing that part of purchase price went to the retailer. It seemed exquisitely insane to me. You sell deception and buy mistrust, to no advantage. The retailer in fact earns his 25-40% by tiresome work, but the prevailing attitude makes him out a clever crook. Ignorance institutionalized. Would you mind leaving the room, we're talking about money.

So along with shit, fuck, cunt, and the rest, I wanted to say among my friends, money, not to swear but to honor function.

You may or may not think capitalism is nice, and I don't know if it's nice. But we should both know that the WHOLE EARTH CATALOG is made of it. Capital was invested by my parents and parents'-parents'-parents in such activities as iron-mining in Minnesota and Eastman Kodak. They paid nicely enough, and by family attentiveness-to-business and flat-out parental generosity, I wound up with a bundle of money without having done a lick of work for it. Stock had been bought in my name; my parents handled it but it was mine to work with; it's a good system, like giving your kid a tough horse to ride when he's young.

By the time I was 29 the stock came to over $100,000. I had ignored it all through my twenties, living in $20 apartments and not travelling much, occasionally wage-earning in photography, design, Army. I suspect I felt guilty about the money. I know I felt stupid about it. So it sat, and I sat, and alienation was a cozy room. Garrett Hardin has written that alienation and irresponsibility are parents of invention. James Watson says that boredom is a prime incentive to creativity. They're right.

The idea for the CATALOG hit me plenty hard, but I think I could never have raised the money for it. Certainly not by grant— I did know about foundations by then. I doubt if I had the brass to steal the money, or deal dope for it. Honest labor would have taken too long for my short attention span.

So I invested, comrade. I took the profits from old investments and put em into a new one, a brand new naive hopeful unlikely business with ditto in charge. Investing in yourself has hard truthful edges; I hope you get a crack at it, and can stay as sweet as you were as a dependent.

Why am I saying all this? Because many who applaud the CATALOG and wholeheartedly use it, have no applause for the uses of money, of ego, of structure (read uptightness), of competition, of business as usual. All the things, plus others, which make the CATALOG, and make the selective applauders into partial liars, and me one too if I aid the lie.

The CATALOG is advantage-seeking, all right. It gains advantage half as far as it gives it. 50% efficiency is about the best nature can do, says Odum (p. 8).

I am also saying all this by way of thanks to my parents. It's as Dick Alpert used to say: It's love money that underwrites this sort of venture every time. Which suggests that if foundations and governments want to do the job they say they do, they should retain the services of better lovers.

The figures. I thought it would cost $10,000 for April-December of the first year, (I didn't even think about it until Dick Raymond mildly asked me). I would loan money to the CATALOG at 8% interest, to be paid back when and if we were money ahead. (This "self-dealing" is now illegal, reasonably. Assholes with tax-evasive non-profit corporations pour money back and forth within the corporation and collect personal tax-free interest. Borrowing now, I'd have to use a bank, and they'd get the interest.)

Well, that first nine months cost $12,780, with no noticeable income. On that hopeful note we started the store ($450/month rent) and started buying stock, too late for the Christmas rush— most book stores do 1/3 of their year's business in November-December. By February 1969 the CATALOG and Truck Store had gone through $28,260, of which $21,425 was loaned by me and Lois. We had 340 subscribers, had sold 800 copies of the Fall 68 CATALOG and were printing a second thousand of them. By May '69 we'd spent $42,550, of which $27,425 was loaned. We stopped loaning. Income kept growing, and by early Fall 1969 we went from red to black. We'd paid for the past.

At the time, in fact, finances were not particularly on my mind. How To Make Money was not the design problem. (I'd heard and bought Ken Kesey's advice that you don't make money by making money: you have that in mind early on, but then you forget it and concentrate entirely on good product; the money comes to pass.) The problem was How to Generate a Low-Maintenance High-Yield Self-Sustaining Critical Information Service.

Easy. You name what you know is good stuff and indicate exactly where to get it. You do this on newsprint, which costs 1/2 of the next higher page stock. Low overhead every step. Employ stone amateurs with energy and enthusiasm. Build furniture out of scrap doors, light tables out of scrap plywood, work in whatever space you have. Pay your pros $5/hr (no raises) and the beginners $2/hr with 25¢ /hr raises every couple months. Employees fill out their own time sheets. If they get dishonest about that— or anything that hurts service, fire them. Spread responsibility as far as it will go, credit too.

If you're doing a clear public service you may get non-profit tax-exempt status. (We pay State taxes on store property, and State and Federal taxes on the store and mail order operation. The CATALOG is non-profit— this was helped by our lowering the price of the CATALOG twice, and by our plan to stop, which indicated we weren't kidding about being primarily an educational prototype. Even so the IRS is grumbling and may change our classification, which could endanger Portola Institute.)

To ensure in-house quality control, acquire low-cost maximum-flexibility tools. For us that was the IBM Selectric Composer for type-setting, the Polaroid MP-3 camera for line and half-tone graphics, and Pitney-Bowes mailing machine and scale for the mail order operation. Lease where you can. What must be bought can be owned by individuals who get depreciation tax advantage that the non-profit corporation can't get.

As Fuller advises; Always promise less than you deliver, and let customers, business associates, staff come to their own conclusions about you. Small business is based on earned trust. Send cash-with-order in your first dealings with another firm. Pay bills scrupulously on time. Keep exact, open books on all your accounting. Small businessmen respond faster to honesty than any other kind of person: most of them couldn't care less what you wear, smoke, or think if you're straight with them and don't care what they wear, smoke, or think.

What you're trying to do is nourish and design an organism which can learn and stay alive while it's learning. Once that process has its stride, don't tinker with it; work for it, let it work for you. Make interesting demands on each other.

Our stopping is primarily an economic experiment. Rather than do the usual succession things we prefer to just cease supply, let demand create its own new sources. Our hope is that those sources will be more diverse and better than we have been or could have been if we continued.

There's money in this business. We made some in spite of ourselves. To really clean up we could have:

Had a private sale of stock at the beginning like Rolling Stone *and Zomeworks.*

Sold expensive advertising space in the CATALOG.

Kept the cover price at $4.

Gone for mass distribution.

Franchised Whole Earth Truck Stores around the world.

Developed a line of Whole Earth tools.

Sold the name and momentum of the CATALOG for a princely sum.

The expenses on this LAST CATALOG will take us back down to zero and probably past it. We're footing most of the $200,000 printing bills and we won't get any income from Random House until November. It looks like we'll have to go into a second printing before then. Eventually we'll be money ahead again, and I'll be responsible for doing something interesting with it.

Here's a rough estimate of what happens to the $5 you paid for this CATALOG. (It's true only at the instant that all 200,000 copies of the first printing have been sold and no further have been paid for.)

$5	
$2.00	bookseller
.50	jobber
.45	Random House
1.00	printing and binding
.15	production salaries, supplies, research
.10	shipping and miscellaneous
.064	Gurney Norman (8% of net)
.0736	Don Gerrard (10% of what's left)
.0662	Portola Institute (tithe) (10% of what's left)
.5962	The Future (all slacks and surpluses taken up here)

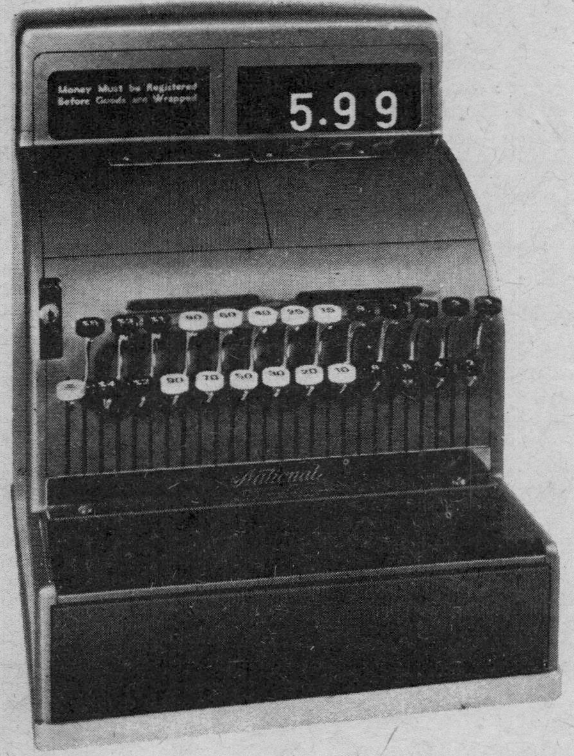

Money Must be Registered Before Goods are Wrapped
5.99

Here's the current state of our books:

Exhibit 1

Whole Earth Division of
Portola Institute
Balance Sheet
April 30, 1971
(Unaudited)

Assets

Current assets:		
Cash - Bank of California, commercial account		$ 24,714.40
- Bank of California, restricted account		35,052.30
- Wells Fargo Bank, savings accounts		1.00
- Bay View Federal Savings & Loan		120,624.85
		180,392.55
Accounts receivable, catalogue & mail order	$ 158,407.18	
Accounts receivable, other	10,484.68	
Advances, Whole Earth, Inc.	5,000.00	173,891.86
Inventories		39,827.16
Prepaid expenses		1,078.94
Deposit on catalogue printing		40,000.00
Total current assets		435,190.51
Property and equipment:		
Furniture and equipment	8,932.39	
Less: Accumulated depreciation	734.50	8,197.89
Total Assets		$ 443,388.40

Liabilities and Capital

Current liabilities:		
Accounts payable, trade		$ 30,215.63
Payroll and sales taxes payable		2,897.70
Total liabilities		33,113.33
Capital:		
Surplus, June 1, 1970	$ 187,571.47	
Net income and surplus, Exhibit 2	222,703.60	410,275.07
Total Liabilities and Capital		$ 443,388.40

This Balance Sheet as at April 30, 1971 and the accompanying Statement of Income were not audited by me and, accordingly, I cannot express an opinion of them.

Vernon M. John

Exhibit 3

Whole Earth Division of
Portola Institute
Departmental Statement of Operating Income or Surplus
June 1, 1970 to April 30, 1971

	Mail Order / Store		Catalogues	
	April, 1971	Year To Date	April, 1971	Year To Date
Income:				
Sales	$ 20,985.08	$ 263,881.35	$ 27,719.95	$ 498,052.43
Cost of sales:				
Salaries	4,155.12	33,872.54	5,554.83	38,352.23
Merchandise	14,269.80	179,929.65		
Printing			14,905.85	132,098.75
Distribution	1,000.00	2,324.07	1,848.39	29,052.78
Outside services		529.87	650.00	11,195.87
Supplies and Miscellaneous	257.51	1,272.93	450.47	7,818.73
Depreciation	49.50	393.50	16.50	33.00
Travel and auto. expenses	15.68	15.68		1,224.39
Utilities	62.76	110.68	62.76	167.77
Rent	225.00	450.00	275.00	1,643.66
	20,035.37	218,898.92	23,763.80	221,587.18
Gross profit	949.71	44,982.43	3,956.15	276,465.25
General and administrative expenses:				
Telephone	101.43	121.34	195.56	236.67
Office supplies and misc.	367.41	315.11	859.59	865.19
Insurance		559.50		186.50
Legal and accounting		70.00	190.00	343.75
Donations				200.00
Division charges	2,000.00	2,000.00		3,000.00
In-house projects costs			495.00	527.03
Receipts (over) and under	238.58	723.55	(189.90)	192.90
Adminis. expenses previously applied		33,510.90		66,602.13
	2,707.42	37,300.40	1,551.14	72,154.17
Net operating income or surplus	$ (1,757.71)	$ 7,682.03	2,405.01	$ 204,311.08

This Statement has not been audited by me and, accordingly, I cannot express an opinion of it.

Vernon M. John Certified Public Accountant

And here's to you, customers, contributors, colleagues, successors. Don't take any wooden nickels.

—SB

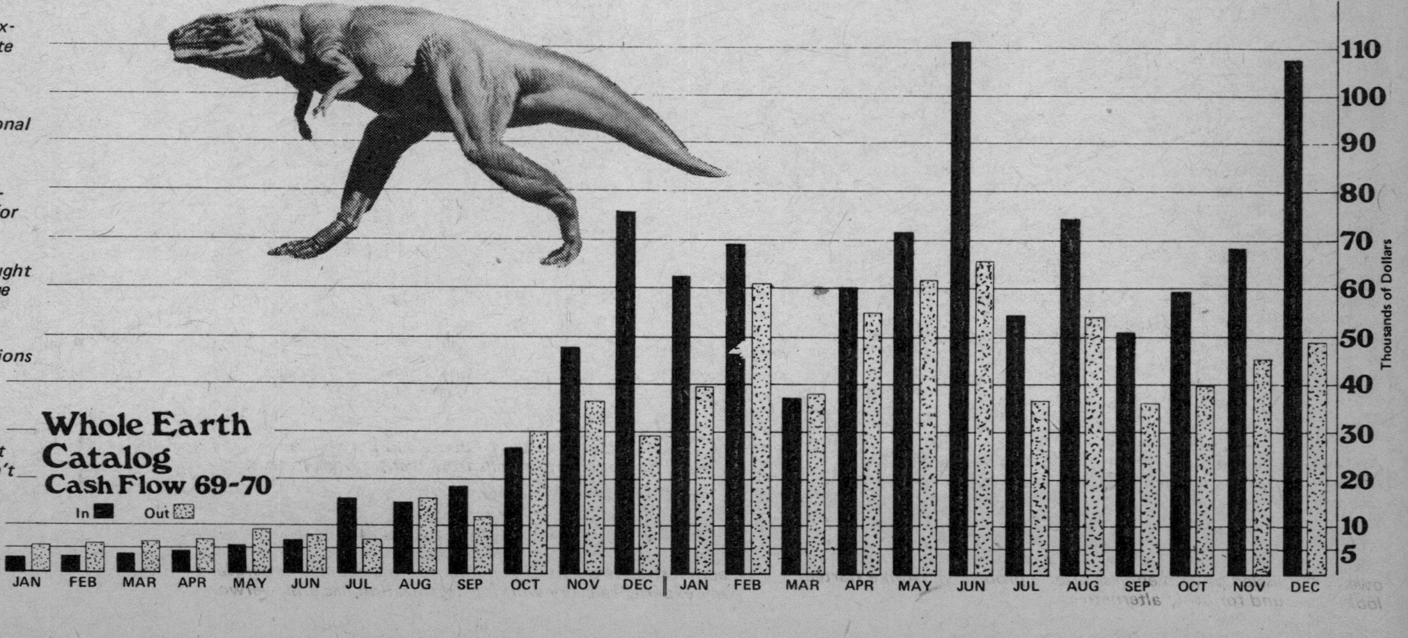

Whole Earth Catalog Cash Flow 69-70
In
Out
110
100
90
80
70
60
50
40
30
20
10
5
Thousands of Dollars
JAN FEB MAR APR MAY JUN JUL AUG SEP OCT NOV DEC
JAN FEB MAR APR MAY JUN JUL AUG SEP OCT NOV DEC

History

Some of what happened around here for the last three years.

The WHOLE EARTH CATALOG got started in a plane over Nebraska in March 1968. I was returning to California from my father's long dying and funeral that morning in Illinois. The sun had set ahead of the plane while I was reading Spaceship Earth by Barbara Ward. Between chapters I gazed out the window into dark nothing and slid into a reverie about my friends who were starting their own civilization hither and yon in the sticks and how could I help. The L. L. Bean Catalog of outdoor stuff came to mind and I pondered upon Mr. Bean's service to humanity over the years. So many of the problems I could identify came down to a matter of access. Where to buy a windmill. Where to get good information on bee-keeping. Where to lay hands on a computer without forfeiting freedom. . .

Shortly I was fantasizing access service. A Truck Store, maybe, traveling around with information and samples of what was worth getting and information where to get it. A Catalog too, continuously updated, in part by the users. A Catalog of goods that owed nothing to the suppliers and everything to the users. It would be something I could put some years into.

Amid the fever I was in by this time, I remembered Fuller's admonition that you have about 10 minutes to act on an idea before it recedes back into dreamland. I started writing on the end papers of Barbara Ward's book (never did finish reading it).

The next morning I approached Dick Raymond at Portola Institute with the idea. I'd been desultorily working for him for abut a half a year, had helped instigate one costly failure (an 'Education Fair' which aborted), and was partly into another doomed project, I called E-I-E-I-O (Electronic Interconnect Educated Intellect Operation).

I told him this Access Catalog was what I wanted to do now. Dick listened gravely and asked a few questions I had no answers for (Who do you consider as the audience for this 'catalog'? What kind of expenses do you think you'll have in the first year? What will be in the catalog? How often would you publish it? How many copies?). All I could tell him was that I felt serious enough about the project to put my own money into it, but not for a while yet. I wanted to move into the scheme gradually, using Portola's office, phone, stationery, and finances (which were Dick's personal savings, dwindling fast). He said okay.

For over a year Portola Institute had been nothing but Dick, a secretary he shared, his office, and a few expensive projects with big ideas and little to show. So he rented a nearby set of cubicles that some architects were moving out of, to give us more room to make mistakes in. I was working in my cubicle several weeks later when Dick leaned in the door and asked, "By the way, what do you think you'll call it?" My head filled with the last success I'd had, a 1966 photograph-of-the-whole-Earth campaign, which I felt was still incomplete. I told him, "I dunno, Whole Earth Catalog, or something."

My activities at this time were mostly visiting book stores and looking at books. One of Dick's friends at the Checkered Frog bookstore in Pacifica told me I could get single copies of books from publishers if I joined the American Booksellers Association, a commitment of $25. Shortly after that I made the big step and (holding my breath) spent $60 on note-o-gram stationery from Modern Business Forms. Dick helped me open a commercial account at a bank.

*I was operating without pay but keeping track of my time, to pay myself back-wages of $5/hr if we ever started to make money. In July 68 I printed up a mimeographed 6-page "partial preliminary booklist" of what I'd gathered so far (*Tantra Art, Cybernetics The Indian Tipi, Recreational Equipment*, about 120 items). With samples of each in the back of our truck Lois and I set out to visit the market — familiar communes in New Mexico and Colorado. In about a month the Whole Earth Truck Store did a stunning $200 of business. No profit, but it didn't cost too much and was good education.*

On return in August I hired an employee, Sandra Tcherepnin, who came around part-time to type and buoy my conviction that something was going on. In September Lois and I moved into Ortega Park (formerly Rancho Diablo), 70 acres and house newly leased by Portola Institute as a teachers' laboratory. She was housekeeper and I was caretaker in an empty mansion. It was a plush time.

Dick Raymond had introduced me to Joe Bonner, a talented teenage artist looking for work. He preferred to do layout than janitor for Portola so I took him to Gordon Ashby's design studio in San Francisco for a 10-minute course in layout. In October 68 we started production on the first WHOLE EARTH CATALOG in the garage at Ortega. Sandy fell in love with the IBM composer while Joe nailed together light tables out of scrap plywood. We got some electric heaters and started work. Joe did layout, Sandy typed, and I researched, reviewed, edited, and photographed. Whenever the typewriter, heaters, camera lights, and fry-pan of wax were on simultaneously the electricity went out. We'd spend an hour on projects like making an exotic border with the composer. A leisurely production. A month or so for 64 white-spacey pages.

We had the contents printed at Nowels Publications, a newspaper press just down the street from Portola Institute, and the cover printed at East Wind in San Francisco (using the picture from a Whole Earth poster we'd already had them print), and the binding done at another place, with us doing the transporting between. It was a terrible arrangement. The 1000 copies we printed were a huge chore to cart around.

Our real luck was in finding Nowels Publications and Bob Parks. I've never met a man I'd rather do business with, and to find a printer who is fast, thorough, cooperative, creative, honest, and inexpensive is just unheard of. We had one CATALOG printed elsewhere and regretted it.

I only dimly recall what we did with that first CATALOG. We sent them to the 50 or so subscribers we'd got with mailers and personal contact. We carted some around to stores, who didn't want them, not even on consignment ("Too big. Too expensive. What is it?") We traded some with other publications like This Magazine is About Schools, Explorers Trademart Log, *and* Green Revolution.

Meanwhile we were starting a store. Dick Raymond had had his eye on the building at 558 Santa Cruz, just across the alley from the cubicles he'd rented. Formerly a USO, then a Salvation Army store, then a printer's , the place had apartments upstairs and 4000 sq. ft. of big rooms downstairs and a nice store front. The printer had failed and the building was going to be sold. Dick got with the likeliest buyer and worked out a 5-year lease for the downstairs part at $450/month. We felt like we were really into the soup now. Five years! That's 1973.

At Thanksgiving we'd met a girl from New York named Annie Helmuth who had some familiarity with the publishing world, mostly on the publicity end. She was hired to take on publicity and help with research and typing since Sandy had left for woolier pastures. We soon found out that handling our own distribution was going to be impossible (bookstores wouldn't pay what they owed and hassled us with endless bizarre problems). Annie started looking around for other alternatives.

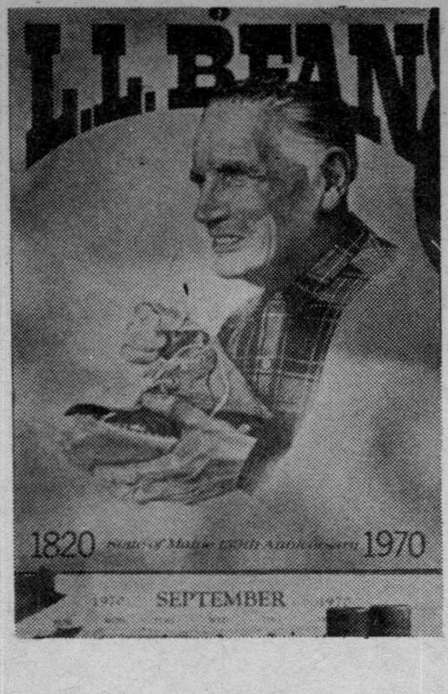

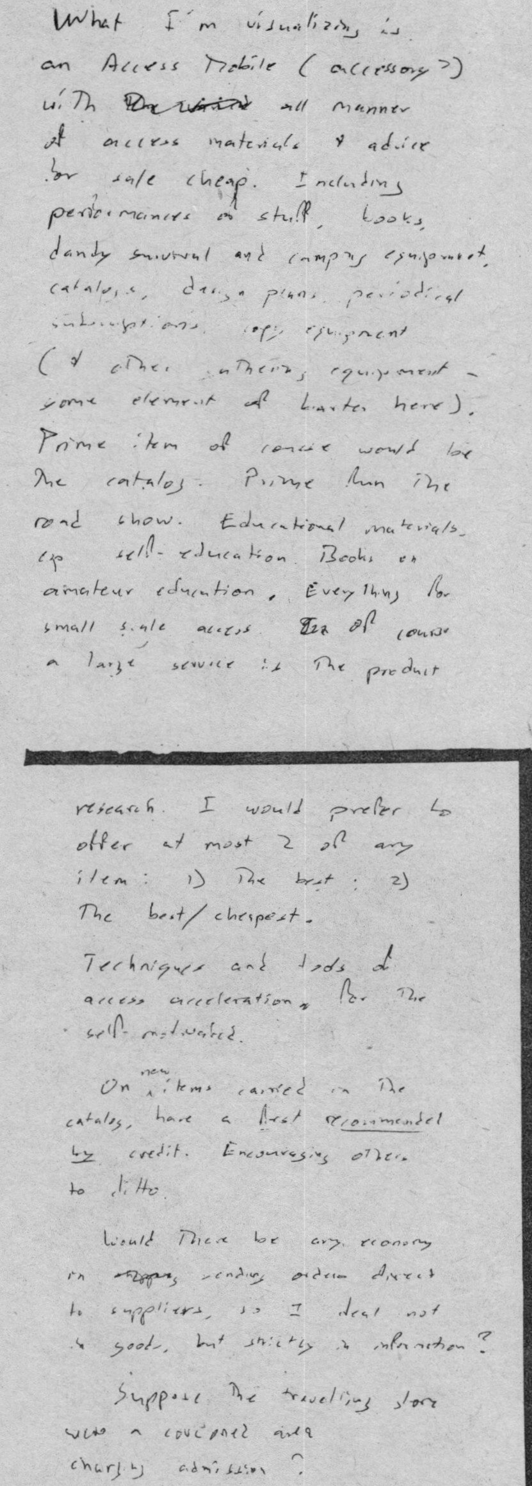

What I'm visualizing is an Access Mobile (accessory?) with all manner of access materials & advice for sale cheap. Including performances of stuff, books, dandy survival and camping equipment, catalogs, design plans, periodical subscriptions, copy equipment (& other authoring equipment — some element of barter here). Prime item of concern would be the catalog. Prime fun the road show. Educational materials, esp self-education. Books on amateur education. Everything for small scale access. Of course a large service is the product

research. I would prefer to offer at most 2 of any item: 1) The best; 2) The best/cheapest.

Techniques and tools of access acceleration, for the self-motivated.

On new items carried in the catalog, have a first recommended by credit. Encouraging others to ditto.

Would there be any economy in sending orders direct to suppliers, so I deal not in goods, but strictly in information?

Suppose the travelling store were a covered area charging admission?

The Whole Earth appendix to *Spaceship Earth*

In December 68 we moved into 558 Santa Cruz. There wasn't much to move — a chair and some books. Joe set to work with free scrap wood making the store a funky pleasant wooden place. We sublet an office in the front to Dave Shapira and a space in the back to lawyer Jim Wolpman. That cut our rent to $250/month. Joe made desks and tables out of doors and 2 x 4's. We never got around to changing the walls from institutional green.

From the beginning the pretty little Indian girl Lois, who still has to show her ID to bartenders, was the hard core of the business. She applied her math background to our bookkeeping, and her sharp tongue to our lazinesses and forgotten promises. She had the administrative qualities you look for in a good First Sergeant. In my experience every working organization has one overworked

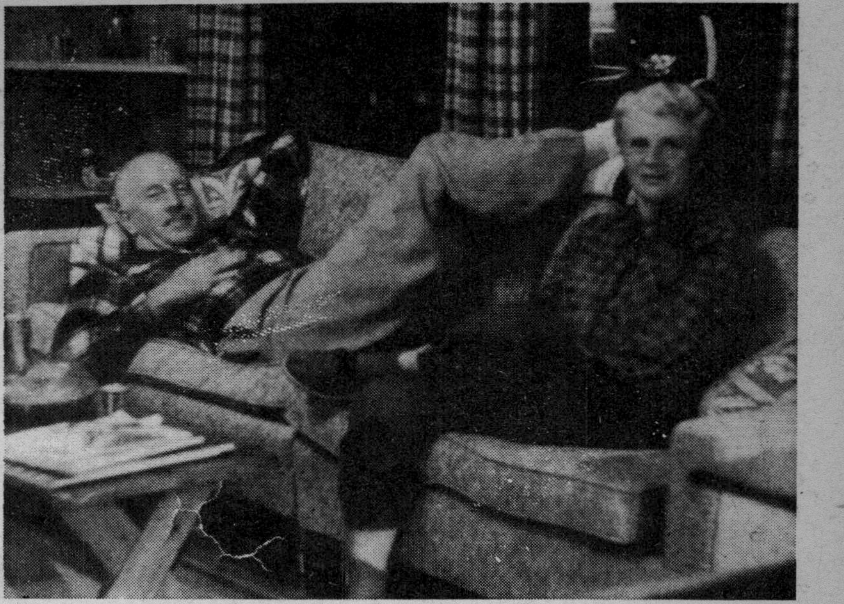

Arthur and Julia Brand

underpaid woman in the middle of things carrying most of the load. None of the rest of us ever cleaned the bathrooms. Lois cleaned the bathrooms.

Annie was at the City Lights Bookstore in San Francisco one day talking to Shig the manager about where to look for a distributor. Shig suggested a new long-haired outfit in Berkeley called Book People. Annie went to them and was immediately taken with Don Gerrard and Don Burns. Pretty soon Book People was our distributor, and that was a big relief. We made no contracts or vows, but the CATALOG stayed with Book People as sole distributor until the March 71 Supplement (when the Realist *took half the distribution).*

In January we had a grand opening party at the store, though we'd been open for a couple weeks ("There's a customer in the store!" we'd whisper in the back room.) Annie and I invited all the newspapers and were surprised and hurt when none of them showed up. It was a nice party anyway. The readership was a small sort of cult then, most of whom seemed to know each other, or wanted to.

Also in January we produced our first "Difficult But Possible Supplement to the Whole Earth Catalog". It was a 32-page newsprint collection of friends' letters, old pamphlets like Abbie Hoffman's "Fuck the System," a solar heater, new CATALOG suggestions. We made it at the Store.

About this time Tom Duckworth joined the scene. He lived in a truck with Connie and their kids and soon had a place to park at Ortega. His dream was to really do a travelling truck store. In March we gave him a shake-down cruise to New Mexico when the Whole Store caravanned to ALLOY (p. 111). If I had to point at one thing that contains what the CATALOG is about, I'd have to say it was ALLOY. We put it in the March Supplement, *along with how much the* Supplement *cost to make, which Steve Baer had suggested at ALLOY. A good practice. We've never regretted it.*

When we started the CATALOG I imagined that it would be a month of work, then an easy month to travel around and get the news, then a month of work, then. . .but it wasn't working out like that. None of us knew how to run a store and we were learning the hard way. We couldn't seem to find a mailing house that would do an even half-decent job of serving the subscribers. We had to try three places, each at big expense.

Our hassle with the Post Office, which continues to this very day, was in its surreal beginnings. (We're a periodical, in every spiritual and legal sense. Periodicals are mailed Second Class, a faster, surer, and cheaper service than Third Class, which is Junk Mail. The classifications man in San Francisco said, "It says Catalog *right here on the cover. Catalogs go Third Class." Dick Raymond cleared his throat, "*The Rolling Stone,*" he said, "is not a stone." Through endless appeals the thing has ambled, letters to our Congressman Pete McCloskey, rulings, and re-rulings, to current result: We have to send this LAST CATALOG to you Third Class. When a mail truck gets stuck in the mud, Third Class is what they throw under the wheels.)*

(continued) →

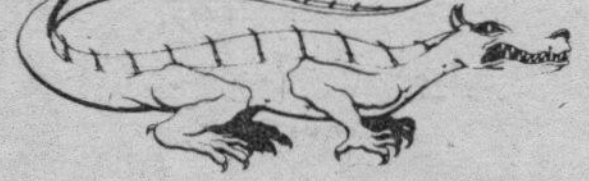

THURSDAY: PHONE CALL

By morning, though, D.R. was thoroughly animated again, restless and filled with an energy that just knew there'd be a letter for him in the mail that day. He felt it so strongly he couldn't get his mind on any work he tried around the place. At ten thirty he gave up trying and took off half-running down the hill to the store.

And sure enough, waiting at the post office was a letter from the Anaheim Flash.

Divine Right,

1. **Man, you have blown me out.**
2. **The telephone is more civilized than letters.**
3. **Letter-writing closes up my centers.**
4. **Estelle has been at Angel's place the last couple of weeks.**
5. **She may not be there now.**
6. **But I sent your letter on to Angel's place anyhow.**
7. **That's all I know.**
8. **Here's 200 bucks.**
9. **Don't spend it all in one place.**
10. **And for Christ's sake, use the phone next time.**

(signed) A. Flash, Esquire

Right on, said D.R. to himself.

(continued) →

History (continued)

About this time Lois and I started living in the store. Joe and Annie and I, with editorial help from Lloyd Kahn, did the Spring 69 CATALOG production amid the busy din of the store, a bad mistake. The CATALOG was twice as big and a dollar cheaper. To clear my head after production I hitchhiked to New Mexico for what turned out to be the Great Bus Race (p 245). Joe and Annie also headed for the desert, pending rendezvous in Albuquerque for the July Supplement production.

You should know that all this time Portola Institute was going through continual interesting changes that someone else is going to have to write about. Dick Raymond did one especially nice thing for us: he protected us from the vicissitudes.

Store and mailorder business was gradually picking up, so we hired Hal Hershey, a friend of the Duckworths who had worked in bookstores. We also hired Diana Shugart, a close buddy of Lois' and mine. At the store we had a chart on the wall that showed our income and expenses for each month. The income was gradually catching up.

While we were having a good July production at Steve and Holly Baer's house in Albuquerque, Hal and Diana were starting to face a heavy current in Menlo Park ("52 subscriptions today!"). Philip Morrison had written kindly of us in the June 69 Scientific American. We were being mentioned in a lot of underground papers such as the East Village Other. And then Nicholas von Hoffman wrote a full piece on the CATALOG that got syndicated all over the U.S. We were caught. We were famous.

(One interesting note. Of all the press notices we eventually got, from Time and Vogue to Hotcha!— in Germany— to the big article in Esquire, nothing had the business impact of one tiny mention in "Uncle Ben Sez" in the Detroit Free Press, where some reader asked, "How do we start a farm?" and Uncle Ben printed our address. We got hundreds and hundreds of subscriptions from that.)

Hal and Diana hired more people. Deposits at the bank were more frequent: the bank officers got more polite.

In September Joe and I returned to Ortega garage to work on the September Supplement. Annie had stayed on at Lama, so we hired a Kelly Girl to do the typing. As I was driving up the hill to work one day it suddenly hit me that I didn't want to. Instead of golden opportunity the publication was becoming a grim chore. I considered the alternatives of taking my medicine like a good boy or setting about passing on my job to somebody else. I'm sure I

Richard Raymond, President of Portola Institute

sighed unhappily. And then this other notion glimmered. Keep the job, finish the original assignment, and then stop. Stop a success and see what happens. Experiment going as well as coming. We printed in the September 69 Supplement that we would cease publication with a big CATALOG in Spring 71.

Meanwhile business was still growing. The morning mail was a daily heavy Santa Claus bag. We hired Tracy McCallum, Peter Ratner, Mary McCabe (a bit of uptown glamour amid the Hair), and a guy named Fred Richardson who had amazing talent for handling the world's hardware. Bernie Sproch and Megan Raymond came in periodically to handle our increasing load of filing and flyer-mailing and other chores. We were having group lunch at the store by now, Lois and Diana dishing it up.

I actually thought I could fit LIFERAFT EARTH (p. 35) in between the September Supplement and the fall CATALOG. Setting up the event was even harder than production. Then starving for a week was no way to recuperate. Dumb.

I went from the LIFERAFT straight into Fall CATALOG production. We were late, so we had to do it in two weeks. Fred was going to take over the camera. We had a hot new typist, Cappy McClure. We had a big new Stat-King that wasn't worth it. Joe brought in his brother Jay to double our layout speed. We worked 80 hours a week. We got to the printer on time.

Then Christmas was on us like a cat on a mouse. Everybody was overloaded at the store. In January we had another burst of hiring, practically whoever came in the door. Les Rosen the book-keeping ex-Marine, John Clark, Russell Bass, Jerry Fihn, Alan Burton, Leslie Acoca, the booklover Laura Besserman. Pam Smith was cooking lunch. When Tracy left to Canada, Pam's husband JD came in as manager. JD instituted a fine addition to the Storefront— a Free Box ("take or leave"). Everybody should have one; they really get used.

About this time I went over some edge. Minor tasks became in-surmountable obstacles. The thought of another production filled me with hopeless dread. I couldn't walk right. It was a nervous breakdown, garden variety. I'd never had one before so I thought I was dying, which stirred up a snowflurry of phobias that took more than a year to disperse. I'm not happy to mention this, but it seems an important part of the bookkeeping we're doing here.

In retrospect what I particularly appreciate was Dick Raymond's help and comfort, which was none at all. He's an unusually merciful soul. He said out loud to Esquire, "You have to let people have their own nervous breakdowns." Correct.

(continued)

Modern Business Forms

A good source of cheap, functional business stationery, note-o-grams, address labels, business notebooks, etc. Catalog free.

—SB

The Drawing Board, Inc.
256 Regal Row
Dallas, Texas 75221

Sound Criticism

What in the Hell is the Big Idea, anyway, threatening to cease publication of the Whole Earth Catalog?!! Why, you characters have hardley even started! What if all the telephone companies suddenly

Fidelity Executive

A good source of cheap, functional cardboard files and bins. Also other office equipment.

—SB

Fidelity Products Co.
705 Pennsylvania Ave. So.
Minneapolis, Minnesota 55426

decided to stop printing the yellow pages next year? What if Sweets suddenly decided they'd stop updating those huge catalogs each year or so? Where would we be? And don't put forth the argument that "Well, we'd probably be better off because somebody'd probably start a new Yellow Pages that would probably be better than the last ones. . ." because only You know how much Money, Time, Effort, Logistics, B.S., and Tears are required to compile and operate such an Information Processing Centre— and now that you've got the first touch of momentum in the Machine you're going to turn it off and like some child of itinerant interests create some new plaything to amuse yourselves and depress a lot of the rest of your followers because just as we get the hang of it and start Magnifying your Outer Ripples you'll Cop Out on us. If there was ever an Evil Plan, a commitment to Irresponsible Action, it's the decision to cease publication of the Catalog in 1971 which MR Brand had the audacity to suggest in a recent interview with TIME Magazine. What if Mother said after 3 months or so of Carrying The Weight: "Well, if Baby can't go it on his own from here I haven't been much use—!" But as I hope You have noticed, really responsible mothers hang on for at least 9 months if not 15 years and then, knowing when to shut up, they do it.

I don't know how much it's coming through to you guys yet or not but your not just titillating the Folks down on The Farm— you've pioneered a whole new concept in Information selection and distribution: "The Catalog With A Soul" And as you might gather from your sales increases over the last few issues there are a hell of a lot of other eyes gomming your rags. For example, there isn't a single school (particularly those tied up old design schools) that isn't absolutely fertile ground for you to pitch your Circus on. . .! The kind of Design Mentality which in your format and attitude you've begun to succeed in showing is possible and enviable on nearly everybody's scale— and the kind of Gospel of Self-Reliance en famille you've preached is so goddamned vital you just can't give up without realizing the Full Implications, the Total Possibilities of the Little Bomb you've set off.

If you had the nerve to call it The Whole Earth Catalog, why the hell isn't It going to BE a WHOLE EARTH CATALOG— a World Source with a World circulation, a World Exposure, a World of Contributors (have you considered the prospect of a WEC in every U.S. Embassy as a start)— A World Institution; Sears and Roebuck did it with a much smaller heart— and you don't even have to stock the merchandise! Here I am in Soggy Olde England and I've sold the Catalog to the First Five people I've shown it to except they query "Where can I get these goodies in England?"

1971 is not the year for you to fold up; 1971 is the year for you to start a New Growth Phase— to show that your concern is even more generous, even more thought-out than you'd have us believe at the moment. How about that: twice a year an Expanding Universe in my mail box! What New Forms can the Whole Earth Catalog take on? Maybe a separate edition for each major category of information, sources, and items as reviewers and contributors expand the range. Or how about a Telex station at WEC so that the backlog of old information from old issues and reviews which will surely pile up at an astounding rate could be tapped by a subscriber anywhere in the World when he needs source material and, as well, reviewers might click in a review when the P.O. eventually proves too slow. The Supplements: in addition to the sort of Interface they are now, could continue to be sort of Reporters-At-Large for us Lookers and Builders but on a much Broader Scale, reaching beyond the Western United States and extending our knowledge of Process/ Ideas by connecting up with other Farmers of the World. (You know that the first European Conference on The Environment was just held in Strassbourg?)

You see, of course, it is just as important that you publish the Catalog as what you put in IT— you are a vital Priority Distillery: Education, Tools, and Appliances for Self-Reliance and you document that very process of distillation thereby endorsing Design as one entire side of the Evolutionary Coin. Now, as never before, because of Extraordinary Devices, one man's Special Sight can be shared by many more who see a little better because of his efforts; in our struggle to become ever less Blind, all the Vehicles which bring the Possibilities of these Special Sights to us are like much needed lenses or Aids: extra eyes and extra ears to help us make our Way in the Dark. As any designer knows— you cut off the Source, the Inspirator— and you cripple the Product, you trip up the Effort.

So, goddamnit, GROW UP. (or at least justify your suicide.)

Very Sincereley Yours,

Gregory Groth Jacobs
London

Every noon, volleyball at the store.

I jittered through the January 70 production and then asked Gurney Norman to handle March. He did, and with bells on. Guest editorship had come to Whole Earth. Joe Bonner left on the mystical road, and I was worried, but Hal Hershey more than filled his shoes on layout.

In January Fred built a volleyball court in back of the store. I was too fucked up to play on it for a while, which grieved me, because volleyball instantly became a valuable part of the store routine. We played two games after lunch every day. It improved our health, got us out in the weather, loosened our tensions, and — honest to God — built character.

Since we were playing on paid-for time, we naturally tried to stretch out the two games, so each day the players spontaneously arranged themselves into always different but equal teams. Lunch and volleyball kept us well acquainted. That, and the morning mail-opening scene. We had some newcomers — Mary Jo Morra, Soni Stoye the good cook, Austin Jenkins of good cheer.

On the Spring CATALOG we went up to 144 pages and lowered the price further to $3. (Later a friend at Stanford Research Institute said he made the calculations one afternoon and figured out we would make the most money with a $4 price tag. Or $3.95, as they say.) A new face on Spring production was Steamboat, who seldom spoke but could draw volumes. (Tuesday's Child on p. 23 is his. So are the dragons.)

In July Lois and I left to see the world and Expo and the Bakers in Japan. My old (and favorite) employer Gordon Ashby took on the July Supplement and totally changed our layout ways.

JD, Nebraska's Marlon Brando, kept a strong crew busy at the Store and started gathering material for the Fall 70 CATALOG he was going to edit.

In September 70 Gurney came back from a summer in Kentucky with Wendell Berry and put out what came to be known as the Cracker issue of the Supplement. The BD-4 airplane kit we'd ordered started to arrive, and Fred and later Troll and Doug and Bob sawed and filed and puzzled and riveted at it in the back room. Don Gerrard had left Book People and among his other projects was trying to find a big distributor for the LAST CATALOG. We wanted a contract by Christmas. Nobody in New York seemed very interested.

There were strong family feelings in the Store by now and a desire to do something else together. A restiveness. When the teacher's lab at Ortega finally failed and quit, JD and I pressed to get it as a home for most of the Truck Store staff, a commune. Idealism

filled the air. It was never a very successful commune; it was a plenty educational one.

As Fall production went on up the hill in the garage there were new laborers in the store. Herald Hoyt, Dudley DeZonia, Francine Slate, Terry Gunesch, Diane Erickson. People's children were in the store more often now. Marilyn's kids, Francine's, Diane's, Pam's. I was buried in the back office starting the long haul toward the LAST CATALOG.

At Christmas there were memorable parties.

In January 71 some of us safaried to a remote unnamed desert hot springs for an adventurous Supplement production.

Don Gerrard had gotten good offers from Dutton and Random House for distribution of the LAST CATALOG. We decided to go with Random.

I asked Richard Brautigan, Ken Kesey, and Paul Krassner if any of them would like to edit the March Supplement. Brautigan said he was already involved in a quaint project, writing a novel. Kesey said he would edit if Krassner would, and new levels of offense and tooldom were leveled at our readers.

The LAST CATALOG you know about.

A lot of other stuff happened too, ask anybody who was there. Ask Bernie Sproch to show you his Whole Earth stamp collection. It's quite a collection.

Fame

I/we've been subject to some, and you're partially responsible, so I thought you ought to know a little about it. Everything bad you've heard about fame is quite true. It can throw a personality into positive feedback, where audience demands drive his character past caricature and off the deep end. Its over-rewards can jade a palate permanently. It wakes you up in the middle of the night with phone calls from whining strangers.

Worst of all is the classic bind of the successful do-gooder. If you do good well, your opportunities to do more increase, as your stamina to do any decreases. You should relax, yes you should, relax, with guilt yammering in your ear. FUCK EM ALL! is no answer either.

Some think they're strong, some think they're smart,
Like butterflies they're pulled apart.
America can break your heart.
You don't know all, sir, you don't know all.

W. H. Auden

Krassner is right to note that celebrityhood is mainly a matter of convenience for people. There's no reason to take it personally.

I will say a couple of good words for fame. It accelerates access if you want access. You can hang around with famous people, which is fun sometimes. Your credit is good with strangers, it's never hard to meet people. It's usually easy to find work, make some money. If you've withstood fame there's some things you're strong at that you might not be otherwise.

The main problem with fame, or any kind of success, is the insulation it packs around you. You don't get all those little course-correcting signals from the universe. In part they're drowned out by all the people telling you what they think and what you ought to think. Also the signals just can't prick you; when a red danger light goes on, you can simply bribe the machine until the light goes off, and the danger grows unheeded.

The voices that you need to hear, whisper, slowly and infrequently. The only way to hear them is listen. Gaze at something until it's nothing. And then at nothing until it's something.

There's a difference between intention driving us on, and mystery pulling us on. Mystery will always educate and correct. Intention can go off the end of its own limb.

If it's all right with you, I'm going back to the tree. We get asked a lot, "What's in the future for you folks," as if we knew. Well, let's see. We'll clean up the garage and sell the production equipment, maybe to Kesey who wants to start a travelling magazine called Spit in the Ocean. Us out-of-work production people will draw our two weeks severance pay. We'll keep the Truck Store going in Menlo Park, and maybe try some new things with it in relation to Portola Institute. We'll have our DEMISE party that Scott Beach has set up at the Exploratorium in San Francisco. We'll do some travelling. We'll take a ride on Patchen's coda:

Pause.

And begin again.

—SB
May 31, 1971

Whole Earth Truck Store

The Whole Earth Truck Store is alive and quite well in Menlo Park. New ventures under way. Old CATALOGS and Supplements available. Come by.

And we still Mail Order.

Hours: Monday—Saturday, 9:30 am - 6 pm
Thursday, 9:30 am - 9 pm

540 Santa Cruz Avenue, Menlo Park, CA 94025

Phone: (415) 323-0313

Portola Institute was established in 1966 as a non-profit corporation to encourage, organize, and conduct innovative educational projects. The Institute relies for support on private foundations and public agencies, to whom specific project proposals are submitted.

Because Portola Institute is a private organization with no need to produce profits or guarantee "success", it can experiment with new and unusual educational projects that would be difficult to administer within more structured organizations. For this reason the staff and facilities of the Institute are deliberately kept small and flexible.

Within its framework a wide variety of projects dealing with innovative education can be created as people with ideas are able to interest people with funds. New projects are always being considered, both within the existing divisions and programs, and within as yet unexplored realms of the learning experience.

Whole Earth Truck Store and Catalog is one division of Portola Institute. Other current activities include:

Briarpatch Review
Alternative Economics
Right Livelihood, including a special 3 yr. program in industrial democracy and education

And he left the store and the people there and went around to Roxie's house to place a collect call to the Flash in California.
"Yal-low?"
"Flash, this is D.R."
"Stop right there," said the Flash. "Before you say another word, I want you to tell me a phone number where I can call you. I would of called you days ago . . ."
"Listen, man, have you heard from Estelle yet?"
"Tell me your phone number and I'll answer that question."
D.R. told the Flash Leonard's phone number. There was a little silence while he wrote it down.
"That's better," said the Flash. "People might as well be lost in outer space without a phone number. Estelle's in San Francisco."
"She's where?"
"She's with these friends of Angel's in the mountains, south of San Francisco. Down toward Santa Cruz."
"What the hell's she doing in San Francisco?"
"What are you doing in Kentucky?" asked the Flash. "What am I doing in Anaheim? It shifts, friend. It shifts and moves around. You should know."
"But San Francisco . . ."
"She's not in San Francisco," said the Flash. "She's south of there . . ."
"Did Angel tell you that?" D.R. asked. "When did you talk to Angel?"
"Yesterday, the day before yesterday, and about a week ago. I would of called you if I'd had your number. Always have a telephone number, D.R. It facilitates communication."
"So go on with it. What did Angel say?"
"She said Estelle had split. She said Estelle stayed with them two weeks, and day before yesterday took off, hitch-hiking south. Angel told her to stop off and stay a few days with these friends of hers who live in this dome in the mountains. Estelle said she'd probably do that, and if she did, then we can find her."
"What about my letter?"
"It got there the day Estelle left. Angel read it, and that's why she called me."
"I'm sorry she's hitch-hiking," said D.R.
"Angel said that was what she wanted to do. Besides that, she was broke."
"Oh shit. What else did she say? Did she say how she was, how she felt?"
"She's kind of down, I think. I'm not supposed to tell you that, so don't tell Angel I told you. She's already convinced you're a rat. I don't want her to think I'm one too."
"Jesus. Did she say what was wrong? Did she say . . ."
"No. But listen; don't sweat it. The Anaheim Flash is swinging into action. If my little scheme works out, you'll be talking to Estelle this afternoon."
"You going to call her? Can I call her?"
"I'm going to set it up. There's no phone in this dome she's supposed to be visiting. But I know a guy up there, in Menlo Park, and he'll fetch her to a phone if I ask him to. Then you guys can hate each other voice to voice, or groove on each other, or whatever weird thing it is you all are trying to get on. What the hell is going on, if I may ask?"
D.R. grinned into the telephone. "I've started a new corporation," he said.

(continued)

CONTENTS

SUBJECT INDEX

TITLE INDEX

This type-face indicates book titles and CATALOG items.

This type-face indicates other materials such as letters, comments, etc.

"A what?"

"A corporation."

"You're crazy. What are you doing, dealing?"

"I'm President of Magic Rabbit, Incorporated," D.R. said.
"You're a vice president, and chief cohort."

"The hell I am," said the Flash.

"It's true. I've written you all about it. My truest and grandest scheme."

"Well I'm hot to hear it," said the Flash. "But listen, man: no more letters from me, okay? You got the money, I guess."

"Got it. And many thanks for it, too."

"The interest is six per cent," said the Flash.

"Fair enough," said D.R. "But listen: if you get Estelle and me together on the telephone, I'll do better than that. I'll make you a full president of Magic Rabbit."

"Can't beat that," said the Flash. "Hang around that phone, now, son. If you don't get a call by tonight some time, call me back, okay?"

"Will do," said D.R.

When he hung up he ran out of Roxie's house yelling "Yip-eee!".

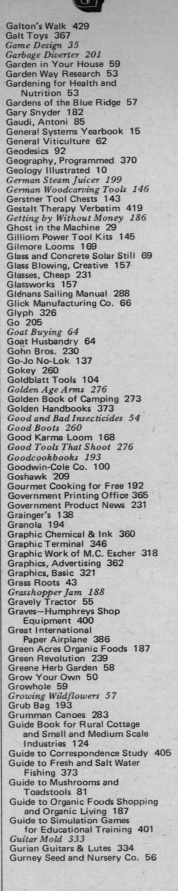

Austin, Cappy, Mark

J

K

L

M

Bernie Sproch

Opening the mail, reading aloud, disbursing. Mary, Cappy, John. Most of these photos are by Sam Falk.

RIP-SNORTER

Okay folks, hold onto your hats. This is Gurney Norman the author speaking, bringing you the end of this folk tale, and it's a rip-snorter. The guy in California that the Anaheim Flash sent to fetch Estelle to the telephone was me. I live here in Menlo Park where the Whole Earth Truck Store is, where Stewart and the production crew are wild in the final stages of the Last Catalog, and I'm wild in the final stages of this here tale.

As a matter of fact, I'm so pushed for time I wasn't at all sure I was going to be able to get away from the desk long enough to go up to Troll's and Marilyn's dome on Skyline and find Estelle. But I did, and it all worked out okay.

As the Flash indicated, Estelle was a little down. She'd been pretty blue since she and D.R. split up in Cincinnati; her trip since then had been pretty much of a bummer. She was nervous and jumpy, and half-hostile when she asked me who the hell I was. I said I was a friend of the Anaheim Flash's, and that he'd called and asked me to get her to a telephone so she could call D.R., who was most desperate to hear from her.

Estelle seemed a little suspicious of the whole thing, but she went with me to Skylonda, where there was a phone booth. I loaned her a dime and she went in, and stayed a long time, talking to D.R. I didn't hear what they said, but apparently it was a pretty groovy conversation because she came out all smiles, and announced that she was going to Kentucky.

I asked her how.

She said the fastest way possible.

That means through the air, I said, and off we went to the San Francisco airport, where I bought her a one-way ticket to Cincinnati, and gave her twenty dollars for bus fare from there south into the hills, to Blaine, Kentucky. (All on the assumption, of course, that I'm to be reimbursed in full by our mutual friend and benefactor, the Anaheim Flash).

By the time the passengers were ready to board the plane, Estelle had mellowed toward me some. Just before she started down the loading ramp she gave me this incredible kiss right on the mouth, and I mean to tell you, it was fine. That D.R. is one lucky fellow, as I think he himself must realize by now.

(continued)

Francine, Accounts Receivable

X— Three Years of Research, and Nothing
   Beginning with X.

By the time Estelle's plane was east of the Sierras I was back at
my desk again, where D.R. was still in raptures from the phone
call. He was so stoned out by the whole thing he gave up all
attempts at serious work, and spent the afternoon wandering
around the homeplace in a daze. He forgot supper entirely. He
tried to get into Stranger In A Strange Land again, but he couldn't
focus on it, so he set it aside and picked up the I Ching again.

It was dark by now. D.R. was sitting at the kitchen table,
casting the coins by lamplight.

He threw a broken line. A solid line. A broken line. A solid
line. Another broken line, and then a final solid line.

Wei Chi/Before Completion

"This hexagram indicates a time when the transition from
disorder to order is not yet complete. The change is indeed
prepared for, since all the lines in the upper trigram are in relation
to those in the lower. However, they are not yet in their places.
While the preceding hexagram offers an analogy to autumn, which
forms the transition from summer to winter, this hexagram presents
a parallel to spring, which leads out of winter's stagnation into the
fruitful time of summer. With this hopeful outlook the Book of
Changes comes to its close."

And so does Divine Right's Trip. D.R. had only one more run
to make, to Blaine, in Urge, bright and shining, freshly washed and
cleaned-up Urge, to meet Estelle's bus, coming in from Lexington
late that night.

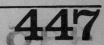

THE WEDDING

There are no guarantees, of course.

There are no guarantees.

But if it could work.

If it looks like it's worth the risk,

The leap.

If there's even a chance for the two of them there, then what D.R. and Estelle will do is have a most marvelous wedding.

One day late in the summer.

Or early in the fall.

All day long,

From morning to night, a celebration.

And people they love will come.

The Flash will come.

He will have to come because he's the presiding minister.

All the way from California, driving his silver Lotus.

The Flash in his silver jumpsuit.

The Flash with his silver hair.

The Flash with his silver eyebrows, and little silver ring in the side of his nose.

Silver boots, with pointy silver toes, and silver buttons down the sides,

And buttons on his jumpsuit, silver,

And silver scarf and silver gloves and sunglasses, on both sides,

Silver.

The Flash had his silver helmet with him too, but as he parked the Lotus in front of Godsey's Store he thought: I probably shouldn't overdo this silver bit. So he left the helmet on the seat and clambered out, uncoiling his five foot, four inch frame as Barry Berry came rolling by in his wheelchair.

"My name's Barry Berry," Barry said.

"I'm the Anaheim Flash," said the Flash, and he got behind Barry's chair and pushed him up the Trace Fork road behind a band of freaks and weirdos, strewing colored ribbons in the weeds.

"I'm Barry Berry." said Barry as they rolled by. "And this is the Anaheim Flash."

"Morning," said J.D. "I'm J.D."

And Pam said she was Pam.

Barry shook hands with them every one, Diane and Jerry and Amy and Barbara and Dudley and John and B. Anne and Peter and Laura and Soni and Doug and Terry and Francine and Bernie.

And Shera was filming it all.

She'd moved down the road a ways from the party to catch the new arrivals, coming up.

She filmed the Flash and Barry Berry.

And Dick Raymond escorting Mrs. Godsey up the road.

She filmed them all passing, and then from low in the yard she filmed Angel's band of Oregonians, Ken and Fay and Babbs and Gretch and Hassler and Paula and Zodiac and Sky and some others, decorating the front porch steps as an altar where the bride and groom would stand.

"The surest test if a man be sane is if he accepts life whole, as it is," he read.

And just then the Flash appeared.

"Excuse me," he said. "But I happened to overhear that little exchange. And what I'm wondering is, would you folks mind reading those scriptures in the wedding ceremony after while."

She filmed Reverend Bagby and some men from the church, building a table across the yard.

Fifteen sawhorses, covered with boards, then women spreading sheets as tablecloths, and tacking on red and blue crepe.

She filmed Fred and George and Mike and Evelyn and Steamboat and Stewart, asleep in a people pile, with Lois and Steve and Holly and Lloyd and Sarah trying to wake them up to rap a while as The Captain, an utter freak in purple velvet and long mustache and conductor's hat too small for his shaggy head sneaked up with his tape recorder to catch what the people said.

"Deliverance. Release from tension," said George.

"No shit!" said Fred.

"And Neptune and Jupiter are in conjunction in Sagittarius," said Mike.

"Be well," said Stewart.

"Hey Mike, I just felt the baby kick," said Evelyn.

"Huh? Oh, the wedding!" said Steamboat.

And The Captain recorded it all.

He recorded the Scott boys, Henry and Tommy from Second Creek, making bird sounds with their mouths.

The Captain tuned in on a conversation among some women carrying dishes to the table. One was Marilyn, of Troll and Marilyn, big and beautiful and pregnant, saying "It'll be a natural childbirth. I'm going to have it at home."

"I had all my younguns at home," said Mrs. Thornton. "Tended by a granny-woman. Old Aunt Dicey Pace from Turkey Creek. She's dead now, bless her soul."

And over by the Kool-Aid table Elmer the mailman was rapping with a leather and denim freak from San Diego, who hadn't said what his name was yet.

"I think ginseng is the answer to about half of mankind's problems," the freak said, and Elmer replied, "My daddy picked 'sang for a living, when I was a boy. It's as native to these hills as it is to over yonder in China."

The Captain recorded that.

And he recorded Maybeline Monday from the Organic Sunflower Commune in California, telling Mrs. Jennings of Jennings Branch that she was doing her own weaving now. And making quilts, and canning her own vegetables.

"We live in a commune, on the land, you see. We're opposed to the nuclear family."

"Lord, child," said Mrs. Jennings. "I've been weaving since I was nine years old. And ever quilt in our old house is hand-made. I had thirteen brothers and sisters, and then nine younguns of my own. We all live over yonder on Jennings Branch, you ought to come see us before you leave."

He recorded the musicians warming up,

Doug and Soni and Diane were setting out bowls of beans and corn and pickled beets and kraut and casseroles and pies and cakes and puddings and plates of biscuits and cornbread with jams and jellies, fruit-jello and salads. The dancers writhed and turned as they moved through the crowd toward some square dancers Wheeler had formed. The rising tempo of the music whirled the dancers around and around and around and around, all in one big circle now.

And people watching began to clap and then to join in.

Shera had to move almost up to the barn to get the whole thing in her lens. Dudley and Barbara had their cameras going too, shooting stills of faces as they came by.

Then Barbara turned to shoot Leonard's face too, and Doyle's, sweating over the charcoal fire.

She shot the Captain as he came over to record Leonard yelling to the Anaheim Flash, "Ten more minutes, Flash! And the chickens'll all be done."

Ten more minutes.

The Flash nodded to Leonard, then nodded to the band, and the music and the dancers slowed down.

Down, down.

It all slowed down.

The people heard the Flash call out, "It's time for the wedding, folks. It's time to gather around."

Gather around.

Gather around the front porch steps where the alter has been arranged.

The best man, Leonard, walked through the crowd to stand at the side of Angel the maid of honor.

When the Flash came down the steps to join them, the scene became quiet and still.

"Wow, man," said the Swami. "Far out!" But Mrs. Godsey declined. "Get Brother Bagby to read my part," she said. "I've got to go in the kitchen and help out."

The Captain recorded that, and then tuned into the band again. J.D. had joined it with his autoharp, and Steamboat with his drums. Two other fellows that no one knew came in with a banjo and flute. Their exotic sound, which they had already dubbed Hillbilly Hindu Rock, lured Chloe and fourteen dancers in tie-dyed leotards out of the house and down the steps, a winding snake of movement through the crowd. They circled around the charcoal pit where Leonard and Doyle and Troll were baking potatoes and barbecuing fifty chickens. They wound around the long, white table where Roxie and Marcella and Mrs. Thornton and Peter and

Dorothy Thornton with her dulcimer, Cecil and Claudine Turner with guitar and mandolin, and Terry sitting in with his new sitar, leading now as they break into an old Mac Wiseman song called Rainbow In The Valley.

The Captain was getting it all.

Armed with a fresh cassette, he moved to the shady side of the house where Swami High-Time from Santa Cruz, carrying the Book of Tao, was into a heavy theological rap with Mrs. Godsey, who as usual held her Bible in her hand.

"A double-minded man is unstable in all his ways," she said. "That's scripture, brother. James one, eight."

The Swami smiled and nodded and turned to chapter twenty one in the Book of Tao.

At last, when all had settled, D.R. and Estelle came through the screen door, across the porch and down the steps to where they were supposed to stand.

D.R. had his leathers on, leather pants and leather shirt, and coonskin cap with tail.

Estelle had her ankle-length gingham on.

There were no flowers.

Estelle's bouquet was simply D.R.'s hand in her own.

They stood there together, grinning at the people who grinned at them, waiting for the Flash to begin.

The Flash moves now to the third step up, so he can see over Leonard's head. He has a book with him, and a large brown bag filled with something, which he rests on the step by his foot. The book is the I Ching. He opens it to After Completion and clearing his throat, he reads:

"The transition from the old to the new time is already accomplished. In principle, everything stands systematized, and it is only in regard to details that successs is still to be achieved. In respect to this, however, we must be careful to maintain the right attitude. Everything proceeds as if of its own accord, and this can all too easily tempt us to relax and let things take their course without troubling over details. Such indifference is the root of all evil. Symptoms of decay are bound to be the result. Here we have the rule indicating the usual course of history. But this rule is not an inescapable law. He who understands it is in position to avoid its effects by dint of unremitting perseverance and caution."

The Flash closes the book and places it on a step behind him.

Then he calls upon the Reverend Bagby to read the little passage from the Book of Tao.

"The surest test if a man is sane is if he accepts life whole, as it is," says Reverend Bagby.

And then the Flash calls upon Swami High-Time to read from the Book of James.

"A double-minded man is unstable in all his ways," says Swami High-Time.

As he and Reverend Bagby step back into the crowd, the Flash reaches into his pocket and takes out two rings. He hands one each to Leonard and Angel, who in turn hand them to D.R. and Estelle.

They face each other.

They hold out their left hands, and simultaneously slip the rings on one another's fingers.

Then they come together in a long and fullsome kiss.

And the Flash says, "As a minister in good standing of the Universal Life Church, I pronounce you guys husband and wife. And I pronounce everybody here at this wedding hereby married to one another."

The Flash reaches into the bag at his feet then, and from it he begins to fling rice out over the gathered people.